NUMERICAL LIST OF CHAPTERS

ACCOUNTANTS' HANDBOOK

Seventh Edition

SUBSCRIPTION NOTICE

This Wiley product is updated on a periodic basis (e.g., annual supplements) to reflect important changes in the subject matter. If you purchased this product directly from John Wiley & Sons, we have already recorded your subscription for this update service.

If, however, you purchased this product from a bookstore and wish to receive any current update at no additional charge, and future updates, revised, or related volumes billed separately with a 30-day examination review, please send your name, company name (if applicable), address, and the title of the product to:

Supplement Department
John Wiley & Sons, Inc.
One Wiley Drive
Somerset, NJ 08875
1-800-225-5945

ACCOUNTANTS' HANDBOOK

Seventh Edition

Edited by

D. R. CARMICHAEL, PhD, CPA
Bernard M. Baruch College, City University of New York

STEVEN B. LILIEN, PhD, CPA
Bernard M. Baruch College, City University of New York

MARTIN MELLMAN, PhD, CPA
Bernard M. Baruch College, City University of New York

JOHN WILEY & SONS

New York • Chichester • Brisbane • Toronto • Singapore

In recognition of the importance of preserving what has been written, it is a policy of John Wiley & Sons, Inc., to have books of enduring value published in the United States printed on acid-free paper, and we exert our best efforts to that end.

Library of Congress Cataloging in Publication Data:

Accountant's handbook / edited by D. R. Carmichael, Steven B. Lilien,
   Martin Mellman. — 7th ed.
      p.   cm.
   Includes bibliographical references.
   ISBN 0-471-61979-5
      1. Accounting. I. Carmichael, D. R. (Douglas R.), 1941–
II. Lilien, Steven B.   III. Mellman, Martin.   IV. Series.
HF5621.A22   1991
657—dc20   90-37693

Printed in the United States of America

10 9 8 7 6 5 4 3 2

ABOUT THE EDITORS

D. R. Carmichael, PhD, CPA, is the Wollman Distinguished Professor of Account-ancy at Bernard M. Baruch College, City University of New York. Until 1983, he was the Vice President, Auditing, at the AICPA, where he was directly involved in the development of accounting and auditing standards. Dr. Carmichael has written 12 books and numerous articles on accounting and auditing. He acts as a consultant on auditing and control matters to CPA firms, attorneys, government agencies, and financial institutions.

Steven B. Lilien, PhD, CPA, is Chairman of the Department of Accountancy at Bernard M. Baruch College, City University of New York. He has served as a consultant on financial accounting and auditing for international and regional firms of CPAs as well as for government agencies and law firms. His articles have appeared in the *Accounting Review, Financial Analysts Journal, Journal of Accounting and Economics, Journal of Accounting, Auditing and Finance, The CPA Journal,* and *Management Accounting.* He has coauthored books on financial accounting and auditing practice and standards and on discovery of accounting information in litigation actions.

Martin Mellman, PhD, CPA, is Professor of Accountancy at Bernard M. Baruch College, City University of New York. He was Chairman of the Department of Accountancy from 1972 to 1981. He has served as a consultant on financial and cost accounting to an international CPA firm as well as to law firms and governmental agencies. His articles have appeared in numerous professional and academic journals, including *Accounting Review, Journal of Accountancy, The CPA Journal, Management Accounting, Journal of Accounting, Auditing and Finance,* and *St. John's Law Review.* He has coauthored books on accounting theory, financial accounting and auditing standards and practice, discovery of accounting informa-tion in litigation actions, and financial management of marketing activities.

CONTRIBUTORS

James R. Adler, PhD, CPA, is the senior technical partner at Checkers, Simon & Rosner. He has served on several committees of the Illinois CPA Society, provided litigation and investigative services to numerous firms, served as an expert witness, and was a university professor.

Vincent Amoroso, FSA, is a principal in the employee benefits section of KPMG Peat Marwick's Washington National Tax Practice. He has published and spoken frequently in the employee benefits accounting area, both on pensions and retiree medical care.

Pauline Appleby, CPA, is a senior audit manager in the New York office of Price Waterhouse and a member of the Financial Services Industry Practice specialty group. Her diverse client responsibilities have included money center, regional, and international banks.

J. T. Ball, PhD, CPA, is assistant director of research and technical activities of the Financial Accounting Standards Board. He was research associate for accounting interpretations for the AICPA, where he authored interpretations of APB Opinions on behalf of the Accounting Principles Board, including the book of interpretations of APB Opinion No. 15, "Computing Earnings per Share." Ball has also been a member of the accounting faculty of University of Florida in Gainesville.

Richard J. Behrens, CPA, is a partner at Price Waterhouse and full-time national chairman of the firm's Real Estate Industry Services Group. He serves on the AICPA's Real Estate Committee and is his firm's representative to several real estate industry organizations.

Martin Benis, PhD, CPA, is a professor at and former chairman of the Department of Accountancy at the Bernard M. Baruch College, City University of New York. He is currently a consultant on accounting and auditing matters to more than 50 accounting firms and organizations throughout the United States. His articles have appeared in major accounting and auditing journals.

Val R. Bitton, CPA, is a senior audit manager in the Salt Lake City office of Deloitte & Touche and was formerly a manager of the accounting research department in the firm's executive office. In addition, he specializes in the financial institutions, health care, and broadcasting industries.

Mimi Blanco-Best, CPA, is a technical manager of the AICPA's Auditing Standards Division and has served as an adjunct professor at New York University. She has published several articles in professional journals.

Peter T. Chingos is the national practice director of KPMG Peat Marwick's Compensation and Human Resource Consulting Practice. He has served as a consultant for all major industries, embracing a wide range of compensation and human resource issues, and is a frequent speaker on compensation.

Richard D. Dole, CPA, is a general practice partner and chairman of the National Energy and Natural Resources Program at Coopers & Lybrand, and Southwest regional director of the firm's Financial Advisory Services. He participated in developing the firm's response to the Financial Accounting Standards Board and the SEC's oil and gas rules, is a published author on accounting and industry issues, and is a frequent speaker and writer on many energy industry topics.

Joseph V. Falanga, CPA, is a tax manager in the New York office of the international accounting firm Spicer & Oppenheim. He specializes in securing trusts, estates, high net worth individuals, closely held businesses, and charitable entities.

Robert A. Flaum, CPA, is an audit partner in the New York office of Price Waterhouse and a member of the Financial Services Industry Practice specialty group. His extensive financial service company experience includes savings and loan organizations and regional and foreign banks. He has presented a number of speeches on financial institution accounting issues, particularly asset securitization.

Dennis F. Galletta, PhD, CPA, is an assistant professor of business administration at the Joseph M. Katz Graduate School of Business with research interests in human–computer interaction, user training, accounting information systems, and end-user computing. He is author of *COBOL with an Emphasis on Structured Program Design* (Prentice-Hall, 1985) and has published several MIS articles in various magazines.

Dale L. Gerboth, CPA, is a partner in the National Accounting Services Department of Ernst & Young. He is coauthor of the AICPA's Accounting Research Monograph No. 1, *Accounting for Depreciable Assets,* and has written and spoken extensively on accounting matters.

Irwin Goldberg, CPA, is a partner in the New York office of Deloitte & Touche specializing in real estate, leasing, and mergers and acquisitions. He is a contributor to the *Real Estate Accounting and Reporting Manual* (Warren, Gorham, & Lamont, 1990), as well as to the *Handbook of Accounting and Auditing* (Warren, Gorham, & Lamont, 1989).

Dan M. Guy, PhD, CPA, is vice-president of auditing at the AICPA. He is a coauthor of *Guide to Compilation and Review Engagements* (Practitioners Publishing Company, 1988) and has published numerous articles in professional journals and two auditing textbooks.

Philip M. Herr, JD, is a tax manager in the New York office of the international accounting firm Spicer & Oppenheim. As an attorney, he specializes in estates and trusts as well as in employee benefit plans.

Henry R. Jaenicke, PhD, CPA, is the C.D. Clarkson Professor of Accounting at Drexel University. He is the author of *Survey of Present Practices in Recognizing Revenues, Expenses, Gains, and Losses* (FASB, 1981) and is a coauthor of the 11th edition of *Montgomery's Auditing* (John Wiley & Sons, 1990). He has served as director to several AICPA committees.

Daniel W. Jones, CPA, is a national consulting partner at Deloitte & Touche in their Wilton, Connecticut, national office, and formerly of the Salt Lake City and Dallas executive offices. He responds to inquiries on business combinations, leasing, financial institutions, real estate, and revenue recognition.

Allyn A. Joyce is senior vice president for appraisals at Management Planning, Inc., of Princeton, New Jersey. He has appeared before various courts as a valuation expert witness.

Jeffrey H. Kinrich, CPA, is a partner in the Litigation Services practice at Price Waterhouse in Los Angeles. He specializes in the application of finance, statistics, and accounting to problems in damage quantification, forensic accounting, business valuation, and other litigation matters.

Terry A. Klebe, CPA, is a senior manager in the Houston office of Ernst & Young. He spent two years in the firm's National Accounting Services Department, where he consulted on complex and emerging accounting issues, including asset impairment and the accounting for depreciable assets.

Richard F. Larkin, CPA, is a senior manager in the Not-for-Profit Industry Services Group of Price Waterhouse. He is extensively involved in the development of accounting standards for not-for-profit organizations, is the chairman of the AICPA's Not-for-Profit Audit Guide task force, and is a member of the FASB Not-for-Profit Accounting Issues task force.

Sherwood P. Larkin, CPA, is a partner in the New York office of BDO Seidman specializing in financial services. He serves many of his firm's public clients and has written and spoken extensively on SEC requirements and accounting regulations.

John J. Mahoney, CPA, is a partner at Ernst & Young. He is a frequent writer and speaker on accounting topics and has served in Ernst & Young's National Accounting office.

Benjamin A. McKnight III, CPA, is a partner in Arthur Andersen & Company's Chicago office. He specializes in services to regulated enterprises, is a frequent speaker, and provides expert testimony on utility and telecommunication accounting topics.

John R. Miller, CPA, is a partner and national director of Government Services at KPMG Peat Marwick. He is chairman of the American Institute of CPA's Government Accounting and Auditing Committee and is a recognized authority on governmental financial management.

Paul B. W. Miller, PhD, CPA, is a professor of accounting at the University of Colorado at Colorado Springs. He has served on the staffs of the Financial Accounting Standards Board and the Office of the Chief Accountant of the Securities and Exchange Commission and is the coauthor of *The FASB: The People, the Process, and the Politics,* Second Edition (Irwin, 1988).

Mary Ellen Morris, CPA, has had more than 10 years of public accounting experience servicing small businesses and their principals and other high-net-worth individuals. She is currently employed by Porter and Travers, a New York City law firm.

Anthony J. Mottola, CPA, is the president and chief executive officer of Johnson, Shuart, and Darrow, Inc. Prior to that he was a senior partner in the international accounting firm Spicer & Oppenheim. He is coauthor of *Financial Disclosure Practices of the American Cities II: Closing the Communication Gap* (Coopers & Lybrand, 1978) and served as special assistant to New York City's Deputy Mayor for Finance. He was the first practice fellow at the Financial Accounting Standards Board.

Gordon A. Ndubizu, PhD, is an associate professor of accounting at Drexel University. He serves on the editorial board of *Advances in Accounting* and the *International Journal of Finance.*

Dennis S. Neier, CPA, is a partner at Deloitte & Touche and is the director of Litigation and Support Services. He is responsible for handling all phases of the litigation process and renders litigation consulting, support, and forensic accounting services to in-house counsel, lawyers in private practice, and insurance companies. He has authored several articles and is a frequent lecturer on accounting, auditing, business management, and litigation consulting and support services subjects.

Grant W. Newton, PhD, CPA, CMA, is a professor of accounting at Pepperdine University. He is the author of the two-volume set *Bankruptcy and Insolvency Accounting (Practice and Procedures; Forms and Exhibits),* Fourth Edition (John Wiley & Sons, 1989), and coauthor of *Bankruptcy Taxation* (John Wiley & Sons, 1991). He is a frequent contributor to professional journals and has lectured widely to professional organizations on bankruptcy-related topics.

Don M. Pallais, CPA, has his own practice in Richmond, Virginia, and is a member of the AICPA Auditing Standards Board. A former director at the AICPA, he has written a host of books, articles, and CPE courses on accounting topics.

Ronald J. Patten, PhD, CPA, is the dean of the College of Commerce and a professor of accounting at DePaul University. He was the first director of research for the Financial Accounting Standards Board and, recently, he has worked with Arthur D. Little International in the Eastern Caribbean.

M. Freddie Reiss, CPA, is a partner at Price Waterhouse specializing in litigation and reorganization services. He has served as an expert witness in bankruptcy and damage trials and often conducts forensic and fraud analyses for creditors' committees, trustees, and others.

Jacob P. Roosma is a senior manager specializing in business valuation with the New York office of Deloitte & Touche. He was previously vice president of Management Planning, Inc.

Steven Rubin, CPA, is director of quality control at Weissbarth, Altman & Michaelson, CPAs, New York City, and adjunct assistant professor of accounting at Brooklyn College of the City University of New York. For nearly 10 years, he held key staff positions at the AICPA and has published many books, articles, and other publications on accounting and reporting matters.

Angel Saez, CPA, is a senior manager in the San Juan, Puerto Rico, office of Price Waterhouse, currently on a two-year assignment in New York. He is a member of the Financial Services Industry specialty group. His experience includes savings and loan and money center banks.

Mona E. Seiler, CPA, is an associate professor of accountancy at Queensborough Community College of the City University of New York. She was on the staff of an international CPA firm and was affiliated with an international banking organization. Her articles have appeared in *The CPA Journal* and the *Journal of Accounting, Auditing, and Finance*. She is coauthor of the *1990 Accounting and Auditing Update Handbook* (AICPA, 1989).

Richard J. Shapiro, JD, is the national director of taxes and a principal in the international firm Spicer & Oppenheim. Before joining the firm, he practiced as a tax attorney with major New York City law firms.

E. Raymond Simpson, CPA, is a project manager at the Financial Accounting Standards Board. He served as project manager for SFAS No. 96, "Accounting for Income Taxes," and SFAS No. 52, "Foreign Currency Translation."

Raymond S. Sims, CPA, is a partner of Management Consulting Services in the Chicago office of Price Waterhouse. He has served as an expert witness and consultant in a wide range of litigation matters involving analysis and evaluation of financial data for determining the extent of damages.

Ashwinpaul C. Sondhi, PhD, is an associate professor at the Leonard N. Stern School of Business, New York University, and a member of Financial Analysts Policy Committee of the Financial Analysts Federation. His research interests include financial statement analysis, evaluation of accounting regulations, and the use of accounting data in financial markets.

Reed K. Storey, PhD, CPA, has more than 25 years' experience on the framework of financial accounting concepts, standards, and principles, working with both the Accounting Principles Board, as Director of Accounting Research of the AICPA, and the Financial Accounting Standards Board, as Senior Technical Advisor. He also has been a member of the accounting faculties of the University of California,

Berkeley, the University of Washington, Seattle, and Bernard M. Baruch College of the City University of New York, and a consultant in the executive offices of Coopers & Lybrand and Haskins & Sells (now Deloitte & Touche).

Anthony D. Todd, CPA, is a partner in the Investment Company Services Group of Price Waterhouse in New York. He previously worked in his firm's London and San Francisco offices and in the national office in New York, where he was responsible for resolving complex accounting issues.

Michael J. Walters, CPA, is a partner at KPMG Peat Marwick and is on assignment to Peat Marwick's Executive Office in New York City. He has been a frequent speaker and has authored a number of publications on the subject of executive compensation and capital accumulation plans.

Shawn Warren, CPA, is a senior manager and assistant to the National Director of Government Services of KPMG Peat Marwick. He is a frequent speaker on governmental accounting and financial reporting and has authored and taught training courses on these topics.

William Warshauer, Jr., CPA, is a partner at Price Waterhouse and chairman of the firm's Not-for-Profit Industry Services Group. He is coauthor of *Financial and Accounting Guide for Nonprofit Organizations,* Third Edition (John Wiley & Sons, 1982).

Gerald I. White, CFA, is the president of Grace & White, Inc., an investment counsel firm located in New York City, and an adjunct associate professor of accounting at the Leonard N. Stern School of Business, New York University. During the past 20 years, he has engaged in numerous professional activities relating to the use of accounting information in making investment decisions.

Jan R. Williams, PhD, CPA, is the Ernst & Young Professor and head of the department of accounting and business law at the University of Tennessee. He frequently contributes to academic and professional literature on financial reporting and accounting education and speaks at professional and continuing education programs.

Paul Ray Williams, CPA, is an audit manager with Coopers & Lybrand specializing in the oil and gas industry. His clients include public exploration and production companies as well as nonpublic entities. He is a contributing author to *Montgomery's Auditing* and various other Coopers & Lybrand publications, including the *Energy Newsletter*.

Alan J. Winters, PhD, CPA, is the Friends of Accounting–Donald H. Cramer Professor of Accounting at the University of South Carolina. Previously the director of auditing research at the AICPA, he has written many articles for professional journals and an auditing textbook. He is a member of the AICPA's Accounting and Review Services Committee.

Paul C. Wirth, CPA, is a partner in the Department of Professional Practice in KPMG Peat Marwick's executive office. In addition to providing consultation to Peat Marwick's operating offices on technical accounting and reporting issues, he is a frequent lecturer on such topics.

Lester Wolosoff, CPA, is a partner in the New York office of Grant Thornton. He was previously a regional director of Accounting and Auditing and has served on several committees of the AICPA and the New York State Society of CPAs.

Everett D. Wong, FAS, MAAA, EA, is a senior manager in the Employee Benefits Consulting Group of KPMG Peat Marwick's New York office. He has published articles on mergers and acquisitions and on supplemental executive retirement plans and has lectured on pension accounting and nonqualified retirement plans.

PREFACE

The seventh edition of the *Accountant's Handbook* has the same goal as the first edition, written nearly 70 years ago: to provide in a single reference source an answer to all reasonable questions on accounting and financial reporting that might be asked by accountants, auditors, executives, bankers, lawyers, financial analysts, and other users and preparers of accounting information.

The *Accountants' Handbook* is accounting's oldest handbook and has the longest tradition of providing comprehensive coverage of the field to both accounting professionals and professionals in other fields who have a need or desire to obtain a quick, understandable, and thorough exposure to a complex accounting-related subject.

Several changes have been made to make this edition handier and easier to use. The *Handbook* is presented in one streamlined volume of 36 chapters. To provide a single resource with the encyclopedic coverage that has been the hallmark of this *Handbook,* this edition has focused on financial accounting and related topics that are the common ground of interest for accounting and business professionals. Certain other topics such as independent auditing, data processing, and management information systems have been confined to single chapters. In contrast, coverage of financial and business accounting topics has been expanded.

The explosion in the scope and complexity of accounting principles and practice that dominated the preparation of the sixth edition has not abated. Although the FASB has continued as the primary source of authoritative accounting guidance, other sources of guidance have become very prominent. Pronouncements by the AICPA, SEC, GASB, and EITF have considerable importance in particular areas. After a brief stint of codifying existing specialized industry guidance under its own imprimatur, the FASB has apparently recognized the impossibility of being the originator of specialized accounting guidance. Within specialized areas today, it is necessary to look to guidance provided by the EITF and AICPA SOPs and guides. All of these sources of accounting guidance are included in this edition of the *Handbook.*

The seventh edition of the *Handbook* has been divided into the following convenient parts:

I. *Structure of Accounting Standards and Authoritative Rule-Making Organizations.* A comprehensive review of the framework of accounting guidance today and the organizations involved in its development.

II. *Financial Statements—Presentation and Analysis.* A compendium of specific guidance on general aspects of financial statement presentation, disclosure, and analysis.

III. *Financial Statement Areas.* Encyclopedic coverage of each specific financial statement area from cash through shareholders' equity.

IV. *Specialized Industries.* Comprehensive single-source coverage of the specialized environmental and accounting considerations for key industries.

V. *Compensation and Benefits.* In-depth coverage of accounting standards applying to pension, retirement plans, and employee stock compensation and other capital accumulation plans. Extensive coverage is provided for the application of measurement principles pertaining to executive compensation and capital accumulation plans.

VI. *Special Areas of Accounting.* A diverse blend of special topics from special entities (such as partnerships and estates and trusts) to specialized topics such as valuation and forensic accounting.

VII. *Topics in Auditing and Management Information Systems.* Focused but detailed coverage of these accounting-related areas.

This edition of the *Handbook* contains several new chapters about specialized industries or areas. Chapters on regulated utilities and financial institutions have been added to round out the section on specialized industries. Chapters have also been added in the special areas of prospective financial statements (forecasts and projections), personal financial statements, and forensic accounting and litigation consulting services.

For ease of use, lists of chapter titles, in both numerical and alphabetical order, appear on the inside front cover; a list of acronyms used in the book appears on the inside back cover.

For convenience the pronoun "he" has been used in this book to refer nonspecifically to the accountant and the person in business. We are aware that many women are also active in accounting practice and business. We did not intend to exclude them through the traditional choice of pronoun.

The specialized expertise of the individual authors remains the critical element of this edition as it was in the prior editions. The editors have worked closely with the authors, reviewing and critically editing their manuscripts. However, in the final analysis, each chapter is the work and viewpoint of the individual author or authors.

At one time, it was common for a handbook such as this to be prepared almost exclusively by university professors. That is no longer the case. Over two-thirds of the chapters in this edition are prepared by partners in accounting firms, financial executives, or financial analysts. Every major international accounting firm is represented among the authors. In the coverage of their chapters, these professionals bring to bear their own and their firms' experiences in dealing with accounting practice problems. All of the 58 authors are recognized authorities in their fields and have made significant contributions to the seventh edition of the *Handbook*.

Our greatest debt is to these 58 authors of the 36 chapters of this edition. We deeply appreciate the value and importance of their time and effort. We must also acknowledge our debt to the editors of and contributors to the six earlier editions of the *Handbook*. This edition draws heavily on the accumulated knowledge of those earlier editions. Finally, we wish to thank Joan Thompkins for handling the many details of organizing and coordinating this effort and our other colleagues at Baruch College, CUNY, for providing advice and support.

D. R. Carmichael
Steven B. Lilien
Martin Mellman

New York, New York
October 1990

CONTENTS

PART I

STRUCTURE OF ACCOUNTING STANDARDS AND AUTHORITATIVE RULE-MAKING ORGANIZATIONS

CHAPTER 1

THE FRAMEWORK OF FINANCIAL ACCOUNTING CONCEPTS AND STANDARDS

Reed K. Storey, PhD, CPA

Financial Accounting Standards Board

CONTENTS

Expressions of individual views by members of the Financial Accounting Standards Board and its staff are encouraged. The views expressed here are those of Mr. Storey. Official positions of the FASB on accounting matters are determined only after extensive due process and deliberation.

Mr. Storey wishes to acknowledge the assistance of Sylvia Storey, MBA, in the research for and writing of this chapter.

FINANCIAL ACCOUNTING AND REPORTING

The principal role of financial accounting and reporting is to serve the public interest by providing information that is useful in making business and economic decisions. That information facilitates the efficient functioning of capital and other markets, thereby promoting the efficient and equitable allocation of scarce resources in the economy. To undertake and fulfill that role, financial accounting in the 20th century has evolved from a profession relying almost exclusively on the experience and practice of a handful of illustrious practitioners into one replete with a set of financial accounting standards and an underlying conceptual foundation.

An underlying structure of accounting concepts was deemed necessary to provide to the institutions entrusted with setting accounting principles or standards the requisite tools for resolving accounting problems. Financial accounting now has a foundation of fundamental concepts and objectives in the Financial Accounting Standards Board's "Conceptual Framework for Financial Accounting and Reporting," which is intended to provide a basis for developing the financial accounting standards that are promulgated to guide accounting practice.

The FASB's conceptual framework and its antecedents constitute the major subject matter of this chapter. Some of the significant members of the cast of characters of this chapter, and of the *Accountants' Handbook,* need to be identified or briefly introduced. They already may be familiar acquaintances, if not old friends, of most readers or will become so in due course.

1.1 THE FASB AND GENERAL PURPOSE EXTERNAL FINANCIAL ACCOUNTING AND REPORTING.   **Financial accounting and reporting** is the familiar name of the branch of accounting whose precise but somewhat imposing full proper name is **general purpose external financial accounting and reporting.** It is the branch of accounting concerned with general purpose financial statements of business enterprises and not-for-profit organizations. General purpose financial statements are possible because several groups, such as investors, creditors, and other resource providers, have common interests and common informational needs. General purpose financial reporting provides information to users who are outside a business enterprise or not-for-profit organization and lack the power to require the entity to supply the accounting information they need for decision making; therefore, they must rely on information made available to them by the entity's management. Other groups, such as taxing authorities and rate-regulators, have specialized informational needs but also have the authority to require entities to provide the information they specify.

General purpose external financial reporting is the sphere of authority of the **Financial Accounting Standards Board,** the private sector organization that since 1973 has established **generally accepted accounting principles** in the United States. General purpose external financial accounting and reporting provides information that is based on generally accepted accounting principles, which result and have resulted primarily from the authoritative pronouncements of the FASB and its predecessors, and is audited by independent certified public accountants. It is also the branch of accounting on which the *Handbook* focuses.

The FASB's standards pronouncements—Statements of Financial Accounting Standards (often abbreviated FASB Statement, SFAS, or FAS)* and FASB Interpretations (often abbreviated FIN)*—are recognized as authoritative by both the **Securities and Exchange Commission** and the **American Institute of Certified Public Accountants** (Chapters 2 and 3 of the *Handbook*).

The FASB succeeded the **Accounting Principles Board,** whose authoritative pronouncements were the APB Opinions. In 1959 the APB had succeeded the **Committee on Accounting Procedure,** whose authoritative pronouncements were the **Accounting Research Bulletins** (often abbreviated ARB), some of which were designated as **Accounting Terminology Bulletins** (often abbreviated ATB).

With respect to the long name "general purpose external financial reporting," this chapter does what the FASB also has done: For convenience, it uses the term "financial reporting."

1.2 OTHER KINDS OF ACCOUNTING.   Financial accounting and reporting is only part of the broad field of accounting. The following paragraphs briefly note other significant kinds of accounting.

(a) Management Accounting.   Management accounting is internal accounting designed to meet the informational needs of managers, whose responsibilities for making decisions and planning and controlling operations at various administrative levels of a business enterprise or not-for-profit organization require more detailed information than is considered necessary or appropriate for external financial reporting even though the same accounting system usually accumulates, processes, and disseminates both management and financial accounting information. Management accounting includes information that is normally not provided outside an organization and is usually tailored to meet specific management information needs.

Aspects of management accounting are discussed in the following chapters:

- "Executive Compensation," Chapter 27.
- "Data Processing and Management Information Systems," Chapter 36.

(b) Tax Accounting.   Tax accounting is concerned with providing appropriate information needed by individuals and corporations for preparing the various returns and reports required to comply with tax laws and regulations, especially the Internal Revenue Code. It is based generally on the same procedures that apply to financial reporting. There are some significant differences, however, and taxing authorities have the statutory authority to prescribe the specific information they want taxpayers to submit as a basis for assessing the amount of income tax owed and do not need to rely on information provided to other groups.

Tax accountants are important participants in the administration of domestic tax laws, which are to a large extent self-assessing. Thus they need to be intimately familiar with federal, state, and local tax laws and regulations.

A tax accountant may be a public accountant who prepares a client's tax return and, if it is contested, defends it. Private accountants may supervise the tax departments and activities of an organization. Various taxing agencies employ accountants who participate in the assessing and collection of taxes and who audit tax returns. Tax accountants work closely with tax lawyers in matters such as estate planning or contested tax cases.

Taxation of estates and trusts, as well as other accounting aspects of those entities, are

---

*In the remaining chapters the acronyms SFAS and FIN will be used for these FASB pronouncements.

discussed in Chapter 31, "Estates and Trusts." The relationship of tax accounting and financial accounting is explained in Chapter 17, "Accounting for Income Taxes."

(c) Not-for-Profit Accounting.   Entities included in the general category of not-for-profit accounting are governmental, educational, and charitable, or eleemosynary, organizations. Since the primary goals of those organizations differ in some respects from those of business enterprises, their financial accounting and financial statements also differ in some ways. For example, not-for-profit organizations commonly use what is known as fund accounting.

Chapters in the *Handbook* that deal with not-for-profit accounting are:

- "State and Local Government," Chapter 24.
- "Not-for-Profit Organizations," Chapter 25.
- "Pension and Retirement Plans," Chapter 26.

(d) Some Specialized Areas of Accounting.   Within financial accounting and reporting, some industries and other areas have special accounting or reporting problems that require accounting standards or practices to supplement the general guidance.

Four chapters of the *Handbook* explain accounting matters for specialized industries:

- "Oil, Gas, and Other Natural Resources," Chapter 20.
- "Real Estate and Construction," Chapter 21.
- "Financial Institutions," Chapter 22.
- "Regulated Industries," Chapter 23.

Two other chapters explain certain accounting aspects of the partnership form of organization and entities that have been unable to pay their liabilities:

- "Partnerships," Chapter 30.
- "Bankruptcy," Chapter 33.

(e) International Accounting.   Aspects of international accounting include comparative study of accounting theory as it has developed in different countries, financial accounting and reporting needed to provide financial statements of multinational or transnational companies, and efforts to harmonize financial accounting standards issued by authoritative bodies in different countries. Those matters are discussed in Chapter 7, "Consolidation, Translation, and the Equity Method."

(f) National Income Accounting.   National income accounting is somewhat more statistically oriented than other areas already noted. It is a function of the Bureau of Economic Analysis of the U.S. Department of Commerce.

National income accounting provides information about the operation of a nation's economic system in terms of specific activities such as production, consumption, and capital formation. The national income accounts show effects of transactions between enterprises, households, governments, and the rest of the world. The gross output of the economy, or gross national product (GNP), is shown in terms of purchases made for private and public consumption, capital formation, and net sales abroad. GNP is balanced against how funds generated by productive activity are distributed to individuals for their roles in the production process or to government for taxes and other payments or are retained by producers.

National income accounts serve as the basis for a country's fiscal and monetary policy, provide information on growth and inflation rates, and show interrelationships among households, government, and foreign trade.

WHY WE HAVE A CONCEPTUAL FRAMEWORK

"Accounting principles" has proven to be an extraordinarily elusive term. To the nonaccountant (as well as to many accountants) it connotes things basic and fundamental, of a sort which can be expressed in few words, relatively timeless in nature, and in no way dependent upon changing fashions in business or the evolving needs of the investment community. (The Wheat Study Group, AICPA, 1972)

Principle. A general law or rule adopted or professed as a guide to action; a settled ground or basis of conduct or practice. (Accounting Research Bulletin No. 7)

A recurring theme in financial accounting in the United States in the 20th century has been the call for a comprehensive, authoritative statement of basic accounting **principles.** It has reflected a widespread perception that something more fundamental than rules or descriptions of methods or procedures was needed to form a basis for, explain, or govern financial accounting and reporting practice. A number of organizations, committees, and individuals in the profession have developed or attempted to develop their own variations of what they have diversely called **principles, standards, conventions, rules, postulates,** or **concepts.** Those efforts met with varying degrees of success, but by the 1970s none of the codifications or statements had come to be accepted or relied on in practice as the definitive statement of accounting's basic principles.

The pursuit of a statement of accounting principles has reflected two distinct schools of thought: that accounting principles are generalized or drawn from practice without reference to a systematic theoretical foundation; or that accounting principles are based on a few fundamental premises that together with the principles provide a framework for solving specific problems encountered in practice. Early efforts to codify or develop accounting principles were dominated by the belief that principles are essentially a "distillation of experience," a description generally attributed to George O. May, one of the most influential accountants of his time, who used it in the title of a book, *Financial Accounting: A Distillation of Experience* (1943). However, as accounting has matured and its role in society has increased, momentum in developing accounting principles has shifted to accountants and others who have come to understand what has been learned in many other fields: that reliance on experience alone leads only so far because environments and problems change; that until knowledge gained through experience is given order and discipline—purpose, direction, internal consistency, etc.—by a conceptual anchor, fundamentals must be reargued interminably and practice is blown in various directions by the winds of changing perceptions and proliferating accounting methods; and that only by studying and understanding the foundations of practices can the path of progress be discovered and the hope of improving practice be achieved.

The conceptual framework project of the Financial Accounting Standards Board thus far represents the most comprehensive effort to establish a structure of objectives and fundamentals to underlie financial accounting and reporting practice. To understand what it is, how it came about, and why it took the form and included the concepts that it did requires some knowledge of its antecedents, which extend back almost 50 years.

1.3 SPECIAL COMMITTEE ON CO-OPERATION WITH STOCK EXCHANGES.   The origin of the use of **principle** in financial accounting and reporting can be traced to a special committee of the American Institute of Accountants (American Institute of Certified Public Accountants since 1957). The Special Committee on Co-operation with Stock Exchanges, chaired by George O. May, gave the word special significance in the attest function of accountants. That significance is still evident in audit reports signed by members of the Institute and most other CPAs attesting that the financial statements of their clients present fairly, or do not present fairly, the client's financial position, results of operations, and cash flows "in conformity with generally accepted accounting principles." The committee laid the foundation that has been the basis of both subsequent progress in identifying or developing and enunciating accounting principles and many of the problems that have accompanied the resulting principles.

In 1930 the Institute undertook a cooperative effort with the New York Stock Exchange aimed at improving financial disclosure by publicly held enterprises. It was widely believed that inferior accounting and reporting practices had contributed to the stock market decline and depression that began in 1929. The Exchange was concerned that its listed companies were using too many different accounting and reporting methods to reflect similar transactions and that some of those methods were questionable. The Institute wanted to make financial statements more informative and authoritative, clarify the authority and responsibility of auditors, and educate the public about the conventional nature of accounting and the limitations of accounting reports.

The Exchange's Committee on Stock List and the Institute's Special Committee on Cooperation with Stock Exchanges exchanged correspondence between 1932 and 1934. The special committee's report, comprising a series of letters that passed between the two committees, was issued to Institute members in 1934 under the title, *Audits of Corporate Accounts* (reprinted in 1963). The key part was a letter dated September 22, 1932, from the Institute committee.

(a) "Accepted Principles of Accounting."   The special committee recommended that an authoritative statement of the broad accounting principles on which "there is a fairly general agreement" be formulated in consultation with a small group of qualified persons, including accountants, lawyers, and corporate officials. Within that framework of "accepted principles of accounting," each company would be free to choose the methods and procedures most appropriate for its financial statements, subject to requirements to disclose the methods it was using and to apply them consistently. Audit certificates (reports) for listed companies would state that their financial statements were prepared in accordance with "accepted principles of accounting." The special committee anticipated that its program would improve financial reporting because disclosure would create pressure from public opinion to eliminate less desirable practices.

The special committee did not define "principles of accounting" but it illustrated what it had in mind. It gave two explicit examples of accepted broad principles of accounting:

> It is a generally accepted principle that plant value should be charged against gross profits over the useful life of the plant. . . .

> Again, the most commonly accepted method of stating inventories is at cost or market, whichever is lower; . . . (*Audits of Corporate Accounts*, 1934, p. 7)

It also listed five principles that it presumed would be included in the contemplated statement of "broad principles of accounting which have won fairly general acceptance":

1. Unrealized profit should not be credited to income account of the corporation either directly or indirectly, through the medium of charging against such unrealized profits amounts which would ordinarily fall to be charged against income account. Profit is deemed to be realized when a sale in the ordinary course of business is effected, unless the circumstances are such that the collection of the sale price is not reasonably assured. An exception to the general rule may be made . . . [for industries in which trade custom is to take inventories at net selling prices, which may exceed cost].

2. Capital surplus [other paid-in capital], however created, should not be used to relieve the income account of the current or future years of charges which would otherwise fall to be made thereagainst. This rule might be subject to the exception that . . . [permits use of quasi-reorganization].

3. Earned surplus [retained earnings] of a subsidiary company created prior to acquisition does not form a part of the consolidated earned surplus of the parent company and subsidiaries; nor

can any dividend declared out of such surplus properly be credited to the income account of the parent company.

4. While it is perhaps in some circumstances permissible to show stock of a corporation held in its own treasury as an asset, if adequately disclosed, the dividends on stock so held should not be treated as a credit to the income account of the company.

5. Notes or accounts receivable due from officers, employees, or affiliated companies must be shown separately and not included under a general heading such as Notes Receivable or Accounts Receivable. (*Audits of Corporate Accounts*, 1934, p. 14. Lengthy exceptions in items 1 and 2 are summarized rather than quoted in full.)

The Institute submitted the committee's five principles for acceptance by its members in 1934, and they are now in ARB No. 43, "Restatement and Revision of Accounting Research Bulletins" (Ch. 1A, pars. 1–5).

The special committee's use of the word *principle* set the stage not only for the Institute's efforts to identify "accepted principles of accounting" but also for future confusion and controversy over what accountants mean when they use the word principle.

(i) But Were They "Principles"?   The special committee's examples of broad principles of accounting were much less fundamental, timeless, and comprehensive than what most people perceive to be principles. They had little or nothing in them that made them more basic or less concrete than conventions or rules. Moreover, the special committee itself referred to them as rules in describing exceptions to them, the Institute characterized them as rules in submitting them for approval by its members, and the chairman of the special committee later conceded that they were nothing more than rules:

> When the committee ... undertook to lay down some of the basic principles of modern accounting, it found itself unable to suggest more than half a dozen which could be regarded as generally acceptable, and even those were rules rather than principles, and were, moreover, admittedly subject to exception. (May, "Improvement in Financial Accounts," 1937, p. 335)

Not surprisingly, the special committee's use of "principles" was soon challenged. In a contest sponsored by the Institute for its 50th anniversary celebration in 1937, Gilbert R. Byrne's essay entitled "To What Extent Can the Practice of Accounting Be Reduced to Rules and Standards?" won first prize for the best answer to the question posed in the title. He complained about accountants' propensity to downgrade "principle" by equating it with terms such as "rule," "convention," and "procedure":

> [R]ecent discussions have used the term "accounting principles" to cover a conglomeration of accounting practices, procedures, conventions, etc.; many, if not most, so-called "principles" may merely have to do with methods of presenting items on financial statements or technique of auditing, rather than matters of fundamental accounting principle. (p. 366)

Stephen Gilman made the same point in his careful analysis of terms in five chapters of his book, *Accounting Concepts of Profit* (1939):

> With sublime disregard of lexicography, accountants speak of "principles," "tenets," "doctrines," "rules," and "conventions" as if they were synonymous. (p. 169)

Gilman also quoted an excerpt from the *Century Dictionary* that he thought pertinent "because of the confusion noted in some accounting writings [about] the distinction between 'principle' and 'rule' ":

> There are no two words in the English language used so confusedly one for the other as the words *rule* and *principle*. You can make a *rule;* you cannot make a *principle;* you can lay down a *rule;* you

cannot, properly speaking, lay down a *principle*. It is laid down for you. You can establish a *rule;* you cannot, properly speaking, establish a *principle*. You can only declare it. *Rules* are within your power, *principles* are not. A *principle* lies back of both *rules* and *precepts;* it is a general truth, needing interpretation and application to particular cases. (p. 188)

Byrne, Gilman, and others, pointed out that the form of accountant's report recommended by the special committee made accountants look foolish by requiring them to express opinions based on the existence of principles they actually could not specify. In that form of report, an accountant expressed the opinion that a client's financial statements "fairly present, *in accordance with accepted principles of accounting consistently maintained by the company during the year under review,* its position . . . and the results of its operations. . . ." According to Byrne, that opinion presumed that accepted principles of accounting actually existed and accountants in general knew and agreed on what they were. In fact, "While there have been several attempts to enumerate [those principles], to date there has been no statement upon which there has been general agreement" (p. 368).

That diagnosis was confirmed by Gilman as well as by Howard C. Greer:

[T]he entire body of precedent [the "accepted principles of accounting"] has been taken for granted.

It is as though each accountant felt that while he himself had never taken the time nor the trouble to make an actual list of accounting principles, he was comfortably certain that someone else had done so. . . .

. . . [T]he accountants are in the unenviable position of having committed themselves in their certificates [reports] as to the existence of generally accepted accounting principles while between themselves they are quarreling as to whether there are any accounting principles and if there are how many of them should be recognized and accepted. (Gilman, 1939, pp. 169–171)

There is something incongruous about the outpouring of thousands of accountants' certificates [reports] which refer to accepted accounting principles, and a situation in which no one can discover or state what those accepted accounting principles are. The layman cannot understand. (Greer, 1938, p. 25)

Byrne argued that lack of agreement on what constituted accepted accounting principles resulted "in large part because there is no clear distinction, in the minds of many, between that body of fundamental truths underlying the philosophy of accounts which are properly thought of as *principles,* and the larger body of accounting rules, practices and conventions which derive from principles, but which of themselves are not principles" (p. 368). His prescription for accountants was to use "principle" in its most commonly understood sense of being more fundamental and enduring than rules and conventions:

If accounting, as an organized body of knowledge, has validity, it must rest upon a body of principles, in the sense defined in Webster's New International Dictionary: "A fundamental truth; a comprehensive law or doctrine, from which others are derived, or on which others are founded; a general truth; an elementary proposition or fundamental assumption; a maxim; an axiom; a postulate." (p. 368)

Accounting principles, then, are the fundamental concepts on which accounting, as an organized body of knowledge, rests. . . . [T]hey are the foundation upon which the superstructure of accounting rules, practices and conventions is built. (p. 372)

Gilman, in contrast, could find no principles that fit Byrne's definition. He concluded that most, if not all, of the propositions that had been put forth as principles of accounting should be relabeled "as doctrines, conventions, rules, or mere statements of opinion" (p. 257). His prescription was that accountants should admit that there were no accounting principles in the fundamental sense and should waste no more time and effort on attempts to identify and state them but should concentrate on more fruitful propositions, such as conventions, doctrines, and rules.

(ii) May's Attempts to Rectify "Considerable Misunderstanding."   In several articles and a book, George O. May responded to those and other criticisms of "accounting principles" and explained what the special committee, as well as several other Institute committees of which he was chairman, had done and why. He detected, in the criticisms and elsewhere, what he described as considerable misunderstanding of both the nature of financial accounting and the committees' work on accounting principles and thought it necessary to get the matter back on the right track.

Although he acknowledged that "In the correspondence the [special] Committee had used the words 'rules,' 'methods,' 'conventions,' and 'principles' interchangeably" (*Financial Accounting,* 1943, p. 42), May considered questions such as whether the propositions should be called rules or principles not to be "of any real importance." As Byrne had pointed out, if there were any principles that fit his definition, "they must be few in number and extremely general in character (such as 'consistency' and 'conservatism')." Thus, they would afford less precise guidance than the more concrete principles illustrated by the special committee (May, "Principles of Accounting" [a comment on Byrne's essay], 1937, p. 424). Those who scolded the special committee for misusing "principles" were just barking up the wrong tree: ". . . accounting rules and principles are founded not on abstract theories or logic, but on utility" (May, 1942, p. 35).

May urged the profession and others to focus efforts to improve financial accounting, as had the special committee, on the questions "of real importance"—the consequences of the necessarily conventional nature of accounting and the limitations of accounting reports. He explained the philosophy underlying the recommendation of the special committee and summarized that philosophy in the introductory pages of his book:

> In 1926, . . . I decided to relinquish my administrative duties and devote a large part of my time to consideration of the broader aspects of accounting. As a result of that study I became convinced that a sound accounting structure could not be built until misconceptions had been cleared away, and the nature of the accounting process and the limitations on the significance of the financial statements which it produced were more frankly recognized.
>
> It became clear to me that general acceptance of the fact that accounting was utilitarian and based on conventions (some of which were necessarily of doubtful correspondence with fact) was an indispensable preliminary to real progress. . . .
>
> Many accountants were reluctant to admit that accounting was based on nothing of a higher order of sanctity than conventions. However, it is apparent that this is necessarily true of accounting as it is, for instance, of business law. In these fields there are no principles, in the fundamental sense of that word, on which we can build; and the distinctions between laws, rules, standards, and conventions lie not in their nature but in the kind of sanctions by which they are enforced. Accounting procedures have in the main been the result of common agreement between accountants, . . . (May, *Financial Accounting,* 1943, pp. 2–3)

He also reiterated and amplified a number of points the special committee had emphasized in *Audits of Corporate Accounts* concerning what the investing public already knew or should understand about financial accounting and reporting, such as, that because the value of a business depended mainly on its earning capacity, the income statement was more important than the balance sheet and should indicate to the fullest extent possible the earning capacity of the business during the period on which it reported; that because the balance sheet of a large modern corporation was to a large extent historical and conventional, largely comprising the residual amounts of expenditures or receipts after first determining a proper charge or credit to the income account for the year, it did not, and should not be expected to, represent an attempt to show the present values of the assets and liabilities of the corporation; and that because financial accounting and reporting was necessarily conventional, some variety in accounting methods was inevitable.

(iii) The Special Committee's Definition of Principle.   May not only identified the definition of "principle" the special committee had used but also explained why it had chosen that particular meaning. In his comment on Byrne's essay, he recalled the committee's discussion and searching of dictionaries before choosing the "perhaps rather magniloquent word 'principle'. . . in preference to the humbler 'rule.' " The definition of principle in the *Oxford English Dictionary* that came closest to defining the sense in which the special committee used the word was:

> A general law or rule adopted or professed as a guide to action; a settled ground or basis of conduct or practice; . . .

The time and effort spent in searching dictionaries was fruitful—the committee found exactly the definition for which it was looking:

> [The] . . . sense of the word "principle" above quoted seemed . . . to fit the case perfectly. Examination of the report as a whole will make clear what the committee contemplated; namely, that *each corporation should have a code of "laws or rules, adopted or professed, as a guide to action* [emphasis added]," and that the accountants should report, first, whether this code conformed to accepted usages, and secondly, whether it had been consistently maintained and applied." (May, "Principles of Accounting," 1937, pp. 423–424)

Thus, the special committee opted for the lofty "principle" rather than the more precise "rule" or "convention" because the definition that precisely fit the committee's needs was a definition of principle, albeit an obscure one, not a definition of rule or convention. Moreover, "rule" and "convention" carried unfortunate baggage:

> [T]he word "rules" implied the existence of a ruling body which did not exist; the word "convention" was regarded as not appropriate for popular use and in the opinion of some would not convey an adequate impression of the authority of the precepts by which the accounts were judged. (May, *Financial Accounting,* 1943, p. 42)

Whereas "principle" conveyed desirable implications:

> It used to be not uncommon for the accountant who had been unable to persuade his client to adopt the accounting treatment that he favored, to urge as a last resort that it was called for by "accounting principles." Often he would have had difficulty in defining the "principle" and saying how, why, and when it became one. But the method was effective, especially in dealing with those (of whom there were many) who regarded accounting as an esoteric but well established body of learning and chose to bow to its authority rather than display their ignorance of its rules. Obviously, the word "principle" was an essential part of the technique; "convention" would have been quite ineffective. (May, *Financial Accounting,* 1943, p. 37)

Rules were elevated into principles because the committee thought it necessary to use a word with the force or power of "principle" to prevent the auditor's authority from being lost on the client.

(b) The Best Laid Schemes . . .   The special committee's program focused on what individual listed companies and their auditors would do. Each corporation would choose from "accepted principles of accounting" its own code of "laws or rules, adopted or professed, as a guide to action" and within that framework would be free to choose the methods and procedures most appropriate for its financial statements, but would disclose the methods it was using and would apply them consistently. An auditor's report would include an opinion on whether each corporation's code consisted of accepted principles of accounting and was applied consistently. The Stock Exchange would enforce the program by requiring each listed corporation to comply in order to keep its listing.

The Institute was to sponsor or lead an effort in which accountants, lawyers, corporate officials, and other "qualified persons" would formulate a statement of "accepted principles of accounting" to guide listed companies and auditors, but it was not to get into the business of specifying those principles. The special committee had explicitly considered and rejected "the selection by competent authority out of the body of acceptable methods in vogue today [the] detailed sets of rules which would become binding on all corporations of a given class" (*Audits of Corporate Accounts,* 1934, p. 8). The special committee also had avoided using "rule" because the word implied a rule-setting body that did not exist, and it had no intention of imposing what it considered an unnecessary and impossible burden on anyone. "Within quite wide limits, it is relatively unimportant to the investor what precise rules or conventions are adopted by a corporation in reporting its earnings if he knows what method is being followed and is assured that it is followed consistently from year to year" (*Audits of Corporate Accounts,* 1934, p. 9). Moreover, no single body could adequately assess and allow for the varying characteristics of individual corporations, and the choice of which detailed methods best fit a corporation's circumstances was best left to each corporation and its auditors. Because financial accounting was essentially conventional and required estimates and allocations of costs and revenues to periods, the utility of the resulting financial statements inevitably depended significantly on the competence, judgment, and integrity of corporate management and independent auditors. Although there had been a few instances of breach of trust or abuse of investors, the committee had confidence in the trustworthiness of the great majority of those responsible for financial accounting and reporting.

In the end, the special committee's recommendations were never fully implemented. Nonaccountants were not invited to participate in developing a statement of accepted accounting principles. In fact, although the Institute submitted the special committee's five principles for acceptance by its members (pp. 1.6–1.7), it attempted no formulation of a statement of broad principles, even by accountants. Nor did the Exchange require its listed companies to disclose their accounting methods.

(c) The Special Committee's Heritage. The only recommendation to survive was that each company should be permitted to choose its own accounting methods within a framework of "accepted principles of accounting." The committee's definition of "principle" also survived, and "accepted principles of accounting" became "generally accepted."

The special committee's definition of principle—"A general law or rule adopted or professed as a guide to action; a settled ground or basis of conduct or practice"—was incorporated verbatim in Accounting Research Bulletin No. 7, "Reports of the Committee on Terminology," (George O. May, chairman) in 1940, but it was attributed to the *New English Dictionary* rather than to the *Oxford English Dictionary.* When Accounting Research Bulletin Nos. 1–42 were restated and revised in 1953, the same definition of principle, by then attributed only to "Dictionaries," was carried over to Accounting Terminology Bulletin No. 1.

"Generally" was added to the special committee's "accepted principles of accounting" in *Examination of Financial Statements by Independent Public Accountants,* published by the Institute in 1936 as a revision of an auditing publication, *Verification of Financial Statements* (1929). According to its chairman, Samuel J. Broad, the revision committee inserted "generally" to answer questions such as ". . . accepted by whom? business? professional accountants? the SEC? I heard of one accountant who claimed that if a principle was accepted by him and a few others it was 'accepted' " (Zeff, 1972, p. 129).

In retrospect, the legacy of institutionalizing that definition of "principle" has been that the terms *principle, rule, convention, procedure,* and *method* have been used interchangeably, and imprecise and inconsistent usage has hampered the development and acceptance of subsequent efforts to establish accounting principles. Moreover, the combination, within the context of so broad a definition of "principle," of the latitude given management in choosing accounting methods; the failure to incorporate into financial accounting and reporting the discipline that would have been imposed by the profession's adopting a few, broad, accepted accounting principles; and the failure to enforce the requirement that companies disclose their accounting methods gave refuge to the continuing use of many different methods and procedures, all justified as "generally accepted principles of accounting," and encouraged the proliferation of even more "generally accepted" accounting methods.

Finally, despite the reluctance of the Institute to become involved in principle- or rule-setting, it eventually assumed that responsibility after the U.S. Securities and Exchange Commission was created and given authority to prescribe accounting practices.

(d) Securities Acts and the SEC—"Substantial Authoritative Support."   The Securities Exchange Act of 1934 established the Securities and Exchange Commission and gave it authority to prescribe accounting and auditing practices to be used by companies in the financial reports required of them under that Act and the Securities Act of 1933. The SEC, like the Stock Exchange before it, became increasingly concerned about the variety of accounting practices approved by auditors. Carman G. Blough, first Chief Accountant of the SEC, told a round-table session at the Institute's 50th anniversary celebration in 1937 that unless the profession took steps to develop a set of accounting principles and reduce the areas of difference in accounting practice, the Commission would take over the process.

In April 1938, the Chief Accountant issued Accounting Series Release No. 4, "Administrative Policy on Financial Statements," requiring registrants to use only accounting principles having "substantial authoritative support." That made official and reinforced Blough's earlier message: If the profession wanted to retain the ability to determine accounting principles and methods, the Institute would have to issue statements of principles that could be deemed to have "substantial authoritative support." Through ASR No. 4, the Commission reserved the right to say what had "substantial authoritative support" but also opened the way to give that recognition to recommendations on principles issued by the Institute.

1.4 COMMITTEE ON ACCOUNTING PROCEDURE—1938–1959.   The Institute expanded significantly its committee on accounting procedure (not principles) and gave it responsibility for accounting principles and authority to speak on them for the Institute—to issue pronouncements on accounting principles without the need for approval of the Institute's membership or governing Council. The committee was intended to be the principal source of the "substantial authoritative support" for accounting principles sought by the SEC.

The president of the Institute was the nominal chairman of the committee on accounting procedure. Its vice chairman and guiding spirit was George O. May.

(a) No Comprehensive Statement of Principles by Institute.   The course the committee would follow for the next 20 years was set at its initial meeting in January 1939. Carman G. Blough, who had left the Commission and become a partner of Arthur Andersen & Co. and who was a member of the committee, recounted in a paper at a symposium at the University of California at Berkeley in 1967 how the committee chose its course:

> At first it was thought that a comprehensive statement of accounting principles should be developed which would serve as a guide to the solution of the practical problems of day to day practice. . . .
>
> After extended discussion it was agreed that the preparation of such a statement might take as long as five years. In view of the need to begin to reduce the areas of differences in accounting procedures before the SEC lost patience and began to make its own rules on such matters, it was concluded that the committee could not possibly wait for the development of such a broad statement of principles. (Blough, 1967, pp. 7–8)

The committee thus decided that the need to deal with particular problems was too pressing to permit it to spend time and effort on a comprehensive statement of principles.

(i) Statements of Accounting Principles by Others.   Although the Institute attempted no formulation of a statement of broad accounting principles, two other organizations did. Both statements were written by professors and were early representations of the two schools of thought about the nature and derivation of accounting principles.

AAA's Theoretical Basis for Accounting Rules and Procedures.   "A Tentative Statement of Accounting Principles Underlying Corporate Financial Statements," by the Executive Committee of the American Accounting Association in 1936, was based on the assumption "that a corporation's periodic financial statements should be continuously in accord with a single coordinated body of accounting theory" (p. 188). The phrase "Accounting Principles Underlying Corporate Financial Statements" emphasized that improvement in accounting practice could best be achieved by strengthening the theoretical framework that supported practice. The "Tentative Statement" was almost completely ignored by the Institute, and its effect on accounting practice at the time was minimal. However, two of its principles (one a corollary of the other) and a monograph by W. A. Paton and A. C. Littleton based on it proved to have long-lasting influence and are described shortly.

Sanders, Hatfield, and Moore's Codification of Accounting Practices.   In contrast to the AAA's attempt to derive a coordinated body of accounting theory, *A Statement of Accounting Principles*, by Thomas Henry Sanders, Henry Rand Hatfield, and Underhill Moore, two professors of accounting and a professor of law, respectively, was a compilation through interviews, discussions, and surveys of "the current practices of accountants" and reflected no systematic theoretical foundation. It was prepared under sponsorship of the Haskins & Sells Foundation and was published in 1938 by the Institute, which distributed it to all Institute members as "a highly valuable contribution to the discussion of accounting principles."

The report was excoriated for its virtually exclusive reliance on experience and current practice as the basis for principles, its reluctance to criticize even the most dubious practices, and its implication that accountants had no greater duty than to ratify whatever management wanted to do with its accounting as long as it was legal and properly disclosed. Many, perhaps most, of the characteristics criticized were inherent in what the authors were asked to do— formulate a code of accounting principles based on practice and the weight of opinion and authority. Even so, the report tended to strike a dubious balance between auditors' independence and duty to exercise professional judgment on the one hand and their deference to management on the other.

It was, nevertheless, "the first relatively complete statement of accounting principles and the only complete statement reflecting the school of thought that accounting principles are found in what accountants do. . . ." It was a successful attempt to codify the methods and procedures that accountants used in everyday practice and "was in fact a 'distillation of practice'" (Storey, 1964, p. 31). Moreover, since the committee on accounting procedure adopted and pursued the same view of principles and incorporated existing practice and the weight of opinion and authority in its pronouncements, *A Statement of Accounting Principles* probably was a good approximation of what the committee would have produced had it attempted to codify existing "accepted principles of accounting."

Sets of Principles by Individuals.   Three less ambitious efforts—eight principles in Gilbert R. Byrne's prize-winning essay (1937), nine accounting principles and conventions in D. L. Trouant's book *Financial Audits* (1937), and six accounting principles in A. C. Littleton's "Tests for Principles" (1938)—provided examples, rather than complete statements, of principles. Each described what "principles" meant and gave some propositions to illustrate the nature of principles or to show how propositions could be judged to be accepted principles. The resulting principles were substantially similar to those of the special committee. For example, all three authors included the conventions that revenue usually should be realized (recognized) at the time of sale and that cost of plant should be depreciated over its useful life. An interesting exception was Trouant's first principle—"Everything having a value has a claimant"—and the accompanying explanation: "In this axiom lies the basis of double-entry bookkeeping and from it arises the equivalence of the balance-sheet totals for assets and liabilities" (p. 5). Not only was that proposition more fundamental than most "principles" of the time but also was distinctive in referring to the world in which accounting takes place rather than to the accounting process.

(ii) Principles from Resolving Specific Problems.   None of those five efforts to state principles of accounting seem to have had much effect on practice, although Sanders, Hatfield, and Moore's *A Statement of Accounting Principles* may indirectly have affected the decision of the committee on accounting procedure to tackle specific accounting problems first: "[A]nyone who read it could not fail to be impressed with the wide variety of procedures that were being followed in accounting for similar transactions and in that way undoubtedly it helped to point up the need for doing something to standardize practices" (Blough, 1967, p. 7).

In any event, the committee on accounting procedure decided that to formulate a statement of broad accounting principles would take too long and elected instead to use a problem-by-problem approach in which the committee would recommend one or more alternative procedures as preferable to other alternatives for resolving a particular financial accounting or reporting problem. The decision to resolve pressing and controversial matters that way was described by members of the committee as "a decision to put out the brush fires before they created a conflagration" (Blough, 1967, p. 8).

(b) The Accounting Research Bulletins.   The committee's means of extinguishing the threatening fires were the Accounting Research Bulletins. From September 1939 through August 1959 it issued 51 ARBs on a variety of subjects. Among the most important or most controversial (or both) were: No. 2, "Unamortized Discount and Redemption Premium on Bonds Refunded" (1939); No. 23, "Accounting for Income Taxes" (1944); No. 24, "Accounting for Intangible Assets" (1944); No. 29, "Inventory Pricing" (1947); No. 32, "Income and Earned Surplus [Retained Earnings]" (1947); No. 37, "Accounting for Compensation in the Form of Stock Options" (1948); No. 40 and No. 48, "Business Combinations" (1950 and 1957); No. 47, "Accounting for Costs of Pension Plans" (1956); and No. 51, "Consolidated Financial Statements" (1959).

Each ARB described one or more accounting or reporting problems that had been brought to the committee's attention and identified accepted principles (conventions, rules, methods, or procedures) to account for the item(s) or otherwise to solve the problem(s) involved, sometimes describing one or more principles as preferable. Because each Bulletin dealt with a specific practice problem, or a set of related problems, the committee developed or approved accounting principles (to use the most common descriptions) case-by-case, ad hoc, or piecemeal.

(i) Piecemeal Principles Based on Practice, Experience, and General Acceptance.   As a result of the way the committee operated and the bases on which it decided issues before it, the Accounting Research Bulletins became classic examples of George O. May's dictum that "The rules of accounting, even more than those of law, are the product of experience rather than of logic" (May, *Financial Accounting*, 1943, p. vii). Despite having "research" in the name, the Accounting Research Bulletins, rather than being the products of research or theory, were much more the products of existing practice, the collective experience of the members of the committee on accounting procedure, and the need to be generally accepted.

Since the committee had not attempted to codify a comprehensive statement of accounting principles, it had no body of theory against which to evaluate the conventions, rules, and procedures that it considered. Although individual ARBs sometimes reflected one or more theories apparently suggested or applied by individual members or agreed on by the committee, as a group they reflected no broad, internally consistent, underlying theory. On the contrary, they often were criticized for being inconsistent with each other. The committee used the word consistency to mean that a convention, rule, or procedure, once chosen, should continue to be used in subsequent financial statements, not to mean that a conclusion in one Bulletin did not contradict or conflict with conclusions in others.

The most influential unifying factor in the ARBs as a group was the philosophy that underlay *Audits of Corporate Accounts* (American Institute of Accountants, 1934), a group of propositions that May and the special committee on co-operation with stock exchanges had described as pragmatic and realistic—not theoretical and logical. For example, the Bulletins clearly were based on the propositions that the income statement was far more important than the balance sheet; that financial accounting was primarily a process of allocating historical costs and revenues to periods rather than of valuing assets and liabilities; that the particular rules or conventions used were less significant than consistent use of whichever ones were chosen; and that some variety in accounting conventions and rules, especially in the methods and procedures for applying them to particular situations, was inevitable and desirable.

Most of the work of the committee on accounting procedure, like that of most Institute committees, was done by its members and their partners or associates, and the ARBs reflected their experience. The experience of Carman G. Blough also left its mark on the Bulletins after he became the Institute's first full-time director of research in 1944. The Institute had established a small research department with a part-time director in 1939, which did some research for the committee but primarily performed the tasks of a technical staff, such as providing background and technical memoranda as bases for the Bulletins and drafting parts of proposed Bulletins. Committee members and their associates did even more of the committee's work as the research department also began to provide staff assistance to the committee on auditing procedure in 1942 and then increasingly became occupied with providing staff assistance to a growing number (44 at one time) of other technical committees of the Institute.

The accounting conventions, rules, and procedures considered by the committee on accounting procedure and given its stamp of approval as principles in an ARB were already used in practice, not only because the committee had decided to look for principles in what accountants did but also because only principles that were already used were likely to qualify as "generally accepted." General acceptance was conferred by use, not by vote of the committee. Each Bulletin, beginning with ARB No. 4 in December 1939, carried this note about its authority: "Except in cases in which formal adoption by the Institute membership has been asked and secured, the authority of the bulletins rests upon the general acceptability of opinions . . . reached." The committee was authorized by the Institute to issue statements on accounting principles, which the Institute expected the SEC to recognize as providing "substantial authoritative support," but the committee had no authority to require compliance with the bulletins. It could only add a warning "that the burden of justifying departure from accepted procedures must be assumed by those who adopt other treatment."

(ii) Decision to Issue Principles Piecemeal Reaffirmed.   The need for a comprehensive statement or codification of accounting principles continued to be raised occasionally, and the committee on accounting procedure periodically revisited the question. Each time it decided against a project of that kind.

In 1949, however, the committee reconsidered its earlier decisions and began work on a comprehensive statement of accounting principles but again abandoned the project as not feasible. Instead, it issued ARB No. 43, "Restatement and Revision of Accounting Research Bulletins," in 1953. ARB No. 43 superseded the first 42 ARBs, except for 3 that were withdrawn as no longer applicable and 8 that were reports of the committee on terminology and were reviewed and published separately in Accounting Terminology Bulletin No. 1, "Review and Résumé." Although ARB No. 43 brought together the earlier bulletins and grouped them by subject matter, "this collection retained the original flavor of the bulletins, i.e., a group of separate opinions on different subjects" (Storey, 1964, p. 43).

Thus, the decision of the committee on accounting procedure at its first meeting to put out brush fires as they flared up rather than to codify accepted accounting principles to provide a basis for solving financial accounting and reporting problems set the course that the committee pursued for its entire 21-year history. All 51 ARBs reflected that decision.

(iii) Influence of the American Accounting Association.   During the 21 years that the committee on accounting procedure was issuing the ARBs, the AAA revised its 1936 "A Tentative Statement of Accounting Principles Underlying Corporate Financial Statements" in 1941, 1948, and 1957, including eight Supplementary Statements to the 1948 Revision. In the "Tentative Statement," as already noted, the executive committee of the AAA emphasized that improvement in accounting practice could best be achieved by strengthening the theoretical framework that supported practice and attempted to formulate a comprehensive set of concepts and standards from which to derive and by which to evaluate rules and procedures. Principles were not merely descriptions of procedures but standards against which procedures might be judged.

The executive committee of the Association, like the committees of the Institute concerned with accounting principles, regarded the principles as being derived from accounting practice, although the means of derivation differed—distillation or compilation by the Institute and theoretical analysis by the Association. Thus, the "Tentative Statement" set forth 20 principles, each a proposition embodying "a corollary of this fundamental axiom":

> Accounting is . . . not essentially a process of valuation, but the allocation of historical costs and revenues to the current and succeeding fiscal periods. (p. 188)

Although the AAA's intent was to emphasize accounting's conceptual underpinnings, the "Tentative Statement" was substantially less conceptual and more practice-oriented than might appear, not only because its principles were derived from practice but also because its "fundamental axiom" was essentially a description of existing practice. The same description of accounting was inherent in the report of the special committee on co-operation with stock exchanges, was voiced by George O. May at the annual meeting of the Institute in October 1935 (May, 1936, p. 15), and was evident in most of the ARBs.

That the principles in the Statements of the AAA were significantly like those in the ARBs should come as no surprise. "Inasmuch as both the Institute and the Association subscribed to the same basic philosophy regarding the nature of income determination, it was more or less inevitable that they should reach similar conclusions, even though they followed different paths" (Storey, 1964, p. 45).

The AAA's 1941 and 1948 revisions generally continued in the direction set by the 1936 "Tentative Statement." Some changes began to appear in some of the Supplementary Statements to the 1948 Revision and the 1957 Revision. They probably were too late, however, to have had much effect on the ARBs, even if the committee on accounting procedure had paid much attention.

Long-lasting influence on accounting practice of the "Tentative Statement," as noted earlier, came some time after it was issued and mostly indirectly through two of its principles on "all-inclusive income" (one a corollary of the other) and a monograph by W. A. Paton and A. C. Littleton (1940).

"ALL-INCLUSIVE INCOME" AND "DISTORTION OF PERIODIC INCOME."   "A Tentative Statement of Accounting Principles Underlying Corporate Financial Statements" strongly supported what was later called the "all-inclusive income" or "clean surplus" theory. The principle (No. 8, p. 189), which gave the theory one of its names, was that an income statement for a period should include all revenues, expenses, gains, and losses properly recognized during the period "regardless of whether or not they are the results of operations in that period." The corollary (No. 18, p. 191), which gave the theory its other name, was that no revenues, expenses, gains, or losses should be recognized directly in earned surplus (retained earnings or undistributed profits).

The SEC later strongly supported that accounting, and it became a bone of contention between the SEC and the committee on accounting procedure. The committee generally favored the "current operating performance" theory of income, which excluded from net income extraordinary and nonrecurring gains and losses "to avoid distorting the net income for the period." Net income was judged to be a highly significant number whose determination was deemed to be the primary function of financial accounting. The committee and the SEC worked out a number of compromises, but each proved unsatisfactory to one or both parties, leading them to try still another compromise.

Eventually the Accounting Principles Board adopted an all-inclusive income statement. That accounting and reporting has since been modified by admitting some significant exceptions, primarily by FASB Statement No. 12, "Accounting for Certain Marketable Securities," and FASB Statement No. 52, "Foreign Currency Translation." Thus, net income reported under current generally accepted accounting principles cannot accurately be described as "all-inclusive income," but the idea of "all-inclusive income" is still generally highly regarded and many still see it as a desirable goal to which to return.

"MATCHING OF COSTS AND REVENUES" AND "ASSETS ARE COSTS."   Two members of the executive committee that issued "A Tentative Statement of Accounting Principles Underlying Corporate Financial Statements" in 1936 undertook to write a monograph to explain its concepts. The result, *An Introduction to Corporate Accounting Standards,* by W. A. Paton and A. C. Littleton (1940), easily qualifies as the academic writing that has been most influential in accounting practice. Although the monograph rejected certain existing practices—such as LIFO and cost or market, whichever is lower—it generally rationalized existing practice, providing it with what many saw as a theoretical basis that previously had been lacking.

The monograph accepted two of the premises that underlay the ARBs: (1) that periodic income determination was the central function of financial accounting—"the business enterprise is viewed as an organization designed to produce income" (p. 23)—and (2) that (in the words of the "fundamental axiom" of the AAA's 1936 "Tentative Statement") accounting was "not essentially a process of valuation, but the allocation of historical costs and revenues to the current and succeeding fiscal periods."

> The fundamental problem of accounting, therefore, is the division of the stream of costs incurred between the present and the future in the process of measuring periodic income. The technical instruments used in reporting this division are the income statement and the balance sheet. . . . The income statement reports the assignment [of costs] to the current period; the balance sheet exhibits the costs incurred which are reasonably applicable to the years to come. (p. 67)

The monograph described the periodic income determination process as the "matching of costs and revenues," giving it not only a catchy name but also strong intuitive appeal—a process of relating the enterprise's efforts and accomplishments. The corollary was that most assets were "deferred charges to revenue," costs waiting to be "matched" against future revenues:

> The factors acquired for production which have not yet reached the point in the business process where they may be appropriately treated as "cost of sales" or "expense" are called "assets," and are presented as such in the balance sheet. It should not be overlooked, however, that these "assets" are in fact "revenue charges in suspense" awaiting some future matching with revenue as costs or expenses.

> The common tendency to draw a distinction between cost and expense is not a happy one, since expenses are also costs in a very important sense, just as assets are costs. "Costs" are the fundamental data of accounting, . . . (p. 25)

> The balance sheet thus serves as a means of carrying forward unamortized acquisition prices, the not-yet-deducted costs; it stands as a connecting link joining successive income statements into a composite picture of the income stream. (p. 67)

Not surprisingly, those who had supported the accounting principles developed in the ARBs but were uncomfortable with those principles' apparent lack of theoretical support found highly attractive the theory that "matching costs and revenues" not only determined periodic net income but also justified the practice of accounting for most assets at their historical costs or an unamortized portion thereof.

However, just as the institutionalizing of a broad definition of accounting principles later caused problems for the committee on accounting procedure itself and for the Accounting Principles Board, the institutionalizing of "matching costs with revenues," "costs are assets," and "distorting periodic income" also later caused problems for the Financial Accounting Standards Board in developing a conceptual framework for financial accounting and reporting. The Board found those expressions not only to be ingrained in accountants' vocabularies and widely used as reasons for or against particular accounting or reporting procedures but also to be generally vague, highly subjective, and emotion laden. They have proved to be of minimum help in actually resolving difficult accounting issues.

(c) Failure to Reduce the Number of Alternative Accounting Methods. The Institute's effort aimed at improving accounting by reducing the number of acceptable alternatives actually did improve accounting by culling out some "bad" practices:

> There are those who seem to believe that very little progress has been made towards the development of accounting principles and the narrowing of areas of differences in the principles followed in practice.

> It is difficult for me to see how anyone who has knowledge of accounting as it was practiced during the first quarter of this century and how it is practiced today can fail to recognize the tremendous advances that have taken place in the art. (Blough, 1967, p. 12)

A number of the practices for whose acceptance Sanders, Hatfield, and Moore's *A Statement of Accounting Principles* had been lambasted had disappeared by the time the committee on accounting procedure was 10 years old. It is uncertain how much of that improvement was due to the ARBs and how much to other factors, such as the good professional judgment of auditors or corporate officials or the SEC's rejection of some egregious procedures.

Ironically, the end result was an overabundance of "good" practices that had survived the process. That plethora of sanctioned alternatives for accounting for similar transactions continued to thrive despite the committee's charge to reduce the number of alternative procedures because, to paraphrase Will Rogers, who never met a man he didn't like, the committee rarely met an accounting principle it didn't find acceptable:

> Two factors contributed to the increase in the number of accepted alternatives: (1) the committee on accounting procedure failed to make firm choices among alternative procedures, and (2) the committee was clearly reluctant to condemn widely used methods even though they were in conflict with its recommendations. For example, in its very first pronouncement on a specific problem—unamortized discount and redemption premium on refunded bonds [ARB No. 2]—the committee considered three possible procedures, of which it rejected one and accepted two.

> The committee had a clear preference—it praised the method of amortization of cost over the remaining life of the old bonds as consistent with good accounting thinking regarding the relative

importance of the income statement and the balance sheet. It condemned immediate writeoff as a holdover of balance-sheet conservatism which was of "dubious value if attained at the expense of a lack of conservatism in the income account, which is far more significant" [ARB No. 2, p. 13]. Nevertheless, the latter method had "too much support in accounting theory and practice and in the decisions of courts and commissions for the committee to recommend that it should be regarded as unacceptable or inferior." (p. 20)

. . . The solution turned out to be a "live-and-let-live" policy. The major thing accomplished by the bulletin was the elimination of a method [amortization over the life of the new issue] which was not widely used anyway. And this type of solution was characteristic of the bulletins, rather than exceptional.

The extreme to which this attitude was sometimes carried is exemplified in the Institute's inventory bulletin [ARB No. 29], a classic example of trying to please everyone. The committee accepted almost every conceivable inventory [pricing] procedure, except the discredited base-stock method. The committee therefore passed up the opportunity to narrow the range of acceptable alternative procedures in the area of inventory [pricing]. . . . Instead, the individual practitioner was left with the high-sounding but useless admonition that the method chosen should be the one which most clearly reflected periodic income. (Storey, 1964, pp. 49–50)

The proliferation of accepted alternative principles was probably inherent in an approach that championed disclosure and consistency in use of procedures over specific principles and consistency between principles.

Most of the controversial subjects covered by the Accounting Research Bulletins came back to haunt the Accounting Principles Board. The case-by-case, ad hoc, or piecemeal approach produced few lasting solutions to financial accounting and reporting problems.

1.5 ACCOUNTING PRINCIPLES BOARD—1959–1973. The American Institute of Accountants changed its name to the American Institute of Certified Public Accountants in June 1957, and in October of that year the new president of the AICPA, Alvin R. Jennings, proposed that the Institute reorganize its efforts in the area of accounting principles. His recommendation came at a time when the committee on accounting procedure was under fire for, among other things, failing to reduce the number of alternative accounting procedures. A growing number of Institute members sensed that the committee's fire-fighting approach to accounting principles had gone about as far as it could and expressed an urgent need for the committee to abandon that effort and to do what it had theretofore been reluctant to do—formulate or codify a comprehensive statement of accounting principles. Jennings called for an increased research effort to reexamine the basic assumptions of accounting and to develop authoritative statements to guide accountants. He appointed a special committee on research program, and its report, "Organization and Operations of the Accounting Research Program and Related Activities," in December 1958, provided the basis for the organization of an Accounting Principles Board and an Accounting Research Division. The committee set a lofty goal:

The general purpose of the Institute in the field of financial accounting should be to advance the written expression of what constitutes generally accepted accounting principles, for the guidance of its members and others. This means something more than a survey of existing practice. It means continuing effort to determine appropriate practice and to narrow the areas of difference and inconsistency in practice. In accomplishing this, reliance should be placed on persuasion rather than on compulsion. The Institute, however, can, and it should, take definite steps to lead in the thinking on unsettled and controversial issues. (pp. 62–63)

The Accounting Principles Board in September 1959 replaced the committee on accounting procedure as the senior technical committee of the Institute with responsibility for accounting principles and authority to issue pronouncements on accounting principles without the need for approval of the Institute's membership or governing Council. The Board's 18 members were members of the Institute, and thus CPAs, who, like members of the committee on accounting procedure, continued their affiliations with their firms, companies, and universities while serving without compensation on the Board.

The APB was originally envisioned as the instrument through which a definitive statement of accounting principles would finally be achieved—what the Wheat Study Group's report later called a " 'grand design' of accounting theory upon which all else would rest." The report of the special committee on research program in 1958 outlined a hierarchy of postulates, principles, and rules to guide the APB's work:

> The broad problem of financial accounting should be visualized as requiring attention at four levels: first, postulates; second, principles; third, rules or other guides for the application of principles in specific situations; and fourth, research.
>
> Postulates are few in number and are the basic assumptions on which principles rest. They necessarily are derived from the economic and political environment and from the modes of thought and customs of all segments of the business community. The profession . . . should make clear its understanding and interpretation of what they are, to provide a meaningful foundation for the formulation of principles and the development of rules or other guides for the application of principles in specific situations. . . .
>
> A fairly broad set of co-ordinated accounting principles should be formulated on the basis of the postulates. The statement of this probably should be similar in scope to the statements on accounting and reporting standards issued by the American Accounting Association. The principles, together with the postulates, should serve as a framework of reference for the solution of detailed problems.
>
> Rules or other guides for the application of accounting principles in specific situations, then, should be developed in relation to the postulates and principles previously expressed. Statements of these probably should be comparable as to subject matter with the present accounting research bulletins. They should have reasonable flexibility.
>
> Adequate accounting research is necessary in all of the foregoing. (p. 63)

The report of the special committee on research program contemplated that the APB would quickly concern itself with providing the conceptual context from which would flow the rules or procedures to be applied in specific situations. The APB would then use the postulates and principles in choosing between alternate rules and procedures to narrow the areas of difference and inconsistency in practice.

(a) Postulates and Principles.   Following that prescription, the new accounting research division published Accounting Research Study No. 1, "The Basic Postulates of Accounting," by Maurice Moonitz in 1961, and Accounting Research Study No. 3, "A Tentative Set of Broad Accounting Principles for Business Enterprises," by Robert T. Sprouse and Maurice Moonitz in 1962. Accounting Research Studies were not publications of the APB and thus did not constitute official Institute pronouncements on accounting principles. On the authority of the Director of Accounting Research, Maurice Moonitz, they were issued for wide exposure and comment.

In an article entitled "Why Do We Need 'Postulates' and 'Principles'?" Moonitz explained that postulates and principles were necessary to give accounting "the integrating structure it needs to give more than passing meaning to its specific procedures. It will provide 'experience' with the aid it needs from 'logic' to explain why it is that some procedures are appropriate and others are not" (p. 46). It would provide accounting with a mechanism by which to rid itself of procedures that clearly were not in harmony with the authoritatively stated principles.

Among the most significant contributions of those Accounting Research Studies was their use of the terms "postulates" and "principles," especially postulates, which Moonitz explained in his article:

> "[P]ostulates" is used . . . to denote those basic propositions of accounting which describe the accountant's understanding of the world in which he lives and acts. The propositions are therefore generalizations about the environment of accounting, generalizations based upon a more or less comprehensive view and understanding of that environment. The term "principles" is used to denote those basic propositions which stem from the postulates and refer expressly to accounting issues. (p. 43)

To qualify as a postulate, a proposition had to meet two conditions: It must be "self-evident," an assertion about the environment in which accounting functions that is universally accepted as valid; and it must be "fruitful for accounting," that is, it must "relate to (be inferred from) a world that does exist and not to one that is a fiction." Moonitz also noted that self-evident is not, as some who commented on ARS No. 1 seemed to have believed, the same as trivial (pp. 44–45). An example to which he referred made his point: "**Postulate A-2. Exchange.** Most of the goods and services that are produced are distributed through exchange, and are not directly consumed by the producers." In that straightforward observation lie the reasons that accounting is concerned with production and distribution of goods and services and with exchange prices; if it is further observed that most exchanges are for cash, the reasons that accounting is concerned with cash prices and cash flows become apparent. As Moonitz observed, the "proposition is an extraordinarily fruitful one for accounting" (ARS No. 1, p. 22).

Emphasis on a basis for accounting principles comprising self-evident propositions about the real-world environment in which accounting functions, and on which it reports, constituted a significant shift in thinking. Accountants' earlier emphasis, largely in a conceptual vacuum, had been on the conventional nature of accounting and the resulting necessity for conventional procedures, allocations, opinion, and judgment to produce the numbers in income statements and balance sheets. The latter provided an unstable and uncertain basis for accounting principles:

> Accounting is often described as "conventional" in nature, and its principles as "conventions." The two terms, conventions and conventional, are ambiguous; the statement that accounting is conventional may be true or false depending on which meaning is intended. It is true if it refers to such things as the use of Arabic numerals, the use of the dollar sign, or the sequence in which assets, liabilities, revenues, and expenses are listed in financial statements because other symbols and forms could be used to convey precisely the same message. It is not true if the statement means that any proposition which accountants accept is a valid one. As a farfetched example, assume that all uninsured losses, without exception, were to be converted into "assets" by the expedient of calling them "deferred charges against future operations." This convention would not make assets out of losses; it would merely give the approval of accountants to a false assertion concerning the enterprise that suffered the losses, and would place accountants and accounting in an unfavorable light in the eyes of those who knew what had happened.

> Suppose, however, that the assertion about accounting principles as "conventions" is intended to convey the idea that they are generalizations, inferences drawn from a large body of data, and that they are not intended to be literal descriptions of reality. "Conventions" and "conventional" are clearly valid descriptions, then, but not because accounting is unique. Instead, accounting is like every other field of human endeavor in this one respect: its basic propositions are generalizations or abstractions and not minute descriptions of every aspect of "reality." (Moonitz, 1963, pp. 45–46)

Postulates that were self-evident propositions about the real world and also fruitful for accounting were needed to provide a solid basis for accounting principles and rules—"a platform from which to start," "a place to stand"—and "a place to stand" was prerequisite to real improvement in accounting practice. "Failure by accountants to agree on a 'place to stand' will mean continued operation in mid-air, as unstable and uncertain in the future as in the past'' (p. 45).

In the more than quarter century since the two studies were published, their valuable contributions to accounting thought increasingly have been recognized. Some of the conclusions and recommendations of ARS No. 3, such as use of replacement costs of inventories and plant and equipment and accounting for the effects of changes in the general price level, have remained controversial and still are largely unacceptable to many accountants. In contrast, most of the conclusions of ARS No. 1 long ago became commonplace in accounting literature. For example, the basic idea that the foundation for accounting principles lies in self-evident propositions about the environment in which accounting functions was incorporated into APB Statement No. 4, *Basic Concepts and Accounting Principles Underlying Financial Statements of Business Enterprises,* in 1970. By 1975 it had become an essential part of the FASB's conceptual framework.

When ARS No. 3 was published in April 1962, however, each copy contained a Statement of the Accounting Principles Board (later designated APB Statement No. 1) passing judgment on both studies: ''The Board believes . . . that while these studies are a valuable contribution to accounting thinking, they are too radically different from present generally accepted accounting principles for acceptance at this time.''

It was not the APB's finest hour. Even though general dissatisfaction with the state of existing practice had been the reason for the APB's creation and the new emphasis on research, the Board, and many others, reacted as if they had been caught by surprise that the studies recommended some significant changes in existing practice. Moreover, instead of letting consideration of the studies follow the anticipated course of wide circulation and exposure and receipt of comments from interested readers before the Board considered the studies, the Board reacted first, spoiling any opportunity of receiving unbiased comments on the studies. The experience seems to have affected the Board's approach to postulates and principles for years.

The experience may have made the APB ''disillusioned with, or at least skeptical toward, the potential that fundamental or 'theoretical' research might have for solving accounting problems. . . . [T]he Board seemed to abandon the hope of the Special Committee on Research Program that such research could serve as a foundation for pronouncements on accounting principles'' (Zeff, 1972, pp. 177, 178). In any event, the Board did little or nothing more on accounting postulates and principles until 1965, except to authorize the project that in March 1965 became ARS No. 7, ''Inventory of Generally Accepted Accounting Principles,'' by Paul Grady, the second Director of Accounting Research. In 1965, the Board renewed efforts on basic matters to comply with recommendations to the Institute's governing Council by the Special Committee on Opinions of the Accounting Principles Board (the Seidman Committee), but most Board members seemed to lack enthusiasm for the effort.

By the summer of 1962, when the Board hoped that it had put behind it the fuss over the postulates and principles studies, three years had passed since an Institute committee had issued an accounting pronouncement. The Board turned its attention from postulates and principles and toward solving specific problems, just as had the committee on accounting procedure.

(b) The APB, the Investment Credit, and the Seidman Committee.   When the Board decided to tackle the thorny issue of accounting for the investment credit, which was enacted in federal income tax law for the first time in October 1962, it inadvertently created an ideal scenario for fueling doubts about its effectiveness and authority. The law provided that a company acquiring a depreciable asset other than a building could deduct up to 7% of the cost of the asset from its income tax otherwise payable in the year the asset was placed in service. Two accounting methods sprang up—the ''flow-through'' method, by which the entire reduction in tax was included in income of the year the asset was placed in service, and the ''deferral'' method, by which the tax reduction was included in net income over the productive life of the acquired property.

APB Opinion No. 2, "Accounting for the 'Investment Credit,'" was issued in December 1962, setting forth the Board's choice of the deferral over the flow-through method. Some of the large accounting firms known as the Big Eight almost immediately made it known that they would not expect their clients to abide by the Opinion. The SEC ruled that both methods had substantial authoritative support, making either acceptable and thereby effectively undercutting the Board's position. Fifteen months later, the Board issued APB Opinion No. 4 (Amending No. 2), "Accounting for the 'Investment Credit,'" reaffirming its opinion that the investment credit should be accounted for by the deferral method. It recognized, however, the inevitable effect of the SEC's action on the authority of APB Opinion No. 2:

> [T]he authority of Opinions of this Board rests upon their general acceptability. The Board, in the light of events and developments occurring since the issuance of Opinion No. 2, has determined that its conclusions as there expressed have not attained the degree of acceptability which it believes is necessary to make the Opinion effective.
>
> In the circumstances, the Board believes that . . . the alternative method of treating the credit as a reduction of Federal income taxes of the year in which the credit arises is also acceptable. (pars. 9–10)

The APB's authority had been severely undermined. Did APB Opinions still have to pass the test of general acceptance, as did the ARBs before them, or did they constitute generally accepted accounting principles solely because the APB had issued them? The Board voted to bring the matter to the Executive Committee and the governing Council of the AICPA.

In May 1964, after an extended and heated debate, Council adopted a resolution "That it is the sense of this Council that [audit] reports of members should disclose material departures from Opinions of the Accounting Principles Board, . . ." Pursuant to a directive in the resolution, the Institute formed a Special Committee on Opinions of the Accounting Principles Board to suggest ways of implementing the resolution and to review the entire matter of the status of APB Opinions and the development of accounting principles and practices for financial reporting.

The special committee reported to Council on its first charge in October 1964, and Council adopted a resolution and transmitted it to Institute members in a Special Bulletin, "Disclosure of Departures from Opinions of the Accounting Principles Board." It declared that members of the Institute should see to it that a material departure from APB Opinions (or from ARBs still in effect)—even if the auditor concluded that the departure rested on substantial authoritative support—was disclosed in notes to the financial statements or in the auditor's report. Since Council adopted recommendations that "1. 'Generally accepted accounting principles' are those principles which have substantial authoritative support [and] 2. Opinions of the Accounting Principles Board constitute 'substantial authoritative support[,]'" the authority of APB Opinions no longer depended on their passing a separate test of general acceptability.

The special committee, commonly referred to as the Seidman committee after its chairman, J. S. Seidman, reported to Council on its second charge in May 1965, reiterating that an authoritative identification of generally accepted accounting principles was essential if an independent CPA was to fulfill his or her primary function of attesting to the conformity of financial statements with generally accepted accounting principles. Its **Recommendation No. 1** was that:

> At the earliest possible time, the [Accounting Principles] Board should:
>
> (a) Set forth its views as to the purposes and limitations of published financial statements. . . .
>
> (b) Enumerate and describe the basic concepts to which accounting principles should be oriented.

(c) State the accounting principles to which practices and procedures should conform.

(d) Define such phrases in the auditor's report as "present fairly" and "generally accepted accounting principles." . . .

(f) Define the words of art employed by the profession, such as "substantial authoritative support," "concepts," "principles," "practices," "procedures," "assets," "liabilities," "income," and "materiality." (AICPA, 1965, p. 12)

The committee made that recommendation acknowledging that the special committee on research program had contemplated that the APB would have accomplished the task described by that time in its life but exculpated the Board: "This planned course ran into difficulty because current problems commanded attention and could not be neglected" (p. 13).

However, the need for a solid conceptual foundation for accounting no longer could be neglected either:

[I]t remains true that until the basic concepts and principles are formulated and promulgated, there is no official bench mark for the premises on which the audit attestation stands. Nor is an enduring base provided by which to judge the reasonableness and consistency of treatment of a particular subject. Instead, footing is given to controversy and confusion. (p. 13)

. . . Accounting, like other professions, makes use of words of art. Since accounting talks to the public, the profession's meaning, as distinguished from the literal dictionary meaning, must be explained to the public.

For example, . . .

What is meant by the expression "generally accepted accounting principles"? How is "generally" measured? What are "accounting principles"? Where are they inscribed, and by whom? . . .

By "accepted," is the profession aiming at what is popular or what is right? There may be a difference. The . . . Special Committee on Research Program said that "what constitutes generally accepted accounting principles . . . means more than a survey of existing practice."

Then again, "accepted" by whom—the preparer of the financial statement, the profession, or the user? (pp. 13–14)

The profession has said that generally accepted accounting principles are those with "substantial authoritative support." What does that expression mean? What yardstick is to be applied to the words "substantial" and "authoritative"? What are the guidelines to prevent mere declaration, or use by someone, somewhere, from becoming the standard?

Many other expressions in accounting need explanation and clarification for the public. They include such words as "concepts," "principles," "practices," "procedures," "assets," "liabilities," "income," and "materiality."

Until the profession deals with all these matters satisfactorily, first for itself and then for understanding by the consumer of its product, there will continue to be an awkward failure of communication in a field where clear communication is vital. (p. 15)

(c) APB Statement No. 4. APB Statement No. 4, "Basic Concepts and Accounting Principles Underlying Financial Statements of Business Enterprises," issued in October 1970, was the Board's response to the Seidman committee's recommendations. For those who had hoped for definitive answers to the Seidman committee's questions or a statement of accounting's fundamental concepts and principles, APB Statement No. 4 was a disappointment. The Board gave every indication of having issued it primarily to comply, somewhat grudgingly, with the Seidman committee's recommendations.

The definition of generally accepted accounting principles in APB Statement No. 4 and its description of their nature and how they become accepted, although couched in the careful language that characterized the Statement, merely reiterated what the Institute had been saying about them for over 30 years:

Generally accepted accounting principles incorporate the consensus[38] at a particular time as to . . . [the items that should be recognized in financial statements, when they should be recognized, how they should be measured, how they should be displayed, and what financial statements should be provided].

. . . Generally accepted accounting principles encompass the conventions, rules, and procedures necessary to define accepted accounting practice at a particular time. . . . includ[ing] not only broad guidelines of general application, but also detailed practices and procedures.

Generally accepted accounting principles are conventional—that is, they become generally accepted by agreement (often tacit agreement) rather than by formal derivation from a set of postulates or basic concepts. The principles have developed on the basis of experience, reason, custom, usage, and, to a significant extent, practical necessity. (pars. 137–139)

---

[38]Inasmuch as generally accepted accounting principles embody a consensus, they depend on notions such as *general acceptance* and *substantial authoritative support*, which are not precisely defined. . . .

Generally accepted accounting principles were a mixture of conventions, rules, procedures, and detailed practices, which were distilled from experience and identified as principles primarily by observing existing accounting practice.

The basic concepts in Chapters 3–5 of APB Statement No. 4 were a mixed bag. On one hand, the definitions of assets, liabilities, and other "basic elements of financial accounting" were what George J. Staubus, who gave the Statement a generally positive review, called "The Definitions Mess" (1972, p. 39). All of the definitions were defective because the only essential distinguishing characteristic of an asset (or liability) was that it was "recognized and measured [as an asset (or liability)] in conformity with generally accepted accounting principles," and the other definitions depended on the definitions of assets and liabilities.

On the other hand, the basic concepts also included new ideas (at least for Institute pronouncements) and normative propositions, and at least some of the concepts looked to what financial accounting ought to be in the future, not just to what it already was. These are examples: The basic purpose of financial accounting is to provide information that is useful to owners, creditors, and others in making economic decisions (pars. 40, 73); financial accounting is shaped to a significant extent by the nature of economic activity in individual business enterprises (par. 42); the transactions and other events that change an enterprise's resources, obligations, and residual interest include exchange transactions, nonreciprocal transfers, and other external events as well as production and other internal events (par. 62); certain qualities or characteristics such as relevance, understandability, verifiability, neutrality, timeliness, comparability, and completeness make financial information useful (pars. 23, 87–105); and to make comparisons between enterprises as meaningful as possible, "differences between enterprises' financial statements should arise from basic differences in the enterprises themselves or from the nature of their transactions and not merely from differences in financial accounting practices and procedures" (par. 101). Anyone familiar with the report of the Trueblood Study Group on objectives of financial statements and the FASB's conceptual framework will recognize that those and similar ideas later appeared in one or both of those sources.

Nevertheless, in describing itself, the Statement virtually ignored that it contained anything that was new, normative, or forward-looking, emphasizing instead that it looked only at the present and the past, even in describing its basic concepts. The Board was adamant that it had not passed judgment on the existing structure and apparently was almost equally reluctant to admit that it had broken new ground:

> The Statement is primarily descriptive, not prescriptive. It identifies and organizes ideas that for the most part are already accepted. . . . [T]he Statement contains two main sections that are essentially distinct—(a) Chapters 3 to 5 on the environment, objectives, and basic features of financial accounting and (b) Chapters 6 to 8 on present generally accepted accounting principles.

The description of present generally accepted accounting principles is based primarily on observation of accounting practice. Present generally accepted accounting principles have not been formally derived from the environment, objectives, and basic features of financial accounting [that is, from the basic concepts*].

The aspects of the environment selected for discussion are those that appear to influence the financial accounting process directly. The objectives of financial accounting and financial statements discussed are goals toward which efforts *are presently directed* [emphasis added]. The accounting principles described are those that the Board believes are generally accepted *today*. *The Board has not evaluated or approved present generally accepted accounting principles except to the extent that principles have been adopted in Board Opinions. Publication of this Statement does not constitute approval by the Board of accounting principles that are not covered in its Opinions* [emphasis in the original]. (pars. 3–4)

[———
*"The term *basic concepts* is used to refer to the observations concerning the environment, the objectives of financial accounting and financial statements, and the basic features and basic elements of financial accounting discussed in Chapters 3–5 of the Statement" (par. 1, ftn. 2). For some unexplained reason, the Statement does not use the term *basic concepts* after paragraph 1, using instead the full definition in footnote 2 or some shorter variation of it.]

The expected contribution of the basic concepts in the Statement was generally vague, and still in the future:

The Statement is a step toward development of a more consistent and comprehensive structure of financial accounting and of more useful financial information. It is intended to provide a framework within which the problems of financial accounting may be solved, although it does not propose solutions to those problems and does not attempt to indicate what generally accepted accounting principles should be. Evaluation of present accounting principles and determination of changes that may be desirable are left to future pronouncements of the Board. (par. 6)

Those paragraphs seemed to deflate unduly the most laudable parts of the Statement, almost as if the Board had gone out of its way to disparage the effort or otherwise lower expectations about it. Instead of emphasizing that APB Statement No. 4 had begun to lay a basis for delineating what accounting ought to be and suggesting positive steps needed to build on it, the Board chose to characterize the Statement as primarily descriptive, thereby casting it into the category of uncritical description of what accounting already was. Once again, accounting principles had been defined as being essentially the product of experience.

However, there were by then too many people within and outside the profession who could no longer be satisfied with that view of accounting principles. Principles distilled from experience could lead only so far, and that point had long since been reached. For 15 to 20 years, principles distilled from experience had created more problems than they had solved, and a growing number of people interested in accounting principles had become convinced that principles had to be defined to mean a higher order of things than conventions or procedures. Dissatisfaction with the APB's performance in this area was mounting, and there was increasing pressure for the Board to state "the objectives of financial statements" as a basis for moving forward.

(d) The End of the APB. At the same time, the APB was constantly under pressure from the SEC and others to confront current, specific problems encountered in practice and to issue opinions on subjects seemingly far removed from the domain of principles, such as the presumed overstating of sales prices in some real estate sales with long-term financing, accounting for nonmonetary transactions, and reporting the effects of disposing of a segment of a business.

The SEC's urgency to deal with specific practice problems and widespread criticism of the use of the pooling of interests method influenced the APB and its staff to expend extra effort to produce an opinion on a highly controversial subject—accounting for business combinations—on which the Accounting Research Division had completed two related Accounting Research Studies: No. 5, "A Critical Study of Accounting for Business Combinations," by Arthur R. Wyatt, and No. 10, "Accounting for Goodwill," by George R. Catlett and Norman O. Olson.

Although the Board worked diligently and analyzed the problems about as well as could be expected in the absence of postulates and principles or other conceptual foundation, it became hopelessly deadlocked. It could find no solutions acceptable to a two-thirds majority to the problems of choosing between the purchase and pooling of interest methods for accounting for a business combination and of whether and how to capitalize goodwill and, if capitalized, whether to amortize it. Yet, it felt compelled to issue an opinion because the SEC was almost certain to issue its own rule if the APB failed to do so.

The experience produced two opinions in 1970, APB Opinion No. 16, "Business Combinations," and No. 17, "Intangible Assets," as well as more intense criticism of, and threats of legal action against, the Board. In a section entitled "Opinions 16 and 17—Vesuvius Erupts," Stephen A. Zeff reported that neither the Board's "hard-won compromise" nor the "'pressure-cooker' manner in which it was achieved" pleased anyone. "These two Opinions, perhaps more than any other factor, seem to have been responsible for a movement to undertake a comprehensive review of the procedure for establishing accounting principles" (Zeff, 1972, p. 216).

In January 1971 AICPA President Marshall S. Armstrong convened a conference to consider how the Institute might improve the process of establishing accounting principles, and two study groups were appointed to explore ways of improving financial reporting. The group chaired by Francis M. Wheat was formed to "examine the organization and operation of the Accounting Principles Board and [to] determine what changes are necessary to attain better results faster." The Wheat Group was primarily concerned with the processes and means by which accounting principles should be established. The Accounting Objectives Study Group, under the chairmanship of Robert M. Trueblood, was organized to review the objectives of financial statements and the technical problems in achieving those objectives.

The APB's days were numbered, although that was not yet clear, and perhaps not even suspected, in 1971, and the Board went on with its work. It issued almost half of its total of 31 opinions after wheels were put in motion to develop an alternative structure that would eventually replace it.

Despite the criticisms it received for Opinions 16 and 17 and others and although some of its Opinions provided only partial solutions that would need to be revisited in the future, on balance the APB's Opinions must be characterized as successful. In several problem areas, the APB succeeded in remedying, sometimes almost completely and often to a significant degree, the greatest ill of the time by carrying out the charge it received at its creation: "to determine appropriate practice and to narrow the areas of difference and inconsistency in practice." APB Opinions such as No. 9, "Reporting the Results of Operations"; No. 18, "The Equity Method of Accounting for Investments in Common Stock"; and No. 20, "Accounting Changes," laid to rest longstanding controversies. APB Opinion No. 22, "Disclosure of Accounting Policies," required implementation in 1972 of one of the key recommendations made in *Audits of Corporate Accounts,* in 1932: Each company would disclose which methods it was using. Some of the most controversial APB Opinions—such as, No. 5, "Reporting of Leases in Financial Statements of Lessee"; No. 8, "Accounting for the Cost of Pension Plans"; No. 11, "Accounting for Income Taxes"; No. 16, "Business Combinations"; No. 17, "Intangible Assets"; No. 21, "Interest on Receivables and Payables"; and No. 26, "Early Extinguishment of Debt"—caused some consternation and often fierce opposition, but both industry and public accountants learned to live with them, and later the FASB encountered opposition when it proposed changing some of them.

The Report of the Wheat Group in March 1972, "Establishing Financial Accounting Standards," concluded that many of the APB's problems were grave flaws. The APB was weakened by nagging doubts about its independence, the inability of its part-time members to devote themselves entirely to the important problems confronting it, and the lack of coherence and logic of many of its pronouncements, which resulted from having to compromise too many opposing points of view. The Group's solution was directed toward remedying those flaws, which, in its opinion, required a new arrangement.

Its report proposed establishment of a Financial Accounting Foundation, with trustees whose principal duties would be to appoint the members of a Financial Accounting Standards Board and to raise funds for its operation. The Board would comprise seven members, all of whom would be salaried, full-time, and unencumbered by other business affiliations during their tenure on the Board, and some of whom would not have to be CPAs. The Group recommended **Standards** Board rather than **Principles** Board because:

> [T]he APB (despite the prominence in its name of the term "principles") has deemed it necessary throughout its history to issue opinions on subjects which have almost nothing to do with "principles" in the usual sense [which connotes something fundamental and basic that is relatively timeless and constant and can be expressed in few words]. (AICPA, 1972, p. 13)

Standard—which connotes something established by authority or common consent as a pattern or model for guidance or a basis of comparison for judging quality, quantity, grade, level, and so on, and may need to be spelled out in some detail—was more descriptive than principles for most of what the APB did and what the FASB was expected to do.

The popular diagnosis of the APB's terminal condition was not the only one. Oscar S. Gellein, a member of the APB during its final years and a member of the FASB during its early years, offered a perceptive analysis:

> The conditions most often identified with the problems of the APB were perceived conflicts of interests causing a waffling of positions and part-time effort where full-time effort was needed. In retrospect, those probably were not as significant as the absence of a structure of fundamental notions that would elevate the level at which debate begins and provide assurance of considerable consistency to the standards pronounced. The APB repetitively argued fundamentals. The same fundamentals were argued in taking up projects near the end of its tenure as were argued in connection with early projects. Even the most fundamental of fundamentals—assets, liabilities, revenue, expense—were never defined nor could the definitions be inferred from APB pronouncements. (Gellein, 1986, p. 13)

Thus, it may have been the Board's continual rejection of the ineluctable need to develop an underlying philosophy as a basis for accounting principles in favor of the committee on accounting procedure's "brush fire" approach that most directly contributed to the way it was perceived and ultimately to its demise. The APB had never been able to achieve a consensus on the conceptual aspects of its work, which had effectively been pushed aside by the Board's efforts to narrow the areas of difference in accounting practice by a problem-by-problem treatment of pressing issues. Although the Accounting Research Studies on basic postulates and broad principles of accounting and APB Statement No. 4 had made conceptual contributions that would prove fruitful in the hands of the Study Group on objectives of financial statements and the FASB, the APB steadfastly refused to take credit for, or even acknowledge, those contributions. Thus, accounting was still without a statement of fundamental principles at the end of the APB's tenure, and its absence would continue to plague the profession until the FASB, mostly on its own initiative, did something about it.

1.6 THE FASB FACES DEFINING ASSETS AND LIABILITIES.   The FASB, which was not part of the AICPA, began operations in Stamford, Connecticut, on January 2, 1973, with Marshall S. Armstrong, the first Chairman, and a small staff. The other six Board members and additional staff joined the group during the first half of the year, and the FASB was fully operational by the time it succeeded the APB at midyear.

Meanwhile, the Institute had approved a restated code of professional ethics that in a new Rule 203 covered for the first time infractions of the recommendations adopted by Council in 1964 regarding disclosure of departures from APB Opinions:

> A member shall not express an opinion that financial statements are presented in conformity with generally accepted accounting principles if such statements contain any departure from an accounting principle promulgated by the body designated by Council to establish such principles. . . .

Council at its May 1973 meeting designated the FASB as the body to establish principles covered by Rule 203. The APB issued its final two Opinions—No. 30 and No. 31—and went out of business on June 30, 1973.

Later that year, the SEC's Accounting Series Release No. 150, "Statement of Policy on Establishment and Improvement of Accounting Principles and Standards," reaffirmed the policy set forth 35 years earlier in ASR No. 4 and declared that the Commission would recognize FASB Statements and Interpretations as having, and contrary statements as lacking, substantial authoritative support.

The FASB set its first technical agenda of seven projects in early April 1973, including a project called "Broad Qualitative Standards for Financial Reporting." The Board undertook the project in expectation of receiving the Report of the Trueblood Study Group, noting:

> [A]s [the Board] develops specific standards, and others apply them, there will be a need in certain cases for guidelines in the selection of the most appropriate reporting. . . . [and] the report of the special AICPA committee on objectives of financial statements chaired by Robert Trueblood will be of substantial help in this project. (FASB *Status Report*, June 18, 1973)

The FASB received the Report of the Trueblood Study Group, "Objectives of Financial Statements," in October 1973. The Study Group had concluded:

> Accounting is not an end in itself. . . . [T]he justification for accounting can be found only in how well accounting information serves those who use it. Thus, the Study Group agrees with the conclusion drawn by many others that "The basic objective of financial statements is to provide information useful for making economic decisions." (p. 61)

The Report's other eleven objectives were more specific; for example, the next two identified the purposes of financial statements with the information needs of those with "limited authority, ability, or resources to obtain information and who rely on financial statements as their principal source of information about an enterprise's economic activities" and with the decisions of actual and potential owners and creditors about placing resources available for investment or loan (p. 62). The Report also included a group of seven "qualitative characteristics of reporting" that information "should possess . . . to satisfy users' needs" (p. 57).

Soon afterward, the FASB announced that the scope of "Broad Qualitative Standards for Financial Reporting" had been broadened because:

> The members of the Standards Board believe that the . . . project should encompass the entire conceptual framework of financial accounting and reporting, including objectives, qualitative characteristics and the information needs of users of accounting information. (FASB News Release, December 20, 1973)

The Board also for the first time used the title, "Conceptual Framework for Accounting and Reporting."

(a) Were They Assets? Liabilities?   In the meantime, two of the other original projects confronted the new Board with the key questions of what constituted and what did not constitute an asset or a liability. The FASB's first technical agenda included some unfinished projects inherited from the APB. One was on accounting for research and development and similar costs, which eventually resulted in FASB Statement No. 2 "Accounting for Research and Development Costs" (October 1974), and FASB Statement No. 7, "Accounting and Reporting by Development Stage Enterprises" (June 1975); the other was on accruing for future losses, which eventually resulted in FASB Statement No. 5, "Accounting for Contingencies" (March 1975). Principal questions raised by those projects were: Do expenditures for research and development, start-up, relocation, and the like result in assets? Do "reserves for self-insurance," "provisions for expropriation of overseas operations," and the like constitute liabilities? decreases in assets?

The Board quite naturally turned to pertinent definitions in the authoritative accounting pronouncements, the definitions of assets and liabilities in APB Statement No. 4. The definitions proved to be circular (as explained in section (i) below) and therefore of no use to the FASB in deciding the major questions raised by the projects and of no use to anyone else in trying to anticipate how the Board would decide the issues in the two projects.

The Board had to turn elsewhere for useful definitions of assets and liabilities to resolve the issues in those projects, and Board members learned that an early priority of the Board's conceptual framework project would have to be providing definitions of assets and liabilities and other elements of financial statements to fill a yawning gap in the authoritative pronouncements.

The reasons that the FASB found the definitions of assets and liabilities in APB Statement No. 4 to be useless underlie the Board's subsequent actions on the conceptual framework project. The related topics, the proliferation of "what-you-may-call-its," the pervasive influence of the belief in "proper matching to avoid distorting periodic net income," and the common use of the expressions "assets are costs" and "costs are assets" help explain not only why Board members took the initiative in establishing a conceptual framework for financial accounting and reporting but also why the Board adopted the basic concepts that it did. Robert T. Sprouse used the term "what-you-may-call-its" to describe certain "deferred charges" and "deferred credits" included in balance sheets without much consideration of whether they actually were assets or liabilities (Sprouse, 1966), and the name has become widely used; "proper matching," "nondistortion of periodic net income," and "assets are costs" originated in the 1930s and 1940s, as noted in section 1.4 (b) (iii) of this chapter, and became widely used in the 1950s, 1960s, and 1970s.

(i) Assets, Liabilities, and What-You-May-Call-Its.   The introduction to the definitions of assets and liabilities in APB Statement No. 4 said: "The basic elements of financial accounting— assets, liabilities . . .—are related to the economic resources, economic obligations . . . discussed [earlier]" (par. 130), suggesting that the Statement's discussion of economic resources and obligations provided a basis for the definitions of assets and liabilities. The Statement did define economic resources and economic obligations in a way that both accountants and nonaccountants would understand them to be, or to be synonymous with, what they also generally understood to be assets and liabilities:

> Economic resources are the scarce means (limited in supply relative to desired uses) available for carrying on economic activities. The economic resources of a business enterprise include:
> 1. *Productive resources* . . . the means used by the enterprise to produce its product. . . .
> 2. *Products.* . . . 3. *Money* 4. *Claims to receive money* 5. *Ownership interests in other enterprises.* (par. 57)

> The economic obligations of an enterprise at any time are its present responsibilities to transfer economic resources or provide services to other entities in the future. . . . Economic obligations include: 1. *Obligations to pay money* 2. *Obligations to provide goods or services.* (par. 58)

Moreover, the first sentence of the parallel definitions of assets and liabilities in paragraph 132 did identify assets with economic resources and liabilities with economic obligations:

{*Assets/Liabilities*} economic {resources/obligations} of an enterprise that are recognized and measured in conformity with generally accepted accounting principles. . . .

The second sentence of the definitions broke the relationships between assets and economic resources and between liabilities and economic obligations, however, by including what-you-may-call-its in assets and liabilities:

{Assets/Liabilities} also include certain deferred {charges/credits} that are not {resources/obligations} but that are recognized and measured in conformity with generally accepted accounting principles.

The definitions actually defined nothing: assets were whatever (economic resources and what-you-may-call-its) generally accepted accounting principles recognized and measured as assets, and liabilities were whatever (economic obligations and what-you-may-call-its) generally accepted accounting principles recognized and measured as liabilities. They were circular: Since the FASB was the body responsible for determining generally accepted accounting principles, research and development costs were assets, and self-insurance reserves were liabilities, if the Board said they were.

Nevertheless, APB Statement No. 4's definitions of assets and liabilities actually were descriptions of items recognized as assets and liabilities in practice. But why should balance sheets include as assets and liabilities items that lacked essential characteristics of what most people would understand to be assets and liabilities—items that involved no scarce means of carrying out economic activities, such as consumption, production, or saving, or items that involved no obligations to pay cash or provide goods or services to other entities?

(ii) Proper Matching to Avoid Distorting Periodic Net Income.   The Board issued a Discussion Memorandum—a neutral document that describes issues and sets forth arguments for and against particular solutions or procedures but gives no Board conclusions—for each of the two projects and scheduled public hearings. At the hearings, respondents to the Discussion Memorandums were able to explain or clarify their analyses of the issues, and Board members could ask questions to pursue certain points made in comment letters and otherwise make sure they understood respondents' proposed solutions to the issues raised by the Discussion Memorandum and their underlying reasoning.

The Board discovered in the comment letters and the hearings that many respondents were less interested in what constituted assets and liabilities than in whether capitalizing and amortizing research and development costs and accruing self-insurance reserves "properly matched" costs with revenues and thus did not "distort periodic net income." Many of the respondents argued that "proper matching" required research and development and similar costs to be capitalized and amortized over their useful lives. Similarly, many argued that "proper matching" required self-insurance and similar costs to be accrued or otherwise "provided for" each period, whether or not the enterprise suffered damage from fire, earthquake, heavy wind, or other cause during the period. Unless the Board required proper matching of costs and revenues, many respondents counseled, periodic income of the affected enterprises would be distorted.

Board members were largely frustrated in their attempts to pin down what respondents meant by "proper matching" and "periodic income distortion," but the reasons for the proliferation of what-you-may-call-its emerged clearly. The following four snippets paraphrase what Board members heard at the hearings on research and development and similar costs and accounting for contingencies. Two of them are clear standing alone; two are understandable only if the questions being answered are also included:

1. **Q.** In other words, you would focus on the measurement of income? You would not be concerned about the balance sheet?

   A. Yes. I think that is the major focus.

2. Much of the controversy over accrual of future loss has focused on whether a company had a liability for future losses or not. However, the impact on income should be overriding. The credit that arises from a provision for self-insurance is not a liability in the true sense, but that in and of itself should not keep it out of the balance sheet. APB Opinion 11 recognized deferred tax credits in balance sheets even though all agreed that the credit balances were not liabilities. Income statement considerations were considered paramount in that case, and similar thinking should prevail in accounting for self-insurance.

3. Defining assets does not really solve the problem of accounting for research and development expenditures and similar expenses. If some items that do not meet the definition of an asset are included in expenses of the current period, they may well distort the net income of that period because they do not relate to the revenues of that period. That accounting also may distort the net income of other periods in which the items more properly belong. The Board should focus on deferrability that gets away from the notion of whether or not those costs are assets and concentrates on the impact of deferral on the determination of net income.

4. **Q.** One of your criteria for capitalization is that net income not be materially distorted. Do you have any operational guidelines to suggest regarding material distortion?

   A. The profession has been trying to solve that one for a great many years and has been unsuccessful. I really do not have an answer.

   Q. Then, is material distortion a useful criterion that we can work with?

   A. Yes, I believe it is. Despite the difficulty, I think it is necessary to work with that criterion. It is a matter of applying professional judgment. (*FASB Public Record,* 1974, Vol. I, Part 2, pp. 171–172, 189–190; Vol. III, Part 2, pp. 18–19, 65)

Board members were not satisfied with the kind of answers just illustrated:

> Members of the FASB concluded early that references to vague notions such as "avoiding distortion" and "better matching" were neither an adequate basis for analyzing and resolving controversial financial accounting issues nor an effective way to communicate with one another and with the FASB's constituency. (Sprouse, 1988, p. 127)

Many of the responses indeed were vague, and it soon became clear that proper matching and distortion of periodic net income were, like beauty, largely in the eye of the beholder. Respondents said essentially that although they had difficulty in describing proper matching and distorted income, they knew them when they saw them and could use professional judgment to assure themselves that periodic net income was determined without distortion in individual cases. The thinking and practice described in the comment letters and at the hearings seemed to make income measurement primarily a matter of individual judgment and provided no basis for comparability between financial statements. To Board members, the arguments for including in balance sheets items that could not possibly qualify as assets or liabilities—what-you-may-call-its—sounded a lot like excuses to justify smoothing reported income, decreasing its volatility.

The experience generally strengthened Board members' commitment to a broad conceptual framework—one beginning with objectives of financial statements and qualitative characteristics (the Trueblood Group report) and also defining the elements of financial statements and including concepts of recognition, measurement, and display—and affected the kind of concepts it would comprise.

(b) Nondistortion, Matching, and What-You-May-Call-Its.   The proliferation of what-you-may-call-its and durability of apparently widely held and accepted notions of accounting such as the overriding importance of "avoidance of distortion of periodic income" and "proper matching of costs with revenues" were the legacy of 40 years of accountants' emphasis on the accounting process and accounting procedures instead of on the economic things and events on which financial accounting is supposed to report. As a result, an accounting convention or procedure with narrow application but a catchy name was elevated to the focal point of accounting: Matching of costs and revenues to determine periodic net income for a period became the major function of financial accounting, and whatever was left over from the matching procedure (mostly "unexpired" costs and "unearned" receipts) was carried over to future periods as assets or liabilities, depending on whether they were debits or credits.

Although Paton and Littleton's AAA monograph (1940) popularized the term "matching of costs and revenues" and provided existing practice with what many saw as a theoretical basis that previously had been lacking (as already briefly noted on pp. 1.17–1.18), the roots of the emphasis on proper matching and nondistortion of periodic net income were older. For example, the basic rationale—that the single most important function of financial accounting was determination of periodic net income, and that the function of a balance sheet was not to reflect the values of assets and liabilities but to carry forward to future periods the costs and credits already incurred and received but needed to determine net income of future periods—appeared in the report of the Institute's special committee on co-operation with stock exchanges:

> It is probably fairly well recognized by intelligent investors today that the earning capacity is the fact of crucial importance in the valuation of an industrial enterprise, and that therefore the income account is usually far more important than the balance-sheet. In point of fact, the changes in the balance-sheets from year to year are usually more significant than the balance-sheets themselves.
>
> The development of accounting conventions has, consciously or unconsciously, been in the main based on an acceptance of this proposition. As a rule, the first objective has been to secure a proper charge or credit to the income account for the year, and in general the presumption has been that once this is achieved the residual amount of the expenditure or the receipt could properly find its place in the balance-sheet at the close of the period, the principal exception being the rule calling for reduction of inventories to market value if that is below cost. (*Audits of Corporate Accounts*, 1934, p. 10)

That thinking led in two related directions that came together only later as the argument that proper matching was needed to avoid distorting periodic net income, which was so popular in the comment letters and hearings on whether to defer research and development expenditures or accrue future losses. The nondistortion and matching arguments seem to have developed separately in the 1940s and 1950s and made common cause only later.

(i) Nondistortion and the Balance Sheet as Footnote.   Since the purpose of income measurement was to indicate the earning power of an enterprise as well as to help appraise the performance of the enterprise and the effectiveness of management, periodic income was expected to be an indicator of the long-run or normal trend of income. The usefulness of the net income of a period as a long-run or normal measure was distorted therefore by including in it the effects of unusual or random events—gains or losses with no bearing on normal performance because they were extraordinary, caused by chance, or tended to average out over time—that could cause significant extraneous fluctuations in reported net income.

Emphasis on nondistortion of periodic net income surfaced in discussions of the effects of extraordinary and nonrecurring gains and losses in comparing the current operating performance and all-inclusive or clean-surplus theories of income, briefly described earlier (pp. 1.16–1.17), but also was later applied to accounting for recurring transactions and other events. The emphasis on stability and nondistortion of reported net income seems to have increased in the late 1940s and 1950s. Herman W. Bevis, who described the need to avoid distorting periodic net income in more detail and with more careful terminology than many accountants, set forth the underlying philosophy:

> If the corporation watches the general economy, the latter also watches the corporation. For example, one of the important national economic indicators is the amount of corporate profits (and the dividends therefrom). Fluctuations in this particular index have important implications both for the private sector and with respect to the government's revenues from taxation; they also have

a psychological effect on the economic mood of the nation. There is no doubt that, given a free choice between steadiness and fluctuation in the trend of aggregate corporate profits, the economic well-being of the nation would be better served by the former. Thus . . . society will welcome any contribution that the accounting discipline can make to the avoidance of artificial fluctuations in reported yearly net incomes of corporations. Conversely, the creation by accounting of artificial fluctuations will be open to criticism. (Bevis, 1965, p. 30)

The primary accounting tool for avoiding artificial fluctuations was accrual accounting, which "reflects the fact that the corporation's activities progress much more evenly over the years than its cash outflow and inflow" and "attempts to transfer the income and expense effect of cash receipts and disbursements, other transactions, and other events from the year in which they arise to the year or years to which they more rationally relate" (pp. 94–96). However, accrual accounting was sometimes too general, and further guidance was needed. Bevis described four guidelines for repetitive transactions and events, which had been developed out of long experience, beginning with the transaction guideline and the matching guideline:

1) Record the effect on net income of transactions and events in the period in which they arise unless there is justification for recording them in some other period or periods. (p. 97)
2) Where a direct relationship between the two exists, match costs with revenues. (p. 100)

To Bevis, in contrast to most accountants of the time, who tended to describe matching of costs and revenues very broadly, the matching guideline was of restricted application because "matching attempts to make a direct association of costs with *revenues*." Its application to a merchandising operation was obvious: "Carrying forward of the inventory of unsold merchandise so as to offset its cost against the revenue from its sale is clearly useful in determining the net income of each of the two years," although its use with some costing methods, such as LIFO, was at least questionable. Another clear application was to "the effecting of a sale [which] can be matched with a liability to pay a sales commission." Otherwise, however, "the ordinary business operation is so complex that revenues are the end product of a variety of corporate activities, often over long periods of time; objective evidence is lacking to connect the cost of most of the activities with any particular revenues." To emphasize that the matching guideline applied "to relatively few types of items," Bevis illustrated the kind of situations to which it clearly did not apply: "The matching guideline can become potentially dangerous when it attempts to match *today's real costs* with *hopes of tomorrow's revenues*, as in deferring research and development costs to be matched against hoped-for, but speculative, future revenues" (p. 101).

In viewing matching narrowly, Bevis essentially agreed with George O. May, to whose memory the book was dedicated. May (in a report written with Oswald W. Knauth for the Study Group on Business Income) noted that it had become common, especially in academic circles, "to speak of income determination as being essentially a process of 'matching costs and revenues'" but warned: "Only in part are costs 'matched' against revenues, and 'matching' gives an inadequate indication of what is actually done. . . . [I]t would be more accurate to describe income determination as a process of (1) matching product costs against revenues, and (2) allocating other costs to periods" (Study Group on Business Income, 1952, pp. 28–29).

Bevis also noted that the matching guideline was "sometimes confused with the allocation of costs to periods. Taxes, insurance, or rent, for example, may be paid in advance and properly allocated to the years covered. However, this allocation is to a *period*, and one would be hard-pressed to establish any direct connection between—i.e., to match—these costs and specific sales of the period to which they are allocated." Those kinds of allocations came not under the matching guideline but rather under the much broader systematic and rational guideline:

> 3) Where there is justification for allocating amounts affecting net income to two or more years, but there is no direct basis for measuring how much should be associated with each year, use an allocation method that is systematic and rational. (p. 101)

An essential companion of the systematic and rational guideline was the nondistortion guideline:

> 4) From among systematic and rational methods, use that which tends to minimize distortions of periodic net income. (p. 104)

Illustrations of "specific allocation practices that are designed to avoid or minimize distortions of net income among years" included self-insurance provisions, provisions for costs of dry-docking ships for major overhauls, and provisions for costs of relining of blast furnaces. For all of them, "[a] rational practice is to spread the costs over a reasonable period of time."

All three of the nondistortion practices described were potential what-you-may-call-its— deferred credits that did not qualify as liabilities. They were recognized not because they were liabilities incurred by the enterprise but because they would lessen the volatility of reported net income.

As already noted in describing the hearing on accruing future losses, not even those who advocated accruing self-insurance provisions and reserves argued that the reserves were liabilities. They argued for accruing the reserves to ensure proper matching and to avoid distorting periodic net income despite the fact that the resulting reserves were not liabilities. Similarly, the effect on net income, "to spread the costs over a reasonable period of time," was the principal consideration in accruing provisions for dry-docking ships and relining blast furnaces. An enterprise did not incur a liability for costs that later would be expended in dry-docking a ship or relining a blast furnace by operating the ship or using the furnace. Rather, it probably began to incur the pertinent liabilities only when it dry-docked the ship and began to scrape off the barnacles or otherwise overhaul her or when it shut down the furnace and started the relining, but certainly not before making a contract with one or more other entities to do the work.

Costs of dry-docking a ship or relining a furnace might legitimately be recognized between dry-dockings or relinings by recognizing them as decreases in the carrying amount of the asset because accumulations of barnacles reduced the ship's efficiency or use of the furnace wore out the lining, but proponents of accruing costs to avoid distortion of periodic net income usually have not argued that way. Since their attention has focused almost entirely on the effect on reported net income, they have not been much concerned with "niceties" of whether periodically recognizing the cost increased liabilities or decreased assets. They have been likely to dismiss questions of that kind with something about it being "merely geography" in the financial statements—an insignificant detail. Lack of concern about assets and liabilities was a distinguishing characteristic of true believers in the matching or nondistortion "gospel."

Bevis reflected that kind of focus on nondistortion of periodic net income and lack of concern about the resulting balance sheet:

> [T]he amounts at which many assets and liabilities are stated in the balance sheet are a by-product of methods designed to produce a fair periodic net income figure. The objective is *not* to produce a liquidating value or a current fair market value of assets. This approach is consistent with the primary interest of the stockholder in periodic income, as opposed to liquidating or "pounce" values in a not-to-be-liquidated enterprise. (p. 107)

Indeed, he came up with the most imaginative—and pertinent—description in the entire nondistortion and proper-matching literature of the way proponents see a balance sheet—as a footnote to an income statement:

> [T]wo-thirds of the items on the asset side of the balance sheet [a "Composite Statement of Financial Position" of "100 Large Industrial Corporations" in the Appendix] . . . are not assets in the sense of either being or expected to be directly converted to cash. They represent a huge amount of "deferred costs," mostly past cash expenditures, which are to be included as costs in future income statements. . . . Among all the footnotes explaining and elaborating on the income statement, this makes the balance sheet the biggest footnote of all. (p. 94)

Although Bevis defined matching narrowly and gave it only a limited place in periodic income determination, relying more on the rational and systematic guideline and the nondistortion guideline, his was probably a minority view. Most accountants who have emphasized the need for nondistorting income determination procedures have considered careful timing of recognition of revenues and expenses by proper matching to be critical in avoiding distortion of periodic income.

(ii) Proper Matching and "Assets Are Costs."   In contrast to Bevis's and May's narrow definitions of matching, most accountants have described matching of costs and revenues broadly, making matching either (1) one of two central functions of financial accounting or (2) *the* central function of financial accounting. Either way, matching encompasses allocations of costs using systematic and rational procedures, such as depreciation and amortization.

Accountants of the first group, whose use of matching has been the narrower of the two, have described periodic income determination as a two-step process: revenue recognition or "realization" and matching of costs with revenues (expense recognition). To them, matching not only recognized perceived direct relationships between costs and revenues, such as between cost of goods sold (product costs) and sales, but also recognized perceived indirect relationships between costs and revenues through mutual association with the same period. The latter would include relationships such as those between, on the one hand, costs recognized as expenses in the period incurred and depreciation and other costs allocated to the same period by a rational and systematic procedure and, on the other hand, revenues allocated to the same period by "realization." That is, matching encompassed both matching product costs with specific revenues (Bevis's and May's definitions) and what usually has been called allocation—matching other costs with periods. For example, this definition clearly encompassed both kinds of matching:

> Matching is one of the basic processes of income determination; essentially it is a process of determining relationships between costs . . . and (1) specific revenues or (2) specific accounting periods. (APB Opinion No. 11 (1967), par. 14(d))

Accountants of the second group have used matching of costs and revenues in the broadest possible sense—as a synonym for periodic income determination—making matching *the* central function of financial accounting. To them, matching encompassed both revenue recognition or "realization" and expense recognition. Matching dictated what has been included in income statements, as it did in both of these definitions:

> **matching** 1. The principle of identifying related revenues and expense with the same accounting period. (Kohler, 1975, p. 307)

> By means of accounting we seek to provide these test readings [of progress made] by a periodic matching of the costs and revenues that have flowed past "the meter" in an interval of time. (Paton and Littleton, 1940, p. 15)

The degree to which matching of costs and revenues had become the central function of financial accounting in the minds of many accountants by the time of the FASB's projects on research and development expenditures and similar costs and accruing future losses was indicated by Delmer Hylton's description in 1965, which was by no means an overstatement:

> Concurrent with the ascendency of the income statement in recent years, we have also witnessed increasing emphasis on the accounting convention known as "matching revenue with expense." In fact, it seems that most innovations in accounting in recent years have been justified essentially as better performing this matching process. In the minds of many accountants, this single convention outweighs all others; in other words, if a given procedure can be asserted to conform to the matching concept, nothing else need be said: the matter is settled and the procedure is justified. (Hylton, 1965, p. 824)

That is basically what Board members read and heard in the comment letters and public hearings on accounting for research and development expenditures and similar costs and accruing future losses. The need for proper matching of costs and revenues to avoid distorting periodic net income was the overriding consideration in many letters and in the prepared statements and answers of a significant number of those who appeared at the hearings and responded to Board members' questions. They showed little or no interest in whether research and development expenditures resulted in assets and whether reserves for self-insurance were liabilities.

Rather, those deferred charges and deferred credits belonged in the balance sheet because they were needed for proper matching to avoid distorting periodic net income. And what were most assets, anyway, except deferred or "unexpired" costs, as Paton and Littleton (1940) had said:

> [A]ssets are costs. "Costs" are the fundamental data of accounting, and. . . . it is possible to apply the term "cost" equally well to an asset acquired, a service received, and a liability incurred. Under this usage assets, or costs incurred, would clearly mean charges awaiting future revenue, whereas expenses, or costs applied, would mean charges against present revenue, . . . (pp. 25–26)

> The factors acquired for production which have not yet reached the point in the business process where they may be appropriately treated as "cost of sales" or "expense" are called "assets," and are presented as such in the balance sheet. . . . [T]hese "assets" are in fact "revenue charges in suspense" awaiting some future matching with revenue as costs or expenses. (p. 25)

Long before the time of those FASB projects, however, Paton had recognized that matching had become a sort of gospel (the subject of incantations about proper matching and nondistortion of the sort that the Board heard recited so often). It had been carried much too far and had been the cause of downgrading the meaning and significance of assets:

> For a long time I've wished that the Paton and Littleton monograph ("An Introduction to Corporate Accounting Standards") had never been written, or had gone out of print twenty-five years or so ago. Listening to Bob Sprouse take issue with the "matching" gospel, which the P & L monograph helped to foster, confirmed my dissatisfaction with this publication . . . . The basic difficulty with the idea that cost dollars, as incurred, attach like barnacles to the physical flow of materials and stream of operating activity is that it is at odds with the actual process of valuation in a free competitive market. The customer does not buy a handful of classified and traced cost dollars; he buys a product, at prevailing market price. And the market price may be either above or below any calculated cost. . . .

> For a long time I've been touting the idea that the central element in business operation is the *resources* (in hand or in prospect) and that the main objective of operation is the efficient utilization of the available assets. (Paton, 1971, pp. x, xi)

(c) An Overdose of Matching, Nondistortion, and What-You-May-Call-Its.   Board members had, as former chairman Donald J. Kirk once put it, cut their accounting teeth on matching, nondistortion, assets are costs, and similar notions. Some of them may have entertained some doubts about some of the ideas before serving on the Board, but it was the paramount importance that was attributed to those ideas in early comment letters and at the early hearings that made the Board increasingly uncomfortable with them. Those notions seemed to be open-ended; no one could explain the limits, if any, on matching or nondistortion procedures or how to verify that proper matching or nondistortion had been achieved. The experience made most, if not all, Board members highly skeptical about arguments that the need for proper matching to avoid distortion of periodic net income was the "be-all and end-all of financial accounting" (Sprouse, 1988, p. 127), with little or no concern expressed about whether the residuals left over after matching actually were assets or liabilities.

Among other things, those early experiences had graphically demonstrated to Board members that once accountants had come to perceive assets primarily as costs, they often failed to distinguish assets in the real world from the entries in the accounts and financial statements. What-you-may-call-its were a consequence of the habit of using "costs" and "assets" interchangeably—"assets were costs; costs were assets"—without worrying about whether the costs actually represented anything in the real world.

The "Pygmalion Syndrome" (after the legendary sculptor who fell in love with his statue of a woman) was at work. That name was given by the noted physicist J. L. Synge to "the tendency of many people to confuse conceptual models of real-world things and events with the things and events themselves" (Heath, 1987, p. 1). Perhaps the most common example has been the habit of lawyers, accountants, corporate directors and officers, stockholders, and others to describe a dividend as paid "out of surplus (retained earnings)." That habit led a prominent lawyer to chide:

> Distributions are never paid "out of surplus," they are paid out of assets; surplus cannot be distributed—assets are distributed. No one ever received a package of surplus for Christmas."
> (Manning, 1981, pp. 33–34)

The fact that the matching literature was so full of references to "unexpired" costs that "expired" when matched against revenues also caused a prominent professor of finance to admonish that accountants had confused matters by defining

> . . . depreciation as "expired capital outlay"—in other words, as "expired cost"—thereby transferring the word from a value to a cost category. But this definition was a dodge rather than a solution, and the fact that it still enjoys some currency among accounting writers who must be aware of its spurious character illustrates the tenacity of convenient though specious phrases. For cost does not "expire." What may be said gradually to expire is the economic significance of the asset as it grows older, in short, its utility or its value. "Expired cost" is therefore mumbo jumbo, and a reversion to the old association of depreciation with loss in value would be a far more sensible alternative. (Bonbright, 1961, pp. 195–196)

As Board members began to look at problems likely to come onto the Board's agenda, they began to see more what-you-may-call-its in their future. In addition to self-insurance reserves and provisions for relining blast furnaces or removing barnacles from ships, which have already been described, a significant number of what-you-may-call-its were part of existing practice in the early 1970s, had been or were being proposed to become part of practice, or had recently been proscribed:

- Unamortized debt discount.
- Deferred tax credits and deferred tax charges.
- Deferred gains and losses on securities in pension funds.
- Deferred gains on translating foreign exchange balances (the APB issued in late 1971 an exposure draft of a proposal to permit deferral of losses on foreign exchange balances but dropped the subject without issuing an Opinion).
- Deferred gains or losses or sales of long-term investments.

- Deferred gains on sale-and-leaseback transactions.
- Negative goodwill remaining after reducing to zero the noncurrent assets acquired in a business combination.

Since several of those what-you-may-call-its were part of topics that might well come before the Board within a few years, Board members thought it essential to ensure that the Board would not have to face those kinds of matters without the necessary tools. They were not anxious to repeat their experiences with research and development expenditures and similar costs and accruing future losses. They not only wanted to get in place a broad conceptual framework to provide a basis for sound financial accounting standards but also had some firm ideas of the kinds of concepts that were needed.

Kirk later described his own thinking at the time, and other Board members probably would concur with most of what he said:

> Among the projects on the Board's initial agenda were accounting for research and development costs and accounting for contingencies. The need for workable definitions of assets and liabilities became apparent in those projects and served as a catalyst for the part of the framework projects that became FASB Concepts Statement No. 3, *Elements of Financial Statements of Business Enterprises* (1980). . . .
>
> To me, the definitions were the missing boundaries that were needed to bring the accrual accounting system back under control. The definitions have, I hope, driven a stake part way through the "nondistortion" guideline. But I am realistic enough to know, having dealt with the subjects of foreign currency translation and pension cost measurement, that the aversion to volatility in earnings is so strong that the notion of "nondistortion" will not die easily. (Kirk, 1988, p. 15)

Kirk's reference to volatility of reported net income was not accidental—that has been and will continue to be a major bone of contention between the FASB and its constituents. Managements have been and continue to be concerned that volatility of periodic net income will affect adversely the market prices of their enterprises' securities and hence their cost of capital. The Board's general response to that concern has been that accounting must be neutral, and if financial statements are to represent faithfully an entity's net income, the presence of volatility must be reported to investors and creditors. For example, former Board member Robert T. Sprouse probably expressed the thinking of many Board members:

> I submit . . . that minimizing the volatile results of actual economic events should be primarily a matter for management policy and strategy, not a matter for accounting standards. To the extent volatile economic events actually occur, the results should be reflected in the financial statements. If it is true that volatility affects market prices of securities and the related costs of capital, it is especially important that, where it actually exists, volatility be revealed rather than concealed by accounting practices. Otherwise, financial statements do not faithfully represent the results of risks to which the enterprise is actually exposed.
>
> To me, the least effective argument one can make in opposing a proposed standard is that its implementation might cause managers or investors to make different decisions. . . . The very reason for the existence of reliable financial information for lenders and investors . . . is to help them in their comparisons of alternative investments. If stability or volatility of financial results is an important consideration to some lenders and investors, all the more reason that the degree of stability or volatility should be faithfully reflected in the financial statements. (Sprouse, 1987, p. 88)

That kind of problem is nothing new. For example, Paton made essentially the same point as Sprouse in writing about the effects on income of the choice of inventory methods almost 50 years earlier:

> [Sanders, Hatfield, and Moore] quote, with apparent approval, the following statement from Arthur Andersen: "The practice of equalizing earnings is directly contrary to recognized

accounting principles.'' But . . . they go out of their way to support a European practice, the base-stock inventory method, which . . . has been vigorously revived and sponsored in recent years [in the United States] under the ''last in, first out'' label, which represents nothing more nor less than a major device for equalizing earnings, to avoid showing in the periodic reports the severe fluctuations which are inherent in certain business fields. . . . Actually, we do have good years and bad years in business, fat years and lean years. There is nothing imaginary about this condition—particularly in the extractive and converting fields, where this agitation centers. . . . It may be that in some situations the year is too short a period through which to attempt to determine net income (as surely the month and quarter often are), but if this is the case, the solution lies not in doctoring the annual report, but in lengthening the period. Certainly it is not good accounting to issue reports for a copper company, for example, which make it appear that the concern has the comparative stability of earning power of the American Telephone and Telegraph Co. (Paton, 1938, pp. 199–200)

The earlier description of the experiences of Board members that led them to support a broad conceptual framework project and to develop firm ideas about the kinds of concepts needed has focused on the projects on accounting for research and development expenditures and similar costs and accounting for contingencies, including accruing future losses. Those projects were highly significant experiences for Board members, as the preceding indicates, but later projects have provided additional or similar experiences. As the comments on volatility of income suggest, the education of Board members and members of the constituency is a continuing process in which the Concepts Statements have been both a source of disagreement and controversy and a significant help in setting sound financial accounting standards.

(d) Initiation of the Conceptual Framework. Confronted with the fruits of decades of the profession's lethargy and inability to fashion a statement defining accounting's most basic concepts, the FASB, on its own initiative and motivated by the experiences of its members, decided to undertake the development of that statement. In 1973 it initiated a conceptual framework project that was intended to be at once both the reasoning underlying procedures and a standard by which procedures would be judged.

A deliberative, authoritative body with responsibility for accounting standards finally had decided to do what the committee on accounting procedure and the APB had been implored to do but had never felt strongly was a part of their mission. The FASB concluded that accounting did possess a core of fundamental concepts that were neither subject to nor dependent on the moment's particular, transitory consensus. Accounting had achieved the stage in its development that made it imperative and proper to place before its constituents a definitive statement of its fundamental principles.

THE FASB'S CONCEPTUAL FRAMEWORK

In an open letter to the business and financial community, which prefaced the booklet, ''Scope and Implications of the Conceptual Framework Project'' (December 2, 1976), Marshall S. Armstrong, the first chairman of the FASB, expressed some of the Board's aspirations for the conceptual framework project:

The conceptual framework project will lead to definitive pronouncements on which the Board intends to rely in establishing financial accounting and reporting standards. Though the framework cannot and should not be made so detailed as to provide automatically an accounting answer to a set of financial facts, it will determine bounds for judgment in preparing financial statements. The framework should lead to increased public confidence in financial statements and aid in preventing proliferation of accounting methods.

The excerpt highlighted a significant characteristic of the conceptual framework project. Although Board members were aware of the widespread criticism directed at the Committee on Accounting Procedure and the Accounting Principles Board for their collective inability to provide the profession with an enduring framework for analyzing accounting issues, the FASB's stimulus was entirely different from that of its predecessors. It was not reacting to instructions or recommendations to establish basic concepts by groups such as the AICPA's Special Committees on Research Program or Opinions of the Accounting Principles Board, the Wheat Study Group, or the SEC. Rather, the Board undertook the self-imposed task of providing accounting with an underlying philosophy on which pronouncements on specific issues could be based because Board members had concluded that to discharge their standard-setting responsibilities properly they needed a set of fundamental accounting concepts for their own guidance in dealing with issues brought before the Board for resolution.

The idea that the conceptual framework was intended to benefit the FASB by guiding its ongoing work in establishing accounting standards was embodied in the Preface, entitled "Statements of Financial Accounting Concepts," to each Concepts Statement:

> The Board itself is likely to be the most direct beneficiary of the guidance provided by the Statements in this series. They will guide the Board in developing accounting and reporting standards by providing the Board with a common foundation and basic reasoning on which to consider merits of alternatives.

Armed with the conviction that a coordinated set of pervasive concepts was prerequisite to establishing sound and consistent accounting standards, the FASB in late 1973 formally expanded the scope of its original concepts project, "Broad Qualitative Standards for Financial Reporting," and changed its name. The new title—"Conceptual Framework for Accounting and Reporting: Objectives, Qualitative Characteristics and Information"—for the first time used the words "conceptual framework" by which the project would become identified.

The Board concluded at the outset that it was unrealistic to attempt to devise a complete conceptual framework and adopt it by a single Board action. It already had experienced an urgent need for a definitive statement about some of the most fundamental components of the envisioned conceptual framework—the objectives of financial reporting and definitions of the elements of financial statements. The absence of meaningful definitions of assets and liabilities in the accounting literature had already hindered the FASB's work on the other projects on its agenda.

The project was conceived as comprising six major parts, as illustrated by Exhibit 1.1. The parts were expected to be undertaken in the order shown by moving down the exhibit and from left to right at each level.

The numbers in parentheses in Exhibit 1.1 reflect that although six Concepts Statements (often abbreviated SFAC)* were issued, their numbers did not correspond to the order in the exhibit because (a) the third projected Statement was finished before the second; (b) not-for-profit organizations were included within the scope of the framework, resulting in Concepts Statement No. 4, which pertained only to not-for-profit organizations, and in Concepts Statement No. 6, which amended Concepts Statement No. 2 and replaced Concepts Statement No. 3, making them applicable to not-for-profit organizations; and (c) little conceptual work was actually completed on the topics in the two lower levels of Exhibit 1.1, and what was done on all three topics was included in a single Concepts Statement, No. 5.
* In the remaining chapters the acronym SFAC will be used for FASB Concepts Statements.

Exhibit 1.2 shows the six Concepts Statements by topic and date of issue and explains how they fit together in relation to Exhibit 1.1.

The effects of the FASB Concepts Statements on various assets, liabilities, equity, revenues, expenses, gains, and losses are described in the chapters of the *Handbook* on those subjects.

* In the remaining chapters the acronym SFAC will be used for FASB Concepts Statements.

Exhibit 1.1.   The FASB's Conceptual Framework for Financial Accounting and Reporting.

The conceptual framework itself constitutes the subject matter of the remainder of this chapter, which considers, among other things, the underlying philosophy of and emphases in the framework, the effects on it of matters discussed earlier in the chapter, the ways that it has been and might be used by the FASB and others in improving financial accounting and reporting practice, and a more detailed look at some of the concepts. The discussion is divided into two sections: It looks at the conceptual framework first as a body of concepts that underlies financial accounting and reporting in the United States and then as five interrelated Concepts Statements, each focused on a different part of the framework.

1.7 THE FRAMEWORK AS A BODY OF CONCEPTS.   The Concepts Statements as a group reflect a number of sources and other influences, most of which have already been introduced or otherwise noted, including:

No. 1 "Objectives of Financial Reporting by Business Enterprises" (November 1978)	No. 4 "Objectives of Financial Reporting by Nonbusiness Organizations" (December 1980)
No. 2 "Qualitative Characteristics of Accounting Information" (May 1980)	[No. 2 amended by No. 6 to apply to not-for-profit organizations as well as to business enterprises]
No. 3 "Elements of Financial Statements of Business Enterprises" (December 1980)	No. 6 "Elements of Financial Statements" (December 1985) [No. 3 superseded by No. 6, which applies to both business enterprises and not-for-profit organizations]
No. 5 "Recognition and Measurement in Financial Statements of Business Enterprises" (December 1984)	[No. 5 also briefly covers display in financial statements and disclosure in notes and other means of financial reporting]

Exhibit 1.2.   The Six Concepts Statements.

- The Trueblood Study Group's report, "Objectives of Financial Statements" (October 1973), whose twelve objectives and seven "qualitative characteristics of reporting" and supporting discussion and analysis directly affected the three Concepts Statements on objectives and qualitative characteristics and indirectly affected the others.
- Board members' experiences in trying to set standards in the absence of an accepted conceptual basis, which was a significant factor both in the FASB's having a conceptual framework and in the kinds of concepts it comprises.
- Conceptual work of the APB and Accounting Research Division, primarily Accounting Research Studies No. 1 and No. 3 on basic postulates and broad principles of accounting and the basic concepts part of APB Statement No. 4.
- Conceptual work of others reported in the literature, including the work of individuals, the AAA's concepts and standards statements, and developments in Canada, the United Kingdom, Australia, New Zealand, and other countries.
- Conceptual work of the FASB itself, including preparatory work on its original concepts project and development of discussion memorandums and exposure drafts that led to the Concepts Statements and related projects, such as that on materiality; and the fruits of "due process," such as some excellent comment letters and exchanges of views at a number of hearings.

Some of the most fundamental concepts in the framework had their roots in those sources and influences. The three examples of fundamental concepts in sections 1.7(a), (b), and (c) combine ideas from one or more Concepts Statements and illustrate those connections.

(a) Information Useful in Making Investment, Credit, and Similar Decisions

Financial accounting and reporting is not an end in itself but is intended to provide information that is useful to present and potential investors, creditors, other resource providers, and other users outside an entity in making rational investment, credit, and similar decisions about it.

The FASB generally followed the report of the Trueblood Study Group on objectives of financial statements in focusing the objectives of financial reporting on information useful in investment, credit, and similar decisions, instead of on information about management's stewardship to owners or information based on the operating needs of managers. The description of Concepts Statement No. 1 in this chapter shows the influence of the Trueblood Study Group's objectives on the FASB's objectives.

That focus on information for decision making represented a fundamental change in attitude toward the purposes of financial statements. Before the Trueblood Group report, APB Statement No. 4 was the only AICPA pronouncement identifying financial reporting with the needs of investors and creditors for decision making rather than with the traditional accounting purpose of reporting on management's stewardship. A vocal minority, which still is heard from occasionally, has insisted that the primary function of accounting by an enterprise is to serve management's needs and that the objectives should reflect that purpose. It has never been quite clear why proponents of that view think that a body such as the APB or FASB should be establishing objectives and setting standards for information that is primarily for internal and private use and that management can require in whatever form it finds most useful. The message intended apparently is that management, not the APB, FASB, or similar body, should decide what information financial statements are to provide to investors, creditors, and others.

The Study Group, which may have been influenced to some extent by APB Statement No. 4, emphasized the role of financial statements in investors' and creditors' decisions and identified the purposes of financial statements with the decisions of investors and creditors, existing or prospective, about placing resources available for investment or loan. The Study

Group's recommendations became the starting point for the FASB to build a conceptual framework.

(b) Representations of Things and Events in the Real World Environment

The items in financial statements represent things and events in the real world, placing a premium on representational faithfulness and verifiability of accounting information and neutrality of both standard setting and accounting information.

The FASB's decision to ground its concepts in the environment in which financial accounting takes place and the economic things, events, and activities that exist or happen there, instead of on accounting processes and procedures, was influenced significantly by ARS No. 1 on basic postulates of accounting and the section of APB Statement No. 4 on basic concepts. The postulates in ARS No. 1 were, as already described, self-evident propositions about the environment in which accounting functions—a world that does exist, not one that is a fiction—that were fruitful for accounting. For example, the observation that most of the goods and services produced in the United States are not directly consumed by their producers but are sold for cash or claims to cash suggests both why accounting is concerned with production and distribution of goods and services and with exchange prices and why investors, creditors, and other users of financial statements are concerned with cash prices and cash flows.

That focus of financial accounting on the environment and the things and events in it that are represented in financial statements constituted a fundamental change from the earlier emphasis on the conventional nature of accounting and the conventional procedures and allocations used to produce the numbers in financial statements. Thus, the Concepts Statements devote considerable space to describing activities such as producing, distributing, exchanging, saving, and investing in what they variously call the "real world," "economic, legal, social, political, and physical environment in the United States," or "U. S. economy," and what is involved in representing those economic things and events in financial statements.

(c) Assets and Liabilities—The Fundamental Elements of Financial Statements

The fundamental elements of financial statements are assets and liabilities because all other elements depend on them: equity is assets minus liabilities; investments by and distributions to owners and comprehensive income and its components—revenues, expenses, gains, losses—are inflows, outflows, or other increases and decreases in assets and liabilities. Because liabilities depend on assets—liabilities are obligations to pay or deliver assets—assets is the most fundamental element of financial statements.

The FASB faced the need for definitions of assets and liabilities soon after its inception and found many examples of definitions in the accounting literature that not only seemed to be pertinent but also agreed on the basic characteristics of assets and liabilities.

Those definitions identified assets with economic resources and wealth, emphasizing the service potential, or benefits, and economic values they confer on the holding or owning entity. Similarly, they identified liabilities with amounts or duties owed to other entities, emphasizing the payment or expenditure of assets required of the debtor or owing entity to satisfy the claim. In short, they were definitions that described things that most people would recognize as assets and liabilities because they had experience with them not only in their business activities but also in everyday life.

These three sets of definitions of assets and liabilities, for example, were among the numerous definitions the FASB considered that had those characteristics:

Assets are economic resources devoted to business purposes within a specific	The interests or equities of creditors (liabilities) are claims against the entity

accounting entity; they are aggregates of service-potentials available for or beneficial to expected operations. (AAA, 1957, p. 3)

An asset may be defined as anything of use to future operations of the enterprise, the beneficial interest in which runs to the enterprise. Assets may be monetary or nonmonetary, tangible or intangible, owned or not owned. (Mautz, 1970, p. 1-5)

Asset. Any owned physical object (tangible) or right (intangible) having economic value to its owner; an item or source of wealth, . . . (Kohler, 1975, p. 39)

arising from past activities or events which, in the usual case, require for their satisfaction the expenditure of corporate resources. (AAA, 1957, p. 7)

Liabilities are claims against a company, payable in cash, in other assets, or in service, on a fixed or determinable future date. (Mautz, 1970, p. 1-8)

Liability. 1. An amount owing by one person (a debtor) to another (a creditor), payable in money, or in goods or services: the consequence of an asset or service received or a loss incurred or accrued; . . . (Kohler, 1975, p. 291)

In contrast, the Board also found definitions of assets and liabilities that included not only economic resources and obligations but also some ultimately undefinable what-you-may-call-its—such as deferred tax charges and credits, deferred losses and gains, and self-insurance reserves—items that were not economic resources or obligations of an entity but were included in its balance sheet to achieve "proper" matching of costs with revenues or to avoid distorting periodic net income (section 1.6 of this chapter). The prime example was APB Statement No. 4, par. 132, which, in addition to explicitly including what-you-may-call-its in its definitions of assets and liabilities, had circular definitions, saying in effect that assets and liabilities were whatever the Board said they were:

Assets—economic resources of an enterprise that are recognized and measured in conformity with generally accepted accounting principles. Assets also include certain deferred charges that are not resources but that are recognized and measured in conformity with generally accepted accounting principles.

Liabilities—economic obligations of an enterprise that are recognized and measured in conformity with generally accepted accounting principles. Liabilities also include certain deferred credits that are not obligations but that are recognized and measured in conformity with generally accepted accounting principles.

Whatever doubts Board members may have had about the definitions in APB Statement No. 4 were soon confirmed. The conceptual and practical superiority of definitions of assets and liabilities that described resources and obligations in the real world rather than deferred charges and credits that result from bookkeeping entries was strongly reinforced by Board members' experiences in trying to set financial accounting standards using assets defined as fallout from periodic recognition of revenues and expenses, which they found too vague and subjective to be workable.

Thus, the Board defined assets and liabilities in essentially the same way as the three sets of definitions by the AAA, Mautz, and Kohler, emphasizing the benefits assets confer on their holders and the obligations to others that bind those with liabilities to pay or expend assets:

Assets are probable future economic benefits obtained or controlled by a particular entity as a result of past transactions or events. [Concepts Statement No. 6, par. 25]

Liabilities are probable future sacrifices of economic benefits arising from present obligations of a particular entity to transfer assets or provide services to other entities in the future as a result of past transactions or events. [Concepts Statement No. 6, par. 35]

The definitions that were adopted exclude all what-you-may-call-its.

Although definitions of the kind adopted by the FASB had been common in the accounting literature from the turn of the century to the 1970s, at the time the Board was developing its definitions, the definitions in APB Statement No. 4 actually reflected accounting practice. Thus, the Board's definitions represented a fundamental change from the emphasis on financial accounting as primarily a process of matching costs and revenues. No longer could deferred charges and credits that were to be carried forward for matching in future periods be included in assets and liabilities merely by meeting definitions no more restrictive than "assets are costs" and "liabilities are proceeds" (pp. 1.36–1.37 and 1.75 and 1.77 of this chapter).

(i) Misunderstanding and Controversy about the Conceptual Primacy of Assets and Liabilities. Both of the other fundamental concepts described—that the objective of financial reporting is to provide information useful in making investment, credit, and similar decisions and that items in financial statements represent things and events in the real world environment—also constituted significant changes in perceptions of the purpose and nature of financial accounting and reporting. Both caused concern among many members of the FASB's constituency at the beginning and drew some criticism and opposition. With time, however, both concepts seem to have been understood reasonably well, their level of acceptance has increased, and active opposition has subsided.

In contrast, the third concept—that assets and liabilities are the fundamental elements of financial statements—still is undoubtedly the most controversial, and the most misunderstood and misrepresented, concept in the entire conceptual framework.

The FASB's emphasis on assets and liabilities in the definitions of the elements of financial statements became a focus of controversy in the development of the conceptual framework because it highlighted the tension in accounting thought and practice between two widely held views about income. The Board referred to them as the "asset and liability view of income" and the "revenue and expense view of income" because they reflected differing perspectives about whether reported income results from measuring changes in assets and liabilities or assets and liabilities result from measuring income—whether assets and liabilities or revenues and expenses are more fundamental.

The two views, and why both are views "of income," are briefly explained in this excerpt from the summary of Chapter 2 (page 35) of the FASB Discussion Memorandum on elements of financial statements and their measurement (December 2, 1976). [A third view, the nonarticulation view, is omitted; and to minimize confusion about terms, "assets" has been substituted for "economic resources," and "income" has been substituted for "earnings," which the Board replaced with "comprehensive income" after Concepts Statement No. 1.]

> [Two] views of financial accounting and financial statements—involving two distinct conceptual views of [income]—are advocated by various proponents: (1) the asset and liability view, [and] (2) the revenue and expense view, . . . In the asset and liability view, [income is] determined as a measure of change . . . in net [assets] of a business enterprise for a period. In the revenue and expense view . . . [income is] a direct measure of the effectiveness of an enterprise in using its inputs to obtain and sell outputs and [is] not necessarily based on or limited to changes in net [assets].

Although the Discussion Memorandum tried to make clear that the central conceptual issue in choosing one of the two views as the basis underlying the conceptual framework was selecting the fundamental elements whose precise definitions are the basis for defining the other elements, former Board member Oscar Gellein has explained it more clearly as the issue of identifying the elements that have what he called "conceptual primacy"—that which sets apart the most fundamental concepts in a coordinated set from those that are derived from them:

> Every conceptual formulation in any field that fulfills its purpose of providing order attaches primacy to certain concepts. They are the concepts used to define other concepts. They prevent

the system from being open-ended and potentially circular. They are the concepts that are used to test for unity and maintenance of a consistent direction—they are the anchor. Conceptual primacy has nothing to do with the question of what information is most useful or of how it is measured. It refers only to the matter of definitional dependency. [Gellein, 1986, p. 15]

CONCEPTUAL PRIMACY—A MATTER OF DEFINITIONAL DEPENDENCY. Gellein explained how the accounting profession's half-century search for accounting principles (described in the first half of this chapter) "brought to light" a need for coordinated concepts "to establish direction, to provide unity necessary for order [which] requires discipline." As that description and the name "conceptual framework" both imply, an integrated and internally consistent body of concepts forms a structure in which the parts support and build on each other and contribute to the shape of the whole. Different concepts in a conceptual framework serve different functions, just as the foundation of a building serves a function different from those of the walls, the roof, and the heating system, and some concepts are more fundamental than others.

The Board's choice between the asset and liability view and the revenue and expense view entailed deciding which elements have conceptual primacy:

Candidates for primacy in financial reporting are assets and liabilities, on the one hand, and revenues and expenses, on the other—the fount and the flow from the fount. Does the definition of the fount depend on the definition of the flow, or vice versa? [Gellein, 1986, p. 15]

Gellein also compared and contrasted financial accounting and reporting based on conceptual primacy of assets and liabilities and conceptual primacy of revenues and expenses:

If assets and liabilities have primacy in determining periodic income by matching cost and revenue, items shown in the balance sheet must satisfy the definitions of assets and liabilities. That is the key to the unity necessary for order and, therefore, discipline. If revenue and expense have conceptual primacy in determining periodic income by matching costs and revenue, items shown in the balance sheet are the things that fall out in matching. The unity and the resulting order and discipline necessarily then derive from the restraints on the matching that are not imposed by the nature of balance-sheet elements. Attempts to identify a good match based on the primacy of revenue and expense have been unsuccessful so far. There is a serious question as to whether revenue and expense can be defined independent of assets and liabilities. As pointed out previously, assets are the fount of revenue and their cost measures expense as the fount is "used up." The fount and that which flows are both assets. Can flow then be defined without reference, direct or implied, to assets? [Gellein, 1986, p. 17]

(ii) Asset and Liability View and Conceptual Primacy of Assets and Liabilities. The FASB adopted the asset and liability view of income and rejected the revenue and expense view. Assets and liabilities are the fundamental elements of financial statements in the Board's definitions. All other elements depend on assets and liabilities. Equity is assets minus liabilities. Investments by and distributions to owners and comprehensive income and its components—revenues, expenses, gains, losses—are inflows, outflows, or other increases and decreases in assets and liabilities. Assets actually is the most fundamental element of financial statements because liabilities depend on assets: Liabilities are obligations to pay or deliver assets.

The Board based its definitions of elements of financial statements on the conceptual primacy of assets and liabilities because those definitions provided the unity, order, and discipline needed in its conceptual framework, while definitions based on the conceptual primacy of revenues and expense promised to leave the set of definitions open-ended and potentially circular. However, that decision was to put the Board at odds with many of its constituents.

(iii) Revenue and Expense View and Its Relation to Practice. The revenue and expense view had been the basis for accounting practice and for most authoritative accounting pronounce-

ments for almost fifty years when the Board looked closely at it in the 1970s. The FASB saw clear evidence of its pervasiveness in practice and in accountants' minds in its early projects on research and development expenditures and accruing future losses. An emphasis on the "proper matching of costs and revenues," a concern for avoiding "distortion of periodic net income," and the willingness to allow "what-you-may-call-its" to appear in balance sheets are all characteristics of the revenue and expense view of income. Thus, the revenue and expense view has been described extensively earlier in this chapter, but those descriptions did not refer to it by that name, which is of recent vintage. Most accountants had never heard the terms "revenue and expense view" and "asset and liability view" until the FASB used them in its 1976 Discussion Memorandum on elements of financial statements.

In that Discussion Memorandum, the Board asked respondents to submit for its consideration precise definitions of revenues and expenses that were wholly or partially independent of economic resources and obligations (assets and liabilities) and capable of general application in a conceptual framework. That no one was able to do that without having to resort to subjective guides such as proper matching and nondistortion was a significant factor in the Board's ultimate rejection of the revenue and expense view. That is, the Board found the revenue and expense view to be part of the problem rather than part of the solution.

(iv) Misunderstanding and Digression.   The issue became highly emotional, and many defenders of the revenue and expense view apparently could not, or would not, believe that the Board's primary concern was the need for a set of definitions that worked. That incredulity probably was to have been expected. Definitions of assets and liabilities have not been significant in the revenue and expense view, which has focused on the need to measure performance by relating efforts expended with the resulting accomplishments and has emphasized proper matching and nondistortion of periodic net income as the means of achieving that association of effort and accomplishment. Its proponents might find it difficult to believe that definitions of assets and liabilities could be considered to be highly significant.

Unfortunately, that incredulity led those who did not accept the Board's explanations to look for other explanations for its decision. Thus, although the Board had defined assets and liabilities in a way that could accurately be described as venerable, many members of the Board's constituency found something unusual, perhaps even sinister, in the Board's definitions of elements of financial statements. As a result, the FASB has been charged over and over with having the intent, for example,

- to downgrade the importance of net income and the income statement by making the balance sheet more important than the income statement
- to supplant accounting based on completed transactions and matching of costs and revenues with a new accounting based on the valuation of assets and liabilities at current values or costs.

Since those charges misrepresented what the Concepts Statements say about the relative significance of the income statement and the balance sheet, transactions and matching, and the measurement of assets and liabilities, they are readily refuted by noting pertinent points of the asset and liability view of income as found in the FASB Concepts Statements:

1. Concepts Statement No. 1 is unequivocal in acknowledging that information about income is considered to be the most useful to investors, creditors, and other users: "The primary focus of financial reporting is information about an enterprise's performance provided by measures of [comprehensive income] and its components. Investors, creditors, and others who are concerned with assessing the prospects for enterprise net cash inflows are especially interested in that information" (par. 43; the

concept called "comprehensive income" in all subsequent Statements was called "earnings" in Concepts Statement No. 1).

2. Concepts Statements Nos. 6 and 2 are equally unequivocal that to be useful to investors, creditors, and other users, accounting information about income must represent net increases in assets or net decreases in liabilities in the real world and not merely the result of bookkeeping entries. Since comprehensive income and its components—revenues, expenses, gains, and losses—are defined as increases or decreases in assets or liabilities, neither comprehensive income nor any of its components can result merely from accruals, deferrals, amortization, or other recognition of what-you-may-call-its or changes in them as if they were assets or liabilities.

3. None of the Concepts Statements say anything about how assets or liabilities are to be measured, except No. 5. Moreover, Concepts Statement No. 5 and numerous speeches and articles by Board members while the Concepts Statements were in progress furnish abundant evidence that Board members never were sufficiently of the same mind on the relative merits and weaknesses of current cost or value and so-called historical cost for measuring assets and liabilities for the Board accurately to be characterized as "having the intent" to adopt any particular measurement model for assets and liabilities.

4. The Concepts Statements retain the matching of costs and revenues, although not as the fundamental basis of income measurement, and affirm the significance of transactions. Concepts Statement No. 6 defines matching of costs and revenues as "simultaneous or combined recognition of the revenues and expenses that result directly and jointly from the same transactions or other events" (par. 146). Accounting for transactions is required to report the sources of comprehensive income—revenues, expenses, gains, and losses. That information is significant to those attempting to use financial statements in assessing the stability, risk, and predictability of the various sources. Concepts Statement No. 5 (par. 22) emphasizes the need to avoid a "bottom line mentality," which focuses attention almost exclusively on amounts of net assets, comprehensive income, earnings per share, or other highly simplified condensations. Rather, the individual items, subtotals, or other parts of a financial statement are often more useful than aggregate amounts to those who make investment, credit, and similar decisions.

Thus, to say that the asset and liability view downgrades the significance of net income and the income statement by making the balance sheet more significant than the income statement was untrue and reflected at best misunderstanding of the asset and liability view used by the Board.

The idea that the Board chose the asset and liability view to impose some kind of current value accounting on an unwilling world also reflects the same misunderstanding or misrepresentation. Moreover, since Board members' continual public denials of that kind of intent and their explanations of what the Board actually was trying to accomplish were publicly brushed aside by many members of the Board's constituency, the unfortunate result has been a highly emotional but generally unenlightening digression that made little or no contribution to the conceptual framework. Rather, it has served no purpose except to cast aspersions on Board members' veracity and integrity and to polarize opinion.

The question that commonly has been characterized as current value or current cost versus historical cost remains unresolved. It also remains controversial and will return to haunt financial accounting and reporting the next time prices rise (or perhaps fall) significantly over a short period. However, it is a question that merits serious consideration on its own merits and is not something hidden in the asset and liability view adopted by the FASB in its conceptual framework.

In summary, much of the misunderstanding about the FASB's decision to base its definitions of elements of financial statements on the conceptual primacy of assets and liabilities stems from oversimplified and essentially irrelevant distinctions between the asset and liability and revenue and expense views concerning which financial statement is more useful and which measurement basis goes with which view.

(v) Time and Care Needed to Assimilate Changes and Heal Wounds.   Clearly, the revenue and expense view is still deeply ingrained in many accountants' minds, and their first reaction to an accounting problem is to think about "proper matching of costs and revenues." Some time will be needed for them to become accustomed to thinking first about effects of transactions or other events on assets or liabilities (or both) and then about how the effect on assets and liabilities has affected revenues, expenses, gains, or losses.

Despite the foregoing explanations, the problem will not go away quickly. The Board's definitions restrict or preclude procedures whose effects have been to reduce the volatility of reported net income or otherwise to provide considerable flexibility to management and auditors. Thus, eventually the definitions will significantly affect practice. However, the Board has demonstrated, in FASB Statement No. 87, "Employers' Accounting for Pensions," for example, that it can implement changes gradually to avoid unduly disrupting practice.

(d) Functions of the Conceptual Framework.   The Preface of each FASB Concepts Statement has carried the following, or a similar, description (this excerpt is from Concepts Statement No. 6):

> The conceptual framework is a coherent system of interrelated objectives and fundamentals that is expected to lead to consistent standards and that prescribes the nature, function, and limits of financial accounting and reporting. It is expected to serve the public interest by providing structure and direction to financial accounting and reporting to facilitate the provision of evenhanded financial and related information that helps promote the efficient allocation of scarce resources in the economy and society, including assisting capital and other markets to function efficiently.

> Establishment of objectives and identification of fundamental concepts will not directly solve financial accounting and reporting problems. Rather, objectives give direction, and concepts are tools for solving problems.

The FASB's conceptual framework is intended to be primarily a set of tools to help the Board in setting sound financial accounting standards and to help members of the Board's constituency not only understand and apply those standards but also contribute significantly to their development. It is not expected automatically to provide ready-made, unique, and obviously logical answers to complex financial accounting or reporting problems, but it should help to solve them by

- Providing a set of common premises as a basis for discussion.
- Providing precise terminology.
- Helping to ask the right questions.
- Limiting areas of judgment and discretion and excluding from consideration potential solutions that are in conflict with it.
- Imposing order and discipline.

Those contributions of the conceptual framework have all been introduced at least indirectly earlier in this chapter, and the last two were cited as factors in the FASB's conclusions in the preceding discussion of assets as the fundamental element of financial statements. The following paragraphs add a few points on the first three.

A critical function of the conceptual framework is to provide a set of common premises from which to begin discussing specific accounting problems and developing solutions for them. The accounting profession's earlier efforts to establish accounting principles has shown that if experience is the frame of reference, no one can be sure of the starting point, if one exists at all, because everyone's experience is different. The FASB's predecessors tried to use experience as a common point of departure, but when confronted with the same problems, people with different experiences too often offered widely different solutions, and financial accounting was inundated with multiple solutions to the same problems. The problems of communication and understanding between those supporting the revenue and expense view and those supporting the asset and liability view offer a striking illustration.

A framework of coordinated concepts as the frame of reference, in contrast, can change that picture. The FASB and its constituency start from common ground, vastly increasing the likelihood that they can communicate with and understand each other on the complex and difficult problems that often arise in financial accounting and reporting. A set of common premises does not guarantee agreement, but it does avoid the problems and wasted time caused by people's talking past each other because they are not actually talking about the same thing. It also promotes consensus once a problem is solved. For example, Donald J. Kirk, former chairman of the FASB, noted that the conceptual framework was undertaken "with the expectation that it would articulate definitions and concepts that would diminish the need for and details in standards; it was to be the 'relief' from the so-called 'firefighting approach' for which the FASB's predecessors had been criticized" (Kirk, 1988, p. 11).

A related purpose of the conceptual framework is to provide a precise terminology. Good terminology serves much the same function as a set of common premises: "Loose terminology encourages loose thinking. Precision in the use of words does not solve human controversies, but at least it paves the way for clear thinking" (Scott, 1960, p. 28). The FASB's conceptual framework has contributed significantly to precise terminology through its careful definitions of the elements of financial statements in Concepts Statement No. 6 and the qualitative characteristics of accounting information in Concepts Statement No. 2.

The conceptual framework helps to ask the right questions. Indeed, the FASB has emphasized that contribution as much as any. For example, the definitions of elements of financial statements not only make clear which are the right questions but also the order in which to ask them:

What is the asset?
What is the liability?
Did an asset or liability or its value change?
  Increase or decrease?
  By how much?
  Did the change result from what we call:
    Investment by owners?
    Distribution to owners?
    Comprehensive income?
      Revenue?
      Expense?
      Gain?
      Loss?

To start at the bottom and work up the list will not work. That is what ad hoc accounting has tried to do over many years, resulting in assets and liabilities in balance sheets that cannot meet the definitions.

The conceptual framework does not guarantee logical solutions to accounting problems.

The results depend significantly on those who use the concepts to establish financial accounting standards. But it does provide valuable tools to standard setters:

> Standard setters' instincts alone are not adequate to maintain direction—to discriminate between a solution that better lends usefulness to a standard than another solution, and at the same time maintain consistency. Their instincts need conceptual guidance.
>
> . . . The objectives build on the role of financial reporting and underlie the definitions of financial statement elements. Acceptance of the definitions provides the necessary discipline for order. Instead of arguing about the definitions, the FASB, as well as its constituents, now focuses attention on whether a matter in a given situation meets the conditions of a definition. That contributes to efficiency and furthers the chances of consistency. (Gellein, 1986, p. 13)

1.8 THE FASB CONCEPTS STATEMENTS.   The Concepts Statements set forth the objectives and conceptual foundation of financial accounting that are the basis for the development of financial accounting and reporting standards. This section of the chapter discusses the individual Concepts Statements in a logical order according to their subject matter. The objectives of financial reporting constitute the subject matter of Concepts Statement No. 1, **"Objectives of Financial Reporting by Business Enterprises,"** and Concepts Statement No. 4, **"Objectives of Financial Reporting by Nonbusiness Organizations."** The qualities that make accounting information useful for investment, credit, and other resource allocation decisions are described in Concepts Statement No. 2, **"Qualitative Characteristics of Accounting Information."** Concepts Statements No. 3 and No. 6 define the **"Elements of Financial Statements."** Finally, Concepts Statement No. 5, **"Recognition and Measurement in Financial Statements of Business Enterprises"** describes a complete set of financial statements and what is meant by recognition and measurement.

(a) Objectives of Financial Reporting.   After the FASB received the Report of the Trueblood Study Group in October 1973, it issued a Discussion Memorandum, "Conceptual Framework for Accounting and Reporting: Consideration of the Report of the Study Group on the Objectives of Financial Statements," in June 1974. The Discussion Memorandum was based primarily on the Trueblood Group's twelve objectives of financial statements and seven qualitative characteristics of reporting. The Board held a public hearing in September and began to develop its own conclusions on the objectives.

(i) Concepts Statement No. 1.   In December 1976, the Board published for comment a draft entitled "Tentative Conclusions on Objectives of Financial Statements of Business Enterprises" and a Discussion Memorandum, "Conceptual Framework for Financial Accounting and Reporting: Elements of Financial Statements and Their Measurement." Although the Trueblood Group report included an objective of financial statements for governmental and not-for-profit organizations, the FASB had decided to concentrate its initial efforts on formulating objectives of financial statements of business enterprises. Following a public hearing on those publications the following August, the Board issued an Exposure Draft, "Objectives of Financial Reporting and Elements of Financial Statements of Business Enterprises," in December 1977. Concepts Statement No. 1, "Objectives of Financial Reporting by Business Enterprises," was issued in November 1978.

The change in title between the Tentative Conclusions and the Exposure Draft indicated a change in the Board's perspective from a focus on financial statements to financial reporting. To a significant extent, it reflected comments received on the Tentative Conclusions document. The change also emphasized that financial statements were the primary, but not the only, means of conveying financial information to users. During the Board's consideration of objectives, it had decided that for general purpose external financial reporting, the objectives of financial statements and the objectives of financial reporting were essentially the same, although, as the Statement said, some information was better provided by financial statements and other information was better provided by other means of financial reporting (par. 5).

That brief sketch of the background of the Statement has touched only certain points. Concepts Statement No. 1, like all of the Concepts Statements, contains an appendix on its background (pars. 57–63).

CONCEPTS STATEMENT NO. 1 AND THE TRUEBLOOD GROUP'S OBJECTIVES.   The FASB accepted the starting point and basic objective in the Report of the Trueblood Study Group and, although some differences in direction had begun to appear in the supporting discussion, accepted in a general way the Group's second and third objectives. These excerpts are from the Study Group's report:

> Accounting is not an end in itself. . . .
>
> The basic objective of financial statements is to provide information useful for making economic decisions.
>
> An objective of financial statements is to serve primarily those users who have limited authority, ability, or resources to obtain information and who rely on financial statements as their principal source of information about an enterprise's economic activities.
>
> An objective of financial statements is to provide information useful to investors and creditors for predicting, comparing, and evaluating potential cash flows to them in terms of amount, timing, and related uncertainty. (pp. 61, 62)

These excerpts are from Concepts Statement No. 1:

> Financial reporting is not an end in itself but is intended to provide information that is useful in making business and economic decisions—for making reasoned choices among alternative uses of scarce resources in the conduct of business and economic activities. . . . (par. 9)
>
> The objectives in this Statement. . . . stem primarily from the informational needs of external users who lack the authority to prescribe the financial information they want from an enterprise and therefore must use the information that management communicates to them. (par. 28)
>
> Potential users of financial information most directly concerned with a particular business enterprise are generally interested in its ability to generate favorable cash flows because their decisions relate to amounts, timing, and uncertainties of expected cash flows. To investors, lenders, suppliers, and employees, a business enterprise is a source of cash in the form of dividends or interest and perhaps appreciated market prices, repayment of borrowing, payment for goods or services, or salaries or wages. They invest cash, goods, or services in an enterprise and expect to obtain sufficient cash in return to make the investment worthwhile. They are directly concerned with the ability of the enterprise to generate favorable cash flows and may also be concerned with how the market's perception of that ability affects the relative prices of its securities. . . . (par. 25)
>
> Financial reporting should provide information that is useful to present and potential investors and creditors and other users in making rational investment, credit, and similar decisions. . . . (par. 34)

None of the other nine objectives of the Study Group were adopted in recognizable form in Concepts Statement No. 1. Many of them were about matters that the Board had decided to include in the recognition, measurement, and display parts of the conceptual framework.

(ii) Concepts Statement No. 4.   By 1977 the fiscal problems of a number of large cities, including New York and Cleveland, had prompted public officials and private citizens increasingly to question the relevance and reliability of financial reporting by governmental and not-for-profit organizations. That concern was reflected in many legislative initiatives

and widely publicized allegations of serious deficiencies in the financial reporting of various kinds of not-for-profit organizations.

The Board began to consider concepts underlying general purpose external financial reporting by not-for-profit organizations by commissioning a research report to identify the objectives of financial reporting by organizations other than business enterprises. That report, "Financial Accounting in Nonbusiness Organizations," by Robert N. Anthony, was published in May 1978. Rather than delay progress on the objectives of financial reporting by business enterprises by attempting to include not-for-profit organizations within its scope, the Board decided to proceed with two separate objectives projects. It issued a Discussion Memorandum based on the Research Report, followed by an Exposure Draft. Then, "Objectives of Financial Reporting by Nonbusiness Organizations" was issued as Concepts Statement No. 4 in December 1980. After Concepts Statement No. 4 was issued, the FASB changed the key term from "nonbusiness" to "not-for-profit" organizations.

(iii) Effects of Environment and Information Needs of Resource Providers.   Concepts Statement No. 1 and Concepts Statement No. 4 have the same structure. Both sets of objectives are based on the fundamental notion that financial reporting concepts and standards should be based on the information needs of users of financial statements who make decisions about committing resources to either business enterprises or not-for-profit organizations with the expectation of pecuniary reward or to not-for-profit organizations for reasons other than expectations of monetary return of or return on resources committed. From that broad focus, the Statements narrow the focus, on the one hand, to the primary interest of investors, creditors, and other users in the prospects of receiving cash from their investments in or loans to business enterprises and the relationship of their prospects to those of the enterprise, and on the other hand, to the needs of resource providers for information about a not-for-profit organization's services, its ability to continue to provide them, and the relationship of management's stewardship to the organization's performance. Finally, both Statements focus on the kinds of information that financial reporting can provide to meet the respective needs of both groups.

The objectives of financial reporting cannot be properly understood apart from the environmental context in which they have been developed—the real world in which financial accounting and reporting takes place. They are affected by the economic, legal, political, and social environment of the United States. The objectives "stem largely from the needs of those for whom the information is intended, which in turn depend significantly on the nature of the economic activities and decisions with which the users are involved" (Concepts Statement No. 1, par. 9). Thus, Concepts Statement No. 1 describes the highly developed exchange economy of the United States, in which:

- Most goods and services are exchanged for money or claims to money instead of being consumed by their producers.
- Most productive activity is carried on through investor-owned business enterprises whose operations are controlled by directors and professional managers acting in the interests of investor-owners.
- Well-developed securities markets tend to allocate scarce resources to enterprises that use them efficiently.
- Productive resources are generally privately- rather than government-owned, although government intervenes in the resource allocation process through taxation, borrowing and spending for government operations and programs, regulation, subsidies, or monetary and fiscal policy.

Cash is important in the economy "because of what it can buy. Members of the society carry out their consumption, saving, and investment decisions by allocating their present and expected cash resources" (Concepts Statement No. 1, par. 10). Entities' efficient allocation of cash and other economic resources is a means to the desired end of a well-functioning, healthy economy. The following excerpt from Concepts Statement No. 1 describes how financial reporting can contribute to achieving that social good. It refers to reporting about business enterprises, but its premise relates as well to the objectives of financial reporting of not-for-profit organizations:

> The effectiveness of individuals, enterprises, markets, and government in allocating scarce resources among competing uses is enhanced if those who make economic decisions have information that reflects the relative standing and performance of business enterprises to assist them in evaluating alternative courses of action and the expected returns, costs, and risks of each. The function of financial reporting is to provide information that is useful to those who make economic decisions about business enterprises and about investments in or loans to business enterprises. (par. 16)

Business enterprises and not-for-profit organizations have both similarities and differences in their operating environments that affect the information needs of those who make decisions about them and thus affect the objectives of financial reporting. Both kinds of entities have transactions with suppliers of goods and services who expect to be paid for what they provide, with employees who expect to be paid for their work, and with lenders who expect to be repaid with interest. Both entities may sell the goods or services they produce, although to survive, business enterprises charge prices sufficient to cover their costs, usually plus a profit, whereas not-for-profit organizations often may sell below cost or at nominal prices or may even give their outputs to beneficiaries without charge.

Not-for-profit organizations commonly need certain kinds of control arrangements more than do business enterprises. Although not-for-profit organizations must often compete not only with each other but also with business enterprises for goods and services, employees, and lendable funds, the operating performance of business enterprises generally is subject to the discipline of market controls to a greater extent than is the performance of not-for-profit organizations because business enterprises must compete in equity markets for funds to finance their operations while not-for-profit organizations do not. Spending mandates and budgets to control uses of resources are significant factors in obtaining and allocating resources for not-for-profit organizations to compensate for the lesser influence of direct market competition.

Business enterprises and not-for-profit organizations also differ in their relationships to some significant resource providers. Business enterprises have stockholders or other owners who invest with the expectation of receiving profits commensurate with the risks incurred. In contrast, not-for-profit organizations have no owners in the same sense as business enterprises and often receive significant amounts of resources by gift or donation from those who do not expect pecuniary returns. Those contributors are interested in the services the organizations provide and receive compensation for their contributions by nonfinancial means, such as by seeing the purposes and goals of the organizations advanced.

(iv) Objectives of Financial Reporting by Business Enterprises.   The objectives of financial reporting by business enterprises are derived from the information needs of investors, creditors, and others outside an enterprise who generally lack the authority to prescribe the information they want and thus must rely on information that management communicates to them. They are the primary users of the information provided by general purpose external financial reporting, whose primary objective is to

> provide information that is useful to present and potential investors and creditors and other users in making rational investment, credit, and similar decisions. (Concepts Statement No. 1, par. 34)

The objectives of general purpose external financial reporting are not derived from and do not comprehend satisfying the information needs of all potential users. Regulatory and taxing authorities, for example, have needs for special kinds of financial information that is not normally provided by financial reporting but also have the statutory authority to obtain the specific information they need. Thus they do not have to rely on information provided to other groups. Management is interested in the information provided by external financial reporting but also has ready access not only to that information but also to a great deal of internal information that is normally unavailable to those outside the enterprise. Management's primary role in external financial reporting is that of a provider or communicator of information for use by investors, creditors, and others outside the enterprise who must rely on management for information.

In emphasizing the information needs of investors, creditors, and similar users, the FASB recognized that external financial reporting cannot satisfy the particular and perhaps diverse needs of various individual users who look to the information provided by financial reporting for assistance in making resource allocation decisions. However, those who make investment, credit, and similar decisions do have common, overlapping interests in the ability of a business enterprise to generate favorable cash flows. It is the common interest in an enterprise's cash flow potential that the objectives of external financial reporting seek to satisfy.

The objectives in Concepts Statement No. 1 focus financial reporting on a particular kind of economic decision—the decision to commit or to continue to commit cash or other resources to a business enterprise with the expectation of payment or of future return of and return on the investment, usually in cash but sometimes in other goods and services. That kind of decision is made by investors, creditors, suppliers, employees, and other potential users of financial information, and they are interested in net cash inflows to the enterprise because their own prospects for receiving cash flows from investments in, loans to, or other participation in an enterprise depend significantly on its ability to generate favorable cash flows.

> Financial reporting should provide information to help present and potential investors and creditors and other users in assessing the amounts, timing, and uncertainty of prospective cash receipts from dividends or interest and the proceeds from the sale, redemption, or maturity of securities or loans. The prospects for those cash receipts are affected by an enterprise's ability to generate enough cash to meet its obligations when due and its other cash operating needs, to reinvest in operations, and to pay cash dividends and may also be affected by perceptions of investors and creditors generally about that ability, which affect market prices of the enterprise's securities. Thus, financial reporting should provide information to help investors, creditors, and others assess the amounts, timing, and uncertainty of prospective net cash inflows to the related enterprise. (Concepts Statement No. 1, par. 37)

Concepts Statement No. 1 explicitly recognizes that financial reporting does not and cannot provide all of the information needed by those who make economic decisions about business enterprises. It is but one source. Information provided by financial reporting needs to be combined with information about, among other things, the general economy, political climate, and prospects for an enterprise's particular industry.

The objectives ultimately focus on the kind of information that fulfills the users' needs described and that the accounting system can provide better than other sources: information about assets, liabilities, and changes in them. Thus financial reporting should

> provide information about the economic resources of an enterprise, the claims to those resources (obligations of the enterprise to transfer resources to other entities and owners' equity), and the effects of transactions, events, and circumstances that change resources and claims to those resources. (Concepts Statement No. 1, par. 40)

That includes information about an enterprise's assets, liabilities, and owners' equity; information about enterprise performance provided by measures of comprehensive income (called "earnings" in Concepts Statement No. 1) and its components; information about liquidity, solvency, and funds flows; information about management stewardship and performance; and management's explanations and interpretations (pars. 41–54).

(v) Objectives of Financial Reporting by Not-For-Profit Organizations. The objectives of financial reporting by not-for-profit organizations are derived from the information needs of external resource providers who, like investors and creditors of business enterprises, generally cannot prescribe the information they want and thus must rely on information that management communicates to them. They are the primary users of the information provided by general purpose external financial reporting, whose primary objective is to

> provide information that is useful to present and potential resource providers and other users in making rational decisions about the allocation of resources to those organizations. (Concepts Statement No. 4, par. 35)

Resource providers encompass those who receive direct compensation for providing resources, including lenders, suppliers, and employees, as well as members, contributors, taxpayers, and others who are concerned with a not-for-profit organization's activities but who are not directly and proportionately compensated financially for their involvement.

The objectives flow from the common interests of those who provide resources to not-for-profit organizations in the services those organizations provide and in their continuing ability to provide services. Because the goals of not-for-profit organizations are to provide services rather than to generate profits,

> Financial reporting should provide information to help present and potential resource providers and other users in assessing the services that a [not-for-profit] organization provides and its ability to continue to provide those services. They are interested in that information because the services are the end for which the resources are provided. The relation of the services provided to the resources used to provide them helps resource providers and others assess the extent to which the organization is successful in carrying out its service objectives. (Concepts Statement No. 4, par. 38)

The kinds of controls imposed on the operations of not-for-profit organizations to compensate for the reduced influence of markets significantly affect the objectives of their financial reporting. Alternative controls, such as specific budgetary appropriations that may limit the amount an organization is allowed to spend for a particular program or donor-imposed restrictions on the use of resources, usually place a special stewardship responsibility on managers to ensure that resources are used for their intended purposes. Those kinds of spending mandates tend to have a pervasive effect on the conduct and control of the activities of not-for-profit organizations. Because of the nature of the resources entrusted to managers of not-for-profit organizations, Concepts Statement No. 4 identifies the evaluation of management stewardship and performance information as an objective of the financial reporting of not-for-profit organizations:

> Financial reporting should provide information that is useful to present and potential resource providers and other users in assessing how managers of a [not-for-profit] organization have discharged their stewardship responsibilities and about other aspects of their performance. (Concepts Statement No. 4, par. 40)

Management stewardship is of concern to investors and creditors of business enterprises and resource providers of not-for-profit organizations. Both kinds of resource providers hold management accountable not only for the custody and safekeeping of an organization's resources but also for their efficient and effective use. Concepts Statement No. 1 identifies comprehensive income (called "earnings" in the Statement) as the common focus for assessing management's stewardship or accountability (par. 51). Since profit figures are not available for not-for-profit organizations, Concepts Statement No. 4 instead delineates information about an organization's performance as the focus for assessing management stewardship. It says that financial reporting can provide information about the extent to which managers have acted in accordance with provisions specifically designated by donors. Information about departures from budget mandates or donor-imposed stipulations that may adversely affect an organization's financial performance or its ability to provide a satisfactory level of services is important in assessing how well managers have discharged their stewardship responsibilities.

The objectives of not-for-profit organizations, like those of business enterprises, ultimately focus on the kind of information that the accounting system can provide better than other sources:

> Financial reporting should provide information about the economic resources, obligations, and net resources of an organization and the effects of transactions, events, and circumstances that change resources and interests in those resources. (Concepts Statement No. 4, par. 43)

Resources are the lifeblood of an organization in the sense that it must have resources to render services. Since resource providers tend to direct their interest to information about how an organization acquires and uses its resources, financial reporting should provide information about an organization's assets, liabilities, and net assets; information about its performance, such as about the nature of and relation between resource inflows and outflows and about service efforts and accomplishments; information about liquidity; and managers' explanations and interpretations (pars. 44–55).

(vi) Keeping the Objectives in Perspective.   Financial accounting information is not intended to measure directly the value of a business enterprise. Nor is it intended to determine or influence the decisions that are made with information it provides about business enterprises and not-for-profit organizations. Its function is to provide the neutral or unbiased information that investors, creditors, various resource providers, and others who are interested in the activities of business enterprises and not-for-profit organizations can use in making those decisions. If financial information were directed toward a particular goal, such as encouraging the reallocation of resources toward particular business enterprises or industries or in favor of certain programs or activities of not-for-profit organizations, it would not be serving its broader objective of providing information useful for resource allocation decisions.

Moreover, as Concepts Statement No. 1 says, financial reporting is not financial analysis:

> Investors, creditors, and others often use reported [income] and information about the components of [income] in various ways and for various purposes in assessing their prospects for cash flows from investments in or loans to an enterprise. For example, they may use [income] information to help them (a) evaluate management's performance, (b) estimate "earning power" or other amounts they perceive as "representative" of long-term earning ability of an enterprise, (c) predict future [income], or (d) assess the risk of investing in or lending to an enterprise. They may use the information to confirm, reassure themselves about, or reject or change their own or others' earlier predictions or assessments. Measures of [income] and information about [income] disclosed by financial reporting should, to the extent possible, be useful for those and similar uses and purposes.

> However, accrual accounting provides measures of [income] rather than evaluations of management's performance, estimates of "earning power," predictions of [income], assessments of risk, or confirmations or rejections of predictions or assessments. Investors, creditors, and other users of the information do their own evaluating, estimating, predicting, assessing, confirming, or rejecting. For example, procedures such as averaging or normalizing reported [income] for several periods and ignoring or averaging out the financial effects of "nonrepresentative"

transactions and events are commonly used in estimating "earning power." However, both the concept of "earning power" and the techniques for estimating it are part of financial analysis and are beyond the scope of financial reporting. (pars. 47–48; "income" has been substituted for "earnings," which the Board replaced with "comprehensive income" after Concepts Statement No. 1)

(b) Qualitative Characteristics of Accounting Information.   "The objectives of financial reporting underlie judgments about the qualities of financial information, for only when those objectives have been established can a start be made on defining the characteristics of the information needed to attain them" (Concepts Statement No. 2, par. 21). Having concluded in Concepts Statement No. 1 that to provide information useful for making investment, credit, and similar decisions is the primary objective of financial reporting, the FASB elaborated on the corollary to that objective in Concepts Statement No. 2: that the usefulness of financial information for decision making should be the primary quality to be sought in determining what to encompass in financial reporting. The qualities that make accounting information useful have been designated its "qualitative characteristics." The term was originally used by the Trueblood Study Group, but the idea of articulating the qualities of information that contribute to its usefulness in decision making has its genesis in the authoritative literature in APB Statement No. 4. That Statement described them as "qualitative objectives," which "aid in determining which resources and obligations and changes should be measured and reported and how they should be measured and reported to make the information most useful" (par. 84).

Both APB Statement No. 4 and the Trueblood report are direct antecedents of the FASB Concepts Statements because emphasis on decision making by investors and creditors represented a departure from the AICPA's traditional view that financial statements primarily reported to present stockholders on management's stewardship of the corporation. Unless stewardship means mere custodianship, however, stockholders need essentially the same information for that purpose as they do for making investment decisions (Concepts Statement No. 1, pars. 50–53).

(i) Concepts Statement No. 2.   Concepts Statement No. 2, "Qualitative Characteristics of Accounting Information," is described as a bridge between Concepts Statement No. 1 and the other statements on elements of financial statements, recognition and measurement, and display. It connects the statements on objectives, which concern the purposes of financial reporting, with the later Concepts Statements and Standards Statements, which deal with how to attain those purposes, by sharing "with its constituents [the Board's] thinking about the characteristics that the information called for in its standards should have. It is those characteristics that distinguish more useful accounting information from less useful information" (par. 1).

When Concepts Statement No. 2 was issued, the Board noted that its discussion of the qualitative characteristics referred primarily to business enterprises but that it had tentatively concluded that the qualities also applied to the financial reporting of not-for-profit organizations. In Concepts Statement No. 6, in 1985, the Board formally amended Concepts Statement No. 2 to apply to both business enterprises and not-for-profit organizations by giving it a new paragraph 4:

> The qualities of information discussed in this Statement apply to financial information reported by business enterprises and by not-for-profit organizations. Although the discussion and the examples in this Statement are expressed in terms commonly related to business enterprises, they generally apply to not-for-profit organizations as well. "Objectives of financial reporting by business enterprises," "investors and creditors," "investment and credit decisions," and similar terms are intended to encompass their counterparts for not-for-profit organizations, "objectives of financial reporting by not-for-profit organizations," "resource providers," "resource allocation decisions," and similar terms.

Accountants are required to make a surprisingly large number of choices—about the criteria by which assets and liabilities and revenues and expenses are to be recognized and the attribute(s) of assets and liabilities to be measured; about methods of allocation; about the level of aggregation or disaggregation of the information to be disclosed in financial reports. Accounting standards issued by the designated standard-setting body narrow the scope for individual choice, but accounting choices will always have to be made, whether between choices for which no standard has been promulgated or between alternative ways of implementing a standard:

> To maximize the usefulness of accounting information, subject to considerations of the cost of providing it, entails choices between alternative accounting methods. Those choices will be made more wisely if the ingredients that contribute to "usefulness" are better understood. (Concepts Statement No. 2, par. 5)

By defining the qualities that make accounting information useful, Concepts Statement No. 2 is intended to enable the Board and its staff to provide direction for developing accounting standards consistent with the objectives of financial reporting, which are oriented toward providing useful information for making investment, credit, and similar decisions:

> The central role assigned here to decision making leads straight to the overriding criterion by which all accounting choices must be judged. The better choice is the one that, subject to considerations of cost, produces from among the available alternatives information that is most useful for decision making. (Concepts Statement No. 2, par. 30)

(ii) A Hierarchy of Accounting Qualities.   Concepts Statement No. 2 examines the characteristics that make accounting information useful, and the FASB has gone to considerable effort to lay out what "usefulness means." Usefulness for making investment, credit, and similar decisions is the most important quality in its "Hierarchy of Accounting Qualities," "[t]he characteristics of information that make it a desirable commodity [and that] guide the selection of preferred accounting policies from among available alternatives. . . . Without usefulness, there would be no benefits from information to set against its costs. The hierarchy is represented in [Exhibit 1.3]" (Concepts Statement No. 2, par. 32).

Usefulness is a high-level abstraction. To serve as a meaningful criterion or standard against which to judge the results of financial accounting, usefulness needs to be made more concrete and specific by analyzing it into its components at lower levels of abstraction. The two primary components of usefulness are relevance and reliability. Although those concepts are more concrete than usefulness, they are still quite abstract. That is why Concepts Statement No. 2 focuses at a still more concrete level, where the concepts of predictive value and feedback value, timeliness, representational faithfulness, verifiability, neutrality, and comparability together serve as criteria for determining information's usefulness.

For accounting standard setting, usefulness cannot be interpreted to mean whatever a particular individual interprets it to mean. A judgment that a piece of information is useful must be the result of a careful analysis that confirms first that the information possesses the qualities at the most concrete level of the hierarchy. Is it timely and does it have predictive or feedback value or both? Is it representationally faithful, verifiable, and neutral? If it has those characteristics, it is relevant and reliable. Only then, if information has survived that kind of examination, can it be deemed useful.

The chart also shows two constraints, primarily quantitative rather than qualitative in nature. The "pervasive constraint" is that the benefits of information should exceed its cost. Information that would be useful for a decision may be just too expensive to justify providing it. The second constraint is a "materiality threshold," meaning that "[t]he requirement that information be reliable can still be met even though it may contain immaterial errors, for errors that are not material will not perceptibly diminish its usefulness" (par. 33).

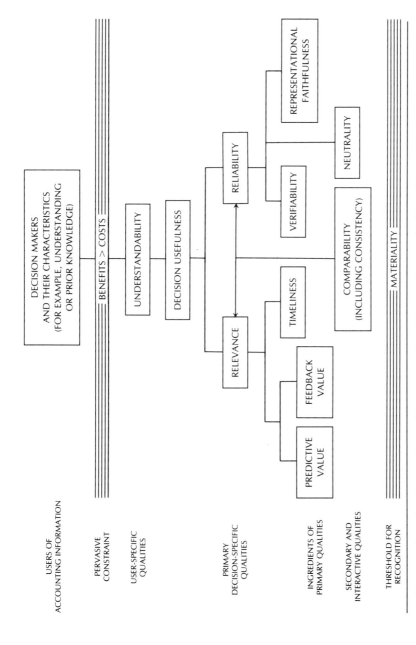

Exhibit 1.3. Hierarchy of accounting qualities. *Source:* Financial Accounting Standards Board, Statement of Financial Accounting Concepts No. 2, par. 32.

The hierarchy distinguishes between user-specific and decision-specific qualities because whether a piece of information is useful to a particular decision by a particular decision maker depends in part on the decision maker. Usefulness depends on a decision maker's degree of prior knowledge of the information as well as on his or her ability to understand it:

> The better informed decision makers are, the less likely it is that any new information can add materially to what they already know. That may make the new information less useful, but it does not make it less relevant to the situation. If an item of information reaches a user and then, a little later, the user receives the same item from another source, it is not less relevant the second time, though it will have less value. For that reason, relevance has been defined in this Statement (paragraphs 46 and 47) in terms of the capacity of information to make a difference (to someone who does not already have it) rather than in terms of the difference it actually does make. The difference it actually does make may be more a function of how much is already known (a condition specific to a particular user) than of the content of the new messages themselves (decision-specific qualities of information). (Concepts Statement No. 2, par. 37)

Similarly, the ability to understand a pertinent piece of information relates more to the characteristics of users for whom the information is intended than to the information itself. Even though information may be relevant to a decision, it will not be useful to a person who cannot understand it.

In Concepts Statement No. 1, the Board said that information provided by financial reporting "should be comprehensible to those who have a reasonable understanding of business and economic activities and are willing to study the information with reasonable diligence" (par. 34). But information's relevance may transcend the ability of a user to recognize its import:

> Financial information is a tool and, like most tools, cannot be of much direct help to those who are unable or unwilling to use it or who misuse it. Its use can be learned, however, and financial reporting should provide information that can be used by all—nonprofessionals as well as professionals—who are willing to learn to use it properly. Efforts may be needed to increase the understandability of financial information. Cost-benefit considerations may indicate that information understood or used by only a few should not be provided. Conversely, financial reporting should not exclude relevant information merely because it is difficult for some to understand or because some investors or creditors choose not to use it. (Concepts Statement No. 1, par. 36)

> Understandability of information is governed by a combination of user characteristics and characteristics inherent in the information, which is why understandability and other user-specific characteristics occupy a position in the hierarchy of qualities as a link between the characteristics of users (decision makers) and decision-specific qualities of information. (Concepts Statement No. 2, par. 40)

The two primary decision-specific qualities that make accounting information useful for decision making are relevance and reliability. If either is missing completely from a piece of information, the information will not be useful. In choosing between accounting alternatives, one should strive to produce information that is both as relevant and reliable as possible, but at times it may be necessary to sacrifice some degree of one quality for a gain in the other.

(iii) Relevance. "To be relevant to investors, creditors, and others for investment, credit, and similar decisions, accounting information must be capable of making a difference in a decision by helping users to form predictions about the outcomes of past, present, and future events or to confirm or correct expectations" (par. 47). That definition of relevance is more explicit than the dictionary meaning of relevance as "bearing upon or relating to the matter in hand." As alluded to earlier, prior knowledge of information may diminish its value but not its relevance, and hence, its usefulness, for it is information's ability to "make a difference" that makes it relevant to a decision.

Statements about relevance of financial statement information must answer the question "relevant to whom for what purpose?" For information to be judged relevant, an object to which it is relevant must always be understood.

PREDICTIVE VALUE AND FEEDBACK VALUE.   To be relevant, information must have predictive value or feedback value or both. Relevant information has the capacity to assist investors, creditors, and similar users in forming, confirming, or changing expectations about future events or outcomes involving cash flows and in evaluating their previous predictions to attempt to improve their future ones:

> Usually, information does both at once, because knowledge about the outcome of actions already taken will generally improve decision makers' abilities to predict the results of similar future actions. Without a knowledge of the past, the basis for a prediction will usually be lacking. Without an interest in the future, knowledge of the past is sterile. (Concepts Statement No. 2, par. 51)

David Solomons, consultant on and major contributor to Concepts Statement No. 2, said in his book, *Making Accounting Policy (1986),* that "[w]hereas predictive value is forward-looking and is derived directly from its power to guide decisions, feedback value is derived from what information tells about the past." He gives as an example of a balance sheet item with predictive value the allowance for uncollectible receivables, which is the amount of accounts receivable that is not expected to produce future cash flows. The most important figure in financial statements with feedback value is the earnings figure which "conveys information about the success of the ventures that have been invested in and also about the performance of the managers who have been responsible for running the business" (p. 90).

To say that accounting information has predictive value is not to say that in itself it constitutes a prediction. Predictive value means value as an input into a predictive process, not value directly as a prediction. It is "the quality of information that helps users to increase the likelihood of correctly forecasting the outcome of past or present events" (Concepts Statement No. 2, Glossary). Information about the present state of economic resources or obligations or about an enterprise's past performance is commonly a basis for expectations. Information is relevant if it can reduce the uncertainty surrounding a decision. It is relevant "if the degree of uncertainty about the result of a decision that has already been made is confirmed or altered by the new information; it need not alter the decision" (Concepts Statement No. 2, par. 49).

TIMELINESS.   To be relevant, information also must be timely. Timeliness means "having information available to decision makers before it loses its capacity to influence decisions." Information that is not available when it is needed or becomes available only long after it has value for future action is useless. "Timeliness alone cannot make information relevant, but a lack of timeliness can rob information of relevance it might otherwise have had" (par. 56).

(iv) Reliability.   Reliability is the quality of information that allows those who use it to depend on it with confidence. "The reliability of a measure rests on the faithfulness with which it represents what it purports to represent, coupled with an assurance for the user, which comes through verification, that it has that representational quality" (par. 59). The hierarchy of qualities decomposes reliability into two components, representational faithfulness and verifiability, with neutrality shown to interact with them.

REPRESENTATIONAL FAITHFULNESS.   Representational faithfulness is "correspondence or agreement between a measure or description and the phenomenon it purports to represent. In accounting, the phenomena to be represented are economic resources and obligations and the transactions and events that change those resources and obligations" (par. 63). The FASB's conceptual framework emphasizes that accounting is a representational discipline. It represents things in the financial statements that exist in the real world. Therefore the correspondence between the measure of the representation and the thing being represented is critical.

Concepts Statement No. 2 uses an analogy with map-making to illustrate what it means by representational faithfulness:

> A map represents the geographical features of the mapped area by using symbols bearing no resemblance to the actual countryside, yet they communicate a great deal of information about it. The captions and numbers in financial statements present a "picture" of a business enterprise and many of its external and internal relationships more rigorously—more informatively, in fact— than a simple description of it. (Concepts Statement No. 2, par. 24)

Just as the lines and shapes on a road map represent roads, rivers, and geographical boundaries, so also descriptions and amounts in financial statements represent cash, property, sales, and a host of things owned or owed by an entity as well as transactions and other events and circumstances that affect them or their values. The items in financial statements have a higher degree of reliability as quantitative representations of economic things and events in the real world—and therefore more usefulness to investors and other parties interested in an entity's activities—if they faithfully represent what they purport to represent. Since the benefit of the information is representational and not aesthetic, to take "artistic license" with the data decreases rather than increases its benefit. Just as a cartographer cannot add roads, bridges, and lakes where none exist, an accountant cannot add imaginary items to financial statements without spoiling the representational faithfulness, and ultimately, the usefulness, of the information.

Striving for representational faithfulness does not comprehend creating an exact replica of the activities of an enterprise. Perfect information is as beyond the reach of accountants as it is of nonaccountants:

> The financial statements of a business enterprise can be thought of as a representation of the resources and obligations of an enterprise and the financial flows into, out of, and within the enterprise—as a model of the enterprise. Like all models, it must abstract from much that goes on in a real enterprise. No model, however sophisticated, can be expected to reflect all the functions and relationships that are found within a complex organization. To do so, the model would have to be virtually a reproduction of the original. In real life, it is necessary to accept a much smaller degree of correspondence between the model and the original than that. One can be satisfied if none of the important functions and relationships are lost. . . . The mere fact that a model works— that when it receives inputs it produces outputs—gives no assurance that it faithfully represents the original. Just as a distorting mirror reflects a warped image of the person standing in front of it. . . so a bad model gives a distorted representation of the system that it models. The question that accountants must face continually is how much distortion is acceptable. . . . (Concepts Statement No. 2, par. 76)

COMPLETENESS.   Completeness of information is an important aspect of representational faithfulness, and thus of reliability because, if financial statements are to faithfully represent an enterprise's financial position and changes in financial position, none of the significant financial functions of the enterprise or its relationships can be lost or distorted. Completeness is defined as "the inclusion in reported information of everything material that is necessary for faithful representation of the relevant phenomena" (Concepts Statement No. 2, Glossary). Financial statements are incomplete, and therefore not representationally faithful, if, for example, an enterprise owns an office structure but reports no "building" or similar asset on its balance sheet.

Completeness also is necessary to relevance, the other primary quality that makes accounting information useful:

> Relevance of information is adversely affected if a relevant piece of information is omitted, even if the omission does not falsify what is shown. For example, in a diversified enterprise a failure to disclose that one segment was consistently unprofitable would not, before the issuance of FASB

Statement No. 14, *Accounting for Segments of a Business Enterprise*, have caused the financial reporting to be judged unreliable, but that financial reporting would have been (as it would now be) deficient in relevance. (Concepts Statement No. 2, par. 80)

Although completeness implies showing what is material and feasible, it must always be relative. Financial statements cannot show everything or they would be prohibitively expensive to provide.

VERIFIABILITY.   "Verifiability" is what most people typically mean when they use the words "reliability" and "objectivity." Verifiability is only part of reliability; moreover, verifiability is a more precise term than objectivity, which means being independent of the observer. The sooner "objectivity" is replaced in accountants' vocabularies by "verifiability" the better.

Concepts Statement No. 2 defines verifiability as one component of reliability, "the ability through consensus among measurers to ensure that information represents what it purports to represent or that the chosen method of measurement has been used without error or bias" (Glossary). The purpose of verifiability is to confirm the representational faithfulness of accounting information.

Accounting information may not be representationally faithful because of two kinds of bias: measurer bias or measurement bias. Measurer bias is introduced if a measurer, unintentionally through lack of skill or intentionally through lack of integrity, or both, wrongly applies the chosen measurement method. It is detected and eliminated by duplicating the measurement and getting the same result. Measurement bias occurs if the resulting measurement fails to represent what it is intended to represent. Solomons says that "the essence of verification is agreement among a number of independent observers. Such agreement is the best, perhaps the only, defense against bias in measurement" (*Making Accounting Policy,* 1986, p. 91).

Since verification entails consensus and to reach agreement is easier on measures of cash than of depreciable assets, accountants may mean either that an accounting measure itself has been verified or that only the procedures used to obtain the measure have been verified, when they speak of verification. The price paid for property, plant, or equipment is usually directly verifiable, whereas the amount of depreciation for a period is normally only indirectly verifiable by checking the allocation method, the calculations used, and the consistency of application. Merely rechecking the mechanics does not verify the representational faithfulness of the measure, leaving some doubt about its reliability:

> In summary, verifiability means no more than that several measurers are likely to obtain the same measure. It is primarily a means of attempting to cope with measurement problems stemming from the uncertainty that surrounds accounting measures and is more successful in coping with some measurement problems than others. (Concepts Statement No. 2, par. 89)

NEUTRALITY.   Neutrality is concerned with bias and thus is a factor in reliability of accounting information. It is the "absence in reported information of bias intended to attain a predetermined result or to induce a particular mode of behavior" (Concepts Statement No. 2, Glossary). Accounting information is neutral if it "report[s] economic activity as faithfully as possible, without coloring the image it communicates for the purpose of influencing behavior in *some particular direction*" (par. 100).

A common perception and misconception is that displaying neutrality means treating everyone alike in all respects. It would not necessarily show a lack of neutrality to require less disclosure of a small company than of a large one if it were shown that an equal disclosure requirement placed an undue economic burden on the small company. Solomons says that neutrality "does not imply that no one gets hurt." His response to the argument that accounting policy can never be neutral because in any policy choice someone gets his or her preference and someone else does not clarifies the meaning of neutrality:

> The same thing could be said of the draft, when draft numbers were drawn by lot. Some people were chosen to serve while others escaped. It was still, by and large, neutral in the sense that all

males of draft age were equally likely to be selected. It is not a necessary property of neutrality that everyone likes the results; the absence of intentional bias is at the heart of the concept. (1986, p. 234)

Neutrality requires that information should be free from bias toward a predetermined result, but that is not to say that standard setters or those who provide information according to promulgated standards should not have a purpose in mind for financial reporting. Accounting should not be without influence on human behavior, but it should not slant information to influence behavior in a particular way to achieve a desired end:

Neutrality in accounting is an important criterion by which to judge accounting policies, for information that is not neutral loses credibility. If information can be verified and can be relied on faithfully to represent what it purports to represent—*and if there is no bias in the selection of what is reported*—it cannot be slanted to favor one set of interests over another. (Concepts Statement No. 2, par. 107)

In an article entitled "Accounting Standards and the Professional Auditor" (1989), former Board member, Arthur R. Wyatt, commented on the crucial nature of the quality of neutrality in Concepts Statement No. 2 to the FASB's process and to the widespread acceptability of its resulting standards:

Early on, . . . the FASB undertook work to develop a conceptual framework, in part so that it could develop standards that had a logical cohesion, and in part so that the results of its deliberations could be evaluated to assess whether the resulting standards flowed from logical premises or may have been the result of lobbying activities or pressure politics. (p. 97)

The Board unequivocally rejected the view that financial accounting standards should be slanted to foster a particular government policy or to favor one economic interest over another:

The notion of neutrality within the Board's conceptual framework is that in resolving issues the Board will attempt to reach conclusions that result in reliable and relevant information and not conclusions that favor one segment of society to the detriment of one or more other segments. . . . [T]he notion of neutrality emphasizes that in developing the standard the Board . . . is not overtly striving to reallocate resources for the benefit of one group to the detriment of others. (Wyatt, 1989, p. 97)

On several occasions Donald J. Kirk, former Board chairman, also made the point that neutrality is essential to fulfilling the objective of providing relevant and reliable information to investors, creditors, and other users, and to prevent standard setting from becoming an exercise in directing resources to a preferred group. For example:

[N]eutrality of information keeps financial reporting standards as a part of a measurement process, rather than a purposeful resource allocation process. . . . It is the emphasis on neutrality of information, as well as the independence of the standard setters from undue influence, that ensures the continued success of private sector standard setting. (Kirk, 1988, p. 13)

To protect the public interest in useful accounting information, what is needed is *not* "good business sense," *nor* even "good public policy," but rather "neutrality" (i.e., "absence in reported information of bias intended to attain a predetermined result or to induce a particular mode of behavior"). The chairman of the SEC made the point about the importance of neutrality in his statement on oil and gas accounting:

If it becomes accepted or expected that accounting principles are determined or modified in order to secure purposes other than economic measurement—even such virtuous purposes as energy production—we assume a grave risk that confidence in the credibility of our financial information system will be undermined.* (Kirk, "Reflections on a 'Reconceptualization of Accounting,' " 1989, p. 95).

*Excerpt quoted from Harold M. Williams, "Accounting Practices for Oil and Gas Producers," Washington, DC, 1978, p. 12).

Neutrality in standard setting is so significant that it has been incorporated into the FASB's Mission Statement, and Concepts Statement No. 2 itself explains why neutrality is so critical to the Board and to the standard-setting process. The first and last words in the section entitled "Neutrality" are:

> Neutrality in accounting has a greater significance for those who set accounting standards than for those who have to apply those standards in preparing financial reports, but the concept has substantially the same meaning for the two groups, and both will maintain neutrality in the same way. Neutrality means that either in formulating or implementing standards, the primary concern should be the relevance and reliability of the information that results, not the effect that the new rule may have on a particular interest. (par. 98)

> The Board's responsibility is to the integrity of the financial reporting system, which it regards as its paramount concern. (par. 110)

(v) Comparability.   Comparing alternative investment or lending opportunities is an essential part of most, if not all, investment or lending decisions. Investors and creditors need financial reporting information that is comparable, both for single enterprises over time and between enterprises at the same time. Comparability is a quality of the relationship between two or more pieces of information—"the quality of information that enables users to identify similarities in and differences between two sets of economic phenomena" (Concepts Statement No. 2, Glossary). Comparability is achieved if similar transactions and other events and circumstances are accounted for similarly and different transactions and other events and circumstances are accounted for differently.

Comparability has been the subject of much disagreement among accountants. Some have argued that enterprises and their circumstances are so different from one another that comparability between enterprises is an illusory goal, and to include it as an aim of financial reporting is to promise to investors and creditors something that ultimately cannot be delivered. In that view, the best that can be hoped for is that individual enterprises will use their chosen accounting procedures consistently over time to permit comparisons with other enterprises and that honorable auditors will be able to attest to the consistent application of "generally accepted accounting principles".

The problem with that view of comparability is that it allows an excessive degree of latitude in reporting practice. It was the dominant view during the 1930s and 1940s, did permit, or even encouraged, a very wide latitude in reporting practice, and was responsible for the proliferation of alternative accounting procedures that characterized the period, many in situations in which few significant differences in enterprises or circumstances were ever reasonably substantiated. The result was an intolerable lack of comparability, which was responsible for much of the criticism directed toward financial accounting and eventually led to the replacement of the Committee on Accounting Procedure by the Accounting Principles Board.

Today, with the objectives of financial reporting focused on decision making, comparability is one of the most essential and desirable qualities of accounting information. Investors and creditors can no longer be expected to tolerate blanket claims of differences in circumstances to justify undue use of alternative accounting procedures. Only differences in transactions and other events and circumstances warrant different accounting.

Concepts Statement No. 2 notes that the need for comparable information is a fundamental rationale for standard setting:

> The difficulty in making financial comparisons among enterprises because of the use of different accounting methods has been accepted for many years as the principal reason for the development of accounting standards. (par. 112)

Some critics have focused on the standard setter's pursuit of comparability, calling it "uniformity," and mistakenly implying that standards are issued to require that all enterprises use the same accounting methods despite underlying differences. Comparability is, however, the antithesis of uniformity:

> Comparability should not be confused with identity, and sometimes more can be learned from differences than from similarities if the differences can be explained. The ability to explain phenomena often depends on the diagnosis of the underlying causes of differences or the discovery that apparent differences are without significance. . . . Greater comparability of accounting information, which most people agree is a worthwhile aim, is not to be attained by making unlike things look alike any more than by making like things look different. (Concepts Statement No. 2, par. 119)

In fact, uniformity of practice may be a greater threat to comparability than is too much flexibility in choice of accounting method. Investors and creditors can often discern and compensate for lack of comparability caused by alternative procedures, but they usually have no way of detecting a lack of comparability caused by forced uniformity of practice.

Consistency, meaning "conformity from period to period with unchanging policies and procedures" (Concepts Statement No. 2, Glossary), has long been regarded as an important quality of information provided by financial statements. For example, it was an explicit part of the recommendation of the special committee on co-operation with stock exchanges in 1932 (section 1.3). Auditors are required to point out changes in accounting principles or in the method of their application that have a material effect on the comparability of a client's financial statements.

Consistent use of accounting methods, whether from one period to another within a single firm or within a single period across firms, is a necessary but not a sufficient condition of comparability. Consistency in applying accounting methods over time contributes to comparability, provided that the methods consistently applied were reasonably comparable to begin with. Lack of comparability will never be transformed into comparability by consistent application. If what is measured and reported has representational faithfulness, an accurate analysis of similarities and differences will be possible, and comparability is enhanced. However, in the same way that lack of timeliness can deprive information of relevance it might otherwise have had, inconsistent use of comparable information can ruin whatever comparability the information might otherwise have had.

Concern for consistency does not mean that accountants should not be open to new and better methods and standards. A change need not inhibit comparability if its effects are properly disclosed.

(vi) Conservatism.   A word needs to be said about "conservatism," an important doctrine in most accountants' minds, but not a separate qualitative characteristic in the FASB's hierarchy of qualities that make accounting information useful. The FASB has described conservatism as "a prudent reaction to uncertainty to try to ensure that uncertainty and risks inherent in business situations are adequately considered" (Concepts Statement No. 2, par. 95). That is quite different from the traditional meaning of conservatism in financial reporting, which usually connoted deliberate, consistent understatement of net assets and profits, summed up by the admonition to "anticipate no profits but anticipate all losses." That view developed during a time when balance sheets were considered the primary (and often only) financial statement, and bankers or other lenders were their principal external users. Since

understating assets was thought to provide a greater margin of safety as security for loans and other debts, deliberate understatement was considered a virtue.

The traditional application of conservatism introduced into reporting a preference "that possible errors in measurement be in the direction of understatement rather than overstatement of net income and net assets" (APB Statement No. 4, par. 171). In practice that often meant depressing reported net income by excessive depreciation or undervaluation of inventory or deferring recognition of income until long after sufficient evidence of its existence became available.

That kind of conservatism has now become discredited because it conflicts with the information's comparability, with its representational faithfulness and neutrality, and thus with its reliability. Any kind of bias, whether overly conservative or overly optimistic, influences the timing of recognition of net income or losses and may mislead investors as they attempt to evaluate alternative investment opportunities. Information that adds to uncertainty is inimical to informed and rational decision making and betrays the fulfillment of the objectives of financial reporting:

> The appropriate way to treat uncertainty is to disclose its nature and extent honestly, so that those who receive the information may form their own opinions of the probable outcome of the events reported. That is the only kind of conservatism that can, in the long run, serve all of the divergent interests that are represented in a business enterprise. It is not the accountant's job to protect investors, creditors, and others from uncertainty, but only to inform them about it. Any attempt to understate earnings or financial position consistently is likely to engender skepticism about the reliability and the integrity of what is reported. Moreover, it will probably be ultimately self-defeating. (Solomons, *Making Accounting Policy*, 1986, p. 101)

(vii) Materiality.   The final item on the hierarchy, characterized as a constraint or "threshold for recognition," is materiality, which is a *quantitative,* not a qualitative, characteristic of information. Materiality judgments pose the question: "Is this item large enough for users of the information to be influenced by it?" (Concepts Statement No. 2, par. 123). Materiality means:

> The magnitude of an omission or misstatement of accounting information that, in the light of surrounding circumstances, makes it probable that the judgment of a reasonable person relying on the information would have been changed or influenced by the omission or misstatement. (Concepts Statement No. 2, Glossary)

Popular usage of "material" often makes it a synonym for "relevant," but the two are not synonymous in Concepts Statement No. 2. Information may be relevant in the sense that it is capable of making a difference and yet the amounts involved are immaterial—too small to matter in a decision. To illustrate the difference between materiality and relevance, Concepts Statement No. 2 (par. 126) provides an example of an applicant for employment who is negotiating with an employment agency. On one hand, information about the nature of the duties, salary, hours, and benefits is relevant, as well as material, to most prospective employees. On the other hand, whether the office floor is carpeted and whether the cafeteria food is of good quality are relevant, but probably not material, to a decision to accept the job. The values placed on them by the applicant are too small to influence the decision.

However, materiality judgments go beyond magnitude itself to the nature of the item and the circumstances in which the judgment has to be made. Items too small to be thought material if they result from routine transactions may be considered material if they arise in abnormal circumstances. Therefore, one must always think in terms of a threshold over which an item must pass, considering its nature and the attendant circumstances as well as its relative amount, that separates material from immaterial items.

Where the threshold for recognition occurs with regard to a materiality decision is a matter of judgment. Many accountants would like to have more quantitative guidelines or criteria for materiality laid down by the SEC, the FASB, or other regulatory agency. The FASB's view has been that materiality judgments can best be made by those who possess all the facts. In recognition of the fact that materiality guidance is sometimes needed, the appendices to Concepts Statement No. 2 include a list of quantitative guidelines that have been applied both in the law and in the practice of accounting. However, if and when those guidelines specify some minimum size stipulated for recognition of a material item, they do not preclude recognition of a smaller segment. There is still room for individual judgment in at least one direction.

(viii) Costs and Benefits.   Information is subject to the same pervasive cost–benefit constraint that affects the usefulness of other commodities: Unless the benefits to be derived from information equal or exceed the cost of acquiring it, it will not be pursued. Financial information is unlike other commodities, however, in being a partly private and partly public good since "the benefits of information cannot always be confined to those who pay for it" (Concepts Statement No. 2, par. 135), and the balancing of costs and benefits cannot be left to the market.

Cost–benefit decisions about accounting standards generally have to be made by the standard-setting body—now the FASB. Both costs and benefits of accounting standards cut across the whole spectrum of the Board's constituency, with the benefits only partly accruing to those who bear the costs and the balance between costs and benefits reacting very imperfectly to supply and demand considerations. Moreover, individuals, be they providers, users, or auditors of accounting information, are not in a position to make cost–benefit assessments due to lack of sufficient information as well as probable biases on the matter.

Cost–benefit decisions are extremely difficult because both costs and benefits often are subjective and difficult or impossible to measure reliably. Cost–benefit analysis is at best a fallible tool. Although the Board is committed to doing the best it can in making cost–benefit assessments, and Board members indeed have taken the matter seriously in facing the question in several standards in which it has arisen, cost–benefit measures and comparisons are too unreliable to be the deciding factor in crucial standards-setting decisions.

(ix) Impact of the Qualitative Characteristics.   In the almost 20 years since the Trueblood Study Group, and later the FASB, authoritatively clarified the objectives of financial reporting and the consequent primacy of usefulness of financial information for decision making, an evolution in accounting thought has slowly taken place:

> Once decision making is seen as the primary objective of financial reporting, it is inevitable that the usefulness of financial information for making decisions should be the primary quality to be sought in deciding what is to be reported and how that reporting is to be done. This is not quite the truism that it seems to be, for . . . only a minority of the respondents to an FASB inquiry in 1974 favored the adoption of that objective. Since 1974 there has been a striking change in attitude among persons interested in financial reporting, and decision usefulness has become widely accepted as the most important quality that financial information should have. (Solomons, *Making Accounting Policy,* 1986, p. 86)

The qualitative characteristics have also had an impact on practice. Former FASB vice chairman, Robert T. Sprouse, in an appearance at a Harvard Business School conference entitled "Conceptual Frameworks for Financial Accounting" in October 1982, described their contribution to accounting debate:

> I must confess that initially, although it was clear that certain identified qualitative characteristics of accounting information constituted an essential component of a conceptual framework for general purpose, external financial reporting, I was skeptical about their contribution to the standard setting process. It seemed to go without saying that accounting information should be relevant and reliable; I doubted that explicit acknowledgment of such qualities would be very

useful to preparers, auditors, users, and standard setters in making decisions about financial reporting issues. I was wrong.

The qualitative characteristics project has proven to be extremely valuable, particularly in improving communications among the many and varied organizations and individuals who are involved in resolving financial reporting issues. Statement No. 2 has established a language that has significantly enhanced the degree of precision and level of understanding in discussions of those matters. Increasingly, position papers and comment letters submitted to the FASB refer to specific qualitative characteristics to support positions that are advocated, recommendations that are proffered, and criticisms that are aimed at Board proposals. Similarly, in Board discussions and deliberations it is no longer sufficient to argue that something is relevant or irrelevant and reliable or unreliable. One must specify whether it is predictive value that is enhanced or lacking or whether representational faithfulness would be achieved or be absent, or whether it is some other aspect of relevance or reliability that is affected. The result has been greater precision in thinking about issues and greater understanding in communicating about them. (Sprouse, 1982, p. 33)

(c) Elements of Financial Statements.   Concepts Statement No. 1 said that "financial reporting should provide information about the economic resources of an enterprise, the claims to those resources (obligations of the enterprise to transfer resources to other entities and owners' equity), and the effects of transactions, events, and circumstances that change resources and claims to those resources" (par. 40). Concepts Statement No. 6 (and previously Concepts Statement No. 3) provides the means for carrying out that objective. It defines the elements of financial statements—the economic resources of an entity, the claims to those resources, and changes in them—about which information is relevant to investors, creditors, and other users of financial statements for investment, credit, and similar decisions:

> The elements defined in this Statement are a related group with a particular focus—on assets, liabilities, equity, and other elements directly related to measuring performance and status of an entity. Information about an entity's performance and status provided by accrual accounting is the primary focus of financial reporting. . . . (Concepts Statement No. 6, par. 3)

(i) Concepts Statement No. 3.   Concepts Statement No. 3, "Elements of Financial Statements of Business Enterprises," issued in December 1980, defined ten elements: assets, liabilities, equity, investments by owners, distributions to owners, and comprehensive income and its components—revenues, expenses, gains, and losses. The Statement introduced the term "comprehensive income," the name adopted by the Board for the concept that was called "earnings" in Concepts Statement No. 1 and the other conceptual framework documents previously issued, including the "Tentative Conclusions on Objectives of Financial Statements of Business Enterprises" (December 1976); the Discussion Memorandum, "Conceptual Framework for Financial Accounting and Reporting: Elements of Financial Statements and Their Measurement" (December 1976); and the Exposure Draft, "Objectives of Financial Reporting and Elements of Financial Statements of Business Enterprises" (December 1977). As its title shows, the first Exposure Draft in the conceptual framework project dealt with both objectives and elements.

During 1978, the Board divided the subject matter of the Exposure Draft. One part developed into Concepts Statement No. 1 on objectives, and another part became the basis for a revised Exposure Draft, "Elements of Financial Statements of Business Enterprises," which was issued in December 1979. The substance of that Exposure Draft became Concepts Statement No. 3.

The Board's work on not-for-profit reporting was advancing concurrently, and Concepts Statement No. 4, "Objectives of Financial Reporting by Nonbusiness Organizations," was issued with Concepts Statement No. 3 in December 1980. The four Concepts Statements constituted a single conceptual framework for financial accounting and reporting by all entities. The Board voiced its expectation in Concepts Statements No. 2 and No. 3 that the qualitative characteristics and definitions of elements of financial statements should apply to both business enterprises and not-for-profit organizations:

> Although the discussion of the qualities of information and the related examples in this Statement refer primarily to business enterprises, the Board has tentatively concluded that similar qualities also apply to financial information reported by nonbusiness organizations. (Concepts Statement No. 2, par. 4)

> Assets and liabilities are common to all organizations, and the Board sees no reason to define them differently for business and nonbusiness organizations. The Board also expects the definitions of equity, revenues, expenses, gains, and losses to fit both business and nonbusiness organizations. (Concepts Statement No. 3, par. 2)

The Board saw no need for separate statements on elements as it had for the objectives.

To solicit views on applying the qualitative characteristics and definitions of elements to both business enterprises and not-for-profit organizations, the Board issued an Exposure Draft, "Proposed Amendments to FASB Concepts Statement 2 and 3 to Apply Them to Nonbusiness Organizations," in July 1983. The Board reaffirmed the conclusion that the qualitative characteristics applied to not-for-profit organizations and issued a revised Exposure Draft, "Elements of Financial Statements," in September 1985. Concepts Statement No. 6, "Elements of Financial Statements," was issued in December 1985, superseding Concepts Statement No. 3 and extending that Statement's definitions to not-for-profit organizations. Most of Concepts Statement No. 3 was carried over into the parts of Concepts Statement No. 6 concerned with business enterprises or with both kinds of entities. Paragraph numbers were changed, however, because Concepts Statement No. 6 has numerous paragraphs that relate only to not-for-profit organizations or that explain how the definitions in Concepts Statement No. 3 apply to not-for-profit organizations.

(ii) Concepts Statement No. 6.   Concepts Statement No. 6 defines the same ten elements of financial statements that Concepts Statement No. 3 had defined: Seven are elements of the financial statements of both business enterprises and not-for-profit organizations—assets, liabilities, equity (business enterprises) or net assets (not-for-profit organizations), revenues, expenses, gains, and losses; and three are elements of financial statements of business enterprises only—investments by owners, distributions to owners, and comprehensive income. The Statement also defines three classes of net assets of not-for-profit organizations, characterized by the presence or absence of donor-imposed restrictions, and the changes in those classes during a period—changes in permanently restricted, temporarily restricted, and unrestricted net assets. For business enterprises, equity is defined only in total.

To try to avoid later confusion, the Statement is precise about what is an element and what is not. For example, cash, inventories, land, and buildings are items that fit the definition of assets, but they are not elements. Assets is the element:

> Elements of financial statements are the building blocks with which financial statements are constructed—the classes of items that financial statements comprise. *Elements* refers to broad classes, such as assets, liabilities, revenues, and expenses. Particular economic things and events, such as cash on hand or selling merchandise that may meet the definitions of elements are not elements as the term is used in this Statement. Rather, they are called *items* or other descriptive names. This Statement focuses on the broad classes and their characteristics instead of defining particular assets, liabilities, or other items. (Concepts Statement No. 6, par. 5)

Paragraph 6 then emphasizes that the elements in financial statements stand for things and events in the real world:

> The items that are formally incorporated in financial statements are financial representations (depictions in words and numbers) of certain resources of an entity, claims to those resources, and

the effects of transactions and other events and circumstances that result in changes in those resources and claims. That is, symbols (words and numbers) in financial statements stand for cash in a bank, buildings, wages due, sales, use of labor, earthquake damage to property, and a host of other economic things and events pertaining to an entity existing and operating in what is sometimes called the "real world."

The definitions are of the real world things and events, not of what is recognized in financial statements. That is, the definition of assets, for example, refers to assets such as the inventory in the warehouse, not to the word "inventory" and the related amount in the balance sheet.

A thing or event and its representation in financial statements commonly are called by the same name. For example, both the amount deposited in a checking account and its representation in the balance sheet are called "cash in bank."

Elements of financial statements are of two types: those that constitute financial position or status at a moment in time and those that are changes in financial position over a period of time. Assets, liabilities, and equity or net assets describe levels or amounts of resources or claims to or interests in resources at a moment in time. All other elements—revenues, expenses, gains, and losses (and for business enterprises, comprehensive income, and investments by and distributions to owners)—describe the effects of transactions and other events and circumstances that affect an entity over a period of time. The interrelation between the two types of elements is called "articulation":

> The two types of elements are related in such a way that (a) assets, liabilities, and equity (net assets) are changed by elements of the other type and at any time are their cumulative result and (b) an increase (decrease) in an asset cannot occur without a corresponding decrease (increase) in another asset or a corresponding increase (decrease) in a liability or equity (net assets). Those relations are sometimes collectively referred to as "articulation." They result in financial statements that are fundamentally interrelated so that statements that show elements of the second type depend on statements that show elements of the first type and vice versa. (Concepts Statement No. 6, par. 21)

The elements of financial statements are defined in relation to particular entities, which may be business enterprises, not-for-profit organizations, other economic units, or people. For example, items that qualify as assets under the definition are assets of particular entities.

(iii) Definition of an Asset.   There is no more fundamental concept in accounting than asset. Assets, or economic resources, are the lifeblood of both business enterprises and not-for-profit organizations. Without assets—to exchange for, combine with, or transform into other assets—those entities would have no reason to exist.

> Economic resources or assets and changes in them are central to the existence and operations of an individual entity. Both business enterprises and not-for-profit organizations are in essence resource or asset processors, and a resource's capacity to be exchanged for cash or other resources or to be combined with other resources to produce needed or desired scarce goods or services gives it utility and value (future economic benefit) to an entity. (Concepts Statement No. 6, par. 11)

> Since resources or assets confer their benefits on an enterprise by being exchanged, used, or otherwise invested, changes in resources or assets are the purpose, the means, and the result of an enterprise's operations, and a business enterprise exists primarily to acquire, use, produce, and distribute resources. (Concepts Statement No. 6, par. 15)

Because assets are so fundamental, one would think that the issue of what is or is not an asset would have been settled long ago. All accountants claim to know an asset when they see one; yet differences of opinion arise about whether some items called assets are assets at all and should be included in balance sheets. Those differences of opinion surfaced at the

FASB's first hearings, as already described, and those experiences convinced early Board members that workable definitions of assets and liabilities were imperative.

The FASB decided on the conceptual primacy of assets and liabilities, meaning that the definitions of all the other elements of financial statements are derived from the definitions of assets and liabilities. Since the assets definition is critical, Concepts Statement No. 6 provides a carefully worded definition with three essential facets, adds an explanation of the characteristics of assets, and devotes a significant part of Appendix B to the Statement to elaborating the concept of assets. All of those sections are part of the definition of assets.

The definition of an asset is in paragraph 25:

> Assets are probable future economic benefits obtained or controlled by a particular entity as a result of past transactions or events.

Paragraph 26 then describes the trio of characteristics that qualify an item as an asset:

> An asset has three essential characteristics: (a) it embodies a probable future benefit that involves a capacity, singly or in combination with other assets, to contribute directly or indirectly to future net cash inflows, (b) a particular entity can obtain the benefit and control others' access to it, and (c) the transaction or other event giving rise to the entity's right to or control of the benefit has already occurred.

The definition indicates the appropriate questions to ask in trying to decide whether or not a particular item is an asset: Is there a future economic benefit? If so, to which entity does it belong? What made it an asset of that entity?

FUTURE ECONOMIC BENEFITS.   Assets commonly are items that can also be characterized as economic resources—the scarce means through which people and other economic units carry out economic activities such as consumption, production, and exchange. All economic resources or assets have "service potential" or "future economic benefit," the scarce capacity to provide services or benefits to the people or other entities that use or hold them.

The capacity to be exchanged for something else of value, to be used to produce something else of value, or to be used to settle liabilities are all evidence of an asset's future economic benefit:

> The most obvious evidence of future economic benefit is a market price. Anything that is commonly bought and sold has future economic benefit. . . . Similarly, anything that creditors or others commonly accept in settlement of liabilities has future economic benefit, and anything that is commonly used to produce goods or services, whether tangible or intangible and whether or not it has a market price or is otherwise exchangeable, also has future economic benefit. (Concepts Statement No. 6, par. 173)

If someone is willing to pay for something—to give up money or something else of value to possess it—that something has future economic benefit. However, the absence of a market price or exchangeability of an asset does not negate future economic benefit that can be obtained by use of the asset instead of by its exchange, although it may cause recognition and measurement problems.

At least two questions need to be asked about the presence or absence of future economic benefit to determine whether or not an entity has an asset: Did the item obtained by an entity truly represent a future economic benefit in the first place, and does all or any of the future economic benefit to the entity remain at the time the issue of its being an asset is considered?

The pervasiveness of uncertainty in business and economic affairs often obscures the fact that some items have the capacity to provide future economic benefits to an entity and thus should be recognized as assets. Expenditures for research and development, advertising, training, development of new markets, relocation, and goodwill are examples of items for which management's intent clearly is to obtain or augment future economic benefits but for which uncertainty about the extent, if any, to which it succeeded in creating or increasing future economic benefits leads to their recognition as expenses or losses rather than as assets. If research and development or advertising costs actually result in new or greater future economic benefit, that benefit qualifies as an asset. The practical problems are in determining whether future economic benefit is actually present and in quantifying it, especially if realization of benefits is far down the road, or perhaps never. (This paragraph summarizes the conclusions of FASB Statement No. 2, "Accounting for Research and Development Costs," whose development raised questions that helped Board members decide that a definition of assets was essential.)

Concepts Statement No. 6 says that most assets presently included in financial statements qualify as assets under its definition because they have future economic benefits. They include cash, accounts and notes receivable, interest and dividends receivable, and investments in the securities of other entities. Inventories of raw materials, work-in-process, and finished goods and productive resources such as property, plant, and equipment also qualify as assets but are mentioned separately from cash, receivables, and investments because they have often been described in accounting literature as "deferred costs" or "deferred charges" to revenues (for reasons described earlier).

Future economic benefits are obtained by incurring costs, but incurring of costs is not sufficient evidence of the existence of an asset:

> Although an entity normally incurs costs to acquire or use assets, costs incurred are not themselves assets. The essence of an asset is its future economic benefit rather than whether or not it was acquired at a cost. However, costs may be significant to applying the definition of assets in at least two ways: as evidence of acquisition of an asset or as a measure of an attribute of an asset. (Concepts Statement No. 6, par. 179)

Economic activity is rife with instances in which costs were incurred without receiving any future economic benefits. Moreover, entities often obtain assets without incurring costs; business enterprises may receive investment in kind by owners, and not-for-profit organizations often acquire assets such as marketable securities and buildings from donors.

Services provided by other entities can be assets of an entity only momentarily as they are received and used, but they may be used to create or add value to other assets. The right to receive services for specified or determinable future periods can be an asset.

CONTROL BY A PARTICULAR ENTITY.   The definition defines assets in relation to specific entities. An asset is an asset of some entity. No asset can simultaneously be an asset of more than one entity, although some physical assets may provide future economic benefits to two or more entities at the same time. That is, some assets comprise separable bundles of benefits that may be unbundled and held simultaneously by two or more entities. For example, a building may provide future economic benefits to its owner, an entity that leases space in it, and an entity that holds a mortgage on it. All have interests in different aspects of the same asset. Most expect to receive cash flows from having one or more of the bundles of benefits.

An entity must control an item's future economic benefit to be able to consider the item as its asset. To enjoy an asset's benefits, an entity generally must be in a position to deny or regulate access to that benefit by others, for example, by permitting access only at a price:

> Thus, an asset of an entity is the future economic benefit that the entity can control and thus can, within limits set by the nature of the benefit or the entity's right to it, use as it pleases. The entity having an asset is the one that can exchange it, use it to produce goods or services, exact a price for others' use of it, use it to settle liabilities, hold it, or perhaps distribute it to owners. (Concepts Statement No. 6, par. 184)

An entity usually gains the ability to control an asset's future economic benefits through a legal right. However, an entity still may have an asset without having an enforceable legal right to it if it can obtain and control the benefit some other way, for example, by maintaining exclusive access to the asset's benefits by keeping secret a formula or process.

OCCURRENCE OF A PAST TRANSACTION OR EVENT.   Items become assets of an entity as the result of transactions or other events or circumstances that have already occurred. An entity has an asset only if it has the present ability to obtain that asset's future economic benefits. If an entity anticipates that it may in the future control an item's future economic benefits but as yet does not have that control, it cannot claim that item as its asset because the transaction, other event, or circumstance conferring that control has not yet occurred:

> Since the transaction or event giving rise to the entity's right to the future economic benefit must already have occurred, the definition excludes from assets items that may in the future become an entity's assets but have not yet become its assets. An entity has no asset for a particular future economic benefit if the transactions or events that give it access to and control of the benefit are yet in the future. (Concepts Statement No. 6, par. 191)

Similarly, once acquired, an asset continues as an asset of an entity as long as the transactions, other events, or circumstances that use up or destroy its future economic benefit or deprive the entity of its control are in the future.

(iv) Definition of a Liability.   The definition of a liability in paragraph 35 of Concepts Statement No. 6 has the same structure as the asset definition. The parallelism of the two definitions was deliberate:

> Liabilities are probable future sacrifices of economic benefits arising from present obligations of a particular entity to transfer assets or provide services to other entities in the future as a result of past transactions or events.

Paragraph 36 describes the three characteristics that an item must possess to be a liability:

> A liability has three essential characteristics: (a) it embodies a present duty or responsibility to one or more other entities that entails settlement by probable future transfer or use of assets at a specified or determinable date, on occurrence of a specified event, or on demand, (b) the duty or responsibility obligates a particular entity, leaving it little or no discretion to avoid the future sacrifice, and (c) the transaction or other event obligating the entity has already happened.

The definition prompts the following questions when trying to decide if a particular item constitutes a liability: Is there an obligation requiring a future sacrifice of assets? If so, which entity is obligated? What past transaction or event made it a liability of that entity?

REQUIRED FUTURE SACRIFICE OF ASSETS.   Liabilities commonly arise as the consequence of financial instruments, contracts, and laws, invented to facilitate the functioning of a highly developed economy by permitting delays in payment and delivery in return for interest or other compensation as the price for enduring delay. Entities routinely incur liabilities to acquire the funds, goods, and services they need to operate and just as routinely settle the liabilities they incur, usually by paying cash. For example: borrowing cash results in an obligation to repay the amount borrowed, usually with interest; using employees' knowledge, skills, time, and effort results in an obligation to pay compensation for their use; or selling products with warranties results in an obligation to pay cash or to repair or replace the products that prove defective. Liabilities come in a vast array of forms, but they all entail a present obligation requiring a nondiscretionary future sacrifice of some future economic benefit:

> The essence of a liability is a duty or requirement to sacrifice assets in the future. A liability requires an entity to transfer assets, provide services, or otherwise expend assets to satisfy a

responsibility to one or more other entities that it has incurred or that has been imposed on it. (Concepts Statement No. 6, par. 193)

Although most liabilities arise from exchanges between entities, most of which are contractual in nature, some obligations are imposed by laws or governmental regulations that require sacrificing assets to comply.

Receipt of proceeds—cash, other assets, or services—without an accompanying cash payment is often evidence that a liability has been incurred, but it is not conclusive evidence. Other transactions and events generate proceeds—cash sales of goods or services or other sales of assets, cash from donor contributions, or cash investments by owners—without incurring liabilities. Liabilities can be incurred without any accompanying receipt of proceeds, for example, by imposition of taxes. It is the obligation to sacrifice future economic benefits that signifies a liability, not whether proceeds were received by incurring it.

Most liabilities presently included in financial statements qualify as liabilities under the definition because they require a future sacrifice of assets. They include accounts and notes payable, wages and salaries payable, long-term debt, interest and dividends payable, and obligations to honor warranties and to pay pensions, deferred compensation, and taxes. Subscriptions or rents collected in advance or other "unearned revenues" from deposits and prepayments received for goods or services to be provided are also liabilities because they obligate an entity to give up assets or provide services to other entities. Those kinds of items sometimes have been referred to as "deferred credits" or "reserves" in the accounting literature.

Obligation of a Particular Entity

To have a liability, an entity must be obligated to sacrifice its assets in the future—that is, it must be bound by a legal, equitable, or constructive duty or responsibility to transfer assets or provide services to one or more other entities. (Concepts Statement No. 6, par. 200)

A liability entails an obligation—legal, moral, or ethical—to one or more other entities to give them assets or provide them with services in the future. Not all probable future sacrifices of assets are liabilities of an entity. An intent or expectation to enter into a contract or transaction to transfer assets does not constitute a liability until an obligation to another entity is taken on.

The obligation aspect of liabilities is not emphasized as strongly in the definition in the Concepts Statement as it perhaps might have been. The Board became enamored with making the one-sentence definitions of assets and liabilities parallel to accentuate the symmetry between future benefits of assets and future sacrifices of liabilities.

The definition of an asset emphasizes its "service potential" or "future economic benefit," "the scarce capacity to provide services or benefits to the entities that use them" (par. 28), the common characteristic possessed by all assets. The definition of a liability puts first "future sacrifices of assets" to make it parallel with the asset definition, but it would have been more precise to focus on an entity's "obligation" to another entity to transfer assets or to provide services to it in the future. Future sacrifices of assets, after all, are the consequence—not the cause—of an obligation to another entity. Liabilities are present obligations of a particular entity to transfer assets or provide services to other entities in the future, requiring probable future sacrifices of economic benefits as a result of past transactions or events.

Some kinds of assets and liabilities are mirror images of one another. Receivables and payables are the most obvious example. Entity X has an asset (a receivable) because Entity Y has a liability (a payable) to transfer an asset (most commonly cash) to Entity X. Unless Entity Y has the liability, Entity X has no asset. Those relationships hold for rights to receive and obligations to pay or deliver cash, goods, or services. In fact, they hold for most contractual relationships involving a right to receive and an obligation to deliver. Receivables and payables cancel each other out in national income accounting, for example, leaving land, buildings, equipment, and similar assets as the stock of productive resources of the economy.

Most kinds of assets are not receivables, and a host of assets have no liabilities as mirror images. For example, the benefit from owning a building does not stem from an obligation of another entity to provide the benefit. The building itself confers significant benefits on its owner. The owner may, of course, enhance the benefits from the building by obtaining the right to services provided by others, who incur corresponding obligations, but that is a separate contractual arrangement involving both rights and obligations for the contracting parties.

Consequently, the Board's concern with the symmetry between the future benefits of assets and the future sacrifices of liabilities tended to overshadow the obligation to another entity that is the principal distinguishing characteristic of a liability. The definition of liabilities in Concepts Statements No. 3 and No. 6 and the accompanying explanations might well have profited from a brief description such as that in FASB Statement No. 5, "Accounting for Contingencies" (par. 70):

> The economic obligations of an enterprise are defined in paragraph 58 of *APB Statement No. 4* as "its present responsibilities to transfer economic resources or provide services to other entities in the future." Two aspects of that definition are especially relevant to accounting for contingencies: first, that liabilities are *present* responsibilities and, second, that they are obligations to *other entities*. Those notions are supported by other definitions of liabilities in published accounting literature, for example:
>
>> Liabilities are claims of creditors against the enterprise, arising out of past activities, that are to be satisfied by the disbursement or utilization of corporate resources. (AAA, 1957, p. 16)
>>
>> A liability is the result of a transaction of the past, not of the future. (Moonitz, 1960, p. 44)

OCCURRENCE OF A PAST TRANSACTION OR EVENT.   Items become liabilities of an entity as the result of transactions or other events or circumstances that have already occurred. An entity has a liability only if it has a present obligation to transfer assets to another entity. Budgeting the payments required to enact a purchase results neither in acquiring an asset nor in incurring a liability because no transaction or event has yet occurred that gives the entity access to or control of future economic benefits or binds it to transfer assets.

Once incurred, a liability remains a liability of an entity until it is satisfied, usually by payment of cash, in another transaction or other event or circumstance affecting the entity.

(v) Nonessential Characteristics of Assets and Liabilities.   The word "probable" is included in the asset and liability definitions with its general, not accounting or technical, meaning: "that which can reasonably be expected or believed on the basis of available evidence or logic but is neither certain nor proved" (*Webster's New World Dictionary of the American Language,* 1982, p. 1132). Its use was intended to indicate that something does not have to be certain or proved to qualify as an asset or liability. The first Exposure Draft did not contain the word "probable." It said:

> [A]ssets (liabilities) are future economic benefits (sacrifices of economic benefits) obtained or controlled by a particular entity (arising from present obligations of a particular entity to transfer assets or provide services to other entities in the future) as a result of past transactions or events.

The Board received many comment letters that said, in essence, "Nothing can ever be an asset or liability because you have said that it has to be certain, and everything except cash is uncertain."

The Board thus inserted "probable" into the definition, but perhaps "expected" would have been a better word. As long as someone thinks that an item has value and is willing to pay for it, the item has value, even if the expectation turns out to have been mistaken. It is easy to read more into the use of "probable" than was intended. "Probable" is not really an essential part of the definitions; its function is to acknowledge the presence of uncertainty and to say that the future economic benefits or sacrifices do not have to be certain to qualify the items in question as assets and liabilities, *not* to specify a characteristic that must be present.

Although the application of the definitions of assets and liabilities commonly requires some assessment of probabilities, degrees of probability are not part of the definitions. The degree of probability of a future economic benefit (or of a future cash outlay or other sacrifice of future economic benefits) and the degree to which its amount can be estimated with reasonable reliability, both of which are required to recognize an item as an asset (or a liability), are recognition and measurement matters.

The asset and liability definitions screen out items that lack one or more of the three essential characteristics that assets and liabilities, respectively, must possess. Assets and liabilities have other features that help identify them. Assets may be acquired at a cost, tangible, exchangeable, or legally enforceable. Liabilities usually require the obligated entity to pay cash to one or more entities and are also legally enforceable. However, the difference between those features and the three characteristics identified by Concepts Statement No. 6 as essential to assets and liabilities is that the absence of a "nonessential" feature, by itself, is not sufficient to disqualify an item from being an asset or liability, whereas the absence of even one of the three essential characteristics does preclude an item from being an asset or liability. For example:

> [A]n item does not qualify as an asset of an entity under the definition in paragraph 25 if (a) the item involves no future economic benefit, (b) the item involves future economic benefit, but the entity cannot obtain it, or (c) the item involves future economic benefit that the entity may in the future obtain, but the events or circumstances that give the entity access to and control of the benefit have not yet occurred (or the entity in the past had the ability to obtain or control the future benefit, but events or circumstances have occurred to remove that ability). Similarly, an item does not qualify as a liability of an entity under the definition in paragraph 35 if (a) the item entails no future sacrifice of assets, (b) the item entails future sacrifice of assets, but the entity is not obligated to make the sacrifice, or (c) the item involves a future sacrifice of assets that the entity will be obligated to make, but the events or circumstances that obligate the entity have not yet occurred (or the entity in the past was obligated to make the future sacrifice, but events or circumstances have occurred to remove that obligation). (Concepts Statement No. 6, par. 168)

(vi) Equity or Net Assets.   Equity of business enterprises and net assets of not-for-profit organizations have the same definition.

> Equity or net assets is the residual interest in the assets of an entity that remains after deducting its liabilities. (Concepts Statement No. 6, par. 49)

Since equity or net assets constitutes what remains after liabilities are deducted from assets, it depends on a business enterprise's profitability or a not-for-profit organization's success at fund raising or in conducting its major operations.

(vii) Equity of Business Enterprises.   Equity of business enterprises differs from net assets of not-for-profit organizations because it represents the ownership interests of those who invest funds in a business enterprise with the expectation of obtaining a return on their investment as a result of the enterprise's operating at a profit. Equity is often referred to as "risk capital," for in an uncertain world owners first bear the risk that an enterprise may be unprofitable. It may be increased and decreased by profits and losses and through investments by and distributions to owners:

> Investments by owners are increases in equity of a particular business enterprise resulting from transfers to it from other entities of something valuable to obtain or increase ownership interests

(or equity) in it. Assets are most commonly received as investments by owners, but that which is received may also include services or satisfaction or conversion of liabilities of the enterprise. (Concepts Statement No. 6, par. 66)

Distributions to owners are decreases in equity of a particular business enterprise resulting from transferring assets, rendering services, or incurring liabilities by the enterprise to owners. Distributions to owners decrease ownership interest (or equity) in an enterprise. (Concepts Statement No. 6, par. 67)

A business enterprise may make discretionary distributions to owners, usually by the formal act of declaring a dividend, but it is not obligated to do so. Many enterprises have several classes of equity, each with different priority claims on enterprise assets in the event of liquidation, depending on the degree to which they bear relatively more of the risk of unprofitability. However, all classes of equity depend to some extent on enterprise profitability for distributions of assets, and no class has an unconditional right or absolute claim to the assets of an enterprise except in the event of liquidation of the enterprise, and even then, owners must stand behind creditors, who have a priority right to enterprise assets.

Liabilities and equity are mutually exclusive claims to or interests in an enterprise's assets by other entities, and liabilities take precedence over ownership interests. Although the line between equity and liabilities is clear in concept, it has been increasingly obscured in practice with the introduction of financial instruments having the characteristics of both liabilities and equity. Convertible debt instruments and redeemable preferred stock are common examples of securities with both debt and equity characteristics, which may present problems in accounting for them.

Since equity ranks after liabilities as a claim to or interest in the assets of the enterprise, it is a *residual* interest. Changes in it result from increases and decreases from nonowner sources as well as from investments by and distributions to owners:

Equity in a business enterprise is the ownership interest, and its amount is the cumulative result of investments by owners, comprehensive income, and distributions to owners. That characteristic, coupled with the characteristic that liabilities have priority over ownership interest as claims against enterprise assets, makes equity not determinable independently of assets and liabilities. Although equity can be described in various ways, and different recognition criteria and measurement procedures can affect its amount, equity always equals net assets (assets minus liabilities). That is why it is a residual interest. (Concepts Statement No. 6, par. 213)

(viii) Comprehensive Income of Business Enterprises

Equity is originally created by owners' investments in an enterprise and may from time to time be augmented by additional investments by owners. Equity is reduced by distributions by the enterprise to owners. However, the distinguishing characteristic of equity is that it inevitably is affected by the enterprise's operations and other events and circumstances affecting the enterprise (which together constitute comprehensive income . . .). (Concepts Statement No. 6, par. 63)

Concepts Statement No. 1 says that "[t]he primary focus of financial reporting is information about an enterprise's performance provided by measures of [comprehensive income] and its components" (par. 43). Investors, creditors and others focus on comprehensive income to help them assess an enterprise's prospects for generating net cash inflows because, in the long run, it is through comprehensive income that investors, creditors, and others obtain a return on their investments, loans, or other association with an enterprise.

Concepts Statement No. 6 (par. 70) defines comprehensive income:

Comprehensive income is the change in equity of a business enterprise during a period from transactions and other events and circumstances from nonowner sources. It includes all changes in equity during a period except those resulting from investments by owners and distributions to owners.

Paragraph 74 describes the sources of comprehensive income:

> Comprehensive income of a business enterprise results from (a) exchange transactions and other transfers between the enterprise and other entities that are not its owners, (b) the enterprise's productive efforts, and (c) price changes, casualties, and other effects of interactions between the enterprise and the economic, legal, social, political, and physical environment of which it is part. An enterprise's productive efforts and most of its exchange transactions with other entities are ongoing major activities that constitute the enterprise's central operations by which it attempts to fulfill its basic function in the economy of producing and distributing goods or services at prices that are sufficient to enable it to pay for the goods and services it uses and to provide a satisfactory return to its owners.

Comprehensive income and investments by and distributions to owners account for all changes in equity of a business enterprise during a period.

With the definition of comprehensive income, the set of definitions of the elements of financial statements necessary to show financial position and to account for all changes in financial position is complete. Six elements—assets, liabilities, equity, investments by owners, distributions to owners, and comprehensive income—are mutually exclusive and sufficient to make the set complete. However, to satisfy the objectives of financial reporting, that is, to provide information intended to be useful to investors and creditors in assessing an enterprise's performance or profitability, requires information about the components of comprehensive income:

> Information about various components of comprehensive income is usually more useful than merely its aggregate amount to investors, creditors, managers, and others who are interested in knowing not only that an entity's net assets have increased (or decreased) but also *how* and *why*. The amount of comprehensive income for a period can, after all, be measured merely by comparing the ending and beginning equity and eliminating the effects of investments by owners and distributions to owners, but that procedure has never provided adequate information about an entity's performance. Investors, creditors, managers, and others need information about the causes of changes in assets and liabilities. (Concepts Statement No. 6, par. 219)

REVENUES, EXPENSES, GAINS, AND LOSSES.   Investors and creditors want and need to know how and why equity has changed, not just the amount that it has changed. The sources of comprehensive income are therefore significant to those attempting to use financial statements to help them with investment, credit, and similar decisions.

The primary source of comprehensive income is an enterprise's major or central operations, but income can also often be generated by peripheral or incidental activities in which an enterprise engages. Moreover, the economic, legal, social, political, and physical environment in which an enterprise operates creates events and circumstances that can affect comprehensive income but that may be partly or wholly beyond the control of individual enterprises and their managements.

Those various sources result in receipts that may differ in stability, risk, and predictability. Thus the desire for information about the various sources of comprehensive income underlies the distinctions between revenues, expenses, gains, and losses.

The components of comprehensive income are defined in the following paragraphs of Concepts Statement No. 6:

> Revenues are inflows or other enhancements of assets of an entity or settlements of its liabilities (or a combination of both) from delivering or producing goods, rendering services, or other activities that constitute the entity's ongoing major or central operations. (par. 78)

> Expenses are outflows or other using up of assets or incurrences of liabilities (or a combination of both) from delivering or producing goods, rendering services, or carrying out other activities that constitute the entity's ongoing major or central operations. (par. 80)

> Gains are increases in equity (net assets) from peripheral or incidental transactions of an entity and from all other transactions and other events and circumstances affecting the entity except those that result from revenues or investments by owners. (par. 82)

> Losses are decreases in equity (net assets) from peripheral or incidental transactions of an entity and from all other transactions and other events and circumstances affecting the entity except those that result from expenses or distributions to owners. (par. 83)

Distinctions between revenues and gains and expenses and losses are not significant in determining comprehensive income. Since comprehensive income is determined by changes in assets and liabilities, it can be derived without separating it into its various components. Revenues and expenses can be determined merely by separating the positive and negative components of income. Gains and losses are the part of income not explained by revenues and expenses.

Revenues and expenses represent actual or expected cash inflows and outflows usually associated with the ongoing major operations and earning and financing activities of an enterprise, leaving other more peripheral and incidental changes in equity to be described as various kinds of gains and losses:

> Revenues and gains are similar, and expenses and losses are similar, but some differences are significant in conveying information about an enterprise's performance. Revenues and expenses result from an entity's ongoing major or central operations and activities—that is, from activities such as producing or delivering goods, rendering services, lending, insuring, investing, and financing. In contrast, gains and losses result from incidental or peripheral transactions of an enterprise with other entities and from other events and circumstances affecting it. Some gains and losses may be considered "operating" gains and losses and may be closely related to revenues and expenses. Revenues and expenses are commonly displayed as gross inflows or outflows of net assets, while gains and losses are usually displayed as net inflows or outflows. (Concepts Statement No. 6, par. 87)

> Distinctions between revenues and gains and between expenses and losses in a particular entity depend to a significant extent on the nature of the entity, its operations, and its other activities. Items that are revenues for one kind of entity may be gains for another, and items that are expenses for one kind of entity may be losses for another. For example, investments in securities that may be sources of revenues and expenses for insurance or investment companies may be sources of gains and losses in manufacturing or merchandising companies. Technological changes may be sources of gains or losses for most kinds of enterprises but may be characteristic of the operations of high-technology or research-oriented enterprises. . . . (Concepts Statement No. 6, par. 88)

Revenues, expenses, gains, and losses, while useful for constructing income statements to show how comprehensive income is obtained, are not needed to derive it. Different components of income are useful to distinguish revenue generated from the production and sale of products from return on investments in marketable securities in an income statement. The primary purpose of separating comprehensive income into revenues and expenses and gains and losses is to make the display of information about an enterprise's sources of comprehensive income as useful as possible.

(ix) Net Assets of Not-for-Profit Organizations.   A not-for-profit organization has no ownership interests that can be sold, transferred, or that convey entitlement to a share of a residual distribution of resources in the event of liquidation of the organization. It thus does not receive investments of assets by owners and is generally prohibited from distributing assets as dividends to its members or officers. Increases in its net assets result from receipt of assets from resource providers who expect to receive neither repayment nor return on the assets. However, some resource providers may impose permanent or temporary restrictions on the uses of the assets they contribute to be able to influence an organization's use of those assets.

Thus net assets of not-for-profit organizations is divided into three mutually exclusive classes—permanently restricted net assets, temporarily restricted net assets, and unrestricted net assets. Restrictions restrain the organization from using part of its resources for purposes other than those specified, for example, to settle liabilities or to provide services outside the purview of the restrictions.

Briefly, permanently restricted net assets is the part of net assets resulting from inflows of assets whose use by the organization is limited by donor-imposed stipulations that neither expire nor can be satisfied or otherwise removed by any action of the organization. Stipulations that require resources to be permanently maintained but that permit the organization to use the income derived from the donated assets are often called endowments.

Temporarily restricted net assets is the part of net assets governed by donor-imposed stipulations that can expire or be fulfilled or removed by actions of the organization in accordance with those stipulations. Once the stipulation is satisfied, the restriction is gone.

Unrestricted net assets is the part of net assets resulting from all revenues, expenses, gains, and losses that are not changes in permanently or temporarily restricted net assets. The only limits on unrestricted net assets are the broad limits encompassing the nature of the organization, which are specified in its articles of incorporation or bylaws, and perhaps limits resulting from contractual agreements (for example, loan covenants) entered into by the organization in the course of its operations.

Although a not-for-profit organization does not have ownership interests or comprehensive income in the same sense as a business enterprise, to be able to continue to achieve its service and operating objectives, it needs to maintain net assets such that resources made available to it at least equal the resources needed to provide services at levels satisfactory to resource providers and other constituents. To assess an organization's success at maintaining net assets, resource providers need information about the components of changes in net assets—revenues, expenses, gains, and losses. The definitions of revenues, expenses, gains, and losses of business enterprises also apply to not-for-profit organizations and

> include all transactions and other events and circumstances that change the amount of net assets of a not-for-profit organization. All resource inflows and other enhancements of assets of a not-for-profit organization or settlements of its liabilities that increase net assets are either revenues or gains and have characteristics similar to the revenues or gains of a business enterprise. Likewise, all resource outflows or other using up of assets or incurrences of liabilities that decrease net assets are either expenses or losses and have characteristics similar to expenses or losses of business enterprises. (Concepts Statement No. 6, par. 111)

A not-for-profit organization's central operations—its service-providing efforts, fund-raising activities, and most exchange transactions—by which it attempts to fulfill its service objectives, are the sources of its revenues and expenses. Gains and losses result from activities that are peripheral or incidental to its central operations and from interactions with its environment, which give rise to price changes, casualties, and other effects that may be largely beyond the control of an individual organization and its management.

(x) Accrual Accounting and Related Concepts.   Concepts Statement No. 6 also defines several "terms of art" or significant financial accounting and reporting concepts that are used extensively in the conceptual framework.

TRANSACTIONS, EVENTS, AND CIRCUMSTANCES.   "Transactions and other events and circumstances" affecting an entity is a phrase used throughout the conceptual framework to describe the sources or causes of changes in assets, liabilities, and equity. Real world occurrences that are reflected in financial statements divide into two categories: events and circumstances. They can be further divided into this hierarchy:

Events
    Transactions
        Exchanges
        Nonreciprocal transfers
    Other external events
    Internal events
Circumstances

Events are by far the most important, encompassing external happenings, including transactions, and internal happenings. The breakdown of events into those various components highlights differences that are important to financial accounting:

> An event is a happening of consequence to an entity. It may be an internal event that occurs within an entity, such as using raw materials or equipment in production, or it may be an external event that involves interaction between an entity and its environment, such as a transaction with another entity, a change in price of a good or service that an entity buys or sells, a flood or earthquake, or an improvement in technology by a competitor. (Concepts Statement No. 6, par. 135)

Transactions are external events that include reciprocal transfers of assets and liabilities between an entity and other entities called "exchanges" and "nonreciprocal transfers" between an entity and its owners or between an entity and entities other than its owners in which one of the participants is often a passive beneficiary or victim of the other's actions:

> A transaction is a particular kind of external event, namely, an external event involving transfer of something of value (future economic benefit) between two (or more) entities. The transaction may be an exchange in which each participant both receives and sacrifices value, such as purchases or sales of goods or services; or the transaction may be a nonreciprocal transfer in which an entity incurs a liability or transfers an asset to another entity (or receives an asset or cancellation of a liability) without directly receiving (or giving) value in exchange. Nonreciprocal transfers contrast with exchanges (which are reciprocal transfers) and include, for example, investments by owners, distributions to owners, impositions of taxes, gifts, charitable or educational contributions given or received, and thefts. (Concepts Statement No. 6, par. 137)

Investments by and distributions to owners are nonreciprocal transfers because they are events in which an enterprise receives assets from owners and acknowledges an increased ownership interest or disperses assets to owners whose interests decrease. They are not exchanges from the point of view of the enterprise because it incurs no obligations nor sacrifices any of its assets in exchange for owners' investments, and it receives nothing of value to itself in exchange for the assets it distributes with the payment of a dividend.

Circumstances, in contrast, are not events but the results of events. They provide evidence of often imperceptible events that may already have happened but that are discernible only in retrospect by the resulting state of affairs. They are important in financial reporting because they often have accounting consequences:

> Circumstances are a condition or set of conditions that develop from an event or a series of events, which may occur almost imperceptibly and may converge in random or unexpected ways to create situations that might otherwise not have occurred and might not have been anticipated. To see the circumstance may be fairly easy, but to discern specifically when the event or events that caused it occurred may be difficult or impossible. For example, a debtor's going bankrupt or a thief's stealing gasoline may be an event, but a creditor's facing the situation that its debtor is bankrupt or a warehouse's facing the fact that its tank is empty may be a circumstance. (Concepts Statement No. 6, par. 136)

ACCRUAL ACCOUNTING.   The objectives of financial reporting are served by accrual accounting, which generally provides a better indication of an entity's performance than does information about cash receipts and payments. Accrual accounting is defined in paragraph 139 of Concepts Statement No. 6:

> Accrual accounting attempts to record the financial effects on an entity of transactions and other events and circumstances that have cash consequences for the entity in the periods in which those transactions, events, and circumstances occur rather than only in the periods in which cash is received or paid by the entity. Accrual accounting is concerned with an entity's acquiring of goods and services and using them to produce and distribute other goods or services. It is concerned with the process by which cash expended on resources and activities is returned as more (or perhaps less) cash to the entity, not just with the beginning and end of that process. It recognizes that the buying, producing, selling, distributing, and other operations of an entity during a period, as well as other events that affect entity performance, often do not coincide with the cash receipts and payments of the period.

Accrual accounting is based not only on cash transactions but also on all the transactions, events, and circumstances that have cash consequences for an entity but involve no concurrent cash movement. By accounting for noncash assets, liabilities, and comprehensive income, accrual accounting links an entity's operations and other transactions, events, and circumstances that affect it with its cash receipts and outlays, thereby providing information about its assets, liabilities, and changes in them that cannot be obtained by accounting only for its cash transactions.

Concepts Statement No. 6 also provides technical definitions of the following procedures used to apply accrual accounting:

> **Accrual** is concerned with expected future cash receipts and payments: it is the accounting process of recognizing assets or liabilities and the related liabilities, assets, revenues, expenses, gains, or losses for amounts expected to be received or paid, usually in cash, in the future. **Deferral** is concerned with past cash receipts and payments—with prepayments received (often described as collected in advance) or paid: it is the accounting process of recognizing a liability resulting from a current cash receipt (or the equivalent) or an asset resulting from a current cash payment (or the equivalent) with deferred recognition of revenues, expenses, gains, or losses. Their recognition is deferred until the obligation underlying the liability is partly or wholly satisfied or until the future economic benefit underlying the asset is partly or wholly used or lost. (par. 141, bold type added)

> **Allocation** is the accounting process of assigning or distributing an amount according to a plan or a formula. It is broader than and includes **amortization,** which is the accounting process of reducing an amount by periodic payments or write-downs. Specifically, amortization is the process of reducing a liability recorded as a result of a cash receipt by recognizing revenues or reducing an asset recorded as a result of a cash payment by recognizing expenses or costs of production. (par. 142, bold type added)

> **Realization** in the most precise sense means the process of converting noncash resources and rights into money and is most precisely used in accounting and financial reporting to refer to sales of assets for cash or claims to cash. . . . **Recognition** is the process of formally recording or incorporating an item in the financial statements of an entity. (par. 143, bold type added)

> **Matching** of costs and revenues is simultaneous or combined recognition of the revenues and expenses that result directly and jointly from the same transactions or other events. In most entities, some transactions or events result simultaneously in both a revenue and one or more expenses. The revenue and expense(s) are directly related to each other and require recognition at the same time. In present practice, for example, a sale of product or merchandise involves both revenue (sales revenue) for receipt of cash or a receivable and expense (cost of goods sold) for sacrifice of the product or merchandise sold to customers. . . . (par. 146, bold type added)

That is a narrow definition of matching, similar to the definitions of Herman W. Bevis and

George O. May (pp. 1.34–1.35 of this chapter). The definition excludes from matching the systematic and rational allocation of revenues or costs to periods by a formula and makes matching a single process in measuring comprehensive income, not a synonym for the entire periodic income determination process, as it has been in many accountants' minds (pp. 1.36–1.37).

Concepts Statement No. 6 also includes an example on debt discount, premium, and issue cost (pars. 235–239) to illustrate precise technical differences between some of those terms.

(d) Recognition and Measurement.   Recognition and measurement originally had been viewed as separate components of the conceptual framework. Two research studies on recognition matters were commissioned by the FASB: "Recognition of Contractual Rights and Obligations: An Exploratory Study of Conceptual Issues" (1980), by Yuji Ijiri, and "Survey of Present Practices in Recognizing Revenues, Expenses, Gains, and Losses" (1981), by Henry R. Jaenicke. Those studies focused, respectively, on the timing of the initial recognition of assets and liabilities and on the related subsequent timing of recognition of revenues and expenses. A third study, "Recognition in Financial Statements: Underlying Concepts and Practical Conventions," by L. Todd Johnson and Reed K. Storey, was published in 1982.

Meanwhile, a project on "Financial Reporting and Changing Prices" was to consider measurement. The direction of the original measurement project was changed, however, because of the urgency caused by the increasing prices of the late 1960s and 1970s and the SEC's issuance of ASR No. 190, "Notice of Adoption of Amendments to Regulation S-X Requiring Disclosure of Certain Replacement Cost Data," which required certain publicly held companies to disclose replacement cost information about inventories, cost of sales, productive capacity, and depreciation. Instead of remaining part of the conceptual framework, it resulted in FASB Statement No. 33, "Financial Reporting and Changing Prices" (1979).

(i) Concepts Statement No. 5.   Recognition decisions often cannot be separated from measurement decisions, particularly if the decision relates to when to recognize changes in assets and liabilities. Recognition and measurement were eventually combined in the conceptual framework because most of the Board became convinced that certain recognition questions, which were among the most important to be dealt with, were so closely related to measurement issues that it was unproductive to try to handle them separately. The product of that union was Concepts Statement No. 5, entitled "Recognition and Measurement in Financial Statements of Business Enterprises," issued in December 1984.

(ii) Financial Statements.   Concepts Statement No. 5 includes concepts that relate recognition and measurement to the earlier Concepts Statements. For example, it is the part of the conceptual framework in which the FASB describes the financial statements that should be provided and how those financial statements contribute to the objectives of financial reporting:

> Financial statements are a central feature of financial reporting—a principal means of communicating financial information to those outside an entity. In external general purpose financial reporting, a financial statement is a formal tabulation of names and amounts of money derived from accounting records that displays either financial position of an entity at a moment in time or one or more kinds of changes in financial position of the entity during a period of time. Items that are recognized in financial statements are financial representations of certain resources (assets) of an entity, claims to those resources (liabilities and owners' equity), and the effects of transactions and other events and circumstances that result in changes in those resources and claims. The financial statements of an entity are a fundamentally related set that articulate with each other and derive from the same underlying data. (Concepts Statement No. 5, par. 5)

To satisfy the objectives of financial reporting—to provide information that is useful to investors and creditors and other users in making rational investment, credit, and similar decisions; to provide information to help them assess the amounts, timing, and uncertainty of prospective net cash inflows to an enterprise; and to provide information about the economic resources, claims to those resources (obligations to transfer resources to other entities and owners' equity), and changes in and claims to those resources—requires a full set of articulated financial statements, comprising:

- A statement of financial position at the end of the period.
- A statement of earnings (net income) for the period.
- A statement of comprehensive income (total nonowner changes in equity) for the period.
- A statement of cash flows during the period.
- A statement of investments by and distributions to owners during the period. (par. 13)

A full set of financial statements provides information about an entity's financial position and changes in its financial position. Financial position, as depicted in a balance sheet, is determined by the relationship between an entity's economic resources (assets) and obligations (liabilities), leaving a residual (net assets or owners' equity). In addition, information about earnings, comprehensive income, cash flows, and transactions with owners are different kinds of information about the effects of transactions and other events and circumstances that change assets and liabilities during a period—that is, they are information about different kinds of changes in financial position.

Not all information useful for investment, credit, and similar decisions that financial accounting is able to provide can be provided by financial statements. Concepts Statement No. 5 includes a diagram (Exhibit 1.4) illustrating the many kinds of information that investors and creditors may contemplate consulting when deciding whether to invest in or loan funds to an enterprise. Financial statements provide only part of the information useful for investment, credit, and similar decisions. Financial reporting also encompasses notes to financial statements and parenthetical disclosures, which provide information about accounting policies or explain information recognized in the financial statements. Supplementary information about the effects of changing prices or management discussion and analysis provides information that may also be relevant for making decisions but that does not meet the criteria necessary for recognition in financial statements. Financial statements are unique because the information they provide is distinguished by its capacity and need to withstand the scrutiny of accounting recognition.

Concepts Statement No. 5, expanding the one-sentence definition in Concepts Statement No. 3, defines recognition as

the process of formally recording or incorporating an item into the financial statements of an entity as an asset, liability, revenue, expense, or the like. Recognition includes depiction of an item in both words and numbers, with the amount included in the totals of the financial statements. For an asset or liability, recognition involves recording not only acquisition or incurrence of the item but also later changes in it, including changes that result in removal from the financial statements. (par. 6)

A slight shift in emphasis discloses another characteristic of recognition: "Recognition attempts to represent or depict in financial statements the effects on an entity of real-world economic things and events" (Johnson and Storey, 1982, p. 2). That description is congruent with the idea expressed throughout the conceptual framework that financial reporting is concerned with providing information about things and events that occur in the real world in which accounting takes place.

Concepts Statement No. 5 affirms the value of information disclosed in notes or other supplementary information as essential to understanding the information recognized in

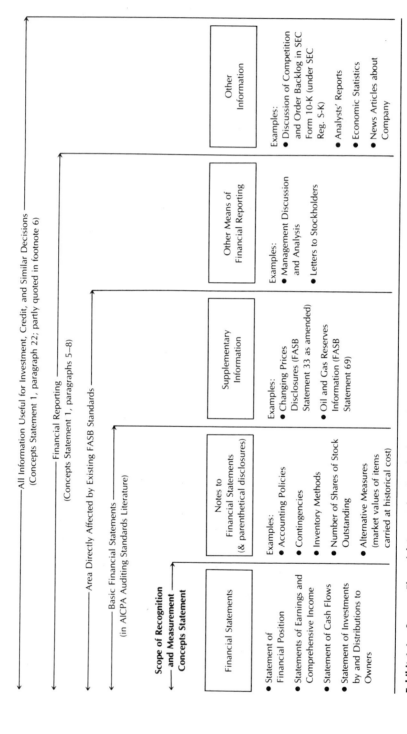

Exhibit 1.4. *Source:* **Financial Accounting Standards Board, Statement of Financial Accounting Concepts No. 5, par. 8.**

financial statements, but it also makes it clear that disclosure by other means is *not* recognition:

> Disclosure of information about the items in financial statements and their measures that may be provided by notes or parenthetically on the face of financial statements, by supplementary information, or by other means of financial reporting is not a substitute for recognition in financial statements for items that meet recognition criteria. Generally, the most useful information about assets, liabilities, revenues, expenses, and other items of financial statements and their measures (that with the best combination of relevance and reliability) should be recognized in the financial statements. (par. 9)

Although information provided by notes to financial statements or by other means is valuable and ought to be made available to investors, creditors, and other users, it is not a substitute for recognition in the body of financial statements with the amounts included in the financial statement totals.

EARNINGS AND COMPREHENSIVE INCOME.   Concepts Statement No. 5 says that a full set of financial statements should include both a statement of earnings and a statement of comprehensive income. Comprehensive income was defined in Concepts Statement No. 3 as an all-inclusive income concept:

> Comprehensive income is the change in equity (net assets) of an entity during a period from transactions and other events and circumstances from nonowner sources. It includes all changes in equity during a period except those resulting from investments by owners and distributions to owners. (par. 56. The same definition was carried over into Concepts Statement No. 6, par. 70.)

That concept was called "earnings" in Concepts Statement No. 1, but afterward the Board changed the name to comprehensive income and reserved the term earnings for possible use to designate a component part of comprehensive income (Concepts Statement No. 3 [and also Concepts Statement No. 6], par. 1, ftn. 1). Later, Concepts Statement No. 5 did use the term "earnings" to describe a component part of comprehensive income that corresponds to net income in current practice, except that it excludes the so-called "catch-up adjustment" required by APB Opinion No. 20, "Accounting Changes" (par. 19(b)), to be included in net income.

Concepts Statement No. 5 describes how earnings relates to comprehensive income at present:

> Earnings and comprehensive income have the same broad components—revenues, expenses, gains, and losses—but are not the same because certain classes of gains and losses are included in comprehensive income but are excluded from earnings. Those items fall into two classes that are illustrated by certain present practices:
>
> (a) Effects of certain accounting adjustments of earlier periods that are recognized in the period, such as the principal example in present practice—cumulative effects of changes in accounting principles—which are included in present net income but are excluded from earnings as set forth in this Statement. . .
>
> (b) Certain other changes in net assets (principally certain holding gains and losses) that are recognized in the period, such as some changes in market values of investments in marketable equity securities classified as noncurrent assets, some changes in market values of investments in industries having specialized accounting practices for marketable securities, and foreign currency translation adjustments. (par. 42)

Concepts Statement No. 5 describes but does not define earnings. Earnings cannot be defined because it results from applying generally accepted accounting principles and is determined by what is done in practice at a particular time—its meaning changes with changes in generally accepted accounting principles. For example, paragraph 35 of the Statement says:

> The Board expects the concept of earnings to be subject to the process of gradual change or evolution that has characterized the development of net income. Present practice has developed over a long time, and that evolution has resulted in significant changes in what net income reflects, such as a shift toward what is commonly called an "all-inclusive" income statement. Those changes have resulted primarily from standard-setting bodies' responses to several factors, such as changes in the business and economic environment and perceptions about the nature and limitations of financial statements, about the needs of users of financial statements, and about the need to prevent or cure perceived abuse(s) in financial reporting. Those factors sometimes may conflict or appear to conflict. For example, an all-inclusive income statement is intended, among other things, to avoid discretionary omissions of losses (or gains) from an income statement, thereby avoiding presentation of a more (or less) favorable report of performance or stewardship than is justified. However, because income statements also are used as a basis for estimating future performance and assessing future cash flow prospects, arguments have been advanced urging exclusion of unusual or nonrecurring gains and losses that might reduce the usefulness of an income statement for any one year for predictive purposes.

Those kinds of arguments also have been advanced urging exclusion of recurring gains and losses that increase the volatility of reported net income. For example, FASB Statement No. 12, "Accounting for Certain Marketable Securities" (1975), and FASB Statement No. 52, "Foreign Currency Translation" (1981), exclude from net income certain holding gains and losses (gains and losses from holding assets or owing liabilities while their prices change). Those provisions are described more fully in, respectively, Chapter 11 and Chapter 7 of this *Handbook* but, briefly, FASB Statement No. 12 requires the carrying amount of a marketable equity securities portfolio to be the lower of its aggregate cost and market value but requires that changes in the carrying amount of a noncurrent marketable equity securities portfolio "be included in the equity section of the balance sheet [that is, not included in net income] and shown separately." Similarly, FASB Statement No. 52 provides that "translation adjustments [as defined in the Statement] are not included in determining net income for the period but are disclosed and accumulated in a separate component of consolidated equity. . . ." As a result, net income is less all-inclusive than it was, say, after issuance of APB Opinion No. 30, "Reporting the Results of Operations—Reporting the Effects of Disposal of a Segment of a Business, and Extraordinary, Unusual and Infrequently Occurring Events and Transactions" (1973).

Since gains and losses of that kind are included in comprehensive income, that concept generally has attracted more criticism than net income or earnings. For example, John W. March's dissent to Concepts Statement No. 5 reflects a common view that periodic income determination should focus on performance rather than report gains and losses from all sources. These are the first and penultimate paragraphs of his dissent:

> Mr. March dissents from this Statement because (a) it does not adopt measurement concepts oriented toward what he believes is the most useful single attribute for recognition purposes, the cash equivalent of recognized transactions reduced by subsequent impairments or loss of service value—instead it suggests selecting from several different attributes without providing sufficient guidance for the selection process; (b) it identifies all nonowner changes in assets and liabilities as comprehensive income and return on equity, thereby including in income, incorrectly in his view, capital inputs from nonowners, unrealized gains from price changes, amounts that should be deducted to maintain capital in real terms, and foreign currency translation adjustments; (c) it uses a concept of income that is fundamentally based on measurements of assets, liabilities, and changes in them, rather than adopting the Statement's concept of earnings as the definition of income; and (d) it fails to provide sufficient guidance for initial recognition and derecognition of assets and liabilities.

> The description of earnings (paragraphs 33–38) and the guidance for applying recognition criteria to components of earnings (paragraphs 78–87) is consistent with Mr. March's view that income

should measure performance and that performance flows primarily from an entity's fulfillment of the terms of its transactions with outside entities that result in revenues, other proceeds on resource dispositions (gains), costs (expenses) associated with those revenues and proceeds, and losses sustained. However, Mr. March believes that those concepts are fundamental and should be embodied in definitions of the elements of financial statements and in basic income recognition criteria rather than basing income on measurements of assets, liabilities, and changes in them.

As March suggested, paragraphs 34 and 38 of Concepts Statement No. 5 contain good, brief descriptions of the goal of periodic income determination in the minds of those who think it should focus on performance:

> Earnings is a measure of performance for a period and to the extent feasible excludes items that are extraneous to that period—items that belong primarily to other periods.

> Earnings focuses on what the entity has received or reasonably expects to receive for its output (revenues) and what it sacrifices to produce and distribute that output (expenses). Earnings also includes results of the entity's incidental or peripheral transactions and some effects of other events and circumstances stemming from the environment (gains and losses).

One reason for the confusion about the relationship between comprehensive income and its component part called "earnings" is that the Board has done nothing more about its conclusion that a full set of financial statements includes a statement of comprehensive income (par. 13). Most people have, to their knowledge, never seen one and may have difficulty picturing it and the relation of earnings to it.

Since the FASB has not required a statement of comprehensive income, pronouncements such as FASB Statements No. 12 and No. 52 have made it possible for many U.S. enterprises to report periodic income that reflects their domestic and foreign operations as less risky than they actually are.

(iii) Capital Maintenance.   Maintenance of capital is a financial concept or abstraction needed to measure comprehensive income. Since comprehensive income is a residual concept, not all revenues of a business enterprise for a period are comprehensive income because the sacrifices necessary to produce the revenues must be considered. Capital used up during the period must be recovered from revenues or other increases in net assets before any of the return may be considered comprehensive income. An enterprise receives a return only after its capital has been maintained or recovered, therefore the concept of capital maintenance is critical for distinguishing an enterprise's return *on* investment from return *of* investment.

Two major concepts of capital maintenance exist, the financial capital concept and the physical capital concept (which is often described as maintaining operating capability, that is, maintaining the capacity of an enterprise to provide a constant supply of goods or services).

In Concepts Statement No. 5, the Board decided that the concept of financial capital maintenance is the basis for a full set of articulated financial statements:

> A return on financial capital results only if the financial (money) amount of an enterprise's net assets at the end of a period exceeds the financial amount of net assets at the beginning of the period after excluding the effects of transactions with owners. The financial capital concept is the traditional view and is the capital maintenance concept in present financial statements. (par. 47)

Financial capital maintenance can be measured either in units of money (for example, nominal dollars) or in units of constant purchasing power (for example, 1972 or 1992 dollars).

The Board rejected the physical capital concept, which holds that:

> [A] return on physical capital results only if the physical productive capacity of the enterprise at the end of the period (or the resources needed to achieve that capacity) exceeds the physical productive capacity at the beginning of the period, also after excluding the effects of transactions with owners. (par. 47)

The general procedure for maintaining physical capital is to value assets, such as inventories, property, plant, and equipment at their current replacement costs and to deduct expenses, such as cost of goods sold and depreciation, at replacement cost from revenues to measure periodic return on capital. The increases and decreases in replacement costs of those assets while they are held by the enterprise are included in owners' equity as a "capital maintenance adjustment" rather than in return on capital as "holding gains and losses." The idea underlying the measurement of return on capital in the physical capital concept is that increases in wealth that are merely increases in prices of things that an enterprise must continue to hold to engage in operations do not constitute return *on* capital but return *of* capital.

The principal difference between the two concepts is in the treatment of holding gains and losses resulting from the effects of price changes during a period on assets while held and on liabilities while owed:

> Under the financial capital concept, if the effects of those price changes are recognized, they are conceptually holding gains and losses . . . and are included in the return on capital. Under the physical capital concept, those changes would be recognized but conceptually would be capital maintenance adjustments that would be included directly in equity and not included in return on capital. Both earnings and comprehensive income as set forth in this Statement, like present net income, include holding gains and losses that would be excluded from income under a physical capital maintenance concept. (Concepts Statement No. 5, par. 48)

To illustrate, if the physical capital maintenance concept were applied to investments in marketable securities, all price appreciation would be considered to be return *of* capital, and only interest and dividends received would be return *on* capital.

(iv) Measurement and Attributes.   Recognition by definition includes the depiction of an item in both words and numbers. The need to quantify the information about an item to be recognized introduces the issue of its measurement. Concepts Statement No. 5 says that

> Measurement involves choice of an attribute by which to quantify a recognized item and choice of a scale of measurement (often called "unit of measure"). (par. 3)

"Attribute" is defined and explained in footnote 2 to paragraph 2 of Concepts Statement No. 1:

> "Attributes to be measured" refers to the traits or aspects of an element to be quantified or measured, such as historical cost/historical proceeds, current cost/current proceeds, etc. Attribute is a narrower concept than measurement, which includes not only identifying the attribute to be measured but also selecting a scale of measurement (for example, units of money or units of constant purchasing power). "Property" is commonly used in the sciences to describe the trait or aspect of an object being measured, such as the length of a table or the weight of a stone. But "property" may be confused with land and buildings in financial reporting contexts, and "attribute" has become common in accounting literature and is used in this Statement.

Since recognition often involves recording changes in assets and liabilities, it often raises the question of whether the amount of an attribute should be changed or whether a different attribute should be used in its place. In any event, since the changes in an asset or liability and in the attribute occur at the same time, it is often difficult to separate recognition from measurement problems.

Five different attributes of assets and liabilities are used in present accounting practice. The following is based on paragraph 67 of Concepts Statement No. 5, which describes the attributes and gives examples of the kinds of assets for which each attribute is commonly reported:

1. *Historical Cost*. The amount of cash or its equivalent paid to acquire an asset, usually adjusted after acquisition for amortization or other allocations (for example, property, plant, equipment, and most inventories).

2. *Current Cost*. The amount that would have to be paid if the same or an equivalent asset were acquired currently (for example, some inventories).

3. *Current Market Value*. The amount that could be obtained by selling an asset in orderly liquidation. Generally used for assets expected to be sold at prices lower than previous carrying amounts (for example, marketable securities).

4. *Net Realizable Value*. The nondiscounted amount into which an asset is expected to be converted in due course of business less direct costs necessary to make that conversion (for example, short-term receivables).

5. *Present (or Discounted) Value of Future Cash Flows*. The present value of future cash inflows into which an asset is expected to be converted in due course of business less present values of cash outflows necessary to obtain those inflows (for example, long-term receivables).

(v) Recognition and Measurement—Description Rather than Concepts.   The preceding pages have described several areas in which Concepts Statement No. 5 has furthered the conceptual framework, at least to some extent—in identifying what a full set of financial statements comprises, in expanding and clarifying what constitutes recognition, in explaining the relationship between comprehensive income and its component part, earnings, and in endorsing financial capital maintenance.

Although the Statement's name implies that it gives conceptual guidance on recognition and measurement, its conceptual contributions to financial reporting are not really in those two areas. As the result of compromises necessary to issue it, much of Concepts Statement No. 5 merely describes present practice and some of the reasons that have been used to support or explain it but provides little or no conceptual basis for analyzing and attempting to resolve the controversial issues of recognition and measurement about which accountants have disagreed for years.

Recognition and measurement are considered by many to be the most critical parts of the conceptual framework. Each component of the framework—the objectives, the qualitative characteristics, the elements of financial statements, recognition and measurement—is successively less abstract and more concrete than the one before. Recognition and measurement are the most concrete and least abstract of the components because they are necessarily at the point at which concepts and practice converge. They are the components in which practicing accountants have been most interested because they determine what actually gets into the numbers and totals in the financial statements. Whereas few practitioners may be interested in what they may see as abstractions—such as objectives, qualitative characteristics, and definitions—most are interested in a change in revenue recognition or the measured attribute of an asset, or perhaps in reporting the effects of inflation, and they usually feel that they have a vested interest in the Board's decisions regarding recognition and measurement and in resisting changes that may adversely affect their future reporting.

Accountants have strongly held, and ultimately polarizing, views about which is the most relevant and reliable attribute to be measured and about the circumstances needed for recognizing changes in attributes and changes in the amounts of an attribute. Proponents of the present model—which often is mislabeled "historical cost accounting" because it is actually a mixture of historical costs, current costs, current exit values, net realizable values, and present values—fiercely defend it and broach no discussion of alternatives for fear that any change would portend its abandonment in favor of "current value accounting," a term that is used generically to refer to the continuous use of any attribute other than historical cost. Similarly, proponents of various current cost or current value models are equally unyielding, often almost as critical of other current value or current cost models that compete with their own favorite model as they are of the current model for its failure to recognize the realities of changing values and changing prices.

The Board was as badly split on recognition and measurement as the constituency. Although most Board members could see the deficiencies in the current model, a majority of the Board could not accept a current value or current cost measurement system, even at a conceptual level. Therefore, instead of indicating a preferred accounting model or otherwise offering conceptual guidance about measurement, Concepts Statement No. 5 merely acknowledged that present practice consists of a mix of five attributes for measuring items in financial statements and said that the Board "expects the use of different attributes to continue" (par. 66). Beyond that, it said that "information based on current prices should be recognized if it is sufficiently relevant and reliable to justify the costs involved and more relevant than alternative information" (par. 90), which was extremely weak guidance. Whereas a neutral exposition of alternatives was appropriate for a Discussion Memorandum, a Concepts Statement seems to have been a curious choice for a document describing a litany of present measurement practices with neither conceptual analysis or evaluation nor guidance for making choices.

In merely describing current practice, Concepts Statement No. 5 seems to be a throwback to statements of accounting principles produced by the "distillation of experience" school of thought, an essentially practical, not a conceptual, effort. And its prescriptions for improving practice are reminiscent of those of the Committee on Accounting Procedure or the Accounting Principles Board: Measurement problems will be resolved on a case-by-case basis. Unfortunately, that approach worked only marginally well for those now-defunct bodies.

Oscar Gellein called the discussion of recognition in the Exposure Draft that ultimately became part of Concepts Statement No. 5 "a helpful distillation of current recognition practices." However, he also saw that the Statement would not advance financial reporting in the area of recognition and measurement:

> The umbrella is broad enough to cover virtually all current practices, but not conceptually directed toward either narrowing those practices or preventing their proliferation. . . . Recognition is the watershed issue in the conceptual framework in the sense that hierarchically it is the ultimate stage of conceptual concreteness. Without that kind of conceptual guidance, there is the risk of reversion to ad hoc rules in determining accounting methods. (Gellein, 1986, p. 14)

David Solomons has criticized Concepts Statement No. 5 for distorting the process of formulating future accounting standards. He noted that in several places it asserts that concepts are to be developed as the standard-setting process evolves, citing these examples:

> The Board expects the concept of earnings to be subject to the process of gradual change or evolution that has characterized the development of net income. (par. 35)

> Future standards may change what is recognized as components of earnings. . . . Moreover, because of the differences between earnings and comprehensive income, future standards also may recognize certain changes in net assets as components of comprehensive income but not as components of earnings. (par. 51)

> The Board believes that further development of recognition, measurement, and display matters will occur as the concepts are applied at the standards level. (par. 108)

Solomons was not at all persuaded by the Board's apparent argument, represented by those excerpts, that concepts could be a by-product of the standard-setting process:

> These appeals to evolution should be seen as what they are—a cop-out. If all that is needed to improve our accounting model is reliance on evolution and the natural selection that results from the development of standards, why was an expensive and protracted conceptual framework project necessary in the first place? It goes without saying that concepts and practices should

evolve as conditions change. But if the conceptual framework can do no more than point that out, who needs it? And, for that matter, if progress is simply a matter of waiting for evolution, who needs the FASB? (Solomons, ''The FASB's Conceptual Framework: An Evaluation,'' 1986, p. 122)

Concepts Statement No. 5 almost seems to have anticipated the challenges to its legitimacy as a statement of concepts and capitulated in its second paragraph, which could serve as its epitaph:

> The recognition criteria and guidance in this Statement are generally consistent with current practice and do not imply radical change. Nor do they foreclose the possibility of future changes in practice. The Board intends future change to occur in the gradual, evolutionary way that has characterized past change.

Concepts Statement No. 5 does make some noteworthy conceptual contributions—they are just not on recognition and measurement.

INVITATION TO LEARN MORE

This chapter has been more of a generous introduction to the FASB's conceptual framework than a comprehensive description or analysis of it. About half of the chapter was concerned with the antecedents of the conceptual framework, why the FASB undertook it, and why it contains the particular set of concepts that it does. The framework cannot really be understood without that background. The descriptions of the various Concepts Statements emphasized their major conclusions and some of the explanation they provide but did not go into them deeply enough to provide a substitute for reading them. Readers are urged to study the Concepts Statements themselves.

The FASB has used the completed parts of the framework with considerable success. The Board's constituents also have learned to use the framework, partly at least because they have discovered that they are more likely to influence the Board if they do. Both the Board and the constituents have also found that at times the concepts appear to work better than at other times, and undoubtedly they sometimes could have been more soundly applied. As much of the chapter suggests, parts of the conceptual framework are still controversial, partly at least because long-held views die hard. The framework remains unfinished, although the Board gives no sign of completing it in the near future.

Despite the fact that the Board has left it incomplete, the FASB's conceptual framework

- is the first reasonably successful effort by a standards-setting body to formulate and use an integrated set of financial accounting concepts,
- has fundamentally changed the way financial accounting standards are set in the United States, and
- has provided a model for the International Accounting Standards Committee and several national standards-setting bodies in other English-speaking countries, which not only have set out their own concepts but also have clearly been influenced by the FASB's Concepts Statements, sometimes to the point of adopting the same or virtually the same set of concepts.

SOURCES AND SUGGESTED REFERENCES

American Accounting Association, Committee on Concepts and Standards Underlying Corporate Financial Statements, ''*Accounting and Reporting Standards for Corporate Financial Statements and Preceding Statements and Supplements,* AAA, Iowa City, IA, 1957.

——, Executive Committee, "A Tentative Statement of Accounting Principles Underlying Corporate Financial Statements," *The Accounting Review*, June 19, 1936, pp. 187–191. Reprinted in *Accounting and Reporting Standards for Corporate Financial Statements and Preceding Statements and Supplements*, AAA, Iowa City, IA, 1957.

American Institute of Accountants, *Audits of Corporate Accounts: Correspondence between the Special Committee on Co-operation with Stock Exchanges of the American Institute of Accountants and the Committee on Stock List of the New York Stock Exchange, 1932–1934*. American Institute of Accountants, New York, 1934. Reprinted AICPA, New York, 1963, and in Zeff, *Forging Accounting Principles in Five Countries* (full reference below), pp. 237–247.

American Institute of Certified Public Accountants, "Restatement and Revision of Accounting Research Bulletins, Accounting Research Bulletin No. 43, AICPA, New York, 1953.

——, "Establishing Financial Accounting Standards," *Report of the Study on Establishment of Accounting Principles* (often called the Wheat Study Report, after its chairman, Francis M. Wheat, a former SEC commissioner), AICPA, New York, March 29, 1972.

——, "Objectives of Financial Statements," *Report of the Study Group on the Objectives of Financial Statements* (often called the Trueblood Report, after its chairman, Robert M. Trueblood), AICPA, New York, October 1973.

——, *Report of Special Committee on Opinions of the Accounting Principles Board*, AICPA, New York, Spring 1965.

——, Special Bulletin, "Disclosure of Departures From Opinions of the Accounting Principles Board, AICPA, New York, 1964. Reprinted in Zeff, *Forging Accounting Principles in Five Countries* (full reference below), pp. 266–268.

——, "Basic Concepts and Accounting Principles Underlying Financial Statements of Business Enterprises," Statement of the Accounting Principles Board No. 4, AICPA, New York, 1970.

Anton, Hector R., "Objectives of Financial Accounting: Review and Analysis," *The Journal of Accountancy*, January 1976, pp. 40–51.

Bevis, Herman W., *Corporate Financial Reporting in a Competitive Environment*, Macmillan, New York, 1965.

Blough, Carman G., "Development of Accounting Principles in the United States," *Berkeley Symposium on the Foundations of Financial Accounting*, University of California Press, Berkeley, 1967, pp. 1–14.

Bonbright, James C., *Principles of Public Utility Rates*, Columbia University Press, New York, 1961.

Byrne, Gilbert R., "To What Extent Can the Practice of Accounting be Reduced to Rules and Standards?" *Journal of Accountancy*, November 1937, pp. 364–379. Reprinted in Moonitz, Maurice, and Littleton, A. C., eds., *Significant Accounting Essays*, Prentice-Hall, Englewood Cliffs, NJ, 1965.

Carey, John L., *The Rise of the Accounting Profession to Responsibility and Authority, 1937–1969*, AICPA, New York, 1970.

Chambers, R. J., "Why Bother with Postulates?" *Journal of Accounting Research*, Spring 1963, pp. 3–15. Reprinted in Zeff, *The Accounting Postulates and Principles Controversy* (full reference below).

Chatfield, Michael, "Postulates and Principles," *A History of Accounting Thought*, rev. ed., Krieger Publishing, Huntington, NY, 1977, pp. 286–306.

Financial Accounting Standards Board, "Conceptual Framework for Financial Accounting and Reporting: Elements of Financial Statements and Their Measurement," Discussion Memorandum, FASB, Stamford, CT, December 2, 1976.

——, *Financial Accounting Standards Board Public Record*, 1974—Volume I, "Discussion Memorandum on Accounting for Research and Development and Similar Costs," dated December 28, 1973, Part 2, Transcript of Public Hearing, held March 15, 1974; 1974—Volume III, "Discussion Memorandum on Accounting for Future Losses," dated March 13, 1974, Part 2, Transcript of Public Hearing, held March 15, 1974.

——, Scope and Implications of the Conceptual Framework Project, FASB, Stamford, CT, 1976.

Gellein, Oscar S., "Financial Reporting: The State of Standard Setting," *Advances in Accounting*, Vol. 3, Bill N. Schwartz, ed., JAI Press, Greenwich, CT, 1986.

——, "Periodic Earnings: Income? or Indicator?" *Accounting Horizons*, June 1987.

Gilman, Stephen, *Accounting Concepts of Profit*, Ronald Press, New York, 1939, pp. 167–257.

Greer, Howard C., "What Are Accepted Principles of Accounting?" *The Accounting Review*, March 1938, pp. 25–30.

Heath, Loyd C., "Accounting, Communication, and the Pygmalion Syndrome," *Accounting Horizons*, March 1987, pp. 1–8.

Hylton, Delmer, "On Matching Revenue with Expense," *The Accounting Review*, October 1965, p. 824.

Johnson, L. Todd, and Storey, Reed K., "Recognition in Financial Statements: Underlying Concepts and Practical Conventions," FASB Research Report, FASB, Stamford, CT, 1982.

Kirk, Donald J., "Commentary on the Limitations of Accounting—A Response [to Eugene H. Flegm]," *Accounting Horizons*, September 1989, pp. 98–104.

———, "Looking Back on Fourteen Years at the FASB: The Education of a Standard Setter," *Accounting Horizons*, March 1988, pp. 8–17.

———, "Reflections on 'Reconceptualizations of Accounting': A Commentary on Parts I–IV of Homer Kripke's Paper, 'Reflections on the FASB's Conceptual Framework for Accounting and on Auditing,' " *Journal of Accounting, Auditing & Finance*, Winter 1989, pp. 83–105.

Kohler, Eric L., *A Dictionary for Accountants*, 5th ed., Prentice-Hall, Englewood Cliffs, NJ, 1975.

Littleton, A. C., "Tests for Principles," *The Accounting Review*, March 1938, pp. 16–24.

Luper, Oral L., and Rosenfield, Paul, "The APB Statement on Basic Concepts and Principles," *The Journal of Accountancy*, January 1971, pp. 46–51.

Manning, Bayless, *A Concise Textbook on Legal Capital*, 2nd ed., The Foundation Press, Mineola, NY, 1981, pp. 33–34.

Mautz, Robert K., "Basic Concepts of Accounting," *Handbook of Modern Accounting*, Sidney Davidson, ed., McGraw-Hill, New York, 1970, pp. 1-1—1-15.

May, George O., *Financial Accounting: A Distillation of Experience*, Macmillan, New York, 1943.

———, "Improvement in Financial Accounts," *The Journal of Accountancy*, May 1937, pp. 333–369.

———, "The Influence of Accounting on the Development of an Economy," *The Journal of Accountancy*, January 1936, pp. 11–22.

———, "The Nature of the Financial Accounting Process," *The Accounting Review*, July 1943, pp. 189–193.

———, "Principles of Accounting," *The Journal of Accountancy*, December 1937, pp. 423–425.

———, "Terminology of the Balance Sheet," *The Journal of Accountancy*, January 1942, pp. 35–36.

Moonitz, Maurice, "The Changing Concept of Liabilities," *The Journal of Accountancy*, May 1960, pp. 41–46.

———, "Why Do We Need 'Postulates' and 'Principles'?" *The Journal of Accountancy*, December 1963, pp. 42–46. Reprinted in Zeff, *The Accounting Postulates and Principles Controversy* (full reference below).

———, "The Basic Postulates of Accounting," Accounting Research Study No. 1, AICPA, New York, 1961. Reprinted in Zeff, *The Accounting Postulates and Principles Controversy* (full reference below).

———, "Obtaining Agreement on Standards in the Accounting Profession," Studies in Accounting Research No. 8, AAA, Sarasota, FL, 1974.

Paton, William A., "Comments on 'A Statement of Accounting Principles,' " *The Journal of Accountancy*, March 1938.

———, "Introduction," *Foundations of Accounting Theory: Papers Given at the Accounting Theory Symposium, University of Florida, March 1970*, Williard E. Stone, ed., University of Florida Press, Gainesville, 1971.

———, and Littleton, A. C., *An Introduction to Corporate Accounting Standards*, AAA, Ann Arbor, MI, 1940.

"Report to Council of the Special Committee on Research Program," *The Journal of Accountancy*, December 1958, pp. 62–68. Reprinted in Zeff, *Forging Accounting Principles in Five Countries*, pp. 248–265, and in Zeff, *The Accounting Postulates and Principles Controversy* (full reference below).

Sanders, Thomas Henry, Hatfield, Henry Rand, and Moore, Underhill, *A Statement of Accounting Principles*, American Institute of Accountants, New York, 1938. Reprinted AAA, Columbus, OH, 1959.

Schattke, R. W., "An Analysis of Accounting Principles Board Statement No. 4," *The Accounting Review*, April 1972, pp. 233–244.

Scott, Austin Wakeman, *Abridgement of the Law of Trusts,* Little Brown, Boston, 1960.

Sherman, H. David, ed., *Conceptual Frameworks for Financial Accounting,* (Proceedings of a conference at the Harvard Business School, October 1–2, 1982), President and Fellows of Harvard College, Cambridge, circa 1984.

Solomons, David, "The FASB's Conceptual Framework: An Evaluation," *The Journal of Accountancy,* June 1986, pp. 114–124.

———, *Making Accounting Policy: The Quest for Credibility in Financial Reporting,* Oxford University Press, New York, 1986.

Sprouse, Robert T., "Accounting for What-You-May-Call-Its," *The Journal of Accountancy,* October 1966, pp. 45–53.

———, "Commentary on Financial Reporting—Developing a Conceptual Framework for Financial Reporting," *Accounting Horizons,* December 1988, pp. 121–127.

———, "Commentary on Financial Reporting—Economic Consequences: The Volatility Bugaboo," *Accounting Horizons,* March 1987, p. 88.

———, and Moonitz, Maurice, *"A Tentative Set of Broad Accounting Principles for Business Enterprises,"* Accounting Research Study No. 3, AICPA, New York, 1962.

Staubus, George J., "An Analysis of APB Statement No. 4," *Journal of Accountancy,* February 1972, pp. 36–43.

Storey, Reed K., "Conditions Necessary for Developing a Conceptual Framework," *FASB Viewpoints,* March 3, 1981. Excerpted in *The Journal of Accountancy,* June 1981, and in *Financial Analysts Journal,* (with unauthorized revisions by the editor, some of which changed the meaning), May–June 1981, pp. 51–58.

———, *The Search for Accounting Principles,* AICPA, New York, 1964. Reprinted Scholars Book Co., Houston, TX, 1977.

Study Group on Business Income, *Changing Concepts of Business Income,* Macmillan, New York, 1952.

Trouant, D. L., *Financial Audits,* American Institute Publishing, New York, 1937.

Webster's New World Dictionary of the American Language, 2nd College ed., Simon & Schuster, New York, 1982.

Wyatt, Arthur R., "Accounting Standards and the Professional Auditor," *Accounting Horizons,* June 1989, pp. 96–102.

Zeff, Stephen A., *The Accounting Postulates and Principles Controversy of the 1960s,* Garland Publishing, New York & London, 1982.

———, *Forging Accounting Principles in Five Countries: A History and an Analysis of Trends,* Stipes Publishing, Champaign, IL, 1972.

CHAPTER 2

FINANCIAL ACCOUNTING REGULATION AND ORGANIZATIONS

Paul B. W. Miller, PhD, CPA

University of Colorado at Colorado Springs

CONTENTS

THE SOCIAL ROLE OF FINANCIAL ACCOUNTING

This chapter provides background on the environment in which financial accountants carry on their activities, including the specific organizations that regulate or otherwise affect those activities. Although the accounting profession is largely self- governed, its members are also regulated by a variety of external organizations. No financial accountant can properly practice without understanding these organizations and how they not only constrain but also assist the performance of financial accounting and reporting services.

2.1 THE OBJECTIVE OF FINANCIAL ACCOUNTING.   An important beginning point for understanding the social role and importance of financial accounting is the identification of the objective that it should meet. Although there are many opinions as to what the **objectives** should be, the most authoritative and influential is this **definition** provided by the FASB in its **Conceptual Framework** project, which was intended to develop a unified theory of accounting (see section 2.8(e)):

> **Financial reporting** should provide information that is useful to present and potential investors and creditors and other users in making rational investment, credit, and similar decisions.

Thus, according to this definition, the goal is to provide information that allows its users to reach better decisions than they would without it. (For simplicity, the FASB used the term "financial reporting" to encompass the activities of "financial accounting and reporting," which include presenting both financial statements and the additional financial information that accompanies them. This chapter uses the term "financial accounting" in this broader sense.)

Usefulness may exist at the individual company level when its management provides reports to investors and creditors in the course of seeking financing or fulfilling various stewardship reporting responsibilities. Although this perspective undoubtedly explains why some aspects of accounting are regulated, it does not really provide an adequate basis for understanding the substantial governing structure. Instead, an economy-wide view is needed.

2.2 AN ECONOMY-WIDE PERSPECTIVE.   The diagram in Exhibit 2.1 summarizes the discussion that follows. It shows the links between a **society's well-being** and the availability of useful financial statements.

The success of a society in providing for its members' well-being involves many different factors. One of the most fundamental and important of these ingredients is the society's **economy.** Without a sound economy, the physical needs and wants of the populace are not met. Because, for example, inferior standards of living tend to create anxiety and a sense of repression, unrest may increase, and injustice and inequity may be more likely to exist. On the other hand, a sound economy will promote higher standards of living and greater opportunities. A society that has economic stability and meets citizens' needs can more easily direct its attention to addressing other social issues.

Although a variety of things contribute to a sound economy, such as an abundance of natural resources, a stable political system, and an appropriate work ethic, one of the most critical is the availability of sufficient **capital resources.** Without adequate capital, manufactured goods and services cannot be produced or distributed to persons who want or need them. Without adequate capital resources, these consumers will not be able to acquire the goods or services that have been produced.

In turn, sufficient capital resources are made available through **effective capital markets** in which those who need capital can obtain it from those who are ready to provide it. If these market participants can conduct their activities in an environment free from excessive mistrust or other similar uncertainties, they will be able to establish fair prices for the capital

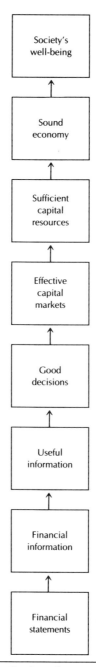

Exhibit 2.1.   The role of financial accounting in society.

in the form of expected returns. And, fair prices will encourage the flow of more capital into the markets.

In order for the markets to be effective, their participants must reach **good decisions** about where to invest or obtain capital under appropriate terms for the risks involved. If decisions are made haphazardly, capital will not be allocated at a fair price to those who will use it most appropriately, and the economy will not contribute as much to social well-being.

A number of elements affect the ability to reach good decisions, and one of these is **useful information.** If capital market participants have no information or only false, misleading, or late information, then their decisions are not likely to be good. With useful information, they can assess the risks associated with alternative strategies and establish the appropriate price for the capital.

Naturally, many different kinds of information are useful to decision makers. Some may relate to a particular company, an industry, or the national and world economies. Some kinds may be rooted in past events, whereas others are predictions of future events and conditions. Of particular importance to the capital markets is **financial information,** which consists of monetary measures of factors related to alternative strategies.

Finally, one source of financial information is the **financial statements** (and other information) that users of capital resources distribute to capital market participants. Although this information by itself is insufficient for making the capital markets work well, it is generally considered to be helpful. Furthermore, the existence of a regular system brings discipline to the reporting process. Because financial accountants know that efforts to mislead the market will generally be revealed when the statements are published, they are less likely to present fabrications.

The important economic role of financial statements causes society to be correctly concerned about the activities of financial accountants, and justifies setting up controls and other regulatory devices to help ensure the availability and usefulness of the information. As should be expected, these controls are aimed at preventing irregularities in the financial reporting system.

2.3 THE PARTICIPANTS IN THE FINANCIAL REPORTING SYSTEM.   Financial accounting is not conducted impersonally or in a sterile arena; rather, the people who conduct it have very real but quite different interests in the process and its outcome.

The primary communication channel is between financial statement **preparers** and financial statement **users.** Generally, preparers are accountants who work for corporations or other entities that need capital resources or that have stewardship reporting responsibilities. Users are investors, creditors, or advisors to those who want to commit resources to an entity or who have already done so. The self-interests of preparers and users clearly are in potential conflict.

Preparers want the reporting system to provide information that will help them get low cost capital or that will cause them to appear to have lived up to their responsibilities. Preparers are also concerned about the costs of preparing and distributing the reports and thus prefer reporting less information to fewer people.

Users, in contrast, are looking for truthful, inexpensively obtained, and dependable information that will enable them to make new decisions or evaluate old ones. They are not well served by information that misleads them through deliberate or inadvertent bias. If users receive unreliable information, the cost of capital will rise to compensate them for the added risks. If this mistrust is widespread, the economy will suffer because the capital markets will not be as effective. Users also tend to want more information and to have it readily available. (This tendency is counterbalanced by the desire to have unique information, which is a key to earning higher returns.)

To reduce the uncertainty about the dependability of the statement, the services of **auditors** partially assure users that the preparers have not abused the reporting system by providing biased, incomplete, or otherwise misleading information. In effect, the auditors increase the credibility of financial statements. However, like the other participants, auditors have self-interests. In particular, they prefer dealing with information that can be verified with minimum risk because they are concerned (and reasonably so) about the possibility of litigation or other recrimination from users who suffer losses after using audited information that turns out to have been false or misleading.

In summary, the three main participating groups have highly conflicting interests. In general, preparers want information that can be cheaply produced and will make them look good; users want plentiful useful information at low cost; and auditors want information that can be successfully defended. In contrast, society needs the capital market to have widely available decision-useful information. Because of these conflicts, financial accounting and financial accountants have been and will continue to be subject to regulation.

This need for protecting society's interest has also led to regulating the activities of users through prohibitions against trading securities on the basis of inside or other misappropriated information. These rules are designed to assure all market participants that they are playing a fair game, so that they are less likely to add undeserved risk penalities to the returns that they will accept from their investments.

2.4 TYPES OF REGULATIONS FOR ACCOUNTANTS.   There are three general categories of regulations for financial accounting: standards for **practice,** standards for **competence,** and standards for **behavior.**

(a) Standards for Practice.   One useful regulatory device is to establish rules governing the choice of accounting practices used in preparing financial statements. When companies use uniform accounting policies, they generate more comparable information than when each company makes its own choices. Reduction or elimination of alternative policies will also reduce or eliminate discretionary choices by preparers who are trying to present more favorable pictures. In addition, a set of practice standards gives auditors a basis for defending their clients' choices.

The standards used in financial accounting are known collectively as "generally accepted accounting principles" (**GAAP**). Originally, "general acceptance" denoted a consensus among a relatively small population of accountants that a particular practice was more common than others and therefore presumably more useful. However, as practices grew more complex and required more complete control, "general acceptance" has come to include designation by an authoritative body that they are suitable for use. Principles lacking this authoritative support are considered inappropriate.

A similar need exists for the conduct of audit procedures. Correspondingly, the practices to be applied in audits are known collectively as "generally accepted auditing standards" (**GAAS**). "General acceptance" here was also originally indicative of a consensus among practitioners but has come to mean authoritative support.

Although the obvious main purpose of GAAP and GAAS is to provide guidance to practitioners, the standards also provide some assurance to statement users about the quality of the information they receive. In addition, they serve as an after-the-fact basis for evaluating the decisions of preparers or auditors. If policies or practices prove to have been contrary to generally accepted standards, the persons who made the decisions can be more easily held responsible for injury resulting from those choices. Of course, knowledge of GAAP and GAAS should help users understand (1) what the statements do and do not describe and (2) how much reliance should be placed on them.

(b) Standards for Competency.   In addition to controlling accountants' practices, society also regulates the **competence** of individual accountants. By distinguishing between those who are or are not competent and by empowering only the competent to perform critical tasks, useful information is more likely to be delivered to the capital markets. In addition, providing unique identification simplifies the search for a competent accountant.

In the United States, the most common competence indicator is the license to practice as a **Certified Public Accountant** (CPA). This license is granted by individual states and other jurisdictions, such as the District of Columbia, through an agency often called the "State Board of Accountancy." Because of this diverse authority and because a person can be licensed by more than one state, it is difficult to determine exactly how many CPAs actually exist. Nonetheless, in 1990, the number was estimated to be between 350,000 and 400,000.

Even though each state requires a candidate to pass the Uniform CPA Examination, there is substantial diversity in the additional requirements because the license is granted under state statutes. Most states, but not all, require a college degree, and some require even more education. Most states, but not all, grant certificates only after a candidate completes 1, 2, or more years of experience in public accounting. Some states also distinguish between certification and the license to practice. In addition to the initial hurdles, most states impose "continuing professional education" requirements designed to maintain the quality and currentness of the CPA's competence. Some accountants in some states carry the designations **Public Accountant** or **Registered Accountant.** These individuals hold licenses that predate the creation of existing CPA requirements, particularly those involving formal education. In effect, they were "grandfathered" when new laws were passed and were allowed to continue practicing public accounting without the regular CPA license. ("Public accounting" has been difficult to define precisely, but it is generally recognized as the offering of accounting services for fees to the public in general as opposed to the performing of accounting services while employed by an entity or government agency.)

The CPA designation is not lost when the individual leaves public practice and is an important credential on the résumés of many accountants who work for corporations and government agencies. Other designations have been developed to provide additional evidence of the competence (or to provide evidence for those who choose not to qualify as CPAs) of accountants who are not in public practice.

The **Certified Management Accountant** certificate was developed by the IMA, which is affiliated with the NAA. Although there is a rigorous "CMA" examination and a requirement for experience as a management accountant, this designation does not grant the holder any special privileges or licenses to do anything not granted to ordinary citizens. Nonetheless, it is a sought after and respected title. CMAs are also required to complete ongoing continuing professional education requirements in order to maintain their competency.

The **Certified Internal Auditor** certificate is similar to the CMA, and is administered by the Institute of Internal Auditors. This designation does not grant any special statutory rights or responsibilities to persons who hold it. It is proving to be an important credential for advancement in the internal auditing profession.

(c) Standards for Behavior. In addition to standards for practice and competence, financial accountants are also subject to standards for behavior in the form of **codes of ethics** or **codes of conduct.** These standards distinguish between good and bad actions by accountants. To be meaningful, the codes must require more of accountants than other laws or morals demand of nonaccountants.

The accountancy laws in the various states generally incorporate a set of ethical standards. If the state authority determines a CPA has violated these standards, it may revoke or suspend the license to practice. In other situations (generally involving some technical error), the authority may merely require remedial education.

Nongovernmental **professional** organizations have also established ethic codes to apply to their members. Under this arrangement, membership carries a higher standard of performance than would be faced without it. It also exposes the member to another investigative and sanctioning authority. The return to the member is a higher perceived level of ethics and some protection against the misdeeds of other less ethical practitioners. The most significant of these bodies is the **American Institute of Certified Public Accountants** (AICPA). There are other societies (also associations and institutes) at the state level. The Institute of Management Accounting also sanctions unethical CMAs.

2.5 REGULATORY AGENCIES AND ORGANIZATIONS. Regulations and standards concerning practices and behavior are created by various agencies and organizations, some of which have already been mentioned. They also often have the power to enforce the rules that they (or other organizations) have produced. These agencies can be classified into three categories: governmental agencies, standards setting organizations, and professional societies.

(a) **Governmental Agencies.**   The greatest regulatory power over financial accountants is held by governmental agencies established by legislative action to protect the public interest.

The most significant of these agencies is the federal **Securities and Exchange Commission** (SEC), which was created by the Securities Exchange Act of 1934. Among other powers, it was granted authority to establish accounting and auditing standards, and to discipline accountants (including preparers and auditors) who do not live up to those standards or to other professional standards of conduct. Although the SEC's jurisdiction extends only to the management, accountants, and other agents of companies whose securities are registered with it (approximately 11,000 in 1990), its influence is great because these registrants include the largest corporations in the United States. Furthermore, their accountants (internal and external) compose the most influential and powerful segments of the profession. Substantial additional information about the SEC is presented in section 2.6 of this chapter.

As mentioned earlier, each CPA falls under the jurisdiction of a state board of accountancy (see section 2.7). CPAs must meet the requirements established at this level in order to obtain or keep the license.

(b) **Standards Setting Organizations.**   In a unique blend of public statutory authority and private voluntary submission, two nongovernmental, nonprofit organizations—the **Financial Accounting Standards Board** (FASB) and the **Governmental Accounting Standards Board** (GASB)—create financial accounting standards. Both organizations are located in Norwalk, Connecticut, and operate under the funding and management of the **Financial Accounting Foundation.**

The FASB has power and influence through its designation in 1973 by the SEC as the authoritative source of accounting principles to be used in financial statements filed by SEC's registrants. The FASB also gains authority through other organizations' endorsements, most notably state boards of accountancy, the AICPA, and state professional societies. An additional avenue of influence is through the participation in its deliberative processes by others affected by financial accounting, most notably statement preparers and users. Despite the importance of the FASB to the SEC (and to the effectiveness of capital markets), the Board does not receive funds directly from the federal government. However, contributions to the FASB by individuals and corporations are tax-deductible, with the result that the Board is essentially subsidized through reduced costs for the donors.

The GASB's influence is limited to the establishment of accounting principles used uniquely by state and local (but not federal) government entities. Its power comes through its endorsement by a variety of professional organizations composed of governmental accountants and governmental agencies, including state legislators and state auditors. Unlike the FASB, the GASB is partially funded through amounts appropriated by a number of state legislatures. It also receives some funds from the federal government, specifically the General Accounting Office (GAO).

More details about these unique and important Boards are presented in sections 2.8 and 2.9.

(c) **Professional Societies.**   Of the voluntary professional societies regulating the practices of accountants, the largest by far is the **American Institute of Certified Public Accountants,** with 280,000 members. This size allows it to have a large permanent staff of several hundred individuals who are responsible for regulating and providing services to the membership. The AICPA also depends on an even larger number of the members to carry out its tasks through various committees. Institute membership is entirely voluntary but is virtually obligatory for CPAs who wish to stay informed and to practice at the highest levels in the profession.

Although similar to the AICPA, state societies of CPAs are separately funded and operated entities. They are also a curious blend of regulatory authority and service providers. Individuals who want to influence the profession in their state consider membership to be essential.

Other national societies exist, including several that are fairly large. Two of these are the **National Association of Accountants** (NAA) and the **Financial Executives Institute** (FEI), both of which generally consist of individuals who are not in public practice. Indeed, they can be characterized as organizations representing the interests of statement preparers.

Another national organization is the **American Accounting Association** (AAA), which was originally created as a professional society for accounting educators. Through the middle of the century, the membership became more eclectic and included not only instructors but a fairly large number of practitioners. However, during the 1970s and 1980s, the AAA lost a large number of the practicing accountants and became more and more oriented toward academic issues and services. Apart from the influence of individual members and the AAA's participation as a "sponsoring organization" of the FASB, it does not affect accounting practice to any great degree.

GOVERNMENTAL AGENCIES

2.6 SECURITIES AND EXCHANGE COMMISSION.   Although the SEC's jurisdiction is limited to publicly held corporations meeting minimum size criteria (in 1989, registration was required for companies having at least $5 million in assets and at least 500 stockholders), its role as the primary regulator and protector of the country's capital markets has given it substantial influence over financial accounting practice.

(a) Background of the SEC.   The Commission was established by the Securities Exchange Act of 1934 and was charged with enforcement of not only that statute but also the Securities Act of 1933. Previously, the 1933 Act had been administered by the Federal Trade Commission.

The SEC's prime mission is to achieve and maintain stable and effective capital markets for securities traded in interstate commerce. The nature of today's capital markets and communications networks makes it difficult to issue a security that is **not** traded across state borders.

The SEC uses a variety of methods to accomplish its mission. The most basic is regulation of the activities of those corporations that have issued or would like to issue securities. Under the 1933 Act, securities must be "registered" before they can be issued to the public. The purpose of registration is to establish a complete and widely available public record of information about the registrant and the securities. For example, registration creates a substantial amount of public information about the officers, directors, and other agents of the corporation, including promoters and underwriters. It also publicizes the company's plans for using the capital raised by issuing the securities. In the case of a company that has existed previously, registration also requires the presentation of financial statements and other financial data.

If the company meets the reporting requirements, the securities are allowed to "go public," regardless of their inherent riskiness. Thus, the registration process is designed to accomplish **disclosure** about the securities rather than to evaluate their **merits.** Although some states conduct merit reviews for securities traded within their borders, this approach would be very difficult to accomplish on a national level. Furthermore, many individuals believe that the capital markets should be as free as possible, as long as fraud and other forms of deceit are prohibited.

The 1934 Act went beyond the initial registration to require substantial ongoing disclosures about the corporation, its officers and directors, and its financial condition and results of operations and other activities. Thus, companies that have securities registered under the 1933 Act must provide quarterly and annual reports to the Commission, as well as ad hoc reports when critical events occur. Again, the goal is to allow the capital markets to work effectively by getting information to market participants. The Commission staff may review the filed information for its compliance with the disclosure requirements, but there is no review of the **merits** of the management's behavior as described in the reports. For example, nothing in the SEC's processes prevents managers from paying large salaries to themselves, **as long as** the amount is disclosed. The idea is that disclosure will allow the market itself to discipline those managers who abuse their fiduciary duties. Of course, the disclosure requirement may very well have the side effect of deterring behavior because the management would expect to have to suffer the consequences.

The 1934 Act also gave authority to the Commission to regulate securities exchanges (such as the NYSE and the ASE) and those brokers and dealers who belong to them or otherwise conduct business for buyers and sellers of securities. This authority was expanded through the Investment Advisers Act of 1940 to encompass all who offer investment counseling. The fundamental goal of this dimension of regulation is to increase market participants' confidence by reducing the likelihood of incompetence, fraud, or deceit. The line of reasoning is that if these problems can be reduced, more people are likely to invest, and if more people invest, the competition will bring about a more effective allocation of capital.

Other legislation has given the SEC additional authorities and jurisdiction in the capital markets, but their contents are generally beyond the scope of this discussion, which focuses on the effect of the SEC on financial accounting. Section 2.6(f) will identify the specific categories of regulations and publications that affect financial accountants and their clients.

It is especially important to note that the 1934 Act gave the SEC specific authority to establish accounting principles to be used by registrants in filed financial statements. This authority led to the issuance of **ASR No. 4** in 1938, which stated that the principles used in the filings would have to enjoy "substantial authoritative support." It also stated that disclosure of a departure from such supported principles would not be an acceptable substitute for applying them. Thus, unlike the overall regulatory theory described before, the Commission determined to have a merit review with respect to the accounting policies used in public financial statements. The effect of ASR No. 4 on the accounting profession is described in section 2.8(a).

(b) Structure of the SEC.   Because the SEC is an independent agency, it does not exist within any of the three traditional branches of government (executive, legislative, or judicial). All five commissioners are appointed by the President and are confirmed by the Senate. In order to help maintain balance, and thereby boost public confidence in the capital markets, no more than three commissioners can be members of the same political party. The basic term for a commissioner is 5 years with the possibility of unlimited reappointments. However, history shows that it is unusual for a commissioner to complete an entire term. Most commissioners are attorneys by training, although occasionally some come from other backgrounds. One commissioner is designated by the President to serve as the chairman and has special administrative responsibilities and acts as a spokesperson for the entire commission. However, the chairman has only one vote, and thus actually has no more authority than the other commissioners. In 1990, commissioners received an annual salary of approximately $82,500, with some variation according to how long they had been in government service.

As is true with most major organizations, a large professional staff supports the work of the commissioners. The SEC has over 2,000 employees at its Washington, D.C., headquarters and its regional offices. A number of divisions and offices deal with particular regulatory activities. The three that financial accountants are most likely to come into contact with are:

- The Division of Corporation Finance.
- The Office of the Chief Accountant.
- The Division of Enforcement.

In dealing with their responsibilities, all three report directly and independently to the Commission. However, they also work closely with one another to coordinate their activities and to avoid contradictions and confusion. Exhibit 2.2 is a diagram of their interrelationships and the points of usual interface with the public.

(c) Division of Corporation Finance. With a staff of several hundred people, the largest of the three sections of the SEC is the Division of Corporation Finance (Corp Fin). Its fundamental responsibility is to process filed documents received from registrants to determine whether they comply with the appropriate disclosure regulations. The Corp Fin staff consists of attorneys, accountants, and financial analysts, and is organized by industry specialties. The Director of Corp Fin is advised by a Chief Accountant for the Division, who is not the same person as the Commission's Chief Accountant.

In the process of reviewing filings, the staff encounters questions about the propriety of the accounting principles applied to registrants' transactions or situations. Some registrants are careful to raise these kinds of questions **before** they file documents in order to determine the principles that the staff believes are applicable. In either situation, the Corp Fin staff often resolves these questions using published GAAP or precedents established in earlier cases. In more complicated or groundbreaking situations, the Corp Fin chief acountant consults with the Commission's Office of the Chief Accountant.

(d) Office of the Chief Accountant. The Commission's primary adviser on financial accounting issues and policy is the Chief Accountant, who is appointed by the Chairman and serves at his or her discretion. The Office of the Chief Accountant (OCA) is supported by a staff of approximately 15 professionals, all of whom are experienced accountants, except for

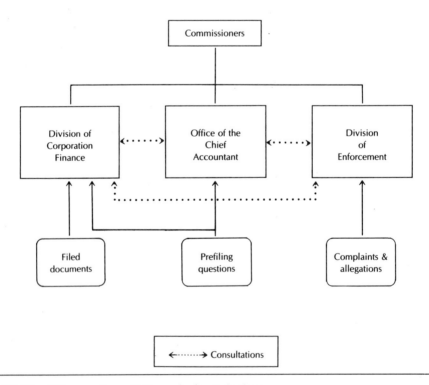

Exhibit 2.2.   SEC accounting activities and suborganizations.

one attorney. As indicated in Exhibit 2.2, the OCA works with the Corp Fin chief accountant to resolve issues raised in filings or by prefiling questions. The diagram also shows that some of these prefiling questions may come directly to the OCA.

In order to identify the accounting and auditing practices that have "substantial authoritative support," the OCA first tries to determine what the authoritative literature says about the issue, turning to its own pronouncements and interpretations only when that literature is silent or ambiguous. In conducting their research, the OCA staff frequently consult with the FASB staff. It is also common for the registrant who raised the question to meet with the SEC staff to explain the facts and circumstances surrounding the issue and to present its point of view. When the question cannot be resolved satisfactorily from the literature, the OCA develops an answer with the goal of providing "full and fair disclosure." To present a united position on the issue, the OCA and Corp Fin establish together what ought to be done. If the registrant does not agree with the answer, the procedures allow it to appeal to the full Commission. However, as a practical matter, registrants seldom make this appeal because the Commissioners virtually always support the staff.

In addition to dealing with situation-specific issues, OCA also advises the Commission on major policy matters affecting financial reporting. This role involves preparing recommendations that new rules be created for registrants. It also involves **overseeing** standards setters, specifically the FASB and the Auditing Standards Board of the AICPA. In this oversight capacity, the OCA avoids dictating to the standards setters either the issues that they should consider or the positions that they should take in resolving them, but it often does explain what sorts of answers would be preferable or acceptable.

(e) Division of Enforcement. The third segment of the SEC staff that commonly interfaces with financial accountants is the Division of Enforcement, which is charged with investigating violations of the statutes and regulations and recommending disciplinary action. Information about possible violations comes from a wide variety of sources, including the OCA and Corp Fin, as well as news reports and direct complaints from individuals. When violations appear to be other than merely inadvertent or technical, "Enforcement" is responsible for determining whether and how to pursue a case and for discovering the facts. In some situations, Enforcement may recommend that the Commission reach a settlement with the alleged offenders without a judicial finding. Although the findings are made public, the subjects neither admit nor deny the allegations, even though some discipline may be accepted (such as suspension or permanent disbarment from practicing before the Commission). In far fewer situations, the Commission orders cases to be turned over to a U.S. Attorney's Office for prosecution in a federal court. Naturally, the Enforcement staff cooperates fully with the attorneys in pursuing these cases.

On violations of statutes or regulations involving accountants, Commission procedures require that the Chief Accountant of Enforcement consult with the OCA to ensure that the proper facts have been uncovered and that the authoritative literature has indeed been violated. These violations typically include failure to maintain proper books and records, preparing financial statements that do not comply with GAAP, issuing an unqualified audit opinion on statements that do not comply with GAAP, or conducting an audit without complying with GAAS. Although Enforcement does not have to obtain concurrence from the OCA to go ahead with a case involving accounting or accountants, a lack of concurrence would make it difficult to persuade the Commission that a violation occurred.

(f) Regulations and Publications. Because the SEC is a government agency, its accounting literature is structured differently from the pronouncements published by the FASB and other standards setters. This discussion provides an overall view of that structure in order to help the reader understand the SEC's regulations and publications. Those interested in more detailed descriptions of SEC financial reporting requirements will need to consult materials developed by one of several reporting services or large accounting firms. Like other agencies, the Commission publishes its pronouncements in the **Federal Register,** which are then compiled and republished by proprietary organizations for sale to practicing accountants and attorneys, as well as libraries and others.

Exhibit 2.3 presents a diagram of the SEC's literature, showing four levels of materials: **statutes, regulations and forms, Commission releases,** and **staff advice** (Miller & Robertson, 1989).

The two main sources of the SEC's authority over accounting are the Securities Act of 1933 and the Securities Exchange Act of 1934. Five other statutes also affect accounting, but less directly. They include the Public Utility Holding Company Act of 1935, the Trust Indenture Act of 1939, the Investment Company Act of 1940, the Investment Advisor Act of 1940, and the Security Investor Protection Act of 1970.

These statutes give the SEC the authority to create **rules and regulations** that interpret the requirements to be met by companies under its jurisdiction. (As a matter of terminology, a regulation is merely a set of related rules.) The SEC has also created **forms,** which are rules specifying items of information to be made public. Unlike income tax forms, the SEC's forms are not rigidly formatted blank sheets to be filled in by the registrant. They are more like checklists that the registrant's accountants should follow in preparing the filings.

The regulations and forms developed to implement the 1933 and 1934 Acts are included in Title 17 of the **Code of Federal Regulations** and are thus cited under the designation "17 CFR." As shown in Exhibit 2.3, the rules under the 1933 Act have been published as 17 CFR 230 and 17 CFR 239. The regulations in 17 CFR 230 are further broken down into general rules (including definitions and administrative matters) and into six other regulations (labeled A through F). The forms to be used by registrants complying with this Act are described in 17 CFR 239. Some of them are:

1-A	Offering statement under Regulation A
D	Notification under Regulation D
S-1, S-2, S-3	Registration statements, general form
S-4	Registration of securities issued in business combination transactions
S-8	Securities offered to employees
S-18	Optional registration form for $5 million or less

The requirements under the 1934 Act have been published as 17 CFR 240 and 17 CFR 249. The former includes various rules, such as 10a-1 through 10a-2 on short sales of securities, 10b-1 through 11Ac1-2 on manipulative and deceptive devices and contrivances, 12b-1 through 12b-37 on registration and reporting, 13b2-1 through 13b2-2 on maintenance of records and preparation of reports, 13d-1 through 13d-101 on completing Schedule 13D for acquisition of a 5% or greater interest, and 13e-1 through 13e-100 on completing Schedule 13E-3 for going private transactions.

Among the forms described in 17 CFR 249 are:

8-K	Current reports
10-K	General form of annual report
10-Q	Quarterly report
11-K	Annual report of employee stock purchase plan
13-F	Report of institutional investment managers

For accountants, the most familiar regulations under these two Acts are **Regulation S-X** (17 CFR 210) and **Regulation S-K** (17 CFR 229). As Exhibit 2.3 indicates, they both implement the authority created under the 1933 and 1934 Acts.

Regulation S-X describes the accounting and auditing requirements that registrants must meet, including not only the financial statements but also the qualifications (including

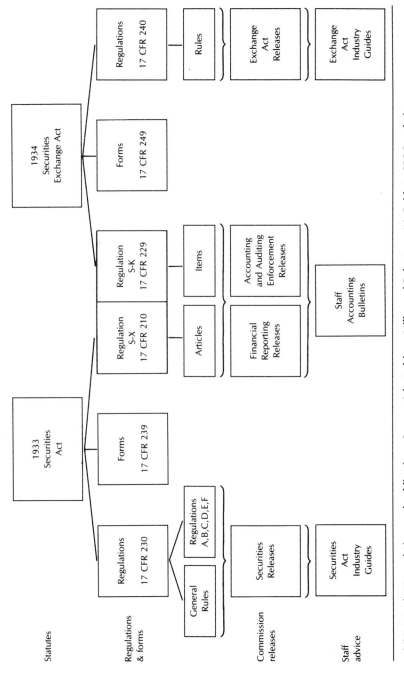

Exhibit 2.3. SEC regulations and publications. *Source:* Adapted from Miller and Robertson, "A Guide to SEC Regulations and Publications— Mastering the Maze," *Research in Accounting Regulation,* Vol. 3, 1989, p. 242.

independence) of and reports filed by accountants who practice before the Commission. It consists of 13 Articles, including:

1	Application of Regulation S-X
2	Qualifications and reports of accountants
3	General instructions for financial statements
3A	Consolidated and combined financial statements
10	Interim financial statements
12	Form and content of schedules

Regulation S-K includes a large number of "Items" about which a registrant must provide information (in addition to the financial statements) in registration statements, annual reports, and proxy solicitations. Some of the Items are:

101	Description of business
201	Market price of and dividends on common equity
303	Management's discussion and analysis
304	Changes in and disagreements with accountants
402	Management remuneration
404	Certain relationships and related party transactions
504	Use of proceeds
702	Indemnification of officers and directors

Some registrants are not required to comply with Regulation S-K; for example, small companies that fall under Regulation D of 17 CFR 230 are exempt, as are investment advisers.

At the next level below regulations and forms are **Commission Releases,** which are essentially official communications between the SEC and the public. They announce changes in the regulations and forms, interpret the regulations, describe various Commission enforcement activities, or declare general Commission policy. The SEC issues these publications only after a majority vote of the Commissioners.

As indicated in Exhibit 2.3, several types of releases are related to the statutes and regulations. Releases concerning matters under the 1933 Act are called **Securities Releases.** When they are published in the *Federal Register,* they are given a number with a "33-" prefix. Releases concerning the 1934 Act are called **Exchange Act Releases,** and have a "34-" prefix in the *Register*. Releases concerned with Regulations S-X and S-K fall into two categories. As might be expected, **Financial Reporting Releases** announce changes and interpretations of these two Regulations. They are published with a "FR-" prefix, although they are commonly identified in the accounting literature as "FRR." It is possible for a single release to have more than one designation. In fact, it is not uncommon to find a release carrying all three.

Accounting and Auditing Enforcement Releases announce enforcement or other disciplinary actions against individuals, firms, and registrants who have been alleged or proven to be in violation of the federal securities laws or who have otherwise fallen under the SEC's disciplinary powers. They are published under the prefix of "AAER."

Until 1982, the Commission issued **Accounting Series Releases** ("ASR"), concerning both financial reporting matters and enforcement actions. In that year, the separate FR and AAER series were created to avoid the confusion of dealing with the two different kinds of actions in one series. The effective portions of the ASRs were codified in FR-1.

The fourth level of literature, **staff advice,** is strictly from the SEC staff to registrants and other interested parties with regard to its interpretation of the regulations and forms. To help avoid arbitrary or otherwise inconsistent policies, these communications are generally subjected to substantial internal review involving two or more divisions or offices, including, for example, the OCA, Corp Fin, and the Office of the General Counsel.

Although staff advice lacks the official standing of Commission releases, a registrant faces substantial difficulty in successfully opposing it in a filing. As with every staff decision, the registrant can appeal to the Commissioners for an exception, but history has shown that few are willing to go to the expense and trouble, and fewer still succeed in overturning the staff's position.

The bottom section of Exhibit 2.3 shows three categories of staff advice that are of interest to accountants. **Staff Accounting Bulletins** are probably the most familiar. They are issued by Corp Fin and the OCA. A **SAB** is published to describe an interpretation that the staff has made either for a series of filings with similar facts and situations or for one filing that dealt with an unusual situation or that took a novel approach to the authoritative literature. The SAB assists registrants through a troubled area or lets them know that a particular approach will not pass the staff's review.

For certain filings under the 1933 Act, the staff has developed six **Securities Act Industry Guides** for implementing the regulations for particular industry-related reporting and disclosure situations. Given that the guides were issued by the same staff that reviews filings, most registrants find that it makes sense to comply with the advice. For certain filings under the 1934 Act, the staff has developed four **Exchange Act Industry Guides** for the same purposes.

(g) Summary.   Even though the SEC has jurisdiction over only public corporations, without doubt it has exerted, and will continue to exert, a substantial influence on financial accounting by private corporations as well. The philosophy of "fair and full disclosure" permeates the practice of financial accounting for all companies, and the SEC's standards for independence and competence of auditors are fairly well established throughout the profession. The enforcement activities of the SEC are also important because they establish and defend norms of behavior expected of financial accountants.

Affiliating with a corporation registered with the SEC puts special demands on its internal and external accountants. No one should venture into this type of practice without substantial training and experience or without competent legal counsel. The requirements are extensive and complicated, and the penalties for not meeting the standards are considerable.

2.7 STATE BOARDS OF ACCOUNTANCY.   The other main category of governmental agencies affecting the practice of financial accounting comprises the 54 **State Boards of Accountancy** in the United States. (One board exists in each of the 50 states, the District of Columbia, Puerto Rico, the Virgin Islands, and Guam.) They have three primary regulatory missions: granting the initial license to practice public accounting, ensuring the maintenance of competency through continuing education, and disciplining licensees who fail to maintain their competency or who act in an unethical manner.

Because of the variety of forms (and names) for the boards, it is difficult to draw generalities. Some boards are separate freestanding agencies, whereas others are part of larger state regulatory bodies that license other professions and service providers. Funding for boards comes from general budget appropriations, dedicated credits from licensing fees, or some combination. Some boards are permanent and others are subject to periodic "sunset" reviews designed to avoid overregulation.

An accountancy board's first responsibility is to award the license to practice, which may do no more than allow the licensees to identify themselves as CPAs. In many states, the license is a legal requirement for performing the attest function (audit or review) for financial statements. The Internal Revenue Service accepts the CPA's license as sufficient qualification to practice before it in the representation of clients in the audit and appeals procedures.

All states require candidates to successfully complete the Uniform CPA Examination prepared, administered, and graded by the AICPA. In a few states, it is possible to be merely "certified" by passing the CPA examination, without being licensed. The license is granted only after the candidate has completed an experience requirement. Other states do not differentiate between certification and licensing. Most states have an experience requirement, but some do not. Most also allow the substitution of advanced college course work or degrees for some or all of the practical experience. A few states require the completion of an additional year's course work beyond the bachelor's degree before certification.

Most state boards require their licensees to participate in formal continuing professional education (CPE). Typically, CPAs need 40 hours of class time per year to continue practicing, although individuals not in public practice may get by with fewer or even none. Some boards regulate CPE by specifying minimum hours in certain topics or by recognizing only courses offered by authorized providers, whereas others require only a report of hours completed.

A majority of state boards promulgate ethical standards of conduct through regulations interpreting the authorizing statutes; others have incorporated the ethics rules directly into their statutes. By and large, the ethics codes of state boards are virtually the same as the AICPA's Code of Conduct, although local political factors often create slight differences. Because most states do not grant their boards sufficient funds to support a full-time investigative staff for allegations of unethical behavior, they must compete with other agencies for investigators' time and effort. In extreme cases, a finding of a violation will lead to revoking the individual's CPA license; however, boards do not mete out this punishment very often. Rather, they impose some rehabilitative discipline, such as a temporary suspension or the completion of additional CPE. In virtually all states, individuals automatically lose their licenses if they are convicted of a felony.

State boards are typically composed of unpaid volunteer practitioners who serve for 3 to 5 years. It is often true that at least one of the board members is not an accountant but represents the general public. This arrangement lends more credibility to the board, which may suffer from a "fox in the hen house" image caused by having only accountants regulate accountants. A difficulty in using volunteers is that the boards tend to get only part-time effort. Larger states achieve more continuity and sustained effort by having a full-time executive director and staff.

In order to gain by shared effort and to provide services efficiently, state boards have formed their own trade organization, the **National Association of State Boards of Accountancy** (NASBA). This group (which includes all 54 U.S. licensing authorities) provides a forum for developing unified positions on issues that can be used in individual states more effectively. For example, the NASBA directors agreed in 1989 to change the specifications for the Uniform CPA Examination. They also have developed a model code of ethics and a model accountancy law to apply in each state. These documents could be (and were) used to persuade state law makers to bring their statutes and regulations up to a national norm. NASBA also assists state boards faced by legislative threats of closure under sunset reviews. In 1989, NASBA proposed serving as a central registry for CPE courses by enrolling all authorized providers. The goal was to prevent unethical submission of inappropriate CPE credit and to protect accountants against inadequate CPE courses. Not all states were enthused by this proposal.

Although the dispersion of certification authority across all states has inefficiencies and inconsistencies, this arrangement is compatible with the policy of protecting states' rights against federal domination. Some professionals believe that this arrangement has outlived its usefulness, particularly for disciplining unethical accountants. Until such time as a federal agency is given a national licensing authority, however, financial accountants wanting to practice as auditors will need to be certified by one or more state boards.

STANDARDS SETTING ORGANIZATIONS

2.8 FINANCIAL ACCOUNTING STANDARDS BOARD.   The **Financial Accounting Standards Board** has a unique status as a private organization charged with protecting the public interest (the GASB, a related organization, is discussed in section 2.9). The SEC endorses it through ASR No. 150 (now codified within FRR No. 1) as the source of "substantial authoritative support" for determining the acceptability of accounting practices for filings with the Commission. It has also been endorsed at the state level to the extent that state boards of accountancy include a requirement for complying with FASB pronouncements in their ethics codes. The FASB does not receive funds directly from either the SEC or the state boards, but the tax deductibility of contributions acts as a de facto subsidy.

Although other private sector bodies, such as the AICPA and the Financial Executives Institute, endorse and finance the FASB, it is, by intent and design, independent of any of them. Of course, the governmental endorsements are contingent on the Board's maintaining an attitude of protecting the public interest.

(a) **Brief History.**   Beginning in 1938 with the issuance of ASR No. 4, the SEC has given the accounting profession a loose rein to establish GAAP.

Shortly after ASR No. 4's release, the American Institute of Accountants (the forerunner of the AICPA) upgraded the level of funding, staffing, and activity of its **Committee on Accounting Procedures.** Over the next 20 years, it produced 51 **Accounting Research Bulletins,** including the all-encompassing ARB No. 43. The CAP did not survive because it suffered from two political shortcomings. First, it never was given authority by the Institute's council to establish standards that would be binding on the membership. Second, it was housed within the Institute, which created at least the appearance that auditors' interests (and their clients' interests) were likely to be preferred to the public interest.

In response to criticism, the AICPA formed the **Accounting Principles Board** in 1958 and again increased the funding and staffing over the previous levels. During the next 15 years, the APB issued 31 **Opinions** and 4 **Statements.** In an effort to establish credibility, the APB's initial membership consisted of the top managing partners of major firms and other comparably influential accountants. Over time, the membership level slipped somewhat into lower levels of management, but highly competent technical experts continued to serve on the Board. In 1964, the AICPA Council acted to correct one of the deficiencies carried forward from the CAP by requiring members of the Institute to identify and justify their clients' departures from principles established by the APB. However, the second weakness still existed in that the Board was perceived as elevating auditors' and clients' interests above the interest of the general public in achieving "full and fair disclosure" for more effective capital markets.

In response to growing sentiments and suggestions that the APB needed to be replaced by a government agency, the AICPA, in 1971, organized the Study Group on Establishing Financial Accounting Standards, under the chairmanship of Francis M. Wheat. During the following year, the Wheat Study Group recommended creating an autonomous standards setting body that would overcome the weaknesses of the CAP and the APB. That is, it would be granted authority to establish binding GAAP but it would not be housed within the AICPA. Thus, it would be more likely to escape the appearance of dominance by the interests of auditors and their clients. The proposal was accepted by six sponsoring organizations, who provided adequate funding and other support to get the FASB established and operating in 1973. The original six sponsors were the AICPA, the Financial Executives Institute, the National Association of Accountants, the American Accounting Association, the Securities Industry Association, and the Financial Analysts' Federation. A critical event of the first year was the SEC's issuance of ASR No. 150.

Initially, the Board was still heavily dependent on the Institute and auditors for its funding and credibility. However, the previous concerns of dominance were raised in Congressional hearings in 1975 and 1976, and the Board's bylaws were changed to make it less subject to the appearance of control by auditors and preparers.

The first chairman was a respected practitioner Marshall Armstrong, who had been a member of the APB from 1963 through 1969. He was succeeded in 1978 by Donald J. Kirk, who had been a charter member of the FASB. Kirk served as chairman through the end of 1987, when he was replaced by Denny Beresford.

(b) **Structure of the FASB.**   The FASB actually is only one part of a three-part organization, which also consists of the **Financial Accounting Foundation** (FAF) and the **Financial Accounting Standards Advisory Council** (FASAC). The relationships between these entities, the

GASB, and the Governmental Accounting Standards Advisory Council (GASAC) are diagrammed in Exhibit 2.4.

The Foundation is a nonprofit, tax-exempt Delaware corporation, managed by an 18-member Board of Trustees. They are responsible primarily for (1) raising operating funds and (2) appointing members of the two Boards and their Advisory Councils. A third unofficial function of the FAF is to shield the Board members from the kinds of pressures to compromise the public interest that shut down the CAP and the APB. Most of the trustees are appointed by the governing boards of the sponsoring organizations, and the remainder are selected by the other trustees. The creation of the GASB caused expansion of the Trustees' group to include three members selected by a consortium of organizations involved with local and state governments.

The Foundation bylaws strictly forbid trustees from tampering with the Boards' procedures in order to affect the standards that they issue. Of course, their control of appointments and reappointments gives the trustees substantial indirect influence.

The **FASAC** was conceived as an experienced and informed microcosm of the Board's constituencies with the sole duty of providing feedback. It has operated that way with a membership ranging from 20 to 35 members, who serve up to three 1-year terms. Only the full-time chairman receives compensation. The Council has no fund-raising responsibilities and does not attempt to take a vote or reach a consensus on the issues. Rather, its job has been to offer advice on the projects to add to the agenda and on preliminary positions for existing projects.

The **FASB** itself has seven full-time members who sever their relationships with their previous employers or partnerships. Each is appointed for a 5-year term and can be reappointed for another. A member appointed to fill an unscheduled vacancy, however, is still allowed to serve two additional full terms. The FAF trustees designate the chairman, who has significant administrative responsibilities, including the leadership of Board meetings. In addition, the chairman is the Board's most visible spokesperson. The chairman's annual salary in 1989 was $360,000; other Board members received $290,000.

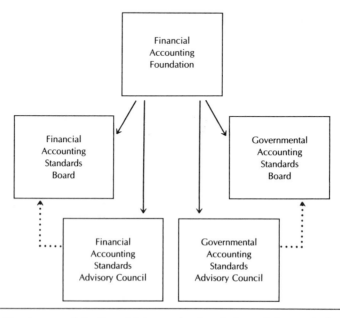

Exhibit 2.4.   The structure of the Financial Accounting Foundation and the Standards Boards.

The **Research and Technical Activities (RTA) staff** assists the Board; it comprises approximately 40 experienced accountants. Selected by the chairman, the staff director is also a spokesperson for the Board and receives the same compensation as a Board member. This equivalent status indicates the importance the FASB attaches to the research underlying its efforts.

In addition to its facilities in Norwalk, Connecticut, the FASB maintains a small office in Washington, D.C., for the dual purposes of informing the Board about events in the capital and representing the Board and its interests to regulators, legislators, and others. The Chairman, Vice Chairman, and RTA Director frequently visit Washington to meet directly with the SEC, its Chief Accountant, and the OCA staff. For example, the concern in the late 1980s over accounting for postemployment health care benefits called for a substantial presence in Washington of Board and staff members, particularly in Congressional committee hearings.

The FASB's annual operating expenditures exceeded $13.7 million in 1989, with 74% being spent on personnel. Sales of Board publications covered 54% of the total expenses and 34% came from donations. The $1.6 million remainder came from accumulated reserves. Of the donated funds, approximately 54% came from the preparer community and 46% came from auditors. Virtually no donations were received from financial statement users. This imbalance has created at least the appearance of domination of preparers' and auditors' interests over those of users and the public.

(c) Board Publications.   Although the FASB exists primarily to create financial accounting standards, it also interprets standards where they are not completely clear. In addition, it was given the assignment of developing broad theoretical concepts of financial accounting. Its position in the regulatory process and the demand from many accountants for detailed rules combine to create the need for implementation guidance. As might be expected, the FASB's publications reflect these tasks.

The main category of publications consists of **Statements of Financial Accounting Standards** (SFASs). They are numbered consecutively, and 105 of them had been issued as of early 1990. ASR No. 150 specifically recognizes the authority of these pronouncements, and they receive similar support in state accountancy statutes and regulations. In addition, they are recognized by the Council of the AICPA as GAAP for the membership; any member not treating them as such will have violated Ethics Rule 203. Thus, financial statements must be prepared in accordance with these standards if they are to receive an unqualified audit opinion. Issuance of an SFAS requires support by a simple majority of the Board members.

Another category of publication, **Interpretations** (FINs), also establishes GAAP. However, none has been issued since 1984, primarily because of the emphasis placed on other media for providing the kind of guidance that interpretations were initially created to provide. Interpretations were numbered consecutively, and 38 have been issued. They are passed only after receiving a majority vote from Board members.

A third category of Board document is the **Statement of Financial Accounting Concepts,** (SFAC). These statements describe broader underlying concepts that the Board has determined to use in developing its standards. The statements do **not** constitute GAAP, and accordingly they are not identified as such by regulatory bodies or ethics codes. Nonetheless, knowledge of these statements is helpful for understanding the content of standards and for anticipating the direction of future standards. For these reasons, the Board's conceptual framework is described in section 2.8(e). Concepts statements are also numbered consecutively, and six were issued between 1978 and 1985. SFAC No. 6 replaced SFAC No. 3, with the result that only five are in effect. With the exception of SFAC No. 6, which had a single dissent, all the concepts statements were passed unanimously, even though a simple majority would have been adequate.

A fourth FASB category of publication comprises **Technical Bulletins** (FTBs), which are actually issued by the RTA staff. They are narrow in scope and interpret the existing authoritative literature (i.e., ARBs, APBOs, SFASs, and FINs) to apply to situations not covered in it directly. Although Board members have the ability to prevent issuance of proposed FTBs, they do not formally vote to authorize their publication. Technical Bulletins are numbered in annual series, such as "85-3," which was the third one issued in 1985. The Board initiated FTBs in order to systematize informal advice that the RTA staff was disseminating by telephone and letters; the use of FTBs expanded in the mid-1980s to reduce the earlier practice of issuing many highly detailed standards and interpretations. This change also allowed Board members to focus their efforts on more substantive issues.

To mitigate the need for narrow Board pronouncements while still providing quick responses to new problems (called "timely guidance" in FASB jargon), the **Emerging Issues Task Force** (EITF) was created in 1984. The director of the RTA staff chairs this group, which consists of approximately 15 technical experts from major and regional accounting firms and large corporations. It meets every 6 weeks to tackle complex new problems by applying the existing literature. Transactions and events that have already transpired are the source of some issues, whereas others are based on proposed transactions. The SEC's Chief Accountant is an active participant in the discussions, although he is officially identified as only an "observer." He and his staff are the prime beneficiaries of the EITF's activity because it addresses the issues that previously were brought to the OCA by registrants and their accountants.

When the EITF faces an issue, it seeks a "consensus," which is considered to exist if no more than two or three members object to a proposed solution. If more object, there is no consensus, with the consequence that the Chief Accountant is left to implement his own views. Alternatively, the Task Force may recommend that the full Board consider dealing with the issue. Prior to 1988, **EITF Consensuses** were not published, although minutes of the meetings were available from the Board. In 1988, the FASB began to publish highly condensed summaries of the issues and their resolutions. These summaries are presented more or less as a public service because the outcomes are not necessarily the opinion of either a majority of the Board or the RTA staff. Although they have not been endorsed as authoritative, they have attained adequate status to be considered a source of GAAP. A consensus is acceptable for SEC filings as long as the OCA does not have a serious objection to its outcome. Like TBs, EITF issues are numbered in annual series. Over 225 of them have been dealt with through 1990.

In addition to the above documents, the FASB also produces numerous other publications. **Research Reports** are developed in response to staff or consultant efforts to identify a problem, review the literature related to a set of issues, or propose answers. **Discussion Memorandums** and **Invitations to Comment** solicit views from the Board's constituents in early stages of deliberations. Three newsletters inform the public of the Board's activities: **Action Alert, Status Report,** and **Highlights.** Another widely distributed item is **Facts about FASB,** which describes the Board's mission, procedures, and membership.

(d) Due Process Procedures.   Like many other regulatory agencies, the FASB has established procedures to ensure that (1) parties affected by new regulations have an opportunity to express their views on the issues and (2) all possible positions on the issues are uncovered. A desirable side effect is that the public's participation may bolster the credibility of the output. Although the term "due process" may imply a rigid set of procedures, there is actually enough flexibility to allow the Board some freedom in determining how extensively to pursue various activities. Certain steps, however, must always be followed.

As shown in the flowchart in Exhibit 2.5, the following six basic steps take place:

- Admission to the agenda.
- Preliminary deliberations.
- Tentative resolution.

- Further deliberations.
- Final resolution.
- Subsequent review.

All these steps are public. Board meetings take place at the headquarters in Norwalk, Connecticut, and are open to all who want to attend, up to the room's capacity. Under the FASB's "sunshine" policy, Board members are not allowed to discuss the issues privately in groups consisting of more than three persons. This arrangement was adopted in the mid-1970s after criticism that the previous policy of "closed door" meetings caused some constituents to feel that their views were not being considered. The following paragraphs describe these six steps.

A project is **added to the agenda** only after substantial preliminary debate. The set of problems to be addressed in the project must meet several criteria. First, there must be diverse practice. Second, the diversity must create significant differences in financial statements, such that there is a potential for users to be misled or to incur excessive analysis costs.

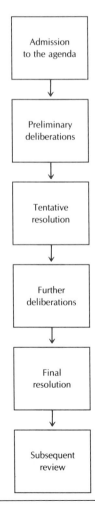

Exhibit 2.5.   The steps in the FASB's due process.

Third, there must be a sufficiently high probability that the issues can be resolved in a manner that justifies the application of Board resources. Of course, the agenda decision involves a certain amount of political activity. Ideas for problems come from the Board and staff, but more often from constituents and the SEC. The EITF deliberations have also created some projects. Apart from a **Research Report,** it is unusual for a publication to be issued in this phase.

The next step is to engage in **early deliberations.** Early during this stage, the RTA staff attempts to frame the issues and sound out Board members and constituents. For major projects, the staff may create a **Task Force** of interested experts from various constituencies to assist its inquiries. Occasionally, the Board will publish a **Discussion Memorandum** or an **Invitation to Comment** at this phase. There may be **public hearings** for especially significant or controversial projects, in order to allow constituents to express their views and to allow Board members and staff to question persons who testify. Board meetings will generally be devoted to questions from the members to the staff and to each other. As the phase draws to a close, the staff efforts turn to helping the members find the common ground on which to build a majority vote.

The third phase is the **tentative resolution.** At this point, a majority of the Board has voted to issue an **Exposure Draft** (ED), which is a proposed standard (or concepts statement or interpretation). The ED is exposed for comment for at least 6 weeks and occasionally for a longer period. More controversial projects may have another round of public hearings. Dissenting Board members' views are included in the ED, as well as a summary of the basis for the majority's conclusions.

During the **further deliberations** step of the due process, the staff and Board attempt to digest the comments received in response to the ED. Because the prior efforts have been thorough, it is very unusual for the comments to bring anything really new to the table. Many persons have a poor understanding of this situation, particularly if they offered views that are subsequently not incorporated in the final standard. The Board's disagreement with them may be misinterpreted as failing to listen when, in fact, the presentation simply failed to persuade a majority of the Board. During this phase, Board member efforts generally aim at fine-tuning the proposal to deal with unanticipated minor glitches. If significant changes are needed in order to keep majority support, a second ED may be necessary.

The **final resolution** phase is short and consists merely of taking votes from the Board members either for or against the "ballot draft" of the standard (or other pronouncement). The published document includes not only the majority's view but also the dissenters', if any. It also describes the comments from the constituents and the Board's reactions to them. Many standards also include an appendix illustrating the application of the requirements. Once this point is reached, the staff's efforts turn to responding to implementation problems. Recent years have seen several **Question and Answer** implementation guides that the Board prepares and distributes.

If substantial problems remain, or if a standard produces new problems, the Board may enter into a **subsequent review** phase of the due process. In 1976, following the issuance of SFAS No. 12, the staff tried to put in place a formalized process for conducting this review. However, it did not survive. Generally, all involved with a project (Board, staff, and constituents) are reluctant to get back into a controversy once it has been resolved. In some cases, a later **Research Report** may attempt to assess the impact of a standard, but this practice has not been common.

In summary, the due process is molded to fit the situation. It can be prolonged in order to help the Board find its consensus and to gain the support of the constituency. It can also be accelerated to get an answer on the street as quickly as possible. Nonetheless, the purposes remain the same: to identify the problem, to uncover the answers, to develop a majority view, and to develop constituent support for that view. The Board specifically disavows any notion that the due process allows it to "count noses" to determine what a majority of the constituency wants. Its role is more judicial than legislative, and the Board members must reach a conclusion as to what is best for the economy as a whole, even if particular groups are strongly opposed to the new accounting standard.

(e) The Conceptual Framework.   An important key to understanding the overall direction of the FASB's efforts to change financial accounting is its project to identify a coherent theory of financial reporting, called the **conceptual framework.**

Because the CAP and APB were criticized for not developing a unified theoretical basis for resolving issues, the FASB's inaugural agenda included the task of identifying concepts that it could use in setting standards.

A critical initial decision in the project was to develop the framework from the "top-down" by identifying the objectives of financial reporting and then working down to more specific concepts. This approach (also called "deductive") had been tried before, most notably by Sprouse and Moonitz in the AICPA's ARS No. 3, "A Tentative Set of Broad Accounting Principles for Business Enterprises" (1962), and by the Trueblood Study Group in its report, "Objectives of Financial Statements" (AICPA, 1973). The opposite approach (called "bottom-up" or "inductive") of looking at practice and identifying common threads had also been tried, most notably in APB Statement No. 4, "Basic Concepts and Accounting Principles Underlying Financial Statements of Business Enterprises" (1970). Although there are several advantages and disadvantages to the two approaches, the main difference between them is that the bottom-up tends to encourage applying old solutions to new problems, whereas the top-down tends to lead to new solutions to old problems. Thus, the determination of the Board to pursue a top-down framework created a substantially greater likelihood that significant change in GAAP could be created. Accordingly, the framework project was (and has continued to be) controversial.

SFAC No. 1, **"Objectives of Financial Reporting by Business Enterprises,"** was issued in 1978. It presented a hierarchy of objectives, the most important being the providing of:

> . . . information that is useful to present and potential investors and creditors and other users in making rational investment, credit, and other decisions.

However obvious this objective might seem on the surface, it is politically significant because it establishes that the interests of financial statement users are to be ranked above the interests of auditors and preparers.

SFAC No. 2, **"Qualitative Characteristics of Accounting Information,"** was issued in 1980. It identifies qualities of information that make it useful for meeting the objective described in SFAC No. 1. The three primary qualities are **relevance, reliability,** and **comparability.** The important point to observe is that the Board chose qualities that reflect the users' needs instead of the needs of auditors (who prefer defensible information) and preparers (who prefer controllable and inexpensive information).

The third phase of the framework culminated in 1980 with the issuance of SFAC No. 3, **"Elements of Financial Statements of Business Enterprises."** It was superseded in 1985 by SFAC No. 6, **"Elements of Financial Statements,"** which also encompasses the elements of financial statements for not-for-profit entities. The business elements identified by the Board included the familiar assets, liabilities, owners' equity, revenues, expenses, gains, and losses; however, its decision to make the assets and liabilities the keystone elements was enormously significant. That is, all the other elements, including "comprehensive income," were defined in terms of assets and liabilities. With this decision, the Board essentially turned away from the familiar "matching" concept of income that had dominated practice for decades with its emphasis on the income statement and its deemphasis of the balance sheet. Instead, under the conceptual framework, income is measured by changes in assets and liabilities because both the income statement and balance sheet are considered useful and important. There are tremendous practical implications in this choice, some of which have already been seen in SFAS No. 87 on accounting for pensions by employers and in SFAS No.

96 on accounting for income taxes. In both cases, the reporting company looks to changes in assets and liabilities to determine its income instead of attempting to match costs with revenues in accordance with a predetermined or otherwise systematic or desired fashion.

SFAC No. 4, **"Objectives of Financial Reporting by Nonbusiness Organizations,"** was also issued in 1980. (Subsequent to issuing SFAC No. 4 but before issuing SFAC No. 6, the FASB determined that the term "not-for-profit" was preferable to "nonbusiness." In particular, the managers of a number of these entities complained that they did not like the inference that they were not "businesslike" in the way they operated.) It was the outgrowth of the FASB's decision to deal with all private entities, even though there had been no mandate from the SEC for doing so. This statement broke new ground because there had not been a significant effort to establish concepts in this area from the top-down. As might be expected, the main objective is similar to the one in SFAC No. 1; specifically, it says that the financial statements of not-for-profit organizations should provide:

> . . . information that is useful to present and potential resource providers and other users in making rational decisions about the allocation of resources to those organizations.

By starting with this objective, the Board again put into place the potential for substantial reform because it would be necessary to show how existing practices met this objective. Because there has been little actual effort to do much in the not-for-profit area, it will not be discussed further here.

The Board encountered major roadblocks when it entered into the project's next phase, "recognition and measurement," because it was here that decisions would be reached on whether, when, and at what amount assets, liabilities, and changes in them should be reflected in the financial statements. The fundamental issue was whether there should be a movement toward including more current value information in the statements. Naturally, this phase of the project attracted much attention and created substantial controversy. In 1985, after more than 3 years of debate, six Board members (one dissented because he wanted to go back to the matching concept of earnings) agreed to issue SFAC No. 5, **"Recognition and Measurement in Financial Statements of Business Enterprises,"** which was clearly a compromise. It says that things recognized in the statements should be elements and that the amount reported for them should be relevant and reliable. In effect, all that was accomplished was to reaffirm the contents of the preceding concepts statements. SFAC No. 5 also identified the cash flow statement as a conceptual member of the set of financial statements, and the Board eventually issued SFAS No. 95, which requires its presentation. SFAC No. 5 also identified two possible income statements, one of which would focus on earnings, whereas the other would report comprehensive income, which might include changes in current value. Nothing has been done to implement this suggestion.

What, then, is the significance of the conceptual framework? It really needs to be interpreted from a political perspective more than from a theoretical one. First, it sets in place the possibility for significant changes in GAAP. Second, it puts users' needs (and thus the public interest) at the highest priority level. Third, it establishes that the statement of financial position should not merely be a resting place for debit and credit balances waiting to be "matched" in the future; rather, it should provide useful information about assets and liabilities. Fourth, the framework rejects matching in favor of reporting changes in assets and liabilities as income, thus raising the possibility that gains and losses from price changes could be recognized as income. Finally, it defines a number of important terms that are used in the Board's communications with its constituents, and in its internal discussions. Far from being an empty academic theoretical exercise, the framework is perhaps the most significant set of pronouncements that the FASB has issued. The more that practitioners know about it, the more they will be capable of dealing with the Board and the changes that its pronouncements will bring about.

(f) The Political Environment and the FASB's Future.   As established in the opening section of this chapter, and confirmed above, political factors very much affect financial accounting. Because accounting standards have the potential for changing the allocation of wealth among various groups and individuals in society, people are willing to spend time, effort, and money to try to establish the standards that they find advantageous. Because the interests of preparers, users, auditors, regulators, and the public can be in serious conflict, efforts to create or change standards naturally create disagreement, controversy, and dissatisfaction.

One pervasive political problem that just will not go away is **standards overload.** Originally, this phrase described the issuance of numerous detailed standards, but more recently it has come to encompass the issuance of complex standards that are difficult to implement, especially by smaller nonpublic companies. Exhibit 2.6 symbolizes the politics of this situation, showing that the FASB is the custodian of power from the SEC to establish GAAP for use by public companies while, **at the same time,** it has received authority from state boards and the AICPA to establish GAAP for use by private companies.

The FASB's dilemma is that too much emphasis on SEC registrants seems to ignore the constraints affecting private companies, yet too much emphasis on private companies ignores the needs of the SEC and the public for effective capital markets. Because the SEC exerts the greatest influence, it seems likely that FASB will continue to focus on the needs of more sophisticated users and will issue standards that may be difficult for private companies to implement. This choice leaves the state boards and the AICPA in a difficult relationship with some of their constituents and members, but there does not appear to be any way out of this dilemma. Some have suggested application of different standards according to whether the company is private or public, but survey responses have consistently shown that GAAP for the private companies would be perceived as being inferior, and that users would probably demand that the public company principles be applied in the private companies' statements. Thus, it does not appear as if the Board will be able to change its position.

Another political problem for the FASB exists in its relationships with the SEC, Congress, and the preparer community. Beginning with ASR No. 150, the SEC has virtually always supported the FASB's efforts, with the exception of SFAS No. 19 on oil and gas accounting. The Board's existence allows the Commission to meet its own needs without appropriating public funds. It also allows the SEC to divert criticism to the FASB when a problem is being solved, or even after a standard has been issued. Thus, it seems unlikely that the SEC will

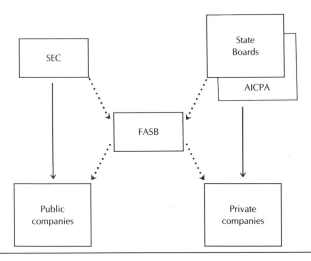

Exhibit 2.6.   Conflicting authorities and standards overload.

seek to move standards setting authority into the federal government. Two particularly strong statements were issued by federal officials in 1988 and 1989 in support of the present arrangement. One came from SEC Chairman David Ruder when he expressed great satisfaction with the Board's efforts and results in a speech to an AICPA conference on SEC matters and in a letter to the **Business Roundtable.** (The Roundtable is an association of the chief executive officers of approximately 200 of the largest corporations in the U.S. It is primarily a lobbying organization to help ensure the protection and promotion of the member companies' interests). The other came from Congressman John Dingell of Michigan in a letter to Ruder, in which he fundamentally stated that he liked the existing system, and if the SEC did not protect FASB against attack, then the Congress would.

Despite this support, members of the Roundtable continued to call for fundamental reform in FASB's structure and activities on the basis that it was "too theoretical" for practice, "unresponsive to its constituents," and "out of control." In reaction to these pressures, the **Groves Committee** was formed by the FAF trustees to identify weaknesses and to recommend changes. In 1989, the trustees accepted a recommendation that they engage in more active supervision of the Board's activities. The specific response was to form an Oversight Subcommittee that will meet with Board members and others to assess performance of both the organization and individual members.

In a sense, the Board was at a crossroads in 1990: Would it continue to try to advance the public interest or would it submit to the special interests of the preparer community? From the discussion in this chapter, it should be clear that the economy needs an independent Board, which can look at all positions on the issues and then resolve them with the public interest in the forefront. Although standards setting by a government agency has many disadvantages, the authority may be driven there if the Board's independence is compromised.

2.9 GOVERNMENTAL ACCOUNTING STANDARDS BOARD.   In response to needs expressed by various groups, a study was undertaken in the early 1980s to consider how to establish financial accounting standards for state and local governmental units. (The federal government's uniqueness has caused the application of governmental accounting standards to be limited to state and local entities.) Standards were being established through professional organizations composed of governmental accountants, but they had not been endorsed by the Council of the AICPA, with the consequence that there was some concern over whether they constituted GAAP. The study group's report recommended the creation of the **Governmental Accounting Standards Board,** which would be under the administration of the FAF. After several years of discussion and opposition, the trustees agreed to set up the GASB, and it began operations in 1984.

The constituencies of GASB overlap those of the FASB, but only to a limited extent. The preparers consist of elected and appointed officials who are accountable to the voting public for the use and safekeeping of funds appropriated or otherwise entrusted to them, and thus they do not coincide with the preparers regulated by the FASB. The auditor constituency is essentially the same as for the FASB, although the actual individuals are likely to be different because of specialization. Some of the users of the financial statements of governmental units are different from the users of business statements, whereas others are the same. In effect, when governmental units go into the capital markets to obtain debt funding, they are competing with corporations for investors' attention. There is no regulatory agency comparable to the SEC with jurisdiction over governmental units, with the consequence that the GASB has no constituent like the Commission. State boards are interested in the GASB's efforts because their licensees act as auditors for governmental units.

The authority of GASB for setting standards is not quite as clear-cut, then, as that of the FASB. It does have power, however, because a variety of professional societies, including the AICPA, endorse its efforts. It also has increased influence because of its indirect affiliation with the FASB.

(a) The Structure of the GASB. The GASB has five members; only the chairman serves in his capacity on a full-time basis. The chairman's salary in 1990 was $185,000. As of that time, the vice-chairman doubled as the director of the Board's research staff, which is separate from the FASB's. His salary was $160,000. The other three members serve part-time and commute to Connecticut for meetings and consultations. Their salaries were $39,000. The Board's headquarters are located in the same building with the FASB and the FAF. Although some of the administrative facilities and activities (such as the Board meeting room, the library, and the accounting and human relations services) are shared, the two Boards operate independently.

The GASB is also funded separately from the FASB. Like the FASB, it depends on sales of its publications and donations for its revenues. Its expenditures for 1989 totaled $2.4 million, of which 65% came from donations and 28% from publications. Also like the FASB, the GASB consumed some of its reserves in 1989 in financing its $305,000 operating deficit. Unlike the FASB, the GASB does receive appropriated funds from governmental units, including a number of state legislatures and city councils, as well as the federal General Accounting Office. Donations from taxpayers are, of course, subsidized by their deductibility for federal income taxes.

In 1989, a committee of the FAF trustees and others completed a study of the GASB in compliance with the arrangement that created it. This committee recommended that the Board continue to operate, with some changes in its structure. Specifically, it recommended that all five Board members be required to sever their ties with their employers and serve the GASB full-time. It was also recommended that there be a full-time director of the research staff, who would not be a member of the Board. When this chapter was written, none of these recommendations had been implemented.

The **Governmental Accounting Standards Advisory Committee** serves the same purpose as the FASAC, but it is not as large and does not have a full-time chairman.

The GASB's due process process procedures are essentially the same as the FASB's and include similar steps. Some of the deliberations are more difficult to accomplish because of the geographical dispersion of the members, but they nonetheless take place.

(b) The Jurisdiction Issue. A persistent problem in the relationship between FASB and GASB has been the overlapping of their jurisdictions in some segments of the economy. In fact, the issue of who should provide standards for these segments was the major stumbling block to the GASB's establishment.

Some organizations subject to the overlapping jurisdiction are utilities and providers of educational and health services. For example, some universities are operated by governments, others are private, and still others are combinations. The same situation exists for utilities, hospitals, and nursing homes, with the additional twist that many are operated for profit by publicly held corporations. The jurisdiction issue turned first on the question of whether all these entities should be required to use the same accounting principles in order to achieve comparability. If so, the next question was which Board should establish those principles.

As long as there were no conflicts over the principles to be used, the jurisdiction dispute did not cause a practical problem. However, that situation did not exist for long because the two Boards reached opposing conclusions concerning the recognition of depreciation. Thus, the unresolved issue continued to chafe both organizations and to confuse their constituents.

It was resolved in late 1989 when the FAF's trustees first voted to implement and then shortly thereafter rejected a recommendation offered by two Special Committees that reviewed the structures of FASB and GASB. The final resolution left the jurisdiction as it had originally been defined, with GASB holding power over state and local government entities, whereas the FASB was given responsibility for all others. In addition, it was agreed that GASB would give careful consideration to the need for comparability when setting standards for public sector entities in industries that also include private companies.

The first resolution was controversial because it removed certain key public sector entities from the GASB's jurisdiction and thereby reduced its influence and status. In reaching their recommendations, the two Special Committees had determined that the jurisdiction was better defined by the user groups than by the preparer groups. That is, they felt that the fact that private and government entities provide the same service does not necessarily mean that their financial statements are used by the same people for the same purposes. Indeed, in most cases, the user groups are far more likely to be different than similar. In those relatively rare situations where the user groups do coincide, such as when a governmental agency goes into the capital market to borrow funds, the Committees recommended that reporting entities use FASB Standards. GASB standards would still have been applied by the public sector entities for financial reports prepared for governmental purposes. In other words, the jurisdictional issue would have been resolved on the basis of who **uses** the statements instead of who **prepares** them. Although this arrangement would have caused some organizations to maintain two sets of records, it might have furthered the objective of providing useful information for rational decisions.

The trustees' decision to reverse their position by rejecting the committees' recommendations and adopting the alternative of a more sensitive due process does not really deal with the heart of the jurisdiction issue, and it seems clear that it will return to the forefront again.

PROFESSIONAL ORGANIZATIONS

2.10 AMERICAN INSTITUTE OF CERTIFIED PUBLIC ACCOUNTANTS.   Of the several professional accounting organizations, the largest and most influential is the American Institute of Certified Public Accountants. Each member must be licensed as a CPA by some jurisdiction, but need not practice as a public accountant. In fact, less than half (46.5%) of the 280,000 membership in 1990 were in public practice, with the majority working in industry, government, or education.

(a) Structure.   In response to assertions from Congressional staff, the AICPA undertook a major restructuring in 1977 to establish a more rigorous self-governance. Even though the concern over the alleged shortcomings was not backed up by enacted legislation, the Institute created a **Division for CPA Firms,** whereas previously it had only individual memberships. Members of this division commit themselves to higher standards of quality and quality control, including triennial **peer reviews** of their quality control systems. The Division is further broken down into two sections: the **Securities and Exchange Commission Practice Section** (SECPS) and the **Private Companies Practice Section** (PCPS). Interestingly, more than half the members of the SECPS do not have any SEC registrants as clients; apparently they joined because of the desire to meet the higher standards. Virtually all major SEC registrants are audited by SECPS firms (studies by the SEC staff and others have shown that 99 + % of the sales revenue dollars of SEC registrants are audited by SECPS members). A five-member **Public Oversight Board,** composed of highly reputable individuals, monitors the effectiveness of the SECPS peer review system. The system is also supported by the work of the **Quality Control Investigation Committee** (formerly the **Special Investigations Committee**). This committee examines the facts and circumstances surrounding all litigation naming SECPS member firms as defendants in order to determine whether information needs to be brought to the attention of the peer reviewers, and to assess the effectiveness of past peer reviews.

As a result of a major change in policy approved by the Institute membership in 1988, all members in public practice will be subject to quality control reviews, even if they do not belong to the Division for CPA Firms. However, these reviews will not be as extensive as full peer reviews, and the AICPA will not release the results to the public as with reviews applied to SECPS firms.

The most significant services provided by the AICPA to its members and the public are discussed below.

(b) Technical Standards. Despite the discontinuation of the APB and the creation of the FASB, the Institute still carries on standards setting activities through the **Accounting Standards Executive Committee** (AcSEC) and the **Auditing Standards Board** (ASB).

AcSEC examines accounting issues that have not reached the FASB's agenda, or that the FASB has decided against adding to its agenda. Accordingly, AcSEC and the FASB are in frequent contact, and FASB staff members attend AcSEC meetings. The primary form of output from AcSEC is a **Statement of Position** (SOP), which must be followed by Institute members. The Committee is composed of between 15 and 18 individuals representing various levels and segments of the profession. Beyond lengthy discussion and research, AcSEC does not have an elaborate set of due process procedures.

The ASB is the only organization that creates authoritative generally accepted auditing standards (GAAS). It issues **Statements on Auditing Standards** (SAS). This 15-member group is composed of senior auditing specialists from major and other auditing firms, as well as from industry and education. It uses a thorough due process, including the issuance of exposure drafts of proposed standards. Because audits are important to the credibility of financial statements, and because financial statements are important to the effectiveness of the capital markets, the SEC oversees the ASB's activities closely, including quarterly meetings between the ASB's leadership and the Chief Accountant and his staff. In 1988, the ASB issued a series of new pervasive standards designed to close a so-called Expectations Gap between what the public seemed to be expecting and what auditors seemed to be delivering. One motivating factor for the standards was the increased amount of litigation alleging auditors' failures to protect the public against fraud and business collapses. Included among the new pronouncements was one changing the language of the standard auditor's opinion for the first time in four decades.

Senior AICPA committees for specific industries provide other technical guidance. Their output is in the form of **Industry Accounting and Auditing Guides.** A member is obliged to follow the provisions of these guides in auditing a client that belongs to one of the covered industries.

In addition to these activities, the Institute staff also provides **technical assistance** to members who have encountered questions in conducting their accounting, auditing, and tax practices. Specifically, members can call or write the Institute staff with their questions and receive guidance on how to resolve them. In many cases, all that is needed is to steer the member to the right portion of the authoritative literature. In other cases, the members are seeking concurrence with a position they have reached on their own. Both services are especially valuable to sole practitioners who do not have a colleague to double-check their research.

(c) Examinations. The AICPA produces, administers, and grades the **Uniform CPA Examination** under contract to individual state boards of accountancy. This service includes writing the exam to specifications established through NASBA, maintaining security over the questions, enrolling candidates and accepting their fees, delivering the exams to the sites, and reading and grading the papers. The Institute then sends the results to the state board, which, in turn, notifies the candidates. Subsequently, the AICPA publishes the questions and unofficial answers to help future candidates prepare for examinations. The CPA exam is administered twice each year, in May and November, and includes four sections: Practice, Theory, Auditing, and Law. A fifth section covering professional ethics is not uniformly required by all states.

The Institute also develops and makes available various levels of **Achievement Tests** that are used by some schools to assess the progress made by their students in comparison to national norms.

(d) Ethics Enforcement.   The AICPA provides substantial effort and leadership concerning the development and enforcement of the Institute's **Code of Conduct,** which replaced the predecessor Code of Professional Ethics early in 1988. Because the AICPA Code serves as the basic model for most state societies and state boards, changes in it are usually incorporated by them in their own codes.

The 1970s and 1980s saw unprecedented challenges to long-standing provisions of the code. The first to come under attack were the rules that prohibited advertising, encroaching on the practices of other accountants, otherwise soliciting clients, and competitive bidding. They were rendered unenforceable by actions of the FTC as unfair restraints of trade. A similar fate was met by a rule that did not allow one accountant to contact another accountant's staff members concerning possible employment.

Contingent fees and fees in the form of commissions had long been forbidden as inconsistent with public accountants' integrity and independence. It was believed that making the fee proportional to an outcome would create a temptation for modifying that outcome, and that the conflict of interest would make the accountant's advice less reliable and useful. The commission policy was challenged once accountants began to offer personal financial planning and found that their ''fee only'' arrangements caused them to lose clients to non-CPAs who did not charge a fee but collected commissions from purchases of financial products by the client. Again, the FTC took an interest and challenged the Institute's rule. In 1989, a settlement was reached that allows commissions in all cases except where the accountant performs an attestation for the client. The contingent fee rule was still unsettled.

Another potential problem that needed resolution involved the vote by the Institute membership to subject all members to the full code. Prior to 1988, those members not in practice were bound only to have integrity and to avoid discrediting the profession. However, the change requires all members, even those employed by others, to not subordinate their judgment to other persons. As of 1990, the AICPA's Ethics Executive Committee had not been able to determine just how this rule applies to employed CPAs who disagree with their superiors and cannot persuade them to go along. It does not seem likely, for example, that a controller would have to resign when the Chief Financial Officer determines that LIFO should be used instead of FIFO, which is the controller's preference. This and similar situations happen far too frequently to require either a resignation or an ethics proceeding.

Through the **Joint Ethics Enforcement Program** (JEEP), the Ethics Division staff works with state societies and members of Institute ethics subcommittees to conduct investigations of alleged violations or to concur with findings conducted at the state level. These investigations attempt to establish only **prima facie** evidence that a section of the Code of Conduct was violated without trying to determine whether the member intended to violate it. JEEP leverages the expertise of the Institute staff to improve the quality of the work done at the state level. This quality control helps ensure that the investigations protect the rights of the respondents while gathering the appropriate evidence. Information about possible violations comes from other CPAs, clients, enforcement agencies, and public information, such as the **Wall Street Journal,** the **Public Accounting Report,** and SEC **Accounting and Auditing Enforcement Releases.** Despite the large investment in ethics enforcement, the most extreme disciplinary action that the AICPA can take is to revoke membership, in which case the CPA is no longer subject to the Institute's authority. However, the embarrassment may be substantial.

(e) Washington, D.C., Office.   The Institute operates a large office on Pennsylvania Avenue in Washington, D.C. This office is responsible for informing the Institute membership and leaders of events that may affect them, and for contacting regulators, administrators, and legislators in order to protect and promote the interests of the profession and the public. Thus, AICPA representatives often appear before Congress (either informally or at hearings) and meet with the Commissioners and staff of the SEC and other regulatory bodies. In addition to accounting matters, the Washington office closely follows developments in income tax legislation and administration.

(f) Member Services.   In addition to the above, the Institute provides other services to its members and the public.

A major division of the AICPA develops and markets **CPE courses.** Seminar courses are available to state societies for offering to their members, and self-study courses are sold directly to members.

The AICPA produces and distributes a variety of **publications,** including **The Journal of Accountancy** and **The Tax Adviser,** as well as **The CPA Letter.** Other information available to members includes brochures and videotapes about accounting as a career and criteria for selecting an accountant. Prepared speeches are available to members for modification and delivery to local audiences.

Another popular service is low-cost **life insurance** for members and their spouses, **disability insurance,** and **professional liability insurance.**

2.11 STATE SOCIETIES, ASSOCIATIONS, AND INSTITUTES.   All states also have their own professional organizations, which are called **societies, associations,** or **institutes,** according to local preference. They duplicate and complement the activities of the AICPA by offering CPE, publishing newsletters and journals, and providing opportunities for service and leadership through committee membership. Substantial ethics enforcement activity occurs at the state level, and it is controlled through JEEP. Recent years have seen state organizations playing a more active part in representing the profession's interests in state legislatures.

2.12 NATIONAL ASSOCIATION OF ACCOUNTANTS.   The **National Association of Accountants** (NAA) was originally called the "National Association of Cost Accountants," and it still draws most of its membership from management accountants. Nonetheless, it has played a leadership role in financial accounting standards setting through its position as one of the sponsoring organizations of the FASB. The primary units of NAA are its local chapters, which operate autonomously in order to best meet the interests of their own members. The NAA publishes a monthly journal, called **Management Accounting,** and offers CPE courses to its members. The Association also has developed a set of **Standards of Ethical Conduct for Management Accountants,** which requires the accountant to tell the truth to all who receive financial reports, including management and external users. The Institute of Management Accounting administers the CMA examination twice each year and awards the CMA certificate to persons meeting all the requirements.

2.13 FINANCIAL EXECUTIVES INSTITUTE.   The **Financial Executives Institute** (FEI) is smaller than the NAA because it draws its membership from only those accountants who have substantial responsibilities in the financial area of their companies, including reporting. In fact, the FEI limits the number of members from any given company, and is thus much smaller than NAA. However, because FEI members occupy higher level positions, it often has more influence, particularly in dealing with the FASB as another of the sponsoring organizations.

2.14 AMERICAN ACCOUNTING ASSOCIATION.   As the major organization of accounting educators, the **American Accounting Association** (AAA) has a substantial influence on the long-term development of financial and other kinds of accounting. To this end, the greatest emphasis of the Association has been on promoting and disseminating research in accounting and finance. The AAA publishes three journals, **The Accounting Review, Accounting Horizons,** and **Issues in Accounting Education.** The **Review** tends to include arcane articles that lack broad appeal to accountants and are unlikely to significantly affect practice. **Horizons,** on the other hand, publishes applied articles and is more likely to be useful to practicing accountants. The AAA is a sponsoring organization of the FASB, and one Board member seat has always been occupied by an academic accountant. However, the Association does not have substantial influence on accounting standards because its members do not have the financial or political power possessed by others, such as the AICPA, the FEI, and the Business Roundtable.

SUMMARY

This chapter has shown how financial accounting is important to society through its contribution to the economy in helping the capital markets operate more effectively. Because of the importance of this social goal, and because history has shown that abusive accounting tends to occur as preparers attempt to gain unfair advantages, financial accounting is significantly regulated by governmental agencies, by private standards setting bodies that are endorsed and supported by governmental agencies, and by professional organizations. This regulation deals with reporting standards, competency standards, and ethical standards.

The regulation of accounting involves politics because of the conflicting interests among financial statement preparers, auditors, users, and regulators. The tension among these interests helps bring about change and improvement, but only at the risk of not fully serving the public interest. The present structure has evolved with what appears to be the central goal of protecting the public, but that mission will be attained only through careful vigilance and oversight.

SOURCES AND SUGGESTED REFERENCES

Accounting Principles Board, "Basic Concepts and Accounting Principles Underlying Financial Statements of Business Enterprises," APB Statement No. 4, AICPA, New York, 1970.

American Institute of Certified Public Accountants, "Objectives of Financial Statements," Report of the Study Group on the Objectives of Financial Statements, AICPA, New York, 1973.

Financial Accounting Foundation, *Report of Special Advisory Group,* FAF, Norwalk, CT, March 1989.

Financial Accounting Standards Board, "Objectives of Financial Reporting by Business Enterprises," Statement of Financial Accounting Concepts No. 1, FASB, Stamford, CT, 1978.

——"Qualitative Characteristics of Accounting Information," Statement of Financial Accounting Concepts No. 2, FASB, Stamford, CT, 1980.

——"Elements of Financial Statements of Business Enterprises," Statement of Financial Accounting Concepts No. 3, FASB, Stamford, CT, 1980.

——"Objectives of Financial Reporting by Nonbusiness Organizations," Statement of Financial Accounting Concepts No. 4, FASB, Stamford, CT, 1980.

——"Recognition and Measurement in Financial Statements of Business Enterprises," Statement of Financial Accounting Concepts No. 5, FASB, Stamford, CT, 1980.

——"Elements of Financial Statements," Statement of Financial Accounting Concepts No. 6, FASB, Stamford, CT, 1985.

Miller, Paul B. W. and Redding, Rodney J., *The FASB: The People, the Process, and the Politics,* Irwin, Homewood, IL, 1988.

Miller, Paul B. W., and Robertson, Jack C., "A Guide to SEC Regulations and Publications—Mastering the Maze," *Research in Accounting Regulation,* Vol. 3, 1989, pp. 239–249.

Skousen, Fred, *An Introduction to the SEC* (5th ed.), South-Western Publishing, Cincinnati, OH, 1990.

Sprouse, Robert and Moonitz, Maurice, "A Tentative Set of Broad Accounting Principles for Business Enterprises," Accounting Research Study No. 3, AICPA, New York, 1962.

CHAPTER 3

SEC REPORTING REQUIREMENTS

Sherwood P. Larkin, CPA

BDO Seidman

CONTENTS

THE SECURITIES AND EXCHANGE COMMISSION

3.1 CREATION OF THE SEC.   Congress created the Securities and Exchange Commission (the SEC, or the Commission) through the Securities Exchange Act of 1934 (the 1934 Act). The Securities Act of 1933 (the 1933 Act) was administered by the Federal Trade Commission before the SEC was established.

The 1933 Act and 1934 Act (the Securities Acts) are the main securities statutes of importance to accountants. The Commission also administers the Public Utility Holding Company Act of 1935, the Trust Indenture Act of 1939, the Investment Company Act of 1940, and the Investment Advisers Act of 1940. The SEC publishes a brief, self-descriptive pamphlet titled "The Work of the Securities and Exchange Commission," which can be obtained without charge by writing to the Securities and Exchange Commission, Washington, DC 20549.

3.2 ORGANIZATION OF THE SEC.   The Commission is an independent agency of five commissioners. No more than three may be of the same political party. They are appointed by the President (with advice and consent of the Senate) to 5-year terms, one term expiring each year.

One commissioner is designated by the President to act as chairman. The Commission has a professional staff, consisting of lawyers, accountants, engineers, financial analysts, economists, and administrative and clerical employees, which is organized into 10 divisions and offices (other than administrative offices). The following are the divisions and offices and their responsibilities:

1. *Division of Corporate Regulation.* Administers the Commission's regulatory functions under the Public Utility Holding Company Act of 1935 and assists the SEC in its advisory functions in reorganization proceedings under the Bankruptcy Act and the Bankruptcy Code.

2. *Division of Market Regulation.* Regulates securities exchanges, national securities associations, and brokers-dealers, and administers the statistical functions.

3. *Division of Enforcement.* Supervises enforcement activities under the statutes administered by the Commission. Institutes civil, administrative, and injunctive actions. Refers criminal prosecution to the Justice Department in collaboration with the General Counsel.

4. *Division of Investment Management.* Administers the Investment Company Act of 1940 and the Investment Advisors Act of 1940. Investigates and inspects broker-dealers and deals with problems of the distribution methods, services, and reporting standards of investment firms.

5. *Division of Corporation Finance.* Accountants will deal primarily with this division on SEC matters. This division is described in greater detail in section 3.3.

6. *Office of Administrative Law Judges.* Rules on admissibility of evidence and makes decisions at hearings held on the various statutes administered by the Commission. The decision, when appealed, is reviewed by the Commission.

7. *Office of Opinions and Review.* Helps the Commission prepare findings, opinions, and orders in cases before the Commission.

8. *Office of the General Counsel.* The General Counsel is the chief law officer of the Commission. Coordinates the SEC's involvement in judicial proceedings and provides legal advice and assistance.

9. *Office of the Chief Accountant.* The Chief Accountant, currently Edmund Coulson, is the Commission's principal adviser on accounting and auditing matters. The Office of the Chief Accountant:

   a. Develops policy with respect to accounting and auditing matters and financial statement requirements.

   b. Supervises implementation of policies on accounting and auditing matters.

   c. Reviews complex, new, or controversial accounting and auditing problems of registrants.

   d. Considers registrants' appeals of decisions by the Division of Corporation Finance on accounting matters.

   e. Is liaison with professional societies (FASB, AICPA, CASB, GASB, and FEI) and federal and state agencies.

   f. Considers accountants' independence.

   g. Prepares Financial Reporting Releases, Accounting and Auditing Enforcement Releases, and (in conjunction with the Division of Corporation Finance) Staff Accounting Bulletins.

   h. Assists counsel in administrative proceedings relating to accounting and auditing matters.

10. *Directorate of Economic and Policy Analysis.* Assists the Commission in formulating regulatory policy and prepares statistical information relating to the capital markets. There is an economic monitoring system within the Directorate to provide timely and useful economic information about the effects of certain SEC regulations on issues, investors, broker-dealers, and other participants in the capital markets. This program focuses on the impact of key rules on the ability of small businesses to raise capital.

The main offices of the Commission are located at 450 Fifth Street NW, Washington, DC 20549. There are also nine regional and six branch offices.

1. The regional offices serve as the field representatives of the Commission. It is their responsibility to process and review the various filings of registered broker-dealers and other filings (e.g., Form S-18).
2. Each branch office is generally under the supervision of the regional office within its zone. The primary function of branch offices is to assist the Commission in its investigative activities.

3.3 DIVISION OF CORPORATION FINANCE.   Because accountants generally deal more with the Division of Corporation Finance than with the other SEC divisions, its duties and operations are considered here in greater detail.

(a) Responsibilities.   The Division's principal responsibility is to ensure that financial information included in SEC filings is in compliance with the rules and regulations of the SEC. Its duties include:

1. Setting standards for information to be included in filed documents.
2. Reviewing and processing filings under the applicable securities acts.
3. Reviewing and processing proxy statements.
4. Reviewing reports of insider trading in equity securities of registrants.
5. Determining compliance with the applicable statutes.
6. Preparing Staff Accounting Bulletins in conjunction with the Office of the Chief Accountant.

The SEC does not pass on the merits of any proposed security issue. Although the SEC sets accounting and disclosure requirements that, in some cases, may be over and above those required by generally accepted accounting principles, it does not generally prescribe the use of specific auditing procedures other than those related to certain regulated industries. It is the responsibility of the independent public accountant to determine whether the financial statements included in the filing have been audited in accordance with generally accepted auditing standards.

(b) Organization.   The Division is supervised by a director who is aided by a senior associate director, 4 associate directors, 7 assistant directors, and 12 examining branches.

The Division also has a chief counsel who interprets the securities laws, and a chief accountant who supervises compliance in accounting and auditing matters. The chief accountant does not set policy; in novel or complex accounting situations, he may confer with the Commission's Chief Accountant.

Each branch is headed by a branch chief, who reports to an assistant director, and it is staffed by attorneys, accountants, and examiners. A branch is responsible for certain specific industries, so that each reviewer will be familiar with a registrant's type of business and will treat accounting and reporting matters consistently. A registrant is assigned to an industry group and then to a particular branch based on the company's primary SIC Code.

Once a company's initial filing is assigned to a branch for review, all subsequent matters relating to that company are generally handled by that branch. To determine the name of the appropriate branch chief, the Office of the Associate Director (Operations) of the Division of Corporation Finance may be called at (202) 272-3269.

The branches have access to the Office of Engineering for assistance in technical areas such as mining and valuation.

(c) Review Procedures. Filings with the Division are customarily reviewed by a branch accountant, attorney, and examiner. The branch accountant's review will be directed toward determining adequate disclosure and compliance with generally accepted accounting principles and the applicable rules of the SEC. This review will also determine the appropriateness of the accounting and disclosures based on information in the textual section of the filing.

Comments from the review may result in issuing the registrant a "deficiency letter" or "letter of comments." The branch chief approves comments made by the attorney or examiner, and the chief accountant of the Division clears comments made by the branch accountant. If there are troublesome accounting problems, the division's chief accountant may confer with the Office of the Chief Accountant. In unusual situations, the Office of the Chief Accountant may bring the matter to the Commission's attention.

To minimize SEC comments regarding potential problem areas in the filing, the registrant may request a prefiling conference with the Commission's staff. Such conferences may also be held after the filing to resolve matters in the letter of comment. Before any meeting, it is usually beneficial to submit written background information on the problem area for SEC review.

The registrant also may refer matters to the Office of the Chief Accountant and, in rare instances, to the Commission. This can occur either before filing, or after receipt of the letter of comments.

Because of the significant volume of filings it receives on an annual basis, the Division has adopted a selective review program. Registration and proxy statements are given priority over the 1934 Act reports because of the tight time schedules associated with such filings. The selective review criteria are directed at reviewing all key filings, and registrants should expect all registration statements for initial public offerings to be thoroughly reviewed. If a registration or proxy statement is selected for review, the registrant will be notified.

Normally the Division attempts to review a registration statement and provide initial comments within 30 days after the filing date. Reviews of Form S-18 are often performed in a regional office and generally take somewhat less time. No matter where the document is filed, the review period will vary depending on the workload of the branch or regional office at the time of filing. Comments are generally provided in writing. However, a reviewer may agree to read them over the phone and confirm them in writing in many instances.

Periodic reports under the 1934 Act may be reviewed on a selective basis after the filing date. In most cases, changes arising from SEC comments on periodic reports are required to be implemented only in future filings.

The 1934 Act permits the SEC to suspend trading in any security "for a period not exceeding 10 days" if it is in the public interest and is necessary to protect investors. Based on a Supreme Court decision, the SEC does not have the authority to issue suspensions beyond the initial 10 days.

(d) EDGAR—Electronic Filing System. In its efforts to reduce paperwork and review time, the Commission has developed the Electronic Data Gathering, Analyses, and Retrieval System (EDGAR). The EDGAR pilot program began in September 1984 and operated for 2 years. The Commission concluded that the pilot project demonstrated the feasibility of electronic filing. Bids have been received for the implementation of "Operational" EDGAR. When fully operational, EDGAR will allow the filing and review of documents, transmittal of review comments and responses, and access to filings by investors, all by computer. The SEC's time schedule is for all public companies to file electronically by 1993.

(e) Extension of Time to File. The time of filing for 1934 Act reports is governed by the date of receipt, rather than date of postmark. If a filing is not expected to be made on a timely basis, the SEC rules require that companies submit a notification on Form 12b-25 indicating the reason for extension, no later than one business day after the due date of the report. In addition, the rules provide relief where reports are not timely filed if a timely filing would involve unreasonable effort or expense. Under this provision, a report will be considered to be filed on a timely basis if:

1. The required notification on Form 12b-25 (*a*) discloses that the reasons causing the inability to file on time could not be eliminated without unreasonable effort or expense, and (*b*) undertakes that the document will be filed no later than the 15th day following the due date (by the 5th day with respect to Form 10-Q).

2. There is a statement, attached as an exhibit to Form 12b-25, from any person other than the registrant (e.g., the independent accountant) whose inability to furnish a required opinion, report, or certification was the reason the report could not be timely filed without unreasonable effort or expense.

3. The report is filed within the represented time period.

This procedure does not require a response by the SEC.

Periodic reports that are filed late with the SEC may (1) prevent the registrant from using short-form registration statements on Forms S-2 and S-3, (2) cause injunctive action to compel filing, (3) make Rule 144 unavailable for the sale of shares by company officers, directors, or insiders (thus requiring registration of those shares before they can be sold), or (4) result in suspension of trading in the registrant's securities.

3.4 RELATIONSHIP BETWEEN THE ACCOUNTING PROFESSION AND THE SEC.   The SEC and the accounting profession have cooperated with each other in developing generally accepted accounting principles. Through its FRRs and SABs, the SEC has informed the accounting profession of its opinions on accounting and reporting. In addition, the Chief Accountant and certain members of his staff attend meetings of the FASB (including the EITF) and technical committees of the AICPA.

In turn, as stated in FRR No. 1 (§ 101):

> . . . the Commission intends to continue its policy of looking to the private sector for leadership in establishing and improving accounting principles and standards through the FASB with the expectation that the body's conclusions will promote the interests of investors. For the purpose of this policy, principles, standards and practices promulgated by the FASB in its Statements and Interpretations will be considered by the Commission as having substantial authoritative support, and those contrary to such FASB promulgations will be considered to have no such support.

Over the past few years the Commission has attempted to eliminate, wherever possible, the differences between SEC accounting and reporting requirements, and GAAP and GAAS requirements. For example, FRR No. 15 was issued in response to SFAS No. 76, "Extinguishment of Debt," (1983) and ASR No. 115 (Accounting Series Release, i.e., the predecessor of FRRs) was rescinded after the SEC reevaluated its prohibition against most "going-concern" opinions in 1933 Act filings.

Although the SEC and FASB have cooperated with each other in many areas, the SEC has also maintained its independent position in the standard-setting process. The SEC continues to initiate accounting and reporting policies in areas it believes the accounting profession has not adequately addressed.

3.5 SELF-REGULATION OF THE ACCOUNTING PROFESSION.   In response to congressional criticism of the accounting profession, and to strengthen the profession's self-regulation process, the AICPA established the Division for CPA Firms, consisting of (1) the SEC Practice Section (SECPS) and (2) the Private Companies Practice Section (PCPS). The SECPS regulates CPA firms performing services for companies required to file audited financial statements with the SEC. The PCPS, among other things, monitors the quality of services CPA firms provide to privately held companies.

The principal objective of the SECPS is the effective self-regulation of member CPA firms. The Public Oversight Board (POB), an independent body appointed by the Executive Committee of the SECPS, monitors the activities of the section and issues annual public reports on the effectiveness of the section.

The SECPS has established certain membership requirements for CPA firms, such as (1) engagement review procedures by a second audit partner for all SEC engagements, (2) rotation of audit partners on SEC engagements every 7 years (for firms with at least 5 SEC audit clients and 10 partners), and (3) triennial peer reviews. The Executive Committee of the SECPS is empowered to impose sanctions on member firms that do not meet the section's standards.

The POB has cited two important aspects of the SECPS, the peer review and the special investigative process, as having helped to reduce the number of audit failures by fostering and improving quality control systems of the member firms. The POB also noted that these accomplishments are virtually unknown by the public and a significant portion of the accounting profession, suggesting that the results be better publicized. As a result, the Division for CPA Firms has undertaken an extensive advertising campaign directed at CPA firms, lawyers, bankers, and business people.

The SEC proposed (Release No. 33-6695, April 1, 1987) to require that financial statements included in filings be audited by an independent accountant who has undergone a peer review of his or her accounting and auditing practice within the past 3 years. However, the Commission decided not to proceed immediately to a final rule. Thereafter the AICPA adopted a program of mandatory quality review for its members that requires a quality review every 3 years and a requirement that all CPA firms with one or more SEC clients join the AICPA's Division for Firms, SEC Practice Section.

3.6 CONGRESSIONAL HEARINGS ON THE ACCOUNTING PROFESSION AND THE SEC.
The SEC's reliance on the accounting profession's self-regulation has recently come under attack by the House Energy and Commerce Oversight and Investigations Subcommittee, chaired by Congressman John Dingell (D-Mich.). The subcommittee has held hearings on the accounting profession and its ability to regulate itself in light of recent audit failures, increased price competition, and expansion of services outside the audit function. The subcommittee has also focused on the increased reliance being placed on the self-regulation process by the SEC at a time when the Commission is focusing its attention on accounting fraud.

In 1986, Congressman Ron Wyden (D-Oreg.), to a member of Congressman Dingell's subcommittee, proposed legislation to establish a comprehensive and integrated system for assuring the detection and reporting of financial fraud. This proposed legislation would have required that auditors report instances of fraudulent activity, as defined by the legislation, to a corporation's management and to the audit committee of the board of directors. In the event that management and the audit committee failed to act responsibly to correct any material fraud or illegality within 90 days of such report, the auditors would have been required to report the matter to the appropriate regulatory and law enforcement authorities.

This legislation was not acted upon by the House before the end of the 1986 congressional session and has not been reintroduced. Periodically, Congressman Wyden has announced that he might reintroduce similar legislation but to date he has chosen to wait until he can determine the impact of the AICPA's "expectation gap" (SASs 53 to 61), which were issued by the AICPA's Auditing Standards Board in May 1988. (See Chapter 35 for discussion of these SASs.)

3.7 NATIONAL COMMISSION ON FRAUDULENT FINANCIAL REPORTING.   For almost 2 years, the National Commission on Fraudulent Financial Reporting, headed by former SEC Commissioner James C. Treadway, studied both the factors that tend to cause fraudulent financial reporting and possible steps to reduce its occurrence. In October 1987, the

Commission issued its final report (National Commission on Fraudulent Financial Reporting, 1987), which includes a number of recommendations for public companies, independent public accountants, regulators, and educators. Although the recommendations are too numerous to include here, some of the more significant ones are:

For the public company:

- Companies should maintain an effective internal audit function.
- The SEC should mandate audit committees composed solely of independent directors.
- The SEC should mandate management reports on internal controls, including management's assessment of the effectiveness of those controls.
- Management should advise the audit committee when it seeks a second opinion on a significant accounting issue.

For the independent public accountant:

- The profession should take affirmative steps to assess the potential for fraudulent financial reporting and design tests to reasonably assure detection.
- The SEC should require outside auditors to review quarterly financial data of public companies before release to the public.
- The profession should modify the standard auditor's report to better communicate the auditor's role and the extent of testing.

For regulators and others:

- The SEC should be granted additional enforcement remedies, including civil money penalties.
- Criminal prosecution of fraudulent financial reporting should be increased.
- The SEC should require all public accounting firms that audit public companies to be members of an SECPS-type organization that has a peer review function and independent public oversight.
- The SEC should be given increased resources to help prevent, detect, and deter fraudulent financial reporting.

For educators:

- Curricula should be revised to foster knowledge and understanding of factors that may cause fraudulent financial reporting and of strategies that can lead to its reduction.
- Continuing education courses should include a study of the forces and opportunities that contribute to fraudulent financial reporting and of the relevant ethical and technical standards.

As can be seen, the National Commission's report is a wide-ranging, and often dramatic, response to the problem of fraudulent financial reporting. Some of those recommendations are already included in the previously mentioned SASs. Additionally, the SEC is taking actions, such as the previously discussed peer review proposal, to respond to the recommendations.

3.8 QUALIFICATIONS AND INDEPENDENCE OF PUBLIC ACCOUNTANTS PRACTICING BEFORE THE SEC.   To qualify for practice before the SEC, the public accountant auditing the financial statements must be independent, in good standing in the profession, and entitled to practice under the laws of his place of residence or principal office (Rule 2-01 of Regulation S-X). A proposed rule would also require that the accountant be peer reviewed.

The SEC's current independence rules substantially conform with those of the AICPA. However, the SEC prohibits the accountant who reports on the financial statements from performing bookkeeping and data-processing services for the registrant, whereas the AICPA permits both those areas of service to be provided under certain circumstances.

Over the years, the SEC staff has maintained a file of correspondence with accounting firms dealing with independence questions. Many of these letters have been summarized in the Codification of Financial Reporting Releases, but the letters themselves were not made publicly available. However, the SEC later decided that doing so might help disseminate the staff's views; accordingly, independence letters dated after November 30, 1982, are now available for inspection and copying at the Commission's public reference room 30 days after the staff has given its response.

3.9 FOREIGN CORRUPT PRACTICES ACT.   The Foreign Corrupt Practices Act of 1977 (FCPA) deals with (1) payments to foreign officials and (2) internal accounting control.

(a) Payments to Foreign Officials.   The act makes it illegal to offer anything of value to any foreign official, foreign political party, and so on (other than employees of foreign governments, etc., whose duties are ministerial or clerical), for the purpose of exerting influence in obtaining or retaining business. The prohibition against payments to foreign officials, as stated in this law, applies to all U.S. domestic concerns regardless of whether they are publicly or privately held. The act may also apply to foreign subsidiaries of U.S. companies.

(b) Internal Accounting Control.   The FCPA makes it illegal for companies subject to SEC jurisdiction to fail to:

- Keep books and records, in reasonable detail, that accurately and fairly reflect the transactions and disposition of the company's assets.
- Devise and maintain a system of internal accounting controls that will provide reasonable assurance that:

    Transactions are properly recorded in accordance with management's authorization.

    Financial statements are prepared in conformity with generally accepted accounting principles and accountability for assets is maintained.

    Access to company assets is permitted only with management's authorization.

    The recorded assets are checked and differences reconciled at reasonable intervals.

Shortly after the act became effective, the SEC issued ASR No. 242, which states: "It is important that issuers subject to the new requirements review their accounting procedures, systems of internal accounting controls and business practices in order that they may take any actions necessary to comply with requirements contained in the Act." To aid management in evaluating internal accounting control (which could be beneficial in judging whether a company complies with the accounting requirements of the FCPA), the AICPA formed a Special Advisory Committee on Internal Accounting Control. This committee issued a report that defines internal accounting control, develops related objectives (categorized by the committee as authorization, accounting, and asset safeguarding), and discusses what management should be doing with respect to an evaluation of these controls.

According to the committee's report, the internal accounting control environment should be a significant factor in management's assessment of the company's system. Along those lines, the report of the Special Advisory Committee on Internal Control (1979) states: "It is unlikely that management can have reasonable assurance that the broad objectives of internal accounting control are being met unless the company has an environment that establishes an appropriate level of control consciousness."

The role of top management and the board of directors in establishing an appropriate internal accounting control environment is significant. The report considers the factors that shape such an environment to include "creating an appropriate organizational structure, using sound management practices, establishing accountability for performance, and requiring adherence to appropriate standards for ethical behavior, including compliance with applicable laws and regulations."

A strong control environment may include, for example, clearly defined accounting policies and procedures, clearly established levels of responsibility and authority, periodic evaluations of employees to determine that their performance is consistent with their responsibilities, budgetary controls, and an effective internal audit function. A strong control environment will provide more assurance that the company's internal accounting control procedures are followed. On the other hand, a poor internal accounting control environment could negate the effect of specific controls (e.g., employees may hesitate to challenge management override of control procedures).

After assessing the control environment, management should evaluate the internal accounting control system. There are several approaches to such an evaluation, depending, for example, on the organizational structure of the company and its type of business. The report uses a "cycle" approach in illustrating an evaluation of internal accounting control, although other approaches may be acceptable (e.g., by function or operating unit). Under the cycle approach, transactions are grouped into convenient cycles (e.g., revenues, expenditures, production or conversion, financing, and external financial reporting) and appropriate internal accounting control criteria are identified for each cycle. In addition, the existing control procedures and techniques used by the company to meet the related criteria should be evaluated.

Meeting internal accounting control criteria generally reduces the risk of material undetected errors and irregularities. Of course, there are inherent limitations to any system of internal accounting control. Even though internal accounting control procedures are performed and the related criteria are met, collusion or override can circumvent existing procedures. Even a strong system of internal accounting control can provide only reasonable assurance for the timely detection of errors or irregularities. However, nonachievement of criteria increases the likelihood that (1) transactions not authorized by management will occur, (2) transactions will not be properly recorded, and (3) assets will be subject to unauthorized access.

The FCPA's legislative history recognizes that the aggregate cost of specific internal controls should not exceed the expected benefits to be derived. Therefore, the report concludes that if it is determined that an internal accounting control criterion is not met, management should evaluate the "cost/benefit" considerations of modifying existing procedures or adding new ones. In determining the aggregate cost, consideration should be given to the direct and indirect dollar cost (e.g., additional personnel, new forms), and whether the new or modified procedure slows the decision-making process or has other deleterious effects on the company. To measure the expected benefit, management should evaluate the likelihood that an error or irregularity could result in a loss to the company or in a misstatement in its financial statements, and evaluate the extent of such loss or misstatement.

Because the system of internal accounting control depends on employees' performing their assigned duties, the report indicates that management should establish a program to obtain reasonable assurance that the controls continue to function properly. The nature of the monitoring program will vary from company to company and will depend on the company's size and organizational structure, the degree of managerial involvement in its day-to-day operations, and the complexity of its accounting system. Ordinarily, monitoring occurs through supervision, representations, audits, or other compliance tests, and so on.

3.10 AUDIT COMMITTEES.   Companies whose securities are traded on the New York Stock Exchange are required by the exchange to have audit committees comprising independent members of the board of directors. This requirement is a condition for original and continued listing. Directors who are members of present management or who serve the company in an advisory capacity, such as consultants or legal counsel, and relatives of executives are not considered independent directors. Former company executives who serve as directors can serve on the audit committee if, in the opinion of the board, that person will exercise independent judgment and will materially aid and assist the function of the committee.

The American Stock Exchange has strongly recommended that all companies listed on that exchange have audit committees comprising independent directors only. However, because of the burden that creating audit committees might place on smaller companies, and because increasing numbers of companies are establishing audit committees on their own, Amex decided not to mandate such committees at the present time. A substantial majority of Amex companies have audit committees.

As previously mentioned, the *Report of the National Commission on Fraudulent Financial Reporting* (1987) recommends that audit committees comprising only independent directors be required for all public companies.

3.11 CONTACT WITH SEC STAFF.   Contact with the staff of the SEC can be both formal and informal and can occur in three situations:

1. *Investigation.* The SEC staff can make an **informal investigation** when they believe the securities laws have been violated. Such investigations may be prompted by market activity in a stock that is not justified by publicly available information, or by news accounts of possible wrongdoing, complaints from the investing public, references from stock exchanges and the National Association of Securities Dealers, or references from other law enforcement agencies. Persons do not have to assist the staff in their investigation and instead can force the staff to proceed immediately to a **formal investigation,** authorized by the Commission when justified. The **formal order of investigation** will name the SEC staff members who are authorized to issue subpoenas for the production of witnesses and documents.

2. *Registration.* SEC review of **1933 Act registration statements** is described later. The company issuing the securities, and its lawyers, underwriters, and accountants, work closely with SEC staff to produce a document that the SEC will not contend lacks full disclosure.

3. *Interpretation.* As a general rule, the U.S. legal system does not allow persons to obtain interpretations of the law before an act is committed. Only through litigation can a person know whether a violation has occurred. However, administrative agencies often provide some exceptions to the rule.

A formal interpretation from the SEC is obtained by receiving a **no-action letter.** This communication is a staff promise not to recommend to the Commission that it take action if the facts submitted by the applicant and described in the letter are found to be accurate. The Commission has always honored its staff's no-action letters. Typical no-action letters involve exemption from 1933 Act registration and refusals by corporations to include a stockholder proposal in the company's proxy material.

Informal interpretations from the SEC abound. Most of the regional offices have **interpretation branches** that offer some help in finding legal sources. More important is direct communication with staff members in the office or division of the SEC that has direct responsibility for administering the matter at hand. In these communications, callers will fare better if they are personally acquainted with the staff members, in which case they may be able to avoid mentioning the name of their firm, company, or client when presenting the facts in question. Some SEC releases name a staff member who should be contacted for interpretations of the matters covered in the release.

3.12 CURRENT REFERENCE SOURCES.   To keep abreast of SEC developments, accountants and others mainly consult the following publications:

- The **SEC Docket** is a weekly compilation of the full text of all SEC releases, including Accounting Series Releases, and the SEC **News Digest** is a daily summary of important SEC developments. Both can be ordered from the Superintendent of Documents, Government Printing Office, Washington, DC 20402.
- The **Federal Securities Law Reporter,** published by Commerce Clearing House (New York), is a loose-leaf service containing all federal securities laws, SEC rules, forms, interpretations and decisions, and court decisions on securities matters.
- The **Securities Regulation and Law Reports,** published by the Bureau of National Affairs, Inc. (Washington, DC), presents weekly summaries of most of the information of the kind contained in Commerce Clearing House publications with the full text of some releases and court decisions.

THE SECURITIES ACT OF 1933

3.13 TRANSACTIONS COVERED.   The preamble to the 1933 Act states that the Act is intended "to provide full and fair disclosure of the character of securities sold in interstate and foreign commerce and through the mails, and to prevent frauds in the sale thereof, and for other purposes."

This statement is misleadingly broad. The 1933 Act does not cover the most common sale of securities: sales of issued and outstanding securities. Those transactions, on a stock exchange, in the OTC market or otherwise, are regulated by the 1934 Act. The 1933 Act covers only the original sale of the security by the issuer, along with sales by persons in control of an issuer.

There are two **primary aspects** to the 1933 Act regulation of securities offerings:

1. The sale must be **registered** with the SEC, and purchasers must be furnished with much of the information contained in the **registration statement** in the form of a prospectus (1933 Act, §§ 5,6).
2. Purchasers of the securities who suffer losses within a specified time period may recover their losses if the registration statement contained a **materially misleading statement** (1933 Act, § 11). Recovery can be obtained from the issuer. However, the proceeds from the sale may have been squandered; therefore recovery is permitted from **directors, underwriters,** and any **expert,** such as an **accountant,** if the material misrepresentation was in the audited financial statements. All defendants, other than the issuer, may avoid liability by proving their **due diligence** in reviewing the registration statement.

3.14 AUDITORS' RESPONSIBILITIES.   As to the **audited financial statements,** auditors must prove that they had, "after reasonable investigation, reasonable ground to believe, and did believe, at the time . . . the registration statement became effective, that the statements [in the audited financial statements] were true and that there was no omission to state a material fact required to be stated therein or necessary to make the statements therein not misleading

. . ." (1933 Act, § 11(b)(3)). The Act states: "The standard of reasonableness shall be that required of a prudent man in the management of his own property" (1933 Act, § 11(c)).

The *BarChris* case (*Escott v. BarChris Construction Corp.*, 283 F. Supp. 643, U.S. District Court, Southern District of New York, 1968) was the first, and remains the most important, case regarding liability for a misleading 1933 Act registration statement. A major accounting firm was among the defendants found not to have fulfilled due diligence requirements. The court stated: "Accountants should not be held to a standard higher than that recognized in their profession." However, the court relied heavily on the failure of the firm to follow its own guidelines for reviewing events since the date of the statements for the purpose of ascertaining whether the audited financial statements were misleading at the time the registration statement became effective. The complete text of the *BarChris* case appears in *Regulating Transactions in Securities* (Wiesen, 1975). An excellent analysis of *BarChris* is given by Folk (1969).

3.15 MATERIALITY.   When the securities acts require plaintiffs to prove that information was false, untrue, or misleading, they must also show that the information was **material** to investors. In general, neither the statutes nor the SEC's rules and regulations offer quantitative tests or useful verbal descriptions of the meaning of "materiality." For example, as to the information required to be filed in a 1933 Act registration statement, information is material if "an average prudent investor ought reasonably to be informed [of it]" (1933 Act, Rule 405).

Many cases involve attempts to further define materiality. In the *BarChris* case, the judge used the test of "a fact which if it had been correctly stated or disclosed would have deterred or tended to deter the average prudent investor from purchasing the securities in question." Starting in the mid-1970s, some courts admitted that they would have to apply materiality standards in a flexible manner, reflecting the context in which the misleading statement was made (e.g., a 1933 Act registration statement, a 1934 Act registration statement or periodic report, a proxy statement, a case involving insider trading or tipping, etc.).

3.16 EXEMPTIONS FROM REGISTRATION.   The following is a discussion of the exemptions from the registration process and the simplified filings available to a company contemplating an offering under the 1933 Act.

The 1933 Act gives to the SEC the authority to establish rules for exempting securities from registration, if offered in small issues or if offered to a limited number of investors. Rules 501 through 506 of the 1933 Act, referred to as Regulation D, cover limited offerings and sales of securities, whereas Rules 251 through 264, called Regulation A, cover the small offering exemptions.

(a) Regulation D.   Regulation D was adopted in 1982 to allow small businesses to raise capital without the burdens imposed by the registration process.

The regulation comprises six Rules (501–506). Rules 501–503 contain definitions, terms, and conditions that generally apply throughout the regulation. Rules 504–506 provide the three exemptions from registration under Regulation D as follows:

- Rule 504 related to offerings where the aggregate sales price does not exceed $500,000 in a 12-month period. This exemption is not available to companies subject to the 1934 Act reporting requirements or to an investment company registered under the Investment Company Act of 1940.
- Rule 505 relates to offerings up to $5 million in a 12-month period to an unlimited number of "accredited" investors (defined below) and to a limit of 35 other purchasers not meeting the accredited investor definition. This exemption is unavailable to registered investment companies.
- Rule 506 permits offerings, without regard to the dollar amount, to no more than 35 purchasers meeting certain sophistication standards, and an unlimited number of

accredited investors. This exemption requires, among other things, that the issuer reasonably believe that the nonaccredited purchaser, or representative, has adequate knowledge and experience in finance and business to evaluate the merits and risks of the securities offered. This rule has no qualifications as to the issuer.

(i) Accredited Investor.   An **accredited investor** includes institutions or individuals who come within, or whom the issuer reasonably believes come within, any of the following categories:

1. An institutional investor, such as a bank, insurance company or an investment company registered under the Investment Company Act of 1940.
2. A private business development company, as defined in the Investment Advisers Act of 1940.
3. An employee benefit plan qualifying under the Employee Retirement Income Security Act (ERISA) with total assets over $5 million, if the plan's investment decisions are made by a bank, insurance company, or registered investment advisor.
4. A tax-exempt organization under the Internal Revenue Code with total assets in excess of $5 million.
5. Any director, executive officer, or general partner of the issuer.
6. A purchaser of at least $150,000 of securities, provided the purchase price is payable within 5 years and does not exceed 20% of the investor's net worth or joint net worth with spouse at the time of sale.
7. A person whose individual net worth or joint net worth with spouse at the time of the purchase exceeds $1 million.
8. A person whose individual income for each of the 2 most recent years is in excess of $200,000 and reasonably expects income in excess of $200,000 in the current year.
9. Any entity in which all the equity owners are accredited investors.

(ii) Disclosure Requirements.   The disclosure requirements of Regulation D depend on the nature of the issuer and the size of the offering:

1. An issuer offering securities under Rule 504 or to only accredited investors is not required to furnish disclosures.
2. Companies **not subject** to the 1934 Act reporting requirement must furnish:
   - For offerings up to $5 million (Rule 505), the same information required by Part I of Form S-18 (see below) or other registration statement, if the issuer is not qualified to use Form S-18. Generally, financial statements for the 2 latest years are required, with only the most recent year audited.
   - For offerings over $5 million (Rule 506), the same information specified in Part I of Form S-18, Form S-1, or other registration statement that would be required in a full registration.

   Certain reduced disclosures may be permitted by the SEC if obtaining an audit would result in "unreasonable effort and expense" to the company.

   Limited partnerships may furnish income tax basis financial statements if their preparation in conformity with generally accepted accounting principles would be unduly burdensome or costly.
3. Companies **subject** to the 1934 Act reporting requirements are required to furnish:
   - Either: The latest annual stockholders' report, related proxy statement and, if requested, Form 10-K,
     Or: The information (but not the Form itself) contained in the most recent Form 10-K or registration statement on Form S-1 or Form 10.
   - Most recent interim filings.

If the securities are offered to even one nonaccredited investor, the issuer is liable to provide the information required in item 2 or item 3 above to all potential purchasers.

(iii) Conditions to Be Met.   In addition to the qualifications to be met by issuers under Rules 504 and 505, Regulation D includes the following limitations and conditions:

- Except as provided in Rule 504, no form of general solicitation or general advertising can be used by the issuer or any person acting on its behalf to offer the securities. The issuer or the person acting on its behalf (e.g., an underwriter) must have a preexisting relationship with the offeree.
- Securities sold under Regulation D will be "restricted" securities with limited transferability. Each stock certificate issued should include a legend stating the security is restricted as to transferability.

(b) Regulation A.   Regulation A, the small issues exemption, governs offerings not exceeding $1.5 million. Although Regulation A is technically an exemption from registration under the 1933 Act, the SEC requires the filing of an offering statement and additional information establishing that the offering is exempt. The offering statement differs from most 1933 Act registration statements in that the textual portion does not have to comply with Regulation S-K and the financial information does not have to be presented in accordance with Regulation S-X.

The Offering Circular, which is an abbreviated version of a prospectus filed under the 1933 Act, is distributed to the investors. Financial statements are not required to be audited if the issuer is not subject to the reporting requirements of the 1934 Act. Otherwise, the most recent fiscal year must be audited.

Regulation A filings have declined in recent years, and represent less than 1% of the dollar volume of all securities offerings. Underwriters or state securities laws may require audited financial statements or more detailed disclosures than would be required under Regulation A. Also the availability of Form S-18, which allows an issuer to raise up to $7.5 million in capital without being subject to the full financial statement and disclosure requirements of the 1933 Act, has diminished the use of Regulation A.

(c) Other Exemptions.   Other exemptions from the registration requirement are:

- Offerings restricted to residents of the state in which the issuer is organized and does business, provided the issuer has at least 80% of its revenue and assets within the state and at least 80% of the net proceeds of the offering are used within the state (Rule 147).
- Securities of some governmental agencies.
- Offerings of small business investment companies (Regulation E).

3.17 FORM S-18.   Form S-18 is a simplified form designed to meet the needs of smaller companies going public for the first time. The form may be used to register securities in cash offerings under the 1933 Act if the offering price does not exceed $7.5 million. Form S-18 is available only to companies that are not subject to the reporting requirements of the 1934 Act and that are not subsidiaries of companies that are themselves ineligible to use Form S-18.

The form requires only one audited balance sheet as of the end of the most recent fiscal year and statements of income, shareholders' equity, and cash flows for each of the 2 most recent fiscal years. Unaudited comparative interim financial statements should also be provided, where applicable. The financial statements do not have to comply with Regulation S-X (except companies engaged in oil- and gas-producing activities, which are required to comply with Rule 4-10 of Regulation S-X).

In addition, the financial statement requirements for the initial Form 10-K are also simplified for an issuer using Form S-18. Form S-18 filed with the SEC in Washington will be processed by the Division of Corporate Finance's Office of Small Business Policy. Form S-18 may alternatively be filed at the applicable SEC regional office.

3.18 "GOING PRIVATE" TRANSACTIONS.   In recent years, an increasing number of companies have repurchased their shares from the public and, in turn, have become privately held. "Going private" transactions include leveraged buyouts, in which a group of investors (normally including company officers) borrows money to purchase company stock, using the assets of the acquired company as collateral for the loan.

In response to numerous complaints from shareholders about going private transactions, the SEC adopted Rule 13e-3, which prohibits going private transactions that are fraudulent, deceptive, or manipulative. Under the rule, companies are required to state whether the transaction is fair to stockholders unaffiliated with management and to provide a detailed discussion of the material factors on which that belief is based. Among the factors that should be addressed are (1) whether the transaction is structured so that approval of at least a majority of unaffiliated stockholders is required and (2) whether the consideration offered to unaffiliated stockholders constitutes fair value in relation to current and historical market prices, net book value, going concern value, liquidation value, purchase price in previous purchases, and any report, opinion, or appraisal obtained on the fairness of the consideration.

Rule 13e-4, relating to an issuer's tender offer for its own securities, also imposes stringent disclosure requirements and other responsibilities on registrants. The rule requires that (1) an issuer's tender offer remain open for at least 20 business days, (2) a shareholder tendering his stock have the right to withdraw within the first 15 business days or after 40 business days following the announcement if the company has not acted on its offer, (3) officers, directors, and major shareholders disclose all their stock transactions during the 40 business days preceding the purchase offer and (4) an issuer accept tendered securities on a pro rata basis if a greater number of securities is tendered than the issuer is obliged to accept within 20 days of an offer.

3.19 INITIAL FILINGS.   The information requirements for initial and annual filings have tended to merge in recent years. The rules applicable to Form 10-K now require much of the same financial statement information required in a registration statement. As a result, the Form 10-K has been referred to as a "mini S-1." However, there are some unique aspects of initial filings.

The following are the most commonly used forms for registration under the 1933 Act:

S-1	General form to be used when no other form is specifically prescribed. Disclosures are similar to those required for Form 10-K.
S-2	For companies that have been reporting to the SEC for 3 or more years but do not meet a "float" test ($150 million or more of voting stock is held by nonaffiliates or, alternatively, the aggregate market value of the voting stock held by nonaffiliates is $100 million or more *and* the annual trading volume is at least 3 million shares). Certain Form S-2 disclosure obligations can be satisfied by delivering the annual report to stockholders along with the prospectus. The more complete information in Form 10-K is incorporated by reference into the prospectus.
S-3	For companies that have been reporting to the SEC for 3 or more years and meet the above float test. Form S-3 allows maximum incorporation by reference and requires the least disclosure in the prospectus.
S-4	For securities to be issued in certain business combinations and that are to be redistributed to the public.
S-6	For unit investment trusts registered under the Investment Company Act of 1940 on Form N-8B-2.
S-8	For securities to be offered to employees under certain stock option, stock purchase, or similar plans.

S-11   For registration of securities issued by certain real estate investment trusts and by companies whose primary business is holding real estate.

S-18   Simplified form for certain domestic and Canadian issuers for securities with cash offerings up to $7.5 million.

F-1, F-2, F-3,   Registration of the securities of certain foreign private issuers.
    and F-4

THE SECURITIES EXCHANGE ACT OF 1934

3.20 SCOPE OF THE ACT.   The 1934 Act has six principal parts:

1. Creation and operation of the SEC.
2. Regulation of stock exchanges and the OTC market.
3. Regulation of brokers and dealers.
4. Corporate disclosure requirements.
5. Regulation of corporate managers, large stockholders, and preparers of filed statements.
6. Prohibition against fraud in securities transactions.

3.21 CORPORATE DISCLOSURE REQUIREMENTS

(a) Registration of Securities.   Unlike the registration of securities transactions under the 1933 Act, registration under the 1934 Act is a one-time registration for an issue of securities.

Issuers of securities registered on a national securities exchange (listed securities), and companies that have assets exceeding $1 million and 500 or more shareholders of record, must register by filing Form 10. This form requires the following items of information:

1. Description of business.
2. Summary of operations.
3. Properties.
4. Parents and subsidiaries.
5. Security ownership of certain beneficial owners and management.
6. Directors and executive officers.
7. Management remuneration and transactions.
8. Legal proceedings.
9. Number of equity security holders.
10. Nature of trading market.
11. Recent sales of unregistered securities.
12. Capital stock to be registered.
13. Debt securities to be registered.
14. Other securities to be registered.
15. Indemnification of directors and officers.
16. Financial statements and exhibits.

(b) Periodic Reports.   Registrants under the 1934 Act (as defined earlier), or any issuer that ever sold securities pursuant to an effective 1933 Act registration statement and has 300 or more shareholders of record, must file **periodic reports** with the Commission. Principally, these reports are **Form 10-K** (an annual report), **Form 10-Q** (a quarterly report), and **Form 8-K** (a special events report).

FORM 10-K AND REGULATIONS S-X AND S-K

Form 10-K is the annual report required to be filed by companies whose securities are registered with the SEC. The due date of the filing is 90 days after the end of the registrant's fiscal year.

The filings are reviewed by the Division of Corporation Finance. As indicated in section 3.3(c), the staff may review Form 10-K on a selective basis after the filing date. However, the filings that are reviewed are subjected to close scrutiny.

The SEC issues a set of instructions concerning the preparation of Form 10-K. Form 10-K is prepared using Regulation S-X, which prescribes requirements for the form, content, and periods of financial statements and for the accountant's reports, and Regulation S-K, which prescribes the other disclosure requirements.

The Form 10-K text (as distinguished from financial statements and related notes) generally is prepared by the company's attorneys, or by the company with assistance, if necessary, from the attorneys.

The accountant should read the entire Form 10-K text for the omission of pertinent information in the financial statements and to avoid inconsistencies between the financial statements and the text. Also, he may become aware of information in the text that he believes to be misleading (see SAS No. 8).

Form 10-K and related documents must be filed on $8^{1}/_{2}$- × -11-inch paper; legal-size paper is not permitted. This rule also applies to other filings with the Commission.

3.22 REGULATION S-X.   The form and content of and requirements for financial statements included in filings with the SEC are set forth in Regulation S-X. Regulation S-X rules, in general, are consistent with GAAP but contain certain additional disclosure items not provided for by GAAP, as discussed later.

Regulation S-X is organized into 13 articles as follows:

Article 1—Application of Regulation S-X. Contains certain definitions that are used throughout Regulation S-X.

Article 2—Qualifications and Accountants' Reports. Contains the SEC rules on the qualification and independence of accountants and the technical requirements for accountants' reports.

Article 3—General Instructions as to Financial Statements. Contains the instructions as to the various types of financial statements (e.g., registrant, businesses acquired or to be acquired, significant unconsolidated subsidiaries) required to be filed, and the periods to be covered.

Article 3A—Consolidated and Combined Financial Statements. Governs the preparations of consolidated or combined financial statements by a registrant.

Article 4—Rules of General Application. Contains certain disclosure requirements not provided for by GAAP and also contains accounting rules for registrants engaged in oil- and gas-producing activities.

Article 5—Commercial and Industrial Companies. Contains the instructions as to the contents of and disclosures for the balance sheet and income statement line items for commercial and industrial companies as well as the requirements for financial statement schedules.

Articles 6 to 9. Contains financial statement and schedule instructions, in a manner similar to Article 5, for certain special types of entities as follows:

Article 6	Registered Investment Companies
Article 6A	Employee Stock Purchase, Savings, and Similar Plans
Article 7	Insurance Companies
Article 9	Bank Holding Companies

Note that Article 8 on Committees issuing certificates of deposit was removed in 1985.

Article 10—Interim Financial Statements. Contains instructions as to the form and content of the interim financial statements required by Article 3.

Article 11—Pro Forma Financial Information. Contains presentation and preparation requirements for pro forma financial statements and certain financial forecasts.

Article 12—Form and Content of Schedules. Sets out the detailed requirements for the various financial statement schedules required by Articles 5, 6, 6A, 7, and 9.

3.23 ACCOUNTANTS' REPORTS.   The form and content of accountants' reports are prescribed by Rule 2-02 of Regulation S-X.

In those situations where other independent accountants have audited the financial statements of any branch or consolidated subsidiary of the registrant, Rule 2-05 of Regulation S-X sets forth the reporting requirements. Section 543 of the AICPA's Statement on Auditing Standards No. 1 requires disclosure in accountants' reports that exceed the requirements of Rule 2-05. Therefore, that Statement should govern the form of accountants' reports when another auditor makes part of the examination.

Where part of an audit is made by an independent accountant other than the principal accountant and his report is referred to by the principal accountant, or when the prior period's financial statements are audited by a predecessor accountant, the separate report of the other accountant must be included in the filing. However, such separate reports are not required to be included in annual reports to stockholders.

The SEC generally will not accept opinions that are qualified for scope or departures from GAAP. However, an audit report will be accepted that contains a fourth explanatory paragraph describing material uncertainties, such as future events that are beyond the control of the registrant (FRR No. 1, § 607).

The SEC will also accept an audit report with an explanatory paragraph that refers to a "going concern" problem if the filing contains full and fair disclosure as to the registrant's financial difficulties and the plans to overcome them. Also, an audit report with a fourth explanatory paragraph describing an accounting change is acceptable.

The accountant's report must be manually signed on at least one copy of the filed 10-K and must include the city and state where issued (locations of CPA firm or principal office for multioffice firms).

3.24 GENERAL FINANCIAL STATEMENT REQUIREMENTS.   Article 3 of Regulation S-X establishes uniform instructions governing the periods to be covered for financial statements included in most registration statements and reporting forms filed with the SEC and annual reports to stockholders furnished pursuant to the proxy rules as follows:

1. Audited balance sheets as of the end of the last 2 fiscal years.
2. Audited statements of income, stockholders' equity, and changes in financial position for each of the last 3 fiscal years.

Additionally, for 1933 Act filings, Article 3, in general, requires in specified circumstances unaudited interim financial statements for a current period along with financial statements for the comparable period of the prior year.

Article 3 codifies the staff position that 1933 Act filings by companies that have not yet completed their first fiscal year must include audited financial statements as of a date within 135 days of the date of the filing.

3.25 CONSOLIDATED FINANCIAL STATEMENTS.   Rule 3A-02 requires a registrant to file consolidated financial statements that clearly exhibit the financial position and results of operations of the registrant and its subsidiaries. A brief description of the principles followed in consolidating the financial statements and in determining the entities included in consolidation is required to be disclosed in the notes to the financial statements. If there has been a change in the entities included in the consolidation or in their fiscal year-ends, such changes should also be disclosed.

Consolidated subsidiaries must have their latest fiscal year ending within 93 days of the registrant's fiscal year-end. Disclosure is required of the year-end of unconsolidated subsidiaries that differ from the parent's year-end.

In May 1986, the SEC revised Rule 3A-02 of Regulation S-X to clarify the importance of accounting for the substance of the parent–subsidiary relationship when determining the entities for consolidation. Under the revised Rule, registrants must look to both their percentage ownership of an entity and to "the existence of a parent–subsidiary relationship by means other than record ownership of voting stock." Previously, Rule 3A-02 prohibited a registrant from consolidating any subsidiary that was not majority owned.

3.26 REGULATION S-X MATERIALITY TESTS.   The following summarizes some of the additional disclosures required by Rules 5-02 and 5-03 of Regulation S-X, based on stated levels of materiality. These disclosures may be made either on the face of the financial statements or in a note.

1. *Notes Receivable.* Show separately if amount represents more than 10% of aggregate receivables.
2. *Other Current Assets and Other Assets.* State separately any amount in excess of 5% of total current assets and total assets, respectively.
3. *Other Current Liabilities and Other Liabilities.* State separately any amount in excess of 5% of total current liabilities and total liabilities, respectively.
4. *Net Sales and Gross Revenues.* State separately each component representing 10% of total sales and revenues.

3.27 CHRONOLOGICAL ORDER AND FOOTNOTE REFERENCING.   The SEC has no preference as to the chronological order (i.e., left to right or right to left) used in presenting the financial statements. However, the same order must be used consistently throughout the filing, including numerical data in narrative sections.

The financial statements are not required to be referenced to applicable notes unless it is appropriate for an effective presentation.

3.28 ADDITIONAL DISCLOSURES REQUIRED BY REGULATION S-X.   Regulation S-X requires certain significant disclosures to the financial statements not required by GAAP. The following is a summary of the most common additional requirements (exclusive of those relating to specialized industries).

1. *Assets Subject to Lien (Rule 4-08(b)).* The nature and approximate amount of assets mortgaged, pledged, or subject to liens and an identification of the related obligation.
2. *Preferred Shares (Rule 4-08(d)).* Disclosure on the face of the balance sheet of the involuntary liquidation preference for preferred shares if different from their par or stated value, and footnote disclosure of any related restrictions on retained earnings.
3. *Restrictions on the Payment of Dividends (Rule 4-08(e)).* A description of the most restrictive limit on the payment of dividends by the registrant and the amount of retained earnings or net income restricted or free of restrictions. Additionally, the amount of consolidated retained earnings representing the undistributed earnings of 50%-or-less-owned equity method investees must be disclosed.

   As discussed in more detail later in this chapter, disclosure may also be required of restrictions on the ability of subsidiaries to transfer funds to the parent, and in some cases separate parent-company-only financial information may be required. The disclosure requirements are based on specified materiality tests.

4. *Financial Information of Unconsolidated Subsidiaries and 50%-or-Less-Owned Equity Method Investees (Rules 3-09 and 4-08(g)).* This requirement is discussed in detail later in this section.

5. *Warrants and Rights Outstanding (Rule 4-08(i)).* Disclosure of the amount and exercise provisions of outstanding warrants or rights for the purchase of a class of the registrant's or subsidiaries' securities.

6. *Related Party Transactions (Rules 1-02(t) and 4-09(1)).* Regulation S-X requires disclosure of material related party balances on the face of the balance sheet, income statements, and statement of cash flows (in addition to the footnote disclosures required by SFAS No. 57).

7. *Income Taxes (Rule 4-08(h)).* The additional SEC disclosures relating to income taxes are discussed in section 3.31.

8. *Notes Payable and Long-Term Debt (Rules 5-02(19) and (22)).* Disclosure of the general character of amounts payable or debt, the amount and terms of unused lines of credit, and, for long-term debt, the details of interest rate, maturity, contingent principal or interest, priority, and, if convertible, the basis.

9. *Redeemable Preferred Stock (Rule 5-02(28)).* The presentation and disclosure requirements for preferred stocks or other equity securities having certain mandatory redemption features are discussed in section 3.32.

3.29 RESTRICTIONS ON TRANSFER BY SUBSIDIARIES AND PARENT-COMPANY ONLY FINANCIAL INFORMATION.   Regulation S-X emphasizes the disclosure of restrictions on subsidiaries' ability to transfer funds to the parent by requiring the following disclosures in certain instances:

- Footnote disclosure describing and quantifying the restrictions on the subsidiaries (Rule 4-08(e)).
- Condensed parent-company only financial information as a financial statement schedule (Rules 5-04 and 12-04).

The following footnote disclosures are required when the sum of (1) the proportionate share of subsidiaries' consolidated and unconsolidated net assets (after intercompany eliminations) that are restricted from being loaned or advanced, or paid as a dividend to the parent without third party consent *and* (2) the parent's equity in undistributed earnings of 50%-or-less-owned equity method investees exceed 25% of consolidated net assets as of the latest fiscal year-end:

- Any restrictions on all subsidiaries' ability to transfer funds to the parent in the form of cash dividends, loans, or advances.
- The separate total amounts of consolidated and unconsolidated subsidiaries' restricted net assets at the end of the latest year.

In addition, the rules require presentation of condensed parent company financial position, results of operations, and cash flows in a financial statement schedule (Schedule III) when the restricted net assets of **consolidated** subsidiaries exceed 25% of consolidated net assets at the end of the latest year (Rules 5-04 and 12-04). The condensed data may be in Form 10-Q format and should disclose, at a minimum, material contingencies, the registrant's long-term obligations and guarantees, cash dividends paid to the parent by its subsidiaries and investees during each of the last 3 years, and a 5-year schedule of maturities of the parent's debt.

   In determining the amount of restricted net assets, where the limitations on funds that may be loaned or advanced differ from any dividend restriction, the **least** restrictive amount should be used in the computation. For example, if a subsidiary is prohibited from paying dividends, but can loan funds to the parent without limitation, the subsidiary's net assets will be considered unrestricted. Illustrations of situations involving restrictions may include loan agreements that require a subsidiary to maintain certain working capital or net assets levels. The amount of the subsidiary's restricted net assets should not exceed the amount of its net assets included in consolidated net assets (acquisition of a subsidiary in a "purchase" transaction can result in significant difference in this regard). Furthermore, consolidation adjustments should be "pushed down" to the subsidiary for the purpose of this test.

In computing net assets, redeemable preferred stock and minority interests should be excluded from equity.

3.30 FINANCIAL INFORMATION REGARDING UNCONSOLIDATED SUBSIDIARIES AND 50%-OR-LESS-OWNED EQUITY METHOD INVESTEES.   Depending on their significance, Regulation S-X can require the presentation of:

- Footnote disclosure of summarized financial statement information for unconsolidated investees and 50%-or-less-owned equity method investees.
- In addition to the footnote disclosure, the presentation of separate financial statements for one or more unconsolidated subsidiaries or 50%-or-less-owned equity method investees.

It should be noted that SFAS No. 94, "Consolidation of All Majority-Owned Subsidiaries," has reduced the number of unconsolidated subsidiaries to a relatively narrow group of subsidiaries for which control is temporary or ineffectual.

Summarized financial statement footnote information as to assets, liabilities, and results of operations of unconsolidated subsidiaries and 50%-or-less-owned equity method investees is required when any one of the following tests (significant subsidiary tests of Rule 1-02(v)) are met on an individual or aggregate basis (Rule 4-08(g)).

- *Asset Test.* The amount of the registrant's and its other subsidiaries' (1) investments in and advances to, or (2) proportionate share of the total assets (after intercompany eliminations) of such subsidiaries and other companies exceeds 10% of the total assets of the parent and its consolidated subsidiaries as shown in the most recent consolidated balance sheet. For a proposed business combination to be accounted for as a pooling of interests, this condition is also met when the number of common shares exchanged or to be exchanged exceeds 10% of the registrant's total common shares outstanding at the date the combination is initiated.
- *Income Test.* The registrant's and its other subsidiaries' equity in the income from continuing operations before income taxes and extraordinary items and cumulative effect of an accounting change of such subsidiaries or other companies exceeds 10% of the income of the registrant and its consolidated subsidiaries for the most recent fiscal year. However, if such consolidated income is at least 10% lower than the average of such income for the last 5 fiscal years, then the average income may be substituted in the determination. Any loss year should be excluded when computing average income. Additionally, when preparing the income statement test on an aggregate basis, unconsolidated subsidiaries and 50%-or-less-owned equity method investees that report losses should not be aggregated with those reporting income.

The summarized information should include (Rule 1-02(aa)):

- *For Financial Position.* Current and noncurrent assets and liabilities, redeemable preferred stock and minority interests. In the case of specialized industries where classified balance sheets ordinarily are not presented, the major components of assets and liabilities should be shown.

- *For Results of Operations.* Gross revenues or net sales, gross profit, income (loss) from continuing operations before extraordinary items and cumulative effect of accounting changes, and net income (loss).

The summarized data is required for the same periods as the audited consolidated financial statements (insofar as it is practicable). In presenting the data, unconsolidated subsidiaries should not be combined with 50%-or-less-owned investees. Furthermore, if the significant subsidiary test is met, the summarized information should be provided for *all* such companies; requests to omit some entities on the basis of immateriality (i.e., less than 10%) will not be routinely granted by the Commission.

In addition to the requirement for footnote disclosure of summarized financial information, separate financial statements are required for any unconsolidated subsidiary or 50%-or-less-owned equity method investee that individually meets the Rule 1-02(v) test using 20% instead of 10%. These separate statements should cover, insofar as is practicable, the same periods as the audited consolidated financial statements and should be audited for those periods in which the 20% test is met.

Combined or unconsolidated financial statements may be presented when two or more unconsolidated subsidiaries, or two or more 50%-or-less-owned investees, meet the 20% test.

The inclusion of those separate financial statements required by Rule 3-09 does not eliminate the need to present summarized footnote information pursuant to Rule 4-08(g), and the existence of one 20% entity will also automatically trigger the footnote disclosure of summarized information for all entities on an aggregate basis.

The following represent informal interpretations by the SEC staff of the significant subsidiary test under Rule 1-02(v)(2):

1. Rule 1-02(v)(2) of Regulation S-X states that a subsidiary is significant if the parent's (registrant's), and its other subsidiaries' proportionate share of the total assets (after intercompany eliminations) of the subsidiary exceeds 10% of consolidated assets.

   The following interpretations are directed to the phrase "after intercompany eliminations." The term "tested subsidiary" (used below), refers to the subsidiary being tested to determine whether it is a significant subsidiary. Receivables of the tested subsidiary from **members of the consolidated group should** be eliminated before determining the consolidated group's proportionate share of total assets of the tested subsidiary. Receivables from **unconsolidated subsidiaries and 50%-or-less-owned persons** of the tested subsidiary **should not** be eliminated before determining the consolidated group's proportionate share of total assets of the tested subsidiary.

   No adjustments would be made to consolidated assets included in the denominator of the fraction, because all appropriate intercompany eliminations are already made in consolidation. Although the phrase "after intercompany eliminations" is not used in Rule 1-02(v)(3), adjustments to income from continuing operations before income taxes for intercompany profits should be made to the entity being tested similar to those made in recording earnings of the entity in consolidation.

2. Rule 1-02(v)(3) states that a subsidiary is significant if the parent's and its other subsidiaries' equity in the income from continuing operations before income taxes, extraordinary items and cumulative effect of an accounting change of the subsidiary exceeds 10% of such income of the parent and its consolidated subsidiaries, provided that if such income of the parent and its consolidated subsidiaries is at least 10% lower than the average of such income for the last 5 fiscal years such average may be substituted in the determination.

   The alternative 5-year average income substitution is only applicable to the parent and its consolidated subsidiaries, and is not applicable to the subsidiary being tested. In computing the 5-year average income, loss years should be omitted from the computation.

In situations where there is a loss figure for one but not both sides of the equation in the computation of the income test, the income test should be made by determining the percentage effect of the parent's and its other subsidiaries' equity in the income or loss from continuing operations before income taxes, extraordinary items, and the cumulative effect of an accounting change of the tested subsidiary on the income or loss of the parent and its subsidiaries, excluding the income or loss of the tested subsidiary.

3.31 DISCLOSURE OF INCOME TAX EXPENSE. Rule 4-08(h) of Regulation S-X requires detailed disclosures relating to income tax expense. The primary purposes of the rule are to enable readers of financial statements to:

1. Evaluate current and potential cash drains that may result from the payment of income taxes.
2. Distinguish between one-time and continuing tax advantages enjoyed by the company.

The income statement or related footnotes must disclose domestic and foreign pretax income (if 5% or more of pretax income) and the components of income tax expense including:

1. Taxes currently payable.
2. The net tax effect of timing differences. The reasons for timing differences should be included in a separate schedule. If no individual difference is 5% or more of the tax computed at the statutory rate, this separate schedule may be omitted.

Those portions of the above components 1 and 2 that represent U.S. federal, foreign, and other income taxes should be shown separately. Amounts applicable to foreign or other income taxes need not be separately disclosed if each is less than 5% of the total of the related component.

In some cases, income tax expense will be included in more than one caption in the income statement. For example, income taxes may be allocated to continuing operations, discontinued operations, extraordinary items, and cumulative effect of an accounting change. In that event, it is not necessary to disclose the components of income tax expense (e.g., currently payable, deferred, foreign) included in each caption. Instead, there may be an overall summary of such components, together with a listing of the total amount of income taxes included in each income statement caption. (The totals of the "overall summary" and the "listing" should be in agreement.) An example of footnote disclosure in this situation is contained in SAB Topic 6-I.

The rule requires the registrant to provide a reconciliation (in percentages or dollars), between the reported income tax expense (benefit), and the amount computed by multiplying pretax income (loss) by the statutory federal income tax rate. If none of the individual reconciling items exceeds 5% of such amount, and the total difference to be reconciled is less than 5% of such amount, the reconciliation may be omitted. Even if the 5% test is not met, the reconciliation still should be submitted to the extent that it is considered significant in evaluating the trend of earnings, or if similar information is presented in the reconciliation for another period. When an item is reported on a net of tax basis (e.g., extraordinary item), the taxes attributable to that item should also be reconciled with the statutory federal income tax rate.

In those cases where the registrant is a foreign entity, the statutory rate prevailing in the foreign country should be used in making the computations outlined above.

3.32 DISCLOSURE OF COMPENSATING BALANCES AND SHORT-TERM BORROWING ARRANGEMENTS. Regulation S-X calls for disclosure of compensating balances (Rule 5-02(1)) and short-term borrowing arrangements (Rule 12-10). The purpose of the rules is to provide information on:

1. Liquidity of the registrant (i.e., short-term borrowings and maintenance of compensating balances).
2. Cost of short-term borrowing.

(a) Disclosure Requirements for Compensating Balances.   A compensating balance is that portion of any demand deposit (i.e., certificate of deposit, checking account balance) maintained by a company as support for existing or future borrowing arrangements.

Compensating balances that are legally restricted under an agreement should be segregated on the balance sheet. An example is a situation where a certificate of deposit must be held for the duration of a loan. If the compensating balance is maintained against a short-term borrowing arrangement, it should be included as a current asset; if held against a long-term borrowing arrangement, it should be treated as a noncurrent asset.

The existence of a compensating balance arrangement, regardless of whether the balance is legally restricted and even if the arrangement is **not reduced to writing,** requires the following disclosures in the notes to financial statements for the latest fiscal year:

1. A description of the arrangement.
2. The amount of the compensating balance, if determinable (e.g., a percentage of short-term borrowings, a percentage of unused lines of credit, an agreed-upon average balance).
3. The required balance, under certain arrangements, may be expressed as an average over a period of time. The average required amount may differ materially from that held at year-end.
4. Material changes in amounts of compensating balance arrangements during the year.
5. Noncompliance with a compensating balance requirement, and possible bank sanctions whenever such sanctions may be immediate and material.
6. Compensating balances maintained for the benefit of affiliates, officers, directors, principal stockholders, or similar parties.

There is a materiality guideline for determining whether disclosure or segregation is required. Usually, compensating balances that exceed 15% of liquid assets (current cash balances and marketable securities) are considered material.

Some considerations in computing compensating balances include the following:

1. A compensating balance may include funds that would be held in any case as a minimum operating balance. Such operating balances should not be subtracted from the compensating balance. It may be desirable, however, to disclose the dual purpose of such amounts in the footnotes.
2. Amounts disclosed or segregated in the financial statements should be on the same basis as the cash amounts shown in those statements. However, the book amounts and bank amounts for cash may differ because of outstanding checks, deposits in transit, and funds subject to collection. To reconcile the book and bank accounts, the compensating balance amount agreed to by the bank should be adjusted by the estimated ''float'' (i.e., outstanding checks less deposits in transit).

(b) Disclosures Requirements for Short-Term Borrowings.   Schedule IX (Rule 12-10 of Regulation S-X) should include the following disclosures for short-term borrowings:

1. The maximum amount of borrowings outstanding at any month-end during each period for which an income statement is required.
2. The approximate average aggregate borrowings outstanding during the periods.

3. The approximate weighted average interest rate for the periods and a brief description of the means for computing such average.

4. The weighted average interest rate and general terms of each category of aggregate borrowings reflected in each balance sheet required.

The notes to financial statements should disclose the amount and terms of unused lines of credit (Rule 5-02(19)). There must be separate disclosure for lines that support a commercial paper borrowing or similar arrangement. If a line of credit may be withdrawn under certain circumstances, this situation also must be disclosed.

A company may maintain lines of credit with a number of banks. If the aggregate amount of credit lines exceeds the debt limit under any one agreement, only the usable credit should be disclosed.

3.33 REDEEMABLE PREFERRED STOCK. Rule 5-02(28) requires that amounts relating to equity securities should be separately classified as (1) preferred stock with mandatory redemption requirements, (2) preferred stock without mandatory redemption requirements, and (3) common stock. For those companies with redeemable preferred stock or another type of stock with the same characteristics, this presentation eliminates the general heading of "stockholders' equity." The three classes of equity securities would not be totaled. Other stockholders' equity captions, such as additional paid-in capital and retained earnings, should also be separately classified.

The rule defines redeemable preferred stock as any class of stock (not just preferred) that (1) the issuer undertakes to redeem at a fixed or determinable price on a fixed or determinable date or dates, (2) is redeemable at the option of the holder, or (3) has conditions for redemption that are not solely within the control of the issuer, such as provisions for redemption out of future earnings.

The rule also requires registrants to provide a general description of each issue of redeemable preferred stock, including its redemption terms, the combined aggregate amounts of expected redemption requirements each year for the next 5 years, and other significant features similar to those for long-term debt.

The rules do not require any change in the calculation of debt/equity ratios for the purpose of making materiality computations to determine if an item requires disclosure or for determining compliance with existing loan agreements. However, where ratios, or other data involving amounts attributable to stockholders' equity are presented, such ratios or other data should be accompanied by an explanation of the calculation. If the amounts of redeemable preferred stock are material and the ratios presented are calculated treating the redeemable preferred stock as equity, the ratios should also be presented as if the redeemable preferred stock were classified as debt.

According to SAB, Topic 3-C, when preferred stock is issued for less than its mandatory redemption value, the stated value should be increased periodically by accreting the difference, using the interest method, between stated value and the redemption value. The periodic accretions should be included with cash dividend requirements of preferred stock in computing income applicable to common stock unless the preferred stock is a common stock equivalent.

3.34 REGULATION S-X SCHEDULES. The schedules required by Regulation S-X support information presented in the financial statements and can be filed 120 days after the balance sheet date as an amendment on Form 8. Each schedule has detailed instructions as to what information is required. It is essential to understand these instructions and tie the schedules into the related items in the financial statements. The information required by any schedule may be included in the financial statements and related notes, in which case the schedule may be omitted.

The schedules are required to be audited if the related financial statements are audited.

In addition to Schedule IX (short-term borrowings) discussed previously, three of the most often required schedules are:

- *Schedule V—Property and Equipment.* Details the changes in the property and equipment accounts and is required for any year in which net property and equipment equals or exceeds 25% of total assets at the beginning or end of the year.
- *Schedule VI—Accumulated Depreciation, Depletion, and Amortization of Property, Plant, and Equipment.* Details the changes in these accounts during the year and is required whenever Schedule V is required.
- *Schedule X—Supplemental Income Statement Information.* Sets forth the amounts of maintenance and repairs, amortization of intangible assets, taxes (other than payroll and income), royalties, and advertising costs charged to expense during the year. The disclosure may be omitted for any amount that did not exceed 1% of total revenues.

The S-X schedules are required in Forms 10-K, S-1, and S-4, but are not required in Forms S-2, S-3, and S-18.

3.35 REGULATION S-K.   Regulation S-K contains the disclosure requirements for the "textual" (nonfinancial statement) information in filings with the SEC. Regulation S-K is divided into the following nine major classifications:

1. *General.* Including the Commission's policy on projections.
2. *Business.* Including a description of property and legal proceedings (Items 101, 102, and 103).
3. *Securities of the Registrant.* Including market price and dividends (Items 201 and 202).
4. *Financial Information.* Including selected financial data, supplementary financial information, management's discussion and analysis of financial condition and results of operations (MD&A), and disagreements with accountants (Items 301–304).
5. *Management and Certain Security Holders.* Including directors, executive officers, promoters, and control persons; executive compensation; security ownership of certain beneficial owners and management; and certain relationships and related transactions (Items 401–404).
6. *Registration Statement and Prospectus Provisions* (Items 501–512).
7. *Exhibits* (Item 601).
8. *Miscellaneous* (Items 701 and 702).
9. *List of Industry Guides* (Items 801 and 802).

3.36 STRUCTURE OF FORM 10-K.   Form 10-K comprises four parts that are structured to facilitate incorporation by reference from the annual stockholders' report and the proxy statement for the election of directors. This format reflects the SEC's ongoing program of promoting the integration of reporting requirements under the 1933 and 1934 Acts.

PART I

Item 1	Business
Item 2	Properties
Item 3	Legal Proceedings
Item 4	Submission of Matters to a Vote of Security Holders

PART II

| Item 5 | Market for Registrant's Common Equity and Related Stockholder Matters |
| Item 6 | Selected Financial Data |

Item 7   Management's Discussion and Analysis of Financial Condition and Results of
                   Operations
Item 8   Financial Statements and Supplementary Data
Item 9   Disagreements on Accounting and Financial Disclosures

PART III

Item 10   Directors and Executive Officers of the Registrant
Item 11   Executive Compensation
Item 12   Security Ownership of Certain Beneficial Owners and Management
Item 13   Certain Relationships and Related Transactions

PART IV

Item 14   Exhibits, Financial Statement Schedules, and Reports on Form 8-K

(a) Part I of Form 10-K.   The information called for by Parts I and II *may* be incorporated by reference from the annual stockholders' report if that report contains the required disclosures. Where information is incorporated by reference, Form 10-K should include a cross-reference schedule indicating the item numbers incorporated and the related pages in the referenced material. The cross-referencing would be included on the cover page and in Item 14 of Form 10-K.

(i) Item 1—Business (Item 101 of Regulation S-K).   This caption requires the disclosures specified by Regulation S-K relating to the description of business, which are segregated into the following major categories:

- General development of the business during the latest fiscal year. The registrant should discuss any bankruptcy proceedings, business combinations, acquisitions or dispositions of material assets not in the ordinary course of business, or any changes in the method of conducting its business.
- Financial information about industry segments for the last 3 fiscal years (or for each year the registrant has been engaged in business, whichever period is shorter). If significant trends relating to segments are identified in the 5-year Selected Financial Data required under Item 6, it may be advisable to include the segment data for the additional years in Item 1.

(ii) Item 2—Properties (Item 102 of Regulation S-K).   A description of the principal properties owned or leased should be identified. The registrant should briefly discuss the location and general character of the property and indicate any outstanding encumbrances. The industry segments in which the properties are used should be included.

The suitability, adequacy, capacity, and utilization of the facilities should be considered. The SEC has indicated this Item will be read in conjunction with the staff's review of the discussion of "capital resources" in the MD&A (Item 7 of Form 10-K).

Additional information is required for registrants engaged in oil- and gas-producing activities.

(iii) Item 3—Legal Proceedings (Item 103 of Regulation S-K).   This caption primarily requires disclosure of legal proceedings that are pending or that were terminated during the registrant's fourth quarter, and involve claims for damages in excess of 10% of consolidated current assets. Environmental actions brought by a governmental authority are required to be disclosed unless the registrant believes that any monetary sanctions will be less than $100,000. Any material bankruptcy, receivership, or similar proceeding of the registrant should also be described.

(iv) Item 4—Submission of Matters to a Vote of Security Holders.   Matters submitted during the **fourth quarter** to security holders' vote, through the solicitation of proxies or otherwise, must

be reported under this caption. The date of the meeting held, names of officers elected, description of other matters voted on, and the voting results, where applicable, would be included.

(b) Part II of Form 10-K

(i) Item 5—Market for Registrant's Common Equity and Related Stockholder Matters (Item 201 of Regulation S-K).   The following information is required under this caption:

- The registrant should provide information relating to principal trading markets and common stock prices for the last 2 years. If the principal market is an exchange (i.e., New York, American, or other stock exchange), the quarterly high and low sales prices should be disclosed. Where there is no established public trading market, a statement should be furnished to that effect.
- The approximate number of shareholders for each class of common stock as of the latest practicable date is required to be disclosed.
- The frequency and amount of any cash dividends declared on common stock during the past 2 years and any restrictions on the registrant's present ability to pay dividends are required. If no dividends have been paid, the registrant should so state.

(ii) Item 6—Selected Financial Data (Item 301 of Regulation S-K).   This item is intended to highlight significant trends in the registrant's financial condition, as well as its results of operations. The following summary should be provided, in columnar form, for the last 5 fiscal years (or shorter period, if applicable) and any additional years necessary to keep the information from being misleading:

- Net sales (or operating revenues).
- Income (loss) from continuing operations and related earnings per common share data.
- Total assets.
- Long-term obligations (including long-term debt, capital leases and preferred stock subject to mandatory redemption features).
- Cash dividends declared per common share (if a dividend was not declared, the registrant should state so).

    In complex earnings per share situations, an exhibit of the computation must be filed in Item 14, unless the computation is obvious from the information in the selected financial data. The computation of fully diluted earnings per share also must be shown in an exhibit, even though dilution may be less than the 3% guideline mentioned in APB Opinion No. 15.

A registrant may provide additional information to enhance the understanding of, or highlight trends in, its financial position or results of operations.

(iii) Item 7—Management's Discussion and Analysis of Financial Condition and Results of Operations (MD&A) (Item 303 of Regulation S-K).   The SEC expects each registrant to tailor the MD&A to its own specific circumstances. As a result there are no prescribed methods of disclosing the required information. The primary focus is centered on the company's earnings, liquidity, and capital resources for the 3-year period covered by the financial statements. MD&A may also include other relevant information that promotes an understanding of a registrant's financial condition, changes in financial condition, or results of operations.

    The use of boilerplate analysis is discouraged. MD&A should not merely repeat numerical data, such as dollar or percentage changes, contained in or easily derived from the financial statements. Instead, the registrant should provide meaningful commentary as to *why* changes in liquidity, capital resources, and operations have occurred. The reasons an expected change did not occur should also be included. The emphasis should be on trends, regardless of whether they are favorable.

The discussion on each topic should not be solely from a historical perspective. A registrant should focus specifically on events and uncertainties that could cause past performance to be different from future operating results or future financial position, such as unusually large promotional expenses, large price increases, and strikes.

The SEC has recently completed an MD&A project that was intended to study MD&As in actual filings to determine what could be done to improve the information therein. An interpretive release (FRR No. 36) providing guidance for the improvement of MD&A was issued on May 18, 1989. FRR No. 36 and ASR No. 299 contain examples illustrating particular points that the staff believes require emphasis. The following discussion of the financial areas that are to be addressed in MD&A incorporates this guidance.

- *Liquidity and Capital Resources*

  Liquidity and capital resources may be discussed together because of their interrelationship. Disclosure is required of internal and external sources of liquidity.

  In this context, liquidity relates to a company's ability to generate sufficient cash flow on both a long-term and short-term basis. The liquidity discussion should go beyond a review of working capital at specific dates. It should cover sources of liquidity, trends, or unusual demands indicating material changes in liquidity, and remedial action required to meet any projected deficiencies. The discussion of liquidity should not be limited to cash flow. The registrant should consider changes in other working capital items and future sources of liquidity, such as financing capabilities and securities transactions.

  Any expected substantial excess of cash outlay for income taxes over income tax expense for any of the next 3 years should also be discussed in the liquidity section. In order to determine this information, the registrant must estimate future timing differences, as well as reversals of prior years' timing differences.

  Indicators of liquidity should be disclosed in the context of the registrant's particular business. For example, working capital may be an appropriate measure of liquidity for a manufacturing company, but might not be so for a bank. Even if working capital is considered to be a measure of a company's liquidity, indicators ordinarily should go beyond working capital. Depending on the nature of the company, liquidity indicators may also include unused credit lines, debt-equity ratios, bond ratings, and debt covenant restrictions.

  If the financial statements, as required by Regulation S-X, disclose restrictions on the ability of subsidiaries to transfer funds to the parent, the liquidity discussion should indicate the impact of these restrictions on the parent.

  Capital resources are not specifically defined by the Commission but equity, debt, and off-balance sheet financing arrangements are used as examples. MD&A should describe any material commitments for capital expenditures, their purpose, and the planned source of funds to pay for those capital items. Trends in capital resources, including anticipated changes between the mix of equity, debt, and any off-balance sheet financing arrangements, should be discussed.

  Forward-looking information, such as the total anticipated cost of a new plant or the company's overall capital budget, is encouraged by the SEC but not required. Although this information would be useful and is expressly covered by the SEC's safe harbor rule for projections, the advisability of including such information ordinarily should be reviewed with legal counsel. Known data that will have an impact on future operations (e.g., known increases in labor or material costs, commitments for capital expenditures), is not considered forward-looking data and is required to be disclosed.

- *Results of Operations*

A description is required of any unusual or infrequent events or transactions and any trends or uncertainties that are expected to affect future sales or earnings. The extent to which sales changes are attributable to volume and prices also should be described. In addition, events that management expects to cause a material change in the relationship between costs and revenues should be discussed, along with the expected change. Furthermore, for the latest 3 years, the effect of inflation and price changes should be discussed (because SFAS No. 33 has been eliminated by the FASB, Item 303's reference to the requirements of that statement is no longer relevant, unless the registrant elects to continue to disclose such information).

Disclosure of the impact of inflation in MD&A generally has not been extensive and, in many cases, has not been adequate. ASR No. 299 points out several examples of good disclosure that should be considered in preparing and reviewing MD&A in connection with Commission filings.

The SEC believes that, in some cases, a discussion of **interrelationships** may be the most helpful way of describing the reasons for changes in several individual items. For example, certain costs may be directly related to sales so that a discussion of the reasons for a change in sales may also serve to explain the changes in a related item. A repetition of the same explanation is neither required nor useful.

A discussion of segments is called for only if considered appropriate to an understanding of the registrant's business. In addition, projections are encouraged, but not required.

The Commission has stated that its focus on MD&A disclosures will continue, and principal targets of enforcement will include the failure of companies to address continued operating trends and financial institutions not candidly addressing loan loss problems. The SEC has also warned that the antifraud provisions applicable to filings under the securities acts also apply to all public statements made by persons speaking on behalf of the registrant. Therefore, company spokesmen should exercise care when making statements that can reasonably be expected to be made known to the financial community and ultimately relied upon by the public investor.

FRR No. 26, dated October 23, 1986, indicates that the provisions of the Tax Reform Act of 1986 will have an impact on the timing and amount of taxes payable upon the reversal of deferred tax amounts that have previously been provided and may also affect the future financial position, liquidity, and results of operations for certain registrants. Registrants should discuss the potential effects of the Tax Act in MD&A in connection with the discussion of known or expected future events that they reasonably expect to have a material impact on liquidity or income from continuing operations. If registrants elect to quantify the effects of the Tax Act as part of their discussion, they should apply the provisions of the SFAS No. 96 "Accounting for Income Taxes." If registrants elect not to quantify the effects, their MD&A should include a discussion of the potential effect on deferred taxes of both the new Tax Act and SFAS No. 96. Comment letters on filings with the Commission since the issuance of FRR 26 have consistently reminded filers of these requirements.

The SEC has circulated a Concepts Release on Management's Discussion and Analysis of Financial Condition and Operations (Release No. 33-6711). This release seeks comments concerning the adequacy of the current rules and the cost and benefits of requiring disclosure of business risks and uncertainties, as well as additional board of director scrutiny and independent auditor association with the disclosures. The Concepts Release was prepared in response to recommendations from members of the accounting profession.

(iv) Item 8—Financial Statements and Supplementary Data

- *Financial Statements*

   Article 3 of Regulation S-X contains uniform instructions governing the periods to be covered by financial statements included in annual stockholders' reports and in most 1933 Act and 1934 Act filings. The basic financial statement requirements for Form 10-K are:

      Audited balance sheets as of the end of the most recent two fiscal years.

      Audited statements of income, changes in stockholders' equity, and cash flows for the most recent 3 fiscal years.

   A registrant filing a Form 10-K for the first fiscal year after a registration statement on Form S-18 becomes effective may prepare financial statements in accordance with the simplified requirements outlined in the general instructions to Form 10-K.

   These financial statements may be incorporated into the 10-K by reference from the annual stockholders' report.

   The financial statement schedules required by Regulation S-X, as well as any separate financial statement required by Rule 3-09, are not included in Item 8 but instead are presented in Item 14.

- *Supplementary Financial Information* (Item 302 of Regulation S-K)

   SELECTED QUARTERLY FINANCIAL DATA

   Companies that:

      Are listed on a national securities exchange *or* are quoted on the National Association of Securities Dealers Automated Quotation System (NASDAQ) and meet specified criteria, including those related to market makers and number of stockholders and shares, *and*

      Have either (*a*) consolidated net income (after taxes and discontinued operations) before extraordinary items and cumulative effect of an accounting change of at least $250,000 for each of the last 3 fiscal years, *or* (*b*) consolidated total assets of at least $200 million for the last fiscal year-end

   are required to disclose certain quarterly financial data in SEC filings containing financial statements. The SEC urges public companies who are exempt from the amendments to comply on a voluntary basis. This information should also be included in annual reports sent to stockholders.

   Companies that were exempt from the disclosure rule when their financial statements were originally filed with the SEC because they did not meet the trading and size criteria will not be required to retroactively include the specified quarterly financial data for the prior year if they are no longer exempt in the current year or if a retroactive adjustment results in their exceeding the materiality criteria for the prior year.

   The $250,000 net income criterion for each of the last 3 years should be based on current financial statements that include those years, giving effect to any restatements of prior years' data.

   The following data is required to be disclosed for each full quarter within the latest 2 fiscal years and any subsequent interim periods for which income statements are presented:

      Net sales, gross profit, income (loss) before extraordinary items and cumulative effect of a change in accounting, net income (loss), and per share data based upon such income (loss) (primary and fully diluted). It may be desirable also to disclose per share data for discontinued operations and extraordinary items. SAB Topic 6-G-1 states that companies in specialized industries should, in lieu of "gross profit," present quarterly data in the manner most meaningful to their industry.

A description of the effect of any disposals of segments of a business and extraordinary, unusual, or infrequently occurring items.

The aggregate effect and nature of year-end or other adjustments that are material to the results of the quarter.

An explanation, in the form of a reconciliation, of differences between amounts presented in this item and data previously reported on Form 10-Q filed for any quarter (e.g., where a pooling of interests occurs or where an error is corrected).

The interim data disclosures are not required for parent-company-only financial statements that are presented in a schedule in Item 14 of Form 10-K. The data also need not be included for supplemental financial statements for unconsolidated subsidiaries or 50%-or-less-owned companies accounted for by the equity method unless the subsidiary or affiliate is a registrant that does not meet the conditions for exemption from the disclosure rule.

Auditors will be required to perform certain review procedures in accordance with SAS No. 36 with respect to the quarterly data. If the auditor does not apply such review procedures to the quarterly data, he should expand his report to disclose such restriction, unless that fact is stated in the text containing the quarterly data. In addition, the auditor's report should be expanded if (1) the quarterly data does not conform with generally accepted accounting principles or (2) the data indicates that a review was performed, but fails to state that the review is substantially less in scope than an audit. Although the rules do not require auditors' involvement with quarterly reports on Form 10-Q prior to their filing, many registrants may request their auditors to review the interim data on a prefiling basis in order to permit early consideration of significant accounting matters and early modification of accounting procedures that might be improved and to minimize the necessity of revising the quarterly data when year-end financial statements are prepared.

INFORMATION ON THE EFFECTS OF CHANGING PRICES

Larger registrants that were previously subject to the reporting provisions of SFAS No. 33 and various other inflation-related pronouncements were required to present information on the effects of changing prices in accordance with those statements. Since the FASB has made compliance with SFAS No. 33 voluntary, the SEC has not revised its requirement to include such information as Supplementary Financial Information. However, if a registrant adequately discusses the impacts of inflation in its MD&A, the lack of such supplementary information will not result in a review comment from the staff.

INFORMATION ABOUT OIL- AND GAS-PRODUCING ACTIVITIES

Information specified in paragraphs 9–34 of SFAS No. 69 is required to be provided for significant oil- and gas-producing activities (as defined in Rule 4-10(a) of Regulation S-X).

(v) *Item 9—Disagreements on Accounting and Financial Disclosures (Item 304 of Regulation S-K).* The SEC has long been concerned about the relationships between the registrant and its independent accountants. During the 1980s, the growing number of allegations about "opinion shopping" encouraged the SEC to adopt new disclosure requirements to provide increased public disclosure of possible opinion-shopping situations. In FRR No. 31, dated April 7, 1988, the Commission stated:

The auditor must, at all times, maintain a "healthy skepticism" to ensure that a review of a client's accounting treatment is fair and impartial. The willingness of an auditor to support a proposed accounting treatment that is intended to accomplish the registrant's reporting objectives, even though that treatment might frustrate reliable reporting, indicates that there may be a lack of such skepticism and independence on the part of the auditor. The search for such an auditor by management may indicate an effort by management to avoid the requirements for an independent examination of the registrant's financial statements. Engaging an accountant under such circumstances is generally referred to as "opinion shopping." Should this practice result in false or misleading financial disclosure, the registrant and the accountant would be subject to enforcement and/or disciplinary action by the Commission.

In 1986 and 1988, the SEC made significant amendments to Item 304 to require additional disclosures about changes in and disagreements with accountants. Disagreements and "other reportable events" are required to be disclosed in Form 8-K and in proxy statements sent to shareholders. The same disclosures are generally required in Form 10-K.

(c) Part III of Form 10-K. The information required in this Part *must* be incorporated by reference from the proxy statement relating to election of directors if such statement is to be filed within 120 days after year-end. If the information is omitted from the Form 10-K and the proxy statement ultimately is not filed within the 120-day period, it will be necessary to amend the Form 10-K by filing a Form 8 to include the omitted information. The reportable information and captions are described in the following subsections.

(i) Item 10—Directors and Executive Officers of the Registrant (Item 401 of Regulation S-K).   The information reportable under this caption includes a listing of directors and executive officers, and information about each individual. Directors would include all persons nominated or chosen to become directors.

The SEC defines executive officers as the president, secretary, treasurer, vice-president in charge of a principal function or business, or any person with policy-making functions affecting the entire entity even if he has no title. Production managers, sales managers, and research scientists who make or are expected to make important contributions to the registrant's business are examples of "significant employees" who would be disclosed in Item 10.

(ii) Item 11—Executive Compensation (Item 402 of Regulation S-K).   Item 402 requires the disclosure of the cash compensation of each of the five most highly paid executive officers of the registrant and its subsidiaries exceeding $60,000 for the last fiscal year. In addition, the total cash compensation for all executive officers as a group (stating the number of persons without naming them) is to be disclosed.

The registrant is allowed flexibility in determining the individuals to be disclosed in order to ensure that key policy-making members of management are covered. Also, in some cases, it might be appropriate to omit an individual falling within the disclosure parameters from specific mention (e.g., he received an unusually large bonus or his services were performed largely overseas).

(iii) Item 12—Security Ownership of Certain Beneficial Owners and Management (Item 403 of Regulation S-K).   The information reportable under this caption is required for owners of more than 5% of any class of voting securities and for all officers and directors. The name and address of the owner, the amount and nature of beneficial ownership, and the class and percentage ownership of stock should be presented in the prescribed tabular form.

(iv) Item 13—Certain Relationships and Related Transactions (Item 404 of Regulation S-K).   Certain transactions in excess of $60,000 must be disclosed that have taken place during the last fiscal year or are proposed to take place, directly or indirectly, between the registrant and any of its directors (including nominees), executive officers, more-than-5% stockholders, or any member of their immediate family. In addition, special rules apply to disclosure of payments between the registrant and entities in which directors have an interest (including significant customers, creditors, and suppliers, and law firms or investment banking firms where fees exceeded 5% of the firm's gross revenues).

If the registrant is indebted, directly or indirectly, to any individual mentioned above, and such indebtedness has exceeded $60,000 at any time during the last fiscal year, Item 13 requires that the individual, nature of the liability, the transaction in which the liability was incurred, the outstanding balance at the latest practicable date and other pertinent information be disclosed.

(d) Part IV of Form 10-K

(i) Item 14—Exhibits, Financial Statement Schedules, and Reports on Form 8-K.   This item relates to Regulation S-X schedules, the financial statements required in Form 10-K but not in the annual stockholders' report (i.e., financial statements of unconsolidated subsidiaries of 50%-or-less-owned equity method investees, or financial statements of affiliates whose securities are pledged as collateral), and exhibits required by Item 601 of Regulation S-K (including a list of the registrant's significant subsidiaries).

All financial statements and schedules filed should be listed under this item. Where any financial statement, financial statement schedule, or exhibit is incorporated by reference, the incorporation by reference should be set forth in a schedule included in this item.

The financial statement schedules at Item 14 must be covered by an accountant's report. If the financial statements in Item 8 have been incorporated by reference from the annual stockholders' report, Item 14 should include a separate accountant's report covering the schedules. Such a report usually makes reference to the report incorporated by reference in Item 8, indicates that the examination referred to in that report also included the financial statement schedules, and expresses an opinion on whether the schedules present fairly the information required to be presented therein. When the financial statements are *not* incorporated by reference from the annual report, the 10-K must include an opinion on both the financial statements required by Item 8 and the financial statement schedules required by Item 14. This is accomplished by either of two methods:

- The report appearing in Item 8 may cover only the financial statements with a separate report included in Item 14 on the financial statement schedules.
- The report appearing in Item 8 may cover both the financial statements and financial statement schedules by including the schedules in the scope paragraph and by adding a third paragraph that contains an opinion on the schedules.

In addition, the registrant should state whether any reports on Form 8-K have been filed during the last quarter, listing the items reported, any financial statements filed, and the dates of the reports.

(e) Signatures.   The required signatories include the principal executive officer, principal financial officer, controller or principal accounting officer, and at least a majority of the board of directors.

(f) Relief for Certain Wholly Owned Subsidiaries.   When a registrant has certain wholly owned subsidiaries, themselves registrants, such subsidiaries are permitted to omit certain data from their own Form 10-K filings (Items 4, 6, 7, 10, and 11) provided they disclose, among other things, an MD&A (similar to the type of MD&A required for Form 10-Q) (see section 3.38(a)(ii)).

(g) Variations in the Presentation of Financial Statements in Form 10-K.   Form 10-K may be presented in various ways, including the following:

- The annual stockholders' report is incorporated by reference in Form 10-K. This approach is encouraged by the SEC.

- The entire Form 10-K (text and financial information) is included in the annual stock-holders' report.
- Bound copies of the financial statements and schedules are attached to the text.

3.37 ANNUAL REPORT TO STOCKHOLDERS.   In recent years, the information included in annual reports to stockholders has moved toward compliance with the reporting require-ments of Form 10-K.

Rules 14a-3 and 14c-3 of the 1934 Act give the SEC the right to regulate the financial statements included in the stockholders' annual report. Although an annual stockholders' report must be sent to the SEC, technically it is not a "filed" document. Therefore the annual stockholders' report is not subject to the civil liability provisions of § 18 of the 1934 Act unless it is an integral part of a required filing, such as when incorporated by reference in Form 10-K. Yet, an annual stockholders' report is subject to the antifraud provisions set forth in § 10b and Rule 10b-5 of the 1934 Act. The trend toward conforming the annual stockholders' report with Form 10-K is part of the Commission's integrated disclosure system, which requires annual stockholders' reports to contain the following:

- Selected quarterly financial data for certain registrants and disagreements with account-ants (Items 302 and 304 of Regulation S-K).
- Selected 5-year financial data (Item 301 of Regulation S-K).
- Management's discussion and analysis of the company's financial condition and operat-ing results (Item 303 of Regulation S-K).
- Information called for by Item 201 of Regulation S-K regarding dividend policy and market prices.

The similar disclosure requirements allow registrants to use extensive incorporation by reference to the annual stockholders' report in SEC filings. As such, the annual stockholders' report is often expanded to meet the disclosure requirements of Items 1 through 4 of Form 10-K to allow incorporation by reference. In some cases, the Form 10-K and the annual report are even combined into one document.

The annual stockholders' report also must contain a statement, in boldface, that the company will provide the annual report on Form 10-K, without charge, in response to written requests and must indicate the name and address of the person to whom such a written request is to be directed. The statement may alternatively be included in the proxy statement.

(a) Financial Statements Included in Annual Report to Stockholders.   Audited balance sheets for the latest 2 years and statements of income and cash flows for the latest 3 years are required.

The financial statements are required to be in accordance with Regulation S-X except that Articles 3 and 11, other than Rules 3-03(e) and 3-04, do not have to be followed. (Article 3 sets forth the financial statements to be included in SEC filings. Article 11 deals with pro forma information. Rule 3-03(e) requires the business segment disclosure of SFAS No. 14, and Rule 3-04 covers changes in other stockholders' equity.) The financial statements must be as large and legible as 8-point modern type and the notes must be at least 10-point modern type.

Financial statement schedules and exhibits, which may otherwise be required in Form 10-K, may be omitted.

If the financial statements for a prior period have been audited by a predecessor accountant, the separate report of the predecessor may be omitted in the annual report to stockholders if it is referred to in the successor accountant's report. The separate report of the predecessor accountant would, however, be required in the Form 10-K, in Part II, or in Part IV as a financial statement schedule.

(b) Content of Annual Report to Stockholders. The SEC has long recognized that the annual stockholders' report is the most effective method of communicating financial information to stockholders. It believes these reports should be readable and informative and prefers that they be written without boilerplate. The SEC allows registrants to use their discretion in determining the format of the annual stockholders' report, as long as the information required is included and can easily be located. To improve the presentation of data, the SEC encourages the use of charts and other graphic illustrations, as long as they are consistent with the information in the financial statements.

Under APB Opinion No. 28, publicly traded companies that neither separately report fourth-quarter results to stockholders nor disclose the results for that quarter in the annual report are required to disclose the following information in a note to the financial statements: (1) disposals of segments of a business and extraordinary, unusual, or infrequently occurring items recognized in the fourth quarter, and (2) the aggregate effect of year-end adjustments that are material to the results of that quarter.

(c) Reporting on Management and Audit Committee Responsibilities in the Annual Report to Stockholders.

The National Commission on Fraudulent Financial Reporting (1987) has recommended the following:

1. All public companies should be required by the SEC to include in an annual stockholders' report, a report signed by top management, acknowledging management's responsibilities for the financial statements and internal controls and providing management's assessment of the effectiveness of the internal controls.
2. All public companies should be required by the SEC to include in an annual stockholders' report, a letter from the chairman of the audit committee describing its activities.

Similar recommendations have been made by both the AICPA and the Financial Executives Institute in the past. Many companies already include "management reports" containing information similar to that suggested by the National Commission.

(d) Summary Annual Reports. The concept of "summary annual reports" has been discussed by the Financial Executives Institute for several years. The basic argument is that the annual report contains much information that is not relevant or meaningful to the average investor; therefore, an alternative reporting vehicle should be permitted by the SEC. For various reasons, the Commission rejected such proposals until January 20, 1987 when it issued a "no-action letter" in response to a proposal by General Motors. In that letter, the SEC staff did not object to the GM proposal to provide a "glossy report" to its shareholders separate from its SEC filings and to include the required annual report as a part of the proxy material and Form 10-K. The glossy report would include summary financial data similar to, though more extensive than, that contained in a quarterly report. It would also include a discussion of significant accounting events in a financial narrative section and an opinion of the public accountants covering the summary financial information. The proxy material and the Form 10-K would then become "stand alone" documents with no incorporation by reference from the glossy report. In its explanation, the SEC staff focused on the following factors in GM's proposal, which is likely to set a precedent for other registrants attempting to prepare such summary annual reports:

1. The release of the full audited financial statements with the earnings press release, and the extensive circulation of the release to the market.
2. The filing of Form 10-K with the Commission at or prior to the release of the glossy report.

3. The proposed auditors' report on the financial information to be included with the summary financial data in the glossy report.

4. Inclusion of the annual report to shareholders, as required by Rule 14a-3(b) in both the Form 10-K and an appendix to the annual election of directors proxy statement.

5. Inclusion of a statement in the glossy report, as well as the proxy statement, to provide the Form 10-K upon request.

GM did not implement its new glossy report for its 1986 year-end.

FORM 10-Q

In addition to the comprehensive annual report on Form 10-K, the Commission requires a registrant to file a Form 10-Q for each of the first three quarters of its fiscal year. Form 10-Q is due 45 days after the end of the quarter; one is not required for the fourth quarter. If the registrant is a listed company, it also must file Form 10-Q with the appropriate stock exchange. The following are the basic requirements of Form 10-Q:

- The form is required to be filed by any company (1) whose securities are registered with the SEC, and (2) which is required to file annual reports on Form 10-K.
- Information must be submitted on a consolidated basis.
- Summarized income statement information should be given for unconsolidated subsidiaries or other companies when separate statements are required by Form 10-K.

A uniform set of instructions for interim financial statements is included in Article 10 of Regulation S-X, as an extension of the SEC's integrated disclosure program. In addition, certain requirements for the current Form 10-Q are contained in FRR §§ 301, 303, 304, and 305. Interpretations of the rules are provided in SAB Topic 6-G.

A registrant may elect to incorporate by reference all of the information required by Part I to a quarterly stockholder report containing the information. The SEC permits a combined quarterly report and Form 10-Q *if* all of the information in Part I is incorporated by reference. Other information also may be incorporated by reference in answer or partial answer to an item in Part II, provided the incorporation by reference is clearly identified.

3.38 STRUCTURE OF FORM 10-Q.   Form 10-Q consists of two parts. Part I contains financial information, and Part II contains other information such as legal proceedings and changes in securities.

(a) Part I—Financial Information

(i) Item 1—Financial Statements.   The financial statements should be prepared in accordance with Rule 10-01 of Regulation S-X, APB Opinion No. 28 and SFAS No. 3. An understanding of these requirements is essential in preparing Form 10-Q.

The financial statements may be condensed and should include a condensed balance sheet, income statement, and statement of cash flows for the required periods. The statements are not required to be audited or reviewed by independent accountants.

Balance sheets as of the end of the latest quarter and the end of the preceding fiscal year are required. A comparative balance sheet as of the end of the previous year's corresponding interim date need only be included when, in the registrant's opinion, it is necessary for an understanding of seasonal fluctuations.

Only the major captions set forth in Article 5 of Regulation S-X are required to be disclosed, except that the components of inventory (raw materials, work-in-process, finished goods) shall also be presented on the balance sheet or in the notes. Thus, even if a company uses the gross profit method or similar method to determine cost of sales for interim periods, management will have to estimate the inventory components.

There is also a materiality rule for disclosure of major balance sheet captions. Those that are less than 10% of total assets *and* that have not changed by more than 25% from the preceding fiscal year's balance sheet may be combined with other captions.

Income statements for the latest quarter and the year to date and for the corresponding periods of the prior year are to be provided. Statements may also be presented for the 12-month period ending with the latest quarter and the corresponding period of the preceding year.

For example, if a company reports on a November 30, 1990 fiscal year-end, its Form 10-Q for the quarter ended August 31, 1990 would include comparative income statements for the 9 months ended August 31, 1990 and 1989 and for the three months ended August 31, 1990 and 1989.

Only major captions set forth in Article 5 of Regulation S-X are required to be disclosed. However, a major caption may be combined with others if it is less than 15% of average net income for the latest 3 fiscal years *and* has not changed by more than 20% as compared to the related caption in the income statement for the corresponding interim period of the preceding year (except that bank holding companies must present securities gains or losses as a separate item, regardless of the amount or percentage change). In computing average net income, only the amount classified as "net income" should be used. Loss years should be excluded unless losses were incurred in all 3 years, in which case the average loss should be used. As with the balance sheet, retroactive reclassification of the prior year is required to conform with the current year's classification in the income statement.

Statements of cash flows for the year to date and for the corresponding period of the prior year are to be presented. In addition, the statement may be presented for the 12-month periods ending with the latest quarter and the corresponding period of the prior year.

Other important provisions of the rules relating to financial information are as follows:

1. Detailed footnote disclosures and Regulation S-X schedules are not required. However, disclosures must be adequate so as not to make the presented information misleading. It would appear that the two preceding sentences are contradictory. There is, however, a presumption that financial statement users have read or have access to the audited financial statements containing detailed disclosures for the latest fiscal year, in which case, most continuing footnote disclosures could be omitted.

   Regulation S-X specifically requires disclosure of events occurring since the end of the latest fiscal year having a material impact on the financial statements, such as changes in:
   a. Accounting principles and practices.
   b. Estimates used in the statements.
   c. Status of long-term contracts.
   d. Capitalization, including significant new borrowings, or modification of existing financing arrangements. If material contingencies exist, disclosure is required even if significant changes have not occurred since year-end. In addition, based on existing pronouncements and informal statements by the SEC, the following matters, if applicable, should be considered for disclosure:
   a. Significant events during the period (i.e., unusual or infrequently occurring items, such as material write-downs of inventory or goodwill).
   b. Significant changes in the nature of transactions with related parties.
   c. The basis for allocating amounts of significant costs and expenses to interim periods if different from those used for the annual statements.
   d. The nature, amount, and tax effects of extraordinary items.

   e. Significant variations in the customary relationship between income tax expense and income before taxes.

   f. The amount of any LIFO liquidation expected to be replaced by year-end or the effect of a material liquidation during the quarter.

   g. Significant new commitments or changes in the status of those previously disclosed. Although it is not mentioned in the rules, registrants may consider it desirable to indicate with a legend on Form 10-Q that the financial statements are condensed and do not contain all GAAP-required disclosures that are included in a full set of financial statements.

2. The interim financial statements should contain a statement representing that they reflect all normally recurring adjustments that are, in management's opinion, necessary for a fair presentation in conformity with GAAP. Such adjustments would include estimated provisions for bonuses and for profit-sharing contributions normally determined at year-end.

3. The registrant may furnish additional information of significance to investors, such as seasonality of business, major uncertainties, significant proposed accounting changes, and backlog. In that connection, it would ordinarily be appropriate to include a statement that the interim results are not necessarily indicative of results to be obtained for the full year.

4. If there has been a business combination accounted for as a pooling of interests, the combined amounts of the pooled companies must be shown for all periods presented. For disposals of a significant portion of the business or for combinations accounted for as purchases, the effect on revenues and net income (including earnings per share), must be disclosed. In addition, in the case of purchases, pro forma disclosures in accordance with APB Opinion No. 16 are required.

5. If the prior period information has been retroactively restated after the initial reporting of that period, disclosure is required of the effect of the change.

6. Disclosure is required of earnings and dividends per share of common stock, the basis of the computation, and the number of shares used in the computation for all periods presented. The registrant must file an exhibit, showing in reasonable detail, the computation of earnings per share in complex situations.

7. If an accounting change was made, the date of the change and the reasons for making it must be disclosed. In addition, in the first Form 10-Q filed after the date of an accounting change, a letter from the accountants (referred to as a preferability letter) must be filed as an exhibit in Part II, indicating whether they believe the change to be a preferable alternative accounting principle under the circumstances. If the change was made in response to an FASB requirement, no such letter need be filed.

   The SEC staff acknowledges that where objective criteria for determining preferability have not been established by authoritative bodies, the determination of the preferable accounting treatment should be based on the registrant's business judgment and business planning (e.g., expectations regarding the impact of inflation, consumer demand for the company's products, or a change in marketing methods). The staff believes that the registrant's judgment and business planning, unless they appear to be unreasonable, may be accepted and relied on by the accountant as the basis of the preferability letter.

   If circumstances used to justify a change in accounting method become different in subsequent years, the registrant may not change back to the principle originally used without again justifying that the original principle is preferable under current conditions.

(ii) Item 2—Management's Discussion and Analysis of Financial Condition and Results of Operations (Item 303(b) of Regulation S-K).   The MD&A must be provided pursuant to Item 303(b) of Regulation S-K and should discuss substantially the same issues covered in the

MD&A for the latest Form 10-K, specifically focusing on:

- Material changes in financial condition for the period from the latest fiscal year-end to the date of the most recent interim balance sheet and, if applicable, the corresponding interim period of the preceding fiscal year.
- Material changes in results of operations for the most recent year-to-date period, the current quarter, and the corresponding periods of the preceding fiscal year.

In preparing the discussion, companies may presume that users of the interim financial information have access to the MD&A covering the most recent fiscal year. The MD&A should address any seasonal aspects of its business affecting its financial condition or results of operations. The impact of inflation does not have to be discussed.

The MD&A should be as informative as possible. As discussed, the registrant should avoid the use of boilerplate analysis and not merely repeat numerical data easily derived from the financial statements.

(b) Part II—Other Information. The registrant should provide the following information in Part II under the applicable captions. Any item that is not applicable may be omitted *without* disclosing that fact.

(i) Item 1—Legal Proceedings (Item 103 of Regulation S-K). A legal proceeding has to be reported in the quarter in which it first becomes a reportable event or in subsequent quarters in which there are material developments. For terminated proceedings, information as to the date of termination and a description of the disposition should be provided in the Form 10-Q covering that quarter.

(ii) Item 2—Changes in Securities. Any changes to any class of registered securities and the effect that the changes have on the shareholder rights should be disclosed. Changes in working capital restrictions and limitations on dividend payments would constitute a "change."

(iii) Item 3—Defaults on Senior Securities. Disclosure is required of a default (with respect to principal or interest) not cured within 30 days of the due date, including any grace period, if the related indebtedness exceeds 5% of consolidated assets. A default relating to dividend arrearages on preferred stock should also be disclosed.

(iv) Item 4—Submission of Matters to a Vote of Security Holders. Matters submitted to security holders' vote, through the solicitation of proxies or otherwise, must be reported under this caption.

(v) Item 5—Other Information. Events not previously reported on Form 8-K may be reported under this caption. Such information would not be required to be repeated in a report on Form 8-K.

(vi) Item 6—Exhibits and Reports on Form 8-K. This caption should include a listing of exhibits filed with Form 10-Q (Item 601 of Regulation S-K) and a listing of Form 8-K reports filed during the quarter, showing the dates of any such reports, items reported, and financial statements filed.

Inapplicable exhibits may be omitted without referring to them in the index. Where exhibits are incorporated by reference, that fact should be noted.

(c) Omission of Information by Certain Wholly Owned Subsidiaries. Certain wholly owned subsidiaries are permitted to omit Items 2, 3, and 4 of Part II provided certain conditions are met.

(d) Signatures.   The form must be signed by the principal financial officer or chief accounting officer of the registrant, as well as another duly authorized officer. If the principal financial officer or chief accounting officer is also a duly authorized signatory, one signature is sufficient provided the officer's dual responsibility is indicated.

3.39 PROPOSED EXPANSION OF FORM 10-Q FILINGS.   In Release No. 33-6514, the SEC proposed that a registrant provide interim segment reporting of revenue, operating income, and identifiable assets by specific industry and geographic segments in its Form 10-Q filings. The proposal also would have required the registrant to focus its MD&A in Form 10-Q, as well as in Form 10-K, on segments to the extent necessary to explain material changes during the period.

The proposal received an unusually large number of comment letters that generally questioned the cost/benefit relationship of the proposed disclosures.

In response, the Commission issued a second release (No. 33-6551) requesting additional information about the costs of the information requested. Additionally, the Commission ordered its Directorate of Economic Policy and Analysis to study the costs and benefits of the proposed rule.

FORM 8-K

3.40 OVERVIEW OF FORM 8-K REQUIREMENTS.   A company that is required to file annual reports on Form 10-K is required to file current reports on Form 8-K, if any of specified reportable events take place. If the registrant is a listed company, it must also file the Form 8-K with the appropriate stock exchange.

Form 8-K is required to report the occurrence of the events specified in Items 1–4 and 6 below, and it must be filed with the SEC within 15 days after the occurrence of the earliest event reported. A report covering an event in Item 5 is to be filed "promptly" (because the filing of Form 8-K for events includable in Item 5 is optional, there is no mandatory filing deadline). FRR 18 has amended the filing requirements of Form 8-K by providing an extension of up to 60 days to file financial statements of acquired businesses that are reportable in Item 2 (see below).

If substantially the same information required for Form 8-K has been previously reported by the registrant in a filing with the SEC (such as in Part II of Form 10-Q), there is no need to include it on a Form 8-K.

If a registrant issues a press release or other document within the specified period above, which includes the information meeting some or all of the requirements of Form 8-K, the information may be incorporated by reference to the document. The document incorporated by reference should be included as an exhibit to Form 8-K.

3.41 EVENTS TO BE REPORTED

(a) Item 1—Changes in Control of Registrant.   Detailed information is required as to a change in control of the registrant, including the identity of acquiring or selling parties, source and amount of consideration, date and description of transaction, percentage of ownership of acquiring party, terms of loans and pledges, and any arrangements or understanding among the parties (see Item 403(c) of Regulation S-K).

(b) Item 2—Acquisition or Disposition of Assets.   Disclosure is required of any acquisitions or dispositions of a significant amount of assets, other than in the ordinary course of business. Disclosures would include the transaction date, description of the assets, the purchase or sales price, the parties involved and any relationships between them, sources of funds used, and the use of assets acquired or sold.

An acquisition or disposition is "significant" if:

1. The net book value of the assets or the purchase price or sales price exceeds 10% of the registrant's consolidated assets before the transaction, *or*
2. The business (100% interest) bought or sold meets the test of a significant subsidiary, *or*
3. The purchase or sale involves an interest (less than 100%) in a business that meets the test of a significant subsidiary, and is required to be accounted for by the equity method.

Financial statements may be required to be filed for the acquired business, depending on its relative significance. The determination of significance is made by applying the significant subsidiary tests in comparing the latest annual financial statements of the acquired business to the registrant's latest annual consolidated financial statements filed at or before the acquisition (Rule 3-05 of Regulation S-X). For pooling of interests transactions, the significant subsidiary tests include a comparison of the number of common shares exchanged with the registrant's common shares outstanding at the date the transaction is initiated. The income and asset test should be as of the latest fiscal year; *provided, however,* that if the registrant has, since the end of the most recent fiscal year, consummated an acquisition for which historical and pro forma financial information has been filed on Form 8-K, then the pro forma amount in that Form 8-K for the latest fiscal year may be used. (Note: Registrants who believe their specific circumstances warrant the use of later financial information in other situations should consult with the Division of Corporation Finance, which will evaluate such requests on a case-by-case basis.)

- If based on such tests, none of the conditions exceeds 10%, financial statements are not required.
- If any condition exceeds 10%, but none exceeds 20%, financial statements are required for the latest year prior to acquisition (audited) and for any interim periods required by Rule 3-02 of Regulation S-X (unaudited).
- If any condition exceeds 40%, financial statements are required for the 3 latest years (audited), as required in Form 10-K, and for any interim periods (unaudited).

Regulation S-X governs the form and content of these financial statements. S-X schedules are not required.

If a portion of a business is being acquired, such as a division or a single product line, the registrant should provide audited financial statements only on the portion of the business acquired. Therefore, the registrant may, depending on the circumstances, present a "statement of assets acquired and liabilities assumed" (excluding amounts not included in the acquisition, such as intercompany advances) instead of a balance sheet and a "statement of revenues and direct expenses" for the business acquired instead of an income statement. A registrant, when acquiring a division or product line whose operations are included in the consolidated financial statements of a larger entity, should determine as soon as possible if the accountant reporting on the consolidated financial statements of the seller is able to report on the portion being acquired.

A significant acquisition or disposition under Item 2 will also require presentation of **pro forma** financial information, giving effect to the event. The purpose of pro forma data is to provide investors with information about the continuing impact of a transaction and assist them in analyzing future prospects of the registrant. The main provisions of the rule (Regulation S-X, Article 11) are as follows:

- The pro forma financial statements should consist of a condensed balance sheet as of the end of the most recent period and condensed income statements for the latest fiscal year and the interim period from the latest fiscal year end to the date of the pro forma balance sheet (interim data for the corresponding period of the prior year is optional). For pooling of interests transactions, the pro forma income statements are required for 3 years.

- Only the major captions of Article 5 of Regulation S-X need be presented. For the balance sheet, captions that amount to less than 10% of total assets may be combined; income statement captions less than 15% of average net income for the latest 3 years may likewise be combined.

- The pro forma statements should be preceded by an introductory paragraph describing the transaction and should be accompanied by explanatory notes.

- Ordinarily, the statements should be in columnar form, presenting historical statements, pro forma adjustments, and the pro forma totals. Care should be taken in combining pro forma adjustments to the same line item. Sufficient detail must be provided to allow for a clear understanding of amount and nature of required adjustments.

- If the acquired business's fiscal year differs from that of the registrant by more than 93 days, the income statement of the acquired business for the latest year should be updated, if practicable. This could be done by adding and deducting comparable interim periods. In that case, there should be disclosure of the periods combined and the revenues and income for periods excluded or for periods included more than once (e.g., an interim period included both as part of the fiscal year and subsequent interim period).

- The pro forma income statement should end with income (loss) from continuing operations before nonrecurring charges or credits directly related to the transaction (e.g., severance pay, gain or loss on the transaction, professional and printing costs). Material nonrecurring items and related tax effects that will affect net income within the next 12 months should be disclosed separately. Nonrecurring items excluded from the pro forma income statement should, nevertheless, be reflected in the pro forma balance sheet.

  If the assets acquired include assets relating to operations that the acquirer intends to dispose of, the staff will not object to the presentation of those assets as a single line item in the pro forma balance sheet, provided the operations are not expected to be continued for more than a short period (i.e., 12 months) prior to disposal.

- Adjustments to the pro forma income statement should assume the transaction was consummated at both the beginning of the fiscal year and latest interim period and should include factually supportable adjustments that are directly attributable to the transaction and expected to have a continuing effect. Adjustments to the balance sheet should assume the transaction had occurred at the balance sheet date. For transactions accounted for as a purchase, the adjustments should reflect goodwill amortization, depreciation, other effects of APB Opinion No. 16, and interest on debt incurred to make the acquisition.

  If an acquired entity was previously part of another entity, adjustments might be necessary when corporate overhead, interest, or income taxes had not been allocated by management on a reasonable basis. Similarly, if the acquired business was an S corporation or a partnership, adjustments should be made to reflect estimated officer salaries and income taxes. For dispositions, the adjustments should include deletion of the divested business and adjustments of expenses incurred on behalf of that business (e.g., advertising costs).

  Tax effects of pro forma adjustments should be shown separately and ordinarily should be calculated at the statutory rate in effect during the periods presented.

  In certain unusual instances, there may only be a limited number of clearly understandable adjustments, in which case a narrative description of the transaction may be substituted for the pro forma statements.

- Per share data, including the number of shares used in the computation, should be disclosed on the face of the pro forma income statement. If common shares are to be issued in the transaction, the per share data should be adjusted to reflect assumed issuance at the beginning of the period presented.

- A financial forecast may be presented in lieu of the pro forma income statement. The forecast should be in the same detail as the pro forma income statements and should cover at least 12 months from the date of the most recent balance sheet included in the filing or the estimated consummation date of the transaction, whichever is later. Historical information for a recent 12-month period should be presented in a parallel column. The forecast should be presented in accordance with AICPA guidelines, with clear disclosure of underlying assumptions.

The determination of what constitutes a "business" for the purpose of determining whether financial statements are required to be included in the filing is a "facts and circumstances" test. This would require an evaluation of whether there is sufficient continuity of the acquired entity's operations before and after the transaction so that presentation of prior financial data is meaningful for an understanding of future operations. There is a presumption that a subsidiary or division is a business, although a smaller component or an entity also could qualify. Among the matters to be considered are:

- Whether the type of revenue-producing activity will remain generally the same.

- Whether physical facilities, employee base, marketing system, sales force, customer base, operating rights, production methods, or trade names will remain.

If it is impractical to file the required historical or pro forma financial statements for an acquired business within the 15-day filing period, Form 8-K provides for an extension of up to 60 days to file the information. The extension is available when (1) providing the information within 15 days is impractical, (2) the registrant states so in Form 8-K, (3) the registrant states the date the financial statements are expected to be filed and (4) the registrant provides the financial information as soon as practical within the 60-day period.

In stating that an extension of time is required, the registrant would provide all available information required under Items 2 and 7 for the business acquisition. The registrant may, at its option, include unaudited financial statements in the initial report on Form 8-K. No further extensions beyond the 60 days will be considered. The SEC has emphasized that the availability of the extension should not be an invitation for nontimely filing of the required information.

In certain **rare** instances, the SEC will consider a request for waiver of some or all of the required financial information of the acquired operations. It has emphasized that a waiver will be considered only where the circumstances are so rare as to constitute a "unique occurrence in the life of the registrant."

The Division of Corporation of Finance will administer the waiver on a case-by-case basis after considering the size of the acquisition relative to the registrant, the reasons why statements cannot be obtained, and the financial information that can be provided.

The SEC has noted that impossibility would be considered a relevant reason why statements cannot be provided; however, the cost of an audit alone generally would not be sufficient for a waiver.

If a waiver is not granted and the required financial statements are not supplied in the prescribed time, the SEC has noted that the deficiency may affect the registrant's current status for both the 1933 and 1934 Acts and, if appropriate, enforcement action would be taken.

(c) Item 3—Bankruptcy or Receivership. If a receiver or similar agent has been appointed for the registrant in a bankruptcy proceeding, disclosure is required concerning the proceeding, the receiver, the court involved, and certain other matters.

(d) Item 4—Changes in Registrant's Independent Accountants. Certain disclosures are required in Form 8-K as a result of the resignation by (or declination to stand for reelection after completion of the current audit) or dismissal of a registrant's independent accountant, or the engagement of a new accountant. Such changes in the accountant for a significant subsidiary on whom the principal accountant expressed reliance in his report would also be reportable events.

The Commission has become increasingly concerned about changes in accountants and the potential for opinion shopping. The 8-K disclosure requirements about changes in accountants were significantly changed in 1988 by FRR No. 31. Then the timing requirements for 8-K filings involving Item 4 were changed in 1989 by FRR No. 34.

When an independent accountant who was the principal accountant for the company or who audited a significant subsidiary and was expressly relied on by the principal accountant resigns (or declines to stand for reelection) or is dismissed, the registrant must disclose:

1. Whether the former accountant resigned, declined to stand for reelection, or was dismissed, including the date thereof.

2. Whether there was an adverse opinion, disclaimer of opinion, or qualification or modification of opinion as to uncertainty, audit scope, or accounting principles issued by such accountant for either of the 2 most recent years, including a description of the nature of the opinion.

3. Whether the decision to change accountants was recommended by or approved by the audit committee or a similar committee or by the board of directors in the absence of such special committee.

4. Whether during the 2 most recent fiscal years and any subsequent interim period preceding the resignation, declination, or dismissal there were any disagreements with the former accountant on any matter of accounting principles or practices, financial statement disclosure, or auditing scope or procedure, which disagreement(s), if not resolved to the satisfaction of the former accountant, would have caused the account-ant to make reference to the subject matter of the disagreement(s) in connection with his or her report.

   The term "disagreements" should be interpreted broadly but should not include preliminary differences of opinion that are "based on incomplete facts" if the differ-ences are resolved by obtaining more complete factual information.

5. Whether there were any "reportable events" during the 2 most recent fiscal years or any subsequent interim period preceding the resignation, declination, or dismissal, including:

   a. The auditor having advised the registrant that the internal controls necessary to develop reliable financial statements do not exist.

   b. The auditor having advised the registrant that information has come to the auditor's attention that led him or her to no longer be able to rely on management's representations or that has made him or her unwilling to be associated with the financial statements.

   c. The auditor having advised the registrant that there is a need to significantly expand the audit scope or that information has come to the auditor's attention during the last 2 fiscal years and any subsequent interim period that, if further investigated, may (1) materially impact the fairness or reliability of either a previously issued audit report or the underlying financial statements or the financial statements issued or to be issued for a subsequent period or (2) cause the auditor to be unwilling to rely on management's representations or to be associated with the financial statements and due to the change in auditors, the auditor did not expand his scope or conduct a further investigation.

d. The auditor having advised the registrant that information has come to the auditor's attention that he or she has concluded materially impacts the fairness or reliability of either (1) a previously issued audit report or the underlying financial statements or (2) the financial statements relating to a subsequent period and, unless the matter is resolved to the auditor's satisfaction, the auditor would be prevented from rendering an unqualified report and, due to the change in auditors, the matter has not been resolved.

Disagreements and reportable events are intended to be communicated to the registrant orally and in writing. Because these are sensitive areas that may impugn the integrity of management, communication will have to be handled with extreme care on the part of all involved.

In early 1989, the Commission finalized its "early warning release," which significantly reduced the time period permitted in filing a Form 8-K relating to a change in accountants. FRR 34 reduced the time period for filing the Item 4 disclosure from 15 calendar days to 5 business days. It also provided (1) that the letter from the registrant's former independent accountant must be filed within 10 business days after the filing that disclosed the change, (2) that the registrant must file such letter within 2 business days of receipt, and (3) that the former accountant may provide an interim letter to the registrant, which also must be filed within 2 business days of receipt. In late 1989, the AICPA's SEC Practice Section adopted a rule requiring member CPA firms to notify the SEC within 5 business days of terminating a relationship with a registrant-client. A notification letter is sent simultaneously to the registrant-client and the Chief Accountant of the SEC.

Additionally, Item 304 of Regulation S-K requires the registrant to disclose similar information about auditor changes during the 2 years preceding the filing of Forms S-1 or S-18 for initial public offerings.

The National Commission on Fraudulent Financial Reporting has recommended that when a change in accountants takes place, SEC rules should require disclosure of all material issues discussed with the prior and successor accountants during the prior 3 years.

(e) Item 5—Other Events.   The registrant may, at its option, report any information that it believes to be important to the stockholders but that is not specifically required to be reported on Form 8-K. Examples would be the commencement of material litigation, plant closings due to fire or strike, the discovery of mineral resources, and any important new products or product lines.

(f) Item 6—Resignation of Registrant's Directors.   A Form 8-K should be filed if a director has resigned or declines to stand for reelection because of a disagreement with management related to the company's operations and has furnished the company with a letter describing the disagreement and requesting the event be disclosed.

The registrant should summarize the disagreement and may include a statement presenting its views if it considers the director's description incorrect or incomplete. The director's letter should be filed as an exhibit with Form 8-K.

(g) Item 7—Financial Statements, Pro Forma Financial Information, and Exhibits.   Financial statements of acquired businesses, if applicable, and all required pro forma information should be included as discussed earlier. The exhibits outlined in Item 601 of Regulation S-K should also be furnished.

(h) Signatures.   The Form 8-K requires the signature of one duly authorized officer of the registrant.

PROXY STATEMENTS

3.42 OVERVIEW.   Because of the geographic dispersion of the owners of a public company, it is unlikely that a quorum could be obtained at any meeting that required a vote of the shareholders. As a result, the use of proxies and proxy statements developed to facilitate such votes. A proxy is broadly defined as any authorization given to someone by security holders to act on their behalf at a stockholders' meeting. The term "proxy" also refers to the document used to evidence such authorization. Persons soliciting proxies must comply with Regulation 14A and the 1934 Act, which prescribes the content of documents to be distributed to stockholders before, or at the same time, such solicitation occurs.

The informational content of the proxy statement provided to the stockholders depends on the action to be taken by the stockholders. Schedule 14A prescribes the informational content required based on the specific circumstances.

When the vote is solicited for (1) an exchange of one security for another, (2) mergers or consolidations, or (3) transfers of assets, the transaction constitutes an "offer to sell securities." As such, a registration statement is required under the 1933 Act and can be filed on Form S-4 (Form F-4 for foreign private issuers in similar transactions).

3.43 REGULATION 14A.   The SEC derives its authority to regulate the solicitation of proxies from the Exchange Act and from the Investment Company Act of 1940. Section 14(a) of the Exchange Act states:

> It shall be unlawful for any person, by the use of the mails or by any means or instrumentality of interstate commerce or of any facility of a national securities exchange or otherwise, in contravention of such rules and regulations as the Commission may prescribe as necessary or appropriate in the public interest or for the protection of investors, to solicit or to permit the use of his name to solicit any proxy or consent or authorization in respect of any security (other than an exempted security) registered pursuant to Section 12 of this title.

Based on this statutory authority, the SEC established Regulation 14A to regulate proxy solicitations. Regulation 14A comprises the following Rules:

14a-1	Definitions
14a-2	Solicitations to Which Rules 14a-3 to 14a-14 Apply
14a-3	Information to Be Furnished to Security Holders
14a-4	Requirements as to Proxy
14a-5	Presentation of Information in Proxy Statements
14a-6	Filing Requirements
14a-7	Mailing Communications for Security Holders
14a-8	Proposals of Security Holders
14a-9	False or Misleading Statements
14a-10	Prohibition of Certain Solicitations
14a-11	Special Provisions Applicable to Election Contests
14a-12	Solicitation Prior to Furnishing Required Proxy Statement
14a-13	Obligation of Registrants in Communicating with Beneficial Owners
14a-14	Modified or Superseded Documents

Because of the complexity of these rules, most are not discussed in detail here. However, it is important to remember that proxies and proxy statements are different from other SEC filings because they are required to be sent directly to the security holders. Registration statements are filed directly with the SEC. Annual reports on Form 10-K are filed with the SEC and are furnished to the shareholder only on request. Typically, the proxy materials must be given to the shareholders at least 20 days prior to the meeting date. Companies listed on the New York Stock Exchange provide shareholders 30 days to review the materials.

The proxy rules require companies to provide shareholders with proxy cards to give them more opportunity to participate in corporate elections. Shareholder proxy cards must (1) indicate whether the proxy is solicited on behalf of the board of directors, (2) enable shareholders to abstain from voting on directors and other proxy matters, as well as to approve or disapprove each matter, and (3) allow shareholders to vote for or against each nominee for the board of directors or to abstain from voting for one or more nominees.

In addition, if 5% or more of the shares cast in the previous proxy solicitations were withheld or were negative with respect to any incumbent director, those results must be disclosed in the current proxy solicitation.

3.44 SEC REVIEW REQUIREMENTS.   Except as noted below, Rule 14a-6 requires that preliminary copies of the proxy statements and related materials be filed with the SEC at least 10 calendar days prior to the date definitive copies of such material are first sent or given to security holders. Such materials should be appropriately marked as "Preliminary Copies" and the date definitive materials are to be mailed to the shareholders must be stated in the filing. Earlier submission (usually more than 20 days) is advisable to allow time for any changes that may be required as a result of the SEC's selective review process.

In 1988, the SEC provided some relief in the area of proxy material review. Preliminary proxy materials need not be filed with the Commission if the solicitation relates to any meeting of security holders at which the only matters to be acted on are:

1. The election of directors.
2. The election, approval, or ratification of accountant(s).
3. A security holder proposal included pursuant to Rule 14a-8.
4. With respect to a registered investment company or business development company, a proposal to continue, without change, any advisory or other contract or agreement that has been the subject of a proxy solicitation for which proxy material has previously been filed.
5. With respect to an open-end registered investment company, a proposal to increase the number of shares authorized to be issued.

Information in preliminary proxy material will be made available to persons requesting it after the definitive proxy is filed, unless an application for confidential treatment for such information is made at the time of filing the preliminary proxy material and approved by the SEC. Such preliminary material will also be made available to persons requesting it if no definitive filing is anticipated.

Before the registrant files the preliminary material, the accountant should read the entire text and compare it with the financial statements. This procedure is intended to avoid inconsistencies and misleading comments of which the accountant may have knowledge and to ascertain that the financial statements include disclosures mentioned in the text that are appropriate for a fair presentation of the financial statements in conformity with GAAP.

A manually signed independent accountant's report is required to accompany the preliminary material if the accountant's audit has been completed. If the audit has not been completed, the SEC requires that a letter from the independent accountant accompany the preliminary material. The letter should state that the accountant has considered the preliminary material and will allow the use of his or her report on the financial statements. This letter is addressed to the registrant, who, in turn, submits it to the SEC. When preparing the letter, the accountant should avoid using general terms such as "considered" or "reviewed" in describing the work and should avoid expressing approval, either directly or indirectly, of the sufficiency of disclosures in the text. The accountant should state that he or she has read the preliminary proxy statements and will upon completion of the audit allow use of the report on the financial statements. The financial statements covered by the report, and the date of the report, should be specified in the letter. When a proxy statement is prepared for a proposed merger, the letter should relate only to the company with which the accountant is familiar.

One copy of the definitive material and the accountant's report must be manually signed. Copies of the definitive material that are mailed to stockholders should be filed with the SEC.

If changed circumstances or new events arising between the time the proxy solicitation is mailed and the stockholders' meeting date cause the proxy material to be materially false and misleading, the corrected material should be disseminated promptly to the stockholders.

SOURCES AND SUGGESTED REFERENCES

BDO Seidman, *Guide to Going Public,* BDO Seidman, New York, 1987.

Financial Accounting Standards Board, ''Extinguishment of Debt,'' Statement of Financial Accounting Standards No. 76, FASB, Stamford, CT, 1983.

National Commission on Fraudulent Financial Reporting, *Report of the National Commission on Fraudulent Financial Reporting,* October 1987.

SEC Compliance, Financial Reporting and Forms, Prentice-Hall, Englewood Cliffs, NJ, annual.

''Securities Regulation and Law Report,'' Bureau of National Affairs, Washington, DC, weekly reporting service.

Special Advisory Committee on Internal Control, *Report of the Special Advisory Committee on Internal Control,* AICPA, New York, 1979.

Warren, Gorham & Lamont, Inc., Boston, monthly newsletter.

Wendell, Paul J. (ed.), *SEC Accounting Report,* Warren, Gorham, & Lamont, NY, continuing reporting service.

Wiesen, J. L., *Regulating Transactions in Securities,* West Publishing Co., St. Paul, MN, 1975.

PART **II**

FINANCIAL STATEMENTS— PRESENTATION AND ANALYSIS

CHAPTER 4

FINANCIAL STATEMENTS: FORM AND CONTENT

Jan R. Williams, PhD, CPA

College of Business Administration, University of Tennessee

CONTENTS

INTRODUCTION

Financial statements are one of management's primary means of communicating with external parties about the financial activities of the enterprise. Through financial statements, interested parties outside a company are able to learn a great deal about the financial effects of various business transactions and the accumulated resources and obligations of the reporting enterprise.

This chapter presents an overview of the form and content of financial statements as a means of introducing these important communication tools. The purpose is not to cover these statements in depth but rather to introduce them, to illustrate how they interrelate or articulate with each other, and to suggest the types of information that can be gleaned from them. Later chapters will develop in more depth the specific content and underlying accounting principles of specific financial statements.

The following sections review the objectives of financial reporting, including financial statements, and identify the principles supporting the preparation of financial statements. Next there are individual reviews and illustrations of the primary financial statements—the balance sheet, the income statement, the statement of stockholders' equity, and the statement of cash flows. Articulation of financial statements is then covered, followed by a discussion of the role of supplemental and note disclosure. The chapter ends with a discussion of some of the limitations of financial statements as communication tools.

PRINCIPLES UNDERLYING FINANCIAL STATEMENTS

4.1 OBJECTIVES OF FINANCIAL REPORTING.   The FASB has established several objectives of financial reporting. Financial reporting is a broad term used to identify all means by which investors, creditors, and other interested parties learn about the financial activities of an enterprise. One of the most important parts of the financial reporting environment is the preparation and distribution of financial statements, particularly statements that are audited by an independent CPA.

Three primary objectives of financial reporting, which are carried out in part through the preparation of financial statements, are as follows:

1. To provide information that is useful to present and potential investors and creditors and other users in making rational investment, credit, and similar decisions (SFAC No. 1, par. 34).
2. To provide information to help present and potential investors and creditors and other users assess the amounts, timing, and uncertainty of prospective cash receipts from dividends and interest and the proceeds from the sale, redemption, or maturity of securities or loans (SFAC No. 1, par. 37).
3. To provide information about the economic resources of the enterprise, claims to those resources and the effects of transactions, events, and circumstances that change resources and claims to resources (SFAC No. 1, par. 40).

In expanding on these objectives, the FASB points out that information provided should be comprehensible to those who have a reasonable understanding of business and economic activities and are willing to study the information with reasonable diligence. Thus, the orientation of financial statements is toward the reasonably informed user of financial information—neither the extreme highest in terms of knowledge (e.g., professional financial analysts) nor the extreme lowest (e.g., the naive investor with little knowledge of business activities).

4.2 SELECTED UNDERLYING PRINCIPLES.   Many broad principles underlie the preparation of financial statements. The following paragraphs briefly set forth several principles that are important to an introductory understanding of the financial statements.

(a) Multiple Sources of Information.   Financial statements are only one of many sources of financial information about a reporting enterprise. Management may communicate financial and other information to interested parties in a variety of ways, some of which are through governmental organizations such as the SEC. News releases and direct contact with owners and others are other means of communication within the financial reporting framework. Many times these include financial statements or refer to information taken from financial statements.

(b) Approximate Measures.   The content of financial statements results, in part, from approximate rather than precise measures of business activities. Many estimates and assumptions are required in order to partition ongoing business activities into relatively short periods of time, such as one year. Although the financial statements have an appearance of precision because items are measured in terms of a monetary unit, determining many of those numbers requires judgments that impose uncertainty and imprecision into the resulting financial-statement items.

(c) Historical Orientation.   The orientation of financial statements is primarily historical inasmuch as they report activities and events that have already occurred. Reporting on historical events, however, sometimes requires estimates of the future.

(d) General Purpose Financial Statements.   The primary financial statements are general purpose in nature in that they are designed to meet the information needs of a wide variety of financial statement users and are not specifically tailored to the unique needs of any particular user group. These general purpose statements are designed primarily for external users who lack the authority to dictate the specific information they receive. Users who do have the authority to dictate the nature of such information are not the primary audience of general purpose financial statements.

(e) Accrual Accounting.   Financial statements are based on accrual accounting principles. Accrual accounting attempts to measure the financial impact of events and transactions when they occur and not simply when the cash consequences of those events and transactions take place. The cash effects of certain transactions may occur earlier or later than the transaction itself and accountants attempt to report at the time of the substantive financial effects rather than only the cash effects.

(f) Explanatory Notes and Disclosures.   The usefulness of financial statements is believed to be enhanced by explanations and details outside the body of the statements themselves. For this reason, financial statements are frequently accompanied by notes and other supplemental disclosures providing a variety of information that would otherwise not be available. A discussion of supplemental and note disclosure is presented later in this chapter.

A complete set of financial statements generally includes a balance sheet, an income statement, a statement of stockholders' equity, and a statement of cash flows. In the following sections, each of these statements is illustrated and described. Because of the overview nature of this chapter, all of the disclosures that would normally accompany the statements are not presented. Rather, the focus is on the basic structure of each statement, the definitions of the primary elements of the statements, and the interrelationship of the statements.

BALANCE SHEET

A balance sheet, also called a **statement of financial position,** is a listing of the quantifiable resources that an enterprise has to operate with as well as a listing of claims against those resources represented by both creditors and owners. In the **report form** of the statement, the

MORRISTOWN PRODUCTS, INC.
Balance Sheet
December 31, 1987, 1988, and 1989
(In thousands of dollars)

	1987	1988	1989
Assets			
Current assets			
Cash	$ 10	$ 13	$ 8
Marketable securities	5	5	6
Accounts receivable	45	40	50
Merchandise inventory	75	90	100
Prepaid expenses	5	4	7
	$140	$152	$171
Property, plant, and equipment			
Equipment	$100	$100	$100
Building	200	200	250
Land	50	60	60
	$350	$360	$410
Less: accumulated depreciation	(75)	(90)	(105)
	275	270	305
Investments	50	67	67
Total assets	$465	$489	$543
Liabilities			
Current liabilities			
Accounts payable	$ 40	$ 45	$ 52
Accrued expenses	35	32	40
	$ 75	$ 77	$ 92
Noncurrent liabilities			
Bonds payable	200	200	200
Total liabilities	$275	$277	$292
Stockholders' equity			
Preferred stock	$ 20	$ 20	$ 20
(500 shares @ $40 par value)			
Common stock	100	110	110
(10,000 shares @ $10 par value			
in 1987; 11,000 shares @ $10			
par value in 1988 and 1989)			
Additional paid-in capital	30	35	35
Retained earnings	40	47	86
Total stockholders' equity	190	212	251
Total liabilities and			
stockholders' equity	$465	$489	$543

Exhibit 4.1. Sample balance sheet.

quantifiable resources, called assets, are first listed, followed by the claims of creditors and owners. In the **account form** of the statement, the assets are typically presented on the left and the claims to the assets on the right side of the statement. An important relationship in the balance sheet is that the claims to the assets equal or "balance" exactly the amount of the assets presented.

Another way to view the balance sheet is that it represents the quantifiable resources of the enterprise and a description of the three primary sources from which those resources have been garnered. The first source is creditors—those who have loaned resources to the company for its use, expecting a return on those loaned amounts as well as eventual repayment of them. The second source is the owners, called stockholders in a corporation, who have committed resources to the company, expecting some combination of return and enhanced value of the investment through the effective employment of resources by the enterprise. The third source also is considered an owner source but results from the assets earned by the enterprise having been retained for its future use rather than having been distributed back to the owners on a periodic basis.

Exhibit 4.1 illustrates a balance sheet for the hypothetical Morristown Products, Inc. It is prepared in the report form, first listing assets, followed by liabilities and stockholders' equity. This is a **classified balance sheet,** with the various major categories further categorized as described below.

4.3 ASSETS.   Assets are defined as probable future economic benefits obtained or controlled by the enterprise as a result of past transactions or events (SFAC No. 6, par. 25). Assets have three essential characteristics: (1) They embody a probable future economic benefit in the form of a direct or indirect future net cash inflow; (2) a particular enterprise (e.g., the owner) can obtain the benefit and control others' access to it; and (3) the transaction or other event giving rise to the enterprise's right to control the benefit has already occurred (SFAC No. 6, par. 26). Assets are typically presented in the balance sheet in terms of current and noncurrent classifications.

(a) Current Assets.   Current assets are assets that are expected to become cash, sold, or consumed in the near future (ARB No. 43, Ch. 3, par. 4). These assets are considered "liquid" in that they represent cash or near-cash resources from which the company can satisfy obligations as they become due. The primary purpose of listing current assets is to communicate information about the various stages of a company's short-term cash-to-cash cycle, including the amount invested in each stage of that cycle. Exhibit 4.2 depicts a typical short-term cash cycle for a company that invests cash in merchandise inventory. That inventory is held until sold to customers on credit, thus creating accounts receivable that are

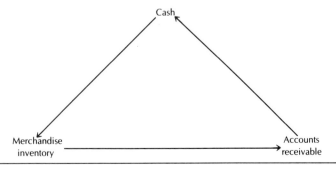

Exhibit 4.2.   Short-term operating cycle.

subsequently converted into cash. Assuming the purchase of inventory takes place at a dollar amount below the price of the sale of that same inventory, the eventual addition to cash is greater than the original reduction in cash when the item was purchased. This short-term or operating cycle is intended to be a primary source of increased cash, which is then available for future use in continued operations.

Current assets are typically listed in their order of liquidity in the balance sheet, beginning with cash itself. Some companies hold certain highly liquid investments as **cash equivalents** and combine them with cash as a current asset in the balance sheet. In Exhibit 4.1 cash is followed by marketable securities, accounts receivable, merchandise inventory, and prepaid expenses, in that order. **Marketable securities** are considered current assets if management invests in them when excess cash is available and disinvests when that cash is again needed for operating purposes. If the intent of management is to retain the investment for a longer period of time, the securities would not be classified as current. Marketable securities presented in the current asset section of a balance sheet may be thought of as secondary sources of cash that are readily available to the company when needed. **Accounts receivable** represent the result of credit sales transactions that have not yet been collected in cash. **Merchandise inventory** represents the company's investment in assets held for resale and expected to be sold in the near future. **Prepaid expenses** represent advance payments of items that will be used by the company in the coming accounting period. They are unlike other current assets in that they will not become cash in the near future. On the other hand, because they exist at any point in time, future cash is conserved. Thus, they are considered current assets.

The time period for distinguishing current assets from other assets is usually 1 year. Some companies, however, have a short-term cash-to-cash cycle, or operating cycle, of more than 1 year. For example, if inventory is required to be held through an aging process, the time between the initial investment of cash in inventory and the eventual return of that cash through the sale of the inventory may be quite long. If a company's operating cycle is longer than 1 year, the longer period of the cycle is used to identify current assets. If the company has several cycles within a year, a year is used.

(b) Noncurrent Assets.   Noncurrent assets are assets that do not meet the definition of current assets. These may represent a variety of resources available to the enterprise and may vary considerably between enterprises, depending on the nature of the business activity in which the enterprise is involved. Many companies require **property, plant, and equipment,** sometimes referred to as fixed or plant assets, in order to operate. In Exhibit 4.1, Morristown Products, Inc., presents equipment, buildings, and land under a property, plant, and equipment caption. The amounts so presented represent the cost of those assets to the enterprise. Over time that cost is recognized as an expense in the income statement of the enterprise, a subject covered in section 4.7 of this chapter. The accumulation of those expense amounts is identified in the balance sheet as "accumulated depreciation" and is subtracted from the cost of the assets. Moving through time, the accumulated depreciation would ordinarily increase in amount as illustrated in Exhibit 4.1.

A variety of other noncurrent assets may be held by a company at any particular point in time. The balance sheet of Morristown Products, Inc., illustrates one such asset, **investments.** These are most likely securities of other enterprises that the company is holding with the intent of not converting to cash in the near future. Thus, they are properly identified as other than current assets.

4.4 LIABILITIES.   Liabilities are probable future sacrifices of economic benefits arising from present obligations of a particular enterprise to transfer assets or provide services to other entities in the future as a result of past transactions or events (SFAC No. 6, par. 35). As with assets, liabilities have three essential characteristics: (1) They embody a present duty or responsibility that is expected to be settled by probable future transfer of assets; (2) the duty or responsibility obligates a particular enterprise; and (3) the transaction or event obligating the enterprise has already occurred (SFAC No. 6, par. 36). Liabilities are typically presented in the balance sheet in terms of current and noncurrent classifications.

(a) Current Liabilities.   Current liabilities are liabilities that are expected to be satisfied with the use of current assets (ARB No. 43, Ch. 3, par. 7). Ordinarily, current assets are those that will be due within 1 year or operating cycle, if longer. There are instances where such short-term obligations are not presented as current liabilities, however, because they are not expected to be satisfied using current assets. For example, if a company has a long-term debt obligation outstanding and throughout the period of the debt provides for repayment by investing in a fund for that purpose, the debt obligation is not a current liability in its last year, because the asset source used for repayment is not a current asset.

In Exhibit 4.1, two examples of current liabilities are illustrated—**accounts payable** and **accrued expenses.** The former most likely results from the purchase of merchandise inventory from suppliers and represents debts to those suppliers that will be paid within a very short time. Accrued expenses may arise from a variety of sources related to the application of accrual accounting procedures and may represent the enterprise's obligation to pay wages to employees, interest to creditors, taxes to government, and other similar items.

(b) Noncurrent Liabilities.   Noncurrent liabilities are liabilities that do not meet the definition of current liabilities. They are part of the long-term financing of the enterprise and are expected to be repaid at some distant date. **Bonds payable** is used as an example of such an arrangement in Exhibit 4.1.

4.5 STOCKHOLDERS' EQUITY.   Equity is the residual interest in the enterprise after deducting liabilities from assets (SFAC No. 6, par. 49). A corporate organization titles that equity as "stockholders' equity." Other forms of business organization, such as sole proprietorships and partnerships, commonly refer to it simply as "owners' equity."

(a) Contributed Equity.   Corporations sell stock as evidence of ownership in the company. This stock may be labeled **preferred** or **common stock.** Although a detailed discussion of these types of stock is beyond the scope of this chapter, preferred stock will receive distributions of assets to owners, called dividends, before common stock. Also, should the company liquidate, preferred stockholders have a preference in receiving assets over common stockholders. The stocks typically have an identified **par** or **stated value** at which they are carried in the corporate balance sheet, as illustrated in Exhibit 4.1 ($40 par for preferred and $10 par for common).

Because preferred and common stock will not necessarily sell to stockholders at precisely their par values, additional accounts may be found in the stockholders' equity section of the balance sheet representing those additional sources of assets. In Exhibit 4.1, the account "additional paid-in capital" is an example of such an account. The preferred stock, common stock, and additional paid-in capital accounts combined represent the contributed or paid-in equity of the enterprise—those amounts that have been committed to the enterprise by owners for the enterprise's use.

(b) Retained Earnings.   The final item in stockholders' equity is **retained earnings.** This amount represents a source of enterprise assets from profitable past operations beyond the amount of such assets that have been distributed to owners in the form of dividends. Typically companies do not distribute assets to stockholders that are equal to the amount of their earnings. Rather, they withhold a portion of earned assets for future operations, including expansion of business activities and other uses.

The balancing feature can be seen in Exhibit 4.1 inasmuch as the assets equal the total of the liabilities and stockholders' equity (e.g., $543,000 in 1989). The balance sheet is based on this primary underlying principle, and it represents a basic tenet of financial reporting. The balance sheet has been described as a still photograph of a business at a point in time, in terms of its assets, liabilities, and owners' equity—a simple but appropriate analogy that identifies what this important financial statement attempts to communicate.

INCOME STATEMENT

Continuing the analogy of the balance sheet as a still photograph of an enterprise at a point in time, the income statement must then be described as a motion picture that identifies certain dimensions of the enterprise over a period of time. Exhibit 4.3 shows the relationship of the balance sheet and the other financial statements, including the income statement in terms of the passage of time. Exhibit 4.4 provides an income statement for Morristown Products, Inc., for the years 1988 and 1989. This income statement relates to, or articulates with, the balance sheet presented earlier in Exhibit 4.1. It describes the profit-seeking activities of the company in terms of its revenues and expenses, leading to a final figure of net income or net loss.

4.6 REVENUES.   Revenues are inflows or other enhancements of assets of an enterprise or settlement of its liabilities from delivering or producing goods, rendering services, or carrying out other activities that constitute the entity's ongoing major or central operations (SFAC No. 6, par. 78). The nature of an enterprise's revenues depends on the type of business activity. For a manufacturing enterprise, revenues may consist of sales of its manufactured product to retailers or other enterprises that will sell to the ultimate consumer. For service enterprise, revenues may represent the value of the services provided to its customers or clients for a period of time. Revenues are typically the first items listed in an income statement, as is the case in Exhibit 4.4 with the "sales" figure for Morristown Products, Inc.

4.7 EXPENSES.   Expenses are outflows or other using up of assets or incurrences of liabilities from delivering or producing goods, rendering services, or carrying out other activities that constitute the entity's ongoing major or central operations (SFAC No. 6, par. 80). Sacrifices are necessary in order for an enterprise to create revenues. These sacrifices are in the form of asset outflows or creation of liabilities that, in turn, will result in asset outflows when those liabilities are eventually paid. Expenses attempt to measure these asset outflows or reductions. Many expense categories are presented in the typical income statement of a business enterprise, as is the case in Exhibit 4.4—**cost of sales, selling and administrative, depreciation, interest, provision for income taxes.** All of these represent various types of expenses that are required to create the asset enhancements or revenues related to these expenses.

The income statement is based on an accounting principle called **matching.** Revenues ordinarily can be readily associated with specific business activity that relates to specific periods of time. Once the revenues for a period of time have been identified, the accountant

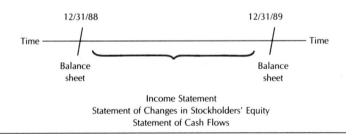

Exhibit 4.3.   Relationship of financial statements.

MORRISTOWN PRODUCTS, INC.
Income Statement
For years ended December 31, 1988 and 1989
(In thousands of dollars)

	1988	1989
Sales	$400	$500
Cost of sales	180	240
Gross margin	$220	$260
Expenses:		
Selling and administrative	$155	$135
Depreciation	15	15
	170	150
Income from operations	$ 50	$110
Interest expense	20	20
Income before income taxes	$ 30	$ 90
Provision for income taxes	9	27
Net income	$ 21	$ 63
Earnings per share	$1.87	$5.60

Exhibit 4.4.   Sample income statement.

then attempts to associate with those revenues all expenses that relate to (1) that same period of time and/or (2) the generation of those specific revenues. These amounts are then matched, meaning that the expenses are subtracted from the revenues, to determine the results of operations for the period. The result is called **net income** if revenues exceed expenses; it is called **net loss** if expenses exceed revenues.

4.8 PRESENTATION ISSUES.   In a **multiple-step income statement,** illustrated in Exhibit 4.4, several subtotals appear within the statement. Examples are "gross margin," "income from operations," and "income before income tax." These discretionary descriptions are intended to help the reader of the statement understand the important relationships that underlie the statement. **Gross margin** measures the difference between sales and cost of sales. Cost of sales is the direct cost of acquiring (or manufacturing) the items sold. Gross margin is the broadest concept of profit in that it deducts from sales only the direct cost of those items sold and does not include other costs of business operations that are necessary, but more indirect. **Income from operations** attempts to measure the excess of sales over those expenses that are most closely tied to ongoing business operations. In the case of Morristown Products, Inc., in Exhibit 4.4, interest payments on borrowings and income taxes have been omitted from the determination of income from operations on the basis that they are less closely related to ongoing business activities than are the other expenses identified earlier in the statement—cost of sales, selling and administrative, and depreciation. **Income before income taxes** indicates the profitability of the company after recognizing all related expenses except income tax. Net income is the final indication of profitability for the period of time covered. The subtotals preceding net income in Exhibit 4.4 are not found in all income statements but are placed there at the discretion of the preparer for the convenience and understanding of the financial statement reader. An income statement that omits these subtotals is called a **single-step income statement.**

Earnings per share (EPS), is an indication of the net income recalculated on a per-share-of-common-stock basis. Referring again to Exhibit 4.4, in 1988 net income per share of common stock was $1.87, and for 1989 the amount was $5.60. This figure is calculated by taking the amount of net income, reducing it by any dividend requirements for preferred stock, and dividing the result by the weighted average number of shares of common stock outstanding for the year.

Income statements may include gains and losses other than those illustrated in Exhibit 4.4. Gains and losses may result from a variety of peripheral business activities: that is, they do not relate to the primary, ongoing central activities of the enterprise. These types of gains and losses occur less frequently than revenues and expenses that are defined in terms of the enterprise's primary revenue-producing activities. They are discussed in greater detail in Chapter 5.

STATEMENT OF STOCKHOLDERS' EQUITY

A required disclosure in a complete set of financial statements of a corporation is an identification of the changes in stockholders' equity in terms of dollars by major category and numbers of shares of stock (APB Opinion No. 12, par. 10). This disclosure can be made in several different forms, such as a note or supplemental schedule to the other financial statements, or a separate financial statement. Because many companies today make this presentation in the form of a separate financial statement, Exhibit 4.5 takes that approach in Morristown Products, Inc.'s statement of stockholders' equity.

Like the income statement, the statement of stockholders' equity covers a period of time rather than a specific point in time. The columns represent the major categories of stockholders' equity: contributed equity—preferred stock, common stock, and additional paid-in capital—and retained earnings. The statement begins with the balance at the end of the period prior to that covered in the statement. In Exhibit 4.5, the statement covers 1988 and 1989, so the statement begins with the balances in the stockholders' equity accounts at the end of 1987.

The rows in the statement indicate activities that resulted in changes in the major categories of stockholders' equity—sale of common stock, net income, and dividends. Notice that the sale of common stock affects only the contributed equity accounts inasmuch as they are intended to include those amounts contributed to the enterprise by stockholders. In this case, common stock increased by the par value of the shares sold, $10,000, and additional paid-in capital increased by $5,000. This means that the stock sold for 1.5 times its

---

MORRISTOWN PRODUCTS, INC.
Statement of Stockholders' Equity
For years ended December 31, 1988 and 1989
(In thousands of dollars)

	Contributed Equity			Retained Earnings
	Preferred Stock	Common Stock	Additional Paid-in Capital	
Dec. 31, 1987	$ 20	$100	$ 30	$ 40
Sale of 1000 shares of common stock		10	5	
Net income				21
Dividends				(14)
Dec. 31, 1988	$ 20	$110	$ 35	$ 47
Net income				63
Dividends				(24)
Dec. 31, 1989	$ 20	$110	$ 35	$ 86

Exhibit 4.5.   Sample statement of stockholders' equity.

par value, or $15 per share. The increase in the number of shares is disclosed in the caption to the left describing the sale of common stock.

Net income and dividends affect only retained earnings, as illustrated in Exhibit 4.5. Net income increases the retained earnings balance, and dividends decrease that balance.

Exhibit 4.5 shows the relationship of the financial statements covered earlier to the statement of stockholders' equity. For example, the net income amount included in the retained earnings column of Exhibit 4.5 is taken directly from the income statement for each year as indicated in Exhibit 4.4. Also, the various stockholders' equity accounts at December 31 of each year correspond to the amounts presented in the company's balance sheet at the end of each year in Exhibit 4.1. For example, the December 31, 1989, balances of preferred stock ($20,000), common stock ($110,000), additional paid-in capital ($35,000), and retained earnings ($86,000) in the balance sheet correspond to the amounts in the final row of the statement of stockholders' equity in Exhibit 4.5, the latter statement describing the changes that resulted in these ending balances.

STATEMENT OF CASH FLOWS

One of the central objectives of financial reporting is to provide information that is useful to external parties in assessing the amount, timing, and uncertainty of prospective cash flows to them. One factor of particular importance in this assessment is the cash position of the enterprise itself. As a result, the fourth financial statement is the statement of cash flows.

The statement of cash flows presents information about an enterprise's cash receipts and payments during a period of time (SFAS No. 95, par. 4). This statement is similar in concept to the income statement and statement of stockholders' equity in that it covers a period of time rather than a point in time, as does the balance sheet. In its simplest form, the statement of cash flows simply indicates the enterprise's primary sources of cash and the primary ways the enterprise used that cash. These changes are presented in a manner that reconciles the change in cash from the beginning to the end of the accounting period.

The statement of cash flows for Morristown Products, Inc., is included in Exhibit 4.6. This statement is presented in three categories—**cash flows from operating activities, cash flows from investing activities,** and **cash flows from financing activities.** At the bottom of the statement, the net change in cash is presented as a reconciling figure to show how the cash balance either increased or decreased between the beginning and ending of the accounting period covered by the statement.

4.9 OPERATING ACTIVITIES.   Cash flows from operating activities describe the cash-flow effects of those transactions presented in the enterprise's income statement. Because the income statement is prepared on an accrual basis, revenues and expenses reported in that statement may not represent the cash implications of those transactions. For example, revenues are generally recognized at the point of sale, but cash may not be received from the sale until the company collects the related receivable at a later date. Expenses, on the other hand, may have been paid before or after the period in which the expense is recognized in the income statement. Depreciation, for example, represents an expense attempting to measure the cost of services rendered during a period of time by the enterprise's plant assets. The cash to purchase those assets may have been paid in an earlier accounting period.

The following are types of cash inflows from operating activities that should be presented in the statement of cash flows, as appropriate (SFAS No. 95, par. 22):

1. Cash receipts from sales of goods or services.
2. Cash receipts from returns on loans to and investments in other enterprises.
3. Other cash receipts that do not stem from transactions classified as investing and financing activities.

MORRISTOWN PRODUCTS, INC.
Statement of Cash Flows
For the years ended December 31, 1988 and 1989
(In thousands of dollars)

	1988	1989
Cash Flows from Operating Activities		
Cash received from customers	$ 405	$ 490
Cash paid to suppliers	(190)	(243)
Cash paid for selling and administrative expenses	(157)	(130)
Cash paid for interest	(20)	(20)
Cash paid for income taxes	(9)	(27)
Net cash provided by operating activities	$ 29	$ 70
Cash Flows from Investing Activities		
Payment to purchase land	$(10)	
Payment to purchase investments	(17)	
Payment to purchase marketable securities		$(1)
Payment to purchase building		(50)
Net cash used in investing activities	(27)	(51)
Cash Flows from Financing Activities		
Sale of common stock	$ 15	
Payment of dividends	(14)	(24)
Net cash provided by (used in) financing activities	1	(24)
Net increase (decrease) in cash	$ 3	$(5)
Cash at beginning of year	10	13
Cash at end of year	$ 13	$ 8
Reconciliation of Net Income to Net Cash Provided by Operating Activities		
Net income	$ 21	$ 63
Adjustments to reconcile net income to net cash provided by operating activities:		
Depreciation	$ 15	$ 15
Change in current assets and liabilities:		
Accounts receivable	5	(10)
Inventory	(15)	(10)
Prepaid expenses	1	(3)
Accounts payable	5	7
Accrued expenses	(3)	8
	8	7
Net cash provided by operating activities	$ 29	$ 70

Exhibit 4.6. Sample statement of cash flows.

Cash outflows from operating activities typically presented in the statement of cash flows are (SFAS No. 95, par. 23):

1. Cash payments to acquire goods for manufacture or sale.
2. Cash payments to suppliers and employers for goods or services.
3. Cash payments to governments for taxes, duties, fines, and other fees or penalties.
4. Cash payments to lenders and other creditors for interest.
5. Other cash payments that are not classified as investing and financing cash outflows.

The types of cash flows from operating activities of a particular enterprise depend on the nature of that enterprise's activities. Exhibit 4.6 presents the cash flows from operating activities first in the statement of cash flows in five categories that are deemed appropriate for this enterprise's particular business activities. The result is a figure of net cash flows from operating activities (e.g., $70,000 for 1989), implying a netting of positive and negative cash flows within that category.

The relationship of net cash flows from operating activities to the company's net income is shown in a disclosure presented as part of the statement of cash flows. In that disclosure, net income is adjusted for noncash items to show the reader of the statement why net income and net cash flows from operating activities are different amounts. For example, for 1989 the former amount was $63,000 and the latter amount was $70,000 because of several noncash items that affected net income but did not provide or use cash during the year.

4.10 INVESTING ACTIVITIES.   Cash flows from investing activities present the enterprise's cash-flow activities in terms of investments in assets. Specifically, cash inflows are ordinarily presented in the following categories (SFAS No. 95, par. 16):

1. Receipts from collections or sales of loans made by the enterprise to other enterprises.
2. Receipts from sales of equity instruments of other enterprises.
3. Receipts from the sales of property, plant and equipment, and other productive assets.

Cash outflows from investing activities are typically presented in the following categories (SFAS No. 95, par. 17):

1. Payments for loans made to other enterprises and investments in other enterprise's debt instruments.
2. Payments to acquire equity instruments of other enterprises.
3. Payments to purchase property, plant and equipment, and other productive assets.

In Exhibit 4.6, the cash flow from investing activities is presented for Morristown Products, Inc., resulting in negative cash flow of $51,000 for 1989. During the year the company had only two types of transactions in investing category—purchase of marketable securities and purchase of building—both of which represent negative cash flows.

4.11 FINANCING ACTIVITIES.   Financing activities represent positive and negative cash flows of the enterprise from debt and equity financing transactions. Typical cash inflows from financing activities are (SFAS No. 95, par. 19):

1. Proceeds from selling stock.
2. Proceeds from issuing bonds, mortgages, notes, and other debt instruments.

Negative cash flows from financing activities are (SFAS No. 95, par. 20):

1. Payments of dividends or other distributions to owners.
2. Repayments of amounts borrowed.

Referring again to Exhibit 4.6, the third major section of the statement of cash flows of Morristown Products, Inc., is the cash flows from financing activities. For 1989 the net amount is a reduction of $24,000, resulting from a single transaction—payment of dividends. For 1988, on the other hand, the net amount from financing activities is a positive $1,000 amount when the amount received from the sale of common stock ($15,000) is offset by the amount of dividends paid ($14,000).

ARTICULATION OF FINANCIAL STATEMENTS

Reference has been made several times to the relationship of the four financial statements in the above presentation. Selected specific examples have shown where the items in one of the statements relate directly to the items in another financial statement.

The four financial statements are derived from the same underlying transactions and the same financial measurements of those transactions. The statements present different types of information about the enterprise's activities during a period of time and thus are not alternatives to each other. All are necessary for the reader to get as complete an understanding as is possible through the medium of financial statements.

Attempting to demonstrate the articulation of financial statements in a single illustration is an impossible undertaking. Exhibit 4.7 does illustrate, however, several of the most important relationships that underlie the four financial statements presented earlier—the balance sheet, the income statement, the statement of stockholders' equity, and the statement of cash flows. These relationships are numbered in Exhibit 4.7 and are summarized in the following list.

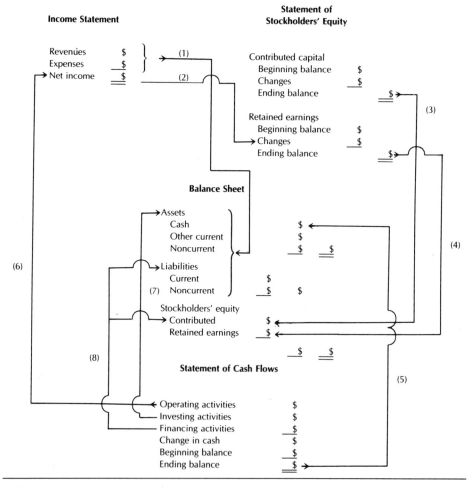

Exhibit 4.7.   Important relationships in financial statements.

1. Revenues and expenses, presented in the income statement, result in changes in assets and liabilities in the balance sheet.

2. Net income flows into the statement of stockholders' equity and is an important determinant of the end-of-period balance in retained earnings.

3. The ending balances of contributed equity accounts in the statement of stockholders' equity correspond to the same amounts in the stockholders' equity section of the balance sheet.

4. The ending balance of retained earnings in the statement of stockholders' equity corresponds to the balance in retained earnings in the stockholders' equity section of the balance sheet.

5. The ending cash balance in the statement of cash flows corresponds to the amount of cash presented on the balance sheet.

6. Cash flows from operating activities in the statement of cash flows reflects the cash effects of those transactions included in the determination of net income. A reconciliation of net income and net cash flows from operating activities is presented as part of the statement of cash flows.

7. Investing activities in the statement of cash flows reflect positive and negative cash flows from changes in assets whose ending balances are included in the balance sheet.

8. Financing activities in the statement of cash flows reflect positive and negative cash flows from debt and equity financing transactions. The end-of-period balances in debt and equity are presented in the balance sheet.

FINANCIAL STATEMENT DISCLOSURE

One of the underlying principles of financial statement preparation is **adequate or fair disclosure.** This means that financial statements and the notes and other supplemental information accompanying them must include all available relevant information to keep them from being misleading. In determining whether a specific item of information should be disclosed, the accountant must judge whether that information would make a difference in the decision of a reasonably prudent reader of the financial statements. If the information would be important to such a person, it should be disclosed.

Many disclosure requirements are specified in the authoritative accounting literature, such as the Statements of Financial Accounting Standards of the FASB. Because of the extensive nature of these requirements, accountants frequently use checklists to ensure that they have not overlooked important information. An example excerpt from such a checklist is found in Exhibit 4.8 for the asset category Property and Equipment. The parenthetical references within the checklist refer to the authoritative literature from which the disclosure requirement is derived. The three columns to the right indicate the alternative responses: "Yes" (disclosure has been made), "No" (disclosure has not been made, but is required), and "N/A" (disclosure is not applicable in this case).

Disclosure takes several forms. The strongest form of disclosure is to include the information in the body of the financial statements. In fact, the statements themselves are a form of disclosure. Including certain words, phrases, and dollar amounts in the statement is one means of disclosing the information. Classification within the financial statements is also an important form of disclosure.

A great deal of information is presented in conjunction with financial statements but outside the body of the statements. This information is typically labeled as **notes** to the financial statements. These notes include both text and numerical information that intend to further inform the reader of the financial statements about matters that have been included in summary fashion in the statements or have been excluded entirely from the financial statements. Notes to the financial statements should not be interpreted by the reader as

	Yes	No	N/A
G. Property and Equipment			
1. For depreciable assets, do the financial statements or notes thereto include disclosure of:			
a. Depreciation expense for each period? [APB 12, par. 5a (AC D40.105a)]	___	___	___
b. Balances of major classes of depreciable assets by nature or function? [APB 12, par. 5b (AC D40.105b)]	___	___	___
c. Accumulated depreciation, either by major classes of assets or in total? [APB 12, par. 5c (AC D40.105c)]	___	___	___
d. The method or methods used in computing depreciation with respect to major classes of depreciable assets? [APB 12, par. 5d (AC D40.105d); APB 22, par. 13 (AC A10.106)]	___	___	___
e. Investment credit, method followed, and amounts involved when material? [APB 4, par. 11 (AC I32.103); FASBI 25 (AC B50.153–.154, I32.107, .114–.115, .117–.120 and I37.109)]	___	___	___
2. Are net assets and liabilities of discontinued segments segregated from the assets and liabilities of continuing operations? [APB 30, par. 18d (AC I13.108d)]	___	___	___
3. Are capitalized interest costs appropriately determined and reported? [SFAS 34, pars. 6–23 (AC I67.102–.103, .105–.107 and .109–.118) as amended by SFAS 42, par. 4 (AC I67.104); SFAS 58, pars. 5–7 (AC I67.105c, .106c–.106e and .117); SFAS 62, par. 5 (AC I67.106)]	___	___	___

Exhibit 4.8.   Sample financial statement disclosure checklist. *Source:* Adapted from American Institute of Certified Public Accountants, *Audit and Accounting Manual,* "Financial Statements and Notes Checklist," par. 8400.05.

secondary or unimportant. In fact, notes often occupy more page space than the statements themselves and frequently include very important information that would not be available if the reader were limited to the information that can be contained in the financial statements themselves.

4.12 BROAD DISCLOSURE REQUIREMENTS.   The following paragraphs discuss several areas of broad disclosure requirements that do not relate to any one financial statement element. Rather, they are more pervasive in nature and apply to the financial statements as a whole.

(a) Accounting Policies.   The basic elements of the financial statements are identified and measured by applying accounting policies, many of which have been established by the FASB and other policy-setting bodies within the accounting profession. In some areas, alternative policies are available, and companies are required to disclose to readers of financial statements those policies that have been adopted in the preparation of the financial statements (APB Opinion No. 22, par. 8).

The inventory accounting policy statement is particularly important because of the disclosure about the accounting method used in determining the amount of inventories. Companies may account for inventories by a variety of techniques, such as FIFO, LIFO, and several averaging methods. The method used in determining the amount of inventory may have an important impact on the amounts in the income statement, balance sheet, and other financial statements and is frequently an important piece of information in interpreting financial statements.

(b) Related Party Transactions.   Related parties are individuals or companies with the ability to influence the financial transactions of each other. Disclosure of related party transactions may be important for a complete understanding of the financial statements of companies engaged in such transactions.

Notes to financial statements should include a description of transactions between related parties, such as transactions between a principal stockholder and the company, between a corporate officer and the company and between a subsidiary company and its parent company (SFAS No. 57, par. 2).

(c) Subsequent Events.   Financial statements cover a specific time period or point in time. These statements are not immediately available at the end of the accounting period but are usually published several weeks later. The period of time between the end of the accounting period and the issuance of the financial statements is called the subsequent period.

During the subsequent period, events may occur or information may become available that should be communicated in the financial statements. If the information reflects conditions that existed at the end of the previous accounting period, the items and amounts in the financial statements may require adjustment in order to appropriately reflect the company's financial position and results of operations for the previous period (SAS No. 12, par. 3). If the information reflects conditions that arose after the end of the previous accounting period, it may be necessary to disclose that information in the form of notes to the statements so that they reflect all relevant information (SAS No. 12, pars. 5–6).

(d) Pervasive Uncertainties.   Financial statements are typically prepared on the assumption that the enterprise is a going concern. This means that, in the absence of information to the contrary, it is reasonable to expect the company to continue in existence for at least the foreseeable future.

Should accountants preparing the financial statements determine that this assumption is not reasonable and that a significant question about continued existence exists, that information must be disclosed in notes to the financial statements (SAS No. 59, par. 10).

(e) Contingent Liabilities.   Contingent liabilities are liabilities that involve a great deal of uncertainty as to their existence and amount. They frequently exist as a result of lawsuits against an enterprise or other situations that may, in the future, require the enterprise to transfer assets in settlement of a claim.

If certain conditions are met, contingent liabilities should actually be entered into the accounting records and become a formal part of the financial statements. Many contingent liabilities, however, are less certain and are required to be disclosed in notes to the financial statements. This is frequently the case with pending lawsuits where the certainty of loss, including the amount of loss, is unknown when the financial statements are issued. Disclosure in this manner puts the reader on notice as to the possible negative consequences of events that have already taken place but do not meet the objectivity standards necessary for inclusion in the body of the financial statements (SFAS No. 5, par. 10).

4.13 DISCLOSURES RELATED TO SPECIFIC FINANCIAL-STATEMENT ELEMENTS.
Whereas the examples of disclosure discussed above are broad in nature and do not
relate to specific financial-statement elements, other disclosures focus attention on individual items in the balance sheet, income statement, or other financial statements. Examples of several of these disclosures are briefly identified and discussed in the following
subsections.

(a) Marketable Securities.   Companies, as a result of having invested cash in the stocks and
bonds of other enterprises, may have marketable securities in the balance sheets. Accepted
accounting procedures call for dividing these securities into two portfolios—current and
noncurrent—based primarily on the intent of management. If management intends to hold the
securities for a long period of time, they are classified in the balance sheet as a noncurrent
asset. If management views the marketable securities as a secondary cash source, investing
excess funds as they are available and disinvesting them as cash is needed, then the
marketable securities are classified in the balance sheet as a current asset.

Because marketable securities may appear in two places in the balance sheet and each
portfolio represents a group of individual investment assets, information must be presented in
the financial statements about the securities in the portfolios. This information includes their
end-of-period value, increases and decreases in the value of securities included in the
portfolios, and the accounting method used in identifying those securities that were sold
during the accounting period (SFAS No. 12, par. 12).

(b) Inventories.   In addition to disclosing information about the accounting policy employed
in accounting for inventories, detailed information about the dollar amounts of inventories
must be disclosed. For example, a manufacturing company may have several types of
inventories—raw materials, work-in-process, and finished goods. The financial statements
or related notes should include an indication of the dollar amounts of each of these types of
inventories (ARB No. 43, Ch. 4, par. 3).

(c) Plant Assets and Depreciation.   Plant assets include land, buildings, equipment, furniture,
fixtures, and other long-lived assets that are required to accomplish the business purposes of
an enterprise. Plant assets are subject to depreciation whereby a portion of the cost of the
asset is written off as an expense during those years in which the asset is used. The remaining
unamortized cost is presented in the balance sheet as an asset.

Information about the amount of plant assets in individual categories, such as equipment
and fixtures, is believed to be important to readers of financial statements. In addition,
information about the historical cost of those assets and the portion of the cost that has been
written off as depreciation to date is also important. This information may be presented in the
body of the financial statements but is often found among notes to the financial statements
(APB Opinion No. 12, par. 5).

(d) Long-Term Debt.   The amount of long-term debt is presented in the enterprise's balance
sheet. That amount may be made up of many different debt issues, having different interest
rates, maturity dates, and other characteristics. Information about the details of individual
debt issues that make up the total of long-term debt is frequently found among the notes to
financial statements in order to avoid unnecessary details in the statements themselves.

(e) Capital Stock.   A corporation may have one or more types of preferred and common stock
in its capital structure. Information about the characteristics of individual issues of capital
stock, such as the number of shares the corporation is authorized to issue, the par or stated
value, and the dividend rate, is disclosed in the financial statement or related notes.

The above are a few examples of the types of information that are usually disclosed in
notes to the financial statements. Disclosures in a variety of other areas, such as leases,

pensions, and income taxes, can be quite long and complex. They include a great deal of information that would otherwise be unknown to the user of the financial statements.

4.14 SPECIAL DISCLOSURES OF PUBLICLY HELD COMPANIES. Publicly held companies must adhere to a higher disclosure standard in certain areas than companies that are not publicly held. The accounting profession has been concerned with **standards overload**—a situation that arises where accounting standards developed for large publicly held companies are then extended to all companies. Concern has been expressed that this situation has led to an unreasonable disclosure burden for small, privately held companies. In partial response to this situation, the FASB has limited certain disclosure requirements to publicly held companies. Several of these are briefly discussed in the following paragraphs.

(a) Segment Disclosures. Segment disclosures are required in three areas: (1) product lines or industry segments, (2) geographic segments, and (3) major customers. In all three areas, where certain materiality tests are met, the reporting enterprise must separate out the numbers in the financial statements on a disaggregated basis so that the reader may become more aware of the risks of the enterprise in the three specified areas (SFAS No. 14, par. 3).

(b) Earnings per Share. EPS figures are required only in the income statements of publicly held companies. These are presented as part of the income statement and indicate the amount of net income attributable to each share of outstanding common stock, after providing for dividends that would be required on preferred stock. Nonpublic companies are not required to make these disclosures in their income statements (SFAS No. 21, par. 12).

(c) Interim Reporting. Companies may provide information to their stockholders and others on a more frequent basis than annually. Many companies provide information regularly on a quarterly basis.

Publicly held companies that report regularly on an interim basis must meet certain specific disclosure standards. These standards specify the information that must be presented, as a minimum, in these reports (APB Opinion No. 28, par. 30).

LIMITATIONS OF FINANCIAL STATEMENTS

Financial statements are important means of communications between management and external parties, primarily investors and creditors. These statements are subject to certain limitations, several of which are introduced in this final section.

4.15 STABLE MONETARY UNIT ASSUMPTION. Financial statements are prepared with an underlying assumption of a stable monetary unit. Accountants recognize that the monetary unit does, in fact, change in value over time. In the United States, the monetary unit is the dollar and in recent years the changes in value have been declines as the general level of prices has risen consistently. Experiments have been undertaken to attempt to measure the impact of changing prices on the financial statements. To date, however, no single approach has been accepted, nor is any adjustment for changing prices required in financial statements prepared in accordance with accepted accounting principles.

Perhaps the best way to describe the underlying assumption is not as a stable monetary unit but rather as a monetary unit with changes in value from period to period that are not large enough to have a material impact on the financial statements. Undoubtedly this will continue to be a controversial issue in accounting, and experimentation with different methods of accounting for the impact of changing prices will continue to take place. In the meantime, astute readers of financial statements should be generally aware that some distortion may exist because of the impact of changing prices and that the failure to adjust for such changes represents a limitation of financial statements.

4.16 HISTORICAL ORIENTATION.   Financial statements are essentially historical representations of business activity. They are frequently used to anticipate the future and their historical orientation imposes a limitation on their value in this regard. Despite the historical orientation of the statements, accountants must consider the future to make many of the judgments that are required in reporting about past activities. For example, in determining an appropriate amount of depreciation on a plant asset for an accounting period, the accountant must make an assumption concerning how long the reporting entity will use that asset.

4.17 JUDGMENT AND ESTIMATION.   Despite the precise appearance of the financial statements, they are tentative in nature and require a great deal of judgment and estimation. Any attempt to partition ongoing business activity into relatively short periods of time, such as a year or quarter, requires judgment and estimation about future events and about the outcome of incomplete past events. Although accountants attempt to apply an objectivity standard to the extent possible, in many instances they must resort to judgment and estimation to determine important amounts that affect the elements of the financial statements.

4.18 MANAGEMENT ABILITY TO INFLUENCE CONTENT.   Within limits, management has the ability to influence the content of financial statements. Employment of certain end-of-period activities can have an important impact on the relationships that investors and creditors consider particularly important in assessing the financial activities of the enterprise.

4.19 UNRECORDED ITEMS.   The accounting system does not attempt to capture all aspects of business activity that may be important factors in the success of the enterprise. One example of an item that may be very important to the future well-being of the enterprise is its human resources. For many companies, its management personnel and labor force may be its most valuable "asset," but nowhere in the balance sheet does this item appear.

Financial statements are limited to those elements that can be measured with reasonable objectivity and that are required by GAAP. They should be viewed as only partial representations, rather than complete representations, of the business enterprise.

4.20 FLEXIBILITY VERSUS UNIFORMITY.   An ongoing debate in the accounting profession is flexibility versus uniformity. This controversy asks the question: Should enterprises have latitude in the manner in which they identify and measure the elements of the financial statements (i.e., flexibility), or should all enterprises follow precisely the same rules and procedures in preparing statements (i.e., uniformity)?

At present, elements of both flexibility and uniformity exist in GAAP. In some areas, enterprises have great latitude in accounting for and presenting certain items in their financial statements. In other areas, enterprises are essentially limited to a single process or procedure. The FASB seeks to identify areas of financial reporting where unjustified differences exist in practice. One objective of the FASB is to narrow these areas of difference in practice so that all enterprises account for similar transactions in essentially the same manner. This is a very long process, however, and undoubtedly both flexibility and uniformity in different areas of accounting will exist for years to come.

SOURCES AND SUGGESTED REFERENCES

Accounting Principles Board, "Omnibus Opinion—1967," APB Opinion No. 12, AICPA, New York, 1967.

——, "Disclosure of Accounting Policies," APB Opinion No. 22, AICPA, New York, 1972.

——, "Interim Financial Reporting," APB Opinion No. 28, AICPA, New York, 1973.

American Institute of Certified Public Accountants, Accounting Research Bulletin No. 43, Ch. 3, "Working Capital," AICPA, New York, 1953.

———, Accounting Research Bulletin No. 43, Ch. 4, "Inventory Pricing," AICPA, New York, 1953.

———, AICPA Financial Statement Preparation Manual: Nonauthoritative Practice Aids, AICPA, New York, 1989.

———, "Subsequent Events," Statement on Auditing Standards No. 12, AICPA, New York, 1972.

———, "The Auditor's Consideration of an Entity's Ability to Continue as a Going Concern," Statement on Auditing Standards No. 59, AICPA, New York, 1988.

Financial Accounting Standards Board, "Objectives of Financial Reporting by Business Enterprises," Statement of Financial Accounting Concepts No. 1, FASB, Stamford, CT, 1978.

———, "Elements of Financial Statements," Statement of Financial Accounting Concepts No. 6, FASB, Stamford, CT, 1985.

———, "Accounting for Contingencies," Statement of Financial Accounting Standards No. 5, FASB, Stamford, CT, 1975.

———, "Accounting for Certain Marketable Securities," Statement of Financial Accounting Standards No. 12, FASB, Stamford, CT, 1975.

———, "Financial Reporting for Segments of a Business Enterprise," Statement of Financial Accounting Standards No. 14, FASB, Stamford, CT, 1976.

———, "Suspension of the Reporting of Earnings Per Share and Segment Information by Nonpublic Enterprises," Statement of Financial Accounting Standards No. 21, FASB, Stamford, CT, 1978.

———, "Related Party Disclosures," Statement of Financial Accounting Standards No. 57, FASB, Stamford, CT, 1982.

———, "Statement of Cash Flows," Statement of Financial Accounting Standards No. 95, FASB, Stamford, CT, 1987.

CHAPTER 5

INCOME STATEMENT PRESENTATION AND EARNINGS PER SHARE

Irwin Goldberg, CPA

Deloitte & Touche

CONTENTS

OFFICIAL PRONOUNCEMENTS ON INCOME STATEMENT PRESENTATION

An enterprise reports its results of operations in a set of financial statements that includes an income statement. The format of the income statement and its components of income have been the subject of controversy, and as a result numerous pronouncements of professional accounting bodies have addressed related issues. For the most part the central issues discussed in these pronouncements involve the distinction between normal recurring items of profit and loss and other items that affect the determination of income.

One such pronouncement, APB Opinion No. 9, "Reporting the Results of Operations," states that net income reported on an income statement should reflect all items of profit and loss recognized during the period with the exception of **prior period adjustments.** The APB also refined the appropriate reporting format in APB Opinion No. 30, "Reporting the Results of Operations—Reporting the Effects of Disposal of a Segment of a Business, and Extraordinary, Unusual and Infrequently Occurring Events and Transactions." Both of these Opinions required that extraordinary items, as defined on page 5.4, be segregated from the results of continuing and ordinary operations of the entity. Opinion No. 30 expanded the categories to be segregated from continuing and ordinary operations by specifying the treatment of **discontinued operations** and **unusual or infrequently occurring items.**

In addition to the segregated items referred to above, APB Opinion No. 20, "Accounting Changes," stated that the effects of specified **changes in accounting principles** should be disclosed on the income statement between the captions, extraordinary items, and net income.

DISCONTINUED OPERATIONS

In general, the term **discontinued operations** refers to the operations of a "segment of a business" which has been or is planned to be abandoned or otherwise disposed of. The term **segment of a business** is defined as a component of an entity whose operations encompass a separate major line of business or class of customer. A component can be a subsidiary, division, joint venture, or unconsolidated investee. This definition of segment of a business should not be confused with the use of the term "segment" in SFAS No. 14, "Financial Reporting for Segments of a Business Enterprise."

5.1 MEASUREMENT DATE.   The component should be reported as discontinued during the first reporting period in which management having the requisite authority commits itself to a formal plan of disposal. This is referred to as the **measurement date.** Once the decision to dispose of the component has been made, the component's operating results prior to the measurement date should be presented on the income statement as a separate category before extraordinary items. Any financial statements for a prior period, presented for comparative purposes, should be restated to conform to this presentation.

The formal plan of disposal should include (1) an identification of the major assets to be disposed, (2) the expected method of disposal, (3) the expected period required to complete the disposal, (4) an estimate of the results of operations from the measurement date to the disposal date (phaseout period) and (5) the estimated proceeds to be realized by disposal.

5.2 DISPOSAL DATE.   The **disposal date** is the closing date if a sale is contemplated. Any gain or loss on the actual disposal of the segment, combined with the operating results of the discontinued operations should be disclosed separately on the face of the income statement or in a note. Income taxes applicable to both items should also be disclosed on the face of the income statement or in a note to the financial statements.

5.3 EXAMPLES OF DISCONTINUED OPERATIONS.   APB Opinion No. 30 states that the discontinuance of a part of a segment of a business, that is the phasing out of a product line or class of service, or a shift in production or marketing emphasis or location is incidental to the evolution of an entity and, accordingly, does not qualify for treatment as a **discontinued operation.** Although in theory the criteria may seem straightforward, accountants have had difficulty interpreting these broad criteria in practice. Recognizing this difficulty, the AICPA issued "Accounting Interpretation of APB Opinion No. 30" in November 1973 to provide guidance on the classifications found in Opinion No. 30. The interpretations provide the following situations as examples that qualify as discontinued operations:

1. The sale of a major division that represents an entity's only activity in a specific industry; the assets and results of operations of the division are clearly separable.
2. The sale by a meat-packing company of a 25% interest in a professional ball club that they had accounted for under the equity method.
3. The sale by a communications company of all its radio stations (constituting 30% of total consolidated revenues). The remaining activities are television stations and a publishing company. The assets and results of operations of the radio station are clearly separable both physically and operationally.
4. The disposal by a food distributor of one of its two food divisions, which use significantly different channels of distribution. One division sells food wholesale primarily to supermarket chains, and the other division sells food through its chain of fast food restaurants, some of which are franchised and some of which are company-owned. Although both divisions are in the business of distribution of food, the sale of food through fast food outlets is vastly different in nature from wholesaling food to supermarket chains. Thus, by having two major classes of customers, the company has two segments of business.

5.4 RECORDING DISCONTINUED OPERATIONS.   The method of recording the discontinuation or disposition of a business segment is determined by whether there is a gain or a loss. A gain should be recognized when it is realized, usually at the disposal date. Losses, on the other hand, should be anticipated and recorded at the measurement date. The gain or loss on disposal is calculated at the measurement date, using estimates of the results of operations during the phaseout period. The APB was concerned that the gain or loss on disposal could conceal normal write-downs on a going-concern basis, for example, inventory or receivable adjustments. Thus it stated that such write-downs should be included in results of operations prior to the measurement date unless clearly and directly associated with the disposal decision. The EITF in Issue No. 85-36, "Discontinued Operations with Expected Gain and Interim Operating Losses,"considered the need for clarification of APB Opinion No. 30 and the related interpretations thereof in accounting for any expected losses from the measurement date to the disposal date when a gain on disposal was expected. The Task Force consensus stated that estimated losses from operations should only be deferred until the disposal date if there is reasonable assurance that a net gain will be realized. The Task Force also reached consensus on two underlying issues. The first consensus applied the previous consensus to sales that do not meet the criteria of a segment. Second, it stated that all multiple disposals of segments under the same formal plan should be reported as a combined amount. However, if the criteria for discontinued segments are not met, these disposals, such as a portion of a line of business, should not be combined.

5.5 ALLOCATION OF COSTS AND EXPENSES.   The EITF also considered the questions of whether interest or general corporate overhead could be allocated to a discontinued operation. The Task Force reached a consensus that general corporate overhead may not be allocated. Interest may be allocated although it is not required to be allocated. If interest is allocated, the calculation of the method to be used is described in EITF Issue No. 87-24 "Allocation of Interest to Discontinued Operations." The SEC observer indicated that public companies must clearly disclose the accounting policy to allocate interest, the method used to determine the amount of interest allocated and the amount allocated to premeasurement date and estimated predisposal date periods.

5.6 DISCLOSURE OF DISCONTINUED OPERATIONS.   Certain disclosures are required for the periods from the measurement date to the disposal date.

1. Identification of the discontinued segment.
2. Expected disposal date and manner of disposal (sale or abandonment).
3. Remaining assets and liabilities of segment at the balance sheet date.
4. Results of operations and any proceeds from disposal of the segment during the period from the measurement date to the balance sheet date (and a comparison with any prior estimates).

Disclosure of per share data, although not separately required for discontinued operations, is commonly given on the face of the income statement or in the notes.

EXTRAORDINARY ITEMS

An extraordinary item is an event or transaction that meets two criteria: it must be both unusual in nature and infrequent in occurrence. Otherwise, an event or transaction is generally presumed to be either an ordinary or a usual activity of the entity. Being either unusual in nature or infrequent in occurrence does not qualify it as an extraordinary item (see section 5.11).

5.7 UNUSUAL NATURE.   As mentioned above, the first criteria an item must meet to be considered extraordinary is to be **unusual.** The underlying event or transaction should be clearly unrelated to the ordinary and typical activities of the entity. This definition encompasses the specific characteristics of the entity, including, for example, the industry in which it operates, the geographical location of its operations, and the extent of government regulation. Thus an event or transaction may be unusual for one industry but normal for another.

5.8 INFREQUENTLY OCCURRING.   The second criterion for an extraordinary item to meet is that the event or transaction is not reasonably expected to recur in the foreseeable future and is not considered to be frequently occurring. This definition considers the same features as items of unusual nature, such as industry, geographical location, and government regulation. Thus this criterion may be met by one company whereas the same underlying event would not be infrequent to another company. Past history of the company provides evidence to assess the probability of recurrence of an event.

5.9 APPLICATION OF CRITERIA.   Certain gains and losses are, by definition (APB Opinion No. 30, par. 23), considered **not extraordinary items,** such as:

1. Write-down of receivables, inventories, equipment leased to others, or intangible assets.
2. Gains or losses from foreign exchange transactions or translations (including major devaluations and revaluations).
3. Gains or losses on the disposal of a segment of a business (discontinued operations).
4. Gains or losses from the sale or abandonment of property, plant, or equipment used in a business.
5. Effects of a strike (including an indirect effect such as a strike against a major supplier).
6. Adjustment of accruals on long-term contracts.

Only in rare instances, may an event or transaction included in item 1 or 4 above clearly meet the criteria and be included in extraordinary items. Such instances would occur if the gain or loss on such an event or transaction is the direct result of a major casualty, an expropriation, or a prohibition under a newly enacted law.

5.10 EXCEPTIONS TO CRITERIA.   Some items that apparently would not meet the criteria of an extraordinary item may be classified as such under existing authoritative literature. Two such items that fit this description are gains and losses on early extinguishment of debt as cited in SFAS No. 4 ''Reporting Gains and Losses from Extinguishment of Debt,''and gain on the restructuring of debt in a troubled situation as discussed in SFAS No. 15, ''Accounting by Debtors and Creditors for Troubled Debt Restructurings.'' The accounting and reporting for early extinguishments and troubled debt restructurings are discussed in Chapter 18.

5.11 REPORTING AN EXTRAORDINARY ITEM.   The effect of an extraordinary item should be segregated if its effect is material to income before extraordinary items, to the trend in earnings before extraordinary items, or to other appropriate criteria. The materiality of individual events or transactions is considered separately and not aggregated unless the effects result from a single identifiable transaction or event that meets the criteria of an extraordinary item. The preference expressed in APB Opinion No. 30 is for individual description captions and amounts for each extraordinary event or transaction on the face of the income statement. However, disclosure in the notes to financial statements describing the nature of the event or transaction comprising the extraordinary item and the principal items entering the calculation of the gain or loss is acceptable. The extraordinary item should be shown net of applicable income taxes.

Per share amounts for income before extraordinary items and net income should be given on the face of the income statement. There is no requirement to give the per share amount of the extraordinary items, but such disclosure is common.

MATERIAL GAINS AND LOSSES—UNUSUAL OR INFREQUENTLY OCCURRING, NOT EXTRAORDINARY

A material event or transaction that is either unusual or infrequently occurring, but not both, is by definition not an extraordinary item. Material gains or losses of this nature should be shown separately on the face of the income statement as a component of income from continuing operations. These items are not shown net of tax, nor is per share disclosure permitted on the face of the income statement. However, note disclosure may be given that presents the item net of tax and discloses the per share effects. The discussion that follows covers four special items, not extraordinary, and their reporting: disposal of part of a segment, restructuring charges, takeover defense, and sale of stock by a subsidiary.

5.12 DISPOSAL OF PART OF A SEGMENT OF A BUSINESS.   The gain or loss on the disposal of part of a segment of a business is not an extraordinary item or a discontinued operation. Thus it may be reported as a separate component of continuing operations. The measurement principles used to calculate gain or loss on disposal are identical to those for **discontinued operations.** The results of operations prior to the measurement date should not, however, be shown separately on the income statement. This information may be disclosed in the notes to financial statements along with per share data.

Some examples of situations not qualifying as discontinued operations that were also given in the interpretations of APB Opinion No. 30 are:

1. Sale of a major subsidiary in one country by an entity that has other activities in the same industry in other countries.
2. Sale of an interest in an equity investee in the same line of business as the investor.
3. Sale of assets related to the manufacture of wool suits when the entity manufactures suits from synthetic products elsewhere (considered only product line disposal.)

5.13 RESTRUCTURING CHARGES.   During the middle-to-late 1980s, enterprises began to restructure their operations. These corporate restructurings involved sales of equipment or facilities, severance of employees, and relocation of operations. The EITF considered the income statement presentation (ordinary or extraordinary) of such restructurings but was unable to reach a consensus in EITF Issue No. 86-22, "Display of Business Restructuring Provisions in the Income Statement". It only stated that entities should use their own judgment. The SEC subsequently addressed this issue in SAB No. 67, "Income Statement Presentation of Restructuring Charges," issued in December 1986. The SEC position stated that restructuring charges should be shown as a component of continuing operations and separately disclosed if material. Since SABs do not apply to nonpublic companies, the EITF considered in Issue No. 87-4, "Restructuring of Operations: Implications of SEC Staff Accounting Bulletin No. 67" whether the SEC position was GAAP for nonpublic companies. The Task Force indicated that following the SAB provisions is not required for nonpublic enterprises to be in accordance with GAAP. The Task Force agreed that consistent with its views expressed in Issue No. 86-22, nonpublic companies should exercise judgment in selecting the most meaningful income statement presentation.

The SEC observer later provided clarification of the extent of SAB No. 67, such as:

1. SAB No. 67 was not intended to address the presentation of a sale of assets or a portion of a line of business.

2. The SAB restates the position of the SEC observer that showing "earnings from operations before provisions for restructuring of operations," which is acceptable under EITF Issue No. 86-22 is not acceptable for SEC registrants.

5.14 TAKEOVER DEFENSE.   A question created by the takeover surge is the appropriate presentation of takeover defense expenses on the income statement. The FASB issued FTB No. 85-6, which states:

1. A company should not classify the cost to defend itself from a takeover or the costs attributable to a "standstill" agreement as an extraordinary item.

2. If a company repurchases shares for a price significantly in excess of current market from an unwanted suitor, it must include stated or unstated rights. Accordingly, only the amount representing fair value should be accounted for as the cost of Treasury shares, any excess should be accounted for according to its substance, presumably charged to expense. The SEC has stated that in applying FTB No. 85-6 quoted market represents fair value; use of appraised values that differ from public market values is not acceptable.

5.15 SALES OF STOCK BY A SUBSIDIARY.   Prior to the issuance in 1983 of SAB No. 51, "Accounting for Sales of Stock by a Subsidiary," most parent companies had accounted for the effects on its equity in the subsidiary of a sale of additional stock by a subsidiary as a capital transaction. In SAB No. 51, the SEC indicated that it had reconsidered this position where the sale of such shares by the subsidiary is not part of a broader corporate reorganization. The SEC, in its reconsideration, stated that it accepts the advisory conclusions of the AICPA issues paper "Accounting in Consideration for Issuances of a Subsidiary's Stock," which indicates that profit or loss should be recognized in these situations. The SEC concluded that if gains (losses) are recognized from issuances of a subsidiary's stock as income statement items, they should be shown as a separate line item (without regard for materiality) and clearly designated as nonoperating. In a recent meeting of the SEC Regulations Committee of the AICPA, the chief accountant of the SEC indicated that SAB No. 51 might be modified. Subsequently SAB No. 81, "Gain Recognition on the Sale of a Business or Operating Assets to a Highly Leveraged Entity," was issued in 1989, indicating that gain recognition may not be appropriate where a subsidiary is sold to a highly leveraged entity. Further, SAB No. 84, "Accounting for Sales of Stock by a Subsidiary," which was also issued in 1989, gives additional guidance on recognizing a sale of stock by a subsidiary as a gain.

ACCOUNTING CHANGES

The APB stated in Opinion No. 20, "Accounting Changes," that:

> A change in accounting by a reporting entity may significantly affect the presentation of both financial position and results of operations for an accounting period and the trends shown in comparative financial statements and historical summaries. The change should therefore be reported in a manner which will facilitate analysis and understanding of the financial statements.

APB Opinion No. 20 defines the term **accounting change** to mean a change in (1) principle, (2) estimate, and (3) reporting entity. This opinion also defines and discusses "corrections of errors" in previously issued financial statements, although it concludes that an item of this nature is not an accounting change.

5.16 GENERAL CHANGES IN ACCOUNTING PRINCIPLE.   A change in accounting principle involves the adoption of a generally accepted accounting principle different from the one previously used for reporting purposes. Thus a change in accounting principle involves a choice among two or more generally accepted accounting principles and the method of applying the chosen principle. It does not include (1) initial adoption of an accounting principle to report first-time or previously immaterial events or transactions, or (2) adoption or modification of an accounting principle because of events or transactions that are clearly different in substance from previously occurring events or transactions.

The APB presumed that, once an accounting principle had been adopted by an entity, it should not be changed unless the alternative accounting principle was preferable in the particular circumstances. Accordingly, note disclosure is required describing the nature of a change in accounting principle and justifying the new method as preferable.

(a) Cumulative Effect Changes.   Most changes in accounting principles, except for **special changes** (explained later), should be recognized by showing the cumulative effect of the change at the beginning of the year as a single-line item between extraordinary items and net income. The effect of the change on income before extraordinary items and net income (including per share amounts) should be disclosed, usually in a note. The cumulative effect of an accounting change is calculated by taking the difference between (1) retained earnings at the beginning of the year in which the change is made, and (2) the calculated amount of such retained earnings had the change been retroactive, adjusted for any related income tax effect.

A pro forma calculation of income before extraordinary items and net income (including primary and fully diluted per share amounts) is required to be shown on the face of the income statement as if the new accounting principle had been adopted retroactively. This pro forma calculation is required when periods prior to the change are shown in the income statement. The pro forma calculation should include the effect of any nondiscretionary adjustments based on income, such as profit-sharing and bonus amounts, net of related income tax effect. The purpose of the pro forma presentation is to show the earnings pattern of the enterprise as if the new principle had been adopted retroactively.

Some changes in accounting principle may be adopted for identifiable long-lived assets on a go forward basis. For example, an entity may adopt the straight-line depreciation method for newly acquired assets but continue to use an accelerated method for previously acquired assets. This type of change does not entail a cumulative-effect adjustment; however, the nature and the effect of the change on income before extraordinary items and net income (including per share amounts) must be disclosed. If the new depreciation method (in this example, straight-line) is adopted for previously acquired assets, it is a cumulative-effect type change, requiring the disclosures applicable thereto.

(b) Cumulative Effect of a Change Unknown.   If the cumulative and pro forma effects of a change in accounting principle cannot be determined, they may be omitted. However, the effect on the results of operations for the period of change and the reason for omitting the cumulative and pro forma effects must be disclosed. This situation should be rare.

A common example of a change in which the effect is indeterminable is a change from the first-in, first-out (FIFO) method of accounting for inventory to the last-in, first-out (LIFO) method. The prior year's ending inventory (on FIFO) may be assumed to the current year's beginning inventory (on LIFO), and there will be no effect of the change; however, this answer will vary depending on which year is considered the initial year of adoption of the LIFO method. If it is possible to calculate the cumulative effect but not the pro forma effect on individual years, the reason for the omission of pro forma information must be disclosed.

5.17 SPECIAL CHANGES IN ACCOUNTING PRINCIPLE.   In certain instances, the restatement of prior financial statements is required when changing an accounting principle. These special situations are (1) a change from LIFO to any other method of inventory pricing, (2) a change in the method of accounting for long-term construction type contracts, and (3) a change to or from the "full cost" method used in the extractive industries. For these changes, the nature, justification, and effects must be disclosed, as well as the effect on income before extraordinary items, net income, and per share data for all prior periods presented.

(a) Going Public Exemption.   Another accounting principle change which should be effected in a retroactive manner is one adopted in an initial public distribution. It is referred to as the "going public exemption" and occurs when an entity first issues its financial statements to (1) obtain additional equity capital from investors, (2) effect a business combination, or (3) register securities. The exemption is available only once and cannot be taken by companies whose securities are widely held.

(b) Authoritative Pronouncement Exemption.   APB Opinion No. 20's general rules on reporting the effects of accounting changes do not apply when an authoritative body issues a pronouncement that creates a new accounting principle or expresses a preference for an existing one. In that case, issuance of the pronouncement is adequate justification for the change. Also, if the manner of implementing the change is indicated in the pronouncement, that method should be followed. For example, a retroactive change was mandated in 1987 by SFAS No. 94, "Consolidation of All Majority-Owned Subsidiaries."

5.18 CHANGES IN ACCOUNTING ESTIMATE.   Changes in accounting estimates are a normal part of the operations of an entity and the estimation of the effects of future events is an inherent part of preparing financial statements. Accounting estimates involve the judgments that management of the entity must make concerning incomplete transactions or events on the basis of the information presently available. Obviously these estimates change as new or better information becomes available or new events occur. Examples of items that require estimates are (1) uncollectible receivables, (2) inventory obsolescence, (3) service lives and salvage value of depreciable assets, (4) warranty costs, (5) amortization period of deferred charges, and (6) recoverable mineral reserves.

Changes in estimates are sometimes difficult for the accountant to distinguish from an accounting principle change as they cannot clearly be classified as either one or the other. For example, a change from deferral and amortization of an expense item to expensing as incurred, when the future benefits of the deferred item are doubtful, may have been made in partial or complete recognition of a change in estimated future benefits. Such changes in principle which are inseparable from changes in estimate are treated as changes in estimate.

The effects, if material, of a change in estimate on income before extraordinary items and net income (including per share amounts) for the current year and for future years, if applicable, should be disclosed in a note describing the change. A change in estimate should not be accounted for retroactively or by reporting pro forma amounts. Disclosure of changes in estimates made in the ordinary course of business (e.g., uncollectible receivables, percentage complete on long-term contracts, or inventory obsolescence) is not required; however, it is recommended if the effect of a change in estimate is material.

5.19 CHANGES IN REPORTING ENTITY.   A change in reporting entity is a special type of change in accounting principle reported by retroactive restatement. This type of change results in financial statements of a different reporting entity and usually is limited mainly to (1) presenting consolidated or combined financial statements in place of financial statements of individual reporting entities, (2) changing specific subsidiaries or companies included in the financial statements of the consolidated or combined group of companies, and (3) changing among cost, equity, and consolidation methods of accounting for subsidiaries or other investments in common stock. The financial statements for the period of a change in reporting entity should disclose the nature and reason for the change and the effect on income before extraordinary items and net income (including per share amounts). A change in reporting entity due to a pooling of interests should be reported as provided in APB Opinion No. 16, "Business Combinations."

5.20 CORRECTION OF AN ERROR.   Although not an accounting change, the correction of an error in previously issued financial statements involves factors similar to those encountered in reporting a change in accounting principle. Errors arise from (1) mathematical mistakes, (2) oversight or misuse of facts existing at the time when financial statements are prepared, and (3) mistakes in the application of accounting principles including a change from an unacceptable accounting principle to a generally accepted accounting principle.

Corrections of errors should be reported as prior period adjustments (see "Prior Period Adjustments" below). The nature of the error and the effect on income before extraordinary items and net income (including per share amounts) should be disclosed in the period when the error was discovered and corrected.

5.21 MATERIALITY.   Materiality, applicable to accounting changes and corrections of errors, is considered in relation to both the effects of individual changes and the aggregate effect of all changes. A change or correction may be material to (1) income before extraordinary items or net income of the current year, or (2) the trend in earnings. In both cases the disclosures referred to above should be made. If the change or correction is not material according to these criteria but is reasonably certain to have a material effect in later periods, disclosure of the change or correction should be made whenever the period of change is presented. SAB No. 40 stated that, if retroactive application of an accounting change is required but prior periods' income statements are not restated because the amounts are immaterial, the cumulative effect of the change should be included in the determination of income for the period in which the change was made. However, if the cumulative effect is material to the current period's income, or to the trend in earnings, prior period income statements would have to be adjusted.

5.22 DISCLOSURES REQUIRED FOR CHANGES IN ACCOUNTING.   The following disclosures are required when an entity effects a change in accounting:

1. Nature and justification for change.
2. Per share effect of cumulative change in accounting on face of income statement.
3. Dollar amount and per share effect on current period in notes.
4. Pro forma amount per share effect as if retroactive restatement on face of income statement.
5. If future periods affected, dollar amount and per share effect on current period.
6. Nature, amount, and per share effect on previously issued financial statements.

5.23 PREFERABILITY LETTER.   The first Form 10Q, quarterly financial statements, filed with the SEC subsequent to an accounting change, must include a preferability letter prepared by the company's accountants. A preferability letter for a change made in the fourth quarter of the fiscal year may be submitted in the company's annual report on Form 10K. If this is not done, the preferability letter must be submitted when filing the next Form 10Q.

Disclosure of a change in accounting principle should include an explanation of why the new accounting principle is preferable. Auditing standards require that the accountant assess the reasonableness of management's justification for the change in accounting principle before concurring. In FRR No. 1 (ASR No. 177) the SEC issued requirements beyond those specified in professional standards. By amending Form 10Q, FRR No. 1 (ASR No. 177) requires the accountant to issue a letter indicating whether the newly adopted accounting principle is preferable under the circumstances. A letter need not be issued, however, if the change in accounting principle was mandated by the FASB.

PRIOR PERIOD ADJUSTMENTS

The items of profit and loss which should be reported as prior period adjustments, as specified in paragraph 10 of SFAS No. 16, "Prior Period Adjustments," are (1) corrections of errors, and (2) realization of income tax benefits of preacquisition operating loss carryforwards of purchased subsidiaries. The disclosure of their effects, both gross and net of taxes, on net income of prior periods is required in the financial statements for the year of the adjustment. Disclosure of the effects on each prior period presented and on per share earnings are also required.

In the deliberations leading to the issuance in 1977 of SFAS No. 16, questions arose as to the statement's applicability to interim as well as annual financial statements. The FASB concluded that certain practices regarding interim information and prior period adjustments should be continued and others should be discontinued. A section entitled "Adjustments Related to Prior Interim Periods of the Current Fiscal Year" was included in SFAS No. 16. Interim reporting is covered in Chapter 9.

REPORTING OF UNUSUAL EVENTS AND TRANSACTIONS

The following listings should provide guidance to accountants in the reporting of events and transactions as extraordinary, or material gains and losses not considered extraordinary, and accounting changes. The reporting of these items requires considerable judgment.

A listing for discontinued operations is not presented because the reporting of this type of event does not vary in practice. Furthermore, the issuance of SFAS No. 16 has restricted the type of items to be reported as prior period adjustments to the extent that such a listing is not necessary.

The primary sources used to obtain this listing are: "Accounting Trends and Techniques," (AICPA, 1987, 1988) and *Updated Illustrations of Reporting Accounting Changes* (Clark and Lorenson, 1987).

EXTRAORDINARY ITEMS

Adjustment of prior period extraordinary item.

Debt extinguishments.

Expropriation.

Major casualties (fire).

Tax loss carryforwards (Under APB Opinion No. 11).

MATERIAL GAINS AND LOSSES NOT CONSIDERED EXTRAORDINARY

Diminished value of intangibles.

Discontinuance of part of a business.

Excess insurance proceeds.

Gain from sale of assets.

Gain on sale of equity interest in subsidiary.

Partial closing of operation facility.

Plant relocation expenses.

Provision for plant closing.

Realignment of operations.

Reduction in plant closing provision.

Restructuring costs.

Sale of investments.

Settlement of antitrust litigation:
  Expense.
  Income.

Settlement of claims.

Strike expense.

Takeover defense.

ACCOUNTING CHANGES

Cumulative-Effect Type Change

Change from flow-through to deferral method for certain costs.

Change in depreciation method.

Change in method of determining inventory costs.

Retroactive-Restatement Type Change

Change from the full-cost method to successful efforts method of oil and gas properties.

Change from LIFO method to FIFO method of inventory valuation.

Change to conform to FASB statements which require or permit retroactive restatement.

Correction of an Error

Change from unacceptable principle to GAAP.

Computational error.

Subsequent discovery of facts existing at date of accountants' report.

Change in Reporting Entity

Change from equity basis to consolidated basis (SFAS No. 94).

Poolings of interests.

Cumulative Effect Not Determinable or Required

Change from FIFO cost to LIFO method inventory valuation.

Change in depreciation method for new assets only.

Change in Estimate

Of allowance for doubtful accounts.

Of depreciable lives.

Of income taxes.

Of restructuring costs.

SEC INCOME STATEMENT PRESENTATION REQUIREMENTS FOR SPECIFIC INDUSTRIES

5.24 RETAIL COMPANIES.   The SEC expressed its views in SAB No. 1 (codified in 1981 in SAB No. 40) on including leased or licensed departments' revenues in the caption "Total revenues" as is common in the financial statements of department stores. The SEC stated that this practice is acceptable but the amounts should be disclosed separately in the income statement or notes thereto. Further, the service fee income from finance subsidiaries of retail companies should be separately disclosed in the income statement or a note.

5.25 UTILITIES.   SFAS No. 90 "Regulated Enterprises-Accounting for Abandonments and Disallowances of Plant Costs," issued in 1986, implies a utility must charge a portion of the cost of an abandoned power plant to expense. In addition, any costs of a completed plant expected to be disallowed should also be charged to expense. The SEC was asked if these charges could be shown as extraordinary. The SEC responded in SAB No. 72 "Classification of Charges for Abandonments and Disallowances," issued in 1987, that these costs do not meet the criteria of APB Opinion No. 30 for unusual and infrequently occurring and should be shown as part of continuing operations.

5.26 CASINO-MOTELS.   In 1987 the SEC stated in SAB No. 69, "Income Statement Presentation," that registrants having casino and hotel operations should show the income from these operations separately. Thus, casino, hotel, and restaurant operations are commonly disclosed separately.

EARNINGS PER SHARE

EPS is a statistic that has evolved as a tool for comparing the performances of corporations of different size and capital structure and also for comparing the year-to-date results of operations of a single company whose size and capital structure are changing.

5.27 OFFICIAL PRONOUNCEMENTS.   The computation and presentation of EPS are governed principally by APB Opinion No. 15, "Earnings per Share." Additional guidance is provided in the AICPA publication *Computing Earnings per Share* (Ball, 1970) and in an additional interpretation of Opinion No. 15, published in 1970. APB Opinion No. 15 was amended by SFAS No. 21, "Suspension of the Reporting of Earnings per Share and Segment Information by Nonpublic Enterprises," which suspended its applicability to nonpublic companies.

5.28 APB OPINION NO. 15.   APB Opinion No. 15 requires a publicly held corporation to present EPS data on the face of its income statement for each period covered by the income statement. At a minimum, **income (or loss) before extraordinary items per share** and **net income (or net loss) per share** must be presented. Though not expressly required, most companies also present the amount of the **extraordinary items per share.** Additional per share amounts are required if the income statement includes any of the following "below the line" items: **cumulative effect of change in accounting principle, results of discontinued operations, and gain or loss from disposal of a business segment.**

If a company's capital structure is such that per share data could be materially reduced (diluted) in the event that outstanding options or warrants were exercised, convertible securities were converted, or contingently issuable shares were issued, then a dual presentation of **primary EPS** and **fully diluted EPS** is required for each of the items listed in the preceding paragraph.

5.29 APB OPINION NO. 15 EXEMPTIONS.   In addition to the exemption for nonpublic companies granted by SFAS No. 21, the following types of enterprises do not have to present EPS data: mutual companies that do not have common stock (such as mutual savings banks, cooperatives, and credit unions); registered investment companies (mutual funds); government-owned corporations; and nonprofit corporations. Also, EPS data need not be presented in parent company financial statements, wholly owned subsidiaries' financial statements and special purpose financial statements that do not purport to present results of operations.

Although APB Opinion No. 15 does not expressly state it, EPS is not normally presented in combined financial statements of two or more corporations under common control.

5.30 TERMS RELATING TO EPS

(a) Dilution.   A reduction in EPS (or an increase in net loss per share) is a dilution if it results from one of the following assumptions: Convertible securities have been converted, options and warrants have been exercised, or other contingently issuable shares have been issued in fulfillment of certain conditions.

(b) Antidilution.   An increase in EPS (or a reduction in net loss per share) is an antidilution if it results from assumptions similar to those for dilution.

(c) Single Presentation.   This is a presentation, on the face of the income statement for all periods reported therein, of only one type of EPS data, reflecting no adjustment for potential dilution.

(d) Dual Presentation.   A presentation, with equal prominence on the face of the income statement for all periods reported therein, of two types of EPS data, known as primary EPS and fully diluted EPS, is a dual presentation. Each reflects appropriate adjustments for potential dilution.

(e) Primary EPS.   This term refers to the amount of earnings attributable to each share of common stock outstanding plus **dilutive** common stock equivalents. Antidilutive common stock equivalents are ignored. A common stock equivalent is an outstanding potentially dilutive security that is regarded as equivalent, in substance, to common shares.

(f) Fully Diluted EPS.   EPS data reflecting the maximum potential dilution that could result from all dilutive conversions, exercises, and other contingent issuances constitute fully diluted EPS. Antidilutive securities are ignored in computing fully diluted EPS unless actually issued.

(g) Simple Capital Structure.   If a company's capital structure is simple (i.e., no potentially dilutive security was outstanding during a particular accounting period), single presentation of EPS data is appropriate for that period. However, if income statements covering two or more periods are presented together for comparative purposes and dual presentation is required for one or more of these periods, dual presentation is required for all periods.

(h) Complex Capital Structure.   If a company's capital structure is complex (i.e., a potentially dilutive security was outstanding during a particular accounting period), dual presentation is required for that period, with two exceptions. One exception is for immateriality reasons: If computation of both primary and fully diluted EPS results in less than 3% dilution, single presentation may be used (though dual presentation is also acceptable). The second exception is for antidilution: If each and every potentially dilutive security is antidilutive (i.e., would increase EPS or reduce net loss per share), single presentation is appropriate.

EPS COMPUTATION AND PRESENTATION

The following discussion presents a summary of the computation and presentation requirements for EPS data under APB Opinion No. 15.

5.31 SINGLE PRESENTATION, NO DILUTION.   If the single presentation of EPS reflecting no adjustment for potential dilution is appropriate, the EPS computation is relatively simple. Basically, it is net income divided by the number of shares outstanding. More precisely, it is:

$$\frac{\text{Net income after deducting dividends on preferred stock and other claims of senior securities}}{\text{weighted average number of common shares outstanding during the period after appropriate adjustments}}$$

Adjustments are required for stock dividends or splits (including those effected after the balance sheet date but prior to issuance of the financial statements) and after adjustments to reflect the number of shares issued in poolings of interest retroactively to the beginning of year.

The following example illustrates the computation of the weighted average number of shares outstanding. Assume that the changes in a company's outstanding common shares during a year are as follows:

Date	Change in Common Shares	Number of Shares
January 1	Outstanding at start of year	900
January 16	Issued on exercise of options	100
April 1	Issued as 10% stock dividend	100
August 11	Issued in pooling of interests	500
September 2	Repurchase of treasury shares	(200)
October 19	Issued for cash	400
December 31	Outstanding at end of year	1,800

Computation of the weighted average number of shares on a "days outstanding" basis would be as follows:

Date	Increase (Decrease)	Cumulative Total	Days Outstanding	Shares Days
January 1		900		
Plus adjustments for:				
10% stock dividend	+ 90			
Shares issued in pooling	+500			
January 1 adjusted		1,490 ×	15	= 22,350
January 16 issuance of options	100			
Plus adjustment for:				
10% stock dividend	+ 10	1,600 ×	229	= 366,400
September 2 Treasury repurchase	− 200	1,400 ×	47	= 65,800
October 19 cash issuance	+400	1,800 ×	74	= 133,200
			365	587,750

The weighted average number of shares outstanding for the year would be

$$\frac{587,750}{365} = 1,610 \text{ shares}$$

In computing the weighted average number of outstanding shares, 90 of the 100 shares issued on April 1 as a 10% stock dividend are treated as outstanding retroactively to January 1, and 10 of the 100 stock dividend shares are treated as outstanding retroactively to January 16 (the date on which the options to which those shares related were exercised), for the following reason. When a stock dividend occurs, ownership in the company has been divided into a greater number of shares, each of which represents a proportionately smaller piece of the company. Retroactive recognition of the stock dividend for EPS computation purposes simply equates the prestock dividend shares with the poststock dividend shares. A stock split would be handled similarly. Prior years' EPS would also be restated for stock dividends and splits.

The 500 shares issued on August 11 in a business combination accounted for as pooling of interests are treated as outstanding retroactively to January 1 (with recomputation of prior years' EPS) because the earnings of the combining companies are pooled retroactively.

5.32 DUAL PRESENTATION, FULLY DILUTED EPS.   Dual presentation includes, with equal prominence, primary EPS and fully diluted EPS.

(a) Primary EPS.   These three steps are followed in computing primary EPS (earnings per common share and common equivalent share) for a period:

1. Identify all potentially dilutive securities that were outstanding during any part of the period. If not convertible within the next 10 years, ignore the security in computing both primary and fully diluted EPS. If convertible only after 5 but less than 10 years, ignore convertible securities in computing primary EPS only. The principal examples of potentially dilutive securities are:
   - Convertible debt or preferred stock.
   - Options and warrants.
   - Contingent issuance agreements.
   - Two-class common stocks or participating securities.

2. Determine which of the foregoing are **common stock equivalents,** according to the following rules:
   - Convertible debt and convertible preferred stock are common stock equivalents if their effective yield rate at issuance is less than 66.6% ($^2/_3$) of the average Aa. corporate bond yield.
   - Stock options and warrants are always common stock equivalents. Convertible securities, options, and warrants issued by a subsidiary but convertible into or exercisable for the parent's common stock must be regarded as potentially dilutive securities in computing the parent's EPS.
   - Contingent issuance agreements are common stock equivalents (a) if the shares are issuable based on attaining a specified earnings level or market price and (b) the specified earnings level or market price is currently being attained.
   - Participating securities and two-class common stocks are common stock equivalents if their holders share in the earnings potential of the issuing company on substantially the same basis as common stock even though the holder may not have the right to exchange his or her shares for common stock. These cases are relatively rare; APB Opinion No. 15 (pars. 27, 59, and 60) provides further guidance.
3. Compute dilutions from common stock equivalents. Ignore any antidilutive common stock equivalents.

(b) Fully Diluted EPS.   The same steps followed for computing primary EPS are followed in computing fully diluted EPS (earnings per common share assuming the maximum potential dilution):

1. Identify all potentially dilutive securities that were outstanding during any part of the period.
2. Compute dilution from the foregoing potentially dilutive securities ignoring any antidilutive securities.

5.33 DILUTION FROM OPTIONS AND WARRANTS.   The most common potentially dilutive securities are options and warrants. In EPS calculations it is assumed that the options or warrants were exercised at the beginning of the period (or at the time of their issuance, if later) and that any proceeds to the company on the assumed exercise were used to purchase treasury shares (1) at the average market price during the period, for primary EPS, and (2) at the greater of the average or the end-of-period market price, for fully diluted EPS. This is known as the "treasury stock method." If a company's common stock is not traded and the market price is therefore not available, use an estimate of the fair value of the common in applying the treasury stock method.

(a) Exercised Options and Warrants.   When using the treasury stock method for computing dilution from options or warrants that have been exercised during the current period, the following steps are required:

Primary EPS. Assume repurchase of treasury shares at the average market price for the portion of the period prior to exercise.

Fully Diluted EPS. Assume repurchase of treasury shares at the market price on the date of exercise, regardless of whether that price is higher or lower than average.

(b) Canceled Options and Warrants.   When using the treasury stock method for computing dilution from options or warrants that expire or are canceled during the period the following steps are required:

Primary EPS. Assume repurchase of treasury shares at the average market price for the portion of the period prior to expiration (cancellation).

Fully Diluted EPS. Assume repurchase of treasury shares at the greater of (1) the average market price during the portion of the period prior to expiration (cancellation) or (2) the market price on the date of expiration (cancellation).

Although options or warrants that expire are generally antidilutive (option price greater than market price), some are dilutive, and canceled options or warrants can be dilutive. The requirement that dilution from an option or warrant that has expired or was canceled must be recognized in computing EPS is expressly set forth in an interpretation of APB Opinion No. 15. The theory is that EPS is a historical (retrospective) ratio, and the option or warrant was potentially dilutive during that portion of the period prior to its expiration or cancellation.

5.34 STOCK COMPENSATION PLANS.   The treasury stock method can be applied to stock compensation plans. It requires measurement of the amount of proceeds that the company is presumed to use to purchase treasury stock. Some stock compensation plans give employees the right to acquire shares because of the increase in the market price of the company's stock over time. In some cases, a cash payment from the employee is required to acquire the stock and in other cases the shares are issued as payment for recognized compensation expense. Sometimes, the amount of the stock compensation is not determinable until after the date of grant or award.

In February 1980, the FASB issued FIN No. 31, "Treatment of Stock Compensation Plans in EPS Computations," which states that the proceeds to be used in applying the treasury stock method are the sum of the cash to be received by the company on exercise, the compensation related to the options or rights that will be charged to expense in the future, and any "windfall" tax benefit that the company gets as a result of a tax deduction for compensation in excess of compensation expense recognized for financial reporting purposes.

5.35 QUARTERLY VERSUS YEAR-TO-DATE COMPUTATIONS.   Because the "average" and "end-of-period" market prices used in applying the treasury stock method may change depending on the length of the period, it can happen that EPS amounts computed on year-to-date basis (i.e., for a 6-month, 9-month, or 12-month period) may not equal the sum of the EPS amounts computed for the individual quarterly periods within the year-to-date period.

5.36 CONTINGENT ISSUANCES.   Shares issuable at a future date based simply on the passing of time are included in both primary and fully diluted EPS computations as additions to the weighted average number of shares actually outstanding. Shares that would be issued if the market price at the end of the current period were to continue indefinitely into the future should be treated in a similar manner. For the shares issuable based on attainment of future higher levels of earnings, the following rules apply:

Primary EPS. Assume that the current period earnings level will continue indefinitely into the future; any shares thus issuable should be reflected in primary EPS computations as additions to the weighted average number of shares actually outstanding.

Fully Diluted EPS. Include at a minimum the same number of shares as is included for primary EPS. In addition, if still more shares would be issued on the basis of an earnings level not currently being attained, assume that those shares are issued and increase actual current earnings to the requisite level; however, do not do this if the effect is antidilutive.

5.37 TWO-CLASS COMMON STOCKS.   When computing two-class common stock, deduct from net income (1) the claims of senior securities (preferred stock) and (2) dividend distributions to holders of *both* classes of common stock, to arrive at undistributed earnings applicable to the two classes of common stock equivalents. The per share distributions to one of the two classes of common stock are added to the resulting per share amount to arrive at earnings per share for that class of common.

EPS-RELATED DISCLOSURES

In addition to requiring the disclosure of EPS numbers on the face of a company's income statement, Opinion No. 15 requires some related disclosures, including (1) disclosures that explain the EPS computations, (2) disclosures concerning the company's capital structure, and (3) certain supplemental disclosures. As mentioned earlier, SFAS No. 21 suspended all of these disclosures for nonpublic companies.

5.38 EXPLANATION OF EPS COMPUTATION.   Disclosures that are required by Opinion No. 15 to explain the bases on which both primary and fully diluted EPS are computed include:

- Identification of securities regarded as common stock equivalents.
- Identification of other potentially dilutive securities.
- Description of all assumptions and adjustments used in deriving the EPS data.
- Claims of senior securities entering into EPS computations.

5.39 COMPANY CAPITAL STRUCTURE.   Disclosures about a company's capital structure are required by APB Opinion No. 15 to be sufficient to explain the pertinent rights and privileges of the various securities outstanding and should include:

- Dividend preferences.
- Liquidation preferences.
- Participation rights.
- Call prices and dates.
- Conversion rates and dates.
- Exercise prices and dates.
- Sinking fund requirements.
- Unusual voting rights.
- Number of shares issued on conversion or exercise, or on meeting the conditions for a contingent issuance.
- Stock dividends, stock splits, reverse splits, or recapitalizations occurring during the period or after the end of the period but before the financial statements are issued.
- Per share and aggregate amount of cumulative preferred dividends in arrears.

Note that APB Opinion No. 12, "Omnibus Opinion—1967" (pars. 9 and 10) prescribes a number of related disclosures, namely, changes in the separate accounts making up stockholders' equity and changes in the number of shares of equity securities outstanding.

5.40 SUPPLEMENTAL DISCLOSURES.   APB Opinion No. 15 also requires supplemental EPS disclosures in the following situations:

- If convertible securities were converted during the period (or shortly after its end), supplemental EPS should be computed as if those conversions had taken place at the beginning of the period if primary or fully diluted EPS would have changed (upward or downward) by more than 3%.
- If common stock or common stock equivalents were sold during the period (or shortly after its end) and the proceeds therefore were (or intended to be) used to retire preferred stock or debt, supplemental EPS should be computed as if those retirements had taken place at the beginning of the period if primary or fully diluted EPS would have changed (upward or downward) by more than 3%.

• If results of operations of a prior period have been restated, the per share effect of the restatement and the restated prior period EPS amounts should be disclosed.

The supplemental EPS amount would be disclosed and described in a note to the financial statements. Both APB Opinion No. 15 and Opinion No. 16, "Business Combinations," require certain EPS disclosures relating to business combinations (whether accounted for by the pooling-of-interest method or the purchase method). Also, APBO No. 20, "Accounting Changes," requires certain pro forma calculations of EPS.

SPECIAL EPS REPORTING REQUIREMENT FOR COMPANIES REGISTERED WITH THE SEC

The staff of the Commission enforces the Opinion for the purpose of computing and reporting EPS data in SEC filings. Additionally, item 601 of Regulation S-K requires an exhibit to the principal filing forms (Forms S-1, S-2, S-4, S-11, 10, 10-Q, and 10-K) as follows: a statement setting forth in reasonable detail the computation of per share earnings, unless the computation can be clearly determined from the material in the registration statement or report. Since Opinion No. 15 does not **expressly** require disclosure of either the number of shares used in computing EPS or the computation itself, and since the SEC requirement to show the computation does not contain an immateriality exemption, the SEC's instruction goes beyond the requirements of the Opinion. Thus many SEC registrants file the computational exhibit which, being an exhibit, is submitted to the SEC as supplemental information but is not included in the published prospectus or in the body of Form 10-K. In addition, SAB No. 40 requires explanatory disclosure of material changes in EPS amounts that are due principally to changes in the number of shares outstanding rather than to changes in net income. For example, disclosure is required if EPS increases materially as a result of the purchase of treasury shares by the issuer, even though aggregate earnings may remain relatively unchanged. Such disclosure would be made in "Management's Discussion and Analysis of the Summary of Earnings," which SEC registrants are required to present.

Where an **initial public offering** (IPO) is occurring and stock, options, warrants, and other potentially dilutive securities have been granted or issued during the period of the IPO and the exercise or issuance price is less than the public offering price, the SEC, in SAB No. 64 "Appliability of Guidance in Staff Accounting Bulletins; Reporting Income or Loss Applicable to Common Stock; Accounting for Redeemable Prefered Stock; Issuances of Shares Prior to an Initial Public Offering," issued in 1986, stated that all EPS calculations should be made assuming use of the treasury stock method as if these securities had been outstanding for all periods. However, the SEC will amend this requirement if (1) the registrant can demonstrate that the instruments were issued for their estimated fair value on the dates issued and (2) the staff will presume that instruments issued within one year of an IPO were issued in contemplation thereof. The SEC, in SAB No. 83, "Earnings per Share Computations in an Initial Public Offering," added that the inclusion of potentially dilutive securities in an IPO (as required by SAB No. 64) does not change the registrant's responsibility under GAAP to determine if compensation expense should be recorded.

EPS COMPUTATIONS—CASE ILLUSTRATION

The following case illustrates the computation of earnings per share. The corporation's capital structure includes outstanding warrants that are common stock equivalents and two convertible bond issues, only one of which meets the test of a common stock equivalent. The other convertible bond issue is included in the fully diluted earnings per share computation. The case also illustrates the computation for antidilution and situations where treasury stock that could be purchased on the exercise of warrants exceeds the 20% limit for use of the treasury stock method.

5.41 CALCULATION OF EARNINGS PER SHARE—HYPOTHETICAL CORPORATION.
The calculation of primary and fully diluted earnings per share is based on the following facts:

1. Net income is $1,300,000.
2. Using the weighted average method, the average number of common shares outstanding during the year as 540,000.
3. The corporation has two classes of convertible bonds outstanding, both of which were sold at par in 19X8. (There were no underwriting discounts and commissions or expenses of sale.) At the time of sale, the Aa corporate bond rate was 8%.

   The two classes of convertible bonds are:

   A. $2,000,000 of 4% bonds, convertible into 40,000 shares of common stock.

   B. $3,000,000 of 7% bonds, convertible into 80,000 shares of common stock.
4. There are outstanding warrants, all exercisable, which will produce a net dilution for both primary and fully diluted calculations of 20,000 shares. (The treasury stock method was used to arrive at this number.)
5. Hypothetical Corporation's federal income tax rate is 50%.

Exhibit 5.1 shows how this information is utilized in the calculations for Hypothetical Corporation.

(a) Calculations Using Additional Facts.   Using the following information, the treasury stock method showed a net dilution of 20,000 shares resulting from the outstanding warrants.

1. There are 100,000 warrants outstanding, each representing the right to purchase one common share.
2. For all quarters, the average market price of common stock is $75 per share.
3. The exercise price of each warrant is $60.
4. The ending market price is below the average market price.

Net dilution of 20,000 shares would be determined as follows:

Proceeds of sale if 100,000 warrants are exercised:		
$60 × 100,000 =	$6,000,000	
Number of shares repurchased at $75:		
$6,000,000 − $75 =		80,000 shares
Net dilution:		
Total issued upon exercise	100,000 shares	
Amount purchased with proceeds	80,000 shares	
Net dilution	20,000 shares	

(b) Further Considerations.   The calculation would differ if the 4% bonds were convertible into 10,000 shares of common rather than 40,000 shares.

The calculation would be quite different in this situation. The effect of their conversion on earnings per share would be antidilutive. $40,000 interest net of tax divided by 10,000 shares yields an effect on earnings per share of $4. Since this would raise the earnings per share, they are dropped from the calculation.

	Primary	Fully Diluted
Shares Outstanding		
Average common outstanding[a]	540,000	540,000
Warrants[b]	20,000	20,000
4% bonds[c]	40,000	40,000
7% bonds[d]		80,000
Common and Equivalent	600,000	
Fully Diluted		680,000
Earnings		
Net income[a]	$1,300,000	$1,300,000
Interest 4% bonds (net of Tax)[c]	40,000	40,000
Interest 7% bonds (net of Tax)[d]		105,000
Adjusted Income for Primary	$1,340,000	
Adjusted Income for Fully Diluted		$1,445,000
Shares	600,000	680,000
Earnings per share	$2.23	$2.12

[a]Net income and average common shares outstanding is given.
[b]All warrants are common stock equivalents: dilution is 20,000 shares.
[c]The 4% bonds are convertible into 40,000 shares. The test of common stock equivalency depends upon the relationship of the effective yield (the same as the coupon rate because the bonds were sold at par) to the Aa corporate bond rate.

A security is a common stock equivalent if its effective yield to the holder at time of issuance was less than $2/3$ of the then current Aa corporate bond rate. In this case, the yield is only 50% of the corporate rate, so the security is a common stock equivalent. Common stock equivalents enter into the calculation of both primary and fully diluted earnings per share. The 40,000 shares appears under primary and fully diluted in the shares outstanding tabulations.

Because this is a common stock equivalent, there would not be $80,000 in interest expense (4% × $2,000,000). This should be added to the net income, net of the 50% tax rate. $40,000 appears under primary and fully diluted in the earnings tabulation.

[d]The second class of convertible bonds is handled differently. Although sold at par, its yield compared to the Aa corporate bond rate is $87^1/_2$%, which means it does not qualify as a common stock equivalent and does not affect the calculation of primary earnings per share.

Fully diluted earnings per share shows all contingent issuances that individually reduce earnings per share. These securities therefore qualify for inclusion in that figure.

As with the 4% bonds, shares are increased by the common shares into which the bonds are convertible, while fully diluted earnings are increased by the interest, net of tax, that would not have been incurred had conversion taken place.

Exhibit 5.1.   Calculation of Primary and Fully Diluted Earnings Per Share

The calculation of the dilution from warrants would also be significantly different if there were 390,000 average shares outstanding rather than 540,000.

APB Opinion No. 15 (par. 38) modifies the treasury stock method by limiting the number of shares assumed purchased for the treasury to 20% of the outstanding common shares.

Because of the 20% limit, the maximum number of shares assumed purchased would be 20% of 390,000 or 78,000, rather than the 80,000 purchased in this question. New dilution, using the treasury stock method, is 22,000 shares:

Total conversion	100,000	shares
Less purchase, up to limit	78,000	shares
	22,000	shares

The balance of the proceeds from the assumed exercise of warrants is applied to reduce, first, any short-term or long-term borrowings and, second, to purchase U.S. government securities and commercial paper, with appropriate recognition of any income tax effect. This increases earnings for the earnings per share computation.

The remaining $150,000 proceeds could be assumed to reduce short-term 10% notes. Interest expense would then decrease $15,000 (10% of $150,000) or $7,500 net of tax effect.

Application of $6,000,000 proceeds would be as follows:

Purchase of 78,000 common shares at $75 market price	$5,850,000
Reduction of debt	150,000
	$6,000,000

SOURCES AND SUGGESTED REFERENCES

Accounting Principles Board, "Reporting the Results of Operations," APB Opinion No. 9, AICPA, New York, 1966.

———, "Accounting for Income Taxes," APB Opinion No. 11, AICPA, New York, 1967.

———, "Omnibus Opinion," APB Opinion No. 12, AICPA, New York, 1967.

———, "Earnings Per Share," APB Opinion No. 15, AICPA, New York, 1969.

———, "Business Combinations," APB Opinion No. 16, AICPA, New York, 1970.

———, "Accounting Changes," APB Opinion No. 20, AICPA, New York, 1971.

———, "Reporting the Results of Operations—Reporting the Effects of Disposal of a Segment of a Business, and Extraordinary, Unusual and Infrequently Occurring Events and Transactions," APB Opinion No. 30, AICPA, New York, 1973.

American Institute of Certified Public Accountants, "Accounting Trends and Techniques," AICPA, New York, 1987.

———, "Accounting Trends and Techniques," AICPA, New York, 1988.

———, "Reporting Results of Operations," Accounting Interpretation of APB Opinion No. 30, AICPA, New York, 1973.

Ball, J.T. Computing Earnings per Share, AICPA, New York, 1970.

Clark Hal G., and Lorensen, Leonard, Updated Illustrations of Reporting Accounting Changes, AICPA, New York, 1987.

Financial Accounting Standards Board, "Discontinued Operations with Expected Gain and Interim Operating Loss, EITF Issue No. 85-36, FASB, Stamford, CT, 1985.

———, "Display of Business Restructuring Provisions in the Income Statement, EITF Issue No. 86-22, FASB, Stamford, CT, 1986.

———, "Restructuring of Operations: Implications of SEC Staff Accounting Bulletin No. 67," EITF Issue No. 87-4, FASB, Stamford, CT, 1987.

———, "Allocation of Interest to Discontinued Operations," EITF Issue No. 87-24, FASB Stamford, CT, 1987.

———, "Treatment of Stock Compensation in EPS Computations," FASB Interpretation No. 31, FASB, Stamford, CT, 1980.

———, "Reporting Gains and Losses from Extinguishment of Debt," Statement of Financial Accounting Standards No. 4, FASB, Stamford, CT, 1975.

———, "Financial Reporting for Segments of a Business Enterprise," Statement of Financial Accounting Standards No. 14, FASB, Stamford, CT, 1976.

———, "Accounting by Debtors and Creditors for Troubled Debt Restructuring," Statement of Financial Accounting Standards No. 15, FASB, Stamford, CT, 1977.

———, "Prior Period Adjustments," Statement of Financial Accounting Standards No. 16, FASB, Stamford, CT, 1977.

———, "Suspension of the Reporting of Earnings per Share and Segment Information by Nonpublic Enterprises," Statement of Financial Accounting Standards No. 21, FASB, Stamford, CT, 1978.

———, "Regulated Enterprises—Accounting for Abandonments and Disallowances of Plant Costs," Statement of Financial Accounting Standards No. 90, FASB, Stamford, CT, 1986.

———, "Consolidation of All Majority-Owned Subsidiaries," Statement of Financial Accounting Standards No. 94, FASB, Stamford, CT, 1987.

———, "Accounting for a Purchase of Treasury shares at a price Significantly in Excess of the Current Market Price of Shares and the Income Statement Classification of costs incurred in Defending against a Takeover Attempt," FASB Technical Bulletin No. 85-6, FASB, Stamford, CT, 1985.

Securities and Exchange Commission, "Codification of SAB Nos, 1–38," Staff Accounting Bulletin No. 40, SEC, Washington, DC, 1981.

———, "Accounting for Sales of Stock by a Subsidiary," Staff Accounting Bulletin No. 51, SEC, Washington, DC, 1983.

———, "Applicability of Guidance in Staff Accounting Bulletins; Reporting Income or Loss Applicable to Common Stock; Accounting for Redeemable Preferred Stock; Issuances of Shares Prior to an Initial Public Offering," Staff Accounting Bulletin No. 64, SEC, Washington, DC, 1986.

———, "Income Statement Presentation of Restructuring Charges," Staff Accounting Bulletin No. 67, SEC, Washington, DC, 1986.

———, "Income Statement Presentation," Staff Accounting Bulletin No. 69, SEC, Washington, DC, 1987.

———, "Classification of Charges for Abandonments and Disallowances," Staff Accounting Bulletin No. 72, SEC, Washington, DC, 1987.

———, "Gain Recognition on the Sale of a Business or Operating Assets to a Highly Leveraged Entity," Staff Accounting Bulletin No. 81, SEC, Washington, DC, 1989.

———, "Earnings per Share Computations in an Initial Public Offering," Staff Accounting Bulletin No. 83, SEC, Washington, DC, 1989.

———, "Accounting for Sales of Stock by a Subsidiary," Staff Accounting Bulletin No. 84, SEC, Washington, DC, 1989.

———, "Codification of Financial Reporting Polices," Financial Reporting Release No. 1 (ASR No. 177), SEC, Washington, DC, 1982.

———, "Integrated Disclosure Rules," Regulation S-K, SEC, Washington, DC, 1982, Updated.

CHAPTER 6

ACCOUNTING FOR BUSINESS COMBINATIONS

Daniel W. Jones, CPA

Deloitte & Touche

Val R. Bitton, CPA

Deloitte & Touche

CONTENTS

POOLING VERSUS PURCHASE ACCOUNTING

The APB found merit in both the pooling of interests method and the purchase method of accounting for business combinations. However, the APB concluded that the two methods were not alternative methods for the same business combination. As a result, the APB created a very specific, although somewhat arbitrary, set of rules that must be met in order to account for a combination as a pooling of interests. A combination that meets all of the conditions for a pooling **must** be accounted for as a pooling of interests. All other combinations are accounted for by the purchase method.

POOLING OF INTERESTS

The APB intended the pooling of interests method to be used in situations where the entities involved form a single entity and the owners of the entities share in the rights and risks of the combined entity. This concept of mutual sharing of substantially all of the rights and risks of ownership of the combined entity is critical to the underlying concept of a pooling. Accordingly, the intent and initial actions of the combining entities, as well as the end result, must be considered in determining whether the combination should be accounted for as a pooling. In addition, the pooling concept precludes combining only selected assets or interests of the combining entities. In theory, the determination of which of the entities in the combination acts as the issuer is simply a matter of convenience. As the mutual interests of both entities are brought together, there is no acquisition of additional ownership rights of one group of shareholders to the exclusion of another group; thus, the designation of the parties in a pooling as acquiror and acquiree are avoided. The accounting for the pooling transaction incorporates the concept of continuity of the combined interests by combining the assets, liabilities, and equity of the entities involved at their previous carrying values.

The following discussion identifies the specific requirements established by the APB relating to the characteristics of the combining companies, the form and substance of the actual combination, and pre- and postcombination transactions of the combining companies. The discussion also describes specific situations that may create violations of the pooling of interests requirements.

6.1 PARTIES TO THE BUSINESS COMBINATION

(a) The Autonomy Concept.   Paragraph 46a of APB Opinion No. 16, "Business Combinations" ("the Opinion"), requires that both of the companies involved in the combination be autonomous and not to have been a subsidiary or division of another company within 2 years before the combination is initiated. As a practical matter, this requirement also applies through the consummation date as explained in AICPA Accounting Interpretations of APB Opinion No. 16 (Interpretation) No. 36.

The purpose of the autonomy requirement is to protect the concept of mutual risk sharing inherent in a pooling of interests business combination. The sharing of risks and rewards in the pooling context assumes completeness. Accordingly, pooling with only a portion of a larger entity is contrary to the notion of risk sharing. The autonomy requirement is designed to prevent a company from spinning off part of its operations into a new entity that is then pooled with another company, or spinning off operations that the other company in the combination is not interested in acquiring.

Exceptions to the autonomy rule are limited and are generally based on substance over form rather than exceptions to the autonomy concept.

(i) Newly Incorporated Companies.   For purposes of the autonomy rule, a new company incorporated within the preceding 2 years is considered autonomous unless it is a successor to a previously existing company or is part of a company that would not itself be considered autonomous.

(ii) Wholly Owned Subsidiaries in a Pooling.   A wholly owned subsidiary may be involved in a pooling transaction as the issuing company by distributing voting common stock of its parent. Interpretation No. 18 defines "wholly owned" to include subsidiaries in which the parent owns "substantially all of the subsidiary's outstanding voting stock." The Interpretation would apply to situations in which the subsidiary has a very few minority shareholders, principally directors or management, because certain states require directors of a corporation to own a limited or de minimis number of shares.

(iii) Autonomy of a Company Divested under a Government Order.   The Opinion permits pooling accounting for an entity that is a divested subsidiary or a new company formed to hold certain assets divested under a government order irrespective of the 2-year autonomy rule.

However, the government order requiring the divestiture must be outside the control of the parties to the business combination and may not give the divesting company an alternative to divestiture, such as would be the case if the government order gave the divesting company the option of infusing additional capital into a regulated subsidiary or divesting itself of the subsidiary. This exception to the autonomy rule is provided in order not to preclude a pooling of interests transaction in a situation where a subsidiary is divested as a result of a governmental action outside the control of the combining companies.

(iv) Autonomy of Entities under Common Control.   Interpretation No. 27 states, "An individual who owns two separate businesses organized as corporations theoretically is a 'parent' with two 'subsidiaries'." In a business combination that involves only a portion of an affiliated group of companies, an evaluation must be made to determine whether, in substance, the combination fragments the ownership interests of the control group or

whether the particular component of the affiliated group is, in substance, an autonomous company for purposes of applying pooling of interests accounting.

Interpretation No. 27 uses the example of a single individual with two companies and concludes that, if both companies are grocery stores, both companies must be a party to the combination to effect a pooling of interests and that the two separate legal organizations should be ignored. However, if one company is a grocery store and the other is an automobile dealership, a combination involving only one of the companies could be accounted for as a pooling of interests if all of the other conditions for a pooling are met since the two companies' operations are demonstrably unrelated.

Generally, a company owned by a control group is considered autonomous, if it operates in a separate line of business, distinct from other companies in the affiliated group, although it may operate in the same general industry. It is important to consider the relationship of the company to the other companies in the affiliated group to determine if there are other conditions, such as significant intercompany transactions, which indicate that the company is not autonomous with regard to other companies within the affiliated group. Some factors to consider in determining whether companies are autonomous include:

- The nature of the products produced or services provided by each company.
- The nature of each company's production process.
- The markets and marketing methods used by each company.
- Whether the separate companies could operate as viable economic entities in the absence of a relationship with each other. Particularly important to the determination of viability of an individual company is the extent of its revenues from or sales to other members of the affiliated group and the extent of any borrowings from them.

(v) Personal Holding Companies and Similar Tax-Driven Structures.   Personal holding companies are, by form, a "parent company" to one or more operating subsidiaries. However, this form of operation isn't always indicative of the normal parent–subsidiary relationship. Accordingly, questions frequently arise as to whether subsidiaries of a personal holding company may be involved in a pooling. Interpretation No. 28 addresses the issue of subsidiaries of personal holding companies and requires an evaluation of the substance of the parent–subsidiary relationship over the form of the personal-holding-company structure. The Interpretation indicates that, in some cases, a valid parent–subsidiary relationship may exist, precluding accounting for a business combination involving the subsidiary as a pooling of interests. The Interpretation also indicates that, in other cases, the personal-holding-company structure may simply be a tax convenience, and the personal holding company may have no direct management influence or provide no services directly to the subsidiary. In those cases, the personal-holding-company structure may be disregarded, and the subsidiaries of the personal holding company may be considered autonomous for purposes of applying the pooling of interests method. However, consideration should be given to the provisions of Interpretation No. 27, discussed above, to determine if other subsidiaries of the common parent operate in the same line of business as the subsidiary in question and, therefore, must be considered as part of the subsidiary for purposes of a pooling of interests.

(b) Independence.   Paragraph 46b of the Opinion requires that each of the combining companies be independent from the others in the combination. As clarified by Interpretation No. 3, the Opinion requires that, from the date of initiation through consummation of the combination, none of the combining companies hold as intercorporate investments more than 10%, in total, of the outstanding voting common stock of any of the combining companies. For purposes of measuring intercorporate investments, voting common stock that is acquired after the initiation date in exchange for the voting common stock issued to effect the combination is excluded.

Immaterial intercorporate investments are considered with other "technical violations" of the pooling rules in the Opinion to arrive at an aggregate 90% test, which must be met for the combination to be accounted for as a pooling of interests. These violations, and the 90% test, are discussed in section 6.2 (b) (ix) of this chapter.

Once it is determined that the parties to the combination are autonomous and independent of each other, the specific combination in question must be evaluated to determine if the pooling of interests method is applicable.

6.2 COMBINING INTERESTS.   The essence of a pooling of interests combination is the mutual sharing of risks and rights of ownership in the combined company. Accordingly, the form and substance of the combination and related transactions must be evaluated to ensure that the concept of mutual sharing is preserved in the combination. Any agreements with stockholders, or alterations of stockholder rights, that give one stockholder group preference over another group in the combination may preclude a pooling.

(a) Single Transaction Completed within One Year after Initiation Date.   To be accounted for as a pooling, the combination must be completed within one year of the initiation date unless any delay is beyond the control of the combining companies, as would be the case if the companies were awaiting federal or state regulatory approval or settlement of litigation, such as a Justice Department antitrust suit or a suit by dissenting shareholders (see Interpretation No. 5).

(b) Offer and Issuance of Stock in the Combination

(i) Accidental Poolings Prohibited.   The Opinion requires that the issuing company **offer and issue** only voting common stock with rights identical to the majority class of the issuing company's voting common stock. The offer and intent of the companies are important parts of the pooling transaction, because the application of the pooling of interests method is not based solely on the results of the combination; it is also affected by the nature of the offer and the intent of the parties involved. Accordingly, a company may not offer cash (except, as provided by the Opinion, for the acquisition of fractional shares and dissenter shares), preferred stock, or a combination of common stock and other consideration in exchange for the common stock of the combining company, even if the actual result is an exchange of only common stock with rights identical to those of the majority class of the issuer in exchange for substantially all of the stock of the combining company. The EITF briefly discussed the concept of accidental poolings as part of its discussion of Issue No. 86-10, "Pooling with 10 Percent Cash Payout Determined by Lottery," which is discussed below. No consensus was reached with regard to accidental poolings; however, a majority of the EITF (including the FASB staff and the Chief Accountant of the SEC) agreed that pooling of interests accounting is not appropriate unless there is clearly an offer of voting common stock in exchange for the common stock of the combining company.

(ii) Pooling with a 10% Cash Lottery.   At its March 1986 meeting, the EITF addressed Issue No. 86-10. In the example discussed, the merger agreement provided that cash would be paid to shareholders for fractional shares and to dissenters as long as not more than 10% of the total shares of the acquired company were acquired for cash. In the event that shareholders holding more than 10% of the total shares of the combining company elected to receive cash, a lottery would be held to reduce the cash paid to dissenters to no more than 10% of the shares. The EITF reached a consensus that the 10% cash lottery would not preclude a pooling, provided all other pooling requirements were met, because the initial offer to issue controlling class of voting common stock was for all or substantially all of the stock of the combining company (i.e., at least 90%). In this instance, the exchange of 90% or more of the combining company's shares did not occur as a result of an accident nor did it differ from the original

offer, but rather was a result of a planned pooling transaction in which the offer as well as the result was the issuance of shares of common stock in exchange for 90% or more of the combining company's outstanding common stock.

(iii) All Shares Must Be Exchanged to Pool.   Interpretation No. 25 indicates that a stockholder may not elect to exchange some shares for the issuing company's shares and retain some shares as minority interest or sell shares to the issuing company for cash. This "all or none" approach to the exchange of shares is consistent with the mutual sharing of rights and risks in a pooling transaction. It is fundamentally inconsistent for a shareholder both to participate in and to dissent from the same transaction.

This provision of the Opinion may appear to provide an easy way to avoid pooling of interests accounting in instances where purchase accounting is preferred by the combining companies. However, simply providing that one or several shareholders retain a number of shares as a minority interest or sell a number of shares to the issuing company while exchanging the remainder of the shares for stock of the issuing company would not necessarily permit the companies to account for the transaction as a purchase. As with all aspects of business combinations, the substance of the combination and related transactions should be evaluated carefully and the ultimate accounting should be determined on the basis of that evaluation, rather than simply on the form of the transaction, which may provide for an insignificant violation contrived solely to violate the pooling rules.

(iv) Identical Shareholder Rights and a Right of First Refusal.   Another required characteristic of the stock issued in a pooling is that it have rights identical to the rights attached to the majority class of the issuing company's common stock (i.e., the class of stock that has voting control of the company).

FTB No. 85-5 indicates that retention by the issuing company of a **right of first refusal** to repurchase the shares issued to effect the business combination would preclude a pooling, because the shares issued to effect the combination would not have rights identical to the issuing company's majority class of voting stock. Even though the only difference in rights may be a condition stating to whom the stockholder may sell his shares, if he decides to sell, the shares issued are not considered identical to the issuing company's majority class of common stock.

(v) Restricted Stock Issued in a Pooling.   Interpretation No. 11 provides guidance on the issuance of restricted stock in a pooling transaction, and indicates that a restriction other than one related to governmental regulation and registration of securities may create rights and risks different from those associated with the issuing company's majority class of voting common stock.

Interpretation No. 6 concludes that issuance of unrestricted or registered stock of the issuing company for common stock of a combining company that is restricted as to voting or sale would not preclude a pooling. The factors to be considered in determining whether the stock issued in a pooling meets the requirements of paragraph 47 of the Opinion are:

- The common stock issued has rights identical to the majority class (i.e., voting control) of common stock of the issuer.
- The common stock issued gives the shareholders of the combining company at least the same rights in relation to other shareholders of the combined company as they had before the combination. Issuing common stock with more or enhanced rights (e.g., registered shares issued in exchange for restricted shares) does not preclude a pooling.

(vi) Carryover of Preexisting Restrictions on Combining Company Stock Exchanged in the Business Combination.   A combining company may have restricted common stock (e.g.,

junior stock or stock issued with vesting provisions) outstanding prior to the initiation of the business combination. Such restrictions may be carried through a combination and attached to the stock issued by the issuing company in exchange for the restricted shares of the combining company. This position is consistent with paragraph 47b of the Opinion, which permits an exchange of substantially identical securities for outstanding equity and debt securities of the combining company.

(vii) Determination of the Majority Class of Common Stock.   The Opinion states that the issuing company in a pooling must issue only common stock with rights identical to those of the majority of its outstanding voting common stock. The Opinion also states that a "class of stock that has voting control of a corporation is the majority class."

Assume Company X has two classes of common stock outstanding. The characteristics of the two classes are identical except for voting rights. Class A shares each receive one vote. Class B shares each receive ten votes.

	Class A Common	Class B Common
Shares issued and outstanding	10,000	1,000
Votes per share	1	10
Votes per class of common stock	10,000	10,000

If there were no adjustment to the outstanding shares, this company would not have a controlling class of common stock. However, if we assume that the Class B shares, as a class, are entitled to elect three-fourths of the board of directors, such a change in terms would create a controlling class of stock.

Company X in this example could be the combining company in a pooling of interests combination as long as both Class A and Class B shares are acquired by the issuing company in exchange for common stock with rights identical to those of the issuing company's majority voting common stock. Company X could only be the issuing company by issuing Class B common stock. Even though the voting rights of the two classes of stock are approximately equal, Class B stock has the right to elect a majority of the board of directors and thereby is deemed to be the majority class of voting stock.

(viii) Two-Class Common Stock in a Pooling.   Interpretation No. 13 addresses a situation where the issuing company designates shares issued in the pooling as a different class of stock. It concludes that, as long as the rights are identical to those of the issuer's majority class of common stock, such a designation is not a violation of the pooling requirements. The problem of two-class common stock becomes more complicated when the issuing company has two classes of common stock with different voting rights or has classes of preferred stock with voting rights.

EITF Issue No. 87-27, "Poolings of Companies That Do Not Have a Controlling Class of Common Stock," addresses examples where voting control is spread among common stock, as well as one or more classes of voting preferred stock. At its November 1987 meeting, the EITF reached a consensus that a business combination involving a combining company without a controlling class of common stock may be accounted for as a pooling of interests only if the issuing company exchanges its common stock for substantially all of the voting common stock and voting preferred stock of the combining company.

The EITF also reached a consensus that a company without a controlling class of common stock could create a controlling class of common stock by issuing shares of its common stock in exchange for a sufficient number of voting preferred shares (or another class of common stock outstanding) so as to create a controlling class of common stock and not violate paragraph 47c of the Opinion, which generally prohibits changes in equity interests in contemplation of a business combination. Once the controlling class of common stock has been created, the company could then act as the issuing company in a pooling of interests business combination.

(ix) Calculation of "Substantially All." The Opinion requires that 90% or more of outstanding common stock of the combining company be exchanged for the issuer's common stock. The following example illustrates how the 90% test would be applied in the case of intercorporate investments, tainted treasury stock (discussed in section 6.2 (d) of this chapter), fractional shares acquired for cash, and minority interest remaining outstanding after the consummation date.

Assume that A is the issuing company and B is the combining company. B has 100,000 shares of common stock issued at the consummation date. The exchange ratio in the combination is one share of A's stock for two shares of B's stock. At the initiation date, A held 900 shares of B's stock as an investment and B held 1,100 shares of A's stock. A and B have tainted treasury stock of 600 and 750 shares, respectively. A acquires a total of 1,700 shares of B's stock for cash as fractional and dissenter shares and, at consummation, holders of 4,300 shares of B's stock elect not to participate in the exchange. Computation of the 90% test is performed as follows:

Common shares of B issued at the consummation date		100,000
Less B's treasury stock		(750)
Common shares of B outstanding at the consummation date		99,250
90% of outstanding shares		× .9
Number of shares required to be exchanged for A's common stock		89,325
B's common shares outstanding at the consummation date		99,250
Less:		
Shares of B held by A at the initiation date	900	
Fractional shares acquired for cash	1,700	
Minority interest remaining outstanding at consummation	4,300	6,900
B's common shares to be exchanged for A's common stock		92,350
Adjustments:		
Equivalent B shares for B's investment in A		
(1100 shares × 2)	2,200	
Tainted treasury stock of B	750	
Equivalent B shares for A's tainted treasury stock		
(600 shares × 2)	1,200	4,150
Computed shares for purposes of the 90% test		88,200

As can be seen from the above example, even though more than 90% of B's outstanding shares were exchanged for A's common shares, the combination fails the 90% test because of the extent of B's tainted treasury stock, B's investment in A, and A's tainted treasury stock.

The EITF considered the relationships of these requirements in Issue No. 87-16, "Whether the 90 Percent Test for a Pooling of Interests Is Applied Separately to Each Company or on a Combined Basis." At its December 17, 1987, meeting, a consensus was reached regarding the application of the 90% test to business combinations involving two companies and to business combinations involving the use of a new corporation formed to issue stock that effects the combination.

(x) New Corporation Formed to Issue Stock to Effect the Combination. The Opinion provides two conditions that must be met when a new company is formed to issue stock to combine two or more companies in a business combination that is to be accounted for as a pooling of interests. They are:

- The number of shares of each company exchanged to effect the combination is not less than 90% of its voting common stock outstanding at the date the combination is consummated.
- The requirements of paragraph 47b would have been met had any one of the combining companies issued its stock to effect the combination on essentially the same basis.

(xi) Other Securities Acquired for Cash or Other Consideration.   The Opinion permits "the issuing company to assume debt securities of the combining company or to exchange substantially identical securities or voting common stock for the outstanding equity and debt securities of the other combining company." Although it may redeem callable or redeemable securities for cash, Interpretation No. 19 requires that only common stock be issued in exchange for debt or equity securities that were issued by the combining company in exchange for the combining company's common stock within 2 years preceding the initiation date.

At its May 9, 1985, meeting, the EITF discussed Issue No. 85-14, "Securities That Can Be Acquired for Cash in a Pooling of Interests." This issue involved whether options, warrants or convertible securities could be acquired for cash or whether such securities must always be exchanged for common stock or substantially identical securities. The EITF reached a consensus that "not all convertible securities need to be considered the equivalent of common shares for a pooling of interests." An assessment of which securities need to be exchanged for common stock in a pooling needs to be made on a case-by-case basis, with the primary focus on whether such securities are essentially "residual equity interests."

(c) Change in Equity Interests in Contemplation of a Business Combination.   The Opinion prohibits changes in equity interests that are presumed to be in contemplation of a combination because such changes violate the mutual sharing of risks and rights and the related combination of mutual interests inherent in a pooling of interests combination. Proscribed changes in equity interests generally include unusual distributions to shareholders, additional issuances of equity securities (including options, warrants and similar instruments) or other equity transactions preferential to a particular group of shareholders.

(i) Mutual/Cooperative to Stock Conversions.   For purposes of applying paragraph 47c, a change in legal form of one of the combining companies within 2 years of a pooling of interests business combination does not generally represent a change in equity interests. FTB No. 85-5 specifically indicates that a change from a cooperative or mutual form of ownership to a stock form of ownership is not proscribed by the Opinion.

(ii) Noncompetition and Employment Agreements.   An issuing company may enter into a variety of noncompetition, employment, or consulting agreements with a principal officer/shareholder of a closely held company acquired in a stock-for-stock exchange. Interpretation No. 31 indicates that an employment agreement does not automatically violate the pooling rules and that the determining factor in evaluating such contracts is the reasonableness of the arrangement and the validity of the business purpose for the agreement. Likewise, the substance of the agreement is more important than its form in determining whether the contract has a valid business purpose and is reasonable compensation for services rendered, or whether it constitutes a disproportionate distribution to the benefit of a particular stockholder or serves to distribute both cash and stock to a particular shareholder in exchange for his shares in the combining company. Some elements of the employment or consulting arrangement to consider in evaluating its substance include:

- Prior compensation of the individual.
- Compensation of other executives of the combined company in similar positions.

- Compensation of executives in similar positions in comparable companies.
- The nature of services to be provided by the employee.

(iii) Standstill Agreements.   Occasionally a company enters into a standstill agreement with a significant shareholder, which prohibits the shareholder from acquiring additional shares of the company's stock for a specified period of time. The EITF addressed Issue No. 87-15, "Effect of a Standstill Agreement on Pooling of Interests Accounting," at its July 9, 1987, meeting and reached a consensus that a standstill agreement with less than a majority shareholder would not preclude pooling of interests accounting if the agreement was not made in contemplation of the combination. The consensus further indicated that a standstill agreement, entered into in contemplation of the business combination, would preclude pooling of interests accounting if made with a more-than-10% shareholder. If the standstill agreement is made with a less-than-10% shareholder in contemplation of the business combination, the number of shares under the standstill agreement should be considered with dissenters' rights, tainted treasury shares, and other technical violations of paragraph 47 to determine if the 90% test (discussed in section 6.2 (b) (ix) of this chapter) is met.

(iv) Transactions between Shareholders.   Interpretation No. 21 indicates that continuity of ownership is not a requirement for a pooling of interests and that shareholder transactions do not violate the pooling rules as long as the combined companies do not use their resources to **bail out** former shareholders of the combining companies. Judgment must be used in evaluating the actions of shareholders, particularly significant shareholders of closely held companies, to determine the substance of the shareholder transactions.

In such situations, actions by individual shareholders may, in substance, be actions of one of the combining companies and, therefore, should be evaluated as if the company were entering into the stock transaction with the other shareholder involved.

(v) Transactions by Affiliates (SAB Nos. 65 and 76).   The SEC's FRR 201.01, formerly ASR No. 135, indicates that pooling of interests accounting will be permitted for SEC registrants if no affiliate (as defined by the SEC) of either combining company disposes of any of that affiliate's shares in the combined company until financial results covering at least 30 days of postmerger combined operations have been published. For purposes of applying ASR No. 135, published results of operations may take the form of a posteffective amendment to a registration statement, a filed Form 10-Q or 8-K (if it reports the required combined net sales and net income) or the issuance of an earnings release or other public issuance wherein combined sales and net income are reported. SAB No. 65 indicates that the restrictions on disposition of shares by affiliates set forth in ASR No. 135 apply to transactions by affiliates of either company to the merger shortly prior to consummation of the combination, as well as for the period subsequent to the acquisition specified in ASR No. 135. An exception to this SEC position applies when there is an unusually long delay between initiation and consummation of the transaction while the companies await regulatory approval. In such cases, the SEC staff generally will not question disposition of shares by affiliates prior to 30 days before the consummation date.

In January 1988, the SEC issued SAB No. 76 which further clarifies the SEC's position on transactions by affiliates. It supplements SAB No. 65 and indicates that the SEC will not question the use of the pooling of interests method because of de minimis sales by affiliates within the SAB No. 65 and ASR No. 135 holding periods. The SAB defines **de minimis** and states:

> . . . (i) the sales by an affiliate must not be greater than 10 percent of the affiliate's pre-combination (or equivalent post-combination) shares, and (ii) the aggregate sales by all affiliates of a combination company must not exceed the equivalent of 1 percent of that Company's pre-combination outstanding shares.

The SAB may also require that outstanding stock options be considered as outstanding shares owned by the affiliate for purposes of computing the 10% and 1% tests described above, depending on an assessment of the specific facts and circumstances. Consideration should be given to the following factors in assessing outstanding stock options:

- The relationship of the option price to the market value of the stock.
- The imminence of exercisability and/or expiration of the options.
- The number of options held by an affiliate in relation to the number of shares owned by the affiliate.
- The effect, if any, the consummation of the combination will have on the terms of the options.

(vi) Options Issued to Shareholders/Officers of the Combined Company.   As with employment-related contracts, stock options may be granted to former stockholders of the combining company or issued by one of the combining companies prior to the combination. Interpretation No. 32 addresses this issue in a manner similar to its analysis of employment contracts discussed above. Options issued as current compensation by the combined company to former shareholder/officers of the combining company as part of the combined company's option plan for its employees and directors would not be a violation of the pooling rules. However, an option that, in substance, constitutes a disproportionate distribution or a contingency payment to those shareholders/officers receiving the options would violate paragraphs 47c and 47g.

(vii) New Stock Option Plans or Grants under Existing Plans Made within 2 Years of the Initiation Date of a Business Combination.   New incentive stock option plans implemented within 2 years of a business combination or grants under existing stock option plans within 2 years of the initiation date are presumed to be a change in equity interests in contemplation of a combination. Accordingly, evaluation of the facts and circumstances surrounding a new option plan is required to determine that a reasonable business purpose existed for implementing the plan or making the grants and that the grants are not just a means of providing an additional distribution to shareholders/officers in the business combination. The factors to evaluate include:

- The nature and extent of the proposed option plan or grant compared with existing plans or previous grants of the company.
- The nature and extent of the proposed option plan compared with plans of similar companies.
- The proximity of the initiation of the plan or date of grant options to the inception of negotiations of the business combination.
- Reasonableness of the compensation awarded under the option plans compared with services rendered by the eligible employees.

A systematic pattern of granting options would provide evidence that the grants were of a normal nature and related to a valid business reason apart from the business combination. Likewise, an option plan that succeeds an expired plan would provide evidence of the company's intent and experience in using equity securities as a form of compensation to shareholders/officers.

In addition, evidence of grant awards in recognition of identified achievements set forth in predetermined goals or business plans would provide further evidence that the grants or initiation of the plan were not in contemplation of a business combination.

(viii) Acceleration of Option Exercise Dates.   Acceleration of the exercise dates or vesting dates of stock options would generally be considered a change in equity interests in contemplation of effecting a business combination and, therefore, would be a violation of the pooling requirements. Absent persuasive evidence to the contrary (e.g., existence of acceleration provisions in a plan implemented more than 2 years prior to the initiation date of the business combination), it is difficult to overcome the presumption that changes in the characteristics of the outstanding options were made in contemplation of a business combination.

(ix) Stock Splits, Dividends, and New Issuances of Stock.   A company may elect to effect a stock split, declare a stock dividend or raise capital through an issuance of common stock within 2 years prior to the initiation of a business combination. These transactions would generally not represent a change in equity interests in contemplation of the business combination if the company can demonstrate that there was a valid business purpose for the split, dividend, or issuance of stock.

In the case of a stock split or dividend, all shareholders receive a proportionate distribution, and the value of the total stock outstanding is adjusted to reflect the split or dividend. Accordingly, a stock split or stock dividend generally does not result in an alteration of equity interests in contemplation of a business combination.

(d) Treasury Stock Transactions

(i) Treasury Stock Acquired Prior to the Pooling of Interests.   Paragraph No. 47d of the Opinion prohibits any of the combining companies from reacquiring its voting common stock except for reacquisitions for purposes other than business combinations. The Opinion specifically mentions reacquisitions of shares for use in stock option and compensation plans as being a reason other than for business combinations. Interpretation No. 20 explains that other purposes for acquiring treasury stock that would not be presumed to be in contemplation of a business combination to be accounted for as a pooling of interests would include shares acquired for:

- Issuance under a stock dividend declared.
- Use in, or reserved for, a specific purchase business combination.
- Issuance to resolve a contingent share agreement in a purchase business combination.

In addition, the SEC's ASR No. 146-A identifies other reacquisitions that would not be considered tainted for purposes of a pooling of interests business combination. These situations include shares acquired to:

- Satisfy the exercise requirements of outstanding warrants or convertible securities.
- Comply with an agreement to purchase stock upon the death of a shareholder.
- Settle a claim or lawsuit relating to the original issuance of the common stock.
- Repossess stock pledged as collateral for a shareholder receivable or other contractual obligation.
- Repurchase stock from employees pursuant to contractual rights or obligations.

Such reacquisitions to settle contractual obligations to shareholders or employees must be supported by the existence of a contract or a claim against the company providing persuasive evidence that the reacquisitions were not made in contemplation of a business combination.

However, even in the case of treasury shares acquired for the purposes mentioned above, particularly for stock option plans and for use in meeting the exercise requirements of warrants or other convertible securities, the treasury shares would be considered tainted unless they are acquired in a systematic pattern of reacquisition established at least 2 years before the combination is initiated. The only exception to the requirement that the systematic reacquisition pattern be established more than 2 years prior to the initiation date of the business combination is when the inception of a systematic reacquisition plan coincides with adoption of a new stock option plan or new issuance of convertible securities, warrants, or similar instruments.

All reacquired shares are presumed to be tainted for purposes of a pooling of interests business combination unless the systematic pattern test is met or it can otherwise be demonstrated that the shares were reacquired for reasons other than for use in business combinations. Such tainted treasury stock should be considered with other violations of paragraph 47 in making the 90% test required by paragraph 47b. Specifically, FRR 201.02 (ASR No. 146) sets forth the SEC's position on treasury stock acquisitions and indicates that shares reacquired because management believes the company is overcapitalized or considers the "price is right" do not overcome the presumption that they were acquired in contemplation of a pooling.

The SEC does not consider an action by the board of directors to reserve reacquired shares for a specific purpose to be "persuasive evidence that they were not reacquired in contemplation of a pooling of interests." The SEC will ordinarily focus on the actual and intended subsequent distribution of shares to determine whether they were reacquired for purposes other than business combinations. ASR No. 146 provides further guidance on the SEC's determination of whether there is a reasonable expectation that the reacquired shares will be issued for the stated purpose.

The following are examples in which a company acquires shares for a valid business purpose other than business combinations but, because of the nature of the reacquisition, such shares are considered tainted:

- Shares acquired in a large block to fill options or warrants exercisable over the next several months or years. Even if a systematic plan of reacquisition exists (e.g., the acquisition of 1,000 shares per month over an extended period of time), a significant block of shares acquired outside the systematic pattern or a block of shares that significantly exceeds the number of shares normally acquired in that time period under the systematic acquisition plan or where shares systematically reacquired substantially exceed expected needs of the next couple of years would be considered tainted.

- A reacquisition plan designed to obtain a specified number of shares of stock as quickly as possible within the legal restrictions. Such a plan would generally not constitute a systematic pattern of reacquisition.

- Sporadic acquisition of shares of stock that are unrelated to a specific plan approved by company management and that are not objectively related to an approved plan of reacquisition.

- Acquisition of a large block of shares on the open market following a substantial broad-based decline in stock prices in an effort to add support to the stock's price. Subsequent to the October 1987 decline in the stock market, the SEC staff was asked whether, in light of the extraordinary conditions in the stock market, consideration was being given by the SEC to relaxing the rules on tainted shares in relation to the reacquisition associated with a broad-based precipitous market decline. The SEC staff indicated that they had discussed the matter and that they had no intention, at that time, of reconsidering the requirements of ASR No. 146.

(ii) Curing the Taint on Tainted Treasury Shares.   Interpretation No. 20 indicates that, in order to cure an existing taint, the treasury shares must be reissued or sold prior to the consummation of a business combination. Interpretation No. 20 also indicates that a company may specifically reserve treasury shares for the purpose for which they were reacquired. How-

ever, in ASR No. 146, the SEC indicates that it believes board designation or reservation of treasury shares lacks substance and does not remove the taint or prevent the taint on treasury shares acquired outside a systematic pattern of reacquisition.

A reissuance or sale of tainted treasury shares must be substantive and must not be a contrived transaction in order to circumvent the prohibition of the Opinion and ASR No. 146 on reacquiring treasury shares in contemplation of a business combination. ASR No. 146 also specifically indicates that the treasury stock taint cannot be cured merely by retiring treasury shares.

(iii) Treasury Stock Acquired after a Pooling of Interests.   Reacquisition of voting common stock by the combined company after a business combination accounted for as a pooling of interests may have the same substance as a tainted treasury stock acquisition prior to the business combination. Paragraph 48 of the Opinion prohibits the combined company from agreeing directly or indirectly to retire or reacquire the shares issued in the combination or to enter into other financial arrangements for the benefit of a particular shareholder or group of shareholders.

The SEC set forth its position regarding treasury stock acquisitions subsequent to the business combination in FRR 201.02 (ASR No. 146) which states that "significant reacquisitions closely following a combination which otherwise qualifies as a pooling of interests may invalidate the applicability of that method."

In a meeting with the AICPA, the SEC interpreted ASR Nos. 146 and 146-A by indicating that a reacquisition of shares that occurs more than 90 days after the consummation date of the business combination would not violate the pooling requirements; however, an acquisition of shares within 30 days after the combination would. The SEC did not address periods of between 30 and 90 days; a practice has developed, however, of using 90 days as the shortest period between the consummation date and treasury stock transactions not considered a violation of ASR No. 146. This 90-day rule applies only to acquisitions not contemplated by the merger agreement and does not limit the prohibition on direct or indirect agreements by the combined entity to retire or reacquire shares issued to effect the combination as described in paragraph 48 of the Opinion.

Some companies will seek to obtain representations from its affiliates that they will not sell shares within the ASR No. 135 holding period. In other cases, the issuing and combining companies may actually restrict the affiliates from selling their shares during the ASR No. 135 holding period in order to preserve pooling of interests accounting for the combination. Such a restriction on affiliate shares technically creates different rights on those shares than the rights associated with the issuing company's majority class of voting common stock. However, such a restriction would not generally preclude the use of the pooling of interests method of accounting as long as the restriction is limited to the ASR No. 135 holding period and is solely a means of assuring that the combination will qualify as a pooling of interests.

Interpretations No. 34 and No. 37 both indicate that any requirements for a shareholder to sell or any provisions requiring a bailout of a shareholder would constitute a violation of the pooling rules. Any condition that requires a shareholder either to sell or not to sell (with the exception of a disposition of shares required by a government order) is contrary to the concept of mutual sharing of risks and rights in a pooling of interests business combination.

Accordingly, in order to avoid violating the pooling requirements, the acquisition of treasury stock subsequent to the business combination must:

- Consist of an acquisition from the public markets or from a tender offer to all share-holders so as not to violate paragraphs 48a and 48b of the Opinion with regard to preferential treatment of a group of shareholders or agreements to reacquire or retire shares issued in the pooling.
- Not be a condition of the merger.

- Meet the 90-day test of ASR No. 146, and not result in a reacquisition of affiliate shares before the ASR No. 135 holding period has been met. However, shares acquired during the ASR No. 146 holding period pursuant to a "systematic pattern of reacquisition" would not be considered a violation of paragraph 48 or ASR No. 146.

An acquisition not meeting the above tests would be considered with other violations of paragraph 47 in much the same way as tainted treasury stock acquired by the issuing company prior to the business combination in order to assess whether the pooling requirements had been met.

In addition, Interpretation No. 21 indicates that, although continuity of ownership interest is not a criterion for the pooling of interests method, the critical factor in meeting the conditions of paragraphs 48a and 48b is that the voting common stock of the combined corporation remain outstanding and outside the combined company without arrangements on the part of any of the companies involved to use their financial resources to bail out former shareholders of the combining company or to induce others to do so.

Finally, shares acquired subsequent to a pooling outside an existing plan that meets the systematic pattern of reacquisitions would be tainted for future business combinations. Provisions of the Opinion and ASR Nos. 135 and 146 with regard to treasury stock transactions before and after a business combination relate to preserving a completed pooling transaction and do not remove or prevent the taint for future poolings.

(e) Contingencies in a Business Combination.   Paragraph 47g of the Opinion requires that the combination be resolved as of the consummation date and that no provisions of the plan be pending. This paragraph prohibits the combining companies from establishing earnings contingencies or stock price contingencies that act as a guarantee of the investment of one group of shareholders in preference to another group. Such guarantees are contrary to the mutual sharing of risks and rights in a pooling. The Opinion, therefore, prohibits agreements whereby the issuing company will issue additional shares or give other consideration to the former shareholders of a combining company at a later date.

(i) Specific Contingencies Permitted in a Pooling of Interests.   Interpretation No. 14 indicates that the only contingent arrangements permitted under paragraph 47g (other than general management representations discussed below) relate to settlement of litigation pending at the consummation date and additional taxes related to examination by the taxing authority for open income tax years. These contingencies are permitted, since they preserve the concept of mutual sharing of risks and rights of ownership interests after the combination without exposing the shareholders of the issuing company to the risks associated with specific identifiable transactions or events (e.g., litigation and tax liabilities) that occurred prior to the consummation date but are not settled as of that date. Accordingly, shares escrowed for specific contingencies must relate to a contingency that is identifiable and known to exist as of the consummation date but whose outcome is not sufficiently predictable to permit recording of the event, although there may be a reasonable possibility of an adverse material effect. In addition, the number of shares reserved or placed in escrow for a specific identifiable contingency must be reasonable in relation to the risks associated with the contingency.

Escrow arrangements would generally be questioned where the number of shares escrowed exceeds 10% of the shares issued to effect the business combination, even though the escrowed shares relate to a specific identifiable contingency.

With regard to specific contingencies, the contingency provisions of the Opinion generally only allow for contingencies known at the date of consummation that, if they had been resolved, would result in the recording of the transaction by the combining company.

(ii) General Management Representations.   Interpretation No. 30 discusses general management representations that are common in business combinations. These representations

relate to the general existence of the combining company's assets and liabilities and its right to title or its obligations associated therewith. The Interpretation specifically permits these types of management representations in a pooling and an escrow of shares of up to 10% for settlement of these contingencies. The Opinion indicates that the contingencies must be resolved within a relatively short time, generally "within a few months following the consummation of the combination." The maximum period permitted by the Interpretation to resolve general management representation contingencies is the period from the consummation date through the date of issuance of the first independent audit report on the company making the representations following consummation of the business combination. However, the SEC has generally taken the position that the maximum period for settlement of general management representations is one year from the consummation date.

In the case of escrowed shares, the shareholders of the combining company must be allowed to vote those shares until the contingency is resolved and the shares are distributed or otherwise settled. If the final resolution of the general management or specific contingencies for which the shares were escrowed results in a change in the actual number of shares issued to effect the combination, stockholders' equity should be adjusted to the number and value of common shares outstanding and the combined company's paid-in capital.

In evaluating the effect of contingencies on a business combination to be accounted for as a pooling of interests, a distinction must be made between general management representations and specific contingencies. Merely describing all contingencies involved in the combination does not make them specific contingencies as contemplated by paragraph 47g of the Opinion. The specific contingencies contemplated by Interpretation No. 30 are those that exist and are pending at the consummation date. Such contingencies are known to exist, but their outcome is not sufficiently predictable to permit recording, although there is a reasonable possibility of an adverse material effect. General management representations are those of a more subjective nature, such as collectibility of receivables, exposure under product liability claims, pollution standard violations, fair labor practices, and other types of ongoing exposure as a result of the general nature of the combining company's business.

(f) Absence of Planned Transactions.   Paragraph 48a of the Opinion prohibits the combined company from agreeing directly or indirectly to retire or reacquire all or part of the common stock issued to effect the combination. As discussed previously in connection with acquisition of treasury stock subsequent to a pooling, such acquisitions cannot be a condition of the combination. Likewise, the combining company cannot guarantee a price or market for the stock after the combination.

(i) Planned Transactions That Benefit Former Stockholders of a Combining Company.   The Opinion prohibits arrangements between combining companies and its shareholders or between significant shareholders of closely held companies upon which a combination is dependent. The Opinion gives the example of a guarantee by a combined corporation of loans secured by the stock issued in the combination. The effect of such a guarantee and payment of cash by the combined corporation if there is a default by the shareholder would be, in substance, the acquisition of the combining companies' shares in exchange for stock and cash.

Interpretation No. 37 precludes the accounting for a business combination as a pooling when it is contingent upon purchase by a third party or parties of any of the voting stock to be issued in the combination or other arrangements whereby shareholders of the combining company receive a guaranteed market or a guaranteed price (i.e., bailout) for the stock received in the exchange.

Other arrangements with shareholders may require careful evaluation in order to determine that the substance of the transaction is not a bailout or other preferential arrangement for a particular group of shareholders. Employment contracts, noncompetition agreements, and consulting agreements would normally not be considered bailouts or other preferential arrangements where the compensation under such agreements is reasonable in comparison to the company's employment history or other similar arrangements in its industry and where there is a sound business purpose for such agreements in connection with a business combination.

(ii) Planned Disposal of Significant Assets of the Combining Companies.   Paragraph 48c of the Opinion prohibits the combined corporation from disposing of a significant part of the assets of the combining companies within 2 years after the combination. The Opinion does allow disposals in the ordinary course of business of the formerly separate companies and to eliminate duplicate facilities or excess capacity. In addition, Interpretation No. 22 permits the disposition of assets to comply with an order of a governmental authority or judicial body or to avoid circumstances that, on the basis of available evidence, would result in the issuance of such an order.

Generally, a spinoff of assets to shareholders is considered conceptually equivalent to a disposition of assets.

(iii) Disposals of Assets Prior to the Consummation of the Business Combination.   Disposals of assets prior to the business combination should be considered in light of the guidance provided by paragraph 48c of the Opinion. Depending on the individual facts and circumstances, the period of time prior to the combination in which disposition of a combining company's assets would affect the pooling of interests treatment should be relatively short.

Several factors should be considered in determining whether a distribution of assets in contemplation of a business combination represents a change in equity interests that violates the conditions for pooling of interests accounting treatment. Such factors might include the nature and significance of the assets distributed and the business purpose for the distribution.

Any distribution of assets that are other than extraneous (i.e., are integral to the business of one of the combining companies) would preclude pooling of interests accounting treatment. Such disposition would be inconsistent with the pooling concept of combining the existing voting common stock interests and the operations of the two previously unrelated companies.

6.3 CONFORMING ACCOUNTING PRINCIPLES OF THE COMBINING COMPANIES. The Opinion permits a change in accounting method to conform the accounting principles used by the combining companies if a change to the new method would have been appropriate for the separate company. Such changes in accounting principles should be applied retroactively through the restatement and combining process for the precombination financial statements of the combining companies.

6.4 EXPENSES RELATED TO THE COMBINATION.   The Opinion indicates that all costs related to a pooling of interests combination should be expensed by the combined corporation in the period in which the expenses are incurred. Those expenses may include registration fees, proxy solicitation costs, fees paid to finders and consultants, and costs and losses of combining operations of the previously separate companies.

6.5 DISCLOSURE IN FINANCIAL STATEMENTS.   The Opinion requires that the following information be disclosed for a pooling of interests:

1. A combined corporation should disclose in its financial statements that a combination that is accounted for by the pooling of interests method has occurred during the period. The basis of current presentation and restatements of prior periods may be disclosed in the financial statements by captions or by references to notes.

2. Notes to financial statements of a combined corporation should disclose the following for the period in which a business combination occurs and is accounted for by the pooling of interests method:

a. Name and brief description of the companies combined, except a corporation whose name is carried forward to the combined corporation.

b. Method of accounting for the combination—that is, by the pooling of interests method.

c. Description and number of shares of stock issued in the business combination.

d. Details of the results of operations of the previously separate companies for the period before the combination's consummation that are included in the current combined net income.

e. Descriptions of the nature of adjustments of net assets of the combining companies to adopt the same accounting practices and of the effects of the changes on net income reported previously by the separate companies and now presented in comparative financial statements. This requirement applies if, prior to the combination, the separate companies have recorded assets and liabilities under different methods of accounting.

f. Details of an increase or decrease in retained earnings from changing the fiscal year of a combining company.

g. Reconciliations of amounts of revenue and earnings previously reported by the corporation that issues the stock to effect the combination with the combined amounts currently presented in financial statements and summaries. A new corporation formed to effect a combination may instead disclose the earnings of the separate companies that comprise combined earnings for prior periods.

3. Notes to the financial statements should disclose details of the effects of a business combination consummated before the financial statements are issued but either is incomplete as of the date of the financial statements or was initiated after that date.

PURCHASE ACCOUNTING

The predominant method of accounting for business combinations is the purchase method, which is used in all situations where the combination does not qualify to use the pooling of interests accounting. Accounting for business combinations using the purchase method is based on the principles of historical cost accounting. Specifically, assets are recorded at the price paid for them, provided the price is validated in an arms-length transaction. This section expands on the basic principle for recording **purchase** business combinations.

6.6 DETERMINING THE ACQUIRING COMPANY.   Determining which company in a purchase business combination is the acquiror requires the evaluation of all the facts and circumstances surrounding the acquisition and subsequent operations of the combined companies. This identification is made from a legal standpoint as well as an accounting standpoint. The equity section of the balance sheet of the combined companies must reflect certain attributes of the **legal acquiror** whereas other amounts in the balance sheet are dependent on the identification of the **accounting acquiror.**

The legal acquiror is usually clearly identified in the purchase or merger agreement. Terms such as **purchaser, surviving corporation** or **parent** are frequently used. In most cases, the **legal acquiror** and **accounting acquiror** are the same.

In some cases, the legal acquiror may not be self-evident or in fact may not even exist. For example, two companies may merge to form a new company with the shareholders of each of the two companies receiving shares in the new corporation. Paragraph 70 of the Opinion provides guidance for determining which party to such a combination is the accounting acquiror and indicates, in part, that:

> . . . the Board concludes that presumptive evidence of the acquiring corporation in combinations effected by an exchange of stock is obtained by identifying the former common stockholder interests of a combining company which either retain or receive the larger portion of the voting

rights in the combined corporation. That corporation should be treated as the acquiror unless other evidence clearly indicates that another corporation is the acquiror.

SAB Topic 2, Item A.2, provides additional guidance in determining the acquiring company and indicates that other factors must also be considered in determining which company is the acquiror. These considerations include:

- Restrictions on the ability of the former officers or directors of one of the companies to solicit proxies or to participate in voting matters of the combined company.
- Predominant control by the management and board of directors of one of the combining companies of management and the board of directors of the combined company.
- The extent to which the assets, revenues, net earnings, and current market value of one of the combining companies significantly exceed those of the other combining companies.
- The market value of the securities to be received or retained by the former common stockholders of the companies involved in the combination.
- The nature of the combined company's business operations compared with operations of the separate entities.

The application of the guidance in paragraph 70 and SAB Topic 2 may result in treating the legal acquiror as the acquiree for purchase accounting purposes. Such is the case in a reverse acquisition as described below.

(a) Reverse Acquisitions.   The term **reverse acquisition** refers to a business combination accounted for by the purchase method in which the company that issues its shares or gives other consideration to effect a business combination is determined to be the acquiree. This is typically based on the fact that the shareholders of the issuer will have less than a majority of voting control of the combined entity. Reverse acquisitions often involve a shell company or a blind pool created for the purpose of raising capital and using such assets to acquire an interest in an operating company by issuing its shares to **acquire** all of the stock of an operating company. A reverse acquisition is frequently characterized by the continued operations of the operating company under its precombination management, with little or no management involvement by officers and directors of the shell or blind pool.

In a reverse acquisition, the legal acquiror continues in existence as the legal entity whose shares represent the outstanding common stock of the combined company. In some instances, the legal acquiror is a public company whose shares are listed on an exchange. By effecting a reverse acquisition, the accounting acquiror can thereby gain access to the public market without going through an initial public offering.

(b) Applying Purchase Accounting to a Reverse Acquisition.   In applying purchase accounting to a reverse acquisition, the assets of the legal acquiror must be revalued and the purchase price allocated to those assets acquired and liabilities assumed. The equity section of the combined company's balance sheet should reflect the legal acquiror's equity securities outstanding. The retained earnings or accumulated deficit of the accounting acquiror should carry over to the combined company, and the difference resulting from purchase price adjustments and adjustments to the legal acquiror's common stock and other equity securities is charged or credited to paid-in capital.

For example, a blind investment pool, P, acquired all of a company's (A's) outstanding common stock in exchange for 48 newly issued shares of P's common stock. As a result of the combination, A's former shareholders hold approximately 70% of the outstanding shares of the combined company. In addition, the operations of A continue to be the principle operations of the combined company, and the management and the board of directors of A continue as the predominant management and the board of directors of the combined company. (Assume the disposition of shares by an affiliate of A violates the use of pooling of interests accounting.) The separate balance sheets and consolidated statements of P and A would be as follows:

	Company P		Company A	
	Historical Cost	*Fair Value*	*Historical Cost*	*Fair Value*
Assets				
Cash	$ 95	$ 95	$ 20	$ 20
Receivables			40	40
Inventory			30	40
Fixed assets—net			75	85
Other assets	5		15	15
Total assets	$100	$ 95	$180	$200
Liabilities and Equity				
Payables	$ 10	$ 10	$ 25	$ 25
Accrued liabilities			15	15
Debt	50	50	70	65
Common stock	20	20	25	25
Paid-in capital	30	30	25	25
Retained earnings	(10)	(15)	20	45
Total liabilities and equity	$100	$ 95	$180	$200

Consolidating Balance Sheet

	P	A	Adjustments	*Consolidated P&A*
Assets				
Cash	$ 95	$ 20		$115
Receivables		40		40
Inventory		30		30
Fixed assets—net		75		75
Other assets	5	15	$ (5)[a]	15
Total assets	$100	$180	$ (5)	$275
Liabilities and Equity				
Payables	$ 10	$ 25		$ 35
Accrued liabilities		15		15
Debt	50	70		120
Common stock	20	25	$ 23[b]	68
Paid-in capital	30	25	(38)[a,b,c]	17
Retained earnings	(10)	20	10[c]	20
Total liabilities and equity	$100	$180	$ (5)	$275

[a]To reflect reduction in fair value of P's other assets.
[b]To reflect issuance of 48 shares of P common stock to A's shareholders for A's common stock.

P shareholders	20 shares (30% of outstanding common stock)
A shareholders	48 shares (70% of outstanding common stock)
	68 shares

[c]To reflect elimination of beginning accumulated deficit of P.

6.7 DETERMINING THE COST OF AN ACQUIRED COMPANY.   The cost of an acquired company is required to be measured by the fair value of the consideration given or the fair value of the acquired company, whichever is the more clearly evident. The fair value of the consideration given will generally be more clearly evident because of the difficulties associated with measuring the fair value of the acquired company. Although the fair value of the individual assets acquired and liabilities assumed must be determined in connection with the accounting for a business combination by the purchase method, it is often difficult to value goodwill or other intangible assets separately or to determine the existence of negative goodwill.

(a) Fair Value of Consideration Given.   Many business combinations are effected through the issuance of cash or other assets or securities, the incurrence or assumption of liabilities, or a combination thereof. Frequently, information required to measure the value of the consideration given is readily available. Cash is measured at its face amount and assets, such as marketable securities, at fair value. Paragraph 74 of the Opinion requires that consideration also be given to the market price of securities for a reasonable period before and after the date the terms of the combination are agreed to and announced. Liabilities are measured at the present value of future cash payments.

Situations frequently encountered where valuation issues arise are those where the consideration given includes securities that are closely held, restricted or thinly traded, preferred stock, debentures, or treasury stock. The valuation of securities that are not readily traded is typically performed by someone with an appropriate level of expertise to make such judgments, such as a reputable investment banker. The following three paragraphs discuss various considerations in these situations.

Preferred stock issued to effect a business combination may have characteristics of debt securities or equity securities, or it may have significant characteristics of both types of securities. Consideration should be given to the fair value of the acquiree and the debt-versus-equity characteristics of the preferred stock, including:

- The stated dividend rate of the preferred stock compared with market rates for similar securities.
- The tax implications to the holders of the securities and the effect of such implications on the value of similar securities.
- Redemption, liquidation, or conversion rights that will affect the valuation of the stock.
- Any other factors that may have a unique bearing on the fair value of such securities.

Debentures or other debt instruments issued to effect an acquisition should be recorded at their fair value (i.e., present value based on market rates of interest determined in accordance with APB Opinion No. 21) and a premium or discount recorded if the stated interest rate differs materially from the current yield for a comparable security.

When the consideration given in a business combination includes treasury stock, the principles of fair value still apply. That is, the purchase price is measured by the fair value of the securities given as consideration following the requirements of paragraph 74 of the Opinion as previously discussed. In all likelihood, this fair value will differ from the carrying value or cost of the treasury shares. Thus, a charge or credit to additional paid-in capital will be necessary for the difference between the value and the recorded cost of the treasury shares.

The cost of a purchase business combination is generally determined at the initiation date of the combination with recognition that security prices may need a short period of time to reflect market valuations associated with the proposed combination.

(b) Options of the Acquiree.   The acquiree in a business combination may have options outstanding at the initiation date. In such instances, the acquiror may assume the obligation of the acquiree to issue shares upon exercise of the options, it may require the acquiree to redeem all of the outstanding options, or it may permit the options to remain outstanding without change. If the options are permitted to remain outstanding without change, their existence ordinarily has no impact on the purchase price because it is assumed that the purchase price reflects any dilution expected to result from their exercise. The exercise of the options will result in creation of, or addition to, minority interest in the acquired company. Accordingly, consideration would need to be given to the outstanding options in the allocation of the purchase price. If the acquiror assumes the acquiree's obligation to issue shares upon exercise of the options, an adjustment of the purchase price is required.

If the options are assumed by the acquiror, an amount equal to the difference between the exercise price and the fair value of the securities at the acquisition date, issuable by the acquiree upon exercise, should be recorded as a part of the purchase price. However, the exercise of such options should not be assumed in recording the shares issuable in connection with the business combination. Such shares may be common stock equivalents or other potentially dilutive securities and consideration should be given to them in the computation of earnings per share of the combined company in accordance with APB Opinion No. 15. However, only the difference between the exercise price and the fair value of the securities issuable should be recorded on the acquisition date. For example, if the fair value of the acquiror's stock is determined to be $100 per share and the exercise price of outstanding options is $45 per share, the difference, $55 per share, should be included in the computation of the purchase price with a corresponding credit to additional paid-in capital. The $45 option exercise price should not be recorded until the option is exercised.

The EITF discussed Issue No. 85-45, "Business Combinations: Settlement of Stock Options and Awards," at its February 6, 1986, meeting and reached the following consensus:

> . . . APB Opinion No. 25, "Accounting for Stock Compensation Plans" requires that, if the target company settles stock options voluntarily, at the direction of the acquiring company, or as part of the plan of acquisition, the settlement should be accounted for as compensation expense in the separate financial statements of the target company.

Accordingly, if the acquiror settles outstanding options for cash or stock, or by assuming the obligation for these options, the consideration given results in an adjustment to the purchase price of the acquisition. If, on the other hand, the acquiree settles the options for cash or other consideration before, after, or as part of the acquisition, compensation expense would be recorded by the acquiree.

(c) Fair Value of the Acquired Company.   As noted earlier, there may be instances where the fair value of the company acquired is more clearly evident than the fair value of the consideration given. For example, this might be the case where the acquiree is a shell company or a blind pool where assets are essentially monetary assets subject to reasonable independent valuations. In other situations where the purchase price must be determined based on the value of the assets acquired, reference should be made to industry price/earnings ratios, opinions of investment bankers, independent appraisals of the acquiree's net assets (including intangibles and goodwill), the value indicated by the negotiations, recent security transactions for both companies to the combination, and any other indicators of value that are available.

6.8 DIRECT COSTS OF ACQUISITION.   The Opinion states in paragraph 76:

> The cost of a company acquired in a business combination accounted for by the purchase method includes the direct costs of acquisition. Costs of registering and issuing equity securities are a reduction of the otherwise determinable fair value of the securities. However, indirect and general expenses related to acquisitions are deducted as incurred in determining net income.

Direct costs of acquisitions have typically been held to mean those costs that would not have been incurred if the acquisition had not been initiated.

Interpretation No. 33 indicates that only "out-of-pocket" or incremental costs (costs of services provided from sources outside the company) should be included in the purchase price because internal costs ordinarily involve an allocation of costs that would have been incurred whether or not the acquisition had taken place.

If a business combination is effected through the issuance of equity securities, the cost of the acquired company should be measured by the fair value of those equity securities. The resulting credit to shareholders' equity should be reduced by the cost of registration and issuance of those securities.

Interpretation No. 35 requires that, if registration costs will not be incurred or paid until after the acquisition date, such costs should be accrued as a liability with a corresponding reduction in the amount credited to additional paid-in capital. The result of this adjustment will generally be recognized as a charge to goodwill.

Typical direct costs of acquisition include:

- Debt placement and other bank related fees in connection with debt incurred to finance the acquisition.
- Refinancing fees associated with the acquiree's debt that require refinancing upon a change in ownership.
- Prepayment penalties associated with the acquiree's debt that is prepaid in order to restructure the financing of the combined company and provide the acquisition lender with the first mortgage on all assets of the combined company.
- Fees paid to investment bankers (see also discussion of SAB No. 77 below).
- Fees paid for outside accounting, legal, engineering, or appraisal services.

In March 1988, the SEC issued SAB No. 77, which addresses the treatment of certain debt issue costs incurred in connection with financing used in a business combination accounted for by the purchase method. The SAB uses the example of a company that retained an investment banker to provide the following services:

- Advisory services in structuring the acquisition.
- Arrangement of "bridge financing" on an interim basis.
- Structuring of "permanent financing" at a subsequent date.

The SAB requires that the investment banker's fees (whether separately billed or not) be allocated to the services provided and that the fees for the bridge financing and permanent financing be accounted for as debt issue costs rather than direct costs of the acquisition.

(a) Acquisition Costs Incurred by the Acquiree.   An acquiree may incur accounting, legal, engineering, and other consulting fees in connection with a business combination. These costs would normally be expensed by the acquiree unless it can be demonstrated that the costs are nonduplicative direct costs of the acquisition and are clearly incurred by the acquiree for the benefit of the acquiror. Nonduplicative acquisition costs are those that are more clearly associated with the distinct activities of the acquiror rather than with the costs that benefit the combined companies or the acquiree's stockholders; such costs would normally have been incurred by the acquiror absent an arrangement between the parties for the acquiree to pay such costs.

In the absence of a reimbursement arrangement between the acquiror and the acquiree, costs incurred by the acquiree incidental to the acquisition should be expensed. These acquisition costs must be evaluated based on the facts and circumstances of the specific acquisition.

(b) Plant Closing Costs and Employee Severance Costs.   Subparagraph 88(i) of the Opinion indicates that, in allocating the purchase price to the assets acquired and liabilities assumed, a liability should be recorded for plant closing expenses incidental to the acquisition. FASB Technical Bulletin No. 85-5 addresses the costs of closing duplicate facilities resulting from an acquisition. It distinguishes between costs of closing plants owned by the acquiree and costs of closing the acquiror's plants. It indicates that only the direct costs of an acquisition should be included in the cost of the acquired company. It does not permit the cost of closing the acquiror's facilities, which become duplicative as a result of the acquisition, to be considered part of the cost of acquisition. Such plant closing costs would include employee severance costs, relocation costs, and other costs incidental to the closing of duplicate facilities. The Technical Bulletin also indicates that plant closing expenses, in general, are not part of the direct costs of the acquisition which are added to the value of securities or assets given to effect the acquisition in arriving at the total purchase price. Rather, a plant closing liability is one factor to be considered in allocating the cost of the acquired company to the individual assets acquired and liabilities assumed. It is ordinarily assumed that the costs of plant closing, employee relocation and severance plans were comprehended in the negotiations and are an integral part of the bargained purchase price in a business combination. The costs of such plant closing, employee relocation, and severance plans should, therefore, be an allocation of the purchase price and not an additional cost of the acquisition.

(c) Payments to Employees: Acquisition Cost versus Employee Compensation Arrangements. An acquisition agreement may include provisions for consideration to be paid to employees of the acquiree. The intent of such arrangements may be to compensate employees of the acquiree for past services, to act as a ''golden handcuff'' in retaining key executives of the acquiree during a specified period subsequent to the acquisition, or to serve as additional consideration in the purchase acquisition.

Payments made, or to be made, to employees of an acquiree should be evaluated carefully to determine if the substance of the transaction is compensation for services performed subsequent to the acquisition or a cost of the acquisition. Many of the considerations discussed earlier in this chapter with regard to employee/shareholder arrangements in a pooling should be considered in determining the purchase price in a business combination accounted for by the purchase method.

A provision that requires employees to remain in the service of the combined company for a specified extended period of time before payments are received, or where such payments seem to approximate normal compensation levels for the employees, generally indicates that the substance of such payments is compensation for services to be rendered in the period subsequent to the acquisition rather than additional cost of the acquisition.

Conversely, if only a short service period is required for the employees to vest, it could indicate that little or no benefit will be received in a period subsequent to the acquisition. Payments significantly in excess of employees' normal compensation may also indicate that the substance of the payments may represent compensation for services rendered prior to the acquisition or an additional cost of acquiring the target company.

Employee payments determined to be part of the acquisition cost represent a liability assumed in the acquisition rather than a direct cost of the acquisition that increases the total purchase price.

6.9 CONTINGENT CONSIDERATION.   A purchase or merger agreement may include provisions for additional consideration, such as cash payments or the issuance of additional stock, in the event that one or more future events occur. In such situations, the ultimate purchase price may vary depending on the outcome of these contingencies. This presents an accounting problem in initially recording the acquisition.

The Opinion requires that ''cash and other assets distributed and securities issued unconditionally and amounts of contingent consideration which are determinable at the date of acquisition should be included in determining the cost of an acquired company and recorded at that date.'' Other consideration that is issuable upon resolution of a contingency should be disclosed but not recorded as a liability unless the outcome of the contingency is ''determinable beyond a reasonable doubt.''

To the extent a contingent consideration liability is recognized, it should be recorded at its present value. The discount should be accreted over the remaining terms of the contingency period in accordance with the provisions of APB Opinion No. 21.

(a) Contingencies Based on Earnings. The Opinion requires that additional consideration that is contingent upon maintaining or achieving specified levels of earnings be recorded when resolved. These types of contingencies result in an adjustment to the purchase price of the acquiree based on the fair value of the consideration issued or issuable, with the fair value measured as of the date the contingency is resolved. The fair value of the consideration issued should be allocated to the assets acquired, generally as an adjustment to goodwill or negative goodwill.

The Opinion does not address whether such contingencies should be recorded at present values or at the total amount to be paid to settle the contingency. The FASB considered a similar question when it issued SFAS No. 38, ''Accounting for Preacquisition Contingencies of Purchased Entities,'' and, in paragraph 33, concluded that it would not specify a requirement to discount the estimated settlement to present value ''. . . because the timing of payment or receipt of a contingent item seldom would be sufficiently determinable to permit the use of a present value technique on a reasonable basis.'' The FASB did not, however, prohibit the use of present value techniques in situations where, based on available information, their use is appropriate.

As with all aspects of a business combination, evaluation should be made of the substance of contingency arrangements as well as their form.

(b) Contingencies Based on Security Prices. Another type of contingency arrangement addressed by the Opinion is one in which the acquiror guarantees attainment of a specified price for its stock or maintenance of a specified security price during the contingency period. If the contingency price is not met, additional consideration in the form of cash, equity, or debt securities is given upon resolution of the contingency to make the current value of the total consideration equal the specified amount. The Opinion's use of the term **specified amount** refers to the total guaranteed value of the acquisition, including the value of the contingency. For example, if Company A proposes to acquire Company B for stock value at $10 million and cash of $50 million, but guarantees that the stock will have a value of $15 million after 3 years or Company A will pay cash or issue additional shares of stock sufficient to meet the $15 million guaranteed value, then the purchase price of Company B would be $65 million, represented by the $50 million cash exchanged, plus the $15 million of guaranteed stock value.

The authoritative literature does not provide guidance on discounting the guaranteed portion to be paid at the end of the contingency period. In practice discounting has been used in some situations and not used in others. The SEC has taken the position in certain cases, primarily where the guarantee is issuable in stock rather than cash or other consideration, that acquisition cost associated with a guaranteed price contingency for stock should be determined without regard to discounting.

(c) Earnings per Share Consequences of Contingent Share Arrangements. Paragraphs 61 through 63 of APB Opinion No. 15 provide guidance on the appropriate accounting for earnings per share under contingent share arrangements. In general terms, the Opinion requires that both primary and fully diluted earnings per share be adjusted to reflect contingently issuable shares when the conditions that give rise to the issuance of such contingent shares are currently being met. Additionally, if the conditions are not currently being met or must be met over a period of years, the contingently issuable shares should be considered in fully diluted earnings per share provided such inclusion is dilutive. Previously reported earnings per share data should not be restated to give retroactive effect to shares subsequently issued as a result of attainment of a specified increased earning level.

In computing earnings per share under the guidance provided by APB Opinion No. 15, consideration should also be given to the impact the issuance of additional shares would have on earnings for the period. For example, if the earnings contingency is given effect in calculating the number of shares outstanding, the impact of the amortization of additional goodwill (or negative goodwill) which would have arisen had the contingent shares actually been issued should also be considered in the earnings per share calculation.

Paragraph 63 of APB Opinion No. 15, which provides guidance on accounting for shares contingently issuable based on market price of the stock at a future date, states:

> The number of shares contingently issuable may depend on the market price of the stock at a future date. In such a case, computations of earnings per share should reflect the number of shares which would be issuable based on the market price at the close of the period being reported on. Prior period earnings per share should be restated if the number of shares issued or contingently issuable subsequently changes because the market price changes.

6.10 ACQUISITION OF MINORITY INTERESTS.   The discussion to this point has been concerned with various types of business combinations. An acquisition of stock held by minority stockholders of a subsidiary is not a business combination; paragraph 43 of the Opinion, however, requires such acquisitions to be accounted for by the purchase method. Use of the purchase method of accounting is required whether the stock is acquired by the parent, the subsidiary itself, or other subsidiaries of the same parent. Additionally, the purchase method should be used if the effect of a transaction, irrespective of its form, is to reduce or eliminate the minority interest in a subsidiary. The adjustments necessary to give effect to the application of the purchase method are not ordinarily recognized in the separate financial statements of the subsidiary and, accordingly, shares purchased directly by the subsidiary, or by the parent or other companies controlled by the parent and contributed to the subsidiary, should be accounted for as a capital transaction by the subsidiary. A more comprehensive discussion of the effects of purchase accounting on the separate financial statements of an acquired company (pushdown accounting) is included in section 6.13.

The purchase of fractional shares or shares held by dissenting stockholders as part of a plan of combination is not an acquisition of minority interest. In this circumstance, the general provisions of the Opinion would apply.

Interpretation No. 26 provides additional guidance on the acquisition of minority interest and indicates that purchase accounting is applicable when:

- A parent exchanges its common stock, assets, or debt for common stock held by minority shareholders of its subsidiary.
- The subsidiary buys as treasury stock the common stock held by minority shareholders.
- Another subsidiary of the parent exchanges its common stock or assets or debt for common stock held by the minority shareholders of an affiliated subsidiary.

The above examples of acquisitions of minority interests raise questions regarding the appropriate accounting in certain circumstances when considered in relation to Interpretation No. 39, which discusses combinations and exchanges between entities under common control. FTB No. 85-5 addresses the issues of downstream mergers and stock transactions between companies under common control. FTB No. 85-5 emphasizes the point made in Interpretation No. 26 that acquisition of minority interest through a downstream merger should be accounted for by the purchase method, even though some would argue that such transactions may represent a combination of entities under common control.

FTB No. 85-5 also discusses in detail the accounting for stock transactions between companies under common control in relation to the acquisition of the minority interest of one subsidiary by issuing stock of another subsidiary. The accounting for such transactions between subsidiaries under common control depends on **whether the minority shareholders are party to the exchange of shares.** Paragraph 6 of the Technical Bulletin indicates that, if shares owned by minority shareholders are exchanged by the minority shareholders for shares of ownership in another subsidiary of the parent, the transaction is recognized by the parent company as the acquisition of a minority interest and should be accounted for by the purchase method. If, however, minority shareholders are not party to an exchange of shares between the two subsidiaries (assuming one partially owned subsidiary issues its shares in exchange for the parent's shares of another subsidiary), the minority interest in the issuing subsidiary remains outstanding. This transaction should be accounted for in a manner similar to that for a pooling of interests under the guidance of Interpretation No. 39, because the substance of the transaction is simply a rearrangement of the parent's investment in its subsidiaries without change in the composition of any of the existing minority interests.

As can be seen from the above example, although the minority stockholders' interest in net assets of the subsidiaries has changed in each case, the accounting will depend on whether the minority shareholders participated in the transaction or if the exchange of shares occurred only between the parent and/or its subsidiaries.

6.11 ALLOCATION OF PURCHASE PRICE.   The bookkeeping mechanics of allocating the purchase price may be accomplished in several ways depending in part on the structure of the transaction (i.e., purchase of stock or assets) and of the continuing organization (i.e., parent/subsidiary or parent only) and future reporting requirements.

In the case of an asset purchase, the assets and liabilities acquired are recorded on the acquiror's books. In the case of a stock purchase to be operated as a wholly owned subsidiary, the parent company could record the purchase as an investment and apply the equity method to account for future activities of the subsidiary. The purchase price allocation in this case would be accomplished **off the books** and only recorded with consolidating entries as part of the consolidation process. Alternatively, the purchase price allocation could be **pushed down** to the subsidiary's books. Under pushdown accounting, all subsidiary assets (tangible and intangible) and liabilities are adjusted to fair market value at the time of the acquisition with an offsetting adjustment to the subsidiary's equity accounts resulting in agreement between the total of these equity accounts and the parent's investment account. The applicability of pushdown accounting is further discussed in section 6.13.

Paragraph 87 of the Opinion provides general guidance on the allocation of the purchase price to the assets acquired and liabilities assumed of an acquired company. It requires that all of the identifiable assets acquired, including intangible assets, be allocated a portion of the cost of the acquired company, normally equal to the asset's fair value at the date of acquisition. The Opinion requires that the excess of cost of the acquired company over the sum of the amounts assigned to tangible and identifiable intangible assets acquired, less values assigned to liabilities assumed, be recorded as goodwill. Paragraph 88 of the Opinion provides specific guidance on the assignment of fair values to individual assets acquired and liabilities assumed in the acquisition.

(a) Negative Goodwill.   In the event that the purchase price is less than the value of the net assets acquired, a **credit excess** or negative goodwill should be recorded. Paragraph 91 indicates that a credit excess should first be applied to reduce the value assigned to noncurrent assets. The Opinion makes an exception for the allocation of a credit excess to long-term marketable securities, because it is not intended that a company would realize gains from the subsequent disposal of marketable securities because of a reduction in the otherwise determinable fair value of such securities through application of a credit excess. Likewise, it is generally considered inappropriate to use a credit excess to reduce the fair value assigned to other noncurrent assets that are scheduled to be disposed of subsequent to the combination or to noncurrent monetary assets such as loans or notes receivable.

Any remaining credit excess, after reduction of noncurrent assets not to be disposed of, should be classified as a deferred credit and amortized systematically to income, consistent with the guidance provided on amortization of goodwill in APB Opinion No. 17. Although not specifically covered under APB Opinion No. 17, the guidance for amortization of intangible assets should be considered in setting an appropriate amortization period. The guidance in APB Opinion No. 17 is based principally on amortizing such amounts over the period estimated to be benefited.

(b) Purchase Price Allocated to Inventories. The objective of allocating the purchase price to the various components of inventories is to assure that the acquiror recognizes only profits associated with value added to the acquired inventory subsequent to the acquisition date and does not recognize profit associated with purchased value of the inventories. Accordingly, in assigning the purchase price to finished goods and work-in-process inventories, the Opinion requires that the valuation be based on selling price less the sum of (1) costs to complete, if applicable; (2) costs of disposal; and (3) a reasonable profit margin for the selling effort and the postacquisition completion effort. It is generally not appropriate to assign the acquiree's carrying value to the cost of acquired inventories, because the acquiree's cost does not reflect the manufacturing profit that is recognized by the acquiree through the normal selling process. This manufacturing profit should be considered as part of the fair value assigned to the inventory.

Raw materials should be valued at replacement cost on the date of the acquisition, because no value has been added to the raw materials through manufacturing or holding. Replacement cost of raw materials inventories should be determined as of the business combination acquisition date because significant changes in replacement cost could have occurred subsequent to the original purchase of the raw materials by the acquiree.

Care should be taken in evaluating the various types of inventory to assure that inventories are valued according to their appropriate classification: raw materials, work-in-process, or finished goods. For example, Company A acquired the olive distribution operations of Company B. The acquisition date was in February. Spot market prices for raw olives as of February were used to value the raw olive inventories of the olive-processing operation. Traditionally, the olive company purchased its olive inventories in September and October when the olive harvests occurred and distilled them for a period of approximately 6 months prior to sale to distributors. Because the valuation of the olive inventories occurred in February during a period when raw olives were at a premium because of low supply, the value assigned to the olives was significantly higher than the company's normal cost of olives and the subsequent selling price of the distilled olives. As a result, sales in the subsequent year resulted in substantial losses to the company. In this case, the nature of the olive market is so seasonal that the February spot price was an inappropriate valuation for the olive inventories. In addition, the olives should have been valued as work-in-process inventories, since the distillation process was under way. A valuation based on estimated selling price during the following selling season, discounted for cost of completing the distillation process, and selling the olives through the company's distribution network was the appropriate method of valuing the olive inventories.

(c) LIFO Inventories. Paragraph 88c of the Opinion requires that fair value be assigned to the inventories based on the nature of the inventories involved. This requirement is applicable to all inventories regardless of method of accounting for inventories by the acquiror or the acquiree. Accordingly, inventories accounted for under the LIFO method by the acquired company should be valued at fair value in accordance with the provisions of the Opinion at the acquisition date. This fair value of the acquired inventories thereby becomes the LIFO base layer valuation for postacquisition purposes. Carryover of the acquiree's LIFO basis inventories for book purposes is not permitted. The effect of differences between book and tax bases arising from the allocation of purchase price is discussed in section 6.11 (i) of this chapter.

(d) Determining Costs to Complete, Selling Costs, and Normal Profit Margin.   The valuation of finished goods and work-in-process inventories requires consideration of costs to complete, selling costs, and normal profit margin for the completion and selling effort. The calculation of a normal profit margin should be based on an allocation of a normal gross profit among the preacquisition and postacquisition activities associated with the inventories. One guideline for determining the reasonable profit allowance (spoken of in par. 88c) is to identify a reasonable dollar value profit margin for the particular item of inventory for the industry. This amount should then be reduced by the estimated selling costs associated with the product. The resulting amount should then be allocated between the preacquisition and postacquisition activities based on the ratio of selling expenses and completion costs to total manufacturing costs plus selling expenses.

(e) Allocation to Noncurrent Tangible and Intangible Assets.   The appraised value of noncurrent tangible and identifiable intangible assets is generally the best measure of fair value for allocating the purchase price of the acquisition. The Opinion specifically suggests the following three methods for allocating purchase price to plant and equipment, depending on the type of expected future use for those assets:

- If the equipment is to be used for an extended period, the valuation should be based on current replacement costs for similar capacity, unless the expected future use of the assets indicates a lower value to the acquiror. The use of appraisal information or relevant published indices would be appropriate to establish replacement cost.
- Equipment to be sold or held for later sale rather than used in postacquisition operations should be valued at current net realizable value.
- Equipment to be used temporarily should be valued at current net realizable value, taking into account future depreciation for the expected period of use.

The Opinion requires that intangible assets that can be identified and named should be valued separately from goodwill and other identifiable assets acquired in the acquisition. Intangible assets typically found in an acquisition include supply or purchase contracts, patents, franchises, customer and supplier lists, and favorable leases. FIN No. 9 provides additional guidance for identification of intangible assets acquired in connection with a business combination involving a savings and loan association or similar institution. These intangibles may include capacity of existing savings and loan accounts to generate future income (core deposits), capacity of existing savings and loan accounts to generate additional business or new business, and the nature of the territory served. The critical factor in assessing whether a particular intangible asset should be valued separately in an acquisition is whether the intangible asset can be separately identified and its value reasonably determined.

If the intangible asset is not separately identifiable and/or not subject to reasonable valuation, the amount should be included in goodwill. However, goodwill should not be used to capture **excess cost** that the acquiror either does not want to allocate to the acquired assets or elects not to allocate because of a desire to forgo the fair valuation process.

(f) Assignment of Purchase Price to Leases.   FIN No. 21, "Accounting for Leases in a Business Combination," provides guidance on valuing capital leases acquired. The Interpretation indicates that the acquiror shall retain the previous classification of leases acquired in a business combination unless the provisions of the leases are modified as indicated in paragraph 9 of SFAS No. 13, "Accounting for Leases." The amounts assigned to the asset and liability as a capital lease in a purchase combination should be determined independently of each other. The liability should be equal to the present value of the remaining lease payments, discounted at an appropriate current interest rate as of the acquisition date. The capital lease asset should be valued based on the underlying value of the asset itself. One method of estimating such a value in a situation in which the remaining useful life of the asset exceeds the lease terms would be to calculate the present value of the current fair rental value for similar used equipment using an appropriate current interest rate as of the acquisition date. The Interpretation also indicates that subsequent to the initial recording, the leases should be accounted for in accordance with SFAS No. 13.

(g) Research and Development Acquired.   FIN No. 4 indicates that identifiable assets resulting from research and development activities of an acquired company should be recorded in the business combination and that the purchase price should be allocated to the research and development asset. Some research and development assets acquired might include patents received or applied for, blueprints, formulas and specifications, designs for new products or processes, materials and supplies, equipment and facilities, and projects in process.

After allocation of the purchase price, an evaluation should be made to determine whether the identifiable R&D assets are to be used in the general research and development activities of the combined enterprise or will be used in a particular research and development project and have no alternative future use. Paragraph 12 of SFAS No. 2 indicates that costs of research and development activities should be expensed unless the asset has alternative future use.

The EITF addressed Issue No. 86-14, "Purchased Research and Development Projects in a Business Combination," at its July 1986 and May 1987 meetings. The Task Force agreed that FIN No. 4 required a portion of the purchase price to be allocated to the R&D projects in process that have value and that the amount allocated to the R&D project would be charged to expense as a research and development cost if the project does not have an alternative future use. Some Task Force members questioned whether the rationale for such allocation of purchase price and subsequent write-off should be reconsidered by the FASB. At the May 1987 meeting, the FASB staff indicated that the Board does not favor reconsidering the guidance in FIN No. 4 or SFAS No. 2. Accordingly, Fin No. 4 continues to require an allocation of purchase price to identifiable results of research and development.

(h) Allocation of Purchase Price to Assets to Be Sold.   EITF Issue No. 87-11, "Allocation of Purchase Price to Assets to Be Sold," addresses several questions regarding the allocation of purchase price to a subsidiary of an acquiree when the acquiror plans to sell the subsidiary within one year of the acquisition date and use the proceeds from the sale to reduce the acquisition debt. At its November 1987 meeting, the EITF reached a consensus that the allocation of purchase price should reflect the acquiror's intent to sell the subsidiary and that this action, if taken within one year of the acquisition, should not result in any impact on the acquiror's consolidated statement of operations as a result of the cash flows from (1) the subsidiary's postacquisition operations, (2) interest on the portion of the acquisition debt used to acquire the subsidiary or (3) proceeds of the sale. **This consensus applies solely to net assets that are expected to be sold within one year of the date of acquisition.**

Prior to this consensus, the SEC had required that the acquiror have a firm contract to sell the assets at the acquisition date before it would permit discounting of the net realizable value. The SEC staff accepted the EITF consensus and will **require** the accounting described above for those instances where the operations to be sold were identified as of the purchase date and, as of that date, there was a reasonable expectation that the operations would be sold within one year. At the December 17, 1987, EITF meeting, the SEC representative indicated that the SEC staff would also require the following disclosures in the financial statements and pro forma information that cover the reporting periods in which the consensus is applied:

- A description of the operations held for sale, a description of the method used to assign amounts to those assets, the expected disposal date, and the method used to account for those assets.
- Disclosures of the operation's profit or loss during the period that has been excluded from the consolidated income statement, together with a schedule reconciling that amount to the earnings received or losses funded by the parent that have been accounted for as an adjustment to the carrying amount of the assets. Allocated interest cost should be separately identified.
- Disclosure of any gain or loss on the ultimate disposition that has been treated as an adjustment of the original purchase price allocation.

In addition, the SEC expects registrants to review differences between actual and estimated cash flow and the estimated sales proceeds in order to determine if a loss should be reported for events that occur during the holding period.

(i) Allocation of Purchase Price to Pensions.   SFAS No. 87 requires that business combinations accounted for by the purchase method include recognition of a liability to the extent the projected benefit obligation exceeds plan assets or, alternatively, recognition of an asset to the extent the plan assets exceed the projected benefit obligation. In applying the guidance of SFAS No. 87, any previously existing unrecognized net gain or loss, unrecognized prior-service cost, and unrecognized net obligation or net asset existing at the date of initial application of SFAS No. 87 are eliminated. Postacquisition pension expense for the acquired plan is based only on service cost, interest cost, and the actual return on assets until such time as unrecognized gains or losses and unrecognized prior service costs arise through the postacquisition operations of the plan. The liability or asset recorded for acquired pension costs is amortized or accreted based on the difference between pension funding and pension expense. If it is anticipated that the plan will be terminated or curtailed, the effects of such actions should be taken into consideration in measuring the projected benefit obligation used to determine the appropriate amount of the asset or liability to be recorded.

The SFAS No. 87 approach to allocation of purchase price to a pension liability or asset may result in a significantly larger liability or asset than would have been recognized under the Opinion, because it takes into consideration the total projected benefit obligation, which includes the effect of future salary increases and comprehends both vested and nonvested benefits.

The effect of this increased allocation to the pension liability will usually result in the recognition of a greater amount of goodwill in most business combinations. This will result in additional charges to income subsequent to the acquisition.

The pension assets and liabilities to be recorded in the acquisition of a company with both overfunded and underfunded plans should not be offset in allocating the purchase price.

(j) Postemployment Benefits of the Acquiree.   The FASB's proposed SFAS on accounting for postretirement benefits other than pensions may affect the allocation of purchase price for such benefits of an acquired entity. Currently, SFAS No. 81 provides guidance on disclosure of postretirement health care and life insurance benefits, however, no formal guidance has been provided on the appropriate accounting for such benefits on an ongoing basis by plan sponsors or for a company offering postemployment benefits acquired in a business combination.

The EITF addressed Issue No. 86-20, ''Accounting for Other Postemployment Benefits of an Acquired Company,'' at its July 24, 1986, meeting. The Task Force agreed that it was preferable to recognize a liability for postemployment benefits of the acquiree, but that it was not explicitly required by the existing literature and that practice varied. The Task Force also reached a consensus that, if a liability is established in the business combination, the acquiree would not be required to use the accrual method prospectively for newly arising postemployment benefit liabilities.

Any liability for postemployment benefits recorded as part of the acquisition should be reduced for payments relating to the specific employees and the specific amounts and types of benefits included in the calculation of the liability recorded at the purchase date. The EITF reached a consensus that changes in the original estimate of the liability at the acquisition date should be recognized in the income statement.

(k) Assignment of Purchase Price to Liabilities Existing at the Acquisition Date. The Opinion requires that liabilities assumed in the acquisition be recorded at their fair value. Such liabilities include warranty accruals, vacation pay, deferred compensation, unfavorable leases, contracts, and commitments, as well as accounts and notes payable and other forms of long-term debt. Liabilities should be recorded at the present value of amounts to be paid and discounted at current interest rates. The objective of allocating fair value to liabilities assumed in the acquisition is to arrive at amounts assigned as though the acquiror had incurred the liabilities as of the acquisition date.

Certain components of equity should also be evaluated to determine if the substance of the security is more closely related to debt than to equity. For example, mandatory redeemable preferred stock, which is typically classified outside of the equity section due to the redemption characteristics, should generally be recorded at fair value at the date of acquisition. The amount of cash the preferred shareholders will receive is fixed, as in a debt arrangement, and generally the other redemption and dividend terms are fixed as well. There is little difference in substance between assuming long-term debt of a target company and assuming mandatorily redeemable preferred stock. Both types of securities represent potential claims against the company for cash.

The EITF discussed Issue No. 84-35a, "Liabilities Accrued in a Purchase Business Combination," at its February 1985 meeting. Several types of liabilities were discussed, and no consensus was reached as to individual types of liabilities that should be accrued. However, the FASB staff expressed its belief that the literature is clear: Liabilities that exist at the acquisition date should be accrued at their fair values.

(l) Income Tax Effects on the Purchase Price Allocation. The following discussion of accounting for income taxes in connection with business combinations accounted for by the purchase method is based on the guidance provided in SFAS No. 96, "Accounting for Income Taxes," which was issued in December 1987 and is effective for fiscal years beginning after December 15, 1991.

Under SFAS No. 96, a deferred tax liability or asset is recognized at the acquisition date for the income tax consequences of differences between the assigned values and the tax bases of the assets acquired and the liabilities assumed. This change from APB Opinion No. 11 may seem to imply nothing more than a requirement to **gross up** the tax effects that were previously recognized under the Opinion on a **net-of-tax** basis. The change, however, is much more significant:

- The amount recognized as a deferred tax asset or liability is based on the recognition and measurement criteria required by SFAS No. 96. Thus, the timing of the reversals of the temporary differences, tax-planning strategies, and the existence of NOL and tax credit carryforwards will all affect the amounts to be recognized.
- SFAS No. 96 does not permit discounting of the income tax consequences of temporary differences. Under previous practice, discounting was often used.
- In certain situations, recognition is given to the tax benefits of the acquiror's NOL and tax credit carryforwards existing at the acquisition date. Under both APB Opinion No. 16 and APB Opinion No. 11, no recognition was given to an acquiror's carryforwards.

Consistent with prior practice, no deferred income taxes are recorded for the difference between the value assigned to and the tax basis of **goodwill.** Also, deferred income taxes are not recorded for the difference between the value assigned to and the tax basis of leveraged leases acquired in a purchase business combination.

The foregoing principles apply to both taxable and nontaxable purchase business combinations. A taxable business combination is distinguished from a nontaxable one in that, in a taxable transaction, the purchase price is assigned to the assets acquired and liabilities assumed both for income-tax and financial-reporting purposes. However, amounts assigned to the individual assets acquired and liabilities assumed for financial-statement purposes are often different from the amounts assigned for income-tax purposes. A deferred income tax liability or asset is recognized for these differences, using the recognition and measurement criteria of SFAS No. 96.

The following example from paragraph 68 of SFAS No. 96 illustrates the recognition and measurement of a deferred tax liability in a business combination and the effect of an acquired loss carryforward on that calculation:

Assumptions:

a. The enacted tax rate is 40% for all future years.

b. The purchase price is $20,000. The tax basis of the identified net assets acquired is $5,000, and the assigned value is $12,000 (i.e., there are $7,000 of temporary differences that will result in taxable amounts in future years). The acquired enterprise also has a $16,000 operating loss carryforward which, under the tax law, may be used by the acquiring enterprise in the consolidated tax return.

c. The acquiring enterprise has a liability for the deferred tax consequences of temporary differences that will result in $30,000 of net taxable amounts in future years.

d. All temporary differences of the acquired and acquiring enterprises will result in taxable amounts before the end of the acquired enterprise's loss carryforward period.

The $16,000 operating loss carryforward will offset:

(1) The $7,000 of net taxable amounts that will result from future recovery of the assigned value of the acquired net assets referred to in (b) above.

(2) Another $9,000 [$16,000 operating loss carryforward less $7,000 referred to in (1) above] of net taxable amounts attributable to the acquiring enterprise's deferred tax liability.

The amounts recorded to account for the purchase transactions are as follows:

Assigned value of the identified net assets acquired	$12,000
Reduction of acquiring enterprise's deferred tax liability [40% of the $9,000 of nex taxable amounts atributable to the acquiring enterprise's deferred tax liability referred to in (2) above]	3,600
Goodwill	4,400
Purchase price of the acquired enterprise	$20,000

If the benefits of a net operating loss or tax credit carryforward are not recognized at the acquisition date (as is the case in the above example), such benefits are recognized in subsequent years when the benefits can be used to reduce a deferred tax liability or actual taxes payable by first reducing to zero any goodwill and other noncurrent intangible assets arising from the acquisition, and then reducing income tax expense.

(m) Remeasurement of Business Combinations upon Adoption of SFAS No. 96. SFAS No. 96 permits restatement of an entity's financial statements for fiscal years before the effective date of the Statement. If the financial statements for prior years are restated, the entity must remeasure all purchase business combinations that were consummated in those prior years using the tax rates and circumstances in effect at the date of the business combination.

For business combinations not remeasured, because they were consummated prior to the earliest year restated upon adoption of SFAS No. 96, no adjustments should be made to the remaining balances of assets or liabilities that were recorded on **net-of-tax** basis under paragraph 89 of the Opinion. SFAS No. 96 requires that any differences between book and tax bases of these assets or liabilities at the date of adoption SFAS No. 96 be recognized as temporary differences pursuant to the provisions of the Statement as of the beginning of the year for which the Statement is first applied. The effect of the adjustment should be included in the cumulative effects of the change in accounting principle required in the year in which the Statement is first applied.

(n) Deferred Taxes Associated with Acquired Identifiable Intangible Assets with No Tax Basis. Differences in the tax and book bases of purchased intangible assets give rise to temporary differences under SFAS No. 96 even if the asset has no tax basis or if the amortization of the asset is not currently deductible for tax purposes. This is often the case in a tax-free business combination where, for accounting purposes, a significant portion of the purchase price is allocated to identifiable intangible assets such as franchise rights, patents, mortgage servicing rights, or other intangible assets with no tax basis.

The FASB staff and its SFAS No. 96 Implementation Task Force agreed, at the Task Force's January 1988 meeting, that these intangible assets should not be treated in a manner similar to goodwill. SFAS No. 96 (par. 23) states, in part:

> A deferred tax liability or asset shall be recognized in accordance with the requirements of this Statement for differences between the assigned values and the tax bases of the assets and liabilities (except goodwill, unallocated "negative goodwill" and leveraged leases) recognized in a purchase business combination.

Paragraph 23 (quoted above) indicates that "unallocated negative goodwill" does not represent a temporary difference. However, negative goodwill that is allocated to (as a reduction of) the fair value of noncurrent assets will affect the deferred tax liability associated with the difference between book and tax bases for those assets. Accordingly, in determining the deferred tax liability for a business combination in which negative goodwill is allocated to noncurrent assets, the negative goodwill must be computed simultaneously with the deferred tax liability.

6.12 PREACQUISITION CONTINGENCIES. SFAS No. 38 provides guidance on the accounting for preacquisition contingencies in purchase business combinations. The Statement defines a **preacquisition contingency** as, "a contingency of an enterprise that is acquired in a business combination accounted for by the purchase method and that [the contingency] is in existence before the consummation of the combination."

The guidance of SFAS No. 5, "Accounting for Contingencies," should be used in determining whether a condition, situation, or set of circumstances constitutes a contingency of the acquiree at the date of acquisition. Contingencies arising from the acquisition itself are not preacquisition contingencies (e.g., litigation over the acquisition or the tax effects of the acquisition). These contingencies are the acquiring company's contingencies rather than preacquisition contingencies.

In the allocation of the purchase price, preacquisition contingencies should be assigned a value based on their fair value if that can be determined during the allocation period or based on a reasonable estimate. After the one-year allocation period suggested by SFAS No. 38, the resolution of a preacquisition contingency should be recorded as an adjustment to income in the period of resolution. Discounting the estimated settlement amount is not required by SFAS No. 38 because the Board concluded that the timing of the settlement or receipt of the contingent settlement would generally not be sufficiently determinable to permit present valuing. However, as explained in paragraph 33 of SFAS No. 38, the use of present value techniques is not prohibited if sufficient information is available to justify their use.

The passage of time, in and of itself, does not change the resolution of a preacquisition contingency from an adjustment of purchase price to an income statement adjustment. For example, assume Company A purchased Company B in June 1986. In the purchase allocation, a liability of $10 million was recorded as "a provision for possible IRS adjustments and other contingencies." As of December 1986, it was determined that the most probable amount due the IRS was $2 million, based on the status of "in-process" IRS examinations. In July 1987, all of the preacquisition contingencies were settled and the total amount to be paid was approximately $2 million. In this case, the allocation period would basically end in December 1986, because the company is no longer waiting for information in order to make the allocation of purchase price required by paragraph 5 of SFAS No. 38. On the basis of the information available in December 1986, Company A could allocate the purchase price using a reasonable estimate of the fair value of the preacquisition contingency. Accordingly, income statement recognition in July 1987 for resolution of the liability would be inappropriate, and the final adjustment should be reflected as an adjustment to the purchase price.

6.13 PUSHDOWN ACCOUNTING. In October 1979 the AICPA Accounting Standards Executive Committee (AcSEC) prepared an Issues Paper entitled "Pushdown Accounting." The Issues Paper's advisory committee dealt with determining the percentage **change in ownership** that would justify a new basis of accounting.

Members of AcSEC supported 90% as a minimum change of ownership that would justify pushdown accounting. At the time ACSEC decided to support pushdown accounting, it was not supported by practice or by other authoritative accounting or regulatory bodies. In January 1983, the Federal Home Loan Bank Board issued guidance in R-Memorandum No. 55 (which was superseded by R-55a in 1986) consistent with the Issues Paper, which permits but does not require pushdown accounting. The SEC also agreed in SAB No. 54 which indicates that "the Staff believes that purchase transactions that result in an entity becoming substantially wholly-owned (as defined in Rule 1-02(z) of Regulation S-X) establish a new basis of accounting for the purchased assets and liabilities."

Accordingly, it would appear that a new basis of accounting in the separate financial statements of an acquired entity may be applied when the change in ownership is at least 90%. In the case of a step acquisition, pushdown accounting may be applied when an individual, company, or control group obtains 90% ownership or more of the acquired entity. Although instances of pushdown accounting have occurred in changes of ownership approaching 80%, the use of pushdown below 90% is still somewhat controversial.

As noted above, the SEC's position on pushdown accounting has been based on an entity becoming "substantially wholly-owned" rather than the "substantial change in ownership" concept discussed in the 1979 AcSEC Issues Paper. The SEC staff has indicated that SAB No. 54 was intended to require pushdown accounting when an entity became "substantially wholly-owned" even if accomplished through a step acquisition that takes a number of years to complete. In addition, the SEC will address each situation on an individual "facts and circumstances" basis.

In June 1985, the EITF discussed Issue No. 85-21, "Changes of Ownership Resulting in a New Basis of Accounting." Several accounting issues regarding the application of pushdown accounting were discussed. No consensus views were reached by the EITF, and the EITF chairman indicated that pushdown issues would be dealt with in the standards phase of the FASB's consolidations project to the extent that it was addressed in the AcSEC Issues Paper on pushdown accounting.

As with all aspects of business combinations, an evaluation should be made of the change in ownership that results in the application of pushdown accounting to assure that the substance of the acquisition and the change in ownership, not just the legal form, determine the appropriate accounting. For example, 80% of a company (X) is owned by the public (Group A) and 20% is owned by two individuals, the president and a board member (Group B). Two unrelated individuals propose to form a holding company (HC) and capitalize it with

$1 million. Then through a series of transactions with Group A and Group B shareholders, HC will acquire 90% of X's stock. HC will be 78% owned by the two unrelated individuals which formed HC and 22% by Group B. Even though X is 90% owned by HC, the application of pushdown accounting would be questionable. In evaluating the acquisition, one should look at the total change in ownership of X held by the two unrelated individuals after the transaction. After the acquistition, the unrelated individuals that formed HC own 78% of HC's 90% ownership interest in X, or approximately 70%. Between the Group A shareholders and Group B shareholders, there is a continuing ownership interest in X of 30%. It is unlikely that one could argue that a 70% change in ownership justifies the use of pushdown accounting.

(a) Pushdown of Parent Company Debt.   In applying the concepts of pushdown accounting, questions often arise regarding the pushdown of the acquiror's debt to its subsidiary. For example, a company (A) forms a subsidiary to acquire the net assets of another company. A has borrowed 100% of the purchase price, which exceeds the recorded basis of the net assets acquired. A intends to service this debt from the earnings of the subsidiary, whose cash flows are expected to be sufficient to cover the debt service on the loan. Should A's debt be pushed down to the subsidiary?

The subject of pushdown of parent company debt to a subsidiary was discussed by the EITF without reaching a consensus. In December 1987, the SEC released SAB No. 73, "Pushdown Basis of Accounting for Parent Company Debt Related to Subsidiary Acquisition." The SAB requires that debt incurred or mandatory redeemable preferred stock issued by a parent to acquire substantially all of the common stock of a subsidiary should be pushed down along with the related purchase price adjustment if:

1. The subsidiary is to assume the debt of the parent in a current or planned transaction.
2. The proceeds of a debt or equity offering of the subsidiary will be used to retire all or part of the parent company's debt, or
3. The subsidiary pledges its assets as collateral or otherwise guarantees the parent company's debt.

(b) Exceptions to Pushdown of Parent Company Debt.   The SAB does not require debt to be pushed down to the subsidiary if only the subsidiary's stock is pledged as collateral for the debt since, in the case of default, such a pledge would not give the parent's debtholders priority over the subsidiary's debtholders but rather would simply transfer the parent's common stock investment to the parent's debtholders. In addition, the SAB provides guidance on the required disclosures in the notes to financial statements and the registrant's "Management's Discussion and Analysis of Financial Condition and Results of Operations."

The SEC has also indicated, in regards to the pushdown of parent-company debt to the separate financial statements of a subsidiary when pushdown accounting itself is not required because of the specific exclusions outlined in SAB No. 54, that pushdown of parent-company debt generally becomes an issue only when pushdown accounting is applied. However, the SEC may require pushdown accounting (and pushdown of the related parent-company debt) in situations where there is public debt, preferred stock, or significant minority interest, depending on the individual facts and circumstances.

6.14 ALLOCATION PERIOD.   The Opinion does not specifically address the period of time subsequent to the acquisition date over which the research and fact gathering must be accomplished and the purchase price allocated. The reasonableness of the allocation period should be determined through an analysis of the specific facts and circumstances surrounding the business combination, including:

• The size and complexity of the entity acquired.
• Information available to the acquiror prior to the consummation date.

- The acquiror's management's knowledge of and expertise in the acquiree's business.
- Demonstration by management of its ongoing efforts to avail itself of relevant information.

In connection with the accounting for preacquisition contingencies (discussed in section 6.12 of this chapter), paragraph 4(b) of SFAS No. 38 defines the "allocation period for preacquisition contingencies" as follows:

> Although the time required will vary with the circumstances, the allocation period should usually not exceed one year from consummation of the business combination.

It is not unusual for a company to acquire another company in a business combination to be accounted for by the purchase method at or near the end of a reporting period or its fiscal year. In such cases, the allocation of the purchase price may not be completed by the date the acquiror's financial statements are issued. In such cases, a preliminary allocation should be made and disclosure should be made in the financial statements that further adjustments may arise as a result of finalization of the ongoing study. Changes subsequent to the issuance of financial statements in the allocation of purchase price should then be evaluated by determining (1) if the original allocation, as reported, was the result of preliminary evaluation of an ongoing data-gathering and evaluation process, which in management's opinion was not expected to differ significantly upon finalizing the study; and (2) whether the study was finalized in a reasonable period of time subsequent to the acquisition. Adjustments to preliminary amounts generally result in corresponding adjustments to goodwill.

6.15 SAB NO. 61.   In May 1986, the SEC issued SAB No. 61, "Adjustments to Allowances for Business Combination Loan Losses-Purchase Method Accounting." The SAB indicates that, with rare exceptions, the SEC does not believe changes in allowances for loan losses are necessary as part of the allocation process in applying purchase accounting adjustments. The SEC believes that, assuming the appropriate methodology is followed by each party to the business combination, each company's estimate of the uncollectible portion of a loan portfolio would fall within a range of acceptability.

However, the SEC concedes that a purchase accounting adjustment may be required to reflect a difference in valuation of a portfolio of loans or receivables if the acquiror's intent with regard to ultimate recovery of the loans or receivables is demonstrably different from the plans or assumptions used by the acquiree in estimating its loan loss reserve. For example, the acquiree may have intended to hold the loans to maturity or to assist a troubled borrower through a long-term workout on the loan, whereas the acquiror plans to sell such loans or foreclose on the underlying collateral. The net carrying value of the loans recorded in purchase allocation should therefore be based on the acquiror's plan of recovery.

Loan losses and allowances for uncollectible accounts and similar reserves are typically not considered preacquisition contingencies. Reasonable methods of estimating such losses or allowances should be used by the acquiree and evaluated by the acquiror at the date of acquisition. Subsequent adjustments to the allowances to reflect the ultimate outcome or resolution of the receivables is presumed to be based on changes in the economic factors surrounding the particular receivable, the nature of the receivable, and the evaluation of the collectibility of the receivables in light of events occurring subsequent to the business combination. Accordingly, such changes in the related valuation accounts should not be accounted for as adjustments to the cost of the business combination.

The provisions and guidance of SAB No. 61 have also been applied to other assets acquired in a purchase business combination. The SEC staff has indicated the guidance should be interpreted broadly with its provisions applied to items such as warranty reserves, inventory obsolescence reserves, and bad debt reserves of nonfinancial institutions, among others.

6.16 DATE USED TO RECORD THE ACQUISITION.   Paragraph 93 of the Opinion indicates that the date of the acquisition is ordinarily the date of consummation of the acquisition (i.e., the date assets are received and other assets are given or securities are issued). Accordingly, such date is normally used for purposes of recording the business combination. The Opinion also provides for the use of a **convenience date,** whereby the parties to the combination may designate as the effective date the end of an accounting period that falls between the initiation date and the consummation date. One condition for using a convenience date is that the written agreement for the acquisition provides that effective control of the acquired company is transferred to the acquiror by the effective date without restriction, except for those restrictions required to protect the stockholders of the acquiree. The restrictions permitted are those that prohibit significant changes in operations or disposal of assets, require normal payment of dividends, and the like.

In the event a convenience date is used, the Opinion requires that adjustments be made to the cost of the acquired company and net income for imputed interest at an appropriate current rate on the assets given, liabilities incurred, or stock issued as of the transfer date to acquire the company.

Factors that should be evaluated in determining if control has passed to the acquiror include the following:

- The combination has been approved by both companies' boards of directors.
- The acquiree does not do anything between the effective date and consummation date outside the ordinary course of business.
- Management of the combined entity takes over the day-to-day operations of the acquiree.
- Only one set of postacquisition accounting records is maintained from the effective date forward.
- Combined operational meetings involving employees of both companies are held.

Use of a convenience date subsequent to the consummation date is not provided for in the Opinion.

6.17 DISCLOSURE IN FINANCIAL STATEMENTS.   Paragraph 96 of the Opinion requires that pro forma results of operations be presented as supplemental information for the period in which the companies are combined and, if comparative statements are presented, for the immediately preceding period.

6.18 ILLUSTRATIONS OF POOLING AND PURCHASE.   Two cases are presented to illustrate pooling and purchase accounting. In the first case, Exhibit 6.1, Issuing Company acquires Combining Company in a pooling of interests that is taxable. In the second case, Exhibit 6.2, given the same data as in the first case, the business combination must be treated as a purchase combination because the action of a 15% shareholder immediately following the combination (sale of shares) violates the pooling criteria.

SAMPLE POOLING
Consolidated Balance Sheet
Date of Combination ($ in thousands)

Assume two companies decide to combine. In the merger negotiations, the companies agree to exchange common stock for common stock. The larger of the two companies (Issuing Co.) agrees to exchange one of its shares for 5.333 shares of the smaller company (Combining Co.). Combining Co. has been fair-valued at $15,000,000 by a reputable investment banker. Issuing Co. will pay $15/share in cash for fractional shares. All criteria of structuring a business combination as a pooling of interests have been met. Approximately 5% of Combining Co.'s shareholders have dissented to the transaction. The transaction is accounted for as a taxable pooling.

| | Historical | | Adjustments | |
	Issuing	Combining	Dr. (Cr.)	Consolidated
Assets				
Current Assets:				
Cash and cash equivalents	$ 3,746	$ 2,469	$(717) (b)	$ 5,498
Accounts receivable	7,511	4,728		12,239
Inventories	4,293	2,253	467 (a)	7,013
Total current assets	15,550	9,450	(250)	24,750
Property, plant and equipment:				
Land	2,704	402		3,106
Buildings and improvements	9,688	2,796		12,484
Machinery and equipment	10,068	8,965	——	19,033
	22,460	12,163		34,623
Less accumulated depreciation	7,210	2,663	——	9,873
Property, plant and equipment—net	15,250	9,500		24,750
Notes receivable	2,591	1,116		3,707
Cost in excess of net assets acquired	2,368	474		2,842
Other assets	1,741	960	——	2,701
Total assets	$37,500	$21,500	$(250)	$58,750
Liabilities and Shareholders' Equity				
Current Liabilities:				
Accounts payable	$ 2,884	$ 1,469		$ 4,353
Accrued liabilities	3,150	2,772		5,922
Current portion of long-term debt	1,673	603		2,276
Current taxes payable	1,043	1,381	——	2,424
Total current liabilities	8,750	6,225	——	14,975
Long-term debt	9,500	2,970		12,470
Deferred income taxes	3,650	1,005	$230 (d)	4,425
Shareholders' Equity:				
Common stock	500	1,000	643*	857
Paid-in capital	2,275	4,375	(156)**	6,806
Retained earnings	12,825	5,925	(467) (a)	19,217
Total shareholders' equity	15,600	11,300	20	26,491
Total liabilities and shareholders' equity	$37,500	$21,500	$250	$58,750

Exhibit 6.1.   Pooling-of-Interests.

(a) Adjustment to conform accounting policy of Combining Co. ("C") with Issuing Co. ("I"). C used LIFO Inventory methodology to account for certain raw materials while I used FIFO for all inventories. The LIFO reserve at date of combination was $467.

(b) Acquisition of 47,800 shares of C, $1 par value, common stock not tendered by dissenting or fractional shareholders for cash totaling $717.

(c) 178,538 shares of I, $2 par value, common stock were exchanged for the remaining 952,200 shares of C common stock.

(d) Adjustment to reflect tax benefits of deferred tax consequences of different temporary differences, credits and unrecognized tax benefits of I and C.

	*		**	
	(357) (c)		3706	(c)
	952 (c)		669	(b)
	48 (b)		(4301)	(c)
	643		(230)	(d)
			(156)	

Exhibit 6.1. *Continued.*

SAMPLE PURCHASE
Consolidated Balance Sheet
Date of Combination ($ in thousands)

Assume the same facts as in the previous transaction; however, a 15% shareholder sold his shares immediately after the exchange and thus, violated the pooling of interests criteria. Accordingly, the transaction has been accounted for as a purchase combination.

	Historical		Adjustments	
	Acquiror	Acquiree	Dr. (Cr.)	Consolidated
Assets				
Current Assets:				
Cash and cash equivalents	$ 3,746	$ 2,469	$ (717) (a)	$ 5,498
Accounts receivable	7,511	4,728		12,239
Inventories	4,293	2,253	467 (c)	7,013
Total current assets	15,550	9,450	(250)	24,750
Property, plant and equipment:				
Land	2,704	402	1,148 (c)	4,254
Buildings and improvements	9,688	2,796	54 (c)	
Machinery and equipment	10,068	8,965	35 (c)	19,068
	22,460	12,163	1,237	35,860
Less accumulated depreciation	7,210	2,663	2,663 (c)	7,210
Property, plant and equipment—net	15,250	9,500	3,900	28,650
Notes receivable	2,591	1,116	34 (c)	3,741
Cost in excess of net assets acquired	2,368	474	(474) (c)	2,368
Other assets	1,741	960	(282)*	2,419
Total assets	$37,500	$21,500	$ 2,928	$61,928
Liabilities and Shareholders' Equity				
Current Liabilities:				
Accounts payable	$ 2,884	$ 1,469		4,353
Accrued liabilities	3,150	2,772		5,922
				(continued)

Exhibit 6.2. Purchase Accounting.

	Historical		Adjustments	
	Acquiror	**Acquiree**	**Dr. (Cr.)**	**Consolidated**
Current portion of long-term debt	1,673	603		2,276
Current taxes payable	1,043	1,381		2,424
Total current liabilities	8,750	6,225		14,975
Long-term debt	9,500	2,970	$ (450) (c)	12,920
Deferred income taxes	3,650	1,005	505**	4,150
Shareholders' Equity:				
Common stock	500	1,000	643***	857
Paid-in capital	2,275	4,375	(9,551)****	16,201
Retained earnings	12,825	5,925	5,925 (c)	12,825
Total shareholders' equity	15,600	11,300	(2,983)	29,883
Total liabilities and shareholders' equity	$37,500	$21,500	$(2,928)	$61,928

(a) Acquisition of 47,800 shares of Acquiree, $1 par value, common stock not tendered by dissenting or fractional shareholders for cash totaling $717.

(b) To reflect the issuance of 178,538 shares of Acquiror $2 par value common stock to effect the combination with Acquiree. Such stock has been independently valued at $14,283.

(c) To reflect the fair value of assets and liabilities of Acquiree obtained in exchange for stock and cash:

	Fair Value
Cash and cash equivalents	$ 2,469
Accounts receivable	4,728
Inventories	2,720
Land	1,550
Buildings and improvements	2,850
Machinery and equipment	9,000
Accumulated depreciation	0
Notes receivable	1,150
Cost in excess of net assets acquired	0
Other assets	178
Accounts payable	(1,469)
Accured liabilities	(2,772)
Current portion of long-term debt	(603)
Current taxes payable	(1,381)
Long-term debt	(3,420)
Deferred Income taxes	0
	15,000
Less: Cash paid [see (a)]	(717)
Fair value of stock exchanged [see (b)]	(14,283)
	$ 0

(d) Adjustment to reflect the impact of the readjustment of tax basis of assets of Acquiree and tax differences of Acquiree utilized by the combination entity.

				***		****	
*	(782) (c)	**	1,005 (c)		48 (a)		669 (a)
	500 (d)		(500) (d)		(357) (b)		(13,926) (b)
	(282)		505		952 (c)		3,706 (c)
					643		(9,551)

Exhibit 6.2. *Continued.*

LEVERAGED BUYOUT (LBO)

6.19 DEFINITION.   Authoritative accounting literature does not provide a definition of an LBO transaction. However, an LBO can best be described as a financing technique for acquiring a company wherein a large portion of the purchase price is derived from borrowings, often some or all of which are secured by the underlying assets of the entity being acquired. In most LBO transactions, management of an existing company (OLDCO) and one or more new investors form a holding company (NEWCO) to acquire all of OLDCO's outstanding common stock.

6.20 STRUCTURE.   There is no predetermined manner in which to structure an LBO; a structure is designed to meet the requirements of each transaction, giving appropriate consideration to existing and forecasted cash flows, capital expenditure and working capital needs, income tax considerations, potential dispositions, and lender requirements. There are, however, common elements in the structure of each LBO transaction.

(a) Legal Form.   NEWCO's are generally formed to acquire OLDCO. Typically, there is no real economic incentive or disincentive to form NEWCO, although for practical purposes many companies acquired in an LBO transaction are publicly owned and are acquired through a tender offer and a NEWCO is generally formed to hold the tendered OLDCO shares prior to the closing of the tender offer. NEWCO may also be used to effect a **squeeze-out** merger, which is a mechanism used to acquire untendered shares. Depending on OLDCO's state of incorporation, a squeeze-out can generally be accomplished after two-thirds of OLDCO's stockholders have tendered their OLDCO stock to NEWCO. At that point, NEWCO may have the legal right to effect a merging of NEWCO into OLDCO, without shareholder approval, and force an exchange of cash or NEWCO securities for the untendered OLDCO stock.

Nonpublic companies acquired in an LBO generally have a limited number of stockholders; therefore, establishing NEWCO simply to acquire shares may be regarded as an unnecessary expense. However, for accounting purposes, the need to form NEWCO to acquire OLDCO is very important. That is, without forming NEWCO, the transaction can only be accounted for as a restructuring-recapitalization for which no change in accounting basis is appropriate.

(b) Management Participation.   In most if not all LBOs, management has the critical role of managing OLDCO's assets to assure repayment of borrowings and maximize value to NEWCO's stockholders. Accordingly, management's involvement in structuring the LBO transaction and, more importantly, their continued involvement in managing OLDCO after the acquisition is often crucial to the success of the LBO transaction. Accordingly, key members of OLDCO management are generally given a substantive incentive to assure the continued successful operation of OLDCO. This is typically accomplished through management's investment in NEWCO.

Management may be granted options to acquire additional NEWCO stock, generally at a price based on the fair market value of the stock at the date of the LBO transaction. A vesting period of several years is often required before management is entitled to receive unrestricted ownership of the stock. The options and warrants provide the stockholders of NEWCO with a mechanism by which to assure continued employment of key management. The granting of options and warrants also provides management the ability to acquire NEWCO equity at bargain rates (assuming that the fair market value of the stock rises) at a future date, thus obviating the need for them to make up-front cash investments.

(c) Financing Arrangements.   The borrowing required to fund an LBO may come from a variety of sources: commercial banks, insurance companies, other financial institutions, public investment, and so on. As mentioned above, financing arrangements are dependent upon cash flow needs for operations, debt service, and dividend distributions. Frequently, however, the financing consists of bank and institutional term loans, private investor debt and equity investments placed by investment bankers, and a bridge loan. The bridge loan is made available by the lenders until less expensive permanent financing is obtained.

Another factor that may affect the legal form of the transaction is the nature of the security required by lenders. That is, NEWCO as the acquiror generally incurs the indebtedness to acquire OLDCO. One or more lending institutions, however, may desire more security on their loans than a pledge of OLDCO stock owned by NEWCO. More specifically, some lending institutions require their loans to be placed in the legal entity that contains the operating assets, that is, OLDCO.

A number of LBO transactions have also included financing through the issuance of debt and/or equity securities to the former owners of OLDCO. Certain securities in an LBO may take the form of what is known as **paid-in-kind** (PIK) securities. These securities, for a specified period of years, pay interest or dividends by issuing additional securities. Such securities provide NEWCO relief from its cash flow needs in the early years following the LBO.

Numerous LBOs have also issued NEWCO common stock to OLDCO shareholders. This provides such shareholders with the potential for large profits frequently generated from postacquisition sales of assets, or public offerings of NEWCO stock at prices in excess of the LBO acquisition price.

(d) Tax Considerations.   A multitude of factors affect the taxability of the transaction to OLDCO and its stockholders. There are, however, some common strategies to minimize income taxes to both parties. For example, OLDCO's management may wish to exchange part or all of its equity interest in OLDCO for an equity interest in NEWCO without paying tax on the appreciation in the OLDCO stock. This can be accomplished through the use of an acquisition holding company to which management transfers its OLDCO stock in exchange for NEWCO stock.

As another example, if a corporate seller of OLDCO has been filing a consolidated return, the buyer and seller may jointly make a § 338(h)(10) election, the effect of which is to treat a stock acquisition as an asset purchase for tax purposes. This will allow higher depreciation deductions to offset postacquisition taxable income. The election may be beneficial to both the seller and the buyer for nontax reasons since the transaction is actually a stock rather than an asset transfer.

Other tax strategies will depend on the specific facts and circumstances of the entities and individuals involved in the transaction.

6.21 HISTORICAL PERSPECTIVE.   The determination of whether an LBO transaction was a purchase business combination, a step-acquisition, or a treasury stock transaction was a difficult accounting problem that accountants increasingly had to solve as the pace of LBO transactions increased. In an LBO transaction in which OLDCO shareholders become NEWCO shareholders, the price paid by NEWCO to acquire their OLDCO stock could be considered as purchase price, a capital transaction, or a mixture of both.

GAAP was not clear regarding the accounting for LBO transactions, and accountants were required to make some difficult decisions regarding the proper manner in which to account for the transactions. Not surprisingly, the decisions produced a variety of accounting results that often meant the difference between the write-up of assets to fair value, or a reduction of equity. In many cases, a reduction of equity resulted in NEWCO reporting a negative net worth. Although the underlying economics of LBO transactions are not changed based on whether the accounting results produce a write-up of assets or a reduction of equity, it is almost undeniable that a company attempting to raise capital will have an easier time doing so if it has positive, rather than negative, equity.

The SEC staff, along with the accounting profession, naturally became concerned regarding the diversity in accounting results and in the proper accounting for LBO transactions. Therefore, while the SEC staff internally adopted guidelines for determining the circumstances in which an LBO transaction should be accounted for as a purchase business combination, they raised the issue of accounting for LBO transactions at the EITF's May 1986 meeting so that the accounting profession would be more directly involved in establishing accounting guidance. The SEC staff and the profession were especially interested in resolving this issue because of its significance to investors, particularly when OLDCO shareholders become NEWCO shareholders.

The EITF reached a consensus on Issue No. 86-16, "Carryover of Predecessor Cost in Leveraged Buyout Transactions," in July 1987. This consensus, however, did not address the accounting for transactions in which an OLDCO shareholder decreased his ownership interest in NEWCO relative to what he owned in OLDCO (these situations are sometimes referred to as **leveraged sell-offs**). At about the same time, the SEC staff communicated to the EITF that LBO transactions seemed to be evolving and that they may not resemble the LBO transaction described in Issue No. 86-16.

In June 1988, the FASB staff raised Issue No. 88-16, "Basis in Leveraged Buyout Transactions When the Previous Owner's Interest Declines." In dealing with Issue 88-16, the EITF formed a working group to formulate a proposal to deal with the varied matters covered by this issue. In the course of the various EITF and working group meetings, it was decided that one comprehensive consensus should be prepared that would encompass the matters addressed in Issue Nos. 86-16 and 88-16. In doing so, the EITF's conclusions were largely influenced by a desire on the part of the SEC staff to limit diversity in practice, prevent potential accounting abuses, and limit the number of circumstances requiring consultation with the SEC staff. The result of the EITF's efforts, reached by consensus at its May 1989 meeting, is predominantly an objective set of rules that define the accounting for all LBO transactions.

6.22 ACCOUNTING FOR THE LBO TRANSACTION.   EITF Issue No. 88-16 indicates that the substance of the LBO transaction must be evaluated to determine whether it constitutes:

1. a financial restructuring-recapitalization for which no change in accounting basis would be appropriate,
2. a step acquisition for which a partial change in accounting basis would be appropriate, or
3. a purchase by new controlling investors for which a partial or complete change in basis, based on the fair value of the transaction, would be appropriate.

The EITF's consensus guidance consists of an elaborate set of criteria that define when a new accounting basis is appropriate (situations 2 and 3 above), and how to determine that new accounting basis.

In the context of basis adjustments to assets and liabilities acquired, LBOs are considered to be analogous to purchase business combinations discussed previously in this chapter.

The EITF consensus is divided into three sections. The first section addresses the circumstances in which a change in control has occurred, the second section addresses the calculation of NEWCO's recorded investment in OLDCO, and the third section addresses limitations on recording the basis otherwise calculated in the second section.

6.23 CHANGE IN CONTROL.   The EITF consensus specifies this general provision:

> A partial or complete change in accounting basis is appropriate only when there has been a change in control of voting interest; that is, a new controlling shareholder or group of shareholders must be established.

This provision stems from the underlying assumption that the establishment of a new controlling shareholder or control group results in a transaction similar to a purchase business combination, as opposed to a recapitalization-restructuring for which a change in basis is not appropriate.

The consensus guidance establishes specific objective and subjective criteria to be evaluated in determining whether a new controlling shareholder or control group (defined below) has been established. Included in this determination is a definition of which shareholders are part of the control group. The consensus guidance also describes the accounting result if a change in control has not occurred.

(a) Objective Criteria.   Except for the most straightforward circumstance under which a change in control has occurred, that is, a single new shareholder gains the ability to unilaterally exercise control over NEWCO, the guidance in this section is based on two underlying assumptions:

1. New shareholders that meet the definition for inclusion in the NEWCO control group will act in concert to exercise control over NEWCO. This assumption concludes that by virtue of (a) the significance of the shareholders' economic interests in NEWCO, and (b) the contemporaneous acquisition of NEWCO interests, such shareholders have similar goals and will consistently act together to control NEWCO.

2. Members of management have a commonality of interest among themselves that distinguishes them from being "typical" shareholders. This commonality of interest is derived from management's shared responsibility to achieve the objectives of the enterprise, and their authority to establish policies and make decisions by which those objectives will be pursued.

The foregoing assumptions address circumstances wherein there has been a step-acquisition by one or more parties. However, the EITF also recognized that there were some circumstances in which certain shareholders in the NEWCO control group had a step-acquisition while other shareholders in the NEWCO control group decreased their ownership interest in NEWCO in relation to their percentage ownership interest in OLDCO. In this latter situation, it was not always clear whether there had been a change in control. Accordingly, the EITF provided explicit guidance to address this issue. This particular portion of the EITF consensus guidance was heavily debated because, in some circumstances, following the guidance could produce a potentially contentious result. For example, as Exhibit 6.3 demonstrates, Investor 2 has been excluded from the NEWCO3 control group for the reason indicated, yet Investors 1 and 2 clearly have a majority ownership in OLDCO and in NEWCO. The question follows then, if Investors 1 and 2 could have controlled OLDCO *and* NEWCO, has there actually been a change in control?

In applying the objective tests for determining whether there has been a change in control, the NEWCO shareholders were divided into three groups—management, shareholders with a greater percentage of residual interest in NEWCO than they held in OLDCO, and shareholders with the same or lower percentage of residual interest in NEWCO than they held in OLDCO. Each group of shareholders was believed to have characteristics distinct from the other groups.

Management shareholders are **presumed** to be part of the control group because they are presumed to have the ability to significantly influence the terms of the LBO transaction and the operations of OLDCO after the LBO transaction. Further, their participation in the LBO transaction indicates a commonality of interest between them and other members of the control group. However, in some instances, management has clearly not participated with the other members of the control group in promoting the LBO transaction, such as when management has pursued its own bid to acquire OLDCO and loses its quest to a rival bidder.

The following examples illustrate the change in control criterion as described in Section 1(a) of the consensus (all ownership interests are fully diluted).

	OLDCO	NEWCO1	NEWCO2	NEWCO3	NEWCO4
Management	20%	60%	30%	0	40%
Investor 1	40	40	10	45	20
Investor 2	40	0	0	15	0
Investor 3	0	0	30	20	20
Investor 4	0	0	30	20	20
Total	100%	100%	100%	100%	100%

NEWCO1 would qualify as a change in control under the criterion in Section 1(a)(i) of the consensus guidance (management obtains unilateral control of NEWCO1).

NEWCO2 would qualify as a change in control under the criterion in Section 1(a)(ii) of the consensus guidance because Investors 3 and 4, who are members of the NEWCO2 control group, obtain unilateral control of NEWCO2.

Assuming Investor 2 is not a member of the NEWCO3 control group, for example, because Investor 2 has no capital at risk in NEWCO other than a common stock interest, NEWCO3 would qualify as a change in control under the criterion in Section 1(a)(iii) of the consensus guidance.

NEWCO4 would not qualify as a change in control because management and Investor 1 are in NEWCO4's control group. A subset of the NEWCO4 control group (management and Investor 1) owned a majority voting interest in OLDCO. See Section 1(c) of the consensus guidance for the criteria for inclusion in the control group.

Exhibit 6.3.   Examples of the change in control criterion used in the EITF consensus on Issue 88-16. Reprinted from Exhibit 88-16B of the EITF consensus.

Therefore, in those unusual circumstances, the EITF believed that the commonality of interest linking management with the other members of the control group was absent, and management should not be presumed part of the NEWCO control group.

When the presumption that management is part of the NEWCO control group has been overcome, management is nevertheless considered a single shareholder in applying other tests required by the EITF consensus because management is still considered to have a commonality of interest among themselves. This logic would seem to be borne out in situations such as the competing management bid described above.

When management is included in the NEWCO control group, they are included without regard to their ownership interest in NEWCO. That is, there is no de minimus exception provided because of the significant influence that management is deemed to have in controlling NEWCO.

NEWCO shareholders that have increased their ownership interest in relation to the percentage ownership interest that they had in OLDCO are divided into two groups based upon their percentage ownership in NEWCO. This division was made so that shareholders representing the passive investing public could be excluded from the control group.

NEWCO shareholders that have *decreased* their relative ownership interest were generally perceived as trying to pass control of OLDCO on to new shareholders. For example, the President of OLDCO owns 100% of OLDCO's outstanding stock and desires to retire, but either has an interest in retaining an "equity kicker" or the new owners are unable to borrow sufficient funds to buy out all of the President's equity in OLDCO. However, there were other examples in which it appeared that control was not being passed on to new owners. Accordingly, the EITF devised two tests designed to determine whether a shareholder was aligned with other members of the control group and, therefore, should be included in or excluded from the control group.

The first test, a **voting-interest test,** is applied to each individual shareholder. It determines whether a shareholder is aligned with other control group members based upon the significance of that shareholder's voting ownership interest in NEWCO. This test employs a complicated set of criteria for determining what constitutes a voting interest.

For the individual shareholder being tested, all dilutive securities owned by that shareholder must be considered exercised when calculating the percentage voting interest. This fully-diluted amount represents the maximum ownership interest that can be obtained by the shareholder. Dilutive securities held by other shareholders are treated as having been exercised when their terms are no less favorable than the terms of the dilutive securities held by the shareholder being tested. However, the effect of dilution cannot reduce the continuing shareholder's voting interest percentage below that which he can currently exercise.

Rights held by a continuing shareholder to purchase NEWCO stock at fair value at the time of exercise need not be considered in the voting-interest test if such rights are not exercisable for a substantive period of time (currently at least 1 year).

The second test, a **capital-at-risk test,** is also applied to individual shareholders. It determines whether a shareholder is aligned with other control group members based upon the significance of the shareholder's economic interest in NEWCO. Although authoritative accounting literature defines control and significant influence based upon the percentage of voting interest, many believe that a person holding a significant economic interest does have significant influence or may effectively control an entity.

(b) Subjective Criteria.   A basic tenet of accounting theory is that the substance of the transaction, rather than merely its legal form, should prevail in recording the event. For example, the EITF believed it would be inappropriate for a new shareholder to form NEWCO, have NEWCO acquire 100% of the outstanding common stock of OLDCO, sell 100% of NEWCO's common stock back to the original OLDCO stockholders, and conclude that a change in control had occurred. Accordingly, the EITF identified a number of factors that should be considered in assessing whether the change in control, determined as a result of applying the objective guidance, is truly a substantive change in control.

(c) No Change in Control.   The consensus guidance states the following when a change in control has not occurred:

> If a change in control is deemed not to have occurred as a result of applying the above guidance, the transaction should be considered a recapitalization-restructuring for which a change in accounting basis is not appropriate.

In other words, the transaction is accounted for as what is alternatively referred to as a redemption, distribution or effective dividend.

6.24 DETERMINING THE CARRYING AMOUNT OF NEWCO'S INVESTMENT IN OLDCO. The EITF consensus sets forth this general provision:

> The form of a transaction by which the investor obtains its interest in NEWCO does not change the accounting to be applied. In general, if an investor in NEWCO owned a residual interest in OLDCO, then the lesser of that investor's residual interest in OLDCO or NEWCO is carried over at the investor's predecessor basis.

Again, although the acquisition of OLDCO by NEWCO could take many different forms as a result of legal, tax or other implications, the EITF concluded that the substance of the transaction should provide the basis for recording the transaction.

The following paragraphs describe the calculation of the carrying amount of NEWCO's investment in OLDCO. It addresses OLDCO interests acquired from all continuing shareholders (i.e., those OLDCO shareholders who have acquired a NEWCO interest), differentiating between those who are, and those who are not, part of the NEWCO control group.

Continuing shareholders who are part of the NEWCO control group are viewed as having acquired OLDCO in step-fashion. Accordingly, the historical cost accounting principles applicable to a step-acquisition are applied. To the extent that a shareholder owns the same percentage of residual interest in NEWCO as in OLDCO, no recordable event has occurred with respect to that residual interest; that is, no exchange has taken place, and the historical cost basis in the OLDCO investment should not be changed. If there is a net increase in ownership, then the carrying amount of NEWCO's investment in OLDCO is generally determined in a manner that is similar to a step-acquisition, and the increase in ownership is recorded at fair value.

Some continuing shareholders who are members of the NEWCO control group, however, actually **decrease** their relative ownership interests. These continuing shareholders are viewed as having retained a portion of their original interest in OLDCO. The portion of the OLDCO investment that has not been disposed of is one in which no exchange has taken place. Accordingly, the proportional historical cost basis for that portion of the investment that is retained is not changed.

Continuing shareholders who are not part of the NEWCO control group are further subdivided between those who own less than 5% of NEWCO and those who own 5% or more of NEWCO, but who own no more of NEWCO (as a percentage) than they held in OLDCO. (This latter group of shareholders was previously excluded from the control group because they had less than a 20% voting interest or less than 20% of the cumulative capital-at-risk in NEWCO.)

The first group, the passive investing public, is not considered parties to the step-acquisition of OLDCO. Therefore, their OLDCO interests acquired by NEWCO may be valued at fair value. The latter group of shareholders cannot, by prior definition, be considered the passive investing public since they own 5% or more of NEWCO. Although these individuals were excluded from the NEWCO control group under the "Change in Control" section discussed above, they, if viewed as a group, could have significant influence as NEWCO investors. Accordingly, their OLDCO interests will be valued by NEWCO at their predecessor basis if they **collectively** have significant influence (i.e., they own 20% or more) of NEWCO. If they do not collectively have significant influence over NEWCO, then their OLDCO interests may be valued at fair value.

OLDCO interests acquired by NEWCO from noncontinuing shareholders may be valued at fair value as an exchange has clearly taken place.

6.25 LIMITATION ON THE CARRYING AMOUNT OF NEWCO'S INVESTMENT IN OLDCO.

The following paragraphs address the valuation of OLDCO based upon the ability to validate the value of NEWCO securities issued to acquire OLDCO. Notwithstanding any conclusion reached under the previous section, this section may limit NEWCO's ability to record all or a portion of its investment in OLDCO at fair value. The EITF's general provision is stated as follows:

> The fair value of any securities issued by NEWCO to acquire OLDCO should be objectively determinable. Fair value should not be used, whether or not the NEWCO securities are publicly traded, unless at least 80 percent of the fair value of consideration paid to acquire OLDCO equity interests comprises monetary consideration (the monetary test).

The EITF consensus defines the element of the numerator and denominator in determining what percentage of the consideration paid by NEWCO constitutes monetary consideration.

If less than 80% of the total consideration paid by NEWCO to acquire OLDCO constitutes monetary consideration, then the OLDCO value as reported by NEWCO is limited to the percentage of monetary consideration paid. Accordingly, NEWCO may be required to

- For purposes of this example, "public" is a group of unrelated shareholders in which none of the individual shareholders owns 5 percent or more of the residual interests of OLDCO or NEWCO.
- Each member of management has the same predecessor basis of $110 per share.
- The presumption that management is part of the NEWCO control group is not overcome.
- The term "management" refers to management as a group.
- Both OLDCO and NEWCO have outstanding 100 shares of voting common stock. The fair value of OLDCO shares is $120 per share, and the fair value of NEWCO shares is $48 per share.
- NEWCO incurs debt of $7,200 and uses the entire proceeds to acquire outstanding OLDCO stock of public shareholders.
- All OLDCO shares acquired from management are acquired in exchange for NEWCO stock. All other OLDCO interests are acquired for cash and stock on a pro rata basis.
- Management's predecessor basis is $110 per share.
- Ownership interests before and after the transactions are presented below.

| | OLDCO | | | NEWCO | |
	Shares	Book Value	Fair Value	Shares	Fair Value
Management	24	$ 2,400	$ 2,880	60	$ 2,880
Public	76	7,600	9,120	40	1,920
Total	100	$10,000	$12,000	100	$ 4,800

Method of Acquisition of OLDCO Interest

Source of cash:	
Debt	$ 7,200
Cash paid to public	$ 7,200
NEWCO common stock issued to public in exchange for OLDCO common stock (40 shares × $48)	1,920
NEWCO common stock issued to management in exchange for OLDCO common stock (60 shares × $48)	2,880
OLDCO fair value	$12,000

Application of the 80% Monetary Test

Monetary consideration	$ 7,200
Total consideration	$12,000
Portion monetary	60%

Accounting

The transaction meets the criteria of Section 1(a) of the consensus (management obtains unilateral control); therefore, a change in basis is appropriate.

Management's 24 percent interest should be recorded at predecessor basis in accordance with Section 2 of the consensus. The monetary test in Section 3 of the consensus is not met; therefore, only 60 percent of the OLDCO interests acquired should be recorded at fair value. The remaining interest acquired from OLDCO public shareholders should be recorded based on OLDCO's book value as a surrogate for public's predecessor basis.

(continued)

Exhibit 6.4. Example of the application of the EITF consensus on Issue 88-16. Reprinted from Exhibit 88-16F of the EITF consensus.

	Percent	Amount
Summary of Accounting		
Valuation:		
Predecessor basis (24 shares × $110)	24%	$ 2,640
OLDCO book value [(76% − 60%) × $10,000]	16%	1,600
Fair value (60% × $12,000)	60%	7,200
Total investment in OLDCO		11,440
Less NEWCO debt		(7,200)
NEWCO equity		$ 4,240
Analysis of NEWCO Equity Account		
Stock issued to management valued at predecessor basis		$ 2,640
Stock issued to public valued at OLDCO book value		1,600
NEWCO equity		$ 4,240

Exhibit 6.4. *Continued.*

record a larger portion of its investment in OLDCO at predecessor basis (that is, larger than that which otherwise results from the application of step-acquisition accounting principles) as a result of an inability to objectively and reliably measure the value of the transaction.

The EITF consensus also addresses circumstances in which NEWCO equity interests have been acquired from OLDCO assets and, therefore, cannot result in NEWCO equity. For example, the controlling NEWCO shareholder may obtain his NEWCO equity interest from OLDCO assets by way of a loan or unusual bonus or other payment. In these circumstances, the cash paid results in a debit to NEWCO equity and a credit to the value of the OLDCO investment.

6.26 LBO ACCOUNTING ILLUSTRATED.   Exhibit 6.4 illustrates the application of the EITF consensus guidance. This example is reprinted from Example 5 of Exhibit 88-16F of the EITF consensus. The consensus contains several additional examples of accounting for LBOs.

SOURCES AND SUGGESTED REFERENCES

Accounting Principles Board, "Earnings per Share," APB Opinion No. 15, AICPA, New York, 1969.

———, "Business Combinations," APB Opinion No. 16, AICPA, New York, 1970.

———, "Intangible Assets," APB Opinion No. 17, AICPA, New York, 1970.

———, "Interest on Receivables and Payables," APB Opinion No. 21, AICPA, New York, 1971.

———, "Accounting for Stock Issued to Employees," APB Opinion No. 25, AICPA, New York, 1972.

———, "Business Combinations: Accounting Interpretations of APB Opinion No. 16," Interpretations Nos. 1–39, AICPA, New York, 1970–1973.

American Institute of Certified Public Accountants, "Pushdown Accounting," Issues Paper, AICPA, New York, 1979.

Federal Home Loan Bank Board, "Pushdown Accounting," R-Memorandum No. 55, FHLBB, Washington, DC, 1983.

Financial Accounting Standards Board, "Business Combinations: Sale of Duplicate Facilities and Accrual," EITF Issue No. 84-35, FASB, Stamford, CT, 1984.

——, "Liabilities Accrued in a Purchase Business Combination," EITF Issue No. 84-35a, FASB, Stamford, CT, 1984.

——, "Securities That Can Be Acquired for Cash in a Pooling of Interests," EITF Issue No. 85-14, FASB, Stamford, CT, 1985.

——, "Changes of Ownership Resulting in a New Basis of Accounting," EITF Issue No. 85-21, FASB, Stamford, CT, 1985.

——, "Business Combinations: Settlement of Stock Options and Awards," EITF Issue No. 85-45, FASB, Stamford, CT, 1986.

——, "Pooling with 10 Percent Cash Payout Determined by Lottery," EITF Issue No. 86-10, FASB Stamford, CT, 1986.

——, "Purchased Research and Development Projects in a Business Combination," EITF Issue No. 86-14, FASB, Stamford, CT, 1986.

——, "Carryover of Predecessor Cost in Leveraged Buyout Transactions," EITF Issue No. 86-16, FASB, Stamford, CT, 1986.

——, "Accounting for Other Postemployment Benefits of an Acquired Company," EITF Issue No. 86-20, FASB, Stamford, CT, 1986.

——, "Allocation of Purchase Price to Assets to Be Sold," EITF Issue No. 87-11, FASB, Stamford, CT, 1987.

——, "Effect of a Standstill Agreement on Pooling of Interests Accounting," EITF Issue No. 87-15, FASB, Stamford, CT, 1987.

——, "Whether the 90 Percent Test for a Pooling of Interests Is Applied Separately to Each Company or on a Combined Basis," EITF Issue No. 87-16, FASB, Stamford, CT, 1987.

——, "Poolings of Companies That Do Not Have a Controlling Class of Common Stock," EITF Issue No. 87-27, FASB, Stamford, CT, 1987.

——, "Basis in Leveraged Buyout Transactions When the Previous Owner's Interest Declines," EITF Issue No. 88-16, FASB, Norwalk, CT, 1988.

——, Applicability of FASB Statement No. 2 to Business Combinations Accounted for by the Purchase Method," FASB Interpretation No. 4, FASB, Stamford CT, 1975.

——, "Applying APB Opinions No. 16 and 17 When a Savings and Loan Association or a Similar Institution Is Acquired in a Business Combination Accounted for by the Purchase Method," FASB Interpretation No. 9, FASB, Stamford, CT, 1976.

——, Accounting for Leases in a Business Combination," FASB Interpretation No. 21, FASB, Stamford, CT, 1978.

——, "Accounting for Research and Development Costs," Statement of Financial Accounting Standards No. 2, FASB, Stamford, CT, 1974.

——, "Accounting for Contingencies," Statement of Financial Accounting Standards No. 5, FASB, Stamford, CT, 1975.

——, "Accounting for Leases," Statement of Financial Accounting Standard No. 13, FASB, Stamford, CT, 1976.

——, "Accounting for Preacquisition Contingencies of Purchased Enterprises," Statement of Financial Accounting Standards No. 38, FASB, Stamford, CT, 1980.

——, "Disclosure of Postretirement Health Care and Life Insurance Benefits," Statement of Financial Accounting Standards No. 81, FASB, Stamford, CT, 1984.

——, "Employers' Accounting for Pensions," Statement of Financial Accounting Standards No. 87, FASB, Stamford, CT, 1985.

——, "Accounting for Income Taxes," Statement of Financial Accounting Standards No. 96, FASB, Stamford, CT, 1987.

——, "Issues Relating to Accounting for Business Combinations," FASB Technical Bulletin No. 85-5, FASB, Stamford, CT, 1985.

Securities and Exchange Commission, "Determination of the Acquiring Corporation," Staff Accounting Bulletins Topic 2, Item A-2, (SAB No. 40), SEC, Washington, DC, 1981.

——, "Application of Pushdown Basis of Accounting in Financial Statements of Subsidiaries Acquired by Purchase," Staff Accounting Bulletin No. 54, SEC, Washington, DC, 1983.

———, "Adjustment of Allowances for Business Combination Loan Losses—Purchase Method Accounting," Staff Accounting Bulletin No. 61, SEC, Washington, DC, 1986.

———, "Views on ASR Nos. 130 and 135 Regarding Risk Sharing in Business Combinations Accounted for as a Pooling-of-Interests," Staff Accounting Bulletin No. 65, SEC, Washington, DC, 1986.

———, "Pushdown Basis of Accounting for Parent Company Debt Related to Subsidiary Acquisition," Staff Accounting Bulletin No. 73, SEC, Washington, DC, 1987.

———, "Effect of Certain De Minimus Sales by Affiliates in Compliance with the Requirements of ASR Nos. 130 and 135," Staff Accounting Bulletin No. 76, SEC, Washington, DC, 1988.

———, "Views Regarding Allocation of Debt Issue Costs in a Business Combination Accounted for as a Purchase," Staff Accounting Bulletin No. 77, SEC, Washington, DC, 1988.

———, "Pooling of Interests Accounting," Accounting Series Release No. 130, SEC, Washington, DC, 1972.

———, "Revised Guidelines for the Application of Accounting Series Release No. 130," Accounting Series Release No. 135, SEC, Washington, DC, 1973.

———, "Effect of Treasury Stock Transactions on Accounting for Business Combinations," Accounting Series Release No. 146, SEC, Washington, DC, 1973.

———, "Statement of Policy and Interpretations in Regard to Accounting Series Release No. 146," Accounting Series Release No. 146-A, SEC, Washington, DC, 1974.

CHAPTER 7

CONSOLIDATION, TRANSLATION, AND THE EQUITY METHOD

Steven Rubin, CPA

Weissbarth, Altman & Michaelson, CPAs

CONTENTS

OVERVIEW

Consolidation, translation, and the equity method are related sets of accounting practices used mainly in the preparation of consolidated financial statements.

7.1 CONSOLIDATION. Consolidated financial statements present the financial position, results of operations, and cash flows of a consolidated group of companies essentially as if the group were a single enterprise with one or more branches or divisions. With limited exceptions, a consolidated group of companies includes a parent company and all subsidiaries in which the parent company has a direct or indirect controlling financial interest. Because the reporting entity for consolidated financial statements transcends the legal boundaries of single companies, consolidated financial statements have special features, which require consideration in preparing and interpreting them.

(a) Control. Consolidation is required when one company, the parent, owns—directly or indirectly—more than 50% of the outstanding voting shares of another company, unless control is likely to be temporary or does not rest with the parent. For instance, a majority-owned subsidiary is not consolidated if it (1) is in legal reorganization or bankruptcy or (2) operates under foreign exchange restrictions, controls, or other governmentally imposed uncertainties so severe that they cast doubt on the parent's ability to control the subsidiary. Majority-owned subsidiaries excluded from consolidation because control is likely to be temporary or does not rest with the parent are called unconsolidated subsidiaries.

Investments in unconsolidated subsidiaries, like other investments that give an investor the ability to exercise significant influence over the investee's operating and financial activities, are accounted for by the equity method, which is discussed below.

(b) Irrelevant Factors. The fact that a particular subsidiary is located in a foreign country, has a large minority interest, or engages in principal activities substantially different from those of its parent is irrelevant to the consolidation requirement. That was not always the case, however. Until the year 1988, those factors were quite relevant and, indeed, were considered to be legitimate reasons for excluding a particular subsidiary from consolidation. The rules were changed by the issuance of SFAS No. 94, "Consolidation of All Majority-Owned Subsidiaries," and that no longer is the case. SFAS No. 94 requires consolidation of all majority-owned subsidiaries unless control is temporary or does not rest with the majority owners.

A difference in fiscal periods of a parent and a majority-owned subsidiary does not in itself justify the subsidiary's exclusion from consolidation. In that case, the subsidiary has to prepare, for consolidation purposes, financial statements for a period that corresponds with or closely approaches the parent's fiscal period.

If, however, the difference between the parent's and the subsidiary's fiscal periods does not exceed about 3 months, the subsidiary's financial statements may be consolidated with those of the parent even though they cover different periods. In that case, recognition has to be given in the consolidated financial statements by disclosure or otherwise of this fact and the effect of any intervening events that materially affect consolidated financial position or results of operations.

(c) Intercompany Amounts. Only legal entities can own assets, owe liabilities, issue capital stock, earn revenues, enjoy gains, and incur expenses and losses. A group of companies as such cannot do those things. So the elements of consolidated financial statements are the elements of the financial statements of the members of the consolidated group of companies—the parent company and its consolidated subsidiaries. They are the assets owned by the member companies, the liabilities owed by the member companies, the equity of the member companies, and the revenues, expenses, gains, and losses of the member companies.

Some elements of the financial statements of member companies are not elements of the consolidated financial statements, however. The elements of the financial statements of a reporting entity are relationships and changes in relationships between the reporting entity and outside entities. But some elements of the financial statements of members of a consolidated group are relationships and changes in relationships between member companies, called **intercompany amounts.** (They would more accurately be described as **intragroup amounts.**) Intercompany amounts are excluded from consolidated financial statements.

As discussed and illustrated in sections 7.19–7.24, it is convenient to prepare consolidated financial statements by starting with the financial statements of the member companies, which include intercompany amounts. The intercompany amounts are removed by adjustments and eliminations in consolidation. The items are:

Intercompany Stockholdings. Ownership by the parent company of capital stock of the subsidiaries and ownership, if any, by subsidiaries of capital stock of other subsidiaries or of the parent company.

Intercompany Receivables and Payables. Debts of member companies to other member companies.

Intercompany Sales, Purchases, Fees, Rents, Interest, and the Like. Sales of goods or provision of services from member companies to other member companies.

Intercompany Profits. Profits recorded by member companies in transactions with other member companies reflected in recorded amounts of assets of member companies at the reporting date.

Intercompany Dividends. Dividends from members of the consolidated group to other members of the consolidated group.

After the intercompany amounts are eliminated, the consolidated financial statements present solely relationships and changes in relationships with entities outside the consolidated reporting entity. They present:

Amounts receivable from and amounts payable to outside entities.

Investments in outside entities.

Other assets helpful in carrying out activities with outside entities.

Consolidated equity equal to the excess of those assets over those liabilities.

Changes in those assets, liabilities, and equity, including profits realized or losses incurred by dealings with outside entities.

Consolidated financial statements present the financial affairs of a consolidated group of companies united for economic activity by common control.

(d) Other Considerations. The **authoritative** accounting literature does not specifically require a company to consolidate an investment in a partnership or an investment of 50% or less of the outstanding voting shares of another company, even if the first company controls the second. Whether consolidation in these circumstances is appropriate is an unresolved issue. The **nonauthoritative** accounting literature, however, strongly suggests that consolidation is appropriate in many of those circumstances and, as a result, a number of companies do consolidate those investments. But, in the absence of a requirement to do so, many companies do not. Conditions that indicate that control exists other than by direct or indirect ownership include a contract, a lease, an agreement with other investors, or a court decree.

(e) Disclosures. Consolidation policy, that is, the composition of the consolidated group, needs to be disclosed in the notes to the consolidated financial statements. Also, a member of a consolidated group that files a consolidated tax return discloses the following information related to income taxes in its own separately issued financial statements:

- The amount of current and deferred tax expense for each statement of earnings presented and any tax-related balances due to or from other group members as of each balance sheet date.
- The principal provisions of the method by which the consolidated amount of current and deferred tax expense is allocated to members of the consolidated group and the nature and effect of any changes in that method.

7.2 BUSINESS COMBINATIONS. A company can start a subsidiary by having it incorporated and investing resources in it. Including such a subsidiary in consolidated financial statements presents no special problem. The amount of the investment recorded by the parent company equals the initial equity of the subsidiary, each of which is eliminated in consolidation.

(a) Types of Business Combinations. Most parent and subsidiary relationships, however, are formed by **business combinations,** events in which separate, active companies become related as parent company and subsidiary. Accounting for business combinations is discussed and illustrated in sections 7.8–7.9 and 7.19–7.24. Business combinations occur in several ways, for example:

Purchase of Stock for Cash. The parent company buys for cash a majority of the capital stock of another company from the other company's stockholders, and the other company becomes a subsidiary.

Purchase of Assets for Cash and the Assumption of Liabilities. The parent company buys for cash the assets of another company, assumes its liabilities, and forms a new company to assume the business of the other company as a subsidiary.

Stock for Stock. The parent company issues some of its capital stock to stockholders of another company and receives from them a majority of the capital stock of the other company, which becomes a subsidiary.

Some business combinations occur in one event; others occur in a series of events, complicating accounting for the combinations.

(b) Methods to Account for Business Combinations. Alternative views on the nature of the events that occur in business combinations and how best to account for them have led to two different methods of accounting for the combinations, the **purchase method** and the **pooling of interests method.** Differences between the financial statement results of applying the method applicable to a business combination and the results that would have been obtained had the other method been applicable are ordinarily substantial for current statements and those of many years following the combination.

Business combinations accounted for by the purchase method usually produce balance sheet amounts referred to as **goodwill on consolidation.** Such purchased goodwill is measured by the excess of the amount paid or the fair market value of the stock issued by the parent company to acquire the subsidiary over the fair values of the identifiable assets and liabilities of the subsidiary at the date of combination.

7.3 TRANSLATION. Financial statements of a parent company are stated in the domestic unit of currency, such as the U.S. dollar for U.S. parent companies. Financial statements of a foreign subsidiary are stated in a foreign unit of currency, a unit of currency other than the domestic unit of currency, such as the U.K. pound for U.K. subsidiaries. Such foreign currency financial statements cannot be consolidated with domestic currency financial statements; the result would be a set of financial statements stated in more than one unit of currency, which would make them unintelligible.

Before the financial statements of a foreign subsidiary can be consolidated with the financial statements of its parent company, therefore, the amounts in its foreign currency financial statements are changed to amounts stated in the domestic unit of currency. Changing the amounts from those stated in the foreign unit of currency to those stated in the domestic unit of currency is called **translation,** analogous to translation from one language to another. Translation is discussed and illustrated in sections 7.10–7.18.

Translation uses foreign exchange rates. Such rates are ratios of exchange, prices of units of one kind of currency in terms of units of another kind of currency, such as $(U.S.) 1.50 for £(U.K.) 1. Foreign exchange rates change, as all other prices do. That causes two problems in translation: (1) how to select the foreign exchange rates to use for translation; and (2) how to treat translation differences, items unique to translated financial statements caused by translating amounts in a single set of financial statements at two or more foreign exchange rates.

7.4 EQUITY METHOD. The equity method is used to account for investments that give an investor the ability to exercise significant influence over the investee's operating and financial activities, including investments in majority-owned subsidiaries that do not qualify for consolidation. The investee may be a corporation, a partnership, or a joint venture. An investment accounted for by the equity method is initially recorded at cost. After that, the investment's carrying amount is increased or decreased for the investor's share of changes in the underlying net assets of the investee and for certain other transactions and other events. Principles relating to the equity method are discussed in sections 7.25–7.28.

7.5 COMBINED FINANCIAL STATEMENTS.   Circumstances exist in which combined financial statements of commonly controlled corporations are likely to be more meaningful than their separate financial statements. Such circumstances include, for example, ownership by one person of a controlling interest in several corporations related in their operations.

If combined financial statements are prepared, they present only relationships and changes in relationships with entities outside the combined group. That means that intercompany sales and purchases, profit, and receivables and payables are eliminated. Intercompany stockholdings, if any, are eliminated.

The separate components of equity of each corporation are aggregated with the corresponding separate components of the other corporations. Presentation of a table showing each corporation's portion of each component of combined equity in either the balance sheet or the notes, though not required by the authoritative accounting literature, would likely enhance the usefulness of the combined statements.

7.6 CONSOLIDATING STATEMENTS.   If all else fails to present information on a group of related companies in a helpful way, **consolidating** statements are often used as an effective means of presenting the pertinent information. Such statements are essentially presentations as in worksheets used to derive consolidated financial statements, illustrated in sections 7.19–7.24, together with notes and other kinds of necessary disclosures.

7.7 SEC RULES AND REGULATIONS ON CONSOLIDATED FINANCIAL STATEMENTS. Beyond the concepts and procedures involving all consolidated financial statements, the SEC, in its Regulation S-X, has published regulations for registrants that file their consolidated financial statements with the commission.

(a) Selection of Reporting Entity.   The rules require that the application of principles for inclusion of subsidiaries in consolidated financial statements "clearly exhibit the financial position and results of operations of the registrant and its subsidiaries." A company not majority owned may not be consolidated. A subsidiary whose financial statements are as of a date or for periods different from those of the registrant may not be consolidated unless all the following conditions apply:

The difference is not more than 93 days.
The closing date of the subsidiary's financial information is expressly indicated.
The necessity for using different closing dates is briefly explained.

Due consideration must be given to consolidating foreign subsidiaries operating under political, economic, or currency restrictions. If such foreign subsidiaries are consolidated, the effects, if determinable, of foreign exchange restrictions on the consolidated financial position and results of operations must be disclosed.

(b) Intercompany Items and Transactions.   Intercompany items and transactions between members of a consolidated group generally are eliminated in consolidated financial statements, and unrealized intercompany profits and losses on transactions with investees accounted for by the equity method are also eliminated. If such items are not eliminated, the registrant is required to state its reason for not doing so.

(c) Other Disclosures.   The SEC rules require brief descriptions in the notes to consolidated financial statements of the principles of consolidation followed and any changes in principles or in the composition of the companies constituting the consolidated group since the last set of consolidated financial statements was filed with the commission.

The rules require that consolidated financial statements also present:

An explanation and reconciliation of differences between (1) the amount at which investments in consolidated subsidiaries are carried on the registrant's books and (2) the equity of the registrant in the assets and liabilities of the subsidiaries.

An explanation and reconciliation between (1) dividends received from unconsolidated subsidiaries and (2) earnings of unconsolidated subsidiaries.

An analysis of minority interest in capital stock, in retained earnings, and in net income of consolidated subsidiaries.

ACCOUNTING FOR BUSINESS COMBINATIONS

The two generally accepted methods of accounting for business combinations are the **pooling of interests method** and the **purchase method.** They are not alternatives. A business combination that meets all 12 conditions relating to (1) attributes of the combining companies before the combination, (2) the manner in which the companies are combined, and (3) the absence of certain types of planned transactions, as set forth in paragraphs 45 to 48 of APB Opinion No. 16, "Business Combinations," is accounted for by the pooling of interests method. A business combination that fails to meet even one of the 12 conditions is accounted for by the purchase method. Transfers of assets and liabilities or securities between companies owned by the same parties, including newly formed corporations, are not considered business combinations for purposes of APB Opinion No. 16. However, Interpretation 39 of APB Opinion No. 16 provides that in those circumstances the assets and liabilities so transferred are accounted for at their recorded amounts.

7.8 THE POOLING OF INTERESTS METHOD. The pooling of interests method accounts for a business combination as the uniting of the ownership interests of two or more companies resulting from a transfer of equity securities. Preexisting ownership interests continue (in modified form), preexisting bases of accounting are retained, and preexisting recorded amounts of assets and liabilities are carried forward to the consolidated financial statements.

(a) Conditions for the Pooling of Interests Method. A business combination that meets all 12 conditions is accounted for by the pooling of interests method. The following discusses the 12 conditions. Though more than two companies may be combined at the same time, the conditions are discussed in terms of a business combination of two entities.

(i) Attributes of the Combining Companies. Two of the 12 conditions pertain to attributes of the combining companies:

1. The combining companies are autonomous, meaning neither has been a subsidiary or division of another company within the 2 years immediately preceding the date the plan of combination is initiated.
   - A plan of combination is considered to be initiated on (a) the date the major terms of a plan, including the ratio of transfer of stock, are announced publicly or are otherwise formally made known to the stockholders of either combining company or, if earlier, (b) the date stockholders of a combining company are notified in writing of a transfer offer.
   - A combining company is considered autonomous though it was a subsidiary of another company (not one of the combining companies) within the 2 years immedi-

ately preceding the date the plan of combination is initiated if it was divested as a result of a governmental order.

2. The combining companies are independent of each other, meaning that, at the date the plan of combination is initiated and at the date the plan of combination is consummated neither combining company owns more than 10% of the outstanding voting common stock of the other combining company acquired before the date the plan of combination is initiated.

   • A plan of combination is considered to be consummated on the date ownership interests are transferred. The date the plan is consummated is often called the **date of combination.**

(ii) Manner in Which Companies Are Combined.   Seven of the 12 conditions pertain to the manner in which the companies are combined:

3. The companies are combined in a single transaction or in accordance with a specific plan within 1 year after the plan of combination is initiated.

   • Altering the terms of the transfer of stock after the plan of combination is initiated renders the original plan void and causes a new plan of combination to be initiated (unless earlier transfers of stock reflect the new ratio).

   • A business combination may be consummated more than 1 year after the plan of combination is initiated and not violate this condition if proceedings of a governmental body or litigation beyond the control of the combining companies caused the delay.

4. One combining company offers and issues only common stock with rights identical to those of the majority of its outstanding voting common stock and receives substantially all, that is, 90% or more, of the voting common stock of the other company.

   • The plan of combination may include provisions for the company issuing stock to distribute cash or other consideration for fractional shares and for shares held by stockholders not participating in the combination.

5. Neither combining company changes the equity interest of the voting common stock in contemplation of the combination within the 2 years immediately preceding the date the plan of combination is initiated until the date the plan is consummated.

   • Changes in equity interests include distributions by a combining company to its stockholders, declarations of dividends, or additional issuances, transfers, or retirements of securities other than in the ordinary course of business.

6. If either combining company reacquires shares of voting common stock, it does so only for purposes other than the business combination, and it does not reacquire more than a normal number of shares between the date the plan of combination is initiated and the date it is consummated.

   • Stock reacquired for purposes other than the business combination includes shares reacquired for stock option and other compensation plans and other recurring distributions, if such plans have existed for at least 2 years preceding the date the plan of combination is initiated.

7. The ratio of an individual common stockholder's interest in a combining company to those of other common stockholders in a combining company remains the same after the transfer of stock that combines the companies.

   • Each common stockholder in a combining company who transfers stock retains the same relative interest as before the combination. For example: M owns 75% of S and J owns 25% of S. If they transfer all their shares to P for P's shares, M will receive three shares for each share J receives.

8. After the combination, the voting rights of the common stock ownership interests in the combining company that issues stock are not restricted in any way.

9. The combination is resolved at the date the plan of combination is consummated with no provisions of the plan pending that relate to the issue of securities or other consideration.

   • At the time of combination, the combining companies issue stock or have already issued stock and agree to issue no additional shares and to distribute no other consideration at a later date to the former stockholders of either combining enterprise, either directly or through an escrow account. Notwithstanding that, a plan may provide that the number of shares issued to combine the companies may be revised for the later settlement of contingencies that existed at the date the combination is consummated.

(iii) Absence of Planned Transactions. Three of the 12 conditions pertain to the absence of planned transactions:

10. The company issuing stock agrees not to retire or to reacquire, either directly or indirectly, any of the common stock issued to combine the companies.

11. Each combining company agrees not to enter into any other financial arrangements for the benefit of former stockholders of a combining company, for example, to guarantee loans secured by stock issued to combine the companies.

12. Neither combining company intends to dispose of a significant part of the assets of either combining company within the 2 years immediately after the combination other than in the ordinary course of business or to eliminate duplicate facilities or excess capacity.

(b) Accounting for Combinations by the Pooling of Interests Method. Section 7.19 illustrates procedures to prepare consolidating worksheets at the date of a business combination accounted for by the pooling of interests method. Section 7.22 illustrates procedures to prepare consolidating worksheets after the date of such a business combination. Those procedures are affected by concepts discussed in this section.

(i) Assets and Liabilities. Under the pooling of interests method, the assets and liabilities of the consolidated group generally are stated initially in the financial statements of the group at the amounts at which they were stated in the separate financial statements of the member companies, except for items of intercompany relationships—intercompany stockholdings, debt, and profit—eliminated because they do not represent relationships or transactions with outside entities.

The combining enterprises may have had accounting policies different from each other. For example, one may have determined the cost of its inventories on the FIFO method and another may have determined the cost of its inventories on the LIFO method. Though not required, the existing recorded amounts of the assets and liabilities of one combining company may be adjusted to conform its accounting principles to those of the other combining company.

(ii) Equity. The individual components of equity—common stock, preferred stock, additional paid-in capital, retained earnings, and so forth—of each member company are aggregated under the pooling of interests method with the corresponding individual components of equity of the other member company, except for items of intercompany relationships, which are eliminated. The aggregated common stock and additional paid-in capital may include amounts attributable to minority interests.

(c) Reporting Combined Results of Operations in the Period of Combination.   Results of operations for the entire period in which a business combination accounted for by the pooling of interests method is consummated are reported as though the companies had been combined at the beginning of that period, regardless of when during the period they were combined. Items of intercompany transactions—intercompany sales, purchases, and profit—are eliminated for the entire period. Indeed, retained earnings of all members of the consolidated group accounted for by the pooling of interests method are treated as the retained earnings of the consolidated group, as though the companies had always been combined.

Expenditures incurred for a business combination accounted for by the pooling of interests method, such as legal fees, accounting fees, registration fees, and so forth, are charged to expense in the consolidated income statements in the periods in which they are incurred.

A member of the consolidated group may dispose of assets after the combination. If such assets are part of duplicate facilities or excess capacity, a resulting gain or loss from disposition is included in income from operations. If such assets are not part of duplicate facilities or excess capacity, however, a resulting gain or loss from disposition is normally included in income from extraordinary items.

Though a consolidated group may be reasonably assured that a business combination initiated but not consummated will qualify for the pooling of interests method, it applies the purchase method in its consolidated financial statements prepared between the date a controlling interest is acquired and the date the plan of combination is consummated. Once the combination qualifies for the pooling of interests method, that method is applied retroactively in financial statements issued on or after that date.

Comparative consolidated financial statements of prior years presented with the consolidated financial statements of the year in which the combination accounted for by the pooling of interests method is consummated are restated as if the combination had been consummated in the earliest year presented.

(d) Disclosures under the Pooling of Interests Method.   A consolidated group that applies the pooling of interests method in accounting for a business combination discloses the following information in its financial statements or related notes for the period in which the combination is consummated:

- The fact that a combination accounted for by the pooling of interests method was consummated.
- The basis of current presentation and restatements of prior periods.
- The names and brief descriptions of the companies combined, except those of a company whose name is carried forward to the consolidated group.
- A description of stock issued and the number of shares issued in the combination.
- Details included in current consolidated net income of the results of operations of the previously separate companies for the portion of the year before the combination is consummated. The details include revenues, extraordinary items, net income, and other changes in equity and the amounts of intercompany transactions and the manner of accounting for them.
- Descriptions of adjustments to assets and liabilities of a combining company to conform its accounting principles to those of the consolidated group and descriptions of the effects of the changes on net income reported previously by the separate companies and presented in comparative financial statements.
- Details of an increase or decrease in retained earnings from changing the fiscal year of a combining company. The details include, at a minimum, revenues, expenses, extraordinary items, net income, and other changes in equity for the period excluded from the reported results of operations.

- Reconciliations of amounts of revenues and earnings reported before the combination by the company that issues the stock to combine the companies with the consolidated amounts currently presented in financial statements and summaries. A new company formed to combine the companies may instead disclose the earnings of the separate companies for prior periods.

7.9 THE PURCHASE METHOD.   A business combination not meeting all 12 conditions discussed in section 7.8(a) is accounted for by the purchase method. The purchase method, in effect, accounts for the combination as the acquisition of a controlling interest in a company by another company. The assets and liabilities of the acquired company are initially reported in consolidation at their fair values at the date of combination. A difference between the aggregate of those amounts and the cost incurred by the acquiring company to acquire the controlling interest is treated as goodwill, or, in some rare instances, negative goodwill.

(a) Method of Acquisition.   In a business combination accounted for by the purchase method, one enterprise, for example, Corporation P, can acquire the voting stock of another enterprise, Corporation S, in several ways:

1. For cash.
2. In exchange for noncash assets.
3. By incurring debt.
4. By issuing its own stock.
5. In a combination of two or more of those ways.

S makes no entry, because it has given up nothing and received nothing. It merely updates its list of stockholders. P records these entries based on various facts:

1. In the simplest type of acquisition, P acquires S's voting stock for cash. If P buys all 100,000 shares of S's voting stock for $10 a share, P makes this entry:

Investment in Corporation S	$1,000,000	
Cash		$1,000,000

2. P acquires for cash 90% of S's voting stock, 90,000 shares, for $9 a share plus a $1 a share commission:

Investment in Corporation S	$ 900,000	
Cash		$ 900,000

3. P acquires all the voting stock of S, 100,000 shares, by paying $5 a share now and agreeing to pay $5 a share to S's former stockholders 2 months from now:

Investment in Corporation S	$1,000,000	
Cash		$ 500,000
Payable		500,000

4. P acquires 80% of S's voting stock, 80,000 shares, in exchange for parcels of land it owns. The book value of the land is $700,000 and its fair value at the date of the exchange is $800,000. The market value of S's stock is not readily discernible, because S is a private, closely held corporation. According to APB Opinion No. 29, "Accounting for Nonmonetary Transactions" (par. 18), the fair values of the assets received or of the assets given, whichever is more clearly evident, are used to record such a barter transaction. This entry records the exchange:

Investment in Corporation S	$ 800,000	
Land		$ 700,000
Gain on disposal		100,000

5. P acquires S by issuing 10,000 shares of its $100 par value voting common stock to S's stockholders who, in turn, transfer to P all their 100,000 $100 par value voting shares of S. Neither security has a readily discernible market value:

Investment in Corporation S	$1,000,000	
Common stock		$1,000,000

6. The facts are the same as number 5 except P's shares have a readily discernible market value of $110 a share:

Investment in Corporation S	$1,100,000	
Common stock		$1,000,000
Additional paid-in capital		100,000

(b) Costs of Acquisition.   Direct costs of a business combination accounted for by the purchase method, such as legal fees, accounting fees, registration fees, and so forth, are considered part of the purchase price of the assets acquired and liabilities assumed.

(c) Allocation of Purchase Price.   The parent company's cost to acquire the subsidiary (its investment) by the purchase method comprises two pieces:

1. The total of the fair values of the subsidiary's assets and liabilities as determined under APB Opinion No. 16.
2. Purchased goodwill.

APB Opinion No. 16 provides the following guidance on how the fair values of the subsidiary's assets and liabilities are determined:

TYPE OF ASSET OR LIABILITY	AMOUNT AT WHICH SUBSIDIARY'S ASSETS OR LIABILITIES ARE INITIALLY INCLUDED IN CONSOLIDATION
Marketable securities	Current net realizable value
Receivables	Discounted amount of expected future net cash inflows
Inventories	
a. Finished goods	Current net realizable value
b. Work in process	Current net realizable value
c. Raw materials	Current replacement cost
Buildings and equipment	
a. Used in operations	Current replacement cost
b. To be sold or held for sale	Current net realizable value
c. Used only temporarily in operations	Current net realizable value, recognizing expected depreciation
Patents, trademarks, copyrights, customer lists, and the like	Appraisal value
Land, natural resources, and nonmarketable securities	Appraisal value
Accounts payable, notes payable, obligations under capital leases, accrued expenses, and the like	Discounted amount of expected future net cash outflows
Deferred income taxes	Zero

Operating loss carryforwards	Expected tax savings only if realization is assured beyond a reasonable doubt
Preacquisition contingencies (other than operating loss carry forwards)	Discounted amount of expected future net cash inflows or outflows, if determinable. The effects of preacquisition contingencies resolved after the combination at amounts different from those at which they are recorded in the combination are charged or credited to income in the periods in which they are resolved.
Research and development costs	Zero. But assets resulting from research and development activities such as formulas, blueprints, and the like are recorded at appraisal value.

The following describe some of the terms used:

Current Net Realizable Value. The amount of cash (or its equivalent) expected to be derived from sale of an asset, net of costs required to be incurred as a result of the sale.

Current Replacement Cost. The amount of cash (or its equivalent) that would have to be paid to acquire currently the best asset available to undertake the function of the asset owned (less depreciation or amortization, if appropriate).

Discounted Amount of Expected Future Net Cash Inflows or Outflows. The discounted amount of expected future cash inflows into which the asset is expected to be converted in due course of business less the discounted amount of expected future cash outflows necessary to obtain those inflows.

Fair Value. The price at which an asset could be exchanged in a transaction, within a reasonably short time, between a buyer and a seller each of whom is well informed and willing to buy or sell and neither of whom is under a compulsion to buy or sell.

Sections 7.20–7.21 illustrate procedures to prepare a consolidating worksheet at the date of a business combination accounted for by the purchase method. Sections 7.23–7.24 illustrate procedures to prepare consolidating worksheets after the date of such a business combination. Those procedures are affected by concepts discussed in this section.

(d) Effects of Differences between Book and Tax Bases. The amounts initially assigned in consolidation to a subsidiary's assets and liabilities for financial reporting purposes may differ from the amounts allowable for tax purposes. These differences are temporary differences, which are subject to deferred tax accounting. Chapter 17 discusses the accounting for deferred taxes on these and other temporary differences that arise in practice.

(e) Purchased Goodwill. Purchased goodwill is measured by the difference between (1) the cost of the parent company's investment accounted for by the purchase method and (2) the fair values of the subsidiary's assets and liabilities as determined under APB Opinion No. 16 at the date of the combination. Subsequent accounting for goodwill depends on whether (1) equals (2), in which case there is no goodwill; (1) exceeds (2), in which case there is goodwill; or (1) is less than (2), in which case there is negative goodwill resulting from a bargain purchase. Those three possibilities take the form shown in Exhibit 7.1.

(i) Accounting for Purchased Goodwill. Goodwill is initially reported in the consolidated balance sheet as an intangible asset and is subsequently amortized to income over the periods expected to be benefited or 40 years, whichever is shorter. The straight line method is typically used.

	1 = 2	1 > 2	1 < 2
Fair values of subsidiary's assets	$500,000	$500,000	$500,000
Fair values of subsidiary's liabilities	200,000	200,000	200,000
Net	300,000	300,000	300,000
Amount of investment	300,000	400,000	200,000
Amount of goodwill	$ -0-	$100,000	
Amount of negative goodwill			$100,000

Exhibit 7.1.   The two types of goodwill compared.

APB Opinion No. 17, "Intangible Assets" (par. 27), identifies the following factors to be considered in determining the estimated useful life of goodwill or other intangible assets:

a. Legal, regulatory, or contractual provisions may limit the maximum useful life.
b. Provisions for renewal or extension may alter a specified limit on useful life.
c. Effects of obsolescence, demand, competition, and other economic factors may reduce a useful life.
d. A useful life may parallel the service life expectancies of individuals or groups of employees.
e. Expected actions of competitors and others may restrict present competitive advantages.
f. An apparently unlimited useful life may in fact be indefinite and benefits cannot be reasonably projected.
g. An intangible asset may be a composite of many individual factors with varying effective lives.

(ii) Negative Goodwill.   Negative goodwill is allocated to reduce proportionately the fair values initially assigned to noncurrent assets (except for long-term investments in marketable securities). If the allocation reduces the affected noncurrent asset amounts to zero, the remainder is classified in the consolidated balance sheet as a deferred credit and, like goodwill, discussed above, is amortized to income over the periods expected to be benefited or 40 years, whichever is shorter. The straight line method is typically used. To illustrate: The fair values assigned S's noncurrent assets other than long-term investments total $300,000 and there is $100,000 in negative goodwill. The negative goodwill is allocated as shown in Exhibit 7.2.

If the unadjusted fair values of noncurrent assets totaled less than $100,000, they would be reduced to zero and the remaining negative goodwill would be accounted for as discussed above.

(f) Comparative Financial Statements.   Comparative financial statements of prior years presented with the financial statements of the year in which a combination accounted for by the purchase method occurs are not restated.

	Fair Values of Noncurrent Assets (unadjusted)	Negative Goodwill Allocation	Adjusted Fair Values
Buildings and equipment	$100,000	$ (33,333)	$ 66,667
Land	200,000	(66,667)	133,333
	$300,000	$(100,000)	$200,000

Exhibit 7.2.   Allocation of negative goodwill.

(g) Disclosures under the Purchase Method. A consolidated group that applies the purchase method discloses the following information in its consolidated financial statements or related notes for the period in which the parent company acquired a controlling interest in a subsidiary:

- That there was a business combination accounted for by the purchase method.
- The name and a brief description of the acquired company.
- The period for which results of operations of the acquired company are included in the consolidated income statement.
- The cost to acquire the subsidiary, including, if applicable, the number of shares of stock the parent company issued to acquire the subsidiary.
- A description of the plan for amortizing goodwill (method and period).
- Contingent payments, options, or commitments specified in the acquisition agreement and the proposed accounting treatment.

A consolidated group whose parent company's stock trades publicly also discloses as supplemental pro forma information:

- Results of operations for the current period as though the member company had been combined at the beginning of the period (unless the members were combined near the beginning of the period).
- Results of operations for the immediately preceding period as though the members had been combined from the beginning of that period.

FOREIGN CURRENCY TRANSLATION

A subsidiary or another unit within a consolidated group of companies (or within a company or an affiliated group of companies), such as a joint venture, a division, or a branch, may be a foreign operation, an operating unit that prepares foreign currency financial statements. Before such statements can be included in domestic currency consolidated financial statements, they ordinarily have to be translated into the domestic currency used in the consolidated financial statements, the currency of the parent company's country. SFAS No. 52, "Foreign Currency Translation," sets forth current GAAP for translation.

7.10 OBJECTIVES OF TRANSLATION. SFAS No. 52 states objectives to be achieved in translation in the face of changes in foreign exchange rates, ratios of exchange between two currencies. The principles in SFAS No. 52 were adopted with the intention of achieving those objectives. The basic objective is:

Compatibility with Expected Effects. Information concerning foreign operations should be generally compatible with the expected effects of changes in foreign exchange rates on the parent company's cash flows and equity. If a change in an exchange rate is expected to have an overall beneficial effect, translation should reflect that. If a change is expected to have an overall adverse effect, translation should likewise reflect that. The expected effects of a change in a foreign exchange rate on the carrying amounts of all assets and liabilities of a foreign operation should therefore be recognized currently.

Other major objectives are:

Conformity with GAAP. Translation should produce amounts that conform with GAAP. For example, inventories and land, buildings, and equipment should be stated at acquisition cost after translation.

Retaining Results and Relationships. The financial results and relationships in the foreign currency financial statements of a foreign operation should be retained in its statements after translation. Profits should translate into profits and losses should translate into losses. Relationships before translation such as a current ratio of two to one or a ratio of gross profit to sales of 35% should be the same after translation.

7.11 ASSUMPTIONS CONCERNING TRANSLATION.   SFAS No. 52 states these assumptions concerning translation on which the principles in the statement are based:

Two Types of Foreign Operations. Foreign operations are of two types, which differ from each other so much that translation procedures for the two types have to differ. The two types are (1) self-contained and integrated foreign operations and (2) components or extensions of the parent company's domestic operations.

Self-Contained and Integrated Foreign Operations. A foreign operation may be relatively self-contained and integrated in a foreign country. Such an operation should be treated in consolidated financial statements as a net investment of the parent company. The entire net investment, not merely certain assets and liabilities of the foreign operation, is exposed to the risk of changes in the exchange rate between the currency of the foreign country and the domestic currency. Though such changes affect the parent company's net investment, they do not affect its cash flows. The effects of such changes on a foreign operation should therefore be excluded from reported consolidated net income unless the parent company sells part or all of its investment in the foreign operation or completely or substantially liquidates its investment in the foreign operation.

Components or Extensions of Parent Company Domestic Operations. A foreign operation may be a direct and integral component or an extension of the parent company's domestic operations, such as an import or export business. It should be treated as an integral part of the parent company's operations. Changes in the exchange rate between the currency of the country in which the foreign operation is conducted and the domestic currency directly affect certain individual assets and liabilities of the foreign operation, for example, its foreign currency receivables and payables, and thereby affect the parent company's cash flows. The effects should be recognized currently in reported consolidated net income.

Functional Currencies. The most meaningful measuring unit for the assets, liabilities, and operations of a foreign operation is the currency of the primary economic environment in which the operation is conducted, its functional currency. Consolidated financial statements should therefore use one measuring unit for each functional currency of the operating units in the consolidated group of companies, including the domestic currency, which is the functional currency of the parent company. If only one measuring unit were used, the resulting information generally would be incompatible with the expected effects of changes in foreign exchange rates on the parent company's cash flows and equity. It would therefore be contrary to the basic objective of translation.

Highly Inflationary Economies. Currencies of countries with highly inflationary economies are unsatisfactory as measuring units for financial reporting. A highly inflationary economy is one that has cumulative inflation of approximately 100% or more over 3 years. An operation in the environment of such a currency should be treated as if the domestic currency were its functional currency.

Effective Hedges. Some contracts, transactions, and balances are, in effect, hedges of foreign exchange risks. They should be treated that way regardless of their form.

7.12 TASKS REQUIRED FOR TRANSLATION.   SFAS No. 52 (par. 69) states that to achieve the objectives of translation and to conform with its assumptions, these major tasks are required for each foreign operation:

a. Identifying the functional currency of the [operation's] economic environment.

b. Measuring all elements of the financial statements in the functional currency.

c. Using the current exchange rate for translating from the functional currency to the reporting currency, if they are different.

d. Distinguishing the economic impact of changes in exchange rates on a net investment from the impact of such changes on individual assets and liabilities that are receivable or payable in currencies other than the functional currency.

(a) Identifying the Functional Currency. SFAS No. 52 indicates that identifying the functional currency of a foreign operation by determining the primary economic environment in which the operation is conducted is essentially a matter of management judgment. Management assesses the economic facts and circumstances pertaining to the foreign operation in relation to the objectives of translation, discussed above. Economic factors are considered both individually and collectively to determine the functional currency, so that the financial results and relationships are measured with the greatest degree of relevance and reliability.

Exercise of management's judgment is simplified if a foreign operation is either clearly self-contained and integrated in a particular foreign country, so that the currency of that country obviously is its functional currency, or clearly a direct and integral component or extension of the parent company's operations, so that the domestic currency obviously is its functional currency.

The functional currency of a foreign operation normally is the currency of the environment in which it primarily generates and expends cash. But sometimes observable facts are ambiguous in pointing to the functional currency. For example, if a foreign operation conducts significant amounts of business in two or more currencies, its functional currency might not be easily identifiable. For those operations, individual economic facts and circumstances need to be assessed.

Appendix A of SFAS No. 52 provides guidance for making those assessments in particular circumstances. The guidance is grouped in sets of indicators: cash flow indicators, sales price indicators, sales market indicators, expense indicators, financing indicators, and intercompany transactions and arrangements indicators.

(b) Measuring in the Functional Currency. Most foreign operations prepare their financial statements in their functional currencies. Some, however, prepare their financial statements in other foreign currencies. Before the financial statements of a foreign operation are translated from its functional currency to the domestic currency, its foreign currency financial statements obviously have to be stated in its functional currency. If its financial statements are stated in another currency because its records are maintained in the other currency, they have to be remeasured into the functional currency before translation.

SFAS No. 52 (par. 10) distinguishes between remeasurement and translation. It states the goal of remeasurement to be "to produce the same results as if the . . . books of record had been maintained in the functional currency."

Remeasurement requires, as does translation, use of foreign exchange rates. For remeasurement, they are the rates between the foreign currency in which the financial statements of a foreign operation are stated and its foreign functional currency. Unlike translation, however, remeasurement requires the use of historical foreign exchange rates in addition to the current foreign exchange rate. Historical rates are rates at dates before the reporting date as of which certain financial statement items are recorded, such as items recorded at acquisition cost.

Remeasurement takes three steps. First, amounts to be remeasured at historical rates are distinguished from amounts to be remeasured at current rates. Second, the amounts are remeasured using the historical and current rates, as appropriate. Third, all exchange gains and losses identified by remeasurement are recognized currently in income. Such gains and losses are identified by remeasuring amounts at rates current at the reporting date, mainly monetary assets and liabilities not denominated in the functional currency, that differ from rates current at the preceding reporting date or an intervening date at which they were acquired.

Amounts remeasured at historical rates generally are amounts stated in historical terms, such as acquisition cost, and related revenue and expenses, such as depreciation.

SFAS No. 52 specifies that amounts resulting from interperiod income tax allocation and amounts related to unamortized policy acquisition costs of stock life insurance companies are to be remeasured using the current rate.

To remeasure an amount recorded in a currency other than the functional currency at the lower of cost and market, its cost in the foreign currency is first remeasured using the historical exchange rate. That amount is compared with market in the functional currency, and the remeasured amount is written down if market is lower than remeasured cost. If the item had been written down in the records because market was less than cost in the currency in which it was recorded, the write-down is reversed if market in the functional currency is more than remeasured cost.

If an item is written down to market in the functional currency, the resulting amount is treated as cost in subsequent periods in which it is held in applying the lower of cost and market rule.

The financial statements of a foreign operation in a highly inflationary economy are remeasured to the domestic currency the way they would be remeasured were the domestic currency its functional currency.

(c) Translation Using the Current Rate. Amounts remeasured into the domestic currency need not be translated, because the domestic currency is used as the reporting currency in the consolidated financial statements. Amounts measured in a foreign currency or remeasured into a foreign currency are all translated using the current foreign exchange rate between the foreign currency and the domestic currency.

For assets and liabilities, that is the rate at the reporting date. For income statement items, that is the rates as of the dates during the reporting period at which the items are recorded. An appropriately weighted average rate may be used to translate such items if they are numerous.

(d) Translation Adjustments. Translation adjustments result from translating all amounts in foreign currency financial statements at rates current at the reporting date or during the reporting period different from rates current at the previous reporting date or during the previous reporting period. Remeasurement of a foreign operation's foreign currency financial statements involves recognition in current income of exchange gains and losses. In contrast, translation adjustments are not recognized in current income but are accumulated in a separate component of equity.

The translation adjustments pertaining to a foreign operation are transferred from equity to gain or loss on disposition of the foreign operation when it is partly or completely sold or completely or substantially liquidated.

7.13 TREATMENT OF FOREIGN COMPONENTS OR EXTENSIONS OF PARENT COMPANY OPERATIONS. The functional currency of a foreign operation that is a component or extension of the parent company's operations is the domestic currency. If it prepares its financial statements in a foreign currency, those financial statements are remeasured into the domestic currency by procedures discussed above. No translation is required for such a foreign operation.

7.14 TREATMENT OF FOREIGN CURRENCY TRANSACTIONS. Some transactions of a unit in a consolidated group of companies may take place in a currency other than the functional currency of the unit. For example, a unit whose functional currency is the Mexican peso may buy a machine on credit for U.K. pounds or may sell securities on credit for French francs. Except in a forward exchange contract (discussed below), the amounts in such a

			U.S. Dollars
Liability			
January 1, 19C		£1,000,000 × $1.60/£1 =	$1,600,000
December 31, 19C		£1,000,000 × $1.50/£1 =	1,500,000
	Transaction gain		$ 100,000

Exhibit 7.3.   Corporation P, transaction gain on forward exchange contracts for the year 19C.

foreign currency transaction are measured at the transaction date at the foreign exchange rate at that date—in the example, between the peso and the pound or between the peso and the franc.

At the next reporting date or at an intervening date at which the receivable or payable is settled, the receivable or payable is remeasured at the rate current at that date. Changes in its amount as measured in the functional currency since the previous reporting date or an intervening date at which it was acquired are transaction gains or losses, to be included in current reported consolidated net income, except as discussed later.

To illustrate: Corporation P, whose functional currency is U.S. dollars, borrowed £(U.K.)1,000,000 on January 1, 19C, and agreed to repay £100,000 on December 31, 19C, and £1,100,000 on December 31, 19D. Exchange rates were $1.60/£1 at January 1, 19C, and $1.50/£1 at December 31, 19C.

The payment of £100,000 on December 31, 19C, is remeasured as interest expense of $150,000. The liability in dollars at December 31, 19C, is remeasured for the change in exchange rate and a transaction gain of $100,000 is determined, for presentation in P's income statement for the year 19C, as shown in Exhibit 7.3.

7.15 FORWARD EXCHANGE CONTRACTS.   Forward exchange contracts are contracts that require currencies of two countries to be traded in specified amounts at specified future dates and specified rates, called **forward rates.** Such contracts are foreign currency transactions that require special treatment.

(a) Discounts or Premiums on Forward Exchange Contracts.   A forward exchange contract may involve a discount or premium, a difference between the foreign exchange rate specified in the contract and the rate at the date the contract is entered into, multiplied by the amount of foreign currency specified in the contract. Ordinarily, a discount or premium is allocated to income over the duration of the forward exchange contract. However, a discount or premium may be treated differently in these circumstances:

> If the contract is designated as and is effective as a hedge of a net investment in a foreign operation (discussed further on). If so, the discount or premium may be included with translation adjustments and thus not be reported in income.

> If the contract meets the tests of a hedge of an identifiable foreign currency commitment (also discussed further on). If so, the discount or premium may be included in the amount at which the foreign currency transaction related to the commitment is stated.

(b) Gains or Losses on Forward Exchange Contracts.   A gain or loss on a forward exchange contract to be reported in the current reporting period is computed by multiplying the amount of the foreign currency to be exchanged by the difference between (1) the foreign exchange rate at the reporting date and (2) the rate (a) on the date on which the contract was made or (b) the previous reporting date, whichever is later. A gain or loss on a forward exchange contract is recognized in income as a transaction gain or loss in the period of the gain or loss, unless it is in one of the categories of transaction gains and losses excluded from net income, discussed later.

To illustrate a forward exchange contract: On January 1, 19B, P and Q enter into a contract in which Q agrees to buy £(U.K.)1,000,000 from P for $(U.S.)1,550,000, incorporating a forward rate of $1.55/£1, on December 31, 19C. The exchange rate at January 1, 19B, is $1.60/£1. The contract therefore involves a premium to P and a discount to Q of £1,000,000 × ($1.60/£1 − $1.55/£1) = $50,000. Q makes this entry:

Foreign currency receivable	$1,600,000	
Payable to P		$1,550,000
Discount on foreign exchange contract		50,000

P makes this entry:

Receivable from Q	$1,550,000	
Premium on foreign exchange contract	50,000	
Foreign currency payable		$1,600,000

P and Q allocate the $50,000 to forward exchange gain or loss over the years 19B and 19C. P makes this entry in each of the 2 years:

Amortization of premium on forward exchange contract	$ 25,000	
Premium on forward exchange contract		$ 25,000

Q makes this opposite entry in each of the 2 years:

Discount on forward exchange contract	$ 25,000	
Amortization of discount on forward exchange contract		$ 25,000

The exchange rate changes to $1.50/£1 at December 31, 19B, and $1.45/£1 at December 31, 19C. P records these entries based on the changes in the exchange rate:

December 31, 19B		
Foreign currency payable	$ 100,000	
Forward exchange gain		$ 100,000
£1,000,000 × ($1.60/£1 − $1.50/£1) = $100,000		
December 31, 19C		
Foreign currency payable	$ 50,000	
Forward exchange gain		$ 50,000
£1,000,000 × ($1.50/£1 − $1.45/£1) = $50,000		

Q records these opposite entries based on the changes in the exchange rate:

December 31, 19B		
Forward exchange loss	$ 100,000	
Foreign currency receivable		$ 100,000
December 31, 19C		
Forward exchange loss	$ 50,000	
Foreign currency receivable		$ 50,000

On settlement of the contract on December 31, 19C, P makes this entry:

Foreign currency payable	$1,450,000	
Cash	$ 100,000	
Receivable from Q		$1,550,000

	Gain by P, Loss by Q, U.S. Dollars
Foreign exchange gain or loss on contract:	
The year 19B—£1,000,000 × ($1.60/£1 − $1.50/£1) =	$100,000
The year 19C—£1,000,000 × ($1.50/£1 − $1.45/£1) =	50,000
	150,000
Premium or discount on contract	(50,000)
Net gain or loss over the life of the contract	$100,000

Exhibit 7.4. Corporation P or Corporation Q, gain or loss on forward exchange contracts beginning in the year 19B.

To record payment of $1,450,000 to buy £1,000,000 to give to Q, receipt of $1,550,000 from Q, and cancellation of the forward exchange receivable from Q.

Q makes this opposite entry:

Payable to P	$1,550,000	
Foreign currency receivable		$1,450,000
Cash		100,000

To record receipt of $1,450,000 on sale of £1,000,000 received from P, payment of $1,550,000 to P, and cancellation of the forward exchange payable to P.

The contract may be summarized as shown in Exhibit 7.4.

The net gain of P and loss of Q of $100,000 equal the difference between the forward rate and the rate on the settlement date times the amount of currency transferred:

$$(\$1.55/£1 - \$1.45/£1) \times £1,000,000 = \$100,000$$

7.16 EXCLUSION OF TRANSACTION GAINS AND LOSSES FROM INCOME. Gains and losses on some foreign currency transactions are not recognized in income when they occur.

(a) Treatment as Translation Adjustments. SFAS No. 52 (par. 20) requires amounts that otherwise fit the definition of gains and losses on foreign currency transactions to be treated as translation adjustments if

a. [They] are designated as, and are effective as, economic hedges of a net investment in a foreign entity, commencing as of the designation date [or]

b. [They are] intercompany foreign currency transactions that are of a long-term investment nature (that is, settlement is not planned or anticipated in the foreseeable future), when the [units that are parties] to the transaction[s] are consolidated, combined, or accounted for by the equity method in the reporting [entity's] financial statements.

(b) Deferral of Transaction Gains and Losses. Recognition of transaction gains and losses in consolidated income is deferred for such gains and losses resulting from transactions intended to hedge identifiable foreign currency commitments; they are included in accounting for the transaction resulting from the commitment. However, recognition of losses is not deferred if deferral would lead to recognition of losses in subsequent periods.

SFAS No. 52 (par. 21) states two conditions that have to be met for a foreign currency transaction to be considered a hedge of an identifiable foreign currency commitment:

a. The foreign currency transaction is designated as, and is effective as, a hedge of a foreign currency commitment.

b. The foreign currency commitment is firm.

7.17 OTHER TOPICS IN FOREIGN CURRENCY TRANSLATION. Other topics concerning translation by the current rate method include income tax considerations, intercompany profit eliminations, selection of exchange rates, approximations, and required disclosures.

(a) Income Tax Considerations. Treatment of foreign operations involves these special income tax accounting treatments:

Unremitted Earnings. Deferred taxes are not recognized on translation adjustments that meet the tests in APB Opinion No. 23, ''Accounting for Income Taxes—Special Areas,'' concerning unremitted earnings.

Intraperiod Allocation. Income taxes related to transaction gains and losses or translation adjustments reported in separate components of the income statement or the statement of changes in equity are allocated to the separate components.

(b) Intercompany Profit Eliminations. An exception in the current rate method to the use of the current exchange rate for translation is the method to eliminate intercompany profits on transactions between combined or consolidated companies or between affiliates accounted for by the equity method. They are eliminated at the rates at the dates of the transactions, because those are the rates at which the profits are embedded in the recorded amounts. Such eliminations precede applying the current exchange rates to the foreign currency amounts.

To illustrate: Corporation P, a domestic parent company, sold a parcel of land last year to Corporation S, its foreign subsidiary, at a profit of $24,000, when the exchange rate was $1/Z8 (Polish zlotys). S recorded the land in zlotys. The current exchange rate is Z6 = $1. The profit is eliminated at Z8/$1. The remaining amount at which S has the land recorded is translated at Z6/$1. However, exchange restrictions between dollars and zlotys may be severe enough to call into question the soundness of including S in the consolidated reporting entity.

(c) Selection of Exchange Rates. The current foreign exchange rate is used for most translation required by SFAS No. 52. Circumstances in which the rates at the dates of transactions are used instead are discussed above. These are other special considerations in selecting exchange rates:

If the two currencies involved could not be exchanged on the date of the transaction or the reporting date, the rate at which they could be exchanged at the first succeeding date is used.

If the inability to exchange the two currencies is not merely temporary, including the foreign operation in a consolidated group or accounting for it by the equity method is questioned.

Foreign currency transactions are translated at the rates at which they could have been settled at the dates of the transactions. Resulting receivables and payables are translated subsequently at the rates at which they could be settled at the reporting dates.

If there is more than one rate at a particular date, the rate at which foreign currency could be exchanged for domestic currency to remit dividends is used.

If the reporting date of the foreign currency financial statements being translated differs from the reporting date of the reporting entity in which the foreign operation is included, the current rate is the rate in effect on the reporting date of the foreign currency financial statements.

(d) Approximations.   Approximations of the results of applying the required translation principles are acceptable if the cost of applying them to every detail exceeds the benefits of such precision and the results do not materially differ from what they would be by applying them to every detail. Judgment is required to determine whether to use approximation, because determining the extent of the differences precisely would require the very calculations to be avoided by approximations.

7.18 DISCLOSURES CONCERNING FOREIGN OPERATIONS.   These disclosures are required concerning foreign operations:

- The total transaction gains or losses, including, for this purpose, gains and losses on forward contracts other than those excluded from income.
- An analysis of the changes in the separate component of equity for translation adjustments, including at least:

    The beginning and ending accumulated balances.

    The net change from translation adjustments and gains and losses from hedges and intercompany balances treated the way translation adjustments are treated.

    Income taxes allocated to translation adjustments.

    Transfers from the equity component into income because of the partial or complete sale of an investment in a foreign operation or the complete or substantial liquidation of a foreign operation.

CONSOLIDATED BALANCE SHEET AT THE DATE OF BUSINESS COMBINATION

Amounts that would be presented in a consolidated balance sheet at the date of a business combination are determined for use in presenting a consolidated balance sheet as of that date or for use in consolidated financial statements for subsequent periods.

The separate balance sheets of the combining companies at the date of the combination include intercompany stockholdings and may include intercompany receivables and payables, all of which are eliminated in consolidation. The eliminating entries are recorded only on a consolidating worksheet, not in the books of any of the companies.

Sections 7.19–7.21 illustrate worksheet procedures to prepare consolidated balance sheets at the date of a business combination under three different sets of circumstances:

- Pooling of interests method: 90% transfer of stock.
- Purchase method: 90% acquisition of stock for cash.
- Purchase method: 80% acquisition of stock by transfer of stock.

7.19 POOLING OF INTERESTS METHOD: 90% TRANSFER OF STOCK.   P acquires 90% of S's voting stock (900 shares) on December 31, 19A, by issuing 1,000 shares of its $100 par value common stock to those of S's stockholders who transfer to P their voting stock in S. The combination qualifies for the pooling of interests method. Also, S owes P $3,000.

| Investment in Corporation S | $100,000 | |
| Common stock | | $100,000 |

The December 31, 19A, balance sheets of P and S immediately after the combination are as shown in the two left-hand columns of Exhibit 7.5 and the December 31, 19A, balance sheets are consolidated as shown in the column on the far right.

	P	S	Eliminations Dr.	Eliminations Cr.	Consolidated Balance Sheet
Cash	$500,000	$ 50,000			$550,000
Accounts receivable (net)	50,000	20,000		$ 3,000 (2)	67,000
Inventories	100,000	60,000			160,000
Buildings and equipment (net)	150,000	20,000			170,000
Investment in S	100,000			100,000 (1)	
	$900,000	$150,000			$947,000
Current liabilities	$ 20,000	$ 10,000	$ 3,000 (2)		$ 27,000
Long-term liabilities	140,000	20,000			160,000
Common stock	500,000	100,000	90,000 (1)		510,000*
Retained earnings	240,000	20,000	10,000 (1)		250,000**
	$900,000	$150,000	$103,000	$103,000	$947,000

(1) To eliminate intercompany stockholding: investment of $100,000 in 90% of S's stock charged first against common stock—$90,000—and the excess—$10,000—charged against retained earnings.
(2) To eliminate intercompany debt.
*Includes $100,000 × 10% = $10,000 of S's common stock owned by outsiders (minority interest).
**Includes $20,000 × 10% = $2,000 of retained earnings attributable to minority interest.

Exhibit 7.5. Corporation P and Corporation S, worksheet to develop consolidated balance sheet, December 31, 19A (just after combination accounted for by the pooling of interests method: 90% transfer of stock).

7.20 PURCHASE METHOD: 90% ACQUISITION OF STOCK.   P acquires 90% of S's voting stock (900 shares) on December 31, 19A, for $150,000. The combination does not qualify for the pooling of interests method, so the purchase method is used. Also, S owes P $3,000.
   P makes the following entry to record the purchase of S's stock:

     Investment in Corporation S $150,000
        Cash $150,000

The December 31, 19A, balance sheets of P and S immediately after the combination are as shown in Exhibit 7.6. For its $150,000, P acquired 90% of the fair value of S's assets and

	P	S
Cash	$350,000	$ 50,000
Accounts receivable (net)	50,000	20,000
Inventories	100,000	60,000
Buildings and equipment (net)	150,000	20,000
Investment in S	150,000	
	$800,000	$150,000
Current liabilities	$ 20,000	$ 10,000
Long-term liabilities	140,000	20,000
Common stock	400,000	100,000
Retained earnings	240,000	20,000
	$800,000	$150,000

Exhibit 7.6.   Corporation P and Corporation S, balance sheets, December 31, 19A (just after combination accounted for by the purchase method: 90% acquisition of stock).

	Fair Values	Book Values(i)	Excess of Fair Values over Book Values	90% of Excess of Fair Values over Book Values
Cash	$ 50,000	$ 50,000	$ -0-	$ -0-
Accounts receivable (net)	20,000	20,000	-0-	-0-
Inventories	80,000	60,000	20,000	18,000
Buildings and equipment (net)	30,000	20,000	10,000	9,000
Current liabilities	(10,000)	(10,000)	-0-	-0-
Long-term liabilities	(26,000)	(20,000)	(6,000)	(5,400)
	144,000	120,000	24,000	$21,600
	×90%	×90%	×90%	
	129,600	$108,000	$21,600	
Amount of investment	150,000			
Goodwill ·	$ 20,400			

Equity:		Total	90% Acquired
Common stock		$100,000	$ 90,000
Retained earnings		20,000	18,000
Totals, as above		$120,000	$108,000

(i) From Exhibit 7.6.

Exhibit 7.7. Corporation P and Corporation S, book values, fair values, and calculation of goodwill, December 31, 19A (combination accounted for by the purchase method: 90% acquisition of stock).

	P(i)	S(i)	Eliminations Dr.	Eliminations Cr.	Consolidated Balance Sheet
Cash	$350,000	$ 50,000			$400,000
Accounts receivable (net)	50,000	20,000		$ 3,000 (2)	67,000
Inventories	100,000	60,000	$ 18,000 (1)		178,000
Buildings and equipment (net)	150,000	20,000	9,000 (1)		179,000
Investment in S	150,000			150,000 (1)	
Goodwill			20,400 (1)		20,400
	$800,000	$150,000			$844,400
Current liabilities	20,000	10,000	3,000 (2)		27,000
Long-term liabilities	140,000	20,000		5,400 (1)	165,400
Common stock	400,000	100,000	90,000 (1)		410,000*
Retained earnings	240,000	20,000	18,000 (1)		242,000**
	$800,000	$150,000	$158,400	$158,400	$844,400

(i) From Exhibit 7.6.
(1) To eliminate intercompany stockholding, adjust S's assets and liabilities to their fair values, and record the difference as goodwill, from Exhibit 7.7.
(2) To eliminate intercompany debt.
*Includes $100,000 × 10% = $10,000 of S's common stock owned by outsiders (minority interest).
**Includes $20,000 × 10% = $2,000 of retained earnings attributable to minority interest.

Exhibit 7.8. Corporation P and Corporation S, worksheet to develop consolidated balance sheet, December 31, 19A (just after combination accounted for by the purchase method: 90% acquisition of stock).

	P	S
Cash	$500,000	$ 50,000
Accounts receivable (net)	50,000	20,000
Inventories	100,000	60,000
Buildings and equipment (net)	150,000	20,000
	$800,000	$150,000
Current liabilities	$ 20,000	$ 10,000
Long-term liabilities	140,000	20,000
Common stock	400,000	100,000
Retained earnings	240,000	20,000
	$800,000	$150,000

Exhibit 7.9.   Corporation P and Corporation S, balance sheets, December 31, 19A (just before combination accounted for by the purchase method: 80% acquisition of stock).

liabilities for $129,600, and goodwill, whose acquisition cost is calculated to be $20,400, as shown in Exhibit 7.7. The December 31, 19A, balance sheets are consolidated as shown in Exhibit 7.8.

7.21 PURCHASE METHOD: 80% ACQUISITION OF STOCK (FOR STOCK).   P acquires 80% (800 shares) of S's outstanding voting stock on December 31, 19A, by issuing 600 shares of its own $100 par value common stock to S's stockholders, who, in turn, transfer S's voting shares to P. The combination does not qualify for the pooling of interests method, so the purchase method is used. The market value of P's stock is not readily discernible, but S's stock is selling for $140 a share. Also, S owes P $3,000. Just before the combination, the December 31, 19A, balance sheets of P and S are as shown in Exhibit 7.9.

The investment in S is recorded at $112,000, the fair value of S's shares (800 shares at $140 = $112,000). P issues 600 shares of its $100 par value stock, for a total of $60,000. The $52,000 difference is credited to additional paid-in capital.

	P	S
Cash	$500,000	$ 50,000
Accounts receivable (net)	50,000	20,000
Inventories	100,000	60,000
Buildings and equipment (net)	150,000	20,000
Investment in S	112,000	
	$912,000	$150,000
Current liabilities	$ 20,000	$ 10,000
Long-term liabilities	140,000	20,000
Common stock	460,000	100,000
Additional paid-in capital	52,000	
Retained earnings	240,000	20,000
	$912,000	$150,000

Exhibit 7.10.   Corporation P and Corporation S, balance sheets, December 31, 19A (just after combination accounted for by the purchase method: 80% acquisition of stock).

	Fair Values	Book Values(i)	Excess of Fair Values over Book Values	80% of Excess of Fair Values over Book Values
Cash	$ 50,000	$ 50,000	$ -0-	$ -0-
Receivables (net)	20,000	20,000	-0-	-0-
Inventories	80,000	60,000	20,000	16,000
Buildings and equipment (net)	30,000	20,000	10,000	8,000
Current liabilities	(10,000)	(10,000)	-0-	-0-
Long-term liabilities	(30,000)	(20,000)	(10,000)	(8,000)
	140,000	120,000	20,000	$16,000
	× 80%	× 80%	× 80%	
	112,000	$ 96,000	$16,000	
Amount of investment	112,000			
Goodwill	$ -0-			

Equity:		Totals	80% Acquired
Common stock		$100,000	$80,000
Retained earnings		20,000	16,000
Totals, as above		$120,000	$96,000

(i) From Exhibit 7.10.

Exhibit 7.11.   Corporation P and Corporation S, book values, fair values, and calculation of goodwill, December 31, 19A (combination accounted for by the purchase method: 80% transfer of stock).

	P(i)	S(i)	Eliminations Dr.	Eliminations Cr.	Consolidated Balance Sheet
Cash	$500,000	$ 50,000			$550,000
Receivables (net)	50,000	20,000		$ 3,000 (2)	67,000
Inventories	100,000	60,000	$ 16,000 (1)		176,000
Buildings and equipment (net)	150,000	20,000	8,000 (1)		178,000
Investment in S	112,000			112,000 (1)	
	$912,000	$150,000			$971,000
Current liabilities	$ 20,000	$ 10,000	3,000 (2)		$ 27,000
Long-term liabilities	140,000	20,000		8,000 (1)	168,000
Common stock	460,000	100,000	80,000 (1)		480,000*
Additional paid-in capital	52,000				52,000
Retained earnings	240,000	20,000	16,000 (1)		244,000**
	$912,000	$150,000	$123,000	$123,000	$971,000

(i) From Exhibit 7.10.
(1) To eliminate intercompany stockholding and adjust S's assets and liabilities to their fair values, from Exhibit 7.11.
(2) To eliminate intercompany debt.
*Includes $100,000 × 20% = $20,000 of S's common stock owned by outsiders (minority interest).
**Includes $20,000 × 20% = $4,000 of retained earnings attributable to minority interest.

Exhibit 7.12.   Corporation P and Corporation S, worksheet to develop consolidated balance sheet, December 31, 19A (just after combination accounted for by the purchase method: 80% acquisition of stock).

P makes this entry:

Investment in Corporation S	$112,000	
Common stock		$ 60,000
Additional paid-in capital		52,000

The December 31, 19A, balance sheets of P and S immediately after the combination are as shown in Exhibit 7.10. For its $112,000 investment, P acquired 80% of the fair values of S's assets and liabilities, which equals $112,000. There is no goodwill. Exhibit 7.11 presents calculations of the fair values. P's and S's December 31, 19A, balance sheets are consolidated as shown in Exhibit 7.12.

CONSOLIDATED FINANCIAL STATEMENTS AFTER THE DATE OF BUSINESS COMBINATION

The financial statements of member companies of a consolidated group after the date of a business combination include elements that represent relationships and the effects of transactions between member companies, which are adjusted or eliminated in consolidation. The items are:

Intercompany stockholdings.

Intercompany receivables and payables.

Intercompany sales, purchases, fees, rents, interest, and the like.

Intercompany profits.

Intercompany dividends.

Eliminations and adjusting entries are recorded only in the consolidating worksheets, not in the books of any member company.

This section illustrates worksheet procedures to prepare consolidated balance sheets, income statements, and statements of changes in retained earnings 1 year and 2 years after the date of a business combination under the three different sets of circumstances illustrated in sections 7.19–7.21.

In all the following illustrations, the investment in S is accounted for by the cost rather than the equity method, which is discussed in sections 7.25–7.29. If P presents the investment at equity in its financial statements, the investment in S is nevertheless kept at cost in the consolidating worksheet. The consolidating entries parallel the entries that would be made in P's investment account to keep it on the equity method.

7.22 POOLING OF INTERESTS METHOD: 90% TRANSFER OF STOCK.   This section illustrates the procedures to develop consolidated financial statements for the year 19B and the year 19C, 1 year and 2 years after a business combination accounted for by the pooling of interests methods involving a 90% transfer of stock, using the facts in the related illustration in section 7.19.

The financial statements of P and S for the year 19B, 1 year after the business combination, are shown in Exhibit 7.13. During the year 19B, P sold merchandise to S for $25,000, including a profit of $5,000 on inventory on hand at December 31, 19B. S paid a cash dividend of $10,000. At the end of the year, P owes S $15,000. The financial statements for the year 19B are consolidated as shown in Exhibit 7.14.

The financial statements of P and S for the year 19C, 2 years after the business combination, are as shown in Exhibit 7.15. There were no intercompany sales or dividends. There is no intercompany debt at year-end. The inventory S sold to P at a $5,000 profit the

	P	S
Income Statement		
Sales	$250,000	$150,000
Cost of goods sold	(150,000)	(75,000)
Investment revenue	20,000	
Other expenses	(70,000)	(40,000)
Net income	$ 50,000	$ 35,000
Statement of Changes in Retained Earnings		
Retained earnings, beginning of year	$250,000	20,000
Net income	50,000	35,000
Dividends	(40,000)	(10,000)
Retained earnings, end of year	$250,000	$ 45,000
Balance Sheet		
Cash	$460,000	$ 90,000
Accounts receivable (net)	60,000	35,000
Inventories	100,000	50,000
Buildings and equipment (net)	160,000	15,000
Investment in S	100,000	
	$880,000	$190,000
Current liabilities	$ 30,000	$ 15,000
Long-term liabilities	100,000	30,000
Common stock	500,000	100,000
Retained earnings	250,000	45,000
	$880,000	$190,000

Exhibit 7.13. Corporation P and Corporation S, financial statements for the year 19B (1 year after combination accounted for by the pooling of interests method: 90% transfer of stock).

previous year is still on hand at December 31, 19C. The financial statements for the year 19C are consolidated as shown in Exhibit 7.16.

7.23 PURCHASE METHOD: 90% ACQUISITION OF STOCK.   This section illustrates the procedures to develop consolidated financial statements for the years 19B and 19C, 1 year and 2 years after a business combination accounted for by the purchase method involving a 90% acquisition of stock, using the facts in the related illustration in section 7.20.

The financial statements of P and S for the year 19B, 1 year after the business combination, are as shown in Exhibit 7.17. During the year 19B, S sold merchandise to P for $25,000, including a profit of $5,000 on inventory on hand at December 31, 19B. S paid a cash dividend of $10,000. At the end of the year, P owed S $15,000. The financial statements for the year 19B are consolidated as shown in Exhibit 7.18.

The financial statements of P and S for the year 19C, 2 years after the business combination, are as shown in Exhibit 7.19. There were no intercompany sales or dividends. There is no intercompany debt at year-end. The financial statements for the year 19C are consolidated as shown in Exhibit 7.20.

7.24 PURCHASE METHOD: 80% ACQUISITION OF STOCK (FOR STOCK).   This section illustrates the procedures to develop consolidated financial statements for the year 19B and the year 19C, 1 year and 2 years after a business combination accounted for by the purchase

	P(i)	S(i)	Adjustments and Eliminations Dr.	Adjustments and Eliminations Cr.	Consolidated Statements
Income Statement					
Sales	$250,000	$150,000	$ 25,000 (2)		$375,000
Cost of goods sold	(150,000)	(75,000)	5,000 (3)	$ 25,000 (2)	(205,000)
Investment revenue	20,000		9,000 (4)		11,000
Other expenses	(70,000)	(40,000)			(110,000)
Net income	$ 50,000	$ 35,000	$ 39,000	$ 25,000	$ 71,000*
Statement of Changes in Retained Earnings					
Retained earnings, beginning of year	$240,000	$ 20,000	$ 10,000 (1)		$250,000
Net income	50,000	35,000	39,000 (A)	$ 25,000 (A)	71,000
Dividends	(40,000)	(10,000)		9,000 (4)	(41,000)
Retained earnings, end of year	$250,000	$ 45,000	$ 49,000	$ 34,000	$280,000**
Balance Sheet					
Cash	$460,000	$ 90,000			$550,000
Receivables (net)	60,000	35,000		$ 15,000 (5)	80,000
Inventories	100,000	50,000		5,000 (3)	145,000
Buildings and equipment (net)	160,000	15,000			175,000
Investment in S	100,00			100,000 (1)	
	$880,000	$190,000			$950,000
Current liabilities	$ 30,000	$ 15,000	$ 15,000 (5)		$ 30,000
Long-term liabilities	100,000	30,000			130,000
Common stock	500,000	100,000	90,000 (1)		510,000***
Retained earnings	250,000	45,000	49,000 (B)	34,000 (B)	280,000
	$880,000	$190,000	$154,000	$154,000	$950,000

(i) From Exhibit 7.13.
(1) To eliminate intercompany stockholding, from Exhibit 7.5.
(2) To eliminate intercompany sales/purchases.
(3) To eliminate intercompany profit from inventory.
(4) To eliminate intercompany dividends.
(5) To eliminate intercompany receivables/payables.
(A) From the income statements.
(B) From the statements of changes in retained earnings.
*Includes $35,000 × 10% = $3,500 of net income attributable to minority interest.
**Includes $45,000 × 10% = $4,500 of retained earnings attributable to minority interest.
***Includes $100,000 × 10% = $10,000 of S's common stock owned by outsiders (minority interest).

Exhibit 7.14. Corporation P and Corporation S, worksheet to develop consolidated financial statements for the year 19B (1 year after combination accounted for by the pooling of interests method: 90% transfer of stock).

	P	S
Income Statement		
Sales	$240,000	$140,000
Cost of goods sold	(140,000)	(65,000)
Investment revenue	10,000	
Other expenses	(70,000)	(30,000)
Net income	$ 40,000	$ 45,000
Statement of Changes in Retained Earnings		
Retained earnings, beginning of year	$250,000	$ 45,000
Net income	40,000	45,000
Dividends	(30,000)	
Retained earnings, end of year	$260,000	$ 90,000
Balance Sheet		
Cash	$460,000	$105,000
Receivables (net)	70,000	45,000
Inventories	90,000	60,000
Buildings and equipment (net)	150,000	10,000
Investment in S	100,000	
	$870,000	$220,000
Current liabilities	$ 20,000	$ 10,000
Long-term liabilities	90,000	20,000
Common stock	500,000	100,000
Retained earnings	260,000	90,000
	$870,000	$220,000

Exhibit 7.15. Corporation P and Corporation S, financial statements for the year 19C (2 years after combination accounted for by the pooling of interests method: 90% transfer of stock).

	P(i)	S(i)	Adjustments and Eliminations Dr.	Adjustments and Eliminations Cr.	Consolidated Statements
Income Statement					
Sales	$240,000	$140,000			$380,000
Cost of goods sold	(140,000)	(65,000)			(205,000)
Investment revenue	10,000				10,000
Other expenses	(70,000)	(30,000)			(100,000)
Net income	$ 40,000	$ 45,000			$ 85,000*
					(continued)

Exhibit 7.16. Corporation P and Corporation S, worksheet to develop consolidated financial statements for the year 19C (2 years after combination accounted for by the pooling of interests method: 90% transfer of stock).

	P(i)	S(i)	Adjustments and Eliminations Dr.	Adjustments and Eliminations Cr.	Consolidated Statements
Statement of Changes in Retained Earnings					
Retained earnings, beginning of year	$250,000	$ 45,000	$ 10,000 (1) 5,000 (2)		$280,000
Net income	40,000	45,000			85,000
Dividends	(30,000)				(30,000)
Retained earnings, end of year	$260,000	$ 90,000	$ 15,000		$335,000**
Balance Sheet					
Cash	$460,000	$105,000			$565,000
Receivables (net)	70,000	45,000			115,000
Inventories	90,000	60,000		$ 5,000 (2)	145,000
Buildings and equipment (net)	150,000	10,000			160,000
Investment in S	100,000			100,000 (1)	
	$870,000	$220,000			$985,000
Current liabilities	20,000	10,000			$ 30,000
Long-term liabilities	90,000	20,000			110,000
Common stock	500,000	100,000	90,000 (1)		510,000***
Retained earnings	260,000	90,000	15,000 (A)		335,000
	$870,000	$220,000	$105,000	$105,000	$985,000

(i) From Exhibit 7.15.
(1) To eliminate intercompany stockholding, from Exhibit 7.5.
(2) To eliminate prior year's intercompany profit from inventory.
(A) From the statements of changes in retained earnings.
*Includes $45,000 × 10% = $4,500 of net income attributable to minority interest.
**Includes $90,000 × 10% = $9,000 of retained earnings attributable to minority interest.
***Includes $100,000 × 10% = $10,000 of S's common stock owned by outsiders (minority interest).

Exhibit 7.16. *Continued.*

	P	S
Income Statement		
Sales	$250,000	$150,000
Cost of goods sold	(150,000)	(75,000)
Investment revenue	20,000	
Other expenses	(70,000)	(40,000)
Net income	$ 50,000	$ 35,000
		(continued)

Exhibit 7.17. Corporation P and Corporation S, financial statements for the year 19B (1 year after combination accounted for by the purchase method: 90% acquisition of stock).

	P	S
Statement of Changes in Retained Earnings		
Retained earnings, beginning of year	$240,000	$ 20,000
Net income	50,000	35,000
Dividends	(40,000)	(10,000)
Retained earnings, end of year	$250,000	$ 45,000
Balance Sheet		
Cash	$310,000	$ 90,000
Accounts receivable (net)	60,000	35,000
Inventories	100,000	50,000
Buildings and equipment (net)	160,000	15,000
Investment in S	150,000	
	$780,000	$190,000
Current liabilities	$ 30,000	$ 15,000
Long-term liabilities	100,000	30,000
Common stock	400,000	100,000
Retained earnings	250,000	45,000
	$780,000	$190,000

Exhibit 7.17. *Continued.*

			Adjustments and Eliminations		Consolidated
	P(i)	S(i)	Dr.	Cr.	Statements
Income Statement					
Sales	$250,000	$150,000	$25,000 (3)		$375,000
Cost of goods sold	(150,000)	(75,000)	18,000 (2)	$25,000 (3)	(223,000)
			5,000 (4)		
Investment revenue	20,000		9,000 (5)		11,000
Other expenses	(70,000)	(40,000)	669 (2)		(110,669)
Net income	$ 50,000	$ 35,000	$57,669	$25,000	$ 52,331*
Statement of Changes in Retained Earnings					
Retained earnings, beginning of year	$240,000	$ 20,000	$18,000 (1)		$242,000
Net income	50,000	35,000	57,669 (A)	$25,000 (A)	52,331
Dividends	(40,000)	(10,000)		9,000 (5)	(41,000)
Retained earnings, end of year	$250,000	$ 45,000	$75,669	$34,000	$253,331**

(i) From Exhibit 7.17.
(1) To eliminate intercompany stockholding, adjust S's assets and liabilities to their fair values, and record the difference as goodwill at the date of the combination, from amounts in Exhibit 7.7.
(2) To amortize P's proportionate share of the excess of fair values of S's assets and liabilities over their book values and goodwill, from the information derived in Exhibit 7.7.

(continued)

Exhibit 7.18. Corporation P and Corporation S, worksheet to develop consolidated financial statements for the year 19B (1 year after combination method: 90% acquisition of stock).

	90% Excess Fair Values and Goodwill (ii)	Assumed Remaining Life	Amount Attributed to Current Year	
			Cost of Goods Sold	Other Expenses
Inventories	$18,000	None	$18,000	
Buildings and equipment	9,000	10 years		$ 900
Long-term debt	(5,400)	3 years		(1,800)
Goodwill	20,400	13 years		1,569
			$18,000	$ 669

	P(i)	S(i)	Adjustments and Eliminations		Consolidated Statements
			Dr.	Cr.	
Balance Sheet					
Cash	$310,000	$ 90,000			$400,000
Receivables (net)	60,000	35,000		$ 15,000 (6)	80,000
Inventories	100,000	50,000	$ 18,000 (1)	5,000 (4)	145,000
				18,000 (2)	
Buildings and equipment (net)	160,000	15,000	9,000 (1)	900 (2)	183,100
Investment in S	150,000			150,000 (1)	
Goodwill			20,400 (1)	1,569 (2)	18,831
	$780,000	$190,000			$826,931
Current liabilities	$ 30,000	$ 15,000	$ 15,000 (6)		$ 30,000
Long-term liabilities	100,000	30,000	1,800 (2)	$ 5,400 (1)	133,600
Common stock	400,000	100,000	90,000 (1)		410,000***
Retained earnings	250,000	45,000	75,669 (B)	34,000 (B)	253,331
	$780,000	$190,000	$229,869	$229,869	$826,931

(ii) From Exhibit 7.7.

In each subsequent year, an entry is made to record the cumulative amounts of annual amortization previously recorded, but those subsequent entries affect consolidated retained earnings directly, not consolidated income.

(3) To eliminate intercompany sales/purchases.
(4) To eliminate intercompany profit from inventory.
(5) To eliminate intercompany dividends.
(6) To eliminate intercompany receivables/payables.
(A) From the income statements.
(B) From the statements of changes in retained earnings.
*Includes $35,000 × 10% = $3,500 of net income attributable minority interest.
**Includes $45,000 × 10% = $4,500 of retained earnings attributable to minority interest.
***Includes $100,000 × 10% = $10,000 of S's common stock owned by outsiders (minority interest).

Exhibit 7.18. Continued.

	P	S
Income Statement		
Sales	$240,000	$140,000
Cost of goods sold	(140,000)	(65,000)
Investment revenue	10,000	
Other expenses	(70,000)	(30,000)
Net income	$ 40,000	$ 45,000
Statement of Changes in Retained Earnings		
Retained earnings, beginning of year	$250,000	$ 45,000
Net income	40,000	45,000
Dividends	(30,000)	
Retained earnings, end of year	$260,000	$ 90,000
Balance Sheet		
Cash	$310,000	$105,000
Accounts receivable (net)	70,000	45,000
Inventories	90,000	60,000
Buildings and equipment (net)	150,000	10,000
Investment in S	150,000	
	$770,000	$220,000
Current liabilities	$ 20,000	$ 10,000
Long-term liabilities	90,000	20,000
Common stock	400,000	100,000
Retained earnings	260,000	90,000
	$770,000	$220,000

Exhibit 7.19. Corporation P and Corporation S, financial statements for the year 19C (2 years after combination accounted for by the purchase method: 90% acquisition of stock).

	P(i)	S(i)	Adjustments and Eliminations Dr.	Adjustments and Eliminations Cr.	Consolidated Statements
Income Statement					
Sales	$ 240,000	$140,000			$380,000
Cost of goods sold	(140,000)	(65,000)			(205,000)
Investment revenue	10,000				10,000
Other expenses	(70,000)	(30,000)	669 (2)		(100,669)
Net income	$ 40,000	$ 45,000	$ 669		$ 84,331*
					(continued)

Exhibit 7.20. Corporation P and Corporation S, worksheet to develop consolidated financial statements for the year 19C (2 years after combination accounted for by the purchase method: 90% acquisition of stock).

	P(i)	S(i)	Adjustments and Eliminations Dr.	Adjustments and Eliminations Cr.	Consolidated Statements
Statement of Changes in Retained Earnings					
Retained earnings, beginning of year	$ 250,000	$ 45,000	$41,669 (1)		$253,331
Net income	40,000	45,000	669 (A)		84,331
Dividends	(30,000)				(30,000)
Retained earnings, end of year	$ 260,000	$ 90,000	$42,338		$307,662**

(i) From Exhibit 7.19.
(1) To eliminate intercompany stockholding, adjust S's assets and liabilities to their fair values at the date of the combination, and record the difference as goodwill, from Exhibit 7.7, reduced by amounts amortized in prior years:

	Excess of Fair Values over Book Values		
	At Date of Combination	Charged in Prior Years	Balance at Beginning of Current Year
Inventories	$18,000	$18,000	$ -0-
Buildings and equipment (net)	9,000	900	8,100
Long-term debt	(5,400)	(1,800)	(3,600)
Goodwill	20,400	1,569	18,831
		$18,669	$23,331
Intercompany profit still in inventory		5,000	
Retained earnings acquired at date of combination		18,000	
Total charge to retained earnings		$41,669	

	P(i)	S(i)	Adjustments and Eliminations Dr.	Adjustments and Eliminations Cr.	Consolidated Statements
Balance Sheet					
Cash	$310,000	$105,000			$415,000
Receivables (net)	70,000	45,000			115,000
Inventories	90,000	60,000		$ 5,000 (1)	145,000
Buildings and equipment (net)	150,000	10,000	$ 8,100 (1)	900 (2)	167,200
Investment in S	150,000			150,000 (1)	
Goodwill			18,831 (1)	1,569 (2)	17,262
	$770,000	$220,000			$859,462
					(continued)

Exhibit 7.20. *Continued.*

	P(i)	S(i)	Adjustments and Eliminations Dr.	Adjustments and Eliminations Cr.	Consolidated Statements
Balance Sheet					
Current liabilities	$ 20,000	$ 10,000			$ 30,000
Long-term liabilities	90,000	20,000	$ 1,800 (2)	$ 3,600 (1)	111,800
Common stock	400,000	100,000	90,000 (1)		410,000***
Retained earnings	260,000	90,000	42,338 (B)		307,662
	$770,000	$220,000	$161,069	$161,069	$859,462

(2) To amortize the excess of the fair values of S's assets and liabilities over their book values and goodwill:

	Excess Fair Values and Goodwill	Remaining Life †	Charge to Other Expenses
Buildings and equipment	$ 9,000	10 years	$ 900
Long-term debt	(5,400)	3 years	(1,800)
Goodwill	20,400	13 years	1,569
			$ 669

†At time of combination.
(A) From income statements.
(B) From statements of changes in retained earnings.
*Includes $45,000 × 10% = $4,500 of net income attributable minority interest.
**Includes $90,000 × 10% = $9,000 of retained earnings attributable to minority interest.
***Includes $100,000 × 10% = $10,000 of S's common owned by outsiders (minority interest).

Exhibit 7.20. *Continued.*

	P	S
Income Statement		
Sales	$250,000	$150,000
Cost of goods sold	(150,000)	(75,000)
Investment revenue	20,000	
Other expenses	(70,000)	(40,000)
Net income	$ 50,000	$ 35,000
Statement of Changes in Retained Earnings		
Retained earnings, beginning of year	$240,000	$ 20,000
Net income	50,000	35,000
Dividends	(40,000)	(10,000)
Retained earnings, end of year	$250,000	$ 45,000
		(continued)

Exhibit 7.21. Corporation P and Corporation S, financial statements for the year 19B (1 year after combination accounted for by the purchase method: 80% acquisition of stock).

	P	S
Balance Sheet		
Cash	$460,000	$ 90,000
Accounts receivable (net)	60,000	35,000
Inventories	100,000	50,000
Buildings and equipment (net)	160,000	15,000
Investment in S	112,000	
	$892,000	$190,000
Current liabilities	$ 30,000	$ 15,000
Long-term liabilities	100,000	30,000
Common stock	460,000	100,000
Additional paid-in capital	52,000	
Retained earnings	250,000	45,000
	$892,000	$190,000

Exhibit 7.21. *Continued.*

			Adjustments and Eliminations		Consolidated
	P(i)	S(i)	Dr.	Cr.	Statements
Income Statement					
Sales	$250,000	$150,000	$25,000 (3)		$375,000
Cost of goods sold	(150,000)	(75,000)	16,000 (2)	$25,000 (3)	(221,000)
			5,000 (4)		
Investment revenue	20,000		8,000 (5)		12,000
Other expenses	(70,000)	(40,000)		1,867	(108,133)
Net income	$ 50,000	$ 35,000	$54,000	$26,867	$ 57,867*
Statement of Changes in Retained Earnings					
Retained earnings, beginning of year	$240,000	$ 20,000	$16,000 (1)		$244,000
Net income	50,000	35,000	54,000 (A)	$26,867 (A)	57,867
Dividends	(40,000)	(10,000)		8,000 (5)	(42,000)
Retained earnings, end of year	$250,000	$ 45,000	$70,000	$34,867	$259,867**

(i) From Exhibit 7.21.
(1) To eliminate intercompany stockholding, adjust S's assets and liabilities to their fair values, and record the difference as goodwill at the date of the combination, from Exhibit 7.11.
(2) To amortize P's proportionate share of the excess of fair values of S's assets and liabilities over their book values, from the information derived in section 7.11:

(continued)

Exhibit 7.22. Corporation P and Corporation S, worksheet to develop consolidated financial statements for the year 19B (1 year after combination accounted for by the purchase method: 80% acquisition of stock).

	80% Excess Fair Values (ii)		Assumed Remaining Life	Amount Attributed to Current Year	
				Cost of Goods Sold	Other Expenses
Inventories	$16,000		None	$16,000	
Buildings and equipment	8,000		10 years		$ 800
Long-term debt	(8,000)		3 years		(2,667)
				$16,000	$(1,867)

			Adjustments and Eliminations		Consolidated
	P(i)	S(i)	Dr.	Cr.	Statements
Balance Sheet					
Cash	$460,000	$ 90,000			$550,000
Receivables (net)	60,000	35,000		$ 15,000 (6)	80,000
Inventories	100,000	50,000	$ 16,000 (1)	5,000 (4)	145,000
				16,000 (2)	
Buildings and equipment (net)	160,000	15,000	8,000 (1)	800 (2)	182,200
Investment in S	112,000			112,000 (1)	
	$892,000	$190,000			$957,200
Current liabilities	$ 30,000	$ 15,000	$ 15,000 (6)		$ 30,000
Long-term liabilities	100,000	30,000	2,667 (2)	$ 8,000 (1)	135,333
Common stock	460,000	100,000	80,000 (1)		480,000***
Additional paid-in capital	52,000				52,000
Retained earnings	250,000	45,000	70,000 (B)	34,867 (B)	259,867
	$892,000	$190,000	$191,667	$191,667	$957,200

(ii) From Exhibit 7.11.
In each subsequent year, an entry is made to record the cumulative amounts of annual amortization previously recorded, but those future entries affect consolidated retained earnings directly, not consolidated income.
(3) To eliminate intercompany sales/purchases.
(4) To eliminate intercompany profit from inventory.
(5) To eliminate intercompany dividends.
(6) To eliminate intercompany receivables/payables.
(A) From the income statements.
(B) From the statements of changes in retained earnings.
*Includes $35,000 × 20% = $7,000 of net income attributable minority interest.
**Includes $45,000 × 20% = $9,000 of retained earnings attributable to minority interest.
***Includes $100,000 × 20% = $20,000 of S's common stock owned by outsiders (minority interest).

Exhibit 7.22. *Continued.*

7 · 39

	P	S
Income Statement		
Sales	$240,000	$140,000
Cost of goods sold	(140,000)	(65,000)
Investment revenue	10,000	
Other expenses	(70,000)	(30,000)
Net income	$ 40,000	$ 45,000
Statement of Changes in Retained Earnings		
Retained earnings, beginning of year	$250,000	$ 45,000
Net income	40,000	45,000
Dividends	(30,000)	
Retained earnings, end of year	$260,000	$ 90,000
Balance Sheet		
Cash	$460,000	$105,000
Accounts receivable (net)	70,000	45,000
Inventories	90,000	60,000
Buildings and equipment (net)	150,000	10,000
Investment in S	112,000	
	$882,000	$220,000
Current liabilities	$ 20,000	$ 10,000
Long-term liabilities	90,000	20,000
Common stock	460,000	100,000
Additional paid-in capital	52,000	
Retained earnings	260,000	90,000
	$882,000	$220,000

Exhibit 7.23.   Corporation P and Corporation S, financial statements for the year 19C (2 years after combination accounted for by the purchase method: 80% acquisition of stock).

method involving an 80% acquisition of stock (for stock), using the facts in the related illustration in section 7.21.

The financial statements of Corporation P and Corporation S for the year 19B are as shown in Exhibit 7.21. During the year 19B, S sold merchandise to P for $25,000, including a profit of $5,000 on inventory on hand at December 31, 19B. S paid a cash dividend of $10,000. At the end of the year, P owed S $15,000. The financial statements of P and S for the year 19B are consolidated as shown in Exhibit 7.22.

The financial statements of P and S for the year 19C, 2 years after the business combination, are as shown in Exhibit 7.23. There were no intercompany sales or dividends. There is no intercompany debt at year-end. The inventory S sold to P at a $5,000 profit the previous year is still on hand at December 31, 19C. The financial statements of P and S for the year 19C are consolidated as shown in Exhibit 7.24.

THE EQUITY METHOD

The **equity method**, which is the focus of APB Opinion No. 18, is used to account for investments in unconsolidated subsidiaries, corporate joint ventures, and common stock that provide the investor with the ability to exercise significant influence over the operating and

	P(i)	S(i)	Dr.	Cr.	Consolidated Statements
			Adjustments and Eliminations		
Income Statement					
Sales	$ 240,000	$140,000			$380,000
Cost of goods sold	(140,000)	(65,000)			(205,000)
Investment revenue	10,000				10,000
Other expenses	(70,000)	(30,000)		1,867 (2)	(98,133)
Net income	$ 40,000	$ 45,000		$1,867	$ 86,867*
Statement of Changes in Retained Earnings					
Retained earnings, beginning of year	$250,000	$ 45,000	$35,133 (1)		$259,867
Net income	40,000	45,000		$1,867 (A)	86,867
Dividends	(30,000)				(30,000)
Retained earnings, end of year	$260,000	$ 90,000	$35,133	$1,867	$316,734**

(i) From Exhibit 7.23.

(1) To eliminate intercompany stockholding, adjust S's assets and liabilities to their fair values at the date of the combination, from Exhibit 7.11, reduced by amounts amortized in prior years:

	Excess of Fair Values over Book Values		
	At Date of Combination (ii)	Charged in Prior Years	Balance at Beginning of Current Year
Inventories	$16,000	$16,000	$ -0-
Buildings and equipment (net)	8,000	800	7,200
Long-term debt	(8,000)	(2,667)	(5,333)
	$16,000	$14,133	$1,867
Intercompany profit still in inventory		5,000	
Retained earnings acquired at date of combination		16,000	
Total charge to retained earnings		$35,133	

(ii) From Exhibit 7.11.

(2) To amortize the excess of the fair values of S's assets and liabilities over their book values:

(continued)

Exhibit 7.24. Corporation P and Corporation S, worksheet to develop consolidated financial statements for the year 19C (2 years after combination accounted for by the purchase method: 80% acquisition of stock).

| | P(i) | S(i) | Adjustments and Eliminations | | Consolidated Statements |
			Dr.	Cr.	
Balance Sheet					
Cash	$460,000	$105,000			$565,000
Receivables (net)	70,000	45,000			115,000
Inventories	90,000	60,000		$ 5,000 (1)	145,000
Buildings and					
equipment (net)	150,000	10,000	$ 7,200 (1)	800 (2)	166,400
Investment in S	112,000			112,000 (1)	
	$882,000	$220,000			$991,400
Current liabilities	$ 20,000	$ 10,000			$ 30,000
Long-term liabilities	90,000	20,000	$ 2,667 (2)	$ 5,333 (1)	112,666
Common stock	460,000	100,000	80,000 (1)		480,000***
Additional paid-in					
capital	52,000				52,000
Retained earnings	260,000	90,000	35,133 (B)	1,867	316,734
	$882,000	$220,000	$125,000	$125,000	$991,400

	Excess Fair Values	Remaining Life †	Charge to Other Expenses
Buildings and equipment	$8,000	10 years	$ 800
Long-term debt	(8,000)	3 years	(2,667)
			$(1,867)

†At time of combination.
(A) From income statements.
(B) From statements of changes in retained earnings.
*Includes $45,000 × 20% = $9,000 of net income attributable to minority interest.
**Includes $90,000 × 20% = $18,000 of retained earnings attributable to minority interest.
***Includes $100,000 × 20% = $20,000 of S's common owned by outsiders (minority interest).

Exhibit 7.24. *Continued.*

financial policies of the investee. Other long-term investments in common stock are accounted for by the method required by SFAS No. 12, "Accounting for Certain Marketable Securities," discussed in section 7.29.

Under the equity method, an investor initially records an investment at cost. It adjusts the carrying amount of the investment at the end of the period in which it is acquired and in succeeding periods by the investor's proportionate share of changes in the investee's assets and liabilities and for the effects of intercompany profits. The principles for determining the cost of an investment accounted for by the equity method are essentially the same as those for determining the cost of an investment leading to a business combination accounted for by the purchase method, discussed in section 7.9.

7.25 DIFFERENCES BETWEEN CONSOLIDATION AND THE EQUITY METHOD.   An investor's net income for a period and its equity at a point in time with its investment accounted for by the equity method are generally the same as they are with the investee consolidated. Application of three statements—SFAS No. 12, SFAS No. 34, "Capitalization of Interest Cost," and SFAS No. 58, "Capitalization of Interest Cost in Financial Statements That Include Investments Accounted for by the Equity Method"—cause differences, however.

(a) SFAS No. 12. In applying SFAS No. 12, the portfolios of marketable equity securities held by investees accounted for by the equity method are kept separate from the portfolios of such securities held by the investor or other investees, for purposes of determining the consolidated lower of cost and market adjustment. In contrast, the portfolios of marketable equity securities held by investees that are consolidated are combined with the portfolios of such securities held by the parent company and other members of the consolidated group for purposes of determining the consolidated lower of cost and market adjustment.

(b) SFAS Nos. 34 and 58. Under SFAS No. 34, the total amount of interest cost capitalized in a set of consolidated financial statements cannot exceed the total amount of interest cost incurred by all the members of the consolidated group after intercompany amounts are eliminated. Under SFAS No. 58, however, for investments accounted for by the equity method, the total amount of interest cost capitalized in the investor's financial statements cannot exceed the total amount of interest cost incurred solely by the investor. That is, interest costs incurred by an investee accounted for by the equity method are excluded in accounting for amounts in the investor's financial statements on which interest is capitalized. Interest cost incurred by the investee can be capitalized only on amounts in the investee's financial statements.

7.26 USING THE EQUITY METHOD. An investor generally uses the equity method to account for each of the following types of investments.

(a) Unconsolidated Subsidiaries. If a subsidiary does not qualify for consolidation, its financial statement elements are not combined with corresponding elements of the parent company line by line, but are instead reported in the parent company's balance sheet and income statement on one line on each statement, the one called **investment in unconsolidated subsidiary** or the like and the other called **investment revenue** or the like.

(b) Joint Ventures. An enterprise may be formed and operated by a number of other enterprises as a joint venture—a separate business or means to carry out a specific project for the benefit of its investors, also called **venturers.** The venturers pool their resources, knowledge, and talents and share risks for the purpose of ultimately sharing rewards. In many joint ventures, each venturer has more than just a passive interest or investment; each participates—either directly or indirectly—in managing the venture. Investments in joint ventures are generally accounted for by the equity method.

(c) Investments in Common Stock Involving Significant Influence. In the absence of evidence to the contrary, an investor with an investment of from 20% to 50% of the voting common stock of an investee is presumed to have the ability to exercise significant influence over the financial and operating policies of the investee and, because of that, uses the equity method to account for such an investment. Conversely, in the absence of evidence to the contrary, an investor with an investment of less than 20% of the common stock of an investee is presumed not to have the ability to exercise significant influence over the financial and operating policies of the investee and, therefore, does not use the equity method to account for such an investment but uses the method discussed in section 7.29.

The ability to exercise significant influence may be inferred from, for example:

- Representation on the investee's board of directors.
- Participation in policy-making processes.
- Material intercompany transactions.
- Interchange of managerial personnel.
- Technological dependency.

The inability to exercise significant influence may be inferred from, for example:

- Opposition by the investee that challenges the investor's ability to exercise significant influence, such as litigation or complaints to government authorities.
- An agreement by the investor surrendering significant rights as a stockholder.
- Concentration of the majority ownership of the investee among a few stockholders, who operate the investee without regard to the views of the investor.
- Inability of the investor to obtain representation on the investee's board of directors after attempting to do so.
- Inability of the investor to obtain financial information necessary to apply the equity method after attempting to do so.

No one item in either of those lists is the sole determining factor as to whether an investor has the ability to exercise significant influence over the investee. Instead, all items are considered collectively.

If an investor owns two investments of, say, 20% each in unrelated corporations, one investment might qualify for the equity method and the other not, because their circumstances differ. Judgment is always necessary in determining whether an investment gives an investor the ability to exercise significant influence over the investee.

7.27 APPLYING THE EQUITY METHOD.   Application of the equity method is discussed and illustrated below.

Under the equity method, the investor's initial investment, in essence, comprises three bundles:

Bundle A. A proportionate share of the book values of the investee's assets and liabilities on the date of the purchase.

plus

Bundle B. A proportionate share of the differences between the book values and the fair values of the investee's assets and liabilities on the date of the initial investment (commonly referred to as **net unrealized appreciation** or **unrealized depreciation**). The principles for determining the fair values of the investee's assets and liabilities parallel the principles in applying the purchase method of accounting for business combinations, discussed in section 7.9.

plus

Bundle C. Goodwill, which is the excess at the date of purchase of (1) the cost of the investment over (2) the investor's proportionate share of the fair values of the investee's assets and liabilities (the sum of $A + B$) at the date of the purchase. If (2) exceeds (1), this bundle is negative goodwill. The principles of accounting for goodwill and negative goodwill under the equity method parallel the principles to account for them in consolidation, discussed in section 7.9.

The investor adjusts the carrying amount of the investment in succeeding periods by its proportionate share of changes in each bundle and for the effects of intercompany profits.

(a) Bundle A.   Changes in the investee's equity are caused by earnings or losses from operations, extraordinary items, prior period adjustments, the payment of cash or property dividends, and other transactions by the investor or the investee in stock of the investee.

The investor charges the investment account for its proportionate share of the investee's earnings from operations and credits investment revenue. If the investee reports a loss, the investor credits the investment account for its proportionate share of the investee's loss from operations and charges investment revenue. A negative balance in the investment revenue account for a reporting period is disclosed as a loss from investment. The investor adjusts its investment account for its proportionate share of the investee's prior period adjustments and extraordinary items and correspondingly charges or credits prior period adjustments and extraordinary items in its own financial statements.

An investor recognizes receipt of a cash dividend by crediting its investment account.

(b) Bundle B.   The portion of the investment that represents the investor's proportionate share of the differences between the fair values and the book values of each of the investee's assets and liabilities at the date of the investment (unrealized appreciation or depreciation) is amortized to investment revenue over the remaining estimated useful lives of the underlying assets and liabilities.

(c) Bundle C.   The portion of the investment that represents goodwill or negative goodwill is amortized to investment revenue over the period expected to be benefited or 40 years, whichever is shorter.

(d) Intercompany Profit or Loss.   Intercompany profit or loss on assets bought from or sold to an investee is eliminated in the period of sale by adjusting the investment and the investment revenue accounts. That entry is reversed in the period in which the asset is sold to unrelated parties. The amount of unrealized profit or loss to be eliminated depends on whether the underlying transactions are considered to be at arm's length. If the transactions are not considered to be at arm's length, all the intercompany profit or loss is eliminated. If, however, the underlying transactions are considered to be at arm's length, only the investor's proportional share of the unrealized profit or loss is eliminated.

(e) Special Considerations.   Applying the equity method sometimes involves the following special considerations.

(i) Preferred Dividends.   An investor computes its proportionate share of the investee's net income or loss after deducting cumulative preferred dividends, regardless of whether they are declared.

(ii) Investee's Capital Transactions.   An investor accounts for transactions between the investee and its stockholders (for example, issuances and reacquisitions of its stock) that directly affect the investor's proportionate share of the investee's equity in the same way that such transactions of a consolidated subsidiary are accounted for.

(iii) Time Lag.   An investor's reporting period may differ from that of the investee or the financial statements of the investee may not be available in time for an investor to record in its financial statements the information necessary to apply the equity method currently. In either case, the investor applies the equity method using the investee's most recent available financial statements. The same lag in reporting is used each period for consistency.

(iv) Permanent Decline in Value.   The recorded amount of an investment accounted for by the equity method is normally not reduced for declines in market value. But if the decline brings that market value below the carrying amount of the investment and is judged to be permanent, the investment is written down to its recoverable amount, usually market value, and a loss is charged to current income. The distinction between a decline that is permanent and one that is not is often not clear. However, evidence of a permanent decline might be demonstrated by, for example, the investor's inability to recover the carrying amount of the investment, the investee's inability to sustain an earnings capacity that would justify the carrying amount of the investment, or a history of losses or market values substantially below cost.

To illustrate: On January 1, 19D, Corporation P accounts for its investment in Corporation S by the equity method. The carrying amount is $24,000 and the market value of the investment is $13,000. If the decline is judged to be permanent, P discontinues applying the equity method and records this entry to reduce the investment to its recoverable amount, in this case market value:

Investment loss	$11,000	
Investment in Corporation S		$11,000

If the market subsequently recovers, $13,000, not $24,000, is the basis at which to resume applying the equity method.

(v) Excessive Losses.   A company that accounts for an investment by the equity method ordinarily discontinues applying that method when the carrying amount of the investment in and net advances to the investee is reduced to zero, unless the investor has guaranteed obligations or is otherwise committed to providing further financial support for the investee. An investor resumes applying the equity method after the investee returns to profitable operations and the investor's proportionate share of the investee's subsequent net income equals the proportionate share of net losses the investor did not recognize during the period that application of the equity method was suspended.

(vi) Changed Conditions.   If an investment no longer qualifies for the equity method because the investor no longer has the ability to exercise significant influence over the investee, the investor stops applying the equity method and starts applying the method described in SFAS No. 12 from that point on as described in section 7.29. The investor does not retroactively adjust the carrying amount of the investment to reflect what the carrying amount of the investment would have been had that method been applied since the investment was acquired.

To illustrate: On January 1, 19D, Corporation P's investment in Corporation S ceases to give P the ability to exercise significant influence over S. On that date the investment in Corporation S is reported in P's financial statements at $28,000. That becomes the investment's cost for purposes of applying SFAS No. 12 from that point on.

If an investment accounted for by the method in SFAS No. 12 subsequently qualifies for the equity method because the investor subsequently gains the ability to exercise significant influence over the investee, the investor stops applying the SFAS No. 12 method and starts applying the equity method from that point on. In that case, in contrast, the investor does retroactively adjust the carrying amount of the investment to what it would have been had it been accounted for by the equity method starting with its first acquisition by the investor, in a manner consistent with the accounting for a step-by-step acquisition of a subsidiary.

To illustrate: P acquired stock of S on January 1, 19C, for $24,000. The investment did not give P the ability to exercise significant influence over S. The investment is reported in P's balance sheet on December 31, 19C, at $24,000, in accordance with SFAS No. 12. Had the investment previously qualified for the equity method, the investment in S would have been reported in P's balance sheet at $32,000.

On January 1, 19D, P gains the ability to exercise significant influence over S without a change in its holding of S's stock. P therefore increases its investment account to $32,000, as follows:

Investment in Corporation S	$8,000	
Retained earnings		$8,000

It applies the equity method from then on the way it would have been applied had P first obtained the ability to exercise significant influence when it first acquired the investment.

7.28 DISCLOSURES CONCERNING THE EQUITY METHOD.   The following information about investments accounted for by the equity method, as applicable, is disclosed on the face of the financial statements, in the notes to the financial statements, or in supporting schedules or statements:

- The names of the investees and the percentages of ownership.
- Reasons investments of 20% or more of the voting stock of an investee are not accounted for by the equity method.
- Reasons investments of less than 20% of the voting stock of an investee are accounted for by the equity method.
- The amounts of net unrealized appreciation or depreciation and how the amounts are amortized.
- The amounts of goodwill and how they are amortized.
- The quoted market prices of the investments, if available.
- Summarized information about the assets, liabilities, and results of operations of investments in unconsolidated subsidiaries or in corporate joint ventures, if they are material individually or collectively in relation to the financial position or results of operations of the investor. The information can be either about each investment accounted for by the equity method or combined information of all investments accounted for by the equity method.
- Descriptions of possible conversions, exercises of warrants or options, or other contingent issuances of stock of investees that may significantly affect the investor's shares of reported earnings.

7.29 INVESTMENTS NOT QUALIFYING FOR CONSOLIDATION OR THE EQUITY METHOD.   Long-term investments in equity securities not qualifying for consolidation or the equity method are ordinarily accounted for in accordance with SFAS No. 12. Under that statement, an investor initially records an investment at cost but does not subsequently adjust the carrying amount, except for writedowns for permanent impairments in value. The investor charges cash and credits investment revenue when it receives cash dividends from the investee but in no other way reflects its proportionate shares of changes in the investee's equity.

Under SFAS No. 12, the aggregate cost of long-term investments in equity securities is compared to their aggregate market value at each reporting date. If the aggregate market value is lower than aggregate cost, an allowance for market declines account is credited and deducted from the cost of the long-term portfolio in the financial statements and a charge is made directly to equity equal to the credit.

The balance in the allowance account is adjusted whenever financial statements are presented, so the net of the aggregate cost and the valuation allowance equals the lower of its aggregate cost and aggregate market value.

If a permanent decline in the value of an individual investment in long-term equity securities is deemed to have occurred, the carrying amount is written down to its recoverable amount, usually market value. Considerations in determining whether to recognize a permanent decline for an investment accounted for in accordance with SFAS No. 12 are essentially the same as those for an investment accounted for by the equity method.

SUMMARY OF MAJOR PRONOUNCEMENTS

The following sections summarize the major pronouncements that deal with the topics covered in this chapter.

7.30 CONSOLIDATION

- ARB No. 43, Chapter 12, "Foreign Operations and Foreign Exchange," provides criteria for the treatment of foreign subsidiaries in consolidated financial statements.
- ARB No. 51, "Consolidated Financial Statements," describes the purpose of consolidated financial statements and selection of a consolidation policy, and it discusses concepts underlying consolidation and procedures to prepare consolidated financial statements.
- SFAS No. 94, "Consolidation of All Majority-Owned Subsidiaries," amends ARB No. 51 to require consolidation of all majority-owned subsidiaries unless control is temporary or does not rest with the majority owners.
- EITF Issue No. 85-12, "Retention of Specialized Accounting for Investments in Consolidation," concludes that the accounting principles a subsidiary uses to account for its own investments should be retained in the consolidated financial statements of the subsidiary and its parent even if the parent does not itself use those specialized accounting principles.
- EITF Issue 87-15, "Effect of a Standstill Agreement on Pooling-of-Interests Accounting," holds that the existence of a standstill agreement does not by itself preclude an otherwise qualifying business combination from being accounted for by the pooling of interests method. A standstill agreement is an agreement that prohibits a more-than-10-% shareholder from acquiring additional shares of the enterprise or its successors for a specified period.
- EITF Issue 87-27, "Poolings of Companies That Do Not Have a Controlling Class of Common Stock," concludes that a business combination may still qualify for the pooling of interests method even if the issuing company has to convert voting preferred stock into voting common stock so as to create a controlling class of common stock.
- EITF Issue 88-27, "Effect of Unallocated Shares in an ESOP on Accounting for Business Combinations," specifies the circumstances in which unallocated shares held by an employee stock option plan should and should not be considered "tainted" for purposes of determining whether a business combination should be accounted for by the pooling of interests method.
- FTB No. 85-5, "Issues Relating to Accounting for Business Combinations, Including Costs of Closing Duplicate Facilities of an Acquirer; Stock Transactions between Companies under Company Control; Downstream Mergers; Identical Common Shares for a Pooling of Interests; Pooling of Interests by Mutual and Cooperative Enterprises," clarifies the following matters:

   That costs incurred to close duplicate facilities as a result of a business combination should not be considered part of the cost of the business combination.

   How a parent company should account for minority interest in an exchange of stock between two of its subsidiaries.

That an exchange by a partially owned subsidiary of its common stock for the outstanding common stock of its parent should be accounted for under the purchase method.

That the pooling of interests method may not be used to account for a business combination in which one company issues common stock identical to other outstanding common shares except that the issuer retains a right of first refusal to reacquire the shares issued in certain specified circumstances.

That the conversion of a mutual or cooperative enterprise to a stock company within 2 years of a business combination does not by itself bar the combination from being accounted for by the pooling of interests method.

7.31 BUSINESS COMBINATIONS

- APB Opinion No. 16, "Business Combinations," describes the conditions for each of the two methods of accounting for business combinations and the accounting principles that apply to each method.
- AICPA interpretations of APB Opinion No. 16 were issued by the AICPA to elaborate on some points made in the Opinion.
- SFAS No. 38, "Accounting for Preacquisition Contingencies of Purchased Enterprises," amends APB Opinion No. 16 to clarify how an acquiring enterprise should account for contingencies of an acquired enterprise that existed at the time of a business combination.
- SFAS No. 79, "Elimination of Certain Disclosures for Business Combinations by Nonpublic Enterprises," amends APB Opinion No. 16 to eliminate the requirement for nonpublic companies to disclose the following information in financial statements of the period in which a business combination accounted for by the purchase method occurs: (1) Results of operations for the current period as though the enterprises had combined at the beginning of the period, unless the acquisition was at or near the beginning of the period, and (2) Results of operations for the immediately preceding period as though the enterprises had combined at the beginning of that period if comparative financial statements are presented.
- EITF Issue 85-14, "Securities That Can Be Acquired for Cash in a Pooling of Interests," specifies that not all convertible securities need be considered common share equivalents for purposes of determining whether a business combination should be accounted for as a pooling of interests and that the assessment of which securities should be so considered is to be made on a case-by-case basis.
- EITF Issue 86-10, "Pooling with 10 Percent Cash Payout Determined by Lottery," states that a business combination that otherwise qualifies for the pooling of interests method would still qualify even if there is a 10%-or-less cash payout determined by a lottery.
- EITF Issue 86-20, "Accounting for Other Postemployment Benefits of an Acquired Company," points out that practice is mixed in this area, because some acquirors allocate a portion of the purchase price in a business combination to a liability for other postemployment benefits whereas others do not.

7.32 FOREIGN CURRENCY TRANSLATION

- ARB No. 43, Chapter 12, "Foreign Operations and Foreign Exchange," provides criteria for the treatment of foreign subsidiaries in consolidated financial statements.
- SFAS No. 52, "Foreign Currency Translation," specifies the accounting for foreign operations reported in the financial statements of a domestic company. It super-

sedes SFAS No. 8, ''Accounting for the Translation of Foreign Currency Transactions and Foreign Currency Financial Statements.''

- FIN No. 37, ''Accounting for Translation Adjustments upon Sale of Part of an Investment in a Foreign Entity,'' prescribes that the accounting in SFAS No. 52 that applies to a sale or complete or substantially complete liquidation of an investment in a foreign entity also applies to a partial disposal by an enterprise of its ownership interest.

7.33 EQUITY METHOD

- APB Opinion No. 18, ''The Equity Method of Accounting for Investments in Common Stock,'' specifies the circumstances in which an investment in common stock should be accounted for by the equity method of accounting and the principles that apply to the method.
- SFAS No. 58, ''Capitalization of Interest Cost in Financial Statements That Include Investments Accounted for by the Equity Method,'' specifies the circumstances in which investments accounted for by the equity method should be considered qualifying assets for purposes of interest capitalization.
- FIN No. 35, ''Criteria for Applying the Equity Method of Accounting for Investments in Common Stock,'' clarifies that the presumptions concerning the applicability of the equity method may be overcome by predominant evidence to the contrary, based on an evaluation of all facts and circumstances relating to the investment.
- FTB No. 79-19, ''Investor's Accounting for Unrealized Losses on Marketable Securities Owned by an Equity Method Investee,'' emphasizes that an investor should not combine the portfolios of its marketable securities with the portfolios of the marketable securities of its investees that are accounted for by the equity method, for purposes of determining the investor's unrealized losses on marketable securities.

7.34 PUSH DOWN ACCOUNTING

- EITF Issue 86-9, ''IRC 338 and Push Down Accounting,'' concluded that push down accounting has to be applied by publicly held companies but need not be applied by nonpublic companies. Under push down accounting, a new basis of accounting is used in the separate financial statements of an acquired entity, based on the purchase price of that entity. The separate financial statements of a subsidiary present the amounts at which its assets and liabilities are recognized in consolidation.

SOURCES AND SUGGESTED REFERENCES

(In addition to the pronouncements listed in sections 7.30–7.34, the following references are suggested.)

Accounting Principles Board, ''Intangible Assets,'' APB Opinion No. 17, AICPA, New York, 1970.

———, ''Accounting for Income Taxes—Special Areas,'' APB Opinion No. 23, AICPA, New York, 1972.

———, ''Accounting for Nonmonetary Transactions,'' APB Opinion No. 29, AICPA, New York, 1973.

Bergstein, Sol, ''More on Pooling of Interest,'' *Journal of Accountancy,* March 1972, pp. 83–86.

Dewherst, John F., ''Accounting for Business Combinations—The Purchase vs. Pooling of Interests Issue,'' *CA Magazine,* September 1972, pp. 17–23.

Donaldson, Howard, and Reinstein, Alan, "Implementing FAS No. 52: The Critical Issues," *Financial Executive*, June 1983, pp. 23–28.

Financial Accounting Standards Board, "Accounting for Certain Marketable Securities," Statement of Financial Accounting Standards No. 12, FASB, Stamford, CT, 1975.

————, "Capitalization of Interest Cost," Statement of Financial Accounting Standards No. 34, FASB, Stamford, CT, 1979.

————, "Capitalization of Interest Cost in Financial Statements That Include Investments Accounted for by the Equity Method," Statement of Financial Accounting Standards No. 58, FASB, Stamford, CT, 1982.

Pacter, Paul, "Applying APB Opinion 18—Equity Method," *Journal of Accountancy*, September 1971, pp. 37–42.

Rosenfield, Paul, and Rubin, Steven, *Consolidation, Translation, and the Equity Method: Concepts and Procedures*, Wiley, New York, 1985.

Rosenfield, Paul, and Rubin, Steven, "Minority Interest: Opposing Views," *Journal of Accountancy*, March 1986, pp. 78–89.

CHAPTER **8**

STATEMENT OF CASH FLOWS

Mona E. Seiler, CPA
Queensborough Community College
City University of New York

CONTENTS

NATURE AND BACKGROUND OF THE STATEMENT OF CASH FLOWS

8.1 PRONOUNCEMENTS ON THE STATEMENT OF CASH FLOWS.   SFAS No. 95, "Statement of Cash Flows," issued in December 1987, establishes standards for providing a **statement of cash flows** in general purpose financial statements. SFAS No. 95 superseded APB Opinion No. 19, "Reporting Changes in Financial Position," issued in 1971, which first elevated the funds statement to the status of a basic financial statement. SFAS No. 95 changes the focus of the funds statement from one based on various definitions of funds, principally working capital or cash, to a focus on changes in cash. Under APB Opinion No. 19, funds were defined variously as cash, cash and short-term investments, quick assets, or working capital. The current uniform focus on cash should result in greater financial statement comparability. The cash focus also conforms more closely to the underlying concepts of SFAC No. 5, "Recognition and Measurement in Financial Statements of Business Enterprises," issued in 1984. SFAC No. 5 (par. 13) states that a full set of financial statements for a period should show among other things, cash flows during the period. Paragraph 52 points out:

> A statement of cash flows directly or indirectly reflects an entity's cash receipts classified by major sources and its cash payments classified by major uses during a period. It provides useful information about an entity's activities in generating cash through operations to repay debt, distribute dividends; or reinvest to maintain or expand operating capacity; about its financing activities, both debt and equity; and about its investing or spending of cash. Important uses of information about an entity's current cash receipts and payments include helping to assess factors such as the entity's liquidity, financial flexibility, profitability, and risk.

The change in emphasis of the funds statement from working capital to cash actually predates SFAS No. 95. In 1981, the FEI encouraged its members to change the focus of the funds statement to cash and cash equivalents. By 1987, "Accounting Trends and Techniques" (AICPA, 1987), which surveys the financial accounting and reporting practices of 600 corporations, observed that in 1980 approximately 90% of the funds statements used a working capital concept of funds. By 1986, only 34% followed that approach, whereas 66% had adopted a form of cash approach.

8.2 BACKGROUND.   Historically, the funds statement was often prepared by accountants to explain the discrepancy between an enterprise's reported net income and the funds available for dividends, debt repayment, and capital expenditure. However, the funds statement was not recognized by managers and financial analysts to be a significant analytic tool until after World War II. During the 20 years that followed, it began to appear in a growing number of annual reports, but great diversity remained in terminology, content, and form. In 1963, APB Opinion No. 3, "The Statement of Source and Application of Funds," provided some guidelines for preparation and presentation of the funds statement; this Opinion, however, only recommended presenting the statement of changes in financial position as supplementary information. The growing number of companies presenting a funds statement in their annual reports and the requirement by several regulatory agencies that a funds statement be included in reports filed with them, finally prompted the APB to issue Opinion No. 19. Opinion No. 19, however, permitted but did not require enterprises to report cash flow information in the statement of changes in financial position. Since that Opinion was issued, the significance of information about an enterprise's cash flows has increasingly been recognized. Nevertheless, certain problems continued to limit the utility of the statement:

- Ambiguity of terms such as funds.
- Lack of comparability arising from diversity in focus.
- Differences in definition of funds flow from operations (cash or working capital).
- Differences in the format of the statement (sources and uses format or activity format).

The diversity in the form and content of the statement has been attributed to the lack of clear objectives for the statement.

The FASB's initial involvement in cash flow reporting started in December 1980, with the publication of a Discussion Memorandum, "Reporting Funds Flows, Liquidity, and Financial Flexibility," which discussed funds flow reporting issues. This was followed in November 1981 by an Exposure Draft of a Proposed Concepts Statement, "Reporting Income, Cash Flows, and Financial Position of Business Enterprises," which discussed the role of a funds statement and guides for reporting components of funds flows, and concluded that the focus should be cash rather than working capital. However, a Statement was not issued. Further work led to the issuance of SFAC No. 5, followed by an Exposure Draft, "Statement of Cash Flows," in July 1986, and the issuance in 1987 of SFAS No. 95.

8.3 OBJECTIVES OF THE STATEMENT OF CASH FLOWS.   SFAS No. 95 (par. 4) sets forth the primary purpose of a statement of cash flows—"to provide relevant information about the cash receipts and cash payments of an enterprise during a period." The statement of cash flows should help investors, creditors, and others to:

- Assess the enterprise's ability to generate positive future net cash flows.
- Assess the enterprise's ability to meet its obligations, its ability to pay dividends, and its needs for external financing.
- Assess the reasons for differences between net income and associated cash receipts and payments.
- Assess the effects on an enterprise's financial position of both its cash and noncash investing and financing transactions during the period.

According to the FASB, these objectives would be achieved by a statement of cash flows that reports the **cash effects** during a period of a company's **operations,** and its **investing** and **financing transactions,** supplemented by a **reconciliation of net income and operating cash flows.** Additionally, noncash financing and investing activities should be reported because they may result in future cash flows.

There are limits to the extent to which a statement of cash flows can be used to assess future cash flows. A cash flows statement shows the details of an enterprise's **current** cash receipts and cash payments. However, a cash flows statement, according to SFAC No. 5 (par. 24),

> . . . provides an incomplete basis for assessing prospects for future cash flows because it cannot show interperiod relationships. Many current cash receipts, especially from operations, stem from activities of earlier periods, and many current cash payments are intended or expected to result in future, not current, cash receipts. Statements of earnings and comprehensive income, especially if used in conjunction with statements of financial position, usually provide a better basis for assessing future cash flow prospects of an entity than do cash flow statements alone.

· However, the reconciliation of net income to net cash flows from operations called for by SFAS No. 95 may further the utility of the statement as a vehicle for assessing future cash flows from operations. The prescribed reconciliation reveals the nature and amounts of differences between net income and net operating cash flows. A time series analysis of such differences studied in conjunction with changes in net income and changes in cash flows from operations may provide a useful tool for assessing future cash flows from operations.

8.4 SCOPE OF SFAS NO. 95.   SFAS No. 95 (par. 3) requires that a business enterprise providing a set of financial statements that reports both financial position and results of operations should provide a statement of cash flows for each period that presents results of operations. This requirement applies to all business enterprises including financial institutions, investment companies, and small businesses.

(a) Financial Institutions.   Financial institutions, especially banks, contended that a cash flows statement would not be meaningful for them because cash is the "product" of their earning activities and is therefore the equivalent of inventory. The Board took the view that "to survive, a bank, like a manufacturer, must generate positive (or at least neutral) cash flows from its operating, investing, and financing activities over the long run" (SFAS No. 95, par. 59). Banks obtain cash from deposits, money market operations and other purchases of funds, issuing long-term debt and equity securities, loan repayments by borrowers, investment sales and maturities, and net interest and fees earned. Banks cash outflows cover deposit withdrawals, liability maturities, loan commitments, expenditures for investment and other purposes, and operating costs. The Board's view is that those activities are integral to a bank's operating, investing, and financing activities and should be disclosed in its financial statements.

(b) Not-for-Profit Organizations.   SFAS No. 95 does not include not-for-profit organizations within its scope. The FASB has indicated that after completing a joint study with the AICPA on financial statement display for not-for-profit organizations, it will decide whether to add to its agenda a project on financial statement display for not-for-profit organizations.

(c) Exemption of Defined Benefit Plans from SFAS No. 95 Requirements.   In February 1989, the FASB amended SFAS No. 95 with SFAS No. 102, "Statement of Cash Flows— Exemption of Certain Enterprises and Classification of Cash Flows from Certain Securities Acquired for Resale." SFAS No. 102 exempts from the requirements of SFAS No. 95 defined benefit pension plans that present financial statements in accordance with SFAS No. 35, "Accounting and Reporting by Defined Benefit Pension Plans." The Board concluded that SFAS No. 35 presents a comprehensive list of basic financial statements that defined benefit pension plans are required to provide; SFAS No. 95 was not intended to modify SFAS No. 35. Additionally, other employee benefit plans that are not covered by SFAS No. 35, such as health and welfare plans, that present financial information similar to the information required by SFAS No. 35 (including the presentation of assets at fair value) are likewise not required to provide a statement of cash flows. The Board noted, however, that a statement of cash flows would provide relevant information if the plan invests in assets that are not highly liquid (real estate) or obtains financing for its investments.

(d) Exemption of Investment Companies.   In SFAS No. 95, the Board concluded that information about cash flows is relevant for investment companies and that such companies should not be exempted from a requirement to provide a statement of cash flows. After further study, the Board reconsidered its earlier conclusion and in SFAS No. 102 decided that a highly liquid investment company that provides a statement of change in net assets would be providing much of the same information contained in a statement of cash flows. Therefore, requiring such companies to provide additionally a statement of cash flows would not be cost-effective. SFAS No. 102 (par. 6) states that a statement of cash flows is not required to be provided by:

(a) an investment company that is subject to the registration and regulatory requirements of the Investment Company Act of 1940 (1940 Act),

(b) an investment enterprise that has essentially the same characteristics as those subject to the 1940 Act, or

(c) a common trust fund, variable annuity account, or similar fund maintained by a bank, insurance company, or other enterprise in its capacity as a trustee, administrator, or guardian for the collective investment and reinvestment of moneys.

To be exempt, an enterprise must meet all of the following conditions in SFAS No. 102 (par. 7):

(a) During the period, substantially all of the enterprise's investments were highly liquid. (For example, marketable securities and other assets for which a market is readily available.)

(b) Substantially all of the enterprise's investments are carried at market value.

(c) The enterprise had little or no debt, based on average debt outstanding during the period, in relation to average total assets.

(d) The enterprise provides a statement of change in net assets.

8.5 FOCUS ON CASH AND CASH EQUIVALENTS. The decision of the Board to focus the statement of cash flows on **flows of cash** rather than on flows of working capital was based on the belief that the cash approach is more consistent with the objectives of the statement and is reinforced by the actual trend in accounting practice toward a cash approach and away from a working capital approach.

Cases have demonstrated that a positive working capital does not necessarily indicate liquidity. Furthermore, decisions of investors, creditors, and others focus on assessments of future cash flows. In focusing on cash, the Board decided to include **cash equivalents,** that is short-term highly liquid investments in which companies frequently invest cash in excess of immediate needs.

(a) Cash. Cash includes currency on hand, demand deposits with banks and other financial institutions, and other accounts that have the general characteristics of demand deposits, which allow deposits and withdrawals at any time and without prior notice or penalty.

(b) Cash Equivalents. To ensure a measure of uniformity in the focus on flows of cash, the Board provided guidance on the short-term, highly liquid investments that would qualify as cash equivalents. SFAS No. 95 (par. 8) states that cash equivalents are short-term highly liquid investments that are both:

a. Readily convertible to known amounts of cash
b. So near their maturity that they present insignificant risk of changes in value because of changes in interest rates.

Paragraph 8 states further, "Generally only investments with original maturities of 3 months or less qualify under that definition." Original maturity is further defined as maturity to the entity holding the investment. The Statement clarifies that the maturity date must be 3 months from the date of its acquisition by the entity. Thus, a Treasury note purchased 3 years ago and held does not become a cash equivalent when its remaining maturity is 3 months.

Cash equivalents include Treasury bills, commercial paper, money market funds, and federal funds sold (for an enterprise with banking operations). The purchase and the sale of those investments are viewed as part of an entity's cash management activities and not as cash flow activities, that is operating, investing, or financing activities. Thus, the details of such transactions need not be reported in the statement of cash flows.

Although the Board provided guidance on what may be included in cash equivalents, SFAS No. 95 does not require *all* cash equivalents to be classified as "cash and cash equivalents." For example, an enterprise could decide to include cash equivalents as investments, especially where its operation consists of investing in short-term, highly liquid investments. The Board decided that items meeting the definition of cash equivalents that are part of a larger pool of investments properly considered investing activities need not be segregated and treated as cash equivalents. Banks and other financial institutions carry 'T' bills and so on in their trading and investment accounts. For these reasons the Board requires an enterprise to disclose its policy for determining which items are treated as cash equivalents. A change in policy of classifying cash equivalents is considered a change in accounting principle to be effected by restating financial statements for earlier years presented for comparative purposes.

(c) Correspondence to Balance Sheet Cash Amount.   The total amount of cash and cash equivalent at the beginning and end of the period in the statement of cash flows must be the same amounts as similarly titled line items or subtotals in the statement of financial position as of those dates.

(d) Restricted Cash.   Cash or cash equivalents may be restricted by management for some noncurrent purpose. Under these circumstances, the cash or cash equivalent should be classified as noncurrent on the basis of management intent. The amount would be reported as a use of cash and classified as operating, investing, or financing depending on intended application.

8.6 GROSS AND NET CASH FLOWS.   SFAS No. 95 adopted the position that reporting **gross cash flows** is more informative and relevant than reporting net cash flows. Thus, the repayment of a loan and the borrowing on a new loan should be reported separately as a cash outflow and a cash inflow, rather than being offset and reported on a net cash flow basis. However, exceptions to this principle appear in paragraph 13, which states:

> Items that qualify for net reporting because their turnover is quick, their amounts are large, and their maturities are short are cash receipts and payments pertaining to (a) investments (other than cash equivalents), (b) loans receivable, and (c) debt providing that the original maturity of the asset or liability is three months or less.

Falling under this exclusion would be short-term debt such as revolving credit arrangements and commercial paper obligations. For certain other items, such as demand deposits of a bank and customer accounts payable of a broker-dealer, the enterprise is essentially holding or disbursing cash for its customers. Knowledge of gross changes of such items is not necessary to an understanding of an entity's cash flows. The Board also decided that cash flows from credit card receivables may be reported net.

Presenting cash flows from operating activities by the **indirect method,** which is permitted by SFAS No. 95, results in net reporting of operating cash receipts and cash payments.

8.7 CLASSIFICATION OF CASH RECEIPTS AND CASH PAYMENTS.   SFAS No. 95 requires that cash receipts and cash payments be classified into **investing, financing,** or **operating activities.** The Board decided that grouping cash flows in this manner enables evaluation of relationships within and among the three kinds of activities. The Statement provides guidelines to ensure comparability across enterprises, and it defines investing and financing activities. Operating activities include all transactions and other events that are not defined as investing or financing activities.

(a) Investing Activities.   Investing activities include the following cash outflows and cash inflows.

Cash outflows for:

- Acquisition of property, plant, and equipment or other productive assets.
- Purchase of debt instruments not designated as cash equivalents or entity instruments.
- Investments in another company.
- Loans made to another entity.

Cash inflows from:

- Proceeds from the disposal of property, plant, and equipment, as well as other productive assets.
- Proceeds from the sale or collection of loans and debt (not cash equivalents).
- Sale or return of investments on equity instruments.
- Collections on loans.

Exhibit 8.1 provides a survey abstracted from 1988 annual reports of transactions related to investing activities, including disposition of segments, discontinued operations, investments in related parties, life insurance proceeds received from officers, and other related-party additions to other accounts receivable.

(b) Financing Activities.   Financing activities include the following cash inflows and cash outflows.

Cash inflows from:

- Proceeds from the sale or issuance of equity securities.
- Proceeds from the issuance of bonds, mortgages, notes, and other short- or long-term debt instruments.

Cash outflows for:

- Payment of dividends to shareholders.
- Other distributions to owners.
- Outlays for repurchase of equity securities.
- Repayment of short- or long-term borrowings.

Exhibit 8.2 provides a survey abstracted from 1988 annual reports of transactions related to financing activities, including proceeds from warrants, principal payments on loans payable to shareholders, payments received from ESOP, and proceeds from sale and leaseback under operating leases.

(c) Operating Activities.   Operating activities comprise all transactions and other events that are not investing and financing activities, including the following cash inflows and outflows.

Cash inflows from:

- Receipts from the sale of goods or services, or the collection or sale of receivables arising from those sales.
- Interest on investment in debt securities and loans.
- Dividends on investments in equity securities.

Acquisition of franchises

Additions to equipment and leasehold improvements

Additions to long-term notes receivable (Super Valu Stores)

Additions to other accounts receivable

Additions to preopening costs

Additions to software products

Capital contributions to unconsolidated subsidiaries

Capital expenditures

Cash proceeds from divestiture and restructuring

Cash proceeds from sale of investments

Change in other assets

Collections of notes receivable

Contributions to 50%-or-less owned affiliates

Disposals of leased assets

Disposition of assets related to discontinued developmental activities

Dissolution of investment in affiliate

Distributions to minority interests (McFaddin Ventures)

Dividends received (First Cities Industries, Inc.)

Equity investments

Expenditures on suspended construction project

Expenses and income taxes related to sale of segment (Quantum Chemical Corporation)

(Increases) decreases in marketable securities

Increase in deferred acquisition cost

Increase in deferred turnarounds and charges and other assets

Investments in joint venture

Investments in life insurance policies

Investments in preferred stock

Investments in related parties

Investments in unconsolidated subsidiaries

Net change in cattle breeding herd

Notes receivable advances to ESOP (Frozen Food Express Industries)

Nuclear fuel expenditures

Nuclear fuel sales to lessors

Payments on long-term notes receivable (Super Valu Stores)

Payments received from officers and other related parties

Proceeds from collection of notes receivable

Proceeds from disposition of carried interest

Proceeds from dispositions of unconsolidated subsidiaries

Proceeds from insurance claims related to investments

Proceeds from sale of insurance subsidiary

Proceeds from sale of property

Proceeds from sale of property, plant, and equipment

Proceeds from sale of segment

Proceeds from sale of technology, net of expenses

Purchase of another company

Purchase of patents and other assets

Purchase of tax benefits

Reduction of investments in related companies

Reduction of restricted investment in marketable securities

(Restriction) release of short-term investments

Short-term investments

Exhibit 8.1. Types of investing transactions appearing in corporate annual reports.

- Receipts on other transactions not defined as investing or financing.

Cash outflows for operating activities include:

- Payments for the acquisition of inventory.
- Payments to employees for services.
- Payments for taxes.
- Interest payments, reduced by amounts capitalized.
- Payments to suppliers for other expenses.
- Payments on other transactions not defined as investing or financing.

(d) Components of Cash Flows from Operating Activities. Cash flows from operating activities are the cash effects of transactions and other events that bear on income determination. Interest received on loans and dividends received on equity securities are included in cash flows from operating activities, although they are investment related. Interest paid on loans is included as a cash flow from an operating activity, although the expenditure itself is finance related. Capitalized interest, however, is part of the cost of the nonmonetary asset and is treated as investment related.

Cash transactions costs of exchange	Payments of short-term debt assumed in acquisitions
Cost of issue debentures	
Cost of refinancing debt	Principal payments on capital lease obligations
Decrease in convertible subordinated debenture as result of extinguishment	Principal payments on loans payable shareholders
	Principal payments on notes payable and installment contracts
Dividends to minority shareholders	
Dividends paid	Proceeds from exercise of stock options
Exercise of stock options, including income tax benefit	Proceeds from issuance of long-term debt
	Proceeds from issuance of pollution control bonds
Exercise of warrants	Proceeds from revolving bank loans
Issuance of preferred stock	Proceeds from sale and leaseback under operating lease, less deferred gains
Loan to ESOP	
Net borrowings under working capital facilities	Purchases of treasury stock
Net increase in privately placed paper	Redemption of common stock
Net payments under line of credit	Redemption of common stock warrants
Net proceeds from public offerings	Redemption of preferred stock
Payments to acquire treasury stock	Redemption of revolving bank loan
Payments of long-term debts, including current maturities	Retirement of common stock, purchase of treasury stock, and other equity transactions
Payments received from ESOP	Stock option plan

Exhibit 8.2.   Types of financing transactions appearing in corporate annual reports.

All income taxes paid are treated as operating cash flows. Allocation of income taxes among activities is considered to be arbitrary and, therefore, is not required.

(e) Additional Classification Guidance.   If a cash inflow or outflow relates to more than one activity category, the classification will be determined according to the item's predominant source of cash flow. For instance, the acquisition, production, and sale of equipment used or rented by a firm is generally investment related. This presumption is overcome, however, if such equipment is used or rented for a short period and then sold. Under such circumstances, the acquisition or production of such an asset as well as the subsequent sale, is classified as part of operating activities.

All cash payments from customers or payments made to suppliers, including cash arising from installment sales, are classified as operating cash flows. This is a change from the exposure draft, which treated only those cash flows occurring soon after a sale or purchase as operating activities.

Each cash flow is classified according to its nature, even if it is intended as a hedge. For example, the purchase or sale of a futures contract is an investing activity, regardless of whether that contract is intended to hedge a firm commitment or purchase inventory.

SFAS No. 104, "Statement of Cash Flows—Net Reporting of Certain Cash Receipts and Cash Payments and Classification of Cash Flows from Hedging Transactions," amends SFAS No. 95 to permit cash flows resulting from futures, forward, option, or swap contracts that are accounted for as hedges of identifiable transactions or events to be classified in the same category as the cash flows from the items being hedged provided there is disclosure of accounting policy. Cash flows from an instrument that is not accounted for as a hedge or from an instrument that does not hedge an identifiable transaction or event should be classified based on the nature of the instrument.

Gains and losses resulting from the redemption of a firm's own debt are financing related and are categorized as cash flows related to the retirement of outstanding debt.

Gains and losses resulting from asset disposals are investment related. Receipts from the disposal of property, plant, or equipment include the proceeds of an insurance settlement.

Advance payments on the purchase of productive assets are considered to be investing cash flows. Any debt to the seller of the productive asset is a financing transaction.

All principal payments on mortgages, including seller-financed mortgages or debt on productive assets, are classified as financing cash flows.

Cash proceeds from business interruption insurance should be classified as an operating activity, whereas insurance proceeds to recover damages to plant and equipment are classified as an investing activity.

Ordinary dividends received are classified as an operating activity. On the other hand, liquidating dividends received would be classified as an investing activity. When a note is repaid, the difference between the amount paid and the carrying value should be reported as interest.

Insurance paid should be classified as an operating activity even if required to obtain a loan.

Accounts payable may need to be separated if it contains financing activities, as for example accounts payable for factory equipment purchased, which should be considered financing in nature.

GUIDANCE ON STATEMENT PRESENTATION

The statement of cash flows for a period reports separately the net cash provided for or used by operating, investing, and financing activities. The cash flows reconcile beginning and ending amounts of cash and cash equivalents. Separate disclosure of cash flows pertaining to extraordinary or discontinued items is no longer required.

The new Statement permits the use of either the **direct** or **indirect method** of presenting cash flows from operating activities. However, companies are encouraged to present cash flows from operating activities using the direct method.

Supporters of the direct approach point out that the presentation is consistent with that of investing and financing cash flows (that is gross operating cash receipts and cash payments are presented). Moreover, information about operating cash receipts and payments is useful when making credit decisions and assessing a company's ability to service existing debt.

The indirect approach (which reconciles net income with net operating cash flows) is favored by some (Mahoney et al., 1988) because

- It provides a useful link between the statement of cash flows and the income statement and balance sheet.
- Financial statement users are more familiar with it.
- It is generally less expensive.
- The direct approach, which presents income statement on a cash rather than an accrual basis, may erroneously suggest that net cash flow from operating activities is as good as, or better than, net income as a measure of performance.

8.8 DIRECT METHOD.   This method involves showing the major classes of operating cash receipts (cash collected from customers or earned on investments) and cash payments (cash paid to suppliers or to creditors for interest). The net cash flow from operating activities is the difference between cash received from operations and cash payments for operations.

Companies reporting under the direct method are required to report separately the following classes of operating cash receipts and payments:

- Cash collected from customers, including lessees and licensees.
- Interest and dividends received.

- Other operating cash receipts, if any.
- Cash paid to employees and other supplies of goods and services.
- Interest paid.
- Income taxes paid.
- Other operating payments.

Companies are also encouraged to provide additional breakdowns beyond the minimum items required under the direct method. For instance, a manufacturer can separate purchases of inventory from selling, general, and administrative expenditures.

Exhibit 8.3 illustrates the direct approach used in the 1988 annual report of Russ Togs, Inc.

8.9 INDIRECT METHOD. Companies choosing not to use the direct method must calculate net cash from operating activities indirectly by adjusting from net income for the effects of these major classes of reconciling items:

- Deferrals of past cash receipts and cash payments (inventory, deferred income, prepaid expenses, and deferred expenses).
- Accruals of expected future cash receipts and payments (accounts receivable and notes receivable from sales transactions; interest receivable; accounts payable and notes payable from transactions with suppliers; interest payable; taxes payable; excess of income under the equity method over dividends; and other accruals).
- Investing or financing-related items and noncash expenses (depreciation; amortization; provision for bad debts; goodwill; gains and losses on the extinguishment of debt; gains and losses on the disposal of property, plant, and equipment, and gains and losses on the disposal of discontinued operations).

This technique is referred to as the indirect or reconciliation method.

8.10 RECONCILIATION OF NET CASH FLOWS FROM OPERATING ACTIVITIES TO NET INCOME. A reconciliation of net cash flows from operating activities to net income must be provided only if the direct method is used. The reconciliation separately reports major classes of reconciling items. At a minimum, changes in inventory, payables, and receivables that are related to operating items are separately reported; however, enterprises are encouraged to provide further breakdowns of reconciling items. For instance, changes in receivables from the sale of goods might be reported separately from other receivables.

If the direct method is employed, the reconciliation is to be provided in a separate schedule. If the indirect method is used, the reconciliation may be included in a separate schedule or within the statement of cash flows. Additionally, under the indirect method, both income taxes paid and interest paid (exclusive of capitalized amounts) must be separately disclosed. In determining net cash from operating activities, all adjustments to net income are to be clearly identified as reconciling items.

Exhibit 8.4 illustrates the indirect approach using the presentation contained in the 1987 annual report of Tyler Corporation.

8.11 SURVEY OF ADJUSTMENTS UNDER THE INDIRECT METHOD. Exhibit 8.5 provides a survey abstracted from 1988 annual reports of reconciling items in converting net income to net cash flow from operations under the indirect method. Under the indirect method shown in the exhibit, there are a number of gain and loss adjustments, including gain on sale of investments, gain on debt extinguishments, and gain on sale of hedges. Other adjustments typically are extraordinary items, cumulative effect of accounting changes, and discontinued operations.

RUSS TOGS, INC.
Consolidated Statement of Cash Flows

($000)	1988	1987	1986
Cash flows from operating activities:			
Cash received from customers	$272,026	$275,474	$283,613
Cash paid to suppliers and employees	(265,383)	(258,440)	(265,771)
Interest and other income received	2,327	2,977	3,195
Interest paid	(1,535)	(1,209)	(1,448)
Income taxes paid	(8,444)	(14,512)	(8,446)
Net cash provided by (used in) operating activities	(1,009)	4,290	11,143
Cash flows from investing activities:			
Proceeds from sale of property and equipment		116	430
Capital expenditures	(1,701)	(2,190)	(1,503)
Reduction in investment in direct financing lease			675
Net cash used in investing activities	(1,701)	(2,074)	(398)
Cash flows from financing activities:			
Net borrowings (repayments) under line of credit agreement	3,810	2,480	(907)
Principal payments on long-term debt	(63)	(783)	(1,009)
Cost of shares of common stock acquired for treasury	(4,134)	(1,512)	(2,914)
Dividends paid	(4,585)	(4,152)	(4,290)
Proceeds from exercise of stock options	141		
Cash paid in lieu of fractional shares on three-for-two stock split	(11)		
Net cash used in financing activities	(4,842)	(3,967)	(9,120)
Net increase (decrease) in cash and cash equivalents	(7,552)	(1,751)	1,625
Cash and cash equivalents—beginning of year	16,547	18,298	16,673
Cash and cash equivalents—end of year	$ 8,995	$ 16,547	$ 18,298
Reconciliation of net earnings to net cash provided by operating activities:			
Net earnings	$ 9,290	$ 13,819	$ 10,986
Adjustments to reconcile net earnings to net cash provided by activities:			
Depreciation and amortization	1,985	1,870	1,938
(Gain) loss on sale of property and equipment	19	(21)	78
Decrease (increase) in:			
Accounts receivable	1,506	1,142	6,798
Inventories	(10,227)	(6,303)	(7,446)
Income tax refunds receivable	(286)		
Prepaid expenses and other current assets	(1,617)	(4,029)	(93)
Other assets	253	(84)	1,166
Increase (decrease) in:			
Accounts payable	6,420	(1,860)	(5,358)
Accrued expenses and taxes	(4,948)	166	1,071
Income taxes	(3,187)	(468)	2,599
Deferred compensation	(393)	70	61
Deferred taxes	176	(12)	(657)
Total	(10,299)	(9,529)	157
Net cash provided by (used in) operating activities	$ (1,009)	$ 4,290	$ 11,143

NOTES TO FINANCIAL STATEMENTS

Note A (in part): Summary of Significant Accounting Policies:
7. In 1988, the Company adopted FASB No. 95 and, accordingly, has presented a statement of cash flows. Prior financial statements have been restated to present a comparative format.

The Company considers all highly liquid debt instruments purchased with a maturity of three months or less to be cash equivalents for purposes of the consolidated statement of cash flows.

Exhibit 8.3. Sample annual report using the direct method.

TYLER CORPORATION
Consolidated Statement of Cash Flows

($000)	1987	1986	1985
Cash flows from operating activities			
Income before extraordinary charge	$16,849	$11,945	$15,363
Extraordinary charge, net of tax benefit	(4,831)	—	—
Net income	12,018	11,945	15,363
Adjustments to reconcile net income to net cash provided by operating activities			
Extraordinary charge—loss on early extinguishment of subordinated notes	8,052	—	—
Depreciation and amortization	23,700	23,145	22,174
Provision for losses on accounts receivable	5,965	6,663	5,484
Deferred income tax	4,379	3,249	6,762
(Increase) decrease in accounts receivable	(30,572)	(17,022)	5,400
(Increase) decrease in inventories	(13,454)	(10,674)	5,357
(Increase) decrease in prepaid expense	87	(545)	(1,477)
Increase (decrease) in accounts payable	2,672	13,241	(3,528)
Increase (decrease) in accrued liabilities	6,367	1,409	(794)
Increase (decrease) in income tax	(330)	2,247	(1,445)
Net cash provided by operating activities	18,884	33,658	53,296
Cash flows from investing activities			
Additions to property, plant and equipment	(25,477)	(29,415)	(35,776)
Undepreciated value of asset disposals	3,499	7,155	1,809
Reduction of investment in tax benefit transfer lease	—	2,579	24
Other	(3,263)	(6,343)	1,430
Net cash used in investing activities	(25,241)	(26,024)	(32,513)
Cash flows from financing activities			
Long-term borrowings	39,671	41,147	6,020
Reduction of long-term debt	(10,896)	(13,104)	(16,944)
Issuance of 11% senior subordinated debentures	96,629	—	—
Retirement of 12⅞% subordinated notes	(100,000)	—	—
Reduction of 10½% subordinated debentures	(3,750)	(3,265)	(300)
Issuance of common stock	72	376	602
Purchase of treasury shares	(7,830)	(8,170)	(6,465)
Redemption of detachable common stock purchase warrants	—	(14,999)	—
Cash dividends	(7,248)	(7,298)	(7,356)
Net cash provided (used) by financing activities	6,648	(5,313)	(24,443)
Net increase (decrease) in cash and cash equivalents	291	2,321	(3,660)
Cash and cash equivalents at beginning of year	3,394	1,073	4,733
Cash and cash equivalents at end of year	$ 3,685	$ 3,394	$ 1,073

NOTES TO CONSOLIDATED FINANCIAL STATEMENTS

Summary of Significant Accounting Policies (in part): The accompanying consolidated statements of cash flows are presented in accordance with Statement of Financial Accounting Standards No. 95—Statement of Cash Flows (SFAS No. 95) issued by the Financial Accounting Standards Board in November 1987. Prior years' statements have been restated to comply with SFAS No. 95. For purposes of the statements of cash flows, the Company considers all highly liquid debt instruments purchased with a maturity of three months or less to be cash equivalents. The Company paid interest of $27,180,000 in 1987, $23,708,000 in 1986 and $22,286,000 in 1985.

Income Tax (in part): The Company paid income tax of $5,503,000 in 1987, $6,618,000 in 1986 and $4,547,000 in 1985. In addition the Company received refunds of prior years' income tax of $814,000 in 1987, $6,600,000 in 1986 and $60,000 in 1985.

Exhibit 8.4. Sample annual report using the indirect method.

Accounts payable	Extraordinary item, net of deferred income taxes
Accretion of note discount	Gain on discontinued development activities
Accrued compensation and employee benefits	Gain on discontinued operations
Accrued income taxes	Gain on extinguishment of debt
Accrued interest payable	Gain on foreign currency hedge
Accrued liabilities	Gain on partial sale of subsidiary
Accrued retirement benefits	Gain on sale of investments
Advanced revenue	Impairments
Allowance for funds used during construction	Income tax benefit from stock option plans
Amortization of deferred gains	Increase in cash surrender value of life insurance
Amortization of goodwill	Increase in deferred items
Amortization of restricted award shares	Increase in escrow bonding arrangement
Amortization of software products	Inventories
Amount due from affiliate	Issuance of common stock in settlement of litigation
Assets held for resale	
Changes in certain noncash, assets and liabilities, net of effects of businesses acquired, and noncash transactions	Issuance of debt in payment of interest on debt
	Loss from discontinued operations
	Loss on disposal property and equipment
Common shares awarded under restricted stock plan	Loss on equity investments
	Manufacturing consolidation accrual
Common stock portion of class action settlement	Minority interest in subsidiaries' earnings
Cumulative effect of change in method of accounting for income taxes	Net earnings from discontinued operations
	Pension settlement gain
Customer advances	Prepaid expenses and other current assets
Decrease in refundable federal and local taxes	Prepaid income taxes
Deferred compensation	Provision for losses on accounts receivable
Deferred contract research and development revenue from related parties	Provision for losses on direct financing leases
	Provision for losses on short-term investments
Deferred income taxes	Provision for possible losses on disposition of restaurant
Deferred investment credit, net	
Deferred revenue	Provision for self-insurance reserve
Depletion	Rate deferrals
Depreciation	Receivables
Employee stock award program	Restructuring charge
Equity in unremitted earnings of unconsolidated affiliates in excess of dividends received from unconsolidated affiliates	Restructuring costs
	Share of related-party losses
	Sublease revenues and other credits
Extraordinary credit resulting from use of net operating loss carryforwards	Writedown of assets and related termination costs

Exhibit 8.5.   Types of adjustments used under the indirect method in arriving at net cash provided by operating activities appearing in annual reports.

8.12 NONCASH TRANSACTIONS.   Noncash transactions—for example, nonmonetary exchanges, the conversion of debt to equity, the acquisition of a machine by incurring a liability—are to be reported in related disclosures. These disclosures may be either narrative or summarized within a schedule. The objective of these disclosures is to clearly relate cash and noncash aspects of transactions involving similar items. If a transaction is part cash and part noncash, only the cash portion is reported in the statement of cash flows.

Exhibit 8.6 provides an example of a narrative presentation of noncash activities used by Allied Signal, Inc.

Tosco Corporation (Exhibit 8.7) uses a schedule to present its noncash activities.

(a) Survey of Noncash Items in Cash Flow Disclosures.   Exhibit 8.8 provides a survey abstracted from 1988 annual reports of common types of noncash items appearing in corporate annual reports. Among the types of noncash items are fair value of treasury stock

ALLIED SIGNAL, INC.
1988 Annual Report
Supplemental Cash Flow Information

In 1988 the Company adopted SFAS No. 95—"Statement of Cash Flows," and amounts for 1987 and 1986 have been reclassified for comparative purposes.

Cash payments during the years 1988, 1987, and 1986 included interest of $258 million, $283 million, and $197 million and income taxes of $134 million, $192 million, and $138 million, respectively.

Debt assumed by the purchasers of businesses in 1988 and 1987 was approximately $52 million and $159 million, respectively.

In May 1988 the Company formed a process technology and catalyst joint venture with Union Carbide. The joint venture was formed by each of the companies contributing the assets and the joint venture assuming the liabilities of both companies' business units in exchange for a 50 percent interest. In addition, the Company received consideration that reflects the difference in the value of the Company's business compared to that of Union Carbide. As a result of the transactions, the Company recorded an after-tax gain of $24 million, or $.16 a share, based on the recorded amount of the-business contributed. The transactions had the following noncash impact on the Company's balance sheet:

	Amount
Current assets	$ (94)
Property, plant and equipment-net	(71)
Investments and long-term receivables	253
Intangible assets	(129)
Current liabilities	41

In 1986 in noncash transactions shareholders exchanged convertible preferred stock of $55 million for common shares.

In May 1986 the Company distributed a special noncash dividend of one share of common stock of Henley for each four shares of the Company's publicly held common stock to its shareholders, which resulted in a charge of $2,370 million to additional paid-in capital and a credit in the same amount to the investments and long-term receivables account.

Exhibit 8.6. Sample narrative presentation of noncash activities.

issued for businesses acquired, surrender of leases and release from debt and other obligations on discontinuing development activities, bank borrowings and subsequent loan of proceeds to ESOPs, transfer of property including debt to a real estate trust in exchange for trust shares, abandonment of a plant, bank foreclosures on real estate, dividends declared but unpaid, the exchange of nonmonetary assets, and acquisition of subsidiaries or nonmonetary assets by issuing equity securities.

TOSCO CORPORATION
1987 Annual Report
Supplemental Schedule of Noncash Investing and Financing Activities

Thousands of Dollars	1987	1986	1985
Sale of property, plant and equipment for notes receivable (net of cash received)	$1,676	$ 5,000	$7,300
Sale of secured assets held for sale (net of cash received) for assumption of debt			7,500
Purchase of property, plant and equipment (net of cash paid) for notes	6,356	2,553	
Issuance of Common Stock in payment of Floating Rate Subordinated Notes	7,991	4,382	
Extraordinary gain from refinancing of debt		74,000	
Surrender of Series C Preferred Stock		70,845	

Exhibit 8.7. Sample schedule of noncash activities.

(b) Noncash Items Not Disclosed.   Not all noncash items are required to be disclosed. For example, if operating activities are presented under the direct method, then the following noncash items are not disclosed in the statement, although they will appear in the reconciliation of net income to net operating cash flow under the indirect method:

- Depreciation of plant and equipment.
- Amortization of intangibles.
- Amortization of bond discount and premium.
- Increase in investments carried at equity.

Some noncash transactions may affect only operating items and may not be disclosed at all, such as exchange of inventory for services.

Other transactions not disclosed are stock dividends and stock splits.

8.13 CASH FLOWS FROM DISCONTINUED OPERATIONS.   Separate disclosure of cash flows from discontinued operations is not required. However, a company may segregate, within the operating section of the statement of cash flows, its cash flows from discontinued operations from cash flows related to continuing operations. If so, this form of presentation should be made for each comparative period included within the statement of cash flows. Income taxes paid need not be allocated between continuing and discontinued operations.

On discontinuing an operation, certain losses and expenses related to disposal are typically identified. These might include anticipated losses on disposal including pension and other postemployment-related events such as termination and severance-related costs. To the extent these anticipated losses and expenses have no immediate cash impacts or are investment related, these items will be included in the reconciliation of net income to net cash flows from operations under the indirect method.

Cash received on the disposal of the discontinued operations is an investment activity, and the related disposal gains and losses are reconciling items in deriving net cash from operating activities. Separation of operating cash paid or generated by a discontinued segment both

Acquisition of company by contributing property, investments, and working capital	Issuance of common stock in payment of floating rate subordinated notes
Acquisition of equity interests of minority shareholders in subsidiaries	Liabilities assumed in business acquisition
	Note received on sale of business
Acquisition of limited partner interests in exchange for common shares	Preferred stock converted into common stock
Borrowing from a bank and subsequently loaning proceeds to ESOP	Purchase of property, plant, and equipment for notes
Capital lease obligations entered into for new lease	Reclassification of current marketable securities to noncurrent stock issued to employees
Common stock dividends paid on convertible stock	Reclassification of short-term borrowings of commercial paper and bank loans
Common stock exchanged for treasury stock	Sale of property, plant, and equipment for notes
Conversion of convertible subordinated debenture	Sale of secured assets held for sale for assumption of debt
Deferred compensation from awarding restricted stock awards	Surrender of leases and release from debt and other obligations on discontinuing development activities
Fair value of treasury stock issued for businesses acquired	Transfer of real property, including debt assumed to a real estate trust in exchange for trust shares
Issuance of common shares on conversion of director's note payable	Treasury stock issued for compensation plans
	Treasury stock issued on conversion of debentures

Exhibit 8.8. Types of noncash transactions disclosed in corporate annual reports.

before and after the measurement date, as defined under APB Opinion No. 30, from net cash provided or used in the disposal of the segment is clearly difficult and somewhat arbitrary. As part of a disposal of a segment, the cash flows attributable to transactions such as cash reversions accompanying pension plan terminations and settlements and payments of termination benefits on severance are all operating activities. All income taxes paid regardless of whether related to continuing or discontinued operations are classified as operating.

Operating cash flow from discontinued operations according to some should be reported as an operating activity even though income or loss between the measurement date and disposal date is included in the gain or loss on disposal. However, cash flows from discontinued operations may be shown separately from cash flow from continuing operations on a pretax basis, followed by a single amount for income taxes paid. This step avoids allocating the tax paid between the two groups.

First City Industries, Inc., in its 1987 annual report, shows a gain on the sale of discontinued operations as a reconciling adjustment to net income in deriving net cash from operating activities. There is a single line item under investments for proceeds received in 1986 and 1987 from the disposal. No separate amount is being provided for cash flows from operating activities associated with the segment disposal.

The 1987 statement of cash flow of Melville Corporation reports separately $7,341 of cash flows required for discontinued operations, under net cash flow by operating activities, and $46,993 of proceeds from discontinued operations, under investment-related activities.

K Mart Corporation, in its 1988 annual report, separates continuing and discontinued operations in its statement of cash flows from operations (Exhibit 8.9). K Mart includes cash provided or used by discontinued operations as an operating cash flow and, in addition, shows reconciling adjustments to income to derive cash flows from discontinued operations.

K MART CORPORATION
Reconciliation of Net Income to
Net Cash Flow from Operating Activities

(Millions)	1988	1987	1986
Operations			
Income from continuing retail operations	$692	$570	$ 472
Noncash charges (credits) to earnings:			
Depreciation and amortization	401	377	344
Deferred income taxes	12	58	90
Undistributed equity income	(36)	(23)	(23)
Increase in other long-term liabilities	67	52	44
Other—net	56	13	20
Cash provided by (used for) current assets and current liabilities:			
(Increase) decrease in inventories	(418)	(677)	387
Increase (decrease) in accounts payable	102	312	(65)
Other—net	90	(59)	129
Total provided by continuing retail operations	966	623	1,398
Discontinued operations			
Gain (loss) from discontinued operations	—	28	(251)
Items not affecting cash—net	—	(95)	249
Cash provided by (used for) discontinued operations	(58)	214	—
Total provided by (used for) discontinued operations	(58)	147	(2)
Net cash provided by operations	$908	$770	$1,396

Exhibit 8.9. **Sample annual report showing separate disclosure of cash flows from discontinued operations.**

8.14 EXTRAORDINARY ITEMS.   Companies having extraordinary items need not separately disclose cash provided from or used by those extraordinary items as was required under earlier pronouncements.

A company can choose to show separately the cash flows from extraordinary items within operating activities, using a treatment similar to that for discontinued operations.

The cash settlement of litigation that qualifies as an extraordinary item would be classified as an operating activity and could be shown separately in the statement of cash flow as an extraordinary operating activity.

Extraordinary items are classified according to the underlying nature of the transaction. Accordingly, a gain or loss on the extinguishment of debt is a reconciling adjustment to net income and is related to financing activities. Extraordinary gains without a cash impact on operations or those that are investment or financing related show up as reconciling adjustments to net income in deriving net cash from operating activities.

Exhibit 8.10 shows the treatment of an extraordinary item by Mapco, Inc., in its 1987 annual report. In a separate schedule Mapco shows other items not requiring cash to include an extraordinary loss from debt extinguishment, which is a reconciling item in arriving at net cash from operating activities. Cash used for redemption of debt is included in financing-related activities of 1986.

In contrast to the Mapco presentation, which adjusted net income for loss on extinguishment of debt, Tosco Corporation, in Exhibit 8.7, shows an extraordinary gain on debt refinancing under noncash investing and financing activities. The adjustment as a reconciling item in operating cash flow is unnecessary in Tosco's case because for each comparative period Tosco presents income before extraordinary items as a starting point in its operating cash flow section, whereas Mapco starts with net income.

8.15 ACCOUNTING CHANGES AND PRIOR PERIOD ADJUSTMENTS.   The cumulative effect of accounting changes not involving cash are reconciling adjustments to net income in arriving at net cash from operating activities. Mapco, Inc., in its 1987 annual report, shows a reconciling adjustment for the cumulative impact of adopting SFAS No. 96 in 1985.

Taxes incurred in connection with an accounting change or prior period adjustment are an operating item. If there is a cash effect of an accounting error, it may be desirable to report it separately in the cash flow statement.

8.16 BUSINESS COMBINATIONS.   In reporting business combinations, the statement of cash flow should reflect a single item under investing activities, for example, "Cash paid to

---

MAPCO, INC.
1987 Annual Report
Schedule of Reconciling Items of Operating Cash Flow

	Years Ended December 31		
	1987	**1986**	**1985**
Loss on sales of property, plant, and equipment	$10,493	$1,157	$ 3,491
Pension income	(5,199)	(5,247)	
Loss of unconsolidated affiliate	$ 2,103	$3,891	$ 4,625
Provision for losses on trade accounts receivable	830	1,884	1,834
Extraordinary loss from debt extinguishment		4,133	
Other noncash income and expense items	543	1,879	292
	$ 8,770	$7,697	$10,242

Exhibit 8.10.   Treatment of extraordinary items.

purchase a company (net of cash acquired)." If a business is sold, then the line item would indicate "Cash received from sale of business (net of cash sold)."

Certainteed Corporation, in its 1987 annual report disclosed:

During 1987, the Company purchased all of the stock of Bay Mills Limited for $98.1 million. In connection with the acquisition, liabilities were assumed as follows:

(Dollars in Thousands)	
Fair value of assets acquired	$116,305
Cash paid for the capital stock	(98,072)
Liabilities assumed	$ 18,233

In its statement of cash flow, Certainteed shows the following under investing activities:

Cash flows from investing activities:	
Purchase of Bay Mills Limited	(98,072)
Cash balances of Bay Mills Limited	3,408

Other companies show the cash paid in the purchase acquisition net of cash received.

A business combination under the pooling method of accounting would be a noncash transaction except for the cash received in the combination, which would appear as an investing activity.

WORKSHEET TECHNIQUE

The format of the statement of cash flows may be differentiated by the approach used to present cash flows from operations—direct method or the indirect method. If the direct method of presentation is adopted (as recommended by SFAS No. 95), the worksheet technique requires the use of a preclosing trial balance for the current period. On the other hand, a postclosing trial balance for the current period is more suitable for the indirect method. It is essential to understand both techniques because SFAS No. 95 requires a reconciliation of net income to net cash flow from operations as supplementary disclosure when the direct method is used in the statement of cash flows. However, Exhibit 8.13, later in this chapter, illustrates a short-cut technique for converting cash flow from operations prepared under the indirect method to the direct method. Preparation of the statement of cash flows requires an analysis of the annual changes in balance sheet accounts and the increases in income and expenses of the period in order to identify all cash flows from operating, investing, and financing activities. Revenue and expense accounts must be adjusted from the accrual basis to a cash basis. Cost of goods sold should also be analyzed for inventory adjustments, and so on. The adjustment for depreciation should be for the total amount incurred and the change in inventories should be inclusive of the amount of depreciation capitalized in inventory. These amounts reconcile with balance sheet changes, although not with APB Opinion No. 12, requiring disclosure of depreciation expense. Gains and losses must be adjusted to reflect the underlying nature and amount of cash effects, that is investing, financing or operating. Noncash transactions are either eliminated (depreciation) or are disclosed separately (acquisition of long-lived assets for debt or stock) as noncash activities.

8.17 DIRECT METHOD.   Exhibit 8.11 illustrates the application of the worksheet technique using the direct method. In Column 1, the 12/31/88 balances of Baruch Corporation reflect postclosing figures. The balances as of 12/31/89, shown in Column 4, are those of the preclosing trial balance. Columns 2 and 3 reflect those entries needed to determine cash flows from operating, financing, and investing activities and to reconcile the changes in account balances from 12/31/88 to 12/31/89 (letters in parentheses refer to list on pp. 8.20 and 8.22).

An analysis of the accounts for 1989 revealed the following:

INCOME ACCOUNTS

Depreciation expense	
Selling expense	$1,500
G & A expenses	2,000
Patent amortization in G & A expenses	500
Amortization of bond discount in interest expense	250
Loss on sale of plant assets in selling expense	2,000

OTHER TRANSACTIONS

Purchases of equipment	$15,000
Equipment sold for $8,000, cost $12,500, accumulated depreciation—$2,500, loss of $2000 included in selling expense	
Gain on bond retirement	
Bonds retired	
Face value	$12,000
Book value	11,000
Cash paid	9,100
(Tax on gain included in income tax expense—$600)	
Bonds converted to common stock	
Face value	$19,000
Book value	18,000
Converted into $1,650 shares of $10 par value capital stock	
Paid in 1989	
Dividend payable 12/31/88	$ 6,000
Notes payable 12/31/88	23,000
Accounts receivable are all from merchandise customers	
Accounts payable are all from inventory suppliers	

Based on the foregoing analysis of changes in the accounts, the following worksheet entries are needed to determine cash flows from the three activities for 1989 (letters correspond to relevant entries in Exhibits 8.11 and 8.12).

A. To record operating activity—cash inflow from customers, $449,750. Includes sales, $440,000, plus decrease in accounts receivable, $9,750. (The provision for bad debts would also need to be analyzed but is not included in this illustration.)

B. To record operating activity—cash paid to suppliers. Includes cost of goods sold, $220,000, plus increase in inventory, $5,000, and decrease in accounts payable, $750.

C. To eliminate the noncash depreciation charge of $3,500 from selling expense, $1,500, and administrative expense, $2,000.

D. To eliminate the noncash charge for patent amortization of $500 from administrative expense.

E. To record operating activity—cash paid for interest expense, $17,500, less $250 amortization of discount.

F. To record investing activity—proceeds on sale of equipment, $8,000; to eliminate loss of $2,000 from selling expense; and to reconcile cost of equipment, $12,500, and accumulated depreciation, $2,500, with changes in those accounts.

G. To record investing activity—cash purchase of equipment, $15,000.

H. To record financing activity—cash paid to retire bonds, $9,100; to reflect change in bonds payable, $12,000, and reduction of unamortized bond discount, $1,000; and to eliminate extraordinary gain of $1,900.

I. To eliminate the effects of a noncash transaction—conversion of bonds payable to common stock, which will be reported separately among the noncash changes. Bonds

Accounts	Balances 12/31/88 DR (CR)	Changes DR	Changes CR	Balances 12/31/89 DR (CR)
Accounts				
Cash	$ 25,000	$ 18,750 (Q)		$ 43,750
Accounts receivable, net	22,500		$ 9,750 (A)	12,750
Inventory	67,500	5,000 (B)		72,500
Property, plant, and equipment	100,000	15,000 (G)	12,500 (F)	102,500
Accumulated depreciation	(19,000)	2,500 (F)	3,500 (C)	(20,000)
Patents, net	4,000		500 (D)	3,500
Unamortized bond discount	3,000		250 (E)	750
			1,000 (H)	
			1,000 (I)	
	$203,000			$215,750
Accounts payable	$(14,000)	750 (B)		$ (13,250)
Accrued G & A expenses payable	(1,000)	1,000 (M)		0
Dividends payable	(6,000)	6,000 (J)	5,000 (K)	(5,000)
Income taxes payable	(18,000)		7,500 (P)	(25,500)
Notes payable	(23,000)	23,000 (L)		0
Convertible bonds payable	(47,000)	12,000 (H)		(16,000)
		19,000 (I)		
Deferred income taxes	(7,500)	1,000 (P)		(6,500)
Capital stock	(56,000)		16,500 (I)	(72,500)
Additional contributed capital	(12,500)		1,500 (I)	(14,000)
Retained earnings	(18,000)			(18,000)
Dividends		5,000 (K)		5,000
	$203,000			$165,750
Sales			440,000 (A)	$(440,000)
Cost of goods sold		220,000 (B)		220,000
Selling expenses		1,500 (C)		91,000
		2,000 (F)		
		87,500 (N)		
G & A expenses		2,000 (C)	1,000 (M)	42,500
		500 (D)		
		41,000 (O)		
Interest expense		17,500 (E)		17,500
Income tax expense		20,900 (P)		20,900
Extraordinary gain on debt extinguishment (before tax)			1,900 (H)	(1,900)
				50,000
				$215,750
Operating Activities				
Cash collected from customers		449,750 (A)		
Cash paid to suppliers			225,750 (B)	
Cash paid for selling expenses			87,500 (N)	
Cash paid for G & A expenses			41,000 (O)	

(continued)

Exhibit 8.11. Sample worksheet showing direct method.

	Balances 12/31/88	Changes		Balances 12/31/89
	DR (CR)	DR	CR	DR (CR)
Cash paid for interest expense			$ 17,250 (E)	
Cash paid for income taxes			14,400 (P)	
		$449,750	385,900	
Investing Activities				
Sale of equipment		8,000 (F)		
Purchase of equipment			15,000 (G)	
Dividends paid			6,000 (J)	
		8,000	21,000	
Financing Activities				
Cash paid to retire convertible bonds			9,100 (H)	
Payment of notes payable			23,000 (L)	
			32,100	
Net change in cash			18,750 (Q)	
		$959,650	$959,650	
Noncash disclosures—items (I) and (K)				

Exhibit 8.11.   *Continued.*

payable reduced by $19,000, unamortized bond discount reduced by $1,000, and capital stock and additional contributed capital increased by $16,500 and $1,500, respectively.

J. To record investing activity—payment of dividends of $6,000.

K. To eliminate the effects of a noncash transaction—declaration of dividends of $5,000, to be reported separately.

L. To record financing activity—the repayment of notes payable, $23,000.

M. To increase G & A expenses to reflect the payment of accrued G & A expenses payable.

N. To record operating activity—payment of selling expenses.

O. To record operating activity—payment of G & A expenses.

P. To record operating activity—payment of income taxes determined as follows:

12/31/88 Balance—Income tax payable		$18,000
Add: Income tax expense	$20,900	
Decrease in deferred income tax	1,000	21,900
		39,900
Income tax paid		14,400
12/31/89 Balance—Income tax payable		$25,500

Q. To reflect the increase in cash of $18,750 as a balancing amount.

8.18 INDIRECT METHOD.   Although SFAS No. 95 recommends the use of the direct method, it permits the use of the indirect method. Furthermore, if the direct method is used,

SFAS No. 95 requires, in a separate schedule, a reconciliation of net income to net cash flow, which is the indirect method.

The worksheet for the indirect method starts with postclosing trial balances for both the prior period and the current period. Net income is then adjusted to net cash flow from operations by removing the effects of accruals and deferrals, and adjusting for the effects of all items whose cash effects are either investing or financing cash flows or are noncash transactions.

The major classes of accounts to portray operating cash flows under the indirect method are the following:

Net change in receivables, payables, and inventory.

Net change in interest and dividends earned but not received.

Net change in interest accrued but not paid.

Depreciation and amortization.

Net change in deferred taxes.

Net gain or loss on sale of property.

The worksheet is illustrated in Exhibit 8.12 using the same data as in Exhibit 8.11. After an initial adjustment (keyed (X)) to remove net income from the change in retained earnings, which sets up the amount as a starting point for cash flow from operations, the remaining adjustments and eliminations track those of the direct method except that the adjustments for operating items are to net income rather than revenues and expenses (letters refer to list on pp. 8.20 and 8.22). After the initial adjustment, entries are keyed in the same manner as explanations to adjustments that appear on Exhibit 8.11.

BARUCH CORPORATION
Worksheet for Statement of Cash Flows—Indirect Method
12/31/89

Accounts	Balances 12/31/88 DR (CR)	Changes DR	Changes CR	Balances 12/31/89 DR (CR)
Cash	$ 25,000	$18,750 (Q)		$ 43,750
Accounts receivable, net	22,500		$ 9,750 (A)	12,750
Inventory	67,500	5,000 (B)		72,500
Property, plant, and equipment	100,000	15,000 (G)	12,500 (F)	102,500
Accumulated depreciation	(19,000)	2,500 (F)	3,500 (C)	(20,000)
Patents, net	4,000		500 (D)	3,500
Unamortized bond discount	3,000		250 (E)	750
			1,000 (H)	
			1,000 (I)	
	$203,500			$215,750
Accounts payable	$ 14,000	750 (B)		$(13,250)
Accrued expenses payable	1,000	1,000 (M)		0
Dividends payable	6,000	6,000 (J)	5,000 (K)	(5,000)
Income taxes payable	18,000		7,500 (P)	(25,500)
Notes payable	23,000	23,000 (L)		0
Convertible bonds payable	47,000	12,000 (H)		(16,000)
		19,000 (I)		
				(continued)

Exhibit 8.12.   Sample worksheet for statement of cash flows showing indirect method.

	Balances 12/31/88	Changes		Balances 12/31/89
	DR (CR)	DR	CR	DR (CR)
Deferred income taxes	$ 7,500	$1,000 (P)		$ (6,500)
Capital stock	56,000		$ 16,500 (I)	(72,500)
Additional contributed capital	12,500		1,500 (I)	(14,000)
Retained earnings	18,000	5,000 (K)	50,000 (X)	(63,000)
	$203,500			$215,750

Operating Activities

Net income		50,000 (X)	
Depreciation		3,500 (C)	
Patent amortization		500 (D)	
Amortization of bond discount		250 (E)	
Gain on retirement of convertible bonds			1,900 (H)
Loss on sale of equipment		2,000 (F)	
Decrease in accounts receivable		9,750 (A)	
Increase in inventory			5,000 (B)
Decrease in accrued expense payable			1,000 (M)
Decrease in accounts payable			750 (B)
Decrease in deferred income taxes			1,000 (M)
Increase in income taxes payable		7,500 (P)	
		73,500	9,650

Investing Activities

Sale of equipment		8,000 (F)	
Purchase of equipment			15,000 (G)
Dividends paid			6,000 (J)
Net cash outflow from investing activities		8,000	21,000

Financing Activities

Cash paid to retire convertible bonds			9,100 (H)
Payment of notes payable			23,000 (L)
			32,100
Net change in cash			18,750 (Q)
		$190,500	$190,500

Noncash disclosures—items (I) and (K)

Exhibit 8.12. *Continued.*

8.19 CONVERSION OF INDIRECT TO DIRECT METHOD OF OPERATING CASH FLOW.
Exhibit 8.13 illustrates a short-cut technique for converting operating cash flows from one
method to the other. Thus, there is no need to prepare two separate worksheets. Once an
initial worksheet is completed, under the indirect method, showing cash flows from operating, investing, and financing activities, then the operating cash flow data and the relevant
adjustments on that worksheet can be used to prepare operating cash flow under the direct
method in Exhibit 8.13.

FOREIGN CURRENCY CASH FLOWS

8.20 CONSOLIDATING FOREIGN OPERATIONS.   SFAS No. 95 requires companies with
foreign operations or foreign currency transactions to include in the consolidated statement
of cash flows the reporting currency equivalent of foreign currency cash flows using exchange
rates in effect at the time of the cash flows. Weighted average exchange rates may be used if
the results are not materially different from those rates at the cash flow dates.

The procedure would require companies with foreign operations to prepare a separate
statement of cash flows in the foreign currency for each foreign operation or by groups of
companies using the same foreign currency, translate them into the reporting currency, and
then consolidate those statements with the statement of cash flows for domestic operations.

The procedures to prepare the statement of cash flows apply irrespective of whether the
functional currency is the local foreign currency or the reporting currency (U.S. dollars).

**8.21 PRESENTATION OF THE EFFECTS OF EXCHANGE RATE CHANGES ON CASH BAL-
ANCE.**   The effect of exchange rate changes on cash balances held in foreign currencies are
not cash flows, but they must be included in the statement of cash flows because they affect
the consolidated balance sheet change in cash and cash equivalents. To facilitate the
reconciliation of the change in cash and cash equivalents, SFAS No. 95 requires that the
effect of exchange rate changes on cash balances held in foreign currencies be reported as a
separate item in the statement of cash flows. The item does not represent an operating,
financing, or investing activity. Therefore, in the statement the item should follow those
activities and precede the net change in cash and cash equivalents. Engelhard Corporation, in
its 1987 annual report, shows the effects of exchange rate changes on cash to arrive at the net
increase in cash for the year.

	1987	1986	1985
Effect of exchange rate changes on cash	$ 5,735	$ 3,284	$ 473
Net increase (decrease) in cash	37,797	(4,030)	51,438
Cash at beginning of year	82,823	86,853	35,415
Cash at end of year	$120,620	$82,823	$86,853

8.22 EXCHANGE RATE GAINS OR LOSSES.   Exchange rate gains or losses recognized in
the income statement and not relating to cash flows are presented as a reconciling item in the
reconciliation of net income and net cash flow from operating activities, similar to the
presentation of other noncash gains or losses.

8.23 DETERMINING EXCHANGE GAIN OR LOSS MODIFIED BY SFAS NO. 95.   The
following simplified example illustrates the method required by SFAS No. 95 for determining
exchange rate gain or loss.

Assume that:

Inactive Overseas Company, a foreign subsidiary whose functional currency is the foreign
currency (FC), had little activity in 19X7. In fact, the only event occurring was the sale of land on
June 30, 19X7, for (FC) 20 which was at the book value.

BARUCH CORPORATION

Worksheet to Convert Cash Flow from Operations from Indirect to Direct Method

			Income Statement		(DR) CR		
	Net Income	Sales	Cost of Goods Sold	Selling and G&A Expenses	Interest Expense	Income Taxes	Gain on Debt Retirement
Net income	$50,000	$440,000	$(220,000)	$(133,500)	$(17,500)	$(20,900)	$1,900
Depreciation	3,500			3,500			
Patent amortization	500			500			
Amortization of bond discount	250				250		
Decrease in deferred income taxes	(1,000)					(1,000)	
Gain on retirement of convertible bonds	(1,900)						(1,900)
Loss on sale of equipment	2,000			2,000			
Decrease in accounts receivable	9,750	9,750					
Increase in inventory	(5,000)		(5,000)				
Decrease in accrued expense payable	(1,000)			(1,000)			
Decrease in accounts payable	(750)		(750)				
Increase in income taxes payable	7,500					7,500	
Net cash inflow from operations	$63,850	$449,750	$(225,750)	$(128,500)	$(17,250)	$(14,400)	$ 0
		Cash Received from Customers	Cash Paid to Suppliers	Cash Paid for Selling and G&A Expenses	Cash Paid for Interest	Cash Paid for Taxes	

Exhibit 8.13. Sample worksheet converting operating cash flows from indirect to direct method.

Other Information:
Cash January 1, 19X7:   (FC) 100
Cash December 31, 19X7:   (FC) 120

Exchange rates from FC to U.S. dollars were .12 at January 1, 19X7, .13 at June 30, 19X7, and .15 at December 31, 19X7.

When preparing the statement of cash flows, the dollar amount used in reporting sale of land and exchange rate gain or loss as follows:

DOLLAR AMOUNT FOR REPORTING SALE OF LAND

	Foreign Currency	Exchange Rate	Translated Amount (Amount Reported)
Investing activities:			
Cash from sale of land	20FC	.13	$2.60
Exchange gain			3.40

Prior to SFAS No. 95, SFAS No. 52, "Foreign Currency Translation," provided no guidance for the preparation of the statement of changes in financial position. One solution that had been used in practice is as follows:

EXCHANGE RATE GAIN OR LOSS

	Foreign Currency	Exchange Rate	Translated Amount (Amount Reported)
Investing activities:			
Cash from sale of land	20FC	.15	$3.00
Exchange gain			3.00

The $3 exchange gain presented under past practice was calculated by holding $100 over the entire year ($100)(.15 − .12). SFAS No. 95 translates cash inflows and outflows using the exchange rate at the date of the transaction: 20FC (.13). Accordingly, the exchange gain is calculated as the sum of the exchange gain from holding 100FC for the year and 20FC for half a year: 100FC (.15 − .12) + 20FC (.15 − .13) = $340. The exchange gain must be identified separately in the statement of cash flows.

8.24 FOREIGN CURRENCY TRANSACTIONS. Foreign currency transactions are transactions denominated in a currency other than the local currency of the entity engaging in the transaction. The reporting currency equivalent of foreign currency cash flows should be classified in the statement of cash flows according to the nature of the transaction. Companies will have to analyze the foreign currency transaction gains and losses to determine whether they should be presented as reconciling items in arriving at cash flow from operations.

For example, in a repayment of foreign currency denominated debt, a realized exchange gain or loss would be a reconciling item in operating cash flow, whereas the repayment would be classified as a financing activity.

8.25 TRANSLATION OF FOREIGN OPERATIONS—A CASE. Exhibit 8.14 (Parts A–D), which illustrates translation of foreign operations, is reproduced with permission from Ernst & Young's 1988 booklet, "Statement of Cash Flows—Understanding and Implementing FASB Statement No. 95."

DISCLOSURE

8.26 SUMMARY OF REQUIRED DISCLOSURES. SFAS No. 95 requires the following disclosures supplementary to the statement of cash flows:

A statement of company policy in classifying cash equivalents.

Details of noncash investing and financing transactions.

OVERSEAS COMPANY
Balance Sheets

To illustrate how to prepare a local currency statement of cash flows and translate it to the reporting currency equivalent of the local currency cash flows, assume the following financial information for Overseas Company, a wholly owned West German subsidiary of a U.S. company with cash flows in Deutsche marks (DM).

	December 31		Increase/
	19X7	**19X6**	**(Decrease)**
Assets			
Current Assets			
Cash and equivalents	752,222 DM	535,784 DM	216,438 DM
Accounts receivable	1,400,000	1,685,000	(285,000)
Inventories	1,500,000	1,600,000	(100,000)
Prepaid expenses	75,000		75,000
	3,727,222	3,820,784	(93,562)
Property and Equipment	2,400,000	2,250,000	150,000
Accumulated depreciation	(410,000)	(260,000)	(150,000)
	1,990,000	1,990,000	
	5,717,222 DM	5,810,784 DM	(93,562) DM
Liabilities and Shareholder's Equity			
Current Liabilities			
Accounts payable and accrued expenses	2,036,281 DM	1,740,429 DM	295,852 DM
Due to parent	867,052	946,372	(79,320)
	2,903,333	2,686,801	216,532
Long-Term Debt	1,600,000	2,000,000	(400,000)
Deferred Income Taxes	60,000	45,000	15,000
Shareholder's Equity			
Capital stock	600,000	600,000	
Paid-in capital	200,000	200,000	
Retained earnings	353,889	278,983	74,906
	1,153,889	1,078,983	74,906
	5,717,222 DM	5,810,784 DM	(93,562) DM

Exhibit 8.14.   Foreign currency cash flows: Preparing and translating a foreign currency statement of cash flows (Part A). Source: Ernst & Young, "Statement of Cash Flows—Understanding and Implementing FASB Statement No. 95," 1988. Used by permission.

A reconciliation of net income and net cash flow from operating activities if the direct method is used to present operating cash flows, or net cash flow from operations is presented as a single amount in the statement.

Disclosure of interest paid (net of interest capitalized) and income taxes paid if the indirect method is used to present cash flow from operations.

8.27 CASH FLOWS PER SHARE.   SFAS No. 95 specifies that cash flow per share is not to be reported. The FASB concluded that the reporting of cash flow per share information "would falsely imply that cash flow, or some component of it, is a possible alternative to earnings per

OVERSEAS COMPANY
Statement of Income and Retained Earnings
Year Ended December 31, 19X7

Sales	7,800,000 DM
Other income	31,211
	7,831,211
Costs and expenses	
Cost of goods sold	6,410,000
General and administrative	650,000
Depreciation	150,000
Interest	220,000
	7,430,000
	401,211
Foreign currency transaction gain	79,320
Income before income taxes	480,531
Income taxes	
Current	290,625
Deferred	15,000
	305,625
Net income	174,906
Retained earnings at beginning of year	278,983
	453,889
Less dividends paid	100,000
Retained earnings at end of year	353,889 DM

Assume the following additional information:

The exchange rate of DM to U.S. dollars was .317 at 12/31/X6, .406 at 12/31/X7, and the weighted average rate for 19X7 was .346.

The only change in property and equipment was a purchase at the beginning of the year; the increase in the amount due to parent was because of changes in exchange rates for U.S. dollar denominated intercompany debt; the decrease in long-term debt was because of repayments during the year; and the dividends of DM 100,000 were paid at year end. Changes in all other balances occurred ratably during the year.

Exhibit 8.14.   Foreign currency cash flows: Preparing and translating a foreign currency statement of cash flows (Part B).

share as a measure of performance.'' This conclusion is consistent with an earlier SEC prohibition against reporting cash flow per share in filings with the Commission. In FRR Section 202.04, (ASR No. 142) the Commission expressed the view that cash flow per share could be misleading, especially since at that time there were no standards for computing that amount.

APPLICATION OF STATEMENT OF CASH FLOWS TO SPECIAL INDUSTRIES

The principles of SFAS No. 95 apply to enterprises other than commercial entities, including financial institutions, insurance companies, health care entities, and investment companies.

OVERSEAS COMPANY
Statement of Cash Flows
Year Ended December 31, 19X7

Foreign Currency as Functional Currency

Assuming the functional currency is the Deutsche mark, the statement of cash flows using the indirect approach would appear as follows in DM and U.S. dollars:

	Local Currency	Exchange Rate	Reporting Currency
Operating Activities			
Net income	174,906 DM	.346 (1)	$ 60,517
Adjustments to reconcile net income to net cash provided by operating activities:			
Depreciation	150,000	.346 (1)	51,900
Deferred taxes	15,000	.346 (1)	5,190
Decrease in accounts receivable	285,000	.346 (1)	98,610
Decrease in inventories and prepaid expenses	25,000	.346 (1)	8,650
Increase in accounts payable and accrued expenses	295,852	.346 (1)	102,365
Foreign currency transaction gain	(79,320)	.346 (1)	(27,445)
NET CASH PROVIDED BY OPERATING ACTIVITIES	866,438		299,787
Investing Activities			
Purchases of property and equipment	(150,000)	.317 (2)	(47,550)
NET CASH USED BY INVESTING ACTIVITIES	(150,000)		(47,550)
Financing Activities			
Repayment of long-term debt	(400,000)	.346 (1)	(138,400)
Cash dividends to parent	(100,000)	.406 (2)	(40,600)
NET CASH USED BY FINANCING ACTIVITIES	(500,000)		(179,000)
Effect of exchange rate changes on cash	N/A		62,321
Increase in Cash and Equivalents	216,438		135,558
Cash and cash equivalents at beginning of year	535,784	.317 (3)	169,844
CASH AND CASH EQUIVALENTS AT END OF YEAR	752,222 DM	.406 (3)	$305,402

(1) Weighted average rate.
(2) Rate at time of transaction. Note: This example assumes all purchases of property and equipment were made at the beginning of the year to demonstrate the statement of cash flow implications. More commonly companies will purchase property and equipment throughout the year and will translate these purchases using a weighted average rate.
(3) Rate at respective period end.

Exhibit 8.14.   Foreign currency cash flows: Preparing and translating a foreign currency statement of cash flows (Part C).

Not-for-profit organizations are not included in the scope of SFAS No. 95 because the Board has not yet decided whether not-for-profit organizations should be required to provide a statement of cash flows. SFAS No. 95 also does not apply to governmental entities. However, because certain funds, such as proprietory and similar trust funds, follow the financial reporting practices of similar private-sector enterprises, most implementation issues faced by these governmental entities are not unique. Thus, such funds may present a statement of cash flows.

The amount reported as the effect of exchange rate changes on cash and cash equivalents can be viewed as a "plug" figure in the statement, but it can be proved this way:

Effect on beginning cash balance		
Beginning cash balance in local currency	535,784 DM	
Net change in exchange rate during year		
(.406–.317)	.089	$ 47,684
Effect from operating activities		
Cash provided in local currency	866,438	
Year-end exchange rate	.406	351,774
Less: U.S. dollar operating cash flows reported		299,787
		51,987
Effect from investing activities		
Cash used in local currency	(150,000)	
Year-end exchange rate	.406	(60,900)
Less: U.S. dollar investing cash flows reported		(47,550)
		(13,350)
Effect from financing activities		
Cash used in local currency	(500,000) DM	
Year-end exchange rate	.406	(203,000)
Less: U.S. dollar financing cash flows reported		(179,000)
		(24,000)
Effect of exchange rate changes on cash		$ 62,321

Cash provided by operating activities using the direct method would be presented this way:

Cash received from customers	8,085,000 DM	(1)	.346 (2)	$2,797,410
Other cash received	31,211		.346 (2)	10,799
Cash paid to suppliers and employees	(6,744,773)	(1)	.346 (2)	(2,333,692)
Interest paid	(230,000)	(3)	.346 (2)	(79,580)
Income taxes paid	(275,000)	(3)	.346 (2)	(95,150)
	866,438 DM			$ 299,787

(1) This amount could be derived using the same methodology illustrated in Section 4.

(2) Weighted average exchange rate during the year.

(3) Difference between these amounts and corresponding amounts reported as expenses in the statement of income are due to changes in beginning and end of year interest and income tax accruals included in accounts payable and accrued expenses.

Exhibit 8.14.   Foreign currency cash flows: Preparing and translating a foreign currency statement of cash flows (Part D).

SFAS No. 102, Appendix B, which is partially reproduced here in Exhibit 8.15, presents a statement of cash flows and the reconciliation of net income to net cash flows provided by operating activities for a financial institution. Note that the gross concept of cash flows is applicable to financial institutions, which is a change from past practice of certain institutions of showing the net change in investments, loans, and deposit accounts in the statement of change in financial position. Exhibit 8.15 offers additional guidance on the requirements of SFAS No. 95 for financial institutions in presenting cash flow data. SFAS No. 104 amends SFAS No. 95 to permit banks, savings institutions, and credit unions to report to a statement

The statement of cash flows and the reconciliation of net income to net cash provided by operating activities for Financial Institution, Inc., provided in paragraph 147 of SFAS No. 95 are superseded by the following:

Increase (Decrease) in Cash and Cash Equivalents

Cash flows from operating activities:		
Interest received	$ 5,350	
Fees and commissions received	1,320	
Proceeds from sales of trading securities	20,550	
Purchase of trading securities	(21,075)	
Financing revenue received under leases	60	
Interest paid	(3,925)	
Cash paid to suppliers and employees	(795)	
Income taxes paid	(471)	
Net cash provided by operating activities		$ 1,014
Cash flows from investing activities:		
Proceeds from sales of investment securities	2,225	
Purchase of investment securities	(4,000)	
Net increase in credit card receivables	(1,300)	
Net decrease in customer loans with maturities of 3 months or less	2,250	
Principal collected on longer term loans	26,550	
Longer term loans made to customers	(36,300)	
Purchase of assets to be leased	(1,500)	
Principal payments received under leases	107	
Capital expenditures	(450)	
Proceeds from sale of property, plant, and equipment	260	
Net cash used in investing activities		(12,158)
Cash flows from financing activities:		
Net increase in demand deposits, NOW accounts, and savings accounts	3,000	
Proceeds from sales of certificates of deposit	63,000	
Payments for maturing certificates of deposit	(61,000)	
Net increase in federal funds purchased	4,500	
Net increase in 90-day borrowings	50	
Proceeds from issuance of nonrecourse debt	600	
Principal payment on nonrecourse debt	(20)	
Proceeds from issuance of 6-month note	100	
Proceeds from issuance of long-term debt	1,000	
Repayment of long-term debt	(200)	
Proceeds from issuance of common stock	350	
Payments to acquire treasury stock	(175)	
Dividends paid	(240)	
Net cash provided by financing activities		10,965
Net decrease in cash and cash equivalents		(179)
Cash and cash equivalents at beginning of year		6,700
Cash and cash equivalents at end of year		$ 6,521

(continued)

Exhibit 8.15. Illustration of statement of cash flow for a financial institution.

Reconciliation of Net Income to Net Cash Provided by Operating Activities:

Net income		$ 1,056
Adjustments to reconcile net income to net cash provided by operating activities:		
Depreciation	$ 100	
Provision for probable credit losses	300	
Provision for deferred taxes	58	
Loss on sales of investment securities	75	
Gain on sale of equipment	(50)	
Increase in trading securities (including unrealized appreciation of $25)	(700)	
Increase in taxes payable	175	
Increase in interest receivable	(150)	
Increase in interest payable	75	
Decrease in fees and commissions receivable	20	
Increase in accrued expenses	55	
Total adjustments		(42)
Net cash provided by operating activities		$ 1,014

Exhibit 8.15. *Continued.*

of cash flows certain net cash receipts and cash payments for (1) deposits placed with other financial institutions and withdrawals of those deposits, (2) time deposits accepted and repayments of those deposits, and (3) loans made to customers and principal collections of those loans.

SOURCES AND SUGGESTED REFERENCES

Accounting Principles Board, "The Statement of Sources and Application of Funds," APB Opinion No. 3, AICPA, New York, 1963.

——,"Omnibus Opinion," APB Opinion No. 12, AICPA, New York, 1967.

——, "Reporting Changes in Financial Position," APB Opinion No. 19, AICPA, New York, 1971.

American Institute of Certified Public Accountants, "Accounting Trends and Techniques," AICPA, New York, 1987.

Clark, H. G., and Lorensen, L., "Illustrations of Cash-Flow Financial Statements," AICPA, New York, 1989.

Ernst & Young, "Statement of Cash Flows—Understanding and Implementing FASB Statement No. 95," Ernst & Young, Cleveland, OH, January 1988.

Financial Accounting Standards Board, "Reporting Funds Flows Liquidity, and Financial Flexibility," Discussion Memorandum, FASB, Stamford, CT, 1981.

——, "Reporting Income, Cash Flows, and Financial Position of Business Enterprises," Exposure Draft of Proposed Concepts Statement, FASB, Stamford, CT, 1981.

——, "Recognition and Measurement in Financial Statements of Business Enterprises," Statement of Financial Accounting Concepts No. 5, FASB, Stamford, CT, 1984.

——, "Accounting and Reporting by Defined Benefit Pension Plans," Statement of Financial Accounting Standards No. 35, FASB, Stamford, CT, 1980.

——, "Foreign Currency Translation," Statement of Financial Accounting Standards No. 52, FASB, Stamford, CT, 1981.

——, "Statement of Cash Flows," Statement of Financial Accounting Standards No. 95, FASB, Stamford, CT, 1987.

——, "Statement of Cash Flows—Exemption of Certain Enterprises and Classification of Cash Flows from Certain Securities Acquired for Resale," Statement of Financial Accounting Standards No. 102, FASB, Norwalk, CT, 1989.

————, "Statement of Cash Flows—Not Reporting of Certain Cash Receipts and Cash Payments and Classification of Cash Flows from Hedging Transactions," Statement of Financial Accounting Standards No. 104, FASB, Norwalk, CT, 1989.

Mahoney, J. J., Sever, M. V., and Theis, J. A., "Cash Flow: FASB Opens the Floodgates," *Journal of Accountancy,* May 1988, pp. 25–38.

Securities and Exchange Commission, "Reporting Cash Flow, per Share Information," Accounting Series Release No. 142, § 202.04, SEC, Washington, DC, 1982.

CHAPTER 9

INTERIM FINANCIAL STATEMENTS

Anthony J. Mottola, CPA

Johnson, Shuart & Darrow, Inc.

CONTENTS

IMPORTANCE OF INTERIM FINANCIAL INFORMATION: TIMELY DISCLOSURE

The sensitivity of securities markets to the release of interim financial data and the emphasis on timely disclosure of such data by the SEC and other regulatory authorities indicate the increasing significance of interim reporting. Publication of financial information at interim dates enables users to assess a company's current performance and to revise or confirm their expectations of future performance. Interim financial information also provides users with a perspective for evaluating the potential impact of national or industry-wide conditions on a company.

Although the great preponderance of effort in the development of GAAP has been devoted to resolving problems associated with annual reporting, many substantive issues affect the preparation and presentation of interim financial information.

APPLICATION OF GAAP TO INTERIM FINANCIAL STATEMENTS

9.1 ALTERNATIVE VIEWS. The fundamental issue is whether interim financial statements are to be viewed as a presentation of an autonomous period or as an integral part of the annual reporting period. If interim statements are considered to be an autonomous presentation of financial data—**the discrete view**—deferrals and accruals should be determined following the same accounting principles and practices that apply to annual periods. If, however, such statements are deemed to be an integral part of the annual period—**the integral view**— reporting at the end of each interim period is affected by judgments made at that date as to results of operations for the balance of the year.

(a) The Discrete View. The premise that expenses should be matched with revenue creates allocation problems in applying the discrete view. Some enterprises, such as outdoor construction contractors, sports arenas, and resorts, have highly seasonal revenue yet incur fixed costs throughout the year. Sophisticated cost allocation techniques have to be developed to enable management to reasonably estimate total costs and profit margins so that each interim period reflects expenses in direct proportion to the revenue generated.

In some industries, significant expenditures normally associated with an annual period, such as the costs of major repairs or advertising campaigns, may benefit more than one interim period. However, under the discrete view such expenditures affect interim earnings when incurred. Furthermore, some business costs, such as volume discounts to customers or an employer's share of social security taxes, may be incurred in one interim period but relate to activities of all interim periods.

(b) The Integral View. The integral view minimizes short-term fluctuations in reported interim earnings that reverse or are offset in later interim periods. However, the integral view introduces another source of volatility—the limitations of the estimation process.

The prediction and estimation required of management in preparing interim statements following the integral view may result in errors that distort operating results in later interim periods. For example, revenue from an advertising campaign conducted during a prior interim period may be substantially below the original estimate, and the deferral of advertising costs to the current interim period may further depress current reported earnings. Conversely, if accruals made in early interim periods for costs that are not incurred, such as major repairs that are postponed, are reversed in a later interim period, higher reported earnings will be reflected.

9.2 CONCERNS COMMON TO BOTH VIEWS. Few companies have developed and refined procedures to accumulate information to prepare interim financial statements. Many companies have no formal closing procedures. Thus accounting estimates, such as allowances for doubtful receivables and losses from commitments and contingencies, are not based on detailed information. Physical inventories are generally not taken because such procedures cannot be cost justified. Management must balance its needs for additional evidence against the desirability of releasing interim results on a timely basis. Also, the potential for imprecision in interim financial statements is greater since estimates are subject to the same range of error as those in annual statements, but the numbers associated with the shorter period are smaller.

9.3 CURRENT VIEW OF APPLICATION OF GAAP TO INTERIM REPORTING. Present practice is governed by the conclusions set forth in paragraphs 9 and 10 of APB Opinion No. 28, "Interim Financial Reporting," wherein the Board essentially adopted the integral view:

> The usefulness of [interim] information rests on the relationship that it has to the annual results of operations. Accordingly, the Board has concluded that each interim period should be viewed primarily as an integral part of an annual period.

. . . However, the Board has concluded that certain accounting principles and practices followed for annual reporting purposes may require modification at interim reporting dates so that the reported results for the interim period may better relate to the results of operations for the annual period.

The FASB will undoubtedly consider issues concerning interim reporting in future pronouncements as it continues to develop the conceptual framework underlying GAAP.

MEASUREMENT PRINCIPLES FOR INTERIM REPORTING

9.4 REVENUE.   As stated in paragraph 11 of APB Opinion No. 28, "revenue from products sold or services rendered should be recognized as earned during an interim period on the same basis as followed for the full year." Revenue is recognized when realized, that is, when the earnings process is complete or virtually complete and when an exchange has taken place. In some situations, this approach may distort interim results. For example, major plant repairs or the need to retool equipment, a strike, or a serious material shortage may cause distortion. These situations require disclosure in interim financial statements so that the statements will not be misleading; however, they do not constitute a justification for departing from the basic principle of revenue recognition.

9.5 COSTS AND EXPENSES.   Since revenue recognition practices are the same for annual and interim reporting, differences in earnings measurements hinge on how the remaining components of the operating statement are recognized and displayed in interim financial statements. In SFAC No. 5, "Recognition and Measurement in Financial Statements of Business Enterprises" (pars. 85–87), the Board provides further recognition guidance by stating: "expenses and losses are generally recognized when an entity's economic benefits are used up in delivering or producing goods, rendering services, or other activities that constitute its ongoing major or central operations or when previously recognized assets are expected to provide reduced or no further benefits." The Board also set forth two principles which specify the basis for recognizing the expenses and losses that are deducted from revenue to determine income or loss. They are "consumption of benefits" and "loss or lack of future benefit."

Under the consumption of benefits principle, the relationship between expenses and revenue is presumed to be either direct or related to revenue recognized during the period. For example, expenses such as cost of goods sold are matched with revenue. Similarly, expenses such as selling and administrative salaries are recognized during the period in which cash is spent or liabilities are incurred for goods and services that are used up either immediately or soon thereafter. Determining the cost of products sold involves several assumptions regarding the flow of costs (LIFO, FIFO, etc. . . .) and the interrelationship between inventory and costs of goods sold.

Costs that do not have a direct cause and effect relationship with revenue, but that clearly provide benefits to more than one accounting period, should be allocated as expenses in a systematic and rational manner to the periods during which the related assets are expected to provide benefits. Examples of such costs include depreciation of fixed assets, amortization of intangible assets, and allocation of rent and prepaid insurance. These types of expenses involve assumptions about the pattern of benefits and the relationship between expenses and benefits. The period(s) over which such expenses are allocated and the allocation method should appear reasonable to an unbiased observer and should be consistent from period to period.

Under the loss or lack of future benefit principle, "An expense or loss is recognized if it becomes evident that previously recognized future economic benefits of an asset have been reduced or eliminated, or that a liability has been incurred or increased without associated economic benefits."

Therefore, costs recognized immediately as expenses are: (1) costs incurred currently that provide no discernible future benefits; (2) costs incurred previously and deferred that no longer provide discernible benefits; and (3) other costs for which allocation among several periods would serve no useful purpose. Examples include officers' salaries and amounts paid to settle lawsuits.

9.6 COSTS ASSOCIATED WITH REVENUE.   Paragraph 13 of APB Opinion No. 28 is consistent with the pervasive principles cited above. It states: "Those costs and expenses that are associated directly with or allocated to the products sold or to the services rendered for annual reporting purposes (including, for example, material costs, wages and salaries and related fringe benefits, manufacturing overhead, and warranties) should be similarly treated for interim reporting purposes." However, Opinion No. 28 also recognizes the propriety of certain departures from annual inventory pricing practices, as described below.

(a) Gross Profit Estimation.   For many companies that do not maintain perpetual inventory records, a physical inventory at the end of each reporting period would be cost prohibitive. Also, the time required to take and price the inventory and to summarize the results might cause unacceptable delays in the release of interim financial information. Thus management determines the cost of goods sold (and inventory) at interim dates by applying estimated gross profit rates to revenue recognized during the interim period. This technique is based on an assumption that the percentage of gross profit (or a composite rate for the different classes of products sold) will be the same in successive accounting periods. Estimated gross profit rates should be reasonably determined from results of prior periods and current budgets. Although use of gross profit rates or other estimation techniques different from those used for the annual determination of inventory and cost of goods sold may be justified, users of interim financial data should be advised that a different method involving a greater degree of judgment was employed. Thus Opinion No. 28 requires that companies disclose the method used at interim dates and any significant adjustments resulting from reconciliations with the annual physical inventory.

(b) LIFO.   As discussed in Chapter 13, the LIFO method associates the most recent inventory acquisitions with the most recent sales for purposes of determining the cost of goods sold. If inventory quantities remain stable from year to year, the value of inventory will also remain stable and the "current" year's costs will be associated with the "current" year's revenue.

The AICPA addressed the problems of applying LIFO for interim reporting in an issues paper entitled "LIFO and Interim Financial Reporting." In particular, the issues paper presents the problems and different approaches involved in estimating the interim effect of LIFO and determining the appropriate balance sheet presentation of the provision to offset the effect of an interim, temporary LIFO inventory liquidation. The paper points out the difficulty of implementing LIFO for interim reporting because LIFO is, by tax law definition, an annual calculation.

Since an estimate for the interim cost of sales must be computed, several approaches for making this estimate are used:

Approach A. Specify quarterly calculation of the LIFO effect based on year to date amounts.

Approach B. Project the expected annual LIFO cost and allocate that projection to the quarters equally or in relation to certain operating criteria.

Approach C. Make a complete quarterly LIFO determination; that is, determining an appropriate LIFO index at the end of each quarter, applying that price change to specifically determined inventories at the end of each quarter and using that information to make discrete quarterly computations, including determination of quarterly increments and decrements (few, if any, companies are believed to use this approach due to cost, effort and time involved).

The AICPA task force concluded, "Only the first two approaches are acceptable as long as the application results in reasonable matching of most recently incurred costs with revenues, considering such things as the effects of significant changes in prices, operating levels, and mix."

APB Opinion No. 28 (par. 14) requires that interim earnings not reflect a LIFO inventory liquidation if management expects to replenish that inventory by year end. According to the LIFO issues paper, the authoritative literature does not state how the adjustment should be treated in the balance sheet. Possible accounting treatments of the adjustment for interim balance sheet purposes include:

Treatment X. Record the pretax income effect of the LIFO inventory liquidation as a deferred credit in the balance sheet's current liabilities section, with inventory reflecting the liquidation.

Treatment Y. Record as a liability (perhaps included in accounts payable) an amount sufficient to reinstate the inventory balance to the amount before liquidation plus the amount necessary to offset the income statement liquidation effect.

Treatment Z. Record as a credit to inventory (in rare circumstances the credit could be greater than the inventory balance), the effect of which in some cases is to do nothing.

The task force believes for practical considerations that either Treatment X and Z is reasonable. Regarding the issue of increments expected to be liquidated by year-end, the task force believes companies using specific goods LIFO should adjust interim costs if temporary interim inventory increments occur, to produce a reasonable matching of most recently incurred costs with current revenues.

Finally, in the case where a LIFO liquidation is not expected to be reinstated by year-end, the interim statements can reflect the effect of the liquidation. The task force believes that "to the extent it can be reasonably determined considering the cost-benefit factors involved, a company should recognize the effect of an interim LIFO inventory liquidation not expected to be reinstated by year-end in the period in which it occurs." However, the task force also believes a company using a dollar value LIFO and Approach B (described above) may spread the expected effect of the liquidation using an approach similar to the one it uses for allocating the LIFO adjustment (normally a charge).

(c) Illustrations of LIFO Liquidation.   Exhibit 9.1 illustrates the accounting for a LIFO liquidation where as of March 31, 19X2, management does not expect to replenish a LIFO liquidated layer. A sample footnote is provided. Additionally, the case reviews the year-end reporting under the assumption management was incorrect and inventory is replenished.

(d) Market below Cost.   Normally, inventory is presented in annual financial statements at cost or market value, whichever is lower. A write-down to market value establishes a new "cost basis" which is not adjusted for subsequent recoveries. For the purposes of interim reporting, this general practice is modified to conform to the integral view of interim statements. If the market value of inventory declines below cost at an interim date, but the loss can reasonably be expected to be recovered either before the inventory is sold or, in the case of LIFO inventory, inventory amounts will be restored by year-end, the loss need not be recognized in interim results of operations since no loss is expected to be incurred in the annual period. So-called temporary market declines not requiring immediate recognition tend to result from unusual circumstances, such as a temporary oversupply in the market, or relate to a product with an established pattern of seasonal price fluctuations. On the other

ZZ COMPANY
Condensed Consolidated Balance Sheets
(Interim)

	March 31, 19X2	March 31, 19X1	December 31, 19X1
Assets:			
Cash	$ 30,000	$ 15,000	$ 19,000
Receivables	100,000	150,000	125,000
Inventories	80,000*	80,000	90,000
Total Assets	$210,000	$245,000	$234,000
Liabilities:			
Accounts Payable	65,000	40,000	50,000
Deferred Credit	15,000*	0	0
Accrued Expenses	5,000	15,000	18,000
	85,000	55,000	68,000
Stockholders' Equity	125,000	190,000	166,000
Total Liabilities and Stockholders' Equity	$210,000	$245,000	$234,000

ZZ COMPANY
Condensed Consolidated Balance Sheets
(Annual)

	December 31, 19X2	December 31, 19X1
Assets:		
Cash	$ 35,000	$ 19,000
Receivables	140,000	125,000
Inventories	65,000**	90,000
Total Assets	$240,000	$234,000
Liabilities:		
Accounts Payable	50,000	50,000
Accrued Expenses	10,000	18,000
	60,000	68,000
Stockholders' Equity	180,000	166,000
Total Liabilities and Stockholders' Equity	$240,000	$234,000

*LIFO liquidation occurs at interim, but management expects to reinstate that inventory at year-end. During the first 3 months of 19X2, a liquidation of LIFO inventory occurred, but it is expected that the reduction will reverse at year-end. Therefore, a deferred credit of $15,000 is established, which is the difference between the cost to replace this temporary inventory reduction and the LIFO cost assigned to the quantities.

**At year-end, management is incorrect, and inventory is not reinstated. During 19X2, a reduction of inventory quantities resulted in a liquidation of LIFO inventory layers carried at costs prevailing in prior years, which are lower than current costs. Had these inventory layers been replaced, the higher cost of replacement would have been charged to cost of sales, thereby decreasing net income by $15,000.

Exhibit 9.1. Accounting for a LIFO liquidation where management does not expect to replenish the LIFO layer.

hand, if management is unable to conclude that it is reasonable to expect a market recovery before either the inventory is sold or, in the case of LIFO inventory, before year-end, the inventory loss should be recognized in the current interim period. Any recovery of such losses in subsequent interim period of the same annual period should be reported as a gain.

Exhibit 9.2 illustrates the accounting for a LIFO liquidation where as of March 31, 19X2,

XYZ COMPANY
Condensed Consolidated Balance Sheets
(Interim)

	March 31, 19X2	March 31, 19X1	December 31, 19X1
Assets:			
Cash	$ 30,000	$ 15,000	$ 19,000
Receivables	100,000	150,000	125,000
Inventories	65,000*	80,000	90,000
Total Assets	$195,000	$245,000	$234,000
Liabilities:			
Accounts Payable	50,000	40,000	50,000
Accrued Expenses	5,000	15,000	18,000
	55,000	55,000	68,000
Stockholders' Equity	140,000	190,000	166,000
Total Liabilities and Stockholders' Equity	$195,000	$245,000	$234,000

XYZ COMPANY
Condensed Consolidated Balance Sheets
(Annual)

	December 31, 19X2	December 31, 19X1
Assets:		
Cash	$ 30,000	$ 19,000
Receivables	140,000	125,000
Inventories	80,000**	90,000
Total Assets	$250,000	$234,000
Liabilities:		
Accounts Payable	30,000	50,000
Accrued Expenses	25,000	18,000
	55,000	68,000
Stockholders' Equity	195,000	166,000
Total Liabilities and Stockholders' Equity	$250,000	$234,000

*LIFO liquidation occurred at interim, but management expects that inventory will not be reinstated. During the first 3 months of 19X2, a reduction of inventory quantities resulted in a liquidation of LIFO inventory layers carried at costs prevailing in prior years, which are lower than current costs. Had these inventory layers been replaced, the higher cost of replacement would have been charged to cost of sales, thereby decreasing net income by $15,000.

**At year-end, management is incorrect and inventory is reinstated. No footnote disclosure is required.

Exhibit 9.2.   Accounting for a LIFO liquidation where management expects to replenish the LIFO layer.

management expects to replenish the LIFO layer. At year-end, management proves incorrect and inventory has been liquidated.

(e) Standard Cost.   Companies that use standard cost accounting systems for determining product costs generally should defer at interim reporting dates purchase price and capacity variances that are expected to be absorbed by the end of the annual period. Unanticipated variances should be reported at the end of an interim period in a manner consistent with practices used at year-end.

All these modifications of annual practices involve a high degree of judgment on the part of management, and methods should be established by management to obtain the data necessary to make informed decisions.

9.7 OTHER COSTS AND EXPENSES.   Costs other than product costs are recognized as expenses in annual periods based on expenditures made in the period, accruals for expenditures to be incurred in subsequent periods, or amortization of expenditures made previously that benefit more than one period. In paragraph 15 of APB Opinion No. 28, the Board concluded that the following standards should apply to such costs in interim periods:

1. Costs and expenses should be charged to income in interim periods as incurred, or be allocated among interim periods based on an estimate of time expired, benefit received, or activity associated with the periods. Procedures adopted for assigning specific cost and expense items to an interim period should be consistent with those followed in reporting annual results of operations. However, when a specific item charged to expense for annual reporting purposes benefits more than one interim period, it may be allocated among the interim periods in question.
2. Costs and expenses incurred in an interim period that cannot be readily identified with the activities or benefits of other interim periods should be charged to the interim period in which they are incurred. The nature and amount of such costs should be disclosed, unless items of a comparable nature are included in both the current interim period and the corresponding interim period of the preceding year.
3. Such costs and expenses should not be arbitrarily assigned to an interim period.
4. Gains and losses arising in an interim period that would not be deferred at year-end should not be deferred to later interim periods.

As the foregoing indicates, there is sufficient latitude in the standards for interim reporting to allow for different treatment of similar items among companies. However, it would be inappropriate to believe that the Accounting Principles Board intended to permit an entity to treat a particular type of cost, in the same circumstances, one way in one interim report and another way in a subsequent interim report. Rather, the need for alternative methods can be attributed to differences in the circumstances of business enterprises, including the ability to gather information necessary to determine whether costs should be accrued or deferred.

If allocation is appropriate, it should be based on a "systematic and rational" method consistently applied. Acceptable allocation methods are (1) ratably over time, (2) proportionately as benefits are received, and (3) in relation to the activity associated with the interim period, perhaps in light of anticipated activity for the annual period. For example, insurance expense should be allocated ratably over the life of the policy; advertising expense should be allocated to the periods when benefits are received; and royalty expense should be allocated on the basis of activity during the interim period. In the last example, if royalty rates vary based on aggregate volume for the annual period, amounts accrued at interim dates will be based on anticipated annual volume.

Although Opinion No. 28 illustrates the application of the standards outlined above, the number of examples given is limited. The following illustrations provide further clarification:

1. Expenses for which a liability is accrued should be allocated based on time expired. *Examples:* interest, rent, property taxes, franchise taxes not based on income, vested vacation pay, and pension expense.

2. Nondiscretionary expenditures incurred randomly that benefit the whole year should be allocated to all interim periods, usually on a time basis. *Examples:* normal recurring repairs, cost of printed annual reports, and normal recurring professional fees (audit, legal, etc.).

3. Expenditures for which a liability is incurred late in the year but that relate to activity during the year should be estimated and accrued, usually on a revenue basis. *Examples:* quantity sales discounts based on annual sales volume, and incentive compensation and bonus plans.

4. Expenses resulting from accounting judgments that are susceptible to interim approximations should be estimated and accrued, on either a time or revenue basis. *Examples:* provisions for bad debts, change in useful lives or fixed assets, provisions for product warranty, and provisions for obsolete inventory.

5. Expenses resulting from amortization of balance sheet amounts should usually be allocated on a time basis. *Examples:* fixed asset depreciation and amortization of deferred charges.

6. Expenses connected with random, unexpected losses should be expensed as incurred. *Examples:* losses on contracts and casualty losses.

9.8 INCOME TAX PROVISIONS.   Determining an appropriate provision for income taxes in interim periods is complex.

An enterprise should develop its best estimate of the effective tax rate for the full year and use that rate in providing for taxes in interim statements. See Chapter 17, "Accounting for Income Taxes," for a discussion of interperiod tax allocation.

As is true of other aspects of interim financial reporting, the selection of an effective tax rate should be neither arbitrary nor static. It should reflect the company's tax posture, budgets, and intentions regarding operations during the annual period, and should be reevaluated and modified at each interim reporting date in the light of current information.

SFAS No. 96 amended certain aspects of income tax provisions under APB Opinion No. 28. For example, in selecting an effective tax rate, the following must be considered: effects of new tax legislation cannot be recognized prior to enactment; tax benefits can now be recognized for the amount of taxes paid in prior years that are refundable by carryback of a loss of the current year: and, an asset cannot be recognized for a loss carryforward at the end of a fiscal year regardless of the probability that the enterprise will generate profits in future years.

SFAS No. 96 requires the entire effect of a change in tax rate on existing deferred income taxes to be recognized in the period in which the change in the rate occurs and not be spread as an adjustment of the tax rate for the remainder of the year. Also the ability to recognize a tax benefit for losses that cannot be carried back is limited to situations where realization in subsequent **interim** periods is assured beyond any reasonable doubt (similar tax benefits existing at the end of a year cannot be recognized under SFAS No. 96).

Exhibit 9.3 illustrates the calculation of income tax expense assuming a tax rate change occurring in the second quarter. A suggested footnote is also included with the example.

9.9 DISPOSAL OF A SEGMENT OF A BUSINESS AND EXTRAORDINARY ITEMS.   APB Opinion No. 30, "Reporting the Results of Operations," requires that extraordinary items and the effects of disposing of a segment of a business be reported separately from the results of operations and net of their tax effect. Events of an abnormal nature that do not meet the criteria for an extraordinary item should also be reported separately from income from continuing operations. This facilitates the comparison of reported earnings with those of prior periods.

CALCULATION OF INCOME TAX EXPENSE

Assume:

The effective tax rate is 40% in the first quarter and 30% in the second quarter

First Quarter:

	3 Months Ended
Income before income taxes	$500 (Assumed)
Provision for income taxes (40%)	200
Net Income	300

Second Quarter:

	6 Months Ended
Income before income taxes	$800
Provision for income taxes (30%)	240
Net Income	560

Interim F/S would appear as follows:

	6 Months Ended June 30, 19X2	Second Quarter	First Quarter (As Previously Reported)
Income before income tax	$800	$300	$500
Provision for income tax	240	40	200
Net Income	$560	$260	$300

The difference in effective tax rates is reported in the second quarter under SFAS No. 96. The footnote disclosure might be as follows:

> The provision for income taxes, and the related liability, have been reduced to give effect to the decline in federal income tax rates from 40% to 30% from January 1, 19X2, the effective date of the rate change. (If applicable, a similar adjustment would be made to any deferred tax balances.)

Exhibit 9.3.   Calculation of income tax expense with a tax rate change in the second quarter from 40% to 30%, applying SFAS No. 96.

These matters are accorded substantially the same treatment in interim statements, although the measurement of materiality is somewhat more complex. In paragraph 21 of Opinion No. 28, the APB specified that the measurement of materiality with respect to extraordinary items should relate to estimated income for the full year. It seems reasonable and consistent with the integral view to apply the same measurement criteria to the disposal of a segment of a business. Consequently, if disposals of business segments and extraordinary items are not material to estimated income for the annual period, they should not be reported separately, on a net-of-tax basis, in interim statements. However, if those items are material to the results of operations for the interim period or to the trend in interim earnings, they should be separately identified in the income statement and explained in a note.

Contingencies such as pending or threatened litigation and other major uncertainties should be reconsidered for each interim report. The accounting and disclosure requirements relating to contingencies are the same for interim as for annual reporting when a complete set of interim financial statements is presented.

9.10 ACCOUNTING CHANGES.   Any change in accounting principles or practices in the current interim period from those applied in (1) the comparable interim period of the prior year, (2) preceding interim periods of the current year, and (3) the prior annual report should be disclosed in the current interim report in accordance with the provisions of APB Opinion No. 20, "Accounting Changes," and SFAS No. 3, "Reporting Accounting Changes in Interim Financial Statements."

Accounting changes requiring restatement of prior annual financial statements also require restatement of previously issued interim financial information. Examples of such changes include a change from the LIFO method of inventory pricing, a change to the percentage-of-completion method of accounting for long-term construction contracts, corrections of errors, and changes in the companies included in combined financial statements. In addition to an explanation of the nature and justification of the change, its effect on income from continuing operations, net income, and related per share amounts should be disclosed for all periods presented.

Repeated restatement of financial statements after their initial issuance could potentially reduce public confidence in financial reports. Accordingly, in paragraph 18 of Opinion No. 20 the APB concluded that most accounting changes should be reported in the period when the change is adopted, and the cumulative effect of the change on previous periods should be reported as a separate component of results of operations. Companies have been urged to adopt accounting changes in the first interim period of the fiscal year because changes adopted in subsequent interim periods complicate the communication process.

When an accounting change other than a change requiring restatement is made in the first interim period of the year, the cumulative effect of the change on retained earnings at the beginning of the period should be included in the determination of net income of the interim period and the following should be disclosed:

1. The nature and justification for the change, including a clear explanation of why the change is preferable (see Chapter 5 of this *Handbook*).
2. The effect of the change on income from continuing operations, net income, and related per share amounts for the interim period.
3. The disclosures in item 2, on a pro forma basis, for any interim periods of prior fiscal years for which financial information is presented. Even if no prior interim period data are presented, disclosure must be made of the actual and pro forma income from continuing operations, net income, and related per share amounts for the corresponding interim period of the preceding year.

When cumulative-effect type accounting changes are made subsequent to the first interim period of a fiscal year, prechange interim periods should be restated to reflect the newly adopted principle; the cumulative effect on retained earnings at the beginning of the fiscal year should be reported as part of the net income of the first interim period. In addition, the disclosures in items 2 and 3 above should be made for each interim period preceding the period of change, as well as for each interim period of prior fiscal years presented for comparative purposes.

Disclosures for interim periods in the year of change subsequent to the period in which the change was adopted should include the disclosures in item 2 above. Some companies present interim information on a year-to-date or 12-months-to-date basis. If such presentations encompass an interim period in which a cumulative-effect type accounting change was adopted, the disclosures set forth in items 1 to 3 above should be made.

In a few instances, most notably a change to the LIFO method of inventory pricing, data for periods preceding the current annual period cannot be determined, and pro forma disclosures need not be made.

Changes in accounting practices related solely to interim financial reporting, such as effective income tax rates—except for the effects of retroactive tax legislation—and certain inventory pricing techniques, constitute changes in accounting estimates. Changes in accounting estimates do not require restatement of, or pro forma disclosures with respect to, prior interim or annual periods. The effect of such changes on results of operations of the current period should be reported in the period of change and in subsequent periods if material or necessary to avoid misleading comparisons.

In determining the materiality of a cumulative-effect type accounting change or correction of an error, amounts should be related to estimated annual income and the effect of the earnings trend. Changes that are not judged material by these criteria but that have a material effect on the interim period should be separately disclosed.

DISCLOSURE OF INTERIM FINANCIAL INFORMATION

9.11 VARIATIONS IN DISCLOSURE.   The nature and the extent of disclosure of financial information by business enterprises at interim dates vary considerably. Owner-managers of closely held corporations may conclude that they obtain sufficient information from their day-to-day involvement in company affairs. Conversely, a company may need to prepare a complete set of financial statements each quarter to, for example, comply with provisions of credit agreements. Obviously, there are a variety of possible alternatives within this range. Even in the absence of specific requirements for external reporting at interim dates, private companies should be mindful of the potential need to prepare interim data on a comparative basis if and when they seek wider distribution of their securities.

9.12 MINIMUM DISCLOSURE FOR PUBLIC COMPANIES.   The APB recognized the need for a balance between completeness of presentation and timeliness of dissemination of interim information. Thus in paragraph 30 of Opinion No. 28 the Board set forth the following as minimum disclosures to be made by public companies to their security holders:

1. Sales or gross revenue, provision for income taxes, extraordinary items (including related income tax effects), cumulative effect of a change in accounting principles or practices, and net income.
2. Primary and fully diluted earnings per share for each period presented, determined in accordance with the provisions of APB Opinion No. 15, "Earnings per Share."
3. Seasonal revenue, costs, or expenses.
4. Significant changes in estimates or provisions for income taxes.
5. Disposal of a segment of a business and extraordinary, unusual, or infrequently occurring items (with explanation).
6. Contingent items.
7. Changes in accounting principles or estimates.
8. Significant changes in financial position (i.e., liquid assets, net working capital, long-term liabilities, or stockholders' equity).

The foregoing data should be presented for the current quarter and current year to date or last 12 months to date, together with comparable data for the preceding year.

To avoid inappropriate inferences by users about fourth-quarter earnings when separate reports for this quarter are not issued, the APB requires that the annual financial statements include a note containing either the data specified above or, at a minimum, (1) disposals of segments of a business; (2) extraordinary, unusual, or infrequently occurring items; and (3) the aggregate effect of year-end adjustments that are material to the results of the quarter. The latter item identifies the cumulative impact of the results of the estimation process during the year.

The APB based these minimum requirements on the presumption that users of summarized interim financial data will have read the latest published annual report, including the annual financial statements, and that interim disclosures will be viewed in that context. This presumption carries the integral view into the reporting process.

9.13 DISCLOSURE REQUIREMENTS OF STOCK EXCHANGES.   The interim information required to be disclosed by companies whose securities trade in the major domestic securities markets is generally less extensive than the minimum set forth in APB Opinion No. 28. Thus the minimum disclosures of Opinion No. 28 apply.

The NYSE and the AMEX require listed companies to release interim financial information on a quarterly basis. Exceptions to quarterly filings are granted in unusual cases where quarterly filings would be impracticable or misleading. Fourth quarter reports are not required since that period is covered by the annual financial statements.

The quarterly information must be released to the exchanges on a timely basis. The NYSE assumes that a listed company will provide the information "as soon as it is available and following a pattern of major companies in its industry." The AMEX requires the information be submitted within 45 days. The interim data must also be distributed as a press release to major newspapers of general circulation (at least in New York), to national newswire services, and to Dow Jones & Company, Inc. Distribution to security holders is encouraged but not mandatory. Copies of all releases should also be filed with the appropriate exchange. See Exhibit 9.4 for an example of a press release.

The National Association of Securities Dealers (NASD), the self-regulatory organization for the OTC market, requires companies whose securities are publicly traded to file with it a copy of the quarterly report mandated by the SEC no later than 2 weeks after its SEC filing date.

From: John Doe   James Smith
    ABC Company   XYZ Public Relations Co.
    1 Main Street   2 Main Street
    Anytown, U.S.A.   Anytown, U.S.A.

FOR IMMEDIATE RELEASE

ABC COMPANY REPORTS HIGHER FIRST QUARTER EARNINGS
REVENUES INCREASE 10%; EARNINGS PER SHARE UP 15%

Anytown, U.S.A., (Date) ABC Company reported higher revenues, net earnings, and earnings per share for the first 3 months of the year. In making the announcement John Doe, chief financial officer, reported that first-quarter revenues rose to $11,000,000, an increase of 10% over the $10,000,000 in the same period last year. Net earnings rose 15% to $1,500,000 versus $1,304,348 for the first 3 months of last year. Similarly, earnings per share for the quarter were $1.50, a 15% increase from the $1.30 reported last year.

Unit sales of widgets were up, reflecting the Company's increasing share of the market. Mr. Doe noted that the Company had opened an additional manufacturing facility which increased the Company's productive capacity by 10%.

	For the Quarters Ended June 30		
	19X2	**19X1**	**% Increase**
Operating revenues	$11,000,000	$10,000,000	10
Earnings before income taxes	3,000,000	2,608,696	15
Federal and other income taxes	1,500,000	1,304,348	15
Net earnings	1,500,000	1,304,348	15
Earnings per share of common stock (based on the weighted average number of shares outstanding)	$1.50	$1.30	15

Exhibit 9.4.   Example of a press release of quarterly results.

ABC COMPANY
Condensed Statement of Financial Condition

	June 30	
	19X2	19X1
Assets:		
Cash	$ 2,000	$ 2,500
Receivables	5,000	3,500
Inventory	5,000	4,500
Other Current Assets	3,000	2,500
Property, Plant & Equipment, Net	6,000	5,500
Other Assets	2,000	2,500
Total Assets	$23,000	$21,000
Liabilities:		
Accounts Payable	1,000	1,500
Notes Payable	3,000	2,500
Accrued Expenses and Other Liabilities	2,000	2,500
Bonds Payable	8,000	6,500
Total Liabilities	14,000	13,000
Stockholders' Equity:		
Common Stock	2,000	2,000
Paid-in Capital	3,000	3,000
Retained Earnings	4,000	3,000
Total Stockholders' Equity	9,000	8,000
Total Liabilities and Stockholders' Equity	$23,000	$21,000

ABC COMPANY
Condensed Statements of Income and Retained Earnings
For the 3 months and 6 months ended June 30, 19X2

	3 Months Ended June 30, 19X2	6 Months Ended June 30, 19X2
Sales	$10,000	$20,000
Cost of goods sold	8,550	17,150
Gross profit	1,450	2,850
Selling and administrative expenses	150	250
Income before taxes	1,300	2,600
Provision for income taxes	300	600
Net income	1,000	2,000
Retained earnings beginning of period	3,500	3,000
Dividends	500	1,000
Retained Earnings June 30, 19X2	$ 4,000	$ 4,000
Earnings per share (assume 2,000 shares)	$ .50	$ 1.00
		(continued)

Exhibit 9.5. Examples of SEC requirements for interim reporting.

ABC COMPANY
Condensed Statement of Cash Flows

	3 Months Ended June 30, 19X2	6 Months Ended June 30, 19X2
Cash provided by operations	$ 1,000	$ 2,000
Cash flows from investing:		
Capital expenditures	$(1,500)	$(3,500)
Cash used in investing	(1,500)	(3,500)
Cash flows from financing:		
Proceeds from issuance of long-term debt	$ 500	$ 1,500
Dividends	(500)	(1,000)
Cash from financing	-0-	500
Increase (decrease) in cash	(500)	(1,000)
Cash, beginning of period	2,500	3,000
Cash, end of period	$ 2,000	$ 2,000
Interest paid in period	$ 250	$ 450
Income taxes paid in period	$ 300	$ 600

Exhibit 9.5.   *Continued.*

9.14 SEC REQUIREMENTS FOR INTERIM REPORTING.   The SEC promulgates financial accounting and disclosure requirements that it deems to be in the public interest or necessary for the protection of investors. In addressing the need for disclosure between annual periods, the Commission has accepted the concept that interim results should be viewed as an **integral** part of the annual period. Thus, for example, (FRR No. 1 ASR No. 177) "Notice of Adoption of Amendments to Form 10-Q and Regulation S-X Regarding Interim Financial Reporting," states, "The Commission . . . believes that detailed footnote disclosures required annually need not be updated quarterly in the absence of highly unusual circumstances."

The SEC requires public companies to file with it quarterly information on Form 10-Q. In addition, unusual or significant events occurring within a quarter, for example, changes in control of the company, a major acquisition or disposal of assets, a change in independent accountants, and other events deemed to be materially important to security holders are to be reported monthly on Form 8-K. In the case of a material acquisition or disposition of assets, audited interim financial statements are required. When a company changes its independent accountant, any disagreement between the company and the former accountant that would have resulted in a modified audit report if not satisfactorily resolved must also be reported to the SEC on Form 8-K. Additionally, the independent accountant must provide a letter to the company, within 10 business days of the date the accountant receives the company's disclosure, expressing his views regarding the company's disclosure to the SEC. The accountant's letter should ordinarily not exceed 200 words.

The information to be filed quarterly with the SEC for the current and immediately preceding periods includes:

1. A condensed balance sheet at the end of the quarter.
2. Condensed statements of income, retained earnings, and cash flows for the quarter and the year to date.
3. An exhibit setting forth the earnings per share computation in reasonable detail.

4. Notes describing in detail any material events (e.g. lawsuit settlements, etc.) or other changes deemed to be materially important to shareholders.

Exhibit 9.5 illustrates some of these requirements. Management must also discuss the reasons for material changes in the amounts of revenue and expense in (1) the current quarter, compared to both the preceding quarter and the corresponding quarter of the prior year; and (2) the current year to date compared to the corresponding period of the prior year.

Regulation S-X, Article 10, Rule 10-01 outlines the Commission's requirements for interim financial statements. Essentially, interim financial statements follow the general form and content of the presentation prescribed for annual reporting. The exceptions, however, include:

- Interim financial statements may be unaudited.
- Interim balance sheets and statements of income shall only include major captions.
- The statement of changes in financial position may be abbreviated.
- Disclosures shall be included to make the information presented not misleading.
- If the registrant entered into a business combination, treated for accounting purposes as a pooling of interests, the interim financial statements shall reflect the combined results of the pooled businesses.
- Where a material business combination is accounted for as a purchase occurs during the current fiscal year, pro forma disclosure shall be made of the results of operations for the current year up to the date of the most recent interim balance sheet provided as though the companies had combined at the beginning of the period being reported on.
- The registrant must state the date of any material accounting change and the reasons for making it.

In response to the National Commission on Fraudulent Financial Reporting (the "Treadway Commission"), the SEC recently made available for comment a concept release that considers whether publicly held companies should be required to subject their interim financial filings—both registration statements and quarterly SEC filings—to timely review by their auditors. At issue is whether the benefits of additional reviews by auditors outweigh the costs involved. As of this printing, no consensus has been reached by the SEC.

The SEC requires companies seeking to register securities for sale to the public to file registration statements including financial statements. Under Regulation S-X, the SEC does not require interim financial data more current than the most recent quarterly reporting date. Additionally, the Commission allows data to be presented in condensed financial statements in the same degree of detail as in Form 10-Q.

ROLE OF THE INDEPENDENT AUDITOR

9.15 ACCOUNTING CHANGES.   Consistency in the application of accounting principles facilitates meaningful comparisons of a company's performance over time. Although new circumstances affecting a company or general business conditions may make modifications in accounting principles desirable, changes cannot be made arbitrarily. In FRR No. 1 [ASR No. 177], the SEC stated,

> Since a substantial burden of proof falls upon management to justify a change, the Commission believes that the burden has not been met unless the justification is sufficiently persuasive to convince an independent accounting expert that in his judgment the new method represents an improved method of measuring business operations in the particular circumstances involved.

Thus the independent auditor must provide the company with a letter, to be filed as an exhibit to the first Form 10-Q filed after adoption of an accounting change, indicating whether the change is to an alternative principle that, in his judgment, is preferable in the circumstances.

See Exhibit 9.6 for a sample letter from an accountant. The subject of preferability letters is discussed further in Chapter 5.

9.16 REVIEWS OF INTERIM FINANCIAL INFORMATION.   The SEC believes that auditor involvement with interim financial data enhances the reliability of quarterly reports and reduces the potential abuses from deferral of certain judgments until the end of the year. A company may elect to have its independent accountant perform a **limited review** of interim financial information before it is filed with the SEC. If such an election is made, the company may so indicate and include a copy of the accountant's report. Because a limited review is significantly more restricted in scope than an audit, the accountant's report refers to whether the accountant became aware of a need for material modifications that should be made to the company's interim financial data to conform with GAAP. See Exhibit 9.7 for a sample report on a limited review of interim financial data.

Regardless of whether independent accountants make a limited review of quarterly reports, companies must include certain summarized quarterly data in a note to the annual financial statements. The note, which is labeled "unaudited," must include data regarding quarterly results of operations for each of the latest 2 years, as well as the aggregate effect and the nature of year-end audit adjustments material to the quarterly results. Because the note is included in audited financial statements, independent accountants are associated with the interim data and normally review these data. However, the auditor's report on the examination of the annual financial statements will not be modified unless (1) the note was not labeled "unaudited"; (2) the interim data were not reviewed; (3) the scope of the accountant's review was restricted; or (4) a material modification of the data should have been made.

---

mm/dd/yy

Basic Corporation
6 Main Street
Anytown, U.S.A.

Gentlemen:

We are providing this letter to you for inclusion as an exhibit to your Form 10-Q filing pursuant to Item 601(b)(18) of Regulation S-K.

We have read management's justification for the change in accounting for inventories from the first-in first-out method to the last-in first-out method contained in the Company's Form 10-Q for the quarter ended March 31, 19X2. Based on our reading of the data and discussions with Company officials of the business judgment and business planning factors relating to the change, we believe management's justification to be reasonable. Accordingly, in reliance on management's determination as regards elements of business judgment and business planning, we concur that the newly adopted accounting principle described above is preferable in the Company's circumstances to the method previously applied.

We have not examined any fiscal statements of Basic Corporation as of any date or for any period subsequent to December 31, 19X1, nor have we audited the application of the change in accounting principle disclosed in Form 10-Q of Basic Corporation for the quarter ended March 31, 19X2; accordingly, our comments are subject to revision on completion of an audit of the financial statements that include the accounting change.

Very truly yours,

Adam, Bailey & Clarke

Exhibit 9.6.   Illustrative letter from independent accountant concurring with accounting change adopted by management.

To the Board of Directors and Stockholders
of Basic Corporation:

We have made a review of the consolidated interim financial information of Basic Corporation and consolidated subsidiaries as of March 31, 19X2 and 19X1, and for the 3-month periods then ended, appearing on pages 21 to 25 of the Report to Stockholders, in accordance with standards established by the American Institute of Certified Public Accountants.

A review of interim financial information consists principally of obtaining an understanding of the system for the preparation of interim financial information, applying analytical review procedures to financial data, and making inquiries of persons responsible for financial and accounting matters. It is substantially less in scope than an examination in accordance with generally accepted auditing standards, the objective of which is the expression of an opinion regarding the financial statements taken as a whole. Accordingly, we do not express such an opinion.

Based on our review, we are not aware of any material modifications that should be made to the accompanying financial information for it to be in conformity with generally accepted accounting principles.

FIXIT SERVICE CO.

Anytown, U.S.A.
April 15, 19X2

Exhibit 9.7.   Accountant's report on review of interim financial statements.

See Chapter 35 on the review of interim financial information and the form of the accountant's report.

SOURCES AND SUGGESTED REFERENCES

Accounting Principles Board, "Earnings per Share," APB Opinion No. 15, AICPA, New York, 1969.

————, "Accounting Changes," APB Opinion No. 20, AICPA, New York, 1971.

————, "Interim Financial Reporting," APB Opinion No. 28, AICPA, New York, 1973.

————, "LIFO and Interim Financial Reporting," Identification and Discussion of Certain Financial Accounting and Reporting Issues Concerning LIFO Inventories, AICPA Issues Paper, AICPA, New York, November 30, 1984.

————, "Reporting the Results of Operations," APB Opinion No. 30, AICPA, New York, 1973.

————, "Basic Concepts and Accounting Principles Underlying Financial Statements of Business Enterprises," APB Statement No. 4, AICPA, New York, 1970.

————, "Review of Interim Financial Information," Statement on Auditing Standards No. 24, AICPA, New York, 1979.

Bows, Albert J., and Wyatt, Arthur R., "Improving Interim Financial Reporting," *Journal of Accountancy*, Vol. 136, 1973.

Carlson, T. E., "Needed: A New Interpretation for Interim Reports," *Management Accounting*, Vol. 59, 1978.

Financial Accounting Standards Board, "Recognition of Inventory Market Declines at Interim Reporting Dates," EITF Abstracts Issue No. 86-13, FASB, Stamford, CT, May 1, 1986.

————, "Objectives of Financial Reporting by Business Enterprises," Statement of Financial Accounting Concepts No. 1, FASB, Stamford, CT, 1978.

————, "Recognition and Measurement in Financial Statements of Business Enterprises," Statement of Financial Accounting Concepts No. 5, FASB, Stamford, CT, December 1984.

————, "Elements of Financial Statements (a replacement of FASB Concepts Statement No. 3—incorporating an amendment of FASB Concepts Statement No. 2)," Statement of Financial Accounting Concepts No. 6, FASB, Stamford, CT, December 1985.

——, "Interim Financial Accounting and Reporting," Discussion Memorandum, FASB, Stamford, CT, 1978.

——, "Accounting for Income Taxes in Interim Periods: An Interpretation of APB Opinion No. 28," FASB Interpretation No. 18, FASB, Stamford, CT, 1977.

——, "Reporting Accounting Changes in Interim Financial Statements: An Amendment of APB Opinion No. 28," Statement of Financial Accounting Standards No. 3, FASB, Stamford, CT, 1974.

——, "Financial Reporting for Segments of a Business Enterprise—Interim Financial Statements: An Amendment of FASB Statement No. 14," Statement of Financial Accounting Standards No. 18, FASB, Stamford, CT, 1977.

——, "Accounting for Income Taxes," Statement of Financial Accounting Standards No. 96, FASB, Stamford, CT, December 1, 1987.

Kigir, Edward C., "Some Auditing Issues of Interim Financial Statements," *CPA Journal,* Vol. 44, 1974.

Rappaport, Louis H., *SEC Accounting Practice and Procedure,* Wiley, New York, 1972.

Schiff, Michael, *Accounting Reporting Problems,* Financial Executives Institute, New York, 1978.

Securities and Exchange Commission, "Notice of Adoption of Amendments to Form 10-Q and Regulation S-X Regarding Interim Financial Reporting," Accounting Series Release No. 177, SEC, Washington, DC, 1975.

——, "Codification of Financial Reporting Policies," Financial Reporting Release No. 1, SEC, Washington, DC, April 1982.

——, "Interim Financial Statements," Rule 10-01, Article 10, Regulation S-X, Bowne, New York, June 1987.

——, "Interpretation of Accounting Series Release No. 177," Staff Accounting Bulletin No. 6, SEC, Washington, DC, 1976.

"SEC seeking views on whether to propose timely review of interim financial data," *Securities Regulation & Law Report,* BNA Publishing, Washington, DC, June 23, 1989.

Securities Exchange Act of 1934, Regulation 14A: Solicitation of Proxies, SEC, Washington, DC, 1978.

CHAPTER 10

ANALYZING FINANCIAL STATEMENTS

Gerald I. White, CFA

Grace & White, Inc.

Ashwinpaul C. Sondhi, PhD

Leonard N. Stern School of Business
New York University

CONTENTS

SCOPE OF FINANCIAL STATEMENT ANALYSIS

10.1 EXTERNAL USERS OF PUBLISHED FINANCIAL STATEMENTS.   This section is concerned with the techniques of financial analysis employed by users of financial statements who are external to the company. As such, the techniques described are generally limited to analysis of published financial statements or similar statements privately circulated. Principal emphasis is on the financial statements of companies whose shares are publicly traded. Chapter 32 of this *Handbook* is concerned with the **valuation** of companies whose shares are not publicly traded.

Management has available far more extensive internal financial data for control of the business and deployment of resources. In many respects it may employ the same analytical approaches as the external user, but in greater detail.

The common characteristic of external users is their general lack of authority to prescribe the information they want from an enterprise. They depend on general-purpose external financial reports provided by management. The objectives of these external users are aptly described by the FASB in SFAC No. 1, "Objectives of Financial Reporting by Business Enterprises," (par. 34):

INFORMATION USEFUL IN INVESTMENT AND CREDIT DECISIONS

Financial reporting should provide information that is useful to present and potential investors and creditors and other users in making rational investment, credit, and similar decisions. The information should be comprehensible to those who have a reasonable understanding of business and economic activities and are willing to study the information with reasonable diligence.

10.2 USER GROUPS AND THEIR ANALYTICAL OBJECTIVES.   External users of financial information encompass a wide range of interests but can be classified in three general groups: (1) **investors**—both creditors and equity investors; (2) **government**—regulatory bodies, tax authorities, the executive and legislative branches; and (3) the general public and special interest groups—labor unions, consumer groups, and so on. Each group has a particular objective in financial statement analysis but, as the FASB stated, the primary users are **equity investors** and **creditors.** The information supplied to investors and creditors, however, is likely to be generally useful to other user groups as well. Hence financial accounting standards are geared to the purposes and perceptions of investors. That is the group for whom the analytical techniques in this chapter are geared.

The **underlying objective of financial analysis** is the comparative measurement of **risk** and **return** in order to make investment or credit decisions. These decisions are based on some estimates of the future, be it a month, a year, or a decade. General-purpose financial statements, which describe the past, provide one basis for projecting future cash flows. Many of the techniques used in this analytical process are broadly applicable to all types of decisions, but there are also specialized techniques concerned with specific investment interests or, put another way, specific risks and returns.

(a) Equity Investors. The equity investor is primarily interested in the **long-term earning power** of the company and its ability to pay **dividends**. Since the equity investor bears the residual risk in an enterprise, his analysis is the most comprehensive of any user and encompasses techniques employed by all other external users. Because the residual risk is the greatest and most volatile, the equity investor has focused increasing attention on measuring comparative risks and diversifying these risks in investment portfolios.

(b) Creditors. This subgroup of investors emphasizes several specialized analytical approaches. Short-term creditors, such as banks and trade creditors, place more emphasis on the immediate **liquidity** of the business because they seek an early payback of their investment. Long-term investors in bonds, such as insurance companies and pension funds, are primarily concerned with the **long-term asset position** and earning power of the company. They seek assurance of the payment of interest and the capability of retiring or refunding the obligation at maturity. Creditor risks are usually less than equity risks and are more easily quantifiable.

10.3 SOURCES OF FINANCIAL INFORMATION. The term "financial statements" normally encompasses four statements: the income statement, the balance sheet, the statement of changes in stockholders' equity (or changes in retained earnings), and the statement of cash flows. The notes to the financial statements are an integral part of the entire set and provide substantial amounts of supplementary information, such as the operations of major segments of the business, the financial position of pension plans, and off-balance-sheet obligations.

These statements are presented in both the annual and the quarterly reports to shareholders and in filings with the SEC. SEC filings (registration statements for new security offerings, the 10-K annual report, and the 10-Q quarterly report) often contain additional valuable information not presented in reports to shareholders. Shareholder reports, on the other hand, often contain useful supplementary financial and statistical data and a narrative report by management. Therefore, any comprehensive analysis of a company should review both of these basic sources.

Industry data and other information about a company also may be obtained from sources outside the company. This discussion is confined to company-originated financial data.

10.4 FRAMEWORK FOR ANALYSIS. Investment analysis should begin with an evaluation of macroeconomic conditions including trends in the GNP, personal consumption, and capital expenditures along with other relevant macrovariables. This analysis should be developed on a domestic and international level for insights into the relative investment potential across countries and industrial sectors. The competitive, economic, and technological factors affecting selected industries should be analyzed next; finally, there should be a comprehensive analysis of various firms in these industries. The analysis framework to achieve forecasts of earning power and market value can be outlined as follows:

1. Economywide factors.
    Gross National Product.
    Personal consumption expenditures.
    Capital expenditures.
    Interest rates.
    Currency rates.
    Other relevant macrovariables.

2. Industrywide factors.

Product life cycle—Sales and earnings.
Unit cost and unit sales price.
   Trends over time.
   Relative to other firms.
Economic and technological forces affecting industry competition.
   Threat of new entrants.
   Bargaining power of buyers.
   Rivalry among existing competitors.
   Threat of substitute products.
   Bargaining power of suppliers.

3. Firm-specific analyses.

Firm strategies in given economic and industrywide environment.
Earning power.
Leverage analysis.

INCOME STATEMENT ANALYSIS

This section discusses the evaluation of earning power and risk through analyses of the revenue and expense components of the income statements. Various analytical techniques used to study trends and variability in revenues and the impact of costs incurred on risk are described.

10.5 THE CONCEPTS OF EARNING POWER AND RISK.   In the long run, earning power is the basis for credit and the source of cash return (interest or dividends) to the investor. The analyst seeks to project earning power over some future period associated with the length of the **risk period.** Therefore, it is the focus of income statement analysis.

Earning power is an analytical concept and cannot be separately identified in the income statement. It is defined as the ability of a company to generate continuing earnings from the operating assets of the business over a period of years. Its characteristics include normality, stability (or variability), and growth. **Normality** is the normal level of earnings, absent strikes, floods, and other unusual nonrecurring events. It excludes extraordinary items such as accounting adjustments and nonrecurring capital gains or charges. **Stability** is the absence of variation around a trend line. **Growth** is the rate of change in the trend line of earnings over a defined period. Generally, earning power is better represented by operating earnings than by total net income, which often includes unusual or random elements. The analyst normalizes and averages operating earnings data to determine earning power, which he then projects and capitalizes.

The **risk element** in earning power is the variability between actual and expected earnings, or the predictability of earnings. The earnings of some companies may fluctuate with some regularity in a cyclical pattern, whereas for others the fluctuations are irregular and unpredictable. Fluctuation is tantamount to uncertainty, which increases as fluctuations become increasingly irregular and unpredictable. Thus, stocks of copper companies are considered more risky than, say, those of household product companies, because their earnings are much less predictable.

10.6 SALES AND REVENUE ANALYSIS.   Sales and other operating revenues are the lifeblood of a business. The analyst compares the company's revenue factors with the industry and with competing companies and seeks to associate economic changes with internal company trends. He makes comparisons by analysis of trend and variability and attempts to ascertain the relative importance of price and volume.

Year	Company A Steady Growth		Company B Cyclical Pattern		Company C Unusual Development	
	Amount	% Change	Amount	% Change	Amount	% Change
1	$ 21.5		$ 18.1		$ 20.5	
2	23.0	7.0	23.6	30.4	21.5	4.9
3	24.0	4.3	28.1	19.1	23.0	7.0
4	25.7	7.1	35.7	17.0	24.5	6.5
5	28.1	9.3	29.0	(18.8)	26.0	6.1
6	29.6	5.3	27.5	(5.2)	26.5	1.9
7	31.3	5.7	26.0	(5.4)	28.0	5.7
8	34.5	10.2	29.0	11.5	29.0	3.6
9	35.0	1.4	32.0	10.3	40.0	10.3
10	36.3	3.7	40.0	25.0	50.0	25.0
10-year Total	$289.0		$289.0		$289.0	
% change Years 1–10		68.8		121.0		143.9
Compound growth rate years 1–10 (%)		6.0		9.2		10.4
Least squares growth rate (%)		6.0		4.8		9.1
Standard deviation		5.3		6.1		9.2

Exhibit 10.1.   Measures of sales trends.

(a) Trend Analysis. The most appropriate measure of a trend is determined by the revenue pattern. A stable trend is easily measured by a compound annual growth rate calculated on the end point values, but a highly variable pattern is better measured by a least squares calculation. Three patterns of sales trends are illustrated in Exhibit 10.1.

Company A shows fairly steady growth, and a compound growth rate calculated between years 1 and 10 is a reasonable measure of trend. It can be presumed to have some predictive power, subject to an analysis of all factors affecting sales.

Company B shows a cyclical pattern with a compound growth rate calculated from year 1 to year 10 of 9.2%, although total sales for 10 years are the same as Company A. Obviously, a growth rate calculated from the bottom of one cycle to the peak of another one does not provide a sound basis for prediction. Two better methods can be used. One is to measure from one peak to the next peak (or from trough to trough). Thus year 1 (trough) to year 7 (trough) shows a compound growth rate of 6.0%; or year 4 (peak) to year 10 (peak) a rate of 1.9%. A second method is to fit a least squares trend line to the data. The slope of this line shows a growth rate of 4.8%, which is probably a more realistic long-term measure for this company.

Company C experiences an explosive sales growth at the end of the decade, enabling it to attain the same 10-year total as companies A and B. The compound growth rate over the whole period is 10.4%, and the least squares growth rate is 9.1%. When it is realized that the growth rate in the first 8 years is only 5.1% compared with 31.3% in the last 2, the 10-year compound growth fails to describe the sales trend. In fact there is no satisfactory measure to project the sales trends of Company C in comparison with the other companies. The company's recent sales experience must be analyzed before any projection can be made.

(b) Variability. These three companies illustrate widely differing sales patterns, leading to different levels of confidence in their persistence in future years. One indication of variability is the simple year-to-year percentage change in sales. Company A's year-to-year increases are close to the 10-year compound growth rate, whereas Company B swings widely above and below its 10-year trend line growth of 4.8% annually. The standard deviation is the statistical tool that measures the variation from the trend line. For Company A it can be expected that about two-thirds of the expected values will fall within ± 5.3, or 18% of the mean, whereas for Company C the range is ± 9.2, or 32% of the mean. A's variability is less, and the certainty of its sales trend is greater, although not absolute.

(c) Components of Sales Trends.   A sales trend can be understood better if the components of price and volume can be separated. Not many companies provide such information, but it often can be derived indirectly. If Company A sells a single product, the price of which is known, volume can be easily computed. For Company A, for example, the price rose at a 4.0% annual rate during the 10-year period.
   Volume growth can be calculated as follows:

$$\text{Volume growth over 10 years} = \frac{\text{Sales (year 10)}}{\text{Price (year 10)}} - \frac{\text{Sales (year 1)}}{\text{Price (year 1)}}$$

   By dividing year 10 sales by year 10 price we obtain a volume figure for that year. A similar exercise for the base year (year 1) provides a comparable figure. Conversely, volume may be known (e.g., steel production), so price can be derived from this equation, substituting volume for price.
   Occasionally the components of sales change are presented in a **variance analysis** in an annual report. This is illustrated as follows:

Total sales increase in year 2	$150,000
Increase due to price ((Price 2 − Price 1) × Volume 1)	86,000
Increase due to volume ((Volume 2 − Volume 1) × Price 2)	64,000

In large diversified companies, gross sales are an aggregate of many diverse activities and many other components of sales should be analyzed. In recent years companies have been required to report sales (and earnings and other data) of the principal segments and geographic sources of the business.
   Within a single product line or segment there are also differences in the **characteristics of sales components.** One example is sales versus service revenues, or sales versus leasing. Most companies provide this breakdown where it is important. Sales of an expensive machine (e.g., a computer) may be expected to fluctuate from year to year, but service revenues will tend to build up steadily as the number of installed machines increases. Alternatively, buyers may shift between buying and leasing, although product shipments remain unchanged. The volatility and the current profitability of these revenue streams are quite different, and both must be analyzed to fully understand the sales trend.
   When examining sales trends, the analyst must be wary of the effects of acquisitions and divestitures as well as the effects of changes in exchange rates. These issues are discussed in sections 10.17 and 10.19.

(d) Comparative Trend Analysis.   A company cannot be analyzed in a vacuum. The outside forces affecting it and its responses are an important aspect of financial analysis. Sales can be tested against competition in the company's markets and general economic trends. There are a number of ways to do this, none very difficult. Exhibit 10.2 is illustrative. Company D is gaining a share of the market. Company E had an earlier cyclical recovery but merely maintained its position relative to the economy over the full business cycle. Its greater cyclical variability is an important aspect of the appraisal of the company. Company F's slow revenue growth is due to lagging volume compared to its industry.
   Although the comparison of similar companies is a necessary part of analysis, it is fraught with peril. No two companies are identical. Differences in sales trends may result from any of

Year	Company D Sales % Industry	Company E Sales % GNP	Company F Volume Index[a]	
			Company	Industry
1	23.5	.00065	100	100
2	27.4	.00072	105	105
3	28.1	.00075	112	117
4	29.3	.00070	113	120
5	30.2	.00068	115	123
5-year average	27.7	.00070	109	113

[a]Year 1 = 100.

Exhibit 10.2.   Comparative sales trend analysis.

the following:

- End markets may have different growth or cyclical characteristics.
- Major customers may differ; differences in customer sales trends will be reflected in new orders.
- Companies who are considered secondary suppliers will show greater variability than "primary" suppliers.
- Some companies have greater vertical integration than others in the same industry.
- In industries with high transportation costs, regional conditions may vary greatly (e.g., cement).

10.7 COST AND EXPENSE ANALYSIS.   Many of the same analytical techniques applied to revenue analysis can also be utilized in expense analysis, but the predominant technique is profit margin analysis. The great diversity of business operations precludes any general standard for such ratios; they are best used in internal trend analysis and company comparisons.

(a) Classification of Costs.   In a typical industrial company the principal expense categories are cost-of-goods-sold and selling, general, and administrative expenses. Sometimes these categories are subdivided. Sometimes depreciation is shown separately rather than included in other categories. Because of these and other classification problems, these categories are rarely comparable from company to company.

For purposes of analysis, one should focus on gross profit (sales less cost-of-goods-sold) or on operating income (before other income and expense, interest income and expense, and income taxes). Using income before interest charges facilitates the comparison of companies with different financial structures.

(b) Margin Analysis.   A company's ability to control costs in relation to revenues is an important factor in earning power. Five ratios or margins are generally used to measure cost control in industrial companies, as follows:

1. Gross margin $= 1 - \dfrac{\text{Cost of goods sold}}{\text{Sales}}$

2. Expense ratio $= \dfrac{\text{Selling, general and administrative expenses}}{\text{Sales}}$

3. Operating margin $= \dfrac{\text{Operating income}}{\text{Sales}}$

4. Pretax margin $= \dfrac{\begin{array}{c}\text{Income before income tax}\\\text{(Operating income + other income − interest)}\end{array}}{\text{Sales}}$

5. Profit margin $= \dfrac{\text{Net income before extraordinary items}}{\text{Sales}}$

These ratios must be interpreted in relation to other companies in the same industry and over time within the company. Any given ratio has little meaning out of context. Margins must also be related to other facets of the business such as the capital required and the turnover ratio, as will be explained in a later part of this section.

For example, a **retail food chain** typically will show a low operating margin because it rapidly passes through a high volume of products at a very low unit cost. Although a low operating margin would normally suggest considerable uncertainty about the continuity of operating income, the rapid turnover provides more opportunity to keep selling prices in line with costs.

In contrast, a **capital intensive industrial company** may have a much wider operating margin, but typically it will have a higher proportion of fixed costs and more volatile sales. An **electric utility company** will show both a wide operating margin and steady sales, but its capital costs (e.g., interest) are also large.

Some lines of business have a very low gross margin, that is, the cost of the product is a high percentage of sales, meaning that value added by the company is modest. In such cases, the dynamics of expenses can be related better to the gross margin than to sales. Today, **commercial banks** offset interest costs, which are far larger than any other expense, against interest income to derive a net interest margin. In effect, this spread is the real measure of a bank's revenue from its lending and investing activities. Other expenses are measured against the total of net interest income and other revenues, such as trust fees.

(c) Analytical Adjustments. When possible, nonrecurring items should be removed from earnings prior to analysis. These items include the following:

- Gains or losses from refinancing.
- Capital gains or losses on asset sales.
- Write-offs or special provisions for loss.
- Transitional impacts of new accounting standards.
- Results of discontinued operations.
- Foreign currency translation gain or loss.
- Settlement in a major law suit.

These items may or may not have great significance for cash flow, but usually they are nonrecurring or infrequent, and therefore cannot be projected in an assessment of future earning power. A loss on a facility closedown is largely an accounting adjustment that in effect recognizes a prior loss of earning power. It will not affect future years except perhaps indirectly in sales and costs. Foreign currency translation gains and losses are accounting adjustments arising from fluctuations in foreign exchange and their economic significance to the business is often hard to judge. A gain from debt retirement is really a capital transaction unrelated to the operations of the business.

(d) Operating Leverage. The analyst should attempt to separate variable, semivariable, and fixed costs. This will permit better analysis of cost control in a fluctuating business environ-

	Company X			Company Y		
	Year 1	Year 2	Year 3	Year 1	Year 2	Year 3
Sales	$1000	$1100	$900	$1000	$1100	$900
Expense						
Variable[a]	$ 500	$ 550	$450	$ 200	$ 220	$180
% of sales	50.0	50.0	50.0	20.0	20.0	20.0
Semivariable[b]	200	205	195	300	315	280
% of sales	20.0	18.6	21.7	30.0	28.6	31.1
Fixed[c]	200	200	200	400	400	400
% of sales	20.0	18.2	22.2	40.0	36.4	44.4
Total expense	900	955	845	900	935	860
% of sales	90.0	86.8	93.9	90.0	85.0	95.5
Operating income	$ 100	$ 145	$ 55	$ 100	$ 165	$ 40
% of sales	10.0	13.2	6.1	10.0	15.0	4.5

[a]Variable costs: direct labor, materials and supplies.
[b]Semivariable costs: administrative expense, fuel, maintenance.
[c]Fixed costs: depreciation, rents, and interest.

Exhibit 10.3.   Operating leverage.

ment. Companies usually do not reveal this information, but an analysis of cost and expense movement over a business cycle may give a general indication. All costs are variable in the long run, but over a business cycle high fixed costs have a leverage effect on operating income.

In Exhibit 10.3, Company X's variable costs are a steady 50% of sales, whereas its fixed costs average only 20% of sales. Company Y has only 20% in variable costs but 40% in fixed costs and 30% in semivariable costs. In year 1, sales and profit margins are the same. With 10% increase in sales in year 2, Company Y shows a 65% gain in operating income compared with 45% for X. In the third year sales drop 18%, and Y suffers a 76% drop in operating income compared with 62% for X. Company Y has a more highly leveraged operating structure, making its income more sensitive to a change in sales.

(e) Fixed Charges.   Fixed charges consist of **interest** and related expense and an interest factor on **capitalized leases,** both of which are contractual commitments and are deductible for income taxes. Preferred stock dividends are a fixed charge ahead of the common stock, but they lack the firm contractual commitment of debt and they are not deductible for income taxes.

The key measure of the burden of fixed charges is the **interest coverage ratio.** This is calculated as follows:

$$\text{Interest coverage ratio} = \frac{\text{Income before interest and taxes}}{\text{Fixed charges}}$$

This is expressed as "times fixed charges covered," for example, 2.75× (times).

If there are senior and subordinated classes of debt, the coverage ratio for the senior debt is calculated separately by using only the interest cost of the senior debt as the divisor. Coverage for the subordinated debt is calculated on an overall basis, as above.

Interest on borrowed funds used for large construction and development projects is now required to be capitalized under SFAS No. 34, "Capitalization of Interest Cost." However, such **capitalized interest** should be added to interest expense in computing coverage ratios. Nor should interest earned be deducted from interest payable, although it can be included with other income. The bondholder is interested in earnings protection for all interest, regardless of accounting reductions.

The quality perception of fixed income securities is heavily influenced by the coverage ratio. But here again the ratio must be related to the type of business. A ratio of 2.50 times for an electric utility is satisfactory because earnings are stable and it is a regulated monopoly providing a basic service. For an industrial company, a ratio of 5.00× or 6.00× would be more appropriate for a highly rated issue because of more variable earnings in competitive markets.

The **margin of safety** is another ratio used to measure the adequacy of protection for fixed charges.

$$\text{Margin of safety} = \frac{\text{Income after fixed charges before income taxes}}{\text{Sales}}$$

It is simply the percentage of revenues remaining after fixed charges or, in other words, the pretax margin. In terms of a bond it shows the percentage by which revenue can decline without endangering full coverage of interest expense. It is useful in conjunction with the coverage ratio. For example, a company may have a small debt and a correspondingly high interest coverage ratio, but a low margin of safety. This could indicate that any adversity could quickly wipe out interest coverage despite the low debt.

(f) Preferred Dividend Coverage.   The coverage of preferred dividends should be calculated on a comprehensive basis, using the following formula:

$$\text{Preferred dividend coverage} = \frac{\text{Income before interest and taxes}}{\text{Fixed charges} + \text{Pretax preferred dividends}}$$

Because preferred dividends are paid out of income after income taxes, they must be "grossed up" before being inserted in the formula. Preferred dividends must be divided by (1

Debt

$50, senior: Annual interest charges @ 10% = $5
$25, junior (subordinated): Annual interest charges @ 12% = $3
1 million shares of preferred stock: Annual dividend @ $1/share = $1

Partial Income Statement

Income before interest and taxes	$16
Interest: Senior debt	(5)
Junior debt	(3)
Pretax income	$ 8
Taxes @ 37.5%	3
Net income	5
Preferred dividend	(1)
Net income available for common stock	$ 4

Coverage Ratios

Senior debt: 16 ÷ 5 = 3.2×
Total debt: 16 ÷ 8 = 2.0× (Not 11 ÷ 3 = 3.67)
Preferred: 16 ÷ (5 + 3 + (1 ÷ .625)) = 16 ÷ 9.6 = 1.67× (Not 4 ÷ 1 = 4.0)

Exhibit 10.4.   Fixed charge coverage ratios for Company P ($ in millions).

minus the marginal income tax rate) to compute the pretax earnings needed to pay the preferred dividend.

The prior deductions method, which simply divides net income by preferred dividends is not a permissible method unless there is no interest expense. Otherwise this method gives a misleading indication of coverage (see Exhibit 10.4 for fixed charge coverage ratios).

10.8 INCOME TAX ANALYSIS.   Given the complexities of the income tax law, some analysis of income tax accruals is often necessary in determining earning power. Effective tax rates sometimes vary considerably from year to year, leading to significant changes in net income. A starting point is the reconciliation between the statutory rate and the effective rate provided in the annual report. If there is a significant difference, the key factors should be examined to determine whether they are continuing or nonrecurring. This may give clues to any permanent tax advantages enjoyed by the company.

Note also the amount of deferred taxes that arises from the difference in depreciation accounting for financial reporting and tax returns. In the short run the result is a quasi-free government contribution to capital. Will it be permanent or will deferred taxes have to be paid (in an accounting sense) in the future? This question may be worth analysis in longer term projections of a company's financial position.

10.9 EARNING POWER ANALYSIS.   Having analyzed reported net income, the analyst can proceed to the comparison of one company with another and to the projection of future earnings. The types of ratio and trend analysis already discussed are applicable here:

- Net income margin on sales.
- Trend over last 5 and 10 years, measured by compound growth rate, least squares trend, or averages for periods.
- Variability over the same period as measured by the standard deviation from trend, or between cyclical peaks and troughs.

These measures can be used to compare the company with others in the same industry and with companies in other industries. These comparisons will usually reveal which companies have the most favorable trends in earning power.

ACCOUNTING AND REPORTING ISSUES

The impacts of various accounting and reporting issues on reported earnings, analyses of risk and earning power are discussed below.

10.10 THE QUALITY OF EARNINGS.   Financial statements prepared in accordance with GAAP may fall short of meeting the needs of investment analysts for various reasons. GAAP-based financial reporting provides a record of significant accounting events but does not report all relevant economic events. The selection and quantification of economic events qualifying for accounting recognition is highly variable across firms. Within GAAP, managements have considerable latitude in their choice of methods (LIFO vs. FIFO; accelerated vs. straight-line depreciation) and estimates (service lives; residual values) resulting in inconsistencies and measurement biases across firms and over time. Thus, an evaluation of the "Quality of Earnings" is an essential component of a comprehensive analysis of financial statements.

Bernstein and Siegel (1979) define quality of earnings as a measure (qualitative) of the comparative integrity, reliability, and predictive ability of reported earnings. Thus, the quality of earnings is determined by the degree to which selected accounting policies reflect economic reality and represent future earning power. This determination must be made across firms and over time for the firm, allowing an assessment of comparability (similarity of accounting policies between companies) and consistency (continuity over time). Various accounting issues requiring particular attention are discussed in the following sections.

10.11 INVENTORY.   Two principal methods of valuing inventories are FIFO and LIFO, which are more fully explained in Chapter 13. LIFO accounting results in lower reported income, lower current taxes, and better forecasts of future earnings when price levels are increasing and inventory quantities are constant or increasing. Despite tax benefits, many major industrial companies have not adopted LIFO. Earnings comparisons across firms can be misleading if no adjustment is made for differences in inventory accounting. The LIFO earnings of a FIFO firm may be approximated by computing the LIFO effect as follows:

$$\text{LIFO effect} = \text{FIFO beginning inventory} \times \text{percent change in specific}$$
$$\text{price level (for major segment(s) of the firm)}$$

The LIFO effect is the difference in cost of goods sold between the LIFO and FIFO methods. Given the effective tax rate for the firm, the impact on income taxes and reported income can be determined. It is easier to determine the FIFO earnings of a LIFO firm since it will disclose the LIFO reserve or the difference between LIFO and FIFO ending inventories. The difference between two consecutive LIFO reserves is the LIFO effect for that time period. The LIFO reserve should be added to the LIFO ending inventory balance to approximate the current cost of inventories on hand. Earnings reported using LIFO will generally not reflect the same trend/growth rate represented by the same earnings stream under FIFO. A liquidation of LIFO layers will increase reported income and current taxes. This impact on net income is generally disclosed in the footnotes. However, liquidations may signal changes in future earnings and/or investment in the affected segment. The analyst should not confuse liquidations with declines in the LIFO reserve that are a result of decreases in inventory prices.

The traditional LIFO method is a "unit LIFO" procedure—generally used in industries with very few basic products. However, LIFO may be used in conjunction with "pools" of products. The pools include products that are substantially identical, that is, similar as to materials, use, or interchangeability. Different pooling approaches will affect comparability across firms and over time within the same firm.

10.12 DEPRECIATION.   Periodic depreciation expense allocates the cost of long-lived assets to operating periods during which the assets are used in production. The expense is a function of the chosen depreciation method, asset lives, and residual values. Although a substantial number of companies use accelerated depreciation methods for income tax reporting, few do so for financial reporting. Those that do so will report lower and more conservative net income. The cash impact of depreciation is due to the tax savings generated by the depreciation method used for income tax reporting. The use of different depreciation methods in tax and financial reporting results in a difference between the tax liability and reported tax expense—that is, a deferred tax expense, which is disclosed in the footnotes. This deferred tax amount divided by the federal statutory tax rate gives an approximation of the difference in depreciation expense and can be used to adjust reported net income. Since depreciation expense is based on historical cost, it tends to overstate income when price levels are increasing. Thus, accelerated depreciation methods may provide a reasonable approximation of replacement or current cost depreciation.

Asset lives also affect reported depreciation expense. Management has some latitude in the determination of asset lives since judgment and experience are used in this choice. Footnote disclosure of depreciation policies can be used to compare asset lives of similar companies in the same industry. A comparison of the ratio of depreciation expense to gross fixed assets will frequently eliminate the effects of different depreciation curves and different useful lives.

The average age of fixed assets used in operations may be computed by dividing the accumulated depreciation by depreciation expense. The ratio of gross property, plant, and equipment to depreciation expense reflects the average life assumption used in reporting. Increasing investment due to expansion or declining investment due to deteriorating business conditions will distort these ratios suggesting the need for caution in interpreting trends in these ratios over time and across firms.

The analyst should use Schedules V and VI of SEC 10-K to obtain data needed for these ratios. Schedule V reports capital expenditures, retirements, and foreign currency translation effects for the period. Schedule VI gives the transactions that affect the accumulated depreciation accounts, including the depreciation charged to costs during the period. In contrast, the depreciation expense reported in the income or cash flow statement is sometimes reported net of other accounting adjustments.

Changes in depreciation methods and asset lives should be evaluated carefully for their effect on the quality of earnings. The depreciation policy adopted for idled/underutilized facilities should be analyzed for inferences regarding the quantification and timing of unamortized costs expected to be recovered through future operations. Changes in depreciation policy may mask a deteriorating financial condition or pervasive asset impairment.

10.13 EXPENSE DEFERRALS.   Various discretionary costs are subject to management control, and they may be reduced by deferral to later periods or by capitalization. Preopening and certain types of developmental expenses fall into this category. Interest incurred during construction was variously expensed or capitalized before the FASB adopted SFAS No. 34, which requires the capitalization of qualifying interest. Although this rule is less conservative, it promotes greater comparability in financial reporting. However, it cannot adjust for differences in capital structure and ultimately lowers the quality of all earnings. Goodwill generated through acquisitions may be amortized over periods as long as 40 years and should be evaluated for comparability across similar firms and validity of amortization period for the firm in light of business conditions and competing technologies.

Analysts should track various discretionary costs over time and across firms. Examples are advertising costs, research and development expenditures, repairs and maintenance costs, and the allowance for bad debts from receivables.

10.14 REVENUE RECOGNITION.   Revenue is generally recognized when goods are sold or as services are rendered. Since the activities of one period may generate cash flows in subsequent periods both the quantification and timing of revenue recognition present problems. The timing of sales and services, uncertainties regarding the collection of expected inflows and expected future costs of providing services should be evaluated in the context of the firm's operations and compared to prevailing industry practices. Various specialized industries including franchising, real estate, motion pictures, and television require particular attention. The increasing emphasis on fee-based services in the financial sector of the economy and the growth of leasing also present challenging revenue recognition problems.

10.15 DISCONTINUED OPERATIONS, EXTRAORDINARY GAINS (LOSSES), AND UN-USUAL ITEMS.   The assessment of future earning power is a function of the predictability of income statistics. Thus, analysts are concerned with revenues and expenses directly related to the normal and recurring operations since they reflect future earning power. The inclusion of unusual or nonrecurring events would distort the predictability of reported income. Inconsistently applied definitions or interpretations of recurring versus nonrecurring events would reduce comparability across firms and may provide a basis for manipulation or smoothing of income. However, unusual and extraordinary data may be relevant to the evaluation of managerial efficiency.

Existing reporting standards require separate reporting of material, unusual, *and* infrequent events in the income statement. These events are evaluated with reference to the specific and similar firms in the same industry in light of the firm's environment. Qualifying extraordinary items are reported separately, net of tax effects, after operating income. The related earnings-per-share amounts also are disclosed separately. Examples include expropriation of assets by foreign governments and gains or losses due to debt extinguishment.

Events that are either unusual or infrequent but not both may be reported on a separate line in the income statement but cannot be reported net of taxes. Impairment of long-lived assets and material write-offs or write-downs may be reported on a separate line in the income statement. Additional footnote disclosure often accompanies these events, and it may provide insights into their effect on future earning power and cash flows.

The operating results of and the gain (loss) due to disposal of qualifying discontinued segments also must be reported separately, net of taxes, after income from continuing operations. The related earnings-per-share effects also are presented separately. Discontinued segments are reported separately if their assets, results of operations, and other activities can be clearly segregated from the assets, results of operations, and other activities of the firm. This segregation must be accomplished physically, operationally, and for financial reporting purposes.

10.16 CHANGING PRICES.   As financial statements are largely based on historical costs, price changes tend to reduce the usefulness of such statements. Whereas periods of high inflation have ushered in attempts to provide inflation-adjusted data, most recently with SFAS No. 33, most financial statements provide little assistance to the user in gauging the effects of inflation on the enterprise.

Past approaches have taken one of two competing tracks. Constant dollar accounting, whereby financial statements are adjusted for changes in the purchasing power of the reporting currency, has the advantages of ease of preparation and ease of audit. Unfortunately there is little evidence that such data has any utility, and financial statement users have shown little interest in constant dollar data.

Current cost data appears to have more relevance to financial statement analysis, despite the softness of the data and inconsistent application of past standards. Many users seek to replace historical cost financial statements with ones based on current values. The merger and acquisition boom of recent years has increased interest in current value statements.

In the case of monetary assets, adjustment is generally not required because price changes have little direct impact on the fair value of such assets. The areas of interest are generally "physical assets," especially inventories, fixed assets, and investments.

When the LIFO method of inventory valuation is used, the analyst can use required disclosures to make the necessary adjustments. Adding back the LIFO reserve (which must be disclosed) provides a reasonable estimate of the current value of inventories. When FIFO or average cost is used, inventories are already stated at close to current value.

The current cost of fixed assets is more difficult to estimate. Although both ASR No. 190 and SFAS No. 33 required estimates of such current cost from companies subject to their requirements, there was considerable leeway in application. Going back to such data (SFAS No. 33 data was last required in 1985) may provide a starting point, but great care must be taken. Some data were arrived at by simply indexing original cost using general construction cost indicators. Such approximations will fail to capture the true value of real estate holdings.

For public companies, the 10-K annual report filed with the SEC may contain a considerable amount of information about the location and extent of real estate holdings. For some categories (shopping centers, hotels, etc.) industry rules of thumb may enable one to translate physical data (e.g., square footage) into market value data.

Clues may be available in the financial statements. Real estate taxes paid may indicate assessed values. When borrowings are secured by specific holdings, some inference about value can be made. The income (or cash flow) generated by real estate investments may be an indication of value. Assets acquired via a purchase method acquisition can be assumed to have been written up at that time; if goodwill was created, one can assume that the write-up was the maximum possible.

When natural resources are included in fixed assets, additional information may be provided. Companies with reserves of oil and natural gas are required (SFAS No. 69) to provide information about the physical quantities and their discounted present value based on current costs and prices. Although such data are based on estimates and preparers strongly discourage their use, these data are widely used in the financial community to value such reserves. For other natural resource holdings (coal, precious metals, etc.) only physical data must be disclosed. The analyst must make assumptions in order to value these holdings, but the result is usually closer to fair value than the historical cost of such holdings.

Investments may also require adjustment. If investee financial statements are available, they can be used to value the holding, perhaps by comparison with public companies in the same industry. In making such comparisons, the user should take care to adjust for differences in accounting methods and financial leverage. When investments include holdings of public companies, current market value can be used in place of cost.

The discussion thus far has focused on balance sheet valuation. However the income statement should also be adjusted for changing prices. To the extent that income includes "holding gains" resulting from price increases, whether realized or unrealized, the financial markets may discount reported earnings.

In the area of inventories, the use of LIFO removes the effect of rising prices from reported earnings. For non-LIFO inventories an approximation must be made. If the company is in one line of business, a government or private price index may be employed to estimate the inflation component. The percentage price change should be multiplied by the starting inventory, and the result (after tax) should be subtracted from operating net income. For multiple lines of business, this should be done on a segmented basis when possible.

Current cost depreciation may be difficult to estimate because of the required assumptions. If the amount of capital spending that does not create higher capacity can be estimated, it may be the best answer. This is because economic depreciation can be defined as the expenditures necessary to leave end-of-year capacity equal to that at the beginning of the period.

10.17 FOREIGN OPERATIONS.   Financial statements of companies with operations outside of the United States are made more complex by the effects of changing currency rates. Despite some opinion to the contrary, SFAS No. 52 **did not** result in the removal of all such impacts from financial statements.

The functional currencies chosen by a company for its foreign operations have an important effect on how currency changes affect reported earnings. Assets and liabilities of foreign subsidiaries are remeasured from local currencies into functional currencies using the principles of SFAS No. 8. Thus, all translation gains and losses resulting from the remeasurement process are included in earnings immediately. In some cases, where the U.S. dollar has been chosen as the functional currency for all foreign operations, there is considerable potential earnings volatility.

Under SFAS No. 52, the translation of functional currency balance sheets into the reporting currency (U.S. dollar for U.S. companies) generates gains or losses that are deferred to a separate component of stockholders equity. Such gains or losses accumulate indefinitely unless a foreign subsidiary is sold or impairment is recognized.

The U.S. dollar must be used as the functional currency in a hyperinflationary economy (defined as 3-year cumulative inflation exceeding 100%). As a result translation gains and losses are included in earnings.

The difference between remeasurement (SFAS No. 8) and translation (SFAS No. 52) is not simply that of recognition of gains and losses. The balance sheet exposure is defined differently as well. Remeasurement uses the temporal method. For most companies, this means that inventories and fixed assets are translated using historical rates; almost all other assets and liabilities are translated at current exchange rates. The exposure to currency fluctuation under SFAS No. 8 is, in practice, the net monetary asset position. Under SFAS

No. 52, in contrast, the exposure is the net investment, regardless of the composition of assets and liabilities. It is, therefore, quite possible for a currency rate change to result in gains under remeasurement (SFAS No. 8) but losses under translation (SFAS No. 52).

Unfortunately, the disclosure requirements of SFAS No. 52 are minimal. Unless the financial statement preparer is willing to provide additional information about functional currencies, the analyst must resort to guessing.

Even when the translation effects of foreign currency changes are excluded from the income statement, reported sales and earnings may be materially affected by such changes. Revenues and costs incurred in foreign currencies are translated into the reporting currency using average exchange rates for the period. When the reporting currency rises, for example, foreign currency earnings and sales will appear to be smaller. Given the large fluctuations of the dollar against other major currencies in recent years, these impacts have had a significant impact on the apparent sales and earnings trends of companies with large foreign operations.

Prior to the effective date of SFAS No. 95, cash flow statements were often distorted by currency rate changes. Real changes and translation effects were mixed together, reducing the usefulness of cash flow data. SFAS No. 95, however, requires that reporting currency cash flow statements be translated directly from functional currency statements. As a result, translation impacts are excluded. Use of average exchange rates still has an impact on the trend of cash flow data, however.

The analysis of foreign operations cannot be confined to looking at the accounting consequences of exchange rate changes. Such changes may have real economic consequences that are quite different from the accounting impacts.

For foreign operations that are completely isolated from external influences, it may be possible to ignore the economic consequences of currency rate changes. In such cases, changes in the U.S. dollar equivalent of the subsidiary net worth may be a fair indicator of changes in economic net worth.

For most foreign operations, however, changing exchange rates do have an impact on local operations. To the extent that local operations compete with imports from or exports to other countries, currency rate changes will affect real profitability. Regardless of whether operations are accounted for using SFAS No. 8 or SFAS No. 52, it is unlikely that the accounting impacts will mirror the economic changes. In some cases (e.g., import competitive), the two may diverge; a rising local currency will increase the translated net worth while decreasing the real profitability (and hence real net worth) of the foreign subsidiary.

Analysis of a company with foreign operations, therefore, requires two types of analysis. First, the user must understand how the reported results of foreign operations have been affected by the rate changes. Second, he must examine the underlying economic relationships in order to understand the trend of real profitability of such operations.

10.18 POSTEMPLOYMENT BENEFITS.   Companies with defined benefit pension plans must account for such plans in accordance with SFAS No. 87 issued in 1985. As current accounting standards permit considerable latitude in making actuarial assumptions and provide for deferred recognition of differences between assumptions and realized results, both income statement and balance sheet may contain considerable "noise."

The balance sheet generally includes only the cumulative differences between accrued pension cost and contributions actually made. The best measure of pension fund status is normally the difference between the fair value of fund assets and the projected benefit obligation. The gap between the amounts reflected on the balance sheet and the funded status results from deferred recognition of actuarial gains and losses, plan amendments, and the initial impact of SFAS No. 87.

Replacing the amounts actually recognized with the funded status will reflect the actual plan status, as if the plan had been consolidated with the corporate parent. In some cases, when plan termination can be assumed, the accumulated benefit obligation may be a better measure of the liability. Note that both liability measures are highly sensitive to the choice of discount rate. That rate can vary from company to company and (for the same company) from year to year.

Pension cost, an operating expense, consists of four components. Service cost, interest on the projected benefit obligation, and assumed return on assets may be considered the "normal" portion of pension cost. Amortization components vary from year to year. Note that even the "normal" costs are sensitive to the choice of discount rate and assumed rate of return on assets. Comparability and consistency cannot be assumed.

Postemployment life and health benefits have historically been accounted for on a "pay-as-you-go" basis by most companies. Given the rapidly rising cost of medical care, the cost of retiree health care has increased dramatically. The FASB is currently considering a requirement that other retiree benefits be accounted for using the accrual method employed by SFAS No. 87. The transition period is likely to be quite long. Nonetheless, financial statement analysis should be taking the liabilities for such benefits into account.

Because few retiree benefit plans (other than pensions) are funded, there is normally only a liability to consider. In the absence of better data, rules of thumb of 15–30 times the latest annual expense are often used. This liability would be a reduction to net worth. For mature companies (high ratio of retirees to active employees) the multiple will tend to be lower; for less mature companies (few retirees), it may be much higher.

Income statement adjustments are also difficult in the absence of data. Some companies have estimated that annual cost under the proposed FASB standard will be 3–6 times current cost. This figure would include amortization of the liability resulting from initial implementation of the new standard. Here again the effect is greater for less mature companies.

10.19 MERGERS AND ACQUISITIONS.   Companies that make significant acquisitions transform their financial statements as a result. Analysis of such companies must attempt to understand the impact of these transactions.

When the pooling-of-interests method has been used, the financial statements of the two entities are combined both retroactively and prospectively. This has the advantage of preserving comparability over time.

One disadvantage from the analyst's perspective is the creation of a fictitious "past history." An acquisition made even after the close of a fiscal year results in inclusion of the acquired entity in the financial statements for that year. Earnings, cash flow, or other desirable attributes can be made to appear the result of the acquirer's management effort. Companies whose shares sell at relatively high price–earnings ratios find it especially easy to "bootstrap" themselves to higher reported earnings.

Another disadvantage of pooling is the suppression of the true purchase price. The acquired entity's balance sheet is merged, without any adjustment, into the balance sheet of the acquirer. Undervalued assets may be sold, and such "gains" will be considered to be income. Yet these assets were almost certainly paid for by the acquiring company.

The purchase method has a different set of pluses and minuses. Under this method, the assets and liabilities of the acquired entity are revalued to current market; any excess of purchase price over fair value of assets acquired becomes goodwill. The income statement reflects the operating results of the acquiree only following the acquisition date.

Under this method, the purchase price is explicitly recognized as to the acquiree only. The asset and liability accounts of the postmerger enterprise contain a mixture of original cost and revalued components. Ratios will be distorted as compared with the postmerger balance sheet under the pooling method.

The existence of goodwill tells the analyst that the assets acquired have been written up as far as possible. For tax reasons (goodwill amortization is normally not tax-deductible) acquirers prefer to allocate purchase cost to tangible assets to the greatest extent possible. Thus recently acquired assets are unlikely to have fair values above their revalued carrying amounts. Goodwill and other intangibles are normally deducted from net worth by analysts prior to computation of book value.

As the operating results of the acquired company are included only after the acquisition date, an "illusion" of growth may be created. This is especially true when many small acquisitions are made; it becomes impossible for the outsider to track the contribution of each acquisition to future operating results. When an acquisition is significant, and in a different line of business, the SFAS No. 14 segment data may permit rough adjustments for the acquisition.

The operations of acquired businesses will also be affected by the accounting adjustments resulting from the revaluation of assets and liabilities. Depreciation and cost-of-goods-sold are frequently increased by the amortization of asset revaluations, and debt incurred for acquisition purposes will generate additional interest cost.

10.20 PUSH DOWN ACCOUNTING.   When an entity that has been acquired in an acquisition accounted for by the purchase method issues its own financial statements, those statements may reflect that transaction. In most cases the purchase method adjustments will be "pushed down" into the financial statements of the acquiree.

This is often seen when an acquired company has publicly held debt or preferred stock and, therefore continues to publish separate financial statements. Such statements may also be presented to bank lenders, creditors, and customers.

The footnotes of these financial statements will normally show the effect of the purchase method adjustments. Users of such statements should bear in mind that the purchase method adjustments will distort ratios derived from both balance sheet and income statement data.

When companies that have been taken private through leveraged buyouts are taken public again, their statements will usually reflect "push down" accounting. Comparisons of such entities with others that have not gone through the revaluation process must take into account the effects of "push down" on the balance sheet and income statement.

10.21 ANALYSIS OF SEGMENT DATA.   Public companies with more than one line of business are required by SFAS No. 14 to provide data on each segment of their business. This data, despite limitations, is generally helpful in assessing the firm's operating results.

Companies subject to SFAS No. 14 guidelines must provide sales, operating income, depreciation expense, capital spending, and total assets for each line of business. Some companies provide more detailed information. Sears Roebuck & Company, for example, provides full financial statements for each major business segment.

The trend of sales and earnings for each business segment should be examined closely. In some cases, poorly performing businesses mask the impact of other segments with superior sales and earnings growth. The depreciation and capital spending data give some indication of how management is allocating capital. The trend of gross assets may also reflect management decisions about the allocation of capital.

When companies enter a new line of business via an acquisition, the segment data may enable the analyst to track the acquired company's results over time.

Segment data is not required to be reported on an interim basis. Many companies do provide such data voluntarily. When available, interim segment data can provide early warning of changes in business trends.

Emhart Corporation provides an excellent example of how the analysis of segment data can improve the understanding of corporate results. As shown in Exhibit 10.5, Emhart reports sales and operating income for five segments. Corporate sales and operating income increased by 32% and 39% respectively over the period 1986–1988. The performance of individual segments varied widely over this period.

Information and Electronic Systems accounted for virtually all of the sales increase; the gain in all other segments combined was less than 3%. Sales of the machinery segment actually fell by one-third. Information and Electronic Systems accounted for nearly half of the 2-year increase in operating income.

EMHART CORPORATION

	1988	1987	1986
Revenues			
Industrial			
Components	$ 641.8	$ 671.9	$ 653.9
Fastening Systems	640.5	638.8	576.3
Machinery	279.0	291.1	419.2
	1,561.3	1,601.8	1,649.4
Information and Electronic Systems	653.7	438.3	39.3
Consumer	547.5	414.4	405.6
Total	$2,762.5	$2,454.5	$2,094.3
Operating Income (loss)			
Industrial			*
Components	$ 63.8	$ 65.7	$ 48.2
Fastening Systems	74.8	78.7	68.3
Machinery	42.7	34.1	44.4
	181.3	178.5	160.9
Information and Electronic Systems	37.2	22.3	2.0
Consumer	84.8	68.3	60.4
Total	303.3	269.1	223.3
Corporate Expense	(35.0)	(32.9)	(30.3)
Total	$ 268.3	$ 236.2	$ 193.0

Change in Trade Revenues

1988 versus 1987	Foreign Exchange Translation	Acquisition/ Divestiture Activity—Net	Price	Volume/ Mix/New Products	Total
Industrial					
Components	$ 10	$ (64)	$ 7	$17	$ (30)
Fastening Systems	19	(38)	17	4	2
Machinery	11	(44)	9	12	(12)
	40	(146)	33	33	(40)
Information and Electronic Systems		197		18	215
Consumer	6	84	20	23	133
	$ 46	$ 135	$53	$74	$ 308

*1986 before provision for restructuring.

Exhibit 10.5. Revenues, operating income (loss), and change in trade revenues ($ in millions).

1987 versus 1986	Foreign Exchange Translation	Acquisition/ Divestiture Activity—Net	Price	Volume/ Mix/New Products	Total
Industrial					
Components	$ 46	$ (56)	$ 7	$21	$ 18
Fastening Systems	40	(16)	23	15	62
Machinery	26	(155)	10	(9)	(128)
	112	(227)	40	27	(48)
Information and Electronic Systems		388		11	399
Consumer	4	(5)	10		9
	$116	$ 156	$50	$38	$ 360

Exhibit 10.5. *Continued.*

Further insight is obtained from Exhibit 10.5. The data, which are not required disclosure, show the sources of changes in revenues. From this data it is evident that price changes, the decline in the U.S. dollar, and acquisition/divestiture activity played major roles. The sales increase for Information and Electronic Systems, for example, resulted almost completely from acquisitions. Divestitures accounted for the drop in machinery sales.

10.22 ANALYSIS OF INTERIM RESULTS.   When analyzing a company's financial statements, the latest annual data are normally supplemented by subsequent interim reports. Although use of interim data is essential because of its timeliness, some caution must be exercised.

For public companies, the user should always obtain the 10-Q quarterly reports filed with the SEC. Shareholder reports are often highly abbreviated. The 10-Q will contain financial statements that may be the equivalent of those found in the annual report except for footnotes.

The lack of footnotes sometimes limits the usefulness of interim reports. Whereas major accounting changes should be disclosed in the 10-Q, changes in estimates may not be. Some of the financial data may be condensed as well.

However, the major reason for caution in the use of interim data is the possibility of drawing misleading conclusions. Companies with a high degree of seasonality will produce interim results that are not an indicator of annual performance. Retailers, for example, produce a disproportionate part of earnings in the quarter that includes the Christmas selling period. A secondary peak around Easter is also normal. Interim results of seasonal companies should, therefore, be compared with the interim results of the corresponding period for prior years.

Accounting for income taxes may create some difficulty in interpreting interim results. As income tax expense is determined on an annual basis, interim tax expense must be estimated based on assumptions about the full year. Income tax expense for the first quarter, for example, must be determined by using the estimated tax rate for the full year. This rate must be reestimated each quarter. Changes in the estimated tax rate may distort quarterly results.

LIFO inventory accounting is also determined on an annual basis and depends on prices and physical inventory levels at the end of the year. Here again, quarterly results depend on estimates of the year-end position, and a new estimate must be made each quarter.

More generally, there is more scope for companies to "manage" earnings on a quarterly basis. Expenses can be deferred (or accrued) in ways that would not be permitted at a fiscal year-end. In addition, transactions may be accounted for differently once the auditors have had their say.

10.23 INTERNATIONAL REPORTING DIFFERENCES.   Differences in accounting and reporting standards among countries may result in a significant lack of comparability between U.S. financial statements and those of other countries. Although the IASC and national standards setters have made considerable efforts to narrow these differences, the user of financial statements must be alert. Major areas of concern include:

- Tax-book conformity, often absent in the United States, is frequently required in foreign jurisdictions.
- Full consolidation has not been common practice outside the United States. However IASC Standard 27 requires full consolidation effective in 1990.
- LIFO is almost never used outside of the United States for reporting purposes but may, at times, be allowed for tax purposes, especially when inflation is high.
- Accounting for foreign operations may vary considerably from SFAS No. 52.
- Goodwill arising from purchase method acquisitions may be written off immediately or amortized rapidly in some non-U.S. jurisdictions.
- Revaluation of assets may be permitted. In the past revaluation has been limited to physical assets, but there is a recent trend toward revaluing brand names and other intangibles.
- Undefined reserves, forbidden to U.S. companies by SFAS No. 5, is permitted in many foreign jurisdictions.
- The distinction between "operating" and "extraordinary" items is drawn differently in different countries.
- Because of national differences in social security systems, as well as different accounting requirements, postemployment benefits may differ widely among jurisdictions.

When comparing companies from different jurisdictions, every effort must be made to identify and adjust for all such differences. Unless this is done, conclusions drawn may be biased by inconsistent data.

BALANCE SHEET ANALYSIS

10.24 ELEMENTS OF THE BALANCE SHEET.   The balance sheet reports the status of the company's financial position at a point in time, in contrast to the income statement, which reflects the flow of operating and earning activities during a period. Because earnings are essential for an enterprise's financial health, primary analytical emphasis has focused on earning power, but balance sheet analysis is equally important for a comprehensive understanding of a company's financial position and progress.

The main components of the balance sheet are the enterprise's assets or financial resources and the equities or claims against those resources. Assets represent probable future economic benefits obtained or controlled by the enterprise as a result of past transactions or events. Assets may be physical or tangible, for example, inventories, plant and equipment, and natural resources. Some assets are intangible in that they represent legal claims or rights to economic resources, for instance, patents and copyrights.

Equities are either external claims against the enterprise's resources (i.e., liabilities), or they represent the "residual" interests of the firm's owners, called stockholders' or owners' equity. Liabilities are probable future sacrifices of economic resources because of the enterprise's present obligations to transfer resources or provide services to external claimants in the future as a result of past transactions or events. Examples are accounts payable, taxes, and bonds payable.

Owners' equity is the residual interest of the owners of the enterprise and represents the excess of the assets over liabilities. It includes preferred and common stock, additional paid-in capital, and the earnings retained in the enterprise. Owners' equity represents the capital invested in the firm by its owners.

Assets and liabilities are defined as economic resources and claims against these resources. However, the financial reporting system emphasizes the recording of accounting events, rather than economic events. Many relevant economic events receive no recognition in financial statements; for example, the impact of price-level changes on reported quantifications of assets and liabilities is virtually ignored since financial statements are based on historical costs.

The selection of economic events that receive accounting recognition is discretionary and highly variable across firms. Leases, which in substance may be installment purchases of assets, may not receive accounting recognition if the lease contract is structured to avoid capitalization criteria in accounting standards. Managements may also select from different methods and use different estimates in quantifying selected accounting events, for example, inventory valuation, depreciation methods, service lives, and pension costs. These factors lead to significant inconsistencies and measurement biases in the financial statements of different firms and of the same firm over time.

The explosive growth in off-balance-sheet financing transactions such as sales or securitization of receivables, take-or-pay contracts, and leases has increased the divergence between reported accounting and economic assets and liabilities. These transactions are generally structured as executory contracts thereby avoiding accounting recognition (see section 10.26(g)).

Balance sheet classification of reported assets and liabilities is based on their respective time cycles for realization. Current assets and liabilities are expected to be realized or paid within a 12-month period or within the normal operating cycle of the firm, whichever is longer. Long-term assets are intended for use in the business, such as plant and equipment, or are not intended for sale, such as investments in affiliates. Long-term liabilities such as bonds payable are due after one year. Owners' equity represents the residual interest and as such is the permanent capital invested in the firm. Balance sheet analysis revolves around the interrelationships among its various components.

10.25 LIQUIDITY ANALYSIS.   Short-term lenders, suppliers, and creditors focus on the liquidity of the firm in their assessment of its risk level. The evaluation concerns the firm's ability to meet its maturing obligations at a given point in time; equally important are changes in that ability over time. Cash or cash equivalents become available through liquidation of short-term debt and equity instruments, collection of receivables, and conversion of inventories into receivables through sales, thence into cash. In ongoing businesses, continuing operations require new investments in inventories and receivables to replace those converted to cash. Thus, receivables and inventories are to a considerable extent "permanent capital," not liquid assets, except for seasonal businesses that experience troughs and peaks. However, as financial markets evolve, securitization of receivables and more effective inventory financing and management techniques may erode the "permanence" of capital invested in these liquid assets.

(a) Analytical Ratios.   Two ratios are traditionally used in the assessment of short-term liquidity and financial flexibility—the current ratio and the quick ratio. They apply primarily to industrial, merchandising, and service companies rather than to utilities or financial services companies. These ratios are defined as follows:

1. Current ratio $= \dfrac{\text{Current assets (cash and equivalents, receivables and inventories)}}{\text{Current liabilities (payables, accruals, taxes and debt due in 1 year)}}$

2. Quick ratio $= \dfrac{\text{Cash and equivalents plus receivables}}{\text{Current liabilities}}$

	A	B	C
Cash	$10,000	$ 10,000	$25,000
Receivables	20,000	35,000	20,000
Inventory	20,000	55,000	20,000
Current assets	$50,000	$100,000	$65,000
Bank loan	—	35,000	—
Payables	5,000	15,000	5,000
Accruals	10,000	15,000	10,000
Taxes	10,000	10,000	15,000
Current liabilities	25,000	75,000	30,000
Net working capital	$25,000	$ 25,000	$35,000
Ratios			
1. Current ratio	2.00	1.33	2.17
2. Quick ratio	1.20	0.60	1.50

Exhibit 10.6.   Liquidity ratios for Company N.

The application of these ratios is illustrated in Exhibit 10.6.

Company N begins the year (column A) with a current ratio of 2.0, which reflects an ample margin of current assets over current liabilities; the quick ratio of 1.2 indicates that liquid assets alone exceed all current liabilities. The quick ratio is a more conservative measure of relative liquidity in that it assumes liquidity is provided only by cash, cash equivalents, and receivables that normally can be realized in the short run without loss. Inventories usually are further removed from realization and may be subject to loss. Inventories of actively traded commodities, for example, wheat, can be very liquid and should be included among liquid assets in the quick ratio for relevant industries.

(i) Using the Ratios.   The measures of liquidity provide an indication of the firm's short-run ability to meet its obligations, but they are superficial standing alone, are limited in that they provide a picture at a specific point in time, and may be distorted at year-end.

The year-to-year trends and business characteristics also must be analyzed along with continued evaluation of the trend of earnings. A good liquidity position and financial flexibility can erode rapidly with losses and vice versa. If Company N's liquidity position changes in 1 year from column A to column B, an obvious deterioration has occurred. All liquidity ratios are lower, and receivables and inventory are higher, increasing the current assets. Current liabilities have increased since short-term bank debt has been used to finance the increase in current assets.

The analyst and short-term creditor should review the trends in and impact on operating cash flow and earnings through an analysis of trends in sales (by segments, where possible), the collectibility of receivables, and the salability of inventories to evaluate sources of increase in risk and decrease in financial flexibility. The ratio of operating cash flow to average current liabilities may provide insights into causes of changes in the current ratio:

$$\text{Operating cash flow to current liabilities} = \frac{\text{Cash provided by operations}}{\text{Average current liabilities}}$$

Empirical research by Casey and Bartczak (1985) suggests that healthy firms exhibit ratios of 40% or better.

However, the changes in and trends of liquidity ratios should be interpreted with caution. When the current ratio exceeds 1.00, equal increases (decreases) in current assets and current liabilities will decrease (improve) the current ratio but need not reflect a decline (improvement) in financial flexibility. Temporary plant shutdowns or recessions may reduce current liabilities or allow the firm to use up inventories with a resulting improvement in current ratios. In contrast, the firm may build up inventories, financing the increase with short-term debt in anticipation of increased sales. These actions may be appropriate but would depress current ratios.

The firm's liquidity position is also susceptible to manipulation. At year-end, purchases may be delayed or receivables sold and proceeds used to retire short-term debt. The use of averages in the ratios and a comparison of ratios over time will mitigate this problem to some extent. Acquisitions and divestitures also significantly distort current ratios. However, some disclosures required by SFAS No. 95, "Statement of Cash Flows" will allow analysts to adjust for these effects.

Lenders providing short-term bank debt and publicly traded long-term debt generally control the liquidity risk by imposing requirements for maintenance of minimum current ratios or working capital. These indenture restrictions or debt covenants are disclosed in footnotes to financial statements and often are included in filings with the SEC 10-K reports. The analyst should monitor the firm's maintenance of liquidity ratios specified in debt covenants and evaluate accounting changes, for example, switching to FIFO inventory valuation from LIFO, which may mask deteriorating financial conditions.

The analyst should use footnote disclosures of significant accounting policies to adjust published figures to a more realistic basis. If the LIFO method is used for inventory accounting, the reported book value of inventories may well be far below current value. Footnote disclosures of LIFO reserves should be used to gross up LIFO inventories to equivalent FIFO amounts, improving the current ratio and augmenting comparability with FIFO companies. The marketable securities also should be adjusted from book to market values allowing for tax effects. These adjustments would make the current assets more representative of the firm's liquidity position.

(ii) Seasonal and Cyclical Factors.   Most seasonal businesses have fiscal years ending at the conclusion of the sales cycle when the financial position is most liquid. At interim periods the current ratios may change considerably from the previous year-end without any change in net working capital and financial flexibility.

Assume that Company N in Exhibit 10.6 is in the Christmas trade and columns A and C represent its financial position at successive January 31 fiscal year-ends, whereas column B reflects its position on October 31. To build inventories for the seasonal peak, the company borrows from its bank, and finances receivables by allowing payables and accruals to build up in the normal course of business. At year-end, inventories are liquidated, receivables collected, bank loans repaid, and net profit of $10,000 is added to the net working capital or liquidity position. During the year, Company N also increases long-term debt to expand the plant.

Although the ratios in column B are the same as in the trend analysis in the first case, the circumstances are different. The lower liquidity ratios reflect a temporary condition just before the inventories begin to move into sales. At the end of the season (column C) the liquidity position has returned to "normal" with some improvement due to profitable operations. The analyst should evaluate firm performance relative to the normal pattern of the Christmas trade and industry performance. If the merchandise does not move at Christmas, the year-end position will be column B, rather than column C.

Highly cyclical industries or building contractors may display this same pattern of change over a longer period as volume increases and then subsides.

(iii) A Fast Turnover Business.   A retail grocery chain, for example, is mostly a cash business and usually has few or no receivables. It can operate adequately on a current ratio of less than 2.0. Cash is being received as quickly as sales are made, and payables and accruals accumulate and turn over at longer intervals. High daily cash receipts and quick inventory turnover allow such firms to raise cash for unanticipated needs very quickly.

(iv) A Slow Turnover Business.   A steel company, on the other hand, will have very large inventories and receivables and typically will have a current ratio of 3.0, 4.0, or higher. However, the receivables and inventory are necessary for operations and may not be immediately available to meet current obligations. Hence, a steel company may be no more liquid than the retail grocery chain despite its nominally higher current ratio.

Companies with diverse businesses may include fast and slow turnover segments, manufacturing, retail, and financial operations and divisions with different or conflicting restrictions on current ratios. To the extent possible, the analyst should adjust for these differences using information in footnotes and segment reports.

(b) Activity Ratios.   Liquidity analysis can be augmented by an assessment of how effectively the firm uses its liquid assets. Various activity ratios are used to analyze the operating cycle, that is, the flow of materials into finished merchandise into receivables into cash.

The inventory turnover ratio provides an indicator of the efficiency of the firm's operations. It is calculated as follows:

$$\frac{\text{Cost of goods sold}}{\text{Average inventory}}$$

The number of days that inventory is on hand can be calculated as:

$$\frac{365}{\text{Inventory turnover}}$$

The turnover ratio and the number of days that inventory is on hand should be analyzed for trends over time and compared to similar firms in the industry. The latter comparison requires an adjustment for any differences in inventory methods. Ideally, for industries experiencing rising prices, the cost of goods sold should be stated in LIFO terms and the inventory balances should reflect current costs (FIFO). Thus both numerator and denominator would reflect current costs. Use of LIFO inventory cost to compute turnover will inflate that ratio, especially if the LIFO reserve is high relative to LIFO cost.

The receivables turnover and the average number of days that receivables are outstanding indicate the effectiveness of the firm's credit policies and the length of time it takes to convert the receivables to cash:

$$\text{Receivables turnover} = \frac{\text{Net credit sales}}{\text{Average receivables}}$$

$$\text{Number of days receivables are outstanding} = \frac{365}{\text{Receivables turnover}}$$

This ratio is only meaningful when compared to credit terms used by the firm and, if possible, similar firms in the industry. If the credit terms are net 30 days but receivables are outstanding for 50 days on average, the collections are slow. When, receivables have been sold, the analyst should use footnote data to adjust turnover calculations (see section 10.26(g)).

The total number of days that inventories are on hand and the number of days that receivables are outstanding indicate the length of the operating cycle of the firm—the amount of time it takes the firm to convert materials into cash. A review of these ratios over time and with similar companies would allow a cash flow forecast and indicate whether short-term obligations can be met with cash flows from operations. Thus, activity ratios are particularly relevant to short-term creditors such as banks. Creditors should also monitor the earnings power, which is essential to maintain solvency and meet maturing obligations. Without adequate margins, the operating cycle will not produce the cash required to repay debts.

10.26 ANALYSIS OF LONG-TERM ASSETS AND LIABILITIES.   Generally, noncurrent assets are stated at their historical cost book values adjusted for depreciation and as such rarely reflect their economic worth. However, noncurrent assets represent the firm's investments in manufacturing technologies and are relevant to an analysis of its growth prospects.

Investments in nonaffiliated companies are reported at acquisition costs and may well be marketable securities, in which case their current market value can be added to liquid assets that are a part of current assets. Investments in affiliated enterprises and joint ventures are reported at cost plus the proportionate interest in the investee's undistributed earnings. They may represent investments in emerging technologies or acquisitions of operating capacity in partnership with other firms. These investments usually are not available for sale, but they should be analyzed for elements of value different from carrying value. Footnotes often provide separate financial data for such investees. Direct borrowing may support these investments, or the firm may provide indirect guarantees of underlying debt. Since the investor reports its proportionate interest in the net assets of these investees, the debt component of these investments requires analysis. (See discussion on off-balance sheet financing techniques.)

Property, plant, and equipment normally represent permanent investment, and their value to the firm is best measured by their contribution to income. The net carrying value is based on historical cost, which provides some idea of relative magnitude but usually is not indicative of current value. Supplementary disclosures under SFAS No. 33 provide some measure of current value. However, these disclosures are no longer mandatory, making analysis difficult if not impossible.

Some types of property have a degree of liquidity, and secondary markets may provide current market values. Substituting these values for net book values may provide insights into a company's economic worth. Reserves of natural resources and commercial real estate are examples.

Oil and gas companies disclose the present values of their reserves of oil and gas; the analyst can use these data to derive an indication of market value. The adjusted valuations have a more practical analytical use than historical book values. Coal reserves and the timber content of forest properties are other examples of natural resource properties to which a similar analysis can be applied. Real estate investment trusts and hotel companies sometimes report the market value of their commercial properties and the change in those values as a measure of income, supplementing their standard historical cost accounts.

Deferred charges are accounting numbers that do not represent assets but are incurred expenditures not yet reflected in income. Normally these have minor significance, but they should be examined carefully when they are large or increasing. Reported income may be overstated in such instances.

(a) Fixed Asset Turnover Ratio.   A measure of the efficiency of capital investment can be derived as follows:

$$\frac{\text{Net sales}}{\text{Average fixed assets}}$$

This ratio reflects the sales generated by investments in productive capacity. Some caveats should be noted. Growing companies would report increasing investments in fixed assets resulting in a relatively low turnover. Significant acquisitions accounted for under the purchase method may also lower the turnover. In contrast, cutbacks in investments, discontinued operations, and write-offs will improve the ratio but with possibly negative implications for earning power. Finally, increased reliance on leasing accounted for as operating leases would have a favorable but comparatively misleading impact on this turnover ratio.

(b) Capitalization Analysis.   The analysis of a company's capital structure—the amount of debt relative to equity—is essential for an evaluation of its use of financial leverage and the measurement of its ability to meet its long-term obligations. The use of debt in the capital structure adds fixed costs through contractual interest payments exerting a leverage effect on the residual return to stockholders. The higher the rate of return on assets relative to the fixed after-tax cost of debt capital, the higher the residual return accruing to stockholders. However, the fixed nature of interest payments has an adverse effect on this return during recessions or declines in demand as the rate of return on assets falls. Given the priority of debt claims relative to equity, a highly leveraged capital structure will have a negative impact on equity holders when adversity strikes. Conservative debt ratios enhance access to capital markets and improve the investment quality of the common stock.

The firm's ability to meet fixed interest and principal repayment obligations is a function of its earnings and cash-generating ability. The proportion of debt to equity capital and the stability of earnings and operating cash flows determine the riskiness of the firm's capital structure.

Long-term creditors use bond covenants to limit debt levels. Covenants that restrict dividend payments based on measures of cumulative profitability or net worth serve to restrict the firm's ability to strengthen stockholders' position relative to that of bondholders. The analyst should monitor the firm's maintenance of various ratios and relationships specified by bond covenants. The recent wave of highly leveraged mergers and recapitalizations and their impact on bondholders emphasizes the importance of a detailed analysis of the protection implied by debt covenants.

(c) Capitalization Table.   The capital structure of a company is usually presented in a capitalization table derived from the balance sheet. It shows the position and proportion of capital issues in relation to each other and the total capital of the company. Exhibit 10.7 illustrates such a table.

(d) Debt Ratios.   Three ratios (defined below) are used to evaluate the relationship between debt and equity. A comprehensive definition of debt includes current debt, long-term debt, capitalized lease obligations, and contractual obligations not afforded accounting treatment as liabilities, for example, take-or-pay payments and certain operating leases. Sections 10.26(f) and (g) discuss the analysis of these off-balance-sheet financing transactions. Preferred stock may have some characteristics of debt and should be evaluated for the most appropriate classification. A detailed discussion of preferred stock follows this section. All subsidiary debt should be included in total capitalization to determine the total debt supported by the company's capital.

Debt ratios that are based on the balance sheet may be calculated as:

$$\text{Debt to total capital ratio} = \frac{\text{Total current and long-term debt} + \text{capitalized leases}}{\text{Total capital (total debt} + \text{leases} + \text{stockholder's equity)}}$$

This figure expresses debt as a percentage of total capital. Exhibit 10.7 shows that this ratio is 34% for Deere & Company. It is 62% of total capital when subsidiary debt is included.

The debt-to-equity ratio is defined as:

$$\frac{\text{Total current and long-term debt} + \text{capitalized leases}}{\text{Total stockholders' equity}}$$

DEERE & COMPANY, OCTOBER 31, 1988
Capitalization Table[a]
($ in millions)

Debt	As Reported		Consolidated	
	Amount	% of Total	Amount	% of Total
Notes payable and current maturities of long-term debt	$ 477.0	12.5	$2,248.0	34.0
Long-term debt and capitalized lease obligations	817.0	21.5	1,408.0	22.0
Claims and policy benefit reserves[b]	—	—	362.0	6.0
Total debt and fixed obligations	1,294.0	34.0	4,018.0	62.0
Common equity	2,507.0	66.0	2,507.0	38.0
Total capitalization	$3,801.0	100.0	$6,525.0	100.0
Common at market (3/31/89)	$3,554.0			

[a]This table shows the impact of consolidating Deere and its finance, insurance, and health-care subsidiaries. Proportionate shares of the 20%–50%-owned affiliated companies are included. The analyst should include preferred stock, if any, at liquidation or redemption value, and the common equity should be charged the difference between the carrying amount and the liquidating value. Goodwill also should be charged to common equity.

[b]Claims and policy benefit reserves represent obligations of Deere's captive insurance and health-care subsidiaries. In some cases, these obligations may represent claims senior to other debt and fixed obligations. In 1988, claims and reserves were 6% of total capitalization. Total debt would be 59% of capitalization if claims and reserves were excluded from capitalization.

Exhibit 10.7.   Sample capitalization table.

This ratio is often used interchangeably with the debt-to-capital ratio, which is preferred. This ratio is 52% for Deere (160% when consolidated).

Total debt at book value should also be compared to the market value of total capital instead of book value:

$$\frac{\text{Total debt at book value}}{\text{Total debt and preferred stock} + \text{common stock at market}}$$
(27% for Deere & Company as of 3/31/89)

When the market value of total capital is well above book value, the debt ratio will be lower than the book value-based ratio; it will be presumed that the company's earning power and/or market conditions are favorable for issuance of debt to raise needed capital or refund existing debt. However, a continued trend of market value of equity at less than book value may signal deteriorating credit and restricted financial flexibility. Although this ratio will vary because of market fluctuations, it is a useful analytical tool.

These derivations can be altered to focus on senior debt, for example, mortgage bonds and bank debt, when the capital structure includes junior debt, for example, debentures or subordinated debt. The junior debt is subtracted from the numerator and added to the denominator, thereby becoming a part of the capital base that supports the senior debt. The debt ratio for senior debt alone is thus more favorable than for the entire debt.

The debt ratios must be viewed in context. The type of business, the variability and trend of earnings and other relevant factors must be evaluated. For example, a finance company, which has liquid financial assets, and an electric utility, which may be a regulated monopoly providing a basic service, will normally carry higher debt ratios than a cyclical manufacturing company.

(e) Preferred Stock Ratios. Preferred stock also has a claim on assets prior to the common stock, and its position and leverage effect are easily shown in the capitalization table. The preferred stock ratio can be classified by seniority, that is, senior preferred stock and junior preference stock.

Adjustments may be necessary for the correct balance sheet presentation of preferred stocks. For purposes of analysis, preferred stock should be shown at liquidating value rather than at stated value because this is the true measure of its claim on assets. Any excess of liquidating value over stated value should be charged against retained earnings in the common equity.

A second issue is the classification of preferred stock subject to mandatory redemption. The SEC now requires that such stock be shown apart from stockholders' equity. This is based on the notion that mandatory redemption through a sinking or purchase fund makes the preferred stock a "temporary" form of capital analogous to debt. Stockholders' equity is considered "permanent" capital.

Preferred stock may be considered permanent capital (i.e., stockholders' equity) on legal grounds because failure to make dividend or sinking fund payments will normally not cause default or bankruptcy, as with a bond. The principal effect of such failure probably would be to block dividends on the common stock. This common equity nature is stronger in the case of convertible preferred, especially when conversion can be forced by calling the preferred.

However, nonconvertible, mandatorily redeemable preferred has the economic characteristics of debt. Thus, it should be treated as subordinated debt for purposes of analysis.

(f) Off-Balance-Sheet (OBS) Obligations. Balance sheet based analyses of capital structure and leverage may understate firm risk because OBS activities and executory contracts do not receive accounting recognition. OBS transactions are designed to transfer or share the risk of the firm's operations, and they have real current or future cash flow consequences. For example, long-term lease contracts may be, in substance, installment purchases of long-term assets, but they have been structured to avoid capitalization requirements of accounting standards, thereby eliminating balance sheet recognition of the asset and the related liability. Nonrecognition in the financial statements limits the usefulness of capital structure and risk indicators unless proper adjustments are made.

Executory contracts involve commitments to purchase or pay for a commodity or service over a period of time. No liability is recognized since no accounting obligation arises until an exchange transaction is completed. This legalistic definition of liabilities has contributed to their nonrecognition in financial statements.

Firms may engage in these transactions to avoid reporting adverse debt-to-equity ratios and to reduce the probability of technical default under restrictive covenants in debt indentures. Historical cost basis financial statements, which suppress the current value of assets, increase the incentive to engage in OBS transactions to keep liabilities off the books. A detailed review of footnote disclosures of OBS transactions and executory contracts is essential for a comprehensive analysis of capital structure.

(g) Examples of OBS Financing Techniques. The most common examples of the use of OBS financing techniques follow. When analyzing a company, the analyst must watch for such transactions and make the appropriate adjustments when computing financial ratios.

(i) Accounts Receivable. Legally separate, wholly owned finance subsidiaries are often created to purchase receivables from the parent, which uses the proceeds to retire debt. When such subsidiaries are unconsolidated, the parent firms report significantly lower debt–equity ratios. Parent companies in the past used the "equity" method to account for their

finance subsidiaries, that is, the consolidated balance sheet reported the parent's net investment in these units, suppressing the debt used to finance receivables. The FASB eliminated this nonconsolidation option (SFAS No. 94), and all post-1987 financial statements must consolidate the assets and liabilities of controlled finance subsidiaries (after relevant intercompany eliminations). The analyst should compute consolidated debt–equity ratios because the parent generally supports finance subsidiary borrowings through extensive income-maintenance agreements and direct or indirect guarantees of its debt.

Receivables also may be financed by sale (or securitization) to unrelated parties with proceeds used to reduce debt. These transactions are effectively collateralized borrowing when receivables are transferred with recourse to the "seller." Footnote disclosures should be analyzed to determine whether the risks and rewards of controlling these receivables have been transferred to the "buyer." Where the "seller" retains these risks and rewards, the analyst should reinstate the receivables and treat the proceeds as debt in computing the debt–equity ratio as well as the current ratio, receivables turnover, and the return on average total capital.

(ii) Inventories. Firms may finance inventory and raw material purchases through take-or-pay commitments whereby they contract to purchase or pay for minimum quantities over a specified time period. The present value of these future obligations should be included in computing debt ratios. Companies typically use take-or-pay contracts to ensure supplies of raw materials or availability of manufacturing capacity. Natural resource companies may use through-put contracts to guarantee distribution needs by contracting with pipelines to purchase or transport minimum quantities. Firms organize joint ventures with related companies or third parties where the take-or-pay commitments effectively guarantee the joint venture's long-term debt service requirements. In some cases, direct guarantees of joint venture or related companies debt are disclosed in footnotes. The obligations under take-or-pay and through-put arrangements and the direct guarantees should be included in the computation of debt–equity ratios.

Natural resource firms may finance inventories through commodity-indexed debt where interest and/or principal repayments are a function of the price of underlying commodities. Changing commodity prices should be monitored to determine their impact on these liabilities and the debt–equity ratios.

(iii) Fixed Assets. Firms acquire rights to fixed assets through lease contracts structured to avoid capitalization criteria in accounting standards. Footnote disclosure of these operating leases details minimum payments for each of the next 5 years and the total payments thereafter. Where this payment schedule depicts relatively stable and long-term payments over a period roughly equivalent to the average economic/useful life of similarly owned long-term assets or those under capitalized leases, the analyst should capitalize these operating leases to adjust reported debt levels. The reported fixed assets, depreciation expense, and interest expense also should be adjusted in order to correctly calculate various affected ratios.

(iv) Joint Ventures. Firms acquire, control, or obtain access to distribution and manufacturing capacity through joint ventures and/or investments in affiliated and nonaffiliated companies. In some cases the joint venture offers economies of scale and needed capacity or provides for a negotiated sharing of technologies, raw materials, or financial risk. The owners of these ventures enter into take-or-pay or through-put arrangements where the minimum, guaranteed payments are designed to cover required debt service obligations. These agreements constitute the collateral for the venture's borrowings in the absence of substantial equity investments by various parties to the joint venture. Direct or indirect guarantees of venture's debt may also be present.

Generally, the firms account for their investment in the joint ventures using the equity method, since no single firm holds a controlling interest. Thus, the balance sheet reports only the nominal net investment in the venture. Footnotes may disclose the assets, liabilities, and results of operations of the venture in a summarized format. These disclosures should be used for proportionate consolidation of the joint venture with the firm. Any direct or indirect guarantees of venture debt should be evaluated for adjustment to reported debt levels.

(v) Investments.   Some firms have issued long-term debt convertible into the common stock of related firms, held as investments. Potential motives for these transactions include lower interest costs on debt, benefits of tax deductibility of interest payments, the 80% exclusion from taxable income of dividends received from eligible investments, and control of the amount and timing of capital gains on conversion.

(vi) Currency- and Interest-rate Exposure.   Long-term debt in foreign currency denominations may increase the firm's exchange-risk exposure. The mix of fixed and variable rate debt exposes the firm to interest-rate risk.

Some firms also engage in interest rate and/or currency swaps related to outstanding debt. For example, a bond may be issued payable in fixed-rate Austrialian dollars and the proceeds swapped for variable-rate Swiss francs. The foreign–currency-denominated debt may also be convertible into commodities or natural resources. Footnote disclosures vary widely, ranging from an acknowledgment of swap transactions to detailed analyses of the effect of swaps on currency- and interest-rate exposure. The analyst should monitor these disclosures to evaluate risk exposure.

Exhibit 10.8 ties together this discussion of OBS techniques, using Ashland Oil, Inc., as an example. Ashland makes extensive use of joint ventures, operating leases, and other OBS

CAPITALIZATION TABLE, SEPTEMBER 30, 1988
Ashland Oil, Inc., and Subsidiaries
($ in thousands)

Debt	Amount	% of Total
Short-term debt	$ 44,852	2.0
Long-term debt	765,050	34.5
Capitalized lease obligations	77,018	3.5
Claims and reserves of captive insurance companies	88,206	4.0
Total debt and obligations	$ 975,126	44.0
Stockholders' Equity		
Common Equity	$1,245,101	56.0
Total Capitalization	$2,220,227	100.00
Common at market (1/31/89)	$2,073,158	

NOTE: The adjustments and analysis of disclosures for OBS transactions follow.

(A) Adjustments to Reported Equity

Reported equity	$1,245,101
Deduct: Costs in excess of net assets of acquired companies	(80,157)
Add: LIFO reserves	346,302
: Excess of present value of discounted cash flows over capitalized costs of oil and gas reserves. ($211,200 − 193,759)	17,441
Adjusted equity	$1,528,687

(continued)

Exhibit 10.8.   Adjustment of capitalization based on footnote disclosure of off balance sheet obligations.

No adjustments were made for investments in cash equivalents and investments of captive insurance companies. These are stated at cost plus accrued interest, which is reported to approximate market value. Any excess of market value over cost would be added to equity. The excess of market value over acquisition cost of Ashland's proportionate share of coal reserves in Ashland Coal and Arch Mineral also constitute valid adjustments.

(B) Adjustments to Reported Debt and Fixed Obligations

Reported debt and fixed obligations	$975,126
Add: Unconsolidated affiliates' debt	
1. 50% share of Arch Mineral Corp's noncurrent liabilities	202,234
2. 46% share of Ashland Coal's liabilities and redeemable preferred stock	43,568
3. 20% share of LOOP Inc. and LOCAP Inc.'s liabilities	132,939
4. Ashland's contingent liabilities for Ashland Coal's debt and lease obligations	9,936

(C) Operating Lease Commitments

Capitalized at 10%—based on rate implicit in capitalized lease obligations	$ 267,000

(D) Adjusted Capitalization Ratio

Adjusted debt and fixed obligations	$1,630,803
Adjusted total capitalization	$3,159,490
Adjusted debt and fixed obligations as a % of total capitalization	51.62%
Adjusted debt to equity ratio	1.07:1

Exhibit 10.8.   *Continued.*

techniques. Adjustment for these obligations increases debt from $975 million to $1631 million or 67%. Even after adjustment for understated equity, the debt-to-capital ratio increases from 44% to 52%.

(h) Property Analysis.   The long-term capital of the company is often compared with its permanent investment in property and equipment. This is analogous to the ratio of mortgage loan to value in the financing of residential and commercial buildings. Since plant and equipment is carried at historical cost and normally is not available for sale, this ratio has limited practical significance. A better measure is the ratio of debt to total net tangible assets including net current assets.

A debt-to-property analysis may be more useful in the case of natural resource companies or companies with large real estate holdings. Frequently, the market value of natural resources holdings exceeds historical cost book values. Theoretically this market value is an indicator of funds available to support debt in an emergency. For some companies these excess market values can be significant, and may augment the potential value of the entire company in an acquisition.

CASH FLOW ANALYSIS

Effective in 1987, SFAS No. 95 replaced the "funds statement" with a statement of cash flows. From an analytic viewpoint, the change is most beneficial. The funds statement generally added little information to that available from the balance sheet and income statement.

In contrast, the statement of cash flows provides significant additional data for analysis. This improvement is mainly due to the provisions of SFAS No. 95 requiring that:

1. The effect of acquisitions be removed from the balance sheet changes used to compute cash flows.
2. The effects of changes in exchange rates be removed from balance sheet changes used to compute cash flows.
3. Cash flows be separated into operating, investing, and financing activities.

The first two requirements result in cash flow data that are unclouded by the effects of acquisitions and exchange rate factors. The third requirement means that such accounts as accounts receivable, accounts payable, accrued liabilities, long-term liabilities, and accounts labeled "other" or "miscellaneous" must be segregated into operating, investing, and financing functions by the financial statement preparer. As a result of these requirements, the statement of cash flows is far more accurate than the "do it yourself" estimates that were formerly necessary (Sondhi, Sorter, and White, 1988).

10.27 DIRECT VERSUS INDIRECT METHODS.   SFAS No. 95 permits the statement of cash flows to be prepared using either the direct or indirect methods. Although the indirect method is used by virtually all preparers, the direct method is more suitable for analysis. In most cases, therefore, direct method statements must be prepared by the analyst. This can be done by rearranging the data given in the indirect method format. For example, combining sales with the change in operating accounts receivable produces cash receipts (Livnat and Sondhi, 1989).

As there is some evidence that the components of cash flow from operating activities are better indicators than the total, the analyst should use whatever detail is available. The ratio of each component to cash receipts, for example, should be looked at over time.

Cash flow used for investments should be compared with cash flow from operations. The difference is often called "free cash flow," and may be a useful indicator of the cash-generating ability of the enterprise. However, the analyst must compare the results of this exercise with the a priori expectations based on the type of business. For example, a company experiencing rapid growth may have little or no operating cash flow and "free cash flow" may be negative. In this case the analyst would be primarily concerned with how this cash deficit was being financed. A proper balance between debt and equity should be struck.

On the other hand, a "cash cow" should generate cash flow from operations well in excess of capital needed for investment purposes. In this case the analyst would be concerned with the use of the excess cash flow. If the "free cash flow" generated did not conform to the prior expectation, this would also be a cause for concern.

10.28 COMPARING CASH FLOWS.   Cash flow analysis is best done using data for a number of years. Cash flow for one period may be distorted by random events (strikes, abnormal volume due to price changes, etc.). Also keep in mind that, for cyclical companies, the business cycle will affect cash flows. Cyclical expansions generally require additional working capital; contractions generate cash as working capital is reduced.

For periods of less than one year, additional caution is required because of seasonality. The statement of cash flows for less than one year should be compared only with the statement for the corresponding period of prior years when the business is at all seasonal. Otherwise, normal seasonal working capital variations will dominate any real trends.

When comparing different companies, allowance must be made for differences in financial structure. Under the provisions of SFAS No. 95, cash flow from operating activities includes income from investments and interest expense (but not dividends paid). In order to facilitate intercompany comparisons, interest expense (after-tax) should be removed from operating cash flow and included in financing cash flow. When income from investments is significant, it should be removed (after-tax) from operating cash flow and included in investing cash flow. With these adjustments, cash flow from operations can be evaluated, and companies can be compared with the effects of financing decisions removed.

INTEGRATED ANALYSIS OF FINANCIAL STATEMENTS

A company's return on assets provides a comprehensive measure of its profitability during a given period of time and is calculated as follows:

$$\text{Return on assets} = \frac{\text{Net income}}{\text{Average total assets}}$$

The trends in this ratio allow an evaluation of the company's performance over time. It also should be compared with the ratio for similar firms over time and with an industry average. This return measure is affected by accounting and tax policy choices and the degree of leverage used by a firm over time and across firms. A measure using earnings before interest and income taxes [EBIT] overcomes these limitations and provides a measure of operating profitability unaffected by differences in leverage and tax effects. It is calculated as:

$$\frac{\text{Earnings before interest and taxes}}{\text{Average total assets}}$$

Further insights into operating performance over time may be obtained by evaluating the components of these return measures. One component is the net income (or EBIT) margin, which is a measure of the profitability in relation to sales. The second component, the asset turnover ratio, evaluates the effectiveness of the firm's use of assets in generating sales. Each component can be analyzed in greater detail to determine the underlying relationships affecting current return and their potential impact on returns over time. The net income (or EBIT) margin can be decomposed further to evaluate changes in different sources of revenues and proportions of various expense categories over time. Inventory, receivables, and fixed asset turnover ratios can be analyzed to evaluate trends in the fixed asset turnover:

Net income margin or EBIT margin	× Asset turnover =	Return on assets
$\dfrac{\text{Net income}}{\text{Net sales}}$		$\dfrac{\text{Net income}}{\text{Average total assets}}$
or	$\times \dfrac{\text{Net sales}}{\text{Average total assets}} =$	or
$\dfrac{\text{EBIT}}{\text{Net sales}}$		$\dfrac{\text{EBIT}}{\text{Average total assets}}$
↓	↓	
Analysis of relevant revenue and expense breakdowns	Analysis of inventory, receivables and fixed asset turnover	

Exhibit 10.9 shows that Merck's return on assets has improved from 13.50% in 1978 to 20.44% in 1988. (EBIT return was 32.99% in 1988 compared to 23.32% in 1978.) From 1979 through 1984, Merck reported declines in return with substantial improvement beginning in 1986 and continuing through 1988. An analysis of the components shows that asset turnover was at its lowest in 1985. Both the asset turnover and net income (EBIT) margins improved steadily from 1985 through 1988.

	1988	1987	1986	1985	1984	1983	1982	1981	1980	1979	1978
$\dfrac{\text{Net Income}}{\text{Sales}}$ (%)	20.32	17.91	16.37	15.22	13.85	13.89	13.55	13.60	15.19	16.01	15.52
$\dfrac{\text{Sales}}{\text{Average total assets}}$ (×)	1.01	.94	.83	.75	.81	.82	.88	.94	.98	.97	.87
$\dfrac{\text{Net income}}{\text{Average total assets}}$ (%)	20.44	16.81	13.50	11.37	11.20	11.46	11.91	12.80	14.95	15.50	13.50
$\dfrac{\text{Average total assets}}{\text{Average common equity}}$ (×)	2.37	2.32	1.94	1.85	1.79	1.71	1.68	1.63	1.59	1.60	1.59
$\dfrac{\text{Net income}}{\text{Average common equity}}$ (%)	48.54	38.92	26.25	21.06	20.01	19.65	19.96	20.85	23.83	24.79	21.41

$$\frac{\text{Net income}}{\text{Sales}} \times \frac{\text{Sales}}{\text{Average total assets}} \times \frac{\text{Average total assets}}{\text{Average common equity}} = \frac{\text{Net income}}{\text{Average common equity}}$$

Net Income—Growth Rates

	1978–1983 %	1983–1988 %	1978–1988 %
% Change	46.63	167.64	291.46
Compound growth rate	7.96	21.73	14.64
Least squares growth rate	8.34	22.26	15.30
Standard deviation	9.20	10.93	12.25

(continued)

Exhibit 10.9. Analysis of return on equity. (*Note*: Numbers in this table do not multiply out precisely because of rounding; the ratios in the table were derived from data reported in Merck's annual reports.)

	1988	1987	1986	1985	1984	1983	1982	1981	1980	1979	1978
$\dfrac{\text{EBIT}}{\text{Sales}}$ (%)	32.79	28.80	27.08	26.07	24.68	24.04	21.68	21.47	25.27	26.62	26.82
$\dfrac{\text{Sales}}{\text{Average total assets}}$ (×)	1.01	.94	.83	.75	.81	.82	.88	.94	.98	.97	.87
$\dfrac{\text{EBIT}}{\text{Average total assets}}$ (%)	32.99	27.10	22.34	19.49	19.96	19.83	19.04	20.21	24.86	25.76	23.32
$\dfrac{\text{Interest expense}}{\text{Average total assets}}$	1.30	1.05	0.89	1.43	2.09	2.14	1.82	1.38	1.34	1.15	1.13
$\dfrac{\text{Average total assets}}{\text{Average common equity}}$ (×)	2.37	2.32	1.94	1.85	1.79	1.71	1.68	1.63	1.59	1.60	1.59
$\dfrac{\text{EBIT}}{\text{Average common equity}}$ (%)	75.25	60.34	41.69	33.93	31.93	30.33	28.89	30.68	37.49	39.35	35.20

$$\frac{\text{EBIT}}{\text{Sales}} \times \frac{\text{Sales}}{\text{Average total assets}} = \frac{\text{EBIT}}{\text{Average total assets}}$$

$$\left(\frac{\text{EBIT}}{\text{Average total assets}} - \frac{\text{Interest}}{\text{Average total assets}}\right) \times \frac{\text{Average total assets}}{\text{Average common equity}} = \frac{\text{Earnings before taxes}}{\text{Average common equity}}$$

Exhibit 10.9. *Continued.*

Investors should also calculate the firm's return on equity (ROE) as:

$$\frac{\text{Net income}}{\text{Average common equity}}$$

The ROE should be analyzed over time and across firms, and compared to an average ROE for the industry in which the firm operates. Merck's ROE ratio doubled from 21.41% in 1978 to 48.54% in 1988. The 1979–1983 period shows a decline from 24.79% in 1979 to a low of 19.65% in 1983. However, growth accelerated over the 1984–1988 period with ROE climbing steadily to 48.54% in 1988.

The trends in ROE can be further analyzed in terms of its components:

$$\text{ROE} = \frac{\text{Net income}}{\text{Average total assets}} \times \frac{\text{Average total assets}}{\text{Average common equity}}$$

or

$$= \text{Profit margin} \times \text{Asset turnover} \times \text{Leverage ratio}$$

$$= \frac{\text{Net income}}{\text{Net sales}} \times \frac{\text{Net sales}}{\text{Average total assets}} \times \frac{\text{Average total assets}}{\text{Average common equity}}$$

An analysis of these components shows that the decline in ROE during 1979–1983 can be traced to a lower return on assets during this period. The components of the return-on-assets ratio, that is, the profit margin and the asset turnover ratio, also show declines. The profit margin improved in 1985, however, and thereafter climbed steadily. The asset turnover ratio reached its lowest level in 1985 but rebounded subsequently. As a result of rising profit margins and asset turnover, ROE rose sharply during the 1984–1989 period.

The third component, assets/equity, is a measure of leverage: the higher the ratio, the lower the proportion of assets financed by common equity. This ratio climbed steadily over the entire 1979–1988 period, and reached 2.37 in 1988, from 1.61 reported in 1979. At the same time, however, the debt level was being reduced to 37% of its 1983 peak amount. And during 1987, the firm repurchased shares, reducing equity by 40% and contributing to the high leverage ratio in 1988. Improved operating efficiency and higher margins have enabled the firm to generate higher operating cash flows, allowing a substantial reduction in debt and equity, and leading to significantly higher returns on assets and equity.

An analysis of Merck's earnings growth rate over the 1978–1988 period confirms these findings. Over this 10-year period, net income has grown at a 15.30% annual rate. However, during the 1978–1983 period, earnings grew at a more moderate 8.34% rate, whereas they grew at more than 22% over the most recent 5 years, 1983–1988.

FIXED INCOME ANALYSIS

Investors in fixed income securities are concerned with the safety of the expected interest payments and redemption of debt at maturity. The safety of interest payments is a function of the margin of earnings in excess of interest so that an unexpected decline in earnings will not jeopardize payment. Redemption at maturity depends on internal cash flows, the relationship of debt to equity, and other industry- and economywide factors. Thus, fixed-income investors need a comprehensive analysis of all financial statements to develop insights into the investment risk relative to expected return.

10.29 EARNINGS PROTECTION.   The key ratios are fixed charge coverage and the margin of safety, which are discussed in section 10.7(e). The adequacy of the coverage ratio depends on the volatility of earnings. The greater the volatility, the higher the ratio necessary to assure protection under adverse circumstances. A low ratio, say $2\frac{1}{2}$ times, is adequate for a finance company, whose earnings are stable. In fact, captive finance subsidiaries (i.e., those conducting at least 70% of their operations with the parent) have income-maintenance agreements with the parent whereby it guarantees coverage ratios from 1.05 to 1.50 times fixed charges. A much higher ratio, 5–6 times, is desirable for an industrial company whose earnings fluctuate because of the business cycle.

Another test of earnings adequacy is earning power—the return before interest expense on the total invested capital. This is given by the following equation:

$$\text{Return on invested capital} = \frac{\text{Earnings before interest and taxes}}{\text{Average invested capital}}$$

This is a useful long-term measure of strength. The margin of safety provided by the return on investment depends on the cost of debt. A return of 14% on invested capital is adequate when rates are 5–7%, but not at substantially higher rates. The current trend toward recapitalization using high-yield debt significantly increases vulnerability and reduces the protection available to the creditors if it is not accompanied by a sustained increase in return on total invested capital.

Redemption at maturity should be evaluated by the analysis of cash flows and the balance sheet in conjunction with the income statement to determine the assurance of payment at maturity. First, the maturity schedule of the outstanding debt, as given in footnotes to the financial statements, must be reviewed. The company may have a continuing run of maturing obligations, including sinking funds, or it may have a few widely spaced larger maturities. The analyst should evaluate the firm's ability to meet the specified repayment schedule and amounts through internally generated funds, that is, operating cash flows. The measure is as follows:

$$\text{Years to pay} = \frac{\text{Total fixed obligations}}{\text{Operating cash flows}}$$

This ratio states the number of years required to pay off all debt by application of all internally generated cash flows. The logic is that debt maturities will have the first priority on all available funds. Normally this ratio ought to be in a range of 3 to 5 years. At 8 to 10 years the repayment burden could be onerous. The recent trend toward increased use of debt has increased the ratio relative to past experience. High levels of internally generated cash flows will signify low years-to-pay and high credit standing.

In summary, whereas actual appropriation of all internal cash flow to debt reduction for several years would hamper the future growth of the business and be tantamount to liquidation, a high ratio of cash flow to debt gives a company considerable flexibility in financing its business internally and/or externally and therefore is a good indicator of credit quality. A useful adjustment to this ratio would require a deduction from operating cash flows of capital expenditures required to maintain productive capacity, a crude measure of which may be provided by the current cost equivalent of depreciation. The resulting ratio is more conservative but would facilitate a more comprehensive analysis. The analyst should also compute this ratio after adjusting for all OBS obligations. These adjustments would enable the anlayst to compare different reported and OBS-inclusive capital structures.

The company's overall credit standing should be reviewed on the expectation that a new issue can be sold to refund a large maturing issue or recapitalize the firm. Here again, the investor should evaluate long-term earning power, interest coverage, the ratio of debt to total capital, OBS financing activities, and bond covenants to determine whether a refunding issue or recapitalization would be accepted in the marketplace. Many industrial bonds have sinking funds that retire most of the issue by maturity, but that is not the case for most utilities. Utilities must maintain a balanced capital structure and adequate coverage in order to maintain continued access to the bond market.

Exhibit 10.10 details Bond Protection ratios for Deere & Company over the 1984–1988

DEERE & COMPANY[a]

Year	Fixed Charge Coverage	Margin of Safety	EBIT as % Average Invested Capital	Debt to Operating Cash Flow (yrs)	Fixed Obligations as % of Average Invested Capital	Current Assets to Total Debt	Net Tangible Assets to Fixed Obligations
1984	1.27×	2.2%	8.51%	13.40	61%	1.71×	2.13×
1985	1.04	0.2	6.13	18.06	63	1.62	2.04
1986	NM[b]	NM	NM	12.12	65	1.49	1.90
1987	0.50	NM	2.81	NM	65	1.48	1.94
1988	2.07	5.7	11.37	11.89	65	1.57	2.07

[a]Includes retail finance, leasing, insurance, and health-care subsidiaries, and incorporates affiliated companies on a pro rata consolidation basis.
[b]NM = Not meaningful.

Exhibit 10.10. Bond protection ratios for an industrial company.

period. The firm's retail finance, leasing, insurance, and health-care subsidiaries have been consolidated with the parent, and affiliated companies are incorporated on a pro rata consolidation basis. All measures of protection and safety for creditors show the deterioration over the 1984–1987 period. Substantial improvements are reported in these ratios for 1988.

FINANCE COMPANY DEBT ANALYSIS

Finance companies have a large body of oustanding debt, and its quality is measured by slightly different criteria adapted to the special circumstances of this business, which involves the financing of sales and receivables of their parents and that of other, unaffiliated companies. Finance company assets are composed largely of financial obligations of third parties that are self-liquidating through relatively frequent payments of both principal and interest, allowing significantly greater leverage than that observed for industrial companies. Earnings depend on the loss experience on loans, the interest rate spread between loans and borrowings, and expense control. Finance subsidiaries and their industrial parents also have extensive operating agreements that call for income maintenance and direct or indirect parent guarantees of subsidiary debt, augmented by extensive debt covenants. The ratios used to measure these factors are fundamentally the same as for other businesses, but they are usually expressed in a different form, and the standards are different. The analyst should also evaluate the operating agreement and bond covenants to evaluate finance company debt risk (for detailed analysis, see Ronen and Sondhi, 1989).

SFAS No. 94 requires the consolidation of leasing and finance subsidiaries that were previously reported under the equity method because of their nonhomogeneous operations. The standard requires continued disclosure of disaggregated information on finance subsidiaries. To the extent possible, the analyst should evaluate separate finance company data to evaluate the riskiness of finance company debt. An analysis of the parent–subsidiary contractual relationship is necessary for an evaluation of recourse to the parent. Lenders to the parent are concerned with both the risk in parent debt and the degree of support the parent is contractually obligated to provide to its subsidiaries. The effect of consolidation on traditional ratios will not always be in the expected direction and of anticipated magnitude because of differences between parent and subsidiary size, profitability, and growth rates over time and across firms. Disaggregated disclosures are necessary for a separate evaluation of finance company and parent debt. To the extent that continued availability of disaggregated disclosure is affected by FASB actions with respect to consolidated financial reporting, analysts will need to monitor these developments.

10.30 THE OPERATING AGREEMENT. Operating agreements govern the transactions between the parent and its financing subsidiary. An income maintenance agreement is used to provide a parent guarantee that the subsidiary's net income will be a prespecified multiple of its fixed charges; direct payments to the subsidiary are required when this multiple is not reached, thereby protecting investments in subsidiary debt. Operating agreements require that receivables be sold to subsidiaries at discounts competitive with those prevailing in the financial markets. Uncollectibles are charged to the parent, and the subsidiary often has the right to withhold a predetermined portion of the purchase price (a holdback reserve), which is refunded when receivables have been collected. Some agreements contain provisions for repossession and payments in the event of default.

In summary, the operating agreement serves to reduce the volatility and risk in subsidiary earnings and cash flows, thereby enhancing the protection available to the finance company's debt holders.

10.31 ASSET PROTECTION RATIOS.   Since receivables are the principal assets of finance companies, asset protection for the debt is measured by the proportion of receivables to debt, as follows:

$$\frac{\text{Gross receivables} - \text{unearned finance charges}}{\text{Total debt}}$$

This ratio should range from 110% to 120%, and it indicates the margin of liquid or financial assets over total debt. A similar ratio should also be calculated on senior debt. Refunding and call provisions in debt covenants provide additional protection. Generally, significant declines in receivables trigger a requirement to redeem outstanding debt at specified premiums. This covenant also limits investment in nonfinancial assets, which may be constrained by other, direct covenants.

10.32 RESERVE AND LOSS RATIOS.   The quality of financial assets is critical to the earning power and credit quality of a finance company. This quality is measured by the rate of losses on collection of receivables and the adequacy of balance sheet reserves to absorb losses. The level of holdback reserves also indicates the continued parent equity in the subsidiary. Loss as a percentage of average receivables is defined as:

$$\frac{\text{Net losses on charge-offs for the year}}{\text{Average receivables (gross receivables} - \text{unearned finance charges)}}$$

This ratio will vary depending on the type of business (retail vs. wholesale; mix of products financed). A rising trend is an important signal. Losses can also be measured against net interest income on a trend basis.

Reserves as a percentage of receivables is defined as:

$$\frac{\text{Reserve for losses}}{\text{Gross receivables} - \text{unearned finance charges}}$$

The reserve is used to absorb losses, and is replenished by charges to operations. To provide a proper cushion, the reserve should be $1\frac{1}{4}$ to 2 times annual losses.

10.33 LOAN SPREADS.   Earnings in the finance (and banking) industry are developed by lending funds at a higher rate than that paid on borrowed funds (i.e., the net interest earned). This spread should be evaluated against the net investment in receivables to derive a rate of return:

$$\frac{\text{Net interest earned (interest revenues} - \text{interest expense)}}{\text{Average receivables (gross receivables} - \text{unearned charges)}}$$

10.34 LIQUIDITY.   Finance companies are constantly in the market, rolling over short-term paper, refunding longer issues, and selling new debt. Liquidity therefore becomes a function of an adequate balance of debt between all sectors of the money market without an undue concentration of maturities, coupled with adequate bank lines of credit. To maintain the confidence of the market to accept paper under various economic conditions, consistent earnings trends, controlled operations, and debt levels are designed to accomplish these objectives, and the analyst should monitor these ratios and covenants over time to manage risk and return tradeoffs.

BENEFICIAL CORPORATION AND SUBSIDIARIES

Year	Fixed Charge Coverage	Margin of Safety	Loan Interest Spread	Senior Debt to Capital Base	Losses % Average Receivables	Reserve % Total Receivables	Receivables % Total Debt
1984	1.31×	12.28%	10.58%	4.76×	.84%	3.94%	89.01%
1985	1.27	10.42	10.24	4.39	.77	4.09	91.90
1986	1.28	11.00	10.17	5.41	1.07	3.78	91.98
1987	1.43	15.95	9.71	4.03	1.08	3.63	116.06
1988	1.31	11.84	9.43	4.45	1.05	3.34	114.88

Exhibit 10.11. Bond protection ratios for a finance company.

10.35 CAPITALIZATION.   Subordinated debt is usually a significant segment of the finance company's capital structure and must be evaluated separately from senior debt. Subordinated debt and equity together represent the capital base supporting the high levels of debt observed in finance companies. Senior debt is normally restricted to a multiple of the capital base, the aggregate of total debt, the liquid net worth, or a multiple of net worth. Covenants also contain similar restrictions on allowed subordinated debt. The ratio of senior debt to the capital base is frequently $2^1/_2$:1 to $3^1/_2$:1 for independent finance companies. Captives may use higher ratios because of access to parent company capital and some guarantees of minimum earnings. Bank credit departments use a similar ratio—"borrowing ratio"—which eliminates nonliquid assets from the capital base. The ratio of senior debt to capital is:

$$\frac{\text{Total senior debt}}{\text{Subordinated debt + net worth}}$$

Thus, the allowed debt (senior and subordinated) is restricted to some multiple of equity or, in the case of subsidiaries, to the parent's equity investment, and may incorporate subordinated debt owed to parent in the capital base. Along with requirements to maintain receivables levels, these covenants preserve collateral available in the finance company. The ratios described above and the covenants should be monitored by the analyst to evaluate finance company debt.

10.36 APPLICATION OF RATIOS.   The use of ratios in a finance company analysis is illustrated in Exhibit 10.11.

Beneficial Corporation's fixed charge coverage and margin of safety declined over the 1984–1986 period and improved slightly in 1987, before declining to earlier levels in 1988. However, its earnings have declined over these 5 years as shown by the interest spread. Losses as a percentage of receivables have increased from .84 to 1.05, whereas the reserves have declined from 3.94% to 3.34% over the same period. This deterioration may be problematic despite the improvement in protection afforded by the increase in receivables as a percentage of total debt from 89% to nearly 115%. The trends in these ratios should be evaluated relative to comparable firms and with reference to expected economic conditions.

GLOSSARY

Liquidity Analysis

1. Current ratio $= \dfrac{\text{Current assets (cash and equivalents, receivables and inventories)}}{\text{Current liabilities (payables, accruals, taxes and debt due in 1 year)}}$

2. Quick ratio $= \dfrac{\text{Cash and equivalents plus receivables}}{\text{Current liabilities}}$

3. Operating cash flow to current liabilities $= \dfrac{\text{Cash provided by operations}}{\text{Average current liabilities}}$

Activity Ratios

4. Inventory turnover $= \dfrac{\text{Cost of goods sold}}{\text{Average inventory}}$

The number of days inventory is on hand can be calculated as:

$$\frac{365}{\text{Inventory turnover}}$$

5. Receivables turnover $= \dfrac{\text{Net credit sales}}{\text{Average receivables}}$

6. Number of days receivables are outstanding $= \dfrac{365}{\text{Receivables turnover}}$

7. Fixed asset turnover ratio $= \dfrac{\text{Net sales}}{\text{Average fixed assets}}$

Margin Analysis

8. Gross margin $= 1 - \dfrac{\text{Cost of goods sold}}{\text{Sales}}$

9. Expense ratio $= \dfrac{\text{Selling, general, and administrative expenses}}{\text{Sales}}$

10. Operating margin $= \dfrac{\text{Operating income}}{\text{Sales}}$

11. Pretax margin $= \dfrac{\begin{array}{c}\text{Income before income tax}\\ \text{(Operating income + other income − interest)}\end{array}}{\text{Sales}}$

12. Profit margin $= \dfrac{\text{Net income before extraordinary items}}{\text{Sales}}$

Debt Ratios

13. Interest coverage ratio $= \dfrac{\text{Income before interest and taxes}}{\text{Fixed charges}}$

14. Margin of safety $= \dfrac{\text{Income after fixed charges before income taxes}}{\text{Sales}}$

15. Preferred dividend coverage $= \dfrac{\text{Income before interest and taxes}}{\text{Fixed charges + pretax preferred dividends}}$

16. Debt to total capital ratio $=$

$$\dfrac{\text{Total current and long-term debt + capitalized leases}}{\text{Total capital (total debt + leases + stockholders' equity)}}$$

17. Debt-to-equity ratio $=$

$$\dfrac{\text{Total current and long-term debt + capitalized leases}}{\text{Total stockholders' equity}}$$

or

$$\dfrac{\text{Total debt at book value}}{\text{Total debt and preferred stock + common stock at market}}$$

Integrated Analysis of Financial Statements

18. Return on assets $= \dfrac{\text{Net income}}{\text{Average total assets}}$

or

19. $\dfrac{\text{Earnings before interest and taxes}}{\text{Average total assets}}$

Decomposition of Margin and Return Ratios

20.
$$
\begin{array}{c}
\text{Net income margin} \\
\text{or} \\
\text{EBIT margin}
\end{array}
\quad \times \text{ Asset turnover } = \quad \text{Return on assets}
$$

$$
\begin{array}{c}
\dfrac{\text{Net income}}{\text{Net sales}} \\[2ex]
\text{or} \\[1ex]
\dfrac{\text{EBIT}}{\text{Net sales}}
\end{array}
\quad \times \dfrac{\text{Net sales}}{\text{Average total assets}} =
\begin{array}{c}
\dfrac{\text{Net income}}{\text{Average total assets}} \\[2ex]
\text{or} \\[1ex]
\dfrac{\text{EBIT}}{\text{Average total assets}}
\end{array}
$$

$$\downarrow \qquad\qquad\qquad \downarrow$$

Analysis of relevant revenue and expense breakdowns

Analysis of inventory, receivables and fixed asset turnover

21. Return on equity (ROE) $= \dfrac{\text{Net income}}{\text{Average common equity}}$

Decomposition of ROE

22. ROE $= \dfrac{\text{Net income}}{\text{Average total assets}} \times \dfrac{\text{Average total assets}}{\text{Average common equity}}$

or

$=$ Profit margin $\times$ Assets turnover $\times$ Leverage ratio

$= \dfrac{\text{Net income}}{\text{Net sales}} \times \dfrac{\text{Net sales}}{\text{Average total assets}} \times \dfrac{\text{Average total assets}}{\text{Average common equity}}$

Other Earnings and Asset Protection Ratios

23. Return on invested capital $= \dfrac{\text{Earnings before interest and taxes}}{\text{Average invested capital}}$

24. Number of years to pay off debt by application of internally generated cash flows $=$

$$\dfrac{\text{Total fixed obligations}}{\text{Operating cash flows}}$$

25. Asset protection ratio $= \dfrac{\text{Gross receivables } - \text{ unearned finance charges}}{\text{Total debt}}$

26. Reserve and loss ratio $=$

$$\dfrac{\text{Net losses on charge-offs for the year}}{\text{Average receivables (gross receivables } - \text{ unearned finance charges)}}$$

27. Reserves as a percentage of receivables =

$$\frac{\text{Reserve for losses}}{\text{Gross receivables} - \text{unearned finance charges}}$$

28. Loan spreads $= \dfrac{\text{Net interest earned (interest revenues} - \text{interest expense)}}{\text{Average receivables (gross receivables} - \text{unearned charges)}}$

29. Ratio of senior debt to capital $= \dfrac{\text{Total senior debt}}{\text{Subordinated debt} + \text{net worth}}$

SOURCES AND SUGGESTED REFERENCES

Bernstein, L. A., and Siegel, J. G., "The Concept of Earnings Quality," *Financial Analysts Journal,* July–August 1979. Vol. 35, No. 4, pp. 72–75.

Casey, C. J., and Bartczak, N. J., "Using Operating Cash Flow Data to Predict Financial Distress: Some Extensions," *Journal of Accounting Research,* Spring, 1985, pp. 384–401.

Financial Accounting Standards Board, "Objectives of Financial Reporting by Business Enterprises," Statement of Financial Accounting Concepts No. 1, FASB, Stamford, CT, 1978.

——, "Accounting for the Translation of Foreign Currency Transactions and Foreign Currency Financial Statements," Statement of Financial Accounting Standards No. 8, FASB, Stamford, CT, 1975.

——, "Financial Reporting for Segments of a Business Enterprise," Statement of Financial Accounting Standards No. 14, FASB, Stamford, CT, 1986.

——, "Financial Reporting and Changing Prices," Statement of Financial Accounting Standards No. 33, FASB, Stamford, CT, 1979.

——, "Capitalization of Interest Cost," Statement of Financial Accounting Standards No. 34, FASB, Stamford, CT, 1979.

——, "Foreign Currency Translation," Statement of Financial Accounting Standards No. 52, FASB, Stamford, CT, 1981.

——, "Disclosures about Oil and Gas Producing Activities," Statement of Financial Accounting Standards No. 69, FASB, Stamford, CT, 1982.

——, "Employers' Accounting for Pensions," Statement of Financial Accounting Standards No. 87, FASB, Stamford, CT, 1985.

——, "Consolidation of All Majority-Owned Subsidiaries," Statement of Financial Accounting Standards No. 94, FASB, Stamford, CT, 1987.

——, "Statement of Cash Flows," Statement of Financial Accounting Standards No. 95, FASB, Stamford, CT, 1987.

International Accounting Standards Committee, "Consolidated Financial Statements and Accounting for Investments in Subsidiaries," International Accounting Standard 27, IASC, London, England, 1988.

Livnat, J., and Sondhi, A. C., "Estimating the Components of Operating Cash Flows," Working Paper, New York University, December 1989.

Ronen, J., and Sondhi, A. C., "Debt Capacity and Financial Contracting: Finance Subsidiaries," *Journal of Accounting Auditing and Finance,* Spring 1989, pp. 237–265.

Securities and Exchange Commission, "Notice of Adoption of Amendments to Regulation S-X Requiring Disclosure of Certain Replacement Cost Data," Accounting Series Release No. 190, SEC, Washington, DC, 1976.

Sondhi, A. C., Sorter, G. H., and White, G. I., "Cash Flow Redefined: FAS 95 and Security Analysis," *Financial Analysts Journal,* November–December 1988, pp. 19–20.

FINANCIAL STATEMENT AREAS

CHAPTER 11

CASH AND INVESTMENTS

Anthony D. Todd, CPA

Price Waterhouse

CONTENTS

GENERAL ASPECTS OF CASH

11.1 NATURE AND IMPORTANCE OF CASH.   Cash is both the beginning and the end of the operating cycle (cash–inventory–sales–receivables–cash) in the typical business enterprise, and almost all transactions affect cash either directly or indirectly. Cash transactions are probably the most frequently recurring type entered into by a business because (except for barter transactions) every sale leads to a cash receipt and every expense to a cash disbursement.

Cash derives its primary importance from its dual role as a medium of exchange and a unit of measure. As a medium of exchange, it has a part in the majority of transactions entered into by an enterprise. Assets are acquired and realized, and liabilities are incurred and liquidated, in terms of cash. Thus, cash is generally the most active asset possessed by a business firm. As a unit of measure, it sets the terms on which all properties and claims against the enterprise are stated in its financial statements. Once thought to have a fixed value, cash is now recognized as fluctuating in value as general and specific price levels rise and fall. Under SFAS No. 89, "Financial Reporting and Changing Prices" such changes in the value of cash may be disclosed in financial statements on a supplementary basis.

11.2 DEFINITION OF CASH.   Cash exists both in physical and book entry forms: physical in the form of coin and paper currency as well as other negotiable instruments of various kinds, and book entry in various forms such as commercial bank deposits and savings deposits. In addition to coin and paper currency, other kinds of physical cash instruments that are commonly reported as cash for financial accounting purposes include certificates of deposit, bank checks, demand bills of exchange (in some cases), travelers' checks, post office or other money orders, bank drafts, cashiers' checks, and letters of credit.

All these forms of cash involve credit and depend for their ready acceptance on the integrity and liquidity of some person or institution other than those offering or accepting them as cash. This is true even for coin and paper currency which is, ultimately, dependent on the credit of the government issuing it. Given this integrity and liquidity, the book entry forms and other physical instruments are properly viewed as cash because of their immediate convertibility into cash in its currency form at the will of the holder. Convertibility in the case of savings accounts, certificates of deposit, and other time deposits may be something less than immediate depending on stipulated conditions imposed by the depository but the assurance of such convertibility makes these items a generally accepted form of cash.

11.3 PROBLEMS OF CASH ACCOUNTING AND CONTROL.   The major problem in accounting for cash in most enterprises is that of maintaining adequate control over the great variety and quantity of cash transactions. Cash receipts may come from such diverse sources as cash sales, C.O.D. transactions, collections on accounts and notes, bank loans, security issues, income from investments, and sales of such properties as retired assets, scrap, and investments. Disbursements may be made for a variety of expense items, for cash purchases and in payment of various liabilities, for dividends and for taxes. Thus, the variety of cash transactions in itself presents inherent problems.

The quantity of cash transactions constitutes another source of difficulty. To handle expeditiously the volume of cash transactions in many companies calls for appropriate equipment, careful organization and segregation of duties, planning of procedures, and design of appropriate forms. Information as to available cash balances is of daily interest to the management of every business and this information must be accurate and prompt if it is to be useful.

TREATMENT OF CASH IN PUBLISHED FINANCIAL REPORTS

11.4 PROBLEMS OF PRESENTATION.   The presentation of cash in the balance sheet is largely an issue of appropriate classification and description. Because of its importance in any appraisal of financial condition, cash must be stated as accurately as possible. This calls for careful analysis of each component of cash so that no items will improperly be included in, or excluded from, current assets. In this connection, ARB No. 43, "Restatement and Revision of Accounting Research Bulletins" (Ch. 3, pars. 4–6), states:

> For accounting purposes, the term current assets is used to designate cash and other assets or resources commonly identified as those which are reasonably expected to be realized in cash or

sold or consumed during the normal operating cycle of the business. Thus the term comprehends in general such resources as (a) cash available for current operations and items which are the equivalent of cash. . . .

This concept of the nature of current assets contemplates the exclusion from that classification of such resources as: (a) cash and claims to cash which are restricted as to withdrawal or use for other than current operations, are designated for expenditure in the acquisition or construction of noncurrent assets, or are segregated for the liquidation of long-term debts. . . .

11.5 FORM OF PRESENTATION.   As the one asset that is completely liquid, that is, expendable with no intermediary transactions or conversions, cash assumes the position of prime importance in the balance sheet and is generally presented as the first item among the assets of the enterprise. Examples of presentation are:

1. Cash (includes time deposits and certificates of deposit, $3,000,000) $8,000,000
2. Cash, including time deposits and certificates of deposit $8,000,000
3. Cash in banks and on hand $8,000,000
4. Cash $8,000,000

Generally, the form shown in example 4 above is widely used, but the important point is that cash subject to withdrawal restrictions should not be combined with cash of immediate availability. In this regard, Defliese, Johnson, and Macleod (1985) state: "Unless otherwise stated, the cash captions on the balance sheet should include cash on hand and cash in banks that is immediately available for any purpose."

11.6 BANK OVERDRAFTS.   Closely related to the presentation of cash in the balance sheet is the presentation of what may be termed the absence of cash—in other words, a bank overdraft. Overdrafts may be of two kinds: (1) an actual *bank* overdraft, resulting from payment by the bank of checks in an amount exceeding the balance available to cover such checks; (2) a *book* overdraft, arising from issuance of checks in an amount in excess of the balance in the account on which drawn, although such checks have not cleared through the bank in an amount sufficient to exhaust the account.

Bank overdrafts represent the total of checks honored by the bank without sufficient funds in the account to cover them; such an overdraft is the bank's way of temporarily (or normally, as in Europe) loaning funds to its customer. Accordingly, bank overdrafts (other than those that arise in connection with a "zero-balance" or similar arrangement with a bank) represent short-term loans and should be classified as liabilities regardless of whether positive cash balances may exist in other accounts with the same bank.

Book overdrafts representing outstanding checks in excess of funds on deposit should generally be classified as liabilities and cash reinstated at the balance sheet date. Such credit book balances should not be viewed as offsets to other cash accounts except where the legal right of offset may exist within the same bank due to the existence of other positive balances in that bank.

FTB No. 88-2, effective for transactions entered into after December 31, 1988, provides additional guidance on when a recognizable right of offset exists. Where right of offset does not exist, the credit balance can be viewed as a reinstatement of the liabilities that were cleared in the bookkeeping process. When outstanding checks in excess of funds on deposit are reclassified, it is preferable that they be separately classified; if they are included in accounts payable, the amounts so included should be disclosed, if material. Reclassifying as a liability *all* outstanding checks (including those covered by funds on deposit in the bank account concerned) is not generally considered acceptable.

11.7 RESTRICTED CASH.   Cash restricted as to use by agreement, such as amounts deposited in escrow or for a specified purpose subject to release only at the order of a person other than the depositor, should not be classified in the balance sheet as cash and, unless deposited to meet an existing current liability, should presumably be excluded from current assets. Cash is sometimes received from customers in advance payment for work being performed under contract or under similar circumstances. Such cash is properly designated as cash in the balance sheet, but may be properly classified as a current asset only if the resulting customer's deposit is classified as a current liability. Cash restricted as to withdrawal because of inability of the depository to meet demands for withdrawal (such as deposits in banks in receivership) is not a current asset and should not be designated in the balance sheet as cash without an appropriate qualifying caption.

In regard to cash awaiting use for construction or other capital purposes or held for the payment of long-term debt, Defliese, Johnson, and Macleod (1985) state:

> Cash sometimes includes balances with trustees, such as those for sinking funds, or other amounts that are not immediately available, such as those restricted to uses other than current operations, designated for acquisition or construction of noncurrent assets, or segregated for the liquidation of long-term debt. Restrictions are considered effective if the company clearly intends to observe them, even though the funds are not actually set aside in special bank accounts. The facts pertaining to those balances should be adequately disclosed, and the amounts should be properly classified as current or noncurrent.

11.8 FOREIGN BALANCES.   Cash in foreign countries may properly be included in the balance sheet as cash if stated at its equivalent in United States currency at the prevailing rate of exchange and if no exchange restrictions exist to prevent the transfer of such monies to the domicile of the owner. Depending on circumstances and the extent to which such cash balances may be subject to exchange control or other restrictions, the amount of cash so included should be considered for disclosure, either by being stated separately, parenthetically or otherwise. The question of exchange restrictions (or economic conditions) preventing transfer of cash across national boundaries is of prime importance, and cash in foreign countries should be classified as a current asset only if appropriate review establishes that no significant restrictions or conditions exist with respect to the amounts involved. If restrictions exist but ultimate transfer seems probable, the cash may be included in the balance sheet in a noncurrent classification.

Difficulty in stating foreign cash balances at their equivalent in United States currency occurs when more than one rate of exchange exists. In this situation, the use of an exchange rate related to earnings received from the foreign subsidiary for the purpose of translating foreign currency accounts is recommended. SFAS No. 52 (pars. 26–28) provides guidance on the selection of exchange rates.

11.9 MISREPRESENTED CASH BALANCES.   Companies sometimes distort their cash balance to improve the appearance of their financial condition. This practice is sometimes called "window dressing." Smith and Skousen (1990) describe this practice as follows:

> Certain practices designed to present a more favorable financial condition than is actually the case may be encountered. For example, cash records may be held open for a few days after the close of a fiscal period and cash received from customers during this period reported as receipts of the preceding period. An improved cash position is thus reported. If this balance is then used as a basis for drawing predated checks in payment of accounts payable, the ratio of current assets to current liabilities is improved. The current ratio may also be improved by writing checks in payment of obligations and entering these on the books even though checks are not to be mailed until the following period.

11.10 COMPENSATING CASH BALANCES.   It is not uncommon for banks to require that a current or prospective borrower maintain a compensating balance on deposit with the bank. Frequently, the required compensating balance is based on the average outstanding loan balance. A compensating deposit balance may also be required to assure future credit availability (including maintenance of an unused line of credit). The compensating balance requirement may be (1) written into a loan or line of credit agreement, (2) the subject of a supplementary written agreement, or (3) based on an oral understanding. In some instances, a fee is paid on an unused line of credit (or commitment) to ensure credit availability.

The SEC originally defined compensating balances in ASR No. 148 as follows:

> A compensating balance is defined as that portion of any demand deposit (or any time deposit or certificate of deposit) maintained by a corporation (or by any other person on behalf of the corporation) which constitutes support for existing borrowing arrangements of the corporation (or any other person) with a lending institution. Such arrangements would include both outstanding borrowings and the assurance of future credit availability.

For SEC registrants, requirements for the disclosure of restrictions on the withdrawal or use of cash and cash items, such as compensating balance arrangements, are set forth in Rule 5-02.1 of Regulation S-X. Guidelines and interpretations for disclosure are in FRP No. 203 and SAB Topic 6H. These provide useful information in evaluating the need for segregation and disclosure of compensating balance arrangements, including determination of the amount to be disclosed. Cash float and other factors should be considered.

Although no other authoritative literature requires SEC-mandated compensating balance disclosures in the financial statements of non-SEC registrants, disclosure of material compensating balances will usually be necessary for fair presentation of the financial statements in accordance with GAAP. Consequently, the disclosure of material compensating balance arrangements in financial statements of non-SEC reporting companies, whether maintained under a written agreement or under an informal agreement confirmed by the bank, is usually considered necessary as an "informative disclosure" under the third standard of reporting. It should be noted that compensating balances may also relate to an agreement or an understanding relative to **future credit availability** (including unused lines of credit). Compensating balances related to future credit availability should be disclosed as well as those related to outstanding borrowings.

As indicated in FRP No. 203.02.b, when a company is not in compliance with a compensating balance requirement at the balance sheet date, that fact should generally be disclosed together with actual or possible sanctions if such sanctions could be material. Regardless of whether a company has met the compensating balance requirement, it is desirable to disclose any sanctions for noncompliance under the compensating balance arrangement. Such disclosure may be stated, for example, as "Compensating balance deficiencies are subject to interest charges at the average rate for 91-day Treasury Bills." Further, some borrowing arrangements do not prohibit the withdrawal of compensating balances, but as a practical matter, future credit availability may be dependent on the maintenance of compensating balances. It may be desirable to disclose such arrangements in a note, for example, that "The compensating balances may be withdrawn but the availability of short-term lines of credit is dependent on maintenance of such compensating balances."

(a) Note Disclosure Method of Compensating Balances.   In circumstances where compensating balances relative to outstanding loans and future credit availability are not legally restricted as to withdrawal, note disclosure is appropriate.

(b) Segregation in the Balance Sheet.   Cash which is not subject to withdrawal should be classified as a noncurrent asset to the extent such cash relates to the noncurrent portion of the debt which causes its restriction. To the extent legally restricted cash relates to short-term borrowings, it may be included with unrestricted amounts on one line in financial statements of non-SEC reporting companies provided the caption is appropriate and there is disclosure of the restricted amounts in the notes, for example, "Cash and restricted cash (Note 3)." Rule 5-02.1 of Regulation S-X requires SEC-reporting companies to "disclose separately" funds legally restricted as to withdrawal, but FRP No. 203.02.b is more specific in its requirement to **segregate** all legally restricted cash in the balance sheet.

No single example is appropriate for the disclosure of all compensating balance arrangements and future credit availability (including unused lines of credit) because the terms of loan agreements vary greatly. However, the following hypothetical examples illustrate methods of disclosing the details of compensating balance agreements and future credit availability.

The following is an example of disclosure where withdrawal of the compensating balance was legally restricted at the date of the balance sheet.

CASH ITEMS DISCLOSED ON BALANCE SHEET

SEC-Reporting Companies

Current assets
  Cash $3,500,000
  Restricted cash
    compensating balances (Note X)   6,000,000

Non-SEC Reporting Companies

Current assets
  Cash and restricted cash (Note X) $9,500,000

Note X. Compensating Balances

A maximum of $100,000,000 is available to the company under a revolving credit agreement. Under the terms of the agreement, the company is required to maintain on deposit with the bank a compensating balance, restricted as to use, of 10% of the outstanding loan balance. At December 31, 19XX, $6,000,000 of the cash balance shown in the balance sheet was so restricted after adjusting for differences of "float" between the balance shown by the books of the company and the records of the bank.

For SEC-reporting companies, the following disclosure should be added to the above note:

This "float" amount consisted of $3,000,000 of unpresented checks less $500,000 of deposits of delayed availability at the agreed-upon schedule of 1.5 days' deposits.

The following is an example of disclosure for both SEC and non-SEC reporting companies where withdrawal of the compensating balance was not legally restricted at the date of the balance sheet.

Current assets
  Cash (Note X) $10,000,000

Note X. Compensating Balances

Under an informal agreement with a lending bank, the company maintains on deposit with the bank a compensating balance of 5% of an unused line of credit and 10% of the outstanding loan balance. At December 31, 19XX approximately $5,800,000 of the cash balance shown in the balance sheet represented a compensating balance.

11.11 DISCLOSURE OF UNUSED LINES OF CREDIT.   Rules 5-02.19 and 22 of Regulation S-X require that the amount and terms (including commitment fees and the conditions under which commitments may be withdrawn) of unused lines of credit or unused commitments for financing arrangements be disclosed in the notes to the financial statements if significant and that the amount of these lines of credit that supports a commercial paper borrowing arrangement or similar arrangement be separately identified.

The term **unused lines of credit** is used for short-term financing arrangements; the term **unused commitments** refers to long-term financing arrangements.

Many future credit arrangements are informal. Even formal arrangements may be withdrawn by lending institutions on very short notice, usually resulting from an adverse change in the financial position of a company. Therefore, limitations relating to the subsequent use of such lines of credit make it particularly difficult to provide informative and adequate disclosure so that the reader does not get a more favorable picture than is warranted. Because of the uncertainty of the duration of some lines of credit, disclosure of these types of lines of credit in financial statements requires the exercise of individual judgment based on the facts of the particular situation, and disclosures should include the limitations and conditions of subsequent use. Unused lines of credit or commitments that may be withdrawn at the mere option of the lender need not be disclosed but, if disclosed, the nature of the arrangement should be disclosed as well.

Disclosure of lines of credit and other borrowing arrangements prescribed in FRP No. 203 is generally not considered to be essential information in financial statements of non-SEC reporting companies. In certain cases, however, such as when unused lines of credit support outstanding commercial paper, this type of information may be significant in evaluating financial position. Where this is so, disclosure of future credit availability under written or informal agreements would be necessary for a "fair presentation," provided the unused credit may not be withdrawn solely at the option of the would-be lender. A fee paid on an unused line of credit or commitment would provide evidence of a binding agreement, as would maintenance of a compensating balance for this purpose.

(a) Fee Paid for Future Credit Availability.   A commitment fee has an effect on the cost of borrowing that is similar to that of a compensating balance. If a fee is paid to a lending bank for an unused line of credit or commitment, such fee should be disclosed if significant (Rule 5-02.19b of Regulation S-X).

(b) Disclosure of Unused Lines of Credit.   The following is an example of disclosure of binding bank credit arrangements. Information of this nature may be combined with note disclosure of indebtedness.

Note X. Unused Lines of Credit

Bank lines of credit under which notes payable of $105,000,000 were outstanding at December 31, 19XX, aggregated $152,500,000. The use of these lines generally is restricted to the extent that the Company is required periodically to liquidate its indebtedness to individual banks for 30 to 60 days each year. Borrowings under such agreements are at interest rates ranging from $\frac{1}{4}$ to $\frac{1}{2}$ of 1% above the prime rate, plus a commitment fee of $\frac{1}{4}$ to $\frac{1}{2}$ of 1% on the unused available credit. Commitments by the banks generally expire one year from the date of the agreement and are generally renewed.

For SEC-reporting companies the following disclosure should be added to the above note:

Total commitment fees paid on the unused lines of credit amounted to $175,000 for 19XX, $195,000 for 19XW, and $180,000 for 19XV.

CONTROL OF CASH FUNDS

11.12 IMPORTANCE OF CONTROL OF CASH.   From the standpoint of internal control structure, cash is among the most difficult and important of the assets for which to account. Smith and Skousen (1990) indicate that

Because of the characteristics of cash—its small bulk, its lack of owner identification and its immediate transferability—it is the asset most subject to misappropriation, intentional or otherwise. Losses can be avoided only by careful control of cash from the time it is received until the time it is spent.

11.13 CONTROL OF CASH ON HAND AND CASH BALANCES. Included within the requirements for adequate control of cash on hand are the following:

1. Designation of specific responsibility for custody of each fund.
2. Limitation, insofar as possible, of the number of employees who have access to cash.
3. Bonding of all employees who have access to significant cash funds.
4. Physical protection of all funds through the use of bank facilities, vaults, locked cash drawers, cashiers' cages, and so on.
5. Holding cash on the premises to an absolute minimum so that superior protective features of banking institutions can be used as fully as possible.
6. Separation of the duty of custody of cash balances from the functions of accounting and record keeping.
7. Periodic examination and count or other review of balances by employees who do not handle or record cash.

11.14 ASSIGNMENT OF RESPONSIBILITY FOR CASH. In the corporate form of business enterprise, the treasurer should be the general custodian of all cash belonging to the business. Heckert and Willson (1963) write:

> With respect to the planning and control of cash, a very close and cooperative relationship must exist between the controller and treasurer. Duties and responsibilities vary in different firms. However, in most industrial or commercial concerns the treasurer is the custodian of cash funds and exercises supervision over the receipts and disbursements. He may select the depository, subject to the approval of the president or other designated authority. Usually it is he who maintains the necessary relationships with banks and other financial agencies.

> Because of the assumed close relationship between cash and cash records, the duties of the treasurer often extend to prescribing the methods of recording cash transactions. In practice, however, with the concurrence of the treasurer, the cash receipts and disbursements procedures are established and periodically reviewed by the controller. This ties in with his usual responsibility for maintaining the corporate, general, and cost accounting records of the company.

In a proprietorship, the proprietor has final responsibility as custodian; in a partnership, it is one of the partners. Various employees may be assigned responsibility under the general custodian for specific funds, but general responsibility should be vested in a single officer.

The custodian of cash is generally called on to make periodic reports of all cash receipts, disbursements, and balances.

11.15 COMPOSITION OF CASH. Cash owned by a business may be represented by a number of different accounts, of which the more common are:

1. Office petty cash or working funds.
2. Store and warehouse change funds.
3. Cash receipts held awaiting deposit.
4. Bank accounts:
   a. Commercial accounts.
   b. Savings accounts.
   c. Time deposits or certificates of deposit.

As an ordinary precaution against loss, no well-run business keeps any more cash on hand than the minimum required for making change and handling miscellaneous transactions over the counter, petty disbursements, and so on. This means that, apart from petty cash and change funds (which are usually nominal in amount) and the current day's receipts, all cash will be represented by bank accounts. Furthermore, widespread acceptance of credit cards diminishes the need to rely on large ready cash funds.

11.16 PETTY CASH AND WORKING FUNDS.   Each petty cash or working fund should be in the sole custody of a single employee, responsible to the treasurer. The number of such funds should be restricted to a minimum, but practical requirements often demand that funds be maintained at a number of locations. Petty cash funds should be established by withdrawals from the general bank account and should be kept under general ledger control. Once established, each fund should be maintained on an imprest basis, which means that the amount of the fund remains constant and that the custodian is reimbursed by check on the general bank account for amounts paid out of the fund upon presentation and surrender of satisfactory evidence of such disbursements. The amount of the reimbursing check should always be for the exact amount of the disbursements made from the fund.

Reimbursement need be made only as frequently as the fund requires replenishing (except that reimbursement is often made at the close of each accounting period in connection with the practice of charging the amount of the reimbursing check directly to the accounts representing the various expenditures). Each petty cash fund should be balanced periodically by the custodian; the frequency of balancing is dependent somewhat on the size of the fund and the volume of transactions but should occur at least as often as the fund is reimbursed. Satisfactory control requires that, at irregular but reasonably frequent intervals, the treasurer, or someone designated by him, make a surprise count of the petty cash funds to assure that they are intact and that evidences of disbursements held therein, in lieu of cash, are proper.

The practice of cashing checks out of the petty cash fund for the convenience of employees and others offers opportunity for manipulation and should be restricted to a minimum. Any checks that may be cashed should be presented to the bank for payment as promptly as possible and the cash should be returned to the fund. Retention of cashed checks in the fund for a period longer than necessary to cash them should be forbidden. If it is necessary to cash checks on a large scale, a special fund for this purpose could be established and cleared of cashed checks daily. Acceptance of postdated checks for cashing should not be permitted.

Change funds are established and controlled in the same manner as are petty cash funds, but these are strictly revolving funds and require no replenishment. The number of change funds will vary with the number of cash registers or with the number of locations at which cash sales are made or collections are made on account. The amount of each change fund remains constant, and that amount is withheld at the close of each day from the total cash in the register or cash drawer as the fund with which to begin the following day; the remaining cash in the register or drawer is turned in as representing the current day's receipts. Thus, if the total cash at the close of the day does not agree with the sum of the established change fund and the recorded receipts, the difference is considered to affect the day's receipts and not the fund. Large stores frequently keep a number of change funds, or "banks," in reserve to be issued to extra employees during periods of increased business activity. The usual practice is to provide for each change fund a locked container, appropriately identified, in which the fund is placed and delivered to a place of safekeeping during nonbusiness hours, to be returned to the custodian employee upon resumption of business. The person charged with responsibility for a change fund should have sole access to it. A duplicate key may be kept in a sealed envelope, signed across the seal by the employee, for use in emergencies. When this key is used, access to the funds should be witnessed by a second employee and the key replaced in an envelope signed across the seal by the employees who accessed the funds. The person responsible for the fund should count it in the presence of a witness to assure that it is intact, then take sole custody of the fund again by placing the duplicate key in a sealed envelope with his signature across the seal.

Under no circumstances should cash receipts be retained with the change fund after the close of the business day, and never with the petty cash fund.

11.17 CASH HELD FOR DEPOSIT.   Custody of cash receipts held awaiting deposit is generally a temporary responsibility that is renewed daily, for, as explained in the discussion of the receipt of cash, all cash received should be deposited intact as promptly as possible, preferably at the close of each business day. Pending such deposit, however, the cash should be retained in the cash registers or in the cashier's department and should be inaccessible to any but properly authorized employees.

11.18 RETURNED CHECKS.   Checks that are returned by the bank unpaid because of insufficient funds or for other reasons should be charged back immediately to the customer from whom received or, if it is found that the reason for nonpayment has been eliminated, should be redeposited without delay. Arrangements should be made with the bank so that returned checks are delivered to someone other than the employee responsible for their deposit, and in that way any fictitious checks deposited to cover temporary shortages may be brought to light. It is not good practice to carry such checks as cash items in the cashier's department or as a part of a petty cash or change fund.

11.19 POSTDATED CHECKS.   Occasionally, postdated checks are presented, or a debtor presents a check of a current date but requests that it not be presented to the bank for payment until some future date. Such checks do not constitute cash and, if accepted, should not be entered in the cash records until such time as they become negotiable. In the interim, they should be retained by the treasurer or cashier and safeguarded as if they were cash. It is good procedure to subject such items to general ledger control by crediting the customer and charging a "postdated check" account. When the checks are ready for deposit, they are entered as cash receipts and credited to the postdated check account, credit to the customer already having been made.

11.20 BANK ACCOUNTS.   In ordinary circumstances, the major portion of a company's cash is in the form of commercial bank accounts. The fact that the cash is not in the physical possession of the business does not, however, lessen the responsibilities of custodianship. If the depositor is a corporation, the bank will require a formal resolution designating the individuals authorized to make withdrawals of amounts deposited. The number of individuals authorized should be limited to the minimum consistent with expeditious operations. This may call for establishing separate accounts for such special purposes as payrolls and dividends, with a stated maximum on single withdrawals so that subordinate employees may be given a disbursement function without having access to the company's general cash account. The bank accounts, and relations with banks generally, should be the responsibility of the treasurer, and his custodianship entails a number of duties, the most important of which are outlined below.

(a) Deposits.   The cashier's department, through which all incoming cash must clear, should be under the direct control of the treasurer, and the bank deposits should be prepared and transmitted to the banks under his supervision. Acknowledged duplicate deposit slips should be obtained from the bank and retained on file in the treasurer's office. Any bank passbooks should also be retained under the control of the treasurer.

(b) Maintenance of Proper Balance.   Custody of the bank accounts entails the responsibility of maintaining balances sufficient to meet the needs of the business. To facilitate this, the treasurer's office should be furnished each day with a cash report showing the deposits and withdrawals for the previous day for each depository and the balance on deposit at the close of the day, in order that the treasurer may determine the sufficiency of the amounts available to meet future requirements, arrange for bank loans if required, or make transfers between depositories if the situation requires it. In order that the treasurer may maintain adequate balances in each depository, he must frequently review information as to the approximate nature, amount, and maturity or discount date of all obligations that must be met within a reasonable future period (see "Maintaining Optimum Cash Balances," section 11.44).

(c) **Disbursements.**   Although the disbursement of cash generally originates outside the treasurer's department, it is in that department that the responsibility rests, and it is there that final approval should be given. The treasurer or his representative should sign checks only after investigating the propriety of the proposed disbursement by examination of the underlying supporting data, authorization, and so on. To afford better internal checks, most businesses require that checks over a certain amount (usually excepting payroll checks) be signed and countersigned; one signature should be that of the treasurer or his representative.

11.21 REVIEW OF ACCOUNTABILITY.   The custodian of every fund is responsible for the integrity of that fund, and the discharge of that responsibility should be reviewed periodically. For petty cash, working, and change funds, this consists of surprise counts by independent employees, preferably on a supervisory level. For bank accounts it consists of reconciliation of the bank and general or subsidiary ledger balances. Reconciliation of bank and book balances is intended to discover any errors or irregularities in either the bank's or the company's record of the company's cash on deposit. Thus, it is an important feature of internal control over cash and should be performed with care.

The reconciliation should be prepared under the direction of the chief accountant by employees having no other duties relating to the receiving or disbursing of cash or the maintenance of cash records. The bank statement and paid checks should be delivered to the person responsible for reconciliation directly from the bank, unopened, and should remain in their control until the reconciliation has been completed. Any errors or irregularities discovered should be reported directly to a responsible officer for investigation.

11.22 RECONCILIATION OF BANK AND BOOK BALANCES.   Reconciling bank and book balances forces a review of all the cash transactions and provides a means of examining the accuracy of the accounting records of these transactions. With appropriate assignment of responsibility and employment of proper procedures, reconciliation enhances control of cash.

(a) **Reconciliation Procedure.**   The standard method of reconciling a bank account consists of the following steps:

1. Compare paid checks returned by bank with debits shown on bank statement.
2. Arrange checks in numerical sequence.
3. Compare checks returned with list of checks outstanding at close of previous month as shown by previous month-end reconciliation and with checks issued during the month as shown by cash disbursements record, noting all checks outstanding or issued that were not returned. This comparison should include check number, name of payee, and amount.
4. Scrutinize each check for proper endorsement. Any checks not properly endorsed should be returned to the bank immediately with a request that such endorsement be obtained.
5. List, by date, number, name, and amount, all checks that have not been paid by the bank as disclosed by the comparison of the checks returned with the previous month's list of checks outstanding and the cash disbursements record.

6. Ascertain that any amounts appearing in the previous month's reconciliation as deposits not credited by the bank appear as credits on the current month's bank statement.

7. Ascertain that all reconciling items other than checks outstanding and deposits not credited by the bank that appeared in the previous month's reconciliation have been accounted for either as corrections by the bank during the current month or by appropriate entry to the general ledger cash account.

8. Compare amounts transmitted to the bank for deposit with deposit amounts shown by the bank statements and list any that have not been credited by the bank.

9. Ascertain what charges and credits, if any, have been made by the bank during the month that have not been entered in the accounting records.

(b) Reconciliation Form. A bank reconciliation may take two different forms. The first form (Exhibit 11.1) agrees the balance per the bank statement to the balance per the books.

The second form (Exhibit 11.2) emphasizes the correct cash balance by reconciling both the bank balance and the book balance to the correct balance.

(c) Accounts with Large Quantities of Checks. If the quantity of checks issued against a single bank account is too great for satisfactory reconciliation as described, it is possible to facilitate the reconciliation procedure through the use of computers. Imprinting checks in such a way as to make the checks suitable input media for a computer permits constructing a computer program enabling the computer to compare checks returned by the bank to the checks issued, to determine the checks still outstanding. Alternatively, it may be possible to provide to the bank a computer tape or file of checks issued, for matching by the bank against checks paid and subsequent reporting to the company of checks paid and unpaid.

A "batch" method of reconciliation is also in use. With this method, checks are grouped and sorted by day or other period of issue ("batched"), and totals for paid checks are compared to totals for checks issued. Use of the batch method eliminates detailed comparison of paid checks with the check register, with a consequent saving of time.

Some firms use multiple bank accounts, usually in the same bank, and rotate their deposits

THADEUS, INC.
Bank Reconciliation
April 30, 19XX

Balance per bank statement, April 30, 19XX		$18,487.19
Add:		
Receipts for April 30 not yet deposited	$11,827.42	
Charge for interest made by bank in error	72.00	
Bank service charges not recorded in books	21.50	
Customer's check deposited April 19 and returned as		
uncollectible	427.19	12,348.11
		30,835.30
Deduct outstanding checks:		
No. 4172 $ 827.16		
No. 4180 94.22		
No. 4181 416.87		
No. 4186 1,319.27	2,657.52	
Check No. 4184 for $348 recorded in books as $384 in error	36.00	
Wire transfer received by bank on April 30 not in books	2,400.00	5,093.52
Balance per books April 30, 19XX		$25,741.78

Exhibit 11.1.   Reconciliation of bank balance to book balance.

THADEUS, INC.
Bank Reconciliation
April 30, 19XX

Balance per bank statement, April 30, 19XX		$18,487.19
Add:		
Receipts for April 30 not yet deposited	$11,827.42	
Charge for interest made by bank in error	72.00	11,899.42
		30,386.61
Deduct outstanding checks:		
No. 4172	$ 827.16	
No. 4180	94.22	
No. 4181	416.87	
No. 4186	1,319.27	2,657.52
Corrected bank balance		$27,729.09
Balance per books, April 30, 19XX		$25,741.78
Add:		
Wire transfer received by bank on April 30	$ 2,400.00	
Check No. 4184 for $348 recorded in books as $384 in error	36.00	2,436.00
		28,177.78
Deduct:		
Bank service charges	$ 21.50	
Customer's check deposited April 19 and returned as uncollectible	427.19	448.69
Corrected book balance		$27,729.09

Exhibit 11.2.   Reconciliation of bank and book balances to corrected balance.

and check issuances from account to account. Rotation leaves first one account, then another dormant long enough to permit all, or nearly all, transit items to clear and thus, in most cases, returns the balance of the account to zero or a predetermined amount. This system eliminates the need for a reconciliation or makes it very simple.

(d) Checks Long Outstanding.   With respect to checks that have been outstanding for protracted periods, Defliese, Johnson, and Macleod (1985) suggest:

> Outstanding checks should not be listed indefinitely on bank reconciliations. A sound practice is to stop payment after a year has elapsed, return the amounts to cash, and record a liability for the unpaid amounts. The liability should be credited to income after expiration of the applicable statute of limitations unless state laws require other disposition. Dividend checks may require special treatment because the laws of some states distinguish between the liability for uncashed dividend checks and that for other uncashed checks.

(e) Approval of Reconciliations.   Bank reconciliations should be reviewed and approved by the controller or some other official whose duties do not include the handling of cash. After such review and approval, appropriate entries should be prepared to reflect in the accounts all reconciling items other than deposits in transit and outstanding checks. Any reconciling items that represent errors by the bank should be reported to the bank for correction.

CONTROL OF CASH RECEIPTS

11.23 GENERAL REQUIREMENTS.   Sales lead to routine cash receipts in forms such as counter receipts, mail receipts, route collections, branch collections, receipts from decentralized collection offices, and receipts from outside collecting agents. Nonroutine cash receipts include proceeds from borrowing, issuance of stock, and asset retirements. To control its cash receipts from all these varied sources, a firm must control incoming mail, cashiers and their records, collectors other than cashiers, and bank deposits. Meigs, Larsen, and Meigs (1988) include the following items applicable to control of cash receipts:

1. Do not permit any one employee to handle a transaction from beginning to end.
2. Separate cash handling from record keeping.
3. Centralize receiving of cash as much as possible.
4. Record cash receipts immediately.
5. Encourage customers to obtain receipts and observe cash register totals.
6. Deposit each day's cash receipts intact.

To the fullest extent possible, a firm should employ systematized routines for handling and recording cash received. This includes assigning duties and responsibilities to individuals and providing evidence of the discharge of these duties and responsibilities. Adequate supervision and training should also be part of the routine. Unless employees know "why" as well as "how," lack of understanding may defeat the purpose of the routine. Adequate physical safeguards are also essential for proper control of cash receipts. This means safeguarding cash instruments during the interim between receipt and deposit and protecting records of cash receipts from alteration or destruction through use of cash registers, vaults, and locked file cabinets.

The possibility of collusion is a difficult obstacle to cope with in establishing control of cash receipts. Control techniques are available that help to prevent or detect collusion, and assist in coping with other abuses as well. Rotation of jobs and forced vacations strengthen control generally and may either deter or lead to detection of collusion. Other controls that relate to cash receipts include investigation of customer complaints, confirmation of accounts receivable balances, and surprise cash counts.

Bonding employees who handle or control substantial amounts of cash is also a fundamental part of controlling cash receipts. It is important to note that indemnification against loss is a part of, not a substitute for, a control system. In addition, cash coverage is expensive and repeated claims will result in increased premiums.

(a) Initial Record of Cash Receipts. Insofar as possible, cash receipts should be listed immediately on entry into the company's control by someone who will have no further control over cash handling or accounting. This listing establishes the accountability of all those who subsequently handle the cash and provides a basis for comparison with amounts actually deposited. If the employee who prepares the listing has no access to accounts receivable or other accounting records, he has no opportunity to conceal any failure to account for all cash received.

(b) Mail Receipts. Mail should be opened promptly on arrival and all remittances should be listed in detail by the mail clerk. The list may be prepared in triplicate, one copy being sent to the cashier for entry to the cash records, one copy being sent to the accounting department for posting to **accounts receivable** and other accounts, and one copy being forwarded to the treasurer for later comparison with daily deposit slips. The cash may be sent to the cashier or to the treasurer as circumstances dictate. The cashier should not be permitted to open mail, and posting to accounts receivable should not be made from the checks received on account.

(c) Counter Receipts. Cash receipts should be listed by cash register tape, cash sales ticket, remittance advice, or other means, and forwarded at least daily to the cashier's department. If cash is taken in by several cashiers, sales clerks, or others, some plan should be established for checking the receipts of each employee each day. Thus a supervisor might count each cash drawer, reconciling the total counted with the sum of the day's recorded receipts plus the basic change fund. The day's receipts should then be sent on to the cashier's department and a release of some kind given to the employee by the supervisor to establish a record of the actual amount turned in.

Once cash receipts have been listed so that subsequent accounting can be performed without reference to the cash itself, all cash may be merged for deposit. It is important in processing cash receipts that as few employees as possible be given access to them, that the responsibility for the receipts at each point of transfer be clearly established, and that each employee be bonded.

11.24 CASH REGISTERS.   Cash registers provide an effective and simple method of controlling the recording of cash receipts. In general, they provide (1) a locked-in record of the amount of cash entered on the register, (2) a printed ticket to be given to the customer or a visible record of the amount registered for the customer's examination, and (3) a safe place for holding a change fund and undeposited receipts. They can be used both for cash sales and for counter collections on account.

Most retail businesses employ cash registers as the first step in accounting for the receipt of cash. For most effective use, the register should, in addition to affording the customer a visible indication of the amount of the sale being registered, furnish the customer with a printed ticket showing the amount paid and produce a continuous printed and totaled record of the amounts registered, classified to the extent desired (within limits) as to the category of merchandise sold or department from which sold, salesperson making sale, cashier making collection, and so on, all of which can be designated by appropriate symbols on the record tape locked in the register. Where there are large numbers of cash registers, such as in a retail chain store, control of the cash registers themselves is important.

Some of the electronic cash registers used in many companies are on-line computer terminals. This expands the number of functions that can be performed at the point of sale and makes it possible to handle charge sales through the cash register with an automatic check of the customer's account before the sale is completed. In addition, accounts receivable and inventory records can be updated from this input. To reduce transcription errors, some systems use an electronic scanner to read data from price tags and customers' charge cards.

Cash registers for use at cashier's windows of public utilities offices and so on, may be designed to perforate or print a customer's receipt on the bill submitted for payment simultaneously with the recording of the payment on the register and at the same time produce a locked-in tape recording all payments received.

11.25 SALES TICKETS.   For statistical and other accounting and control purposes, some retail enterprises require a written record of each individual sale that is more detailed than the record produced by the traditional cash register. Such a record is prepared by the salesperson at the point of sale on a sales slip or ticket. These are available in a variety of forms, all of which have certain features in common, for example:

1. Slips must be consecutively prenumbered.
2. They must be supplied in bound pads or books of convenient size.
3. They must provide space for the customer's name and address (for charge sales), a description of the merchandise, individual selling prices, and total amount of sale.

Space may also be provided for recording date of sale, name, initials, or symbol of salesperson, and department in which sale is made, although those last items may be obtained by proper control over the serial numbers of books of tickets at time of issuance to the sales departments. Sales slips are usually bound in triplicate. The original copy is retained by the store for accounting and control purposes, the duplicate is given to the customer, and the triplicate is a tissue copy that remains bound in the book as a permanent record.

To control sales tickets, some companies use an autographic forms register. Stettler (1982) describes these registers as follows:

> These machines automatically feed a three-copy form into an open writing space. The clerk then writes the sales check, turns a crank, and the machine ejects two copies of the sales check and deposits the audit copy into a locked drawer. The audit copy is thus tamperproof, and there is less possibility that abstracted cash receipts can be concealed by showing different information on the customer's copy and the store's copy of the sales check.

11.26 DAILY AUDIT OF RECEIPTS.   The original sales slips are retained by the employee who prepared them until the close of the business day, when they are turned over to a central cashier together with all cash received during the day on cash sales. The tape printed in the cash register should be accessible only to a designated employee of the sales audit or controller's department (in small stores or branch stores, the manager, proprietor, or an office employee) and should not be accessible to the salespeople using the register. At the close of the business day, the employees having access to the registers should unlock and "read" each one, clear it for the following day, thus automatically recording on the tape the total of the current day's cash receipts, and remove the tape from the register. Such tapes should be retained for independent comparison with the total of the related cash sales slips and with the total cash turned in from the respective registers.

The cash turned in from the registers should be counted immediately (usually on the following morning) by the cashier's department and the bank deposit prepared. A list showing the amount removed from each register should be prepared for the sales audit department to compare with the register tapes and the sales slips. All differences between amounts obtained from the three sources must be explained. To obtain effective internal control, this comparison and accounting should be done by employees who have no access to the related cash. Concurrent with this accounting for daily cash sales, all sales slip serial numbers (both cash and charge) should be accounted for, the daily sales total determined, and the charge sales slips turned over to the bookkeeping department for posting to the specific customer accounts.

Collections on accounts receivable or miscellaneous cash receipts in a department store or other retail establishment should be handled in much the same manner as in any other business enterprise, that is, through a cashier's department, not through the cash sales receipts channels.

11.27 DECENTRALIZED COLLECTIONS.   Businesses operating through a chain of stores or through a number of branches usually require procedures for proper handling of cash receipts that differ somewhat from those appropriate to a business operating in a single location. Such is particularly the case if the branch is a sales outlet only and all accounting records are maintained at a main office. One common arrangement is to decentralize billing but request that customers remit directly to the central office.

(a) Branch Cash Sales.   If the branch is one whose receipts are exclusively from cash sales, the immediate recording may best be handled through a cash register system as heretofore explained. If the branch is close to the main office, the receipts may be delivered to the main office daily for deposit, or may be picked up by a main office messenger, together with the daily sales report. If this is not practicable, the daily receipts should be deposited intact in a bank convenient to the branch in an account designated for that specific purpose, subject to withdrawal only by the main office. A receipted duplicate deposit slip should be obtained by the branch from the bank and forwarded immediately to the main office with the related daily sales report and cash register tapes if the latter are used. Comparison of the amount deposited with the sales reported should be made at the main office and the cash entered in the general cash receipts records. Under such a plan, the branch bank account should be used exclusively for the deposit of branch receipts, and withdrawals therefrom should be only for transfer of funds to the general bank accounts.

A number of systems are employed to effect such transfers. Irrespective of the method followed, bank statements of the branch account should be obtained by the main office directly from the bank, and under no circumstances is it desirable to make disbursements from such accounts except for transfers of funds to other bank accounts.

(b) Branch Collections on Account.   Where a branch receives collections on account in addition to receipts from cash sales, the procedure will be identical with that followed by the branch having cash sales receipts only, except that a detailed daily collection report must be submitted to the main office together with the daily sales report. Data for posting to the individual customers' accounts at the main office must be obtained from the collection report. If the branch is one that not only receives collections on account but maintains the accounts with its customers, it is not necessary to send a detailed collection report to the main office (see also the discussions of the lockbox system and concentration banking in section 11.50).

11.28 BANK DEPOSITS.   Cash and checks received should be deposited in the bank intact, as frequently as is expedient, preferably daily. Checks should be endorsed "for deposit only" as soon as they are received. Under such a plan, the entire amount received in any one day would be deposited as of the close of that day. Under no circumstances should disbursements be made from cash received for deposit.

Upon entry of the cash in the cash receipts records, the cashier should prepare the bank deposit. Ideally, the bank deposit slip should show all checks in detail as to source as well as amount, and a duplicate should be prepared to be acknowledged by the bank and retained on file by the treasurer. However, because of the volume of receipts, it may be impractical to indicate all such information on the deposit slip, and the slip may be prepared as a simple adding machine listing of the checks deposited.

(a) Comparison of Receipts and Deposits.   Comparison of the cash received each day, as summarized from the cash register tapes or other listings prepared when the cash is first received, with daily deposits as shown in the bank statement, received at least monthly, should be an integral part of the internal control program for cash receipts. This comparison should reveal any failure to deposit receipts in full, any tendencies to hold cash instead of depositing it promptly, and any restitution of amounts taken previously. It should be performed by someone not connected in any way with the processing or recording of cash receipts.

(b) Alternative Ways of Proving Cash Receipts.   Although most businesses rely on a well-designed system of internal checks to assure proper accounting for incoming cash, there are other ways to verify cash receipts. Businesses selling relatively few types of "one-price" merchandise in readily ascertainable units may depend on periodic physical inventories to determine the correctness of the cash received. Gasoline service stations, for example, by means of physical inventories taken daily or more often, are able to determine the amount of cash for which the operators are responsible. Chain clothing stores sometimes employ comparable methods to determine that all incoming cash is being properly handled and recorded.

CONTROL OF CASH DISBURSEMENTS

11.29 GENERAL REQUIREMENTS.   Kieso, Mautz, and Moyer (1989) list the following as essential to adequate control over cash disbursements:

1. All disbursements of material amount should be made by check.
2. Checks should be signed only on presentation of satisfactory documentary evidence that the disbursement is proper.

3. The imprest system should be used for minor cash disbursements and, where applicable, for payrolls, branch office expenses, and the like.
4. The function of purchasing and approving purchases should be separated from receiving and storing, and check signing should be separated from voucher preparation.

All general cash disbursements should be made by check in order to utilize the internal control features inherent in the check method of disbursement. These include (1) limitation of the disbursement function to specifically authorized persons, (2) definite fixing of responsibility for disbursements made, (3) a record of every disbursement, (4) possibility of separation of duties with respect to check preparation, signing, and mailing, and (5) elimination of the need for carrying large amounts of currency on hand to meet daily requirements. Checks may be prepared in a number of departments, but principally and preferably only in the accounts payable and payroll departments, wherein are kept the records relating to transactions requiring the disbursement of cash.

11.30 CHECKS PRODUCED BY COMPUTER.   Consolidation of activities and integration of functions is the expected condition in systems that employ computers. Writing checks and accounting for disbursements would normally be combined with such activities as processing invoices, inventory control, accounts payable, and possibly other functions. Check preparation and disbursement accounting thus become the final steps of a related series of activities surrounding a purchase. The computer generally produces checks and remittance statements that are ready for mailing as soon as they have been signed and separated, with names and addresses positioned to appear in the window of an envelope. It also prepares a cash disbursements register.

11.31 SAFEGUARDS IN ISSUING CHECKS.   All checks should be serially prenumbered to permit their full accountability. (This presumes that the checks have been specially printed and designed for the use of the business. If the checks used are the standard forms furnished by the bank to its depositors, prenumbering loses some of its advantages.) Checks should be written with care to prevent their fraudulent alteration. For example, no space should be left that would permit the insertion of either figures or written amounts to increase the amount of a check above that for which it was drawn by the issuer. Most businesses pass all checks through a "protector" that imprints the amount thereon in some ineradicable and unalterable manner.

The development of sophisticated copy machines with the capability of reproducing documents in color presents the possibility that a validly issued check may be reproduced several times and the copies and the original presented for payment. To protect checks from this risk, special checks have been developed that will cause the word "Void" to appear on any copies of the checks made on a color copier. The checks are further protected through two additional features. First of all, the face of the original check has a colored background that cannot be reproduced by a color copier, and this fact is stated on the top of the check. Second, the reverse side of the check has an artificial watermark that is impossible to reproduce on a copier because it can be read only when the check is held at an angle.

Checks should be prepared only on the basis of a properly authorized written instrument, such as an invoice, check requisition or approved payroll; checks should never be prepared on the basis of oral authority only. After checks have been prepared, they should be submitted to the authorized officials for signature, accompanied by the underlying data indicating the authority for, and propriety of, the check being issued. No check should be signed unless it is accompanied by its supporting data or until such supporting data have been reviewed for propriety by the signing official and compared with the check. After such review and comparison, the supporting data should be canceled in such a manner as to preclude their subsequent use in support of a duplicate or fraudulent disbursement. This cancellation should be done by or under the direction of the signing official, before the data are returned for filing in the department in which the check originated.

(a) Check Signatures.   Checks should ordinarily be signed by the treasurer or an assistant treasurer. To improve the effectiveness of internal control structure, many businesses require that checks also be countersigned. Those authorized to sign checks should not be the same persons who prepare the checks or authorize their issuance, or the employees who maintain the cash receipts and disbursement records. At least one of the signatures on the check should be manual. If a countersignature is affixed mechanically, the check-signing machine must be under the careful control of, and used only in the presence of, an official authorized to sign. This control is doubly important if the only signature is one mechanically affixed, as is often the case with payroll and dividend checks. Under no circumstances should blank checks be signed in advance of their preparation. If frequent absence of signing officials makes it difficult to obtain signatures when checks are due for issuance without resort to this procedure, additional officials or employees should be authorized to sign.

(b) Mailing.   Checks should be mailed directly from the treasurer's office, or turned over by the treasurer's office directly to the mailing department, without being returned to the department in which prepared.

(c) Spoiled Checks.   Checks spoiled in the course of preparation should be mutilated in a manner to prevent their issuance but should not be destroyed. The originals should be filed in numerical sequence with the paid checks returned by the bank, and the duplicates, if such are used, should likewise be retained in their proper numerical sequence. If for some reason checks that have been signed and entered in the disbursements record are not transmitted to the payee, they should be taken up as cash received and redeposited. This practice is preferable to cancellation of the check, because it avoids the necessity for a journal entry to the cash account or for a reversal entry in the check register.

11.32 CHECKBOOKS.   Checks may be obtained from the bank in bound form, each with a perforated stub on which to note, as a permanent record, the significant data with respect to the check for accounting purposes. Check stubs also provide for the recording of amounts deposited and for showing a running balance of the amount on deposit. The check stub, however, is often inadequate to meet the accounting requirements of even the small business enterprise, and in its stead, a check register or cash disbursements journal must be employed. The use of such a journal makes it unnecessary to use the check stub, and the checks in general business use are furnished with no stub attached.

11.33 CHECK REGISTER.   The typical form of check register provides for the listing in numerical sequence of all checks issued, showing date issued, check number, payee, amount disbursed, cash discount taken, and the account or accounts to be charged with the disbursement and the respective amount or amounts to be charged thereto. A manual check register may include a "money" column for each of the accounts most frequently charged with disbursements, and a single column for the disbursements that affect accounts other than those covered by the specially designated columns. If more than one bank account is in use, the number of "bank" columns should be expanded to provide one for each bank, or a separate check register should be used for each bank. The latter alternative is often more desirable as it facilitates the accounting for the numerical sequence of checks issued and simplifies the periodic reconciling of the bank accounts. Through variation of the number of columns and of the column headings, a check register can be adapted to a wide variety of situations. Entries in a register of the type described would usually be made directly from the checks themselves and the accompanying remittance advices to be transmitted to the payee, or would be prepared by a computer using the same source data that was used to prepare the checks.

11.34 VOUCHER CHECK.   Probably the most widely used form of check for general business purposes is one of a type that incorporates with the check a remittance advice on which to detail the items paid thereby, to be detached by the payee before the check is cashed. A check of this type is generally provided in duplicate or triplicate (the carbon copies bear the check number but are unsigned and distinguished from the original by differences in color). The duplicate copy can then be bound or filed in numerical sequence as a continuous record of checks drawn. The triplicate can be attached to the invoices or other data paid by the check to serve as a convenient means of identification or filing reference.

The use of a voucher check permits the numerically arranged duplicate copies to be used as a check register and eliminates the duplication of work required if all checks drawn must be transcribed in detail to a check register of the type previously discussed. If checks are issued in any considerable volume, the saving in time resulting from the use of the duplicate check as the check register is considerable. Under this plan, a total is obtained of the checks issued each day (indicating the check numbers included), which is entered in a cash disbursements summary distributed to the accounts affected by the disbursement. Monthly postings to the general ledger accounts are made from the cash disbursements summary. A plan of this kind can be used most advantageously if all items to be paid by check are distributed first by credit to "vouchers payable" or "accounts payable," permitting all debits from the check register to be made to a single account.

11.35 CHECKS INTEGRATED INTO VOUCHER SYSTEM. A check of the voucher type may readily be adapted to serve as an integral part of a voucher system. Such adaptation precludes using prenumbered checks. As invoices are received and approved for payment, a check is prepared immediately, except for insertion of the amount, and the invoice is listed on the remittance advice portion of the check. The check is then filed under the date of issuance, and this file constitutes the record of vouchers payable. (The invoices listed may or may not be attached to the check while it awaits issuance.) As additional invoices are received from the same vendors, they are listed on the check already prepared (provided they are payable on the same date). Separate checks must, of course, be prepared for each payment or discount date involved. Daily, the vouchers that are payable on that day are removed from the file, the total of the invoices listed on each check and the remittance to be made are determined, and the checks are filled in as to amount and consecutively numbered. Procedures thereafter are as previously described insofar as signatures, check register, and so on, are concerned.

11.36 CHECK REQUISITIONS. It has been previously stated that no check should be issued except on the basis of written authority. If the disbursement to be made is one not represented by an invoice or some other documentary evidence from the payee, a check requisition should be presented. This requisition should be prepared by the department or individual requiring the check, it should give all necessary information for preparing the check and determining the accounting distribution, and it should be approved by an appropriate official. The requisition serves in lieu of, and should be handled in every way as though it were, an invoice.

11.37 DIVISION OF DUTIES. Control of cash disbursements can be made very effective if all payments are made by check under a well-designed voucher system, excepting minor petty cash disbursements from an imprest fund. For maximum effectiveness, the disbursement functions should be separated completely from the duties of receiving cash and of approving invoices and other items for payment. The disbursement functions themselves should be separated, as far as is expedient, along the following lines:

1. Preparation of checks.
2. Entry of checks in register.
3. Signing of checks and comparison with underlying documents.
4. Transmittal of checks to payees.
5. Reconciling of bank accounts.

It is particularly important that checks be signed by individuals other than those who approve the underlying data and that bank accounts be reconciled by employees who have no other duties relating to the cash records.

11.38 PETTY CASH DISBURSEMENTS.   A satisfactory system of control of disbursements from petty cash funds requires the use of a formal prenumbered voucher to be filled out in ink and approved by an authorized official or employee other than the custodian of the fund before any disbursement is made from the fund. A separate voucher should be used for each disbursement from the fund, and supporting data, such as invoices, freight bills, and receipts, should be used as supplementary to, not in lieu of, the voucher. Such supporting data should be attached to each voucher and should accompany it when vouchers are surrendered for reimbursement. Upon reimbursement of the fund, every voucher (and all related supporting data) covered by the reimbursing check should be canceled in such a manner as to preclude subsequent use to evidence an unauthorized disbursement. Prior to issuance of the reimbursing check, the serial numbers of all petty cash vouchers used since the date of the previous reimbursement should be accounted for by someone other than the custodian of the fund to assure that all such vouchers have been properly used and that no disbursements covered thereby are permitted to remain undistributed as cash items constituting a part of the fund.

11.39 REIMBURSEMENT OF PETTY CASH.   The petty cash fund is reimbursed by a check drawn on the general bank account for the exact amount of petty cash disbursed. The total amount of the reimbursement is listed in the invoice journal as an account payable to the custodian of the fund, in the same manner as an invoice rendered by an outside supplier. The reimbursing check is then issued to the order of the custodian of the fund and charged to accounts payable. The check thus becomes a part of the fund and is presented by the custodian to the bank to obtain cash for replenishment. No entries are made to the general ledger petty cash account as long as the total amount of the fund remains unchanged.

11.40 PAYROLL AND DIVIDEND PAYMENTS.   Control of certain types of disbursement can be improved if they are made from special bank accounts reserved for such purposes. Salaries and wages are generally paid from special payroll bank accounts maintained on an imprest basis. Deposits are made to the account each pay period by a check drawn on the general bank account in the exact amount of the wages to be paid, and the general ledger balance of the payroll bank account remains at a constant figure (usually zero). The payroll record itself usually serves as the check register for the payroll bank account by the simple expedient of inserting opposite the name of each employee the number of the check issued thereto. If the earnings are determined and the payrolls prepared and approved in a department separate from that which prepares the payroll checks and distributes them to employees, control over the payroll disbursements is usually sufficient to permit the checks to be issued with a single signature, often not that of an official. However, an independent reconciliation of the payroll bank account is required.

Dividends are customarily paid from a separate bank account, deposits to which have been made in the exact amount of the dividend declared.

When a deposit is made to a special bank account, the sole effect is the transfer of cash from an unrestricted to a restricted status. The corporate liability is not liquidated by the deposit but must await disbursement from the special bank account. If a balance sheet is prepared between the dates of deposit and payment, the special bank account and the corporate obligation should not be offset; rather, each account should be appropriately classified as to its asset and liability characteristics.

Although control of payroll disbursements is most effective if these are made by check, payment in currency is required or desired in some situations. Currency for this purpose should be withdrawn from the general bank account in the exact amount required to meet the payroll, in such denominations as will most conveniently fill the respective pay envelopes.

11.41 BRANCH OFFICE DISBURSEMENTS.   Disbursements by branches may be controlled in a number of ways, depending on the size of the branch and the nature of the branch operation. Probably the most satisfactory, if conditions permit, is to maintain at the branch only an imprest fund for petty disbursements, to be reimbursed by the main office, and to pay all other branch items from the main office general bank account. Almost equally satisfactory is a system under which the branch has an imprest bank account on which it is permitted to draw. A report of all checks issued is submitted to the main office, accompanied by the data in support of such checks, and the imprest bank account is reimbursed by check on the main office bank account in the amount of the branch disbursements reported. Under such a system, it is advisable to have the bank statement of the imprest account mailed directly to the main office for reconciliation of balances. Other situations may require that the branch operate its own payroll account, on an imprest basis, but that all other expenditures, except from petty cash, be made from the main office bank account.

A branch should not be permitted to make disbursements from the account in which it deposits receipts from sales and collections, as explained in the discussion of cash receipts, unless it is a branch maintaining its own general accounting system with the attendant general bank accounts.

11.42 PURCHASE ORDER DRAFTS.   One example of a purchase order draft system involves the issuance of blank checks to selected suppliers for small purchases at the time the purchase order is mailed. The supplier ships the goods, fills in the check, including remittance information, and deposits the check in its bank account. When the check clears, it is used as the basis for recording the cash disbursement. Control is exercised by printing on the front of the check that it is not valid after 90 days or for amounts in excess of a certain amount, perhaps $500. In addition, the words "for deposit only to the account of payee" are printed on the reverse of the check so that the check is worthless to unauthorized persons.

The only significant cost of the system is the advancement in the liquidation of current liabilities when the system is initiated. Advantages claimed for it include reduction in total paperwork, elimination of any risk of losing cash discounts, reduction in back orders, facility in the automation of small dollar purchases, and increased goodwill from small vendors.

The system may also be applied to the payment of freight on outbound shipments and to reimbursing employees for business expenses paid out of their personal funds. If a postreview of transactions and documents is made a part of the system, it will provide adequate control in most circumstances.

CASH MANAGEMENT

11.43 RESPONSIBILITY FOR CASH MANAGEMENT.   In the *Price Waterhouse/Euromoney International Treasury Management Handbook* (1986) treasury (cash) management is defined as:

> . . . the management of the liquidity of the business to ensure that the right amount of funds in the right currency are in the right place at the right time. The management of liquidity should be undertaken in such a way as to maximize yields and minimize costs subject to security, liquidity, interest and currency risk constraints.

In addition to handling the problems of cash accounting and control, effective cash management involves speeding the collection and handling of cash receipts, proper timing of cash disbursements, maintaining optimum cash balances, borrowing on the most favorable terms possible, and efficient usage of excess cash.

In recent years, there have been significant developments in the area of sophisticated treasury management systems available to the corporate treasurer. Today, many computerized systems are available, from packages designed to handle one particular facet of the cash management function to complete **treasury workstations** intended as management decision support systems for the entire corporate treasury function. These systems are available both from banks and from independent software vendors or, in some cases, have been custom designed for a particular entity.

The treasurer and his staff usually have responsibility for the treasury function, including custody of cash funds, supervision of receipts and disbursements, maintaining relationships with financial agencies, and administering the investment portfolio. To perform these functions effectively, the treasurer's office must prepare cash forecasts and other cash reports, ordinarily based on information and profit projections supplied by the controller. Cooperation between the treasurer and the controller is essential for achieving the objectives of cash management.

Effective cash management frequently requires quick action. For this reason, it is preferable to vest authority for various aspects of cash management in individuals. It is appropriate for higher authority and/or committees to establish guidelines and limits for the individual(s) who has operating responsibility for cash management, but operating responsibility must vest in individuals to avoid delays that result in lost opportunities.

11.44 MAINTAINING OPTIMUM CASH BALANCES.   Idle cash is not a productive asset. For this reason, an optimum cash balance is the minimum amount required to meet financial obligations when and as they occur. Lundquist (1964) identifies four reasons for maintaining cash balances:

1. To meet obligations, including payrolls, creditors' bills, taxes, dividends.
2. To provide funds for recognized future needs.
3. To provide protection against business fluctuations.
4. To maintain good relations with banks.

In order to determine the amount of cash required to fill the first two needs, the cash manager needs the assistance of both short- and long-term cash forecasts. Protection against business fluctuations is the responsibility of top management, and the cash manager's actions in this area are guided by company policy. Closely related to this third problem is the maintenance of good relations with banks. In deciding on the amount to be kept on deposit over and above any minimum balance required by the bank, it should be kept in mind that banks tend to favor good customers when money is scarce.

11.45 DAILY CASH REPORT.   Sound administration of cash and other liquid assets requires that accurate information as to all available cash balances be supplied to the company's financial management currently. Daily cash reports vary considerably in arrangement but generally provide for showing the location of all cash that is available, the balance in each bank, and a summary of the day's cash transactions. Many major banks offer a daily cash reporting service whereby they collect balance and transaction information for all of a company's bank accounts, regardless of where located, and make it available to the cash manager on a terminal in his or her office. In addition to providing the raw data in bank accounts, some reporting services compare these data to target balances and suggest money movements that should be made to reach the targets. The cash manager can usually transmit money transfer instructions directly to the bank's money transfer department and receive confirmation that the transfer has been made, as well as a transfer identification number, all through a terminal in his office.

11.46 CASH RECEIPTS AND DISBURSEMENTS STATEMENT.   A cash receipts and disbursements statement summarizes prior cash transactions for a given period of time. The statement serves a dual purpose: (1) it provides a review of the sources of cash and the nature of cash disbursements, and (2) it furnishes a basis for estimating future cash needs and probable sources. A cash receipts and disbursements statement shows the beginning cash balance and lists by sources all cash received, all cash disbursed, and the ending cash balance. In essence, the statement represents an analysis of the cash account for a certain period of time.

11.47 THE CASH BUDGET.   Adequate cash to meet daily needs should be kept available at all times. On the other hand, it is unwise to carry larger balances of cash on hand or in checking accounts than are likely to be required by the actual needs of the company. This may call for short-term borrowing in those portions of the year when the need for cash is greatest and for temporarily investing cash in short-term government or other securities when the cash balance is excessive. In order that the treasurer may foresee the need for loan and investment transactions and plan accordingly, a cash budget or forecast should be prepared. Systematic and regular forecasting of cash flows, coupled with subsequent comparisons of actual performance with those forecasts, will also aid in identifying surprises that may have occurred in the past but have not been documented. Most important will be the identification of disbursements and receipts that can be controlled in order to improve cash flow and thereby increase the amount of investible funds.

(a) Nature of the Cash Budget.   A cash budget is not an operating statement. It is a prediction, based on careful analysis of past experience and anticipated conditions, of the flow of cash through the company. All noncash expenses, such as depreciation and amortization, are eliminated from consideration. Attention is directed only at those transactions that actually affect the company's cash balance. With the growing emphasis on cash management, the cash budget assumes ever greater significance. It is restricted to estimated cash transactions only.

Neither is the budget intended as a means of forecasting financial results. It is a method of organizing and using estimated cash receipt and disbursement data to facilitate adjustments in financial plans and policies as business developments make such modification necessary.

(b) Uses of the Cash Budget.   The primary purpose of a cash budget is to plan for the sources of cash necessary to meet cash requirements during a given period of time. A significant corollary purpose is to control the flow of cash funds through a company.

(c) Time Period of a Cash Budget.   Normally, a cash budget is prepared for each month of the budget period, but it is not uncommon for the budget to be prepared on a weekly or daily basis. A typical procedure is to prepare a cash budget for the next 10 days or 2 weeks with a subsequent breakdown by months.

A short-term cash budget covers a period of one year or less, whereas a long-term cash forecast or budget covers a period beyond a year. The former is particularly useful for planning daily operations; the latter is of value in formulating overall financial policies for a firm. Long-term forecasts are more tentative and contain less detail than do short-term forecasts. To achieve its maximum value, a long-term cash forecast should be integrated into a long-term company plan, which should include a forecast of earnings and plans for capital expansion.

11.48 CASH FORECASTING METHODS.   The specific procedures to be employed in the preparation of a cash budget must be adapted to the individual enterprise. The methods commonly used are (1) Cash receipts and disbursements method, and (2) Adjusted net income method. Each method produces the same end product—the expected cash balance at a particular point of time—but they differ in the basic sources of information and in the amount of detail that is made available in the budget.

(a) Cash Receipts and Disbursements Method.   This method, which is most frequently used, is essentially a projection of the cash records. Under this method, the forecast contains a detailed listing of the sources of cash receipts and the nature of cash disbursements, thereby providing a complete picture of expected cash transactions. The cash forecast under this method is an effective instrument of control, because individual cash receipts and disbursements can be compared with budgeted amounts. Companies that experience seasonal fluctuations and operate on small cash balances find this method of forecasting to be ideal for their needs.

In estimating cash receipts, consideration must be given to all sources of cash. The sales budget is particularly helpful in estimating cash sales. Past records and experience of the company plus knowledge of future plans and trends will provide information for forecasting cash receipts from interest, dividends, rents and royalties, proceeds from sale of investments, and fixed assets. Special care is required in predicting collections from customers. The company's collection experience must be reviewed in the light of prevailing business trends, seasonal influences, terms of sale, and discount and credit policies. Individual percentage estimates of collections should be made of each month's sales. These percentages can then be applied to the budgeted credit sales of other months to arrive at the total cash collections of each month.

In forecasting cash disbursements, recourse should be made to (1) other budgets (the operating budget, the raw materials budget, the plant and equipment budget, etc.), (2) contractual commitments, and (3) board action. The determination of total cash payments to vendors is frequently a problem. Only in a few instances are materials and services purchased for cash; however, a firm, with the assistance of its purchasing department's information about probable delivery dates and a knowledge of its procedures for processing disbursements, should be able to estimate the lags with reasonable accuracy. Design of the disbursement system should ensure qualification for cash discounts, and the effect of these discounts should be considered in estimating cash disbursements.

Initially, only operating transactions are included in the cash budget. This affords management an opportunity to measure the cash position necessary to, and resulting from, daily operations. From these findings, management can then formulate policy concerning financial activities—short-term and long-term borrowing, voluntary debt reduction, replacement or expansion of capacity, and dividends—for later incorporation into the overall cash budget.

(b) Adjusted Net Income Method.   The estimated statement of income and expense provides the starting point for this method. The expected net income is first adjusted for all noncash transactions to arrive at estimated income or loss on a cash basis; second, this amount is adjusted for cash transactions that do not affect the income calculation. For example, depreciation expense is added to estimated earnings, because it does not require a cash outlay, and the amount of expected capital expenditures is deducted from earnings; similarly, the excess of expected collections over sales for the period is also added to adjusted earnings in determining total expected cash receipts.

The adjusted net income method is particularly suitable for long-term forecasts because it highlights changes taking place in all the components of the company's working capital rather than focusing only on changes in cash. Under the adjusted net income method, cash receipts and disbursements are not forecasted item by item, with the result that effective control over cash is seldom possible. Only companies that forecast future earnings can use this procedure, and the accuracy of the cash forecast is directly proportionate to the accuracy of the estimated earnings.

11.49 RELATIONSHIPS WITH BANKS.   Banks perform many services for their customers, for some of which they make no specific charge. To have good relationships with banks, firms must maintain bank balances that are adequate to compensate banks for these services and to fulfill minimum balance requirements on loan and line-of-credit arrangements. In addition to lending money, banks provide many other services, including investing money and acting as an investment advisor; transferring money; assisting in the issuance of bonds and stock; acting as registrars and transfer agents; acting as trustee of a bond indenture; acting as trustee of a retirement fund; assisting in mergers and acquisitions; obtaining credit and other confidential information; performing data processing and related services; and reconciling bank accounts.

A cash manager's objective is to maintain a bank balance that is satisfactory to the bank, yet not excessive. To achieve this objective, he must keep informed about each bank used with regard to its practices in analyzing depositors' accounts for profitability. Most banks compute a loanable balance for a depositor by reducing the balance of the depositor's account for reserve requirements and float. A bank's reserve requirement is the fraction of its deposits it must retain in cash and/or redeposit in a Federal Reserve bank. Float is the delay in collecting transit items deposited in an account. After allowing for earnings at a given rate on the loanable balance, banks usually deduct an estimate of the cost of the services provided to the depositor.

11.50 TECHNIQUES TO PERMIT RELEASE OF CASH FOR INVESTMENT.   To be effective, a cash management program should place appropriate emphasis on day-to-day money transactions, including speeding up collections, controlling payables and controlling bank balances. To speed up collections, companies use two major techniques—lockbox systems and concentration banking.

(a) Lockbox System.   A **lockbox system** shortens the time between a customer's payment of funds and the deposit of those funds to a firm's bank account. A firm using a lockbox system regionalizes its markets and asks customers in each region to send payments to a post office box designated for the region. A bank, acting as the firm's agent, collects from the post office box several times each day. The bank credits the firm's account, forwards checks to the banks on which they are drawn, and mails lists of checks or copies of the checks and/or remittance advices to the firm. A lockbox system lessens the delay of cash availability by 1 to 3 days, but it is usually economic only for firms with a high volume of checks for substantial amounts. High cost, occasional customer resistance, and delay in receiving credit control information are disadvantages of a lockbox system. A lockbox should be used only by companies that have sound accounting and accounts receivable operations. Banks are well equipped to handle large volumes of "clean" payments accompanied by remittance advices; however, they are not equipped to assist in identifying which account should be credited with a payment.

(b) Concentration Banking.   Concentration banking is an arrangement with banks that permits automatic transfers between local banks and regional banks, and between regional banks and the headquarters bank(s) on the basis of predetermined target balances. When a balance in a local or regional bank is above the target amount, the overage is transferred to the next higher level, and the flow reverses when a balance falls below the target amount. The system frees cash for investment that might otherwise by trapped in banks that serve each local unit. Concentration banking may be coupled with a lockbox system or used in lieu of a lockbox system. This method of speeding up collections is especially beneficial to companies that have many service or retail outlets that take in small collections.

(c) Payables Management.   To control payables, two approaches in general use are **centralized management of payments** and **administrative bank accounts.** The advantages of centralized management of payments are that it provides better control over the timing of payments, it increases the employment of excess funds, and it permits streamlining of banking relationships.

Three types of administrative bank account are:

1. *Imprest Account*. The account operates on a fixed maximum balance, usually based on average disbursements for a period of time. At the end of the time period, the account is reimbursed on the basis of receipted bills furnished to the company's headquarters.
2. *Zero Balance Accounts*. A separate clearing account is maintained for each division at a zero balance. As the division's checks are presented for payment, the bank will automatically transfer, from a central account, enough funds to cover them.
3. *Automatic Balance Account*. An account is maintained at a balance predetermined as the appropriate working level for a division. The bank is authorized to transfer (or "sweep") funds above this balance to the company's general bank account, and is authorized to draw funds from the general account if the account balance is below the predetermined level.

Bank balances can be controlled through the following means: (1) Using drafts, (2) Playing the float, or (3) Using money market funds.

Disbursement of cash is delayed by using drafts instead of checks. Even though a draft is dated on the due date, payment does not take place until the draft is presented for acceptance. As compared with disbursement by check, there can be a delay in payment of up to 3 days. Funds in a bank account can then be limited to those anticipated to meet current draft presentations. A firm can achieve the same advantage by making disbursements with checks and playing the float. This means that a firm is taking advantage of the difference between the bank balance and the book balance that results from the delay required to process checks written. Use of drafts rather than checks simply eliminates the risk of having a bank overdraft. Some firms arrange in advance for loans that are automatically credited to their bank account whenever the balance falls below a predetermined amount. This arrangement eliminates the risk of an overdraft and may be more convenient than using drafts.

A money market fund is a mutual fund that invests in short-term money market instruments. It permits withdrawals at any time on demand, without penalty, usually provided the amount of the withdrawal exceeds a minimum amount of, say, $500 or $1,000. A company can write checks on its funds and have them continue to earn interest until the check is presented to the fund for payment. The only significant differences between using a bank and a money market fund are that (1) deposits in a money market fund are not insured as bank deposits are, and (2) there are minimum-denomination requirements to meet on initial deposits and on certain types of withdrawals.

11.51 UTILIZATION OF CASH ASSETS.   For most companies excess cash should consist only of amounts required to meet short-term fluctuations. It is usually advantageous to invest any additional cash in the company's own operations or else use it to repay debt. Debt structure is not always flexible enough to allow partial or early retirement, and opportunities for a firm to invest in its own operations may not coincide with cash availability. Moreover, amounts required to meet short-term fluctuations are often substantial, so cash managers frequently face responsibility for productive utilization of a substantial cash balance. This calls for investment policies that are as imaginative and progressive as their counterparts in the production and distribution functions.

(a) Objectives in Managing Cash and Near-Cash Investments.   An organization has four basic objectives in managing cash and near-cash investments: (1) safety of principal, (2) liquidity of principal, (3) yield, and (4) convenience in handling. The relative importance attached to each of the four objectives will vary with an organization's immediate circumstances and with the attitudes and preferences of top management.

(b) Instruments for Utilizing Cash.   There are a wide variety of investment media that can be used to absorb short-term cash:

1. U.S. Treasury securities, which are generally divided into Treasury bills, which are due in 3-month, 6-month, and 1-year maturities; Treasury notes, which have a maturity of 1 to 10 years when issued; and Treasury bonds, which have an original maturity of 10 years or more.

2. Federal agency securities, which include such organizations as the Federal Home Loan Bank System, the Government National Mortgage Association, the Banks for Cooperatives, the Federal Land Banks, and the Federal Intermediate Credit Banks. These securities have the de facto backing of the federal government. They have a slightly higher yield than U.S. government securities because they are less liquid.

3. Eurodollar securities, which are those issued by foreign corporations and banks and foreign branches of United States banks. These securities are denominated in U.S. dollars. A Eurodollar deposit is simply dollars deposited in a bank outside the United States.

4. Certificates of deposit, which are obligations issued by banks that can be traded in a secondary market if funds are required before maturity of the deposit. This can only be done if the original certificates were issued in negotiable form.

5. Commercial paper, which is unsecured promissory notes issued by industrial and manufacturing firms and finance companies. The maximum maturity for which commercial paper can be sold is 270 days, because paper with a longer maturity would have to be registered with the SEC.

6. Bankers' acceptances, which are short-term, non-interest-bearing notes sold at a discount and redeemed by the accepting bank at maturity for full face value.

7. Repurchase agreements, which involve the purchase of securities for a particular price with a simultaneous agreement by the seller to repurchase the securities in the future, usually 1 or 7 days later, at a higher price (the increased price reflecting interest on the funds used).

8. Municipal notes and bonds, which are debt securities issued by state and local governments that are attractive because the interest income is exempt from federal taxation and usually also from any income taxes levied within the state where they are issued.

9. Money market mutual funds, which themselves invest in a variety of the above instruments. The money market funds provide a convenient vehicle for short-term investment of available cash; by the end of 1988, there were over 400 different funds available, with aggregate assets in excess of $300 billion.

ELECTRONIC FUNDS TRANSFER SYSTEMS

11.52 NATURE AND IMPORTANCE OF ELECTRONIC FUNDS TRANSFER SYSTEMS. Improvements in communications and technological advances have made it possible to execute funds transactions quickly and accurately without the use of extensive amounts of paperwork. Such transactions are handled through several different electronic networks, all of which are generally referred to as **electronic funds transfer systems (EFTS).**

To some, EFTS means a system to replace checks, cash, and credit card vouchers with a nationwide or worldwide network of computer-linked terminals that instantaneously keep track of each penny spent everywhere. To others, it simply means getting cash out of a machine. In one way or another, EFTS refers to the application of computer and telecommunication technology in making or processing payments.

EFTS is the primary method used to transfer funds in terms of dollar value, although it is relatively small in terms of number of transactions. The reason for this is that EFTS is the primary method used by business for large dollar transactions, whereas retail transactions, which are relatively low in dollar amount but very high in volume, tend to be made by check.

11.53 EFTS IN THE CORPORATE ENVIRONMENT.   EFTS has found ready acceptance by corporations because it provides the capability to implement cash management techniques with swift, accurate movement of money to areas where it can be productive. In addition, EFTS permits corporations to keep funds invested longer, because payments can be made on the date they are due. There are two basic types of EFTS in use by corporations—single-transfer messages and multiple-transfer messages.

(a) Single-Transfer Messages.   Where high dollar values are involved, corporations generally use single-transfer messages, which involve the sending of one message for each fund transfer. In executing single-transfer messages for their customers, banks have three primary systems available: Fed wire, CHIPS, and SWIFT.

Fed wire is the electronic network that connects banks that are members of the Federal Reserve System through the 12 Federal Reserve Banks and their branches. When a bank uses this system, it provides for immediate transfer of funds from its account at a Federal Reserve bank to the account of another bank at a Federal Reserve bank. Because these transactions are handled through accounts at Federal Reserve banks, the funds received are immediately available for use by the receiving corporation. There is no wait for the funds to "clear" the banking system.

CHIPS, established in 1970, is an acronym for **Clearing House Interbank Payments System,** which is the electronic network that connects banks that have elected to use this service with each other through a private telecommunication system. CHIPS is responsible for approximately 90% of all international interbank dollar transfers. The system is operated by the New York Clearing House Association, which comprises 12 major New York banks. In addition to these banks, 10 other banks are "settling banks" and these banks, together with banks outside of New York and branches and agencies of foreign banks, bring the number of participants to around 100. The "settling banks" are simply those that settle for themselves or through whom other participants must settle transactions. At the end of each day, all transfer messages are totaled by the CHIPS system and a net amount is debited or credited to an account with one of the 22 "settling" members. At the end of each day, settlement is made through a special CHIPS settlement account at the Federal Reserve Bank in New York. Those banks that have a debit position settle by making a payment to the special CHIPS account by 5:45 PM; as soon as all debtor settling banks have made the required payments, the funds are released to the accounts at the Federal Reserve Bank of those settling banks having credit positions. At the end of the day, the balance of the special settlement account is zero.

SWIFT is the acronym for the **Society for Worldwide Interbank Financial Telecommunication,** the private electronic network that enables participating banks to send funds transfer messages and administrative messages to each other. Originally established in 1973, SWIFT has grown to a point where over 1,500 banks in more than 60 countries now participate, covering almost the entire globe, with the exception of parts of Eastern Europe and the Middle East. SWIFT is headquartered in Brussels and owned by the member banks that use its services. The original SWIFT system involved centralized processing of transactions through data centers in Europe and the United States; SWIFT II, an enhanced system that began to be operational in 1985, involves distributed data processing through centers geographically dispersed around the globe. The SWIFT system is available 24 hours a day, 7 days a week and provides superior transaction processing in terms of speed, cost, and security.

When transferring funds, corporations do not have to specify to their banks which system is to be used. They simply instruct the banks where to transfer the funds (bank name and account number), when the funds are to be available, and the amount. The bank chooses the appropriate system to carry out the instructions.

To further expedite this type of funds transfer and to reduce the number of manual errors, several banks are providing their corporate customers with direct access to their domestic money transfer systems through machines located in the customers' offices. Corporations send a message directly to the bank's transfer system and receive confirmation that the transaction has been executed without the need to go through bank personnel.

(b) Multiple-Transfer Messages.   Where low dollar values are involved, corporations generally use multiple-transfer messages, which involve the sending of one message for many fund transfers. This is a substitute for the present check collection system. Essentially, it functions by collecting paperwork at the initial point of transfer, converting the data to machine-readable format, and processing the transfers electronically. The paperwork remains at the point where the transfers were initiated. This is in contrast to check processing, where the paperwork (check) must physically move through the collection system. The systems available for multiple transfer messages are similar to those available for check clearing.

In direct delivery systems, a magnetic tape is sent from one bank to another, either physically or through an electronic message. This tape identifies the names and account numbers to be charged for each transfer and the identity of the sending bank whose account is to be credited.

When transfers are made through an **automated clearing house (ACH),** the information is delivered through a magnetic tape either physically or through an electronic message similar to that used in a direct delivery system. The tape, however, includes transfers to all banks that are members of the ACH. This is similar to the delivery of checks to a clearing house for further delivery and settlement at the banks on whom the checks are drawn. There are a number of ACHs located throughout the United States; each ACH transfers funds among its members and the members of other ACHs through an interregional ACH exchange. Transactions executed through the interregional exchange provide funds availability on the day after the transfer message.

Two types of transfers are handled through multiple transfer messages:

- **Credit transfers.** Electronic version of a deposit.
- **Debit transfers.** Electronic version of a typical check transaction.

Credit transfers that are corporation- or government-initiated include payroll or commission payments; pension, annuities, and Social Security payments; and payment of dividends and interest.

In a credit transaction, the corporation instructs its bank to credit various accounts at one or more banks and charge its account. For example, in processing a payroll, the corporation instructs the bank to move funds from its account to the accounts of its employees. This eliminates the need to prepare checks for the corporation and relieves the employees of the need to visit their bank to deposit payroll checks. Employees receive payroll slips showing the calculation of gross pay to net pay. These slips serve as notification that the net amount has been deposited to their accounts. One of the most successful uses of credit transactions through a multiple-transfer message mode has been the direct deposit of Social Security checks by the U.S. government. The recipient furnishes a bank name and account number to the government and is assured that a deposit will be made in the account on the 3rd day of each month.

Debit transfers that are corporation- or financial institution-initiated include various types of repetitive payments (e.g., mortgage payments, insurance, etc.); variable amount payments for which the consumer is notified before payment takes place (e.g., monthly utility payments, etc.); and drawdown of funds deposited throughout the United States (e.g., concentration of funds from retail stores in a chain making daily deposits throughout the United States).

11.54 EFTS IN THE RETAIL ENVIRONMENT.   In the retail, or consumer, environment, EFTS can be grouped into the following three major functional areas, all of which require the consumer to initiate the transaction:

- Remote-banking services.
- Retail point-of-sale services.
- Direct-deposit and preauthorized payment services.

Remote-banking services are transacted through the use of remote-banking terminals (**automated teller machines,** or **ATMs**) or touch-tone telephones. A customer interacts with an ATM in the same way that he would interact with a teller in a bank. First, he identifies himself by inserting a plastic card into the machine and pushing buttons that represent his **personal identification number (PIN).** After the computer has verified that the card and the PIN correspond, the customer can push certain buttons to carry out various types of transactions, including deposits, withdrawals, transfers between accounts, bill paying, and inquiry on account status.

Where a touch-tone telephone is used, the same procedures are followed. However, the customer can perform only the last three transactions in the preceding list, because there is no way to physically transfer cash between the customer and the bank for a deposit or withdrawal.

Retail point-of-sale services are provided through the use of **point-of-sale (POS)** terminals. These terminals have the capability of transferring money from a customer's account to the store's account. The customer presents his debit card (as distinguished from a credit card that is used to extend credit) to the retail clerk, who enters the card into the POS terminal. The customer enters his PIN on an enclosed numeric keypad on his side of the terminal, and the transaction is then handled in the same manner as a remote-banking transaction.

Direct-deposit and preauthorized payment services originate with the customer but are executed by a corporation or a financial institution as described earlier. The direct deposit of a payroll amount can be made only if authorized by the employee. In the same manner, a debit transfer, which involves the charging of a customer's account by a corporation, can be made only if the customer has authorized the corporation to execute the transaction.

Customer acceptance of remote-banking services has generally been good because the customer has been provided with the ability to do normal banking transactions 24 hours a day without any significant additional cost. The use of POS terminals has expanded slowly; generally, consumers do not see an incentive to adopt these systems because of the way checks and credit cards are priced. Free or low-priced checking services are used to attract customers. In addition, check payments are deducted from the customer's account when the check clears the banking system, thus providing the consumer with float. The customer can use this float to take advantage of interest-bearing or interest-saving alternatives for the duration of the float. Therefore, POS will gain wider acceptance only when the customer perceives that it offers some personal gain.

ACCOUNTING FOR INVESTMENTS

11.55 AUTHORITATIVE PRONOUNCEMENTS FOR INVESTMENTS.   SFAS No. 12, "Accounting for Certain Marketable Securities," governs the accounting for investments in the securities specified therein. The FASB has also issued five Interpretations of this Statement (FIN Nos. 10–13 and 16) and FTB No. 79-19. FIN No. 10 has been superseded by SFAS No. 83. This section describes the accounting for investments in securities held by for-profit enterprises in industries that do not have specialized accounting practices with respect to investments in securities. It covers both those security investments accounted for under

SFAS No. 12 and other marketable securities. It does not apply to enterprises in industries that have specialized accounting practices with respect to investments in securities, to not-for-profit organizations (unless required by other authoritative literature) or to employee benefit plans; accounting for investments of these entities is covered elsewhere in authoritative literature, as is the accounting for investments by the equity method.

In general, SFAS No. 12 requires that marketable equity securities be recorded at the lower of aggregate cost or aggregate market value. Lower of cost or market adjustments applicable to securities classified as current are reflected in income; similar adjustments for securities classified as noncurrent or securities in unclassified balance sheets are recorded directly in shareholders' equity. SFAS No. 12 also requires that when write-downs have been made because the market value is lower than cost and such write-downs are judged to be temporary, subsequent recoveries in market value should be recorded to the extent that the resulting carrying amount of the portfolio does not exceed cost.

11.56 TYPES OF SECURITIES

(a) Marketable Equity Securities.   SFAS No. 12 (par. 7) defines marketable equity securities. Under a literal interpretation of paragraphs 7a and 7b, investments such as open-end investment companies would not be considered marketable because sales or bid and asked prices are not available on a national securities exchange or in the over-the-counter market (securities are purchased from and redeemed directly by the fund). It appears unlikely that this interpretation was intended and, accordingly, such investments should be considered as marketable equity securities for purposes of applying SFAS No. 12. The essential point is whether market values are ascertainable from an active market.

A consensus of the EITF (Issue No. 86-40) states that a financial institution should report its investment in an open-end investment company that invests only in obligations of, or obligations guaranteed by, the U.S. government or its agencies at the lower of cost or market following SFAS No. 12. It would appear appropriate for all entities (except those that follow specialized accounting practices) reporting investments in open-end investment companies to apply the guidance in SFAS No. 12.

Generally, an equity security is not marketable if price quotations specified by SFAS No. 12 (par. 7b) are not available on the balance sheet date. This would occur in the following three situations:

- Trading in the security on a national securities exchange has been suspended.
- No quotation is available from NASDAQ.
- Quotations from fewer than three dealers are available.

However, a temporary lack of trades or price quotations for a security at the balance sheet date does not make it nonmarketable if the required market prices are available on days closely preceding and following the balance sheet date. It should also be noted that bid and ask prices are frequently available on a national securities exchange even if the security did not trade on a particular day. FIN No. 16 provides guidance where there is a temporary lack of quotations by NASDAQ or dealers.

(b) Restricted Stock.   SFAS No. 12 defines restricted stock as ". . . securities for which sale is restricted by a governmental or contractual requirement except where such requirement terminates within one year or where the holder has the power by contract or otherwise to cause the requirement to be met within one year." Even if the probability that the power to terminate the restriction will be exercised is remote (or the holder does not intend to exercise the power), the security would be deemed unrestricted.

FIN No. 16 (par. 7) states that if marketable equity securities, for example, common shares, collateralize a loan (due date after one year, thereby causing the shares to be restricted) and the enterprise, at its option, can substitute securities other than common shares as collateral or can sell the collateral and use the proceeds to repay the loan, the common shares should be considered unrestricted if the enterprise has the financial ability to effect a substitution. However, if the loan agreement prohibits sale or substitution, the securities would be considered restricted if the loan has a maturity of greater than one year.

If an investor owns equity securities that are subject to registration with the SEC and the investor cannot require that a registration statement be filed, the securities should be considered unrestricted only:

- If a registration statement covering the securities is expected to be filed and become effective within one year from the balance sheet date.
- If and to the extent that the securities can be qualified for sale within one year under Rule 144 of Section 4 of the Securities Act of 1933 or similar rules of the SEC. Rule 144 specifies that if certain conditions are met, a security may be sold to the public without an effective registration statement on file with the SEC, subject to a limitation on the number of shares that may be sold during a given time period.

If an investor can require that a registration statement covering the securities be filed, the securities should be considered unrestricted if it can reasonably be expected that a registration statement could become effective within one year from the date of the financial statements, regardless of the investor's intent with respect to requiring the filing of a registration statement.

Shares held because of a regulatory requirement (e.g., FNMA shares held by mortgage bankers) should be deemed restricted only to the extent of the regulatory requirement.

(c) Other Securities.   Securities other than marketable equity securities include restricted shares, debt, convertible debt, and certain redeemable preferred shares of all types of issuers. Cash equivalents (e.g., certificates of deposit) and treasury shares are not considered to be investments (other securities) as contemplated by this section.

11.57 CLASSIFICATION AND AGGREGATION OF SECURITIES

(a) Classification of Securities.   SFAS No. 12 specifies the accounting and reporting requirements for those marketable equity securities classified as current, noncurrent or included in an unclassified balance sheet. It did not alter GAAP with respect to the appropriate classifications of such securities. Proper classification is essential to the application of SFAS No. 12 because adjustments of cost to market of securities classified as current generally are recorded in income whereas similar adjustments (except where the decline in value is other than temporary) for noncurrent securities or securities included in an unclassified balance sheet are recorded directly in equity. SFAS No. 12 provides examples of disclosure requirements.

(i) Current Assets.   ARB No. 43 (Ch. 3A, par. 4) states:

. . . the term *current assets* is used to designate cash and other assets or resources commonly identified as those which are reasonably expected to be realized in cash or sold or consumed during the normal operating cycle of the business. Thus the term comprehends in general such resources as . . . marketable securities representing the investment of cash available for current operations. . . .

(ii) Noncurrent Assets.   ARB No. 43 (Ch. 3A, par. 6) states, in part:

This concept of the nature of current assets contemplates the exclusion from that classification of such resources as . . . investments in securities (whether marketable or not) or advances which have been made for the purpose of control, affiliation, or other continuing business advantage. . . .

Particular consideration should be given to the entity's ability to hold the security as well as its present intent. Where evidence indicates that as a result of factors such as diminished financial position or working capital, it is unlikely that the security can be held beyond one year, GAAP require that the security be classified as current with the corresponding lower of cost or market adjustment, if any, reflected in income.

SFAS No. 12 (par. 9) requires that marketable equity securities in unclassified balance sheets be treated as noncurrent assets. An exception to this general rule may apply to financial institutions where unclassified balance sheets are issued. Banks historically have made the distinction between trading and investment accounts to determine whether a write-down with respect to current securities should be charged to income. The AICPA Industry Audit Guide "Audits of Banks" states that securities classified as trading ("current") should be reported at market value, with the required adjustment reflected in income.

(iii) Trading versus Investment.   A task force of the AICPA Accounting Standards Executive Committee has proposed an (SOP) "Reporting by Financial Institutions of Debt securities Held as Assets." The proposed SOP would require that financial institutions designate debt securities held as assets, at the time of acquisition and at each subsequent balance sheet date, as (1) investments, (2) assets held for sale, or (3) trading assets. Debt securities should be designated as investments and reported at amortized cost only if the institution currently has the ability to hold the securities to maturity and it intends to hold them for the foreseeable future, as defined in the SOP. Debt securities should be designated as trading assets if they are held for the purpose of selling them in the short term, generally involving active buying and selling of the securities; such securities should be carried at market value. Debt securities that do not meet the criteria for classification as investments or trading assets should be reported in a separate category as assets held for sale and recorded at the lower of their amortized cost or market value. A decline in the value of debt securities that is other than temporary should be charged to operations, and it results in a new historical cost basis for the debt securities.

(b) Aggregation of Securities.   SFAS No. 12 (par. 9) requires that all marketable equity securities within a consolidated group (except as discussed below) be aggregated into one current and one noncurrent portfolio.

Portfolios of marketable equity securities owned by investees accounted for by the equity method should not be combined with portfolios of any other entity in the financial statements. Such entities are subject to SFAS No. 12 standing alone. When the equity section of an equity investee's balance sheet contains a charge attributable to a valuation allowance for a marketable equity securities portfolio, the investor should reduce its investment in the investee and record a charge in its equity section equal to its proportionate share of the investee's valuation allowance (see FTB No. 79-19, par. 6).

Where the parent follows specialized industry practices and two or more consolidated subsidiaries do not, the subsidiaries' marketable equity securities should be aggregated (exclusive of the portfolios of the parent) as required by SFAS No. 12 (par. 19).

SFAS No. 12 does not require subsidiaries and investees accounted for by the equity method to conform their accounting practices with respect to marketable equity securities to the parent's practices. However, it does require that subsidiaries and investees include realized gains and losses in income if the parent's policy is to include them in income.

FIN No. 13 requires that securities owned by consolidated subsidiaries that have different year-ends from that of the parent should be aggregated with those of the parent based on the subsidiaries' year-ends. For example, the cost and market value of securities owned by a subsidiary with a November 30 year-end should be included as of that date when aggregating those securities with those of the parent at December 31.

It would not be appropriate to combine with marketable equity securities those other securities recorded (by industry practice or otherwise) at the lower of cost or market, as to do so would violate the requirement of SFAS No. 12 with respect to marketable equity securities. Such other securities should be considered separately. The provisions of SFAS No. 12 allowing declines in market value to be charged to equity should not be followed for such other securities.

11.58 ACCOUNTING FOR MARKETABLE EQUITY SECURITIES

(a) Classified as Current.   Current marketable equity securities should be recorded at the lower of aggregate cost or aggregate market value. Valuation adjustments should be recorded in income and as a valuation allowance. Subsequent increases in market value should be reflected in income to the extent original aggregate cost is not exceeded. SFAS No. 12 (par. 7) (see also FIN No. 12) defines cost as original cost less adjustments reflecting impairments of value deemed other than temporary. Adequate detailed records must be maintained to prevent the recording of market increases in excess of cost. This would entail details of securities on hand at the beginning of the period, securities purchased, sold, transferred from noncurrent or from a restricted category, and securities permanently impaired. SFAS No. 12 (including the Appendices) provides examples of disclosure requirements.

(b) Classified as Noncurrent.   Noncurrent marketable equity securities should be recorded at the lower of aggregate cost or aggregate market value. Valuation adjustments should be recorded directly in shareholders' equity (as a separate line item) and as a valuation allowance. Subsequent increases in market value should be reflected in equity to the extent aggregate original cost (as defined in SFAS No. 12, par. 7) is not exceeded. The comments above regarding the maintenance of detailed records apply equally to noncurrent marketable equity securities. SFAS No. 12 provides examples of disclosure requirements.

(c) Transfers between Categories.   Changes in classification should occur only when justified by the facts and circumstances within the concepts of ARB No. 43 (Ch. 3A). SFAS No. 12 (par. 10) requires that transfers between current and noncurrent categories be made at the lower of cost or market with any corresponding adjustment reflected in income. This requirement prevents the reclassification of a security to noncurrent in order to prevent a downward market adjustment from being reflected in income. It should be noted that SFAS No. 12, requires the lower of cost or market adjustment to be made for each individual security and not with respect to aggregate securities that may be transferred. If market value of a transferred security is less than cost, the market value becomes the new cost basis.

(d) Changes from Marketable to Nonmarketable.   FIN No. 16 discusses the treatment of marketable equity securities that change status from marketable to nonmarketable or vice versa (such as with the imposition or expiration of restrictions). This situation could arise whether the security is current or noncurrent and could involve a coincident change in classification from current to noncurrent or vice versa. The example below assumes a current marketable security becomes a noncurrent nonmarketable security as the result of an imposition of restrictions.

Current securities at December 31, 19XX

Security	Cost	Market
A	$10,000	$ 4,000
B	8,000	15,000
C	5,000	2,000
Aggregate amounts	$23,000	$21,000

The unrealized loss (and valuation allowance) at December 31, 19XX is $2,000. During 19XY, no changes in market values or the portfolio occur except that on November 1, 19XY, Security B becomes restricted and the restriction is expected to extend beyond one year.

Even though the valuation allowance is derived by the lower of aggregate cost or market, it represents individual unrealized gains and losses. Although Security B was a current marketable equity security, its unrealized gain of $7,000 "protected" that amount of unrealized losses on Securities A and C from being charged to income. Because Security B at November 1, 19XY is not longer a current marketable equity security, its gain is unavailable to cover the unrealized loss on Securities A and C and the valuation allowance should be increased by $7,000 at that date by a charge to income.

The fact that Security B becomes noncurrent coincident with its change in status to nonmarketable is of no particular consequence in this case because market exceeds cost at the time of the change in classification. Security B would be recorded at cost, which would be subject to continuing evaluation as to impairment pursuant to GAAP. However, if Security B had an unrealized loss, its cost basis would be reduced to market value at the time of the change in classification to noncurrent.

If Security B were noncurrent at the time it became nonmarketable because of the imposition of restrictions, GAAP for investments other than marketable equity securities require that it be recorded at cost unless there is a decline in value considered to be other than temporary. SFAS No. 12 did not change GAAP in this regard, providing disclosures are adequate. However, a careful evaluation should be made of whether the decline in value is temporary.

(e) Changes in Market Value Subsequent to Balance Sheet Date.   SFAS No. 12 (par. 13) states that an entity's financial statements should not be changed for realized gains or losses or changes in market prices with respect to marketable equity securities that occur subsequent to year-end. If significant, such subsequent events should be disclosed. Securities sold subsequent to year-end but prior to the issuance of the financial statements would generally indicate that the securities should be classified as current at year-end. Accordingly, if at year-end, the securities were classified as noncurrent, a reclassification to current would likely be required and the related valuation allowance at year-end would be transferred from equity to income.

With respect to marketable equity securities for which the effect of a change in carrying amount is included in shareholders' equity rather than in net income, sales of those securities at a loss subsequent to year-end but prior to the issuance of financial statements would be a consideration, along with other factors, that the decline in value was other than temporary and should have been reflected in income. The amount of the loss reflected in income at year-end would be the lesser of the realized loss or the unrealized loss at year-end (see FIN No. 11).

Changes in market value after year-end should be evaluated to ascertain whether such changes are compatible with judgments made as to whether declines in value for particular securities at year-end were temporary.

(f) Parent Company (Only) Financial Statements.   SFAS No. 94 precludes the use of parent company (only) financial statements as "the financial statements of the primary reporting entity." SFAS No. 12, (par. 3c, fn. 1) limits that statement's applicability to parent company financial statements prepared for issuance as the financial statements of the primary reporting entity. Consequently, when parent company (only) financial statements to be used for other purposes include depreciated marketable equity securities, and a subsidiary that is consolidated in the consolidated financial statements has appreciated marketable equity securities, a question arises as to whether the parent company (only) financial statements should reflect the depreciation with no effect given to the appreciation of the subsidiary's marketable securities. There is no clear-cut answer to this question.

The effect of reflecting the depreciation while ignoring the appreciation would cause the sum of the results of the parent company (only) and its subsidiary to be different from consolidated results. In the circumstances described above, it would probably be inappropriate to reflect the depreciation of its marketable equity securities without reflecting the appreciation of the subsidiary's marketable equity securities in the parent's equity in such subsidiary.

11.59 ACCOUNTING FOR OTHER SECURITIES.   ARB No. 43 (Ch. 3A, par. 9) states:

> In the case of marketable securities where market value is less than cost by a substantial amount and it is evident that the decline in market value is not due to a mere temporary condition, the amount to be included as a current asset should not exceed the market value.

Rule 5-02.12 of Regulation S-X includes the following with respect to other investments:

> With respect to other security investments (i.e., other than marketable equity securities) and any other investment, state, parenthetically or otherwise, the basis of determining the aggregate amounts shown in the balance sheet, along with the alternate of the aggregate cost or aggregate market value at the balance sheet date.

From the foregoing, it is evident that the only specific requirement in either ARB No. 43 or Regulation S-X for the mandatory adjustment of other securities to market value (whether classified as current or noncurrent or not classified) where such amount is less than cost is when the decline in market value is considered to be other than temporary. Otherwise, disclosure of the aggregate market value is the only requirement.

(a) Troubled Debt Restructurings—Debt Securities.   SFAS No. 15, "Accounting by Debtors and Creditors for Troubled Debt Restructurings," sets standards for accounting and reporting by a creditor for modification of the terms of debt in situations where the creditor grants relief to a debtor in view of the debtor's financial difficulties. The definition of debt as used in SFAS No. 15 encompasses debt securities that are held as an investment. In accounting for debt securities in troubled debt situations, a conflict exists between the provisions of ARB No. 43 and SFAS No. 15. Circumstances may arise where an issuer of debt securities is experiencing financial difficulties and is in the process of offering (or is expected to offer) the holders of the debt securities a modification of the terms of the debt. ARB No. 43 requires that the investment be adjusted to market value in cases where the decline in market value is judged to be other than temporary. However, as provided in SFAS No. 15 (pars. 30–31), no adjustment of a debt security that is restructured only by modification of its terms in a troubled debt situation is required unless the recorded amount of the investment (exclusive of any allowance for estimated uncollectible amounts or other valuation account) is greater than the total amount of future cash to be received under the modified terms. If the recorded amount of the investment is greater than the specified future cash receipts, the investment is adjusted to the amount of future cash to be received under the modified terms.

In practice, very few situations will arise where application of ARB No. 43 will coincide with the consummation of a restructuring. In the absence of assurance of the final terms of a restructuring agreement, the provisions of ARB No. 43 should be applied. The financial statement disclosures required by SFAS No. 15 are applicable when a troubled debt restructuring has been consummated even though no further adjustment of the recorded amount of the investment is required.

(b) Sale of Marketable Securities with a Put.   The EITF has considered sales of marketable securities with a put. EITF Consensuses on related Issues Nos. 84-5, 85-25, 85-30, and 85-40 are reflected in the following discussion.

This type of transaction involves sale of a security having a fixed maturity date to a third party with the latter having an option to "put" the security back to the seller in the future for a fixed price. Because of the put option, the seller generally receives a premium price for the security. The accounting should be based on an assessment of the probability that the put will be exercised. If it is probable that the put will be exercised, the transaction should be accounted for as a borrowing. Any difference between the "sale" proceeds and the put price would be accrued as interest expense over the period to the first date the securities are eligible to be put back, with additional accruals if subsequent put prices are higher. Impairment of the underlying security would generally not be recognized. If it is not probable that the put will be exercised, the asset should be removed from the balance sheet. For a transaction that, if reported as a sale, would involve recognition of a gain, such gain should be deferred because the gain represents a contingency that, under SFAS No. 5, should not be recognized until the contingency is resolved by expiration of the put without exercise. If the transaction is accounted for as a borrowing, there should be a continual reassessment of the probability that the put will be exercised, with a change in the accounting if appropriate. If a transaction is initially recorded as a sale but exercise of the put later becomes probable, the company should immediately accrue any losses expected upon exercise of the put, periodically adjust the estimated loss accrual, and ultimately record the repurchased security at the lower of cost or market.

Factors to be considered in assessing whether it is probable the put will be exercised include the relationship of the put price to market price, the length of time the put is outstanding in relation to the term of the security, and the difference, if any, between the put price and the sale proceeds. The longer the put period, the less likely it is that the put will be exercised because the fair value of the security increases over time as it approaches maturity. Accordingly, a transfer of a security with a put that extends beyond 50% of the expected remaining life of the security should be recognized as a sale. In an arrangement involving multiple put dates, if **any** put extends beyond 50% of the expected remaining life of the security, the transaction should be recognized as a sale. The greater the spread between the put price and the market value of the security or the put price and the sales proceeds, the more likely it is that the buyer (lender) will exercise the put.

It should be recognized that the EITF specifically restricted the application of its consensus to transactions involving marketable securities. It did not address the accounting for sales with put arrangements that would involve assets other than marketable securities.

11.60 INCOME TAX ACCOUNTING RELATED CONSIDERATIONS

(a) Under APB Opinion No. 11.   SFAS No. 12 (par. 22) requires that the provisions of APB Opinion No. 11 be applied to unrealized gains and losses and provides that tax benefits of unrealized capital losses not be recorded unless realization is assured beyond a reasonable doubt.

Assurance beyond a reasonable doubt would exist, for example, if the entity had capital gains in the current and immediately preceding 2 years in amounts at least equal to its realized and unrealized capital losses. The concept of assurance does not require that the entity manifest an intent to dispose of the security (and thereby realize the loss) but, rather, depends on whether the tax benefit would be realized if the security were sold. Present U.S. tax laws permit capital losses of corporations to be carried back 3 years. For purposes of assessing assurance, the carry-back period should be limited to the immediately preceding 2 years because the opportunity to carry back to the 3rd preceding year would lapse on the first day of the ensuing fiscal year.

Even though SFAS No. 12 requires the aggregation of marketable equity securities, the opportunity for any tax benefits of unrealized losses to be deemed realizable requires an assessment of each tax reporting entity's individual income tax situation. In other words, assurance of a tax benefit may be contingent upon each tax reporting entity having sufficient capital gains. It is inappropriate to offset an unrealized capital loss of one tax reporting entity against an unrealized capital gain of a different tax reporting entity in determining the realizability of the tax benefits.

With respect to noncurrent valuation adjustments, SFAS No. 12 and APB Opinion No. 11 state that any tax effects should be recorded directly against the valuation adjustment and not included with the provision for income taxes.

Although SFAS No. 12 (par. 22) specifically requires that the provisions of APB Opinion No. 11 be applied to valuation adjustments, SFAS No. 12 is silent as to whether APB Opinion No. 23 also applies. Because no specific reference is made to APB Opinion No. 23, a question arises as to whether the individual entities' unrealized gains and losses that cumulatively result in the aggregate valuation adjustments required by SFAS No. 12 should be added to or deducted from the individual entities' "other" undistributed earnings for purposes of applying APB Opinion No. 23 provisions. A similar question arises as to whether such individual unrealized gains and losses should be added to or deducted from the individual entities' income statement and balance sheet accounts, as applicable, for the financial reporting of balance sheet and income statement information by geographical location (SFAS No. 14). The relevant literature would seem to require the assignment of the individual unrealized gains and losses to the individual entities for both APB Opinion No. 23 and financial reporting purposes even though SFAS No. 12 specifies that the valuation adjustments be derived from aggregate amounts. Of course, the adequacy of disclosures must be carefully assessed as it is possible, for example, that the foreign subsidiaries have unrealized gains that are more than offset by the U.S. parent's unrealized losses.

(b) Under SFAS No. 96. Unrealized gains and losses on marketable securities should be included in the SFAS No. 96 scheduling exercise in a manner that is not inconsistent with the current or noncurrent classification of the securities. A current classification would require reversal in the first subsequent year; a noncurrent classification would require reversal based on the period in which management intends to sell the securities and should be consistent with the operating plans of the company. Tax planning strategies as defined in SFAS No. 96 would then be taken into account as would capital gain and loss carryback and carryforward provisions of the tax law.

The SFAS No. 96 amendment of SFAS No. 12 (par. 22) also eliminated the APB Opinion No. 11 concept of recognition of an unrealized capital loss only when there exists "assurance beyond a reasonable doubt" that the benefit will be realized. Such recognition of an unrealized capital loss is now governed by SFAS No. 96; that is, the benefit will be recognized when the future capital loss (1) offsets capital gain temporary differences arising in the scheduling process in future years or (2) is recoverable by a carryback refund of taxes paid in the current or prior year.

11.61 VALUATION PROBLEMS

(a) Determination that Decline in Value Is Other than Temporary. As a general rule, **all** adjustments to reflect a diminution in value deemed other than temporary must be recorded in income. Equity securities so adjusted are not to be subsequently written up to original cost should the market recover, regardless of classification.

The determination as to whether a decline in value of marketable equity securities is temporary must be made with care. SFAS No. 12 (par. 21) prohibits the recording of subsequent market recoveries of securities for which the decline in value is deemed to be other than temporary and requires additional downward adjustments to market if necessary. Such additional downward adjustments must also be analyzed to ascertain whether they are other than temporary. As SFAS No. 12 requires that lower of cost or market computations be applied to aggregate securities amounts while prohibiting the recording of subsequent market recoveries, the need for adequate detailed records is readily apparent.

In assessing whether a decline in value is other than temporary under SFAS No. 12 (or under ARB No. 43, for securities not covered by SFAS No. 12), it is important to consider the difference between a decline in market value that results from a change in the investment quality of the issue itself and a decline that results from a downward movement of the market as a whole. It is also important to consider the investor's intention to hold or sell particular securities.

Whether a decline in value is other than temporary will frequently be difficult to determine and obviously may be viewed differently by different individuals. No fixed set of rules can be given to use in making this determination and the decision will require consideration of all of the circumstances in each situation. Factors that may be pertinent are listed below.

The following factors may indicate that a decline in value is temporary:

1. Stock market has declined generally but securities owned continue to have reasonable earnings and dividends.
2. Bond interest or preferred stock dividend rate (on cost) is lower than rates for similar securities issued currently but quality of investment is not adversely affected.
3. Specific, recognizable, short-term factors have affected the market value.
4. Financial condition, market share, backlog, and other key statistics indicate growth.

The following factors may indicate that a decline in value is other than temporary:

1. Issuer is experiencing depressed and declining earnings in relation to competitors, erosion of market share, and deteriorating financial position.
2. Issuer has lowered dividend payments or its securities ratings have dropped.
3. Issuer has suffered catastrophe-type loss or exhaustion of natural resources.
4. Issuer is in bankruptcy or auditor's report on its financial statements indicates it has an uncertain future.

In SAB Topic 5M, the staff of the SEC expressed its view that the phrase "other than temporary" as used in SFAS No. 12 in connection with impairment in value of noncurrent marketable equity securities should not be interpreted to mean "permanent" impairment. The SEC staff also cited the following factors that it believes should be considered in evaluating whether a write-down of the carrying amount of such an investment is required:

1. Duration and extent to which the market value has been less than cost.
2. Financial condition and near-term prospects of the issuer including any specific events that may influence the operations of the issuer, such as changes in technology that may impair the earnings potential of the investment or the discontinuance of a segment of the business that may offset the future earnings potential.
3. Ability and intent of the holder to retain its investment for a period of time sufficient to allow for any anticipated recovery in market value.

The Chief Accountant of the SEC has stated that the above-mentioned factors are not all-inclusive, that judgment is required in assessing whether the decline in market value of a noncurrent marketable equity security is other than temporary, and that a registrant should use all available evidence to support the realizable value of its investments. Although SAB Topic 5M does not change existing authoritative literature, it clearly sets forth the SEC staff's views that a registrant should be prepared to demonstrate why a decline in market value of a noncurrent marketable equity security is temporary and that a charge to income is not required.

The SEC's position on accounting for noncurrent marketable equity securities, as set forth in SAB Topic 5M, raised several questions with respect to previously existing practice in this area. These questions, which were discussed by the EITF in Issue No. 85-39 included (1) Whether SAB Topic 5M represents a significant change in current guidance included in Statement 12 and related interpretations and how they have been applied in practice in determining whether a charge to income is required in connection with a write-down of noncurrent marketable equity securities, (2) the factors that might be considered as evidence to support a realizable value equal to or greater than the current carrying value of the investment, (3) the implications SAB Topic 5M has beyond accounting for noncurrent marketable equity securities, and (4) in applying SAB Topic 5M, how a company should report the write-down of marketable equity securities if that write-down includes amounts that may have been charged to earnings in prior years had the provisions of SAB Topic 5M been applied in those prior years.

Several EITF members expressed a view that SAB Topic 5M takes a stronger stance on when a write-down should be charged to income than previously existing authoritative literature. Some members commented that the criteria for not recognizing a write-down— evidence that supports a realizable value equal to or greater than the carrying value of the investment—is virtually impossible to meet short of experiencing market price increases. The SEC Observer indicated that he does not view SAB Topic 5M as a change in existing literature but as a reminder that applicable literature does require consideration when market declines have occurred. He also stated that the SEC staff intends that judgment be used in evaluating the specific events attributable to the market decline and that the company should consider all available evidence to evaluate the realizable value of its investments, including specific conditions of the issuer. He also stated that the SEC staff does not intend for SAB Topic 5M to have broader implications as to other kinds of asset write-downs. As to the application of SAB Topic 5M, he indicated that recognizing the write-down as a charge to current period income is acceptable when a write-down is deemed to be appropriate even though all or part of the write-down could have been recognized in a prior period if SAB Topic 5M had been applied in that period. If the registrant can demonstrate that the write-down should have occurred in a prior period, however, recognition as a correction of previously issued financial statements would be acceptable.

In circumstances in which industrial companies have substantial investments in securities other than marketable equity securities, provisions should be made for market losses, where material, if the investments are classified as current assets. If these investments are classified as noncurrent or included in unclassified balance sheets and if the company clearly intends (or the purpose of the investment indicates the necessity) to hold the securities either until maturity or for a reasonably long period of time, disclosure of the aggregate market value of the securities is sufficient unless there is evidence of a decline in value of the investment that is other than temporary. This position recognizes that classification as a current asset carries with it a presumption that the carrying amount generally should not exceed net realizable value and that there is a possibility of sale in the course of the operating cycle. Conversely, classification as a noncurrent asset carries a presumption that losses that would be sustained if the investment were sold at current market prices will not occur in the near future because there is no present intention to sell.

(b) Other Security Valuation Problems. Market quotations of registered securities may not be appropriate for use in valuing similar but unregistered securities (see FRP No. 404). Some discount based on the conditions yet to be met to permit salability is often required where any restrictions on immediate sale are present. In addition, consideration should also be given, in valuing securities, to large block holdings, the disposition of which could depress market prices. Care should also be exercised in assessing market values when evidence indicates securities are thinly traded.

For securities other than marketable equity securities recorded at the lower of cost or market, it would generally be appropriate to compare aggregate cost with aggregate market.

Although not all authorities agree, it seems reasonable that subsequent market recoveries be reflected in income to the extent of prior reductions below cost unless such prior reductions reflected a decline in value that was considered to be other than temporary.

FRP No. 404 comments on the valuation of investment securities by registered investment companies and certain of the procedures that the independent accountant should apply in examining financial statements that involve security valuations and the attendant reporting problems, especially in circumstances where securities are valued by the directors in the absence of readily available market quotations.

11.62 INTERIM REPORTING OF INVESTMENTS.   The provisions of SFAS No. 12 apply to interim as well as annual reporting periods (par. 23).

A determination should be made as to whether any unusual or significant fourth quarter adjustments arising from the application of SFAS No. 12 require special disclosure.

SOURCES AND SUGGESTED REFERENCES

American Institute of Certified Public Accountants, *Accounting Trends and Techniques,* 43rd ed., AICPA, New York, 1989.

———, "Audit Considerations in Electronic Funds Transfer Systems," *Computer Services Guidelines,* AICPA, New York, 1978.

———, Committee on Accounting Procedure, "Restatement and Revision of Accounting Research Bulletins," Accounting Research Bulletin No. 43, AICPA, New York, 1953.

Bank Administration Institute, *Security, Audit, and Control Considerations in the Design of Electronic Funds Transfer Systems,* BAI, Park Ridge, IL, 1977.

Bort, Richard, *Corporate Cash Management Handbook,* Warren, Gorham & Lamont, Boston, 1989.

Conference Board, *Cash Management,* Conference Board, Inc., New York, 1973.

Defliese, Philip L., Johnson, Kenneth P., and Macleod, Roderick K., *Montgomery's Auditing,* 10th ed., Ronald Press, New York, 1985.

Financial Accounting Standards Board, "Application of FASB Statement No. 12 to Personal Financial Statements (an interpretation of FASB Statement No. 12)," FASB Interpretation No. 10, FASB, Stamford, CT, 1976.

———, "Changes in Market Value After the Balance Sheet Date (an interpretation of FASB Statement No. 12)," FASB Interpretation No. 11, FASB, Stamford, CT, 1976.

———, "Accounting for Previously Established Allowance Accounts (an interpretation of FASB Statement No. 12)," FASB Interpretation No. 12, FASB, Stamford, CT, 1976.

———, "Consolidation of a Parent and Its Subsidiaries Having Different Balance Sheet Dates (an interpretation of FASB Statement No. 12)," FASB Interpretation No. 13, FASB, Stamford, CT, 1976.

———, "Clarification of Definitions and Accounting for Marketable Equity Securities That Become Nonmarketable (an interpretation of FASB Statement No. 12)," FASB Interpretation No. 16, FASB, Stamford, CT, 1976.

———, "Accounting for Certain Marketable Securities," Statement of Financial Accounting Standards No. 12, FASB, Stamford, CT, 1975.

———, "Accounting by Debtors and Creditors for Troubled Debt Restructurings," Statement of Financial Accounting Standards No. 15, FASB, Stamford, CT, 1977.

———, "Foreign Currency Translation," Statement of Financial Accounting Standards No. 52, FASB, Stamford, CT, 1981.

———, "Financial Reporting and Changing Prices," Statement of Financial Accounting Standards No. 89, FASB, Stamford, CT, 1986.

———, "Consolidation of All Majority-Owned Subsidiaries," Statement of Financial Accounting Standards No. 94, FASB, Stamford, CT, 1987.

———, "Accounting for Income Taxes," Statement of Financial Accounting Standards No. 96, FASB, Stamford, CT, 1987.

Heckert, J. Brooks, and Willson, James D., *Controllership,* 2nd ed., Ronald Press, New York, 1963.

Hunt, Alfred L., *Corporate Cash Management,* AMACOM, New York, 1978.

Johnson, Glen L., and Gentry, James A., Jr., *Finney and Miller's Principles of Accounting* (Intermediate) 7th ed., Prentice-Hall, Englewood Cliffs, NJ, 1974.

Kieso, Donald E., Mautz, R. K., and Moyer, C. A., *Intermediate Principles of Accounting,* 6th ed., Wiley, New York, 1989.

Lundquist, William H., "Fundamentals of Short and Long-Term Cash Forecasting," *National Association of Accountants Bulletin,* April 1964.

Lyons, Norman R., "Segregation of Functions in EFTS," *Journal of Accountancy,* October 1978.

Meigs, Walter B., Larsen, E. John, and Meigs, Robert F., *Principles of Auditing,* 9th ed., Irwin, Homewood, IL, 1988.

Morley, James E., Jr., "Cash Management—Working for the Extra 1% or 2%," *Management Accounting,* October 1978.

Price Waterhouse/Euromoney International Treasury Management Handbook, Volumes I and II, Euromoney Publications, London, England, 1986.

Richardson, Dana R., "Auditing EFTS," *Journal of Accountancy,* October 1978.

Schaller, Carol A., "The Revolution of EFTS," *Journal of Accountancy,* October 1978.

Securities and Exchange Commission, "Notice of Adoption of Amendments to Regulation S-X and Related Interpretations and Guidelines Regarding Disclosure of Compensating Balances and Short-Term Borrowing Arrangements," Accounting Series Release No. 148, SEC, Washington, DC, November, 1973.

Smith, Jay M., Jr., and Skousen, K. Fred, *Intermediate Accounting,* 10th ed., South-Western Publishing Co., Cincinnati, OH, 1990.

Stettler, Howard F., *Auditing Principles,* 5th ed., Prentice-Hall, Englewood Cliffs, NJ, 1982.

Welsch, Glenn A., Zlatkovich, Charles T., and Harrison, Walter T., Jr., *Intermediate Accounting,* 8th ed., Irwin, Homewood, IL, 1988.

CHAPTER 12

REVENUES AND RECEIVABLES

Henry R. Jaenicke, PhD, CPA

Drexel University

Gordian A. Ndubizu, PhD

Drexel University

CONTENTS

The authors wish to acknowledge the comments received from Bhaskar H. Bhave and the editorial assistance provided by Myra D. Cleary.

NATURE AND MEASUREMENT OF REVENUE

12.1 DEFINITION AND COMPONENTS OF REVENUE.   SFAC No. 6, "Elements of Financial Statements" (pars. 78, 79, and 82), issued in December 1985, defines revenues and gains as follows:

> Revenues are inflows or other enhancements of assets of an entity or settlements of its liabilities (or a combination of both) from delivering or producing goods, rendering services, or other activities that constitute the entity's ongoing major or central operations.

> Revenues represent actual or expected cash inflows (or the equivalent) that have occurred or will eventuate as a result of the entity's ongoing major or central operations. The assets increased by revenues may be of various kinds—for example, cash, claims against customers or clients, other goods or services received, or increased value of a product resulting from production. Similarly, the transactions and events from which revenues arise and the revenues themselves are in many forms and are called by various names—for example, output, deliveries, sales, fees, interest, dividends, royalties, and rent—depending on the kinds of operations involved and the way revenues are recognized.

> Gains are increases in equity (net assets) from peripheral or incidental transactions of an entity and from all other transactions and other events and circumstances affecting the entity except those that result from revenues or investments by owners.

SFAC No. 6 (pars. 87–89) addresses the distinction between revenues and gains (and between expenses and losses) as follows:

Revenues and gains are similar, and expenses and losses are similar, but some differences are significant in conveying information about an enterprise's performance. Revenues and expenses result from an entity's ongoing major or central operations and activities—that is, from activities such as producing or delivering goods, rendering services, lending, insuring, investing, and financing. In contrast, gains and losses result from incidental or peripheral transactions of an enterprise with other entities and from other events and circumstances affecting it. Some gains and losses may be considered "operating" gains and losses and may be closely related to revenues and expenses. Revenues and expenses are commonly displayed as gross inflows or outflows of net assets, while gains and losses are usually displayed as net inflows or outflows.

The definitions and discussion of revenues, expenses, gains, and losses in this Statement give broad guidance but do not distinguish precisely between revenues and gains or between expenses and losses. Distinctions between revenues and gains and between expenses and losses in a particular entity depend to a significant extent on the nature of the entity, its operations, and its other activities. Items that are revenues for one kind of entity may be gains for another, and items that are expenses for one kind of entity may be losses for another. For example, investments in securities that may be sources of revenues and expenses for insurance or investment companies may be sources of gains and losses in manufacturing or merchandising companies. Technological changes may be sources of gains or losses for most kinds of enterprises but may be characteristic of the operations of high-technology or research-oriented enterprises. Events such as commodity price changes and foreign exchange rate changes that occur while assets are being used or produced or liabilities are owed may directly or indirectly affect the *amounts* of revenues or expenses for most enterprises, but they are *sources* of revenues or expenses only for enterprises for which trading in foreign exchange or commodities is a major or central activity.

Since a primary purpose of distinguishing gains and losses from revenues and expenses is to make displays of information about an enterprise's sources of comprehensive income as useful as possible, fine distinctions between revenues and gains and between expenses and losses are principally matters of display or reporting.

This chapter does not distinguish between gains and revenues because the distinction is not important in resolving the major issues of revenue recognition and measurement. The distinction is significant, however, in considering income statement presentation of earnings, particularly whether asset inflows and outflows should be shown gross or net and where gains and losses should be reported.

12.2 CLASSIFICATION OF REVENUE.   O'Reilly, Hirsch, Defliese, and Jaenicke (1990, p. 371) note that:

Most companies have one or more major sources of revenues and several less significant types of miscellaneous revenues, commonly referred to as "other income." The term used for a given type of revenue usually depends on whether it is derived from one of the enterprise's principal business activities. For example, sales of transformers by an electrical supply company would be "sales," while such transactions would be "other income" to an electric utility. Conversely, interest and dividends from investments would be "other income" to almost all enterprises except investment companies, for which interest and dividends are a primary source of revenues.

12.3 MEASUREMENT, EARNING, REALIZATION, AND RECOGNITION OF REVENUE. There is general agreement on the meaning of the terms "measurement" and "earning" as they apply to revenue. However, there is disagreement regarding usage of two other terms— realization and recognition—that are significant in establishing the accounting period in which revenue should be recognized.

(a) Measurement of Revenue.   There is widespread agreement that revenue is measured by the exchange value of the goods or services produced by the enterprise. The measurement criterion, coupled with the FASB definition of revenues, thus excludes from revenues those items commonly referred to as "revenue adjustments," such as bad debts, discounts, returns, and allowances. (See the discussion below under "Revenue Adjustments and Aftercosts.") In certain circumstances, the time value of money should be acknowledged, and interest implicit in a revenue transaction should be classified separately.

Depending on the point in the transaction at which revenue is recognized, the measurement process requires varying degrees of estimation. The later revenue is recognized in the earning process, the less need there is to use estimates in measuring it.

(b) Earning of Revenue.   Agreement also exists on the question of when revenue is "earned." According to SFAC No. 5 (par. 83.b) "Recognition and Measurement in Financial Statements of Business Enterprises," revenues are not recognized until earned. An entity's revenue-earning activities involve delivering or producing goods, rendering services, or other activities that constitute its ongoing major or central operations. Revenues are considered to have been earned when the entity has substantially accomplished what it must do to be entitled to the benefits represented by the revenues. Understanding revenue recognition rules in certain industries may thus require a knowledge of the nature of the specific earning process in those industries.

(c) Revenue Realization and Recognition.   To "recognize" revenue means to report it in the entity's financial statements or to record it in the entity's accounts by crediting a revenue account and simultaneously recording an increase in an asset or a decrease in a liability. At the time revenue is recognized, closely related expenses (such as cost of goods sold) also are recorded, although the particular accounting system (e.g., a periodic inventory system) may cause the actual bookkeeping entry to be made later in the accounting period. At the point of revenue recognition, the accounting for related assets switches from recording entry values, that is, amounts based on purchase prices (such as the historical cost of an asset), to recording exit values, that is, amounts based on selling prices (such as the selling price of an asset sold in the ordinary course of business). "In traditional accounting terminology, the accountant is said to 'recognize revenue' when he switches from one measurement approach to the other" (Staubus, 1977, p. 172).

The **realization principle** is often described in relation to the recognition of revenue. Unfortunately, use of the term "realization" is not uniform, and for that reason some authors prefer to avoid it. The term is so deeply embedded in accounting terminology, however, that it cannot be ignored.

Some authors use realization in a very broad sense to mean that the necessary conditions for recognizing revenue have been met. The 1957 revision of the AAA's *Accounting and Reporting Standards for Corporate Financial Statements* (p. 3), for example, states: "The essential meaning of realization is that a change in an asset or liability has become sufficiently definite and objective to warrant recognition in the accounts." Under this broad view, the point of realization (recognition) is movable, and specific rules must be provided to define when it occurs in different types of revenue transactions and earning processes.

A more widely held view, however, is that realization takes place at a single specific point in time, such as the sale date, and recognition of revenue at all other points in time is a departure from or an exception to the realization principle. Some departures or exceptions are considered acceptable in specific circumstances, based on the presence of certain characteristics. APB Statement No. 4, "Basic Concepts and Accounting Principles Underlying Financial Statements of Business Enterprises" (pars. 150–152), illustrates this view of the realization principle:

> Revenue is conventionally recognized at a specific point in the earning process of a business enterprise, usually when assets are sold or services are rendered. This conventional recognition is the basis of the pervasive measurement principle known as realization.
>
> **P-2 Realization.** Revenue is generally recognized when both of the following conditions are met: (1) the earning process is complete or virtually complete, and (2) an exchange has taken place.

The exchange required by the realization principle determines both the time at which to recognize revenue and the amount at which to record it. Revenue from sales of products is recognized under this principle at the date of sale, usually interpreted to mean the date of delivery to customers. Revenue from services rendered is recognized under this principle when services have been performed and are billable. Revenue from permitting others to use enterprise resources, such as interest, rent, and royalties is also governed by the realization principle. Revenue of this type is recognized as time passes or as the resources are used. Revenue from sales of assets other than products is recognized at the date of sale. Revenue recognized under the realization principle is recorded at the amount received or expected to be received.

Revenue is sometimes recognized on bases other than the realization rule. For example, on long-term construction contracts revenue may be recognized as construction progresses. This exception to the realization principle is based on the availability of evidence of the ultimate proceeds and the consensus that a better measure of periodic income results. Sometimes revenue is recognized at the completion of production and before a sale is made. Examples include certain precious metals and farm products with assured sales prices. The assured price, the difficulty in some situations of determining costs of products on hand, and the characteristic of unit interchangeability are reasons given to support this exception.

A third meaning of realization restricts the term to its dictionary meaning of "conversion into actual money," or in slightly modified form, "conversion of nonmonetary assets into monetary assets." This meaning of the term is divorced completely from any notion of revenue recognition, although revenues may, coincidentally, be recognized when cash ("actual money") or other monetary assets are received. The FASB uses the term essentially in this third sense in SFAC No. 6 (par. 143):

Realization in the most precise sense means the process of converting noncash resources and rights into money and is most precisely used in accounting and financial reporting to refer to sales of assets for cash or claims to cash. The related terms *realized* and *unrealized* therefore identify revenues or gains or losses on assets sold and unsold, respectively. Those are the meanings of realization and related terms in the Board's conceptual framework. Recognition is the process of formally recording or incorporating an item in the financial statements of an entity.

12.4 ALTERNATIVE BASES OF REVENUE RECOGNITION.   Revenue could possibly be recognized at various points in the earning process, depending on the circumstances. The use of each basis in different circumstances is discussed below. The general criteria for recognizing revenue and specific factors to be considered in applying those criteria are considered later in this chapter under "Criteria for Recognizing Revenue."

(a) Sale Basis.   Recognizing revenue on the basis of the time a product is delivered or service rendered is most common and most supported in the authoritative literature. Paton and Littleton (1940, pp. 53–54) state:

For the great majority of business enterprises the sale basis of measuring revenue clearly meets the requirements of accounting standards more effectively than any other possible basis. Revenue is the financial expression of the product of business operation and hence should be gauged in terms of the decisive stage or step in the stream of activity. Revenue, moreover, should be evidenced and supported by new and dependable assets, preferably cash or near-cash. These fundamental requirements are well met by adopting the completed sale as the test of the realization of revenue.

For most concerns engaged in making or dealing with tangible goods the sale is the most conclusive, and the most financially significant, of the chain of events making up the business process; the sale is the capstone of activity, the end toward which all efforts are directed. . . .

If product is in the form of service, as in transportation, banking, etc., the act or process of furnishing service may be viewed as the equivalent of sale for the purpose of measuring revenue. . . .

One of the six rules adopted by the membership of the AICPA in 1934, and reprinted in ARB No. 43 (Ch. 1, § A, par. 1), states: "Profit is deemed to be realized when a sale in the ordinary course of business is effected, unless the circumstances are such that the collection of the sale price is not reasonably assured." The APB reaffirmed that view in 1966 in APB Opinion No. 10 (par. 12), stating: "Revenues should ordinarily be accounted for at the time a transaction is completed, with appropriate provision for uncollectible accounts."

George O. May (1943, pp. 30–31) stated the rationale behind the widespread use of the sale basis as long ago as 1943:

> The problem of allocation of income to particular short periods obviously offers great difficulty—indeed, it is the point at which conventional treatment becomes indispensable, and it must be recognized that some conventions are scarcely in harmony with the facts. Manifestly, when a laborious process of manufacture and sale culminates in the delivery of the product at a profit, that profit is not attributable, except conventionally, to the moment when the sale or delivery occurred. The accounting convention which makes such an attribution is justified only by its demonstrated practical utility.
>
> It is instructive to consider how it happens that a rule which is violative of fact produces results that are practically useful and reliable. The explanation is, that in the normal business there are at any one moment transactions at every stage of the production of profit, from beginning to end. If the distribution were exactly uniform, an allocation of income according to the proportion of completion of each unit would produce the same result as the attribution of the entire profit to a single stage.
>
> A number of conclusions immediately suggest themselves: first, that the convention is valid for the greatest variety of purposes where the flow of product is most uniform; second, that it is likely to be more generally valid for a longer than for a shorter period; and, third, that its applicability is seriously open to question for some purposes where the final consummation is irregular in time and in amount. Thus, the rule is almost completely valid in regard to a business which is turning out a standard product in relatively small units at a reasonable stable rate of production. It is less generally valid—or, to put it otherwise, the figure of profit reached is less generally significant—in the case of a company engaged in building large units, such as battleships, or carrying out construction contracts.

(i) Exceptions to the Sale Basis.   In certain circumstances, variations from the sale basis of revenue recognition are regarded as acceptable.

Revenue may be recognized **before the time of sale** (i.e., before delivery or full performance) (1) for construction contracts for which total profit can be estimated with reasonable accuracy and ultimate realization is reasonably assured, and (2) for commodities that have a wide and ready market and meet other conditions. Those exceptions to the sale basis are discussed below in some detail, under "Recognition before Sale."

Revenue may also be recognized **after the time of sale,** most commonly for certain installment sales in which the customer receives the goods and agrees to pay for them in a series of periodic payments, or "installments." The seller may recognize the revenue when the goods are delivered (sale basis) or, in circumstances described below, use the cash basis, under which revenue is recognized as the installments are collected (cost recovery or installment methods).

(ii) Objections to the Sale Basis.   Use of the sale as the time of revenue recognition is not without shortcomings. Paton and Paton (1955, pp. 278–279) noted the following objections that others have raised to this basis as a measure of revenue:

a. Accounts receivable may become uncollectible.
b. Collection expenses and other costs may be incurred subsequent to sale.
c. Merchandise returns and allowances may be made.

d. Accounts receivable are not the equivalent of cash and hence do not represent immediately disposable funds.

e. Revenue is earned through the entire process of production and hence it is unduly conservative to postpone recognition until the time of sale.

The first three objections can be overcome through periodic adjustment for uncollectible accounts, anticipated expenses, and returns and allowances.

The fourth objection reflects confusion between income and cash flows. Under the accrual basis of accounting, revenue is not equated with cash receipts, as is implied by the objection. Moreover, that net income may not be disposable need not invalidate the sale as the basis of revenue recognition. The measurement of income (results of operations) and the administration of funds generated by those operations are separate and distinct.

The fifth objection—that is, the sale basis is unduly conservative because revenue is earned through the entire production process—suggests that there should be no distinction between the earning and the recognition of revenue. Revenue is recognized during the entire earning process, as in the percentage-of-completion method, only when certain conditions, discussed below and in Chapter 21, are present. If those conditions are not present, a more conservative approach is appropriate.

(b) Recognition before Sale.   As indicated above, in certain industries the recognition of revenue may occur prior to the time of sale. Revenue may be recognized during production, as in the construction industry, or at completion of production, as in farming.

(i) Construction Contracts.   In the construction industry, revenue may be recognized on the completed contract or the percentage-of-completion (production) basis. (See the detailed discussion in Chapter 21.) Recognizing revenue in construction projects on the basis of production is regarded as a desirable departure from the sale basis if total revenue and cost can be reliably estimated.

Accounting for revenue by the **completed contract method**—that is, when the contract has been fully performed—is appropriate if estimates of revenue and expenses are not reliable. This method, which is the equivalent of the sale basis, is conservative, since it eliminates the possibility of cancellation of the contract after revenue and profit have been recognized. Also, the amount of profit can be more accurately determined, since the need for estimates is greatly reduced. The principal limitation of this basis in connection with long-term contracts is that periodic operating reports do not reveal what is happening in the enterprise if revenue is recognized in the period of completion rather than as the work progresses. Revenue is recognized only sporadically, when contracts are completed, despite continuous performance.

For long-term contracts, as in the construction of roads, buildings, ships, and so forth, the recognition of revenue using the **percentage-of-completion method** generally results in periodic net income that is more nearly related to the earning of revenue. The use of that basis is justified, however, only if there is reasonable assurance of the profit margin and its ultimate realization. The term "percentage of completion" ordinarily refers to the relationship between costs incurred and the total estimated cost of the completed project, although a percentage based on time or physical units of production may be used.

The percentage-of-completion method, as developed in the construction industry, has been applied, sometimes improperly, to seemingly analogous situations in other industries. The method is also widely used to recognize revenue from production-type contracts and certain service transactions.

(ii) Extractive Industries and Agriculture.   The production basis of recognizing revenue is regarded as acceptable in certain extractive industries and agriculture in which the com-

modities are immediately salable at quoted market prices. The mining of precious metals and growing of crops such as wheat, cotton, and oats are examples. Revenue is recognized before sale by valuing inventory of products on hand at market value (Kieso and Weygandt, 1989, p. 886).

The AICPA (ARB No. 43, "Restatement and Revision of Accounting Research Bulletins," Ch. 4, par. 16) sanctions this procedure, as follows:

> It is generally recognized that income accrues only at the time of sale, and that gains may not be anticipated by reflecting assets at their current sales prices. For certain articles, however, exceptions are permissible. Inventories of gold and silver, when there is an effective government-controlled market at a fixed monetary value, are ordinarily reflected at selling prices. A similar treatment is not uncommon for inventories representing agricultural, mineral, and other products, units of which are interchangeable and have an immediate marketability at quoted prices and for which appropriate costs may be difficult to obtain. Where such inventories are stated at sales prices, they should of course be reduced by expenditures to be incurred in disposal, and the use of such basis should be fully disclosed in the financial statements.

Despite the support for recognition prior to sale that is found in the authoritative accounting literature, in practice revenue is generally recognized on mineral products when they are sold. The authoritative literature is silent on the appropriateness of recognizing revenue on agricultural products still in the growth or production stage, even if they are readily marketable at quoted prices (Kieso and Weygandt, p. 887).

(iii) Accretion Basis. Paton and Littleton (1940, p. 52) rejected considering accretion (increase in value from natural growth or aging process) as revenue:

> Allied to the question of the significance of production in relation to revenue is the problem of increase resulting from growth and other natural processes. . . . In this situation there is no doubt that assets have increased, and the amount of the physical increase is subject to objective verification. The technical process of production, however, remains to be undertaken, followed by conversion into new liquid assets. Assuming that the final product of the enterprise is lumber, it is clearly incorrect to treat accretion as revenue.

They added, however, that there is no serious objection to disclosing measurable increases from accretion as supplementary information, provided cost is not obscured and the resulting credit is clearly labeled as unrealized income. Since revenue from accretion is not recognized, the costs incurred for the purpose of encouraging accretion should, theoretically at least, be added to the growing product and recognized as expenses when revenues are recognized at the time the timber, nursery stock, or other property is sold.

Hendriksen (1982, p. 181) concludes that from an economic point of view, recognition of accretion may be justified, but from a practical standpoint, "the present discounted value [required to make the necessary comparative inventory valuations] is difficult to determine because it depends upon expectations regarding future market prices and expectations regarding future costs of providing for growth and future costs of harvesting and getting the product ready for market." Periodic recognition of accretion as revenue has not been adopted in practice.

(iv) Appreciation Basis. Accounting authorities for many years have generally agreed that appreciation of property values attributable to market changes does not constitute revenue. Paton and Littleton (1940, pp. 46 and 62) summarize the proposition, as follows:

> Appreciation in its various forms is not income. The case for introducing estimated appreciation (or "declination") into the accounts and reports otherwise than as supplementary data is not strong. . . .

Without doubt the movement of prices has an important bearing on the economic significance of existing business assets, but there is little warrant for the view that sheer enhancement of market value, however determined, represents effective income. Appreciation, in general, does not reflect or measure the progress of operating activity; appreciation is not the result of any transaction or any act of conversion; appreciation makes available no additional liquid resources which may be used to meet obligations or make disbursements to investors; appreciation has little or no legal standing as income.

In recent years, several authorities have expressed approval, to varying degrees, of certain departures from historical practice and the adoption of alternative approaches to income recognition. SFAS No. 33, ''Financial Reporting and Changing Prices,'' provides a good example. However, its requirements were subsequently amended by SFAS Nos. 82 and 89; the latter makes the supplementary disclosure of current cost/constant purchasing power information voluntary.

(v) Cost Savings versus Revenue.   Savings resulting from efficient operation or fortunate purchases generally are classified as reductions of costs, not as revenue. Edwards and Bell (1965, p. 93) define the term ''cost saving'' as ''an increase in the current cost of assets held.'' That usage of the term has not been widely accepted and is not adopted in this chapter.

(c) Recognition after Sale.   As noted earlier, in certain circumstances revenue may be recognized after the time of sale. Methods used include the **deposit method** (which is really a nonrecognition method), the **cost recovery method,** and the **installment method.** Both the cost recovery and installment methods are referred to as **cash bases of revenue recognition.**

The cash basis of revenue recognition should not be confused with the **cash basis of accounting.** As Paton and Littleton (1940, p. 59) noted more than 50 years ago,

Placing revenue on a cash basis when such treatment is appropriate, it is hardly necessary to say, does not imply that expense should be measured by expenditure. Revenue is the controlling element; expense is the cost of the amount of revenue acknowledged. If receipts from customers are viewed as revenue the applicable expense is the cost of producing such receipts, not the cash disbursements made during the period.

Under the cash basis of accounting, revenue is measured by cash receipts and expense is measured by cash disbursements.

It is important to distinguish between an installment sale and the method used to recognize revenue, expense, and income from that type of sale. In installment sales, the purchaser agrees to pay for the purchase in a series of periodic payments, usually, but not always, preceded by an initial payment customarily termed a ''down payment.'' The vendor may account for installment sales in the same manner as other charge sales, that is, by recognizing income at the time of sale, or may recognize income either proportionally as the installments are collected or after all costs have been recovered. The latter methods, known as the installment method and cost recovery method, respectively, are acceptable if certain conditions (discussed below) are present.

(i) Installment Method and Cost Recovery Method.   When the APB (APB Opinion No. 10, par. 12) expressed the view ''that revenues should ordinarily be accounted for at the time a transaction is completed . . . ,'' it also (in a note to that paragraph) recognized that:

[T]here are exceptional cases where receivables are collectible over an extended period of time and, because of the terms of the transactions or other conditions, there is no reasonable basis for estimating the degree of collectibility. When such circumstances exist, and as long as they exist, either the installment method or the cost recovery method of accounting may be used. (Under the cost recovery method, equal amounts of revenue and expense are recognized as collections are made until all costs have been recovered, postponing any recognition of profit until that time.)

(ii) Deposit Accounting. In some circumstances, such as in contracts that do not qualify to be recorded as sales in retail land transactions, **deposit accounting** should be used (SFAS No. 66, "Accounting for Sales of Real Estate," pars. 65–67). In deposit accounting, a liability is recorded when cash is received, and no amounts are reflected in revenue until the period has expired during which the customer may cancel and receive a full refund.

(d) Differences in Revenue Recognition for Accounting and Tax Purposes. SFAS No. 96, "Accounting for Income Taxes," contains a detailed description of differences between income and its components for accounting purposes and for federal income tax purposes. Those differences include **permanent differences** and **temporary differences.** Permanent differences between revenue (or gain) recognized for accounting purposes and revenue (or gain) recognized for tax purposes result, for example, from the nontaxability of municipal bond interest and of proceeds from insurance policies on lives of officers. SFAS No. 96 (par. 10) provides examples of temporary differences involving revenue:

- *Revenues or gains that are taxable after they are recognized in financial income.* An asset (for example, a receivable from an installment sale) may be recognized for revenues or gains that will result in future taxable amounts when the asset is recovered.
- *Revenues or gains that are taxable before they are recognized in financial income.* A liability (for example, subscriptions received in advance) may be recognized for an advance payment for goods or services to be provided in future years. For tax purposes, the advance payment is upon the receipt of cash. Future sacrifices to provide goods or services (or future refunds to those who cancel their orders) will result in future tax deductible amounts when the liability is settled.

NATURE AND SIGNIFICANCE OF RECEIVABLES

12.5 RECEIVABLES DEFINED. "Receivables" is a broad designation applicable to claims for future receipt of money, goods, and services. This broad designation thus includes deposits for purchases and payments for services to be rendered in the future such as insurance, advertising, and utilities. This chapter uses the more restrictive, but common, definition of "receivables" as a designation for claims collectible in money. Claims collectible in goods or services are termed "prepayments."

The general classification of receivables depends on whether they are evidenced by a written statement. Thus, receivables are either:

1. *Accounts Receivable*. Receivables for which no written statement acknowledging the obligation has been received from the obligor.
2. *Notes Receivable*. Receivables for which a written statement acknowledging the obligation has been received from the obligor.

In addition, receivables may be due for purchases of goods and services charged on credit cards issued by the entity itself or by a financial institution or other organization. The types of receivables are further classified by the situation in which the receivable arose (origin), whether a security interest was obtained with the receivable, and the time of expected receipt of the money.

12.6 TYPES OF ACCOUNTS RECEIVABLE. Accounts receivable are first classified by the situation giving rise to the receivable. The most frequent situation is the delivery of goods. In practice, the term "accounts receivable" is normally used to designate the book amounts owed by trade customers. Other items are used to designate accounts receivable arising from revenue recognition in the normal course of business in various industries. Examples of such designations are "revenues receivable" (used by public utilities), "rents receivable" (used by real estate agencies), and "subscriptions receivable" (used by publishers).

12.7 TYPES OF NOTES RECEIVABLE.   The term "notes," used broadly, includes two types of instruments: promissory notes and bills of exchange or drafts. (Lease receivables required to be accounted for as receivables in accordance with SFAS No. 13, "Accounting for Leases," are discussed in Chapter 16.) Promissory notes and bills of exchange are defined by Raphael (1967, p. 97) as follows:

> **A promissory note** is a promise made by one person, called the "maker," to pay to the order of another person, called the "payee" (or to bearer) a certain sum of money on demand or at a definite future time.
>
> **A draft** or bill of exchange is an instrument in which one person called the "drawer" orders another person called the "drawee" to pay a certain sum of money to another person called the "payee" (or to bearer), on demand or at a definite future time. The drawer and drawee may be the same person. The drawer and payee may be the same person.

To be "negotiable" within the meaning of the Uniform Commercial Code [§ 3-104(1)], all such instruments must meet the following conditions:

a. Be signed by the maker or drawer;
b. Contain an unconditional promise or order to pay a certain sum in money and no other promise, order, obligation or power given by the maker or drawer except as authorized by this Article 131;
c. Be payable on demand or at a definite time; and
d. Be payable to order or to bearer.

A distinctive feature of the typical commercial bill or draft, as compared with a note, is that the former is initiated by the creditor rather than by the debtor. Bills are "orders" to pay; notes are "promises" to pay. Bills arising in domestic commerce are usually referred to as "commercial drafts"; the term "bills of exchange" is generally restricted to instruments used in foreign commerce.

12.8 CREDIT CARD RECEIVABLES.   A retail business that accepts credit card drafts in payment of purchases may accept one of three types: (1) bank credit cards, (2) travel and entertainment credit cards, and (3) company credit cards (also called "in-house" credit cards). Each of these requires separate treatment by the retailer. Issuers of travel and entertainment and bank credit cards treat credit card receivables in the same fashion as a retailer treats company credit card receivables (except, of course, that the receivables are forwarded by a retailer rather than being direct sales).

For the retailer, bank and travel and entertainment credit card drafts are receivables from the issuer of the credit card. Although procedures for individual card issuers vary slightly, they generally require that the credit card drafts be accumulated and forwarded periodically to the issuer. There is usually a merchant's charge (discount) for the credit card drafts, which may be recorded at the time of forwarding the accumulated drafts or when the payment is received from the issuer of the card. Company credit card drafts are receivables under a credit card agreement. These agreements vary, but normally they provide for a minimum payment with interest on the unpaid balance.

CRITERIA FOR RECOGNIZING REVENUE

12.9 GENERAL CRITERIA.   As discussed earlier in this chapter, the general criteria for recognition follow the realization principle stated in APB Statement No. 4, namely, that the revenue has been earned and an exchange has taken place. One of the most difficult tasks the accountant faces is applying those general criteria to specific transactions and events for the purpose of determining the most appropriate time in the earning process to recognize all or part of the revenue. For some transactions and events and for some industries, authoritative or quasi-authoritative literature provides, on an ad hoc basis, more specific criteria—and sometimes conditions—that must be met before revenue is recognized; those instances are described in sections 12.16 and 12.17. The paragraphs below provide guidance for selecting the appropriate method of revenue recognition in the absence of specific authoritative or quasi-authoritative pronouncements.

12.10 ATTRIBUTES MEASURED BY ENTRY AND EXIT VALUES.   As noted earlier, recognizing revenue results in a shift from accounting for **entry values** to accounting for **exit values.** In theory, two attributes of assets can be measured using entry values: historical cost and current cost. Similarly, three attributes can be measured using exit values: current selling price in orderly liquidation, expected selling price in due course of business, and present value of expected cash flows (FASB Discussion Memorandum, "An Analysis of Issues Related to Conceptual Framework for Financial Accounting and Reporting: Elements of Financial Statements and Their Measurement," p. 194).

In general, the existing accounting model measures historical cost before revenue and related expenses are recognized. When revenue is recognized, the attribute measured becomes expected selling price in due course of business, that is, net realizable value. For example, inventory is usually accounted for at historical cost until it is sold. At that time, the cost of inventory is recognized as an expense, and the inventory disappears from the balance sheet. The inventory is replaced by a new asset, often a receivable, which is accounted for at net realizable value, and an equal amount of revenue is recognized.

Of course, other attributes of elements of financial statements besides historical cost or proceeds and expected selling price in due course of business can be measured. The significant point is that when revenue is recognized, a switch is made from some entry to some exit value. Unless otherwise specified, however, this discussion assumes that the entry value is historical cost or proceeds and the exit value is net realizable value—that is, "the historical cost model."

12.11 CONCEPTUAL FRAMEWORK AND REVENUE RECOGNITION.   SFAC No. 1, "Objectives of Financial Reporting by Business Enterprises" (pars. 34 and 37), states the first two **objectives of financial reporting** by business enterprises, as follows:

> Financial reporting should provide information that is useful to present and potential investors and creditors and other users in making rational investment, credit, and similar decisions.

> Financial reporting should provide information to help present and potential investors and creditors and other users in assessing the amounts, timing, and uncertainty of prospective cash receipts from dividends or interest and the proceeds from the sale, redemption, or maturity of securities or loans. The prospects for those cash receipts are affected by an enterprise's ability to generate enough cash to meet its obligations. . . . Thus, financial reporting should provide information to help investors, creditors, and others assess the amounts, timing, and uncertainty of prospective net cash inflows to the related enterprise.

SFAC No. 5 (par. 6) defines recognition as "the process of formally recording or incorporating an item into the financial statements of an entity as an asset, liability, revenue, expense, or the like." Paragraph 63 specifies "fundamental recognition criteria" for recognizing a financial statement element:

> An item and information about it should meet four fundamental recognition criteria to be recognized and should be recognized when the criteria are met, subject to a cost–benefit constraint and a materiality threshold. Those criteria are:

> *Definitions*—The item meets the definitions of an element of financial statements.

Measurability—It has a relevant attribute measurable with sufficient reliability.

Relevance—The information about it is capable of making a difference in user decisions.

Reliability—The information is representationally faithful, verifiable, and neutral.

All four criteria are subject to a pervasive cost–benefit constraint: the expected benefits from recognizing a particular item should justify perceived costs of providing and using the information. Recognition is also subject to a materiality threshold; an item and information about it need not be recognized in a set of financial statements if the item is not large enough to be material and the aggregate of individually immaterial items is not large enough to be material to those financial statements.

The measurability criterion states that the financial statement element "must have a relevant attribute that can be quantified in monetary units with sufficient reliability. Measurability must be considered together with both relevance and reliability" (par. 65). The qualities of relevance and reliability sometimes conflict with each other and require that trade-offs be made. Generally, the sooner that reliable information about revenue transactions can be conveyed to financial statement users, the more relevant it will be to them. By the same token, the earlier in the earning process revenue is recognized, the greater the likelihood of a divergence between the information and the underlying economic reality. Accordingly, the later in the earning process revenue is recognized, the greater the likelihood that the information presented will be reliable, but the lesser the likelihood that it will be relevant for users' decisions.

SFAC No. 5 also provides guidance for applying the fundamental criteria to recognizing revenues. Paragraph 83 specifies that revenue recognition involves consideration of two factors, namely, being realized or realizable, and being earned. Revenues are realized when products or other assets are exchanged for cash or claims to cash, and revenues are realizable when assets received or held are readily convertible to known amounts of cash or claims to cash; revenues are earned when the entity has substantially completed what it was required to do to be entitled to the benefits represented by the revenues. The Concepts Statement presents examples of how those two factors may be helpful in determining when revenue should be recognized (especially from sales transactions). Many accountants believe, however, that the recognition and criteria application guidance set forth in SFAC No. 5 are not sufficiently prescriptive to be helpful in determining the appropriate point of recognition in complex earning processes.

12.12 SPECIFIC RECOGNITION CRITERIA.   The specific criteria discussed below have been suggested by various individuals or groups as being significant to the timing of revenue recognition. They address characteristics of the event or transaction that gives rise to the revenue, characteristics of the asset received in the transaction, and characteristics of the revenue recognized (see Exhibit 12.1). Despite some degree of overlap in the criteria, the classification scheme seems useful, particularly in resolving problems that are not addressed by authoritative pronouncements.

12.13 CHARACTERISTICS OF THE REVENUE EVENT OR TRANSACTION.   The event or transaction should be nonreversible, and the risks and rewards of ownership should be transferred before revenue is recognized. Both criteria should be applied on the basis of substance, not merely form. APB Statement No. 4 (par. 127) discusses substance over form as one of the basic features of financial accounting:

> **F-13. Substance over form.** Financial accounting emphasizes the economic substance of events even though the legal form may differ from the economic substance and suggest different treatment.

Characteristics of the Revenue Event or Transaction

1. The economic substance of the transaction that precedes the recognition of revenue should be such that:
   a. Reversal of the transaction is remote—that is, the revenue recognized has permanence.
   b. If ownership of property has changed hands, the risks and rewards of ownership should also be transferred.
2. Either an event that serves as the basis of recognizing revenue should not be within the control of the entity, or it should be verifiable by external evidence.

Characteristics of the Asset Received

The asset recorded in a revenue transactions should be:
1. Liquid.
2. Free from significant obligations and restrictions.
3. Collectible.
4. Reliably measurable.

Characteristics of the Revenue Recognized

The revenue should be "earned" to the extent that it has been recognized. If the earning process is not complete or substantially complete, either the critical event in the earning process should have occurred or measurable progress should have been made toward the completion of the earning process before revenue is recognized.

Exhibit 12.1.   Specific criteria for recognizing revenue.

Usually the economic substance of events to be accounted for agrees with the legal form. Sometimes, however, substance and form differ. Accountants emphasize the substances of events rather than their form so that the information provided better reflects the economic activities represented.

SAB No. 30, "Interpretation Regarding Divestitures in Connection with a Sale of a Subsidiary," states that "economic substance rather than legal form should determine the accounting and reporting of a transaction." Although the literature provides such guidance for determining the economic substance of particular transactions in specific industries, it provides little guidance for applying the substance over form notion in general. That may well be because, as noted in SFAC No. 2, "Qualitative Characteristics of Accounting Information" (par. 160), "[S]ubstance over form is, in any case, a rather vague idea that defies precise definition" (see Jaenicke, 1981, for further discussion).

(a) Nonreversibility.   If revenue is recognized on the basis of a particular event or transaction and subsequent events or transactions reverse the effect of the earlier one, the problem is not that revenue has been recognized in the wrong accounting period—it should never have been recognized at all because the definition of revenue or asset (or both) has not been met. Thus, in addition to affecting the timing of revenue recognition, the possibility of reversal of the revenue transaction also affects the determination of whether the revenue exists. Windal (1961, p. 252) states that "for an item to be sufficiently definite [to warrant recognition], it must appear unlikely to be reversed. We might say it must appear to have permanence."

In some cases, as in sales with right of return, the possibility of the transaction being permanent exists, and the likelihood of reversal may be predictable. In those cases, revenue should be recognized and appropriate allowances recorded for the estimated returns. In other cases, as in many product financing arrangements that contain repurchase agreements, the possibility of permanence is zero or extremely remote. If the economic substance of the "sale" rather than its formal designation is judged and the "sale" transaction is found to be fictitious, completion of the transaction and permanence of the revenue are absent and no revenue should be recognized. As another example, the receipt of a small down payment and small periodic payments, with a large final "balloon" payment, often suggests that an option to buy an asset has been sold, not the asset itself; the sale of the asset itself may never take place.

"Bill and hold" sales represent another type of transaction that, depending on the underlying circumstances, could be reversible. According to SEC Exchange Act Release No. 17878 (June 22, 1981), in a bill and hold transaction "a customer agrees to purchase the goods but the seller retains physical possession until the customer requests shipment to designated locations." In that release, the SEC sanctioned recognizing revenue from bill and hold sales when the buyer has made an absolute purchase commitment, but is unable to accept delivery because of a compelling business reason.

In SEC Accounting and Auditing Enforcement Release No. 108 (August 5, 1986), the SEC specified the conditions that a bill and hold transaction should meet in order to qualify for revenue recognition:

1. The risks of ownership must have passed to the buyer;
2. The customer must have made a fixed commitment to purchase the goods, preferably reflected in written documentation;
3. The buyer, not the seller, must request that the transaction be on a bill and hold basis. The buyer must have a substantial business purpose for ordering the goods on a bill and hold basis;
4. There must be a fixed schedule for delivery of the goods. The date for delivery must be reasonable and must be consistent with the buyer's business purpose (e.g., storage periods are customary in the industry);
5. The seller must not have retained any specific performance obligations such that the earning process is not complete;
6. The ordered goods must have been segregated from the seller's inventory and not be subject to being used to fill other orders; and
7. The equipment must be complete and ready for shipment.

The above listed conditions are the important conceptual criteria which should be used in evaluating any purported bill and hold sale. This listing is not intended as a check list. In some circumstances, a transaction may meet all the factors listed above but not meet the requirements for revenue recognition.

In applying the above criteria to a purported bill and hold sale, the individuals responsible for preparation and filing of the financial statements should also consider the following factors:

1. The date by which the seller expects payment, and whether it has modified its normal billing and credit terms for this buyer;
2. The seller's past experiences with and pattern of bill and hold transactions;
3. Whether the buyer has the expected risk of loss in the event of a decline in the market value of the goods;
4. Whether the seller's custodial risks are insurable and insured;
5. Whether APB Opinion No. 21, pertaining to the need for discounting the related receivable, is applicable; [a] and
6. Whether extended procedures are necessary in order to assure that there are no exceptions to the buyer's commitment to accept and pay for the goods sold, i.e., that the business reasons for the bill and hold have not introduced a contingency to the buyer's commitment.

---

[a]Once the individuals responsible for preparation and filing of the financial statements have ascertained that the revenue may be properly recognized, they of course, have an on-going obligation to review for collectibility of the bill and hold receivable.

(b) Transfer of the Risks and Rewards of Ownership.

The criterion that the risks and rewards of ownership should be transferred before revenue is recognized appears in several places in the accounting literature. For example, SFAS No. 13 (par. 60) states: "[T]he provisions of this Statement derive from the view that a lease that transfers substantially all of the benefits and risks incident to the ownership of property should be accounted for as the acquisition of an asset and the incurrence of an obligation by the lessee and as a sale or financing by the lessor." SAB No. 30 states that in resolving the issue discussed, "[T]he principal consideration must be an assessment of whether the risks and other incidents of ownership have been transferred to the buyer with sufficient certainty." In practice, however, applying the criterion does not always yield a definitive answer because in many transactions the risks and rewards are divided between the two parties (see Jaenicke, 1981, for further discussion).

Determining that the "risks and other incidents of ownership" have been transferred to the buyer requires an examination of the underlying facts and circumstances. The following circumstances may raise questions about the transfer of risks:

1. A continuing involvement by the seller in the transaction or in the assets transferred, such as through the exercise of managerial authority to a degree usually associated with ownership, perhaps in the form of a remarketing agreement or a commitment to operate the property.
2. Absence of significant financial investment by the buyer in the asset transferred, as evidenced, for example, by a token down payment or by a concurrent loan to the buyer.
3. Repayment of debt that constitutes the principal consideration in the transaction dependent on the generation of sufficient funds from the asset transferred.
4. Limitations or restrictions on the purchaser's use of the asset transferred or on the profits from it.
5. Retention of effective control of the asset by the seller.

The first three items on the list are suggested by SAB No. 30; the last two are found in ASR No. 95, "Accounting for Real Estate Transactions Where Circumstances Indicate That Profits Were Not Earned at the Time the Transactions Were Recorded."

Some of the circumstances above may also be useful in assessing whether other criteria noted in Exhibit 12.1 have been met. For example, a continuing involvement by the seller may affect the criteria that the asset received be free of significant obligations, that the earning process be substantially complete, and that the asset received be measurable.

(c) Recognition Based on Events.   Revenues are sometimes recognized on the basis of events rather than transactions. For example, production that precedes revenue recognized on the percentage-of-completion basis is more properly described as an event than as a transaction because it need not involve a transfer of something of value between two or more entities. An event occurring within the enterprise that precedes the recognition of revenue, such as production, should be verifiable by evidence external to the enterprise, such as an increase in market price or the existence of a firm contract. If revenue recognition is based on an event external to the enterprise, such as a price increase, the event should not be within the control of the enterprise.

12.14 CHARACTERISTICS OF THE ASSET RECEIVED.   Many accountants believe that revenue recognition is based on the presumption that, to some degree at least, the asset received is liquid, free from significant obligations or restrictions, collectible, and objectively measurable. Those tests would be relevant in addition to any characteristics of assets included in the FASB's definition of asset in SFAC No. 6.

(a) Asset Liquidity.   Asset liquidity has long been suggested as a prerequisite for recognizing revenue. Canning (1929, p. 102) observed that one of the usual conditions for recognizing revenue is that "the future receipt of money within one year has become highly probable." Paton and Littleton (1940, p. 49) stated: "[R]evenue is realized, according to the dominant view, when it is evidenced by cash receipts or receivables, or other new liquid assets." The liquidity criterion is also generally interpreted as having been met if the financial flow is in the form of a reduction of liabilities that would obviate the subsequent use of liquid assets.

Contrary to the views expressed above, however, the APB did not consider asset liquidity a significant condition for revenue recognition. APB Opinion No. 29, "Accounting for Nonmonetary Transactions" (par. 18), states:

> In general accounting for nonmonetary transactions should be based on the fair values of the assets (or services) involved which is the same basis as that used in monetary transactions. Thus, the cost of a nonmonetary asset acquired in exchange for another nonmonetary asset is the fair value of the asset surrendered to obtain it, and a gain or loss should be recognized on the exchange.

The same opinion states, however, that illiquidity of the nonmonetary asset may prevent its fair value from being determinable (i.e., measurable) and thus prevent the recognition of gain or loss.

> Accounting for a nonmonetary transaction should not be based on the fair values of the assets transferred unless those fair values are determinable within reasonable limits. (par. 20)

> Fair value should be regarded as not determinable within reasonable limits if major uncertainties exist about the realizability of the value that would be assigned to an asset received in a nonmonetary transaction accounted for at fair value. . . . If neither the fair value of a nonmonetary asset transferred nor the fair value of a nonmonetary asset received in exchange is determinable within reasonable limits, the recorded amount of nonmonetary asset transferred from the enterprise may be the only available measure of the transaction. (par. 26)

Horngren (1982, p. 330) contended that the receipt of liquid assets per se should not be a condition for recognizing revenue, but should serve as evidence that the measurability criterion has been met. (Horngren was also on the APB at the time of Opinion No. 29.) To some extent, however, the widespread criticism of the accounting profession during the 1970s was caused by recognition of income long before the receipt of the only asset possessing absolute liquidity—cash.

A strict liquidity test presents two problems, however. It implicitly establishes a hierarchy of asset worth based on relative liquidity, which does not have authoritative support. Also, to the extent that management can control the kind of asset received in revenue transactions and the conversion of one asset type to another, a strict liquidity test would give management "control" over the timing of income, that is, an ability to "manage earnings."

(b) Absence of Obligations and Restrictions.   The absence of obligations and restrictions as a criterion was expressed by Vatter (1947, p. 25) as follows: "Revenue differs from other asset-increasing transactions in that the new assets are completely free of equity restrictions other than the residual equity of the fund itself." The obligations and restrictions that Vatter had in mind—repayment obligations, obligations to share income, voting rights, dividend preferences—characterize debt and equity financing. Under this view, sales and excise taxes collected by an enterprise should be recognized as liabilities, not as revenue, because the amounts collected are earmarked for remittance to a governmental agency.

There are presently no known instances of improper revenue recognition resulting from the recording of assets with obligations and restrictions attached. It is conceivable, however, for the "buyer" to impose such conditions on the asset as to suggest that the risks and rewards of the asset's ownership are not transferred to the "seller." This condition, then, would be analogous to the condition (discussed above) that the seller's risks and rewards of ownership should transfer to the buyer if revenue is to be recognized.

(c) Asset Collectibility.   As noted above, the earliest authoritative statement of revenue recognition emphasized the collectibility criterion when the asset received is other than cash: "Profit is deemed to be realized when a sale in the ordinary course of business is effected, unless the circumstances are such that the collection of the sale price is not reasonably assured" (ARB No. 43, Ch. 1, par. 1). As discussed in the subsequent material on authoritative and quasi-authoritative pronouncements about typical revenue recognition issues and specialized industry problems, much of the literature in recent years has been concerned with defining and refining the collectibility criterion in specific circumstances, such as for retail land sales. Little discussion of collectibility in general exists in the pronouncements of authoritative bodies; however, the collectibility criterion is rarely questioned.

From the case-by-case approach to collectibility taken by rule-making bodies, the following conditions may suggest doubtful collectibility:

- Evidence of financial weakness of the purchaser.
- Uncertainty resulting from the form of consideration or method of settlement, for example, nonrecourse notes and purchaser's stock.
- Small or no down payment.
- Concurrent loans to purchasers, presumably to finance the down payment.

This list comes from ASR No. 95. Although the release is titled "Accounting for Real Estate Transactions Where Circumstances Indicate That Profits Were Not Earned at the Time the Transactions Were Recorded," the circumstances discussed have wider applicability and appear in slightly different versions in AICPA Accounting Guides issued in the 1970s and subsequently incorporated into FASB statements. If the conditions above are present, an event or transaction may also fail to meet other recognition criteria, particularly the "transfer of risks and rewards of ownership" test.

(d) Asset Measurability.   This criterion was suggested by Canning (1929), as well as by a committee of the AAA. Canning noted (p. 102) that the measurability criterion has two aspects—first, that "the amount to be received can be estimated with a high degree of reliability" and second, that "the expenses incurred or to be incurred in the (income) cycle can be estimated with a high degree of accuracy."

The AAA 1964 Concepts and Standards Research Committee on the Realization Concept noted in "The Realization Concept" (pp. 314–315):

> It is difficult to be precise about what is the current prevailing practice, but it appears that presently accepted tests for realization require receipt of a current (or liquid) asset capable of objective measurement in a market transaction for services rendered. . . . The committee would stress measurability, and not liquidity, as the essential attribute required for recognition of realized revenue.

The measurability criterion is related to the verifiability, and hence the objectivity, of evidence supporting the amount of revenue to be recognized. Thus the FASB (Discussion Memorandum, 1976, p. 158) has stated:

> Verifiability . . . generally means that independent measurers using the same methods obtain essentially the same result. Verifiability is in one sense a measure of the objectivity (freedom from bias) of financial statement measures because the more the measure reflects the characteristics of the object or event measured, the more likely that different measurers will agree.

For revenue to be recognized, the asset received should be measurable with a degree of verifiability such that approximately the same amount would be used by all accountants and it would thus be free from measurer bias—that is, it would be objective. As discussed previously, measurability is one of the four recognition criteria provided in paragraph 63 of SFAC No. 5 and is defined in terms of a financial statement item having "a relevant attribute measurable with sufficient reliability."

The measurability of the asset received, and thus of the revenue recognized, is enhanced if the asset received is liquid. Measurability is also related to the nonreversibility and collectibility criteria discussed earlier. Those criteria suggest that possible later reductions in recorded revenue should be small; the measurability criterion suggests that any such reductions be capable of reasonable estimation.

12.15 CHARACTERISTICS OF THE REVENUE RECOGNIZED. One of the most commonly suggested criteria for recognizing revenue is that it be "earned" before it is recognized. SFAC No. 5 (par. 83) states that "revenues are not recognized until earned." This criterion takes several forms.

The first form requires completion or **substantial completion** of the earning process. As noted earlier, APB Statement No. 4 (par. 150) states: "Revenue is generally recognized when both of the following conditions are met: (1) the earning process is complete or virtually complete, and (2) an exchange has taken place." Paragraph 153 notes that the earning requirement

> usually causes no problems because the earning process is usually complete or nearly complete by the time of the required exchange. The requirement that revenue be earned becomes important, however, if money is received or amounts are billed in advance of the delivery of goods or rendering of services.

APB Statement No. 4 then suggests that the substantial completion test is not always followed and that revenue is sometimes recognized, as on long-term construction contracts, on the basis of **recognizable progress** toward completion of the earning process, a second form of the criterion. A third variation of the earning criterion, first suggested by Meyers in 1959 (p. 528), suggests that recognition be related to the **critical event** in the earning process.

Waiting until the earning process is substantially complete may, depending on the nature of the transaction, delay the recognition of revenue more than either the "recognizable progress" or the "critical event" form of the earning criterion, thus minimizing the risk of error from incorrectly identifying the critical event or the extent of progress. Moreover, at the point of "substantial completion," the costs associated with the revenue transaction are known with more certainty than under the other two approaches because those costs have already been incurred.

The critical event form of the earning requirement permits greater flexibility in the timing of revenue, depending on the nature of the event or transaction. The recognizable performance version is based on the economic reality that revenue is, in fact, not earned at a single point in time. Since these two forms of the earning criterion may result in revenue recognition earlier than would the substantial completion form, their use could provide information that is more relevant to the needs of users than that attainable from the substantial completion form, but at a possible sacrifice of reliability.

Determining either the point of substantial completion or the critical event may be difficult if there are continuing obligations by the seller after the initial transfer of the asset. Thus the criterion that the principal risks and rewards of ownership be transferred is related to the criterion that the revenue be earned. For example, special warranties by the seller, remarketing agreements, or the seller's commitment to operate the property not only may raise the question of whether the critical event or substantial completion has taken place, but may also call into question the transfer of the risks and rewards of ownership.

TYPES OF REVENUE TRANSACTIONS

12.16 SPECIAL REVENUE RECOGNITION PROBLEMS.   Special revenue recognition problems are posed by events and transactions in which the source of revenue is something other than the sale of a product or the rendering of service in a transaction that is completed over a relatively short period. In several cases, authoritative or quasi-authoritative pronouncements have addressed the issue of the proper timing of revenue recognition. In other cases, such pronouncements do not exist, and the proper recognition policies can be determined only by reference to the specific criteria suggested earlier in this chapter. Specialized industry practices are discussed in section 12.17.

(a) Revenue Recognition Problems Discussed in Other Chapters.   To avoid duplication, the special revenue recognition problems that are discussed elsewhere in this *Handbook* are listed below, with the relevant chapter number.

Income from Equity Investments. Revenue recognition under the cost and equity methods, as well as income from investments in both incorporated and unincorporated joint ventures, is the subject of several APB opinions and AICPA accounting interpretations. These are discussed in Chapter 7.

Installment Sales. Revenue from installment sales contracts extending over more than one accounting period may be recognized at the time of sale, on the installment basis, or on the cost recovery basis, depending on circumstances. This issue is further discussed in Chapter 21.

Nonmonetary Exchanges of Fixed Assets. APB Opinion No. 29 specifies the conditions under which gain and loss should be recognized on the exchange of nonmonetary assets; the required accounting varies according to whether a gain or a loss should be recognized, whether the assets exchanged are similar or dissimilar, and whether "boot" is received. Those cases are discussed in Chapter 14.

Sale and Leaseback Transactions. Recognition or deferral of gain by the seller-lessee in a sale and leaseback transaction is specified in SFAS No. 13, "Accounting for Leases," as modified by SFAS No. 98, "Accounting for Leases: Sale-Leaseback Transactions Involving Real Estate." This issue is further discussed in Chapter 16.

Sales-type Leases. Accounting for leases by a lessor is prescribed by SFAS No. 13. Leases that are classified in SFAS No. 13 as sales-type leases result in recognition of revenue by the lessor at the inception of the lease; Chapter 16 discusses sales-type leases.

(b) Sales of Receivables with Recourse.   SFAS No. 77, "Reporting by Transferors for Transfers of Receivables with Recourse" (par. 5), requires that a transfer of receivables with recourse be recognized as a sale if all of the following conditions are met:

a. The transferor surrenders control of the future economic benefits embodied in the receivables.
b. The transferor's obligation under the recourse provisions can be reasonably estimated.
c. The transferee cannot require the transferor to repurchase the receivables except pursuant to the recourse provisions.

If the above conditions are not met, the proceeds from the transfer should be reported as a liability.

(c) Grants Received from Governments.   In 1979 an AICPA committee concluded that, except as specified below, grants received from governments should be recorded as income (Accounting Standards Division, "Accounting for Grants Received from Governments").

Grants related to revenue should be recognized as revenue in the period in which the revenue is earned; grants related to expenses should be treated as reductions of those expenses. Grants that should not be taken into income currently, but should be deferred and reflected in income of future periods, include grants related to expenses of future periods, grants related to depreciable fixed assets, and grants received before the recipient fulfills the conditions of the grant. A grant that will probably be refunded or repaid should be reported as a liability.

(d) Product Financing Arrangements. SFAS No. 49, "Accounting for Product Financing Arrangements," establishes accounting and reporting standards for product financing arrangements. A product financing arrangement is a transaction in which an enterprise sells and agrees to repurchase inventory with the repurchase price equal to the original sale price plus carrying and financing costs, or other similar terms. SFAS No. 49 requires that a product financing arrangement be accounted for as a borrowing rather than as a sale.

Under SFAS No. 49 (par. 3), product financing arrangements include agreements in which a company seeking to finance a product (referred to as a sponsor):

a. Sells the product to another entity, and in a related transaction agrees to repurchase the product (or a substantially identical product);
b. Arranges for another entity to purchase the product on the sponsor's behalf and, in a related transaction, agrees to purchase the product from the other entity; or
c. Controls the disposition of the product that has been purchased by another entity in accordance with the arrangements described in either (a) or (b) above.

Other characteristics that commonly exist in product financing arrangements but that are not necessarily present in all such arrangements are specified in paragraph 4:

a. The entity that purchases the product from the sponsor or purchases it directly from a third party on behalf of the sponsor was established expressly for that purpose or is an existing trust, nonbusiness organization, or credit grantor.
b. The product covered by the financing arrangement is to be used or sold by the sponsor, although a portion may be sold by the other entity directly to third parties.
c. The product covered by the financing arrangement is stored on the sponsor's premises.
d. The debt of the entity that purchases the product being financed is guaranteed by the sponsor.

According to paragraph 8 of SFAS No. 49, product financing arrangements that require the sponsor to repurchase the product or a substantially identical product at specified prices, adjusted to cover all costs incurred by the other entity in purchasing and holding the product, should be accounted for by the sponsor as follows:

If a sponsor sells a product to another entity and, in a related transaction, agrees to repurchase the product (or a substantially identical product) or processed goods of which the product is a component, the sponsor shall record a liability at the time the proceeds are received from the other entity to the extent that the product is covered by the financing arrangement. The sponsor shall not record the transaction as a sale and shall not remove the covered product from its balance sheet.

If the sponsor is party to an arrangement whereby another entity purchases a product on the sponsor's behalf and, in a related transaction, the sponsor agrees to purchase the product or processed goods of which the product is a component from the entity, the sponsor shall record the asset and the related liability when the product is purchased by the other entity.

(e) Revenue Recognition When Right of Return Exists. SFAS No. 48, "Revenue Recognition When Right of Return Exists," establishes accounting and reporting standards for sales of an enterprise's product in which the buyer has a right to return the product. Revenue from those sales transactions should be recognized at time of sale only if all of the following conditions are met (par. 6):

a. The seller's price to the buyer is substantially fixed or determinable at the date of sale.

b. The buyer has paid the seller, or the buyer is obligated to pay the seller and the obligation is not contingent on resale of the product.

c. The buyer's obligation to the seller would not be changed in the event of theft or physical destruction or damage of the product.

d. The buyer acquiring the product for resale has economic substance apart from that provided by the seller.

e. The seller does not have significant obligations for future performance to directly bring about resale of the product by the buyer.

f. The amount of future returns can be reasonably estimated.

SFAS No. 48 (pars. 6–7) states that if sales are recognized because the above conditions are met, provision should be made immediately for any costs or losses that may be expected in connection with any returns. Amounts of sales revenue and cost of sales reported in the income statement should exclude the portion for which returns are expected. Transactions for which sales recognition is postponed should be recognized as sales when the return privilege has substantially expired.

The ability to reasonably predict the amount of future returns depends on many factors. Although circumstances vary from one case to the next, the existence of the following factors would appear to impair the ability to make a reasonable prediction (SFAS No. 48, par. 8):

a. The susceptibility of the product to significant external factors, such as technological obsolescence or changes in demand.

b. Relatively long periods in which a particular product may be returned.

c. Absence of historical experience with similar types of sales of similar products, or inability to apply such experience because of changing circumstances, for example, changes in the selling enterprise's marketing policies or relationships with its customers.

d. Absence of a large volume of relatively homogeneous transactions.

(f) Service Transactions.   The FASB added the project "Accounting for Certain Service Transactions" to its agenda in 1978, and published an "Invitation to Comment" based on a draft Statement of Position of the AICPA's Accounting Standards Division on that topic. Among the types of business mentioned that offer services rather than products are correspondence schools, health spas, retirement homes, cemetery associations, perpetual care societies, engineering firms, service and maintenance contractors, electronic security companies, advertising agencies, and computer service organizations. (The list is not intended to be all-inclusive.)

The FASB "Invitation to Comment" summarizes, on pages 2–4, the conclusions of the AICPA Accounting Standards Division and is reproduced below. The FASB has not issued a statement on accounting for service transactions generally, although parts of the "Invitation to Comment" were incorporated into SFAC No. 5.

> The AICPA draft Statement of Position sets forth conclusions on (1) the guidelines to apply to transactions in which both services and products are provided, (2) the appropriate manner of revenue recognition, (3) the classification of costs as initial direct costs, direct costs, and indirect costs and the accounting for each, and (4) the accounting for initiation and installation fees. . . .
>
> A service transaction may involve a tangible product that is sold or consumed as an incidental part of the transaction or is clearly identifiable as secondary or subordinate to the rendering of the service. The following guidelines apply to transactions in which both services and products are provided:

1. If the seller offers both a service and a product in a single transaction and if any product involved is not separately stated in such a manner that the total transaction price would vary as a result of the inclusion or exclusion of the product, the product is incidental to the rendering of the service and the transaction is a service transaction.

2. If the seller offers both a product and a service in a single transaction and any service involved is incidental and is provided or available to all purchasers, the transaction is a product transaction.

3. If the seller of a product offers a related service to purchasers of the product but separately states the service and product elements in such a manner that the total transaction price would vary as a result of the inclusion or exclusion of the service, the transaction consists of two components; a product transaction and a service transaction, and each should be accounted for separately.

Revenue from service transactions should be recognized based on performance, because performance determines the extent to which the earnings process is complete or virtually complete. Performance is the execution of a defined act or acts or occurs with the passage of time. Accordingly, revenue from service transactions should be recognized under one of the following methods:

1. *Specific performance method*—Performance consists of the execution of a single act and revenue should be recognized when that act takes place.

2. *Proportional performance method*—Performance consists of the execution of more than one act and revenue should be recognized based on the proportionate performance of each act. For example, if the service transaction involves a specified number of similar acts, an equal amount of revenue should be recognized for each act. If the transaction involves a specified number of defined but not similar acts, revenue recognized for each act should be based on the ratio of the seller's direct costs to perform each act to the total estimated direct costs of the transaction. If the transaction involves an unspecified number of similar acts with a fixed period for performance, revenue should be recognized on the straight-line method over the performance period.

3. *Completed performance method*—If services are performed in more than a single act, the proportion of services to be performed in the final act may be so significant in relation to the service transaction taken as a whole that performance cannot be deemed to have taken place until execution of that act. Revenue should be recognized when that act takes place.

4. *Collection method*—If there is a significant degree of uncertainty surrounding realization of service revenue (for example, many personal services), revenue should not be recognized until collection.

The following classifications related to costs have been developed by the Division for purposes of the draft Statement of Position:

1. *Initial direct costs* are costs incurred that are directly associated with negotiating and consummating service agreements.

2. *Direct costs* are costs that have a clearly identifiable beneficial or causal relation (i) to the services performed or (ii) to the level of services performed for a group of customers.

3. *Indirect costs* are all costs other than initial direct costs and direct costs.

The principles set forth in the professional literature for recognizing costs state, in general, that costs should be charged to expense in the period in which the revenue with which they are associated is recognized as earned. Costs are not deferred, however, unless they are expected to be recoverable from future revenues.

1. *Cost recognition under the specific performance and completed performance methods*—If revenues are recognized under the specific performance or completed performance methods, all initial direct costs and direct costs should be charged to expense at the time revenues are recognized. Indirect costs should be charged to expense as incurred.

2. *Cost recognition under the proportional performance method*—Generally there is a close correlation between the amount of direct costs incurred and the extent of performance achieved. Since revenues are recognized in a manner related to performance achieved, direct costs should be charged to expense as incurred. Initial direct costs should be deferred and allocated over the term of service performance in proportion to the recognition of service revenue. Indirect costs should be charged to expense as incurred.

3. *Cost recognition under the collection method*—If the degree of uncertainty surrounding realization of service revenue is so significant that revenues are recognized only when collected, all costs (initial direct, direct, and indirect) should be charged to expense as incurred.

A service transaction may involve the charge of a nonrefundable initiation fee with subsequent periodic payments for future services or a nonrefundable fee for installation of equipment essential to providing the future services with subsequent periodic payments for the services. Initiation and installation fees also may in substance be wholly or partly an advance charge for future services.

The accounting for initiation and installation fees are discussed below:

1. *Initiation fees*—If there is an objectively determinable value of the franchise or privilege granted by the initiation fee itself, that value should be considered revenue, and the related direct costs should be charged to expense at the initiation date. If the value of the initiation fee cannot be determined objectively, the fee should be considered an integral part of the service transaction including the future services and should be recognized using the appropriate method of revenue recognition.

2. *Installation fees*—If the equipment and its installation costs are essential for the service to be provided and are not normally offered for separate sale, the installation fee should be considered an advance charge for future services and recognized as revenue over the estimated period future services are to be provided. Costs of installation and installed equipment should be deferred and amortized over the period the installation is expected to provide revenue. If the customer is able to purchase the installation separately, the installation fee is not a service transaction.

(g) Troubled Debt Restructurings.   SFAS No. 15, "Accounting by Debtors and Creditors for Troubled Debt Restructurings," establishes standards of financial accounting and reporting by the debtor and by the creditor in a troubled debt restructuring. A troubled debt restructuring may include one or more of the following (par. 5):

a. Transfer from the debtor to the creditor of receivables from third parties, real estate, or other assets to satisfy fully or partially a debt (including a transfer resulting from foreclosure or repossession).

b. Issuance or other granting of an equity interest to the creditor by the debtor to satisfy fully or partially a debt unless the equity interest is granted pursuant to existing terms for converting the debt into an equity interest.

c. Modification of terms of a debt, such as one or a combination of:
    1. Reduction (absolute or contingent) of the stated interest rate for the remaining original life of the debt.
    2. Extension of the maturity date or dates at a stated interest rate lower than the current market rate for new debt with similar risk.
    3. Reduction (absolute or contingent) of the face amount or maturity amount of the debt as stated in the instrument or other agreement.
    4. Reduction (absolute or contingent) of accrued interest.

A debtor should account for a troubled debt restructuring according to the type of restructuring, as follows:

- A debtor that transfers assets to a creditor in full settlement of a payable should recognize a gain on restructuring of payables, measured by the excess of the carrying amount of the payable over the fair value of the assets transferred. If material, the gain, net of related taxes, is classified as an extraordinary item. A difference between the fair value and the carrying amount of the assets transferred is a gain or loss on assets transferred; whether it is an extraordinary item is determined by whether it meets the criteria in APB Opinion No. 30, "Reporting the Results of Operations."
- A debtor that settles fully a payable by issuing an equity interest should recognize a gain (extraordinary item, if material) on restructuring of payables equal to the difference between the fair value of the equity interest and the carrying amount of the payable.
- If the troubled debt restructuring involves only modification of the terms of a payable, not a transfer of assets or grant of an equity interest, the carrying amount of the payable should not be changed (and thus no gain should be recognized) unless it exceeds the total cash payments specified by the new terms. In the latter event, the carrying amount of the payable should be reduced to the total cash payments specified by the new terms, and a gain (extraordinary, if material) should be recognized equal to the reduction.
- SFAS No. 15 also specifies the debtor's accounting when the new restructuring involves a combination of two or more of the above mentioned types.

A creditor should account for a troubled debt restructuring according to the type of restructuring, as follows:

- A creditor that receives assets (including an equity interest in the debtor) in full satisfaction of a receivable should account for those assets at their fair value. A loss would be recognized that, to the extent not offset against allowances for uncollectibles or other valuation accounts, would be an extraordinary item only if it met the conditions of APB Opinion No. 30.
- If the troubled debt restructuring involves only modification of the terms of a receivable, the creditor's accounting parallels that of the debtor.
- SFAS No. 15 also specifies the creditor's accounting when there is a combination of types.

This subject is discussed further in Chapter 33, "Bankruptcy." The taxability of gains or losses from foreclosures and from forgiveness of debt is also addressed by the IRC.

12.17 SPECIALIZED INDUSTRY PROBLEMS.   Many problems of when to recognize revenue are specific to entire industries. For example, all franchisors face the problem of when to recognize as revenue the initial fees from the sale of franchises. As with nonindustry-specific revenue recognition problems, the source of the difficulty is the relatively long period, often several accounting periods, over which the earning of revenue (in its broadest sense, extending through total performance and collection) takes place. In many instances, authoritative or quasi-authoritative pronouncements have specified the appropriate timing of revenue in various circumstances. In others, the accountant must still rely solely on judgment; in those cases the specific criteria suggested earlier may be helpful.

(a) Specialized Industries Discussed in Other Chapters. To avoid duplication of material, the industries that are discussed elsewhere in this *Handbook* are listed below with the relevant chapter number:

Construction industry. Revenue may be recognized when long-term construction contracts are completed (completed contract method) or as construction progresses (percentage-of-completion method), depending on the circumstances surrounding each contract. Those methods and their applicability in varying circumstances are discussed in Chapter 21.

Nonprofit enterprises. The recognition of revenue from pledges and donated services continues to be controversial, despite AICPA pronouncements on those issues. Chapter 25 reviews current practice.

Real estate industry. Revenue recognition from the sale of real estate and from retail land sales depends largely on the buyer's assuming the normal risks and rewards of ownership, often evidenced by the size of the down payment, and on the seller's performance under the terms of the sales agreement. Those conditions and other related criteria for recognizing revenue are discussed in SFAS No. 66 and Chapter 21 of this book.

(b) Cable Television Companies. SFAS No. 51, "Financial Reporting by Cable Television Companies," discusses revenue recognition and other accounting problems of cable television companies. SFAS No. 51 suggests that costs incurred during construction before the first subscriber hookup and a portion of certain costs after the first subscriber hookup, but before construction of the entire system is complete, usually may be capitalized. During that period, all revenues except those from hookups should be reported as system revenues, and the portion of costs, depreciation, and amortization charged to expense, as well as specified period costs, should be included in appropriate categories of costs of services. According to SFAS No. 51 (par. 11), "[I]nitial hookup revenue shall be recognized as revenue to the extent of direct selling costs incurred. The remainder shall be deferred and amortized to income over the estimated average period that subscribers are expected to remain connected to the system."

(c) Franchising Companies. The major franchise accounting problem concerns the recognition of revenue from the initial franchise fee. SFAS No. 45, "Accounting for Franchise Fee Revenue," establishes accounting and reporting standards for franchisors. It requires that franchise fee revenue from individual and area franchise sales be recognized only when all material services or conditions relating to the sale have been substantially performed or satisfied by the franchisor. SFAS No. 45 also discusses accounting for continuing franchise fees, continuing product sales, agency sales, repossessed franchises, franchising costs, commingled revenue, and relationships between a franchisor and a franchisee.

(d) Record and Music Industry. SFAS No. 50, "Financial Reporting in the Record and Music Industry," requires the licensor of a record master or music copyright to recognize the licensing fee as revenue if the licensor:

1. Has signed a noncancelable contract.
2. Has agreed to a fixed fee.
3. Has delivered the rights to the licensee, who is free to exercise them.
4. Has no remaining significant obligations to furnish music or records.
5. Collectibility of the full licensing fee is reasonably assured.

(e) Mortgage Banking Industry.   SFAS No. 65, "Accounting for Certain Mortgage Banking Activities," discusses alternative methods of recognizing revenue from loan fees. SFAS No. 65 concludes that loan origination fees, to the extent they represent reimbursement of loan origination costs, should be recognized as revenue when the loan is made. Loan commitment fees should be recognized as revenue when the loans are sold to permanent investors. Fees for services performed by third parties and loan placement fees should be recognized as revenue when all significant services have been performed. Land acquisition, development, and construction loan fees and standby and gap commitment fees should be recognized as revenue over the combined commitment and loan periods.

(f) Motion Picture Films; Broadcasting Industry.   SFAS No. 53, "Financial Reporting by Producers and Distributors of Motion Picture Films," discusses revenue recognition for exhibition rights transferred under license agreements for television program material. According to paragraph 6, a licensor should recognize revenue from a license agreement for television program material when the license period begins and all of the following conditions have been met:

a. The license fee for each film is known.
b. The cost of each film is known or reasonably determinable.
c. Collectibility of the full license fee is reasonably assured.
d. The film has been accepted by the licensee in accordance with the conditions of the license agreement.
e. The film is available for its first showing or telecast. Unless a conflicting license prevents usage by the licensee, restrictions under the same license agreement or another license agreement with the same licensee on the timing of subsequent showings shall not affect this condition.

Once the above conditions have been met, revenue should be recognized unless significant factors raise doubt about the obligation or ability of either party to perform under the agreement.

SFAS No. 63, "Financial Reporting by Broadcasters," concludes that broadcasters' accounting for television film license agreements should parallel accounting by the licensor and, accordingly, assets and liabilities should be recorded for the rights acquired and the obligations incurred under the agreement.

SFAS No. 63 also establishes standards of reporting by broadcasters for transactions in which unsold advertising time is bartered for products or services. According to paragraph 5:

> Those costs shall be allocated to individual programs within a package on the basis of the relative value of each to the broadcaster, which ordinarily would be specified in the contract. The capitalized costs shall be amortized based on the estimated number of future showings, except that licenses providing for unlimited showings of cartoons and programs with similar characteristics may be amortized over the period of the agreement because the estimated number of future showings may not be determinable.

REVENUE ADJUSTMENTS AND AFTERCOSTS

12.18 NATURE OF REVENUE ADJUSTMENTS AND AFTERCOSTS.   Revenue adjustments include **sales returns and allowances, discounts,** and **bad debts; warranties and guarantees** may be treated either as future revenue or as "aftercosts," depending on the circumstances; obligations related to product defects should be treated as expenses.

Practice does not always clearly distinguish between events and transactions that give rise to expenses and those that are more properly treated as adjustments or valuations of revenue.

Alternative definitions of revenue were presented at the beginning of this chapter; expenses are outflows or expirations of assets sold or liabilities incurred in the process of earning revenue (as "earning" was previously defined). Hendriksen (1977, p. 193) notes that:

> Sales returns and allowances are normally treated as revenue offsets, and rightly so. On the other hand, sales discounts and bad debt losses have been treated conventionally as expenses. In the opinion of the author, however, it is more logical to classify them as offsets to revenue than as expenses. Sales discounts do not represent the use of goods or services. A small part of such discounts may represent the monetary discount or interest equal to the cost of waiting in the absence of uncertainty. But if the discount is taken, the net price represents the price of the goods: the discount is a reduction of the revenue and not a cost of borrowing funds. Likewise, bad debt losses do not represent expirations of goods or services but rather reductions of the amount to be received in exchange for the product.

12.19 SALES RETURNS.   Merchandise returned by a customer is, in effect, a cancellation of the original sales transaction, in whole or in part, and should be treated as a direct offset to gross sales rather than as a revenue adjustment. However, to maintain a record of sales returns as well as of the amount of gross sales, returns are ordinarily recorded in a contra sales account, "sales returns." A special problem arises if the returned merchandise has been used or has deteriorated to a point substantially below its original value. In those cases, the returned goods should be recorded at their net realizable value in the light of their present condition and estimated costs of making them available for resale. This accounting also recognizes losses attributable to returned goods.

12.20 SALES ALLOWANCES.   Allowances to customers fall into two general classes, as follows:

1. Specific allowances on certain products, such as those for shortages in shipments, breakage, spoilage, inferior quality, failure to meet specifications, or errors in billing or handling of freight.
2. Policy allowances, or allowances that the company makes only because of the possible loss of volume it would suffer in related lines if it refused.

Allowances falling in the first class should clearly be treated as a direct offset to gross sales. Allowances in the second class are generally classified as revenue deductions.

12.21 DISCOUNTS.   In general, discounts may be defined as deductions from gross invoice prices, order quotations, or published price lists.

(a) Cash Discounts.   Credit terms usually allow customers a cash discount for payment of invoices within a certain period. In the past, cash discounts were sometimes viewed as interest allowances to customers for prompt payment. Sales discounts taken were thus treated as financial expenses; discounts not taken were implicitly included in gross revenue. This interpretation and handling can still be found in the accounting literature. The preferred method, however, is to regard cash discounts as sales adjustments, either by deducting discounts taken from sales on the income statement or by initially recording the sales at net prices and treating forfeited discounts as additional revenue. As a practical matter, the amounts involved are usually not material to the financial statements.

(b) Trade Discounts.   Cooper and Ijiri (1983, p. 510) define a trade discount as follows:

> The discount allowed to a class of customers on a list price before consideration of credit terms; as a rule, invoice prices are recorded in the books of account net after the deduction of trade and quantity discounts.

In effect, trade discounts are deductions from list prices, allowed to customers for quantities purchased or for the purpose of establishing price levels for classes of customers, such as wholesalers or retailers. The trade discount is also employed to enable vendors to change the effective prices of articles included in catalogs or similar sales publications by the relatively simple process of issuing a revised discount sheet.

(c) Employee Discounts.   Employees are often allowed special discounts on purchases made through the company. The discount may be limited to the company's ordinary product or merchandise, or it may extend to clothing, food, and other commodities carried in a general company store for the benefit of employees and sold to them at cost. If the sales are not recorded net of discounts initially, the total discounts should generally be treated as a sales deduction. If a discount is in substance additional compensation, it should be treated as an operating expense.

12.22 UNCOLLECTIBLE RECEIVABLES.   Uncollectible receivables are amounts that will probably not be collected in the future. Providing an allowance for uncollectible receivables is required under SFAS No. 5 when a loss is probable and can be reasonably estimated. Under the **allowance method,** an allowance account is used to indicate the estimated uncollectible amount of receivables. The allowance account is reflected as a contra to the controlling receivables account, and the individual subsidiary accounts are left intact. When it is decided that a specific amount is uncollectible, it is charged against the allowance account. Bad debt expense is charged when the allowance account is increased. Although not acceptable for financial statements prepared in conformity with GAAP, a method acceptable for income tax purposes is the **direct write-off method.** Under this method, no allowance is required; instead, uncollectible accounts are written off during the period in which they are determined to be uncollectible. The loss is charged directly to bad debt expense.

Bad debts are classified on the income statement as (1) a financial expense or loss, (2) an operating expense (either selling or administrative), or (3) a sales adjustment. The first view assumes that all customers' claims are initially valid in the amount of their face value and that subsequent lack of collection is a loss that must be borne by the business as a whole. Under the second interpretation, the department that has the responsibility for controlling bad debts is considered to include such losses with its other costs and expenses. The third alternative recognizes at the outset that a certain percentage of customers' claims will become uncollectible, that total credit sales are therefore tentative and subject to subsequent adjustment, and that, consequently, no asset has expired or liability been incurred.

When an allowance account is used, there are three methods for estimating the credit to the account: (1) percentage-of-sales method, (2) percentage-of-receivables method, and (3) aging method.

(a) Percentage-of-Sales Method.   The percentage-of-sales method can be used with both accounts and notes receivable, either together or separately. As a practical matter, however, this method can be used advantageously with notes *only* when the notes are numerous and arise as a regular credit term granted at the time of the sale. Although the uncollectible expense percentage should be based on and applied to charge sales, substantially the same result is attained by using a smaller percentage applied to total sales (assuming the relationship of cash sales to charge sales remains fairly constant). The allowance account may become excessive or inadequate unless there are periodic reviews of probable losses and consequent adjustments of the allowance account as necessary.

(b) Percentage-of-Receivables Method.   The percentage-of-receivables method requires a determination of collection experience. The total of expected uncollectibles is thus ascertained by applying the loss percentage to total receivables. The allowance account is then credited by the amount necessary to increase the existing balance to the required amount.

The percentage-of-receivables method can also be used with both accounts and notes receivable. When the notes held are relatively few in number and originate in the process of collection of accounts receivable or through loans and advances, the percentage-of-receivables method is an appropriate means of valuing notes receivable.

This method results in a fairly accurate approximation of expected net realizable value of receivables. In terms of bad debt expense on the income statement, however, the method may be deficient in that bad debts are related to all open receivables irrespective of the origin of the claims, with the result that uncollectible receivable losses may not be charged to the period in which the sale is made.

(c) Aging-of-Receivables Method.   The aging-of-receivables method is a variation of the percentage-of-receivables method. The basis for using this method is that the older the receivable, the less likely it is to be collected. The first step in aging receivables is classifying them as to time since (1) billing, (2) end of regular credit period granted, (3) payment due date, or (4) date of last payment. The amount of expected uncollectibles as determined by the aging process becomes the balance to be reflected in the allowance account. Accordingly, bad debt expense is debited and the allowance account is credited for an amount necessary to bring the present balance of the allowance account into agreement with the required balance.

If properly applied, the aging method, including use of appropriate supplemental information, provides the most accurate approximation of the expected net realizable value of receivables. However, like the percentage-of-receivables method described above, the aging method may fail to allocate losses to the period in which they arise. In the aging process, bad debt losses are related to impairment-of-asset values irrespective of the time of the sales activity. Claims resulting from the most recent sales, for example, may be regarded as fully collectible in the aging process, only to prove uncollectible in the subsequent period. The aging method is costly and time-consuming when many accounts are involved.

(d) Allowance for Collection Expense.   As stated by Edwards, Hermanson, and Salmonson (1967, p. 105), ''The expenses incurred to collect accounts receivable, such as the expenses of a credit department, a collection department, and legal fees connected with the collection, rightfully are expenses of the period in which the sales were made which gave rise to the receivables being collected.'' The estimated costs applicable to the handling and collection of receivables outstanding at the close of the period should therefore be accrued and charged against revenue if income is to be properly measured. A liability account or a contra account to accounts receivable should be credited. In practice, this adjustment is usually not made; most entities follow a modified cash system in handling such costs and charge them against revenue in the period in which they are incurred, on the theory that their amount is usually insignificant.

12.23 WARRANTIES AND GUARANTEES.   SFAS No. 5 (pars. 24 and 25) states:

A warranty is an obligation incurred in connection with the sale of goods or services that may require further performance by the seller after the sale has taken place. Because of the uncertainty surrounding claims that may be made under warranties, warranty obligations fall within the definition of a contingency. . . . Losses from warranty obligations shall be accrued when the conditions in paragraph 8 are met. [See below.] Those conditions may be considered in relation to individual sales made with warranties or in relation to groups of similar types of sales made with warranties. If the conditions are met, accrual shall be made even though the particular parties that will make claims under warranties may not be identifiable.

If, based on available information, it is possible that customers will make claims under warranties relating to goods or services that have been sold, the condition in paragraph 8(a) [see below] is met at the date of an enterprise's financial statements because it is probable that a liability has been incurred. Satisfaction of the condition in paragraph 8(b) [see below] will normally depend on the experience of an enterprise or other information. In the case of an enterprise that has no experience of its own, reference to the experience of other enterprises in the same business may be appropriate. Inability to make a reasonable estimate of the amount of a warranty obligation at the time of sale because of significant uncertainty about possible claims (i.e., failure to satisfy the condition in paragraph 8(b)) precludes accrual and, if the range of possible loss is wide, may raise a question about whether a sale should be recorded prior to expiration of the warranty period or until sufficient experience has been gained to permit a reasonable estimate of the obligation.

Paragraph 8 states:

An estimated loss from a loss contingency . . . shall be accrued by a charge to income if both of the following conditions are met:

a. Information available prior to issuance of the financial statements indicates that it is probable that an asset had been impaired or a liability had been incurred at the date of the financial statements.

b. The amount of the loss can be reasonably estimated.

Kieso and Weygandt (1989, pp. 605–606) note that the accrual of losses from warranty obligations can be accomplished using two different accounting treatments—the expensed warranty treatment and the sales warranty treatment.

The expensed warranty treatment charges the estimated future warranty costs to operating expense in the year of sale or manufacture. It is the generally accepted method and should be used whenever the warranty is an integral and inseparable part of the sale and is viewed as a loss contingency. The sales warranty treatment defers a certain percentage of the original sales price until some future time when actual costs are incurred or the warranty expires.

The sales warranty treatment is applicable to companies that sell warranty contracts separately from the product. . . . A liability in the form of unearned revenue would be recorded at the time of the sale, and the warranty revenues, costs, and any income would be recognized in the periods in which the services, repairs, and replacements under the warranty were performed.

Business managers commonly view warranty costs simply as additional expenses of selling or manufacturing the product rather than as additional sales. It is normally assumed that the selling price of a product covers costs of warranty, not that the warranty is something to be sold separately. Many accountants believe that the deferred warranty revenues must be recognized in the period the sale is made rather than when the cost of repair or replacement is incurred. Neither the expensed warranty nor the sales warranty treatment is allowable for income tax purposes.

12.24 OBLIGATIONS RELATED TO PRODUCT DEFECTS.   SFAS No. 5 (par. 26) states:

Obligations other than warranties may arise with respect to products or services that have been sold, for example, claims resulting from injury or damage caused by product defects. If it is probable that claims will arise with respect to products or services that have been sold, accrual for losses may be appropriate. The condition in paragraph 8(a) would be met, for instance, with respect to a drug product or toys that have been sold if a health or safety hazard related to those products is discovered and as a result it is considered probable that liabilities have been incurred. The condition in paragraph 8(b) would be met if experience or other information enables the enterprise to make a reasonable estimate of the loss with respect to the drug product or the toys.

ANCILLARY REVENUE

12.25 DIVIDENDS.   Generally, cash dividends and dividends paid in property from retained earnings of the payer corporation are classified as "other income" unless the dividends are a major source of income to the recipient; then they are classified as operating revenue.

Dividends received in property of the payer corporation are recorded as revenue in amounts equivalent to the fair market value of the property (APB Opinion No. 29, par. 18). The date a stockholder becomes entitled to receive a dividend is the accepted time for recognizing it as revenue. In practice, organizations often record the revenue when the dividend is actually received.

As indicated by the AICPA (ARB No. 43), stock dividends consisting of shares received on holdings of the same class of stock do not represent income to the recipient, since there is no "distribution, division, or severance of corporate assets."

Liquidating dividends do not normally result in income until their cumulative total exceeds the recipient's cost of the investment to which they apply.

12.26 INTEREST.   Interest generally is classified as "other income," unless, as in financial institutions, it is a major source of income; then it is classified as operating revenue. Interest on obligations of debtors generally should be recorded as it accrues. If collectibility of interest is doubtful, the recognition of interest income should be postponed until the interest is received or its collection becomes reasonably certain.

Interest on long-term investments purchased at a premium is subject to reduction by the amount of the amortization of the premium from the date of purchase to the earliest call date or maturity. The amount of discount on investments purchased at less than face value should be similarly amortized and included in income. If collection of the principal amount of the obligation is uncertain, the discount should not be amortized.

12.27 PROFITS ON SALES OF MISCELLANEOUS ASSETS.   Profits on sales of miscellaneous assets—those not regularly and customarily offered for sale in the normal conduct of the business—are usually recognized as "other income." Such profits frequently include profits on sales of securities, real estate, machinery and equipment, automobiles and trucks, furniture and fixtures, and sundry salvaged materials. Profits on those sales are generally recorded "net"; that is, the selling price is not recorded as revenue and the carrying value of the asset sold is not shown as expense.

12.28 RENTS.   Rents receivable should be recorded as revenue in the accounting period during which they accrue. Rents received in advance should be deferred and included in revenue in the period to which they apply.

12.29 ROYALTIES.   Royalties may be broadly defined as a compensation or a portion of the proceeds paid to the owner of a right for its use. The compensation may be in the form of a share in kind of the product or the right that is exploited or in the form of monetary compensation at agreed rates based on units produced, used, or sold or the equivalent of their market value. The types of property for which royalties may be paid include forests, mineral and oil lands, copyrights, patents, processes, and equipment.

Royalties should be recognized as revenue as they accrue. Periodic royalty reports from the user of the property customarily form the basis for determining the amount to be accrued. Amounts collected as advance royalties or as minimum periodic royalties should be deferred to the extent that such collections may be applied in settlement of royalties accruing in a period subsequent to the period of receipt.

12.30 BY-PRODUCT, JOINT PRODUCT, AND SCRAP SALES.   Horngren (1982, p. 539) states: "[T]he distinction among joint products, by-products, and scrap is largely influenced by the relative sales values of the products in question. However, these distinctions are not firm; the variety of terminology and accounting practice is bewildering."

Horngren (p. 532) defines joint products as follows: "When a group of individual products is simultaneously produced, with each product having a significant relative sales value, the outputs are usually called joint products." By-products are (p. 540):

> [M]ultiple products that have minor sales value as compared with that of the major or chief product(s). . . . The distinction between scrap and by-products is often difficult to establish. A view that is sometimes helpful is that by-products (a) have relatively more sales value than scrap, (b) are often subject to additional costs beyond the split-off point, whereas scrap is usually sold outright. The basic accounting for scrap and for by-products is the same. The net realizable values of both are best treated as deductions from the cost of the main product.

Joint product sales are normally recorded in the same manner as the principal sources of revenue. The major accounting problem in this connection is determining the proportionate share of total product costs to be assigned to joint products.

12.31 PURCHASE DISCOUNTS.   Purchase discounts are treated in practice either as financial revenue or as a reduction of purchases. Kieso and Weygandt (1989, p. 355) note that the latter method has more theoretical support because revenue should not be recognized before the sale of goods.

STATEMENT PRESENTATION

The income statement should disclose sales for the period, usually net of discounts, returns, and allowances. The basis for presentation of receivables in the balance sheet is the time of their collection. Receivables expected to be collected within the next operating cycle or fiscal year, whichever is longer, are ordinarily classified as current assets. There are several exceptions allowed by ARB No. 43, which are discussed below. Specialized reporting requirements are also discussed below.

Kieso and Weygandt (1989, p. 316) summarize the general rules for statement presentation in the receivables section of the balance sheet:

> (1) [S]egregate the different receivables that an enterprise possesses, if material; (2) insure that the valuation accounts are appropriately offset against the proper receivable accounts; (3) determine that receivables classified in the current assets section will be converted into cash within the year or the operating cycle, whichever is longer; (4) disclose any loss contingencies that exist on the receivables; and (5) disclose any receivables assigned or pledged as collateral.

12.32 PRESENTATION OF SINGLE-PAYMENT ACCOUNTS RECEIVABLE.   Ordinarily accounts receivable are classified in the balance sheet as **current assets.** Noncurrent amounts that will not be collected until the next operating cycle or fiscal year, however, should be shown under the **investment** caption. In the interest of full disclosure, it is considered desirable to limit the "accounts receivable" designation to current claims attaching to trade customers and to identify separately other major types of accounts receivable, such as amounts due from officers and employees, prepayments, and stock subscriptions receivable.

12.33 PRESENTATION OF INSTALLMENT RECEIVABLES ARISING FROM SALES.   ARB No. 43 (Ch. 3, par. 4) specifically provides for the inclusion within *current assets* of "installment or deferred accounts and notes receivable if they conform generally to normal trade practices and terms within the business." Thus installment contracts may be classified as current regardless of the length of the collection period. Designation of annual maturity dates by separate listing of contracts receivable or by parenthetical or note disclosure is recommended to enable readers to ascertain the current position.

Conflicting opinions exist as to the proper classification of the **deferred gross profit account** related to installment receivables. The AICPA (''Accounting for Retail Land Sales'') recommends that deferred gross profit be treated as an asset valuation account for installment land sales. Since deferred gross profit is part of revenue from installment sales not yet realized, the related receivable will be overstated unless deferred gross profit is deducted. Another alternative is to report deferred gross profit as a deferred credit in the liability section. This alternative has been criticized, however, because the credit is not an obligation to an outsider.

SFAS No. 32, ''Specialized Accounting and Reporting Principles and Practices in AICPA Statements of Position and Guides on Accounting and Auditing Matters,'' specifies that the accounting in the AICPA industry accounting guide is preferable for retail land sales, although it is not required.

In preparing an income statement, installment sales, cost of sales, and realized revenues may be shown in the statement, or only the realized profit may be reported, with sales and cost of sales reflected in a separate supporting schedule.

12.34 INTEREST ON RECEIVABLES.   Notes receivable arise in many situations in which the legal form of the note specifies an interest rate (including lack of an interest rate) that varies from prevailing interest rates. APB Opinion No. 21, ''Interest on Receivables and Payables,'' requires that, in these situations, the note receivable be recorded at its present value and that interest be imputed at an appropriate rate. The resulting discount or premium is amortized over the life of the note. APB Opinion No. 21 (par. 3) exempts the following receivables:

 a. Receivables arising from transactions with customers in the normal course of business which are due in customary trade terms not exceeding approximately one year.
 b. Receivables from the customary cash lending activities of financial institutions.
 c. Receivables where interest rates are affected by the tax attributes or legal restrictions prescribed by a governmental agency.
 d. Receivables from a parent, subsidiary, or another firm with a common parent.

12.35 INTERNATIONAL ACCOUNTING STANDARD ON REVENUE RECOGNITION. The IASC issued IAS No. 18, ''Revenue Recognition,'' in December 1982. The standard is concerned with the recognition of revenue arising in the course of an enterprise's ordinary activities from (1) the sale of goods, (2) the rendering of services, and (3) the use of other enterprise resources yielding interest, royalties, and dividends. Financial statements prepared in conformity with U.S. GAAP will comply with the international standard in all material respects.

SOURCES AND SUGGESTED REFERENCES

Accounting Principles Board, ''Omnibus Opinion—1966,'' APB Opinion No. 10, AICPA, New York, 1966.

――――, ''Interest on Receivables and Payables,'' APB Opinion No. 21, AICPA, New York, 1971.

――――, ''Accounting for Nonmonetary Transactions,'' APB Opinion No. 29, AICPA, New York, 1973.

――――, ''Reporting the Results of Operations,'' APB Opinion No. 30, AICPA, New York, 1973.

――――, ''Basic Concepts and Accounting Principles Underlying Financial Statements of Business Enterprises,'' APB Statement No. 4, AICPA, New York, 1970.

American Accounting Association, Committee on Accounting Concepts and Standards, *Accounting and Reporting Standards for Corporate Financial Statements (1957) Revision,* AAA, Sarasota, Florida, 1957.

――――, 1964 Concepts and Standards Research Committee on the Realization Concept, ''The Realization Concept,'' *Accounting Review,* April 1965.

American Institute of Certified Public Accountants, Accounting Standards Division, "Accounting for Grants Received from Governments," Draft of an Issues Paper, AICPA, New York, 1979.

———, Committee on Accounting Procedure, "Restatement and Revision of Accounting Research Bulletins," Accounting Research Bulletin No. 43, AICPA, New York, 1953.

———, Committee on Land Development Companies, "Accounting for Retail Land Sales," Industry Accounting Guide, AICPA, New York, 1973.

Canning, J. B., *The Economics of Accounting,* Ronald Press, New York, 1929.

Cooper, W. W., and Ijiri, Y., eds., *Kohler's Dictionary for Accountants,* 6th ed., Prentice-Hall, Englewood Cliffs, NJ, 1983.

Edwards, E. O., and Bell, P. W., *The Theory and Measurement of Business Income,* University of California Press, Berkeley and Los Angeles, 1965.

Edwards, J. O., Hermanson, R. H., and Salmonson, R. F., *Accounting,* Vol. II, Irwin, Homewood, IL, 1967.

Financial Accounting Standards Board, "An Analysis of Issues Related to Conceptual Framework for Financial Accounting and Reporting: Elements of Financial Statements and Their Measurement," Discussion Memorandum, FASB, Stamford, CT, 1976.

———, "Accounting for Certain Service Transactions," Invitation to Comment, FASB, Stamford, CT, 1978.

———, "Objectives of Financial Reporting by Business Enterprises," Statement of Financial Accounting Concepts No. 1, FASB, Stamford, CT, 1978.

———, "Qualitative Characteristics of Accounting Information," Statement of Financial Accounting Concepts No. 2, FASB, Stamford, CT, 1980.

———, "Recognition and Measurement in Financial Statements of Business Enterprises," Statement of Financial Accounting Concepts No. 5, FASB, Stamford, CT, 1984.

———, "Elements of Financial Statements," Statement of Financial Accounting Concepts No. 6, FASB, Stamford, CT, 1985.

———, "Accounting for Contingencies," Statement of Financial Accounting Standards No. 5, FASB, Stamford, CT, 1975.

———, "Accounting for Leases," Statement of Financial Accounting Standards No. 13, FASB, Stamford, CT, 1977.

———, "Financial Reporting for Segments of a Business Enterprise," Statement of Financial Accounting Standards No. 14, FASB, Stamford, CT, 1976.

———, "Accounting by Debtors and Creditors for Troubled Debt Restructurings," Statement of Financial Accounting Standards No. 15, FASB, Stamford, CT, 1977.

———, "Disclosure of Information about Major Customers," Statement of Financial Accounting Standards No. 30, FASB, Stamford, CT, 1979.

———, "Specialized Accounting and Reporting Principles and Practices in AICPA Statements of Position and Guides on Accounting and Auditing Matters," Statement of Financial Accounting Standards No. 32, FASB, Stamford, CT, 1979.

———, "Financial Reporting and Changing Prices," Statement of Financial Accounting Standards No. 33, FASB, Stamford, CT, 1979.

———, "Accounting for Franchise Fee Revenue," Statement of Financial Accounting Standards No. 45, FASB, Stamford, CT, 1981.

———, "Revenue Recognition When Right of Return Exists," Statement of Financial Accounting Standards No. 48, FASB, Stamford, CT, 1981.

———, "Accounting for Product Financing Arrangements," Statement of Financial Accounting Standards No. 49, FASB, Stamford, CT, 1981.

———, "Financial Reporting in the Record and Music Industry," Statement of Financial Accounting Standards No. 50, FASB, Stamford, CT, 1981.

———, "Financial Reporting by Cable Television Companies," Statement of Financial Accounting Standards No. 51, FASB, Stamford, CT, 1981.

———, "Financial Reporting by Producers and Distributors of Motion Picture Films," Statement of Financial Accounting Standards No. 53, FASB, Stamford, CT, 1981.

———, "Financial Reporting by Broadcasters," Statement of Financial Accounting Standards No. 63, FASB, Stamford, CT, 1982.

———, "Accounting for Certain Mortgage Banking Activities," Statement of Financial Accounting Standards No. 65, FASB, Stamford, CT, 1982.

———, "Accounting for Sales of Real Estate," Statement of Financial Accounting Standards No. 66, FASB, Stamford, CT, 1982.

———, "Reporting by Transferors for Transfers of Receivables with Recourse," Statement of Financial Accounting Standards No. 77, FASB, Stamford, CT, 1983.

———, "Financial Reporting and Changing Prices: Elimination of Certain Disclosures," Statement of Financial Accounting Standards No. 82, FASB, Stamford, CT, 1984.

———, "Financial Reporting and Changing Prices," Statement of Financial Accounting Standards No. 89, FASB, Stamford, CT, 1986.

———, "Accounting for Income Taxes," Statement of Financial Accounting Standards No. 96, FASB, Stamford, CT, 1987.

———, "Accounting for Leases: Sale-Leaseback Transactions Involving Real Estate," Statement of Financial Accounting Standards No. 98, FASB, Norwalk, CT, 1988.

Hendriksen, E. S., *Accounting Theory,* 3rd ed., Irwin, Homewood, IL, 1977.

———, *Accounting Theory,* 4th ed., Irwin, Homewood, IL, 1982.

Horngren, C. T., *Cost Accounting: A Managerial Emphasis,* 5th ed., Prentice-Hall, Englewood Cliffs, NJ, 1982.

———, "How Should We Interpret the Realization Concept?" *Accounting Review,* April 1965.

International Accounting Standards Committee, "Revenue Recognition," International Accounting Standard No. 18, AICPA, New York, 1982.

Jaenicke, Henry R., "Survey of Present Practices in Recognizing Revenues, Expenses, Gains, and Losses," FASB, Stamford, CT, January 1981.

Kieso, D. E., and Weygandt, J. J., *Intermediate Accounting,* 6th ed., Wiley, New York, 1989.

May, G. O., *Financial Accounting: A Distillation of Experience,* Macmillan, New York, 1943.

Meyers, J. H., "The Critical Event and the Recognition of Net Profit," *Accounting Review,* October 1959.

O'Reilly, V. M., Hirsch, M. B., Defliese, P. L., and Jaenicke, H. R., *Montgomery's Auditing,* 11th ed., Wiley, New York, 1990.

Paton, W. A., and Littleton, A. C., *An Introduction to Corporate Accounting Standards,* AAA, Sarasota, FL, 1940.

Paton, W. A., and Paton, W. A., Jr., *Corporation Accounts and Statements,* Macmillan, New York, 1955.

Raphael, J. S., The *Uniform Commercial Code Simplified,* Ronald Press, New York, 1967.

Staubus, G. J., *Making Accounting Decisions,* Scholars Book Co., Houston, 1977.

Securities and Exchange Commission, Accounting and Auditing Enforcement Release No. 108, SEC, Washington, DC, 1986.

———, "Accounting for Real Estate Transactions Where Circumstances Indicate That Profits Were Not Earned at the Time the Transactions Were Recorded," Accounting Series Release No. 95, SEC, Washington, DC, 1972.

———, "Interpretation Regarding Divestitures in Connection with a Sale of a Subsidiary," Staff Accounting Bulletin No. 30, SEC, Washington, DC, 1979.

———, "Order Instituting Proceedings and Opinion and Order Pursuant to Rule 2(e) of the Commission's Rules of Practice *In the Matter of Arthur Andersen & Co.,*" Exchange Act Release No. 17878, SEC, Washington, DC, 1981.

Vatter, W. J., *The Fund Theory of Accounting and Its Implications for Financial Reports,* University of Chicago Press, Chicago, 1947.

Windal, Floyd W., "The Accounting Concept of Realization," *Accounting Review,* April 1961.

CHAPTER 13

INVENTORY

John J. Mahoney, CPA

Ernst & Young

CONTENTS

OVERVIEW

Accounting for inventory has been guided more by practice than by pronouncement. As advances in manufacturing processes have occurred, accounting practices have evolved to identify the applicable costs to be allocated to inventory. Authoritative accounting literature related to inventory accounting and financial reporting is not extensive. The accounting profession has made it clear that examining individual facts and circumstances is important when valuing inventory and applying the established standards.

Historical cost is the normal starting point to record inventory as an asset. In determining inventory cost, a cost flow assumption must be selected. Alternate valuation methods that are exceptions to the historical cost convention are used for certain specialized types of inventory (e.g., sales price less cost of disposal for precious metals, and net realizable value for trade-in inventory). The write-down of inventory to amounts below cost may be necessary due to factors such as damage or changing market conditions.

This chapter addresses inventory costing in greater detail by identifying the pertinent guidance in the authoritative accounting literature and by citing examples that illustrate the practical application of the fundamental principles. The chapter also explains the various types of inventory and practical ways to determine inventory quantities. Finally, the chapter explores effective internal control techniques and financial statement disclosure requirements.

ESSENTIAL INVENTORY CONCEPTS

13.1 INVENTORY AS AN ASSET.   SFAC No. 6, "Elements of Financial Statements," describes assets as "probable future economic benefits obtained or controlled by a particular entity as a result of past transactions or events." Inventory generally is acquired or produced for subsequent exchange. This utility or **service potential** justifies the classification of inventory as an asset of the enterprise that controls it. Normally, inventory is converted into cash or other assets during the operating cycle of the business. In fact, this process is what establishes the operating cycle. As a result, inventory typically is classified as a current asset for purposes of preparing a classified balance sheet.

13.2 DEFINITION OF INVENTORY.   The primary authoritative guidance addressing financial reporting for inventory is ARB No. 43, Chapter 4, "Inventory Pricing." It defines inventory of mercantile and manufacturing enterprises as:

> The aggregate of those items of tangible personal property which (1) are held for sale in the ordinary course of business, (2) are in process of production for such sale, or (3) are to be currently consumed in the production of goods or services to be available for sale.

This definition makes it clear that the trading merchandise of a retailer or wholesaler—and the finished goods, work in process, and raw materials of a manufacturer—constitute inventory.

The Bulletin specifically excludes from inventory long-term assets subject to depreciation accounting. Fixed assets such as buildings and equipment provide benefits that generally extend beyond the operating cycle and, therefore, are classified as noncurrent assets. ARB No. 43 notes that such assets should not be classified as inventory even if they are retired and held for sale.

13.3 OBJECTIVES OF ACCOUNTING FOR INVENTORY.   The sale of inventory to customers is often the most significant component of revenue for a business enterprise. Matching inventory costs with the revenues received from the sale of the goods in order to determine periodic income is the major objective of inventory accounting. Incurred inventory costs that have not been charged against operations represent the carrying amount of inventory on the balance sheet. The costs allocated to goods on hand should not, however, exceed the utility of those goods. In other words, the recorded inventory balance should not exceed the total revenues less selling costs that will result when those goods are sold.

The methods used to determine and measure the flow of inventory costs should be consistent from period to period. The methods should be objective so that comparable results are produced by similar transactions, to allow for independent verification and to prevent manipulation of results of operations. Adequate disclosure should be made regarding the nature of the inventory and the basis on which it is stated.

TYPES OF INVENTORY

13.4 RETAIL–WHOLESALE.   Wholesalers and retailers typically acquire merchandise that is ready for resale to customers. Acquisition cost becomes the basis for carrying the inventory until it is sold.

13.5 MANUFACTURING.   In a manufacturing operation, a production process creates goods for sale to customers or for use in other operations. Manufacturing inventories often are categorized by stage of completion.

(a) Raw Materials.   Goods to be incorporated into a product or used in the production process that have not yet entered the process are referred to as raw materials inventory. The output from one process can become the raw material for another process (e.g., subassemblies).

(b) Work in Process.   Goods typically are classified as work in process inventory as soon as they are drawn from raw materials stock and enter the manufacturing process.

(c) Finished Goods.   Products that are complete and ready for sale are considered finished goods inventory.

(d) Supplies.   Materials necessary for the manufacturing operation but not a significant component of the final product are known as supplies inventory. For example, small incidental screws may be considered supplies inventory, or oil used to lubricate a grinding machine may be considered supplies inventory. ARB No. 43 specifically mentions manufacturing supplies as a type of inventory and notes that the fact that a small portion of the supplies may be used for purposes other than production does not require separate classification.

13.6 CONSIGNMENT.   Arrangements for marketing, storage, distribution, and finishing of a company's products can result in goods' being held by a party other than the owner. The consignee (party holding the goods) generally is precluded from recording the inventory because legal title is retained by the consignor and no exchange has taken place. The consignment inventory balance frequently is combined with the work in process or finished goods inventory shown on the consignor's financial statements. Examples include inventories held for sale in a retail store that have been consigned by the manufacturer, and components held by an outside machine shop to be used in a larger product by the consignor.

13.7 TRADE-IN. Some companies obtain goods accepted from customers in connection with sales of other products. These goods may or may not be similar to the items sold or other products of the seller. An example is a memory board accepted in trade by a computer manufacturer when upgrading customer equipment. Trade-in inventory should be valued at net realizable value, defined as estimated selling price less costs of disposal. The discount or allowance deducted from the list price of the goods sold is not an appropriate value to assign to the trade-in inventory, because the discount often pertains to marketing strategy and other factors not related to the trade-in items.

13.8 REPOSSESSED. In connection with its collection efforts, a company may repossess its product from a customer. Companies that provide consumer financing often deal with repossessed inventory. The physical condition of the property may vary widely and will affect the company's decision regarding disposition (e.g., rework, offer for sale at a discount, scrap). Replacement cost is the primary method of valuing repossessed inventory. If replacement cost cannot realistically be determined, net realizable value should be used. Recording a repossessed item at the outstanding balance of the receivable from the customer is not appropriate, because this approach does not consider the condition and utility of the repossessed item.

13.9 CONTRACT PRODUCTION. A company may enter into a contract under which the customer provides specifications for producing goods, constructing facilities, or providing services. Chapter 21 deals with this topic in detail.

13.10 PRODUCTS MATURING IN MORE THAN ONE YEAR. Certain products—such as tobacco, spirits, livestock, and forest products—are held for an extended period of time until they are mature for sale or inclusion in a finished product. Recognized trade practice is to classify such inventory items as current assets despite the required aging process.

13.11 SPARE PARTS. To service their customers, many companies (particularly equipment dealers and manufacturers) maintain a supply of spare parts for their products. Also, transportation companies hold spare parts to allow their fleets to operate continuously. Spare parts often are classified as inventory. When many small-value items are involved, companies amortize the related costs on a systematic basis. For more valuable spare parts, quantities are tracked and values are determined by the conventional inventory methods discussed in this chapter.

FINANCIAL REPORTING EXAMPLE

TEXAS AIR CORPORATION AND SUBSIDIARIES
Consolidated Balance Sheet
(Dollars in thousands)

Assets	December 31 1988	December 31 1987
Current Assets:		
Cash	$ 76,905	$ 50,275
Marketable securities, at lower of cost or market	812,122	736,389
Accounts receivable, less allowance for doubtful receivables ($30,270 and $16,906)	862,377	863,939
Inventories of spare parts and supplies, less allowance for obsolescence ($53,583 and $37,239)	446,868	366,001

TEXAS AIR CORPORATION AND SUBSIDIARIES

Notes to Consolidated Financial Statements

(c) Spare parts and supplies—Flight equipment expendable parts and supplies are valued at average cost. An allowance for obsolescence is accrued to allocate the costs of these assets over the useful lives of the related aircraft and engines to an estimated residual value.

13.12 MISCELLANEOUS.   Many other types of products may be classified as inventory for financial reporting purposes. Examples include by-products (secondary products that result from the manufacturing process, particularly in the chemicals and the oil and gas industries), reusable items (such as beverage containers), and extractive products.

DETERMINING PHYSICAL QUANTITIES

13.13 INTRODUCTION.   An important aspect of inventory accounting is to establish quantities. This section discusses the two basic methods used to determine the quantities of goods on hand, the periodic system and the perpetual system. In practice, hybrid methods often are used. Also, a company may use a periodic system for certain types of inventories and a perpetual system for others. For example, a steel company may use a perpetual system for work in process and for finished steel products but a periodic system for raw, bulk commodities such as iron ore.

A periodic system employs physical counts to determine physical quantities on hand. A perpetual system maintains detailed records to track quantities based on additions and usage. A perpetual system provides greater internal accounting control because it allows the user to identify and investigate differences between actual quantities on hand and the amounts the records indicate. The additional record-keeping requirements of a perpetual system generally are justified by the additional control given over high-value and off-site inventories. The increased inventory holding costs arising from relatively high interest rates in recent periods and the greater availability and variety of automated systems have led to a proliferation of perpetual inventory systems.

Companies may use less sophisticated methods to determine inventory quantities at interim dates, compared to those used in connection with the year-end inventory valuation.

13.14 PERIODIC SYSTEM.   The most direct means of determining the physical quantity of inventory on hand is to count it. An inventory system that establishes quantities on the basis of recurring counts is known as a periodic system. After establishing quantities on hand, each unit is multiplied by its unit cost to determine its inventory value. Cost of sales is a residual amount obtained by subtracting the ending inventory amount from the cost of goods available for sale:

$$
\begin{array}{l}
\quad \text{Beginning Inventory} \\
+ \ \underline{\text{Purchases and Costs of Production}} \\
\quad \text{Goods Available for Sale} \\
- \ \underline{\text{Ending Inventory}} \\
\quad \overline{\underline{\text{Cost of Sales}}}
\end{array}
$$

A periodic system is most likely to be used by a small company or for a department with low-value items that do not warrant more elaborate control procedures. A periodic system also is used for inventories for which reliable usage data cannot practicably be generated (e.g., certain supplies and extractive materials).

(a) Physical Count Procedures.   Written instructions that describe the procedures to be performed by the individuals participating in the count are an important part of the effort and should be prepared and distributed well in advance of the physical inventory date.

The instructions should cover each phase of the procedures and address these matters:

1. Names of persons drafting and approving the instructions.
2. Dates and times of inventory taking.
3. Names of persons responsible for supervising inventory taking.
4. Plans for arranging and segregating inventory, including precautions taken to clear work in process to cutoff points.
5. Provisions for control of receiving and shipping during the inventory-taking period and, if production is not shut down, the plans for handling inventory movements.
6. Instructions for recording the description of inventory items and how quantities are to be determined (e.g., count, weight, or other measurement).
7. Instructions for identifying obsolete, damaged, and slow-moving items.
8. Instructions for the use of inventory tags or count sheets (including their distribution, collection, and control).
9. Plans for determining quantities at outside locations.
10. Instructions for review and approval of inventory by department heads or other supervisory personnel.
11. Method for transcribing original counts to the final inventory sheets or summaries.

Physical inventory count teams should be familiar with the inventory items. The counts should be checked, or recounts should be performed, by persons other than those making the original counts.

(b) Cutoff.   The process to ensure that transactions are recorded in the proper accounting period is known as cutoff. For inventory, the general rule is that all items owned by the entity as of the inventory date should be included, regardless of location. For goods in transit, if they are shipped f.o.b. destination, ownership does not pass from the seller to the purchaser until the purchaser receives the goods from the common carrier. For goods shipped f.o.b. shipping point, title passes from the seller to the purchaser once the seller turns the goods over to the common carrier.

In practice, purchases are recorded upon receipt, based on the date indicated on the receiving report. Inventory generally is relieved for items sold as of the date of shipment. In this manner, the accounting entries to record the purchase and sale of inventory correspond to the physical movement of the goods at the company. Assuming an accurate physical count of goods on hand is achieved, companies effectively eliminate cutoff errors by verifying that purchases have been recorded in the period of receipt and sales have been recorded in the period of shipment. This usually is accomplished by matching accounts payable invoices to receiving reports, and matching sales invoices to shipping documents. The procedure described above guarantees that both sides of the accounting entry are recorded in the same period. The inventory amount is recorded through the physical count and valuation, whereas the accounts payable/cost of sales amount is recorded through the matching procedure. This method implies all purchases are f.o.b. destination and all sales are f.o.b. shipping point. Although this is unlikely to be the case, the approach works in practice because goods in transit are typically not significant, and the procedure is applied consistently. Companies that have a significant volume of goods in transit and varying terms regarding transfer of ownership should scrutinize the inventory cutoff calculations. For example, an f.o.b. destination sale that was in transit at period end would be recorded prematurely using the method described above. As a result, pretax income would be overstated by the gross margin on the sale, accounts receivable would be overstated, and inventory would be understated. Such a situation normally is considered more of a revenue recognition issue (discussed in Chapter 12) than an inventory issue. The effect of a similar situation for a purchase would merely affect the balance sheet, because there is no margin involved for the buyer. In situations where a strict legal determination of ownership is impractical or other cutoff questions arise, the terms of the sales agreement, the intent of the parties involved, industry practices, and other factors should be considered.

Achieving an accurate cutoff is enhanced by controlling the shipping, receiving, and transfer activity during the physical count. Also, source documents (e.g., receiving reports, shipping reports, bills of lading) pertaining to goods shipped and received around the inventory date must be reviewed closely to verify that transactions have been recorded in the proper period.

13.15 PERPETUAL SYSTEM. Many businesses require frequent information regarding the quantity of goods on hand or the value of their inventory. A perpetual inventory system meets this need by maintaining records that detail the physical quantity and dollar amount of current inventory items. Technological advances such as scanners and low-cost computer applications have made automated perpetual inventory systems more practical and more popular. Their ease of use and their control over inventory quantities have enhanced the productivity of users. The records are updated constantly to reflect inventory additions and usage. Physical inventory counts are performed periodically to check the accuracy of the perpetual records. Discrepancies between the physical count and the quantities shown on the perpetual records should be investigated to determine the causes. Assuming an accurate physical count was achieved, the accounting records should be adjusted to reflect the results of the count. This entry is commonly referred to as the **book to physical adjustment.** The ability to isolate the book to physical adjustment is a perpetual system control feature not present in a periodic system.

(a) Record-Keeping Procedures. In a perpetual inventory system, detailed records are maintained on an ongoing basis for each inventory item. The inventory balance is increased as items are purchased or inventoriable costs are incurred, and the balance is reduced as items are sold or transferred. Cost of sales reflects actual costs relieved from inventory. The level of sophistication of the records can vary dramatically, from manual entries posted directly to the general ledger to refined automated systems that use standard costs and detailed subsidiary records.

Cycle counting may be used with a perpetual inventory system to supplement other control procedures and to spread the physical counting effort throughout a period. A cycle count involves physically counting a portion of the inventory and comparing the quantity to that indicated by the perpetual records. Cycle counts test the reliability of the perpetual records. In connection with the ABC method of inventory control, in which higher-cost items receive a greater degree of continuous control than other items, cycle counts are performed more frequently for high-cost items. Successful results from interim cycle counts can justify reliance on the perpetual records, and thereby eliminate the need to perform a company-wide physical inventory at the fiscal year-end date. This approach generally is recommended in situations where no unusual book to physical adjustments has been identified during the interim cycle counts.

(b) Cutoff. The points made above about periodic inventory system cutoff are equally applicable to a perpetual system. In fact, the detailed record-keeping procedures regularly performed in a perpetual system generally make the period-end cutoff process less burdensome.

13.16 PROCEDURES TO CONTROL INVENTORY QUANTITIES. Implementation of effective accounting procedures and internal accounting controls over inventory quantities can protect the company's investment and reduce costs. A key objective is that goods or services are purchased only with proper authorization. To achieve this objective, some or all of the following control procedures may be helpful:

1. Approval by designated personnel within specified dollar limits is required for requisitions and purchase orders.
2. Receiving, accounts payable, and stores personnel are denied access to purchasing records (e.g., blank purchase orders).
3. Purchasing personnel are denied access to blank receiving reports and accounts payable vouchers.
4. Purchase orders are compared to a control list or a file of approved vendors.
5. Purchase orders are issued in prenumbered order; sequence is independently checked.
6. Records of returned goods are matched to vendor credit memos.
7. Goods are compared to purchase orders or other purchase authorization before acceptance.
8. Unmatched receivers are investigated; unauthorized items are identified for return to the vendor.
9. Receipts under blanket purchase orders are monitored; quantities exceeding the authorized total are returned to the vendor.
10. Overhead expense budget is approved by management; variances from budgeted expenditures are analyzed and explained.

Another control objective is to prevent or detect promptly the physical loss of inventory. The following controls may help to achieve this objective:

1. Responsibility for inventories is assigned to designated storekeepers; written stores requisition or shipping order is required for all inventory issues.
2. Perpetual records are regularly checked by cycle count or complete physical count.
3. Where no perpetual records are maintained, quantities are determined regularly by physical count, costing, and comparison to the inventory accounts.
4. Inventory counts and record-keeping are independent of storekeepers.
5. Written instructions are distributed for inventory counts; compliance is checked.
6. Formal policies exist for scrap gathering, measuring, recording, storing, and disposal/recycling; compliance is reviewed periodically.
7. Cost of scrap, waste, and defective products is regularly reviewed and standards are adjusted.
8. Inventory adjustments are documented and require management approval.
9. Complete production is reconciled to finished goods additions.
10. Guards and/or alarm system are used.
11. Employees are identified by badge, card, and so on.
12. Employees are bonded.
13. Storage areas are secured against unauthorized admission and protected against deterioration.
14. Off-site inventories are stored in bonded warehouses.
15. Materials leaving premises are checked for appropriate shipping documents.
16. Estimation methods are used for retail inventories.

VALUATION METHODS

13.17 COST. The cost principle that underlies today's financial accounting model holds that historical cost is the appropriate basis for recording and valuing assets. ARB No. 43 states:

> The primary basis of accounting for inventories is cost, which has been defined generally as the price paid or consideration given to acquire an asset. As applied to inventories, cost means in principle the sum of the applicable expenditures and charges directly or indirectly incurred in bringing an article to its existing condition and location.

A later section of this chapter deals with the write-down of inventory to amounts below cost by applying the lower of cost or market concept. In such circumstances, the reduced amount is considered cost for subsequent accounting periods.

ARS No. 13, "The Accounting Basis of Inventories," states that "inventories are to be priced at cost, excluding nonmanufacturing costs." Determining what costs are inventoriable is a matter of professional judgment based on the broad guidance in the authoritative literature referred to above. ARB No. 43 contains these additional comments pertaining to the determination of inventory costs:

> Selling expenses constitute no part of inventory costs.
>
> The exclusion of all overheads from inventory costs does not constitute an accepted accounting procedure.
>
> Items such as idle facility expense, excessive spoilage, double freight, and rehandling costs may be so abnormal as to require treatment as current period charges rather than as a portion of the inventory cost.
>
> General and administrative expenses should be included as period charges, except for the portion of such expenses that may be clearly related to production and thus constitute a part of inventory costs (product charges).

(a) Job-Order Costing. Products produced in individual units or batches, and requiring varying amounts of materials and labor (often to customer specifications) compared to other products, normally are costed using the job-order method. This technique is common in the furniture, printing, and robotics industries.

FINANCIAL REPORTING EXAMPLE
NEC CORPORATION AND CONSOLIDATED SUBSIDIARIES

Notes to Consolidated Financial Statements

Work in process made to customer specification represents accumulated production costs of job orders.

Costs of direct material and direct labor are assigned to specific jobs, based on actual usage. Usage information frequently is obtained from material requisition forms and labor time cards. Overhead typically is applied using a predetermined annual rate adjusted periodically to approximate actual costs.

(b) Process Costing. Products produced in large quantities are normally costed using an averaging method called process costing. Companies in the textile, chemical, mining, and glass industries typically use process costing. Production runs are costed based on standard costs, which are the costs expected under efficient operating conditions. The total of all standard costs reported during each period is compared to actual costs incurred, based on general ledger account totals used to capture each cost category. Variances between standard costs and actual costs are analyzed and may be included in inventories or charged to expense, depending on the cause of the variance. No attempt is made to match costs of specific materials and labor to inventory units, because doing so would be highly impractical. A standard cost system can be effective in a process costing environment because of the relative predictability of unit costs. Standard costs can be developed based on each product's bill of materials and engineering specifications.

(c) Direct Material Component.   Materials contained in and traceable to a finished product are designated as direct materials. Because direct materials are a physical component of inventory items, and their cost is based on invoices from vendors, accounting for direct material costs is not difficult as long as quantities are tracked accurately. Freight and other costs of receiving materials also are inventoriable. Generally, freight-in is included as a portion of direct material, whereas receiving costs are included in the overhead pool. Paton & Paton (1971) indicate the cost of materials should be recorded net of related purchase discounts under the theory that income is not generated as a result of acquiring goods or services.

For operational purposes, material price variances and usage variances are identified to highlight deviations from standard amounts. Use of the lower of cost or market criteria described later in this chapter determines whether unfavorable variances or other factors such as spoilage require a write-down of the carrying amount for financial accounting purposes.

(d) Direct Labor Component.   Payroll costs of employees incurred in the technical operations of converting raw materials to finished product are considered direct labor. It is more difficult to associate labor costs directly with inventory than to associate material costs in that way. Labor reporting systems are often the most cumbersome part of collecting inventory costs. Labor price variances and labor efficiency variances are identified to highlight the reasons for deviations from standard costs.

(e) Overhead Component.   Overhead, often referred to as factory overhead or indirect manufacturing costs, consists of all costs—other than direct material and direct labor—directly related to and adding value to the manufacturing process.

Costs typically included in the overhead pool are:

1. Indirect labor (e.g., factory supervision and maintenance).
2. Factory depreciation (plant and machinery).
3. Receiving department.
4. Factory insurance.
5. Factory property taxes.
6. Factory utilities.
7. Other plant maintenance and repairs.

Other, less obvious costs appropriate to charge to the overhead pool include:

1. Rework, scrap, and spoilage that are not unusual or excessive.
2. Pension costs for production personnel.
3. Personnel department costs to the extent they relate to such activities as hiring and administering benefits of production personnel.
4. Purchasing department costs that relate to the acquisition of raw materials, supplies, and goods for resale.
5. Data processing costs related to manufacturing and cost accounting.
6. Legal costs incurred for labor relations or workers' compensation issues.
7. Officers' salaries directly related to the production process.

The authoritative literature does not specify how to apply overhead costs to inventory. As described above, certain costs such as selling expenses, abnormal costs, and a defined portion of general and administrative costs are to be excluded from inventory and charged to operations as incurred. ARS No. 13 suggests relevant costs to be allocated to the overhead pool should be determined by considering a "cause-effect" relationship. "Causes are actions taken to manufacture products or to maintain the facilities and organization to manufacture products. The effects are the costs." The Research Study indicates that in conventional practice all costs associated with the selling function generally are treated as expenses of the period in which incurred, as are costs of general administration (excluding factory administration), finance, and general research. SFAS No. 2, "Accounting for Research and Development Costs," requires that all research and development costs encompassed by the Statement be charged to expense when incurred. SFAS No. 86, "Accounting for the Costs of Computer Software to Be Sold, Leased, or Otherwise Marketed," requires that all costs incurred to establish the technological feasibility of a computer software product be charged to expense as research and development. Once technological feasibility is established, software production costs are capitalized and amortized on a product-by-product basis. Capitalization of computer software costs ends when the product is available for general release to customers. Costs related to maintenance and customer support are expensed as incurred or when the related revenue is recognized, whichever occurs first. Costs incurred to duplicate the software, documentation, and training materials and to physically package the product for distribution are capitalized as inventory.

Selling costs are appropriately charged to expense as incurred, because such costs typically cannot be identified with individual sales and relate to goods previously sold rather than to inventory on hand. The question of deferring certain selling and marketing costs that relate to transactions not yet recognized for accounting purposes (i.e., in order to record the expense in the same period as the related revenue) is controversial and beyond the scope of this chapter. Nevertheless, if such costs are deferred, they should not be included with or classified as inventory.

Numerous other types of costs raise questions about whether they should be included in the overhead pool or treated as a period cost. These costs include purchasing and other costs of ordering, quality control, warehousing, cost accounting, and carrying costs such as interest and insurance (on the inventory items and on the warehouse). The decision to include a cost in the overhead pool requires considerable judgment. In addition to using the "cause–effect" approach described earlier, to challenge whether the cost adds value to the product is often useful. Observation of current practice indicates all of the above items except interest are included in the overhead pool by some companies and excluded by others. SFAS No. 34, "Capitalization of Interest Cost," states, "Interest cost shall not be capitalized for inventories that are routinely manufactured or otherwise produced in large quantities on a repetitive basis because in the Board's judgment, the informational benefit does not justify the cost of so doing."

Including judgmental-type costs in inventory increases current assets and shareholders' equity. The effect on income of a particular period can be in either direction, depending on the relative inventory balances at the beginning and end of the period. However, for a growing company, a broadly defined overhead pool generally serves to increase income reported each period.

Before an overhead application rate is determined, consideration should be given to whether any overhead costs related to idle or excess capacity should be removed from the overhead pool and charged directly to current period operations. ARS No. 13 describes the **Idle Excess Capacity Cost Concept** this way:

> The idea of not allocating costs of excess manufacturing capacity to production of the fiscal year is essentially the notion that they are costs of not producing and therefore should be expenses of the year in which the capacity is idle.

Identifying the cost of idle capacity usually requires segregating the overhead into fixed and variable components. Variable costs change in proportion to production volume, and therefore, generally are not incurred as a result of excess capacity. Fixed costs (such as depreciation, insurance, and property taxes) are incurred (at least in the short term) regardless of production volume. As explained above, the fixed components of overhead that relate to excess productive capacity should be excluded from the overhead pool and charged to expense in the year incurred.

(f) Overhead Allocation.   There are several means of allocating overhead costs to inventory and cost of sales. The traditional method has been to develop an overhead rate based on overhead cost per direct labor hour or direct labor dollar. This method allocates overhead to inventory and cost of sales in proportion to the amount of labor used. Other allocation bases may be more logical in certain circumstances. For instance, use of machine-hours may be a preferable method of overhead allocation for highly automated processes. Recording overhead costs by function and department can significantly improve the cost allocation process. Logical statistical methods can be established to allocate indirect costs. Such refinements can produce more meaningful results than use of a single plant-wide overhead rate. Increased accuracy and control results from using more specific and relevant overhead allocation methods.

Possible methods of allocating indirect costs include:

Indirect Cost	Allocation Basis
Materials handling	Quantity or weight of materials
Occupancy (depreciation, rent, property taxes, etc.)	Square-footage occupied
Employment-related	Number of employees, labor hours, or labor dollars

The level of sophistication in allocating indirect costs and determining overhead absorption rates can profoundly affect the inventory valuation and such other important matters as product margins and pricing.

FIN No. 1, "Accounting Changes Related to the Cost of Inventory," indicates a change in composition of the elements of cost included in inventory is an accounting change. Reporting of such changes should conform with APB Opinion No. 20, "Accounting Changes." Preferability should be based on an improvement in financial reporting, not on the basis of the income tax effect alone.

13.18 LOWER OF COST OR MARKET.   GAAP require reducing the carrying amount of inventory below cost whenever the selling price less cost of disposal of the goods is less than their cost. Impairment of inventory can occur through damage, obsolescence (technological changes or new fashions have reduced or eliminated customer interest in the product), deterioration, changes in price levels, excess quantities, and other causes. The lower of cost or market valuation method is designed to eliminate the deferral of unrecoverable costs and to recognize the reduction in the value of inventory when it occurs. Of the 600 companies included in the AICPA Accounting Trends and Techniques 1987 survey, 90% disclosed lower of cost or market as the method used to value at least some portion of their inventories.

The concept of writing down inventories so they are not carried in excess of amounts expected to be realized is recognized by International Accounting Standards. IAS No. 2 and the IASC's Framework for the Preparation and Presentation of Financial Statements identify the valuation method of lower of historical cost and net realizable value as the appropriate means for accomplishing this effect. Net realizable value is the estimated normal selling price less costs of completion and less costs necessary to make the sale.

The U.S. guidelines for calculating the lower of cost or market adjustment differ from and are more complex than, the international rules. ARB No. 43 states:

> As used in the phrase "lower of cost or market," the term "market" means current replacement cost (by purchase or by reproduction, as the case may be) except that:
>
> (1) Market should not exceed the net realizable value (i.e., estimated selling price in the ordinary course of business less re asonably predictable costs of completion and disposal); and
>
> (2) Market should not be less than net realizable value reduced by an allowance for an approximately normal profit margin.

Use of replacement cost as the starting point for the market valuation is intended to reflect the utility of the goods based on the cost required to produce equivalent goods currently. Replacement cost also is more practical than net realizable value for establishing a market value for raw materials and component parts because these items may not be sold separately or in their existing condition.

The ceiling of the market valuation described above is related to net realizable value to ensure that replacement cost valuation does not defer costs that will not be recovered by the ultimate selling price. For example, an inventory item with a net realizable value of $10 would not be carried above that amount even if its replacement cost exceeded $10. The floor of the market valuation is intended to eliminate any write-off of costs that will be recovered from the customer even though the replacement cost of the inventory is lower. For example, an item with a normal profit margin of 20% to be sold to a customer for $10 would not be carried at less than $8 even if its replacement cost was less than $8.

The lower of cost or market adjustment may be recorded for each inventory item or may be aggregated for the total inventory or for major inventory categories. The choice depends on the nature of the inventory and should be the one that most clearly reflects periodic income. Once selected, the same method should be applied consistently. Any comparisons of aggregate cost and market offset unrealized gains on certain inventory items against expected losses on other items (if such loss items exist), and therefore, reduce the amount of the inventory write-down compared to the amount calculated on an item-by-item basis. Notwithstanding the principle of conservatism, the aggregate approach may be preferable when there is only one type of inventory or when no loss is expected on the sale of all goods because price declines of certain components are offset by adequate margins on other components. Similarly, the lower of cost or market procedure should be applied on an individual item basis for unrelated items and for inventories that cannot practically be classified into categories. Profitable margins on one product line should not be used to eliminate a lower of cost or market write-down for other unrelated products. ARB No. 43 specifically requires use of the item-by-item method of applying the lower of cost or market principle to excess inventory stock (quantity of goods on hand exceeds customer demand).

ARB No. 43 also states that "if a business is expected to lose money for a sustained period, the inventory should not be written down to offset a loss inherent in the subsequent operations."

Controls that can provide reasonable assurance that obsolete, slow-moving, or overstock inventory is prevented or promptly detected and provided for include:

1. Perpetual records show date of last usage; stock levels and usability are regularly reviewed.
2. Physical storage methods are regularly reviewed for sources of inventory deterioration.
3. Purchase requisitions are compared to preestablished reorder points and economic order quantities.

4. Potential overstock is identified by regularly comparing quantities on hand with historical usage.

5. Production and existing stock levels are related to forecasts of market and technological changes.

6. Bill of materials and part number systems provide for identification of common parts and subassemblies; discontinued products are reviewed for reusable components.

7. Work in process is periodically reviewed for old items.

Regular preparation and review of product line income statements can identify products that are losing money and may warrant a lower of cost or market write-down. Another procedure to highlight potential lower of cost or market concerns is to compare product carrying amounts to selling prices. A company can minimize lower of cost or market adjustments at year-end by periodically comparing the carrying value of inventory items to net realizable value and adjusting to the lower figure.

The EITF reached a consensus on Issue No. 86-13, "Recognition of Inventory Market Declines at Interim Reporting Dates" that inventory should be written down to the lower of cost or market at an interim date unless:

1. Substantial evidence exists that market prices will recover before the inventory is sold.

2. In the case of LIFO inventories, inventory levels will be restored by year-end.

3. The decline is due to seasonal price fluctuations.

13.19 RETAIL METHOD.   The retail method offers a simplified, cost-effective alternative of inventory valuation for department stores and other retailers selling many and varied goods. By using estimates of inventory cost based on the ratio of cost to selling price, it generally eliminates the procedure of referring to invoice cost to value each item. This ratio is often referred to as the cost ratio or cost complement. To avoid distortions arising from differing product mix and margins, a separate calculation is generally performed for each department. This step produces more accurate departmental costs and operating results. Also, because the types of products that constitute the inventory on hand at the balance sheet date may differ significantly from the proportion in which goods were purchased during the period, use of departmental cost ratios reduces the likelihood that these differences will improperly affect the inventory valuation.

Definitions of certain key terms used in the retail industry and important to the retail inventory method are:

Original Retail. The price at which merchandise is first offered for sale.

Markon. The difference between the retail price and the cost of merchandise sold or in inventory.

Markup. An addition to the original retail price.

Markdown. A reduction of original retail price.

Markup Cancellation. A reduction in marked-up merchandise that does not reduce retail price below the original retail price.

Markdown Cancellation. An addition to marked-down merchandise that does not raise retail price above the original retail price.

Physical inventory counts (such as for year-end inventory taking) are initially priced at retail value (i.e., selling prices) and converted to cost using the cost ratio. The retail method also allows for periodic determination of inventory and cost of sales without the need for a physical count by means of a calculation similar to that shown in Exhibit 13.1. Retailers regularly use this type of calculation to value inventory at interim periods.

To perform the retail inventory calculations in a manner similar to that shown in Exhibit 13.1, a record of the cost and the retail value of the beginning inventory and of the current period purchases is kept (often referred to as the stock ledger). Net markups (markups less markup cancellations) are added to these amounts to determine the total goods available for sale on both the cost and retail bases. The cost ratio or cost complement calculated by dividing total cost of purchases by total selling price is used to reduce inventory at retail to cost. The markon percentage can be obtained by subtracting the cost ratio from 100%. The ending inventory at retail is obtained by subtracting current period sales, net markdowns (markdowns less markdown cancellations), and other reductions from the total goods available for sale on the retail basis. Finally, the ending inventory at retail is multiplied by the cost ratio to obtain the ending inventory at cost.

Note that the calculation in the exhibit excludes net markdowns from the computation of the cost ratio. Markdowns are deducted from the retail amount after the cost ratio is computed. This method values the ending inventory at an estimate of the lower of cost or market. ARB No. 43 acknowledges that this method is acceptable provided adequate markdowns are currently taken.

In contrast, the retail method is considered to approximate average costs if the calculation includes net markdowns in the computation of the cost ratio. This inclusion reduces the cost ratio denominator and thereby increases the ending inventory figure compared to the lower of

	Department A Traditional Sleepwear		Department E Cosmetics	
	Cost	Retail	Cost	Retail
Beginning inventory—1/31/X2	$200,000	$ 400,000	$170,000	$ 285,000
Purchases(1)	450,000	865,000	575,000	950,000
Markups	—	5,500	—	3,500
Markup cancellations	—	(500)	—	(1,000)
Total available	650,000	1,270,000	745,000	1,237,500
Cost complement		51.18%		60.20%
Markon		48.82%		39.80%
Sales		720,000		918,000
Employee discounts		7,500		5,500
Shrinkage		11,500		14,900
Markdowns		78,000		1,100
Markdown cancellations		(1,000)		—
Promotional markdowns		10,000		—
		826,000		939,500
Ending inventory—1/31/X3				
at retail		$ 444,000		$ 298,000
at lower of cost or market	$227,239	51.18%	$179,396	60.20%

(1) The *National Retail Merchants Association Accounting Manual* states that, for department stores, markon is based on the delivered cost of merchandise and original selling price, adjusted for errors in pricing and additional markups. Markdowns and markdown cancellations do not enter into the calculation of the cost complement. Most accounting references suggest that cash purchase discounts should not be credited to purchases but should be separately accounted for, and a pro rata share of discounts should be netted against the closing inventory. As a practical matter, many retailers either run cash purchase discounts through the purchase journal or record purchases net of discount. *Source:* Wilson and Christensen, LIFO for Retailers, 1985.

Exhibit 13.1.   Example of retail inventory calculation.

cost or market methodology. To illustrate, the following calculations use the figures for Department A in the exhibit to compute the retail method variation that approximates average costs:

	Cost	Retail
Beginning inventory	$200,000	$ 400,000
Purchases	450,000	865,000
Markups		5,500
Markup cancellations		(500)
Markdowns		(78,000)
Markdown cancellations		1,000
Total available	650,000	1,193,000
Cost complement		54.48%
Sales		720,000
Employee discounts		7,500
Shrinkage		11,500
Promotional markdowns		10,000
		749,000
Ending inventory		
at retail		$ 444,000
at average cost	$241,891	54.48%

Note that the ending inventory calculated using the retail method average cost variation amounts to $241,891, which is $14,652 higher than the ending inventory calculated using the retail method lower of cost or market variation.

Retail FIFO is another derivation of the retail method and is obtained in the same way as the average cost computation, except that the beginning inventory is excluded from the calculation of the cost ratio.

The retail LIFO valuation method is discussed in section 13.28 (g).

13.20 ABOVE COST.   In certain cases, inventory items possess such widely accepted value and immediate marketability that an exception is made to the normal requirement that an exchange (e.g., sale) must occur for income to be recognized. Examples of inventories often valued above cost (i.e., at sales price less costs of disposal) include precious metals, farm products, minerals, and certain other commodities. It has become standard practice in these industries to value inventories based on selling prices rather than on cost. This is a practical solution to the difficulty of determining product cost for goods that are obtained from the ground rather than from manufacture.

FINANCIAL REPORTING EXAMPLE
AMERICAN BARRICK RESOURCES CORPORATION

Notes to Consolidated Financial Statements
(Tabular dollar amounts in thousands of United States dollars)

(c) **Inventories**

Gold bullion inventory is valued at net realizable value.

ARB No. 43 indicates that to be valued above cost, inventory items must meet these criteria:

1. Inability to determine appropriate approximate costs.
2. Immediate marketability at quoted market price.
3. Unit interchangeability.

Note that when inventory valuations are based on selling price, holding gains are recognized when the selling price increases, and holding losses are recorded when the selling price decreases. When inventories are stated above cost, disclosure of this policy should be made in the financial statements.

Companies often hedge their exposure to commodity price fluctuations by entering into futures contracts or forward contracts. Theoretically, any gain or loss in the market value of the hedged item is directly offset by a change in the market value of the futures or forward contract. SFAS No. 80, "Accounting for Futures Contracts," recognizes that hedging activities reduce risk and, as a result, gains and losses on contracts that meet the criteria of a hedge should be deferred.

FINANCIAL REPORTING EXAMPLE
HARKEN ENERGY CORPORATION AND SUBSIDIARIES

Notes to Consolidated Financial Statements

Commodities Trading—In the normal course of business, Harken engages in futures and options transactions for the purpose of hedging existing inventory positions and inventory purchase requirements or taking advantage of pricing differentials in the markets for such commodities. For transactions which qualify as a hedge of an existing asset or anticipated transaction, any gain or loss on the transaction is deferred until the related asset sale or purchase transaction is completed.

Deferral of contract gains or losses is not appropriate if the hedged item is carried at market value. Inventories of commodities—particularly grain—that have been hedged through the use of such contracts are often carried at market value. The related contracts also are adjusted to the market value. In this way, if a perfect hedge has been obtained, the market value adjustments will offset each other so the inventory is effectively carried at cost.

13.21 REPLACEMENT COST.   As described above, replacement cost is the starting point for determining market value under the lower of cost or market valuation method. Replacement cost also is the primary method of valuing repossessed goods.

13.22 NET REALIZABLE VALUE.   Certain inventory items for which cost or replacement cost is not determinable or is inappropriate for valuation purposes are valued at net realizable value, defined as estimated selling price in the ordinary course of business less reasonably predictable costs of completion and disposal. Scrap, by-products, and trade-in inventory are regularly valued at net realizable value.

FINANCIAL REPORTING EXAMPLE
AILEEN, INC.

Notes to Financial Statements

Obsolete inventory items are carried at net realizable value.

13.23 GROSS MARGIN METHOD.   A frequently used technique to estimate the inventory balance without performing a physical count is the gross margin method. Although the gross margin method generally is not acceptable as the inventory valuation method for financial reporting purposes because of its reliance on estimated rather than actual cost information, it is useful for a variety of purposes, such as:

1. *Estimating the Inventory Balance at Regular Interim Periods.* This might be required to calculate operating results and to calculate borrowing limits on loans collateralized by inventory. Companies with complicated manufacturing operations may not be able to take a complete physical inventory every quarter and, therefore, might require an estimating technique such as the gross margin method.

2. *Preparing Budget Information*. Budgets usually are centered on sales forecasts. The gross margin method is useful to estimate the cost of goods sold and inventory amounts based on the sales forecast.

3. *Estimating the Value of Inventory Destroyed by a Casualty, Such as a Fire*. Such calculations may be required to support insurance claims related to the loss.

4. *Checking the Reasonableness of an Inventory Balance Determined Using a More Sophisticated Valuation Method*.

This method assumes the gross margin percentage can be predicted with reasonable accuracy, based on results of prior periods or other calculations. This example demonstrates the estimation of an inventory balance using the gross margin method:

Cost of Goods Sold	
Sales	$100,000
× Gross margin percentage	× 25%
Gross margin	$ 25,000
Sales	$100,000
Less: Gross margin	25,000
Cost of goods sold	$ 75,000
Ending inventory	
Beginning inventory	$300,000
Purchases	80,000
Cost of goods available for sale	380,000
Less: Cost of goods sold	75,000
Ending inventory	$305,000

APB Opinion No. 28, "Interim Financial Reporting," recognizes that some companies use the gross margin method to estimate inventory and cost of goods sold for interim reporting purposes (e.g., quarterly reporting to the SEC). Such companies must disclose that this method is used and disclose any significant adjustments that result from reconciliations with the annual physical inventory.

FINANCIAL REPORTING EXAMPLE
ZALE CORPORATION AND SUBSIDIARIES

Notes to Condensed Consolidated Financial Statements (Unaudited)

Inventories

Substantially all inventories are valued using the last-in first-out (LIFO) method, which results in a better matching of current costs with current revenues. During interim periods, the valuation of inventories at LIFO and the resulting cost of sales must be based on various assumptions, including projected year-end inventory levels, anticipated gross margin percentages, and estimated inflation rates. Changes in economic events that are not presently determinable may lead to changes in the assumptions upon which the interim LIFO inventory valuation was made, which in turn could significantly affect the results of future interim quarters.

13.24 IN CONNECTION WITH A PURCHASE BUSINESS COMBINATION. The following general guidelines for assigning amounts to inventories acquired in a purchase business combination are contained in APB Opinion No. 16, "Business Combinations":

1. Finished goods and merchandise are valued at estimated selling prices less the sum of (a) costs of disposal and (b) a reasonable profit allowance for the selling effort of the acquiring enterprise.

2. Work in process is valued at estimated selling prices of finished goods less the sum of (a) costs to complete, (b) costs of disposal, and (c) a reasonable profit allowance for the completing and selling effort of the acquiring enterprise, based on profit for similar finished goods.

3. Raw materials are valued at current replacement costs.

The criteria set forth in APB Opinion No. 16 for distinguishing between a pooling of interests and a purchase differ from the criteria for deciding whether a business combination is a taxable transaction. As a result, some business combinations accounted for as purchases are nontaxable. In those circumstances, if the acquired company accounted for inventories using the LIFO method and the acquiring company continues that LIFO election, the amounts reported as LIFO inventories for financial statement and for tax purposes will likely differ in the year of combination and in subsequent years.

FINANCIAL REPORTING EXAMPLE
BRUNSWICK CORPORATION

Notes to Financial Statements

At December 31, 1988 and 1987, the book basis of LIFO inventories exceeded the tax basis by approximately $3.5 million and $6.1 million, respectively, as a result of applying the provisions of Accounting Principles Board Opinion No. 16 in various purchase business combinations.

Some business combinations accounted for as purchases are also taxable transactions. In those instances, the portion of the purchase price allocated to inventories for financial reporting purposes may differ from that allocated to inventories for tax purposes. For example, when a "bargain purchase" is made, APB Opinion No. 16 requires current values to be assigned to all current assets and the "bargain purchase" credit to be used to reduce the amounts otherwise assigned to noncurrent assets (except marketable securities). For income tax purposes, on the other hand, the "bargain purchase" credit usually is allocated to most of the assets acquired, including inventory.

13.25 CONTROL PROCEDURES TO HELP ACHIEVE A PROPER INVENTORY VALUA-TION. To record inventory amounts accurately and ensure costs are assigned to inventory in accordance with the stated valuation method, controls should be implemented. These control procedures can be effective:

1. Cost accounting subsidiary records are balanced regularly to the general ledger control accounts.
2. Standard unit costs are compared to actual material prices, quantities used, labor rates and hours, overhead expenses, and proper absorption rate.
3. Variances, including overhead, are analyzed periodically and allocated to inventory and cost of sales; results are submitted to management for review.
4. Written policies exist for inventory pricing; changes are appropriately documented, quantified as to effect, and approved prior to change.

To provide assurance that goods and services are recorded correctly as to account, amount, and period, a company may select control procedures such as these:

1. Goods are counted, inspected, and compared to packing slips before acceptance.
2. Receiving reports are issued by the receiving/inspection department in prenumbered order; sequence is checked independently or unused receivers are otherwise controlled.
3. Services received are acknowledged in writing by a responsible employee.

4. Receiving documentation, purchase order, and invoice are matched before the liability is recorded.

5. Invoice additions, extensions, and pricing are checked.

6. Unmatched receiving reports and invoices are investigated for inclusion in the estimated liability at the close of the period.

7. Account distribution is reviewed when recording the liability or when signing the check.

8. Vendor statements are regularly reconciled.

In addition to valuing inventory properly at periodic reporting dates, an important objective is that the usage and movement of inventory be recorded correctly by account, amount (quantities and dollars), and period. To achieve this objective, these controls should be considered:

1. Periodic comparisons of actual quantities to perpetual records are made for raw materials, purchased parts, work in process, subassemblies, and finished goods.

2. Documentation is issued in prenumbered order for receiving, stores requisitions, production orders, and shipping (including partial shipments); sequence is checked independently.

3. Shipments of finished goods are checked for appropriate shipping documents.

4. Shipping, billing, and inventory records are reconciled on a regular basis.

5. Records are maintained for inventory on consignment (in and out), held by vendors, or in outside warehouses; these records are reconciled to reports received from outsiders.

6. Inventory accounts are adjusted for results of periodic physical counts.

7. Inventory adjustments are documented and require approval.

FLOW OF COSTS

13.26 INTRODUCTION.   For cost-based inventory valuation methods, it is necessary to select an assumption of the flow of costs to value the inventory and cost of sales systematically. The reason is that the unit cost of items typically varies over time, and a consistent method must be adopted for allocating costs to inventory and cost of sales. As items are accumulated in inventory at different costs, a basis must be established to determine the cost of each item sold. The cost flow does not always match the physical movement of the inventory goods. ARB No. 43 recognizes that several cost flow assumptions are acceptable and that the major objective in selecting a method is to reflect periodic income most clearly. This emphasis on operating results rather than on financial position is contrary to the current direction of the FASB, which has, more recently, emphasized the balance sheet over the income statement in its SFACs and recent pronouncements. The Bulletin also states that in some cases it may be "desirable to apply one of the acceptable methods of determining cost to one portion of the inventory or components thereof and another of the acceptable methods to other portions of the inventory."

13.27 FIFO.   The FIFO method assumes that costs flow through operations chronologically. Cost of sales reflects older unit costs whereas inventory is valued at most recent costs. In periods of rising prices, FIFO can result in holding gains (also known as inventory profits) because older costs are matched against current sales. ARS No. 13 concludes "that FIFO is the most logical assumed flow of costs if specific identification is not practicable." This conclusion is based on the pattern of the physical flow of goods, and the valuation of inventory as close to current cost as is reasonably possible under the historical cost basis of accounting. The FIFO method is also relatively simple to apply.

In practice, the FIFO method is applied by valuing inventory items at the most recent costs of acquisition or production. For example, assume a dealer made these purchases of Item A during the year:

Date	Quantity	Unit Cost
Jan. 6	1,000	$4.00
Aug. 12	3,000	5.00
Dec. 18	2,000	6.00

If 4,000 units of Item A were held in inventory at December 31, under the FIFO method they would be valued this way:

2,000 units @ $6.00 each = $12,000
2,000 units @ $5.00 each =   10,000
                           $22,000

Note that, unlike the LIFO method, the FIFO method produces the same results whether the periodic or the perpetual inventory system is used.

13.28 LIFO.   The LIFO method assumes the most recent unit costs are charged to operations. This values inventory at older costs. In periods of increasing prices, LIFO produces a higher cost of sales figure than FIFO and, accordingly, a lower income amount. Advocates of the LIFO method point out that in periods of continuous inflation, LIFO provides a better matching of costs and revenues than other cost flow assumptions because it matches current costs with current revenues in the income statement. In addition, LIFO often improves the company's cash flow because it results in lower income taxes. This situation is attractive to companies seeking to reduce their income tax liability, and as a result, many companies use the LIFO method for income tax purposes. The IRS regulations contain a "conformity requirement" that companies using LIFO for tax purposes must use LIFO for external financial reporting purposes. IRS regulations have historically had a significant impact on LIFO techniques used for financial reporting purposes. The AICPA Accounting Trends and Techniques 1987 Survey of 600 companies indicates 66% of those companies use LIFO for at least some portion of their inventories. Also noteworthy is that some of the survey companies that are reported as not using LIFO have no inventories.

As mentioned previously, LIFO causes the inventory amount on the balance sheet to be carried at older costs. The theory supporting this method is that because a company needs certain levels of inventory to operate its business, carrying inventories at their initial cost is consistent with the historical cost principle. Under the LIFO concept, inventory levels are carried on the balance sheet at their original LIFO cost until they are decreased. Any increases (i.e., new layers) are added to the inventory balance at the current cost in the year of acquisition and are carried forward at that amount to subsequent periods. A liquidation occurs when the quantity of an inventory item or pool decreases. The liquidation causes older costs to be charged to operations, failing to achieve the LIFO objective of matching current costs and revenues. To summarize, as long as inventory quantities are maintained (i.e., not decreased), the older, generally low-cost layers are preserved. If inventory quantities decrease, older layers are liquidated and charged to operations, generally increasing earnings.

LIFO is more complex than other inventory valuation methods, principally because of the involved calculations related to inventory pools and layers. To date, LIFO has been governed largely by IRS rules and regulations. As a result, LIFO may result in higher record-keeping costs and require more management attention and planning. Certain companies, particularly those publicly held, may be concerned with investor reaction to the lower earnings reported under LIFO when prices are rising. The IRS rules that permit companies to make supplemental disclosures of FIFO earnings may help alleviate this concern.

FINANCIAL REPORTING EXAMPLE

CHELSEA INDUSTRIES, INC. AND SUBSIDIARIES

Notes to Consolidated Financial Statements

The following information summarizes the effect on income of use of the LIFO as compared to the FIFO accounting method and is presented in order to facilitate the comparison of the Company with other companies exclusively on the FIFO method. Had the Company reported its LIFO inventories at values approximating current cost, as would have resulted from using the FIFO method, and had the statutory tax rates for each year been applied to the resulting changes in income, net income would have been $3,996 ($1.90 per share) in 1988, $2,213 ($.99 per share) in 1987, and $7,072 ($2.73 per share) in 1986.

Studies have indicated that market prices of the common stock of companies that changed from FIFO to LIFO actually increased slightly on average after the change was announced. This data suggests investors understand the potential cash flow benefit of using LIFO.

(a) Specific Goods Method. The specific goods method is normally the simplest LIFO approach to apply and understand. Inventory quantities and costs are measured in terms of individual units. Each item or group of similar items is treated as a separate inventory pool.

The advantage of the specific goods method is that it is easy to conceptualize because LIFO costs are associated with specific items in inventory. This method has been used most frequently by companies that have basic inventory items, such as steel or commodities, and deal with a relatively low volume of transactions.

There are disadvantages, however, in using the specific goods method, especially if the inventory has a wide variety of items or if items change frequently (e.g., for technological reasons). In such circumstances, the specific goods method might become complicated, may prove costly to administer, and may produce unwanted LIFO liquidations.

(b) Dollar-Value Method. The dollar-value LIFO method measures inventory quantities in terms of fixed dollar equivalents (base-year costs), rather than of quantities and prices of individual goods. Similar items of inventory are aggregated to form inventory pools. Increases or decreases in each pool are identified and measured in terms of the total base-year cost of the inventory in the pool, rather than of the physical quantities of items.

One of the most important aspects of dollar-value LIFO is selecting the pools to be used in the computations. Generally, the fewer the pools, the lower the likelihood of a liquidation and the lower the resulting taxable income. Fewer pools also minimize the administrative burden associated with accounting for LIFO inventories. The IRS frequently challenges the nature and number of pools selected; both must be specified when a company applies to the IRS for an accounting change to the LIFO inventory method. Once a company has established the number of pools it will use in the year LIFO is adopted, changes can be made only with permission from the IRS. A method of pooling is considered an accounting method for tax purposes. Therefore, any change in the method of poolings requires IRS approval.

The broadest definition of a pool is the natural business unit pool. This includes in a single pool, all inventories, including raw materials, work in process, and finished goods. This method is only available to companies—generally manufacturers and processors—whose operations consist of a single product line, or more than one if they are related. The natural business unit pool is attractive to many companies because the use of a single pool simplifies the LIFO calculations and reduces the number of layer liquidations.

Companies that do not qualify for natural business unit pooling or that wish to elect LIFO for only a portion of their inventory may elect the multiple pool method. Each of the multiple pools should consist of "substantially similar" inventory items.

There are two basic ways to apply the dollar-value method—the double-extension technique and the link-chain technique. Both techniques have the objective of determining the base-year cost of the current-year inventory. The double-extension technique converts current-year amounts directly to base-year costs. The link-chain technique achieves the objective indirectly by developing an index based on the current-year cost increases and multiplying that index by the prior-year cumulative index.

(c) Double-Extension Technique.   The double-extension technique extends ending inventory quantities twice—once at current-year costs (unit costs for the current period, determined using another method, typically FIFO) and once at base-year costs. This double extension procedure provides the current-year index (total current-year cost divided by total base-year cost).

To determine the net inventory change for the year, the ending inventory expressed in terms of base-year costs is compared to the beginning-of-the-year inventory expressed in terms of base-year costs. If the ending inventory at base-year costs exceeds the beginning inventory at base-year costs, a new LIFO layer has been created and is converted to LIFO cost by multiplying the base-year cost increase by the current-year index. If the ending inventory at base-year costs is less than beginning inventory at base-year costs, a LIFO liquidation has occurred. When a liquidation has occurred, decrements in base-year costs are deducted from the layers of earlier years beginning with the most recent prior year.

When an item enters the inventory for the first time, a company must either use its current cost or determine its base-year cost. Under IRS regulations, current cost must be used unless the company is able to reconstruct a base-year cost. The use of manufacturing specifications or other methods may allow a company to determine what the cost of a new item would have been in the base year. This effort may be worthwhile, because it may calculate a base-year cost that is lower than the current-year cost, most likely due to inflation in the cost of materials and labor. Use of a lower base-year cost in the LIFO calculations increases the current-year index, and thereby, lowers the inventory balance and pretax income. In other words, by reconstructing a base-year cost for new items, the impact of LIFO is normally maximized.

Companies that use the double-extension technique must retain indefinitely a record of base-year unit costs of all items in inventory at the beginning of the year in which LIFO was adopted, as well as any base-year unit costs developed for new items added in subsequent years. Exhibit 13.2 is an example of the LIFO double-extension technique.

The double-extension technique can prove cumbersome, particularly when the base year extends back a number of years. Changes in product specifications and manufacturing

---

The following example illustrates the application of the double-extension technique of dollar-value LIFO for one pool. Assume that the company's opening inventory on January 1, 19X1 (the date LIFO is adopted), totaled $150,000. Ending inventory for the next 3 years follows:

Item	Quantities in Ending Inventory	Base-Year Cost Unit Cost	Base-Year Cost Amount	Current-Year Cost Unit Cost	Current-Year Cost Amount	Index
Year Ended December 31, 19X1						
A	8,000	$ 1.00	$ 8,000	$ 1.15	$ 9,200	
B	7,000	4.00	28,000	4.30	30,100	
C	10,000	7.00	70,000	7.60	76,000	
D	12,000	6.00	72,000	6.35	76,200	
			$178,000		$191,500	107.58
						(continued)

Exhibit 13.2.   Example of LIFO double-extension technique.

Item	Quantities in Ending Inventory	Base-Year Cost Unit Cost	Base-Year Cost Amount	Current-Year Cost Unit Cost	Current-Year Cost Amount	Index
Year Ended December 31, 19X2						
A	12,000	$ 1.00	$ 12,000	$ 1.30	$ 15,600	
B	6,000	4.00	24,000	4.75	28,500	
C	7,000	7.00	49,000	8.15	57,050	
D	15,000	6.00	90,000	6.80	102,000	
E	7,000	9.00	63,000	10.30	72,100	
			$238,000		$275,250	115.65
Year Ended December 31, 19X3						
A	18,000	$ 1.00	$ 18,000	$ 1.50	$ 27,000	
D	17,000	6.00	102,000	7.50	127,500	
E	10,000	9.00	90,000	11.20	112,000	
F	5,000	8.00	40,000	9.75	48,750	
G	3,000	10.00	30,000	12.35	37,050	
			$280,000		$352,300	125.82

Computation of LIFO Cost

	Base-Year Cost	Index	LIFO Cost
December 31, 19X1			
January 1, 19X1, base	$150,000	100.00	$150,000
December 31, 19X1, increment	28,000	107.58	30,122
	$178,000		$180,122
December 31, 19X2			
January 1, 19X1, base	$150,000	100.00	$150,000
December 31, 19X1, increment	28,000	107.58	30,122
December 31, 19X2, increment	60,000	115.65	69,390
	$238,000		$249,512
December 31, 19X3			
January 1, 19X1, base	$150,000	100.00	$150,000
December 31, 19X1, increment	28,000	107.58	30,122
December 31, 19X2, increment	60,000	115.65	69,390
December 31, 19X3, increment	42,000	125.82	52,844
	$280,000		$302,356

Exhibit 13.2. *Continued.*

methods are common in many industrial companies. The link-chain method eliminates the burden of reconstructing base-year costs and so is a more efficient means of computing LIFO cost. In determining a LIFO index, an IRS rule of thumb holds that at least 70% of the total value of the pool should be matched to the prior-year costs to achieve a representative sample. If a statistical, random sampling technique is used, fewer items may be matched to obtain acceptable results.

(d) Link-Chain Technique.   Under the link-chain technique, the ending inventory is double-extended at both current-year unit costs and prior-year unit costs. The respective extensions are then totaled, and the totals are used to compute a current-year index. This current-year index is multiplied by the prior-year cumulative LIFO index to obtain a current-year cumulative index. Total current-year costs are divided by the current-year cumulative index to determine base-year costs. If ending inventory stated at base-year cost exceeds beginning inventory stated at base-year cost, a new LIFO layer has been created. The new layer is valued using one of the approaches described later in this chapter. If ending inventory stated at base-year cost is less than beginning inventory stated at base-year cost, a LIFO liquidation has occurred.

When a liquidation has occurred, decrements in base-year costs are deducted from the layers of earlier years, beginning with the most recent prior year.

If new items are included in the calculation of an index under the link-chain method, a unit cost would be reconstructed using prior-year, rather than base-year, costs. The reason is that the link-chain current-year index attempts to measure inflation for the most recent year. Exhibit 13.3 is an example of the LIFO link-chain technique and compares the results obtained to those calculated using the double-extension technique in Exhibit 13.2.

The following example, which uses the same inventory items and unit costs as in Exhibit 13.2, is intended to illustrate the link-chain technique and to compare the results with those achieved using the double-extension technique. Because this example involves only a few items, the entire inventory has been double extended. A representative sample also may be used with the link-chain technique. As in the double-extension example, assume that the company's opening inventory on January 1, 19X1 (the date LIFO is adopted), totals $150,000.

Item	Quantities in Ending Inventory	Prior-Year Cost		Current-Year Cost		Index	
		Unit Cost	Amount	Unit Cost	Amount	Current Year	Cumulative
Year Ended December 31, 19X1							
A	8,000	$ 1.00	$ 8,000	$ 1.15	$ 9,200		
B	7,000	4.00	28,000	4.30	30,100		
C	10,000	7.00	70,000	7.60	76,000		
D	12,000	6.00	72,000	6.35	76,200		
			$178,000		$191,500	107.58	107.58
					÷107.58		
			Base-Year Cost		$178,000		
Year Ended December 31, 19X2							
A	12,000	$ 1.15	$ 13,800	$ 1.30	$ 15,600		
B	6,000	4.30	25,800	4.75	28,500		
C	7,000	7.60	53,200	8.15	57,050		
D	15,000	6.35	95,250	6.80	102,000		
E	7,000	9.60	67,200	10.30	72,100		
			$255,250		$275,250	107.84	116.01
					÷116.01		
			Base-Year Cost		$237,264		

(continued)

Exhibit 13.3.   Example of LIFO link-chain technique.

Item	Quantities in Ending Inventory	Prior-Year Cost		Current-Year Cost		Index	
		Unit Cost	Amount	Unit Cost	Amount	Current Year	Cumulative
Year Ended December 31, 19X3							
A	18,000	$ 1.30	$ 23,400	$ 1.50	$ 27,000		
D	17,000	6.80	115,600	7.50	127,500		
E	10,000	10.30	103,000	11.20	112,000		
F	5,000	9.15	45,750	9.75	48,750		
G	3,000	11.60	34,800	12.35	37,050		
			$322,550		$352,300	109.22	126.71
					÷126.71		
			Base-Year Cost		$278,036		

Computation of LIFO Cost

	Base-Year Cost	Index	LIFO Cost Using Link-Chain	LIFO Cost Using Double-Extension (From Exhibit 13.2)
December 31, 19X1				
January 1, 19X1, base	$150,000	100.00	$150,000	$150,000
December 31, 19X1, increment	28,000	107.58	30,122	30,122
	$178,000		$180,122	$180,122
December 31, 19X2				
January 1, 19X1, base	$150,000	100.00	$150,000	$150,000
December 31, 19X1, increment	28,000	107.58	30,122	30,122
December 31, 19X2, increment	59,264	116.01	68,752	69,390
	$237,264		$248,874	$249,512
December 31, 19X3				
January 1, 19X1, base	$150,000	100.00	$150,000	$150,000
December 31, 19X1, increment	28,000	107.58	30,122	30,122
December 31, 19X2, increment	59,264	116.01	68,752	69,390
December 31, 19X3, increment	40,772	126.71	51,662	52,844
	$278,036		$300,536	$302,356

Exhibit 13.3. *Continued.*

(e) Valuing the Current-Year Layer. Regardless of the technique used to compute LIFO values, an approach to price any newly created current-year LIFO layer must be selected and used consistently. Alternative approaches include:

1. *Latest Acquisition Cost.* This approach is attractive because it frequently is the easiest to apply. Many companies on LIFO maintain their internal inventory records on FIFO because of its simplicity and because it is a logical starting point for calculating LIFO. If the latest acquisition-cost approach is used, current-year unit costs are available from the FIFO inventory valuation. A disadvantage of this approach is that it results in the highest value for the new layer (and therefore, the highest taxable income) if costs have

been consistently rising throughout the year. Another disadvantage is that the company must wait until after year-end to compute current-year cost.

2. *Earliest Acquisition Cost.* In periods of steadily increasing prices, this approach prices new layers at lower costs than the other approaches do. The result is the lowest tax liability. Another advantage is that current-year unit costs may be computed in the early part of the year. The major disadvantage of this approach is that it may require additional effort, because it generally involves a separate calculation. The separate calculation usually requires double-extending a sample of inventory items at earliest current-year costs to obtain the earliest acquisition-cost index.

3. *Average Acquisition Cost.* The results obtained from this approach represent a middle ground between the other two approaches. However, this approach may require even more involved calculations than the earliest acquisition approach.

In addition, any other method that in the opinion of the IRS clearly reflects income may be used to price current-year LIFO layers.

(f) Other LIFO Matters. In the year LIFO is adopted, any market write-downs or other valuation allowances must be restored so that the opening inventory is stated at cost. Also, because the prior year's ending inventory (presumably at FIFO or average cost) becomes the opening LIFO inventory, there is no adjustment for any cumulative effect of a change in accounting principle or disclosure of pro forma amounts for prior years. APB Opinion No. 20 cites the change in inventory pricing from FIFO to LIFO as an example of a change in accounting principle for which the cumulative effect adjustment and pro forma disclosures may be omitted.

In 1984, the AcSEC of the AICPA approved an issues paper, "Identification and Discussion of Certain Financial Accounting and Reporting Issues Concerning LIFO Inventories." In SAB No. 58, the SEC staff endorsed the issues paper, saying it represents an accumulation of existing acceptable LIFO accounting practices, and companies and their auditors should refer to it for guidance. The issues paper recommends that all companies using LIFO follow these LIFO-related disclosures required for SEC registrants:

1. The effect on net income of LIFO quantities liquidations.

2. For companies that have not fully adopted LIFO, the extent to which LIFO is used (e.g., the portion of ending inventory priced at LIFO and the portion priced under other methods).

3. For LIFO inventories, the amount and basis for determining the excess of replacement or current cost over the stated LIFO value.

The issues paper also provides practical implementation guidance on expanded supplemental non-LIFO disclosures (such as notes to the financial statements and other supplemental information that disclose the "pro forma" effects of using FIFO or some other acceptable inventory method), and the use of LIFO applications for financial reporting purposes that differ from the applications used for income tax purposes.

Practice Bulletin No. 2, "Elimination of Profits Resulting from Intercompany Transfers of LIFO Inventories," issued by the AcSEC of the AICPA, which also deals with LIFO, indicates intercompany profits arising from LIFO liquidations caused by transfers between or from LIFO pools within a reporting entity should be deferred until such profits are realized by the reporting entity through dispositions outside the consolidated group.

In ASR No. 293, the SEC indicated LIFO accounting has been unduly influenced by IRS rules, and the amended IRS regulations that allow companies to compute LIFO differently for financial reporting and tax purposes are viewed very positively by the Commission. In this manner, companies can select for financial reporting purposes LIFO techniques (from those described above) that best reflect the company's circumstances, rather than being forced to use IRS-mandated methods that dictate the income tax return calculations. The SEC also indicated its concern that supplemental income disclosures based on non-LIFO methods may be misleading. This concern is mitigated when these additional disclosures are made:

1. Clearly state that the use of LIFO results in a better matching of costs and revenues.
2. State the reason supplemental income disclosures are provided.
3. Provide essential information about the supplemental income calculation to enable users to appreciate the quality of the information.

As a result of this SEC release, publicly held companies that disclose supplemental income information based on non-LIFO methods also regularly make the three additional disclosures recommended by the SEC.

Written policies and procedures for performing LIFO computations and determining LIFO pools can improve the quality and consistency of the results. Because of the complexity of the calculations, a thorough detailed review by someone other than the preparer is worthwhile.

(g) Retail LIFO Method. Like the retail inventory method described earlier, the retail LIFO method is used most frequently by department stores and other retailers that sell many and varied goods. Use of retail LIFO permits these companies to match most recent costs against current revenues and, as a result, values inventory at older costs. The retail method of LIFO is an adaptation of the dollar-value LIFO method. However, the retail method differs from other applications of dollar-value LIFO because in recording inventory input and output retail sales values are used rather than cost. Items in the closing inventory are initially priced at retail value (i.e., intended sales value), and the retail value of the closing inventory in each department is converted to cost by applying a factor reflecting the relationship of those values to cost.

Most retailers that adopt LIFO continue to maintain their books for internal merchandise management and accounting purposes at the lower of non-LIFO cost or market, following the retail method described earlier in this chapter. The internal records are converted to LIFO only for external financial reporting and tax purposes.

The retail LIFO method requires that retail selling prices be adjusted for markdowns to state inventories at approximate cost rather than at the lower of cost or market, as frequently followed under the non-LIFO retail method. To state the inventory at cost, the cost complement under the retail LIFO method includes the effects of markdowns. However, temporary or promotional markdowns are not included in the cost complement calculation, because the physical inventory would never reflect such markdowns (i.e., they are applied separately at the time of sale).

Department stores using the retail LIFO method are allowed to use price indexes published by the IRS based on information furnished by the Bureau of Labor Statistics. Other entities are required to generate their own indexes in much the same way as nonretail organizations that use dollar-value LIFO. Exhibit 13.4 is an example of the retail LIFO computation.

13.29 AVERAGE COST. Another fairly common cost flow assumption uses an average cost per unit to determine cost of sales and the inventory value. A weighted average cost (including the cost of the beginning inventory and current period purchases and production) is used in connection with a periodic inventory system. A moving average cost typically is used with a perpetual inventory system. The average cost method is used by companies in many industries and is often viewed as producing results similar to those obtained from the FIFO method. The reason is that the inventory balance is directly influenced by current costs.

The example below illustrates the calculation of LIFO using the retail method. (Calculation of the indexes is not shown because those principles have been discussed in section 13.28.) The example illustrates the calculation for one department for the first 3 years the company is on LIFO.

Step No.	Item or Computation	First Year	Second Year	Third Year
1	Purchases at cost	$1,400,000	$1,600,000	$1,800,000
2	Purchases at retail, including markups	$2,900,000	$3,400,000	$3,700,000
3	Less permanent markdowns applicable to purchases	100,000	150,000	200,000
4	Net purchases at retail	$2,800,000	$3,250,000	$3,500,000
5	Cost complement percentage (1 ÷ 4)	50%	49.23%	51.43%
6	Ending inventory at retail	$ 800,000	$ 900,000	$ 950,000
7	Index (computed or BLS)	104.5	109.1	112.3
8	Inventory at base-year retail (6 ÷ 7)	765,550	824,931	845,948
9	Base-year retail, previous year	700,000	765,550	824,931
10	Current-year increment at base-year retail (8 − 9)	65,550	59,381	21,017
11	Valuation of current-year increment (7 × 10)	68,500	64,785	23,602
12	Current-year increment at cost (11 × 5)	34,250	31,894	12,138
13	Prior LIFO basis inventory	350,000*	384,250	416,144
14	LIFO cost of inventory (12 + 13)	$ 384,250	$ 416,144	$ 428,282

*For purposes of this example, assume the cost complement percentage for the beginning inventory also was 50% (assumed opening inventory of $700,000 × 50% = $350,000).
   If there had been a decrement or liquidation in any of the years, it would have been handled in the same manner as other LIFO methods (i.e., applied to most recent layer).

LIFO Reserve

In order to disclose the LIFO reserve (i.e., the difference between the inventory amount calculated using the retail method and the inventory amount calculated using the retail LIFO method), it is necessary to calculate the cost complement percentage as though the retailer used the retail method. As mentioned earlier, however, this usually is easily derived from the internal records, because most retailers on LIFO maintain their records on the retail method. The following illustrates this calculation for the above example:

	Cost	Retail	Retail Cost Complement
First Year			
Opening inventory	$ 350,000	$ 700,000	
Purchases including markups	1,400,000	2,900,000	
Goods available	$1,750,000	$3,600,000	48.61%
Second Year			
Opening inventory	$ 388,800	$ 800,000	
Purchases including markups	1,600,000	3,400,000	
Goods available	$1,988,800	$4,200,000	47.35%

(continued)

Exhibit 13.4. Example of retail LIFO computation.

	Cost	Retail	Retail Cost Complement
Third Year			
Opening inventory	$ 426,150	$ 900,000	
Purchases including markups	1,800,000	3,700,000	
	$2,226,150	$4,600,000	48.39%

The retail cost method complement percentage above (48.61% in the first year, for example) is lower than the LIFO cost complement percentage (50% in the first year) because the retail method is a lower-of-cost-or-market method. Conversely, the LIFO method is a cost method. The LIFO reserve disclosure should represent the difference between LIFO cost and the lower of current cost or market.

	First Year	Second Year	Third Year
Summary of LIFO Reserve			
Inventory at retail	$800,000	$900,000	$950,000
Cost complement percentage	48.61%	47.35%	48.39%
Inventory at retail method	388,880	426,150	459,705
Inventory at LIFO cost above	384,250	416,144	428,282
LIFO reserve	$ 4,630	$ 10,006	$ 31,423

Exhibit 13.4. *Continued.*

13.30 SPECIFIC IDENTIFICATION. Companies in a limited number of industries track the cost of individual items and retain costs in inventory until the related physical goods are sold using the specific identification method. This method is commonly used for large or expensive items such as automobiles or precious gems. Theoretically, this approach is preferable because it matches costs and revenues based on the actual physical flow of specific goods. However, to implement it is often difficult or impossible, because the cost of individual inventory items cannot be determined, or the expense of tracking cost by item is not justified by increased accuracy. Also, when the approach is used in situations where inventory items are not unique, manipulation of recorded amounts is possible. For example, a company having similar inventory items with different costs can record in inventory and cost of sales the item that yields the most favorable current results.

13.31 OTHER ASSUMPTIONS. Other cost flow assumptions not commonly used for external reporting but possibly useful for internal purposes include:

1. Next-In, First-Out.
2. Cost-of-Last-Purchase.
3. Base Stock Method (similar to LIFO in that it assumes a certain minimum level of inventory is required to operate a business. The base stock is carried at initial cost.).

These methods are not considered to be within GAAP. However, they may assist companies in identifying current product-profit margins, because they match current costs against current sales.

CONTROL OBJECTIVES AND PROCEDURES

13.32 GENERAL CONTROL PROCEDURES. For most manufacturing and merchandising companies, inventory represents a significant asset, valuable to others as well as to the company. As a result, it is important that proper internal controls are in place to protect this investment. General controls provide an environment that enhances safeguarding the inventory in a planned and systematic manner.

(a) Physical Safeguards.   The use of locks, guards, restricted access, and other physical means to secure valuable inventory items improves control and discourages theft. In addition, proper shelter and storage facilities reduce deterioration and spoilage. As with most control measures, a cost/benefit evaluation should be performed to determine the extent to implement physical safeguards.

(b) Written Policies.   Documentation of the procedures and policies authorized by management for inventory control should exist and be updated regularly for changes. The documentation should be readily available to and understood by employees who perform these procedures. Systems documentation is particularly useful for training new employees and minimizing disruption from other changes in personnel.

(c) Reconciliations.   Regular comparisons of physical goods to the accounting records and reconciliations of various source documents can improve control by identifying losses, problems, or other matters warranting management's timely attention. A perpetual inventory system is required to make effective use of reconciliations as a control. Reconciliations should be reviewed by the individual who supervises the person that prepares them. Many specific inventory reconciliation procedures are included in the lists of specific control procedures presented in sections 13.15 and 13.16.

(d) Budgets.   In the inventory area, the use of budgets is most effective for fixed and semifixed costs. Comparison of actual costs to the budgeted amounts can identify matters for further investigation. Explanations of budget variances can assist management in determining whether to record actual costs or standard costs as the inventory amount.

(e) Use of Standard Costs and Analysis of Variances.   For variable costs, the use of regularly updated standard costs and the related variance analysis can identify differences between actual costs and standard costs, regardless of the level of volume. These differences should be examined to ascertain what caused them and what corrective action may be required.

13.33 SPECIFIC CONTROL PROCEDURES.   To support the general control procedures in achieving an effective system of internal control over inventory, specific control procedures must be implemented. Several lists of potential specific control procedures related to inventory are in sections 13.15 and 13.16.

IMPACT OF TAX REGULATIONS

13.34 INTRODUCTION.   In many situations, governmental requirements for the treatment of inventory and related items in an entity's income tax return can influence the accounting and financial reporting. In some cases, these requirements result in two sets of accounting records. In the United States, IRS regulations have had a significant impact on several major aspects of inventory accounting. The previous section of this chapter on the LIFO cost flow assumption describes the impact of IRS regulations on the LIFO computations. This section describes other areas of inventory accounting significantly affected by IRS requirements.

13.35 CAPITALIZATION OF INDIRECT COSTS.   After many years of uncertainty and litigation regarding the types of indirect costs that must be included in inventories, the Treasury Department in 1973 issued regulations mandating the **full absorption** method for all manufacturers. Under this method all direct material and labor costs were allocated to inventories, whereas the treatment of indirect production costs varied according to the nature of the cost.

Indirect costs were separated into three categories under the full absorption regulations. Category I costs were required to be allocated to inventory; Category II costs were not required to be inventoried; and Category III costs were inventoried only for financial reporting purposes.

The full absorption rules required allocating indirect costs to inventory only if they were directly related and added utility to goods in inventory. Because this is not inconsistent with the criteria for capitalizing indirect costs under GAAP, the full absorption rules usually did not result in differences between book and tax inventories.

The Tax Reform Act of 1986 requires inventory for tax purposes to include a number of costs that may have been expensed under the previous IRS rules that mandated full absorption costing. The Act affects all taxpayers that account for inventories and requires the use of "uniform capitalization rules" by any producer of tangible property and by any taxpayer that acquires and holds property for resale. Because some of these costs cannot be capitalized for financial reporting purposes, many companies are required to maintain separate inventory cost records for book and tax purposes. The EITF reached a consensus on Issue No. 86-46, "Uniform Capitalization Rules for Inventory under the Tax Reform Act of 1986," concluding that the fact that a cost is capitalizable for tax purposes does not indicate that it is preferable—or even appropriate—to capitalize that cost for financial reporting purposes. The EITF did not indicate which costs that must be capitalized for tax purposes may also be capitalized for financial reporting purposes. That determination can be made only after an analysis of the individual facts and circumstances, and it involves considerable judgment. The section of this chapter on the overhead component provides additional guidance for making these decisions. Examples of costs that would be capitalized to inventory for tax purposes, but not for financial reporting purposes, are tax depreciation in excess of book depreciation, interest costs, and costs of disposal such as warehousing and disposal where those costs are not an integral aspect of bringing the goods to a saleable condition.

Any differences between book and tax inventories resulting from application of the uniform capitalization rules are temporary differences that generally will create deferred income taxes for financial reporting purposes.

13.36 WRITE-DOWNS. As a result of the Supreme Court decision in the case of *Thor Power Tool Co. v. IRS Commissioner* (1979), the IRS did not permit a write-down of excess inventory using a percentage or aging formula and prohibits the write-down of inventory to scrap value until the goods are disposed of. Once again, any resulting differences between inventory for book and for tax purposes are temporary differences that generally will create deferred income taxes for financial reporting purposes. In practice, many companies check their facilities shortly before the fiscal year-end to make sure all inventory to be scrapped is disposed of before the balance sheet date. In spite of such efforts, many companies record nondeductible reserves for excess inventory that has not been disposed of.

FINANCIAL STATEMENT DISCLOSURE REQUIREMENTS

13.37 GAAP REQUIREMENTS. The primary GAAP disclosure requirements for inventory are specified in ARB No. 43 and include:

1. The basis of stating inventories (e.g., lower of cost or market).
2. The method of determining inventory cost (e.g., FIFO).

3. Whether inventories are stated above cost.

4. Amount of net losses on firm purchase commitments.

APB Opinion No. 22, "Disclosure of Accounting Policies," requires disclosure of the policies relating to inventory pricing.

The 1984 AICPA Issues Paper, "Identification and Discussion of Certain Financial Accounting and Reporting Issues Concerning LIFO Inventories," recommends that all companies using LIFO make several LIFO-related disclosures required for SEC registrants. These include:

1. The effect on net income of LIFO quantity liquidations.

> FINANCIAL REPORTING EXAMPLE
> ARMCO INC.
>
> **Notes to Financial Statements**
> *(Dollars in millions, except per share amounts)*
>
> During 1988, 1987 and 1986, certain inventory quantity reductions caused liquidation of LIFO inventory values. These liquidations increased net income for 1988 and 1987 by $4.9 and $2.8 or $.06 and $.04 per share and decreased the net loss for 1986 by $11.2 or $.16 per share.

2. For companies that have not fully adopted LIFO, the extent to which LIFO is used (e.g., the portion of ending inventory priced at LIFO and under other methods).

> FINANCIAL REPORTING EXAMPLE
> CHAMPION SPARK PLUG COMPANY
>
> **Notes to Financial Statements**
>
> **Inventories**
>
> Inventories, valued at the lower of cost or market, are summarized as follows:
>
> | (In millions) | 1988 | 1987 |
> |---|---|---|
> | LIFO basis | $ 80.8 | $ 94.3 |
> | FIFO or average cost basis | 90.0 | 95.6 |
> | | $170.8 | $189.9 |

3. For LIFO inventories, the amount and basis for determining the excess of replacement or current cost over stated LIFO value (in most cases, the basis for determining current cost is FIFO).

SFAS No. 86 requires these disclosures:

1. Unamortized computer software costs included in each balance sheet presented.

2. The total amount charged to expense in each income statement presented for amortization of capitalized computer software costs and for amounts written down to net realizable value.

FINANCIAL REPORTING EXAMPLE
ON-LINE SOFTWARE INTERNATIONAL, INC. AND SUBSIDIARIES

Consolidated Balance Sheets

As of May 31
(In thousands)

	1989	1988
Assets		
Current Assets		
Cash	$ 1,275	$ 300
Short-term investments	8,743	15,133
Trade receivables, including lease receivables, net	28,910	29,873
Prepaid income taxes and other current assets	1,635	4,205
Total Current Assets	40,563	49,511
Purchased and Capitalized Proprietary Software, less		
accumulated amortization	33,539	31,428

ON-LINE SOFTWARE INTERNATIONAL, INC. AND SUBSIDIARIES

Notes to Consolidated Financial Statements

Software Development and Acquisition Costs. The Company capitalizes certain software development costs in conformity with the requirements of Financial Accounting Standards Board Statement No. 86. The Statement requires that software development costs be capitalized under specified circumstances.

The cost of Purchased Proprietary Software is amortized over the shorter of its useful life or seven years. Capitalized Software is amortized over the shorter of its useful life or five years.

7. *Purchased and Capitalized Proprietary Software.* Purchased Proprietary Software has been recorded at cost based upon purchase agreements for the proprietary products. Certain agreements also provide for the Company to pay commissions averaging approximately 5% to 20% of revenue derived from the license of these products. The cost of Purchased Proprietary Software has been reduced by accumulated amortization of $12,109,000 and $7,165,000 at May 31, 1989 and 1988, respectively.

For the years ended May 31, 1989, 1988 and 1987, the Company capitalized $4,541,000, $4,296,000 and $2,295,000 of development costs, respectively. Related amortization expense was $777,000 in 1989, $354,000 in 1988 and $18,000 in 1987.

13.38 SEC REQUIREMENTS. Rule 5-02.6 of SEC Regulation S-X indicates that inventories typically are classified as current assets and requires these disclosures:

1. If practicable, disclose the major classes of inventories such as finished goods, inventoried cost relating to long-term contracts and programs, work in process, raw materials, and supplies.

FINANCIAL REPORTING EXAMPLE
ALLIED PRODUCTS CORPORATION AND CONSOLIDATED SUBSIDIARIES

Consolidated Balance Sheets

	December 31	
Assets	*1987*	*1988*
Current assets:		
Cash and marketable securities	$ 945,000	$ 7,878,000
Notes and accounts receivable, less allowances of $4,100,000 and $3,348,000, respectively	$166,632,000	$186,042,000

Inventories—		
Raw materials	$ 43,829,000	$ 51,862,000
Work in process	40,084,000	45,516,000
Finished goods	50,914,000	52,716,000
	$134,827,000	$150,094,000

If inventories are presented using the LIFO method and the calculation method does not allow for the practical determination of amounts assigned to major classes of inventory, the amounts of those classes may be stated under another cost flow assumption (e.g., FIFO) with the excess of this amount over the aggregate LIFO inventory amount shown as a reduction.

2. The basis of determining the inventory amounts shall be stated.

3. If the cost method is used, disclose the nature of the cost elements included in inventory, and the method by which amounts are removed from inventory (i.e., cost flow assumption).

4. If any general and administrative costs are charged to inventory, state in a note to the financial statements the aggregate amount of the general and administrative costs incurred in each period and the actual or estimated amount remaining in inventory at the date of each balance sheet. The most common examples of these disclosures are those made by defense and other long-term contractors in accordance with ASR No. 164.

FINANCIAL REPORTING EXAMPLE
MARTIN MARIETTA CORPORATION AND CONSOLIDATED SUBSIDIARIES

Notes to Financial Statements

Selling, general, and administrative costs in connection with production under long-term government contracts were charged to inventories as incurred in the amounts of $271,830,000 in 1988 and $249,900,000 in 1987. The estimated amounts remaining in inventories were $34,390,000 at December 31, 1988, and $19,440,000 at December 31, 1987.

5. For LIFO inventories, disclose the amount and basis for determining the excess of replacement or current cost over stated LIFO value, if material. ASR No. 141 indicates that in determining replacement or current cost for the purpose of this disclosure, any inventory method may be used (such as FIFO or average cost) which derives a figure approximating current cost.

FINANCIAL REPORTING EXAMPLE
BARRY WRIGHT CORPORATION AND SUBSIDIARIES

Notes to Consolidated Financial Statements

If the inventories stated on the LIFO method were valued at FIFO (which approximates replacement cost in each year), they would have been $6.5 million and $5.7 million higher than reported at December 31, 1988 and 1987, respectively.

SAB No. 40 requires the disclosure of the amount of income, if material, that has been recorded because a LIFO inventory liquidation took place.

SOURCES AND SUGGESTED REFERENCES

Accounting Principles Board, "Business Combinations," APB Opinion No. 16, AICPA, New York, 1970.

———, "Accounting Changes," APB Opinion No. 20, AICPA, New York, 1971.

——, "Disclosure of Accounting Policies," APB Opinion No. 22, AICPA, New York, 1972.

——, "Interim Financial Reporting," APB Opinion No. 28, AICPA, New York, 1973.

Accounting Standards Executive Committee, "Elimination of Profits Resulting from Intercompany Transfers of LIFO Inventories," Practice Bulletin No. 2, AICPA, New York, 1987.

——, "Identification and Discussion of Certain Financial Accounting and Reporting Issues Concerning LIFO Inventories," AICPA, New York, 1984.

American Institute of Certified Public Accountants, *Accounting Trends and Techniques,* AICPA, New York, 1987.

——, "Inventory Pricing," Accounting Research Bulletin No. 43, AICPA, New York, 1953.

——, "The Accounting Basis of Inventories," Accounting Research Study No. 13, AICPA, New York, 1973.

Financial Accounting Standards Board, "Recognition of Inventory Market Declines at Interim Reporting Dates," EITF Issue No. 86-13, FASB, Stamford, CT, 1986.

——, "Uniform Capitalization Rules for Inventory under the Tax Reform Act of 1986," EITF Issue No. 86-46, FASB, Stamford, CT, 1986.

——, "Accounting Changes Related to the Cost of Inventory," FASB Interpretation No. 1, FASB, Stamford, CT, 1974.

——, "Elements of Financial Statements," Statement of Financial Accounting Concepts No. 6, FASB, Stamford, CT, 1985.

——, "Accounting for Research and Development Costs," Statement of Financial Accounting Standards No. 2, FASB, Stamford, CT, 1974.

——, "Capitalization of Interest Cost," Statement of Financial Accounting Standards No. 34, FASB, Stamford, CT, 1979.

——, "Accounting for Futures Contracts," Statement of Financial Accounting Standards No. 80, FASB, Stamford, CT, 1984.

——, "Accounting for the Costs of Computer Software to Be Sold, Leased, or Otherwise Marketed," Statement of Financial Accounting Standards No. 86, FASB, Stamford, CT, 1985.

International Accounting Standards Committee, "Framework for the Preparation and Presentation of Financial Statements," IASC, London, 1989.

——, "Valuation and Presentation of Inventories in the Context of the Historical Cost System," International Accounting Standard No. 2, IASC, London, 1975.

Paton, W. A., and Paton, W. A., Jr., *Assets—Accounting and Administration,* Roberts & Roehl, Warren, MI, 1971.

Securities and Exchange Commission, "LIFO Method of Accounting for Inventories," Financial Reporting Releases, § 205 (ASR No. 141), SEC, Washington, DC, 1973.

——, "Improved Disclosures Related to Defense and Other Long-Term Contract Activities," Financial Reporting Releases, § 206, (ASR No. 164), SEC, Washington, DC, 1974.

——, "LIFO Method of Accounting for Inventories," Financial Reporting Releases, § 205 (ASR No. 293), SEC, Washington, DC, 1981.

——, "Codification of SAB Nos. 1–38," Staff Accounting Bulletin No. 40, SEC, Washington, DC, 1981.

——, "LIFO Inventory Practice," Staff Accounting Bulletin No. 58, SEC, Washington, DC, 1985.

——, "Inventories," Rule 5-02.6, Regulation S-X, SEC, Washington, DC, 1974, Updated.

Thor Power Tool Co. v. IRS Commissioner, 439 U.S. 522, 1979.

Wilson, P. W., and Christensen, K. E., *LIFO for Retailers,* Wiley, New York, 1985.

CHAPTER 14

PROPERTY, PLANT, AND EQUIPMENT AND DEPRECIATION

Dale L. Gerboth, CPA
Ernst & Young

Terry A. Klebe, CPA
Ernst & Young

CONTENTS

NATURE OF PROPERTY, PLANT, AND EQUIPMENT

14.1 DEFINITION.   Property, plant, and equipment are presented as **noncurrent assets** in a classified balance sheet. The category includes land, buildings, equipment, furniture, fixtures, tools, and machinery. It excludes intangibles and investments in affiliated companies.

14.2 CHARACTERISTICS.   Property, plant, and equipment have several important characteristics:

1. A relatively long life.
2. The production of income or services over its life.
3. Tangibility—having physical substance.

COST

Property, plant, and equipment are usually recorded at cost, defined as the amount of consideration paid or incurred to acquire or construct an asset and put it into use. Cost consists of several elements. Welsch and Zlatkovich (1989) explain:

> The capitalizable costs include the invoice price (less discounts), plus other costs such as sales tax, insurance during transit, freight, duties, ownership searching, ownership registration, installation, and break-in costs.

14.3 DETERMINING COST.   APB Opinion No. 16, ''Business Combinations'' (par. 67), states three principles for determining the cost of an asset:

   a. An asset acquired by exchanging cash or other assets is recorded at cost—that is, at the amount of cash disbursed or the fair value of other assets distributed.
   b. An asset acquired by incurring liabilities is recorded at cost—that is, at the present value of the amounts to be paid.
   c. An asset acquired by issuing shares of stock of the acquiring corporation is recorded at the fair value of the asset—that is, shares of stock issued are recorded at the fair value of the consideration received for the stock.

(a) Acquisition by Exchange.   Property, plant, and equipment may be acquired by exchange, as well as by purchase. In that case, the applicable accounting requirements are set forth in APB Opinion No. 29, ''Accounting for Nonmonetary Transactions,'' which defines an exchange (par. 3c) as ''a reciprocal transfer between an enterprise and another entity that results in the enterprise's acquiring assets or services or satisfying liabilities by surrendering other assets or services or incurring other obligations.''

After defining nonmonetary assets (par. 3b) to include property, plant, and equipment, APB Opinion No. 29 goes on to state (par. 18) the general rule:

> Accounting for nonmonetary transactions should be based on the fair values of the assets (or services) involved. . . . Thus, the cost of a nonmonetary asset acquired in exchange for another nonmonetary asset is the fair value of the asset surrendered to obtain it, and a gain or loss should be recognized on the exchange. The fair value of the asset received should be used to measure the cost if it is more clearly evident than the fair value of the asset surrendered.

However, the Opinion recognizes (par. 21) an exception to its general rule if an exchange of nonmonetary assets ''is not essentially the culmination of an earning process.'' In that case, the accounting ''should be based on the recorded amount (after reduction, if appropriate, for an indicated impairment of value) of the nonmonetary asset relinquished.''

Among the exchanges of nonmonetary assets that do not culminate the earning process, the Opinion includes (par. 21b) ''an exchange of a productive asset [defined to include property, plant, and equipment] not held for sale in the ordinary course of business for a similar productive asset or an equivalent interest in the same or similar productive asset.''

However, the rule about basing exchanges of productive (nonmonetary) assets on recorded amounts has its own exception if the exchange includes monetary consideration. In that case, the Opinion (par. 22) states:

> The Board believes that the recipient of the monetary consideration has realized gain on the exchange to the extent that the amount of the monetary receipt exceeds a proportionate share of the recorded amount of the asset surrendered. The portion of the cost applicable to the realized amount should be based on the ratio of the monetary consideration to the total consideration received (monetary consideration plus the estimated fair value of the nonmonetary asset received) or, if more clearly evident, the fair value of the nonmonetary asset transferred. The Board further believes that the entity paying the monetary consideration should not recognize any gain on [an exchange not culminating the earning process] but should record the asset received at the amount of the monetary consideration paid plus the recorded amount of the nonmonetary asset surrendered. If a loss is indicated by the terms of [an exchange not culminating the earning process], the entire indicated loss on the exchange should be recognized.

The FASB's Emerging Issues Task Force later reached a consensus (EITF Issue No. 86-29) that an exchange of nonmonetary assets should be considered a monetary (rather than nonmonetary) transaction if monetary consideration is significant, and agreed that ''significant'' should be defined as at least 25% of the fair value of the exchange.

(b) Acquisition by Issuing Debt.   If property, plant, and equipment are acquired in exchange for payables or other contractual obligations to pay money (referred to collectively as "notes"), APB Opinion No. 21, "Interest on Receivables and Payables" (par. 12), states:

> There should be a general presumption that the rate of interest stipulated by the parties to the transaction represents fair and adequate compensation to the supplier for the use of the related funds.

However, the Opinion continues:

> That presumption . . . must not permit the form of the transaction to prevail over its economic substance and thus would not apply if (1) interest is not stated, or (2) the stated interest rate is unreasonable . . . or (3) the stated face amount of the note is materially different from the current cash sales price for the same or similar items or from the market value of the note at the date of the transaction.

In any of these circumstances, both the assets acquired and the note should be recorded at the fair value of the assets or at the market value of the note, whichever can be more clearly determined. If the amount recorded is not the same as the face value of the note, the difference is a discount or premium, which should be accounted for as interest over the life of the note. If there is no established price for the assets acquired and no evidence of the market value of the note, the amount recorded should be determined by discounting all future payments on the note using an imputed rate of interest.

In selecting the imputed rate of interest to be used, APB Opinion No. 21 (par. 14) states that consideration should be given to:

> (a) An approximation of the prevailing market rates for the source of credit that would provide a market for sale or assignment of the note; (b) the prime or higher rate for notes which are discounted with banks, giving due weight to the credit standing of the maker; (c) published market rates for similar quality bonds; (d) current rates for debentures with substantially identical terms and risks that are traded in open markets; and (e) the current rate charged by investors for first or second mortgage loans on similar property.

(c) Acquisition by Issuing Stock.   Assets acquired by issuing shares of stock should be recorded at either the fair value of the shares issued or the fair value of the property acquired, whichever is more clearly evident.

Smith and Skousen (1987) further explain:

> When securities do not have an established market value, appraisal of the acquired assets by an independent authority may be required to arrive at an objective determination of their fair market value. If satisfactory market values cannot be obtained for either securities issued or the assets acquired, values may have to be established by the board of directors for accounting purposes. The source of the valuation should be disclosed on the balance sheet.

(d) Mixed Acquisition for Lump Sum.   Several assets may be acquired for a lump-sum payment. This type of acquisition is often called a **basket purchase.** It is essential to allocate the joint cost carefully, because the assets may include both depreciable and nondepreciable assets, or the depreciable assets may be depreciated at different rates.

Welsch and Zlatkovich (1989) discuss the methods of allocating **joint costs:**

> The allocation of the purchase price should be based on some realistic indicator of the relative values of the several assets involved, such as current appraised values, tax assessment, cost savings, or the present value of estimated future earnings.

(e) Donated Assets.   Property, plant, and equipment may be donated by shareholders or by governmental or civic groups. Such donations are dealt with in APB Opinion No. 29 as

nonreciprocal transfers. Paragraph 18 of the Opinion concludes that property, plant, and equipment received in nonreciprocal transfers should be recorded at the fair value of the assets received.

A donation may be contingent on some act to be performed by the donee. In that case, Smith and Skousen (1987) recommend:

> The contingent nature of the asset and the capital item should be indicated in the account titles. Account balances should be reported "short" or a special note should be made on the balance sheet. When conditions of the gift have been met, both the increase in assets and in owners' equity should be recognized in the accounts and on the financial statements.

14.4 OVERHEAD ON SELF-CONSTRUCTED ASSETS.   Companies often construct their own buildings and equipment. Materials and labor directly identifiable with the construction are part of its cost.

As to whether overhead should be included in the cost of construction, Lamden, Gerboth, and McRae (1975) suggest:

> In the absence of compelling evidence to the contrary, overhead costs considered to have "discernible future benefits" for the purpose of determining the cost of inventory should be presumed to have "discernible future benefits" for the purpose of determining the cost of a self-constructed depreciable asset.

Mosich and Larsen (1986) agree and go on to discuss two alternative views as to what overhead should be included:

> **Allocate Only Incremental Overhead Costs to the Self-Constructed Asset.** This approach may be defended on the grounds that incremental overhead costs represent the relevant cost that management considered in making the decision to construct the asset. Fixed overhead costs, it is argued, are period costs. Because they would have been incurred in any case, there is no relationship between the fixed overhead costs and the self-constructed project. This approach has been widely used in practice because it does not distort the cost of normal operations.
>
> **Allocate a Portion of All Overhead Costs to the Self-Constructed Asset.** The argument for this approach is that the proper function of cost allocation is to relate all costs incurred in an accounting period to the output of that period. If an enterprise is able to construct an asset and still carry on its regular activities, it has benefited by putting to use some of its *idle capacity*, and this fact should be reflected in larger income. To charge the entire overhead to only a portion of the productive activity is to disregard facts and to understate the cost of the self-constructed asset. This line of reasoning has considerable merit.

14.5 INTEREST CAPITALIZED.   SFAS No. 34, "Capitalization of Interest Cost," (par. 6) states:

> The historical cost of acquiring an asset includes the costs necessarily incurred to bring it to the condition and location necessary for its intended use. If an asset requires a period of time in which to carry out the activities necessary to bring it to that condition and location, the interest cost incurred during that period as a result of expenditures for the asset is a part of the historical cost of acquiring the asset.

Paragraph 9 describes the assets that qualify for interest capitalization:

  a. Assets that are constructed or otherwise produced for an enterprise's own use (including assets constructed or produced for the enterprise by others for which deposits or progress payments have been made).
  b. Assets intended for sale or lease that are constructed or otherwise produced as discrete projects (e.g., ships or real estate developments).

The amount of interest capitalized is computed by applying an interest rate to the average amount of accumulated expenditures for the asset during the period. To the extent that specific new borrowings are associated with the asset, the interest rate on those borrowings may be used. Otherwise, the interest rate should be the weighted average rate applicable to other borrowings outstanding during the period. In no event should the total interest capitalized exceed total interest costs incurred for the period. Imputing interest costs on equity is not permitted.

Descriptions of capitalized interest are often seen in footnotes, such as the following example from 1989 financial statements:

DELTA AIR LINES, INC.

NOTES TO CONSOLIDATED FINANCIAL STATEMENTS

Note 1. Summary of Significant Accounting Policies

Interest Capitalized—Interest attributable to funds used to finance the acquisition of new aircraft and construction of major ground facilities is capitalized as an additional cost of the related asset. Interest is capitalized at the Company's average interest rate on long-term debt or, where applicable, the interest rate related to specific borrowings. Capitalization of interest ceases when the property or equipment is placed in service.

14.6 EXCESS COST.   Assets are normally acquired through arms' length transactions between parties presumed to be acting in their own interests. When that is the case, the full cost of the asset is usually presumed to benefit future periods and is capitalized accordingly. However, evidence may indicate that the cost actually incurred exceeds the cost of acquiring a similar asset from other sources. This excess arises most often in the case of self-constructed assets. When the cost of constructing an asset exceeds the cost that would have been incurred to purchase the same asset, Welsch and Zlatkovich (1989) suggest that "the company should include the excess cost in expense (or loss) of the period in which the self-construction is completed. Failure to do so carries forward cost elements that have no future benefit." Others disagree, arguing that no accounting principle requires that an asset be recorded at its lowest possible cost. If the cost actually incurred can be recovered through future operations, they contend, that cost is the amount at which the asset should be recorded. Practice is mixed.

A variation of this issue arises when a company does not take advantage of **discounts** on purchases paid for within a specified time. Some authorities believe that all discounts, whether taken or not, should be accounted for as reductions in cost. Failing to take advantage of a discount, they argue, does not increase an asset's value; it is a loss due to poor financing practices. Others disagree, and practice is mixed.

14.7 COST OF LAND.   Determining the cost of land presents particular problems, as described by Pyle and Larson (1984):

When land is purchased for a building site, its cost includes the amount paid for the land plus real estate commissions. It also includes escrow and legal fees, fees for examining and insuring the title, and any accrued property taxes paid by the purchaser, as well as expenditures for surveying, clearing, grading, draining, and landscaping. All are part of the cost of the land. Furthermore, any assessments incurred at the time of purchase or later for such things as the installation of streets, sewers, and sidewalks should be debited to the Land account since they add a more or less permanent value to the land.

Excavation of land for building purposes, however, is chargeable to buildings rather than to land.

See Chapter 21 for a discussion of the accounting for land acquired as part of a real estate operation.

(a) Purchase Options.   If a company acquires an option to purchase land and later exercises that option, the cost of the option generally becomes part of the cost of the land. Even if an option lapses without being exercised, its cost can be capitalized if the option is one of a series of options acquired as part of an integrated plan to acquire a site. In that case, if any one of the options is exercised, the cost of all may be capitalized as part of the cost of the site.

(b) Interest.   SFAS No. 34 (par. 11) describes the proper accounting for interest cost related to land:

> Land that is not undergoing activities necessary to get it ready for its intended use is not [an asset qualifying for interest capitalization]. If activities are undertaken for the purpose of developing land for a particular use, the expenditures to acquire the land qualify for interest capitalization while those activities are in progress. The interest cost capitalized on those expenditures is a cost of acquiring the asset that results from those activities. If the resulting asset is a structure, such as a plant or a shopping center, interest capitalized on the land expenditures is part of the acquisition cost of the structure. If the resulting asset is developed land, such as land that is to be sold as developed lots, interest capitalized on the land expenditures is part of the acquisition cost of the developed land.

(c) Other Carrying Charges.   SFAS No. 67, "Accounting for Costs and Initial Rental Operations of Real Estate Projects" (par. 6), states:

> Costs incurred on real estate for property taxes and insurance shall be capitalized as property cost only during periods in which activities necessary to get the property ready for its intended use are in progress. Costs incurred for such items after the property is substantially complete and ready for its intended use shall be charged to expense as incurred.

Even though the scope of the Statement excludes "real estate developed by an enterprise for use in its own operations, other than for sale or rental," this guidance is followed in capitalizing carrying charges generally.

14.8 COST OF ASSETS HELD FOR RESEARCH AND DEVELOPMENT ACTIVITIES. Although SFAS No. 2, "Accounting for Research and Development Costs" (par. 12), generally requires that research and development costs be charged to expense when incurred, it makes an exception (par. 11a) for "the costs of materials (whether from the enterprise's normal inventory or acquired specially for research and development activities) and equipment or facilities that are acquired or constructed for research and development activities and that have alternate future uses (in research and development projects or otherwise)." These costs, the Statement says, "shall be capitalized as tangible assets when acquired or constructed."

IMPAIRMENT OF VALUE

Accounting literature provides only limited guidance for deciding whether a company has the ability to recover the carrying amount of its property, plant, and equipment from future operations and, if it does not, for deciding what accounting recognition should be given to the resulting value impairment.

14.9 AUTHORITATIVE PRONOUNCEMENTS.   SFAS No. 5, "Accounting for Contingencies," (par. 31) recognizes the issue but does not resolve it:

> In some cases, the carrying amount of an operating asset not intended for disposal may exceed the amount expected to be recoverable through future use of that asset even though there has been no physical loss or damage of the asset or threat of such loss or damage. For example, changed

economic conditions may have made recovery of the carrying amount of a productive facility doubtful. The question of whether, in those cases, it is appropriate to write down the carrying amount of the asset to an amount expected to be recoverable through future operations is not covered by this Statement.

APB Statement No. 4, "Basic Concepts and Accounting Principles Underlying Financial Statements of Business Enterprises" (par. 183), recognizes that impairment is sometimes, but not always, recorded:

> In unusual circumstances persuasive evidence may exist of impairment of the utility of productive facilities indicative of an inability to recover cost although the facilities have not become worthless. The amount at which those facilities are carried is sometimes reduced to recoverable cost and a loss recorded prior to disposition or expiration of the useful life of the facilities.

In 1980 the AcSec sent the FASB an AICPA Issues Paper, "Accounting for the Inability to Fully Recover the Carrying Amount of Long-Lived Assets," containing the following advisory conclusions:

1. The inability to fully recover the carrying amount of long-lived assets should be reported in financial statements.
2. The concept of permanent decline is unsatisfactory and an alternative concept should be sought.
3. The probability test in SFAS No. 5 is a workable alternative to the concept of permanent decline.
4. Judgment is necessary in selecting the asset measurement that best predicts future economic benefits, as it is difficult to select one measurement that would be appropriate in all circumstances.
5. If the inability to fully recover the carrying amounts of a long-lived asset is recorded in the accounts, future upward adjustments should be permitted if evidence indicates a recovery.

14.10 EXISTING PRACTICE.   In practice, the conclusions of the AICPA Issues Paper have generally been followed, except for the last one. The Securities and Exchange Commission has consistently rejected registrants' proposals to reverse previous impairment write-downs.

Most impairment write-downs have been in the oil and gas industry, where depressed conditions in the 1980s resulted in asset-carrying amounts far in exces of amounts expected to be recovered through future operations. In fact, the only formal rules for determining the amount of an impairment write-down are the SEC rules for oil and gas companies using the full-cost method of accounting. Those rules prescribe a discounted cash flow analysis for determining the maximum carrying amounts of oil and gas properties.

The following is an example, appearing in 1987 financial statements, of impairment determined by a discounted cash flow analysis in the oil and gas industry.

STRADA CORPORATION

CONSOLIDATED BALANCE SHEET

	1987	1986
	(in thousands)	
Property and equipment:		
Proved oil and gas properties (using successful efforts accounting)		
Producing, net of allowance for impairments of $5,872,000 and $8,673,000 in 1987 and 1986, respectively	7,914	8,511
Undeveloped, net of allowance for impairments of $901,000 and $968,000 in 1987 and 1986, respectively	125	125
Pipelines and compressors, net of allowance for impairments of $2,580,000 and $2,577,000 in 1987 and 1986, respectively	1,078	1,078

CONSOLIDATED STATEMENT OF OPERATIONS

	1987	1986	1985
Expenses			
Provision for impairment of proved oil and gas properties	143	5,165	5,833

NOTES TO CONSOLIDATED FINANCIAL STATEMENTS

Note 1. Basis of Presentation

Property and Equipment:

During 1987, 1986, and 1985, the Company provided write-downs of its capitalized costs that exceeded the future net cash flows from proved oil and gas properties (See Note 15).

Note 15. Oil and Gas Reserve Information (unaudited)

Standardized Measure of Discounted Future Net Cash Flows and Changes Therein Relating to Proved Oil and Gas Reserves

	1987	1986	1985
		(in thousands)	
Future cash inflows	$10,182	$13,291	$20,064
Future production costs	(7,295)	(8,489)	(11,115)
Future income tax expenses			
Future net cash flows	2,887	4,802	8,949
10% annual discount for estimated timing of flows	(393)	(958)	(2,777)
Standardized measure of discounted future net cash flows	$ 2,494	$ 3,844	$ 6,172

Future net cash flows were computed using year-end prices and costs and year-end statutory tax rates (adjusted for permanent differences) that relate to existing proved oil and gas reserves in which the Company has mineral interests. Pricing and cost assumptions used do not necessarily reflect current conditions due to changing economic factors within the industry. The standardized measure of future net cash flows is not intended to represent the fair market value of proved oil and gas reserves.

The discounted future net cash flows reflect the standardized measure of oil and gas reserves as follows:

	Oil and Gas Reserves	Reduction for Pipeline	Total
1987	$3,637	$(1,143)	$2,494
1986	4,978	(1,134)	3,844
1985	7,332	(1,160)	6,172

The Company's pipeline is considered to be support equipment in the standardized measure of discounted net cash flows. Historically, compression and transportation revenues from third parties have provided net income to the Company. Management expects that the pipeline operation will continue to provide net income through compression and transportation charges to third parties and continuing cost controls. Such net income will mitigate the impact of the indicated negative effect of the pipeline on oil and gas reserve values.

The principal sources of change in the standardized measure of discounted future net cash flows are as follows:

	1987	1986	1985
		(in thousands)	
Sales and transfers of oil and gas produced, net of production costs	$(1,177)	$(1,450)	$(2,203)
Net changes in prices and production costs	(179)	(2,395)	(3,602)
Reserves sold or abandoned	(157)	(47)	(2,316)
Development costs incurred during the period			(464)
Revisions of previous quantity estimates	(51)	1,197	(5,915)
Accretion of discount	214	367	1,944
Net change in income taxes			2,176
	(1,350)	(2,328)	(10,380)
Standardized measure of future net cash flows at beginning of year	3,844	6,172	16,552
Standardized measure of future net cash flows at end of year	$2,494	$3,844	$6,172

During 1987, 1986, and 1985, the Company's provisions for impairment of capitalized costs were recorded based on the future net cash flows from proved developed reserves before discounting.

Outside the oil and gas industry, write-downs or disclosures of impairment have been limited. Examples are contained in a 1987 AICPA Financial Report Survey, "Illustrations of Accounting for the Inability to Fully Recover the Carrying Amounts of Long-Lived Assets." The following example is taken from 1985 financial statements.

RAYMARK CORPORATION

NOTES TO FINANCIAL STATEMENTS

Note F. Restructuring

In the third quarter of 1985, the Company implemented a restructuring program to reduce operating costs, dispose of underutilized assets, and to recognize an impairment in the carrying value of a production facility at Manheim. Accordingly, the Company recognized a charge of $10,900 or $3.81 per share. This charge consists of a write-down of certain manufacturing facilities and related inventories to their estimated net realizable value amounting to $5,000 and $3,400 respectively. Additionally, the Company recorded a charge of $2,500 for accrued termination benefits resulting from senior management changes and administrative reductions. These charges are included in the following captions in the consolidated statement of operations: other expenses $5,000; cost of sales $3,400; and selling and administrative expenses $2,500.

Impairment has been considered once by the EITF. Issue No. 84-28 asked, "In assessing the impairment of productive assets, what are the generally accepted accounting principles for determining whether a write-down of those productive assets should be recorded?"

The EITF was unable to reach a consensus. However, the Task Force made the following general observations: (1) Current practice indicates that write-downs as a result of economic impairment are permissible, (2) practice is to not write down assets below a break-even point, based on future cash flows measured either on a gross basis or on a discounted basis, and (3) once written down, the assets are not subsequently written back up. The EITF noted that the dominant practice is to recognize only permanent impairments.

The SEC observer at the EITF meeting noted that when the facts and circumstances suggest that an asset may be impaired and the write-down would be material, the Commission requires a write-down if it is probable that estimated undiscounted future cash flows will be less than the net book value of an asset. However, he stated that the Commission will also accept recognition of impairment based on the discounted value of future cash flows.

Respondents to a 1986 FEI "Survey of Unusual Charges" stated that they used four bases for determining the amount of an impairment write-down: net realizable value, undiscounted expected cash flow, discounted expected cash flow, and a combination of net realizable value and discounted cash flow. Most respondents stated that they use a break-even assumption for determining the new carrying value.

In November 1988, the FASB added to its agenda a project to address the issue of impairment.

EXPENDITURES DURING OWNERSHIP

14.11 DISTINGUISHING CAPITAL EXPENDITURES FROM OPERATING EXPENDITURES. After property, plant, and equipment have been acquired, additional expenditures are incurred to keep the assets in satisfactory operating condition. Certain of these expenditures—capital expenditures—are added to the asset's cost. The remainder—operating expenditures (sometimes called **revenue expenditures**—are charged to expense.

Kohler (1983) defines a capital expenditure as follows:

1. An expenditure intended to benefit future periods, in contrast to a revenue expenditure, which benefits a current period; an addition to a capital asset. The term is generally restricted to expenditures that add fixed-asset units or that have the effect of increasing the capacity, efficiency, life span, or economy of operation of an existing fixed asset.

2. Hence, any expenditure benefiting a future period.

Although the distinction is important, immaterial capital expenditures can be charged to expense.

Expenditures during ownership fall into four categories: (1) maintenance and repairs; (2) replacements, improvements, and additions; (3) rehabilitation; (4) rearrangement and reinstallation.

14.12 MAINTENANCE AND REPAIRS.   The terms maintenance and repairs are generally used interchangeably. However, Kohler (1983) defines them separately, and his definitions are useful in identifying expenditures that should be accounted for as maintenance and repairs.l He defines maintenance (p. 315) as follows:

The keeping of property in operable condition; also, the expense involved. Maintenance costs include outlays for (a) labor and supplies; (b) the replacement of any part that constitutes less than a retirement unit; and (c) major overhauls the items of which may involve elements of the first two classes. Items falling under (a) and (b) are always regarded as operating costs, chargeable to current expense directly or through the medium of a maintenance reserve. . . . Costs under (c) are similarly treated unless they include the replacement of a retirement unit the outlay for which is normally capitalized.

He defines repairs (p. 428) as follows:

The restoration of a capital asset to its full productive capacity, or a contribution thereto, after damage, accident, or prolonged use, without increase in the asset's previously estimated service life or productive capacity. The term includes maintenance primarily "preventive" in character, and capitalizable extraordinary repairs.

(a) Accounting Alternatives.   As Kohler states, except for extraordinary repairs (or major overhauls), discussed below, maintenance and repairs expenditures are accounted for in two ways:

- Charge to expense when the cost is incurred.
- Charge to a maintenance allowance account.

Charge to Expense When the Cost Is Incurred. Since ordinary maintenance and repairs expenditures are regarded as operating costs, they are usually charged directly to expense when incurred.

Charge to a Maintenance Allowance Account. The charge to expense may be accomplished through an allowance account. In some cases, the purpose of an allowance account is to equalize monthly repair costs within a year. Total repair costs are estimated at the beginning of the year, and the total is spread evenly throughout the year. The difference between the estimated and actual amounts at the end of the year is usually spread retroactively over all months of the year rather than being absorbed entirely by the last month. In the balance sheet, this allowance account may be treated as a reduction of the related asset account.

This latter approach is supported by APB Opinion No. 28, "Interim Financial Reporting," (par. 16a):

> When a cost that is expensed for annual reporting purposes clearly benefits two or more interim periods (e.g., annual major repairs), each interim period should be charged for an appropriate portion of the annual cost by the use of accruals or deferrals.

In other cases, the purpose of a maintenance allowance account is to charge the costs of major repairs over the entire period benefited, which may be longer than 1 year. When airlines acquire new aircraft, for example, they begin immediately to accrue the cost of the first engine overhaul, which usually is scheduled for more than 1 year hence. As illustrated by the following example from 1987 financial statements, the accrual charges are credited to a maintenance allowance account, which is then charged for cost of the overhaul.

STATESWEST AIRLINES, INC. AND SUBSIDIARIES

NOTES TO CONSOLIDATED FINANCIAL STATEMENTS

Summary of Significant Accounting Policies

Engine Overhaul Reserve. For all the leased aircraft, the Company accrues maintenance expense, on the basis of hours flown, for the estimated cost of engine overhauls.

(b) Extraordinary Repairs. Welsch, Anthony, and Short (1984) define extraordinary repairs as repairs that

> . . . occur infrequently, involve relatively large amounts of money, and tend to increase the economic usefulness of the asset in the future because of either greater efficiency or longer life, or both. They are represented by major overhauls, complete reconditioning, and major replacements and betterments.

Since expenditures for extraordinary repairs increase the future economic usefulness of an asset, they benefit future periods and are therefore capital expenditures. Ordinarily, they are added to the related asset account, as illustrated in the following example from 1987 financial statements.

AIR MIDWEST, INC. AND SUBSIDIARIES

NOTES TO CONSOLIDATED FINANCIAL STATEMENTS

Note 1. Summary of Significant Accounting Policies

d. Maintenance and Repairs

Major renewals and betterments are capitalized and depreciated over the remaining useful life of the asset.

Some authorities recommend that the expenditures for extraordinary repairs be charged against the accumulated depreciation account. The rationale for charging accumulated depreciation is provided by Smith and Skousen (1987):

> Often it is not possible to identify the cost related to a specific part of an asset. In these instances, by debiting accumulated depreciation, the undepreciated book value is increased without creating a build-up of the gross asset values.

Other authorities argue against debiting accumulated depreciation for extraordinary repairs because the accumulated depreciation on the asset may be less than the cost of the repairs and because the practice allows the original cost of any parts replaced to remain in the asset account.

14.13 REPLACEMENTS, IMPROVEMENTS, AND ADDITIONS. Replacements, improvements, and additions are related concepts. Kohler (1983) defines a replacement as "the substitution of one fixed asset for another, particularly of a new asset for an old, or of a new part for an old part." He defines an improvement (which he calls a "betterment") as "an expenditure having the effect of extending the useful life of an existing fixed asset, increasing its normal rate of output, lowering its operating cost, increasing rather than merely maintaining efficiency or otherwise adding to the worth of benefits it can yield." Improvements ordinarily do not increase the physical size of the productive facility. Such an increase is an addition.

The distinctions between replacement, improvement, and addition notwithstanding, the accounting for all three is substantially the same. Expenditures for them are capital expenditures, that is, additions to property, plant, and equipment. (In practice, immaterial amounts are often charged to expense.) The cost of existing assets that are replaced, together with their related accumulated depreciation accounts, is eliminated from the accounts.

14.14 REHABILITATION. Expenditures to rehabilitate buildings or equipment purchased in a run-down condition with the intention of rehabilitating them should be capitalized. Normally the acquisition price of a rundown asset is less than that of a comparable new asset, and the rehabilitation expenditures benefit future periods. Capitalization of the expenditures is therefore appropriate. However, the total capitalized cost of the asset should not exceed the amount recoverable through operations.

When rehabilitation takes place over an extended period, care should be taken to distinguish between the cost of rehabilitation and the cost of maintenance.

14.15 REARRANGEMENT AND REINSTALLATION. Kieso and Weygandt (1986) describe rearrangement and reinstallation costs and the accounting for them:

> Rearrangement and reinstallation costs, which are expenditures intended to benefit future periods, are different from additions, replacements and improvements. An example is the rearrangement and reinstallation of a group of machines to facilitate future production. If the original installation cost and the accumulated depreciation taken to date can be determined or estimated, the rearrangement and reinstallation cost can be handled as a replacement. If not, which is generally the case, the new costs if material in amount should be capitalized as an asset to be amortized over those future periods expected to benefit. If these costs are not material, if they cannot be separated from other operating expenses, or if their future benefit is questionable, they instead should be expensed in the period in which they are incurred.

DISPOSALS

Asset disposals may be voluntary, through retirement, sale, or trade-in, or involuntary, from fire, storm, flood, or other casualty. In general, these terms have the same meaning for accounting purposes as they do in ordinary discourse. The one exception is retirement, which for accounting purposes, means the removal of an asset from service, whether or not the asset is removed physically. This is clear from Kohler's definition (1983) of retirement as "the removal of a fixed asset from service, following its sale or the end of its productive life, accompanied by the necessary adjustment of fixed asset and depreciation-reserve accounts."

14.16 RETIREMENTS, SALES, AND TRADE-INS. Davidson, Stickney, and Weil (1988) describe the accounting for retirements, which applies also to assets that are sold or traded in:

> When an asset is retired from service, the cost of the asset and the related amount of accumulated depreciation must be removed from the books. As part of this entry, the amount received from the sale or trade-in and any difference between that amount and book value must be recorded. The difference between the proceeds received on retirement and book value is a gain (if positive) or a loss (if negative).

As discussed below, when composite or group rate depreciation is used, no gain or loss on disposal is recognized.

When an asset is traded in, the amount that should in theory be recorded as received from the trade-in is the asset's fair market value (which is not necessarily the amount by which the cash purchase price of the replacement asset is reduced). However, in practice, a reliable market value for the old asset may not be available. In that case, the usual practice is to recognize no gain or loss on the exchange, but to record as the acquisition cost of the replacement asset the net book value of the old asset plus the cash or other consideration paid.

14.17 CASUALTIES. Casualties, the accidental loss or destruction of assets, can give rise to gain or loss, even when the assets are replaced. FIN No. 30, "Accounting for Involuntary Conversions of Nonmonetary Assets to Monetary Assets" (par. 2), makes this clear:

> Involuntary conversions of nonmonetary assets to monetary assets are monetary transactions for which gain or loss shall be recognized even though an enterprise reinvests or is obligated to reinvest the monetary assets in replacement nonmonetary assets.

DEPRECIATION

Property, plant, and equipment used by a business in the production of goods and services, is a **depreciable asset.** That is, its cost is systematically reduced by charges to goods produced or to operations over the asset's estimated service life. That meaning is captured by IAS No. 4, "Depreciation Accounting," which defines depreciable assets as assets that (a) are expected to be used during more than one accounting period, and (b) have a limited useful life, and (c) are held by an enterprise for use in the production or supply of goods and services, for rental to others, or for administrative purposes."

14.18 DEPRECIATION DEFINED. Despite its widespread used, **depreciation** has no single, universal definition. Economists, engineers, the courts, accountants, and others have definitions that meet their particular needs. Seldom are the definitions identical.

The generally accepted accounting definition is set forth in Accounting Terminology Bulletin No. 1:

> Depreciation accounting is a system of accounting which aims to distribute the cost or other basic value of tangible capital assets, less salvage (if any), over the estimated useful life of the unit (which may be a group of assets) in a systematic and rational manner. It is a process of allocation, not of valuation. Depreciation for the year is the portion of the total charge under such a system that is allocated to the year.

As the definition says, the depreciation accounting is "a process of allocation, not of valuation." That is, its purpose is to allocate the net cost (cost less salvage) of an asset over time, not to state the asset at its current or long-term value.

Depreciation, as accountants use the term, applies only to buildings, machinery, and equipment. It is thus distinguished first from depletion, which is a process of allocating the cost of wasting resources, such as mineral deposits, and second from amortization, which is a process of allocating the cost of intangible assets.

14.19 BASIC FACTORS IN THE COMPUTATION OF DEPRECIATION.   Three basic factors enter in the computation of depreciation:

1. The estimate of the service life (sometimes called the useful life) of the asset.
2. The determination of the depreciation base.
3. The choice of a depreciation method.

SERVICE LIFE

14.20 SERVICE LIFE AS DISTINGUISHED FROM PHYSICAL LIFE.   Depreciation allocates the net cost of an asset over its service life, not its physical life. The service life of an asset represents the period of usefulness to its present owner. The physical life of an asset represents its total period of usefulness, perhaps to more than one owner. For any given asset, and any given owner, physical and service life may be identical, or service life may be shorter. For example, a company that supplies automobiles to its sales force may replace its automobiles every 50,000 miles. An automobile's physical life is usually longer than 50,000 miles. But to this particular company, the service life of an automobile is 50,000 miles, and the company's depreciation policies would seek to allocate the net cost of its automobiles over 50,000 miles.

14.21 FACTORS AFFECTING SERVICE LIFE.   Factors affecting service life may be physical or functional:

1. Physical factors:
   a. Wear and tear.
   b. Deterioration and decay.
   c. Damage or destruction.

2. Functional factors:
   a. Inadequacy.
   b. Obsolescence.

(a) Physical Factors.   Mosich and Larsen (1986) discuss physical factors:

Physical deterioration results largely from wear and tear from use and the forces of nature. These physical forces terminate the usefulness of plant assets by rendering them incapable of performing the services for which they were intended and thus set the maximum limit on economic life.

Wear and tear and **deterioration and decay** act gradually and are reasonably predictable. They are ordinarily taken into consideration in estimating service life. **Damage** or **destruction,** on the other hand, usually occurs suddenly, irregularly, infrequently, and unpredictably. It is ordinarily not taken into consideration in estimating service life. Its effects are therefore usually not recognized in the depreciation charge but as a charge to expense when the damage or destruction occurs.

(b) Functional Factors.   Asset **inadequacy** may result from business growth, requiring the company to replace existing assets with larger or more efficient assets. Or assets may become inadequate because of changes in the market, in plant location, in the nature or variety of products manufactured, or in the ownership of the business. For example, a warehouse may be in good structural condition, but if more space is needed and cannot be economically provided by adding a wing or a separate building, the warehouse has become inadequate, and its remaining service life to its present owner is ended.

Obsolescence usually arises from events that are more clearly external, such as **progress, invention,** and **technical improvement.** For example, the Boeing 707 and the Douglas DC-8 jet aircraft made many propeller-driven airplanes obsolete, at least as to major airlines, because propeller-driven planes were no longer economical in long-range service.

A distinction should be made between **ordinary obsolescence** and **extraordinary obsolescence.** Ordinary obsolescence is due to normal, reasonably predictable technical progress; extraordinary obsolescence arises from unforeseen events that result in an asset being abandoned earlier than expected.

The AAA publication, "A Statement of Basic Accounting Theory" (1966), states: "Obsolescence, to the extent it can be quantified by equipment replacement studies or similar means, should be recognized explicitly and regularly." Thus ordinary obsolescence, like wear and tear, should be considered in estimating useful life so that it can be recognized in the annual depreciation charge. But extraordinary obsolescence, like damage or destruction, is recognized outside depreciation accounting as an extraordinary charge when it occurs.

14.22 THE EFFECT OF MAINTENANCE.   As Welsch and Zlatkovich (1989) note, "The useful life of operational assets also is influenced by the repair and maintenance policies of the company." The expected effect of a company's maintenance policy is therefore considered in estimating service lives.

14.23 STATISTICAL METHODS OF ESTIMATING SERVICE LIVES.   In several industries, notably utilities, estimates of service lives have been based on historical analyses of retirement rates for specific groups of assets, such as telephone or electric wire poles. These analyses have resulted in the development of statistical techniques for predicting retirement rates and service lives. Utilities have used such techniques in defending depreciation practices, replacement needs and policies, and investment valuations for rate-making purposes. Statistical techniques are appropriate for any group of homogeneous assets where estimating individual service lives is not possible or practical (e.g., mattresses and linens in a hotel, overhead and underground cables of telephone companies, and rails and ties for railroads).

Grant and Norton (1955) mention other statistical approaches to determining service lives:

1. Actuarial methods, which aim at determining survivor curves and frequency curves for annual retirements, as well as giving estimates of average life. These methods are generally similar to the methods developed by life insurance actuaries for the study of human mortality. They require plant records in sufficient detail so that the age of each unit of plant is known at all times.

2. Turnover methods, which aim only at estimating average life. Since turnover methods require only information about additions and retirements, they require less detail in the plant records than do actuarial methods.

14.24 SERVICE LIVES OF LEASEHOLD IMPROVEMENTS.   Leasehold improvements are depreciated over the shorter of the remaining term of the lease or the expected life of the asset. Lease renewal terms are usually not considered unless renewal is probable.

14.25 REVISIONS OF ESTIMATED SERVICE LIVES.   Service life estimates should be reviewed periodically and revised as appropriate. The NAA Statement on Management Accounting Practices No. 7, "Fixed Asset Accounting: The Allocation of Costs," suggests that reviews of estimates involve operations, management, engineering, and accounting personnel.

A change in the estimated useful lives of depreciable assets should be accounted for as a change in an accounting estimate. As prescribed by APB Opinion No. 20, "Accounting Changes," the change is recognized in the period of change and in future periods affected. If future periods are affected, the Opinion also requires disclosure of the effect on income before extraordinary items, on net income, and on related per-share amounts of the current period. The following is an example of this disclosure from 1987 financial statements:

CROWN CENTRAL PETROLEUM CORPORATION

NOTES TO CONSOLIDATED FINANCIAL STATEMENTS

Note N. Change in Accounting Estimate

In the second quarter of 1987, the Company increased the estimated remaining useful lives of its refinery units based on available technology and anticipated severity of service. Remaining asset lives that averaged 9 years were increased to an average of 20 years. The effects of this change in accounting estimate were to decrease 1987 depreciation expense by approximately $3,224,000 and increase net income by approximately $1,799,000, or $.25 per primary share, ($.18 per fully diluted share).

Accounting changes are discussed in greater detail in Chapter 5.

DEPRECIATION BASE

The cost to be depreciated, otherwise known as the depreciation base, is the total cost of an asset less its estimated net salvage value. When immaterial, net salvage value is commonly ignored.

14.26 NET SALVAGE VALUE.   Kohler's Dictionary for Accountants (1983) defines salvage as: "Value remaining from a fire, wreck, or other accident or from the retirement or scrapping of an asset." Salvage value may be determined by reference to quoted market prices for similar items or to estimated reproduction costs, reduced by an allowance for usage. Salvage value reduced by the cost to remove the asset is net salvage value.

In some cases, for example the retirement of a nuclear power plant, removal cost may exceed salvage value, giving rise to **negative salvage value.** Adding a negative salvage value to the cost of an asset would cause total depreciation to exceed cost, producing at the end of the asset's life a negative carrying value. To avoid that result, depreciation should be limited to the original cost of the asset, with net removal costs accrued separately.

Net salvage value can be taken into account in either of two ways: directly, by reducing the depreciation base; or, indirectly, by adjusting the depreciation rate.

To illustrate the latter, assume an asset with a total cost of $1,000, a service life of 10 years, and an estimated net salvage value of $250. A 7 1/2% rate applied to the cost will yield the same annual depreciation charge as a 10% rate applied to cost less estimated net salvage value. This point should be borne in mind in interpreting stated rates of depreciation; the rates may be applied to the asset cost or to cost less net salvage value.

17.27 PROPERTY UNDER CONSTRUCTION.   Assets usually are not depreciated during construction, which includes any necessary pilot testing or breaking in. Such assets are not in service, and the purpose of depreciation accounting is to allocate the cost of an asset over its service life.

An exception to the general rule arises when an asset under construction is partially used in an income-producing activity. In that case, the part in use should be depreciated. An example is a building that is partially rented while still under construction.

14.28 IDLE AND AUXILIARY EQUIPMENT.   NAA Statement on Management Accounting Practices No. 7 recommends that depreciation be continued on idle, reserve, or standby assets. When the period of idleness is expected to be long, the assets should be set forth separately in the balance sheet, but depreciation should continue.

EITF Issue No. 84-28 raises the question of how idle facilities or facilities operating significantly below normal operating levels should be depreciated. Some EITF members stated that they were aware of a limited number of cases in which the depreciation method for such assets was changed to one of the usage methods (see below), but none expressed knowledge of cases in which depreciation of the assets was totally suspended. The EITF reached no consensus.

14.29 USED ASSETS.   The depreciation base of a used asset is the same as for a new asset, that is, cost less net salvage value. The carrying value of a used asset in the accounts of the previous owner should not be carried over to the accounts of the new owner. See, however, Chapter 6 for the accounting for assets acquired in a business combination.

DEPRECIATION METHODS

Assets are depreciated by a variety of methods, including the following:

1. Straight-line method.
2. Usage methods:
   a. Service-hours method.
   b. Productive-output method.
3. Decreasing-charge methods:
   a. Sum-of-digits method.
   b. Fixed-percentage-of-declining-balance method.
   c. Double-declining-balance method.

4. Interest methods:
   a. Annuity method.
   b. Sinking-fund method.
5. Other methods:
   a. Appraisal method.
   b. Retirement method.
   c. Replacement method.
   d. Arbitrary assignment.

14.30 STRAIGHT-LINE METHOD.   This method recognizes equal periodic depreciation charges over the service life of an asset, thereby making depreciation a function solely of time without regard to asset productivity, efficiency, or usage. The periodic depreciation charge is computed by dividing the cost of the asset, less net salvage value, by the service life expressed in months or years:

$$\frac{\text{Cost} - \text{Net salvage value}}{\text{Service life}} = \text{Depreciation charge per period}$$

Assuming an asset cost $15,000 and has an estimated net salvage value of $750 (5% of cost) and a service life of 10 years, the annual depreciation charge would be $1,425, calculated as follows:

$$\frac{\$15,000 - \$750}{10 \text{ years}} = \$1,425$$

When the use or productivity of an asset differs significantly over its life, the straight-line method produces what some believe is a distorted allocation of costs. For example, if an asset is more productive during its early life than later, some view an equal amount of depreciation in each year as distorted. Nevertheless, the method is widely used because of its simplicity.

A survey reported by Lamden, Gerboth, and McRae (1975) showed that the straight-line method is most frequently used for financial statement purposes by companies with the following characteristics:

1. Relatively large investments in depreciable assets.
2. Relatively high depreciation charges.
3. Stock traded on one of the major stock exchanges or in the over-the-counter market.
4. Managements with a high level of concern for (a) matching costs with revenues and (b) maintaining comparability with other firms in the industry.
5. Managements with a low level of concern for conforming depreciation for financial statement to depreciation for tax purposes.

14.31 USAGE METHODS.   Two other methods, the service-hours method and the productive-output method, vary the periodic depreciation charge to recognize differences in asset use or productivity.

(a) Service-Hours Method.   This method assumes that if an asset is used twice as much in period 1 as in period 2, the depreciation charge should differ accordingly. The depreciation rate is calculated as it is for the straight-line method, except that service life is expressed in terms of hours of use:

$$\frac{\text{Cost} - \text{Net salvage value}}{\text{Service life}} = \text{Rate per hour of use}$$

If an asset cost $15,000 and had an estimated net salvage value of $750 and an estimated service life of 38,000 hours, the calculation would be as follows:

$$\frac{\$15,000 - \$750}{38,000 \text{ hours}} = \$0.375 \text{ per hour of use}$$

If the asset is used 4,000 hours in the first year, the annual depreciation charge would be $1,500 (4,000 hours × $0.375 per hour).

Welsch and Zlatkovich (1989) state, "The service hours method usually is appropriate when obsolescence is not a primary factor in depreciation and the economic service potential of the asset is used up primarily by running time."

(b) Productive-Output Method.   This method is essentially the same as the service-hours method, except that service life is expressed in terms of units of production rather than hours of use. If the asset described above had a service life of 95,000 units of production rather than 38,000 hours of use, the depreciation rate would be calculated as follows:

$$\frac{\$15,000 - \$750}{95,000 \text{ units}} = \$0.15 \text{ per unit of product}$$

Depreciation by the productive-output method is illustrated by the following example from 1987 financial statements:

MCDERMOTT INTERNATIONAL, INC.

NOTES TO CONSOLIDATED FINANCIAL STATEMENTS

Note 3. Change in Depreciation Method

Effective April 1, 1986, McDermott International changed the method of depreciation for major marine vessels from the straight-line method to a units-of-production method based on the utilization of each vessel. Depreciation expense calculated under the units-of-production method may be less than, equal to, or greater than depreciation expense calculated under the straight-line method in any period. McDermott International employs utilization factors as a key element in the management of marine construction operations and believes the units-of-production method, which recognizes both time and utilization factors, accomplishes a better matching of costs and revenues than the straight-line method. The cumulative effect of the change on prior years at March 31, 1986, of $25,711,000, net of income taxes of $17,362,000 ($0.70 per share), is included in the accompanying Consolidated Statement of Income (Loss) and Retained Earnings for the fiscal year ended March 31, 1987. The effect of the change on the fiscal year ended March 31, 1987, was to increase Income from Continuing Operations before Extraordinary Items and Cumulative Effect of Accounting Change and decrease Net Loss $6,556,000 ($0.18 per share). Pro forma amounts showing the effect of applying the units-of-production method of depreciation retroactively, net of related income taxes, are presented in the Consolidated Statement of Income (Loss) and Retained Earnings.

The productive-output method is sometimes used to adjust depreciation calculated by the straight-line method, when asset usage varies from normal. The adjustment may be limited to a specified range, as illustrated in the following example drawn from 1986 financial statements:

WHEELING-PITTSBURGH STEEL CORPORATION

NOTES TO FINANCIAL STATEMENTS

Note G. Property, Plant, and Equipment

The Corporation utilizes the modified units-of-production method of depreciation which recognizes that the depreciation of steelmaking machinery is related to the physical wear of the equipment as well as a time factor. The modified units-of-production method provides for straight-line depreciation charges modified (adjusted) by the level of production activity. On an annual basis, adjustments may not exceed a range of 60% (minimum) to 110% (maximum) of related straight-line depreciation. The adjustments are based on the ratio of actual production to a predetermined norm. Eighty-five percent of capacity is considered the norm for the Corporation's primary steelmaking facilities; 80% of capacity is considered the norm for finishing facilities. No adjustment is made when the production level is equal to norm. In 1986 depreciation under the modified units of production method exceeded straight-line depreciation by $1.5 million or 3.2%. For 1985 and 1984 aggregate straight-line depreciation exceeded that recorded under the modified units-of-production method by $10.1 million or 18.3%, $7.0 million or 12.6%, respectively.

The productive-output method recognizes that not all hours of use are equally productive. Therefore, the theory underlying the preference for a usage method, would point to the productive-output method as the better of the two.

14.32 DECREASING-CHARGE METHODS.   Decreasing-charge methods allocate a higher depreciation charge to the early years of an asset's service life. These methods are justified on the following grounds:

- Most equipment is more efficient (hence more productive) in its early life. Therefore, the early years of service life should bear more of the asset's cost.
- Repairs and maintenance charges generally increase as an asset gets older. Therefore, depreciation charges should decrease as the asset gets older so as to produce a more stable total charge (repairs and maintenance plus depreciation) for the use of the asset during its service life.

(a) Sum-of-Digits Method.   This method applies a decreasing rate to a constant depreciation base (cost less net salvage value). The rate is a fraction. The denominator is the sum of the digits representing periods (years or months) of asset life. The numerator, which changes each period, is the digit assigned to the particular period. Digits are assigned in reverse order. For example, if an asset has an estimated service life of 5 years, the denominator would be 15, calculated as follows:

$$1 + 2 + 3 + 4 + 5 = 15$$

In the first year the rate fraction would be $5/_{15}$, in the second year $4/_{15}$, in the third year $3/_{15}$, and so on. The denominator may be calculated by means of the following formula, where n is the service life in years or months:

$$\frac{n + 1}{2} \times n = \text{Denominator}$$

For example, if the service life is estimated to be 25 years:

$$\frac{25 + 1}{2} \times 25 = 325$$

(b) Fixed-Percentage-of-Declining-Balance Method.   This method produces results similar to the sum-of-digits method. However, whereas the sum-of-digits method multiplies a declining rate times a fixed balance, the fixed-percentage-of-declining-balance method multiplies a fixed rate times a declining balance. The rate is calculated by means of the following formula, where n equals the service life in years:

$$\text{Depreciation rate} = 1 - \sqrt[n]{\frac{\text{Net salvage value}}{\text{Cost}}}$$

The rate thus determined is then applied to the cost of the asset, without regard to salvage value, reduced by depreciation previously recognized. The result is to reduce the cost of the asset to its estimated net salvage value at the end of the asset's service life. (Some salvage value must be assigned to the asset, since it is not possible to reduce an amount to zero by applying a constant rate to a successively smaller remainder. In the absence of an expected salvage value, a nominal value of $1 can be assumed.)

To illustrate, assume an asset with a cost of $10,000, an estimated salvage value of $1,296, and an estimated service life of 4 years:

$$\text{Depreciation rate} = 1 - \sqrt[4]{\frac{\$1,296}{\$10,000}} = 1 - \frac{6}{10} = 40\%$$

The first year's depreciation will be $4,000 ($10,000 × 40%), the second year's $2,400 [($10,000 − $4,000) × 40%], and so on, leaving at the end of the fourth year a net asset of $1,296.

(c) Double-Declining-Balance Method.   The double-declining-balance method was introduced into the income tax laws in 1954. Since then, it has gained increased acceptability for financial reporting as well. This method differs from the fixed-percentage-of-declining-balance method by specifying that the fixed rate should be twice the straight-line rate. Otherwise the two methods are identical: The fixed rate is applied to the undepreciated book value of the asset—a declining balance.

To illustrate, assume an asset with a cost of $15,000, an estimated net salvage value of $750, and an estimated service life of 10 years. Twice the straight-line rate would be 20%. Exhibit 14.1 shows the calculation for the first 4 years.

Year	Book Value Beginning of Period	Rate (%)	Annual Depreciation Charge	Book Value End of Period
1	$15,000	20%	$3,000	$12,000
2	12,000	20	2,400	9,600
3	9,600	20	1,920	7,680
4	7,680	20	1,536	6,144

Exhibit 14.1. Depreciation using the double-declining-balance method.

Note that, as with the fixed-percentage-of-declining-balance method, the rate is applied to the cost of the asset without regard to net salvage value. This means that by the end of the asset's estimated service life, some amount of undepreciated book value will be left in the asset account. But since the depreciation rate is determined without regard to estimated net salvage value, the undepreciated amount left in the account will likely differ from net salvage value. For example, at the end of the 10-year service life of the asset illustrated in Exhibit 14.1, the asset's book value would be $1,611, which is $861 greater than estimated net salvage value. To avoid such differences, companies usually switch from the double-declining-balance method to the straight-line method sometime during an asset's service life. For tax purposes, the switch does not require prior IRS approval.

To calculate the straight-line depreciation charge at the time of the switch, the net book value (cost less accumulated depreciation), less estimated net salvage value, is divided by the estimated remaining service life. For example, if an asset has a remaining depreciation base (cost less estimated net salvage value) of $4,620 and 7 years of remaining service life, a straight-line charge of $660 for the next 7 years will depreciate the asset to its net salvage value.

The optimal time to make a switch is when the year's depreciation computed using the straight-line method exceeds depreciation computed using the double-declining-balance method. That is usually sometime after the midpoint of the asset's life.

Exhibit 14.2 compares the annual depreciation charges computed by the straight-line method, the sum-of-digits method, and the double-declining-balance method with switch to straight-line.

Note that although all three methods charge the same total amount to expense over the same service life, the amounts charged at the midpoint of the asset's service life differ:

Year	Straight-Line	Sum-of-Digits	Double-Declining-Balance, Switch to Straight-Line
1	$ 1,425	$ 2,591	$ 3,000
2	1,425	2,332	2,400
3	1,425	2,073	1,920
4	1,425	1,814	1,536
5	1,425	1,555	1,229
6	1,425	1,295	983
7	1,425	1,036	796
8	1,425	777	796
9	1,425	518	795
10	1,425	259	795
	$14,250	$14,250	$14,250

Exhibit 14.2. Comparison of annual depreciation charges: straight-line, sum-of-digits, and declining-balance with switch to straight line.

1. Straight-line has charged 50% of the total.
2. Sum-of-digits has charged nearly 73%.
3. Double-declining-balance with switch to straight-line has charged about 71%.

14.33 INTEREST METHODS.   Two methods, the annuity method and the sinking-fund method, compute depreciation using compound interest factors. Both methods produce an increasing annual depreciation charge. Neither method is used much in practice.

(a) Annuity Method.   The annuity method equalizes each year's sum of depreciation and an imputed interest charge calculated at a constant rate on the asset's undepreciated book value. Each year's sum of depreciation and imputed interest is calculated by the following formula, where n is the estimated service life of the asset in years and i is the imputed rate of interest:

$$\frac{\text{Cost of asset less present value of net salvage value}}{\text{Present value of an ordinary annuity of } n \text{ payments of 1 at } i}$$

Assume, for example, that an asset with an economic life of 5 years and a net salvage value of $67,388 is acquired at a cost of $800,000. Using an imputed rate of interest of 10%, each year's sum of depreciation and imputed interest would be computed as follows:

$$= \frac{\$800,000 - (\$67,388 \times 0.620921^*)}{3.790787}$$

$$= \frac{\$800,000 - \$41,843}{3.790787}$$

$$= \$200,000$$

*Present value of $1 for five periods at 10%.

The result is presented in Exhibit 14.3.
Imputed interest is computed only for purposes of computing depreciation; it is not charged to expense.

(b) Sinking-Fund Method.   The sinking-fund method produces a depreciation pattern that is identical to that of the annuity method but by means of a different rationale and a different

Year	Combined Depreciation and Imputed Interest	Imputed Interest (10% of Carrying Amount)	Depreciation	Accumulated Depreciation	Carrying Amount of Asset
0					$800,000
1	$ 200,000	$ 80,000	$120,000	$120,000	680,000
2	200,000	68,000	132,000	252,000	548,000
3	200,000	54,800	145,200	397,200	402,800
4	200,000	40,280	159,720	556,920	243,080
5	200,000	24,308	175,692	732,612	67,388
	$1,000,000	$267,388	$732,612		

Exhibit 14.3.   Depreciation using the annuity method. *Source:* Mosich and Larsen, *Intermediate Accounting,* McGraw-Hill, 1986, p. 627 (adapted).

formula. Under the sinking-fund method, the amount of annual depreciation is equal to the increase in a hypothetical interest-earning asset replacement fund. The increase in the fund consists of assumed equal periodic deposits to the fund plus interest at the assumed rate on the fund balance.

Each year's depreciation charge is calculated by the following formula, where n is the remaining service life of the asset in years and i is the assumed rate of interest:

$$\text{Depreciation} = \frac{\text{Cost of asset less net residual value}}{\text{Ordinary annuity of } n \text{ payments of 1 at } i}$$

Using the same facts as in Exhibit 14.3 (an asset cost of $800,000, a 5-year life, a net salvage value of $67,388, and a 10% interest rate) the first year's depreciation would be computed as follows:

$$\text{Depreciation} = \frac{\text{Cost of asset less net residual value}}{\text{Ordinary annuity of 5 payments of 1 at 10\%}}$$

$$= \frac{\$800,000 - \$67,388}{6.1051}$$

$$= \$120,000$$

14.34 OTHER METHODS.   The other methods described below attempt to distribute the net cost of an asset over its service life. But none are, properly speaking, depreciation methods.

(a) Appraisal Method.   This method reduces the asset's book value to an appraised value at the end of each year. As such, it is a method of asset valuation, not of cost allocation, and thus is not a method of depreciation accounting. It is also hard to apply in practice, since a going-concern appraisal value can seldom be determined with enough accuracy to result in an objective measurement.

(b) Retirement and Replacement Methods.   Neither of these methods is a depreciation method, since they do not distribute the cost of an asset over its estimated useful life. The retirement method writes off the entire depreciation base in the period in which the asset is retired from service. The replacement method charges depreciation for the cost of replacement assets. Under both methods, no depreciation is charged until the first retirement takes place.

Also under both methods, the property accounts on the balance sheet carry gross costs. Under the retirement method, the property accounts show the gross cost of any asset currently in use. Under the replacement method, the accounts show the gross cost of the original plant acquisitions.

Retirement and replacement methods have been used by utilities because of the practical problems encountered in depreciating large numbers of interrelated items, such as rails, ties, poles, and pipe sections, whose individual cost is small. In such situations, service life is hard to estimate, and the distinction between maintenance and replacement is often unclear.

(c) Arbitrary Assignment.   Arbitrary assignment is not a method of depreciation, since it is not "systematic and rational." It is also highly subjective and open to abuse.

14.35 DEPRECIATION FOR PARTIAL PERIODS.   Since assets are acquired and disposed of throughout the year, companies must compute depreciation for partial periods. Five computation alternatives are found in practice:

1. Depreciation is recognized to the nearest whole month. Assets acquired on or before the 15th of the month or sold after the 15th are reduced by a full month's depreciation; assets acquired after the 15th or sold on or before the 15th are excluded from the month's depreciation computation.

2. Depreciation is recognized to the nearest whole year. Assets acquired during the first 6 months or sold during the last 6 months are reduced by a full year's depreciation; assets acquired during the last 6 months or sold during the first 6 months are excluded from the year's depreciation computation.

3. One-half year's depreciation only is recognized on all assets purchased or sold during the year.

4. No depreciation is recognized on all assets purchased or sold during the year.

5. A full year's depreciation is recognized on assets acquired during the year; none is recognized on assets retired during the year.

14.36 CHANGE IN DEPRECIATION METHOD.   A change in depreciation method is a change in an accounting principle. In accordance with APB Opinion No. 20 (par. 18), the cumulative effect of the change is recognized in net income of the period of change. Accounting changes are discussed more fully in Chapter 5.

DEPRECIATION RATES

14.37 SOURCES OF DEPRECIATION RATES.   Information concerning depreciation rates for various classes of business property is available from several sources. Depreciation rates have been given attention by authors of manuals on accounting, engineering, management, rate making, and other aspects of the business process. They have been the subject of special investigation by industry through individual studies and studies conducted under the auspices of manufacturing and other trade associations.

The choice of depreciation rates has also been influenced by the requirements of tax law and regulation, discussed later in this chapter.

14.38 GROUP AND COMPOSITE RATES.   A group of assets may be depreciated at a single rate. Assets of electrical utilities and hotels are sometimes depreciated in this manner. The two most common methods of depreciating asset groups are the group depreciation method and the collective depreciation method.

(a) Group Depreciation.   Mosich and Larsen (1986) define group depreciation as the "process of averaging the economic lives of a number of plant assets and computing depreciation on the entire class of assets as if it were an operating unit." Smith and Skousen (1987) elaborate:

> Because the accumulated depreciation account under the group procedure applies to the entire group of assets, it is not related to any specific asset. Thus, no book value can be calculated for any specific asset and there are no fully depreciated assets. To arrive at the periodic depreciation charge, the depreciation rate is applied to the recorded cost of all assets remaining in service, regardless of age.

To illustrate, assume that a company purchased a group of 100 similar machines having an average expected service life of 5 years at a total cost of $200,000. Of this group, 30 machines are expected to be retired at the end of 4 years, 40 at the end of 5 years, and the remaining 30 at the end of 6 years. Under the group depreciation method, dpreciation is based on the average expected service life of 5 years, which converts to an annual depreciation rate of 20%. This rate is applied to those assets in service each year. Assuming the machines are retired as expected, the charges for depreciation and the changes in the group asset and accumulated depreciation accounts are summarized in Exhibit 14.4.

It should be noted that the depreciation charge per machine-year is $400—one-fifth of the unit price of $2,000. In each of the first 4 years, 100 machines are in use, and the annual depreciation charge is $40,000. In the 5th year, when the number of machines in use drops to 70, the charge is $28,000. In the 6th year, when only 30 units are in use, the charge is $12,000.

When an asset in the group is disposed of, no gain or loss is recognized. The asset's cost is removed from the group asset account, and the difference between the cost and the asset's actual net salvage value is removed from the accumulated depreciation account.

The advantage of group depreciation, according to Smith and Skousen (1987) is "an annual charge that is more closely related to the quantity of productive facilities being used. Gains and losses due solely to normal variations in asset lives are not recognized, and operating results are more meaningfully stated."

But what Smith and Skousen see as an advantage, Geiger (1963) sees as a weakness:

> Since, for all practical purposes, the actual depreciation rate of an item is unknown and is not used, the true gain or loss at time of its sale or disposal cannot be computed. Accordingly, gain or loss on disposal of fixed assets is not recognized in the income accounts.

But Smith and Skousen (1987) counter: "With normal variations in asset lives, the losses not recognized on early retirements are offset by the continued depreciation charges on those assets still in service after the average life has elapsed."

(b) Composite Depreciation.   Composite depreciation applies group depreciation procedures to groups of dissimilar assets with varying service lives.

Exhibit 14.5 illustrates the calculation of composite rates. The composite life of the assets is 9.96 years; the resulting composite depreciation rate is 9.2%. To determine the annual depreciation, the composite rate of 9.2% is applied to the asset account balance at the beginning of the year. The total acquisition cost of $30,000 is thus reduced to the estimated salvage value of $2,500 in 9.96 years.

As in group depreciation, when an asset is disposed of, no gain or loss is recognized. The asset's cost is removed from the group asset account, and the difference between cost and actual net salvage value is removed from the accumulated depreciation account.

Once a composite rate has been established, it is usually continued until a significant event indicates the need for a new rate. Such an event may be a material change in the service lives of the assets included in the group, a major asset addition, or a major asset retirement. Composite depreciation is based on the assumptions that assets are regularly retired near the end of their service lives and that the retired assets are replaced with similar assets. If

End of Year	Depreciation (20% of cost)	Asset			Accumulated Depreciation			Asset Book Value
		Debit	Credit	Balance	Debit	Credit	Balance	
		$200		$200				$200
1	$ 40			200		$ 40	$40	160
2	40			200		40	80	120
3	40			200		40	120	80
4	40		$ 60	140	$ 60	40	100	40
5	28		80	60	80	28	48	12
6	12		60	—	60	12	—	—
	$200	$200	$200	$200	$200	$200		

Exhibit 14.4.   Group depreciation (all amounts in thousands).

Asset Item	Cost	Net Salvage Value	Depreciation Base	Annual Rate	Depreciation
A	$ 2,000	$ —	$ 2,000	20.0%	$ 400
B	5,000	500	4,500	12.0	540
C	8,000	1,000	7,000	10.0	700
D	15,000	1,000	14,000	8.0	1,120
Group	$30,000	$2,500	$27,500		$2,760

Composite life: $27,500 ÷ $2,760 = 9.96 years.
Composite rate: $2,760 ÷ $30,000 = 9.2%.

Exhibit 14.5. Composite depreciation.

replacements do not take place according to the assumptions, if the service lives of replacement assets differ substantially from the service lives of the assets replaced, or if the cost of replacement assets differs materially from the cost of the assets replaced, continued use of the same composite rate is inappropriate.

Mosich and Larsen (1986) discuss the advantages and disadvantages of composite depreciation:

> The primary disadvantage . . . is that the averaging procedure may obscure significant variations from average. The accuracy of the . . . composite depreciation rate may be verified by recomputing depreciation on the straight-line basis for individual plant assets. Any significant discrepancies between the two results require a change in the composite depreciation rate.

> The advantages . . . are simplicity, convenience, and a reduction in the amount of detail involved in plant asset records and depreciation computations. The availability of computers has reduced the force of this argument.

14.39 THE EFFECT OF REPLACEMENTS, IMPROVEMENTS, AND ADDITIONS. As stated in section 14.13, major expenditures that extend the service lives of assets or otherwise benefit future years are capitalized. Such expenditures require new depreciation computations. The new periodic depreciation charge is found by dividing the asset's new book value by the new remaining service life, illustrated for straight-line depreciation, as follows:

Original asset cost (original estimated life, 10 years)	$8,000
Six years' depreciation	−4,800
Net book value before capital expenditure	3,200
Net increase in book value resulting from capital expenditure	2,400
New book value (new estimated life, 8 years)	$5,600
New annual depreciation charge ($5,600 ÷ 8)	$ 700

Retroactive adjustment of previous years' depreciation is not appropriate, since the expenditures benefit future years only.

14.40 TOOLS AND RELATED ASSETS. Tools are sometimes divided into two classes: semidurable (lives of 5 years or more) and perishable. The cost of semidurable tools is capitalized and depreciated, usually at a group or composite rate. The rate is usually high because tools are hard to control.

Perishable tools may be handled in a variety of ways. Their cost may be charged directly to the appropriate expense or production cost account. Or the cost may be capitalized, often at some arbitrarily reduced amount, and written down when periodic inventories reveal shrinkage and deterioration. A third method is to capitalize the original cost and charge all subsequent expenditures for replacements to expense.

DEPRECIATION FOR TAX PURPOSES

Tax regulations contain their own depreciation requirements. Before 1954, the Internal Revenue Service generally allowed only the straight-line method of depreciation. Subsequently, the tax laws and regulations have been amended several times to permit accelerated depreciation methods and arbitrarily short asset lives. As a result, depreciation for financial reporting purposes and depreciation for tax purposes commonly differ. The difference between an asset's tax and accounting basis is a temporary difference that requires interperiod tax allocation under SFAS No. 96, "Accounting for Income Taxes" (see Chapter 17).

14.41 CURRENT REQUIREMENTS.   Depreciation for tax purposes is currently determined under the **accelerated cost recovery system** (ACRS), enacted in the Economic Recovery Act of 1981, and the **modified accelerated cost recovery system** (MACRS), enacted in the Tax Reform Act of 1986. ACRS abandoned the term "depreciation" and replaced it with a cost recovery charge. MACRS provides for accelerated write-offs. In many cases, the asset service lives allowable for tax purposes under ACRS and MACRS are shorter than the realistic economic service lives used for financial reporting purposes.

14.42 MACRS.   MACRS is mandatory for most tangible depreciable property placed in service after December 31, 1986, but not if the taxpayer uses a depreciation method, such as the service-hours method, based on a service life expressed other than in years.

Under MACRS, property other than real estate is depreciated over 3, 5, 7, 10, 15, or 20 years, depending on its classification. Real estate is classified as residential rental property, which is depreciated over 27.5 years, or nonresidential real property, which is depreciated over 31.5 years.

Most property can be depreciated using an alternate method, which computes depreciation using the straight-line method with no salvage value over the applicable MACRS class life.

14.43 ADDITIONAL FIRST-YEAR DEPRECIATION.   The Internal Revenue Code also allows, with certain limitations, up to $10,000 of qualified tangible personal property to be deducted as an expense in the year acquired. The additional expense must be deducted from cost to determine the asset's depreciable base for tax purposes.

FINANCIAL STATEMENT PRESENTATION AND DISCLOSURE

14.44 GENERAL REQUIREMENTS.   APB Opinion No. 12, "Omnibus Opinion—1967" (par. 5), requires the following disclosures in the financial statements or notes:

1. Depreciation expense for the period.
2. Balances of major classes of depreciable assets, by nature or function, at the balance sheet date.
3. Accumulated depreciation, either by major asset classes or in total, at the balance sheet date.
4. A general description of the method or methods used in computing depreciation for major classes of depreciable assets.

Special disclosures may include the method of accounting for fully depreciated assets and liens against property. Ordinarily, the **basis of valuation** is also disclosed. Chapter 3 discusses the SEC's requirements.

14.45 CONSTRUCTION IN PROGRESS.   Payments to contractors for construction in progress are usually recorded as advances, since the payor does not acquire ownership until completion of the construction. Self-constructed assets are normally classified separately as construction in progress until construction is complete.

14.46 GAIN OR LOSS ON RETIREMENT.   Under APB Opinion No. 30, "Reporting the Results of Operations" (par. 23), gains or losses from the sale or abandonment of property, plant, or equipment used in the business are usually not reported as extraordinary items. They are expected to recur as a consequence of customary and continuing business activities. Exceptions are recognized for gains and losses that are "a direct result of a major casualty (such as an earthquake), an expropriation, or a prohibition under a newly enacted law or regulation" and that clearly meet both criteria of unusual nature and infrequency of occurrence.

14.47 FULLY DEPRECIATED AND IDLE ASSETS.   Many authorities recommend that the cost and accumulated depreciation of fully depreciated assets still in use be kept in the accounts until the assets are sold or retired. Stettler (1982) recommends disclosure not only of fully depreciated assets in use, but also of idle assets:

> Disclosure should also be made if there are material amounts of fully depreciated assets still in use or material amounts of assets still subject to depreciation that are not currently in productive use.

14.48 SEGMENT INFORMATION.   SFAS No. 14, "Financial Reporting for Segments of a Business Enterprise," requires disclosure of two items of information about property, plant, and equipment for each reportable segment:

- The aggregate amount of "identifiable assets," which includes all tangible assets, for each reportable segment (par. 26).
- The aggregate amount of depreciation, depletion, and amortization expense and the amount of capital expenditures for each reportable segment (par. 27).

SOURCES AND SUGGESTED REFERENCES

Accounting Principles Board, "Omnibus Opinion—1967" APB Opinion No. 12, AICPA, New York, 1967.

———, "Business Combinations," APB Opinion No. 16, AICPA, New York, 1970.

———, "Accounting Changes," APB Opinion No. 20, AICPA, New York, 1971.

———, "Interest on Receivables and Payables," APB Opinion No. 21, AICPA, New York, 1971.

———, "Interim Financial Reporting," APB Opinion No. 28, AICPA, New York, 1973.

———, "Accounting for Nonmonetary Transactions," APB Opinion No. 29, AICPA, New York, 1973.

———, "Reporting the Results of Operations," APB Opinion No. 30, AICPA, New York, 1973.

———, "Basic Concepts and Accounting Principles Underlying Financial Statements of Business Enterprises," Statement of the Accounting Principles Board No. 4, AICPA, New York, 1970.

American Accounting Association, "A Statement of Basic Accounting Theory," AAA, Sarasota, FL, 1966.

American Institute of Certified Public Accountants, "Accounting Research and Terminology Bulletins—Final Edition," AICPA, New York, 1961.

———, "Accounting for the Inability to Fully Recover the Carrying Amount of Long-Lived Assets," Issues Paper, AICPA, New York, July 15, 1980.

———, "Illustrations of Accounting for the Inability to Fully Recover the Carrying Amounts of Long-Lived Assets," AICPA, New York, April 1987.

Bendel, C. W. "Streamlining the Property Accounting Procedures," *NACA Bulletin*, Vol. 31, No. 11, 1950.

Davidson, Sidney, Stickney, Clyde P., and Weil, Roman L., *Financial Accounting, An Introduction to Concepts, Methods and Uses*, 5th ed., Dryden Press, Hinsdale, IL, 1988.

Financial Accounting Standards Board, "Impairment of Long-Lived Assets and Depreciation of Idle Facilities," EITF Issue No. 84-28, FASB, Stamford, CT, October 18, 1984, December 19, 1985, and February 6, 1986.

———, "Nonmonetary Transactions: Magnitude of Boot and the Exceptions to the Use of Fair Value," EITF Issue No. 86-29, FASB, Stamford, CT, December 3–4, 1986, January 15, 1987, and February 26, 1987.

———, "Applicability of FASB Statement No. 2 to Business Combinations Accounted for by the Purchase Method" FASB Interpretation No. 4, FASB, Stamford, CT, 1975.

———, "Accounting for Involuntary Conversions of Nonmonetary Assets to Monetary Assets," FASB Interpretation No. 30, FASB, Stamford, CT, 1979.

———, "Accounting for Research and Development Costs," Statement of Financial Accounting Standards No. 2, FASB, Stamford, CT, 1974.

———, "Accounting for Contingencies," Statement of Financial Accounting Standards No. 5, FASB, Stamford, CT, 1975.

———, "Financial Reporting for Segments of a Business Enterprise," Statement of Financial Accounting Standards No. 14, FASB, Stamford, CT, 1976.

———, "Capitalization of Interest Cost," Statement of Financial Accounting Standards No. 34, FASB, Stamford, CT, 1979.

———, "Accounting for Costs and Initial Rental Operations of Real Estate Projects," Statement of Financial Accounting Standards No. 67, FASB, Stamford, CT, 1982.

———, "Accounting for Income Taxes," Statement of Financial Accounting Standards No. 96, FASB, Stamford, CT, 1987.

Financial Executives Institute, "Survey of Unusual Charges," Morristown, NJ, September 26, 1986.

Geiger, H. Dwight, "Composite Depreciation under Depreciation Guidelines," *NAA Bulletin*, Vol. 44, No. 11, July 1963.

Grant, E., and Norton, P., *Depreciation*, Ronald Press, New York, 1955.

International Accounting Standards Committee, "Depreciation Accounting," International Accounting Standards No. 4, IASC, London, 1977.

Kieso, Donald E., and Weygandt, Jerry J., *Intermediate Accounting*, 5th ed., Wiley, New York, 1986.

Kohler, Eric Louis, *Kohler's Dictionary for Accountants*, 6th ed., Prentice-Hall, Englewood Cliffs, NJ, 1983.

Lambert, S. J., III, and Lambert, Joyce C., "Concepts and Applications in APB Opinion No. 29," *Journal of Accountancy* March 1977, pp. 60–68.

Lamden, Charles, Gerboth, Dale L., and McRae, Thomas, "Accounting for Depreciable Assets," Accounting Research Monograph No. 1, AICPA, New York, 1975.

Mosich, A. N., and Larsen, E. John, *Intermediate Accounting*, 6th ed., McGraw-Hill, New York, 1986.

National Association of Accountants, Management Accounting Practices Committee, "Fixed Asset Accounting: The Capitalization of Costs," Statement on Management Accounting Practices No. 4, NAA, New York, 1973.

———, "Fixed Asset Accounting: The Allocation of Costs," Statement on Management Accounting Practices No. 7, NAA, New York, 1974.

Pyle, William W., and Larson, Kermit D., *Fundamental Accounting Principles*, 10th ed., Irwin, Homewood, IL, 1984.

Smith, Jay M., and Skousen, K. Fred, *Intermediate Accounting, Comprehensive Volume*, 9th ed., South-Western Publishing, Cincinnati, OH, 1987.

Stettler, Howard F., *Auditing Principles*, 5th ed., Prentice-Hall, Englewood Cliffs, NJ, 1982.

Welsch, Glenn A., Anthony, Robert N., and Short, Daniel G., *Fundamentals of Financial Accounting*, Irwin, Homewood, IL, 1984.

———, and Zlatkovich, Charles T., *Intermediate Accounting*, 8th ed., Irwin, Homewood, IL, 1989.

CHAPTER 15

INTANGIBLE ASSETS

Lester Wolosoff, CPA
Grant Thornton

CONTENTS

CHARACTERIZATION OF INTANGIBLE ASSETS

Intangibles are generally defined as economic resources having no physical existence. Although accounts receivable seem to fit this definition, they are classified as tangible assets. Deferred charges have the same characteristics and are considered to be intangible assets.

One way in which APB Opinion No. 17, "Intangible Assets," classifies intangible assets is based on the ability to identify a specific asset. Identifiable intangible assets include patents, copyrights, trademarks and trade names, franchises, royalty and license agreements, customer and supplier lists, noncompete agreements, favorable leases, and secret formulas and processes. Goodwill, the unidentifiable intangible asset, is defined in APB Opinion No. 17 as the excess cost of an acquired company over the sum of identifiable net assets.

Intangible assets can also be classified by methods other than identifiability. APB Opinion No. 17 (par. 10) indicates that intangible assets can be alternatively categorized by:

1. Manner of acquisition—acquired singly, in groups, or in business combinations or developed internally.
2. Expected period of benefit—limited by law or contract, related to human or economic factors, or indefinite or indeterminate duration.
3. Separability from an entire enterprise—rights transferable without title, salable, or inseparable from the enterprise or a substantial part of it.

GENERAL PRINCIPLES OF ACCOUNTING FOR INTANGIBLE ASSETS

15.1 INITIAL VALUATION.   APB Opinion No. 17 requires that the cost of intangible assets acquired from others be recorded as assets. Cost is generally measured by the amount of cash disbursed. However, when other than cash is used, the fair value of assets distributed, the present value of amounts to be paid for liabilities incurred, the fair value of consideration received for stock issued or the fair value of stock issued, whichever is more reliable, should be used to measure the cost of the asset.

(a) Valuation of Intangibles in Business Combinations.   Under APB Opinion No. 16, "Business Combinations," in a business combination accounted for as a purchase, identified and named intangible assets should be recorded at fair value. If such assets have a tax basis different from the cost otherwise appropriate to assign, the future tax effects of the differences should be considered in recording the fair value of the assets. The impact of these tax effects depends on numerous factors, as stated in APB Opinion No. 16 (par. 89), including the imminence or delay of realization of the asset value and the possible timing of tax consequences. Prior to the promulgation of SFAS No. 96, "Accounting for Income Taxes," differences in tax basis and the fair value of intangible assets acquired in a purchase transaction were not recorded in deferred tax accounts.

This has been amended by SFAS No. 96 (par. 23), under which a deferred tax liability or asset is recognized as prescribed according to the rules of SFAS No. 96 for differences between the assigned values and the tax bases of the assets and liabilities (except for goodwill, unallocated negative goodwill and leveraged leases). The net of tax accounting required by APB Opinion No. 16 and the custom of discounting the tax effects are eliminated for years after the adoption of SFAS No. 96. As a result, retroactive adoption of SFAS No. 96 to years of or prior to a major business combination can produce materially significant differences in the valuation of intangibles. Adoption of SFAS No. 96 is not required until fiscal years beginning after December 15, 1991.

(b) Valuation of Internally Developed Intangibles.   APB Opinion No. 17 does not specify the initial valuation of identifiable intangible assets that are developed internally. However, some specific intangibles are covered by other authoritative literature such as SFAS No. 2, "Accounting for Research and Development Costs," which requires the expensing of research and development costs as incurred.

SFAS No. 86, "Accounting for the Costs of Computer Software to Be Sold, Leased, or Otherwise Marketed," establishes criteria for the expensing or capitalization of internally developed costs and purchased software to be sold, leased, or otherwise marketed.

Other intangible assets that are internally developed, such as patents and trademarks, may result in a recorded asset to the extent that direct costs are incurred although they are not specifically covered by authoritative literature. For example, in obtaining a patent, legal fees, filing fees, and other expenses may be capitalized.

(c) Valuation of Goodwill.   The cost of unidentifiable assets (goodwill) is deferred only if acquired from others. Deferral of the costs of developing, maintaining, or restoring intangible assets that are not specifically identifiable (goodwill) is prohibited by APB Opinion No. 17 (par. 24).

Goodwill is usually acquired as part of a group of assets or as part of the purchase of a business as a whole. In a purchase transaction, goodwill is measured by the difference between the total cost of the assets acquired and the sum of the costs assigned to specifically identifiable tangible and intangible assets less the liabilities assumed. Accordingly, the principal difference between measuring costs for identifiable intangible assets and costs for goodwill is that identifiable intangibles are valued directly, but goodwill is valued as a "residual."

When the fair value of the net assets acquired exceeds the cost, the residual is referred to as "negative goodwill." Determination of this residual may result in a reduction in the values assigned to the identifiable tangible and intangible assets acquired in the transaction with the remaining balance reflected as a deferred credit on the balance sheet.

15.2 AMORTIZATION.   Amortization of intangibles differs for those that have a limited life and those that have an unlimited life. Limited life intangibles include such items as patents, licenses, and franchises with a fixed term. Unlimited life intangibles include goodwill, trademarks, secret processes and formulas, and perpetual franchises. APB Opinion No. 17

(par. 23) requires minimum and maximum amortization periods for all intangibles. This conclusion is based on the assumption that the value of all intangible assets, whether their lives are limited or unlimited, becomes zero at some point, even though the requirement for minimum and maximum amortization is necessarily arbitrary. Amortization is required whether the asset was acquired or internally developed.

The cost of intangible assets acquired from others cannot be charged against income in the period of acquisition, nor can any intangible assets be amortized over a period longer than 40 years. APB Opinion No. 17 (par. 27) indicates that the cost of each intangible asset should be amortized over the estimated period of benefit of that specific asset. Several factors noted by APB Opinion No. 17 should be considered in estimating the useful life:

1. Legal, regulatory, or contractual provisions may limit the maximum useful life.
2. Provisions for renewal or extension may alter a specified limit on useful life.
3. The effects of obsolescence, demand, competition and other economic factors may reduce a useful life.
4. A useful life may parallel the service life expectancies of individuals or groups of employees.
5. Expected actions of competitors and others may restrict present competitive advantages.
6. An apparently unlimited useful life may in fact be indefinite and benefits cannot be reasonably projected.
7. An intangible asset may be a composite of many individual factors with varying effective lives.

For intangible assets with indeterminate lives that are likely to exceed 40 years, costs should be amortized over the maximum period of 40 years. In practice, goodwill is often amortized over shorter periods. Specific rules applicable to banks and thrifts are discussed in section 15.23.

APB Opinion No. 17 (par. 30) requires that the straight-line method of amortization be used unless another systematic method appears more appropriate. However, except for some specialized industries, such as banks and thrifts, methods other than straight-line are rarely encountered. Generally, in computing amortization, no residual value is associated with intangibles and such assets are usually amortized to zero.

Periodically, management should reevaluate the estimated useful life of the intangible asset to determine whether intervening economic events and circumstances have affected the remaining useful life. If it appears that the remaining useful life of the asset should be revised, this change in estimate is reflected on a prospective basis under APB Opinion No. 17 (par. 31) by a change in the amortization rate.

APB Opinion No. 16 (par. 91) requires that the deferred credit resulting from negative goodwill be amortized systematically to income over the period expected to be benefited but not in excess of 40 years. In practice it is invariably amortized over shorter periods. The credit may not be added directly to stockholders' equity at the date of acquisition.

15.3 WRITE-OFFS.   Write-offs of intangible assets may be required because of declines in value or disposal.

APB Opinion No. 17 (par. 28) prohibits writing off intangible assets in the period of acquisition. However, the remaining unamortized costs should be written off or down against income in the period in which it is determined that the intangible asset has reduced or has no remaining future benefit.

Caution must be exercised in making the determination to write off unamortized costs of intangible assets. A single loss year or even a few loss years do not necessarily indicate that intangible assets have declined in value. Often some additional economic factor is necessary to show that a decline has occurred. For example, the competitive advantage giving rise to the value of the intangible assets may have disappeared as a result of a change in consumer buying patterns or the availability of substitute products. If the value of the intangible asset was related to service lives of personnel, employee or management turnover may result in a decline in value.

The unamortized cost of specifically identifiable intangible assets is written off when the assets are disposed of by transfer of their special rights or benefits to another party. For example, the transfer or sale of a license to another party results in the remaining unamortized cost of the license being written off as a cost of the sale or transfer.

Goodwill (APB Opinion No. 17, par. 32) cannot be disposed of separately from the enterprise. All or a portion of the unamortized costs of goodwill should be included in the cost of assets sold if a large segment or separable group of the related assets or the acquired enterprise as a whole, is disposed of or if operations are terminated.

15.4 PRE-NOVEMBER 1, 1970, ASSETS.   APB Opinions No. 16 and 17 are effective for intangible assets acquired after October 31, 1970. Intangible assets existing on October 31, 1970, continue to be subject to the requirements of Chapter 5 of ARB No. 43, "Restatement and Revision of Accounting Research Bulletin."

ARB No. 43, as opposed to the APB Opinion No. 17 classification method of identifiability, divides intangibles into two classes—those with a limited term of existence and those with an unlimited term. Intangibles with an unlimited term of existence are not required by ARB No. 43 (Ch. 5, par. 6) to be amortized, unless it becomes evident that the periods benefited by such intangibles have become limited.

If intangible assets existed as of October 31, 1970, but were not being amortized, APB Opinion No. 17 (par. 35) encourages, but does not require, prospective application of the amortization requirement.

In the case of a step acquisition, an AICPA interpretation of APB Opinion No. 17 indicates that, when blocks of stock of an acquired company were purchased both prior to and after October 31, 1970, only the intangibles related to the purchases subsequent to October 31, 1970, are required to be amortized. Amortization of intangibles related to the stock acquired prior to October 31, 1970, is encouraged, but not required.

15.5 FINANCIAL STATEMENT PRESENTATION AND DISCLOSURE

(a) Balance Sheet Presentation of Intangibles.   Each material intangible asset should be separately identified on the face of the balance sheet. However, if there are many intangible assets, greater detail regarding the amount of each specific type may be given in a note. Intangible assets are generally shown in a noncurrent asset section of the balance sheet after tangible assets such as property, plant, and equipment.

Accumulated amortization is generally deducted directly from the asset account. However, it is also permissible to reflect the accumulated amortization in a separate valuation account that is shown as a deduction from the original cost of the asset on the face of the balance sheet or in the notes.

If the allocation of an excess of net assets acquired over cost, negative goodwill, reduces the noncurrent assets to zero value (except long-term investments in marketable securities), the remainder of the excess over cost should be classified as a deferred credit.

(b) Income Statement Presentation of Intangibles.   Amortization of intangible assets may be included in cost of sales or another operating expense category, as applicable.

APB Opinion No. 30 (par. 23) specifically indicates that write-offs of intangible assets should generally not be reported as extraordinary items because they are usual in nature or may be expected to recur in the future. However, write-offs of intangible assets may be classified as extraordinary items if they are a direct result of a major casualty, an expropriation, or a prohibition under a newly enacted law or regulation that meets both the unusual nature and infrequency of occurrence tests of APB Opinion No. 30. APB Opinion No. 17 (par. 31) further requires that the reason for any write-off of intangible assets be disclosed.

(c) Cash Flow Statement Presentation of Intangibles.   SFAS No. 95, "Statement of Cash Flows," (par. 28) notes that, under the indirect or reconciliation method of reporting cash flow from operating activities, net income would be adjusted to remove the effect of, among other items, amortization of goodwill. The cash portion of an acquisition of a business would be reported as an investing activity in the statement of cash flows; the noncash portion is disclosed in a supplemental schedule of noncash investing activities.

(d) Disclosure Requirements for Intangibles.   APB Opinion No. 22, "Disclosure of Accounting Policies" (par. 13), requires that the policy with respect to amortization of intangible assets be included in an accounting policies note. APB Opinions No. 16 (par. 95) and 17 (par. 30) require that both the method and period of amortization be disclosed. The method and period of negative goodwill amortization should also be disclosed, as required by APB Opinion No. 16 (par. 91).

Regulation S-X (Rule 5-02.15) requires that each class of intangible asset which is in excess of 5% of the total assets be stated separately along with the basis of determining the respective amounts. Any significant addition or deletion must be explained in a note.

(e) Segment Reporting Presentation of Intangibles.   For public companies subject to SFAS No. 14, "Financial Reporting for Segments of a Business Enterprise" (par. 10), intangible assets are normally identified with specific segments to the extent possible. Intangible assets to be identified with specific segments include goodwill acquired in connection with the purchase of a particular segment or part of the segment.

For public companies subject to the segment reporting requirements of SFAS No. 14, amortization of intangibles is normally included in the operating income of the individual segments.

15.6 TAX CONSIDERATIONS.   An intangible must have a tax basis before it can be amortized for income tax purposes. An intangible will have a tax basis equal to its cost if it is acquired in a transaction that is treated for tax purposes as a purchase of assets or if amounts expended in its development are deferred for tax purposes.

The tax basis of an intangible may differ from its accounting basis. For example, a corporation may acquire all of the assets of another corporation in a purchase transaction that is classified as a nontaxable acquisition for tax purposes. Normally, in a nontaxable transaction, the acquired corporation's tax basis in the transferred assets becomes the acquiring corporation's tax basis. Accordingly, regardless of what basis is allocated to an intangible for accounting purposes, the intangible will not have a tax basis to the acquiring corporation unless it had a tax basis to the acquired corporation.

In a taxable acquisition of an intangible asset, a specific allocation of part of the purchase price to the intangible in an arm's-length contract is the best proof of the cost of the purchased intangible. Detailed cost records are usually accepted as establishing the tax basis of developed intangibles.

Before an intangible with a tax basis can be amortized for tax purposes, it must have a limited useful life, the length of which can be estimated with reasonable accuracy unless the IRC specifies otherwise. Examples of intangibles with a limited life for tax purposes are patents, copyrights, noncompete agreements, favorable leases, and, when a termination period is provided, franchise, royalty, and license agreements.

Although an intangible's life may readily be measured by an objective standard, a shorter useful life for tax purposes may be proper if justified by the surrounding facts and circumstances. To illustrate, by law a U.S. patent has a legal life of 17 years, but in an area of rapid technological development a particular patent may become economically obsolete in a much shorter period.

If the life of an intangible cannot be reasonably estimated, the tax write-off of its cost must be deferred until existing facts establish that its useful life has ended. Examples of intangibles whose lives cannot be reasonably estimated for tax purposes include goodwill, secret formulas and processes, and trademarks and trade names. Customer and supplier lists are usually included in the group of intangibles without reasonable estimated lives, but there may be exceptions based on the actual circumstances.

The IRC provides that research and experimental costs may be expensed currently or, alternatively, amortized over not less than 60 months. The costs of organizing a corporation may be amortized over a period of not less than 60 months. The IRS has ruled that the cost of developing computer software may be expensed currently or, alternatively, amortized over the shorter of its useful life or 5 years.

Usually the term "amortization" is preferred over "depreciation" as a designation for the periodic decline in value of intangibles. When the periodic expensing of the cost of an intangible is allowable for tax purposes, the IRS generally requires the use of the straight-line method over the remaining life of the asset. The use of the declining balance and sum-of-the-years digits methods is specifically prohibited.

IDENTIFIABLE INTANGIBLE ASSETS

15.7 COPYRIGHTS.   A copyright is the exclusive right to reproduce, publish, and sell a literary product or artistic work. The term of the copyright in the United States is now the life of the author plus 50 years. Until January 1, 1978, the period was 28 years plus renewal for an additional 28 years. As in the case of a patent, the rights to a copyright may be assigned, licensed, or sold.

(a) Capitalizable Amounts for Copyrights.   The costs of developing copyrights and the costs of purchased copyrights may be substantial and should be deferred. For a copyright developed internally, costs include expenditures for government filing fees and attorneys' fees and expenses, as well as outlays for wages and materials in the preparation of the material to be copyrighted and expenditures incurred to establish the right. If a copyright is purchased, the initial valuation includes the acquisition price plus any costs incurred in establishing the right.

(b) Amortization of Copyrights.   Copyrighted materials often do not have an active market past the first few years after the issuance of the copyright, and it is usually advisable to write off capitalized costs early in the copyright's legal life, sometimes during the first printing or other use. Amounts are amortized over such a short term because of the difficulty of determining which periods the copyright will benefit. In some cases, rather than writing off costs over an original printing or other use, costs are amortized over the number of years in which sales or royalties related to the copyright can be expected.

Continuing review of the status of copyrights is essential to determine whether they have continuing value. If they do not, they should be written off.

(c) Financial Statements Presentation for Copyrights.   If material, copyrights should be presented separately on the balance sheet at cost less accumulated amortization. The financial statements should disclose the amortization period and method.

15.8 CUSTOMER AND SUPPLIER LISTS.   Customer and supplier lists can be particularly valuable to a business as they represent groups of customers or suppliers with whom business relations have been established. The value of such lists is based on the assumption of continuing business, as well as possibly reducing the marketing costs that would otherwise be necessary.

(a) Capitalizable Amounts for Customer and Supplier Lists.   Customer or supplier lists are often developed internally, and the cost specifically identified with development is generally impossible to determine. Such costs are not deferred, but when lists are purchased from others, the acquisition cost should be deferred.

(b) Amortization of Customer and Supplier Lists.   The value of customer or supplier lists decreases as customers or suppliers are lost or cease to exist. The cost of the list might be written off based on these factors, but in practice it is often difficult to precisely track lost customers or suppliers. Since this particular asset has an otherwise unlimited life, the cost should be written off over a period not to exceed 40 years, with shorter periods advisable in practice. Any remaining unamortized costs should be written off immediately when it is determined that the lists no longer have any value.

(c) Financial Statements Presentation for Customer and Supplier Lists.   Amounts assigned to customer and supplier lists should be presented separately on the balance sheet, if material, at cost less accumulated amortization. The amortization method and period should be disclosed.

15.9 FRANCHISES.   Franchises may be granted by governmental units, individuals, or corporate entities. Public utilities are granted franchises by the communities they serve. These franchises establish the right to operate and specify the conditions under which utilities must function. Such franchises usually place certain restrictions on the enterprise concerning rates and operating conditions, but they also confer certain privileges, ranging from those of a minor nature to the granting of a monopoly. Private franchises are contracts for the exclusive right to perform certain functions or to sell certain (usually branded) products or services. Such agreements involve the use by the franchisee of a trademark, trade name, patent, process, or know-how of the franchisor for the term of the franchise. For example, a manufacturer may grant a dealer a franchise to market a product within a given territory and agree not to allow other dealers to market the same product in that area.

(a) Capitalizable Amounts for Franchise and Amortization Period.   Costs of obtaining a franchise include any fees paid to the franchisor, as well as legal and other expenditures incurred in obtaining the franchise. If a franchise agreement covers a specified period of time, the cost of the franchise should be written off systematically over that period unless the economic life is anticipated to be less. If the franchise is perpetual, the costs should be written off over a period not to exceed 40 years, subject to economic life considerations. If the franchise is revocable at the option of the grantor, it is ordinarily accounted for as if perpetual, although some believe that the cost should be written off over a short period of time. In any event, the unamortized costs assigned to a franchise should be written off when it become evident that the franchise is worthless. Additional periodic payments based on revenues or other factors may be required in addition to initial fees. These period costs are expensed as incurred because they relate only to the current period and represent no future benefit. The franchise agreement may also require certain property improvements that should be capitalized and included in property, plant, and equipment.

(b) Reacquisition of Franchise.   The accounting for the reacquisition of a franchise by a franchisor is governed by SFAS No. 45, "Accounting for Franchise Fee Revenue." If the franchisor refunds the consideration received, revenue previously recognized is to be accounted for as a reduction of revenue in the period the franchise is repossessed. If no refund is made, estimated uncollectible receivables are to be provided for and any retained revenue that was not previously recognized must be reported as current revenue.

If a business combination is, in substance, a cancellation of an original franchise, it is to be accounted for as indicated in the previous paragraph.

(c) Financial Statements Presentation for Franchise.   Franchises should be presented on the balance sheet at cost less accumulated amortization. The financial statements should also disclose the amortization method and term.

15.10 FAVORABLE LEASES AND LEASEHOLD RIGHTS.   A favorable lease is one in which the property rights obtained under the lease could presently be obtained only at a higher rental. This concept is not to be mistaken for the issue of capitalized leases or capital additions classified as leasehold improvements. Favorable leases may be recognized when a business is purchased or when a payment is made to an existing lessee for the right to sublease.

(a) Capitalizable Amounts for Favorable Leases and Leasehold Rights.   The favorable lease is usually measured by the present value of the cost differential between the terms of the lease and the amount that could be obtained currently in an arm's-length transaction.

(b) Amortization of Favorable Leases and Financial Statements Presentation.   The cost assigned to a favorable lease is amortized over the lease term. A lump-sum payment at the inception of the lease should be amortized to rent expense over the life of the lease. The amortization period is the life of the lease without consideration of renewal options.

Favorable leases and leasehold rights should be presented in the balance sheet at cost less accumulated amortization. The amortization method and period should be described.

15.11 NONCOMPETE AGREEMENTS.   Contracts for the purchase of a business often contain an agreement that the seller will not engage in a competing business in a certain area for a specified time period. This provides protection for the buyer from competition from the seller until the buyer can become established in the business. Employment agreements or contracts may also contain such covenants. Assignment of costs to noncompete agreements should be made to reduce the amounts otherwise assignable to goodwill in the purchase of a business. It is also advantageous to the buyer to identify these costs because amortization of a covenant not to compete is deductible for federal income tax purposes, whereas amortization of goodwill is not.

(a) Capitalizable Amounts for Noncompete Agreement.   The amount to be assigned to noncompete agreements should be specified in contracts for sales of businesses to avoid disputes with taxing authorities. If it is not, a reasonable amount of the purchase price should be allocated to the noncompete agreement. It is ordinarily not possible to assign a value to a noncompete agreement contained in an employment contract or agreement, however, since no separate payment is made.

(b) Amortization Period and Financial Statements Presentation.   The cost of a covenant not to compete should be amortized over the period covered by the covenant, unless the estimated economic life is expected to be less. The straight-line method of amortization ordinarily is used.

Noncompete agreements should be presented separately on the balance sheet, if material, at cost less accumulated amortization. The amortization method and term should be disclosed.

15.12 ORGANIZATION COSTS.   Organization costs are expenditures made to promote and organize a concern, including costs of establishing the entity's existence. Such expenses are considered to benefit the future operations of the entity and are not regarded as a current loss or expense.

(a) Capitalizable Amounts for Organization Costs.   Costs to be capitalized include attorney's fees for drafting corporate charters and bylaws, expenses of organizational meetings of directors and shareholders prior to an organization's actual creation, and incorporation fees.

(b) Amortization and Financial Statements Presentation for Organization Costs.
Organization costs have an indeterminate life and thus may be amortized over a period not to exceed 40 years. However, such costs are usually written off over a short period, commonly 5 years, the deductible period for tax purposes.

Deferred organization costs should be presented separately on the balance sheet, if material, at cost less accumulated amortization. The amortization method and period should be disclosed, as well as any unusual write-offs during the period.

15.13 PATENTS.   Accounting for patents is affected by the laws governing the legal rights of a patent holder. A U.S. patent is a nonrenewable right granted by the government of the United States that enables the recipient to exclude others from the manufacture, sale, or other use of an invention for a period of 17 years from the date of the grant. Enforceability of a patent begins only upon the grant of the patent, and the exclusive right of use is not retroactive. However, the filing of a patent application provides protection from the claims of a later inventor for the same item so that, in effect, the period of protection may be considered to extend from the date of the original application. Also, the effective period of competitive advantage may extend beyond the original 17-year patent term if additional patents are obtained as improvements are made. The rights to a patent may be assigned in whole or in part, as well as the right to use the patent (i.e., licenses under the patent) on a royalty or other basis.

(a) Capitalizable Amounts for Patents.   Patents may be purchased from others or developed internally as a result of research and development activities. The cost of a purchased patent includes the purchase price and any related expenditures, such as attorney's fees and other uncovered costs of successful legal actions to protect the patent. If a patent is developed internally, its cost includes legal fees in connection with patent applications, patent fees, litigation fees, litigation costs, costs of sale or licensing, and filing fees. Any related research, experimental and developmental expenditures, including the cost of models and drawings not specifically required for a patent application, are research and development costs and should be expensed as incurred in accordance with SFAS No. 2.

The grant of a patent through the U.S. Patent Office is no guarantee of protection. It is often necessary to defend the patent in court tests of the patent's validity and alleged infringement of other patents, as well as infringement of the patent by others. The costs of successful court tests are generally deferred as these costs establish the patent's validity and enforceability.

However, if the litigation is unsuccessful, the costs of the litigation and any other costs of the affected patent should be written off immediately as the patent obviously no longer has value.

(b) Amortization of Patents.   A U.S. patent has a specified legal life. It provides protection for 17 years, and that is the maximum amortization period. The period used in practice is often less because of technological or market obsolescence, the issuance of new patents to competitors, improved models, substitutes, or general technological progress. These factors must be taken into account in determining the original useful life and its subsequent reviews of remaining economic life. The amortization period should not extend beyond the market life of the product with which the patent is associated, unless the patent can also be used in other applications. However, if it is possible to extend a patent's economic life by obtaining additional patents, it is permissible to amortize the remaining balance of the costs of the old patent over the estimated economic lives of the new ones. Once it is determined that the monopolistic advantage offered by use and ownership of the patent no longer exists, the remaining unamortized balance should be written off. Also, any increases in deferred costs, due to such factors as an additional lawsuit establishing the validity of the patent, should be written off over the remaining estimated economic life of the patent.

(c) Financial Statements Presentation for Patents. If material, patents should be presented separately in the balance sheet, stated at cost less accumulated amortization. Classification of the amortization charge in the income statement depends on the nature and use of the patent. For example, patents related to manufacturing activities are charged to manufacturing expense, whereas patents used in packaging activities may be included in marketing expense. The financial statements should also disclose the method and period of amortization.

15.14 REGISTRATION COSTS. The SEC staff in SAB Topic 5A stated that specific incremental costs directly attributable to a proposed or actual offering of securities may properly be deferred and charged against the gross proceeds of the offering. Management salaries or other general and administrative expenses may not be allocated as costs of the offering. Costs of an aborted offering may not be deferred and charged against a subsequent offering. A postponement of up to 90 days does not represent an aborted offering.

15.15 RELOCATION COSTS. Until recently, there were no guidelines in accounting literature governing the accounting for moving costs. EITF Issue No. 88-10, "Costs Associated with Lease Modification or Termination," dealt with the question of whether moving costs incurred by the lessee in connection with changing from one lease to another lease may be deferred and amortized over the new lease term. The Task Force did not reach a consensus but its members agreed that the predominant practice is to charge the costs of moving to expense as incurred. The SEC observers at their meeting noted that as a general rule the SEC staff would object to the deferral of moving costs.

Subsequent to the EITF consideration of this issue, the FASB issued FTB No. 88-1, "Issues Relating to Accounting for Leases." Paragraph 8 states that "The lessee's immediate recognition of expenses or losses, such as moving expenses, . . . is not changed by this Technical Bulletin." Even if the costs of moving are assumed by the new lessor, the lessee should expense the relocation costs and establish a corresponding deferred credit that is written off over the term of the new lease.

15.16 RESEARCH AND DEVELOPMENT COSTS. SFAS No. 2, "Accounting for Research and Development Costs," (par. 12) requires that research and development costs be charged to expense when incurred:

> Research is planned search or critical investigation aimed at discovery of new knowledge with the hope that such knowledge will be useful in developing a new product or service . . . or a new process or technique . . . or in bringing about a significant improvement to an existing product or process.

> Development is the translation of research findings or other knowledge into a plan or design for a new product or process or for a significant improvement to an existing product or process whether intended for sale or use. It includes the conceptual formulation, design, and testing of product alternatives, construction of prototypes, and operation of pilot plants. It does not include routine or periodic alterations to existing products, production lines, manufacturing processes, and other on-going operations even though those alterations may represent improvements and it does not include market research or market testing activities.

SFAS No. 2 does not apply to R&D costs incurred for others under a contractual agreement or to costs incurred in activities unique to the extractive industries.

Research and development costs, according to SFAS No. 2 (par. 11), include the following elements:

> *Materials, Equipment and Facilities.* The cost of materials . . . and equipment or facilities that are acquired or constructed for research and development activities and that have alternative future uses . . . shall be capitalized as tangible assets when acquired or constructed. The cost of such materials consumed in research and development activities and the depreciation of such

equipment or facilities used in those activities are research and development costs. However, the costs of materials, equipment, or facilities that are acquired or constructed for a particular research and development project and that have no alternative future uses . . . are research and development costs at the time the costs are incurred.

Personnel. Salaries, wages and other related costs of personnel engaged in research and development activities shall be included in research and development costs.

Intangibles Purchased from Others. The costs of intangibles that are purchased from others for use in research and development activities and that have alternative future uses . . . shall be capitalized and amortized as intangible assets in accordance with APB Opinion No. 17. . . . The amortization of those intangible assets used in research and development activities is a research and development cost. However, the costs of intangibles that are purchased from others for a particular research and development project and that have no alternative future uses . . . are research and development costs at the time the costs are incurred.

Contract Services. The costs of services performed by others in connection with the research and development activities of an enterprise, including research and development conducted by others in behalf of the enterprise, shall be included in research and development costs.

Indirect Costs. Research and development costs shall include a reasonable allocation of indirect costs. However, general and administrative costs that are not clearly related to research and development activities shall not be included as research and development costs.

SFAS No. 2 (par. 12) requires that all costs of activities identified as R&D be charged to expense as incurred. The only exception is that government-regulated enterprises may be required to defer certain costs for rate-making purposes. This occurs when the rate regulator reasonably assures the recovery of R&D costs by permitting the inclusion of the costs in allowable costs for rate-making purposes. SFAS No. 2 (par. 13) also requires disclosure of total R&D costs charged to expense in each period.

Intangibles to be used in R&D activities may be acquired through a business combination accounted for by the purchase method. FIN No. 4, "Applicability of FASB Statement No. 2 to Business Combinations Accounted for by the Purchase Method" (par. 4), states the following requirements:

[C]osts shall be assigned to all identifiable tangible and intantible assets, including any resulting from research and development activities of the acquired enterprise or to be used in research and development activities of the combined enterprise. Identifiable assets resulting from research and development activities of the acquired enterprise might include, for example, patents received or applied for, blueprints, formulas, and specifications or designs for new products or processes. Identifiable assets to be used in research and development activities of the combined enterprise might include, for example, materials and supplies, equipment and facilities, and perhaps even a specific research project in process. In either case, the costs to be assigned under APB Opinion No. 16 are determined from the amount paid by the acquiring enterprise and not from the original cost to the acquired enterprise.

Subsequent accounting by the combined enterprise for the costs allocated to assets to be used in R&D activities is prescribed by SFAS No. 2, that is, costs assigned to assets to be used in particular R&D projects and having no alternative future uses are charged to expense at the date of acquisition.

15.17 ROYALTY AND LICENSE AGREEMENTS.   Royalty and license agreements are contracts allowing the use of patented, copyrighted, or proprietary (trade secrets) material in return for royalty payments. An example is the licensing of a patented chemical process for use in a customer's operating system.

The costs to be assigned to royalty and license agreements include any initial payments required plus legal costs incurred in establishing the agreements. Royalty or usage fees are expensed as incurred, because they relate to services of products and not to future benefits.

The capitalized costs of royalty and license agreements should be amortized over the life of the agreement or the expected economic life, whichever is less. Unamortized costs of royalty and license agreements should be written off when it is determined that they have become worthless.

Royalty and license agreements should be stated at original cost less accumulated amortization on the balance sheet and, if material, should be presented separately. The notes to financial statements should disclose the amortization term and method, as well as royalty terms.

15.18 SECRET FORMULAS AND PROCESSES.   A formula or process known only to a particular producer may be a valuable asset, even if not patented. As in the case of a patent, the value of a trade secret is derived from the exclusive control that it gives. Trade secrets, like patents and copyrights, are recognized legal property and are transferable.

Costs that can be directly identified with secret formulas and processes are properly capitalized, except that costs of activities constituting research and development as defined by SFAS No. 2 must be expensed. Costs are normally assigned to secret formulas and processes only as a result of a business combination. Because secret formulas and secret processes have unlimited lives in a legal sense, costs capitalized are to be written off over a period not to exceed 40 years or the estimated economic life, whichever is less. A write-off is required when the value of the formula or process is impaired because of lack of demand for the related product, development of a substitute product or process, loss of exclusivity, or other factors.

Reporting and disclosure of capitalized costs of secret formulas and processes are similar to those of other intangible assets. They should be stated separately in the balance sheet, if material, at cost less accumulated amortization, and the financial statements should disclose the amortization period and method.

15.19 START-UP AND PREOPERATING COSTS.   Start-up and preoperating costs include all nonrecurring, noncapital manufacturing and other costs, such as promotional expenses, incurred in preparing for the operation of new or expanded facilities.

Capitalization of start-up and preoperating costs is supported on the basis that they benefit future periods and should be matched with the revenues of those periods. The start-up or preoperating period ordinarily continues, in the case of manufacturing operations, until a commercially salable product is manufactured and product specifications are met or, in other situations, until normal commercial product specifications start. Start-up and preoperating costs differ from organizational costs in that they relate to the beginning of operations rather than to the establishment of the entity's existence.

Deferral of start-up and preoperating costs is not routine because of the difficulty of assigning benefits to future periods and the possibility that costs will not be recovered from future operations. Deferral of start-up and preoperating costs can be particularly questionable for development stage enterprises.

Costs incurred by an established company entering an established market, such as preopening costs of a new store incurred by an established chain of retail stores, have a greater probability of recovery from future operations. Preopening or preoperating costs that may be deferred comprise those identified and documented as directly related to the specific events.

(a) Capitalizable Amounts for Start-up and Preoperating Costs.   Costs to be deferred include the costs of attorney's fees, site selection, movement of equipment and other property, recruitment and movement of personnel, development of information systems to serve new locations, and cost of production during the start-up phase in excess of predetermined average costs. It is essential to distinguish between start-up and preoperating costs and losses from normal operations. Under no circumstances should continuing operating losses be deferred to future periods.

(b) Amortization of Start-up Costs and Financial Statements Presentation.   Start-up and preoperating costs theoretically benefit the entire period when a facility is used or a product is produced and thus could be amortized over a period not to exceed 40 years. In practice, however, such costs are rarely amortized over a period greater than 10 years and are ordinarily written off over a much shorter period. The straight-line method of amortization can be used, but the unit of production method or other methods are also used. The unamortized balance of start-up and preoperating costs should be written off when it is reasonably evident that the costs have no remaining value or will not be recovered.

Deferred start-up and preoperating costs should be separately stated on the balance sheet, if material, at cost less accumulated amortization. The basis for capitalization and the method and period of amortization should be disclosed.

15.20 TOOLING COSTS.   Initial tooling costs are sometimes treated as an intangible asset, but they are more often considered an element of property, plant, and equipment or, in the case of certain long-term contracts, inventory. SFAS No. 2 (par. 9) states that the design of tools, jigs, molds, and dies involving new technology is a research and development cost, which must be expensed as incurred. However, routine design of those items is not research and development, and the cost may be deferred and amortized over the periods expected to benefit. Deferred tooling may be written off over a period of time (generally less than 5 years, with shorter periods used when tooling relates to products with frequent style or design obsolescence) or anticipated production (using the unit-of-production method). Replacements of parts of tooling for reasons other than changes in the product are usually expensed.

If deferred initial tooling costs are material, the accounting policy regarding those costs should be disclosed. SEC registrants are required to state, if practicable, the amount of unamortized deferred tooling costs applicable to long-term contracts or programs (Regulation S-X, Rule 5.02-6(d)(i)).

15.21 TRADEMARKS AND TRADE NAMES.   Broadly defined, a trademark is any distinguishing label, symbol, or design used by a concern in connection with a product or service. A trade name identifies the entity.

Trademarks can be registered with the U.S. Patent Office to provide access to the federal courts for litigation and to serve as notice of ownership. Proof of prior and continuing use of the trademark is required to obtain and retain the right to use the registered item. Protection of trademarks and trade names that cannot be registered or are not registered can also be sought through common law. These assets have an unlimited life as long as they are used continuously, although technically the term of registration at the U.S. Patent Office is 20 years with indefinite renewal for additional 20-year periods. They may also be registered under the laws of most states. It is customary to consider trademarks and trade names as being of value only as long as they are used. The value of a trademark or trade name consists of the product differentiation and identification that it provides, which theoretically contributes to revenue by enabling a business to sell such products at a higher price than unbranded products. Although closely related to goodwill, trademarks and trade names are property rights that are separately identifiable and, as such, can be assigned or sold.

(a) Capitalizable Amounts for Trademarks and Trade Names Costs.   The cost of a trademark or trade name developed internally consists of legal fees associated with successful litigation involving the trademark or trade name, registration fees, and all developmental expenditures that can be reasonably associated with trademarks, such as payments to design firms. The cost of a purchased trademark or trade name is its purchase price and any other costs required to maintain exclusive use of the mark or name. Obviously, much of the value of a trademark or trade name is established by continuing operations that create a reputation with customers. Some of that reputation, however, may have been gained through the use of advertising and other marketing techniques. The determination of the portion of advertising or marketing expenditures to be considered costs of developing trademarks or trade names and, therefore, potentially capital in nature is generally so subjective that these expenditures should be recorded as current expenses.

(b) Amortization of Trademarks and Trade Names and Financial Statements Presentation. Because of the legal status of trademarks and trade names, established trademarks and trade names have unlimited legal lives as long as they are used. There is no specified statutory life that restricts the amortization period. Thus the general provisions of APB Opinion No. 17 apply, and costs should be written off over a period not to exceed 40 years.

If trademarks or trade names are no longer used or are considered to have no continuing value, unamortized amounts should be written off.

Trademarks and trade names should be shown separately on the balance sheet, if material, at cost less accumulated amortization. The amortization method and period should be disclosed. Trademarks and trade names sometimes are stated at nominal value when costs are expensed as incurred.

INTANGIBLE ASSETS IN SPECIALIZED INDUSTRIES

Intangible assets are particularly significant or receive unique accounting treatment in certain industries.

15.22 AIRLINES. AICPA Industry Audit Guide, Audits of Airlines, as amended by Statement of Position 88-1, "Accounting for Developmental and Preoperating Costs, Purchases and Exchanges of Take-off and Landing Slots, and Airframe Modifications," permits the capitalization of preoperating costs related to integration of new types of aircraft. Amortization of the costs should begin when the new aircraft is ready to be placed in service. The costs of acquiring take-off and landing slots, whether by exchange of stock or through purchase, are identifiable intangible assets to be amortized in conformity with APB Opinion No. 17. Developmental costs related to preparation of new routes should no longer be capitalized as previously permitted by the Audit Guide.

15.23 BANKING AND THRIFTS. APB Opinion No. 17 was amended by SFAS No. 72, "Accounting for Certain Acquisitions of Banking or Thrift Institutions." In banking or thrift acquisitions, goodwill that is created by an excess of the fair value of liabilities assumed over the fair value of tangible and identified intangible assets acquired is to be amortized by the interest method over a period no greater than the estimated remaining life of the long-term, interest-bearing assets acquired. If the assets acquired do not include a significant amount of long-term, interest-bearing assets, such goodwill is to be amortized over a period not exceeding the estimated average life of the existing customer (deposit) base acquired. SFAS No. 72 did not address the amortization period for goodwill arising from excess of cost over net assets acquired, thereby leaving APB Opinion No. 17 as the governing literature for amortization of such remaining goodwill. However, the SEC staff in SAB Topics 2-A3 and 2-A4 stated that, for the remaining goodwill acquired in business combinations after December 23, 1981, the automatic selection of a 40-year amortization period is not appropriate and, for goodwill acquired in business combinations initiated after September 30, 1982, 25 years is the maximum acceptable life.

15.24 BROADCASTING INDUSTRY. The principal intangible assets in the broadcasting industry are Federal Communications Commission licenses, broadcast rights (license agreement to program material) and network affiliation agreements. Television and radio stations may not operate without an FCC license, which specifies, for example, the frequency to be used. A broadcasting license is granted for a 5-year period and is renewable for additional 5-

year periods. The FCC is reluctant to issue new broadcasting licenses unless there is a proven need for an additional station in a particular area. Accordingly, broadcasting licenses are limited as to availability and generally increase in value with the passage of time. Historically, revocations and nonrenewals of licenses have been rare, but there is no guarantee that this situation will continue. Several license renewals have been challenged recently.

Generally, network affiliations make a station more valuable than an independent station in the same geographical area because of the access to network programming and other resources. The contracts effectively have an unlimited life since cancellations and nonrenewals are unusual.

FCC licenses and network affiliation agreements generally are amortized over a period not exceeding 40 years, rather than their legal lives, because of the historical experience of renewal.

(a) Broadcast Rights. Broadcast rights result from a contract or license to exhibit films, programs, or other works and permit one or more exhibitions during a specified license period. Compensation is ordinarily payable in installments over a period shorter than the period of the licensing contract, but it may also take the form of a lump-sum payment at the beginning of the period. The license expires at the end of the contract period. The accounting for broadcast rights is specified in SFAS No. 63, "Financial Reporting by Broadcasters." Amounts recorded for broadcasting rights are to be segregated on the balance sheet as current and noncurrent assets based on estimated usage within one year. Rights should be amortized based on the estimated number of future showings. Items which may be used on an unlimited basis, rather than a limited number of showings, may be amortized over the period covered by the agreement. An accelerated method of amortization is required when the first showing is more valuable than reruns, as is usually the case. Straight-line amortization is allowable only when each telecast or broadcast is expected to generate approximately the same revenue. Feature programs are to be amortized on a program-by-program basis; however, amortization as a package may be appropriate if it approximates the amortization that would have been provided on a program-by-program basis.

The capitalized costs of rights to program material should be reported in the balance sheet at the lower of unamortized cost or estimated net realizable value on a program-by-program, series, package, or daypart basis, as appropriate. If management's expectations of the programming usefulness of a program, series, package, or daypart are revised downward, it may be necessary to write down unamortized cost to estimated net realizable value. Daypart is defined in SFAS No. 63 as an aggregation of programs broadcast during a particular time of day (for example daytime, evening, late night) or programs of a similar type (for example sports, news, children's shows). A write-down from unamortized cost to a lower estimated net realizable value establishes a new cost basis.

(b) Revoked or Nonrenewed Broadcast Licenses. When broadcasting licenses are not renewed or are revoked, unamortized balances should be written off. If a network affiliation is terminated and is not immediately replaced or under agreement to be replaced, the unamortized balance of the amount originally allocated to the network affiliation agreement should be charged to expense. If a network affiliation is terminated and immediately replaced or under agreement to be replaced, a loss is recognized to the extent that the unamortized cost of the terminated affiliation exceeds the fair value of the new affiliation. Gain is not to be recognized if the fair value of the new network affiliation exceeds the unamortized cost of the terminated affiliation.

15.25 CABLE TELEVISION. Cable television companies experience a long preoperating and development period. SFAS No. 51, "Financial Reporting by Cable Television Companies," defines the prematurity period as the period when a cable television system is partially under construction and partially in service. Costs incurred during this period that relate to both current and future operations are partially expensed and partially capitalized. In a cable system, portions or segments that are in the prematurity period and can be clearly distinguished from the remainder of the system should be accounted for separately. Costs incurred to obtain and retain subscribers and general and administrative expenses incurred during the prematurity period are to be expensed as period costs. Programming costs and other system costs that will not vary significantly regardless of the number of subscribers are allocated between current and future operations. The amount currently expensed is based on a relationship of subscribers during the current month (as prescribed in the SFAS) and the total number of subscribers expected at the end of the prematurity period. The capitalized portions decrease each month as the cable company progresses toward the end of the prematurity period. Prior to the prematurity period, system-related costs are capitalized; subsequent thereto, none of these costs are deferred. Capitalized costs should be amortized over the same period used to depreciate the main cable television plant.

Costs of successful franchise applications are capitalized and amortized in accordance with APB Opinion No. 17. Costs of unsuccessful applications and abandoned franchises are charged to expense.

15.26 COMPUTER SOFTWARE.   SFAS No. 86, "Computer Software to Be Sold, Leased, or Otherwise Marketed," prescribes the accounting for the costs of computer software purchased or internally developed as a marketable product by itself. Costs incurred to establish the technological feasibility are charged to expense when incurred. Technological feasibility is established on completion of all planning design, coding, and testing activities necessary to establish that the product can be produced. The completion of a detailed program design or completion of a working model provides evidence of the establishment of technological feasibility. Costs incurred subsequent to the establishment of technological feasibility are capitalized. Software used as an integral part of product or process is not capitalized until both technological feasibility has been established and all research and development activities for the other components have been completed. When the product is available for release to customers, capitalization ceases. Costs of maintenance and customer support are expensed when the related revenue is recognized or when the costs are incurred, whichever occurs first. Purchased software that has alternative future uses should be capitalized but subsequently accounted for according to its use.

Amortization of capitalized software costs is based on the ratio that current gross revenues bear to the total current and anticipated revenues with a minimum amortization equivalent to straight-line over the remaining estimated economic life of the product. The excess of unamortized capitalized costs over a product's net realizable value is written off (and not subsequently restored).

The unamortized computer costs included in the balance sheet, the total amortization charged to expense in each income statement presented and amounts written down to net realizable value should be disclosed.

FIN No. 6 (par. 4) states that, to the extent the acquisition, development, or improvement of a process for use in selling and administrative activities includes costs for computer software, these costs are not research and development costs. Examples given of excluded costs are the development by an airline of a computerized reservation system or the development of a general management information system. SFAS No. 86 does not cover accounting for costs of software used internally. The Board, in Appendix B of SFAS No. 86 (par. 26), stated that it recognized that the majority of companies expense all costs of developing software for internal use and the Board was not persuaded that their predominant practice is improper. It further stated that SFAS No. 86 establishes a high capitalization threshold that is likely to be applied to costs incurred in developing software for internal use as well as for sale or lease to others.

15.27 EXTRACTIVE INDUSTRIES.   Intangible assets in the extractive industries include leased or purchased rights to exploit mineral and other natural resources based on lump-sum, periodic, or production-based payments. The rights are usually included in the property section of the balance sheet. A comprehensive discussion of the accounting for these and other assets in the extractive industries is given in Chapter 20, "Accounting for Oil and Gas Activities."

15.28 PUBLIC UTILITIES.   The general provisions of accounting for intangible assets of various types apply to public utilities. However, since public utilities are required by regulatory agencies to maintain their accounts in accordance with accounting practices that may vary from GAAP, certain differences in treatment may result. An example is research and development costs, which certain regulatory agencies allow to be deferred.

The rate regulator may reasonably assure the existence of an asset by permitting the inclusion of a cost in allowable costs for rate-making purposes. SFAS No. 71, "Accounting for the Effects of Certain Types of Regulation" (par. 9), states the two criteria to be met in order for a utility to capitalize a cost that would otherwise be expensed:

1. It is probable that future revenue in an amount at least equal to the capitalized cost will result from inclusion of that cost in allowable costs for rate-making purposes.
2. Based on available evidence, the future revenue will be provided to permit recovery of the previously incurred cost rather than to provide for expected levels of similar future costs. If the revenue will be provided through an automatic rate-adjustment clause, this criterion requires that the regulator's intent clearly be to permit recovery of the previously incurred cost.

With regard to goodwill, a regulator may permit a utility to amortize purchased goodwill over a specified period, may direct a utility not to amortize goodwill acquired after October 30, 1970, or may direct the utility to write off goodwill. SFAS No. 71 (par. 30) requires the goodwill to be amortized for financial reporting purposes over the period during which it will be allowed for rate-making purposes. If the regulator either excludes amortization from allowable costs for rate-making purposes or directs the utility to write off goodwill, the value of the goodwill may be reduced or eliminated. The goodwill would be amortized for financial reporting purposes but continually evaluated to determine whether it should be reduced significantly by a charge to income in accordance with APB Opinion No. 17.

15.29 RECORD AND MUSIC INDUSTRY.   Significant intangible assets in the record and music industry include record masters, recording artist contracts, and copyrights. Accounting for copyrights generally follows that used in other industries, but the accounting for record masters and recording artist contracts is unique.

SFAS No. 50, "Financial Reporting in the Record and Music Industry," is the primary source of accounting principles in this area. Costs of producing a record master include the costs of musical talent; technical talent for engineering, directing, and mixing; equipment to record and produce the master; and studio facility charges. When past performance of an artist provides a reasonable basis for estimating that the cost of a record master borne by the record company will be recovered from future sales, that cost should be recorded as an asset and, when material, should be separately disclosed. The cost of record masters should be amortized by a method that reasonably relates the cost to the net revenue expected to be realized. Ordinarily, amortization occurs over a very short period. Unamortized amounts should be written off when it becomes apparent that they will not be recovered through future sales. The cost of the record master recoverable from the artist's royalties is to be accounted for as an advance royalty.

A recording artist contract is a contract for personal services. A major portion of the artist's compensation consists of participation in earnings (measured by sales and license fee income, commonly referred to as a "royalty") or of a nonrefundable advance against royalties. Advances should be recorded as an asset (as a prepaid royalty, classified as current or noncurrent depending on when amounts are expected to be realized) if it is anticipated that they will be recovered against royalties otherwise payable to the artist. When it is determined that a prepayment will not be recovered, the balance should be written off.

15.30 TIMBER INDUSTRY.   Companies in the forest products industry may make lump-sum payments for timber-cutting rights, which allow them to remove trees for a specified period or in specified quantities. Lump-sum payments made at the inception of an agreement are properly deferred and amortized over the period of the agreement or on the basis of estimates of recoverable timber. Periodic or production-based payments are expensed as they do not represent future benefits. Cutting rights are ordinarily included in the Property section of the balance sheet and are stated at cost less amortization. The amortization policy should be disclosed.

15.31 TRUCKING INDUSTRY.   The Motor Carrier Act of 1980 substantially reduced interstate trucking regulations and allows much easier entry into the industry. One result was a significant reduction of the value of operating rights.

SFAS No. 44, "Accounting for Intangible Assets of Motor Carriers," requires the unamortized costs of motor carrier intangible assets representing interstate rights to transport goods with limited competition to be charged to income. Other identifible intangible assets and goodwill relating to motor carrier operations are not affected. However, the cost of intrastate operating rights are accounted for in accordance with SFAS No. 44 if a state deregulates motor carriers with effects similar to those of the 1980 Act.

UNIDENTIFIABLE INTANGIBLE ASSETS (GOODWILL)

15.32 INITIAL VALUATION.   APB Opinions No. 16 and No. 17 define accounting for purchased goodwill. APB Opinion No. 16 (par. 68) indicates that the difference between the sum of the assigned values of tangible and identifiable intangible assets acquired less the liabilities assumed and the cost of the groups of assets is evidence of unspecified intangible values. This excess of costs should be recorded as goodwill. For accounting purposes, purchased goodwill is the residual cost remaining after all other identifiable assets and liabilities have been valued.

Although purchased goodwill is generally a residual, sometimes it may be necessary to compute goodwill directly. APB Opinion No. 16 (par. 75) indicates the following:

> If the quoted market price [of an equity security issued] is not the fair value of stock, either preferred or common, the consideration received should be estimated even though measuring directly the fair values of assets received is difficult. Both the consideration received, including goodwill, and the extent of the adjustment of the quoted market price of the stock issued should be weighted to determine the amount to be recorded.

APB Opinion No. 16 (par. 88) identifies the valuation method for the assets to be recorded in a purchase transaction. Specifically excluded as a separate asset to be recorded is any goodwill previously recorded by the acquired company. The only goodwill that should be recorded by the acquiring company is that which resulted from the purchase transaction.

15.33 AMORTIZATION AND WRITE-OFF.   APB Opinion No. 17 (pars. 28–29) requires that goodwill be amortized over its estimated period of benefit. However, the period of benefit should not exceed 40 years. APB Opinion No. 17 also indicates that if the estimated period of benefit exceeds 40 years, the amortization period should be 40 years and not some arbitrary shorter period. In practice, goodwill is often amortized over periods shorter than 40 years (see section 15.23).

APB Opinion No. 17 also specified that the method of amortization is to be straight-line, unless it can be demonstrated that another systematic amortization method is more appropriate. In practice, the straight-line method of amortization is normally used.

Periodically, the remaining expected period of benefit should be reviewed. If the review of the remaining period of benefit results in a change in useful life, the rate of amortization in the future should be adjusted accordingly. Retroactive adjustment of goodwill amortization is not permitted. Any increase in the estimated useful life of the goodwill should not extend beyond 40 years from the date of acquisition.

If the review of the remaining period of benefit determines that a significant reduction in the value of goodwill has occurred, a charge for part or all of the unamortized goodwill should be made to income. However, any write-off of goodwill should not be arbitrary. Even a loss year or several loss years would not, by themselves, be sufficient evidence under the requirements of APB Opinion No. 17 (par. 31) to indicate that the goodwill has been reduced in value. Usually it is necessary to show that the economic conditions and factors that gave rise to the goodwill no longer exist, or the period of benefit of such factors and conditions has expired because of some unexpected event.

Goodwill cannot be disposed of apart from the enterprise as a whole (APB Opinion No. 17, par. 32). If a large segment or separable group of assets of an acquired company, or the entire acquired company is sold or otherwise disposed of, the unamortized cost of goodwill should be included in the cost of assets sold.

15.34 CONTINGENT CONSIDERATION.   Often, in a business combination accounted for by the purchase method, the acquisition agreement provides for contingent consideration. Such contingent consideration can be based on future security prices or future earnings. APB Opinion No. 16 (par. 79) provides that, if the contingent consideration is based on future security prices, any such consideration paid does not change the recorded cost of the acquisition. On the other hand, if the contingent consideration is based on future earnings, any such consideration paid is an additional element of the acquisition cost. Because goodwill is the residual recorded in a purchase acquisition, its cost is generally affected by the payment of contingent consideration based on future earnings. Any change in the goodwill originally recorded as a result of the payment of contingent consideration should be amortized over the remaining estimated period of benefit of the goodwill. Amortization of the goodwill originally recorded in the transaction should not be restated.

Also, any interest or dividends paid with respect to the contingent consideration while in escrow, less any related tax effects of such consideration, are an adjustment to goodwill. These adjustments are also amortized on a prospective basis.

15.35 ADJUSTMENTS TO PURCHASE PRICE.   Under the asset valuation rules of APB Opinion No. 16 (par. 88), the acquiring company generally cannot record the tax benefit of net operating loss carryforwards of an acquired company that exist on the date of acquisition. However, if tax benefits from those loss carryforwards are eventually realized, such benefits should be recognized by reducing retroactively the goodwill recorded in the purchase transaction. A retroactive adjustment of goodwill will also affect previously recorded amortization. Under SFAS No. 96 (par. 23), however, the tax benefits of an acquired operating loss or tax credit carryforwards for financial reporting that are recognized in financial statements after the acquisition date are first applied to reduce goodwill and other noncurrent assets to zero. Any additional tax benefit reduces income tax expense. There is no retroactive adjustment. SFAS No. 96 is effective for years beginning after December 15, 1991.

SFAS No. 38, "Accounting for Preacquisition Contingencies of Purchased Enterprises," provides for a retroactive allocation of the cost of an acquired enterprise during the "allocation period" for contingent assets and liabilities. Although the time period may vary based on the particular circumstances, the allocation period would usually not exceed one year from the date the purchase was consummated. Any such retroactive reallocation of cost would affect previously recorded amounts of goodwill and related amortization.

15.36 PRESENTATION AND DISCLOSURE.   Purchased goodwill, if material, should be shown as a separate noncurrent asset on the balance sheet. Captions to describe goodwill being used in practice include "goodwill, less accumulated amortization," "excess of cost over net assets of subsidiaries purchased," and "excess of cost over tangible value of businesses acquired."

Amortization of purchased goodwill should generally be reflected in the income statement as an operating expense. APB Opinion No. 30 (par. 23) specifically prohibits reflecting write-offs of intangibles, such as goodwill, as extraordinary items. However, if the write-off results from a major casualty, expropriation, or prohibition under a new law or regulation (which new law or regulation must be both unusual in nature and infrequent in occurrence as these items are defined in APB Opinion No. 30), it may be reflected as a extraordinary item.

Also, the write-off of goodwill associated directly with the disposal of a segment of a business is appropriately classified in the income statement as part of the gain or loss on disposal. However, the write-off of goodwill should not include amortization that should have occurred in the normal course of business, prior to the disposal.

In the statement of cash flows, amortization of goodwill is normally a noncash adjustment to net earnings in arriving at cash provided from operating activities.

The notes to financial statements normally disclose the method of amortization and the period of years over which purchased goodwill is being amortized. Also, the notes should disclose the reasons for any write-offs of goodwill during the period.

15.37 NEGATIVE GOODWILL.   Occasionally, the fair value of the assets acquired will exceed the purchase price. The residual is often called "negative" goodwill.

APB Opinion No. 16 (par. 87) recognizes that the sum of the market or appraisal values of identifiable assets acquired, less liabilities assumed, may sometimes exceed the cost of the acquired company. In this circumstance, the excess over cost should be allocated to reduce proportionately the values assigned to noncurrent assets, except long-term investments in marketable securities. If the allocation reduces all noncurrent assets to zero value, any remaining excess should be classified as a deferred credit. APB Opinion No. 16 (par. 92) indicates that no part of the excess should be added directly to stockholders' equity at the date of acquisition.

APB Opinion No. 16 (par. 91) requires that the deferred credit remaining after all noncurrent assets have been reduced to zero be amortized systematically to income over the period estimated to be benefited, but not in excess of 40 years. This deferred credit is frequently amortized to income over a period considerably less than 40 years. In fact, amortization periods as short as 5 years have been used.

There are no specific rules in the authoritative accounting literature governing the write-off and disposal of negative goodwill. However, it can be reasonably assumed that the principles governing the write-off and disposal of positive goodwill are appropriate in this case too. In general, negative goodwill should not be written off unless the economic factors and conditions that give rise to the existence of this deferred credit have changed. However, such a conclusion would be difficult in light of the inability to specifically define the nature of this deferred credit. It can also be presumed that the disposal of this deferred credit cannot occur without the disposal of a substantial portion of the acquired assets.

Negative goodwill, that is, the deferred credit remaining after all noncurrent assets have been reduced to zero, should be identified separately in the balance sheet, if material. This credit will appear in a noncurrent liability section of the balance sheet, appropriately captioned as "excess of fair value of net assets acquired over cost" or some similar designation. It is not appropriate to offset negative goodwill against positive goodwill of prior acquisitions on the balance sheet.

Amortization of negative goodwill is generally reflected as a reduction of operating expenses. The write-off or disposal of negative goodwill should not be reflected as an extraordinary item. It may be appropriate, however, to reflect the negative goodwill as part of disposal of a segment of the business.

It is advisable to describe the circumstances giving rise to negative goodwill, including disclosure of any excess value over cost allocated to noncurrent assets, in a note to the financial statements of the period of acquisition. The notes, as required by APB Opinion No. 16 (par. 91), should also disclose the method and period of amortization for negative goodwill. The circumstances surrounding any write-off or disposal of negative goodwill should be disclosed.

15.38 PUSH DOWN ACCOUNTING.   Push down accounting refers to the reflection, in the separate financial statements of the acquired subsidiary, of the fair value of the assets purchased and the liabilities assumed by the parent. The parent's cost as allocated to the assets and liabilities of the acquired company (the subsidiary) is accordingly pushed down to the subsidiary. Where push down accounting is applied, goodwill and other intangibles acquired by the parent would be reflected in the subsidiary's separate financial statements. The Accounting Standards Division of the AICPA discussed push down accounting in the Issues Paper, "Push Down Accounting," dated October 30, 1979. The FASB is addressing the issue in its project on consolidation accounting. The SEC, in SAB Topic 5J, has stated that, where the purchase transaction results in an entity becoming substantially wholly owned, a new basis of accounting for the purchased assets and liabilities should be pushed down to the subsidiary's separate financial statements.

SOURCES AND SUGGESTED REFERENCES

Accounting Principles Board, "Business Combinations," APB Opinion No. 16, AICPA, New York, 1970.

———, "Intangible Assets," APB Opinion No. 17, AICPA, New York, 1970.

———, "Disclosure of Accounting Policies," APB Opinion No. 22, AICPA, New York, 1973.

———, "Reporting the Results of Operations," APB Opinion No. 30, AICPA, New York, 1973.

———, "Restatement of Revision of Accounting Research Bulletins," Accounting Research Bulletin No. 43, AICPA, New York, 1968.

American Institute of Certified Public Accountants, "Push Down Accounting," Issues Paper, AICPA, New York, 1979.

———, "Accounting for Developmental and Preoperating Costs, Purchases and Exchanges of Take-off and Landing Slots, and Airframe Modifications," Statement of Position 88-1, AICPA, New York, 1988.

———, "Unofficial Accounting Interpretations of APB Opinion No. 17," AICPA, New York, 1973.

Financial Accounting Standards Board, "Costs Associated with Lease Modifications or Termination," EITF Issue No. 87-10, FASB, Norwalk, CT, 1988.

———, "Applicability of FASB Statement No. 2 to Business Combinations Accounted for by the Purchase Method (an interpretation of FASB Statement No. 2)," FASB Interpretation No. 4, FASB, Stamford, CT, 1975.

———, "Applicability of FASB Statement No. 2 to Computer Software (an interpretation of FASB Statement No. 2)," FASB Interpretation No. 6, FASB, Stamford, CT, 1975.

———, "Accounting for Research and Development Costs," Statement of Financial Accounting Standards No. 2, FASB, Stamford, CT, 1974.

———, "Financial Reporting for Segments of a Business Enterprise," Statement of Financial Accounting Standards No. 14, FASB, Stamford, CT, 1976.

———, "Accounting for Preacquisition Contingencies of Purchased Enterprises" (an amendment of APB Opinion No. 16), Statement of Financial Accounting Standards No. 38, FASB, Stamford, CT, 1980.

———, "Accounting for Intangible Assets of Motor Carriers," Statement of Financial Accounting Standards No. 44, FASB, Stamford, CT, 1980.

———, "Accounting for Franchise Fee Revenue," Statement of Financial Accounting Standards No. 45, FASB, Stamford, CT, 1981.

———, "Financial Reporting in the Record and Music Industry," Statement of Financial Accounting Standards No. 50, FASB, Stamford, CT, 1981.

———, "Financial Reporting by Cable Television Companies," Statement of Financial Accounting Standards No. 51, FASB, Stamford, CT, 1981.

———, "Financial Reporting by Broadcasters," Statement of Financial Accounting Standards No. 63, FASB, Stamford, CT, 1982.

———, "Accounting for the Effects of Certain Types of Regulation," Statement of Financial Accounting Standards No. 71, FASB, Stamford, CT, 1982.

———, "Accounting for Certain Acquisitions of Banking or Thrift Institutions," Statement of Financial Accounting Standards No. 72, FASB, Stamford, CT, 1983.

———, "Accounting for the Costs of Computer Software to Be Sold, Leased, or Otherwise Marketed," Statement of Financial Accounting Standards No. 86, FASB, Stamford, CT, 1985.

———, "Statement of Cash Flows," Statement of Financial Accounting Standards No. 95, FASB, Stamford, CT, 1987.

———, "Accounting for Income Taxes," Statement of Financial Accounting Standards No. 96, FASB, Stamford, CT, 1987.

———, "Issues Relating to Accounting for Leases," FASB Technical Bulletin No. 88-1, FASB, Norwalk, CT, 1988.

Securities and Exchange Commission, "Acquisitions Involving Financial Institutions," Staff Accounting Bulletin Topic 2-A3, SEC, Washington, DC, 1981.

———, "Amortization of Goodwill by Financial Institutions upon Becoming SEC Registrants," Staff Accounting Bulletin Topic 2-A4, SEC, Washington, DC, 1985.

———, "Expenses of Offering," Staff Accounting Bulletin Topic 5A, SEC, Washington, DC, 1975.

———, "Push Down Basic of Accounting Required in Certain Limited Circumstances," Staff Accounting Bulletin Topic 5J, SEC, Washington, DC, 1983.

CHAPTER 16

LEASES

James R. Adler, PhD, CPA
Checkers, Simon & Rosner

CONTENTS

INTRODUCTION AND BACKGROUND INFORMATION

A lease is an agreement conveying the right to use property, plant, or equipment, usually for a stated period of time. Since World War II, the leasing industry has become a major economic force, and leasing has become a method by which to finance acquisitions of property.

According to the *U.S. News and World Report* (August 14, 1989, p. 45), the U.S. Commerce Department lacks an exact measure of the total revenue developed in the economy by the leasing industry. However, the biggest part of this industry is equipment leasing, a $117-billion business that doubled itself between 1985 and 1989. The rapid growth created by the demand to lease everything from equipment to automobiles, furniture, and even people has caused a highly price-competitive environment.

Lessors earn their profits by buying equipment at lower prices than ordinary buyers, charging brokerage fees, and getting tax deductions for equipment write-offs. The 1986 Tax Reform Act has wiped out tax credits, removing some of the traditional cash flow advantages that lessors could gain upon initiating a leasing transaction.

Traditionally, lessees prefer to have operating leases rather than capital leases so that the future lease payment obligations do not appear on the balance sheet as a liability.

16.1 FINANCING ADVANTAGES OF LEASING. The financing advantages associated with leasing include the following:

- Leasing permits 100% financing, whereas a normal equipment loan may require a 20% to 40% initial down payment. Leasing can thereby conserve cash and working capital.
- Longer terms than are normally available with loans can be arranged for leasing many types of capital equipment.
- Financing of initial acquisition costs is possible because these costs can be included in a lease. Such costs, for example, delivery charges, interest on advance payments, sales or use taxes, and installation costs, are not normally financed under other methods of equipment financing.
- Leasing offers greater convenience than either debt or equity financing because of the reduced documentation.
- The risk of obsolescence can be avoided by the lessee as compared with the risk he would assume on the purchase of such equipment.

16.2 FINANCING DISADVANTAGES OF LEASING. Some of the financing disadvantages associated with leasing are as follows:

- The effective interest rate is generally greater than if the lessee obtained a bank loan for the same term. This may not be true, however, for leveraged leases.
- The lessee suffers the loss of residual rights to the property at the termination of the lease.
- The lessee does not enjoy the tax benefits of accelerated depreciation and interest expense.

ACCOUNTING ISSUES AND PRONOUNCEMENTS

Exhibit 16.1 lists the technical accounting pronouncements concerning leases. These numerous pronouncements are an indication of the complexity and controversy surrounding the accounting for leases. The manufacturer or dealer is concerned with the issue of when a lease becomes a sale with the respective profit and loss recognition. Other lessors are perceived as either renting out their asset or providing financing for the acquisition of this asset by a lessee, depending on the circumstances. Likewise, the lessee either has an asset and a liability or is committed to an obligation to rent an asset. The accounting issues can then be summarized as follows:

1. On whose balance sheet should the leased asset appear?
2. What is the timing of financial statement recognition of lease events?
3. How are measurements made for both balance sheet and income statement effects of leases?
4. What disclosures should be made in the financial statements?

FASB Statements

13	Accounting for Leases
22	Changes in the Provisions of Lease Agreements Resulting from Refundings of Tax-Exempt Debt
23	Inception of the Lease
27	Classification of Renewals or Extensions of Existing Sales-Type or Direct Financing Leases
28	Accounting for Sales with Leasebacks
29	Determining Contingent Rentals
76	Extinguishment of Debt
77	Reporting by Transferors for Transfers of Receivables with Recourse
91	Accounting for Nonrefundable Fees and Costs Associated with Originating or Acquiring Loans and Initial Direct Costs of Leases
94	Consolidation of All Majority-Owned Subsidiaries
96	Accounting for Income Taxes
98	Accounting for Leases:

- Sale-Leaseback Transactions Involving Real Estate
- Sales-Type Leases of Real Estate
- Definition of the Lease Term
- Initial Direct Costs of Direct Financing Leases

FASB Interpretations

19	Lessee Guarantee of the Residual Value of Leased Property (SFAS No. 13)
21	Accounting for Leases in a Business Combination (SFAS No. 13)
23	Leases of Certain Property Owned by a Governmental Unit or Authority (SFAS No. 13)
24	Leases Involving Only Part of a Building (SFAS No. 13)
26	Accounting for Purchase of a Leased Asset by the Lessee During the Term of the Lease (SFAS No. 13)
27	Accounting for a Loss on a Sublease (SFAS No. 13 and APB Opinion No. 30)

FASB Technical Bulletins

79-10	Fiscal Funding Clauses in Lease Agreements
12	Interest Rate Used in Calculating the Present Value of Minimum Lease Payments
13	Applicability of FASB Statement No. 13 to Current Value Financial Statements
14	Upward Adjustment of Guaranteed Residual Values
15	Accounting for Loss on a Sublease Not Involving the Disposal of a Segment
16R	Effect of a Change in Income Tax Rate on the Accounting for Leveraged Leases

(continued)

Exhibit 16.1.   Technical pronouncements on lease accounting.

79-17   Reporting Cumulative Effect Adjustment from Retroactive Application of FASB Statement No. 13
79-18   Transition Requirements of Certain FASB Amendments and Interpretations of FASB Statement No. 13
85-3   Accounting for Operating Leases with Scheduled Rent Increases
86-2   Accounting for an Interest in the Residual Value of a Leased Asset:
         • Acquired by a Third Party or
         • Retained by a Lessor That Sells the Related Minimum Rental Payments
88-1   Issues Relating to Accounting for Leases:
         • Time Pattern of the Physical Use of the Property in an Operating Lease
         • Lease Incentives in an Operating Lease
         • Applicability of Leveraged Lease Accounting to Existing Assets of the Lessor
         • Money-Over-Money Lease Transactions
         • Wrap Lease Transactions

Emerging Issues Task Force Issues

The EITF has discussed and published issue papers on leases as follows:

84-12   Operating Leases with Scheduled Rent Increases
         Status: Consensus reached; nullified by FTB No. 85-3. Additional guidance provided by FTB No. 88-1.
84-25   Offsetting Nonrecourse Debit with Sales-Type or Direct Financing Lease Receivables
         Status: Resolved by FTB No. 86-2 and SAB No. 70.
84-37   Sale-Leaseback Transaction with Repurchase Option
         Status: Partially resolved by SFAS No. 98.
85-16   Leveraged Leases
         a. Real Estate Leases and Sale-Leaseback Leases
         b. Delayed Equity Contributions by Lessors
         Status: Consensus reached. Additional guidance provided by SFAS No. 98.
85-27   Recognition of Receipts From Made-Up Rental Shortfalls
         Status: Consensus reached.
85-32   Purchased Lease Residuals
         Status: Consensus nullified by FTB No. 86-2.
86-17   Deferred Profit on Sale-Leaseback Transaction with Lessee Guarantee of Residual Value
         Status: Consensus reached. Additional guidance provided by SFAS No. 98.
86-33   Tax Indemnification in Lease Agreements
         Status: Consensus reached.
86-43   Effect of a Change in Tax Law on Rates in Leveraged Leases
         Status: Consensus reached.
86-44   Effect of a Change in Tax Law on Investments in Safe Harbor Leases
         Status: Consensus reached.
87-7   Sale of an Asset Subject to a Lease on Nonrecourse Financing: Wrap Lease Transactions
         Status: Consensus reached. Additional guidance provided by FTB No. 88-1.
87-8   Tax Reform Act of 1986: Issues Related to the Alternative Minimum Tax
         Status: Consensus partially nullified by SFAS No. 96.
88-3   Rental Consensus Provided by Landlord
         Status: Resolved by FTB No. 88-1.
88-10   Costs Associated with Lease Modification or Termination
         Status: Consensus reached.
88-21   Accounting for the Sale of Property Subject to the Seller's Preexisting Lease
         Status: Consensus reached.
89-16   Consideration of Executory Costs in Sale-Leaseback Transactions
         Status: Consensus reached.
89-20   Accounting for Cross Border Tax Benefit Leases
         Status: Consensus reached.

Exhibit 16.1. *Continued.*

The FASB issued SFAS No. 13 in November 1976 to resolve the issues. SFAS No. 13 superseded all preceding technical literature and established the primary current standard in accounting for leases. Under this pronouncement when substantially all of the risks and rewards of ownership have passed from the lessor to the lessee, the leased property transfers from the lessor to the lessee. The question of whose asset it is and the related income statement effect are answered by establishing where the substantial risks and rewards of ownership lie. Timing is at the inception of the lease, and measurement is usually at the fair value of the leased property to the lessor at that date.

In January 1990, the FASB released a **codification of the authoritative pronouncements on lease accounting** issued through January 1990. Essentially, the codification is a reproduction of the lease accounting section included in the FASB Current Text. All of the FASB Statements, Interpretations, and Technical Bulletins were utilized and integrated into this publication. However, the discussion of issues by the EITF concerning lease accounting were not included in the codification. When a consensus is reached by the Task Force, the agreement represents current thoughts where no lease accounting standards exist. Additional decisions and issues will be considered by the Task Force in the future and any such consensus previously reached is subject to change. A summary of the proceedings of the Task Force on each lease accounting issue is published by the FASB in the EITF Abstracts.

16.3 LEASE ACCOUNTING CLASSIFICATION—LESSEE.   From the standpoint of the lessee, a lease may be classified as either a **capital lease** or an **operating lease.** If the lease meets any one of the following criteria, then the lessee should classify and account for the arrangement as a capital lease:

1. The lease transfers ownership of the property to the lessee at the end of the lease term.
2. The lease contains a bargain purchase option.
3. The lease term is equal to at least 75% of the estimated economic life of the property. (If the beginning of the lease term falls within the last 25% of the total estimated life including earlier use, this criterion should not be used.)
4. The present value of the minimum lease payments at the beginning of the lease term, excluding that portion of the payments representing executory costs, is 90% or more of the fair value of the leased property to the lessor at the inception date, less any related investment tax credit retained by and expected to be realized by the lessor. The discount rate that the lessee used in computing the present value of the lease payments is the lessee's incremental borrowing rate, defined in SFAS No. 13 as "The rate that, at the inception of the lease, the lessee would have incurred to borrow the funds necessary to buy the leased asset on a secured loan with repayment terms similar to the payment schedule called for in the lease." However, if the lessee knows the implicit rate used by the lessor and that rate is less than the lessee's borrowing rate, SFAS No. 13 requires use of the implicit rate. (If the beginning of the lease term falls within the last 25% of the total estimated life including earlier use, this criterion should not be used.)

Leases that do not meet any of these criteria are classified as operating leases by the lessee.

16.4 LEASE ACCOUNTING CLASSIFICATION—LESSOR.   SFAS No. 13 specifies the following classifications of leases for lessors:

- Direct financing.
- Sales type.
- Operating.
- Leveraged.

A lease is classified as a **direct financing lease** if it meets any one of the four lease classification criteria and, in addition, meets both of the following criteria:

1. Collectibility of the minimum lease payments is reasonably predictable.
2. No important uncertainties surround the amount of unreimbursable costs yet to be incurred by the lessor under the lease.

A lease is classified as a **sales-type lease** if it qualifies as a direct financing lease and, in addition, has a fair market value in excess of the property's carrying value. Sales-type leases are generally associated with dealers and manufacturing lessors. Leases that do not meet these criteria are classified as operating leases. **Leveraged leases** are covered in section 16.17.

16.5 DEFINITIONS OF LEASE TERMS.   The following technical terms have been defined in accounting pronouncements on leases:

1. *Bargain Purchase Option.* A provision allowing the lessee, at the lessee's option, to purchase the leased property for a price that is sufficiently lower than the expected fair value of the property at the date the option becomes exercisable so that exercise of the option appears, at the inception of the lease, to be reasonably assured.
2. *Bargain Renewal Option.* A provision allowing the lessee, at the lessee's option, to renew the lease for a rental sufficiently lower than the fair rental of the property at the date the option becomes exercisable so that exercise of the option appears, at the inception of the lease, to be reasonably assured.
3. *Capital Lease.* A lease that must be capitalized by a lessee because it meets one of the four SFAS No. 13 lease classification criteria.
4. *Contingent Rentals.* The increases or decreases in lease payments that result from changes occurring subsequent to the inception of the lease in the factors (other than the passage of time) on which lease payments are based, except as provided in the following sentence. Any escalation of minimum lease payments relating to increases in construction or acquisition cost of the leased property or for increases in some measure of cost or value during the construction or preconstruction period shall be excluded from contingent rentals. Lease payments that depend on a factor directly related to the future use of the leased property, such as machine hours of use or sales volume during the lease term, are contingent rentals and, accordingly, are excluded from minimum lease payments in their entirety.

   However, lease payments that depend on an existing index or rate, such as the consumer price index or the prime interest rate, shall be included in minimum lease payments based on the index or rate existing at the inception of the lease; any increases or decreases in lease payments that result from subsequent changes in the index or rate are contingent rentals and thus affect the determination of income as accruable.
5. *Direct Financing Leases.* A lease that meets any one of the four SFAS No. 13 lease classification criteria for a lessor plus two additional criteria:
   a. Collectibility of minimum lease payments must be reasonably predictable.
   b. No uncertainties may surround the amount of unreimbursable costs to be incurred by the lessor under the lease.
6. *Estimated Economic Life of Leased Property.* The estimated remaining period during which the property is expected to be economically usable by one or more users, with normal repairs and maintenance, for the purpose for which it was intended at the inception of the lease, without limitation by the lease term.
7. *Estimated Residual Value of Leased Property.* The estimated fair value of the leased property at the end of the lease term.

8. *Executory Costs.* Those costs such as insurance, maintenance, and taxes incurred for leased property, whether paid by the lessor or lessee. Amounts paid by a lessee in consideration for a guarantee from an unrelated third party of the residual value are also executory costs. If executory costs are paid by a lessor, any lessor's profit on those costs is considered the same as executory costs.

9. *Fair Value of the Leased Property.* The price for which the property could be sold in an arm's-length transaction between unrelated parties. The following are examples of the determination of fair value:

   a. When the lessor is a manufacturer or dealer, the fair value of the property at the inception of the lease will ordinarily be its normal selling price, reflecting any volume or trade discounts that may be applicable. However, the determination of fair value shall be made in light of market conditions prevailing at the time, which may indicate that the fair value of the property is less than the normal selling price and, in some instances, less than the cost of the property.

   b. When the lessor is not a manufacturer or dealer, the fair value of the property at the inception of the lease will ordinarily be its cost, reflecting any volume or trade discounts that may be applicable. However, when there has been a significant lapse of time between the acquisition of the property by the lessor and the inception of the lease, the determination of fair value shall be made in light of market conditions prevailing at the inception of the lease, which may indicate that the fair value of the property is greater or less than its cost or carrying amount, if different.

10. *Finance Lease.* A financing device by which a user can acquire use of an asset for most of its useful life. Rentals are net to the lessor, and the user is responsible for maintenance, taxes, and insurance. Rent payments over the life of the lease are sufficient to enable the lessor to recover the cost of the equipment plus interest on its investment.

11. *Inception of the Lease.* The date of the lease agreement or commitment, if earlier. For purposes of this definition, a commitment shall be in writing, signed by the parties in interest to the transaction, and shall specifically set forth the principal provisions of the transaction. If any of the principal provisions is yet to be negotiated, such a preliminary agreement or commitment does not qualify for purposes of this definition.

12. *Initial Direct Costs.* Only those costs incurred by the lessor that are (a) costs to originate a lease incurred in transactions with independent third parties resulting directly from and essential to acquiring that lease and which would not have been incurred had that leasing transaction not occurred, and (b) certain costs directly related to specified activities performed by the lessor for that lease. Those activities include evaluating the prospective lessee's financial condition; evaluating and recording guarantees, collateral, and other security arrangements; negotiating lease terms; preparing and processing lease documents; and closing the transaction. The costs directly related to those activities include only that portion of the employees' total compensation and payroll-related fringe benefits directly related to time spent performing those activities for that lease and other costs related to those activities that would not have been incurred but for that lease. Initial direct costs do not include costs related to activities performed by the lessor for advertising, soliciting potential lessees, servicing existing leases, and other ancillary activities related to establishing and monitoring credit policies, supervision, and administration. They also do not include administrative costs, rent, depreciation, any other occupancy and equipment costs and employees' compensation and fringe benefits related to ancillary activities, unsuccessful origination efforts, and idle time.

13. *Interest Rate Implicit in the Lease.* The discount rate that, when applied to (a) the minimum lease payments, excluding that portion of the payments representing executory costs to be paid by the lessor, together with any profit thereon, and (b) the unguaranteed residual value accruing to the benefit of the lessor causes the aggregate

present value at the beginning of the lease term to be equal to the fair value of the leased property to the lessor at the inception of the lease, minus any investment tax credit retained by the lessor at the inception of the lease and minus any investment tax credit retained by the lessor and expected to be realized by him. (This definition does not necessarily purport to include all factors that a lessor might recognize in determining his rate of return.)

14. *Lease*. An agreement conveying the right to use property, plant, or equipment (land or depreciable assets or both) usually for a stated period of time.

15. *Lease Term*. The fixed noncancelable term of the lease plus:

   a. All periods, if any, covered by bargain renewal options.
   b. All periods, if any, for which failure to renew the lease imposes a penalty on the lessee in such amount that a renewal appears, at the inception of the lease, to be reasonably assured.
   c. All periods, if any, covered by ordinary renewal options during which a guarantee by the lessee of the lessor's debt directly or indirectly related to the leased property is expected to be in effect or a loan from the lessee to the lessor directly or indirectly related to the leased property is expected to be outstanding.
   d. All periods, if any, covered by ordinary renewal options preceding the date as of which a bargain purchase option is exercisable.
   e. All periods, if any, representing renewals or extensions of the lease at the lessor's option. However, in no case shall the lease term be assumed to extend beyond the date a bargain purchase option becomes exercisable.

A lease that is cancelable only upon the occurrence of some remote contingency, only with the permission of the lessor, only if the lessee enters into a new lease with the same lessor, or only if the lessee incurs a penalty in such amount that continuation of the lease appears, at inception, reasonably assured shall be considered "noncancelable" for purposes of this definition.

16. *Lessee's Incremental Borrowing Rate*. The rate that, at the inception of the lease, the lessee would have incurred to borrow over a similar term the funds necessary to purchase the leased asset.

17. *Leveraged Lease*. A lease that meets the definition as a direct financing lease for a lessor and, in addition, has all the following characteristics:

   a. At least three partners are involved: a lessee, a lessor, and a long-term lender.
   b. The financing provided by the lender is substantial to the transaction and without recourse to the lessor.
   c. The lessor's net investment declines during the early years of the lease and rises during the latter years of the lease.

18. *Minimum Lease Payments*

   a. From the standpoint of the lessee: The payments that the lessee is obligated to make or can be required to make in connection with the leased property. Contingent rentals are excluded from minimum lease payments. However, a guarantee by the lessee of the lessor's debt and the lessee's obligation to pay (apart from the rental payments) executory costs in connection with the leased property shall be excluded. If the lease contains a bargain purchase option, only the minimum rental payments over the lease term and the payment called for by the bargain purchase option shall be included in the minimum lease payments. Otherwise, minimum lease payments include the following:
      i. The minimum rental payments called for the lease over the lease term.
      ii. Any guarantee by the lessee or any party related to the lessee of the residual value at the expiration of the lease term, whether or not payment of the guarantee constitutes a purchase of the leased property. When the lessor has

the right to require the lessee to purchase the property at termination of the lease for a certain or determinable amount, that amount shall be considered a lessee guarantee. When the lessee agrees to make up any deficiency below a stated amount in the lessor's realization of the residual value, the guarantee to be included in the minimum lease payments is the stated amount, rather than an estimate of the deficiency to be made up.

   iii. Any payment that the lessee must make or can be required to make upon failure to renew or extend the lease at the expiration of the lease term, whether or not the payment would constitute a purchase of the lease property. In this connection, it should be noted that the definition of lease term includes "all periods, if any, for which failure to renew the lease imposes a penalty on the lessee in an amount such that renewal appears, at the inception of the lease, to be reasonably assured." If the lease term has been extended because of that provision, the related penalty is not included in minimum lease payments.

   b. From the standpoint of the lessor: The payments described above plus any guarantee of the residual value or of rental payments beyond the lease term by a third party unrelated to either the lessee or the lessor, provided the third party is financially capable of discharging the obligations that may arise from the guarantee.

19. *Net Lease.* In a net lease, executory costs in connection with the use of the equipment are to be paid by the lessee and are not a part of the rental. For example, taxes, insurance, and maintenance are paid directly by the lessee. Most finance leases are net leases.

20. *Nonrecourse Financing.* Lending or borrowing activities in which the creditor does not have general recourse to the debtor but rather has recourse only to the property used for collateral in the transaction or other specific property.

21. *Operating Lease.* A lease that does not meet any of the lease classification criteria of a capital lease (lessee) or direct financing lease (lessor). Also describes a short-term rental agreement by which a user can acquire use of an asset for a fraction of the useful life of that asset.

22. *Penalty.* Any requirement that is imposed or can be imposed on the lessee by the lease agreement or by factors outside the lease agreement to disburse cash, incur or assume a liability, perform services, surrender or transfer an asset or rights to an asset or otherwise forego an economic benefit, or suffer an economic detriment. Factors to consider when determining if an economic detriment may be incurred include, but are not limited to, the uniqueness of purpose or location of the property, the availability of a comparable replacement property, the relative importance or significance of the property to the continuation of the lessee's line of business or service to its customers, the existence of leasehold improvements or other assets whose value would be impaired by the lessee vacating or discontinuing use of the leased property, adverse tax consequences, and the ability or willingness of the lessee to bear the cost associated with relocation or replacement of the leased property at market rental rates or to tolerate other parties using the leased property.

23. *Related Parties.* A parent company and its subsidiaries, an owner enterprise and its joint ventures (corporate or otherwise) and partnerships, and an investor (including a natural person) and its investees, provided that the parent company, owner enterprise, or investor has the ability to exercise significant influence over operating and financial policies of the related party. In addition to the foregoing examples of significant influence, significant influence may be exercised through guarantees of indebtedness, extensions of credit, or through ownership of warrants, debt obligations, or other securities. If two or more enterprises are subject to the significant influence of a parent company, owner enterprise, investor (including a natural

person), or common officers or directors, those enterprises shall be considered related parties with respect to each other.

24. *Renewal or Extension of a Lease*. The continuation of a lease agreement beyond the original lease term including a new lease under which the lessee continues to use the same property.

25. *Sale-Leaseback Accounting*. A method of accounting for a sale-leaseback transaction in which the seller-lessee records the sale, removes all property and related liabilities from its balance sheet, recognizes gain or loss from the sale, and classifies the leaseback as a financing or operating lease as appropriate.

26. *Sales Recognition*. Any method to record a transaction involving real estate, other than the deposit method, or the methods to record transactions accounted for as financing, leasing, or profit-sharing arrangements. Profit recognition methods commonly used to record transactions involving real estate include, but are not limited to, the full accrual method, the installment method, the cost recovery method, and the reduced profit method.

27. *Sales-Type Lease*. A direct financing lease that also contains a dealer or manufacturer's profit; the fair market value of the property at lease inception exceeds the related carrying value.

28. *Unguaranteed Residual Value*. The estimated residual value of the leased property exclusive of any portion guaranteed by the lessee or by a third party unrelated to the lessor.

OPERATING LEASES

16.6 LESSEE ACCOUNTING FOR OPERATING LEASES.   Normally, rental on an operating lease is charged to expense over the lease term as it becomes payable. If rental payments are not made on a straight-line basis, rental expense nevertheless is recognized on a straight-line basis unless another systematic and rational basis is more representative of the time pattern in which use benefit is derived from the leased property, in which case that basis would be used (see section 16.9).

16.7 LESSEE DISCLOSURES FOR OPERATING LEASES.   The following information with respect to operating leases must be disclosed in the lessee's financial statements or the notes thereto.

1. For operating leases having initial or remaining noncancelable lease terms in excess of 1 year:
   a. **Future minimum rental payments** required as of the date of the latest balance sheet presented, in the aggregate and for each of the 5 succeeding fiscal years.
   b. The total of minimum rentals to be received in the future under noncancelable subleases as of the date of the latest balance sheet presented.

2. For all operating leases, rental expense for each period for which an income statement is presented, with separate amounts for **minimum rentals, contingent rentals,** and **sublease rentals.** Rental payments under leases with terms of a month or less that were not renewed need not be included.

3. For all operating leases, a general description of the lessee's leasing arrangements including, but not limited to, the following:
   a. The basis on which contingent rental payments are determined.
   b. The existence and terms of renewal or purchase options and escalation clauses.

c. Restrictions imposed by lease agreements, such as those concerning dividends, additional debt, and further leasing.

16.8 LESSOR ACCOUNTING FOR OPERATING LEASES.   Operating leases are accounted for by the lessor as follows:

1. Leased property is included with or displayed near other property, plant, and equipment in the balance sheet.
2. Depreciation is recorded following the lessor's normal depreciation policy for like assets, and accumulated depreciation is displayed as a reduction of the leased property.
3. Rent is recorded as income over the lease terms as it becomes receivable under the provisions of the lease. However, if the rentals vary from the straight-line basis, the income is recognized on a straight-line basis unless another systematic and rational basis is more representative of the time pattern in which the benefit from the leased property is diminished, in which case that basis is used.
4. Initial direct costs are deferred and allocated over the lease term in proportion to revenue recognition under the lease. However, these costs may be expensed when incurred if the effect is not materially different from that which would have resulted from the use of the method prescribed above.

16.9 AN EXAMPLE OF OPERATING LEASES.   The Williams Company leases property with a cost and fair value of $5,000 and a life of 10 years to the Scotts Company for 4 years with a rental of $2,000 per year for years 1 and 2 and $1,000 per year for years 3 and 4.

WILLIAMS COMPANY

Years 1 and 2		
Cash	$2,000	
Rent Income		$1,500
Deferred Rent Income		500
Depreciation Expense	500	
Accumulated Depreciation		500
$5,000/10 years = $500		
Years 3 and 4		
Deferred Rent Income	500	
Cash		1,000
Rent Income		1,500
Depreciation Expense	500	
Accumulated Depreciation		500
$5,000/10 years = $500		

SCOTTS COMPANY

Years 1 and 2		
Rent Expenses	$1,500	
Prepaid Rent	500	
Cash		$2,000
Years 3 and 4		
Rent Expense	1,500	
Prepaid Rent		500
Cash		1,000

This example assumes that some other time pattern other than straight line of benefit to the lessee and dimunition of benefit to the lessor does not exist. For simplicity, the straight-line depreciation method was used although other methods could be selected by the lessor.

CAPITAL LEASES

16.10 ACCOUNTING FOR CAPITAL LEASES.   For capital leases, the lease transaction is viewed as a form of financing in which an asset is acquired and a liability is incurred. The lessee records a capital lease as an asset and a liability on the balance sheet. The amount recorded on the balance sheet is the **present value of the minimum lease payments.** Executory costs such as insurance, maintenance, and taxes to be paid by the lessor are excluded from the minimum payments. However, the amount recorded as an asset and liability must not exceed the fair value of the leased property.

The lessee will record depreciation expense and interest expense on capitalized leases. A capitalized asset should be depreciated by the lessee in a manner consistent with the lessee's normal depreciation policy. The depreciation period to be used is the lease term, unless there is a bargain purchase or transfer of ownership at the end of the lease term, in which case the depreciation is over the life of the assets, as if owned.

Interest expense is recognized by the lessee in proportion to the remaining balance of the capitalized lease obligation. This is accomplished by allocating each minimum lease payment between interest expense and reduction of lease obligation so as to produce a constant periodic rate of interest on the remaining lease obligation. This method is called the effective interest method.

16.11 DISCLOSURE FOR CAPITAL LEASES.   The following information on capital leases must be disclosed.

1. The gross amount of assets recorded under capital leases as of the date of each balance sheet presented by major classes according to nature or function. This information may be combined with the comparable information for owned assets.

2. Future minimum lease payments as of the date of the latest balance sheet presented, in the aggregate and for each of the 5 succeeding fiscal years, with separate deductions from the total for the amount representing executory costs, including any profit thereon, included in the minimum lease payments and for the amount of the imputed interest necessary to reduce the net minimum lease payments to present value.

3. The total of minimum sublease rentals to be received in the future under noncancelable subleases as of the date of the latest balance sheet presented.

4. Total contingent rentals actually incurred for each period for which an income statement is presented.

5. Assets recorded under capital leases and the accumulated amortization thereon shall be separately identified in the lessee's balance sheet or in notes thereto. Likewise, the related obligations shall be separately identified in the balance sheet as obligations under capital leases and shall be subject to the same considerations as other obligations in classifying them with current and noncurrent liabilities in classified balance sheets. Unless the charge to income resulting from amortization of assets recorded under capital leases is included with depreciation expense and the fact that it is so included is disclosed, the amortization charge shall be separately disclosed in the financial statements or notes thereto.

16.12 AN EXAMPLE OF CAPITAL LEASE—LESSEE.   SFAS No. 13 offers an example illustrating classification and accounting for leases. Assume that lessee and lessor sign a lease with the following provisions:

- The lease has a noncancelable term of 30 months, and payments of $135 are due at the beginning of each month.
- The equipment costs $5,000, has a 5-year economic life, and has a residual value guaranteed by lessee of $2,000.

- Lessee receives any excess of the sales price over the guaranteed amount.
- Lessee pays executory costs.
- Lessee's incremental borrowing rate is $10\frac{1}{2}\%$.
- The interest rate implicit in the lease is unknown to the lessee because the lessor's unguaranteed residual value assumption is unknown to the lessee.
- Lessee depreciates similar equipment on a straight-line basis.
- No investment tax credit is available.

(a) Minimum Lease Payments.   Minimum lease payments for both lessee and lessor are calculated as follows:

Payments $135 × 30 months	$4,050
Residual value guarantee	2,000
Total minimum lease payments	$6,050

(b) Lease Classification.   The lease is classified by reviewing the four lease capitalization criteria presented in section 16.3.

1. *Not Met.* The lease does not transfer ownership.
2. *Not Met.* The lease does not contain a bargain purchase option.
3. *Not Met.* The lease is not for a term equal to or greater than 75% of the economic life of the property.
4. *Met.* For the lessee, the present value of the minimum lease payments using the lessee's incremental borrowing rate exceeds 90% of the fair value of the property at the inception of the lease (calculations below). Even if the lessee knows the implicit rate, he uses his incremental borrowing rate because it is lower. Therefore lessee classifies the lease as a capital lease.

Present values using the lessee's incremental borrowing rate of 10.5% are as follows:

Present value:	
Rental payments (present value of $135 at 0.875% per month for 29 months)	$3,580
Residual guarantee (present value of $2,000 in 30 months at 0.875% per month)	1,540
Total	$5,120

Although the lessee's incremental borrowing rate produces a present value of $5,120 for lease classification criteria, SFAS No. 13 stipulates that the lease is not to be capitalized in excess of fair value, or $5,000 in this example. When the present value is adjusted to total $5,000, the interest rate raises to 12.036% or 1.003% per month as follows:

Present value:	
Rental payments (present value of $135 at 1.003% per month for 29 months)	$3,517
Residual guarantee (present value of $2,000 in 30 months at 1.003% per month)	1,483
Total	$5,000

(c) Lessee Accounting at Inception.   At the beginning of the lease, the lessee's journal entries are:

Equipment under capital lease	$5,000	
Capital lease obligation		$5,000
The first month's payment is recorded as:		
Capital lease obligation	135	
Cash		135
Interest Expense	49	
Accrued Interest		49

Then at the beginning of the second month:

Capital lease obligation	86	
Accrued Interest	49	
Cash		135

(d) Lessee Depreciation.   Depreciation would be taken on a straight-line basis over 30 months. Total depreciation to be taken equals the capitalized lease value of $5,000, less its estimated residual value of $2,000. Each month's depreciation would be recorded as follows:

Depreciation expense	$100	
Accumulated depreciation—		
Equipment under capital lease		$100

(e) Lease Payments.   Each lease payment contains both interest and principal, and SFAS No. 13 requires that interest be calculated on the effective interest method, as follows:

Payment Number	Lease Payment	Interest (1.003%) on Principal	Reduction of Principal	Net Lease Obligation
1	$135	-0-	-0-	$4,865
2	135	$49	$86	4,779
3	135	48	87	4,692
4	135	47	88	4,604
5	135	46	89	4,515

DIRECT FINANCING LEASES

16.13 ACCOUNTING FOR DIRECT FINANCING LEASES.   In a direct financing lease, a lessor accounts for the investment in the lease as a receivable. A direct financing lease is accounted for by recording the following:

- *Gross Investment.* The minimum lease payments (excluding executory costs paid by the lessor) plus any unguaranteed residual value accruing to the lessor are recorded as the gross investment in finance leases.
- *Unearned Income.* The difference between the gross investment and the cost or carrying amount of the leased property is recorded as unearned income. This unearned income, reduced by an amount equal to initial direct costs, is amortized to income over the lease term, applying the effective interest method to produce a constant rate of return on the net investment in the lease.
- *Net Investment.* The net investment consists of the gross investment less the unearned income.
- *Initial Direct Costs.* These costs are expensed as incurred.
- *Earned Income.* Earned income consist of two elements:

    An amount equal to initial direct costs, which is recorded at the inception of the lease.

    The remaining unearned income, which is amortized to income over the lease term using the effective interest method.

16.14 AN EXAMPLE OF DIRECT FINANCING LEASES.   Assume that a lessor executes the same lease described earlier. In addition, for simplicity, assume that there were no initial direct costs.

This lease does not meet the first three criteria for a direct finance lease, but it does meet the 90% of fair value test. Having met this test and assuming that the collectibility and uncertainty tests are also met, the lessor will classify this lease as a direct financing lease.

The interest rate implicit in this lease is the internal rate of return that discounts the minimum lease payments ($135 × 30 plus $2,000 residual value) to the fair value of the property at the inception of the lease ($5,000). That rate is 12.036% or 1.003% per month.

In this case, the rate is shown by adding the present values of the components of return:

Present value of 29 payments of $135 at 1.003% per month	$3,382
Plus $135 for first payment	135
Equals present value of rental payments	$3,517
Plus present value of $2,000 in 30 months at 1.003% per month	1,483
	$5,000

The lessor uses this rate to calculate the present value of the minimum lease payments in the 90% of fair value test, as follows:

Present value:		
Rental payments	$3,517	
Residual guarantee	1,483	
Total	$5,000	
Fair value of property at inception of lease		$5,000
Present value of minimum lease payments as percentage of fair value		100%

In all direct financing leases where an unguaranteed residual value is recorded, the fair value of property will exceed the present value of minimum lease payments. This is because the unguaranteed residual value is excluded from the lessor's present value calculation. The lessor must produce the following information to record the lease:

1. Gross investment is $6,050. Payments of $135 × 30 plus $2,000 guaranteed residual value.
2. Unearned income is $1,050. Gross investment less $5,000 cost of equipment.
3. Net investment is $5,000. The gross investment less the unearned income.

The entries for the lessor at the inception of the lease are:

Minimum lease payments receivable	$6,050	
Equipment		$5,000
Unearned income		1,050
Monthly lease payments would be recorded as:		
Cash	135	
Minimum lease payments receivable		135

Earned income (excluding any applicable income to cover initial direct costs) for the first month would be recorded as:

Unearned income	$ 49	
Earned income		$ 49

A similar pattern is followed for the remainder of the lease term.

The following table summarizes the income recognition and net investment of the lessor over the term of the lease.

Payment Number	Payment	Interest Income on Net Investment	Principal Reduction	Net Investment Beginning of Month
1	$ 135	$ -0-	$ 135	$4,865
2	135	49	86	4,779
3	135	48	87	4,692
4	135	47	88	4,604
—	—	—	—	—
—	—	—	—	—
—	—	—	—	—
30	135	21	114	1,980
	-0-	20	(20)	2,000
	$4,050	$1,050	$3,000	

SALES-TYPE LEASES

The major difference between a direct financing lease and a sales-type lease is the presence of a manufacturer's profit in a sales-type lease; for example, the fair market value of the property is greater than the carrying value of such property.

16.15 ACCOUNTING FOR SALES-TYPE LEASES.   A sales-type lease is accounted for by recording the following:

1. *Gross Investment*. The minimum lease payments (excluding executory costs paid by the lessor) plus any unguaranteed residual value accruing to the lessor are recorded as the gross investment in finance leases.
2. *Unearned Income*. The difference between the gross investment and the cost or carrying amount of the leased property is recorded as unearned income. This unearned income is amortized to income over the lease term, applying the effective interest method to produce a constant rate of return on the net investment in the lease.
3. *Net Investment*. The net investment consists of the minimum lease gross investment less the unearned income.
4. *Cost of Goods Sold or Cost of Sales*. The cost or carrying amount of the lease property less the present value of any unguaranteed residual value accruing to the benefit of the lessor.

16.16 AN EXAMPLE OF SALES-TYPE LEASES.   In the case presented in section 16.14, assume that the lessor produces the equipment for a cost of $4,000. The information needed to record the sales-type lease is as follows:

1. Gross investment is $6,050 ($4,050 of lease payments plus $2,000 of guaranteed residual value).
2. Unearned interest income is $1,050 (gross investment of $6,050 less $5,000).
3. Sales price is $5,000 (present value of minimum lease payments).
4. Cost of goods sold is $4,000 less the present value of any unguaranteed residual value accruing to the benefit of the lessor. Because there is no unguaranteed residual value, the cost of goods sold equals the lessor's cost to produce the equipment under lease.

The transaction is recorded by the lessor as follows:

Lease payments receivable	$6,050
Cost of goods	4,000

Sales revenue	$5,000
Equipment	4,000
Unearned income	1,050

Thereafter, the accounting for lessors would follow the example of the direct financing lease.

BALANCE SHEET PRESENTATION—CAPITAL LEASE—LESSEE

Long-lived assets:	
Leased property under capital leases less accumulated amortization	$XXX
Current liabilities:	
Obligations under capital leases	$XXX
Long-term liabilities:	
Obligations under capital leases	$XXX

BALANCE SHEET PRESENTATION—CAPITAL LEASE—LESSOR

Current assets:	
Net investment in direct financing and sales-type leases—current portion	$XXX
Noncurrent assets:	
Net investment in direct financing and sales-type leases	$XXX
Long-lived assets:	
Property on operating leases and property held for leases net of accumulated depreciation	$XXX

LEVERAGED LEASES

16.17 LEVERAGED LEASE ACCOUNTING. Leveraged leases derive their name from a characteristic of the transaction, namely that the lessor tends to have a small equity in the leased property and borrows or otherwise finances a large part of the cost of owning the asset. Frequently the lessor's equity is reduced by an immediate return from investment tax credits related to the leased property, which offsets income taxes otherwise payable by the lessor. The lessor (equity participant) is frequently a financial institution able to finance the leverage at a relatively low cost. This combination, together with the security of a high-quality lessee (or lease), tends to produce a comparatively low usage cost of the asset to the lessee.

The lessor's investment in a finance lease may be zero or even negative at certain times during the lease period. The concept of recognizing a profit during a period of negative investment caused some theoretical problems in determining the proper accounting for leveraged leases.

(a) Characteristics of a Leveraged Lease. SFAS No. 13 defines a leveraged lease to be one having all of the following four characteristics:

1. It meets the definition of a direct financing lease.
2. It involves at least three parties: a **lessee,** a **long-term creditor,** and a lessor (commonly called the **equity participant**).
3. The financing provided by the long-term creditor is nonrecourse as to the general credit of the lessor (although the creditor may have recourse to the specific property leased and the unremitted rentals relating to it), and the amount of the financing is sufficient to provide the lessor with substantial "leverage" in the transaction.
4. The lessor's net investment declines during the early years once the investment has been completed and rises during the later years of the lease before its final elimination.

Provided the lease meets these requirements and the investment tax credit, if any, is not accounted for using the flow-through method, the lease is treated as a leveraged lease.

(b) Lessee Accounting.   From the viewpoint of the lessee, leveraged leases are classified and accounted for in the same manner as nonleveraged leases.

(c) Lessor Accounting for Investment.   The lessor records the investment in a leveraged lease net of the nonrecourse debt. The net balance of the following accounts represents the initial and continuing investment in leveraged leases:

1. Rentals receivable, net of that portion of the rental applicable to principal and interest on the nonrecourse debt.
2. A receivable for the amount of the investment tax credit to be realized on the transaction.
3. The estimated residual value of the leased asset.
4. Unearned income (the remaining amount of estimated pretax lease income or loss and investment tax credit to be allocated to income over the lease term, after deducting initial direct costs).

(d) Lessor Recognition of Income.   The lessor in a leveraged lease transaction recognizes income by use of the investment with separate phases method. Under this method, lease income is recognized at a level aftertax rate of return on net investment in those years in which the net investment at the beginning of the period is positive. Deferred taxes should be used to calculate the net investment for use in computing income from the lease. However, deferred taxes should not be offset against the investment in the lease for balance sheet presentation. Usually, the lessor's net investment in a leveraged lease is as follows:

* *Early Period.* Positive, due to the initial investment in leased property.
* *Middle Period.* Negative, due to income tax reductions provided by accelerated depreciation, interest on nonrecourse debt, and investment tax credits, the cash flows are shielded from payment of taxes. In this period, the lessor has not only recovered his initial investment but has received additional funds, which are temporarily invested in other operations.
* *Later Period.* Positive, due to a transfer from a tax shelter position to a tax-paying position arising primarily from reduced depreciation and interest charges.
* *Final Period.* Zero, when the residual value is realized on sale of the property.

The investment with separate phases method identifies two separate and distinct types of earnings: primary earnings and earnings from reinvestment. Primary earnings consist of three elements: pretax lease income, tax effect of pretax lease income, and investment tax credit. The income that is recognized at a level rate of return in the years in which the net investment is positive consists only of the primary earnings from the lease.

In the middle years of a leveraged lease, the net investment is typically negative. The lessor has recovered his initial investment and has the further use of cash that is shielded from tax by high depreciation and interest expense charges. The earnings from the reinvestment of excess funds are taken into income during the years when the net investment is negative and are independent of the reporting of the leveraged lease income.

The result is that lease income is recognized at a level rate of return on the net investment (cost of property less nonrecourse debt and less the investment tax credit) in the years in which the net investment is positive at the beginning of the year. During the years when the net investment is negative, only the earnings from the reinvested funds are realized.

16.18 LEVERAGED LEASE DISCLOSURES.   When leasing activities, exclusive of leveraged leasing, are a significant part of the lessor's business activities in terms of revenue, net income, or assets, the following information with respect to leases should be disclosed in the financial statements or notes.

1. For sales-type and direct financing leases:

    a. The components of the net investment in sales-type and direct financing leases as of the date of each balance sheet presented:

        i. Future minimum lease payments to be received, with separate deductions for amounts representing executory costs, including any profit thereon, included in the minimum lease payments and the accumulated allowance for uncollectible minimum lease payments receivable.

        ii. The unguaranteed residual values accruing to the benefit of the lessor.

        iii. For direct financing leases only, initial direct costs.

        iv. Unearned income.

    b. Future minimum lease payments to be received for each of the 5 succeeding fiscal years as of the date of the latest balance sheet presented.

    c. Total contingent rentals included in income for each period for which an income statement is presented.

2. For operating leases:

    a. The cost and carrying amount, if different, of property on lease or held for leasing by major classes of property according to nature or function, and the amount of accumulated depreciation in total as of the date of the latest balance sheet presented.

    b. Minimum future rentals on noncancelable leases as of the date of the latest balance sheet presented, in the aggregate and for each of the 5 succeeding fiscal years.

    c. Total contingent rentals included in income for each period for which an income statement is presented.

3. A general description of the lessor's leasing arrangements.

REAL ESTATE LEASES

Leases involving real estate can be categorized as follows:

1. Land only lease.
2. Land and building leases.
3. Real estate and equipment leases.
4. Leases involving part of a building.

The same criteria are used to determine classification as an operating or capital lease.

16.19 LEASES INVOLVING LAND ONLY. If land is the only item of property leased and the lease transfers ownership of the property or contains a bargain purchase option, the lessee should account for the lease as a capital lease; because ownership of the land is expected to pass to the lessee, the asset recorded under the lease is not normally amortizable. If the lease does not meet either of those criteria, the lease is an operating lease.

If the lease transfers ownership and meets the requirements of collectibility and uncertainty, the lessor accounts for the lease as either a sales type or a direct financing lease, whichever is appropriate. If the lease does not meet those requirements, it is an operating lease. The lessor does not use the bargain purchase option criterion to classify the lease.

16.20 LEASES INVOLVING LAND AND BUILDINGS. When the lease either transfers ownership or contains a bargain purchase option, there are two forms of accounting:

1. *Lessee's Accounting.* If the lease transfers ownership or contains a bargain purchase option, the land and the buildings are separately capitalized by the lessee. The present value of the minimum lease payments is apportioned between land and buildings in

relation to their fair values at the inception of the lease. The building should be amortized under the normal accounting policies of the lessee.

  2. *Lessor's Accounting.* If the lease transfers ownership and meets both the collectibility and uncertainty tests, the lessor accounts for the lease as a single unit. If there is a manufacturer or dealer profit, the lease would be a sales-type lease. Without such profit, it would be a direct financing lease or leveraged lease, as appropriate. If the lease does not meet these tests, the lessor accounts for the lease as an operating lease. The lessor does not use the bargain purchase option criterion to classify the lease.

When the lease neither transfers ownership nor contains a bargain purchase option, whether the land and the building are considered together or separately depends on the relation of the fair value of the land to the total fair value of the leased property.

If the fair value of the land is less than 25% of the total fair value of the leased property, both the lessee and the lessor must consider the land and the building as a single unit, the economic life of the building.

If the lease term is at least 75% of the property's estimated economic life or if the present value of the minimum lease payments is 90% or more of the fair value of the property, the lessee capitalizes the land and buildings as a single unit and amortizes it. If the lease does not meet those requirements, it is accounted for as an operating lease.

If the lease term is at least 75% of the property's economic life or if the present value of minimum lease payments is 90% or more of the fair value of the property and both the collectibility and uncertainty tests are met, the lessor accounts for the lease as a single unit, a sales-type lease, a direct financing lease, or a leveraged lease. If the lease does not meet those requirements, it is accounted for as an operating lease.

If the building in the lease meets the economic life or 90% fair value tests, the building is accounted for as a capital lease by the lessee. The land element of the lease is separately accounted for as an operating lease. However, if the building element in the lease meets neither the economic life nor the fair value test, both the building and the land are accounted for as a single operating lease by the lessee.

If the building in the lease meets the economic life or fair value test as well as the criteria for uncertainty and collectibility, the lessor accounts for the building elements as a sales-type lease, a direct financing lease, or a leveraged lease, as appropriate. The land is accounted for as an operating lease. As with lessees, if the building does not meet the economic life or fair value tests and does not meet the tests for collectibility, both the building and the land are accounted for collectively as a single operating lease.

16.21 LEASES INVOLVING LAND AND EQUIPMENT. If a lease involves land and equipment, the portion of the minimum lease payments applicable to the equipment is estimated by whatever means are appropriate and reasonable. The equipment is then to be treated separately for purposes of applying the criteria and accounted for separately according to its classification by both lessee and lessor.

16.22 LEASES INVOLVING ONLY PART OF A BUILDING. When the leased property is part of a larger entity, its cost and fair value may not be objectively determinable as, for example, if a floor in an office building was leased. If the cost and fair value of the leased property are objectively determinable, both the lessee and the lessor should classify and account for the lease as described above. Unless both the cost and the fair value are objectively determinable, the lease is classified and accounted for as follows:

  1. *Lessee.* If the fair value of the leased property is not objectively determinable, the lessee shall classify the lease pursuant to whether it meets the 75% of economic life test.

  2. *Lessor.* If either the cost or the fair value of the property is not objectively determinable, the lessor shall account for the lease as an operating lease.

SELECTED ISSUES IN LEASE ACCOUNTING

16.23 PARTICIPATION BY THIRD PARTIES.   The sale or assignment of a lease or property subject to a lease to a third party does not change the original accounting for the lease. Any profit or loss on the sale should be recognized at the time of the transaction, unless the transaction is between related parties (see section 16.24) or is sold with recourse (see SFAS No. 77, "Reporting by Transferors for Transfers of Receivables with Recourse" for guidance).

16.24 RELATED PARTY LEASES.   In general, related party leases are classified in accordance with the same criteria as all other leases, unless it is clear that the terms of the transaction have been significantly affected by the relationship of the lessees and lessor. The economic substance of such a transaction may cause the accounting for such leases to be modified from that which would be suggested by the strict terms of the lease.

16.25 SUBLEASES.   If the original lease was classified as a capital lease because of transfer of title or a bargain purchase option, the sublease by the lessee should be treated as a new lease and classified according to the same criteria as any other lease. If the original lease was classified as a capital lease because of the economic life or 90% fair value tests, only the economic life test should be used to classify the sublease except where the lessee who is now becoming a lessor was really only an intermediary between the new lessee and original lessor. In that event, the 90% fair value test should also be used. If the original lease was an operating lease, the sublease must also be an operating lease.

16.26 CHANGES IN THE PROVISIONS OF LEASES.   From the standpoint of the lessor, three changes can take place as follows:

1. The change does not give rise to a new agreement. A new agreement is defined as a change that, if in effect at the inception of the lease, would have resulted in a different classification.
2. The change does give rise to a new agreement that would be classified as a direct financing lease.
3. The change gives rise to a new agreement classified as an operating lease.

If either (1) or (2) occurs, the balance of the minimum lease payment receivable and the estimated residual value are adjusted to reflect the effect of the change. The net adjustment is to be charged (or credited) to the unearned income account, and the accounting for the lease adjusted to reflect the change.

If the new agreement is an operating lease, then the remaining net investment (lease receivable less unearned income) is to be removed from the books and the leased asset shall be recorded at the lower of its cost, present fair value, or carrying value. The net adjustment resulting from these entries is charged (or credited) to the income of the period. Thereafter, the new lease is accounted for as any other operating lease.

16.27 RENEWAL, EXTENSION, OR TERMINATION OF LEASES.   A renewal or extension involves one of two circumstances that affect the accounting for an existing lease:

- A guarantee or penalty is rendered inoperative.
- A new agreement exists.

In both circumstances, the lessee in a capital lease adjusts the current balance of the leased asset and obligation to the present value of the future minimum lease payments based upon the implicit interest rate in the original lease. If a new agreement exists and it is classified as an operating lease, then the lessee continues to account for the existing capital lease until the end of the term. The renewal or extension is an operating lease and is accounted for as such.

In both circumstances, the lessor in a direct financing lease would adjust the lease receivable and estimated residual value charging or crediting unearned income for the difference. An upward revision to estimated residual value is prohibited, however. If a renewal or extension constitutes a new agreement and is an operating lease, then the lessor continues to account for the existing lease until the end of the term and accounts for the renewal/extension as an operating lease. If the new agreement is a sales-type lease, the renewal or extension is accounted for as a sales-type lease providing the renewal/extension occurred at or near the end of the existing lease term.

In a termination, the lessor eliminates the remaining net investment and records the leased asset at its lower of present fair value, current book value, or historical cost. The net difference is reflected in the income statement of the current period. The lessor in a capital lease will eliminate the asset and obligation from the financial statements recording a gain or loss on termination. In an operating lease, no adjustment is required.

16.28 LEASES AND BUSINESS COMBINATIONS.   If, in connection with a business combination, the provisions of a lease are modified such that the revised lease is essentially a new agreement, this new lease should be classified as any new lease would be.

In a pooling of interests, unless the lease has been modified as above, no changes should be made in the accounting for the leases in effect.

In a purchase, unless the terms of the lease have been changed, the previous classification would remain in effect. However, the amounts assigned to the assets and liabilities arising from the accounting for leases should be determined in accordance with the guidelines under APB Opinion No. 16, ''Business Combinations.''

16.29 CHANGE IN RESIDUAL VALUE.   A lessor should at a minimum annually review the estimated residual values in any leasing transactions. For any decline in value that is deemed to be permanent, a loss should be recognized in the period of decline and the residual value should be revised. For any declines that are deemed to be temporary, no such action need be taken. No change in residual values is ever recognized for estimated increases in such values.

16.30 SALE AND LEASEBACK.   A sale and leaseback transaction is one involving the sale of property by the owner (seller-lessee), who simultaneously leases it back from the new owner. Sale and leaseback transactions are frequently entered into as a means of raising additional cash from assets that are owned and used by a company. For example, a company may sell a building it owns and simultaneously lease it back. The facilities of the building are still available to the company. The cash received can be invested in the company's productive process or business at a relatively high rate of return. Since real estate investors, who purchase and lease the building, frequently accept lower rates of return than are available to the company from its normal operations, overall rate of return is improved. In effect, the company transfers funds invested in real estate (or similar) assets to higher yielding, more active investments. The lease in a sale and leaseback transaction is frequently a net lease, which provides that the lessee remains liable for all executory costs, taxes, maintenance, and so on.

(a) Lessee Accounting.   If the lease meets one of the criteria for treatment as a capital lease, the seller–lessee accounts for it as a captial lease. If the lease does not meet one of the criteria, then it is an operating lease. In general, any profit or loss on the sale is deferred and recognized in proportion to the amortization of the leased asset in a captial lease or to the gross rental expense in an operating lease. The exceptions to the general rule are as follows:

1. The seller–lessee relinquishes rights to substantially all of the property sold, retaining only a minor portion. Both the sale and leaseback are treated as separate transactions unless they require an adjustment due to the unreasonable amount of rentals called for by the leaseback compared to market conditions.
2. The seller–lessee retains more than a minor part of the property but less than substantially all. Only the profit on the sale in excess of the present value of the minimum lease payments or recorded value of the leased asset is recognized at the date of sale.
3. The fair value of the property is less than its net book value, in which case a loss should be immediately recognized.

(b) Lessor Accounting. If the lease meets any one of the lease classification criteria and both criteria for collectibility and uncertainty, the purchaser-lessor must record the transaction as a purchase and a direct financing lease. If the lease does not meet these criteria, the lessor records the transaction as a purchase and an operating lease.

(c) Sale-Leaseback for Real Estate. A sale-leaseback for real estate involves any transaction that involves real estate, including real estate with equipment or furniture and fixtures, regardless of the relative value of the equipment or furniture and fixtures and the real estate. Sale-leaseback can be used by a seller-lessee only if the agreement includes all of the following:

1. A normal leaseback.
2. Payment terms and provisions adequately demonstrating the buyer-lessor's initial and continuing investment in the property. (See SFAS No. 66, "Accounting for Sales of Real Estate," (FASB, 1982)).
3. Payment terms and provisions transferring all of the other risks and rewards of ownership as demonstrated by the absence of any other continuing involvement by the seller-lessee.

A normal leaseback involves active use of the property by the seller-lessee in exchange for the payment of rent except for minor subleasing (10% or less of the fair value). Terms and provisions substantially different than those that an independent lessor or lessee would normally accept are considered an exchange of unstated rights or privileges that should be considered in evaluating continuing involvement by the seller-lessee. These may include sales price or interest rate. A sale-leaseback that does not qualify for a normal leaseback because of the continuing involvement by the seller-lessee should be accounted for by the deposit method or as a financing.

Continuing involvement includes:

1. Sale-leaseback of property improvements or equipment without leasing the underlying land.
2. Buyer-lessor shares the future appreciation of the property with the seller-lessee.
3. Seller-lessee has an option or obligation to repurchase.
4. Seller-lessee guarantees buyer-lessor's investment or return on investment for some period of time.
5. Guarantee by the seller-lessee such as fair value of property at end of lease, providing nonrecourse financing, remaining as liable on obligation, and so on.

Disclosures required include the terms of the sale-leaseback, the obligation for future minimum lease payments in the aggregate and for each of the 5 succeeding fiscal years, and the total of minimum sublease rentals in the aggregate and for each of the 5 succeeding fiscal years.

EXAMPLES OF LEASE DISCLOSURE

Exhibits 16.2 and 16.3 provide comprehensive illustrations of lease disclosure. Exhibit 16.2 presents a lessee's disclosure of capital and operating leases. Exhibit 16.3 presents a lessor's disclosure.

NOTES TO CONSOLIDATED
FINANCIAL STATEMENTS
Note L—Lease Obligations

Certain airport and other retail facilities, a cruise ship, buses and bus terminals (primarily subleased), plants, offices and equipment are leased. The leases expire in periods ranging from one to 46 years, and some provide for renewal options ranging from one to 25 years. Also, certain leases contain purchase options. Leases which expire are generally renewed or replaced by similar leases.

Capital leases included in the cost of property and equipment aggregate $40,992,000 and $79,395,000 at December 31, 1988 and 1987, respectively, with related accumulated depreciation of $28,704,000 and $45,656,000, respectively.

At December 31, 1988, future minimum payments and related sublease rentals receivable with respect to capital leases and noncancelable operating leases with terms in excess of one year, are as follows:

(000 omitted)	Capital Leases	Operating Leases				
		Airport Terminal Concessions	Buses	Cruise Ship	Other	Total
1989	$ 4,621	$ 42,942	$20,138	$12,949	$ 37,144	$113,173
1990	4,570	42,116	19,479	12,949	33,763	108,307
1991	4,973	46,125	19,466	12,949	30,720	109,260
1992	4,858	47,174	17,996	12,949	25,188	103,307
1993	4,641	49,354	7,048	12,949	22,078	91,429
Thereafter	41,002	93,239		23,742	133,183	250,164
Total future minimum lease payments	64,665	$320,950	$84,127	$88,487	$282,076	$775,640
Less imputed interest	27,795					
Present value of future minimum capital lease payments	$36,870					

Rentals Receivable under Subleases
(000 omitted)

	Subleased Buses	Other (Principally Airport Concessions)	Total
1989	$21,727	$ 16,628	$ 38,355
1990	21,043	16,546	37,589
1991	21,043	17,424	38,467
1992	19,576	17,290	36,866
1993	7,325	15,632	22,957
Thereafter		39,622	39,622
	$90,714	$123,142	$213,856

(continued)

Exhibit 16.2.   Lessee disclosure.

Information regarding net operating lease rentals for the three years ended December 31, 1988, is as follows:

(000 omitted)	1988	1987	1986
Minimum rentals	$130,795	$ 88,120	$50,617
Contingent rentals	38,925	18,676	12,179
Sublease rentals	(55,753)	(32,285)	(1,112)
Total net rentals	$113,967	$ 74,511	$61,684

Contingent rentals on operating leases are based primarily on sales and revenues for buildings and leasehold improvements and usage for other equipment.

Exhibit 16.2. *Continued.*

SUN COMPANY, INC.
NOTES TO CONSOLIDATED FINANCIAL STATEMENTS
8 (in part): Long-Term Receivables and Investments

	December 31	
	1987	1986
	(millions of dollars)	
Investment in:		
Leveraged leases	$ 85	$ 79
Direct financing and sales-type leases	276*	271
	361	350
Accounts and notes receivable	114	68
Investments in and advances to affiliated companies	27	34
Other investments, at cost	19	12
	$521	$464

*Includes $129 million used with $26 million of other assets as collateral for $87 million recourse long-term debt—leasing notes associated with sales-type leases (Note 12).

Sun, as lessor, has entered into leveraged, direct financing and sales-type leases of a wide variety of equipment including oceangoing vessels, aircraft, mining equipment, railroad rolling stock and various other transportation and manufacturing equipment. The components of Sun's investment in these leases at December 31, 1987 and 1986 are set forth below (in millions of dollars):

	Leveraged Leases December 31		Direct Financing and Sales-Type Leases December 31	
	1987	1986	1987	1986
Minimum rentals receivable	$63*	$50*	$401	$417
Estimated unguaranteed residual value of leased assets	61	61	60	55
Unearned and deferred income	(39)	(32)	(185)	(201)
Investment in leases	85	79	$276	$271
Deferred taxes arising from leveraged leases	(60)	(54)		
Net investment in leveraged leases	$25	$25		

*Net of principal of and interest on related nonrecourse financing aggregating $234 and $247 million in 1987 and 1986, respectively.

(continued)

Exhibit 16.3. **Lessor disclosure.**

The following is a schedule of minimum rentals receivable by years at December 31, 1987 (in millions of dollars):

	Leveraged Leases	Direct Financing and Sales-Type Leases
Year ending December 31:		
1988	$ 4	$ 51
1989	5	49
1990	5	48
1991	4	46
1992	6	37
Later years	39	170
	$63	$401

Exhibit 16.3.   *Continued.*

SOURCES AND SUGGESTED REFERENCES

Arthur Andersen & Co., *Accounting for Leases,* Chicago, 1986.

Bisgay, Louis, "FASB Issues Statement 98," *Management Accounting,* Vol. 70, Aug. 1988, p. 63.

Byington, J. Ralph, Moores, Charles, T., and Munter, Paul H., "How Initial Direct Costs Affect Lessors" *The CPA Journal,* Vol. 58, Feb. 1988, pp. 67–69.

Financial Accounting Standards Board, Statement of Financial Accounting Standards No. 66, "Accounting for Sales of Real Estate," FASB, Stamford, CT, 1982.

"Firms Now Lease Everything But Time," *U.S. News & World Report,* August 14, 1989, p. 45.

Johnson, James M., *Fundamentals of Finance for Equipment Lessors: A Transaction Orientation,* American Association of Equipment Lessors, Arlington, VA, 1986.

McMeen, Albert R., *Treasurer's and Controller's New Equipment Leasing Guide,* Prentice-Hall, Englewood Cliffs, NJ, 1984.

Vernor, James D., "Comparative Lease Analysis Using a Discounted Cash Flow Approach," *Appraisal Journal,* Vol. 56, July 1988, pp. 391–398.

ACCOUNTING FOR INCOME TAXES

J. T. Ball, PhD, CPA
Financial Accounting Standards Board

E. Raymond Simpson, CPA
Financial Accounting Standards Board

CONTENTS

The Financial Accounting Standards Board encourages its members and staff to express their individual views. The views expressed in Chapter 17 are those of Dr. Ball and Mr. Simpson. Official positions of the FASB on accounting matters are determined only after extensive due process and deliberation.

ACCOUNTING RECOGNITION OF INCOME TAXES

17.1 THE BASIC PROBLEM.   Accounting for income taxes is one of the most complex and controversial accounting subjects in this country. The basic problem is that transactions and events may be reported in different years for financial reporting and for income tax purposes. This may be because different accounting methods are used for each purpose, for example, accrual accounting versus cash basis accounting, straight-line depreciation versus an accelerated depreciation method, the percentage-of-completion versus the completed contract methods on long-term contracts, or revenue recognition at time of sale versus the installment method. It may also be because a different estimated useful life is elected for depreciation or amortization. These differences may occur because the income tax reporting requirements and generally accepted accounting principles are different for a particular event or transaction or because a taxpayer is able to elect to report differently.

The accounting procedure employed to recognize the tax effects of amounts that are reported in different years for financial reporting and for income tax reporting has been known as **interperiod income tax allocation** or **tax effect accounting.** The more neutral description of "recognition" of income taxes is used in this chapter and the other terms are not generally used.

Several different approaches to the recognition of income taxes have been used at various times in the United States. An income statement approach known as the **deferred method** of interperiod income tax allocation was adopted in 1967 in APB Opinion No. 11, "Accounting for Income Taxes." Under that method, amounts reported in different years for financial reporting and for income tax reporting are known as **timing differences.** Using accelerated depreciation on the income tax return and straight-line depreciation in the income statement, for example, causes a timing difference to originate each year during the early life of an asset; the timing difference reverses or "turns around" during the later life of the asset. Other items, known as **permanent differences,** are not considered taxable income, are not tax deductible, or are special deductions for income tax reporting purposes. Because they always differ for financial and income tax reporting purposes, there is a permanent, nonrecurring difference. For example, interest income from state and local government bonds is financial revenue that is not taxable under the federal income tax.

SFAS No. 96, "Accounting for Income Taxes," is a balance sheet approach to accounting for income taxes, known as the **liability method.** Under that method, differences between the amounts reported in the balance sheet for assets and liabilities and the income tax bases of those assets and liabilities are known as **temporary differences.** Thus, whereas the difference between the amount of depreciation on the tax return and in the income statement in a single year is a timing difference under APB Opinion No. 11, the cumulative difference at the balance sheet date between the tax basis of the asset and its cost (or other amount) reported in the balance sheet is a temporary difference under SFAS No. 96. Temporary differences may also result from causes other than cumulative timing differences (see section 17.4(a)).

Because the concepts underlying timing differences and temporary differences are so different, the term "timing difference" will be used in this chapter only in the explanation of APB Opinion No. 11 and earlier accounting requirements; elsewhere the more current term "temporary difference," which originated in SFAS No. 96, will be used.

17.2 TAX RECOGNITION CONCEPTS.   Income taxes are seldom, if ever, paid completely in the period to which they relate. Thus the **cash basis** is not acceptable under GAAP. Income taxes, like other expenses, should be recognized on an **accrual basis** of accounting. Although there is agreement that, at a minimum, income tax expense should include income taxes paid and payable for a period as determined on the income tax return for the period, the **taxes payable method** ignores timing and temporary differences and is not acceptable under GAAP.

(a) Development in the United States.   There has long been general agreement in this country on the need for, at a minimum, recognition of deferred taxes for nonrecurring material differences that will reverse in a relatively short period. That partial recognition position was taken in 1944 in ARB No. 23, "Accounting for Income Taxes," carried forward in 1953 in ARB No. 43, "Restatement and Revision of Accounting Research Bulletins," and reaffirmed in 1954 in ARB No. 44, "Declining-Balance Depreciation." In 1958 ARB No. 44 (Revised), "Declining-Balance Depreciation," further called for tax allocation even though depreciation differences were of a recurring nature, or a plant was expanding, so there would be long-term deferral of an increasing tax balance. That comprehensive recognition approach extended the applicability of the interperiod income tax allocation procedure to depreciation differences to which it had not previously been broadly applied. In 1962 APB Opinion No. 1, "New Depreciation Guidelines and Rules," further extended the applicability of that procedure to differences arising from adoption of shorter lives for income tax depreciation in relation to those used for financial reporting.

Whether the concepts in those pronouncements applied for timing differences other than depreciation was uncertain, however, and interperiod income tax allocation was not literally required for most timing differences until APB Opinion No. 11 became effective in 1968. That opinion also generally resolved the question of which method should be applied in favor of the deferred method with comprehensive allocation. Although the deferred method was preferred in the earlier pronouncements mentioned previously, the liability and net-of-tax methods were also acceptable. In the research study published by the AICPA before APB Opinion No. 11 was issued, Black (1966) discussed those methods in detail. They are summarized below.

(i) Deferred Method.   The deferred method is an income statement approach to interperiod income tax allocation that seeks to match the tax effects of revenues and expenses with those items in the period for which they are recognized for financial reporting purposes. Deferred taxes are determined on the basis of tax rates in effect when timing differences originate and are not adjusted for changes in tax rates or for new taxes. The tax effect of a timing difference that reduces income tax currently payable is reported as an increase in income tax expense in the income statement and as a deferred tax credit in the balance sheet; conversely, the tax effect of a timing difference that increases income tax currently payable is reported as a reduction in income tax expense in the income statement and as a deferred tax charge (or reduction of deferred tax credits) in the balance sheet. Because the beginning amount of income tax expense in the income statement is based on taxes currently payable, in concept the deferred method adjusts tax expense as if originating timing differences for the period were included in taxable income. The tax effects of reversing timing differences likewise adjust tax expense, but in concept at the tax rates in effect when those timing differences originated. Paragraph 57 of APB Opinion No. 11 states that "deferred charges and deferred credits relating to timing differences represent the cumulative recognition given to their tax effects and as such do not represent payables or receivables in the usual sense."

(ii) Liability Method.   The liability method is a balance sheet approach to accounting for income taxes. The method seeks to determine the liability for income taxes payable in the future or the asset for prepaid income taxes and, accordingly, measures the tax effect of a temporary difference at the tax rate or rates in effect when the difference will reverse. If tax rates change or new taxes are imposed, the balance sheet accounts are adjusted with a corresponding adjustment to income tax expense.

(iii) Net-of-Tax Method.   The net-of-tax method is a method of valuing an asset or liability and the related revenue or expense by recognizing that those amounts are worth more or less because of their tax status. Under this method, if straight-line depreciation is used for financial reporting and accelerated depreciation is used for income tax reporting, the tax effect of the difference is an adjustment to depreciation expense and to the allowance for depreciation. Accordingly, in the early years of an asset's life, the net book value of the asset is less (in relation to what it would be under other methods) because of the increased allowance. In later years, depreciation expense and the addition to the allowance are less each year than straight-line depreciation. The theory is that as an asset's *tax* depreciability is used up, it is worth less and its book value should reflect that fact. Tax effects under the net-of-tax method may be determined using either a deferred or a liability approach.

(iv) Comprehensive Recognition.   Under comprehensive recognition of deferred taxes, the tax effects of all timing and temporary differences are recognized. Thus recurring transactions will have both originating and reversing timing or temporary differences that may offset in the tax return but nevertheless leave temporary differences in the balance sheet. In this case the deferred taxes in the balance sheet "roll over" in a "revolving account," as do accounts receivable or accounts payable. Recurring timing or temporary differences of continually increasing amounts cause deferred income taxes in the balance sheet to likewise continually increase. An expanding company using various elections to defer income taxes currently payable on recurring transactions will have an increasing balance of deferred income taxes under comprehensive recognition.

(v) Partial Recognition.   Partial recognition of deferred taxes ignores recurring timing or temporary differences and timing or temporary differences that will not reverse for long periods. Income tax expense is based on income taxes currently payable, adjusted for the tax effects of nonrecurring timing or temporary differences that will materially increase or decrease income taxes payable in a relatively short period, such as 5 years. Accordingly, balance sheet amounts for deferred income taxes would be considerably less for most companies under partial recognition than under comprehensive recognition of deferred taxes.

Although APB Opinion No. 11 was generally a comprehensive approach to accounting for income taxes, exceptions were made for several special areas. Although some of these exceptions continue, SFAS No. 96 eliminates some significant exceptions, and the exceptions discussed later in this section are the only items for which SFAS No. 96 allows partial recognition. Because APB Opinion No. 11 only considered the tax effects of timing differences in any single year, other tax effects of basis differences were ignored, such as an increase in the tax basis of assets in a taxable business combination accounted for as a pooling of interests when the former book values of the assets are carried forward for financial reporting. SFAS No. 96 considers such differences temporary differences for which deferred taxes must be recognized and eliminates those exceptions to tax allocation that existed under APB Opinion No. 11.

(b) Move to the Liability Method.   The FASB issued SFAS No. 96 adopting the liability method in December 1987 as the culmination of a 6-year project to reconsider the accounting for income taxes. For various reasons, preparers, auditors, users, and educators had strongly supported moving from the deferred method to the liability method when the FASB undertook the project and while it was in process. Some objected to the increasing amounts of deferred taxes reported in balance sheets under APB Opinion No. 11 even though corporate income tax rates had been declining. Others believed income tax allocation under APB Opinion No. 11 had become too complex and viewed the liability method as a simpler approach. Still others thought the results obtained from applying the deferred method could only be explained procedurally and believed the liability method would be conceptually superior.

(c) Delay and Reconsideration. Some companies adopted SFAS No. 96 in their 1987 financial statements before they were required to do so, but others complained that the statement was too complex and difficult to apply and disagreed with some of the results of applying it. In December 1988, the FASB issued SFAS No. 100, "Accounting for Income Taxes—Deferral of the Effective Date of FASB Statement No. 96," to delay the required application of SFAS No. 96 by 1 year to 1990. In large part, the delay was to permit the FASB to provide implementation guidance. At the same time, the FASB began considering requests to simplify the application of SFAS No. 96, to relax its requirements for recognizing a deferred tax asset, and to modify several other specific requirements. In December 1989, the FASB issued SFAS No. 103, "Accounting for Income Taxes—Deferral of the Effective Date of FASB Statement No. 96," further delaying the required application of SFAS No. 96 until 1992 to continue consideration of those requests. The principal modifications being considered are to reduce complexity by eliminating the need to schedule and apply many tax planning strategies, which would simplify application of the statement, or to adopt a probability approach for the recognition of deferred tax assets, which would permit more tax assets to be recognized. The application of SFAS No. 96 described in this chapter would be modified if the FASB amends the statement to adopt any of those approaches. In the meantime, until SFAS No. 96 becomes effective (perhaps in an amended form) or a company voluntarily applies the statement, APB Opinion No. 11 and its amendments and interpretations remain in effect.

17.3 GENERAL APPROACH TO RECOGNITION OF INCOME TAXES AND EXCEPTIONS. The GAAP for recognition of income taxes are specified by SFAS No. 96. The statement, however, did not change a limited number of long-standing exceptions to its recognition principles and provided some specific exceptions.

(a) General Approach to Recognition. SFAS No. 96 requires comprehensive recognition of the effects of income taxes for temporary differences by the liability method. Under that method, the **tax effect** of a temporary difference is computed by multiplying the difference by the enacted tax rate(s) scheduled to be in effect for the year(s) the difference is expected to be reported in an income tax return(s). The tax effect may be either a deferred tax asset or a deferred tax liability. The statement, however, provides certain exceptions.

(b) Net Tax Debits Not Recognized. Although not an exception to its basic principle of comprehensive recognition, SFAS No. 96 does not permit the recognition of a net deferred tax asset except when it could be recovered by a tax refund from carryback of net deductible temporary differences against taxable income in the carryback period. This is strict application of tax law rather than an exception to the basic principle of comprehensive recognition and is discussed in section 17.5(a)(ii).

(c) Goodwill and Leveraged Lease Exceptions. SFAS No. 96 prohibits recognition of a deferred tax liability related to goodwill (or a deferred tax asset related to unallocated negative goodwill). This was a practical decision because recognizing a deferred tax liability would increase goodwill by a like amount since goodwill is merely the amount of the purchase price that cannot be allocated to identifiable assets in a business combination accounted for as a purchase. Not changing the accounting specified by SFAS No. 13, "Accounting for Leases," for income taxes related to leveraged leases also represented a practical decision. Although that accounting is not consistent with SFAS No. 96, the FASB concluded that changing it would require reconsidering the accounting for leveraged leases.

(d) Exceptions for Special Areas.   SFAS No. 96 continues APB Opinion No. 11's exceptions to recognition of deferred taxes in the areas addressed by APB Opinion No. 23, "Accounting for Income Taxes—Special Areas." Those areas are undistributed earnings of subsidiaries, "bad debt reserves" of savings and loan associations, "policyholders' surplus" of stock life insurance companies, and an investor's income from a corporate joint venture accounted for by the equity method. APB Opinion No. 23 explains that in the four special areas addressed, payment of income taxes may be postponed indefinitely or the taxes may never have to be paid because of special provisions in the federal tax laws. Accordingly, recognition of deferred taxes is not required in those four areas if the company is able to demonstrate that the payment of income taxes related to the item in question can be postponed indefinitely. If circumstances change and it appears that taxes will subsequently be paid, they must be accrued as tax expense at that time and may not be classified as an extraordinary item.

Although not addressed by APB Opinion No. 23, deposits in statutory reserve funds by U.S. steamship companies had some similar characteristics to those special areas and were not addressed by APB Opinion No. 11. They are likewise not addressed by SFAS No. 96, but in practice they are treated the same as the other special areas (see section 17.4).

APPLYING SFAS NO. 96

17.4 BASIC PRINCIPLES.   The objective of accounting for income taxes under SFAS No. 96 is to recognize all income taxes payable or available for refund for all events recognized in the financial statements. Income taxes payable or available for refund are measured by applying the enacted tax laws for each jurisdiction in which the company is subject to tax.

Most transactions and events are reported at the same time and in the same manner in the financial statements and in the tax return, and income taxes currently payable or refundable are determined from the tax return. Some items reported in the financial statements, however, are never reported in the tax return. Interest income from municipal bonds is not taxable on a U.S. federal income tax return, for example, and fines paid are not deductible.

Items that are reported partially or completely in different periods or in different amounts in the financial statements and in the tax return create temporary differences. For example, a temporary difference between the reported amount of depreciable assets and their tax basis is created when depreciation is deducted sooner in the tax return than the expense is reported in the income statement. A deferred tax liability or asset is recognized for the amount of taxes payable or refundable in future years as a result of temporary differences between the reported amount of an enterprise's assets and liabilities and their tax basis. The deferred tax liability or asset is measured (applying enacted tax law), in concept, as though tax returns were prepared for each future year in which temporary differences will result in taxable or deductible amounts after obtaining the most favorable tax position by applying **tax planning strategies.** However, the tax effect of earning income or incurring losses or expenses in future years is not anticipated.

The only exceptions permitted by SFAS No. 96 are (1) those addressed by APB Opinion No. 23 for the undistributed earnings of a subsidiary or corporate joint venture included in consolidated income, "bad debt reserves" of S&Ls, and "policyholders' surplus" of stock life insurance companies, (2) statutory reserves of U.S. steamship companies, (3) leveraged leases, and (4) goodwill.

(a) Temporary Differences.   Tax laws and financial accounting standards differ as to when or how some items are recognized or measured. Consequently, items may be reported sooner or later or in different amounts on the tax return than in the financial statements. Examples are:

1. *Revenue or Gain That Is Recognized in Income before It Is Taxable.* The receivable for an installment sale is a temporary difference that becomes taxable when collected.

2. *Expense or Loss That Is Recognized in Income before It Is Deductible for Taxes.* A liability for product warranty cost is a temporary difference that becomes deductible when settled.

3. *Revenue or Gain That Is Taxable before It Is Recognized in Income.* Prepaid rental income is taxable when cash is received. The liability for financial reporting is a temporary difference that becomes deductible (or results in nontaxable income) when the liability is settled.

4. *Expense or Loss That Is Deductible before It Is Recognized in Income.* An asset may be expensed or depreciated by an accelerated method on the tax return but depreciated straight-line for financial reporting. The amount by which the undepreciated cost exceeds the tax basis is a temporary difference that becomes taxable when the undepreciated cost is recovered.

5. *Differences Caused by Tax Credits.* Investment tax credit (ITC) or other tax credits may reduce the tax basis of an asset, and deferred ITC reduces the cost of the related asset for financial reporting. In either case, the difference between the accounting cost and tax basis is a temporary difference.

6. *Purchase Business Combinations.* The amounts assigned to assets and liabilities in a business combination accounted for by the purchase method may differ from their tax bases. Those differences are temporary differences.

7. *Differences in Accounting.* A U.S. company using the dollar as its functional currency for foreign operations under SFAS No. 52, "Foreign Currency Translation," will have temporary differences from remeasuring nonmonetary assets and liabilities after a change in exchange rates. If tax law allows assets to be indexed for inflation, temporary differences result if they are not also inflation adjusted for financial reporting (which is not currently permitted by GAAP).

8. *Transfers of Assets.* For purposes of consolidated financial statements, the excess of tax basis over the cost (as reported in the consolidated financial statements) of inventory and other assets that have been transferred between companies that are not included in the same consolidated tax return is a temporary difference. Questions 23–25 in the FASB special report on implementation of SFAS No. 96 (Simpson, Cassel, Giles, and Jonas, 1989) address this issue.

A difference between the tax basis of an asset or liability and the amount at which it is reported in the balance sheet is a temporary difference. It will be deductible or taxable in some future year when the related asset is recovered or the related liability is settled. An assumption inherent in financial statements prepared in accordance with GAAP is that amounts reported for assets will be recovered and for liabilities will be settled. A tax liability or asset is recognized for the deferred tax consequences of temporary differences. Earning income or incurring losses or expenses in future years are events that are not inherently assumed in financial statements for the current year. Under SFAS No. 96, the tax consequences of those future events are recognized in the future and do not affect the amount of taxes recognized currently for temporary differences.

A few temporary differences do not relate to a particular asset or liability on the balance sheet. For example, research and development costs are charged to expense as incurred under SFAS No. 2, "Accounting for Research and Development Costs," but may be deferred and amortized for tax reporting. Also, a contract accounted for by the percentage-of-completion method for which amounts billed have been collected but reported by the completed-contract method for tax purposes is a temporary difference for which no identifiable amount appears in the balance sheet. In those situations, there is an asset or liability for tax purposes and none for financial reporting.

(b) Annual Computation and Scheduling.   The first step in determining the net deferred tax asset or liability for all temporary differences at the date of the financial statements is to acquire information about when those differences will be deductible or taxable in the future, that is, when they are expected to be reported on a tax return. How precise that information needs to be will vary depending on particular circumstances. A separate computation of deferred taxes is prepared for each tax jurisdiction involved, such as federal, state, local, and foreign, applying the tax laws of each jurisdiction. A net capital loss expected in a future year would not be applied against ordinary income of that year, for example, in a tax jurisdiction in which capital losses are deductible only from capital gains. Provisions in the tax law regarding loss carryback and carryforward determine whether net deductions in a particular year offset net taxable amounts in earlier or later years.

Tax laws do not usually treat income and losses the same way. A tax payment is due for taxable income but a refund is not received for a tax loss unless it can be carried back and applied against taxable income of a prior year. Similarly, SFAS No. 96 prohibits recognition of a tax benefit for deductible temporary differences (and for an operating loss or tax credit carryforward) that do not offset taxable temporary differences or for which a loss carryback refund could not be recovered. However, SFAS No. 96 does require a company to recognize the effects of qualifying tax-planning strategies that would increase the extent of offsetting. Most qualifying strategies involve actions that would accelerate or delay the recovery of an asset or settlement of a liability and thereby accelerate or delay the reversal of the related temporary difference. A tax-planning strategy changes the future year(s) in which a temporary difference results in a taxable or deductible amount so as to achieve offsetting that otherwise would not occur and thereby reduces the deferred tax liability or increases the deferred tax asset that can be recognized to the greatest extent possible.

To be a qualifying tax-planning strategy, a strategy must be prudent and feasible and not involve significant cost to implement. Although the company may never actually have to use the strategy, management must both be able and intend to use it, if necessary, to reduce taxes. For example, a company with an operating loss carryforward scheduled to expire unused in the following year could not recognize a tax benefit (asset) for it. If the company had a taxable temporary difference for an installment receivable due in a later future year, however, an acceptable strategy might be to sell the receivable at its recorded amount in the year the carryforward would expire so as to accelerate taxable income to that year, resulting in eliminating the taxes otherwise payable for the temporary difference for the installment receivable. A strategy to accelerate the recovery of an installment receivable ordinarily would not involve a significant cost to implement. It would, however, if the receivable could only be sold at less than its recorded amount, that is, if sale of the receivable would result in recognizing a significant loss.

17.5 RECOGNITION AND MEASUREMENT.   A deferred tax liability or asset is recognized and measured under SFAS No. 96 by applying enacted tax laws and rates to the taxable or deductible amounts that will occur in future years as a result of temporary differences that exist at the date of the financial statements. Discounting is not permitted.

(a) Recognition of a Deferred Tax Liability or Asset.   The tax law in most jurisdictions is often viewed as asymmetrical because taxable income always results in tax payments but tax losses often do not result in tax refunds. Under tax law, the current tax benefit of a loss carryforward is zero. Any future tax benefit will be a consequence of earning taxable income in some future year. The requirements of SFAS No. 96 for recognition and measurement of a deferred tax liability or asset are symmetrical with the tax law. Because a gain may be taxed but a refund may not be made for a loss, SFAS No. 96 likewise requires recognition of a deferred tax liability but may not allow recognition of a deferred tax asset.

(i) Deferred Tax Liability.   SFAS No. 96 requires recognition of a liability for the deferred tax consequences of temporary differences that will result in net taxable amounts in future years. The net taxable or deductible amount for each future year is determined by first offsetting deductible and taxable amounts that will occur in the same future years and then by applying any loss carryback and carryforward provisions of the tax law to determine the net taxable amounts in each future year. Those net taxable amounts are multiplied by the enacted tax rates applicable to each future year. The result is then reduced by any allowable tax credit carryforwards to determine the amount of the deferred tax liability to be recognized at the balance sheet date for which the computation is made.

The following example illustrates an annual computation if scheduling is required. The tax law in this jurisdiction permits a 1-year loss carryback and a 2-year loss carryforward. The enacted tax rate is 34% for future years.

	Temporary Differences	Future Years				
		Year 2	Year 3	Year 4	Year 5	Year 6
Taxable differences	$600	$100	$100	$200	$100	$100
Deductible differences	(500)		(400)	(100)		
	$100	100	(300)	100	100	100
Loss carryback		(100)	100			
Loss carryforward			200	(100)	(100)	
Net taxable amount		$ -0-	$ -0-	$ -0-	$ -0-	$100
Deferred tax liability						$ 34

(ii) Deferred Tax Asset.   SFAS No. 96 requires recognition of a tax benefit for temporary differences that will result in deductible amounts in future years by:

1. Reducing a deferred tax liability to the extent that those deductible amounts will offset taxable amounts resulting from other temporary differences (the offsetting procedure described above for determining a deferred tax liability).
2. Recognizing a deferred tax asset to the extent that the tax law would permit carryback of those deductible amounts for a refund of taxes paid in the current or preceding years.

SFAS No. 96 prohibits recognition of a deferred tax asset for any additional amount of deductible temporary differences. In effect, any additional amount of deductible temporary differences is the same as an operating loss carryforward. Prior to earning income in future years, the current tax benefit (as measured based on tax law) of an operating loss carryforward is zero. Any future tax benefit will be a consequence of earning income in future years. Under GAAP, income that is expected in future years cannot be recognized in financial statements for the current year. Under SFAS No. 96, the tax consequences of income that is expected in future years cannot be recognized in financial statements for the current year.

The following example illustrates an annual computation that results in recognition of a deferred tax asset. The tax law in this jurisdiction permits a 1-year loss carryback and a 2-year loss carryforward.

	Current Year	Future Years		
		Year 2	Year 3	Year 4
Taxable income	$300			
Taxable differences		$200	$100	$100
Deductible difference		(900)		
	300	(700)	100	100
Loss carryback	(300)	300		
Loss carryforward		200	(100)	(100)
Operating loss carryforward	$ -0-	$(200)	$ -0-	$ -0-

A tax benefit is recognized for $700 of the $900 deductible temporary difference that reverses in year 2 by (1) offsetting the $400 of taxable temporary differences that reverse in years 2–4 and (2) recognizing a deferred tax asset for the amount of income taxes that would be refundable based on a $300-loss carryback from year 2 to the current year. No tax benefit is recognized for the remaining $200 that in effect is the same as the operating loss carryforward.

As noted above, a deferred tax asset for deductible temporary differences is the amount of refund that could be recovered by loss carryback. Measured in that manner, tax rates in effect during the carryback years are one factor in determining the amount of the deferred tax asset. Some have objected to this requirement because they expect that a tax benefit for a deductible temporary difference will usually be realized by offsetting taxable income earned in a future year. If so, the benefit will be realized at the tax rate applicable to that future year rather than at the tax rate of the carryback year. That is, the tax benefit of a $1,000 net deductible amount for a future year in which the tax rate is 34% might be measured by carryback to a year in which the tax rate was 46% and, accordingly, reported as a deferred tax asset of $460 rather than the $340 expected to be realized by offsetting taxable income earned in that future year. That issue is addressed by questions 21 and 22 in the FASB special report on implementation of SFAS No. 96 (Simpson, Cassel, Giles, and Jonas, 1989).

Others have objected to SFAS No. 96's prohibition against recognizing a deferred tax asset for a net carryforward when they believe the company will earn enough taxable income in future years to realize a tax benefit for the net deductible amount. Both of these objections, however, arise from SFAS No. 96's reliance on tax law and its prohibition against anticipating taxable income beyond that resulting from recovery of the carrying amount of an enterprise's assets and settlement of the carrying amount of an enterprise's liabilities as reported in the enterprise's financial statements. Supporters of SFAS No. 96 point out that future income may be virtually certain from contracts or orders on hand at the date of the financial statements, but if GAAP do not allow that income to be recognized, they believe a tax asset dependent on that income should not be recognized either.

(iii) Offset of Taxable and Deductible Amounts. Tax law determines which amounts can offset each other and, accordingly, which deductible temporary differences can offset which taxable temporary differences in any future period. If capital losses can only be offset against capital gains, for example, deductible temporary differences related to capital assets (as defined by tax law) cannot be offset against other types of taxable temporary differences in computing deferred taxes under SFAS No. 96. Or the deductible temporary difference may result in a capital loss deduction or an ordinary deduction depending on whether the carrying amount of the capital asset will be recovered by sale or by use. Any limitations imposed on certain deductions by tax law must be observed in applying SFAS No. 96.

(iv) Pattern of Taxable or Deductible Amounts. Whether detailed information about the pattern in which temporary differences will result in taxable or deductible amounts is necessary depends on a company's particular circumstances (see discussion of "Aggregate

Calculation'' in section 17.5(f)). When necessary, however, determination of that pattern for some temporary differences requires estimating when the related asset will be recovered or the related liability (such as a warranty obligation) will be settled. Questions 8–19 in the FASB special report on implementation of SFAS No. 96 provide guidance on the pattern of taxable or deductible amounts for various types of temporary differences.

When temporary differences related to depreciable and intangible assets will become taxable or deductible is readily predictable but may require considering new temporary differences that will arise from existing depreciable and intangible assets for which there are no temporary differences at the date of the financial statements; this would be the case, for example, when new depreciable assets have been acquired at the close of the period that will give rise to new ''yet unborn'' temporary differences while existing temporary differences are ''playing out.'' The response to question 14 in the FASB special report on implementation of SFAS No. 96 (Simpson, Cassel, Giles, and Jonas, 1989) states that:

> Consideration of future originating depreciation or amortization differences and their subsequent reversal may sometimes result in (a) net deductible amounts for which a tax benefit cannot be recognized for some years and (b) taxable amounts that increase a deferred tax liability for other years. That result could occur because of limitations on the carryback or carryforward of net deductible amounts to other years, or it could occur if the deductible amounts are capital losses that can only reduce capital gains and there are no capital gain temporary differences that can be offset.

> A first-in, first-out (FIFO) pattern should be used for **all** depreciable and amortizable assets in a particular tax jurisdiction if consideration of future originating differences results in creating net deductible amounts for which a tax benefit cannot be recognized and thereby either increases a deferred tax liability or reduces a deferred tax asset. In other words, there is a limitation on consideration of future originating differences if, as a result, future taxable income is greater than it otherwise would be based on consideration of only the **net** amount of temporary differences that exist at the date of the financial statements.

Temporary differences related to assets and liabilities that are measured at present values will require the consistent application of various assumptions from period to period to establish the pattern by which those temporary differences will become taxable or deductible. This will be the case, for example, for the temporary difference related to a receivable from an installment sale measured at present value that involves the collection of both principal and interest. Either of two methods, known as the loan amortization method and the present value method, may be used. The same method for a particular category of temporary difference in a particular tax jurisdiction should be used consistently from year to year, and a change in method is a change in accounting principle.

The following example illustrates both of those methods. The assumptions are as follows:

1. An installment sale occurs on the last day of year 1.
2. The amount of the installment receivable is $1,000 for financial reporting and its tax basis is zero.
3. The interest rate is 10%. Five annual payments of $264 are due starting at the end of year 2. The amortization schedule is as follows:

Year	Interest	Principal	Balance
At inception			$1,000
2	$100	$164	836
3	84	180	656
4	66	198	458
5	46	218	240
6	24	240	—

Under the loan amortization method, each future cash receipt of $264 is allocated first to interest and then the remainder to reversal of the $1,000 temporary difference. Under the present value method, the reversal pattern is considered to be the present value of each of those $264 cash receipts. As of the end of year 1, the pattern of taxable amounts under each method is as follows:

	Future Years				
	Year 2	Year 3	Year 4	Year 5	Year 6
Loan amortization method	$164	$180	$198	$218	$240
Present value method	240	218	198	180	164

(v) Temporary Differences for Foreign Assets and Liabilities.   A foreign asset or liability can have a temporary difference for the difference between its foreign currency carrying amount and tax basis the same as a domestic asset or liability. In addition, a company that uses the U.S. dollar as the functional currency for measuring its foreign operations under SFAS No. 52, "Foreign Currency Translation," has another source of temporary differences when exchange rates change. That is, after a change in exchange rates, recovering the U.S. dollar cost of a foreign nonmonetary asset would require more or fewer units of foreign currency. The change in exchange rates creates a temporary difference between the foreign currency equivalent of the U.S. dollar cost of that nonmonetary asset and its foreign currency tax basis. For example, if a foreign subsidiary purchases FC1,200 of inventory when the exchange rate is FC1 = $1US, the U.S. dollar historical cost is $1,200. If the exchange rate changes to FC1.20 = $1US, revenues of FC1,440 are required to recover the $1,200 U.S. dollar historical cost of that inventory. Since the tax basis of that inventory is only FC1,200, there is a FC240 (FC1,440 minus FC1,200) taxable temporary difference.

(b) Measurement of a Deferred Tax Liability or Asset.   The deferred tax liability or asset for each future year is measured at the date of the financial statements based on enacted tax laws and rates applicable to those years or the current and prior years if a carryback is involved. The measurements also consider all elections that are expected to be made for tax purposes.

   Graduated tax rates may pose a problem to some companies in the computation described above because a deferred tax liability is measured as though temporary differences at the date of the financial statements will be the only taxable amounts in future years. Such a company is permitted to use an estimated average tax rate for measurement if it deals separately with any unusual situation, such as an unusually large temporary difference that will become taxable in a single year, to which an average rate would not appropriately apply.

(c) Operating Losses and Tax Credit Carryforwards and Carrybacks.   Carrybacks and carryforwards are treated differently under SFAS No. 96 just as they are generally treated differently under tax law.

(i) Recognition of a Tax Benefit for Carrybacks.   Items that can be carried back under tax law, such as operating losses and tax credits, will produce a current refund of taxes paid in the prior years to which they are carried. SFAS No. 96 applies the same approach to net deductible temporary differences. Therefore, a net deductible temporary difference can be recognized as a deferred tax asset to the extent that it could result in a refund of taxes paid in prior years to which it would be carried back. Whether the net deductible temporary difference will, in fact, be carried back will depend on future income and tax deductions that are combined with the difference on a tax return. If net taxable income is reported on the tax return for that future year, the actual tax benefit of those net deductible temporary differences will be realized at tax rates in effect in that future year rather than at rates in the carryback period. The change in the amount of the tax benefit, however, is a consequence of earning income in that future year and it is reported in that future year under SFAS No. 96.

(ii) Recognition of a Tax Benefit for Carryforwards.   Recognition of the tax consequences of earning future income is prohibited when applying SFAS No. 96. Consequently, a tax benefit is recognized for a tax loss carryforward only if it reduces a deferred tax liability based on offsetting temporary differences that become taxable during the carryforward period.

(iii) Reporting the Tax Benefit of Operating Loss Carryforwards or Carrybacks.   With certain exceptions, the tax benefits recognized for an operating loss carryforward or carryback are reported based on the source of the income or loss in the current year and not by the source of the carryforward or taxes paid in a prior year. (Those exceptions are carryforwards from a purchase business combination, quasi reorganization, and employee stock options, which are discussed in section 17.6.) Thus, the tax benefit of an operating loss carryforward reduces income tax expense from continuing operations if realization of the tax benefit results from income from continuing operations or is reported as an extraordinary item if realization is from an extraordinary item, irrespective of the source of the operating loss carryforward.

(d) Carryforwards for Tax Purposes and for Financial Reporting.   If the company has an operating loss carryforward for tax purposes, its operating loss for financial reporting is that amount (1) reduced to the extent that it offsets temporary differences that will result in net taxable amounts during the carryforward period and (2) increased by temporary differences that will result in net tax deductions for which a tax benefit cannot be recognized in the financial statements. If there is no operating loss carryforward for tax purposes, the last amount, listed as in (2) above, will be the operating loss carryforward for financial reporting.

(e) Tax-Planning Strategies.   When all temporary differences have been scheduled and carrybacks and carryforwards have been used to apply deductible amounts to the greatest extent possible to reduce taxable amounts for all future years, some years may have net deductible amounts for which a deferred tax asset cannot be recognized under SFAS No. 96. If those net deductible amounts could occur in other, different years in which there are net taxable amounts or vice versa, however, the company's net deferred tax liability might be reduced or eliminated or a deferred tax asset might be recognizable. Changing the future years in which temporary differences will result in taxable or deductible amounts is possible by employing tax-planning strategies.

The following example illustrates the effect of tax-planning strategies. The assumptions are as follows:

1. The tax law permits a 3-year loss carryback and a 15-year loss carryforward.
2. An enterprise has only two temporary differences. Absent tax-planning strategies, one will result in a $1,000 taxable amount in year 5, and the other will result in a $400 deductible amount in year 10.
3. There is a qualifying tax-planning strategy to accelerate the $400 deductible amount from year 10 to year 5.

	Future Years	
	Year 5	Year 10
Net taxable (deductible) amounts before tax-planning strategy	$1,000	$ (400)
Tax-planning strategy	(400)	400
Net taxable amount after tax-planning strategy	$ 600	$ -0-

Absent a qualifying tax-planning strategy, the enterprise would recognize a deferred tax liability for the $1,000 taxable amount in year 5 and could not recognize a tax benefit for the $400 deductible amount in year 10 because of the 3-year limitation on loss carryback.

Companies frequently employ tax-planning strategies to reduce taxes payable in the current year (by deferring revenues or accelerating deductions) or to preserve the benefit of an expiring loss or tax credit carryforward (by selling assets at a gain whose tax is offset by use of the carryforward and purchasing similar assets with a higher tax basis that will provide larger tax deductions in the future than the deduction for the assets sold).

(i) Limits on Strategies.   For purposes of accruing a deferred tax liability or asset under the requirements of SFAS No. 96, tax-planning strategies are limited to (1) actions that management would take to accelerate or delay the recovery of an asset or the settlement of a liability so that the related temporary difference would result in a taxable or deductible amount in a different future year, (2) the manner in which an asset is recovered or a liability is settled if that affects the type of taxable or deductible amount (for example, ordinary income or capital gain) that will result from a temporary difference, and (3) elections for tax purposes (for example, to claim either a deduction or tax credit for foreign taxes paid). Strategies that involve earning income or incurring losses or expenses in future years are prohibited.

(ii) Use of Strategies Required.   SFAS No. 96 requires recognition of the effect of qualifying tax-planning strategies that would move amounts among years to minimize a deferred tax liability or to maximize a deferred tax asset for temporary differences at the date of the financial statements. Such strategies might be to (1) sell an installment receivable to accelerate taxable income, (2) sell and leaseback assets to accelerate taxable income, (3) settle an estimated liability sooner than usual to accelerate a tax deduction, or (4) dispose of obsolete inventory to accelerate a tax deduction. The strategy must be an action that is prudent and feasible and over which management has discretion and control. It cannot involve significant cost to implement. Although the strategy may never need to be actually used, management must have both the ability and intent to use the strategy, if necessary, to reduce taxes. Note that the use of tax-planning strategies is not optional under SFAS No. 96 but, rather, is required. Questions 52–68 in the FASB special report on implementation of SFAS No. 96 (Simpson, Cassel, Giles, and Jonas, 1989) provide guidance about the requirements for tax-planning strategies.

(f) Aggregate Calculation.   All companies need some understanding of the pattern and timing of reversals of temporary differences, but the level of detail may vary depending on a company's particular circumstances. That understanding is necessary because of the requirements for balance sheet classification, recognition of tax benefits based on offsetting, and measurements based on enacted tax laws and rates.

However, some companies may not need to do extensive scheduling and consideration of tax-planning strategies in order to satisfy those requirements of SFAS No. 96. For example, a company with only net taxable temporary differences or with sufficient taxable temporary differences to use any operating loss carryforward before it would expire may be able to compute its deferred tax liability on an aggregate basis (i.e., by multiplying the net taxable temporary difference by the enacted tax rate). Likewise, a company with large amounts that will not be deductible for many years without carryback benefit and that cannot be moved by a qualifying tax-planning strategy could ignore those deductible temporary differences and make an aggregate computation for near-term taxable temporary differences. Alternatively, the existence of a qualifying tax-planning strategy to accelerate those deductible amounts to earlier years could also justify an aggregate computation. Estimates may be required in these situations if there are phased-in changes in tax law or tax rates or if the company would be significantly affected by graduated tax rates in some years (see section 17.5(b), "Measurement of a Deferred Tax Liability"). Questions 1–7 in the FASB special report on implementation of SFAS No. 96 provide guidance on use of an aggregate calculation and the need for scheduling.

17.6 SPECIAL APPLICATIONS.   SFAS No. 96 provides for a number of special applications.

(a) Regulated Companies.   SFAS No. 71, "Accounting for the Effects of Certain Types of Regulation," provides special accounting rules for companies that are rate regulated, such as utilities. A company subject to SFAS No. 71, for example, may be required to capitalize a cost that other companies would charge to expense. If capitalization of that cost creates a temporary difference, a deferred tax liability is recognized. If it is probable that future revenue will be provided for the payment of that deferred tax liability, a new asset is recognized for that probable future revenue. That asset and the deferred tax liability are shown as an asset and liability and are not offset. Similar accounting also may result from other special accounting rules for rate-regulated companies such as those for (1) the equity component of the allowance for funds used during construction, (2) tax benefits that are flowed through to customers when temporary differences originate, and (3) adjustments of a deferred tax liability or asset for an enacted change in tax law or rates (see Chapter 23, "Regulated Utilities").

(b) Leveraged Leases.   SFAS No. 13, "Accounting for Leases," and FIN No. 21, "Accounting for Leases in a Business Combination," specify special accounting for the tax benefits associated with a leveraged lease. SFAS No. 96 does not change that special accounting (except to substitute temporary difference for timing difference) (see Chapter 16, "Leases").

Deferred tax credits related to leveraged leases may be offset, subject to certain limitations, by temporary differences (not related to leveraged leases) that result in net deductible amounts or by an operating loss or tax credit carryforward if a tax benefit could not otherwise by recognized for those items.

(c) Business Combinations.   SFAS No. 96 significantly changes the accounting for the income tax effects of business combinations. Under APB Opinion No. 16, "Business Combinations," the tax effect of a difference between the fair value and the tax basis of an asset acquired or a liability assumed in a purchase business combination was recognized in the accounting cost assigned to the asset or liability, that is, it was recorded on a net-of-tax basis. Sometimes the tax effect was discounted. Also any difference between the tax basis and recorded amount of an asset or liability was not a timing difference under APB Opinion No. 11. Questions 30–35 in the FASB special report on implementation of SFAS No. 96 address business combinations.

(i) Nontaxable Business Combinations.   A purchase business combination may be accomplished in a tax-free exchange so the tax bases of assets and liabilities carry over. Differences between the amounts assigned and the tax bases are temporary differences and a deferred tax liability or asset is recognized except for temporary differences related to goodwill (positive or negative) and leveraged leases.

The following example illustrates the accounting for a nontaxable business combination that is accounted for as a purchase. The assumptions are as follows:

1. The purchase price is $30,000.
2. The acquired company's only assets are depreciable assets with a pretax fair value of $28,000 and a tax basis of $20,000. The only liability is the deferred tax liability for the temporary difference related to those depreciable assets.
3. The enacted tax rate is 34% for all years.

The amounts recorded to account for the purchase transaction would be as follows:

Depreciable assets	$28,000
Deferred tax liability (34% of the $8,000 temporary difference between the assigned value and the tax basis of the depreciable assets)	(2,720)
Goodwill	4,720
Purchase price	$30,000

(ii) Taxable Business Combinations.   The amounts assigned to various assets and liabilities may differ for tax and accounting in a taxable purchase business combination. Those differences are temporary differences and a deferred tax liability or asset is recognized except for temporary differences related to goodwill (positive or negative) and leveraged leases. Likewise, a taxable business combination may be accounted for as a pooling-of-interests. The differences resulting from increases in tax bases are temporary differences. Tax benefits attributable to the increase in tax basis that are recognized at the combination date are allocated to contributed capital; those recognized thereafter reduce income tax expense.

(iii) Carryforwards—Purchase Method.   If (1) the combining companies expect to file a consolidated tax return and (2) the tax law permits an operating loss or tax credit carryforward of one company to offset taxable income of the other company, an operating loss or tax credit carryforward of either company is recognized as a reduction of the deferred tax liability of the other as of the acquisition date. The effect is to reduce positive goodwill in the acquisition (or produce negative goodwill that reduces noncurrent assets other than marketable securities before being recorded).

(iv) Carryforwards—Pooling-of-Interests Method.   A combining company in a tax-free pooling may have operating loss or tax credit carryforwards that can be used to reduce a deferred tax liability of the other combining company subsequently if a consolidated income tax return is filed. The tax benefit of the carryforward is recognized in that circumstance as part of the adjustment to restate financial statements for prior periods on a combined basis.

(v) Subsequent Recognition of Carryforwards.   Tax benefits of acquired carryforwards that were not recognized at the date of a purchase business combination, when subsequently recognized by reducing a deferred tax liability or taxes payable, are first applied to reduce any goodwill and other noncurrent intangible assets from the acquisition to zero, and any remaining tax benefits are recognized as a reduction of income tax expense.

The tax benefits of net deductible temporary differences and operating loss or tax credit carryforwards that arise after the combination date are recognized as a reduction of income tax expense. Whether subsequently recognized tax benefits are attributable to items existing at the combination date or arising thereafter is determined by the tax rules for the sequence in which those items are utilized for tax purposes. If not determinable by reference to the tax law, tax benefits are prorated between (1) a reduction of goodwill and other noncurrent intangible assets and (2) income tax expense.

A carryforward from a prior year may sometimes offset taxable income attributable to an originating deductible temporary difference in the current year, for example, a temporary difference related to a liability for unearned rental income or for subscriptions received in advance. In effect, the carryforward at the beginning of the year is replaced by a deductible temporary difference at the end of the year. Recognition of a tax benefit depends on whether that deductible temporary difference meets the criteria for recognition of tax benefits.

(d) Quasi Reorganizations.   In a quasi reorganization, charges or credits go directly to contributed capital and any deficit in retained earnings is eliminated by a charge to contributed capital. Because a quasi reorganization is considered an accounting "fresh start," the tax benefits of operating loss or tax credit carryforwards existing at the time of the quasi reorganization are credited directly to contributed capital if subsequently recognized. However, some reorganizations have involved only a deficit reclassification from retained earnings; the tax benefits of carryforwards for them are reported in income normally and then are reclassified to contributed capital.

(e) Comprehensive Alternative Tax Systems—Alternative Minimum Tax.   Some tax jurisdictions may have parallel tax systems with the tax liability for each period determined by computing taxes under both systems; usually, there is a requirement that the company pay the higher tax so determined.

In the United States, the alternative minimum tax (AMT) is such a parallel tax system. The tax rules for regular tax and for AMT are different. As a result, a particular type of temporary difference, such as depreciation temporary differences, may be one amount for regular tax and a different amount for AMT. Future reversal patterns (timing and amount) may also be different. Or a temporary difference may exist for one and not the other system. Thus, accrual of a U.S. federal deferred tax liability or asset requires regular tax and AMT calculations for future years. The amount accrued is the higher of regular tax or AMT in future years. An AMT credit can be carried forward indefinitely. It may be recognized in deferred tax calculations by reducing a future year's regular tax to the tentative minimum tax for that future year. A deferred tax asset cannot be recognized for any additional amount of AMT credit carryforward.

Future originating depreciation or amortization temporary differences can sometimes create a book income adjustment that may be eliminated if there is a qualifying tax-planning strategy to accelerate the recovery of those depreciable or amortizable assets. Another effect of that tax-planning strategy might be to reduce the extent of scheduling. In applying each system, the same strategies or assumptions must be used for temporary differences that exist under both systems.

ACCOUNTING FOR THE INVESTMENT TAX CREDIT

17.7 BACKGROUND.   The investment tax credit was first provided by the Revenue Act of 1962. Since then, some features of the credit have been modified, the credit has been discontinued and reinstated and discontinued again. Some other countries have similar programs, but they have not generated nearly as much controversy over accounting treatment. The credit was introduced as an inducement to increase business investment in productive assets and thereby stimulate the economy; how to account for it immediately caused strong differences of opinion in and among the accounting profession, industry, and government agencies.

The first APB opinion on how to account for the credit was largely ignored by industry, and the SEC effectively suspended it before the APB modified the opinion to make either of two methods acceptable. Nearly a decade later, when the investment credit was being reinstated in the tax system, the APB again sought to establish a single method to account for the credit; Congress intervened and wrote into the Revenue Act authorizing the new credit a provision that prohibited the APB or any other such body, such as the SEC, from mandating a single method to account for the investment tax credit.

17.8 CONCEPTUAL APPROACHES AND THE RESULTING CONTROVERSY.   When the investment tax credit was first enacted, the APB considered three approaches in APB Opinion No. 2 on how to account for the credit:

1. **Contribution to capital** in the form of a subsidy from the government to the taxpayer.
2. **Tax reduction** that reduces a company's income tax expense in the year the credit is received; this approach views the credit as a selective reduction in income tax rates.
3. **Cost reduction** that should be recognized in income over the productive life of the asset to which the credit relates:
   a. Through reduced depreciation, or
   b. Through reduced tax expense.

The first approach, viewing the credit as a subsidy to be treated as contributed capital, was rejected by the APB and has received no serious consideration in this country since. The question, therefore, is not whether the credit should be included in income but rather when— in the year "earned" or over the life of the property.

By a narrow margin, the APB adopted the cost reduction approach in APB Opinion No. 2 ("Accounting for the 'Investment Credit'"). Under the Revenue Act of 1962, the investment credit reduced the tax basis of the related asset, thus reducing the amount of depreciation a taxpayer could claim over the life of the asset. The APB favored the same approach for financial reporting—that is, reduce the carrying amount of the asset by the amount of the credit and thereby recognize the credit in income over the life of the asset through reduced depreciation—but other approaches that would achieve the same result were also acceptable. For example, an investment credit could be carried as a deferred credit that would be amortized to income over the life of the asset. Also, under Opinion No. 2, the amount of credit to be recognized was limited to the amount realized as a reduction of income taxes payable; investment credit carryforwards were not to be recognized as assets.

When Opinion No. 2 was issued (December 1962), APB opinions relied on "general acceptability" for authority, and that opinion was not well received. To the contrary, many companies indicated they would not follow the opinion. In January 1963 the SEC issued ASR No. 96, "Accounting for the 'Investment Credit,'" which indicated that the SEC would allow companies subject to its jurisdiction to report the investment credit in income over the productive life of the property or by the "48–52%" method, or in certain cases as a reduction of income tax expense in the year the credit arises.

The Revenue Act of 1964 eliminated the requirement to reduce the tax basis of the property by the amount of the investment credit. In March 1964 the APB issued Opinion No. 4 ["Accounting for the 'Investment Credit'" (Amending APB No. 2)], indicating that the method specified by Opinion No. 2 should be considered preferable but that the alternative of reducing income tax expense by the amount of the credit in the year the credit arises is also an acceptable method.

Because of a "booming" economy later in the 1960s, Congress suspended the investment credit in 1966, reinstated it in 1967, and eliminated it in 1969. Then, to stimulate investment in the recession that occurred in the early 1970s, Congress began considering the possibility of reinstating the investment credit. In an attempt to resolve the accounting for the credit, the APB rushed out an exposure draft of an opinion proposing to require that the credit be recognized in income over the life of the asset rather than in the year it reduces income taxes payable. In enacting the credit in the Revenue Act of 1971, however, Congress included in the Act a provision that no one could require a particular method of accounting to be followed in reports to federal agencies, including the SEC. As a result, the APB did not issue another opinion addressing the accounting for the investment tax credit, and APB Opinions No. 2 and No. 4 continue in force.

Although not so described in Opinions No. 2 and No. 4, the two methods of accounting for the investment tax credit allowed by those two opinions are known in practice as the **deferral** method and the **flow-through** method, respectively. (The deferred method of interperiod income tax allocation is also sometimes called the "deferral" method and should not be confused with the deferral method of accounting for the investment credit.)

17.9 DEFERRAL METHOD.   Although the deferral method (APB Opinion No. 2) was deemed the preferable method of accounting for the investment tax credit by the APB, it is less widely used in practice. The deferral method is used most widely by financial institutions, such as banks and leasing companies, to account for investment credits retained on property leased on financing leases (sales-type, direct financing, and leveraged leases under SFAS No. 13). In essence, such institutions often consider the investment credit as part of the yield on a financing lease, that is, like interest on a note receivable.

Although APB Opinion No. 2 encouraged reducing the carrying amount of the asset by the amount of the credit, ASR No. 96, "Accounting for the 'Investment Credit,'" prohibited that approach for companies subject to SEC jurisdiction. The usual approach in practice under the deferral method now is to carry the investment credit as a deferred credit and to amortize the credit to income on some systematic and rational basis. Amortization might be (1) in proportion to depreciation on the related asset, (2) by the interest method described in APB Opinion No. 21, "Interest on Receivables and Payables," for a financing lease, or (3) as the credit is no longer subject to recapture, for tax purposes. Opinion No. 2 also encourages including the amortization of the investment credit as a component of accounting income before income taxes, but the credit is now generally treated as a reduction of income tax expense except when it is treated as part of the yield on a financing lease.

17.10 FLOW-THROUGH METHOD AND RECOGNITION OF THE CREDIT.   The flow-through method of accounting for investment tax credits, which is recognized as an acceptable method under APB Opinion No. 4, is widely used in practice. Under this method, the amount of the credit recognized in a year is treated as a reduction of income tax expense of that year.

In addition to investment tax credits realized as a reduction of income taxes payable on a company's income tax return, including investment credits carried back and realized as a refund of income taxes previously paid, the company may also be able to recognize all or part of any additional investment tax credit carryforward available as a reduction of its deferred income tax liability. A tax credit carryforward functions the same as an operating loss carryforward under SFAS No. 96. That is, the tax credit carryforward reduces deferred income tax liabilities related to net taxable temporary differences scheduled during the tax credit carryforward period. Any existing or enacted future limitations on recognition of the credit apply, such as a limitation allowing only a percentage of the tax due for any year to be offset by the credit.

Although the investment tax credit was eliminated by the 1986 Revenue Act, various other tax credits remain available. Those credits are treated the same as the investment credit in applying SFAS No. 96. Further, given the history of the investment tax credit in this country, it could be reinstated the next time Congress decides to use the tax system to encourage companies to purchase new production equipment as a means of stimulating the economy.

17.11 INVESTMENT CREDITS IN FINANCING LEASES.   SFAS No. 13, "Accounting for Leases," specifically addresses the accounting for the investment tax credit only in paragraphs 42–44 concerning a lessor's accounting for leveraged leases. One condition for accounting for a lease as a leveraged lease under that statement is that the investment tax credit be accounted for as specified by those paragraphs. In essence, an investment tax credit to be realized on a leveraged lease transaction must be recorded as a receivable and as unearned income. The unearned income is then recognized in income over the term of the lease only in the years the lessor's net investment in the lease is positive.

SFAS No. 13 does not address the accounting for investment tax credit retained by a lessor on leases of other types, and either the deferral or the flow-through method may be used for a sales-type, direct financing, or operating lease. Frequently, however, financial institutions, such as banks and leasing companies, account for the investment credit by the deferral method and consider it as part of the "yield" on the lease receivable for a financing lease.

FINANCIAL REPORTING

17.12 TAX ALLOCATION WITHIN A PERIOD.   The process of allocating income taxes among income from continuing operations and other items within a period is known as **intraperiod tax allocation.** (This should not be confused with tax allocation among interim periods of a year, which is discussed later in this section.) Intraperiod income tax allocation is the apportionment of total income tax for the period among income from continuing operations, disposal of a segment of a business, extraordinary items, prior period adjustments, and direct entries to stockholders' equity.

The first step in intraperiod income tax allocation under SFAS No. 96 is to determine the tax expense or benefit related to income or loss from continuing operations as though that were the only amount in pretax financial income or loss. The difference between that amount and total tax expense or benefit is the incremental tax effect to be allocated to all of the other items listed above. If there is only one other item (for example, an extraordinary item), the incremental tax effect is allocated to it. If there is more than one item, the incremental tax effect is allocated between (or among) them as follows:

1. Determine the incremental tax benefit of all items with a loss.
2. Allocate the incremental tax benefit for all loss items pro rata among those items.
3. Allocate the difference between (a) the tax expense or benefit determined earlier for income or loss from all items other than continuing operations and (b) the incremental tax benefit determined in (1) above for all items with a loss (c) pro rata among all items with a gain.

Questions 41–43 in the FASB special report on implementation of SFAS No. 96 provide guidance on intraperiod income tax allocation.

17.13 FINANCIAL STATEMENT PRESENTATION AND DISCLOSURE. SFAS No. 96 requires deferred tax liabilities or assets to be classified as current and noncurrent in a classified balance sheet. The classification is determined for each tax jurisdiction, and offset of liabilities and assets attributable to different tax jurisdictions is not permitted. The current amount of the deferred tax liability or asset is the net deferred tax consequences of temporary differences (1) that will result in net taxable or deductible amounts within one year, (2) that are related to an asset or liability classified as current because the operating cycle is longer than one year, or (3) that are not related to an asset or liability on the balance sheet (for example, deferred taxable income when the completed contract method is used for tax but not financial reporting) but other related assets or liabilities are classified as current because the operating cycle is longer than 1 year.

The income statement or notes must disclose the following components of income tax expense for continuing operations for each income statement presented:

1. Current tax expense or benefit (not including any interest or penalties assessed on deficiencies).
2. Deferred tax expense or benefit, not including the effects in "(6)" below.
3. Investment tax credits.
4. Government grants that reduce income tax expense.
5. Benefits of operating loss carryforwards.
6. Adjustments of deferred tax assets or liabilities for changes in tax laws, tax rates, or tax status (i.e., the company becomes taxable or tax exempt).

Disclosure is also required for the tax expense or benefit allocated to continuing operations, discontinued operations, extraordinary items, the cumulative effect of accounting changes reported as a "catch-up adjustment," prior period adjustments, gains or losses reported directly in capital (such as from marketable equity securities or foreign currency translation), and capital transactions for each year whenever those items are reported.

An amount or percentage reconciliation of the income tax expense for continuing operations to the comparable tax that would result from applying domestic federal statutory tax rates is required (regular tax rates if there are alternative tax systems). Public companies must disclose the nature and estimated amount of each significant reconciling item; nonpublic companies may omit the amount. A public company not subject to income tax because its income is taxed directly to its owners (such as a publicly held limited partnership) must disclose that fact and the net difference between its reported assets and liabilities and their tax bases.

The types of temporary differences that relate to significant portions of a reported deferred tax asset or liability must be disclosed. Companies that have not recognized a deferred tax liability for any of the exceptions listed in section 17.3(d) must disclose:

1. The type of temporary difference involved and what would cause it to become taxable.
2. The cumulative amount of the temporary difference.
3. The amount of the unrecognized tax liability. (If determination of the amount related to unremitted earnings is not practicable, that fact and the amount of withholding taxes that would be payable on remittance may be disclosed instead.)

Disclosure is required of the amounts and expiration dates of operating loss and tax credit carryforwards (1) for financial reporting and (2) for tax purposes. If significant, the amount of carryforwards for which any recognized tax benefits will be applied to reduce goodwill and other noncurrent intangible assets must also be disclosed.

In separately issued financial statements, a company that is included in a consolidated tax return must disclose:

1. The current and deferred tax expense for each income statement presented and any tax-related amounts due to or from affiliates for each balance sheet presented.
2. How the consolidated tax expense is allocated to members of the group and the nature and effect of any change in the method of allocation or determining amounts to or from affiliates for the periods included in (1) above.

Questions 36–40 in the FASB special report on implementation of SFAS No. 96 provide guidance on classification and disclosure.

When this chapter was prepared, the SEC's disclosure requirements in Rule 4-08(h) of Regulation S-X related to the accounting for income taxes continued to be those required in connection with APB Opinion No. 11. On February 17, 1989, in Release 33-6818, however, the SEC proposed amendments to reflect the issuance of SFAS No. 96, so the SEC's disclosure requirements are subject to change. At this time, however, the SEC has indicated that a registrant that has adopted SFAS No. 96 should make the following disclosures that are not required by that statement:

1. Domestic and foreign pretax accounting income if income (loss) from operations located outside the registrant's home country is 5% or more of total pretax accounting income.
2. The tax related to the amounts disclosed under (1) if 5% or more of total tax expense.
3. The amount of each significant component of a deferred tax asset or liability (unless included in the "types of temporary differences" disclosure required by SFAS No. 96).

As does SFAS No. 96, the SEC requires a reconciliation of tax expense to what tax expense would be at federal domestic statutory tax rates. If the statutory rate used is not the U.S. federal corporate income tax rate, the rate used and the basis for using that rate must be disclosed.

17.14 OTHER DISCLOSURES.   APB Opinions No. 2 and No. 4 call for disclosure of the method used to account for the investment tax credit and any material amounts involved, including unused credits.

ACCOUNTING FOR INCOME TAXES IN INTERIM PERIODS

17.15 RELEVANT PRONOUNCEMENTS.   APB Opinion No. 28, "Interim Financial Reporting" (pars. 19–20), specifies the general concepts for accounting for income taxes and investment tax credits in interim periods. Essentially, Opinion No. 28 adopted the integral approach for income taxes and credits by requiring that they be determined for interim periods by using an estimated annual effective tax rate. However, income taxes and credits associated with significant unusual or extraordinary items are reported in the interim period in which they occur. FIN No. 18, "Accounting for Income Taxes in Interim Periods—An Interpretation of APB Opinion No. 28," explains those general concepts and illustrates how to compute income taxes for an interim period in various circumstances. SFAS No. 16, "Prior Period Adjustments," addresses adjustments related to prior interim periods of the current fiscal year. The pronouncements described elsewhere in this chapter that specify how to determine the appropriate annual provision for income taxes must also be applied to determine tax expense for an interim period.

17.16 ESTIMATED ANNUAL EFFECTIVE TAX RATE.   For convenience, FIN No. 18 (par. 5) defines certain terms that are used in special ways for interim period income taxes as follows:

    a. "Ordinary" income (or loss) refers to "income (or loss) from continuing operations before income taxes (or benefits)" excluding significant "unusual or infrequently occurring items." Extraordinary items, discontinued operations, and cumulative effects of changes in accounting principles are also excluded from this term. The term is **not** used in the income tax context of ordinary income v. capital gain. [Footnote omitted.]

    b. Tax (or benefit) is the total income tax expense (or benefit), including the provision (or benefit) for income taxes both currently payable and deferred. [Words in parentheses are deleted in the following discussion.]

    The estimated annual effective tax rate is the estimated income tax for the year allocated to ordinary income divided by the estimated ordinary income for the year. The estimated income tax for the year includes anticipated investment tax credits accounted for by the flow-through method, foreign taxes and credits, the effect of items that receive special income tax treatment, such as percentage depletion and long-term capital gains, and other available tax planning alternatives.

    In theory, the estimated income tax for the year is determined by forecasting what the balances of income taxes payable and deferred income taxes will be at year end and adjusting for beginning of the year balances. Forecasting year-end balances requires scheduling temporary differences and applying tax planning strategies for each tax jurisdiction the same as when determining any other end of the year tax balance. In practice, estimates of tax for the year may suffice. Having estimated income tax for the year, the procedures described in this section for intraperiod income tax allocation are used to allocate the estimated income tax for the year between ordinary income and the items that are treated separately (e.g., unusual, infrequently occurring, and extraordinary items, discontinued operations, and cumulative effects of accounting changes). A new estimate of the annual effective tax rate should be made whenever assumptions change significantly.

17.17 INTERIM PERIOD TAX.   The income tax for the current interim period is determined in several steps. First, the year-to-date ordinary income is multiplied by the current estimated annual effective tax rate to determine the applicable year-to-date tax. Second, the total tax applicable to ordinary income for prior interim periods of that fiscal year is subtracted to determine tax applicable to ordinary income for the current interim period. Third, income tax allocated to unusual or infrequently occurring items and similar items included in income from continuing operations but handled on a discrete basis is added. The result is the income tax applicable to income from continuing operations for the current interim period.

Procedures such as the "realization assured beyond any reasonable doubt" test, recognition of the tax benefit of a loss or tax credit carryforward through "draw down" of deferred tax credits, and intraperiod tax allocation must all be properly applied when applicable in computing the estimated annual effective tax rate to correctly determine interim period income taxes.

17.18 SPECIAL INTERIM PERIOD PROBLEMS.   FIN No. 18, addresses several special interim period problems.

First, it may not be possible to make a reliable estimate of the annual effective tax rate. In those situations, the actual effective tax rate for the year to date may be the best estimate of the annual effective tax rate. Also, if components of ordinary income or the related tax cannot be reliably estimated, those components may be excluded from the overall estimated annual effective tax rate and handled on an actual effective tax rate for the year to date.

Second, several estimated annual effective tax rates may have to be computed for one company. For example, a company that is subject to income tax in several jurisdictions may have losses in some jurisdictions for which no tax benefit can be recognized. Separate annual effective tax rates must be estimated for those loss jurisdictions. Another example is a U.S. company that has foreign operations and is unable to make a reliable estimate *in dollars* of the ordinary income or of the related tax for the foreign operations. Those amounts must be reported on a discrete basis.

Third, new tax legislation poses special problems for reporting income taxes in interim periods. In the past, some companies have anticipated the effect of proposed tax legislation, but SFAS No. 96 amended paragraph 20 of APB Opinion No. 28 to make it clear that the tax effects of new legislation, such as a change in tax rates, are not recognized prior to enactment.

COMPARISON OF U.S. GAAP TO THOSE OF OTHER COUNTRIES

17.19 GENERAL COMPARISON.   In the United States, comprehensive recognition of deferred taxes has applied rather broadly since 1968. The United States differs from other countries in methods used, the extent to which they are used, and how long they have been used.

The results of a 1979 survey of accounting practices in 64 countries by Price Waterhouse International (Fitzgerald, Stickler, and Watts, 1979) are shown in Exhibit 17.1, with respect to the breakdown in accounting for income taxes.

Prior to SFAS No. 96, the United States and Canada had very similar accounting requirements for interperiod income tax allocation. The United Kingdom also adopted comprehensive allocation by the deferred method but subsequently modified that requirement.

	Comprehensive Allocation	Partial Allocation	No Tax Allocation	Liability Method	Deferred Method
Required	5*	2	5	1	4*
Predominant practice	6	1	41	15	5
Minority practice	20	15	7	9	18
Rarely or not found	23	33	1	28	29
Not accepted or permitted	8	11*	8*	4*	1
Not applicable	2	2	2	7	7
Totals	64	64	64	64	64

*Includes United States and Canada.

Exhibit 17.1.   Tax allocation practices in 64 countries.

17.20 UNITED KINGDOM.   In 1975 the Accounting Standards Committee (ASC) in the United Kingdom issued SSAP 11, "Accounting for Deferred Taxation," which called for comprehensive interperiod income tax allocation by the deferred method. The following year the ASC announced that it was reviewing SSAP 11 and implementation was deferred. In 1977 the ASC issued ED 19, "Accounting for Deferred Taxation," which called for tax allocation by the liability method for short-term timing differences that normally reverse the following year and took an approach similar to APB Opinion No. 23, by not calling for tax allocation for certain kinds of timing differences for which it could be demonstrated that payment of taxes could be postponed indefinitely.

In 1978 the ASC issued SSAP 15, "Accounting for Deferred Taxation," which required tax allocation for short-term timing differences and for other originating timing differences unless it could be demonstrated that (1) there will be no tax liability for timing differences that would reverse within 3 years and (2) the situation was not likely to change. If tax allocation was required, partial allocation might be appropriate. Unlike ED 19, SSAP 15 (pars. 26–30) did not specify the liability method but rather allowed either the liability or the deferred method.

SSAP 15 was revised in May 1985. The revised Statement specifies the liability method and calls for timing differences to be accounted for only if based on reasonable assumptions it is probable that a liability or asset will "crystallise." Assessing whether a tax liability will "crystallise" is based on a review of financial plans or projections for 3 to 5 years for a regular pattern of timing differences and a longer period for an irregular pattern.

17.21 INTERNATIONAL STANDARDS.   IAS 12 ("Accounting for Taxes on Income"), which became effective in 1981, calls for a blend of interperiod income tax allocation (which it calls "tax effect accounting") that is a combination of the approaches taken in APB Opinion No. 11, APB Opinion No. 23, and SSAP 15. That is, although much of the international standard is similar to the two APB opinions, it permits either the deferred or the liability method and permits partial allocation; tax allocation is not required for timing differences that will not reverse for at least 3 years. The international standard is not binding unless it is made so by the appropriate body in a country, but it may influence other countries to move from the cash basis and taxes payable method, although that may be partial allocation.

In January 1989, the IAS Committee issued an exposure draft of a Proposed Statement, E33, to adopt the liability method to account for income taxes. E33 states a preference for comprehensive application (including taxes on undistributed earnings of subsidiaries and associates) but would allow disclosure only for timing differences that will not reverse for at least 3 years and will be replaced by equivalent timing differences when they reverse. It would allow disclosure only for taxes on undistributed earnings of subsidiaries and associates until it is probable the earnings will be distributed. The benefit of a tax loss carryforward would be recognized in the current period only if there is assurance beyond any reasonable doubt that the benefit will reduce future taxes.

PROSPECTS FOR CHANGE IN U.S. GAAP— RECONSIDERATION OF SFAS NO. 96

The FASB has received and considered a number of requests to amend SFAS No. 96, most of which fall into two categories. One category is to relax the criteria for recognition and measurement of deferred tax assets so as to anticipate, in certain circumstances, the tax consequences of future income. The other category is to exempt certain types of temporary differences (primarily temporary differences that were not timing differences under APB Opinion No. 11) from the requirements of SFAS No. 96. In addition, SFAS No. 96 is criticized for the complexity of the requirements for scheduling and for consideration of tax-planning strategies.

As this chapter goes to production, the FASB has issued SFAS No. 103 to defer the effective date of SFAS No. 96 to fiscal years beginning after December 15,1991. The principal reason for the deferral is to study whether to amend SFAS No. 96 to reduce the complexity of scheduling and tax-planning strategies and to change the criteria to allow recognition of more deferred tax assets. The nature of any changes that will be made to the requirements of SFAS No. 96 cannot be predicted at this time.

SOURCES AND SUGGESTED REFERENCES

Accounting Principles Board, "Accounting for the 'Investment Credit,'" APB Opinion No. 2, AICPA, New York, 1962.

——, "Accounting for the 'Investment Credit,'" APB Opinion No. 4 (Amending No. 2), AICPA, New York, 1964.

——, "Accounting for Income Taxes," APB Opinion No. 11, AICPA, New York, 1967.

——, "Business Combinations," APB Opinion No. 16, AICPA, New York, 1970.

——, "Accounting for Income Taxes—Special Areas," APB Opinion No. 23, AICPA, New York, 1972.

——, "Interim Financial Reporting," APB Opinion No. 28, AICPA, New York, 1973.

Accounting Standards Committee, "Accounting for Deferred Taxation," Statement of Standard Accounting Practice No. 15, The Institute of Chartered Accountants in England and Wales, London, 1978, revised 1985.

American Institute of Accountants, "Accounting for Income Taxes," Accounting Research Bulletin No. 23, AIA (now AICPA), New York, 1944.

——, "Restatement and Revision of Accounting Research Bulletins," Accounting Research Bulletin No. 43, AIA (now AICPA), New York, 1953.

——, "Declining-Balance Depreciation," Accounting Research Bulletin No. 44, AIA (now AICPA), New York, 1954.

——, "Declining-Balance Depreciation," Accounting Research Bulletin No. 44 (Revised), AIA (now AICPA), New York, 1958.

American Institute of Certified Public Accountants, "New Depreciation Guidelines and Rules," APB Opinion No. 1, AICPA, New York, 1962.

Black, Homer A., "Interperiod Allocation of Corporate Income Taxes," Accounting Research Study No. 9, AICPA, New York, 1966.

Financial Accounting Standards Board, "Accounting for Income Taxes in Interim Periods—An Interpretation of APB Opinion No. 28," FASB Interpretation No. 18, FASB, Stamford, CT, 1977.

——, "Accounting for Leases in a Business Combination," FASB Interpretation No. 21, FASB, Stamford, CT, 1978.

——, "Accounting for Research and Development Costs," Statement of Financial Accounting Standards No. 2, FASB, Stamford, CT, 1974.

——, "Accounting for Leases," Statement of Financial Accounting Standards No. 13, FASB, Stamford, CT, 1977.

——, "Prior Period Adjustments," Statement of Financial Accounting Standards No. 16, FASB, Stamford, CT, 1977.

——, "Foreign Currency Translation," Statement of Financial Accounting Standards No. 52, FASB, Stamford, CT, 1981.

——, "Accounting for the Effects of Certain Types of Regulation," Statement of Financial Accounting Standards No. 71, FASB, Stamford, CT, 1982.

——, "Accounting for Income Taxes," Statement of Financial Accounting Standards No. 96, FASB, Stamford, CT, 1987.

——, "Accounting for Income Taxes—Deferral of the Effective Date of FASB Statement No. 96," Statement of Financial Accounting Standards No. 100, FASB, Norwalk, CT, 1988.

————, "Accounting for Income Taxes—Deferral of the Effective Date of FASB Statement No. 96," Statement of Financial Accounting Standards No. 103, FASB, Norwalk, CT, 1989.

Fitzgerald, R. D., Stickler, A. D., and Watts, T. R., Editors, Price Waterhouse International, *International Survey of Accounting Principles and Reporting Practices,* Butterworth & Co. (Canada) Ltd., Scarborough, Ontario, 1979.

International Accounting Standards Committee, "Accounting for Taxes on Income," IAS 12, IASC, London, 1978.

————, "Accounting for Taxes on Income," E33, IASC, London, 1989.

Securities and Exchange Commission, "Accounting for the 'Investment Credit'," Accounting Series Release No. 96, SEC, Washington, DC, 1963.

————, "Amendments to Rules, Forms, and Codification of Financial Reporting Policies," Securities Act of 1933 Release No. 33-6818, SEC, Washington, DC, February 17, 1989.

————, "Form and Content of and Requirements for Financial Statements," Regulation S-X, Part 210 of Title 17 of the Code of Federal Regulations, SEC, Washington, DC, as amended through October 1989.

Simpson, E. Raymond, Cassel, Jules M., Giles, Jill Peperone, and Jonas, Gregory J., "Special Report: A Guide to Implementation of Statement 96 on Accounting for Income Taxes—Questions and Answers," FASB, Norwalk, CT, 1989.

CHAPTER 18

LIABILITIES

Martin Mellman, PhD, CPA

Bernard M. Baruch College
City University of New York

Steven B. Lilien, PhD, CPA

Bernard M. Baruch College
City University of New York

CONTENTS

NATURE OF LIABILITIES

18.1 DEFINITION OF LIABILITIES.   SFAC No. 6, "Elements of Financial Statements," defines liabilities as:

> [P]robable future sacrifices of economic benefits arising from present obligations of a particular entity to transfer assets or provide services to other entities in the future as a result of past transactions or events.

Probable is used with its usual general meaning and refers to that which can reasonably be expected on the basis of available evidence but is not certain. Obligation is broader than "legal obligation," referring to duties imposed legally or socially and to that which one is bound to do by contract, promise, or moral responsibility. SFAS No. 6 (par. 36) elaborates that a liability has three essential characteristics:

(a) [I]t embodies a present duty or responsibility to one or more other entities that entails settlement by probable future transfer or use of assets at a specified or determinable date, on occurrence of a specified event, or on demand,

(b) the duty or responsibility obligates a particular entity, leaving it little or no discretion to avoid the future sacrifice, and

(c) the transaction or other event obligating the entity has already happened.

The dividing line between equity and liabilities may be clear in concept. SFAS No. 6 defines equity as net assets, that is, the residual interest that remains in the assets of an entity after deducting its liabilities. In practice, however, the difference may be obscured. Certain securities issued by business enterprises seem to have characteristics of both liabilities and equity in varying degrees, or the name given to some securities may not accurately describe their essential characteristics. Examples are convertible debt instruments that have both liability and residual-interest characteristics. Preferred stock may also have both debt and equity characteristics, and some preferred stocks may have mandatory redemption requirements.

A broader connotation is suggested by the accepted definition of the AICPA, in Accounting Terminology Bulletin No. 1, which defines a liability in relation to the balance sheet as "Something represented by a credit balance that is or would be properly carried forward upon a closing of the books of account according to the rules or principles of accounting, provided such credit balance is not in effect a negative balance applicable to an asset." Thus, in addition to debts or obligations in the usual sense, this definition includes such items as capital stock and related elements of proprietorship.

The AAA in "Accounting and Reporting Standards for Corporate Financial Statements" (1957) suggests referring to the creditor and shareholder interest as equities. The right side of the balance sheet is then divided into two parts: the liabilities, or the equities of creditors, and the equity of owners. The "conventional" view of liabilities, was given by the APB in 1964. APB Statement No. 4 (par. 132) says that liabilities are:

> [E]conomic obligations of an enterprise that are recognized and measured in conformity with generally accepted accounting principles. Liabilities also include certain deferred credits that are not obligations but that are recognized and measured in conformity with generally accepted accounting principles.

Ijiri (1967), in a generally mathematical approach, defines liabilities as **negative assets:** "When goods are received from a supplier whom the entity has not paid, but to whom the entity expects to deliver cash in the future, the entity is allowed to recognize its negative control over the cash."

Normally, a liability arises through the furnishing by the creditor of funds, goods, or services with a value or cost corresponding to the initial amount of the liability. The amounts involved may be due or accrued, or they may represent fixed or variable claims payable at a future date or dates. In the case of a corporation, liabilities may arise by action of the board of directors in the declaration of a dividend. Liabilities for **taxes** may be considered somewhat of an exception to the general rule. With taxes the liability arises from the existence of the definite legal obligation to make a payment, rather than from the receipt of a specific benefit to the corporation.

Whether the existence of a **contract** requiring specific payments in the future gives rise to a liability is not clear. The AICPA (in APB Opinion No. 5) stated: "[T]he rights and obligations related to unperformed portions of executory contracts are not recognized as assets and liabilities in financial statements under generally accepted accounting principles as presently understood." This notion was overturned by the adoption of SFAS No. 13, which requires that both the rights and obligations related to capital leases be included in the balance sheet as assets and liabilities.

It is common under product financing arrangements for companies to sell inventory, at cost, to financial institutions. The sale is accompanied by a firm repurchase agreement that obligates the company to reacquire the inventory from the financial institution, generally at a price consisting of the original cost plus compound interest on the purchase cost. Common practice was to omit both the sold inventory and the liability for repurchase (as well as accrued interest) from the financial statements of the selling company. In 1981, the FASB issued SFAS No. 49, "Accounting for Product Financing Arrangements," which required that product financing agreements be reflected on the books of the selling company by continuing to include the inventory in the balance sheet, establishing a liability for the repurchase price, and accruing imputed interest.

On the other hand, **firm purchase commitments,** unaccompanied by a previous sale, remain unrecognized as liabilities in balance sheets.

As a practical matter, a clear definition of liabilities, consistent with past and present practice and with the uses to which liabilities figures are put by users of financial statements, has continued to elude accountants. Almost all the criteria offered suffer from a lack of universality. A criterion such as inevitability of payment fails when it is realized that many ongoing business costs, such as future wages, are more certain of payment than some legal liabilities. Notions of symmetry—requiring that the liability on the company's books be matched by a receivable recorded by some other party—would, if consistently applied, spell the end of concepts such as deferred income taxes. The government, of course, settles its accounts with taxpayers annually and shows no receivable for the enormous amounts of deferred taxes on the right-hand side of corporate balance sheets.

18.2 OFFSETTING LIABILITIES AGAINST ASSETS.   Generally accepted accounting principles do not permit the offsetting of a liability against an asset so that only the net amount appears in the financial statements. This rule holds even in the case of an asset that is **pledged as security** for a debt. In such circumstances, disclosure of the relationship between the asset and liability should be accomplished by footnotes or a brief mention associated with the balance sheet caption.

However, some exceptions exist to the general rule against offset accounting. FTB 88-2, "Definition of a Right of Setoff," issued in 1988, defines a right of setoff as "a debtor's legal right, by contract or otherwise, to discharge all or a portion of the debt owed to another party by applying against the debt an amount that the other party owes to the debtor," and specifies the following conditions (par. 2):

- Each of the two parties owes the other determinable amounts.
- The reporting party has the right to set off the amount owed with the amount owed by the other party.
- The reporting party intends to set off.
- The right of setoff is enforceable at law.

The Bulletin discusses various pronouncements, such as SFAS No. 87, that incorporate setoffs in the reporting process. The Bulletin does not alter those treatments.

In other examples, a company with an overdraft in a bank account at a particular bank may offset the overdraft against a cash balance in another account at the same institution. However, such offsetting is not permitted when the cash balances and overdrafts exist at different banks. Similarly, customers' credit balances should not be offset against accounts receivable except when the balance is applied to the same customer.

Companies engaged in large-scale construction projects frequently receive **progress payments** from customers while having, at the same time, billed or unbilled receivables. If such balances apply to the same customer, offset accounting is theoretically permissible. Nevertheless, since the amounts are frequently significant to an evaluation of the financial condition of the construction company, separate presentation of the assets and liabilities, even when related to the same customer, is recommended.

Although not covered in authoritative accounting pronouncements, the logic of the arguments related to offset accounting might reasonably be extended to a situation in which a debt (or debt security) can be satisfied by the tendering of another, specific security. Offset accounting is also effectively sanctioned in paragraph 57 of APB Opinion No. 11, which requires that the *net* current and *net* noncurrent amounts of deferred tax charges and credits be shown. For example, if a company has a noncurrent deferred tax charge of $100,000 and a noncurrent deferred tax credit of $150,000, the financial statements should reflect the *net* $50,000 credit. The APB gave no explanation for this required offset accounting, other than to note that deferred tax items "do not represent receivables or payables in the usual sense." The legal arguments usually cited for offset accounting would not seem to apply here, since there are no actual accounts with the government for these supposed tax items.

Under SFAS No. 96 the net deferred tax asset or liability in each tax jurisdiction is presented in two classifications—a net current asset or liability and a net noncurrent asset or liability.

18.3 MEASUREMENT OF LIABILITIES.   SFAC No. 5 (par. 67) recognized that items currently reported in financial statements are measured by different attributes, depending on the nature of the item. Liabilities that involve obligations to provide goods or services to customers are generally reported at historical proceeds, which is the amount of cash, or its equivalent, received when the obligations were incurred and may be adjusted after acquisi- tion for amortization or other allocations. Some liabilities that involve marketable com- modities and securities, for example, the obligation of writers of options or sellers of common shares who do not own the underlying commodities or securities, are reported at current market value. Liabilities that involve known or estimated amounts of money payable at unknown future dates, for example, trade payable or warranty obligations, generally are reported at their net settlement value. This value is nondiscounted. On the other hand, long- term payables are reported at their present value, discounted at the implicit or historical rate, which is the present value of future outflows required to settle the liability.

The AAA, in "Accounting and Reporting Standards for Corporate Financial State- ments," states that liabilities are measured initially by ". . . cash received, or by the established price of non-cash assets or services received, or by estimates of a definitive character when the amount owing cannot be measured more precisely." The reference to "estimates of a definitive character" emphasizes that the necessity for estimating the amount of a liability does not impair its validity or reduce its status to that of a contingency. In general, a clear distinction must be drawn between an actual liability of uncertain amount and a condition that may result in a future liability. Often situations arise, such as with service warranties, in which the amount of the liability is an estimate and there is uncertainty as to the parties who will receive payment. These amounts are liabilities nevertheless and should be shown on the balance sheet as such, accompanied by a note explaining the assumptions on which the estimate is based. The use of the word "reserve" to describe such items is not considered good practice.

An alternative situation is that the possible payee is known, but the amount and/or probability of payment is not certain. Such contingencies are covered by SFAS No. 5, discussed below.

Chambers (*Accounting, Evaluation and Economic Behavior*) suggests another dimension of the measurement problem: "The monetary measurement of an asset or a liability at a point of time is its **current cash equivalent** at that time." This definition of the measurement process introduces the time dimension; that is, a liability might have a different absolute value at different times. The question of **discounting liabilities** is discussed in greater length in connection with long-term liabilities.

18.4 GOING CONCERN CONCEPTS OF LIABILITIES.   In recent years questions have been raised as to whether certain liabilities, which are clearly susceptible to measurement in terms of amount, should actually be considered liabilities on a going-concern basis. Such questions have arisen principally in connection with accounting for deferred federal income taxes and unfunded prior service pension costs. The **fundamental argument** is: If a liability constantly revolves, or rolls over, from one period to the next, the ultimate payment is indefinitely deferred; hence there is no liability. APB Opinion No. 11 recognizes this argument in connection with **deferred income taxes** but prefers the conventional view: "The fact that when the initial differences reverse other initial differences may offset any effect on the amount of taxable income does not . . . nullify the fact of the reversal." This viewpoint was reaffirmed by the FASB in SFAS No. 96.

Taking the opposite view, however, British accountants ended deferred tax accounting (with SSAP No. 19, published by the Institute of Chartered Accountants in England and Wales) except when reversal in a short period was certain.

18.5 EXECUTORY CONTRACTS AS LIABILITIES.   As noted above, the furnishing of goods, services, or money to a firm is normally a prerequisite for the recording of a liability. The opinion is held, however, that the existence of a firm, verifiable, and measurable **commitment to make future payments** adequately constitutes a liability, even in the absence of prior consideration or the furnishing of services or money to the entity. The AAA (1966) notes:

> [I]nformation about . . . contracts is clearly relevant to a host of decisions involving stewardship, changes in management, credit extension and investment decisions. Recording of these events would also result in greater uniformity of reporting essentially similar events where the only difference lies in the form of obligation assumed. Therefore, the committee recommends the reporting of all long-term leases, material and nonrepetitive commitments, pension plans, and executive compensation contracts including stock options or deferred payments and the like in dollar terms in the regular framework of the statements.

The AAA recommendation was implemented with SFAS No. 13, which requires certain leases to be placed in the balance sheet. SFAS No. 49, requires obligations under certain repurchase agreements to be shown as liabilities.

18.6 CREDIT BALANCES THAT ARE NOT LIABILITIES.   Items such as **minority interest** and **excess of equity in consolidated subsidiaries over cost** (negative goodwill) are sometimes found on the right side of balance sheets. On occasion, such items are confused with liabilities. Neither minority interest nor negative goodwill is a liability, and the presentation of these items in financial statements should be such as to clearly segregate them from any long-term liabilities.

18.7 CURRENT AND LONG-TERM LIABILITIES.   The traditional distinction between current and long-term liabilities is clearly presented by the SEC Regulation S-X (Rule 4-05):

> If a company's normal operating cycle is longer than one year, generally recognized trade practices should be followed with respect to the inclusion or exclusion of items in current assets or current liabilities. An appropriate explanation of the circumstance should be made and if practicable an estimate given of the amount not realizable or payable within one year. The amounts maturing in each year (if practicable) along with the interest rates or range of rates also shall be disclosed.

Although the **one-year rule** has the advantages of consistency, simplicity, and tradition, it represents merely an arbitrary time period and in certain cases might produce misleading inferences regarding current position. The AICPA (ARB No. 43) notes:

> It should be emphasized that financial statements of a going concern are prepared on the assumption that the company will continue in business. Accordingly, the views expressed in this section represent a departure from any narrow definition or strict one-year interpretation of either current assets or current liabilities; the objective is to relate the criteria developed to the operating cycle of a business.

As a practical matter, however, the one-year cutoff for current liabilities is virtually the only rule followed. The **operating cycle concept** has achieved acceptance only in those rare industries where the total operating cycle is in excess of one year.

Under APB Opinion No. 11 ("Accounting for Income Taxes"), **deferred taxes** are classified as current or noncurrent depending on the assets and liabilities they relate to. Thus, if installment receivables are a current asset, the related deferred tax credit should also be classified as current. This position was amplified in SFAS No. 37, "Balance Sheet Classification of Deferred Income Taxes." It states that the APB Opinion No. 11 treatment holds, if there is a relationship to a specific asset or liability. If, however, there is no such relationship, the current or noncurrent classification follows the treatment accorded other assets and liabilities. (In addition, see Chapter 17.)

SFAS No. 96, which is effective for fiscal years beginning after December 15, 1991, would classify as current the net deferred tax consequences of temporary difference that will result in net taxable or deductible amounts during the next year. It would also classify as current the temporary differences related to an asset or a liability classified as current because the operating cycle is longer than one year. If not related to a specific asset or liability, then the determination would be based on other related items that are classified based on the longer operating cycle.

(a) Long-Term Obligations Approaching Maturity.   Grady (ARS No. 7) states:

> If part of the [long-term] liability matures or otherwise becomes payable within one year after the balance sheet date (e.g., serial maturities on long-term debt) accountants classify that portion as a current liability.

In the case of bonds or similar long-term debt, the reclassification of a portion as a current liability provides no problems. However, the same theory requires current liability classification of portions of other long-term liabilities, such as **capitalized lease obligations.** In the case of capitalized leases, the *amount* to be reclassified is unclear. SFAS No. 13 merely implies that the reclassification should be made, but does not stipulate the amount. One notion would suggest classifying as current an amount equal to the following period's cash payments. Another theory suggests considering the present value of that amount as current. Limited observations by the authors suggest that in practice, the reduction in the present value of the future lease payments that will occur in the next period is the amount classified as current. This figure is equal to the amortization of the capitalized lease liability that will be made in the following year and might be considered as equivalent to the following period's principal repayment on a debt.

(b) Short-Term Obligations to Be Refinanced.   During the 1970s, some companies treated short-term obligations that were continuously refinanced or "rolled over" as long-term in their balance sheets. This practice was substantially restricted when the FASB issued SFAS No. 6 in 1975, "Classification of Short-Term Obligations Expected to Be Refinanced."

SFAS No. 6 allows short-term obligations to be classified as long-term only if:

1. The enterprise intends to refinance the obligations on a long-term basis.
2. The intent to refinance on a long-term basis is evidenced either by an actual post-balance sheet issuance of long-term debt or equity or by the enterprise having entered into a firm agreement to make an appropriate refinancing.

In FIN No. 8, issued in 1976, the FASB elaborated on SFAS No. 6. The interpretation addresses the situation of a company that intends to refinance short-term obligations with long-term ones, thereby conforming to the requirements of SFAS No. 6. However, because of an excess of cash, the company actually pays off the short-term debt before the long-term debt is issued. The long-term debt is then issued as planned. The FASB took the position that since the payment of the short-term debt actually used current assets, the original debt must be classified as short term.

(c) Classification of Obligations Callable by the Creditor.   SFAS No. 78 "Classification of Obligations That Are Callable by the Creditor," states that current liability classification includes obligations that are due on demand or that will be due on demand within one year (or operating cycle, if longer) from the balance sheet date, even though liquidation may not be expected within that period.

Current classification also applies to long-term obligations that are or could become callable by the creditor either because the debtor's violation of a provision of the debt agreement at the balance sheet date makes the obligation callable or because the violation, if not cured within a grace period, will make the obligation callable. However, long-term classification is appropriate if the creditor has waived or subsequently lost the right to demand repayment for more than a year, or if it is probable that the violation will be cured within a grace period. In the latter case disclosure is required of the circumstances.

(d) Demand Notes.   Loan agreements may specify the debtor's repayment terms but may also enable the creditor, at his discretion, to demand payment at any time. The loan arrangement may have wording such as "the term note shall mature in monthly installments as set forth therein or on demand, whichever is earlier," or "principal and interest shall be due on demand, or if no demand is made, in quarterly installments beginning on . . ." The EITF in Issue No. 86-5 concluded that such an obligation should be considered a current liability in accordance with SFAS No. 78. Further, the demand provision is not a subjective acceleration clause as discussed in FTB 79-3.

(e) Subjective Acceleration Clause in Long-Term Debt Agreements.   SFAS No. 6 defines a subjective acceleration clause contained in a financing agreement, as one that would allow the cancellation of an agreement for the violation of a provision that can be evaluated differently by the parties. The inclusion of such a clause in an agreement that would otherwise permit a short-term obligation to be refinanced on a long-term basis would preclude that short-term obligation from being classified as long-term. SFAS No. 6 does not address financing agreements related to long-term obligations. In FTB 79-3, the Board concluded that the treatment of long-term debt with a subjective acceleration clause would vary depending on the circumstances. In some situations only disclosure of the existing clause would be required. Neither reclassification nor disclosure would be required if the likelihood of the acceleration of the due date were remote, such as when the lender historically has not accelerated due dates in similar cases, and the borrower's financial condition is strong and its prospects are good.

(f) Classes of Current Liability.   The principal classes of current liability are:

1. Accounts payable and accrued expenses.
2. Short-term notes payable.
3. Dividends payable.
4. Deferred income or revenue.
5. Advances and deposits.
6. Withheld amounts.
7. Estimated liabilities.

Accounts payable includes all trade payable arising from purchases of merchandise or services. In published balance sheets this classification normally also includes **accrued expenses** where services are being acquired on a time basis, that is, estimated amounts payable for wages and salaries, rent, and royalties. Accrued interest and taxes are also normally included under this caption. Federal income taxes payable are frequently shown separately. The traditional distinction between accounts payable and accrued expenses has tended to disappear, and the common practice today is to include the two items in one heading.

In most cases, **notes payable,** if shown as a separate category, refers to a definite borrowing of funds, as distinguished from goods purchased through the use of trade acceptances. In this latter case, relatively rare today, notes payable may be presented as part of accounts payable. **Dividends payable,** the liability to shareholders representing dividend declarations, has traditionally been viewed as a distinct type of obligation. **Deferred revenues** appear when collection is made in whole or part prior to the actual furnishing of goods or services. A common example is found in the insurance field, where premiums are regularly collected in advance. Tickets, service contracts, and subscriptions are other deferred revenue items.

Advances and deposits required to guarantee performance and returnable to the depositor are current liabilities. The **returnable containers** used in many industries are sometimes included in this category. **Withheld amounts,** also referred to as **agency obligations,** result from the collection or acceptance of cash or other assets for the account of a third party. By far the most common items today are federal, state, and local income taxes and payroll taxes withheld from wages.

Estimated liabilities refer to obligations where the amount may be uncertain but the existence of the liability is unquestioned. Examples include product and service guarantees and warranties.

(g) Classes of Long-Term Liability.   The most common types of long-term liability are **bonds, long-term notes,** and other similar financial obligations.

A **mortgage** refers to the security for a debt, not to the debt itself. The term "mortgage payable" as a liability caption is, nevertheless, occasionally found in financial statements.

Installment purchase contracts are a popular means of financing asset acquisitions. In the typical case, the buyer secures possession upon making a down payment and agrees to pay the balance in a series of installments, usually with interest, over an extended period. In some cases, buyers with excellent credit ratings are not required to provide down payments. Transfer of title is often deferred until payment of the final installment.

Long-term **borrowings on open account** from affiliated corporations or other parties are a type of long-term liability and should normally be shown separately. **Long-term advances** received for future use of property or merchandise, or for service to be rendered, represent a liability on the books of the party obligated to furnish property or render the service. Classification of this type of item as a "deferred credit" is not recommended.

Deferred income taxes, caused principally by temporary differences in tax and book depreciation, have constituted one of the more significant term liabilities appearing on corporate financial statements. The present value of long-term lease obligations also appears as a long-term liability in corporate financial statements. The criteria requiring lease capitalization are discussed in Chapter 16.

18.8 ACCOUNTS PAYABLE: TRADE.   In some cases the term "accounts payable" is restricted to trade creditors' accounts, represented by unpaid invoices for the purchase of merchandise or supplies. In other cases "accounts payable" includes all unpaid invoices, regardless of their nature. In the accounting system, of course, accounts payable will normally be limited to those transactions where the company has received an invoice. For financial statement presentation purposes it is common to include "accrued expenses" in the same balance sheet caption.

Accounts payable may be recorded at gross invoice price, that is, including **discounts offered for prompt payment;** or they may be shown net. The latter treatment, though often deemed to be more theoretically correct, is rarely found in practice. As a practical matter, the theoretical appropriateness of either treatment depends on an interpretation of the nature of the discount. In some industries the discount is normally deducted from invoices regardless of when they are paid, whereas in others the terms of payment are strictly enforced and any invoices paid after the discount period must be paid in full. In theory, if the discount is always deducted, it amounts to a purchase price reduction and should be accounted for as such. If it is only available within the discount period then it appears to be more in the nature of a financial item.

The practical difficulties of apportioning small discounts to a series of items on one invoice lead most companies to account for discounts separately from the purchase price of merchandise. Inventory is recorded at the gross price, and the credit balances resulting from the discount is normally netted against the total year's purchases. In principle, year-end adjustments should be made for that portion of the purchases that remains in inventory, but in practice this is rarely done.

Some companies consider that the rate of interest implicit in the usual trade discount is so large that substantial efforts should be devoted to assuring that it is not lost. When conditions preclude the taking of the discount, the difference between the gross price actually paid and the net price that would have been paid may be accounted for as **"discount lost."** The balance of this account may be interpreted as a financial expense or as evidence of inefficiency in the accounts payable operation.

OTHER CURRENT LIABILITIES

18.9 NOTES PAYABLE: BANK.   Bank loans evidenced by secured or unsecured notes payable to commercial banks are a common method of short-term financing. Ordinarily the notes are interest bearing, and in such cases the amount borrowed and the liability to be recorded is the face amount of the note.

In some instances, however, non-interest-bearing or "discount" paper is issued. In such transactions, the bank deducts the interest in advance from the amount given to the borrower, who subsequently repays the full amount of the note.

Assume, for example, that the X Company gives the bank a $1,000 non-interest-bearing 2-month note on a 12% basis. The customary entry to record the borrowing is as follows:

Cash	$980	
Prepaid interest	20	
Notes payable—bank		$1,000

The customary treatment of the discount as "prepaid interest" has been objected to on the ground that the company has borrowed only $980 and that, therefore, the $20 asset is in no way a prepaid item. Essentially the same problem arises on a long-term basis when bonds are issued at a discount. This matter is discussed in section 18.25.

In some cases bank loans or notes are taken for short periods, but with the intent on the part of both borrower and lender that the note will be **continuously refinanced.** At one time, the intent to renew the short-term loan was the controlling factor and it was common to classify such loans as long-term liabilities. In SFAS No. 6, however, the FASB established stricter conditions. To have a loan classified as a long-term liability, the company must have a firm agreement from the bank that the loan will be renewed to a maturity running to more than one year after the balance sheet date.

18.10 NOTES PAYABLE: TRADE AND OTHERS.   Short-term notes payable often arise directly or indirectly from purchases of merchandise, materials, or equipment. When such notes arise directly from purchases they may be classified in the financial statements with accounts payable. However, if the notes arise indirectly, or have substantially different payment dates from the usual trade payables, they should be shown separately. Such notes normally run from a month to a year or longer and generally bear interest at a specified rate. It is customary to record the liability at the **face value** of the note, if the interest rate is appropriate.

When promissory **notes are given in direct exchange for assets** other than cash, the usual treatment assumes the cost of assets received to be the equivalent of the face value of the obligation. This interpretation is not permitted, however, if the notes are "non-interest-bearing" or when the stated interest rate is such that the market value of the note differs from its face value. Proper interpretation of these transactions calls for a recognition of an **implicit interest factor** calculated at the market rate, and careful segregation of interest and financing costs from the cost of the assets received. APB Opinion No. 21 provides the appropriate methodology and manner of determining the right interest rate. See "Issue of Bonds and Notes for Other than Cash," below, for a full discussion of the requirements of APB Opinion No. 21. It should be noted that the necessity to discount non-interest-bearing obligations applies also to accounts receivable and in other situations. For example, when the value of a **motion picture license** for television exhibition is recorded in the financial statements (generally at the inception of the license period), if the payments are to be received (made) over an extended period, the face amount of the contract should be discounted like any other non-interest-bearing loan. SFAS No. 53, "Financial Reporting by Producers and Distributors of Motion Picture Films," specifies (par. 9) that the present value of the license fee, computed in accordance with APB Opinion No. 21, generally should be used as the sales price for each film.

18.11 ACCRUED EXPENSES.   An accounts payable figure can be determined at the balance sheet date from the control account, even though it is normally necessary to review all invoices paid for a reasonable period subsequent to the balance sheet date (**search for unrecorded liabilities**) to assure that all amounts actually payable at the balance sheet date are properly recorded. In contrast, although some part of the balance of accrued expenses may be determined from recurring expense accruals, in general it is necessary to make a thorough review of all the company's relevant expense accounts—rent, salaries, and so on—to determine the appropriate amount at year-end. Thus accrued liabilities (expenses) arise principally only when financial statements are prepared. When preparing the accruals for the different expenses, it is well to keep in mind a sense of balance between the possibility of producing financial statements with every conceivable accrual determined precisely and the added economic value of such precision. In many cases the amount of extra work necessary to estimate certain accruals with extreme accuracy may not be justified by their value to a user of the financial statements. For such **immaterial items** relatively rough estimates may suffice.

(a) Interest Payable.   Outside of financial institutions, it is usually not deemed necessary to accrue interest liabilities from day to day, but it is essential that such liabilities be fully recognized at the close of each period. **Accrued interest** must be calculated in terms of the various outstanding obligations that bear interest such as accounts, notes, bonds, and capitalized leases. In the case of notes and similar instruments issued or granted at par or face value, the problem of figuring interest is a simple arithmetical matter, the amount of work required depending on the number of contracts involved. In some forms of note registers columns are provided for periodic interest accruals, and in certain instances periodic accruals are calculated in advance for the entire life of the interest-bearing contract. In the case of **annuities, land contracts,** and similar obligations, where each payment includes an item of principal as well as interest, care must be exercised to confine the accrued liability to the interest element (since principal already appears in full as a liability). This suggestion does not preclude a transfer from the main liability account to a special temporary account of that part of the liability due currently.

(b) Accrued Payrolls.   Full recognition of the liability for wages and salaries earned, but not paid, should be made at the close of each accounting period. Accruals should include not only hourly wages and salaries up to the close of business on the last day of the period, but also estimates of bonuses accrued, commissions earned, employer share of Social Security, and so on. To avoid the necessity for making a detailed calculation of the wages, salaries, and Social Security taxes applicable to each employee for the accrual period, it is satisfactory to apply a fraction (whose numerator is the number of days in the accrual period and whose denominator is the total number of days that will be worked during the payroll period in which the end of the accounting period falls) to the total amount of the payroll for that pay period. Unless there are sharp distortions in overtime or other factors, this represents a reasonable approximation to the appropriate accrual.

The liability for **unclaimed wages** is a related item usually of minimal size but of some legal significance. Unclaimed pay envelopes should be redeposited and credited to a special liability account. Payroll checks that have been outstanding for a period should be restored to the bank account and credited to unclaimed wages. In many states the amount of unclaimed wages escheats to the state after a number of years and therefore should be carefully accounted for until such payment is made. In other states the balance of unclaimed wages should be credited to income after a reasonable period of time.

(c) Vacation Pay.   Prior to SFAS No. 43, practice related to accruing for vacation pay varied. Most companies did not make such accruals, but a minority did. The prevalent practice was to record compensation for vacation pay as paid. SFAS No. 43, issued November, 1980, modified accounting practice by requiring an employer to accrue a liability for employee's right to receive compensation for future absenses if **all** of the following conditions are met:

- The employee's obligation relating to employees' rights to receive compensation for future absences is attributable to services the employee has already rendered.
- The obligation relates to rights that vest or accumulate. "Accumulate" means that earned but unused rights to compensated absences may be carried forward to one or more periods subsequent to that in which they are earned, even though there may be a limit to the amount that may be carried forward.
- Payment of the compensation is probable.
- The amount can be reasonably estimated.

If a company meets the first three conditions but does not accrue the cost because of an inability to reasonably estimate the amount, that fact must be disclosed.

SFAS No. 43 does not apply to severance or termination pay, postretirement benefits, deferred compensation, stock or stock options issued to employees, or other long-term disability pay. Furthermore, accrual is not required for nonvesting accumulating rights of employees to receive sick pay benefits.

(d) Commissions and Fees.   All liabilities for commissions, fees, and similar items should be accrued at any time when financial statements are prepared. The principal problem is the determination of the precise amount to be accrued as of a given date. In the case of **salespeople's commissions,** which are in no sense contingent or conditional, and where all sales have been recorded, the precise amount is readily determinable. However, where salespeople are operating under bonus plans and commissions are subject to reduction in the event of cancellation, uncollectibility, or other contingencies, it is not possible to make an exact determination of the liability. In such circumstances a reasonable estimate should be made, taking into consideration the maximum liability based on performance to date, reduced by the expected amount, based on past experience, of adjustments due to cancellations, and similar contingencies.

In the case of **professional services,** such as those furnished by accountants and lawyers, the client often finds it difficult to determine the amount due or earned as of a given date. When billing from accountants or lawyers is based on hourly or per diem rates, a statement to date can be obtained and no difficulty is involved in setting up the proper liability. If, however, the engagement has been undertaken for a lump sum, or if the fee will not be determined until the outcome is known, as is common in legal services, the accrual may be very difficult to estimate. In such circumstances it is more appropriate to make a reasonable determination of a fair presentation of the liability than to ignore the amount entirely. If no reasonable determination can be made, and the amount is material, it should be clearly mentioned in the notes to the financial statements.

(e) Payroll Taxes.   Proper accounting requires that payroll tax liabilities applicable to all payrolls up to the date of the balance sheet be recorded. Although some of the payroll taxes reflect the employer's share and other parts are withholding of amounts from employees, there is no logical necessity to segregate the two portions. However, because of the high priority of the government's lien for such amounts (and the penalties that may fall if timely remittance is not made) the amounts of payroll taxes payable should be segregated from other payables.

(f) Income Tax Withholding.   Amounts withheld from employee wages for employee federal, state, or city income taxes are not properly thought of as a payroll tax, since the employer merely acts as a collecting agent for the government. Nevertheless, the separate liability for such taxes is usually recognized at the time of accrual of the payroll.

It is the employer's responsibility to withhold an appropriate amount of income taxes in accordance with government withholding schedules. If the employer underwithholds and the employee subsequently fails to pay the taxes due, the employer may be held responsible.

(g) Federal Income Taxes.   The determination of the precise liability for federal corporate income taxes is a complex process. In the rush accompanying preparation of year-end financial statements and annual reports, it is not uncommon to obtain an automatic extension for the filing of a **tax return (Form 4868) and to delay** the preparation of the return, hence determination of the precise tax liability, until after the financial statements have been prepared. It is necessary, under such circumstances, to make an estimate of the income taxes payable and to record that estimate as a liability in the financial statements.

In some instances, there may be income tax items for which the appropriate tax treatment is not clear. Attitudes toward the treatment of such items vary, but many companies will tend to resolve them in their own favor and await possible disallowance by IRS examining agents. The question then arises as to whether the liability for income taxes should include an amount for the possible disallowances. A specific provision for a contentious item could precipitate a disallowance or be used later in court. Although not technically in accord with GAAP and SFAS No. 5, many companies provide, as a practical matter, a "cushion" in the tax provision for such items, without specific identification of the reason.

If the estimate of the tax liability proves to be reasonably accurate, small corrections are usually adjusted to the expense account in the following period.

The determination of the federal income tax liability in **interim statements** is a far more difficult problem, since it requires an estimate of the year's tax burden. Proper interpretation of LIFO depletions within the year, and of items such as the investment tax credit, cannot be clearly stipulated. For a complete discussion of treatment of tax provisions in interim statements, see Chapter 9.

(h) Property Taxes.   Tax laws, income tax regulations, and court decisions have mentioned various dates on which property taxes may be said to **accrue legally.** Such dates include assessment date, date on which tax becomes a lien on the property, and date or dates tax is payable, among others. The IRS holds that property taxes accrue on the assessment date, even if the amount of tax is not determined until later.

The legal liability for property taxes must be considered when title to property is transferred at some point during the taxable year in order to determine whether buyer or seller is liable for the taxes and to adjust the purchase price accordingly. For normal accounting purposes, however, the legal liability concept is held to be secondary to the general consideration that property taxes arise ratably over time. The AICPA (ARB No. 43) states the following:

> Generally, the most acceptable basis of providing for property taxes is monthly accrual on the taxpayer's books during the fiscal period of the taxing authority for which the taxes are levied. The books will then show, at any closing date, the appropriate accrual or prepayment. . . .
>
> An accrued liability for real or personal property taxes, whether estimated or definitely known, should be included among current liabilities. . . .

(i) Rent Liabilities.   Where property is held under a lease agreement with cash rents payable currently to the lessor and the lease is classified as an operating lease under SFAS No. 13, rent should be accrued ratably with occupancy as an expense and any unpaid portions shown as current liabilities. For treatment of other lease liabilities, see Chapter 16.

Rent advanced by a tenant represents deferred revenue on the books of the lessor and should also be classed as a liability. Generally, tenants' deposits and sureties should be recorded as separate items. In some jurisdictions, interest must be paid on tenants' deposits and should be accrued.

18.12 ADVANCES FROM OFFICERS AND EMPLOYEES.   In the FRR Codification, § 602.01 (ASR 37) the Commission noted that Rule 2-01 codifies principles to be applied by the Commission in considering questions of independence. The Commission determined that it was desirable to incorporate these principles in the published rules and regulations, in view of cases in which substantial amounts due from officers and directors were shown separately in balance sheets filed with the Commission but, in the balance sheet contained in the annual report to stockholders, were included without disclosure under the caption "Accounts and notes receivable, less reserves."

Underlying the Commission's requirement that clear disclosure be made of the amounts from officers, directors, and principal stockholders is the principle that such persons have obligations and responsibilities comparable to those of a fiduciary, and that therefore the financial statements should clearly reveal amounts due from such persons, accompanied, where the amounts involved are substantial, by appropriate supporting details. Where an indebtedness results from a transaction between the company and one or more of the management, as individuals, the certifying accountants should employ every means at their disposal to insist on full disclosure by the company and, failing persuasion of the company, should as a minimum qualify their certificate or disclose therein the information not set forth in the statements. Perhaps the most critical test of the actuality of an accountant's independence is the strength of his insistence on full disclosure of transactions between the company and members of its management as individuals; accession to the wishes of the management in such cases must inevitably raise a serious question as to whether the accountant is in fact independent. Moreover, in considering whether an accountant is in fact independent, such accession to the wishes of the management is no less significant when it occurs with respect to the financial statements included in an annual report to security holders or otherwise made public than when it occurs with respect to statements required to be filed with the Commission. (See also Regulation S-K Item 404(c) Indebtedness of management.)

The SEC, however, normally excludes from the strict requirement amounts arising from travel and other expenses and for other items arising in the normal course of business in a similar manner for all employees. Even in non-SEC companies, however, care should be taken to assure that liabilities to (or receivables from) officers and employees are clearly disclosed.

18.13 PROPRIETARY CURRENT ACCOUNTS.   In unincorporated enterprises there is some difficulty in clearly categorizing the nature of the credit balances in partners' salary or current accounts as liabilities or equity. Where such amounts are subject to withdrawal without restriction and clearly do not represent profits or other funds that are in effect being retained in the business as capital, they may reasonably be accounted for as liabilities. In other cases there is a presumption that they are of an equity nature. Whether a particular balance of this type can be better viewed as a liability or as a proprietary item depends on the circumstances.

18.14 DIVIDENDS PAYABLE.   The amount of cash dividends declared, but unpaid, is commonly treated as a current liability in balance sheets. See Chapter 19 for a discussion of the nature and treatment of dividends.

  Stock dividends declared, constituting only a rearrangement of the equity accounts, are not recorded as a liability.

18.15 DEFERRED REVENUES.   Advances by customers or clients that are to be satisfied by the future delivery of goods or performance of services are liabilities and should be shown as such. These items are often labeled ''deferred revenues'' or ''deferred credits.'' It is better disclosure to provide a title that clearly describes the nature of the item, such as **''advances from customers.''** Commonly such accounts are payable in goods or services rather than in cash, and as a rule a margin of profit will emerge in making such payment. For a discussion of timing of the recognition of income associated with this type of transaction, see Chapter 12, ''Revenues and Receivables.''

18.16 ESTIMATED AND CONTINGENT LIABILITIES.   There is often some confusion between estimated liabilities and contingent liabilities. Hendriksen (1965, p. 361) makes the following distinction:

> [T]he difference between an estimated liability and a contingent liability is that a liability has a positive most probable value even though this must be estimated; a contingent liability will probably not result in a specific obligation, but there is a chance that a specific obligation may arise if an event or events occur. For example, obligations under warranties are definite liabilities because it is highly probable that some payments will be required even though the total amount must be estimated. A legal suit against the company for damages, however, is a contingent liability if it appears likely that the firm will lose the case. If it is almost certain that the case will be lost, a liability exists and the main problem is in estimating the most probable amount of damages to be awarded. . . .

SFAS No. 5, ''Accounting for Contingencies'' (1975), served to institutionalize Hendriksen's distinction. Essentially, estimated liabilities are now those **loss contingencies** that should be accrued under SFAS No. 5. As noted below, for accrual to be required, estimated liabilities must meet two conditions of certainty. Loss contingencies, on the other hand, that do not meet these standards of certainty are generally disclosed, rather than accrued for.

  In SAB No. 87 the SEC gives an example in which specific uncertainties involving an individual claim or group of related claims result in a loss contingency that the staff believes requires disclosure:

> A property-casualty insurance company (the company ''C'') underwrites product liability insurance for an insured manufacturer which has produced and sold millions of units of a particular product which has been used effectively and without problems for many years. Users of the product have recently begun to report serious health problems that they attribute to long term use of the product and have asserted claims under the insurance policy underwritten and retained by the company C. To date, the number of users reporting such problems is relatively small, and there is presently no conclusive evidence that demonstrates a causal link between long term use of the product and the health problems experienced by the claimants. However, the evidence generated

to date indicates that there is at least a reasonable possibility that the product is responsible for the problems and the assertion of additional claims is considered probable, and therefore the potential exposure of the company C is material. While an accrual may not be warranted since the loss exposure may not be both probable and estimable in view of the reasonable possibility of material future claim payments, the staff believes that disclosure made in accordance with SFAS 5 would be required under these circumstances.

It is interesting to note that SFAS No. 5 does not specifically require the disclosure that a provision has been made for a loss. Thus there is the theoretical (and apparently practical) possibility that a company could avoid disclosure of an event that is in the nature of a loss contingency by making an undisclosed accrual.

(a) Contingencies. In SFAS No. 5 (par. 1), the FASB defines a contingency as:

[A]n existing condition, situation, or set of circumstances involving uncertainty as to possible gain or loss to an enterprise that will ultimately be resolved when one or more future events occur or fail to occur. Resolution of the uncertainty may confirm the acquisition of an asset or the reduction of a liability or the loss or impairment of an asset or the incurrence of a liability.

Obviously, not all the uncertainties inherent in the accounting process result in the type of **contingencies** foreseen by SFAS No. 5. **Estimates,** such as those required in the determination of useful lives, do not make depreciation a contingency. Similarly, a requirement that the amount of a liability be estimated does not produce a contingency as long as there is no uncertainty that the obligation has been incurred. Thus amounts owed for services received, such as advertising and utilities, are not contingencies, although the amounts actually owed may have to be estimated at the time financial statements must be prepared.

(b) Likelihood of Contingencies. SFAS No. 5 indicates that the likelihood of contingencies occurring may vary and stipulates different accounting depending on that likelihood. The standard (par. 3) suggests three possibilities:

1. *Probable*. The future event or events are likely to occur.
2. *Reasonably Possible*. The chance of the future event or events occurring is more than remote but less than likely.
3. *Remote*. The chance of the event or future events occurring is slight.

(c) Examples of Loss Contingencies. Among the types of loss contingency suggested by SFAS No. 5 are:

1. Collectibility of receivables.
2. Obligations related to product warranties and product defects.
3. Risk of loss or damage of enterprise property by fire, explosion, or other hazards.
4. Threat of expropriation.
5. Pending or threatened litigation.
6. Actual or possible claims or assessments.
7. Risk of loss from catastrophes assumed by property and casualty insurance companies.
8. Guarantees of indebtedness of others.
9. Obligations of commercial banks under "standby letters of credit."
10. Agreements to repurchase receivables (or to repurchase the related property) that have been sold.

(d) Accrual of Loss Contingencies.   In SFAS No. 5 the FASB requires that an estimated loss from a loss contingency be accrued by a charge to income if **both** the following conditions are met:

1. Information available prior to the issuance of the financial statements indicates that it is **probable** that an asset had been impaired or a liability had been incurred at the date of the financial statements. This condition implies that it must be probable that one or more future events will occur confirming the fact of the loss.
2. The amount of loss can be **reasonably estimated.**

These criteria support traditional accounting for estimated losses from the collectibility of accounts receivable and the cost of fulfilling obligations related to conventional product warranties.

(e) Estimating Amounts to Be Accrued.   As noted immediately above, SFAS No. 5 requires that an estimated loss be accrued when (1) it appears that an asset has been impaired and (2) the amount of the loss can be **reasonably estimated.**

Obviously, the term "reasonably estimated" is susceptible to interpretation. In many cases, particularly with litigation and claims, estimates of the amount of the loss may be difficult. Since SFAS No. 5 (issued in March 1975) did not define "reasonably estimated" specifically, the FASB issued FIN No. 14, "Reasonable Estimation of the Amount of a Loss," in September 1976 in an attempt to define the term more clearly.

FIN No. 14 indicates that if a reasonable estimate of the loss is a **range,** the "reasonably estimated" criterion is satisfied. If no value in the range is more likely than any other, the minimum amount should be accrued. Thus if the loss from a contingency is probable and will be within a range of $4 million to $6 million, and there is no better estimate within that range, $4 million should be accrued. On the other hand, if within the $4 million to $6 million range, $5.5 million is the most likely outcome, that latter amount should be accrued.

As a practical matter, it does not appear that the somewhat complex semantics of FIN No. 14 improved the understanding or application of SFAS No. 5. Companies still are generally reluctant to make and accrue estimates of future losses unless such estimates are quite firm. Auditors have tended to rely more on full disclosure than accruals to suffice in difficult situations.

(f) Disclosure of Loss Contingencies.   In many circumstances a loss contingency exists but does not satisfy the two conditions calling for accrual. In such cases SFAS No. 5 directs that disclosure of the loss contingency be made. Disclosure is required when there is at least a **reasonable possibility** that a loss or an additional loss may have occurred. The disclosure should indicate the nature of the contingency and should give an estimate of the possible loss or range of loss or, if appropriate, it should state that such an estimate cannot be made. SFAS No. 5 provides a number of examples and suggests appropriate accounting. Nevertheless, in application, clear answers have not always been forthcoming.

FIN No. 34, "Disclosure of Indirect Guarantees of Indebtedness of Others," clarifies SFAS No. 5 with regard to disclosure of guarantees of indebtedness of others to include indirect guarantees of indebtedness of others. FIN No. 34 defines an indirect guarantee as one that "obligates one entity to transfer funds to a second entity upon the occurrence of a specified event, under conditions whereby (a) the funds are legally available to the creditors of the second entity and (b) those creditors may enforce the second entity's claims against the first entity under the agreement."

In FRR No. 23, issued in December 1985, the SEC concluded, on the basis of applicable accounting literature, that oral statements, which are in substance guarantees, are contingent liabilities that may, under certain circumstances, require disclosure. The commission emphasized that the substance of oral agreements should be considered by financial institutions and others in completing audit confirmations.

(g) Uninsured Risks. Enterprises may decide to insure against certain risks by specifically obtaining coverage. In other cases risks may be borne by the company either through use of deductible clauses in insurance contracts or through the failure to purchase insurance at all. Insurance policies purchased through a subsidiary or investee, to the extent that policies have not been reinsured with an independent insurer, are considered not to constitute insurance. Some risks such as a decline in business, may not be insurable. Self-assumption of this type of risk is required.

SFAS No. 5 states that the absence of insurance does not mean that an asset has been impaired or that a liability has been incurred at the date of the enterprise's financial statements. Therefore, exposure to uninsured risks does not constitute a contingency requiring either disclosure or accrual.

However, if an **event has occurred,** such as an accident, for which the enterprise is not insured and for which some liability is suggested, the proper accounting or disclosure of that event must be considered within the framework of the standard.

(h) Litigation, Claims, and Assessments. The most complex area under SFAS No. 5 has been related to ligitation, either actual or possible. Problems that arise in this area involve the probability of payment, estimates of amounts, and in a particularly sensitive area, the reluctance of companies to disclose information that may be actually or potentially adverse. Full disclosure or the accrual of a loss contingency, when litigation is threatening or pending, may well be seized on by an opposing party as evidence to support its case.

When there has been an actual **adjudication,** it is appropriate to accrue a loss when it is reasonably certain that the company has lost (the litigation) and that a reasonable estimate can be made of the damages that will be payable. As a practical matter, however, the initial verdicts by lower courts are often appealed and frequently overturned, with the result that even an unfavorable verdict and a damages amount does not necessarily satisfy the standards of SFAS No. 5. In recent major litigation, companies have disclosed that they have lost in **lower courts** and also have disclosed the amounts of damages assessed but have tended not to accrue provisions for losses until verdicts and the amounts have been upheld on **appeal.**

Clearly, litigation in process in lower courts does not warrant accrual but does warrant disclosure. The same considerations apply to an action that has been brought against the company but has not yet come to trial.

Among the most difficult issues to resolve is that of **unasserted claims.** An unasserted claim exists, for example, when the company knows that an event such as a product failure has occurred, but no actions have yet been brought against the company. It is conceivable that disclosure of the event, along with a discussion indicating the possibility of claims being asserted, could trigger litigation adverse to the company that might not have been brought, absent the company's own disclosure. SFAS No. 5 (par. 10) takes a somewhat ambiguous position: "Disclosure is not required of a loss contingency involving an unasserted claim or assessment when there has been no manifestation by a potential claimant of an awareness of a possible claim or assessment unless it is considered probable that it will be asserted and there is a reasonable possibility that the outcome will be unfavorable."

(i) General Reserves for Contingencies Not Permitted. In the past, some companies have provided, sometimes through income, reserves for general contingencies. In other cases, such reserves have been established as appropriations of retained earnings. SFAS No. 5 does not permit such general contingency reserves to be charged to income, nor does it permit retained earnings to be so appropriated.

(j) Warranty Obligations.   The obligation to satisfy a product warranty, incurred in connection with the sale of goods or services, is a loss contingency of the type that requires accrual under SFAS No. 5. That is, future obligations under warranties should be estimated and provided for. Such estimates may be difficult, particularly if new products or changed warranty terms are involved. Still, an effort should be made to determine the liability. If necessary, reference may be made to the experiences of other companies.

If there is inadequate information to permit a reasonable estimate of an appropriate accrual for warranties, the propriety of recording a sale of the goods until the warranty period has expired should be questioned.

(k) Write-Downs of Operating Assets.   SFAS No. 5 explicitly states (par. 32) that it does not cover the situation of whether an operating asset should be written down when its carrying value exceeds or may exceed the amount that is recoverable from future revenues. There have been indications that this exclusion has been misinterpreted. If the carrying value of an operating asset has been permanently impaired, the asset must be written down to recoverable value. SFAS No. 5 does not change this basic rule; it does not deal with the situation.

18.17 TRANSLATION OF LIABILITIES IN FOREIGN CURRENCIES.   When a domestic corporation consolidates a foreign branch or subsidiary or when an importer purchases goods or incurs liabilities expressed in foreign currencies, the problem arises of translating these liabilities into U.S. dollar amounts.

If there has been no change in the exchange rate between the foreign currency and the dollar, the translation of foreign currency amounts presents no difficulties. However, when exchange rates fluctuate, several questions arise: At what rate should foreign currency liabilities be translated, and what is the appropriate disposition of any amounts of gain or loss that appear on translation?

Accounting principles in this area have undergone considerable change in recent years and are discussed fully in Chapter 7.

18.18 STATEMENT PRESENTATION OF CURRENT LIABILITIES.   As previously indicated, obligations expected to be liquidated within the next operating cycle by the use of current assets or the creation of other current obligations should be classified as current liabilities.

(a) Balance Sheet Classification.   The SEC (Regulation S-X, Rule 5.02(19)) requires the following classification in balance sheets:

Accounts and notes payable. State separately amounts payable to:

1. Banks for borrowings.
2. Factors or other financial institutions for borrowings.
3. Holders of commercial paper.
4. Trade creditors.
5. Related parties.
6. Underwriters promoters, and, employees (other than related parties).
7. Others.

Rule 5.02(19) also requires disclosure of the amount and terms of unused lines of credit for short-term financing.

(b) Other Current Liabilities.   Regulation S-X, Rule 5.02(20), requires the separate statement in the balance sheet or in a note thereto, of any item in excess of 5% of total current liabilities. Such items may include, but are not limited to, accrued payrolls, accrued interest, taxes,

NOTE 7. SHORT-TERM DEBT

The Company borrows on a short-term basis, as necessary, by the issuance of commercial paper and by obtaining short-term bank loans. The maximum and average amount of short-term borrowings during 1988 were $112 million and $56 million, respectively, at a weighted average interest rate of 7.77%. The Company has an agreement for a line of credit for up to $200 million through December 1991. No short-term debt was outstanding at December 31, 1988. The line of credit is on a fee basis.

Exhibit 18.1.   Sample presentation of short-term liabilities as required by the SEC. *Source:* **Oklahoma Gas & Electric Co., 1988 Annual 10K Report.**

indicating the current portion of deferred income taxes, and the current portion of long-term debt. Remaining items may be shown in one amount.

In addition to the above-required disclosures in the balance sheet. Regulation S-X (Rule 12.10) states that the notes to the financial statements must include the weighted average interest rate and the general terms (including maturities) for each class of short-term borrowing—banks, financial institutions, and commercial paper—shown in the balance sheet at the balance sheet date and the weighted average interest for such borrowings during the period ending with the balance sheet. In addition, disclosure is required of the average amount of short-term borrowings during the period and the maximum amount of such borrowings in any one month during the period. The amount and terms (including fees and conditions) of any unused lines of credit for such borrowings should also be disclosed.

Many companies disclose arrangements for compensating balances in the note covering short-term debt, although these are covered in Regulation S-X under requirements related to cash.

An example of a note that presents the required SEC information is given in Exhibit 18.1.

In the less detailed form used in published reports to shareholders, it is common to present current liabilities as follows:

Payable to banks.

Accounts payable and accrued expenses.

Federal income taxes payable.

Current portion of long-term debt.

As a general rule, current liabilities should not be offset against related assets. For example, an overdraft at one bank should not be canceled against a debit balance at another bank; such offsetting distorts the current ratio. An exception to the general rule is indicated by APB Opinion No. 10 ("Omnibus Opinion—1966") in the instance of short-term government securities "when it is clear that a purchase of securities (acceptable for the payment of taxes) is in substance an advance payment of taxes that will be payable in the relatively near future. . . ."

Supplemental disclosure should be used to indicate partially and fully secured current claims, overdue payments, and special conditions of future payment (see section 18.2).

NATURE AND ISSUE OF BONDS PAYABLE

18.19 BONDS DEFINED.   Bonds are essentially long-term notes issued under a formal legal procedure and secured either by the pledge of specific properties or revenues or by the general credit of the issuer. In the last case, the bonds are considered "unsecured." The most common bonds are those issued by corporations, governments, and governmental agencies. A significant difference, from the point of the holder although not the issuer, is that most obligations of state and local governmental units are free of federal income taxes on interest and sometimes of state taxes, as well. Both state and local government bonds are usually called **municipals. Agency bonds** are obligations of government agencies and frequently carry a form of guarantee from the government unit. The typical bond contract calls for a series of "interest" payments semiannually and payment of principal or face amount at maturity. Bonds differ from individual notes in that they represent fractional shares of participation in a group contract, under which a trustee acts as intermediary between the corporation and holders of the bonds. The terms are set forth in the **trust indenture** covering the entire issue. **Indentures** are frequently long and complex documents and normally contain various conditions and restrictions related to the operations of the borrower.

The conditions and restrictions referred to as covenants may include restrictions on dividend payments and an agreement to maintain a minimum amount of working capital. Failure to comply with covenants would lead to default and acceleration of the due date of the debt. This event may trigger default on other obligations of the corporation under cross-covenant provisions.

Bonds, like stocks, are a means of providing the funds required for the long-run operation of the corporation and have been used for this purpose on a large scale, particularly in the utility field. The primary difference between the two broad classes of securities is that bonds represent a **contractual liability,** whereas stocks represent a residual equity. Failure to pay interest and principal as agreed under the bond contract usually results in definite legal action to protect the rights of the bondholder. As long as the corporation meets all obligations as prescribed, the bondholder has little or no influence on the administration of the company. However, if the issuer violates one or more of the restrictive convenants in the indenture, the power of the holders may substantially increase.

Bonds are normally long-term securities and are often issued for periods of 10 years or longer. Maturities vary with industry and with general conditions at the time of issue. Recent high rates of inflation have tended to reduce maturities. Intermediate-term securities, with maturities of 1 to 5 years, like bonds in every other respect, are normally called notes. Whereas bonds are usually issued in units of $1,000, prices are quoted of multiples of $100. Thus a bond quoted at $85 would actually be priced at $850. Alternatively, bond prices may be quoted in terms of their interest yield.

18.20 BONDS CLASSIFIED.   Bonds may be classified in a number of different ways. Typical of the more traditional writers, Dewing (1953) has stated: "[I]t is in the character of the security that bonds differ fundamentally among themselves." The security given in connection with the bond may range from a first or senior lien on specific physical property, such as a first mortgage bond or an equipment obligation, to securities that are a general lien, such as debentures, and finally to conditional promises with no lien, such as income bonds. Graham, Dodd, and Cottle (*Security Analysis*) argue emphatically, however, against "even the establishment of any sharply defined standards or requirements which favor secured bonds over debentures." The **analysis of bonds** is treated in detail in Chapter 10.

The traditional distinction between bonds and stocks became blurred through the increasing use of hybrid types such as convertible bonds, bonds with stock-purchase warrants attached, and redeemable preferred stocks. Similarly, the popularity of **serial bonds,** in which a portion of the issue matures each year, has blurred distinctions based on maturities.

For financial statement purposes, clear identification of bonds that are "secured" and similarly clear labeling of the assets involved are absolute requirements.

(a) Convertible Bonds.   During the 1960s, it became increasingly common to offer bonds that partake to some degree of the characteristics of both the typical senior security and the typical common stock. The most common form of **privileged issue** is the convertible bond, which includes a provision giving the right to the holder to exchange the bond for common stock on certain stipulated terms. Another method of introducing an equity element into a bond is the **bond with warrants attached,** under which holders of the bond may purchase common shares in amounts, at prices and during periods that are stipulated in advance. In the postwar "bull market" such issues achieved a high degree of popularity and were offered by both relatively speculative companies and well-established organizations.

Some measure of the popularity of these hybrids appeared to stem from the failure of generally accepted accounting principles to require adequate accounting for the equity features, particularly the potential dilution in per share earnings that could result from conversion. With the issuance of APB Opinions No. 14 and 15, the accounting advantages were removed. With the decline in securities prices during the 1970s, such issues became less popular. Chapter 5 includes a complete discussion of the effects of warrants and conversion features on per share earnings computations.

These privileged issues have created several other problems in accounting. Aside from the accounting required upon conversion, the existence of warrants or a conversion feature provides difficulties in the determination of the amount of discount. These points are considered in sections 18.29 and 18.44.

(b) Serial Bonds and Sinking Funds. Graham, Dodd, and Cottle (1962) state (p. 335):

> In its modern form a sinking fund provides for the periodic retirement of a certain portion of a senior issue through payments made by the corporation. The precise manner of acquiring the bonds for retirement varies and is not of material significance. The benefits of a sinking fund are of a twofold nature. The continuous reduction in the size of the issue makes for increasing safety and the easier repayment of the balance at maturity. Also important is the support given to the market for the issue through the repeated appearance of a substantial buying demand. In recent years increasing emphasis has been laid upon the desirability of a sinking fund, and few long-term senior issues of any type are now offered without such a provision.

Generally, the same type of protection sought by a sinking fund can be obtained by the use of **serial bonds,** issues that mature in installments. For most serial bonds, coupon interest rates differ with each maturity, and the issue price is relatively similar for all maturities. Serial retirement, however, does not provide the market demand for the issue as does a sinking fund. In principle, a default of any issue in a serial maturity or a failure to make a sinking fund payment causes the entire issue to become due and payable. In practice, as long as the issuer continues to meet interest payments, some remedy short of total default is normally arranged.

18.21 AUTHORITY TO ISSUE BONDS. The general right of a corporation to create a bonded indebtedness is found in the power to borrow funds granted by statute, and specific authorization of such action is usually included in the charter or **bylaws.** However, the authority of the directors to place a mortgage on corporate assets may be subject to shareholder approval. Securing such approval is often advisable, even if not required, in the event of a heavy borrowing program, in view of the effect of such a program on the shareholders' position. Under some statutes, corporate borrowing is subject to **general restrictions** (e.g., limitation to a certain percentage of total capital stock).

18.22 OUTLINE OF ISSUING PROCEDURE. Following is an outline of steps when bonds are issued through investment bankers:

1. Directors authorize management to proceed with negotiations.
2. Investment bankers are interviewed by corporation's representatives.
3. Propositions of investment bankers are submitted to board of directors, and board approves a particular proposal.
4. Plan is submitted to corporation's attorneys.
5. Meeting of shareholders is called, and resolution is passed approving the bond issue.

6. Appraisers and certified public accountants, acceptable to bankers, are instructed to make an investigation and submit reports.
7. Attorneys examine titles and arrange legal details.
8. An underwriting agreement with investment bankers is drawn up.
9. Trust indenture is prepared and trustee is appointed.
10. Application for registration is made to the SEC if bonds are to be marketed outside the state of origin.
11. Application is made to state commissions of states in which bonds are to be sold.
12. Certificates are printed and prepared for delivery.
13. Bonds are signed by corporate officers and trustee.
14. Bonds are delivered to underwriter and money is received by corporation.

18.23 RECORDING ISSUE OF BONDS. If the entire issue is "sold" to the underwriters, which is the most frequent procedure, and the corporation has no responsibility with respect to the process of distribution, the entries covering the issue boil down to a charge to the underwriters—or directly to "cash," if payment is made upon delivery—and a credit to "bonds payable." If the corporation disposes of the bonds through the efforts of its own organization, the accounting will be more extended and may include the recording of **subscriptions.**

Assume, for example, that a company authorizes debenture bonds in the par amount of $1,000,000 and undertakes to dispose of the bonds at par through its own office. Assume, further, that subscriptions are taken at par for 700 bonds of $1,000 each. The following general entries are required:

Subscriptions to bonds	$700,000	
Debenture bonds subscribed		$700,000

Assuming cash is received in full for 500 bonds, the entries are:

Cash	$500,000	
Subscriptions to bonds		$500,000

When the bonds are issued, the account with bonds subscribed is charged and the regular liability account, "bonds payable," is credited.

When bond subscriptions are collected on the **installment plan,** it may be advisable to set up separate accounts for each installment receivable, as a means of controlling collections and segregating balances past due. In any event detailed records of each subscription must be maintained.

On the balance sheet, bond subscriptions are preferably shown as a receivable, with bonds subscribed reported as a form of liability.

(a) Origin of Bond Discount and Premium. Bond discount is defined as the excess of face or maturity value over the amount of cash or equivalent paid in by the original bondholder, and, conversely, premium is defined as the excess of cash paid in over maturity value. The explanation of this excess is fact that in the discount case, the **nominal** or **"coupon" rate** of interest stated on the bond is less than the market or **effective rate.** In this case the investor is unwilling to pay maturity value for the bond, since this price would yield only the coupon rate. Instead, the price of the bond is set at some lower point at which the yield to the buyer is the same as the market rate of interest on comparable securities. In the case of a premium, the coupon interest rate exceeds the market rate, and the price of the bond is set at a point above maturity value that will yield to the investor only the market rate of interest.

Until the 1950s it was common for companies to issue bonds with low, even-percentage coupons (such as 4%) to demonstrate the solidity of the company. The result, frequently, was large amounts of discount, accompanied by major accounting disputes over proper treatment. More recently, it has become common to state the nominal rate of interest on bonds in rather precise fractions. An attempt is usually made to align the nominal rate as closely as possible with the market or effective rate, and the absolute magnitude of the discount or premium tends to be small. This condition does not simplify the accounting for discount and premium, but it does suggest that in many cases theoretical arguments will be disposed of on grounds of materiality.

(b) Issue of Bonds at Discount and Premium. Bonds are recorded in the main liability account at par or maturity value. If issued for less than par, the difference is charged to a discount account, illustrated as follows:

Cash	$ 97,550	
Discount on bonds payable	2,450	
Bonds payable		$100,000

Or, if subscriptions are involved,

(1)

Bond subscriptions	97,550	
Discount on bonds payable	2,450	
Bonds subscribed		100,000
To record taking of subscriptions.		

(2)

Cash	97,550	
Bond subscriptions		97,500
To record collection of subscriptions.		

(3)

Bonds subscribed	100,000	
Bonds payable		100,000
To record issue of certificates to bondholders.		

An account "discount on bond subscriptions" may be used to reflect the discount until the bond subscriptions are collected in full, at which time the account will be transferred to "discount on bonds payable."

If bonds are issued for cash in excess of the face amount of the bonds, the excess is credited to a premium account as follows:

Cash	$102,700	
Bonds payable		$100,000
Premium on bonds payable		2,700

The entries for bond subscriptions at a premium would correspond with the discount illustration shown above.

The practice of recording the face amount of the bonds and discount (or premium) in separate accounts is thoroughly established, in spite of the fact that on the investors' books it is good practice to record the purchase of the bond at cost without regard to face or maturity value. The discussion below indicates that it is theoretically correct to credit "bonds payable" with the proceeds of the bond issue, but the practice illustrated above is not objectionable, provided it is properly interpreted and reported.

(c) Issue of Bonds or Notes for Assets Other than Cash. When bonds or notes are exchanged for property, goods, or services in a bargained, arm's-length transaction, there is a general presumption that the rate of interest stipulated by the parties to the transaction is fair and adequate. If the presumption is correct, the bonds or notes are entered at par value and the asset account is charged with the par amount of the bonds.

However, the presumption of a fair interest rate cannot be allowed to prevail over the economic substance of the transaction. Thus if the bonds or notes issued in a noncash transaction carry no interest rate or an interest rate that appears unreasonable in the circumstances, they should not be recorded at face amount. Instead, in these circumstances APB Opinion No. 21 states: "[T]he note, the sales price, and the cost of the property, goods or service exchanged for the note should be recorded at the fair value of the property, goods, or service or at an amount that reasonably approximates the market value of the note, **which ever is more clearly determinable**" (emphasis added).

If the face amount thus arrived at for the notes or bonds differs from the amount appropriately recorded, discount or premium should be computed and accounted for as an element of interest over the life of the note, in accord with the methods set forth elsewhere in this section.

(d) Determining an Interest Rate.   APB Opinion No. 21 states that the determination of the appropriate value for the bonds should be made by reference first to the value of the related property, goods, or services, using the best evidence available to establish such values. However, if no valid measure of the **value of the property** can be determined, Opinion No. 21 suggests determining value of both the notes and the property by discounting the notes at an appropriate rate of interest. The carrying value of the assets would then be derived from the resulting present value of the notes.

The selection of the appropriate rate of interest should be made by reference to interest rates on **similar instruments** of the same or comparable issuers, with similar maturities, security, and so on. Published rates such as the prime rate and the market rates should also be considered. APB Opinion No. 21 notes that the objective is "to approximate the rate that would have resulted if an independent borrower and an independent lender had negotiated a similar transaction under comparable terms and conditions with the option to pay the cash price upon purchase or to give a note for the amount of purchase which bears the prevailing rate of interest to maturity."

Consider, for example, the issue of $1,000,000 of 5-year, non-interest-bearing notes in exchange for a piece of property. Since no interest has been provided for, it is clear that the provisions of APB Opinion No. 21 apply.

APB Opinion No. 21 suggests that an attempt first be made to determine the fair value of the property. Assume that the property is appraised at $600,000. The property would then be entered on the books at $600,000. The bonds would be entered at $1,000,000 less a discount of $400,000. The interest rate can be determined through the use of a financial calculator by entering $1,000,000 as a future value, $600,000 as a present value, and 5 as the number of periods. Solving for the interest rate yields 10.76% as the rate for computing interest expense (amortization of the discount).

Alternatively, no valid appraisal may be available, but evidence indicates that the company could borrow at 11% in a comparable transaction. Entering $1,000,000 as future value in a financial calculator, 11% as the interest rate, and 5 as the number of periods, a present value of $593,451 is obtained. The asset would then be entered at that value and the bonds at $1,000,000 less a discount of $406,549.

In the event that neither a valid appraisal nor a comparable interest rate can be determined, a reasonable estimate of the fair value of the property should be made by the personnel most capable of doing so. The valuation of the properties and the bonds at fair value cannot be avoided.

(e) Segregation of Bond Issue Costs.   Charges connected with the issue of new bonds—such as legal expenses in preparing the bond contract and mortgage, cost of printing certificates, registration costs, and commission to underwriters—are costs of the use of capital obtained for the whole life of the issue and should be capitalized and written off over that period.

It is common practice to lump these costs with actual discount (or net them against premium, as the case may be). Good accounting requires careful distinction between a true asset and bond discount, which is properly an offset to the maturity value of the bonds. Offset of issue costs against the premium liability is likewise objectionable.

Occasionally the amount of bond issue costs is difficult to determine. This is particularly true where bonds are sold through underwriters who share expenses. As a **general rule,** the difference between the amount paid in by the first bona fide bondholders and maturity value represents premium or discount. The difference between this amount paid in and net proceeds to the issuer represents bond issue cost.

For example, if bonds with a face value of $1 million are issued through underwriters to original holders at a price of $100\frac{1}{2}$, and if the net proceeds to the issuer are $98\frac{1}{4}$, out of which bond issue costs amounting to $15,000 are paid, the entries are:

(1)

Cash	$982,500	
Bond issue costs	22,500	
Bonds payable		$1,000,000
Premium on bonds payable		5,000
To record receipt of bond proceeds from underwriters.		

(2)

Bond issue costs	15,000	
Cash		15,000
To record payment of other bond issue costs.		

Bond issue costs of $37,500 are classified on the balance sheet as an intangible asset and amortized over the life of the bond issue on a straight-line basis.

(f) Allocation of Debt–Issue Costs in a Business Combination.   In SAB No. 77, the SEC's staff took the position that fees paid to an investment banker for advisory services, including financing services, must be allocated between direct costs of the acquisition and debt issue costs. This position is consistent with APB Opinion No. 16, "Business Combinations," which states that debt issue costs are an element of the effective interest cost of the debt, and neither the source of the debt financing nor the use of the debt proceeds changes the nature of such costs. The allocation would apply whether the services were billed as a single amount or separately. Tests of reasonableness should consider such factors as fees charged by investment bankers in connection with other recent bridge financings and fees charged for advisory services when obtained separately. The allocation should result in an effective debt service cost and interest and amortization of debt issue costs that are comparable to the effective cost of other recent debt issues of similar investment risk and maturity.

The bridge financing costs should be amortized over the estimated interim period preceding the placement of the permanent financing; any unamortized amounts should be charged to expense if the bridge loan is repaid prior to the expiration of the estimated interim period.

(g) Bonds Issued between Interest Dates.   When a bond is sold after the stated issue date, the price paid by the purchaser will include interest accrued at the coupon rate from the issue date on the bond. At the outset this accrued interest represents a liability to the issuer covering the amount of interest advanced by the investor, in view of the date of purchase, and payable at the next interest date.

For example, 10% bonds in maturity amount of $100,000 and dated January 1 are marketed at par and accrued interest one month after the stated date. The entries to record the sale and the initial payment of interest are:

	February 1	
Cash	$100,833.34	
Bonds payable		$100,000.00
Bond interest payable		833.34

	July 1	
Bond interest payable	833.34	
Bond interest charges	4,066.66	
Cash		5,000.00

When a bond is finally sold after one or more interest coupons have matured, the matured coupons are detached by the issuing company and the buyer is charged only with interest accrued since the last interest payment date.

Cases involving discount and premium are discussed below.

18.24 DETERMINATION OF BOND ISSUE PRICE.   When an investor buys a bond, he acquires two rights: (1) the right to receive periodic interest payments from the date of purchase to maturity and (2) the right to receive face value at maturity date. It follows that the current price of the bond is the sum of (1), the present value of the interest payments, plus (2), the present value of the face amount.

For example, a corporation plans to issue $1,000,000 face value, 20-year bonds. The bonds bear interest (coupon rate) of 9%, payable semiannually. If the market yield (rate of interest) on securities of this quality is 10% at the date of issue, the sale price of the bond is the sum of:

1. The present value of 40 semiannual payments of $45,000 each.

2. The present value, 40 periods hence, of $1,000,000.

Here both present values are calculated to yield 10% per annum (or more precisely, 5% each 6 months, since interest is compounded semiannually).

The present value of item 1, an annuity of $45,000 for 40 periods at 5%, is $772,158.89. The present value of the maturity payment of $1,000,000, payable in 20 years at 10% is $142,045.68. Thus we can compute the value of the bond and the discount as:

Present value of interest payments	$772,158.89
Present value of principal	+ 142,045.68
Value of the bond	914,204.57
Less face value of bond	−(1,000,000.00)
Discount on issue	$ 85,795.43

The effect of various yield rates on the issue price of this bond issue can be shown by calculating the bond issue price at various yields, as shown in the following table:

(1) Assumed Semiannual Yield Rate	(2) Present Value of Interest Payments	(3) Present Value of Payment at Maturity	(4) Present Issue Price (col. 2 + col. 3)
7%	$599,926.90	$ 66,780.38	$ 666,707.28
6	677,083.36	97,222.19	774,305.55
5	772,158.89	142,045.68	914,204.57
$4^1/_2$	828,071.30	171,928.70	1,000,000.00
4	890,674.82	208,289.04	1,098,963.86

As shown in the $4\frac{1}{2}\%$ line of the table above, when the yield rate is the same as the coupon rate, the investor pays face value for the bonds.

In some cases the issue price of the bonds is determined first; then the problem arises of estimating the effective rate established by such price. More sophisticated financial calculators are capable of determining the yield under such conditions. If a direct result cannot be obtained, successive approximation will produce an adequate result.

18.25 BOND DISCOUNT AND PREMIUM IN THE BALANCE SHEET. It was standard practice for many years to show bond discount on the balance sheet as a deferred charge and bond premium as a deferred credit, with the bond liability account remaining at face value throughout the life of the bonds.

A debate over this accounting practice raged for decades. However, it was ended by APB Opinion No. 21, which stated: "[D]iscount or premium resulting from the determination of present value in cash or non-cash transactions is not an asset or liability separable from the note which gives rise to it."

APB Opinion No. 21 calls for the presentation in the balance sheet of discount or premium as direct deduction or addition to the face amount of the note. Such an amount should not be classified as a deferred charge or credit.

Examples in APB Opinion No. 21 show discount presented either in parenthetical form in the caption for a note or as a separate statement amount deducted from the outstanding balance of the note. The Opinion notwithstanding, some companies apparently classify discount or premium in some other account when the amount is inconsequential. As noted earlier, this is frequently the case when coupon values are almost identical to market interest rates.

BOND INTEREST PAYMENTS, PREMIUM AMORTIZATION, AND DISCOUNT ACCUMULATION

18.26 ACCRUAL OF BOND INTEREST. Interest payment dates may not coincide with accounting period dates, and in such circumstances it is necessary to accrue interest on outstanding bonds to secure the proper charge to the income statement and recognition of the interest liability. And even when the stated date of payment and the end of the accounting period are the same, systematic accrual of income deduction and liability is good procedure, especially since interest money may be deposited prior to the interest date and payment of all coupons may not be effected on such date. A regular **monthly accrual** is usually desirable.

For example, if 12% bonds in the par amount of $1,000,000 are issued at par on June 1, the issuing company may well make entries at the end of each month throughout the life of the bonds as follows:

Bond interest charges	$10,000.00	
Bond interest payables		$10,000.00

18.27 PAYMENT OF INTEREST. Bond interest is ordinarily paid semiannually. Thus the regular cash requirement for interest on an issue of $1,000,000 of 12% bonds is 6% or $60,000 every 6 months. Interest may be paid directly by the issuer or through the trustee. In the former case, the issuer mails checks to all registered holders and makes a deposit in some specified bank sufficient to cover all outstanding coupons (or, in some instances, makes payments by check or in actual cash to parties presenting coupons). In the latter case, the issuer deposits the required interest money with the **trustee,** and depends on the trustee to carry out the actual process of paying the individual bondholders. Assuming that deposit with the trustee is tantamount to payment, the entries covering such deposit are, for example:

Bond interest payable	$60,000	
Cash		$60,000

However, a more complete and satisfactory treatment is to charge the trustee with the money deposit and cancel the liability when payment of coupons has been reported (or coupons have been returned). Thus:

(1)

Interest fund—Blank Trust Co.	$60,000	
Cash		$60,000

(2)

Bond interest payable	60,000	
Interest fund—Blank Trust Co.		60,000

The amount of **unredeemed coupons** due at any time is represented by the balance of "bond interest payable," and the amount available for payment is the balance of the interest fund. If desired, the amount of past-due coupons may be transferred to a distinct account.

Paid or **canceled coupons** should be systematically filed either by the issuing company or by the trustee.

(a) Interest on Treasury Bonds. Any matured coupons attached to treasury bonds (either unissued or reacquired) should be removed, canceled, and filed. The interest entries should be confined to bonds actually outstanding. When payment is made by the trustee, coupons on bonds in the treasury may be forwarded with the check for interest on outstanding bonds, or they may be filed by the company with notice to the trustee that the bonds are in the treasury.

(b) Interest on Bonds Held by Trustee. Bonds of the company's own issue in the hands of the trustee are not truly outstanding, and any "interest" payments on such bonds required by the trust agreement should not be permitted to affect the interest accounts of the issuer. A requirement that "interest" be deposited on bonds already held by the trustee is simply a means of accelerating the accumulation of the sinking fund.

Assume, for example, that 10% of an issue on which the total semiannual interest is $20,000 is in the hands of the trustee, and that the agreement calls for deposit of the entire amount. The appropriate entries are:

(1)

Bond interest charges	$18,000	
Bond interest payable		$18,000
To record accrual of interest on outstanding bonds.		

(2)

Interest and sinking fund—Blank Trust Co.	20,000	
Cash		20,000
To record periodic payment to trustee.		

(3)

Bond interest payable	18,000	
Interest and sinking fund—Blank Trust Co.		18,000
To record payment of coupons by trustee.		

18.28 PREMIUM AMORTIZATION AND DISCOUNT ACCUMULATION. APB Opinion No. 21 requires that bond discount or premium be charged systematically to income as interest expense or income over the life of the bond issue. The effect on the income statement of systematic amortization of premium or accumulation of discount is to show interest expense at the effective amount.

In the past there were two common methods of amortizing bond discount or premium: the **straight-line method** and the **interest method.** The straight-line method was utilized more commonly by industrial and commercial companies, whereas financial institutions favored the interest method. In APB Opinion No. 12, the AICPA favored the interest method.

However, in APB Opinion No. 21 (1971), the AICPA took the position that only the interest method was acceptable for amortization of discount or premium. The opinion does, however, permit the use other methods that provide results that are not materially different from the results given under the interest method. In practice, it appears that some issuers have used a sum-of-the-digits method, sometimes referred to as **"rule of 78,"** which is the sum of the month's digits in a year. Amortization on a sum-of-the-digits basis will usually provide more accelerated amortization than the interest method, which many accountants would consider "conservative." As a practical matter, it appears that companies using sum-of-the-digits now were doing so when APB Opinion No. 21 was introduced and have continued in the name of consistency. There seems to be no reason to adopt the method for a new operation.

As an illustration of the interest method, assume a $1,000,000 issue of 5-year bonds with 8% annual interest (payable semiannually), priced to yield 10% to investors, for a market price of $922,782.65.

The interest method is a procedure for absorbing the discount or premium in accord with the ordinary mathematical interpretation of the composition of the issue price; it provides for spreading of the total interest charge in terms of the effective or market rate of interest. For the illustrative issue, the entry to record interest and the amortization of discount for the first period is:

Bond interest expense (5% × $922,782.65)	$46,139.13	
Discount on bonds payable		$ 6,139.13
Bond interest payable (4% × $1,000,000)		40,000.00

In each subsequent period bond interest expense will be charged with the effective rate of interest times the carrying value of the bonds, and the periodic amortization will be the difference between this amount and the bond interest liability. The amortization of premium is given similar treatment.

An **accumulation table** for the bonds above for the first 3 years under the interest method is as follows:

Half-Year Period	Carrying Value of Bonds	Interest Expense	Interest Payments	Accumulation of Discount
1	$922,782.65	$46,139.13	$40,000.00	$6,139.13
2	928,921.78	46,446.09	40,000.00	6,446.09
3	935,367.87	46,768.39	40,000.00	6,768.39
4	942,136.26	47,106.81	40,000.00	7,106.81
5	949,243.07	47,462.15	40,000.00	7,462.15
6	956,705.22	47,835.26	40,000.00	7,835.26

In practice, it is common to develop such tables when bonds are first issued, to provide a basis for subsequent accounting. Since interest dates are not likely to coincide with financial reporting dates, tables are frequently developed on a monthly or daily basis to permit correct entries whenever financial statements are prepared. Similar entries and tables result for the amortization of bond premium.

18.29 DISCOUNT ON CONVERTIBLE BONDS AND BONDS WITH WARRANTS.   Bonds that may eventually be converted into a certain number of shares of common stock and bonds that have warrants attached, permitting the purchase of common stock at a fixed price, have achieved considerable popularity. The attraction to the buyer of such issues is obvious—they provide the fixed income of bonds along with the opportunity to participate in an equity increase. An attraction of such issues to the issuing corporation is that they are typically sold at interest rates below those that would be required for similar securities in the absence of the equity privileges. In some cases, the corporation's credit may be such that debt could not be issued at all without the conversion privilege or warrants.

Traditional accounting permitted the recording of such securities by the issuer as if they were really straight debt and has ignored the existence of the privileges until conversion, exercise, or refunding. That the corporation, when it issues such privileged securities, is actually selling two instruments, (1) a straight bond plus (2) a call on its stock at some time in the future, received scant attention in accounting literature until the APB issued Opinion Nos. 14 and 15.

In Opinion No. 14, the AICPA affirmed that the amount of discount that would be attributable to bonds with warrants should be treated in a manner similar to the usual bond discount, that is, amortized to income. The amount of discount attributable to the warrant feature is determined by reference to the price of an equivalent "straight" bond of the same or a comparable issuer. See section 18.47 for a more complete discussion of this subject. No discount, however, is to be recognized as being related to the conversion privilege of convertible bonds. In Opinion No. 15, the AICPA recognized the dilutive effects of warrants and the conversion privilege and called for appropriate adjustment in per share earnings calculations (see Chapter 5).

18.30 BLOCKS ISSUED AT DIFFERENT RATES.   In some cases bonds of a particular class and series are marketed at different times and at different prices. Assume, for example, that of an issue with a maturity amount of $1,000,000 the first $600,000 is sold at 102 and the second $400,000 at 105. Under such conditions two **alternative procedures** are available. The two blocks of the issue may be accounted for separately and the premium on each block may be amortized at the effective rate involved. The alternative is to combine both blocks in the accounts and to apply an overall approximate rate, determined in the light of the conditions under which the two blocks were issued. Separate computations are generally advisable where considerable time elapses between issue dates and there is a substantial difference between the effective rates involved.

18.31 TREATMENT OF SERIAL BONDS.   In the rare case of various maturities of serial bonds being issued at the same yield rate, this rate can be applied to the net book value of the entire issue to determine accumulation or amortization as in the interest method illustrations above.

In the much more common case of serial bonds that are issued with different yields on each maturity, the interest method of amortization of discount or premium should be applied to each maturity, treating it as if it were a separate issue. Formerly, such treatment was considered "too complex," but the development of sophisticated financial calculators obviates that argument. However, if all the bonds in a series have the same yield, the bonds-outstanding method would probably be acceptable, since, as illustrated below, it tends to give a result that is not materially different from the interest method sanctioned by APB Opinion No. 21. However, as noted above, there seems to be no practical reason to use this method, except consistency.

(a) Bonds-Outstanding Method.   Under the bonds-outstanding method, the periodic amortization is determined by multiplying the total premium or discount by a fraction, the numerator of which is the par value of bonds outstanding during the year and denominator the sum total of the par value of bonds outstanding over the life of the issue.

For example, assuming that a $50,000 issue of 8% bonds are issued on January 1 for $52,625.45 and that $10,000 mature at the end of each year, the amortization schedule is:

End of Year	Bonds Outstanding	Fraction	Premium Amortization
1	$ 50,000	$5/_{15}$	$ 875.15
2	40,000	$4/_{15}$	700.12
3	30,000	$3/_{15}$	525.09
4	20,000	$2/_{15}$	350.06
5	10,000	$1/_{15}$	175.03
	$150,000		$2,625.45

The bonds-outstanding method provides for the recognition of uniform amounts of amortization in terms of the par value of bonds outstanding. The method has the same advantages and disadvantages that are inherent in the straight-line method for term bonds.

(b) Interest Method. Under the interest method the periodic amortization is the difference between the interest due and effective rates of interest applied to the carrying value of bonds outstanding at the interest date.

For example, the amortization schedule under the interest method, using the data in the preceding illustration, which yields a 6% rate to the investor, is as follows:

End of Year	Interest Payment (8% of Par)	Effective Interest (6% of Carrying Value)	Premium Amortization
1	$ 4,000.00	$3,157.53	$ 842.47
2	3,200.00	2,506.98	693.02
3	2,400.00	1,865.40	534.60
4	1,600.00	1,233.32	366.68
5	800.00	611.32	188.68
	$12,000.00	$9,374.55	$2,625.45

BOND REDEMPTION, REFUNDING, AND CONVERSION

18.32 PAYMENT AT MATURITY. No special accounting problems arise when bonds are paid as agreed at maturity, assuming that items of bond issue cost and of discount or premium have been disposed of systematically.

The amount of any matured bonds not presented for redemption by the holder at maturity date should be segregated in a special account. This balance should be carried as a current liability except where a special fund—not reported in current assets—is maintained to redeem the bonds when they are presented. Interest does not accrue on matured bonds not in default.

18.33 SETTLEMENT AFTER MATURITY. When default occurs at maturity, no special entries are required prior to the settlement made through reorganization procedure, although the fact that the liability has matured but remains unpaid should be indicated in the balance sheet. Occasionally, creditors consent to a postponement of payment provided the corporation continues to pay interest at a specified rate. When the liability is scaled down through a **reorganization procedure,** the difference between the amount paid and maturity amount constitutes a special credit to retained earnings or deficit, although such difference will often be absorbed by revision of recorded asset values. Where a special settlement following default at maturity provides for issue of new securities to replace the defaulted bonds, the book value assigned to such securities will presumably equal the maturity amount of the bonds (plus any unpaid interest accruing since maturity), except as conditions clearly warrant some other treatment.

18.34 DEFAULTED BONDS. Default of bonds prior to maturity creates a situation similar to that of default at maturity. Generally, no entries are called for, but the condition of default should be clearly described in the statements. **Interest** continues to accrue on defaulted bonds under conditions prescribed in the contract and should be recorded.

Since the par amount ordinarily becomes due and payable at default, it may be argued that any balance of **discount** or **premium** on the books should be immediately written off, but there is little point in such action if actual payment is unlikely. Rather, the regular schedule of accumulation or amortization, as well as amortization of bond issue costs, should be continued during the period of default. In case of refunding or redemption as a part of reorganization procedure, complete write-off of any unabsorbed balance is recommended.

18.35 CLASSIFICATION OF OBLIGATIONS WHEN A VIOLATION IS WAIVED BY THE CREDITOR.   In Issue No. 86-30 the EITF considered whether the waiver of a lender's rights resulting from the violation of a covenant with retention of the periodic covenant test represents, in substance, a grace period. If viewed as a grace period, the borrower must classify the debt as current under SFAS No. 78, unless it is probable that the borrower can cure the violation (comply with the covenant) within the grace period. The Task Force's consensus was that unless the facts and circumstances would indicate otherwise, the borrower should classify the obligation as noncurrent unless (1) a covenant violation has occurred at the balance sheet date or would have occurred absent a loan modification and (2) it is probable that the borrower will not be able to cure the default at measurement dates that are within the next 12 months.

18.36 COMPOSITIONS WITH CREDITORS.   Compositions with creditors in the event of financial weakness often involve a scaling down of acknowledged liabilities, either through actual cancellation of the claims or through issue of stock to cover some element of the total debt. Chapter 11 of the **Bankruptcy Act** is designed to facilitate such agreements, to eliminate losses due to forced sale of property, and to prevent cash payments to dissenting minorities when a revision in the debt structure is agreed to by a substantial majority of claimants of the same class. These procedures tend to encourage continued operations under the same management when this seems desirable (see Chapter 33).

(a) Troubled Debt Restructurings.   When a debtor has difficulty making scheduled payments on debts, usually as evidenced by notes to one creditor, rather than by bonds, a restructuring of the debt may be arranged. That is, the creditor will agree to alter the payments of interest and/or principal in such a manner as to make it more likely that the debtor can make the payments. Restructurings usually include reductions in the original interest rate, deferral of interest payment, and extension of the time for payment of principal or a combination of all three. On the other hand, they rarely include a reduction in the absolute value of the principal amount. If the debtor cannot eventually pay the principal, lenders tend to "close in," that is, to call the loan.

Debt restructurings of the type noted above traditionally did not call for any accounting entries by debtor or creditor, since the results were viewed as being prospective. However, with the substantial increase in such arrangements, particularly as precipitated by the financial difficulties of real estate companies and REITs, the FASB issued SFAS No. 15, "Accounting by Debtors and Creditors for Troubled Debt Restructurings" (June 1977).

The exposure draft of SFAS No. 15 caused a great deal of controversy, since it appeared to require that creditors report losses on restructurings, equal in amount to the decline in present value of the stream of cash flows expected to come from eventual repayment of the loan by the debtor. After much debate, the original notion was scaled back. SFAS No. 15, as issued, stated that creditors would record losses on restructurings (and debtors would record gains) only when the discounted present values of the restructured interest and principal payments were less than the original, absolute (undiscounted) value of the principal. Arithmetically, this means that unless the amount of the principal is reduced—and it is rarely reduced—there will be no gain recorded by the debtor and no loss by the creditor.

Interest expense, subsequent to a restructuring, is recorded by the debtor so that a constant effective interest rate is applied to the carrying amount of the payable at the beginning of the period between the restructuring and maturity. This is, in substance, the method prescribed by APB Opinion No. 21 (par. 15) and described elsewhere in this chapter (section 18.23(c)).

SFAS No. 15 requires disclosure of the principal features of a restructuring, of any gain or loss, and of the per share impacts.

FTB No. 80-2, "Classification of Debt Restructurings by Debtors and Creditors," emphasizes that a debt restructuring is very much an individual entity event. That is, a debtor could have a restructuring even though the related creditor does not have a troubled debt restructuring. The debtor and creditor must individually apply SFAS No. 15 to the specific facts and circumstances. The Statement establishes tests for applicability that are not symmetrical. For example, FTB No. 80-2 illustrates a case where a creditor purchases a note at a deep discount. Settlement by the debtor at less than his carrying value could nevertheless exceed the carrying value of the existing creditor. Thus it could be a troubled debt restructuring only from the standpoint of the debtor.

FTB No. 81-6, "Applicability of FASB Statement 15 to Debtors in Bankruptcy Situations," indicates that the principles of troubled debt restructuring of SFAS No. 15 do not apply where a company is involved in a Chapter 11 bankruptcy proceeding that will result in a restatement of all of its indebtedness, say at 50 cents on the dollar. However, SFAS No. 15 would apply to an isolated troubled debt restructuring by a debtor involved in a bankruptcy proceeding as long as it did not result in a general restatement of the debtor's liabilities.

(b) Restructurings Involving Exchanges of Property.   The same real estate industry conditions that prompted the type of debt restructurings discussed immediately above also produced instances of creditors who accepted properties and accounts receivable in full or partial settlement of debts. To avoid the recording of losses by creditors, the value of the properties taken by the creditors was often stipulated to be equal to the loan balance settled.

SFAS No. 15 also attacked this situation. It requires that property transferred in such settlements be recorded at fair value. The **debtor records** any difference between the carrying value of the payable and the fair value of the assets transferred to the creditor as a gain or loss. The debtor also records any difference between the carrying value of the assets transferred to the creditor and the fair value of those assets as a gain or loss, as provided in APB Opinion No. 30, "Reporting the Results of Operations." (See Chapter 5 for further materials on reporting unusual gains and losses.)

(c) Troubled Debt Restructuring Distinguished from Early Extinguishment.   The EITF recently considered the issue of whether a creditor can recognize a gain on debt extinguishment for a modification of debt terms when the debtor is experiencing financial difficulty (EITF Issue No. 89-15). Under the terms of the proposed exchange the creditor would receive new debt whose terms are more favorable to the creditor than the terms of the existing debt. However, the terms of the new debt are not representative of and are less favorable to the creditor than the prevailing terms for new borrowings by enterprises with similar credit ratings. The Task Force reached a consensus that no gain should be recognized in the described circumstances. The terms of the exchange were deemed to involve concessions to the debtor by the creditor. Therefore, the EITF concluded that the transaction should be accounted for by both parties as a modification of an existing obligation under the provisions of SFAS No. 15.

18.37 REDEMPTION BEFORE MATURITY.   Many bond contracts provide for the calling of any portion, usually selected by random draw, or all of the issue at the option of the company at a stated price, usually above par, to allow the corporation to reduce its debt before maturity as the occasion arises. In periods of high interest rates, buyers of new bonds prefer indentures that restrict the **call privilege.** Also, bonds are often retired piecemeal through **sinking fund operations,** or acquired by the issuer on the open market.

SFAS No. 76, "Extinguishment of Debt," provides guidance to debtors as to when debt should be considered extinguished for financial reporting. See section 18.43 for a discussion of SFAS No. 76.

As interest rates rose in the 1970s, some corporations retired older, low interest bonds (and, in some cases, low-yielding convertible bonds), to increase earnings by passing the gain on retirement through income. In many cases, these retirements appeared to be uneconomic, suggesting that earnings creation was the principal reason. See below, under "Gains and Losses from Extinguishment of Debt," for a more complete discussion.

Outstanding bonds acquired by the issuer may be permanently retired or—if the conditions of acquisition permit—they may be held in the corporate treasury for reissue at some later date. If the bonds were issued at par and are redeemed at par, the only special problem is the absorption of any bond issue costs remaining on the books. Additional problems arise when there is unabsorbed discount or premium on the books at the time of redemption, or where the redemption price differs from the maturity value.

Assuming **outright redemption,** all balances relating to the bonds redeemed should be eliminated.

The M Co., for example, has outstanding a bond issue of $100,000 maturity amount. On the books related to this issue are unamortized bond issue costs of $2,000 and unaccumulated discount of $3,000. At this point the entire issue is called at 105, and costs are incurred in the carrying out of this transaction of $1,500. The summarized entries are:

Bonds payable	$100,000	
Loss on redemption of bonds	11,500	
Bond issue costs		$ 2,000
Discount on bonds payable		3,000
Cash		106,500

When bonds are redeemed by **purchase on the market,** a book profit may result.

Assume conditions as in the preceding example except that instead of calling the entire issue, the M Co. bought bonds in par amount of $20,000 on the market at a total expenditure, including all charges, of $15,000. The summarized entries are:

Bonds payable	$ 20,000	
Bond issue costs		$ 400
Discount on bonds payable		600
Cash		15,000
Gain on redemption of bonds		4,000

In this case, with 20% of the issue retired, the write-off of issue costs and discount is restricted to 20%.

(a) Gains and Losses from Extinguishment of Debt.   Losses resulting from unamortized bond issue costs, unamortized discount, calll premium, or a combination of these factors and gains or losses resulting from market conditions, upon retirement, should be recognized currently as income of the period in which the debt extinguishment takes place. SFAC No. 4 states: "Gains and losses from extinguishment of debt that are included in the determination of that income shall be aggregated and if material classified as an extraordinary item, net of related income tax effect."

The requirement to classify gains and losses on extinguishment of debt as extraordinary items does not apply to required purchases for sinking funds before their scheduled maturity. Debt maturing serially is not considered to have the characteristics of sinking fund requirements, and gain and loss from extinguishment of a serial debt is classified as an extraordinary item.

The history of accounting for early extinguishment of debts is long and full of contention. For many years, accountants attempted to distinguish between extinguishments of debt followed by a refunding, debts permanently retired, and other cases involving extinguishment. Various treatments were prescribed, and there was frequently little uniformity.

Finally, APB Opinion No. 26, "Early Extinguishment of Debt," which became effective for extinguishments of debt occurring on or after January 1, 1973, stated:

> All extinguishments of debt before scheduled maturities are fundamentally alike. The accounting for such transactions should be the same regardless of the means used to achieve the extinguishment.
>
> A difference between the reacquisition price and the net carrying amount of the extinguished debt should be recognized currently in income of the period of extinguishment as losses or gains.

A period followed the issuance of APB Opinion No. 26 during which gains and losses on extinguishment of debt were reported under the criteria stipulated in APB Opinion Nos. 9 and 30. The AICPA (1973) appeared to preclude classifying gains or losses from early extinguishment of debt as extraordinary, and this resulted in the inclusion of these items in net income.

With rises in interest rates during the late 1970s, an increasing number of companies entered into early extinguishments of debt and reported large profits, included in net income, from the transactions. Disclosure was frequently less than complete. Eventually, complaints of financial statement users and the SEC forced a reconsideration of the issue, and SFAS No. 4 was promulgated, requiring disclosure of the following items:

1. A description of the distinguishment of transaction, including the sources of any funds used to extinguish debt if it is practicable to identify the sources.
2. The income tax effect in the period of extinguishment.
3. The per share amount of the aggregate gain or loss net of related income tax effect.

The treatment stipulated by APB Opinion No. 26, carrying all gains and losses on extinguishment of debt to income applies to all debt, including **convertible debt.**

SFAS No. 64, "Extinguishments of Debt Made to Satisfy Sinking-Fund Requirements," amended SFAS No. 4, "Reporting Gains and Losses from Extinguishment of Debt," so that gains and losses from extinguishment of debt made to satisfy sinking-fund requirements that an enterprise must meet within one year of the date of extinguishment are not required to be classified as extraordinary items. This classification is to be determined without regard to the means used to achieve the extinguishment, that is, cash purchase, debt exchange, or stock for debt. SFAS No. 64 does not apply to debt maturing serially.

(b) Noncash Early Extinguishments.   FTB No. 80-1, "Early Extinguishment of Debt through Exchange for Common or Preferred Stock," indicates that APB Opinion No. 26 applies to all early extinguishments of debt effected by issuance of common or preferred stock, including redeemable and fixed maturity preferred stock, unless the extinguishment is a troubled debt restructuring or a conversion by the holder pursuant to conversion privileges contained in the original debt issue. The reacquisition price is determined by the value of the common or preferred stock issued or the value of the debt, whichever is more clearly evident.

18.38 TREATMENT AND REISSUE OF TREASURY BONDS.   Bonds acquired by the corporation as a result of call or purchase may be canceled by formal action, or they may be held in substantially the same category as authorized bonds that have never been issued. The most common modern form of presentation is to show only the net amount of bonds outstanding on the balance sheet and to indicate the existence of treasury bonds in a note to the statements.

It follows from this that the acquisition by a corporation of its own bonds amounts to redemption of those bonds, and disposition of any balances of unamortized premium or discount, or bond issue costs, should follow the recommendations presented above under

"Gains and Losses from Extinguishment of Debt," permitting recognition of book gain or loss.

The SEC (Regulation S-X, Rule 4-06) states:

> Reacquired evidences of indebtedness shall be deducted from the appropriate liability caption. However, reacquired evidences of indebtedness held for pension and other special funds not related to the particular issues may be shown as assets; provided that there be stated the amount of such evidences of indebtedness, the cost thereof, and the amount at which stated, and the purpose for which acquired.

Where the recommendations above for accounting for acquisition of treasury bonds have been followed, accounting for reissue is essentially the same as for bonds that have never before been outstanding. If the par amount of the treasury bonds is carried in a special account, this account is credited at par when the bonds are issued.

18.39 USE OF SINKING FUNDS.   Retirement of bonds through the operation of a special fund is familiar financial practice. The fund procedure may be a plan adopted by the issuing corporation and entirely within its control, or it may be an arrangement provided by contract, involving a **trustee.**

Most commonly, the sinking fund is an arrangement rather than an actual fund. That is, the bond indenture requires the borrowing corporation to make specific, periodic payments to the trustee, who then acquires the necessary bonds. Whether the sinking fund actually holds the bonds or arranges for their retirement is actually a moot question, since when held by the sinking fund, the bonds are effectively retired. In the past, sinking funds might actually consist of a fund, holding assets other than the debt in question. Since the purpose of the sinking fund arrangement is to provide gradual retirement of the debt, there is no reason for the fund to undertake the risk of holding securities of another issuer. In another common arrangement the company may acquire bonds in the open market or through calls, hold them as treasury bonds, then deposit them in satisfaction of sinking fund requirements at appropriate dates. In the case of some convertible debt, the conversion of enough bonds may satisfy the sinking fund requirements.

When the trustee has used the funds to acquire the corporation's bonds, either at or before maturity, the bonds so acquired are in effect retired and should be reported as such on the balance sheet of the corporation. Accounting for corporation bonds acquired by a sinking fund trustee should follow the same procedures described in section 18.38. This treatment is proper even when the bonds are kept "alive" by the trustee for the purpose of accumulating "interest" from the corporation issuer. "Interest" payments by the corporation to the trustee on the corporation's own bonds held in the fund should be treated simply as additional deposits.

18.40 PAYMENT BY REFUNDING.   In the utility field, in particular, the funded debt is often viewed as a permanent part of the **capital structure.** This means that corporate policy is not always directed toward the permanent retirement of long-term liabilities; instead, the usual procedure is to secure the funds to meet maturing obligations by floating new loans.

A distinction should be drawn between retirement of bonds through an exchange and payment by refunding or refinancing. In the typical refunding operation a new bond issue, with new terms, is floated through investment channels, and the funds so provided as specifically employed to retire the preceding bond issue. However, in some cases the holders of the old issue are given the opportunity to exchange their bonds directly for bonds of the new issue. To the extent that **direct exchange** can be arranged by the issuing corporation, the cost of refinancing is minimized.

No additional accounting problems are encountered when bonds are refunded at maturity. The retirement of the old bonds and the issue of the new bonds are separate transactions.

18.41 DETERMINING WHEN TO REFUND.   Ignoring effect on taxes and other special factors, there is no object in refunding prior to maturity except when more favorable terms can be secured, particularly with respect to interest rate. However, the bare fact that the market rate has fallen does not justify refunding. To retire a complete issue of outstanding bonds prior to maturity ordinarily necessitates exercise of right of call, and this means payment of a redemption premium, usually substantial. Moreover, the **costs of refunding** must be considered. When the old issue is called before maturity, the trustee will require a fee for additional services. There will be legal and accounting fees, taxes, and printing costs. More serious are the added costs of registration and marketing the issue. Another factor that may be important is the additional interest charge required by the overlapping of the two issues.

There has been considerable discussion in financial circles as to the proper method of **computing the saving**—if any—to be realized by refunding under a specified set of conditions. Probably the most significant approach is that which compares the present values at the prevailing effective rate of the cash requirements of the two programs, considering the new issue to run for only the remaining life of the old. (It is pure speculation to make the comparison for a longer term.)

For example, the M Company has outstanding $1,000,000, maturity amount, of 6% bonds, with 10 years yet to run. These bonds are callable at any interest date at 105. Assume that the effective market rate of interest for this class of security is at the present time only 4%, for loans of 10 years or longer. The service costs of various kinds required to call the old bonds and float the new loan are estimated at $30,000. The present cash value of the obligations under the old contract is found as follows:

Present value of amount due in 20 periods (10 years) at 2% per period	$ 672,971.33
Present value of annuity of $30,000 per period for 20 periods at 2%	490,543.00
	$1,163,514.33

The amount of cash required to meet these claims through the medium of a new loan is $1,080,000 (including redemption premium of $50,000 and costs of $30,000). By comparison it appears that an advantage is realized by refunding.

It is important to note that the question of **book loss** realized on redemption has no bearing on the determination of the financial advantage of a refunding program over continuation of the existing contract.

However, as noted above in connection with early retirement of bonds and notes, some companies have undertaken early retirement to produce reported earnings, even though the transactions are inherently uneconomical.

With a high level of corporate income and profits taxes prevailing, the desire to realize a book loss for tax purposes in the form of unamortized discount and expense may be an important or even a decisive factor in bringing about a decision to refund. It is even possible for a situation to develop in which a refunding might seem to be advantageous, in view of the tax angle, although no saving in interest charges results.

18.42 DEBTOR'S ACCOUNTING FOR A MODIFICATION OF DEBT TERMS.   When interest rates decline, debtors may consider transactions that would use the leverage of an existing call provision to reduce the higher interest rate on an older debt issue. For example, the debtor may exchange new noncallable debt with a lower interest rate for old callable debt or have the creditor pay a fee in return for an agreement not to exercise the call provision for the life of the debt or for a shorter period. In Issue No. 86-18, the Task Force reached a consensus that the exchange of a new noncallable debt instrument for an older callable debt instrument should be accounted for by the debtor as the extinguishment of the older debt issue. The Task Force expressed diverse views regarding the accounting for fees paid for a waiver. But they agreed that any fees paid would be included in an analysis of the revised cash flows under the modified terms.

18.43 IN-SUBSTANCE DEFEASANCE.   SFAS No. 76, ''Extinguishment of Debt,'' provides guidance to debtors as to when debt should be considered to be extinguished for financial reporting purposes and provides special criteria for the recognition of in-substance defeasance of debt. SFAS No. 76 (par. 3), states that a debtor shall consider debt to be extinguished for financial reporting in the following circumstances:

a. The debtor pays the creditor and is relieved of all its obligations with respect to the debt. This includes the debtor's reacquisition of its outstanding debt securities in the public securities markets, regardless of whether the securities are canceled or held as so-called treasury bonds.

b. The debtor is legally released from being the primary obligation under the debt either judicially or by the creditor and it is probable that the debtor will not be required to make future payments with respect to that debt under any guarantees.

c. The debtor irrevocably places cash or other assets in a trust to be used solely for satisfying scheduled payments of both interest and principal of a specific obligation and the possibility that the debtor will be required to make future payments with respect to the debt is remote. In this circumstance the debt is extinguished even though the debtor is not legally released from being the primary obligor under the debt obligations.

Paragraph 4 of SFAS No. 76 establishes restrictions on the nature of assets to be held by the trust to effect an in-substance defeasance under paragraph 3(c). Only monetary assets that are essentially risk-free as to the amount, timing, and collection of interest and principal qualify. For debt denominated in U.S. dollars, investments must be limited to (par. 4):

(1) Direct obligations of the U.S. government

(2) Obligations guaranteed by the U.S. government

(3) Securities that are backed by U.S. government obligations as collateral under an arrangement by which the interest and principal payments on the collateral generally flow immediately through to the holder of the security.

The cash flow from the investments should approximately coincide as to timing and amount with the scheduled interest and principal payments on the debt. The amount invested should also cover trustee costs if they are to be paid by the trust.

If debt is considered extinguished under an in-substance defeasance arrangement, a general description of the transaction and the amount of debt that is considered extinguished at the end of the period should be disclosed as long as the debt remains outstanding.

In FRR No. 15, the SEC commented on SFAS No. 76 with respect to four points:

1. Although SFAS No. 76 does not have any specific eligibility requirements for the trustee of the trust created pursuant to paragraph 3(c) of SFAS No. 76, the Commission stated that the standard contemplates the trustee being independent with respect to the company.

2. SFAS No. 76 limits investments by the trust to the three categories itemized above. The SEC expressed the view that very few securities of the type listed in (2) and (3) above can satisfy the essential risk-free requirements, particularly because the requirements for the assets to be risk-free as to timing of collection applies to the risk of late as well as early payments. The Commission stressed that a guaranty that provides for the ultimate collection, but not for the collection of principal and interest in sufficient time to ensure payments on the defeased debt as they become due, would not qualify.

3. Assessments as to the debtor being required to make future payments with respect to the debt must be made not only because of an inadequacy of trust assets attributable to a failure to realize scheduled cash flows, but also because of acceleration of the debt's maturity. An acceleration may occur because of the violation of a covenant of another debt or because of cross-default provisions.

4. The Commission concluded that the trust must be designed so that neither the corporation nor its creditors or others can rescind or revoke it, or obtain access to its assets.

FTB No. 84-4, "In-Substance Defeasance of Debt," clarifies a number of issues that have arisen in applying SFAS No. 76.

(a) Instantaneous Defeasance Transactions.   FTB 84-4 takes the position that borrow-and-invest activities cannot result in debt extinguishment. Thus, if assets that the debtor places in trust were acquired at or about the time that the debt was incurred, or were acquired as part of a series of investment activities initiated at the time the debt was incurred, or if debt was incurred pursuant to a forward contract entered into at or about the time the debtor acquired the assets being irrevocably placed in trust, an in-substance defeasance cannot be recognized. The Board based this conclusion on the fact that any gain or loss on extinguishing previously outstanding debt reflects in large measure the effect of past changes in interest rates for the debtor, whereas the gain or loss related to borrow-and-invest activities reflects principally the concurrent differences in interest rates when the debt was issued. Borrow-and-invest activities, in effect, hedge the debtor against the risk of changes in interest rates.

(b) Assessing Remoteness of Risk of Trust Assets.   SFAS 76 requires that the cash inflow to the trust in an in-substance defeasance be essentially risk-free. Specified criteria are established that focus on the nature of the monetary assets placed in trust rather than on possible external events. Thus callable securities are not risk-free (see SFAS No. 76, pars. 4(a), 31, 32). Variations from the specified criteria are not permitted on the basis that any related risks are remote. Areas where remoteness of contingencies in determining whether the cash inflows to the trust from its assets are essentially risk-free would include the likelihood of a default by the sovereign government or the imposition of currency controls and the like.

(c) Callable Debt.   FTB 84-4 concludes that a debtor's retention of an option to purchase the debt through a call provision is not, in itself, an impediment to an in-substance defeasance. The option creates no risk that the debtor will be required to make further payments with respect to the debt because the exercise is at the debtor's option. Thus, callable debt does not violate the requirement of SFAS No. 76 that it apply only to debt with specified maturities and fixed payment schedules. The assets placed in trust must, however, meet the planned or anticipated call schedule.

18.44 BOND CONVERSION.   When convertible bonds issued at par are converted into stock at par, dollar for dollar, the conversion is ordinarily assumed to be the equivalent of the payment of the liability and the issue of additional stock at par. The entries necessary to recognize conversion under these conditions, accordingly, consist essentially of a charge to bonds outstanding and a corresponding credit to capital stock. In the case of the conversion of bonds issued at a premium into stock on a par-for-par basis, the **unamortized premium** on the date of conversion is preferably treated as a form of stock premium. Similarly, an **unaccumulated discount** attaching to bonds converted into stock on a par-for-par basis should be set up as a type of stock discount, although such discount would presumably not represent an amount that might be collected from shareholders by assessment. The schedule of accumulation of discount or amortization of premium set up for convertible bonds should disregard the possibility of conversion, and such schedule should be adhered to until conversion takes place.

When bonds are convertible into stock at some specified price other than par or stated value, the book value of the bonds converted is generally made the basis of the credit to capital stock.

Assume, for example, that a company has outstanding an issue of debenture bonds in the par amount of $1,000,000, with applicable unaccumulated discount of $50,000, and that such bonds are convertible into the common stock of the company on any interest date at a price of $25 per share, or on the basis of 40 shares of stock for each bond in the maturity amount of $1,000. The shares of this class of stock outstanding have a stated-value of $10 each. At this point 10% of the bond issue is presented for conversion, and shares are issued in accordance with the exchange ratio. The summarized entries are:

Debenture bonds—Maturity amount	$100,000	
Discount on debenture bonds		$ 5,000
Capital stock—Stated value		40,000
Capital stock—Contributions in excess of stated value		55,000

In some cases the specified **conversion price** of the stock increases in terms of stated periods. The contract may also provide for termination of the conversion privilege at a specified date. A minor complication arises when the exchange ratio is such that conversion calls for issue of fractional shares. In this situation the converting bondholder may pay in sufficient cash to entitle him to a whole number of shares, the corporation may make an appropriate cash payment, or the corporation may actually issue the fractional shares.

The treatment of **unamortized bond issue cost** on conversion date is something of a problem. As a matter of convenience, such cost may be absorbed in the conversion entries in the same manner as bond discount. However, a better treatment would be to retain the balance of issue cost as in effect a cost of stock financing. A convertible bond is potential capital stock and may become actual stock at any time the bondholder elects. As long as the bonds are outstanding, the schedule of amortization of issue costs based on the total life of the bonds should be maintained, as conversion is not assured and is beyond the control of the issuer. Upon conversion, nevertheless, the contingency becomes controlling, and the balance of bond issue cost becomes a cost of issuing stock.

The assumption made in the foregoing discussion that the **net book value** of the bonds converted determines the issue price does not receive acceptance from all parties. The AAA (1957) emphatically disagrees:

> When a liability is discharged by conversion to a stock equity, the market value of the liability is ideally the measure of the new equity created. However, if a reliable market price for the liability is not available, the market value of the stock issued may be used.

In practice the net book value method has achieved the greatest acceptance. However, it should be noted that the **total capital** of the corporation will be unaffected by the choice of method. But since in most cases conversion is made when the market value of the stock is in excess of the book value of the bond, to the extent that an increased loss on conversion is recognized there will be a transfer between retained earnings and capital surplus.

18.45 INDUCED CONVERSION. SFAS No. 84, "Induced Conversions of Convertible Debt," which amends APB Opinion No. 26, "Early Extinguishment of Debt," specifies that when a convertible debt is converted to equity securities of the debtor pursuant to an inducement offer, the debtor should recognize an expense (not extraordinary) equal to the fair value of all securities and other consideration transferred in excess of the fair value of securities issuable pursuant to the original conversion terms.

Measurement of the fair value of the securities should be as of the date the inducement is accepted. Usually this is when conversion takes place or a binding agreement is signed.

Inducement includes changes made by the debtor to the conversion privileges for purposes of inducing conversion. The Statement applies only to conversions occurring pursuant to a change in conversion privileges that are exercisable for a limited period of time and include the issuance of all of the equity securities issuable pursuant to conversion privileges included in the terms of the debt at issuance for each debt instrument that is converted. Inducements include reducing the original conversion price, issuing warrants or other securities not included in the original terms, or payment of cash.

18.46 ACCRUED INTEREST UPON CONVERSION OF CONVERTIBLE DEBT. In Issue No. 85-17, the EITF concluded that when accrued but unpaid interest is forfeited at the date of conversion of convertible debt, either because the conversion date falls between interest payment dates or because there are no interest payment dates (a zero coupon convertible instrument), interest should be accrued or imputed to the date of conversion of the debt instrument. Accrued interest from the last interest payment date, if applicable, to the date of conversion, net of related income tax effects, if any, should be charged to expense and credited to capital as part of the cost of the securities issued. Thus accrued interest is accounted for in the same way as the principal amount of the debt and any unamortized issue or premium discount.

18.47 SUBSCRIPTION RIGHTS AND WARRANTS SOLD WITH BONDS. Bonds are sometimes sold with warrants or subscription rights attached. The rights or warrants permit their holder to purchase other securities, normally common shares, at some fixed or determinable price in a future period at a certain future date. The warrants are essentially calls or options on the common stock, at a fixed price. The theory, of course, is that the combination of the warrant and the bond enables the company to market the bond at a lower interest rate.

Such securities achieved considerable popularity in the period before the issuance of APB Opinion Nos. 14 and 15. Until then, companies were not required to (and did not) give recognition to the dilutive effect of the warrants on the per share earnings attributable to the outstanding common stock. Thus companies could issue a form of equity without diluting reported earnings, until the warrants were exercised.

APB Opinion Nos. 14 and 15 (1969) sharply changed this situation, with the result that bonds with warrants have become considerably less popular. APB Opinion No. 15 requires giving consideration to the dilutive effect of the warrants. See Chapter 5 of this *Handbook* for a complete discussion of the appropriate computations. APB Opinion No. 14 requires:

1. Separate accounting for the fair values of the bond and the warrants.
2. Attributing debt discount to the fair value of the warrants and amortizing that discount.

The result of item 2 above is a reduction in reported income, equal to the amount of the amortization of debt discount. Since convertible bonds can be designed to provide essentially the same mixture of debt and equity as a bond with warrants, and since the conversion feature does not give rise to debt discount, companies interested in such securities have tended to issue convertibles instead of debt with warrants.

As an illustration of the accounting for a bond with warrants, consider the following example. A company issues a bond at par with an $8^3/_4\%$ yield. Each bond has a warrant attached that permits the holder of the warrant to purchase a share of the company's stock for $20, within 5 years. The common shares are presently selling for $50. It is determined that the company's bond, without the warrant attached (a straight bond), could have been sold for 95, that is, $950 per bond.

The underwriter handling the issue estimates that the warrant will be worth about $75 when issued. Note that APB Opinion No. 14 calls for this valuation (and that of the comparable straight bond) to be made "at the time of issuance," which it defines as "the date when agreement as to terms has been reached and announced." This is not the actual date of issue of the securities, when relative market values for the two securities could be determined. The date given in APB Opinion No. 14 is earlier. Thus the fair value will be approximated or estimated by someone, probably the underwriter.

The allocation required under APB Opinion No. 14 is as follows:

$$\frac{\text{Value of bonds}}{\text{Value of bonds without warrants} + \text{value of warrants}} \times \text{Purchase price} = \text{Value assigned to bonds}$$

$$\frac{\$950}{\$950 + \$75} \times \$1,000 = \$927.00$$

$$\frac{\text{Value of warrants}}{\text{Value of bonds without warrants} + \text{value of warrants}} \times \text{Purchase price} = \text{Value assigned to warrants}$$

$$\frac{\$75}{\$950 + \$75} \times \$1,000 = \$73.00$$

The entries, for the issuance assuming one bond, would be:

Cash	$927	
Discount on bonds	73	
Bonds payable		$1,000
Cash	73	
Paid-in capital		73

This accounting applies to warrants that are "separable" from the bonds, which is the most common situation. If the warrants were required to trade with the bond, the issue would be almost identical to a convertible bond and should be accounted for as a convertible.

OTHER LONG-TERM LIABILITIES

18.48 MORTGAGES AND LONG-TERM NOTES.   A **mortgage is essentially a pledge of title to physical property as security for repayment of a loan.** A **promissory note** usually accompanies the granting of a mortgage. On the balance sheet the liability should appear as "Mortgage Notes Payable" or "Notes Payable—Secured" with brief reference to the property pledged.

If mortgages are payable on the **installment plan,** the liability account is charged each payment date with the amount of principal paid. When the periodic installments are fixed amounts covering both payment on principal and accrued interest, apportionment between principal and interest must be made (see "Purchase Contracts," below).

With respect to individual mortgages and accompanying notes, the borrower usually receives cash in the face amount of the note, in which case the face amount is the true liability and discount or premium is not involved. However, when the consideration for the note is in the form of property, as is the case when a mortgage is given on the property purchased or when "points" are given, the liability may be more or less than the face of the note. **Points** are the analogue, in mortgage financing, of original issue discount for bonds. They raise the effective interest rate above that specified in the note. A point is 1% of the face of the note. For example, if a 20-year mortgage note for $100,000 face were signed, but the banker demanded four points, the borrower would receive 4% less than $100,000 or $96,000. If the note carried an interest rate of $10^3/_4\%$, for example, the borrower would still be obligated to make the monthly payments on $100,000, that is, $1,015 per month. Since he received only $96,000, the borrower's effective interest rate is increased to about 12.3% on the money he received. Accounting for this transaction would follow the reasoning outlined in section 18.23.

18.49 PURCHASE CONTRACTS. Land or durable equipment is often purchased on a contract under which title rests with the vendor until the condition of the contract have been met. In the meantime the purchaser has use of the property. Proper accounting requires showing the asset at full cost and the balance of the contract payable as a liability.

Purchase contracts are commonly payable in equal **periodic installments.** The regular installment may include both interest on the contract balance and a payment on the principal, or it may apply entirely to principal, with interest paid separately.

To illustrate the first plan, assume a contract covering the purchase of equipment for $5,000, with interest at 12%, which provides for semiannual payments of $500 each until the entire obligation has been discharged. The division of these payments between interest and retirement of principal, at an interest rate of 12%, compounded semiannually, is shown in the accompanying table within section 18.49.

The entries in this case for the first semiannual payment (assuming no interim accrual of interest) are:

Purchase contract payable	$200	
Interest on purchase contract	300	
Cash		$500

Half-Year Period	Balance of Debt	Interest 6% per Period	Payment	Amortization of Debt
1	$5,000.00	$ 300.00	$ 500.00	$ 200.00
2	4,800.00	288.00	500.00	212.00
3	4,588.00	275.28	500.00	224.72
4	4,363.28	261.80	500.00	238.20
5	4,125.08	247.50	500.00	252.50
6	3,872.58	232.36	500.00	267.64
7	3,604.94	216.30	500.00	283.70
8	3,324.24	199.27	500.00	300.73
9	3,020.51	181.23	500.00	318.77
10	2,701.74	162.10	500.00	337.90
11	2,363.84	141.83	500.00	358.17
12	2,005.67	120.34	500.00	379.66
13	1,626.01	97.56	500.00	402.44
14	1,223.57	73.41	500.00	426.59
15	796.98	47.82	500.00	452.18
16	344.80	20.69	365.49	344.80
		$2,865.49	$7,865.49	$5,000.00

In this example, the fair value of the property is assumed to be the full contract price of $5,000, since interest is provided at a presumably adequate rate. If no interest were provided the provisions of APB Opinion No. 21 would apply.

18.50 LONG-TERM LEASES. Leasing, as a means of financing the acquisition of long-term assets, has seen a rapid expansion in the United States and other countries since World War II. It was not until the 1960s, however, that authoritative accounting pronouncements began to significantly affect lease accounting. There now exist several major pronouncements and many interpretations. The related accounting is extremely complex. Chapter 16 is entirely devoted to lease accounting, from both the lessee and lessor points of view.

18.51 DEFERRED REVENUE OBLIGATIONS. "Deferred revenue" is the term often applied to liabilities that arise from the receipt of payment in advance of furnishing the service for which the funds are received. Usually deferred revenues are current, in that the service will be rendered in the next accounting period and the obligation discharged. A more complete discussion of accounting for deferred revenue is given above in connection with current liabilities. In some cases, however, payments are received covering a period of years, and here it is necessary to reduce the obligation each period by an appropriate amount, with a concurrent credit to revenue. Such long-term collections in advance should be shown as long-term liabilities in the balance sheet, under an appropriate title. The amount to be discharged in the following accounting period should be classed as current, with only the balance shown as a long-term liability.

Casualty insurance premiums are frequently collected 3 to 5 years in advance, and the long-term portions of such premiums represent long-term liabilities on the books of the insurer.

18.52 LONG-TERM EXPENSE ACCRUALS. Although most accruals of expenses are properly classified as current liabilities, there are some commitments such as 3-to-5-year product and service warranties, self-insurance programs, and pension plans that deserve classification as long-term obligations. The amount of the obligation is estimated in the light of a company's past experience and is established by an expense charge. That the amount is estimated and the identity of the specific obligee may be unknown at the time the obligation is recognized do not affect the propriety of the entry. Subsequently, when payment or service is made, the long-term liability account is eliminated.

The extent to which **inflation** should be recognized in long-term expense accruals is not clear. If, for example, a company gives a 5-year repair warranty on a product, it is reasonable to assume that the labor cost of repair work performed in 5 years will be considerably higher than it is today. It is not clear whether the accrual of the liability for the warranty work should be made at current prices or at estimated future prices. As discussed in Chapter 26, the FASB rejected a provision for future inflation in the determination of the present value of future pension benefits, in SFAS No. 35. Nevertheless, it seems preferable to make other long-term accruals giving consideration to inflation.

In the past it was common to refer to such long-term expense accruals as **operating** or **liability reserves,** which, on occasion, were located ambiguously between the liability and equity sections of the balance sheets. These amounts are clearly liabilities and should be presented as such. The use of the term **reserve** in this context is not good practice.

18.53 PENSION PLANS AND DEFERRED COMPENSATION CONTRACTS. Plans for payment of employee pensions and other retirement allowances involve assumption of obligations that are deferred until employee retirement dates. Accounting for pension plans, both by the plan itself and by sponsors has undergone great change in recent years. Accounting for retirement plans is the subject of Chapter 26. Deferred compensation is covered in Chapter 27.

18.54 FUTURE FEDERAL INCOME TAXES. The AICPA (APB Opinion No. 11) holds that:

> Comprehensive interperiod tax allocation is an integral part of the determination of income tax expense. The tax effects of those transactions which enter into the determination of pre-tax accounting income either earlier or later than they become determinants of taxable income should be recognized in the period in which the differences between pre-tax accounting income and taxable income arise and in the periods in which the differences reverse.

In SFAS No. 96, "Accounting for Income Taxes," the FASB continues the concept of comprehensive interperiod tax allocation. However, SFAS No. 96 adopts an assets and liability view of deferred taxes:

> The objective in accounting for income taxes on an accrual basis is to recognize the amount of current and deferred taxes payable or refundable at the date of the financial statements (a) as a result of all events that have been recognized on the financial statements and (b) as measured by the provisions of enacted tax laws. Other events not yet recognized in the financial statements may affect the eventual tax consequences of some events that have been recognized in the financial statements. But that change in tax consequences would be a result of those other later events, and the Board decided that the tax consequences of an event should not be recognized until that event is recognized in the financial statements.

Comprehensive tax allocation recognizes the tax effects of temporary differences between the tax basis and accounting basis of assets and liabilities resulting from the use of different accounting methods for the two objectives.

The most common example of the tax differences occurs when a company utilizes an accelerated method of depreciation for tax purposes and the straight-line method for book purposes. The FASB's position in that the deferred tax constitutes a future tax payable and should be set up on the credit side of the balance sheet. A complete discussion of this subject is in Chapter 17 of this *Handbook*.

18.55 STATEMENT PRESENTATION OF LONG-TERM LIABILITIES.   There is general agreement about the nature of information that should be presented on the balance sheet concerning long-term liabilities.

In reporting long-term liabilities on the balance sheet, the nature of the liabilities, maturity dates, interest rates, methods of liquidation, conversion privileges, collateralized property, covenant restrictions and other significant matters should be indicated. Disclosure is also required for each of the 5 years following the balance sheet date of the combined aggregate of maturities and sinking fund requirements for all long-term borrowings, and other significant matters should be indicated.

Some writers insist that the description of a bond issue should include the nature of the underlying security. Grady (ARS No. 7) states:

> The balance sheet should clearly indicate the nature and amount of the securities supporting the liabilities. While this information is usually included in the liability section of the balance sheet in the description of the liability account, it is sometimes indicated in the asset section also, in order to identify the assets which are pledged and therefore not available for the payment of other liabilities.

Grady appears to take a somewhat stronger position on disclosing security than does the SEC in Regulation S-X (Rule 4-08(b)). Assets mortgaged, pledged, or otherwise subject to lien, and the approximate amounts thereof shall be designated and the obligations collateralized briefly identified.

General requirements of the SEC for disclosure of long-term debt are stated in Regulation S-X (5-02(22)):

> Bonds, mortgages and other long-term debt . . . (a) State separately in the balance sheet or in a note thereto, each issue or type of obligation and such information as will indicate (1) the general character of each type of debt including the rate of interest; (2) the date of maturity, or if maturing serially, a brief indication of the serial maturities . . . ; (3) if the payment or principal or interest is contingent, an appropriate indication of such contingency; (4) a brief indication of priority; (5) if convertible, the basis.

Other disclosures called for by the SEC in Regulation S-X include:

Rule 4.08(c). Defaults.

Rule 4.08(f). Significant changes in bonds, mortgages and similar debt.

Rule 5.02(23). Indebtedness to Related Parties.

Rule 12.05. Schedule of indebtedness of and to related parties not current.

Rule 12.29. Scheduled mortgage loans on real estate.

An example of a note that presents the required SEC information is given in Exhibit 18.2.

If contingencies are considered to be highly significant, they may be disclosed through the use of the caption "contingent liabilities" with no dollar figure provided but with a reference to the appropriate note to the financial statements. In other cases contingencies are disclosed by a note in the financial statements.

NOTE 7. LONG-TERM DEBT

Under the terms of the Company's first mortgage indenture and the indentures supplemental thereto, and relative to all series of first mortgage bonds, the Company on May 1 of each year is required to make annual sinking fund payments equal to one percent of the maximum amount outstanding during the preceding calendar year. The Company has satisfied such requirements through the year 1988 by allocating an amount of additional property and expects to continue such practice in succeeding years. Rockland Electric Company is required under the terms of its sixth supplemental indenture to make an annual sinking fund payment on June 14 of each year of $240,000 with respect to its Series "F" Bonds and, pursuant to its seventh supplemental indenture, is required to make sinking fund payments of $333,000 on January 31 of each year with respect to its Series "G" Bonds. During 1988, cash payments totaling $573,000 were made to satisfy such sinking fund requirements of Rockland Electric Company. Pike County Light & Power Company is required, pursuant to its first mortgage indenture, to make annual sinking fund payments in the amount of $9,500. The sinking fund requirements of Pike County Light & Power Company for 1988 were satisfied by the allocation of an amount of additional property.

Details of long-term debt at December 31, 1988 and 1987 are as follows:

	December 31	
	1988	**1987**
	(Thousands of Dollars)	
Orange and Rockland Utilities, Inc.:		
First Mortgage Bonds:		
Series F, 4¹/₂% due June 15, 1988	$ —	$ 10,000
Series G, 4⁷/₈% due April 15, 1991	12,000	12,000
Series H, 4⁷/₈% due August 15, 1995	17,000	17,000
Series I, 6¹/₂% due October 1, 1997	23,000	23,000
Series J, 9¹/₄% due February 1, 2000	20,000	20,000
Series K, 7¹/₂% due April 1, 2001	21,000	21,000
Series L, 8% due December 1, 2001	12,000	12,000
Series M, 8¹/₂% due May 15, 2003	25,000	25,000
Series N, 9¹/₈% due March 1, 2004	30,000	30,000
Promissory Notes (unsecured) 10.75%–13.45% due through December 15, 1993	80	65
Promissory Notes (unsecured) 10¹/₄% due October 1, 2014	55,000	55,000
Promissory Notes (unsecured) 9% due August 1, 2015	44,000	44,000
Rockland Electric Company:		
First Mortgage Bonds:		
Series B, 4⁵/₈% due August 15, 1988	—	2,000
Series C, 4⁵/₈% due August 15, 1995	2,000	2,000
		(*continued*)

Exhibit 18.2.   Sample presentation of long-term debt as required by the SEC. *Source:* **Orange and Rockland Utilities, Inc. 1988, Annual 10K Report.**

	December 31	
	1988	1987
Series D, 9¹/₈% due February 15, 2000	5,000	5,000
Series E, 7⁷/₈% due April 15, 2001	6,000	6,000
Series F, 8.95% due June 15, 2004	4,640	4,880
Series G, 10% due February 1, 1997	3,002	3,335
Pike County Light & Power Company:		
First Mortgage Bonds:		
Series A, 9% due July 15, 2001	884	884
Nonutility Operations	8,183	5,136
	288,789	298,300
Less: Amount due within one year	899	12,597
	287,890	285,703
Unamortized (discount) premium on long-term debt	(327)	(315)
Total Long-Term Debt	$287,563	$285,388

The aggregate amount of maturities and sinking fund requirements, a portion of which will be satisfied by the allocation of additional property under sinking fund requirements, for each of the five years following 1988, is as follows: 1989—$2,208,600; 1990—$2,206,700; 1991—$14,074,000; 1992—$2,071,000; 1993—$2,072,000.

Substantially all of the utility plant and other physical property is subject to the liens of the respective indentures securing the First Mortgage Bonds of the Company and its utility subsidiaries.

Investments in the wholly owned utility subsidiaries, costing $11,828,700, which have been eliminated from the consolidated balance sheet, are pledged under the Second Supplemental Indenture to the Company's First Mortgage Indenture.

Exhibit 18.2. *Continued.*

18.56 DISCLOSURE OF UNCONDITIONAL PURCHASE AND OTHER LONG-TERM OBLIGATIONS.

SFAS No. 47, "Disclosure of Long-Term Obligations," requires that an enterprise disclose its commitments under unconditional purchase obligations, such as take-or-pay contracts or through-put contracts, that are associated with suppliers' financing arrangements. Such arrangements result in obligations to transfer funds in the future for fixed or minimum amounts or quantities of goods or services at fixed or minimum prices.

If not recorded on the purchaser's balance sheet, disclosure is required of an unconditional purchase obligation that (par. 6):

a. Is noncancelable, or cancelable only

(1) Upon the occurrence of some remote contigency or

(2) With the permission of the other party or

(3) If a replacement agreement is required between the same parties or

(4) Upon payment of a penalty in an amount such that continuation of agreement appears reasonably assured

b. Was negotiated as part of arranging financing for the facilities that will provide the contracted goods or services or for costs related to those goods or services

c. Has a remaining term in excess of one year

For such unrecorded obligations, the required disclosures, which may be combined for similar or related obligations, include (par. 7):

a. The nature and the term of the obligation(s)

b. The amount of the fixed and determinable portion of the obligation(s) as of the date of the latest balance sheet presented in the aggregate and, if determinable, for each of the five succeeding fiscal years

   c. The nature of any variable components of the obligation(s)

   d. The amounts purchased under the obligation(s) for each period for which an income statement is presented.

The discount rate to determine the present value of the obligation(s) should be the interest rate of the borrowings that financed the facilities to provide the goods or services, if known by the purchaser. If not, the rate should be the purchasers' incremental borrowing rate at the date the obligation is entered into.

Disclosure under this Statement is not required for leases disclosed under SFAS No. 13.

If certain unconditional purchase obligations are presently recorded as liabilities, they should continue to be so recorded. Disclosure is not an appropriate substitute for accounting recognition if in substance a liability has been incurred.

When the obligation(s) has been recorded, the following disclosures should be made for each of the 5 years following the latest balance sheet date (par. 10):

   a. The aggregate amount of payments for unconditional purchase obligations that meet the criteria of paragraph 6 and that have been recognized on the purchaser's balance sheet

   b. The combined aggregate amount of maturities and sinking fund requirements for all long-term borrowings.

18.57 REDEEMABLE PREFERRED STOCK. SFAS No. 47 also requires similar disclosure for capital stock with mandatory redemption requirements. Specifically, paragraph 10(c) requires disclosure of:

The amount of redemption requirements for all issues of capital stock that are redeemable at fixed or determinable dates, separately by issue or combined.

FINANCIAL INSTRUMENTS

18.58 INTRODUCTION. The FASB is currently considering the accounting issues pertaining to financial instruments. Such a project became necessary because of the explosion of new instruments created in response to the volatile financial markets, tax law changes, deregulation, the desire to take advantage of current accounting measurement rules, and other stimuli. Some areas of the newer financial instruments reflect either an absence of accounting rules or conflicting guidance.

In excess of 50% of the issues addressed by the EITF have dealt with financial instruments, financial institutions, and off-balance-sheet financing. A major source of concern is the inconsistent practices and standards for handling the complex transactions and financial instruments that have evolved over recent years. The FASB divided the project into the following three phases:

- Disclosure.
- Recognition and measurement.
- Distinguishing between liability and equity instruments.

The first phase of the project resulted in SFAS No. 105, "Disclosure of Information about Financial Instruments with Off-Balance-Sheet Risk and Financial Instruments with Concentrations of Risk." An initial exposure draft on disclosures about financial instruments was issued in November 1987, which would have required extensive disclosures about financial instruments including (1) credit risks, probable and reasonably possible credit losses, and individual, industry, or geographic concentrations; (2) contractual future cash receipts and payments; (3) interest rates; and (4) current market values. Following the FASB's deliberations, including the evaluation of constituent responses to the initial exposure draft, a revised exposure draft more limited in scope was issued March 1988. The revised draft dealt only with financial instruments having off-balance sheet risk. SFAS No. 105, which conforms to the revised draft establishes disclosure requirements for those instruments with off-balance-sheet risk. The remaining disclosures that were addressed in the first exposure draft will be reexamined as a part of a separate component of the project's disclosure phase.

The recognition and measurement phase of the project will focus on:

- Whether financial instruments are considered sold if there is recourse.
- Accounting for financial instruments that attempt to transfer market and credit risk.
- How to measure financial instruments—that is, market value, lower of cost or market.

The liability–equity phase of the project addresses accounting for financial instruments that have liability and equity characteristics such as accounting for convertible debt instruments and mandatorily redeemable preferred stock. These last two phases of the project will be initiated by the issuance of discussion memorandums.

18.59 SFAS NO. 105—DISCLOSURE OF INFORMATION ABOUT FINANCIAL INSTRUMENTS WITH OFF-BALANCE-SHEET RISK AND FINANCIAL INSTRUMENTS WITH CONCENTRATIONS OF CREDIT RISK

(a) Scope.   The focus of SFAS No. 105 is on disclosure of information about financial instruments having the risk of accounting losses in excess of amounts recognized in the balance sheet. Such risk is referred to as **off-balance-sheet risk.** The pronouncement also addresses disclosures for financial instruments with concentrations of risk.

(b) Excluded from Scope of SFAS No. 105.   The statement does not apply to the following financial instruments:

Insurance contracts, other than financial guarantees and investment contracts.

Lease contracts (disclosures about concentration of risk still required).

Unconditional purchase obligations.

Employers' obligations for pension benefits, postretirement health care and life insurance benefits, employee stock option and stock purchase plans, and other forms of deferred compensation arrangements.

Substantially extinguished debt.

Payables and other financial instruments denominated in a foreign currency except those with other risks in addition to foreign exchange risk and obligations under foreign exchange contracts (disclosures about concentration of risk still required).

Financial instruments of a pension plan including plan assets accounted for under SFAS No. 87.

(c) Financial Instruments Defined.   Financial instruments are defined in SFAS No. 105 as:

Cash, evidence of ownership in an entity, or a contract that is both:

A (recognized or unrecognized) contractual right of one entity to receive cash or another financial instrument from another entity or to exchange other financial instruments on potentially favorable terms with another entity.

A (recognized or unrecognized) contractual obligation of another entity to deliver cash or another financial instrument to another entity or to exchange financial instruments on potentially unfavorable terms with another entity.

(d) Components of Accounting Risk.   In determining the extent of off-balance-sheet risk, it is first necessary to define components of accounting risk. A financial instrument is then defined

	Off-Balance-Sheet (OBS) Risk of Accounting Loss					
	Holder[a]			Issuer[b]		
		Type of OBS Risk[c]			Type of OBS Risk[c]	
Financial Instrument	OBS Risk[d]	CR	MR	OBS Risk[d]	CR	MR
Traditional items:						
Cash	No					
Foreign currency	No					
Time deposits (non-interest bearing, fixed rate, or variable rate)	No			No		
Bonds carried at amortized cost (fixed or variable rate bonds, with or without a cap)	No			No		
Bonds carried at market (in trading accounts, fixed or variable rate bonds, with or without a cap)	No			No		
Convertible bonds (convertible into stock of the issuer at a specified price at option of the holder; callable at a premium to face at option of the issuer)	No			No		
Accounts and notes receivable/payable (non-interest bearing, fixed rate, or variable rate)	No			No		
Loans (fixed or variable rate, with or without a cap)	No			No		
Refundable (margin) deposits	No			No		

Accrued expenses receivable/payable (wages, etc.)	No		No
Common stock (equity investments—cost method or equity method)[e]	No		No
Preferred stock (convertible or participating)	No		No
Preferred stock (nonconvertible or nonparticipating)	No		No
Cash dividends declared	No		No
Obligations arising from financial instruments sold short	No	X	Yes

Note: Credit risk and market risk are present for many of the instruments included in this illustration. However, only those instruments with off-balance-sheet credit or market are denoted with an "X" (refer to footnote c).

[a] Holder includes buyer and investor.

[b] Issuer includes seller, borrower, and writer.

[c] An "X" in any of the columns (CR or MR) denotes the presence of the respective *off-balance-sheet* risk of accounting loss. The types of risk included are:
1. *Credit risk* (CR)—the possibility that a loss may occur from the failure of another party to perform according to the terms of a contract
2. *Market risk* (MR)—the possibility that future changes in market prices may make a financial instrument less valuable or more onerous

[d] A "Yes" in this column denotes the presence of off-balance-sheet risk of accounting loss; a "No" denotes no off-balance-sheet risk of accounting loss.

[e] Many joint ventures or other equity method investments are accompanied by guarantees of the debt of the investee. Debt guarantees of this nature present off-balance-sheet risk of accounting loss due to credit risk and should be evaluated with other financial guarantees.

(continued)

Exhibit 18.3. Illustration applying the definition of a financial instrument with off-balance-sheet risk. *Source:* **Financial Accounting Standards Board, SFAS No. 105, "Disclosure of Information about Financial Instruments with Off-Balance-Sheet Risk and Financial Instruments with Concentrations of Credit Risk." The illustration presents some financial instruments that have and that do not have off-balance-sheet risk of accounting loss; it does not illustrate *all* financial instruments that are included in the scope of this Statement. Off-balance-sheet risk of accounting loss for similar financial instruments may differ among entities using different methods of accounting.**

Financial Instrument	Off-Balance-Sheet (OBS) Risk of Accounting Loss					
	Holder			Issuer		
		Type of OBS Risk			Type of OBS Risk	
	OBS Risk	CR	MR	OBS Risk	CR	MR
Innovative items:						
Increasing rate debt	No			No		
Variable coupon redeemable notes	No			No		
Collateralized mortgage obligations (CMOs):						
CMO accounted for as a borrowing by issuer	No			No		
CMO accounted for as a sale by issuer	No			No[f]		
Transfer of receivables:						
Investor has recourse to the issuer at or below the receivable carrying amount—accounted for as a borrowing by issuer	No			No		
Investor has recourse to the issuer—accounted for as a sale by issuer	No			Yes	X	
Investor has recourse to the issuer and the agreement includes a floating interest rate provision—accounted for as a sale by issuer	No			Yes	X	X
Investor has no recourse to the issuer—accounted for as a sale by issuer	No			No		
Securitized receivables	Same as transfer of receivables					
(Reverse) Repurchase agreements:						
Accounted for as a borrowing by issuer	No			No		
Accounted for as a sale by issuer	No			Yes	X	X

	No	Yes		
Put option on stock (premium paid up front):				
Covered option	No	Yes		X
Naked option	No	Yes		X
Put option on interest rate contracts[g] (premium paid up front):				
Covered option	No	Yes	X	X
Naked option	No	Yes	X	X
Call option on stock, foreign currency, or interest rate contracts (premium paid up front):				
Covered option	No	Yes		X
Naked option	No	Yes		X
Loan commitments:				
Fixed rate	No	Yes	X	X
Variable rate	No	Yes	X	
Interest rate caps	No	Yes		X
Interest rate floors	No	Yes		X
Financial guarantees	No	Yes	X	
Note issuance facilities at floating rates	No	Yes	X	
Letters of credit (also standby letters of credit) at floating rates	No	Yes	X	

[f]Issuer refers to both the trust and the sponsor.
[g]Put options on interest rate contracts have credit risk if the underlying instrument that might be put (a particular bond, for example) is subject to credit risk.

(continued)

Exhibit 18.3. *Continued.*

Off-Balance-Sheet Risk of Accounting Loss

Financial Instrument	OBS Risk	Both Counterparties[h] Type of OBS Risk	
		CR	MR
Interest rate swaps—accrual basis:			
In a gain position	Yes	X	X
In a loss position	Yes	X	X
Gain or loss position netted: right of setoff exists[i]	Yes	X	X
Interest rate swaps—marked to market:			
In a gain position	Yes	X	X
In a loss position	Yes	X	X
Gain or loss position netted: right of setoff exist[j]	Yes	X	X
Currency swaps	Same as interest rate swaps		
Financial futures contracts—hedges (marked to market and gain or loss deferred—			
Statement 52 or 80 accounting):			
In a gain position	Yes		X
In a loss position	Yes		X
Multiple contracts settled net	Yes		X

Financial futures contracts—nonhedges (marked to market—Statement 52 or 80 accounting):		
In a gain position	Yes	X
In a loss position	Yes	X
Multiple contracts settled net	Yes	,
Forward contracts—hedges (marked to market and gain or loss deferred):		
In a gain position	Yes	X
In a loss position	Yes	X
Gain or loss position netted: right of setoff exists[i]	Yes	X
Forward contracts—nonhedges (marked to market and gain or loss recognized):		
In a gain position	Yes	X
In a loss position	Yes	X
Gain or loss position netted: right of setoff exists[i]	Yes	X
Forward contracts—not marked to market	Yes	X

[h]Swaps, forwards, and futures are two-sided transactions; therefore, the holder and issuer categories are not applicable. Risks are assessed in terms of the position held by the entity.

[i]Netting of receivable and payable amounts when right of setoff does not exist is in contravention of APB Opinion No. 10, *Omnibus Opinion—1966*, paragraph 7, and FASB Technical Bulletin No. 88-2, *Definition of a Right of Setoff*.

Exhibit 18.3. *Continued.*

to have off-balance-sheet risk if the risk of accounting loss to the entity exceeds the amount recognized, if any, in the balance sheet. The risk of accounting losses on a financial instrument includes:

1. *Credit Risk.* The possibility of loss, even if remote, from the failure of another party to perform according to the terms of a contract.
2. *Market Risk.* The possibility that future changes in market price may make a financial instrument less valuable or less desirable.
3. *Risk of Theft or Physical Loss.*

Only the first two risks are dealt with in the new Statement.

(e) Survey of Extent of Off-Balance-Sheet Risk.   SFAS No. 105 provides the following analysis of the extent to which financial instruments have off-balance-sheet risk (see Exhibit 18.3). Risk is broken into its components, and a determination is made whether there is off-balance-sheet risk to the holder/issuer or both counterparties. Off-balance-sheet risk exists only if the risk of accounting loss exceeds the amount recorded on the books. Many traditional instruments do not have such risk, since the maximum loss is already reflected on the books. Financial instruments such as swaps, forward contracts, and futures contracts create risk to both parties. Financial instruments such as loan commitments, letters of commitment, and options present off-balance-sheet risk only to the issuer.

(f) Required Disclosures about Off-Balance-Sheet Risk.   Within the body of financial statements or accompanying footnotes for entities with off-balance-sheet credit risk, the following disclosures are required:

- Information about the extent, nature, and terms of financial instruments with off-balance-sheet risk including face, contract, or notional principal amount (if without face or contract amount), cash requirements of those instruments, and a discussion of related credit and market risks and the relevant accounting policies under APB No. 22, "Disclosure of Accounting Policies."
- Amount of accounting loss that would be incurred due to counterparty failure to perform according to terms of contract.
- Entity's policy for recognizing collateral or other security for financial instruments with credit risk.

(g) Required Disclosures about Financial Instruments with Concentration of Credit Risk.   In the body of the financial statements or accompanying footnotes for entities with concentrations of credit risk, the following is to be disclosed:

- Where there are concentrations of credit risk resulting from exposures with individual counterparties and/or groups of counterparties, information should be provided for each significant concentration about shared activity, region, or identifying economic characteristics.
- For each area of significant concentration, credit risk information should be identical to that for provided for financial instruments with off-balance-sheet risk.

(h) Sample Disclosures.   Exhibits 18.4 and 18.5 illustrate the required disclosures for off-balance-sheet risk and concentrations of credit risk.

NOTE Y: FINANCIAL INSTRUMENTS WITH OFF-BALANCE-SHEET RISK*

The Corporation is a party to financial instruments with off-balance-sheet risk in the normal course of business to meet the financing needs of its customers and to reduce its own exposure to fluctuations in interest rates. These financial instruments include commitments to extend credit, options written, standby letters of credit and financial guarantees, interest rate caps and floors written, interest rate swaps, and forward and futures contracts. Those instruments involve, to varying degrees, elements of credit and interest rate risk in excess of the amount recognized in the statement of financial position. The contract or notional amounts of those instruments reflect the extent of involvement the Corporation has in particular classes of financial instruments.

The Corporation's exposure to credit loss in the event of nonperformance by the other party to the financial instrument for commitments to extend credit and standby letters of credit and financial guarantees written is represented by the contractual notional amount of those instruments. The Corporation uses the same credit policies in making commitments and conditional obligations as it does for on-balance-sheet instruments. For interest rate caps, floors, and swap transactions, forward and futures contracts, and options written, the contract or notional amounts do not represent exposure to credit loss. The Corporation controls the credit risk of its interest rate swap agreements and forward and futures contracts through credit approvals, limits, and monitoring procedures.

Unless noted otherwise, the Corporation does not require collateral or other security to support financial instruments with credit risk.

	Contract or Notional Amount (in millions)
Financial instruments whose contract amounts represent credit risk:	
Commitments to extend credit	$ 2,780
Standby letters of credit and financial guarantees written	862
Financial instruments whose notional or contract amounts exceed the amount of credit risk:	
Forward and futures contracts	815
Interest rate swap agreements	10,520
Options written and interest rate caps and floors written	950

Commitments to extend credit are agreements to lend to a customer as long as there is no violation of any condition established in the contract. Commitments generally have fixed expiration dates or other termination clauses and may require payment of a fee. Since many of the commitments are expected to expire without being drawn upon, the total commitment amounts do not necessarily represent future cash requirements. The Corporation evaluates each customer's creditworthiness on a case-by-case basis. The amount of collateral obtained if deemed necessary by the Corporation upon extension of credit is based on management's credit evaluation of the counter-party. Collateral held varies but may include accounts receivable, inventory, property, plant, and equipment, and income-producing commercial properties.

Standby letters of credit and financial guarantees written are conditional commitments issued by the Corporation to guarantee the performance of a customer to a third party. Those guarantees are primarily issued to support public and private borrowing arrangements, including commercial paper, bond financing,

(continued)

---

*Placement within financial statements of the information that describes the extent of involvement an entity has in financial instruments with off-balance-sheet risk and the related nature, terms, and credit risk of those instruments is at the discretion of management. The example illustrates information that would be provided in a note "Financial Instruments with Off-Balance-Sheet Risk." An entity may decide, however, to disclose this information in several separate notes.

Exhibit 18.4.   Illustration of required disclosures about financial instruments with off-balance-sheet risk.
Source: Financial Accounting Standards Board, SFAS No. 105, "Disclosure of Information about Financial Instruments with Off-Balance-Sheet Risk and Financial Instruments with Concentrations of Credit Risk."

and similar transactions. Except for short-term guarantees of $158 million, most guarantees extend for more than 5 years and expire in decreasing amounts through 20XX. The credit risk involved in issuing letters of credit is essentially the same as that involved in extending loan facilities to customers. The Corporation holds marketable securities as collateral supporting those commitments for which collateral is deemed necessary. The extent of collateral held for those commitments at December 31, 19XX varies from 2 percent to 45 percent; the average amount collateralized is 24 percent.

Forward and futures contracts are contracts for delayed delivery of securities or money market instruments in which the seller agrees to make delivery at a specified future date of a specified instrument, at a specified price or yield. Risks arise from the possible inability of counterparties to meet the terms of their contracts and from movements in securities values and interest rates.

The Corporation enters into a variety of interest rate contracts—including interest rate caps and floors written, interest rate options written, and interest rate swap agreements—in its trading activities and in managing its interest rate exposure. Interest rate caps and floors written by the Corporation enable customers to transfer, modify, or reduce their interest rate risk. Interest rate options are contracts that allow the holder of the option to purchase or sell a financial instrument at a specified price and within a specified period of time from the seller or "writer" of the option. As a writer of options, the Corporation receives a premium at the outset and then bears the risk of an unfavorable change in the price of the financial instrument underlying the option.

Interest rate swap transactions generally involve the exchange of fixed and floating rate interest payment obligations without the exchange of the underlying principal amounts. Though swaps are also used as part of asset and liability management, most of the interest rate swap activity arises when the Corporation acts as an intermediary in arranging interest rate swap transactions for customers. The Corporation typically becomes a principal in the exchange of interest payments between the parties and, therefore, is exposed to loss should one of the parties default. The Corporation minimizes this risk by performing normal credit reviews on its swap customers and minimizes its exposure to the interest rate risk inherent in intermediated swaps by entering into offsetting swap positions that essentially counterbalance each other.

Entering into interest rate swap agreements involves not only the risk of dealing with counterparties and their ability to meet the terms of the contracts but also the interest rate risk associated with unmatched positions. Notional principal amounts often are used to express the volume of these transactions, but the amounts potentially subject to credit risk are much smaller.

Exhibit 18.4. *Continued.*

NOTE Z: SIGNIFICANT GROUP CONCENTRATIONS OF CREDIT RISK

Most of the Corporation's business activity is with customers located within the state. As of December 31, 19XX, the Corporation's receivables from and guarantees of obligations of companies in the semiconductor industry were $XX million.

As of December 31, 19XX, the Corporation was also creditor for $XX of domestic loans and other receivables from companies with high debt to equity ratios as a result of buyout transactions. The portfolio is well diversified, consisting of XX industries. Generally, the loans are secured by assets or stock. The loans are expected to be repaid from cash flow or proceeds from the sale of selected assets of the borrowers. Credit losses arising from lending transactions with highly leveraged entities compare favorably with the Corporation's credit loss experience on its loan portfolio as a whole. The Corporation's policy for requiring collateral is **[state policy, along with information about the entity's access to that collateral or other security and a description of collateral]**.

Exhibit 18.5. Illustration of required disclosure of concentrations of credit risk. *Source:* **Financial Accounting Standards Board, SFAS No. 105, "Disclosure of Information about Financial Instruments with Off-Balance-Sheet Risk and Financial Instruments with Concentrations of Credit Risk."**

18.60 ACCOUNTING FOR SELECTED FINANCING INSTRUMENTS.   In recent years numerous modifications to traditional debt instruments have required the EITF to address the accompanying accounting issues. In one instance, a traditional convertible debt instrument was modified by giving the buyer the option to put (sell) the issue back to the issuer at a premium. Other modifications to traditional debt have included debt issuances that have altered the traditional way in which interest rates are set. There have been issuances of debt with increasing interest rates and deferral of the setting of interest rates as well as issuances of debt instruments that provide not only for principal repayment, but also contingent payments. Companies have also sold their marketable securities granting the buyer the right to sell those assets back to the issuer. These modifications have led to such fundamental questions as whether the transaction is a sale or a borrowing, the amount of liability to be accrued, the amount of interest expense and pattern of interest recognition, and the method of accounting for possible impairments. The following section summarizes both the accounting issues that have arisen from these financial instrument modifications and the EITF consensus agreements on acceptable accounting.

(a) EITF Issue No. 85-29—Convertible Bonds with a Premium Put.   The EITF considered convertible bonds issued at par value with a put allowing the bondholder to require that the corporation redeem the bonds at a future date for cash at a premium to the bond's par value. At the date of issue, the par value of the bonds exceeds the market value of the common stock into which they are convertible.

The questions addressed in Issue No. 85-29 are as follows:

- Should a liability be accrued for the put premium and, if so, over what period?
- Should the liability continue to be booked if the value of debt or equity changes, making exercise of the put unlikely?
- If the put expires unexercised, should the put be recognized as income or paid-in capital, amortized as a yield adjustment, or continue to be carried as part of debt?

The EITF reached the following consensus:

- The issuer should accrue the put premium over the period from the date of issuance to the first put date. The accrual should continue even though changes in market value of the bond or underlying common stock indicate put will not be exercised.
- If the put expires unexercised, the amount accrued should be credited to additional paid-in capital if the market value of the common stock exceeds the put price. Otherwise, if the put price exceeds the market value of the common stock, the put premium should be amortized as a yield adjustment over the remaining life of the bonds.

(b) EITF Issue No. 86-15—Increasing-Rate Debt.   The EITF dealt with debt that matures three months from date of issuance but may be extended at the discretion of the issuer for an additional period at each maturity date until final maturity. The rate of interest increases each time the note's maturity is extended.

Issue No. 86-15 addressed the following:

- How should the borrower's interest expense be determined and what maturity date should be used in establishing that rate?
- How should the debt be classified?
- What period is to be used for amortization?
- If debt is paid at an earlier date than that assumed in arriving at the interest rate, how should the excess accrual be accounted for?

The EITF reached the following consensus:

- The lender's periodic interest rate should be based on an average interest rate using the estimated term of the borrowing. Plans, intent, and ability to service debt should be considered in estimating the term of the debt.
- Classification of debt as current or noncurrent should reflect the borrower's anticipated source of repayment and is not necessarily identical to the time period used to establish periodic interest rate. That is, if short-term debt is expected to be used to refinance the debt, then the original debt is current. If SFAS No. 6 requirements are met, the debt is noncurrent.
- Debt issuance costs should be amortized over the same period used in interest cost determination.
- If debt is redeemed at par value before estimated maturity, the excess interest expense accrual is an adjustment to interest and is not an extraordinary item.

(c) EITF Issue No. 84-14—Deferred Interest Rate Setting.   The EITF considered an arrangement where the borrower, at the same time as issuing debt at a fixed rate, enters into a deferred interest-rate-setting arrangement with an investment banker. An agreement is made to base the interest rate for the debt on conditions prevailing at some later period in time. When the rate is set, if the rates have been declining, the investment banker pays the issuer a one-time amount representing the present value of the interest differential. If the rates have increased, the borrower pays the investment banker the present value of the spread.

The issue here is:

- How to account for the one-time amount received or paid when the rate is determined?

The EITF's consensus was:

If the deferred rate-setting agreement is an integral part of the original issuance of the debt, the amounts received or paid are recognized over the term of the debt as an adjustment to interest yield over the term of the debt.

(d) EITF Issue No. 86-26—Using Forward Commitments as a Surrogate for Deferred Rate Setting.   A company issues fixed-rate debt and simultaneously enters into a short-term forward commitment to purchase treasury bonds having a maturity and interest rate equal to the debt.

The issues here are:

- How to account for the change in value of the forward commitment entered into at the same time as the issuance of fixed-rate debt?
- Are changes in value of forward commitments accounted for as modification to interest expense over the life of the debt?

No consensus was reached on these issues. Many Task Force members felt that the forward commitment was a separate transaction and should be accounted for separately. The SEC Observer said registrants could not treat the forward commitment as an adjustment of interest expense on the debt.

(e) EITF Issue No. 86-28—Accounting Implications of Indexed Debt Instruments.   The Task Force considered debt instruments with contingent and guaranteed payments. The contingent payments were linked to the price of specific commodities or to the S&P 500. In some instances, the right to the contingent payment is separable from the debt instrument.

The issues are:

- Should the proceeds be allocated between the debt liability and the right to receive the contingent payment?
- How should the issuer account for changes in the underlying commodity or index values?

The EITF reached the following consensus:

If the investor's right to a contingent payment is separable, the issuer should allocate the proceeds between the debt instrument and the right. The discount on the debt instrument should be accounted for in accordance with ABP No. 21. No consensus was reached on situations where the contingent payments are not separable.

Whether or not there is any initial allocation of proceeds to the contingent payment, if the index changes so that the issuer would have to pay the investor a contingent payment at maturity, the issuer must recognize a liability. The amount recognized is measured by the extent to which the contingent payment exceeds the amount, if any, originally allocated to that feature. When no proceeds are allocated to the contingent payment, the additional liability is an adjustment to the carrying amount of the debt. No consensus was reached on the applicability of hedge accounting to this area.

Some Task Force members would require expense recognition when the index increases to a level requiring liability accrual. Other members would not require such accrual when contingent payments are settled using physical commodities.

(f) EITF Issue No. 84-5—Sale of Marketable Securities with a Put Option.   The EITF reviewed the sale of a marketable security with an option to put the security back to the seller at a future date. The seller receives a premium for the security to induce the transaction.

The issues are:

- Should the seller account for the transaction as a sale or a borrowing?
- How should impairments be recognized?

The EITF's consensus is as follows:

The transaction should be based on a probability assessment of whether the put option will be exercised. If it is probable that the put will be exercised, the transaction should be accounted for as a borrowing; otherwise it is to be treated as a sale. If the transaction is treated as a borrowing, the difference between the put price and the sales proceeds should be accrued as interest expense. Also, continual reassessments of the probability that the put will be exercised should be accounted for as a change in accounting resulting from a change in circumstances. Where it is not probable that the put will be exercised, the transaction should be accounted for as a sale, and the marketable security should be removed from the books of the seller.

If the transaction is originally accounted for as a sale and it becomes probable that the put will be exercised, the expected losses that would result from exercise of the put should be immediately accrued. The estimated loss accrual should then be periodically adjusted.

In assessing the probability that the put will be exercised or the possibility of recording the transaction as a sale, one must consider the put price and sales price and the term of the put relative to the life of the marketable security. If the put period extends beyond one-half of the marketable security's remaining life, the transaction must be recorded as a sale.

(g) EITF Issue No. 85-30—Sale of Marketable Securities at a Gain with a Put Option.   The Task Force considered sale of a marketable security to a third-party buyer having a put option. The carrying amount of the marketable securities is below the current market price.

The issue here is:

- Do the criteria for recording gains on marketable securities with put options differ from the criteria for recording losses?

The task force did not reach consensus. Some maintained no gain on sale can be recognized.

(h) EITF Issue No. 85-40—Comprehensive Review of Sales of Marketable Securities with Put Arrangements.   The Task Force reviewed the same issues that were considered in Issue Nos. 84-5 and 85-30.

A consensus was reached that if the transaction results in a gain and is reported as a sale, the asset should be removed from the balance sheet, but the gain should be deferred because it is a gain contingency that will only be resolved by the expiration of the put without exercise.

(i) EITF Issue No. 86-35—Debentures with Detachable Stock Purchase Warrants.   The EITF considered a situation in which notes are issued with detachable warrants that include a put. The notes mature in about 7 years. The detachable warrants give the holder the right to purchase 6,250 shares of stock for $75 per share and also the right to sell back (put) these warrants to the firm for $2,010 per warrant at a date several months after the notes mature.

The issues are:

- Should the proceeds received at date of issuance be allocated between the debt and warrant?
- Should the carrying amount of the warrants be accrued to the put price?
- If there is an accrual, should the charge be to interest expense or immediately to retained earnings associated with the equity instrument?

The EITF's consensus is:

The proceeds should be allocated between warrants and debt, and the discount should be amortized using the effective interest rate approach under APB No. 21.

An accrual should be made that is sufficient to bring the carrying amount of the warrant to the put price.

Because the put price is so high relative to the value of the warrant without such a feature, any accrual is to be treated as interest expense and the warrant is to be treated as a debt instrument.

18.61 ASSET-SECURITIZATION TRANSACTIONS.   Typically, asset securitization transactions involve isolating assets and then issuing debt securities that designate the isolated assets as the payment of the required principal and sole source of interest. Typically, such transactions are initiated to reduce financing costs. Additionally, when such asset securitizations are properly structured, they provide off-balance-sheet financing.

A variety of techniques accomplish asset securitization transactions. For instance, a company issues bonds secured by mortgage-backed securities or mortgage loans in a transaction structured so that all collections of principal and interest from the underlying collateral are paid to the holders of the bonds. To accomplish this transaction, the sponsoring parent corporation sets up a special entity (the issuer), and this entity acquires from the parent the mortaged-backed securities or mortage loans that secure the obligation. The special entity then issues the bonds to investors and turns over the acquired instruments to an independent trustee for the benefit of the bondholders until obligations under the bond covenants are satisfied. The bondholders' only recourse for payment is to the trusteed assets. This type of instrument is referred to as a **collaterized mortgage obligation** (CMO).

The two applicable standards of the FASB associated with securitization transactions are FTB No. 85-2, "Accounting for Collateralized Mortgage Obligations," and SFAS No. 77, "Reporting by Transferors for Transfers of Receivables with Recourse."

18.62 FTB NO. 85-2—COLLATERIZED MORTGAGE OBLIGATIONS.   In a CMO transaction, the collaterized assets and the associated borrowings are removed from the balance sheet and gains and losses are recognized if:

(1) The future economic benefits from the collaterized assets are surrendered by the issuer of the obligation and its affiliates.

(2) The investor can look only to the collaterized assets or third-party guarantees for repayment of interest and principal on the instruments.

(3) The issuer and affiliated entities are not secondarily liable.

(a) Substitution of Collateral or the Obtaining of Collateral by Calling Obligation.   Ordinarily, the issuer and related affiliates cannot substitute collateral or reacquire collateral by calling the outstanding bonds. However, to keep the cost of servicing underlying mortgage loans reasonable, a call provision can be included in the CMOs allowing the issuer to redeem any outstanding CMOs when the remaining amount of such obligations is minor. In such circumstances the call provision does not preclude removal of the collateral from the books.

(b) Partial Interest in Collateral Retained by Issuer or Its Affiliates.   Excess residual interest in collateral as measured by present value of amounts reverting to issuer or its affiliates must be nominal, before collateral can be removed from books. Fees in excess of normal amounts for servicing the underlying mortgage-backed securities or underlying mortgage loans are included as part of the expected residual interest computation. Retention by an affiliate of the issuer of a partial ownership interest in mortgage-backed securities or mortage loans precludes removing collateral from the books.

(c) Collateral Removed from Books Because Conditions Are Met.   Where the collateral is removed from the books, any expected residual interest is not recognized as an asset; rather, these interests are accrued as they benefit the issuer or its affiliates.

(d) Obligatory Redemption of CMO by Issuer or Its Affiliates.   Required redemptions of CMOs prior to maturity other than through normal payment through collections from underlying collateral precludes removal of debt from books.

(e) Financial Statements of Majority-Owned Special Entities Issuing CMOs.   The financial statements of special entities should be consolidated with that of the sponsor.

(f) CMOs Recorded as Liabilities.   Where conditions for removal of the debt are not met, the liability on the books of the issuer is not offset against the assets used as collateral when presenting the balance sheet.

18.63 SFAS NO. 77—RECEIVABLES SOLD WITH RECOURSE.   An alternative to a borrowing using receivables as collateral is the sale of receivables with recourse. Sales of receivables with recourse share characteristics similar to those of loans collateralized by receivables. Distinctions between the two are not clear, and some maintain that in bankruptcy, sales with recourse could be treated as a secured borrowing.

Transfers of receivables with recourse are treated as sales when:

(1) The seller surrenders control of the future economic benefits from the receivables.

(2) The seller's obligations under recourse provisions are capable of being reasonably estimated.

(3) The buyer cannot require seller to reacquire receivables except under normal recourse provisions.

Where the seller possesses the option to reacquire the receivables at fair value, control that precludes sales accounting has not been surrendered.

(a) Accounting for Transfers of Receivables.   In transfers accounted as sales, the difference between the sales prices and carrying amount of net receivables is a gain or loss. The sales price is adjusted for accruals of recourse-related obligations. If the seller continues to service the receivables, the sales price is adjusted to reflect situations where the stated servicing rate differs from those currently being charged for such service. The current servicing rate should not be less than estimated costs to service the receivables. The sales price should also reflect the market interest rate at the transfer date when receivables are sold subject to floating rates. Subsequent changes in interest rates are changes in an estimated sales price accounted for under APB Opinion No. 20.

(b) Allocation of Recorded Investment When a Loan or Part of a Loan Is Sold—EITF Issue No. 88-11.   Upon the sale of an interest in a securitized loan, the seller should allocate the investment in recorded receivables between that which is retained and that which is sold. The allocation is based on relative fair market values of those portions on the date that the loan was acquired, adjusted for payments and other activities subsequent to date of acquisition. In performing the allocation, amounts included in allowance for loan losses should be disregarded. Where it is impractical to ascertain fair values as of the date of acquisition, the allocation should be based on relative fair values of the portion retained and the portion sold on the date of sale. The amount of gain recognized should not exceed the gain that would be recognized if the entire receivable were sold.

After a partial sale, the seller should evaluate the allowance for losses considering the collectibility of the remaining receivable balance and recourse obligations related to that balance.

SOURCES AND SUGGESTED REFERENCES

Accounting Principles Board, "Omnibus Opinion–1966," APB Opinion No. 10, AICPA, New York, 1966.

———, "Accounting for Income Taxes," APB Opinion No. 11, AICPA, New York, 1967.

———, "Accounting for Convertible Debt and Debt Issued with Stock Purchase Warrants," APB Opinion No. 14, AICPA, New York, 1969.

———, "Earnings per Share," APB Opinion No. 15, AICPA, New York, 1969.

———, "Interest on Receivables and Payables," APB Opinion No. 21, AICPA, New York, 1971.

———, "Early Extinguishment of Debt," APB Opinion No. 26, AICPA, New York, 1972.

American Accounting Association, "Accounting and Reporting Standards for Corporate Financial Statements," AAA, Sarasota, FL, 1957.

———, "A Statement of Basic Accounting Theory," AAA, Sarasota, FL, 1966.

American Institute of Certified Public Accountants, "Accounting Interpretations," *Journal of Accountancy,* Vol. 136, No. 15, November 1973, pp. 82–85.

———, Committee on Accounting Procedure, "Working Capital," Accounting Research Bulletin No. 43, Chapter 3, AICPA, New York, 1953.

Canning, John B., "Liabilities and Net Proprietorship," *The Economics of Accountancy,* Ronald Press, New York, 1929.

Dewing, Arthur Stone, *The Financial Policy of Corporations,* 5th ed., Ronald Press, New York, 1953.

Financial Accounting Standards Board, "Sale of Marketable Securities with a Put Option," EITF Issue No. 84-5, FASB, Stamford, CT, 1984.

———, "Deferred Interest Rate Setting," EITF Issue No. 84-14, FASB, Stamford, CT, 1984.

———, "Convertible Bonds with a Premium Put," EITF Issue No. 85-29, FASB, Stamford, CT, 1985.

———, "Sale of Marketable Securities at a Gain with a Put Option," EITF Issue No. 85-30, FASB, Stamford, CT, 1985.

———, "Comprehensive Review of Sales of Marketable Securities with Put Arrangements," EITF Issue No. 85-40, FASB, Stamford, CT, 1985.

———, "Increasing-Rate Debt," EITF Issue No. 86-15, FASB, Stamford, CT, 1986.

———, "Debtor's Accounting for a Modification of Debt Terms," EITF Issue No. 86-18, FASB, Stamford, CT, 1986.

———, "Using Forward Commitments as a Surrogate for Deferred Rate Setting," EITF Issue No. 86-26, FASB, Stamford, CT, 1986.

———, "Accounting Implications of Indexed Debt Instruments," EITF Issue No. 86-28, FASB, Stamford, CT, 1986.

———, "Classification of Obligations When a Violation Is Waived by the Creditor," EITF Issue No. 86-30, FASB, Stamford, CT, 1986.

———, "Debentures with Detachable Stock Purchase Warrants," EITF Issue No. 86-35, FASB, Stamford, CT, 1986.

———, "Allocation of Recorded Investment When a Loan or Part of a Loan Is Sold," EITF Issue No. 88-11, FASB, Norwalk, CT, 1988.

———, "Classification of a Short-Term Obligation Repaid Prior to Being Replaced by a Long-Term Security," FASB Interpretation No. 8, FASB, Stamford, CT, 1976.

———, "Reasonable Estimation of the Amount of a Loss," FASB Interpretation No. 14, FASB, Stamford, CT, 1976.

———, "Disclosure of Indirect Guarantees of Indebtedness of Others," FASB Interpretation No. 34, FASB, Stamford, CT, 1981.

———, "Elements of Financial Statements," Statement of Financial Accounting Concepts No. 6, FASB, Stamford, CT, 1985.

———, "Reporting Gains and Losses from Extinguishment of Debt," Statement of Financial Accounting Standards No. 4, FASB, Stamford, CT, 1975.

———, "Accounting for Contingencies," Statement of Financial Accounting Standards No. 5, FASB, Stamford, CT, 1975.

———, "Classification of Short-Term Obligations Expected to Be Refinanced," Statement of Financial Accounting Standards No. 6, FASB, Stamford, CT, 1975.

———, "Accounting for Leases," Statement of Financial Accounting Standards No. 13, FASB, Stamford, CT, 1976.

———, "Accounting by Debtors and Creditors for Troubled Debt Restructurings," Statement of Financial Accounting Standards No. 15, FASB, Stamford, CT, 1977.

———, "Balance Sheet Classification of Deferred Income Taxes," Statement of Financial Accounting Standards No. 37, FASB, Stamford, CT, 1980.

———, "Accounting for Compensated Absences," Statement of Financial Accounting Standards No. 43, FASB, Stamford, CT, 1980.

———, "Disclosure of Long-Term Obligations," Standard of Financial Accounting Standards No. 47, FASB, Stamford, CT, 1981.

———, "Accounting for Product Financing Arrangements," Statement of Financial Accounting Standards No. 49, FASB, Stamford, CT, 1981.

———, "Extinguishments of Debt Made to Satisfy Sinking-Fund Requirements," Statement of Financial Accounting Standards No. 64, FASB, Stamford, CT, 1982.

———, "Extinguishment of Debt," Statement of Financial Accounting Standards No. 76, FASB, Stamford, CT, 1983.

——, "Reporting by Transferors for Transfers of Receivables with Recourse," Statement of Financial Accounting Standards No. 77, FASB, Stamford, CT, 1983.

——, "Classification of Obligations That Are Callable by the Creditor," Statement of Financial Accounting Standards No. 78, FASB, Stamford, CT, 1983.

——, "Accounting for Income Taxes," Statement of Financial Accounting Standards No. 96, FASB, Stamford, CT, 1987.

——, "Disclosure of Information about Financial Instruments with Off-Balance-Sheet Risk and Financial Instruments with Concentrations of Credit Risk," Statement of Financial Accounting Standards No. 105, FASB, Stamford, CT, 1987.

——, "Early Extinguishment of Debt through Exchange for Common or Preferred Stock," Technical Bulletin No. 80-1, FASB, Stamford, CT, 1980.

——, "Classification of Debt Restructurings by Debtors and Creditors," Technical Bulletin No. 80-2, FASB, Stamford, CT, 1980.

——, "Applicability of FASB Statement 15 to Debtors in Bankruptcy Situations," Technical Bulletin No. 81-6, FASB, Stamford, CT, 1981.

——, "In-Substance Defeasance of Debt," Technical Bulletin No. 84-4, FASB, Stamford, CT, 1984.

——, "Accounting for Collateralized Mortgage Obligations," Technical Bulletin No. 85-2, FASB, Stamford, CT, 1985.

——, "Definition of a Right of Setoff," Technical Bulletin No. 88-2, FASB, Norwalk, CT, 1988.

Grady, Paul, "Inventory of Generally Accepted Accounting Principles for Business Enterprises," Accounting Research Study No. 7, AICPA, New York, 1965.

Graham, Benjamin, Dodd, David L., and Cottle, Sidney, *Security Analysis-Principles and Technique*, 4th ed., McGraw-Hill, New York, 1962.

Henderson, M. S., "The Nature of Liabilities," *Australian Accountant*, Vol. 44, No. 6, July 1974, pp. 328–334.

Hendriksen, Eldon S., *Accounting Theory*, Irwin, Homewood, IL, 1965.

Ijiri, Yuji, *The Foundations of Accounting Measurement—A Mathematical, Economic, and Behavioral Inquiry*, Prentice-Hall, Englewood Cliffs, NJ, 1967.

Jacobsen, Lyle E., "Liabilities and Quasi Liabilities," in *Modern Accounting Theory*, Morton Backer, Ed., Prentice-Hall, Englewood Cliffs, NJ, 1966, pp. 232–249.

Ma, Ronald, and Miller, Malcolm C., "Conceptualizing the Liability," *Accounting and Business Research*, Vol. 8, No. 32, Autumn 1978, pp. 258–265.

Moonitz, Maurice, "The Changing Concept of Liabilities," *Journal of Accountancy*, Vol. 109, No. 5, May 1960, pp. 41–46.

Securities and Exchange Commission, "The Significance of Oral Guarantees to the Financial Reporting Process," Financial Reporting Release No. 23, Codification of Financial Reporting Releases, Section 104, SEC, Washington DC, 1985.

——, "Form and Content of Financial Statements," Regulation S-X, SEC, Washington DC, 1974 Updated.

——, "Allocation of Debt Issue Costs in a Business Combination," Staff Accounting Bulletin No. 77, SEC, Washington DC, 1988.

Sprouse, Robert T., "Accounting for What-You-May-Call-Its," *Journal of Accountancy*, Vol. 122, No. 4, October 1966, pp. 45–53.

——, and Moonitz, Maurice, "A Tentative Set of Broad Accounting Principles for Business Enterprises," Accounting Research Study No. 3, AICPA, New York, 1962.

Trumbull, Wendell P., "What Is a Liability?" *Accounting Review*, Vol. 38, No. 1, January 1963, pp. 46–51.

CHAPTER 19

SHAREHOLDERS' EQUITY

Martin Benis, PhD, CPA

Bernard M. Baruch College
City University of New York

CONTENTS

THE CORPORATION

19.1 DEFINITION.   A corporation is a statutory form of organization created under rules promulgated by the legislature of the state in which it is incorporated. It is "an artificial being, invisible, intangible, and existing only in contemplation of law. Being the mere creature of law, it possesses only those properties which the charter of its creation confers upon it" (*The Trustees of Dartmouth College v. Woodward,* 4 Wheaton 518; 4 L. Ed. 629 (1819)). Thus, a corporation is a distinct and unique entity, separate from the personal affairs and other interests of its owners.

19.2 ADVANTAGES OF CORPORATE FORM.   The important advantages of doing business as a corporation are the following:

1. Continuity of life.
2. Limited liability for owners.
3. Ease of transferability of ownership.

The combination of these three advantages provides the corporation with the ability to raise large sums of capital. It is the sources of this capital and the claims on it that are of concern to the accountant.

19.3 OWNERS' INTERESTS.   Since the corporation is separate and distinct from its owners, owners merely have claims against its net assets. These claims and their nature and origin are presented in the shareholders' equity section of the corporate balance sheet. Shareholders' equity generally comprises three broad categories:

1. Capital stock or legal capital.
2. Additional paid-in capital.
3. Retained earnings (deficit).

The reporting of transactions affecting these classifications is influenced by legal as well as by accounting principles.

19.4 CERTIFICATE OF INCORPORATION.   In order to form a corporation, incorporators— usually at least three—file articles of incorporation with the secretary of state in the state of incorporation. The Model Business Corporation Act (MBCA), prepared by the American Bar Association and adopted in a majority of states, lists in § 54 the required provisions of the articles. Those of relevance to this section are the following:

1. The aggregate number of shares which the corporation shall have authority to issue; if such shares are to consist of one class only, the par value of each of such shares, or a statement that all of such shares are without par value; or, if such shares are to be divided into classes, the number of shares of each class, and a statement of the par value of the shares of each such class or that such shares are to be without par value.
2. If the shares are to be divided into classes, the designation of each class and a statement of the preferences, limitations and relative rights in respect of the shares of each class.
3. If the corporation is to issue the shares of any preferred or special class in a series, then the designation of each series and a statement of the variations in the relative rights and preferences as between series. . . .

When the secretary of state determines that the articles of incorporation conform to law, he issues a certificate of incorporation, after which corporate life commences.

SHARES OF STOCK

19.5 CERTIFICATES REPRESENTING SHARES.   Shares of a corporation are represented by stock certificates that state the following:

1. The state in which the corporation was organized.
2. The date of issuance of the stock.
3. The name of the person to whom issued.
4. The certificate number.
5. The class of shares, and the designation of the series, if any, which the certificate represents.

6. The par value of each share represented by the certificate, or a statement that the shares are without par value.
7. The name of the issuing corporation.
8. The number of shares represented by the certificate.
9. The number and classes of shares authorized.
10. The rights of each class of stock.

Certificates for shares may not be issued until the full amount of consideration has been received; however, New York and other states provide an exception to this rule for shares purchased under employee stock option plans (New York Business Corporation Law, § 505(e)). Neither promissory notes nor future services constitute payment or part payment for shares of a corporation.

Shares of stock are classified as either preferred or common with subclassifications within each of these two major classifications.

19.6 COMMON STOCK.   A corporation has the power to create and issue the number of shares for the various classes of stock stated in its certificate of incorporation. Holders of shares have the right to vote, the right to share in profits through dividend distributions, and the right to share in assets distributed in full or partial liquidation. Traditionally, common shareholders had **preemptive** rights, such as the right to maintain their proportionate interest when more shares are issued. More recently, however, the cost of satisfying this requirement has led many corporations to eliminate it. The certificate of incorporation may limit these rights; however, limitation of the rights of any class is precluded unless one class has no such limitations.

Preferred stock generally contains limitations of all of the above rights. Because of these limitations, the holders are given various preferences as to dividends and in liquidation. Common stock contains no limitations as to voting, dividend distributions, or liquidation distributions. However, the shares represent residual interests; preferred shares must receive dividends first, and in liquidation all obligations, including those to preferred shareholders, must be satisfied before the common shareholders receive anything.

Generally, a corporation has only one class of common stock. However, some corporations, such as Ford Motor Co., have two or more classes of common stock with each class reflecting different voting or dividend rights.

19.7 PREFERRED STOCK.   Preferred stock is given preference over common stock as to distributions of corporate earnings and distributions of assets in the event of corporate liquidations. Sometimes, in involuntary liquidations, the preference is in excess of the par or stated value of the shares. APB Opinion No. 10, "Omnibus Opinion—1986" (par. 10), recommends that in these situations "the liquidation preference of the stock be disclosed in the equity section of the balance sheet in the aggregate, either parenthetically or in short, rather than on a per share basis or by disclosure in notes." In exchange for these preferences, preferred shareholders usually relinquish certain rights, such as the right to vote.

Preferred stock generally has a fixed dividend rate and usually has a par value of $100. In some aspects it is similar to a bond; however, dividends on preferred stock are not deductible for income tax purposes; whereas interest on bonds is tax deductible. Therefore, capital obtained through the issuance of preferred stock is expensive. Nevertheless, corporations may use this method at times because of the following circumstances:

1. A high debt to equity ratio may adversely affect bond ratings.
2. Investors, such as pension funds, prefer this type of investment.

3. Banks and insurance companies that desire to minimizes the risks inherent in equity securities favor preferred stock. Although an investment in bonds minimizes risks even further, interest is fully taxable to most corporate investors; whereas, 70% of preferred dividends is excluded from corporate taxable income.

In recent years, preferred stock has acquired even more of the characteristics of bonds because of mandatory redemption provisions.

(a) Preferred Stock Subject to Mandatory Redemption.   A corporation, at its option, may redeem its stock at the market price or at a price stated in the stock certificate. However, recently, corporations have issued preferred stock with mandatory redemption provisions. The FASB has not provided guidance as to how the issuing corporation should classify this type of stock. It has, however, in SFAS No. 47, "Disclosure of Long-Term Obligations" stated that for each of the 5 years following the date of the latest balance sheet presented, the corporation shall disclose "the amount of redemption requirements for all issues of capital stock that are redeemable at fixed or determinable prices on fixed or determinable dates, . . ."

(b) Classification Requirements for Mandatory Redeemable Preferred Stock.   The FASB has been silent about classification requirements of the issues of mandatory redeemable preferred stock. It did state, however, in SFAS No. 12, "Accounting for Certain Marketable Securities," that a preferred stock "that must be redeemed by the issuing enterprise or is redeemable at the option of the holder is not, **from the standpoint of the holder,** an equity security" (par. 7).

The SEC, on the other hand, has been rigorous in its requirements for issuers of mandatory redeemable preferred stock. In 1979, the Commission amended Regulation S-X to modify the financial statement presentation of preferred stocks subject to mandatory redemption requirements or whose redemption is outside the control of the issuers. Companies having these types of securities outstanding are required to present separately in their balance sheets amounts applicable to the following three general classes of securities:

1. Preferred stocks subject to mandatory redemption requirements or whose redemption is outside the control of the issuer.

2. Preferred stocks which are not redeemable or are redeemable solely at the option of the issuer.

3. Common stocks.

A general heading, "Stockholders' Equity," is prohibited as is presentation of a combined total for equity securities, inclusive of mandatorily redeemable preferred stock.

Companies have been reporting mandatory redeemable preferred stock on their balance sheets between the last liability account and the equity section. The SEC suggests that in these circumstances the equity section be captioned "Non-Redeemable Preferred Stocks, Common Stocks, and Other Stockholders' Equity."

In addition to the above, the SEC requires disclosure in the notes to financial statements. The note should be captioned "Redeemable Preferred Stocks" and should include (1) terms of redemption, (2) 5-year maturity date, and (3) changes in these securities. Aggregate redemption amounts are required to be presented on the face of the balance sheet.

(c) Dividends on Mandatory Redeemable Preferred Stock.   The SEC has not established whether this type of preferred stock is, in fact, debt, therefore, there is no change in the calculation of debt equity ratios. In addition, dividends paid on these securities are accounted for in the same manner as dividends paid on other equity securities—a reduction of retained earnings.

(d) Carrying Amount of Mandatory Redeemable Preferred Stock.   When mandatory redeemable preferred stock is issued, it should be recorded at its fair value at date of issue. If the fair value of the security at date of issue is less than the mandatory redemption amount, its carrying amount should be increased by periodic accretions, using the interest method, so that the carrying amount will equal the redemption amount at the mandatory redemption date. The corresponding entry for the periodic accretion is a reduction of retained earnings.

(e) Callable Preferred Stock.   Since preferred stock is a burden of which corporations want to be relieved, many preferred issues contain a callable feature. This feature gives the corporation the right to call in the preferred stock at a stated redemption price, generally in excess of the par value or issue price of the stock. This excess is to compensate the owner for his involuntary loss. When preferred stock is called, all dividend arrearages must be satisfied.

APB Opinion No. 10 (par. 11) requires financial statements to disclose either on the face of the balance sheet or in the notes to financial statements "the aggregate or per share amounts at which preferred shares may be called or are subject to redemption through sinking fund operations or otherwise; . . . ."

(f) Cumulative Preferred Stock.   Generally, preferred stock contains a cumulative provision whereby dividends omitted in previous years must be paid before dividends on other outstanding shares may be paid. Inasmuch as dividends do not become a corporate liability until declared, dividend arrearages should be disclosed. APB Opinion No. 15, "Earnings per Share" (par. 50), requires financial statements to disclose the aggregate and per share amounts of arrearages in cumulative preferred stock.

(g) Fully Participating Preferred Stock.   Participating preferred stock is entitled to dividends in excess of its specified rate after the common stock has received the same rate. Preferred stock may be fully or partially participating. If it is fully participating with a 5% dividend rate, then, after the common stockholders receive 5% dividends, both the common and the preferred shareholders receive additional dividends on a pro rata basis. The dividend rate is based on the par values of the stocks, and the allocation of excess dividends between common and preferred stockholders is based on the total par values of the classes of stock involved.

(h) Partially Participating Preferred Stock.   If preferred stock is partially participating, it shares with common stock dividends in excess of its specified rate, limited by its participation percentage. If 5% preferred stock is partially participating up to a maximum of an additional 10%, it and the common stock may receive up to 15% on par value; after which, the common shareholders receive all additional dividends.

Participating preferred stock is not common today; the overwhelming majority of preferred stock currently issued is nonparticipating.

(i) Convertible Preferred Stock.   Convertible preferred stock may be converted into common shares at a specified ratio at the option of the shareholder. It is issued in order to make the preferred stock more attractive to investors while at the same time reducing the dividend rate. Under certain conditions, convertible preferred is considered to be a common stock equivalent for the computation of earnings per share (see Chapter 5).

When conversion occurs, a realignment of the components of stockholders' equity takes place. This realignment may result in an increase in additional paid-in capital or a decrease in retained earnings; it may not result in an increase in retained earnings.

At the time of conversion, the company must reduce its preferred stock and additional paid-in capital-preferred stock accounts for the amount originally received for the stock. This amount is then credited to the common stock and additional paid-in capital-common stock accounts. For example, if a $100 par value preferred share, convertible into 6 shares of $1 par value common, was issued at $103, the journal entry to record the conversion is as follows:

Preferred stock—$100 par value	$100	
Capital in excess of par value—preferred stock	3	
Common stock—$1 par value		$ 6
Capital in excess of par value—common stock		97

If, however, the par value of the common stock was $20, the journal entry to record the conversion would be as follows:

Preferred stock—$100 par value	$100	
Capital in excess of par value—preferred stock	3	
Retained earnings	17	
Common stock—$20 par value		$120

(j) Increasing-Rate Preferred Stock—SAB No. 68.   SAB No. 68, published in May 1987, expresses the staff's views regarding accounting for increasing-rate preferred stock. Essentially, increasing-rate preferred stock is cumulative preferred and carries either a zero dividend rate in the early years after issuance or a low dividend rate, which increases over time to a higher "permanent" rate. The higher dividend rate is usually a market rate for dividend yield given the preferred's characteristics, other than scheduled cash dividend entitlements (voting rights, liquidation preference, and the like), as well as the registrant's financial condition and future prospects. Therefore, the issue price is well below the amount that could be expected, based on the future permanent dividend.

(i) Balance Sheet Treatment.   The staff's view is that the increasing-rate preferred stock should be recorded initially at its fair value at the date of issuance. Thereafter, the carrying amount should be increased periodically.

(ii) Amortization of Discount.   It is unacceptable to recognize the dividend costs according to their stated schedules. Any discount due to the absence of dividends, or gradually increasing dividends, for an initial period represents prepaid, unstated dividend cost. The discount is based on the price the stock would have sold for had the permanent dividend been in effect from the date of issuance. The discount should be amortized over the periods preceding commencement of the perpetual dividend by charging imputed dividend cost against retained earnings and increasing the carrying amount of the preferred stock by a corresponding amount.

(iii) Computation of Discount and Amortization.   The discount at the time of issuance should be computed as the present value of the difference between (1) any dividends that will be payable in the periods preceding commencement of the perpetual dividend and (2) the perpetual dividend amount for a corresponding number of periods, discounted at a market rate for dividend yield on preferred stocks that are comparable (other than with respect to dividend payment schedules) from an investment standpoint.

The amortization in each period should be the amount which, together with any stated dividend for the period, results in a constant rate of effective cost relative to the carrying amount of the preferred stock (the market rate that was used to compute the discount). The staff believes that this approach is consistent with APB Opinion No. 21, "Interest on Receivables and Payables."

The imputed dividends would be considered an adjustment of net income in the computation of earnings per common share during the amortization period.

If stated dividends on an increasing-rate preferred stock are variable, computations of the initial discount and subsequent amortization should be based on the value of the applicable index at the date of issuance and should not be affected by subsequent changes in the index.

(k) Voting Rights of Preferred Stock.   Each share of stock, regardless of classification, is entitled to one vote. The corporation may, however, in its articles of incorporation deny voting rights to any class of stock. This, usually, is done with preferred stock.

The denial of voting rights to preferred stock is generally contingent on the maintenance of dividends. The NYSE will deny listing to any preferred issue that does not give holders the right to elect at least two members of the board of directors if six quarterly dividends are passed. Some companies will make the following disclosure in the financial statements:

> Holders of the series of preferred stock will not have voting rights, except that if six quarterly dividends shall be in arrears in part or in full, . . . , holders of preferred stock voting separately as a class . . . will be entitled to elect two directors of the Company until such time as all such dividends . . . in arrears on all outstanding shares of preferred stock have been satisfied.

19.8 PAR AND NO PAR VALUE STOCK.   Prior to 1912, all shares of corporate stock contained a par value—an arbitrarily assigned amount below which the stock could not be issued. The function of the par value was to provide an upper limit to the shareholder's liability, while at the same time indicating to creditors the minimum amount of permanent capital of the corporation.

In the late 1800s and early 1900s, corporations generally issued stock with high par values. However, as corporations split their stock, par values declined so that today the par value of the common stock of IBM is $1.25 and that of General Motors is $1.67. In addition, many states assess corporate taxes based on the par value of a company's stock; thereby providing an incentive for low par value stock.

In 1912, New York State enacted a law permitting corporations to issue no par value stock. Most states quickly followed New York and enacted similar laws. When no par value stock is issued, the board of directors may give it a stated value after which, for accounting purposes, it is reported in a manner similar to par value stock.

19.9 RECORDING THE ISSUANCE OF STOCK.   When par value stock is issued at par value, the stock account is increased by the amount of the proceeds. When par value stock is issued at a price in excess of par value, the excess is included in the additional paid in capital of that class of stock. Section 18 of the MBCA states that shares may be issued for not less than their par values; however, in states where there is not mandated, shares may be issued for a price below par value and the difference, **the discount,** is reported as a deduction in the stockholders' equity section of the balance sheet. The discount is the amount the stockholders who paid less than par value for the stock may be forced to ultimately pay to the corporation.

When no par value stock with a **stated value** is issued, the consideration in excess of the stated value increases the additional paid in capital for that class of stock. When no par value stock **without a stated value** is issued, the entire proceeds are included in the account of that class of stock.

19.10 STATED CAPITAL.   Section 2(j) of the MBCA defines stated capital as the sum of the following:

1. The par value of all shares of the corporation having a par value that have been issued.
2. The amount of the consideration received by the corporation for all shares of the corporation without par value that have been issued, except such part of the consideration therefrom as may have been allocated to capital surplus in a manner permitted by law.

3. Such amounts not included (above) . . . as have been transferred to stated capital of the corporation, whether upon the issue of shares as a share dividend or otherwise, minus all reductions from such sum as have been effected in a manner permitted by law.

Thus the stated or legal capital of the corporation represents the permanent investment of the shareholders; it is that portion of the net assets which cannot be distributed legally to stockholders prior to partial or total liquidation.

19.11 BALANCE SHEET PRESENTATION.   Below is the shareowners' equity section of Eastman Kodak Company, a company with one class of par value stock outstanding, as presented in its December 27, 1987, balance sheet.

(dollars in thousands)	1987	1986
Shareowners' equity:		
Common stock, par value $2.50 per share	$ 933	$ 622
500,000,000 shares authorized; issued		
at December 27, 1987—373,379,570		
at December 28, 1986—248,705,111		
Additional capital paid or transferred from retained earnings	—	314
Retained earnings	7,139	6,533
	8,072	7,469
Less Treasury stock at cost	2,059	1,081
at December 27, 1987—49,008,666 shares		
at December 28, 1986—34,007,309 shares		
Total shareowners' equity	$6,013	$6,388

The stockholders' equity section of a company with no par value common stock and authorized but unissued preferred stock is presented in the balance sheet as follows:

	19X1	19X0
Stockholders' equity:		
Preferred stock, no par value authorized		
1,000,000 shares, none issued	$ —	$ —
Common stock, no par value, authorized		
8,000,000 shares, shares issued and outstanding of		
2,688,198 in 19X1 and 2,347,074 in 19X0	10,320,000	5,673,000
Retained earnings	19,726,000	17,014,000
Total stockholders' equity	$30,046,000	$22,687,000

Although no preferred stock has been issued, it is reported on the balance sheet. Rule 5-02 of Regulation S-X requires the disclosure of all classes of stock and the number of shares authorized and issued or outstanding, as appropriate. The stockholders' equity section also indicates that the no par value stock does not have a stated value since there is no additional paid in capital.

The stockholders' equity section of a company with both preferred stock and common stock outstanding is presented in the balance sheet as follows:

	19X1	*19X0*
Stockholders' equity:		
Senior preferred stock, without par or stated value		
Authorized 3,000,000 shares, issued and outstanding		
1,600,000 shares, preference in liquidation—$40,000	$ 40,000	
Preferred stock, without par or stated value		
Authorized 1,000,000 shares, issued and outstanding		
204,000 shares, preference in liquidation—$10,200	7,132	$ 7,132
Common stock, par value $1 per share		
Authorized 20,000,000 shares, issued and outstanding		
9,908,000 and 6,024,000 shares respectively	9,908	6,024
Additional paid-in capital	71,370	53,438
Retained earnings	38,925	7,966
Total stockholders' equity	$167,335	$74,560

As required by APB Opinion No. 10 (par. 10), the liquidation preference of each class of preferred stock is disclosed in the equity section of the balance sheet in the aggregate, rather than on a per share basis or by disclosure in notes.

ISSUANCE OF STOCK

19.12 AUTHORIZED CAPITAL STOCK.   The maximum number of shares of stock a corporation is authorized to issue is specified in its articles of incorporation. However, a corporation may, with stockholder approval, amend its articles to increase the number of its authorized shares.

Rule 5-02 of Regulation S-X of the SEC requires the corporate balance sheet to state, for each class of stock, the following:

1. The title of the issue.
2. The number of shares authorized.
3. The number of shares issued or outstanding, as appropriate.
4. The dollar amount of the shares issued or outstanding.

A company may issue its shares immediately for full consideration or it may receive payments in installments and not issue its shares until all installments have been collected.

19.13 COST OF ISSUING STOCK.   When a corporation issues stock, it incurs certain costs such as printing of certificates; security registration and listing fees; legal and accounting fees; and commissions, fees, and expenses of its investment bankers and underwriters. Usually, these costs are accounted for as a deduction from the gross proceeds of the sale of stock; however, under Rule 5-02 of Regulation S-X, these costs may be classified as an intangible asset and amortized into income over some arbitrary number of years.

Section 507 of the New York Business Corporation Law states:

The reasonable charges and expenses of formation or reorganization of a corporation, and the reasonable expenses of and compensation for the sale of underwriting of its shares may be paid or allowed by the corporation out of consideration received by it in payment for the shares without thereby impairing the fully paid and nonassessable status of such shares.

If a corporation withdraws shares it intended to issue, the costs incurred for the contemplated sale are charged to income in the year of withdrawal. The charge is *not* an extraordinary item.

19.14 ISSUANCE OF SHARES FOR CASH. From an accounting perspective, the par value or stated value of capital serves one purpose only—that amount, and only that amount, appears in the stock account of the corporate records. The excess is included in an appropriate additional paid-in capital account. Thus, if common stock with a par value of $10 is issued for $12 and the consideration is cash, the entry is as follows:

Cash	$12	
Common stock		$10
Capital in excess of par value—common stock		2

The consideration for the issuance of shares may be paid, in whole or in part, in other than cash.

19.15 ISSUANCE OF SHARES FOR PROPERTY OR SERVICES. Under the MBCA, in the absence of fraud, the judgment of the board of directors or the shareholders as to the value of consideration received for shares shall be conclusive. APB Statement No. 4, "Basic Concepts and Accounting Principles Underlying Financial Statements of Business Enterprises" (par. 182) states:

> Measurements of owners' investments is generally based on the fair value of the assets or the discounted present value of liabilities that are transferred. The market value of stock issued may be used to establish an amount at which to record owners' investments but this amount is only an approximation when the fair value of the assets transferred cannot be measured directly.

Thus, when a publicly held corporation issues its stock for property or services, the market value of the stock issued may be used to approximate the fair value of the consideration received. However, a closely held corporation will have to rely on its board of directors to determine the fair value of consideration other than cash received for its stock.

19.16 SUBSCRIPTION FOR SHARES. Sale of stock on a subscription basis generally occurs when a closely held corporation sells stock either to outsiders or to employees or when a publicly held corporation offers stock to its employees. When stock is sold on a subscription basis, the full price of the stock is not received and the stock generally is not issued until full payment is made.

(a) Recording Subscription. When stock is sold on a subscription basis, two accounts are set up—Subscriptions Receivable and Capital Stock Subscribed. For example, if common stock with a par value of $10 is subscribed to for $12 the entry would be:

Subscriptions receivable	$12	
Common stock subscribed		$10
Additional paid-in capital		2

The common stock subscribed account is similar to the common stock account in that only the par value or stated value of the stock is entered in this account. As cash is collected on the subscription, the receivable is reduced, and when the final payment is made, the common stock subscribed account is reduced and the common stock account is increased by a similar amount.

(b) Balance Sheet Presentation.   If common stock subscribed has not been issued, it is still reported on the balance sheet as part of stockholders' equity, either as a separate caption or as part of the common stock with appropriate disclosure.

Subscriptions receivable may be presented in the balance sheet as an asset or as a deduction from stockholders' equity. However, Rule 5-02 of Regulation S-X requires a company to show the total dollar amount of capital shares subscribed but unissued, reduced by subscriptions receivable in the capital shares section of stockholders' equity. Below is the shareholders' equity section of the balance sheet of a company that has stock subscriptions receivable.

Shareholders' equity:
Common stock, $.10 per value, authorized
5,000,000 shares; outstanding 1,769,500 shares subscribed 57,000 shares $ 182,650
Capital surplus   4,612,598

                                                                                            4,795,248
Less—Common stock subscriptions receivable   (114,000)

                                                                                         $4,681,248

The total shares of 1,769,500 outstanding plus 57,000 subscribed equal 1,826,500 shares. This number multiplied by the par value of 10 cents equals the common stock amount of $182,650.

(c) Defaulted Subscriptions.   The disposition of the cash received before default is determined by state law. Under the New York Business Corporation Law, if the subscriber paid at least 50% of the subscription price, the shares subscribed for must be offered for sale for cash. The offering price must be sufficient to pay the full balance owed by the subscriber plus all expenses incidental to the sale. Excess proceeds realized must be remitted to the delinquent subscriber.

If less than 50% of the subscription price has been paid, or if there is no cash offer sufficient to pay expenses plus the full balance owed by a delinquent subscriber who paid at least 50% of the subscription price, the shares subscribed for must be canceled. Under these conditions, payments previously made by the subscriber are forfeited to the corporation and credited to an additional paid-in capital account.

19.17 STOCK PREMIUM AND STOCK DISCOUNT.   The accounting treatment for stock issued at a premium is covered in ATB No. 1, "Review and Resume." Paragraph 66 states:

These [stockholder] interests include the entire proprietary capital of the enterprise, frequently divided further, largely on the basis of source, as follows:

(1) Capital stock, representing the par or stated value of the shares.

(2) Capital surplus, representing (a) capital contributed for shares in excess of their par or stated value or (b) capital contributed other than for shares.

In a subsequent paragraph, however, the Bulletin states that the use of the term "surplus" should be discontinued and in its place should be the term "capital contributed for, or assigned to, shares in excess of such par on stated value."

Rule 5-02 of Regulation S-X requires separate captions in the stockholders' equity section for paid-in additional capital and other additional capital.

It is rare today for stock to be issued at a discount; however, if it is, the discount is reported in the balance sheet as a deduction from capital contributed. The discount is a liability of the shareholder to the creditors of the corporation; not to the corporation. Below is the stockholders' equity section of the balance sheet of a company that has issued stock in excess of par value and below par value.

	19X1	19X0
Stockholders' equity		
Capital stock:		
Preferred—$100 par value, authorized		
260,000 shares, issued 99,817 shares, less discount		
of $1,500,000	$ 8,482,000	$ 8,482,000
Common—$.625 par value, authorized		
7,500,000 shares, issued 5,795,061 shares	3,622,000	3,622,000
Capital in excess of par value	6,246,000	6,246,000
Retained earnings	40,892,000	33,812,000
Less—common stock in treasury,		
311,503 and 328,753 shares respectively	(2,090,000)	(2,206,000)
Total stockholders' equity	$57,152,000	$49,956,000

COMMON STOCK ADJUSTMENTS

19.18 STOCK SPLITS. Corporations can achieve wider distribution of shares or maintain the market price of shares within a specified range by means of stock splits. Chapter 7B of ARB No. 43, "Restatement and Revision of Accounting Research Bulletins" defines a split as the issuance ". . . by a corporation of its own common shares to its common shareholders without consideration and under conditions indicating that such action is prompted mainly by a desire to increase the number of outstanding shares for the purpose of effecting a reduction in their unit market price and thereby, of obtaining wider distribution and improved marketability of the shares."

(a) Split with Change in Par Value.   Generally, a stock split is executed by changing the par value of the stock. In the early part of 1979, the stock of IBM was selling for approximately $300 a share. The stockholders approved a 4 for 1 split of its stock when the par value of the shares was $5. After the split, the shares traded at approximately $75 and the par value was reduced to $1.25 a share. This type of stock split requires no monetary entry on the corporation's books; however, a memorandum entry should be made to note the change in the number of shares outstanding and the change in the par value.

(b) Split with No Change in Par Value.   A corporation may execute a stock split without changing the par value of its stock; it may transfer from additional paid-in capital to common stock an amount equal to the additional shares issued multiplied by the par value. For example, if 1 million shares of common stock with a par value of $10 are split 2 for 1 without adjusting the par value, $10 million will be transferred from additional paid-in capital to common stock. A corporation may also increase the number of its shares outstanding by means of a stock dividend. This adjustment is explained in the discussion of dividends.

(c) Reverse Splits.   At times, a corporation may wish to raise the market price of its shares and reduce the number of shares outstanding. This may be accomplished by means of a reverse split, in which the number of shares outstanding is reduced and the par value is increased proportionately. For example, if a company with 1 million shares of its $5 par value stock outstanding desires to reduce the number of outstanding shares, it may execute a 1 for 2 reverse split. The outstanding shares would be reduced to 500,000 and the par value would be increased to $10.

REACQUISITION AND RETIREMENT OF CAPITAL STOCK

19.19 TREASURY STOCK. Treasury shares are shares that were issued by a corporation and subsequently reacquired that have not been canceled or restored to the status of authorized but unissued shares. Treasury shares are issued but not outstanding and may be resold below par value without liability attaching to their purchase.

A corporation may purchase its own shares unless restricted by its certificate of incorporation or the corporation law of its state of incorporation. Section 513 of the New York Business Corporation Law applies to the purchase or redemption by a corporation of its own shares. It states the following:

1. A corporation may purchase its own shares or redeem its redeemable shares out of surplus except when the corporation is insolvent or would be made insolvent by the purchase.
2. A corporation may redeem or purchase its redeemable shares out of stated capital except when the corporation is insolvent or would be made insolvent by the transaction.

(a) Restrictions on Retained Earnings. The corporation laws of most states provide that distributions from retained earnings—in some states, retained earnings plus additional paid-in capital—are restricted to the extent of the cost of treasury shares until the shares are either disposed of or canceled. APB Opinion No. 6, "Status of Accounting Research Bulletins," (par. 13) requires the disclosure of these restrictions.

(b) Agreements to Purchase. Several states allow a corporation to contract to purchase its own shares, even though at the time of the agreement it is unable to pay for them because of the insolvency provisions of the law. Section 514 of the New York Business Corporation Law permits such an agreement, if at the time of partial or full payment, the corporation is solvent and the payment will not render it insolvent.

19.20 BALANCE SHEET PRESENTATION OF TREASURY STOCK. Under paragraph 12(b) of APB Opinion No. 6, a corporation may report its treasury stock as follows:

1. The cost of acquired stock may be shown separately as a deduction from the total capital stock, additional paid-in capital and retained earnings.
2. The stock may be accorded the treatment appropriate for retired stock.
3. In some circumstances, treasury shares may be shown as an asset.

Generally, treasury shares are reported as described in (1) and (2) above. Treasury stock is rarely reported as an asset because it is difficult to justify classifying what is essentially equivalent to unissued stock as an asset. However, occasionally corporations acquire their own stock to satisfy a specific obligation and classify these reacquired shares as assets. The SEC staff has indicated that asset classification of treasury stock is appropriate only if the shares repurchased are expected to be reissued promptly (within 1 year) under existing stock plans.

Reporting the cost of reacquired shares as a deduction from the total stockholders' equity is commonly known as the cost method or the single-transaction and unallocated deduction method. Treating reacquired shares as retired stock is commonly known as the par value method or the two-transaction and contraction of capital method.

19.21 REPORTING TREASURY STOCK TRANSACTIONS—COST METHOD. The cost method is more frequently used than the par value method in reporting treasury stock transactions. *Accounting Trends and Techniques* (Shohet and Rikert, 1988) noted that in

1987, of the 600 annual reports reviewed, 391 disclosed treasury stock. Of these, 366 reported treasury shares under the cost method, 21 under the par value method, 2 under other methods, and 2 as noncurrent assets.

Under the cost method, the acquisition of treasury shares is treated as the initial step of a financing operation that will culminate in the resale of these shares, that is, the purchase and sale are viewed as one continuous transaction. As a result, treasury stock assumes the status of a capital element in suspense, and the ultimate disposition of the shares marks the time for recognizing any adjustment among the various capital elements. A treasury stock account is debited for the cost of the shares purchased, and on resale the account is credited for the cost. If possible, the cost of each acquisition should be accounted for separately. When the treasury stock is resold, it should be reissued on the basis of specific identification. If specific identification is not possible, the stock may be assigned a cost on the basis of FIFO or, as a last resort, average cost.

(a) Disposition of Treasury Stock.   When treasury stock is sold for less than its cost, the charge for the loss depends on the laws of the state of incorporation and the status of shareholders' equity accounts in excess of legal or stated capital. It is customary to assign losses on treasury stock transactions to the following accounts in the order given: capital in excess of par value from previous treasury stock transactions of the same class of shares, capital in excess of par value from original sale of the same class of shares, pro rata, and retained earnings.

When treasury stock is sold for more than its cost, the gain is credited to additional paid-in capital, treasury stock transactions for that class of stock.

(b) Treasury Stock Retired.   When reacquired stock is retired, the stock account is debited for the amount credited when the stock was issued originally, the treasury stock account is credited at cost, and if the difference is a gain, it is credited to Capital in Excess of Par Value— Retired Stock. If the retirement results in a loss, it is debited to the following accounts in the order given:

1. Capital in Excess of Par Value to the extent of the credit when the stock was issued.
2. Capital in Excess of Par Value from previous treasury stock transactions of the same class of stock.
3. Retained Earnings.

APB Opinion No. 9, ''Reporting the Results of Operations'' (par. 28), reaffirmed the provisions of Chapter 1B of ARB No. 43 and stated:

> . . . the following should be excluded from the determination of net income or the results of operations under all circumstances: (a) adjustments or charges or credits resulting from transactions in the company's own stock. . . .

Under both GAAP and provisions of the IRC, gains and losses on treasury stock transactions are not included in determining income and, therefore, do not affect provisions for income taxes.

19.22 REPORTING TREASURY STOCK TRANSACTIONS—PAR VALUE METHOD.   Under the par value method for treasury stock, the reacquisition is viewed as the termination of the contract between the corporation and the shareholder, requiring the elimination of all capital elements identified with these shares. As a result, any adjustment between the retiring and remaining equityholders is made at the time of acquisition. The subsequent disposition of the treasury shares is regarded as a completely independent transaction. The purchase and resale of stock constitutes two transactions. Although accounting practitioners have turned increasingly to the cost method, the par value method has received more theoretical support.

Under the par value method, the acquisition of treasury shares has essentially the same effect on paid-in capital as the purchase and retirement of the stock. The treasury stock account is debited for the par (or stated) value of the stock acquired. The related capital in excess of par (or stated) value accounts are debited for the same amount as was identified with the stock when originally sold. If the reacquisition cost exceeds the original sales proceeds, the excess is charged to retained earnings. When the original sales proceeds exceed the reacquisition price, the difference is credited to Capital in Excess of Par (or Stated) Value—Treasury Stock. If the company cancels the reacquired stock, proper accounting requires that the balance in the treasury stock account be transferred to the account credited when the stock was originally sold.

The subsequent resale of acquired stock is accounted for in a manner similar to that for the sale of unissued stock. The treasury stock account is credited for par (or stated) value. Any proceeds from the sale in excess of the par (or stated) value should be credited to Capital in Excess of Par (or Stated) Value—Treasury Stock. Should the proceeds be less than par (or stated) value, the difference is debited to retained earnings because no discount liability attaches to the sale of treasury stock.

19.23 DONATED TREASURY STOCK.   In situations not so common today, shareholders may donate shares of company stock to the company. Whatever the reasons for the donation, it does not affect either total assets or total stockholders' equity. Kieso and Weygandt (1989) discuss the following three methods of accounting for donated stock when it is received:

1. Treasury Stock is debited and Donated Capital is credited for the current market value of the donated shares. When the donated treasury shares are received, they are accounted for in the same manner as other treasury stock applying the cost method.

2. Treasury Stock is debited for the par or stated value (or if it is true no-par stock, the average price paid in may be used), Paid-in Capital in Excess of Par or Stated Value is debited for the original premium paid in at the time of issuance, and Donated Capital is credited for the sum of the two debits. When the donated shares are reissued, they are accounted for in the same manner as other treasury stock applying the par value method, that is, as newly issued shares.

3. The donated shares are assumed to have no cost. Only a memorandum record is made indicating the number of shares received. The entire proceeds from reissuance of the donated treasury shares would be credited for Donated Capital.

19.24 CONTRAST IN ACCOUNTING FOR TREASURY STOCK TRANSACTIONS UNDER THE COST AND PAR VALUE METHODS.   The cost and par value methods of accounting for treasury stock transactions are illustrated below. Assume the following facts:

Common stock, $10 par value; issued and outstanding 1,000 shares	$10,000
Capital contributed in excess of par value	1,000
Retained earnings	9,000
Total Stockholders' Equity	$20,000

Furthermore, assume the following:

1. Company acquired 200 shares of its stock, 100 at $12 and 100 at $9.
2. (a) Sold the 200 shares for $13.
   (b) Sold the 200 shares for $7.

The journal entries are as follows:

	Cost Method		Par-Value Method
1. To record purchase of shares at $12 and $9			
Treasury stock	$1,200		$1,000
Capital contributed in excess of par value			100
Retained earnings			100
Cash		$1,200	$1,200
Treasury stock	$ 900		$1,000
Capital contributed in excess of par value			
Treasury stock transactions			$ 100
Cash		$ 900	900
2(a). To record sales of shares at $13			
Cash	$2,600		$2,600
Contributed capital, Treasury stock transactions		$ 500	$ 600
Treasury stock		2,100	2,000
2(b). To record sale of shares at $7			
Cash	$1,400		$1,400
Capital contributed in excess of par value	200		100
Capital in excess of par value, Treasury stock transactions			100
Retained earnings	500		400
Treasury stock		$2,100	$2,000

19.25 PRESENTATION OF TREASURY STOCK IN SHAREHOLDERS' EQUITY.   Below are the shareholders' equity sections of the balance sheets of two companies showing the usual manner of reporting treasury stock under both methods.

COST METHOD
Shareholders' equity (dollars in thousands):

Preference stock	$ 248
Common stock, par value $2.50 per share; authorized 100,000,000 shares; issued 28,988,757 shares	72,472
Additional paid-in capital	206,316
Retained earnings	734,020
	1,013,056
Less common stock in treasury, at cost; 1,249,110 shares	68,440
Total shareholders' equity	$ 944,616

PAR VALUE METHOD
Shareholders' equity:

Capital stock	
Common stock; authorized 10,000,000 shares of $2.50 par value each; issued 4,316,045 shares	$ 10,790,000
Less: treasury stock—157,611 shares	394,000
Outstanding—4,158,434 shares	$ 10,396,000
Capital in excess of par value	35,487,000
Retained earnings	108,297,000
Total shareholders' equity	$154,180,000

In its notes to the consolidated financial statements, this company indicated that its capital in excess of par value is increased for the proceeds of the sale of treasury stock in excess of par value and decreased by the cost in excess of par value of treasury stock purchased.

Other companies using the par value method for reporting treasury stock merely report the number of shares outstanding and parenthetically state the number of shares held in the treasury.

19.26 PURCHASE OF TREASURY SHARES AT A PRICE SIGNIFICANTLY IN EXCESS OF CURRENT MARKET PRICE.   Recently, companies that have been targets of unfriendly takeover attempts have paid prices in excess of market for its stock to persons holding the stock and attempting the takeover. These payments have been called **greenmail.** FTB No. 85-6 requires the company to allocate the cost of the reacquired stock to treasury stock for the market price of the stock and to other elements of the transaction for the balance. The other elements should be accounted for according to their substance.

FTB No. 85-6 requires disclosure of the allocation of the cost of the reacquired stock and the accounting treatment of the allocated costs.

STOCK EQUIVALENTS

19.27 USE OF STOCK EQUIVALENTS.   Corporations attempt to make debt more appealing but less costly, stock more desirable and employees more committed. Stock equivalents are used to achieve these goals. Tax incentives also have served to enhance the use of stock equivalents. For purposes of this section, stock equivalents comprise the following:

1. Stock warrants and stock rights.
2. Employee stock options.
3. Employee stock ownership plans (ESOPs).

19.28 STOCK WARRANTS AND STOCK RIGHTS.   Stock warrants are issued in conjunction with and attached to debt securities, are sold separately, or are given to investment bankers, stockbrokers, and attorneys as compensation for services rendered in the issuance of the company's stock. Stock warrants entitle the holder to purchase the company shares, generally its common stock, at a specified price, either within a given period or for an indefinite period.

(a) Issued with Debt.   When stock warrants are issued with debt or any other security, they may be either detachable or nondetachable. APB Opinion No. 14, "Accounting for Convertible Debt and Debt Issued with Stock Purchase Warrants" (par. 16), states that "the portion of the proceeds of debt securities issued with detachable stock purchase warrants which is allocable to the warrants should be accounted for as paid-in capital." The allocation is based on the relative fair values of the two securities at time of issuance, and the amount allocated to the warrant either increases the bond discount or reduces the bond premium. If, however, the warrant is not detachable, no allocation is made and the proceeds are attributed entirely to the debt.

Fair values may not be readily determinable when the company's securities are not publicly traded. In these circumstances, the company should estimate what the interest rate on the debt would be without the accompanying warrant. This rate would naturally be higher than the rate on the debt and warrant. The future cash flows from the payment of the debt and the interest payments should be discounted to the present. The difference between this amount and the amount received for the debt and the warrant is attributable to the warrant.

(b) Sale of Warrants.   When stock warrants are sold, the transaction is reported in a manner similar to the sale of stock; that is, the proceeds are credited to a paid-in capital account, generally Stock Warrants Outstanding.

(c) Issued for Services.   When stock warrants are issued for services, the fair market value of the services or the warrants, whichever is more clearly determinable, should be credited to paid-in capital.

(d) Exercise of Warrants.   When the stock warrant is exercised, part of the cost of the stock is considered to be the value allocated to the warrant. Therefore, this amount is removed from the stock warrants outstanding account and, together with the cash received, credited to the stock account for the par or stated value. Any excess is credited to the capital in excess of par value account.

(e) Stock Rights.   Stock rights and stock warrants are, for all practical purposes, the same. The differences are essentially mechanical. Stock warrants may be sold alone; whereas stock rights are usually sold in conjunction with a debt or equity security. Generally, one warrant, but more than one right, is required to acquire one share of stock. Whatever the esoteric differences may be between stock rights and stock warrants, they are reported in a similar manner for accounting purposes.

(f) Lapsed Warrants and Rights.   When stock warrants and stock rights lapse, the accounts should be closed and a paid-in capital account should be credited. The following stockholders' investment section of a company's comparative balance sheets shows the results of a lapse of warrants.

	1989	1988
Stockholders' Investment:		
Common stock—$.10 per value,		
5,000,000 shares authorized, 1,816,318 shares issued and		
outstanding	$ 181,632	$ 181,632
Warrants outstanding	—	15,000
Paid-in capital	982,833	967,833
Retained earnings (deficit)	693,834	(676,867)
	$1,858,299	$ 487,598

In 1988, the warrants expired and the $15,000 was added to paid-in capital.

(g) Tax Consequence of Lapsed Warrants.   A company may have taxable income when its warrants lapse. In these circumstances, the company could avoid adverse tax consequences by extending the expiration date of the warrants. Before any action is taken, however, the company should consult with its tax advisor.

(h) Reacquisition of Warrants.   When stock warrants are reacquired, the amount paid in excess of the amount assigned to the warrants at issuance is charged to retained earnings. If the warrants are reacquired at a price less than the amount originally assigned to them the difference is credited to additional paid-in capital.

(i) Contingent Warrants.   Occasionally, a company will issue warrants to certain of its customers to purchase its stock at a specified price. These warrants become exercisable only if those customers purchase specified amounts of the company's product. These warrants are contingent warrants. The SEC in SAB No. 57 stated that the warrants should not be valued or recorded until the customer had made the specified amount of sales and any other uncertainties were resolved. However, the company should periodically determine whether it is probable (as defined in SFAS No. 5, "Accounting for Contingencies") that the customers will make purchases sufficient to earn the warrants. Sales made subsequent to the date that a probable cost will occur should be charged with a pro rata amount of the estimated ultimate cost of the warrants.

19.29 EMPLOYEE STOCK OPTIONS.   Stock options are nontransferable rights granted by a corporation to its employees to purchase shares of the corporation at a stated price, either at a specified date or during a specified period. Stock options may be either compensatory or noncompensatory. Chapter 13B of ARB No. 43 states that "to the extent that such options and rights involve a measurable amount of compensation, this cost of services received should be accounted for as such . . ."

(a) Compensatory Stock Options.   Stock options involving an element of compensation generally arise when the employee has the right to purchase the company's stock at a price below market value at the measurement date. Paragraph 10(b) of APB Opinion No. 25, "Accounting for Stock Issued to Employees," states:

> The measurement date for determining compensation cost in stock option, purchase, and award plans is the first date on which are known both (1) the number of shares that an individual employee is entitled to receive and (2) the option or purchase price, if any. That date for many or most plans is the date an option is granted.

Compensation is the difference between the market price of the stock at the measurement date and the amount, if any, that the employee is required to pay. The amount allocated to compensation costs is credited to a paid-in capital account. Kieso and Weygandt (1989) illustrate the accounting and reporting of a compensatory stock option plan with the following example.

On January 1, 1989, a company grants options to its officers for 10,000 shares of its $1 par value common stock. The options may be exercised at any time within the next 10 years, commencing two years after the date of the grant. At the time of the grant, the market price of the stock is $70 a share and the option price for the stock is $60; therefore, there is an element of compensation in this option to the extent of $100,000 ($10 × 10,000). The company will record the following entries in 1989:

January 1, 1989		
Deferred compensation expense	$100,000	
Paid-in capital-stock options		$100,000
December 31, 1989		
Compensation expense	$ 50,000	
Deferred compensation expense		$ 50,000

At December 31, 1989, the Stockholders' Equity section of the company's balance sheet is as follows:

Stockholders' equity:		
Common stock, $50 par, 20,000 shares issued and outstanding		$1,000,000
Paid-in capital-stock options	$100,000	
Less deferred compensation	50,000	50,000
Total stockholders' equity		$1,050,000

At December 31, 1990, the remaining $50,000 to the deferred compensation account is written off and charged to income. If 20% or 2000 of the 10,000 options were exercised on June 1, 1992, the following entry would be recorded:

Cash (2000 × $60)	$120,000	
Paid-in capital-stock option (20% × $100,000)	20,000	
Common Stock (2,000 × $1)		$ 2,000
Paid-in Capital in Excess of Par		138,000

If the remaining stock options lapse, the balance in the "Paid-in Capital—Stock Option" account is transferred to a new account, "Paid-in Capital—Expired Stock Options."

(b) Disclosure Requirements.   ARB No. 43 (Ch. 13B, par. 15; see also *FASB Accounting Standards—Current Text—General Standards as of June 1, 1989,* par. C47.123) states the disclosure requirements for stock options. Disclosure is required as to the status of the plan at the balance sheet date including the following:

1. Number of shares under option.
2. Option price.
3. Number of shares for which options were exercisable.
4. Options exercised during the period, number of shares involved, and option price thereof.

The notes to the 1988 financial statements of McDonald's Corporation describe the company's stock option plan as follows:

STOCK OPTIONS

Under the company's employee stock option plans, options to purchase common stock are granted at prices not less than fair market value of the stock at date of grant. Substantially all of these options become exercisable cumulatively in four equal biennial installments, commencing one year from date of grant and expire ten years from date of grant. At December 31, 1988 12,440,833 shares of common stock were reserved for issuance under employee stock option plans.

	1988	*1987*	*1986*
Options outstanding at January 1	9,617,700	10,160,159	10,719,248
Options granted	1,820,790	1,777,150	2,236,551
Options exercised	(1,738,285)	(1,892,050)	(2,011,560)
Options forfeited	(429,011)	(427,559)	(784,080)
Options outstanding at December 31	9,271,194	9,617,700	10,160,159
Options exercisable at December 31	2,988,549	3,116,677	3,803,435
Common Shares reserved for future grants at December 31	3,169,639	4,561,418	5,911,009
Option prices per common share			
Exercised during the year	$9 to $51	$9 to $40	$9 to $30
Outstanding at year-end	$9 to $52	$9 to $60	$9 to $44

19.30 EMPLOYEE STOCK OWNERSHIP PLANS, REPORTING THE ESOP.   An ESOP is a plan under which employees acquire stock of their employer. It is also a means by which the corporation can obtain additional capital. Generally, the ESOP borrows from the bank and uses the proceeds to buy the company's shares, either from the corporation or from shareholders with significant holdings. The corporation guarantees the loan made to the

ESOP, and the ESOP repays the loans from tax-deductible contributions made to it by the corporation.

Financial reporting by the corporation of its ESOP is determined by the provisions of *SOP No. 76-3,* "Accounting Practices for Certain Employee Stock Ownership Plans," issued by the Accounting Standards Division of the AICPA. It requires the following:

1. The ESOP obligation guaranteed by the corporation must be recorded as a liability by the corporation with an offsetting reduction in shareholders' equity section.

2. The amount of the liability and the offsetting reduction in the shareholders' equity section are reduced as the ESOP makes payments on its debt.

Therefore, under the ESOP and variations of it, such as a Tax Reduction Act Stock Ownership Plan (TRASOP), the stockholders' equity section of the company reports a deduction to the extent of the ESOP outstanding debt that it guaranteed.

19.31 OTHER STOCK COMPENSATION PLANS.   The extent of stock compensation plans is limited only by the imagination and ingenuity of company management. Because of the proliferation of these plans, the FASB has been studying the subject of employee stock compensation plans and the method of accounting for them. In its 1984 *Invitation to Comment,* "Accounting for Compensation Plans Involving Certain Rights Granted to Employees," the FASB classified these plans as follows:

1. Market performance plans. These are plans in which the amounts involved are solely a function of the market price of the company's stock. Examples of these plans are the following:
   a. Incentive stock options.
   b. Nonqualified stock options.
   c. Stock appreciation rights.
   d. Phantom stock units.
   e. Restricted stock awards.
   f. Restricted stock purchase rights.
   g. Qualified employee stock purchases.
2. Enterprise performance plans. These are plans in which the amounts involved are solely a function of enterprise performance based on established criteria, such as earnings per share, but not based on the market price of the company's stock. Examples of these plans are the following:
   a. Performance units.
   b. Book value units.
   c. Book value purchase rights.
3. Market/enterprise performance plans (combination plans). These are plans in which the amounts involved are a function of both market performance and enterprise performance. Examples of these plans are the following:
   a. Performance share units.
   b. Stock appreciation rights with performance requirements.
   c. Stock options with performance requirements.

Accounting for these plans is explained in Chapter 27 of the *Handbook.* Authoritative pronouncements that provide guidance are:

1. APB Opinion No. 25, "Accounting for Stock Issued to Employees."
2. FIN No. 28, "Accounting for Stock Appreciation Rights and Other Variable Stock Option or Award Plans."
3. FIN No. 31, "Treatment of Stock Compensation Plans in EPS Computations."

RETAINED EARNINGS

19.32 DEFINITION.   The MBCA states that the retained earnings of a corporation is

> equal to its net profits, income, gains and losses from the date of incorporation or from the latest date when a deficit was eliminated by an application of its capital surplus or stated capital or otherwise, after deducting subsequent distributions to shareholders and transfers to stated capital and capital surplus. . . .

A corporation is an entity separate and distinct from its shareholders, and legally it cannot make a distribution to shareholders from permanent capital. Therefore, a credit balance in the retained earnings account represents the maximum potential claim which the shareholders have against the net assets of the corporation. The claim is no longer potential when, and to the extent that, the company's board of directors declares a dividend.

The board of directors may declare a dividend except when the corporation is insolvent or when the dividend payment would render the corporation involvent. Dividends may be declared only out of the unreserved and unrestricted retained earnings of the corporation; however, in some states, dividends may also be declared out of additional paid-in capital.

19.33 EVENTS AFFECTING RETAINED EARNINGS.   The balance in the retained earnings account is increased by net income and reduced by net loss. In addition, the balance is affected by the following:

1. Prior period adjustments.
2. Dividends.
3. Recapitalizations and reorganizations.
4. Treasury stock transactions.
5. Stock redemptions.

Treasury stock transactions and stock redemptions were discussed earlier in this section. The first three items are discussed below.

19.34 PRIOR PERIOD ADJUSTMENTS.   The theoretical undesirability of prior period adjustments has been acknowledged for many years:

> . . . it is plainly desirable that all costs, expenses, and losses, and all profits of a business, . . . be included in the determination of income. If this principle could in practice be carried out perfectly, there would be no charges or credits to earned surplus [retained earnings] except those relating to distributions and appropriations of final net income. This is an ideal upon which all may agree, but because of conditions impossible to foresee it often fails of attainment. (ARB No. 43, ch. 2B, par. 3)

Although Chapter 2B has been superseded, the undesirability of prior period adjustments is still recognized. Conditions under which prior period adjustments may be recorded have been narrowed so that except for items specifically noted in authoritative pronouncements, only one item may be accounted for as a prior period adjustment and recorded directly in the retained earnings account.

(a) Correction of an Error in Prior Period Financial Statements.   SFAS No. 16, "Prior Period Adjustments," as amended, states that "an item of profit and loss related to the correction of an error in the financial statements of a prior period . . . shall be accounted for and reported as a prior period adjustment and excluded from the determination of net income for the current period."

"Errors in financial statements result from mathematical mistakes, mistakes in the application of accounting principles, or oversight or misuse of facts that existed at the time the financial statements were prepared" (APB Opinion No. 20, "Accounting Changes," par. 13).

(b) Reporting Prior Period Adjustments.   SFAS No. 16 (par. 16a) states that "those items that are reported as prior period adjustments shall, in single period statements, be reflected as adjustments of the opening balance of retained earnings." When comparative income statements are presented, the previously issued statements, if affected by the adjustment, shall be restated. If the prior period adjustment affects years prior to those being presented, the opening retained earnings of the earliest year must be adjusted.

19.35 OTHER PRIOR PERIOD ADJUSTMENTS.   In addition to the adjustment of retained earnings required by SFAS No. 16, other events require an adjustment of retained earnings.

The FASB has made many of its pronouncements effective on a retroactive basis. This requires restatements of all prior years' statements presented and, if applicable, an adjustment of the opening retained earnings of the earliest year presented.

In addition to FASB requirements for retained earnings adjustments, APB Opinion No. 20 (pars. 27 and 29) provides examples of changes in accounting principle requiring retroactive application. In those situations, balances in retained earnings must be adjusted.

19.36 DIVIDENDS.   Dividends are pro rata distributions of company assets to its shareholders, limited by business considerations, availability of resources and, in most states, the amount of retained earnings. They represent the portion of the accumulated earnings that the board decides it can distribute without adversely affecting the operations of the company.

Although shareholders have the right to share in the earnings of the company, they are not entitled to receive the earnings or any part thereof without action by the board of directors. The declaration by the board and the distribution by the corporation of dividends involve three dates:

1. The declaration date.
2. The record date.
3. The payment date.

Dividends are of the following types:

1. Cash.
2. Stock.
3. Property.
4. Scrip or liability.
5. Liquidating.

19.37 DIVIDEND DATES.   For dividends other than stock dividends, the corporation incurs a liability at the time of declaration. This is the date when the board of directors meets and votes the dividend. At this meeting, the board also establishes the record date and the payment date for the dividend. When a stock dividend is declared, the board may **rescind** it prior to distribution.

At **declaration date** for other than a stock dividend, the company reduces its retained earnings by the amount of the dividend and records a liability. The **record date** does not affect the corporation. It must pay dividends on the number of shares outstanding; the record date merely established who will receive the dividend. For stocks that are publicly traded, generally the stock is traded **ex-dividend**—without the dividend—4 or 5 days prior to the record date.

On the **record date,** the person responsible for distributing the dividend determines the individuals who will receive the dividend, and on the payment date the dividend is remitted to the stockholder. On the record date, no entry is required on the corporate books; on the **payment date** the corporation eliminates its liability by distributing the assets necessary to satisfy the liability.

19.38 CASH DIVIDENDS.   Declaration of a **cash dividend** is the usual manner in which the board initiates a distribution to the shareholders. The declaration is usually quarterly and may be stated as either a percentage of the par value of the shares or a dollar amount per share. However stated, at the date of declaration the corporation has assumed a liability and must therefore record it with a corresponding reduction of retained earnings.

As noted earlier, the company makes no entry in recognition of the record date of the dividend. On the payment date, the corporation satisfies its liability by distributing the cash.

19.39 STOCK DIVIDENDS.   ARB No. 43 (Ch. 7B, par. 1) defines a stock dividend as follows:

> An issuance by a corporation of its own common shares to its common shareholders without consideration and under conditions indicating that such action is prompted mainly by a desire to give the recipient shareholders some ostensibly separate evidence of a part of their respective interests in accumulated corporate earnings without distribution of cash or other property which the board of directors deems necessary or desirable to retain in the business.

A stock dividend is the second most common type of dividend, and it is the only one which, when declared, does not create a legally enforceable corporate liability. The declaration of a stock dividend is not a commitment to distribute corporate assets; it merely indicates an intent to **realign** the accounts constituting stockholders' equity by issuing additional stock to current shareholders.

(a) Small Stock Dividend.   ARB No. 43 (Ch. 7B) indicates that a distribution less than 20% to 25% of the shares previously outstanding would be considered a **small** stock dividend. Recipients of small stock dividends view them as distributions of corporate earnings, usually in an amount equal to the fair value of the shares received. ARB No. 43 (Ch. 7B, par. 10) states:

> [I]t is to be presumed that such views of recipients are materially strengthened in those instances, which are by far the most numerous, when the issuances are so small in comparison with the shares previously outstanding that they do not have any apparent effect upon the share market prices and, consequently, the market value of the shares previously held remains substantially unchanged. The committee therefore believes that when these circumstances exist the corporation should in the public interest account for the transaction by transferring from earned surplus to the category of permanent capitalization (represented by the capital stock and capital surplus accounts) an amount equal to the fair value of the additional shares issued.

Therefore, when a small stock dividend is declared or distributed (see below for time of recording), the corporation must do the following:

1. Reduce retained earnings by the fair value of the shares.
2. Increase the common stock account by the par or stated value of the shares.
3. Increase capital paid in excess of par or stated value by the difference between such value and the amount determined in (1) above.

If no par value stock is distributed, its total market value should be credited to the common stock account.

(b) Large Stock Dividend.   A distribution of 20% to 25% or more of the shares previously outstanding is considered a **large** stock dividend; therefore it is reasonable to assume a reduction in the market value of outstanding shares. Under these circumstances, the retained earnings account is reduced and the stock account increased by the par or stated value of the shares. If no par value stock is distributed, the amount is computed by multiplying the number of shares distributed by the average amount per share paid in.

(c) Closely Held Corporation.   For closely held corporations, market value is not a factor in determining the amount of the stock dividend. Under these circumstances, "there is no need to capitalize earned surplus other than to meet legal requirements" (ARB No. 43, Ch. 7B, par. 12). Therefore, the par or stated value of the shares distributed determines the amount of the reduction of retained earnings.

(d) Record Date.   Since there is no legally enforceable obligation at the declaration date to issue the stock, the dividend should be recorded at the market value on the date the stock is distributed. However, many accountants prefer to record the dividend at the date of declaration. When this is done, the corporation establishes a new account, Stock Dividend Distributable, which, at the date of declaration, is credited for the par or stated value of the shares to be distributed.

(e) Reasons for Stock Dividends.   Stock dividends usually are declared for the following reasons:

1. To permanently retain earnings in the business by capitalizing a portion of accumulated earnings.
2. To maintain a record of paying dividends without affecting corporate assets.
3. To increase the number of shares outstanding without affecting the market price significantly.
4. To take advantage of the nontaxability of stock dividends.

The last reason is significant since not only are stock dividends not taxable on receipt, but also the stock is assumed to have the same holding period as the shares on which the dividend was declared.

19.40 PROPERTY DIVIDENDS.   Occasionally, a corporation will pay a dividend in kind, that is, it will pay the dividend in property, inventory, real estate, marketable securities of other corporations. Prior to the adoption of APB Opinion No. 29, "Accounting for Nonomonetary Transactions," dividends of this nature were accounted for at book value.
APB Opinion No. 29 (par. 18) states:

A transfer of a nonmonetary asset to a stockholder or to another entity in a nonreciprocal transfer should be recorded at the fair value of the asset transferred, and a gain or loss should be recognized on the disposition of the asset.

However, if the transfer is a spinoff or other form of reorganization or liquidation, it should be recorded at book value, not market value.
The recording of a property dividend is explained in the following example. Assume that a corporation owns 1,000 shares of "X" Corp. stock which it acquired at $10 a share and which now has a market value of $25. If it declares a property dividend of 600 shares, it must record a gain on the disposal of the 600 shares. Therefore, at the declaration date, it increases its investment by $9,000 (600 shares × $15) and credits an account, Gain on Disposal of Investment. It then reduces retained earnings by $15,000 (600 shares × $25) and records its liability. The $9,000 gain is reported in the income statement; however, for income tax

purposes, this gain is not taxable. Since this item does not have tax consequences, it is not considered when computing income taxes under the provisions of SFAS No. 96, "Accounting for Income Taxes."

19.41 SCRIP OR LIABILITY DIVIDENDS.   Although it is rarely done, a corporation may pay a dividend in scrip—a note. The accounting and reporting is the same as for a cash dividend, except that the corporation records notes payable rather than dividends payable as the liability. Notes payable for dividends bear interest which, when accrued, is charged to the interest expense account.

One reason for scrip dividends is that the shareholders may want a cash dividend; however, at the time of declaration, the corporation wishes to conserve its cash. After the shareholders receive the notes for the dividend, they can discount them and thereby obtain the desired cash.

19.42 LIQUIDATING DIVIDENDS.   A liquiding dividend is any dividend not based on profits; therefore it must be recorded as a reduction of paid-in capital. Dividends of this nature are common in industries involved in natural resources. Section 45(b) of the MBCA recognizes the possibility of this kind of dividend. It states:

> If the articles of incorporation of a corporation engaged in the business of exploiting natural resources so provide, dividends may be declared and paid in cash out of the depletion reserves, but each such dividend shall be identified as a distribution of such reserves and the amount per share paid from such reserves shall be disclosed to the shareholders receiving the same concurrently with the distribution thereof.

Liquidating dividends also may be declared as a result of contraction of a corporation's operations. For example, a corporation may dispose of a division or a subsidiary and decide not to reinvest the proceeds.

When a liquidating dividend is declared and stock is not redeemed, accounts other than the retained earnings and capital stock accounts must be reduced. These accounts are capital in excess of par value, donated capital, capital arising from treasury stock transactions or some similar capital account.

19.43 QUASI REORGANIZATION.   In the early years of a corporation's existence, it is not unusual for the corporation to be unprofitable and build up an accumulated deficit. When the corporation becomes profitable, it will not be able to pay dividends until this deficit is eliminated. One way of eliminating the deficit is a reorganization—an adjustment of the financial structure of the company.

Reorganizations may be formal and be subject to the provisions of the Federal Bankruptcy Law and the jurisdiction of the bankruptcy courts, or they may be informal. Informal reorganizations, generally called **quasi reorganizations,** adjust the corporate capital structure without recourse to the courts. In addition to speeding up the reorganization process, a quasi reorganization is less costly than the more formal court-supervised reorganization.

GAAP state that "capital surplus, however created, should not be used to relieve the income account of the current or future years of charges which would otherwise . . . be made . . . (ARB No. 43, Ch. 1A, par. 2)." However, exceptions to this rule are provided for in the case of a quasi reorganization.

(a) Procedures in a Quasi Reorganization.   Chapter 7A of ARB No. 43 explains the procedures used in a quasi reorganization. Assets are revalued downward to fair value at the date of adjustment; however, upward adjustments of items within the same asset classification are permitted so long as the net effect of the adjustments does not result in a write-up of the net assets (see SAB No. 78). The net reduction in assets is a charge to the accumulated deficit of the corporation. After all asset adjustments are completed, the accumulated deficit is written off against any additional paid-in capital accounts. If the total in these accounts is not sufficient to absorb the accumulated deficit, additional paid-in capital should be created by means of a reduction in the par or stated value of the stock.

(b) Retained Earnings after Readjustment.   "When the readjustment has been completed, the company's accounting should be substantially similar to that appropriate for a new company" (ARB No. 43, Ch. 7B, par. 9). Therefore, retained earnings **must** be zero and thereafter, whenever a balance sheet is prepared, the retained earnings should be dated to indicate from which date these earnings have been accumulated. ARB No. 46 indicates that generally this dating should continue over a period of 10 years, although there may be exceptional circumstances where dating may cease before 10 years.

Dating of retained earnings may be done either on the face of the balance sheet or in the notes to financial statements. In its 1988 balance sheet, Genentech, Inc., reported the following:

	1988	1987
Shareholders' Equity:		
Preferred stock, $.02 per value; authorized 100,000,000 shares; none issued	$ —	$ —
Common stock, $.02 per value; authorized 297,00,000 shares; outstanding; 1988—82,924,439; 1987—78,739,896	1,658	1,575
Earnings convertible restricted stock $.02 per value; authorized 3,000,000 shares; outstanding: 1988—none; 1987—2,927,260	—	59
Additional paid-in capital	366,518	336,267
Notes receivable from sale of stock	—	(320)
Retained earnings (since October 1, 1987, quasi reorganization in which a deficit of $329,457 was eliminated)	31,119	17,831
Total stockholders' equity	399,295	355,412
Total liabilities and stockholders' equity	$668,755	$618,973

In its notes to financial statements explaining its reorganization, the Company stated:

> On February 18, 1988 the Company's Board of Directors approved the elimination of the Company's accumulated deficit through an accounting reorganization of its stockholders' equity accounts (quasi-reorganization) effective October 1, 1987. The quasi-reorganization did not involve any revaluation of assets or liabilities. The effective date of the quasi-reorganization (October 1, 1987) reflects the beginning of the quarter in which the Company received approval for and commenced marketing of its second major product, and as such, marks a turning point in the Company's operations. The accumulated deficit was eliminated by a transfer from additional paid-in capital in an amount equal to the accumulated deficit. The Company's stockholders' equity accounts at October 1, 1987 before and after the quasi-reorganization, are reflected in the consolidated statements of stockholders' equity. The tax benefits recognized subsequent to the quasi-reorganization that relate to items occurring prior to the quasi-reorganization have been reclassified from retained earnings to additional paid-in capital.

(c) Tax Loss Carryforwards.   A corporation that undertakes a quasi reorganization probably has operating loss or tax credit carryforwards that have not been recognized as assets. When the benefits of these carryforwards are realized subsequent to the quasi reorganization, they should be reported as a direct addition to contributed capital. If, however, the quasi reorganization involved only the elimination of the accumulated deficit by a reduction in contributed capital, subsequent recognition of prior operating loss or tax credit carryforwards should be accounted for as if the quasi reorganization had not occurred. That is, it should be recognized in the income statement. However, after this recognition, the tax benefit should be reclassified from retained earnings to contributed capital (SFAS No. 96, par. 54).

19.44 RESTRICTIONS OF RETAINED EARNINGS.   Although retained earnings indicates the maximum which may be distributed to shareholders, this amount may be subject to certain constraints and restrictions. Paragraph 199 of APB Statement No. 4 states that information about restrictions on assets and of owners' equity should be disclosed.

Restrictions of retained earnings are classified as follows:

1. Legal.
2. Contractual.
3. Voluntary.

(a) Legal Restrictions.   A legal restriction on retained earnings was noted in section 19.19, which discussed treasury stock. Under § 6 of the MBCA, a corporation has the right to acquire its stock but only to the extent of unreserved or unrestricted retained earnings. The section further states:

> To the extent that earned surplus or capital surplus is used as the measure of the Corporation's right to purchase its own shares, such surplus shall be restricted so long as such shares are held as treasury shares. . . .

(b) Contractual Restrictions.   Bond indentures and loan agreements with banks usually contain restrictions on retained earnings. Typical of these restrictions and the related disclosure is the note in the 1987 financial statements of Occidental Petroleum Corporation:

> At December 31, 1987, under the most restrictive covenants of certain financing agreements, the capacity for the payment of all cash dividends and other distributions on, and for acquisitions of, capital stock was approximately $2.2 billion, assuming that such dividends, distributions or acquisitions were made without incurring additional borrowing. The net assets of certain subsidiaries of Occidental are restricted from being advanced, loaned or dividended to Occidental and its affiliates by certain financing agreements. At December 31, 1987, net assets of consolidated subsidiaries so restricted were approximately $1.1 billion.

(c) Voluntary Restrictions.   Occasionally a corporation will voluntarily restrict the distribution of dividends because of some loss contingency that does not qualify for deduction on the income statement or because of future plans for major construction or renovation. In these situations, the corporation is merely informing the user of its financial statements that it has voluntarily restricted the payment of dividends.

(d) Liquidating Value of Preferred Stock.   The question of whether the excess of the liquidating value of preferred stock over its par value is a restriction on retained earnings is a legal determination. When state law is unclear, the uncertainty should be disclosed.

19.45 APPROPRIATIONS OF RETAINED EARNINGS.   Usually, restrictions of retained earnings are disclosed in the notes to financial statements and recorded on the books by means of a memorandum entry. Sometimes, by action of the board of directors, retained earnings may be appropriated; that is, total retained earnings is reduced and a new account, Appropriated Retained Earnings, is established. However, the total retained earnings remains the same. Rarely is appropriated retained earnings reported on the balance sheet.

19.46 LOSS CONTINGENCIES.   Appropriated retained earnings may not relieve the income statement of an expense. SFAS No. 5 (par. 15) states:

> Some enterprises have classified a portion of retained earnings as "appropriated" for loss contingencies. . . . Appropriation of retained earnings is not prohibited by this Statement provided that it is shown within the stockholders' equity section of the balance sheet and is clearly identified as an appropriation of retained earnings. Costs or losses shall not be charged to an appropriation of retained earnings, and no part of the appropriation shall be transferred to income.

When the event for which the appropriation was established has passed, the appropriated retained earnings account is reduced by the amount originally established and the retained earnings account increased by a similar amount.

OTHER ITEMS AFFECTING STOCKHOLDERS' EQUITY

19.47 MINORITY INTERESTS.   When consolidated financial statements are prepared in situations where the parent company does not own 100% of the stock of its subsidiary, the minority interest in the subsidiary usually is presented between long-term debt and stockholders' equity. The presentation represents essentially a proprietary theory approach and implies that the minority interest is a liability. However, minority interests do not represent liabilities any more than the interests of the majority shareholders do. Under the **entity theory** of consolidated statements, controlling shareholder and minority interests should be accorded the same reporting treatment.

Griffin, Williams and Larson (1980) state:

> The acceptance of the entity notion for consolidated statements carries with it the obligation to regard all shareholders equal per share claimants to the combined resources of the affiliated companies. The presentation of shareholders' interests should be made in such a manner as to clearly indicate the values attributable to controlling and noncontrolling interests, *but without reference to legal preference or implications as to hierarchical status.* Clearly, according to this view, an identification of minority interests as liabilities in consolidated statements is inappropriate; it may also be argued that the compromise consolidated position between the liabilities and the controlling stockholders' equity divisions violates the spirit of the entity theory.

General Telephone & Electronics Corporation has always recognized the entity theory of consolidated financial statements. Its 1987 balance sheet reported the following:

	1987	1986
	(thousands of dollars)	
Shareholders' equity:		
GTE Corporation—		
Preferred stock	$ 544,030	$ 22,153
Common stock—shares issued 340,549,668 and		
331,464,120	34,055	33,146
Amounts paid in, in excess of par value	4,769,391	4,457,642
Foreign currency translation adjustment	(83,685)	(141,069)
Reinvested earnings	3,637,926	3,372,738
Foreign currency translation adjustment	(83,685)	(141,069)
Reinvested earnings	3,637,926	3,372,738
Common stock held in treasury—15,000,000 and	(598,428)	(59,336)
1,506,000 shares, at cost		
	8,303,289	7,885,274
Minority interests in equity of subsidiaries	780,583	732,865
Total shareholders' equity	$9,083,872	$8,618,139

19.48 COMBINED FINANCIAL STATEMENTS. Consolidated financial statements are required when one company owns more than 50% of the outstanding voting shares of another company. However, a group of independent companies may have common controlling shareholders. For example, an individual may have controlling interest in two or more corporations or a parent company may have more than one subsidiary. When these commonly controlled companies present financial information, "combined financial statements . . . are more meaningful than . . . separate statements" (ARB No. 51, "Consolidated Financial Statements," par. 22).

When combined financial statements are presented, intercompany transactions and profits or losses must be eliminated. When combining balance sheets, all components are combined except for the outstanding stock of the separate entities, which is presented separately. The shareholders' equity section of the 1983 combined balance sheet of AMP Incorporated and Pamcor, Inc. and their subsidiaries was presented as follows:

	1983	1982
Shareholders' equity:		
AMP Incorporated		
Common stock, without par value—		
Authorized 50,000,000 shares, issued 37,440,000 shares	$ 12,480	$ 12,480
Pamcor, Inc.		
Common stock, par value $1.00 per share—		
Authorized and issued, 20,000 shares	20	20
Other capital	27,235	26,262
Cumulative translation adjustments	(39,439)	(24,665)
Retained earnings	853,845	748,085
	854,141	762,182
Less—Treasury stock, at cost	53,288	47,685
Total shareholders' equity	$ 800,853	$ 714,497

In the notes to combined financial statements, the principles of combination were explained as follows:

> The financial statements of AMP and Pamcor and their subsidiaries (all wholly owned with one exception) are combined, as each company is owned beneficially by identical shareholders. Intercompany and affiliated company accounts are eliminated in the combination.

19.49 INVESTOR AND INVESTEE TRANSACTIONS. There are situations where a parent–subsidiary relationship exists and the subsidiary issues additional shares to someone other than its parent. In these circumstances, the parent's percentage interest in the subsidiary decreases, and the book balance of its investment may change, depending on the price at which the new stock is sold.

Assume that on January 2, 1989, Company "P" owns a 90% interest in Company "S" whose balance sheet on that date is as follows:

Assets	$10,000
Liabilities	$ 1,000
Stockholders' equity	9,000
Total	$10,000

Company "S" has outstanding 1,000 shares of which Company "P" owns 900 shares; each share has a book value of $9 ($9,000 ÷ 1,000). Further assume that, when Company "P" acquired its shares, there was no goodwill; therefore at January 2, 1989, its investment account has a balance of $8,100 (90% × $9,000).

(a) Investee Sale at Book Value. Assume Company "S" sells 500 shares to the public on January 2, 1989 at its book value of $9 a share or $4,500. The outstanding shares therefore increase to 1,500 and the balance sheet of Company "S" is as follows:

Assets	$14,500
Liabilities	$ 1,000
Stockholders' equity	13,500
Total	$14,500

Company "P's" ownership dropped to 60% (900 shares of 1,500 outstanding) but 60% of $13,500 still equals $8,100, and the transaction does not affect the carrying value of the investor's investment.

(b) Investee Sale in Excess of Book Value. If Company "S" sells the 500 shares for $10 a share ($1 over book value) or $5,000, the result is different. After the sale, the balance sheet of Company "S" is as follows:

Assets	$15,000
Liabilities	$ 1,000
Stockholders' equity	14,000
Total	$15,000

Under these circumstances, Company P's investment account should reflect a balance of 60% of $14,000 or $8,400. The increase represents 60% of $500 (the amount paid in excess of book value). This increase is not an item of income nor is it an item to be credited to retained earnings. It is a capital transaction; the investment account must be increased by $300 and the corresponding credit is to an additional paid-in capital account.

(c) Investee Sale below Book Value. If Company "S" sells the 500 shares below book value— $7 a share or $3,500—a different situation exists. After the sale, the balance sheet of Company "S" is as follows:

Assets	$13,500
Liabilities	$ 1,000
Stockholders' equity	12,500
Total	$13,500

Under these circumstances, Company "P's" investment account should reflect a balance of 60% of $12,500 or $7,500. The decrease represents 60% of $1,000 (the amount paid below book value). Company "P" therefore must reduce its investment account by $600 and reduce additional paid-in capital by a similar amount. If there is not a sufficient balance in the additional paid-in capital account of Company "P," the excess must be applied to a reduction of retained earnings.

(d) SAB No. 51. The SEC, in this bulletin, stated that where the investee sales are not part of a planned reorganization, it would permit the investor to recognize the gain or loss in its income statement as a separate line item.

(e) No Parent Subsidiary Relationship. If the investor company owns more than 20% but 50% or less of the outstanding voting stock of the investee, the same treatment must be accorded investee transactions in its own stock. However, if the investor's interest falls below 20%, no adjustment is made to the investment account (APB Opinion No. 18, "The Equity Method of Accounting for Investments in Common Stock," par. 19(b)).

If an investor company initially owns less than 20% of the voting stock of the investee and in a subsequent period increases its percentage ownership to 20% or more, either by its actions or by the actions of the investee, "the investment, results of operations (current and prior periods presented), and retained earnings of the investor should be adjusted retroactively in a manner consistent with the accounting for a step-by-step acquisition of a subsidiary" (APB Opinion No. 18, par. 19(m)). The mechanics of a step-by-step acquisition of a subsidiary are explained in ARB No. 51 (par. 10) and reported in Chapter 7 of the *Handbook*.

19.50 ACCOUNTING FOR CERTAIN MARKETABLE SECURITIES. SFAS No. 12 prescribes the accounting for marketable securities if the investor has less than a 20% interest in the investee and therefore does not follow the provisions of APB Opinion No. 18. The Statement requires the investor to calculate the total cost and the total market value at the balance sheet date for all marketable securities classified as long-term and to make a similar calculation for these securities that are classified as current. If the total market value of the securities classified as long term is less than their total cost, a valuation allowance must be established to reflect the temporary decline in value of this long-term portfolio.

If a valuation allowance is established, paragraph 11 of SFAS No. 12 requires that:

> Accumulated changes in the valuation allowance for a marketable equity securities portfolio included in non-current assets or in an unclassified balance sheet shall be included in the equity section of the balance sheet and shown separately.

19.51 TRANSLATION ADJUSTMENTS. SFAS No. 52, "Foreign Currency Translation," states that when translating foreign currency financial statements where that currency is the functional currency into the reporting currency, a translation adjustment results. This adjustment (gain or loss) is reported as a separate component in the stockholders' equity section.

19.52 PENSION LIABILITIES. SFAS No. 87, "Employers' Accounting for Pensions," requires that companies recognize in their balance sheet an additional minimum liability for pension costs in certain circumstances. In these circumstances, an intangible asset is recognized but not in excess of any unrecognized prior service cost. The difference between the intangible asset and the additional minimum liability, net of any tax benefits, is a debit to stockholders' equity, reported as a separate component.

DISCLOSURE OF CHANGES IN STOCKHOLDERS' EQUITY

APB Opinion No. 12, "Omnibus Opinion—1967" (par. 10), requires that:

> When both financial position and results of operations are presented, disclosure of changes in the separate accounts comprising stockholders' equity (in addition to retained earnings) and of the changes in the number of shares of equity securities during at least the most recent annual fiscal period . . . is required to make the financial statements sufficiently informative. Disclosure of such changes may take the form of separate statements or may be made in the basic financial statements or notes thereto.

HARSCO CORPORATION
Consolidated Statements of Changes in Shareholders' Equity
for the years 1988, 1987, and 1986

	Common Stock		Additional Paid-in	Cumulative Translation	Retained
	Issued	Treasury	Capital	Adjustments	Earnings
	(All dollars in thousands, except per share)				
Balances, January 1, 1986 (issued 31,383,914 shares; treasury 1,536,914 shares)	$39,230	$ 14,808	$67,640	$(6,642)	$382,267
Net income					46,401
Cash dividends declared, $.94 per share					(27,903)
Translation adjustments, net of $405 deferred income taxes				438	
Acquired during the year, 556,437 shares		13,934			
Stock options exercised, 59,453 shares	67		622		
Other, 25 shares, net	7	(9)	(1)		
Balances, December 31, 1986 (issued 31,442,989 shares; treasury 2,092,948 shares)	39,304	28,733	68,261	(6,204)	400,765
Net income					63,289
Cash dividends declared, $1.03 per share					(29,371)
Translation adjustments, net of $1,720 deferred income taxes				2,375	
Acquired during the year, 2,229,800 shares		66,239			
Stock options exercised, 43,757 shares	54		473		
Other, 395 shares, net		(10)	1		
Balances, December 31, 1987 (issued 31,486,746 shares; treasury 4,322,353 shares)	39,358	94,962	68,735	(3,829)	434,683
Net income					31,103
Cash dividends declared, $1.14 per share					(30,197)
Translation adjustments, net of $(38) deferred income taxes				(65)	
Acquired during the year, 744,000 shares		23,860			
Stock options exercised, 14,525 shares	19		256		
Other, 906 shares, net		(22)	3		
Balances, December 31, 1988 (issued 31,501,271 shares; treasury 5,065,447 shares)	$39,377	$118,800	$68,994	$(3,894)	$435,589

See accompanying notes to consolidated financial statements (notes not provided in this illustration).

Exhibit 19.1. Statement of changes in shareholders' equity.

Companies disclose changes in stockholders' equity in various ways. A method which corporations are using more frequently is the statement of changes in shareholders' equity. Exhibit 19.1 is an example of this statement.

An alternative method is to present a statement of income and retained earnings and to disclose in the notes to financial statements a schedule of the changes in the other components of stockholders' equity.

SOURCES AND SUGGESTED REFERENCES

Accounting Principles Board, "Status of Accounting Research Bulletins," APB Opinion No. 6, AICPA, New York, 1965.

——, "Reporting the Results of Operations," APB Opinion No. 9, AICPA, New York, 1966.

——, "Omnibus Opinion—1966," APB Opinion No. 10, AICPA, New York, 1966.

——, "Omnibus Opinion—1967," APB Opinion No. 12, AICPA, New York, 1967.

——, "Accounting for Convertible Debt and Debt Issued with Stock Purchase Warrants," APB Opinion No. 14, AICPA, New York, 1969.

——, "Earnings per Share," APB Opinion No. 15, AICPA, New York, 1969.

——, "The Equity Method of Accounting for Investments in Common Stock," APB Opinion No. 18, AICPA, New York, 1971.

——, "Accounting Changes," APB Opinion No. 20, AICPA, New York, 1971.

——, "Interest on Receivables and Payables," APB Opinion No. 21, AICPA, New York, 1971.

——, "Accounting for Stock Issued to Employees," APB Opinion No. 25, AICPA, New York, 1972.

——, "Accounting for Nonmonetary Transactions," APB Opinion No. 29, AICPA, New York, 1973.

——, "Basic Concepts and Accounting Principles Underlying Financial Statements of Business Enterprises," APB Statement No. 4, AICPA, New York, 1970.

American Bar Association, Committee on Corporate Laws of Section of Corporation, Banking and Business Law: Model Business Corporation Act, American Law Institute—American Bar Association Committee on Continuing Professional Education, Philadelphia, PA, 1975.

American Institute of Ceritified Public Accountants, "Restatement and Revision of Accounting Research Bulletins," Accounting Research Bulletin No. 43, AICPA, New York, 1953.

——, "Review and Resume," Accounting Terminology Bulletin No. 1, AICPA, New York, 1953.

——, "Discontinuance of Dating Earned Surplus," Accounting Research Bulletin No. 46, AICPA, New York, 1956.

——, "Consolidated Financial Statements," Accounting Research Bulletin No. 51, AICPA, New York, 1959.

——, "Accounting Practices for Certain Employee Stock Ownership Plans," Statement of Position 76-3, AICPA, New York, 1976.

Financial Accounting Standards Board, "Accounting for Stock Appreciation Rights and Other Variable Stock Option or Award Plans," FASB Interpretation No. 28, FASB, Stamford, CT, 1978.

——, "Treatment of Stock Compensation Plans in EPS Computations," FASB Interpretation No. 31, FASB, Stamford, CT, 1980.

——, "Determining the Measurement Date for Stock Option, Purchase, and Award Plans Involving Junior Stock," FASB Interpretation No. 38, FASB, Stamford, CT, 1984.

——, "Accounting for Compensation Plans Involving Certain Rights Granted to Employees," Invitation to Comment, FASB, Stamford, CT, 1984.

——, "Objectives of Financial Reporting by Business Enterprises," Statement of Financial Accounting Concepts No. 1, FASB, Stamford, CT, 1978.

——, "Qualitative Characteristics of Accounting Information," Statement of Financial Accounting Concepts No. 2, FASB, Stamford, CT, 1980.

——, "Recognition and Measurement in Financial Statements of Business Enterprises," Statement of Financial Accounting Concepts No. 5, FASB, Stamford, CT, 1984.

——, "Elements of Financial Statements," Statement of Financial Accounting Concepts No. 6, FASB, Stamford, CT, 1985.

——, "Accounting for Contingencies," Statement of Financial Accounting Standards No. 5, FASB, Stamford, CT, 1975.

——, "Accounting for Certain Marketable Securities," Statement of Financial Accounting Standards No. 12, FASB, Stamford, CT, 1975.

——, "Prior Period Adjustments," Statement of Financial Accounting Standards No. 16, FASB, Stamford, CT, 1977.

——, "Disclosure of Long-Term Obligations," Statement of Financial Accounting Standards No. 47, FASB, Stamford, CT, 1981.

——, "Foreign Currency Translation," Statement of Financial Accounting Standards No. 52, FASB, Stamford, CT, 1981.

——, "Employer's Accounting for Pensions," Statement of Financial Accounting Standards No. 87, FASB, Stamford, CT, 1985.

——, "Accounting for Income Taxes," Statement of Financial Accounting Standards No. 96, FASB, Stamford, CT, 1987.

——, "Accounting for the Conversion of Stock Options into Incentive Stock Options as a Result of the Economic Recovery Tax Act of 1981," FASB Technical Bulletin No. 82-2, FASB, Stamford, CT, 1982.

——, "Accounting for a Purchase of Treasury Shares at a Price Significantly in Excess of the Current Market Price of the Shares and the Income Statement Classification of Costs Incurred in Defending against a Takeover Attempt," FASB Technical Bulletin No. 85-6, FASB, Stamford, CT, 1985.

Griffin, Charles H., Williams, Thomas H., and Larson, Kermit D., *Advanced Accounting,* 4th ed., Irwin, Homewood, IL, 1980.

Kieso, Donald E., and Weygandt, Jerry J., *Intermediate Accounting,* 6th ed., Wiley, New York, 1989.

Melcher, Beatrice, "Stockholders' Equity," Accounting Research Study No. 15, AICPA, New York, 1973.

Securities and Exchange Commission, "Accounting Rules," Regulations S-X, SEC, Washington, DC.

——, "Accounting for Sales of Stock by Subsidiary," Staff Accounting Bulletin No. 51, SEC, Washington, DC, 1983.

——, "Views Concerning Accounting for Contingent Warrants in Connection with Sales Agreements with Certain Major Customers," Staff Accounting Bulletin No. 57, SEC, Washington, DC, 1984.

——, "Increasing Role Preferred Stock," Staff Accounting Bulletin No. 68, SEC, Washington, DC, 1987.

——, "Views Regarding Certain Matters Relating to Quasi Reorganizations, Including Deficit Eliminations," Staff Accounting Bulletin No. 78, SEC, Washington, DC, 1988.

Shohet, Jack, and Rikert, Richard, eds., *Accounting Trends and Techniques,* 42nd ed., AICPA, New York, 1988.

PART **IV**

SPECIALIZED INDUSTRIES

CHAPTER 20

OIL, GAS, AND OTHER NATURAL RESOURCES

Paul Ray Williams, CPA

Coopers & Lybrand

Richard D. Dole, CPA

Coopers & Lybrand

CONTENTS

INTRODUCTION

Accounting for oil and gas activities can be extremely complex because it encompasses a wide variety of business strategies and vehicles. The industry's diversity developed in response to the risk involved in the exploration process, the volatility of prices, and the fluctuations in supply and demand for oil and gas. In addition to having a working knowledge of accounting procedures, the oil and gas accountant should be familiar with the operating characteristics of companies involved in oil and gas activities and understand the impact of individual transactions.

Oil and gas activities cover a wide spectrum—ranging from exploration activities to the refining, transportation, and marketing of products to consumers. Since SEC accounting rules regulate exploration and production activities more stringently, this chapter deals primarily with the SEC aspect of oil and gas accounting. Accounting for refining activities is similar in many ways to other process manufacturing businesses. Likewise, transportation and marketing do not differ significantly from one end product to another.

OIL AND GAS EXPLORATION AND PRODUCING OPERATIONS

Oil- and gas-producing activities begin with the search for prospects—parcels of acreage that management thinks may contain economically viable oil or gas formations. For the most likely prospects, the enterprise may contract with a geological and geophysical (G&G) company to test and assess the subsurface formations and their depths. Based on the G&G studies, the enterprise evaluates the various prospects, rejecting some and accepting others as suitable for acquisition of lease rights (prospecting may be done before or after obtaining lease rights).

Specialists called **landmen** may be used to obtain lease rights. A landman is in effect a lease broker who searches titles and negotiates with property owners. Although the landman may be part of the company's staff, oil and gas companies often acquire lease rights to properties through independent landmen. Consideration for leasing the mineral rights usually includes a bonus (an immediate cash payment to the lessor) and a royalty interest retained by the lessor (a specified percentage of subsequent production minus applicable taxes).

Once the leases have been obtained and the rights and obligations of all parties have been determined, exploratory drilling begins. Because drilling costs run to hundreds of thousands or millions of dollars, many companies reduce their capital commitment and related risks by seeking others to participate in **joint venture arrangements.** Participants in a joint venture are called **joint interest owners;** one owner, usually the enterprise that obtained the leases, acts as operator. The operator manages the venture and reports to the other, nonoperator participants. The operator initially pays the drilling costs and then bills those costs to the nonoperators. In some cases, the operator may collect these costs from nonoperators in advance.

The operator acquires the necessary supplies and subcontracts with a drilling company for drilling the well. The drilling time may be a few days, several months, or even a year or longer depending on many factors, particularly well depth and location. When the hole reaches the desired depth, various instruments are lowered that "**log the well**" to detect the presence of oil or gas. The joint interest owners evaluate the drilling and logging results to determine whether sufficient oil or gas can be extracted to justify the cost of completing the well. If the evaluation is negative, the well is plugged and abandoned as a **dry hole.** If sufficient quantities of crude oil or natural gas (hydrocarbons) appear to be present, the well is completed and equipment is installed to extract and separate the hydrocarbons from the water coming from the underground reservoir. Completion costs often equal or exceed the initial drilling costs.

Before production begins (sometimes even before the well is drilled), the enterprise selects oil and gas purchasers and negotiates sales contracts. To transport the oil or gas from the well, a trunk line may be built to the nearest major pipeline; crude oil also may be stored in tanks at the production site and removed later by truck. Generally, the various parties prepare and sign division orders, which are revenue distribution contracts specifying each party's share of revenues. If the division order specifies that the purchaser is to pay all revenues to the operator, the operator must distribute the appropriate amounts to the other joint interest owners and the lessor(s).

20.1 FACTORS DETERMINING SUCCESS OR FAILURE OF EXPLORATION ACTIVITIES.
The various factors that determine the success or failure of oil and gas exploration activities

include many uncertainties, some of which are discussed below. These factors set the oil and gas industry apart from other capital-intensive industries.

- *Anticipated Success of Drilling.* According to figures compiled by the American Petroleum Institute and the American Association of Petroleum Geologists, only 15% to 20% of exploratory wells have traditionally been successful, whereas the success rate for development wells (wells in areas known to contain oil or gas) approximates 80%. In addition to the risks associated with finding commercial quantities of oil and gas, exploration activities are affected by drilling risks such as stuck drill pipes, blowouts, and improper completions.

- *Taxation.* A substantial portion of the revenues from the sale of crude oil and natural gas goes directly or indirectly to the federal and state governments in the form of severance taxes, ad valorem taxes, and income taxes. In the late 1970s, Congress enacted the **Windfall Profit Tax** on domestic crude oil. On August 25, 1988, the Windfall Profit Tax was repealed for all crude oil removed after that date. After the various taxes, royalties to the landowner, and production costs have been deducted, the producer's income from the sale of crude oil and natural gas may be only a small percentage of gross revenues.

- *Product Price and Marketability.* U.S. producers typically do not encounter problems selling the oil they produce. Although the price received is not controlled by the U.S. government, it is dependent, in part, on prices set by the **Organization of Petroleum Exporting Countries (OPEC)**. The OPEC countries control a very high percentage of the free world's oil reserves, thus giving them significant impact on the price of oil. The increase of oil prices in the late 1970s and early 1980s had twofold impact—conservation was encouraged and exploration for oil reserves outside the OPEC countries increased. As a result, OPEC's market share of world oil sales dropped significantly from 1973 to 1986. With the new reserves in the North Sea, Mexico, and the North Slope displacing OPEC sales, the OPEC countries were forced to curtail production in order to support the price of oil on the world market.

  Currently, OPEC does not appear to have the ability to force oil prices to the levels seen in 1981; however, should OPEC be unable to enforce production limitation on the member countries, the result could be significantly lower prices. The price volatility in 1986 was the result of such a situation.

  Marketability of natural gas varies significantly in different areas of the United States. Producers of natural gas are dependent on the needs of the pipeline company that purchases and transports natural gas in the area. In the past, the pipeline companies have curtailed or completely stopped purchasing natural gas from some wells during periods of excess supply. The U.S. government no longer regulates the price of most natural gas. Since natural gas is not as easily stored as oil and transportation methods are also more limited, the price may vary significantly depending on the time of year. For example, the demand for natural gas is usually much stronger during winter, and prices may increase during this period. Natural gas prices are controlled to some extent by oil prices because a large proportion of users can switch back and forth between oil and gas, depending on prices.

- *Timing of Production.* How quickly oil and gas are produced directly affects the payback period of an investment and its financial success or failure. The timing of production varies with the geologic characteristics of the reservoir and the marketability of the product. Reservoirs may contain the same gross producible reserves, yet the timing of production causes significant differences in the present value of the future revenue stream.

- *Acreage and Drilling Costs.* The availability of quality exploration acreage, drilling personnel, and supplies has increased, whereas the related costs have dropped significantly since the boom period of the late 1970s and early 1980s.

ACCOUNTING FOR JOINT OPERATIONS

Oil- and gas-producing activities are recorded in the same general manner as most other activities that use manual or automated revenue, accounts payable, and general ledger systems. There are significant differences in the data gathering and reporting requirements, however, depending on whether the entity is an operator or a nonoperator. The two major accounting systems unique to oil- and gas-producing activities are the **joint interest billing system** and the **revenue distribution system.** The operator's joint interest billing system must properly calculate and record the operator's net cost as well as the costs to be billed to the nonoperators. Likewise, the revenue distribution system should properly allocate cash receipts among venture participants; this entails first recording the amounts payable to the participants and later making the appropriate payments.

As discussed previously, joint interest operations evolved because of the need to share the financial burden and risks of oil- and gas-producing activities. Joint operations typically take the form of a simple joint venture evidenced by a formal agreement, generally referred to as an operating agreement. The operating agreement defines the geographic area involved, designates which party will act as operator of the venture, defines how revenue and expenses will be divided, and sets forth the rights and responsibilities of all parties to the agreement. The agreement also establishes how the operator is to bill the nonoperators for joint venture expenditures and provides nonoperators with the right to conduct "**joint interest audits**" of the operator's accounting records.

Accounting for joint operations is basically the same as accounting for operations when a property is completely owned by one party, except that in joint operations, revenues and expenses are divided among all of the joint venture partners. The following section discusses accounting for joint operations, first from the operator's standpoint and then from the nonoperators' perspective.

20.2 OPERATOR ACCOUNTING. The operator typically records revenue and expenses for a well on a 100%, or "gross," basis and then allocates the revenue and expenses to the nonoperators based on ownership percentages maintained in the division order and joint interest master files. The usual approach is first to record the full invoice or remittance advice amount and then to use a contra or clearing account that sets up the amounts due from or to the nonoperators. Recording transactions by means of contra accounts facilitates generation of information that management uses to review operations on a gross basis.

Before drilling and completing a well, the operator prepares an **authorization for expenditure (AFE)** itemizing the estimated costs to drill and complete the well. Although AFEs are normally required by the operating agreement, they are so useful as a capital budgeting tool that they are routinely used for all major expenditures by oil and gas companies, even if no joint venture exists. In addition to AFEs, the operator's field supervisor or engineer at the well site prepares a daily drilling report, which is an abbreviated report of the current status and the drilling or completion activity of the past 24 hours. That report may be compared with a drilling report prepared by the drilling company (also called a "tour" report). Some daily drilling reports indicate estimated cumulative costs incurred to date.

For shallow wells that are quickly and easily drilled, the AFE subsidiary ledger, combined with the daily drilling report, may provide the basis for the operator's estimate of costs incurred but not invoiced. For other wells, however, the engineering department prepares an estimate of cumulative costs incurred through year-end as a basis for recording the accrual and, if material, the commitments for future expenditures. Since an oil and gas company's accruable liabilities are primarily costs related to wells in progress, the engineering estimates may in some instances replace the auditor's usual tests for unrecorded liabilities in this area.

The operator normally furnishes the nonoperators with a monthly summary billing that shows the amount owed the operator on a property-by-property basis. The summary billing is accompanied by a separate joint operating statement for each property. The joint operating statement contains a description of each expenditure and shows the total expenditures for the property. The statement also shows the allocation of expenditures among the joint interest participants. The operator does not always furnish copies of third-party invoices supporting items appearing on the joint interest billing, but the third-party invoices can be examined and copied during the nonoperators' audit of the joint account. The operator may also furnish the nonoperators a production report and at a later date remit checks to the nonoperators for their share of production.

20.3 NONOPERATOR ACCOUNTING.   From the nonoperators' standpoint, the accounting for joint operations is basically the same as that followed by the operator. It is not unusual for a company to act as an operator on some properties and a nonoperator on others. To be able to make comparisons and evaluations that include both types of properties, nonoperators should also record items on a gross basis. A nonoperator should develop a control procedure for reviewing the joint operating statement to determine whether the operator is complying with the joint operating agreement, is billing the nonoperator only valid charges at the appropriate percentages, and is distributing the appropriate share of revenue.

20.4 OTHER ACCOUNTING PROCEDURES.   The operating agreement may permit the operator to charge the joint venture a monthly fixed fee to cover its internal costs incurred in operating the joint venture. Alternatively, the agreement may provide for reimbursement of the operator's actual costs.

The parties in a joint operation may agree either to share costs in a proportion that is different from that used for sharing revenue or to change the sharing percentages after a specific event takes place. Typically, that event is "**payout,**" the point at which certain venturers have recovered their initial investment. All parties involved in joint operations encounter payout situations at some time. Controls must be designed to monitor payout status to ensure that all parties are satisfied that items have been properly allocated in accordance with the joint operating agreement.

ACCEPTABLE ACCOUNTING METHODS

20.5 THE SUCCESSFUL EFFORTS METHOD

(a) Basic Rules.   The following points summarize the major aspects of the **successful efforts method** of accounting for oil and gas property costs:

- The costs of all G&G studies conducted before acquiring a property are charged to expense as incurred.
- Lease acquisition costs for **unproved** properties are initially capitalized. Unproved properties are those on which no economically recoverable oil or gas has been demonstrated to exist. Unproved properties are to be assessed for impairment at least annually.
- If an unproved property becomes **impaired** because of such events as pending lease expiration or an unsuccessful exploratory well (dry hole), the loss is recognized and a valuation allowance is established to reflect the property's impairment.
- Once proved reserves are found on a property, the property is considered **proved** and the costs are amortized over the property's producing life based on total proved reserves.
- If both oil and gas are produced from the property, the capital costs are amortized (depleted) on a **unit-of-production** basis. For a property containing both oil and gas reserves, the unit is normally equivalent barrels or mcfs, whereby gas is converted to

equivalent barrels (or barrels are converted to equivalent mcfs) based on relative energy content. The common conversion factor is 6 mcfs to 1 equivalent barrel.

- For a property containing both oil and gas, the unit may reflect either oil or gas if:

    The relative property of oil and gas extracted in the current period is expected to continue in the future, or

    The reflected mineral clearly dominates the other for both current production and reserves.

- Carrying costs required to retain rights to unproved properties (delay rentals, ad valorem taxes, etc.) are charged to expense.

- Exploratory wells are capitalized initially as wells-in-progress and expenses if proved reserves are not found. Successful exploratory wells are capitalized, as are their completion costs (setting casing and other costs necessary to begin producing the well).

- Costs of drilling development wells (even the rare dry ones) are capitalized.

- Costs of successful exploratory wells, along with the costs of drilling development wells on the lease, are amortized over the property's proved developed reserves on:

    A property-by-property basis

    The basis of some reasonable aggregation of properties with a common geologic or structural feature or stratigraphic condition, such as a reservoir or field

    Once production has begun, all regulated production costs are charged to expense.

(b) Exploratory versus Development Well Definition.   Because Reg. S-X requires that the costs of dry exploratory wells be charged to expense, whereas the costs of dry development wells are capitalized, it is important to properly classify wells. Reg. S-X, Rule 4-10, defines the two categories of wells as follows:

- Development Well. A well drilled within the proved area of an oil or gas reservoir to the depth of a stratigraphic horizon known to be productive.

- Exploratory Well. A well drilled to find and produce oil or gas in an unproved area, to find a new reservoir in a field previously found to be productive of oil or gas in another reservoir, or to extend a known reservoir. Generally, an exploratory well is any well that is not a development well, a service well, or a stratigraphic test well.

These definitions may not coincide with those that have been commonly used in the industry (typically, the industry definition of a development well is more liberal than Reg. S-X, Rule 4-10. This results in two problems:

- Improper classification of certain exploratory dry holes as development wells (the problem occurs primarily with stepout or delineation wells drilled at the edge of a producing reservoir.

- Inconsistencies between the drilling statistics found in the forepart of Form 10-K (usually prepared by operational personnel) and the supplementary financial statement information required by SFAS No. 69 (usually prepared by accounting personnel).

(c) Treatment of Costs of Exploratory Wells Whose Outcome Is Undetermined.   As set out below, Reg. S-X, Rule 4-10, effectively curtails expended deferral of the costs of an exploratory well whose outcome has not yet been determined:

(g) *Accounting for the costs of exploratory wells and exploratory-type stratigraphic test wells if the successful efforts method of accounting is followed.* The costs of drilling exploratory wells and the costs of drilling exploratory-type stratigraphic test wells shall be capitalized as part of the reporting entity's uncompleted wells, equipment, and facilities pending determination of whether the well has found proved reserves. If the well has found proved reserves, the capitalized costs of drilling the well shall become part of the entity's wells and related equipment and facilities (even though the well may not be completed as a producing well); if, however, the well has not found proved reserves, the capitalized costs of drilling the well, net of any salvage value, shall be charged to expense. The determination of whether proved reserves are found is usually made on or shortly after completion of drilling the well and the capitalized costs shall either be charged to expense or be reclassified as part of the costs of wells and related equipment facilities at that time. Information that becomes available after the end of the period covered by the financial statements but before those financial statements are issued shall be taken into account in evaluating conditions that existed at the balance sheet date. Occasionally, an exploratory well or an exploratory-type stratigraphic test well may be determined to have found oil and gas reserves, but classification of those reserves as proved cannot be made when drilling is completed. In those cases, one of three subparagraphs set forth below shall apply. Paragraphs (g)(1) and (2) are intended to prohibit, in all cases, the deferral of the costs of exploratory wells that find some oil and gas reserves merely on the chance that some event totally beyond the entity's control will occur, e.g., on the chance that the selling prices of oil and gas will increase sufficiently to result in classification of reserves as proved that are not commercially recoverable at current prices.

(1) *Exploratory wells that find oil and gas reserves in an area requiring a major capital expenditure, such as a trunk-pipeline, before production could begin.* On completion of drilling, an exploratory well may be determined to have found oil and gas reserves, but classification of those reserves as proved depends on whether a major capital expenditure can be justified which, in turn, depends on whether additional exploratory wells find a sufficient quantity of additional reserves. In that case, the cost of drilling the exploratory well shall continue to be carried as an asset pending determination of whether proved reserves have been found only as long as both of the following conditions are met: (i) the well has found a sufficient quantity of reserves to justify its completion as a producing well if the required capital expenditure is made, an (ii) drilling of additional wells is underway or firmly planned for the near future. Otherwise, the exploratory well shall be assumed to be impaired, and its costs shall be charged to expense.

(3) *Exploratory-type stratigraphic test wells that find oil and gas reserves.* On completion of drilling, such a well may be determined to have found oil and gas reserves, but classification of those reserves as proved depends on whether a major capital expenditure (usually a production platform) can be justified which, in turn depends on whether additional exploratory-type stratigraphic test wells find a sufficient quantity of additional reserves. In that case, the cost of drilling the exploratory-type stratigraphic test well shall continue to be carried as an asset pending determination of whether proved reserves have been found only as long as both of the following conditions are met: (i) The well has found a quantity of reserves that would justify its completion for production had it not been simply a stratigraphic test well, and (ii) drilling of the additional exploratory-type stratigraphic test well is underway or firmly planned for the near future. Otherwise, the exploratory-type stratigraphic test well shall be assumed to impaired, and its costs shall be charged to expense.

(d) Successful Efforts Impairment Test. SFAS No. 19 and Reg. S-X, Rule 4-10, address this issue, but they do not require that an impairment provision be recognized for proved properties. SFAS No. 19 (pars. 184 and 209) states the following:

184. Limiting capitalized costs to the estimated value of reserves, which is an integral part of the full cost method of accounting, requires estimation of reserve quantities, production quantities, development costs, production costs, the timing of development and production, selling prices and appropriate discount rates. The uncertainties inherent in those estimates and projections tend to make estimates of reserve values highly subjective, and estimates of value made by trained experts can differ markedly. Under the successful efforts method, the need to limit capitalized costs is much less crucial because the costs of unsuccessful effort, which may represent a large part of the total capitalized costs under the full cost method, will have been charged to expense as incurred or recognized as a loss when the effort was determined to be unsuccessful.

209. As explained in paragraphs 190 and 191, a cost center is not the primary consideration in the capitalized/expense decision under the approach to successful efforts accounting adopted by the Board in this Statement. Under that approach, the assets to which the capitalized acquisition,

exploratory drilling and development costs related are properties, wells, equipment, and facilities. The question of whether to write down the carrying amount of productive assets to an amount expected to be recoverable through future use of those assets is unsettled under present generally accepted accounting principles. This is a pervasive issue that the Board has not addressed. Consequently, this Statement is not intended to change practice by either requiring or prohibiting an impairment test for proved properties or for wells, equipment and facilities that constitute part of an enterprise's oil and gas producing systems.

A number of independent accountants and the SEC believe that some impairment test should be made. They recognize that the following different methods currently in use are considered acceptable:

- Lease-by-lease, prospect-by-prospect, or some other reasonable aggregation.
- Market basket or "successful efforts pool."

Both methods may be computed using the discounted/undiscounted future net revenues. Once a method having a material impact on the financial statements has been applied, the method should be disclosed and applied consistently. Informally, the SEC suggests that the impairment test be based on undiscounted future net revenues.

20.6 THE FULL COST METHOD

(a) Basic Rules.   Under Reg. S-X, Rule 4-10, oil and gas property costs are accounted for as follows:

- All costs associated with property acquisition, exploration and development activities shall be capitalized by *country-wide* cost center. Any internal costs that are capitalized shall be limited to those costs that can be *directly* identified with the acquisition, exploration and development activities undertaken by the reporting entity for its own account, and shall not include any costs related to production, general corporate overhead or similar activities.
- Capitalized costs within a cost center shall be amortized on the unit-of-production basis using proved oil and gas reserves, as follows:

  Costs to be amortized shall include (A) all capitalized costs, less accumulated amortization, excluding the cost of certain unevaluated properties not being amortized; (B) the estimated future expenditures (based on current costs) to be incurred in developing proved reserves; and (C) estimated dismantlement and abandonment costs, net of estimated salvage values.

  Amortization shall be computed on the basis of physical units, with oil and gas converted to a common unit of measure on the basis of their approximate relative energy content, unless economic circumstances (related to the effects of regulated prices) indicated that use of revenue is a more appropriate basis of computing amortization. In the latter case, amortization shall be computed on the basis of current gross revenues from production in relation to future gross revenues (excluding royalty payments and net profits disbursements) based on current prices from estimated future production of proved oil and gas reserves (including consideration of changes in existing prices provided for only by contractual arrangements). The effect on estimated future gross revenues of a significant price increase during the year shall be reflected in the amortization provision only for the period after the price increase occurs.

  In some cases it may be more appropriate to depreciate natural gas cycling and processing plants by a method other than the unit-of-production method.

  Amortization computations shall be made on a consolidated basis, including investees accounted for on a proportionate consolidation basis. Investees accounted for on the equity method shall be treated separately.

(b) Exclusion of Costs From Amortization.   Under Reg. S-X, Rule 4-10, **as originally written** and prior to the issuance of FRR No. 14), the costs of **unusually significant** investments in unproved properties and major development projects could be excluded from capitalized costs to be amortized, subject to the following:

- Costs of acquiring and evaluating unproved properties could be excluded only if the costs incurred were unusually significant in relation to the aggregate costs to be amortized (e.g., the costs of acquiring major offshore leases). All costs of acquiring such properties and related exploration costs could be excluded from the amortization computation until it was determined whether proved reserves were attributable to the properties. Until such a determination was made, the properties were to be assessed individually to ascertain whether impairment had occurred. If the results of the assessment indicated impairment, the amount of the impairment was to be added to the costs to be amortized.
- Costs of major development projects could be excluded from amortization only if unusually significant development cost had to be incurred prior to ascertaining the quantities of proved reserves attributable to the properties under development (e.g., the installation of an offshore drilling platform from which development wells were to be drilled, the installation of improved recovery programs, and similar major projects undertaken in the expectation of significant additions to proved reserves). In such cases, a portion of the development costs identified with such a project could be excluded from the costs to be amortized until the proved reserves added as result of the project were ascertainable or until it was determined that impairment had occurred.

This rule created significant problems and controversy within the industry, principally in defining what constituted an **unusually significant** property. Various positions were taken regarding exclusion:

- Exclusion of only those individual unproved properties whose **acquisition** cost was significant (at least 15% of the net full cost pool).
- Exclusion of individual unproved properties if the acquisition and **related exploration costs to be incurred** in total exceeded 15% of the net full cost pool.
- Exclusion of individual insignificant unproved properties acquired in a bulk purchase where the total cost relating to the unproved properties was significant.

As a result of the controversy over this issue, the SEC amended its original rules in September 1983. FRR No. 14 amended the SEC full cost rules to provide for two alternative methods of computing the amortization base. The amendment is to be applied prospectively for costs incurred in fiscal years beginning after December 15, 1983. The two alternatives are:

- Immediate inclusion of all costs incurred in the amortization base.
- Temporary exclusion of **all** acquisition and exploration costs incurred that directly relate to unevaluated properties and certain costs of major development projects.

Costs incurred in previous fiscal years will continue to be accounted for in the same manner as in prior financial statements. Restatement of previously issued full cost financial statements to conform to the amended rules is not permitted (i.e., a company cannot go back and exclude unproved properties that were previously being amortized). Unevaluated properties are defined as those for which no determination has been made of the existence or nonexistence of proved reserves. Costs that may be excluded are all those costs **directly** related to the unevaluated properties (i.e., leasehold acquisitions costs, delay rentals, G&G, exploratory drilling, and capitalized interest). The cost of exploratory dry holes should be included in the amortization base as soon as the well is deemed dry.

These excluded costs must be assessed for impairment annually, either:

- Individually for each significant property (cost exceeds 10% of the net full cost pool), which conforms to the old rule.
- In the aggregate for insignificant properties using the successful efforts approach discussed in Rule 4-10(c)(1) (i.e., by transferring the excluded property costs into the amortization base ratably on the basis of such factors as the primary lease terms of the properties, the average holding period, and the relative proportion of properties on which proved reserves have been found previously).

(c) The Full Cost Ceiling Test

(i) For each cost center capitalized costs, less accumulated amortization and related deferred income taxes, shall not exceed an amount (the cost center ceiling) equal to the sum of: (A) the present value of the future net revenues from estimated production of proved oil and gas reserves as defined in paragraph (k)(6) of this section; plus (B) the cost of properties not being amortized pursuant to paragraph (i)(3)(ii) of this section; plus (c) the lower of cost or estimated fair value of unproved properties included in the costs being amortized; less (D) income tax effects related to differences between the book and tax basis of the properties involved.

(ii) If unamortized costs capitalized within a cost center, less related deferred income taxes, exceed the cost center ceiling, the excess shall be charged to expense and separately disclosed during the period in which the excess occurs. Amounts thus required to be written off shall not be reinstated for any subsequent increase in the cost center ceiling.

Two other unique aspects of the full cost ceiling test are:

- *Ceiling Test Exemption for Purchases of Proved Properties.* The client might purchase proved properties for more than the present value of estimated future net revenues, causing net capitalized costs to exceed the cost center ceiling on the date of purchase. To avoid the writedown, the client may request from the SEC staff a temporary (usually one year) waiver of applying the ceiling test. The client must be prepared to demonstrate that the purchased properties' additional value exists beyond reasonable doubt. For more details see SAB No. 47, Topic 12, D-3a.

  The avoidance of a writedown must be adequately disclosed, but the subsequent events should not be considered in the required disclosures of the client's proved reserves and future net revenues. For more details, see SAB No. 47, Topic 12, D-3b.

NATURAL GAS BALANCING

Accounting techniques are basically the same whether revenue is generated by selling crude oil or natural gas. However, the following unique situations arise in accounting for natural gas revenue:

- Operating agreements that permit joint venture participants to take their proportional share of gas production "in-kind" may result in multiple purchase contracts for a single well's production.
- Differences in marketing strategy may result in one joint venture participant's electing to sell gas on the spot market whereas other joint venture participants elect not to sell at the prevailing spot price.
- Unitization of gas properties can result in multiple purchase contracts, giving rise to production "in-kind" issues.

The above situations can cause a production imbalance situation. For example, if the joint venture participants own equal working interests in a well, and one company decides to sell gas on the spot market but the other company declines to sell due to a low spot price (or other factors), the company selling gas will receive 100% of revenue after paying the royalty interests. The selling company is in an overproduced capacity with respect to the well (the company is entitled to 50% of the gas after royalties but will receive 100%).

Natural gas balancing is rapidly becoming one of the most important accounting issues in the oil and gas industry. Gas-producing companies must choose between the following methods in accounting for gas revenues:

- Sales method.
- Entitlements method.

20.7 SALES METHOD.   Under the sales method, the company recognizes revenue and a receivable for the volume of gas sold, regardless of ownership of the property. For example, if Company A owns a 50% net revenue interest in a gas property but sells 100% of the production in a given month, the company would recognize 100% of the revenue generated. In a subsequent month, if Company A sells no gas (and the other owners "make up" the imbalance), Company A would recognize zero revenue.

Although this method is rather simple from a revenue accounting standpoint, it presents other problems. Regardless of the revenue method chosen, the operator will issue joint interest billing statements for expenses based on the ownership of the property. Depending on the gas-balancing situation, the sales method may present a problem with the matching of revenues and expenses in a period. If a significant imbalance exists at the end of an accounting period, the accountant may be required to analyze the situation and record additional expenses (or reduce expenses depending on whether the property is overproduced or underproduced).

20.8 ENTITLEMENTS METHOD.   Under the entitlements method, the company recognizes revenue based on the volume of sales to which it is entitled by its ownership interest. For example, if Company A owns a 50% net revenue interest but sells 100% of the production in a given month, the company would recognize 50% of the revenue generated. Company A would recognize a receivable for 100% of the revenue with the difference being recorded in a deferred revenue account. When the imbalance is corrected, the deferred revenue account will be zero, thus indicating that the property is "in balance."

This method correctly matches revenues and expenses but presents another accounting issue. If a property is significantly imbalanced, Company A may find itself in a position that reserves are insufficient to bring the well back to a balanced condition. If Company A is underproduced in this situation, a deferred charge may be recorded in the asset category that has a questionable realization. In addition, the company is really under- or overproduced in terms of volumes (measured in cubic feet) of gas. A value per cubic foot is assigned based on the sale price at the period of imbalance. If the price is significantly different when the correction occurs, the deferred revenue may not show a zero balance in the accounting records.

20.9 GAS BALANCING EXAMPLE

Facts: Company A owns a 50% net revenue.
  Gas sales for January are 5,000 mcf @ $2.00.
  Gas sales for February are 5,000 mcf @ $2.00.
  In January, Company A sells 100% of gas production to its purchaser.
  In February, Company sells zero gas to its purchaser.

JANUARY ACCOUNTING ENTRIES

Under the Sales Method	Debit	Credit
Accounts receivable, gas sales	$10,000	
Gas revenue		$10,000

Under the Entitlements Method

Accounts receivable, gas sales	$10,000	
Gas revenue		$ 5,000
Deferred revenue		$ 5,000

FEBRUARY ACCOUNTING ENTRIES

Under the Sales Method	No entries are recorded

Under the Entitlements Method

Deferred revenue	$ 5,000	
Gas revenue		$ 5,000

FINANCIAL STATEMENT DISCLOSURES

SFAS No. 69 details supplementary disclosure requirements for the oil and gas industry, most of which are required only by public companies. Both public and nonpublic companies, however, must provide a description of the accounting method followed and the manner of disposing of capitalized costs. Audited financial statements filed with the SEC must include supplementary disclosures, which fall into three categories:

- Historical cost data relating to acquisition, exploration, development, and production activity.
- Proved reserve quantities.
- Standardized measure of discounted future net cash flows relating to proved oil and gas reserve quantities (also known as SMOG [standardized measure of oil and gas]).

The supplementary disclosures are required of companies with significant oil- and gas-producing activities; significant is defined as 10% or more of revenue, operating results, or identifiable assets. The statement provides that the disclosures are to be provided as supplemental data; thus they need not be audited. The disclosure requirements are described in detail in the statement, and examples are provided in an appendix to SFAS No. 69. If the supplemental information is not audited, it must be clearly labeled as unaudited. Various SASs impose certain responsibilities on the auditor, as the following discussion points out.

Because of the reliance placed on the supplementary reserve information by financial statement users and because certain audited information (i.e., amortization and impairment information) is derived directly from the reserve data, the auditor should have a basic understanding of how reserve data are developed and of the inherent risks involved.

Proved oil and gas reserves are the estimated quantities of crude oil, natural gas, and natural gas liquids that have been demonstrated with reasonable certainty, based on geological and engineering data, to be recoverable in future years from known reservoirs under existing economic and operating conditions (i.e., using prices and costs in effect on the date of the estimate). Proved reserves are inherently imprecise because of the uncertainties and limitations of the data available.

Most large companies and many medium-sized companies have qualified engineers on their staffs to prepare oil and gas reserve studies. Many also use outside consultants to make independent reviews. Other companies, which do not have sufficient operations to justify a full-time engineer, engage outside engineering consultants to evaluate and estimate their oil and gas reserves. Usually, reserve studies are reviewed and updated at least annually to take into account new discoveries and adjustments of previous estimates.

Auditors of oil and gas companies generally use the reserve studies prepared by petroleum engineers. Because of the expertise required to estimate reserve quantities, however, the auditor typically does not have the necessary qualifications to fully evaluate an engineer's estimate. Therefore, as required by SAS No. 11 (AU § 336), and a related Auditing Interpretation (AU § 9336.03), the auditor ordinarily should be satisfied as to the reputation and independence of the outside engineer or the qualifications and experience of the in-house engineer who estimates the reserve quantities. The auditor should also understand the engineer's methods and assumptions used in preparing the reserve estimates, test the accounting data provided to the engineer, and consider whether the engineer's report supports the related information in the financial statements.

In addition, if the supplementary reserve information required by SFAS No. 69 is included in the financial statements being reported on, SAS No. 27 (AU § 553), as supplemented by SAS No. 45 (AU § 557), requires that the auditor:

- Inquire about management's understanding of the specific requirements for disclosure of supplementary oil and gas reserve information.
- Inquire about the qualifications of the person who estimated the reserve quantity information.
- Compare recent production with reserve estimates for significant properties and inquire about disproportionate ratios.
- Compare reserve quantity information with information used for the amortization computation and inquire about differences.
- Inquire about the methods used to calculate the SMOG disclosures.
- Inquire whether the methods and bases for estimating reserve information are documented and whether the information is current.

SOURCES AND SUGGESTED REFERENCES

American Institute of Certified Public Accountants, "Statements on Auditing Standards," New York, 1989.

Financial Accounting Standards Board, "Financial Accounting and Reporting by Oil and Gas Producing Companies," Statement of Financial Accounting Standards No. 19, FASB, Stamford, CT, 1977.

———, "Disclosures about Oil and Gas Producing Activities," Statement of Financial Accounting Standards No. 69, FASB, Stamford, CT, 1982.

O'Reilly, V. M., *Montgomery's Auditing,* 11th ed., Wiley, New York, 1990.

Securities and Exchange Commission, "Oil and Gas Producers—Full Cost Accounting Practices; Amendment of Rules," Financial Reporting Release No. 14, SEC, Washington, DC, 1983.

———, "Interpretations Relating to Oil and Gas Accounting," Staff Accounting Bulletin No. 47, SEC, Washington, DC, 1982.

———, "Financial Accounting and Reporting for Oil and Gas Producing Activities Pursuant to the Federal Securities Laws and the Energy Policy and Conservation Act of 1975," Regulation S-X, Rule 4-10, SEC, Washington, DC, 1975.

CHAPTER 21

REAL ESTATE AND CONSTRUCTION

Richard J. Behrens, CPA
Price Waterhouse

CONTENTS

THE REAL ESTATE INDUSTRY

21.1 OVERVIEW. The real estate industry does not easily lend itself to definition. It encompasses a variety of interests (developers, investors, lenders, tenants, homeowners, corporations, etc.) with a divergence of objectives (tax benefits, security, long-term appreciation, etc.). The industry is also a tool of the federal government's income tax policies (evidenced by the rules on mortgage interest deductions and restrictions on "passive" investment deductions).

Although the industry consists primarily of many private developers and builders, the economic dynamics of the 1980s have brought new forces to the real estate industry. The most important of these forces are:

1. *The U.S. Government.* The savings and loan and bank crises have left the federal government the single largest property owner in the United States.

2. *Foreign Investment.* Long-term growth, stability, and favorable exchange rates have led many foreign investors to U.S. real estate. Notwithstanding the recent publicity given the influx of Japanese investment, European investors, who have been in the United States for a longer time, outpace the amount of Japanese investment and will probably continue to do so for the foreseeable future.

3. *U.S. Pension Funds and Insurance Companies.* Driven by similar forces as the foreign investors, these companies have been increasing the amount of their funds invested in real estate. The amount to be invested in real estate in the next 10 years has been estimated to be in excess of $100 billion.

4. *Corporations.* In response to the pressures on corporate management to increase shareholder value, many corporations have been forced to focus more attention on their real estate assets. This is easy to understand because occupancy (real estate) costs are generally the second largest expense for a company after personnel costs. In fact, many of the takeovers of the 1980s were based upon the underutilization of the target corporations' assets.

As we move through the 1990s, many uncertainties face the real estate industry. Overbuilding and the extent of repossessed assets held by the U.S. government will continue to plague the recovery of many real estate markets. The sources and extent of available capital for financings and construction will continue to be a concern. This concern will be centered on the ability and willingness of the financing institutions in various markets to reenter the real estate lending arena and the willingness of foreign investors to fill a void left by the financial institutions.

SALES OF REAL ESTATE

21.2 ANALYSIS OF TRANSACTIONS. Real estate sales transactions are generally material to the entity's financial statements. "Is the earnings process complete?" is the primary question that must be answered regarding such sales. In other words, assuming a legal sale, have the risks and rewards of ownership been transferred to the buyer?

21.3 ACCOUNTING BACKGROUND. Prior to 1982, guidance related to real estate sales transactions was contained in two AICPA Accounting Guides: "Accounting for Retail Land Sales" and "Accounting for Profit Recognition on Sales of Real Estate." These guides had been supplemented by several AICPA Statements of Position that provided interpretations.

In October 1982, SFAS No. 66, "Accounting for Sales of Real Estate," was issued as part of the FASB project to incorporate, where appropriate, AICPA Accounting Guides into FASB Statements. This Statement adopted the specialized profit recognition principles of the above guides.

The FASB formed the Emerging Issues Task Force (EITF) in 1984 for the early identification of emerging issues. The EITF has dealt with many issues affecting the real estate industry, including issues that clarify or address SFAS No. 66.

Regardless of the seller's business, SFAS No. 66 covers all sales of real estate, determines the timing of the sale and resultant profit recognition, and deals with seller accounting only. This Statement does not discuss nonmonetary exchanges, cost accounting and most lease transactions or disclosures.

The two primary concerns under SFAS No. 66 are:

- Has a sale occurred?
- Under what method and when should profit be recognized?

The concerns are answered by determining the buyer's initial and continuing investment and the nature and extent of the seller's continuing involvement. The guidelines used in determining these criteria are complex and, within certain provisions, arbitrary. Companies dealing with these types of transactions are often faced with the difficult task of analyzing the exact nature of a transaction in order to determine the appropriate accounting approach. Only with a thorough understanding of the details of a transaction can the accountant perform the analysis required to decide on the appropriate accounting method.

21.4 CRITERIA FOR RECORDING A SALE.   SFAS No. 66 (pars. 44–50) discussed separate rules for Retail Land Sales (see section 21.9). The following information is for all real estate sales other than retail land sales. To determine whether profit recognition is appropriate, a test must first be made to determine whether a sale may be recorded. Then there are additional tests related to the buyer's investment and the seller's continued involvement.

Generally, real estate sales should not be recorded prior to **closing.** Since an exchange is generally required to recognize profit, a sale must be consummated. A sale is consummated when all the following conditions have been met:

- The parties are bound by the terms of a contract.
- All consideration has been exchanged.
- Any permanent financing for which the seller is responsible has been arranged.
- All conditions precedent to closing have been performed.

Usually all those conditions are met at the time of closing. On the other hand, they are not usually met at the time of a **contract to sell** or a preclosing.

Exceptions to the "conditions precedent to closing" have been specifically provided for in SFAS No. 66. They are applicable where a sale of property includes a requirement for the seller to perform future construction or development. Under certain conditions, partial sale recognition is permitted during the construction process because the construction period is extended. This exception usually is not applicable to single-family detached housing because of the shorter construction period.

Transactions that should not be treated as sales for accounting purposes because of **continuing seller's involvement** include the following:

- The seller has an option or obligation to repurchase the property.
- The seller guarantees return of the buyer's investment.
- The seller retains an interest as a general partner in a limited partnership and has a significant receivable.
- The seller is required to initiate or support operations or continue to operate the property at its own risk for a specified period or until a specified level of operations has been obtained.

If the criteria for recording a sale are not met, either the deposit, financing, lease, or profit sharing (co-venture) methods should be used, depending on the substance of the transaction.

21.5 ADEQUACY OF DOWN PAYMENT.   Once it has been determined that a sale can be recorded, the next test relates to the **buyer's investment.** For the seller to record full profit recognition, the buyer's down payment must be adequate in size and in composition.

(a) Size of Down Payment.   The minimum down payment requirement is one of the most important provisions in SFAS No. 66. Appendix A of this pronouncement, reproduced here as Exhibit 21.1, lists minimum down payments ranging from 5% to 25% of sales value based on usual loan limits for various types of properties. These percentages should be considered

	Minimum Initial Investment Payment Expressed as a Percentage of Sales Value
Land:	
Held for commercial, industrial, or residential development to commence within two years after sale	20%
Held for commercial, industrial, or residential development after two years	25%
Commercial and industrial property:	
Office and industrial buildings, shopping centers, and so forth:	
Properties subject to lease on a long-term lease basis to parties having satisfactory credit rating; cash flow currently sufficient to service all indebtedness	10%
Single-tenancy properties sold to a user having a satisfactory credit rating	15%
All other	20%
Other income-producing properties (hotels, motels, marinas, mobile home parks, and so forth):	
Cash flow currently sufficient to service all indebtedness	15%
Start-up situations or current deficiencies in cash flow	25%
Multifamily residential property:	
Primary residence:	
Cash flow currently sufficient to service all indebtedness	10%
Start-up situations or current deficiencies in cash flow	15%
Secondary or recreational residence:	
Cash flow currently sufficient to service all indebtedness	10%
Start-up situations or current deficiencies in cash flow	25%
Single-family residential property (including condominium or cooperative housing)	
Primary residence of buyer	5%[a]
Secondary or recreational residence	10%[a]

[a]As set forth in Appendix A, "if collectibility of the remaining portion of the sales price cannot be supported by reliable evidence of collection experience, the minimum initial investment shall be at least 60% of the difference between the sales value and the financing available from loans guaranteed by regulatory bodies, such as the FHA or the VA, or from independent financial institutions.

This 60% test applies when independent first mortgage financing is not utilized and the seller takes a receivable from the buyer for the difference between the sales value and the initial investment. If independent first mortgage financing is utilized, the adequacy of the initial investment on sales of single-family residential property should be determined in accordance with SFAS No. 66 (par. 53).

Exhibit 21.1.   Minimum initial investment requirements. *Source:* **SFAS No. 66, "Accounting for Sales of Real Estate" (Appendix A), FASB, 1982.**

as specific requirements because it was not intended that exceptions be made. Additionally, EITF consensus No. 88-24 "Effect of Various Forms of Financing under FASB Statement No. 66," discusses the impact of the source and nature of the buyer's down payment on profit recognition. Exhibit A to EITF 88-24 has been reproduced here as Exhibit 21.2.

If a newly placed permanent loan or firm permanent loan commitment for maximum financing exists, the minimum down payment must be the higher of (1) the amount derived from Appendix A or (2) the excess of sales value over 115% of the new financing. However, regardless of this test, a down payment of 25% of the sales value of the property is usually considered sufficient to justify the recognition of profit at the time of sale.

Situation	Cash Received by Seller at Closing	Components of Cash Received by Seller at Closing		Assumption of Seller's Nonrecourse Mortgage
		Buyer's Initial Investment	Buyer's Independent 1st Mortgage	
1.	100	20	80	
2.	100	0	100	
3.	20	20		80
4.	0	0		100
5.	20	20		
6.	20	20		
7.	80	20	60	
8.	20	20		60
9.	20	20		
10.	0	0		
11.	0	0		
12.	0	0		
13.	80	0	80	
14.	10	10		
15.	10	10		
16.	90	10	80	
17.	10	10		80
18.	10	10		

[1] First or second mortgage indicated in parentheses.
[2] Seller remains contingently liable.
[3] The profit recognized under the reduced profit method is dependent on various interest rates and payment terms. An example is not presented due to the complexity of those factors and the belief that this method is not frequently used in practice. Under this method, the profit recognized at the consummation of the sale would be less than under the full accrual method, but normally more than the amount under the installment method.

Assumptions:
1. Sales price: $100.
2. Seller's basis in property sold: $70.
3. Initial investment requirement: 20%.
4. All mortgage obligations meet the continuing investment requirements of Statement 66.

Exhibit 21.2.   Examples of the application of the EITF consensus on Issue No. 88-24. *Source:* EITF Issue No. 88-24, "Effect of Various Forms of Financing under FASB Statement No. 66," (Exhibit 88-24A), FASB, 1988.

An example of the down payment test—Appendix A compared to the newly placed permanent loan test—is given below:

ASSUMPTIONS

Initial payment made by the buyer to the seller on sale of an apartment building	$ 200,000
First mortgage recently issued and assumed by the buyer	1,000,000
Second mortgage given by the buyer to the seller at prevailing interest rate	200,000
Stated sales price and sales value	$1,400,000
115% of first mortgage (1.15 × $1,000,000)	1,150,000
Down payment necessary	$ 250,000

Seller Financing[1]	Assumption of Seller's Recourse Mortgage[2]	Recognition under Consensus Paragraph	Profit Recognized at Date of Sale[3]		
			Full Accrual	Installment	Cost Recovery
		#1	30		
		#1	30		
		#1	30		
		#1	30		
80(1)		#2	30		
	80	#2	30		
20(2)		#2	30		
20(2)		#2	30		
20(2)	60	#2	30		
	100	#3		0	0
100(1)		#3		0	0
20(2)	80	#3		0	0
20(2)		#3		10	10
90(1)		#3		3	0
	90	#3		3	0
10(2)		#3		20	20
10(2)		#3		20	20
10(2)	80	#3		3	0

RESULT

Although the down payment required under Appendix A is only $140,000 (10% of $1,400,000), the $200,000 actual down payment is inadequate because the test relating to the newly placed first mortgage requires $250,000.

The down payment requirements must be related to **sales value,** as described in SFAS No. 66 (par. 7). Sales value is the stated sales price increased or decreased for other consideration that clearly constitutes additional proceeds on the sale, services without compensation, imputed interest, and so forth.

Consideration payable for development work or improvements that are the responsibility of the seller should be included in the computation of sales value.

(b) Composition of Down Payment.   The primary acceptable down payment is cash, but additional acceptable forms of down payment are:

- Notes from the buyer (only when supported by irrevocable letters of credit from an independent established lending institution).
- Cash payments by the buyer to reduce previously existing indebtedness.
- Cash payments that are in substance additional sales proceeds, such as prepaid interest that by the terms of the contract is applied to amounts due the seller.

Other forms of down payment that are not acceptable are:

- Other noncash consideration received by the seller, such as notes from the buyer without letters of credit or marketable securities. Noncash consideration constitutes down payment only at the time it is converted into cash.
- Funds that have been or will be loaned to the buyer builder/developer for acquisition, construction, or development purposes or otherwise provided directly or indirectly by the seller. Such amounts must first be deducted from the down payment in determining whether the down payment test has been met. An exemption from this requirement was provided in paragraph 115 of SFAS No. 66, which states that if a future loan on normal terms from a seller who is also an established lending institution bears a fair market interest rate and the proceeds of the loan are conditional on use for specific development of or construction on the property, the loan need not be subtracted in determining the buyer's investment.
- Funds received from the buyer from proceeds of priority loans on the property. Such funds have not come from the buyer and therefore do not provide assurance of collectibility of the remaining receivable; such amounts should be excluded in determining the adequacy of the down payment. In addition, EITF consensus No. 88-24 provides guidelines on the impact that the source and nature of the buyer's initial investment can have on profit recognition.
- Marketable securities or other assets received as down payment will constitute down payment only at the time they are converted to cash.
- Cash payments for prepaid interest that are not in substance additional sales proceeds.
- Cash payments by the buyer to others for development or construction of improvements to the property.

(c) Inadequate Down Payment.   If the buyer's down payment is inadequate, the accrual method of accounting is not appropriate, and either the deposit, installment, or cost recovery method of accounting should be used.

When the sole consideration (in addition to cash) received by the seller is the buyer's assumption of existing nonrecourse indebtedness, a sale could be recorded and profit recognized if all other conditions for recognizing a sale were met. If, however, the buyer assumes recourse debt and the seller remains liable on the debt, he has a risk of loss comparable to the risk involved in holding a receivable from the buyer, and the accrual method would not be appropriate.

EITF consensus No. 88-24 states that the initial and continuing investment requirements for the full accrual method of profit recognition of SFAS No. 66 are applicable unless the seller receives one of the following as the full sales value of the property:

- Cash, without any seller contingent liability on any debt on the property incurred or assumed by the buyer.
- The buyer's assumption of the seller's existing nonrecourse debt on the property.

- The buyer's assumption of all recourse debt on the property with the complete release of the seller from those obligations.
- Any combination of such cash and debt assumption.

21.6 RECEIVABLE FROM THE BUYER.   Even if the required down payment is made, a number of factors must be considered by the seller in connection with a receivable from the buyer. They include:

- Collectibility of the receivable.
- Buyer's continuing investment—amortization of receivable.
- Future subordination.
- Release provisions.
- Imputation of interest.

(a) Assessment of Collectibility of Receivable.   Collectibility of the receivable must be reasonably assured and should be assessed in light of factors such as the credit standing of the buyer (if recourse), cash flow from the property, and the property's size and geographical location. This requirement may be particularly important when the receivable is relatively short term and collectibility is questionable because the buyer will be required to obtain financing. Furthermore, a basic principle of real estate sales on credit is that the receivable must be adequately secured by the property sold.

(b) Amortization of Receivable.   Continuing investment requirements for full profit recognition require that the buyer's payments on its total debt for the purchase price must be at least equal to level annual payments (including principal and interest) based on amortization of the full amount over a maximum term of 20 years for land and over the **customary term of a first mortgage** by an independent established lending institution for other property. The annual payments must begin within 1 year of recording the sale and, to be acceptable, must meet the same composition test as used in determining adequacy of down payments. The customary term of a first mortgage loan is usually considered to be the term of a new loan (or the term of an existing loan placed in recent years) from an independent financial lending institution.

All indebtedness on the property need not be reduced proportionately. However, if the seller's receivable is not being amortized, realization may be in question and the collectibility must be more carefullly assessed. Lump-sum (balloon) payments do not affect the amortization requirement as long as the scheduled amortization is within the maximum period and the minimum annual amortization tests are met.

For example, if the customary term of the mortgage by an independent lender required amortizing payments over a period of 25 years, then the continuing investment requirement would be based on such an amortization schedule. If the terms of the receivable required principal and interest payments on such a schedule only for the first 5 years with a balloon at the end of year 5, the continuing investment requirements are met. In such cases, however, the collectibility of the balloon payment should be carefully assessed.

If the amortization requirements for full profit recognition as set forth above are not met, a reduced profit may be recognized by the seller if the annual payments are at least equal to the total of:

- Annual level payments of principal and interest on a maximum available first mortgage.
- Interest at an appropriate rate on the remaining amount payable by the buyer.

The reduced profit is determined by discounting the receivable from the buyer to the present value of the lowest level of annual payments required by the sales contract excluding

---

Assumptions:

Down payment (meets applicable tests)		$ 150,000
First mortgage note from independent lender at market rate of interest (new, 20 years—meets required amortization)		750,000
Second mortgage notes payable to seller, interest at a market rate is due annually, with principal due at the end of the 25th year (the term exceeds the maximum permitted)		100,000
Stated selling price		$1,000,000

Adjustment required in valuation of receivable from buyer:

Second mortgage payable to seller	$100,000	
Less: present value of 20 years annual interest payments on second mortgage (lowest level of annual payments over customary term of first mortgage—thus 20 years not 25)	70,000	30,000
Adjusted sales value for profit recognition		$ 970,000

The sales value as well as profit is reduced by $30,000.
In some situations profit will be entirely eliminated by this calculation.

Exhibit 21.3.   Calculation of reduced profit.

requirements to pay lump sums. The present value is calculated using an appropriate interest rate, but not less than the rate stated in the sales contract.

The amount calculated would be used as the value of the receivable for the purpose of determining the reduced profit. The calculation of reduced profit is illustrated in Exhibit 21.3.

The requirements for amortization of the receivable are applied cumulatively at the closing date (date of recording the sale for accounting purposes) and annually thereafter. Any excess of down payment received over the minimum required is applied toward the amortization requirements.

(c) Receivable Subject to Future Subordination.   If the receivable is subject to future subordination to a future loan available to the buyer, profit recognition cannot exceed the amount determined under the cost recovery method unless proceeds of the loan are first used to reduce the seller's receivable. Although this accounting treatment is controversial, the cost recovery method is required because collectibility of the sales price is not reasonably assured. The future subordination would permit the primary lender to obtain a prior lien on the property, leaving only a secondary residual value for the seller, and future loans could indirectly finance the buyer's initial cash investment. Future loans would include funds received by the buyer arising from a permanent loan commitment existing at the time of the transaction unless such funds were first applied to reduce the seller's receivable as provided for in the terms of the sale.

The cost recovery method is not required if the receivable is subordinate to a previous mortgage on the property existing at the time of sale.

(d) Release Provisions.   Some sales transactions have provisions releasing portions of the property from the liens securing the debt as partial payments are made. In this situation, full profit recognition is acceptable only if the buyer must make, at the time of each release, cumulative payments that are adequate in relation to the sales value of property not released.

(e) Imputation of Interest.   Careful attention should be given to the necessity for imputation of interest under APB Opinion No. 21, "Interest on Receivables and Payables," since it could have a significant effect on the amount of profit or loss recognition. As stated in the first paragraph of APB Opinion No. 21: "The use of an interest rate that varies from prevailing interest rates warrants evaluation of whether the face amount and the stated interest rate of a note or obligation provide reliable evidence for properly recording the exchange and subsequent related interest."

If imputation of interest is necessary, the mortgage note receivable should be adjusted to its present value by discounting all future payments on the notes using an imputed rate of interest at the prevailing rates available for similar financing with independent financial institutions. A distinction must be made between first and second mortgage loans because the appropriate imputed rate for a second mortgage would normally be significantly higher than the rate for a first mortgage loan. It may be necessary to obtain independent valuations to assist in the determination of the proper rate.

(f) Inadequate Continuing Investment.   If the criteria for recording a sale has been met but the tests related to the collectibility of the receivable as set forth herein are not met, the accrual method of accounting is not appropriate and the installment or cost recovery method of accounting should be used. These methods are discussed in section 21.10 of this chapter.

21.7 SELLER'S CONTINUED INVOLVEMENT.   A seller sometimes continues to be involved over long periods of time with property legally sold. This involvement may take many forms such as participation in future profits, financing, management services, development, construction, guarantees, and options to repurchase. With respect to profit recognition when a seller has continued involvement, the two key principles are as follows:

- A sales contract should not be accounted for as a sale if the seller's continued involvement with the property includes the same kinds of risk as does ownership of property.
- Profit recognition should follow performance and in some cases should be postponed completely until a later date.

(a) Participation Solely in Future Profits.   A sale of real estate may include or be accompanied by an agreement that provides for the seller to participate in future operating profits or residual values. As long as the seller has no further obligations or risk of loss, profit recognition on the sale need not be deferred. A receivable from the buyer is permitted if the other tests for profit recognition are met, but no costs can be deferred.

(b) Option or Obligation to Repurchase the Property.   If the seller has an **option or obligation to repurchase** property (including a buyer's option to compel the seller to repurchase), a sale cannot be recognized (SFAS No. 66, par. 26). However, neither a commitment by the seller to assist or use his best efforts (with appropriate compensation) on a resale nor a right of first refusal based on a bona fide offer by a third party would preclude sale recognition. The accounting to be followed depends on the repurchase terms. EITF consensus No. 86-6 discusses accounting for a sale transaction when antispeculation clauses exist. A consensus was reached that the contingent option would not preclude sale recognition if the probability of buyer noncompliance is remote.

When the seller has an obligation or an option that is reasonably expected to be exercised to repurchase the property at a price higher than the total amount of the payments received and to be received, the transaction is a **financing arrangement** and should be accounted for under the financing method. If the option is not reasonably expected to be exercised, the deposit method is appropriate.

In the case of a repurchase obligation or option at a lower price, the transaction usually is, in substance, a lease or is part lease, part financing and should be accounted for under the lease method. Where an option to repurchase is at a market price to be determined in the future, the transaction should be accounted for under the deposit method or the profit-sharing method.

(c) General Partner in a Limited Partnership with a Significant Receivable. When the seller is a general partner in a limited partnership and has a significant receivable related to the property, the transaction would not qualify as a sale. It should usually be accounted for as a profit-sharing arrangement. A significant receivable is one that is in excess of 15% of the maximum first lien financing that could be obtained from an established lending institution for the property sold.

(d) Lack of Permanent Financing. The buyer's investment in the property cannot be evaluated until adequate permanent financing at an acceptable cost is available to the buyer. If the seller must obtain or provide this financing, obtaining the financing is a prerequisite to a sale for accounting purposes. Even if not required to do so, the seller may be presumed to have such an obligation if the buyer does not have financing and the collectiblity of the receivable is questionable. The deposit method is appropriate if lack of financing is the only impediment to recording a sale.

(e) Guaranteed Return of Buyer's Investment. SFAS No. 66 (par. 28) states: ''If the seller guarantees return of the buyer's investment, . . . the transaction shall be accounted for as a financing, leasing or profit-sharing arrangement.''

Accordingly, if the terms of a transaction are such that the buyer may expect to recover the initial investment through assured cash returns, subsidies, and net tax benefits, even if the buyer were to default on debt to the seller, the transaction is probably not in substance a sale.

(f) Other Guaranteed Returns on Investment—Other than Sale-Leaseback. When the seller guarantees cash returns on the buyer's investment, the accounting method to be followed depends on whether the guarantee is for an extended or limited period and whether the seller's expected cost of the guarantee is determinable.

(i) Extended Period. SFAS No. 66 states that when the seller contractually guarantees cash returns on investments to the buyer for an extended period, the transaction should be accounted for as a financing, leasing, or profit-sharing arrangement. An ''extended period'' was not defined but should at least include periods that are not limited in time or specified lengthy periods, such as more than 5 years.

(ii) Limited Period. If the guarantee of a return on the buyer's investment is for a limited period, SFAS No. 66 indicates that the deposit method of accounting should be used until such time as operation of the property covers all operating expenses, debt service, and contractual payments. At that time, profit should be recognized based on performance (see section 21.10). A ''limited period'' was not defined but is believed to relate to specified shorter periods, such as 5 years or less.

Irrespective of the above, if the guarantee is determinable or limited, sale and profit recognition may be appropriate if reduced by the maximum exposure to loss as described below.

(iii) Guarantee Amount Determinable. If the amount can be reasonably estimated, the seller should record the guarantee as a cost at the time of sale, thus either reducing the profit or increasing the loss on the transaction.

(iv) Guarantee Amount Not Determinable. If the amount cannot be reasonably estimated, the transaction is probably in substance a profit-sharing or co-venture arrangement.

(v) Guarantee Amount Not Determinable But Limited.   If the amount cannot be reasonably estimated but a maximum cost of the guarantee is determinable, the seller may record the maximum cost of the guarantee as a cost at the time of sale, thus either reducing the profit or increasing the loss on the transaction. Alternatively, the seller may account for the transaction as if the guarantee amount is not determinable. Implications of a seller's guarantee of cash flow on an operating property that is not considered a sale-leaseback arrangement are discussed in section 21.7 (j).

(g) Guaranteed Return on Investment—Sale-Leaseback.   A guarantee of cash flow to the buyer sometimes takes the form of a leaseback arrangement. Since the earnings process in this situation has not usually been completed, profits on the sale should generally be deferred and amortized.

Accounting for a sale-leaseback of real estate is governed by SFAS No. 13, "Accounting for Leases," as amended by SFAS No. 28, "Accounting for Sales with Leasebacks," SFAS No. 98, "Accounting for Leases: Sale-Leaseback Transactions Involving Real Estate," and SFAS No. 66. SFAS No. 98 specifies the accounting by a seller-lessee for a sale-leaseback transaction involving real estate, including real estate with equipment. SFAS No. 98 provides that:

- A sale-leaseback transaction involving real estate, including real estate with equipment, must qualify as a sale under the provisions of SFAS No. 66 as amended by SFAS No. 98, before it is appropriate for the seller-lessee to account for the transaction as a sale. If the transaction does not qualify as a sale under SFAS No. 66, it should be accounted for by the deposit method or as a financing transaction.

- A sale-leaseback transaction involving real estate, including real estate with equipment, that includes any continuing involvement other than a normal leaseback in which the seller-lessee intends to actively use the property during the lease should be accounted for by the deposit method or as a financing transaction.

- A lease involving real estate may not be classified as a sales-type lease unless the lease agreement provides for the transfer of title to the lessee at or shortly after the end of the lease term. Sales-type leases involving real estate should be accounted for under the provisions of SFAS No. 66.

(i) Profit Recognition.   Profits should be deferred and amortized in a manner consistent with the classification of the leaseback:

- If the leaseback is an operating lease, deferred profit should be amortized in proportion to the related gross rental charges to expense over the lease term.

- If the leaseback is a capital lease, deferred profit should be amortized in proportion to the amortization of the leased asset. Effectively, the sale is treated as a financing transaction. The deferred profit can be presented gross; the author's preference is to offset the deferred profit in the balance sheet against the capitalized asset.

In situations where the leaseback covers only a minor portion of the property sold or the period is relatively minor compared to the remaining useful life of the property, it may be appropriate to recognize all or a portion of the gain as income. Sales with minor leasebacks should be accounted for based on the separate terms of the sale and the leaseback unless the rentals called for by the leaseback are unreasonable in relation to current market conditions. If rentals are considered to be unreasonable, they must be adjusted to a reasonable amount in computing the profit on the sale.

The leaseback is considered to be minor when the present value of the leaseback based on reasonable rentals is 10% or less of the fair value of the asset sold. If the leaseback is not considered to be minor (but less than substantially all of the use of the asset is retained through a leaseback) profit may be recognized to the extent it exceeds the present value of the minimum lease payments (net of executory costs) in the case of an operating lease or the recorded amount of the leased asset in the case of a capital lease.

(ii) Loss Recognition. Losses should be recognized immediately to the extent that the undepreciated cost (net carrying value) exceeds the fair value of the property. Fair value is frequently determined by the selling price from which the loss on the sale is measured. Many sale-leasebacks are entered into as a means of financing, or for tax reasons, or both. The terms of the leaseback are negotiated as a package. Because of the interdependence of the sale and concurrent leaseback, the selling price in some cases is not representative of fair value. It would not be appropriate to recognize a loss on the sale that would be offset by future cost reductions as a result of either reduced rental costs under an operating lease or depreciation and interest charges under a capital lease. Therefore, to the extent that the fair value is greater than the sale price, losses should be deferred and amortized in the same manner as profits.

(h) Services without Adequate Compensation. A sales contract may be accompanied by an agreement for the seller to provide management or other services without adequate compensation. Compensation for the value of the services should be imputed, deducted from the sales price, and recognized over the term of the contract. See discussion of implied support of operations in section 21.7 (j) below if the contract is noncancelable and the compensation is unusual for the services to be rendered.

(i) Development and Construction. A sale of undeveloped or partially developed land may include or be accompanied by an agreement requiring future seller performance of development or construction. In such cases, all or a portion of the profit should be deferred. If there is a lapse of time between the sale agreement and the future performance agreement, deferral provisions usually apply if definitive development plans existed at the time of sale and a development contract was anticipated by the parties at the time of entering into the sales contract.

In addition, SFAS No. 66 (par. 41) provides that "The seller is involved with future development or construction work if the buyer is unable to pay amounts due for that work or has the right under the terms of the arrangement to defer payment until the work is done."

If the property sold and being developed is an operating property (such as an apartment complex, shopping center, or office building) as opposed to a nonoperating property (such as a land lot, condominium unit, or single-family detached home), section 21.7 (j) below may also apply.

(i) Completed Contract Method. If a seller is obligated to develop the property or construct facilities and total costs and profit cannot be reliably estimated (e.g., because of lack of seller experience or nondefinitive plans), all profit, including profit on the sale of land, should be deferred until the contract is completed or until the total costs and profit can be reliably estimated. Under the completed contract method, all profit, including profit on the sale of land, is deferred until the seller's obligations are fulfilled.

(ii) Percentage of Completion Method (Cost-Incurred Method). If the costs and profit can be reliably estimated, profit recognition over the improvement period on the basis of costs incurred (including land) as a percentage of total costs to be incurred is required. Thus, if the land was a principal part of the sale and its market value greatly exceeded cost, part of the profit that can be said to be related to the land sale is deferred and recognized during the development or construction period.

The same rate of profit is used for all seller costs connected with the transaction. For this

Assumptions:

1. Sale of land for commercial development—$475,000.
2. Development contract—$525,000.
3. Down payment and other buyer investment requirements met.
4. Land costs—$200,000.
5. Development costs $500,000 (reliably estimated)—$325,000 incurred in initial year.

Calculation of profit to be recognized in initial year:

Sale of land	$ 475,000
Development contract price	525,000
Total sales price	1,000,000
Costs:	
Land	200,000
Development	500,000
Total costs	700,000
Total profit anticipated	$ 300,000
Cost incurred through end of initial year:	
Land	$ 200,000
Development	325,000
Total	$ 525,000
Profit to be recognized in initial year − 525,000 ÷ 700,000 × 300,000 =	$ 225,000

Exhibit 21.4.   Percentage of completion, or cost-incurred, method.

purpose, the cost of development work, improvements, and all fees and expenses that are the responsibility of the seller should be included. The buyer's initial and continuing investment tests, of course, must be met with respect to the total sales value. Exhibit 21.4 illustrates the cost incurred method.

(j) Initiation and Support of Operations.   If the property sold is an operating property, as opposed to a nonoperating property, deferral of all or a portion of the profit may be required under SFAS No. 66 (pars. 28–30). These paragraphs establish guidelines not only for **stated support** but also for **implied support.**

Although the implied support provisions do not usually apply to undeveloped or partially developed land, they do apply if the buyer has commitments to construct operating properties and there is stated or implied support.

Assuming that the criteria for recording a sale and the test of buyer's investment are met, the following sets forth guidelines for profit recognition where there is stated or implied support.

(i) Stated Support.   A seller may be required to support operations by means of a guaranteed return to the buyer. Alternatively, a guarantee may be made to the buyer that there will be no negative cash flow from the project, buy may not guarantee a positive return on the buyer's investment. For example, EITF consensus No. 85-27 ''Recognition of Receipts from Made-Up Rental Shortfalls,'' considers the impact of a master lease guarantee. The broad exposure that such a guarantee creates has a negative impact on profit recognition.

(ii) Implied Support.   The seller may be presumed to be obligated to initiate and support operations of the property sold, even in the absence of specified requirements in the sale

contract or related document. The following conditions under which support is implied are described in footnote 10 of SFAS No. 66:

- A seller obtains an interest as general partner in a limited partnership that acquires an interest in the property sold.
- A seller retains an equity interest in the property, such as an undivided interest or an equity interest in a joint venture that holds an interest in the property.
- A seller holds a receivable from a buyer for a significant part of the sales price and collection of the receivable is dependent on the operation of the property.
- A seller agrees to manage the property for the buyer on terms not usual for the services to be rendered and which is not terminable by either seller or buyer.

(iii) Stated or Implied Support.   When profit recognition is appropriate in the case of either stated or implied support, the following general rules apply:

- Profit is recognized on the ratio of costs incurred to total costs to be incurred. Revenues for gross profit purposes include rent from operations during the rent-up period; costs include land and operating expenses during the rent-up period as well as other costs.
- As set forth in SFAS No. 66 (par. 30):

  [S]upport shall be presumed for at least two years from the time of initial rental unless actual rental operations cover operating expenses, debt service, and other contractual commitments before that time. If the seller is contractually obligated for a longer time, profit recognition shall continue on the basis of performance until the obligation expires.

- Estimated rental income should be adjusted by reducing estimated future rent receipts by a safety factor of $33^1/_3\%$ unless signed lease agreements have been obtained to support a projection higher than the rental level thus computed. As set forth in SFAS No. 66 (par. 29), when signed leases amount to more than $66^2/_3\%$ of estimated rents, no additional safety factor is required but only amounts under signed lease agreements can be included.

(k) Partial Sales.   A partial sale includes the following:

- A sale of an interest in real estate.
- A sale of real estate where the seller has an equity interest in the buyer (e.g., a joint venture or partnership).
- A sale of a condominium unit.

(i) Sale of an Interest in Real Estate.   Except for operating properties, profit recognition is appropriate in a sale of a partial interest if all the following conditions exist:

- Sale is to an independent buyer.
- Collection of sales price is reasonably assured.
- The seller will not be required to support the property, its operations, or related obligations to an extent greater than its proportionate interest.
- Buyer does not have preferences as to profits or cash flow. (If the buyer has such preferences, the cost recovery method is required.)

In the case of a sale of a partial interest in operating properties, if the conditions set forth in the preceding paragraph are met, profit recognition must reflect an adjustment for the implied presumption that the seller is obligated to support the operations.

(ii) Seller Has Equity Interest in Buyer.   No profit may be recognized if the seller controls the buyer. If seller does not control the buyer, profit recognition (to the extent of the other investors' proportionate interests) is appropriate if all other necessary requirements for profit recognition are satisfied. The portion of the profit applicable to the equity interest of the seller/ investor should be deferred until such costs are charged to operations by the venture. Again, with respect to a sale of operating properties, a portion of the profit relating to other investors' interests may have to be spread as described in section 21.7 (j) because there is an implied presumption that the seller is obligated to support the operations.

21.8 SALES OF CONDOMINIUMS.   Although the definition of "condominium" varies by state, the term generally is defined as a multiunit structure in which there is fee simple title to individual units combined with an undivided interest in the common elements associated with the structure. The common elements are all areas exclusive of the individual units, such as hallways, lobbies, and elevators.

A **cooperative** is contrasted to a condominium in that ownership of the building is generally vested in the entity, with the respective stockholders of the entity having a right to occupy specific units. Operation, maintenance, and control of the building are exercised by a governing board elected by the owners. This section covers only sales of condominium units.

(a) Criteria for Profit Recognition.   The general principles of accounting for profit on sales of condominiums are essentially those previously discussed for sales of real estate in general. The following criteria must be met prior to recognition of any profit on the sale of a dwelling unit in a condominium project:

- All parties must be bound by the terms of the contract. For the buyer to be bound, the buyer must be unable to require a refund. Certain state and federal laws require appropriate filings by the developer before the sales contract is binding; otherwise, the sale may be voidable at the option of the buyer.
- All conditions precedent to closing, except completion of the project, must be performed.
- An adequate cash down payment must be received by the seller. The minimum down payment requirements are 5% for a primary residence and 10% for a secondary or recreational residence.
- The buyer must be required to adequately increase the investment in the property annually; the buyer's commitment must be adequately secured. Typically, a condominium buyer pays the remaining balance from the proceeds of a permanent loan at the time of closing. If, however, the seller provides financing, the same considerations as other sales of real estate apply concerning amortization of the buyer's receivable.
- The developer must not have an option or obligation to repurchase the property.

(b) Methods of Accounting.   Sales of condominium units are accounted for by using the closing (completed contract) method or the percentage of completion method. Most developers use the **closing method.**

Additional criteria must be met for the use of the **percentage of completion** method:

- The developer must have the ability to estimate costs not yet incurred.
- Construction must be beyond a preliminary stage of completion. This generally means at least beyond the foundation stage.
- Sufficient units must be sold to assure that the property will not revert to rental property.
- The developer must be able to reasonably estimate aggregate sales proceeds.

(i) Closing Method.   This method involves recording the sale and related profit at the time a unit closes. Since the unit is completed, actual costs are used in determining profit to be recognized.

All payments or deposits received prior to closing are accounted for as a liability. Direct selling costs may be deferred until the sale is recorded. Where the seller is obligated to complete construction of common areas or has made guarantees to the condominium association, profit should be recognized based on the relationship of costs already incurred to total estimated costs, with a portion deferred until the future performance is completed.

(ii) Percentage of Completion Method.   This method generally involves recording sales at the date a unit is sold and recognizing profit on units sold as construction proceeds. As a result, this method allows some profit recognition during the construction period. Although dependent on estimates, this method may be considered preferable for some long-term projects. A lack of reliable estimates, however, would preclude the use of this method.

Profit recognition is based on the percentage of completion of the project multiplied by the gross profit arising from the units sold. Percentage of completion may be determined by using either of the following alternatives:

- The ratio of costs incurred to date to total estimated costs to be incurred. These costs could include land and common costs or could be limited to construction costs. The costs selected for inclusion should be those that most clearly reflect the earnings process.
- The percentage of completed construction based on architectural plans or engineering studies.

Under either method of accounting, if the total estimated costs exceed the estimated proceeds, the total **anticipated loss** should be charged against income in the period in which the loss becomes evident so that no anticipated losses are deferred to future periods. See further discussion of this method in the section entitled "Construction Contracts."

(c) Estimated Future Costs.   As previously mentioned, future costs to complete must be estimated under either the closing method or the percentage of completion method. Estimates of future costs to complete are necessary to determine net realizable value of unsold units. Estimated future costs should be based on adequate architectural and engineering studies and should include reasonable provisions for:

- Unforeseen costs in accordance with sound cost estimation practices.
- Anticipated cost inflation in the construction industry.
- Costs of offsite improvements, utility facilities, and amenities (to the extent that they will not be recovered from outside third parties).
- Operating losses of utility operations and recreational facilities. (Such losses would be expected to be incurred for a relatively limited period of time—usually prior to sale of facilities or transfer to some public authority.)
- Other guaranteed support arrangements or activities to the extent that they will not be recovered from outside parties or be the responsibility of a future purchaser.

Estimates of amounts to be recovered from any sources should be discounted to present value as of the date the related costs are expected to be incurred.

Estimated costs to complete and the allocation of such costs should be reviewed at the end of each financial reporting period, with costs revised and reallocated as necessary on the basis of current estimates, as recommended in SFAS No. 67, "Accounting for Costs and Initial Rental Operations of Real Estate Projects." How to record the effects of changes in estimates depends on whether full revenues have been recorded or whether reporting of the revenue has been deferred due to an obligation for future performance or otherwise.

When sales of condominiums are recorded in full, it may be necessary to accrue certain estimated costs not yet incurred and also related profit thereon. Adjustments of accruals for costs applicable to such previously recognized sales, where deferral for future performance was not required, must be recognized and charged to costs of sales in the period in which they become known. See section 21.8 (b) (ii) for further discussion.

In many cases, sales are not recorded in full (such as when the seller has deferred revenue because of an obligation for future performance to complete improvements and amenities of a project). In these situations, the adjustments should not affect previously recorded deferred revenues applicable to future improvements but should be recorded prospectively in the current and future periods. An increase in the estimate of costs applicable to deferred revenues will thus result in profit margins lower than those recorded on previous revenues from the project.

An exception exists, however, when the revised total estimated costs exceed the applicable deferred revenue. If that occurs, the total anticipated loss should be charged against income in the period in which the need for adjustment becomes evident.

In addition, an increase in estimated costs to complete without comparable increases in market value could raise questions as to whether the estimated total costs of the remaining property exceed the project's net realizable value.

APB Opinion No. 20, "Accounting Changes," has been interpreted to permit both the cumulative catch-up method and the prospective method of accounting for changes in accounting estimates. It should be noted that SFAS No. 67 (pars. 42–43) requires the prospective method.

21.9 RETAIL LAND SALES.   Retail land sales, a unique segment of the real estate industry, is the retail marketing of numerous lots subdivided from a larger parcel of land. The relevant accounting guidance originally covered by the AICPA Industry Accounting Guide, "Accounting for Retail Land Sales," and now included in SFAS No. 66, applies to retail lot sales on a volume basis with down payments that are less than those required to evaluate the collectibility of casual sales of real estate. Wholesale or bulk sales of land and retail sales from projects comprising a small number of lots, however, are subject to the general principles for profit recognition on real estate sales.

(a) Criteria for Recording a Sale.   Sales should not be recorded until:

- The customer has made all required payments and the period of cancellation with refund has expired.
- Aggregate payments (including interest) equal or exceed 10% of contract sales price.
- The selling company is clearly capable of providing land improvements and offsite facilities promised as well as meeting all other representations it has made.

If these conditions are met, either the accrual or the installment method must be used. If the conditions are not met, the deposit method of accounting should be used.

(b) Criteria for Accrual Method.   The following tests for the use of accrual method should be applied on a project-by-project basis:

- The seller has fulfilled the obligation to complete improvements and to construct amenities or other facilities applicable to the lots sold.
- The receivable is not subject to subordination to new loans on the property, except subordination for home construction purposes under certain conditions.

- The **collection experience** for the project indicates that collectibility of receivable balances is reasonably predictable and that 90% of the contracts in force 6 months after sales are recorded will be collected in full. A down payment of at least 20% shall be an acceptable indication of collectibility.

To predict collection results of current sales, there must be satisfactory **experience on prior sales** of the type of land being currently sold in the project. In addition, the collection period must be sufficiently long to allow reasonable estimates of the percentage of sales that will be fully collected. In a new project, the developers' experience on prior projects may be used if they have demonstrated an ability to successfully develop other projects with the same characteristics (environment, clientele, contract terms, sales methods) as the new project.

Collection and **cancellation experience** within a project may differ with varying sales methods (such as telephone, broker, and site visitation sales). Accordingly, historical data should be maintained with respect to each type of sales method used.

Unless all conditions for use of the accrual method are met for the entire project, the installment method of accounting should be applied to all recorded sales of the project.

(c) Accrual Method.   Revenues and costs should be accounted for under the accrual method as follows:

- The **contract price** should be recorded as gross sales.
- Receivables should be discounted to reflect an appropriate interest rate using the criteria established in APB Opinion No. 21.
- An **allowance for contract cancellation** should be recorded and deducted from gross sales to derive net sales.
- Cost of sales should be calculated based on net sales after reductions for sales reasonably expected to cancel.

(d) Percentage of Completion Method.   Frequently, the conditions for use of the accrual method are met, except the seller has not yet completed the improvements, amenities, or other facilities required by the sales contract. In this situation the percentage of completion method should be applied provided both of the following conditions are met:

- There is a reasonable expectation that the land can be developed for the purposes represented.
- The project's improvements have progressed beyond preliminary stages, and there are indications that the work will be completed according to plan. Indications that the project has progressed beyond the preliminary stage include the following:

    Funds for the proposed improvements have been expended.

    Work on the improvements has been initiated.

    Engineering plans and work commitments exist relating to the lots sold.

    Access roads and amenities such as golf courses, clubhouses, and swimming pools have been completed.

In addition, there shall be no indication of significant delaying factors such as the inability to obtain permits, contractors, personnel, or equipment, and estimates of costs to complete and extent of progress toward completion shall be reasonably dependable.

The following general procedures should be used to account for revenues and costs under the percentage of completion method of accounting:

- The amount of revenue recognized (discounted where appropriate pursuant to APB

Opinion No. 21) is based on the relationship of costs already incurred to the total estimated costs to be incurred.

- Costs incurred and to be incurred should include land, interest and project carrying costs incurred prior to sale, selling costs, and an estimate for future improvement costs.

Estimates of future improvement costs should be reviewed at least annually. Changes in those estimates do not lead to adjustment of deferred revenue applicable to future improvements that has been previously recorded unless the adjusted total estimated costs exceeds the applicable revenue. When cost estimates are revised, the relationship of the two elements included in the revenue not yet recognized—cost and profit—should be recalculated on a cumulative basis to determine future income recognition as performance takes place. If the adjusted total estimated cost exceeds the applicable deferred revenue, the total anticipated loss should be charged to income. When anticipated losses on lots sold are recognized, the enterprise should also consider recognizing a loss on land and improvements not yet sold.

Future performance costs such as roads, utilities, and amenities may represent a significant obligation for a retail land developer. Estimates of such costs should be based on adequate engineering studies, appropriately adjusted for anticipated inflation in the local construction industry, and should include reasonable estimates for unforeseen costs.

(e) Installment and Deposit Methods.   If the criteria for the accural or percentage of completion methods are not satisfied, the installment or deposit method may be used. See section 21.10 below for a general discussion of these methods.

When the conditions required for use of the percentage of completion method are met on a project originally recorded under the installment method, the percentage of completion method of accounting should be adopted for the entire project (current and prior sales). The effect should be accounted for as a change in accounting estimate due to different circumstances. See section 21.8 (c) for further discussion of methodology.

21.10 ALTERNATE METHODS OF ACCOUNTING FOR SALES.   As previously discussed, in some circumstances the accrual method is not appropriate and other methods must be used. It is not always clear which method should be used or how it should be applied. Consequently, it is often difficult to determine the appropriate method and whether alternative ones are acceptable.

The methods prescribed where the buyer's initial or continuing **investment is inadequate** are the deposit, installment, cost recovery, and reduced profit methods.

The methods prescribed for a transaction that cannot be considered a sale because of the **seller's continuing involvement** are the financing, lease, and profit sharing (or co-venture) methods.

(a) Deposit Method.   When the substance of a real estate transaction indicates that a sale has not occurred, for accounting purposes, as a result of the buyer's inadequate investment, recognition of the sale should be deferred and the deposit method used. This method should be continued until the conditions requiring its use no longer exist. For example, when the down payment is so small that the substance of the transaction is an **option arrangement,** the sale should not be recorded.

All cash received under the deposit method (including down payment and principal and interest payments by the buyer to the seller) should be reported as a deposit (liability). An exception is interest received that is not subject to refund may appropriately offset carrying charges (property taxes and interest on existing debt) on the property. Note also the following related matters:

- Notes receivable arising from the transaction should not be recorded.

- The property and any related mortgage debt assumed by the buyer should continue to be reflected on the seller's balance sheet, with appropriate disclosure that such properties and debt are subject to a sales contract. Even nonrecourse debt assumed by the buyer should not be offset against the related property.
- Subsequent payments on the debt assumed by the buyer become additional deposits and thereby reduce the seller's mortgage debt payable and increase the deposit liability account until a sale is recorded for accounting purposes.
- Depreciation should be continued.

Under the deposit method, a sale is not recorded for accounting purposes until the conditions in SFAS No. 66 are met. Therefore, for purposes of the **down payment tests,** interest received and credited to the deposit account can be included in the down payment and sales value at the time a sale is recorded.

If a buyer defaults and forfeits his nonrefundable deposit, the deposit liability is no longer required and may be credited to income. The circumstances underlying the **default** should be carefully reviewed since such circumstances may indicate **deteriorating value** of the property. In such a case it may be appropriate to treat the credit as a valuation reserve. These circumstances may require a provision for additional loss. See sections 21.23 and 21.26 for further discussion.

(b) Installment Method.   When the substance of a real estate transaction indicates that a sale has occurred for accounting purposes, but that **collectibility** of the total sales price cannot be reasonably estimated (i.e. inadequate buyer's investment), the installment method may be appropriate. However, circumstances may indicate that the cost recovery method is required or is otherwise more appropriate. For example, when the deferred gross profit exceeds the net carrying value of the related receivable, profit may have been earned to the extent of such excess.

Profit should be recognized on cash payments, including principal payments by the buyer on any debt assumed (either recourse or nonrecourse), and should be based on the ratio of total profit to total sales value (including a first mortgage debt assumed by the buyer, if applicable). Interest received on the related receivable is properly recorded as income when received.

The total sales value (from which the deferred gross profit should be deducted) and the cost of sales should be presented in the income statement. Deferred gross profit should be shown as a deduction from the related receivable, with subsequent income recognition presented separately in the income statement.

(c) Cost Recovery Method.   The cost recovery method must be used when the substance of a real estate transaction indicates that a sale has occurred for accounting purposes but no profit should be recognized until costs are recovered. This may occur when (1) the receivable is subject to future subordination, (2) the seller retains an interest in the property sold and the buyer has preferences, (3) uncertainty exists as to whether all or a portion of the cost will be recovered, or (4) there is uncertainty as to the amount of proceeds. As a practical matter, the cost recovery method can always be used as an alternative to the installment method.

Under the cost recovery method, no profit is recognized until cash collections (including principal and interest payments) and existing debt assumed by the buyer exceed the cost of the property sold. Cash collections in excess of cost should be recorded as revenue in the period of collection.

Financial statement presentation under the cost recovery method is similar to that for the installment method.

(d) Reduced Profit Method.   When the substance of a real estate transaction indicates that a sale has occurred for accounting purposes, but the continuing investment criteria for full profit recognition is not met by the buyer, the seller may sometimes recognize a reduced profit at the time of sale (see additional discussion in section 21.6(b)). This alternative is rarely used since a full accrual of anticapted costs of continuing investment will permit full accrual of the remaining profit.

(e) Financing Method.   A real estate transaction may be, in substance, a financing arrangement rather than a sale. This is frequently the case when the seller has an **obligation to repurchase** the property (or can be compelled by the buyer to repurchase the property) at a price higher than the total amount of the payments received and to be received. In such a case the financing method must be used.

Accounting procedures under the financing method should be similar to the accounting procedures under the deposit method, with one exception. Under the financing method, the difference between (1) the total amount of all payments received and to be received and (2) the repurchase price is presumed to be interest expense. As such, it should be accrued on the interest method over the period from the receipt of cash to the date of repurchase. As in the deposit method, cash received is reflected as a liability in the balance sheet. Thus, at the date of repurchase, the full amount of the repurchase obligation should be recorded as a liability.

In the case of a **repurchase option,** if the facts and circumstances at the time of the sale indicate a presumption or a likelihood that the seller will exercise the option, interest should be accrued as if there were an obligation to repurchase. This presumption could result from the value of the property, the property being an integral part of development, or from management's intention. If such a presumption does not exist at the time of the sale transaction, interest should not be accrued and the deposit method is appropriate.

(f) Lease Method.   A real estate transaction may be, in substance, a lease rather than a sale. Accounting procedures under the lease method should be similar to the deposit method, except as follows:

- Payments received and to be received that are in substance deferred rental income received in advance should be deferred and amortized to income over the presumed lease period. Such amortization to income should not exceed cash paid to the seller.
- Cash paid out by the seller as a guarantee of support of operations should be expensed as paid.

The seller may agree to make **loans** to the **buyer** in support of operations, for example, when cash flow does not equal a predetermined amount or is negative. In such a situation, deferred rental income to be amortized to income should be reduced by all the loans made or reasonably anticipated to be made to the buyer, thus reducing the periodic income to be recognized. Where the loans made or anticipated exceed deferred rental income, a loss provision may be required if the collectibility of the loan is questionable.

(g) Profit-Sharing or Co-Venture Method.   A real estate transaction may be, in substance, a profit-sharing arrangement rather than a sale. For example, a **sale** of **real estate** to a **limited partnership** in which the seller is a general partner or has similar characteristics is often a profit-sharing arrangement. If such a transaction does not meet the tests for recording a sale, it usually would be accounted for under the profit-sharing method. This accounting method should also be followed when it is clear that the buyer is acting merely as an agent for the seller.

Under the profit-sharing method, giving consideration to the seller's continued involvement, the seller would be required to account for the operations of the property through its income statement as if it continued to own the properties.

COST OF REAL ESTATE

21.11 CAPITALIZATION OF COSTS.   In October 1982, the FASB issued SFAS No. 67. This Statement incorporates the specialized accounting principles and practices from the AICPA SOPs No. 80-3, "Accounting for Real Estate Acquisition, Development and Construction Costs," and No. 78-3, "Accounting for Costs to Sell and Rent, and Initial Rental Operations of Real Estate Projects," and those in the AICPA Industry Accounting Guide, "Accounting for Retail Land Sales," that address costs of real estate projects. SFAS No. 67 establishes whether costs associated with acquiring, developing, constructing, selling, and renting real estate projects should be capitalized. Guidance is also provided on the appropriate methods of allocating capitalized costs to individual components of the project.

SFAS No. 67 also established that a rental project changes from nonoperating to operating when it is substantially completed and held available for occupancy, but not later than one year from cessation of major construction activities.

What are the general precepts? Costs incurred in real estate operations range from "brick and mortar" costs that clearly should be capitalized to general administrative costs that clearly should not be capitalized. Between these two extremes lies a broad range of costs that are difficult to classify. Therefore, judgmental decisions must be made as to whether such costs should be capitalized.

21.12 PREACQUISITION COSTS.   These costs include payments to obtain options to acquire real property and other costs incurred prior to acquisition such as legal, architectural, and other professional fees, salaries, environmental studies, appraisals, marketing and feasibility studies, and soil tests. Capitalization of costs related to a property that are incurred before the enterprise acquires the property, or before the enterprise obtains an option to acquire it, is appropriate provided all of the following conditions are met:

- The costs are directly identifiable with the specific property.
- The costs would be capitalized if the property had already been acquired.
- Acquisition of the property or of an option to acquire the property is probable (that is, likely to occur). This condition requires that the prospective purchaser is actively seeking acquisition of the property and has the ability to finance or obtain financing for the acquisition. In addition, there should be no indication that the property is not available for sale.

Capitalized preacquisition costs should be included as project costs on acquisition of the property or should be charged to expense when it is probable that the property will not be acquired. The charge to expense should be reduced by the amount recoverable by the sale of the options, plans, and so on.

21.13 LAND ACQUISITION COSTS.   Costs directly related to the acquisition of land should be capitalized. These costs include option fees, purchase cost, transfer costs, title insurance, legal and other professional fees, surveys, appraisals, and real estate commissions. The purchase cost may have to be increased or decreased for **imputation of interest** on mortgage notes payable assumed or issued in connection with the purchase, as required under APB Opinion No. 21.

21.14 LAND IMPROVEMENT, DEVELOPMENT, AND CONSTRUCTION COSTS.   Costs directly related to improvements of the land should be capitalized by the developer. They may include:

- Land planning costs, including marketing and feasibility studies, direct salaries, legal and other professional fees, zoning costs, soil tests, architectural and engineering studies, appraisals, environmental studies, and other costs directly related to site preparation and the overall design and development of the project.

- Onsite and offsite improvements, including demolition costs, streets, traffic controls, sidewalks, street lighting, sewer and water facilities, utilities, parking lots, landscaping, and related costs such as permits and inspection fees.
- Construction costs, including onsite material and labor, direct supervision, engineering and architectural fees, permits, and inspection fees.
- Project overhead and supervision, such as field office costs.
- Recreation facilities, such as golf courses, clubhouse, swimming pools, and tennis courts.
- Sales center and models, including furnishings.

General and administrative costs not directly identified with the project should be accounted for as period costs and expensed as incurred.

Construction activity on a project may be suspended before a project is completed for reasons such as insufficient sales or rental demand. These conditions may indicate an impairment of the value of a project that is other than temporary, which suggests valuation problems. See section entitled "Valuation Problems" below.

21.15 INTEREST COSTS. Prior to 1979, many developers capitalized interest costs as a necessary cost of the asset in the same way as "bricks and mortar" costs. Others followed an accounting policy of charging off interest cost as a period cost on the basis that it was solely a financing cost that varied directly with the capability of a company to finance development and construction through equity funds. This long-standing debate on capitalization of interest cost was resolved in October 1979 when the FASB published SFAS No. 34, "Capitalization of Interest Cost," which provided specific guidelines for accounting for interest costs. The guidelines set forth herein are based to a large extent on the provisions of SFAS No. 34.

SFAS No. 34 requires capitalization of interest cost as part of the historical cost of acquiring assets that need a period of time in which to bring them to that condition and location necessary for their intended use. The objectives of capitalizing interest are to obtain a measure of acquisition cost that more closely reflects the enterprise's total investment in the asset and to charge a cost that relates to the acquisition of a resource that will benefit future periods against the revenues of the periods benefited. Interest capitalization is not required if its effect is not material.

(a) Assets Qualifying for Interest Capitalization. Qualifying assets include real estate constructed for an enterprise's own use or real estate intended for sale or lease. Qualifying assets also include investments (equity, loans, and advances) accounted for by the equity method while the investee has activities in progress necessary to commence its planned principal operations, but only if the investee's activities include the use of such to acquire qualifying assets for its operations.

Capitalization is not permitted for assets in use or ready for their intended use, assets not undergoing the activities necessary to prepare them for use, assets that are not included in the consolidated balance sheet, or investments accounted for by the equity method after the planned principal operations of the investee begin. Thus land that is not undergoing activities necessary for development is not a qualifying asset for purposes of interest capitalization. If activities are undertaken for developing the land, the expenditures to acquire the land qualify for interest capitalization while those activities are in progress.

(b) Capitalization Period. The capitalization period commences when:

- Expenditures for the asset have been made.

- Activities that are necessary to get the asset ready for its intended use are in progress.
- Interest cost is being incurred.

Activities are to be construed in a broad sense and encompass more than just physical construction. All steps necessary to prepare an asset for its intended use are included. This broad interpretation includes administrative and technical activities during the pre-construction stage (such as developing plans or obtaining required permits).

Interest capitalization must end when the asset is substantially complete and ready for its intended use. A real estate project should be considered substantially complete and held available for occupancy upon completion of major construction activity, as distinguished from activities such as routine maintenance and cleanup. In some cases, such as in an office building, tenant improvements are a major construction activity and are frequently not completed until a lease contract is arranged. If such improvements are the responsibility of the developer, SFAS No. 67 indicates that the project is not considered substantially complete until the earlier of (1) completion of improvements or (2) one year from cessation of major construction activity without regard to tenant improvements. In other words, a one-year grace period has been provided to complete tenant improvements.

If substantially all activities related to acquisition of the asset are suspended, interest capitalization should stop until such activities are resumed. However, brief interruptions in activities, interruptions caused by external factors, and inherent delays in the development process do not necessarily require suspension of interest capitalization.

Under SFAS No. 34, interest capitalization must end when the asset is **substantially complete** and **ready for its intended use.** For projects completed in parts, where each part is capable of being used independently while work continues on other parts, interest capitalization should stop on each part that is substantially complete and ready for use. Examples include individual buildings in a multiphase or condominium project. For projects that must be completed before any part can be used, interest capitalization should continue until the entire project is substantially complete and ready for use. Where an asset cannot be used effectively until a particular portion has been completed, interest capitalization continues until that portion is substantially complete and ready for use. An example would be an island resort complex with sole access being a permanent bridge to the project. Completion of the bridge is necessary for the asset to be used effectively.

Interest capitalization should not stop when the capitalized costs exceed net realizable value. In such instances, a valuation reserve should be recorded or appropriately increased to reduce the carrying value to net realizable value (see section 21.23).

(c) Methods of Interest Capitalization.   The basic principle is that the amount of interest cost to be capitalized should be the amount that theoretically could have been avoided during the development and construction period if expenditures for the qualifying asset had not been made. These interest costs might have been avoided either by foregoing additional borrowing or by using the funds expended for the asset to repay existing borrowings in the case where no new borrowings were obtained.

The amount capitalized is determined by applying a **capitalization rate** to the average amount of accumulated capitalized expenditures for the asset during the period. Such expenditures include cash payments, transfer of other assets, or incurrence of liabilities on which interest has been recognized, and they should be net of progress payments received against such capitalized costs. Liabilities such as trade payables, accruals, and retainages, on which interest is not recognized, are not expenditures. Reasonable approximations of net capitalized expenditures may be used.

The author's preference is for the capitalization rate to be based on the weighted average of the rates applicable to borrowings outstanding during the period. Alternatively, if a specific new borrowing is associated with an asset, the rate on that borrowing may be used. If the average amount of accumulated expenditures for the asset exceeds the amounts of specific new borrowings associated with the asset, a weighted average interest rate of all other borrowings must be applied to the excess. Under this alternative, judgment will be required to select the borrowings to be included in the weighted average rate so that a reasonable measure will be obtained of the interest cost incurred that could otherwise have been avoided. It should be remembered that the principle is not one of capitalizing interest costs incurred for a specific asset, but one of capitalizing interest costs that could have been avoided if it were not for the acquisition, development, and construction of the asset.

The amount of interest cost capitalized in an accounting period is limited to the total amount of interest cost incurred in the period. However, interest cost should include amortization of premium or discount resulting from imputation of interest on certain types of payables in accordance with APB Opinion No. 21 and that portion of minimum lease payments under a capital lease treated as interest in accordance with SFAS No. 13.

(d) Accounting for Amount Capitalized. Interest cost capitalized is an integral part of the cost of acquiring a qualifying asset, and therefore its disposition should be the same as any other cost of that asset. For example, if a building is subsequently depreciated, capitalized interest should be included in the depreciable base the same as bricks and mortar.

In the case of interest capitalized on an investment accounted for by the equity method, its disposition should be made as if the investee were consolidated. In other words, if the assets of the investee were being depreciated, the capitalized interest cost should be depreciated in the same manner and over the same lives. If the assets of the investee were developed lots being sold, the capitalized interest cost should be written off as the lots are sold.

21.16 TAXES AND INSURANCE. Costs incurred on real estate for property taxes and insurance should be treated similarly to interest costs. They should be capitalized only during periods in which activities necessary to get the property ready for its intended use are in progress. Costs incurred for such items after the property is substantially complete and ready for its intended use should be charged to expense as incurred.

21.17 INDIRECT PROJECT COSTS. Indirect project costs that relate to a specific project, such as costs associated with a project field office, should be capitalized as a cost of that project. Other indirect project costs that relate to several projects, such as the costs associated with a construction administration department, should be capitalized and allocated to the projects to which the cost related. Indirect costs that do not clearly relate to projects under development or construction should be charged to expense as incurred.

The principal problem is defining and identifying the cost to be capitalized. It is necessary to consider all of the following points:

- Specific information should be available (such as timecards) to support the basis of allocation to specific projects.
- The costs incurred should be incremental costs; that is, in the absence of the project or projects under development or construction, these costs would not be incurred.
- The impact of capitalization of such costs on the results of operations should be consistent with the pervasive principle of matching costs with related revenue.
- The principle of conservatism should be considered.

Indirect costs related to a specific project that should be considered for capitalization include direct and indirect salaries of a field office and insurance costs. Costs that are not directly related to the project should be charged to expense as incurred.

21.18 GENERAL AND ADMINISTRATIVE EXPENSES. Real estate developers incur various types of general and administrative expenses, including officers' salaries, accounting and legal fees, and various office supplies and expenses. Some of these expenses may be closely associated with individual projects, whereas others are of a more general nature. For example, a developer may open a field office on a project site and staff it with administrative personnel, such as a field accountant. The expenses associated with the field office are directly associated with the project and are therefore considered to be overhead. On the other hand, the developer may have a number of expenses associated with general office operations that benefit numerous projects and for which specifically identifiable allocations are not reasonable or practicable. Those administrative costs that cannot be clearly related to projects under development or construction should be charged to current operations.

21.19 AMENITIES.   Real estate developments often include **amenities** such as golf courses, utilities, clubhouses, swimming pools, and tennis courts. The accounting for the costs of these amenities should be based on management's intended disposition as follows:

- *Amenity to Be Sold or Transferred with Sales Units.* All costs in excess of anticipated proceeds should be allocated as common costs because the amenity is clearly associated with the development and sale of the project. Common costs should include estimated net operating costs to be borne by the developer until they are assumed by buyers of units in the project.
- *Amenity to Be Sold Separately or Retained by Developer.* Capitalizable costs of the amenity in excess of its estimated fair value on the expected date of its substantial physical completion should be allocated as common costs. The costs capitalized and allocated to the amenity should not be revised after the amenity is substantially completed and available for use. A later sale of the amenity at more or less than the determined fair value as of the date of substantial physical completion, less any accumulated depreciation, should result in a gain or loss in the period in which the sale occurs.

21.20 ABANDONMENTS AND CHANGES IN USE.   Real estate, including rights to real estate, may be abandoned, for example, by allowing a mortgage to be foreclosed or by allowing a purchase option to lapse. Capitalized costs, including allocated common costs, of real estate abandoned should be written off as current expenses or, if appropriate, to allowances previously established for that purpose. They should not be allocated to other components of the project or to other projects, even if other components or other projects are capable of absorbing the losses.

Donation of real estate to municipalities or other governmental agencies for uses that will benefit the project are not abandonment. The cost of real estate donated should be allocated as a common cost of the project.

Changes in the intended use of a real estate project may arise after significant development and construction costs have been incurred. If the change in use is made pursuant to a formal plan that is expected to produce a higher economic yield (as compared to its yield based on use before change), the project costs should be charged to expense to the extent the capitalized costs incurred and to be incurred exceed the estimated value of the revised project when it is substantially completed and ready for its intended use.

If no formal plans exist, the project costs should be charged to expense to the extent they exceed the estimated net realizable value of the property based on the assumption it will be sold in its present state.

21.21 SELLING COSTS.   Costs incurred to sell real estate projects should be accounted for in the same manner as, and classified with, construction costs of the project when they meet both of the following criteria:

- The costs incurred are for tangible assets that are used throughout the selling period or for services performed to obtain regulatory approval for sales.

- The costs are reasonably expected to be recovered from sales of the project or incidental operations.

Examples of costs incurred to sell real estate projects that ordinarily meet the criteria for capitalization are costs of model units and their furnishings, sales facilities, legal fees for the preparation of prospectuses, and semipermanent signs.

SFAS No. 67 states that other costs incurred to sell real estate projects should be capitalized as prepaid costs if they are directly associated with and their recovery is reasonably expected from sales that are being accounted for under a method of accounting other than full accrual. Costs that do not meet the criteria for capitalization should be expensed as incurred.

Capitalized selling costs should be charged to expense in the period in which the related revenue is recognized as earned. When a sales contract is canceled (with or without refund) or the related receivable is written off as uncollectible, the related unrecoverable capitalized selling costs are charged to expense or to an allowance previously established for that purpose.

ALLOCATION OF COSTS

After it has been determined what costs are capitalized, it becomes important to determine how the costs should be allocated, because these costs will enter into the calculation of cost of sales of individual units. Although a number of methods of allocation can be used in different circumstances, judgment often must be used to make sure that appropriate results are obtained.

21.22 METHODS OF ALLOCATION.   Capitalized costs of real estate projects should first be assigned to individual components of the project based on specific identification. If specific identification on an overall basis is not practicable, capitalized costs should be allocated as follows:

- Land costs and all other common costs should be allocated to each land parcel benefitted. Allocation should be based on the relative fair value before construction.
- Construction costs should be assigned to buildings on a specific identification basis and allocated to individual units on the basis of relative value of each unit.

In the usual situation, sales prices or rentals are available to compute relative values. In rare situations, however, where relative value is impracticable, capitalized costs may be allocated based on the area method/or the relative cost method as appropriate under the circumstances.

The followng sections describe the specific identification, value, and area methods of cost allocation.

(a) Specific Identification Method.   This method of cost allocation is based on determining actual costs applicable to each parcel of land. It rarely is used for land costs because such costs usually encompass more than one parcel. However, it frequently is used for direct construction costs because these costs are directly related to the property being sold. This method should be used wherever practicable.

(b) Value Method.   The relative value method is the method usually used after costs have been assigned on a specific identification basis. Under this method, the allocation of common costs should be based on relative fair value (before value added by onsite development and construction activities) of each land parcel benefitted. In multiproject developments common costs are normally allocated based on estimated sales prices net of direct improvements and selling costs. This approach is usually the most appropriate because it is less likely to result in deferral of losses.

With respect to condominium sales, certain units will usually have a higher price because of location. With respect to time-sharing sales, holiday periods such as Easter, Fourth of July, and Christmas traditionally sell at a premium. Depending on the resort location, the summer or winter season will also sell at a premium as compared with the rest of the year. Caution should be exercised to ensure that the sales values utilized in cost allocation are reasonable.

(c) Area Method.   This method of cost allocation is based on square footage, acreage, or frontage. The use of this method will not always result in a logical allocation of costs. When negotiating the purchase price for a large tract of land, the purchaser considers the overall utility of the tract, recognizing that various parcels in the tract are more valuable than others. For example, parcels on a lake front are usually more valuable than those back from the lake. In this situation, if a simple average based on square footage or acreage was used to allocate costs to individual parcels, certain parcels could be assigned costs in excess of their net realizable value.

Generally, the area method should be limited to situations where each individual parcel is estimated to have approximately the same relative value. Under such circumstances, the cost allocations as determined by either the area or value methods would be approximately the same.

VALUATION PROBLEMS

21.23 NET REALIZABLE VALUE.   The overbuilding and financial institutions' crises of the mid to late 1980s have revived the issues related to accounting for the net realizable value (NRV) of real estate projects. Much of the attention of late has focused on the valuation utilized by lenders related to recording foreclosed properties.

No specific action has been taken by the AICPA or the FASB on the matter of NRV in the 1980s. However, in October 1982 the FASB issued SFAS No. 67, which, in the glossary, defines net realizable value as "the estimated selling price in the ordinary course of business less estimated costs of completion (to the stage of completion assumed in determining the selling price), holding and disposal." SFAS No. 67 (par. 24) also states the general principle that the carrying amount of a real estate project should not exceed NRV on an individual project basis.

The following discussion of NRV incorporates the principal matters contained in SFAS No. 67; however, it should be noted that the FASB has placed an impairment of assets project on its agenda (November 1988). The current schedule calls for a discussion memorandum to be issued in 1990. Accordingly, new guidance on this subject may be issued.

As a general principle, real estate held for sale, or development and sale, should be included in the balance sheet at the lower of cost or net realizable value. The major questions that arise in applying this principle are:

- What types of real estate should be subject to NRV guidelines?
- How should the principle of lower of cost or NRV be applied to real estate projects?
- How should estimated selling prices be determined?
- Should cost of completion include the cost (especially interest cost) to carry the inventory to date of sale?

If the cost of the project exceeds NRV an allowance should be provided. However, the capitalization of costs should not cease, but an additional allowance should be provided.

21.24 INVENTORY VERSUS LONG-TERM INVESTMENT.   Real estate held for sale, or for development and sale, generally falls into the category of inventory. This includes such properties as land (including raw land and land under development), condominiums, and single-family housing, as well as income properties held for sale. Inventories do not include:

- Income properties held for long-term investment.
- Real property used in the business.
- Land held for future development or construction of property as a long-term investment or as property used in the business.

It is not appropriate for income properties to be declared to be held for investment solely to avoid losses that otherwise would have to be recorded under rules for inventories.

Factors that should be considered in the evaluation of real estate held for sale or for development and sale are:

- The company's financial ability to hold or to develop the properties in question.
- The company's plans for the properties, including information about its past practices and experience.
- The company's plans for the timing of development and sale.
- Appraisals of the property prepared either by independent appraisers or by the company staff.

21.25 INDIVIDUAL OR GROUP BASIS.   As a general rule, due to the low volume and high dollar value of the individual sales transactions in the real estate industry—and as required by SFAS No. 67—the lower of cost or net realizable value test should be determined on the basis of an evaluation of the individual unit.

21.26 DETERMINATION OF NET REALIZABLE VALUE

(a) Selling Price.   The estimated selling price should usually be determined on the basis of a sale in the ordinary course of business, which would allow a reasonable time to find a willing purchaser under normal market conditions, exclusive of any adjustment for anticipated inflation. If, however, the intention is to dispose of the property on an immediate sale basis or if the owner does not have the financial ability to hold the property, the estimated selling price should be determined on an immediate liquidation basis.

The nature of the property will affect the method used to determine its selling price. Selling prices for bulk undeveloped land should ordinarily be based on comparable sales prices, allowing a reasonable time to find a purchaser.

Certain future events, such as prospective developments or possible future legislation, should not be factored into the determination of the estimated selling prices except to the extent that such events are being recognized currently in the marketplace. Possible future zoning should not be considered unless it is reasonably certain that it can be obtained.

In determining selling prices for property under development (such as retail lots, single-family homes, and condominiums) current sales prices should be used. Where experience is lacking or where there has been relatively low sales volume, selling prices of comparable transactions in the local area should be used.

Income properties usually are valued on the basis of their estimated future net cash flow and a capitalization (or discount) rate, which varies with the type of project and the financial markets. Estimated future cash flow should be based on full or stabilized operations with appropriate reductions for the estimated cash flow shortfalls prior to stabilization. When using this approach to determine estimated selling prices, pro forma operating costs should be based on costs that are comparable to the estimated future revenues rather than on historical averages. For example, future net cash flow should be adjusted to reflect recent increases in utility costs.

(b) Cost of Completion, Including Interest and Property Taxes.   The total cost of completion of properties being evaluated should include all additional costs to be incurred to complete the properties to be sold. These costs should include the effects of inflation and should be determined on a basis consistent with the determination of costs that are capitalizable or included in inventory.

There has been considerable controversy as to whether future interest costs should be considered in determining NRV. It has long been the author's view that the future interest costs should be included in the calculation if such interest costs were capitalized as a part of the cost of the project. The FASB issued, in October 1979, SFAS No. 34, which requires the capitalization of interest cost as part of the historical cost of development and construction of real estate projects. (See section 21.15 for further discussion of SFAS No. 34.) The thrust of the Statement is that interest costs during the improvement period should not be treated differently from bricks and mortar. In addition, SFAS No. 67 states that capitalization should not stop when accounting principles require recognition of a lower carrying value for the asset. The allowance required to reduce the acquisition cost to a lower carrying value should be established or increased appropriately.

Although SFAS No. 34 does not directly address the question of what, if any, interest costs should be included in the computation of net realizable value, the only logical conclusion from the statement is that the estimated future capitalizable interest costs should be included in this computation. The controversy, however, has not been resolved over whether to include other future interest costs in determining net realizable value. Other future interest costs would include such costs until the estimated time of sale with respect to undeveloped land or, for developed real estate, after substantial completion. The author's view is that such additional interest costs should not be included.

There have been two approaches generally used to include future interest costs in the calculation of net realizable value. One method, which is consistent with SFAS No. 34, is to include the interest cost in the estimated aggregate cost of the property. To the extent that it exceeds the estimated future sale proceeds, interest cost is recognized currently in the loss provision. Another method indirectly reflects future interest costs by discounting estimated future sales proceeds (net of estimated cash disbursements exclusive of interest) to present value. The resulting amount is compared to costs accumulated to date to determine any loss provision required. Effectively, the former method measures the loss as the difference between total estimated costs to be incurred and estimated proceeds at the future date, while the latter measures the loss as the difference in cost and value at a current date. The latter method is illustrated in the Appendices to AICPA SOP No. 75-2, "Accounting Practices of Real Estate Investment Trusts" and is therefore used by these entities as well as savings and loan associations, as specified in the AICPA *Accounting Guide*. Although that statement requires an interest rate based on an average cost of capital (i.e., total interest cost divided by the aggregate of debt and equity), it should be noted that the FASB rejected that approach for purposes of interest capitalization in SFAS No. 34.

How should future property taxes, insurance and indirect project costs be accounted for in the determination of NRV? Similar to interest, to the extent that these future costs are expected to be capitalized, such costs should be included in the estimated cost of completion.

(c) Costs of Disposal.   Such costs include marketing, selling, advertising, points, fees, and commissions.

21.27 REVERSAL OF RESERVES.   Because of the many factors that can affect recoverability of investments in real estate, the estimated loss on an individual unit or project may not be the same as the ultimate loss sustained on the disposition of the property. Where the valuation is based on estimates, the reduction in value is treated as a valuation reserve that could be adjusted periodically based on a relatively complete reevaluation.

If the valuation has been determined based on known losses caused by specific sales contracts or commitments, the property should be written down to net realizable value. In both instances, once a reserve has been established, the project may not be "written up" to original cost, as the reserve establishes a new cost basis.

CONSTRUCTION CONTRACTS

Although most real estate developers acquire land in order to develop and construct improvements for their own use or for sale to others, some develop and construct improvements solely for others. There are also many general contractors whose principal business is developing and constructing improvements for others and rarely, if ever, do they own the land.

This section covers guidelines for accounting for development and construction contracts where the contractor does not own the land but is providing such services for others. The principal issue in accounting for construction contracts is when to record income. Construction contracts are generally of two types: fixed price and cost-plus. Under fixed price contracts, a contractor agrees to perform services for a fixed amount. Although the contract price is fixed, it may frequently be revised as a result of change orders as construction proceeds. If the contract is longer than a few months, the contractor usually receives advances from the customer as construction progresses.

Cost-plus contracts are employed in a variety of forms, such as cost plus a percentage of cost or cost plus a fixed fee. Sometimes defined costs may be limited and penalties provided in situations where stated maximum costs are exceeded. Under cost-plus agreements, the contractor is usually reimbursed for its costs as costs are incurred and, in addition, is paid a specified fee. In most cases, a portion of the fee is retained until the construction is completed and accepted. The method of recording income under cost-plus contracts generally is the same as for fixed price contracts and is described below.

21.28 AUTHORITATIVE LITERATURE.   In 1955 the AICPA Committee on Accounting Procedures issued ARB No. 45 "Long-Term Construction-Type Contracts." This document described the generally accepted methods of accounting for long-term construction-type contracts for financial reporting purposes and described the circumstances in which each method is preferable.

In 1981 the AICPA issued SOP No. 81-1, "Accounting for Performance of Construction-Type and Certain Production-Type Contracts." This Statement culminated extensive reconsideration by the AICPA of construction-type contracts. The recommendations set forth therein provide guidance on the application of ARB No. 45 but do not amend that bulletin. In 1982, the FASB issued SFAS No. 56, "Contractor Accounting" which states that the specialized accounting and reporting principles and practices contained in SOP No. 81-1 are preferable accounting principles for purposes of justifying a change in accounting principles.

Prior to the issuance of SOP 81-1, authoritative accounting literature used the terms "long-term" and "short-term" in identifying types of contracts. SOP No. 81-1 chose not to use those terms as identifying characteristics because other characteristics were considered more relevant for identifying the types of contracts covered. The guidelines set forth below are based largely on SOP No. 81-1.

21.29 METHODS OF ACCOUNTING.   The determination of the point or points at which revenue should be recognized as earned and costs should be recognized as expenses is a major accounting issue common to all business enterprises engaged in the performance of construction contracting. Accounting for such contracts is essentially a process of measuring the results of relatively long-term events and allocating those results to relatively short-term accounting periods. This involves considerable use of estimates in determining revenues, costs, and profits and in assigning the amounts to accounting periods. The process is complicated by the need to continually evaluate the uncertainties that are inherent in the performance of contracts and by the need to rely on estimates of revenues, costs, and the extent of progress toward completion.

There are two generally accepted methods of accounting for construction contracts: the percentage of completion method and the completed contract method. The determination of the preferable method should be based on an evaluation of the particular circumstances as the two methods are not acceptable alternatives for the same set of circumstances. The method used and circumstances describing when it is used should be disclosed in the accounting policy footnote to the financial statements.

(a) Percentage of Completion Method.   The use of this approach depends on the ability of the contractor to make reasonably dependable estimates. The percentage of completion method is the author's preference as an accounting policy in circumstances in which reasonably dependable estimates can be made and in which all the following conditions exist:

- The contract is clear about goods or services to be provided, the consideration to be exchanged, and the manner and terms of settlement.
- The buyer can be expected to pay for the services performed.
- The contractor can be expected to be able to perform his contractual obligations.

The percentage of completion method is the author's preference because this method presents the economic substance of activity more clearly and timely than the completed contract method. It should be noted that estimates of revenues, costs and percentage of completion are the primary criteria for income recognition. Billings may have no real relationship to performance and generally are not a suitable basis for income recognition.

(b) Completed Contract Method.   This method may be used in circumstances in which an entity's financial position and results of operations would not vary materially from those resulting from the percentage of completion method. The completed contract method is the author's preference in circumstances in which estimates cannot meet the criteria for reasonable dependability or in which there are inherent hazards that caused forecasts to be doubtful.

(c) Consistency of Application.   It is possible that a contractor may use one method for some contracts and the other for additional contracts. There is no inconsistency, since consistency in application lies in using the same accounting treatment for the same set of conditions from one accounting period to another. The method used, and circumstances when it is used, should be disclosed in the accounting policy footnote to the financial statements.

21.30 PERCENTAGE OF COMPLETION METHOD.   This method is the author's preference because it recognizes the legal and economic results of contract performance on a timely basis. Financial statements based on the percentage of completion method present the economic substance of a company's transactions and events more clearly and more timely than financial statements based on the completed contract method, and they present more accurately the relationships between gross profit from contracts and related period costs. The percentage of completion method informs the users of the general purpose financial statements concerning the volume of a company's economic acitivity.

In practice, several methods are used to measure the extent of progress toward completion. These methods include the cost-to-cost method, the efforts-expended method, the units-of-delivery method and the units-of-work-performed method. These methods are intended to conform to the recommendations of ARB 45 (par. 4), which states:

> . . . that the recognized income be that percentage of estimated total income, either:
>
> **a.** that incurred costs to date bear to estimated total costs after giving effect to estimates of costs to complete based upon most recent information, or
>
> **b.** that may be indicated by such other measure of progress toward completion as may be appropriate having due regard to work performed.

One generally accepted method of measuring such progress is the stage of construction, as determined through engineering or architectural studies.

When using the "cost incurred" approach, there may be certain costs that should be exluded from the calculation. For example, substantial quantities of standard materials not unique to the project may have been delivered to the job site but not yet utilized. Or engineering and architectural fees incurred may represent 20% of total estimated costs whereas only 10% of the construction has been performed.

The principal disadvantage of the percentage of completion method is that it is necessarily dependent on estimates of ultimate costs that are subject to the uncertainties frequently inherent in long-term contracts.

The estimation of total revenues and costs is necessary to determine estimated total income. Frequently a contractor can estimate total contract revenue and total contract cost in single amounts. However, on some contracts a contractor may be able to estimate only total contract revenue and total contract cost in ranges of amounts. In such situations, the most likely amounts within the range should be used, if determinable. If not, the least favorable amounts should be used until the results can be estimated more precisely.

(a) Revenue Determination. Estimating revenue on a contract is an involved process. The major factors that must be considered in determining total estimated revenue include the basic contract price, contract options, change orders, claims, and contract provisions for incentive payments and penalties. All these factors and other special contract provisions must be evaluated throughout the life of a contract in estimating total contract revenue.

(b) Cost Determination. At any time during the life of a contract, total estimated contract cost consists of two components: costs incurred to date and estimated cost to complete the contract. A company should be able to determine costs incurred on a contract with a relatively high degree of precision. The other component, estimated cost to complete, is a significant variable in the process of determining income earned and is thus a significant factor in accounting for contracts. SOP No. 81-1 states that the following practices should be followed in estimating costs to complete:

a. Systematic and consistent procedures that are correlated with the cost accounting system should be used to provide a basis for periodically comparing actual and estimated costs.

b. In estimating total contract costs the quantities and prices of all significant elements of cost should be identified.

c. The estimating procedures should provide that estimated cost to complete includes the same elements of cost that are included in actual accumulated costs; also, those elements should reflect expected price increases.

d. The effects of future wage and price escalations should be taken into account in cost estimates, especially when the contract performance will be carried out over a significant period of time. Escalation provisions should not be blanket overall provisions but should cover labor, materials, and indirect costs based on percentages or amounts that take into consideration experience and other pertinent data.

e. Estimates of cost to complete should be reviewed periodically and revised as appropriate to reflect new information.

(c) Revision of Estimates.   Adjustments to the original estimates of the total contract revenue, cost, or extent of progress toward completion are often required as work progresses under the contract, even though the scope of the work required under the contract has not changed. Such adjustments are changes in accounting estimates as defined in APB Opinion No. 20. Under this Opinion, the cumulative catch-up method is the only acceptable method. This method requires the difference between cumulative income and income previously recorded to be recorded in the current year's income.

The following example illustrates the percentage of completion method.

A contracting company has a lump-sum contract for $9 million to build a bridge at a total estimated cost of $8 million. The construction period covers 3 years. Financial data during the construction period is as follows:

	Year 1	Year 2	Year 3
	(thousands of dollars)		
Total estimated revenue	$9,000	$9,100	$9,200
Cost incurred to date	$2,050	$6,100	$8,200
Estimated cost to complete	6,000	2,000	—
Total estimated cost	$8,050	$8,100	$8,200
Estimated gross profit	$ 950	$1,000	$1,000
Billings to date	$1,800	$5,500	$9,200
Collections to date	$1,500	$5,000	$9,200
Measure of progress	25%	75%	100%

The amount of revenue, costs, and income recognized in the three periods would be as follows:

	To Date	Recognized Prior Year	Current Year
		(thousands of dollars)	
Year 1 (25% completed)			
Earned revenue ($9,000,000 × 0.25)	$2,250.0		$2,250.0
Cost of earned revenue			
($8,050,000 × 0.25)	2,012.5		2,012.5
Gross profit	$ 237.5		$ 237.5
Gross profit rate	10.5%		10.5%
Year 2 (75% completed)			
Earned revenue ($9,100,000 × 0.75)	$6,825.0	$2,250.0	$4,575.0
Cost of earned revenue			
($8,100,000 × 0.75)	6,075.0	2,012.5	4,062.5
Gross profit	$ 750.0	$ 237.5	$ 512.5
Gross profit rate	11.0%	10.5%	11.2%
Year 3 (100% completed)			
Earned revenue	$9,200.0	$6,825.0	$2,375.0
Cost of earned revenue	8,200.0	6,075.0	2,125.0
Gross profit	$1,000.0	$ 750.0	$ 250.0
Gross profit rate	10.9%	11.0%	10.5%

Source: AICPA.

21.31 COMPLETED CONTRACT METHOD.   This method recognizes income only when a contract is completed or substantially completed, such as when the remaining costs to be incurred are not significant. Under this method, costs and billings are reflected in the balance sheet but there are no charges or credits to the income statement.

As a general rule, a contract may be regarded as subtantially completed if remaining costs and potential risks are insignificant in amount. The overriding objectives are to maintain consistency in determing when contracts are substantially completed and to avoid arbitrary acceleration or deferral of income. The specific criteria used to determine when a contract is substantially completed should be followed consistently. Circumstances to be considered in determining when a project is substantially completed include acceptance by the customer, departure from the site, and compliance with performance specifications.

The completed contract method may be used in circumstances in which financial position and results of operations would not vary materially from those resulting from use of the percentage of completion method (for example, in circumstances in which an entity has primarily short-term contracts). In accounting for such contracts, income ordinarily is recognized when performance is substantially completed and accepted. For example, the completed contract method, as opposed to the percentage of completion method, would not usually produce a material difference in net income or financial position for a small contractor that primarily performs relatively short-term contracts during an accounting period.

The completed contract method is the author's preference in circumstances in which estimates cannot meet the criteria for reasonable dependability under the percentage of completion method or where there are inherent hazards of the nature of those discussed in SOP No. 81-1. However, for circumstances in which there is an assurance that no loss will be incurred on a contract (for example, when the scope of the contract is ill-defined but the contractor is protected by a cost-plus contract or other contractual terms), the percentage of completion method based on a zero profit margin, rather than the completed contract method, should be used until more precise estimates can be made.

The significant difference between the percentage of completion method applied on the basis of a zero profit margin and the completed contract method relates to the effects on the income statement. Under the zero profit margin approach to applying the percentage of completion method, equal amounts of revenue and cost, measured on the basis of performance during the period, are presented in the income statement and no gross profit amount is presented in the income statement until the contract is completed. The zero profit margin approach to applying the percentage of completion method gives the users of general purpose financial statements an indication of the volume of a company's business and of the application of its economic resources.

The principal advantage of the completed contract method is that it is based on results as finally determined, rather than on estimates for unperformed work that may involve unforeseen costs and possible losses. The principal disadvantage is that it does not reflect current performance when the period of the contract extends into more than one accounting period. Under these circumstances, it may result in irregular recognition of income.

21.32 PROVISION FOR LOSSES.   Under either of the methods above, provision should be made for the entire loss on the contract in the period when current estimates of total contract costs indicate a loss. The provision for loss should represent the best judgment that can be made in the circumstances.

Other factors that should be considered in arriving at the projected loss on a contract include target penalties for late completion and rewards for early completion, nonreimbursable costs on cost-plus contracts, and the effect of change orders. When using the completed contract method and allocating general and administrative expenses to contract costs, total general and administrative expenses that are expected to be allocated to the contract are to be considered together with other estimated contract costs.

21.33 CONTRACT CLAIMS.   Claims are amounts in excess of the agreed contract price that a contractor seeks to collect from customers or others for customer-caused delays, errors in specifications and designs, unapproved change orders, or other causes of unanticipated additional costs. Recognition of amounts of additional contract revenue relating to claims is apropriate only if it is probable that the claim will result in additional contract revenue and if the amount can be reliably estimated.

These requirements are satisfied by the existence of all the following conditions:

- The contract or other evidence provides a legal basis for the claim.
- Additional costs are caused by circumstances that were unforeseen at the contract date and are not the result of deficiencies in the contractor's performance.
- Costs associated with the claim are identifiable and are reasonable in view of the work performed.
- The evidence supporting the claim is objective and verifiable.

If the foregoing requirements are met, revenue from a claim should be recorded only to the extent that contract costs relating to the claim have been incurred. The amounts recorded, if material, should be disclosed in the notes to the financial statements.

Change orders are modifications of an original contract that effectively change the provisions of the contract without adding new provisions. They may be initiated by either the contractor or the customer. Many change orders are unpriced; that is, the work to be performed is defined, but the adjustment to the contract price is to be negotiated later. For some change orders, both scope and price may be unapproved or in dispute. Accounting for change orders depends on the underlying circumstances, which may differ for each change order depending on the customer, the contract, and the nature of the change. Priced change orders represent an adjustment to the contract price and contract revenue, and costs should be adjusted to reflect these change orders.

Accounting for unpriced change orders depends on their characteristics and the circumstances in which they occur. Under the completed contract method, costs attributable to unpriced change orders should be deferred as contract costs if it is probable that aggregate contract costs, including costs attributable to change orders, will be recovered from contract revenues. For all unpriced change orders, recovery should be deemed probable if the future event or events necessary for recovery are likely to occur. Some factors to consider in evaluating whether recovery is probable are the customer's written approval of the scope of the change order, separate documentation for change order costs that are identifiable and reasonable, and the entity's favorable experience in negotiating change orders (especially as it relates to the specific type of contract and change order being evaluated). The following guidelines should be used in accounting for unpriced change orders under the percentage of completion method:

- Costs attributable to unpriced change orders should be treated as costs of contract performance in the period in which the costs are incurred if it is not probable that the costs will be recovered through a change in the contract price.
- If it is probable that the costs will be recovered through a change in the contract price, the costs should be deferred (excluded from the cost of contract performance) until the parties have agreed on the change in contract price or, alternatively, they should be treated as costs of contract performance in the period in which they are incurred, and contract revenue should be recognized to the extent of the costs incurred.
- If it is probable that the contract price will be adjusted by an amount that exceeds the costs attributable to the change order and the amount of the excess can be reliably estimated, the original contract price should also be adjusted for that amount when the costs are recognized as costs of contract performance if its realization is probable. However, since the substantiation of the amount of future revenue is difficult, revenue in excess of the costs attributable to unpriced change orders should only be recorded in circumstances in which realization is assured beyond a reasonable doubt, such as

circumstances in which an entity's historical experience provides assurance or in which an entity has received a bona fide pricing offer from the customer and records only the amount of the offer as revenue.

If change orders are in dispute or are unapproved in regard to both scope and price, they should be evaluated as claims.

OPERATIONS OF INCOME-PRODUCING PROPERTIES

21.34 RENTAL OPERATIONS.   Operations of income-producing properties represent a distinct segment of the real estate industry. Owners are often referred to as "real estate operators." Income-producing properties include office buildings, shopping centers, apartments, industrial buildings, and similar properties rented to others. A lease agreement is entered into between the owner/operator and the tenant for periods ranging from one month to many years, depending on the type of property. Sometimes an investor will acquire an existing income-producing property or alternatively will have the builder or developer construct the property. Some developers, frequently referred to as "investment builders," develop and construct income properties for their own use as investment properties.

SFAS No. 13 is the principal source of standards of financial accounting and reporting for leases. Under SFAS No. 13, a distinction is made between a **capital lease** and an **operating lease.** The lessor is required to account for a **capital lease** as a sale or a financing transaction. The lessee accounts for a capital lease as a purchase. An **operating lease,** on the other hand, requires the lessor to reflect rent income, operating expenses, and depreciation of the property over the lease term; the lessee must record rent expense.

Accounting for leases is discussed in Chapter 16 and therefore is not covered in depth here. Certain unique aspects of accounting for leases of real estate classified as operating leases, however, are covered below.

21.35 RENTAL INCOME.   Rental income from an operating lease should usually be recorded by a lessor as it becomes receivable in accordance with the provisions of the lease agreement.

FTB No. 85-3 provides that the effects of scheduled rent increases, which are included in minimum lease payments under SFAS No. 13, should be recognized by lessors and lessees on a straight-line basis over the lease term unless another systematic and rational allocation basis is more representative of the time pattern in which the leased property is physically employed. Using factors such as the time value of money, anticipated inflation, or expected future revenues to allocate scheduled rent increases is inappropriate because these factors do not relate to the time pattern of the physical usage of the leased property. However, such factors may affect the periodic reported rental income or expense if the lease agreement involves contingent rentals, which are excluded from minimum lease payments and accounted for separately under SFAS No. 13, as amended by SFAS No. 29.

A lease agreement may provide for scheduled rent increases designed to accommodate the lessee's projected physical use of the property. In these circumstances, FTB No. 88-1 provides for the lessee and the lessor to recognize the lease payments as follows:

a. If rents escalate in contemplation of the lessee's physical use of the leased property, including equipment, but the lessee takes possession of or controls the physical use of the property at the beginning of the lease term, all rental payments including the escalated rents, should be recognized as rental expenses or rental revenue on a straight-line basis in accordance with paragraph 15 of Statement No. 13 and Technical Bulletin 85-3 starting with the beginning of the lease term.

b. If rents escalate under a master lease agreement because the lessee gains access to and control over additional leased property at the time of the escalation, the escalated rents should be considered rental expense or rental revenue attributable to the leased property and recognized in proportion to the additional leased property in the years that the lessee has control over the use of the additional leased property. The amount of rental expense or rental revenue attributed to the additional leased property should be proportionate to the relative fair value of the additional property, as determined at the inception of the lease, in the applicable time periods during which the lessee controls its use.

(a) Cost Escalation.   Because of increased inflation, more lessors require that the lessee pay operating costs of the leased property such as utilities, real estate taxes, and common area maintenance. Some lessors require the lessee to pay for such costs when they escalate and exceed a specified rate or amount. In some cases, the lessee pays these costs directly. More commonly, however, the lessor pays the costs and is reimbursed by the lessee. In this situation, the lessor should generally record these reimbursement costs as a receivable at the time the costs are accrued, even though they may not be billed until a later date. Since these costs are sometimes billed at a later date, collectibility from the lessee should, of course, be considered.

(b) Percentage Rents.   Many retail leases, such as those on shopping centers, enable the lessor to collect additional rents, based on the excess of a stated percentage of the tenant's gross sales over the specified minimum rent. While the minimum rent is usually payable in periodic level amounts, percentage rents (sometimes called "overrides") are usually based on annual sales, often with a requirement for periodic payments toward the annual amount.

SFAS No. 29 (par. 13), "Determining Contingent Rentals," states: "Contingent rentals shall be includable in the determination of net income as accruable."

21.36 RENTAL COSTS.   The following considerations help determine the appropriate accounting for project rental costs.

(a) Chargeable to Future Periods.   Costs incurred to rent real estate should be deferred and charged to future periods when they are related to and their recovery is reasonably expected from future operations. Examples include initial direct costs such as commissions, legal fees, costs of credit investigations, and costs of preparing and processing documents for new leases acquired, and that portion of compensation applicable to the time spent on consummated leases. Other examples include costs of model units and related furnishings, rental facilities, semipermanent signs, grand openings, and unused rental brochures, but not rental overhead, such as rental salaries (see "Period Costs" below).

For leases accounted for as operating leases, deferred rental costs that can be directly related to revenue from a specific operating lease should be amortized over the term of the related lease in proportion to the recognition of rental income. Deferred rental costs that cannot be directly related to revenue from a specific operating lease should be amortized to expense over the period of expected benefit. The amortization period begins when the project is substantially completed and held available for occupancy. Estimated unrecoverable deferred rental costs associated with a lease or group of leases should be charged to expense when it becomes probable that the lease(s) will be terminated.

For leases accounted for as sales-type leases, deferred rental costs must be charged against income at the time the sale is recognized.

(b) Period Costs.   Costs that are incurred to rent real estate projects that do not meet the above criteria should be charged to expense as incurred. SFAS No. 67 specifically indicates that rental overhead, which is defined in its glossary to include rental salaries, is an example of such period costs. Other examples of expenditures that are period costs are initial indirect costs, such as that portion of salaries and other compensation and fees applicable to time spent in negotiating leases that are not consummated, supervisory and administrative expenses, and other indirect costs.

21.37 DEPRECIATION.   Under GAAP, the costs of income-producing properties must be depreciated. Depreciation, as defined by GAAP, is the systematic and rational allocation of the historical cost of depreciable assets (tangible assets, other than inventory, with limited lives of more than 1 year) over their useful lives.

In accounting for real estate operations, the most frequently used methods of depreciation are straight-line and decreasing charge methods. The most common **decreasing charge methods** are the declining balance and sum-of-the-years-digits methods. **Increasing charge methods,** such as the sinking fund method, are not generally accepted in the real estate industry in the United States. There is much merit to the sinking fund method (which is accepted in Canada) particularly for long-term leases, but it needs further study and authoritative literature before it should be considered acceptable in the real estate industry here.

The major components of a building, such as the plumbing and heating systems, may be identified and depreciated separately over their respective lives. This method, which is frequently used for tax purposes, usually results in a more rapid write-off.

21.38 INITIAL RENTAL OPERATIONS.   When a real estate project is substantially complete and held available for occupancy, the procedures listed here should be followed:

- Rental revenue should be recorded in income as earned.
- Operating costs should be charged to expense currently.
- Amortization of deferred rental costs should begin.
- Full depreciation of rental property should begin.
- Carrying costs, such as interest and property taxes, should be charged to expense as accrued.

If portions of a rental project are substantially completed and occupied by tenants or held available for occupancy and other portions have not yet reached that stage, the substantially completed portions should be accounted for as a separate project. Costs incurred should be allocated between the portions under construction and the portions substantially completed and held available for occupancy.

21.39 RENTAL EXPENSE.   Rental expense under an operating lease normally should be charged to operations by a lessee over the lease term on a basis consistent with the lessor's recording of income, with the exception of periodic accounting for percentage rent expense, which should be based on the estimated annual percentage rent.

ACCOUNTING FOR INVESTMENTS IN REAL ESTATE VENTURES

21.40 ORGANIZATION OF VENTURES.   The joint venture vehicle—the sharing of risk—has been widely utilized for many years in the construction, mining, and oil and gas industries as well as for real estate developments. Real estate joint ventures are typically entered into in recognition of the need for external assistance, for example, financing or market expertise. The most common of these needs is capital formation.

Real estate ventures are organized either as corporate entities or, more frequently, as partnerships. Limited partnerships are often used because of the advantages of limited liability. The venture is typically formed by a small group, with each investor actively contributing to the success of the venture and participating in overall management, and with no one individual or coporation controlling its operations. The venture is usually operated separately from other activities of the investors. Regardless of the legal form of the real estate venture, the accounting principles for recognition of profits and losses should be the same.

21.41 ACCOUNTING BACKGROUND.   Accounting practices in the real estate industry in general and, more specifically, accounting for investments in real estate ventures, have varied. The result was lack of comparability and, in some cases, a lack of comprehension. Therefore the following relevant pronouncements were issued:

- *APB Opinion No. 18.* In response to the wide variation in accounting for investments, the APB, in March 1971, issued Opinion No. 18, "The Equity Method of Accounting for Investments in Common Stock." This opinion became applicable to investments in unincorporated ventures, including partnerships, because of an interpretation promulgated in November 1971.
- *AICPA Statement of Position No. 78-9.* The AICPA recognized the continuing diversity of practice and in December 1978 issued SOP No. 78-9, "Accounting for Investments in Real Estate Ventures." This statement was issued to narrow the range of alternative practices used in accounting for investments in real estate ventures and to establish industry uniformity.
- *SFAS No. 94.* In response to the perceived problem of off-balance sheet financing, of which unconsolidated majority-owned subsidiaries were deemed to be the most significant aspect, the FASB issued SFAS No. 94, "Consolidation of All Majority-Owned Subsidiaries," in October 1987. SFAS No. 94 eliminated the concept of not consolidating nonhomogeneous operations and replaced it with the concept that the predominant factor in determining whether an investment requires consolidation should primarily be control rather than ownership of a majority voting interest. This Statement is also applicable to investments in unincorporated ventures, including partnerships.
- *AICPA Notice to Practitioners, ADC Loans, February 1986.* Recognizing that financial institutions needed guidance on accounting for real estate acquisition, development, and construction (ADC) arrangements, the AICPA issued the above notice (also known as the Third Notice). The notice provides accounting guidance on ADC arrangements that have virtually the same risks and potential rewards as those of joint ventures. It determined that accounting for such arrangements as loans would not be appropriate and provides guidance on the appropriate accounting.

  The SEC incorporated the notice into SAB No. 71 "Views Regarding Financial Statements of Properties Securing Mortgage Loans." SAB No. 71, and its amendment SAB No. 71A, provide guidance to registrants on the required reporting under this notice. Also, EITF Issue Nos. 84-4 and 86-21, as well as SAB No. 71, extend the provisions of this notice to all entities, not just financial institutions. It should be noted that a Task Force of the AICPA, formed in early 1990, is considering several aspects of accounting by lenders for ADC loans.

21.42 INVESTOR ACCOUNTING PROBLEMS.   The accounting literature mentioned above covers many of the special problems investors encounter in practice. The major areas are:

- Investor accounting for results of operations of ventures.
- Special accounting problems related to venture losses.
- Investor accounting for transactions with a real estate venture, including capital contributions.
- Financial statement presentation and disclosures.

A **controlling investor** should account for its income and losses from real estate ventures under the principles that apply to investments in subsidiaries, which usually require **consolidation** of the venture's operations. A **noncontrolling investor** should account for its share of income and losses in real estate ventures by using the equity method. Under the equity method, the initial investment is recorded by the investor at cost; thereafter, the carrying amount is increased by the investor's share of current earnings and decreased by the investor's share of current losses or distributions.

In accounting for transactions with a real estate venture, a controlling investor must **eliminate all intercompany profit.** When the investor does not control the venture, some situations require that all intercompany profit be eliminated, whereas in others, intercompany profit is eliminated by the investor only to the extent of its ownership interest in the venture. For example, as set forth in AICPA SOP No. 78-9, even a noncontrolling investor is precluded from recognizing any profit on a **contribution of real estate or services** to the venture. Accounting for other transactions covered by SOP 78-9 includes sales of real estate and services to the venture, interest income on loans and advances to the venture, and venture sales of real estate or services to an investor.

With regard to **financial statement presentation,** a controlling investor is usually required to consolidate venture operations. A noncontrolling investor should use the equity method, with the carrying value of the investment presented as a single amount in the balance sheet and the investor's share of venture earnings or losses as a single amount in the income statement. The proportionate share approach, which records the investor's share of each item of income, expense, asset, and liability, is not considered acceptable except for legal undivided interests.

The material above is only a very brief summary of comprehensive publications, and there are exceptions to some of those guidelines. In accounting for real estate venture operations and transactions, judgment must be exercised in applying the principles to assure that economic substance is fairly reflected no matter how complex the venture arrangements.

FINANCIAL REPORTING

21.43 FINANCIAL STATEMENT PRESENTATION. There are matters of financial statement presentation—as opposed to footnote disclosures—that are unique to the real estate industry. The financial reporting guidelines in this section are based on the principles set forth in authoritative literature and reporting practice.

(a) Balance Sheet. Real estate companies frequently present nonclassified balance sheets; that is, they do not distinguish between current and noncurrent assets or liabilities. This is because the operating cycle of most real estate companies exceeds one year.

Real estate companies normally list their assets on the balance sheet in the order liquidity, in the same manner as other companies. A second popular method, however, is to list the real estate assets first, to demonstrate their importance to the companies. In either case, **real estate assets** should be disclosed in the manner that is most demonstrative of the company's operations. These assets are often grouped according to the type of investment or operation as follows:

- Unimproved land.
- Land under development.
- Residential lots.
- Condominium and single-family dwellings.
- Rental properties.

(b) Statement of Income. Revenues and costs of sales are generally classified in a manner consistent with that described for real estate investments. In 1976 the Financial Accounting Standards Board issued SFAS No. 14, "Financial Reporting for Segments of a Business Enterprise," which states that the financial statements of an enterprise should include certain information about the industry segments of the enterprise. An industry segment is defined in paragraph 10(a) as ''a component of an enterprise engaged in providing a product or service or a group of related products and services primarily to unaffiliated customers (i.e. customers outside the enterprise) for profit.'' Some developers, however, have traditionally considered themselves to be in only one line of business.

21.44 ACCOUNTING POLICIES.   Because of the alternatives currently available in accounting for real estate developments, it is especially important to follow the guidelines of APB Opinion No. 22, ''Disclosure of Accounting Policies.'' The Opinion states (par. 12) that disclosures should include the accounting principles and methods that involve any of the following:

A selection from existing acceptable alternatives.

Principles and methods peculiar to the industry in which the reporting entity operates, even if such principles and methods are predominantly followed in that industry.

Unusual or innovative applications of generally accepted accounting principles (and, as applicable, of principles and methods peculiar to the industry in which the reporting entity operates).

The following lists certain accounting policy disclosures that are appropriate in the financial statements of a real estate company, as opposed to a manufacturing or service enterprise.

1. *Profit Recognition*. The accounting method used to determine income should be disclosed. Where different methods are used, the circumstances surrounding the application of each should also be disclosed. Similarly, a comment should be included indicating the timing of sales and related profit recognition.
2. *Cost Accounting*. The method of allocating cost to unit sales should be disclosed (e.g., relative market values, area, unit, specific identification). Financial statement disclosure should include, where applicable, capitalization policies for property taxes and other carrying costs, and policies with respect to capitalization or deferral of start-up or preoperating costs (selling costs, rental costs, initial operations).
3. *Net Realizable Value*. Inventory is required to be carried at the lower of cost or NRV. The method of determining NRV should preferably be disclosed.
4. *Investment in Real Estate Ventures*. Disclosures of the following accounting policies should be made:
   a. Method of inclusion in investor's accounts (e.g., equity or consolidation).
   b. Method of income recognition (e.g., equity or cost).
   c. Accounting principles of significant ventures.
   d. Profit recognition practices on transactions between the investor and the venture.

21.45 FOOTNOTE DISCLOSURES.   The following list describes other financial statement disclosures that are appropriate in the footnotes to the financial statements of a real estate developer.

Real Estate Assets. If a breakdown is not reflected on the balance sheet, it should be included in the footnotes. Disclosure should also be made of inventory subject to sales contracts that have not been recorded as sales and the portion of inventory serving as collateral for debts.

Inventory Write-Downs. Summarized information or explanations with respect to significant inventory write-downs should be disclosed in the footnotes because write-downs are generally important and unusual items.

Nonrecourse Debt. Although it is not appropriate to offset nonrecourse debt against the related asset, a note to the financial statements should disclose the amount and interrelationship of the nonrecourse debt with the cost of the related property.

Capitalization of Interest. SFAS No. 34 requires the disclosure of the amount of interest expensed and the amount capitalized.

Deferral of Profit Recognition. When transactions qualify as sales for accounting purposes but do not meet the tests for full profit recognition and, as a result, the installment or cost recovery methods are used, disclosure should be made of significant amounts of profit deferred, the nature of the transaction, and any other information deemed necessary for complete disclosure.

Investments in Real Estate Ventures. Typical disclosures with respect to significant real estate ventures include names of ventures, percentage of ownership interest, accounting and tax policies of the venture, the difference, if any, between the carrying amount of the investment and the investor's share of equity in net assets and the accounting policy regarding amortization of the difference, summarized information as to assets, liabilities, and results of operations or separate financial statements, and investor commitments with respect to joint ventures.

Construction Contractors. The principal reporting considerations for construction contractors relate to the two methods of income recognition: the percentage of completion method and the completed contract method.

When the completed contract method is used, an excess of accumulated costs over related billings should be shown in a classified balance sheet as a current asset, and an excess of accumulated billings over related costs should be shown as a current liability. If costs exceed billings on some contracts, and billings exceed costs on others, the contracts should ordinarily be segregated so that the asset side includes only those contracts on which costs exceed billings, and the liability side includes only those on which billings exceed costs.

Under the percentage of completion method, assets may include costs and related income not yet billed, with respect to certain contracts. Liabilities may include billings in excess of costs and related income with respect to other contracts.

The following disclosures, which are required for SEC reporting companies should generally be made by a nonpublic company whose principal activity is long-term contracting:

- Amounts billed but not paid by customers under retainage provisions in contracts, and indication of amounts expected to be collected in various years.

- Amounts included in receivables representing the recognized sales value of performance under long-term contracts where such amounts had not been billed and were not billable at the balance sheet date, along with a general description of the prerequisites for billing and an estimate of the amount expected to be collected in one year.

- Amounts included in receivables or inventories representing claims or other similar items subject to uncertainty concerning their determination or ultimate realization, together with a description of the nature and status of principal items, and amounts expected to be collected in one year.

- Amount of progress payments (billings) netted against inventory at the balance sheet date.

SOURCES AND SUGGESTED REFERENCES

Accounting Principles Board, "The Equity Method of Accounting for Investments in Common Stock," APB Opinion No. 18, Interpretation No. 18-2, AICPA, New York, November 1971.

———, "The Equity Method of Accounting for Investments in Common Stock," APB Opinion No. 18, AICPA, New York, March 1971.

———, "Accounting Changes," APB Opinion No. 20, AICPA, New York, 1971.

———, "Interest on Receivables and Payables," APB Opinion No. 21, AICPA, New York, August 1971.

———, "Disclosure of Accounting Policies," APB Opinion No. 22, AICPA, New York, April 1972.

American Institute of Certified Public Accountants, "Inventory Pricing," "Restatement and Revision of Accounting Research Bulletins," Accounting Research Bulletin No. 43, AICPA, New York, June 1953.

———, "Long-Term Construction-Type Contracts," Accounting Research Bulletin No. 45, AICPA, New York, October 1955.

———, "Audit and Accounting Guide for Construction Contractors," Accounting Guide, AICPA, New York, 1981.

———, "Guide for the Use of Real Estate Appraisal Information," Accounting Guide, AICPA, New York, 1987.

———, Issues Paper on "Accounting for Allowances for Losses on Certain Real Estate and Loans and Receivables Collaterialized by Real Estate," AICPA, New York, June 1979.

———, "Accounting Practices of Real Estate Investment Trusts," Statement of Position No. 75-2, AICPA, New York, June 27, 1975.

———, "Accounting for Costs to Sell and Rent, and Initial Real Estate Operations of, Real Estate Projects," Statement of Position No. 78-3, AICPA, New York, 1978.

———, "Accounting for Investments in Real Estate Ventures," Statement of Position No. 78-9, AICPA, New York, December 29, 1978.

———, "Accounting for Real Estate Acquisition, Development and Construction Costs," Statement of Position No. 80-3, AICPA, New York, 1980.

———, "Accounting for Performance of Construction-Type and Certain Production-Type Contracts," Statement of Position 81-1, AICPA, New York, July 15, 1981.

———, Third Notice to Practitioners, "Accounting for Real Estate Acquisition, Development, and Construction Arrangements," AICPA, New York, February 10, 1986.

Financial Accounting Standards Board, "Acquisition, Development, and Construction Loans," EITF Issue No. 84-4, FASB, Stamford, CT, 1984.

———, "Recognition of Receipts from Made-Up Rental Shortfalls," EITF Issue No. 85-27, FASB, Stamford, CT, 1985.

———, "Antispeculation Clauses in Real Estate Sales Contracts," EITF Issue No. 86-6, FASB, Stamford, CT, 1986.

———, "Application of the AICPA Notice to Practitioners Regarding Acquisition, Development, and Construction Arrangements to the Acquisition of an Operating Property," EITF Issue No. 86-21, FASB, Stamford, CT, 1986.

———, EITF Abstracts: A Summary of Proceedings of the FASB Emerging Issues Task Force, "Profit Recognition on Sale of Real Estate with Insurance Mortgages on Surety Bonds," EITF Issue No. 87-9, FASB, Norwalk, CT, 1988.

———, "Effect of Various Forms of Financing under FASB Statement No. 66," EITF Issue No. 88-24, FASB, Norwalk, Conn., 1988.

———, "Accounting for Leases," Statement of Financial Accounting Standards No. 13, FASB, Stamford, CT, November 1976.

———, "Financial Reporting for Segments of a Business Enterprise," Statement of Financial Accounting Standards No. 14, FASB, Stamford, CT, 1976.

———, "Accounting for Sales with Leasebacks (an amendment of FASB Statement No. 13)," Statement of Financial Accounting Standards No. 28, FASB, Stamford, CT, 1979.

———, "Determining Contingnent Rentals (an amendment of FASB Statement No. 13)," Statement of Financial Accounting Standards No. 29, FASB, Stamford, CT, 1979.

———, "Capitalization of Interest Cost," Statement of Financial Accounting Standards No. 34, FASB, Stamford, CT, October 1979.

———, "Designation of AICPA Guide and Statement of Position (SOP) 81-1 on Contractor Accounting and SOP 81-2 Concerning Hospital-Related Organizations as Preferable for Purposes of Applying APB Opinion 20," Statement of Financial Accounting Standards No. 56, FASB, Stamford, CT, February 1982.

———, "Accounting for Sales of Real Estate," Statement of Financial Accounting Standards No. 66, FASB, Stamford, CT, October 1982.

———, "Accounting for Costs and Initial Rental Operations of Real Estate Projects," Statement of Financial Accounting Standards No. 67, FASB, Stamford, CT, October 1982.

———, "Consolidation of all Majority-Owned Subsidiaries," Statement of Financial Accounting Standards No. 94, FASB, Stamford, CT, October 1987.

———, "Statement of Cash Flows," Statement of Financial Accounting Standards No. 95, FASB, Stamford, CT, November 1987.

———, "Accounting for Leases," Statement of Financial Accounting Standards No. 98, FASB, Norwalk, CT, May 1988.

———, "Accounting for Operating Leases with Scheduled Rent Increases," FASB Technical Bulletin No. 85-3, FASB, Stamford, CT, November 1985.

———, "Issues Relating to Accounting for Leases," FASB Technical Bulletin No. 88-1, FASB, Norwalk, CT, December 1988.

Klink, James J., *Real Estate Accounting and Reporting: A Guide for Developers, Investors, and Lenders,* 2nd ed., Wiley, New York, 1985.

Price Waterhouse, "Accounting for Condominium Sales," New York, 1984.

———, "Accounting for Sales of Real Estate," New York, 1983.

———, "Cost Accounting for Real Estate," New York, 1983.

———, "Investor Accounting for Real Estate Ventures," New York, 1979.

Securities and Exchange Commission, "Reporting Cash Flow and Other Related Data," Financial Reporting Policy 202, SEC, Washington, DC.

———, "Requirement for Financial Statements of Special Purpose Limited Partnerships," Financial Reporting Policy 405, SEC, Washington, DC.

———, "Preparation of Registration Statements Relating to Interests in Real Estate Limited Partnerships," Guide 5, SEC, Washington, DC.

———, "Special Instructions for Real Estate Operations to Be Acquired," Regulation S-X, Article 3, Rule 3-14, SEC, Washington, DC.

———, "Consolidation of Financial Statements of the Registrant and its Subsidiaries," Regulation S-X, Article 3A, Rule 3A-02, SEC, Washington, DC.

———, "Views on Financial Statements of Properties Securing Mortgage Loans," Staff Accounting Bulletin 71-71A (Topic No. 1I), SEC, Washington, DC.

———, "Offsetting Assets and Liabilities," Staff Accounting Bulletin Topic No. 11D, SEC, Washington, DC.

CHAPTER 22

FINANCIAL INSTITUTIONS

Robert A. Flaum, CPA

Price Waterhouse

Pauline Appleby, CPA

Price Waterhouse

Angel L. Saez, CPA

Price Waterhouse

CONTENTS

OVERVIEW

22.1 EVOLUTION.   Financial institutions have evolved over the centuries from the rudimentary functions of the money changer to the vast array in existence today. They range from commercial banks, which offer a broad base of financial services, to entities that specialize in specific functions and services, such as investment companies and securities brokers and dealers. These institutions have evolved in the main part to deal in one common commodity, money, which primarily exists only as book entries in the records of these financial institutions. The volume of money represented by actual coin and currency is dwarfed by the volume that exists in the book entry medium.

As economies developed and trade increased in volume and velocity on a worldwide basis, there was a greater need to develop a financial system to service these economies. Financial institutions have evolved to fill this need. Their continued development is in response to new challenges and, probably more compellingly, profit opportunities in the marketplace.

22.2 ROLE IN THE ECONOMY.   Financial institutions in their basic role provide a medium of exchange; however, they may also serve as a tool to regulate the economy. In a complex financial and economic environment, the regulation of financial institutions—directly and indirectly—is used to impact economic activity.

22.3 TYPES OF FINANCIAL INSTITUTIONS.   Many kinds of financial institutions exist. Some of the more important types are described below.

(a) Commercial Banks.   The once unique feature of these institutions—the ability to accept demand deposits—was significantly eroded as a result of the relaxation of the regulations restricting this activity to commercial banks. These institutions typically offer a broad range of financial services to their customers, including individuals, commercial organizations, and agricultural entities.

(b) Thrift Institutions. These institutions focus primarily on lending to individuals to finance residential properties and are funded by various forms of deposit accounts of individuals. Known as both savings and loan associations and also savings banks, there are two primary forms of organization—mutual and capital stock companies.

(c) Investment Banks. Investment banks or merchant banks deal with the financing requirements of corporations and institutions. They may be organized as corporations or partnerships.

(d) Securities Brokers and Dealers. Securities dealers buy and sell securities with customers and other dealers for their own account, that is, acting as principal. Securities brokers act only in an agency capacity, buying and selling on behalf of their customers in return for a commission on such activity. Brokers and dealers may perform other services, including underwriting of securities, offering investment advisory services, and acting as a depository for securities.

(e) Credit Unions. These organizations focus on individual borrowers and savers. They are typically sponsored by the individual's employer, which may provide the credit union with subsidized administration or other services. Credit unions are owned by their members/depositors.

(f) Investment Companies. These companies are a vehicle for investors to obtain the benefits of professional investment management at a low cost. These companies sell shares and invest the proceeds in specified investments as defined in the offering prospectus, primarily securities. Certain types of investment companies, so-called **mutual funds,** provide a liquid form of investment vehicle.

(g) Insurance Companies. These companies provide two major types of insurance—life, and property and liability. Benefit and claim coverage is provided to policyholders in return for premium payments, which are invested by the insurance companies to fund future payments. The premiums are determined based on projected payments derived using such factors as historical data and assumptions regarding projected interest and expense costs. There are two basic forms of insurance company—mutual and stock companies. The latter issue shares like many other companies, whereas mutual companies are owned by the insurance policyholders.

(h) Real Estate Investment Trusts. These organizations invest in real estate as either an equity owner or a lender and are funded by borrowing from other financial institutions and/or through the raising of share capital.

The distinctions between these types of institutions are becoming less clear as regulations evolve and, in some instances, disappear and competition increases. Significant changes in federal and state laws, including the change in reserving requirements under the Depository Institution Deregulation and Monetary Control Act of 1980 and the Depository Institution Amendments Act of 1982, have resulted in more homogeneity of financial institutions. In view of the range and diversity of financial institutions, this chapter will focus only on three major types—commercial banks, thrift institutions, and investment companies.

22.4 UNIQUE CHARACTERISTICS OF FINANCIAL INSTITUTIONS. Certain unique characteristics are common to most financial institutions, including the risks associated with their business activities. These business activities result in certain unique accounting matters which have led to the development of a body of accounting guidance that may differ from regulatory reporting treatment.

(a) Risks. Financial institutions are inherently risky—since it is by taking risks, to a greater or lesser extent, that profits are made. These risks may include:

Credit Risk. The risk that the counterparties to a transaction will be unwilling or unable to fulfill their obligations. This risk is one of the most fundamental risks faced by many financial institutions and is inherent in both on- and off-balance sheet transactions.

Interest Rate Risk. The risk that adverse movements in interest rates may result in loss of profits since financial institutions routinely borrow funds at one rate and lend them at another, higher rate.

Liquidity Risk. The risk that an institution may be unable to meet its obligations as they become due. An institution may acquire funds short-term and lend funds long-term to obtain favorable interest rate spreads thus creating liquidity risk if depositors or creditors demand repayment.

Currency Risk. The risk of loss arising from adverse movements in foreign exchange rates.

Market Risk. The exposure arising from movements in the market prices of financial assets. Rapid changes in market values may result in significant losses.

Operational Risk. This risk is not unique to financial institutions but is increased as a result of the high volume and value of the often complex transactions processed.

(b) Internal Accounting Control Systems. In view of the numerous risks inherent in their business, financial institutions need well-developed control systems to manage and control such risks. These risks are exacerbated by the high volume and value of transactions and the fungibility of the basic medium of most transactions—money. The internal accounting control systems can range from the most sophisticated artificial intelligence systems to the maintenance of a fundamental segregation of duties. There is often a highly regulated system of review and approval and a strong emphasis on exception transaction monitoring and reporting.

(i) Proof. A key element in this control environment, particularly for banks, is the proof function. Each department must prove the results of the accounting entries passed in a day to ensure that the records of the bank are in balance. This is especially important since banks generally close their records every day to monitor compliance with regulatory requirements. The proof process is complicated by the banks' use of one-sided entries in processing transactions that may result in imbalances if strict controls are not maintained to ensure both sides of the transaction are processed.

(ii) Internal Audit. Many institutions, particularly banks, have established internal audit functions that may be an important element in the system of internal accounting control. This department is normally charged with reviewing compliance with the control systems on an ongoing basis. This emphasis on internal accounting control is also in response to the high degree of regulation in many sectors of the financial services industry. Banks and certain other institutions are subject to examination by various supervisory agencies that focus on the controls in place to safeguard the institution, its assets, and its customers.

(c) Electronic Data Processing Systems. In view of the volume and velocity of transactions that may be processed, there is often a high utilization of computerized information processing by financial institutions. This reliance on data processing is generally far greater in financial institutions than other companies of a comparable size. Transactions may be initiated, processed, and executed with minimal manual intervention. Furthermore, with the increased emphasis on maintenance of electronic records, paper trails of transactions may be minimal or nonexistent. This environment will normally affect the type and extent of internal accounting control systems since greater reliance will be placed on them.

(d) Unique Accounting Matters

(i) Financial Statement Presentation.   In view of the unique operations of many types of financial institutions, certain specialized formats have evolved that are used by certain industry segments. For example, banking institutions place heavy emphasis on spread management, that is, the difference between the rates at which funds are borrowed and lent by the institution. Accordingly, a specialized format has evolved that focuses on the result of these activities, that is, net interest income. Exhibit 22.1 illustrates a typical statement of income for a commercial bank. Supplemental income statement information may be provided separately to show the impact of investing in certain tax-exempt securities. Such "taxable equivalent" data purports to illustrate pro forma summary income statement data as if such tax-exempt securities were fully taxable.

The balance sheets of financial institutions are not classified into short-term and long-term categories for assets and liabilities but are generally presented in descending order of maturity. Supplemental information is also presented by many banking institutions showing average balances of assets and liabilities and the associated income or expense and average rates earned or paid to better reflect the return on the balance sheet components.

The presentation of the statements of cash flows for certain financial institutions is affected by two amendments to SFAS No. 95, "Statement of Cash Flows," which allow these institutions, primarily banks and securities brokers and dealers, to net the cash flows for selected activities. These amendments, set forth in SFAS No. 102 and SFAS No. 104, permit the netting of trading, deposit taking, and loan activities, respectively.

SEC registrants are required to comply with certain industry-specific financial statement requirements set forth in Regulation S-X, for example, Article 6 for Registered Investment Companies and Article 9 for Bank Holding Companies. In addition, they must comply with other, often extensive, nonfinancial disclosures required by Regulation S-K, for example, Guide 3 for Bank Holding Companies.

Certain pervasive issues arise in accounting for financial institutions, including the recording of transactions on- or off-balance sheet and questions of valuation.

(ii) On/Off-Balance Sheet.   Financial institutions offer a variety of services and instruments. Depending on the nature of these transactions, they may not appear on the balance sheet and are only disclosed in a footnote to the financial statements. Consideration of such factors as (1) the capacity in which these transactions are undertaken, that is, as principal or only in an agency capacity (e.g., trust assets of a bank); (2) the type of instrument, that is, whether it is an asset or merely the right to acquire an asset (e.g., an option) or liability to fund a commitment (e.g., letter of credit); and (3) current industry conventions. There is little guidance in this area, and it is a focus for financial institutions, the accounting profession, and the regulators.

(iii) Valuation.   The issue of valuation is challenging not only from the perspective of ascertaining whether a historical cost or a market value is the more appropriate methodology but also because there are no true standard methodologies for valuing many instruments. There is increasing pressure from both the regulators and the accounting profession to move toward market value accounting for those industry segments that do not already present their financial statements on this basis. For example, the balance sheets of banks are presented in the main part on a historical cost basis reflecting the nontrading aspect of most of their activities, whereas securities brokers and dealers record the majority of their assets and liabilities on a market value basis reflecting the trading nature of their activities.

EXAMPLE BANK
Statement of Income
Years Ended December 31, 19X1 and 19X2

	19X2	19X1
Interest income:		
Interest and fees on loans	$17,147,500	$13,817,500
Interest on investment securities:		
U.S. Treasury securities	1,778,400	2,006,400
Obligations of other U.S. government agencies and corporations	483,600	696,800
Obligations of states and political subdivisions	1,560,000	1,570,000
Other securities	139,200	100,800
Interest on trading securities	574,600	626,600
Interest on deposits in banks	830,000	262,500
Interest on federal funds sold and securities purchased under reverse repurchase agreements	206,400	172,800
	22,719,700	19,253,400
Interest expense:		
Interest on deposits	16,115,000	13,350,000
Interest on federal funds purchased and securities sold under repurchase agreements	607,200	187,200
Interest on short-term borrowings	208,000	208,000
Long-term debt	125,000	125,000
	17,055,200	13,870,200
Net interest income	5,664,500	5,383,200
Provision for loan losses	150,000	170,000
Net interest income after provision for loan losses	5,514,500	5,213,200
Other income:		
Trust department income	467,500	415,000
Service fees	254,400	247,200
Trading asset revenues	452,400	174,200
Foreign exchange revenues	175,000	171,000
Other	185,000	192,500
	1,534,300	1,199,900
Other expense:		
Salaries	1,744,800	1,723,200
Pensions and other employee benefits	382,500	325,000
Occupancy expenses, net	890,000	760,000
Equipment	500,000	465,000
Other operating expenses	1,792,800	1,555,200
	5,310,100	4,828,400
Income before income taxes	1,738,700	1,584,700
Applicable income taxes	200,000	120,000
Net income	$ 1,538,700	$ 1,464,700

Exhibit 22.1.   Statement of income for a commercial bank.

(e) Accounting Guidance.   In addition to the main body of professional accounting literature that comprises GAAP discussed elsewhere in this volume, more specific industry guidance is provided in the industry-specific Audit Guides published by the AICPA, for example, "Audits of Banks" (1984) and "Savings and Loan Associations" (1987). A significant portion of the matters discussed by the EITF of the FASB relates to financial institutions and financial instruments, due to the rapidly evolving nature of this industry. However, there is significant diversity in accounting treatment for many financial instruments and products for which there is no authoritative guidance.

(f) GAAP and RAP. Many financial institutions are highly regulated by various bodies that promulgate specified reporting practices and procedures referred to collectively as regulatory accounting practices (RAP) which may differ from GAAP. Although the regulators generally prefer conformity of accounting between GAAP and RAP, the primary objective of the regulators is to monitor the safety and soundness of the financial institution and therefore there are differing accounting methodologies for certain transactions. It is noteworthy that the Financial Institutions Reform, Recovery and Enforcement Act of 1989 (FIRREA) directed federal banking regulators to adopt a single comprehensive accounting framework by August 1990.

REGULATION AND SUPERVISION

22.5 BACKGROUND. As a result of the financial repercussions of the Great Depression, the government took certain measures to maintain the stability of the country's financial system. Several new regulatory and supervisory agencies were created to promote economic stability, particularly in the banking industry, and strengthen the regulatory and supervisory agencies that were in existence at the time. Among the agencies created were the FDIC, the SEC, the FHLBB and the FSLIC. The agencies that were strengthened included the OCC and the FRS. These entities were responsible for designing and establishing policies and procedures for the regulation and supervision of national and state banks, foreign banks doing business in the United States, and other depository institutions. This regulatory and supervisory structure, created during the 1930s, was in place for almost 60 years. However, during 1989, as the result of the serious problems being experienced by the thrift industry, Congress enacted FIRREA, which changed the regulatory and supervisory structure of thrift institutions. FIRREA eliminated the FHLBB and the FSLIC. In their place, it created the OTS as the primary regulator of the thrift industry and the Savings Association Insurance Fund (SAIF) as the thrift institutions' insurer to be administered by the FDIC.

Even though several of the aforementioned federal agencies have overlapping regulatory and supervisory responsibilities over depository institutions, in general terms, the OCC has primary responsibility for national banks; the FRS has primary responsibility over state banks that are members of the FRS and all bank holding companies; the FDIC has primary responsibility for all state-insured banks that are not members of the FRS (nonmember banks); and the OTS has primary responsibility for thrift institutions. Exhibit 22.2 tabulates these regulatory responsibilities.

22.6 SECURITIES AND EXCHANGE COMMISSION. The SEC was created by Congress in 1934 to administer the Securities Act of 1933 (1933 Act) and the Securities Exchange Act of 1934 (1934 Act). The SEC is an independent agency of the U.S. government, consisting of five commissioners appointed by the President, subject to Senate confirmation.

The 1933 Act requires companies to register securities with the SEC before they may be sold, unless the security or the transaction is exempt. Banks are exempt from the registration requirements of the 1933 Act; however, bank holding companies are not. The 1934 Act, among other things, requires extensive and continuous reporting by companies that issue securities listed on the national exchanges or by companies with more than 500 security holders and more than $5 million in assets. Banks are not exempt from the requirements of the 1934 Act. However, the registration and reporting provisions related to banks are administered by the federal bank regulatory agencies instead of the SEC.

	OCC	State Banking Department	Federal Reserve	FDIC
Bank Classifications				
National banks	X			
State banks and trust companies				
Federal Reserve		X	X	
Nonmembers				
FDIC insured		X		X
Noninsured		X		X
Bank holding companies			X	

- All national banks are members of the Federal Reserve System.

- All national banks and state chartered member banks are insured by the FDIC.

Exhibit 22.2.   Regulatory supervision.

22.7 OFFICE OF THE COMPTROLLER OF THE CURRENCY.   The OCC was created in 1863 by the National Currency Act, later renamed the National Bank Act. The OCC is under the general direction of the Secretary of the Treasury. The Comptroller is appointed by the President, subject to Senate confirmation. The OCC shares the responsibility for regulating and supervising the banking industry with the FRS and the FDIC. Its primary objective is to promote safety and stability within the national banking system by regulating, supervising, and assessing the condition of national banks.

A national bank must obtain the approval of the OCC before it can be organized to do business. Once created, national banks must report continuously to the OCC and submit to its extensive regulating activities. The regulatory and supervisory functions of the OCC include:

- Examining national banks as often as it deems necessary.
- Overseeing the organization, conversion, merger, establishment of branches, relocation, and dissolution of national banks.
- Determining insolvency and referring insolvent banks to the FDIC.
- Administering the registration and reporting requirements of the 1934 Act as applied to national banks.

22.8 FEDERAL RESERVE SYSTEM.   The FRS was created by Congress in 1913 by the Federal Reserve Act. The primary role of the FRS is to establish and conduct monetary policy, as well as to regulate and supervise a wide range of financial activities. The structure of the FRS includes a Board of Governors, the Federal Reserve banks, and the member banks. The Board of Governors consists of seven members appointed by the President, subject to Senate confirmation. National banks must be members of the FRS. State banks are not required to, but may elect to become members. The member banks and other financial institutions are required to keep reserves with the FRS and member banks must subscribe to the capital stock of the reserve bank in the district to which they belong.

Since all national banks are supervised by the OCC, the FRS primarily regulates and supervises member state banks, including administering the registration and reporting requirements of the 1934 Act.

The regulatory and supervisory functions and other services provided by the FRS include:

- Examining the Federal Reserve banks, state member banks, bank holding companies, and their nonbank subsidiaries.

- Requiring reports of member and other banks.
- Setting discount rate.
- Issuing loans to members and other depository institutions.
- Approving or denying FRS membership applications and applications for branches, mergers, or creation of bank holding companies.
- Supplying currency when needed.
- Regulating foreign transactions of its member banks and the transactions of foreign banks doing business in the United States.
- Enforcing legislation and issuing rules and regulations dealing with "truth in lending."
- Issuing regulations to prevent deceptive and unfair bank practices.
- Providing procedures for transfer of funds throughout the country.

22.9 FEDERAL DEPOSIT INSURANCE CORPORATION.   The FDIC was created under the Banking Act of 1933. The main purpose for its creation was to insure bank deposits in order to maintain economic stability in the event of bank failures. FIRREA restructured the FDIC during 1989 to carry out broadened functions by insuring thrift institutions as well as banks. Therefore, the FDIC now insures all depository institutions except credit unions.

The FDIC is an independent agency of the U.S. government, managed by a five-member board of directors, consisting of the Comptroller of the Currency, the Director of the Office of Thrift Supervision, and three other members appointed by the President, subject to Senate confirmation.

The FDIC insures deposits under two separate funds—the Bank Insurance Fund and the Savings Association Insurance Fund. From its Bank Insurance Fund, the FDIC insures national and state banks that are members of the FRS. These institutions are required to be insured. Also insured from this fund are state nonmember banks and branches of foreign banks, which are not required to be insured by the FDIC, but may elect to do so.

From its SAIF, the FDIC insures all federal savings and loan associations and federal savings banks. These institutions are required to be insured. The state thrift institutions are also insured from this fund.

Currently, each account in a depository institution is insured to a maximum of $100,000. Other responsibilities of the FDIC include:

- Administering the registration and reporting requirements of the 1934 Act as applied to state nonmember banks.
- Supervising the liquidation of insolvent insured depository institutions.
- Providing financial support and additional measures to prevent insured depository institution failures.
- Supervising state nonmember insured banks by conducting bank examinations, regulating bank mergers, consolidations, and establishment of branches and establishing other regulatory controls.

22.10 OFFICE OF THRIFT SUPERVISION.   During 1989, FIRREA created the OTS under the Department of the Treasury. The OTS regulates federal and state thrift institutions and thrift holding companies. As a principal rule maker, examiner, and enforcement agency, OTS exercises primary regulatory authority to grant federal thrift institution charters, approve branching applications and allow mutual-to-thrift charter conversions. OTS is headed by a presidentially appointed director. The 12 district Federal Home Loan Banks continue to be the primary source of credit for thrift institutions.

COMMERCIAL BANKS

22.11 BACKGROUND. Commercial banks range from the multinational giants to single office entities. Other financial institutions now offer many of the services provided by commercial banks, including the extension of loans and the acceptance of deposits. The permissible activities of banks are governed by federal and state regulations, which in some cases prohibit the conduct of interstate banking. These restrictions gave rise to the development of bank holding companies during the early part of the century. The Bank Holding Act of 1956 (1956 Act) was enacted to regulate the types of services these companies could offer that are broader in scope than those permissible under banking regulations. Under this 1956 Act, bank holding companies may engage in various activities, in addition to the more traditional banking functions, including:

- Mortgage banking.
- Finance companies for general, consumer and commercial activities.
- Leasing.
- Investment, financial, and economic advisory services.
- Discount brokerage.
- Underwriting and dealing in commercial paper, municipal revenue bonds, mortgage and consumer receivable related securities.
- Underwriting insurance for credit life, credit accident, and health.

22.12 CAPITAL REQUIREMENTS. Banks are required to meet certain minimum capital standards. Since 1985 they have been required to maintain a minimum ratio of 6% of total capital to total assets. This simple formula did not consider off-balance sheet instruments or the relative risks of assets and liabilities. In July 1988, the Bank for International Settlements through the Committee on Banking Regulations and Supervisory Practices issued guidelines for minimum capital standards and measuring capital adequacy. These guidelines have been applied to commercial banks and are being phased in under transitional rules during 1990 and 1991 with full implementation required by the end of 1992.

These new 1992 "risk-based capital standards" establish two forms of capital—Tier I and Tier II. Banks are required to maintain a minimum of 8% of total capital to risk-weighted assets and at least half the amount (4%) should be in Tier I.

Tier I capital comprises common stockholders' equity (common stock, surplus, and retained earnings); any goodwill is deducted from Tier I capital. Banks may also include noncumulative preferred stock as Tier I capital. Bank holding companies may include preferred stock, both cumulative and noncumulative, up to 25% of Tier I capital.

Tier II capital includes general loan loss reserves, cumulative perpetual preferred stock, long-term preferred stock, hybrid capital instruments, subordinated debt, and intermediate preferred stock subject to certain qualifications. In particular, the allowance for loan losses will be includable up to a limit of 1.25% of risk-weighted assets.

Risk-weighted assets are determined by assigning specified percentages to assets and off-balance sheet activities. These percentages range from 0% for low risk assets, such as cash and U.S. government securities, to 100% for most of the loan portfolio. Off-balance sheet activities are first converted to a balance sheet **credit equivalent amount,** again ranging from 100% to 0% based on perceived risk, and then are assigned a percentage based on obligor, collateral, or guarantor.

22.13 LOANS. Lending of funds is one of the most significant activities of a commercial bank. A bank's ability to generate profits is largely based on its ability to generate a spread, that is, the difference between interest earned on money lent by the bank and interest earned on funds borrowed by the bank.

In response to customer requirements and the bank's assessment of the risks of lending, a variety of loan products have developed. Loans vary by type of security (or lack thereof), term, interest rate basis, and currency. Loans are extended in accordance with certain defined terms and covenants with which the borrower must comply. Loans may be extended on a secured or unsecured basis, payable on demand, at certain preestablished maturity dates, or may be "evergreen" revolving credits, which are renewed periodically.

Loan covenants are structured to establish requirements with which the borrower must comply. The bank may "call" the loan (i.e., demand payment) if these requirements are not complied with throughout the duration of the loan term. Typically, these requirements include minimum levels of working capital, earnings, and equity, and restrictions on the disposition of assets. Many agreements require evidence of a review of such covenants on a periodic basis to ascertain continued compliance.

(a) Types of Loans.   Unsecured loans are extended based on the bank's assessment of such factors as the financial condition and debt service capability of the borrower. Such loans generally have recourse to the assets and liabilities of the borrower only after secured claims are met. As such, these loans usually have higher risk characteristics and require a detailed knowledge of the borrower's other obligations, sources of revenue, and timing of cash flows to mitigate this risk.

Secured loans are structured in a variety of ways—the security is intended to minimize risk of loss if adverse circumstances develop, but it is not intended to be a source of repayment. Banks generally prefer to avoid taking possession of and liquidating collateral since it is often neither practical nor economic to do so if a viable alternative exists.

A security interest in collateral is a form of fixed or floating claim over assets, or it comprises a mortgage interest, which must be established in compliance with varying federal, state, and local requirements to ensure a valid interest is created or perfected. Typical forms of security interests include:

A **lien** is a right to retain property until the debt has been repaid. It may be evidenced by physical possession of evidence of ownership, for example, title deed, certificate of ownership. A mortgage is a lien on real property.

Assignment is the transfer of the right to receive benefit from a third party.

Hypothecation is a charge over items but does not comprise ownership. It is an indirect legal title.

A **guarantee** is the acceptance of responsibility by a third party. Such guarantees may be written or oral and their enforceability may significantly vary based on the legal jurisdiction.

A **pledge** is an express agreement confirming possession but not ownership of specific goods.

Loans may be classified in many ways—by their terms or by their purpose. Some of the most common types of loan classifications are described below.

Demand loans may be **called** (repayment demanded by the bank) at any time and are often unsecured. A demand loan is typically extended for a short duration, for example, 90–180 days, and is intended to fund short-term needs, with the principal usually being repaid at maturity.

Term loans are usually extended for longer periods and may be repaid in installments over the life of the loan or at maturity.

Commercial loans are, as their name implies, extended to commercial entities for a variety of purposes and under varying terms. An essential element in the administration of these types of credits is an understanding of the entity to which the loan is being extended and whether the entity is empowered to engage in the borrowing.

Real estate mortgage loans are normally secured by first mortgage liens on improved property, both commercial and residential. They are extended to both individuals for home purchases and also to companies for commercial purposes. Repayments are usually based on a level monthly amortization method which includes a principal and an interest portion. Such payments may also include amounts for the payment of insurance and tax payments, which the bank will then remit to the appropriate party. These latter payments are referred to as **escrow** payments and are required in the case of certain loans that are guaranteed by the FHA and the VA. Real estate mortgage loans are extended based on a percentage of the appraised value of the property being financed and normally are not for the full value of the loan. This policy allows for any possible deterioration in the value of the collateral if real estate markets decline.

Construction loans are extended to fund the construction of a property. As such, the loan is normally extended in a series of payments, with each payment only being disbursed to the borrower after a certain minimum level of construction is reached to provide collateral protection. Many banks may not finance construction loans unless a commitment is in place to provide permanent financing after the construction phase is complete. However, the bank itself may provide this permanent financing.

Consumer loans are payable on demand, single payment or in installments. They may have a fixed maturity or be a revolving credit line. They are normally small in size and may be of relatively short duration. As such, it is essential that the bank achieves economies of scale in order to effectively and profitably conduct this type of lending. Banks may originate the loan directly with the customer (direct loans) or may purchase them from a third party—typically the vendor of the goods being purchased by the loan proceeds, for example, automobile dealers—who will originate the loans.

(b) Regulation.   Lending activities of commercial banks are heavily regulated both from the perspective of protecting the soundness of the institution and also the customer's rights.

Legal limitations exist for banks with respect to:

Funding Limitations. There is an overall limitation on loans to one borrower which is based on a percentage (generally 15%) of the bank's capital position.

Executive Officers. National banks may only make loans to executive officers on an arm's length basis in accordance with certain criteria.

Stock Purchase. The Federal Reserve Board Regulation U restricts amounts that may be loaned for purchasing or financing securities.

Consumer Credit. Numerous regulations that are beyond the scope of this chapter are in effect to control the lending of credit to consumers. For example, the so-called **truth in lending** regulations require the consumer to be notified of the **true cost** of credit, that is, the actual effective interest rate, which may differ from the stated coupon rate.

(c) Accounting for Loans.   Most loans are recorded at their face value, that is, the value of the funds originally disbursed. Certain loans are recorded on a discounted basis, that is, interest and other payments (e.g., insurance premiums) are added to the amount advanced. Unearned income is then recorded as a contra asset to the loan balance. The loan portfolio is presented net of a reserve for uncollectible accounts in the financial statements.

Loan commitments, which represent loans that the bank has agreed to extend but has not yet disbursed, are recorded in memorandum accounts and are disclosed in the footnotes to the financial statements.

Interest is accrued on the principal amount in accordance with the loan terms. Usually interest is accrued daily. Unearned income on discounted loans is amortized to income over the life of the loan, using some form of interest method, to result in a level yield on the loan balance.

The accrual of interest is usually suspended on loans that are in excess of 90 days past due, unless the loan is both well secured and in the process of collection. When a loan is placed on such nonaccrual status, interest that has been accrued but not collected is reversed, and interest subsequently received is recorded on a cash basis or applied to reduce the principal balance depending on the bank's assessment of ultimate collectibility of the loan. An exception to this rule is that many banks do not place certain types of consumer loans on nonaccrual since they automatically charge off such loans within a relatively short period of becoming delinquent—generally within 180 days.

(i) Loan Fees.   Various types of fees are collected by banks in connection with lending activities. SFAS No. 91, "Accounting for Nonrefundable Fees and Costs Associated with Originating or Acquiring Loans and Initial Direct Costs of Leases," requires that the majority of such fees and associated direct origination costs be offset. The net amount must be deferred as part of the loan (and reported as a component of loans in the balance sheet) and recognized in interest income over the life of the loan and/or loan commitment period as an adjustment of the yield on the loan. The requirements for cost deferral under this standard are quite restrictive and require direct linkage to the loan origination process. Activities for which costs may be deferred include (1) evaluating the borrower, guarantees, collateral, and other security; (2) preparation and processing of loan documentation for loan origination; and (3) negotiating and closing the loan. Certain costs are specifically precluded from deferral, for example, advertising and solicitation, credit supervision and administration, costs of unsuccessful loan originations and other activities not **directly** related to the extension of a loan.

Loan fees and costs for loans originated or purchased for resale are deferred and are recognized when the related loan is sold.

Commitment fees to purchase or originate loans, net of direct origination costs, are generally deferred and amortized over the life of the loan when it is extended. If the commitment expires, then the fees are recognized in other income on expiration of the commitment. There are two main exceptions to this general treatment:

- If past experience indicates that the extension of a loan is unlikely, then the fee is recognized over the commitment period.
- Nominal fees, which are determined retroactively, on a commitment to extend funds at a market rate, may be recognized in income at the determination date.

Certain fees may be recognized when received, primarily loan syndication fees. Generally, the yield on the portion of the loan retained by the syndicating bank must at least equal the yield received by the other members of the syndicate. If this is not the case, a portion of the fees designated as a syndication fee must be deferred and amortized to income to achieve a yield equal to the average yield of the other banks in the syndicate. The distinctions between syndications and participations are becoming less distinct; as a result, EITF Issue No. 88-17 provides guidance with respect to criteria for **in substance** syndications. According to the EITF consensus, generally if at least 50% of the loan balance is sold within 60 days of origination and the risks and rewards of the seller and purchaser are shared proportionately from the date of sale, then the transaction can be considered to be a syndication, with appropriate fee recognition principles applied.

Purchased loans are recorded at cost net of fees paid/received. The difference between this recorded amount and the principal amount of the loan is amortized to income over the life of the loan to produce a level yield. Acquisition costs are not deferred, but are expensed as incurred.

(ii) Acquisition, Development, and Construction Arrangements.   Certain transactions that appear to be loans are considered effectively to be investments in the real estate property financed. These transactions are required to be presented separately from loans and accounted for as real estate investments using the guidance set forth in the AICPA Notice to Practitioners dated February 1986. Factors indicating such treatment include arrangements whereby the financial institution:

1. Provides substantially all financing to acquire, develop and, construct the property, that is, borrower has little or no equity in the property.
2. Funds the origination or commitment fees through the loan.
3. Funds substantially all interest and fees through the loan.
4. Has security only in the project with no recourse to other assets or guarantee of the borrower.
5. Can recover its investment only through sale to third parties, refinancing, or cash flow of the project.
6. Is unlikely to foreclose on the project during development since no payments are due during this period and therefore the loan cannot normally become delinquent.

(iii) Troubled Debt Restructurings.   Banks may routinely restructure loans to meet a borrower's changing circumstances. The new loan terms are reflected in the financial statements essentially as if a new loan has been made. However, if "a creditor for economic or legal reasons related to the debtor's financial difficulties grants a concession . . . that it would not otherwise consider," then SFAS No. 15, "Accounting by Debtors and Creditors for Troubled Debt Restructurings," applies. This standard defines what constitutes a **troubled debt restructuring,** which may include one or more of the following:

- Transfers of assets of the debtor or an equity interest in the debtor to partially or fully satisfy a debt.
- Modification of debt terms, including reduction of one or more of the following (1) interest rates with or without extensions of maturity date(s), (2) face or maturity amounts, and (3) accrued interest.

Generally, a troubled debt restructuring is not indicated if the assets received at least equal the recorded value of the debt, interest rate and maturity date changes are reflective of current market conditions, and the debtor can obtain third party financing at approximately market rates. However, if the SFAS No. 15 criteria are met, the bank is required to compare the expected cash flows under the new terms to the recorded loan balance. Any deficiency is recorded as a charge-off. A difference in the expected cash flows between the original terms and the renegotiated terms is recorded prospectively on a level yield basis provided such cash flows are in excess of the recorded balance.

(iv) Other Real Estate Acquired in Settlement of Loans.   Borrowers may experience such severe financial problems that the bank's only source of repayment is to repossess the collateral securing the loan. Real estate is the most common type of collateral that is repossessed. The bank records the repossessed property at its estimated fair value, net of disposition costs. Such property is recorded as an **other asset** and is classified as **other real estate.** Bank regulators restrict the length of time that repossessed property may be held—typically 5 years.

(v) In Substance Foreclosure.   In some instances, as a result of declining values, the bank is deemed to have taken **in substance repossession** of collateral securing a loan. The SEC FRR No. 28 provides guidance on the criteria for such treatment, including:

1. The debtor has little or no equity in the collateral.
2. Repayment of the loan is expected only from sale or operation of the collateral.
3. The debtor has either (1) formally or effectively abandoned control over the collateral or (2) retained control, but it is doubtful that the debtor can either rebuild equity or repay the loan in the foreseeable future.

Loans that are considered to be in substance repossessions are accounted for at fair value in accordance with SFAS No. 15, that is, in the same manner as repossessed collateral.

(vi) Sale of Loans. Banks may originate and sell loans for a variety of reasons—to diversify risk by retaining a smaller exposure to a borrower or to retain a portion of the interest on the loan while not retaining the loan balance on the balance sheet. This latter motivation is becoming increasingly important in view of the recent introduction of the risk-based capital rules. Loans held for resale are recorded at the lower of cost or current market value. Loan sales to other institutions are typically referred to as participations, and the loan balance is recorded net of the amount participated or sold, provided there is no recourse to the selling bank. The bank records a gain or loss calculated based on the difference between the sale proceeds and the recorded value of the loan. If there are any recourse provisions, then these provisions must be evaluated under the following requirements of SFAS No. 77, "Reporting by Transferors for Transfers of Receivables with Recourse":

- The selling bank transfers the future economic benefits associated with the receivables and has no option to repurchase them at a future date.
- A reasonable estimate can be made of the recourse obligation. The recourse, including collectibility of the receivable and related repossession and collection costs, must be quantifiable and will enter into the calculation of the gain or loss on sale.
- The selling bank cannot be required to repurchase the receivable except under the recourse provisions. This prohibition does not cover a de minimis repurchase provision when the receivables balances have reached a minimum level.

If these provisions are not met, then the transaction must be recorded as a financing.

Loan participations are differentiated from syndications since under participations the bank owns the whole loan and subsequently sells a portion, whereas under syndications the bank never owns those portions of the loan that are syndicated to other banks. In practice these distinctions become somewhat less distinct.

(vii) Securitization. A newly emerging area is that of securitization where loans are sold to a separate entity that then finances the purchase through the issuance of debt securities or undivided interests in the loans. Securitization typically involves some form of recourse, and therefore the provisions of SFAS No. 77 apply in accounting for these transactions. No recourse is allowed in order to record a sale for regulatory purposes. However, sale treatment for regulatory purposes may be achieved if the recourse requirements are funded through the future cash flows of the transaction. Therefore, a portion of the periodic payments from the receivables is designated to fund the recourse provision. The regulators are currently examining the concept of what constitutes recourse, emphasizing the substance of recourse over form. Many of these transactions limit the amount of total possible recourse by purchasing a letter of credit from a highly rated financial institution. The selling bank often retains the servicing rights to the sold loans for which it receives a servicing fee.

The gain or loss on sale of the loans is calculated as the difference between the recorded cost and the sales price, including future expected cash flows, after adjusting for estimated recourse costs, normal servicing fees (in accordance with industry costs), and costs of securitization.

(viii) Syndications. Loan syndications are generally formed when a group of banks come together to finance a credit that a single bank would be unwilling or unable to finance. Typically, one bank will organize the syndication for which a separate fee will be received. The accounting treatment for this fee differs markedly than for other loan origination fees as discussed above, since it may be recorded in income at the time of the syndication.

(d) Allowance for Loan Losses. The allowance for loan losses is "the estimated amount of losses in the bank's portfolio" (AICPA, 1984). The allowance is increased by provisions that are charged to the statement of income and is decreased by charge-offs (write-offs) of loans that are deemed to be uncollectible. Any recoveries on previously charged-off loans are generally applied to the allowance. The assessment of the adequacy of the allowance for loan losses is necessarily highly judgmental. Banks use various methodologies to assess the adequacy, including a review of delinquent loans, prior experience, and the quality of the current portfolio. The assessment of the factors to be considered in evaluating the adequacy of the reserve for loan losses is discussed in the AICPA publication "Auditing the Allowance for Credit Losses of Banks."

22.14 DIRECT LEASE FINANCING AND ACCOUNTING FOR LEASES. Leasing is a form of debt financing similar to term lending with the same type of inherent risks. This topic is discussed in more length in Chapter 16 of this book. Certain unique factors for banks include the tax treatment of the lease, that is, which party (borrower or lender) obtains the benefit of depreciation of the asset and which party will own the financed asset at maturity of the lease.

Lease financings may be accounted for as a financing lease (i.e., a loan), which will be recorded on the balance sheet net of unearned income and expected residual value in accordance with the requirements of SFAS No. 13, "Accounting for Leases."

22.15 INVESTMENTS AND TRADING. Banks use a variety of financial instruments for three basic purposes: investing, trading, and hedging activities.

Investing activities are undertaken for one or more of the following primary reasons: liquidity, asset risk diversification, income, and meeting of regulatory requirements to secure certain deposits through pledging. Since the primary purpose is to meet liquidity requirements, investment instruments must be readily convertible into cash in case the holders of liabilities, including deposit account holders, request repayment. Although some level of sales and purchases of such investments would appear to be acceptable within the context of their liquidity function, high levels of activity would indicate that these assets are of a trading nature. This area is a focus of much attention from the regulators and the accounting profession, and the requirements for recording assets as investment securities is expected to become more restrictive.

Trading activity, by contrast, involves speculation in certain instruments by taking positions with the goal of profiting from price movements. If the price of an instrument is expected to increase, the bank will go **long** (i.e., purchase the instrument) with the intent to resell it at a profit at a later date. If the price is expected to decrease, the bank will go **short** (i.e., sell the instrument) with the intention of repurchasing it at a lower price at a later date.

Hedging activities are designed to reduce risk. If a bank owns an asset that is vulnerable to risk, for example, interest rate or foreign currency risk, then it may enter into a financial instrument contract, such as a futures contract or forward foreign exchange contract, to mitigate or offset the exposure.

Since the bank may enter into a variety of instruments for each of the three activities—investing, trading, and hedging—it is essential that the rationale for the activity be clearly defined and segregated by type to ensure appropriate accounting treatment is applied in each case. The principal types of instruments include certain permissible securities and bonds, contracts for foreign exchange, financial futures, swaps, and options instruments.

The accounting guidance with respect to many of the instruments used by banks continues to evolve. The FASB is pursuing a project addressing the accounting for traditional and innovative financial instruments and off-balance sheet financing. This three-phase project, which is expected to span several years, is addressing disclosure, recognition, and measurement, and distinguishment between liability and equity instruments.

(a) Accounting for Investment and Trading Securities.   Banks are restricted as to the types of securities which they can own. Essentially banks may only own and deal in U.S. government securities, municipal bonds, and certain other bonds, notes, and debentures. The banking industry is pressing to repeal or relax the restrictions on securities activities. Some selective exceptions have been granted to certain banks as a preliminary step in this process. Under Regulation 20 a number of banks have established separate subsidiaries that are permitted to underwrite certain types of securities subject to a cap on the income that may be generated by this type of activity (10% of revenue at the time of the writing of this chapter). These subsidiaries are required to be separately capitalized from the bank and must establish **firewalls** around the subsidiaries to protect the bank in the event of financial loss to the subsidiaries.

Investment and trading portfolios are presented separately in the financial statements and the activities should be carefully segregated. Transfers between the portfolios require appropriate accounting treatment, that is, a transfer between the investment portfolio and the trading portfolio must be marked to market.

Historically, investment securities have been recorded at cost, with any difference from the face amount being recorded as a premium or discount, which is amortized to income using an interest method over the period held.

Historically, banks have not recognized changes in the market value of these securities if they have the intent and ability to hold them to maturity.

Although investment securities and trading securities are required to be recorded on a trade date basis, in practice they are usually recorded on a settlement date which is generally 5 days later. This use of settlement date accounting is considered acceptable provided that the results are not materially different.

Trading account securities are held for resale and therefore the accounting treatment is different. Trading securities are recorded at market value.

Interest income on investment and trading securities is recorded separately as a component of interest income, whereas gains and losses are recorded as a separate component of noninterest income or loss. Trading gains and losses include both realized and also unrealized (valuation) gains and losses.

Gains and losses on investment securities represent the results of actual sales of investment securities. Certain transactions, so-called **wash sales** may not be considered to be completed transactions if securities are sold and substantially similar securities are repurchased within a short period of time. In these cases no gain or loss is recorded. In order for a transaction to have taken place, there must be a reasonable period between the sale and purchase of substantially similar securities and during which the bank must have been at risk.

(b) Accounting for Other Financial Instruments.   Banks use other financial instruments for both trading and hedging activity. Many of these instruments are traded on established exchanges, on the interbank market and also in private transactions between the bank and its customers. The principal amounts of these transactions are not recorded on the balance sheet of the bank but are recorded in memorandum accounts in view of the nature of these transactions. The most common types are discussed in (c) through (f) below.

(c) Accounting for Foreign Exchange Contracts.   These contracts are used both to provide a service to customers and as part of the bank's trading activities. The bank profits by maintaining a margin between the purchase and sales price. Contracts may be for current trades (spot contract), future dates (forward contract), or swap contracts. The bank may also enter into these contracts to hedge a foreign currency exposure.

The accounting for foreign exchange contracts is set forth in SFAS No. 52, "Foreign Currency Translation," which requires mark to market accounting for trading contracts (i.e., the difference between the contracted rate for the contract and the currently available rate for the same maturity date). The realized and unrealized gains on these contracts are therefore recorded as a component of other income. No separate accounting recognition is given to the premium or discount for these contracts.

Certain contracts are accounted for differently provided they meet the required criteria under SFAS No. 52 for hedge accounting, including such factors as the contract being designated and effective as a hedge of the hedged item or commitment. For these transactions a discount or premium is calculated at inception which comprises the difference between the spot and forward rates at that date. Typically, this premium or discount is then amortized to income over the life of the hedged item irrespective of the recognition of gain or loss on the hedge contract. Gains and losses on hedge contracts (i.e., the difference between the spot rate at the balance sheet date and the spot rate at inception) generally follow the gains and losses on the hedged item and therefore are recorded in income, when incurred, over the life of the hedged item. (Exceptions to these general rules apply for hedges of foreign currency commitments and investments in foreign entities.)

(d) Accounting for Financial Futures.   A financial futures contract is an agreement to make or take delivery of a financial instrument (interest rate instrument, currency, and certain stock indices) at a future date. Most futures contracts are closed out prior to the delivery date by entering into an offsetting contract. Banks use futures for both trading and hedging purposes.

The accounting for futures contracts is set forth in SFAS No. 80, "Accounting for Futures Contracts," which requires that all contracts that do not meet certain very stringent criteria for hedge accounting should be marked to market with realized and unrealized gains and losses recorded in other income. Although the criteria for hedge accounting are more stringent than those under SFAS No. 52, SFAS No. 80 is more flexible in that it allows hedging of anticipated transactions. SFAS No. 80 requires that:

- The item to be hedged exposes the bank to price or interest rate risk.
- The hedge reduces the exposure and is designated as a hedge. There must be a high correlation between changes in the value of the hedged item and the type of futures contract used for hedging.

The effect of changes in the value of the futures contract is recognized as an adjustment of the value of the hedged item or is deferred and recognized in its measurement in the case of a futures transaction.

(e) Accounting for Swaps.   These are contracts between parties to exchange sets of cash flows based on a predetermined **notional** principal. Only the cash flows are exchanged (usually on a net basis) with no principal exchanged; it is merely a reference point to determine the amounts of the cash flows. Swaps are used to change the nature or cost of existing transactions, for example, exchanging fixed rate debt cash flows for floating rate cash flows. The principal types of swaps are interest rate swaps and currency swaps.

There is no authoritative guidance for the accounting for swap transactions and there is some diversity in practice between institutions. However, predominant practice appears to be that trading swaps are marked to market, whereas hedge swaps are accounted for on an accrual basis over the life of the swap, that is, the net cash inflow or outflow is recorded as a component of net interest income on a normal accrual basis.

(f) Accounting for Options.   Options contracts provide the purchaser with the right, but not the obligation, to buy a specified instrument, such as currencies, interest rate products, or futures. They also put the seller under the obligation to deliver the instrument to the buyer but only at the buyer's option.

Accounting guidance is provided by the AICPA March 1986 Issues Paper, "Accounting for Options," which provides recommendations but is not intended to establish standards. This paper concludes that trading options should be marked to market and the resultant unrealized gains and losses included in trading income. Premiums paid or received are recorded in the balance sheet as trading account assets and other liabilities. When options are exercised, liquidated, or expire, the value of the premium paid or received remaining on the balance sheet enters into the calculation of the gain or loss on the option position. If the following specified criteria are met, then hedge accounting may be used:

- The option must reduce exposure created by the transaction being hedged. (This differs from the more stringent SFAS No. 80 requirement to assess enterprise risk.)
- High correlation between changes in the market value of the hedged item and the option must be probable.
- The price of the hedged item and the option must have a clear relationship.
- The option must be designated as a hedge.

Hedge accounting can only be used to the extent of the premiums received on options sold, and hedge accounting cannot be used if the hedged item is an asset carried at cost.

22.16 MONEY MARKETS.   Money markets are the wholesale markets for short-term financial instruments that banks use to borrow or lend money. There are several primary types of instruments used, including interbank placements, certificates of deposit, federal funds, sale and repurchase agreements, commercial paper, bankers' acceptances, and treasury bills.

Interbank placements are made between banks to provide funds or as a source of investment. The most active market is the "Eurocurrency" market, which involves the placement of currency deposits outside the national boundaries of the institution.

(a) Accounting for Certificates of Deposit.   Certificates of deposit are negotiable instruments issued by a bank for a fixed period of time. They are usually recorded at par value, and interest is accrued in accordance with the terms of the instrument. As there is an active secondary market, these deposits are generally liquid.

(b) Accounting for Federal Funds.   U.S. banks are required to maintain reserve accounts at the Federal Reserve Bank to collateralize certain types of deposit accounts maintained by customers. Since these reserve account deposits are noninterest-bearing, banks attempt to maintain the minimum required. Any excess or deficiency may be purchased or sold to other institutions to maintain their reserve requirements. Such purchases and sales may be overnight or for longer periods and are recorded as lendings or borrowings, with interest income or expense recorded in accordance with the terms of the transaction between the banks.

(c) Accounting for Sale and Repurchase Agreements.   These transactions are structured as sales and repurchases of securities that are substantially the same. For accounting purposes they are treated as short-term loans or borrowings secured by collateral in the form of securities that are expected to be repurchased. The security that secures the loan or borrowing remains on the balance sheet, and the "repo" is also recorded. The difference in price between the purchase and sale of the repo represents the interest charge that is recorded for the use of funds borrowed or lent.

(d) Accounting for Commercial Paper. Commercial paper is an unsecured form of borrowing and therefore is only available to entities with a high credit rating. It is usually issued and recorded on a discount basis even when issued in interest-bearing form.

22.17 ACCOUNTING FOR DEPOSITS. Deposit accounts are funds held by the bank for another party, which may be a company, an individual, or another bank. In many instances, deposit accounts are the most significant form of funding for the bank. There are varying forms of deposit account—both interest-bearing and noninterest-bearing, payable on demand and payable at agreed dates.

Demand deposits are commonly referred to as **checking accounts.** Although they are an attractive form of funding for banks because they are noninterest-bearing, they are potentially highly volatile since they are subject to withdrawal at any time.

Savings accounts are interest-bearing and may have certain features similar to demand deposits. For example, **NOW** accounts and money market accounts are interest-bearing variations of the demand deposit accounts but have certain requirements, such as maintenance of minimum balances. Other types of savings accounts may have restrictions as to withdrawal and access.

Time deposit accounts are repaid after a specified period and are generally in one of two forms—certificates of deposit and open time deposits.

Deposit accounts are recorded based on the amounts deposited, with interest expense being accrued in accordance with the deposit terms.

22.18 ACCOUNTING FOR TRADE FINANCE. Trade finance instruments are designed to finance trade activities by substituting the credit of the bank for that of the importer of the goods. Many forms of letters of credit have evolved to meet various needs. In its simplest form an importer requests a bank to issue a letter of credit guaranteeing payment of a specified amount on receipt of certain documents (typically documents evidencing satisfactory shipment of goods in accordance with the agreed-upon contract between the parties). Such payment by the importer's bank will often result in the creation of a loan to that customer. The exporter's bank usually acts as the advising bank and will eventually receive payment from the issuing bank for the account of the exporter. The advising bank may remit payment to the exporter immediately on the shipment of goods and therefore **accepts** the credit risk of receiving future payment from the importer's bank.

Standby and performance letters of credit, unlike other trade letters of credit, are not expected to have funds drawn against them. They are used to provide assurance that the issuing bank will provide financing if the principal party does not perform under the contractual terms of an agreement. The bank will then in turn obtain reimbursement from the principal party. These types of letters of credit are used for a variety of purposes, including construction contracts and issuances of commercial paper by various companies.

A banker's acceptance is created when a purchaser of goods requests that a bill of exchange be drawn and **accepted** by its bank, that is, the bank guarantees payment at a specified maturity date. Such instruments are readily marketable on the secondary markets since they rely on the creditworthiness of the issuing bank for payment and are bearer paper.

Letters of credit are considered to be contingent liabilities of the bank until accepted and as such are recorded in memorandum accounts only and are disclosed in the footnotes to the financial statements.

Bankers' acceptances are recorded as both an asset and a liability—the asset being the receivable from the bank's customer and the liability being the liability of the bank to make payment under the bill of exchange.

The fees charged for providing these types of trade instruments are recorded in income in

1. Brazilian Import Co. agrees to purchase equipment from German Export Co.
2. Import Co. arranges for issuance of Letter of Credit through Brazilian Bank, which is issued to German Bank in favor of Export Co. as beneficiary.
3. German Bank notifies Export Co. of the terms, and Export Co. ships equipment to Import Co.
4. Export Co. presents German Bank with documentary evidence supporting shipment and demands payment.
5. German Bank makes payment to Export Co. and then receives payment from Brazilian Bank, after providing bill of exchange.
6. Brazilian Bank forwards documents to Import Co., which uses it to claim equipment upon arrival in Brazil.

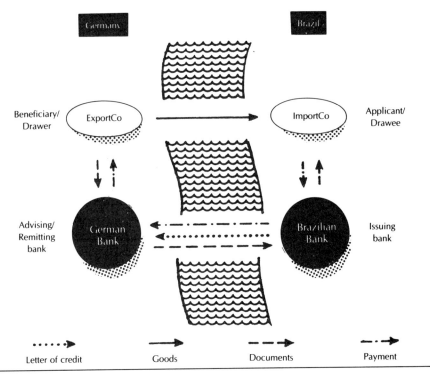

Exhibit 22.3.   Example of a trade finance transaction.

accordance with the requirements of SFAS No. 91. Exhibit 22.3 provides an example of a trade finance transaction.

22.19 ACCOUNTING FOR FIDUCIARY SERVICES.   In their fiduciary capacity, banks must serve their clients' interests and must act in good faith at a level absent in most other banking activities. In view of this high degree of fiduciary responsibility, banks usually segregate the responsibilities of the trust department from that of the rest of the bank. This segregation is designed to maintain a highly objective viewpoint in the fiduciary area. Fiduciary services range from the simple safekeeping of valuables to the investment management of large pension funds.

Custodial, safekeeping, and safe deposit activities involve the receipt, storage, and issuance of receipts for a range of valuable assets. This may involve the holding of bonds, stocks, and currency in escrow pending the performance under a contract, or merely the maintenance of a secure depository for valuables or title deeds. As custodian, the bank may receive interest and dividends on securities for the account of customers.

Investment management may be discretionary, whereby the bank has certain defined powers to make investments, or nondiscretionary, whereby the bank may only execute investment transactions based on customers' instructions. The former obviously involves a higher degree of risk to the institution and creates an obligation to make prudent investment decisions.

Other fiduciary services include trust administration, stock registrar, and bank trustee. Trust administration involves holding or management of property, such as pension funds and estates, for the benefit of others. Stock registrar and bank trustee functions include the maintenance of records and execution of securities transactions, including changes in ownership and payment of dividends and interest.

Since the assets and liabilities of the trust department of the bank are held in an agency capacity, they are not recorded on the balance sheet of the bank. These activities do, however, generate significant fee income, which is recorded when earned in the statement of income.

22.20 ACCOUNTING FOR OTHER FEE INCOME ACTIVITIES. Emphasis on fee income-generating activities has increased in response to both the new risk-based capital rules, which are creating more pressure to reduce the size of the balance sheet, and also a general increase in competition in the financial services industry.

Some of the principal forms of fee-generating activity include:

Underwriting. Banks may guarantee to purchase certain allowable securities if they are not fully subscribed to in an offering.

Brokerage. Banks may arrange for the purchase and sale of securities on behalf of customers in return for a commission.

Corporate and Advisory Services. These activities involve advice on mergers and acquisitions, capital raising, and treasury management in return for a fee.

Private Placements. This activity normally involves the placement of securities on a **best efforts** basis as opposed to an underwriting commitment.

Private Banking. This activity involves investment planning, tax assistance, and credit extensions to wealthy individuals.

Many of the activities, particularly underwriting, are subject to restriction by regulation as to the type of securities that may be transacted, and separately capitalized subsidiaries may be required. These restrictions are subject to change at the current time and may be significantly relaxed in the near future.

These activities generate fee income that is recorded when earned. Certain activities are conducted in conjunction with credit extension activities, and therefore particular attention is required to ensure that fees generated are appropriately recorded. It is essential to distinguish between fees that may be recorded immediately and fees that are essentially loan origination fees to be accounted for over the life of the loan (SFAS No. 91).

22.21 CASH AND CLEARING. The volume of cash transactions that are essentially used to receive and pay obligations is significant for banks. Banks maintain accounts with the Federal Reserve Bank and with other correspondent banks in order to facilitate the clearance of these transactions. Cash includes physical cash on hand, deposits in various other banks, and items in the process of collection from other institutions (float). Such account balances are recorded at their face or par value.

22.22 MONEY TRANSFER. This important activity is not directly reflected on the financial statements of the banks but is the means by which most banking transactions are settled.

Elaborate systems have been established to both transmit payment instructions and actually settle transactions.

22.23 TAXATION. Bank taxation is extremely complex; specific discussion is therefore beyond the scope of this book. However, certain significant factors affecting bank taxation are discussed below.

(a) Loan Loss Reserves. Prior to the Tax Reform Act of 1986 (1986 Act), banks were permitted to deduct loan loss provisions based on either the experience method or on a percentage of certain eligible loans. Under the 1986 Act the tax deduction is limited to loans actually charged off and banks are required to recapture prior excess tax deductions over a 4-year period for larger institutions (over $500 million in average assets) and a longer period for other institutions. As banks record a deduction for provisions for loan losses in the financial statements when provided, this creates a timing (APB Opinion No. 11, "Accounting for Income Taxes") or temporary (SFAS No. 96, "Accounting for Income Taxes") difference giving rise to deferred taxes.

(b) Leasing Activities. Direct financing activities may qualify as financings for tax purposes. As a result, a bank will be able to obtain a tax deduction for the depreciation on the leased asset, whereas it will record none for financial reporting purposes. This will result in a difference between book and tax accounting under both APB Opinion No. 11 and SFAS No. 96.

(c) Tax-Exempt Securities. Banks invest in tax-exempt securities that typically have a lower rate than other comparable securities in view of their tax-exempt nature. This results in a permanent difference between financial reporting and tax accounting income.

THRIFT INSTITUTIONS

22.24 EVOLUTION AND BACKGROUND. Thrift institutions (savings and loan associations and savings banks) developed and diversified as a result of commercial banks' inability to meet the demands for consumer home financing. Before 1980, there were clear distinctions between commercial banks and thrift institutions, where home mortgages were the principal assets of the thrift institutions, as opposed to consumer and commercial lending for commercial banks. During the late 1980s, however, the activities of thrift institutions were more similar to those of commercial banks.

Before 1980, the type of deposits the thrift institutions could accept and the types of loans and investments they could make were limited by their charters and applicable laws. Most of the thrift institutions' assets were oriented toward fixed-rate 30-year mortgage loans, and their deposits were based on interest-bearing savings accounts and time deposits.

However, during the beginning of the 1980s, interest rates reached a record high. Therefore, thrift institutions were paying higher interest on their deposits while saddled with low fixed-rate mortgage loans. This weakened condition of the thrift institutions resulted in deregulation in the industry, offering thrift institutions an opportunity to compete by merging with other institutions or engaging in activities formerly limited to commercial banks. These changes blurred the distinction between thrift institutions and commercial banks. Thrift institutions began investing in riskier instruments and making higher risk lending decisions, promoting abuses and mismanagement in certain institutions. This trend was a product of deregulation and is being reversed by FIRREA, which imposes, among other things, a tighter qualified thrift lender test, requiring that effective, June 30, 1991, at least 70% of their portfolio assets be in qualified thrift investments. This restriction may well push thrift institutions back into the origination of single-family mortgages, reducing their involvement in riskier instruments.

22.25 LEGAL STRUCTURE.   Thrift institutions can be structured in either stock or mutual form. Stock thrifts issue capital stock, which represents equity ownership similar to any other corporation. Mutual thrifts have no capital stock; the voting rights and control of the institutions reside with their depositors and borrowers.

22.26 CAPITAL STANDARDS.   One of the most important regulatory and supervisory requirements introduced as part of FIRREA is the implementation of three capital standards that must be met by the thrift institutions beginning on December 7, 1989, as follows:

Leverage ratio	Core capital must equal at least 3% of total assets
Tangible capital ratio	Tangible capital must equal at least 1.5% of total assets
Risk-based ratio	Total capital must equal at least 6.4% of risk-weighted assets (80% of the December 31, 1992, standard); total capital is core capital plus supplementary capital (not greater in amount than core capital)

Core capital includes common stockholders' equity, noncumulative perpetual preferred stock, and related surplus and minority interest in consolidated subsidiaries. Deductions in arriving at core capital include nonsupervisory goodwill. Taking note of the conflicting legislative history, the OTS regulation views qualifying supervisory goodwill as amounts arising from transactions involving institutions that presented supervisory concerns. Those intangibles for which an independent market value can be established are also deemed to be core capital, but only up to 25% of core capital.

Supplementary capital includes permanent capital instruments such as cumulative perpetual preferred stock and perpetual subordinated debt, maturing capital instruments such as subordinated debt within a few years of maturity, and a limited amount of general valuation loan loss allowances.

Tangible capital equals core capital less most intangible assets. Purchased mortgage servicing rights, generally up to 90% of market value, are tangible assets for capital purposes. Excess mortgage servicing rights are intangible assets.

Total assets for capital purposes are determined on a consolidated basis, excluding those assets that require "dollar for dollar" capital support like nonsupervisory goodwill. Beginning July 1, 1990, institutions must phase out, over 5 years, investments in subsidiaries that engage in activities outside the scope permitted by OTS regulations.

The essential feature of the risk-based rule is the risk weightings assigned to assets. All assets are assigned to one of five risk weight categories. Off-balance sheet transactions are assigned to one of four credit conversion factor categories or to a separate category for interest rate and exchange rate contracts. The full principal amount of assets sold with recourse must be included in an off-balance sheet risk category.

22.27 PRINCIPAL ACTIVITIES AND THEIR ACCOUNTING TREATMENT.   The accounting treatment of thrift institution activities is similar to that of commercial banks previously covered in this chapter. Therefore, this section will focus on specific accounting issues most relevant to thrift institutions.

(a) Real Estate Purchased for Sale or Development.   Real estate purchased for sale or development should be recorded at the lower of cost or estimated net realizable value. Direct holding costs should be capitalized; in the computation of holding costs the thrifts must include cost of capital (debt and equity), whereas banks do not. However, carrying amounts should not exceed estimated net realizable value. Estimated net realizable value means the estimated sales price in cash or cash equivalent upon subsequent disposition reduced by the sum of the following estimates: (1) direct selling expenses such as sales commissions, advertising cost of title policy, and other expenses of disposition; (2) costs of completion or improvement; and (3) direct holding costs including taxes, maintenance, insurance (net of rental or other income), and cost of all capital during the period to be held.

(b) Real Estate Acquired in Settlement of Loans. Real estate acquired in the settlement of loans should be recorded at the lower of fair value at acquisition date or net realizable value.

(c) Mortgage Banking Activities. The concentration of mortgage-related activities in thrift institutions heightens the importance of the specific accounting rules relating to these activities. SFAS No. 65, "Accounting for Certain Mortgage Banking Activities," provides specific guidance on accounting issues relevant to mortgage banking activity. Some of the most relevant accounting issues covered by SFAS No. 65 and other pronouncements follows.

(d) Mortgage Loans and Mortgage-Backed Securities. Mortgage loans are loans granted to debtors for real estate purchases, refinancing, and improvements; the loans are secured by the underlying property. Mortgage-backed securities are securities issued by a governmental agency or corporation (e.g., GNMA or FHLMC) or by private issuer (e.g., FNMA, banks and mortgage banking enterprises). Mortgage-backed securities generally are referred to as mortgage participation certificates or pass-through certificates (PCs). A PC represents an undivided interest in a pool of specific mortgage loans. Periodic payments of FHLMC and FNMA PCs are guaranteed by those corporations but are not backed by the U.S. government. It should be noted that, in accordance with FIRREA, the FHLMC was restructured and privatized.

The valuation of mortgage loans and mortgage-backed securities for financial reporting purposes depends on whether they are held for sale or for investment. Mortgage loans and mortgage-backed securities held for investment should be valued at cost. Mortgage loans and mortgage-backed securities held for sale should be valued at the lower of cost or market, according to the type of mortgage loan or mortgage-backed security. Write-downs, of a mortgage loan or mortgage-backed security to the lower of cost or market, should be included in net income of the period in which the adjustment occurs. After write-downs, write-ups to market values in subsequent periods should be recorded, but total recorded market value may not exceed cost. A mortgage loan or a mortgage-backed security held for sale that is transferred to an investment classification must be transferred at the lower of cost or market value at the date of the transfer. Any difference between the carrying amount of the loan or the security and its outstanding principal balance should be recognized as an adjustment to yield by the interest method.

(e) Loan Origination Fees and Costs. Mortgage loan origination and commitment fees are a significant income component of mortgage banking activity. Based on diversity in practice among financial institutions regarding accounting for nonrefundable fees and costs associated with lending activities, the FASB undertook the loan origination fees and costs project and issued SFAS No. 91, making accounting practices uniform for such fees and costs. Accounting for loan origination and commitment fees and associated costs has been previously discussed in section 22.13.

(f) Servicing Fees. A mortgage banking institution generally retains the right to service mortgage loans it sells to investors. The process of performing loan administration functions (collecting, maintaining mortgage loan records, etc.) is referred to as "servicing." In compensation for this service, a servicing fee is charged based on a percentage of the unpaid principal balance of the loans.

If mortgage loans are sold with servicing retained and the stated servicing fee rate differs materially from a current (normal) servicing fee rate, the sales price should be adjusted for purposes of determining gain or loss on the sale to provide for the recognition of a normal servicing fee in each subsequent year. A current (normal) servicing fee rate is a rate that is representative of servicing fee rates most commonly used in comparable servicing agreements covering similar types of mortgage loans. The amount of the adjustment should be the difference between:

- The actual sales price, and
- The estimated sales price that would have been obtained if a normal servicing fee rate had been specified.

The adjustment and any gain or loss to be recognized should be determined as of the date the mortgage loans are sold. If normal servicing fees are expected to be less than estimated servicing costs over the estimated life of the mortgage loans, the expected loss on servicing the loans should be accrued at the date the mortgage loans are sold.

(g) Servicing Rights. In a bulk purchase of mortgage loans, a purchaser often may pay more than the selling price for the mortgages in order to acquire the right to service the loans. This right is an intangible asset that may be acquired as part of the purchase of loans or a business combination. It may also be acquired directly as a mortgage-servicing contract. The cost of acquiring the servicing rights should be capitalized and amortized over the period of estimated net servicing income (servicing revenue in excess of servicing costs).

When acquired as part of a bulk purchase of loans, capitalization of the portion of the bulk purchase price pertaining to the cost of acquiring the servicing right is subject to the following conditions and limitations:

1. A definite plan for the sale of the mortgage loans must exist when the transaction is initiated, or a commitment is made within a reasonable period (usually not more than 30 days after the purchase date) to sell the mortgage loans, and
2. The plan must include estimates of the purchase price and the selling price.

The amount capitalized should not exceed:

1. The purchase price of the loans, including any transfer fees paid, in excess of the market value of the loans without servicing rights at the purchase date, or
2. The amount by which the present value of estimated future servicing revenue exceeds the present value of expected future servicing costs. The ratios used to determine these present values should be an appropriate long-term interest rate.

(h) Loan Placement Fees. Fees for arranging a commitment directly between a permanent investor and a borrower (loan placement fees) should be recognized as revenue when all significant services have been performed. In addition, if a mortgage banking enterprise obtains a commitment from a permanent investor before or at the time a related commitment is made to a borrower and if the commitment to the borrower will require (1) simultaneous assignment of the commitment to the investor and (2) simultaneous transfer to the borrower of the amount received from the investor, the related fees should also be accounted for as loan placement fees.

INVESTMENT COMPANIES

22.28 BACKGROUND. An investment company (referred to as a "fund" or a "mutual fund") generally pools investors' funds to provide them with professional investment management and diversification of ownership in the securities markets. Typically, an investment company sells its capital shares to the public and invests the net proceeds in stocks, bonds, government obligations, or other securities, intended to meet the fund's stated investment objectives. A brief history of investment companies is included at item 1.7 of "Audits of Investment Companies," the AICPA Audit and Accounting Guide. One of the more notable distinctions between investment companies and companies in other industries is the extremely high degree of compliance to which registered investment companies must adhere.

(a) SEC Statutes.   The SEC is responsible for the administration and enforcement of the following statutes governing investment companies:

> **The Investment Company Act of 1940.** Regulates registered investment companies (having more than 100 shareholders) and provides extensive rules and regulations that govern recordkeeping, reporting, fiduciary duties, and other responsibilities of an investment company's management.
>
> **The Investment Advisers Act of 1940.** Requires persons who are paid to render investment advice to individuals or institutions, including investment companies, to register with the SEC, and regulates their conduct and contracts.
>
> **The Securities Act of 1933.** Relates primarily to the initial public offering and distribution of securities (including the capital shares of investment companies).
>
> **The Securities Exchange Act of 1934.** Regulates the trading of securities in secondary markets after the initial public offering and distribution of the securities under the 1933 Act. Periodic SEC financial reporting requirements pursuant to § 13 or § 15(d) of the 1934 Act are satisfied by the semiannual filing of Form N-SAR pursuant to § 30 of the 1940 Act.

(b) Types of Investment Companies.   Three common methods of classification are (1) by securities law definition, (2) by investment objectives, and (3) by form of organization.

(i) Classification by Securities Law Definition.   Securities law divides investment companies into three types: management companies, face amount certificate companies, and unit investment trusts. The most common classification is the management company. The term "mutual fund" refers to an open-end management company as described under § 5 of the 1940 Act. Such a fund stands ready to redeem its shares at net asset value whenever requested to do so and usually continuously offers its shares for sale, although it is not required to do so. A closed-end management company does not stand ready to redeem its shares when requested (although it may occasionally make tender offers for its shares) and generally does not issue additional shares, except perhaps in connection with a dividend reinvestment program. Its outstanding shares are usually traded on an exchange, often at a premium or discount from the fund's underlying net asset value.

Other management investment companies include SBICs and BDCs. Management companies, at their own election, are further divided into diversified companies and non-diversified companies. A fund that elects to be a diversified company must meet the 75% test required under § 5(b)(1) of the 1940 Act. Nondiversified companies are management companies that have elected to be nondiversified and do not have to meet the requirements of § 5(b)(1).

The 1940 Act also provides for face amount certificate companies, which are rather rare, and unit investment trusts. Unit investment trusts are established under a trust indenture by a sponsoring organization that acquires a portfolio (often tax-exempt or taxable bonds that are generally held to maturity) and then sells undivided interests in the trust. Units of the trust generally are not offered continuously, nor do the trusts generally make any additional portfolio acquisitions. Units remain outstanding until they are tendered for redemption or the trust is terminated.

Separate accounts of an insurance company that underlie variable annuity and variable life insurance products are also subject to the requirements of the 1940 Act. They may be established as management companies or as unit investment trusts. Variable annuities and variable life products are considered to be both securities subject to the 1933 Act and insurance products subject to regulation by state insurance departments.

(ii) Classification by Investment Objectives.   Investment companies can also be classified by their investment objectives or types of investments, for example, growth funds, income funds, tax-exempt funds, global funds, option funds, money market funds, and equity funds. At the end of 1988, the Investment Company Institute, an industry trade association, reported the existence of 2,718 funds, divided among 22 types of funds.

(iii) Classification by Form of Organization.   Investment companies can also be classified by their form of organization. Funds may be organized as corporations or trusts (and, to a lesser extent, as partnerships).

Incorporation offers the advantages of detailed state statutory and interpretative judicial decisions governing operations, limited liability of shareholders, and in normal cases, requires no exemptions to comply with the 1940 Act.

The business trust, or Massachusetts Trust, is an unincorporated business association established by a declaration or deed of trust and governed largely by the law of trusts. In general, a business trust has the advantages of unlimited authorized shares, no annual meeting requirement, and long duration.

22.29 FUND OPERATIONS.   When a new fund is established, it enters into a contract with an investment adviser (often the sponsoring organization) to manage the fund and, within the terms of the fund's stated investment objectives, to determine what securities should be purchased, sold, or exchanged. The investment adviser places orders for the purchase or sale of portfolio securities for the fund with brokers or dealers selected by it. The officers of the fund, who generally are also officers of the investment adviser or fund administrator, give instructions to the custodian of the fund holdings as to delivery of securities and payments of cash for the account of the fund. The investment adviser normally furnishes, at its own expense, all necessary services, facilities, and personnel in connection with these responsibilities. The investment adviser may also act as administrator; administrative duties include preparation of regulatory filings and managing relationships with other service providers. The investment adviser and administrator are usually paid for these services through a fee based on the value of net assets.

The distributor or underwriter for an investment company markets the shares of the fund—either directly to the public ("no-load" funds) or through a sales force. The sales force may be compensated for their services through a direct sales commission included in (deducted from) the price at which the fund's shares are offered (redeemed), through a distribution fee (also referred to as a "12b-1 plan fee") paid by the fund as part of its recurring expenses, or in both ways. Rule 12b-1 under the 1940 Act permits an investment company to pay for distribution expenses, which otherwise are paid for by the distributor and not the fund.

A fund has officers and directors (and in some cases, trustees) but generally has no employees, the services it requires being provided under contract by others. Primary servicing organizations are summarized below.

(a) Fund Accounting Agent.   The fund accounting agent maintains the fund's general ledger and portfolio accounting records and computes the net asset value per share, usually on a daily basis. In some instances, this service is provided by the investment adviser or an affiliate of the adviser, or a nonaffiliated entity may perform this service. The fund accounting agent, or in some cases a separate administrative agent, may also be responsible for preparation of the fund's financial statements, tax returns, semiannual and annual filings with the SEC on Form N-SAR, and the annual registration statement filing.

(b) Custodian.   The custodian maintains custody of the fund's assets, collects income, pays expenses, and settles investment transactions. The 1940 Act provides for three alternatives in selecting a custodian. The most commonly used is a commercial bank or trust company that meets the requirements of §§ 17 and 26 of the 1940 Act. The second alternative is a member firm of a national securities exchange; the third alternative is for the fund to act as its own custodian and utilize the safekeeping facilities of a bank or trust company. Section 17(f) and Rule 17f-2 of the 1940 Act provide for specific audit procedures to be performed by the fund's independent accountant when either alternative two or three is used.

(c) Transfer Agent.   The fund's transfer agent maintains the shareholder records and processes the sales and redemptions of the fund's capital shares. The transfer agent processes the capital share transactions at a price per share equal to the net asset value per share of the fund next determined by the fund accounting agent (forward pricing). In certain instances, shareholder servicing—the direct contact with shareholders, usually by telephone—is combined with the transfer agent processing.

22.30 ACCOUNTING.   The AICPA Audit and Accounting Guide "Audits of Investment Companies" (1987) provides specific guidance on accounting issues relevant to investment companies. The SEC has set forth in ASR No. 118 its views on accounting for securities by registered investment companies.

Because for federal income tax purposes the fund is a conduit for the shareholders, the operations of an investment company are normally influenced by federal income tax considerations, and book reporting that follows the tax treatment is often the most meaningful to the shareholder. Accordingly, conformity between book and tax accounting is usually maintained whenever practicable under GAAP. In general, investment companies carry securities, which is their most significant asset, at current value, not at historical cost. In such a "mark-to-market" environment, conforming book and tax accounting usually has no effect on net asset value and only has a reclassification effect on income. On this basis, the Audit and Accounting Guide permits federal income tax accounting as an acceptable accounting policy in many areas.

Uniquely, most mutual funds close their books daily and calculate a net asset value per share, which forms the pricing basis for shareholders who are purchasing or redeeming fund shares. SEC Rules 2a-4 and 22c-1 set forth certain accounting requirements, including a one cent per share materiality criterion used by funds when pricing shares. Because of this daily closing of the books, mutual funds and their agents must maintain well-controlled and current accounting systems to provide proper records for their highly compliance-oriented industry.

The SEC has promulgated extensive rules under each of the statutes that it administers, including the following:

Article 6 of Regulation S-X (and Rule 3-18 of Article 3 and Rule 12-12 of Regulation S-X). Sets forth requirements as to the form and content of, and requirements for, financial statements filed with the SEC, including what financial statements must be presented and for what periods.

Regulation S-K Item 302—Supplementary Financial Information. Requires disclosure of selected quarterly financial data of closed-end funds meeting specified size and trading requirements.

Financial Reporting Policies. Section 404 relates specifically to registered investment companies.

22.31 FINANCIAL REPORTING

(a) New Registrants.   Any company registered under the 1940 Act that has not previously had an effective registration statement under the 1933 Act must include in its initial registration statement financial statements and per share data and ratios as of a date within 90 days prior to the date of filing. For a company that did not have any prior operations, this would be limited to a **seed capital** statement of assets and liabilities and related notes.

Section 14 of the 1940 Act requires that an investment company have a net worth of at least $100,000. Accordingly, a new investment company is usually incorporated by its sponsor with seed capital of that amount.

(b) General Reporting Requirements.   SEC reporting requirements are outlined in § 30 of the 1940 Act and the related rules and regulations thereunder, which supersede any requirements under § 13 or § 15(d) of the 1934 Act to which an investment company would otherwise be subject. A registered investment company is deemed by the SEC to have satisfied its requirement under the 1934 Act to file an annual report by the filing of semiannual reports on Form N-SAR.

The SEC requires that every registered management company send to its shareholders, at least semiannually, a report containing financial statements and selected per share data and ratios. Only the financial statements and per share data and ratios in the annual report are required to be audited.

Some funds prepare quarterly reports to shareholders, although they are not required to do so. They generally include a portfolio listing; in relatively few cases, they include full financial statements. Closed-end funds listed on the New York Stock Exchange have quarterly reporting requirements under their listing agreements with the Exchange.

(c) Financial Statements.   Article 6 of Regulation S-X deals specifically with investment companies and requires the following statements:

- A statement of assets and liabilities (supported by a separate listing of portfolio securities) or a statement of net assets, which includes a detailed list of portfolio securities at the reporting date.
- A statement of operations for the year.
- A statement of changes in net assets for the latest two years.

SFAS No. 95 provides that a statement of cash flows should be included with financial statements prepared in accordance with GAAP. SFAS No. 102 exempts investment companies from providing a statement of cash flows, provided certain conditions are met. A statement of changes in net assets should be presented even if the statement of cash flows is presented because it presents the changes in shareholders' equity required by GAAP.

22.32 TAXATION.   Investment companies are subject to federal income taxes and certain state and local taxes. However, investment companies registered under the 1940 Act may qualify for special federal income tax treatment as **regulated** investment companies (RICs) under the IRC and may deduct dividends paid to shareholders. If a fund fails to qualify as a RIC, it will be taxed as a regular corporation, and the deduction for dividends paid by the fund is disallowed. Subchapter M (§§ 851 to 855) of the IRC applies to RICs. Chapter 4 of the Audit Guide discusses the tax considerations related to RICs.

To qualify as a RIC, the fund must:

- Be registered under the 1940 Act.
- Derive less than 30% of its gross income from sales of securities held less than 3 months (the so-called short-short test).
- Derive 90% of its total income from dividends, interest, and gross gains on sales of securities.

- Have 50% of its assets composed of cash, U.S. government securities, securities of other funds, and "other issues," as defined.
- Have not more than 25% of the value of its total assets invested in the securities (other than U.S. government securities or the securities of other regulated investment companies) of any one issuer or of two or more issuers controlled by the fund that are determined to be engaged in the same or similar trades or businesses.
- Distribute at least 90% of its net investment company taxable income and net tax-exempt interest income to its shareholders.

Also, to avoid a 4% nondeductible excise tax, a fund must distribute, by December 31 of each year, 98% of its ordinary income measured on a calendar year basis and 98% of its net capital gains measured on a fiscal year basis ending October 31. Actual payment of the distribution must be before February 1 of the following year.

22.33 SEC FILINGS.   SEC registration forms applicable to investment companies include the following:

Form N-8A. The notification of registration under the 1940 Act.

Form N-1A. The registration statement of open-end management investment companies under the 1940 and the 1933 Acts. (It is not to be used by SBICs, BDCs, or insurance company separate accounts.) The Form describes in detail the company's objectives, policies, management, investment restrictions, and similar matters. The Form consists of the prospectus, the statement of additional information (SAI), and a third section of other information, including detailed information on the SEC-required yield calculations. Posteffective amendments on Form N-1A, including updated audited financial statements, must be filed and become effective under the 1933 and 1940 Acts within 16 months after the end of the period covered by the previous audited financial statements if the fund is to continue offering its shares.

Form N-SAR. A reporting form used for semiannual and annual reports by all registered investment companies that have filed a registration statement that has become effective pursuant to the 1933 Act, with the exception of face amount certificate companies and BDCs. Face amount certificate companies file periodic reports pursuant to § 13 or § 15(d) of the 1934 Act.

Management investment companies file the form semiannually; unit investment trusts are only required to file annually. There is no requirement that the form or any of the items be audited. The annual report filed by a management investment company must be accompanied by a report on the company's system of internal accounting controls from its independent accountant. The requirement for an accountant's report on internal accounting controls does not apply to SBICs or to management investment companies not required by either the 1940 Act or any other federal or state law or rule or regulation thereunder to have an audit of their financial statements.

Form N-2. A registration statement for closed-end funds comparable to the N-1A for open-end funds.

Forms N-1, N-3, N-4, N-8B-2, and S-6. The registration statements for various types of insurance-related products including variable annuities and variable life insurance.

Form N-14. The statement for registration of securities issued by investment companies in business combination transactions under the 1933 Act. It contains information about the companies involved in the transaction including historical and pro forma financial statements.

22.34 OFFSHORE FUNDS—SPECIAL CONSIDERATIONS.   Offshore funds may be described generally as investment funds set up to permit international investments with minimum tax burden on the fund shareholders. This is achieved by setting up the fund in countries with lenient tax laws. An offshore fund that invests in U.S. securities is organized outside the United States, and its shares are offered to investors residing outside the United States. An advantage of being offshore is that offshore funds investing in U.S. debt securities issued after July 18, 1984, are not subject to U.S. withholding tax. Also, offshore funds (1) are not subject to SEC registration and reporting requirements and (2) avoid the IRC distribution and other requirements imposed on U.S. funds.

An offshore fund will not be subject to U.S. income taxes applicable to domestic entities if it is not considered as having its principal office in the United States. Pursuant to the provisions of IRS Reg. § 1.864-2(c)(2):

> A foreign corporation which carries on most or all of its investment activities in the U.S. . . . . will not be considered as having its principal office in the U.S. if all or a substantial portion of . . . ten (specified) functions are carried on, at or from an office or offices located outside the U.S.

SOURCES AND SUGGESTED REFERENCES

Accounting Principles Board, "Accounting for Income Taxes," APB Opinion No. 11, AICPA, New York, 1967.

American Institute of Certified Public Accountants, "Auditing the Allowance for Credit Losses of Banks," Auditing Procedure Study, AICPA, New York, 1986.

———, "Accounting for Options," Issues Paper, AICPA, New York, 1986.

———, "Audits of Banks," Industry Audit Guide, AICPA, New York, 1984.

———, "Audits of Investment Companies," Industry Audit Guide, AICPA, New York, 1987.

———, "Savings and Loan Associations," Audit and Accounting Guide, AICPA, New York, 1987.

———, "ADC (Acquisition, development and construction), Arrangements," Notice to Practitioners, *Journal of Accounting,* April 1986, and included in AICPA Practice Bulletin No. 1.

Financial Accounting Standards Board, EITF Abstracts: A Summary of Proceedings of the FASB Emerging Issues Task Force, "Accounting for Fees and Costs Associated with Loan Syndications and Loan Participations," EITF Issue No. 88-17, FASB, Norwalk, CT, 1989.

———, "Accounting for Leases," Statement of Financial Accounting Standards No. 13, FASB, Stamford, CT, 1976.

———, "Accounting by Debtors and Creditors for Troubled Debt Restructurings," Statement of Financial Accounting Standards No. 15, FASB, Stamford, CT, 1977.

———, "Foreign Currency Translation," Statement of Financial Accounting Standards No. 52, FASB, Stamford, CT, 1981.

———, "Accounting for Certain Mortgage Banking Activities," Statement of Financial Accounting Standards No. 65, FASB, Stamford, CT, 1982.

———, "Reporting by Transferors for Transfers of Receivables with Recourse," Statement of Financial Accounting Standards No. 77, FASB, Stamford, CT, 1983.

———, "Accounting for Futures Contracts," Statement of Financial Accounting Standards No. 80, FASB, Stamford, CT, 1984.

———, "Accounting for Nonrefundable Fees and Costs Associated with Originating or Acquiring Loans and Initial Direct Costs of Leases," Statement of Financial Accounting Standards No. 91, FASB, Stamford, CT, 1986.

———, "Statement of Cash Flows," Statement of Financial Accounting Standards No. 95, FASB, Stamford, CT, 1987.

———, "Accounting for Income Taxes," Statement of Financial Accounting Standards No. 96, FASB, Stamford, CT, 1987.

———, "Statement of Cash Flows—Exemption of Certain Enterprises and Classification of Cash Flows from Certain Securities Acquired for Resale,'' Statement of Financial Accounting Standards No. 102, FASB, Norwalk, CT, 1989.

———, ''Statement of Cash Flows—Net Reporting of Certain Cash Receipts and Cash Payments and Classification of Cash Flows from Hedging Transactions,'' Statement of Financial Accounting Standards No. 104, FASB, Norwalk, CT, 1989.

Securities and Exchange Commission, ''Codification of Financial Reporting Policies,'' Financial Reporting Release No. 1 (ASR No. 118), SEC, Washington, DC, 1982.

———, ''Accounting for Loan Losses by Registrants Engaged in Lending Activities,'' Financial Reporting Release No. 28, SEC, Washington, DC, 1985.

CHAPTER 23

REGULATED UTILITIES

Benjamin A. McKnight III, CPA
Arthur Andersen & Co.

CONTENTS

Mr. McKnight wishes to acknowledge the assistance provided by Alan D. Felsenthal and Robert W.
Hriszko, both of Arthur Andersen & Co.

THE NATURE AND CHARACTERISTICS OF REGULATED UTILITIES

23.1 INTRODUCTION TO REGULATED UTILITIES.   Many types of business have their rates for providing services set by the government or other regulatory bodies, for example, utilities, insurance companies, transportation companies, hospitals, and shippers. The enterprises addressed in this chapter are limited to electric, gas, telephone, and water (and sewer) utilities that are regulated on an **individual cost-of-service** basis. Effective business and financial involvement with the utility industry requires an understanding of what a utility is, the regulatory compact under which utilities operate, and the interrelationship between the rate decisions of regulators and the resultant accounting effects.

23.2 DESCRIPTIVE CHARACTERISTICS OF UTILITIES.   Regulated utilities are similar to other businesses in that there is a need for capital and, for private sector utilities, a demand for investor profit. Utilities are different in that they are dedicated to public use—they are obligated to furnish customers service on demand—and the services are considered to be necessities. Many utilities operate under monopolistic conditions. A regulator sets their prices and grants an exclusive service area, which probably serves a relatively large number of customers. Consequently, a high level of public interest typically exists regarding the utility's rates and quality of service.

Only a utility that has a monopoly of supply of service can operate at maximum economy and, therefore, provide service at the lowest cost. Duplicate plant facilities would result in higher costs. This is particularly true because of the capital-intensive nature of utility operations, that is, a large capital investment is required for each dollar of revenue.

Because there is an absence of free market competitive forces such as those found in most business enterprises, regulation is a substitute for these missing competitive forces. The goal of regulation is to provide a balance between investor and consumer interests by substituting regulatory principles for competition. This means regulation is to:

1. Provide consumers with adequate service at the lowest price.
2. Provide the utility the opportunity, **not a guarantee,** to earn an adequate return so that it can attract new capital for development and expansion of plant to meet customer demand.
3. Prevent unreasonable prices and excessive earnings.
4. Prevent unjust discrimination among customers, commodities and locations.
5. Insure public safety.

To meet the goals of regulation, regulated activities of utilities typically include:

1. Service area.
2. Rates.
3. Accounting and reporting.
4. Issuance of debt and equity securities.
5. Construction, sale, lease, purchase, and exchange of operating facilities.
6. Standards of service and operation.

HISTORY OF REGULATION

Some knowledge of the history of regulation is essential to understanding utilities. Companies that are now regulated utilities find themselves in that position because of a long sequence of political events, legislative acts, and judicial interpretations.

Rate regulation of privately owned business was not an accepted practice during the early history of the United States. This concept has evolved because important legal precedents have established not only the right of government to regulate but also the process that government bodies must follow to set fair rates for services. The background and the facts of *Munn v. Illinois* (94 U.S. 113 (1877)) are significant and basic to the development of ratemaking since the case established a U.S. legal precedent for the right of government to regulate and set rates in cases of public interest and necessity.

23.3 *MUNN V. ILLINOIS.* In 1871, the Illinois State Legislature passed a law that prescribed the maximum rates for grain storage and that required licensing and bonding to ensure performance of the duties of a public warehouse. The law reflected the popular sentiment of midwestern farmers at that time against what they felt was a pricing monopoly by railroads and elevators. Munn and his partner, Scott, owned a grain warehouse in Chicago. They filed a suit maintaining that they operated a private business and that the law deprived them of their property without due process.

The case ultimately reached the U.S. Supreme Court. The Court decided that, when private property becomes "clothed with a public interest," the owner of the property has, in effect, granted the public an interest in that use and "must submit to be controlled by the public for the common good." The Court was impressed by Munn and Scott's monopolistic position while furnishing a service practically indispensable to the public.

From the precedent of *Munn*, railroads, a water company, a grist mill, stockyards, and finally gas, electric, and phone companies were brought under public regulation. Thus, when utilities finally came into existence in the 20th century, the framework for regulation already was in place and did not have to be decided by the courts. When state legislatures began to set up utility commissions, it was the *Munn* decision that established beyond question their right to do so.

23.4 CHICAGO, MILWAUKEE & ST. PAUL RY. CO. V. MINNESOTA.   A second important case which began to establish the principle of "due process" in ratemaking is *Chicago, Milwaukee & St. Paul Railroad Co. v. Minnesota ex rel. Railroad & Warehouse Comm.* (134 U.S. 418 (1890)). In this important case the courts first began to address the issue of standards of reasonableness in regulation. The U.S. Supreme Court decided that a Minnesota law was unconstitutional because it established rate regulation but did not permit a judicial review to test the reasonableness of the rates. The Court found that the state law violated the due process provisions of the 14th Amendment because the utility was deprived of the power to charge reasonable rates for the use of its property, and if the utility was denied judicial review, then the company would be deprived of the lawful use of its property, and ultimately, the property itself.

23.5 SMYTH V. AMES.   A third important case, *Smyth v. Ames* (169 U.S. 466 (1898)), established the precedent for the concept of "fair return upon the fair value of property." During the 1880s the state of Nebraska passed a law that reduced the maximum freight rates that railroads could charge. The railroads' stockholders brought a successful suit that prevented the application of the lowered rates. The state appealed the case to the U.S. Supreme Court, which unanimously ruled that the rates were unconstitutionally low by any standard of reasonableness.

In its case, the state maintained that the adequacy of the rates should be tested by reference to the present value, or reproduction cost, of the assets. This position was attractive to the state because the current price level had been declining. The railroad was built during the Civil War, a period that was marked by a high price level and substantial inflation, and the railroad believed that its past costs merited recognition in a "test of reasonableness."

In reaching its decision, the Court began the formulation of the "fair value" doctrine, which prescribed a test of the reasonableness and constitutionality of regulated rates. The Supreme Court's opinion held that a privately owned business was entitled to rates that would cover reasonable operating expenses plus a fair return on the fair value of the property used for the convenience of the public.

The *Smyth v. Ames* decision also established several ratemaking terms still in use today. This was the first attempt by the courts to define ratemaking principles. These terms include:

1. *Original Cost of Construction*. The cost to acquire utility property.
2. *Fair Return*. The amount that should be earned on the investment in utility property.
3. *Fair Value*. The amount on which the return should be based.
4. *Operating Expenses*. The cost to deliver utility services to the public.

Each of these three landmark cases, especially *Smyth v. Ames,* established the inability of the legislative branch to effectively establish equitable rates. They also demonstrated that the use of the judicial branch is an inefficient means of accomplishing the same goal. In *Smyth v.*

Ames, the U.S. Supreme Court, in essence, declared that the process could be more easily accomplished by a **commission** composed of persons with special skills and experience and the qualifications to resolve questions concerning utility regulation.

REGULATORY COMMISSION JURISDICTIONS

A view of the overlays of regulatory commissions will be helpful in understanding their unique position and responsibilities.

23.6 FEDERAL REGULATORY COMMISSIONS.   The interstate activities of public utilities are under the jurisdiction of several federal regulatory commissions. The members of all federal regulatory commissions are appointed by the executive branch and are confirmed by the legislative branch. The judicial branch can review and rule on decisions of each commission. This form of organization represents a blending of the functions of the three separate branches of government.

- The **Federal Communications Commission** (FCC), established in 1934 with the passage of the Communications Act, succeeded the Federal Radio Commission of 1927. At that time the FCC assumed regulation of interstate and foreign telephone and telegraph service from the Interstate Commerce Commission, which was the first federal regulatory commission (created in 1887). The FCC prescribes for communications companies a uniform system of accounts (USOA) and depreciation rates. It also states the principles and standard procedures used to separate property costs, revenues, expenses, taxes, and reserves between those applicable to interstate services under the jurisdiction of the FCC and those applicable to services under the jurisdiction of various state regulatory authorities. In addition, the FCC regulates the rate of return carriers may earn on their interstate business.
- The **Federal Energy Regulatory Commission** (FERC) was created as an agency of the cabinet-level Department of Energy in 1977. The FERC assumed many of the functions of the former Federal Power Commission (FPC), which was established in 1920. The FERC has jurisdiction over the transmission and sale at wholesale of electric energy in interstate commerce. The FERC also regulates the transmission and sale for resale of natural gas in interstate commerce and establishes rates and prescribes conditions of service for all utilities subject to its jurisdiction. The entities must follow the FERC's USOA and file a Form 1 (electric) or Form 2 (gas) annual report.
- The SEC was established in 1934 to administer the Securities Act of 1933 and the Securities Exchange Act of 1934. The powers of the SEC are restricted to security transactions and financial disclosures—not operating standards. The SEC also administers the Public Utility Holding Company Act of 1935 (the 1935 Act), which was passed because of financial and services abuses in the 1920s and the stock market crash and subsequent depression of 1929–1935. Under the 1935 Act, the SEC was given powers to regulate the accounting, financing, reporting, acquisitions, allocation of consolidated income taxes, and parent–subsidiary relationships of electric and gas utility holding companies.

23.7 STATE REGULATORY COMMISSIONS.   All 50 states have established agencies to regulate rates. State commissioners are either appointed or elected, usually for a specified term. Although the degree of authority differs, they have authority over utility operations in intrastate commerce. Each state commission sets ratemaking policies in accordance with its own state statutes and precedents. In addition, each state establishes its prescribed forms of reporting and systems of accounts for utilities. However, most systems are modifications of the federal USOA.

THE RATEMAKING PROCESS

23.8 HOW COMMISSIONS SET RATES.   The process for establishing rates probably constitutes the most significant difference between utilities and enterprises in general. Unlike an enterprise in general, where market forces and competition establish the price a company can charge for its products or services, rates for utilities are generally determined by a regulatory commission. The process of establishing rates is described as **ratemaking.** The administrative proceeding to establish utility rates is typically referred to as a **rate case** or **rate proceeding.** Utility rates, once established, generally will not change without another rate case.

The establishment of a rate for a utility on an individual cost-of-service basis typically involves two steps. The first step is to determine a utility's general level of rates that will cover operating costs and provide an opportunity to earn a reasonable rate of return on the property dedicated to providing utility services. This process establishes the utility's required revenue (often referred to as the **revenue requirement** or **cost-of-service**). The second step is to design specific rates in order to eliminate discrimination and unfairness from affected classes of customers. The aggregate of the prices paid by all customers for all services provided should produce revenues equivalent to the revenue requirement.

23.9 THE RATEMAKING FORMULA.   This first step of rate regulation, on an individual cost-of-service basis, is the determination of a utility's total revenue requirement, which can be expressed as a ratemaking formula:

$$\text{Rate Base} \times \text{Rate of Return} = \text{Return (Operating Income)}$$
$$\text{Return} + \text{Allowable Operating Expenses} = \text{Required Revenue (Cost of Service)}$$

1. *Rate Base.* The amount of investment in utility plant devoted to the rendering of utility service upon which a fair rate of return may be earned.
2. *Rate of Return.* The rate determined by the regulatory agency to be applied to the rate base to provide a fair return to investors. It is usually a composite rate that reflects the carrying costs of debt, dividends on preferred stock, and a return provision on common equity.
3. *Return.* The rate base multiplied by rate of return.
4. *Allowable Operating Expenses.* Merely the costs of operations and maintenance associated with rendering utility service. Operating expenses include:
   a. Depreciation and amortization expenses.
   b. Production fuel and gas for resale.
   c. Operations expenses.
   d. Maintenance expenses.
   e. Income taxes.
   f. Taxes other than income taxes.
5. *Required Revenue.* The total amount that must be collected from customers in rates. The new rate structure should be designed to generate this amount of revenue on the basis of current or forecasted levels of usage.

23.10 RATE BASE.   A utility **earns** a return on its rate base. Each investor-supplied dollar is entitled to such a return until the dollar is remitted to the investor. Some of the items generally included in the rate base computation are utility property and plant in service, a working capital allowance, and in certain jurisdictions or circumstances, plant under construction. Generally, nonutility property, abandoned plant, plant acquisition adjustments, and plant held for future use are excluded. Deductions from rate base typically include the reserve for depreciation, accumulated deferred income taxes, which represent cost-free capital, certain

AVERAGE NET INVESTMENT RATE BASE

	In Millions
Plant in service	$350
Less reserve for depreciation	(100)
Net plant in service	250
Add:	
Working capital allowance	3
Construction work-in-progress	20
Deduct:	
Accumulated deferred income taxes	(14)
Advances in aid of construction	(2)
Average net investment rate base	$257

Exhibit 23.1.   Example of a utility rate base computation.

unamortized deferred investment tax credits, and customer contributions in aid of construction. Exhibit 23.1 provides an example of the computations used to determine a rate base.

23.11 RATE BASE VALUATION.   Various methods are used in valuing rate base. These methods apply to the valuation of property and plant and include:

1. Original cost.
2. Fair value.
3. Weighted cost.

(a) Original Cost.   The original cost method, the most widely used method, corresponds to GAAP, which require historical cost data for primary financial statement presentation. In addition, all regulatory commissions have adopted the USOA, requiring original cost for reporting purposes. Original cost is defined in the FERC's USOA as "the cost of such property to the person first devoting it to public service." This method was originally adopted by various commissions during the 1930s, at which time inflation was not a major concern.

(b) Fair Value.   The fair value method is defined as **not** the cost of assets but rather what they are really worth at the time rates are established. The following three methods of computing fair value are most often used:

1. *Trended Cost.* Utilizes either general or specific cost indices to adjust original cost.
2. *Reproduction Cost New.* A calculation of the cost to reproduce existing plant facilities at current costs.
3. *Market Value.* Involves the appraisal of specific types of plant.

(c) Weighted Cost.   The weighted cost method for valuation of property and plant is used in some jurisdictions as a compromise between the original cost and the fair value methods. Under this method, some weight is given to both original cost and fair value. Regulatory agencies in some weighted cost jurisdictions use a 50/50 weighting of original cost and fair value, whereas others use 60/40 or other combinations.

(d) Judicial Precedents—Rate Base.   In a significant rate base case, *Federal Power Commission v. Hope Natural Gas Co.* (320 U.S. 591 (1944)), the original cost versus fair value controversy finally came to a head. A number of important points came out of this case, including the **Doctrine of the End Result.** The U.S. Supreme Court's decision did not approve original cost or fair value. Instead, it said a ratemaking body can use any method, including no formula at all, so long as the end result is reasonable. It is not the theory but the impact of the theory that counts.

23.12 RATE OF RETURN AND JUDICIAL PRECEDENTS.   The rate of return is the rate determined by a regulator to be applied to the rate base to provide a fair return to investors. In the capital market, utilities must compete against nonregulated companies for investors' funds. Therefore, a fair rate of return to common equity investors is critical.

Different sources of capital with different costs are involved in establishing the allowed rate of return. Exhibits 23.2 and 23.3 show the computations used to determine the rate of return.

The cost of long-term debt and preferred stock is usually the "embedded" cost, that is, long-term debt issues have a specified interest rate, whereas preferred stock has a specified dividend rate. Computing the cost of equity is more complicated because there is no stated interest or dividend rate. Several methods have been used as a guide in setting a return on common equity. These methods reflect different approaches, such as earnings/price ratios, discounted cash flows, comparable earnings, and perceived investor risk.

The **cost** of each class of capital is weighed by the percentage that the class represents of the utility's total capitalization.

Two important cases provide the foundation for dealing with rate of return issues: *Bluefield Water Works & Improvement Co. v. West Virginia Public Service Comm.* (262 U.S. 679 (1923)) and the *Hope Gas* case. The important rate of return concepts that arise from these cases are as follows:

1. A company is entitled to, but not guaranteed, a return on the value of its property.

2. Return should be equal to that earned by other companies with comparable risks.

3. A utility is not entitled to a return such as that earned by a speculative venture.

4. The return should be reasonably sufficient to:
   a. Assure confidence and financial soundness of the utility.
   b. Maintain and support its credit.
   c. Enable the utility to raise additional capital.

5. Efficient and economical management is a prerequisite for profitable operations.

COST OF CAPITAL AND RATE OF RETURN

	In Millions
Capitalization	
Stockholder's equity:	
Common stock ($8 par value, 5,000,000 shares outstanding	$ 40
Other paid-in capital	45
Retained earnings	28
Common stock equity	113
Preferred stock (9% dividend rate)	16
Total stockholders' equity	129
Long-term debt (7.50% average interest rate)	128
	$257

Exhibit 23.2.   Example of a utility capitalization structure.

	Dollars In Millions	Capitalization Ratios	Annual Cost Rate	Weighted Cost
Long-term debt	$128	50	7.5%	3.75%
Preferred stock	16	6	9.0	.54
Common stock equity	113	44	13.0	5.71
Cost of capital	$257	100		10.00%

Exhibit 23.3.   Computation of the overall rate of return.

23.13 OPERATING INCOME.   Operating income for purposes of establishing rates is computed based on **test-year** information, which is normally a recent or projected 12-month period. In either case, historic or projected test-year revenues are calculated based on the current rate structure in order to determine if there is a revenue requirement deficiency. The operating expense information generally includes most expired costs incurred by a utility. As illustrated in Exhibit 23.4, the operating expense information, after reflecting all necessary pro forma adjustments, determines operating income for ratemaking purposes.

Above-the-line and **below-the-line** are frequently used expressions in public utility, financial, and regulatory circles. The above-the-line expenses on which operating income appears are those that ordinarily are directly included in the ratemaking formula; below this line are the excluded expenses (and income). The principal cost that is charged **below-the-line** is interest on debt since it is included in the ratemaking formula as a part of the rate-of-return computation and not as an operating expense. The inclusion or exclusion of a cost above-the-line is important to the utility since this determines whether it is directly includable in the ratemaking formula as an operating expense.

A significant consideration in determining the revenue requirement is that the rate of return computed is the rate **after income taxes** (which are a part of operating expenses). In calculating the revenue required, the operating income (rate of return times rate base) deficiency must be **grossed up** for income taxes. This is most easily accomplished by dividing the operating income deficiency by the complement of the applicable income tax rate. For

COST OF SERVICE INCOME STATEMENT—TEST YEAR
(Twelve Months Ended 12/31/XX)

Operating revenue	$300,000
Operating expenses	
Commercial	45,000
Maintenance	45,000
Traffic	49,000
General and administrative	61,000
Depreciation	60,000
General taxes	6,000
Income taxes	
Federal current and deferred	10,000
State current and deferred	2,000
ITC, net	1,300
Total operating expenses	279,300
Operating income	$ 20,700

Exhibit 23.4.   Example of a utility operating income computation.

RATEMAKING FORMULA

(Rate of Return × Rate Base) + Cost of Service = Revenue Requirement

Test-year operating revenue	$300,000,000
Test-year operating expense	279,300,000
Test-year operating income	20,700,000
Rate base	257,000,000
Desired rate of return	10%
Assumed federal tax rate	46%
Rate base	$257,000,000
× Rate of return	× .10
Operating income requirement	25,700,000
+ Operating Expenses	+ 283,559,259 (A)
Revenue requirement	$309,259,259

(A) $279,300,000 Operating expenses
  4,259,259 Pro forma tax adjustment based on
         $5,000,000 operating income deficiency
         ($25,700,000 − $20,700,000) and 46% tax rate

                                $283,559,259

Exhibit 23.5.   Example of the revenue requirement computation based on Exhibits 1 through 4.

example, if the operating income deficiency is $5,000,000 and the income tax rate is 46%, the required revenue is $5,000,000/.54, or $9,259,259. By increasing revenues $9,259,259, income tax expense will increase by $4,259,259 ($9,259,259 × 46%), with the remainder increasing operating income by the deficiency amount of $5,000,000. This concept is illustrated as part of an example revenue requirement calculation based on the information presented in Exhibit 23.5.

Exhibit 23.6 shows a shortcut method of computing the revenue requirement, which calculates the operating income deficiency and then grosses that up for income taxes. The answer under either method is the same.

When the ratemaking process is complete, the utility will set rate tariffs to recover $309,259,259. At this level, future revenues will recover $283,559,259 of operating expenses and provide a return of $25,700,000. This return equates to a 10% earnings level on rate base. The $25,700,000 operating income will go toward paying $9,600,000 of interest on long-term debt ($128,000,000 × 7.5%) and preferred dividends of $1,440,000 ($16,000,000 × 9%),

---

REVENUE REQUIREMENT

Desired operating income	$ 25,700,000
Actual operating income	20,700,000
Operating income deficiency	$ 5,000,000
Gross up factor for income taxes (1 − 46%)	÷ .54
Revenue deficiency	$ 9,259,259
Test-year operating revenue	300,000,000
Revenue requirement	$309,259,259

Exhibit 23.6.   Shortcut computation of the utility revenue requirement.

leaving net income for the common equity holders of $14,660,000—which approximates the desired 13% return on common equity of $113,000,000. However, the ratemaking process only provides the **opportunity** to earn at that level. If future sales volumes, operating costs, or other factors change, the utility will earn more or less than the allowed amount.

INTERRELATIONSHIP OF REGULATORY REPORTING AND FINANCIAL REPORTING

23.14 ACCOUNTING AUTHORITY OF REGULATORY AGENCIES. Regulatory agencies with statutory authority to establish rates for utilities also prescribe the accounting that their jurisdictional regulated entities must follow. Accounting may be prescribed by a USOA, by periodic reporting requirements, or by accounting orders.

Because of the statutory authority of regulatory agencies over both accounting and rate setting of regulated utilities, some regulators, accountants, and others believe that the agencies have the final authority over the form and content of financial statements published by those utilities for their investors and creditors. This is the case even when the stockholders' report, based on regulatory accounting requirements, would not be in accordance with GAAP.

Actually, this issue has not arisen frequently because regulators have usually reflected changes in GAAP in the USOA that they prescribe. For example, the new USOA of the FCC, effective in 1988, has GAAP as its foundation, with departures being permitted as necessary, because of departures from GAAP in ratemaking. But the general willingness of regulators to conform to GAAP does not answer the question of whether a regulatory body has the final authority to prescribe the accounting to be followed for the financial statements included in the annual and other reports to stockholders or outsiders, even when such statements are not prepared in accordance with GAAP.

The landmark case in this area is the *Appalachian Power Co. v. Federal Power Commission* (328 F.2d 237 (4th Cir.), *cert. denied,* 379 U.S. 829 (1964)). The FPC (now the FERC) found that the financial statements in the annual report of the company were not in accordance with the accounting prescribed by the FPC's USOA. The FPC was upheld at the Circuit Court level in 1964 and the Supreme Court denied a writ of certiorari. The general interpretation of this case has been that the FPC had the authority to order that the financial statements in the annual report to stockholders of its jurisdictional utilities be prepared in accordance with the USOA, even if not in accordance with GAAP.

During subsequent years, the few differences that have arisen have been resolved without court action, and so it is not clear just what authority the FERC or other federal agencies may now have in this area. The FERC has not chosen to contest minor differences, and one particular utility, Montana Power Company, met the issue of FPC authority versus GAAP, by presenting, for several years, two balance sheets in its annual report to shareholders. One balance sheet was in accordance with GAAP, which reflected the ratemaking prescribed by the state commission, and one balance sheet was in accordance with the USOA of the FPC, which had ordered that certain assets be written off even though the state commission continued to allow them in the rate base. The company's auditors stated that the first balance sheet was in accordance with GAAP and that the second balance sheet was in accordance with the FPC USOA.

In a more recent instance, the FERC has allowed a company to follow accounting that the FERC believes reflects the ratemaking even though the accounting does not comply with a standard of the FASB. The SEC has ruled that the company must follow GAAP. As a result, the regulatory treatment was reformulated to meet the FASB standard, and so the conflict was resolved without going to the courts.

On June 21, 1988, a Notice of Inquiry (NOI) with the title "Accounting for Phase-in Plans" was issued by the FERC in Docket No. RM88-22. The NOI announced an inquiry into the interrelationship between the FERC's accounting authority and its USOA and the SEC authority over issuance of financial statements, in light of recent actions by the FASB. The FERC requested comments regarding the potential effects of conflicts that result from the FASB's actions and proposals on regulated enterprises, investors, and ratepayers and the FERC's current regulations, as well as what FERC action, if any, may be appropriate under the circumstances. The comment period ended on September 7, 1988. The FERC has not made a decision as to whether a rulemaking proceeding or another action may be necessary to resolve the subject conflicts.

23.15 SEC AND FASB.   The FASB has no financial reporting enforcement or disciplinary responsibility. Enforcement with regard to entities whose shares are traded in interstate commerce arises from SEC policy articulated in ASR No. 150, which specifies that FASB standards (and those of its predecessors) are required to be followed by registrants in their filings with the SEC. Thus, the interrelationship between the FASB and the SEC operates to achieve, virtually without exception for an entity whose securities trade in interstate commerce, the presentation of financial statements that reflect GAAP. Although this jurisdictional issue is neither resolved nor disappearing, it appears that the SEC currently exercises significant, if not controlling, influence over the general-purpose financial statements of all public companies, including regulated utilities.

23.16 RELATIONSHIP BETWEEN RATE REGULATION AND GAAP

(a) Historical Perspective.   Ratemaking on an individual cost-of-service basis is designed to permit a utility to recover its costs that are incurred in providing regulated services. Individual cost-of-service does not guarantee cost recovery. However, there is a much greater assurance of cost recovery under individual cost-of-service ratemaking than for enterprises in general. This likelihood of cost recoverability provides a basis for a different application of GAAP, which recognizes that ratemaking can affect accounting.

As such, a rate regulator's ability to recognize, not recognize, or defer recognition of revenues and costs in established rates of regulated utilities adds a unique consideration to the accounting and financial reporting of those enterprises. This unique economic dimension was first recognized by the accounting profession in paragraph 8 of ARB No. 44 (Revised), "Declining-Balance Depreciation:"

> Many regulatory authorities permit recognition of deferred income taxes for accounting and/or rate-making purposes, whereas some do not. The committee believes that they should permit the recognition of deferred income taxes for both purposes. However, where charges for deferred income taxes are not allowed for rate-making purposes, accounting recognition need not be given to the deferment of taxes if it may reasonably be expected that increased future income taxes, resulting from the earlier deduction of declining-balance depreciation for income-tax purposes only, will be allowed in the future rate determinations.

A year later, in connection with the general requirement to eliminate intercompany profits, paragraph 6 of ARB No. 51, "Consolidated Financial Statements," concluded:

> However, in a regulated industry where a parent or subsidiary manufactures or constructs facilities for other companies in the consolidated group, the foregoing is not intended to require the elimination of intercompany profit to the extent that such profit is substantially equivalent to a reasonable return on investment ordinarily capitalized in accordance with the established practice of the industry.

(b) The Addendum to APB Opinion No. 2.   In 1962, the APB decided to express its position on applicability of GAAP to regulated industries. The resulting statement initially reported in the

The Journal of Accountancy in December, 1962, later became the Addendum to APB Opinion No. 2, "Accounting for the Investment Credit" (the Addendum), and provided that:

1. GAAP applies to all companies—regulated and nonregulated.
2. Differences in the application of GAAP are permitted as a result of the ratemaking process because the rate regulator creates economic value.
3. Cost deferral on the balance sheet to reflect the ratemaking process is appropriately reflected on the balance sheet only when recovery is clear.
4. A regulatory accounting difference without ratemaking impact does not constitute GAAP. The accounting must be reflected in rates.
5. The financial statements of regulated entities other than those prepared for regulatory filings should be based on GAAP with appropriate recognition of ratemaking consideration.

The Addendum provided the basis for utility accounting for almost 20 years. During this period, utilities accounted for certain items differently than enterprises in general. For example, regulators often treat capital leases as operating leases for rate purposes, thus excluding them from rate base and allowing only the lease payments as expense. In that event, regulated utilities usually treated such leases as operating leases for financial statement purposes. This resulted in lower operating expenses during the first few years of the lease.

Also, utilities capitalize both debt and equity components of funds used during construction, which is generally described as an allowance for funds used during construction (AFUDC). The FASB, under SFAS No. 34, "Capitalization of Interest Cost," allows nonregulated companies to capitalize only the debt cost. Because property is by far the largest item in most utility companies' balance sheets and because they do much of their own construction, the effect of capitalizing AFUDC is frequently very material to both the balance sheet and the statement of income.

Such differences, usually concerning the timing of recognition of a cost, were cited as evidence that the Addendum allowed almost any accounting treatment if directed by rate regulation. There was also some concern that the Addendum applied to certain industries that were regulated, but not on an individual cost-of-service basis. These as well as other issues ultimately led to the FASB issuing SFAS No. 71, "Accounting for the Effects of Certain Types of Regulation," which attempted to:

1. Provide a clear conceptual basis to account for the economic impact of regulation.
2. Emphasize the concept of one set of accounting principles for all enterprises.
3. Enhance the quality of financial reporting for regulated enterprises.

SFAS NO. 71: "ACCOUNTING FOR THE EFFECTS OF CERTAIN TYPES OF REGULATION"

23.17 SCOPE OF SFAS NO. 71.   SFAS No. 71 specifies criteria for the applicability of the Statement by focusing on the nature of regulation rather than on specific industries. As stated in paragraph 5 of SFAS No. 71:

[T]his statement applies to general-purpose external financial statements of an enterprise that has regulated operations that meet all of the following criteria:

1. The enterprise's rates for regulated services or products provided to its customers are established by or are subject to approval by an independent, third-party regulator or by its own governing board empowered by statute or contract to establish rates that bind customers.

2. The regulated rates are designed to recover the specific enterprise's costs of providing the regulated services or products.

3. In view of the demand for the regulated services or products and the level of competition, direct and indirect, it is reasonable to assume that rates set at levels that will recover the enterprise's costs can be charged to and collected from customers. This criterion requires consideration of anticipated changes in levels of demand or competition during the recovery period for any capitalized costs.

Based on these criteria, SFAS No. 71 provides guidance in preparing general-purpose financial statements for most investor-owned, cooperative, and governmental utilities.

The FASB's sister entity, the GASB, has been empowered to set pervasive standards for government utilities to the extent applicable and, accordingly, financial statements issued in accordance with GAAP must follow GASB standards. However, in the absence of an applicable pronouncement issued by the GASB, differences between accounting followed under GASB or other FASB pronouncements and accounting followed for ratemaking purposes should be handled in accordance with SFAS No. 71.

23.18 AMENDMENTS TO SFAS NO. 71.   After the issuance of SFAS No. 71, the FASB became concerned about the accounting being followed by utilities (primarily electric companies) for certain transactions. Significant economic events were occurring, such as:

1. Disallowances of major portions of recently completed plants.
2. Very large plant abandonments.
3. Phase-in plans.

All of these events in one way or another prevented utilities from recovering costs currently and, in some instances, did not allow recovery at all. As a result, the FASB amended SFAS No. 71 in December 1986 with SFAS No. 90, "Regulated Enterprises—Accounting for Abandonments and Disallowances of Plant Costs," and in August 1987 with SFAS No. 92, "Regulated Enterprises—Accounting for Phase-in Plans."

23.19 OVERVIEW OF SFAS NO. 71.   The major issues addressed in SFAS No. 71 relate to the following:

1. Effect of ratemaking on GAAP.
2. Evidence criteria for recording regulatory assets and liabilities.
3. Application of GAAP to utilities.
4. Proper financial statement disclosures.

SFAS No. 71 sets forth (pars. 9–12) general standards of accounting for the effects of regulation. In addition, there are specific standards that are derived from the general standards and various examples (Appendix B) of the application of the general standards.

23.20 GENERAL STANDARDS.   In SFAS No. 71, the FASB recognized that a principal consideration introduced by rate regulation is the cause-and-effect relationship of costs and revenues—an economic dimension that, in some circumstances, should affect accounting for regulated enterprises. Thus, a regulated utility should capitalize a cost (as a regulatory asset) or recognize an obligation (as a regulatory liability) if it is probable that, through the ratemaking process, there will be a corresponding increase or decrease in future revenues.

(a) Regulatory Assets.   Paragraph 9 of SFAS No. 71 states that the "rate action of a regulator can provide reasonable assurance of the existence of an asset." All or part of an **incurred** cost that would otherwise be charged to expense should be capitalized if:

1. It is **probable** that future revenues in an amount approximately equal to the capitalized cost will result from inclusion of that cost in **allowable** costs for ratemaking purposes.

2. The regulator intends to provide for the recovery of that specific incurred cost rather than to provide for expected levels of similar future costs.

Thus, a regulated utility should capitalize a cost that would otherwise be charged to expense if future recovery in rates is probable. This general standard is not totally applicable to regulatory treatment of costs of **abandoned plants** and **phase-in plans.** The accounting accorded abandoned plant costs and phase-in plans is specified in SFAS Nos. 90 and 92.

To illustrate this provision in paragraph 9, assume a regulated utility has an incurred cost of $9 million for terminating a long-term fuel supply contract. The contract buyout was based on the utility's analysis that available alternative sources of fuel made such action economically beneficial to its customers. Further, the affected regulator's historical policy has been to allow similar costs to be recovered through customer rates over a 3-year period, so the utility concludes that future recovery is probable. In this situation, paragraph 9 of SFAS No. 71 should be applied, and a $9 million regulatory asset should be recorded on the utility's balance sheet. The utility will typically request recovery of the $9 million in connection with its next rate case. Once the regulator specifically provides for the amount of and period for recovery, the regulatory asset should be amortized in a consistent manner, above-the-line.

The term **probable** was defined in SFAS No. 71 differently from the way it had been defined in SFAS No. 5, "Accounting for Contingencies." One of the most significant amendments to SFAS No. 71, in SFAS No. 90, is the change in the definition of "probable" from the dictionary definition (better than a 50% certainty) to the SFAS No. 5 definition (likely to occur). The change has a considerable effect on the degree of assurance required, and therefore the timing, for recognizing in financial statements the economic impact of regulation.

The terms **allowable costs** and **incurred costs,** as defined in SFAS No. 71, also required further attention, which was provided by the FASB in SFAS No. 92. The two terms were often applied interchangeably so that, in practice, the provisions of SFAS No. 71, paragraph 9, were interpreted to permit the cost of equity return to be deferred and capitalized for future recovery as a regulatory asset. The FASB, in SFAS No. 92, stated that equity return (or an allowance for earnings on shareholders' investment) is not "an incurred cost that would otherwise be charged to expense. Accordingly, such an allowance shall not be capitalized pursuant to paragraph 9 of SFAS No. 71."

(b) Asset Impairment.   The general standards in paragraph 10 of SFAS No. 71 state that ratemaking actions can reduce or eliminate the value of an asset by the disallowance of the recovery of an asset through the ratemaking process. The carrying amount of any affected asset should be reduced to the extent that it has been **impaired,** as judged the same as for enterprises in general. In practice, this guidance has been generally followed for evaluating **recorded** regulatory assets, as well as other assets recognized under GAAP, as applied by enterprises in general. However, for utilities subject to the provisions of SFAS No. 71, disallowances of costs of recently completed plants, whether direct or indirect, are accounted for in accordance with SFAS No. 90. The application of paragraph 10 in practice was a major reason the FASB issued SFAS No. 90 to amend SFAS No. 71.

(c) Regulatory Liabilities.   The general standards also recognize that the rate action of a regulator can impose a liability on a regulated enterprise, usually to the utility's customers. The following are typical ways in which regulatory liabilities can be imposed:

1. A regulator may require refunds to customers (revenue collected subject to refund).

2. A regulator can provide current rates intended to recover costs that are expected to be incurred in the future. If those costs are not incurred, the regulator will reduce future rates by corresponding amounts.

3. A regulator can require that a gain or other reduction of net allowable costs be given to customers by amortizing such amounts to reduce future rates.

Paragraph 12 of the general standards states that "actions of a regulator can eliminate a liability only if the liability was imposed by actions of the regulator." The practical effect of this provision is that a utility's balance sheet should include all liabilities and obligations that an enterprise in general would record under GAAP, such as for capital leases, pension plans, compensated absences, and (once SFAS No. 96, "Accounting for Income Taxes," is adopted) income taxes.

23.21 SPECIFIC STANDARDS.   SFAS No. 71 also sets forth specific standards for several accounting and disclosure issues.

(a) AFUDC.   Paragraph 15 allows the capitalization of AFUDC, including a designated cost of equity funds, if a regulator requires such a method, rather than using SFAS No. 34 for purposes of capitalizing the carrying cost of construction.

Rate regulation has historically provided utilities with two methods of capturing and recovering the carrying cost of construction:

1. Capitalizing AFUDC for future recovery in rates.
2. Recovering the carrying cost of construction in current rates by including construction work-in-progress in the utility's rate base.

The computation of AFUDC is generally prescribed by the appropriate regulatory body. The predominant guidance has been provided by the FERC and FCC. The FERC has defined AFUDC as "the net cost for the period of construction of borrowed funds used for construction purposes and a reasonable rate on other funds when so used." The term "other funds," as used in this definition, refers to equity capital.

The FERC formula for computing AFUDC is comprehensive and takes into consideration:

1. Debt and equity funds.
2. The levels of construction.
3. Short-term debt.
4. The costs of long-term debt and preferred stock are based on the traditional embedded cost approach, using the preceding year-end costs.
5. The cost rate for common equity is usually the rate granted in the most recent rate proceeding.

The FCC instructions also provide for equity and debt components. In allowing AFUDC, the FERC and FCC recognize that the capital-carrying costs of the investments in construction work-in-progress are as much a cost of construction as other construction costs such as labor, materials, and contractors.

In contrast to regulated utilities, nonregulated companies are governed by a different standard, SFAS No. 34. Under the FASB guidelines:

> [T]he amount of interest to be capitalized for qualifying assets is intended to be that portion of interest cost incurred during the assets acquisition periods that theoretically could have been avoided (for example, by avoiding additional borrowings or by using the funds expended for the assets to repay existing borrowings) if expenditures for the assets had not been made.

Furthermore, the FASB statement allows only debt interest capitalization and does not recognize an equity component.

The specific standard in SFAS No. 71 states that capitalization of such financing costs can occur only if both of the following criteria are met.

1. It is **probable** that future revenue in an amount at least equal to the capitalized cost will result from the inclusion of that cost in allowable costs for ratemaking purposes.
2. The future revenue will be provided to permit recovery of the previously incurred cost rather than to provide for expected levels of similar future costs.

In practice, many have interpreted the standard under SFAS No. 71 to mean that AFUDC should be capitalized if it is reasonably possible (not necessarily probable under SFAS No. 5) that the costs will be recovered. This same reasoning was also applied to the capitalization of other incurred costs such as labor and materials. Thus, capitalization occurred so long as recovery was reasonably possible and a loss was not probable.

As previously indicated, SFAS No. 90 amends the definition of probable included in SFAS No. 71 such that probable is now defined under the stringent technical definition in SFAS No. 5. In addition, paragraph 8 of SFAS No. 90 clarified that AFUDC capitalized under paragraph 15 can occur only if "subsequent inclusion in allowable costs for ratemaking purposes is probable." Accordingly, the standard for capitalizing AFUDC is different from the standard applied to other costs, such as labor and materials.

The FASB also concluded in SFAS No. 92, paragraph 66, that:

> [I]f the specific criteria in paragraph 15 of SFAS No. 71 are met but AFUDC is not capitalized because its inclusion in the cost that will become the basis for future rates is not probable, the regulated utility may not alternatively capitalize interest cost in accordance with SFAS No. 34.

(b) Intercompany Profit.   Paragraph 16 of SFAS No. 71 generally reaffirms the provision in ARB No. 51 that intercompany profits on sales to regulated affiliates should not be eliminated in general-purpose financial statements if the sales price is reasonable and it is probable that future revenues allowed through the ratemaking process will approximately equal the sales price.

(c) Accounting for Income Taxes.   In paragraph 18 of SFAS No. 71, the FASB recognizes that, in some cases, a regulator flows through the tax effects of certain timing differences as a reduction in future rates. In such cases, if it is **probable** that future rates will be based on income taxes payable at that time, SFAS No. 71 does not permit deferred taxes to be recorded in accordance with APB Opinion No. 11, "Accounting for Income Taxes." SFAS No. 71 does require disclosure of the cumulative amount of timing differences for which deferred income taxes have not been provided.

In December, 1987, SFAS No. 71 was amended by SFAS No. 96; when SFAS No. 96 is adopted, paragraph 18 is to be replaced by the following:

> A deferred tax liability or asset shall be recognized for the deferred tax consequences of temporary differences in accordance with FASB Statement No. 96, "Accounting for Income Taxes."

(d) Refunds.   Paragraph 19 of SFAS No. 71 addresses the accounting for significant refunds. Examples include refunds granted gas distribution utilities from pipelines and telephone refunds occurring where revenues are estimated in one period and "trued-up" at a later date or where revenues are billed under bond pending settlement of a rate proceeding.

For refunds recognized in a period other than the period in which the related revenue was recognized, disclosure of the effect on net income and the years in which the related revenue was recognized is required if material. SFAS No. 71 provides presentation guidance that the effect of such refunds may be disclosed by displaying the amount, **net** of income tax, as a line item in the income statement, but not as an extraordinary item.

Adjustments to prior **quarters** of the **current** fiscal year are appropriate for such refunds, provided all of the following criteria are met:

1. The effect is material (either to operations or income trends).
2. All or part of the adjustment or settlement can be specifically identified with and is directly related to business activities of specific prior interim periods.
3. The amount could not be reasonably estimated prior to the current interim period but becomes reasonably estimable in the current period.

This treatment of prior interim periods for utility refunds is one of the restatement exceptions contained in paragraph 13 of SFAS No. 16, "Prior Period Adjustments."

(e) Deferred Costs Not Earning a Return.   Paragraph 20 of SFAS No. 71 requires disclosure of costs being amortized in accordance with the actions of a regulator but not being allowed to earn a return during the recovery period. Disclosure should include the remaining amounts being amortized (the amount of the nonearning asset) as well as the remaining recovery period.

(f) Examples of Application.   Appendix B in SFAS No. 71 contains examples of the application of the general standards to specific situations. These examples, along with the basis for conclusions (Appendix C) are an important aid in understanding the provisions of SFAS No. 71 and the financial statements of utilities.
Items discussed include:

1. Intangible assets.
2. Accounting changes.
3. Early extinguishment of debt.
4. Accounting for contingencies.
5. Accounting for leases.
6. Revenue collected subject to refund.
7. Refunds to customers.
8. Accounting for compensated absences.

SFAS NO. 90: "REGULATED ENTERPRISES—ACCOUNTING FOR ABANDONMENTS AND DISALLOWANCE OF PLANT COSTS"

23.22 CONCERN WITH SFAS NO. 71—DISALLOWANCES AND ABANDONMENTS. After SFAS No. 71 was issued, various regulatory agencies began to question the cost of certain new plants and to discuss major disallowances. Also, several electric generating units in advanced stages of construction were abandoned. In several states, courts ruled that the affected utilities could not recover the costs of those abandoned plants through rates.

The related accounting for these significant economic events was unsettled in practice and viewed by many as being potentially troublesome. For example, large cost disallowances were ordered by regulators, but no losses were being currently reported by affected utilities under the theory that, on an overall basis, the total cost would be recovered. By including the return earned on the **allowed** portion of the new plant, the plant cost would be recovered even though it might earn less than a full return.

To illustrate, say a plant costing $2 billion is placed in service and the regulator disallows $200 million from rate base and depreciation recovery. As long as the future cash flows from the $1.8 billion allowed portion exceed $2 billion, then no write-off would be recorded because the asset was not "impaired" in an accounting sense. This accounting treatment was considered to be consistent with the provisions of SFAS No. 71 (par. 10), which states:

> [T]he carrying amount of any related asset shall be reduced to the extent that the asset has been impaired. Whether the asset has been impaired shall be judged the same as for enterprises in general.

Similarly, as long as cost recovery for abandonments was probable (no matter over how long a time period), no immediate loss was required under GAAP. Thus, if a $3 billion project were abandoned and a regulator allowed recovery of $100 million for 30 years, no write-off would result.

The FASB recognized, in its basis for conclusions included in SFAS No. 90, that the accounting provisions of SFAS No. 71 require regulated utilities "to recognize probable increases in future revenues due to a regulator's actions as assets by capitalizing incurred costs that would otherwise be charged to expense." Accordingly, regulated utilities "should also recognize probable decreases in revenues due to a regulator's actions as reductions in assets." The accounting for disallowances and abandonments discussed above is inconsistent with this conclusion, so SFAS No. 71 was amended by SFAS No. 90.

23.23 SIGNIFICANT PROVISIONS OF SFAS NO. 90.   The provisions of SFAS No. 90 are limited to the narrow area of accounting for abandonments and disallowances of plant costs and not to other assets, regulatory or otherwise.

(a) Accounting for Regulatory Disallowances of Newly Completed Plant.   When a *direct disallowance* of a newly completed plant is **probable** and **estimable,** a loss should be recorded, dollar for dollar, for the disallowed amount. After the write-down is achieved, the reduced asset forms the basis for future depreciation charges. Application of this requirement to the regulatory disallowance situation cited above would result in an immediate write-off for $200 million of the $2 billion plant cost.

An **indirect disallowance** occurs when, in certain circumstances, no return or a reduced return is permitted on all or a portion of the new plant for an extended period of time. To determine the loss resulting from an indirect disallowance, the present value of the future revenue stream allowed by the regulator should be determined by discounting at the most recent allowed rate of return. This amount should be compared with the recorded plant amount and the difference recorded as a loss. Under this discounting approach, the remaining asset should be depreciated consistent with the ratemaking and in a manner that would produce a constant return on the undepreciated asset equal to the discount rate.

(b) Accounting for Plant Abandonments.   In the case of abandonments, when no return or only a partial return is permitted, at the time the abandonment is both **probable** and **estimable** the asset should be written off and a separate new asset should be established based on the present value of the future revenue stream. The entities' incremental borrowing rate should be used to measure the new asset. During the recovery period, the new asset should be amortized to produce zero net income based on the theoretical debt, and interest should be assumed to finance the abandonment.

FTB 87-2, "Computation of a Loss on an Abandonment," supports discounting the abandonment revenue stream using an after-tax incremental borrowing rate. Until SFAS No. 96 is adopted, the tax effects of the abandonment loss should be based on the statutory rate for the year of abandonment. This is the rate supported under APB Opinion No. 11 and APB Opinion No. 20, "Accounting Changes."

(c) Effective Date.   The provisions of SFAS No. 90 became effective for fiscal years beginning after December 15, 1987, unless its application would have caused a violation of a restrictive clause contained in an existing loan indenture or other agreement. In that case, application could be delayed for 1 year beyond the effective date.

(d) Income Statement Presentation. SAB No. 72 (currently cited as SAB Topic 10E) concludes that the effects of adoption of SFAS No. 90 should not be reported as an extraordinary item. SAB No. 72 states that such charges should be reported **gross** as a component of other income and deductions and **not shown net-of-tax.** The following presentation complies with the requirements of SAB No. 72.

Operating income	$XX
Other income (expense)	
Allowance for equity funds used during construction	XX
Disallowed plant cost	(XX)
Income tax reduction for disallowed plant cost	XX
Interest income	XX
Income taxes applicable to other income	XX
Income before interest charges	$XX

SFAS NO. 92: "REGULATED ENTERPRISES—ACCOUNTING FOR PHASE-IN PLANS"

23.24 CONCERN WITH SFAS NO. 71—PHASE-IN PLANS. Subsequent to the issuance of SFAS No. 71, a combination of circumstances has caused traditional ratemaking procedures to result in a phenomenon called "rate spike." Rate spike is a major, one-time increase in rates that can occur from the inclusion of the cost of new plants in rates under traditional ratemaking procedures. Rate spikes have in part been caused by the high cost of nuclear power plants, which escalated far beyond initial expectations. Also, demand for many utilities' services has not grown in recent years to the extent that was expected when the decision was made to construct many of the recently completed plants. As a result, plants that were expected to be necessary to meet demand have created excess capacity. In addition, the increased efficiency of the new plants has not been sufficient to offset the high construction and capitalized capital costs of those plants and the return on investment that would have been included in rates under traditional ratemaking procedures.

Phase-in plans were developed to alleviate the problem of rate spike by:

1. Moderating the initial increase in rates that would otherwise result from placing newly completed plants in service by deferring some of that rate increase to future years and providing the utility with return on investment for those deferred amounts.
2. Creating a pattern of gradually increasing allowable costs for the initial years of the plant's service life instead of the traditional pattern of an increase in allowable costs followed by decreasing allowable costs for utility plants after the plants are placed in service.

The major aspects of phase-in plans that the FASB found troublesome related to the conceptual problems these plans create and these various factors seemed to undermine the credibility of financial reporting under SFAS No. 71. These conceptual concerns include:

1. The mere fact that phase-in plans defer cost recovery to future periods seems to contradict the requirement in SFAS No. 71 that rates set at levels designed to recover a utility's costs are collectible from customers.
2. SFAS No. 71 requires that rates be designed to recover a utility's cost of service. Under a phase-in plan, cost recovery can be deferred to future periods, and consequently, current rates can be based upon criteria other than cost of service.

3. Some phase-in plans provide for capitalization of equity costs **after** a plant begins operations.

The FASB reached two major conclusions about phase-in plans in SFAS No. 92.

1. If such plans result in costs deferred and capitalized for financial reporting purposes, a stringent set of criteria must be met so as to not undermine the credibility of SFAS No. 71.
2. Capitalization of phase-in plan costs should only be permitted if substantial construction of the affected plant occurred before January 1, 1988. If not, no phase-in plan accounting under SFAS No. 92 is permitted for the newly completed plant. This provision affects the newly completed plants of all regulated utilities subject to SFAS No. 71.

23.25 SIGNIFICANT PROVISIONS OF SFAS NO. 92.   A phase-in plan, as defined in SFAS No. 92, is a method of ratemaking that meets all of the following criteria:

1. Adopted **in connection with a major, newly** completed plant of the utility or one of its suppliers or a major plant scheduled for completion in the near future.
2. Defers the rates intended to recover allowable costs beyond the period in which those allowable costs would be charged to expense under GAAP applicable to enterprises in general.
3. Defers the rates intended to recover allowable costs beyond the period in which those rates would have been ordered under ratemaking methods **routinely** used prior to 1982 by that regulator for **similar** allowable costs of that utility.

This definition is **not** limited to **electric** utility plants and encompasses, for example, methods of depreciation slower than straight-line (sinking fund depreciation) and the treatment of a capital lease under SFAS No. 13 as an operating lease for ratemaking purposes. Deferral of costs associated with newly completed plants before a rate order is issued, which is often referred to as a short-term or rate synchronization deferral, is specifically excluded from being defined as a phase-in plan.

(a) Accounting for Phase-in Plans.   SFAS No. 92 requires allowable costs deferred for future recovery under a phase-in plan related to plants completed before January 1, 1988, and plants on which substantial physical construction has been performed before January 1, 1988, to be capitalized if each of four criteria is met. The criteria to determine whether capitalization is appropriate are as follows:

1. The plan has been agreed to by the regulator.
2. The plan specifies when recovery will occur.
3. All allowable costs deferred under the plan are scheduled for recovery within 10 years of the date when deferrals begin.
4. The percentage increase in rates scheduled for each future year under the plan is not greater than the percentage increase in rates scheduled for each immediately preceding year.

If any of these criteria are not met, allowable costs deferred under the plan would not be capitalized for financial reporting purposes. Instead, those costs would be recognized in the same manner as if there were no phase-in plan.

(b) Financial Statement Classification.   From a financial statement viewpoint, costs deferred should be classified and reported as a separate item in the income statement in the section relating to those costs. For instance, if capital costs are being deferred, they should be classified below-the-line. If depreciation or other operating costs are being deferred, the "credit" should be classified above-the-line with the operating costs. Allowable costs capitalized should not be reported net as a reduction of other expenses. Amortization of phase-in plan deferrals typically should be above-the-line (similar to recovering AFUDC via depreciation). This income statement presentation is consistent with guidance provided by the SEC's staff in the "Official Minutes of the Emerging Issues Task Force Meeting" (February 23, 1989, Open Meeting).

(c) AFUDC.   SFAS No. 92 clarifies that AFUDC-equity can be capitalized in general purpose financial statements only during construction (based on par. 15 of SFAS No. 71) or as part of a qualifying phase-in plan. Thus, it is clear that, after January 1, 1988, AFUDC-equity can no longer be capitalized in connection with short-term, rate synchronization deferrals. It should also be noted that, in connection with the adoption of SFAS No. 92, such deferrals can be recorded only when it is probable—based on SFAS No. 5—that such costs will be recovered in future rates. This is consistent with the discussion on SFAS No. 90 relating to capitalizing AFUDC.

(d) Interrelationship of Phase-in Plans and Disallowances.   Amounts deferred pursuant to SFAS No. 92 should also include an allowance for earnings on stockholders' investment. If the phase-in plan meets the criteria in SFAS No. 92 and the regulator prevents the enterprise from recovering either some amount of its investment or some amount of return on its investment, a disallowance occurs that should be accounted for in accordance with SFAS No. 90.

(e) Financial Statement Disclosure.   A utility should disclose in its financial statements the terms of any phase-in plans in effect during the year. If a phase-in plan exists but does not meet the criteria in SFAS No. 92, the financial statements should include disclosure of the net amount deferred for ratemaking purposes at the balance sheet date and the net change in deferrals for ratemaking purposes during the year for those plans. In addition, the nature and amounts of any allowance for earnings on stockholders' investment capitalized for ratemaking purposes but not capitalized for financial reporting are to be disclosed.

(f) Transition and Effective Date.   SFAS No. 92 is effective for fiscal years beginning after December 15, 1987 and interim periods within those fiscal years. Earlier application is encouraged. However, application can be delayed if (1) the company has filed a rate application to have the plan amended to meet the provisions of SFAS No. 92 or intends to do so as soon as practicable, and (2) it is reasonably possible that the regulator will change the terms of the phase-in plan so that it qualifies under the Statement. If these conditions are met, the provisions of the Statement should be applied on the earlier of the date when one of those conditions ceases to be met or the date when a final rate order is received, amending or refusing to amend the phase-in plan.

At the date the Statement is first applied, if such plans do not meet the phase-in plan rules, all allowable costs deferred by the regulator under such plans that have been previously capitalized for financial reporting purposes are to be written off unless the company is able to delay application as described above.

SFAS NO. 101: "REGULATED ENTERPRISES—ACCOUNTING FOR THE DISCONTINUATION OF APPLICATION OF FASB STATEMENT NO. 71"

Deregulation and competition, as well as political pressures, have brought the broader issue of the necessity of SFAS No. 71 into question.

1. Are rates really cost based?
2. If a portion of the business becomes deregulated, is the remainder of the enterprise really individual cost-of-service rate regulated and still subject to SFAS No. 71?

23.26 SIGNIFICANT PROVISIONS OF SFAS NO. 101. SFAS No. 101 deals with the required accounting **once** a utility concludes that it should discontinue application of SFAS No. 71. Although it does not specify **when** a utility should discontinue application, SFAS No. 101 does provide the following examples of potential cause for a utility not meeting the scope criteria in SFAS No. 71, paragraph 5.

1. Deregulation.
2. Regulation that is no longer cost based.
3. Competition that precludes selling utility services at cost-recoverable rates.

23.27 REGULATORY ASSETS AND LIABILITIES. Once a utility concludes that all or a part of a company's operations no longer comes under SFAS No. 71, it should discontinue application of that Statement and report discontinuation by eliminating from its balance sheet the effects of any actions of regulators that had been recognized as assets and liabilities pursuant to SFAS No. 71 but would not have been recognized as assets and liabilities by enterprises in general. The guidance in SFAS No. 101 indicates that all regulatory-created assets and liabilities should be written off unless the right to receive payment or the obligation to pay exists as a result of past events and regardless of expected future transactions.

Examples of such regulatory-created assets and liabilities include:

1. Deferred storm damage.
2. Deferred plant abandonment loss.
3. Receivables or payables to future customers under purchased gas or fuel adjustment clauses (unless amounts are receivable or payable regardless of future sales).
4. Deferred gains or losses or reacquisition of debt.
5. Revenues subject to refund as future sales price adjustments.

23.28 FIXED ASSETS AND INVENTORY. SFAS No. 101 also states:

> However, the carrying amounts of plant, equipment and inventory measured and reported pursuant to SFAS No. 71 should not be adjusted unless those assets are impaired (as measured by enterprises in general), in which case the carrying amounts of those assets should be reduced to reflect that impairment.

The carrying amount of inventories measured and reported pursuant to SFAS No. 71 would not be adjusted—to eliminate, for example, intercompany profit—absent loss recognition by applying the "cost or market, whichever is lower" rule set forth in Chapter 4, "Inventory Pricing," of ARB No. 43, "Restatement and Revision of Accounting Research Bulletins."

Reaccounting is required for **true** regulatory assets that have been **misclassified** as part of plant, such as postconstruction cost deferrals recorded as part of plant, and for systematic underdepreciation of plant in accordance with ratemaking practices.

23.29 INCOME TAXES. An apparent requirement of SFAS No. 101 when SFAS No. 71 is discontinued is that net-of-tax AFUDC should be displayed gross along with the associated deferred income taxes. This requirement is based on the notion that the net-of-tax AFUDC presentation is pursuant to industry practice and not SFAS No. 71. The interaction of this requirement along with the SFAS No. 101 treatment of excess deferred income taxes and the transition provision in paragraph 36 of SFAS No. 96 must be considered in connection with discontinuing the application of SFAS No. 71. In addition, deferred taxes that have not been recorded because of ratemaking practices would have to be recognized on the balance sheet even if SFAS No. 96 has not been adopted. This is a requirement because the sole basis for the omission is the provision in paragraph 18 of SFAS No. 71, which would no longer be available.

23.30 TRANSITION AND EFFECTIVE DATE.   The net effect of the above adjustments should be included in income of the period of the change and classified as an extraordinary item in the income statement.

SFAS No. 101 is effective for discontinuations of application of SFAS No. 71 occurring in fiscal years ending after December 15, 1988, but its adoption may be delayed until the issuance of annual financial statements for the fiscal year that includes December 15, 1989. Retroactive application to discontinuations reported prior to fiscal years ending after December 15, 1988, by restatement of the financial statements for the period including the date of discontinuation and periods subsequent to the date of the discontinuation is permitted but not required.

OTHER SPECIALIZED UTILITY ACCOUNTING PRACTICES

23.31 UTILITY INCOME TAXES AND INCOME TAX CREDITS.   Income tax expense is important to utilities because it generally is one of the largest items in the income statement and usually is a key factor in the determination of cost of service for ratemaking purposes. Deferred income taxes represent a significant element of internally generated funds and a major financing source for the extensive construction programs that utilities have historically experienced. In addition, the complexity of the IRC and of the various regulations to which utilities are subject causes a significant amount of controversy. As a result, the method of accounting for income taxes—"normalization" versus "flow-through" ratemaking—is often a specific issue in rate proceedings. The ratemaking method is an important area of concern to analysts and can be a factor in establishing the cost of equity and new debt offerings.

(a) Interperiod Income Tax Allocation.   The accounting for differences between income before income taxes and taxable income has been and continues to be a subject of much discussion. GAAP, whether under APB Opinion No. 11 or SFAS No. 96, require that a "Provision for deferred taxes" be made for the tax effect of most of such differences. This practice of interperiod tax allocation is referred to in the utility industry as **normalization.**

The term "normalization" evolved because income taxes computed for accounting purposes on the normalization basis would cause reported net income to be a "normal" amount had the utility not adopted, for example, a particular tax return method for a deduction that created the tax-book difference. Under the deferred tax, or normalization concept, the taxes that would be payable, except for the use of the tax return deduction that created the tax-book difference, are merely deferred, not saved. For example, when tax depreciation exceeds book depreciation in the early years of property life, deferred taxes are charged to expense with a contra credit to a reserve. In later years, when the tax write-offs are lower than they otherwise would be, the higher taxes when payable are charged against this reserve. To illustrate the concept, assume the following facts:

	Year 1	Year 2	Year 3
Revenues	$1,000	$1,000	$1,000
Other expenses	600	600	600
Book depreciation	200	200	200
Tax depreciation	300	200	100
Tax rate	34%	34%	34%

DEFERRED TAX ACCOUNTING

	Income Statement	Tax Return	Timing Difference
Revenue	$1,000	$1,000	$ —
Depreciation	(200)	(300)	100
Other expenses	(600)	(600)	—
Income before taxes	$ 200	$ 100	$100
Federal income taxes:			
Payable currently (34% × $100)	$ 34	$ 34	
Deferred (34% × $100)	34		$ 34
Total	$ 68		
Operating income	$ 132		

Exhibit 23.7.   Illustration of "normalized" tax accounting.

Exhibit 23.7 sets forth how normalized (deferred) tax accounting would be recorded in Year 1 for the tax and book depreciation difference of $100.

(b) Flow-Through. "Flow-through" is a cash basis concept wherein the reductions in current tax payments from tax deductions, such as received by using accelerated depreciation, are flowed through to customers via lower cost-of-service and revenue requirements. Under this approach, income tax expense is equal to the currently payable amount only. No recognition (deferred taxes) is given to the tax effect of differences between book income before income taxes and taxable income. Under a "partial" allocation approach, deferred taxes are provided on certain differences but are ignored on others.

The principal argument used by those who support flow-through accounting is that a provision for deferred taxes does not constitute a current cost, and therefore such a deferment should not be made. Income tax expense for the year should only include those taxes legally payable with respect to the tax return applicable to that year, and any provision in excess of taxes payable represents "phantom" taxes or "customer contributed capital." Further, when property additions are growing, as they are for certain utilities, and if no change were made to the tax law, deferred tax provisions **in the aggregate** would continue to grow and would never turn around (or reverse); thereby the tax timing differences are, in fact, "permanent differences."

Exhibit 23.8 sets forth how flow-through tax accounting would be recorded in Year 1 for the tax and book depreciation difference of $100.

Although Exhibit 23.8 shows a "bottom line" impact from the elimination of deferred tax expense, such accounting is not acceptable. GAAP requires deferred tax accounting with SFAS No. 71, permitting departures only when regulators affect revenues. To be acceptable, therefore, the regulator would lower revenue requirements due to the omission of deferred tax expense as an element of the utility's cost-of-service for ratemaking purposes. The action of the regulator in this case is to defer a cost that will be recoverable through increased rates in the future.

As previously discussed, utility regulators determine operating income first and then add allowable expenses to derive operating revenue. In Exhibit 23.7, $132 is presumed to be the result of multiplying rate base × rate of return. The same operating income of $132 in the normalization example would be developed first under the flow-through concept and, with the elimination of deferred tax expense of $34, only $948 of revenue would be required to produce the $132 of operating income under flow-through. The proper application of flow-through is shown in Exhibit 23.9.

"FLOW-THROUGH" ACCOUNTING ASSUMING NO DECREASE IN CUSTOMER RATES

	Income Statement	Tax Return	Timing Difference
Revenue	$1,000	$1,000	$—
Depreciation	(200)	(300)	100
Other expenses	(600)	(600)	—
Income before taxes	$ 200	$ 100	$100
Federal income taxes:			
Payable currently (34% × $100)	$ 34	$ 34	
Deferred (34% × $0)	—		$—
Total	$ 34		
Net Income	$ 166		

Exhibit 23.8.   Illustration of "flow-through" accounting with no impact on customer rates.

This $52 reduction in revenues (by eliminating only $34 of deferred tax expense) is caused by the tax-on-tax effect, which is discussed under the ratemaking formula. In short, the elimination of the deferred tax expense results in a direct reduction of revenues, causing current tax expense also to be reduced. This effect is the primary reason so much attention is focused on normalization versus flow-through ratemaking for income taxes.

The comparison of the normalization and flow-through concepts in Exhibit 23.10 illustrates that operating income continues to be $132 under both methods and that the $52 of savings in revenue requirement in Year 1 due to flow-through is offset by $52 of higher rates in Year 3. For simplicity, this example ignores the rate base reducing effects of deferred taxes.

The comparison illustrates the principal argument for normalization—that revenues are at a level, or normal, amount, whereas revenue varies greatly under flow-through. Advocates of normalization note that normalization distributes income tax expense to time periods, and therefore to customers' revenue requirements, consistently with the costs (depreciation) that are affecting income tax expense. As the ratemaking process necessarily involves the deferral

"FLOW-THROUGH" ACCOUNTING ASSUMING DECREASE IN CUSTOMER RATES

	Income Statement	Tax Return	Timing Difference
Revenue	$948	$948	—
Depreciation	(200)	(300)	$100
Other expenses	(600)	(600)	—
Income before taxes	$148	$ 48	$100
Federal income taxes:			
Payable currently (34% × $48)	16	16	
Deferred	—		—
Total	$ 16		
Net income	$132		

Exhibit 23.9.   Illustration of "flow-through" accounting with a decrease in rates.

COMPARISON OF NORMALIZATION AND FLOW-THROUGH

	Normalization				Flow-Through			
	Year 1	Year 2	Year 3	Total	Year 1	Year 2	Year 3	Total
Revenues	$1,000	$1,000	$1,000	$3,000	$948	$1,000	$1,052	$3,000
Depreciation	(200)	(200)	(200)	(600)	(200)	(200)	(200)	(600)
Other expenses	(600)	(600)	(600)	(1,800)	(600)	(600)	(600)	(1,800)
Income before income taxes	200	200	200	600	148	200	252	600
Income taxes								
Payable currently	34	68	102	204	16	68	120	204
Deferred taxes	34	—	(34)	—	—	—	—	—
	68	68	68	204	16	68	120	204
Operating income	$ 132	$ 132	$ 132	$ 396	$132	$ 132	$ 132	$ 396

Exhibit 23.10. Illustration of normalization versus flow-through differences.

of costs such as plant investment and distribution of these costs over time, normalization is used to produce a consistent determination of income tax expense.

Normalization also recognizes that the "using up" of tax basis of depreciable property (or using up an asset's ability to reduce taxes) creates a cost. This cost should be recognized as the tax payments are reduced. Basing tax expense solely on taxes payable without recognizing the cost of achieving reductions in tax payments is not consistent with accrual accounting. Although flow-through ratemaking ignores this current cost, this cost does not disappear any more than the nonrecognition of depreciation for ratemaking would make that cost disappear.

(c) Provisions of the Internal Revenue Code.   Complicating the regulatory treatment and financial reporting of income taxes for utilities are significant amounts of deferred income taxes that are "protected" under provisions of the I.R.C. That is, normalization is required with respect to certain tax and book depreciation differences if the utility is to remain eligible for accelerated depreciation. A historical perspective of tax incentives and tax legislation, as they relate to the utility industry, is helpful in understanding why the regulatory treatment of income tax is of such importance.

(d) The Concept of Tax Incentives.   The first significant tax incentive that was generally available to all taxpayers was a provision of the 1954 Code that permitted accelerated methods of depreciation. Prior to enactment of this legislation, tax depreciation allowances were generally limited to those computed with the straight-line method, which is traditionally used for financial reporting and ratemaking purposes. The straight-line method spread the cost of the property evenly over its estimated useful life. The accelerated depreciation provisions of the 1954 Code permitted taxpayers to take greater amounts of depreciation in the early years of property life and lesser amounts in later years. Although accelerated methods permit taypayers to recover capital investments more rapidly for tax purposes, deductions are limited to the depreciable cost of property. Thus, only the timing, not the ultimate amount of depreciation, is affected.

Because utilities are capital intensive in nature, accelerated depreciation provisions generate significant amounts of tax deferrals. Additionally, other sources of deferred taxes can be relatively small in some industries but are magnified in the utility industry because of its large construction programs. Among the major differences, generally referred to as **basis differences,** are interest, pensions, and taxes capitalized as costs of construction for book purposes but deducted currently (as incurred) as expenses for tax purposes. Once again, it is the timing, not the ultimate cost, that is affected.

Accelerated methods and lives were intended by the U.S. Congress to generate capital for investment, stimulate expansion, and contribute to high levels of output and employment. The economic benefit to the taxpayer arising from the use of accelerated depreciation and capitalized costs is the time value of the money because of the postponement of tax payments. The availability of what are effectively interest-free loans, obtained from the U.S. Treasury, reduces the requirements for other sources of capital, thereby reducing capital costs. Prior to the Tax Reform Act of 1986, these capitalized overheads represented significant deductions for tax purposes. However, subsequent to that Act, such amounts are now capitalized into the tax basis of the asset and depreciated for tax purposes as well. Thus, the benefits that once resulted from basis differences have, to a large extent, been eliminated.

(e) Tax Legislation.   A brief history of the origin of accelerated tax depreciation and the intent of the U.S. Congress in permitting liberalized depreciation methods is helpful in understanding the regulatory and accounting issues related to income taxes.

(i) Tax Reform Act of 1969.   The accelerated tax depreciation methods initially made available to taxpayers in 1954 were without limitations in the tax law as to the accounting and ratemaking methods used for public utility property. However, in the late 1960s, the U.S.

Treasury Department and Congress became concerned about larger-than-anticipated tax revenue losses as a result of rate regulatory developments. Although both Congress and the Treasury realized that accelerated tax deductions would initially reduce Treasury revenues by the tax effect, they had not anticipated that flow-through would about double (at the then 48% tax rate) the Treasury's tax loss because of the tax-on-tax effect. Depending on the exact tax rate, about one-half the reduction in payments to the Treasury came from the deduction of accelerated depreciation and the other one-half from the immediate reduction in customer rates from the use of flow-through. It was this second one-half reduction of Treasury revenues that was considered unacceptable. Furthermore, immediate flow-through of these incentives to utility customers negated the intended Congressional purpose of the incentives themselves. It was the utility customers who immediately received all of the benefit of accelerated depreciation. Accordingly, the utility did not have all the Treasury "capital" that was provided by Congress for investment and expansion.

Faced with larger-than-anticipated Treasury revenue losses, Congress enacted TRA '69. By adding § 167(1), it limited the Treasury's exposure to revenue losses by making the accelerated depreciation methods available to public utility properties only if specific qualifying standards as to accounting and ratemaking were met. Although § 167(1) did not dictate to state regulatory commissions a ratemaking treatment they should follow with respect to the tax effects of accelerated depreciation, the Act provided that:

1. If a utility had not used accelerated depreciation prior to 1970, it would not be allowed to use accelerated tax depreciation in the future unless it normalized for ratemaking and accounting purposes.
2. Utilities that had been using accelerated tax depreciation and were normalizing for accounting and ratemaking purposes would not be allowed to use accelerated depreciation in the future unless they continued to normalize for accounting and ratemaking purposes.
3. Companies that were currently on a flow-through basis were allowed to continue on a flow-through basis in the future. However, an election was offered to such companies by which they could elect to be in a position where they would lose accelerated depreciation on future expansion additions unless they were normalizing for ratemaking and accounting purposes with respect to such future expansion property additions.

(ii) Revenue Act of 1971. The Revenue Act of 1971, signed into law on December 10, 1971, codified the Asset Depreciation Range (ADR) system for determining depreciation for tax purposes. Under ADR, lives were shortened, thereby accelerating tax depreciation even further. The ADR regulations prescribed the same standards regarding normalization versus flow-through ratemaking as were set forth in TRA '69.

(iii) Economic Recovery Act of 1981. The Economic Recovery Act of 1981, signed into law on August 31, 1981, continued to allow acceleration of depreciation tax deductions and included normalization rules for public utility property with respect to depreciation under the Accelerated Cost Recovery System. Normalization is mandatory under the Act for accelerated depreciation taken on all public utility property placed in service after December 31, 1980.

(iv) Tax Reform Act of 1986. TRA '86 reduced the acceleration of depreciation tax deductions and continued normalization requirements for public utility property. In addition, the maximum federal tax rate for corporations was reduced from 46% to 34%. This reduction in the federal tax rate not only reduces tax payments currently being made, but will also reduce future tax payments (assuming continuation of the present tax rate) that result from the reversal of previously recorded deferred tax amounts—effectively forgiving a portion of the loan from the U.S. Treasury.

TRA '86 (§ 203(e)) provided that deferred taxes related to certain depreciation method and life differences on public utility property in excess of the new 34% statutory rate be used to reduce customer rates using the average rate assumption method. This method generally requires the development of an average rate determined by dividing the aggregate normalized timing differences into the accumulated deferred taxes that have been provided on those timing differences. As the timing differences begin to reverse, the turnaround occurs at this average rate. Under this method, the so-called excess in the reserve for deferred taxes is reduced over the remaining life of the property.

If a regulatory commission requires reduction in the deferred tax balance more rapidly than under this method, book depreciation must be used for tax purposes. There is no provision in TRA '86 for any protection of other deferred taxes, such as book/tax basis differences, life differences on pre-ADR assets, salvage value on ADR assets, repair allowance, and so on. In addition, the deferred taxes on depreciation method and life differences provided at rates in excess of 46% are not protected under the average-rate assumption method.

(f) "Accounting for Income Taxes"—APB Opinion No. 11.

In December 1967 the APB issued Opinion No. 11, which requires that, in general, deferred taxes be provided for all tax-timing differences. Under the deferred method, deferred taxes provided are not meant to be a provision for the taxes that will be payable in the future but, rather, a deferral of the benefit received. Thus, under APB No. 11, deferred tax assets and liabilities are not adjusted when tax rates or other provisions of the income tax law change. Instead, they turn around during the reversal period at the tax rates used when the deferred taxes were originally provided. The deferred method is the professional standard today for all industries, with one major exception. That exception is for those utilities that are regulated on a flow-through basis if certain requirements are met with respect to increased rates being provided to recover higher future taxes. Income tax accounting for regulated enterprises is also addressed in SFAS No. 71 and, under this existing literature, deferred taxes for timing differences flowed through to reduce customer rates typically are not recorded for financial reporting purposes. However, the cumulative net amount of any income tax timing differences for which deferred taxes have not been provided must be disclosed in the footnotes to a utility's financial statements.

(g) "Accounting for Income Taxes"—SFAS No. 96.

In December 1987 the FASB issued SFAS No. 96, which shifts the focus of income tax accounting from the income statement to an asset and liability approach. SFAS No. 96 retains the current requirement to record deferred taxes whenever income or expenses are reported in different years for financial reporting and tax purposes. However, it changes the way companies compute deferred taxes by requiring deferred tax assets and liabilities to be adjusted whenever tax rates or other provisions of the income tax law change. This is referred to as the "liability method" of providing deferred income taxes. SFAS No. 96 also requires utility companies to record tax liabilities for all temporary differences (defined as differences between the book and tax bases of assets and liabilities recorded on their respective balance sheets), even those that have previously been flowed through. For many utilities, these amounts are significant.

The liability method represents a change from the existing "deferred method" embodied in APB Opinion No. 11. However, in most situations, the amounts of the deferred tax provision under each of these concepts would be the same. In addition, ratemaking calculations of income tax expense may continue under an APB No. 11 type approach long after SFAS No. 96 is implemented.

As a result of adopting SFAS No. 96, utilities will adjust their accumulated deferred income tax balances to the level obtained by multiplying the statutory tax rate by existing temporary differences. Because this amount may be more or less than what has been permitted to be recovered through the ratemaking process, regulatory assets or liabilities will also be recorded for financial reporting purposes. These regulatory assets and liabilities represent the future recovery or reduction in revenues as a result of previous income tax policies of regulatory commissions.

To illustrate the unique effects of utilities adopting SFAS No. 96, two significant transactions will be described—recording of amounts previously flowed through as a reduction in customer rates and the effects of a change in tax rates.

1. *Recording of Amounts Previously Flowed Through.* SFAS No. 96 requires utilities to record accumulated deferred taxes using the liability approach for all temporary differences whether normalized or flowed through. Accordingly, paragraph 18 of SFAS No. 71 is superseded when SFAS No. 96 is adopted. Furthermore, the FASB has concluded that the asset (liability) created by a regulatory promise to allow recovery (or require a settlement) of flow-through amounts is best measured by the expected cash flow to be provided as the temporary difference turns around and is recovered (settled) in rates. Thus, a regulatory asset or liability is established at the revenue requirement level, taking into account the tax-on-tax impact. In the Statement, these regulatory assets/liabilities are characterized as "probable future revenue/probable reduction in future revenue."

The corresponding accumulated deferred income tax (ADIT) liability represents the income taxes that would result in connection with recovering both the temporary difference itself and the newly recorded regulatory asset. Accordingly, the computation of the amount to be recorded for prior flow-through is:

> Temporary differences flowed through
> × Gross-up (tax-on-tax) factor
> × Tax rate
> _____
> Dr. Regulatory asset/Cr. ADIT liability

Paragraph 64 of SFAS No. 96 requires the regulatory asset and ADIT liability to be displayed separately for general-purpose financial reporting.

2. *Effects of a Change in Tax Rates.* Under the liability method in SFAS No. 96, the ADIT liability is reported at the enacted settlement tax rate. Thus, deferred tax liabilities or assets established at rates in excess of the current statutory rate (34%) should be reduced to that level. Utilities are required to record the reduction in the ADIT liability but presumably will not immediately recognize the reduction in the results of operations because:

a. The average rate assumption method provision contained in TRA '86 prohibits excess deferred taxes related to protected depreciation differences from being used to reduce customer rates more rapidly than over the life of the asset giving rise to the difference. Under this method, the excess in the deferred tax reserve is not reduced until the temporary differences giving rise to deferred taxes begin to turn around.

b. Regulators may adopt a similar methodology for nonprotected excess deferred taxes.

For these reasons, the credit to offset the reduction in the ADIT liability required by the liability method should be reclassified by regulated utilities as a separate liability. Consistent with the asset recovery scenario discussed previously, the FASB measures this separate liability as the cash flow impact of settling the specific liability (i.e., the future reduction in the revenue requirement). Accordingly, a gross-up factor must be applied to the excess deferred tax liability. The concept is illustrated with the following skeleton entry:

$$
\begin{array}{l}
\text{Temporary difference} \\
\times\ \text{Enacted tax rate} \\
\hline
\text{Required ADIT liability} \\
-\ \text{Existing deferred taxes on temporary difference} \\
\hline
\text{Excess deferred taxes} \\
\times\ \text{Gross-up factor} \\
\hline
\text{Dr. ADIT liability/Cr. Other liabilities}
\end{array}
$$

Other temporary differences that will result in the recording of ADIT and regulatory assets/liabilities are unamortized ITC balances (see next section), amounts recorded on a net-of-tax basis (SFAS No. 96 prohibits such presentations), and AFUDC-equity (previously recorded on an after-tax basis). Considering the large amounts of construction activity, the AFUDC-equity ADIT and regulatory assets may be significant.

At the time of adoption, paragraph 36 of SFAS No. 96 sets forth transitional guidance whereby a single temporary difference between the book and tax bases of **plant in service** may be computed and the net effect recorded on the balance sheet.

The important concept to consider is that implementing SFAS No. 96, in and of itself, does not alter ratemaking/revenue requirements and therefore SFAS No. 71 requires regulatory assets/liabilities for differences in the recognition of the timing of income tax expense via that process. Thus, flow-through of tax expense may continue for regulatory purposes, but SFAS No. 96 will require financial statements to report the deferred income tax liability with an offsetting regulatory asset to recognize that such cost will be recovered at a future date.

(h) Investment Tax Credit.   The accounting and ratemaking aspects of the ITC are discussed separately because the economics and the effect are different from those of the acceleration in the write-off of costs for tax purposes. The ITC represents a permanent savings in taxes rather than a deferral. Although the tax credit should be used to reduce expense, the accounting and ratemaking question is not one of flow-through but rather is a question as to which year's tax expense should be reduced and the benefit passed on to utility customers.

(i) Accounting for ITC.   Based on APB Opinion Nos. 2 and 4, the two accounting methods in use are to:

1. Flow the tax reduction through to income over the life of the property giving rise to the investment tax credit (service-life method), or
2. Reduce tax expense in the current year by the full amount of the credit (initial year flow-through method).

(ii) Tax Legislation and Regulatory Treatment.   The service-life method is required by the I.R.C. in order for many utilities to claim ITC. In 1964, in connection with the investment credit, the U.S. Congress specifically established certain ratemaking requirements, stating that federal regulatory agencies could not use the investment credit to reduce cost of service except over the service life of the related property. Congress also extended the practice of including ratemaking requirements in the tax law when it enacted the job development tax credit in 1971 and provided that, except where a special election was made by a limited number of eligible companies, the benefits of the job development credit were to be shared between consumers and investors and that the consumers' share was to be passed on to them over the life of the property.

If the ratemaking and the accounting are not in accordance with the irrevocable election made by the company pursuant to the 1971 Act, the utility taxpayer can be denied ITC. The four available options were:

1. No portion of the investment credit would be used to reduce cost-of-service for rate purposes, but the unamortized credit could be used to reduce rate base (general rule).
2. The ratemaking authority could reduce the cost-of-service for no more than the annual amortization of the investment credit over the book life of the property giving rise to the credit, and the unamortized balance of the credit could not be used to reduce rate base (ratable flow-through).
3. Utilities that were flow-through for accelerated depreciation under the standards of the Tax Reform Act of 1969 were permitted to elect to continue to follow the flow-through method for the investment credit. This election does not preclude the use of a service-life method of amortization of the credit if the regulatory commission agreed.
4. If the appropriate regulatory agency declared there was a shortage of supply, companies in the natural gas or steam heat business would lose the credit if the ratemaking body either reduced the cost of service or reduced the rate base.

With few exceptions, electric utilities, gas distribution companies, and telephone companies are now on the service-life amortization method for all or most of the investment credit, in most cases using the ratemaking method covered by Option 2 above. Natural gas pipeline companies elected the "shortage of supply" option. As a result, no element of the credit could be passed on to customers. They were in the same position as nonregulated companies and could use either the initial year flow-through or service-life method for accounting purposes. However, in 1986, the FERC determined that there was no longer a shortage of gas supply and these companies would follow Option 1 for any credits subsequently realized.

The 1986 Act repealed the ITC, generally effective for property placed in service after December 31, 1985. The Act requires that a utility continue to follow its present method of accounting for amortizing the ITC. For failure to continue its present method, a utility will be forced to recapture the greater of (1) ITC for all open years or (2) unamortized ITC of the taxpayer or ITC not previously restored to rate base.

23.32 REVENUE RECOGNITION.   Under GAAP as applied in practice, there are three acceptable methods of accounting for utility (principally gas and electric) revenues or related costs of gas and electricity, as follows:

1. To include in revenues the amounts **billed** for service for which meters were read during the period, and to include in expenses the cost of gas or electricity for the period (**billed revenue** method).
2. To include in revenues the estimated amount applicable to gas or electricity **delivered** to customers during the period, whether or not the meters have been read and bills rendered, and to include in expenses the cost of gas or electricity for the period (**unbilled revenue** method).
3. To include in revenues the amounts billed for service for which meters were read during the period, and to include in expenses the cost of gas or electricity applicable to such revenues, that is, to defer the cost of electricity or gas for the period that relates to service rendered during the period for which no revenues have been recognized (**deferred cost** method).

Acceptance of the **billed revenue** method is based on long-standing industry practice. From an accounting and reporting point of view, the **unbilled revenue** method is regarded as preferable and the **deferred cost** method as acceptable.

Prior to 1987, the majority of public utilities did not record unbilled revenues in their financial statements for several reasons, one of which related to income taxes. TRA '86 has prospectively eliminated the favorable tax treatment that was previously accorded unbilled revenues and, consequently, numerous utilities have changed to the unbilled revenue method of accounting for financial statement purposes. Beginning in 1987, all utilities must accrue unbilled revenues for income tax purposes regardless of whether such revenues are accrued for financial statement purposes.

23.33 ACCOUNTING FOR PENSION PLANS.   The application of SFAS No. 87, "Employers' Accounting for Pensions," can result in different pension accounting principles for ratemaking and financial reporting purposes. Paragraph 210 of SFAS No. 87 addresses the issue of rate-regulated enterprises and the applicability of SFAS No. 71 and states that:

> [SFAS No. 71] may require that the difference between net periodic pension cost as defined in this Statement and amounts of pension cost considered for ratemaking purposes be recognized as an asset or a liability created by the actions of the regulator. Those actions of the regulator charge the timing of recognition of net periodic cost as an expense; they do not otherwise affect the requirements of this Statement.

For example, if a regulator continues to allow a higher level of pension expense based on funding determined under APB Opinion No. 8 or some other acceptable actuarial method, a prepaid pension expense and corresponding regulatory liability to ratepayers—displayed broad—should be recorded on the balance sheet for the difference between the amount funded and recovered from customers and the amount to be recognized as pension expense under SFAS No. 87. In this situation, the balance sheet liability must be included in the reconciliation of the funded status of the plan to the reported balance sheet amount. This reconciliation is illustrated in "A Guide to Implementation of Statement No. 87 on Employers' Accounting for Pensions" (Amble and Cassel, 1986, Table 1, p. 8).

The Guide also illustrates how these balance sheet entries and net periodic pension cost should be recorded and classified in the financial statements. The Guide encompasses an unearned revenue notion. The resulting presentation is somewhat foreign to the typical utility income statement display for the effects of regulation because revenues are reduced and operating expenses will not reflect the amount of pension expense that has been included in cost-of-service by the regulator. Because of the potential for confusion and the questionable usefulness of the Guide's income statement treatment for a utility, in practice pension expense in the income statement is typically equal to the amount recovered in rates. In such situations, the disclosures required by SFAS No. 87, as illustrated in the Guide (Table 2, p. 8), should be modified.

Portions of a pension plan footnote might look as follows (required comparative information is not illustrated):

The reconciliation of the funded status of the retirement plans to the pension liability recorded by a utility is as follows as of December 31, 19XX:

Fair value of plan assets	$XXX
Projected benefit obligation	(XXX)
Excess of plan assets over projected benefit obligation	XXX
Unrecognized net loss from past experience Different than that assumed	XXX
Unrecognized net asset	XXX
Regulatory effect recorded	(734)
Pension liability	$XXX

Components of annual net pension expense:

Service cost (benefits earned during the period)	$XXX
Interest cost on projected benefit obligation	XXX
Actual return on plan assets	XXX
Net amortization and deferral	XXX
Regulatory effect based on funding	734
Net pension expense	$XXX

23.34 OTHER FINANCIAL STATEMENT DISCLOSURES

(a) **Purchase Power Contracts.**   Many utilities enter into long-term contracts for the purchase of electric power in order to meet customer demand. The SEC's SAB No. 28 (currently cited as SAB Topic 10D) sets forth the disclosure requirements related to long-term contracts for the purchase of electric power. This release states:

> The cost of power obtained under long-term purchase contracts, including payments required to be made when a production plant is not operating, should be included in the operating expenses section of the income statement. A note to the financial statements should present information concerning the terms and significance of such contracts to the utility company including date of contract expiration, share of land output being purchased, estimated annual cost, annual minimum debt service payment required and amount of related long-term debt or lease obligations outstanding.

(b) **Financing through Construction Intermediaries.**   Utilities using a construction intermediary should include the intermediary's work-in-progress in the appropriate caption of utility plant on the balance sheet. SAB No. 28 (currently cited as SAB Topic 10A) requires the related debt to be disclosed and included in long-term liabilities. Capitalized interest included as part of an intermediary's construction work-in-progress should be recognized as interest expense (with an offset to AFUDC-debt) in the income statement.

A note to the financial statements should describe the organization and purpose of the intermediary and the nature of its authorization to incur debt to finance construction. The note should also disclose the interest rate and amount of interest capitalized for each period in which an income statement is presented.

(c) **Jointly Owned Plants.**   SAB No. 28 (currently cited as SAB Topic 10C) also requires a utility participating in a jointly owned power station to disclose the extent of its interests in such plant(s). Disclosure should include a table showing separately for each interest the amount of utility plant in service, accumulated depreciation, the amount of plant under construction, and the proportionate share. Amounts presented for plant in service may be further subdivided into subcategories such as production, transmission, and distribution. Information concerning two or more generating plants on the same site may be combined if appropriate.

Disclosure should address the participant's share of direct expenses included in operating expenses on the income statement (e.g., fuel, maintenance, other operating). If the entire share of direct expenses is charged to purchased power, then disclosure of this amount, as well as the proportionate amounts related to specific operating expenses on the joint plant records, should be indicated.

(d) **Nuclear Fuel and Decommissioning Costs.**   In January 1978, the SEC published SAB No. 19 (currently cited as Topic 10B), which addressed estimated future costs of storing spent nuclear fuel as well as decommissioning costs of nuclear generating plants. SAB No. 19

requires footnote disclosure of the estimated decommissioning or dismantling costs and whether a provision for these costs is being recorded/recognized in rates. If decommissioning or dismantling costs are not being provided for, disclosure of the reasons for not doing so and the potential financial statement impact should be made.

This SAB suggests disclosure of the estimated future storage or disposal costs for spent fuel recorded as nuclear fuel amortization. The note should also disclose whether estimated future storage or disposal costs and residual salvage value recognized in prior years are being recovered through a fuel clause or through a general rate increase.

A typical footnote is as follows:

(x) Jointly Owned Electric Utility Plant

Under joint ownership agreements with other state utilities, the company has undivided ownership interests in two electric generating stations and related transmission facilities. Each of the respective owners was responsible for the issuance of its own securities to finance its portion of the construction costs. Kilowatthour generation and operating expenses are divided on the same basis as ownership with each owner reflecting its respective costs in its statements of income. Information relative to the company's ownership interest in these facilities at December 31, 19XX, is as follows:

	Unit 1	Unit 2
Utility plant in service	$XXX,XXX	$XX,XXX
Accumulated depreciation	$XXX,XXX	$XX,XXX
Construction work-in-progress	$ XX,XXX	$ XX
Plant capacity—Mw	XXX	XXX
Company's share	XX%	XX%
In-service date	1974	1981

SOURCES AND SUGGESTED REFERENCES

Accounting Principles Board, "Accounting for the 'Investment Credit,'" APB Opinion No. 4, AICPA, New York, 1964.

———, "Accounting for Income Taxes," APB Opinion No. 11, AICPA, New York, 1967.

———, "Accounting Changes," APB Opinion No. 20, AICPA, New York, 1971.

Amble, Joan L., and Cassel, Jules M., "A Guide to Implementation of Statement 87 on Employers' Accounting for Pensions," FASB, Stamford, CT, 1986.

American Institute of Certified Public Accountants, "Restatement and Revision of Accounting Research Bulletins," Accounting Research Bulletin No. 43, AICPA, New York, 1953.

———, "Declining-Balance Depreciation," Accounting Research Bulletin No. 44, AICPA, New York, July 1958.

———, "Consolidated Financial Statements," Accounting Research Bulletin No. 51, AICPA, New York, August 1959.

Financial Accounting Standards Board, "Official Minutes of the Emerging Issues Task Force Meeting," FASB, Norwalk, CT, February 23, 1989.

———, "Accounting for Contingencies," Statement of Financial Accounting Standards No. 5, FASB, Stamford, CT, 1975.

———, "Prior Period Adjustments," Statement of Financial Accounting Standards No. 16, FASB, Stamford, CT, 1977.

———, "Capitalization of Interest Cost," Statement of Financial Accounting Standards No. 34, FASB, Stamford, CT, 1979.

———, "Accounting for the Effects of Certain Types of Regulation," Statement of Financial Accounting Standards No. 71, FASB, Stamford, CT, 1982.

———, ''Regulated Enterprises—Accounting for Abandonments and Disallowances of Plant Costs,'' Statement of Financial Accounting Standards No. 90, FASB, Stamford, CT, 1986.

———, ''Regulated Enterprises—Accounting for Phase-in Plans,'' Statement of Financial Accounting Standards No. 92, FASB, Stamford, CT, 1987.

———, ''Accounting for Income Taxes,'' Statement of Financial Accounting Standards No. 96, FASB, Stamford, CT, 1987.

———, ''Regulated Enterprises—Accounting for the Discontinuation of Application of FASB Statement No. 71,'' Statement of Financial Accounting Standards No. 101, FASB, Norwalk, CT, 1988.

———, ''Computation of a Loss on an Abandonment,'' FASB Technical Bulletin No. 87-2, FASB, Stamford, CT, December 1987.

Securities and Exchange Commission, ''Interpretation Describing Disclosure Concerning Expected Future Costs of Storing Spent Nuclear Fuel and of Decommissioning Nuclear Electric Generating Plants,'' Staff Accounting Bulletin No. 19, SEC, Washington, DC, January 1978.

———, ''Financing by Electric Utilities Through Use of Construction Intermediaries,'' Staff Accounting Bulletin No. 28, SEC, Washington, DC, December 1978.

———, ''Utilities—Classification of Disallowed Costs or Costs of Abandoned Plants,'' Staff Accounting Bulletin No. 72, SEC, Washington, DC, November 1987.

.

CHAPTER 24

STATE AND LOCAL GOVERNMENT ACCOUNTING

John R. Miller, CPA
KPMG Peat Marwick

Shawn Warren, CPA
KPMG Peat Marwick

CONTENTS

INTRODUCTION

The rapid changes that have occurred in the environment of state and local governments during the past few years have prompted sweeping changes to governmental accounting practice and theory. The evolution of governmental accounting and reporting standards has made great strides since the formation of the GASB and the Single Audit Act of 1984. Related to the changes is greater scrutiny by federal and state agencies as they begin to realize the importance of audit quality in the governmental environment. Governmental enterprises are no longer the "shoebox" operations imagined by many people. Rather, government is a large business—a very large business. Officials in government need to be and are much more sophisticated now than similar personnel were only 10 years ago. In other words, the increasing complexity of the governmental environment, the increasing demands for public accountability, and the challenges and opportunities that face today's governments require accounting systems that provide fast, accurate, and timely information to the government's decision makers.

Going forward and dealing with the challenges of issues like deteriorating infrastructure, an aging work force, and public health care, including the AIDS epidemic, are likely to be key concerns of the individuals who operate the state and local governments. However, the nature and organization of a government's daily activities form an important foundation that must be understood in order to deal with the greater challenges of the future.

THE NATURE AND ORGANIZATION OF STATE AND LOCAL GOVERNMENT ACTIVITIES

24.1 STRUCTURE OF GOVERNMENT. For the most part, government is structured on three levels: federal, state, and local. This chapter deals only with state and local governments.

States are specific identifiable entities in their own right, but accounting at the state level is associated more often than not with the individual state functions, such as departments of revenue, retirement systems, turnpike authorities, and housing finance agencies.

Local governments exist as political subdivisions of states, and the rules governing their types and operation are different in each of the 50 states. There are, however, three basic types of local governmental units: **general purpose local governments** (counties, cities, towns, villages, and townships), **special purpose local governments,** and **authorities.**

The distinguishing characteristics of general purpose local governments are that they:

- Have broad powers in providing a variety of government services, for example, public safety, fire prevention, public works.
- Have general taxing and bonding authority.
- Are headed by elected officials.

Special purpose local governments are established to provide specific services or construction. They may or may not be contiguous with one or more general purpose local governments.

Authorities and agencies are similar to special purpose governments except that they have no taxing power and are expected to operate with their own revenues. They typically can issue only revenue bonds, not general obligations bonds.

24.2 OBJECTIVES OF GOVERNMENT. The purpose of government is to provide the citizenry with the highest level of services possible given the available financial resources and the legal requirements under which it operates. The services are provided as a result of decisions made during a budgeting process that considers the desired level and quality of services. Resources are then made available through property taxes, sales taxes, income taxes, general and categorical grants from the federal and state governments, charges for services, fines, licenses, and other sources. However, there is generally no direct relationship between the cost of the services rendered to an individual, and the amount that the individual pays in taxes, fines, fees, and so on.

Governmental units also conduct operations that are financed and operated in a manner similar to private business enterprises, where the intent is that the costs of providing the goods or services be financed or recovered primarily through charges to the users. In such situations, governments have many of the features of ordinary business operations.

24.3 ORGANIZATION OF GOVERNMENT. A government's organization depends on its constitution (state level) or charter (local level) and on general and special statutes of state and local legislatures. When governments were simpler and did not provide as many services as they do today, there was less tendency for centralization. The **commission** and **weak mayor** forms of governments were common. The financial function was typically divided among several individuals.

As government has become more complex, however, the need for strong professional management and for centralization of authority and responsibility has grown. There has been a trend toward the **strong mayor** and **council-manager** forms of government. In these forms, a chief financial officer, usually called the **director of finance** or **controller,** is responsible for maintaining the financial records and preparing financial reports; assisting the CEO in the preparation of the budget; performing treasury functions such as collecting revenues, managing cash, managing investments, and managing debt; and overseeing the tax assessment function. Other functions that may report to the director of finance are purchasing, data processing, and personnel administration.

Local governments are also making greater use of the **internal audit** process. In the past, the emphasis by governmental internal auditors was on **preaudit,** that is, reviewing invoices and other documents during processing for propriety and accuracy. The internal auditors reported to the director of finance. Today, however, governmental internal auditors have been removing themselves from the preaudit function by transferring this responsibility to the department responsible for processing the transactions. They have started to provide the typical internal audit function, that is, conducting reviews to ensure the reliability of data and the safeguarding of assets, and to become involved in **performance auditing** (i.e., reviewing the efficiency and effectiveness of the government's operations). They have also started to report, for professional (as opposed to administrative) purposes, to the CEO or directly to the governing board. Finally, internal auditors are becoming more actively involved in the financial statement audit and single audit of their government.

24.4 SPECIAL CHARACTERISTICS OF GOVERNMENT.   Several characteristics associated with governments have influenced the development of governmental accounting principles and practices:

- Governments do not have any owners or proprietors in the commercial sense. Accordingly, measurement of earnings attributable or accruing to the direct benefit of an owner is not a relevant accounting concept for governments.

- Governments frequently receive substantial **financial inflows** for both operating and capital purposes from sources other than revenues and investment earnings, such as taxes and grants.

- Governments frequently obtain **financial inflows** subject to legally binding **restrictions** that prohibit or seriously limit the use of these resources for other than the intended purpose.

- A government's authority to raise and expend money results from the adoption of a **budget** that, by law, usually must balance (e.g., the estimated revenues plus any prior years' surpluses need to be sufficient to cover the projected expenditures).

- The power to raise revenues through taxes, licenses, fees, and fines is generally defined by law.

- There are usually restrictions related to the tax base that govern the purpose, amount, and type of indebtedness that can be issued.

- Expenditures are usually regulated less than revenues and debt, but they can be made only within approved budget categories and must comply with specified purchasing procedures when applicable.

- State laws may dictate the local government accounting policies and systems.

- State laws commonly specify the type and frequency of financial statements to be submitted to the state and to the government's constituency.

- Federal law, the Single Audit Act of 1984, defines the audit requirements for state and local governments receiving more than $100,000 in federal financial assistance.

In short, the environment in which governments operate is complex and legal requirements have a significant influence on their accounting and financial reporting practices.

SOURCE OF ACCOUNTING PRINCIPLES FOR STATE AND LOCAL GOVERNMENT ACCOUNTING

Governmental accounting principles are not a complete and separate body of accounting principles, but rather are part of the whole body of GAAP. Since the accounting profession's standard-setting bodies have been concerned primarily with the accounting needs of profit-seeking organizations, these principles have been defined primarily by groups formed by the state and local governments. In 1934, the **National Committee on Municipal Accounting** published "A Tentative Outline—Principles of Municipal Accounting." In 1968, the **National Committee on Governmental Accounting** (the successor organization) published *Governmental Accounting, Auditing, and Financial Reporting* (GAAFR), which was widely used as a source of government accounting principles. The AICPA Industry Audit Guide, "Audits of State and Local Governmental Units," published in 1974, stated that the accounting principles outlined in the 1968 GAAFR constituted GAAP for government entities.

The financial difficulties experienced by many governments in the mid-1970s led to a call for a review and modification of the accounting and financial reporting practices used by governments. Laws were introduced in Congress, but never enacted, that would have given the federal government the authority to establish governmental accounting principles. The FASB, responding to pressures, commissioned a research study to define and explain the issues associated with accounting for all nonbusiness enterprises, including governments. This study was completed in 1978 and the Board developed SFAC No. 4 for nonbusiness organizations. The statement defined nonbusiness organizations, the users of the statements, the financial information needs of these users, and the information that is necessary to meet these needs.

24.5 NATIONAL COUNCIL ON GOVERNMENTAL ACCOUNTING (NCGA). The NCGA was the successor of the National Committee reconstituted as a permanent organization. One of its first projects was to "restate," that is, update, clarify, amplify, and reorder the GAAFR to incorporate pertinent aspects of "Audits of State and Local Governmental Units." The restatement was published in March 1979, as NCGA Statement 1, "Governmental Accounting and Financial Reporting Principles." Shortly thereafter, the AICPA Committee on State and Local Government Accounting recognized NCGA Statement 1 as authoritative and agreed to amend the Industry Audit Guide accordingly. This restatement was completed, and a new guide was published in 1986. Thus NCGA Statement 1 became the primary reference source for the accounting principles unique to governmental accounting. However, in areas not unique to governmental accounting, the complete body of GAAP still needed to be considered.

24.6 GOVERNMENTAL ACCOUNTING STANDARDS BOARD (GASB). In 1984, the (FAF) established the GASB as the primary standard setter for GAAP for governmental entities. Under the jurisdictional agreement GASB has the primary responsibility for establishing accounting and reporting principles for government entities. GASB's first action was to issue Statement No. 1, "Authoritative Status of NCGA Pronouncements and AICPA Industry Audit Guide," which recognized the NCGA's statements and interpretations and the AICPA's audit guide as authoritative. The Statement also recognized the pronouncements of the FASB issued prior to the date of the agreement as applicable to governments. FASB pronouncements issued after the organization of GASB do not become effective unless GASB specifically adopts them.

The GASB has operated under this jurisdictional arrangement since 1984. However, the arrangement came under scrutiny during the GASB's mandatory 5-year review conducted in 1988. The Committee to Review Structure of Governmental Accounting Standards released its widely read report in January 1989 on the results of its review and proposed to the FAF, among other recommendations, a new jurisdictional arrangement and GAAP hierarchy for governments. These two recommendations prompted a great deal of controversy within the industry. The issue revolved around the Committee's recommended jurisdictional arrangement for the separately issued financial statements of certain "special-entities." (Special entities are organizations that can either be privately or governmentally owned and include colleges and universities, hospitals, and utilities.) The Committee recommended that FASB be the primary accounting standard-setter for these special entities when they issue separate, stand-alone financial statements and that GASB be allowed to require the presentation of "additional data" in these stand-alone statements. This arrangement would allow for greater comparability between entities in the same industry (e.g., utilities) regardless of whether the entities were privately or governmentally owned and still allow government-owned entities to meet their "public accountability" reporting objective.

This recommendation and a subsequent compromise recommendation were unacceptable to many and especially to the various public interest groups such as the Government Finance Officers Association (GFOA) who, 10 months after the Committee's report, began discussions to establish a new body to set standards for state and local government. These actions prompted the FAF to consider whether a standard-setting schism was in the interest of the public and the users of financial statements. Based on this consideration, the FAF decided that the jurisdictional arrangement established in 1984 should remain intact.

GOVERNMENTAL ACCOUNTING PRINCIPLES AND PRACTICES

24.7 SIMILARITIES TO PRIVATE SECTOR ACCOUNTING.   Since the accounting principles and practices of governments are part of the whole body of GAAP, certain accounting concepts and conventions are as applicable to governmental entities as they are to accounting in other industries:

- *Consistency*. Identical transactions should be recorded in the same manner both during a period and from period to period.
- *Conservatism*. The uncertainties that surround the preparation of financial statements are reflected in a general tendency toward early recognition of unfavorable events and minimization of the amount of net assets and net income.
- *Historical Cost*. Amounts should be recognized in the financial statements at the historical cost to the reporting entity. Changes in the general purchasing power should not be recognized in the basic financial statements.
- *Matching*. The financial statements should provide for a matching, but in government it is a matching of revenues and expenditures with a time period to ensure that revenues and the expenditures they finance are reported in the same period.
- *Reporting Entity*. The focus of the financial report is the economic activities of a discrete individual entity for which there is a reporting responsibility.
- *Materiality*. Financial reporting is concerned only with significant information.
- *Full Disclosure*. Financial statements must contain all information necessary to understand the presentation of financial position and results of operations and to prevent them from being misleading.

24.8 USERS AND USES OF FINANCIAL REPORTS.   Users of the financial statements of a governmental unit are not identical to users of a business entity's financial statements. The GASB Codification § 100.130 identifies three groups of primary users of external governmental financial reports:

- *Those to Whom Government Is Primarily Accountable—The Citizenry.* The citizenry group includes citizens (whether they are classified as taxpayers, voters, or service recipients), the media, advocate groups, and public finance researchers. This user group is concerned with obtaining the maximum amount of service with a minimum amount of taxes and wants to know where the government obtains its resources and how those resources are used.
- *Those Who Directly Represent the Citizens—Legislative and Oversight Bodies.* The legislative and oversight officials group includes members of state legislatures, county commissions, city councils, boards of trustees, and school boards, and those executive branch officials with oversight responsibility over other levels of government. These groups need timely warning of the development of situations that require corrective action, financial information that can serve as a basis for judging management performance, and financial information on which to base future plans and policies.
- *Those Who Lend or Participate in the Lending Process—Investors and Creditors.* Investors and creditors include individual and institutional investors and creditors, municipal security underwriters, bond-rating agencies (Moody's Investors Service, and Standard & Poor's, etc.), bond insurers, and financial institutions.

The uses of a government's financial reports are also different.

GASB Codification § 100.132 also indicates that governmental financial reporting should provide information to assist users in (1) assessing accountability and (2) making economic, social, and political decisions by:

- *Comparing Actual Financial Results with the Legally Adopted Budget.* All three user groups are interested in comparing original or modified budgets with actual results to get some assurance that spending mandates have been compiled with and that resources have been used for the intended purposes.
- *Assisting in Determining Compliance with Finance-Related Laws, Rules, and Regulations.* In addition to the legally mandated budgetary and fund controls other legal restrictions may control governmental actions. Some examples are bond covenants, grant restrictions, and taxing and debt limits. Financial reports help demonstrate compliance with these laws, rules, and regulations.

  Citizens are concerned that governments adhere to these regulations because noncompliance may indicate fiscal irresponsibility and could have severe financial consequences such as acceleration of debt payments, disallowance of questioned costs, or loss of grants.

  Legislative and oversight officials are also concerned with compliance as a follow-up to the budget formulation process.

  Investors and creditors are interested in the government's compliance with debt covenants and restrictions designed to protect their investment.
- *Assisting in Evaluating Efficiency and Effectiveness.* Citizen groups and legislators, in particular, want information about service efforts, costs, and accomplishments of a governmental entity. This information, when combined with information from other sources, helps users assess the economy, efficiency, and effectiveness of government and may help form a basis for voting or funding decisions.
- *Assessing Financial Condition and Results of Operations.* Financial reports are commonly used to assess a state or local government's financial condition, that is, its financial position and its ability to continue to provide services and meet its obligations as they come due.

  Investors and creditors need information about available and likely future financial resources, actual and contingent liabilities, and the overall debt position of a government to evaluate the government's ability to continue to provide resources for long-term debt service.

Citizens' groups are concerned with financial condition when evaluating the likelihood of tax or service fee increased.

Legislative and oversight officials need to assess the overall financial condition, including debt structure and funds available for appropriation, when developing both capital and operating budget and program recommendations.

With the users and the uses of financial reports clearly defined, the GASB developed the following overall objectives of governmental financial reporting:

1. Financial reporting should assist in fulfilling a government's duty to be publicly accountable and should enable users to assess that accountability by:
   a. Providing information to determine whether current-year revenues were sufficient to pay for current-year services.
   b. Demonstrating whether resources were obtained and used in accordance with the entity's legally adopted budget and compliance with other finance-related legal or contractual requirements.
   c. Providing information to assist users in assessing the service efforts, costs, and accomplishments of the governmental entity.
2. Financial reporting should assist users in evaluating the operating results of the governmental entity for the year by providing information:
   a. About sources and uses of financial resources.
   b. About how the governmental entity financed its activities and met its cash requirements.
   c. Necessary to determine whether the entity's financial position improved or deteriorated as a result of the year's operations.
3. Financial reporting should assist users in assessing the level of services that can be provided by the governmental entity and its ability to meet its obligations as they become due by:
   a. Providing information about the financial position and condition of a governmental entity. Financial reporting should provide information about resources and obligations, both actual and contingent, current and noncurrent, and about tax sources, tax limitations, tax burdens, and debt limitations.
   b. Providing information about a governmental entity's physical and other nonfinancial resources having useful lives that extend beyond the current year, including information that can be used to assess the service potential of those resources.
   c. Disclosing legal or contractual restrictions on resources and risks of potential loss of resources.

24.9 SUMMARY STATEMENT OF PRINCIPLES.   Because governments operate under different conditions and have different reporting objectives than commercial entities, 12 basic principles applicable to government accounting and reporting have been developed. These principles are generally recognized as being essential to effective management control and financial reporting. In other words, understanding these principles and how they operate is extremely important to the understanding of governments. The 12 principles defined for state and local government in GASB Codification § 1100 are as follows:

(a) Accounting and Reporting Capabilities.   A governmental accounting system must make it possible both (1) to present fairly the financial position and results of financial operations of the funds and account groups of the governmental unit in conformity with GAAP, which include full disclosure; and (2) to determine and demonstrate compliance with finance-related legal and contractual provisions.

(b) Fund Accounting Systems. Governmental accounting systems should be organized and operated on a fund basis. A "fund" is defined as a fiscal and accounting entity with a self-balancing set of accounts recording cash and other financial resources, together with all related liabilities and residual equities or balances, and changes therein, which are segregated for the purpose of carrying on specific activities or attaining certain objectives in accordance with special regulations, restrictions, or limitations.

(c) Types of Funds. The following types of funds should be used by state and local governments.

(i) Governmental Funds

1. *The General Fund.* To account for all financial resources except those required to be accounted for in another fund.
2. *Special Revenue Funds.* To account for the proceeds for specific revenue sources (other than expendable trusts, or major capital projects) that are legally restricted to expenditures for specified purposes.
3. *Capital Projects Funds.* To account for financial resources to be used for the acquisition or construction of major capital facilities (other than those financed by proprietary funds and trust funds).
4. *Debt Service Funds.* To account for the accumulation of resources for, and the payment of, general long-term debt principal and interest.

The GASB Codification also discusses special assessment funds. However, the issuance of GASB Statement No. 6, "Accounting and Financial Reporting for Special Assessments," in January 1987, eliminated the special assessment fund type for financial reporting purposes. The Statement does, however, allow special assessment funds to exist for budget purposes.

(ii) Proprietary Funds

1. *Enterprise Funds.* To account for operations (1) that are financed and operated in a manner similar to private business enterprises, where the intent of the governing body is that the cost (expenses, including depreciation) of providing goods or services to the general public, on a continuing basis be financed or recovered primarily through user charges; or (2) where the governing body has decided that periodic determination of revenues earned, expenses incurred, and/or net income is appropriate for capital maintenance, public policy, management control, accountability, or other purposes.
2. *Internal Service Funds.* To account for the financing of goods or services provided by one department or agency to other departments or agencies of the governmental unit, or to other governmental units, on a cost-reimbursement basis.

(iii) Fiduciary Funds. Trust and agency funds account for assets held by a governmental unit in a trustee capacity or as an agent for individuals, private organizations, other governmental units, and other funds. These include (1) expendable trust funds, (2) nonexpendable trust funds, (3) pension trust funds, and (4) agency funds.

(d) Number of Funds. Governmental units should establish and maintain those funds required by law and sound financial administration. Only the minimum number of funds consistent with legal and operating requirements should be established, however, since unnecessary funds result in inflexibility, undue complexity, and inefficient financial administration.

(e) Accounting for Fixed Assets and Long-Term Liabilities.   A clear distinction should be made between (1) proprietory and similar trust fund fixed assets and general fixed assets and (2) proprietory and similar trust fund long-term liabilities and general long-term debt.

1. Fixed assets related to specific proprietary funds or similar trust funds should be accounted for through those funds. All other fixed assets of a govenmental unit should be accounted for through the general fixed assets account group.
2. Long-term liabilities of proprietary funds and trust funds should be accounted for through those funds. All other unmatured, general long-term liabilities of the governmental unit should be accounted for through the general long-term debt account group.

(f) Valuation of Fixed Assets.   Fixed assets should be accounted for at cost or, if the cost is not practicably determinable, at estimated cost. Donated fixed assets should be recorded at their estimated fair value at the time received.

(g) Depreciation of Fixed Assets.   Depreciation of general fixed assets should not be recorded in the accounts of governmental funds. Depreciation of general fixed assets may be recorded in cost accounting systems or calculated for cost funding analyses, and accumulated depreciation may be recorded in the general fixed assets account group.

Depreciation of fixed assets accounted for in a proprietary fund should be recorded in the accounts of that fund. Depreciation is also recognized in trust funds where expenses, net income, and/or capital maintenance are measured.

(h) Accrual Basis in Governmental Accounting.   The modified accrual or accrual basis of accounting, as appropriate, should be used in measuring financial position and operating results.

1. Governmental fund revenues and expenditures should be recognized on the modified accrual basis. Revenues should be recognized in the accounting period in which they become available and measurable. Expenditures should be recognized in the accounting period in which the fund liability is incurred, if measurable, except for unmatured interest on general long-term debt, which should be recognized when due.
2. Proprietary fund revenues and expenses should be recognized on the accrual basis. Revenues should be recognized in the accounting period in which they are earned and become measurable; expenses should be recognized in the period incurred, if measurable.
3. Fiduciary fund revenues and expenses or expenditures (as appropriate) should be recognized on the basis consistent with the fund's accounting measurement objective. Nonexpendable trust and pension trust funds should be accounted for on the accrual basis; expendable trust funds, on the modified accrual basis. Agency fund assets and liabilities should be accounted for on the modified accrual basis.
4. Transfers should be recognized in the accounting period in which the interfund receivable and payable arise.

(i) Budgeting, Budgetary Control, and Budgetary Reporting.   An annual budget should be adopted by every governmental unit. The accounting system should provide the basis for appropriate budgetary control. Budgetary comparisons should be included in the appropriate financial statements and schedules for governmental funds for which an annual budget has been adopted.

(j) Transfer, Revenue, Expenditure, and Expense Account Classification. Interfund transfers and proceeds of general long-term debt issues should be classified separately from fund revenues and expenditures or expenses.

Governmental fund revenues should be classified by fund and source. Expenditures should be classified by fund, function (or program), organization unit, activity, character, and principal classes of objects.

Proprietary fund revenues and expenses should be classified in essentially the same manner as those of similar business organizations, functions, or activities.

(k) Common Terminology and Classification. A common terminology and classification should be used consistently throughout the budget, the accounts, and the financial reports of each fund.

(l) Interim and Annual Financial Reports. Appropriate interim financial statements and reports of financial position, operating results, and other pertinent information should be prepared to facilitate management control of financial operations, legislative oversight, and, where necessary or desired, external reporting.

A comprehensive annual financial report covering all funds and account groups of the governmental unit should be prepared and published, including appropriate combined, combining, and individual fund statements; notes to the financial statements; required supplementary information; schedules; narrative explanations; and statistical tables.

General purpose financial statements may be issued separately from the comprehensive annual financial report. Such statements should include the basic financial statements, notes to the financial statements, and any required supplementary information essential to a fair presentation of financial position and operating results and cash flows of proprietary funds and nonexpendable trust funds.

24.10 DISCUSSION OF THE PRINCIPLES. To enable readers to more fully understand the 12 principles of GASB Codification § 1100, a discussion of each of the principles appears below.

24.11 LEGAL COMPLIANCE. **Principle 1** of governmental accounting (GASB Codification § 1100.101) states:

> A governmental accounting system must make it possible both: (a) to present fairly and with full disclosure the financial position and results of financial operations of the funds and account groups of the governmental unit in conformity with generally accepted accounting principles; and (b) to determine and demonstrate compliance with finance-related legal and contractual provision.

Several state and local governments have accounting requirements that differ from GAAP; for example, cash basis accounting is required, and capital projects must be accounted for in the general fund. Because of this situation, the **legal compliance** principle used to be interpreted as meaning that, when the legal requirements for a particular entity differed from GAAP, the legal requirements became GAAP for the entity. This interpretation is no longer viewed as sound. When GAAP and legal requirements conflict, governments should present their basic financial report in accordance with GAAP and, if the legal requirements differ materially from GAAP, the legally required reports can be published as supplemental data to the basic financial report or, if these differences are extreme, it may be preferable to publish a separate legal basis report.

However, conflicts that arise between GAAP and legal provisions do not require maintaining two sets of accounting records. Rather, the accounting records typically would be maintained in accordance with the legal requirements but would include sufficient additional information to permit preparation of reports in accordance with GAAP.

24.12 FUND ACCOUNTING.   Principle 2, fund accounting, is used by governments because of (1) legally binding restrictions that prohibit or seriously limit the use of much of a government's resources for other than the purposes for which the resources were obtained, and (2) the importance of reporting the accomplishment of various objectives for which the resources were entrusted to the government.

GASB Codification § 1100.102, defines a fund for accounting purposes as:

> A fiscal and accounting entity with a self-balancing set of accounts recording cash and other financial resources, together with all related liabilities and residual equities or balances, and changes therein, which are segregated for the purposes of carrying on specific activities or obtaining certain objectives in accordance with special regulations, restrictions, or limitations.

Thus a fund may include accounts for assets, liabilities, fund balance or retained earnings, revenues, expenditures, or expenses. Accounts may also exist for appropriations and encumbrances, depending on the budgeting system used.

24.13 TYPES AND NUMBER OF FUNDS.   Because of the various nature of activities carried on by government, it is often important to be able to account for certain activities separately from others (i.e., when required by law). **Principles 3 and 4** define seven basic fund types in which to account for various governmental activities. The purpose and operation of each fund type differs, and it is important to understand these differences and why they exist. Every fund maintained by a government should be classified into one of these seven fund types:

- General fund.
- Special revenue funds.
- Debt service funds.
- Capital projects funds.
- Enterprise funds.
- Internal service funds.
- Trust and agency funds.

The general fund, special revenue funds, debt service funds, and capital projects funds are considered **governmental funds** since they record the transactions associated with the general services of a local governmental unit (i.e., police, public works, fire prevention) that are provided to all citizens and are supported primarily by general revenues. For these funds, the primary concerns, from the financial statement reader's point of view, are the types and amounts of resources that have been made available to the governmental unit and the uses to which they have been put.

The enterprise funds and internal services funds are considered **proprietary funds** because they account for activities for which the determination of net income is important.

The trust and agency funds are considered **fiduciary funds.** There are basically three types of trust funds: expendable trust funds that operate in a manner similar to governmental funds, nonexpendable trust funds and pension trust funds that operate in a manner similar to proprietary funds, and agency funds that account for funds held by a government entity in an agent capacity. Agency funds consist of assets and liabilities only and do not involve the measurement of operations.

Although a government should establish and maintain those funds required by law and sound financial administration, it should set up only the minimum number of funds consistent with legal and operating requirements. The maintenance of unnecessary funds results in inflexibility, undue complexity, and inefficient financial administration. For instance, in the past, the proceeds of specific revenue sources or resources that financed specific activities as required by law or administrative regulation had to be accounted for in a special revenue fund. However, governmental resources restricted to purposes usually financed through the general fund should be accounted for in the general fund, provided that all legal requirements can be satisfied. Examples include state grants received by an entity for special education. If a separate fund is not legally required, the grant revenues and the grant-related expenditures should be accounted for in the fund for which they are to be used.

Another way to minimize funds is by accounting for debt service payments in the general fund and not establishing a separate debt service fund unless it is legally mandated or resources are actually being accumulated for future debt service payments (i.e., for term bonds or in sinking funds).

Furthermore, one or more identical accounts for separate funds should be combined in the accounting system, particularly for funds that are similar in nature or are in the same fund group. For example, the cash accounts for all special revenue funds may be combined, provided that the integrity of each fund is preserved through a distinct equity account for each fund.

(a) General Fund.   The **general fund** accounts for the revenues and expenditures not accounted for in other funds and finances most of the current normal functions of governmental units—general government, public safety, highways, sanitation and waste removal, health and welfare, culture, and recreation. It is usually the largest and most important accounting activity for state and local governments. Property taxes are often the principal source of general fund revenues, but substantial revenues may also be received from other financing sources.

The general fund balance sheet is typically limited to current assets and current liabilities. The GASB Codification emphasizes this practice by using the terms **expendable assets** and **current liabilities** when describing governmental funds, of which the general fund is one. Thus the fund balance in the general fund is considered available to finance current operations.

A governmental unit, however, often makes long-term **advances** to independent governmental agencies, such as redevelopment authorities or housing agencies, or provides the capital necessary to establish an internal service fund. The advances are recorded in the general fund as an advance receivable. Although in most cases collectibility is assured, repayment may extend over a number of years. The inclusion of a noncurrent asset in the general fund results in a portion of the general fund's fund balance not being readily available to finance current operations.

To reflect the unavailability of an advance to finance current activities, a fund balance reserve is established to segregate a portion of the fund balance from the general fund in an amount equal to the advance that is not considered currently available. Establishing this reserve does not require a charge to operations; rather, it is a segregation of the fund balance in the available general fund and is established by debiting unreserved fund balance and crediting reserved fund balance. The reserve is reported in the fund balance section of the balance sheet.

(b) Special Revenue Funds.   **Special revenue funds** should be established to account for the proceeds of specific revenue sources (other than expendable trusts, or major capital projects) that are legally restricted to expenditure for specified purposes and for which a separate fund is legally required. Examples are parks, schools, and museums, as well as particular functions or activities, such as highway construction or street maintenance.

A special revenue fund may have a definite limited life, or it may remain in effect until discontinued or revoked by appropriate legislative action. It may be used for a very limited purpose, such as the maintenance of a historic landmark, or it may finance an entire function of government, such as public education or highways.

A special revenue fund may be administered by the regularly constituted administrative and financial organization of the government; by an independent body or special purpose local district, such as a park board or the board of directors of a water district; or by a quasi-independent body. In some cases, the fund may be administered by an independent board, but the government maintains the accounting records because the independent board does not have the necessary personnel or other facilities.

Some of the activities mentioned above could also be accounted for in an enterprise fund. Deciding which type of fund to use is often difficult. Basically, unless the government determines that the activity should be financed and operated in a manner similar to that for private business enterprises, the activity should be accounted for as a special revenue fund. A special revenue fund is not appropriate, however, when the costs, including depreciation, of providing goods or services to the general public on a continuing basis are to be financed or recovered primarily through user charges. Also, a special revenue fund is not appropriate when the government has decided that periodic determination of revenues earned, expenses incurred, or net income is appropriate for capital maintenance, public policy, management control, accountability, or other purposes.

(c) Debt Service Funds.   **Debt service funds** exist to account for the accumulation of resources for, and the payment of, long-term debt principal and interest other than that which is issued for and serviced primarily by an enterprise or similar trust fund. A debt service fund is necessary only if it is legally required or if resources are being accumulated for future payment. Although governments may incur a wide variety of debt, the more common types are described below.

Term (or sinking fund) bonds are being replaced by **serial bonds** as the predominant form of state and local government debt. For term bonds, debt service consists of annual additions of resources being made to a cumulative "investment fund" for repayment of the issue at maturity. The additions, also called "sinking fund installments," are computed on an actuarial basis, which includes assumptions that certain rates of interest will be earned from investing the resources accumulating in the investment fund. If the actual earnings are less than the planned earnings, subsequent additions are increased; if the earnings are greater than planned, the excess is carried forward until the time of the final addition of the fund. Because term bond principal is due at the end of the bond's term, the expenditure for repayment of principal is recognized at that time.

Debt service on serial bonds, however, generally consists of preestablished principal payments that are due on an annual basis and interest payments based on either fixed or variable rates that are due on a semiannual basis. No sinking fund is involved in the repayment of serial bonds.

The revenues for a debt service fund come from one or more sources, with property taxes being the predominant source. Taxes that are specified for debt service appear as a **revenue** of the debt service fund. Taxes for general purposes (i.e., not specified but nevertheless used for debt service) are considered to be an operating transfer to the debt service fund from the fund in which the revenue is recorded, oftentimes the general fund.

Enterprise activity earnings may be another resource for servicing general obligation debt. In these instances, the general obligation debt should be classified as enterprise debt (a liability of the enterprise fund), and the debt service payments should be recorded in the enterprise fund as a reduction of the liability, not in the debt service fund. The debt service transactions would be recorded in the debt service fund only if the enterprise fund was not expected to be responsible for repaying the debt on an ongoing basis. Essentially, if the enterprise fund became unable to service the principal and interest and the general governmental unit assumed responsibility for servicing the debt, then the debt service fund would be used.

More recently, governmental units have been exploring alternative financing activities including lease-purchase arrangements and issuance of zero-coupon or deep discount debt. Some of the accounting issues concerning these financing vehicles are being studied currently by the GASB but have not been fully resolved.

The issues surrounding lease-purchase arrangements involve legal questions about whether such arrangements constitute debt of a government since they often do not require voter approval prior to incurring the debt. Zero-coupon and deep discount debt issues center on the manner of presenting and amortizing the bond discount amount in the government's financial statements.

Quite often, a **refunding bond** is issued to replace or consolidate prior debt issues. Determining the appropriate accounting principles to apply to refunding bonds depends primarily on whether the bonds are included in an enterprise fund or in the general long-term debt account group. GASB Statement No. 7, ''Advance Refundings Resulting in Defeasance of Debt,'' outlines the appropriate accounting and reporting principles as discussed below.

For the refunding of debt recorded in the GLTDAG, the proceeds of the refunding issue become an ''other financing source'' of the fund receiving the proceeds of the refunding bond (oftentimes a debt service fund created to service the original issue or a capital projects fund). Since the proceeds are used to liquidate the original debt, an ''other financing use'' is also recorded in the debt service or capital projects fund in an amount equal to the remaining principal, interest, and other amounts due on the original debt. The outstanding principal of the issue being refunded is removed from the GLTDAG, and the principal amount of the new debt is then recorded in the GLTDAG.

EXAMPLE

Assuming the proceeds of the refunding bond issue (new debt) are $10,000,000 and the unpaid principal of the existing debt (old debt) recorded in the GLTDAG is $7,000,000, the following journal entries are needed to record the advance refunding in a debt service fund.

Debt Service Fund

Cash	$10,000,000	
Other financing services—bond proceeds		$10,000,000
To record proceeds of new debt		
Other financing uses—payment to bondholders	7,000,000	
Cash		7,000,000
To record defeasance of old debt		

GLTDAG

Bonds payable	7,000,000	
Amounts to be provided		7,000,000
To record extinguishment of old debt		
Amounts to be provided	10,000,000	
Bonds payable		10,000,000
To record new debt outstanding		

If, as a result of the refunding, the liability to the bondholders is satisfied, the refunding is referred to as a legal defeasance of debt. However, **advance refundings** often do not result in the legal defeasance of debt. These other refundings are referred to as ''in-substance defeasances.'' To qualify for an in-substance defeasance, the proceeds of the refunding bonds are placed in an irrevocable trust and invested in essentially risk-free securities, usually obligations of the U.S. Treasury or other government agencies, so that the risk-free securities, together with any premiums on the defeased debt, and expenses of the refunding operation will be sufficient for the trust to pay off the debt to the bondholders when it becomes due. The accounting for an in-substance defeasance is identical to legal defeasances except that payment is made to a trustee rather than to bondholders. The trustee then pays principal and interest to the bondholders based on the maturity schedule of the bond. In addition, the recording of payments of proceeds to the trustee as another financing use is limited to the amount of proceeds.

Advance refundings of debt recorded in a proprietary fund follow the accounting principles outlined in APB Opinion No. 26. This opinion requires a gain or loss on the defeasance of debt to be recognized in the operating statement of the proprietary fund for the difference between the reacquisition price and the net carrying amount of the defeased debt. This gain or loss should be reported as an extraordinary item, if it is both infrequent and unusual.

Regardless of whether the defeased debt was recorded in the GLTDAG or a proprietary fund, GASB Statement No. 7 requires the disclosure of a description of the refunding transaction; the cash flow gain or loss, which is the difference between the total cash outflow of the new debt (i.e., principal, interest, etc.) and the remaining cash outflow of the old debt; and the economic gain or loss, which is the difference between the present values of the cash flows of the new and old debt.

If the defeasance is an in-substance defeasance, each year after the defeasance, the footnotes to the financial statements should disclose the remaining amount of debt principal that the trustee has to pay to bondholders.

(d) Capital Projects Funds.   The purpose of a **capital projects fund** is to account for the receipt and disbursement of resources used for the acquisition of major capital facilities other than those financed by enterprise funds. Capital projects are defined as outlays for major, permanent fixed assets having a relatively long life (e.g., buildings), as compared with those of limited life (e.g., office equipment). Capital projects are usually financed by bond proceeds, but they can also be financed from other resources, such as current revenues or grants from other governments.

Capital outlays financed entirely from the direct revenues of the general fund or a special revenue fund and not requiring long-term borrowing may be accounted for in the fund providing such resources rather than in a separate capital projects fund. Assets with a relatively short life—hence not capital projects—are usually financed from current revenues or by short-term obligations and are accounted for in the general or special revenue fund.

An individual fund should ordinarily be established for each authorized capital project. If related projects have been combined under a single authorization and were financed through a single bond issue, they may be accounted for in a single fund. Also, if a group of related projects is financed from the general fund or a special revenue fund, it may be accounted for under a single capital projects fund. Projects financed by grants from other governmental units, rather than by borrowing, should be accounted for in a separate fund for each project.

(i) Accounting for Capital Projects Fund Transactions.   Bonds are issued and capital projects are started under a multiyear capital program. In some instances, it is necessary to secure referendum approval to issue general obligation bonds. Obligations are then incurred and expenditures made according to an annual capital projects budget.

When a project is financed entirely from general obligation bond proceeds, the initial entry to be made in the capital projects fund when the bonds are sold is:

Cash	$XXX	
Other financing source—		
Proceeds of general obligation bonds		$XXX

Whereas the proceeds of the bonds are accounted for in the capital projects funds, the liability for the face amount of the bonds is recorded in the general long-term debt account group.

If bonds are sold at a **premium** (i.e., above par value) the premium increases the other financing sources. Oftentimes, the premium is transferred—by a debit to "other financing sources" and a credit to "cash"—to the debt service fund established to service the debt for the project. If the bonds are sold at a **discount** (i.e., below par value), the discount reduces the amount recorded as other financing sources in the capital projects fund. Bond issuance costs either paid out of available funds or withheld from the bond proceeds usually are accounted as debt service expenditures in the capital projects or debt service funds operating statement.

(ii) Bond Anticipation Notes.   Governments sometimes issue **bond anticipation notes** (BANs) prior to the sale of bonds, planning to retire the notes with the proceeds of the bond issue to which the notes are related. The reasons would be:

- The governmental unit wants to accelerate initiation of a project, and issuance of the long-term bonds will require more time than is required to issue BANs.
- The governmental unit does not want to undertake long-term financing until the project is complete and ready for use. Hence bond anticipation notes are used to provide construction financing.
- The current and projected interest rates make it prudent to issue short-term notes first and to defer issuance of long-term bonds.
- The individual capital projects to be financed from the proceeds of the bond sale are so small as to make the sale of bonds to finance each project impracticable.

The cash proceeds and the liabilities resulting from the sale of BANs should be recorded in the capital projects fund as follows:

Cash	$XXX	
Bond anticipation notes payable		$XXX

When the long-term bonds are sold, an "other financing source" should be recorded and the BANs payable debited in an amount equal to the portion of the BANs redeemed as follows:

Bond participation notes payable	$XXX	
Other financing sources		$XXX

If the BANs are not redeemed with long-term bond proceeds or other funds by the end of the year, and the governmental unit has both the intent and the ability (as those terms are defined in SFAS No. 6, "Classification of Short-Term Obligations Expected to Be Refinanced," pars. 10 and 11) to redeem the BANs with long-term debt, the bond anticipation notes payable account should be debited and an "other financing source" should be credited. The BANs payable and the offsetting amount to be provided should be established in the general long-term debt group account. If the governmental unit does not have the intent or ability to redeem the BANs with long-term debt, it is appropriate to leave the liability in the capital projects fund. The ability to redeem the BANs could be demonstrated by a post balance sheet issuance of long-term debt or the entering into of a long-term financing arrangement for the BANs.

(iii) Project Budgets.   When debt is issued to finance an entire capital project, it is usually done so at the beginning of the project in an amount equal to the total estimated project cost. Accordingly, a portion of the proceeds may remain unexpended over a considerable period of time. To the maximum extent possible, these excess proceeds should be invested in interest-bearing investments. However, consideration should be given to the federal arbitrage regulations that limit the amount of interest that can be earned from investing the proceeds of a tax-exempt bond issue. If certain limits are exceeded, the bond's tax-exempt status may be lost or severe penalities could be imposed on the issuer.

Project budgets are typically established for capital projects to control costs and to guard against cost overruns. All expenditures needed to place the project in readiness, that is, indirect as well as direct costs, should be recorded against this budget. The actual expenditures, however, will probably be either less or greater than the amounts authorized. Therefore, in the absence of any legal restrictions, any unspent balance should be transferred to the appropriate sources. If the project was financed only from bond proceeds, the transfer should be to the debt service fund from which the bond issue is to be repaid. If the resources were drawn from more than one source, such as bond proceeds and current revenues, the transfer should be split among the sources in proportion to their contributions. If the expenditures were greater than authorized and a deficit exists, sufficient funds must be transferred to liquidate any commitments.

As construction of the project is completed, the costs should be recorded in the general fixed assets account group with the following entry:

Construction in progress	$XXX	
Investment in general fixed assets		$XXX

When the project is finally completed, the entry in the general fixed assets account group would then be:

Buildings	$XXX	
Construction in progress		$XXX

The amount of construction in progress would be transferred to the buildings account in the general fixed assets account group when the project is completed.

(e) Enterprise Funds. **Enterprise funds** are the funds that governments use to account for services to the public when most of the costs involved are paid for in the form of charges by the users of such services. Examples are electric utilities, water, sanitary sewer, gas, local transportation systems, airports, public housing, parking lots, golf courses, and swimming pools. The substantial federal and state grants to certain types of enterprise activities, however, as well as the rising costs of these services and the public's unwillingness to pay the full amounts, have meant that many of these activities are no longer financed predominantly by user charges. Hence, the activities theoretically would have to be accounted for in the general fund or as special revenue funds, and not enterprise funds.

Nonetheless, in many instances it is still highly desirable to account for many of these activities as enterprise funds, because it is often important to know the full costs of the activities, to monitor the amount of outside support required for them, and to know the extent of costs paid for by **user charges.** Accordingly, the definition of enterprise funds (GASB Codification § 1300.104) addresses these issues. Enterprise funds are used:

> To account for operations (a) that are financed and operated in a manner similar to private business enterprises—where the intent of the governing body is that the costs (expenses, including depreciation) of providing goods and services to the general public on a continuing basis be financed or recovered primarily through user charges; or (b) where the governing body has decided that periodic determination of revenues earned, expenses incurred and/or net income is appropriate for capital maintenance, public policy, management control, accountability, or other purposes.

Enterprise activities are frequently administered by departments of the general purpose government, for example, a municipal water department or a state parks department. They can also be the exclusive function of a local special district, such as a water district, power authority, or bridge and tunnel authority.

User charges are one significant source of enterprise fund resources; revenue bond proceeds are another. Revenue bonds are long-term obligations, the principal and interest of which are paid from the earnings of the enterprise for which the bond proceeds were spent.

The enterprise revenues may be pledged to the payment of the debt, and the physical properties may carry a mortgage that is to be liquidated in the event of default.

Revenue bond **indentures** usually also contain several requirements concerning the use of the bond proceeds, the computation and reporting of revenue bond **coverage,** and the establishment and use of restricted asset accounts for handling revenue bond debt service requirements. For instance, a revenue bond indenture may require the establishment of various bond accounts including a construction account, operations and maintenance account, current debt service account, future debt service account, and revenue and replacement account. This does not necessarily mean establishing individual accounting funds for each bond issue. Instead, the accounting and reporting requirements can be met through the use of various accounts within an accounting fund.

The revenue bond construction account normally represents cash and investments (including interest receivable) segregated by the bond indenture for construction. Construction liabilities payable from restricted assets should be reported as "contracts payable from restricted assets." As with all restricted accounts, construction assets and the liabilities to be paid from them generally should not be classified as current assets and liabilities. The difference between the restricted construction asset and liability accounts is not required to be reported as a reserve in retained earnings.

A revenue bond operations and maintenance account often is established pursuant to a bond indenture. Resources for this account are provided through bond proceeds and/or operating income or net income. This account generally accumulates assets equal to operating costs for one month. Once this account has been established, additional proceeds from future bond issues generally are necessary only to the extent the costs associated with these expanded operations are expected to increase. This account is normally balanced by a reserve for revenue bond operations and maintenance account in retained earnings.

Bond indentures may also include a covenant requiring the establishment of a restricted account for the repayment of bond principal and interest. Resources for this account also are provided through bond proceeds and/or operating income or net income. Normally, assets accumulated for debt service payments (i.e., principal and interest) due within one year are classified in the revenue bond current debt service account. This account is at least partially associated with the bonds payable—current account and the accrued interest payable account. Any difference between the revenue bond current debt service account and related current bonds payable and accrued interest payable should be reported as reserved retained earnings. When accounts are restricted for debt service payments beyond the next 12 months, a revenue bond future debt service account should be established.

The final restricted account typically established pursuant to a covenant within a bond indenture is the revenue bond renewal and replacement account. Bond proceeds and/or net income are often restricted for payments of unforeseen repairs and replacements of assets originally acquired with bond proceeds. Provided that liabilities have not been incurred for this purpose, the revenue bond renewal and replacement account is balanced by the reserve for revenue bond renewal and replacement account in retained earnings.

The following general rule should be considered when determining the amount of retained earnings to reserve in restricted asset accounts: Unless otherwise required by the bond indenture, retained earnings should only be reserved for amounts of restricted assets in excess of related liabilities.

Another restricted asset often found in enterprise funds is the amount resulting from the deposits customers are required to make to ensure payment of their final charges and to protect the utility against damage to equipment located on the customer's property. These funds are not available for the financing of current operations and, generally, the amount, less the charges outstanding against the account, must be returned to the customer upon withdrawing from the system. Also, these deposits may, depending on legal and policy requirements, draw interest at some stipulated rate.

In some instances, revenue bonds are also secured by the full faith and credit of the governmental unit. This additional security enables the bonds to obtain better acceptance in the securities market. If the bonds are to be serviced by the enterprise activity, the cash, liability, principal, and interest payments should be accounted for in the enterprise fund. Even if the bonds are secured only by full faith and credit and not by a revenue pledge, but the intention is to use enterprise revenues to service the bonds, they should be accounted for as if they were revenue bonds. If, however, general obligation bond proceeds are used to finance the enterprise activity and there is no intention to service the bonds with enterprise fund resources, the amounts provided to the enterprise fund should be recorded as a contribution from the fund recording the proceeds of the bond, typically, the general fund.

Other sources of contributions also provide significant resources for enterprise activities. Such resources include contributions of permanent capital by other funds or other governmental bodies; contributions in aid of construction by customers or other members of the general public; the aforementioned proceeds of a bond issue to be repaid from general fund revenues, federal grants, or state grants; connection charges to users of utility services; payments by real estate developers for installing utility lines; and similar receipts.

If such resources are externally restricted for capital acquisitions or construction, they should be reported as **contributed capital.** Fixed assets acquired with these contributions should be capitalized at full cost and depreciated over the estimated useful life of the fixed assets. The depreciation on fixed assets acquired by grants, entitlements, and shared revenues received from other governments may be closed to the appropriate contributed capital account rather than retained earnings. If this option is followed, such depreciation is "added back" to the enterprise fund's net income or loss, thereby increasing the net income or reducing the net loss that is closed to retained earnings.

Another resource is the support provided by or to other funds of the government. For instance, an enterprise fund will frequently use the services or commodities of a central facility operated as an internal service fund. Conversely, the general fund departments will use the services of an electric utility fund.

It is important to handle these relationships on a businesslike basis. All services rendered by an enterprise fund for other funds of the government should be billed at predetermined rates, and the enterprise should pay for all services received from other funds on the same basis that is utilized to determine charges for other users. The latter will often include **payments in lieu of taxes** to the general fund in amounts comparable to the taxes that would have been paid by the enterprise were it privately owned and operated, or an "administrative charge" if the enterprise does not have its own management capacity and instead uses management services provided by the general government. Unless this is done, the financial operations of a government-owned enterprise will be distorted, and valid comparisons of operating results with those for similar privately owned enterprise cannot be made. However, other considerations, such as the amount of planned idle capacity, have an impact on the comparability of public and private enterprise funds.

Interfund operating transfers may also occur between an enterprise fund and governmental funds. Operating subsidy transfers from the general fund or special revenue fund are possible. There may also be transfers from an enterprise to finance general fund expenditures.

Finally, there are the nonoperating income and expenses, which are incidental to, or by-products of, the enterprise's primary service function. Nonoperating income consists of such items as interest earnings, rent from nonoperating properties, intergovernmental revenues, and sale of excess supplies. Nonoperating expenses include items such as interest expense and fiscal agents' fees.

(f) Internal Service Funds.   Internal service funds finance and account for special activities that are performed and commodities that are furnished by one department or agency of a governmental unit to other departments or agencies of that unit or to other governmental units on a cost-reimbursement basis. The services differ from those rendered to the public at large, which are accounted for in general, special revenue or enterprise funds. Examples of activities in which internal service funds are established include central motor pools, duplication services, central purchasing and stores departments, and insurance and risk-management activities.

When an internal service fund is established, resources are typically obtained from capital contributions from other operating funds, such as the general fund or an enterprise fund, or from long-term advances from other funds that are to be repaid from earnings. The entry to be made when the fund is created varies depending on the source of the capital.

The cost of services rendered and commodities furnished, including labor, depreciation on all fixed assets used by the funds other than buildings financed from capital projects, and overhead, are charged to the departments served. These departments reimburse the internal service fund by recording expenditures against their budgeted appropriations. The operating objective of the fund is to recover costs incurred to provide the service, including depreciation. Accordingly, the operations of the fund should not result in any significant profit or loss. Whenever it uses the services of another fund, such as an enterprise fund, the fund pays for and records the costs just as if it had dealt with an outside organization.

Since exact overhead charges are usually not known when bills are prepared, the departments being served are usually billed for direct costs plus a uniform rate for their portion of estimated overhead. Any difference in actual overhead expenses may be charged or credited to the departments at fiscal year-end or adjusted for in a subsequent year. At the end of each fiscal year, net income or loss must be determined. The excess of net billings to the department over costs is closed to the retained earnings account.

(g) Trust and Agency Funds.   The purpose of **trust and agency funds** is to account for assets held by a governmental unit in a trustee capacity or as an agent for individuals, private organizations, other governmental units, or other funds.

(i) Trust Funds.   Usually in existence for an extended period of time, **trust funds** deal with substantial vested interests and involve complex administrative problems. The government's records must provide adequate information to permit compliance with the terms of the trust as defined in the trust document, statutes, ordinances, or governing regulations. For instance, if depreciable property were included in a nonexpendable trust fund, depreciation would have to be recorded as an expense and not included in the distributable income, to keep the principal intact. Similarly, gains and losses on the sale of investments may, unless otherwise specified in the trust agreement, be credited or charged to trust principal.

(ii) Expendable and Nonexpendable Trust Funds.   Within the trust fund category there are **expendable trust funds,** where the principal as well as the income may be expended, and **nonexpendable trust funds,** where the principal must be preserved intact. These funds require a precise determination of revenues and expenditures (expenses) in accordance with the trust document so that only the correct net income will be expended.

(iii) Pension Trust Funds.   Another type of trust fund is the **pension trust fund,** in which governments account for the money held for the future retirement benefit of their employees, that is, their retirement systems. The resources of this fund are the members' contributions, contributions from the government employer, and earnings on investments in authorized securities. The expenses are the authorized retirement allowances and other benefits, refunds of contributions to members who resign prior to retirement, and administrative expenses.

Professional actuaries should make periodic actuarial studies of the retirement systems and compute the amounts that should be provided so that the benefits can be paid as required. The reserve accounts should be periodically adjusted to reflect the current actuarial requirements. If the actuarial requirement is reported as a reservation of fund balances, the existence of a credit balance in the unreserved and undesignated fund balance account on a statement date indicates that a retirement system has assets in excess of the actuarial requirement, whereas a deficit reflects a deficiency that must be financed at some future date.

The proper accounting and reporting for pension trust funds is extremely complex. The GASB Codification § Pe5 identifies the following pronouncements as being acceptable sources of pension accounting and reporting principles for state and local governments: NCGA Statement 1, NCGA Statement 6, SFAS No. 35, GASB Statement No. 5.

Whereas the first three pronouncements establish accounting and disclosure requirements, GASB Statement No. 5 only establishes disclosure requirements. Government employers participating in a public employee retirement system (PERS) as well as the PERS itself are required to make pension disclosures in accordance with GASB Statement No. 5 regardless of which of the three accounting pronouncements is followed. The GASB Statement No. 5 disclosures, which are often lengthy, provide financial statement users with the standardized information needed to assess (1) the funding status of a PERS on a going-concern basis, (2) the progress made in accumulating sufficient assets to pay benefits when due, and (3) whether employers are making actuarially determined contributions.

The key disclosure item in GASB Statement No. 5 is the "pension benefit obligation" (PBO), which is defined as "the actuarial present value of credited projected benefits, prorated on service, and discounted at a rate equal to the expected return on present and future plan assets." However, GASB Statement No. 5 indicates that single-year financial data alone cannot provide sufficient information to accomplish the objectives mentioned above and therefore requires disclosure of 10-year historical trend information as "required supplementary information."

By standardizing a measure of pension obligation, the PBO increases comparability among various employers and PERS. The presentation of required historical information makes it possible to analyze trends, including the accumulation of assets to pay benefits and the relative strength of the PERS over time.

Even though the pension disclosure requirements have been established, the GASB is still deliberating on new pension accounting principles for state and local government employers as outlined in its Exposure Draft (ED) released in January 1990. The ED would establish standards for recognition and measurement of pension expenditure/expense and related liabilities or assets in the financial statements of state and local governmental employers. However, it does not address accounting and financial reporting for PERS and pension trust funds, which will be the subject of a future pronouncement.

In short, for employers participating in defined benefit plans, the ED would require measurement of pension expenditure/expense according to certain "Parameters for Calculating Pension Expenditure/Expense" (the Parameters). The Parameters are a set of criteria for deciding whether the employer's periodic actuarially required contribution (ARC) has been determined in a systematic and rational manner, consistent with the concepts of accrual-basis accounting and interperiod equity, and is, therefore, an acceptable measure of periodic pension expenditure/expense.

If the employer's ARC for an accounting period is determined according to the Parameters, the employer should accrue periodic pension expenditure/expense equal to the ARC. If the employer's ARC is determined in some other manner, or if no ARC is determined, the employer should calculate pension expenditure/expense according to the Parameters and accrue that amount. Any difference between the amount recognized as periodic pension expenditure/expense according to the Parameters and the amount of the employer's actual contribution to the PERS or plan for the same period should be recognized as a pension liability or asset. Balance sheet recognition of the unfunded liability or funding excess of the PERS or plan would not be required.

(iv) Agency Funds.   Used by governments to handle cash resources held in an agent capacity, **agency funds** require relatively simple administration. The typical agency funds used by state and local governments include (1) tax collection funds, under which one local government

collects a tax for an overlapping governmental unit and remits the amount collected less administrative charges to the recipient; (2) payroll withholdings, under which the government collects the deductions and periodically remits them in a lump sum to the appropriate recipient; (3) clearance funds, used to accumulate a variety of revenues from different sources and to apportion them to various operating funds; and (4) deferred compensation plans organized under IRC § 457.

(h) Special Assessment Activities.   Special assessment activities pertain to (1) the financing and construction of certain public improvements, such as storm sewers, which are to be paid for wholly or partly from special assessments levied against the properties benefited by such improvements, or (2) the providing of services that are normally provided to the public as general governmental functions and that would otherwise be financed by the general fund or a special revenue fund. Those services may include street lighting, street cleaning, and snow plowing. The payment by the property owners or taxpayers receiving the benefit distinguishes these activities from activities that benefit the entire community and are paid for from general revenues or general obligation bond proceeds. Sometimes, however, a special assessment bond, which is often used to finance the special assessment improvement, also carries the additional pledge of the full faith and credit of the governmental unit.

It should be emphasized that whereas GASB Statement No. 6 eliminated the requirement to report special assessment funds in an entity's general purpose financial statement, accounting for special assessment activities is still an important part of governmental accounting.

Capital improvement special assessment projects have two distinct and functionally different phases. The initial phase consists of financing and constructing the project. In most cases, this period is relatively short in duration, sometimes lasting only a few months, and rarely more than a year or two. The second phase, which may start at the same time as, during, or after the initial phase, consists of collecting the assessment principal and interest levied against the benefited properties and repaying the cost of financing the construction. The second phase is usually substantially longer than the first.

There are many ways of financing a capital improvement special assessment project. Assessments may be levied and collected immediately. Funds will then be available to pay construction costs, and it will not be necessary to issue special assessment bonds. Alternatively, a project may be constructed using the proceeds from short-term borrowing. When the project is complete and the exact cost is known, special assessment bonds are issued to provide the exact amount of money and the short-term borrowings are repaid. A third—and perhaps the most common—financing alternative is for the government to levy a special assessment for the estimated cost of the improvement, issue bonds to provide the funds, construct the improvement using the bond proceeds, and then collect the assessments over a period of years, using the collections to service the bonds.

Five basic types of transactions are associated with a capital project type special assessment:

1. Levying the special assessment.
2. Issuing special assessment bonds.
3. Constructing the capital project.
4. Collecting the special assessment.
5. Paying the bond principal and interest.

Because the special assessment fund has been eliminated for financial reporting purpose, the transactions related to special assessment activities are typically reported in the same manner, and on the same basis of accounting, as any other capital improvement and financing transaction. Transactions of the construction phase of the project should generally be reported in a capital projects fund, and transactions of the debt service phase should be reported in a debt service fund, if one is required.

At the time of the levy, special assessments receivable should be recognized and offset by deferred revenue; deferred revenue should be reduced as the assessments become measurable and available. The fixed assets constructed or acquired (other than those related to an enterprise fund) should be reported in the general fixed assets account group, and the outstanding long-term debt should be reported in the general long-term debt account group.

The entry to record the special assessment levy is shown below.

Special assessments receivable	$XXX	
Special assessment revenue		$XXX
Deferred special assessment revenue		$XXX

When the current special assessments and the governmental unit's share are collected, the following entry is made:

Cash	$XXX	
Special assessments receivable		$XXX

The issuance of special assessment bonds at par is recorded by the following entries:

Capital Projects Fund

Cash	$XXX	
Other financing sources—bond proceeds		$XXX

GLTDAG

Amounts to be provided	$XXX	
Bonds payable		$XXX

If the bonds are issued at a premium or discount, the debit to "cash" for the proceeds received, and the credit to "other financing sources" would be adjusted accordingly.

The entry for the retirement of special assessment bonds and for the construction of the special assessment project would follow the accounting principles outlined in the discussion on capital projects. The usual entries are made for expenditures and for encumbrances if such a system exits. At the end of the year, the revenues and expenditures should be closed to the fund balance to reflect the balance that may be expended in future periods.

Although the accounting for special assessment construction activities is quite similar to other financing and construction activities, the major issue relating to special assessment activities involves the definition of special assessment debt. Special assessment debt is often defined as those long-term obligations, secured by a lien on the assessed properties, for which the primary source of repayment is the assessments levied against the benefiting properties.

However, the nature and composition of debt associated with special assessment-related capital improvements is not always consistent with this definition. Rather, it can vary significantly from one jurisdiction to another. Capital improvements involving special assessments may be financed by debt that is:

1. General obligation debt that is not secured by liens on assessed properties but nevertheless will be repaid in part by special assessment collections.

2. Special assessment debt that is secured by liens on assessed properties and is also backed by the full faith and credit of the government as additional security.

3. Special assessment debt that is secured by liens on assessed properties and is not

backed by the full faith and credit of the government but is, however, fully or partially backed by some other type of general governmental commitment.

4. Special assessment debt that is secured by liens on assessed properties, is not backed by the full faith and credit of the government, and is not backed by any other type of general governmental commitment; the government is not liable under any circumstance for the repayment of this category of debt, should the property owner default.

In some cases special assessment debt is payable entirely by special assessment collections from the assessed property owners; in other cases the debt may be repaid partly from special assessment collections and partly from the general resources of the government, either because the government is a property owner benefiting from the improvements or because the government has agreed to finance part of the cost of the improvement as a public benefit. The portion of special assessment debt that will be repaid directly with governmental resources is, in essence, a general obligation of the government. If the government owns property that benefits from the improvements financed by special assessment debt as in item 4 above, or if a public benefit assessment is made against the government, the government is obligated for the public benefit portion and the amount assessed against its property, even though it has no liability for the remainder of the debt issue.

Because the special assessment debt can have various characteristics, the extent of a government's liability for debt related to a special assessment capital improvement can also vary significantly. For example, the government may be primarily liable for the debt, as in the case of a general obligation issue; it may have no liability whatsoever for special assessment debt; or it may be obligated in some manner to provide a secondary source of funds for repayment of special assessment debt in the event of default by the assessed property owners. A government is obligated in some manner for special assessment debt if (1) it is legally obligated to assume all or part of the debt in the event of default or (2) the government may take certain actions to assume secondary liability for all or part of the debt—and the government takes, or has given indications that it will take, those actions.

Stated differently, the phrase "obligated in some manner" is intended to include all situations other than those in which (1) the government is prohibited (by constitution, charter, statute, ordinance, or contract) from assuming the debt in the event of default by the property owner or (2) the government is not legally liable for assuming the debt and makes no statement, or gives no indication, that it will, or may, honor the debt in the event of default.

Debt issued to finance capital projects that will be paid wholly or partly from special assessments against benefited property owners should be reported as follows:

1. General obligation debt that will be repaid, in part, from special assessments should be reported like any other general obligation debt.
2. Special assessment debt for which the government is obligated in some manner should be reported in the GLTDAG, except for the portion, if any, that is a direct obligation of an enterprise fund, or that is expected to be repaid from operating revenues of an enterprise fund.
   a. The portion of the special assessment debt that will be repaid from property owner assessments should be reported as "special assessment debt with governmental commitment."
   b. The portion of special assessment debt that will be repaid from general resources of the government (the public benefit portion, or the amount assessed against government-owned property) should be reported and classified in the GLTDAG like other general obligation debt.
3. Special assessment debt for which the government is not obligated in any manner should not be displayed in the government's financial statements. However, if the government is liable for a portion of that debt (the public benefit portion, or as a property owner), that portion should be reported as in subparagraph 2b above.

24.14 FIXED ASSETS: VALUATION AND DEPRECIATION.   Principles 5, 6, and 7 of GASB Codification § 1100 discuss accounting for fixed assets. Governments account for their general fixed assets, that is, the fixed assets not belonging to an enterprise fund, an internal service fund, or a similar trust fund in the **general fixed assets account group.** This account group is established to maintain accountability for the fixed assets even though they do not belong to any individual fund, but rather to the governmental unit as an instrumentality. Furthermore, they do not represent net financial resources available for expenditure, but items for which financial resources have been used. Thus their inclusion in a specific fund would distort the fund balance.

Fixed assets in enterprise funds, internal service funds, and similar trust funds should be accounted for in the respective fund.

To be classified as a fixed asset, a specific piece of property should have three attributes: It should be tangible, have a life at least longer than the current fiscal year, and have a significant value. Reporting of **public domain** or **"infrastructure" fixed assets,** that is, roads, bridges, curbs and gutters, streets, sidewalks, drainage systems, lighting systems, and similar assets that are immovable and have value only to the governmental unit, is optional. General fixed assets acquired through noncancelable leases, as the term is defined by SFAS No. 13, "Accounting for Leases," should be capitalized and a liability for the present value of the future lease payments should be recorded in the general long-term debt account group.

The amount recorded for fixed assets should be historical cost, or estimated historical cost if the original cost is not available. Cost should include not only the purchase price or construction cost, but also all ancilliary charges necessary to place the asset in its intended location ready to use: freight and transportation charges, site preparation expenditures, professional fees, and legal claims directly attributable to the asset's acquisition. If the asset is constructed by the governmental unit's own personnel, the amount recorded should result from a complete accounting of the costs of labor, materials, equipment usage, and overhead. Donated fixed assets should be recorded at their estimated fair value on the date donated.

Capitalization of interest is required for assets constructed in enterprise and similar trust funds if the amount is material. The interest capitalization policy should be disclosed for all assets constructed and capitalized, including assets in the general fixed assets account group.

(a) Accounting for Acquisition and Disposal of Fixed Assets.   The expenditures for general fixed assets are recorded in the general fund, special revenue fund, or capital projects fund. The entry that records the asset is made in the general fixed assets account group as follows:

Buildings	$XXX	
Investment in general fixed assets		$XXX

The debit entry should reflect the asset classification: land, buildings, improvements other than buildings, equipment, construction in progress. The credit is normally made to "investment in general fixed assets."

(b) Subsidiary Property Records.   The maintenance of **subsidiary property records** aids in the control of fixed assets. The subsidiary records should contain such information as classification code, date of acquisition, name and address of vendor, unit charged with custody, location, cost, fund and account from which purchased, method of acquisition, estimated life, and repair and maintenance data.

(c) Disposal or Retirement of Fixed Assets.   In the **disposal or retirement** of a general fixed asset the amount for which the asset is recorded must be removed from the asset side of the general fixed assets account group, and an equal amount must be deducted from the investment in fixed assets. If the asset is sold, the amount obtained in cash or by evidence of indebtedness should be recorded in the appropriate governmental fund. The same amount should be credited to a revenue account, such as sale of fixed assets or miscellaneous revenues or other financing sources.

(d) Depreciation. Depreciation of general fixed assets is not recorded in the operating statements of governmental funds because governmental funds report expenditures and depreciation is an **expense.** Depreciation can be recorded, however, in the cost accounting systems or calculated for purposes of cost analysis. Accumulated depreciation may also be recorded in the general fixed assets account group by increasing the accumulated depreciation account and decreasing the investment in the general fixed asset account.

Depreciation of fixed assets accounted for in a proprietary fund should be recorded in that fund. Depreciation is also recognized in trust funds where expenses, net income, or capital maintenance is measured.

24.15 LONG-TERM LIABILITIES. Principle 5 indicates that all unmatured long-term indebtedness of the government not directly related to or expected to be repaid from proprietary funds, or similar trust funds, is **general long-term debt** and should be accounted for in the **general long-term debt account group.** General long-term debt is not limited to liabilities arising from debt issuances, but may also include lease purchase agreements, long-term portion of compensated absences, judgments and claims, and other commitments that are not current liabilities properly recorded in the governmental funds. Matured long-term indebtedness should be recorded in the debt service fund, if maintained, or another governmental fund. Long-term indebtedness directly related to and expected to be repaid from proprietary or trust fund resources should be included in those funds.

Typically, the general long-term debt of a state and local government is secured by the general credit and revenue-raising powers of the government rather than by the assets acquired for specific fund resources. Furthermore, just as general fixed assets do not represent financial resources available for appropriation and expenditure, the unmatured principal of general long-term debt does not require current appropriation and expenditure of a governmental fund's financial resources. Thus, to include it as a governmental fund liability would be misleading for management control and accountability functions for the current period. However, this issue is being examined by the GASB in its projects on ''Measurement Focus and Basis of Accounting'' and ''Financial Reporting and Display'' as discussed in section 24.25 of this chapter.

General long-term debt should be classified appropriately as term bonds, serial bonds, and other general long-term liabilities (i.e., unpaid sick leave and vacation, unpaid pensions, etc.). Balancing accounts would show the amount available in the debt service funds for payment of debt principal and the amount that must be provided in future years for such payments.

(a) Accounting for Long-Term Debt. The entry to establish the long-term debt payable in the general long-term debt account group is made when the bonds are issued and the proceeds are recorded in a governmental fund. It is as follows:

Amount to be provided for repayment of bonds	$XXX	
Bonds payable		$XXX

When funds are accumulated in the debt service funds for payment of the bonds, the following entry is made in the general long-term debt account group:

Amount available in debt service funds	$XXX	
Amount to be provided for repayment of bonds		$XXX

When the bonds mature, one of the following entries is recorded, depending on whether the matured bonds are paid from current revenues or from accumulated resources in a debt service fund:

Bonds payable	$XXX	
Amount to be provided for repayment of bonds		$XXX
Bonds payable	$XXX	
Amount available in debt service funds		$XXX

The amount to be recorded in the general long-term debt account group for noncurrent liabilities on lease-purchase agreement is generally the lower of the present value at the beginning of the lease term of the minimum lease payments due during the noncancelable lease term excluding executory costs, and the fair value of the leased property at the inception of the lease. This amount should be adjusted at the end of each year to reflect the payments on the lease liability.

(b) Deficit Bonds. **Deficit bonds** result from governments' ending a fiscal year with a deficit and issuing bonds, payable in future years, to finance the deficit. The bonds are classified as "deficit bonds payable" in the general long-term debt account group. The offsetting debit would be the "amount to be provided for repayment of deficit bonds." The credit attributable to the proceeds of the deficit bonds should be to a general fund account entitled "fund balance provided by deficit bonds."

In subsequent years, as these bonds are liquidated from the excesses of revenues over expenditures (prior to consideration of debt service of the deficit bonds), the deficit bonds payable and the amount to be provided for redemption of deficit bonds are reduced. The fund balance provided by deficit bonds should also be reduced by closing the principal portion of debt service payments of the deficit bonds to the account. Thus, at any point, the total amount to be provided for repayment of the deficit bonds in the general long-term debt account group will be equal to "fund balance provided by deficit bonds" in the general fund.

24.16 MEASUREMENT FOCUS AND BASIS OF ACCOUNTING. The accounting and financial reporting treatment applied to a fund is determined by its measurement focus. The measurement focus refers to what is being expressed in reporting an entity's financial performance and position. A particular measurement focus is accomplished by considering not only which resources are measured, but also when the effects of transactions or events involving those resources are recognized (the basis of accounting). **Principle 8** describes the basis of accounting used by governments.

(a) Measurement Focus. All governmental funds and expendable trust funds are accounted for by using a current financial resources measurement focus. With this measurement focus, only current assets and current liabilities are included on the balance sheet. Operating statements of these funds present increases (i.e., revenues and other financing sources) and decreases (i.e., expenditures and other financing uses) in net current assets.

All proprietary funds, nonexpendable trust funds and pension trust funds are accounted for on a flow of economic resources measurement focus. With this measurement focus, all assets and liabilities associated with the operation of these funds are included on the balance sheet. Fund equity (i.e., net total assets) is segregated into contributed capital and retained earnings components. Proprietary fund-type operating statements present increases (e.g., revenues) and decreases (e.g., expenses) in net total assets.

(b) Basis of Accounting. The **basis of accounting** determines when revenues, expenditures, expenses, and transfers—and the related assets and liabilities—are recognized in the accounts and reported in the financial statements. Specifically, it relates to the timing of the measurements made, regardless of the measurement focus. For example, whether depreciation is recognized depends on whether expenses or expenditures are being measured rather than on whether the cash or accrual basis is used.

(i) Cash Basis.   Under the **cash basis** of accounting, revenues and transfers in are not recorded in the accounts until cash is received, and expenditures or expenses and transfers out are recorded only when cash is disbursed.

The cash basis is frequently encountered, but its use is not generally accepted for any governmental unit. With the cash basis, it is difficult to compare expenditures with services rendered, because the disbursements relating to those services may be made in the fiscal period following that in which the services occurred. Also, statements prepared on a cash basis do not show financial position and results of operations on a basis that is generally accepted.

(ii) Accrual Basis.   Under the **accrual basis** of accounting, most transactions are recorded when they occur, regardless of when cash is received or disbursed. Items not measurable until cash is received or disbursed are accounted for at that time.

The accrual basis is considered a superior method of accounting for the economic resources of any organization because it results in accounting measurements that are based on the substance of transactions and events, rather than merely on the receipt or disbursement of cash. Its use is recommended to the fullest extent practical in the governmental environment and is being proposed as the basis of accounting for all fund types in the GASB's project, "Measurement Focus and Basis of Accounting," which is discussed in section 24.25.

(iii) Modified Accrual Basis.   As indicated previously, the financial flows of governments, such as taxes and grants, typically do not result from a direct exchange for goods or services and thus cannot be accrued based on the completion of the earnings process and an exchange taking place. Governments have thus devised the **"susceptible to accrual"** concept as the criterion for determining when inflows are accruable as revenue. A revenue is susceptible to accrual when it is both **measurable** and **available** to finance current operations. An amount is measurable when the precise amount is known because the transaction is completed, or when it can be accurately estimated using past experience or other available information. An amount is available to finance operations when it is (1) **physically available,** that is, collectible within the current period or soon enough thereafter to be used to pay liabilities of the current period; and (2) **legally available,** that is, authorized for expenditure in the current fiscal period and not applicable to some future period.

On the expenditure side, a government's main concern, for governmental funds at least, is to match the financial resources used with the financial resources obtained. This measure of whether current-year revenues were sufficient to pay for current-year services is referred to as interperiod equity. A measure of interperiod equity shows whether current-year citizens received services but shifted part of the payment burden to future-year citizens or used up previously accumulated resources. Conversely, such a measure would show whether current-year revenues were not only sufficient to pay for current-year services, but also increased accumulated net resources.

This adaptation of the accrual basis to the conditions surrounding government activities and financing has been given the term **modified accrual.** Modified accrual is currently used in all governmental fund types (i.e., the general fund, special revenue funds, etc.) where the intent is to determine the extent to which provided services have been financed by current resources.

In proprietary funds the objective is to determine net income, and the accounting should be essentially the same as commercial accounting. Hence, proprietary funds use the economic resources measurement focus and the accrual basis without the need for modification described above.

(c) Revenue Transactions.   The modified accrual basis of accounting is applied in practice for revenue transactions as follows:

1. **Property taxes** are recorded as revenue when the taxes are levied, provided that they apply to and are collected in the current period or soon enough thereafter to finance the current period's expenditures. The period after year-end generally should not exceed 60 days. The amount recorded as revenue should be net of estimated uncollectible taxes, abatements, discounts, and refunds. (Property taxes that are measurable but not available—and hence not susceptible to accrual—should be deferred and recognized as revenue in the fiscal year they become available.)

2. **Taxpayer-assessed income, gross receipts, and sales taxes** should be recorded as revenues when taxpayer liability, measurability, and collectibility have been clearly established.

3. **Miscellaneous revenues** such as **fines and forfeits,** athletic fees, and inspection charges are generally recognized when cash is received because they are usually not measurable and available until they are received.

4. **Grants** should be recorded when the government has an irrevocable right to the grant. If expenditure of funds is the prime factor for determining eligibility for the grant funds, revenue should be recognized when the expenditure is made. A more detailed discussion of grant accounting is provided in section 24.20.

5. **Interest earned on special assessment levies** may be accrued when due rather than when earned if it approximately offsets interest expenditures on special assessment indebtedness that is also recorded when due.

(d) Expenditure Transactions.   Expenditure transactions under the modified accrual basis are treated as follows:

1. **Interest** on long-term debt should be recorded as an expenditure when due.

2. **Inventory items** may be considered expenditures either when purchased (the purchases method) or when used (the consumption method). Under either method significant amounts of inventory at the end of a fiscal year should be reported as an asset on the balance sheet.

3. **Expenditures for insurance** and similar services extending over more than one accounting period need not be allocated between or among accounting periods, but they may be accounted for as expenditures of the period of acquisition.

4. **Interest expenditures** on special assessment indebtedness may be recorded when due if they are approximately offset by interest earnings on special assessment levies that are also recorded when due.

5. **Vacation and sick leave benefits** should be recorded when a liability has been incurred that is payable from expendable available resources.

24.17 BUDGETARY ACCOUNTING.   **Principle 9** describes the requirements related to budgeting. **Budgeting,** or the allocation of scarce resources to enable established objectives to be accomplished, is the central element in a government's planning, financial management, control, and public accountability processes. The **budget** is the financial plan embodied into law, introduced and enacted in the same manner as any other ordinance or statute. Thus it enables governments to demonstrate that they are meeting a major objective of governmental accounting, namely, compliance with the law.

Budgets are the goals of governments in the same way that net income and return on investment are the goals to corporate organizations. A financial report that compares the actual results with the budgeted results is the means by which a governmental unit demonstrates accountability and managerial performance. Accordingly, an annual operating budget is usually developed for and adopted by every governmental fund.

(a) Types of Operating Budgets. Several types of annual operating budgets are used in contemporary public finance. Among the more common are the following:

- Line item budget.
- Program budget.
- Performance budget.
- Zero-base budget.

(i) Line Item Budgeting. Listing the inputs for resources that each organizational unit requests for each **line** (or **object**) of expenditure is referred to as **line item budgeting.** This simple approach produces a budget that governing bodies and administrators can understand, based on their own experience. It provides for tight control over spending and is the most common local government budgeting approach, although this popularity is due primarily to tradition.

Line item budgeting is criticized because it emphasizes inputs rather than outputs, analyzes expenditures inadequately, and fragments activities among accounts that bear little relation to purposes of the government. However, all budgeting systems use objects for the buildup of costs and for execution of the budget.

Overcoming criticisms of a line item budgeting system can be accomplished by:

- Improving the budget structure to encompass all funds and organizational units in a manner that enables the total resources available to a particular organizational unit or responsibility center to be readily perceived.
- Developing a level of detail for the object categories that permits adequate analysis of proposed expenditures and effective control over the actual expenditures.
- Improving the presentation of historical data to stimulate the analysis of trends.
- Providing a partial linking of outputs to the objects of expenditures.

(ii) Program Budgeting. Formulating expenditure requests on the basis of the services to be performed for the various programs the government provides is known as **program budgeting**. A program budget categorizes the major areas of citizen needs and the services for meeting such needs into programs. Goals and objectives are stated for each program, normally in relatively specific, quantified terms. The costs are estimated for the resources required (e.g., personnel and equipment) to accomplish the objective for each program. The governing body can then conduct a meaningful review of budget requests by adding or deleting programs or placing different emphasis on the various programs.

Program budgeting has existed for many years, but relatively few governments have adopted it, partly because line budgeting is so familiar and comprehensible. Lack of acceptance also results from the difficulty of developing operationally useful program budgets that meet the governmental notion of accountability, that is, control of the number of employees and other expense items, rather than achievement of results in applying such resources.

The operational usefulness of program budgeting has also been questioned as a result of the complexity of the **program structure,** the vagueness of goals and objectives, the lack of organizational or individual responsibility for program funds that span several departments or agencies, and the inadequacy of accounting support to record direct and indirect program costs.

Nevertheless, program budgeting can be an extremely effective approach for a government willing to devote the effort. The steps that departments should take to implement the system are:

- Identify programs and the reasons for their existence.
- Define the goals of programs.
- Define kinds and levels of services to be provided in light of **budgetary guidelines** (council- or CEO-furnished guidelines, e.g., budget priorities, budget assumptions, and budget constraints).
- Develop budget requests in terms of resources needed, based on the programs' purposes, the budgetary guidelines, the projected levels of services, and the previous years' expenditure levels for the programs.
- Submit budget requests for compilation, review, and approval.

(iii) Performance Budgeting.   Formulating expenditure requests based on the work to be performed is the primary function of **performance budgeting.** It emphasizes the work or service performed, described in quantitative terms, by an organizational unit performing a given activity; for example, number of tons of waste collected by the Sanitation Department and case work load in the Department of Welfare. These performance data are used in the preparation of the annual budget as the basis for increasing or decreasing the number of personnel and the related operating expenses of the individual departments.

The development of a full-scale performance budget requires a strong budget staff, constructive participation at all levels, special accounting and reporting methods, and a substantial volume of processed statistical data. Primarily for these reasons, performance budgeting has been less widely used than line item budgeting.

The approach to developing a performance budgeting system is as follows:

- Decide on the extent to which functions and activities will be segmented into work units and services for formulation and execution of the budget.
- Define the functions in services performed by the government, and assemble them into a structure.
- Identify and assemble or develop work load and efficiency measures that relate to service categories.
- Estimate the total costs of the functions and services.
- Analyze resource needs for each service in terms of personnel, equipment, and so on.
- Formulate the first-year performance budget. For the first year, set the budget appropriations and controls at a higher level than the data indicate.
- Perform cost accounting for the functional budget category; initiate statistical reporting of the work load measures; match resources utilized to actual results.

(iv) Zero-Base Budgeting.   In the preparation of a budget, **zero-base budgeting** projects funding for services at several alternative levels, both lower and higher than the present level, and allocates funds to services based on rankings of these alternatives. It is an appropriate budgeting system for jurisdictions whose revenues are not sufficient for citizen demands and inflation-driven expenditure increases, where considerable doubt exists as to the necessity and effectiveness of existing programs and services, and where incremental budgeting processes have resulted in existing programs and their funding being taken as a given, with attention devoted to requests for new programs.

Zero-base budgeting can be used with any existing budgeting system, including line item, program, or performance budgeting. The budget format can remain unchanged.

The steps to implement zero-base budgeting are as follows:

- Define **decision units,** that is activities that can be logically grouped for planning and providing each service.
- Analyze decision units to determine alternative service levels, determine the resources required to operate at alternative levels, and present this information in **decision packages.**
- Rank the decision packages in a priority order that reflects the perceived importance of a particular package to the community in relation to other packages.
- Present the budget to the governing body for a review of the ranking of the decision packages.

(b) Budget Preparation. The specific procedures involved in the preparation of a budget for a governmental unit are usually prescribed by state statute, local charter, or ordinance. There are, however, certain basic steps:

- Preparation of the budget calendar.
- Development of preliminary forecasts of available revenues, recurring expenditures, and new programs.
- Formulation and promulgation of a statement of executive budget policy to the operating departments.
- Preparation and distribution of budget instructions, budget forms, and related information.
- Review of departmental budget requests and supporting work sheets.
- Interview with department heads for the purpose of adjusting or approving their requests in a tentative budget.
- Final assembly of the tentative budget, including fixing of revenue estimates and the required tax levy.
- Presentation of the tentative budget to the legislative body and the public.
- Conduction of a public hearing, with advance legal notice.
- Adoption of final budget by the legislative body.

(i) Revenue and Expenditure Estimates. The property tax has been the traditional basic source of revenue for local government. The amount to be budgeted and raised is determined by subtracting the estimated nonproperty taxes and other revenues, plus the reappropriated fund balance, from budgeted expenditures. This amount, divided by the assessed valuation of taxable property within the boundaries of the governmental unit, produces the required tax rate.

Many jurisdictions have legal ceilings on the property tax rates available for general operating purposes. Additionally, taxpayer initiatives like California's Proposition 13 and Massachusett's Proposition $2^1/_2$ have forced governments to seek new revenue sources. Accordingly, governmental units have turned increasingly to other types of revenue, such as sales taxes, business and nonbusiness license fees, charges for services, state-collected, locally shared taxes, and grants-in-aid from the federal and state governments. Department heads, however, ordinarily have little knowledge of revenue figures. As a result, the primary responsibility for estimating these revenues usually lies with the budget officer and the chief finance officer.

Most governmental units, as a safeguard against excessive accumulation of resources, require that any **unappropriated fund balance** in the general fund be included as a source of financing in the budget of that fund for the succeeding fiscal year. Most controlling laws or ordinances provide for inclusion of the estimated surplus (fund balance) at the end of the current year, although many require that the includable surplus be the balance at the close of the last completed fiscal year.

Departmental estimates of expenditures and supporting work programs or performance data generally are prepared by the individual departments, using forms provided by the central budget agency. Expenditures are customarily classified to conform to the standard account classification of the governmental unit and thus permit comparison with actual performance in the current and prior periods.

(ii) Personal Services.   Generally, **personal services** are supported by detailed schedules of proposed salaries for individual full-time employees. Nonsalaried and temporary employees are usually paid on an hourly basis, and the budget requests are normally based on the estimated number of hours of work.

Estimates of materials and supplies and other services, ordinarily quite repetitive in nature, are most often based on current experience, plus an allowance, if justified, for rising costs. Capital outlay requests are based on demonstrated need for specific items of furniture or equipment by individual departments.

In recent years, governmental units, particularly at the county, state, and federal levels, have disbursed substantial sums annually that are unlike the usual current operating expenditures. These sums include welfare or **public assistance payments,** contributions to other governmental units, benefit payments, and special grants. They are properly classified as "other charges." Estimates of these charges are generally based on unit costs for assistance, legislative allotments, requests from outside agencies or governmental units, and specified calculations.

In addition to departmental expenditures, the budget officer must estimate certain nondepartmental or general governmental costs not allocated to any department or organizational unit. Examples include pension costs and retirement contributions, which are not normally allocated, election costs, insurance and surety bonds, and interest on tax notes.

Although most governments still operate under laws that require the budget to be balanced precisely, an increasing number permit a surplus or contingency provision in the expenditure section of the budget. This is usually included to provide a reserve to cover unforeseen expenditures during the budget year.

The expenditure budget may be approved by a board, a commission, or other governing body before presentation to the central budget-making authority.

(iii) Presentation of the Budget.   To present a comprehensive picture of the proposed fund operations for a budget year, a budget document is prepared that is likely to include a budget message, summary schedules and comparative statements, detailed revenue estimates, detailed expenditure estimates, and drafts of ordinances to be enacted by the legislative body.

The contents of a budget message should set forth concisely the salient features of the proposed budget of each fund and will generally include the following: (1) a total amount showing amounts of overall increase and decrease, (2) detailed amounts and explanations of the increases and decreases, and (3) a detailed statement of the current financial status of each fund for which a budget is submitted, together with recommendations for raising the funds needed to balance the budget of each fund. It should identify the relationship of the operating budget to the capital program and capital budget, which are submitted separately.

(iv) Adoption of the Budget.   Most states adopt the budget by the enactment of one or more statutes. Many cities require the formality of an ordinance for the adoption of the budget. In other cases, the budget is adopted by resolution of the governing body.

(v) Appropriations.   Because **appropriations** constitute maximum expenditure authorizations during the fiscal year, they cannot be exceeded legally unless subsequently amended by the legislative body (although some governments permit modifications up to a prescribed limit to be made by the executive branch). Unexpended or unencumbered appropriations may lapse at the end of a fiscal year or may continue as authority for subsequent period expenditures, depending on the applicable legal provisions.

It may be necessary for the legislative agency to adopt a separate appropriation resolution or ordinance, or the adoption of the budget may include the making of appropriations for the items of expenditure included therein. Provision for the required general property tax levy is usually made at this time, either by certifying the required tax rates to the governmental unit that will bill and collect the general property tax or by enacting a tax levy ordinance or resolution.

(c) Budget Execution.   The budget execution phase entails obtaining the revenues, operating the program, and expending the money as authorized. The accounts are usually structured on the same basis on which the budget was prepared. Many governments maintain budgetary control by integration of the budgetary accounts into the general and subsidiary ledger. The entry is as follows:

Estimated revenues	$XXX	
Appropriations		$XXX

If estimated revenues exceed appropriations, a credit for the excess is made to "budgetary fund balance"; if they are less the appropriations, the difference is debited to a "budgetary fund balance."

Individual sources of revenues are recognized in subsidiary revenue accounts. A typical revenue ledger report is illustrated in Exhibit 24.1. This format provides for the comparison, at any date, of actual and estimated revenues from each source.

To control expenditures effectively, the individual amounts making up the total appropriations are recorded in subsidiary expenditures accounts, generally called "appropriation ledgers." Exhibit 24.2 presents an example of an appropriation ledger. It should be noted that this format provides for recording the budget appropriation and for applying expenditures and **encumbrances** (see below) relating to the particular classification against the amount appropriated at any date.

When the managerial control purposes of integrating the budgetary accounts into the general ledger have been served, the budgetary account balances are reversed in the process of closing the books at year-end. Budgetary accounting procedures thus have no effect on the financial position or results of operations of a governmental entity.

(i) Encumbrances.   An **encumbrance,** which is unique to governmental accounting, is the reservation of a portion of an applicable appropriation that is made because a contract has been signed or a purchase order issued. The encumbrance is usually recorded in the accounting system to prevent overspending the appropriation. When the goods or services are received, the expenditure is recorded and the encumbrance is reversed. The entry to record an encumbrance is as follows:

Encumbrances	$XXX	
Reserve for encumbrances		$XXX

The entries that are made when the goods or services are received are:

Reserve for encumbrances	$XXX	
Encumbrances		$XXX
Expenditures	$XXX	
Vouchers payable ,		$XXX

Many governments report encumbrances that are not liquidated at year-end in the same way as expenditures because the encumbrances are another use of budgetary appropriations. The total amount of encumbrances not liquidated by year-end may be considered as a reservation of the fund balance for the subsequent year's expenditures, based on the encumbered appropriation authority carried over.

NAME OF GOVERNMENTAL UNIT
Budget versus Actual Revenue
by Revenue Source
for Accounting Period June 30, 19X2

Fund Type: The General Fund

Revenues	Budgeted	Actual	Variance
015 Real & per. revenue recognized			
0110 Real & p. prop rev. recognized	$459,449,213	$460,004,317	$ (555,104)
Revenue class total	459,449,213	460,004,317	(555,104)
020 Motor vehicle & other excise			
0121 M/V taxes—current year	16,000,000	22,727,905	(6,727,905)
0122 M/V taxes—prior '87'	0	2,886,605	(2,886,605)
0123 M/V taxes—'1986'	0	32,051	(32,051)
0124 M/V taxes—'1985'	0	45,378	(45,378)
0125 M/V taxes—'84 & prior	0	85,393	(85,393)
0126 M/V taxes—'72'-prior	0	2	(2)
0127 Boat excise—cur yr '88	15,000	40,414	(25,414)
0128 Boat excise—'87'	0	155	(155)
0131 M.V. lessor surcharge	200	60	139
Revenue class total	16,015,200	25,817,963	(9,802,764)
025 Local excise taxes			
0129 Hotel/motel room excise	13,500,000	13,580,142	(80,142)
0130 Aircraft fuel excise	12,400,000	12,960,966	(560,966)
Revenue class total	25,900,000	26,541,108	(641,108)
030 Departmental & other revenue			
0133 Penalties & int-prop. taxes	1,000,000	1,746,007	(746,007)
0134 Penalties & int.-M/V taxes	525,000	620,124	(95,124)
0135 Penalties & int.-sidewalk	0	115	(115)
0136 Penalties & interest/tax title	5,000,000	3,835,517	1,164,483
0138 Penalties & int./boat excise	0	3	(3)
3101 Data processing services	100	6,849	(6,749)
3103 Purchasing services	50,000	69,038	(19,038)
3104 Recording of legal instruments	150	291	(141)
3105 Registry division—fees	750,000	761,238	(11,238)
3107 City record/sale of publicatn	10,000	25,353	(15,353)
3108 Assessing fees	1,600	914	686
3109 Liens	400,000	373,410	26,590
3120 City clerk—fees	250,000	231,970	18,030
3130 Election—fees	12,000	10,633	1,367
3140 City council/sale of pubicatn	200	310	(110)
3199 Other general services	35,000	18,691	16,309
3202 Police services	350,000	365,102	(15,102)
3211 Fire services	1,150,000	1,582,355	(432,355)
3221 Civil defense	40,000	161.835	(121,835)
3301 Parking facilities	3,350,000	3,775,810	(425,810)
Revenue class total	$ 12,924,050	$ 13,585,565	$ (661,515)

Exhibit 24.1.   A typical revenue ledger report.

NAME OF GOVERNMENTAL UNIT
Budget Versus Actual Expenditures
and Encumbrances by Activity
for Accounting Period June 30, 19X2

Fund Type: The General Fund

Expenditures		Budgeted	Actual	Variance
1100 Human services				
011-384-0384	Rent equity board	$ 1,330,977	$ 1,274,531	$ 56,446
011-387-0387	Elderly commission	2,534,005	2,289,549	244,456
011-398-0398	Physically handicapped comm	180,283	159,768	20,515
011-503-0503	Arts & humanities office	211,916	207,219	4,697
011-740-0741	Vet serv-veterans serv div	2,871,616	2,506,363	365,253
011-740-0742	Vet serv-veterans graves reg	158,270	146,392	11,878
011-150-1505	Jobs & community services	370,053	369,208	845
Activity total		7,657,120	6,953,030	704,090
1200 Public safety				
011-211-0211	Police department	116,850,000	117,145,704	(295,704)
011-221-0221	Fire department	80,594,068	79,587,423	1,006,645
011-222-0222	Arson commission	189,244	175,670	13,574
011-251-0251	Transportation-traffic div	13,755,915	13,707,890	48,025
011-252-0252	Licensing board	542,007	449,825	92,182
011-251-0253	Transportation-parking clerk	7,520,539	7,474,462	46,077
011-261-0260	Inspectional services dept	10,004,470	10,003,569	901
Activity total		229,456,243	228,544,543	911,700
1300 Public works				
011-311-0311	Public works department	64,900,000	60,281,837	4,618,163
011-331-0331	Snow removal	2,250,000	2,360,326	(110,326)
Activity total		67,150,000	62,642,163	4,507,837
1400 Property & development				
011-180-0180	RPD-general administration div	432,740	416,569	16,171
014-180-0183	Real property dept county	1,027,660	354,328	673,332
011-180-0184	RPD-buildings division	6,010,155	6,038,464	(28,309)
011-180-0185	RPD-property division	1,847,650	1,806,427	41,223
011-188-0186	PFD-code enforcement division	504,013	458,984	45,029
011-188-0187	PFD-administration division	4,677,365	4,697,167	(19,802)
011-188-0188	PFD-construction & repair div	3,063,637	2,808,266	255,371
Activity total		$ 17,563,220	$ 16,580,205	$ 983,015

Exhibit 24.2.   A typical appropriation ledger report.

(ii) Allotments.   Another way to maintain budgetary control is to use an allotment system. With an allotment system, the annual budget appropriation is divided and allotted among the months or quarters in the fiscal year. A department is not permitted to spend more than its allotment during the period.

The International City Managers' Association lists the following purposes of an allotment system:

1. To make sure that departments plan their spending so as to have sufficient funds to carry on their programs throughout the year, avoiding year-end deficiencies and special appropriations.

2. To eliminate or reduce short-term tax anticipation borrowing by making possible more accurate forecast control of cash position throughout the fiscal year.

3. To keep expenditures within the limits of revenues that are actually realized, avoiding an unbalanced budget in the operation of any fund as a whole.

4. To give the chief administrator control over departmental expenditures commensurate with the administrative responsibility, allowing the administrator to effect economies in particular activities as changes in work load and improvements in methods occur.

(iii) Interim Reports.   The last element in the budget execution process is interim financial reports. These are prepared to provide department heads, senior management, and the governing body with the information needed to monitor and control operations, demostrate compliance with legal and budgetary limitations, anticipate changes in financial resources and requirements due to events or developments that are unknown or could not be foreseen at the time the budget was initially developed, or take appropriate corrective action. Interim reports should be prepared frequently enough to permit early detection of variances between actual and planned operations, but not so frequently as to adversely affect practicality and economy. For most governmental units, interim reports on a monthly basis are necessary for optimum results. With smaller units, a bimonthly or quarterly basis may be sufficient. With sophisticated data-processing equipment, it may be possible to automatically generate the appropriate information daily.

Governmental units should prepare interim financial reports covering the following:

Revenues.
Expenditures.
Cash projections.
Proprietary funds.
Capital projects.
Grant programs.

The form and content of these reports should reflect the government's particular circumstances and conditions.

(d) Proprietary Fund Budgeting.   The nature of most operations financed and accounted for through proprietary funds is such that the demand for the goods or services largely determines the appropriate level of revenues and expenses. Increased demand causes a higher level of expenses to be incurred but also results in a higher level of revenues. Thus, as in commercial accounting, **flexible budgets** prepared for several levels of possible activity typically are better for planning, control, and evaluation purposes than are fixed budgets.

Accordingly, budgets are not typically adopted for proprietary funds. Furthermore, even when flexible budgets are adopted, they are viewed not as appropriations but as approved plans. The budgetary accounts are generally not integrated into the ledger accounts because it is considered unnecessary. Budgetary control and evaluation are achieved by comparing interim actual revenues and expenses with planned revenues and expenses at the actual level of activity for the period.

In some instances, fixed dollar budgets are adopted for proprietary funds either to meet local legal requirements or to control certain expenditures (e.g., capital outlay). In such cases, it may be appropriate to integrate budgetary accounts into the proprietary fund accounting system in a manner similar to that discussed for governmental funds.

(e) Capital Budget. Many governments also prepare a **capital budget.** A capital budget is a plan for capital expenditures to be incurred during a single budget year from funds subject to appropriation for projects scheduled under the **capital program.** The annual capital budget is adopted concurrently with the operating budgets of the governmental unit, being subject to a public hearing and the other usual legal procedures.

The capital budget should not be confused with a **capital program** or **capital project budget.** A capital program is a plan for capital expenditures to be incurred over a period of years, usually 5 or 6 years. The capital project budget represents the estimated amount to be expended on a specific project over the entire period of its construction. The capital budget authorizes the amounts to be expended on all projects during a single year. Controlling this amount is important for the proper use of available funds.

24.18 CLASSIFICATION AND TERMINOLOGY. **Principles 10** and **11** establish the requirements surrounding classification and terminology. Governmental fund revenues should be classified by fund and source. The major revenue source classifications are taxes, licenses and permits, intergovernmental revenues, charges for services, fines and forfeits, and miscellaneous. Governmental units often classify revenues by organizational units. This classification may be desirable for purposes of management control and accountability, as well as for auditing purposes, but it should supplement rather than supplant the classifications by fund and source.

(a) Classification of Expenditures. There are many ways to classify governmental fund expenditures in addition to the basic fund classification. Function, program, organizational unit, activity, character, and principal class of object are examples. Typically, expenditures are classified by character (current, intergovernmental, capital outlay, and/or debt service). Current expenditures are further classified by function and/or program.

- *Character Classification.* Reporting expenditures according to the physical period they are presumed to benefit. The major character classifications are (1) current expenditures, which benefit the current fiscal period; (2) capital outlays, which are presumed to benefit both the present and future fiscal periods; and (3) debt service, which benefits prior fiscal periods as well as current and future periods. Intergovernmental expenditures is a fourth character classification that is used when one governmental unit makes expenditures to another governmental unit.
- *Function Classification.* Establishing groups of related activities that are aimed at accomplishing a major service or regulatory responsibility. Standard function classifications are as follows:

  General government.

  Public safety.

  Health and welfare.

  Culture and recreation.

  Conservation of natural resources.

  Urban redevelopment and housing.

  Economic development and assistance.

  Education.

  Debt service.

  Miscellaneous.
- *Program Classification.* Establishing groups of activities, operations, or organizational units that are directed at the attainment of specific purposes or objectives, for example, protection of property, or improvement of transportation. Program classification is used by governmental units employing program budgeting.

- *Organizational Unit Classification.* Grouping expenditures according to the governmental unit's organization structure. Organizational unit classification is essential to responsibility reporting.
- *Activity Classification.* Grouping expenditures according to the performance of specific activities. Activity classification is necessary for the determination of cost per unit of activity, which in turn is necessary for evaluation of economy and efficiency.
- *Object Classification.* Grouping expenditures according to the types of items purchased or services obtained, for example, personal services, supplies, other services and charges. Object classifications are subdivisions of the character classification.

Excessively detailed object classifications should be avoided since they complicate the accounting procedure and are of limited use in financial management. The use of a few object classification is sufficient in budget preparation; control emphasis should be on organization units, functions, programs, and activities rather than on the object of expenditures.

(b) Classifications of Other Transactions.   Certain transactions, although not revenues or expenditures of an individual fund or the governmental entity as a whole, are increases or decreases in the equity of an individual fund. These transactions are classified as **other financing sources and uses** and are reported in the operating statement separately from fund revenues and expenditures. The most common other financing sources and uses are:

- *Proceeds of Long-term Debt Issues.* Such proceeds (including leases) are not recorded as fund liabilities; for example, proceeds of bonds and notes expended through the capital project or debt service funds.
- *Operating Transfers.* These include legally authorized transfers from a fund receiving revenues to the fund through which the resources are to be expended; examples are transfers of tax revenues from a special revenue fund to a debt service fund and transfers from an enterprise fund other than payments in lieu of taxes to finance general fund expenditures.

Other interfund transactions are:

- *Interfund Loans and Advances.* These funds are disbursed by one fund for the benefit of another. If the funds will be repaid shortly, the amount should be reclassified as **due from** other funds by the lending fund and **due to** other funds by the receiving fund. When two funds owe each other, the amounts receivable and payable should not be offset in the accounts. However, for purposes of reporting, current amounts due from and due to the same funds may be offset and the net amounts shown in the respective fund balance sheets.
  If the advance is long-term in nature and the asset will not be available to finance current operations, a fund balance reserve equal to the amount of the advance should be established.
- *Quasi-External Transactions.* These transactions would be treated as revenues, expenditures, or expenses if they involved organizations external to the governmental unit. Examples are payments in lieu of taxes from an enterprise fund to the general fund; internal service fund billings to departments; routine employer contributions from the general fund to a pension trust fund; and a routine service charge for inspection, engineering, utilities, or similar services provided by a department financed from one fund to a department financed from another fund.
  Amounts should be accounted for as revenues in the recipient fund and as expenditures in the disbursing fund.

- *Reimbursements*. These transactions constitute reimbursements of a fund for expenditures or expenses initially made from it that are properly applicable to another fund. An example is an expenditure properly chargeable to a special revenue fund but initially made from the general fund, which is subsequently reimbursed. The transaction should be recorded as an expenditure or expense in the reimbursing fund and as a reduction of an expenditure or expense in the reimbursed fund.

(c) Residual Equity Transfers. Another type of interfund transaction, **residual equity transfers,** is not classified as an other financing source or use because it is a change in fund balance that is not considered in the determination of the results of operations. A **residual equity transfer** is a nonrecurring or nonroutine transfer of equity between funds. Examples are a general fund's contribution of capital to an enterprise fund or an internal service fund; the subsequent return of all or part of such contribution to the general fund; and transfers of residual balances of discontinued funds to the general fund or a debt service fund.

(d) Classification of Fund Equity. Fund equity is the difference between a fund's assets and its liabilities. In the governmental funds, it is called the "fund balance"; in the proprietary funds, it consists of retained earnings and contributed capital.

The important amount in the fund equity account for governmental funds is the amount available for future appropriation and expenditure (i.e., unreserved and undesignated fund balance); therefore governments should clearly delineate amounts that are not available for such purposes. Fund balance can be segregated into reserved and unreserved amounts. Unreserved fund balance can be segregated further into designated and undesignated amounts.

Reservations of fund balance identify (1) third-party claims against resources of the entity that have not materialized as liabilities at the balance sheet date, or (2) the existence of assets that, because of their nonmonetary nature or lack of liquidity, represent financial resources not available for current appropriation or expenditure; for example, inventories, prepaid expenses, and noncurrent assets (usually receivables). Such reserves are not intended as valuation allowances, but merely demonstrate the current unavailability of the subject assets to pay current expenditures.

Designations of fund balance identify tentative plans for or restrictions on the future use of financial resources. Such designations should be supported by definitive plans and approved by either the government's CEO or the legislature. Examples of such designations include the earmarking of financial resources for capital projects and contingent liabilities.

Reserves and designations are established by debiting unreserved, undesignated fund balance and crediting the reserve or designation. The reserve is not established by a charge to operations.

Another type of fund equity, existing only in the proprietary funds, is **contributed capital.** It represents the amount of fund equity or permanent capital contributed to a proprietary fund by another fund or by customers, developers, other members of the general public, or other government bodies toward the cost of capital facilities.

(e) Investment in General Fixed Assets. Although presented in the fund equity section of a governmental unit's balance sheet, **investment in general fixed assets** is not considered fund equity.

(f) Accounting Coding. Charts of accounts in governments range from simple three-digit codes designed for manual accounting systems to multidigit codes that use the logical arrangement of numbers within the codes to signify such things as fund, organizational unit, program, fiscal year, activity, and source of revenue.

24.19 EXTERNAL FINANCIAL REPORTING. Prior to 1979, governments traditionally prepared external financial reports by preparing a balance sheet; a statement of revenues, expenditures, and transfers (or operations); and a statement of changes in fund balance (retained earnings) for every fund (plus a statement of changes in financial position for every enterprise fund) maintained by the government. This often resulted in lengthy financial reports. Principle 12 relates to financial reporting and is discussed below.

(a) Pyramid Concept and General Purpose Financial Statements. GASB Codification § 1900 recommends that governments use the **pyramid concept** for external financial reporting. Specifically, they should prepare **general purpose financial statements** (GPFS) composed of the following:

- Combined balance sheet—all fund types and account groups (Exhibit 24.3).
- Combined statement of revenues, expenditures, and changes in fund balances—all governmental fund types and expendable trust funds (Exhibit 24.4).
- Combined statement of revenues, expenditures, and changes in fund balances—budget and actual—general and special revenue fund types (Exhibit 24.5).
- Combined statement of revenues, expenses, and changes in retained earnings—all proprietary fund types and similar trust funds (Exhibit 24.6).
- Combined statement of cash flows—all proprietary and nonexpendable trust fund types (Exhibit 24.7). (Note: GASB Statement No. 9 requires a combined statement of cash flows—all propriety and nonexpendable trust fund types to be presented in place of a statement of changes in financial position. GASB Statement No. 9 is effective for fiscal periods ending after December 15, 1989.)
- Notes to financial statements.
- Required supplementary information.

Even though the GASB encourages each governmental entity to prepare a **comprehensive annual financial report** (CAFR) the GPFS constitutes fair presentation of financial position and results of operations in accordance with GAAP and could be opined upon as such by an independent auditor. The statements would be suitable for inclusion in an official statement for a securities offering and for widespread distribution to users requiring less detailed information about the governmental unit's finances than is contained in the CAFR described below.

The following should be noted for each recommended GPFS:

- *Combined balance sheet—all fund types and account groups.*

    The term "assets and other debits" is used rather than "assets" because of the nature of the debits in the general long-term debt account group.

    The term "equities" is used for contributed capital, investment in general fixed assets, retained earnings, and fund balances, with the four separated on the balance sheet.

    The fund types and account groups are classified into the following categories: governmental fund types, proprietary fund types, fiduciary fund types, and account groups. (Classifying the fiduciary funds with the governmental and proprietary fund, as appropriate, is an acceptable alternative.)

    The totals of the amounts of all types and account groups may be reported for each caption. If they are reported, the total column should be headed "memorandum only."

    Interfund and similar eliminations may or may not be made in arriving at the total. If eliminations are made, this fact should be disclosed by headings on the statement, and the nature of the elimination should be explained in the accompanying notes (if not obvious from the financial statements).

The presentation of comparative totals for the prior year for each caption is encouraged because this information is useful to the statement.

Comparative data for fund types is not typically presented because such a presentation will unduly complicate the statement.

• *Combined statement of revenues, expenditures, and changes in fund balances—all governmental fund types and expendable trust funds.*

The statement should be classified as follows:

> Revenues
> − Expenditures
> _____
>   Excess of revenues over (under) expenditures
> ± Other financing sources (uses)
> _____
>   Excess of revenues and other sources over
>   (under) expenditures and other uses
> + Fund balance—beginning of period
> _____
>   Fund balance—end of period

Alternatively, such statements may be presented as follows:

> Revenues
> + Other financing sources
> _____
>   Total revenue and other sources
>
> Expenditures
> + Other uses (e.g., operating transfers to other funds)
> _____
>   Total expenditures and other uses
>
>   Excess of revenues and other sources over
>   (under) expenditures and other uses
> + Fund balance—beginning of period
> _____
>   Fund balance—end of period

It is also acceptable to open the statement of revenues, expenditures, and changes in fund balance with "fund balance—beginning of period." For example:

> Fund balance—beginning of period
> _____
> Revenues
> + Other financing sources
> _____
>   Total revenues and other sources
>
> Expenditures
> + Other uses (e.g., operating transfers to other funds)
> _____
>   Total expenditures and other uses
>
>   Excess of revenues and other sources over
>   (under) expenditures and other uses
> _____
>   Fund balance—end of period

NAME OF GOVERNMENTAL UNIT
Combined Balance Sheet—All Fund Types and Account Groups
December 31, 19X2
(With Comparative Totals for December 31, 19X1)

		Governmental Fund Types		
	General	Special Revenue	Debt Service	Capital Projects
Assets				
Cash	$258,500	$101,385	$ 43,834	$ 663,785
Cash with fiscal agent	—	—	102,000	—
Investments, at cost or amoritized cost	65,000	37,200	160,990	—
Receivables (net of allowances for uncollectibles):				
Taxes	58,300	2,500	3,829	—
Accounts	8,300	3,300	—	646,135
Notes	—	—	—	—
Loans	—	—	—	—
Accrued interest	50	25	1,557	350
Due from other funds	2,000	—	—	—
Due from other governments	30,000	75,260	—	640,000
Advances to internal service funds	65,000	—	—	—
Inventory of supplies, at cost	7,200	5,190	—	—
Prepaid expenses	—	—	—	—
Restricted assets:				
Cash	—	—	—	—
Investments, at cost or amortized cost	—	—	—	—
Land	—	—	—	—
Buildings	—	—	—	—
Accumulated depreciation	—	—	—	—
Improvements other than buildings	—	—	—	—
Accumulated depreciation	—	—	—	—
Machinery and equipment	—	—	—	—
Accumulated depreciation	—	—	—	—
Construction in progress	—	—	—	—
Amount available in debt service funds	—	—	—	—
Amount to be provided for retirement of general long-term (debt)	—	—	—	—
Total assets	$494,350	$224,860	$312,210	$1,950,270
Liabilities				
Vouchers payable	$118,261	$ 33,850	$ —	$ 49,600
Contracts payable	57,600	18,300	—	119,000
Judgments payable	—	2,000	—	33,800
Accrued liabilities	—	—	—	10,700
Payable from restricted assets:				
Construction contracts	—	—	—	—
Fiscal agent	—	—	—	—
Accrued interest	—	—	—	—
Revenue bonds	—	—	—	—
Deposits	—	—	—	—
Due to other taxing units	—	—	—	—
Due to other funds	24,189	2,000	—	1,000
Due to student groups	—	—	—	—

Exhibit 24.3. Sample combined balance sheet.

	Proprietary Fund Types		Fiduciary Fund Type	Account Groups		Totals (Memorandum Only)	
Enterprise	Internal Service	Trust and Agency	General Fixed Assets	General Long-term Debt	December 31, 19X2	December 31, 19X1
$ 257,036	$ 29,700	$ 216,701	$ —	$ —	$ 1,570,941	$ 1,258,909
—	—	—	—	—	102,000	—
—	—	1,239,260	—	—	1,502,450	1,974,354
—	—	580,000	—	—	644,629	255,400
29,130	—	—	—	—	686,865	494,635
2,350	—	—	—	—	2,350	1,250
—	—	35,000	—	—	35,000	40,000
650	—	2,666	—	—	5,298	3,340
2,000	12,000	11,189	—	—	27,189	17,499
—	—	—	—	—	745,260	101,400
—	—	—	—	—	65,000	75,000
23,030	40,000	—	—	—	75,420	70,900
1,200	—	—	—	—	1,200	900
113,559	—	—	—	—	113,559	272,968
176,800	—	—	—	—	176,800	143,800
211,100	20,000	—	1,259,500	—	1,490,600	1,456,100
447,700	60,000	—	2,855,500	—	3,363,200	2,836,700
(90,718)	(4,500)	—	—	—	(95,218)	(83,500)
3,887,901	15,000	—	1,036,750	—	4,939,651	3,922,200
(348,944)	(3,000)	—	—	—	(351,944)	(283,750)
1,841,145	25,000	—	452,500	—	2,318,645	1,924,100
(201,138)	(9,400)	—	—	—	(210,538)	(141,900)
22,713	—	—	1,722,250	—	1,744,963	1,359,606
—	—	—	—	210,210	210,210	284,813
—	—	—	—	1,889,790	1,889,790	1,075,187
$6,375,514	$184,800	$2,084,816	$7,326,500	$2,100,000	$21,053,320	$17,059,911
$ 131,071	$ 15,000	$ 3,350	$ —	$ —	$ 351,132	$ 223,412
8,347	—	—	—	—	203,247	1,326,511
—	—	—	—	—	35,800	32,400
16,870	—	4,700	—	—	32,270	27,417
17,760	—	—	—	—	17,760	—
139	—	—	—	—	139	—
32,305	—	—	—	—	32,305	67,150
48,000	—	—	—	—	48,000	52,000
63,000	—	—	—	—	63,000	55,000
—	—	680,800	—	—	680,800	200,000
—	—	—	—	—	27,189	17,499
—	—	1,850	—	—	1,850	1,600

(continued)

	Governmental Fund Types			
	General	**Special Revenue**	**Debt Service**	**Capital Projects**
Liabilities—*Continued*				
Deferred revenue	15,000	—	—	—
Advance from general fund	—	—	—	—
Matured bonds payable	—	—	100,000	555,000
Matured interest payable	—	—	2,000	—
General obligation bonds payable	—	—	—	—
Revenue bonds payable	—	—	—	—
Total liabilities	215,050	56,150	102,000	769,100
Fund Equity				
Contributed capital	—	—	—	—
Investment in general fixed assets	—	—	—	—
Retained earnings:				
Reserved for revenue bond retirement	—	—	—	—
Unreserved	—	—	—	—
Fund balances:				
Reserved for encumbrances	38,000	46,500	—	1,126,500
Reserved for inventory of supplies	7,200	5,190	—	—
Reserved for advance to Internal Service Funds	65,000	—	—	—
Reserved for loans	—	—	—	—
Reserved for endowments	—	—	—	—
Reserved for employees' retirement system	—	—	—	—
Unreserved:				
Designated for debt service	—	—	210,210	46,070
Designated for subsequent years' expenditures	50,000	—	—	—
Undesignated	119,100	117,020	—	8,600
Total fund equity	279,300	168,710	210,210	1,181,170
Total liabilities and fund equity	$494,350	$224,860	$312,210	$1,950,270

The notes to the financial statements are an integral part of this statement.

Exhibit 24.3. *Continued.*

Excessive detail should be avoided in choosing the captions for reporting revenues and expenditures. Appropriate revenue and expenditure captions were discussed in section 24.18 of this chapter.

• *Combined statement of revenues, expenditures, and changes in fund balances—budget and actual—general and special revenue fund types.*

This statement provides the comparison of the budgeted amounts and the actual results for those governmental fund types for which a legally adopted budget was prepared. The budget data should be obtained from the legally adopted budget. If the budget is not a legal document, the amounts may be those that the governing body or management considers its annual budget.

If the budget has been revised, the budget amounts should reflect the latest revised

Proprietary Fund Types		Fiduciary Fund Type	Account Groups		Totals (Memorandum Only)	
Enterprise	Internal Service	Trust and Agency	General Fixed Assets	General Long-term Debt	December 31, 19X2	December 31, 19X1
—	—	—	—	—	15,000	3,000
—	65,000	—	—	—	65,000	75,000
—	—	—	—	—	655,000	420,000
—	—	—	—	—	2,000	—
700,000	—	—	—	2,100,000	2,800,000	2,110,000
1,798,000	—	—	—	—	1,798,000	1,846,000
2,815,492	80,000	690,700	—	2,100,000	6,828,492	6,456,989
1,392,666	95,000	—	—	—	1,487,666	815,000
—	—	—	7,326,500	—	7,326,500	5,299,600
129,155	—	—	—	—	129,155	96,975
2,038,201	9,800	—	—	—	2,048,001	1,998,119
—	—	—	—	—	1,211,000	410,050
—	—	—	—	—	12,390	10,890
—	—	—	—	—	65,000	75,000
—	—	50,050	—	—	50,050	45,100
—	—	134,000	—	—	134,000	94,000
—	—	1,426,201	—	—	1,426,201	1,276,150
—	—	—	—	—	256,280	325,888
—	—	—	—	—	50,000	50,000
—	—	(216,135)	—	—	28,585	106,150
3,560,022	104,800	1,394,116	7,326,500	—	14,224,828	10,602,922
$6,375,514	$184,800	$2,084,816	$7,326,500	$2,100,000	$21,053,320	$17,059,911

budget and the column should be headed "revised budget." If the revised budget differs substantially from the original budget, the original budget should also be reported.

The budget amounts and actual results should be on the same basis of accounting. Often, that basis is in conformity with GAAP. However, if the budget is prepared on a basis not consistent with GAAP, the actual results should be reported in conformity with the basis used to prepare the budget. In addition a reconciliation between the results on a budgeting basis and the results on a GAAP basis should be reported in the statement of revenues, expenditures, and changes in fund balance or in a note to the financial statements.

A note to the financial statements should disclose any material amounts of expenditures over appropriations at the legal level of control in an individual fund that is not disclosed

NAME OF GOVERNMENTAL UNIT
Combined Statement of Revenues, Expenditures, and Changes in Fund Balances—
All Governmental Fund Types and Expendable Trust Funds
For the Fiscal Year Ended December 31, 19X2
(With Comparative Totals for December 31, 19X1)

| | Governmental Fund Types | | | | Fiduciary Fund Type | Total (Memorandum Only) Year Ended | |
	General	Special Revenue	Debt Service	Capital Projects	Expendable Trust	December 31, 19X2	December 31, 19X1
Revenues							
Taxes	$ 881,300	$ 189,300	$ 79,177	$ —	$ —	$1,149,777	$1,137,900
Licenses and permits	103,000	—	—	—	—	103,000	96,500
Intergovernmental revenues	186,500	831,100	41,500	1,490,000	—	2,549,100	1,509,200
Charges for services	91,000	79,100	—	—	—	170,100	160,400
Fines and forfeits	33,200	—	—	—	—	33,200	26,300
Miscellaneous revenues	19,500	71,625	7,140	32,845	200	131,310	111,500
Total revenues	1,314,500	1,171,125	127,817	1,522,845	200	4,136,487	3,041,800
Expenditures							
Current:							
General government	121,805	—	—	—	—	121,805	134,200
Public safety	258,395	480,000	—	—	—	738,395	671,300
Highways and streets	85,400	417,000	—	—	—	502,400	408,700
Sanitation	56,250	—	—	—	—	56,250	44,100
Health	44,500	—	—	—	—	44,500	36,600
Welfare	46,800	—	—	—	—	46,800	41,400
Culture and recreation	40,900	256,450	—	—	—	297,350	286,400
Education	509,150	—	—	—	2,420	511,570	512,000

Capital outlay	—	—	—	1,938,600	—	1,938,600	803,000
Debt service:							
Principal retirement	—	—	60,000	—	—	60,000	52,100
Interest and fiscal charges	—	—	40,240	28,000	—	68,420	50,000
Total expenditures	1,163,200	1,153,450	100,420	1,966,600	2,420	4,386,090	3,039,800
Excess of revenues over (under) expenditures	151,300	17,675	27,397	(443,755)	(2,220)	(249,603)	2,000
Other financing sources (uses)							
Proceeds of general obligation bonds	—	—	—	900,000	—	900,000	—
Operating transfers in	—	—	—	74,500	2,530	77,030	89,120
Operating transfers out	(74,500)	—	—	—	—	(74,500)	(87,000)
Total other financing sources (uses)	(74,500)	—	—	974,500	2,530	902,530	2,120
Excess of revenues and other sources over (under) expenditures and other uses	76,800	17,675	27,397	530,745	310	652,927	4,120
Fund Balances—January 1	202,500	151,035	182,813	650,425	26,555	1,213,328	1,209,208
Fund Balances—December 31	$ 279,300	$ 168,710	$210,210	$1,181,170	$26,865	$1,866,255	$1,213,328

The notes to the financial statements are an integral part of this statement.

Exhibit 24.4.   Combined statement of revenues, expenditures, and changes in fund balances—all governmental fund types and expendable trust funds.

NAME OF GOVERNMENTAL UNIT
Combined Statement of Revenues, Expenditures, and Changes in Fund Balances—Budget and Actual—
General and Special Revenue Fund Types
for the Fiscal Year Ended December 31, 19X2

	General Fund			Special Revenue Funds			Totals (Memorandum Only)		
	Budget	Actual	Variance—Favorable (Unfavorable)	Budget	Actual	Variance—Favorable (Unfavorable)	Budget	Actual	Variance—Favorable (Unfavorable)
Revenues									
Taxes	$ 882,500	$ 881,300	$ (1,200)	$ 189,500	$ 189,300	$ (200)	$1,072,000	1,070,600	$ (1,400)
Licenses and permits	125,500	103,000	(22,500)	—	—	—	125,500	103,000	(22,500)
Intergovernmental revenues	200,000	186,500	(13,500)	837,600	831,100	(6,500)	1,037,600	1,017,600	(20,000)
Charges for services	90,000	91,000	1,000	78,000	79,100	1,100	168,000	170,100	2,100
Fines and forfeits	32,500	33,200	700	—	—	—	32,500	33,200	700
Miscellaneous revenues	19,500	19,500	—	81,475	71,625	(9,850)	100,975	91,125	(9,850)
Total revenues	1,350,000	1,314,500	(35,500)	1,186,575	1,171,125	(15,450)	2,536,575	2,485,625	(50,950)
Expenditures									
Current:									
General government	129,000	121,805	7,195	—	—	—	129,000	121,805	7,195
Public safety	277,300	258,395	18,905	494,500	480,000	14,500	771,800	738,395	33,405
Highways and streets	84,500	85,400	(900)	436,000	417,000	19,000	520,500	502,400	18,100
Sanitation	50,000	56,250	(6,250)	—	—	—	50,000	56,250	(6,250)

Health	47,750	44,500	3,250	—	—	—	47,750	44,500	3,250
Welfare	51,000	46,800	4,200	—	—	—	51,000	46,800	4,200
Culture and recreation	44,500	40,900	3,600	272,000	256,450	15,550	316,500	297,350	19,150
Education	541,450	509,150	32,300	—	—	—	541,450	509,150	32,300
Total expenditures	1,225,500	1,163,200	62,300	1,202,500	1,153,450	49,050	2,428,000	2,316,650	111,350
Excess of revenues over (under) expenditures	124,500	151,300	26,800	(15,925)	17,675	33,600	108,575	168,975	60,400
Other financing sources (uses)									
Operating transfers out	(74,500)	(74,500)	—	—	—	—	(74,500)	(74,500)	—
Excess of revenues over (under) expenditures and other uses	50,000	76,800	26,800	(15,925)	17,675	33,600	34,075	94,475	60,400
Fund Balances—January 1	202,500	202,500	—	151,035	151,035	—	353,535	353,535	—
Fund Balances—December 31	$252,500	$279,300	$26,800	$135,110	$168,710	$33,600	$387,610	$448,010	$60,400

The notes to the financial statements are an integral part of this statement.

Exhibit 24.5. Combined statement of revenues, expenditures, and changes in fund balances—budget and actual—general and special revenue fund types.

NAME OF GOVERNMENTAL UNIT
Combined Statement of Revenues, Expenses, and Changes in Retained Earnings/Fund Balances—All Proprietary Fund Types and Similar Trust Funds
for the Fiscal Year Ended December 31, 19X2
(With Comparative Totals for December 31, 19X1)

	Proprietary Fund Types		Fiduciary Fund Type		Totals (Memorandum Only) Year Ended	
	Enterprise	Internal Service	Nonexpendable Trust	Pension Trust	December 31, 19X2	December 31, 19X1
Operating Revenues						
Charges for services	$ 672,150	$88,000	$—	$—	$ 760,150	$ 686,563
Interest	—	—	2,480	28,460	30,940	26,118
Contributions	—	—	—	160,686	160,686	144,670
Gifts	—	—	45,000	—	45,000	—
Total operating revenues	672,150	88,000	47,480	189,146	996,766	857,351
Operating Expenses						
Personal services	247,450	32,500			279,950	250,418
Contractual services	75,330	400			75,730	68,214
Supplies	20,310	1,900			22,210	17,329
Materials	50,940	44,000			94,940	87,644
Heat, light, and power	26,050	1,500			27,550	22,975
Depreciation	144,100	4,450			148,550	133,210
Benefit payments	—	—		21,000	21,000	12,000
Refunds	—	—		25,745	25,745	13,243
Total operating expenses	564,180	84,750	—	46,745	695,675	605,033
Operating income	107,970	3,250	47,480	142,401	301,101	252,318

Nonoperating Revenues (Expenses)

Operating grants	55,000	—	—	—	55,000	50,000
Interest revenue	3,830	—	—	—	3,830	3,200
Rent	5,000	—	—	—	5,000	5,000
Interest expense and fiscal charges	(92,988)	—	—	—	(92,988)	(102,408)
Net nonoperating revenues (expenses)	(29,158)	—	—	—	(29,158)	(44,208)
Income before operating transfers	78,812	3,250	47,480	142,401	271,943	208,110
Operating transfers in (out)	—	—	(2,530)	—	(2,530)	(2,120)
Net income	78,812	3,250	44,950	142,401	269,413	205,990
Retained Earnings/Fund Balances— January 1	2,088,544	6,550	139,100	1,040,800	3,274,994	3,069,004
Retained Earnings/Fund Balances— December 31	$2,167,356	$9,800	$184,050	$1,183,201	$3,544,407	$3,274,994

The notes to the financial statements are an integral part of this statement.

Exhibit 24.6. Combined statement of revenues, expenses, and changes in retained earnings/fund balances— all proprietary and similar trust fund types.

CITY OF EXAMPLE, ANY STATE
Statement of Cash Flows—All Proprietary Fund Types and Nonexpendable Trust Funds
for the Year Ended December 31, 19X2
(With Comparative Totals for December 31, 19X2)

	Enterprise	Internal Service	Nonexpendable Trust	Totals (Memorandum Only) Year Ended	
				December 31, 19X2	December 31, 19X1
Cash Flows from Operating Activities					
Operating income	$107,970	$ 3,250	$47,480	$158,700	$161,688
Adjustments to Reconcile Operating Income to Net Cash Provided by Operating Activities:					
Depreciation	144,100	4,450	—	148,550	123,611
Change in Assests and Liabilities:					
Decrease in other current liabilities payable from restricted assets	(8,946)	—	—	(8,946)	(6,491)
Increase in other restricted assets	(1,624)	—	—	(1,624)	(1,554)
Decrease in accounts receivable	5,570	—	5,000	10,570	11,681
Increase in inventory of supplies	(11,250)	(14,000)	—	(25,250)	30,068
Increase in prepaid expenses	(460)	—	—	(460)	(540)
Decrease in due from other funds	6,000	8,000	—	14,000	11,000
Increase (decrease) in vouchers payable	72,471	(5,000)	—	67,471	74,868
Increase in other liabilities	12,160	—	—	12,160	18,888
Decrease in contracts payable	(551,653)	—	—	(551,653)	(631,168)
Total adjustments	(333,632)	(6,550)	5,000	(335,182)	(369,637)
Net cash provided (used) by operating activities	(225,662)	(3,300)	52,480	(176,482)	(207,949)

Cash Flows from Noncapital Financing Activities

Retirement of general obligation bonds	(50,000)	(50,000)	—	(50,000)
Interest expense and fiscal charges	(92,988)	(92,988)	—	(104,681)
Operating grants received	55,000	55,000	—	65,000
Operating transfers (to) from other funds	—	(2,530)	(2,530)	3,650
Repayment of advance from general fund	(10,000)	(10,000)	—	(15,000)
Net cash used for noncapital financing activities	(87,988)	(100,518)	(2,530)	(101,031)

Cash Flows from Capital and Related Financing Activities:

Acquisition and construction of capital assets	(324,453)	(331,453)	(7,000)	(285,611)
Proceeds from sale of revenue bonds	127,883	127,883	—	143,344
Retirement on revenue bonds payable	(52,000)	(52,000)	—	(58,000)
Capital contributed by subdividers	672,666	672,666	—	701,168
Rent	5,000	5,000	—	10,000
Net Cash provided (used) by capital and related financing activities	429,096	422,096	(7,000)	510,901

Cash Flows from Investing Activities:

Purchase of investment securities	—	(46,640)	(46,640)	(41,118)
Proceeds from sale and maturities of investment securities	—	1,000	1,000	2,000
Interest and dividends on investments	3,830	3,830	—	4,450
Net cash provided (used) by investing activities	3,830	(41,810)	(45,640)	(34,668)
Net Increase (Decrease) in Cash and Cash Equivalents	119,276	103,286	4,310	167,253
Cash and Cash Equivalents at Beginning of Year	137,760	200,151	12,391	32,898
Cash and Cash Equivalents at End of Year	$257,036	$303,437	$16,701	$200,151

Exhibit 24.7. Statement of cash flows—all proprietary fund types and nonexpendable trust funds.

in the combined statement of revenues, expenditures, and changes in fund balances—budget and actual—general and special revenue fund types.

- *Combined statement of revenues, expenses, and changes in retained earnings—all proprietary fund types and similar trust funds.*

The format for this statement should be as follows:

    Operating revenues
− Operating expenses
       Operating income (loss)

± Nonoperating revenues (expenses)
       Income before operating transfers
± Operating transfers from (to) other funds
       Net income (loss) before extraordinary items
± Extraordinary items
    Net income (loss)

+ Retained earnings—beginning of period
    Retained earnings—end of period

Bond proceeds are not reported in the statement of revenues, expenses, and changes in retained earnings—all proprietary fund types.

Contributed capital represents a contribution of permanent equity capital, not revenue. Hence it is not reported in the statement of revenues, expenses, and changes in retained earnings—all proprietary fund types. Instead, an analysis of activity in the contributed capital account is presented in a note to the financial statements.

If the governmental unit has several enterprise funds involved in diverse activities, the information concerning the individual activities should be segmented in a note to the financial statements. Enterprise fund segment disclosures are required if (1) material long-term liabilities are outstanding, (2) the disclosures provide essential assurance that the GPFS are not misleading, or (3) the disclosures are necessary to assure interperiod comparability.

- *Combined statement of cash flows—all proprietary and nonexpendable trust fund types.*

This statement can be presented on either the direct or indirect method of reporting cash flows. The statement should report net cash provided or used in each of the four categories (operating, investing, capital and related financing, and noncapital financing), as well as the net effect of those flows on cash and cash equivalents during the period in a manner that reconciles beginning and ending cash and cash equivalents.

A comprehensive listing of required footnote disclosures can be found in GASB Codification § 2300. However, typical notes for a government's financial report may provide such disclosures as:

- Summary of significant accounting policies.
- Cash and investments.
- Property taxes.
- Long-term debt and debt refundings.
- Leases.
- Fixed assets.
- Encumbrances.

- Pensions.
- Budget basis of accounting and budget/GAAP reconciliation.
- Deficits in funds and individual fund interfund payables and receivables.
- Segment information.
- Legal violations.
- Commitments and contingencies.
- Litigations.
- Subsequent events.
- Related party transactions.
- Joint ventures.

The summary of significant accounting policies note should contain, among other things, the following items:

- A brief description of the governmental unit and its form of government.
- Criteria used to determine the scope of the reporting entity.
- Identification of any associated governmental units included in the reporting entity or excluded from the entity.
- Basis of presentation.
- Identification and description of the funds maintained by the governmental unit.
- Basis of accounting, including the manner in which the susceptible to accrual concept is applied to the major revenue classification.
- Policies for establishing the budgets.
- Description of encumbrance accounting if used and identification of the funds using encumbrance accounting.
- Investment valuation policy.
- Definition of cash and cash equivalents.
- Inventory valuation policy.
- Fixed assets valuation policy.
- Depreciation policy.
- Lease capitalization policy.
- Interest capitalization policy.
- Infrastructure capitalization policy.
- Basis for the establishment of reserves.
- Vacation and sick leave policy.
- Meaning and nature of any unusual accounts.

Required supplementary information (RSI) should be disclosed as part of the GPFS for governmental employers participating in defined benefit single-employer or agent multiple-employer pension plans and for the financial statements of PERS. Also, certain RSI should be disclosed for risk financing and certain insurance-related activities of state and local government entities. RSI differs from other types of information ouside the basic financial statements because the GASB considers the information an essential part of the financial reporting of certain entities and because authoritative guidelines for the measurement and presentation of the information have been established.

(b) Comprehensive Annual Financial Report.   The **comprehensive annual financial report** (CAFR) differs from the GPFS in the level of detail and the quantity of data presented. The additional data are *not* necessary for fair presentation of financial position or results of operation in accordance with GAAP, but they are useful and informative for certain readers of a government's financial report. Furthermore, the CAFR may be the vehicle for providing the necessary information for fulfilling the legal and other disclosure requirements of higher levels of government, bondholders, and similar groups. It is also useful in demonstrating management's stewardship responsibilities since alongside the comparative budgets, it presents in more detail the use of the available resources.

The recommended contents of the CAFR includes:

- Introductory section.
  Title page. Contains the title "Comprehensive Annual Financial Report," (or "Component Unit Financial Report"), the name of the governmental unit, the period of time covered, and the names of the principal government officials.
  Table of contents. Identifies the presence and location of each item included in the report.
  Transmittal letter. From the government's chief finance officer (or CEO), providing significant aspects of financial operations during the period. The letter may include, for example, changes in financial policies; discussion of internal controls; changes in operating results or expected revenues, expenditures, and debt; significant elements of financial management including cash and risk management; financial problems encountered; budget procedures and current budget; and a preview of the significant developments or changes contemplated in the coming year including economic conditions, outlook, and major initiatives.
  Certificate of Achievement for Excellence in Financial Reporting. If a certificate was awarded from the GFOA for the previous year's CAFR, a reproduction of that certificate should be included in the introductory section.
- Financial section.
  Independent auditor's report.
  General purpose financial statements. Includes all required financial statements and related notes as previously described.
  Combining financial statements. Used when a governmental unit has more than one fund of a given type.
  Individual fund financial statements. Used when this information is not provided in a separate column in a combining statement or it is desirable to present a level of detail that would be excessive for the GPFS or the combining statements. Examples are detail comparisons to budgets that cannot be reflected on the combining statements, comparative data for prior years, or a demonstration of an individual fund's compliance with legal provisions.
  Required supplementary information. Included when disclosure is required by employers and PERS or public risk pools.
  Schedules necessary to demonstrate compliance. Included when such are required by state law or by a bond covenant.
  Other schedules desired by the government. Used for reporting particular kinds of information that are spread throughout the numerous financial statements and that can be brought together and presented in greater detail than in the individual statements, or that show the details of a specific amount or amounts presented in the GPFS, the combining statements, or the individual fund financial statements.
- Statistical section.
  Statistical tables cover a period of several years and contain data drawn from more than just the accounting records. Their purpose is to present social, economic, and financial

trends, and the fiscal capacity of the governmental unit. The following titles indicate recommended statistical tables for a local government's comprehensive annual financial report:

General Governmental Expenditures by Function—Most Recent 10 Fiscal Years.

General Revenues by Source—Most Recent 10 Fiscal Years.

Property Tax Levies and Collections—Most Recent 10 Fiscal Years.

Assessed and Estimated Actual Value of Taxable Property—Most Recent 10 Fiscal Years.

Property Tax Rates-All Overlapping Governments—Most Recent 10 Fiscal Years.

Special Assessment Billings and Collections—Most Recent 10 Fiscal Years.

Ratio of Net General Bonded Debt to Assessed Value and Net Bonded Debt Per Capita—Most Recent 10 Fiscal Years.

Computation of Legal Debt Margin (if not in GPFS).

Computation of Overlapping Debt (if not in GPFS).

Ratio of Annual Debt Service Expenditures for General Bonded Debt to Total General Government Expenditures—Most Recent 10 Fiscal Years.

Revenue Bond Coverage—Most Recent 10 Fiscal Years.

Demographic Statistics.

Property Values, Construction, and Bank Deposits—Most Recent 10 Fiscal Years.

Principal Taxpayers.

Miscellaneous Statistics.

- Single Audit Section.

Although not a required part of a CAFR, it is becoming increasingly popular to include in a separate section the information, including auditor's reports, required by the Single Audit Act of 1984.

(c) Certificate of Achievement Program.   Governmental units may submit their CAFRs to the GFOA (180 North Michigan Avenue, Chicago, IL 60601) for evaluation in accordance with the standards of financial reporting established by the GASB and the GFOA. If the report substantially adheres to these standards, the government is awarded a **Certificate of Achievement for Excellence in Financial Reporting.** The certificate is only valid for one year. It may be reproduced in the government's annual report and should be included in the subsequent year's CAFR. Annually, the GFOA publishes a list of the governments that hold valid certificates.

Many governments endeavor to obtain the certificate. They realize that credit rating agencies and others familiar with governmental accounting and financial reporting recognize that governments holding a certificate typically maintain complete financial records and effectively report their financial information to permit detail analyses to be performed. This characteristic can improve the government's bond rating.

(d) Popular Reports.   Governments also prepare **popular reports** to communicate with persons who are neither interested in a complete set of financial statements or able to review them. Popular reports, also called **condensed summary data,** are at the top of the financial reporting "pyramid."

There are three types of popular reports. The first is an aggregation of the data from the financial statements that disregards the distinction among fund types and account groups and the different bases of accounting and presents the data as if all the assets, liabilities, equities, revenues, and expenditures (expenses) pertain, not to the fund types, but to the government as a whole. This results in a presentation similar to that made by corporations and their subsidiaries. In such cases, the government usually eliminates significant interfund transactions before arriving at totals.

The second approach is to visually present the entity's financial information, for instance, by using pie charts or bar graphs. A common presentation is to present one pie to show the composition of revenue by cutting the pie into slices with each slice representing a major revenue source. The size of the slice would reflect the magnitude of the respective revenue source. Similar pie charts can be used to show the major categories of expenditures, the major categories of assets, and the major categories of liabilities.

The third approach, taken by a few governments, is to issue consolidated financial statements, similar to those proposed by the AICPA in a project on experimental financial reporting. Such a consolidated approach replaces the funds and account groups by a single "fund" that is used to report the financial position and results of operations of the entire oversight unit or reporting entity. Intragovernmental transactions are eliminated in the consolidation process and a single basis of accounting (normally accrual) is used for all transactions.

Consolidated financial statements typically include a balance sheet, operating statement, and statement of cash flows. Because the accrual basis of accounting is normally used, fixed assets are reported in the single fund and depreciated. Also, long-term obligations are reported in the single fund, with the result that debt service principal payments are treated as balance sheet rather than operating statement transactions.

GRANT ACCOUNTING

24.20 DEFINITIONS.   A **grant** is a contribution or gift of cash, or other assets from another government to be used or expended for a specified purpose, activity, or facility. Some grants are restricted by the grantor for the acquisition or construction of fixed assets. These are **capital grants.** All other grants are **operating grants.**

An **entitlement** is the amount of payment to which a government is entitled pursuant to an allocation formula contained in applicable statutes. A **shared revenue** is a revenue levied by one government but shared on a predetermined basis with another government. Grants, entitlements, and shared revenues have become major sources of revenues for governments. Frequently, however, special accounting and reporting requirements are associated with these grants.

24.21 FUND IDENTIFICATION.   All grants, entitlements, and shared revenues should be accounted for in one of the seven fund types. The identity of the fund should be based on the purpose or requirements of the grant. For instance, grants, entitlements, or shared revenues received for purposes normally financed through the general fund may be accounted for within that fund, provided that applicable legal requirements can be appropriately satisfied. Resources received for the payment of principal or interest on general long-term debt may be accounted for in a debt service fund. Capital grants or shared revenues received for capital acquisitions or construction, other than those associated with enterprise and internal service funds, may be accounted for in a capital projects fund. However, it is not always necessary to establish a separate fund for an individual grant, entitlement, or shared revenue. Existing funds should be used to the extent possible in order to comply with the minimal number of funds principle.

If a grant, entitlement, or shared revenue may be used for more than one purpose and the recipient has not determined the purposes for which it intends to use the funds, the resources may be accounted for in an agency fund pending determination of their use. When the determination is made, the assets and revenues should be recognized in the appropriate fund and removed from the agency fund. Since most grants, entitlements, or shared revenues are either unrestricted as to purpose or restricted to a specific purpose, there is seldom a need to use an agency fund.

24.22 REVENUE AND EXPENDITURE (EXPENSE) RECOGNITION.   Grants, entitlements, and shared revenues recorded in governmental funds should be recognized as revenue when they become susceptible to accrual, that is, measurable and available. Legal and contractual requirements should be carefully reviewed. If the restriction is more form than substance, revenue should be recognized at the time of receipt or earlier. If the grant is earned by the recipient government as funds are expended for a specific restricted purpose, revenue should be recognized when the expenditures are made for that purpose. The latter are called **"expenditure-driven" grants.**

Grants, entitlements, and shared revenues received before the revenue recognition criteria are met should be reported as deferred revenue and reported as a liability account in the government's financial statements. Resources not received should be reported as a receivable if the revenue recognition criteria have been met. If the resources have not been received and the revenue recognition criteria have not been met, the grants should not be reported on the balance sheet at all. They may, however, be disclosed in the notes to the financial statements.

Grants, entitlements, and shared revenues that are received by a proprietary fund for operating purposes, or that may be used for operations or capital purposes at the discretion of the recipient government, should be recognized as nonoperating revenue when earned. Resources restricted to the acquisition or construction of capital assets should be recorded as contributed capital.

Operating expenses should include depreciation on all depreciable fixed assets, including assets acquired with contributed capital. Depreciation recognized on assets acquired or constructed with contributed capital may be charged to the contributed capital account by "adding back" the depreciation on such assets to net income before closing it to retained earnings.

AUDITS OF GOVERNMENTAL UNITS

Audits of governmental units with financial statements can be performed in accordance with:

- Generally accepted auditing standards (GAAS).
- *Government Auditing Standards* (the "Yellow Book").
- The Single Audit Act of 1984 and OMB Circular A-128.

When performing an audit in accordance with GAAS, the guidance contained in the *AICPA Professional Standards* (AICPA 1989) is followed. This is the same guidance followed by auditors when auditing the financial statement of commercial entities and typically results in the issuance of an opinion of the financial statements and perhaps a management letter. *Government Auditing Standards,* also known as the "Yellow Book" (U.S. Comptroller General, rev. 1988), establishes the concept of an expanded scope audit that includes both financial and compliance features. According to the Yellow Book, a financial audit can help determine whether:

1. The financial statements of an audited entity present fairly the financial position and the results of financial operations in accordance with GAAP.
2. The entity has complied with laws and regulations that may have a material effect on the financial statements.

The Yellow Book incorporates the AICPA Professional Standards mentioned above and sets forth additional standards and requirements, including the following:

1. A review is to be made of compliance with applicable laws and regulations, as set forth in federal audit guides and other applicable reference sources.
2. Either the auditor's reports on the entity's financial statements or a separate report shall contain a statement of positive assurance on those items of compliance tested and negative assurance on those items not tested. It shall also include material instances of noncompliance and instances or indications of illegal acts found during or in connection with the audit.
3. The auditors shall report on their consideration of the entity's internal control structure made as part of the financial audit.

   They shall identify as a minimum:
   a. Scope of auditor's work in obtaining an understanding of the internal control structure and assessing risk.
   b. The entity's significant internal accounting controls or control structures including those established to ensure compliance with laws and regulations.
   c. The reportable conditions including separate identification of material weaknesses identified as a result of the auditor's work.
4. Auditors performing government audits are required to obtain 80 hours of continuing education every 2 years, of which 24 hours should be directly related to government. At least 20 of the 80 hours should be completed in each year of the 2-year period.
5. Audit organizations performing government audits are required to establish an internal quality control system and participate in an external quality control review program.

The revisions to the Yellow Book including those listed above became effective for *audits conducted* after January 1, 1989.

24.23 THE SINGLE AUDIT ACT OF 1984.   As a result of the Single Audit Act of 1984, many state and local governments are required to obtain a periodic audit of the federal funds they receive—usually once a year. The audits are normally performed by an independent CPA or public accountant, or, in some states, by the government's internal audit personnel. A few jurisdictions have an independently elected or appointed auditor who conducts the audit. Single audits are conducted in accordance with GAAS, *Government Auditing Standards,* and the Single Audit Act and its implementing legislation, OMB Circular A-128.

The objectives of the Act are:

- To improve the financial management of state and local governments with respect to federal financial assistance programs through improved auditing.
- To establish uniform requirements for audits of federal financial assistance provided to state and local governments.
- To promote the efficient and effective use of audit resources.
- To ensure that federal departments and agencies, to the maximum extent practicable, rely on and use audit work performed pursuant to the requirements of the Single Audit Act.

Though the single audit builds on the annual financial statement audit currently required by most state and larger local governments, it places substantial additional emphasis on the consideration and testing of internal controls and the testing of compliance with laws and regulations.

The Single Audit Act and OMB Circular A-128 require the auditor to determine whether:

- The financial statements of the government, department, agency, or establishment present fairly its financial position and the results of operations in conformity with GAAP.
- The organization has internal and other control structures to provide reasonable assurance that it is managing federal financial assistance programs in compliance with applicable laws and regulations.
- The organization has complied with laws and regulations that may have a material effect on its financial statements and on each major federal financial assistance program.

The governmental units that are subject to single audits include those that *receive* $100,000 or more of federal financial assistance in any fiscal year. If a government receives between $25,000 and $100,000 of federal assistance, the entity has the option of having a single audit or separate grant audits performed. For those governments receiving less than $25,000 in assistance, there is an exemption from the Single Audit Act requirements.

The Single Audit Act provides auditors with guidance on the focus of the audit by defining a level of audit work based on the concept of "major" and "nonmajor" federal assistance programs. Major programs (not grants) are typically the larger programs in which an entity participates and are determined on a sliding scale by the relationship between the expenditures of the program and the total federal expenditures of the entity. For most small and medium-sized governments a major program is defined as the larger of $300,000 or 3% of the total federal *expenditures* for all federal programs with expenditures for all programs are less than or equal to $100 million.

For larger governments whose total federal expenditures exceed $100 million, the Single Audit Act defines a major federal financial assistance program based on a sliding scale.

The Single Audit Act and OMB Circular A-128 require the auditor to issue several reports:

For the entity:
- A report on the audit of the general purpose or basic financial statements of the entity as a whole, or the department, agency, or establishment covered by the audit.
- A report on internal control based on an understanding and assessment of the internal control structure obtained as a part of the audit of the general purpose or basic financial statements.
- A report on compliance with laws and regulations that may have a material effect on the financial statements.

For its federal financial assistance programs:
- A report on a supplementary schedule of the entity's federal financial assistance programs, showing total expenditures for each federal assistance program.
- A report on compliance with laws and regulations identifying all findings of non-compliance and questioned costs.
- A report on internal control structure used in administering federal financial assistance programs.
- A report on fraud, abuse, or an illegal act, or indications of such acts, when discovered (a written report is required); normally, such reports are issued separately.

24.24 OTHER CONSIDERATIONS.   Most government officials and auditors of governmental units realize that a good audit should furnish more than an opinion on the financial statements. Other services a governmental auditor can provide are pinpointing the key information upon which decisions should be based and contributing to the presentation of this information in a manner that facilitates decision making; uncovering deficiencies in the accounting system and providing suggestions for improving the efficiency and effectiveness of the system; and obtaining and presenting information useful for marketing securities.

Obtaining a qualified auditor, particularly one who can provide the additional services described above, requires that the selection be based on qualifications and experience, and not solely cost. The National Intergovernmental Audit Forum in its handbook "How to Avoid a Substandard Audit: Suggestions for Procuring an Audit," indicates:

> Public entities should never select auditors without considering five basic elements of an effective audit procurement process:
>
> - planning (determining what needs to be done and when),
> - fostering competition by soliciting proposals (writing a clear and direct solicitation document and disseminating it widely),
> - technically evaluating proposals and qualifications (authorizing a committee of knowledgeable persons to evaluate the ability of prospective auditors to effectively carry out the audit),
> - preparing a written agreement (documenting the expectations of both the entity and the auditor), and
> - monitoring the auditor's performance (periodically reviewing the progress of that performance).

This handbook provides detailed information about the five elements of procurement listed above as well as the use of audit committees in a government environment and other useful information about the auditor procurement process.

(a) Governmental Rotation of Auditors. The **automatic rotation of auditors** after a given number of years is a common practice in many governments; however, it is not always beneficial. Many governments have followed this policy, believing that they will (1) receive a fresh outlook from the audit, (2) spread the work among several firms, and (3) encourage lower fees. In actuality, automatic rotation may be harmful in that it could deprive the government of the extensive knowledge of the entity developed by the current auditor. It may also impair auditing effectiveness since a new auditor may need to spend considerable time learning the government's system—the government may actually incur more cost since its personnel will need to spend time explaining the organization, systems, and data to the new auditors, and the new auditors will need to spend valuable time reviewing information that is already part of the previous auditor's workpapers. Although a government should continuously monitor its auditor's performance to assure that the service obtained is commensurate with the cost, the entity should normally change auditors only because of dissatisfaction with services and not for the sake of receiving a lower fee.

(b) Audit Committees. In recent years, governments have started establishing **audit committees** similar to those in the private sector. Some appropriate tasks for a local government's audit committee are:

- Reviewing significant financial information for reliability, timeliness, clarity, appropriateness of disclosure, and compliance with GAAP and legal requirements.
- Ascertaining that the internal control structure is appropriately designed and functioning effectively.
- Evaluating independent audit firms and selecting one for approval by the appropriate body.
- Overseeing the scope and performance of the independent audit function.
- Ensuring that the auditors' recommendations for improvements in internal controls and operating methods receive management's attention and are implemented on a timely basis.

- Providing an effective communications link between the auditors and the full governing board.

The primary benefit of an audit committee is in assisting the full governing board to fulfill its responsibilities for the presentation of financial information about the governmental unit. There are also secondary benefits: The other parties involved in the issuance of financial information—management and independent and internal auditors—can perform their roles more effectively if an audit committee is involved in the process. Finally, there are advantages for the government's constituencies—in particular, the taxpayers and bond-holders.

PROPOSED CHANGES AND OTHER MATTERS

24.25 MEASUREMENT FOCUS AND BASIS OF ACCOUNTING.   Although the strides made by governmental accounting and reporting over the past 10 years have been great, the next 10 years should bring even further changes. The GASB recently issued a Statement entitled "Measurement Focus and Basis of Accounting—Governmental Fund Operating Statements" (MFBA) that will begin to significantly change governmental accounting and reporting. The Statement establishes new measurement focus and basis of accounting standards for governmental fund types and expendable trust funds.

The Statement mandates the use of the flow of financial resources measurement focus for reporting governmental and expendable trust fund operating results, and accordingly, the operating results will measure the extent to which financial resources obtained during a period were sufficient to cover claims incurred during that period against those financial resources. Financial resources are cash, claims to cash (for example, debt securities of another entity account and taxes receivable), claims to goods or services (for example, prepaid items), consumable goods (for example, supplies inventories), and equity securities of another entity obtained or controlled as a result of past transactions or events. Additionally this measurement focus will employ an accrual basis of accounting rather than the modified accrual basis described in section 24.16 of this chapter. This change will result in transactions or events that affect financial resources being recognized when they take place, regardless of when cash is received or paid. The GASB is using an accrual basis of accounting in order to properly measure interperiod equity and believes that such a measure is important to the users of governmental financial statements because its computation and presentation will allow users to determine whether revenues were raised in an amount sufficient to pay for the services provided.

By employing the flow of financial resources measurement focus and accrual basis of accounting revenues, operating expenditures and interfund operating and residual equity transfers are recorded in the operating statement when the transactions or events that affect financial resources occur. For certain revenue sources such as property taxes, the amounts recognized will typically increase as a result of MFBA since the "60-day" would no longer apply.

Sales and income tax revenue will generally *increase*. The origin of the increase is the fact that taxes due within the fiscal year or within 2 months after the fiscal year (if administrative lead time is built into the tax calendar) and certain delinquent taxes will be recorded as revenue. Currently sales and income taxes are often recorded as revenue on a modified cash basis. Cash received during the fiscal year is recognized as revenue as are taxes due or received after the fiscal year that relate to the current fiscal period. Because the Statement allows slight variations of the revenue calculation for different taxes, the overall revenue increase or decrease needs to be assessed for each government based on the types of revenue sources the government has and the availability of accrual information.

Expenditures can be expected to increase under the provisions of MFBA. This increase will result from the accrual of costs currently accounted for on essentially a cash basis (i.e., compensated absences and other similar operating expenditures). Although MFBA omits specific accounting guidance with respect to certain controversial expenditures (i.e., pension expenditures) the general guidance in the Statement will be applicable. Therefore, it should be expected that pensions, postretirement benefits and the like will be recorded on the accrual basis and result in an increase in reported expenditures. As with revenues, the precise impact of the change in expenditure recognition will depend greatly on the individual government.

The acquisition, disposition, and long-term financing of capital assets and the long-term financing of certain nonrecurring projects or activities that have long-term economic benefit will continue to be recorded in the operating statement when transactions that affect financial resources occur. However, the long-term debt financing of operations will *not* be reported in the operating statement as a transaction affecting financial resources as is currently allowed. This means that the proceeds of operating debt will not be reported in the operating statement, and fund balance will no longer be increased as a result of issuing debt used to finance operations.

24.26 OTHER ISSUES AT THE GASB.   The GASB is dealing with many other issues that require resolution including the presentation of capital assets in the financial statements. The usefulness of the information currently presented is being examined to determine whether it is appropriate. Information being considered for disclosure includes fixed asset capacity, replacement cost, maintenance cost, age, and other items that would enable users to determine the physical condition of a government's fixed assets. In a related project, the GASB is examining the presentation of capital assets and related capital financing activities. Suggested presentations range from maintaining the current presentation (i.e., retaining separate fund types for capital projects and debt service, and retaining the GLTDAG and GFAAG) to combining the capital projects fund, debt service fund, GFAAG and GLTDAG into one fund. Since this project is still in the early stages, no single presentation has wide-ranging support.

The GASB is also dealing with projects covering pension accounting for employers (discussed earlier), compensated absences, service efforts and accomplishments, and others.

24.27 AUDIT QUALITY.   Perhaps one of the hottest topics in the government industry today is audit quality. The results of recent GAO studies of the quality of audits of government units have indicated that audit fieldwork and reporting were deficient in a significant number of audit engagements. Because the auditor is one defense mechanism against improper spending of federal funds, the GAO looks unfavorably on auditors who are performing substandard work and has taken steps to alleviate the problem. *Government Auditing Standards* includes a requirement for auditors performing government audits to meet minimum continuing professional education requirements and for auditing firms to have independent quality control reviews at least once every 3 years.

24.28 SUMMARY.   Governmental accounting and reporting is changing and expanding at an increasing rapid rate. Coupling this with public accountability issues, the federal government's pressure for increased audit quality, and the penalties for substandard audit performance results in increasing levels of audit risk. Government audits, often considered low-risk engagements by many, are quickly becoming areas of extremely high risk. Auditing professionals need to recognize the risk associated with government engagements now and in the future before incurring severe penalties or embarrassment. The technical issues involved in government auditing are on a par with those in the commercial environment but auditors have much less experience and less technical guidance to fall back on.

Dealing with these technical issues requires well-trained, highly motivated individuals and can no longer be left to less experienced members of the audit team. Dealing with the *real* issues governments are facing (e.g., infrastructure, AIDS, prison overcrowding, drugs, etc.)

requires even more from the individuals in the profession. Like it or not, government accounting and reporting is being thrust into the spotlight and will be scrutinized by a multitude of individuals and groups. It is imperative that individuals in the industry realize this fact and begin now to prepare for the future.

APPENDIX 24.1: PRONOUNCEMENTS ON STATE AND LOCAL GOVERNMENT ACCOUNTING

Governmental Accounting Standard Board		*Effective Date*
Statement No. 1	Authoritative Status of NCGA Pronouncements and AICPA Industry Audit Guide	On issuance (7/84)
Statement No. 2	Financial Reporting of Deferred Compensation Plans Adopted under the Provisions of Internal Revenue Code Section 457	Financial statements for periods ending after 2/15/86
Statement No. 3	Deposits with Financial Institutions, Investments (including Repurchase Agreements), and Reverse Repurchase Agreements	Financial statements for periods ending after 2/15/86
Statement No. 4	Applicability of FASB Statement No. 87, "Employers' Accounting for Pensions," to State and Local Governmental Employers	On issuance (9/86)
Statement No. 5	Disclosure of Pension Information by Public Employee Retirement Systems and State and Local Governmental Employers	Financial reports issued for fiscal years beginning after 12/15/86
Statement No. 6	Accounting and Financial Reporting for Special Assessments	Financial statements for periods beginning after 6/15/87
Statement No. 7	Advance Refundings Resulting in Defeasance of Debt	Fiscal periods beginning after 12/15/86
Statement No. 8	Applicability of FASB Statement No. 93, Recognition of Depreciation by Not-for-Profit Organizations, to Certain State and Local Governmental Entities	Fiscal periods beginning after 5/15/87
Statement No. 9	Reporting Cash Flows of Proprietary and Nonexpendable Trust Funds and Governmental Entries, that use Proprietary Fund Accounting	Fiscal periods beginning after 12/15/89
Statement No. 10	Accounting and Financial Reporting for Risk Financing and Related Insurance Issues	Pools—Fiscal periods beginning after 6/15/90 Other—Fiscal periods beginning after 6/15/93
Statement No. 11	Measurement Focus and Basis of Accounting—Governmental Fund Operating Statements	Fiscal periods beginning after 6/15/94
Statement No. 12	Disclosure of Information on Postemployment Benefits Other than Pension Benefits by State and Local Governmental Employers	Fiscal periods beginning after 6/15/90

Governmental Accounting Standard Board—Continued		*Effective Date*
Statement No. 13	Accounting for Operating Leases with Scheduled Rent Increases	Leases with terms beginning after 6/30/90
Interpretation No. 1	Demand Bonds Issued by State and Local Governmental Entities	Fiscal periods ending after 6/15/85
Technical Bulletin No. 84-1	Purpose and Scope of GASB Technical Bulletins and Procedures for Issuance	None
Technical Bulletin No. 87-1	Applying Paragraph 66 of GASB Statement 3	On issuance (1/87)
Concepts Statement No. 1	Objectives of Financial Reporting	None

National Council on Governmental Accounting		*Effective Date*
Statement 1	Governmental Accounting and Financial Reporting Principles	Fiscal years ending after 6/30/80
Statement 2	Grant, Entitlement, and Shared Revenue Accounting by State and Local Governments	Fiscal years ending after 6/30/80
Statement 3	Defining the Governmental Reporting Entity	Prospectively for fiscal years ending after 12/31/82
Statement 4	Accounting and Financial Reporting Principles for Claims and Judgments and Compensated Absences	Fiscal years beginning after 12/31/82; ¶20 extended indefinitely by NCGAI 11
Statement 5	Accounting and Financial Reporting Principles for Lease Agreements of State and Local Governments	Fiscal years beginning after 6/30/83
Statement 6	Pension Accounting and Financial Reporting: Public Employee Retirement Systems and State and Local Government Employers	Extended indefinitely by NCGAI 8
Statement 7	Financial Reporting for Component Units Within the Governmental Reporting Entity	Prospectively for fiscal years ending after 6/30/84
Interpretation 1	GAAFR and the AICPA Audit Guide (Superseded)	Issued 4/86; superseded by NCGAS 1
Interpretation 2	Segment Information for Enterprise Funds	Prospectively for fiscal years ending after 9/30/80
Interpretation 3	Revenue Recognition—Property Taxes	Fiscal years beginning after 9/30/81
Interpretation 4	Accounting and Financial Reporting for Public Employee Retirement Systems and Pension Trust Funds (Superseded)	Fiscal years beginning after 6/15/82; superseded by NCGAS 6 and repealed by NCGAI 8
Interpretation 5	Authoritative Status of Governmental Accounting, Auditing, and Financial Reporting (1968)	On issuance (3/82)
Interpretation 6	Notes to the Financial Statements Disclosure	Prospectively for fiscal years beginning after 12/31/82

National Council on Governmental Accounting—Continued		*Effective Date*
Interpretation 7	Clarification as to the Application of the Criteria in NCGA Statement 3. "Defining the Governmental Reporting Entity"	On Issuance (9/83)
Interpretation 8	Certain Pension Matters	Fiscal years ending after 12/31/83
Interpretation 9	Certain Fund Classifications and Balance Sheet Accounts	Fiscal years ending after 6/30/84
Interpretation 10	State and Local Government Budgetary Reporting	Fiscal years ending after 6/30/84
Interpretation 11	Claim and Judgment Transactions for Governmental Funds	On issuance (4/84)

GASB Exposure Drafts Outstanding 6/11/90

Accounting for Pensions by State and Local Government Employers

The Financial Reporting Entity

SOURCES AND SUGGESTED REFERENCES

American Institute of Certified Public Accountants, APB Opinion No. 26, "Early Extinguishment of Debt," AICPA, New York, 1972.

———, "Audits of State and Local Government Units," Industry Audit and Accounting Guide, AICPA, New York, 1986.

———, "AICPA Professional Standards," AICPA, New York, 1989.

Financial Accounting Standards Board, "Classification of Short-Term Obligations Expected to Be Refinanced," Statement of Financial Accounting Standards No. 6, FASB, Stamford, CT, 1975.

———, "Accounting for Leases," Statement of Financial Accounting Standards Board No. 13, FASB, Stamford, CT, 1975.

———, "Objectives of Financial Reporting by Nonbusiness Organizations," Statement of Financial Accounting Concepts No. 4, FASB, Stamford, CT, 1980.

General Accounting Office, "Government Auditing Standards," GAO, Washington, DC, 1988.

Governmental Accounting Standards Board, "Codification of Governmental Accounting and Financial Reporting Standards," GASB, Stamford, CT, 1987.

Government Finance Officers Association, "Governmental Accounting, Auditing and Financial Reporting," GFOA, Chicago, IL, 1988. (Study guide available)

CHAPTER 25

NOT-FOR-PROFIT ORGANIZATIONS

William Warshauer, Jr., CPA
Price Waterhouse

Richard F. Larkin, CPA
Price Waterhouse

CONTENTS

The authors wish to acknowledge that the exhibits and inspiration for this work were derived from the work *Financial and Accounting Guide for Nonprofit Organizations*, by Price Waterhouse partners Malvern J. Gross, Jr., and William Warshauer, Jr. (John Wiley & Sons, New York, 1983).

THE NOT-FOR-PROFIT ACCOUNTING ENVIRONMENT

Not-for-profit organizations range from the large and complex to the small and simple. They include hospitals, colleges and universities, voluntary social service organizations, religious organizations, associations, foundations, and cultural institutions. All are confronted with accounting and reporting challenges. All are presently covered by authoritative accounting literature. This chapter discusses not-for-profit accounting and reporting conventions and examines accounting pronouncements, auditing concerns, and the regulatory environment applicable to different types of not-for-profit organizations.

25.1 RECENT CHANGES IN ACCOUNTING PRINCIPLES.   Not-for-profit accounting is undergoing a period of profound change. In the recent past, authoritative accounting principles and reporting practices have been established for many not-for-profit organizations that previously had neither.

In 1972, the AICPA issued an Industry Audit Guide for hospitals. In 1973, an Industry Audit Guide for colleges and universities was issued. And in 1974, a third not-for-profit Industry Audit Guide, for voluntary health and welfare organizations, was issued.

In late 1978, the AICPA issued SOP No. 78-10, "Accounting Principles and Reporting Practices for Certain Nonprofit Organizations." SOP No. 78-10 defines accounting principles and reporting practices for all not-for-profit organizations **not** covered by earlier guides.

As the most current broad-scope pronouncement of the accounting profession on not-for-profit accounting, the SOP is the authoritative reference for not-for-profit accounting and reporting questions for the organizations covered, and it may be consulted for guidance by other organizations on questions not addressed in their respective audit guides.

In 1979, the FASB issued SFAS No. 32, which recognizes principles prescribed by AICPA Industry Audit Guides and Statements of Position as preferable when considering a change in accounting principles.

These guides and the SOP had a dramatic effect on not-for-profit accounting, as they represented the first authoritative attempt to codify accounting principles and reporting practices for the not-for-profit industry. However, inconsistencies exist among the four guides, and they frequently contradict one another on key accounting concepts. Also, the accounting principles presented in the guides have limited authority as they constitute GAAP only until formal standards are set on this subject by the FASB. Steps to relieve this confusion are currently in process.

By the early 1980s, persons interested in not-for-profit accounting issues had identified the following key areas of accounting that would have to be considered in unifying the diverse not-for-profit accounting practices.

- Reporting entity (when should controlled and affiliated organizations be included in an entity's financial statements?).
- Depreciation.
- Joint costs of multipurpose activities, particularly those involving a fundraising appeal (on what basis should such costs be divided among the various purposes served?).
- Revenue recognition for expendable/restricted receipts (when, in which fund, and how should such items be reported as revenue?).
- Display (what format should be used to present financial data?).
- Valuation of investments.
- Contributions (how should these be valued, when and how should they be reported?).
- Grants awarded to others (when should these be accrued and expensed by the grantor?).

Before accounting principles could be written, concepts had to be developed. The FASB had originally excluded not-for-profits from concepts development, but later started a separate project for not-for-profits. The first concepts statement under this project was issued in 1980. SFAC No. 4, "Objectives of Financial Reporting by Nonbusiness Organizations," proved to be so similar to the corresponding statement for businesses (SFAC No. 1) that the FASB started thinking in terms of only one set of concepts. Indeed, SFAC No. 2 was amended to include not-for-profits; SFAC No. 6 (Elements of Financial Statements) covers both types of entities, although some parts of this statement deal separately with the two sectors. The FASB is now beginning to develop accounting principles for the not-for-profit sector.

25.2 CURRENT STATUS OF ACCOUNTING PRINCIPLES.   The FASB identified five areas in which it will develop accounting principles for not-for-profits: depreciation, contributions, the reporting entity, financial statement display, and investments:

- Depreciation is the subject of the recently issued SFAS No. 93. Effective in 1990, this requires all not-for-profits to depreciate long-lived tangible assets, except that museum collections and similar assets often considered to be inexhaustible need not be depreciated if verifiable evidence of their inexhaustibility is available.
- Contributions are being studied by the FASB staff, with a timetable of publishing an exposure draft in the third quarter of 1990. The conclusion, in SFAC No. 6, that unspent expendable restricted gifts do not normally meet the definition of a liability will have a major impact on accounting standards in this area.
- Financial statement format is the subject of initial work by an AICPA task force. The division of net assets (formerly called fund balance) into three classes—unrestricted, temporarily restricted, and permanently restricted—as set forth in SFAC No. 6, and other matters discussed in that document, will likely have a significant effect on the format of the financial statements of many not-for-profit organizations. This group prepared a report for consideration by the FASB that was exposed for public comment in 1989.
- The reporting entity is being studied by the FASB as part of a larger project covering businesses as well as not-for-profits.
- Investments are not currently under active study but will eventually be addressed as part of another larger project, also involving businesses.

The AICPA is currently preparing a new audit guide that will cover all not-for-profit entities and supersede existing audit guides and SOP No. 78-10.

25.3 GOVERNMENT AUDIT REQUIREMENTS.   Not-for-profit entities are increasingly subject to audit requirements imposed by government agencies. These requirements are discussed in section 25.33 of this chapter.

NOT-FOR-PROFIT ACCOUNTING PRINCIPLES AND REPORTING PRACTICES

25.4 BASIS OF ACCOUNTING: CASH OR ACCRUAL.   Not-for-profit organizations frequently maintain their records on a **cash basis.** Cash basis accounting is a bookkeeping process that reflects only transactions involving cash. On the other hand, most commercial organizations, as well as many medium and large not-for-profit organizations, keep accounts on an **accrual basis.** In accrual basis accounting, income is recognized when earned and expenses are recognized when incurred. For bookkeeping purposes either basis is acceptable.

Each accounting basis has certain advantages. The principal advantage of cash basis accounting is **simplicity**—its procedures are easy to learn and easy to execute. Because of this simplicity, a cash basis accounting system is **less expensive** to maintain than an accrual basis system. Because there is often no material difference in financial results between cash and accrual basis accounting for small organizations, the incremental cost of an accrual basis system may be unwarranted. In addition, many not-for-profit organizations think it more

prudent to keep their books on a cash basis. They often do not want to recognize income prior to the actual receipt of cash.

The principal advantage of accrual basis accounting is that it portrays financial position and results of operations on a more **realistic** basis—a complex organization with accounts receivable and bills outstanding can present realistic financial results only on the accrual basis. In addition, accrual basis accounting usually achieves a better **matching** of revenue and related expenses. Also, many individuals who use the financial statements of not-for-profit organizations, such as bankers, local businesspeople, and board members, are often more familiar with accrual basis accounting.

Organizations wanting the accuracy of accrual basis accounting, but not wishing to sacrifice the simplicity of cash basis bookkeeping, have several alternatives. They may maintain their books on a cash basis and at year-end record all payables, receivables, and accruals. These adjustments would permit presentation of accrual basis financial statements.

An organization can also keep its books on a cash basis, except for certain transactions that are recorded on an accrual basis. A popular type of ''modified cash basis'' accounting is to record accounts payable as liabilities are incurred, but to record income on a cash basis as received.

25.5 FUND ACCOUNTING.   Fund accounting is the process of segregating resources into sets of self-balancing accounts on the basis of either restrictions imposed by donors or designations imposed by governing boards.

In the past, most not-for-profit organizations have followed fund accounting procedures in accounting for resources. This was done because many organizations regard fund accounting as the most appropriate means of exercising stewardship over funds. Reporting all the details of funds, however, is not required of all not-for-profit organizations, and in many cases is not recommended. Fund accounting, if carried to its logical extreme, requires a separate set of accounts for each restricted gift or contribution; this leads to confusing financial statements that often present an organization as a collection of individual funds rather than as a single entity. Today, many not-for-profit organizations are combining funds and eliminating fund distinctions for reporting purposes to facilitate financial statement users' understanding of the organization as a whole.

An infinite variety of funds is possible. To limit the number of funds reported, broad fund classifications may be used. One scheme commonly used today is classification of resources by type of donor restriction. Another criterion for classifying funds is the degree of control an organization possesses over its resources. Under this approach, funds are combined for reporting purposes into two groupings—**unrestricted** and **restricted.** A third approach classifies resources on the basis of their availability for current expenditure on an organization's programs. Under this approach, funds are combined into two categories, **expendable** and **nonexpendable.**

When resources are classified by type of donor restriction, four fund groupings are commonly used—current unrestricted, current restricted, endowment, and fixed asset funds.

The **current unrestricted fund** contains assets over which the board has total managerial discretion. This fund includes unrestricted contributions, revenue, and other income and can be used in any manner at any time to further the goals of the organization. For all not-for-profit organizations except colleges, ''board-designated'' funds should be included with current unrestricted funds. Board-designated funds are voluntary segregations of unrestricted fund balances approved by the board for specific future projects or purposes.

Current restricted funds are resources given to an organization to be expended for specific operating purposes.

Endowment funds are amounts donated to an organization with the legal restriction that the principal be maintained inviolate and in perpetuity. Investment income on such funds is generally unrestricted and should be reported in the current unrestricted fund. Occasionally, endowment gifts stipulate restricted uses for the investment income, and such restricted income should be reported in the appropriate fund.

The **fixed asset fund** represents the land, buildings, and equipment owned by an organization. Since these assets are usually unrestricted in the sense that the board can employ (or dispose of) them in any manner it wishes to further the goals of the organization, fixed assets need not be reported in a separate fund, and may be reported as part of the current unrestricted fund.

25.6 RECLASSIFICATIONS.   The use of fund accounting necessitates transfers in some situations to allocate resources between funds. Financial statement readers often find it difficult to comprehend such reclassifications. In addition, if not properly presented, transfers may give the impression that an organization is willfully manipulating amounts reported as income.

To minimize confusion and the appearance of deception, transfers must not be shown as either **income** of the receiving fund or **expenses** of the transferring fund. Transfers are merely an internal reallocation of resources and in no way result in income or expense recognition.

Transfers should be presented in the "fund balances" section of a statement of income and expenses, or in a separate statement of changes in fund balances, if one is used. If an organization chooses to present transfers in a statement of income and expenses, they should be presented after the caption "excess of revenue over expenses." (Colleges and voluntary health and welfare organizations often present transfers in a slightly different manner; see sections 25.22–25.25 of this chapter.) Columnar statements, which present the activity of each fund in separate, side-by-side columns, facilitate clear, comprehensive presentation of transfers.

25.7 APPROPRIATIONS.   Appropriations (or designations) are internal authorizations to expend funds in the future for specific purposes. They are neither expenditures nor legal obligations. When appropriation accounting is followed, appropriated funds should be set aside in a separate account as part of the fund balance of an organization.

Appropriation accounting is both confusing and subject to abuse. It is confusing because "appropriation" is an ambiguous term, and many readers do not understand that it is neither a current expenditure nor a binding obligation for a future expenditure. It is subject to abuse because, when treated incorrectly, appropriations can appear to reduce the current year's excess of revenue over expenses to whatever level the board wants. The board can then, at a later date, restore "appropriated" funds to the general use of the organization.

The use of appropriation accounting is not recommended. If an organization wishes to follow appropriation accounting techniques and wants to conform with GAAP, it must be certain that appropriations are not presented as expenses, and that they appear only as part of the fund balance of the organization. Expenses incurred out of appropriated funds should be charged as expenses in the year incurred, and the related appropriations should be reversed once an expense has been incurred.

Disclosure in notes is an alternative to appropriation accounting. Under this approach, an organization does not refer to appropriations in the body of its financial statements but instead discloses such amounts only in notes to the financial statements.

25.8 FIXED ASSETS.   Treatment of fixed assets is one of the most perplexing accounting issues confronting not-for-profit organizations. There are three reasons some not-for-profit organizations have historically not recorded a value for fixed assets on their balance sheets. First, many not-for-profit organizations have not been as interested in matching income and expenses as are businesses. This being the case, management of these organizations has felt no compelling need to record assets and then charge depreciation expense against current income. Second, the principal asset of many not-for-profit organizations is real estate that was often acquired many years previously. In these inflationary times, many organizations do not wish to carry at cost and depreciate assets now worth several times their original purchase price. Third, many not-for-profit organizations plead poverty as a means of raising funds. By not recording fixed assets, they appear less substantial than they in fact are.

Confusion concerning fixed assets is heightened by lack of a universally accepted treatment for fixed assets. Historically, there have been three common alternatives for handling fixed assets: immediate write-off, capitalization (with or without depreciation), and write-off, followed by capitalization.

Immediate write-off is the simplest method of treating fixed assets and is used most frequently for small organizations and those on a cash basis. Under this method, an organization expenses fixed asset purchases immediately on the statement of income and expenses.

The principal advantage of this approach is simplicity—the bookkeeping complexities of capitalization are avoided, and the amount of excess revenue over expenses reported on the statement of income and expenses more closely reflects the amount of money at the board's disposal.

The major disadvantage of immediate write-off is that the historical costs of an organization's fixed assets are not recorded, and its balance sheet does not present the true net worth of the organization. Another disadvantage is that expensing fixed assets may produce fluctuations in net income that are largely unrelated to operations. Finally, this approach does not conform with GAAP.

A second alternative available to an organization is to **capitalize** all major fixed asset purchases. Under this approach, all major fixed assets are reflected on the organization's balance sheet.

The principal advantage of this approach is that it conforms with GAAP and permits an auditor to express an unqualified opinion on an organization's financial statements. It also documents the amount of assets the organization controls, permitting evaluation of management performance, and allows the organization to follow depreciation accounting if it wishes.

The major disadvantage of capitalization is that it renders financial statements more complex. An unsophisticated statement reader may conclude that an organization has more funds available for current spending than it actually has.

A third alternative is to immediately **write off** fixed asset purchases on the statement of income and expenses and **then capitalize** these assets on the balance sheet. This method permits an organization to report expenditures for fixed asset purchases on the statement of income and expenses, thus offsetting any excess of income over expenses that may have been caused by contributions received for fixed assets on its balance sheet. This in turn gives a clearer picture of the net worth of the organization.

However, this approach is very confusing, is inconsistent with other accounting conventions, does not permit depreciation accounting in a traditional sense, and does not constitute GAAP. Accordingly, the use of this approach is strongly discouraged.

25.9 DEPRECIATION. Depreciation has been as thorny a problem for not-for-profit organizations as the problem of fixed assets. If an organization capitalizes fixed assets, it is immediately confronted with the question of whether it should depreciate them: that is, allocate the cost over the estimated useful life of the assets.

Depreciation accounting is rapidly becoming a generally accepted practice for most not-for-profit organizations and as of 1990 it constitutes GAAP for all not-for-profit organizations. (Prior to that year it was optional for colleges.) SFAS No. 93, "Recognition of Depreciation by Not-for-Profit Organizations," (as amended by SFAS No. 99) requires not-for-profit organizations to record depreciation on fixed assets for fiscal years beginning on or after January 1, 1990. Many arguments in favor of recording depreciation, such as the following, are valid for not-for-profit organizations:

1. Depreciation is a cost of operations. Organizations cannot accurately measure the cost of providing a product or service or determine a fair price without including this cost component.

2. Most organizations replace at least some fixed assets out of recurring income. If depreciation is not recorded, an organization may think that its income is sufficient to cover costs when, in reality, it is not.

3. If depreciation is not recorded, income may fluctuate widely from year to year, depending on the timing of asset replacement and the replacement cost of assets.

4. Organizations that are "reimbursed" by a government agency for the sale of goods or services must depreciate fixed assets if they wish to recapture all costs incurred.

5. Some not-for-profit organizations pay federal income tax on "unrelated business income." Depreciation should be reported as an expense to reduce income subject to tax.

Depreciation is computed in the same manner as that used by commercial enterprises. In a single-fund organization, depreciation is reported as an item of expense on the statement of income and expenses, and accumulated depreciation is reported under the "fixed assets" caption on the balance sheet. In a multifund organization with a separate plant fund, it is usually confusing to report depreciation in the current unrestricted fund (to match income and expenses) and record accumulated depreciation in the plant fund. To reduce confusion, it is recommended that multifund organizations that wish to report depreciation expense in the current unrestricted fund include all fixed assets in this fund.

If fixed asset purchases are capitalized but not written down through regular depreciation charges in the statement of income and expenses, it may be necessary to periodically write down their carrying value so that the balance sheet is not overstated. The preferred method of achieving this is to report the write-down as an expense on the statement of income and expenses and to reduce the asset value on the balance sheet.

25.10 INVESTMENT INCOME.   Dividends and interest earned on unrestricted investment funds, including board-designated funds, should be reported as income in the current unrestricted fund.

Unrestricted investment income earned on endowment funds should also be reported as income directly in the current unrestricted fund.

Restricted investment income should be reported directly in the appropriate restricted fund. For example, if the donor of an endowment fund gift specifies that the investment income be used for a particular purpose, investment income should be reported directly in the appropriate restricted fund rather than the current unrestricted fund or the endowment fund.

25.11 GAINS AND LOSSES ON INVESTMENTS.   **Realized gains or losses on unrestricted investment funds** should be reported directly in the current unrestricted fund (colleges treat gains and losses in a different manner, which is discussed in section 25.22(h)). Unrestricted capital gains or losses may be reported in the statement of income and expenses as an income item along with dividends and interest, or they may be reported separately from other investment income, above the caption "excess of income over expenses."

Realized gains or losses on endowment investments have traditionally been treated as adjustments to principal of the endowment fund. They have not been considered as income and were thought to possess the same restrictions as those that are attached to the principal. The legal status of gains or losses on endowment funds—as unrestricted income or as a component of restricted principal—is, however, currently unresolved. Where permitted by state law, such gains or losses should be treated as income and reported with dividends and interest in the current unrestricted fund above the caption "excess of income over expenses." Restricted gains or losses may be treated in a similar manner except that they are reported in the appropriate restricted fund. Different types of not-for-profit organizations have different reporting requirements, which are discussed in section 25.26(h).

Unrealized gains or losses did not pose accounting questions for not-for-profit organizations prior to 1973 because, before that year, investments could be carried only at cost and gains or losses were realized only at the time investments were sold or otherwise disposed of.

After 1973 the tenor of accounting pronouncements on the carrying value of investments and the treatment of unrealized gains or losses changed dramatically. In 1973 and 1974 the AICPA Industry Audit Guides for colleges and universities and voluntary health and welfare organizations permitted those organizations to carry their investments at either cost or market. Hospitals were required in 1978 to carry equity investments at market if the fair value dipped below cost. SOP No. 78-10 permits covered organizations to carry investments at market or the lower of cost or market.

When investments are carried at market, gains and losses are recognized on a continuing basis. Realized and unrealized gains or losses should be reported together in a single caption: "net increase (decrease) in carrying value of investments." It is appropriate to report this increase or decrease in the same section in which investment dividends and interest are reported (except for organizations covered by SOP No. 78-10, which report gains on endowment funds as capital additions).

Even when investments are carried at cost, if market value declines "permanently" below cost, the carrying value of this investment should be written down to the market value. This is accomplished by setting up a "provision for decline in market value of investments" in the statement of income and expenses in the same section where realized gains or losses are presented.

25.12 CONTRIBUTIONS. **Unrestricted contributions** should be reported as income in the statement of income and expenses. They may be reported along with other sources of income or reported separately from operating income. In either case, they are reported above the excess or deficit of income over expenses for the period.

Current restricted contributions are contributions restricted to use for a current purpose or activity. Considerable controversy surrounds the reporting of such income, and three alternative treatments are currently in use.

One approach is to report current restricted gifts as income in the year that the gifts are received. This approach is recommended by "Audits of Voluntary Health and Welfare Organizations," issued by the AICPA, and is widely followed. Under this approach gifts are recognized as income as they are received, and expenses are recognized as they are incurred. Current restricted gifts that are unexpended at year-end are included in the fund balance of the organization.

Another approach is to recognize current restricted gifts as income only at the time they are expended. This approach is recommended by the hospital and the college and university guides. Under this approach current restricted gifts are reported directly in the fund balance section of the balance sheet when received, and they are recognized as income in the statement of income and expenses only when actually expended.

A third approach is to defer current restricted gifts until restrictions have been met. This approach is gaining in popularity and is recommended in SOP No. 78-10 for certain not-for-profit organizations. Under this approach, current restricted gifts are reflected in the liability section of the balance sheet until restrictions are met, at which time they are recognized as income.

Noncurrent restricted contributions are gifts given for specific purposes (usually, for endowment or plant) other than current activities. Depending on the type of organization, methods of recording such contributions differ.

Endowment fund gifts should be included in the endowment fund on the balance sheet. There are several ways to report endowment fund gifts in the statement of income and expenses. If a multifund statement (which intrinsically separates operating income from endowment funds gifts) is used, the gift should be reported directly in the endowment fund. Alternatively, endowment gifts can be reported in a nonexpendable additions section of a single-fund statement of income and expenses, directly following the caption "excess of income over expenses before nonexpendable additions."

Plant fund gifts, depending on the type of organization, should be recognized as income at the time received and should be treated in a manner similar to endowment gifts or deferred until such time as the gift is used to purchase plant fund assets.

25.13 GRANTS. Grants received from third parties to perform specific activities should be recognized as income in the manner discussed above for restricted contributions. If expenses covered by the grant are incurred prior to grant receipt, a receivable should be set up to reflect the grantor's obligation.

25.14 BEQUESTS. When an organization is named as a beneficiary before an estate is probated or distributions are made, the critical question is **when** the bequest should be recorded as an asset and reported as income.

A bequest should be recorded as an asset as soon as an organization knows, with reasonable certainty, the amount of the bequest (usually when the probate court has issued the order permitting transfer of the assets to the beneficiary organization). If there is uncertainty concerning the amount of the bequest that will ultimately be received, note disclosure is appropriate.

Unrestricted bequests or bequests for endowment should be recognized as income when the bequest is recorded as an asset. Bequests restricted for current purposes or for plant additions should be treated in the same manner as other current restricted or plant fund gifts.

25.15 CONTRIBUTED SERVICES AND ASSETS. Generally, contributed services may be recorded under certain conditions, and contributed assets should be recorded at fair value.

(a) Contributed Services. Services contributed by volunteers may be valued and reported as income if all the following criteria, stipulated in SOP No. 78-10, are met:

1. Services provided must constitute an essential element of an organization's activities, which, if not contributed, would be performed by paid staff.
2. Controls must be exercised over volunteer employment.
3. An objective basis to value contributed services must exist.
4. The services must relate to activities benefiting persons outside the organization.

If the above criteria are met, a dollar value for contributed services should be reported on a separate line, in the same section of the statement of income and expenses where unrestricted contributions are reported. The value of contributed services should be reported as an expense directly in the appropriate program or supporting service category. Note disclosure of the nature of contributed services and the valuation method should be made.

(b) Contributed Materials, Plant, and Facilities. Contributed materials, plant, and facilities should be recorded if they are significant in amount and there is an objective basis for valuation. Supplies and equipment should be recorded at the amount an organization would pay to purchase such items if contributed materials were unavailable.

Contributed plant normally requires an independent appraisal to determine its value. If an organization is given the use of a facility, the value recorded should be the rental value of facilities the organization would otherwise rent.

(c) Contributed Investments. Marketable securities should be reported at market value on the date of receipt or, if sold shortly thereafter, at the amount of proceeds actually received.

25.16 PLEDGES. Authoritative not-for-profit accounting literature is divided over the issue of **whether** pledges should be reported in the financial statements, and **when** pledges should be recognized as income (for specific requirements, see discussions of different types of organizations in sections 25.20(j), 25.22(j), 25.24(l), and 25.26(j)).

A pledge should be recorded as an asset only if the pledge is legally enforceable and if it is likely to be collected. Pledges to be received in future years should not be recorded beyond a relatively few periods.

Recognition of pledges as income is a function of the **donor's intention.** If donors are **silent** on their intentions, the organization should presume that they intend their pledges to be used in the period when payment is made. Accordingly, the amount currently due is recognized as income in the current year, and the amount forthcoming in future years is recorded as deferred pledge income in the liabilities section of the balance sheet until received.

If donors specify **when** their gifts should be used, their intentions should govern the timing of income recognition. This is true if a donor wants a contribution to be recognized as income in the current year, even though payment will not be made until the following year.

Organizations recording pledges should set up an allowance for uncollectible pledges. The size of this allowance should reflect historic default rates, economic climate, prospective pledge use, and payment record of the particular pledger.

25.17 RELATED ORGANIZATIONS. Practice varies regarding when not-for-profit entities combine the financial statements of affiliated organizations with those of the central organization. Part of the reason for this is the widely diverse nature of relationships among such organizations, which often creates difficulty in determining when criteria for combination have been met. In general, related entities should be combined when a parent controls an affiliate that exists mainly to further the purposes of the parent. However, exceptions to this are discussed in sections 25.20(k) and 25.25(d).

25.18 CASH FLOWS. SFAS No. 95, which requires businesses to present a statement of cash flows (in lieu of the former statement of changes in financial position), does not yet apply to not-for-profits. Included in the report of the AICPA task force on display are recommendations on how not-for-profits should apply SFAS No. 95. A sample statement of cash flows, following the proposal in this report, is illustrated in Exhibit 25.13 (section 25.27). The FASB will eventually issue standards on financial statement display for not-for-profit entities, which will include a statement of cash flows.

25.19 GOVERNMENTAL VERSUS NONGOVERNMENTAL ACCOUNTING. In 1989, the Financial Accounting Foundation, overseer of the FASB and its counterpart in the governmental sector, the GASB (see discussion in Chapter 24, "State and Local Government Accounting") resolved the question of the jurisdiction of each body. A question related to several types of organizations, mainly not-for-profits, which exist in both governmental and nongovernmental forms. These types include institutions of higher education, museums, libraries, hospitals, and others. The issue is whether it is more important to have, for example, all hospitals follow a single set of accounting principles, or to have all types of governmental entities do so. This matter was resolved by conferring on GASB jurisdiction over all governmental entities.

HOSPITALS

The "Hospital Audit Guide" issued by the AICPA in 1972 is the most authoritative pronouncement of accounting principles and reporting practices for hospitals. The guide has been amended by six AICPA Statements of Position and in 1990 was in the process of revision.

25.20 ACCOUNTING PRINCIPLES.   Hospitals generally follow the same accounting principles as other not-for-profit organizations, but accounting for related organizations and third-party reimbursement may create unusual problems.

(a) Accrual Basis Accounting.   Hospitals should follow accrual basis accounting. Patient receivables should be recorded at their estimated net realizable amount at the time services are rendered. Estimated receivables and payables under contracts subject to adjustments, and investment income should also be accrued.

(b) Fund Accounting.   Not-for-profit hospitals traditionally have used fund accounting for record-keeping and financial reporting purposes. According to the FASB (SFAC Nos. 4 and 6), information about fund groupings is not a necessary part of general purpose external financial reporting, other than to recognize any limitations on equity. Therefore, some hospitals present balance sheets that display assets, liabilities, and equity classified by fund groups. Others use "single fund" reporting, in which all assets, liabilities, and equity amounts are displayed in a single aggregated balance sheet, with fund differentiation indicated by notation in the equity section and disclosure in the notes to the financial statements.

Not-for-profit hospitals use two broad fund groupings: general and donor-restricted. **General funds** are used to account for all resources and obligations not recorded in donor-restricted funds. These include the facility's working capital, assets whose use is limited, and property and equipment related to general operations. The classification "assets whose use is limited" includes assets set aside by the governing board for identified purposes as well as assets whose use is limited under terms of debt indentures, trust agreements such as self-insurance arrangements, agreements with third party payors to meet depreciation funding requirements, or other similar arrangements.

Donor-restricted funds consist of assets that are specifically restricted to use for a particular purpose by a donor or grantor, along with any related obligations. Included are funds restricted for specific operating purposes, funds restricted for additions to property and equipment, endowment funds, term endowment funds, and annuity and life income funds. Although donor restrictions may require such funds to be kept separate for record-keeping purposes, they may be grouped for financial reporting purposes.

(c) Fixed Assets.   Property and equipment pertaining to general operations are recorded in the general fund. Property held for future expansion or investment purposes should be included in general funds, but presented separately from fixed assets used in general operations. Property held by endowment funds should be recorded in the appropriate donor-restricted endowment fund.

(d) Depreciation.   Depreciation should be recorded in the financial statements and reported separately as an expense of operations in the statement of revenue and expenses.

(e) Carrying Value of Investments.   Investments in marketable equity securities should be carried at the lower of aggregate cost or market value, and investments in marketable debt securities should be carried at cost. The market value of all investments should be disclosed either on the financial statements or in the notes.

(f) Investment Income.   The same "peripheral or incidental" conditions that apply to unrestricted contributions and grants (see section 25.20(g)) apply to income from investing activities of the general fund (interest, dividends, rents, and net gains or losses from investment transactions). Such income is usually classified as "nonoperating" because of its "peripheral or incidental" nature; however, in some cases it is classified as "operating."

Specific circumstances in which an operating presentation should be used are enumerated in the audit guide.

Income and losses from investing activities of **restricted** funds should generally be recorded as an addition to or reduction of the appropriate fund balance. Unrestricted income from endowment funds is recorded as revenue of the general fund, and is usually classified as nonoperating because of its peripheral or incidental nature.

(g) Gifts, Bequests, Grants, and Subsidies (cash). Unrestricted gifts, bequests, grants, and subsidies are recorded as operating or nonoperating revenue depending on whether they are central and ongoing or peripheral and incidental to the hospital's operations. As a general rule, income generated from activities that are peripheral or incidental to providing health care services or income stemming from events that may be largely beyond management's control should be classified as "nonoperating" in the statement of revenues and expenses. Unrestricted contributions, grants, tax subsidies, and revenues from fund-raising activities are usually classified as nonoperating because they are considered to meet the "peripheral or incidental" condition. Only in the relatively infrequent situations in which such revenues are deemed to be ongoing major activities by which the hospital attempts to fulfill its basic function of providing healthcare services, should they be classified as "operating."

Resources received from donors or grantors that are **restricted** for specific operating purposes are recorded as additions to the appropriate restricted fund balance when received. When expended for their intended purpose, they are reclassified as revenue of the general fund. To the extent that the revenues offset expenditures included in operating expense, the revenue should be classified as operating. If the contribution was restricted for indigent care, it should be recorded as a reduction of the allowance for charity care.

Resources received from donors or grantors that are restricted for additions to property and equipment are recorded as additions to the appropriate restricted fund balance when received. When expended for their intended purpose, they are reclassified to the general fund balance; they are not reported as revenue.

Endowments are recorded as additions to the appropriate restricted fund balance when received. Endowments may be classified as permanent or term. Permanent endowments may never be expended, so they will always remain in a restricted endowment fund balance. When donor-imposed time or conditional restrictions are satisfied on term endowments, they are reclassified as revenue of the general fund if there is no further restriction on their use; their classification as operating or nonoperating revenue depends on whether they are central and ongoing or peripheral and incidental to the hospital's operations. If they are further restricted, they are reclassified to the appropriate restricted fund balance until expended for their intended purpose.

(h) Donated Services. The value of donated services is generally not recorded unless certain specific criteria are met. These criteria are set forth in the audit guide.

(i) Noncash Donations. Donations of assets other than cash should be recorded at the fair market value of the assets on the date of the contribution. Donations of property and equipment are recorded as additions to the appropriate restricted fund balance when the assets are received. They are reclassified to the general fund balance when the donated property or equipment is placed in service.

Donations of other types of assets (such as investments or supplies) are recorded as revenue if unrestricted or as an addition to the appropriate restricted fund balance if restricted. If unrestricted, their classification as operating or nonoperating revenue depends on whether they are central and ongoing or peripheral and incidental to the hospital's operations.

(j) Pledges.   Pledges should be reported at their estimated net realizable value. Unrestricted and restricted pledges should be treated similarly to unrestricted and restricted contributions.

(k) Related Organizations.   Many hospitals have restructured or diversified into multi-hospital systems. SOP No. 81-2 provides guidance in determining the circumstances in which not-for-profit organizations should be considered to be "related" to a not-for-profit hospital for financial statement purposes, and sets forth the disclosure requirements for those organizations in hospital financial statements. However, this guidance is of limited use, as the SOP did not contemplate the complex organizational structures now being developed (such as multiple not-for-profit organizations and taxable entities under common parents). FASB is currently working on a project that is expected to provide a concept of reporting entity for not-for-profit organizations, but the timetable for its completion is undetermined.

(l) Malpractice Claims.   The ultimate costs of malpractice claims should be accrued when the incidents occur that give rise to the claims, if certain criteria are met, as discussed in SOP No. 87-1, "Accounting for Asserted and Unasserted Medical Malpractice Claims of Health Care Providers and Related Issues." These criteria include a determination that a liability has been incurred and an ability to make a reasonable estimate of the amount of the loss. Further guidance is in SFAS No. 5, "Accounting for Contingencies."

(m) Third-Party Reimbursement Timing Differences.   For financial reporting purposes, third-party payors may reimburse hospitals for certain costs in different accounting periods than those in which the costs were recognized. This results in timing differences that affect the financial statements of the periods in which they arise and the periods in which they reverse. Sometimes changes in third-party payment program provisions or regulations cause temporary timing differences to become permanent. When this occurs, the effect is recorded in the financial statements in the period when it is determined that the timing differences will not be recovered or realized.

(n) Patient Service Revenue.   Patient service revenue is reported net of deductions in the statement of revenues and expenses. The provision for uncompensated care must be disclosed. Other types of deductions such as contractual allowances may also be disclosed if deemed necessary.

25.21 REPORTING PRACTICES.   Hospitals generally prepare four financial statements:

1. Balance sheet.
2. Statement of revenue and expenses.
3. Statement of changes in fund balances.
4. Statement of changes in financial position, or statement of cash flows.

Supplementary statements may be prepared as needed.

(a) Balance Sheet.   A balance sheet, presented in Exhibit 25.1, reports two separate fund groups, **general** and **donor-restricted.**
    A **single** fund balance is reported for all **general** funds, although the composition of the general fund balance may be reported either on the balance sheet, in the statement of changes in fund balances, or in statement notes.
    The **donor-restricted** fund is divided into three self-balancing subfund groups—specific purpose, plant replacement and expansion, and endowment funds.

(b) Statement of Revenue and Expenses.   The statement of revenue and expenses, presented in Exhibit 25.2, reports all **unrestricted** revenue and expenses for the period. Financial

JOHNSTOWN HOSPITAL
Balance Sheet (Condensed)
December 31, 19X2

Assets		Liabilities and Fund Balances	
	General Funds		
Current assets (in total)	$ 1,500,000	Current liabilities (in total)	$1,200,000
Assets whose use is limited:		Deferred third-party	
By board for capital		reimbursement	100,000
improvements	140,000	Long-term debt	400,000
Under trusteed malpractice		Fund balance	5,925,000
self-insurance arrangement	175,000		
Under bond indenture	210,000		
Property, plant and equipment	10,000,000		
Less depreciation	(4,400,000)		
Total	$ 7,625,000	Total	$7,625,000
	Donor-Restricted Funds		
	Specific-Purpose Fund		
Cash	$ 100,000	Fund balance	$ 100,000
	Plant Replacement and Expansion Fund		
Cash	25,000	Fund balance	$ 200,000
Investments	100,000		
Pledges	75,000		
	$ 200,000		$ 200,000
	Endowment Fund		
Cash	$ 25,000	Fund balances:	
Investments	5,000,000	Permanent	$4,500,000
	$ 5,025,000	Term	525,000
			$5,025,000

Exhibit 25.1.   Balance sheet. *Source:* Adapted from Gross and Warshauer, *Financial and Accounting Guide for Nonprofit Organizations,* Wiley, 1983, pp. 236–237. Reproduced by permission.

activity is arranged in the following sequence: Patient revenue **plus** other operating revenue minus operating expenses **plus** nonoperating revenue yields excess (deficit) of revenue over expenses. The statement of revenue and expenses reports the results of operations, as well as the result of total unrestricted financial activity for the period.

(c) Statement of Changes in Fund Balances.   The statement of changes in fund balances, Exhibit 25.3, reports changes in fund balances for general and donor-restricted funds. All changes in fund balances are reported in one statement for the general fund, whereas separate changes in fund balances are reported for the specific purpose, plant replacement and expansion, and endowment fund components of the restricted fund.

(d) Statement of Changes in Financial Position or Cash Flows.   Hospitals should prepare a statement of cash flows or a statement of changes in financial position for the unrestricted fund. The latter statement is similar to the statement of changes in financial position formerly prepared by commercial entities. An example of a statement of changes in financial position is

JOHNSTOWN HOSPITAL
Statement of Revenues and Expenses of General Funds
For the Year Ended December 31, 19X2

Net patient service revenue	$4,000,000
Other operating revenue (including $50,000 from specific-purpose funds)	100,000
Total operating revenue	4,100,000
Operating expenses:	
Nursing services	1,800,000
Other professional services	1,300,000
General services	1,000,000
Fiscal services	200,000
Administrative services (including interest of $18,000)	500,000
Provision for depreciation	200,000
Total operating expenses	5,000,000
Loss from operations	(900,000)
Nonoperating revenue:	
Unrestricted gifts and bequests	600,000
Unrestricted income from endowment funds	300,000
Income and gains from investments whose use is limited:	
By board for capital improvements	20,000
Under indenture agreement	30,000
Total nonoperating revenue	950,000
Excess of Revenue over Expenses	$ 50,000

Exhibit 25.2.   Statement of revenue and expenses. *Source:* Adapted from Gross and Warshauer, *Financial and Accounting Guide for Nonprofit Organizations,* Wiley, 1983, p. 239. Reproduced by permission.

shown in Exhibit 25.12, and an example of a statement of cash flows is provided in Exhibit 25.13.

COLLEGES AND UNIVERSITIES

The AICPA Industry Audit Guide, "Audits of Colleges and Universities," issued in 1973, is the most authoritative pronouncement on accounting principles and reporting practices for colleges and universities. The guide was revised in 1974 by an AICPA SOP, "Financial Accounting and Reporting by Colleges and Universities," which modified certain descriptions and classifications of current funds revenue, expenditures, and transfers.

25.22 ACCOUNTING PRINCIPLES.   Fund accounting is a prominent element of college and university accounting. Treatment of depreciation and treatment of current restricted gifts, in addition, pose special accounting problems.

(a) Accrual Basis of Accounting.   Colleges and universities should follow accrual basis accounting. All accounts should be maintained on an accrual basis unless unrecorded amounts are immaterial, including such often overlooked accruals and deferrals as investment income and interest on student loans. Revenue from and expenditures for summer sessions should be reported in the fiscal year in which most of the session occurs.

(b) Fund Accounting.   Colleges and universities have historically followed fund accounting procedures. Fund accounting continues to find favor at colleges and universities because many gifts and grants that colleges receive possess external restrictions that must be carefully

JOHNSTOWN HOSPITAL
Statements of Changes in Fund Balances

	Year Ended December 31	
	19X2	19X1
General Funds		
Balance, beginning of the year	$5,750,000	$5,630,000
Excess of revenue over expenses	50,000	80,000
Donated medical equipment	100,000	10,000
Transferred from plant replacement and expansion fund to finance property, plant and equipment expenditures	25,000	30,000
Balance, end of the year	$5,925,000	$5,750,000
Donor-Restricted Funds		
Specific-purpose fund:		
Balance, beginning of the year	$ 80,000	$ 75,000
Donor-restricted gifts and bequests	65,000	45,000
Net gain on sale of investments	5,000	—
Transferred to other operating revenue and to offset allowances	(50,000)	(40,000)
Balance, end of the year	$ 100,000	$ 80,000
Plant replacement and expansion fund:		
Balance, beginning of the year	$ 95,000	$ 85,000
Donor-restricted gifts and bequests	100,000	25,000
Income from investments	10,000	10,000
Net gain on sale of investments	20,000	5,000
Transferred to general funds	(25,000)	(30,000)
Balance, end of the year	$ 200,000	$ 95,000
Endowment fund:		
Balance, beginning of the year	$4,825,000	$4,645,000
Donor-restricted gifts and bequests	100,000	150,000
Net gains on sale of investments	100,000	30,000
Balance, end of the year	$5,025,000	$4,825,000

Exhibit 25.3.   Statements of changes in fund balances. *Source:* **Adapted from Gross and Warshauer,** *Financial and Accounting Guide for Nonprofit Organizations,* **Wiley, 1983, p. 241. Reproduced by permission.**

monitored, and also because many colleges voluntarily set aside some current unrestricted funds as "endowment" to produce future income.

The following six fund groupings are generally used by colleges and universities.

Current funds are resources available for carrying out the general activities of an institution. In public reporting, current unrestricted funds are usually reported separately from current restricted funds, that is, funds restricted by donors or grantors for specific current purposes.

Loan funds are resources available for loans to students, faculty, and staff. If only the investment income from restricted endowment funds can be used for loans, only the income should be reported in the loan fund.

Endowment and similar funds consist of three types of endowment resources:

1. **True endowment,** where the donor stipulates that the principal must be maintained inviolate and in perpetuity, and only the income earned thereon may be expended.

2. **Term endowment,** where the donor stipulates that, upon the passage of time or the incidence of an event, the principal may be used for current operations or specific purposes.
3. **Quasi endowment,** where the board of trustees voluntarily retains as principal a portion of current funds to produce current and future income.

Annuity and life income funds are endowment resources of which the college owns only the principal and not the income earned thereon. In accepting an annuity or life income gift, the college agrees to pay the contributor all income earned or a specific amount for a stated period of time.

Plant funds consist of four fund groupings, and separate financial data for each are often reported:

1. **Unexpended plant funds** are used for plant additions or improvements.
2. **Renewal and replacement funds** are transferred from current funds for **future** renewal or replacement of the existing plant. In the absence of depreciation, these funds provide for the future integrity of the physical plant.
3. **Retirement of indebtedness funds** are set aside to service debt interest and principal. It is often appropriate to designate which funds are set aside under mandatory contractual agreements with lenders and which funds are voluntarily designated.
4. **Investment in plant** records the actual cost of all land, buildings, and equipment owned by the college. Donated plant is recorded at market value at the date of the gift.

Agency funds are funds over which an institution exercises **custodial** but not **proprietary** authority. An example is funds that are owned by a student organization but are deposited with the college.

(c) Encumbrance Accounting.   Encumbrance accounting is not acceptable for financial statements of colleges and universities. It is inappropriate to report, as expenditures or liabilities, commitments for materials or services not received by the reporting date. A portion of the current unrestricted fund may be designated to satisfy purchase orders, provided that the designation is made only in the fund balances section of the balance sheet.

(d) Fixed Assets.   Material fixed assets should be capitalized and recorded on the balance sheet. A college cannot write off or "expense" fixed assets as acquired.

(e) Depreciation.   The requirement of the AICPA audit guide is that, once capitalized, fixed assets may **not** be depreciated in a statement of income and expenses or in any statement presenting current financial activity for the period. If the college elects to record depreciation of its fixed assets, this depreciation may be reported in the "investment in plant" section of the plant fund on the balance sheet.

Effective for fiscal years beginning on or after January 1, 1990, private colleges must begin to depreciate fixed assets, in accordance with the requirements of SFAS No. 93 (effective date amended by SFAS No. 99). Because the GASB has no similar requirement, public colleges need not depreciate their fixed assets.

Colleges that depreciate fixed assets in accordance with SFAS No. 93 should report it in accordance with the audit guide, until the FASB issues a final standard on financial statement display.

(f) Investment Income.   Unrestricted investment income, including unrestricted endowment fund income, should be reported as revenue in the current unrestricted fund in the period earned. Restricted investment income should be reported as revenue directly in the fund to which the restrictions pertain.

(g) Carrying Value of Investments. Investments may be carried at either cost or market value. Cost for donated investments is market value at the date of receipt. Whatever carrying basis is selected, it must be applied to all investments.

(h) Gains and Losses on Investments. Realized gains and losses should be included in revenue and reported in the fund holding the investment.

Unrealized gains and losses for colleges carrying investments at market are reported in the same manner as realized gains and losses.

(i) Gifts, Bequests, and Grants. Unrestricted gifts, bequests, and grants should be reported as revenue in the current unrestricted fund in the year received. Once this has been done, the board can, if it wishes, designate a portion of unrestricted gifts, bequests, or grants for specific purposes, and transfer them to the appropriate fund.

Restricted gifts, bequests, and grants should be reported directly in the applicable fund group. Current restricted gifts are reported in the current restricted fund either in their entirety or to the extent expended, depending on the financial statement in question (see section 25.23).

(j) Pledges. If an institution elects, pledges may be reported in the financial statements. If reported, pledges should be recorded at their estimated net realizable value. If unrecorded, note disclosure is appropriate.

25.23 REPORTING PRACTICES. Colleges and universities generally prepare three financial statements:

1. A statement of changes in fund balances.
2. A balance sheet.
3. A statement of current funds revenues, expenditures, and other changes.

Supplementary financial information may be presented at the institutions' discretion.

(a) Statement of Changes in Fund Balances. The statement of changes in fund balances, illustrated in Exhibit 25.4, is the most comprehensive and important statement prepared by colleges and universities. It summarizes the financial activity of all funds of an institution.

The format of Exhibit 25.4 is similar to that of an income statement. Expenditures are ostensibly subtracted from revenue, yielding the net change for the period. However, the statement of changes in fund balances is **not** a statement of income and expenses. "Revenue and other additions" and "expenditures and other deductions" include many items that do not constitute revenue or expense in a strict accounting sense. "Other additions" and "other deductions" include such nonrevenue and nonexpense items as "expended for plant facilities" and "retirement of indebtedness," which would normally be treated as adjustments to the fund balance of particular fund groups or included in a statement of changes in financial position.

All restricted gifts, bequests, and grants received during the period are reported as revenue in the current restricted fund. This treatment differs from that followed in the statement of current funds revenues, expenditures, and other changes (Exhibit 25.6), where restricted gifts, bequests, and grants are reported as revenue only to the extent expended.

Exhibit 25.4 includes a "net increase (decrease) before transfers" caption and a "total all funds" column. Both of these are permitted but not recommended by the audit guide. The

MARY AND
Statement of Changes
For the Year

| | Current Funds | | Loan |
	Unrestricted	Restricted	Funds
Revenues and other additions:			
Unrestricted current fund revenues	$3,385,000		
Gifts and bequests—restricted		$400,000	$10,000
Grants and contracts—restricted		200,000	
Investment income—restricted		10,000	
Realized gains on investments			
Interest on loans receivable			5,000
Expended for plant facilities			
Retirement of indebtedness			
Total	3,385,000	610,000	15,000
Expenditures and other deductions:			
Educational and general expenditures	2,300,000	550,000	
Auxiliary enterprises expenditures	95,000		
Refunded to grantors		10,000	
Expended for plant facilities			
Retirement of indebtedness			
Interest on indebtedness			
Disposal of plant facilities			
Loans written off			3,000
Total	2,395,000	560,000	3,000
Net increase/(decrease) before transfers	990,000	50,000	12,000
Transfers among funds—additions/(deductions):			
Mandatory:			
Principal and interest	(220,000)		
Renewals and replacements	(50,000)		
Unrestricted gifts allocated	(600,000)		
Portion of unrestricted quasi-endowment			
funds investment gains appropriated	40,000		
Total	(830,000)		
Net increase/(decrease) for the year	160,000	50,000	12,000
Fund balance, beginning of year	650,000	85,000	84,000
Fund balance, end of year	$ 810,000	$135,000	$96,000

Exhibit 25.4. Statement of changes in fund balances. *Source:* Gross and Warshauer, *Financial and Accounting Guide for Nonprofit Organizations,* Wiley, 1983, pp. 208–209. Reproduced by permission.

"net increase (decrease) before transfers" caption does not, given the mixed nature of the revenue and expenditure items, represent excess of revenue over expenditures for the period. It does, however, present the activity of each fund prior to transfers. A "total all funds" column is included in the illustration because it facilitates evaluation of a college as a single entity, rather than as a collection of individual funds. In recent years, more accountants prefer, and more institutions are presenting, these items.

Transfers between funds are segregated from the revenues and expenditures sections of the statement. Transfers mandated by contractual agreements should be reported separately from voluntary transfers.

ISLA COLLEGE
in Fund Balances
Ended June 30, 19X1

| Endowment and Similar Funds | Plant Funds | | | | Total All Funds |
	Unexpended	Renewal and Replacement	Retirement of Indebtedness	Investment in Plant	
					$ 3,385,000
$ 160,000	$ 65,000				635,000
					200,000
5,000	20,000	$ 10,000			45,000
150,000					150,000
					5,000
				$ 1,000,000	1,000,000
				170,000	170,000
315,000	85,000	10,000		1,170,000	5,590,000
					2,850,000
					95,000
					10,000
	900,000	100,000			1,000,000
			$170,000		170,000
			50,000		50,000
				85,000	85,000
					3,000
	900,000	100,000	220,000	85,000	4,263,000
315,000	(815,000)	(90,000)	(220,000)	1,085,000	1,327,000
			220,000		
		50,000			
550,000	50,000				
(40,000)					
510,000	50,000	50,000	220,000		
825,000	(765,000)	(40,000)		1,085,000	1,327,000
4,210,000	1,200,000	150,000	100,000	21,615,000	28,094,000
$5,035,000	$ 435,000	$110,000	$100,000	$22,700,000	$29,421,000

A statement of changes in fund balances should contain a "net increase (decrease) for the year" caption. This caption, recommended by the audit guide, communicates the net change in fund balances for the period for each fund and for the institution as a whole.

(b) Balance Sheet. The audit guide permits balance sheet presentation in either a "columnar" or "layered" format. Exhibit 25.5 illustrates a columnar balance sheet, which presents an overview of an entire organization. When the columnar format is used, the nature of restrictions imposed by donors on certain assets must be carefully identified. Layered or "pancake" format, with assets on the left and liabilities and fund balances on the right, and with separate, self-balancing accounts for major fund groupings, is also permissible.

MARY AND
Balance
June 30,

| | Current Funds | | Loan |
	Unrestricted	Restricted	Funds
Assets			
Current assets:			
Cash	$ 910,000	$285,000	$16,000
Short-term investments	930,000		
Accounts receivable	18,000		80,000
Inventories	20,000		
Prepaid expenses	25,000		
Total	1,903,000	285,000	96,000
Long-term investments			
Invested in plant			
Interfund receivable (payable)	(410,000)	(150,000)	
Total assets	$1,493,000	$135,000	$96,000
Liabilities and Fund Balance			
Current liabilities:			
Accounts payable	$ 573,000		
Current portion of debt			
Tuition deposits	110,000		
Total	683,000		
Long-term debt			
Fund balances:			
Restricted		$135,000	$50,000
Unrestricted	810,000		46,000
Total	810,000	135,000	96,000
Total liabilities and fund balance	$1,493,000	$135,000	$96,000

Exhibit 25.5.   Columnar balance sheet. *Source:* Gross and Warshauer, *Financial and Accounting Guide for Nonprofit Organizations,* Wiley, 1983, pp. 214–215. Reproduced by permission.

(c) Statement of Current Funds Revenues, Expenditures, and Other Changes.   Exhibit 25.6 presents a statement of current funds revenues, expenditures, and other changes. This statement reports all activity involving current funds—unrestricted and restricted—that are available for conducting the primary functions of an institution. Although similar in format to a statement of income and expenses, this statement does not present net results of operations for the year. It merely reports revenue and expenditure activity of current operations and amounts transferred between current and other funds.

Three column headings are used: "current unrestricted," "current restricted," and "total." The "current unrestricted fund" column reports all unrestricted revenue received during the period, regardless of when in the period it is received and whether it has been expended. The "current restricted fund" column reports restricted revenue only to the extent expended for restricted purposes. Thus, the amount reported as restricted revenue is equal to the amount reported as restricted expenditures, and is usually different from the amount reported as restricted revenue in the statement of changes in fund balances (Exhibit 25.4).

ISLA COLLEGE
Sheet
19X1

| Endowment and Similar Funds | Plant Funds | | | | Total All Funds |
	Unexpended	Renewal and Replacement	Retirement of Indebtedness	Investment in Plant	
$ 310,000	$ 20,000	$ 60,000			$ 1,601,000
	400,000	50,000	$100,000		1,480,000
					98,000
					20,000
					25,000
310,000	420,000	110,000	100,000		3,224,000
4,215,000					4,215,000
				$23,450,000	23,450,000
510,000	50,000				
$5,035,000	$ 470,000	$110,000	$100,000	$23,450,000	$30,889,000
	$ 35,000				$ 608,000
				$ 170,000	170,000
					110,000
	35,000			170,000	888,000
				580,000	580,000
$2,025,000	210,000	$110,000		22,700,000	25,230,000
3,010,000	225,000		$100,000		4,191,000
5,035,000	435,000	110,000	100,000	22,700,000	29,421,000
$5,035,000	$ 470,000	$110,000	$100,000	$23,450,000	$30,889,000

Included with expenditures on this statement are "mandatory" transfers required under debt and similar contractual agreements. Expenditures and mandatory transfers of auxiliary enterprises that are not central to the primary objectives of an institution, such as bookstores, are also included in the expenditure section.

"Other transfers and additions" are reported separately from expenditures. "Other transfers" are nonmandatory and represent internal shifts of resources between current and other funds.

A "net increase in fund balances" is reported at the bottom of the statement. This caption is not comparable to "excess of revenue over expenditures" for the year, but is merely the amount the board wishes to retain in the current fund.

VOLUNTARY HEALTH AND WELFARE ORGANIZATIONS

The AICPA Industry Audit Guide, "Audits of Voluntary Health and Welfare Organizations," issued in 1974, is the most authoritative pronouncement of accounting principles and reporting practices for voluntary health and welfare organizations. The guide defines

MARY AND ISLA COLLEGE
Statement of Current Funds Revenues, Expenditures, and Other Changes
For the Year Ended June 30, 19X1

	Current Fund		
	Unrestricted	Restricted	Total
Revenues:			
Educational and general:			
Student tuition and fees	$1,610,000		$1,610,000
Governmental appropriations	400,000		400,000
Governmental grants		$200,000	200,000
Gifts	900,000	340,000	1,240,000
Endowment income	350,000	10,000	360,000
Auxiliary enterprises	125,000		125,000
Total current revenues	3,385,000	550,000	3,935,000
Expenditures and mandatory transfers:			
Educational and general:			
Instruction	1,100,000		1,100,000
Research	300,000	550,000	850,000
Academic support	200,000		200,000
Student services	100,000		100,000
Operation and maintenance of plant	500,000		500,000
Institutional support	100,000		100,000
	2,300,000	550,000	2,850,000
Mandatory transfers for:			
Principal and interest	200,000		200,000
Renewals and replacements	50,000		50,000
Total educational and general	2,550,000	550,000	3,100,000
Auxiliary enterprises:			
Expenditures	95,000		95,000
Mandatory transfer for principal and interest	20,000		20,000
Total expenditures and mandatory transfers	2,665,000	550,000	3,215,000
Other transfers and additions:			
Excess of restricted receipts over transfers to revenues		60,000	60,000
Refunded to grantors		(10,000)	(10,000)
Unrestricted gifts allocated to other funds	(600,000)		(600,000)
Portion of quasi-endowment gains appropriated	40,000		40,000
Net increase in fund balance	$ 160,000	$ 50,000	$ 210,000

Exhibit 25.6.   Statement of current funds revenues, expenditures, and other changes. *Source:* **Gross and Warshauer,** *Financial and Accounting Guide for Nonprofit Organizations,* **Wiley, 1983, p. 216. Reproduced by permission.**

voluntary health and welfare organizations as "those not-for-profit organizations that derive their revenue primarily from voluntary contributions from the general public to be used for general or specific purposes connected with health, welfare, or community services."

25.24 ACCOUNTING PRINCIPLES

(a) Accrual Basis Accounting.   Voluntary health and welfare organizations should follow accrual basis accounting if they want to describe their financial statements as prepared in accordance with GAAP. Cash basis statements are permitted, although they are not in accordance with GAAP, unless differences from accrual basis statements are immaterial.

(b) Fund Accounting.   Most voluntary health and welfare organizations employ fund accounting. Five major funds are commonly used:

1. *Current Unrestricted Fund.* Includes all unrestricted resources of an organization, including all board-designated funds. Board designation of unrestricted funds is normally reported only in the fund balance section of the balance sheet. Board-designated funds may not be included with any other fund, but they may be reported as a separate part of the current unrestricted fund.

2. *Current Restricted Fund.* Includes all resources given to an organization for specific purposes that are part of the normal current operations of the organization.

3. *Land, Building, and Equipment Fund.* Includes the organization's net investment in fixed assets, and contributions restricted for fixed asset purchases. Fixed assets may be combined with current unrestricted funds.

4. *Endowment Fund.* Includes all investment gifts containing legal stipulations that only the investment income, and not the investment principal, may be expended for either restricted or unrestricted purposes.

5. *Custodian Fund.* Includes all assets held for and disbursed at the direction of other individuals or organizations. Custodian funds (also called "agency funds") do not constitute assets of the organization holding them.

(c) Appropriations.   An organization may designate a portion of the balance of the current unrestricted fund for a specific future purpose. This designation may appear only in the fund balance section of the balance sheet. The appropriation may not be shown as an expense or deduction in the statement of financial activity for the period.

(d) Fixed Assets.   Fixed assets should be capitalized on the balance sheet at cost if purchased, or at fair market value if donated. Minor fixed asset purchases usually not exceeding some specified maximum limit may be expensed as acquired. When capitalizing currently owned fixed assets for the first time, cost-based appraisal is an appropriate valuation basis if an organization cannot determine the original cost.

(e) Depreciation.   Capitalized fixed assets should be depreciated. Depreciation should be reported in the statement showing financial activity for the period as an element of expense in the fund in which the assets are recorded.

(f) Investment Income.   All **unrestricted** investment income (including income from investments held in board-designated or endowment funds) should be reported when earned as revenue in the current unrestricted fund.

   Restricted investment income should be reported as revenue in the appropriate restricted fund. Investment income restricted to a specific operating purpose should be reported in the current restricted fund. Endowment income, if unrestricted, should be reported in the current unrestricted fund; if endowment income is restricted, it should be reported as revenue in the appropriate restricted fund.

(g) Carrying Value of Investments.   An organization may carry its marketable investments at either cost or market value. If investments are carried at cost, market value should be disclosed in the financial statements; if investments are carried at market value, cost should be disclosed. The same carrying basis should be used for all investments.

(h) Gains and Losses on Investments.   All realized and unrealized gains and losses on investments should be reported in the revenue section of the activity statement of the fund owning the investment, except that legally unrestricted gains on investments held by the current restricted fund should be reported in the current unrestricted fund.

(i) **Gifts.** **Unrestricted** gifts should be reported as income in the current unrestricted fund. The timing of income recognition is governed by the donor's intent. If the donor is silent, the gift should be recognized as income in the year made.

The timing of income recognition for **restricted** gifts is the same as for unrestricted gifts.

Current restricted gifts should be reported in the current restricted fund. Building fund and endowment fund gifts are reported in their respective funds.

(j) **Bequests.** Bequests should be reported as income in the appropriate fund when the organization is reasonably certain of the amount it will receive. In most cases, this will not be known until the estate has been settled. In the meantime, if the organization has been advised that a substantial but uncertain amount will be received, note disclosure is appropriate.

(k) **Noncash Contributions.** A value for **donated services** is normally recorded if amounts are material and all of the following criteria are met:

1. A "measurable basis" exists for valuing the services.
2. Control is exercised over employment.
3. The services performed are a normal part of an organization's activities.

The hourly rate used to value such services is the rate the organization would have to pay someone to do equivalent work.

Donated materials are normally recorded as a contribution at their market value. If amounts are immaterial or if no objective basis for valuation exists, donated materials are not recorded.

Donated securities are valued at market value at the date of receipt and are recorded in the same manner as cash donations.

Donated fixed assets are normally recorded as income in the fixed asset fund at market value at the date of receipt.

(l) **Pledges.** Pledges should be recorded as assets when made; if necessary, an allowance for uncollectible pledges should be established based on the organization's prior collection experience. Pledges should be recognized as income in the period made unless the donor specifies otherwise.

(m) **Allocation of Joint Costs.** One of the most difficult problems faced by not-for-profit organizations has been accounting for **joint costs of multipurpose activities.** The problem stems from the difficulty in determining an objective basis for allocating such costs to the multiple purposes. These costs are often very significant for charities, and state regulators in particular have expressed concern that charities may use allocation methods that understate fund-raising expenses, thus misleading contributors into thinking that more of their gifts go for programs than is actually the case. The AICPA guides were not consistent in their rules for cost allocation: SOP No. 78-10 called for full allocation, whereas the Voluntary Health and Welfare guide leaned toward the so-called "primary purpose" rule (originally set forth in the Black Book) that if fund-raising was the primary purpose of an activity, then all joint costs were charged to fund-raising. The **Black Book** is a publication of the National Health Council, Inc., the National Assembly of National Voluntary Health and Social Welfare Organizations, Inc., and the United Way of America. It was first published in 1964 to attain uniform accounting and reporting by members of those organizations. The AICPA has issued an SOP (No. 87-2) calling for full allocation if certain criteria are met.

25.25 REPORTING PRACTICES. Three financial statements are generally prepared by voluntary health and welfare organizations.

1. Statement of support, revenue, and expenses, and changes in fund balances.

2. Statement of functional expenses.

3. Balance sheet.

(a) Statement of Support, Revenue, and Expenses, and Changes in Fund Balances. A statement of support, revenue, and expenses, and changes in fund balances is presented in Exhibit 25.7.

Expenses should be reported on a functional basis. Amounts spent on program services and supporting services should be separately reported. Within program services, amounts spent on each major program category should be reported. Within supporting services, amounts spent on fund-raising and on management and general activities should be separately reported.

Statement presentation is usually in columnar format; a "total all funds" column is recommended to summarize the financial activity of the organization as a whole. All unrestricted revenues and expenses, including activity of board-designated funds, should be reported in the current unrestricted fund. In addition, a separate plant fund may be presented, or fixed asset activity may be reported in the current unrestricted fund.

If investments are carried at market value, unrealized appreciation (or depreciation) should be reported in the revenue section of the appropriate fund. Realized gains or losses may be combined with unrealized appreciation (depreciation) for reporting purposes. Interfund transfers are reported after the excess (deficit) for the period, under the caption "other changes in fund balances."

(b) Statement of Functional Expenses. Exhibit 25.8 presents a statement of functional expenses, which analyzes the functional expenses as reported in the activity statement in terms of natural expense categories, such as salaries and supplies.

Depreciation should be included as an expense. Depreciation expense may be reported either with other expense categories (as in Exhibit 25.8) or after other expenses are subtotaled.

(c) Balance Sheet. A balance sheet is presented in Exhibit 25.9. Although the audit guide illustrates a "layered" balance sheet, with each fund presented as a separate, self-balancing set of accounts, **columnar** format balance sheets are also permitted. When a columnar format is used, restrictions attached to certain resources should be clearly identified.

One or more columns presenting comparative information for the preceding period may be included.

(d) Related Organizations. Financial data of affiliated organizations should be combined with those of the reporting organization if they all effectively function as a single organization. Criteria that should be considered when deciding whether to combine data include the degree of control exercised by one organization over the other(s), the extent of interorganization financial relationships, the degree of closeness implied in the organizations' fund-raising materials, and the extent to which the activities of the organizations are related.

OTHER NOT-FOR-PROFIT ORGANIZATIONS

Not-for-profit organizations not covered by a specific AICPA Industry Audit Guide are covered by SOP No. 78-10. Issued in 1978, the SOP does not contain an effective date because of the expectation that differences with forthcoming FASB pronouncements on not-for-profit accounting will have to be resolved. Covered organizations are encouraged to follow the SOP, pending the issuance of FASB standards.

NATIONAL ASSOCIATION OF ENVIRONMENTALISTS
Statement of Support, Revenues and Expenses, and Changes in Fund Balances
For the Year Ended December 31, 19X2

	Current Funds		Fixed Asset Fund	Endowment Fund	Total All Funds
	Unrestricted	Restricted			
Support:					
Contributions and gifts	$213,000		$10,000		$223,000
Bequests	60,000			$ 21,500	81,500
Total support	273,000		10,000	21,500	304,500
Revenues:					
Membership dues	20,550				20,550
Research projects	89,500	$38,400			127,900
Advertising income	33,500				33,500
Subscriptions to nonmembers	18,901				18,901
Dividends and interest income	14,607				14,607
Appreciation of investments				33,025	33,025
Total revenues	177,058	38,400		33,025	248,483
Total support and revenues	450,058	38,400	10,000	54,525	552,983

Expenses:					
Program services:					
"National Environment" magazine	108,240		2,260		110,500
Clean-up month campaign	124,308		2,309		126,617
Lake Erie project	83,285	26,164	5,616		115,065
Total program services	315,833	26,164	10,185		352,182
Supporting services:					
Management and general	30,355		3,161		33,516
Fund raising	5,719		250		5,969
Total supporting services	36,074		3,411		39,485
Total expenses	351,907	26,164	13,596		391,667
Excess (deficit) of revenues over expenses	98,151	12,236	(3,596)	54,525	161,316
Other changes in fund balance:					
Equipment acquisitions from unrestricted funds	(30,000)		30,000		—
Transfer of endowment fund gains	50,000			(50,000)	—
Fund balance, beginning of year	17,365	5,915	67,266	230,010	320,556
Fund balance, end of year	$135,516	$18,151	$93,670	$234,535	$481,872

Exhibit 25.7. Statement of support, revenues and expenses, and changes in fund balances. *Source: Gross and Warshauer, Financial and Accounting Guide for Nonprofit Organizations,* Wiley, 1983, p. 186. Reproduced by permission.

NATIONAL ASSOCIATION OF ENVIRONMENTALISTS
Statement of Functional Expenses
For the Year Ended December 31, 19X2

	Total All Expenses	Program Services				Supporting Services		
		"National Environment" Magazine	Clean-up Month Campaign	Lake Erie Project	Total Program	Management and General	Fund Raising	Total Supporting
Salaries	$170,773	$ 24,000	$ 68,140	$ 60,633	$152,773	$15,000	$3,000	$18,000
Payroll taxes and employee benefits	22,199	3,120	8,857	7,882	19,859	1,950	390	2,340
Total compensation	192,972	27,120	76,997	68,515	172,632	16,950	3,390	20,340
Printing	84,071	63,191	18,954	515	82,660	1,161	250	1,411
Mailing, postage, and shipping	14,225	10,754	1,188	817	12,759	411	1,055	1,466
Rent	19,000	3,000	6,800	5,600	15,400	3,000	600	3,600
Telephone	5,615	895	400	1,953	3,248	2,151	216	2,367
Outside art	14,865	3,165	11,700	—	14,865	—	—	
Local travel	1,741	—	165	915	1,080	661	—	661
Conferences and conventions	6,328	—	1,895	2,618	4,513	1,815	—	1,815
Depreciation	13,596	2,260	2,309	5,616	10,185	3,161	250	3,411
Legal and audit	2,000	—	—	—	—	2,000	—	2,000
Supplies	31,227	—	1,831	28,516	30,347	761	119	880
Miscellaneous	6,027	115	4,378	—	4,493	1,445	89	1,534
Total	$391,667	$110,500	$126,617	$115,065	$352,182	$33,516	$5,969	$39,485

Exhibit 25.8. Statement of functional expenses. *Source:* Gross and Warshauer, *Financial and Accounting Guide for Nonprofit Organizations,* Wiley, 1983, p. 192. Reproduced by permission.

NATIONAL ASSOCIATION OF ENVIRONMENTALISTS
Balance Sheet
December 31, 19X2 and 19X1

| | December 31, 19X2 | | | | | December 31, 19X1 |
| | Current Funds | | Endowment Funds | Fixed Asset Funds | Total All Funds | Total All Funds |
	Unrestricted	Restricted				
Assets						
Current assets:						
Cash	$ 52,877	$22,666	$ 8,416	$ 2,150	$ 86,109	$ 11,013
Savings accounts	50,000				50,000	
Accounts receivable	3,117				3,117	918
Investments, at market	76,195		226,119		302,314	269,289
Pledges receivable	4,509	1,000			5,509	769
Total current assets	186,698	23,666	234,535	2,150	447,049	281,989
Fixed assets, at cost				111,135	111,135	72,518
Less: Accumulated depreciation				(19,615)	(19,615)	(6,019)
Net fixed assets				91,520	91,520	66,499
Total assets	$186,698	$23,666	$234,535	$ 93,670	$538,569	$348,488
Liabilities and Fund Balances						
Current liabilities:						
Accounts payable	$ 48,666	$ 1,015			$ 49,681	$ 25,599
Deferred income	2,516	4,500			7,016	2,333
Total current liabilities	51,182	5,515			56,697	27,932
Fund balance	135,516	18,151	$234,535	$ 93,670	481,872	320,556
Total liabilities and fund balances	$186,698	$23,666	$234,535	$ 93,670	$538,569	$348,488

Exhibit 25.9. Balance sheet. *Source:* Gross and Warshauer, *Financial and Accounting Guide for Nonprofit Organizations*, Wiley, 1983, p. 194. **Reproduced by permission.**

25.26 ACCOUNTING PRINCIPLES. It is not always immediately apparent whether some not-for-profit organizations are covered by SOP No. 78-10 or by the "Audits of Voluntary Health and Welfare Organizations." (It is usually clear whether an organization is a college or a hospital.) Since several major differences exist between these two documents that can have a significant effect on financial statements, organizations should consider carefully which document they should properly follow. Organizations covered by the SOP include professional and trade associations, private and community foundations, religious organizations, libraries, museums, private schools, and performing arts organizations.

(a) Accrual Basis Accounting. The SOP requires that not-for-profit organizations **report** on the accrual basis if they wish to describe their financial statements as being prepared in accordance with GAAP. If the difference between cash basis and accrual basis statements is immaterial, an organization may remain on a cash basis and still effectively report on a GAAP basis.

(b) Fund Accounting. The SOP does not require the use of fund reporting by organizations wishing to prepare financial statements in accordance with GAAP. Instead, organizations should properly segregate unrestricted resources from resources possessing externally imposed restrictions. Fund reporting may be used if helpful in achieving this segregation.

(c) Fixed Assets. Fixed assets should be capitalized. Capitalization should be based on cost for purchased assets and fair market value at date of gift for donated fixed assets. If historical cost is unobtainable, another reasonable basis, such as cost-based appraisal value, may be used.

(d) Museum Collections. Museums and similar organizations may capitalize their collections but are not required to do so. Other fixed assets (e.g., buildings) owned by such organizations should be capitalized.

(e) Depreciation. Once capitalized, fixed assets that are exhaustible should be depreciated. Inexhaustible fixed assets, such as landmarks, monuments, and historical treasures, need not be depreciated if the criteria in SFAS No. 93 are met. Houses of worship must be depreciated after the effective date of SFAS No. 93.

(f) Investment Income. **Unrestricted** investment income, including unrestricted endowment income, should be reported in the unrestricted fund as earned.

Reporting of **restricted** investment income depends on how the income is used. If the income is from investment of current restricted funds, restricted plant funds, or endowment funds whose investment income the donor has limited to current restricted purposes, investment income should be deferred in a liability account on the balance sheet until expended for the restricted purpose. The investment income would then be recognized.

If investment income arises from endowment funds with donor-imposed restrictions specifying that investment income must be added to principal, such investment income is reported as a capital addition in the nonexpendable additions section of the statement of activity. (See the discussion of reporting practices in section 25.27.)

(g) Carrying Value of Investments. Marketable securities may be carried either at the lower of cost or market value, or at market value. For marketable debt securities expected to be held to maturity, amortized cost is also an appropriate alternative.

Investments not readily marketable, such as real estate or oil and gas interests, may also be carried at fair value or the lower of cost or fair value.

(h) Gains and Losses on Investments. Unrestricted realized and unrealized gains and losses on investments should generally be reported as current unrestricted revenue, except that unrealized gains (losses) on noncurrent investments carried at the lower of cost or market value are reported as direct additions to (or deductions from) the appropriate fund balance.

Restricted realized and unrealized gains and losses held by current restricted funds should be deferred on the balance sheet until restrictions are met.

Unrealized gains and losses on endowment fund investments carried at market value and all realized gains (losses) on endowment investments should be reported as capital additions or deductions to the endowment fund.

(i) Current Restricted Gifts, Grants, and Bequests. Current restricted gifts, grants, and bequests should be recorded as deferred income in the liability section of the balance sheet until donor-imposed restrictions are met. Once the organization incurs an expense for the purpose specified by the donor, revenue should be recognized to the extent of the expense.

(j) Pledges. Legally enforceable pledges should be recorded as assets on the balance sheet at their estimated net realizable value. The timing of recognizing pledges as income depends on the intentions of the donor. If the donor specifies that the pledge must be expended in the current period, it should be recognized as income in the current period. If the donor designates a future period for expenditure, the pledge should be recorded as deferred income in the current period and recognized as income in the designated future period. If the donor does not indicate a period for expenditure, the pledge should not be recognized as income until the time receipt is expected.

(k) Contributed Services. A value for contributed services should be reported as income and expenses only if all the following criteria are met:

1. Services provided must constitute an essential element of an organization's activities, which, if not contributed, would be performed by paid staff.
2. Controls must be exercised over volunteer employment.
3. An objective basis to value contributed services must exist.
4. The services must relate to activities benefiting persons outside the organization.

The fourth criterion will limit organizations that report a value for contributed services to those providing services for the public.

(l) Subscription and Membership Income. Subscription and membershi income should be recognized in the periods in which the organization provides goods or services to subscribers or members. This usually requires deferring such amounts when received and recognizing them ratably over the membership or subscription period. Special calculations, based on life expectancy, are required when so-called life memberships are involved.

(m) Functional Reporting of Program Services. Organizations that receive a significant level of support in the form of contributions from the general public should report expenses on a functional or program basis. Other organizations may classify expenses on a natural (or object) basis or on a functional basis, as they see fit.

(n) Management and General Expenses. Management and general expenses are defined in SOP No. 78-10 as those costs that cannot be exclusively identified with a single program or activity, but are nonetheless vital to the conduct of the programs and activities of an organization. An appropriate portion of management and general expenses should be allocated to programs or activities receiving benefits.

(o) Fund-Raising Expenses. Fund-raising expenses are defined by the SOP as costs incurred to induce others to contribute resources (e.g., money, time, or materials) without receipt of direct economic benefits in return. Fund-raising costs include a fair allocation of overhead, as well as direct costs. Fund-raising costs should be expensed when incurred. If fund-raising activities are combined with program functions, such as mailing educational literature to prospective contributors, the total cost should be allocated between functions on the basis of how the literature is used, as determined by content, reason for distribution, and expected audience, in accordance with SOP No. 87-2.

(p) Grants to Others.   Organizations that award grants should record a grant as a liability and an expense in the period in which the recipient is entitled to the grant. This is usually the period in which the grant is authorized, even though some of the payments may not be made until later periods.

25.27 REPORTING PRACTICES.   Three primary financial statements are required by SOP No. 78-10:

1. A balance sheet.
2. A statement of activity.
3. A statement of changes in financial position.

A comprehensive statement of changes in financial position was not previously required of any category of not-for-profit organization.

A statement of functional expenses may be presented if desired.

(a) Balance Sheet.   A balance sheet (Exhibit 25.10) should present the amount of assets, liabilities, and fund balances of an organization. Assets and liabilities of different funds may be mingled, provided that the fund balance section of the balance sheet clearly shows separate balances for (1) unrestricted funds, (2) restricted funds, and (3) fixed assets. If an organization has only unrestricted funds, it must designate which assets and liabilities are **current** and which are **noncurrent.** Fixed assets may be reported in a separate fund or combined with unrestricted or restricted funds, as appropriate.

(b) Statement of Activity.   A statement of activity (Exhibit 25.11) should include all revenue and support, expenses, and nonexpendable or capital additions for the period. The statement of activity may have any title that correctly identifies the information contained therein. The amount and source of unrestricted revenue and support, current restricted revenue and support, and nonexpendable additions should be reported. Operating income and expenses should be reported separately from nonexpendable additions. The excess (deficit) of operating income over expenses should be reported both **before** and **after** nonexpendable additions. The statement of activity should contain a fund balance section that reconciles the beginning and end-of-period fund balances. Transfers between funds should be reported in this section, after the caption "fund balance, beginning of year."

(c) Statement of Changes in Financial Position or Cash Flows.   The statement of changes in financial position (Exhibit 25.12) required by the SOP is similar to the one formerly required of commercial entities. It summarizes the resources made available to an organization during a period and the uses made of these resources. Generally, this statement reconciles changes in working capital for a period, but in smaller organizations it may merely present changes in cash balances. Eventually, not-for-profit organizations will present a statement of cash flows, as do businesses. A sample statement of cash flows is illustrated in Exhibit 25.13.

(d) Financial Statement Format.   The SOP does not prescribe a financial statement format. The format selected should be appropriate for presenting the financial condition and activity

---

WAUWATOSA COMMUNITY SERVICE ORGANIZATION
Balance Sheet
June 30, 19X1

Assets

Current assets:		
Cash	$ 79,000	
Pledges receivable	16,000	
Accounts receivable	48,000	
Inventory	25,000	
Total current assets		$168,000
Endowment fund investments, at market		320,000
Building and equipment, less depreciation of $151,000		211,000
Total assets		$699,000

Liabilities and Fund Balances

Current liabilities:		
Accounts payable		$ 24,000
Current portion of mortgage		7,000
Deferred gifts and dues:		
Membership fees	$ 18,000	
Plant fund gifts	25,000	
Restricted gifts	18,000	
Unrestricted gifts	3,000	64,000
Total current liabilities		95,000
Mortgage, 8%, due 2006		75,000
Total liabilities		170,000
Fund balances:		
Unrestricted, available for current operations	80,000	
Invested in fixed assets, net	129,000	
Endowment fund	320,000	
Total fund balances		529,000
Total liabilities and fund balances		$699,000

Exhibit 25.10. Balance sheet. *Source:* **Gross and Warshauer, Wiley,** *Financial and Accounting Guide for Nonprofit Organizations,* **1983, p. 269. Reproduced by permission.**

of a particular organization. The SOP does, however, recommend certain reporting practices.

Use of a "total all funds" column is recommended, but not required, as is presentation of comparative financial statements. Functional reporting of expenses is required of organizations receiving contributions from the general public and is recommended for all organizations.

Preparation of combined financial statements by financially interrelated organizations is required when one organization controls another and when any one of the following criteria is met:

1. A separate entity solicits funds in the name of the reporting organization for use by the reporting organization.

2. A reporting organization transfers resources to another entity to be held for the benefit of the reporting organization.

3. A reporting organization assigns functions to a controlled entity whose funding is derived from sources other than public contributions.

WAUWATOSA COMMUNITY SERVICE ORGANIZATION
Statement of Revenue, Expenses, Capital Additions,
and Changes in Fund Balances
For the Year Ended June 30, 19X1

	Operating	Plant	Endowment	Total
Revenue and support:				
Service fees	$155,000			$155,000
Grants, including $34,000 of				
restricted grants	61,000			61,000
Membership dues	53,000			53,000
Unrestricted contributions and				
bequests	35,000			35,000
Dividends and interest	16,000			16,000
Unrestricted realized and				
unrealized gains	18,000			18,000
Total revenue and support	338,000			338,000
Expenses:				
Program:				
Project A	105,000	$ 10,000		115,000
Project B	95,000	13,000		108,000
Membership services	40,000	4,000		44,000
Total program	240,000	27,000		267,000
Supporting:				
General management	38,000	2,000		40,000
Fund raising	6,000	1,000		7,000
Membership development	7,000	1,000		8,000
Total supporting	51,000	4,000		55,000
Total expenses	291,000	31,000		322,000
Excess of revenue and support over				
expenses	47,000	(31,000)	—	16,000
Nonexpendable additions:				
Restricted gifts		20,000	$ 39,000	59,000
Restricted interest		1,000		1,000
Restricted realized and				
unrealized gains			17,000	17,000
Excess of revenue, support, and				
nonexpendable additions over				
expenses	47,000	(10,000)	56,000	93,000
Fund balances, beginning of period	64,000	108,000	264,000	436,000
Transfers	(31,000)	31,000		—
Fund balances, end of period	$ 80,000	$129,000	$320,000	$529,000

Exhibit 25.11.   Statement of activity. *Source:* **Gross and Warshauer,** *Financial and Accounting Guide for Nonprofit Organizations,* **Wiley, 1983, p. 272. Reproduced by permission.**

Combined financial statements may also be prepared in circumstances other than those above. Religious organizations are exempt from the combination requirement.

AUDIT CONSIDERATIONS FOR A NOT-FOR-PROFIT ORGANIZATION

25.28 GENERAL CONSIDERATIONS.   An audit of the financial statements of a not-for-profit organization is similar to an audit of a for-profit enterprise, and generally accepted

WAUWATOSA COMMUNITY SERVICE ORGANIZATION
Statement of Changes in Financial Position
For the Year Ended June 30, 19X1

Working capital was provided by:		
Current activities:		
Excess of revenue and support over expenses	$16,000	
Nonexpendable additions	77,000	
Excess of revenue, support, and nonexpendable additions over expenses	93,000	
Add—Expenses not requiring outlay of working capital— depreciation	31,000	
Less—Income not providing working capital—unrealized gains	(15,000)	
Net		$109,000
Proceeds of mortgage		10,000
Sale of investments		45,000
Total working capital provided		164,000
Working capital was utilized for:		
Acquisition of fixed assets	(20,000)	
Acquisition of investments	(90,000)	
Repayment of bank loan	(7,000)	
Total working capital utilized		(117,000)
Net increase in working capital		$ 47,000
Components of change in working capital:		
Increases in current assets:		
Cash	$17,000	
Pledges receivable	2,000	
Accounts receivable	6,000	
Inventory	1,000	
		$ 26,000
Decrease (increase) in current liabilities:		
Accounts payable	47,000	
Deferred gifts and dues	(26,000)	
		21,000
		$ 47,000

Exhibit 25.12. Statement of changes in financial position in which all funds are combined. *Source:* Gross and Jablonsky, *Principles of Accounting and Financial Reporting for Nonprofit Organizations,* Wiley, 1979, p. 314.

auditing standards should be followed. A not-for-profit organization, however, seeks to provide an optimal level of services, rather than to maximize profits, and its financial statements, accordingly, focus on the activity and balances of different funds. This in turn, influences the conduct of the audit.

25.29 INTERNAL CONTROL STRUCTURE. Some not-for-profit organizations do not have effective internal control structures. The size of staff may be inadequate to achieve a proper segregation of duties, and the nature of some transactions often precludes sufficient checks and balances. Internal control structure deficiencies are often mitigated by adoption of procedures including the following: (1) involvement of senior management and directors in the operation of the organization; (2) restricting check signing to senior management and directors; (3) implementing effective bank reconciliation procedures; (4) preparing annual

WAUWATOSA COMMUNITY SERVICES ORGANIZATION
Statement of Cash Flows
For the Year Ended June 30, 19XX

Operating cash flows:	
Cash received from:	
Sales of goods and services	$204,000
Investment income	16,000
Gifts and grants:	
Unrestricted	66,000
Restricted	52,000
Cash paid to employees and suppliers	(290,000)
Cash paid to charitable beneficiaries	(42,000)
Interest paid	(7,000)
Net operating cash flows	(1,000)
Capital cash flows:	
Cash received from gifts	59,000
Investment income received	1,000
Net capital cash flows	60,000
Financing cash flows:	
Proceeds from borrowing	10,000
Repayment of debt	(7,000)
Net financing cash flows	3,000
Investing cash flows:	
Purchase of building and equipment	(20,000)
Purchase of investments	(90,000)
Proceeds from sale of investments	65,000
Net investing cash flows	(45,000)
Net increase in cash	17,000
Cash: Beginning of year	62,000
End of year	$ 79,000

Exhibit 25.13.   Statement of cash flows, derived from data included in Exhibit 25.12.

budgets and promptly investigating variances from budget estimates; and (5) depositing investment securities with independent custodians.

25.30 MATERIALITY.   The issue of what is material is equally important for not-for-profit and for-profit organizations. In for-profit enterprises, evaluating materiality involves considering the effect of alternate accounting treatments and disclosures on decisions by investors, and it relates to net income and earnings per share. These measures are generally not applicable to not-for-profit organizations. Instead, evaluating materiality involves considering the effects of accounting treatments and disclosures on decisions by contributors, and it relates to revenue, expenditures, and the cost of individual programs.

25.31 TAXES.   Not-for-profit organizations are generally exempt from income taxes and are often exempt from property and sales taxes. Tax liabilities, however, may arise from tax on unrelated business income, tax on net income resulting from a loss of tax-exempt status, or certain excise taxes applicable to private foundations.

25.32 CONSOLIDATION.   Not-for-profit organizations do not "own" other organizations in the sense that businesses own other businesses. Not-for-profit organizations, however, may exercise effective control over affiliates or related organizations; in such instances, preparation of combined financial statements may be appropriate.

25.33 COMPLIANCE AUDITING. In recent years, federal and state governments have become more active in requiring recipients of government money to submit auditor reports on various aspects of financial operations. These usually include opinions on financial data for the organization as a whole and, for government grants, reports on internal controls and compliance with laws and regulations. The exact requirements may differ depending on the type of recipient (college, hospital, etc.), the agency that made the grant, whether the money was received directly or through another level of government, and the amount of money received. It is important for the auditor to ascertain any compliance auditing requirements prior to beginning fieldwork, so that the auditor can perform the work necessary to issue the required reports. Specific requirements are contained in a number of different documents including SAS No. 63, "Compliance Auditing Applicable to Governmental Entities and Other Recipients of Governmental Financial Assistance"; the Department of Health and Human Services audit guide, "Guidelines for Audits of Federal Awards to Nonprofit Organizations"; various circulars issued by the Office of Management and Budget (principally A-21, A-110, A-122, A-128, A-133); and "Government Auditing Standards," issued by the GAO (generally referred to as the "Yellow Book"). Compliance auditing is discussed further in Chapter 24, "State and Local Government Accounting."

25.34 UNIQUE AUDITING AREAS. Auditing areas unique to not-for-profit organizations include the following:

- **Collections of Museums, Libraries, Zoological Parks, and Similar Organizations.** Auditing considerations include valuation of assets, capitalization, accessions and deaccessions, security, insurance coverage, and observation of inventory.
- **Contributions.** Auditing considerations include ascertaining that amounts reported as contributions are properly stated. Audit tests for noncash contributions include testing their assigned value. Auditors are particularly concerned about the possibility that contributions that were intended for the organization may never have been received and recorded.
- **Fees for Performance of Services, Including Tuition, Membership Dues, Ticket Revenue, and Patient Fees.** Auditing considerations include confirming that revenue is computed at proper rates, collected, and properly recorded for all services provided.
- **Functional Allocation of Expenses.** Auditing considerations include appropriateness of allocations among functions, reasonableness of allocation methods, accuracy of computations, and consistency of allocation bases with bases of prior periods. These considerations are especially important when joint costs of multipurpose activities (discussed above) are involved.
- **Restricted Resources.** Auditing considerations include ascertaining that transactions are for the restricted purpose and are recorded in the proper restricted fund.
- **Grant Awards to Others.** Auditing considerations include confirming grant awards with recipients and ascertaining that grants are recorded in the proper accounting period.
- **Tax Compliance.** Not-for-profits are subject to IRC sections that differ from those regularly applicable to businesses. Auditors must review compliance with these sections. Areas of particular concern are conformity with exempt purpose, unrelated business income, lobbying, status as a public charity (if applicable), and special rules applicable to private foundations.

SOURCES AND SUGGESTED REFERENCES

Adams, J. B., Bossio, R. J., and Rohan, P., *Accounting for Contributed Services: Survey of Preparers and Users of Financial Statements of Not-for-Profit Organizations,* FASB, Norwalk, CT, 1989.

American Institute of Certified Public Accountants, Committee on College and University Accounting and Auditing, "Audits of Colleges and Universities, Including Statement of Position issued by the Accounting Standards Division," Industry Audit Guide, 2nd ed., AICPA, New York, 1975.

———, "Compliance Auditing Applicable to Governmental Entities and Other Recipients of Governmental Financial Assistance," Statement on Auditing Standards No. 63, AICPA, New York, 1989.

———, "Reporting Practices Concerning Hospital-Related Organizations," Statement of Position No. 81-2, AICPA, New York, 1981.

———, "Accounting for Asserted and Unasserted Medical Malpractice Claims of Health Care Providers and Related Issues," Statement of Position No. 87-1, AICPA, New York, 1987.

———"Accounting for Joint Costs of Informational Materials and Activities of Not-for-Profit Organizations That Include a Fund-Raising Appeal," Statement of Position No. 87-2, AICPA, New York, 1987.

———, Committee on Voluntary Health and Welfare Organizations, "Audits of Voluntary Health and Welfare Organizations," Industry Audit Guide, 2nd ed., AICPA, New York, 1988.

———, Subcommittee on Health Care Matters, "Hospital Audit Guide, Including Statements of Position issued by the Accounting and Auditing Standards Divisions," Industry Audit Guide, 6th ed., AICPA, New York, 1987.

———, Subcommittee on Nonprofit Organizations, "Audits of Certain Nonprofit Organizations," including "Accounting Principles and Reporting Practices for Certain Nonprofit Organizations," Statement of Position No. 78-10, 2nd ed., AICPA, New York, 1988.

Anthony, R. N., *Financial Accounting in Nonbusiness Organizations: An Exploratory Study of Conceptual Issues,* FASB, Stamford, CT, 1978.

Anthony, R. N., and Young, D. W., *Management Control in Nonprofit Organizations,* 3rd ed., Irwin, Homewood, IL, 1984.

Cary, W. L., and Bright, C. B., *The Law and the Lore of Endowment Funds—Report to the Ford Foundation,* Ford Foundation, New York, 1969.

Daughtrey, W. H., Jr., and Gross, M. J., Jr., *Museum Accounting Handbook,* American Association of Museums, Washington, DC, 1978.

Financial Accounting Standards Board, "Objectives of Financial Reporting by Business Enterprises," Statement of Financial Accounting Concepts No. 1, FASB, Stamford, CT, 1978.

———, "Qualitative Characteristics of Accounting Information," Statement of Financial Accounting Concepts No. 2, FASB, Stamford, CT, 1980.

———, "Objectives of Financial Reporting by Nonbusiness Organizations," Statement of Financial Accounting Concepts No. 4, FASB, Stamford, CT, 1980.

———, "Accounting for Contingencies," Statement of Financial Accounting Standards, No. 5, FASB, Stamford, CT, 1975.

———, "Elements of Financial Statements," Statement of Financial Accounting Concepts No. 6, FASB, Stamford, CT, 1985.

———, "Specialized Accounting and Reporting Principles and Practices in AICPA Statements of Position and Guides on Accounting and Auditing Matters," Statement of Financial Accounting Standards No. 32, FASB, Stamford, CT, 1979.

———, "Recognition of Depreciation by Not-for-Profit Organizations," Statement of Financial Accounting Standards No. 93, FASB, Stamford, CT, 1987 (Amended by SFAS No. 99, "Deferral of the Effective Date of Recognition of Depreciation by Not-for-Profit Organizations," 1988).

———, "Statement of Cash Flows," Statement of Financial Accounting Standards No. 95, FASB, Stamford, CT, 1987.

———, "Financial Reporting by Not-for-Profit Organizations: Form and Content of Financial Statements," (Invitation to Comment), FASB, Norwalk, CT, 1989.

Evangelical Joint Accounting Committee, "Accounting and Financial Reporting Guide for Christian Ministries," Christian Ministries Management Association, Diamond Bar, CA, 1987.

Gross, J.J., Jr., and Jablonsky, S.F., *Principles of Accounting and Financial Reporting for Nonprofit Organizations*, Wiley, New York, 1979.

———, and Warshauer, W., Jr., *Financial and Accounting Guide for Nonprofit Organizations*, rev. 3rd ed., Wiley, New York, 1983.

Henke, E. O., *Introduction to Nonprofit Organization Accounting*, Kent Publishing, Boston, MA, 1980.

Holck, M., Jr., and Holck, M., Sr., *Complete Handbook of Church Accounting*, Prentice-Hall, Englewood Cliffs, NJ, 1978.

Holder, W. W., *The Not-for-Profit Organization Reporting Entity*, Philanthropy Monthly Press, New Milford, CT, 1986.

National Association of College and University Business Officers, *College and University Business Administration*, Washington, DC, 1982.

National Health Council, National Assembly of National Voluntary Health and Social Welfare Organizations, Inc., and United Way of America, *Standards of Accounting and Financial Reporting for Voluntary Health and Welfare Organizations*, 3rd ed., NHC, NANVHSWO, and UWA, New York, 1988.

Nelson, C. A., and Turk, F. J., *Financial Management for the Arts: A Guidebook for Arts Organizations*, Associated Council of the Arts, New York, 1975.

Ramanathan, K. V., *Management Control in Nonprofit Organizations*, Wiley, New York, 1982.

United States Department of Health and Human Services, "Guidelines for Audits of Federal Awards to Nonprofit Organizations," DHHS, Washington, DC, 1989.

United States General Accounting Office, *Government Auditing Standards*, GAO, Washington, DC, 1988.

United States Office of Management and Budget, "Cost Principles for Educational Institutions," Circular No. A-21, OMB, Washington, DC, 1979.

———, "Grants and Agreements with Institutions of Higher Education, Hospitals, and Other Nonprofit Organizations," Circular No. A-110, OMB, Washington, DC, 1976.

———, "Cost Principles for Nonprofit Organizations," Circular A-122, OMB, Washington, DC, 1980.

———, "Audits of State and Local Governments," Circular A-128, OMB, Washington, DC, 1985.

———, "Audits of Institutions of Higher Education and Other Nonprofit Institutions," Circular A-133, OMB, Washington, DC, 1990.

United Way of America, *Accounting and Financial Reporting: A Guide for United Ways and Not-for-Profit Human Service Organizations*, 2nd ed., UWA, Alexandria, VA, 1989.

Wacht, R. F., *Financial Management in Nonprofit Organizations*, Georgia State University, Atlanta, GA, 1984.

PART V

COMPENSATION AND BENEFITS

CHAPTER **26**

PENSION PLANS AND OTHER POSTEMPLOYMENT BENEFITS

Vincent Amoroso, FSA
KPMG Peat Marwick

Paul C. Wirth, CPA
KPMG Peat Marwick

Everett D. Wong, FSA
KPMG Peat Marwick

CONTENTS

BACKGROUND, ENVIRONMENT, AND OVERVIEW

26.1 INTRODUCTION.   The dramatic transformation that U.S. pension accounting underwent in the 1980s has placed a significant burden on companies and their accountants to understand the intricate concepts of accounting for pension assets, obligations, and periodic pension cost. This chapter has been written to explain those accounting concepts and to assist the reader in understanding and implementing them. The focus will be on the two distinct set of accounting standards that apply to pension and retirement plans—**SFAS No. 35,** "Accounting and Reporting by Defined Benefit Pension Plans," and **SFAS Nos. 87 and 88,** "Employers' Accounting for Pensions" and "Employers' Accounting for Settlements and Curtailments of Defined Benefit Pension Plans and for Termination Benefits." SFAS No. 35 applies to the preparation of financial statements for the pension plan, as an entity. SFAS Nos. 87 and 88, on the other hand, specify the accounting to be followed in the financial statements of the plan sponsor. They also established new standards for measuring a company's annual pension cost and balance sheet pension obligations.

26.2 DEVELOPMENT OF THE PRIVATE PENSION SYSTEM.   Before consideration of the accounting requirements specified by SFAS Nos. 35, 87, and 88, some background information regarding the pension system may be useful. It will outline why companies sponsor retirement programs and how plans are changing in response to a changing environment.

(a) The Past.   The U.S. private pension system traces its origins to 1875 when the first formal plan was established by a company in the railroad industry. In addition to fostering humanitarian objectives, the early plans were established to achieve a well-defined **management goal**—to affect the age composition of the work force. By using such plans, manufacturing firms could ease out older workers who were less productive and service industries were able to provide promotion opportunities for younger employees. Pension plans were typically established in conjunction with mandatory retirement policies. Tax-driven motives were noticeably absent because there were no meaningful tax incentives until 1942 when corporate tax rates were increased dramatically to finance World War II.

The private U.S. pension system started during the **industrial revolution.** Emerging national companies could not continue their past practice of accommodating aged workers with informal ad hoc policies. One by one, big companies with the financial ability to do so adopted formal retirement arrangements to solve this problem. The list includes the Standard Oil Companies, DuPont, U.S. Steel, and Bell Companies. By 1930 nearly 400 major corporations with more than 4 million workers, representing approximately one-sixth of the private work force, had adopted formal pension plans.

The seeds of federal regulation were sown before the Depression. Many plans were implemented and operated by companies to achieve their goals without regard to **employee rights.** Courts viewed these contracts as one-sided and issued decisions that construed plans as gratuities.

(b) The Period of Growth.   Plan sponsors' motives for providing pensions have become less homogeneous since World War II. During this period of unprecedented economic prosperity, companies have responded in droves to **increased taxes** and **union demands** (or threats of organization) by establishing plans. Exhibit 26.1 shows the growth in pension coverage between 1940 and 1980.

Higher tax rates coupled with federal wage controls that had been imposed to stifle war-related inflation triggered a spurt of growth in plan formation during the 1940s. Exhibit 26.1 shows that pension coverage doubled in this decade.

The wide-reaching economic prosperity of the 1950s and 1960s had a profound effect on the pension system; coverage almost tripled during this period (see Exhibit 26.1). Through collective bargaining, unions succeeded in establishing plans in many booming industries. Companies with unfilled orders willingly paid the price of starting a program. In addition, plans were established for nonunion employees to assure parity with unionized co-workers. In companies without unions, plans were developed to ward off organization drives. As the

NUMBER OF WORKERS COVERED BY PRIVATE PENSION PLANS	
Year	Number
1940	4,100,000
1950	9,800,000
1960	18,700,000
1970	26,300,000
1980	35,800,000

Exhibit 26.1.   Growth in pension coverage. *Source:* Alicia H. Munnell, *Economics of Private Pensions,* The Brookings Institution, 1982, p. 11.

economic pie grew, the one-company worker came to expect that he would be rewarded with a secure retirement for his loyal and long service. He was not disappointed. By the dawn of the congressional debates that culminated in the passage of pension reform legislation in 1974, pension plans had been adopted by virtually all established large and medium-sized companies. Pension coverage is still spotty, however, in smaller companies that operate on thin margins.

Small professional corporations have maintained a proliferation of pension plans as tax shelters during the 1980s. Accumulation of assets and tax savings for the proprietor(s) are the usual goals of these plans. In many ways federal pension regulation has been driven by tax authorities' desire to correct perceived abuses in this segment of the pension system.

(c) The Present. The private system is currently under significant **pressure from external forces.** Through repeated changes in the 1980s the federal government is reducing available tax incentives and increasing administrative complexity and, therefore, compliance costs. Foreign competition and corporate restructuring in the recent era of mergers and takeovers have caused many companies to rethink their pension policies. Changes in the make-up of the labor force are also having an effect on the makeup of pension programs.

For now, change in plan design and types of plans used for providing retirement income are the only discernible trends in the responses of plan sponsors. Companies are increasingly turning to so-called **nonqualified plans** (see Sponsor Accounting for Nonqualified Plans). Plans such as 401(k) and thrift or matching programs are becoming an increasingly important part of plan sponsors' deferred compensation policies. Younger employees prefer these savings plans because of their visibility, and the predictability of their annual costs appeals to many employers.

26.3 PLAN ADMINISTRATION.   Employers still establish plans to affect the age composition of its work force by providing income security during employees' retirement years. A plan's level of benefit and other important features—such as early retirement provisions—balance the sponsor's management goals and cost tolerance. Once a program is established, its administration is dictated by specific plan language, which in turn is affected significantly by federal law.

The **Employee Retirement Income Security Act of 1974** (ERISA) established minimum standards applicable to virtually all employee plans. Certain unfunded nonqualified plans are exempted. Through a succession of amendments since 1974, the original legal standards have been modified and are now considerably more detailed. Employers are not required to start pension plans but, once established, ERISA limits a sponsor's freedom in changing benefits or options. The IRS administers most of the minimum standards, including participation, funding, and vesting and accrual of benefits. The DOL is responsible for the fiduciary and reporting and disclosure requirements. In addition, the DOL assists participants by investigating alleged infractions and by bringing civil action to enforce compliance, if necessary. The **Pension Benefit Guaranty Corporation** (PBGC) administers the termination insurance program established by ERISA.

Plan administration can be viewed as three functions—operation, communication, and compliance. Operating a plan in accordance with its terms requires maintaining sufficient data to determine the proper apportionment of benefits to participants, the calculations needed to apply benefits, and an appropriate level of contributions. Communicating information about benefits to participants assists employees' retirement planning and enhances loyalty. Compliance activities include adopting amendments to conform plans to changing federal requirements and to ERISA's reporting and disclosure requirements. The latter include annual and other reporting to the three pension regulatory agencies and to plan participants.

Most defined benefit pension plans are subject to the **termination insurance program** that was codified by Title IV of ERISA. Covered plans pay annual premiums to the PBGC, which in 1989 was $16 per participant plus a surcharge applicable to underfunded plans. Within specified time constraints an employer can terminate a fully funded plan at will. A procedure is prescribed for notifying participants and the PBGC. Underfunded plans maintained by employers in financial distress can transfer responsibility to the PBGC for paying benefits guaranteed by the insurance program.

26.4 EVOLUTION OF PENSION ACCOUNTING STANDARDS.   SFAS Nos. 35, 87, and 88 are the result of approximately 11 years of deliberations by the FASB. However, the controversies concerning the accounting for pension plans well preceded that. As noted in the introduction to SFAS No. 87, since 1956 pension accounting literature has "expressed a preference for accounting in which cost would be systematically accrued during the expected period of actual service of the covered employees."

In 1966, **APB Opinion No. 8,** "Accounting for the Cost of Pension Plans," was issued. Within broad limits, annual pension cost for accounting purposes under APB No. 8 was the same as cash contributions for prefunded plans. Over the years, however, actuarial funding methods have evolved that produce different patterns of accumulating ultimate costs—some are intended to produce level costs, other front-end load costs, and still others tend to back-load costs.

In 1980, the FASB issued SFAS No. 35, which established standards of financial accounting and reporting for the annual financial statements of a defined benefit pension plan. The Statement was considered the FASB's first step in the overall pension project. After SFAS No. 35 was issued, the FASB concluded that the contribution-driven standard prescribed by APB No. 8 was no longer acceptable for employer financial reporting purposes. The proliferation of plans and a total asset pool of nearly $1 trillion (and growing) argued for an accounting approach under which reported costs would be more consistent for a company from one period to the next and more comparable among companies.

SFAS No. 87 and its companion SFAS No. 88 were issued in 1985. These Statements now govern the accounting for virtually all defined benefit pension plans. They prescribe a **single method** for accruing plan liabilities for future benefits that is independent from the way benefits are funded. Standards are prescribed for selecting **actuarial assumptions** used for calculating plan liability and expense components. Most importantly, the discount rate used to calculate the present value of future obligations is market-driven and follows prevailing yields in the bond markets. Taken together, these changes are intended to improve the quality of pension accounting information, but further refinements are possible. SFAS No. 87 states:

> This Statement continues the evolutionary search for more meaningful and useful pension accounting. The FASB believes that the conclusions it has reached are a worthwhile and significant step in that direction, but it also believes that those conclusions are not likely to be the final step in that evolution.

SPONSOR ACCOUNTING

26.5 SCOPE OF SFAS NO. 87.   The goal of the FASB in issuing SFAS No. 87 was to establish objective standards of financial accounting and reporting for employers that sponsor pension benefit arrangements for their employees. The Statement applies equally to single-employer plans and multiemployer plans, as well as pension plans or similar benefit arrangements for employees outside the United States. Any arrangement that is similar in substance to a pension plan is covered by the Statement.

The accounting specified in SFAS No. 87 does not supersede any of the **plan** accounting and reporting requirements of SFAS No. 35 (see Plan Accounting). It does, however, affect sponsor accounting by superseding the accounting requirements to calculate pension cost as described in APB No. 8, and the disclosure requirements as stated in SFAS No. 36, "Disclosure of Pension Information."

The Statement does not apply to pension or other types of plans that provide life and/or health insurance benefits to retired employees, although the sponsor of a plan that provides such benefits may elect to account for them in accordance with the provisions of SFAS No. 87. The accounting for the cost of these other postemployment benefits is the subject of a separate FASB project (see Accounting for Postretirement Benefits Other than Pensions).

26.6 APPLICABILITY OF SFAS NO. 87.   In substance, there are two principal types of single-employer pension plans—**defined benefit plans** and **defined contribution plans.** SFAS No. 87 applies to both kinds of plans; however, most of the provisions of the Statement are directed toward defined benefit plans.

Appendix D of SFAS No. 87 defines these two types of pension plans:

Defined benefit pension plan—A pension plan that defines an amount of pension benefit to be provided, usually as a function of one or more factors such as age, years of service, or compensation. Any pension plan that is not a defined contribution plan is, for purposes of this Statement, a defined benefit plan.

Defined contribution pension plan—A plan that provides pension benefits in return for services rendered, provides an individual account for each participant, and specifies how contributions to the individual's account are to be determined instead of specifying the amount of benefits the individual is to receive. Under a defined contribution pension plan, the benefits a participant will receive depend solely on the amount contributed to the participant's account, the returns earned on investments of those contributions, and forfeitures of other participants' benefits that may be allocated to such participant's account.

The paragraphs that immediately follow address the principal accounting and reporting requirements for a sponsor of a defined benefit pension plan. The provisions of SFAS No. 87 that provide standards for other types of pension plans—defined contribution, multiemployer, and multiple employer plans—are discussed in sections 26.14, 26.16, and 26.17.

For employers with more than one pension plan, SFAS No. 87 generally applies to each plan separately, although the financial disclosures of the plans in the sponsor's financial statements may be aggregated within certain limitations.

26.7 BASIC ELEMENTS OF PENSION ACCOUNTING.   The intention of the FASB in adopting SFAS No. 87 was to specify accounting objectives and results rather than the specific computational means of obtaining those results. Accordingly, the Statement permits a certain amount of flexibility in choosing methods and approaches to the required pension calculations.

One of the reasons for the flexibility is that in a defined benefit pension plan an employer promises to provide the employee with retirement income in future years after the employee retires or otherwise terminates employment. The actual amount of pension benefit to be paid usually is contingent on a number of future events, many of which the employer has no control over. These future events are incorporated into the defined benefit plan contract between the employer and employee, and form the basis of the plan's benefit formula.

The benefit formula within a pension plan generally describes the amount of retirement income an employee will receive for services performed during his employment. Since accounting and financial reporting are intended to mirror actual agreements and transactions, it is logical that sponsor accounting for pensions should follow this contract to pay future benefits—that is the plan's benefit formula. However, two problems arise from this accounting premise: How will the amount and timing of benefit payments be determined, and over what years of service will the cost of those pension benefits be attributed?

(a) Attribution.   When drafting SFAS No. 87, the FASB considered whether the determination of net periodic pension cost should be based on a benefit approach or a cost approach.

The **benefit approach** determines pension benefits attributed to service to date and calculates the present value of those benefits. The benefit approach recognizes costs equal to the present value of benefits earned for each period. Even when an equal amount of benefit is earned in each period, the cost being recognized will nevertheless increase as an employee approaches retirement. The **cost approach,** on the other hand, projects the present value of the total benefit at retirement and allocates that cost over the remaining years of service. Under the cost approach, the cost charged in the early years of an employee's service is greater than the present value of benefits earned based on the plan's benefit formula. In the later years of an employee's service, the cost is less than the present value of benefits earned so that the cumulative cost by the time the employee retires will be the same as that under the benefits approach.

Exhibit 26.2 depicts the two attribution approaches for determining pension cost based on the aggregate projected benefits to be earned during an employee's career.

As noted previously, accounting is intended to mirror actual agreements. In a defined benefit plan contract, the employer's promise to the employee is specified in terms of how benefits are earned based on service. Accordingly, the benefit approach was selected by the FASB and is the single attribution approach permitted by SFAS No. 87. Specifically, the Statement requires:

- For flat benefit plans, the **unit credit actuarial method.**
- For final-pay and career-average-pay plans, the **projected unit credit method.**

Under APB No. 8, any "acceptable actuarial cost method" was permitted for purposes of determining pension cost. Many companies, in an effort to experience more stable costs, among other reasons, chose one of the cost-based methods. A cost-based method tended to front-end load or attribute more cost to the early years of an employee's career, as shown in Exhibit 26.2. Thus, many companies that were funding their pension costs as accrued under the cost attribution approach, accumulated more plan assets than they would have under the benefit attribution approach.

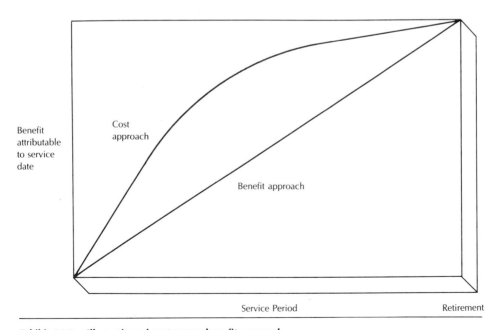

Exhibit 26.2. Illustration of cost versus benefit approach.

(b) Actuarial Assumptions.   The value of plan benefits that form the basis for determining net periodic pension cost are calculated through use of actuarial assumptions. The discount rate reflects the time value of money. Demographic assumptions help determine the probability and timing of benefit payments—for example, assumptions for mortality, termination of employment, and retirement incidence are used to develop expected payout streams. Demographic assumptions are also utilized to establish certain amortization schedules. Prior service costs attributable to plan amendments and experience gains and losses typically are spread over the expected remaining service of active employees. Paragraphs 43–45 of SFAS No. 87 establish standards for selecting assumptions. Each nonfinancial assumption must reflect the **best estimate** of future experience for that assumption.

(c) Interest Rates.   Under SFAS No. 87, employers are required to utilize two interest rates in measuring plan obligations and computing net periodic pension cost—an assumed **discount rate** and an **expected long-term rate of return on plan assets.**

As implied by its name the expected long-term rate of return on assets should reflect the expected long-term yield on plan assets available for investment during the ensuing year, as well as the reinvestment thereof in subsequent years. The discount rate, however, is a "snapshot" rate determined on the measurement date used for financial reporting. It reflects the underlying rate at which the pension benefits could be effectively settled (by purchasing annuities for example). The Statement refers to two indicators that can be used to estimate the settlement rate—high-quality bond yields and annuity rates published by the PBGC. Commercial annuity quotes (the standard in many cases) are based on fixed-income yields available at the time of the offer and, thus change continuously. The interest rate data presented in Exhibit 26.3 are taken from selected Federal Reserve Bulletins and imply the yield curves for U.S. Treasury securities. The corresponding curves for corporate bonds of noted qualities can be inferred by the long-term yields shown.

Variation in the discount rate used by different plan sponsors is inherent in the process prescribed by the Statement for selecting it. There is, at any time, a range of prices quoted by different insurance companies for the same "block of benefit obligations." Discrepancy in price can reflect differences in the underlying settlement of discount rate. Two other levels of variation exist—insurers tend to prefer obligations dominated by benefits that are already in pay status and they prefer bigger blocks of benefits. The best price (with the highest settlement rate), therefore, would be expected from the most aggressive insurer bidding for a

	INTEREST RATES (Percent)					
	U.S. Treasury Securities* Years to Maturity			Long-Term Corporate Bonds** Quality		
Date	1	7	30	Aaa	A	Baa
1/1/84	10.1	11.7	11.8	12.6	13.3	13.8
1/1/85	9.1	11.4	11.5	12.1	12.8	13.4
1/1/86	7.6	8.9	9.3	9.9	11.0	11.4
1/1/87	6.0	7.1	7.5	8.5	9.4	10.0
1/1/88	7.2	8.7	9.0	10.1	10.6	11.2
1/1/89	9.1	9.2	9.0	9.6	10.1	10.7

*Average for the week ending nearest to or coincident with the noted date. *Source:* Federal Reserve Bulletin.
**Averages for the week ending nearest to or coincident with the noted date as determined by Moody's. *Source:* Federal Reserve Bulletin.

Exhibit 26.3.   Interest rate data.

large group of annuities for benefits that are mostly in pay status. Conversely, a lower settlement rate would be expected from a "selective" insurer that is bidding on a small group of annuities for young participants who are not in pay status.

The procedure contemplated by the Statement for selecting a discount rate assumes that there is a reasonable range of rates at any one moment that could be supported. Of course, this range will move as prevailing yields move. Minimizing change in the discount rate used from one measurement date to the next is desirable because that will reduce volatility in the recorded expense. Generally, it is not acceptable, however, to keep the discount rate the same in successive years if settlement rates have shifted even if the discount rate remains within the reasonable range of rates for 2 years. For example, assume that prevailing yields are 8.5% to 10.0% at the prior measurement date and 7.0% to 9.0% at the current measurement date, and a plan sponsor used an 8.75% discount rate on both dates. Although 8.75% falls within an otherwise acceptable range, using it for the second year is inconsistent with the significant decline in prevailing rates that was observed for the interim. There may be mitigating circumstances, however—such as a demographic change in the employee group or a change in the plan's sponsor method for approximating the settlement rate—which, in this example, could support leaving the discount rate the same despite the drop in prevailing rates.

A plan may contain provisions affecting the interest rate at which benefit obligations may be settled. Examples include an optional lump sum payment computed using a low interest rate, and retirement annuities that are required to be purchased from an insurance company at specified rates. The assumed discount rate should properly reflect such plan provisions.

(d) Consistency. The Statement suggests some consistency among the assumptions used to calculate plan liabilities. In practice this means that identical components of financial assumptions generally should be used. For example, the inflation component of the discount rate, the assumed rate of salary increases, and the rate of increase in Social Security benefits or covered earnings should be the same. This suggestion reflects recent strong swings in inflation, productivity, and prevailing yields, which render rule-of-thumb relationships among such variables speculative.

Notwithstanding the preceding paragraph, the Statement does not require an employer to adopt any specific method of selecting the assumptions. Instead SFAS No. 87 requires the assumptions to be the employer's best estimates. Therefore, it is not deemed a change in accounting principle, as defined in APB Opinion No. 20, "Accounting Changes," if an employer should change its basis of selecting the assumed discount rate, for example, from high-quality bond rates to annuity purchase rates.

One of the best indicators of the reasonableness of assumptions is the amount of **unrecognized net gain or loss** under the plan. If the assumptions are reasonable, the gains and losses should offset each other in the long term. Therefore, when a plan has a pattern of unrecognized gains or losses that does not appear to be self-correcting, the assumptions used to measure benefit obligations and net periodic pension cost may be unrealistic. Assumptions, which do not appear on the surface to be unreasonable, may still be unrealistic if not borne out by actual experience.

(e) Actuarial Present Value of Benefits. As noted previously, the FASB determined the SFAS No. 87 accounting would be based on the plan's contractual arrangement—that the projection of ultimate benefits to be paid under a pension plan should be based on the plan's benefit formula. Accordingly, SFAS No. 87 utilizes two different measurements in estimating this ultimate pension liability—the **accumulated benefit obligation** (ABO), and the **projected benefit obligation** (PBO). The ABO comprises two components—**vested and nonvested benefits**—both of which are determined based on employee service and compensation amounts to date. Benefits are vested when they no longer depend on remaining in the service of the employer. The PBO is equal to the ABO plus an allowance for future compensation levels, that is, a projection of the actual salary upon which the pension benefit will be

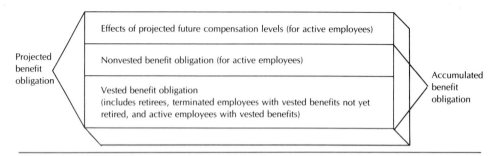

Exhibit 26.4. Relationship of ABO and PBO.

calculated and paid (i.e., projection of the final salary in a "final-pay" plan). The relationship of these two obligations is reflected in Exhibit 26.4.

Consider the example of a plan that provides a retirement pension equal to 1% of an employee's average final 5-year compensation for each year of service. The PBO for an employee with 5 years of service is the actuarial present value of 5% of his projected average compensation at his expected retirement date; whereas his ABO is determined similarly but only taking into account his average compensation to date. Further, assume that this employee would be 60% vested in his accrued benefits if his service is terminated today; then his vested benefit obligation is equal to 60% of his ABO.

Unless there is evidence to the contrary, accounting is based on the **going-concern** concept. Accordingly, the PBO is utilized as the basis for computing the service and interest components of the net periodic pension cost since it is more representative of the ultimate pension benefits to be paid than the ABO.

When evaluating a plan's benefit formula to determine how the attribution method should be applied, SFAS No. 87 specifies that the substance of the plan and the sponsor's history of plan amendments should be considered. For example, an employer that regularly increases the benefits payable under a flat-benefit plan may, in substance, be considered to have sponsored a plan with benefits primarily based on employees' compensation. In such cases, the attribution method should reflect the plan's substance, rather than simply conform to its written terms. Similarly, attribution of benefits (and, therefore, recognition of cost) for accounting purposes may differ from that called for in a plan's benefit formula if the formula calls for deferred vesting ("backloading") of benefits. This by far is one of the more subjective areas of SFAS No. 87. Obviously, the determination that there is a commitment by the sponsor to provide benefits beyond the written terms of the pension plan's benefit formula requires careful evaluation and consideration.

If an employer has committed to making certain **plan amendments,** these amendments should be reflected in the PBO even if they may not have been formally written into the plan or if some of the changes may not be effective until a later date. Collectively bargained pension plans often provide for benefit increases with staggered effective dates. Such a plan may provide a monthly pension equal to $20 per month for each year of service in the first year of a labor contract, $21 in the second year, and $22 in the third. Once the contract has been negotiated, the PBO should be based on the $22 level.

(f) Measurement Date. The date as of which the plan's PBO and assets are measured—for purposes of disclosure in the employer's financial statements and determination of pension cost for the subsequent period—is known as the **measurement date.** Although SFAS No. 87 contemplates that the measurement date coincides with the date of the financial statements, an alternative date not more than 3 months prior may be used. However, a change in the measurement date, for example, from September 30 in one year to December 31 in the next year would constitute a change in accounting principle under APB No. 20. Although most employers have one measurement date each year, some employers remeasure their PBO and select the assumed discount rates on a more frequent basis. The frequency of measurement is part of the employer's accounting methods and may not be changed without proper disclosure of the impact.

Although the projected benefit obligation disclosed in the financial statements is as of the measurement date, it generally is not necessary to determine the PBO using participant data as of that date. Instead the PBO may be estimated from a prior measurement, provided that the result obtained does not differ materially from that if a new measurement is made using current participant data. The fair value of plan assets, on the other hand, should be as of the measurement date.

The period between consecutive measurement dates is known as the measurement period and is used for determining the net periodic pension cost. The cost thus determined is used for the related financial reporting period. Events that occur after the measurement date but still within the financial reporting period generally are excluded from the SFAS No. 87 disclosure requirement. If significant, the cost implications thereof should nevertheless be disclosed in a manner similar to other post year-end events.

26.8 NET PERIODIC PENSION COST.   **Net periodic pension cost** represents the accounting recognition of the consequences of events and transactions affecting a pension plan. The amount of pension cost for a specified period is reported as a single net amount in an employer's financial statements. Under SFAS No. 87, net periodic pension cost comprises the following six components:

- Service cost.
- Interest cost.
- Actual return on plan assets.
- Amount of gain or loss being recognized or deferred.
- Amortization of unrecognized prior service cost.
- Amortization of the unrecognized net obligation or net asset existing at the initial application of the Statement.

(a) Service Cost Component.   A defined benefit pension plan contains a benefit formula that generally describes the amount of retirement income that an employee will receive for services performed during their employment. SFAS No. 87 requires the use of this benefit formula in the measurement of annual service cost. The **service cost** component of net periodic pension cost is defined by the Statement as the actuarial present value of pension benefits attributed by the pension benefit formula to employee service during a specified period. Under SFAS No. 87, attribution (the process of assigning pension benefits or cost to periods of employee service) generally is based on the benefit formula (i.e., the benefit attribution approach).

A simplified example will help illustrate this concept. Assume that a pension plan's benefit formula states that an employee shall receive, at the retirement age of 65, retirement income of $15 per month for life, for each year of credited service. Thus a pension of $15 per month can be attributed to each year of employee service. The actuarial present value of the $15 monthly pension represents the service cost component of net periodic pension cost. Although it is customary to determine the service cost at the end of the year, an equally acceptable practice is to compute the service cost at the beginning of the year and to add the interest thereon at the assumed discount rate to the interest cost component.

In certain circumstances the plan's benefit formula does not indicate the manner in which a particular benefit relates to specific services performed by the employee. In this case SFAS No. 87 specifies that the benefit shall be considered to be accumulated as follows:

- If the **benefit is includable in vested benefits,** the benefit shall be accumulated in proportion to the ratio of total completed years of service as of the present to the total completed years of service as of the date the benefit becomes fully vested. A vested benefit is a benefit that an employee has an irrevocable right to receive. For example, receipt of the pension benefit is not contingent on whether the employee continues to work for the employer.
- If the **benefit is not includable in vested benefits,** the benefit shall be accumulated in proportion to the ratio of completed years of service as of the present date to the total projected years of service. An example of a benefit that is not includable in vested benefits is a death or disability benefit that is payable only if death or disability occurs during the employee's active service.

Some pension plans require contributions by employees to cover part of the plan's overall cost. SFAS No. 87 does not specify how the net periodic pension cost should be adjusted for **employee contributions.** An often-used approach is to reduce the service cost component directly by the employee contributions, thus possibly resulting in a negative service cost. Under this approach the plan's PBO encompasses both benefits to be financed by employee contributions and those financed by the employer.

(b) Interest Cost Component.   In determining the PBO of a plan, SFAS No. 87 gives appropriate consideration to the time value of money, through the use of discounts for interest cost. Therefore, the Statement requires that an employer recognize, as a component of net periodic pension cost, interest on the projected benefit obligation. This **interest cost** component is equal to the increase in the amount of the PBO due to the passage of time. The accretion of interest on the PBO is based on the assumed discount rate.

Since the assumed discount rate is intended to reflect the interest rate at which the PBO currently could be settled, it is imperative that the discount rate assumption be reevaluated each year to determine whether it reflects the best estimate of current settlement rates. As a rule of thumb, if interest rates are in a period of fluctuation, the discount rate generally should change.

(c) Actual Return on Plan Assets Component.   SFAS No. 87 requires that an employer recognize, as a component of net periodic pension cost, the **actual return or loss on pension plan assets** (see section 26.9). The actual return or loss on plan assets equals the difference between the fair value of plan assets at the beginning and end of a period, adjusted for employer contributions and pension benefit payments made during the period. Exhibit 26.5 illustrates the determination of the actual return on plan assets.

A positive return on plan assets decreases the employer's cost of providing pension benefits to its employees, whereas a negative return (loss) increases net periodic pension

Fair value of plan assets, beginning of year	$900
Add contributions	100
Subtract benefit payments	(150)
	850
Fair value of plan assets, end of year	931
Actual return on plan assets	$ 81

Exhibit 26.5.   Illustration of the determination of the actual return on plan assets.

cost. Note that net periodic pension income is a possibility where very positive earnings are experienced for plan assets held during a period, and those earnings more than offset the other net periodic pension cost components.

Although the Statement purports to offset a plan's cost by the actual return on plan assets, the net periodic pension cost is in fact affected by the **expected return** rather than the actual return since the difference between the actual and expected returns is deferred (see section 26.8(d)—Asset gains and losses). The FASB felt that the actual return is an important piece of information that needs to be disclosed, even though the net periodic pension cost for any period is independent of the actual return earned in that period.

The Statement makes no specific allowance for **administrative or investment expenses** paid directly from the pension fund. These expenses may be reflected in the net periodic pension cost as an offset to the actual investment return on plan assets, and in such case, may also be considered in the selection of the expected long-term rate of return on plan assets. If deemed appropriate, administrative expenses may be treated differently than investment expenses and added to the plan's service cost.

(d) Amortization of Unrecognized Net Gains and Losses Component. SFAS No. 87 broadly defines gains and losses as changes in the amount of either the PBO or pension plan assets that generally result from differences between the estimates or assumptions used and actual experience. Gains and losses may reflect both the refinement of estimates or assumptions and real changes in economic conditions. Hence, the **gain and loss** component of SFAS No. 87 consists of the net difference between the estimates and actual results of two separate pension items—actuarial assumptions related to pension plan obligations (liability gains and losses) and return on plan assets (asset gains and losses).

Liability gains and losses (increases or decreases in the PBO) stem from two types of events—changes in obligation-related assumptions (i.e., discount rate, assumed future compensation levels) and variances between actual and assumed experience (i.e., turnover, mortality). Liability gains and losses generally would be calculated at the end of each year as the difference between the projected value of the year-end pension obligation based on beginning of the year assumptions and the actual year-end value of the obligation based on the end-of-year assumptions.

Asset gains and losses represent the difference between the actual and expected rate of return on plan assets during a period. These gains and losses are entirely experience-related. As noted in the previous section, the actual return on pension plan assets is equal to the difference between the fair value of pension plan assets at the beginning and end of a period, adjusted for any contributions and pension benefit payments made during that period. The **expected return on pension plan assets** is a computed amount determined by multiplying the market-related value of plan assets (as defined below) by the expected long-term rate of return. The expected long-term rate of return is an actuarial assumption of the average expected long-term interest rate that will be earned on plan assets available for investment during the period.

In order to reduce the potentially volatile impact of gains and losses on net periodic pension cost from year to year, the FASB adopted various **"smoothing" techniques** in SFAS No. 87—**the netting of gains and losses, the market-related value of plan assets, the initial deferral of net gains and losses,** and **the amortization of the net deferred amount.** The impact of the first smoothing technique is obvious; the other techniques are discussed briefly in the following paragraphs.

As noted previously, the **market-related value of plan assets** is utilized in the determination of the expected return on pension plan assets. The market-related value of plan assets can be either the actual fair value of plan assets or a "calculated" value that recognizes the changes in the fair value of plan assets over a period of not more than 5 years. Employers are permitted great flexibility in selecting the method of calculating the market-related value of plan assets. Any method that averages gains and losses over not longer than a 5-year period would be acceptable under the Statement, provided it met two criteria—that the method be both systematic and rational. In fact, changes in the fair value of assets would not have to be averaged at all but could be recognized in full in the subsequent year's net periodic pension cost provided that the method is applied consistently to all gains and losses (on both plan assets and obligations) and is disclosed. An employer also may use different methods for determining the market-related values of plan assets in separate pension plans and in separate asset categories within each plan, provided that the differences can be supported.

SFAS No. 87 specifies that the net gain or loss resulting from the assumptions or estimates used differing from actual experience be deferred and amortized in future periods. **Deferred gains and losses** (excluding any asset gains and losses subsequent to the initial implementation of SFAS No. 87 that have not yet been reflected in the market-related value of assets) are amortized as a component of net periodic pension cost if they exceed the **"corridor."** The corridor is defined as a range equal to plus or minus 10% of the greater of either the PBO or the market-related value of plan assets. If the cumulative gain or loss, as computed, does not lie outside the corridor, no amount of gain or loss needs to be reflected in net periodic cost for the current period. However, if the cumulative gain or loss does exceed the corridor, only the excess is subject to amortization. To visualize the concept of the corridor refer to Exhibit 26.6.

The **minimum amortization** that is required in net periodic pension cost is the excess amount described above, divided by the average remaining service period of the active employees expected to receive benefits under the plan. Unlike other amortization under SFAS No. 87, the average remaining service period is redetermined each year. The FASB does permit alternative methods of amortization. An employer may decide not to use the corridor method or substitute any alternative amortization method that amortizes an amount

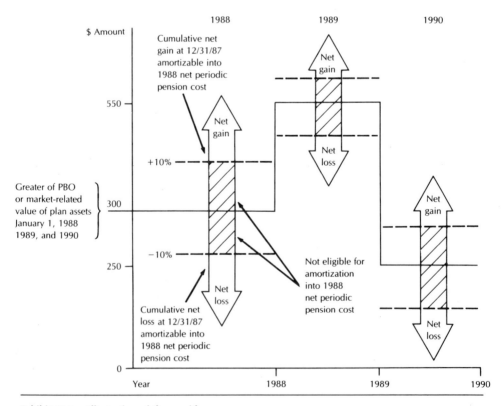

Exhibit 26.6.   Illustration of the corridor.

at least equal to the minimum. Consequently, an alternative method could recognize the entire amount of the current period's gain or loss in the ensuing period. Any alternative amortization method must be applied consistently from year to year and to both gains and losses, and must be disclosed in the employer's financial statements.

The 10% corridor is designed to avoid amortization of relatively small and temporary gains and losses arising in any one year that can be expected to offset each other in the long run. It is not intended to exclude a portion of gains and losses from ever being recognized in the sponsor's income statement. If a substantial amount of net gain or loss remains unrecognized from year to year, or increases in size, it may imply that the PBO and net periodic pension cost have been overstated or understated.

(e) Amortization of Unrecognized Prior Service Cost Component.   Defined benefit pension plans are sometimes amended, usually to provide increased pension benefits to employees. An amendment to a pension plan (or initiation of a pension plan) that grants benefits to employees for services previously rendered generates an increase in the PBO under the plan. This additional PBO is referred to as **prior service cost.** Retroactive pension benefits generally are granted by the employer in the expectation that they will produce future economic benefits, such as increasing employee morale, reducing employee turnover, or improving employee productivity.

Under SFAS No. 87, prior service cost is to be amortized and included as a component of net periodic pension cost. A separate **amortization schedule** is established for each prior service cost based on the expected future service by active employees who are expected to receive employer-provided benefits under the plan. Instead of a declining amortization schedule, a common practice is to amortize the prior service cost on a straight-line basis over the average future service period. Once this amortization schedule has been established, it will generally not be changed unless the period during which the employer expects to realize future economic benefits has shortened or the future economic benefits have become impaired. Decelerating the amortization schedule is prohibited.

If substantially all of the participants of a pension plan are inactive, the prior service cost from a retroactive amendment should be amortized over the remaining life expectancy of those plan participants.

SFAS No. 87 permits the use of alternative amortization methods that more rapidly reduce the amount of unrecognized prior service cost, provided that the alternatives are used consistently. For example, straight-line amortization of unrecognized prior service cost over the average future service period of active employees who are expected to receive benefits under the plan is acceptable. The immediate recognition of prior service cost, however, generally is inappropriate.

As noted previously, a plan amendment typically increases the cost of pension benefits and increases the amount of the PBO. However, there are situations where a plan amendment may decrease the cost of pension benefits, resulting in a decrease in the amount of the PBO. Any decrease resulting from a plan amendment should be applied to reduce the balance of any existing unrecognized prior service cost using a systematic and rational method (i.e., LIFO, FIFO, or pro rata, unless such reduction can be related to any specific prior service cost). Any excess is to be amortized on the same basis as increases in unrecognized prior service cost.

Once the employer has committed to a plan amendment, the net periodic pension cost for the remainder of the year should reflect the additional service cost, interest cost, and amortization related to the amendment. Remeasurement based on the current discount rate may also be called for. Pension cost for any prior periods should not be restated merely on account of the amendment, even if the amendment may be effective retroactively to a prior date.

(f) Amortization of the Unrecognized Net Obligation or Net Asset Component.   The **unrecognized net obligation or net asset** of a pension plan was determined as of the first day of the fiscal year in which SFAS No. 87 was first applied or if applicable, the measurement date immediately preceding that day. The initial unrecognized net obligation or net asset was equal to the difference between the PBO and fair value of pension plan assets (plus previously recognized unfunded accrued pension cost or less previously recognized prepaid pension cost).

A schedule was set up to amortize the initial unrecognized net obligation or net asset on a straight-line basis over the average remaining service period of employees expected to receive benefits under the plan, except under the following circumstances:

- If the average remaining service period was less than 15 years, an employer could elect to use 15 years.
- If the plan was composed of all or substantially all inactive participants, the employer should use those participants' average remaining life expectancy as the amortization period.

26.9 PLAN ASSETS.   **Pension plan assets** generally consist of equity or debt securities, real estate, or other investments, which may be sold or transferred by the plan, that typically have been segregated and restricted in a trust. In contrast to SFAS No. 35, for purposes of SFAS No. 87, plan assets exclude contributions due but unpaid by the plan sponsor. Also excluded are assets that are not restricted to provide plan benefits such as so-called rabbi trusts in which earmarked funds are available to satisfy judgment creditors.

Pension plan assets that are held as an investment to provide pension benefits are to be measured at fair value as of the date of the financial statements or, if used consistently from year to year, as of a date not more than three months prior to that date (this date is defined by the Statement as the measurement date).

In the context of SFAS No. 87, fair value is defined as the amount that a pension plan trustee could reasonably expect to receive from the sale of a plan asset between a willing and informed buyer and a willing and informed seller. The FASB believes that fair value is the appropriate measurement for pension plan assets because it provides the more relevant information in assessing both the plan's ability to pay pension benefits as they become due and the future contributions necessary to provide for unfunded pension benefits already promised.

If an active market exists for a plan investment, fair value is determined by the quoted market price. If an active market does not exist for a particular plan investment, selling prices for similar investments, if available, should be appropriately considered. If no active market exists, an estimate of the fair value of the plan investment may be based on its projected cash flow, provided that appropriate consideration is given to current discount rates and the investment risk involved.

Pension plan assets that are used in the actual everyday operations of a plan—buildings, leasehold improvements, furniture, equipment, and fixtures—should be valued at historical cost less accumulated depreciation or amortization.

26.10 RECOGNITION OF LIABILITIES AND ASSETS.   SFAS No. 87 retained the requirement of APB No. 8 to reflect either a liability (accrued pension cost) or an asset (prepaid pension cost) in an employer's statement of financial condition for the difference between the pension cost accrued by the employer and the amount actually contributed to the pension plan. However, the Statement introduced a radically new concept to sponsor accounting— the recognition of **an additional minimum pension liability.**

An additional minimum pension liability must be recorded to the extent that an unfunded ABO (taking into consideration any contribution paid by the employer between the measurement date and the date of the financial statements) exceeds the liability for unfunded accrued pension cost. If a prepaid pension asset exists, the minimum liability that is recorded equals the sum of the prepaid amount and the unfunded ABO. If an additional minimum liability is recognized, an equal amount of **intangible asset** should be recorded provided the asset recognized does not exceed any unrecognized prior service cost plus any unrecognized net liability (but not net asset) at the date of initial application of SFAS No. 87. If the additional liability exceeds the sum of the preceding two items, the remaining debit balance should be recorded as a separate component of stockholders' equity, net of related tax benefits.

The additional liability, intangible asset, and reduction in stockholders' equity are reestablished at each measurement date, and the amounts previously recorded on the balance sheet are reversed. No amortization of the additional liability or intangible asset is required or permitted.

There is no additional asset if plan assets plus (less) accrued (prepaid) pension cost exceed its ABO. Furthermore, the additional liability is determined separately for each plan, and an employer may not reduce the additional liability for one plan by the excess of plan assets in another.

26.11 INTERIM MEASUREMENTS.   Generally, the determination of interim pension cost should be based on assumptions used as of the previous year-end measurements. Similarly, any additional minimum liability recognized in the year-end financial statements should be carried forward, after adjustment for subsequent accruals and contributions. If, however, more recent measurements of plan assets and pension obligations are available, or if a significant event occurs that ordinarily would call for such measurements (i.e., a plan amendment), that updated information should be used.

26.12 FINANCIAL STATEMENT DISCLOSURES.   The following **disclosures** should be made in the financial statements of an employer who sponsors a defined benefit pension plan:

- A **description of the pension plan,** including the employee groups covered, type of benefit formula, funding policy, types of assets held and significant nonbenefit liabilities (if any), and the nature and effect of significant matters affecting comparability of information for all periods presented. This general information was required by the FASB to enhance the understanding and comparability of sponsor pension plan accounting.

- The **amount of net periodic pension cost** for each period an income statement is presented, detailing the separate amounts for the (1) service cost component, (2) interest cost component, (3) actual return on plan assets for the period, and (4) net total of other components. The net total of other components comprises the net asset gain or loss from the current period deferred for future recognition, amortization of the net gain or loss from earlier periods, amortization of unrecognized prior service cost, and amortization of the unrecognized net obligation or asset at the initial application of SFAS No. 87.

- A **schedule reconciling the funded status of the plan** with amounts reported in the employer's statement of financial position, showing separately:

1. The fair value of plan assets.
2. The PBO, separately identifying the ABO and vested benefit obligation.
3. The amount of unrecognized prior service cost.
4. The amount of unrecognized net gain or loss, including asset gains and losses not yet reflected in market-related values.
5. The **amount of any remaining unrecognized net obligation or net asset** existing at the date of the initial application of SFAS No. 87.
6. The **amount of additional minimum liability** equal to the unfunded ABO plus (minus) any prepaid (accrued) pension cost.
7. The amount of the **net pension asset or liability that has been recognized in the employer's statement of financial position.** This amount must be equal to the total net result of combining the preceding six items. For purposes of SFAS No. 87, different prepaid and accrued pension cost amounts that may have been created at different

times for different reasons may be combined and netted. The portion of accrued pension cost equal to the employer's expected contribution for the next twelve months is classified as a current liability, whereas the remainder should be classified as noncurrent.

Items 1 through 5 are as of the measurement date whereas items 6 and 7 are as of the employer's year-end. When the measurement date precedes the year-end date, plan assets (i.e., item 1) are increased by the amount of contribution paid by the employer during the interim period between the measurement date and the employer's year-end. Except for this modification, the fair value of plan assets should be the actual value as of the measurement date. It is, however, acceptable to estimate the PBO based on a prior measurement such as that done as of the previous measurement date, provided that the result would not be materially different if the PBO had been remeasured using current participant data.

- The **weighted-average assumed discount rate** and, if applicable, the **rate of compensation increase** used in determining the PBO, and the **weighted-average expected long-term rate of return** on pension plan assets. These three assumptions are the most subjective for pension accounting and have the greatest impact on the computations of pension obligations and net periodic pension cost (the assumptions used in measuring the PBO at one fiscal year-end are generally used to determine net periodic pension cost the following fiscal year).

- If applicable, the **amounts and types of securities** of the employer and/or related parties that are included in plan assets, and the approximate **amount of annual benefits of employees and retirees covered by annuity contracts** issued by the employer and related parties. Also, if applicable, the **alternative amortization method used for unrecognized prior service cost** and the **alternative amortization method used to reflect the commitment of an employer to pay more employee benefits than its existing pension benefit formula indicates.**

Though not required, most employers also disclose the measurement date(s) if different from the year-end date.

An employer may combine two or more of its defined benefit pension plans for purposes of financial statement disclosure, including plans with different measurement dates. However, separate reconciliations of funded status are required for plans with assets in excess of ABO and plans with assets less than ABO, and U.S. plans and non-U.S. plans unless they use similar economic assumptions.

26.13 ANNUITY CONTRACTS.   All or part of an employer's obligation to provide pension plan benefits to employees may be effectively transferred to an insurance company by the purchase of annuity contracts. An **annuity contract** is an irrevocable agreement in which an insurance company unconditionally agrees to provide specific benefits to designated individuals, in return for a fixed consideration or premium. Hence, by purchasing an annuity contract, an employer transfers to the insurer its legal obligation, and the attendant risks, to provide pension benefits. For purposes of SFAS No. 87, an annuity contract does not qualify unless the risks and rewards associated with the assets and obligations assumed by the insurance company are actually transferred to the insurance company by the sponsor.

An annuity contract may be participating or nonparticipating. In a **participating annuity** contract, the insurance company's investment experience with the funds received for the annuity contract are shared, in the form of dividends, with the purchaser (the employer or the pension fund). The purchase price of a participating annuity is ordinarily higher than that for a nonparticipating annuity, with the excess representing the value of the participation right (i.e., expected future dividends). This excess should be recognized as a plan asset.

Benefits covered by annuity contracts are excluded from the benefit obligations of the plan. The annuity contracts themselves are not counted as plan assets, except for the cost of any participation rights. If any benefits earned in the current period are covered by annuity contracts, the cost of such benefits is equal to the cost to purchase the annuities less any participation right.

Annuity contracts issued by a captive insurance company are not considered annuities for the purpose of SFAS No. 87, since the risk associated with the benefit obligations remains substantially with the employer. Similarly, if there is reasonable doubt that the insurance company will meet its obligations under the contract, it is not considered an annuity contract.

Insurance contracts that are not in substance annuity contracts are accounted for as pension plan assets and are measured at fair value. If a contract has a determinable cash surrender value or conversion value, that is presumed to be its fair value.

A pension fund may have structured a portfolio of fixed-income investments with a cash flow designed to match expected benefit payment. Known as a **dedicated bond portfolio,** its purpose is to protect the pension fund against swings in interest rates. For the purposes of SFAS No. 87, a dedicated bond portfolio is not an annuity contract even if it is managed to remove all or most of the investment risk associated with covered benefit payments.

26.14 DEFINED CONTRIBUTION PENSION PLANS.   A **defined contribution pension plan** provides for employer contributions that are defined in the plan. A defined contribution plan maintains individual accounts for each plan participant and contains terms that specify how contributions are allocated among participants' individual accounts. Pension benefits are based solely on the amount available in each participant's account at the time of retirement. The amount available in each participant's account at the time of retirement is the total of the amounts contributed by the employer, the returns earned on investments of those contributions, and forfeitures of other participants' accounts that have been allocated to the participant's account.

Under SFAS No. 87, the net periodic pension cost of a defined contribution pension plan is the amount of contributions for the period in which services are rendered by the employees. If a plan calls for contributions after an individual retires or terminates, the estimated cost should be accrued during periods in which the individual performs services.

An employer that sponsors one or more defined contribution pension plans **discloses** the following information separately from its defined benefit pension plan disclosures:

- A **description of the plan(s)** including employee groups covered, the basis for determining contributions, and the nature and effect of significant matters affecting comparability of information for all periods presented.
- The **amount of pension cost** recognized during the period.

For the purposes of SFAS No. 87, any plan that is not a defined contribution pension plan is considered a defined benefit pension plan.

26.15 NON-U.S. PENSION PLANS.   SFAS No. 87 does not make any special provision for **non-U.S. pension plans.** In some foreign countries it is customary or required for an employer to provide benefits for employees in the event of a voluntary or involuntary severance of employment. In this event, if the substance of the arrangement is a pension plan, it is subject to the provisions of SFAS No. 87 (i.e., benefits are paid for substantially all terminations).

Plans in Puerto Rico or other U.S. territories are considered U.S. plans.

26.16 MULTIEMPLOYER PLANS.   A **multiemployer plan** is a plan to which more than one employer contributes, usually pursuant to a labor union agreement. Under these plans, contributions are pooled and separate employer accounts do not exist. As a result, assets contributed by one employer may be used to provide benefits to the employees of other participating employers.

SFAS No. 87 provides no change in the accounting for multiemployer plans. A participating employer should recognize pension cost equal to the contribution required to the plan for the period. The disclosures required by the Statement for multiemployer plans are similar to those for defined contribution pension plans—a description of the plan, including the employee groups covered and type of benefits provided, and the amount of pension cost recognized in the period.

An underfunded multiemployer plan may assess a withdrawing employer a portion of its unfunded benefit obligations. If this **withdrawal liability** becomes either probable or reasonably possible, the provisions of SFAS No. 5, "Accounting for Contingencies," apply.

26.17 MULTIPLE EMPLOYER PLANS. A **multiple employer plan** is similar to a multiemployer plan except that it usually does not include any labor union agreement. It is treated under ERISA as a collection of single-employer plans sponsored by the respective participating employers. If separate asset allocation is maintained among the participating employers (even though pooled for investment purposes), SFAS No. 87 applies individually to each employer with respect to its interest and benefit obligations within the plan. If assets are not allocated among the participating employers (for example, when a number of subsidiaries participate in a plan sponsored by their parent), the organization sponsoring the plan, if one exists, should account for the plan as a single-employer plan, whereas each participating employer should account for this arrangement as a multiemployer plan in its separate financial statements. Disclosure of net periodic pension cost and the reconciliation of the funded status should be for the plan as a whole, with each participating employer further disclosing its own pension cost with respect to this arrangement.

26.18 FUNDING AND INCOME TAX ACCOUNTING. SFAS No. 87 does not address funding considerations, other than to recognize that there may be differences between reported net periodic pension cost and funding. IRS regulations recognize the projected unit credit method as one of several acceptable funding methods. However, when employing the projected unit credit method and the same explicit assumptions used to calculate net periodic pension cost, the range between the permissible maximum and minimum funding amount, may not bracket the net periodic pension cost. This can be caused by the difference in amortization periods for unrecognized pension costs and limitation imposed by the tax law on contributions to relatively well-funded plans. In general, the objective of matching expensing and funding of net periodic pension cost may no longer be appropriate due to tax, legal, and cash flow considerations. In this regard companies must continue to provide deferred taxes, where appropriate, for these differences.

(a) SFAS No. 96. The method of accounting for income taxes—particularly the way deferred taxes are calculated—was changed by SFAS No. 96, "Accounting for Income Taxes." Its focus is on an asset and liability approach, as opposed to an income statement approach. On a simplified basis, deferred taxes are calculated by applying the tax rates enacted for future years to differences between the financial statement carrying amounts and the tax bases of assets and liabilities. These differences are known as temporary differences.

Temporary differences frequently will arise as a result of differences between the tax basis of pension assets and liabilities and the amounts recognized under SFAS No. 87. For example, assuming that a company funds the pension cost to the extent deductible for tax purposes, a pension asset (prepaid pension cost) will be recognized when the amount funded is in excess of pension cost determined under SFAS No. 87. A pension liability (accrued pension cost) will be recognized when the amount funded is less than the pension cost determined under SFAS No. 87. In addition, settlement gains and losses recognized under SFAS No. 88 will create temporary differences because the transactions generally are not taxable or deductible at the date recognized for financial reporting purposes. Because of the complexities of accounting for pensions, numerous other situations will result in temporary differences.

(b) Scheduling of Temporary Differences. On March 31, 1989, the FASB's staff issued a Special Report, "A Guide to Implementation of Statement 96 on Accounting for Income Taxes—Questions and Answers." Question 12 of that Special Report deals exclusively with temporary differences related to pension plans. The Special Report indicates that either of the following two approaches should be used to schedule future taxable and deductible amounts for temporary differences related to pension assets and liabilities.

Under one approach, a temporary difference related to a pension asset would be scheduled to result in a taxable amount in the year(s) that there is expected to be an asset reversion from the pension plan, limited to the amount of the pension asset. The Special Report also states that a qualifying tax-planning strategy could be used to determine the future year(s) when there would be an asset reversion from the pension plan. An excise tax or other penalty charge on withdrawal of plan assets would not be considered a significant cost in evaluating the criteria for tax-planning strategies if the excise tax or penalty rate would be the same regardless of the year of the withdrawal. Under this approach, a temporary difference related to a pension liability would be scheduled to result in deductible amounts based on the pattern of the present values of the estimated tax deductions in future years, limited to the amount of the pension liability.

Under the other approach, the Special Report states that a temporary difference related to a pension asset would be scheduled to result in taxable amounts based on estimated pension expense for financial reporting purposes in future years, limited to the amount of the pension asset. Under this approach, a temporary difference related to a pension liability would be scheduled to result in deductible amounts based on estimated future tax deductions in excess of future interest calculated on the pension liability that is recognized for financial reporting purposes, limited to the amount of the pension liability.

One final note on SFAS No. 96: As this volume goes to press, the FASB is still wrestling with several implementation issues concerning SFAS No. 96. Future guidance on that Statement or revisions thereto, may have an impact on the accounting described above.

26.19 ILLUSTRATION—APPLICATION OF SFAS NO. 87. Exhibit 26.7 illustrates the application of the major accounting requirements of SFAS No. 87 for a hypothetical defined benefit pension plan having a final-pay benefit formula. To assist the reader, the material has been presented under the following headings: Background Information and Assumptions, Components of Pension Cost, Changes in Projected Benefit Obligation, Valuation of Plan Assets, Amortization of Unrecognized Net Gain or Loss, Unrecognized Gains and Losses, Pension-Related Balance Sheet Accounts, and Financial Statement Disclosures.

BACKGROUND INFORMATION AND ASSUMPTIONS

Company X, a calendar year entity, adopted SFAS No. 87 on January 1, 1987, as required by the Statement. In prior years, the Company recognized pension cost equal to the maximum annual amount that could be contributed to the plan for federal income tax purposes. The Company funds its contribution to the plan on December 31 of each year.

The Company utilizes the following practices when calculating pension cost for financial statement purposes:

- *Market-Related Value of Plan Assets.* A computed value that recognizes changes in fair value of plan assets (asset gains and losses) over a 5-year period.
- *Amortization of Gains and Losses.* Amortized on a corridor approach (i.e., unrecognized gain or loss is amortized only if it exceeds 10% of the greater of the PBO or the market-related value of plan assets).
- *Amortization of Prior Service Cost.* Amortized on a straight-line basis over the average remaining service period of active employees expected to receive benefits.
- *Measurement Date.* Year-end financial statement date, December 31.

(continued)

Exhibit 26.7. Application of SFAS No. 87.

The results of annual actuarial valuations and related actuarial assumptions at the date of initial application of SFAS No. 87 and in subsequent years are:

| | December 31 | | | |
	1986	1987	1988	1989
Accumulated benefit obligation	$ 6,900	$ 8,900	$12,600	$13,100
Projected benefit obligation	10,000	12,100	16,000	16,600
Plan assets (fair value)	7,200	9,000	10,700	12,150
Benefits paid (on December 31)	400	450	500	550
Contribution (on December 31)	1,000	1,100	1,200	1,250
Weighted-average settlement rate	9%	8%	7.5%	8%
Expected long-term rate of return on plan assets	10%	10%	10%	10%
Salary progression rate	6.5%	5.5%	5.5%	5.75%

For all years presented, the average remaining service period of active employees expected to receive benefits is estimated to be 14 years. On December 31, 1988, a plan amendment was adopted that granted increased benefits to employees based on services previously rendered.

COMPONENTS OF PENSION COST

| | Year Ended December 31 | | |
	1987	1988	1989
Service cost[1]	$ 600	$ 650	$ 700
Interest cost[2]	900	968	1,200
Return on plan assets[3]			
Actual return	(1,150)	(1,000)	(750)
Deferred gain (loss)	430	134	(284)
Expected return	(720)	(866)	(1,034)
Amortization of unrecognized prior service cost[4]	0	0	130
Amortization of net loss[5]	0	0	15
Amortization of unrecognized net obligation at transition[6]	200	200	200
Net pension cost	$ 980	$ 952	$1,211

[1]This amount is calculated by the actuary, based on the plan's benefit formula, using assumptions and measurements as of the beginning of the year.
[2]The product of the PBO and the assumed discount (settlement) rate as of the beginning of the year.
[3]See Valuation of Plan Assets.
[4]Represents the cost of the retroactive plan amendment adopted December 31, 1988 ($1,820), divided by the average remaining service period of active employees (14 years).
[5]See Amortization of Unrecognized Net Gain or Loss.
[6]Represents the unrecognized net loss at transition—the excess of the PBO ($10,000) over the fair value of plan assets ($7,200)—divided by the average remaining service period of active employees (14 years).

CHANGES IN PROJECTED BENEFIT OBLIGATION

	1987	1988	1989
Accumulated benefit obligation, January 1	$ 6,900	$ 8,900	$12,600
Effect of assumed salary progression	3,100	3,200	3,400
Projected benefit obligation, January 1	10,000	12,100	16,000
			(continued)

Exhibit 26.7. *Continued.*

CHANGES IN PROJECTED BENEFIT OBLIGATION

	1987	1988	1989
Anticipated increase (decrease) in PBO during the year:			
Service cost	600	650	700
Interest cost	900	968	1,200
Benefit payments	(450)	(500)	(550)
Projected benefit obligation, December 31	11,050	13,218	17,350
Increase (decrease) in PBO attributable to revised assumptions at end of year:			
Discount rate	1,100	650	(760)
Salary progression rate	(290)	0	80
Other (turnover, etc.)	240	312	(70)
Net loss (gain) deferred	1,050	962	(750)
Effect of retroactive plan amendment adopted December 31, 1988	0	1,820	0
Actual projected benefit obligation, December 31	$12,100	$16,000	$16,600

VALUATION OF PLAN ASSETS

	Fair Value	Market-Related Value
Fair value of assets, January 1, 1987	$ 7,200	$ 7,200
Expected return for 1987[1]	720	720
Difference between actual and expected return:		
Net gain—fair value	430	
Market-related[2]		86
Benefit payments on December 31	(450)	(450)
Sponsor contribution on December 31	1,100	1,100
Value of assets, January 1, 1988	9,000	8,656
Expected return for 1988	866	866
Difference between actual and expected return:		
Net gain—fair value	134	
Market-related		113
Benefit payments on December 31	(500)	(500)
Sponsor contribution on December 31	1,200	1,200
Value of assets, January 1, 1989	10,700	10,335
Expected return for 1989	1,034	1,034
Difference between actual and expected return:		
Net gain—fair value	(284)	
Market-related		56
Benefit payments on December 31	(550)	(550)
Sponsor contribution on December 31	1,250	1,250
Value of assets, January 1, 1990	$12,150	$12,125

[1]The expected long-term rate of return on plan assets (10%) times the market-related asset value at the beginning of the year.

[2]The market-related value of plan assets is used in calculating the expected return on plan assets. A portion of the cumulative difference between expected and actual return on plan assets (gain or loss) is included each year in the market-related value of plan assets, and the unrecognized gain or loss subject to amortization. Company X's accounting policy states that 20% of the prior year net gain or loss is to be included.

(continued)

Exhibit 26.7. *Continued.*

AMORTIZATION OF UNRECOGNIZED NET GAIN OR LOSS

Under SFAS No. 87, the net gain or loss experienced in the current year is subject to amortization in the following year. Since Company X first applied the Statement in 1987, pension cost for 1987 would not include any amortization. Beginning in 1988 and for each year thereafter, the Company would be required to calculate whether, under the corridor approach, amortization of net unrecognized gains or losses is to be included in the then current year's pension cost.

The corridor calculation for 1988 and 1989 would involve the following:

	1988	1989
Unrecognized net gain (loss) at January 1 subject to amortization[1]	$ (964)	$(1,813)
Corridor = 10% of the greater of the PBO or the market-related value of assets at January 1[2]	1,210	1,600
Unrecognized net gain (loss) in excess of corridor	0	(213)
Divided by average remaining service period (years)	14	14
Amortization of net gain (loss) to be included in pension cost	$ 0	$ (15)

[1]See Unrecognized Gains and Losses.
[2]Applicable amounts are:

	1988	1989
PBO—See Changes in Projected Benefit Obligation	$12,100	$16,000
Market-related value of plan assets—See Valuation of Plan Assets	8,656	10,335

UNRECOGNIZED GAINS AND LOSSES

For purposes of the corridor calculation, the unrecognized net gain or loss excludes those asset gains and losses not yet reflected in the calculated market-related value of plan assets. The schedule below displays the elements of the unrecognized net gain or loss and the interaction between it and the unrecognized net gain or loss to be included in the corridor calculation.

	Unrecognized Net Gain (Loss)	Unrecognized Net Gain (Loss) for Purposes of Corridor
January 1, 1987	$ 0	$ 0
Gains (losses) arising in 1987:		
Increase in PBO[1]	(1,050)	(1,050)
Difference between actual return and expected return on plan assets[2]	430	86
December 31, 1987	(620)	(964)
Amortization of unrecognized net loss[3]	0	0
Gains (losses) arising in 1988:		
Increase in PBO	(962)	(962)
Difference between return on plan assets and expected return	134	113
December 31, 1988	(1,448)	(1,813)
Amortization of unrecognized net loss[3]	15	15
Gains (losses) arising in 1989:		
Decrease in PBO	750	750
Difference between return on plan assets and expected return	(284)	56
December 31, 1989	$ (967)	$ (992)

[1]See Changes in Projected Benefit Obligation.
[2]See Valuation of Plan Assets.
[3]See Amortization of Unrecognized Net Gain or Loss.

(continued)

Exhibit 26.7.   Continued.

PENSION-RELATED BALANCE SHEET ACCOUNTS

The interaction between periodic pension cost and funding can best be demonstrated by:

	1987	1988	1989
Prepaid pension cost, January 1	$ 0	$ 120	$ 368
Pension cost	(980)	(952)	(1,211)
Amount contributed (funded)	1,100	1,200	1,250
Prepaid pension cost, December 31	$ 120	$ 368	$ 407

The difference between the accumulated benefit obligation and the fair value of plan assets at the end of each year is:

	December 31		
	1987	1988	1989
Accumulated benefit obligation	$8,900	$12,600	$13,100
Fair value of plan assets	9,000	10,700	12,150
Unfunded (overfunded) accumulated benefit obligation	$ (100)	$ 1,900	$ 950

Company X, as permitted under SFAS No. 87, waited until 1989 to record an additional minimum liability. On December 31, 1989, the adjustment necessary to reflect this minimum liability was $1,357 (unfunded ABO of $950 plus prepaid pension cost of $407), with a corresponding intangible asset ($1,357) being recorded. The maximum intangible asset would have been $3,890 (unrecognized prior service cost of $1,690 plus unrecognized net obligation at date of initial application of SFAS No. 87 of $2,200).

FINANCIAL STATEMENT DISCLOSURES

The comparative financial statements of Company X for the year ended December 31, 1989, would include the following disclosures regarding its pension plan.

Note X

The Company has a defined pension plan covering substantially all of its employees. Benefits are based on years of service and employee's compensation at the time of retirement. The Company's funding policy is to contribute annually the maximum amount that can be deducted for federal income tax purposes.

Pension cost for 1989, 1988, and 1987 consists of the following components:

	1989	1988	1987
Service cost	$ 700	$ 650	$ 600
Interest cost	1,200	968	900
Actual return on plan assets	(750)	(1,000)	(1,150)
Deferrals and amortization	61	334	630
Net pension cost	$1,211	$ 952	$ 980

The following assumptions were used:

	As of December 31		
	1989	1988	1987
Weighted-average discount rate for projected benefit obligation (%)	8	7.5	8
Rate of increase in compensation levels for projected benefit obligation (%)	5.75	5.5	5.5
Expected long-term rate of return on plan assets—periodic pension cost (%)	10	10	10

(continued)

Exhibit 26.7. *Continued.*

The following table sets forth the plan's funded status and amounts recognized in the Company's statement of financial position at December 31, 1989 and 1988:

	December 31	
	1989	**1988**
Actuarial present value of benefit obligations:		
Vested benefit obligation	$(10,400)	$ (9,700)
Accumulated benefit obligation	(13,100)	(12,600)
Projected benefit obligation	(16,600)	(16,000)
Plan assets at fair value	12,150	10,700
Funded status	(4,450)	(5,300)
Unrecognized net loss (gain)	967	1,448
Unrecognized prior service cost	1,690	1,820
Unrecognized net obligation at date of initial application—		
January 1, 1987	2,200	2,400
Prepaid (accrued) pension cost prior to recognizing additional		
liability	407	368
Adjustment necessary to reflect additional minimum liability	(1,357)	—
Prepaid (accrued) pension cost	$ (950)	$ 368

As SFAS No. 87 permits, the Company waited until 1989 to record an additional minimum liability for unfunded pension benefit obligations. Had the requirement been adopted as of December 31, 1988, prepaid pension assets would have decreased by $368, other accrued liabilities would have increased by $1,900, and an intangible asset of $2,268 would have been recorded.

Plan assets consist of publicly traded stocks and bonds, and U.S. government securities.

Unrecognized prior service cost is amortized on a straight-line basis over the estimated average service period of employees active at the date of the related plan amendment who are expected to receive plan benefits.

Exhibit 26.7.   Continued.

SPONSOR ACCOUNTING FOR NONRECURRING EVENTS

26.20 OVERVIEW.   An integral concept of pension accounting is that certain pension obligations should be recognized over time rather than immediately. They include gains and losses from experience different from that assumed, the effects of changes in actuarial assumptions on the pension obligations, the cost of retroactive plan amendments, and any unrecognized net obligation or asset at transition established when the plan first complied with SFAS No. 87. The premise of this delayed recognition is that plan amendments are made in anticipation of economic benefits that the employer may derive over the future service periods of its employees, and that gains or losses already incurred may be reversed in the future. When events happen that fundamentally alter or eliminate the premise for delayed recognition, immediate recognition of previously unrecognized amounts may be required.

Examples of such special events include **business combinations,** addressed in paragraph 74 of SFAS No. 87; and **settlements, curtailments,** and **termination benefits,** the subjects of **SFAS No. 88,** which is effective simultaneously with SFAS No. 87. Thus an employer generally may not, for instance, follow the SFAS No. 88 accounting for a settlement unless SFAS No. 87 has been adopted. Relevant paragraphs of **APB Opinion Nos. 8 and 16** are superseded by these new statements, as is **SFAS No. 74** in its entirety.

Although prior accounting opinions and statements, such as APB Opinion No. 8, did require immediate recognition of gains or losses in certain situations, they did not define the methodology by which the special pension recognition should be carried out. As a result, widely divergent practices evolved, with differing effects on the affected employers' subsequent pension costs. In contrast, the new accounting provisions for nonrecurring events are based on standardized measurement methods that are applied within the general framework of SFAS No. 87. As with that Statement, SFAS No. 88 focuses on proper accounting of events in the future and generally allows plans to begin with a clean slate at the initial compliance date regardless of how such events were handled previously. There is also an exception for **immaterial items.**

26.21 SETTLEMENT. To constitute a **settlement,** a transaction must (1) be irrevocable, (2) relieve the employer of primary responsibility for a pension benefit obligation, and (3) eliminate significant risks related to the obligations and the assets used to effect the settlement. This is a new accounting concept introduced by SFAS No. 88.

The most common type of settlement is the **purchase of nonparticipating annuities** for or **lump-sum cash payments** to plan participants to discharge all or part of the benefit obligation of the plan, which may or may not be connected with a plan termination. (A participating annuity allows the purchaser to participate in the investment performance and possibly other experience—for example, mortality experience—of the insurance company, through dividends or rate credits. It generally costs more than a nonparticipating annuity, which is based on a fixed price.) Although SFAS No. 88 extends condition (2) in the preceding paragraph to include a transaction that relieves the plan of the responsibility for the benefit obligation, that condition is generally not sufficient, for example, if the benefit obligation is transferred to another plan sponsored by the same or a related employer, or if the annuities are purchased from a subsidiary of the employer.

(a) Timing. The timing of the settlement recognition depends on when all three qualifying conditions for a settlement have been met. For example, a commitment to purchase annuity is not sufficient to constitute a settlement until the benefit obligation risk has been transferred to the insurance company and the premium for the annuities has been paid in cash or in kind, except for minor adjustments. Although a dedicated portfolio designed to match the estimated benefit payments under the plan may eliminate the investment risk on assets backing those payments, it does not constitute a settlement because the plan continues to be exposed to the mortality risk on those payments and also because the portfolio is not irrevocable.

(b) Gain or Loss. The **maximum gain or loss** subject to settlement recognition is the unrecognized net gain or loss in the plan at the date of settlement, plus any remaining unrecognized net asset (but not a net obligation) at transition. The magnitude of the projected benefit obligation to be settled, as determined by the employer prior to the settlement, is generally not the same as the cost to discharge that obligation, such as the premium for the annuities, and must first be set equal to the latter. This adjustment in the projected benefit obligation generates a gain or loss that is added to unrecognized net gain or loss before the settlement recognition is done. The amount of the **settlement gain or loss** is equal to the maximum gain or loss subject to settlement recognition multiplied by the **settlement percentage,** which is the percentage of the projected benefit obligation of the plan being settled. Computations described in this paragraph are generally performed on a plan-by-plan basis rather than by aggregating all of the employer's plans.

(c) Use of Participating Annuities. **Participating annuities** are acceptable instruments to effect a settlement, unless their substance is that the employer remains subject to all or most of the risks and rewards associated with the benefit obligation covered by the annuities or the assets transferred to the insurance company. If the purchase of a participating annuity constitutes a settlement, the maximum gain (but not the maximum loss) must first be reduced by the cost of the participation feature. This means that the participation feature of the annuity contract is excluded from the settlement recognition entirely and its value, which is the present value of the future dividends expected from the insurance company, is carried as a plan asset.

SFAS No. 88 also permits **a de minimis exemption** from settlement recognition if the total cash and annuity settlements in a year do not exceed the sum of the service cost and interest cost components of the net periodic pension cost, provided this accounting practice is followed consistently from year to year.

26.22 CURTAILMENT. A curtailment is an event that significantly reduces the expected years of future service of present employees covered by the plan, or eliminates for a significant number of employees covered by the plan the accrual of defined benefit for some or all of their future services. It is possible for an event, such as a window retirement program, to change significantly the benefit obligation but not the total expected future services and, therefore, not to be a curtailment. Unrelated, individually insignificant reductions in future services do not qualify as a curtailment even if they occur in a single year and are significant in aggregate. Conversely, a series of individually insignificant reductions in future services, which are caused by the same event but take place over more than one fiscal year, should be aggregated to determine if the reduction is sufficiently significant to constitute a curtailment.

Examples of curtailment include reduction in work force, closing of a facility with the employees not employed elsewhere by the employer, disposal of a business segment, window retirement program, termination of a defined benefit plan or freezing of the benefits thereunder. A process known as **termination/reestablishment,** whereby an employer terminates a defined benefit plan, recovers the surplus plan assets, and then establishes a new plan for the same employees that provides the same overall benefits as the terminated plan when benefits from the terminated plan are taken into account, is not a curtailment because the employer's benefit obligation has not been materially altered. Even if the new plan created through the termination/reestablishment process does not reproduce the same overall benefits, the transaction should be treated as a plan amendment and not a curtailment. Similarly, if the employees are covered by multiple plans and the suspension of their benefit accrual under one plan is wholly or partially balanced by increased benefit accrual under another plan of the same or a related employer (e.g., a supplemental retirement plan providing defined benefits, which is offset by the benefits from the suspended plan), the event should be treated not as a curtailment but as simultaneous amendments to the two plans: One reduces benefits and one increases benefits.

The **curtailment gain or loss** to be recognized is the sum of the **prior service cost recognition** and the **projected benefit obligation adjustment,** both determined on a plan-by-plan basis rather than by aggregating all of the employer's plans.

According to statements made by the FASB staff, the **prior service cost recognition** is intended to be the immediate recognition of any unrecognized prior service cost and any remaining unrecognized net obligation (but not a net asset) at transition that relate to those employees whose services have been curtailed. Since these two items are often not available for specific employees or groups of employees, SFAS No. 88 provides a general rule to compute the prior service cost recognition as the product of any unrecognized net obligation at transition, or any prior service cost related to the entire plan, and the applicable **curtailment percentages.** The curtailment percentage is the percentage reduction in the remaining expected future years of service associated with the prior service cost or the net obligation at transition; it is determined separately for each prior service cost and the net obligation at transition. To reduce computational complexity, it is common practice to use an alternative curtailment percentage such as the percentage reduction in future years of service of all employees immediately prior to the curtailment, provided that the results would not be materially distorted.

The **projected benefit obligation adjustment** can be a gain or a loss. If the curtailment reduces the projected benefit obligation, the reduction is applied first against any unrecognized net loss in the plan and the residual amount is recognized as a gain. If the curtailment increases the projected benefit obligation, the increase is applied first against any unrecognized net gain and any remaining unrecognized net asset at transition, and the residual amount is recognized as a loss.

The timing of the curtailment recognition depends on whether the net effect is a gain or a loss. A net gain is recognized when the event has occurred, whereas a net loss is recognized when the event appears probable and its effects are reasonably estimable.

Although Paragraph 31 of **APB Opinion No. 8** had required immediate recognition of any actuarial gains or losses resulting from unusual events, SFAS No. 88 further specifies the conditions necessitating the immediate recognition and the method of determining the amount to be recognized, thus greatly narrowing down the divergence of practice that prevailed prior to SFAS No. 88.

26.23 DISPOSAL OF A BUSINESS.   When an employer disposes of a business segment, its pension plan may experience a **curtailment,** due to the termination of some employees' services, and a **settlement,** if all or part of the benefit obligation is transferred to the purchaser. Certain **termination benefits** such as severance payments may also be involved. The effects of such curtailment, settlement, and termination benefits should be determined in accordance with SFAS No. 88 and then included in the **gain or loss on the disposal** pursuant to paragraphs 15–17 of APB Opinion No. 30, "Reporting the Results of Operations—Reporting the Effects of Disposal of a Segment of a Business and Extraordinary, Unusual and Infrequently Occurring Events and Transactions," except for the following modifications to the SFAS No. 88 measurements: (1) the curtailment recognition is made regardless of whether the reduction in future services is significant; (2) the de minimis exemption for settlements does not apply; and (3) the difference between any benefit obligation and plan assets transferred to the purchaser is recognized in full as a gain or loss before the settlement percentage is determined. However, if the settlement, by purchasing annuities, for example, could have taken place in the absence of the business disposal, the settlement recognition should not be included in the gain or loss on the disposal.

26.24 PLAN MERGER, SPINOFF, AND TERMINATION.   The **merger** of two or more pension plans of the same employer does not require any SFAS No. 88 recognition. Prior service costs should be amortized as before. The remaining unrecognized net obligations or assets at transition should be netted and amortized over a reasonably weighted average of the remaining amortization periods previously used by the separate plans. The unrecognized net gains or losses should be aggregated and the minimum amortization thereof should reflect the average remaining service period of the combined employee group.

Spinoff of a portion of a pension plan to an unrelated employer, as may happen after the sale of a business segment, should be handled as a settlement unless there is reasonable doubt that the purchaser will meet the benefit obligation and the seller remains contingently liable for it. A settlement does not occur if an employer divides a pension plan into two or more plans all sponsored by it. In that case any remaining unrecognized net obligation or asset should be allocated among the plans in proportion to their respective projected benefit obligations, as should any unrecognized net gain or loss. Any unrecognized prior service cost should be allocated on the basis of the participants in the surviving plans.

If one of these surviving plans is further **transferred to a subsidiary,** the employer should reduce its prepaid (accrued) pension cost by the amount of prepaid (accrued) pension cost related to the transferred plan and simultaneously record a decrease (increase) in its stockholders' equity by the same amount. The subsidiary, on the other hand, should record the transferred prepaid (accrued) pension cost as an asset liability and an equal amount as an increase (decrease) in its stockholders' equity.

Prior to SFAS No. 88, the accounting effect of the **termination** of a defined benefit plan was largely based on the amount of surplus assets or deficit in the plan. If surplus assets were returned to the employer and there was no successor defined benefit plan, the previously unrecognized amount was typically reflected in the employer's earnings over a period of 10 to

20 years. SFAS No. 88 changed entirely the accounting concept relating to a plan termination. First of all, any remaining unrecognized gain from a **prior asset reversion,** which had been accomplished through a settlement as defined by SFAS No. 88, was recognized immediately upon the initial application date of the Statement as the effect of a change in accounting principle, to the extent that plan assets plus (minus) accrued (prepaid) pension cost exceeded the projected benefit obligation. There would be no further amortization of the remaining amount since it was already reflected in the size of the unrecognized net obligation or asset at transition. The second change introduced by SFAS No. 88 is that a plan termination is accounted for as a combination of a curtailment (i.e., elimination of further benefit accrual, assuming that there is not a successor defined benefit plan) and a settlement. Indeed, the **asset reversion** is no longer the triggering event, and substantially the same accounting effect has been achieved when the benefit accrual is frozen and the benefit obligation settled, even if the plan is not terminated. Any **excise tax** related to the asset reversion should be recognized at the time of the reversion. As noted in section 26.22, the termination/reestablishment of a defined benefit plan does not constitute a curtailment, but it may nevertheless require a settlement recognition.

Withdrawal from a multiemployer plan may result in additional cost to the employer. The effect of the withdrawal should be recognized when it becomes probable or reasonably possible.

26.25 TERMINATION BENEFITS. SFAS No. 74, "Accounting for Special Termination Benefits Paid to Employees," was issued in 1983, ostensibly to address window retirement programs and shutdown benefits. Although it required recognition of the effects of any changes on the previously accrued expenses for those benefits, no recognition method was defined and compliance with the Statement was not widespread.

SFAS No. 88 superseded SFAS No. 74, and as with that Statement, it deals with both pension and nonpension benefits such as severance payments, supplemental unemployment benefits, and life and health insurance benefits, regardless of whether they are paid by a plan or directly by the employer. The amount to be recognized is the amount of any immediate payments plus the present value of any expected future payments. The cost of **special termination benefits** that are offered only for a short period of time should be recognized when the employees accept the offer and the amount can be reasonably estimated. In contrast, **contractual termination benefits,** which are required by the terms of a plan only if a specified event (such as a plant closing) occurs, should be recognized when it is probable that employees will be entitled to benefits and the amount can be reasonably estimated.

Keep in mind that a situation involving termination benefits often also involves a curtailment. The curtailment recognition is first determined using the benefit obligation without the termination benefits. The effect of the termination benefits is then the difference between the benefit obligations determined with and without the termination benefits.

It is not unusual, in the measurement of the projected benefit obligation and the pension cost of a plan, to assume some probability for events that may give rise to termination benefits. In such a situation, the amount of termination benefits to be recognized under SFAS No. 88 is the difference between the projected benefit obligation including the termination benefits and that measured without any termination benefit. For example, a plan may permit early retirement after age 55 with a reduced pension but provide an unreduced pension regardless of age in the event of a change in control of the employer. When a change in control occurs, the amount of termination benefit to be recognized for an employee who is age 40 is the difference in the value of his unreduced pension commencing immediately and his reduced pension commencing when he will reach age 55. Furthermore, if the situation constitutes a curtailment, the projected benefit obligation adjustment is the difference between the value of his reduced pension commencing at age 55 and his projected benefit obligation determined using the regular actuarial assumptions including, if applicable, an allowance for some probability that change-in-control benefits may be invoked. It would not be reasonable to treat the entire change in projected benefit obligation as a gain or loss or to handle the situation solely as a curtailment, merely because the assumptions used to determine the projected benefit obligation prior to the change of control included some allowance for change-in-control benefits.

26.26 BUSINESS COMBINATION.   No special accounting treatment is needed if the business combination is accounted for as a pooling of interest. However, if the **purchase method** under APB Opinion No. 16 is used, the purchaser should record a liability (accrued pension cost) equal to the excess of the acquired projected benefit obligation over the acquired plan assets, or an asset (prepaid pension cost) equal to the excess of the acquired plan assets over the acquired projected benefit obligation. The liability or asset thus recorded should be net of tax effects, even though the gross pretax amount will be used in subsequent determination of the minimum balance sheet liability with respect to the plan (if SFAS No. 96 is utilized the gross pretax amount will be used and a deferred tax liability (asset) will be recorded). The tax effects of such purchase accounting adjustment are included in the reconciliation of the plan's funded status alongside any prior service cost. Simultaneous with the recording of such purchase accounting liability (asset), **goodwill** is increased (decreased) by an equal amount. Once these adjustments have been made, any previously existing unrecognized prior service cost, net obligation, or asset at transition and net gain or loss are eliminated and no further amortization thereof will be needed. If the acquired company continues to issue its own separate financial statement after the purchase date, its pension cost may be determined without the purchase accounting adjustment and may therefore be different from the pension cost reported by the parent company on its behalf.

The measurement date for the purchase accounting adjustment is the acquisition date, even if the employer customarily uses a measurement date different from its fiscal year-end for all other aspects of SFAS No. 87. In determining the projected benefit obligation at the acquisition date, the effects of certain **postacquisition events** should be reflected. Examples of such events include curtailments (without regard to the significance criterion), termination benefits, and plan amendments that were highly probable at the time of the purchase. To be included in the purchase accounting, these events generally must either occur, or be substantially decided upon, within one year of the acquisition date.

Although not a standard practice, similar purchase accounting adjustments may also be made for **nonpension benefits** such as healthcare benefits for retirees. The **restructuring** of a company, including merger of two or more legal entities, generally does not trigger a purchase accounting adjustment for pension.

26.27 SEQUENCE OF MEASUREMENT STEPS.   In a year containing one of the unusual events described above, the employer's pension cost comprises (1) the net periodic pension cost for the period prior to the event, determined without regard to the event; (2) the effect of the event such as the curtailment or settlement recognition; and (3) the net periodic pension cost for the period subsequent to the event, fully reflecting the changes resulting from the event. The **preevent pension cost** in (1) is generally based on the assumptions, such as the discount rate, used for the previous year-end measurement. **Updated projected benefit obligation and plan assets** are then determined as of the event date as if the event had not taken place, using assumptions that are appropriate at that date, including, if applicable, any adjustment to the projected benefit obligation to reflect the actual cost of settling any benefit obligation. The prepaid (accrued) pension cost, as well as any unrecognized prior service cost, net obligation, or asset at transition and net gain or loss, are brought up to date. The effect of the event is next determined on the basis of the updated projected benefit obligation and plan assets. The **postevent pension cost** in item (3) is based on the projected benefit obligation, plan assets, prior service cost, unrecognized net obligation, or asset at transition and net gain or loss that remain after the event.

In determining the postevent pension cost, the remaining amortization period for any unrecognized net obligation or asset at transition will generally not be changed even though the amount to be amortized may have. Similarly the remaining amortization schedule of any prior service cost will generally remain unchanged, unless the period during which the employer expects to realize future economic benefits from the plan amendment is shorter than originally estimated, or if the future economic benefits have been impaired. Amortization of net gain or loss, on the other hand, should reflect the postevent average remaining service period.

In case of **multiple events** occurring within one fiscal year, the process described in the preceding paragraphs may need to be repeated more than once, taking the events one at a time in chronological order. For simultaneous events it is permissible to establish the presumed sequence unless there is compelling reason against the logic of that sequence, provided that the same approach is followed consistently in the future. The sequence selected can materially affect the amount of gain or loss to be recognized. It is also possible for events that originated from the situation to be recognized in different fiscal years, for example, when a plan is terminated in one year but the benefit obligation is not settled until the following year.

Special considerations are needed when the plan's measurement date differs from the employer's fiscal year-end. It is generally not practical to measure the effect of the special event on any date other than the date of the event, since such measurement typically involves the changes in the projected benefit obligation or plan assets on the event date, such as the amounts of benefit obligation and plan assets being transferred to another employer. One approach is to determine the effect of the event using benefit obligation, plan assets, and net gain or loss as of the event date, even though the preevent pension cost was computed using a measurement date different from the fiscal year-end, and then determine the postevent pension cost for the period from the event date to the fiscal year-end. However, the ensuing year-end measurement may again be done at a measurement date that is consistent with that used in the preceding year.

Gain or loss related to events occurring after the measurement date but prior to the employer's fiscal year-end is generally not recognized in the current period, except when it relates to a disposal of business segment that is reflected in the current year or when it results from the termination of a pension plan without a successor defined benefit plan. Even if not recognized, the effect of the event should be disclosed if it is material. The preceding statements apply to quarterly financial statements as well.

26.28 DISCLOSURE REQUIREMENTS FOR NONRECURRING EVENTS.   An employer that recognizes a gain or loss for curtailment, settlement, or termination benefits shall disclose the **nature of the event** and the **amount recognized.** Despite the nonrecurring nature of these events, such gain or loss is normally not an extraordinary item as defined in paragraphs 20–22 of APB Opinion No. 30. One exception is when the gain or loss is related to the disposal of a business segment.

26.29 ILLUSTRATION—NONRECURRING EVENTS.   Exhibit 26.8 illustrates the application of SFAS No. 88 with respect to settlement, curtailment, and special termination benefits and that of SFAS No. 87 with respect to business combinations accounted for under the purchase method.

BACKGROUND INFORMATION AND ASSUMPTIONS

Company X, which was used to illustrate the application of SFAS No. 87, experienced the following events, all occurring on December 31, 1989, and in the sequence shown below:

- The projected benefit obligation for pensioners was $6,000 on December 31, 1989. Company X purchased participating annuities at a cost of $6,200 to discharge this obligation, $600 of which would be expected to be refunded by the insurance company in the form of dividends in future years.

(continued)

Exhibit 26.8.   Nonrecurring events.

- Company X closed one of its major manufacturing plants and permanently laid off all its workers. These workers would have represented 20% of the future service of all of Company X's employees. The projected benefit obligation with respect to these laid-off workers was $1,500 before the layoff and only $800 after the layoff, ignoring the special benefits described below.
- For those laid-off employees who were eligible for early retirement, Company X offered unreduced early retirement pensions and an additional supplemental pension up to age 62. If not for the plant closing, these employees would have been entitled to a reduced early retirement pension only and no supplement. The value of the supplements and the waiver of the early retirement reduction was $400.
- Also on December 31, 1989, Company X acquired Company Y, which sponsored a defined-benefit pension plan with a projected benefit obligation of $1,000 and plan assets worth $1,400. Company X has not adopted SFAS No. 96.

EFFECT ON FUNDED STATUS ON DECEMBER 31, 1989

	Initial Status	Effect of Settlement[1]	Effect of Curtailment[2]	Special Termination Benefit[3]	Acquisition of Company Y[4]	Revised Status
Projected benefit obligation	$(16,600)	$6,200	$ 700	$(400)	$(1,000)	$(11,100)
Plan assets (fair value)	12,150	(5,600)	0	0	1,400	7,950
Funded status	$ (4,450)	$ 600	$ 700	$(400)	$ 400	$ (3,150)
Unrecognized net loss (gain)	967	(728)	(239)	0	0	0
Unrecognized prior service cost	1,690	0	(338)	0	0	1,352
Unrecognized net obligation at date of initial application	2,200	0	(440)	0	0	1,760
Deferred tax liability from acquisition of Company Y	0	0	0	0	(228)	(228)
Prepaid (accrued) pension cost	$ 407	$ (128)	$(317)	$(400)	$ 172	$ (266)

[1]Although the price of the annuity contract was $6,200, the cost for SFAS No. 87 purposes is only $5,600 since $600 of future dividends are anticipated. The $600 will be carried as a plan asset.

In accounting for the settlement the following steps are followed:

First, the $16,600 PBO needs to be reevaluated because the PBO for pensioners was discovered to be $5,600 instead of $6,200. The revised PBO, therefore, is $16,000, of which $5,600 was settled through the annuity purchase. The settlement percentage is 35%.

Second, the unrecognized net loss is reduced from the $967 before the settlement by the $600 "savings" from the annuity contract, leaving a net loss of $367.

The settlement loss is $128 (i.e., $367 net loss times settlement percentage of 35%). This loss reduces the prepaid pension cost from $407 to $279.

[2]The 20% reduction in future services expected from the employee is significant enough to constitute a curtailment under SFAS No. 88. The curtailment gain/loss consists of two components—the prior service recognition and the PBO adjustment.

(continued)

Exhibit 26.8. *Continued.*

The curtailment loss is calculated as follows:

The remaining unrecognized prior service cost on December 31, 1989, is $1,690 and the remaining transition obligation is $2,200 for a total of $3,890. The prior service cost recognition is 20% (the curtailment percentage) of the $3,890, or a $778 loss.

The PBO is reduced by $700 on account of the plant closing. However, since the plan still carries an unrecognized net loss of $239 at this point, the $700 saving must first be applied to eliminate the $239 unrecognized loss before the remaining $461 may be recognized as a PBO adjustment gain.

The net curtailment loss is $317 (the $778 prior service cost less the $461 PBO gain). This $317 loss results in an accrued pension cost of $38. The amortization of the prior service cost ($130 in 1989) will be $160 in 1990. The respective remaining amortization periods will nevertheless remain unchanged.

[3]The value of the special benefits ($400) is recognized in full immediately and further increases the accrued pension cost from $38 to $438.

[4]Company Y's plan has an excess of $400, the difference between the plan assets of $1,400 and the PBO of $1,000. The $400 excess (less $228 in deferred tax) is recognized in purchase accounting and added to goodwill. Meanwhile the accrued pension cost is reduced by $172, from $438 to $266.

Exhibit 26.8. Continued.

SPONSOR ACCOUNTING FOR NONQUALIFIED PLANS

26.30 QUALIFIED VERSUS NONQUALIFIED PLANS. Qualified pension plans present notable tax advantages to both employer and employee as a form of employee compensation. The immediate advantage to the employer is the ability to deduct currently, within limitations, contributions to the plan. The employee on whose behalf the contribution is made does not, however, have to report the amount as gross income until it is made available to him. This deferral of tax has an added advantage since, in the typical case, benefits are not distributed until retirement, when the employee may be in a lower income tax bracket. The long-term, and perhaps the most important, tax advantage enjoyed by a qualified plan is that the fund or trust that receives and invests the contributions enjoys tax-exempt status. Investments earnings are not taxed until distributed, thus permitting an accelerated rate of growth for the fund.

For a pension plan to be considered qualified for income tax purposes, it must comply with certain IRC requirements, not only in the design of the plan but also in its operations. Some of these requirements are:

- The plan must not discriminate in favor of employees who are officers or shareholders or highly compensated.
- Benefits under the plan must be reasonable in amount when considered with other forms of compensation.
- Plan operations must be conducted in accordance with the plan document and trust agreement.
- The pension fund must be exclusively for the benefit of participants and their beneficiaries.
- The plan must comply with certain minimum funding and reporting requirements.

Over the years these requirements have become increasingly complex and burdensome, thus adding to the costs of administering qualified plans.

It has always been fairly common for an employer to maintain nonqualified retirement plans or to provide individualized deferred compensation arrangements for a selected group of management and highly compensated employees. There is no precise definition of "highly compensated employees" in this context, and it is not linked to the definition of "highly compensated employees" introduced by the Tax Reform Act of 1986. The primary advantages of such nonqualified arrangements are that (1) the coverage can be limited to only a few selected employees; (2) the benefits can be designed to meet the employer's objectives and the employees' needs without having to worry about the myriad of constraints imposed by ERISA and the tax code; and (3) they are exempt from virtually all ERISA reporting and funding requirements except a one-time notice of their existence to the DOL.

During the 1980s, the tax code was repeatedly amended to limit the amount of benefit that can be provided by, and the flexibility in the design of, a qualified plan. As a result nonqualified plans gained increasing importance. Despite these advantages over qualified plans, a nonqualified plan suffers from a serious tax disadvantage. Contributions to the plan, if any, are not currently tax-deductible to the employer as long as the employees' rights to those contributions are subject to a substantial risk of forfeiture. Instead, the employer may deduct the benefits when they are paid. Moreover, there is no tax shelter for any fund that the employer may have set aside to finance the plan. Investment earnings on such fund are taxed directly to the employer, thus retarding the growth of the fund.

An exception to the preceding paragraph is a plan that is funded through a **secular trust** (also known as a vesting trust). In that case the employer's contribution is tax-deductible to the employer and is taxed as income to the employee when the employee's interest has vested. Investment earnings of the trust are generally taxed to the employer unless distributed to the employee. The use of secular trust as the funding vehicle for a nonqualified plan may subject the plan to the reporting, funding, and other requirements of ERISA and the tax code. It is assumed throughout this chapter that the nonqualified plan is not being funded through a secular trust.

26.31 NONQUALIFIED PLAN ASSETS.

For accounting and tax purposes, any fund that an employer may have set aside to finance a nonqualified plan is treated as an asset of the employer and not as an asset of the plan in the context of SFAS Nos. 87 and 88. Indeed some plans must be unfunded in order to be exempt from the ERISA funding and reporting requirements. Therefore, such a fund is accounted for like any other general asset of the employer, whereas the cost of the benefits under the plan is determined in accordance with SFAS Nos. 87 and 88 as if there were no plan assets.

In order to improve the security of benefits to the employees, legal devices such as **rabbi trusts** have been used to prohibit or limit access to the plan fund by the employer or its creditors. Nevertheless the assets of a rabbi trust are still considered assets of the employer, and the trust accounting is consolidated with the employer's accounting.

26.32 NONQUALIFIED DEFINED CONTRIBUTION PLANS.

Pure nonqualified defined contribution plans are relatively uncommon. To constitute a defined contribution plan, the employer's obligation must be limited to its contributions to the plan, with the employees receiving benefits based on those contributions plus investment earnings thereon. Since most nonqualified plans are either unfunded or funded indirectly through vehicles such as corporate-owned life insurance, the mechanism to operate a defined contribution generally does not exist. A deferred compensation plan that promises a certain rate of interest on compensations deferred by employees is not a defined contribution plan, unless the promised rate is equal to the actual after-tax rate of return on the compensations deferred by the employees. This situation is not changed if the promised rate is based, for example, on the projected rate of return on certain life insurance policies used to finance the plan.

The employer's cost for a defined contribution plan is equal to its contribution to the plan.

26.33 NONQUALIFIED DEFINED BENEFIT PLANS.

Both SFAS Nos. 87 and 88 apply to nonqualified plans and to any arrangement that is similar in substance to a pension plan regardless of the form or means of financing. For any other individually designed deferred compensation contract, cost should be accrued in accordance with APB Opinion No. 12 in a systematic and rational manner over the employee's period of active employment, starting from the time the contract is entered into, so that the full cost will have been accrued at the end of the term of active employment.

Examples of nonqualified defined benefit plans are (1) **supplemental retirement plans** for selected employees providing retirement benefits in addition to the employer's qualified pension plans; (2) **benefit restoration plans** to restore to the employees any benefits that may have been restricted by IRC § 401(a) or 415, or by § 401(k) on the maximum amount of compensation that can be deferred; (3) **deferred compensation or termination indemnity plans** promising to credit a rate of interest that is not equal to the after-tax investment return on the assets set aside to finance the plans. **Golden parachutes** are generally accounted for as severance payments. Change-of-control pension provisions in a pension plan, which provides certain special benefits in the event of a change in control of the employer, are handled as termination benefits under SFAS No. 88.

In applying SFAS Nos. 87 and 88 to a nonqualified plan, the following factors should be considered: (1) The discount rate should reflect the effect of any tax liability for annuities that may be purchased to discharge the benefit obligation; (2) there is generally no contribution to the plan since any funds set aside to finance the plan remain assets of the employer, except for benefits paid to the employees or payments made to purchase annuities, for example, to discharge benefit obligations; (3) as a result of (2) above, the expected return on plan assets is zero (whereas the investment return on any assets or funds that may have been appropriated to finance the plan would have already been reported elsewhere as income to the employer); (4) as noted under (2) above, benefit payments are also treated as contributions and, therefore, would reduce the employer's accrued pension cost; and (5) a nonqualified plan linked to a qualified plan, such as a supplemental retirement plan providing benefits that are offset by benefits from a qualified pension plan, should nevertheless be accounted for separately from the qualified plan.

SFAS No. 96 has a particularly adverse impact on nonqualified plans. The sponsor of a nonqualified plan generally is not entitled to tax deductions until benefits are paid to the employees, which may not happen for many years, well beyond the permitted loss carryback period. (In contrast, the sponsor of a qualified plan is entitled to a tax deduction when it makes contributions to the plan.) As a result, SFAS No. 96 may preclude the plan sponsor from recording a deferred tax benefit at the same time that it is accruing a cost for the plan.

26.34 CORPORATE-OWNED LIFE INSURANCE.   No discussion of nonqualified plans can be complete without examining the role played by **corporate-owned life insurance** (COLI). In its simplest form COLI is life insurance taken out by an employer on the lives of its employees, with the employer being the premium payer, owner, and beneficiary of the insurance policies. It is the most widely used financing vehicle for nonqualified plans. COLI can also be owned by a trust established for the plan.

Under current tax laws, even though the insurance premiums paid by the employer are not currently tax-deductible, the insurance proceed payable upon the employee's death is tax-free. More importantly, the growth in the cash value of an insurance policy is not taxed to the employer, except when it is surrendered prior to the employee's death. This creates an indirect tax shelter that can be used to overcome the main tax disadvantage of a nonqualified plan: the lack of tax shelter. However, due to the start-up costs, overheads, and policy cancellation charges typically associated with life insurance policies, the use of COLI as a financing vehicle generally will only succeed if the policies are maintained for an extended period of time, if the employer's own achievable after-tax rate of return stays below that on the COLI policies, and if the preferential treatment of life insurance under the current tax laws will continue.

Another tax advantage offered by COLI has to do with the tax deduction on interest paid on policy loans. Subject to certain conditions, interest paid by the employer on loans taken on COLI policies is tax-deductible (for policies purchased after June 20, 1986, for loans up to

$50,000 in total on all policies on any one employee). Suppose the insurance company charges 10% interest on a $1,000 policy loan and the employer's marginal tax rate is 40%. The interest cost to the employer is $100 gross and $60 net of tax. Suppose further that, for the $100 interest paid on the loan, the insurance company would increase the policy's cash value by $90. The net result of these transactions is that the employer has managed to convert $60 after tax into $90 worth of insurance policy cash value, which it will eventually be able to collect as tax-free insurance proceeds.

Because of these tax advantages, COLI can be a more profitable investment than other investments available to the employer. This profit can be used to offset the cost of a nonqualified plan, thus creating the illusion of a no-cost benefit plan. This line of reasoning is often used to promote the sale of COLI policies and the establishment of nonqualified plans. Techniques known as ratable charge method or zero realization method, for example, have been used to demonstrate that premiums paid on COLI policies need not be charged against earnings if the policies are projected to generate a profit over time, or that the cost of a nonqualified plan need not be accrued because it is less than the projected profit from the COLI policies used to finance it. These methods were rejected by FTB 85-4, "Accounting for Purchase of Life Insurance," which prescribed the cash surrender value method as the only generally accepted method of accounting for COLI policies. Under the cash surrender value method, premiums are charged against the employer's earnings, any change in cash surrender or contract value is recorded as an adjustment of premiums paid, and the cash surrender value is carried as an asset of the employer. SFAS No. 96, "Accounting for Income Taxes," further requires the tax effect on the excess of cash surrender value over premiums paid to be recorded in situations where the employer's intention to maintain the policies till maturity is in doubt.

Any related nonqualified plan that may have been funded using COLI should be separately accounted for under SFAS Nos. 87 and 88, as described in section 26.33. The COLI policies, which have already been included in the assets of the employer, are not considered plan assets in this context. Insurance proceeds are recorded as income to the employer. A policy loan is recorded simultaneously as an increase in cash and a reduction in the net cash value of the COLI policy that is carried as an asset on the employer's balance sheet and therefore does not have an impact on the employer's earnings. Interest paid on a policy loan is charged as expense like any other interest payment.

PLAN ACCOUNTING

26.35 BACKGROUND.   In March 1980 the FASB issued SFAS No. 35, which established for the first time GAAP for the entity defined as a pension plan. The standard is effective for financial statements for fiscal years beginning after December 15, 1980. SFAS No. 35 was developed only after a great deal of controversy and followed a discussion paper, a public hearing, and two exposure drafts over a period of 5 years. It applies to all plans, including private plans and those of state and local governments. Coming under the standard are defined benefit pension plans that are subject to the financial reporting requirements of ERISA as well as those that are not. It does not apply to plans that are being terminated.

For nongovernmental plans with 100 or more participants as of the beginning of the plan year, a comprehensive annual report (Form 5500) must be filed in accordance with ERISA. The annual report must include:

1. A set of financial statements prepared in accordance with GAAP, with an audit and opinion by an independent qualified public accountant.
2. An actuarial report, including the status of the minimum funding standard account, and opinion by an enrolled actuary.

26.36 OBJECTIVE AND CONTENT OF FINANCIAL STATEMENTS.   Under SFAS No. 35, the plan itself is the reporting entity, not the trust. The statement is based on a position that the primary objective of a plan's financial statements is to provide information useful in assessing its present and future ability to pay benefits when due. This objective requires the presentation of information about the economic resources of the plan and a measurement of its participants' accumulated benefits. The Statement leaves unresolved, at least for the time being, the issue of whether accumulated plan benefits are accounting liabilities of the plan. Therefore it allows flexibility in presenting the actuarial information by providing that the plan's annual financial statements must include:

1. A **statement** that includes information regarding **net assets available for benefits**.
2. A **statement** that includes information regarding the **changes in net assets** available for benefits.
3. Information regarding the actuarial **present value of accumulated plan benefits** as of the benefit information date (which can either be at the beginning or end of the year).
4. **Information** regarding the effects, if significant, of certain factors effecting the year-to-year change in the actuarial present value of accumulated plan benefits.

SFAS No. 35 provides that the actuarial information required under items 3 and 4 can be presented in separate statements, in the notes to financial statements, or combined with the other required information on the net assets available for benefits and the year-to-year changes therein (provided the information is as of the same date and/or for the same period.)

26.37 NET ASSETS AVAILABLE FOR BENEFITS.   Plan investments, excluding contracts with insurance companies, must be reported at **fair value.** Contracts with insurance companies must be reported in accordance with the rules required by certain governmental agencies (i.e., primarily the DOL regulations) relating to the plan's annual report filed pursuant to ERISA. Plans not subject to ERISA also would be required to report their contracts with insurance companies as though they had filed that annual report. Exhibit 26.9 is a brief summary of those filing requirements.

Because net assets are the existing means by which a plan can provide benefits, net asset information is necessary to assess a plan's ability to pay benefits when due. Using fair value as the basis to measure a plan's investments provides the most relevant information about resources currently available to pay the participants' benefits. The fair value of an investment is the amount that the plan could reasonably expect to receive for the investment from a current sale between a willing buyer and a willing seller, that is, not in a forced liquidation sale. If there is an active market for the investment, fair value is measured by the **market price** as of the reporting date.

(a) Good Faith Valuations.   Investments that do not have a quoted market price, must be valued "in good faith." In determining a good faith value the following factors should be considered:

• Quoted market prices for similar investments.
• Information about transactions or offers regarding the plan's investment.
• Forecast of expected cash flows for that investment.

(b) Insurance Company Contracts.   Contracts with insurance companies must be valued in accordance with the instructions to either Form 5500 or Form 5500-C/R (herein referred to as **contract value**). The instructions, which are the same for both these forms, provide that contracts under which payments to the insurance companies are allocated to individual participants are **excluded** from plan assets. An **allocated contract** is one under which the insurance company guarantees the benefit payment to the participant, thereby relieving the sponsor, upon payment of the premium, of all risks. **Unallocated insurance contracts,** whereby the plan is responsible for paying benefits to the participants, are included as assets of the plan.

Investments in unallocated contracts must be presented at **contract value,** that is, at the amounts determined by the insurance company and furnished to the plan. The contract value can be, and probably is, different from fair value. However, the FASB decided to require contract value because it is readily available, whereas a fair value approach would necessitate extra calculations that might be extremely complex. Because the FASB did not have sufficient information at the time the statement was developed to reach definitive conclusions concerning insurance contracts, a practical solution was adopted.

A plan can enter into several types of insurance contract with an insurance company. Classification of these contracts is primarily based on whether (1) the contract assets are allocated to specific participants or (2) the premium payments made by the sponsor are accumulated in an unallocated fund and used to meet benefit payments as they become due or to purchase annuities for participants at some future date, such as at retirement. When reviewing different types of insurance contract for accounting purposes, the major consideration is the determination of the party (i.e., the plan or insurance company) ultimately liable for the benefit payments to participants.

(c) Deposit Administration Contracts. A deposit administration contract is an unallocated contract under which a specified interest return is typically guaranteed. In addition, experience credits (dividends) may be declared to the plan at the sole discretion of the insurance company. Typically, when a participant retires, an individual annuity is purchased for that participant, the insurance company guarantees payment of the benefits, and the annuity contract is no longer recorded as an asset of the plan.

Under the deposit administration contract, all funds intended for the future payment of benefits to participants are held in an undivided account, generally referred to as the "active life fund," which is credited with all premium deposits, interest earned on the funds invested, and any dividends or experience credits declared by the insurance company. It is charged with the purchase price of all annuities provided for retired participants and any other benefits paid directly from the account, such as for death or disability, and for all expenses not paid directly by the sponsor. Although the insurance company guarantees an interest return on all funds invested, it does not guarantee that sufficient funds will be available to meet the costs of annuities to be purchased. The contract value of deposit administration contracts is generally the amount in the active life funds as of the reporting date.

(d) Immediate Participation Guaranteed Contracts. An immediate participation guaranteed contract is a variation of the deposit administration contract except that an interest return is not guaranteed by the insurance company (a *low* minimum rate may be guaranteed), nor is a dividend credited to the contract. Instead, income is based on the actual interest rates earned by the insurance company. An immediate participation in the insurer's investment performance is a contract right. In accordance with the terms of the contract, the plan makes contributions to the insurance company, which credits the plan's account for the amount of the deposit. For investment purposes, the money (deposits) in the plan's account are commingled with the other assets of the insurance company. The plan's account is credited with interest based on the actual rates (generally referred to as "new money rates") earned by the insurance company according to the individual year in which the funds are deposited. Expenses charged to the plan's account are specified in the insurance contract, and benefit payments are made directly from the fund to retirees and charged to the plan's account. Alternatively, annuities can be purchased at the time the participants retire and the price of the annuity charged directly to the fund. In this case, the fund is adjusted each year based on the insurer's analysis of mortality, benefits paid, and earnings.

	Pension Plan with 100 or More Participants	Pension Plans with Fewer than 100 Participants	Welfare Benefit Plans — Plans with 100 or More Participants	Welfare Benefit Plans — Plans with Fewer than 100 Participants	One Participant Pension Plan with $100,000 or More of Assets
Basic Annual Return/Report Form	Form 5500	Form 5500-C/R	Form 5500	Form 5500-C/R	Form 5500-EZ
Financial Statements to Be Attached to Basic Form					
Statement of assets and liabilities at current value	Yes	No	Yes	No	No
Statement of income, expense, and changes in net assets	Yes	No	Yes	No	No
Notes to financial statements	Yes	No	Yes	No	No
Financial Information in Attached Schedules					
Assets held for investment:					
At the end of year	Yes	No	Yes	No	No
Both acquired and disposed within the plan year	Yes	No	Yes	No	No
Party-in-interest transactions	Yes	Yes	Yes	Yes	No
Obligations in default	Yes	No	Yes	No	No
Leases in default	Yes	No	Yes	No	No
Reportable transactions	Yes	No	Yes	No	No
Report of Independent Public Accountant	Yes	No	Yes	No	No

Schedules for Attachment to Basic Forms

Schedule A (Insurance Information)[1]	Yes	Yes	Yes	No
Schedule B (Actuarial Information)[2]	Yes	No	No	Yes
Schedule SSA (Separated Participants with Deferred Vested Benefits)	Yes	No	No	No
Annual statement of assets and liabilities of a bank common or collective trust or an insurance company pooled separate account[3]	No	Yes	No	No
Due Date for Filing				
Number of months after close of plan year	7	7	7	7
Additional number of months allowed upon timely filing of a request for extension	$2\frac{1}{2}$	$2\frac{1}{2}$	$2\frac{1}{2}$	$2\frac{1}{2}$

[1]Required if benefits are provided by an insurance carrier.
[2]Required if the plan is subject to the minimum funding standards of ERISA (defined benefit pension plan).
[3]If the bank or insurance company files a copy of the annual report directly with the Department of Labor, a plan filing need not contain a separate copy of the annual report.

Exhibit 26.9.   Employee benefit plans: schedule of DOL filing requirements. *Source:* U.S. Department of Labor.

When an individual annuity contract is not purchased, the insurance company requires the plan to maintain a minimum balance in the account that is referred to as the "retired life fund." This fund must be sufficient to purchase annuities for all retired participants. Although this fund is effectively transferred to the insurance company in return for the insurance company's agreement to provide benefits, the fund is still included in the contract value as a plan asset.

Some insurance companies make a distinction between "book value" and "contract value" with respect to immediate participation guaranteed contracts. As mentioned above, the plan participates in the actual earnings of the insurance company's general asset fund and also may be given an experience credit, which is held by the insurance company until distributed to the plan in a future year. The combined amount of the plan's account and the experience credit that will be distributed in the future is referred to as the **book value.** Contract value, on the other hand, is the amount of the plan's account excluding the experience credits. In reporting the plan's investment in the statement of net assets, the book value is the amount that should be used.

A problem occurs when the plan year is not the same as the contract year, the latter usually being the insurance company's calendar year. Some insurance companies credit the plan's account with an estimated interest amount during the year and adjust that amount to the actual amount as of the insurance company's year-end. In addition, there could be a significant difference (as much as 11 months) between the insurance company's year-end and the date the actual rate is credited to the plan's account. In these instances the plan administrator, or plan trustees, should make certain that the estimated amount credited to the account as of the plan's year-end is reasonable and appropriate disclosure should be made in the notes to the financial statements.

A **separate-separate account** is an investment arrangement with the insurance company whereby funds deposited (contributions) by the plan are invested by the insurance company. The assets of the separate-separate account are the assets of the insurance company, but they are not commingled with the general assets of the insurance company. The separate-separate account provides the plan sponsor with more flexibility in investing the plan's funds. Investments in a separate-separate account are separately identified, and the account is operated similar to a bank trust fund (see below), although the net assets of the account are included in the insurance company's financial statements.

Because the insurance company legally owns the assets, and also because the plan does not have a beneficial interest in the individual assets held in the account, the plan's investments in these accounts should be presented in the statement of net assets available for benefits on a one-line basis appropriately described as investments in an account with the insurance company.

A **pooled separate account** is an account maintained with an insurance company that consists of assets of two or more participating plans, plans of a controlled group being treated as a single account. Each plan's share in the account is determined on a participation unit or variable unit basis, with the value usually adjusted each business day to reflect the investment performance of the account. The plan account provides a cumulative record of the number of participation units credited to it and the number of units allocated or withdrawn from it. The net balance of participation units credited to the account as of the end of the year, multiplied by the current participation unit value, equals the contract value amount that should be reported as an asset of the plan. Such amounts are reported on a one-line basis in the statement of net assets available for benefits, appropriately described such as, "units of interest in XYZ Insurance Co."

(e) Trusteed Assets.   Typically, a plan administrator or a fiduciary will engage a trustee or an investment adviser to assist with the investment activities of the trust. Generally four different types of trustee arrangements are applicable to a plan's investments.

Under a **nondiscretionary trust arrangement** (also referred to as a **directed trust**), the trustee acts as custodian of the plan's investments and is responsible for collecting investment income and handling trust asset transactions, as directed by the party named as having discretion to make investment decisions. Such an arrangement provides the plan with a good degree of control over the accounting transactions, because investment decisions are made by the plan trustee or fiduciary. The plan ordinarily maintains a record of the instructions given to the trustee concerning the specific investment transactions to be executed.

Under a **discretionary trust arrangement** the plan administrator gives the trustee discretionary authority and control over investments. The trustee has the authority to purchase or sell investment assets within the framework of the trust instruments and usually maintains all the detail records concerning the investment transactions and supporting documentation.

In a **common or commingled trust fund** maintained with a bank, the plan acquires investment units, sometimes referred to as **units of participation,** which are roughly equivalent to shares purchased in a mutual fund. The purchase or redemption price of the units is determined periodically by the bank, on the basis of the current fair market values of the underlying assets of the fund. The trust funds are not included in the bank's financial statements. The units of participation shoud be reported in the plan's statement of net assets available for benefits on a one-line basis, appropriately described.

A company that sponsors more than one pension plan, or a controlled group of companies in several plans, may place assets relating to some or all of the plans into one combined trust account, commonly referred to as a **master trust.** Each plan may have an undivided interest in the net assets of the trust account, or ownership may be represented by units of participation. A bank ordinarily is the trustee for a combined trust account for which it acts as custodian, and it may have discretionary control over the assets. Although SFAS No. 35 does not deal with accounting for master trusts, the instructions to Form 5500 (and Form 5500-C/R) require that for master trusts, the plan's pro rata share of each category of assets be presented in the financial statements.

(f) Disclosures for Investments.   Information regarding the plan's investments must be presented in the plan's statement of net assets available for benefits in sufficient detail to identify the general types of investment (e.g., as government securities, short-term securities, corporate bonds, common stocks, mortgages, and real estate). In addition, whether fair values have been measured by quoted price in an active market or determined otherwise must be disclosed.

(g) Operating Assets.   Assets used in the plan's operations must be presented at cost, less accumulated depreciation or amortization. Such assets would include, for example, buildings, equipment, furniture and fixtures, and leasehold improvements. Although the DOL's instructions to Forms 5500 and 5500-C/R require the presentation of all assets at fair value, it is believed that the DOL will not object to this presentation in the financial statements.

(h) Contributions Receivable.   The plan's financial statements should include as contributions receivable all amounts due the plan, as of the reporting date, from the employer, participants, and other sources of funding (e.g., state subsidies or federal grants). These receivables would include amounts due pursuant to formal commitments as well as legal or contractual requirements.

26.38 CHANGES IN NET ASSETS AVAILABLE FOR BENEFITS.   The information about a plan's ability to pay benefits when due, provided by its financial statements, is affected whenever transactions or other events affect the net asset or benefit information presented in those statements. Because a plan's ability to pay participants' benefits normally does not remain constant, users of its financial statements are concerned with assessing the plan's ability to pay participants' benefits not only as of a particular point in time, but also on a continuing basis. For this reason, they need to know the **reasons for changes** in the net asset and benefit information reported in successive financial statements.

The FASB concluded, therefore, that plan financial statements should include (1) information regarding the year-to-year change in net assets available for benefits, and (2) disclosure of the effects, if significant, of certain factors affecting the year-to-year change in benefit information.

SFAS No. 35 requires presentation of the statement of changes in net assets available for benefits in sufficient detail to permit identification of the significant changes during the year. The statement should include, at a minimum:

1. The net change in fair value for each significant class of investments, segregated as between investments whose fair values have been measured by quoted prices in an active market and those whose fair values have been determined otherwise.

2. Investment income, excluding the changes of fair value described in item 1.

3. Contributions from employers, segregated as between cash and noncash contributions.

4. Contributions from participants.

5. Contributions from other identified sources such as state subsidies or federal grants.

6. Benefits paid.

7. Payments to insurance companies to purchase contracts that are excluded from plan assets.

8. Administrative expenses.

In presenting this information, gains and losses from investments sold are not segregated from **unrealized gains and losses** relating to investments held at the plan's year-end.

26.39 ACTUARIAL PRESENT VALUE OF ACCUMULATED PLAN BENEFITS. Accumulated plan benefits are future benefit payments that are attributable, under the plan's provisions, to employees' service rendered prior to the **benefit information date**—the date as of which the actuarial present value of accumulated plan benefits is presented. Accumulated benefits include benefits for retired or terminated employees, beneficiaries of deceased employees, and present employees or their beneficiaries.

The accumulated benefit information may be presented as of the beginning or end of the plan year. If it is presented as of the beginning of the plan year, the prior year statement of net assets available for benefits and changes therein must also be presented. For example, if the plan year-end is December 31, 1990, and the statement of accumulated plan benefits is based on a benefit information date of December 31, 1989, statements of net assets available for benefits and of changes therein also would be presented for 1989.

Measurement of accumulated plan benefits is based primarily on the employees' history of pay, service, and other appropriate factors as of the information date. **Future salary changes** are not considered, nor is a provision for inflation allowed. However, future increases that are guaranteed under a cost-of-living adjustment should be estimated. **Future years of service** are considered only in determining an employee's expected eligibility for benefits of particular types, such as early retirement, death, and disability benefits. To measure the actuarial present value, assumptions are used to adjust the accumulated plan benefits to reflect the time value of money and the probability of payment between the benefit information date and the expected date of payment. An assumption that the plan is ongoing must underlie those assumptions. Benefit information should relate to the benefits reasonably expected to be paid in exchange for employees' service to the benefit information date.

To the extent possible, plan provisions should apply in measuring accumulated plan benefits. If the benefit for each service year is not determinable from the provisions of the plan, the benefit must be considered to accumulate by years of service rendered in proportion to total years required to earn a particular benefit. Normally, the plan provisions will indicate how to measure accumulated plan benefits. Plan amendments occurring subsequent to the date of the calculation must be excluded from the actuarial computation. In addition, benefits that are guaranteed by a contract with an insurance company (i.e., allocated contracts) are also excluded.

(a) Actuarial Assumptions.   The most important decisions in developing the actuarial present value of accumulated plan benefits are in the selection of actuarial assumptions. The **interest return assumption** (analogous to the discount rate assumption in the section "Sponsor Accounting") is the single most important issue. It is used to discount future benefit payments, as well as to determine the anticipated rates of return on current and prospective assets. The concept of a **best estimate** and the principle of an **explicit approach** are integral to the rationale used in developing actuarial assumptions.

The concept of a "best estimate" is used by the FASB in discussing the actuarial assumptions in SFAS No. 35, possibly because the term is included in the ERISA certification required of an **enrolled actuary.** The reason is not critical, but it is important to realize that the best estimate requirement under ERISA is being interpreted in several ways. Its use for plan accounting purposes may be quite different from the best estimate for a funding basis. The section on sponsor accounting discusses the concept further.

Although there is no specific discussion of what the FASB intended by "best estimate," there is a discussion in the Statement of what is meant by **explicit approach.** It is important to recognize that prior to the Omnibus Budget Reconciliation Act of 1987 the explicit approach, although strongly recommended to actuaries by the American Academy of Actuaries, was not required in developing the ERISA requirements under the **minimum funding standard account.** Because of the importance of this issue, part of SFAS No. 35 is reproduced here:

199. This statement requires that each significant assumption used in determining the benefit information reflect the best estimate of the plan's future experience solely with respect to that assumption. That method of selecting assumptions is referred to as an **explicit approach.** An **implicit approach,** on the other hand, means that two or more assumptions do not individually represent the best estimate of the plan's future experience with respect to those assumptions. Rather, the aggregate effect of their combined use is presumed to be approximately the same as that of an explicit approach. The Board believes that an explicit approach results in more useful information regarding (a) components of the benefit information, (b) changes in the benefit information, and (c) the choice of significant assumptions used to determine the benefit information.

200. The following illustrates the preferability of an explicit approach as it relates to measuring components of the benefit information (that is, vested benefits of participants currently receiving payments, other vested benefits, and nonvested benefits). Under an implicit approach, it might be assumed that the net result of assuming no withdrawal before vesting and increasing assumed rates of return by a specified amount would approximate the same actuarial present value of total accumulated plan benefits as that which would result from using assumed rates of return and withdrawal rates determined by an explicit approach. Even if that were true, increasing assumed rates of return to compensate for withdrawal before vesting might significantly misstate components of the benefit information. Withdrawal before vesting relates only to nonvested benefits. Therefore, discounting vested benefits at rates of return that have been adjusted to implicitly reflect that withdrawal understates that component of the benefit information and correspondingly overstates the nonvested benefit information.

201. The disadvantage of an implicit approach with respect to information regarding changes in the benefit information can be similarly illustrated. Assume that under an implicit approach, assumed rates of return are decreased to implicitly reflect the effects of a plan's provision for an automatic cost-of-living adjustment (COLA). In that situation, the effect of a plan amendment relating to the automatic COLA, for example, an amendment to increase the "cap" on the COLA from three percent to four percent, might be obscured. If significant, the effect of such an amendment should, pursuant to the requirements of the Statement, be disclosed as the effect of a plan amendment. If an implicit approach is used, however, assumed rates of return would be adjusted to reflect the effects of that amendment and accordingly, some part or all of the effect might be presented as the effect of a change in an actuarial assumption rather than as the effect of a plan amendment (particularly if assumed rates of return are also changed for other reasons).

202. In addition to the foregoing possible disadvantages, an implicit approach might result in less meaningful disclosure of the significant assumptions used to determine the benefit information. For example, disclosure of the assumed rates of return resulting from the implicit approaches described in paragraphs 200 and 201 could mislead users of the financial statements regarding the plan's investment return expectations and could result in noncomparable reporting for two plans with the same investment return expectations. Users might also draw erroneous conclusions about the relationship between the plan's actual and assumed rates of return.

There are economic actuarial assumptions and noneconomic actuarial assumptions. The key issue in developing a plan's economic assumptions is the forecast of **long-term inflation.** The inflation component should be consistently reflected in all the economic assumptions. For example, if the long-term investment return assumption reflects a 5% inflation compo-nent, then the estimate of future salary increases should also reflect a 5% inflation component. In plan accounting it is not necessary to develop an assumption for future pay increases or future Social Security benefits. Because very few plans provide for automatic postretirement cost-of-living adjustments, that assumption will seldom be required for plan accounting.

It is clear from SFAS No. 35 that the interest assumption used for accounting purposes will frequently, if not usually, be different from that used for funding. The key requirement in developing an interest assumption, and for that matter any other assumption, is to use a sensible rationale. Judgmental elements in the actuary's development of a recommendation should be highlighted and subject to review and approval by the plan's sponsor. The framework and illustration of such a rationale is discussed in "Sponsor Accounting." Although the result may differ as between sponsor and plan accounting, the same approach can be applied in both instances.

The noneconomic assumptions of **mortality, withdrawal, disability, and early (late) retire-ment** are referred to in SFAS No. 35, relating to the probability and timing of benefit payments. They are referred to here as noneconomic because they are usually not influenced by the long-term economic forecast, although short-term economic conditions can have a marked impact on withdrawal and early retirement experience. The mortality and disability assumptions are more highly technical. The typical plan sponsor will have to rely more heavily on the actuary's judgment and recommendations when adopting them. The impact of variations in mortality and disability assumptions on the actuarial value of accumulated benefits is not generally very large. The withdrawal and early retirement assumptions can vary considerably from one organization to another, because they are affected by the personnel practices and business circumstances of the plan sponsor. Accordingly, more input from the plan sponsor is appropriate with respect to these assumptions. The discussion of these assumptions under "Sponsor Accounting" applies here as well.

(b) Disclosures for Actuarial Present Value of Accumulated Plan Benefits.   As previously stated, the accumulated benefit information may be presented as a separate financial statement, in a note to the financial statements, or combined with other information in the financial statements. The information must all be located in one place and must be segregated as follows:

- Vested benefits of participants currently receiving benefits.
- Other vested benefits.
- Nonvested benefits.

If employees contribute to the plan, accumulated employee contributions must be disclosed and, if applicable, accumulated interest credited on the contributions, including the interest rate, must also be disclosed.

(c) Relationship to Disclosures Under SFAS No. 87 and SFAS No. 88.   If the plan sponsor also complies with SFAS No. 87, it is required to disclose at its fiscal year-end the accumulated and vested benefit obligations of its plan. These items are the same as the present values of accumulated and vested plan benefits, if the plan's benefit information date is the same as the sponsor's fiscal year-end. **Schedule B to Form 5500** also discloses the present value of vested and nonvested accrued benefits, which are conceptually similar to the disclosures required under SFAS No. 35, except that Schedule B items do not reflect future indexation of the maximum benefit limitations under IRC § 415. Starting with plan years beginning in 1988, additional conditions were placed on the definition of Schedule B present values and the interest rate that may be used to compute them. As a result, they will often (usually) differ from SFAS No. 35 present values.

26.40 CHANGES IN THE ACTUARIAL PRESENT VALUE OF ACCUMULATED PLAN BENE-FITS.   The FASB requires disclosure of the effects, if significant, of certain factors affecting the year-to-year change in the benefit information. If the **benefit information date** is the beginning of the year, the required information regarding the year-to-year change in the benefit information would also relate to the preceding year. Consistent with the requirement for accumulated benefit information, the changes therein also may be presented as a separate financial statement, combined with other information in the financial statements, or in the notes to the financial statements. In addition, the information can be presented either in a reconciliation format or in a narrative format. As a minimum, significant effects of the following factors must be included in the disclosure of the information:

1. Plan amendments.
2. Changes in the nature of the plan, such as a plan spinoff or a merger with another plan.
3. Changes in actuarial assumptions.

Effects that are individually significant should be separately identified.

If only the minimum required disclosure is presented, presentation in a statement format will necessitate an additional unidentified "other" category to reconcile the beginning and ending amounts. Changes in actuarial assumptions are treated as changes in accounting estimates, and therefore previously reported amounts should not be restated.

26.41 ILLUSTRATIVE PLAN FINANCIAL STATEMENTS.   Exhibit 26.9 gives the DOL's filing requirements for employee benefit plans of various types. More specifically, Exhibits 26.10 through 26.13 illustrate the financial statements of a defined benefit pension plan. Exhibit 26.10 presents a statement of net assets available for benefits. SFAS No. 35 requires the net asset information to be presented as of the end of the plan year. However, if the information regarding the actuarial present value of accumulated plan benefits is presented as of the beginning of the plan year, the net asset information also must be presented as of that date (i.e., presented as of the end of the current and preceding plan years).

Exhibit 26.11 contains a statement of changes in net assets available for benefits, identifying the significant changes during the plan year. If the information regarding accumulated plan benefits is presented as of the beginning of the plan year, the statement of changes in net assets available for benefits must be presented for two years.

Exhibits 26.12 and 26.13 present a statement of accumulated plan benefits and a statement of changes in accumulated plan benefits. This information can be presented as of a benefit information date that is either the beginning or end of the plan year. In addition, the

	December 31, 1989
Assets	
Investments, at fair value	
United States government securities	$ 350,000
Corporate bonds and debentures	3,500,000
Common stock	
ABC Company	690,000
Other	2,250,000
Mortgages	480,000
Real estate	270,000
	7,540,000
Deposit administration contract, at contract value	1,000,000
Total investments	8,540,000
Receivables	
Employees' contributions	40,000
Securities sold	310,000
Accrued interest and dividends	77,000
	427,000
Cash	200,000
Total assets	9,167,000
Liabilities	
Accounts payable	70,000
Accrued expenses	85,000
Total liabilities	155,000
Net assets available for benefits	$9,012,000

Exhibit 26.10.   Statement of net assets available for benefits.

	Year Ended December 31, 1989
Investment income	
Net appreciation in fair value of investments	$ 207,000
Interest	345,000
Dividends	130,000
Rents	55,000
	737,000
Less investment expenses	39,000
	698,000
Contributions	
Employer	780,000
Employees	450,000
	1,230,000
Total additions	1,928,000
Benefits paid directly to participants	740,000
Purchases of annuity contracts	257,000
	997,000
	(continued)

Exhibit 26.11.   Statement of changes in net assets available for benefits.

	Year Ended December 31, 1989
Administrative expenses	65,000
Total deductions	1,062,000
Net increase	866,000
Net assets available for benefits	
Beginning of year	8,146,000
End of year	$9,012,000

Exhibit 26.11. *Continued.*

information can be presented in a combined statement with the related net asset information or included in the notes to the financial statements. The statement presented in Exhibit 26.13 reconciles the year-to-year change in the actuarial present value of accumulated plan benefits. As an alternative to presenting this information in a statement format, disclosure can be made of only the factors significantly changed in accumulated plan benefits. The information can be disclosed in the notes to the financial statements or presented on the face of the statement of accumulated plan benefits. Factors that usually have a significant effect on accumulated plan benefits include plan amendments, changes in the nature of a plan (e.g., a plan spinoff or merger with another plan), and changes in actuarial assumptions.

26.42 ADDITIONAL FINANCIAL STATEMENT DISCLOSURES.   Disclosure of the plan's accounting policies must include a description of the methods and significant assumptions used to determine the fair value of investments and the reported value of contracts with insurance companies. In addition, a description of the method and significant actuarial assumptions used to determine the actuarial present value of accumulated plan benefits must be disclosed in the notes to the financial statements. Such disclosure would include any significant changes of methods or assumptions between benefit information dates.

In addition to disclosing significant accounting policies, SFAS No. 35 requires the following disclosures:

1. A brief general description of the plan agreement, including vesting and benefit provisions.
2. A description of significant plan amendments made during the year. If significant amendments occur between the latest benefit information date and the plan's year-end

	December 31, 1989
Actuarial present value of accumulated plan benefits	
Vested benefits	
Participants currently receiving payments	$ 3,040,000
Other participants	8,120,000
	11,160,000
Nonvested benefits	2,720,000
Total actuarial present value of accumulated plan benefits	$13,880,000

Exhibit 26.12.   Statement of accumulated plan benefits.

	Year Ended December 31, 1989
Actuarial present value of accumulated plan benefits at beginning of year	$11,880,000
Increase (decrease) during the year attributable to:	
Plan amendment	2,410,000
Change in actuarial assumptions	(1,050,500)
Benefits accumulated	895,000
Increase for interest due to the decrease in the discount period	742,500
Benefits paid	(997,000)
Net increase	2,000,000
Actuarial present value of accumulated plan benefits at end of year	$13,880,000

Exhibit 26.13.   Statement of changes in accumulated plan benefits.

and therefore were not reflected in the actuarial present value of accumulated plan benefits, disclosure should be made of this matter.

3. A brief general description of the priority order of participants' claims to the assets of the plan in the event of plan termination and benefits guaranteed by PBGC.

4. Funding policy and any changes in such policy during the plan year.

5. The policy regarding the purchase of contracts with insurance companies that are excluded from plan assets.

6. Tax status of the plan, if a favorable letter of determination has not been obtained or maintained.

7. Identification of individual investments that represent 5% or more of the net assets available for benefits.

8. Significant real estate or other transactions between plan and the sponsor, employers, or employee organizations.

9. Unusual or infrequent events or transactions occurring subsequent to the latest benefit information date but before issuance of the financial statements, such as a plan amendment occurring after the latest benefit information date that significantly increases future benefits that are attributable to employee service rendered before that date.

26.43 DECISION TO PREPARE PLAN FINANCIAL STATEMENTS. The number of accounting decisions required to prepare the plan's financial statements is not large.

For many plans the first and most important decision will be whether to issue a statement at all. Plans subject to ERISA requirements must issue a statement, but public employee plans and ERISA plans with fewer than 100 participants are not required by ERISA to issue statements. The usual reason for not publishing plan financial statements, particularly for smaller employers, will be to avoid the additional expenses of preparing, auditing and distributing the statement. The usual reasons for publishing statements when not required by ERISA will include the following:

1. The employer wishes to present a strong, positive image to employees (or the public) about the administration and financial strength of the plan.

2. The number of participants may not be indicative of the financial values involved. Plan assets could be very significant in relation to the company's net worth.

3. The employer wants to protect the plan's fiduciaries against legal liability.

4. Publication is required by state or local law.

Other reasons for decisions are practical, largely affecting the ease and expense with which financial statements can be prepared. One subtle decision occurs when there have been multiple changes during the year, such as plan amendments and changes in assumptions. The order in which these items are presented can affect the reader's perception of what actually happened during the year. The FASB in SFAS No. 35 commented:

> The Board recognized that the determined effects of factors comprising the net change in the benefit information will vary depending on the order in which the effects are calculated. . . . Thus, the Board concluded that at this time it would not prescribe an order.

This can be cleared up through footnote disclosures as desired. Some of the practical decisions involved include:

1. Whether to use a **benefit information date** other than year-end. Many plans (if not most) will find it more convenient to use a beginning of the year date. However, that approach does require more information to be furnished regarding both net assets available and changes in such assets during the preceding year. Another approach when the regular actuarial valuation (to determine funding) is performed at the beginning of the year is to value the accumulated benefits at that point, and project to year-end, using "reasonable approximation." The FASB makes permissive reference to that type of an approach, provided that the results are substantially the same as those contemplated by SFAS No. 35. For many plans this approach will produce very acceptable results. An employer that discloses the funded status of its pension plan under SFAS No. 87 in its year-end financial statements may find it convenient to satisfy the SFAS No. 35 disclosure requirements by using the accumulated and vested benefit obligations disclosed under SFAS No. 87.
2. Whether to make a more complete **disclosure** of the plan's circumstances. In the interest of doing so, some plan sponsors may wish to present the benefit value information in more than the three minimum categories specified by SFAS No. 35. For example, the other vested benefit category could be expanded to include the value of vested benefits for employees eligible for normal or early retirement.

26.44 DEFINED CONTRIBUTION PLANS.   Although SFAS No. 35 does not cover defined contribution plans, many of the concepts and principles included are applicable to defined contribution plans. Defined contribution plans require the maintenance of **individual accounts** for each participant, to record each one's share of the total net assets of the plan. Typically, a defined contribution plan will require a certain contribution from the employer without specifying the amount of benefits to be provided to the participants. The types and amounts of benefits, as well as the eligibility requirements, are frequently determined by the plan's trustees, who can be totally "unrelated" to the employer; in other cases the employer reserves those rights. Employer contributions are based on a formula that may be a certain rate per hour of work or per unit of production, a function of the employee's contribution, a percentage of the employer's annual profitability, or some other specified method. The employer's obligation here differs from that under a defined contribution plan. With a defined contribution plan, the employer is not obligated to make up any shortfalls in actual versus assumed experience. This can be particularly significant, of course, in the case of the investment experience.

(a) Separate Accounts.   Employer contributions, changes in the value of the plan's net assets, and forfeitures, if any, are allocated to individual participant accounts maintained for each participant. In addition, employee contributions, if any, are credited to the account.

(b) Types of Plan.   Defined contribution plans include:

1. Profit-sharing plans, which provide for an employer contribution based on current or accumulated profits.
2. Money purchase plans, which provide for an employer contribution based on employee compensation, units of production, hours worked, or some criterion other than profits.
3. Stock bonus and employee stock ownership plans which are qualified profit-sharing plans that invest substantially all the plan's assets in the stock of the employer company.
4. Thrift or savings plans, which provide for periodic employee contributions with matching, in whole or in part, by the employer—usually from current or accumulated profits.

(c) Financial Statements.   Financial statements for a defined contribution plan should include a statement of net assets available for benefits and a statement of changes in net assets available for benefits. The disclosures would be similar to those required for a defined benefit pension plan, except for the references to actuarial information.

ACCOUNTING FOR POSTRETIREMENT BENEFITS OTHER THAN PENSIONS

26.45 BACKGROUND.   In February 1989 the FASB issued a proposed statement concerning employers' accounting for postretirement benefits other than pensions (PBOP Exposure Draft). Retiree medical benefits is the proposal's primary focus, but life insurance and other welfare benefits provided to employees after retirement are also included. The specific approach and methodology closely parallel the pension accounting rules issued by the Board in December 1985—SFAS Nos. 87 and 88.

Most employers presently recognize the cost of postretirement benefits other than pensions on the **"pay-as-you-go"** or cash basis. Under the proposed accounting requirements, postretirement benefits are viewed as a form of deferred compensation that should be recognized on an **accrual basis** during the periods that the employees render service.

Three out of four midsize and larger employers provide health care benefits for their retirees. Although some employers provide benefits only until retirees reach age 65 and become eligible for Medicare, many programs provide lifetime benefits. Typically, benefits for retirees are similar to those for active employees. Programs for retirees age 65 and over usually are coordinated with Medicare benefits. Although benefit plans for retirees age 65 and over may appear similar to plans for retirees under age 65, some of the specific details of post-age-65 benefit programs may have significant cost implications.

The practice of providing postretirement health care benefits took root after the Medicare program was established in 1965. Employers found that, for relatively few dollars, **Medicare supplements,** as they were called, bought much employee goodwill. The effect of inflation on medical costs, the trend toward earlier retirement, and longer life expectancies have made these benefits increasingly expensive. During recent decades the cost of medical care has risen at an average rate of more than 40%, which is twice the average inflation rate for the same period. Total medical costs, which were approximately 6% of the gross national product in the mid-1960s, exceeded 11% in 1989 and continue to rise.

26.46 PBOP EXPOSURE DRAFT.   Effective 1992, employers that provide retiree medical or other affected benefits will be required to follow a prescribed method in determining the annual expense charge for such benefits and to provide extensive disclosures in their financial statement. A minimum balance sheet liability standard is also prescribed with a delayed effective date (1997). Generally, as of the financial statement date (measurement date), the discounted value of all future benefits that are expected to be paid is calculated (expected postretirement benefit obligation). For a newly hired employee, this liability is accrued ratably over the period from date of hire until such employee is first eligible to retire with full benefits (service cost). Transition rules, like their pension counterparts, prescribe how the liability for prior service for existing retirees and their dependents and the active work force is amortized (transition obligation).

26.47 QUANTIFICATION OF MEDICAL BENEFITS TO RETIREES.   The basic building block for the expense and liability determinations is the **discounted value of future benefits.**

Unlike the pension model where the monthly benefit is fixed at retirement, future medical benefits depend on the likelihood and cost of future claims. Besides variations due to plan provisions that define the level or richness of benefits provided, claims experience varies significantly by age, sex, occupation, and geographical location. For a given employee population, future retiree medical costs will increase because:

- Medical inflation will continue to outpace overall price increases, but will likely decelerate in the future.
- More active employees will retire.
- Per capita costs will rise as the retiree group ages.
- Advances in medical technology will introduce better and more costly treatment methods.

For example, for the projection year 1992 assume that an employer expects to have 18 retirees as shown below and cash flow of $20,000:

Age	Number of Retirees		Per Capita Cost		Cash Flow
	Males	Females	Males	Females	
60	4	—	$2,100	—	$ 8,400
65	—	8	—	$700	5,600
70	6	—	1,000	—	6,000
				Total	$20,000

This process is repeated for 1993 and each subsequent year to arrive at a stream of expected cash flow. The total value in 1992 of the employer's future liabilities is calculated by discounting this stream of cash flow to 1992 to reflect the time value of money.

The number of retirees or other beneficiaries for each year is projected by applying pensionlike **actuarial assumptions** to the current employee and retiree group. Rates of mortality, disability, retirement, and termination of employment are used to estimate how the current beneficiary group will change from one year to the next.

The **per capita costs** are projected in a similar fashion. Expected future costs are calculated by using actual base year figures and medical trend factors. These factors reflect the expected effects of future price inflation, technological changes, and an individual's propensity to use medical goods and services.

The **expected postretirement benefit obligation** (EPBO) represents the actuarial present value of the future postretirement benefits expected to be paid to or for an employee, including benefits for the employee's beneficiaries and dependents. This differs from the projected benefit obligation in pension accounting in that the EPBO represents the value of all future postretirement benefits, not just those that have been attributed to employees' service as of the reporting date. The service cost is the portion of EPBO attributed to the current period.

The **accumulated postretirement benefit obligation** (APBO) represents the portion of the EPBO that has been attributed to employees' service rendered to date. If all employees have reached their full eligibility date, the APBO would be the same as the EPBO.

The PBOP Exposure Draft specifies that a **transition obligation,** at the date that the new standard is adopted would be measured as the unfunded APBO less any accrued postretirement benefit cost already recognized on the employer's balance sheet. The transition obligation would not be recognized on the balance sheet at transition, but would be recognized in the **net periodic postretirement benefit cost** through **straight-line amortization** over:

- The average remaining service period of active participants, or 15 years if longer.
- The average remaining life expectancy of the participants if almost all participants are retirees.

Additional amortization of the transition obligation would be required if the computed amortization on a cumulative basis is less than cumulative benefit payments. This provision may require additional amortization for certain mature plans with relatively high pay-as-you-go costs.

26.48 STATUS OF EXPOSURE DRAFT.   As this volume goes to press, the Board is deliberating public reaction to the Exposure Draft. Hundreds of written comments were received and dozens of firms provided testimony in public hearings conducted during the fall of 1989. Commentators expressed concern over the transition period (it should be longer), the attribution period (it should extend over the working life) and the medical trend rate (further guidance is necessary). Until a final statement is issued, however, the limited disclosure requirements of SFAS No. 81 remain in effect.

26.49 ILLUSTRATION—POSTRETIREMENT BENEFITS OTHER THAN PENSIONS.   The FASB's proposed accrual method for postretirement benefits other than pensions is illustrated by Exhibit 26.14.

Expected postretirement benefit obligation	$20,000,000
Accumulated postretirement benefit obligation	12,000,000
Transition obligation	12,000,000[1]
Service cost	750,000[2]
Minimum liability	9,000,000[3]
Net periodic postretirement benefit cost:	
Service cost	750,000
Interest cost on APBO	960,000
Return on assets	0[4]
Amortization of transition obligation over 15 years	800,000
Net periodic postretirement benefit cost	2,510,000
Pay-as-you-go cost charged to expense under current practice	$ 700,000

[1]The transition obligation is equal to the APBO because the plan is unfunded and there is no recognized accrued postretirement benefit cost.
[2]Service cost represents the portion of the EPBO that is attributed to employees' service during the current period.
[3]The minimum liability represents the unfunded APBO for retirees and active employees fully eligible for benefits.
[4]This employer continues to operate the plan on a pay-as-you-go basis rather than prefunding it.

Exhibit 26.14. Postretirement benefits other than pensions.

SOURCES AND SUGGESTED REFERENCES

American Academy of Actuaries, "An Actuary's Guide to Compliance with Statement of Financial Accounting Standards No. 87," AAA, Washington, DC, 1986.

———, "Actuarial Compliance Guideline for Statement of Financial Accounting Standards No. 88," Actuarial Standards Board, Washington, DC, 1989.

Accounting Principles Board, "Accounting for the Cost of Pension Plans," APB Opinion No. 8, AICPA, New York, 1966.

———, "Accounting Changes," APB Opinion No. 20, AICPA, New York, 1971.

———, "Reporting the Results of Operation—Reporting the Effects of Disposal of a Segment of a Business, and Extraordinary, Unusual and Infrequently Occurring Events and Transactions," APB Opinion No. 30, AICPA, New York, 1973.

Financial Accounting Standards Board, "Employers' Accounting for Postretirement Benefits Other than Pensions," Exposure Draft, FASB, Norwalk, CT, 1989.

———, "A Guide to Implementation of Statement 87 on Employers' Accounting for Pensions: Questions and Answers," FASB, Stamford, CT, 1986.

———, "A Guide to Implementation of Statement 88: Questions and Answers," FASB, Norwalk, CT, 1988.

———, "Accounting and Reporting by Defined Benefit Pension Plans," Statement of Financial Accounting Standards No. 35, FASB, Stamford, CT, 1980.

———, "Employers' Accounting for Pensions," Statement of Financial Accounting Standards No. 87, FASB, Stamford, CT, 1985.

———, "Employers' Accounting for Settlements and Curtailments of Defined Benefit Pension Plans and for Termination Benefits," Statement of Financial Accounting Standards No. 88, FASB, Stamford, CT, 1985.

———, "Accounting for Income Taxes," Statement of Financial Accounting Standards No. 96, FASB, Stamford, CT, 1987.

Munnell, Alicia H., *Economics of Private Pensions*, The Brookings Institution, Washington, DC, 1982.

CHAPTER **27**

EMPLOYEE STOCK COMPENSATION AND OTHER CAPITAL ACCUMULATION AWARDS

Peter T. Chingos
KPMG Peat Marwick

Michael J. Walters, CPA
KPMG Peat Marwick

CONTENTS

DEFINITION

A capital accumulation plan is defined as a compensation plan under which participating employees are awarded either:

> Capital stock.
> The right to purchase or receive capital stock under specified terms and conditions.
> The right to receive cash under specified terms and conditions.
> A combination of the foregoing.

OBJECTIVES OF CAPITAL ACCUMULATION PLANS

Capital accumulation plans have become increasingly complex over the past several years because of a desire by companies to design and implement plans that are responsive to the objectives of both the employer and the participating employees. The design of such plans requires a thorough understanding of such objectives, as well as an understanding of the relevant accounting principles and current tax laws. With this understanding, a plan can be designed to facilitate attainment of both the employer's and the participating employees' objectives.

Some capital accumulation plans are intended primarily to encourage widespread employee stock ownership and/or to raise equity capital. Other plans are intended primarily to attract, compensate, and retain key employees.

Typical objectives of this latter type of plan, from the employer's viewpoint, include the following:

1. To provide a competitive capital accumulation program for key members of the management team (i.e., managers who are in a position to affect directly the long-term growth and profitability of the enterprise).
2. To provide an integral element of the total compensation program for key managers.
3. To encourage executive retention and performance through deferral of compensation over a specified service period or until specific performance objectives are met.
4. To minimize compensation expense recognized by the employer for financial reporting purposes.

From the employee's viewpoint, typical objectives of participating in such a capital accumulation plan include:

1. To be compensated at a competitive level on the basis of responsibilities and performance.
2. To accumulate capital to supplement income for retirement or other purposes.
3. To have flexibility as to the form of payment and the timing of actual or constructive receipt of compensation earned pursuant to an award.
4. To maximize after-tax earnings.

In an effort to meet one or more of an employer's objectives, it is often necessary to compromise one or more of the objectives of the participants, and vice versa. For example, an employer may wish to incorporate certain features into a plan that will maximize tax deductions for compensation expense. But the inclusion of such features in the plan tends to limit the employees' flexibility in determining the timing of actual or constructive receipt, as employees are generally required to recognize taxable income in the same period, and in the same amount, that the employer is entitled to a deduction for compensation expense.

Prior to enactment of the Tax Reform Act of 1986, an additional key consideration was the distinction between tax rates applicable to capital gains and ordinary income. To the extent awards were structured so as to result in capital gains, as opposed to ordinary income, the employee received the benefit of the substantially lower tax rates applicable to capital gains; however, the employer was denied an income tax deduction for any amounts taxable to the employee as capital gains. If the distinction between capital gains and ordinary income tax rates are reinstated through further tax law changes, this would again become a major consideration in the structuring of awards.

The design of plans to meet as many as possible of the often competing objectives of the employer and the participating employees, as well as the complexity of the relevant accounting principles, have been largely responsible for the evolution of the complex and somewhat exotic capital accumulation plans commonly in use today.

TYPES OF CAPITAL ACCUMULATION PLANS

The three basic categories of capital accumulation plans—appreciation, purchase, and full-value—are shown in Exhibit 27.1.

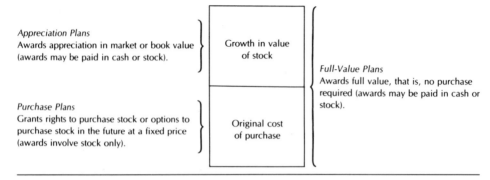

Exhibit 27.1.   Three basic categories of capital accumulation plans.

27.1 APPRECIATION PLANS.   Appreciation plans are capital accumulation plans under which an employer grants employees the right to receive appreciation in shares of the employer's capital stock from the date of the award to a specified future date. Appreciation may be measured on the basis of changes in the quoted market price of the employer's capital stock or on a formula, such as changes in book value of the employer's capital stock. An appreciation plan does not require a participating employee to make an investment in an employer's capital stock.

Stock appreciation rights (SARs) and "phantom stock" are the most common appreciation plans.

27.2 PURCHASE PLANS.   Purchase plans are capital accumulation plans under which an employer grants employees the right to purchase shares of the employer's capital stock immediately (stock purchase rights) or options to purchase shares of the employer's capital stock in the future (stock options).

Stock option plans (SOPs) are the most popular employee purchase plans.

27.3 FULL-VALUE PLANS.   Full-value plans are capital accumulation plans under which an employer awards employees the full value of shares of the employer's capital stock, or units with an assigned value or a value that will be determinable at some future date. Value may be determined based on the quoted market price of an employer's capital stock or on a formula (e.g., book value of the employer's capital stock). Thus, full-value plans do not require a capital outlay by the participants.

The most commonly used full-value plans include restricted stock, performance shares, and performance units plans.

ACCOUNTING FOR CAPITAL ACCUMULATION AWARDS

For accounting purposes, awards granted pursuant to capital accumulation plans ("capital accumulation awards") can be classified as either stock-based or formula-based compensation awards.

27.4 STOCK-BASED COMPENSATION AWARDS.   Compensation arrangements under which participating employees are granted one or any combination of the following awards:

1. Capital stock of an employer.
2. The right to purchase or receive shares of an employer's capital stock under specified terms and conditions.

3. The right to receive cash in lieu of shares of an employer's capital stock under specified terms and conditions, the amount of which is contingent on certain future events (e.g., the quoted market price of an employer's capital stock at the end of a specified period).

The amount of compensation expense to be recognized by an employer for stock-based compensation awards, if any, is based, in whole or in part, on the quoted market price (or, in the absence of a quoted market price, on the otherwise determined fair value), or on changes in the quoted market price, of the employer's capital stock.

27.5 FORMULA-BASED COMPENSATION AWARDS.   Compensation arrangements under which participating employees may be granted one or any combination of the following awards:

1. Capital stock of an employer, with a right to sell the capital stock back to the employer at a specified future date(s) at a price to be determined in accordance with a specified formula.
2. The right to purchase or receive shares of an employer's capital stock under specified terms and conditions and, in some instances, a corresponding right to sell the capital stock so acquired back to the employer at a specified future date(s) at a price to be determined in accordance with a specified formula.
3. The right to receive cash under specified terms and conditions, the amount of which is contingent on future events (e.g., changes in book value of the employer's capital stock).

The amount earned by an employee with respect to a formula-based compensation award is determined by reference to the formula specified in the plan and is not affected by the quoted market price or by changes in the quoted market price of the employer's capital stock.

Stock-based and formula-based awards are similar in many respects. For example, both types of awards may be retention-oriented, performance-oriented, or both retention- and performance-oriented. Further, in many cases, the ultimate amount an employee may receive with respect to either type of award is based on future events; for example, the level of attainment of performance goals specified in the plan or award and/or the market price (or formula price) of an employer's capital stock at a specified future date(s).

For accounting purposes, a significant distinction between stock-based and formula-based compensation awards is the method of determining the amount of compensation cost to be recognized by the employer. For a stock-based compensation award, compensation cost is determined, in whole or in part, by reference to the quoted market price or changes in the quoted market price of the employer's capital stock; however, for a formula-based compensation award the amount of such cost, if any, is determined by reference to factors other than the quoted market price or changes in the quoted market price of the enterprise's capital stock (e.g., book value per share of the employer's capital stock). It should also be noted that there is a difference in the accounting for certain formula-based awards by publicly held and privately held companies (see section 27.10(g), "Settlement of Awards").

Another characteristic of formula-based awards is that they are normally "variable" awards for accounting purposes and, as a result, total compensation cost, if any, to be recognized by the employer for such awards is not determinable until some time subsequent to the date of grant. (Note, however, for certain formula awards granted by privately held companies, no compensation cost is recognized by the employer; see section 27.10(g).)

27.6 TYPES OF STOCK- AND FORMULA-BASED AWARDS.   The types of awards granted pursuant to stock-based and formula-based compensation plans in common use today are summarized in Exhibit 27.2.

TYPES OF CAPITAL ACCUMULATION AWARDS

Type	Stock-Based		Formula-Based (Note)
	Fixed	Variable	
Purchase Awards			
Incentive stock option	X		
Nonstatutory stock option (nondiscounted)	X		
Nonstatutory stock option (fixed discount)	X		
Nonstatutory stock option (variable discount)		X	
Book-value (or other formula) purchase rights (options)			X
Book-value (or other formula) shares			X
Restricted stock purchase rights	X		
Appreciation Awards			
Stock appreciation rights (settled in shares of an employer's capital stock)		X	
Stock appreciation rights (settled by payment of cash)		X	
Phantom stock units		X	
Book value (or other formula) units			X
Full Value Awards			
Restricted stock	X		
Performance share units		X	
Performance units			X

Note: Formula-based awards are generally accounted for as variable awards; however, there are exceptions for certain book-value (or other formula) awards granted by privately held companies. (See discussion under section 27.10(g).)

Exhibit 27.2.   Summary of capital accumulation awards.

Illustrations of the accounting and federal income tax consequences of certain types of capital accumulation awards, including a fixed award, a variable award, and a formula-based award, can be found in the section "Illustrations of the Accounting and Federal Income Tax Consequences of Certain Capital Accumulation Awards."

27.7 OVERVIEW OF ACCOUNTING PRONOUNCEMENTS.   The nature and types of capital accumulation plans and awards have constantly changed over the years. However, the most significant problems in determining the appropriate accounting for capital accumulation awards have remained the same:

1. Measurement of compensation cost (i.e., the determination of total compensation cost to be allocated to expense for financial reporting purposes).
2. Allocation of compensation cost (i.e., the determination of the period(s) over which total compensation cost should be allocated to expense and the method of allocation).

The authoritative accounting literature addresses the accounting for capital accumulation awards in several pronouncements. Although these pronouncements, for the most part, relate specifically to stock-based compensation awards, the general guidance set forth therein in practice, also applies to formula-based awards. The principal pronouncements are as follows:

1. ARB No. 43, Chapter 13B, "Compensation Involved in Stock Option and Stock Purchase Plans," (AICPA, Committee on Accounting Procedure, 1953).

2. APB Opinion No. 25, "Accounting for Stock Issued to Employees" (AICPA, 1972). Also see Interpretation of APB Opinion No. 25, "Accounting for Stock Issued to Employees" (AICPA, 1973).

3. FIN No. 28, "Accounting for Stock Appreciation Rights and Other Variable Stock Option or Award Plans," an interpretation of APB Opinion Nos. 15 and 25 (FASB, 1978).

ARB No. 43, Chapter 13B, issued in 1953, provides guidance in accounting for stock option and stock purchase plans. In 1972, in recognition of the increasing popularity of various types of capital accumulation plans not in general use at the time of the issuance of ARB No. 43, Chapter 13B, the APB (the successor to the Committee on Accounting Procedure) issued APB Opinion No. 25, "Accounting for Stock Issued to Employees."

The second paragraph of APB Opinion No. 25 specifically discusses certain plans not described in ARB No. 43, Chapter 13B:

Among traditional plans not described in Chapter 13B of ARB No. 43 are plans in which an employer corporation awards to employees shares of stock of the corporation for current or future services. Some corporations have replaced or supplemented traditional plans with more complex plans, contracts, and agreements for issuing stock. An arrangement may be based on variable factors that depend on future events; for example, a corporation may award a variable number of shares of stock or may grant a stock option with a variable option price. Other arrangements combine the characteristics of two or more types of plans, and some give an employee an election.

The board encompassed these plans in APB Opinion No. 25 by specifying that the Opinion is applicable "to all stock option, purchase, award and bonus rights granted by an employer corporation to an individual employee after December 31, 1972 under both existing and new arrangements. . . ." The Opinion contains substantial guidance in the application of its provisions to such plans.

Subsequent to the issuance of APB Opinion No. 25, the trend toward the adoption by enterprises of more complex capital accumulation plans and awards continued. Of particular significance was the increase in the number of combination plans—plans that provide for the granting of two or more types of awards to individual employees. In many combination plans, the employee, or the enterprise, must make an election from alternative awards as to the award to be exercised, thereby canceling the other awards granted under the plan.

Following the issuance of APB Opinion No. 25, there was also a significant increase in the number of plans that provide for the granting of variable awards to employees, that is, awards where, at the date the grant is awarded, either (1) the number of shares of stock (or the amount of cash) an employee is entitled to receive, (2) the amount an employee is required to pay to exercise his rights with respect to the award, or (3) both the number of shares an employee is entitled to receive and the amount an employee is required to pay, are unknown. One of the most popular variable awards is the stock appreciation right (SAR). SARs are rights granted that entitle an employee to receive, at a specified future date(s), the excess of the market value of a specified number of shares of the granting employer's capital stock over a stated price, usually the market value of the specified number of shares at the date the rights are granted. The form of payment for amounts earned under an award of SARs may be specified by the award (i.e., stock, cash, or a combination thereof), or the award may permit the employee or employer to elect the form of payment. (Accounting for an SAR award is illustrated in Exhibit 27.7.)

Notwithstanding the guidance provided in Chapter 13B of ARB No. 43 and in APB Opinion No. 25, considerable disagreement continued to exist as to the appropriate method of accounting for variable awards. As a result, significant differences arose in the methods used by employers to account for variable awards, which led to numerous requests of the FASB for clarification. In December 1978 the FASB provided this clarification through the issuance of FIN No. 28, "Accounting for Stock Appreciation Rights and Other Variable Stock Option or Award Plans," an interpretation of APB Opinion Nos. 15 and 25. In paragraph No. 2 of the Interpretation, the FASB specifies that:

> APB Opinion No. 25 applies to plans for which the employer's stock is issued as compensation or the amount of cash paid as compensation is determined by reference to the market price of the stock or to changes in its market price. Plans involving stock appreciation rights and other variable plan awards are included in those plans dealt with by Opinion No. 25.

The Interpretation provides specific guidance in the application of APB Opinion No. 25 to variable awards, particularly in those more troublesome areas where the greatest divergence in accounting existed prior to its issuance.

FASB AND EITF PRONOUNCEMENTS

Year	Issued By	Title
1980	FASB	FIN No. 31: "Treatment of Stock Compensation Plans in EPS Computations," an interpretation of APB Opinion No. 15 and a modification of FASB Interpretation No. 28
1982	FASB	FTB No. 82-2: "Accounting for the Conversion of Stock Options into Incentive Stock Options as a Result of the Economic Recovery Tax Act of 1981"
1984	FASB	FIN No. 38: "Determining the Measurement Date for Stock Option, Purchase, and Award Plans Involving Junior Stock," an interpretation of APB Opinion No. 25
1984	EITF	EITF Issue No. 84-13: "Purchase of Stock Options and Stock Appreciation Rights in a Leveraged Buyout"
1984	EITF	EITF Issue No. 84-18: "Stock Option Pyramiding"
1984	EITF	EITF Issue No. 84-34: "Permanent Discount Restricted Stock Purchase Plans"
1985	EITF	EITF Issue No. 85-10: "Employee Stock Ownership Plan Contribution Funded by a Pension Plan Termination"
1985	EITF	EITF Issue No. 85-11: "Use of an Employee Stock Ownership Plan in a Leveraged Buyout"
1985	EITF	EITF Issue No. 85-45: "Business Combinations: Settlement of Stock Options and Awards"
1986	EITF	EITF Issue No. 86-4: "Income Statement Treatment of Income Tax Benefit for Employee Stock Ownership Plan Dividends"
1986	EITF	EITF Issue No. 86-27: "Measurement of Excess Contributions to a Defined Contribution Plan or Employee Stock Ownership Plan"
1987	EITF	EITF Issue No. 87-6: "Adjustments Relating to Stock Compensation Plans"
1987	EITF	EITF Issue No. 87-23: "Book Value Stock Purchase Plans"
1987	EITF	EITF Issue No. 87-33: "Stock Compensation Issues Related to Market Decline"
1988	EITF	EITF Issue No. 88-6: "Book Value Stock Plans in an Initial Public Offering"
1988	EITF	EITF Issue No. 88-27: "Effect of Unallocated Shares in an Employee Stock Ownership Plan on Accounting for Business Combinations"
1989	EITF	EITF Issue No. 89-8: "Nonlevel Payments of Employee Stock Ownership Plan Debt"
1989	EITF	EITF Issue No. 89-10: "Sponsor's Recognition of Employee Stock Ownership Plan Debt"

Exhibit 27.3.   Post-1978 accounting pronouncements related to stock compensation plans and awards.

However, the three pronouncements discussed above failed to incorporate criteria that can be consistently applied to all types of plans. As a result, as new types of plans have evolved and changes in the tax laws have occurred, new interpretations and guidance have been required, resulting in a steady stream of pronouncements by the FASB and the EITF since 1978, as shown in Exhibit 27.3.

The nature and the frequency of these additional pronouncements underscore the difficulties in applying the primary pronouncements to the myriad of capital accumulation awards that have arisen since their issuance.

The FASB is well aware of this problem and, in 1984, undertook a major project to reconsider the accounting for capital accumulation awards. However, in 1988, after having devoted considerable efforts to this project over a 4-year period, and after having arrived at "tentative conclusions" with respect to many of the basic issues, the FASB announced the termination of the project. Concurrent with the termination of this issue as a discrete project, the FASB added the consideration of accounting for capital accumulation awards to its "Financial Instruments" project. Thus, whereas new, comprehensive guidance that would eliminate the need for constant interpretation may ultimately be issued by the FASB in connection with its Financial Instruments project, neither the timing of issuance of, nor the ultimate conclusions embodied in, such a pronouncement can be predicted with any reasonable degree of comfort.

Pending the issuance of comprehensive new guidance from the FASB, it is likely that, with each significant innovation in plan design, and as tax laws change, additional guidance in the form of further interpretations of the existing literature will be required. Determination of the appropriate accounting for capital accumulation awards, therefore, requires an understanding of the primary accounting literature in this area, as well as of the numerous existing, and any future, interpretations thereof.

APPLICATION OF THE ACCOUNTING PRONOUNCEMENTS

27.8 NONCOMPENSATORY AND COMPENSATORY PLANS.   ARB No. 43, Chapter 13B specifically recognizes that certain stock option and purchase plans are noncompensatory— that is, they are not intended primarily to provide a means of compensating employees, but rather to provide a means to secure equity capital or to induce widespread ownership of an enterprise's stock among employees, or both. The Committee on Accounting Procedure specified that no compensation need be recognized by the employer with respect to noncompensatory plans, as long as the inducements to participating employees are not greater than would reasonably be required to secure an equivalent amount of capital through an offer of shares to all shareholders.

APB Opinion No. 25 provides further clarification on this issue by specifying that a plan must have the following characteristics in order to be considered as noncompensatory:

1. Substantially all full-time employees meeting limited employment qualifications may participate (employees owning a specified percentage of the outstanding stock and executives may be excluded).
2. Stock is offered to eligible employees equally on the basis of a uniform percentage of salary or wages (the plan may limit the number of shares of stock that an employee may purchase through the plan).
3. The time permitted for exercise of an option or purchase right is limited to a reasonable period.
4. The discount from the market price of the stock is no greater than would be reasonable in an offer of stock to stockholders or others.

A compensatory plan is any plan that does not have all four characteristics of a noncompensatory plan. It should be recognized, however, that awards granted under compensatory plans do not necessarily result in recognition of compensation expense by the employer. An employer recognizes compensation expense with respect to awards granted pursuant to a compensatory plan only if the application of the measurement principle, discussed below, results in the determination of compensation cost.

27.9 MEASUREMENT OF COMPENSATION: GENERAL PRINCIPLE. In ARB No. 43, Chapter 13B, the Committee on Accounting Procedure stated, ''In the case of stock options involving compensation, the principal problem is the measurement of the compensation. *This problem involves selection of the date as of which measurement of any element of compensation is to be made and the manner of measurement*'' (emphasis added).

The Committee, in considering both elements of this problem, stated that:

1. In most cases, including situations in which the right to exercise is conditional on continued employment, valuation should be made of the option as of the date of grant.
2. Although there is, from the standpoint of the grantee, a value inherent in a restricted future right to purchase shares at a price at or even above the fair value of shares at the grant date, it is impracticable to measure any such value.

The Committee thus concluded ''that the value to the grantee and the related cost to the corporation of a restricted right to purchase shares at a price below the fair value of the shares at the grant date may . . . be taken as the excess of the then fair value of the shares over the option price.''

Furthermore, although it recognized that quoted market prices of shares covered by a stock option or stock purchase right are an important factor in determining fair value of the stock option or stock purchase right, the Committee indicated that the quoted market prices are not necessarily conclusive evidence of fair values. It specified that other factors should be considered as well, such as the range of quotations over a reasonable period and the avoidance by the corporation of some or all of the expenses that would otherwise be incurred in the sale of shares. In the absence of a ready market, the Committee indicated that other means of arriving at fair value may have to be employed.

The APB also recognized the significance of the measurement problem, particularly in view of the emergence of many plans involving the granting of variable awards, whereby the total compensation cost with respect to an award is based on factors that cannot be finally determined until after the grant or award date. The APB, through the issuance of APB Opinion No. 25, modified the principles covering the determination and measurement of compensation cost as set forth in ARB No. 43, Chapter 13B. Paragraph 10 of APB Opinion No. 25 sets forth the following ''measurement principle'' for the measurement of compensation cost related to stock option, purchase, and award plans:

> *Measurement Principle*—Compensation for services that a corporation receives as consideration for stock issued through employee stock option, purchase, and award plans should be measured by the quoted market price of the stock at the measurement date less the amount, if any, that the employee is required to pay. . . . If a quoted market price is unavailable, the best estimate of the market value of the stock should be used to measure compensation. . . . The measurement date for determining compensation cost in stock option, purchase, and award plans is the first date on which are known both (1) the number of shares that an individual employee is entitled to receive, and (2) the option or purchase price, if any.

When the measurement date for an award granted to an employee under a stock-based compensation plan is the same as the grant date, the award is defined as a **fixed award.** When the measurement date is after the grant date, the award is defined as a **variable award.** As previously noted, all "book value" and other formula awards are variable awards, as the "formula price" the employee will ultimately receive is not determinable at the date of grant.

The measurement principle adopted in APB Opinion No. 25 modified the measurement criterion set forth in ARB No. 43, Chapter 13B in two material respects:

1. Notwithstanding the conclusion set forth in ARB No. 43, Chapter 13B that market quotations of shares of stock covered by a stock option or stock purchase right are not necessarily conclusive evidence of the fair value of a stock option or stock purchase right, the Board concluded that the value of an employee's right to acquire or receive shares of stock is affected by various factors, some of which tend to diminish its value, whereas others tend to enhance its value. Because of the difficulty in measuring such factors, and as a practical solution to the measurement problem, the Board concluded that, for purposes of applying APB Opinion No. 25:

    [T]he unadjusted quoted market price of a share of stock of the same class that trades freely in an established market should be used in measuring compensation, . . . [I]f a quoted market price is unavailable, the best estimate of the market value of the stock should be used to measure compensation.

    Thus, under APB Opinion No. 25, the unadjusted quoted market price of stock covered by a capital accumulation award should be used in measuring compensation cost; adjustments to the quoted market price to reflect trading or other restrictions are clearly inappropriate.

2. The measurement date for determining compensation cost for stock-based compensation awards was changed to "the first date on which are known both (1) the number of shares that an individual employee is entitled to receive, and (2) the option or purchase price, if any."

When both of the factors specified in (2) above are known at the grant or award date (i.e., when the award is a fixed award), total compensation cost for an award is measured at the grant date. However, when either or both of these factors are not known at the grant or award date (i.e., when the award is a variable award), an employer should estimate total compensation cost each period from the date of grant or award to the measurement date based on the quoted market price of the employer's capital stock at the end of each period. This latter point is clarified in FIN No. 28, which defines the compensation related to variable plan awards as:

> The amount by which the quoted market value of the shares of the employer's stock covered by the grant exceeds the option price or value specified, by reference to a market price or otherwise, subject to any appreciation limitations under the plan. Changes, either increases or decreases, in the quoted market value of those shares between the date of grant and the measurement date [as defined in APB Opinion No. 25] result in a change in the measure of compensation for the right or award.

27.10 APPLICATION OF THE MEASUREMENT PRINCIPLE. A proper understanding of the measurement principle of APB Opinion No. 25 (including the clarification set forth in FIN No. 28) is essential to determining the appropriate accounting, including the amount of compensation expense to be recognized, for capital accumulation awards. Paragraphs 11(a) through 11(h) of APB Opinion No. 25, as well as subsequent FASB and EITF pronouncements, contain guidance on the application of the measurement principle, as discussed in the following paragraphs.

(a) Measurement of Compensation Cost Based on Cost of Treasury Stock. Paragraph 11(a) states:

> Measuring compensation by the cost to an employer corporation of reacquired (treasury) stock that is distributed through a stock option, purchase, or award plan is not acceptable practice. The

only exception is that compensation cost under a plan with all the provisions described in paragraph 11(c) may be measured by the cost of stock that the corporation (1) reacquires during the fiscal period for which the stock is to be awarded and (2) awards shortly thereafter to employees for services during that period.

Thus compensation cost of an award of stock for current services may be measured by the cost of reacquired treasury stock only if the above conditions and those specified in paragraph 11(c) (see below) of the Opinion are met. Otherwise, compensation cost should be measured as of the measurement date otherwise determined in accordance with the criterion set forth in paragraph 10 of the Opinion.

(b) Vesting Contingent on Continued Employment.   Paragraph 11(b) states:

The measurement date is not changed from the grant or award date to a later date solely by provisions that termination of employment reduces the number of shares of stock that may be issued to an employee.

This paragraph makes it clear that a requirement that an employee remain employed by the granting enterprise for a specified period of time in order for his rights to become vested under a stock-based compensation award does not preclude a determination, as of the grant or award date, of the total compensation cost to be recognized as an expense by the granting employer.

(c) Designation of Measurement Date.   Paragraph 11(c) states:

The measurement date of an award of stock for current service may be the end of the fiscal period, which is normally the effective date of the award, instead of the date that the award to an employee is determined if (1) the award is provided for by the terms of an established formal plan, (2) the plan designates the factors that determine the total dollar amount of awards to employees for the period (for example, a percent of income), although the total amount or the individual awards may not be known at the end of the period, and (3) the award pertains to current service of the employee for the period.

The effect of this paragraph is to allow the designation of the end of a fiscal period as the measurement date when all of the conditions specified in paragraph 11(c) are met, even though the actual awards to individual employees may not be determined until after the close of the fiscal period.

(d) Impact of Renewals, Extensions, and Other Modifications of Stock Options and Purchase Rights.   Paragraph 11(d) states:

Renewing a stock option or purchase right or extending its period establishes a new measurement date as if the right were newly granted.

This paragraph reflects a very important concept. Its application could result in measurement of compensation cost with respect to outstanding stock option or purchase rights upon their renewal or extension, even though no compensation cost was ascribable to the original award under the measurement principle of APB Opinion No. 25. For example, any excess of the quoted market price of an employer's capital stock over the exercise price of a stock option at the date of renewal or extension is compensation cost; this may require recognition of compensation cost in addition to any compensation cost associated with the original award.

Paragraph 11(d) addresses "renewals" and "extensions" of stock purchase rights. There are modifications other than renewals and extensions that could also have an impact on the accounting for previously granted awards.

For example, FTB No. 82-2, "Accounting of the Conversion of Stock Options into Incentive Stock Options as a Result of the Economic Recovery Tax Act of 1981," indicates that increasing the exercise price of a previously granted option to 100% of the fair market value at the original grant date, for the purpose of converting the option into an "incentive stock option" as permitted by the Economic Recovery Tax Act of 1981, does not change the award from a fixed award to a variable award. Thus, instead of creating a new measurement date at the time the option is repriced (which would require a remeasurement of compensation cost associated with the award, based on the quoted market price of the shares under option at the repricing date, less the revised exercise price), the Bulletin specifies that, in the period the option exercise price is increased, the company should reverse the compensation expense previously recognized.

EITF Issue No. 87-6, "Adjustments Relating to Stock Compensation Plans," addresses, among other issues, "Changes to Stock Plans Arising from the Tax Reform Act of 1986." This issue involves changes to outstanding incentive stock options for the purpose of converting them to nonqualified stop options and thereby providing the company with a tax deduction equal to the excess of the market value at the exercise date over the exercise price. The Task Force reached a consensus on this issue that "minor technical changes linked to the 1986 Act would not create a new measurement date if the aggregate effect on the value of the option is *de minimus* from the perspective of the employee." The Task Force also agreed that "changes to the option beyond the minimum necessary for disqualification would presumptively lead to a new measurement date."

EITF Issue No. 87-33, "Stock Compensation Issues Related to Market Decline," addresses a series of issues related to modifications to stock option and award plans as a result of the October 1987 stock market decline. The EITF's consensus on these issues generally precludes reversals of previously recognized compensation expense when outstanding awards are modified because of market value declines and, in many instances, require measurement and recognition of compensation cost for both the original and the "modified" award.

(e) Transfer of Stock or Assets to a Trustee, Agent, or Other Third Party.   Paragraph 11(e) states:

> Transferring stock or assets to a trustee, agent, or other third party for distribution of stock to employees under the terms of an option, purchase, or award plan does not change the measurement date from a later date to the date of transfer unless the terms of the transfer provide that the stock (1) will not revert to the corporation, (2) will not be granted or awarded later to the same employee on terms different from or for services other than those specified in the original grant or award, and (3) will not be granted or awarded later to another employee.

This paragraph reinforces the principle that the measurement date is the first date on which are known both (1) the number of shares that an individual employee is entitled to receive, and (2) the option or purchase price, if any. The authors are not aware of any awards that have been structured in a manner that has resulted in an acceleration of the otherwise determined measurement date as a result of the application of paragraph 11(e).

(f) Awards of Convertible Stock or Rights.   Paragraph 11(f) states:

> The measurement date for a grant or award of convertible stock (or stock that is otherwise exchangeable for other securities of the corporation) is the date in which the ratio of conversion (or exchange) is known unless other terms are variable at that date (paragraph 10b). The higher of the

quoted market price at the measurement date of (1) the convertible stock granted or awarded or (2) the securities into which the original grant or award is convertible should be used to measure compensation.

Awards to employees of convertible stock or rights to purchase convertible stock are not common. Nevertheless, this paragraph provides guidance in measuring the compensation cost of such awards. Further guidance can be found in FIN No. 38, "Determining the Measurement Date for Stock Option, Purchase, and Award Plans Involving Junior Stock," an interpretation of APB Opinion No. 25.

(g) Settlement of Awards.   Paragraph 11(g) states:

> Cash paid to an employee to settle an earlier award of stock or to settle a grant of option to the employee should measure compensation cost. If the cash payment differs from the earlier measure of the award of stock or grant of option, compensation cost should be adjusted (para. 15). The amount that a corporation pays to an employee through a compensation plan is "cash paid to an employee to settle an earlier award of stock or to settle a grant of option" if stock is reacquired shortly after issuance. Cash proceeds that a corporation receives from sale of awarded stock or stock issued on exercise of an option and remits to the taxing authorities to cover required withholding of income taxes on an award is not "cash paid to an employee to settle an earlier award of stock or to settle a grant of option" in measuring compensation cost.

The intent of this paragraph seems quite clear. If an earlier award of stock or stock options is ultimately settled by cash payment to the employee, the amount actually paid is the final measure of compensation cost to be recognized by the employer, regardless of the amount of compensation cost previously determined. However, in practice, application of this paragraph has often proved difficult and, as a result, a number of EITF Issues have dealt with cash settlements of awards, as discussed in the following paragraph.

(i) EITF Issue No. 84-13, "Purchase of Stock Options and Stock Appreciation Rights in a Leveraged Buyout." This pronouncement sets forth the EITF's consensus that the "target company" in a leveraged buyout should recognize compensation expense in the amount of cash paid by the target company to acquire outstanding stock options and stock appreciation rights.

(ii) EITF Issue No. 85-45, "Business Combinations: Settlement of Stock Options and Awards." Similar to the consensus in EITF Issue No. 84-13, this consensus indicates that when a target company settles outstanding stock options or awards "voluntarily, at the direction of the acquiring company, or as part of the plan of acquisition, Opinion 25 requires that the settlement be accounted for as compensation expense in the separate financial statements of the target company."

(iii) EITF Issue No. 87-6, "Adjustments Relating to Stock Compensation Plans." This consensus addresses stock option plans that contain a cash bonus feature that provides for a reimbursement to employees of the taxes payable as a result of the exercise of a nonqualified stock option (a "tax-offset bonus"). The consensus indicates that awards under such plans are variable awards (with the exception of certain narrowly defined awards outstanding as of April 7, 1987, and which meet very specific criteria set forth in the consensus). Thus, the existence of a tax-offset bonus related to a stock option award requires that the entire award (the stock option *plus* the cash bonus feature) be accounted for as a variable award, as the option and the tax-offset bonus are viewed as a single variable award. This consensus is consistent with footnote 1 to FIN No. 28, "Accounting for Stock Appreciation Rights and Other Variable Stock Option or Award Plans" which states, in part, "Plans under which an employee may receive cash in lieu of stock or additional cash upon the exercise of a stock

option are variable plans for purposes of the Interpretation as the amount is contingent upon the occurrence of future events.'' The significant point here is that two different awards, one being a fixed award and the other a variable award, should be accounted for as a single, variable award unless the two awards are totally independent (i.e., unless the payout under the variable award is unaffected by the existence of the fixed award).

(iv) EITF Issue No. 87-23, "Book Value Stock Purchase Plans."   This consensus provides much-needed guidance in accounting for formula-based plans, under which employees purchase shares, or are granted options to acquire shares, of the employer's common stock at a formula price. The formula price is usually based on book value, a multiple of book value, or earnings. Additionally, the employee must sell the acquired shares back to the employer upon retirement or other termination of employment, at a selling price determined in the same manner as the original purchase price.

An unusual aspect of this consensus is that it distinguishes between privately held and publicly held companies. The consensus includes the following guidance.

Privately held companies only:

1. No compensation expense should be recognized for changes in the formula price during the employment period "if the employee makes a substantive investment that will be at risk for a reasonable period of time." This consensus applies to plans where the employee is allowed to resell all or a portion of the acquired shares to the company at fixed or determinable dates, as well as plans where the shares are resold to the company only upon retirement or other termination of employment.

2. If an ESOP covers all employees and provides that an employee may resell shares acquired through the ESOP for cash, at the formula price, no compensation expense should be recognized when the employee sells shares back to the ESOP or to the employer.

Privately held and publicly held companies:

If **options** are granted to employees to purchase shares at the formula price and the employees can resell the options, or the shares acquired upon exercise of the options, to the company upon retirement or other termination of employment, or at fixed or determinable dates, the consensus of the EITF is the same for both privately held and publicly held companies. The consensus indicates that compensation expense should be recognized for increases in the formula price from the grant date to the exercise date (i.e., the award should be accounted for as a variable award). The consensus further indicates that the expense previously recognized should not be reversed upon exercise of the option, and that "additional expense would be recognized if the shares are sold back to the company shortly after exercise, as required by paragraph 11(g) of APB Opinion 25."

The SEC Observer at the EITF provided the following clarification of the SEC staff's views of book value plans for publicly held companies:

> The SEC Observer indicated that the SEC staff views a book value plan for a publicly held company as a performance plan and noted that it should be accounted for like an SAR. The SEC Observer noted that, for existing book value stock plans, issuances of grants under those plans made prior to January 28, 1988 need not be accounted for like an SAR if such accounting treatment was not being followed prior to that date and the terms of the book value plan had been adequately disclosed.

As previously noted, the difference in accounting for book value purchase (and other formula-based) awards by privately held and publicly held companies is unusual. This difference, of course, raises questions as to the accounting to be applied to these types of awards when a privately held company becomes publicly held. This issue was subsequently addressed by the EITF in EITF Issue No. 88-6, "Book Value Stock Plans in an Initial Public Offering" (see following discussion of EITF Issue No. 88-6).

(v) EITF Issue No. 87-33, "Stock Compensation Issues Related to Market Decline."   This consensus addresses a number of issues related to the October 1987 stock market decline, including "How to account for the repurchase of an outstanding option and the issuance of a 'new' option." The Task Force consensus on this issue was that "paragraph 11(g) of APB Opinion No. 25 does not apply if an existing option is repurchased in contemplation of the issuance of a new option that contains terms identical to the remaining terms of the original option except that the exercise price is reduced. . . ." The consensus also indicates that "the cash paid to repurchase the original option represents additional compensation that should be charged to expense in the current period."

The effect of this consensus is to preclude an employer from decreasing compensation cost associated with a stock option award, by "settling" the award through a cash payment that is less than the amount of compensation cost previously determined, and then granting a "new" option to the same employee that contains terms identical to the remaining terms of the original option except that the exercise price is reduced. In the event such an arrangement were entered into, application of the consensus would (1) require the employer to charge the amount of the cash payment to expense in the current period, (2) proscribe the reversal of any previously recognized expense associated with the original option, (3) require continued amortization of any compensation measured at the original measurement date that had not been amortized and, additionally, could result in the measurement of additional compensation expense associated with the "new" award.

The consensus also requires similar accounting when an option is "repriced," as opposed to the situation described above where an option is canceled and reissued.

(vi) EITF Issue No. 88-6, "Book Value Stock Plans in an Initial Public Offering."   As previously noted, EITF Issue No. 87-23 addresses certain issues related to the accounting for stock purchase awards to employees, where the purchase price is a formula price based on book value or earnings, and where the shares must ultimately be sold back to the company by the employee at a price determined in the same manner as the original purchase price. The consensus set forth in EITF Issue No. 87-23 makes certain distinctions between privately and publicly held companies with respect to the accounting for these types of awards.

In EITF Issue No. 88-6, the Task Force reached a consensus that a book value stock purchase plan of a publicly held company should be viewed as a performance plan, and should be accounted for like an SAR (this is consistent with the SEC Observer's comment noted under the discussion of EITF Issue No. 87-23 above). Thus, for a publicly held company, compensation expense should be recognized for increases in book value (or other formula price based on earnings) on awards outstanding under such a plan. However, the SEC Observer noted that, consistent with the SEC Observer's indications of the SEC staff's views set forth in EITF Issue No. 87-23, grants under existing book value stock purchase or stock option plans "made prior to January 28, 1988 need not be accounted for like an SAR if such accounting treatment was not being followed prior to that date and the terms of the book value plan had been adequately disclosed." For a privately held company, however, under the consensus reached in EITF Issue No. 87-23, no compensation expense would be recognized for such increases in the book value or other formula price, regardless of when the awards were granted.

The Task Force also reached consensuses in EITF Issue No. 88-6 addresses issues related to the recognition and measurement of compensation expense by a privately held company for such awards in the event of a subsequent IPO (i.e., when a privately held company becomes a publicly held company). These consensuses are set forth in Exhibit 27.4.

ACCOUNTING FOR BOOK VALUE OPTIONS AND SHARES
OF A PRIVATELY HELD COMPANY AT TIME OF IPO

Type of Award Outstanding	Status at Time of IPO	Accounting
Book value option	Converts to an option to purchase unrestricted (market value) stock	In addition to compensation expense previously recognized for changes in book value, compensation expense should be recognized on successful completion of the IPO for the difference between market value and book value at the date of the IPO, because conversion of the book value option to a market value option results in a new measurement date. Subsequent to the IPO, no further compensation expense would be recognized, assuming the plan otherwise remains a fixed plan under APB Opinion No. 25.
	Remains a book value option	Any change in book value resulting from successful completion of the IPO should be recognized as compensation expense at the time of the IPO in accordance with variable plan (SAR) accounting. Subsequent to the IPO, the plan should continue to be accounted for like an SAR based on the consensus reached in conjunction with Issue No. 87-23.
Book value shares	Converts to unrestricted (market value) stock	No compensation expense should be recognized at the time of the IPO; however, shares issued under the purchase plan within one year of the IPO are presumed to have been issued in contemplation of the IPO and would result in compensation expense for the difference between the book value of those shares and their estimated fair value at date of issuance. Subsequent to the IPO, no further compensation expense would be recognized, assuming the plan remains a fixed plan under APB Opinion No. 25.
	Remains book value stock	No compensation expense should be recognized upon successful completion of the IPO for any impact that the IPO may have on book value; however, shares issued under the purchase plan within one year of the IPO are presumed to have been issued in contemplation of the IPO, and would result in variable award (SAR) accounting for actual changes in book value of the shares since the date of their issuance. Subsequent to the IPO, compensation expense would be recognized for increases in book value after the IPO (variable award accounting).

Exhibit 27.4. Accounting for book value options and book value shares at time of an IPO.

EITF Issue No. 88-6 also contains certain guidance regarding pro forma disclosures for these types of plans in the event of an IPO, as well as an exhibit that contains "Examples of the Application of Opinion 25 and the EITF Consensus from Issue Nos. 87-23 and 88-6 in an IPO."

As indicated in paragraph 11(g), cash proceeds received by an employer from the sale of stock issued pursuant to a stock option or award plan to cover income taxes required to be withheld are not considered cash paid to settle an award of stock or a stock option granted to an employee. See the discussion under section 27.10(j) regarding the use of stock option shares to cover required tax withholding.

(h) Combination Plans and Awards.　Paragraph 11(h) states:

> Some plans are a combination of two or more types of plans. An employer corporation may need to measure compensation for the separate parts. Compensation cost for a combination plan permitting an employee to elect one part should be measured according to the terms that an employee is most likely to elect based on the facts available each period.

If more than one type of award is granted to an employee under a plan, the measurement principle must be applied to each award for purposes of measuring compensation cost to an employer. Furthermore, if a combination plan permits an employee to elect one award from a number of alternative awards, compensation cost should be measured in terms of the award the employee is considered most likely to elect in view of the facts available each period. In many combination plans involving alternative awards, an employer retains the right to approve or reject an employee's election under certain circumstances, giving the employer significant control over the determination of the award under which compensation cost will be measured.

FIN No. 28 provides additional guidance with respect to combination plans. In that Interpretation, the FASB specifies that in combination plans involving both a variable award (i.e., an SAR or other variable award) and a fixed award (e.g., a stock option), compensation cost should normally be measured and allocated to expense under the presumption that the variable award will be elected by the employee. However, this presumption may be overcome if experience or other factors, such as ceilings on the appreciation available to the employee under the variable feature, provide evidence that the employee will elect to exercise the fixed award.

(i) Stock Option Pyramiding.　Stock option pyramiding is a stock option exercise approach that developed subsequent to the issuance of APB Opinion No. 25. This approach involves the payment by the employee of the option exercise price by transferring to the employer previously owned shares with a current fair value equal to the exercise price. In EITF Issue No. 84-18, "Stock Option Pyramiding," the Task Force reached a consensus that "some holding period" for the exchanged shares is necessary to "avoid the conclusion that the award of the option is, in substance, a variable plan (or a stock appreciation right), thereby requiring compensation charges." A majority of the Task Force members indicated that a 6-month period would satisfy the holding period requirement.

In a subsequent consensus set forth in EITF Issue No. 87-6, "Adjustments Relating to Stock Compensation Plans," the Task Force addressed a "phantom" stock-for-stock exercise arrangement, under which an employee holds "mature" shares meeting the holding period requirement discussed in EITF Issue No. 84-18. In this consensus, the Task Force indicated that if the exercise is accomplished by the enterprise issuing a certificate for the "net" shares (i.e. the shares issuable upon exercise of the option less the number of shares required to be relinquished to pay the exercise price), as opposed to the enterprise accepting the mature shares in payment of the exercise price and then issuing a new certificate for the total number of shares covered by the exercised option, the plan remains a fixed plan.

Thus, even though the "net" number of shares to be issued under either of the arrangements described above is not known at the date of grant, the use of qualifying mature shares to pay the option exercise price does not, under these two consensuses, change a plan that otherwise qualifies as a fixed plan to a variable plan. As a result, the enterprise is not required to recognize compensation expense for appreciation in shares under option subsequent to the date of grant solely because the award allows for payment of the exercise price of an option by surrendering mature shares owned by the employee or through a phantom stock-for-stock exercise involving mature shares owned by the employee.

(j) Use of Stock Option Shares to Cover Required Tax Withholding.   EITF Issue No. 87-6, "Adjustments Relating to Stock Compensation Plans," addresses an issue that is similar to the stock option pyramiding issue discussed under (i) above. The Task Force reached a consensus that "an option that allows the use of option shares to meet tax withholding requirements may be considered a fixed plan if it meets all the other requirements of APB Opinion No. 25. No compensation needs to be recorded for the shares used to meet the tax withholding requirements. The Task Force noted that this treatment would be limited to the number of shares with a fair value equal to the dollar amount of only the *required* tax withholding." Therefore, even though the net number of shares to be issued would not be known at the date of grant under these circumstances (since the shares to be withheld to cover the required tax withholding will not be known until the exercise date), plans with tax withholding features may be accounted for as fixed plans as long as they meet the other requirements for a fixed plan under APB Opinion No. 25.

27.11 ALLOCATION OF COMPENSATION COST: DETERMINING THE SERVICE PERIOD. With respect to the allocation to expense of compensation cost associated with a capital accumulation award, the Committee on Accounting Procedure concluded in ARB No. 43, Chapter 13B that, if the period for which payment for services is being made by the issuance of the stock option or stock purchase right is not specifically indicated in the offer or agreement, the amount of compensation cost should be allocated to expense over the period of service that "seems appropriate in the circumstances."

The APB basically retained the allocation principle set forth in ARB No. 43, Chapter 13B, by indicating that compensation cost related to "stock option, purchase and award plans should be recognized as an expense of one or more periods in which an employee performs services. . . . The grant or award may specify the period or periods during which the employee performs services or the periods may be inferred from the terms or from the past pattern of grants or awards."

FIN No. 28 also indicates that compensation cost with respect to variable awards should be allocated to expense over the period(s) in which the employee performs the related services. However, the FASB went a step further in this Interpretation by specifying that the service period, unless defined in the plan or other agreement (e.g., employment agreement) as a shorter or previous period, is presumed to be the vesting period—normally the period from the date of the grant of the rights or awards to the date(s) they become exercisable. These criteria for determining the service period are considerably more definitive than the guidance provided in APB Opinion No. 25 and, in the authors' view, should be used for determining the service period for awards made pursuant to all capital accumulation awards (i.e., both fixed and variable awards.)

(a) Allocation of Compensation Cost Related to Fixed Awards.   Compensation cost related to fixed awards should normally be allocated to expense over the service period on a straight-line basis. On rare occasions, however, circumstances may arise that would justify allocation on another basis. In any event, the method used should be systematic, reasonable, and consistently applied.

(b) Allocation of Compensation Cost Related to Variable Awards.   Allocating compensation cost related to variable awards to expense is more complex, because the measurement date and, thus, the final determination of compensation cost, occur subsequent to the date of grant. Total compensation cost with respect to a variable award must be estimated from the date of grant to the measurement date, based on the quoted market price of the employer's stock at the end of each interim period. Compensation cost so determined should be allocated to expense in the following manner:

1. If a variable award is granted for current and/or future services, estimated total compensation cost determined at the end of each period **prior to the expiration of the service period** should be allocated to expense over the service period. Changes in the estimated total compensation cost attributable to increases or decreases in the quoted market price of the employer's capital stock **subsequent to the expiration of the service period** (but prior to the measurement date) should be charged or credited to expense each period as the changes occur (see Exhibit 27.8).

2. If a variable award is granted for past services, estimated total compensation cost determined at the date of grant is charged to expense of the period in which the award is granted. Changes in estimated total compensation cost attributable to increases or decreases in the quoted market price of the employer's capital stock subsequent to the date of grant (but prior to the measurement date) should be charged or credited to expense each period as the changes occur.

27.12 CANCELED OR FORFEITED RIGHTS.   APB Opinion No. 25 states in paragraph 15: "If a stock option is not exercised (or awarded stock is returned to the corporation) because an employee fails to fulfill an obligation, the estimate of compensation expense recorded in previous periods should be adjusted by decreasing compensation expense in the period of forfeiture." Application of this paragraph to a situation where an award is canceled or forfeited because employment is terminated prior to vesting of the award is straightforward; the previously accrued compensation should be eliminated by decreasing compensation expense in the period of cancellation or forfeiture.

However, prior to the issuance of FIN No. 28, the application of this paragraph to combination plans was unclear. In a combination plan that permits an employee to elect either a fixed award (e.g., a stock option) or a variable award (e.g., an SAR), FIN No. 28 specifies that compensation cost should be accrued based on the presumption that the employee will elect the variable award, unless there is evidence to the contrary. In cases involving combination plans where the employer has accrued compensation based on the presumption that the employee will elect to exercise the variable award and, due to a change in circumstances, it becomes more likely that settlement will be based on the fixed award (e.g., when appreciation in the quoted market price of the employer's capital stock exceeds the maximum appreciation an employee is entitled to receive upon exercise of an SAR), FIN No. 28 specifies that the compensation accrued with respect to the variable award should not be adjusted by decreasing compensation expense, but should be recognized as consideration for the stock issued upon settlement of the fixed award. However, the Interpretation further specifies that, if both the fixed award and the variable award are forfeited or canceled, accrued compensation should be eliminated by decreasing compensation expense during the period of forfeiture or cancellation.

EITF Issue No. 87-33, "Stock Compensation Issues Related to Market Decline," provides further clarification of APB 25, paragraph 15. That EITF Issue addresses questions regarding the accounting for stock compensation plans that arose because of revisions or contemplated revisions to plan awards as a result of the October 1987 stock market decline (see section 27.10(g)). In EITF Issue No. 87-33, "Task Force members agreed that the reversal of previously measured compensation would be appropriate only if the forfeiture or cancellation of an option or award results from the employee's termination or nonperformance."

27.13 ACCOUNTING FOR INCOME TAXES.   Compensation expense associated with capital accumulation awards is often deductible by the employer for income tax purposes in a different period than such expense is recognized for financial reporting purposes. If the employer company has not implemented SFAS No. 96, "Accounting for Income Taxes," such differences are timing differences and should be accounted for in accordance with APB Opinion No. 11, "Accounting for Income Taxes." If, however, the employer company has implemented SFAS No. 96, such differences are temporary differences and should be accounted for as specified in SFAS No. 96.

In many instances, however, there is a permanent difference between the amount of compensation expense recognized for financial reporting purposes and compensation expense deductible for income tax purposes for capital accumulation awards. These differences generally arise because an employer is normally entitled to an income tax deduction for such awards equal to the amount of compensation reportable as income by the employee, and this amount is often different from the amount of compensation expense recognized by an employer for financial reporting purposes. In addressing this situation, APB Opinion No. 25 specifies that the reduction in income tax expense recorded by an employer with respect to a stock option, purchase, or award plan should not exceed the proportion of the tax reduction related to the compensation expense recognized by the employer for financial reporting purposes. Any additional tax reduction should not be accounted for as a reduction of income tax expense but, rather, should be credited directly to paid-in capital in the period that the additional tax benefit is realized through a reduction of current income taxes payable.

Occasionally, the amount of compensation associated with a capital accumulation award and recognized as expense for financial reporting purposes exceeds the amount of compensation deductible for income tax purposes. In these situations, an employer may, in the period of the tax reduction, deduct from paid-in capital and credit to income tax expense or previously recognized deferred taxes the amount of the additional tax reduction that would have resulted had the compensation expense recognized for financial reporting purposes been deductible for income tax purposes. However, this reduction is limited to the amount of tax reductions attributable to awards made under the same or similar plans that have been previously credited to paid-in capital.

27.14 EARNINGS PER SHARE IMPACT OF CAPITAL ACCUMULATION AWARDS.
Computation of the impact of capital accumulation awards on earnings per share is addressed in two authoritative pronouncements:

1. APB Opinion No. 15, "Earnings per Share."
2. FIN No. 31, "Treatment of Stock Compensation Plans in EPS Computations."

It should also be noted that SFAS No. 21, "Suspension of the Reporting of Earnings per Share and Segment Information by Nonpublic Enterprises" (SFAS No. 21) suspended the requirement for nonpublic enterprises to report earnings per share information in their financial statements. SFAS No. 21 does, however, require that any earnings per share information included in the financial statements of nonpublic enterprises be presented in a manner consistent with the requirements of APB Opinion No. 15. Thus, the discussion of earnings per share in this chapter is applicable to the earnings per share information presented in financial statements of public companies, as required by APB Opinion No. 15, as well as to any earnings per share information that nonpublic enterprises elect to report in their financial statements.

The calculation of the earnings per share impact of certain capital accumulation awards is shown in this chapter in the section "Illustrations of the Accounting and Federal Income Tax Consequences of Certain Capital Accumulation Awards."

Capital accumulation awards influence earnings per share to the extent of compensation expense or credits to compensation expense, net of income tax effects, recognized by the employer for financial reporting purposes. For awards that will be settled by payment of cash to the employee, there is no additional impact on earnings per share, since settlement of the award will not result in the issuance of shares of an employer's common stock. However, when awards will be settled through issuance of shares of common stock, additional dilution in earnings per share may result because of the incremental number of shares of the employer's common stock deemed to be outstanding. In a combination plan involving alternative awards that will be settled by either the issuance of common stock or payment of cash, depending on the election made, additional dilution in earnings per share will result only if compensation is being recognized by the employer based on the presumption that the award will be settled through issuance of common stock.

APB Opinion No. 15 states that "options, warrants and similar arrangements usually have no cash yield and derive their value from their right to obtain common stock at specified prices for an extended period. Therefore, these securities should be considered as common stock equivalents at all times." Accordingly, shares of an employer's common stock that are potentially issuable to settle a capital accumulation award are common stock equivalents. The dilutive impact of common stock equivalents on earnings per share is computed under the treasury stock method, as prescribed by APB Opinion No. 15.

(a) Primary Earnings per Share Calculation. In applying the treasury stock method to a capital accumulation award, the incremental number of shares estimated to be outstanding each period for purposes of computing primary earnings per share is determined as if the shares issuable pursuant to the award were issued at the beginning of the period (or at the date the award was granted, if later), and as if the assumed exercise proceeds were used by the employer to acquire shares of common stock at the average market price during the period. Paragraph 3 of FIN No. 31 defines exercise proceeds as follows:

> In applying the treasury stock method of paragraph 36 of Opinion 15 to stock options, including stock appreciation rights and other variable plan awards, the exercise proceeds of the options are the sum of the amount the employee must pay, the amount of measurable compensation ascribed to future services and not yet charged to expense (whether or not accrued), and the amount of any "windfall" tax benefit[1] to be credited[2] to capital. Exercise proceeds shall not include compensation ascribed to past services.

---

(1) The windfall tax benefit is the tax credit resulting from a tax deduction for compensation in excess of compensation expense recognized for financial reporting purposes. Such credit arises from an increase in the market price of the stock under option between the measurement date (as defined in APB Opinion No. 25, "Accounting for Stock Issued to Employees," and the date at which the compensation deduction for income tax purposes is determinable. The amount of the "windfall" tax benefit shall be determined by a "with-and-without" computation as described in paragraph 36 of APB Opinion No. 11, "Accounting for Income Taxes." [*Note:* If the employer company has implemented SFAS No. 96, the above footnote is amended to delete the words "computation as described in paragraph 36 of APB Opinion No. 11, 'Accounting for Income Taxes'," from the last sentence.]
(2) Paragraph 17 of APB Opinion No. 25 states that there may be instances when the tax deduction for compensation is less than the compensation expense recognized for financial reporting purposes. If the resulting difference in income tax will be deducted from capital in accordance with that paragraph, such taxes to be deducted from capital shall be treated as a reduction of exercise proceeds.

The difference between the shares issuable and the shares deemed to be acquired from the assumed exercise proceeds is the incremental number of shares deemed to be outstanding for purposes of computing primary earnings per share. The number of shares so determined is not included, however, in the computation of primary earnings per share if the effect of inclusion is antidilutive, that is, if the effect of inclusion is to increase the earnings per share or to decrease the loss per share.

(b) Fully Diluted Earnings per Share. The impact of a compensation award on fully diluted earnings per share is computed in the same manner as the impact on primary earnings per share, with one exception. In order to reflect the maximum potential dilution, the market price of the employer's common stock at the end of each period, if higher than the average market price during the period, is used to compute the number of commmon shares deemed to be acquired by the employer with the assumed exercise proceeds. As in the case of primary earnings per share, the incremental number of shares deemed to be outstanding is not included in the computation of fully diluted earnings per share if the effect is antidilutive.

(c) Earnings per Share Computations for Fixed Awards. Computations of the impact of fixed awards on earnings per share are relatively straightforward. At the date an award is granted, both the number of shares that an individual employee is entitled to receive (i.e., the shares issuable pursuant to the award) and the option or purchase price, if any, are known. Thus the number of incremental shares issuable pursuant to the award remains constant until the award is settled by issuance of shares. However, the reduction in the number of incremental shares for common shares deemed to be acquired by an employer with the assumed exercise proceeds will vary each period, because of changes in the assumed exercise proceeds and in the quoted market price of the employer's common stock.

(d) Earnings per Share Computations for Variable Awards. Computations of the impact of variable awards on earnings per share are considerably more complex than computations involving fixed awards. In paragraph 4 of FIN No. 31, the FASB specifies:

> The dilutive effect of stock appreciation rights and other variable plan awards on primary earnings per share shall be computed using the average aggregate compensation and average market price for the period. The market price of an employer's stock and the resulting aggregate compensation used to compute the dilutive effect of stock appreciation rights and other variable plan awards in fully diluted earnings per share computations shall be the more dilutive of the market price and aggregate compensation at the close of the period being reported upon or the average market price and average aggregate compensation for that period.

In the case of variable awards, either (1) the number of shares issuable pursuant to the award, (2) the option or purchase price, if any, or (3) both the number of shares issuable and the option of purchase price are not known at the date the award is granted. For example, in the case of SARs to be settled by issuance of shares of an employer's common stock, there is no option or purchase price. However, the estimated number of shares issuable will vary each period in which an award is outstanding, based in changes in the quoted market price of the employer's common stock. Furthermore, the number of shares deemed to be acquired by the employer from the assumed exercise proceeds will also vary each period in which an award is outstanding, due to changes in (a) the quoted market price of the employer's common stock, and (b) the amount of measurable compensation ascribed to future services and not yet charged to expense.

(e) Earnings per Share Computations Involving Restricted Shares. When restricted shares of an employer's common stock are issued to an employee, the ultimate benefit to be realized by the employee with respect to such shares is dependent on the employee's performance of future services. After the required services have been performed (e.g., continued employment for a specified period), the employee has the unrestricted right to the issued shares. Thus, upon performance of the required services, the issued shares entitle the holder to the same rights and privileges as those held by other common shareholders.

Accountants hold differing views as to the appropriate method of calculating the dilution in earnings per share resulting from outstanding restricted shares. Some argue that all outstanding restricted shares should be included in the computation of earnings per share. Others argue that the number of restricted shares included in the calculation should be determined by application of the treasury stock method. In their view, the number of shares included in computations of earnings per share should equal the total number of restricted shares outstanding, reduced by the number of shares deemed to be acquired by the employer from the assumed exercise proceeds (i.e., the amount of measurable compensation ascribed to future services and not yet charged to expense and the amount of any "windfall" tax benefit to be credited to capital).

In the authors' view, all outstanding restricted shares should be included in computations of earnings per share, since such shares entitle the holder to full dividend and voting rights, and any dividends on the shares are charged directly to retained earnings as opposed to compensation expense. Under this view, no reduction in the number of outstanding restricted shares should be assumed through application of the treasury stock method.

(f) Earnings per Share Computation Including Shares Subject to Reacquisition by the Issuer. When book value shares or other shares subject to reacquisition by the issuer at a formula price (e.g., shares subject to reacquisition at book value, at a multiple of book value, or at a formula price based on earnings) are issued to an employee, the ultimate benefit to be realized by the employee with respect to such shares is dependent on the employee's performance of future services. However, after the specified services have been performed (e.g., continued employment for a specified period), the employee's rights become vested. Further, the employee is normally permitted, or in some instances required, to sell the shares back to the employer, either upon retirement, other termination of employment, or at other fixed or determinable dates.

The appropriate method of calculating the dilution in earnings per share as a result of outstanding book value shares is not clear. Some believe the preferable method is to consider the awarded shares as outstanding shares from the date of their issuance for purposes of computing both primary and fully diluted earnings per share, assuming the shares entitle the holders to the same voting and dividend rights that other common shareholders possess. If this method is used, no reduction in the number of shares outstanding is made for any shares that would be deemed to be acquired by the employer through application of the treasury stock method. Others argue that the number of outstanding shares included in the earnings per share computation should be reduced through application of the treasury stock method. These differing views are similar to the differing views on earnings per share computations involving restricted stock, as previously discussed.

However, for book value and other shares subject to reacquisition by the employer at a formula price, there is also a third view. It suggests that any such shares that will ultimately be sold or "put" back to the employer should be excluded from computations of earnings per share. The rationale for this approach is that such shares are, in effect, mandatorily redeemable securities. This last view finds some support, at least for publicly held companies, in EITF Issue No. 88-6, which includes the following statement:

> For publicly held companies with existing book value stock plans and for privately held companies with book value stock plans that will remain in existence after an IPO, the SEC Observer noted that the SEC staff will require that the redemption amount of the book value stock be classified in the balance sheet outside stockholders' equity, consistent with the requirements of ASR 268, if the plan includes any conditions under which the company must redeem the stock with the payment of cash.

Consistent with this position expressed by the SEC Observer, it would appear to be appropriate for publicly held companies to exclude book value and other shares subject to repurchase by the company at a formula price from stockholders' equity "if the plan includes any conditions under which the company **must** redeem the stock with the payment of cash" (emphasis added). When this presentation is followed, the authors believe it would also be appropriate to exclude such shares from the calculation of earnings per share. However, the other requirements set forth in ASR No. 268 (incorporated into FRR § 211), should be followed, including a requirement to reduce net income by dividends on such shares in computing earnings available for common stock to be used in the earnings per share computation.

ILLUSTRATIONS OF THE ACCOUNTING AND FEDERAL INCOME TAX CONSEQUENCES OF CERTAIN CAPITAL ACCUMULATION AWARDS

This section includes (a) definitions of certain capital accumulation awards; (b) a summary of the accounting consequences of the awards, including the impact on compensation expense and federal income tax expense to be recognized for financial reporting purposes, and the impact on earnings per share; (c) a summary of the federal income tax consequences of the awards to both the employer and the employee; and (d) exhibits illustrating the accounting and federal income tax consequences of hypothetical awards.

The discussion and exhibits demonstrate the application of the principles and concepts discussed in this chapter. Capital accumulation plans and awards, however, tend to be unique; accordingly, the income tax and accounting consequences of any capital accumulation award should be determined based on the specific terms of the award and the authoritative accounting literature and the tax laws and rulings in effect at the time of the award. State and local income tax consequences of capital accumulation awards are not addressed in this section; such consequences should be determined pursuant to the tax laws of the applicable state and local governments. Finally, the exhibits ignore any employer withholding tax requirements; however, an employer should institute measures to ensure compliance with any requirements to withhold income taxes from recipients of awards. Failure to comply with applicable withholding requirements could jeopardize the employer's right to a tax deduction with respect to an award.

The discussion and exhibits address the accounting and income tax consequences of a fixed award, a variable award, and a formula award, as follows:

Fixed Award. Nonstatutory stock option (nondiscounted). Note that nonstatutory stock options (discounted), which can be either a fixed or a variable award, are also defined and discussed; however, Exhibits 27.5 and 27.6 illustrate the accounting and tax consequences of a nonstatutory stock option (nondiscounted).

Variable Award. Stock appreciation right (granted in tandem with a nonstatutory stock option).

Formula Award. Book value share.

27.15 NONSTATUTORY STOCK OPTIONS: DEFINITIONS AND ACCOUNTING BY EMPLOYER

(a) Definition. A nonstatutory stock option is an employee stock option that does not qualify for the special tax treatment afforded incentive stock options under IRC § 422A, or the special tax treatment afforded stock option issued under employee stock purchase plans under IRC § 423.

A nonstatutory stock option (nondiscounted) entitles an employee to purchase shares of the employer's capital stock for an amount equal to the fair market value of the shares as of the grant date. The employee's right is nontransferable and normally vests over a specified period (e.g., 3–5 years) although, in some instances, the right is vested at the date of grant. The right to exercise the option expires after a specified period of time (e.g., 10 years).

A nonstatutory stock option (discounted) is similar to a nonstatutory stock option (nondiscounted), the significant distinction being that a nonstatutory stock option (discounted) entitles the employee to purchase shares of the employer's capital stock at a discount from the fair market value of the stock. The number of shares under option and the exercise price may either be determined at the date of grant (a fixed award), or may be determinable at a date subsequent to the date of grant (a variable award) based on future events.

(b) Accounting by Employer for Compensation Expense. A nonstatutory stock option (nondiscounted) is a fixed award (i.e., both the number of shares the employee is entitled to receive and the option price are known at the date of grant). However, for financial reporting purposes, there is no compensation expense associated with such an award, since the option exercise price is equal to the fair market value of the employer's capital stock at the date of grant.

A nonstatutory stock option (discounted), however, does result in the recognition of compensation expense by the employer. The method of measuring compensation expense depends on whether the award is a fixed award or a variable award.

- For a fixed award, total compensation cost is determined at the date of grant, based on the difference between the exercise price and the fair market value of the shares under option. Compensation cost so determined is allocated to expense over the service period.

- For a variable award, total compensation cost is not determinable until some date subsequent to the date of grant. Until total compensation cost is determinable (i.e., until the "measurement date"), compensation cost must be estimated each period and allocated to expense over the service period (see section 27.16 for a discussion and illustration of the accounting for a variable award).

(c) Accounting by Employer for Federal Income Taxes. Upon exercise by a "non-insider" employee of a nonstatutory stock option, the employer is entitled to an income tax deduction for compensation expense, based on the difference between the option exercise price and the fair market value of the shares acquired through exercise, determined as of the exercise date.

However, for exercises of nonstatutory stock options by "insiders" (i.e., individuals subject to restrictions under § 16(b) of the Securities Exchange Act of 1934), the transfer is treated as having occurred 6 months after the exercise date. Thus, unless an insider makes an election under IRC § 83(b), the employer's income tax deduction for compensation expense resulting from the exercise of a nonstatutory stock option by an insider is based on the difference between the option exercise price and the fair market value of the shares acquired through exercise, determined 6 months after the exercise date; the deduction so computed is deductible by the employer in its taxable year in which the employee's taxable year that includes the income attributable to the option exercise ends. However, if the insider makes an IRC § 83(b) election within 30 days of the option exercise date, the employer's tax deduction is computed under the general rules discussed in the preceding paragraph.

Thus, a difference usually arises between the amount of compensation expense recognized for financial reporting purposes and the amount of compensation expense that is deductible for income tax purposes. Any reduction of income taxes payable resulting from an excess of compensation expense deducted for income tax purposes over compensation expense recognized for financial reporting purposes should be credited to paid-in capital in the period of the reduction.

The federal income tax consequences of a nonstatutory stock option are summarized in Exhibit 27.5.

(d) Accounting by Employer for Earnings per Share. Nonstatutory stock option awards result in a reduction of earnings per share to the extent of compensation expense recognized by the employer with respect to such awards for financial reporting purposes. Additionally, a further reduction of earnings per share occurs as a result of the incremental number of common shares of the employer's stock deemed to be outstanding as a result of such awards. The incremental number of outstanding shares, if any, is computed by the treasury stock method in accordance with APB Opinion No. 15.

(e) Illustration of a Hypothetical Nonstatutory Stock Option Award (Nondiscounted)—Accounting and Federal Income Tax Consequences. Exhibit 27.6 demonstrates the accounting and federal income tax consequences of a hypothetical nonstatutory stock option award (nondiscounted).

27.16 STOCK APPRECIATION RIGHT: DEFINITIONS AND ACCOUNTING BY EMPLOYER

(a) Definition. An SAR is a right granted by an employer to an employee that entitles the employee to receive the excess of the quoted market price of a specified number of shares of the employer's capital stock over a specified value (usually the market price of the specified number of shares of the employer's capital stock at the date the right is granted). An SAR sometimes contains a limitation on the amount an employee may receive upon exercise. Further, an SAR may be the only compensation feature of an award; however, an SAR is often granted as part of a combination award in tandem with a nonstatutory stock option, whereby an employee or the employer must make an election to settle the award pursuant to either (but not both) the SAR or the nonstatutory stock option. The form of payment for amounts earned pursuant to an SAR may be specified by the award (i.e., stock, cash, or a combination thereof), or the award may allow the employee or employer to elect the form of payment. If the award is settled in stock, the number of shares issued to the employee is determined by dividing the amount earned by the fair market value of this stock, determined as of the exercise date. The employee's right to exercise an SAR normally vests after a specified period (e.g., 5 years) and the right to exercise expires after a specified period (e.g., 10 years). In the case of an SAR granted in tandem with a nonstatutory award (or other alternate award), the vesting and expiration dates for both awards are usually identical.

(b) Accounting by Employer for Compensation Expense. An SAR is a variable award, that is, the number of shares, or the amount of cash, an individual is entitled to receive is not known at the date the award is granted. The measurement date and, thus, the determination of total compensation cost associated with an SAR, occur at the exercise date. Total compensation, determined at the exercise date, is equal to the number of rights multiplied by the difference between the quoted market price of the employer's capital stock at the exercise date and the value specified in the award (normally the quoted market price of the employer's capital stock at the grant date).

For purposes of allocating compensation cost to expense of interim periods between the date of grant and the exercise date, compensation cost is estimated as of the end of each interim period by multiplying the number of shares specified in the award times the difference between the quoted market price of the employer's capital stock as of the end of the period and the value specified in the award. During the service period, the amount of compensation cost so determined is allocated to interim periods by recording an expense (or a decrease in expense) in an amount required to adjust accrued compensation at the end of each period to an amount equal to the percentage of the total service period that has elapsed times the estimated compensation cost. For interim periods ending after the service period and up to the exercise date, compensation expense is recorded in an amount sufficient to adjust accrued compensation at the end of each period to the estimated total compensation cost.

In some cases, an SAR awarded to an employee vests over various periods (e.g., 25% per year for 4 years). In these situations, each portion of the SAR that vests on a different vesting date is accounted for as a separate award. Thus, compensation cost attributable to each group should be separately determined and allocated to expense of interim periods from the date of grant to the measurement date in the manner set forth in the preceding paragraph. The accounting for an SAR that vests in this manner is illustrated in Appendix B to FIN No. 28.

FEDERAL INCOME TAX CONSEQUENCES OF A NONSTATUTORY STOCK OPTION

	Federal Income Tax Consequences	
Event	Employer	Employee
Grant of option	None	None
Vesting	None	None
Exercise of option	The amount taxable as compensation to the employee is deductible as compensation expense.	The difference between the amount paid by the employee and the fair market value of the acquired shares, determined as of the exercise date, is taxable as compensation. (However, if the employee is considered to be an insider under § 16(b) of the Securities Exchange Act of 1934, the taxable compensation to the employee is computed in the same manner, except that the fair market value of the required shares used in the computation is determined 6 months from the date of exercise.)
Disposal of shares acquired through exercise of option, held for:		
One year or less	None	The difference between the sales price and the fair market value of the shares as of the exercise date is reportable as a short-term capital gain or loss.
More than one year	None	The difference between the sales price and the fair market value of the shares as of the exercise date is reportable as a long-term capital gain or loss.

Exhibit 27.5.   Effects of a nonstatutory stock option on federal income taxes.

HYPOTHETICAL NONSTATUTORY STOCK OPTION AWARD (NONDISCOUNTED)
Assumptions

Event	Date	Fair Market Value of Employer's Common Stock
Grant of options to acquire common shares	January 1, 1989	$20
Vesting date (i.e., the date options become exercisable)	January 1, 1994	42
Expiration date of unexercised options	December 31, 1998	60
Exercise of options	December 31, 1998	60
Sale by employee of acquired shares	January 1, 2001	65
		(*continued*)

Exhibit 27.6.   Accounting and tax consequences for a nonstatutory stock option award (nondiscounted).

Event	Date	Fair Market Value of Employer's Common Stock
Options granted	100	
Exercise price (options are nondiscounted, so exercise price equals fair market value at date of grant)	$20	
Par value of employer's common stock	$ 5	
Employer's effective tax rate	34%	

The year-end and average market prices of the employer's common stock between the date of grant and the exercise date (required for purposes of determining the impact of the award on earnings per share) are as follows:

	Market Price of Employer's Common Stock	
Year Ended December 31	End of Year	Average During the Year
1989	$25	$24
1990	29	27
1991	27	28
1992	34	30
1993	42	36
1994	43	42
1995	48	45
1996	55	51
1997	57	56
1998	60	59

ACCOUNTING BY EMPLOYER
(Entries required)

Date	Description	Debit	Credit
December 31, 1998	Cash	$2,000	
	Common stock		$ 500
	Paid-in capital		1,500
	To record proceeds from exercise of stock option ($20 × 100)		
December 31, 1998	Income taxes payable	1,360	
	Paid-in capital		1,360
	To record the federal income tax benefit resulting from the deduction of compensation expense [34% ($60–$20) × (100)]		

FEDERAL INCOME TAX CONSEQUENCES

Date	Event	Employer	Employee
January 1, 1989	Grant of options	None	None
January 1, 1994	Vesting of options	None	None
December 31, 1998	Exercise of options	$4,000 deductible as compensation expense [($60–$20) × (100)]	$4,000 taxable as compensation [($60–$20) × (100)]
January 1, 2001	Sale of shares	None	$500 taxable as a long-term capital gain [($65–$60) × (100)]
			(continued)

Exhibit 27.6. *Continued.*

No compensation expense is recognized by the employer with respect to the award of nonstatutory stock options (nondiscounted). Thus the only dilution in earnings per share from the date of grant to the date the options are exercised is the dilution that results from the incremental number of shares deemed to be outstanding, computed under the treasury stock method, as set forth below.

		Incremental Year	
	1989	1990	1991
Primary earnings per share[a]			
Total assumed exercise proceeds (see calculation)	$2,136	$2,238	$2,272
Average market price of employer's common stock	÷24	÷27	÷28
Shares deemed to be acquired with the assumed exercise proceeds	(89)	(83)	(81)
Shares issuable upon exercise	100	100	100
Incremental number of shares[a]	11	17	19
Fully diluted earnings per share[b]			
Total assumed exercise proceeds (see calculation)	$2,170	$2,306	$2,272
Ending or average market price of employer's common stock, whichever is greater	÷25	÷29	÷28
Shares deemed to be acquired with the assumed exercise proceeds	(87)	(80)	(81)
Shares issuable upon exercise	100	100	100
Incremental number of shares[b]	13	20	19

[a]The incremental number of shares determined under this computation is added to the number of shares otherwise included in the computation of primary earnings per share if the effect is dilutive. If the effect is antidilutive, the stock options are ignored in the determination of the average number of shares to be used in the computation of primary earnings per share.

[b]The more dilutive of the incremental number of shares used in the computation of primary earnings per share or the incremental number of shares determined under this computation is used in the computation of fully diluted earnings per share. If the effect is antidilutive, the stock options are ignored in the determination of the average number of shares to be used in the computation of fully diluted earnings per share.

Total assumed exercise proceeds for primary earnings per share are computed as follows:

	Assumed Exercise Proceeds Year		
	1989	1990	1991
Windfall tax benefit to be credited to capital			
Average market price of employer's common stock	$ 24	$ 27	$ 28
Less exercise price	−20	−20	−20
	4	7	8
Shares issuable	×100	×100	×100
Compensation deductible for tax purposes	400	700	800
Effective tax rate	×34%	×34%	×34%
Windfall tax benefit to be credited to capital	136	238	272
Exercise price ($20 × 100)	2,000	2,000	2,000
Total assumed exercise proceeds	$2,136	$2,238	$2,272

Exhibit 27.6. *Continued.*

Number of Shares
Ended December 31

1992	1993	1994	1995	1996	1997	1998
$2,340	$2,544	$2,748	$2,850	$3,054	$3,224	$3,326
÷ 30	÷ 36	÷ 42	÷ 45	÷ 51	÷ 56	÷ 59
(78)	(71)	(65)	(63)	(60)	(58)	(56)
100	100	100	100	100	100	100
22	29	35	37	40	42	44
$2,476	$2,748	$2,782	$2,952	$3,190	$3,258	$3,360
÷ 34	÷ 42	÷ 43	÷ 48	÷ 55	÷ 57	÷ 60
(73)	(65)	(65)	(62)	(58)	(57)	(56)
100	100	100	100	100	100	100
27	35	35	38	42	43	44

for Primary Earnings per Share
Ended December 31

1992	1993	1994	1995	1996	1997	1998
$ 30	$ 36	$ 42	$ 45	$ 51	$ 56	$ 59
− 20	− 20	− 20	− 20	− 20	− 20	− 20
10	16	22	25	31	36	39
× 100	× 100	× 100	× 100	× 100	× 100	× 100
1,000	1,600	2,200	2,500	3,100	3,600	3,900
× 34%	× 34%	× 34%	× 34%	× 34%	× 34%	× 34%
340	544	748	850	1,054	1,224	1,326
2,000	2,000	2,000	2,000	2,000	2,000	2,000
$2,340	$2,544	$2,748	$2,850	$3,054	$3,224	$3,326

(continued)

Total assumed exercise proceeds for fully diluted earnings per share are computed as follows:

	Assumed Exercise Proceeds Year		
	1989	1990	1991
Windfall tax benefit to be credited to capital			
Ending or average market price of employer's common stock, whichever is greater	$ 25	$ 29	$ 28
Less exercise price	− 20	− 20	− 20
Compensation deductible for tax purposes	5	9	8
Shares issuable	× 100	× 100	× 100
	500	900	800
Effective tax-rate	× 34%	× 34%	× 34%
Windfall tax benefit to be credited to capital	170	306	272
Exercise price ($20 × 100)	2,000	2,000	2,000
Total assumed exercise proceeds	$2,170	$2,306	$2,272

Exhibit 27.6.   *Continued.*

(c) Accounting by Employer for Federal Income Taxes.   When the amount earned by an employee under an SAR is settled by payment of cash, the employer is entitled to a tax deduction for compensation expense, in the year of payment, equal to the amount of cash paid. Accordingly, the entire amount of the tax benefit is credited to previously recorded deferred taxes and/or income tax expense.

When the amount earned by an employee under an SAR is settled by issuance of shares of the employer's capital stock, the employer is entitled to a tax deduction for compensation expense in the year in which the shares to be issued are delivered to the transfer agent. The amount of the deduction is equal to the fair market value of the shares, determined as of the date of delivery to the transfer agent. Thus, the deduction for compensation expense for tax purposes may differ from the amount of compensation expense recognized for financial reporting purposes if shares are delivered to the transfer agent after the measurement date (i.e., the exercise date). In this event, any reduction in income taxes in excess of the reduction that would have occurred if the deduction for income tax purposes had been based on compensation expense recognized for financial reporting purposes should be credited directly to paid-in capital, rather than to income tax expense. Correspondingly, in some instances the deduction for income tax purposes will be less than compensation expense recognized for financial reporting purposes. In such situations, to the extent that tax reductions attributable to awards under the same or similar plans have been credited to paid-in capital, the employer may recognize an additional reduction of income tax expense for financial reporting purposes by charging paid-in capital and crediting income tax expense for an amount equal to the additional tax reduction that would have resulted if compensation expense recognized for financial reporting purposes had been deductible for income tax purposes.

The tax consequences of an SAR are summarized in Exhibit 27.7.

(d) Accounting by Employer for Earnings per Share.   Earnings per share are affected each period from the date of the award of an SAR to the measurement (exercise) date as a result of compensation expense (net of related income taxes) recognized for financial reporting purposes. If the award is expected to be settled in cash, there would be no impact on earnings per share other than the impact due to compensation expense charged against earnings. However, if the award is expected to be settled by issuance of shares of the employer's common stock, additional dilution may occur as a result of the incremental number of shares of the employer's common stock deemed to be outstanding. It should be noted that for SARs

**for Fully Diluted Earnings per Share
Ended December 31**

1992	1993	1994	1995	1996	1997	1998
$ 34	$ 42	$ 43	$ 48	$ 55	$ 57	$ 60
− 20	− 20	− 20	− 20	− 20	− 20	− 20
14	22	23	28	35	37	40
× 100	× 100	× 100	× 100	× 100	× 100	× 100
1,400	2,200	2,300	2,800	3,500	3,700	4,000
× 34%	× 34%	× 34%	× 34%	× 34%	× 34%	× 34%
476	748	782	952	1,190	1,258	1,360
2,000	2,000	2,000	2,000	2,000	2,000	2,000
$2,476	$2,748	$2,782	$2,952	$3,190	$3,258	$3,360

FEDERAL INCOME TAX CONSEQUENCES OF AN SAR

Event	Federal Income Tax Consequences	
	Employer	Employee
Grant of SAR	None	None
Vesting of SAR	None	None
Exercise of SAR	The amount paid (or fair market value of shares issued, determined as of the date they are delivered to the transfer agent) to the employee is deductible as compensation expense	The value of the amount received (equal to the amount deductible by the employer as compensation expense) is taxable as compensation
Disposal of shares acquired, assuming shares are held for:		
One year or less	None	The difference between the sales price and the fair market value of the shares as of the date they were delivered to the transfer agent is taxable as a short-term capital gain or loss
More than one year	None	The difference between the sales price and the fair market value of the shares as of the date they were delivered to the transfer agent is taxable as a long-term capital gain or loss

Exhibit 27.7.   Summary of federal income tax consequences of an SAR.

that "are payable in stock or cash at the election of the enterprise or the employee, the decision of whether such rights or awards are common stock equivalents shall be made according to the terms most likely to be elected based on the facts available each period. It shall be presumed that such rights or awards will be paid in stock, but that presumption may be overcome if past experience or a stated policy provides a reasonable basis to believe that the rights or awards will be paid partially or wholly in cash." The incremental number of shares, if any, deemed to be outstanding is computed under the treasury stock method in accordance with APB Opinion No. 15 and FIN No. 31. Appendix B of FIN No. 31, "Treatment of Stock Compensation Plans in EPS Computations," includes illustrations of the computation of earnings per share for variable plan awards.

(e) Illustration of a Hypothetical Award of an SAR (Granted in Tandem with a Nonstatutory Stock Option)—Accounting and Federal Income Tax Consequences. Exhibit 27.8 shows the consequences of a hypothetical SAR award (granted in tandem with a nonstatutory stock option).

HYPOTHETICAL AWARD OF AN SAR

Assumption

General: An SAR is granted in tandem with a nonstatutory stock option. Exercise of any portion of the SAR cancels an equal portion of the option, and vice versa. If the SAR feature is exercised, the award is payable in shares of the employer's common stock.

Event	Date	Fair Market Value of Employer's Common Stock
Grant of SAR/option	January 1, 1989	$20
Vesting of SAR option (i.e., the date SAR/option becomes exercisable)	December 31, 1992	$23
Expiration date of SAR/option	December 31, 1993	No significance
Exercise of SAR and delivery of shares to the transfer agent	December 31, 1993	$29
Disposal of shares by the employee	June 30, 1995	$31
Fair market value of employer's common stock:	January 1, 1989	$20
	December 31, 1989	21
	December 31, 1990	22
	December 31, 1991	26
	December 31, 1992	23
	December 31, 1993	29
	December 31, 1994	28
	June 30, 1995	31
Number of shares/rights covered by award	1,000	
Exercise price of option/ "base price" of SAR	$20	
Par value of employer's common stock	$ 5	
Employer's effective tax rate	34%	
Employee election	It is assumed that the employee will elect to exercise the SAR (i.e., the variable award).	

(continued)

Exhibit 27.8. Accounting and federal income tax consequences for an SAR award.

ACCOUNTING BY EMPLOYER
(Entries required)

Date	Description	Debit	Credit
December 31, 1989	Compensation expense	$ 250	
	Accrued compensation		$ 250
	Deferred income taxes	85	
	Income tax expense		85
December 31, 1990	Compensation expense	750	
	Accrued compensation		750
	Deferred income taxes	255	
	Income tax expense		255
December 31, 1991	Compensation expense	3,500	
	Accrued compensation		3,500
	Deferred income taxes	1,190	
	Income tax expense		1,190
December 31, 1992	Accrued compensation	1,500	
	Compensation expense		1,500
	Income tax expense	510	
	Deferred income taxes		510
December 31, 1993	Compensation expense	6,000	
	Accrued compensation		6,000
	Deferred income taxes	2,040	
	Income tax expense		2,040
	To record compensation expense and the related federal income tax effect for each of the years in the 5-year period ended December 31, 1993 (see computation)		
December 31, 1993	Accrued compensation	9,000	
	Income taxes payable	3,060	
	Common stock		1,550
	Paid-in capital		7,450
	Deferred income taxes		3,060
	To record issuance of 310 earned shares ($9,000 + $29) and the related adjustments to accrued compensation and deferred income taxes		

Computation of compensation expense and the related federal income tax effect:

	Year Ended December 31				
	1989	1990	1991	1992	1993
Increase in fair market value of employer's capital stock over base price	$ 1	$ 2	$ 6	$ 3	$ 9
Shares covered by SAR	× 1,000	× 1,000	× 1,000	× 1,000	× 1,000
Estimated total compensation cost	$1,000	$2,000	$6,000	$ 3,000	$9,000
Service period elapsed (%)	× 25%	× 50%	× 75%	× 100%	× 100%
Cumulative compensation expense	$ 250	$1,000	$4,500	$ 3,000	$9,000
Accrued compensation—beginning of period	—	− 250	− 1,000	− 4,500	− 3,000
Compensation expense—current period	$ 250	$ 750	$3,500	$(1,500)	$6,000
Effective tax rate	× 34%	× 34%	× 34%	× 34%	× 34%
Tax effect	$ 85	$ 255	$1,190	$ (510)	$2,040

(continued)

Exhibit 27.8. *Continued.*

FEDERAL INCOME TAX CONSEQUENCES

Date	Event	Employer	Employee
January 1, 1989	Grant of award	None	None
December 31, 1992	Vesting of award	None	None
December 31, 1993	Exercise of SARs and delivery of shares to the transfer agent	$9,000 deductible as compensation expense [($29−$20) × (1,000)]	$9,000 taxable as compensation [($29−$20) × (1,000)]
June 30, 1995	Disposal of awarded shares	None	$620 taxable as a long-term capital gain [($31−29) × (310)]; see entries required at December 31, 1993, illustrated below, for computation of the number of shares issued (310)

Earnings per Share

Earnings per share are affected each period from the date of the award to the measurement date as a result of compensation expense (or credits to compensation expense), net of related income tax effects, recognized for financial reporting purposes. Additional dilution (assuming the effect is dilutive) occurs as a result of the incremental number of shares deemed to be outstanding, computed under the treasury stock method, as set forth below.

Computation of incremental number of shares for purposes of computing primary earnings per share[a]:

	Year Ended December 31				
	1989	1990	1991	1992	1993
Accrued compensation—end of period	$250	$1,000	$4,500	$3,000	$9,000
Market price of employer's common stock—end of period	÷21	÷22	÷26	÷23	÷29
Incremental number of shares—end of period	12	45	173	130	310
Incremental number of shares—beginning of period	—	+12	+45	+173	+130
Combined incremental number of shares—beginning and end of period	12	57	218	303	440
	÷2	÷2	÷2	÷2	÷2
Incremental number of shares (average)[b]	6	29	109	152	220

[a]The incremental number of shares determined under this computation is added to the number of shares otherwise included in the computation of primary earnings per share if the effect is dilutive. If the effect is antidilutive, the number of shares issuable upon exercise of the SAR is ignored in the computation of primary earnings per share.

[b]The examples in Appendix B to FIN No. 31 illustrate a slightly different method of computing the incremental number of shares; however, a note to Exhibit 1 indicates, "These computations could also be done using other methods of averaging."

(continued)

Exhibit 27.8. *Continued.*

Computation of incremental number of shares for purposes of computing fully diluted earnings per share[c]:

	Year Ended December 31				
	1989	**1990**	**1991**	**1992**	**1993**
Accrued compensation—end of period	$250	$1,000	$4,500	$3,000	$9,000
Market price of employer's common stock—end of period	÷ 21	÷ 22	÷ 26	÷ 23	÷ 29
Incremental number of shares	12	45	173	130	310

[a]The more dilutive of the incremental number of shares included in the computation of primary earnings per share and the incremental number of shares determined under this computation is used in the computation of fully diluted earnings per share. If the effect is antidilutive, the number of shares issuable upon exercise of the SAR is ignored in the computation of fully diluted earnings per share.

Exhibit 27.8.   *Continued.*

27.17 BOOK VALUE SHARES: DEFINITIONS AND ACCOUNTING BY EMPLOYER

(a) Definition.   A book value share is a share of an employer's capital stock purchased by, or awarded to, an employee pursuant to a capital accumulation plan. Book value shares must be sold back to the company upon retirement or earlier termination of employment, and the arrangement may also permit the employee to sell some or all of his shares back to the company at other fixed or determinable dates. The initial purchase price (or, in the case of a full value award where the employee is not required to pay for the shares, the initial measurement of compensation cost) is equal to the book value of the shares. When the shares are subsequently sold back to the company, the selling price is determined in the same manner as the initial valuation (i.e., book value). An employee-holder of book value shares is entitled to the same voting and dividend rights as other holders of the same class of stock. Shares for which the valuations are based on a multiple of book value, or on another formula based on earnings, are similar to book value shares, and the guidance in this illustration is generally applicable to such shares.

(b) Accounting by Employer for Compensation Expense.   As previously discussed, and as addressed in EITF Issue Nos. 87-23 and 88-6, there is a distinction, for accounting purposes, between book value shares of publicly held and privately held companies. EITF Issue No. 88-6 sets forth the EITF's consensus that ''a book value stock purchase plan of a publicly held company should be considered a performance plan and should be accounted for like a stock appreciation right (SAR).'' In that consensus, the SEC Observer noted that ''for existing book value stock purchase or stock option plans, issuances or grants under those plans made prior to January 28, 1988, need not be accounted for like an SAR if such accounting treatment was not being followed prior to that date and the terms of the book value plan had been adequately disclosed.''

Further, with respect to **options** granted to employees to acquire book value shares (as opposed to selling book value shares to emloyees), the Task Force reached a consensus in EITF Issue No. 87-23 that both publicly held and privately held companies should recognize compensation expense ''for any increase in option value from grant date to exercise date'' (variable plan accounting).

Thus, book value shares issued by publicly held companies, and book value options issued by both publicly and privately held companies, should be accounted for as variable awards. For book value shares purchased by employees of privately held companies, the Task Force reached a consensus in EITF Issue No. 87-23 that ''no compensation expense should be recognized for the increase or decrease in book value during the employment period if the employee makes a substantive investment that will be at risk for a reasonable period of time.''

Because of these differences between publicly and privately held companies in accounting for book value shares, the EITF addressed certain issues in EITF Issue No. 88-6 related to ''the recognition and measurement of compensation expense for private company book value stock purchase and stock option plans in connection with an initial public offering (IPO).''

Although not specifically addressed in the applicable accounting pronouncements, the authors believe that dividends on book value shares should be accounted for in a manner consistent with the accounting applied to the book value shares. Thus, for book value shares of privately held companies on which compensation expense for increases in book value is not being recognized, the authors believe that dividends should be charged to retained earnings in the same manner as dividends on other shares of the same class of stock. For book value shares of publicly held companies on which compensation expense is being recognized for increases in book value and which are classified outside of stockholders' equity (see section 27.14(f)), the authors believe that dividends should be charged to compensation expense.

(c) Accounting by Employer for Federal Income Taxes.   For federal income tax purposes, the employer is entitled to a deduction for increases in the value of book value shares occurring from the date of purchase by the employee to the vesting date (i.e., the date the employee is entitled to sell the shares back to the employer). The employer is not entitled to a deduction for increases in the value of the book value shares that occur subsequent to the vesting date. The income tax treatment for dividends on book value shares is parallel to the treatment of changes in book value; the employer is entitled to a deduction for dividends on book value shares prior to the vesting date, but is not entitled to a deduction for dividends subsequent to the vesting date.

The federal income tax consequences of a book value share award are summarized in Exhibit 27.9.

The above discussion and exhibit are based on the presumption that the employee does not make an election under IRC § 83(b) within 30 days after the acquisition of the book value shares. If such an election is made, the federal income tax consequences are considerably different. When an election under IRC § 83(b) is made by an employee, the employer is entitled to a deduction for income tax purposes in the year of the award, based on the book value of the shares as of the award date; however, the employer is not entitled to any further deductions with respect to subsequent increases in book value of, or dividends paid on, the awarded shares (this applies both to the restricted period and the period subsequent to the vesting date).

Reductions in federal income taxes payable as a result of income tax deductions for increases in the value of book value shares and deductions for dividends on book value shares should be accounted for in a manner consistent with the accounting from such increases in book value and dividends. Thus, income tax benefits resulting from deductions for increases in the value of book value shares and dividends on such shares that are being recognized as compensation expense for financial reporting purposes should be credited to income tax expense. Correspondingly, income tax benefits resulting from deductions for increases in the value of book value shares and dividends on such shares that are **not** being recognized as compensation expense for financial reporting purposes should be credited to paid-in capital.

(d) Accounting by Employer for Earnings per Share.   For publicly held companies, (as well as privately held companies if the conditions specified in EITF Issue No. 87-23 are not met), earnings per share are affected each period from the date of the award to the date the book value shares are sold back to the employer by the amount of compensation expense, net of income taxes, recognized for financial reporting purposes as described above. For privately

FEDERAL INCOME TAX CONSEQUENCES

Event	Employer	Employee
Grant of award and acquisition of shares by employee	None	None
Dividend payments before vesting date	Dividends paid are deductible as compensation expense	Dividends received are taxable as compensation
Vesting date (i.e., the date after which the shares may be sold to the employer at their net book value)	The net book value of the shares, determined as of the vesting date, less the amount originally received for the shares upon sale to the employee is deductible as compensation expense	The net book value of the shares determined as of the vesting date, less the amount originally paid for the shares, is taxable as compensation
Dividend payments subsequent to vesting date	None	Dividends received are taxable as dividend income
Sale of shares back to the employer if held for:		
One year or less	None	The difference between the sales price and the net book value of the shares determined as of the vesting date is taxable as a short-term capital gain or loss
More than one year	None	The difference between the sales price and the net book value of the shares determined as of the vesting date is taxable as a long-term capital gain or loss.

Exhibit 27.9.   Summary of tax consequences of a book value share award.

held companies that elect to present earnings per share information in their financial statements, the authors believe that additional dilution results from the inclusion of the book value shares in the earnings per share computation. For publicly held companies, book value shares that are viewed as a form of mandatorily redeemable equity security (see ASR No. 268 and discussion under section 27.14(f)) should be classified outside of stockholders' equity. As a result such shares do not increase the number of shares used in the computation of earnings per share for publicly held companies; however, as discussed at section 27.17(b), the authors believe that dividends paid on such shares should be charged to compensation expense and would thereby result in an additional reduction of earnings per share.

(e) Illustration of a Hypothetical Book Value Purchase Award Made by a Privately Held Company (No. IRC § 83(b) Election)—Accounting and Federal Income Tax Consequences. Exhibit 27.10 illustrates the federal income tax consequences of a hypothetical book value purchase award made by a privately held company (assuming no election is made under IRC § 83(b)).

HYPOTHETICAL BOOK VALUE PURCHASE AWARD
(Privately Held Company)

Assumptions

General: Common shares are acquired by an employee at their net book value. Acquired shares (book-value shares) can be sold back to the employer by the employee at their net book value 3 years from the date of purchase, or at any time thereafter, but must be resold under termination of employment. If employment is terminated prior to 3 years from the date of purchase, the shares must be resold to the employer at a price equal to the lower of their net book value at date of termination or the amount originally paid for the shares.

Employee does not make an election under IRC § 83(b)		
Date of award and acquisition of shares by employee	January 1, 1989	
Vesting date (i.e., the first date on which shares may be sold back to the employer at net book value)	January 1, 1992	
Number of shares acquired	1,000	
Book value per share of employer's common stock	January 1, 1989	$10
	December 31, 1989	11
	December 31, 1990	13
	December 31, 1991	14
	January 1, 1992	14
	September 30, 1992	17
Effective date as of which employee elects to sell shares back to the employer	September 30, 1992	
Date employer acquires shares from employee (based on book value per share as of September 30, 1992)	November 15, 1992	
Par value of employer's common stock	$5	
Employer's effective tax rate	34%	
Dividends		
Paid between the date shares are acquired by the employee and the vesting date	June 30, 1991	$0.50 per share
Paid between the vesting date and the date shares are sold back to the employer	June 30, 1992	0.50 per share

---

ACCOUNTING BY EMPLOYER
(Entries required)

Date	Description	Debit	Credit
January 1, 1989	Cash	$10,000	
	Common stock		$5,000
	Paid-in capital		5,000
	To record issuance of 1,000 book-value shares ($10 × 1,000)		

Date	Event	Employer	Employee
June 30, 1991	Retained earnings	$ 500	
	Cash		$ 500
	Income taxes payable	170	
	Paid-in capital		170
	To record dividends paid on book-value shares ($0.50 × 1,000) and the related tax benefit (34% (500))		
			(continued)

Exhibit 27.10. Illustration of a book value purchase award.

Date	Event	Employer	Employee
January 1, 1992	Income tax payable Paid-in capital To record reduction of taxes payable due to vesting of book value shares ($4,000 × 34%)	1,360	1,360
June 30, 1992	Retained earnings Cash To record dividends paid on book-value shares ($0.50 × 1,000)	500	500
November 15, 1992	Treasury shares Cash To record acquisition of book-value shares	17,000	17,000

FEDERAL INCOME TAX CONSEQUENCES

Date	Event	Employer	Employee
January 1, 1989	Grant of award and acquisition of shares by employee	None	None
June 30, 1991	Dividend payment	$500 deductible as compensation expense ($0.50 × 1,000)	$500 taxable as compensation ($0.50 × 1.000)
January 1, 1992	Vesting date	$4,000 deductible as compensation expense ($14 − $10) × (1,000)	$4,000 taxable as compensation ($14 − $10) × (1,000)
June 30, 1992	Dividend payment	None	$500 taxable as dividend income ($0.50 × 1,000)
September 30, 1992	Employee elects to sell shares back to employer	None	None
November 15, 1992	Employer acquires shares from employee	None	$3,000 taxable as a long-term capital gain ($17 − $14) × (1,000)

Earnings per Share

Earnings per share are diluted as a result of the inclusion of the book value shares (1,000) in the earnings per share computation. There is no additional dilution, since no compensation expense is recognized for financial reporting purposes.

Exhibit 27.10.   *Continued.*

SOURCES AND SUGGESTED REFERENCES

Accounting Principles Board, "Accounting for Income Taxes," APB Opinion No. 11, AICPA, New York, 1967.

———, "Earnings per Share," APB Opinion No. 15, AICPA, New York, 1969.

——, "Accounting for Stock Issued to Employees," APB Opinion No. 25, AICPA, New York, 1972.

American Institute of Certified Public Accountants, Committee on Accounting Procedure, "Compensation Involved in Stock Option and Stock Purchase Plans," Accounting Research Bulletin No. 43, Chapter 13B, AICPA, New York, 1953.

Financial Accounting Standards Board, "Purchase of Stock Options and Stock Appreciation Rights in a Leveraged Buyout," EITF Issue No. 84-13, FASB, Stamford, CT, 1984.

——, "Stock Option Pyramiding," EITF Issue No. 84-18, FASB, Stamford, CT, 1984.

——, "Permanent Discount Restricted Stock Purchase Plans," EITF Issue No. 84-34, FASB, Stamford, CT, 1984.

——, "Employee Stock Ownership Plan Contribution Funded by a Pension Plan Termination," EITF Issue No. 85-10, FASB, Stamford, CT, 1985.

——, "Use of an Employee Stock Ownership Plan in a Leveraged Buyout," EITF Issue No. 85-11, FASB, Stamford, CT, 1985.

——, "Business Combinations: Settlement of Stock Options and Awards," EITF Issue No. 85-45, FASB, Stamford, CT, 1985.

——, "Income Statement Treatment of Income Tax Benefit for Employee Stock Ownership Plan Dividends," EITF Issue No. 86-4, FASB, Stamford, CT, 1986.

——, "Measurement of Excess Contributions to a Defined Contribution Plan or Employee Stock Ownership Plan," EITF Issue No. 86-27, FASB, Stamford, CT, 1986.

——, "Adjustments Relating to Stock Compensation Plans," EITF Issue No. 87-6, FASB, Stamford, CT, 1987.

——, "Book Value Stock Purchase Plans," EITF Issue No. 87-23, FASB, Stamford, CT, 1987.

——, "Stock Compensation Issues Related to Market Decline," EITF Issue No. 87-33, FASB, Stamford, CT, 1987.

——, "Book Value Stock Plans in an Initial Public Offering," EITF Issue No. 88-6, FASB, Norwalk, CT, 1988.

——, "Effect of Unallocated Shares in an Employee Stock Ownership Plan on Accounting for Business Combinations," EITF Issue No. 88-27, FASB, Norwalk, CT, 1988.

——, "Nonlevel Payments of Employee Stock Ownership Plan Debt," EITF Issue No. 89-8, FASB, Norwalk, CT, 1989.

——, "Sponsor's Recognition of Employee Stock Ownership Plan Debt," EITF Issue No. 89-10, FASB, Norwalk, CT, 1989.

——, "Accounting for Stock Appreciation Rights and Other Variable Stock Option or Award Plans," FASB Interpretation No. 28, FASB, Stamford, CT, 1978.

——, "Treatment of Stock Compensation Plans in EPS Computations," FASB Interpretation No. 31, FASB, Stamford, CT, 1980.

——, "Determining the Measurement Date for Stock Option, Purchase, and Award Plans Involving Junior Stock," FASB Interpretation No. 38, FASB, Stamford, CT, 1984.

——, "Accounting for the Conversion of Stock Options into Incentive Stock Options as a Result of the Economic Recovery Tax Act of 1981," FASB Technical Bulletin No. 82-2, FASB, Stamford, CT, 1982.

——, "Suspension of the Reporting of Earnings per Share and Segment Information by Nonpublic Enterprises," Statement of Financial Accounting Standards No. 21, FASB, Stamford, CT, 1978.

——, "Accounting for Income Taxes," Statement of Financial Accounting Standards No. 96, FASB, Stamford, CT, 1987.

Securities and Exchange Commission, "Codification of Financial Reporting Policies," Financial Reporting Release No. 1, § 211 (ASR No. 268), SEC, Washington, DC, 1982.

PART VI

SPECIAL AREAS OF ACCOUNTING

CHAPTER 28

PROSPECTIVE FINANCIAL STATEMENTS

Don M. Pallais, CPA

CONTENTS

TYPES OF PROSPECTIVE FINANCIAL STATEMENTS

28.1 DEFINITIONS. **Prospective financial information** is future-oriented; that is, financial information about the future. **Prospective financial statements** are future-oriented presentations that present, at a minimum, certain specific financial information.

The AICPA *Guide for Prospective Financial Statements* (1986) defines prospective financial statements as presentations of an entity's financial position, results of operations, and changes in financial position for the future. In addition to the AICPA Guide, there is also a Statement on Standards for Accountants' Services on Prospective Financial Information, "Financial Forecasts and Projections" (AICPA, 1986), which establishes standards for accountants' services. Since all the guidance in that statement is duplicated in the AICPA Guide, this chapter refers only to the Guide.

Entity means an individual, organization, enterprise, or other unit for which financial statements could be prepared in conformity with GAAP. It is not necessary for the entity to have been formed at the time the prospective financial statements are prepared—prospective financial statements may be prepared for entities that may be formed in the future. In fact, before committing capital to proposed entities, prospective investors or lenders often insist on seeing prospective financial statements covering the early years of proposed operations.

Although the AICPA Guide defines prospective financial statements as presentations of future financial position, results of operations, and changes in financial position, three full financial statements are not always required. Prospective financial statements may be presented in summarized or condensed form. A presentation of future financial data would be considered to be a prospective financial statement if it disclosed at least the following items, to the extent they apply to the entity and would be presented in the entity's historical financial statements for the period covered:

1. Sales or gross revenue.
2. Gross profit or cost of sales.
3. Unusual or infrequently occurring items.
4. Provision for income taxes.
5. Discontinued operations or extraordinary items.
6. Income from continuing operations.
7. Net income.
8. Primary and fully diluted earnings per share (required only when disclosure is also required for the entity's historical financial statements).
9. Significant changes in financial position (that is, significant balance sheet changes not otherwise disclosed in the presentation).

When an entity chooses to present its prospective financial statements in the format of three full financial statements, a prospective statement of cash flows is generally used instead of a prospective statement of changes in financial position.

The definition of prospective financial statements does not specify the **length** of the future period. For a presentation to be prospective, however, **some** of the period covered must be in the future even though a part of the period may have expired. Thus, a calendar 19X1 presentation done on December 30, 19X1, would still, in theory, be a prospective presentation since there would still be an unexpired day in the period. Determining the period to be covered by prospective financial statements is discussed in more detail in section 28.9(b).

There are two kinds of prospective financial statements: financial forecasts and financial projections. In practice, though, prospective financial statements are often given other names, such as "budgets," "business plans," and "studies."

Although the terms **forecast** and **projections** are sometimes used interchangeably in popular usage, in the technical accounting literature, forecasts and projections differ in what they purport to represent. Forecasts represent expectations, whereas projections are hypothetical analyses.

(a) Financial Forecasts.   Financial forecasts are defined as prospective financial statements that present, to the best of management's knowledge and belief, an entity's expected financial position, results of operations, and changes in financial position based on management's assumptions reflecting conditions it expects to exist and the course of action it expects to take. In some cases forecasts can be prepared by persons other than current management, such as a potential acquirer of the entity, but usually the person (or persons) who takes responsibility for the assumptions is someone who expects to be in a position to influence the entity's operations during the forecast period. The AICPA Guide refers to the person who takes responsibility for the assumptions as the **responsible party.**

Despite the inherent uncertainty of future events and the softness of prospective data, a forecast cannot be prepared without a **reasonably objective basis.** That is, sufficiently objective assumptions must be capable of being developed to present a forecast. Without a reasonably objective basis, management has no grounds for any expectations; all it would have is guesses.

The determination of whether a reasonably objective basis for a forecast exists is primarily an exercise in judgment. The key question is whether assumptions, based on the entity's plans, made by persons who are informed about the industry in which the entity operates would generally fall within a relatively narrow range. If so, there may be a reasonably objective basis for the forecast. On the other hand, if there is so much uncertainty regarding significant assumptions that consensus would be unlikely to be reached, there may not be a reasonably objective basis, precluding preparation of a forecast (although a projection could be developed). For example, there would be no reasonably objective basis to forecast the winnings of a thoroughbred being reared to race.

If prospective financial data are necessary, but no reasonably objective basis exists to present a forecast, management might hypothesize the assumption that is not subject to reasonable estimation and call the presentation a **projection** or quantify only those assumptions that have a reasonably objective basis and prepare a **partial presentation.** However, both of these alternatives are limited in their usefulness (see sections 28.3–28.6 for a further discussion).

Exhibit 28.1 presents factors to consider in determining whether there is a reasonably objective basis to present a forecast.

Occasionally, an entity may need to present a forecast but cannot do so because of an uncertainty about the **actions** the **users** of the forecast may take. For example, an assumption may relate to passage of a referendum when the forecast is to be used by voters deciding on the

SUFFICIENTLY OBJECTIVE ASSUMPTIONS—MATTERS TO CONSIDER		
Basis	**Less Objective**	**More Objective**
Economy	Subject to uncertainity	Stable
Industry	Emerging/unstable—high rate of business failure	Mature/stable
Entity		
• Operating history	New/no operating history	Seasoned company/stable operating history
• Customer base	Diverse, changing customer group	Stable customer group
• Financial condition	Weak financial position Poor operating results	Stong financial position Good operating results
Management Experience With:		
Industry	Inexperienced	Experienced
• The business and its products	Inexperienced/high turnover of key personnel	Experienced
Product or Service		
• Market	New/uncertain market	Existing/stable market
• Technology	Rapidly changing	Relatively stable
• Experience	New products or expanding product line	Relatively stable products
Competing Assumptions	Wide range of possible outcomes	Relatively narrow range of possible outcomes
Dependency of Assumptions on the Outcome of Forecasted Results	More dependency	Less dependency

Exhibit 28.1.   Determining a reasonably objective basis. *Source*: **Financial Forecasts & Projections Task Force, Proposed SOP, "Questions and Answers on *Reasonably Objective Basis* and Other Issues Affecting Prospective Financial Statements."**

referendum. In those cases, despite the high level of uncertainty, management may select one of the alternatives as its assumption and then call the presentation a forecast if:

1. The assumption is subject to only two possible outcomes (an either/or situation).
2. The outcome of that assumption is dependent on the actions of the users of the presentation.
3. The alternative selected is not unreasonable on its face.
4. The presentation discloses that the forecast represents management's expectations only if the prospective action of users takes place.

Regardless of the need for a reasonably objective basis and management's efforts to present its expectations, a forecast is not a **prediction.** A forecast is not judged on whether, in hindsight, it came true. A forecast is a presentation intended to provide financial information regarding management's plans and expectations for the future. It augments information in historical financial statements and other sources of data to help prospective investors, lenders, or others make better financial decisions.

(b) Financial Projections.   Financial projections present, to the best of management's knowledge and belief, an entity's future financial position, results of operations, and changes in financial position given the occurrence of one or more **hypothetical assumptions.** Financial projections are sometimes prepared to analyze alternative courses of action, as in response to a question such as "What would happen if . . . ?"

The hypothetical assumptions in a projection are those that are not necessarily expected to occur but are consistent with the reason the projection was prepared. There is no explicit limit on the number of hypothetical assumptions used in a projection. However, since a projection is a presentation of expectations based on the occurrence of the hypothetical assumptions; a presentation of all hypothetical assumptions (or in which all significant assumptions have been hypothesized) would not be a projection because it depicts no dependent expectations. Thus, at some point the number of hypothetical assumptions may grow so large that the presentation is not a projection.

Hypothetical assumptions need not be reasonable or plausible; in fact, they may even be improbable if their use is consistent with the reason the projection is prepared. For example, it is generally improbable that a hotel would experience 100% occupancy. But use of that occupancy rate as a hypothetical assumption would be appropriate if the projection were prepared to demonstrate the maximum return on investment of a hotel. However, there are special disclosure rules when hypothetical assumptions are improbable (see section 28.13(b)).

All the nonhypothetical assumptions in a projection are expected to occur **if the hypothetical assumption occurred,** which may be different from expecting the nonhypothetical assumption actually to occur. For example, a company may hypothesize adding a new product line and intend to use the resulting projection in deciding whether to do so. As a result of the assumption about a new product line, the projection might include assumptions about hiring new sales personnel. Management may not actually expect to hire new sales personnel, but it would hire them if it started a new product line; thus the assumption is not actually expected, but it is expected given the occurrence of the hypothetical assumption.

28.2 OTHER PRESENTATIONS THAT LOOK LIKE PROSPECTIVE FINANCIAL STATE-MENTS.   A number of presentations look like prospective financial statements but are not, including **presentations for wholly expired periods, partial presentations, pro forma financial statements,** and **financial analyses.**

(a) Presentations for Wholly Expired Periods.   Prospective financial statements are presentations for a future period. If the period covered by a presentation is wholly expired, such as a prior-year budget, it is not a prospective financial statement.

(b) Partial Presentations.   Partial presentations are presentations of prospective financial information that omit one or more minimum items required of prospective financial statements (see section 28.1). They are not subject to the same rules as prospective financial statements.

(c) Pro Formas.   Pro forma financial statements are historical financial statements adjusted for a prospective transaction. Although one transaction has not occurred at the time of presentation, the statements are essentially historical ones. In essence, such statements answer the question "What would have happened if . . . ?" Guidance for accountants' reports on pro forma presentations can be found in the SSAE "Reporting on Pro Forma Financial Information" (1988).

(d) Financial Analyses.   Financial analyses are defined in the AICPA Guide as presentations in which the independent accountant rather than management develops and takes responsibility for the assumptions. Such presentations are normally a by-product of a consulting engagement in which management asks the accountant to analyze a condition and make recommendations about possible or prudent courses of action.

These analyses are not prospective financial statements because the party who takes responsibility for the assumptions (the accountant) is not, and does not expect to be, in a position to influence the entity's operations in the future period. If, however, management adopts the assumptions used, it may present the statements as a forecast or projection.

LIMITATIONS ON THE USE OF PROSPECTIVE FINANCIAL STATEMENTS

28.3 HOW PROSPECTIVE FINANCIAL STATEMENTS ARE USED.   The use of prospective financial statements is neither required nor recommended by AICPA literature. Nonetheless, they are used for many purposes in practice. For example, they are used by management in internal planning, by potential suppliers of capital in making investment decisions, and by government agencies for monitoring or approving an entity's operations.

The AICPA Guide (§ 210) categorizes all the potential uses of prospective financial statements into two broad classes: **general use,** which refers to passive users, and **limited use,** which refers to use by management only or use by persons who are negotiating directly with management.

The AICPA Guide states that forecasts are appropriate for either general or limited use; projections are generally appropriate only for limited use.

Unlike SEC registration rules, the type of use is not dependent on the **number** of users of the prospective financial statements. A user is considered a limited user if it is negotiating directly with the entity; if it is not, it is a general user. Thus, even one passive user would constitute general use; whereas an entity may negotiate directly with numerous users, each of whom can change the terms of the transaction, and each would be considered a limited user.

28.4 GENERAL USE.   General use means use of the prospective financial statements by persons who are **not** negotiating directly with management. General users are passive users; that is, they can review the prospective financial statements to determine their own course of action, but they cannot affect the company's actions or the terms of their investment. For example, after reviewing an entity's prospective financial statements, a potential investor in a limited partnership can decide whether to invest in it and if so, how much to invest, but he cannot change the terms of the investment; thus he would be considered a general user. If he can change the terms of the investment, he would be considered a limited user.

Because general users cannot negotiate the terms of their involvement with the entity, their information needs are much like those of shareholders in a public company. To make informed decisions, general users would ordinarily be served best by a presentation of management's estimate of future financial results—a forecast.

A presentation of results based on a hypothetical assumption that does not reflect management's expectations (that is, a projection) would not serve general users because such a presentation would only tell them what is **not** necessarily expected to happen, not what is. This would be analogous to providing shareholders with pro forma financial statements including transactions that did not occur instead of with historical financial statements.

Accordingly, financial projections are not ordinarily issued to general users unless the projections supplement a forecast **for the period covered by the forecast.** Thus, general users may benefit from an analysis of a hypothetical course of action when it supplements a presentation of management's expectations for that period, but not when it stands alone as the only presentation of prospective results for a period.

That forecasts are appropriate for general use, of course, does not suggest that they will meet all the users' information needs. Potential investors or lenders often need to consider other information as well before making economic decisions, just as they do when presented with historical financial statements.

28.5 LIMITED USE.   Limited use of prospective financial statements means use by the entity itself or use by persons with whom the entity is negotiating directly. **Negotiating** is an active concept. It includes more than the user's ability to ask questions of the entity; it refers to the user's ability to affect the terms of its business with the entity beyond merely deciding whether to participate and the amount of its participation.

There is no limit on the potential number of limited users in a particular circumstance except for the limit of the number of parties that management can practically negotiate with at any one time. It is also unnecessary to specifically identify the limited users at the time the prospective financial statements are prepared.

Because limited users can negotiate the terms of their involvement and challenge or propose changes to the hypothetical assumptions, they can use presentations that don't present management's best estimates. Accordingly, projections are often useful for limited users.

Similarly, because limited users can demand additional information as a condition of their participation (or, when there is a lack of needed information, increase the cost of capital in response to a perceived increase in risk), it may also be appropriate for limited users to use **partial presentations** or **financial analyses.**

Of course, financial forecasts are appropriate for limited users as well as general users.

28.6 INTERNAL USE.   Internal use means use of the prospective financial statements only by the entity itself. It is a type of limited use. Limitation of the prospective financial statements to internal use does not affect the type of statements that are appropriate in the circumstances, but it affects the type of services that an independent accountant can perform on them. This is discussed in more detail in section 28.33.

DEVELOPING PROSPECTIVE FINANCIAL STATEMENTS

28.7 GENERAL GUIDELINES.   Section 300 of the AICPA Guide (1986) presents 11 guidelines for **preparation of prospective financial statements.** Although forecasts and projections can be developed without adhering to those guidelines, using them often results in more reliable prospective data.

The AICPA guidelines are listed in Exhibit 28.2. They apply to projections as well as forecasts, though in many cases they do not apply to the **hypothetical assumptions** in projections.

A general approach to developing prospective financial statements involves three steps:

1. Identifying key factors.
2. Developing assumptions for each key factor.
3. Assembling the prospective financial statements.

28.8 IDENTIFYING KEY FACTORS.   The AICPA Guide (§ 315.01) states: "Key factors are those significant matters upon which an entity's future results are expected to depend. Those factors are basic to the entity's operations and serve as a foundation for the prospective financial statements."

Key factors vary by entity and industry. They are general matters such as manufacturing labor, sales, or capital asset needs. A knowledge of the entity's industry and proposed operations is necessary to identify all the key factors that will form the basis for the prospective financial statements.

Financial forecasts should be prepared in good faith.

Financial forecasts should be prepared with appropriate care by qualified personnel.

Financial forecasts should be prepared using appropriate accounting principles.

The process used to develop financial forecasts should provide for seeking out the best information that is reasonably available at the time.

The information used in preparing financial forecasts should be consistent with the plans of the entity.

Key factors should be identified as a basis for assumptions.

Assumptions used in preparing financial forecasts should be appropriate.

The process used to develop financial forecasts should provide the means to determine the relative effect of variations in the major underlying assumptions.

The process used to develop financial forecasts should provide adequate documentation of both the financial forecasts and the process used to develop them.

The process used to develop financial forecasts should include, where appropriate, the regular comparison of the financial forecasts with attained results.

The process used to prepare financial forecasts should include adequate review and approval by the responsible party at the appropriate levels of authority.

Exhibit 28.2.   Guidelines for preparation of prospective financial statements. *Source:* AICPA, *Guide for Prospective Financial Statements* (§ 300, pp. 22–23).

28.9 DEVELOPING ASSUMPTIONS.   Assumptions are developed for each key factor. In a **forecast,** the assumptions represent management's best estimate of future conditions and courses of action. In a **projection,** the hypothetical assumptions are consistent with the purpose of the projection, and all the other assumptions represent management's best estimate of future conditions and courses of action **given the occurrence of the hypothetical assumptions.**

Approaches to developing assumptions range from highly sophisticated mathematical models to estimates based on personal opinion. Regardless of the approach taken to quantify the assumptions, to determine whether the assumptions are appropriate, management considers whether:

1. There appears to be a rational relationship between the assumptions and the underlying facts and circumstances.
2. Assumptions have been developed for each key factor.
3. Assumptions have been developed without undue optimism or pessimism.
4. Assumptions are consistent with the entity's plans and expectations.
5. Assumptions are consistent with each other.
6. Individual assumptions make sense in the context of the prospective financial statements taken as a whole.

It is not always necessary to obtain support for each significant assumption, but developing support often results in more reliable prospective financial information. In any case, the significant considerations in developing a forecast are (1) whether management has a reasonably objective basis (see section 28.1(a)) to base its expectations on and (2) whether the assumptions are consistent with its expectations.

(a) Mathematical Models.   Forecasts may be based on sophisticated mathematical techniques such as regression analysis. However, merely extrapolating historical results into the future does not result in a forecast. To forecast, management satisfies itself that it has identified the conditions and course of action it intends to take in the future period. If, based on consideration of key factors, management believes that historical conditions are indicative of future results, it then might use an estimation technique based on historical results.

(b) Length of the Prospective Period.   The AICPA Guide does not specify the appropriate **length** of the period to be covered by prospective financial statements. It does state, however, that in determining the appropriate length, management should consider both the needs of the user and its own ability to estimate future financial results.

The AICPA Guide (§ 400.32) states that to be meaningful to users, a forecast or projection should include at least one full year of normal operations. For example, an entity forecasting a major acquisition would present at least the first full year following the acquisition; a newly formed entity would show at least the first full year of normal operations in addition to its start-up period.

When the entity has a long operating cycle or when long-term results are necessary to evaluate the investment consequences involved, it may be necessary to forecast farther into the future to meet the needs of users.

Uncertainty increases as to periods farther in the future. At some point, the underlying assumptions become so subjective that no reasonably objective basis exists to present a forecast.

The AICPA Financial Forecasts and Projections Task Force has proposed an SOP "Questions and Answers on *Reasonably Objective Basis* and Other Issues Affecting Perspective Financial Statements" (1990), which would establish a guideline for the point at which results become too subjective to estimate. The proposed SOP states that it ordinarily would be difficult to establish that a reasonably objective basis exists for a financial forecast extending beyond 3 to 5 years.

The proposed SOP recognizes that, in some cases, forecasts can be presented for longer periods, such as when long-term contracts exist that specify the timing and the amount of revenue and costs can be controlled within reasonable limits (as in the case of real estate projects with long-term leases). It also recognizes that in some cases it may be hard to justify even a 3-year forecast, such as for certain start-up or high technology companies.

The **SEC rules** are generally more restrictive than the AICPA's. For prospective financial statements included in SEC filings, the SEC has stated that "[F]or certain companies in certain industries a [forecast] covering a two or three year period may be entirely reasonable. Other companies may not have a reasonable basis for [forecasts] beyond the current year" (Reg. 229.10(b)(2)).

In determining how far into the future it can forecast, management considers the key factors and resulting assumptions for each future period presented. Considering them in detail for, say, 3 years and merely extrapolating the results for an additional 7 years beyond that does not result in a 10-year forecast, but in a 3-year forecast and a 7-year projection.

28.10 ASSEMBLING THE PROSPECTIVE FINANCIAL STATEMENTS.   Assembling the prospective financial statements involves converting the assumptions into prospective amounts and presenting the amounts and assumptions in conformity with AICPA presentation guidelines. Those guidelines are discussed in more detail in the following sections.

PRESENTATION AND DISCLOSURE OF PROSPECTIVE FINANCIAL STATEMENTS

28.11 AUTHORITATIVE GUIDANCE.   The primary source of guidance for presentation and disclosure of financial forecasts and projections is § 400 of the AICPA Guide. In the absence of FASB pronouncements, the Guide establishes the equivalent of GAAP for prospective financial statements.

Although the Guide establishes guidelines for presentation and disclosure, it does not require or recommend the presentation of prospective financial statements in any circumstance. The decision to present prospective financial statements is generally management's, based on its need and desires and those of potential financial statement users.

Other bodies have also established rules concerning presentation and disclosure of forecasts and projections. For example, the SEC, the North American Security Analysts Association, and individual state securities commissions have established rules that are applicable in certain situations. Issuers of prospective financial statements used in offering statements should be aware of those rules as well, but it is beyond the scope of this chapter to discuss all of them.

Occasionally, potential users of prospective financial statements also require a specific form or content for the statements. For example, users may specify the level of detail presented or the period covered, or they may require the completion of prescribed forms. Issuers of prospective financial statements should consider how those requirements compare with those in the AICPA Guide and whether compliance with the user's requirements may cause difficulties in obtaining an independent accountant's services on the statements.

28.12 FORM OF PROSPECTIVE FINANCIAL STATEMENTS.   Unlike historical financial statements, the **form** of prospective financial statements is flexible. Flexibility is permitted to present the most useful information in the circumstances.

Presenting prospective financial statements in the same form as the historical financial statements expected to be issued at the end of the prospective period facilitates later comparison. Accordingly, if later comparison is expected, an entity may issue a prospective balance sheet, income statement, and statement of cash flows. The AICPA Guide discusses a prospective statement of changes in financial position because it was written before SFAS No. 95, "Statement of Cash Flows" (1987), was issued. However, it is generally acknowledged in practice that disclosure of prospective changes in financial position is accomplished by presenting a prospective statement of cash flows.

If no later comparison is intended, or if more aggregated data are desired, the prospective financial statements may be presented in a summarized or condensed format. The amount of condensation or summarization is flexible as long as the following minimum items, to the extent they are applicable and would be presented in the historical financial statements, are either presented or otherwise derivable from the presentation:

1. Sales or gross revenue.
2. Gross profit or cost of sales.
3. Unusual or infrequently occurring items.
4. Provision for income taxes.
5. Discontinued operations or extraordinary items.
6. Income from continuing operations.
7. Net income.
8. Primary and fully diluted earnings per share.
9. Significant changes in financial position.

Exhibit 28.3 illustrates a condensed format for a financial forecast.

(a) Amounts Presented.   The prospective financial statements may be presented in terms of single-point estimates or ranges.

Ranges are sometimes presented when management wants to present a forecast but cannot refine its estimate of expected results sharply enough to present a single point as its best estimate. If the prospective financial statements are presented in terms of ranges, the range is not selected in a biased manner. That is, one end of the range is not significantly more likely than the other. In addition, the range is not characterized as representing the best and worst cases, since actual results might fall outside of the range.

XYZ COMPANY, INC.
Summarized Financial Forecast
Year Ending December 31, 19X3
(in thousands except per-share amounts)

| | Forecasted 19X3 | Comparative Historical Information* | |
		19X2	19X1
Sales	$101,200	$91,449	$79,871
Gross profit	23,700	21,309	19,408
Income tax expense	3,400	3,267	2,929
Net income	4,500	3,949	3,214
Earnings per share	4.73	4.14	3.37
Significant anticipated changes in financial position:			
Cash provided by operations	4,100	3,103	4,426
Net increase (decrease) in long-term borrowings	3,400	300	(300)
Dividend			
(per share 19X3: $1.50; 19X2: $1.35; 19X1: $1.00)	1,400	1,288	954
Additions to plant and equipment	4,400	2,907	2,114
Increase (decrease) in cash	1,400	(334)	1,017

See accompanying Summary of Significant Forecast Assumptions and Accounting Policies [not illustrated in exhibit].

*Comparative historical information is not part of the minimum presentation.

Exhibit 28.3.   Illustration of condensed format for prospective financial statements. *Source:* **AICPA,** *Guide for Prospective Financial Statements* (§ 410.05, p. 56).

Any of the following formats for a forecast might be acceptable.

Single-point estimate:

Sales	$XXX
Cost of sales	XXX

Range (from X to Z) showing an intermediate point (Y):

	X	Y	Z
Sales	$XXX	$YYY	$ZZZ
Cost of sales	XXX	YYY	ZZZ

Range showing a one line item only; example assumes the range is based on a forecasted range of sales prices and demand is inelastic:

Sales	$XXX—$YYY
Cost of sales	$XXX

(b) Titles.   The **titles** of financial forecasts should include the word "forecast" or "forecasted." Financial projections' titles should refer to the hypothetical assumptions. Titles such as "budget" are avoided since they afford the reader no indication whether the presentation is a forecast or a projection.

28.13 DISCLOSURES.   In addition to the items listed at the beginning of section 28.12, the AICPA Guide requires that the following matters be **disclosed** in prospective financial statements:

1. Description of what the presentation intends to depict.
2. Summary of significant assumptions.
3. Summary of significant accounting policies.

Each page of the prospective financial statements should direct the readers' attention to the summaries of significant assumptions and accounting policies. A legend such as "The accompanying summaries of significant assumptions and accounting policies are an integral part of the financial forecast" or "See accompanying summaries of significant assumptions and accounting policies" is generally used.

(a) Description of the Presentation.   The prospective financial statements should include a description of what management intends the statements to present, a statement that the assumptions are based on management's judgment at the time the prospective information was prepared, and a caveat that the prospective results may not be achieved.

The description is usually presented as the introduction to the summary of significant assumptions.

The **introduction** to the assumptions for a financial forecast would disclose the necessary information as follows:

> This financial forecast presents, to the best of management's knowledge and belief, the Company's expected financial position, results of operations, and cash flows* for the forecast period. Accordingly, the forecast reflects its judgment, as of [date], the date of this forecast, the expected conditions and its expected course of action. The assumptions disclosed herein are those that management believes are significant to the forecast. There will usually be differences between the forecasted and actual results, because events and circumstances frequently do not occur as expected, and those differences may be material.

---

*If the presentation is summarized or condensed, this might read ". . . summary of the Company's expected results of operations and cash flows. . . ."

The introduction to the summary of significant assumptions for a financial projection would be similar to that for a forecast except that it would clearly explain the **special purpose** and **limitations** on the usefulness of the presentation. Such an introduction might read as follows:

> This financial projection is based on sales volume at maximum productive capacity and presents, to the best of management's knowledge and belief, the Company's expected financial position, results of operations, and cash flows* for the projection period if such volume were attained. Accordingly, the projection reflects its judgment, as of [date], the date of this projection, the expected conditions and its expected course of action if such sales volume were experienced. The presentation is designed to provide information to the Company's board of directors concerning the maximum profitability that might be achieved if current production were expanded through the addition of a third production shift and should not be considered to be a presentation of expected future results. Accordingly, this projection may not be useful for other purposes. The assumptions disclosed herein are those that management believes are significant to the projection. Management considers it highly unlikely that the stated sales volume will be experienced during the projection period. Further, even if the stated sales volume were attained, there will usually be

differences between the projected and actual results, because events and circumstances frequently do not occur as expected, and those differences may be material.

_____

*If the presentation is summarized or condensed, this might read ". . . summary of the Company's expected results of operations and changes in financial position. . . ."

If the presentation is shown as a range, the introduction also makes it clear that presentation is shown as a range, that the range represents managements' expectations, and that there is no assurance that actual results will fall within the range. A sample introduction follows:

> This financial forecast presents, to the best of management's knowledge and belief, the Company's expected financial position, results of operations, and cash flows for the forecast period at occupancy rates of 75% and 95% of available apartments. Accordingly, the forecast reflects its judgment, as of [date], the date of this forecast, the expected conditions and its expected course of action at each occupancy rate. The assumptions disclosed herein are those that management believes are significant to the forecast. Management reasonably expects, to the best of its knowledge and belief, that the actual occupancy rates achieved will be within the range shown; however, there can be no assurance that it will. Further, even if the actual occupancy rate is within the range shown, there will usually be differences between the forecasted and actual results, because events and circumstances frequently do not occur as expected, and those differences may be material, and the actual results may be outside the range presented by the forecast.

(b) Significant Assumptions.   The assumptions form the basis for the prospective financial statements; for the statements to be meaningful to users, the assumptions should be disclosed.

Numerous assumptions are made in developing prospective financial statements. Only **significant assumptions** are required to be disclosed. Significance is generally considered to be measured in terms of the magnitude of an assumption's effect on the prospective financial statements.

Assumptions, however, may be considered significant even though they may not have a direct and large dollar effect on the statements. Those assumptions, which need to be disclosed as well, include:

1. Sensitive assumptions, that is, assumptions about which there is a reasonable possibility of the occurrence of a variation that may significantly affect the prospective results.
2. Significantly changed conditions, that is, assumptions about anticipated conditions that are expected to be significantly different from current conditions.
3. Hypothetical assumptions used in a projection.
4. Other matters deemed important to the statements or their interpretation.

The form and placement of assumptions is flexible and can be based on management's judgment in the circumstances. The guiding principle is that the disclosure is understandable by the persons expected to use the statements.

Disclosure of the basis or rationale underlying the assumptions assists users in understanding and making decisions based on prospective financial statements. Such disclosure is recommended, but not required, by the AICPA Guide.

The following examples show the form of disclosure of significant assumptions that might be appropriate in various circumstances.

As a footnote in a formal presentation:

2. *Sales.* Sales of the Company's product in 19X2 are expected to increase 20% over those experienced in 19X1 ($1,000,000).

As a footnote in a formal presentation, including basis and rationale:

2. *Sales.* Based on commitments received and its current expansion into the Midwest market, management expects unit sales to increase by 15% over the number of units sold in 19X1. In addition, the Company expects to increase sales prices by an average of 5% over the year to cover expected increases in raw material costs. Increasing sales prices is not expected to adversely affect units sold since raw material cost increases will affect the entire industry and management anticipates industry-wide price increases. (Disclosure might also include discussion of other product lines, marketing plans, and other related information.)

Informal, shown on the face of the statements:

Sales (units up 15% over 19X1, price up 5%) $1,200,000

Informal, shown as output of factors used in a computer spreadsheet:

Sales = 1.2* 19X1Sal

The appropriateness of each approach would depend on the expected use of the prospective financial statements. The formal presentation that includes the basis and rationale would be most useful for general users; the informal printout of factors from a spreadsheet might be appropriate, and least costly to prepare, for internal use.

The disclosure of significant assumptions should also indicate which assumptions are **hypothetical** and which are **particularly sensitive.**

The **hypothetical** assumptions used in a projection should be specifically identified. In addition, if any of the hypothetical assumptions are considered **improbable,** the disclosure should indicate that.

Particularly sensitive assumptions are those for which there is a relatively high probability of variation that would significantly affect the prospective financial statements. The presentation should indicate which assumptions appeared to be particularly sensitive at the time of preparation of the statements (even though hindsight might indicate that others actually were particularly sensitive).

The disclosure of sensitivity is flexible. Below are examples of disclosures that might be appropriate in the circumstances.

With sensitivity quantified:

9. *Interest Expense.* The forecast assumes that the debt to be placed will carry an interest rate of 10%; however, the rate will not be determined until closing. For each $\frac{1}{4}$ of 1% that the actual interest rate differs from the rate assumed, forecasted income before income taxes would be raised or lowered by $25,000 and after-tax cash flow would change by approximately $16,000. If the rate exceeds $11\frac{1}{4}$%, the forecast would not indicate sufficient cash flow from the new project to service the debt.

Without sensitivity quantification:

9. *Interest Expense.* The forecast assumes the debt to be placed will carry an interest rate of 10%. The actual rate will not be determined until closing and may be higher or lower. To the extent that the actual rate exceeds 10%, forecasted income would be adversely affected.

Informal, printout of factors in computer spreadsheet:

Int exp = 0.1*debt! part. sensitive

(c) Significant Accounting Principles.   The prospective financial statements should include disclosure of the **significant accounting principles** used in the statements. The basis of accounting and the accounting principles used in the prospective statements are generally those that are expected to be used during the prospective period. Thus, if the prospective statements accompany historical financial statements, this disclosure may be accomplished by referring the reader to the appropriate note in the historical statements.

If the basis of accounting used in the prospective statements is a **comprehensive basis of accounting other than GAAP,** the basis used should be disclosed as well as that it is different from GAAP.

If the basis of accounting used is different from that expected to be used in the historical financial statements for the prospective period (such as presenting cash-flow forecast for an entity that uses GAAP for its historical financial statements), the use of a different basis of accounting in the prospective statements should be disclosed. The differences in prospective results that are caused by the use of the different basis would usually be reconciled in the statements unless the reconciliation would not be useful.

If the accounting principles used differ from those expected to be used (such as in a projection that analyzes the effect of a possible change in accounting principles), the use of a different principle in the projection should be disclosed. The results in the projection may also be reconciled to those that would result from using the principle used in the historical financial statements.

If management expects to change an accounting principle during the prospective period, the change in principle should be reflected in the prospective financial statements the same way it would be in the historical financial statements covering the prospective period. Other specific disclosures required for historical financial statements, such as those regarding pensions and income taxes, are not required for prospective financial statements.

(d) Other Matters.   The **date** of preparation of the prospective financial statements should be disclosed. This disclosure provides information to users about how current the information underlying the statements is likely to be. The date is generally disclosed in the introduction to the summary of significant assumptions.

Occasionally, management recognizes that users need information for periods beyond its ability to forecast. For example, management may plan a refinancing of debt or the introduction of new products after the end of the forecast period. Or, management may expect expiration of a significant contract or future adverse tax consequences to investors.

If users are considered limited users, management may present projections or partial presentations for the more distant periods.

If, however, the users are general users, presentation of a projection outside of the forecast period would be considered inappropriate (see section 28.4). In an effort to address this situation, the AICPA Financial Forecasts and Projection Task Force proposed an SOP that would allow disclosure of such long-term results outside of the forecast period. The proposed SOP, "Questions and Answers on *Reasonably Objective Basis* and Other Issues Affecting Projective Financial Statements" was exposed February 5,1990. The SOP would allow this disclosure if the information is less comprehensive than a financial projection and if it includes:

1. A title that indicates that it presents information about periods beyond the forecast period.
2. An introduction that indicates the purpose of the disclosure and that the disclosure is not a financial forecast.
3. Disclosure of significant assumptions underlying the disclosure.
4. A statement that the information is presented for analysis purposes only and that there is no assurance that the events and circumstances described will occur.

The SOP would prohibit presenting this disclosure on the face of the financial forecast or in a summary of investor benefits.

TYPES OF ACCOUNTANTS' SERVICES

28.14 OBJECTIVES OF ACCOUNTANTS' SERVICES.   Companies generally retain independent accountants to provide services on prospective financial statements for one of two reasons: to add credibility to prospective statements expected to be used by third parties or to provide consultation or assistance in developing statements expected to be used primarily by the client. The AICPA performance and reporting standards recognize that the type of service that is appropriate in the circumstances may vary depending on the expected use.

The AICPA Guide provides three standard accountants' services for prospective financial statements expected to be used by third parties: **compilation, examination,** and application of **agreed-upon procedures.** (No review, or moderate-level assurance, service is permitted.) When third-party use is not reasonably expected, the accountant may provide the three standard services or other types of services and reports that more closely reflect the purpose of the engagement.

28.15 STANDARD ACCOUNTANTS' SERVICES.   The accountant is required to either compile, examine, or apply agreed-upon procedures whenever:

1. The presentation includes prospective financial statements.
2. The statements are, or reasonably might be, expected to be used by a third party.
3. The accountant either (a) submits to his client or others statements that he has assembled or assisted in assembling or (b) reports on the statements.

There are three exceptions to this rule:

1. The accountant need not report on **drafts** of prospective financial statements submitted if they are clearly marked as such.
2. The accountant need not provide one of the standard services when the prospective financial statements are used solely in connection with engagements involving potential or pending litigation before a trier of fact in connection with the resolution of a dispute between two or more parties (often called **litigation support services**). In such circumstances the accountant's work is ordinarily subjected to detailed analysis and challenge by each party to the dispute. However, the exception does not apply when the prospective financial statements are used by third parties who do not have the opportunity for such analysis and challenge. For example, creditors may not have that opportunity when a financial forecast is submitted to them to secure their agreement to a plan of reorganization.
3. The accountant who submits interim historical financial statements in a document that also contains prospective financial statements need not provide one of the standard services on the prospective statements if the prospective statements are labeled "budget," they do not extend beyond the end of the current fiscal year, the accountant's report states that he did not apply any of the standard services to them, and the accountant's report disclaims an opinion or any other form of assurance on the statements.

(a) Prospective Financial Statements.   If the presentation doesn't meet the minimum disclosure requirement of prospective financial statements, (see section 28.1), it is a **partial presentation** rather than prospective financial statements. In that case, the accountant is not required to provide a standard service on the prospective data. The AICPA Auditing Standards Division issued in January 1990, SOP 90-1, "Accountants Services on Prospective Financial Statements for Internal Use Only and Partial Presentations," that established guidelines for compilations, examinations, and application of agreed-upon procedures to partial presentations. The SOP does not **require** those services on partial presentations, but provides guidance for the accountant who was engaged to provide them.

(b) Third-Party Use.   Third parties generally are any persons outside the entity presenting the prospective financial statements. Sometimes, however, such persons may not need to be considered third parties for the purpose of determining whether the guidance on accountants' services applies.

The AICPA Guide (§ 500.02) provides the following guidelines for determining whether outsiders are considered third parties:

> In deciding whether a party that is or reasonably might be expected to use an accountant's report is considered to be a third party, the accountant should consider the degree of consistency of interest between [management] and the user regarding the forecast. If their interests are substantially consistent (for example both the [preparer] and the user are employees of the entity about which the forecast is made), the user would not be deemed to be a third party. On the other hand, where the interests of the [preparer] and user are potentially inconsistent (for example, the [preparer] is a nonowner manager and the user is an absentee owner), the user would be deemed a third party. In some cases, this determination will require the exercise of considerable professional judgment.

In considering whether the statements will be restricted to internal use, the accountant may generally rely on management's oral or written representations, unless something leads him to believe that, despite management's representations, the statements are likely to be distributed to a third party.

(c) Assemble and Submit.   **Assembly** means the "manual or computer processing of mathematical or other clerical functions related to the presentation of the prospective financial statements." (AICPA Guide, § 200.16). This refers to converting the assumptions into prospective amounts or putting the amounts into the form of statements. Assembly does not mean merely copying or collating statements prepared by someone else.

28.16 INTERNAL USE.   The accountant may provide compilation, examination, or agreed-upon procedures engagements for internal use if engaged to do so. However, for internal use, the accountant has more flexibility to accommodate the varying circumstances of the engagement. Normally, these engagements involve consulting or planning (such as in management-consulting or tax-planning services) rather than third-party reliance. Common reporting options for internal use include **assembly reports** and **plain paper** prospective financial statements. Internal-use services are discussed in more detail in section 28.33.

28.17 PROHIBITED ENGAGEMENTS.   The AICPA Guide prohibits the accountant from submitting or reporting on prospective financial statements intended for third-party use if those statements omit the disclosure of significant assumptions. Similarly, the accountant is prohibited from submitting or reporting on a projection for third-party use if it does not identify the hypothetical assumption or describe the limitations on the usefulness of the presentation.

The accountant also may not submit or report on a financial projection that is intended for general use (unless it supplements a forecast for the same period) because such use is considered inappropriate (see section 28.4). This prohibition means that the accountant could not assemble and submit such a presentation even if management agreed not to present the accountant's report or refer to him in the document containing the projection that would be presented to general users.

28.18 MATERIALITY. Accountants consider **materiality** in conducting engagements on prospective financial statements much as they do for historical financial statements. The AICPA Guide (§ 500.28) states, however, "Materiality is a concept that is judged in light of the expected range of reasonableness of the information; therefore, users should not expect prospective information (information about events that have not yet occurred) to be as precise as historical information."

It follows, then, that materiality criteria would be higher for prospective statements than for the same company's historical statements. That is, an amount that would be material to the historical statements might not be material to the prospectives. There is no consensus in practice, however, as to just how much higher materiality should be for prospective financial statements.

28.19 SEC PERSPECTIVE. Relevant SEC rules regarding accountants' services on prospective financial statements in filings subject to the SEC's authority include the Safe Harbor Rule for Projections and the Guides for Disclosure of Projections. These rules, however, add relatively little to the requirements for accountants' procedures and reports established by the AICPA Guide. The more significant SEC policies in this area are less formal ones. Two particularly significant positions taken by the SEC involve **compilation services** and **independence rules.**

(a) Compilations in SEC Filings. Although not stated in formal SEC rules, the Commission's staff has been reluctant to accept compilations of prospective financial statements. Thus, although that service is allowed under the AICPA literature for both public and nonpublic entities (unlike compilations of historical statements, which are only appropriate for nonpublic companies), they generally are not an option for filings subject to SEC authority.

(b) Independence. SEC independence rules differ from those established by the AICPA. As a general rule, AICPA literature considers independence impaired when the accountant either has a direct financial interest in the client or when he is acting in the capacity of management or an employee. Thus, providing a service on prospective financial statements would not, in and of itself, affect the auditor's independence for the audit of its historical financial statements or any other service.

The SEC rules, however, are based on a different concept, which the SEC refers to as "mutuality of interest." The SEC considers that the accountant's assistance in preparing prospective financial statements creates a mutuality of interest in the prospective results. Thus, it has stated that, if the accountant actively participates in the preparation of the prospective data, he has lost the independence necessary to examine and report on that prospective data (see SEC Guides, 33-5992 and 34-15305).

In a letter to an accountant, the SEC staff pursued this reasoning even further, stating that active assistance in the preparation of a company's prospective financial statements would also affect the accountant's independence in regard to its **historical financial statements** for the length of the prospective period. This independence impairment would occur regardless of whether the prospective statements were forecasts or projections or whether they were issued to the public or restricted to internal use (see Letter from Chief Accountant to Amper, Politzner, and Mattia, April 14, 1987; CCH, 1990, ¶7986).

28.20 IRS PERSPECTIVE. IRS Circular 230 applies to prospective financial statements included in tax shelter offerings. It states that an accountant who reports on prospective financial statements in such offerings must either provide a **tax shelter opinion** or rely on one issued by another professional, such as another accountant or a lawyer.

A tax shelter opinion under Circular 230 states whether, in the professional's opinion, it is more likely than not that an investor will prevail on the merits of each material tax issue that involves a reasonable possibility of challenge by the IRS and an overall evaluation of the extent to which the material tax benefits are likely to be realized in the aggregate.

COMPILATION SERVICES

28.21 SCOPE OF THE COMPILATION SERVICE. A **compilation** of prospective financial statements is similar to a compilation of historical financial statements performed subject to SSARS No. 1, "Compilation and Review of Financial Statements" (1978). It relies primarily on an informed reading of the statements with an eye for obvious problems, but it doesn't provide any assurance on the statements.

The AICPA Guide states that a compilation of prospective financial statements involves:

1. Assembling, to the extent necessary, the prospective financial statements based on management's assumptions.
2. Performing the required compilation procedures, including reading the prospective financial statements with their summaries of significant assumptions and accounting policies and considering whether they appear to be (a) presented in conformity with AICPA presentation guidelines and (b) not obviously inappropriate.
3. Issuing a compilation report.

28.22 ASSEMBLY. Assembly, which is defined in section 28.15(c), refers to performing the necessary mathematics to turn assumptions into prospective financial data and drafting prospective financial statements in the appropriate form. In some cases, such as when the client has a sophisticated financial reporting function and prepares its own statements, assembly may not be required in a compilation. Often, however, assembly assistance is one of the primary benefits the client receives from the accountant.

Assembly does not include identifying key factors or developing assumptions, although accountants often help clients in these areas in a compilation.

28.23 COMPILATION PROCEDURES. The compilation procedures required by AICPA standards are listed in Exhibit 28.4.

There are two principal differences between the procedures done in a compilation of prospective statements and a compilation of historical statements: the requirement to consider the **actual results** for any expired portion of the prospective period and the requirement to obtain **signed representations** from the client.

Another difference between prospective and historical compilations is that **working papers** are required in a compilation of prospective financial statements. The working papers should be sufficient to show that the compilation was adequately planned and supervised and that the required procedures were performed. Signing off a checklist of procedures similar to Exhibit 28.4 may be considered evidence of both in some cases and may serve as sufficient documentation of the engagement.

28.24 REPORTING ON A COMPILATION. The **standard report** on a compilation of prospective financial statements includes:

1. An identification of the prospective financial statements.
2. A statement that the accountant compiled the statements in accordance with standards established by the AICPA.
3. A statement that a compilation is limited in scope and does not enable the accountant to express an opinion or any other form of assurance on the statements or assumptions.

In performing a compilation of prospective financial statements the accountant should, where applicable—

a. Establish an understanding with the client, preferably in writing, regarding the services to be performed.

b. Inquire about the accounting principles used in the preparation of the prospective financial statements.
- For existing entities, compare the accounting principles used to those used in the preparation of previous historical financial statements and inquire whether such principles are the same as those expected to be used in the historical financial statements covering the prospective period.
- For entities to be formed or entities formed that have not commenced operations, compare specialized industry accounting principles used, if any, to those typically used in the industry. Inquire about whether the accounting principles used for the prospective financial statements are those that are expected to be used when, or if, the entity commences operations.

c. Ask how the responsible party identifies the key factors and develops its assumptions.

d. List, or obtain a list of, the responsible party's significant assumptions providing the basis for the prospective financial statements and consider whether there are any obvious omissions in light of the key factors upon which the prospective results of the entity appear to depend.

e. Consider whether there appear to be any obvious internal inconsistencies in the assumptions.

f. Perform, or test the mathematical accuracy of, the computations that translate the assumptions into prospective financial statements.

g. Read the prospective financial statements, including the summary of significant assumptions, and consider whether—
- The statements, including the disclosures of assumptions and accounting policies, appear to be not presented in conformity with the AICPA presentation guidelines for prospective financial statements.[1]
- The statements, including the summary of significant assumptions, appear to be not obviously inappropriate in relation to the accountant's knowledge of the entity and its industry and, for a— *Financial forecast,* the expected conditions and course of action in the prospective period. *Financial projection,* the purpose of the presentation.

h. If a significant part of the prospective period has expired, inquire about the results of operations or significant portions of the operations (such as sales volume), and significant changes in financial position, and consider their effect in relation to the prospective financial statements. If historical financial statements have been prepared for the expired portion of the period, the accountant should read such statements and consider those results in relation to the prospective financial statements.

i. Confirm his understanding of the statements (including assumptions) by obtaining written representations from the responsible party. Because the amounts reflected in the statements are not supported by historical books and records but rather by assumptions, the accountant should obtain representations in which the responsible party indicates its responsibility for the assumptions. The representations should be signed by the responsible party at the highest level of authority who the accountant believes is responsible for and knowledgeable, directly or through others, about matters covered by the representations.
- *For a financial forecast,* the representations should include a statement that the financial forecast presents, to the best of the responsible party's knowledge and belief, the expected financial position, results of operations, and changes in financial position for the forecast period and that the forecast reflects the responsible party's judgment, based on present circumstances, of the expected conditions and its expected course of action. If the forecast contains a range, the representation should also include a statement that, to the best of the responsible party's knowledge and belief, the item or items subject to the assumption are expected to actually fall within the range and that the range was not selected in a biased or misleading manner.
- *For a financial projection,* the representations should include a statement that the financial projection presents, to the best of the responsible party's knowledge and belief, the expected financial position, results of operations, and changes in financial position for the projection period given the hypothetical assumptions, and that the projection reflects its judgment, based on present circumstances, of expected conditions and its expected course of action given the occurrence of the hypothetical events. The representations should also (i) identify the hypothetical assumptions and describe the limitations on the usefulness of the presentation, (ii) state that the assumptions are appropriate, (iii) indicate if the hypothetical assumptions are improbable, and (iv) if the projection contains a range, include a statement that, to the best of the responsible party's knowledge and belief, given the hypothetical

(continued)

Exhibit 28.4.   Standard compilation procedures. *Source:* **AICPA, "Financial Forecasts and Projections" Statement on Standards for Accountants' Services on Prospective Financial Information, (Appendix B).**

assumptions, the item or items subject to the assumption are expected to actually fall within the range and that the range was not selected in a biased or misleading manner.

j. Consider, after applying the above procedures, whether he has received representations or other information that appears to be obviously inappropriate, incomplete, or otherwise misleading and, if so, attempt to obtain additional or revised information. If he does not receive such information, the accountant should ordinarily withdraw from the compilation engagement.[2] (Note that the omission of disclosures, other than those relating to significant assumptions, would not require the accountant to withdraw).

[1]Presentation guidelines for entities that issue prospective financial statements are set forth and illustrated in the AICPA *Guide for Prospective Financial Statements.*
[2]The accountant need not withdraw from the engagement if the effect of such information on the prospective financial statements does not appear to be material.

Exhibit 28.4. *Continued.*

4. A caveat that the prospective results may not be achieved.

5. A statement that the accountant assumes no responsibility to update the report for events and circumstances occurring after the date of the report (the date of the report is the date of the completion of the compilation procedures).

6. For a projection, a paragraph that describes the limitations on the usefulness of the presentation.

The standard form of compilation report for a financial forecast is as follows:

We have compiled the accompanying forecasted balance sheet, statements of income, retained earnings, and cash flows of XYZ Company as of December 31, 19XX* and for the year then ending in accordance with standards established by the American Institute of Certified Public Accountants.

A compilation is limited to presenting in the form of a forecast information that is the representation of management and does not include evaluation of the support for the assumptions underlying the forecast. We have not examined the forecast, and, accordingly, do not express an opinion or any other form of assurance on the accompanying statements or assumptions. Furthermore, there will usually be differences between the actual and forecasted results, because events and circumstances frequently do not occur as expected, and those differences may be material. We have no responsibility to update this report for events and circumstances occurring after the date of this report.

———
*If the presentation is summarized, the opening sentence of the report would begin, "We have compiled the accompanying summarized forecast of XYZ Company as of December 31, 19XX. . . ."

The standard form of compilation report for a financial projection is as follows:

We have compiled the accompanying projected balance sheet, statements of income, retained earnings, and cash flows of XYZ Company as of December 31, 19XX* and for the year then ending in accordance with standards established by the American Institute of Certified Public Accountants.

The accompanying projection and this report were prepared for [description of the special purpose, e.g., "the DEF National Bank for the purpose of negotiating a loan to expand XYZ Company's plant"] and should not be used for any other purpose.

A compilation is limited to presenting in the form of a projection information that is the representation of management and does not include evaluation of the support for the assumptions underlying the projection. We have not examined the projection, and, accordingly, do not express an opinion or any other form of assurance on the accompanying statements or assumptions. Furthermore, even if [description of the hypothetical assumption, e.g., "the loan is granted and the plant is expanded"], there will usually be differences between the actual and projected results, because events and circumstances frequently do not occur as expected, and those differences may be material. We have no responsibility to update this report for events and circumstances occurring after the date of this report.

---

*If the presentation is summarized, the opening sentence of the report would begin, "We have compiled the accompanying summarized projection of XYZ Company as of December 31, 19XX. . . ."

If the presentation is shown as a range, the accountant's report also includes a paragraph that states that management has shown the results of one or more assumptions as a range. The following is an example of such a paragraph:

As described in the summary of significant assumptions, management of XYZ Company has elected to portray forecasted [description of the financial statement element or elements for which the expected results of one or more assumptions fall within a range, and identification of the assumptions expected to fall within a range, e.g., "revenue at the amounts of $XX and $YY, which is predicated upon occupancy rates of XX% and YY% of available apartments"] rather than as a single-point estimate. Accordingly, the accompanying forecast presents forecasted financial position, results of operations, and cash flows [description of the assumptions expected to fall within a range, e.g., "at such occupancy rates"]. However, there can be no assurance that the actual results will fall within the range of [description of the assumptions expected to fall within a range, e.g., "occupancy rates"] presented.

28.25 PROBLEM SITUATIONS.   Potential problems in a compilation engagement include **scope limitations, deficiencies in the prospective financial statements,** and lack of **independence.**

(a) Scope Limitations.   Scope limitations might include a client's inadequate responses to the limited inquiries required in a compilation or its refusal to supply signed representations. The AICPA Guide does not allow a scope-limitation compilation report. If the accountant cannot apply all the necessary procedures, he cannot complete the engagement and ordinarily should withdraw.

(b) Presentation Deficiencies.   Possible deficiencies in the prospective financial statements might affect either the assumptions or the other required disclosures. If the deficiency affects disclosures **other than assumptions,** the accountant may mention it in his compilation report. For example, if management chose to omit the disclosure of significant accounting policies, the accountant might add the following paragraph to his compilation report:

Management has elected to omit the summary of significant accounting policies required by the guidelines for presentation of a financial forecast established by the American Institute of Certified Public Accountants. If the omitted disclosures were included in the forecast, they might influence the user's conclusions about the Company's financial position, results of operations, and cash flows for the forecast period. Accordingly, this report is not intended for those who are not informed about such matters.

If the deficiency affects the disclosure of **assumptions** and the accountant is unable to have it corrected, he is not permitted merely to mention it in his report. In that case, he ordinarily would withdraw from the engagement.

(c) Independence.   Since a compilation provides no assurance, an accountant may compile prospective financial statements when he is not independent. In that case his report would indicate his lack of independence, but not the reason for it. The following sentence would be added to the compilation report to indicate the lack of independence:

We are not independent with respect to XYZ Company.

EXAMINATION SERVICES

28.26 SCOPE OF AN EXAMINATION.   An examination of prospective financial statements is similar to an audit of historical financial statements. It is based on evidence-gathering procedures and results in positive assurance about the statements. The main difference between the two services involves the evidence-gathering procedures. Because completed transactions do not generally constitute the bulk of the data underlying prospective financial statements, the accountant's procedures generally consist primarily of inquiry and analysis rather than of document inspection and confirmation.

An examination of prospective financial statements involves:

1. Evaluating the preparation of the statements.
2. Evaluating the support underlying the statements.
3. Evaluating the presentation of the statements for conformity with AICPA presentation guidelines.
4. Issuing a report as to whether, in the accountant's opinion,
   a. The prospective financial statements are presented in conformity with AICPA presentation guidelines and
   b. The assumptions provide a reasonable basis for the forecast or, for a projection, whether the assumptions provide a reasonable basis given the hypothetical assumptions.

(a) Evaluating Preparation.   The accountant considers the process that management uses to develop its prospective financial statements to determine how much support he will need to accumulate. This consideration is similar to the consideration an auditor gives to a company's internal control structure in planning and performing an audit of historical financial statements. The better controlled the process of developing the financial statements, the less work the accountant generally needs to do in obtaining support for them.

In judging the process the entity uses in developing its prospective financial statements, the accountant generally compares the process to the guidelines discussed in section 28.7.

(b) Evaluating Assumptions.   The accountant performs procedures to determine whether the assumptions provide a reasonable basis for the prospective financial statements. He can decide that they do if he can conclude that:

1. Management has identified all key factors expected to affect the entity during the prospective period.
2. Management has developed assumptions for each key factor.
3. The assumptions are suitably supported.

To determine whether management has identified all **key factors** and developed assumptions for each one, the accountant needs to possess, or obtain during the engagement, an appropriate knowledge of the industry in which the entity will operate and the accounting principles and practices of that industry.

The accountant can conclude that the assumptions are **suitably supported** if the preponderance of information supports each significant assumption. Preponderance, here, does not imply a statistical majority of information. A preponderance exists if the weight of available information tends to support the assumption. The AICPA Guide states, however, "Because of the judgments involved in developing assumptions, different people may arrive at somewhat different but equally reasonable assumptions based on the same information."

The accountant need not obtain support for the **hypothetical** assumptions in a projection, since they are not necessarily expected to occur. For a projection, the accountant considers whether the hypothetical assumptions are consistent with the purpose of the projection and whether the other assumptions are suitably supported given the hypothetical assumption.

In evaluating the support for the assumptions, the accountant considers:

1. Whether sufficient pertinent sources of information, both internal and external to the entity, have been considered.
2. Whether the assumptions are consistent with the sources from which they are derived.
3. Whether the assumptions are consistent with each other.
4. Whether the historical financial information and other data used in developing the assumptions are sufficiently reliable for that purpose.
5. Whether the historical information and other data used in developing the assumptions are comparable over the periods specified or whether the effects of any lack of comparability were considered in developing the assumptions.
6. Whether the logical arguments or theory, considered with the data supporting the assumptions, are reasonable.

Support for assumptions may include market surveys, engineering studies, general economic indicators, industry statistics, trends and patterns developed from an entity's operating history, and internal data and analysis, accompanied by their supporting logical argument or theory.

The accountant determines whether the assumptions provide a reasonable basis for the statements, but he cannot conclude that any outcome is expected because (1) realization of prospective results may depend on management's intentions, which cannot be examined; (2) there is substantial uncertainty in the assumptions; (3) some of the information accumulated about an assumption may appear contradictory; and (4) different but similarly reasonable assumptions concerning a particular matter might be derived from common information.

(c) Evaluating Presentation.   The accountant compares the presentation of the prospective financial statements to the AICPA presentation guidelines (see sections 28.12–28.13).

28.27 STANDARD EXAMINATION REPORT.   The accountant's **standard report** on an examination of prospective financial statements includes:

1. An identification of the statements presented.
2. A statement that the examination of the statements was made in accordance with AICPA standards and a brief description of the nature of such an examination.
3. The accountant's opinion that the statements are presented in conformity with AICPA presentation guidelines and, for a forecast, that the underlying assumptions provide a reasonable basis for the forecast or, for a projection, that the underlying assumptions provide a reasonable basis for the projection given the hypothetical assumptions.
4. A caveat that the prospective results may not be achieved.
5. A statement that the accountant assumes no responsibility to update the report for events and circumstances occurring after the date of the report, which is the date of the completion of the examination procedures.

6. For a projection, a separate paragraph describing the limitations on the usefulness of the presentation.

The standard report on the examination of a financial forecast is as follows:

We have examined the accompanying forecasted balance sheet, statements of income, retained earnings, and cash flows of XYZ Company as of December 31, 19XX,* and for the year then ending. Our examination was made in accordance with standards for the examination of a forecast established by the American Institute of Certified Public Accountants and, accordingly, included such procedures as we considered necessary to evaluate both the assumptions used by management and the preparation and presentation of the forecast.

In our opinion, the accompanying forecast is presented in conformity with guidelines for presentation of a forecast established by the American Institute of Certified Public Accountants and the underlying assumptions provide a reasonable basis for management's forecast. However, there will usually be differences between the forecasted and actual results, because events and circumstances frequently do not occur as expected, and those differences may be material. We have no responsibility to update this report for events and circumstances occurring after the date of this report.

---

*If the presentation is summarized as discussed in section 28.12, the first sentence would read, in part, "We have examined the accompanying summarized forecast of XYZ Company as of. . . ."

The standard report on the examination of a financial projection is as follows:

We have examined the accompanying projected balance sheet, statements of income, retained earnings, and cash flows of XYZ Company as of December 31, 19XX,* and for the year then ending. Our examination was made in accordance with standards for the examination of a projection established by the American Institute of Certified Public Accountants and, accordingly, included such procedures as we considered necessary to evaluate both the assumptions used by management and the preparation and presentation of the projection.

The accompanying projection and this report were prepared for [description of the special purpose, e.g., "the DEF National Bank for the purpose of negotiating a loan to expand XYZ Company's plant"] and should not be used for any other purpose.

In our opinion, the accompanying projection is presented in conformity with guidelines for presentation of a projection established by the American Institute of Certified Public Accountants, and the underlying assumptions provide a reasonable basis for management's projection [description of the hypothetical assumption, e.g., "assuming the granting of the requested loan for the purpose of expanding XYZ Company's plant as described in the summary of significant assumptions"]. However, even if [description of the hypothetical assumption, e.g., "the loan is granted and the plant is expanded"], there will usually be differences between the projected and actual results, because events and circumstances frequently do not occur as expected, and those differences may be material. We have no responsibility to update this report for events and circumstances occurring after the date of this report.

---

*If the presentation is summarized as discussed in section 28.12, the first sentence would read, in part, "We have examined the accompanying summarized projection of XYZ Company as of. . . ."

When the prospective financial statements are presented as a range, the report also includes a separate paragraph describing the range (see section 28.24 for an example).

28.28 MODIFIED EXAMINATION REPORTS.   There are four types of modified examination reports:

1. A **qualified** report, used when the statements depart from the AICPA presentation guidelines but the deficiency does not affect the assumptions (although if the matter is highly material, the accountant may issue an adverse report).

2. An **adverse** report, used when the statements fail to disclose significant assumptions or when the assumptions do not provide a reasonable basis for the presentation.

3. A **disclaimer** used when the accountant is precluded from applying procedures he considers necessary in the circumstances.

4. A **reference** to another accountant, used when another accountant examines the prospective financial statements of a significant portion of the entity, such as a major subsidiary.

(a) Qualified Opinion. The accountant issues a qualified opinion if there is a material presentation deficiency that does not affect the assumptions. The following is an examination report qualified because of a presentation deficiency:

> We have examined the accompanying forecasted balance sheet, statements of income, retained earnings, and cash flows of XYZ Company as of December 31, 19XX, and for the year then ending. Our examination was made in accordance with standards for the examination of a forecast established by the American Institute of Certified Public Accountants and, accordingly, included such procedures as we considered necessary to evaluate both the assumptions used by management and the preparation and presentation of the forecast.
>
> The forecast does not [description of the presentation deficiency, such as "disclose the significant accounting principles underlying the presentation, which we believe is required by the guidelines for presentation of a forecast established by the American Institute of Certified Public Accountants"].
>
> In our opinion, except for [description of the presentation deficiency, e.g., "the omission of the disclosure of significant accounting policies"] as discussed in the preceding paragraph, the accompanying forecast is presented in conformity with guidelines for presentation of a forecast established by the American Institute of Certified Public Accountants and the underlying assumptions provide a reasonable basis for management's forecast. However, there will usually be differences between the actual and forecasted results, because events and circumstances frequently do not occur as expected, and those differences may be material. We have no responsibility to update this report for events and circumstances occurring after the date of this report.

(b) Adverse Report. If the accountant believes an assumption to be unsupported or not disclosed, he issues an adverse opinion. He may also issue one if he believes that a departure from the presentation guidelines not involving the assumptions is serious enough to warrant it. The following is an example of an adverse report issued by the accountant because he believed an assumption was unreasonable:

> We have examined the accompanying forecasted balance sheet, statements of income, retained earnings, and cash flows of XYZ Company as of December 31, 19XX, and for the year then ending. Our examination was made in accordance with standards for the examination of a forecast established by the American Institute of Certified Public Accountants and, accordingly, included such procedures as we considered necessary to evaluate both the assumptions used by management and the preparation and presentation of the forecast.
>
> [Description of the problem assumption, e.g., "As discussed under the caption "sales" in the summary of significant assumptions, the forecasted sales include, among other things, revenue from the Company's federal defense contracts continuing at the current level. The Company's present federal defense contracts will expire in March 19XX. No new contracts have been signed, and no negotiations are under way for new federal defense contracts. Furthermore, the federal government has entered into contracts with another company to supply the items being manufactured under the Company's present contracts."]
>
> In our opinion, the accompanying forecast is not presented in conformity with guidelines for presentation of a forecast established by the American Institute of Certified Public Accountants because management's assumptions, as discussed in the preceding paragraph, do not provide a

reasonable basis for management's forecast. We have no responsibility to update this report for events and circumstances occurring after the date of this report.

There is no caveat about actual results differing from those forecasted since the accountant believes the forecast assumptions to be unreasonable.

(c) Disclaimer.   If the accountant cannot apply all the procedures he believes necessary to support an opinion on the statements, he issues a disclaimer. An example of a disclaimer follows:

> We have examined the accompanying forecasted balance sheet, statements of income, retained earnings, and cash flows of XYZ Company as of December 31, 19XX, and for the year then ending. Except as explained in the following paragraph, our examination was made in accordance with standards for the examination of a forecast established by the American Institute of Certified Public Accountants and, accordingly, included such procedures as we considered necessary to evaluate both the assumptions used by management and the preparation and presentation of the forecast.
>
> [Description of the scope limitation, e.g., "As discussed under the caption 'income from investee' in the summary of significant assumptions, the forecast includes income from an equity investee constituting 23% of forecasted net income, which is management's estimate of the Company's share of the investee's income to be accrued for the year ending December 31, 19XX. The investee has not prepared a forecast for the year ending December 31, 19XX, and we were therefore unable to obtain suitable support for this assumption."]
>
> Because, [description of the scope limitation, e.g., "as described in the preceding paragraph, we were unable to evaluate management's assumption regarding income from an equity investee and other assumptions that depend thereon"], we express no opinion with respect to the presentation of or the assumptions underlying the accompanying forecast. We have no responsibility to update this report for events and circumstances occurring after the date of this report.

In a disclaimer there is no caveat about differences between actual and forecasted assumptions since the accountant cannot satisfy himself about the reasonableness of the assumptions.

Notwithstanding his scope limitation, if the accountant is aware of material deficiencies in the forecast, those deficiencies should be discussed in the disclaimer.

(d) Divided Responsibility.   When another accountant is involved in the examination, the principal accountant may refer to the work of the other accountant as a basis, in part, for his own report. The reference is done in essentially the same way divided-responsibility reports are done for audits of historical financial statements.

28.29 INDEPENDENCE.   The accountant who examines prospective financial statements is required to be independent. If he is not, the accountant generally issues a compilation report rather than disclaim an opinion after his examination.

AGREED-UPON PROCEDURES

28.30 SCOPE OF SERVICE.   An engagement to apply agreed-upon procedures to prospective financial statements involves applying the procedures specified by the users of the statements and reporting the results of their application. The level of service is flexible; it consists of whatever the users want the accountant to do, but the accountant's report may only be distributed to the users who specified the procedures. Thus, it is a limited-distribution service.

28.31 PROCEDURES.   The procedures applied in an engagement may be limited or extensive, depending on the users' needs. For example, the service may consist of procedures below the level done in a compilation (such as mere assembly) or may be similar to those done in an examination. Alternatively, the service may consist of different levels of procedures applied to different amounts in the statements, such as a high level of work done on forecasted sales and very limited procedures on forecasted expenses.

Any level of procedures is appropriate in an agreed-upon procedures engagement as long as (1) the user takes responsibility for the adequacy of the procedures for his purposes and (2) the procedures are more extensive than a mere reading of the prospective financial statements.

28.32 REPORTS.   The accountant's report on the results of applying agreed-upon procedures:

1. Indicates the statements covered by the report.
2. Indicates that the report is limited in use, intended solely for the specified users, and should not be used by others.
3. Enumerates the procedures performed and refers to conformity with arrangements made with the specified users.
4. If the procedures are less than those that would be performed in an examination, states that the work performed was less in scope than an examination of prospective financial statements in accordance with AICPA standards and disclaims an opinion on whether the presentation of the statements is in conformity with AICPA presentation guidelines and on whether the underlying assumptions provide a reasonable basis for the statements.
5. States the accountant's findings.
6. Includes a caveat that the prospective results may not be achieved.
7. States that the accountant assumes no responsibility to update the report for events and circumstances occurring after the date of the report, which is the date of the completion of the procedures.
8. If the accountant desires, states that the accountant makes no representation about the sufficiency of the procedures for the specified user's purposes.
9. For a projection, includes a paragraph that describes the limitations on the usefulness of the presentation.

The report does not express any form of negative assurance on the statements taken as a whole.

The following is an example of a report on the application of agreed-upon procedures:

Board of Directors—XYZ Corporation

Board of Directors—ABC Company

At your request, we have performed certain agreed-upon procedures, as enumerated below, with respect to the forecasted balance sheet, statements of income, retained earnings, and cash flows of DEF Company, a subsidiary of ABC Company, as of December 31, 19XX, and for the year then ending. These procedures, which were specified by the Boards of Directors of XYZ Corporation and ABC Company, were performed solely to assist you in connection with the proposed sale of DEF Company to XYZ Corporation. It is understood that this report is solely for your information and should not be used by those who did not participate in determining the procedures.

a. With respect to forecasted rental income, we compared the assumptions about expected demand for rental of the housing units to demand for similar housing units at similar rental prices in the city area in which DEF Company's housing units are located.

b. We tested the forecast for mathematical accuracy.

Because the procedures described above do not constitute an examination of prospective financial statements in accordance with standards established by the American Institute of Certified Public Accountants, we do not express an opinion on whether the prospective financial statements are presented in conformity with AICPA presentation guidelines or on whether the underlying assumptions provide a reasonable basis for the presentation.

In connection with the procedures referred to above, no matters came to our attention that caused us to believe that rental income should be adjusted or that the forecast is mathematically inaccurate. Had we performed additional procedures or had we made an examination of the forecast in accordance with standards established by the American Institute of Certified Public Accountants, matters might have come to our attention that would have been reported to you. Furthermore, there will usually be differences between the forecasted and actual results, because events and circumstances frequently do not occur as expected, and those differences may be material. We have no responsibility to update this report for events and circumstances occurring after the date of this report.

INTERNAL USE SERVICES

28.33 SCOPE OF SERVICES.   When the accountant assembles and submits or reports on prospective financial statements for **third-party use,** he must compile, examine, or apply agreed-upon procedures to them. However, for **internal use** the accountant's services and reports can be more flexible.

Internal use services generally are provided in the form of consulting, tax planning, or so-called controllership services. In these types of service the objective of the service is not to lend credibility to the statements and there is no third-party reliance on them, so AICPA guidelines allow the accountant to structure the engagement and report to fit the circumstances.

The accountant **may** provide compilation, examination, or agreed-upon procedures for internal use prospective financial statements, but he is not required to do so.

28.34 DETERMINING WHETHER USE IS INTERNAL.   The accountant may provide internal use services if he believes that third party use is not reasonably expected. In arriving at his belief, the accountant may rely on the oral or written representation of management, unless something comes to his attention to contradict management's representation.

The AICPA Guide (§ 500.02) provides the following guidelines for determining whether outsiders are considered third parties:

In deciding whether a party that is or reasonably might be expected to use an accountant's report is considered to be a third party, the accountant should consider the degree of consistency of interest between [management] and the user regarding the forecast. If their interests are substantially consistent (for example both the [preparer] and the user are employees of the entity about which the forecast is made), the user would not be deemed to be a third party. On the other hand, where the interests of the [preparer] and user are potentially inconsistent (for example, the [preparer] is a nonowner manager and the user is an absentee owner), the user would be deemed a third party. In some cases, this determination will require the exercise of considerable professional judgment.

28.35 PROCEDURES.   The procedures applied in an internal use engagement are usually based on the nature of the engagement. They may focus on developing prospective data, or they may focus on improving operations or financial planning with prospective data being only a by-product of the engagement.

28.36 REPORTS.   The accountant's report for internal use services is flexible. Such reports sometimes speak solely to the prospective financial statements, but often they focus on alternative or recommended courses of action.

The standard compilation, examination, or agreed-upon procedures reports may be utilized for internal use, but often they are not used.

Reports on prospective financial statements for internal use generally take three broad forms: **plain paper, legend,** and **formal.** Where there is a report on the statements, it may stand alone or may be incorporated into another report, such as a consultant's report.

(a) Plain Paper. Plain paper means that the accountant provides neither a report on the statements nor any other written communication that accompanies them. In a plain-paper situation there would be nothing apparent to the reader to associate the accountant with the statements.

(b) Legend. When an accountant's written communication (such as a transmittal letter) accompanies the prospective financial statements, SOP 90-1 "Accountants' Services on Prospective Financial Statements for Internal Use and Partial Presentations" requires that the accountant include (1) a caveat that prospective results may not be achieved and (2) a statement that the prospective financial statements are for internal use only. Many accountants choose to present this as a **legend** on the statement itself.

(c) Formal Report. If the accountant decides to issue a report on a service, he may do so. However, the accountant is not permitted to report on a forecast or projection, even for internal use, if it does not disclose the significant assumptions.

According to the proposed SOP, a report for internal use preferably:

1. Is addressed to management.

2. Identifies the statements being reported on.

3. Describes the character of work performed and the degree of responsibility taken with respect to the statements in a manner that does not appear to vouch for the achievability of the prospective statements.

4. Indicates the restrictions as to the distribution of the statements and report.

5. Is dated as of the date of the completion of the accountant's procedures.

6. For a projection, describes the limitations on the usefulness of the presentation.

The following is an example of a report on an internal use service consisting of assembly of a forecast:

To Mr. John Doe, President
XYZ Company

We have assembled from information provided by management, the accompanying forecasted balance sheet, statements of income, retained earnings, and cash flows of XYZ Company as of December 31, 19XX,* and for the year then ending. We have not compiled or examined the financial forecast and express no assurance of any kind on it. Further, there will usually be differences between the forecasted and actual results, because events and circumstances frequently do not occur as expected, and those differences may be material. In accordance with the terms of our engagement, this report and the accompanying forecast are restricted to internal use and may not be shown to any third party for any purpose.

---

*If the presentation is summarized as discussed in section 28.12, the first sentence would read, in part, "We have assembled . . . the accompanying summarized forecast of XYZ Company. . . ."

An example of a report on the assembly of a projection is as follows:

To Mr. John Doe, President
XYZ Company

We have assembled from information provided by management, the accompanying projected balance sheet, statements of income, retained earnings, and cash flows, and summaries of significant assumptions and accounting policies of XYZ Company as of December 31, 19XX,* and for the year then ending. The accompanying projection and this report were prepared for [description of the special purpose, e.g., "presentation to the Board of Directors of XYZ Company for its consideration as to whether to add a third operating shift"]. We have not compiled or examined the financial projection and express no assurance of any kind on it. Further, even if [description of the hypothetical assumption, e.g., "the third operating shift is added"], there will usually be differences between the projected and actual results, because events and circumstances frequently do not occur as expected, and those differences may be material. In accordance with the terms of our engagement, this report and the accompanying projection are restricted to internal use and may not be shown to any third party for any purpose.

---

*If the presentation is summarized as discussed in section 28.12, the first sentence would read, in part, "We have assembled . . . the accompanying summarized projection of XYZ Company. . . ."

In addition to the above, the accountant's report on prospective financial statements for internal use would:

1. Indicate if he is not independent with respect to the client (the report would not express any assurance on the statements if there is a lack of independence) and
2. Note any disclosures required under the presentation guidelines (see section 28.11) whose omission comes to the accountant's attention (other than omitted assumptions). The report might either describe the omitted disclosures or merely note the omission of disclosures in a manner such as:

> This financial forecast was prepared to help you develop your personal financial plan. Accordingly, it does not include all disclosures required by the guidelines established by the American Institute of Certified Public Accountants for presentation of a financial forecast.

SOURCES AND SUGGESTED REFERENCES

American Institute of Certified Public Accountants, Accounting and Review Services Committee, "Compilation and Review of Financial Statements," Statement on Standards for Accounting and Review Services No. 1, AICPA, New York, 1978.

———, Auditing Standards Board, "Financial Forecasts and Projections," Statement on Standards for Accountant's Services on Prospective Financial Information, AICPA, New York, 1985.

———, "Reporting on Pro Forma Financial Information," Statement on Standards for Attestation Engagements, AICPA, New York, 1988.

———, Guide for Prospective Financial Statements, AICPA, New York, 1986.

———, Financial Forecasts and Projections Task Force, "Accountants' Services on Prospective Financial Statements for Internal Use Only and Partial Presentations," Statement of Position 90-1, AICPA, New York, 1990.

———, "Questions and Answers on Reasonably Objective Basis and Other Issues Affecting Prospective Financial Statements," Proposed Statement of Position, AICPA, New York, 1990.

Commerce Clearing House, SEC Accounting Rules, CCH, Chicago, 1990.

Financial Accounting Standards Board, "Statement of Cash Flows," Statement of Financial Accounting Standards No. 95, FASB, Stamford, CT, 1987.

Pallais, Don, and Holten, Stephen D., Guide to Forecasts and Projections, 5th ed., Practitioners Publishing, Fort Worth, TX, 1990.

CHAPTER 29

PERSONAL FINANCIAL STATEMENTS

Dennis S. Neier, CPA
Deloitte & Touche

Mary Ellen Morris, CPA
Porter & Travers

CONTENTS

GUIDANCE

The authoritative guide in the preparation of personal financial statements is AICPA SOP No. 82-1, ''Accounting and Financial Reporting for Personal Financial Statements.'' This SOP

Mary Ellen Morris, CPA, is an employee of Porter & Travers and her views as expressed in this publication do not necessarily reflect the views of Porter & Travers.

establishes the use of estimated current value rather than historical cost as the basis for measuring assets and liabilities in personal financial statements. It also provides guidance on how to determine estimated current value for several kinds of assets and liabilities.

Accountants are often engaged to compile, review, or audit personal financial statements. The specific guide for such engagements is the AICPA "Personal Financial Statements Guide," which includes SOP No. 82-1.

The general guidance provided by the AICPA in SSARS No. 1, "Compilation and Review of Financial Statements," applies to compilations and reviews of all financial statements, including personal financial statements.

A subsequent AICPA release, SSARS No. 6, "Reporting on Personal Financial Statements Included in Written Personal Financial Plans," allows accountants to prepare personal financial statements that omit disclosures required by GAAP so long as the statement will be used solely in the development of the client's personal financial plan and not to obtain credit or to meet other disclosure requirements. If an accountant prepares a personal financial statement under this exemption, he should issue a written report stating the restricted purpose of the statement and noting that it has not been audited, reviewed, or compiled.

GENERAL DESCRIPTION AND REQUIREMENTS

29.1 DEFINITION.   A personal financial statement presents the personal assets and liabilities of an individual, a husband and wife, or a family. It is not a financial statement on a business owned by the person; in fact, it differs from a business financial statement in several important ways (see Exhibit 29.1).

The essential purpose of a personal financial statement is to measure wealth at a specified date—to take a snapshot of the person's financial position. It does this by presenting:

- Estimated current values of assets.
- Estimated current amounts of liabilities.
- A provision for income taxes based on the taxes that would be owed if all the assets were liquidated and all the liabilities paid on the date of the statement.
- Net worth.

The basic personal financial statement containing this information is called a **statement of financial condition,** not a balance sheet. Values and amounts for one or more prior periods

	Personal	Business
Objective	Measurement of wealth	Reporting of earnings, evaluation of performance
Uses	Facilitation of financial planning; procural of credit; provision of disclosures to the public or the court	Procural of credit, information for shareholders, regulatory requirements
Valuation	Current value	Historical cost
Method of accounting	Accrual	Accrual
Classification	None: assets presented in order of liquidity, liabilities in order of maturity	Assets and liabilities classified current or long-term
Excess of assets over liabilities	Net worth	Retained earnings

Exhibit 29.1.   Personal and business financial statements compared.

may be included for comparison with the current values and amounts, but this is optional. The **statement of changes in net worth** is also optional. It presents the major sources of increase or decrease in net worth (see Exhibit 29.2).

29.2 OWNERSHIP.   A personal financial statement covering a whole family usually presents the assets and liabilities of the family members in combination, as a single economic unit. However, the members may have different ownership interests in these assets or liabilities. For example, the wife may have a remainder interest in a testamentary trust, whereas the husband may own life insurance with a net cash surrender value. It may be useful, especially when the statement is to be used in a divorce case, to disclose each individual's interests separately. This may be done in separate columns within the statement, in the notes to the statement, or in additional statements for each individual.

JAMES AND JANE PERSON
Statements of Financial Condition
December 31, 19X3 and 19X2

	December 31	
	19X3	19X2
Assets		
Cash	$ 3,700	$ 15,600
Bonus receivable	20,000	10,000
Investments		
Marketable securities (Note 2)	160,500	140,700
Stock options (Note 3)	28,000	24,000
Kenbruce Associates (Note 4)	48,000	42,000
Davekar Company, Inc. (Note 5)	550,000	475,000
Vested interest in deferred profit-sharing plan	111,400	98,900
Remainder interest in testamentary trust (Note 6)	171,900	128,800
Cash value of life insurance ($43,600 and $42,900), less loans		
payable to insurance companies ($38,100 and $37,700)		
(Note 7)	5,500	5,200
Residence (Note 8)	190,000	180,000
Personal effects (excluding jewelry) (Note 9)	55,000	50,000
Jewelry (Note 9)	40,000	36,500
	$1,384,000	$1,206,700
Liabilities		
Income taxes—current year balance	$ 8,800	$ 400
Demand 10.5% note payable to bank	25,000	26,000
Mortgage payable (Note 10)	98,200	99,000
Contingent liabilities (Note 11)		
	132,000	125,400
Estimated income taxes on the differences between the estimated		
current values of assets and the estimated current amounts of		
liabilities and their tax bases (Note 12)	239,000	160,000
Net worth	1,013,000	921,300
	$1,384,000	$1,206,700

The notes to financial statements are an integral part of these statements.

(continued)

Exhibit 29.2.   Illustrative financial statements. *Source:* **Reproduced with permission from AICPA, Personal Financial Statements Guide, Appendix E: Statement of Position No. 82-1, "Accounting and Financial Reporting for Personal Financial Statements," 1983, pp. 62–68.**

JAMES AND JANE PERSON
Statements of Changes in Net Worth
For the Years Ended December 31, 19X3 and 19X2

	Year ended December 31	
	19X3	19X2
Realized increases in net worth		
Salary and bonus	$ 95,000	$ 85,000
Dividends and interest income	2,300	1,800
Distribution from limited partnership	5,000	4,000
Gains on sales of marketable securities	1,000	500
	103,300	91,300
Realized decreases in net worth		
Income taxes	26,000	22,000
Interest expense	13,000	14,000
Real estate taxes	4,000	3,000
Personal expenditures	36,700	32,500
	79,700	71,500
Net realized increase in net worth	23,600	19,800
Unrealized increases in net worth		
Marketable securities (net of realized gains on securities sold)	3,000	500
Stock options	4,000	500
Davekar Company, Inc.	75,000	25,000
Kenbruce Associates	6,000	
Deferred profit sharing plan	12,500	9,500
Remainder interest in testamentary trust	43,100	25,000
Jewelry	3,500	
	147,100	60,500
Unrealized decrease in net worth		
Estimated income taxes on the differences between the estimated current values of assets and the estimated current amounts of liabilities and their tax bases	79,000	22,000
Net unrealized increase in net worth	68,100	38,500
Net increase in net worth	91,700	58,300
Net worth at the beginning of year	921,300	863,000
Net worth at the end of year	$1,013,000	$ 921,300

The notes to financial statements are an integral part of these statements.

(continued)

Exhibit 29.2. *Continued.*

Note 1. The accompanying financial statements include the assets and liabilities of James and Jane Person. Assets are stated at their estimated current values, and liabilities at their estimated current amounts.

Note 2. The estimated current values of marketable securities are either (a) their quoted closing prices or (b) for securities not traded on the financial statement date, amounts that fall within the range of quoted bid and asked prices.

Marketable securities consist of the following:

	December 31, 19X3		December 31, 19X2	
	Number of shares or bonds	Estimated current values	Number of shares or bonds	Estimated current values
Stocks				
Jaiven Jewels, Inc.	1,500	$ 98,813		
McRae Motors, Ltd.	800	11,000	600	$ 4,750
Parker Sisters, Inc.	400	13,875	200	5,200
Rosenfield Rug Co.			1,200	96,000
Rubin Paint Company	300	9,750	100	2,875
Weiss Potato Chips, Inc.	200	20,337	300	25,075
		153,775		133,900
Bonds				
Jackson Van Lines, Ltd. (12% due 7/1/X9)	5	5,225	5	5,100
United Garvey, Inc. (7% due 11/15/X6)	2	1,500	2	1,700
		6,725		6,800
		$160,500		$140,700

Note 3. Jane Person owns options to acquire 4,000 shares of stock of Winner Corp. at an option price of $5 per share. The option expires on June 30, 19X5. The estimated current value is its published selling price.

Note 4. The investment in Kenbruce Associates is an 8% interest in a real estate limited partnership. The estimated current value is determined by the projected annual cash receipts and payments capitalized at a 12% rate.

Note 5. James Person owns 50% of the common stock of Davekar Company, Inc., a retail mail order business. The estimated current value of the investment is determined by the provisions of a shareholders' agreement, which restricts the sale of the stock and, under certain conditions, requires the company to repurchase the stock based on a price equal to the book value of the net assets plus an agreed amount for goodwill. At December 31, 19X3, the agreed amount for goodwill was $112,500, and at December 31, 19X2, it was $100,000.

A condensed balance sheet of Davekar Company, Inc., prepared in conformity with generally accepted accounting principles, is summarized below:

(continued)

Exhibit 29.2. *Continued.*

	December 31	
	19X3	**19X2**
Current assets	$3,147,000	$2,975,000
Plant, property, and equipment—net	165,000	145,000
Other assets	120,000	110,000
Total assets	3,432,000	3,230,000
Current liabilities	2,157,000	2,030,000
Long-term liabilities	400,000	450,000
Total liabilities	2,557,000	2,480,000
Equity	$ 875,000	$ 750,000

The sales and net income for 19X3 were $10,500,000 and $125,000 and for 19X2 were $9,700,000 and $80,000.

Note 6. Jane Person is the beneficiary of a remainder interest in a testamentary trust under the will of the late Joseph Jones. The amount included in the accompanying statements is her remainder interest in the estimated current value of the trust assets, discounted at 10%.

Note 7. At December 31, 19X3 and 19X2, James Person owned a $300,000 whole life insurance policy.

Note 8. The estimated current value of the residence is its purchase price plus the cost of improvements. The residence was purchased in December 19X1, and improvements were made in 19X2 and 19X3.

Note 9. The estimated current values of personal effects and jewelry are the appraised values of those assets, determined by an independent appraiser for insurance purposes.

Note 10. The mortgage (collateralized by the residence) is payable in monthly installments of $815 a month, including interest at 10% a year through 20Y8.

Note 11. James Person has guaranteed the payment of loans of Davekar Company, Inc., under a $500,000 line of credit. The loan balance was $300,000 at December 31, 19X3, and $400,000 at December 31, 19X2.

Note 12. The estimated current amounts of liabilities at December 31, 19X3, and December 31, 19X2, equaled their tax bases. Estimated income taxes have been provided on the excess of the estimated current values of assets over their tax bases as if the estimated current values of the assets had been realized on the statement date, using applicable tax laws and regulations. The provision will probably differ from the amounts of income taxes that eventually might be paid because those amounts are determined by the timing and the method of disposal or realization and the tax laws and regulations in effect at the time of disposal or realization.

The estimated current values of assets exceeded their tax bases by $850,000 at December 31, 19X3, and by $770,300 at December 31, 19X2. The excess of estimated current values of major assets over their tax bases are—

	December 31	
	19X3	**19X2**
Investment in Davekar Company, Inc.	$430,500	$355,500
Vested interest in deferred profit-sharing plan	111,400	98,900
Investment in marketable securities	104,100	100,000
Remainder interest in testamentary trust	97,000	53,900

Exhibit 29.2. *Continued.*

Often an individual covered by the statement is one of a group of joint owners of assets, as with community property or property held in joint tenancy. In this case, the statement should include only the individual's interest as a beneficial owner under the laws of the state. If the parties' shares in the assets are not clear, the advice of an attorney may be needed to determine whether the person should regard any interest in the assets as his own, and if so, how much. The statement should make full disclosure of the joint ownership of the assets and the grounds for the allocation of shares.

29.3 USES.   Many individuals or families use personal financial statements for investment, tax, retirement, gift and estate planning, and for obtaining credit. A personal financial statement may also be required for disclosure to the court in a divorce case, or to the public when the individual is a candidate or an incumbent of public office.

29.4 ACCOUNTING BASIS.   SOP No. 82-1 establishes the use of estimated current values and amounts and the accrual basis of accounting as GAAP for personal financial statements. The AICPA "Personal Financial Statements Guide" allows accountants to prepare, compile, review, or audit personal financial statements on other comprehensive bases of accounting, such as historical cost, tax, or cash.

29.5 ORDER OF PRESENTATION.   Assets are presented in order of liquidity, and liabilities in order of maturity. No distinction is made between current and long-term assets and liabilities because there is no operating cycle in a person's financial affairs.

Assets and liabilities of a closely held business that is conducted as a separate entity are not combined with similar personal items in a personal financial statement. Instead, the estimated current net value of the person's investment in the entity is shown as one amount. But if the person owns a business activity that is not conducted as a separate entity, such as a real estate investment with a related mortgage, the assets and liabilities of the activity are shown as separate amounts.

ASSETS

29.6 ESTIMATED CURRENT VALUE.   Assets are presented at their estimated current value. This is defined by SOP No. 82-1 (AICPA, par. 12) as "the amount at which the item could be exchanged between a buyer and a seller, each of whom is well informed and willing, and neither of whom is compelled to buy or sell." Sales commissions and other costs of disposal should be considered if they are expected to be material.

SOP No. 82-1 recognizes that determining the estimated current value of some assets may be difficult, and if the costs of doing so would appear to exceed the benefits, recommends that the person use his judgment.

In general, the best way to determine estimated current value is by reference to recent market prices of similar assets in similar circumstances. If recent market prices are not available, other methods may be used, including the use of appraisals, the adjustment of historical cost by reference to a specific price index, the capitalization of past or prospective earnings, the use of liquidation values, or the use of discounted amounts of projected cash receipts.

Whatever method is used, it should be consistently applied from period to period for the same asset.

29.7 RECEIVABLES.   Receivables are presented at the discounted amounts of cash expected to be collected, using the prevailing interest rate at the date of the statement.

29.8 MARKETABLE SECURITIES.   Marketable securities are stocks, bonds, unfulfilled futures contracts, options on traded securities, CDs, and money market accounts for which market quotations are publicly available. The estimated current value of a marketable security is its closing price on the date of the statement, less the expected sales commission. IRAs and Keogh accounts should be presented net of the penalty charge for early withdrawal.

If the security was not traded on that date, but published bid and asked prices are available,

SOP No. 82-1 states that the estimated current value should be within the range of those prices. Some accountants (Kinsman and Samuelson, 1987, p. 139), however, believe that only the bid price should be used, because "people can ask all they want for an asset, but what matters is what others will pay for it."

If bid and asked prices are not available for the date of the statement, the estimated current value is the closing price on the last day that the security was traded, unless the trade occurred so far back in the past as to be meaningless by the date of the statement.

On over-the-counter securities, unfortunately, the market does not speak with a single voice. Different quotations may be given by the financial press, quotation publications, financial reporting services, and various brokers. In such a case, the mean of the bid prices, of the bid and asked prices, or of the prices quoted by a representative sample of brokers may be used as the estimated current value.

Large blocks of stock may also pose a problem. If a large block of stock were dumped on the market, the price might not hold up. On the other hand, a controlling interest might be worth more, share for share, than a minority interest. Market prices may need to be adjusted for these factors to determine estimated current value. Preparers should consult a qualified stockbroker for an opinion on this problem.

Restrictions on the transfer of a stock are yet another factor that might call for an adjustment of market prices to determine estimated current value.

29.9 LIMITED PARTNERSHIP INTERESTS.   If interests in a limited partnership are actively traded, the estimated current value of such an interest should be based on the prices of recent trades. If interests in the partnership are not actively traded, the current value of the partnership's underlying assets may be used to measure the value of the interest (see sections 29.13 and 29.14). When this method is used, the person should consider discounting the value of the interest for lack of marketability and lack of control over the general partner.

If it is not feasible to estimate the current value of the partnership's underlying assets (and the interests are not actively traded), the estimated current value of the interest may be shown at the amount of cash that the person has invested. If the underlying assets of the partnership are considered to be virtually worthless, however, the interest should be valued at zero.

The person's share of the partnership's negative tax basis, if any, should be included in the computation of the provision for income taxes (see "Provision for Income Taxes" below).

The statement should disclose the person's share of any recourse debts of the partnership, and any commitments for future funding. If the person's interest in the partnership represents a substantial proportion of ownership, it may be useful to disclose summarized financial information about the partnership as an investment in a closely held business (see section 29.13).

29.10 PRECIOUS METALS.   The estimated current value of precious metals, like that of marketable securities, is their closing price on the date of the statement, less the expected sales commission.

29.11 OPTIONS ON ASSETS OTHER THAN MARKETABLE SECURITIES.   Options to buy assets other than marketable securities should first be valued at the difference between the exercise price and the asset's current value. Then this difference should be discounted at the person's borrowing rate over the option period, if this is material. The borrowing rate should reflect the cost of a loan secured by the asset.

29.12 LIFE INSURANCE.   The estimated current value of a life insurance policy is its cash surrender value, less any loans against it. This information may be obtained from the insurance company.

Disclosure of the face value of the policy is required by SOP No. 82-1. It may also be useful to disclose the death benefits that would accrue to family members covered by the statement.

29.13 CLOSELY HELD BUSINESSES.   If the person has a material investment in a closely held business that is conducted as a separate entity, the statement should disclose the name of the company, the person's percentage of ownership, and the nature of the business. It should also disclose summarized financial information on the company's assets, liabilities, and results of operations, based on the company's financial statements for the most recent year. The basis of presentation of these statements, such as GAAP, tax, or cash, should also be disclosed, and so should any significant loss contingencies.

Determining the estimated current value of an investment in a closely held business, whether a proprietorship, partnership, joint venture, or corporation, is notoriously difficult. The objective is to approximate the amount at which the investment could be exchanged, on the date of the statement, between a well-informed and willing buyer and seller, neither of whom is compelled to buy or sell. This value is presented as a single item in the statement of financial condition, and a condensed balance sheet of the company should be presented in the notes.

SOP No. 82-1 recognizes several methods, or combinations of methods, for determining the estimated current value of a closely held business: appraisals, multiple of earnings, liquidation value, reproduction value, discounted amounts of projected cash receipts, adjustments of book value, and cost of the person's share of the equity of the business. If a buy-out agreement exists specifying the amount that the person will receive when he or she withdraws, retires, or sells out, SOP No. 82-1 says that it should be considered but that it does not necessarily determine estimated current value.

A prior question that SOP No. 82-1 does not address is whether an accountant preparing a personal financial statement should try to value a closely held business at all. Competence in valuing businesses requires a considerable degree of concentration on the subject, and some accountants' litigation liability coverage excludes valuations. Qualified appraisers, such as members of the American Society of Appraisers or the Institute of Business Appraisers, are readily available to value the business. Thus, some accountants (Siegel, Lederfich, 1988, p. 67) believe that "the accountant should refrain from valuing the business interest himself."

29.14 REAL ESTATE.   The estimated current value of an investment in real estate or a leasehold may be based on sales of similar properties in similar circumstances; on assessed value for property taxes, considering the basis of the assessment and its relationship to market values in the area; on the discounted amounts of projected cash flows from the property; or on an appraisal from a qualified real estate appraiser.

The estimated current value of a property should be presented net of expected sales commissions and closing costs.

29.15 PERSONAL PROPERTY.   Personal property includes but is not limited to cars, jewelry, antiques, and art. These items should be valued at appraisal values derived from a specialist's opinion or at the values given in published guides such as the *Blue Book* for cars. If the costs of an appraisal seem to outweigh the benefits, historical cost should be used.

29.16 INTANGIBLE ASSETS.   Patents, copyrights, and other intangible assets should be presented at the net proceeds of a current sale of the asset or the discounted amount of cash flow arising from its future use. If the amounts and timing of receipts from the asset cannot be reasonably estimated, the asset should be presented at its purchased cost.

29.17 FUTURE INTERESTS.   The following future interests should be shown in a personal financial statement: guaranteed minimum portions of pensions, vested interests in pension or profit-sharing plans, deferred compensation contracts, beneficial interests in trusts, remainder interests in property subject to life estates, fixed amounts of alimony for a definite future period, and annuities. Any other future interests should also be shown, so long as they are nonforfeitable rights for fixed or determinable amounts; are not contingent on the holder's life expectancy or the occurrence of a particular event, such as disability or death; and do not require future performance of service by the holder.

Such future interests should be presented at their discounted amounts. Suppose, for example, that Sally Smith has an $80,000 interest in her employer's profit-sharing plan, 75% of it vested. She would receive her benefits in a lump sum one year after leaving the company. Since current interest rates on similar investments are 10%, the present value of $1 to be received in one year is $0.9091. Thus, Smith's interest in the profit-sharing plan would be calculated as $80,000 × 0.75 × 0.9091, and would be shown at $54,546.

LIABILITIES

29.18 ESTIMATED CURRENT AMOUNT.   Payables and other liabilities are presented at their estimated current amount. This is the amount of cash to be paid, discounted by the rate implicit in the transaction in which the debt was incurred. APB Opinion No. 21, "Interest on Receivables and Payables," explains how to determine this rate.

Although certain kinds of liabilities are not discounted in business financial statements, all liabilities should be presented at their discounted amounts in personal financial statements. No distinction is made between current and long-term liabilities.

With some home mortgages and other debts, the person may be able to pay off the debt currently at an amount less than the present value of future payments. If this alternative exists, the debt should be presented at the lower amount.

Personal liabilities such as home mortgages are shown separately from investment liabilities such as margin accounts. Obligations related to limited partnership investments should be shown if the person is personally liable for them. Debt that was included in the valuation of an investment in a closely held business, however, should not be shown again here.

29.19 NONCANCELABLE COMMITMENTS.   Child support, alimony, pledges to charities, and other noncancelable commitments to pay future sums should be presented as liabilities at their discounted amounts if they have all of the following characteristics:

- The commitment is for a fixed or determinable amount.
- The commitment is not contingent on someone else's life expectancy or the occurrence of a particular event, such as death or disability.
- The commitment does not require future performance by others, as an operating lease does.

29.20 CONTINGENT LIABILITIES.   Among the contingent liabilities that should be considered for disclosure are personal guarantees on others' loans, liabilities for limited partnership obligations, lawsuits against the person, inadequate medical insurance coverage, and noncoverage for personal liability. SFAS No. 5, "Accounting for Contingencies," provides guidance on whether a contingent liability should be recorded, disclosed in a footnote, or omitted. This pronouncement says, in short, that a liability should be recorded if its amount can be estimated and its occurrence is probable. If its amount cannot be estimated but its occurrence is either probable or possible, the liability should be recognized in a footnote. If its occurrence is remote, neither recording nor footnote recognition is required.

29.21 INCOME TAXES PAYABLE.   Income taxes currently payable include any unpaid income taxes for past tax years, deferred income taxes arising from timing differences, and the estimated amount of income taxes accrued for the elapsed portion of the current tax year to the date of the statement. If the statement date coincides with the tax year-end, there is obviously no difficulty in estimating the amount for the current year. If the dates do not coincide, the estimate should be based on taxable income to date and the tax rate applicable to estimated taxable income for the whole year. The taxes for the current year should be shown net of amounts withheld from pay or paid with estimated tax returns.

PROVISION FOR INCOME TAXES

29.22 DEFINITION.   The personal financial statement presents a provision for the income taxes that would be owed if all of the person's assets were sold, and all of his liabilities paid, on the date of the statement. This provision should be shown under its full title as given in SOP No. 82-1 (par. 30): "Estimated income taxes on the differences between the estimated current values of assets and the estimated current amounts of liabilities and their tax bases." It is presented in the statement as one amount and is shown between liabilities and net worth. A note discloses the methods and assumptions used to compute it (see Exhibit 29.2).

29.23 COMPUTING THE PROVISION FOR INCOME TAXES.   Currently applicable income tax laws and regulations, state and local as well as federal, should be used in computing the provision for income taxes. Negative tax bases of tax shelters, recapture of depreciation, available carryovers, the one-time exclusion for sale of a residence, the deductibility of state income taxes against federal income taxes, and alternative minimum taxes should all be considered.

Because most of these considerations apply to one or two assets or liabilities but not to others, the provision for income taxes should be computed separately for each asset and each liability. It is not necessary, however, to disclose all these computations in the note. For example, note 12 in Exhibit 29.2, which is reproduced from SOP No. 82-1, shows only the excess of estimated current values over the tax bases of major assets.

29.24 TAX BASIS.   It is often difficult to determine the tax basis of an asset or liability acquired long ago, or by inheritance or trade. In such a case the preparer may use a conservative estimate of the tax basis in computing the provision for income taxes, with a note disclosing how the estimate was determined.

29.25 DISCLAIMER.   SOP No. 82-1 (par. 31) requires a statement that "the provision will probably differ from the amounts of income taxes that might eventually be paid because those amounts are determined by the timing and the method of disposal, realization, or liquidation and the tax laws and regulations in effect at the time of disposal, realization, or liquidation." This statement should be made in the note (see Exhibit 29.2, note 12).

STATEMENT OF CHANGES IN NET WORTH

29.26 DEFINITION.   A statement of changes in net worth is an optional supplement to the statement of financial condition. It presents the major sources of change in the person's net worth.

Whereas the statement of financial condition may or may not show amounts for prior periods and thus may not show change in net worth at all, the statement of changes in net worth should present:

- Increases in net worth produced by income, by increases in the estimated current values of assets, by decreases in the estimated current amounts of liabilities, and by decreases in the provision for income taxes.

- Decreases in net worth produced by expenses, by decreases in the estimated current values of assets, by increases in the estimated current amounts of liabilities, and by increases in the provision for income taxes.

The statement of changes in net worth does not attempt to measure net income. It combines income and other changes because the financial affairs of an individual or family are a mixture of business and personal activities.

29.27 USES.   Accountants have often found that lenders do not require a statement of changes in net worth from persons seeking credit; and that credit-seekers, for their part, are not eager to reveal so much information about their standard of living. But a statement of changes in net worth can be very useful in financial planning. As one accountant (Bull, 1984, p. 42) observes, knowing the amounts and sources of increase or decrease in wealth enables the person to estimate how much he will have to increase earnings or decrease consumption to achieve a desired level of wealth—or on the other hand, how much he may decrease earnings or increase consumption and still achieve the same goal.

29.28 FORMAT.   The sample statement of changes in net worth shown in Exhibit 29.2, which is reproduced from SOP No. 82-1, distinguishes realized from unrealized sources of increase or decrease in net worth, thus dividing the sources into four categories: Realized increases, realized decreases, unrealized increases, and unrealized decreases.

DISCLOSURES

A personal financial statement should include sufficient disclosures to make it adequately informative. These disclosures may be made either in the body of the statement or in the notes. The following list, although not exhaustive, indicates the nature and type of information that should ordinarily be disclosed:

- The names of the individuals covered by the statement.
- The fact that assets are presented at their estimated current values and liabilities at their estimated current amounts.
- The methods used to determine current values and amounts, and any change in these methods from one period to the next.
- If any assets shown in the statement are jointly held, the nature of the joint ownership.
- If the person's investments in securities are material in relation to his other assets, and if they are concentrated in one or a few companies or industries, the names of those companies or industries and the estimated current value of each security.
- Information on material investments in closely held businesses, including the name of the company; the person's percentage of ownership; the nature of the business; summarized financial information on the company's assets, liabilities, and results of operations, based on the company's financial statements for the most recent year; the basis of presentation of these statements, such as GAAP, tax, or cash; and any significant loss contingencies.
- Description of intangible assets and their estimated useful lives.
- The face amount of life insurance.
- Nonforfeitable rights, such as pensions based on life expectancy, that were omitted from the statement because they do not have all the characteristics required for inclusion (see section 29.17).

- The following tax information:

    The methods and assumptions used in computing the provision for estimated income taxes on the differences between the estimated current values of assets and the estimated current amounts of liabilities and their tax bases.

    A statement that this provision will probably differ from the amounts of income taxes that might eventually be paid, because these amounts will be determined by the actual timing and method of disposal, realization, or liquidation, and by the tax laws and regulations in effect at the time of disposal, realization, or liquidation.

    Unused operating-loss and capital-loss carryforwards.

    Other unused deductions and credits, with their expiration periods, if applicable.

    The differences between the estimated current values of major assets and the estimated current amounts of major liabilities, or categories of assets and liabilities, and their tax bases.

- Maturities, interest rates, collateral, and other pertinent details on receivables and debt.
- Related-party transactions such as notes receivable or notes payable to other family members.
- Contingencies such as pending lawsuits and loan guarantees.
- Noncancelable commitments, such as operating leases, that do not have all the characteristics required for inclusion (see section 29.19).
- Subsequent events, such as a decline in value of an asset after the statement date.

SOURCES AND SUGGESTED REFERENCES

Accounting Principles Board, APB Opinion No. 21, "Interest on Receivables and Payables," AICPA, New York, 1971.

American Institute of Certified Public Accountants, Accounting and Review Services Committee, "Compilation and Review of Financial Statements," Statement on Standards for Accounting and Review Services No. 1, AICPA, New York, 1979.

———, "Reporting on Personal Financial Statements Included in Written Personal Financial Plans," Statement on Standards for Accounting and Review Services No. 6, AICPA, New York, 1986.

———, "Accounting and Financial Reporting for Personal Financial Statements," Accounting Standards Division, Statement of Position No. 82-1, AICPA, New York, 1982.

———, Personal Financial Statements Task Force, Personal Financial Statements Guide, AICPA, New York, 1983.

Bull, I. O., "Personal Financial Statements—Suggestions for Improvement," *CPA Journal,* December 1984, p. 42.

Financial Accounting Standards Board, "Accounting for Contingencies," Statement of Financial Accounting Standards No. 5, FASB, Stamford, CT, 1975.

Kinsman, M. D., and Samuelson, B., "Personal Financial Statements: Valuation Challenges and Solutions," *Journal of Accountancy,* September 1987, p. 139.

Siegel, J. G., and Lederfich, L., "Accounting and Disclosures for Personal Financial Statements," CPA Journal, February 1988, p. 67.

CHAPTER 30

PARTNERSHIPS

Ronald J. Patten, PhD, CPA

College of Commerce
DePaul University

CONTENTS

NATURE AND ORGANIZATION OF PARTNERSHIP ENTITY

30.1 DEFINITION OF PARTNERSHIP.   The Uniform Partnership Act (UPA), which has been adopted by most of the states, defines a partnership as an association of two or more persons who contribute money, property, or services to carry on as co-owners a business for profit.

A partnership may be "general" or "limited." In the general partnership each partner may be held personally responsible for all the firm's debts, whereas in the limited partnership the liability of certain partners is limited to their respective contributions to the capital of the firm. The limited partnership is composed of a general partner and limited partners with the latter playing no role in the management of the business.

There has been a dramatic increase in the use of limited partnerships in recent years. Passive investors, in particular, use limited partnerships as an investment vehicle, with real estate partnerships and research and development partnerships being very popular. However, as discussed in section 30.3 the Tax Reform Act of 1986 has served to dampen the attractiveness of limited partnerships as a tax shelter.

30.2 ADVANTAGES AND DISADVANTAGES OF PARTNERSHIP.   Bogen (1968, Section 12, p. 5) states:

> The partnership form of organization is superior to the proprietorship because it permits several persons to combine their resources and abilities to conduct a business. It is easier to form than a corporation, and retains a personal character making it more suitable in professional fields.

Historically, the three outstanding disadvantages of the partnership form of organization, as compared with corporate form, were recognized as (1) **unlimited liability of the partners for business debts,** (2) **mutual agency power of each partner as it pertains to business actions,** and (3) **limited life of the partnerships.** More recently, the existence of large partnerships, particularly in the areas of accountancy and investment banking, indicates that these disadvantages may be more apparent than real. The unlimited liability condition, which creates the possibility of loss of personal assets on the part of each partner, is a retardant to many. This is especially important when one considers that each party is assumed to be an agent for all partnership activities, with the power to bind the other partner as a result of his actions. In addition, since the partnership is subject to dissolution upon the death, bankruptcy, insanity, or retirement of a partner—which events do not affect the continuity of a corporation—long-term commitments for the business unit are difficult to obtain. Again, it should be noted that several large partnerships have managed to overcome these presumed difficulties. Some partnership agreements provide for automatic continuation by the remaining partners subject to liquidation of the former partner's interest. In a sense, these partnerships have an unlimited life.

A distinct advantage of a partnership over a corporation is the close relationship between ownership and management. This provides more flexible administration, as well as more management talent with a personal interest in the problems and success of the business.

30.3 TAX CONSIDERATIONS.   Even though a partnership is not considered a separate taxable entity for purposes of paying and determining federal income taxes, it is treated as such for purposes of making various elections and for selecting its accounting methods, taxable year, and method of depreciation.

Under Section 761 (a) of Subchapter K of the Internal Revenue Code of 1954, certain unincorporated organizations may be excluded, completely or partially, from treatment as partnerships for federal income tax purposes. This exclusion applies only to those organizations used (1) for investment purposes rather than as the active conduct of a business, or (2) for the joint extraction, production, or use of property, but not for the purpose of selling the products or services extracted or produced.

The use of limited partnerships because of favorable tax considerations has been significant. The limited partnership, as a form of tax-sheltered investment, has been used in real estate, motion picture production, oil drilling, cable TV, cattle feeding, and research and development. The limited partnership gives investors the tax advantages of the partnership such as the pass-through of losses, while at the same time limiting their liability to the original investment. The Tax Reform Act of 1986 changed the situation considerably, however.

I.R.C. § 465 generally limits a partner's loss to the amount that the partner has "at risk" and could actually lose from an activity. These rules, which apply to individuals and certain closely held corporations, are designed to prevent taxpayers from offsetting trade, business, or professional income with losses from investments in activities that are, for the most part, financed by nonrecourse loans for which they are not personally liable. If it is determined that the loss is deductible under these "at-risk" rules, the taxpayer is subjected to "passive activity" loss rules. Generally, losses from passive trade or business activities, such as in a partnership where the partner is not active, may not be deducted from other types of income such as wages, interest, or dividends according to I.R.C. § 469.

Some substantial tax benefits can still be enjoyed by investing in a triple net lease limited partnership. These partnerships buy buildings that are used by fast-food, auto parts, and other chains and franchises that do not want mortgage debt on their balance sheet. The partnerships collect rent and pass it along to the partners net of three costs—insurance, upkeep, and property taxes—paid by the tenants.

30.4 IMPORTANCE OF PARTNERSHIP.   In the United States, the single proprietorship is the most common form of business organization in terms of number of establishments, and the corporate form does by far the greatest volume of business. Nevertheless, the partnership form of organization holds an important place in both respects and fills a significant need. It is widely employed among the **smaller business units** and in **professional fields** such as medicine, law, dentistry, and accountancy, activities in which the partners are closely identified with the operation of the business or profession. Partnerships are also found in financial lines, such as investment banks. Occasionally a substantial trading or other business is conducted as a partnership.

30.5 FORMATION OF PARTNERSHIP.   The agreement among the copartners that brings the partnership into existence may be oral or written. The latter is much to be preferred. Note the following from Bedford, Perry, and Wyatt (1979):

> Since a partnership is based on a contract between two or more persons, it is important, although not necessarily a legal requirement, that special attention be given to the drawing up of the partnership agreement. This agreement is generally referred to as the "Articles of Copartnership." In order to avoid unnecessary and perhaps costly litigation at some later date, the Articles should contain all of the terms of the agreement relating to the formation, operation, and dissolution of the partnership.

Each partner should sign the Articles and retain a copy of the agreement. It is desirable that a copy of the agreement be filed with the recorder, clerk, or other official designated to receive such documents in the county in which the partnership has its principal place of business. In the case of a limited partnership such filing is imperative. There may also be a requirement that the agreement be published in newspapers.

According to Bogen (1968), the following matters should be covered by the articles:

1. Names of partners and the firm name.
2. Kind of business to be conducted.

3. Capital contribution of each partner.
4. Duration of the partnership contract.
5. The time to be devoted to the business by each, and any limitation upon outside business interests.
6. Method of dividing profits and losses.
7. Restrictions upon the agency powers of the partners.
8. Salaries to be paid partners, or limitations upon the withdrawal of profits.
9. Method of admitting new partners.
10. Provision for insurance on lives of partners for benefit of firm.
11. Procedure to be followed in voluntary dissolution.
12. Procedure upon death or withdrawal of partner, including method of valuation of tangible assets and goodwill, and provision for continuation of the business by the remaining partners.

In the event that contributions of assets other than cash are being made to the new firm, the articles should also cover the matter of **income tax treatment** upon the subsequent disposal of such assets. In general, such assets retain the tax basis of the previous owner so that the taxable gain or loss when ultimately disposed of may be greater or less than the gain or loss to the partnership.

Many partnerships have been plagued, if not entirely destroyed, through disagreements that could have been avoided, or greatly minimized, by the exercising of more care and skill in the drafting of the original agreement.

30.6 INITIAL BALANCE SHEET.   Section 8 of the UPA states that:

1. All property originally brought into the partnership or subsequently acquired by purchase or otherwise, on account of the partnership is partnership property.
2. Unless the contrary intention appears, property acquired with partnership funds is partnership property. . . .

It follows that the initial balance sheet should explicitly identify the assets contributed by partners as belonging to the partnership and assign values to these assets that are agreeable to all partners. Debts assumed by the partnership will receive comparable treatment. The initial balance sheet should also show the total initial proprietorship and the partners' shares therein. According to Moonitz and Jordan (1963):

> The most direct manner of accomplishing this result is to include the initial balance sheet in the partnership agreement itself. If it is not expedient to include it as an integral part of the agreement, reference to the initial balance sheet should be made in the agreement, and the balance sheet, as a separate document, should be signed by each partner.

Unambiguous **identification** of assets and obligations at the inception of the partnership is important for at least two reasons. (1) Partnership creditors have no claim against the assets of individual partners until the partnership assets have been exhausted (special cases are discussed in Parts III and VI of the UPA). (2) Unless specifically provided for in the partnership agreement, partnership assets may be used only for partnership purposes; partners' personal assets are, of course, subject to no such limitations.

ACCOUNTING FOR PARTNERSHIP OPERATIONS

30.7 PECULIARITIES OF PARTNERSHIP ACCOUNTING.   In many respects, the accounting problems of the partnership are the same as those of other forms of business organization. The underlying pattern of the accounting for the various assets and current goods and service costs, including departmental classification and assignment, is not modified by the type of ownership and method of raising capital employed. The same is true of the recording of revenues and the treatment of liabilities. The **special features** of partnership accounting relate primarily to the recording and tracing of capital, the treatment of personal services furnished by the partners, the division of profits, and the adjustments of equities required upon the occasion of reorganization or liquidation of the firm.

30.8 METHODS OF DIVIDING PROFITS AND LOSSES.   As stated in § 18 of the UPA, partnership income is shared equally unless otherwise provided for in the partnership agreement. In some cases the agreement may specify division of profits in an arbitrary ratio (which of course includes the equal ratio already mentioned), referred to elsewhere in this discussion as the **income ratio.** Such a specified ratio (e.g., 60–40, $^2/_3$–$^1/_3$) may or may not be related to the original capital contributions of the respective partners. It is reiterated that the essential point is agreement among the partners as to how they wish profits to be divided.

Another example of profit division by a single set of relationships is afforded by division in **proportion to capital balances.** Since this phrase is ambiguous, the agreement should specify which of the following bases are intended: (1) original capital, (2) capital at the beginning of the year, (3) capital at the end of the year, or (4) average capital. If the last is specified, the method of computation should be outlined.

30.9 EXAMPLE USING AVERAGE CAPITAL RATIO.   The following example shows the division of profits and losses on the basis of average capital ratios.

The Articles of Copartnership of Bracey and Maloney provide for the division of profits on the basis of the average capital balances as shown for the year by the books of the partnership. Effect is to be given to all contributions and withdrawals during the year. The capital accounts for the year appear as follows:

	Bracey		Maloney	
	Debit	Credit	Debit	Credit
January 1		$60,000		$48,000
March 1	$6,000			
April 1			$3,000	
June 1		12,000		
July 1			6,000	
September 1		3,000		21,000
October 1	9,000		9,000	
December 1				6,000

Computation of average capital is as follows:

		Bracey			
	Debits	Credits	Balance	Time Maintained	Dollar-Months
January 1		$60,000	$60,000	2 mos.	$120,000
March 1	$ 6,000		54,000	3	162,000
June 1		12,000	66,000	3	198,000
September 1		3,000	69,000	1	69,000
October 1	9,000		60,000	3	180,000
	$15,000	$75,000	$60,000	12 mos.	$729,000

Average capital ($729,000 ÷ 12) $ 60,750

			Maloney	
	Debits	Credits	Balance	Time Maintained	Dollar-Months
January 1		$48,000	$48,000	3 mos.	$144,000
April 1	$ 3,000		45,000	3	135,000
July 1	6,000		39,000	2	78,000
September 1		21,000	60,000	1	60,000
October 1	9,000		51,000	2	102,000
December 1		6,000	57,000	1	57,000
	$18,000	$75,000	$57,000	12 mos.	$576,000
Average capital ($576,000 ÷ 12)					$ 48,000

If net profit for the year is $36,000, it is distributed as follows:

Bracey	$ 60,750	6,075 ÷ 10,875 × $36,000 =	$20,110.35
Maloney	48,000	4,800 ÷ 10,875 × 36,000 =	$15,889.65
	$108,750		$36,000.00

The method above assumes each month to be of equal significance. If the contributions and withdrawals are dated irregularly, it might be desirable to use days rather than months as the time unit.

30.10 TREATMENT OF TRANSACTIONS BETWEEN PARTNER AND FIRM.   It has often been pointed out that no single profit-sharing ratio can yield equitable results under all circumstances in view of the various contributions of the partners to the firm activities. Accordingly, the articles may well include provisions regarding allowances for (1) interest on invested capital, (2) salaries for services rendered, and (3) bonuses. The ratio for dividing the profit or loss remaining after applying such provisions must, of course, also be specified.

(a) Interest on Invested Capital.   The partnership agreement should cover at least four points in the matter of allowing interest on invested capital:

1. Specific rate or directions for determining the rate.
2. Procedure to be followed if the net income before interest is less than the interest requirement.
3. Procedure to be followed if the partnership experiences a loss.
4. Capital balance (beginning, closing, or average) on which interest is to be allowed (and, if an average balance, method by which the average is to be determined).

The **rate of interest** may be stated specifically or it may be determined by reference to the call money market, the yield of certain governmental obligations, the charge made by local banks for commercial loans, or some other available measure.

If the articles provide for a regular interest allowance, there should be included a statement of how to deal with the cases in which the firm operates at a loss or has a net profit of less than the interest. Following are two ways of dealing with these contingencies: (1) the interest allowance may be dropped or reduced (when there is some profit) for the period in question; (2) the full interest may be allowed and the resulting net debit in the income account apportioned in the income (profit-sharing) ratio. The second procedure is customary for cases in which the articles do not cover the point precisely.

(b) Partners' Salaries.   Each working partner should be entitled to a stated salary as compensation for his services just as each investing partner should receive interest on his capital investment. (The general rule, from a legal standpoint, is that a partner is not entitled to compensation for services in carrying on the business, other than his share in the profits, unless such compensation is specifically authorized in the partnership agreement.) It is always desirable that the articles of partnership specify the amounts of salaries or wages to be paid to partners, or indicate clearly how the amounts are to be determined. The agreement regarding salaries should also cover the contingencies of inadequate income and net losses in particular periods.

Charges for salaries designed to represent reasonable allowances for personal services rendered by the partners are often viewed as **operating expenses,** and this interpretation may be included in the agreement. Under this interpretation, there would seem to be good reason for concluding that regular salaries should be allowed, whether or not the business is operated at a profit. As is the case with interest allowances on capital investments, there is strong presumption that if salaries are authorized in the agreement, they must be allowed, regardless of the level of earnings, in all cases in which a contrary treatment is not prescribed.

Treatment of salary allowances as business expenses is convenient from the standpoint of accounting procedure, particularly in that this treatment facilitates appropriate departmentalization of such charges. On the other hand, it must not be forgotten that partners' salaries, like interest allowances, are essentially devices intended to provide equitable treatment of partners who are supplying unlike amounts of capital and services to the firm; the purpose, in other words, is to secure an equitable apportionment of earnings.

According to Bedford (1962), a distinct rule, "derived from custom and from law," that applies in accounting for partnership owners' equities, is that "the income of a partnership is the income before deducting partners' salaries; partners' salaries are treated as a means of dividing partnership income."

Dixon, Hepworth, and Paton (1966), on the other hand, indicate that the interpretation of partners' salaries should vary with the circumstances:

> Where there are a substantial number of partners, and salaries are allowed to only one or two members who are active in administration, there is practical justification for treating such salaries as operating charges closely akin to the cost of services furnished by outsiders. This is especially defensible where the salaries are subject to negotiation from period to period and are in no way dependent upon the presence of net earnings. Where there are only two partners, and both capital investments and contributions of services are substantially equal, there is less need for salary adjustments; if "salaries" are allowed in such a situation it would seem to be reasonable to interpret them as preliminary distributions of net income—an income derived from a coordination of capital and personal efforts in a business venture. Between these two extremes there lies a range of less clear-cut cases . . . .

(c) Bonuses.   Where a particular partner furnishes especially important services, the device of a bonus—usually expressed as a percentage of net income—may be employed as a means of providing additional compensation. The principal question that arises in such cases is the interpretation of the bonus in relation to the final net amount to be distributed according to the regular income ratio, as illustrated in the following example.

Stark and Bruch share profits equally. Per the partnership agreement, Bruch is to receive a bonus of 20% of the net income of the firm, before allowing the bonus, for special services to the firm. If in a particular year the credit balance of the expense and revenue account is $27,000 before allowing the bonus, profits are divided as follows:

	Stark	Bruch	Total
Bonus, 20% of $27,000		$ 5,400	$ 5,400
Balance equally	$10,800	10,800	21,600
	$10,800	$16,200	$27,000

If the bonus is to be treated as an expense item in the computation of the final net income, the $27,000 credit balance of the expense and revenue account represents both the bonus and the final net income. Hence the $27,000 is 120% of the net income, and the net income is 100% or $22,500. Under this method the profits are divided as follows:

	Stark	Bruch	Total
Bonus, 20% of $22,500		$ 4,500	$ 4,500
Balance equally	$11,250	11,250	22,500
	$11,250	$15,750	$27,000

(d) Debtor–Creditor Relationship. At times, when a partnership is formed, a partner may not be interested in investing more than a certain amount of assets on a permanent basis. He, therefore, may make an advance to the partnership that is viewed as a loan rather than an increase in his capital account. The firm may thus obtain the initial financing it needs without having to negotiate with an outside source on less favorable terms. The loan may be interest bearing and may be repayable in installments. As noted by Meigs, Johnson, and Keller (1966), **interest charges** on such loans should be treated as an expense of the partnership, and the loan itself should be disclosed clearly as a liability of the firm.

Occasionally, a partner may withdraw a sum from the partnership. This type of transaction should be treated in the manner dictated by the circumstances. If the loan is material relative to the partner's net personal assets, if no repayment terms are stipulated, and if the loan has been long outstanding, the loan is, in effect, a **withdrawal** and should be viewed as a contraction of the firm's capital. If, on the other hand, the partner has every intention of repaying the sum, the loan may be regarded as a valid receivable.

(e) Landlord–Tenant Relationship. In some cases, a partner may rent property from or to the partnership. Transactions of this type should be handled exactly as rental agreements with others are handled. The only possible difference in recording this type of event would find the rent receivable from a partner being debited to his drawing or capital account instead of to a "rent receivable" account. If the rent was owed to the partner, the payable could be recorded as a credit to either the partner's drawing or capital account. To minimize the possibility of confusion, it is preferable to record rental transactions with partners in the same manner as other rental agreements.

(f) Statement Presentation. Receivables and payables arising out of transactions between a partner and the firm of which he is a partner should be classified in the balance sheet in the same manner as are receivables and payables arising out of transactions with nonpartners. However, any such receivables and payables included in the balance sheet should be set forth separately; they should not be combined with other receivables and payables. SFAS No. 57 (FASB, 1982) indicates that receivables or payables involving partners stem from a related party transaction and, as such, if material, should be disclosed in such a way as to include:

1. The nature of the relationship(s) involved.
2. A description of the transactions including transactions to which no amounts or nominal amounts were ascribed, for each of the periods for which income statements are presented, and such other information deemed necessary to an understanding of the effects of the transaction on the financial statements.
3. The dollar amounts of transactions for each of the periods for which income statements are presented and the effects of any change in the method of establishing the terms from that used in the preceding period.
4. Amounts due from or to related parties as of the date of each balance sheet presented and, if not otherwise apparent, the terms and manner of settlement.

30.11 CLOSING OPERATING ACCOUNTS.   The operating accounts are closed to the expense and revenue account in the usual manner. That account is then closed by crediting each partner's capital account with his share of the net income or debiting it with his share of the net loss. The drawing account of each partner is then closed to the respective capital account.

(a) Division of Profits Illustrated.   The articles of copartnership of (the fictitious firm of) Ahern and Ciecka include the following provisions as to distribution of profits:

Partners' loans. Loans made by partners to the firm shall draw interest at the rate of 6% per annum. Such interest shall be computed only on December 31 of each year regardless of the period in which the loan was in effect.

Partners' salaries. On December 31 of each year, salaries shall be allowed by a charge to the expense and revenue account and credits to the respective drawing accounts of the partners at the following amounts per annum: Ahern $14,400; Ciecka, $12,000. Partners' salaries are to be allowed whether or not earned.

Interest on partners' invested capital. Each partner is to receive interest at the rate of 6% per annum on the balance of his capital account at the beginning of the year. Such interest is to be allowed whether or not earned.

Remainder of profit or loss. The balance of net income after provision for salaries, interest on loans, and interest on invested capital is to be divided equally. Any loss resulting after provision for the above items is to be divided equally.

On December 31, the books of the partnership show the following balances before recognition of interest and salary adjustments.

Sundry assets	$309,000	
Sundry liabilities		$ 66,000
Ahern, capital		120,000
Ahern, drawings	15,000	
Ciecka, capital		60,000
Ciecka, drawings	9,000	
Ciecka, loan		30,000
Expense and revenue		57,000
	$333,000	$333,000

Balances of the capital accounts on January 1 were: Ahern $105,000; Ciecka $48,000. The loan from Ciecka was made on April 1. Division of profits is as shown in Exhibit 30.1.

AHERN AND CIECKA, PARTNERSHIP Schedule of Division of Net Income For the year ended December 31, 19XX			
	Total	**Ahern**	**Ciecka**
Interest on loan	$ 1,350		$ 1,350
Interest on capital	9,180	$ 6,300	2,880
Salaries allowed	26,400	14,400	12,000
Remainder—equally	20,070	10,035	10,035
Profit earned	$57,000	$30,735	$26,265

Exhibit 30.1.   Division of profits.

AHERN AND CIECKA, PARTNERSHIP
Statement of Partners' Capitals
For the year ended December 31, 19XX

	Total	Ahern	Ciecka
Balances: January 1	$153,000	$105,000	$48,000
Add: additional investments	27,000	15,000	12,000
net income for year—per schedule	57,000	30,735	26,265
Total	$237,000	$150,735	$86,265
Less: withdrawals	24,000	15,000	9,000
Investment, December 31	$213,000	$135,735	$77,265

Exhibit 30.2. Sample statement of partners' capitals.

(b) Statement of Partners' Capitals Illustrated. Formal presentation of the activity of the partners' capital accounts is often made through the **statement of partners' capitals** (Exhibit 30.2).

30.12 INCOME TAXES. According to Hoffman (1978, p. 359):

> Unlike corporations, estates, and trusts, partnerships are not considered separate taxable entities. Instead, each member of a partnership is subject to income tax on their distributive share of the partnership's income, even if an actual distribution is not made. (Section 701 of Subchapter K of the 1954 Code contains the statutory rule that the partners are liable for income tax in their separate or individual capacities. The partnership itself cannot be subject to the income tax on its earnings.) Thus, the tax return (Form 1065) required of a partnership serves only to provide information necessary in determining the character and amount of each partner's distributive share of the partnership's income and expense.

Some states, however, impose an unincorporated business tax on a partnership that for all practical purposes is an income tax.

ACCOUNTING FOR CHANGES IN FIRM MEMBERSHIP

30.13 EFFECT OF CHANGE IN PARTNERS. From a legal point of view, the withdrawal of one or more partners or the admission of one or more new members has the effect of dissolving the original partnership and bringing into being a **new firm.** This means that the terms of the original agreement as such are not binding on the successor partnership. As far as the continuity of the business enterprise is concerned, on the other hand, a change in firm membership may be of only nominal importance; with respect to character of the business, operating policies, relations with customers, etc., there may be no substantial difference between the new firm and its predecessor.

To determine the value of the equity of a retiring partner, or the amount to be paid for a specified share by an incoming partner, a complete **inventory and valuation of firm resources** may be required. Estimation of **interim profits** and unrealized profits on long-term contracts may be involved. In any event, there should be a careful adjustment of partners' equities in accordance with the new relationships established.

A withdrawing partner may continue to be liable for the firm obligations incurred prior to his withdrawal unless the settlement includes specific release therefrom by the continuing partners and by the creditors.

A person admitted as a partner into an existing partnership is liable for all the obligations of the partnership arising before his admission as though he had been a partner when such obligations were incurred, except that this liability shall be satisfied only out of partnership property.

30.14 NEW PARTNER PURCHASING AN INTEREST.   It is possible for a party to acquire the interest of a partner without becoming a partner. A member of a partnership may sell or assign his interest, but unless this has received the **unanimous approval** of the other partners, the purchaser does not become a partner; one partner cannot force his copartners into partnership with an outsider. Under the Uniform Partnership Act, the buyer in such a case acquires only the seller's interest in the profits and losses of the firm and, upon dissolution, the interest to which the original partner would have been entitled. He has no voice in management, nor may he obtain an accounting except in case of dissolution of the business; ordinarily he can make no withdrawal of capital without the consent of the partners.

To illustrate some of the possibilities in connection with purchase of an interest, assume that the firm of Hirt, Thompson, and Pitts negotiates with Davis for the purchase of a capital interest. Data are as follows:

	Capital Accounts	Income Ratio
Hirt	$20,000	50%
Thompson	12,000	40
Pitts	8,000	10
	$40,000	100%

(a) Purchase at Book Value.   If Davis purchases a one-fourth interest for $10,000, it is clear that he is paying exactly book value, and the entry would be:

Hirt, capital	$5,000	
Thompson, capital	3,000	
Pitts, capital	2,000	
Davis, capital		$10,000

The cash payment would be divided in the same manner (i.e., Hirt $5,000, Thompson $3,000, and Pitts $2,000), and would pass directly from Davis to them without going through the firm's cash account.

(b) Purchase at More than Book Value.   Assume now that Davis agrees to pay $12,000 for a one-fourth interest; this is more than book value. In general, two solutions are possible.

(i) Bonus Method.   Under this method, the extra $2,000 paid by Davis is considered to be a bonus to Hirt, Thompson, and Pitts and is shared by them in the income ratio. The entry is:

Hirt, capital	$5,000	
Thompson, capital	3,000	
Pitts, capital	2,000	
Davis, capital		$10,000

The cash payment of $12,000 is divided as follows:

	Hirt	Thompson	Pitts	Total
Capital transferred	$5,000	$3,000	$2,000	$10,000
Premium—in income ratio	1,000	800	200	2,000
Cash received	$6,000	$3,800	$2,200	$12,000

(ii) Goodwill Method.   That Davis is willing to pay $12,000 for a one-fourth interest indicates that the business is worth $48,000. Existing assets are therefore undervalued by $8,000. Under the goodwill or revaluation of assets method, if specific assets can be revalued, this should be done. If not, or if the agreed revaluation is less than $8,000, the difference may be assumed to be goodwill. Dividing the gain in the income ratio results in this entry:

Sundry assets and/or goodwill	$8,000	
Hirt, capital		$ 4,000
Thompson, capital		3,200
Pitts, capital		800

The entry to record Davis' admission would then be:

Hirt, capital	$6,000	
Thompson, capital	3,800	
Pitts, capital	2,200	
Davis, capital		$12,000

The cash payment will be received in amounts equal to the transfer from the capital accounts.

(c) Purchase at Less than Book Value.   Assume next that Davis agrees to pay only $9,000 for a one-fourth interest—that is, less than book value. Again two solutions are possible.

(i) Bonus Method.   Under this method, the same transfers are made from the three partners to Davis' capital account as if he had paid book value, but the difference of $1,000 is apportioned to determine the cash settlement, as follows:

	Hirt	Thompson	Pitts	Total
Capital transferred	$5,000	$3,000	$2,000	$10,000
Loss—in income ratio	500	400	100	1,000
Cash received	$4,500	$2,600	$1,900	$ 9,000

(ii) Revaluation of Assets Method.   This approach reasons that a price of $9,000 for a one-fourth interest indicates that the business is worth $36,000 and that assets should be revalued downward by $4,000. Where a portion of the write-down can be identified with specific tangible assets, the appropriate accounts should be adjusted. Otherwise, existing goodwill should be included in the write-down.

	(1)	
Hirt, capital	$2,000	
Thompson, capital	1,600	
Pitts, capital	400	
Sundry, assets and/or goodwill		$4,000

	(2)	
Hirt, capital	$4,500	
Thompson, capital	2,600	
Pitts, capital	1,900	
Davis, capital		$9,000

30.15 NEW PARTNER'S INVESTMENT TO ACQUIRE AN INTEREST.   The admission of a new partner when he makes an investment in the firm to acquire a capital interest is illustrated by the following cases.

Assume that the capital account balances of the partnership of Andrews and Bell prior to the admission of Cohen are:

	Capital Accounts	Income Ratio
Andrews	$18,000	60%
Bell	12,000	40
	$30,000	100%

(a) Investment at Book Value.   If Cohen invests $10,000 in the firm for a one-fourth interest, the entry is:

Cash (or other assets)	$10,000	
Cohen, capital		$10,000

(b) Investment at More than Book Value.   If Cohen is willing to invest $14,000 for a one-fourth interest, the total capital will be $44,000.

(i) Bonus Method.   Under this method, Cohen's share is one-fourth or $11,000, and the $3,000 premium is treated as a bonus to the old partners by the entry:

Cash (or other assets)	$14,000	
Andrews, capital		$ 1,800
Bell, capital		1,200
Cohen, capital		11,000

(ii) Goodwill Method.   If Cohen invests $14,000 for a one-fourth interest, it would seem that the total worth of the firm should be $56,000. Since total capital is $44,000, under the **goodwill or revaluation of assets method,** there is justification in assuming that existing assets are undervalued to the extent of $12,000. Circumstances may indicate that the $12,000 undervaluation is in the form of goodwill. If it is to be recognized, the entries are as follows:

	(1)	
Goodwill	$12,000	
Andrews, capital		$ 7,200
Bell, capital		4,800

	(2)	
Cash	$14,000	
Cohen, capital		$14,000

If the understatement of the capital of the old partners was attributable to excessive depreciation allowances, land appreciation, an increase in inventory value, or to some combination of such factors, an appropriate adjustment of the asset or assets involved would be substituted for the charge to "goodwill."

(c) Investment at Less than Book Value

(i) Bonus Method.   If Cohen invests $8,000 for a one-fourth interest, it may indicate the willingness of the old partners to give Cohen a bonus to enter the firm.
Since the total capital is now $38,000, a one-fourth interest is $9,500 and the entry is:

Cash	$8,000	
Andrews, capital	900	
Bell, capital	600	
Cohen, capital		$9,500

(ii) Revaluation of Assets Method.   Under this method, the investment by Cohen of only $8,000 for a one-fourth interest may be taken to mean that the existing net assets are worth only $24,000. The overvaluation of $6,000 could be corrected by crediting the overvalued assets and charging Andrews and Bell in the income ratio.

	(1)	
Andrews, capital	$3,600	
Bell, capital	2,400	
Sundry assets		$6,000

	(2)	
Cash	$8,000	
Cohen, capital		$8,000

(iii) Goodwill Method.   A third method sometimes offered to handle this situation is the goodwill method, which assumes that the new partner contributes goodwill (of $2,000 in this case) in addition to the cash, and is credited for the amount of his interest at book value ($10,000 in this case). This seems illogical, however, since it contradicts the original fact that Cohen's investment was to be $8,000.

30.16 SETTLING WITH WITHDRAWING PARTNER THROUGH OUTSIDE FUNDS.   The withdrawal of a partner where settlement is effected by payments made from personal funds of the remaining partners directly to the retiring partner is illustrated by the firm of Adams, Bates, & Caldwell:

	Capital Balances	Income Ratio
Adams	$30,000	50%
Bates	24,000	30
Caldwell	16,000	20
	$70,000	100%

(a) Sale at Book Value.   If Caldwell retires, selling his interest at book value to the other partners in their income ratio and receiving payment from outside funds of Adams and Bates, the entry is:

Caldwell, capital	$16,000	
Adams, capital		$10,000
Bates, capital		6,000

The total payment to Caldwell is $16,000, and payments by Adams and Bates are $10,000 and $6,000, respectively.

(b) Sale at More than Book Value.   If payment to Caldwell exceeds book value, either the bonus or the goodwill method may be used.

(i) Bonus Method.   If total payment to Caldwell is $18,000, the premium of $2,000 may be treated as a bonus to Caldwell. The entry to record the withdrawal of Caldwell is the same as above, and payment would be as follows:

	Adams	Bates	Total
Capital per books	$10,000	$6,000	$16,000
Premium paid	1,250	750	2,000
Cash required	$11,250	$6,750	$18,000

(ii) Goodwill Method.   In the following situation, Adams and Bates are willing to pay a total of $2,000 more than book value for Caldwell's interest. Since the latter receives 20% of the profits, this implies that assets are undervalued by $10,000. Under the **goodwill or revaluation of assets method,** all or part of this amount may be goodwill. The entries to record this situation are:

	(1)	
Goodwill or sundry assets	$10,000	
Adams, capital		$ 5,000
Bates, capital		3,000
Caldwell, capital		2,000

	(2)	
Caldwell, capital	$18,000	
Adams, capital		$11,250
Bates, capital		6,750

(c) Sale at Less than Book Value.   If Caldwell should agree to accept $15,000 for his interest, this is $1,000 less than book value.

(i) Bonus Method.   The $1,000 may be considered to be a **bonus** to Adams and Bates. The entry would be the same as in the first example, but the cash payments would be calculated as follows:

	Adams	Bates	Total
Capital, per books	$10,000	$6,000	$16,000
Less discount allowed	625	375	1,000
Cash required	$ 9,375	$5,625	$15,000

(ii) Revaluation of Assets Method.   In this example, it can be argued under the revaluation of assets approach that the discount of $1,000 for a 20% share in firm profits implies an overstatement of book values of assets by $5,000. If this correction is to be made, the entries to adjust the books and record the subsequent withdrawal of Caldwell are:

	(1)	
Adams, capital	$ 2,500	
Bates, capital	1,500	
Caldwell, capital	1,000	
Sundry assets		$5,000

	(2)	
Caldwell, capital	$15,000	
Adams, capital		$9,375
Bates, capital		5,625

In preceding examples, the so-called bonus method and revaluation of assets method have been presented as alternatives. Although each method results in different capital account balances in the new firm that comes into being, it should be observed that the partners in the new firm are treated relatively the same under either method. This is subject to the basic qualification that the old partners who remain in the new firm must continue to share profits and losses as between themselves in the same ratio as before.

30.17 SETTLEMENT THROUGH FIRM FUNDS.   The withdrawal of a partner where settlement is to be made from funds of the business is illustrated by the firm of Arnold, Brown & Cline.

	Capital Balances	Income Ratio
Arnold	$ 40,000	30%
Brown	50,000	30
Cline	60,000	40
	$150,000	100%

(a) Premium Paid to Retiring Partner.   Payment is to be made to Cline from the assets of the partnership. Payment is $64,000, to be made one-half in cash and the balance in notes payable. Under one treatment, the premium of $4,000 is viewed as chargeable to the remaining partners in their income ratio. The entry is:

Arnold, capital	$ 2,000	
Brown, capital	2,000	
Cline, capital	60,000	
Cash		$32,000
Notes payable		32,000

A second method treats the $4,000 premium as payment for Cline's share of the unrecognized goodwill of the firm. The following entry would be made:

Goodwill	$ 4,000	
Cline, capital	60,000	
Cash		$32,000
Notes payable		32,000

A third possibility for recording the retirement of Cline is to recognize a total goodwill or asset revaluation implied by the premium paid for the retiring partner's share. Since a $4,000 premium was paid for a 40% share, total implied goodwill or asset revaluation is $10,000 and the entries are:

(1)

Goodwill or sundry assets	$10,000	
Arnold, capital		$ 3,000
Brown, capital		3,000
Cline, capital		4,000

(2)

Cline, capital	$64,000	
Cash		$32,000
Notes payable		32,000

Many accountants are inclined to approve of the first treatment on the ground that it is "conservative." Meigs, Johnson, and Keller (1966) state that it is "consistent with the current trend toward viewing a partnership as a continuing business entity, with asset valuations and accounting policies remaining undisturbed by the retirement of a partner." The second treatment is supported by reference to the rule that it is proper to set up goodwill only when it has been purchased. The third interpretation relies on the idea that it is inconsistent to recognize the existence of an intangible asset and then to record it at only a fraction of the proper amount.

The accountant may distinguish between a payment for goodwill and one that represents a partner's share of the increase in value of one or more of the firm's assets. In the latter case, it is generally not reasonable to record only the increase attaching to the retiring partner's equity. Suppose, for example, that an inventory of merchandise has a **market value** on the date of settlement substantially above book value. Clearly, the most appropriate treatment here is that under which the inventory is adjusted to market value—the value at which it is in effect acquired by the new firm; to add to book value only the withdrawing partner's share of the increase would result in figures unsatisfactory from the standpoint both of financial accounting and operating procedure.

(b) Discount Given by Retiring Partner. Assuming that Cline receives $57,000 for his interest in the firm and payment is made by equal amounts of cash and notes payable, two possible accounting treatments are available.

First, the discount of $3,000 may be credited to the remaining partners in their income ratio:

Cline, capital	$60,000	
Cash		$28,500
Notes payable		28,500
Arnold, capital		1,500
Brown, capital		1,500

In the second method the implied overvaluation of assets is recognized. Since Cline's share (40%) was purchased at a discount of $3,000, the total overvaluation of firm assets may be considered as $7,500. The following entries are made:

	(1)	
Arnold, capital	$ 2,250	
Brown, capital	2,250	
Cline, capital	3,000	
Sundry assets		$ 7,500

	(2)	
Cline, capital	$57,000	
Cash		$28,500
Notes payable		28,500

30.18 ADJUSTMENT OF CAPITAL RATIOS.   Circumstances may arise in partnership affairs when it becomes desirable to adjust partners' capital account balances to certain ratios—most often the income ratio. This may happen in connection with the admission of a new partner, the withdrawal of a partner, or at some time when no change in personnel has occurred. Only a simple case involving a continuing firm is illustrated here.

Assume the following data for the firm of Emmett, Frye, and Gable:

	Capital Balances	Income Ratio
Emmett	$50,000	50%
Frye	25,000	30
Gable	15,000	20
	$90,000	100%

If the partners wish to adjust their capital balances to the income ratio without changing total capital, it is obvious that Frye should pay $2,000 and Gable $3,000 directly to Emmett, and that the entry should be:

Emmet, capital	$5,000	
Frye, capital		$2,000
Gable, capital		3,000

Adjustment of the capital balances to the income ratio by the minimum **additional investment**

into the firm (as distinguished from the preceding personal settlement) could, of course, be effected by the additional investment of $5,000 each by Frye and Gable.

INCORPORATION OF A PARTNERSHIP

According to Meigs, Johnson, and Keller (1966):

> Most successful partnerships give consideration at times to the possible advantages to be gained by incorporating. Among the advantages are limited liability, ease of attracting outside capital without loss of control, and possible tax savings.

> A new corporation formed to take over the assets and liabilities of a partnership will usually sell stock to outsiders for cash either at the time of incorporation or at a later date. To assure that the former partners receive an equitable portion of the total capital stock, the assets of the partnership will need to be adjusted to fair market value before being transferred to the corporation. Any goodwill developed by the partnership should be recognized as part of the assets transferred.

> The accounting records of a partnership may be modified and continued in use when the firm changes to the corporate form. As an alternative, the partnership books may be closed and a new set of accounting records established for the corporation. . . .

PARTNERSHIP REALIZATION AND LIQUIDATION

30.19 BASIC CONSIDERATIONS.   A partnership may be disposed of either by selling the business as a unit or by the sale (realization) of the specific assets followed by the liquidation of the liabilities and final distribution of the remaining assets (usually cash) to the partners. A basic principle to be observed carefully in all such cases is that losses (or gains) in realization or sale must first be apportioned among the partners in the income ratio, following which, if outside creditors have been paid in full or cash reserved for that purpose, payments may be made according to the remaining capital balances of the partners.

Discussions of partnership liquidations usually point out that the proper **order of cash distribution** is: (1) payment of creditors in full, (2) payment of partners' loan accounts, and (3) payment of partners' capital accounts. Actually the stated priority of the **partners' loans** appears to be a legal fiction. An established legal doctrine called the **right of offset** requires that any credit balance standing in a partner's name be set off against an actual or potential debit balance in his capital account. Application of this right of offset always produces the same final result as if the loan or undrawn salary account were a part of the capital balance at the beginning of the process. For this reason, no separate examples are given that include loan accounts. If they are encountered, they may be added to the capital account balance at the top of the liquidation statement. (The existence of partners' loan accounts might have an effect on profit sharing, however, in the sense that interest on partners' loans is usually provided for and profits might be shared in the average capital ratio: loans would presumably be excluded from the computation.)

Realization of all assets and liquidation of liabilities may be completed before any cash is distributed to partners. Or, if the realization process stretches over a considerable period of time, so-called **installment liquidation** may be employed.

30.20 LIQUIDATION BY SINGLE CASH DISTRIBUTION.   The illustration below demonstrates the realization of assets, payment of creditors, and final single cash distribution to the partners. Losses are first allocated to the partners in the income ratio, followed by cash payment to creditors and then to partners.

Rogers, Stevens, and Troy are partners with capital balances of $20,000, $15,000 and $10,000, respectively. Profits and losses are shared equally. On a particular date they find that the firm has assets of $80,000, liabilities of $47,000, and undistributed losses of $12,000. At this point the assets are sold for $59,000 cash. The proper distribution of the cash is as follows:

	Total	Rogers	Stevens	Troy
Capital balances	$45,000	$20,000	$15,000	$10,000
Less undistributed losses	12,000	4,000	4,000	4,000
Adjusted balances	$33,000	$16,000	$11,000	$ 6,000
Less loss on sale of assets	21,000	7,000	7,000	7,000
Adjusted balances	$12,000	$ 9,000	$ 4,000	$(1,000)
Payment by Troy for deficiency		1,000		1,000
Balances before distribution	$13,000	$ 9,000	$ 4,000	-0-
Cash available	$60,000			
Paid to creditors	47,000			
Cash paid to partners	$13,000	$ 9,000	$ 4,000	-0-

In this example it was assumed that Troy was financially able to make up the $1,000 deficiency that appeared in his capital account. Only by making this payment does he bear his agreed share of the losses. If Troy had been personally insolvent and therefore unable to make the $1,000 payment, the statement from that point on would have taken the following form:

	Total	Rogers	Stevens	Troy
Adjusted balances	$12,000	$ 9,000	$ 4,000	$(1,000)
Apportion deficiency in income ratio		(500)	(500)	1,000
Balances before distribution	$12,000	$ 8,500	$ 3,500	-0-
Cash available	$59,000			
Paid to creditors	47,000			
Cash paid to partners	$12,000	$ 8,500	$ 3,500	-0-

Troy is now personally indebted to Rogers and Stevens in the amount of $500 each. Just how this debt would rank in the settlement of Troy's personal affairs depends on the state having jurisdiction. Under the UPA his personal creditors (not including Rogers and Stevens) have prior claim to his personal assets; because he was said to have been personally insolvent, the presumption is that Rogers and Stevens would collect nothing. In a common-law state, a deficiency of this sort is considered to be a personal debt and would generally rank along with the other personal creditors. In this event Rogers and Stevens would presumably make a partial recovery of the $500 due each of them.

30.21 LIQUIDATION BY INSTALLMENTS. It is sometimes necessary to liquidate on an installment basis. Two of the many possible cases are illustrated—in the first there is no capital deficiency to any partner when the first cash distribution is made; in the second there is a possible deficiency of one partner at the time of the first cash distribution. The situation involving a final deficiency of a partner is discussed above in the partnership of Rogers, Stevens, and Troy. If this situation should appear in the winding up of an installment liquidation, its treatment would be the same as described there.

The role of the liquidator is especially important in the case of installment liquidation. In addition to his obvious responsibility to see that outside creditors are paid and to convert the various assets into cash with a maximum gain or a minimum loss, he must protect the interests of the partners in their relationship to each other. Other than for reimbursement of liquidation expenses, no cash payment can be made to a partner, even on loan accounts or undrawn profits, except as the total standing to his credit exceeds his share of total possible losses on assets not yet realized. Improper payment by the liquidator might result in personal liability therefor, if recovery could not be made from the partner who was overpaid.

30.22 CAPITAL CREDITS ONLY—NO CAPITAL DEFICIENCY.   Below is the balance sheet of Burns & Mantle as of April 30, when installment liquidation of the firm began. The partners share profits and losses equally.

ASSETS		LIABILITIES AND CAPITAL	
Cash	$ 6,200	Liabilities	$ 56,000
Other assets	350,000	Burns, capital	220,200
		Mantle, capital	80,000
	$356,200		$356,200

During May assets having a book value of $220,000 are sold for cash of $198,000, and $39,000 is paid to creditors. During June the remaining assets are sold for $90,000, the balance due creditors is paid, and liquidation expenses of $8,000 are paid. Distribution of cash to the partners should be made as follows:

	Total	Burns	Mantle
Capital, per balance sheet	$300,200	$220,200	$80,000
Less realization loss in May	22,000	11,000	11,000
Balance after loss	$278,200	$209,200	$69,000
Cash available to partners	148,200		
Possible loss divided	$130,000	65,000	65,000
Balances paid in cash		$144,200	$ 4,000
Balances, June 1		$ 65,000	$65,000
Less realization loss in June	40,000	20,000	20,000
Balances after loss	$ 90,000	$ 45,000	$45,000
Less liquidation expense	8,000	4,000	4,000
Final cash payment	$ 82,000	$ 41,000	$41,000

Cash available to partners at May 31 is calculated as follows:

Cash, per balance sheet	$ 6,200	
Received from sale of assets—May	198,000	$204,200
Paid to creditors—May	$ 39,000	
Reserved for creditors	17,000	56,000
Available for distribution to partners		$148,200

In this example the first payment of $148,200 reduces the capital claims to the profit and loss ratios, and all subsequent charges or credits to the partners' capital accounts are made accordingly.

(a) Capital Credits Only—Capital Deficiency of One Partner.   This situation is illustrated in Exhibit 30.3 using the previous balance sheet but assuming the following liquidation data:

BURNS & MANTLE
Statement of Liquidation
May 1 to July 31

	Total	Burns	Mantle
Capital balances, May 1	$300,200	$220,200	$ 80,000
Less realization loss in May	30,000	15,000	15,000
Balances after loss, May 31[a]	$270,200	$205,200	$ 65,000
Less realization loss in June	40,000	20,000	20,000
Balances after loss, June 30	$230,200	$185,200	$ 45,000
Cash available to partners[b]	60,200		
Possible loss apportioned	$170,000	85,000	85,000
Balances after apportionment		$100,200	$(40,000)
Further possible loss to Burns		(40,000)	40,000
Cash payment to Burns		$ 60,200	
Balances, July 1		$125,000	$ 45,000
Less realization loss in July	25,000	12,500	12,500
Balances after loss, July 31	$145,000	$112,500	$ 32,500
Less liquidation expense	8,000	4,000	4,000
Final cash payment	$137,000	$108,500	$ 28,500

[a]No cash was distributed to partners at May 31 because only $200 was available at that time. The calculation:

Cash, per balance sheet		$ 6,200	
Received from sale of assets—May		50,000	$ 56,200
Paid to creditors—May		$ 39,000	
Reserved for creditors		17,000	$ 56,000
Available to partners—not distributed, May 31			$ 200

[b]This amount is the $200 not distributed at May 31 plus the $60,000 received in June from sale of assets.

Exhibit 30.3. Sample statement of liquidation.

	Assets Sold	Cash Received	Creditors Paid	Expenses Paid
May	$ 80,000	$ 50,000	$39,000	
June	100,000	60,000	17,000	
July	170,000	145,000		$8,000

In Exhibit 30.3 each partner received in total the balance of his capital account per the balance sheet minus his share (50%) of realization losses and expenses, the same as if one final cash payment had been made on July 31. Note that if Mantle had had a loan account of, say, $20,000 and a capital balance of $60,000, the first cash distribution of $60,200 would still have gone entirely to Burns. At this point, after exercising the right of offset, Mantle would still have had a future possible deficiency of $40,000.

(b) Installment Distribution Plan.   A somewhat different approach to the problem of installment liquidation is illustrated below.

Fox, Green, and Harris are partners sharing profits equally. Following is the partnership balance sheet as of December 31, at which time it is decided to liquidate the firm by installments.

ASSETS		LIABILITIES AND CAPITAL	
Cash	$ 3,000	Liabilities	$ 24,000
Other assets	186,000	Fox, capital	79,000
		Green, capital	52,000
		Harris, capital	34,000
	$189,000		$189,000

Using the balance sheet above, computation of correct cash distribution is as follows:

	Total	Fox	Green	Harris
Partners' capital balances	$165,000	$79,000	$52,000	$34,000
Loss that would eliminate Harris, who is least able to absorb	102,000	34,000	34,000	34,000
Balances	$ 63,000	$45,000	$18,000	
Loss that would eliminate Green	36,000	18,000	18,000	
Balances	$ 27,000	$27,000		

The amount of the loss that will extinguish each partner's capital account is determined by dividing his capital account by his percentage of income and loss sharing. Hence, for Harris this amount is $34,000 ÷ 33$\frac{1}{3}$%, or $102,000.

From the computations, it is possible to prepare a schedule for the distribution of cash as follows:

	Cash	Liabilities	Fox	Green	Harris
First	$21,000	$21,000			
Next	27,000		All		
Next	36,000		$\frac{1}{2}$	$\frac{1}{2}$	
All in excess of	84,000		$\frac{1}{3}$	$\frac{1}{3}$	$\frac{1}{3}$

It is assumed that the $3,000 cash on hand on December 31 is used in payment of liabilities. The following liquidation data are given:

	Assets Sold	Cash Received	Creditors Paid
January	$ 64,000	$ 41,000	$24,000
February	60,000	37,000	
March	62,000	54,000	
Totals	$186,000	$132,000	$24,000

Based on these data, the application of the computations already made results in the following payments to creditors and partners:

	Amount	Liabilities	Fox	Green	Harris
January	$ 41,000	$21,000	$20,000		
February	37,000		7,000		
			15,000	$15,000	
March	54,000		3,000	3,000	
			16,000	16,000	$16,000
Totals	$132,000	$21,000	$61,000	$34,000	$16,000

SOURCES AND SUGGESTED REFERENCES

American Institute of Certified Public Accountants, "Related Party Transactions," Statement of Auditing Standards No. 6, AICPA, New York, 1975.

Anderson, R. J., *External Audit,* Pitman Publishing Co., Toronto, Ont., Canada, 1977.

Bedford, Norton M., *Introduction to Modern Accounting,* Ronald Press, New York, 1962.

———, Perry, Kenneth W., and Wyatt, Arthur H., *Advanced Accounting—An Organization Approach,* Wiley, New York, 1979.

Bogen, Jules I., "Advantages and Disadvantages of Partnership," in *Financial Handbook,* 4th ed., Ronald Press, New York, 1968.

Defliese, Philip L., Johnson, Kenneth P., and Macleod, Roderick K., *Montgomery's Auditing,* 9th ed., Ronald Press, New York, 1975.

Dixon, Robert L., Hepworth, Samuel R., and Paton, William A., Jr., *Essentials of Accounting,* Macmillan, New York, 1966.

Financial Accounting Standards Board, "Related Party Disclosures," Statement of Financial Accounting Standards No. 57, FASB, Stamford, CT, 1982.

Hoffman, William H., Jr., Ed., *West's Federal Taxation: Corporations, Partnerships, Estates and Trusts,* West Publishing Co., St. Paul, MN, 1978.

Internal Revenue Service & Internal Revenue Code of 1954, Section 761, Subchapter K.

Meigs, Walter B., Johnson, Charles E., and Keller, Thomas F., *Advanced Accounting,* McGraw-Hill, New York, 1966.

Moonitz, Maurice, and Jordan, Louis H., *Accounting—An Analysis of Its Problems,* 2 vols., rev. ed., Holt, Rinehart, and Winston, New York, 1963.

CHAPTER 31

ESTATES AND TRUSTS

Joseph V. Falanga, CPA
Spicer & Oppenheim

Philip M. Herr, JD
Spicer & Oppenheim

Richard J. Shapiro, JD
Spicer & Oppenheim

CONTENTS

ESTATES—LEGAL BACKGROUND

31.1 EXECUTING A WILL. A **will** is a revocable instrument whereby a person makes a disposition of his property to take effect at death. A prudent person should secure legal advice upon reaching the age of majority (age 18 in many states). If the attorney deems it advisable, such person should execute a will. In the will, the testator (maker) should spell out in detail who is to inherit his property upon his death. The testator may also name a person to administer the estate and select a **guardian** (a protector of the body and property of his children, if any). A will can be very simple or very complex depending on the extent of the testator's property and desires. To be valid, the will must be properly executed according to state law. Such state laws normally require the maker to declare that the document is his last will and testament and to sign it in the presence of at least two witnesses, who also sign. Such witnesses, called **subscribing witnesses,** may later be called upon to testify about the maker's appearance of mental competence at the time of the execution of the will.

31.2 WILL PROVISIONS. Every will provision must be adhered to by the executor and the courts unless it is contrary to law or against public policy.

   A typical will provides for:

    1. **General bequests or legacies** of money or property to named individuals payable out of the general assets of the estate.

2. **Devises** of real property to specified individuals.

3. **Specific bequests or legacies** of specific property. They fail if the property does not exist at the testator's death.

4. **Demonstrative bequests or legacies.** These are gifts of money or property payable out of a particular fund; if the fund is insufficient, the balance becomes a general legacy.

5. Provisions concerning disposal of the **residuary estate.** The residuary estate is all property not otherwise provided for in the will.

6. The duties and powers of the executor (described later in this section).

7. The naming of **fiduciaries** (executors, trustees, guardians, committees for incompetents) and their successors; and often, the exemption of having to post a fidelity bond.

8. Definitions of terms used in the will.

9. Provisions apportioning federal and state death taxes among the various classes of beneficiaries (marital vs. nonmarital, specific vs. residuary, charitable vs. noncharitable).

10. Simultaneous death provision that provides who shall be presumed to have survived whom as between the testator and other beneficiaries taking under the will.

11. The terms of any testamentary trusts that might be established under the will (i.e., for a minor beneficiary).

12. Signature of testator and subscribing witnesses.

31.3 RULES UNDER INTESTACY.   "Intestacy" is defined as the state or condition of dying without having made a valid will, or without having disposed by will of a part of the deceased's property. Thus it arises not only when the deceased died without having made a will, but also if the will is invalid, or if it contains ineffective or no provisions concerning the disposal of the residuary estate.

When an intestacy is present, state law provides who is to receive the property. In effect, state statutes make a will for the deceased. The plan of distribution of the property, sometimes called **intestate succession** or **laws of descent and distribution,** is strictly defined by state statute and is based on degree of relationship to the deceased. New York State, for example, provides that if a decedent dies without a will and leaves a wife and two children, the wife receives one-third of the estate and the children share two-thirds. Under the same circumstances, Oregon allows the spouse one-half of the estate and the children share the other one-half. Distribution plans under state laws vary even more if a spouse or children do not survive the decedent. Distribution plans under intestacy do not take into account financial needs or close bonds of a decedent to certain relatives. It may result in relatives with whom a decedent has had no contact for many years inheriting a portion of the property. Absence of a will can result in fights over the appointment of administrators and in custody battles over the guardianship of minor children and their property. The failure to make a will should be a conscious decision of an informed individual to allow state law to make it for him and not a result of ignorance or procrastination.

31.4 DOMICILE.   Generally most states take the position that the property of a person domiciled in a state at the time of death is subject to court jurisdiction (and the estate and inheritance tax) of that state. **Domicile** is defined as the place where a person has a true, fixed, and permanent home to which, whenever absent, the person has the intention of returning.

In addition, states generally also claim court jurisdiction over (and estate and inheritance tax on) real and tangible personal property located within their boundaries for persons domiciled outside the state at the time of their death.

These two concepts often force an executor or administrator to bring court proceedings in more than one state. Proceedings brought outside the state of domicile are called **ancillary**

proceedings. The distribution by the executor or administrator of ancillary property is governed by the state law of the property's location.

Sometimes more than one state claims that a decedent was domiciled in that state at the time of death. Such a situation can lead to expensive litigation and excessive estate or inheritance tax. A person with dual residences should clearly establish which state he considers to be his domicile. This can be done by consistency in such evidence of domicile as voter registration, automobile registration, state income tax returns, declaration in will, and positions taken in documents executed during life.

31.5 PROBATE PROCEDURES: WILL. The courts having jurisdiction over decedents' estates have different names. Some states call such a court a "probate court"; others, a "surrogate court." Often the same court governs both decedents leaving wills and those dying without wills.

After a decedent's will has been located, it should be presented to the court for **probating,** that is, proving it valid. The named executor (executrix if a female), if qualified and willing to act, is issued **letters testamentary,** that is, a document authorizing him to act on behalf of the estate. In some states temporary letters are issued with formal letters issued at a later date.

31.6 PROBATE PROCEDURES: FAILURE OF EXECUTOR. If the executor named in the will is unqualified because of such factors as age, competency, or residency, any named successor if qualified is allowed to take the executor's place. Should all successors fail to qualify or refuse the appointment, any beneficiary of the estate may petition the court for appointment. State laws generally provide an order of priority, the appointment going first to a qualified surviving spouse, then to qualified children (sometimes in age order), then to qualified grandchildren, and so on.

The person who qualifies and accepts the appointment is called an **administrator** (or **administratrix**) **CTA** (*cum testamento annexo,* that is, "with the will annexed"). The administrator CTA has the same duties and powers as an executor and looks to the will for authority to act.

31.7 PROBATE PROCEDURES: INTESTACY. The death of a person without a will necessitates the appointment of an administrator. As mentioned above, appointments are made by interested parties petitioning the court and the court appointing the first person who can qualify in the order of priority outlined under state law. Letters of administration are issued after compliance with the governing statutes. The administrator must distribute the estate in accordance with the laws of intestacy of the state in which he is appointed.

31.8 SETTLEMENT OF SMALL ESTATES. Most state statutes provide special rules for the settlement of small estates with either no court administrative involvement or some form of an abbreviated procedure. The definition of "small" depends on the gross value of the estate. These values can be as low as $5,000 to $15,000, or as high as $50,000 to $60,000. Utilization of these special rules results in greatly reduced administration costs and a quicker settlement of the estate.

31.9 FIDUCIARY RESPONSIBILITIES

(a) Executor versus Administrator. Although the executor's powers and duties come primarily from the will and secondarily from state law if the will is silent, the administrator of a person dying intestate must look solely to state law for authority to act.

The term **personal representative** or simply **representative** as used in this section encompasses both executors and administrators. The term **fiduciary** includes executors, administrators, guardians, and trustees.

(b) General Duties of Representatives.   Duties of a representative, stated generally, are to collect the decedent's assets, pay creditors, account for all income and expenses, and distribute the assets remaining according to the provisions of the will or in accordance with state law in the absence of will provisions.

In the performance of these duties, the personal representative must use the **"reasonable man" rule,** that is, duties must be exercised with the prudence a reasonable person would exercise with his own property. The representative does not guarantee estate assets against loss. However, he is responsible for acting reasonably and can be asked to make good estate losses should he fail to act reasonably. Since the representative is not required to possess the expertise of an accountant, attorney, or investment counselor (although a decedent may often name such a professional in the will), a representative acting in a "reasonable" manner should determine whether the will or state law authorizes the retention of such advisors whenever necessary.

(c) Preliminary Administration.   Often a death is sudden and unexpected. Determining whether the decedent left a will is sometimes a problem. Finding it and determining whether it is the last will executed may be even bigger problems. A careful search must be made of the decedent's personal papers. If the decedent had an attorney, accountant, or insurance broker, the person may be helpful in ascertaining the existence of a will and locating it. The importance of the will lies not only in carrying out the decedent's plan for distribution of his assets, but also in determining the persons named as executors, trustees, and guardians of minors or others incapable of caring for themselves. Administration of the estate must begin, however, at the moment of death. There are too many important acts, such as carrying out the decedent's instructions for bodily organ donations, arranging for the funeral, and safe-guarding valuable or perishable assets, to await the location of the will or formal appointment of a representative. Someone must take responsibility at once. Should it later turn out that another person was named executor or appointed administrator, an orderly transition of authority can be made.

(d) Specific Duties of Representatives.   Other specific duties of the personal representative are to:

1. Arrange to have all estate assets inventoried and title transferred to the name of the executor or administrator.

2. Obtain possession of the decedent's important papers and personal property and arrange for safekeeping.

3. Arrange for adequate insurance coverage for estate assets.

4. Collect all debts owed to the decedent and litigate if necessary.

5. Arrange for an appraisal of all estate assets by qualified appraisers before distributing any assets.

6. Keep clear and accurate records of all estate receipts and disbursements. This is necessary for tax returns and for accountings to courts and beneficiaries.

7. Determine whether assets coming under the control of representatives are sufficient to meet both claims against the estate and legacies allowed by will and/or state law.

8. Review cash requirements to pay legacies, taxes, debts, and administration expenses, and determine whether assets are sufficiently liquid to pay such claims as they become due.

9. Arrange for the preparation of any payment of tax due on the decedent's final income tax returns, federal estate return, state or foreign estate or inheritance tax returns, and estate income tax returns.

10. Advertise for creditors (publish notification of decedent's death, allowing statutory period for claim presentation) and pay all valid claims against the estate.
11. Pay legacies at times specified under state law and distribute the remainder of the estate after payment of all debts and administration expenses to persons directed by will or by state law in the absence of will direction.
12. Prepare interim and/or final accountings for beneficiaries and courts as required by state law.

A graphic outline of the administration of a decedent's estate is presented in Exhibit 31.1.

(e) Possession of Assets.   After the appointment of the administrator or executor, the next step is to assemble the property belonging to the estate. The representative is required to exercise due diligence in the discovery of assets and must take all proper legal steps to obtain possession of them.

(f) Probate versus Nonprobate Assets.   Probate assets are those assets whose disposition is controlled by the decedent's will. Nonprobate assets pass to the designated beneficiary by either operation of law (i.e., joint tenancy with right to survivorship, tenants by the entirety), or by operation of contract (i.e., designated beneficiary of an insurance policy, qualified retirement plan, or other form of deferred compensation). Although the value of nonprobate

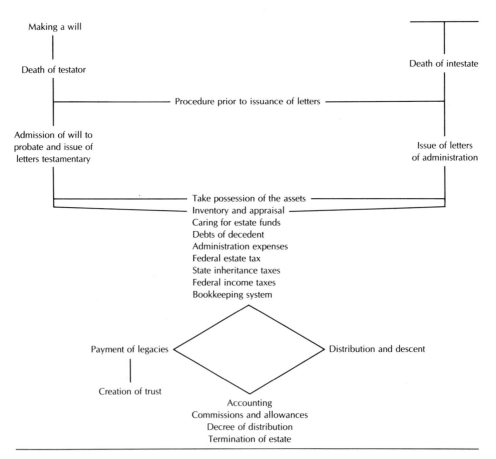

Exhibit 31.1.   Graphic outline of the administration of decedent's estate.

assets is includable in the decedent's gross estate for tax purposes, the administrator or executor is not responsible for the collection of these assets. However, the estate representative's cooperation in assisting a beneficiary obtain possession of these assets is a usual occurrence.

(g) Personal Property Exemptions.   Personal property of the deceased passes directly to the personal representative of the decedent. However, certain items of personal property must be exempted by statute for the benefit of the family of the decedent.

(h) Real Property.   Title to real property passes directly to the heirs, or devisees, and such property does not ordinarily come under the control of the representative unless left to the estate by will, sold by order of the court to pay valid obligations of the estate, or administered by the representative as a requirement of state law. If real estate does come under the control of the representative, it is handled in the same manner as personal property. In some states, the representative may manage the real estate and collect rents during the period of administration. The balance due on a **land contract** receivable is personal property of the estate, although the title to the land passes to the heirs and is retained by them until the contract is paid.

(i) Inventory of Assets.   A detailed inventory of all assets taken over, which will form the basis of the accounting of the representative, should be prepared and filed with the court. Schedules should be prepared of all cash on hand and on deposit; all furniture, fixtures, and articles of personal use; all claims against others **(choses in action)**; all contract rights that do not involve personal services; all unpaid fees, commissions, and salaries; all life insurance policies payable to the estate; all interest in partnerships; all unpaid dividends of record as of the date of death, or other accrued income; all leases; and all other personal property owned by the decedent. The inventory does not include goods or money held by the decedent for others. Claims canceled by will are included in the inventory, as are articles exempted for the decedent's family and articles of no apparent value. No liabilities are mentioned in the inventory, and assets pledged to secure a loan are listed without deduction for the amount of the loan. Accruals are to be computed up to midnight following the death of the decedent.

(j) Valuation of Assets.   The asset values are usually set by appraisers appointed by the court and will presumably be the market values at the time of death. The executor should keep a copy of the inventory and incorporate its details into the bookkeeping system.

(k) Management of Estate Funds.   Generally, the function of the administrator or executor of an estate is to **liquidate,** whereas the role of the trustee or guardian is to manage. Nonetheless, the administrator or executor may have important managerial functions to perform. Perishable goods, speculative investments, and burdensome property should be disposed of promptly. Unless forgiven in the will, every effort should be made to collect all claims due the estate. Articles of a personal nature are usually distributed among legatees or next of kin at their inventory value but may be sold if such a distribution is not feasible.

All **estate funds** should be kept in a separate bank account in the name of the representative, with an indication of the fiduciary relationship, and should not be mingled with those of the representatives (except in the case of a trust company). All **disbursements** should be made by check. Interest should be secured on bank balances if possible. Stock certificates in the name of the decedent should be transferred to the name of the representative in his fiduciary capacity. Adequate insurance should be carried against fire, theft, public liability, and other risks. In general, the representative, to avoid personal liability for loss of funds and property, must care for the assets as diligently as if they were his own, assuming the representative to be a reasonably prudent businessman.

An executor or administrator may not be under legal compulsion to invest the funds of the estate, but it is certainly good business practice to make interim investments in guaranteed obligations, such as short-term U.S. securities or bank savings certificates or savings accounts if significant amounts of cash are accumulated for taxes, expenses, or future distribution. If investments are made, the representative must be guided by the procedure required of trustees (see later discussion).

The representative is not justified in continuing to operate a business owned by the decedent unless authorized to do so by the will. In the case of a closely held business, either a corporation or partnership, the representative will be guided by the provisions, if any, in the partnership or shareholder agreement. The terms of a buy–sell agreement may obligate and bind the representative to sell the decedent's business interest to either the surviving shareholders or partners, or to the corporation or partnership itself. In the absence of any such agreements or provisions, the business should be liquidated by the surviving partners.

(l) Payments of Debts. The administrator or executor has a duty to satisfy himself as to the validity of the claims made against the estate and should interpose objections to any doubtful claims. A judgment cannot be rejected. A doubtful claim may be settled by a reasonable compromise in good faith. A partial payment of a debt barred by the statute of limitations does not revive the debt.

The representative is not required to pay any debt or make any distribution of assets until the expiration of a statutory period of time. If any payment or distribution is made during the period, the representative may be held responsible for the remaining assets not being sufficient to meet the remaining liabilities.

(m) Advertising for Creditors. The representative is permitted to advertise for creditors and should do so for personal protection. Notices are inserted in one or more newspapers published in the county requesting persons who have claims to present them with supporting affidavits and vouchers within a specified time, usually 6 months. Claims not yet due should be presented for proof so that funds will be set aside for their payment.

(n) Order of Debt Payment. When the list of debts is completed and presented to the court, the solvency or insolvency of the estate can be determined. If the estate is solvent, the order of payment is immaterial, but if the liabilities are in apparent excess of the value of the assets, a statutory order must be followed. The following order of payment is, according to Stephenson (Estate and Trusts), representative:

1. Debts that by law have a special lien on property to an amount not exceeding the value of the property.
2. Funeral expenses.
3. Taxes.
4. Debts due to the United States and to the state.
5. Judgments of any court of competent jurisdiction, within the state, docketed and in force, to the extent to which they are a lien on the property of the deceased person at death.
6. Wages due to any domestic servant or mechanical or agricultural laborer for a period of not more than one year immediately preceding the death.
7. Claim for medical services within 12 months preceding death.
8. All other debts and demands.

(o) Source of Funds for Debt Payment. Unless the will directs otherwise, the assets of the estate are used in the following order in the payment of debts:

1. Personal property not bequeathed.

2. Personal property bequeathed generally.
3. Personal property bequeathed specifically.
4. Realty not devised.
5. Realty devised generally.
6. Realty devised specifically.

The sale, lease, or mortgaging of real estate to provide funds for the payment of debts must, in the absence of a provision to the contrary in the will, follow a petition to the court for permission so to use the realty, and the court must approve of the disposition made by the representative. Property descended to heirs is usually used before that distributed by will. Land sold by an heir or devisee before the estate is settled is subject to a possible claim for unpaid debts of the estate. All **dower or curtsey rights** (statutory rights for surviving wife or husband) and estates for life or years are adjusted, and heirs or devisees must be reimbursed if any assets are subsequently discovered from which the debts could have been paid.

(p) Administration Expenses. Reasonable and necessary outlays made by the representative in collecting and distributing assets will be allowed by the court. The representative is personally liable for amounts disallowed. The compensation of the representative, court costs, and an allowance for preparing the accounting are allowed specifically when an accounting is made. Attorney's fees, accountant's fees, fire insurance premiums, necessary repairs to property, collection costs, and other ordinary expenses will be allowed. The character and amount of the estate and the complications of the particular situation will govern the decisions of the courts as to the reasonableness or necessity of a particular expenditure.

(q) Distribution of Estate Assets. After making appropriate provisions for the payment of all claims against the estate, the personal representative proceeds to distribute the remaining assets according to the instructions in the will or in compliance with the laws of descent and distribution.

(r) Payment of Legacies. Legacies are usually payable one year after the death of the testator. General legacies ordinarily draw interest after that date and should be charged with interest for payments prior to the due date. General legacies to the testator's dependent children usually bear interest from the date of death. If the estate appears to be solvent, the executor may pay or deliver legacies at any time but should, for his own protection, take a bond from the legatee providing for a refund to the estate in case the assets prove to be inadequate to meet the prior claims. Otherwise a suit in equity may be necessary to recover the improper payments.

(s) Abatement of Legacies. If there are insufficient assets to meet the debts and other prior claims, the legacies are reduced or abated. A complete revocation is referred to as an **ademption.** The rules governing priority in the abatement of legacies are as follows:

1. A specific legacy takes priority over a general legacy. If the testator bequeaths specific shares of stock to A and $5,000 in cash to B, B's legacy will be diminished or, if necessary, entirely wiped out before the stock left to A is resorted to.
2. A legacy for the support of the testator's widow or children, who are not otherwise adequately provided for, takes priority over legacies to strangers or more distant relatives.
3. In most states, the personal assets of the estate will be used for the payment of debts before resorting to the real estate. As a result, the bequests of money or personal

property may be diminished or wiped out, although the devisees of the real property are not affected.

4. Subject to the foregoing rules, all legacies are reduced pro rata in case of a deficiency.

If the will directs that real estate be sold to pay debts, the sale will take place before any legacies are abated.

(t) Deductions from Legacies.   There may be certain required deductions from legacies, the most common one being state inheritance taxes. A debt due by a legatee to the testator should be deducted, but a debtor who becomes a legatee is not entitled to retain funds applicable to the payment of all charges and legacies.

(u) Lapsed Legacies.   A legacy is said to have "lapsed" if the legatee dies before the testator, and the assets involved revert to the undistributed or residuary portion of the estate. An exception is sometimes made when the deceased legatee is a child or other near relative who has left surviving children; the children then receive the legacy.

The children would receive the legacy on either a **per stirpes** or **per capita** basis. **Per stirpes** means that the children of a deceased parent receive an equal share of the deceased parents' share. **Per capita** means that the children of a deceased parent receive their own share. For example: A's will leaves everything to spouse or A's children should spouse predecease. A's spouse and one adult child predecease A. A is survived by a second adult child (B) and the predeceased child's two children (C and D). A **per stirpes** distribution would leave 50% to B and 25% to each of C and D. A **per capita** distribution would leave $33\frac{1}{3}\%$ to B, C, and D.

(v) Advancement and Hotchpot.   An advancement is a transfer of property by a parent to a child in anticipation of the share of the estate the child would receive if the parent died intestate. If a person indicates in his will that the advances are to be part of the child's legacy, these advances are considered as part of the corpus of the estate and must be taken into account in making the final distribution. An **allowance to a widow** for the support of the family is not an advance, nor is it a direct charge against items devised or bequeathed to her.

If there is no will and the advancement exceeds the child's distributable shares of the estate, the legatee is entitled to no further distribution but is not required to return the excess; if the advancement is less than the child's share, he is entitled to the difference. **Hotchpot** or **collation** is the bringing together of all the estate of an intestate with the advancements made to the children in order that it may be divided in accordance with the statutes of distribution.

(w) Disclaimers.   It is often recommended that an intended legatee or beneficiary forfeit, give up, or disclaim, an estate distribution. In other words, the legatee or beneficiary waives his or her right to receive all or part of their interest in an estate asset or distribution of assets. The effect of a proper disclaimer is that the intended legatee or beneficiary is presumed to have predeceased the decedent, and the asset is distributed to the contingent legatee or beneficiary. Disclaimers are governed both by state statute and the IRC in §§ 2046 and 2518. The requirements of both must be carefully observed in order to obtain the desired result. In general, the following steps must be observed:

1. The disclaimer must be made in writing.
2. It must be received by the executor and filed with the surrogate or probate court that has jurisdiction of the estate within 9 months of the date of death.
3. The intended legatee or beneficiary must renounce all right, title, and interest in the item(s) and must not have received, or be deemed to have received, any economic benefit of the assets being disclaimed.
4. The disclaimed interest must pass to someone other than the disclaiming legatee or beneficiary, and he may not direct to whom the asset will pass in lieu of himself.

(x) Decree of Distribution and Postdecree Procedure.   The principal distribution of estate properties is made after the issuance by the court of a decree of distribution. Upon the filing of an acceptable final accounting (see below) and the expiration of the time for objections by interested parties, the court approves the accounting, allows the expenses of preparing the accounting and the representative's commission, and issues a decree that disposes of the balance of the estate according to the will or according to the statutes of descent and distribution in that jurisdiction.

The representative distributes the estate assets according to the decree, pays his commission, settles any other expenses allowed in the decree, closes his books, presents his vouchers to the court, and asks for a discharge from his responsibilities and for the cancellation of his bond.

(y) Funding of Trusts.   It is not uncommon for part of the estate to be distributed to a testamentary trust or to a preexisting intervivos trust. The distribution to the trust may make up part of a marital, residuary, or charitable bequest. A testamentary trust may also be funded to hold assets for a minor beneficiary. The appointment and approval of the trustee(s), and the distribution of the estate assets to the trust would be included in the courts' decree described above.

31.10 POWERS OF ESTATE REPRESENTATIVE

(a) Executor versus Administrator.   The personal representative's powers, as distinguished from duties, are those acts that he is authorized, rather than required, to perform. As previously mentioned, the powers of an executor or administrator CTA are outlined in the will and are often broader than those allowed to an administrator of an intestate, who must look solely to statutory authority.

The most common statutory and will clause powers of the personal representative are to invest and reinvest estate assets, to collect income and manage the estate property, to sell estate property as he sees fit, to mortgage property (in some states), and to deliver and execute agreements, contracts, deeds, and other instruments necessary to administer the estate. Most properly drawn wills reproduce the statutory powers and add additional desired powers not granted by statute.

(b) Will Powers Not Conferred by Statute.   Using New York State law as outlined by Harris (1984) as an example, the powers listed below, when included in a will of a New York decedent, would grant additional powers not conferred by statute. These powers would not be available to an executor unless enumerated in the will (and never available to an administrator of an intestate):

1. To distribute the estate immediately after death. Many states require the executor to delay any distribution for as much as one year after letters testamentary are issued.
2. To hold property without regard to the limitations imposed by law on the proper investment of estate assets.
3. To make "extraordinary repairs" to estate assets. New York allows the representative to make only "ordinary repairs"; he has to secure the permission of all beneficiaries and possibly of the court to make "extraordinary repairs" such as replacing a heating system on real estate administered by the estate.
4. To charge the cost of agents such as attorneys, accountants, and investment advisors as estate expenses.
5. To continue a business of decedent.
6. To keep funds uninvested or invested in nonincome-producing assets.
7. To abandon, alter, or demolish real estate.

8. To borrow on behalf of the estate and give notes or bonds for the sums borrowed, and to pledge or mortgage any property as security for the borrowing.

9. To pay all necessary or proper expenses and charges from income or principal, or partly from each as the fiduciary deems advisable. (This important power will be expanded on in the discussion of income and principal of trusts.)

10. To do all acts not specifically mentioned as if the fiduciary were the absolute owner of the property.

(c) Will Powers versus Statutory Powers.   It is important to remember that state law is looked to only where the will is silent. Any will provision will be adhered to, even if it is broader or more restrictive than statutory powers, unless such provision is contrary to law or public policy.

31.11 COMMISSIONS OF REPRESENTATIVES.   Many states make executors' and administrators' commissions statutory. However, with an executor, the first step is to look to the will. Testators may specifically provide the amount of commission or prohibit commissions for fiduciaries. These will provisions will be adhered to, although several states allow an executor to renounce the will provisions and receive statutory commissions. Other states force the executor to renounce the appointment and petition to be appointed administrator, thereby becoming eligible for the statutory commissions of an administrator. Some states do not have statutory commission rates, leaving the awarding of commissions to the court's discretion.

It is important to bear in mind that commissions are allowed only on the **probate assets,** that is, assets that come under the administration of the personal representative. As previously mentioned, real property does not generally come under the control of the representative and thus is not usually a probate asset. When real property is a probate asset, the representative is entitled to commissions. In several states, specific bequests and the income thereon are treated as nonprobate and thus noncommissionable assets. In addition, if an asset is secured by a liability, only the net equity should enter into the commission base.

Sometimes a will provides for more than one executor. State law must then be examined to determine whether each is entitled to statutory commission or whether one such commission must be shared.

31.12 TAXATION OF ESTATES

(a) Final Individual Income Taxes.   One of the responsibilities of the personal representative is to file any unfiled federal and state income tax returns, as well as final income tax returns for the short taxable year that ends on the date of death of the decedent. If the deceased left a surviving spouse, the personal representative can elect to file a joint federal tax return for the year of death. A joint return will normally be prepared on the cash basis for the calendar year, including the decedent's income only through the date of death, and the income of the surviving spouse for the full calendar year. An election in the final return to accrue medical expenses unpaid at death that are paid within one year of death may be made. Accrued interest on U.S. Government Series E Bonds owned by the decedent may be included as income in the final federal income tax return. Expert tax advice should be secured by the representative before making these or various other available elections.

Unused capital loss carryforwards and unused charitable contribution carryforwards of decedent are no longer deductible after the final year. Unused passive activity losses are allowed on the final return to the extent they exceed the estate tax value over the decedent's adjusted basis.

If a joint return is being filed, the tax shown on the return must be allocated between the decedent and the surviving spouse. The allocation will take into account the decedent's withholding tax and his actual payments of estimated tax, leaving the estate of the decedent with either an asset (representing overpayment of taxes) or a liability (representing underpayment of taxes). If the surviving spouse had income or paid some portion of the tax, she would owe the estate or be entitled to reimbursement from it, depending on the relationship of her tax payments to the separate tax liability on her income.

(b) Federal Estate Tax.   Decedents with gross estates valued at over $600,000 are required to file a Federal Estate Tax Return, Form 706, regardless of the fact that there may be no federal estate tax liability. The federal estate tax is a tax on the value of the decedent's gross estate less certain deductions. Generally, the tax is paid from the estate property and reduces the amount otherwise available to the beneficiaries. Therefore, in the absence of specific directions in a will or trust, taxes are generally apportioned to the property that causes a tax. If property passes without tax because of a marital or charitable deduction, no taxes are chargeable to the property.

The gross estate for tax purposes includes all of the decedent's property as defined in the IRC, not merely probate property. The following are examples of property that is part of the gross estate for estate tax purposes, though not part of the probate estate and thus not accounted for in the representative's accounting:

1. Specifically devised real property.
2. Jointly owned property passing to the survivor by operation of law.
3. Life insurance not payable to the estate when the decedent possessed "incidents of ownership" such as the right to borrow or change the beneficiary of the policy, and policies transferred within 3 years of death.
4. Lump-sum distributions from retirement plans paid to someone as a result of surviving the decedent.
5. Gift taxes paid by the decedent within 3 years of death.

In putting a value on the gross estate for estate tax purposes, the representative has an election to value the estate as of the date of death or an alternative date. The alternative date is either 6 months after the date of death or at disposition of an asset if sooner. If the election to use the alternative date is not made, all property must be valued as of the date of death; if the alternative date is elected, all property must be valued at the alternative valuation date or dates. Alternate valuation is available only if there is a reduction in estate taxes.

Deductions from the gross estate to arrive at the taxable estate include administration expenses (if an election has not been made to deduct them on estate income tax returns), funeral expenses, debts of the decedent, bequests to charitable organizations, and a marital deduction for property passing to a surviving spouse.

The 1976 Tax Reform Act unified estate and gift tax rates by provisions for a unified table to be applied both to taxable gifts made after 1976 and to taxable estates for persons dying after 1976. In computing estate taxes on the taxable estate, gifts made after 1976 are added to the taxable estate and the unified tax is recomputed with credit given for the gift tax previously paid on such gifts. This computation has the effect of treating gift taxes paid as only payments on account of future estate and gift tax brackets. A marital deduction is now available for 100% of property passing to the surviving spouse. The property may be left in trust with income to the spouse for life, together with either a general power of appointment, or limited power of appointment. The latter may qualify for the marital deduction if the representative makes a Qualified Terminable Interest Property (QTIP) election with the return. Eventually, the property would be taxable in the surviving spouse's estate and the tax thereon would be payable from the property.

Estates are also allowed an unlimited charitable deduction for bequests left directly to charities. A prorated charitable deduction is allowed for a split-interest bequest to charity either in the form of a remainder interest or an income interest.

A **unified credit** is allowed against the computed estate tax. The unified credit is subtracted from the taxpayer's estate or gift tax liability. However, the amount of the credit available at death will be reduced to the extent that any portion of the credit is used to offset gift taxes on lifetime transfers. The amount of the credit is equivalent to a taxable estate of $600,000. Therefore, a decedent can have a taxable estate of up to $600,000 before any estate tax is due. Other credits are also available to estates: the credit for state death taxes, which is based on an IRS table; for foreign estate taxes paid; and, for previously taxed property.

(c) State Estate and Inheritance Taxes.   The estate tax in some states, such as New York, take the form of a tax on the right to transmit wealth that is similar to the federal estate tax. In other states, an inheritance tax is applied to one's right to receive a portion of a decedent's estate. The state inheritance taxes are paid from estate funds by the representative, who will therefore withhold an appropriate amount from each legacy or establish a claim against those beneficiaries responsible for the tax by the terms of the will or by state law. Kinship of the beneficiary to the decedent is usually the controlling factor in determining exemptions and tax rates with close relatives being favored.

Other states such as Florida assess an estate tax based upon the amount of credit for state death taxes claimed on the federal estate tax return.

Almost all states provide for the tax to be at least equal to the federal credit for state death taxes if total inheritance taxes are less.

(d) Generation Skipping Transfer Tax.   The Tax Reform Act of 1986 revised and imposes a new generation skipping transfer tax on most transfers made to individuals two generations (i.e., grandchildren) down from the donor or decedent. Most transfers prior to 1987 are exempt. Direct transfers or distributions from trusts to individuals two generations down will be subject to the tax if the transfer exceeds the allowable exemption.

A donor/decedent has a lifetime exemption of $1,000,000. Transfers in excess of this amount to grandchildren are subject to a flat tax in addition to the estate and gift tax. This flat tax is imposed at the highest marginal estate and gift tax rate, which is currently 55%. Consequently, it is conceivable that transferring $100 could cost $110 in estate/gift and generation skipping taxes. The law is relatively new and complex. Therefore, knowledge of the law and planning are important in order to minimize the impact of the tax.

(e) Estate Income Taxes.   The representative may be responsible for filing annual federal income tax returns for the estate for the period beginning the day after the date of death and ending when the estate assets are fully distributed. The returns are generally prepared on a cash basis and can be prepared on a fiscal year, rather than a calendar year, basis. Such an election is made with the filing of the initial return and is often done to cut off taxable income in the first year of the estate. Maintenance of books on a fiscal year basis and filing the request for an extension of time to file the return will also establish the fiscal year. If returns are not timely filed, the estate will then be required to file on a calendar year basis.

A federal income tax return is due if the estate earns gross income of $600 or more per year. A $600 exemption is allowed in computing the income subject to federal income taxes. Administration expenses such as executor's commission and legal and accounting fees may be deducted if the representative does not elect to take these expenses on the federal estate tax return. If the estate distributes net income (gross income less expenses), such **distributable net income** is taxed to the recipient and the estate is allowed a corresponding deduction in computing its taxable income. Any remaining taxable income after deductions for exemption, expenses, and distributions is taxed at a rate specified in a table to be used exclusively for estates and trusts.

Estates must now make quarterly estimated tax payments in the same manner as individuals, except that an estate is exempt from making such payments during its first 2 taxable years. Accordingly, the penalties for underpayment of income tax are applicable to fiduciaries.

Some states also tax the income of estates, and the representative must see to it that such state statutes are complied with.

ACCOUNTING FOR ESTATES

31.13 GOVERNING CONCEPTS.   The general concepts governing the accounting for decedent's estates are for the most part similar to those applicable to trusts, but there are some differences. The underlying equation expressing the accounting relationship is assets = accountability. However, the representative is concerned, *not* with the long-term management of property for beneficiaries, but rather with the payment of debts and the orderly realization and distribution of the estate properties. The collection and the distribution of income are incidental to the main function of the estate's fiduciary.

Whenever an estate accounting is prepared, a reconciliation of the gross estate as finally determined for estate tax purposes should be made with the schedule of principal received at the date by the representative. Every difference should be explainable.

(a) Accounting Period.   The accounting period of the estate is determined by the dates set by the fiduciary or by the court for intermediate and final accountings; nevertheless, the books must be closed at least once a year for income tax purposes.

(b) Principal and Income.   Unless otherwise provided for, the rules outlined below for the trustee should generally be followed by the representative in the allocation of receipts and disbursements to principal and income. Such distinctions, although not called for under the will, are frequently mandated by requirements of estate, inheritance, and income tax laws and regulations.

(c) Treatment of Liabilities.   The representative picks up only the inventory of assets of the decedent at the inception of the estate. Claims against the estate, after presentation and review, are paid by the representative and are recorded as "debts paid." The payment of such debts reduces in proportion the accountability of the representative.

31.14 RECORD-KEEPING SYSTEM.   No special type of bookkeeping system is prescribed by law, but a complete record of all transactions must be kept with sufficient detail to meet the requirements of the courts, and of the estate, inheritance, and income tax returns. Much of the information may be in memorandum form outside of the formal accounting system.

The federal estate tax law requires information regarding assets beyond those ordinarily under the control of the representative (e.g., real estate). Such information must be assembled in appropriate form by the representative, who has responsibility for the estate tax return.

(a) Journals.   A single multicolumn journal is usually sufficient. It should incorporate cash receipts, cash disbursements and asset inventory adjustments. Further, it is important to note and keep track of the distinction between principal and income.

(b) Operation of a Going Business.   If the decedent was the **individual proprietor** of a going business and if the court or the will instructs the administrator or executor to continue the operation of the business, the bookkeeping procedure becomes somewhat complicated. The books of the business may be continued as distinct from the general estate books, or the transactions of the business may be combined with other estate transactions in one set of records. The best procedure, if the business is of at least moderate size, is to keep the operations of the business in a separate set of books and to set up a controlling accounting in the general books of the executor or administrator.

As soon as the representative takes charge of the business, the assets should be inventoried and the books closed, normally as of the date of death. The liabilities should be transferred to the list of debts to be paid by the representative, leaving the assets, the operating expenses and income, and the subsequently incurred liabilities to be recorded in the books of the company. An account should be opened in the books of the business for the representative that will show the same amount as the controlling account for the business in the books of the representative.

(c) Final Accounting. The "final" accounting is the report to the court of the handling of the estate affairs by the representative, if required. It presents, among other things, a plan for the distribution of the remainder of the assets of the estate and a computation of the commission due the representative for his services. If the court approves the report, it issues a decree putting the proposals into effect.

ESTATE OF JOHN SMITH
Charge and Discharge Statement
A. L. White, Executor
From April 7, 19XX, to December 15, 19XX

First, as to Principal:

The Executor charges himself as follows:

With amount of inventory at the date of death, April 7, Schedule A		$xxx	
With amount of assets discovered subsequent to date of death, Schedule B		xxx	
With gain on realization of assets, Schedule C		xxx	
			$xxx

The Executor credits himself as follows:

With loss on realization of assets, Schedule C		$xxx	
With amount paid for funeral and administrative expenses, Schedule D		xxx	
With amount paid on debts of the estate, Schedule F		xxx	
With distributions to legatees, Schedule G		xxx	
			xxx
Leaving a balance of principal, Schedule C, of			$xxx

Second, as to Income:

The Executor charges himself as follows:

With amount of income received, Schedule H		$xxx	

The Executor credits himself as follows:

With amount of administrative expenses chargeable to income, Schedule D	$xxx		
With distribution of income to legatees, Schedule I	xxx	xxx	
Leaving a balance of income, Schedule J			xxx
Leaving a balance of principal and income of			$xxx

Balance of principal and income to be distributed to those entitled thereto, subject to the deduction of the Executor's commissions, legal fees, and the expenses of this accounting, Schedule K.

Exhibit 31.2.   Sample charge and discharge statement.

31.15 REPORTS OF EXECUTOR OR ADMINISTRATOR.   The form of the reports of the fiduciary will vary according to the requirements of the court and to the character of the estate. In general, however, the representative "charges" himself with all of the property received and subsequently discovered plus gains on realizations, and "credits" (or discharges) himself with all disbursements for debts paid, expenses paid, legacies distributed, and realization losses. Each major item in the charge and discharge statement should be supported by a schedule showing detailed information. At any time during the administration of the estate, the excess of "charges" over "credits" should be represented by property in the custody of the fiduciary. It may be necessary to show the market value of property delivered to a legatee or trustee at the date of delivery, in which case the investment schedule will show the increase or decrease on distribution of assets, as well as from sales. The **income schedule,** when needed, should be organized to show the total income from each investment, the expenses chargeable against income, and the distribution of the remainder.

Exhibit 31.2 is typical of the **charge-and-discharge statement,** each item being supported by a schedule.

TRUSTS AND TRUSTEES—LEGAL BACKGROUND

31.16 NATURE AND TYPES OF TRUSTS.   The trust relationship exists whenever one person holds property for the benefit of another. The **trustee** holds legal title to the property for the benefit of the **beneficiary,** or *"cestui que trust."* The person from whom trust property is received is known as the grantor, donor, settler, creator, or trustor.

An **express trust** is one in which the trustee, beneficiary, subject matter, and method of administration have been explicitly indicated. An **implied** trust may be created whether language of an instrument indicates the desirability of a trust but does not specify the details, or when the trust relationship is assumed in order to prevent the results of fraud, breach of trust, or undue influence. The terms "constructive," "resulting," and "involuntary" trust are sometimes applied to such situations.

A **testamentary trust** is one created by a will. A **living trust,** or *"trust inter vivos,"* is created to take effect during the grantor's lifetime. Trusts are sometimes created by court order, as in the case of a guardianship.

A **private trust** is created for the benefit of particular individuals, while a **public** or **charitable trust** is for the benefit of an indefinite class of persons. Charitable trusts are discussed in Chapter 25.

A **simple trust** directs the trustee to distribute the entire net income of the trust to the named beneficiary. A **complex trust** gives the trustee the discretionary authority to distribute or accumulate the trust net income to or on behalf of the named beneficiary. In some instances, the trust may start off as complex and then convert to a simple trust upon the happening of a specified event, that is, the beneficiary's attainment of age 21 or 25.

A **grantor trust** exists when both the grantor and beneficiary are the same individual. A grantor trust may be implied if the grantor retains sufficient rights or controls over disposition of trust income and/or principal.

A trust may include a **spendthrift clause** that prohibits the beneficiary from assigning his interest before receiving it or prevents creditors from enforcing their claims against the income or principal of a trust fund, or both.

Trusts are often used for business purposes, as when property is transferred by a deed of trust instead of a mortgage, when trustees are appointed to hold title and perform other functions under a bond issue, or when assets are assigned to a trustee for the benefit of creditors. Bankruptcy and insolvency are discussed in Chapter 33.

(a) Limitations on Private Trusts.   A public trust may be established for an indefinite period, but a trust may not suspend indefinitely the power of anyone to transfer the trust property.

The common law rule, otherwise known as the **Rule against Perpetuities,** limits the duration of a private trust to 21 years after the death of some person who is living when the trust is created. Another common limitation in certain states is "two lives in being" at the origin of the trust.

Accumulation of the income of a trust is also restricted by state law. A common provision, for example, is that in the case of a trust created for the benefit of a minor, the income can be accumulated only during the minority of the beneficiary. Even the income of a charitable trust cannot be accumulated for an "unreasonable" period.

(b) Revocation of Trusts. A completed trust cannot be revoked without the consent of all the beneficiaries unless the right to revoke has been expressly reserved by the grantor. Trusts are therefore sometimes classified as "revocable" or "irrevocable."

31.17 APPOINTMENT AND REMOVAL OF TRUSTEES. In general, anyone competent to make a will or a contract is competent to create a trust. The trustee must be one who is capable of taking and holding property and who has the legal capacity and natural ability to execute the trust.

(a) Choice of Trustee. The decedent's will usually names the trustee for a testamentary trust. A grantor who is establishing an inter vivos trust will usually appoint one or more of the following to act as trustee: a relative; his professional advisor, that is, attorney, accountant, broker; a business associate; or an institutional entity, such as a bank or trust company. Each type of trustee has its pros and cons; however, the most important concern is not to choose a trustee that will cause adverse income tax consequences.

(b) Methods of Appointment. Some of the means by which trustees are appointed are:

1. By deed or declaring of trust. The creator of the trust names the trustees in the instrument.
2. By will. The same person may be both executor and trustee under a will, but this dual capacity should be clearly indicated.
3. By agreement.
4. By the court. The court will appoint a trustee when a trust may fail for lack of a trustee, when a trustee refuses to serve or has died, or when a vacancy from any cause exists and no other means have been provided for filing the vacancy.
5. By implication of law.
6. By self-perpetuating boards. When vacancies occur, they are filed by the remaining members of the board.
7. By the exercise of a power of appointment. The instrument creating the trust may give the remaining trustees, beneficiaries, or any other person the power to appoint a trustee to fill a vacancy. Specific instructions should be included in the instrument as to the situation establishing a vacancy, the persons who may be appointed, and the manner of making the appointment.

(c) Acceptance or Disclaimer. Acceptance of an appointment as trustee may be made by positive statement, by qualifying as executor if the appointment is by will, by the acceptance of property of the trust, or by other acts from which acceptance may be presumed. An individual may refuse to accept an appointment as a trustee and should execute and deliver a disclaimer expressing rejection of the appointment.

(d) Resignation of Trustee. According to the Restatement of the Law of Trusts 2d (1 Trusts A.L.I. 234):

A trustee who has accepted the trust cannot resign except (a) with the permission of a proper court; or (b) in accordance with the terms of the trust; or (c) with the consent of all the beneficiaries, if they have capacity to give such consent.

(e) Removal of Trustee. The court has power to remove a trustee and appoint a successor under certain circumstances. Scott (1986) cites, among others, the following grounds upon which trustees have been removed:

1. Failure to exercise discretion.
2. Self-dealing.
3. Failure to keep proper accounts, and mingling with trustee's own funds.
4. Incompetency and neglect of duty.
5. Conversion of trust property.
6. Refusal to obey orders of the court.

31.18 POWERS AND DUTIES OF TRUSTEES. The powers of trustees are obtained both from the provisions and implications of the instrument creating the trust and from the general laws pertaining to the trust relationship. The instrument may either expand or restrict the general powers, except that it may not relieve the trustee from liability for gross negligence, bad faith, or dishonesty. The powers of a trustee may be either (1) imperative or mandatory, or (2) permissive or discretionary. In other words, they must either be exercised definitely and positively within a given length of time or upon the occurrence of some contingency, or they may be exercised at the discretion of the trustee.

(a) General Powers. The general powers of a trustee, which include all necessary incidental powers, are:

1. To take and retain possession of the trust property.
2. To invest trust funds so as to yield a fair income.
3. To sell and reinvest when necessary.
4. To sell and convey real estate when necessary to carry out the provisions of the trust.
5. To release real estate so that it may earn income.
6. To pay for repairs, taxes, and other such expenses in connection with trust property.
7. To sue or defend suits when necessary.
8. To make contracts that are necessary to carry out the purposes of the trust.
9. To pay over and distribute the trust property to those entitled to it.

The trustee secures possession of the trust property and holds title in his own name. All debtors should be notified of the change in ownership of claims against them in order to hold them directly liable to the trustee. All debts due the trust estate should be collected promptly. Trust property must be kept separate from the property of anyone else. The trustee will be liable for any loss occurring as a result of their mingling of funds or other property. An exception is usually made when a trust company is acting as trustee; it may deposit cash in trust funds with itself or may mingle various trust funds and deposit same with designated depositories.

(b) Duties. The duties of the trustee are outlined by Scott (1986) as follows:

1. To administer the trust as long as he continues as trustee.
2. To administer the trust solely in the interest of the beneficiary (the duty of loyalty as a fiduciary).

3. Not to delegate to others the performance of acts which the trustee sought personally to perform.

4. To keep clear and accurate accounts.

5. To give to beneficiaries upon their request complete and accurate information as to the administration of the trust.

6. To exercise such care and skill as a man of ordinary prudence would exercise in dealing with his own property; and if the trustee possesses greater skill than that of an ordinary prudent man, he must exercise the skill he has.

7. To take reasonable steps to secure control of trust property and to keep control of it.

8. To use care and skill to preserve the trust property. The standard of care and skill is that of a man of ordinary prudence.

9. To take reasonable steps to realize on claims which he holds in trust and to defend claims of third persons against the trust estate.

10. To keep the trust property separate from his own property and separate from property held upon other trusts; and to designate trust property as property of the trust.

11. To refrain in ordinary circumstances from lending trust money without security.

12. To invest trust funds so that they will be productive of income.

13. To pay the net income of the trust to the beneficiary at reasonable intervals; and if there are two or more beneficiaries he must deal with them impartially.

14. Where there are several trustees, it is the duty of each of them, unless otherwise provided by the trust instrument, to participate in the administration of the trust, and each trustee must use reasonable care to prevent the others from committing a breach of trust.

31.19 PROPER TRUST INVESTMENTS.   The trustee is under a duty to invest funds in such a way as to receive an income without improperly risking the loss of the principal. The only general rule as to investment is that the trustee is under a duty to make such investments as a prudent man (the **"prudent man" rule** or "Massachusetts" rule) would make of his own property, having primarily in view the preservation of the estate and the amount and regularity of the income to be derived. In some states ("legal-list" states), the legislatures tell trustees in what they must or may invest funds unless the terms of the trust otherwise provide.

Kinds of investments that are almost universally condemned are summarized by Scott (1986) as follows:

1. Purchase of securities on margin.

2. Purchase of speculative shares of stock.

3. Purchase of bonds selling at large discount because of uncertainty of repayment at maturity.

4. Purchase of securities in new and untried enterprises.

5. Use of trust property in the carrying on of a trade or business, even though it is not an untried enterprise.

6. Purchase of land or other things for the purpose of resale, unless authorized by the terms of the trust.

7. Purchase of second and other junior mortgages.

8. Making unsecured loans to individuals or firms or corporations.

Types of investments that are almost universally permitted include:

1. Bonds of the United States or of the state or of a municipality thereof.

2. First mortgages on land.

3. Corporate bonds of a high investment grade.

31.20 TRUSTEE'S PERSONAL LIABILTIES AND LIABILITY FOR ACTS OF CO-TRUSTEE.   A trustee is liable to the beneficiary for failure to fulfill his duties under the statutes, general rules of equity, or the provisions of the trust indenture.

A trustee must be particularly circumspect in all matters affecting his own property or benefit. He is personally liable for torts committed by himself or his agents and, unless his agreement states otherwise, is personally liable on all contracts made on behalf of the trust.

A trustee is not responsible for **loss** by theft, embezzlement, or accident if he has taken all the precautions that a careful businessman takes in guarding his own property, and if he is strictly following his line of duty as a trustee. If a trustee is not insolvent and mixes trust property with his own, the beneficiary may take the whole, leaving the trustee to prove his own part. If the trustee is insolvent, the beneficiary shares with the other creditors unless definite property can be identified as belonging to the trust. Interest will be charged against a trustee who has mingled trust funds with his own. If bank deposits are made in the individual name of the trustee, he will be treated as a guarantor of the solvency of the bank, even though he uses care in his choice of the bank and has not in any way misused the funds.

In general, a trustee is not liable for losses caused by the default or negligence of a co-trustee unless he has cooperated with the trustee who is at fault, or has known of the trustee's misconduct and has not taken any steps to prevent it. If, however, each trustee should have interested himself in the matter in question, such as the proper investment of funds, each would be responsible even though he took no part in or knew nothing of the misconduct. All trustees should act together in handling the trust property and should apply to the court for instructions in case they cannot agree. Unanimity is usually required for all important decisions in the case of private trusts, but a majority of a board of trustees may act for a charitable trust.

31.21 GUARDIANS.   If a person is incompetent to manage his own property because of a disability such as infancy or mental incompetency, a guardian will be appointed by the probate or other appropriate court. The court must approve the appointment of a guardian by will. A guardian is a trustee in the strictest sense of the term. He is directly under the supervision of the court. If possible, only the income from the property should be used for the maintenance and education of the beneficiary; permission must be granted by the court before the principal can be used for this purpose. Any **sale of real estate** must be authorized by the court. A guardian should have the authorization of the court or the direction of a will before paying money to a minor or to anyone for the minor; otherwise he may be compelled to pay the amount again when the minor becomes of age.

31.22 TESTAMENTARY TRUSTEE.   The work of the trustee appointed by a will begins when the executor sets aside the trust fund out of the **estate assets.** One person may serve as both executor and trustee under a will.

The testamentary trustee has slightly more freedom in handling the funds than does the executor, and his responsibility may be made less rigorous by provisions of the will. He holds, invests, and cares for the property, and disposes of it or its income as directed by the will. A trustee should have specific authority of a will or the court, or the consent of everyone interested, before carrying on a business. If there are several executors, one can act alone, but trustees must act jointly.

31.23 COMPENSATION OF TRUSTEES.   Trustees are usually allowed compensation for their work, either by provision of the trust instrument or by statute. The **statutory provision** is usually a graduated percentage of the funds handled.

A trustee is entitled to be repaid expenditures reasonably and properly incurred in the care of trust property. The compensation is usually allocated to principal and income in accordance with the specific provision of the indenture or as provided by statute or rules of law.

31.24 RIGHTS OF BENEFICIARY.   The beneficiary has an equitable title to the trust property, that is, he can bring suit in a court of equity to enforce his rights and to prevent misuse of the property by the trustee. Unless the instrument by which the trust is created provides otherwise, the beneficiary, if of age, can sell or otherwise dispose of his equitable estate in the property.

The beneficiary has the **right to inspect** and take copies of all papers, records, and data bearing on the administration of the trust property and income that are in the hands of the trustee. The beneficiary may have an accounting ordered whenever there is any reason for suspicion, or any failure to allow inspection or to make satisfactory reports and statements. Whenever it seems advisable, a court of equity will order an accounting.

The beneficiary may have an injunction issued to restrain the trustee from proceeding with any unauthorized action, if such action will result in irremediable damage. The beneficiary may present a petition to the court for the removal of a trustee but must be able to prove bad faith, negligence, lack of ability, or other such cause for the removal. The trustee is entitled to a formal trial.

The beneficiary can, if it is possible to do so, follow the trust property and have it subjected to the trust, even if a substitution has been made for the original property, unless it comes into hands of an innocent holder for value. If the trust property cannot be traced or is in the hands of an innocent holder for value, the beneficiary may bring action against the trustee in a court of equity for breach of trust.

If the beneficiary is of age and mentally competent, he may approve or ratify acts of the trustee that would otherwise be a violation of the trustee's duties or responsibilities.

31.25 DISTINCTION BETWEEN PRINCIPAL AND INCOME.   Probably the most difficult problem of the trustee is to differentiate between principal (corpus) and income. The intention of the creator of the trust is binding if it can be ascertained, but in the absence of instructions to the contrary the general legal rules must be followed.

The **life tenant** (the present beneficiary) is entitled to the net income and the **remainderman** (the future beneficiary) to the principal, as legally determined. The principal is the property itself that constitutes the trust fund, and the income is the accumulation of funds and other property arising from the investment or other use of the trust principal. Increases or decreases in the value of the assets that constitute the trust fund affect only the principal. The income determined under these rules is not always the same as taxable income or income as determined by GAAP. The life tenant is entitled to receive only the net income from all sources for the entire term of his tenancy. He is not allowed to select the income from only those investments that are lucrative.

(a) Receipts of Principal.   The following receipts of cash or other property have been held to be part of the **corpus** of the trust and therefore to belong to the remainderman or persons entitled to the corpus:

1. Interest accrued to the beginning of the trust. Bond coupons are not apportioned in the absence of a statute providing for such a division.
2. Rent accrued to the beginning of the trust. Under the common law, rent was not apportioned according to the time expired.
3. Excess of selling price of trust assets over their value in the original inventory or over its purchase price. Appreciation, in general, belongs to the trust corpus.
4. The value of assets existing at the time of the original inventory was taken but not included in the inventory.
5. Dividends (see discussion below).
6. Proceeds of the sale of stock rights.
7. Profit from the completion of executory contracts of a decedent.
8. Profits earned prior to the beginning of the trust on the operations of a partnership or sole proprietorship.
9. Insurance money received for a fire that occurred prior to the date of the beginning of

the trust, or after that date if the property is in the hands of the trustee for the benefit of the trust in general.

10. If trust property is mortgaged, the proceeds may be said to be principal assets, although there is no increase in the equity of the remainderman.

(b) Disbursements of Principal. The following payments, distribution, and exhaustion of assets have been held to be chargeable to the corpus:

1. Excess of the inventory value or purchase price of an asset over the amount realized from its sale.
2. Payment of debts owed, including accruals, at the date of the beginning of the trust.
3. Real estate taxes assessed on or before the date of the beginning of the trust. In the case of special assessments made during the administration of the trust, the remainderman may pay the assessment and the life tenant may be charged interest thereon annually during the life of the trust, or else some other equitable adjustment will be made between them.
4. Any expenditures that result in improvements of the property, except those made voluntarily by a life tenant for his own benefit, and all expenditures on newly acquired property that are necessary to put it into condition to rent or use.
5. Wood on the property that the life tenant uses for fuel, fences, and other similar purposes. The life tenant may operate mines, wells, quarries, and so on, that have been opened and operated on the property.
6. Losses due to casualty and theft of general trust assets.
7. Expenses of administration except those directly pertaining to the administration of income. For example, legal expenses incurred in defending the trust estate are chargeable to principal; however, the expenses of litigation in an action to protest only the income are payable out of income.
8. Trustee's commissions in respect to the receipts or disbursements out of principal. Commissions computed on income are ordinarily payable out of income.
9. Brokerage fees and other expenses for changing investments should generally be chargeable to principal, since they are a part of the cost of purchase or sale.
10. Income taxes on gains made from disposition of principal assets.
11. Carrying charges on unproductive real estate, unless the terms of the trust direct the trustee to retain the property even though it is unproductive.
12. Cost of improvements to property held as part of the principal.

(c) Receipts of Income. The following receipts have been held to be income and to belong to the life tenants or persons entitled to the income.

1. Interest, rent, and so on, accruing after the date of the beginning of the trust. The proceeds of a foreclosed mortgage may be apportionable between principal and income. Interest includes the increment in securities issued at a discount.
2. Increase in value of investments made by the trustee from accumulated undistributed income.
3. Dividends (see discussion below).
4. Crops harvested during the trust.
5. Royalties or other income from operation of mines, quarries, or wells that were made productive prior to the beginning of the trust, or were developed or leased in cooperating with the remainderman.
6. Net profit from the operation of a business.

(d) Disbursements of or Charges to Income.   The following items have been held to be chargeable against the income of the trust:

1. Interest payable, accruing during the life of the trust.
2. Any expenses incurred in earning or collecting income, caring for trust property, or preserving its value, and an appropriate share of administration fees and expenses.
3. Income tax except those levied on gains from sale of principal assets.
4. Premiums on trustee's bond.
5. Provision for amortization of wasting property, including leasehold interests, royalties, oil and gas wells, machinery, and farm implements (see discussion of depreciation below).
6. Provision for amortization of improvements to trust property when such improvements will not outlive the duration of the trust.
7. Losses of property due to the negligence of the life tenant.
8. Losses due to casualty and theft of income assets.

31.26 PRINCIPAL AND INCOME—SPECIAL PROBLEMS.   The distinction between principal and income also involves a consideration of such problems as unproductive property, accruals, dividends, bond premium and discount, and depreciation and depletion.

(a) Unproductive Property.   When the trustee is required to sell unproductive property and the sale is delayed, the net proceeds of the sale should be apportioned between principal and income. The net proceeds are allocated by determining the sum that, with interest thereon at the current rate of return on trust investments, would equal the net proceeds, and the sum so determined is treated as principal and the balance as income (Restatement of Trusts, § 241). Apportionment between principal and income is generally applicable to real estate, but it has been applied in the case of personal property also. It does not matter whether the property is sold at a gain or a loss.

(b) Accruals.   There are two dates at which the matter of accruals becomes significant. The first is the date at which the trust begins. Income and expenses accrued at that date belong to the corpus of the estate. The second date is the one when the life interest terminates. Income and expenses accrued at that date belong to the life tenant or his estate.

Larsen and Mosich (1988) provide a summarization of the general rule of accrual as applied to certain items, from which the following is taken:

1. *Interest.* Interest accrued on receivables and investments at the date the trust is established is considered part of the trust corpus. Exceptions are interest on (a) savings accounts when the interest is paid only if the deposit remains until the end of the interest period, and (b) coupon bonds when the payment is contingent upon the owner presenting the coupon, in which case the date of receipt is controlling. Similar rules apply to the accrual of interest expense.
2. *Rent.* The accrual of rent prior to the beginning of the trust is considered by many states as a portion of a trust corpus. Any rent accruing between the date of the establishment of the trust and the termination of the tenancy belongs to the income beneficiary. Rent expense is handled similarly.
3. *Dividends.* Ordinary cash dividends are not divisible. If the dividend is declared and the date of record has passed before the trust is created, the dividend is a part of the corpus. Otherwise it is considered income to the trust. A stock dividend is treated in the same manner in many states. . . . [For a discussion of special treatment of cash and stock dividends under the Massachusetts and Pennsylvania rules, see below.]
4. *Property taxes.* Taxes which have been levied on trust property prior to the beginning of the trust are charges against the principal. Any taxes assessed on the basis of trust property held for

the benefit of the income beneficiary are chargeable against income. Special assessments made during the administration of the trust are usually paid by the remainderman, although in some cases where the assessment is for improvements which benefit the life tenant, a part or all of the assessment may be charged against income. When the assessment is paid from the corpus, interest on the funds advance may be charged against income.

5. *Profits.* Income earned by a partnership or proprietorship does not accrue. The income which is earned prior to the creation of the trust is considered a part of the principal of the trust. In many cases a partnership is dissolved upon the death of a partner, and there may be no income earned after the trust is established. In the event that the business continues by specific direction of the grantor or provision of the partnership agreement, any income earned after the trust is created is income of the trust.

6. *Executory contracts.* Any profits earned on the completion of an executory contract by the trustee is an addition to the principal of the trust.

7. *Livestock and crops.* Any livestock born during the tenancy under the trust is considered income, except to the extent that the herd must be maintained as directed by the grantor, in which case the increase must be divided between principal and income in a manner which honors this intention. If the principal includes land, any crops harvested during this tenancy are considered income of the trust.

8. *Premium returns.* Any return of premium or dividend on insurance policies which was paid prior to the creation of the trust is a part of the principal. This is considered realization of assets.

9. *Royalties.* Royalties or other income from the operation of mines or other natural resource deposits which were made operative before the trust was created or which were developed in cooperation with the remainderman are income to the trust.

(c) Dividends.   The determination of whether a dividend is principal or income involves a consideration of applicable state laws. Ordinary cash dividends declared during the period of the trust belong to the income beneficiary. An ordinary stock dividend is usually regarded as income except in states that follow the **Massachusetts rule.** This rule holds that all cash dividends are treated as income and that stock dividends are entirely principal.

Some states follow the **Pennsylvania rule,** which holds that, in regard to extraordinary dividends, it is not the form of the dividend but its source that determines whether and to what extent it is income or principal. Generally, under this rule extraordinary dividends are income if declared out of earnings accruing to the corporation during the period of the trust, but they are principal if declared out of earnings accruing prior to the creation of the trust. Thus, if such dividends cause the book value of the corporation's stock to be reduced below the book value that existed at the creation of the trust, that portion of the dividend equivalent to the impairment of book value is principal and only the remainder is income. The present Pennsylvania law provides that stock dividends of 6% or less ''shall be deemed income'' unless the instrument provides to the contrary.

Although there is still wide diversity among the courts and state statutes in the apportionment of corporate distributions, Scott (1986) points out that the recent trend has been in favor of the Massachusetts rule. The Uniform Principal and Income Act (Uniform Laws Annotated, Vol. 9B, § 5) follows the essence of the Massachusetts rule in treating cash and other property dividends as income and stock dividends as principal.

(d) Premium and Discount on Bonds.   The necessity of accumulating bond discount or amortizing bond premium in order to determine the **correct interest income** still gives rise to a great deal of confusion in trust and estate administration. In general, it appears that most courts support the amortization of premium on bonds purchased by the trustee, but there has been little or no support of the accumulation of discount. Any difference between the inventory value and the face value of the bonds taken over by the trustee is usually treated as an adjustment of principal.

In the event of **redemption before maturity,** it has been held that the proper procedure is to amortize the premium to the date of redemption; the unamortized balance is a loss borne by principal. If a bonus is received, it should be credited to principal.

Scott (1986) suggests:

> It might well be held that the whole matter [of amortizing premium and discount] should be left to the discretion of the trustee, and if he is not guilty of an abuse of discretion in unduly favoring some of the beneficiaries at the expense of the others, the court should not interpose its authority. This, of course, is the result reached where such discretion is expressly conferred upon the trustee by the terms of the trust.

(e) Depreciation and Depletion.   In determining whether provision must be made for depreciation and depletion, it is essential to consider carefully the intentions and wishes of the trustor. If the trustor intended to give the full, undiminished income to the life tenant even though the principal would thereby be partially or completely exhausted, no deduction from income for depletion or depreciation is allowed. If, however, there is an expressed or implied intention to preserve the principal intact, the trustee is required to withhold from income an amount sufficient to maintain the original property of the trust.

When the trustor's intentions regarding the receipts from wasting property cannot be determined from the trust instrument, then, according to Scott (1986), the inference is that the trustor did not intend that the life beneficiary should receive the whole income at the expense of the principal. Thus, when the trustee holds wasting property, including royalties, patents, mines, timberlands, machinery, and equipment, he is under a duty to make a provision for amortization of such property. The general rule has been applied to new buildings erected and improvements made by the trustee; however, the courts have generally held that buildings that were part of the trust estate at the beginning of the trust need not be depreciated. The courts have, in effect, refused to treat the buildings as wasting property.

The trend appears to be in the direction of adopting principles of depreciation followed in accounting practice. For example, the position taken in § 13 of the Revised Uniform Principal and Income Act is that, with respect to charges against income and principal, there shall be:

> . . . a reasonable allowance for depreciation under generally accepted accounting principles, but no allowance shall be made for depreciation of that portion of any real property used by a beneficiary as a residence or for depreciation of any property held by the trustee on the effective date of this Act for which the trustee is not then making an allowance for depreciation.

31.27 TAX STATUS OF TRUST.   Unless the trust qualifies as an exempt organization (charitable, educational, etc.), or unless the income of the trust is taxable to the grantor (revocable, or grantor retains substantial dominion and control), the income of the trust is subject to the federal income tax in a manner similar to the case of an individual. In general, the trust is treated as a conduit for tax purposes and is allowed a deduction for its income that is distributed or distributable currently to the beneficiaries. The trust may also be subject to state income taxes, personal property taxes, and so on. A tax service should be consulted for the latest provisions and rulings as to deductions, credits, rates, and filing requirements.

It is important to note that although trusts and estates are taxed similarly, there are two major differences. Trusts must be operated on a calendar year basis, whereas estates may operate on a fiscal year, usually tied to the decedent's date of death. Secondly, trusts must pay estimated taxes in the same fashion as individuals. Estates, on the other hand, are exempt from this requirement; but only for their first 2 tax years.

31.28 TERMINATION OF TRUST.   A trust may be terminated by the fulfillment of its purpose or by the expiration of the period for which the trust was created. A trust may also be terminated under a power reserved by the grantor, or by the consent of all beneficiaries unless continuance of the trust is necessary to carry out a material purpose for which it was created.

When the trust is terminated, the trustee is discharged when he has transferred the property to those entitled to it according to the terms of the trust instrument. The trustee, to protect himself, may secure a formal release of all claims from all who receive any of the property and are competent to consent, may require a bond of indemnity from the beneficiaries, or may refuse to act without a decree of court.

ACCOUNTING FOR TRUSTS

31.29 GENERAL FEATURES. Generally, accounting for a trust is the same as accounting for an estate. The emphasis for a trust, however, is that principal or corpus versus income should be properly distinguished. Two interests, that is, current or life versus future or remainder, usually serve different parties. One party may have a current or income interest whereas another party holds a future or remainder interest. Therefore, allocation between principal and income is important.

(a) Accounting Period. The accounting period for a trust depends somewhat on the nature of the trust and the provisions of the trust instrument. Reports may be required by the court or may be submitted to other interested parties at various intervals during the life of the trust.

(b) Recording Principal and Income. A careful distinction must be made between principal (corpus) and income in recording the transactions. The **legal theory** seems to be that the principal of a trust is not a certain amount of monetary value but is a certain group of assets that must be capable of isolation from the assets that compose the undistributed income. Actual **separation of cash and investments** is difficult because of such factors as accrued interest and amortization of bond premium and discount. Ordinarily it is sufficient to keep one account for cash and one for each type of investment, and to indicate the claims of the principal and income in the total.

Accounts should be kept with the beneficiaries to show the amounts due and paid to each.

The trustee should keep records that will meet both the requirements of the income tax law and regulations and the law relating to principal and income. There are apt to be conflicts at various points in the determination of taxable income and of income belonging to the life tenant. The only solution is to keep sufficiently detailed records so that all of the information is available for both purposes. In some cases, it may be necessary to prepare **reconciliation schedules** in order to keep a record of the differences between the income tax calculation of net income and the application of trust accounting principles of accounting income.

(c) Accounting for Multiple Trusts. Several trusts may be created by a single instrument, such as trusts originating through the provisions of a will, and a single trustee may have to keep his accounts so as to be able to prepare a report of the administration of the estate as a whole and also a separate report of each trust.

(d) Treatment of Liabilities. In some cases, trust property will be encumbered with an unpaid mortgage or other obligation of which the trustee must keep a record. It is also possible that in handling the business of the trust some liabilities will be incurred. These are usually current in character and the entry made at the time of payment, charging the amount to an asset or expense account, is usually sufficient.

31.30 RECORD-KEEPING SYSTEM. The bookkeeping system requirements for the trust, like those for any other enterprise, vary with the complexity of the situation. The trustee should keep a complete record of all transactions relating to the trust in order to protect himself, to make reports to the court, to prepare income tax returns, and to give the beneficiaries of the trust an adequate accounting. No special type of bookkeeping system is prescribed by law, but a complete record of all transactions must be kept in such a way that the reports required by the courts can be prepared. All records should be kept in permanent form and should be carefully preserved and filed for possible future reference.

(a) Journals. In a comparatively simple situation, one multicolumn journal may be satisfactory, but in most cases a set of various journals should be kept.

(b) Principal and Income Accounts. It is necessary to distinguish carefully between principal and income in the administration of trusts. The Trust Principal account and the Undistributed Trust Income account record the net worth or capital of the trust. It will usually be necessary to analyze those accounts for income tax purposes, just as equity is analyzed in corporation accounts to obtain all of the information required for the income tax return. There may be some conflicts between income as defined by the law relating to the administration of trusts and taxable income as defined by the income tax law and regulations.

(c) Opening Books of Account. If an inventory has been filed with the court, such as an executor's or guardian's inventory, the trustee must record the same values in his accounts. If no such inventory was filed, the trustee should have one prepared that will serve as the basis of his property accounting. Whenever possible, the inventory should contain the same values as those required for income tax purposes in determining the gain or loss from the sale of property. In any case a record of such values must be available.

(d) Amortization of Bond Premium or Discount. When bonds are taken over in the inventory at more or less than their face value, the difference between the inventory value and the amount received at maturity is ordinarily treated as a loss or gain on realization; but when bonds are purchased at a premium or discount, the difference between the amount paid and the amount to be received at maturity should be treated as an adjustment of the interest earned and should be written off during the remaining life of the bond. If the amount is not large, the "straight-line" method may be used, that is, the total premium or discount is divided by the number of remaining interest payments to obtain the amount to be written off at each interest date. If the amount is large, amortization tables may be used in which the **effective rate** of interest is applied to the present value of the bond to obtain the income due to the life tenant.

(e) Depreciation. Except for buildings forming part of the inventory at the date of origin of the trust, or in trusts where contrary provisions were intended by the grantor, wasting assets, including buildings and equipment, should be preserved by reflecting depreciation as a charge to income, if allowed by the trust instrument or state law. Many states have no provision for depreciation.

If all of the trust income is distributed to beneficiaries without regard for depreciation, the entire periodic deduction for depreciation is taken for income tax purposes by the beneficiaries, and the trustee has no occasion to record depreciation in his records. In all instances the trustee should be guided by the provisions of the trust instrument or state law in his handling of depreciation.

(f) Payments of Expenses. A distinction must be made between expenses chargeable to principal and income. In the absence of direction in the instrument the fiduciary should rely upon state law as to allocation of trust expenses. Generally if an expense is recurring each year it is usually charged to income. It could also be allocable one-half to principal and one-half to income. If an expense is attributable to corpus, it should be charged to principal. If the expense was to maintain and collect income, then it should be charged to income. For example, capital gains are allocated to principal, and the income tax paid by the trustee on capital gains should also be charged to principal; however, when a bank assesses an annual fee for a custody account, the custody fee could be charged to income or split 50/50 between income and principal.

31.31 TRUSTEE'S REPORTS.   Trustee's reports vary in form and in frequency according to the nature and provisions of the trust, and whether it is being administered under the jurisdiction of a court. Moreover, the form of the report varies among jurisdictions. Before preparing the report, the accountant should ascertain from the court whether a particular form is required. The valuations to be used must always be the same as those appearing on the inventory unless specific permission has been granted to change them. If assets have been written off as worthless, they must nevertheless appear in the new inventory without value.

If income and principal cash accounts have been properly maintained, the balance of the undistributed income would be represented by an equal amount of cash in the bank. If specific investments have been made with the intention that the funds used were still to be considered as undistributed income, the assets acquired should be shown as assets belonging to the trust income account.

The reports consist primarily of an analysis of the principal and income accounts. In addition, a statement showing the changes in the investments, an inventory of the property at the date of the report, and supporting schedules of various items will be required. A reconciliation of cash receipts and disbursements is also often prepared.

SOURCES AND SUGGESTED REFERENCES

Denhard, J. G., Jr., *A Complete Guide to Estate Accounting and Taxes,* 4th ed., Prentice-Hall, Englewood, NJ, 1988.

Ferguson, M. Carr, Freeland, James L., and Stephens, Richard B., *Federal Income Taxation of Estates and Beneficiaries,* Little Brown, Boston, 1970, 1989 Suppl.

Harris, Homer I., *Estates Practice Guide,* 4th ed., Lawyer's Co-Operative Publishing, Rochester, NY, 1984, 1989 Suppl.

Larsen, E. J., and Mosich, A. N., *Modern Advanced Accounting,* 4th ed., McGraw-Hill, New York, 1988.

Nossman, Walter L., Wyatt, Joseph L., Jr., and McDaniel, James R., *Trust Administration and Taxes,* rev. 2nd ed., Matthew Bender, New York, 1988.

Scott, Austin Wakeman, *The Law of Trusts,* 4th ed., Little Brown, Boston, 1986, 1989 Suppl.

Stephenson, G. T., and Wiggins, Norman, *Estates and Trusts,* 5th ed., Appleton-Century-Crofts, New York, 1970.

CHAPTER 32

VALUATION OF NONPUBLIC COMPANIES

Allyn A. Joyce

Management Planning, Inc.

Jacob P. Roosma

Deloitte & Touche

CONTENTS

Mr. Joyce and Mr. Roosma wish to acknowledge the review assistance provided by Philip H. Osborne, David Moomaw, Myrtle Seyfert, and Marilyn Van Kirk, all of Management Planning, Inc.

DEFINITION OF VALUE

32.1 DEFINITION OF NONPUBLIC.   A **public company** is one whose common stock has widespread ownership and investment interest and such active trading that market quotations ordinarily represent fair market value. In contrast, the common stock of a **nonpublic company** generally has concentrated ownership and such few trades that the transactions do not provide reliable indications of fair market value.

32.2 PURPOSES FOR VALUATIONS.   The need for valuing the common stock of a nonpublic or closely held company arises on many occasions. Among the more important situations requiring the valuation of nonpublic stock are filing estate and gift tax returns, estate planning, financial planning, employee stock ownership plan transactions and reports, granting stock options, drawing stock purchase agreements, marital dissolutions, structuring recapitalizations, sales, mergers, and divestitures.

32.3 FAIR MARKET VALUE.   Briefly stated, **fair market value** is that value at which a willing buyer and a willing seller, both well informed and neither under any compulsion to act, would arrive in an arm's-length sale of the asset in question. Such value is always determined as of a specific date and is based on all pertinent facts and conditions that are known or reasonably might be anticipated on that date. The existence of a willing buyer and a willing seller is assumed in the very definition of fair market value.

GENERAL PROCEDURE FOR VALUATION

32.4 COMPILE BACKGROUND INFORMATION ABOUT THE COMPANY.   In valuing the common stock of a nonpublic company it is necessary to become as informed as the well-informed buyer and seller assumed in the definition of value.

The appraiser should review the **history** of the corporation including date and state of incorporation, the products originally made, evolutionary developments to the present, and changes in control over the years. A list of stockholders and a listing of officers' names, salaries, ages, and experience should be obtained.

The appraiser must understand the nature of the company's products, raw materials used, and the methods of manufacture. A facilities tour is helpful. He should inquire as to how technologically advanced (or backward) the company is and review anticipated capital expenditures.

Information on the size of the labor force, the existence of collective bargaining agents, and background information on employee relations, as well as the corporation's strike experience should be obtained. The risk of customer loss during a strike must be evaluated.

The analyst should carefully analyze the structure of the industry, including the identity of existing competitors, barriers to entry and exit, and the bargaining position of customers and suppliers.

Obtain information on the sales force, including its size, structure, methods of compensation and radius of distribution. Information on markets, including principal industries served and principal customers served, is also important. Any material dependence on a single industry (25% or more of sales) or on a single customer (10% or more of sales) should be carefully reviewed and the risk of a sudden loss evaluated. The nature of the markets served (e.g., replacement vs. original equipment market or job shop vs. proprietary) should be examined. The economic forces that give rise to demand for the company's products or services should be understood. Market share data, when available, can be helpful. Price, quality, and service as competitive factors should be assessed. The role of **patents** and proprietary or secret technology in the competitive structure of the industry should be examined, and if these are important, the possible effects of patent expirations should be reviewed. **Research and development** projects underway should be reviewed with management.

Changes in the industry, particularly those of a technological or marketing nature, must be analyzed in terms of the company's outlook. The analyst should obtain a "feel" for **the industry.** Background information can usually be obtained from trade sources. He should compile and analyze long-term sales data on the industry (preferably in terms of both dollars and units), to examine the growth and cyclical characteristics of the industry. He should compare the performance of the company relative to its industry, and he should understand the reasons for any pronounced differences in trends between the company and its industry.

32.5 COMPILE FINANCIAL INFORMATION REGARDING THE COMPANY.   The appraiser should obtain **audit reports** for the past 5 years. If audit reports are not available, he will have to use unaudited statements. Some situations may require a complete audit of the books or even the services of an investigation accountant. In any event, the appraiser must clearly state the source of the financial information upon which he has relied.

The appraiser should prepare a 5-year spreadsheet of the income accounts and should review such areas as officers' compensation, the company's relationship with affiliated entities, and travel and entertainment.

It is helpful to restate the income account in ratios, at least down as far as operating income. This frequently discloses trends in cost–price relationships that should be discussed with management. Margins by product lines should be reviewed for a multiline company. The appraiser should obtain the **latest interim statement** and interview management with regard to the company's outlook for the current fiscal year. It is useful to get the interim statement for the same period of the previous year.

It is helpful to prepare and review a 5-year comparison of the **balance sheets.** Analyze changes that may be occurring in financial position. If the company is growing, evaluate its capacity to finance future growth. The latest balance sheet should be most carefully scrutinized for **nonoperating assets,** which, if substantial, should be segregated and valued separately. Hidden assets or hidden liabilities not adequately disclosed in the statements or notes must be ferreted out in interviews with management. The capital structure must be carefully reviewed, as well as the terms of any stock purchase agreements or stock options.

The appraiser should get sales, income, and dividend data back for a longer period of years, generally 10 to 20 years, if readily available, to review both the **growth and cyclical characteristics** of the company, as well as its long-term dividend policy. It is particularly important to review the long-term outlook with management. Most managements will have given it a great deal of thought and will be very insightful. Some, however, may be quite reticent on the subject, requiring a number of probing questions on the part of the appraiser. It is helpful to get insights from production, finance, and sales and marketing people, as well as the CEO.

32.6 SELECT COMPARATIVE COMPANIES.   Having reviewed the quantitative and qualitative factors discussed above, the appraiser must translate this complex array of facts into value. This requires an analysis of the most relevant facts from the actual marketplace. This is ordinarily done through the selection and analysis of comparative companies that can be used to formulate objective guidelines for the evaluation of the subject company. Comparative companies are publicly held companies that come as close as possible to the investment characteristics of the company being valued. Ideally, they are in the same industry. Frequently, however, there are no public companies in the same industry, so it is necessary to select companies with an underlying similarity of investment characteristics based on markets, products, growth, cyclical variability, and other factors.

Such companies have traditionally been called "comparative companies," a term that seems to connote companies "just like" the company being valued. It is seldom, if ever, possible to find publicly held companies "just like" the company under consideration. Some appraisers use the term "guideline companies" as a more appropriate term than "comparative companies."

The importance of a thorough, objective selection of comparative companies cannot be overestimated. The credibility of any valuation analysis is dependent on the demonstrated objectivity of the selection of comparative companies.

In searching for comparative companies, the best available **sources** are usually *Moody's Industrial Manual* and Standard & Poor's *Standard Corporation Records*. Both manuals are updated annually. The **Directory of Companies Required to File Annual Reports with the SEC** can also be helpful. These sources classify companies by industry, and the appropriate industry groupings can be reviewed for possible comparative companies. If no appropriate industry classification can be found, it is sometimes necessary to review all the companies listed in either Standard & Poor's or Moody's. In recent years many appraisers have switched from printed sources of information on possible comparative companies to computerized databases. It must be recognized that the breadth and depth of coverage and the accuracy of the information contained in such services will affect the results. Although they are far more efficient than the traditional printed sources, if such databases are not comprehensive in the number of companies they cover or in the way they classify businesses, some actively traded companies that meet the criteria established for the selection of comparative companies may be missed.

The appraiser must clearly state the criteria used in selecting comparative companies and prepare a list of all reasonable potential comparative companies. The list should state the reasons for rejecting or retaining the potential companies. A description of each comparative company finally selected should be part of the report.

(a) Compile Data on Comparative Companies.   It is necessary to compile financial and operating data on the comparative companies. Annual reports should be obtained on the comparative companies, and 10-K reports often are helpful. As much information as possible must be gleaned from official reports, trade sources, prospectuses, and so on, regarding products, markets, and customer dependence, for each of the comparative companies. Five-year **balance sheet** and **income account** comparisons are recommended. Where possible, **adjustments** should be made to the income and balance sheets of the comparative companies and/or the subject company to minimize differences in accounting when such differences are material.

Generally, public companies compute **depreciation** on the straight-line basis for financial reporting purposes. If the company being valued uses accelerated depreciation, its income and net worth should be adjusted to a straight-line basis when the difference is substantial (10% or more of average income over the past 5 years).

Adjustments should be considered when there is a difference in **inventory accounting** method between the subject company and the guideline companies. The most common difference is that most or all the comparative companies are on LIFO and the subject company is on FIFO. Most appraisers tend to ignore this difference unless the impact exceeds 10% of income or net worth. Pratt advocates adjusting both the balance sheet and income account of LIFO comparatives to value a FIFO company. This is the most common approach to the problem, but a surprising number of appraisers simply ignore the issue altogether.

When the subject company and all the comparative companies are on LIFO, most appraisers make no adjustments. However, even here, some adjustment of the balance sheet should be considered. If the subject company has been on LIFO for an appreciably longer or shorter time than the comparatives, there may be a substantial difference in the understatement of inventories on the LIFO method. This is readily handled by simply adjusting all balance sheets to a FIFO basis which, in any event, provides a more current measure of the value of inventories. This procedure can be followed even though earnings comparisons are left on a LIFO basis. However, when LIFO inventory liquidations occur, resulting profits should be adjusted out as nonrecurring.

The income accounts of the subject company should be carefully reviewed and the management interviewed with regard to **extraordinary factors** affecting income, such as inventory write-downs, uninsured losses, plant moving expenses, or anything of a substantial and nonrecurring nature. Adjustments should be made to eliminate the effects of these extraordinary, nonrecurring items.

(b) Calculate Market Value Ratios.   Next, the appraiser should calculate the **market values** of the comparative companies by multiplying the number of shares outstanding by the price per share on the valuation date. If the company has preferred stock outstanding, include it in this computation.

It is necessary to compute the **price–earnings ratio.** Generally, but by no means always, a weighted average of earnings over the past 5 years is used. (The weighted average places a weight of five on the earnings of the most recent year, a weight of four to income of the year before that, etc.) When earnings are variable, an unweighted average may be appropriate. The period selected must be the one that best measures the earning power of the subject company relative to the earning power of the comparative group. Generally, median ratios are used to avoid the distorting effect of extremes on the arithmetic average.

Compute the **average cash flow** (net income plus noncash charges) for each of the comparative companies using the same period. Compute the median price-cash flow ratio of the comparative group.

Compute the **price-dividend ratio** of each of the guideline companies. Generally, the dividend of the latest year is suitable for this purpose. However, if there has been an abrupt change in the dividend rate in a recent quarter, the new rate may be more indicative of dividend expectations. Compute the median price-dividend ratio of the comparative group.

Compute market-value-to-book-value ratios and the median of these ratios.

32.7 ESTIMATE DIVIDEND-PAYING CAPACITY.   The use of the price-dividend ratio raises the question of the significance of the actual dividend payments of a nonpublic corporation. In many cases, even though the company has the capacity to pay dividends, it pays small ones, or none at all. This inevitably raises the question of whether actual dividend payments or dividend-paying capacity should be capitalized. That dividend-paying capacity must be considered is quite clearly the position of the IRS (Rev. Rul. 59-60, § 3e), but the courts have not always been as clear.

In estimating dividend-paying capacity, the comparative companies are useful as a guideline. Compute the payout ratio (dividends as a percentage of net income) of the comparative companies and derive the median payout ratio of the group. Then examine the financial position of the company being valued relative to that of the comparative companies. Consider also that the company being valued, as a closely held company, does not have the same **access to capital markets** for equity capital as the comparative companies and must, therefore, rely on the retention of earnings to a greater extent than publicly held companies. As a reasonable rule of thumb, when the company being valued has a financial position roughly similar to that of the comparative companies, construct dividends at a **payout ratio** equal to two-thirds that of the comparative companies. That is, if the comparative companies are paying out 60% of their earnings, a privately held company of similar financial position could be expected to pay out about 40% of earnings. This lesser payout ratio (40% as opposed to 60%) recognizes the nonpublic company's greater reliance on the retention of earnings to finance its business. When the financial position of the company being valued is weaker than that of the comparative companies, the dividend-paying capacity is correspondingly less. If the financial position of the company being valued is significantly stronger than that of the comparative companies, it may have a dividend-paying capacity equal to or greater than that of the comparative companies, despite its inferior access to capital markets.

A second part to this question is, if dividend-paying capacity should be capitalized, how? Does a dollar of dividend that could be paid, but is not paid, have a value to the minority interest investor equal to a dollar of dividend that is actually paid? One reasonable procedure is to capitalize actual dividend payments at the same rate as the comparative companies and capitalize unpaid dividend-paying capacity (the excess of the capacity to pay dividends over the actual dividends paid) at half the multiplier derived from the guideline companies. This procedure recognizes that the minority interest investor does benefit from that unpaid dividend-paying capacity because the company builds its equity base faster than it would if such dividends were paid. However, it also recognizes that the benefit is not as direct nor as immediate as the actual payment of dividends.

32.8 JUDGMENTAL MODIFICATION OF THE VALUATION RATIOS.   These market value ratios provide useful valuation guidelines. However, they are nothing more than guidelines and must inevitably be combined with the appraiser's judgment in arriving at a sound valuation conclusion. The appraiser must, after careful consideration of all relevant factors, come to one of three possible conclusions:

1. Investors would find the subject company to be more attractive than the group of guideline companies. (In this case a premium must be added to the median valuation ratios.)
2. Investors would find the subject company to be less attractive than the comparative companies. (In this case a discount from the median valuation ratios is required.)
3. Investors would regard the subject as being neither more nor less attractive than the group of guideline companies. (In this case the use of the median ratios would be appropriate.)

This decision requires a careful comparative analysis of the subject company and the guideline companies in terms of both qualitative and quantitative differences.

In addition to the basic nature of the product, qualitative considerations may include such factors as **market position, geographic, product, and market diversification, patent protection, depth of management, research and development capabilities,** and many others. Often, but by no means always, public companies are larger and more diversified, and have more professional management. When they are used as comparative companies for the valuation of a smaller, weaker, less diversified company, a judgmental adjustment to the valuation ratios may be necessary. However, in making these judgmental adjustments, care must be taken to avoid "counting the same trick twice." For instance, in valuing a company with low earnings, one should not take a discount for poor management, if it is the poor management that causes the low earnings. That would obviously be "doubling up."

In terms of quantitative differences, one should first look to **long-term trends of sales and income.** Place the sales and income of each of the comparative companies on an index basis, selecting a base period that is not affected by abnormal factors. Determine the median sales index of the group of comparative companies and compare it to the company being valued. Charts of these comparisons are particularly helpful.

Differences in **trends** may be properly reflected in the valuation procedure through the use of a weighted average. However, a pronounced long-term inferiority of sales trend, and particularly of income trend, may require a further discount to the valuation ratios derived from the comparative companies. Conversely, a decided long-term superiority of trends may require an upward adjustment to those valuation ratios.

One should also look to the factor of **variability.** A company with a highly variable earnings trend is less attractive to investors than a company with a stable earnings trend. However, be careful in comparing the trend of earnings of a single company to that of the the group average or median. The averaging process tends to have a stabilizing influence, and it may therefore be desirable to make a comparison on an individual company basis.

A comparison of financial ratios is also recommended. This should include the current ratio (current assets divided by current liabilities), liquidity ratio (current assets as a percentage of total assets), and leverage ratios (total liabilities as a percentage of total assets and net worth as a percentage of total assets). Differences in financial position can be appropriately reflected in the estimation of dividend-paying capacity. In most cases, the use of dividend-paying capacity as a valuation factor makes a reasonable allowance for differences in financial position. When there are extreme differences, some further adjustment may be necessary. The financial position of the company being valued may be so weak that the nonpayment of dividends does not adequately reflect its poor financial position. In this case, an appraiser must make a judgmental negative adjustment to the valuation ratios. On the other hand, a strong financial position is normally adequately reflected through either liberal dividend payments or a strong dividend-paying capacity. A company with an extremely strong financial position relative to the comparative companies represents an unusual situation, which is covered in section 32.20.

Operating ratios, including sales times net worth, net income as a percentage of sales and income as a percentage of net worth, should be computed and charted. These ratios should be reviewed with particular attention to the profit margin. A profit margin that is well below average may indicate a high-cost operation and, when accompanied by highly variable earnings, may require some discount to the valuation ratios. However, frequently a low profit margin is accompanied by a high ratio of sales to net worth, and together these characteristics are symptomatic of integration lesser than that of the comparative companies.

Finally, examine the fundamental assumption in the valuation procedure that the **earnings outlook** of the subject company is roughly similar to that of the comparative companies. If there are strong indications that such an assumption is not reasonable, make an appropriate adjustment to the valuation ratios.

32.9 APPLICATION OF THE MARKET VALUE RATIOS. At this point, the appraiser has derived four valuation ratios that have been derived from the comparative companies: price–net worth ratio, price–earnings ratio, price–cash flow ratio, and price–dividend ratio. The application of the four ratios provides four indicators of value, and there may be considerable variation among them. This inevitably raises the question of their relative importance. There is close to universal acceptance of the notion that, except under unusual circumstances, earnings are the most important valuation factor.

Some appraisers and some courts completely ignore the concept of **cash flow.** The use of cash flow in valuation analysis is most appropriate when the company has large assets that do not necessarily decline in value with time and are not "used up" in production. An obvious example is a real estate holding company. The use of cash flow in the valuation of companies with very little investment in depreciable assets (service companies, for instance) is somewhat redundant, in that cash flow may be almost identical to earnings, and its use is simply a repetition of the price–earnings ratio analysis.

If the subject company is significantly more or less capital intensive than the guideline companies, the cash flow approach should be modified or eliminated.

Some appraisers completely ignore dividends and dividend-paying capacity. Some give no weight to the book value factor.

The necessity of translating these indicators into a value presents a dilemma to the appraiser. If he uses specific weights, he must defend these as reasonable and not constituting a formula. On the other hand, deriving a value from only one of these factors also constitutes a weighting procedure because it assigns a weight of 100% to that one factor and zero to the others. Some appraisers cope with this problem by simply stating that "all things considered, I think the value is X," but they must face the obvious question: What factors did you consider and how much weight did you give to them?"

The following tabulation gives a cross section of the weightings commonly used by business appraisers in valuing industrial corporations.

Valuation Basis	Weights						
Price—Book Value	20	20	10	33$^1/_3$	0	10	0
Price—Earnings	30	40	60	33$^1/_3$	60	90	100
Price—Cash Flow	20	0	0	0	20	0	0
Price—Dividends	30	40	30	33$^1/_3$	20	0	0

For the most part, courts do not specify the weight they accord to these various valuation factors. In the few cases where the courts have been specific, they have tended to ascribe **primary importance to earnings and dividends,** and they have demonstrated a tendency to give more weight to earnings than to dividends. The factor of book value has generally received relatively little weight in court decisions involving industrial companies. However, it is not totally ignored.

Whatever weights are used, the appraiser must thoughtfully analyze the resulting value for **reasonableness.** If this stock were publicly traded at this price, would it be more attractive than the shares of the comparative companies? Would it be significantly less attractive than shares of the guideline companies? If the appraiser can answer both of these questions in the negative, he has probably arrived at a reasonable result.

(a) Discount for Lack of Marketability. The value derived from the comparative analysis is the freely traded price, that is, the price at which the common stock of the subject company would trade if it had an active public market.

Clearly, lack of ready marketability makes a stock considerably less attractive than it would be if it were readily marketable. This was recognized by the IRS in its Rev. Rul. 77-287 when, in discussing the value of unregistered shares of public companies, it stated: "The discount from the market price provides the main incentive for a potential buyer to acquire restricted securities."

In recent years appraisers have generally used transactions in the restricted shares of public companies as the best guideline for determining the appropriate discount for lack of marketability. A number of studies have been made of this market, and they indicate a rather wide dispersion of discounts but most indicate a median discount of about 35%. The two seminal studies, those of Maher (1976) and Moroney (1973) indicated median discounts of 34.73% and 33% respectively. More recent studies have been made by Williamette Management Associates (median 31.2%) and Standard Research Consultants (45%).

Willamette Associates has also analyzed the relationship of original public offering prices to arm's-length trades during the 3 years preceding the public offering, which suggests discounts in the 40% to 60% range.

(b) Discount for Minority Interest. The discount for lack of marketability should not be confused with a discount for minority interest. This chapter has explained the use of publicly held comparative companies in making a judgment as to the value of stock in a nonpublic company. The prices at which the common stocks of those comparative companies sell reflect minority interest values; therefore the comparative analysis enables the appraiser to express an opinion about the price at which the stock of the subject closely held company would trade if it had an active public market (the freely traded value). It is therefore a minority interest value to begin with, and a minority interest discount is inappropriate. However, the stock of a closely held company is lacking in marketability, and a discount for lack of marketability is appropriate.

32.10 DISCOUNTED FUTURE BENEFITS APPROACHES. Discounted future benefits approaches to the determination of fair market value can be done on the basis of projected dividends, earnings, or cash flow. These approaches involve five steps:

1. *The Projection (of dividends, earnings, or cash flow).* Many appraisers base their projections on past growth rates. Others rely on projections prepared by management. In either event, assumptions underlying the projections should be clearly stated.

2. *Determination of the Discount Rate.* The most frequently used reference point in the derivation of equity capitalization rates is the historic premium return on small company stocks as compiled by Ibbotson Associates. This premium is defined as the historic return on small company stocks less the risk-free rate of return. Most appraisers derive a premium based on data between 1926, the first year included in the Ibbotson study, and the year preceding the valuation date. Shorter time periods are sometimes used and can produce substantially different results.

   Ibbotson (1989) states that the arithmetic mean (as opposed to the geometric mean) is appropriate for valuation purposes.

   Most appraisers using this technique add a judgmental increment to the small company stock premium on the theory that the subject company entails greater risk than those companies in the Ibbotson small company stock series.

   The premium must be added to the risk-free rate. Some appraisers use the return on U.S. Treasury bills as the risk-free rate, and others use the return on long-term government bonds as more appropriate because it better reflects the assumed time horizon of the common stock investor.

3. *Determination of the Horizon.* The value of stock is the present value of future benefits in perpetuity. This axiom requires that the future benefits be projected in perpetuity or at least so far into the future that present value increments become insignificant. Most appraisers using this technique solve this problem by using a relatively short time horizon, 5 years being the most common.

4. *Determination of Terminal Value.* The use of a horizon necessitates the determination of a terminal value at the end of the horizon year.

5. *The Determination of Present Value.* Value is computed by discounting to present value the projected terminal value and the projected flow of future benefits up to the end of the horizon year. The rate of return derived in step 2 is used for discounting in step 5.

Generally, a large part of the total value (up to 80% or more) derives from the terminal value discounted to the present. The estimation of the terminal value is little more than "a shot in the dark" and the credibility of this approach is no better than the estimate of terminal value.

In recent years, as discounted future benefits appraisals have been subjected to critical review, exclusive reliance on this technique seems to have waned. Few appraisers now rely entirely on these approaches in valuing established companies. These approaches are generally used as an adjunct to the comparative company approach.

If the comparative company approach and the discounted future benefits approach produce substantially different results, the appraiser should carefully analyze the reasons for the difference and reconcile them.

32.11 USE OF FORMULAS.   Rev. Rul. 59-60, the courts, and the ESOP Association have discredited the use of valuation formulas. The ESOP Association made the point very clearly: "Formula appraisals are totally unacceptable, because they will virtually always result in an unfair, if not absurd, appraisal at some time in the future."

Valuation formulas can be as simple as "Value = net book value," "Value = net asset value," or "Value = 10 × earnings." On the other hand, they can be so complex as to defy comprehension. Doctors and engineers seem particularly enamored of complex valuation formulas.

The most widely employed type of formula still in use by some business appraisers, is the "excess earnings formula." The original formula of this type was ARM-34, which was used for many years by IRS in the valuation of closely held companies.

ARM-34 was as follows:

$$\text{Value} = \text{book value} + \text{capitalized excess earnings}$$

Generally, excess earnings were defined as earnings in excess of 10% of net worth, and a 20% capitalization rate was generally used in capitalizing excess earnings so that, in practice, the formula was:

$$\text{Value} = \text{book value} + 5 \left(\text{earnings} - \frac{\text{book value}}{10} \right)$$

The formula has long since been discredited and abandoned by the IRS as well as the courts because it is arbitrary and not market oriented and can therefore produce very unrealistic values.

However, a variation of ARM-34 is still in use by some appraisers. The basic formula is the same:

$$\text{Value} = \text{book value} + \text{capitalized excess earnings}$$

Excess earnings are defined as the earnings in excess of the industry's average rate of earnings on stockholders' equity. Typically, these excess earnings are capitalized at 20% (or multiplied by 5). The shortcomings of this approach are fundamentally the same as ARM-34. The underlying assumption that a company is worth its book value if it has an average rate of earnings on net worth for its industry is arbitrary and unsupported. In fact, companies in industries marked by low rates of earnings on book value, will tend, on average, to be worth less than book value, whereas companies in industries with high rates of earnings on equity tend, on average, to have values in excess of book value, sometimes by a factor of 4 or 5.

32.12 NET ASSET VALUE APPROACH.   Net asset value is simply computed by adjusting all assets to a market value basis and deducting all liabilities. Fundamentally, this is yet another formula approach, the formula being "Value = net asset value." There is ample evidence in the marketplace that the common stocks of industrial companies can sell appreciably above or below net asset value. This is not surprising because the normal expectation of investors is that the benefits of ownership will be received by them by way of dividends and a rising market price. However, if the liquidation of a company is pending, net asset value is of paramount importance.

Net asset value has greater relevance to the appraisal of holding companies, notably investment companies and real estate holding companies. Even here, however, the evidence of the marketplace is that the stocks of such companies almost always trade below net asset value.

SPECIAL SITUATIONS

32.13 WHOLESALE AND RETAIL COMPANIES.   The valuation of wholesale and retail companies is essentially similar to that of an industrial company as described above. Particular attention should be paid to the factor of **geographic diversification** in valuing distribution companies. For example, a supermarket chain whose stores are concentrated in a single city involves greater investment risk than a regional supermarket company operating in a number of cities, and special allowance should be made for such differences.

32.14 SERVICE COMPANIES.   The valuation of service companies is similar to the valuation of industrial companies, although investors tend to ascribe relatively little weight to the factor of book value and cash flow in the valuation of service companies.

32.15 COMPANIES WITH LOW EARNINGS.   The valuation of a company with a very low rate of earnings on stockholders' equity can present a particular problem. The extreme form of this is a company that over a period of years has had no earnings and no capacity to pay dividends. The use of the valuation procedure described earlier can be misleading in this instance, since primary weight is given to evidence of earning power. Obviously, the company with no earnings has no value based solely on the factor of earning power. These cases must be carefully judged on their own merits. If liquidation is certain, or even probable, **liquidating value** is governing. If not, a going-concern valuation is called for, recognizing that companies that are "worth more dead than alive" because of chronically low earnings may go on for years without liquidating, and the minority interest investor cannot force a liquidation.

In estimating going-concern value, it is helpful to examine the range of the ratios of market value to book value of the comparative companies. Frequently there are, among the comparative companies, two or three companies with low rates of earnings on stockholders' equity (5% or less) and these tend to have low price-book value ratios. In a group where the median price-book value ratios might be 80% or 90%, there may very well be two or three companies earning less than 5% on capital, which may have price-book value ratios of 40% or 50%. Under such circumstances, these data would lead to the conclusion that the company with no earnings at all should be valued below that 40% or 50%.

The influence of judgment in this situation can be reduced through the use of a **statistical regression technique.** Examine the relationship between the market value-book value ratio and the rate of earnings on book value of the comparative companies. Generally there is a definite relationship that can be described precisely through the use of a simple linear correlation. This technique makes it quite clear that the companies with high rates of earnings on stockholders' equity tend to have high price-book value ratios, and the companies with low rates of earnings on stockholders' equity tend to have low market price-book value ratios. The statistical definition of this relationship can constitute a satisfactory basis for the valuation of a company with little or no earnings.

32.16 HOLDING COMPANIES.   The comparative company technique is also used in valuing holding companies, that is, companies whose assets consist largely of securities. Comparative companies must be selected that parallel, to the extent possible, the nature of the assets of the company being valued. If the holding company being valued has a **diversified portfolio of common stocks,** it is desirable to select closed-end diversified investment companies. The analyst can then examine the relationship between the market value of the stocks of such companies and **underlying net asset values.** The relationships of market value to earnings and of market value to dividends should also be reviewed. However, the ratio of market value to net asset value is generally conceded to be the primary determinant of value and, as a practical matter, this ratio generally shows far greater consistency than the price-earnings or price-dividends ratios of closed-end investment companies. In determining the net asset value of the holding company, the **capital gains tax** on unrealized capital gains may be deducted as a way to reflect the tax disadvantage of the holding company vis-à-vis regulated investment companies. However, some simply modify the median price to net asset value derived from comparatives on the theory that the subject company, unlike the comparative companies, may be "locked in" to some investments by virtue of the capital gains tax.

The procedure involving a **nondiversified investment company** is essentially similar to that just described for diversified companies, except that nondiversified investment companies are selected for comparison. The other difference is that some of the nondiversified investment companies may be taxed as ordinary corporations; therefore the holding company may not be at a tax disadvantage relative to such comparative companies.

If the portfolio of the subject company is concentrated in just a few investments, it may be difficult to find public companies so lacking in diversification. Under these circumstances it will be necessary to apply a discount to the ratios derived from the comparative companies.

If the investment portfolio is largely **debt securities** of good quality, one should examine the relationship between market value and underlying net asset value of closed-end bond funds. As a general rule, the market value-net asset value ratio among these companies is quite close to net asset value.

32.17 REAL ESTATE COMPANIES. The valuation of a minority interest in a real estate holding company requires an **appraisal of the underlying assets** by a qualified real estate appraiser.

The **net asset value** of the real estate holding company can then be computed by adjusting stockholders' equity for the difference between the appraisal value of the real estate and net book value.

The appraiser should select publicly held real estate companies owning similar types of real estate, which disclose the estimated appraised value of their assets. This can be used in calculating net asset value. This, in turn, can be used to calculate the price–net asset value relationship. It is also recommended that the relationship between market value and earnings, cash flow, and dividends be examined.

In applying such ratios to the company being valued, primary weight should be given to the market price–net asset value ratio. However, the factors of earnings, cash flow, and dividends certainly should not be ignored.

In applying these ratios, judgment must be brought to bear on qualitative differences between the comparative companies and the subject company. Diversification by property and neighborhood must be considered. A comparison of financial position and the operating record is also important.

32.18 COMPANIES WITH NONOPERATING ASSETS. Industrial companies with large nonoperating assets present a particular valuation problem. The company whose **cash** clearly exceeds its operating needs by a substantial margin is a case in point. Another is a company owning a large portfolio of **securities.** Another example is a company owning valuable **real estate** unrelated to its basic business. In these instances it is best to remove such assets from the balance sheet and deduct the related earnings, with an appropriate tax adjustment, from reported earnings. Dividends must also be adjusted. Value the company as though it did not own the nonoperating assets. It is then necessary to determine the appropriate increment to the value of the stock determined on an operating basis. If the nonoperating assets are securities, the best procedure is that recommended for an investment company (see section 32.16). Similarly, if such assets are real estate, the procedure used in valuing a minority interest in a real estate company is appropriate.

32.19 LIFE INSURANCE PROCEEDS. In valuing common stock for estate tax purposes it is necessary to reflect any windfall to the company arising from any life insurance on the deceased. This may be done by considering the company's improved financial position and its higher earning power related to the proceeds. If the proceeds result in a level of cash beyond the needs of the business, then the excess should be treated as a nonoperating asset, as reviewed above.

If the deceased was a key man it may be necessary to apply a special discount to reflect the higher risk related to his loss.

32.20 COMPANIES WITH AN EXTREMELY STRONG FINANCIAL POSITION. A company with an extremely strong financial position can present a particular valuation problem. An example is a real estate company with no long-term debt. The publicly held companies that might be used for comparative purposes, without exception, have large amounts of long-term debt outstanding. Thus any price–earnings ratio or price–net asset value ratio that can be derived from them reflects the way in which the investing public values a real estate company with significant leverage.

One might approach this problem in the usual way and then adjust the valuation ratios derived from publicly held real estate companies to reflect the superior financial position of the subject company. However, the influence of the appraiser's judgment can be minimized by changing to the **"total invested capital technique,"** to quantify better the effect of extreme superiority in financial position.

In employing the total invested capital technique, the total market value of all preferred and common stock is combined with the total market value of all the outstanding long-term debt of each of the comparative companies. That represents the total market value of the total invested capital. That amount is then related to the book value of that total invested capital (net worth plus long-term debt), adjusted for underlying asset values in the case of real estate companies.

Similarly, the total market value of the total invested capital is related to the earnings available for that total invested capital (net income plus interest on long-term debt), to the cash flow available for that invested capital (net income plus noncash charges, plus interest on long-term debt), and finally it is related to the earnings paid out on that total invested capital (dividends plus interest on long-term debt). The application of these ratios to a company with a decidedly stronger financial position is recommended when the company being valued is stronger than the comparative companies by a very wide margin, a circumstance that tends to occur in the valuation of real estate companies but may be encountered in the valuation of an industrial company.

One important drawback of this technique should be noted. It is necessary to ascertain the market value of the long-term debt of the comparative companies and, when the debt is not publicly traded, it is necessary to estimate its market value. This introduces an element of judgment that the basic procedure does not entail.

32.21 PREFERRED STOCK.   A standard preferred stock is a security which has the following features:

1. The right to receive a stated cumulative cash dividend before any cash dividends are paid to the company's common stock.
2. The right to receive a stated amount upon liquidation of the company before any proceeds are distributed to the company's common stock.
3. No voting rights in normal circumstances.
4. No participation rights in dividends or liquidation proceeds beyond its stated preferences.
5. No conversion rights.
6. No redemption rights at the option of the holder; may be callable by the company.
7. No sinking fund or other feature that provides a definite maturity.

There are two key elements in the valuation of a standard preferred stock.

1. The probability that the company will meet the obligations of the preferred stock. This entails consideration of:
   a. The earnings coverage for the dividend preference.
   b. The asset coverage for the liquidation preference.
   c. The characteristics of the corporation, which could affect these coverages, particularly its prospective growth, financial position, and stability.
2. The yields available from comparable fixed income investments.

The valuation of preferred stock requires the selection and analysis of publicly traded preferred stocks that can be used to formulate the best possible valuation guidelines. There are surprisingly few actively traded standard preferred stocks of industrial companies, and it is not possible to confine comparatives to a single industry. It is necessary to compute the earnings coverage of each of these securities. Earnings coverage is computed as follows:

$$\frac{\text{Earnings before interest and taxes}}{\text{Interest} + \left(\dfrac{\text{preferred dividend requirement}}{1 - \text{tax rate}}\right)}$$

Asset coverage is measured relative to both current assets and total assets and is computed as follows:

$$\text{Current assets coverage:} = \frac{\text{Current assets}}{\text{Total liabilities} + \text{par value of preferred}}$$

$$\text{Total assets coverage:} = \frac{\text{Total assets}}{\text{Total liabilities} + \text{par value of preferred}}$$

Compute the yield (**dividend divided by market price**) on each of these securities, looking for a relationship between the yield and the earnings and asset coverages of the comparative preferreds. Qualitative factors should also be considered. Precise relationships are seldom ascertainable. However, a careful review of the data should provide a good base for the exercise of informed judgment in determining the freely traded value.

A discount to the freely traded value is required. General practice among appraisers is to apply a discount of 15% to 20% for lack of marketability of standard preferred stocks.

It is sometimes necessary to appraise a preferred stock that deviates in significant ways from a standard preferred stock. An exhaustive list of such preferred stocks is not practical. However, a few of the more common variations are as follows:

1. *Noncumulative Preferred Stock.* Some increase in the yield is warranted for the risk that the dividend may be skipped and "gone forever."

2. *Preferred Stock with Share Convertibility.* This is preferred stock that is convertible into a specified number of shares of common stock. It is necessary to determine the fair market value of the common stock into which the preferred is convertible. If the conversion value (the value of the common stock into which the preferred is convertible) is substantially less than the value as a standard preferred, the premium for convertibility is small or even nonexistent. On the other hand, if the conversion value exceeds the value as a standard preferred stock, the market value is equal to the conversion value plus a small premium.

3. *Preferred Stock with Dollar Convertibility.* This type of preferred is typically convertible into an amount of common stock having a specified dollar value, usually $100, on the conversion date. Even though its dividend may not warrant a value of $100, the conversion feature may give it a value close to or at the conversion price, depending on the assurance that the owner of the preferred can convert and receive $100 worth of common stock at any time.

4. *Preferred Stock with Participation Rights.* This type of preferred is entitled to the standard fixed dividend and liquidation preferences **plus** a share of the residual dividends or asset values, or both, which would otherwise pass to the common stock. Such rights give the preferred some of the attributes of a common stock and these attributes should be valued in a similar manner.

5. *Preferred Stock with an Adjustable Dividend Rate*. The dividend rate on such preferreds is typically adjusted quarterly to reflect prevailing market yields. This adjustment feature, depending on its specific structure, generally maintains the value of these preferreds at or near par. Many public companies have issued adjustable rate preferred stocks, but they are uncommon among nonpublic companies.

32.22 EMPLOYEE STOCK OWNERSHIP PLANS. Over the past 15 years there has been an enormous growth in the number of companies with employee stock ownership plans. The trust established under an ESOP requires a determination of fair market value for a variety of reasons, including:

1. Contributions of stock by the company or sales by its stockholders to the ESOT.
2. Sales of stock by the ESOT to third parties.
3. Transfer of shares from the ESOT to a beneficiary.
4. Repurchase of shares from a beneficiary exercising his or her put.
5. Reports required by ERISA.

The appraiser of ESOP shares should be familiar with the Department of Labor proposed regulations regarding ESOP appraisals. These regulations stress the requirement that the appraiser be independent of all parties to the transaction other than the plan. They also stress the requirement of a fully documented appraisal. The proposed regulation affirms Rev. Rul. 59-60 as a reasonable statement of general valuation principles, but the DOL seems to go out of its way to mandate the use of comparative companies.

The valuation of ESOP shares is fundamentally the same as valuation for other purposes except that the put obligation, providing it is enforceable, constitutes a kind of marketability that may reduce or even eliminate the lack of marketability discount that would otherwise be required. The appraiser, in deriving the freely traded value of the shares, will have used publicly held comparative companies as valuation guidelines. If the appraiser concludes that the put gives the beneficiary about the same assurance of marketability that he would enjoy if the trust held stock of the comparative companies, then no discount is appropriate. However, if the business risks of the subject company are such that the assurance of marketability is less, then some discount for lack of marketability is required. The size of such discount depends on the appraiser's assessment of the probability that the company will be financially able to honor its put obligations. This requires an analysis of the company's growth, stability, financial position, and cash flow—all factors that the appraiser will have considered in the basic appraisal process. Consideration should also be given to the timing and size of stock distributions to terminating employees since these factors could affect the company's ability to honor its put obligations.

Some appraisers believe that an additional discount is required for the lack of marketability of the stock in the hands of the trust, because the put does not affect the marketability of shares until they are distributed out of the trust. Others, viewing the trust as a device by which stock is held for ultimate distribution to terminating employees, conclude that the degree of marketability to the trust need not be reflected in valuing the stock.

There has been considerable discussion within the appraisal profession as to the effect that the stock repurchase liability may have on the fair market value of the stock. ("Stock repurchase liability" is not a liability in the normal sense of the word because it is an obligation to purchase an asset at its market value.) To date, no consensus has developed, and most appraisers seem to ignore the issue or list it as "a factor that has been considered."

Leveraged ESOPs present additional problems to the appraiser beyond the scope of this book.

32.23 VALUATIONS FOR MARITAL DISSOLUTIONS. The classic definition of fair market value is not always appropriate for a business valuation to be used in a divorce proceeding. This is particularly true in the case of professional practices that cannot be sold. The standard of value may not be clear from the statutes or the case law. It is imperative that the appraiser get guidance from the attorney with regard to the standard of value and the ways in which that standard can be applied to the case at hand.

The date as of which the marital estate is to be valued frequently is not clear from the statutes or case law and can, in some states, be set at the discretion of the trier of fact.

32.24 RESTRICTIVE AGREEMENTS. The existence of certain restrictive agreements can be determinative of value for estate tax purposes. If such an agreement restricts the sale of the stock during the stockholder's lifetime and obligates the estate to sell after death, and if the price is readily ascertainable from the agreement (and was reasonable at the time the agreement was signed), then the agreement is normally determinative of the value for estate tax purposes. However, where the parties to the agreement are family members, there is the possibility that IRC § 2036(c) will apply and require a different valuation standard. This question should be resolved by the attorney for the estate.

32.25 S CORPORATIONS. There is no consensus among appraisers as to the impact of the Subchapter S election on value. Some appraisers simply adjust the earnings of the S corporation to a C corporation basis. Others develop price earnings ratios from the pretax earnings of guideline companies. These methods assume that the S election has no effect on value. Other appraisers have concluded that the premium can be as much as 100% or more, depending upon the payout ratio (Schackelford, 1988). Still others use a preliminary premium of 52%, derived from two subpremiums. The first premium is 9% and results from the difference between the marginal corporate (34%) and personal (28%) tax rate. (This assumes that the corporation will distribute a minimum of 28% of its taxable income, and such payments should be regarded as "in lieu of taxes." The 9% premium is obtained by dividing the percentage of after-tax income of the S corporation by that of the C corporation—72% ÷ 66% = 1.09.) The second premium is 39% and arises because it takes $1.39 of taxable income from a C corporation to equal $1.00 of income from an S corporation. (The 52% premium is derived from the product of the two premiums—1.09 × 1.39.)

These and other premiums are exaggerated to the extent that they assume that the S advantage will remain unchanged in perpetuity. In fact it can be lost by changes within the legal structure of the company or its ownership or by changes in the tax code. Moreover, because it reduces the type and number of possible purchasers of the stock, an increment to the discount for lack of marketability seems warranted.

32.26 START-UP COMPANIES. Start-up companies are all future, no past; therefore the comparative company approach will be of limited use in appraising a start-up company. Some form of discounted future benefit approach must be used. The projections will be of the utmost importance and, in the case of a high-technology company, the appraiser will need significant input from an expert familiar with the technology and its market potential.

32.27 NONVOTING STOCK. Many corporations have a voting and a nonvoting common stock, which presents a valuation problem. One SEC study indicates a value differential of about 8% between high vote and low vote common shares where voting power is the only difference in the rights of each class.

Courts have been rather erratic on this question. In one case the court held that the voting stock, which constituted 1% of the equity, had 40% of the value. However, in other cases the courts were more moderate, and a number of cases have used relatively modest discounts for nonvoting stock, generally about 5%. A 5% to 10% differential seems reasonable in considering minority interest blocks.

32.28 VALUATION OF A CONTROLLING INTEREST. The ultimate controlling interest is the **100% interest.** The value of such an interest is the greater of the liquidating value of the corporation or the price it would fetch as a going concern in a sale or merger. If the company has relatively low earnings, the liquidating value should be estimated. **Liquidating value** may differ substantially from book value. Receivables may be difficult to collect by a company in liquidation, particularly if the company has granted credit to a large number of small accounts. The value of inventories tends to vary with the complexity of the inventory. An inventory of raw material, steel or copper, for example, has a fairly ascertainable value. On the other hand, a complex inventory of plumbing supplies, for example, can generally be sold only at a deep discount.

An appraisal should be obtained for real estate, as well as machinery and equipment. Standard machinery, a machine tool for instance, has an established market, and an experienced machinery and equipment appraiser can readily ascertain its value. Special machinery may have no more than scrap value. Consideration must be given to operating costs during the wind-up period and to severance pay and **pension obligations** under the Employee Retirement Income Security Act (ERISA). If liquidating value exceeds going-concern value, then the value of the 100% interest is the present value of the estimated proceeds of liquidation.

Most companies are worth more as **going concerns** than they are in liquidation and, under those circumstances, it is necessary to estimate the value of the company as a going concern. This presents essentially the same problem as a minority valuation in the sense that the appraiser must make a judgment as to the proper capitalization of earnings. It is desirable to examine the objective evidence of the marketplace. The preferred approach is to analyze available data on similar companies that have been involved in a sale or merger. There are two good sources of information to be used in obtaining information on such transactions. The first of these is *F&S Index of Corporate Change,* a quarterly published by Predicasts, Inc., which tabulates corporate sales and mergers by SIC number. The second is *Mergers & Acquisitions—The Journal of Corporate Venture,* a quarterly published by Information for Industry, Inc., which summarizes recent merger activity.

These sources should reveal a number of companies of a similar nature that have been sold or merged near the valuation date. Often it is not possible to obtain extensive details on such transactions. However, when the analyst can obtain a minimum of information, such as the sale price of the company, combined with a recent balance sheet and at least one year's income account, the transaction can serve as a useful guideline in the valuation of a 100% interest. When the acquiring company reports to the SEC, 10-K and S-4 reports may contain useful information.

Frequently this "direct approach" to the valuation of a 100% interest is not feasible because there have been no transactions involving similar companies or because information cannot be obtained on the transactions that have occurred. In that case, standard practice is to determine a minority interest value, following essentially the procedure outlined previously. Having determined this minority interest value, it is necessary to apply an appropriate **premium** to derive the value of a 100% interest. A useful guideline in this respect can be developed from the premiums that have been paid for publicly held industrial companies generally in recent months. This premium can be derived by examining the relationship between the sale price of the stock of each company and its stock price before the pending merger was influencing its market value. If this is done on a sufficient number of companies, a useful guideline to an appropriate merger premium for the company being valued can be obtained. However, there tends to be considerable variation among merger premiums, and the appropriate merger premium for the subject company is essentially a matter of judgment. The merger premium analysis is a very rough guideline, but it is a very useful one.

Lesser percentages of ownership can constitute absolute control. In some states 50% plus one share can force the sale, merger, or liquidation of a company. In other states it is two-thirds plus one share. Blocks of stock having legal absolute control are worth a substantial premium over minority interest values. However, some large companies have a policy of avoiding less than 100% acquisitions because they may prevent consolidation for income tax purposes or involve possible minority interest or dissenting stockholder problems. Therefore, a block of stock, substantially less than 100%, but legally constituting absolute control, has a per share value greater than that of a minority interest but somewhat less than that of a 100% interest.

In some states (Illinois, Ohio, Minnesota, and others) a two-thirds majority is required for sale, merger, or liquidation. In these states it is possible to own more than 50% of the voting securities and still not have absolute control. In these states the owner of, for example, 55% of the voting securities has **working control,** but not absolute control. He can control the dividend-paying policy of the company, its operating policies, and its employment policies. The owner of that 55% block is certainly in a better position than the owner of a minority interest. However, because he cannot force the sale or liquidation of the company, the 55% interest is not proportionately as valuable as an interest that can force the sale or merger of the company.

The premium that should be attached to a minority interest value to reflect this kind of working control tends to vary from company to company, and considerable judgment must be used by the appraiser in reflecting this factor. The premium should be 10% or more, but it should be significantly less than the premium for absolute control.

32.29 FIFTY PERCENT INTEREST.   Sometimes it is necessary to value a block of stock that represents exactly 50% of the voting power. Obviously, this block of stock is not a controlling interest. However, 50% of the vote does have "veto power." Although it cannot force any number of basic moves that may be deemed desirable, it can prevent the remaining half from undertaking action it deems to be undesirable. A holder of a 50% interest is in a better position than an owner of a minority interest; therefore a 50% block should have some premium in value over a minority interest value. This premium should be small, certainly no more than 10%.

COURT DECISIONS ON VALUATION ISSUES

The U.S. Tax Court probably hears more business valuation cases than any other court. However, looking to Tax Court opinions for guidance with regard to "factors considered," discounts, premiums, and so on can be a rather frustrating exercise because the opinions are not always clear. The best summary of court decisions related to business valuations is the *Federal Tax Valuation Digest.*

An analysis of cases is beyond the scope of this book. However, two developments in court decisions should be mentioned.

For many years the U.S. Tax Court seemed to reflect a "split it down the middle" attitude, which fostered extreme valuations by the government as well as by taxpayers. This was explicitly changed by a series of decisions in the early 1980s. The most important of these was *Buffalo Tool & Die v. Commissioner* (74 TC 441, 1980), in which the court indicated that it would lean heavily toward the party that presents the better appraisal. Subsequent cases that made the same point include *Donald Strutz v. Commissioner* (40 TCM 757, 1980), *Sirloin Stockade, Inc. v. Commissioner* (40 TCM 928, 1980), and *Hooker Industries v. Commissioner* (44 TCM 258, 1982). The cumulative effect of these cases, together with the imposition of tax penalties for overappraisal or underappraisal (see IRC §§ 6659 and 6660) has been to increase drastically the risk of relying on a poorly documented or poorly reasoned appraisal.

The second development concerns the definition of what constitutes a minority interest, as opposed to a controlling interest, in a family-owned corporation. In the early 1980s the IRS took the position in Rev. Rul. 81-253 that individual minority interest blocks of stock owned by family members in a family-controlled corporation should be valued as parts of a control block. This theory has not been accepted by any court so far (see, e.g., *Estate of Bright v. U.S.*, 658 F. 2d 999 (5th Cir. 1981); *Estate of Andrews*, 79 TC 938 (1982); *Victor J. Minahan v. Commissioner*, 88 TC 492 (1987)). In spite of these decisions, the Service has not yet withdrawn Rev. Rul. 81-253.

Valuations in matrimonial cases vary greatly among jurisdictions and may involve a standard of value different from the classic definition of fair market value.

SAMPLE CONDENSED VALUATION ANALYSIS

32.30 COMPANY BACKGROUND.   The following abbreviated valuation of a company is presented for illustrative purposes. Many of the facts and most of the tables and charts used in a full valuation analysis have been omitted here for the sake of brevity. The subject company and the comparative companies are fictional.

The purpose of the appraisal is to determine the fair market value of a 20% interest in ABC Snack Foods Inc., as of March 31, 1989.

ABC Snack Foods, Inc. (hereinafter referred to as ABC), is a producer of potato chips, tortilla and corn chips, and popcorn. The company has two plants, one of 205,000 sq. ft. in Houston, Texas, and a second of 100,000 sq. ft. in Amarillo, Texas, which was opened in 1988.

Products are distributed through 350 routes, of which 225 are company owned and 125 are independent distributors. In each of its major markets ABC is either the first or second brand. Advertising, which averages 1.75% of sales, is done primarily by TV and radio and, to a lesser extent, by billboards. Promotions normally account for 2.5% of sales. No single customer accounts for more than 5% of sales.

The analysis indicated that ABC was growing somewhat faster than both the potato chip and the popcorn industries. Both the potato chip and popcorn businesses are marked by fairly intense competition in terms of price, promotions, distribution, and advertising. The company competes with several companies that are substantially larger than ABC, as well as with a large number of small local firms, some of which are industry leaders in their locality.

Financial and income data with appropriate adjustments are shown for ABC Snack Foods in Exhibit 32.1.

32.31 SELECTION OF GUIDELINE COMPANIES.   In selecting guideline companies certain criteria were established:

1. The common stock must be publicly held and actively traded.
2. The stock must trade above $2.00 per share. This criterion was established to eliminate very cheap stocks whose prices frequently do not have realistic relationships to basic determinants of value.
3. Comparative companies must be primarily engaged in the production and sale of dessert and snack foods.

In searching for companies that would meet these criteria, we reviewed all companies classified as food companies in *Standard Corporation Records* and in *Moody's Industrial Manual* and *Moody's OTC Industrial Manual*. These sources published financial data concerning virtually all securities in which there is sufficient public interest to warrant such publication. All the companies in the industry classifications listed were reviewed and eight were selected as being the best possible companies that could be used as a valuation

ABC SNACK FOODS, INC.
Condensed Balance Sheets and Computations of Total Net Worth
Net Income, Cash Flow and Dividends
(Figures in Thousands of Dollars)

Fiscal Years Ending March 31,	1984	1985	1986	1987	1988	1989
Condensed Balance Sheets						
Assets:						
Current assets						
Cash and equivalent	$ 3,827	$ 4,818	$ 4,578	$ 3,130	$ 4,259	$ 4,157
Accounts receivable	3,599	5,433	7,627	7,289	7,203	9,552
Inventories	1,385	2,402	2,408	2,236	2,576	3,861
Other current assets	909	419	434	843	914	1,322
Total current assets	9,720	13,072	15,047	13,498	14,360	18,892
Net fixed assets	7,615	8,665	9,254	13,949	17,464	16,875
Net fixed assets	7,615	8,665	9,254	13,949	17,464	16,875
Other assets	131	178	176	1,075	454	426
Other assets	131	178	176	1,075	454	426
Total assets	$17,467	$21,915	$24,477	$28,522	$32,278	$36,193
Capital and liabilities:						
Current liabilities	$ 3,501	$ 4,613	$ 4,008	$ 4,382	$ 4,313	$ 5,070
Current liabilities	3,501	4,613	4,008	4,382	4,313	5,070
Other credits	—	—	—	—	—	—
Other liabilities	784	989	1,103	1,593	2,004	2,524
Total net worth	13,180	16,314	19,369	22,545	25,963	28,599
Total capital and liabilities	$17,465	$21,916	$24,480	$28,520	$32,280	$36,193
Computation of Total Net Worth						
Preferred stock	$ —	$ —	$ —	$ —	$ —	$ —
Common stock	2,045	2,045	2,045	2,045	2,045	2,045
Additional paid-in capital	3,554	3,554	3,554	3,554	3,554	3,554
Retained earnings	7,581	10,716	13,771	16,946	20,365	23,001
Treasury stock	—	—	—	—	—	—
Adjustments:						
Total net worth	$13,180	$16,314	$19,369	$22,545	$25,963	$28,599
Additional Information						
Total liabilities	$ 4,285	$ 5,602	$ 5,111	$ 5,975	$ 6,317	$ 7,594
Net working capital	6,219	8,459	11,040	9,116	10,047	13,822
Net sales	51,581	58,880	62,376	66,037	70,671	76,499
Computation of Adjusted Net Income and Cash Flow						
Reported net income		$ 3,481	$ 3,431	$ 3,679	$ 3,924	$ 4,386
Adjustments:						
Flood loss (net)		—	—	—	—	843
Adjusted net income		3,481	3,431	3,679	3,924	5,229
Depreciation & amortization		1,140	1,479	1,825	2,023	2,197
Cash flow		$ 4,620	$ 4,911	$ 5,504	$ 5,947	$ 7,426
Computation of Total Dividends						
Preferred stock dividends		$ —	$ —	$ —	$ —	$ —
Common stock dividends		342	376	505	505	1,686
Total dividends		$ 342	$ 376	$ 505	$ 505	$ 1,686

Exhibit 32.1. Adjusted financial and income data. *Source:* Management Planning, Inc.

guideline. The reasons for the exclusion of the others were given. A very brief description of each of these companies follows:

Alabaster Ice Cream, Inc., manufactures premium ice cream for distribution throughout the West and in several major cities in the Midwest.

Hi-Grade Enterprises, Inc., manufactures and distributes potato chips, fried pork skins, peanut butter crackers, and popcorn. Products are sold throughout the South.

Hudson Foods Corp., produces meat sticks and beef jerky under the names Slim Jim and Pemmican. Distribution is national.

Interlaken Foods Corp. is primarily a producer of chocolate and confectionary products distributed nationally.

King Foods Inc. produces and markets soft pretzels, baked cookies and muffins, and semifrozen carbonated beverages and frozen juice treats and desserts. Distribution is national.

Munchies, Inc., produces and distributes snack items including peanut butter or cheese-filled cracker sandwiches, cookie sandwiches, potato chips, popcorn, and fried pork skins. Sales are primarily through the company's own sales organization to service stations and drug stores in 35 states, primarily east of the Mississippi River.

Sweetgoods Corp. produces sweet goods, including single portion cakes, frozen cakes and pies, doughnuts, and cookies. Distribution is primarily in 23 eastern and southeastern states.

Tri-State Snacks Corp. is a producer of candy and other snack items, primarily under its own brand names. Products are marketed nationally.

The market value of each of the guideline companies has been computed by simply multiplying the closing price on March 31, 1989, by the number of shares outstanding. That market value appears on Column I of Exhibit 32.2.

Column II shows the weighted average earnings of each company during the 5 years preceding the valuation date. (The weighting procedure places a weight of one on 1984, two on 1985, up to five on the earnings of 1988.) Column III shows the price–earnings ratios. The median price earnings ratio is 16.8. The next column shows the 5-year weighted average cash flow over the same period and shows that the median market price to cash flow ratio is 10.7 times. Column VI shows the dividends of each company in the year preceding the valuation date and this is followed by the price dividend ratio. The median is 41.0. Column VIII shows the payout ratio of each company, indicating that the median payout ratio is 42.5%. Finally we show the total net worth of each company, and that is followed by the market value to net worth percentage.

These market value ratios provide useful guidelines for the valuation of ABC. However, they are nothing more than guidelines and must inevitably be combined with the appraiser's judgment in arriving at a sound valuation conclusion. The appraiser must, after careful consideration of all relevant facts, come to one of three possible conclusions:

1. Investors would find ABC to be more attractive than the group of guideline companies. (In this case a premium must be added to the median valuation ratios.)
2. Investors would find ABC to be less attractive than the guideline companies. (In this case a discount from the median valuation ratios is required.)
3. Investors would regard ABC as being neither more nor less attractive than the group of guideline companies. (In this case the use of the median ratios would be appropriate.)

32.32 QUALITATIVE CONSIDERATIONS. ABC has an excellent trade name in its marketing territory as evidenced by the fact that it is the number one or number two brand in all its major markets. We think that the ABC trade name, in its markets, is as good as some of the guideline companies and inferior to several of them. On balance we think that this is a small negative consideration for ABC.

| | MARKET VALUE RATIOS | | | |
| | I | II | III | IV |
Company	3/31/89 Total Market Value	Latest 5-Year Weighted Average Earnings	Market Value Times Latest 5-Year Weighted Average Earnings	Latest 5-Year Weighted Average Cash Flow
	($000)(a)	($000)		($000)
Alabaster Ice Cream, Inc.	$ 112,258	$ 5,076	22.1	$ 10,252
Hi-Grade Enterprises, Inc.	121,617	6,957	17.5	14,143
Hudson Foods Corp.	63,129	4,153	15.2	6,091
Interlaken Foods Corp.	2,389,938	116,487	20.5	161,127
King Foods Inc.	75,842	4,784	15.9	8,191
Munchies, Inc.	561,257	38,060	14.7	53,736
Sweetgoods Corp.	137,542	7,291	18.9	12,372
Tri-State Snacks Corp.	235,345	14,518	16.2	17,144
Guideline company median			16.8	

NOTE: (a) On a minority interest basis.

Exhibit 32.2.   Market value data for the guideline companies. *Source:* Management Planning, Inc.

In terms of size, ABC is at the low end of the range of the guideline companies and it has less geographic diversification than the group of guideline companies. This is a small negative consideration for ABC.

ABC's new plant in Amarillo positions it to expand geographically and results to date exceed expectations. We think that this is a positive factor.

ABC uses two commodities, potatoes and corn, and both of these commodities are subject to rather considerable price variability. However, some of the guideline companies' businesses are as vulnerable as ABC to price changes of a limited number of commodities.

Mr. A. B. Caldwell, the founder of the company, is 64 and in ill health. Mr. John Grundy, the company's executive vice president has been groomed to succeed Mr. Caldwell. However, there is no one other than Mr. Grundy with the depth of experience needed to run the company. We conclude that ABC has somewhat less depth of management than the guideline companies and that this is a negative consideration.

32.33   QUANTITATIVE CONSIDERATIONS.   A comparison of sales and income growth appears in Exhibit 32.3. The sales of each company were placed on a index basis with the years 1985–1986 equal to 100, and the group median was determined. The upper portion of that chart shows that the sales growth of ABC has been similar to that of the guideline companies.

The lower portion of that chart shows that the long-term trend of ABC's net income has been close to the group of guideline companies.

A comparison of certain operating ratios is shown in Exhibit 32.4. The top section shows that in 1984 and 1985 ABC was generating more sales per dollar of equity capital than the group of guideline companies. However, during the last 3 years ABC has been almost identical to the group median.

The middle portion of the chart shows that ABC's net profit margin has remained fairly constant at about 6%, whereas the guideline companies have declined from 7.7% in 1984 to 5.2% in 1988.

V	VI	VII	VIII	IX	X
Market Value Times Latest 5-Year Weighted Average Cash Flow	Latest Year Dividends	Market Value Times Latest Year Dividends	Latest Year Dividends as a % of Latest 5-Year Weighted Average Earnings	Total Net Worth	Market Value as a % of Net Worth
	($000)			($000)	
10.9	$ 1,421	79.0	28.0	$ 29,888	375.6
8.6	4,097	29.7	58.9	58,914	206.4
10.4	1,537	41.1	37.0	24,935	253.2
14.8	58,530	40.8	50.2	679,284	351.8
9.3	2,037	37.2	42.6	33,113	229.0
10.4	20,999	26.7	55.2	201,593	278.4
11.1	3,096	44.4	42.5	50,651	271.5
13.7	4,077	57.7	28.1	42,693	551.2
10.7		41.0	42.5		275.0

The lower portion of that chart shows that ABC's rate of earnings on stockholders' equity was above the group median in 1984 but has been slightly inferior to the group median since then. Since 1984 the trends have been parallel.

ABC's current ratio of 3.7 times is considerably better than the group median of 2.2 times. Both ABC and the guideline companies have about 50% of their assets in the form of current assets and about 50% in fixed assets. In terms of leverage, ABC is significantly better than the group median. ABC's ratio of total liabilities to total assets is 21%, compared to the group median of 43%. We conclude that the overall financial position of ABC is better than the group of guideline companies.

The quantitative analysis revealed no important differences between ABC and the group of guideline companies that would require modification of the median ratios. Its growth rates were not significantly different. The comparison of operating ratios did not reveal any significant differences that would require adjustment. The analysis did reveal that ABC has significantly less leverage than the guideline companies. However, that low leverage has enabled ABC to pay out about the same percentages of its earnings as the comparative companies (40% vs. 42.5%) despite its inferior access to capital markets. We think that the better financial position is reasonably reflected through the capitalization of dividends.

We summarize as follows:

NEGATIVE DIFFERENCES

1. Slight inferiority in trade name.
2. Inferior depth of management.
3. Less geographic diversification.

POSITIVE DIFFERENCES

1. ABC's promising geographic expansion.

ABC SNACK FOODS, INC.

NET SALES v. THE GUIDELINE COMPANIES

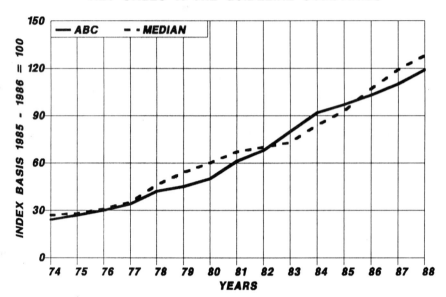

ABC SNACK FOODS, INC.

NET INCOME v. THE GUIDELINE COMPANIES

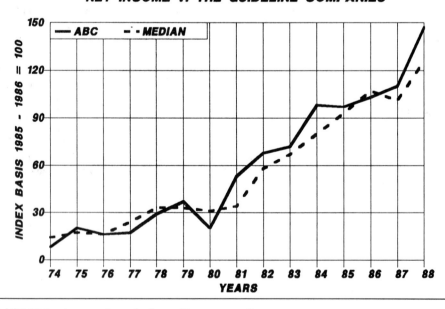

Exhibit 32.3.   A comparison of sales and income growth.

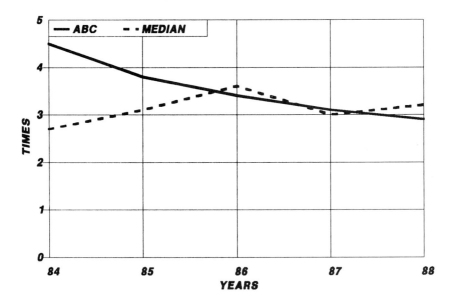

ABC SNACK FOODS, INC.

NET SALES TIMES NET WORTH

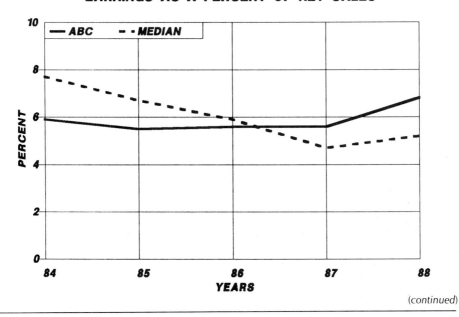

ABC SNACK FOODS, INC.

EARNINGS AS A PERCENT OF NET SALES

(continued)

Exhibit 32.4.   A comparison of certain operating ratios.

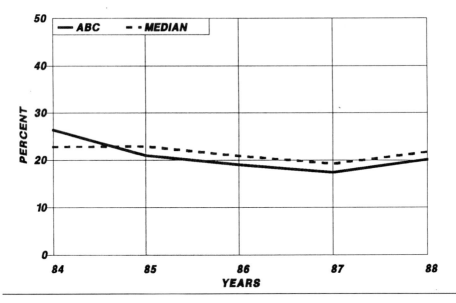

ABC SNACK FOODS, INC.

EARNINGS AS A PERCENT OF NET WORTH

Exhibit 32.4. *Continued.*

We think that, on balance, these differences make ABC somewhat less attractive than the guideline companies and are appropriately reflected by a 10% reduction in the median valuation ratios.

32.34 APPLICATION OF THE VALUATION RATIOS.   The valuation ratios are applied to ABC's own figures on Exhibit 32.5. Primary weight (60%) is applied to the value derived from earnings and 20% each to the values derived from cash flow and dividends. This weighting procedure results in a value of $62,382,000.

It should be noted that the value of $62,382,000 is 218% of ABC's book value of $28,599,000. This is well within the range of the guideline companies and is reasonable. No separate weight has been given to the guideline companies' ratio of market value to book value because we believe that investors give little, if any, weight to book value in appraising the securities of companies with the high rates of earnings on capital that are characteristic of this industry.

It should also be noted that we have not used a discounted future benefits approach because ABC's prospective growth rates are roughly comparable to those of the guideline companies. The adjusted valuation ratios are, therefore, a reflection of both the growth rate and the capitalization rate appropriate to ABC Snack Foods, Inc., on the valuation date.

Dividing the preliminary value of $62,382,000 by the 100,000 shares outstanding results in a freely traded value (the price at which the stock would trade in an active market) of $624 per share.

The fact that the ABC stock lacks ready marketability must be reflected by a discount for lack of marketability. We think that a discount of 30% is appropriate. This results in a value for the common stock of $437 per share.

It is our conclusion that a block of 20,000 shares had a fair market value of $437 per share, as of March 31, 1989, or $8,740,000 for the entire block.

VALUATION OF THE COMMON STOCK OF ABC SNACK FOODS, INC.
Modified Valuation Ratios Derived on Exhibit 32.2

	Median Ratios	Modified Valuation Ratios	
Market value × 1984–1988 weighted average earnings	16.8	15.1	
Market value × 1984–1988 weighted average cash flow	10.7	9.6	
Market value × 1988 dividends	41.0	36.9	
Application of valuation ratios to ABC's earnings, cash flow, and dividends			
15.1 × ABC's 1984–1988 weighted average earnings of $4,214,000 = $63,631,000 × a weight of 60%			$38,179,000
9.6 × ABC's 1984–1988 weighted average cash flow of $6,125,000 = $58,800,000 × a weight of 20%			11,760,000
36.9 × ABC's 1988 dividends of $1,686,000 = $62,213,000 × a weight of 20%			12,443,000
			$62,382,000
Freely traded value per share (based on 100,000 shares issued and outstanding)			$624
Less: Discount for lack of marketability (30%)			187
Fair market value per share			$437

Exhibit 32.5. Valuation of the common stock of ABC Snack Foods, Inc., as of March 31, 1989. *Source: Management Planning, Inc.*

SOURCES AND SUGGESTED REFERENCES

Blackman, L., *The Valuation of Privately-Held Businesses*, Probus Publishing, Chicago, 1986.

Brown, Ronald L., *Valuing Professional Practices and Licenses: A Guide for the Matrimonial Practitioner*, Prentice-Hall, 1987.

Burke, Frank M., Jr., *Valuation and Valuation Planning for Closely-Held Businesses*, Prentice-Hall, 1981.

ESOP Associations, *Valuing ESOP Shares*, ESOP Assoc., Washington, DC, pp. 7–8.

Howitt, Idelle A., Peterson, Shirley D., and Schechter, Susan E., *Federal Tax Valuation Digest*, Warren, Gorham & Lamont, Boston, 1989.

Ibbotson, Roger A., *Stocks, Bonds, Bills and Inflation*, Ibbotson Associates, Chicago, 1989.

Internal Revenue Service, *IRS Valuation Guide for Income, Estate & Gift Taxes*, Commerce Clearing House, Chicago, 1985.

———, Revenue Ruling No. 59-60, U.S. Treasury Dept., Washington, DC.

Maher, J. Michael, "Discounts for Lack of Marketability for Closely-Held Business Interests," *Taxes—The Tax Magazine*, September 1976, pp. 562–571.

Moody's Investors Service, *Moody's Industrial Manual*, Moody's Investors Sevice, New York, annual update.

———, *Moody's OTC Industrial Manual*, Moody's Investors Service, New York, annual update.

Moroney, Robert E., "Most Courts Overvalue Closely Held Stocks," *Taxes—The Tax Magazine*, March 1973, pp. 144–154.

Pratt, Shannon P., Ed., *Readings in Business Valuation*, American Society of Appraisers Educational Foundation, 1986.

———, *Valuing a Business*, 2nd ed., Dow Jones-Irwin, Homewood, IL, 1989, pp. 247–255.

——, *Valuing Small Businesses and Professional Practices,* Dow Jones-Irwin, Homewood, IL, 1986.

Schackelford, Aaron L., "Valuation of S Corporations," Business Valuation Review, December 1988, pp. 159–162.

Schnepper, J. A., *The Professional Handbook of Business Valuation,* Addison-Wesley, Reading, MA, 1982.

Securities and Exchange Commission, *Directory of Companies Required to File Annual Reports with the Securities and Exchange Commission,* SEC, Washington, DC, annual update.

Smith, Gordon V., *Corporate Valuation,* Wiley, New York, 1988.

Standard & Poor's Corporation, *Standard Corporation Records,* Standard & Poor's, New York, annual update.

CHAPTER 33

BANKRUPTCY

Grant W. Newton, PhD, CPA, CMA
Pepperdine University

CONTENTS

OVERVIEW

This chapter contains a brief description of the Bankruptcy Code, a discussion of the services that can be rendered by the accountant, and an introduction to the problems faced by accountants working in the bankruptcy area.

ALTERNATIVES AVAILABLE TO TROUBLED COMPANIES

The debtor's first alternatives are to locate new financing, to merge with another company, or to find some other basic solution to its situation that avoids the necessity of discussing its problems with representatives of creditors. If none of these alternatives is possible, the debtor may be required to seek a remedy from creditors, either informally (out of court) or with the help of judicial proceedings.

33.1 OUT-OF-COURT SETTLEMENTS.   The informal settlement is an out-of-court agreement that usually consists of an extension of time (stretch-out), a pro rata cash payment for full settlement of claims (composition), an issue of stock for debt, or some combination. The debtor, through counsel or credit association, calls an informal meeting of the creditors for the purpose of discussing its financial problems. In many cases, the credit association makes a significant contribution to the out-of-court settlement by arranging a meeting of creditors, providing advice, and serving as secretary for the creditors' committee.

A **credit association** is composed of credit managers of various businesses in a given region. Its functions are to provide credit and other business information to member companies concerning their debtors, to help make commercial credit collections, to support legislation favorable to business creditors, and to provide courses in credit management for members of the credit community.

At the **creditors' meeting** the debtor describes the causes of failure, discusses the value of assets (especially those unpledged) and unsecured liabilities, and answers any questions the creditors may ask. The main objective of this meeting is to convince the creditors that they would receive more if the business were allowed to operate than if it were forced to liquidate, and that all parties would benefit from working out a settlement.

(a) Appointment of Creditors' Committee. To make it easier for the debtor to work with the creditors, a committee of creditors is normally appointed during the initial meeting of the debtor and its creditors, providing, of course, the case is judged to warrant some cooperation by the creditors. It should be realized that the creditors are often as interested in working out a settlement as is the debtor. The **creditors' committee** serves as the bargaining agent for the creditors, supervises the operation of the debtor during the development of a plan, and solicits acceptance of a plan once the committee has approved it. Generally, the creditors' committee meets immediately after appointment for the purpose of selecting a presiding officer and counsel.

(b) Plan of Settlement. Provided there is enough time, it is often advisable that the accountant and the attorney assist the debtor in preparing a suggested **plan of settlement** for presentation and discussion at the first meeting with creditors. Typically only the largest creditors and a few representatives of the smaller creditors are invited so that the group is a manageable size for accomplishing its goals.

There is no set pattern for the form that a plan of settlement proposed by the debtor must take. It may call for 100% payment over an extended period of time, payments on a pro rata basis in cash for full settlement of creditors' claims, satisfaction of debt obligations with stock, or some combination. A carefully developed forecast of projected operations, based on realistic assumptions developed by the debtor with the aid of its accountant, can help creditors determine whether the debtor can perform under the terms of the plan and operate successfully in the future.

33.2 ASSIGNMENT FOR BENEFIT OF CREDITORS. A remedy available under state law to a corporation in serious financial difficulties is an **assignment for the benefit of creditors.** In this instance the debtor voluntarily transfers title to its assets to an assignee, who then liquidates them and distributes the proceeds among the creditors. Assignment for the benefit of creditors is an extreme remedy because it results in the cessation of the business. This informal liquidation device (although court-supervised in many states) is like the out-of-court settlement devised to rehabilitate the debtor, in that it requires the consent of all creditors or at least their agreement to refrain from taking action. The appointment of a custodian over the assets of the debtor gives creditors the right to file an involuntary bankruptcy court petition.

Proceedings brought in the federal courts are governed by the Bankruptcy Code. Normally it is necessary to resort to such formality when suits have been filed against the debtor and its property is under garnishment or attachment or is threatened by foreclosure or eviction.

33.3 BANKRUPTCY COURT PROCEEDINGS. Bankruptcy court proceedings are generally the last resort for the debtor whose financial condition has deteriorated to the point where it is impossible to acquire additional funds. When the debtor finally agrees that bankruptcy court proceedings are necessary, the liquidation value of the assets often represents only a small fraction of the debtor's total liabilities. If the business is liquidated, the creditors get only a small percentage of their claims. The debtor is discharged of its debts and is free to start over; however, the business is lost and so are all the assets. Normally, liquidation proceedings result in large losses to the debtor, the creditors, and the business community in general. Chapter 7 of the Bankruptcy Code covers the proceedings related to liquidation. Another alternative under the Bankruptcy Code is to seek some type of relief so that the debtor, with the help of the bankruptcy court, can work out agreements with creditors and be able to continue operations. Chapters 11, 12, and 13 of the Bankruptcy Code provide for this type of operation.

(a) Title 11—Bankruptcy Code. Title 11 U.S. Code contains the bankruptcy law. The code is divided into eight chapters:

- Chapter 1   General Provisions
- Chapter 3   Case Administration
- Chapter 5   Creditors, the Debtor, and the Estate
- Chapter 7   Liquidation
- Chapter 9   Adjustment of Debts of a Municipality
- Chapter 11   Reorganization
- Chapter 12   Adjustment of Debts of a Family Farmer with Regular Income
- Chapter 13   Adjustment of Debts of an Individual with Regular Income

Chapters 1, 3, and 5 apply to all proceedings under the code except chapter 9, where only specified sections of chapters 1, 3, and 5 apply. A case commenced under the Bankruptcy Code—chapter 7, 9, 11, 12, or 13—is referred to as a **Title 11 case.** Chapter 13, which covers the adjustment of debts of individuals with regular income, is beyond the scope of this presentation because it can be used only by individuals with unsecured claims of less than $100,000 and secured claims of less than $250,000. Provisions relating to chapter 11 are discussed in detail in a separate section.

(b) Chapter 7—Liquidation. Chapter 7 is used only when the corporation sees no hope of being able to operate successfully or to obtain the necessary creditor agreement. Under this alternative, the corporation is liquidated and the remaining assets are distributed to creditors after administrative expenses have been paid. An individual debtor may be discharged from liabilities and entitled to a fresh start. A corporation's debt is not discharged.

The decision as to whether rehabilitation or liquidation is best also depends on the amount that can be realized from each alternative. The method resulting in the greatest return to the creditors and stockholders should be chosen. The amount received from liquidation depends on the resale value of the firm's assets minus the costs of dismantling and legal expenses. The value of the firm after rehabilitation must be determined (net of the costs of achieving the remedy). The alternative leading to the highest value should be followed.

Financially troubled debtors often attempt an informal settlement or liquidation out of court; if it is unsuccessful, they will then initiate proceedings under the Bankruptcy Code. Other debtors, especially those with a large number of creditors, may file a **petition for relief** in the bankruptcy court as soon as they recognize that continuation of the business under existing conditions is impossible.

As soon as the **order for relief** has been entered, the U.S. trustee appoints a disinterested party from a panel of private trustees to serve as the **interim trustee.** The functions and powers of the interim trustee are the same as those of an **elected trustee.** Once an interim trustee has been appointed, the creditors meet to elect a trustee that will be responsible for liquidating the business. If a trustee is not elected by the creditors, the interim trustee may continue to serve in the capacity of the trustee and carry through with an orderly liquidation of the business.

The objective of the trustee is to liquidate the assets of the estate in an orderly manner. Once the property of the estate has been reduced to money and the security claims have been satisfied to the extent allowed, then the property of the estate is distributed to the holders of the claims in the order specified by the Bankruptcy Code. The first order, of course, is priority claims; when they have been established, the balance goes to unsecured creditors. After all the funds have been distributed, the remaining debts of an individual are discharged. As mentioned earlier, if the debtor is a corporation, the debts are not discharged. Thus it is necessary for the corporation to cease existence. Any funds subsequently coming into the corporate shell would be subject to attachment.

(c) Chapter 12—Adjustment of Debt of a Family Farmer with Regular Annual Income. To help farmers resolve some of their financial problems Congress passed chapter 12 of the Bankruptcy Code. It became effective November 26, 1986, and lasts until October 1, 1993. Because chapter 12 is new and relates to a specific class of debtors, Congress will evaluate whether the chapter is serving its purpose and whether there is a need to continue this special chapter for the family farmer. After Congress makes this evaluation it will be able to determine whether to make this chapter permanent. If Congress does not act, chapter 12 will terminate on October 1, 1993. Chapter 12 has been very effective, in the opinion of many users, and as a result it will most likely be extended beyond 1993.

Under current law, a family farmer in need of financial rehabilitation may file either a chapter 11 or 13 petition. Most family farmers, because they have too much debt to qualify, cannot file under chapter 13 and are limited to chapter 11. Many farmers have found chapter 11 needlessly complicated, unduly time-consuming, inordinately expensive, and, in too many cases, unworkable. Chapter 12 is designed to give family farmers an opportunity to reorganize their debts and keep their land. According to legislative history, chapter 12 gives debtors the protection from creditors that bankruptcy provides while, at the same time, it prevents abuse of the system and ensures that farm lenders receive a fair repayment.

In order to file a petition, an individual or an individual and spouse engaged in farming operations must have total debt that does not exceed $1,500,000, and at least 80% of noncontingent, liquidated debts (excluding debt from principal residence unless debt arose out of family operations) on the date the petition is filed must have arisen out of farming. Additionally more than 50% of the petitioner's gross income for the taxable year prior to the filing of the petition must be from farming operations.

A corporation or partnership may file if more than 50% of the outstanding stock or equity is owned by a family and:

1. More than 80% of the value of its assets consist of assets related to farming operations.
2. The total debts do not exceed $1,500,000 and at least 80% of its noncontingent, liquidated debts on the date the case is filed arose out of farming operations.
3. The stock of a corporation is not publicly traded.

Only the debtor can file a plan in a chapter 12 case. The requirements for a plan in chapter 12 are more flexible and lenient than those in chapter 11. In fact, only three requirements are set forth in § 1205 of the Bankruptcy Code. First, the debtor must submit to the supervision and control of the trustee all or such part of the debtor's future income as is necessary for the execution of the plan. Second, the plan must provide for full payment, in deferred cash payments, of all priority claims unless the creditors agree to a different treatment. Third, where creditors are divided into classes, the same treatment must apply to all claims in a particular class. The plan can alter the rights of secured creditors with an interest in real or personal property, but there are a few restrictions. To alter the right of the secured claim holder, the debtor must satisfy one of the following three requirements:

1. Obtain acceptance of the plan.
2. Provide in the plan that the holder of such claim retain the lien and as of the effective date of the plan provide that the payment to be made or property to be transferred is not less than the amount of the claim.
3. Surrender the property securing such claim.

If a holder of an allowed unsecured claim does not accept the plan, then the court may not approve the plan unless:

1. The value of the property to be distributed is equal to at least the amount of the claim.

2. The plan provides that all of the debtor's projected disposable income to be received within 3 years, or longer if directed by the court, after the first payment is made will be a part of the payments under the plan.

To facilitate the operation of the business and the development of a plan, § 1206 of the Bankruptcy Code allows family farmers to sell assets not needed for the reorganization prior to confirmation without the consent of the secured creditor, provided the court approves such a sale.

33.4 THE ACCOUNTANT'S SERVICES IN PROCEEDINGS. One of the first decisions that must be made at an early meeting of the debtor with bankruptcy counsel and accountants is whether it is best to liquidate (under provisions of state law or Bankruptcy Code), to attempt an out-of-court settlement, to seek an outside buyer, or to file a chapter 11 petition. To decide which course of action to take, it is also important to ascertain what caused the debtor's current problems, whether the company will be able to overcome its difficulties, and, if so, what measures will be necessary. Accountants may be asked to explain how the losses occurred and what can be done to avoid them in the future. To help with this determination, it may be necessary to project the operations after a 30-day period over at least the next 3 to 6 months, and to indicate the areas where steps will be necessary in order to earn a profit.

For existing clients, the information needed to make a decision about the course of action to make may be obtained with limited additional work; however, for a new client, it is necessary to perform a review of the client's operations to determine the condition of the business. Once the review has been completed, the client must normally decide to liquidate the business, attempt an informal settlement with creditors, or file a chapter 11 petition, unless additional funds can be obtained or a buyer for the business is located. For example, where the product is inferior, the demand for the product is declining, the distribution channels are inadequate, or other similar problems exist that cannot be corrected, either because of the economic environment or management's lack of ability, it is normally best to liquidate the company immediately.

The decision whether a business should immediately file a chapter 11 petition or attempt an out-of-court settlement depends on several factors. Among them are the following:

1. Size of company.
    a. Public.
    b. Private.
2. Number of creditors.
    a. Secured.
    b. Unsecured.
    c. Public.
    d. Private.
3. Complexity of matter.
    a. Nature of debt.
    b. Prior relationships with creditors.
4. Pending lawsuits.
5. Executory contracts, especially leases.
6. The impact of alternatives selected.
7. Nature of management.
    a. Mismanagement.
    b. Irregularities.

GENERAL PROVISIONS OF BANKRUPTCY CODE

33.5 FILING OF PETITION. A **voluntary case** is commanded by the debtor's filing of a bankruptcy petition under the appropriate chapter.

An **involuntary petition** can be filed by 3 or more creditors (if 11 or fewer creditors, only one creditor is necessary) with unsecured claims of at least $5,000 and can be initiated only under chapter 7 or 11. An indenture trustee may be one of the petitioning creditors. The Court allows a case to proceed only if (1) the debtor generally fails to pay its debts as they become due, provided such debts are not the subject of a bona fide dispute; or (2) within 120 days prior to the petition a custodian was appointed or took possession. The latter excludes the taking of possession of less than substantially all property to enforce a lien.

33.6 TIMING OF PETITION—TAX CONSIDERATIONS. The timing for filing the petition is important. For example, if the debtor delays filing the petition until the creditors are about to force the debtor into bankruptcy, the debtor may not be in a position to effectively control its destiny. On the other hand, if the petition is filed when the problems first develop and while the creditors are reasonably cooperative, the debtor is in a much better position to control the proceeding. If possible, it is best to file the petition near the end of the month, or even better, near the end of the quarter, to avoid a separate closing of the books.

Tax factors should also be considered in deciding when to file the petition. For example, if a debtor corporation that has attempted an unsuccessful out-of-court settlement decides to file a petition, the tax impact of the out-of-court action should be considered. If, in the out-of-court agreement, the debtor transferred property that resulted in a gain and a substantial tax liability, it would be best for the debtor to file the petition after the end of the current taxable year. By taking this action the tax claim is a **prepetition tax claim** and not an administrative expense. If the tax claim is a prepetition claim, interest and penalties stop accruing on the day the petition is filed and the debtor may provide in the plan for the deferral of the tax liability up to 6 years. If the tax claim is an administrative expense, penalties and interest on any unpaid balance will continue to accrue and the provision for deferred payment of up to 6 years does not apply.

33.7 ACCOUNTING SERVICES—ACCOUNTING DATA REQUIRED IN THE PETITION. The accountant must supply the attorney with certain information necessary for filing a Chapter 11 petition. This would normally include the following:

List of Largest Creditors. A list containing the names and addresses of the 20 largest unsecured creditors, excluding insiders, must be filed with the petition in a voluntary case. In an involuntary situation, the list must be submitted after an order of relief is entered. See Bankruptcy Rule 1008 and Bankruptcy Form 9.

List of Creditors. The debtor must file with the court a list of the debtor's creditors of each class, showing the amounts and character of any claims and securities and, so far as is known, the name and address or place of business of each creditor and a notation whether the claim is disputed, contingent, or unliquidated as to amount, when each claim was incurred and the consideration received, and related data.

List of Equity Security Holders. It is necessary to provide a list of the debtor's security holders of each class showing the number and kind of interests registered in the name of each holder and the last known address or place of business of each holder.

Schedules of Assets and Liabilities. The schedules that must accompany the petition are sworn statements of the debtor's assets and liabilities as of the date the petition is filed under chapter 11. These schedules consist primarily of the debtor's balance sheet broken down into detail, and the accountant is required to supply the information generated in the preparation of the normal balance sheet and its supporting schedules. The required information is supplied on Schedules A-1 and A-3, which include a complete statement of liabilities, and Schedules B-1 through B-4, which are a complete statement of assets. It is crucial that this information be accurate and complete because the omission or incorrect listing of a creditor might result in a failure to receive notice of the proceedings, and consequently the creditor's claim could be exempted from a discharge when the plan is later confirmed. Also omission of material facts may be construed as a false statement or concealment.

Statement of Financial Affairs. The **statement of affairs,** not to be confused with an accountant's usual use of the term, is a series of detailed questions about the debtor's property and conduct. The general purpose of the statement of affairs is to give both the creditors and the court an overall view of the debtor' operations. It offers many avenues to begin investigations into the debtor's conduct. The statement (official Form No. 8) consists of 21 questions to be answered under oath concerning the following areas:

1. The nature, location, and name of the business, including the employer's identification number, when the business was begun, where else and under what other names the debtor has conducted business.
2. Books and records, with the name and address of each person who kept and audited them during the preceding 2 years and who has possession of them now.
3. All financial statements issued within the previous 2 years.
4. The total dollar value of the last 2 inventories taken of the debtor's property, the valuation method used, the person who conducted the inventory, and the location of the records.
5. Income received from sources other than business operations.
6. Where and when income tax returns were filed for the last 3 years, tax refunds received or entitled to be received for the last 2 years.
7. All bank accounts and safe deposit boxes, including closed accounts.
8. Property held in trust for another person.
9. Prior bankruptcy proceedings.
10. Prior receiverships, general assignments, and other modes of liquidation.
11. Property of the debtor in the hands of a third person.
12. Suits pending at the time of the filing of the original petition; suits terminated within 1 year; any property attached, garnished, or seized within the year immediately preceding the filing of the original petition.
13. Any loans and installment purchases repaid during the year before the filing of the petition. Sufficient information must be given so as to determine whether any preferences have been made that might be recovered. Related to this will be a determination of the exact date when the debtor was insolvent.
14. Property transferred especially other than in the ordinary course of business during the preceding year. This is important because the transfer might have been fraudulent.
15. Assignment of accounts or other receivables.
16. Property returned or repossessed by a seller or secured party during the preceding year.
17. Business leases and security deposits.
18. Losses from fire, theft, or gambling.
19. Personal withdrawals, including compensation, bonuses, and loans made by officers, directors, insiders, managing executives, or shareholders (partners).
20. Payments or transfers to attorneys.
21. Names and addresses of all officers, directors, insiders, managing executives, and principal stockholders (members of partnership).

Statement of Executory Contracts. This listing of unexpired leases and other unperformed agreements permits the trustee (or the debtor) to consider which of its obligations are burdensome to the estate and should be rejected under § 365. Bankruptcy Rule 1007(b)(1) requires that a statement of executory contracts be filed with the court. Relevant particulars, such as the following, should be listed for each executory contract:

Party contracting with debtor.

Address of party.

Concise characterization of contract (employment agreement, equipment lease, and so on).

Date of contract.

Term of contract, expiration date, options, and so on.

Price or payment of terms of contract.

Balance of any monies owed by the debtor or other condition(s) of default as of the petition date.

Exhibit "A" to the Petition. This is a thumbnail sketch of the financial condition of the business listing total assets, total liabilities, secured claims, unsecured claims, information relating to public trading of the debtor's securities, and the identity of all insiders.

The debtor must also file any additional reports or documents that may be required by local rules or by the U.S. trustee.

33.8 ADEQUATE PROTECTION AND AUTOMATIC STAY.

A petition filed under the Bankruptcy Code results in an automatic stay of the actions of creditors. The **automatic stay** is one of the fundamental protections provided the debtor by the Bankruptcy Code. In a chapter 7 case it provides for an orderly liquidation that treats all creditors equitably. For business reorganizations under chapter 11, 12, or 13, it provides time for the debtor to examine the problems that forced it into bankruptcy court and to develop a plan for reorganization. As a result of the stay, no party, with minor exceptions, having a security or adverse interest in the debtor's property can take an action that will interfere with the debtor or his property, regardless of where the property is located, until the stay is modified or removed. Section 362(a) provides a list of eight kinds of acts and conduct subject to the automatic stay.

The stay of an act against the property of the estate continues, unless modified, until the property is no longer the property of the estate. The stay of any other act continues until the case is closed or dismissed, or the debtor is either granted or denied a discharged. The earliest occurrence of one of these events terminates the stay.

(a) Relief from the Stay. The court may grant relief after notice and hearing, by terminating, annulling, modifying, or conditioning the stay. The court may grant relief for cause, including the lack of adequate protection of the interest of the secured creditor. With respect to an act against property, relief may be granted under chapter 11 if the debtor does not have an equity in the property and the property is not necessary for an effective reorganization.

Section 361 identifies acceptable ways of providing adequate protection. First, the trustee or debtor may be required to make periodic cash payments to the entity entitled to relief as compensation for the decrease in value of the entity's interest in the property resulting from the stay. Second, the entity may be provided with an additional or replacement lien to the extent that the value of the interest declined as a result of the stay. Finally, the entity may receive the indubitable equivalent of its interest in the property.

The granting of relief when the debtor does not have any equity in the property solves the problem of real property mortgage foreclosures where the bankruptcy court petition is filed just before the foreclosure takes place. It was not intended to apply if the debtor is managing or leasing real property, such as a hotel operation, even though the debtor has no equity, because the property is necessary for an effective reorganization of the debtor.

The automatic stay prohibits a secured creditor from enforcing its rights in property owned by the debtor until the stay is removed. Without this right a creditor could foreclose on the debtor's property, collect the proceeds, invest them, and earn income from the investment, even though a bankruptcy petition has been filed. Since the Bankruptcy Code does not allow this action to be taken, the creditor loses the opportunity to earn income on the proceeds that could have been received on the foreclosure. The courts refer to this as **creditor's opportunity costs.** Four circuit courts have looked at this concept of opportunity cost. Two circuits (ninth and fourth) have ruled that the debtor is entitled to opportunity cost, the eighth circuit ruled that under certain conditions opportunity costs may be paid, and the fifth circuit ruled that opportunity cost need not be paid. In January 1988 the Supreme Court held in *In re Timbers of Inwood Forest Associates* (484 U.S. 365 (1988)) that creditors having collateral with a value less than the amount of the debt are not entitled to interest during the period that their property is tied up in the bankruptcy proceeding. Because of the extended time period during which the creditors' interest in the property is tied up in bankruptcy proceedings, this decision will most likely encourage creditors to properly collateralize their claim and may in limited ways restrict the granting of credit.

If **relief from the stay** is granted, a creditor may foreclose on property on which a lien exists, may continue a state court suit, or may enforce any judgment that might have been obtained before the bankruptcy case.

(b) Accounting Services—Determining Equity in Property. The accountant may assist either the debtor or the creditor in determining the value of the collateral to help determine if there is any equity in the property. As a result of the *Timbers* decision the court is more closely considering the prospects for successful reorganization. In cases where there is considerable question about the ability of the debtor to reorganize, courts are now allowing the stay to be removed, providing there is no equity in the property. The debtor, creditors' committee, or secured creditor(s) may ask accountants to provide evidences as to the ability of the debtor to reorganize.

33.9 EXECUTORY CONTRACTS AND LEASES. Section 365(a) provides that the debtor or trustee, subject to court approval, may assume, assign, or reject any executory contract or unexpired lease of the debtor. **Executory contracts** are contracts that are "so far unperformed that the failure of either [the bankrupt or nonbankrupt] to complete performance would constitute a material breach excusing the performance of the other" (see Countryman, 1973). Countryman's definition seems to have been adopted by Congress in the statement that "executory contracts include contracts under which performance remains due to some extent on both sides" (see S. Rep. No. 95-989, 95th Cong., 2nd Sess.____(1977)]. However, before a contract can be assumed, § 361(b) indicates that the debtor or trustee must:

1. Cure the past defaults or provide assurance they will be promptly cured.
2. Compensate the other party for actual pecuniary loss to such property or provide assurance that compensation will be made promptly.
3. Provide adequate assurance of future performance under the contract or lease.

(a) Limitations on Executory Contracts. To be rejected, the contract must still be an executory contract. For example, the delivery of goods to a carrier before the petition is filed, under terms that provide that the seller's performance is completed upon the delivery of the goods to the carrier, would not be an executory contract in chapter 11. Furthermore, the seller's claim would not be an administrative claim. On the other hand if the terms provide that the goods are received on delivery to the buyer, the seller under U.C.C. § 2-705 would have the right to stop the goods in transit and the automatic stay would not preclude such action. If the goods are delivered, payment for such goods would be an administrative expense.

The damages allowable to the landlord of a debtor from termination of a lease of real property are limited to the greater of 1 year or 15% of the remaining portion of the lease's rent due not to exceed 3 years after the date of filing or surrender whichever is earlier. This formula compensates the landlord while not allowing the claim to be so large as to hurt other creditors of the estate. The damages resulting from the breach of an employment contract are limited to 1 year following the date of the petition or the termination of employment, whichever is earlier.

(b) Accounting Services—Rejection of Executory Contracts.   The accountant may render several services relating to the rejection of executory contracts, including the following:

1. Estimating the amount of the damages that resulted from the lease rejection for either the debtor or landlord.
2. Evaluating for the landlord the extent to which the debtor has the ability to make the payments required under the lease.
3. Assisting the debtor in determining (or evaluating for the creditor's committee) the leases that should be rejected. To the extent possible, this assessment should be made at the beginning of the case to help reduce the expenses of administration during the chapter 11 case. Each lease needs to be analyzed to determine if there is equity in the lease or if the debtor needs it to successfully reorganize.

33.10 AVOIDING POWER.   The Bankruptcy Code grants to the trustee or debtor in possession the right to avoid certain transfers and obligations incurred. For example § 544 allows the trustee to avoid unperfected security interest and other interests in the debtor's property. Thus if the creditor fails to perfect a real estate mortgage, the trustee may be able to avoid that security interest and force the claim to be classified as unsecured rather than secured.

The trustee needs these powers and rights to ensure that actions by the debtor or by creditors in the prepetition period do not interfere with the objective of the bankruptcy laws, to provide for a fair and equal distribution of the debtor's assets through liquidation—or rehabilitation, if this would be better for other creditors involved.

In addition the trustee has the power to avoid preferences, fraudulent transfers, and postpetition transfers.

33.11 Preferences.   A **preferential payment** as defined in § 547 of the Bankruptcy Code is a transfer of any of the property of a debtor to or for the benefit of a creditor, for or on account of an antecedent debt made or suffered by the debtor while insolvent and within 90 days before the filing of a petition initiating bankruptcy proceedings, when such transfer enables the creditor to receive a greater percentage of payment than it would receive if the debtor were liquidated under chapter 7. Insolvency is presumed during the 90-day period. A transfer of property to an insider between 90 days and 1 year before the filing of the petition is also considered a preferential payment. Preferences include the payment of money, a transfer of property, assignment of receivables, or the giving of a mortgage on real or personal property.

A preferential payment is not a fraud but rather a legitimate and proper payment of a valid antecedent debt. The voidability of preferences is created by law to effect equality of distribution among all the creditors. The 90-day period (1 year for transactions with insiders) prior to filing the bankruptcy petition has been arbitrarily selected by Congress as the time period during which distributions to the debtor's creditors may be redistributed to all the creditors ratably. During this period, a creditor who accepts a payment is said to have been preferred and may be required to return the amount received and later participate in the enlarged estate to the pro rata extent of its unreduced claim.

(a) Exceptions to Preferential Transfers.   Section 547(b) contains seven exceptions to the power the trustee has to avoid preferential transfers. Five of the assumptions are discussed below.

   1. *Contemporaneous Exchange*. A transfer intended by the debtor and creditor to have a contemporaneous exchange for new value given to the debtor and that is in fact a substantially contemporaneous exchange is exempted. The purchase of goods or services with a check would not be a preferential payment, provided the check is presented for payment in the normal course of business.
   2. *Ordinary Course of Business*. The second exemption protects payments of debts that were incurred in the ordinary course of business or financial affairs of both the debtor and the transferee when the payment is made in the ordinary course of business according to ordinary business terms.
   3. *Purchase Money Security Interest*. The third exception exempts security interests granted in exchange for enabling loans when the proceeds are used to finance the purchase of specific personal property. For example, a debtor borrowed $75,000 from a bank to finance a computer system and subsequently purchased the system. The "transfer" of this system as collateral to the bank would not be a preference provided the proceeds were given after the signing of the security agreement, the proceeds were used to purchase the system, and the security interest was perfected within 10 days after the debtor received possession of the property.
   4. *New Value*. This exception provides that the creditor is allowed to insulate from preference attack a transfer received to the extent that the creditor replenishes the estate with new value. For example, if a creditor receives $10,000 in preferential payments and subsequently sells to the debtor, on unsecured credit, goods with a value of $6,000, the preference would be only $4,000. The new credit extended must be unsecured and can be netted only against a previous preferential payment, not a subsequent payment.
   5. *Inventory and Receivables*. This exception allows a creditor to have a continuing security interest in inventory and receivables (or proceeds) unless the position of the creditor is improved during the 90 days before the petition. If the creditor is an insider, the time period is extended to 1 year. An improvement in position occurs when a transfer causes a reduction in the amount by which the debt secured by the security interest exceeds the value of all security interest for such debt.

   A two-point test is to be used to determine if an improvement in position occurred: The position 90 days (1 year for insiders) prior to the filing of the petition is compared with the position as of the date of the petition. If the security interest is less than 90 days old, then the date on which new value was first given is compared to the position as of the date of the petition. The extent of any improvement caused by transfers to the prejudice of unsecured creditors is considered a preference.

   To illustrate this rule, assume that on March 1, the bank made a loan of $700,000 to the debtor secured by a so-called floating lien on inventory. The inventory value was $800,000 at that date. On June 30, the date the debtor filed a bankruptcy petition, the balance of the loan was $600,000 and the debtor had inventory valued at $500,000. It was determined that 90 days prior to June 30 (date petition was filed) the inventory totaled $450,000 and the loan balance was $625,000. In this case there has been an improvement in position of $75,000, ($600,000 − $500,000) − ($625,000 − $450,000) and any transfer of a security interest in inventory or proceeds could be revoked to that extent.

(b) Accounting Services—Search for Preferential Payments.   The trustee or debtor-in-possession will attempt to recover preferential payments. Section 547(f) provides that the debtor is presumed to be insolvent during the 90-day period prior to bankruptcy. This presumption does not apply to transfers to insiders between 91 days and 1 year prior to bankruptcy. This presumption requires the adverse party to come forth with some evidence to prove the presumption. The burden of proof, however, remains with the party in whose favor the presumption exists. Once this presumption is rebutted, insolvency at the time of payment is necessary and only someone with the training of an accountant is in a position to prove insolvency. The accountant often assists the debtor or trustee in presenting evidence showing whether the debtor was solvent or insolvent at the time payment was made. In cases where new management is in charge of the business or where a trustee has been appointed, the emphasis is often on trying to show that the debtor was insolvent in order to recover the previous payments and increase the size of the estate. The creditors' committee likewise wants to show that the debtor was insolvent at the time of payment to provide a larger basis for payment to unsecured creditors. Of course, the specific creditor recovering the payment looks for evidence to indicate that the debtor was solvent at the time payment was made.

Any payments made within the 90 days preceding the bankruptcy court filing and that are not in the ordinary course of business should be very carefully reviewed to see if the payments were preferences. Suspicious transactions would include anticipations of debt obligations, repayment of officers' loans, repayment of loans that have been personally guaranteed by officers, repayment of loans made to personal friends and relatives, collateral given to lenders, and sales of merchandise made on a countraaccount basis.

In seeking to find voidable preferences, the accountant has two crucial tasks: to determine the earliest date on which insolvency can be established within the 90-day period (1 year for insiders), and to report to the trustee' attorney questionable payments, transfers, or encumbrances that have been made by the debtor after that date. It is then the attorney's responsibility to determine the voidable payments. However, the accountant's role should not be minimized, for it is the accountant who initially determines the suspect payments. See Newton (1989) for a discussion of the procedures to follow in a search for preferences.

33.12 FRAUDULENT TRANSFERS.   **Fraudulent transfers** and **obligations** are defined in § 548 and include transfers that are presumed fraudulent regardless of whether the debtor's actual intent was to defraud creditors. A transfer may be avoided as fraudulent when made within 1 year prior to the filing of the bankruptcy petition, if the debtor made such transfer or incurred such obligation with actual intent to hinder, delay, or defraud existing or real or imagined future creditors. Also avoidable are constructively fraudulent transfers where the debtor received less than a reasonably equivalent value in exchange for such transfer or obligation and (1) was insolvent on the date that such transfer was made or such obligation was incurred, or became insolvent as a result of such transfer or obligation; (2) was engaged in business, or was about to engage in business or a transaction, for which any property remaining with the debtor was an unreasonably small capital; or (3) intended to incur, or believed that the debtor would incur, debts that would burden the debtor's ability to pay as such debts matured.

In the determination of fraudulent transfers, insolvency is defined by § 101(26) as occurring when the present fair salable value of the debtor's property is less than the amount required to pay its debts. The fair value of the debtor's property is also reduced by any fraudulently transferred property, and for an individual, by the exempt property under § 522.

(a) LBO as a Fraudulent Transfer.   A fraudulent transfer may occur in a LBO. For example, in a LBO transaction where the assets of the debtor were used to finance the purchase of the debtor's stock and the debtor became insolvent, operated with an unreasonably small capital, or incurred debt beyond the ability to repay, a fraudulent transfer may have occurred. Note that the transfer may have been made without adequate consideration because the debtor corporation received no benefit from the proceeds from the loan that were used to retire former stockholder's stock.

(b) Accounting Services—Search for Fraudulent Transfers.   It is important for the accountant to ascertain when a fraudulent transfer has in fact occurred because it represents a possible recovery that could increase the value of the estate. It can, under certain conditions, prevent the debtor from obtaining a discharge. To be barred from a discharge as the result of a fraudulent transfer, the debtor must be an individual and the proceedings must be under chapter 7 liquidation or the trustee must be liquidating the estate under a chapter 11 proceeding.

In ascertaining if the debtor has made any fraudulent transfers or incurred fraudulent obligations, the independent accountant would carefully examine transactions with related parties within the year prior to the petition or other required period, look for the sale of large amounts of fixed assets, review liens granted to creditors, and examine all other transactions that appear to have arisen outside the ordinary course of the business.

33.13 POSTPETITION TRANSFERS.   Section 549 allows the trustee to avoid certain transfers made after the petition is filed. To be avoidable, transfers must not be authorized either by the court or by an explicit provision of the Bankruptcy Code.

(a) Adequate Value Received.   The trustee can avoid transfers made under §§ 303(f) and 542(c) of the Bankruptcy Code even though authorized. Section 303(f) authorizes a debtor to continue operating the business before the order for relief in an involuntary case. Section 549 does, however, provide that a transfer made prior to the order for relief is valid to the extent of value received. Thus, the provision of § 549 cautions all persons dealing with a debtor before an order for relief has been granted to evaluate the transfers carefully. Section 542(c) explicitly authorizes certain postpetition transfers of real property of the estate made in good faith by an entity without actual knowledge or notice of the commencement of the case.

(b) Accounting Services—Preventing Unauthorized Transfers.   To prevent unauthorized transfers, the procedures that the accountant should see are operative include the following:

1. Establishing procedures to ensure that prepetition debt payments are made only with proper authorization.
2. Designating an individual to handle all requests for prepetition debt payments.
3. Acquainting accounting personnel with techniques that might be used to obtain unauthorized prepetition debt payments.

33.14 SETOFFS.   Setoff is that right existing between two parties to net their respective debts where each party, as a result of unrelated transactions, owes the other an ascertained amount. The right to setoff is an accepted practice in the business community today. When one of the two parties is insolvent and files a bankruptcy court petition, the right to setoff has special meaning. Once the petition is filed, the debtor may compel the creditor to pay the debt owed and the creditor may in turn receive only a small percentage of the claim—unless the Bankruptcy Code permits the setoff.

The Bankruptcy Code gives the creditor the right to offset a mutual debt, providing both the debt and the credit arose before the commencement of the case. Major restriction on the use of setoff prevents the creditor from unilaterally making the setoff after a petition is filed. The right to setoff is subject to the automatic stay provisions of § 362 and the use of property under § 363. Thus, a debtor must obtain relief from the automatic stay before proceeding with the setoff. This automatic stay and the right to use the amount subject to setoff is possible only when the trustee or debtor in possession provides the creditor with adequate protection. If adequate protection—normally in the form of periodic cash payments, additional or replacement collateral, or other methods that will provide the creditor with the indubitable equivalent of its interest—is not provided, then the creditor may proceed with the offset as provided in § 553.

(a) Early Setoff Penalty.   Section 553(b) contains a penalty for those creditors who, when they see the financial problems of the debtor and threat of the automatic stay, elect to offset their claim prior to the petition. The Code precludes the setoff of any amount that is a betterment of the creditor's position during the 90 days prior to the filing of the petition. Any improvement in position may be recovered by the debtor in possession or trustee. The amount to be recovered is the amount by which the insufficiency on the date of offset is less than the insufficiency 90 days before the filing of the petition. If no insufficiency exists 90 days before the filing of the petition, then the first date within the 90-day period where there is an insufficiency should be used. **Insufficiency** is defined as the amount by which a claim against the debtor exceeds a mutual debt owing to the debtor by the holder of such claim. The amount recovered is considered an unsecured claim.

(b) Accounting Services—Setoffs.   In addition to developing a schedule that helps determine the amount of the penalty, the accountant may assist in determining the amount of debt outstanding.

33.15 RECLAMATION.   One area where the avoiding power of the trustee is limited is in a request for reclamation. Section 546(c) provides that under certain conditions the creditor has the right to reclaim goods if the debtor received the goods while insolvent. To **reclaim** these goods, the seller must demand in writing, within 10 days after their receipt by the debtor, that the goods be returned. The court can deny reclamation, assuming the right is established, only if the claim is considered an administrative expense or if the claim is secured by a lien. A creditor faces some problems in attempting to reclaim goods. One is that the request must be made within 10 days. Requests made after this time period are denied.

Another problem is that the right of reclamation under UCC § 2-702 is basically a right to obtain the physical return of particular goods in the hands of the debtor. If the goods have been sold or used, the ability to obtain the goods may be limited. For example, it is doubtful that the seller could reclaim goods that were sold by the debtor to a purchaser in good faith that had no knowledge of the debtor's financial problems. Also, the reclamation rights of the seller are subject to any superior right of other creditors, which most likely would include the good faith purchaser or buyer in the ordinary course of business.

33.16 U.S. TRUSTEE.   Chapter 30 of Title 28, U.S. Code, provides for the establishment of the U.S. trustee program. The Attorney General is responsible for appointing one U.S. trustee in each of the 21 regions, and one or more assistant U.S. trustees perform the supervisory and appointing functions formerly handled by bankruptcy judges. They are the principal administrative officers of the bankruptcy system.

The U.S. trustee establishes, maintains, and supervises a panel of private trustees that are eligible and available to serve as trustee in cases under chapter 7 or 11. Also, the U.S. trustee supervises the administration of the estate and the trustees in cases under chapter 7, 11, 12 or 13. The intent is not for the U.S. trustee system to replace private trustees in chapters 7 and 11. Rather, the system should relieve the bankruptcy judges of certain administrative and supervisory tasks and thus help to eliminate any institutional bias or the appearance of any such bias that may have existed in the prior bankruptcy system.

The U.S. trustees are responsible for the administration of cases. They appoint the committees of creditors with unsecured claims and also appoint any other committees of creditors or stockholders authorized by the court. If the court deems it necessary to appoint a trustee or examiner, a U.S. trustee makes this appointment (subject to court approval) and also petitions the court to authorize such an appointment.

U.S. trustees monitor applications for compensation and reimbursement for officers and accountants and other professionals retained in the case, raising objections when deemed appropriate. Other responsibilities include monitoring plans and disclosure statements, creditors' committees, and the progress of the case.

HANDLING OF CLAIMS UNDER CHAPTER 11

A claim antedating the filing of the petition that is not a priority claim or that is not secured by the pledge of property is classified as an **unsecured claim.** Claims where the value of the security interest is less than the amount of the claims are divided into a secured and unsecured part.

33.17 PROOF OF CLAIMS.   A proof of claim or interest is deemed filed in a chapter 11 case provided the claim or interest is listed in the schedules filed by the debtor, unless the claim or interest is listed as disputed, contingent, or unliquidated. A creditor is thus not required to file a proof of claim if it agrees with the debt listed in the schedules. It is, however, advisable for creditors to file a proof of claim in most situations. Creditors who for any reason disagree with the amount admitted on the debtor's schedules, such as allowable prepetition interest on their claims, or creditors desiring to give a power of attorney to a trade association or lawyer, should always prepare and file a complete proof of claim. Special attention must also be devoted to secured claims that are undersecured.

33.18 UNDERSECURED CLAIMS.   Section 506 provides that if a creditor is undersecured, the claim will be divided into two parts. The first part is secured to the extent of the value of the collateral or to the extent of the amount of funds subject to setoff. The balance of the claim is considered unsecured. The value to be used to determine the amount of the secured claim is, according to § 506(a), to "be determined in light of the purpose of the valuation and of the proposed disposition or use of such property, and in conjunction with any hearing on such disposition or use or on a plan affecting such creditors' interest." Bankruptcy Rule 3012 provides that any party in interest may petition the court to determine the value of a secured claim.

Thus, the approach used to value property subject to a lien for a chapter 7 may be different from that for a chapter 11 proceeding. Even within a chapter 11 case, property may be valued differently. For example, fixed assets that are going to be sold because of the discontinuance of operations may be assigned liquidation values, whereas assets that will continue to be used by the debtor may be assigned going concern values. Although courts have to determine value on a case-by-case basis, it is clear that the **value** is to be determined in light of the purpose of the valuation and the proposed disposition or use of the property.

Section 1111(b) allows a secured claim to be treated as a claim with recourse against the debtor in chapter 11 proceedings (that is, where the debtor is liable for any deficiency between the value of the collateral and the balance due on the debt) whether the claim is nonrecourse by agreement or by applicable law. This preferred status terminates if the property securing the loan is sold under § 363 or is to be sold under the terms of the plan, or if the class of which the secured claim is a part elects application of § 1111(b)(2).

Another available section under § 1111(b) is that a class of undersecured creditors can elect to have its entire claim considered secured. A class of creditors will normally be only one creditor. For example, in chapter 11 cases where most of the assets are pledged, very little may be available for unsecured creditors after paying administrative expenses. Thus, the creditor might find it advisable to make the § 1111(b)(2) election. On the other hand, if there will be a payment to unsecured creditors of approximately 75 cents per dollar of debt, the creditor may not want to make this election.

The purpose of the election is to provide adequate protection to holders of secured claims where the holder is of the opinion that the collateral is undervalued. Also, if the treatment of the part of the debt that is accorded unsecured status is so unattractive, the holder may be willing to waive his unsecured deficiency claims. The class of creditors making this election has the right to receive full payment for its claims over time. If the members of the class do not approve the plan, the court may confirm the plan as long as the plan provides that each member of the class receives deferred cash payments totaling at least the allowed amount of the claim. However, the present value of these payments as of the effective date of the plan must be at least equal to the value of the creditors' interest in the collateral. Thus, a creditor who makes the election under § 1111(b)(2) has the right to receive full payment over time, but the value of that payment is only required to equal the value of the creditor's interest in the collateral.

33.19 ADMINISTRATIVE EXPENSES. The actual, necessary costs of preserving the estate, including wages, salaries, and commissions for services rendered after the commencement of the case, are considered administrative expense. Any tax including fines or penalties is allowed unless it relates to a tax-granted preference under § 507(a)(7). Compensation awarded a professional person, including accountants, for postpetition services is an expense of administration. Expenses incurred in an involuntary case subsequent to the filing of the petition but prior to the appointment of a trustee or the order for relief are not considered administrative expenses. They are, however, granted second priority under § 507. Administrative expenses of a chapter 11 case that is converted to chapter 7 are paid only after payment of chapter 7 administrative expenses.

33.20 PRIORITIES. Section 507 provides for the following priorities:

1. Administrative expenses.
2. Unsecured claims in an involuntary case arising after commencement of the proceedings but before an order of relief is granted.
3. Wages earned within 90 days prior to filing the petition (or the cessation of the business) to the extent of $2,000 per individual.
4. Unsecured claims to employee benefit plans arising within 180 days prior to filing petition limited to $2,000 times the number of employees covered by the plan less the amount paid in (3) above and the amount previously paid on behalf of such employees.
5. Unsecured claims of grain producers against a grain storage facility or of fishermen against a fish storage or processing facility to the extent of $2,000.
6. Unsecured claims of individuals to the extent of $900 from deposits of money for purchase, lease, or rental of property or purchase of services not delivered or provided.
7. Unsecured tax claims of governmental units:
   a. Income or gross receipts tax, provided tax return was due (including extension) within 3 years prior to filing petition.
   b. Property tax last payable without penalty within 1 year prior to filing petition.
   c. Withholding taxes.
   d. Employment tax on wages, and so forth, due within 3 years prior to the filing of the petition.
   e. Excise tax due within 3 years prior to the filing of the petition.
   f. Customs duty on merchandise imported within 1 year prior to the filing of the petition.
   g. Penalties related to a type of claim above in compensation for actual pecuniary loss.

Priority claims must be provided for in the plan.

33.21 Processing of Claims. Several accounting firms and other businesses have developed models to handle the processing of claims of both small and large debtors. Some of their features include:

1. Capture of all the various formats of claims needed by the bankruptcy court.
2. Information needed for management to review and evaluate each claim.

3. Mailing lists and labels.
4. Creditor statements.
5. On-line update and inquiry capability.
6. Modeling and decision analysis capability that enables management to evaluate settlement alternatives efficiently.

One system uses a multifield data base to help debtors deal with the complexities of a bankruptcy. Creditors' files can be sorted in terms of classes of creditors, priorities of claims, and so on, and then alphabetically within these categories. Notices sent to creditors include all the necessary information, such as the amount of a claim and its current status. Ongoing information that changes over time is constantly updated. This could include the extent to which proofs of claim differ from the recorded debt, the assessment of market values of collateral pledged as security, other assets that are not pledged as security, distributions made during the course of a chapter 11 case, and changes to or withdrawals of claims. Automatically prepared and mailed notices keep creditors current on the proceedings of a case. The system, through automatic mailings, answers telephone inquiries as they are entered.

OPERATING UNDER CHAPTER 11

No order is necessary under the Bankruptcy Code for the debtor to operate the business in chapter 11. Sections 1107(a) and 1108 grant the debtor all the rights, powers, and duties of a trustee, except the right to compensation under § 330, and provide that the trustee may operate the business unless the court directs otherwise. Thus, the debtor will continue to operate the business unless a party in interest requests that the court appoint a trustee. Until action is taken by management to correct the problems that caused the adverse financial condition, the business will most likely continue to operate at a loss. If the creditors believe new management is necessary to correct the problem, they will press for a change in management or the appointment of a trustee. In most large bankruptcies as well as in many smaller cases, the management is replaced, often by **turnaround specialists,** who have particular expertise in taking over troubled companies. They often eliminate the unprofitable aspects of the company's operations, reduce overhead, and find additional financing as part of the turnaround process. Once the plan has been confirmed, turnaround specialists frequently move on to other troubled companies. In small cases where management is also the stockholders, creditors are apt to be uncomfortable with existing management, which may have created the problems.

33.22 USE OF PROPERTY. The debtor or trustee must be able to use a secured party's collateral, or in most situations there would be no alternative but to liquidate the business. Section 363(c) gives the trustee or debtor the right to use, sell, or lease property of the estate in the ordinary course of business without a notice and a hearing. As a result of this provision the debtor may continue to sell inventory and receivables and use raw materials in production without notice to secured creditors and without court approval. The use, sale, or lease of the estate's property other than in the ordinary course of business is allowed only after notice and an opportunity for a hearing.

(a) Cash Collateral. One restriction on the use of the property of the bankruptcy estate is placed on the trustee or debtor where cash collateral is involved. **Cash collateral** is cash, negotiable instruments, documents of title, securities, deposit accounts, or other cash equivalents where the estate and someone else have an interest in the property. Also included would be the proceeds of noncash collateral, such as inventory and accounts receivable and proceeds, products, offspring, and rents, profits, or property subject to a security interest, if converted to proceeds of the type defined as cash collateral, provided the proceeds are subject to the prepetition security interest.

To use cash collateral, the creditor with the interest must consent to its use, or the court, after notice and hearing, must authorize its use. The court may authorize the use, sale, or lease of cash collateral at a preliminary hearing if there is a reasonable likelihood that the debtor in possession will prevail at the final hearing. The Bankruptcy Code also provides that the court is to act promptly for a request to use cash collateral.

(b) Accounting Services—Assisting Debtor in Providing Information to Secured Lender. In many cases, a company cannot operate unless it can obtain use of its cash collateral. For example, cash in bank accounts subject to setoff or collections from pledged receivables and inventory prior to the filing of the petition are not available for use until the company obtains the consent of the appropriate secured creditor or of the court.

Thus, an immediate concern of many companies that need to file a chapter 11 petition is how to procure enough cash to operate for the first week or so after filing the petition. Often the best way to obtain the use of the cash is to get approval from the secured creditor prior to the filing of the petition. Accountants can work with the debtor in putting together information for the secured lender that may result in the pledge of additional property or an extension of a receivable or inventory financing agreement for the release of cash to allow operation of the business once the petition is filed.

33.23 OBTAINING CREDIT.   In most chapter 11 proceedings the debtor must obtain additional financing in order to continue the business. Although the debtor was allowed to obtain credit under prior law, the power granted to the debtor under the Bankruptcy Code is broader. Section 364(a) allows the debtor to obtain unsecured debt and to incur unsecured obligations in the ordinary course while operating the business. This right is automatic unless the court orders otherwise. Also the holder of these claims is entitled to first priority as administrative expenses.

If the debtor is unable to obtain the necessary unsecured debt under § 364(a), the court may authorize the obtaining of credit and the incurring of debt by granting special priority for claims. These priorities may include the following:

1. Giving priority over any or all administrative expenses.
2. Securing the debt with a lien on unencumbered property.
3. Securing the debt with a junior lien on encumbered property.

For the court to authorize the obtaining of credit with a lien on encumbered property that is senior or equal to the existing lien, the debtor must not be able to obtain credit by other means and the existing lien holder must be adequately protected.

Credit obtained other than in the ordinary course of business must be authorized by the court after notice and a hearing. Where there is some question whether the credit is related to the ordinary course of business, the lender should require court approval.

33.24 APPOINTMENT OF TRUSTEES.   The Bankruptcy Code provides that a trustee can be appointed in certain situations based on facts in the case and not related to the size of the company or the amount of unsecured debt outstanding. The trustee is appointed only at the request of a party in interest after a notice and hearing. A party in interest includes the debtor, the trustee (in other contexts), creditors' or stockholders' committees, creditors, stockholders, or indenture trustees. Also, a U.S. trustee, while not a party in interest, may petition the court for an appointment of a trustee.

Section 1104(a) states that a trustee be appointed:

1. for cause, including fraud, dishonesty, incompetence, or gross mismanagement of the affairs of the debtor by current management, either before or after the commencement of the case, or similar cause, but not including the number of holders of securities of the debtor or the amount of assets or liabilities of the debtor; or
2. if such appointment is in the interest of creditors, any equity security holders, and other interests of the estate, without regard to the number of holders of securities of the debtor or the amount of assets or liabilities of the debtor.

The U.S. trustee is responsible for the appointment of the trustee from a panel of qualified trustees, once the appointment has been authorized by the court. It also appears that the U.S. trustee would have the right to replace trustees who fail to perform their functions properly.

33.25 Appointment of Examiner.   Under the Bankruptcy Code, the trustee's major functions are to (1) operate the business, and (2) conduct an investigation of the debtor's affairs. Under certain conditions it may be best to leave the current management in charge of the business, without resolving the need for the investigation of the debtor. The Code provides for the appointment of an examiner to perform this function. Section 1104(b) states that if a trustee is not appointed:

. . . [O]n request of a party in interest, and after notice and hearing, the court shall order the appointment of an examiner to conduct such an investigation of the debtor as is appropriate, including an investigation of any allegations of fraud, dishonesty, incompetence, misconduct, mismanagement, or irregularity in the management of the affairs of the debtor of or by current or former management of the debtor, if

1. Such appointment is in the interest of creditors, any equity security holders, and other interests of the estates; or
2. The debtor's fixed, liquidated, unsecured debts, other than debts for goods, services, or taxes, or owing to an insider, exceed $5 million.

(a) Functions of Examiner.   The function of the examiner is to conduct an investigation into the actions of the debtor, including fraud, dishonesty, mismanagement of the financial condition of the debtor and the operation of the business, and the desirability of the continuation of such business. The report is to be filed with the court and given to any creditors' committee, stockholders' committees, or other entities designated by the court. In addition to these two provisions, § 1106(b) also states that an examiner may perform other functions as directed by the court. In some cases the court has expanded the role of the examiner. For example, the bankruptcy judges may prefer to see additional controls exercised over the management of the debtor, but may not see the need to incur the costs of the appointment of a trustee. These functions are assigned to the examiner.

(b) Accountants as Examiners.   Accountants may serve as examiners, and in some regions U.S. trustees have expressed a preference for appointing accountants in certain situations. Where a financial investigation is needed, an accountant may be the most qualified person to perform as an examiner. In many cases where the role of the examiner has been expanded, accountants were serving as examiners.

33.26 OPERATING STATEMENTS.   Several different types of reports are required while the debtor is operating the business in a chapter 11 reorganization proceeding. The nature of the reports and the time period in which they are issued depend to some extent on local rules and on the type of internal controls of the debtor and the extent to which large losses are anticipated.

Districts establish local bankruptcy rules that generally apply to all cases filed in that particular district. These rules cover some of the procedural matters that relate to the handling of a bankruptcy case, including appearance before the court, forms of papers filed with court, assignment of case, administration of case, employment of professionals, and operating statements. The rules for the filing of operating statements have become primarily the responsibility of the U.S. trustee and, as a result, the specific procedures for these statements are those of the U.S. trustee.

One statement required by all regions is an operating statement—profit and loss statement. This statement may include, in addition to the revenue and expense accounts needed to determine net income on the accrual basis, an aging of accounts payable (excluding prepetition debts) and accounts receivable, status of payments to secured creditors, analysis of tax payments, analysis of insurance payments and coverage, and summary of bankruptcy fees that have been paid or are due.

The U.S. trustee also requires cash receipts and disbursement statements. In some cases it may be necessary to prepare this statement for each bank account of the debtor. For example the U.S. trustee for the central district of California requires that the debtor, in addition to the regular account, establish separate accounts for payroll and taxes. Separate cash receipts and disbursements statements are also required for each account.

An independent accountant may assist the debtor in the preparation of these monthly operating reports. If the accountant is associated with the debtor, a compilation report should be attached to the reports filed. Of course, if the statements have been reviewed or audited, then the appropriate report should be attached.

33.27 REPORTING PROBLEMS.   Companies that have filed chapter 11 face several reporting problems, including how to classify liabilities, what to include in prepetition liabilities, how to account for adjustments to liability accounts as a result of the chapter 11 petition, and how to account for administrative expenses. Each of these problems will be examined in this section.

(a) Classification of Prepetition Claims.   Prepetition claims are currently shown in three ways—as current liabilities, in between current and long-term liabilities, and as long-term liabilities. Chapter 11 debtors are not at all consistent in their manner of disclosing these claims.

In most situations the prepetition claims do not meet the definitions of a current liability—they will not be paid within 1 year and will not require the use of current assets. It appears to this author that the profession should adopt a policy of reporting all prepetition liabilities in a separate category below the current liabilities. If it is known at the time of issuing the statement of financial position that some of the liabilities may be paid within 1 year and will require the use of current assets, such should be disclosed in the note to the statement.

The AcSEC has issued an Exposure Draft for a SOP that would require liabilities that are subject to compromise to be disclosed in a separate category and not to be classified as current or noncurrent.

(b) Content of Prepetition Liabilities.   There is no specific guidance as to the items to include in the prepetition liability account. It appears that it should consist of all liabilities that must be dealt with under the plan. It would not include those liabilities that were incurred after the petition was filed and that will be paid in the normal course of business, such as postpetition trade payables and those liabilities that are not impaired. For example, fully secured debts where the debtor will cure any defaults and continue to make payments as required under the contract should not be included in the prepetition liabilities. On the other hand, undersecured debt must be provided for in the plan and, as a result, the total amount should be included in prepetition liabilities. During the proceeding it may be necessary to adjust the prepetition liability account for several reasons. For example, as the amount of disputed claims is determined, as liabilities for cancellation of executory contracts are determined, and as there are changes in the liabilities that will be considered unimpaired in the proposed plan, adjustments to the prepetition liabilities account should be recorded.

(c) Accounting for Claims Arising from Chapter 11.   According to SFAS No. 5, "Accounting for Contingencies," a claim must be "probable and reasonably estimable" before any amount is recorded. A question arises concerning the handling of claims that arise during the bankruptcy case. For example, when should the debtor accrue, and for what amount, the damages due to the rejection of a lease—operating or capital? The liability arising from the rejection of a lease is a prepetition unsecured claim that is generally classified with other unsecured claims. It would appear that the amount of the damages should be estimated in accordance with SFAS No. 5 and recorded at the time the lease is rejected. Should the amount of the accrual be an estimate of the damages or should it be an estimate of the amount that will be paid? It appears that, since all other unsecured claims are shown at the amount of the claim until a plan is approved that provides for debt discharge, the estimate of the damages should be recorded at the time the lease is rejected. If part of the claim is subsequently discharged, the gain from such a discharge will be reported with other gains from the discharge of unsecured debts.

Thus, at the time leases are rejected or other claims against the estate become known, an amount should be accrued that is a reasonable estimate of the claim that will eventually be allowed by the bankruptcy court.

(d) Accounting for Professional Fees.   A review of current practice indicates that chapter 11 debtors report professional and other related administrative expenses in one of four ways:

1. *Estimation of Fees When Petition Is Filed.* Under this approach an estimate of these costs is written off at the time the petition is filed and a loss contingency (liability) is established.
2. *Recognition of Fees on Approval of Plan.* All costs are deferred until the plan is approved, and then these costs are written off against the gain from debt discharge.
3. *Recognition of Fees as Expenses When Services Are Performed.* Expenses are considered operating items.
4. *Recognition of Fees as Expenses When Services Are Performed Except for Year of Debt Discharge, When These Expenses Are Charged Against Gain from Debt Discharge.* Expenses are considered operating items except in year of discharge, where they are classified as extraordinary items.

It appears that the best alternative is to expense administrative expenses (professional fees) as they are incurred. This conclusion is based on the premise that this approach is the most theoretically viable because these costs are generally period costs and should be charged against income in the period incurred. If this approach is used, nonexistent liabilities will not appear on the balance sheet (accrual at the beginning of the case) and assets will not be reflected where there is considerable uncertainty as to their realization (deferral of cost to confirmation of plan).

Even though most of the professional expenditures will provide substantial future benefits, they are, by their very nature, not of the type that would normally be capitalized, but would generally be charged against the current period's revenue. Even when the policy is followed to expense items as incurred, specific costs related to the reorganization in the form of stock issuance costs and so forth would be charged against the proceeds or, in the case of stock for debt, against income from debt discharge. Some chapter 11 debtors have expensed all of the professional fees in years prior to confirmation and then in the year of confirmation reduced the gain from debt discharge by the amount of the professional fees incurred that year.

It appears that a reader of the financial statements would prefer to see all costs from the reorganization activities separated from the costs associated with the ongoing business activities. Reporting the professional fees and, perhaps, other reorganization expenses in this manner would permit the reader to determine the nonrecurring costs of the current period. Thus, the reader should better understand the probable cost structure of the entity after the plan is confirmed.

The related SOP proposed by the AcSEC follows the above suggestion.

CHAPTER 11 PLAN

The accountant advises and gives suggestions to the debtor and attorney in drawing up a plan. Section 1121 of the Bankruptcy Code provides that only the debtor may file a plan of reorganization during the first 120 days of the case (unless a trustee has been appointed). This breathing period permits the debtor to hold lawsuits and foreclosures in status quo and to determine economic causes of its financial predicament while developing a plan. Using the schedules of assets and liabilities, statement of affairs, and past and projected financial statements, the debtor and its accountant examine the liabilities of the debtor and the value of the business and explore sources of funding for the plan such as enhanced profitability, partial liquidation, issuing debt securities, or outside capitalization. They outline the classes of debt that cannot be deferred or reduced and negotiate with the rest.

33.28 CLASSIFICATION OF CLAIMS.   Section 1122 provides that claims or interests can be divided into classes provided each claim or interest is substantially similar to the others of such class. In addition, a separate class of unsecured claims may be established consisting of claims that are below or reduced to an amount the court approves as reasonable and necessary for administrative convenience. For example, claims of less than $1,000, or those creditors who will accept $1,000 as payment in full of their claim, may be placed in one class and the claimants will receive the lesser of $1,000 or the amount of their claim. All creditors or equity holders in the same class are treated the same, but separate classes may be treated differently.

Generally, all unsecured claims, including claims arising from rejection of executory contracts or unexpired leases, are placed in the same class except for administrative expenses. They may, however, be divided into different classes if separate classification is justified. The Bankruptcy Code does not require placing all claims that are substantially the same in the same class.

Courts have stated that § 1122(a) "does not require that similar claims must be grouped together, but merely that any group created must be homogeneous."

33.29 DEVELOPMENT OF PLAN.   The items that may be included in the plan are listed in § 1123. Certain items are listed as mandatory and others are discretionary. The mandatory provisions are:

1. Designate classes of claims and interests.
2. Specify any class of claims or interest that is not impaired under the plan.
3. Specify the treatment of any class of claims or interest that is impaired under the plan.
4. Provide the same treatment for each claim or interest in a particular class unless the holders agree to less favorable treatment.
5. Provide adequate means for the plans' implementation, such as:
   - Retention by the debtor of all or any part of the property of the estate.
   - Transfer of all or any part of the property of the estate to one or more entities.
   - Merger or consolidation of the debtor with one or more persons.

- Sale of all or any part of the property of the estate, either subject to or free of any lien, or the distribution of all or any part of the property of the estate among those having an interest in such property of the estate.
- Satisfaction or modification of any lien.
- Cancellation or modification of any indenture or similar instrument.
- Curing or waiving any default.
- Extension of a maturity date or a change in an interest rate or other term of outstanding securities.
- Amendment of the debtor's charter.
- Issuance of securities of the debtor, or of any entity involved in a merger or transfer of the debtor's business for cash, for property, for existing securities, or in exchange for claims or interests, or for any other appropriate purpose.

6. Provide for the inclusion in the charter of the debtor, if the debtor is a corporation, or of any corporation referred to in (5) above, of a provision prohibiting the issuance of nonvoting equity securities, and providing, as to the several classes of securities possessing voting power, an appropriate distribution of such power among such classes, including, in the case of any class of equity securities having a preference over another class of equity securities with respect to dividends, adequate provisions for the election of directors representing such preferred class in the event of default in the payment of such dividends.

7. Contain only provisions that are consistent with the interests of creditors and stock-holders and with public policy with respect to the selection of officers, directors, or trustee under the plan.

In addition to these requirements, the plan may also:

1. Impair or leave unimpaired any class of unsecured or secured claims or interests.
2. Provide for the assumption, rejection, or assignment of executory contracts or leases.
3. Provide for settlement or adjustment of any claim or interest of the debtor or provide for the retention and enforcement by the debtor of any claim or interest.
4. Provide for the sale of all of the property of the debtor and the distribution of the proceeds to the creditors and stockholders.
5. Include any other provision not inconsistent with the provisions of the Bankruptcy Code.

In determining the classes of creditors' claims or stockholders' interests that must approve the plan, it is first necessary to determine if the class is **impaired.** Section 1124 states that a class of claims or interest is impaired under the plan, unless the plan leaves unaltered the legal, equitable, and contractual rights of a class, cures defaults that led to acceleration of debts, or pays in cash the full amount of their claims.

33.30 DISCLOSURE STATEMENT.   A party cannot solicit the acceptance or rejection of a plan from creditors and stockholders affected by the plan unless they receive a written disclosure statement containing adequate information as approved by the court. Section 1125(b) requires that the court must approve this disclosure statement, after notice and a hearing, as containing adequate information.

(a) Definition of Adequate Information.   Section 1125(a) states that adequate information means information of a kind, and in sufficient detail, as far as is reasonably practicable in light of the records, that would enable a hypothetical reasonable investor typical of holders of claims or interests of the relevant class to make an informed judgment about the plan. This definition contains two parts. First it defines adequate information and then it sets a standard against which the information is measured. It must be the kind of information that a typical investor of the relevant class, not one that has special information, would need to make an informed judgment about the plan. Section 1125(a)(1) provides that adequate information need not include information about other possible proposed plans.

(b) Content. As noted above, the information disclosed in the statement should be adequate to allow the creditor or stockholder to make an informed judgment about the plan. The following paragraphs describe the types of information that might be included.

1. *Introduction.* The statement should provide information about voting on the plan, as well as background information about the debtor and the nature of the debtor's operations.

2. *Management.* It is important to identify the management that will operate the debtor on emergence from bankruptcy and to provide a summary of their background.

3. *Summary of the Plan of Reorganization.* Typical investors want to receive a description of the terms of the plan and the reasons the plan's proponents believe a favorable vote is advisable.

4. *Reorganization Value.* Included in the disclosure statement should be the reorganization value of the entity that will emerge from bankruptcy. One of the first, as well as one of the most difficult, steps in reaching agreement on the terms of a plan is determining the value of the reorganized entity. Once the parties—debtor, unsecured creditors' committee, secured creditors, and shareholders—agree on the reorganization value, this value is then allocated among the creditors and equity holders. Thus, before determining the amount that unsecured creditors, secured creditors, or equity holders will receive, it is necessary to determine the reorganization value. An unsecured creditors' committee or another representative of creditors or equity holders is generally unable, and often unwilling, to agree to the terms of a plan without any knowledge of the emerging entity's reorganization value. It also appears that if this value is needed by the parties that must agree on the terms of a plan, it is also needed by each unsecured creditor to determine how to vote on the plan. Yet, many disclosure statements fail to disclose reorganization value. One method of presentation is to include these values in the pro forma balance sheet based on the assumption that the plan is confirmed. See discussion of pro forma statements below.

5. *Financial Information.* Among several types of information that may benefit creditors and stockholders considerably in assessing the potential of the debtors' business are the following: audited reports of the financial position as of the date the petition was filed or as of the end of a recent fiscal year, and the results of operations for the past year; a detailed analysis by the debtor of its properties, including a description of the properties, the current values, and other relevant information; and a description of the obligations outstanding with identification of the material claims in dispute. If the nature of the company's operations is going to change significantly as a result of the reorganization, historical financial statements for the past 2 to 5 years are of limited value.

In addition to the historical financial statements, it may be useful to present a **pro forma balance sheet** showing the impact that the proposed plan, if accepted, will have on the financial condition of the company. Included should be the source of new capital and how the proceeds will be used, the postpetition interest obligation, lease commitments, financing arrangements, and so forth.

To provide the information needed by creditors and stockholders for effective evaluation of the plan, the pro forma statement should show the reorganization value of the entity. Thus the assets would be presented at their current values and, if there is any excess of the reorganization value (going concern value) over individual assets, this value would be shown. Liabilities and stockholder's equity should be presented at their discounted values based on the assumption that the plan will be confirmed. If appraisals of the individual assets have not been made, it appears appropriate to reflect the differences between the book value and reorganization value as an adjustment to the asset side of the pro forma balance sheet.

If the plan calls for future cash payments, the inclusion of projections of future operations will help the affected creditors make a decision as to whether they believe the debtor can make the required payments. Even if the plan calls for no future cash payments, it may still be advisable to include the financial information in the disclosure statement that will allow creditors and stockholders to see the business's potential for operating profitably in the future. These projections must, of course, be based on reasonable assumptions, and the assumptions must be clearly set forth in the projections accompanying the disclosure statement.

6. *Liquidation Values.* Included in the disclosure statement should be an analysis of the amount that creditors and equity holders would receive if the debtor was liquidated under chapter 7. In order to effectively evaluate the reorganization alternative, the creditors and equity holders must know what they would receive through liquidation. Also, the court, in order to confirm the plan, must ascertain, according to § 1129 (a)(7), that each holder of a claim or interest who does not vote in favor of the plan must receive at least an amount that is equal to the amount that would be received in a chapter 7 liquidation.

Generally, it is not acceptable to state that the amount provided for in the plan exceeds the liquidation amount. The presentation must include data to support this type of statement.

7. *Special Risk Factors.* In any securities that are issued pursuant to a plan in a chapter 11 proceeding, certain substantial risk factors are inherent. It may be advisable to include a description of some of the factors in the disclosure statement.

33.31 CONFIRMATION OF PLAN. Prior to the confirmation hearing on the proposed plan, the proponents of the plan will seek its acceptance. Once the results of the vote are known, the debtor or other proponent of the plan will request confirmation of the plan.

The holder of a claim or interest, as defined under § 502, is permitted to vote on the proposed plan. Voting is based on the classification of claims and interests. A major change from prior law is that the acceptance requirements are based on those actually voting and not on the total value or number of claims or interests allowed in a particular class. The Secretary of the Treasury is authorized to vote on behalf of the United States when the United States is a creditor or equity security holder.

A class of claim holders has accepted a plan if at least two-thirds in amount and more than one-half in number of the allowed claims for that class that are voted are cast in favor of the plan. For equity interests it is only necessary that votes totaling at least two-thirds in amount of the outstanding securities in a particular class that voted are cast for the plan. The majority in number requirement is not applicable to equity interests.

33.32 CONFIRMATION REQUIREMENTS. Section 1129(a), which contains the requirements that must be satisfied before a plan can be confirmed, is one of the most important sections of the Bankruptcy Code. The provisions follow:

1. *The Plan Complies with the Applicable Provisions of Title 11.* Section 1122 concerning classification of claims and § 1123 on the content of the plan are significant sections.

2. *The Proponents of the Plan Comply with the Applicable Provisions of Title 11.* Section 1125 on disclosure is an example of a section that is referred to by this requirement.

3. *The Plan Has Been Proposed in Good Faith and Is Not by Any Means Forbidden by Law.*

4. *Payments Are Disclosed.* Any payment made or to be made for services, costs, and expenses in connection with the case or plan has been approved by, or is subject to the approval of, the court as reasonable.

5. *There Is Disclosure of Officers.* The proponent of the plan must disclose the persons who are proposed to serve after confirmation as director, officer, or voting trustee of the reorganized debtor. Such employment must be consistent with the interests of creditors and equity security holders and with public policy. Also, names of insiders to be employed and the nature of their compensation must also be disclosed.

6. *Regulatory Rate Has Been Approved.* Any governmental regulatory commission that will have jurisdiction over the debtor after confirmation of the plan must approve any rate changes provided for in the plan.

7. *The Plan Satisfies the Best-Interest-of-Creditors Test.* It is necessary for the creditors or stockholders who do not vote for the plan to receive as much as they would if the business were liquidated under chapter 7.

8. *The Plan Has Been Accepted by Each Class.* Each class of creditors or stockholders impaired under the plan must accept the plan. Section 1129(b), however, provides an exception to this requirement—the **"Cram Down."**

   This section allows the court under certain conditions to confirm a plan even though an impaired class has not accepted it. The plan must not discriminate unfairly, and it must be fair and equitable, with respect to each impaired class of claims or interest that has not accepted the plan. The Code states conditions for secured claims, unsecured claims, and stockholder interests that would be included in the "fair and equitable" requirement. It should be noted that because the word "includes" is used, the meaning of fair and equitable is not restricted to these conditions. A discussion of the "cram down" provision is found in § 5.46 of Newton's *Bankruptcy and Insolvency Accounting: Practice and Procedure* (1989).

9. *Priority Claims Have Been Satisfied.* This requirement provides that priority claims must be satisfied with cash payment as of the effective date of the plan unless the holders agree to a different treatment. An exception to this general rule is allowed for taxes. Taxes must be paid over a period of 6 years from date of assessment with a present value equal to the amount of the claim.

10. *At Least One Class Accepts the Plan.* If a class of claims is impaired under the plan, at least one class that is impaired, other than a class of claims held by insiders, must accept the plan.

11. *Plan Is Feasible.* Confirmation of the plan is not likely to be followed by liquidation or by the need for further financial reorganizaton unless the plan provides for such liquidation or reorganization.

33.33 ACCOUNTING SERVICES—ASSISTANCE TO DEBTOR.   Accountants can provide considerable services to their client relating to the formulation of the plan, some of which are described in the following subsections.

(a) Liquidation Value of Assets.   Section 1129(a)(7) provides that each holder of a claim must either accept that plan or receive or retain interest in property of a value that is at least equal to the amount that would have been received or retained if the debtor were liquidated under chapter 7. Accountants can help the debtor establish these values.

(b) Projections of Future Operations.   Section 1129(a)(11) contains the feasibility standard of chapter 11 requiring that confirmation of the plan of reorganization is not likely to be followed by liquidation or further reorganization (unless contemplated). The accountant may assist the debtor or trustee to formulate an acceptable plan by projecting the ability of the debtor to carry out and perform the terms of the plan. To establish feasibility, the debtor must project the profitability potential of the business. Where the plan calls for installment payments, the accountant may be requested to prepare or review projected budgets, cash flow statements, and statements of financial position. The creditors must be assured by the projected income statement and cash flow statement that the debtor will be in a position to make the payments as they become due. The forecast of the results of operations and financial position should be prepared on the assumption that the proposed plan will be accepted, and the liability and asset accounts should reflect the balance that would be shown after all adjustments are made relative to the debt forgiveness. Thus, interest expense is based on the liabilities that will exist after the discharge occurs.

(c) Reorganization Value. Not only are cash projections needed for the feasibility test as mentioned in the previous paragraph, but they are an important part of the negotiation process. The creditors want to receive the maximum amount possible in any chapter 11 plan and often want the payment in cash as of the effective date of the plan. The creditors realize, however, that if their demands are beyond the ability of the debtor to make payments, the plan will not work and they will not receive the payments provided for in the plan. Cash flow projections assist both parties in developing reasonable conclusions regarding the value of the entity emerging from chapter 11. In some reorganizations, there is considerable debate over cash flow projections and the discount rate to be used in determining the value of the debtor's continuing operations, to which must be added the amount to be realized on the sale of nonoperating assets plus excess working capital. Once the debtor and its creditors' committee can agree on the basic value of the entity, it is easier to negotiate the terms of the plan.

During the formulation of the plan the accountant can assist the debtor considerably by helping to determine the reorganized value of the debtor or by helping the debtor to assess the valuation of an investment banker or other specialists. If the accountant develops the cash projections supporting the valuation, the accountant will be precluded from being independent for SEC purposes. Once the debtor has determined an estimate of the value of the entity that will emerge from bankruptcy, the accountant can provide assistance to the debtor in negotiating the terms of the plan with the creditor.

(d) Pro Forma Balance Sheet. Also of considerable help in evaluating a plan is a pro forma balance sheet showing how the balance sheet will look if the plan is accepted and all provisions of the plan are carried out. By using reorganization models or simulation models, the pro forma balance sheet may be prepared based on several possible courses of action that the debtor could take. The pro forma balance sheet illustrates the type of debt equity position that would exist under different alternatives.

This pro forma balance sheet should reflect the debts at discounted values. Assets are generally presented at their historical cost values unless the debtor has made a decision to apply the concept of quasi reorganization. A pro forma balance sheet that reflects the reorganized values of the entity is of considerable benefit to the debtor in developing the terms for a plan.

Once the terms of the proposed plan have been finalized, the pro forma balance sheet based on historical values reflecting these terms is generally included in the disclosure statement that must be submitted prior to or at the time votes are solicited on the plan. The pro forma balance sheet reflecting reorganized values, however, provides information for the creditors and stockholders that is much more relevant in making an informed judgment about how to vote on the plan.

(e) Reorganization Model.   Accountants can develop a model to help the debtor in developing a plan. The outcome of a reorganization plan depends on a variety of assumptions, including the creditors' willingness to accept different mixes of cash and securities, economic trends, possible sources for financing continuing operations or acquisitions, and many other factors. Using a model, these assumptions can be altered one at a time with all else held constant, and the possible courses of action can be analyzed according to the needs of management. Using this technique, creditors or the debtor can identify potential problem areas and request clarifications. Once these have been received and entered into the system, a new set of comparisons is made and the process is repeated until both sides are satisfied that the most favorable course is being pursued. Breakdowns of reorganization plans by computer models allow debtors and creditors to focus on the financial data most relevant to the case at hand.

33.34 ACCOUNTING SERVICES—ASSISTANCE TO CREDITORS' COMMITTEE.   The following subsections describe several of the services that the accountant can render for the creditors' committee or for a committee of equity holders.

(a) Assistance in the Bargaining Process.   One of the basic functions performed by the creditors' committee is to negotiate a settlement and then make its recommendation to the other creditors. The accountant should be familiar with the bargaining process that goes on between the debtor and the creditors' committee in trying to reach a settlement. Bargaining can be both vigorous and delicate. The debtor bargains, perhaps, for a settlement that consists of a small percentage of the debt, demanding only a small immediate cash outlay, with payments to be made in the future. The debtor may want the debts outstanding to be subordinated to new credit or may ask that the agreement call for partial payment in preferred stock. The creditors want a settlement that represents a high percentage of the debt and consists of a larger cash down payment with the balance to be paid as soon as possible. In cases where there is very little cash available for debt repayment on confirmation, unsecured creditors may be interested in obtaining most of the outstanding stock of the company. In the past 10 years, the creditors of public companies have received an increasing interest in the ownership of the debtor. It is not unusual for the creditors to own between 80% and 95% of the outstanding stock of the emerging entity. For example, Wickes' creditors received 84% ownership, and the existing equity of Emmons Industries retained only 3% interest whereas creditors received the balance.

The services that the accountant may render for the creditors' committee in the negotiations with the debtor vary significantly depending on several factors, including the size of the debtor, the experience of the members of the creditors' committee, the nature of the debtor's operations, and the creditors' committee confidence in the debtor and in the professionals—especially attorneys and accountants—who are helping the debtor. The committee in most cases, to varying degrees, depends on the accountant to help evaluate the debtor's operations, the information provided about those operations, and the terms of a proposed plan. Often accountants may be engaged to perform an audit or to investigate selected aspects of the debtor's operations and to obtain an overall understanding of the debtor's problems and possible solutions.

(b) Evaluation of Debtor's Projections.   Of primary significance to a creditors' committee is determining whether the projections and forecasts submitted by the debtor are realistic. The representatives of the largest unsecured creditors on the committee typically are not accountants and thus may need assistance in evaluating the financial data prepared by the debtor. The accountant for the creditors' committee may be in a strong position to evaluate the debtor's projections and to make recommendations. The intention is not to perform an audit of such data but rather to review the information to determine whether the projections can be supported to some extent by hard evidence. The level of involvement by the accountant for the creditors' committee will vary, depending on the sophistication of the company or of the financial people who prepared the data. The review in some cases could be limited to a discussion of the data with those who prepared the projections, to determine whether the forecasts seem to make sense. In other situations, however, the accountant may find that the preparation of this information has been somewhat loose or vague. In these circumstances, the accountant for the committee may need to get involved in the preparation or to perform a review of the appropriate accounting records to see whether the basic underlying data have some foundation in fact.

(c) Reorganization Value.   In some cases accountants for the creditors' committee develop their own models of the debtor's operations. Cash flow projections can then be prepared for determining the reorganized entity's value. Operational changes made by the debtor are entered in the model as are proposed sales or other major actions, providing a basis for the committee's response to the debtor's proposals. Evaluation by the creditors' committee focuses on the impact these actions will have on the value of the reorganized entity and on the amount of potential settlement.

(d) Review of Plan and Disclosure Statement.   As was noted earlier, the accountant for the debtor provides advice and assistance in the formulation of a plan of reorganization in a chapter 11 proceeding and a plan of settlement in an agreement out of court. An important function of an accountant employed by the creditors is to help evaluate the proposed plan of action. In a chapter 11 case where the debtor has not proposed a plan within 120 days, a proposed plan has not been accepted within 180 days after the petition was filed, or where the trustee has been appointed, the accountant may assist the creditors in developing a plan to submit to the court. The accountant is able to provide valuable assistance to the committee because of familiarity with the financial background, nature of operations, and management of the company gained during the audit. In committee meetings a great deal of discussion goes on between the committee members and the accountant concerning the best settlement they can expect and how it compares with the amount they would receive if the business were liquidated.

The creditors are interested in receiving as much as possible under any reorganization plan. The accountant may work with the creditors' committee to see that the amount proposed under the plan is reasonable and fair based on the nature of the debtor's business. First, it must be determined that the plan provides for at least as much as would be received in a chapter 7 liquidation. Second, the creditors must leave for the debtor enough assets to operate the business after reorganization. If a reasonable basis does not exist for future operations, the judge may not confirm the plan because it is not feasible.

If an audit has not been performed, the accountant for the creditors' committee must rely on the information contained in the disclosure statement and in other reports that have been issued. Thus, the content of the disclosure statement may be most important. Also, since the disclosure statement serves as the basic report used by the creditors to evaluate the plan, it is critical that it be properly prepared and contain the type of information that allows the creditors to effectively evaluate the proposed plan.

The accountant for the creditors' committee may be asked to evaluate the disclosure statement. If, in the accountant's opinion, it does not contain adequate information, the deficiencies may be conveyed to the debtor informally (normally through creditors' committee counsel) prior to submission of the plan to the court, or an objection to the content of the statement may be raised at the disclosure hearing.

In evaluating the information in the disclosure statement, the accountant for the creditors' committee may be asked to review the financial statements contained in the disclosure statement or others that were issued by the debtor. Special consideration must be made in reviewing pro forma and liquidation statements of financial condition. The pro forma statement provides the creditors with an indication of the debtor's likely financial condition if the plan is accepted. This statement should show that the creditors will receive more if they accept the plan than they would receive if the debtor were liquidated. The pro forma statement also should demonstrate that the plan is feasible in that, after satisfying the provisions of the plan, the debtor retains an asset base with which to operate. In reviewing the pro forma statement prepared by the debtor, special consideration must be given to the analysis of the assumptions used to prepare it and to the evaluation of the value of the assets (which may differ from book values). If the pro forma statements are based on historical costs, the accountant for the creditors' committee may want to restate them to reflect the reorganized values of the entity. The creditors' committee will be able to evaluate the terms of the plan more effectively if it can compare the terms to pro forma statements containing the reorganized value of the entity rather than historical values.

Liquidation statements show what the unsecured creditors would receive if the business were liquidated. The assumptions used in the adjustments to book values must be evaluated carefully. The accountant for the creditors' committee may be asked to review statements of this nature and to provide advice as to the reasonableness of the analysis. There may be a tendency for the debtor to understate liquidation values in order to make the terms of the plan more appealing to the unsecured creditors.

33.35 ACCOUNTING FOR THE REORGANIZATION. Several accounting problems arise in accounting for the entity as it emerges from bankruptcy. Among them are the following: Should debt issued or compromised as a result of the proceeding be discounted, should the emergence from bankruptcy be accounted for as a quasi reorganization, or should the deficit in retained earnings be eliminated?

To help resolve some of these reporting issues, the AcSEC issued an Exposure Draft for an SOP entitled "Financial Reporting by Entities in Reorganization under the Bankruptcy Code." The Exposure Draft would require entities emerging with a reorganization plan under chapter 11 to adopt fresh start reporting if

1. The reorganization value of the assets of the emerging entity immediately before the date of confirmation are less than the total of all postpetition liabilities and allowed claims, and

2. The holders of existing voting shares immediately before confirmation receive less than 50% of the voting shares of the emerging entity.

According to the Exposure Draft, if an entity does not meet the above requirement, the liabilities of the debtor should be discounted in accordance with APB Opinion No. 21, "Interest on Receivables and Payables"; forgiveness of debt, if any, should be reported as an extraordinary item; and quasi-reorganization accounting should not be used by the debtor on emerging from chapter 11.

(a) Fresh Start Reporting. Entities that meet the above standard for fresh start reporting should revalue their assets and liabilities on emergence from chapter 11. The Exposure Draft suggests following these principles in allocating the reorganization value:

- The reorganization value of the entity should be allocated to the entity's assets in conformity with the procedures of APB Opinion No. 16, "Business Combinations," for transactions reported on the basis of the purchase method. If any part of the reorganized value cannot be attributable to specific assets, such amounts should be reported as "reorganization value in excess of amounts allocable to identifiable assets."

- Liabilities should be reported at their fair value and determined in the same manner as a note issued in a noncash transaction under APB Opinion No. 21.

- Deferred taxes should be reported in accordance with the provisions of SFAS No. 96, "Accounting for Income Taxes."

Special guidance is provided in the Exposure Draft on to how to account for and disclose the revaluation.

(b) Discounting of Debt. Under current practice some debtors discount their debt and others follow the provisions of SFAS No. 15, "Accounting by Debtors and Creditors for Troubled Debt Restructurings." Footnote 4 to SFAS No. 15 and FTB No. 81-6 indicate that SFAS No. 15 is not applicable to quasi reorganization or corporate readjustment where the debtor restates its liabilities generally. In situations where SFAS No. 15 does not apply, no guidance is given as to how to value the new debt issued. In the late 1970s and early 1980s it was easy to find some debtors that discounted their debt and others that did not. However, an analysis of the annual reports issued by public companies between 1985 and 1988 indicated that most debtors are now discounting the debt. It appears that discounting should be used since it is more in line with the economics of the transaction. If the Exposure Draft for a SOP becomes effective it would require discounting as noted above.

(c) Revaluation of Assets. Currently the only generally accepted manner to write up assets at the time the debtor emerges from bankruptcy is to elect to account for the reorganization as a quasi reorganization. Under a quasi reorganization the assets and liabilities of the debtor are presented at their fair value. However, for public companies the SEC will not allow a net write-up in assets (SAB No. 78). The SEC staff has indicated that they will consider previous write-downs in determining if there has been a net write-up. In a quasi reorganization the deficit in the retained earnings account is eliminated by a charge against paid-in capital.

If the Exposure Draft for the SOP becomes effective it would require that when the reorganization value is less than liabilities and there is a change in ownership, assets and liabilities of the entity emerging from chapter 11 be restated to reflect current values and the fresh start provided for in the Bankruptcy Code. Quasi reorganization would no longer apply to debtors in chapter 11.

(d) Elimination of Deficit. The SEC stated in SAB No. 73 that it is not an acceptable practice for public companies just to eliminate the deficit and not to revalue assets and liabilities (but only to the extent that there is not a net write-up in assets). Thus, a deficit reclassification is considered to be a quasi reorganization requiring the adjustment of the value of assets and liabilities.

SOURCES AND SUGGESTED REFERENCES

Accounting Principles Board, "Business Combinations," Accounting Principles Board Opinion No. 16, AICPA, New York, 1970.

———, "Interest on Receivables and Payables," Accounting Principles Board Opinion No. 21, AICPA, New York, 1971.

Accounting Standards Executive Committee, "Financial Reporting by Entities in Reorganization under the Bankruptcy Code" (Exposure Draft), AICPA, New York, 1990.

Behrenfield, William H., and Biebl, Andrew R., "Bankruptcy/Insolvency," *The Accountant's Business Manual,* AICPA, New York, 1989.

Countryman, "Executory Contracts in Bankruptcy," *Minnesota Law Review,* Vol. 57, (1973), pp. 439, 460.

Financial Accounting Standards Board, "Reporting Gains and Losses from Extinguishment of Debt," Statement of Financial Accounting Standards No. 4, FASB, Stamford, CT, 1975.

———, "Accounting for Contingencies," Statement of Financial Accounting Standards No. 5, FASB, Stamford, CT, 1975.

———, "Accounting by Debtors and Creditors for Troubled Debt Restructurings," Statement of Financial Accounting Standards No. 15, FASB, Stamford, CT, 1977.

King, Lawrence P., ed., *Collier Bankruptcy Manual,* Matthew Bender, New York, 1989.

Newton, Grant W., *Bankruptcy and Insolvency Accounting,* 4th ed., Wiley, New York, 1989.

Securities and Exchange Commission, "Push down" Basis of Accounting for Parent Company Debt Related to Subsidiary Acquisitions," Staff Accounting Bulletin No. 73, SEC, Washington DC, 1987.

———, "Views Regarding Certain Matters Relating to Quasi-Reorganizations, Including Deficit Eliminations," Staff Accounting Bulletin No. 78, SEC, Washington DC, 1988.

Summers, Mark Stevens, *Bankruptcy Explained: A Guide for Businesses,* Wiley, New York, 1989.

CHAPTER **34**

FORENSIC ACCOUNTING AND LITIGATION CONSULTING SERVICES

Jeffrey H. Kinrich, CPA
Price Waterhouse

M. Freddie Reiss, CPA
Price Waterhouse

Raymond S. Sims, CPA
Price Waterhouse

CONTENTS

The authors would like to thank the following Price Waterhouse staff members for their valuable research and editorial assistance: John Bednarski, Gloria Gowan, Jess Hines, Elo Kabe, Albert Lilienfeld, Linda Morris, Neil Murdoch, Leslie Spiller, and Daniel Wray.

Forensic accounting can be broadly defined as the application of accounting principles, theories, and discipline to facts and hypotheses at issue in a legal context. This legal context is generally litigation, but any dispute resolution proceeding (e.g., arbitration or mediation) is a candidate for the application of forensic accounting. Similarly, forensic accounting applies equally to both civil and criminal litigation. The principal focus of this chapter will be civil litigation because it is by far the most frequent dispute resolution proceeding in which the professional accountant will be involved.

The terms "forensic accounting," "litigation support," or "litigation consulting" are sometimes used as synonyms. Attorneys, however, sometimes use "litigation support" to mean automated document management. For purposes of this chapter, forensic accounting includes all financial and accounting analysis performed by a professional accountant to assist counsel in connection with its investigation, assessment, and proof of issues in a dispute resolution proceeding.

This chapter provides a brief description of the litigation process and a discussion of the accountant's role in, and contribution to, that process. It includes a description of the types of cases in which professional accountants typically get involved and a discussion of analytical techniques and approaches that the accountant can apply to these cases. The last section of this chapter, "Testimony" provides suggestions as to how to prepare and deliver deposition and trial testimony.

THE LEGAL CONTEXT

34.1 THE ADVERSARIAL PROCESS.   In civil disputes it is generally up to the parties (the plaintiff and defendant), not the court, to initiate and prosecute litigation, to investigate the pertinent facts, and to present proof and legal argument to the adjudicative body. The court's function, in general, is limited to adjudicating the issues that the parties submit to it, based on the proofs presented by them. The adversarial system is based on the belief that the truth is more likely to emerge from bilateral investigation and presentation, motivated by the strong pull of self-interest, rather than from judicial investigation motivated only by official duty.

34.2 STAGES IN A CIVIL SUIT.   There are three basic phases or stages in a civil suit, barring appeal. These stages are the same for virtually all adversarial proceedings, whether in a federal, state, or administrative court.

(a) Pleadings.   A lawsuit is started by a **complaint** that is filed with the clerk of the trial court and served on the defendants. The complaint lays out the facts and causes of action alleged by the plaintiff. The defendants may file a **motion** to dismiss (arguing that the defendant is not legally liable even if the alleged facts are true) or an **answer** to the complaint. The answer may contain a denial of the allegations or an affirmative defense (e.g., statute of limitations has expired). The defendant also may file a **counterclaim** which presents a claim by the defendant (counterplaintiff) against the plaintiff (counterdefendant).

(b) Pretrial Discovery.   The purpose of pretrial discovery is to narrow the issues that need to be decided at trial and to obtain evidence to support legal and factual arguments. It is essentially an information-gathering process. Evidence is obtained in advance to facilitate presentation of an organized, concise case, as well as to prevent any surprises at trial. This sharing of information often will result in the settlement of the case before trial.

The first step in discovery typically involves the use of **interrogatories** and **document requests**. Interrogatories are sets of formal written questions directed by one party in the lawsuit to the other. They are usually broad in nature and are used to fill in and amplify the fact situation set out in the pleadings. Interrogatories are also used to identify individuals who may possess unique knowledge or information about the issues in the case.

Requests for production of documents identify specific documents and records that the requesting party believes are relevant to its case and that are in the possession of and controlled by the opposing party. The opposing party is only required to produce the specific documents requested. Accordingly, when drafting these requests, care must be taken to be as broad as possible so as to include all relevant documents but narrow enough to be descriptive. It is not unusual for more than one set of interrogatories and document requests to be issued during the course of a lawsuit. The accountant is often involved in developing interrogatories and document requests on financial and business issues.

Depositions are the second step in the discovery process. They are the sworn testimony of a witness recorded by a court reporter. During the deposition, the witness may be asked questions by the attorneys for each party to the suit. The questions and answers are transcribed, sworn to, and signed. The testimony will allow the party taking the deposition to better understand the facts of the case and may be used as evidence in the trial. The accountant expert witness may be heavily involved at this stage, both in being deposed and in developing questions for opposing witnesses.

(c) Trial.   The third stage of the litigation/adversarial process is the trial. It is the judicial examination and determination of issues between the parties to the action. The trial begins with the attorneys for each party making opening statements concerning the facts they expect to prove during the trial. Then the plaintiff puts forth its case, calling all of the witnesses it believes are required to prove its case. Each witness will be subject to direct examination and then cross-examination by the opposing party's attorney. After the plaintiff has called all of its witnesses and presented all of its evidence, the defendant will then present its case in the same manner. The plaintiff then has an opportunity to present additional evidence to refute the defendant's case in a rebuttal. The defendant can respond in a surrebuttal. Finally, each party has the opportunity to make a closing statement before the court.

The U.S. Constitution and most state constitutions provide for the right of trial by jury in most cases. This right does not have to be exercised and many cases are tried without a jury. In most states and in federal courts, one of the parties must request a jury or the right is presumed to be waived.

34.3 REQUIRED PROOFS.   In order for a plaintiff to succeed in a claim for damages, it must satisfy three different but related proofs: liability, causation, and amount of damages. If the burden of proof is not met on any one of these, the claim will fail.

(a) Liability.   The plaintiff must prove that one of its legal rights has been transgressed by the defendant. It will present evidence attempting to prove that the actions of the defendant were in violation of the plaintiff's legal rights. Similarly, the defendant will present evidence in an effort to prove that the plaintiff's rights were not violated, or at least, were not violated by the defendant.

(b) Causation.   If the plaintiff proves that the defendant has violated one of its legal rights, it must be shown that this violation resulted in some harm to the plaintiff. Here, attorneys for the plaintiff and defendant will try to prove or disprove the nexus between the defendant's actions and some harm to the plaintiff.

(c) Damages.   After presenting the evidence relating to the liability and causation issues, the parties' next step in most cases is to prove damages.

Damages are one of a number of remedies that may be available to a prevailing plaintiff. Other types of remedies include specific performance (performance of the act that was promised), injunctions (an order by the court forbidding or restraining a party from doing an act), and restitution (the return of goods, property, or money previously conveyed). Damages are the only type of remedy discussed in this chapter.

The general principle in awarding damages is to put the plaintiff in the same position it would have been if its legal rights had not been transgressed. There are three main categories of damages: compensatory, consequential, and punitive. Compensatory damages compensate the injured party only for injuries or losses actually sustained and proved to have arisen directly from the violation of the plaintiff's rights. Consequential damages are foreseeable damages that are caused by special circumstances beyond the action itself. They flow only from the consequences or results of an action. Punitive damages are intended to penalize the guilty party and to make an example of the party to deter similar conduct in the future. They are awarded only in certain types of cases (e.g. fraud).

The quantification of damages is primarily a question of fact. The burden of proving the damage amount normally falls on the plaintiff. It is in this area that accountants are most frequently utilized. Many different methods can be used to quantify the economic loss. They are discussed in section 34.20.

THE ACCOUNTANT'S ROLE IN THE LITIGATION PROCESS

Typically the accountant is hired by attorneys representing either the plaintiff or the defendant. In some cases, however, an accountant may be engaged directly by one of the parties to the action, often by an audit client. No matter who engages the accountant, a number of possible services might be provided. The accountant can work as either testifying expert or as consultant. The basic difference between the two is discoverability of the accountant's work product.

34.4 THE TESTIFYING EXPERT.   Frequently, the accountant's purpose in the case will be to develop and render an opinion regarding financial or accounting issues. Ordinarily, only facts and firsthand knowledge can be presented by witnesses at trial. The only exception to this rule is the testimony of experts, which can include an expression of the expert's **opinions.**

According to the courts and the law, experts are those who are qualified to testify authoritatively because of their education, special training, and experience. Clearly, a professional accountant can qualify as an expert in issues relating to accounting and financial data.

As discussed in sections 34.14–.18 and 34.19–.22, the accountant as expert may be asked to develop and present evidence in support of any or all of the required proofs. For example, the accountant can review and offer an opinion as to the adequacy of the work performed by another accountant in a professional liability suit (proof of liability). Or, the accountant might review the financial records and the business environment of a company to determine whether a bank's withdrawal of credit caused the company to go out of business (proof of causation). Most commonly, the accountant will be asked to provide an opinion regarding the economic loss suffered by the plaintiff in the case (proof of damages).

34.5 NONTESTIFYING CONSULTANT.   In certain situations, the accountant will be asked to be a consultant rather than a testifying expert. The accountant will take on more of an advisory role and will not provide testimony. The work the accountant performs for the attorney as a consultant is generally protected by the attorney's work product privilege and as such is not discoverable by the opposing party. For this reason, accountants are often engaged initially as consultants. This enables the attorney to explore avenues and conduct analyses from which he might want to shield his testifying expert. However, once the accountant has been designated as an expert, **all** work products may be subject to discovery.

34.6 CASE ANALYSIS AND PLANNING.   Whether in the role as testifying expert or nontestifying consultant, the professional accountant can provide valuable assistance throughout the litigation process.

In many circumstances, the accountant can be of use to the attorney before the complaint is even filed. The accountant can help the attorney understand the accounting, financial, and economic issues involved in the case, and can also assess the potential value of the claim by providing an estimate of the amount of damages. In certain cases, especially those involving accountant's liability, the accountant may actually help to identify causes of action to be included in the complaint.

Once a case has been filed, the accountant can help the attorney understand and evaluate critical accounting, financial, and economic issues and assist with the formulation of an appropriate strategy. Strategy formulation is a continual process; as new information is received and additional issues uncovered, the overall strategy is revised. During the planning phase, the accountant will evaluate alternative approaches and determine the most reasonable approach to take based on all available information. At the same time, the accountant will assess the strengths and weaknesses of the opponent's case. The accountant's involvement in this phase will help the attorney to focus on those issues that have the greatest impact on proving the case.

34.7 DISCOVERY.   Discovery is the information-gathering stage of the litigation process. During discovery each party attempts to identify and obtain all the information and documents necessary to prove its case. The accountant's initial assistance may be in formulating specific accounting and financially oriented questions to be included in interrogatories. The accountant will also assist in drafting document requests by identifying in a very specific manner the types of documents (particularly accounting records and reports) that would be of interest and that the opposing party is likely to have retained. The more specific the requests are, the more likely the response will be useful. The accountant will also be able to assist the attorney with the preparation of **responses** to the opposing party's interrogatories and document requests.

Depositions provide each side with an opportunity to elicit relevant facts and to identify weaknesses in an opponent's argument. The accountant can be helpful in this area by assisting the attorney in identifying subjects to be explored and in developing specific deposition questions, especially when financial executives or experts are being deposed. Frequently, an attorney will request the accounting expert to be present at these key depositions. Here the accountant can help the attorney understand and interpret the deponent's responses and formulate follow-on questions to probe more deeply into the subject area. Having the accountant present at the deposition will enable the attorney to completely understand and consider the financial issues. The accountant who will be a testifying expert may be subject to deposition by the opposing attorney. The opposition will attempt to gain a thorough understanding of the accountant's analysis and conclusions and, when possible, identify weaknesses and lay the groundwork for attack at trial. The importance of giving effective deposition testimony is obvious. The last section of this chapter, "Testimony," presents a description of the deposition process and some pointers for giving deposition testimony.

34.8 SETTLEMENT ANALYSIS. Settlement negotiations can occur at any point during the litigation process. They can be greatly facilitated by the use of an accounting expert. The accountant can be instrumental in evaluating existing alternatives and terms as well as in proposing other strategic approaches. The accountant's evaluation may involve (1) the determination of economic value and feasibility of various strategies, or (2) an analysis of the strengths and weaknesses of the two sides' positions.

When determining value and evaluating feasibility, the accountant can estimate damages under various scenarios and help to assess the probability of occurrence for each, thereby giving the attorney a better understanding of the risks involved. Just as importantly, the accountant can evaluate the true economic value of various settlement alternatives (e.g., structured settlements and noncash settlements) and determine possible tax effects of each. This will enable the attorney and client to make a more informed decision regarding settlement options and perhaps offer alternatives that benefit both parties.

The accountant also can provide an evaluation of the relative strengths and weaknesses of both the plaintiff's and the defendant's positions, thereby helping the attorney strengthen his bargaining position and anticipate potential problems.

34.9 TRIAL. If the case does not settle, the final role of the accountant will be to assist during the trial itself. The accountant's testimony in court is a key part of this role. In testimony, the accountant presents the opinions developed as a result of his information gathering, review, and analysis. This role is clearly the most important one the accountant will play in the process. It is imperative that the accountant present opinions in a straightforward, cogent, and concise manner. The last section of this chapter describes the course of direct testimony and suggests ways to enhance the effectiveness of the testimony.

Although opinion testimony is of paramount importance at the trial stage, the accountant can play other valuable roles. For example, the accountant can be of tremendous value to attorneys during the cross-examination of opposing experts and financial witnesses. The accountant can work with the attorney to prepare cross-examination questions in an effort to undermine the testimony or the credibility of the witness. The accountant will be important in this phase because of his ability to formulate accounting and financially oriented questions that will be difficult for the witness to evade or deflect. More importantly, the accountant will be able to assess the responses and provide follow-on questions to "close the loop" on important issues.

34.10 PROFESSIONAL STANDARDS RELEVANT TO LITIGATION CONSULTING. Throughout the litigation process, the accountant will be asked to provide input, conduct analyses, and offer advice or opinions regarding facts at issue in the case. Clearly, the attorney-client will expect that appropriate standards of care are followed by the accountant during the course of the engagement. However, although the litigation process itself is a formal, structured process with many rules and procedures that must be followed, the nature of the accountant's work is typically very unstructured and loosely defined. For this reason, no formal professional standards have been established applying specifically to litigation engagements, and in fact, the AICPA has established certain exemptions for CPAs engaged as expert witnesses as discussed below. Despite the lack of specifically defined standards, the general standards established by the AICPA form a framework for a responsible practitioner in the role as a forensic accountant. These standards serve as reasonable guidelines to ensure that the accountant does not jeopardize the interests of the attorney or the attorney's client.

No rules or standards are substitutes for professional judgment. The following discussion of selected AICPA standards is by no means all inclusive. The standards and guidelines that follow define a base on which a responsible professional can comfortably rely while conducting litigation services engagements.

Regardless of the service or engagement the accountant is called upon to provide, key elements of the AICPA's Code of Professional Conduct will apply. Notably, Article IV—Objectivity and Independence (AICPA, 1988, pp. 7–8) advises the accountant to be "impartial, intellectually honest and free of conflicts of interest." The attorney and client should not expect less.

(a) Litigation Support Exemptions.   Litigation support services are specifically exempted from the reporting requirements concerning financial forecasts and projections in the Statement on Standards for Accountants' Services on Prospective Financial Information (AICPA, 1985). The basis for this exemption is that prospective financial information in a litigation context is open to challenge, that is, cross-examination. Absent this opportunity for scrutiny and challenge, the professional standard applies.

An additional exemption for litigation engagements is provided for attestation standards in the AICPA's Statement on Standards for Attestation Engagements (AICPA, 1986). A CPA's testimony as an expert is not considered an attest engagement.

Current AICPA definitions and standards for MAS practice do not mention litigation services specifically, but the AICPA is expected to release guidelines defining litigation services as a type of consulting service. Also, guidance on providing litigation services is available in the AICPA Management Advisory Services Technical Consulting Practice Aid No. 7, "Litigation Services," (Wagner and Frank, 1986). This practice aid provides insights into types of engagements, relationships with attorneys and clients, approach to the work, and other unique aspects of this practice.

(b) Conflicts of Interest.   Conflicts of interest warrant special attention and concern by the accountant in a litigation engagement. Not only is the practitioner exposed to conflicts with his general practice clients, but the discovery of a conflict during the litigation engagement could jeopardize the ability of the attorney to serve the client, not to mention cause embarrassment to the accountant and high likelihood that fees will not be collected.

A conflict of interest exists in a litigation engagement when the ability of the accountant to be objective and independent may be affected by prior or current business relationships. The accountant should avoid engagements that involve conflicts of interest. Conflicts may arise from the accountant's ethical obligation to preserve existing client confidences, or from other relationships that may affect the accountant's ability to present adequately an issue for the client. An accountant may decline an engagement on the basis of perceived conflicts or business considerations. Accepting a litigation engagement on behalf of an audit client would not be a conflict; accepting an engagement against an audit client may be a professional conflict and would likely be a business conflict. Often, potential conflicts can be resolved through agreements between the parties, establishment of "chinese walls" (procedural barriers between teams within the firm), or other methods.

Before the accountant accepts a litigation engagement, all current and prior relationships, if any, with all known parties in a litigation must be evaluated for possible conflicts of interest. Known parties include potential clients, opposing parties, and each of their respective counsels. Also, throughout the engagement, potential conflicts of interest could surface, and these situations should be evaluated as if they occurred before the engagement began.

TYPES OF CASES

34.11 GENERAL ROLE OF ACCOUNTANT-EXPERT.   An accountant may be called as an expert in almost any case where there are numbers or dollars in dispute. Since most civil lawsuits are about money, this means that an accountant may be involved in almost any type of litigation.

Accountants are also used as experts in cases that require a knowledge of business records and transactions. However, there are certain types of cases in which the accountant is more likely to be involved.

A lawsuit typically requires proof of liability, causation, and damages. An accountant may be involved in any or all of these areas. Cases requiring an accountant's testimony on liability typically revolve around professional liability (e.g., was the audit performed properly?) or investigatory accounting (e.g., can the accountant determine what really happened?). Damages cases usually involve the computation of lost economic value, including lost profits, lost royalties, or loss of asset value.

34.12 BUSINESS-ORIENTED CASES.   The accountant's work often involves business disputes. This section presents a summary of common types of cases and the accountant's role.

(a) Breach of Contract.   Typically, the plaintiff has a contract with the defendant that the defendant is accused of breaching. For example, the contract may call for the defendant to buy a certain quantity of product for a certain price. The defendant, however, fails to make the required purchases. Or, the defendant may be accused of breaching a warranty on its goods or services. The accountant may be asked to quantify the damages suffered by the plaintiff as a result of the breach. Usually, the damages are measured by lost profits, that is, the additional profits the plaintiff would have earned but for the defendant's breach. Among the issues the accountant may address are lost revenues, avoided costs, available capacity, and possible mitigating actions, including sale of the product to others.

(b) Business Interruption.   A business interruption claim may arise from an accident, fire, flood, strike, or other unexpected event. It may even arise from a contract or warranty claim where the defendant's breach has caused the plaintiff to suspend operations. Typically, these claims are filed by a business against its insurance carrier, though a claim against the entity causing the event is possible. In a business interruption case, the plaintiff claims the event caused the business to suffer losses.

Often, the accountant is asked to quantify the loss. Elements to be considered may include lost profits, loss of tangible assets, loss of intangible assets (including goodwill), loss of an entire business or business line, cost to repair or reestablish the business, cost of downtime, or cost of wasted effort (time spent fixing the problem instead of generating operating profits).

(c) Intellectual Property.   Intellectual property disputes involve the rights to use patents, copyrights, and trademarks. The plaintiff claims that the defendant infringed on the plaintiff's intellectual property by illegally using the patent, copyright, or trademark. For patents, damages are defined by law to be plaintiff's lost profits (if reasonably provable), but not less than a reasonable royalty. Damages in a copyright case are the market value of the infringed work, the profits that the owner lost or will lose as a result of the infringement, or the defendant's profit. In a trademark case, where the mark has been registered with the Patent and Trademark Office, the owner may recover actual damages and also the infringer's profits.

Often computations are made separately for lost profits and for reasonable royalties. Sometimes the accountant can perform both analyses. Other times the accountant's opinion on reasonable royalty may be supplemented by another expert with experience in negotiating royalties in the particular industry.

(d) Antitrust   The plaintiff in antitrust litigation may be either the government or a private party. The government usually brings suit to oppose a merger or to break up a monopolist. Government suits are usually not for monetary damages. Experts in these suits, particularly in liability issues involving monopolistic practices, relevant market share, and the like, are often economists, not accountants.

In a private suit, the plaintiff accuses the defendant of violating antitrust laws, resulting in injury to competition, including (or especially) injury to the plaintiff. The accountant's role again may be the computation of lost profits.

A company may be accused of violating antitrust laws by selling the same goods at different prices to different parties in the same channel of distribution. This ostensibly discriminatory pricing may be refuted if the defendant can show that the price differences are justified by differences in cost of production, service, freight, and so on. An accountant may conduct these cost justification studies.

Accusations of predatory pricing also fall under the antitrust laws. The defendant in a predatory pricing case is accused of pricing so low that competitors lose money and are driven out of business. Once the competition is eliminated, the defendant presumably raises prices and enjoys monopoly profits. One legal standard for predatory pricing is pricing below cost of production. Depending on the law, the standard may be either incremental costs or fully allocated costs. An accountant may help establish or refute this claim by studying product pricing and production costs, and measuring the resulting profit margins.

(e) White Collar Crime and Fraud.   Lawsuits in this area usually relate to actions that resulted in the failure of a venture. Accountants are typically engaged to determine whether the venture was structured, organized, or managed as a conduit to abscond with investor money. Some of the more egregious examples typically are "boiler room" solicitations that appeal to investors because of the promised high return on investment.

Other examples of white collar crime and fraud activities include schemes involving the "penny stock" market and high-yielding investment certificates that may actually be nothing more than "Ponzi" transactions. In a typical Ponzi arrangement, real profits do not exist. Instead, money from new investors is used to pay investment returns to existing investors, giving the impression of profits.

Other types of fraud cases include various schemes by executives, employees, and customers to siphon funds from financial institutions for their personal use, check kiting, lapping, computer fraud, embezzlement, defense procurement fraud, costing fraud, schemes involving kickbacks, insider trading cases, and fraudulent bankruptcy actions.

The accountant's role in white collar crime and fraud cases is usually twofold. First, the accountant may assist counsel in the investigation of the venture to document what happened and establish liability. Second, the accountant may be involved in calculating damages that result from the fraud.

(f) Securities Act Violations.   Lawsuits in this area usually involve alleged violations of the federal acts, specifically §§ 11 and 12(2) of the Securities Act of 1933 and § 10(b) of the Securities and Exchange Act of 1934. These sections concern making false or misleading public statements about a company or omitting a material fact (either in a prospectus or in public statements, including financial statements), resulting in an alleged overvaluing of the company's stock. Typically, when the correct information becomes public, the value of the stock drops. Plaintiffs claim that, but for the misleading statements, they would not have bought the stock or they would have bought at a lower price. These lawsuits are often brought against officers, directors, investment bankers, lawyers, accountants, and others who may have been party to misstatements. Accountants may be involved in the liability, causation, and damages portions of securities cases. Involvement with liability issues is most common when an auditor has been accused of violating § 10(b)5 by failing to perform a GAAS audit and/or by giving a clean opinion to non-GAAP financial statements. The accountant will review the auditor's work papers and other relevant materials to reach a conclusion as to the adequacy of the audit of the financial statements. For more on this topic, see section 34.12(j) below.

The causation and damages phases of securities cases are closely linked. They consist of determining whether the information had any impact on the stock price and quantifying the losses suffered by the plaintiff investors as a result. Typically, this involves determining what the stock price **would have been** if the proper information had been released at the proper time. The methods for doing this are beyond the scope of this chapter; see Wagner and Hurd (1990) for a treatment of this subject.

(g) Bankruptcy.   Bankruptcy matters may require an accountant's services for many different tasks. The role of the accountant and scope of services to be performed is influenced by the size of the company and by whether the accountant is working for the trustee, debtor in possession, secured creditors, or the creditors' committee(s).

Accountants for the debtor in possession may be asked to prepare analyses supporting the solvency or insolvency of the debtor, which may affect creditors' claims, recoveries, or security interests. Such accountants also may be involved in preparing prospective financial information filed with the U.S. Trustee's Office or used in negotiating plans of reorganization with the parties of interest. Another important role may require making analyses to support a debtor's use of cash collateral and analyses showing that adequate protection is available to the secured creditor.

An accountant for the creditors' committee, in addition to reviewing any analyses prepared for the debtor, will have additional responsibilities. The accountant may initially be asked to determine the cause for the business failure and may need to determine quickly whether the debtor's operation may be further depleting the assets available for creditors. The creditors' accountants also may need to investigate the conduct of the debtor. The scope and depth may vary significantly based on the relationship and confidence the creditors have with existing management. At a minimum, a review to determine possible preferential payments, fraudulent conveyances, and insider transactions is usually performed. The roles, definitions, and exceptions to preferences and fraudulent conveyances are detailed in the Bankruptcy Code as well as in Newton (1989).

(h) Lender Liability.   This is an area in which a significant amount of litigation has occurred within the last few years and which has altered the business dealings between banks and their customers. Common law verdicts in numerous states have established a duty requiring banks to act in good faith and to provide a reasonable time period for a customer to arrange alternative financing should the bank no longer wish to continue the relationship. Other cases involve inaccurate or incomplete responses from banks to inquiries by third parties or failure to honor financing commitments. In some situations the bank's activity, either as a member of the business's Board of Directors, or in selecting those members, or the bank's insistence on designating workout consultants, places them in a position of being too close to operating the business; and they may find themselves accountable for its losses or ultimate bankruptcy.

The accountant's role is to assist with liability, causation, and damage issues. With respect to liability issues, the accountant may develop financial data to determine whether the borrower was in compliance with various loan convenants at various intervals during the banking relationship, including at its commencement. A review of debt and equity items in the financial statements could identify differences in definitions or inconsistencies between GAAP and the bank loan document terminology.

Accounting consultants working with defendants to lender liability actions may provide useful information to show the bank was acting prudently in calling a loan or in refusing to extend it based on the results of a financial analysis of the debtor. On the causation issue, the accountant can determine whether the bank's actions caused the business failure, or whether other circumstances were involved.

The accountant's role in damages is important for both the plaintiff and defendant. Damage theories may include both the actual cost of the termination of the credit relationship and more complex damages, including punitive and RICO claims where business failure occurs.

(i) Employment Litigation. Employment litigation typically involves claims of employment discrimination (including discrimination on the basis of age, race, or gender) or wrongful discharge. Claims may involve discrimination in hiring, promotion, or wages.

The accountant may be involved in both liability and damages phases of employment claims. For liability, the accountant may compile hiring rates, promotion rates, salary levels, or similar historical information to prove or refute a claim of differential treatment. This liability work often may be performed in conjunction with a statistician.

On damages, the accountant may determine what the plaintiff's income would have been had the alleged discrimination not occurred. The accountant will consider the proper level of earnings, the likely duration of the earnings, and any offset from amounts actually earned. The issues are very similar to loss of earnings claims in personal injury cases. Although specific approaches are not discussed in this chapter, the methods are logically similar to lost profits claims.

(j) Accountant's Liability. Most litigated claims against accountants have arisen from audit work. Recently, significant litigation has come from compilation, review, and prospective financial statement engagements.

Litigation over audited financial statements generally involves allegations that GAAP was not applied, or that the audit was not conducted in accordance with GAAS, or both. In class action securities litigation, noncompliance with SEC Regulations S-X and S-K as well as Financial Reporting Releases may also be alleged.

The accountant will review and analyze the company's financial records and auditor's work papers to determine if information can be discovered to prove or disprove compliance with GAAP or GAAS.

34.13 NONBUSINESS CASES. Important nonbusiness issues include marital dissolution, partnership dissolution, and personal injury matters.

(a) Marital Dissolution. In many states the financial aspects of a marital dissolution are governed by family law statutes that establish rules for sharing of income and the division of property. The tax laws have also greatly influenced the allocation of income and assets during and after a marital dissolution. Most states divide assets "equitably"; a few states are governed by community property rules. Awareness of the local rules and practices is of critical importance to accountants in their financial analyses.

In community property states the impact of community versus separate property is important. Simply stated, in community property states both spouses share equally in all income earned and property acquired during the marriage using community property funds. Separate property owned prior to marriage or acquired during marriage using separate property assets may retain its distinction. However, where funds and assets are commingled, the ultimate sharing of such items is complicated. The accountant's role is often to trace receipts and disbursements to determine which assets are community property.

Accountants often are asked to determine the value of the assets owned by the litigants as well as the income sources from which spousal and child support can be calculated. The valuation of assets often includes business valuation and, in the case of professionals, the value of their shareholdings or partnership interest. Issues such as professional goodwill or celebrity goodwill are important and contested often in marital dissolution litigation.

(b) Partnership Dissolution. Partnerships sometimes break up in a manner similar to a divorce. The accountant's work is also similar, focusing on tracing, valuation, and fair apportionment of assets and liabilities.

(c) Personal Injury. Personal injury cases stem from automobile accidents, slip-and-falls, and the like. Typically, damage components include medical expenses, pain and suffering, and lost earnings. The accountant is usually involved in the last item only. For identification of the issues involved, see 34.12(i).

THE ACCOUNTANT'S ROLE IN THE LIABILITY ISSUE

Accountants can play a critical role in assisting counsel in issues related to liability. Because attorneys are usually not knowledgeable about accounting or auditing issues, the accounting expert may provide critical insights into the nature of the liability aspects of a case. Although the issues vary by the type of case, the role that an accountant performs frequently focuses on the following areas.

34.14 VIOLATIONS OF GAAP. An accountant is often called on to assess whether there have been violations of GAAP. At one time, GAAP was simply common practice, that is, those principles that were generally used by professionals. GAAP has become more codified with pronouncements from the FASB, the EITF, government bodies (e.g., SEC) and industry organizations. The accounting expert must be cognizant of the literature and must be able to bring knowledge of the ever-increasing corpus of pronouncements and standards that constitute GAAP to the issues of the case.

During the discovery process, the accountant has the opportunity to explore the underlying documents and associate the facts with the accounting pronouncements. The accountant will refer to a company's general accounting records and documents as well as to the work papers of the independent auditor. The ability to review an independent auditor's work papers is essential. Such a review process requires the expert either to be an auditor or to have some auditing background. Issues related to the auditing firm's consideration of GAAP, their consultation with parties in their firm who provide technical expertise, and the extent to which they have researched a specific area of accounting should be documented in the auditor's work papers.

GAAP issues often arise in **securities cases.** In securities class action suits, the company's auditor may be named as a defendant along with the officers and directors of the company. The plaintiff's complaint usually enumerates a number of GAAP violations, centering around the timing and nature of revenues and expenses. That is, the complaint often alleges that the earnings of the defendant company were due to the overrecognition of revenues and the underrecognition of expenses.

For example, a recent securities case involved, in part, the recognition by the company of revenues related to sales of territorial rights for franchisees. The complaint alleged that the defendant recognized the revenue before the earning process was complete and therefore committed a fraud on the market through reporting higher revenues to the public. Another case involved the recognition of production expense related to a film company's extensive inventory of products for the theatrical and ancillary markets. In this instance, the company was alleged to have used accounting methods that were not in conformity with SFAS No. 53. As a result, one of the major allegations in the lawsuit was that the company did not write-down film costs to their net realizable value when supposedly it became known that the company would not realize revenues to cover their unamortized costs.

GAAP is also an issue in disputes over the **contractual purchase** of a company. With such purchases, the audited financial statements are used as the basis for the purchase or condition of the sale. The expert in these cases is called on by the seller to review the working papers of the independent auditor of the financial statements. From these working papers and the notes to the financial statements, the expert can determine what accounting methods were employed and whether they are in conformity with GAAP and common industry practice.

In contractual purchases litigation, the issues center on the valuation of assets or the quantification and disclosure of liabilities. Asset values in dispute may include such issues as proper use of LIFO or FIFO, inventory write-downs, unrecorded liabilities, accounting for impaired assets, amortization of goodwill, replacement cost versus book value, and realizable value of accounts receivable.

Liabilities are of critical importance since the buyer needs to be alerted to all potential and contingent debts and encumbrances. The accountant would determine whether there was adequate disclosure of the liabilities in the financial statements that were either issued or relied on by the buyer. The accountant may also need to evaluate whether subsequent events were reasonably foreseeable.

34.15 VIOLATIONS OF GAAS OR OTHER PROFESSIONAL STANDARDS.   The accountant may review and assess potential violations of GAAS or other applicable professional standards. Such violations may range from the failure of the defendant auditing firm to adequately observe the physical inventory, to not confirming sufficient accounts receivable, to not performing an adequate subsequent events review. GAAS violations are usually alleged in conjunction with GAAP violations. Liability issues related to a failure to perform an audit in accordance with GAAS are usually not unearthed until a review of the auditing firm's work papers has taken place.

Bankruptcy cases often focus on the liability of the auditor of the failed company's financial statements. For example, in the savings and loan industry, independent auditors of some failed institutions have been charged with violations of the ethical rule on independence, with failure to adequately circularize loans, and with inadequately documenting audit findings. In these cases, attorneys for both the plaintiff and defendant have turned to accounting experts to assist them, particularly in determining whether any GAAS violations have occurred.

With the increasing number of authoritative pronouncements being issued by the AICPA in areas related to compilations and reviews, forecasts and projections, the detection of fraud, and the need for auditors to communicate significant deficiencies in internal control structure, the accounting expert may be frequently called on by attorneys to address the issue of compliance with professional standards.

34.16 TRANSACTIONAL ANALYSES.   The accountant provides expertise in several types of transactional disputes.

In **white collar crime** cases where "Ponzi" schemes are suspected, the accountant will want to document how the enterprise was structured and to develop organizational charts and flow charts. Tracing transactions from the receipt of investor funds to its ultimate investment or disposition will be required. Analyses that illustrate the lack of any positive cash flow other than by raising additional investor funds will be useful to the attorney in showing liability. The flow of all cash transactions, identification of all bank accounts, location of any safe deposit boxes, investment accounts, or custodial arrangements are all within the accountant's scope.

The accountant should also analyze cash disbursements to see whether any patterns indicating self-dealing emerge, or to identify possible related entities or personal use or benefit of company assets. Unusual expenses should be vouched and particular attention should be devoted to traditionally sensitive areas such as travel and entertainment expenses. Some suspicious transactions are easily detected. Many illegal activities involve disguised transactions, but it is just as likely that the paid bills and supporting evidence will be fairly explanatory.

In the case of **penny stock fraud** schemes, the accountant may shift greater attention to the financial results and reports to shareholders, press releases and the like, to determine if evidence exists that such data were incorrect or inaccurate. Income recognition abuses or improper capitalization of expenses are typical categories of abuses used by penny stock promoters to misstate the operating results and mislead investors. In addition, the accountant should analyze key contracts, employment agreements, and other consulting arrangements. A time line analysis that reflects all key "publicized events" should be developed and used to determine if such events did occur. From the time line it can be determined whether, in the same time frame, all acquisitions or dispositions of assets and other financial transactions were accounted for properly.

Marital dissolution is another transactional area where the accountant can assist the attorney. Actual "liability" is usually not an issue in marital dissolutions. Most states have no-fault statutes that allow either party to seek a dissolution. The "liability" role of the accountant is to identify all assets and liabilities of the parties so that a fair and equitable distribution of assets results. Most family law courts are equity oriented, so the substance of transactions should carefully be considered when analyzing financial data. The forensic accountant has to examine financial data with concern for diversion of assets, improper cash transactions, and padded payroll and other fringe benefits and perks that may deprive the nonworking spouse of a fair share of the business's net worth as well as a share of spousal support.

If financial statements do not exist for closely held companies, such financial statements may need to be prepared. The accountant must be familiar with the local state family law. The accountant must also be familiar with tax implications of various asset transfers or split-ups so that neither spouse later finds unexpected tax consequences. The accountant should be aware of the proper handling of pension plan assets, individual retirement accounts, 401(k) plans, and the like, so that each party receives a fair share of assets, and so that income tax or excise taxes are not triggered unnecessarily.

In community property states, the existence of separate property and the impact of prenuptial agreements may also require analysis. Significant tracing of funds may become necessary if a total segregation of separate property assets has not been maintained. The marital community may have rights to a contribution for increased value of separate property that arises from services provided by the community after marriage. Lastly, the community may have some interest in separate property if joint tax returns have been filed and no separate tax cost was allocated to each category of assets.

34.17 BANKRUPTCY AND BANKRUPTCY FRAUDS. The work required to establish liability in bankruptcy cases is similar to that discussed in section 34.16 on transactional work, particularly in relation to white collar crime. One difference is that liability issues in bankruptcy have the benefit of explicit rules in the Bankruptcy Code (Title 11 USC, more specifically, §§ 543–549). These sections of the Bankruptcy Code detail the powers of a trustee to avoid transfers that defraud, hinder, or delay creditors, give preferential treatment to certain creditors, or do not give the bankrupt person or entity fair value for the transfer. Since these code sections define the scope of the trustee's power, an accountant engaged by the trustee should first read and understand the relevant provisions before planning the work. In addition, an accountant must obtain an understanding of certain sections of the Uniform Commercial Code and in particular the Uniform Fraudulent Transfer Act of the state where the business is situated. The location of the business may influence the scope of the work since the time period under the bankruptcy statute only allows for recovery one year prior to the bankruptcy, whereas state laws vary from 3 to 10 years.

Once the appropriate time period and scope have been determined, the accountant needs to review all material transactions to gain an understanding as to the economic benefit of the exchange to the bankrupt, including all monetary and nonmonetary exchanges. In addition, the accountant needs to determine the timing and explanation for any liens or other security interest granted or recorded during the time period. This review should include any asset sales, purchases, foreclosures, and tax assessments. Transactions between related entities or commonly controlled entities or their affiliates must be reviewed. Unlike the typical audit where discovery of fraud is not an objective unless it would materially misstate the financial statements, in a bankruptcy case the accountant is trying to develop **any** evidence that might show fraud or fraudulent intent.

A **preferential payment** analysis covers a review of transactions within 90 days (one year for insiders) prior to bankruptcy wherein a creditor is paid for an antecedent debt at a time the debtor is insolvent and such payment is not in the ordinary course of business. The definition of insolvency for this purpose is the fair value of assets compared with the fair value of liabilities—a balance sheet approach. "Ordinary course of business" is not defined except by reference to case precedents. For example, if creditors are routinely paid in 90 days but certain creditors get paid just before bankruptcy within 30 days, such payments are probably **not** in the ordinary course of business.

One area beginning to surface in possible cases of bankruptcy fraud is the **leveraged buyout transaction** (LBO). Certain LBOs have encountered financial difficulty shortly after consummation, and some creditors have used various security law and bankruptcy law theories to unwind these transactions and seek recoveries from selling shareholders, secured creditors, and others.

The accountant's work in establishing or defending liability is critical. Analyses that show the cash flow of the entity before and after the LBO help establish whether sufficient capital or working capital was available to the company. Changes in a company's borrowing, especially where a significant amount of assets have been recently pledged, also illustrate the potential damage to unsecured creditors. The accountant's ability to distinguish operating losses caused by the form and structure of the buyout from losses due to the economy or other competing companies will also assist counsel in determining whether the LBO can be attacked as a fraudulent transfer.

34.18 ECONOMIC FORECASTS AND PROJECTIONS.   Accountants are sometimes retained by attorneys to address liability issues in the areas of economic forecasts, projections, and market definitions. The accountant sometimes works with and assists other experts whose testimony has direct bearing on the financial issues of the case.

In antitrust cases, the accountant's insights into pricing and costs complement the economic expert's development of liability issues surrounding predatory pricing, price discrimination, and monopolistic behavior. Attorneys may use the accountant to assist an economist rather than to testify to these issues. Because of their familiarity with the underlying financial and accounting documents of the company, accounting experts are often used to assist marketing experts in liability issues related to market definition in antitrust cases and product substitution in patent and intellectual property cases.

CAUSATION AND DAMAGES

34.19 PROVING THE CAUSE OF DAMAGES.   The issues of causation and damages arise after the proof of liability. In discussing damages, we rely on the concept of the "but-for" world. The but-for world is the economic and physical environment that would have existed "but for" the actions of the defendant. In other words, it is the "undamaged" world, in contrast to the "actual," damaged world that did occur, and in which the defendant performed the alleged illegal acts.

In proving liability, the plaintiff must prove that the complained-of actions occurred and were illegal. In moving logically from liability toward damages, the plaintiff must demonstrate that the actions caused injury—that the but-for world arises logically out of the liability claims. Only then can the amount of damage be assessed.

This step is often omitted or glossed over. Often, the nexus between liability and damages is clear, and the act of calculating damages is enough to show the relationship. For example, if the lawsuit is over the loss of a specific contract, it may be obvious that damages should be the lost profit on that contract. However, there are situations where, if this step is overlooked, the plaintiff (and its expert accountant acting as damage witness) may not succeed in demonstrating its case.

As an example, consider the following situation. Company P's growth was at 20% during Year 1, and it has grown at that rate for many years. A conspiracy by two competitors, D1 and

D2, to injure P is alleged to have started on January 1, Year 2. This conspiracy consists of sharing internal information between D1 and D2, but does **not** affect market prices, customer perceptions, or any other external matters. Nevertheless, Company P's growth has fallen to 12% during Year 2, and it sues.

Assume that the conspiracy was illegal. It would be inappropriate for a damage expert to measure damages based on the 8% shortfall in expected growth. Growth is determined in the marketplace, and the liability acts do not have a clear relationship to actions by customers. Absent such a showing, whether through logic or quantitative analysis, a damage study based on the 8% shortfall would be flawed.

Often, in proving causation, the accountant must eliminate or take into account possible causes other than the complained-of liability acts. In the example above, the parties may have cut prices (legally), a new competitor may have entered the market, or a specific contract may have been lost (legally). In a securities case, where the allegation is that stock prices fell after bad news was released, it is possible that the entire market or industry declined at the same time. The accountant must analyze the specific facts and discriminate between legal and illegal causes and effects. Only after the link between the correct cause (liability) and effect (damages) is established can the accountant proceed to calculate damages.

34.20 PROVING THE AMOUNT OF DAMAGES

(a) Measures of Damages.   Depending on the case, there are many different standards by which damages are measured:

1. Lost profits (past profits, prospective profits, or both, including increased costs).
2. Lost asset value (the appraised value of identified assets, including goodwill, or other intangibles).
3. Lost personal earnings (wages, salary, etc.).
4. Lost royalties or licensing fees (amounts due for use of the plaintiff's assets or rights).

In most cases, these approaches are all attempts to compute the difference between the but-for world and the actual world. That is, an attempt to measure the difference between what **should have** happened and what **actually did** happen.

Lost profits are the most common standard for business cases. Valuations are used in both business disputes and marital dissolution proceedings. Personal earnings is the damages standard for the economic component of personal injury suits. (Other components are medical costs and pain and suffering.) Reasonable royalty is used in intellectual property disputes, especially patent cases.

The basics of a lost profits computation are discussed below, but valuation methods are beyond the scope of this chapter. Loss of personal earnings was mentioned briefly above; many of the principles of lost profits computation can be applied. Reasonable royalty computations depend to some extent on a lost profits analysis, but the specific requirements of a reasonable royalty analysis are also beyond the scope of this chapter. For more on reasonable royalty, see Frank and Wagner (1987).

(b) Mitigation.   A plaintiff has the obligation to mitigate damages. This means that the plaintiff must take reasonable steps to minimize the damages suffered. More specifically, the courts (and damages experts) will compute damages as if the plaintiff mitigated, whether the mitigation really occurred or not. Consider the following examples of mitigation:

1. Plaintiff company lost a production contract. Plaintiff should lay off staff, sell the product to someone else, cancel subcontractors or purchase orders, and so on. Damages would be lost revenues less unavoidable costs.

2. Plaintiff individual was injured and unable to work at his old job, which involved physical labor. However, his injuries allow him to perform office work. Plaintiff is obligated to look for an appropriate job, commensurate with his abilities and skills, which he is able to perform. Damages would be lost wages less alternative wages which were or should have been earned (plus, of course, damages for medical costs and pain and suffering).

3. Plaintiff had a binding contract with defendant for sale of plaintiff's business. Defendant breached. Plaintiff must make a good faith effort to find a new buyer. Damages would be computed as difference between the contract value and the market value that would be paid by a new buyer, plus any increased costs or time-value-of-money costs caused by the breach.

In many cases, reasonable mitigation will have occurred, and the expert may look at the difference between what should have occurred and what did occur as the measure of damages. After all, the plaintiff's recovery through litigation is uncertain, and plaintiff has every incentive to reduce damages to itself. However, if reasonable mitigation did not occur, the accountant should make the necessary adjustments.

34.21 QUANTIFYING LOSSES UNDER THE LOST PROFITS APPROACH. Basically, the procedure to follow in quantifying losses is to determine lost sales volume and the related incremental revenue, consider the plaintiff's capacity to produce, and compute the costs associated with generating the projected revenue.

Lost profits may be computed using either the **incremental** or **overall** methods. Under the incremental method, all incremental (additional) revenues and costs are computed; the difference between incremental revenues and incremental costs is the lost profit. Under the overall method, the company's overall revenues and costs (historical plus incremental) are computed; lost profits are the difference between historical and but-for profits. For more on the basics of lost profits, see Sims and Haller (1988).

If done carefully, the incremental and overall methods are identical. In practice, errors may occur in applying the incremental method because incremental costs are overlooked. In particular, this may happen when, in the but-for world, the cost of an **historical** activity changes. For example, assume 200 units of raw material were purchased historically for $10 per unit. In the but-for world, 300 units would be required. Due to volume discounts, the material can be purchased at $9 per unit. A pure incremental analysis would compute incremental costs as 100 units times $9 per unit, or $900. This is wrong, for it fails to take into account the cost savings on the 200 historical units. Either an overall analysis or a proper incremental analysis would show the incremental cost to be $(300 \times \$9) - (200 \times \$10) = \$700$.

Quantifying lost profits is essentially a three-step procedure:

(i) Determine Lost Sales Volume and the Related Incremental Revenues. Lost sales volume should be estimated based on the liability theory of the but-for world. Often, certain benchmarks are used to establish lost sales. Some common methods are:

The Direct Approach. In many cases, the facts support a direct computation of lost sales. For example, in a breach of contract matter, the contract may call for a certain quantity of product to be produced.

The Before-and-After Approach. Compare sales or sales growth before the liability act to the comparable figures afterward.

The Yardstick (or Benchmark) Approach. Compare the subject company to other companies or to industry averages. This requires the accountant to conclude that, but for the liability acts, the subject company would have performed as well as the comparable company or the industry average. If the defendant has gained the sales lost by the plaintiff, a comparison to the plaintiff may be appropriate. A variation of this method incorporates the before-and-after approach: Compare the subject company to a standard or the industry average before the liability act; use that relationship to project the but-for world.

The Market Forecast Approach. Project the market or the company's market share directly based on other evidence in the case. Sometimes, prior market forecasts are available. In other circumstances, the accountant may make the forecast or rely on another expert or witness in the case to provide the forecast.

A sales forecast may be made in units or dollars. If units are used, the forecast must be converted into dollars by using an assumed price. The accountant should consider whether the but-for economic environment would result in different prices than the actual environment. If the plaintiff was illegally constraining prices (for example, through predatory pricing or producing goods in violation of a patent), the but-for price may be higher than the historical price. If the plaintiff illegally constrained competition (for example, through antitrust violations), the historical price may be too high.

The combination of the sales forecast and but-for prices yields a but-for revenue projection.

(ii) Consider the Plaintiff's Capacity to Produce.   The plaintiff must be able to produce the projected sales for them to be recoverable as damages. If the plaintiff is selling all it can produce, the incremental sales forecast may not be achievable.

Capacity can always be expanded, but at a cost. Within some production range, there are no significant production constraints. If projected sales are within this range, the analysis may be straightforward. Beyond this range, the plaintiff may only be able to expand production by adding overtime, moving to a second or third shift, or by building additional production facilities. If the plaintiff's claim requires an expansion of production capacity, the accountant must evaluate the increased capacity for three factors: reasonableness, timing, and cost.

Reasonableness may be judged by a company's responses to similar situations. When capacity constraints arose in the past, did the company expand, or did it simply operate with constraints? Were additional shifts or mandatory overtime instituted to expand capacity, or were capital expenditures made? If additional shifts or hours were run, was this a long-term solution, or was it only until additional capacity could be constructed? Is the increased demand permanent, or it is better to lose sales now to avoid excess capacity later? How does increased demand relate to production of the company's other products?

Once reasonableness is established, **timing** must be considered. Can capacity be expanded quickly? What lead time is required? What evidence of increased demand does company management require before committing to an expansion? Are there supply constraints on getting the required capital goods?

Finally, consider **cost.** How much will the expanded capacity cost? If required production is within the usual production range, a special cost analysis may not be needed. If overtime, shift differentials, or capital expenditures are required, their costs should be estimated.

(iii) Compute the Costs Associated with Generating the Projected Revenue.   The accountant must be careful to identify all costs associated with projected revenue. As with revenues, either a total cost or incremental cost approach may be appropriate. Costs include both capacity expansion costs (see above) and ordinary production, selling, and administrative costs.

Costs may be estimated using a variety of techniques. Among the most common are:

Direct Assignment. Costs are specifically identified and associated with the incremental sales. This is often used for direct costs, such as materials and direct labor.

Cost Allocations. Accounting or engineering judgments are used to allocate costs to units. The techniques used are similar to those of cost accounting. In allocating costs, it is important to have a thorough understanding of the magnitude of the incremental volume, and of the related fixed and variable costs. Costs which are considered fixed for a small change in volume may be variable for a larger change.

Statistical Methods. Statistical methods, especially regression analysis, may be used to find the relationship between historical costs and volumes. Once such a relationship is established, it may be used to estimate costs for the but-for volume. These methods are powerful, but require significant training to apply correctly.

For more on cost estimation methods, see Kinrich (1990).

34.22 OTHER ISSUES. Besides the basic procedures for determining lost profits, there are other issues to take into consideration.

(a) Cash Flow. When accountants speak of lost profits, they often mean net income according to GAAP. However, in computing damages, it may be appropriate to measure lost cash flow. The computation of net income includes numerous accounting conventions and techniques (depreciation, LIFO, etc.) that may not reflect actual out-of-pocket losses. Depending on the legal standard, lost cash flow may be more appropriate. Even if net income is the proper standard, cash flow is clearly relevant if interest is to be earned on past damages.

(b) Interest on Damage Awards. Some or all of most damage awards are to compensate for past losses. In order to be made whole in economic terms, it might be supposed that the plaintiff should earn interest on past losses from the date of loss to the date of payment. However, the law does not always allow interest, and when it does, the interest rate is not always the rate applicable to the economic circumstances.

In general, the treatment of interest is governed by the applicable law. The courts distinguish between prejudgment interest (accrued between the date of loss and the date of trial or final judgment) and postjudgment interest (accrued from the date of judgment to the date of payment, which can be years if the judgment is appealed). In some jurisdictions, the rate of interest is set by law, often at a rate between 6% and 10%. Depending on the case, some jurisdictions do not allow prejudgment interest; most allow postjudgment interest.

Some interest awards are within the province of the court. Some judges may allow calculations of interest to go to the jury as part of the damage claim; others may reserve the right to separately compute interest (either at the statutory rate or at a rate depending on proof) after the jury awards damages. If the court allows economic testimony as to the amount of interest, what is the proper approach? The accountant should determine interest by recreating what would have happened to the plaintiff had the money been received at the times the damage claim asserts. The issues to be analyzed include:

The Amount of Cash That Would Have Been Received. This is not necessarily the amount of net income. Adjustments should be made for changes in working capital, capital expenditures, depreciation, repayment of principal, and so on.

The Income Taxes That Would Be Paid on the Income. Interest should be calculated on after-tax cash available for investment, as that is the amount that would be available in the but-for world. Only if net income approximates cash flow would a calculation based on net income be acceptable.

The Interest Rate That Would Have Been Enjoyed by the Defendant. The courts reject any ''speculative'' damage claim, including a speculative interest rate. This means that it is normally inappropriate to treat interest as equivalent to a lost investment opportunity (since the results of that investment may be speculative), thereby computing interest as a return on equity. Appropriate interest rates may include the defendant's borrowing rate (if defendant has debt outstanding), money market rates, short-term or long-term government rates (T-bills or bonds), or the prime rate. The choice of rate depends on circumstances.

Taxes to Be Paid on Interest Earned. Interest earned is subject to taxes. If a before-tax interest rate is used, taxes must be subtracted before compounding the interest in future periods. Alternatively, an after-tax interest rate may be used. For more on the treatment of taxes, see below.

(c) Present Value and Inflation.   Future damages must be discounted to present value. The choice of discount rate depends on circumstances. A nominal discount rate (such as the T-bill rate, the prime rate, or any other market rate) includes both a real rate of interest and an inflation premium. If the damages into the future are computed in constant (uninflated) dollars, then discounting at a real rate (net of inflation) may be appropriate. If inflation has been built into the projected damage figures, a nominal interest rate is correct. In either case, the appropriate discount rate should include an adjustment for risk.

(d) Income Taxes.   Under the law, some damage awards are taxable to the recipient, whereas others are tax-free. In computing damages, the goal is to properly account for taxes so the plaintiff is in the same position as it would have been if the liability act had never occurred.

If the award is taxable, then the damages should be computed on a before-tax basis. The plaintiff then receives the damage award, pays taxes, and is in the proper after-tax position. If the amount is tax-free, only the after-tax amount should be assessed as damages.

Complications arise in the two areas: (1) if prejudgment interest is due, and (2) if tax rates have changed from the damage date to the payment date. As discussed above, prejudgment interest is computed on the after-tax amount, since that is the amount the plaintiff would have had to invest. However, if the award is taxable, the damages must be expressed in pretax dollars. The solution is simple. Compute the entire award, including damages and interest, in after-tax dollars. Then, gross up the award by the tax rate in the year of payment. When the plaintiff receives this amount and pays tax on it, plaintiff will be in the proper after-tax position. This approach, although accurate, has been relatively untested in court.

A similar situation arises if tax rates have changed. If pretax damages are used, the change in tax rates will result in an incorrect after-tax award. The solution is again to compute the after-tax amounts, then gross up the award for the current tax rate.

SUPPORT FOR OPINIONS

34.23 SOURCES OF INFORMATION.   The accountant must be aware of the many facts and statistics that relate to the subject and issues of the case and must have adequate data to authoritatively support opinions or conclusions. The data should be of high reliability since the accountant is subject to cross-examination.

There are two basic sources for data: the litigating parties (either the client or the opposition), and external sources, such as industry publications, economic statistics, and so on. The former is obtained through the discovery phase discussed previously. The latter is discussed here.

Many reference books list sources of business information. Two recommended by Sheppard and Carroll (1990) are *Encyclopedia of Business Information Sources* (Woy, 1988), and *Where to Find Business Information* (Brownstone and Carruth, 1982).

Computer databases are widely available and eliminate the need for data entry as the information can be downloaded into a computer file. Sheppard and Carroll (1990) mention the following computer database references: *Directory of Online Databases* (Cuadra and Elsevier, 1990), *The Computer Data and Database Source Book* (Lesko, 1984), and *Complete Guide to Dial-Up Databases,* (Datapro Research, 1985).

Often, an accountant may need to call on other experts or persons knowledgeable in the particular industry. A few state CPA societies have formed litigation services committees that the accountant may contact. Also, a research library may have an index of experts who can be contacted.

For a more comprehensive list of sources, see Sheppard and Carroll (1990).

34.24 RELIANCE ON OTHERS. The accountant as an expert witness may rely on the work of employees as well as personal research or sources in forming his opinion. Federal Rule of Evidence No. 703 describes permissible bases on which expert testimony may be founded: (1) information acquired through firsthand observation, (2) facts observed by, or presented to, the expert witness at the trial or at the hearing, (3) data considered by the expert witness outside of court. Rule 703 permits an expert to rely on facts that are not normally admissible in evidence if they are of a type reasonably relied on by experts in the field. "Reasonably" means trustworthy. "Type relied on" is left to the discretion of the trial judge. In turn, the judge may question the accountant-witness as to the appropriate degree of reliance.

34.25 DOCUMENTATION. All materials prepared, accumulated, or referred to by the accountant acting as an expert witness in a case may be made available to the opposing side. At the outset the attorney and accountant should develop a clear understanding of exactly what the accountant will be preparing and retaining for the engagement. Then the accountant should carefully control the content of work papers and correct or avoid collecting materials that are irrelevant to forming an opinion. This should be an ongoing process, as the accountant may not be able to remove anything after receiving a subpoena. All work products of an expert may be discoverable and could be thoroughly scrutinized by the opposing party. Errors, inconsistencies, and irrelevant materials may form the basis for an effective challenge to the testimony of the accountant.

34.26 ENGAGEMENT LETTERS. The accountant may feel that it is appropriate to issue an engagement letter specifying the engagement's purpose, the tasks that need to be performed, and the terms of compensation. If the accountant is identified as an expert witness, the opposing party can discover the engagement letter. If, due to subsequent events, tasks enumerated in the engagement letter are not completed or are completed with adverse consequences to the accountant's client, opposing counsel may use this information to imply that the accountant's opinion is defective, or that the accountant did not perform all the analyses required to substantiate the conclusions presented. Accordingly, under many circumstances the engagement letter should describe the tasks in general terms only.

TESTIMONY

Testimony is the ultimate result of expert witness work. This section provides advice on giving testimony and suggestions for the expert.

34.27 GIVING DEPOSITION TESTIMONY. A deposition of an expert witness is part of the discovery process in which counsel seeks to fulfill several major objectives. The most obvious objective is to find out what opinions the expert is going to offer at trial, and why. A deposition is also an opportunity to commit the expert to sworn testimony that can later be used for impeachment purposes, should the expert try to change his opinion. Additionally, counsel will use the deposition to assess the expert's effectiveness as a witness and the strength of the case for purposes of settlement negotiation and development of trial strategy. Consequently, expert depositions may be more important than the trial testimony and should be regarded with due respect.

Adequate preparation is crucial to giving an effective deposition. Naturally, a thorough review of one's opinions and underlying support is in order. The expert should also review any prior writings and testimony for previous positions that may be construed as contradictory. Being caught unaware in an apparent contradiction can have a debilitating effect on the credibility of a deponent's testimony. Know the information and sources relied on, the various analyses performed, the opinions reached, and the strengths as well as the weaknesses of the case. Above all, tell the truth.

Finally, insist on a detailed predeposition briefing with counsel. This briefing should include a conclusion regarding disclosure strategy. If the objective is to cause a settlement to occur, a complete disclosure of all the strengths of the case should be made. If the case is likely to proceed to trial, then a restrictive approach may be called for, in which the expert should answer only the question asked and should not volunteer related issues to opposing counsel.

There are some general rules an expert should follow when giving a deposition:

- *Bring No Documentation unless Required or Advised by Counsel.* To do so will only make opposing counsel more effective in conducting discovery and provide additional avenues of questions. Of course if the deposition is in response to a subpoena, all documents identified in that subpoena must be provided.

- *Think before Answering and Do Not Answer unless You Are Sure You Understand the Question.* Word crafting is an attorney's stock in trade. If a question is not totally understood, at best the answer will be unresponsive. At worst, the *accountant* may fall into a trap. Or, the attorney may not even understand his own question, and the response will only serve to lead the attorney to more effective questioning.

- *Answer Questions Directly—Then Stop.* Do not fill dead air, ramble, or volunteer information. The "pregnant pause" is a favorite gambit to elicit additional information when opposing counsel is not quite sure what to ask next and wants the expert's help.

- *Stop Talking and Listen When Your Counsel Objects.* The question may be improper, or the accountant's counsel may have noticed the infamous "trick" question. Common trick questions include the use of compound questions, double negatives, absolute terms, and prefacing a question with a misstatement of prior testimony.

  Absolute terms are typified by questions such as, "Were those **all** the documents you reviewed?" or, "Are those **all** your opinions regarding this case?" An affirmative answer may preclude a temporarily forgotten item that is important to the case from later being cited at trial. Consequently, if appropriate, qualify with responses such as, "Those are the items that I recall at the present time."

  A misstatement of prior testimony typically starts with, "Earlier you testified. . . ," and ends with a question which is often not directly related to the mischaracterized testimony. By answering the question while failing to correct the mischaracterization, an argument can be made that the witness agrees with the misstatement.

- *Refuse to Engage in Speculation.* Either the expert knows the answer or does not know. Opposing counsel may have the fact in hand and is hoping to trap the expert in a conflict. Being asked to interpret an unfamiliar document can be particularly treacherous. Likewise, an incorrect guess on a forgotten minor detail can be as damaging as an error on a major one. Do not be afraid to respond "I don't know" or "I don't recall." No one knows everything and very few, if any, people have perfect recall.

- *Resist Being Provoked into Anger or Arguing with Counsel.* Chances are the provocation is calculated, and there is no upside potential. Anger will cloud reasoned logic and possibly blind the expert to a trap that is just about to open.

- *Review the Court Reporter's Transcript, Correct All Errors and Typographical Errors, and Sign.* Once the deposition has been completed and the court reporter has prepared a transcript, read your testimony carefully. If you said something you did not mean, now is the only time you will have to change it.

34.28 GIVING TRIAL TESTIMONY

(a) Direct Testimony.   The objective of direct testimony is to present an opinion in a manner such that it will be understood and believed by the judge and jury. The testimony will begin by reviewing the witness's qualifications, which provide the prerequisite skill and training enabling the witness to provide the court with expert testimony.

The expert's opinions then will be solicited. It is imperative that the expert not appear to be an advocate for the plaintiff or defendant, but rather fair and unbiased. The job of advocacy should be reserved for the attorney. Violation of this precept will tend to undermine the expert's credibility.

Finally, the basis for the expert's opinion will be presented. The engagement scope is reviewed, including who retained the expert and why, documents reviewed, interviews conducted, the engagement team, manner of supervision and time spent, compensation, and any engagement scope limitations imposed. Next the methodology employed is explained, which leads to the conclusions and opinions reached. Typically any weaknesses are acknowledged and explained in a preemptive fashion to reduce potential damage on cross-examination.

The key to persuasive and effective testimony is communication. The expert's position may be a technical marvel, but it is worthless if the jury is not convinced. Therefore, the expert should speak English and eliminate accounting and financial jargon. Concepts should be explained by way of common, everyday occurrences. Condescending or patronizing speech is inappropriate. There is an old saying: "If you can't say it in simple English, you don't understand it." You can be sure that if you do not express it in simple terms, the judge or jury will not understand it.

The expert's job is to educate the jury and the court in an interesting fashion. This job can be facilitated by the use of and reference to trial exhibits. It is difficult to devote too much attention to trial exhibits. Trial exhibits are used to lead the jury, court, and oneself through the basis of the opinion, as well as to keep everyone's attention focused. Like the language used in testimony, the exhibits should be kept clear and simple so the point is unmistakable and memorable. In many jurisdictions, the jury cannot take notes, and visual exhibits are the most effective method to ensure a point or conclusion is remembered.

(b) Cross-Examination.   The purpose of cross-examination is to cast doubt on or, if possible, undermine the expert witness's credibility and testimony. One of the simpler ways to accomplish this objective is through impeachment. Consequently, a thorough review of prior testimony, writings, and the deposition transcript is required. Make sure you are not on record as holding a view that is or appears to be contrary to the one you are now presenting, or be able to provide an explanation.

Be calm and polite, even if opposing counsel is manipulating responses. The expert is in the attorney's ballpark, and any anger will be turned against the witness. Cross-examining attorneys will frequently use "yes/no" questions to manipulate an opposing expert. The expert should generally resist the tendency to provide lengthy qualifications to such questions, as a skilled attorney may succeed in having the expert admonished by the court to answer only the question asked. An admonishment will taint the expert in the jury's mind, as well as leave the expert with less maneuvering room during the remainder of cross-examination. However, this is not to suggest the expert should timidly follow the yes/no trail. Make explanations when necessary.

Another favored approach is the hypothetical question. Care must be taken not to appear too defensive or restrictive when answering a hypothetical question. Select the appropriate moment to cleanly sever the link between the hypothetical and the reality of the case at hand. Finally, remember that redirect examination can rehabilitate mischaracterizations by opposing counsel. So even if you must admit something that appears damaging, you will have a chance to explain why the admission is irrelevant in the current context.

If opposing counsel has discovered an error, the expert should acknowledge the error, but not necessarily the implications or conclusions drawn by counsel. Again, redirect examination can salvage errors, especially immaterial errors.

It is important to know the opposing expert's opinion and basis, and the key differences between both experts' work. The ultimate objective of cross-examination is to get the expert to agree with the opposing expert's opinion and basis. Nearly as damaging is an acknowledgment that the opposing expert is a leading expert in the field. Failing this, an admission that reasonable minds can differ is a likely parting shot.

The expert must also be prepared for questions concerning fees and any scope limitations, especially if opposing counsel has not engaged an expert witness. A comfortable, matter-of-fact response is called for. The expert is a professional who has been asked to conduct certain analyses and offer an opinion. This is not unlike any other engagement an accountant conducts, and you should not feel guilty about being compensated for your time and effort.

Finally, the expert must stay within his field of expertise. By straying, the expert will end up in unnecessary difficulties.

(c) Redirect Examination.   The purpose of redirect examination is to rehabilitate points made by the opponent and clarify responses and mischaracterizations. It is generally counterproductive to a witness's credibility to argue with opposing counsel or to resist answering questions which, to the jury, appear reasonable and straightforward. An evasive witness generally is a less credible witness. The expert is back in friendly hands during redirect, and this is the time to mitigate real or perceived damage.

During the redirect examination the attorney will typically select two or three areas where additional explanation is necessary to counter the points made on cross-examination. This is the witness's opportunity to clearly explain **why** the points made during cross-examination are irrelevant and have no bearing on the expert's opinion.

SOURCES AND SUGGESTED REFERENCES

American Institute of Certified Public Accountants, *Code of Professional Conduct*, AICPA, New York, 1988.

——, Auditing Standards Board, *Statement on Standards for Accountants' Services on Prospective Financial Information,* "Attestation Standards," AICPA, New York, 1986.

——, Auditing Standards Board, *Statement on Standards for Accountants' Services on Prospective Financial Information*, "Financial Forecasts and Projections," AICPA, New York, 1985.

Black, Henry C., *Black's Law Dictionary*, 5th ed., West Publishing, St. Paul, MN, 1979.

Brownstone, David M., and Carruth, Gorton, *Where to Find Business Information*, 2nd ed., Wiley, New York, 1982.

Cuadra, Carlos, and Elsevier, *Directory of Online Databases,* Cuadra/Elsevier, New York, 1990.

Datapro Research Corp., *Complete Guide to Dial-Up Databases,* Datapro Research Corp., Delran, NJ, 1985.

Dunn, Robert L., *Recovery of Damages for Lost Profits*, 3rd ed., Lawpress, Tiburon, CA, 1987.

Dykeman, Francis C., *Forensic Accounting: The Accountant as Expert Witness,* Wiley, New York, 1982.

Frank, Peter B., and Wagner, Michael J., "Computing Lost Profits and Reasonable Royalties," *AIPLA Quarterly Journal,* Vol. 15, No. 4, AIPLA, Arlington, VA, 1987, pp. 391–425.

Frank, Peter B., Wagner, Michael J., and Weil, Roman L., eds., *Litigation Services Handbook: The Role of the Accountant As Expert Witness,* Wiley, New York, 1990.

Kinrich, Jeffrey H., "Cost Estimation," in *Litigation Services Handbook: The Role of the Accountant As Expert Witness* by Frank, Peter B., Wagner, Michael J., and Weil, Roman L., eds., Wiley, New York, 1990.

Knapp, Charles L., *Commercial Damages,* Matthew Bender, New York, 1986.

Kraft, Melvin D., *Using Experts in Civil Cases,* Practising Law Institute, New York, 1977.

Lesko, Matthew, *The Computer Data and Database Source Book,* Avon Books, New York, 1984.

Newton, Grant W., *Bankruptcy and Insolvency Accounting,* Wiley, New York, 1989.

Sheppard, Howard R., and Carroll, Susan E., "Where to Get the Data," in *Litigation Services Handbook: The Role of the Accountant As Expert Witness* by Frank, Peter B., Wagner, Michael J., and Weil, Roman L., eds., Wiley, New York, 1990.

Sims, Raymond S., and Haller, Mark W., "Lost Profits: Covering All the Bases in the 'But For' World," *Inside Litigation,* Vol. 2, No. 4, Prentice-Hall Law & Business, New York, February 1988.

Wagner, Michael J., and Frank, Peter B., *Litigation Services: Management Advisory Services Technical Consulting Practice Aid No. 7,* AICPA, New York, 1986.

Wagner, Michael J., and Hurd, Dale R., "Securities Act Violations: Computation of Damages," in *Litigation Services Handbook: The Role of the Accountant As Expert Witness* by Frank, Peter B., Wagner, Michael J., and Weil, Roman L., eds., Wiley, New York, 1990.

Woy, James, ed., *Encyclopedia of Business Information Sources,* 7th ed., Gale Research Inc., Detroit, 1988.

PART VII

TOPICS IN AUDITING AND MANAGEMENT INFORMATION SYSTEMS

CHAPTER 35

AUDITING STANDARDS AND AUDIT REPORTS

Dan M. Guy, PhD, CPA
American Institute of Certified Public Accountants

Alan J. Winters, PhD, CPA
University of South Carolina

Mimi Blanco-Best, CPA
American Institute of Certified Public Accountants

CONTENTS

The views of Mr. Guy and Ms. Blanco-Best, as expressed in this publication, do not necessarily reflect the views of the AICPA. Official positions are determined through certain specific committee procedures, due process, and deliberation.

SERVICES OFFERED BY INDEPENDENT ACCOUNTANTS

35.1 CLASSIFICATION OF SERVICES.   The term **independent accountant** is used interchangeably with **independent auditor** and **independent public accountant.** Generally, the term
is limited to either CPAs or public accountants licensed to perform audits and express
opinions on financial statements under applicable state accountancy laws.

Because they are knowledgeable about accounting principles and accounting systems, tax
matters, and the like, independent accountants provide a wide range of services in addition to
audits. These include accounting and review services, tax services, management advisory
services, personal financial planning, and other types of special service.

35.2 AUDITING SERVICES.   An audit involves the application of a variety of procedures
and techniques to obtain evidential matter sufficient for the independent accountant to
express an informed opinion about whether the financial statements conform with GAAP.
When serving as an auditor, the independent accountant is guided by a Code of Professional
Conduct and a variety of standards promulgated by professional bodies established for that
purpose.

Rule of Conduct 202 of the AICPA's Code of Professional Conduct provides:

A member who performs auditing, review, compilation, management advisory, tax or other professional services shall comply with standards promulgated by bodies designated by . . . [the AICPA].

(a) Generally Accepted Auditing Standards. Ten generally accepted auditing standards (GAAS) are cited by *AICPA Professional Standards* (AU 150):

GENERAL STANDARDS

1. **Competence.** The audit is to be performed by a person or persons having adequate technical training and proficiency as an auditor.
2. **Independence.** In all matters relating to the assignment, an independence in mental attitude is to be maintained by the auditor or auditors.
3. **Due care.** Due professional care is to be exercised in the performance of the audit and the preparation of the report.

STANDARDS OF FIELD WORK

4. **Planning and supervision.** The work is to be adequately planned and assistants, if any, are to be properly supervised.
5. **Internal control.** A sufficient understanding of the internal control structure is to be obtained to plan the audit and to determine the nature, timing, and extent of tests to be performed.
6. **Evidence.** Sufficient competent evidential matter is to be obtained through inspection, observation, inquiries, and confirmations to afford a reasonable basis for an opinion regarding the financial statements under audit.

STANDARDS OF REPORTING

7. **Generally accepted accounting principles.** The report shall state whether the financial statements are presented in accordance with generally accepted accounting principles.
8. **Consistency.** The report shall identify those circumstances in which such principles have been consistently observed in the current period in relation to the preceding period.
9. **Disclosure.** Informative disclosures in the financial statements are to be regarded as reasonably adequate unless otherwise stated in the report.
10. **Expression of opinion.** The report shall either contain an expression of opinion regarding the financial statements, taken as a whole, or an assertion to the effect that an opinion cannot be expressed. When an overall opinion cannot be expressed, the reasons therefor should be stated. In all cases where an auditor's name is associated with financial statements, the report should contain a clear-cut indication of the character of the auditor's work, if any, and the degree of responsibility the auditor is taking.

(b) Statements on Auditing Standards. SASs are pronouncements issued by the Auditing Standards Board (ASB) of the AICPA to guide auditing practice. As Rule 202 indicates, SASs are enforceable under the Code; but perhaps of equal importance, courts generally view adherence to SASs as the standard for assessing an auditor's liability.

SASs specify required auditing procedures, provide guidance on important areas of judgment often encountered in audits, and establish the form and content of the auditor's report. They are issued individually in a numbered series and are codified in a loose-leaf service. Bound versions of the loose-leaf service are issued periodically and provide the most convenient form for use in practice.

(c) Auditing Interpretations. Interpretations of SASs are issued by the AICPA staff but are reviewed by members of the ASB before publication. They deal with the application of SASs to particular circumstances, thus are usually more limited and specific in coverage. After publication, they are included in the loose-leaf service and published in the *Journal of Accountancy*.

35.3 ACCOUNTING SERVICES.   Accounting services include all forms of involvement with financial statements or financial information other than an audit, such as bookkeeping, compilation of financial statements from a trial balance, and review of financial statements.

(a) Nonpublic Company.   The accountant's responsibilities for the unaudited financial statements of a nonpublic company are set forth in Statements on Standards for Accounting and Review Services (SSARS), a numbered series of pronouncements issued by the Accounting and Review Services Committee of the AICPA. Technically, an accountant is not "associated" with the unaudited financial statements of a nonpublic company under SSARS No. 1, "Compilation and Review of Financial Statements" (AR 100) but has a similar reporting obligation:

> An accountant should not consent to the use of his name in a document or written communication containing unaudited financial statements of a nonpublic entity unless (a) he has compiled or reviewed the financial statements and his report accompanies them, or (b) the financial statements are accompanied by an indication that the accountant has not compiled or reviewed the financial statements and he assumes no responsibility for them.

> The accountant should not submit unaudited financial statements of a nonpublic entity to his client or others unless, as a minimum, he complies with the provisions of this statement applicable to a compilation engagement.

Thus the only types of report an accountant may issue in connection with the unaudited financial statements of a nonpublic company are for the accounting services of a compilation or review. These services are defined as follows in SSARS No. 1 (AR 100):

> **Compilation.** Presenting in the form of financial statements information that is the representation of management (owners) without undertaking to express any assurance on the statements.

> **Review.** Performing inquiry and analytical procedures that provide the accountant with a reasonable basis for expressing limited assurance that there are no material modifications that should be made to the statements in order for them to be in conformity with generally accepted accounting principles or, if applicable, with another comprehensive basis of accounting.

An accountant may provide a variety of other accounting services to a nonpublic client, such as preparing a trial balance, assisting in adjusting books, or providing various manual, automated, or electronic bookkeeping services. However, if the accountant issues financial statements as a result of these services, he must issue a compilation report under SSARS No. 1.

(b) Public Company.   A public company is defined by SAS No. 26, "Association with Financial Statements" (AU 504), as:

> [a]ny entity (a) whose securities trade in a public market either on a stock exchange (domestic or foreign) or in the over-the-counter market, including securities quoted only locally or regionally, (b) that makes a filing with a regulatory agency in preparation for the sale of any class of its securities in a public market, or (c) a subsidiary, corporate joint venture, or other entity controlled by an entity covered by (a) or (b).

The accountant looks to pronouncements of the ASB when dealing with the unaudited financial statements (information) of a public company. The unaudited financial statements of a public company may be reviewed in accordance with SAS No. 36, "Review of Interim Financial Information" (AU 722), when they are interim statements. Interim statements include 12-month statements with a closing date other than the normal year-end.

35.4 RELATED SERVICES.   In addition to the typical accounting and auditing services related to financial statements, the training and the experience of independent public accountants qualify them to provide a wide variety of tax services, management advisory services, personal financial planning, and other special services. In carrying out such engagements, a member of the AICPA complies with the general standards for professional competence, due care, planning and supervision, and sufficient relevant data as set forth in Rule 201 of the AICPA's Code of Professional Conduct. Other, more specific standards may apply for particular types of engagements, such as those involving prospective information.

(a) **Tax Services.**   The accountant may be called on to deal with a variety of tax problems, including those involving federal and state income taxes, estate and inheritance taxes, sales and use taxes, payroll taxes, and property taxes. The field of **income taxes** is especially important. The services rendered by the accountant in this area include determination of taxable income, preparation of tax returns and claims for refunds, representation of clients before taxing authorities, and cooperation with lawyers in the settlement of tax suits by litigation. The AICPA publishes Statements on Responsibilities in Tax Practice for the guidance of its members.

(b) **Management Advisory Services.**   The AICPA's Management Services Executive Committee issues pronouncements related to the conduct of so-called management advisory services. Statement on Standards for Management Advisory Services No. 1, "Definition and Standards for MAS Practice," (MS 11) describes management advisory services as "the function of providing advice and technical assistance where the primary purpose is to help the client improve the use of its capabilities and resources to achieve its objectives." Services provided may involve activities such as:

1. Counseling management in its analysis, planning, organizing, operating, and controlling functions.
2. Conducting special studies, preparing recommendations, proposing plans and programs, and providing advice and technical assistance in their implementation.
3. Reviewing and suggesting improvement of policies, procedures, systems, methods, and organizational relationships.
4. Introducing new ideas, concepts, and methods to management.

(c) **Other Special Services.**   The independent public accountant may be called on to make **special investigations** or to **report in connection with the special requirements of a government agency.** Those services may require aspects of tax, management advisory, and accounting and auditing skills.

Special investigations often involve application of agreed-upon procedures to specified elements, accounts, or items of a financial statement. For example, an auditor may apply agreed-upon procedures in connection with a proposed acquisition, claims of a creditor, or costs under government or other contracts under SAS No. 35, "Special Reports—Applying Agreed-Upon Procedures to Specified Elements Accounts or Items of a Financial Statement" (AU 622).

The investigation of a client's merger candidate may involve a full-scale audit, but it often is limited to application of agreed-upon procedures to selected accounts or unaudited financial statements. Procedures requested may entail a review of the candidate's accounting principles and practices, and an evaluation of important assets (e.g., receivables, inventories, and property), liabilities including contingencies, and commitments. The accountant follows the guidance in SAS No. 35 when agreed-upon procedures are applied to selected accounts. This type of engagement is discussed in section 35.16.

An accountant may be requested to apply and describe limited procedures for underwriters when unaudited information is included in a registration statement filed with the SEC. Guidance for such services is found in SAS No. 49, "Letters for Underwriters" (AU 634). Similar services may be provided for unaudited financial statements in connection with acquisition agreements. In that circumstance, SAS No. 26 "Association with Financial Statements" (AU 504) provides that acceptance and performance of such an engagement is appropriate if the applicable requirements for a letter for underwriters are met.

Certain regulatory agencies require that the report of an independent public accountant accompany information filed with them. Those reports may be in connection with specified amounts reflected in filed schedules, such as schedules required by the Federal Power Commission in connection with rate filings. Other reports relate to compliance with a specific regulatory requirement or to systems of internal control. Guidance for such reports may be found in SAS No. 62, "Special Reports" (AU 623), and in SAS No. 30, "Reporting on Internal Accounting Control" (AU 642), both of which are discussed in the section "Other Reports."

THE AUDIT PROCESS

35.5 OBJECTIVE OF THE AUDIT.   *AICPA Professional Standards* (AU 110) states that "the objective of the ordinary audit of financial statements by the independent auditor is the expression of an opinion on the fairness with which they present fairly, in all material respects, financial position, results of operations, and cash flows in conformity with generally accepted accounting principles." The process designed to achieve that objective is complex. It involves the application of numerous procedures and the coordination of many activities. Although those procedures and activities overlap, the audit process encompasses:

1. *Planning.* The development of an overall approach to the conduct of an audit.
2. *Execution.* Steps taken to accomplish the audit plan.
3. *Evaluation.* A critical evaluation of the work carried out on the audit.

35.6 PLANNING THE AUDIT.   Planning is a continuous process that occurs throughout the audit. SAS No. 22, "Planning and Supervision" (AU 311), states that:

Audit planning involves developing an overall strategy for the expected conduct and scope of the audit. The nature, extent, and timing of planning vary with the size and complexity of the entity, experience with the entity, and knowledge of the entity's business. In planning the audit, the auditor should consider, among other matters:

a. Matters relating to the entity's business and the industry in which it operates.
b. The entity's accounting policies and procedures.
c. The methods used by entity to process significant accounting information, including the use of service organizations such as outside service centers.
d. Planned assessed level of control risk.
e. Preliminary judgments about materiality levels for audit purposes.
f. Financial statement items likely to require adjustment.
g. Conditions that may require extension or modification of audit tests, such as the possibility of material errors or irregularities or the existence of related party transactions.
h. The nature of reports expected to be rendered.

Proper planning is essential to efficient and effective auditing. Consequently, seasoned auditors ordinarily are involved in the planning process. Evidence of planning is documented by planning memoranda, work papers dealing with the independent auditor's understanding of the business and internal control structure, and **written audit programs,** including modifications necessary as the audit proceeds.

(a) Engagement Letter.   A clear understanding of the services to be performed ordinarily is established with the client by use of an engagement letter. An engagement letter reduces to writing the understanding of the arrangements concerning services to be provided and helps eliminate potential misunderstandings that otherwise may arise. Use of an engagement letter is not required by professional standards; however, its use is common. Exhibit 35.1 illustrates an audit engagement letter.

Engagement letters are mentioned in several AICPA pronouncements. For example, "Savings and Loan Associations," the Audit and Accounting Guide of the AICPA's Committee on Savings and Loan Associations, includes the engagement letter among the matters to be considered when planning the audit. Moreover, engagement letters may be required on engagements involving government agencies.

(b) Audit Programs.   SAS No. 22, "Planning and Supervision," (AU 311) states: "In planning his audit, the auditor should consider the nature, extent, and timing of work to be performed and should prepare a written audit program (or a set of written audit programs)."

Planning of an audit is reflected in the written audit program. The program forms the basis for time budgets, staff scheduling, and subsequent control of time on the engagement. Audit programs also provide a record of procedures actually applied, an evidential link between the assessed levels of inherent risk and control risk and planned procedures, and a record of individuals who are responsible for the program.

Each audit program is responsive to the particular entity and its internal control structure. Accordingly, the audit program is tailored to the engagement; it ordinarily comprehends all procedures involved in gaining an understanding of the entity's business and its internal control structure, and testing transactions and balances. On larger engagements, the audit program may be made up of several individually complete sections (e.g., inventory and cost of sales; property, plant, and equipment). For smaller engagements, separate sections may not be necessary. Audit procedures may be grouped as to (a) preliminary or interim procedures and (b) year-end procedures. The program provides space for initials of the person who completed the work, and reference to supporting work papers (when appropriate). In many firms, the audit program and subsequent modifications are approved by an audit partner or manager.

(c) Matters Related to the Entity's Business and Industry.   The independent public accountant should acquire a **general knowledge of the industry,** as well as a more detailed **knowledge of the specific business,** including its organizational and operational characteristics and current business developments. According to SAS No. 22 that knowledge:

> should enable him to obtain an understanding of the events, transactions, and practices that, in his judgment, may have a significant effect on the financial statements. The level of knowledge customarily possessed by management relating to managing the entity's business is substantially greater than that which is obtained by the auditor in performing his audit.

Knowledge obtained about the entity's industry encompasses an understanding of the accounting and auditing practices common to that industry, and other unique aspects of the industry. Pertinent information about the industry includes trends and growth patterns; government regulation; unusual accounting, tax, or financing practices; and special audit considerations. Special audit considerations may be necessary because of matters such as industrywide litigation or disclosure of illegal acts by other companies in the industry.

The auditor should be aware of the general state of the economy and its impact on the entity and its industry. Such matters as credit availability, environmental efforts, and the impact on the industry of changes in consumer disposable income can have a significant effect on the client's operations. For example, corporate liquidity may be affected by the level of business activity, high interest rates, and the availability of money.

Good, Better, & Best   Certified Public Accountants

[Date]
Mr. Thomas Tofias, President
Anonymous Company, Inc.
Route 70
Nowhere, New York 10000

Dear Mr. Tofias:

This will confirm our understanding of the arrangements for our audit of the financial statements of Anonymous Company, Inc., for the year ending [date].

We will audit the Company's balance sheet at [date], and the related statements of income, retained earnings, and cash flows for the year then ended, for the purpose of expressing an opinion on them. The financial statements are the responsibility of the Company's management. Our responsibility is to express an opinion on the financial statements based on our audit.

We will conduct our audit in accordance with generally accepted auditing standards. Those standards require that we plan and perform the audit to obtain reasonable assurance about whether the financial statements are free of material misstatement. An audit includes examining, on a test basis, evidence supporting the amounts and disclosures in the financial statements. An audit also includes assessing the accounting principles used and significant estimates made by management, as well as evaluating the overall financial statement presentation. We believe that our audit will provide a reasonable basis for our opinion.

Our procedures will include tests of documentary evidence supporting the transactions recorded in the accounts, tests of the physical existence of inventories, and direct confirmation of receivables and certain other assets and liabilities by correspondence with selected customers, creditors, legal counsel, and banks. At the conclusion of our audit, we will request certain written representations from you about the financial statements and matters related thereto.

Our audit is subject to the risk that material errors and irregularities, including fraud or defalcations, if they exist, will not be detected. However, we will inform you of irregularities that come to our attention, unless they are inconsequential.

If you intend to publish or otherwise reproduce the financial statements and make reference to our firm, you agree to provide us with printers' proofs or masters for our review and approval before printing. You also agree to provide us with a copy of the final reproduced material for our approval before it is distributed.

We will review the Company's federal and state [identify states] income tax returns for the fiscal year ended [date]. These returns, we understand, will be prepared by your controller.

Further, we will be available during the year to consult with you on the tax effects of any proposed transactions or contemplated changes in business policies.

Our fee for these services will be at our regular per diem rates, plus travel and other out-of-pocket costs. Invoices will be rendered every two weeks and are payable on presentation.

We are pleased to have this opportunity to serve you.

If this letter correctly expresses your understanding, please sign the enclosed copy where indicated and return it to us.

Very truly yours,

Good, Better, & Best

_____
        Partner

APPROVED:

By _____

Date _____

Exhibit 35.1.   Illustrative audit engagement letter.

Knowledge of the client's business directs attention to important audit areas and helps avoid perfunctory procedures. It also provides the auditor with a basis for developing the most efficient audit techniques (e.g., use of computer-assisted audit techniques, statistical sampling). SAS No. 22 points out that such knowledge is useful for:

1. Identifying areas that may need special consideration.
2. Assessing conditions under which accounting data are produced, processed, reviewed, and accumulated within the organization.
3. Evaluating the reasonableness of estimates, such as valuation of inventories, depreciation, allowances for doubtful accounts, and percentage of completion of long-term contracts.
4. Evaluating the reasonableness of management representations.
5. Making judgments about the appropriateness of the accounting principles applied and the adequacy of disclosures.

Matters relevant to the nature of the business include ownership and management, organization, numbers and types of employees, the existence of related party transactions, significant accounting policies, and operating characteristics. The activities of most businesses can be categorized into the following functions: sales, production (product or services), and financial. An effective method for obtaining knowledge about the entity's business is to consider a series of key questions about each of these functions and to make inquiries about the entity's information system.

(d) Nature of Assertions.   Financial statements consist of a series of assertions or representations by management. SAS No. 31 (AU 326) classifies the broad categories of assertions embodied in elements of financial statements as follows:

1. *"Existence or occurrence."* Deals with whether assets or liabilities exist at a given date and whether recorded transactions have occurred.
2. *"Completeness."* Deals with whether all transactions and accounts that should be reflected in the financial statements are reflected therein.
3. *"Rights and obligations."* Deals with whether assets are the rights of the entity and liabilities are the obligations of the entity at a given date.
4. *"Valuation or allocation."* Deals with whether all assets, liabilities, revenue, and expense elements have been properly reflected in the financial statements at appropriate amounts.
5. *"Presentation and disclosure."* Deals with whether particular elements of the financial statements are properly classified, described, and disclosed.

The independent auditor designs audit procedures to obtain evidence about financial statement assertions. To be workable, the broad assertions are related to particular accounts or groups of accounts (e.g., for inventory accounts), and procedures are developed to obtain evidence concerning the assertions for that specific account (e.g., the existence of inventory may be tested by observing physical counts, confirmation of goods not on hand, etc.). At this level, the assertion may be restated as an audit objective.

(e) Audit Risk and Materiality.   When determining the nature, timing, and extent of auditing procedures to be applied, SAS No. 47, "Audit Risk and Materiality in Conducting an Audit" (AU 312), requires the auditor to consider audit risk and materiality both in planning the audit and designing audit procedures and in evaluating whether the financial statements, taken as a whole, are fairly presented in accordance with GAAP.

Audit risk is the risk that the auditor may unknowingly fail to appropriately modify his opinion on financial statements that are materially misstated. At the account-balance or class-of-transactions level, audit risk consists of (1) the risk (consisting of inherent risk and control risk) that the balance or class contains misstatements that could be material to the financial statements when aggregated with other misstatements in other balances or classes and (2) the risk (detection risk) that the auditor will not detect such misstatements.

Inherent and control risks are not controlled by the auditor; they are characteristics of the entity that are assessed by the auditor. Inherent risk is the susceptibility of an assertion to a material misstatement, assuming there are no related internal control structure policies or procedures. Control risk is the risk that a material misstatement that could occur in an assertion will not be prevented by the entity's internal control structure policies and procedures. The auditor assesses inherent risk and control risk to determine how effective audit procedures have to be to hold detection risk to an acceptable level. Detection risk is the risk that the auditor will not detect a material misstatement that exists in an assertion. The lower the detection risk the auditor is willing to accept, the more evidence he needs to obtain. The way the auditor considers these component risks and combines them involves professional judgment and depends on his audit approach.

Financial statements are materially misstated when they contain errors or irregularities whose effect, either individually or in the aggregate, is important enough to cause them not to be presented fairly in conformity with GAAP. The auditor's consideration of materiality is a matter of professional judgment and is influenced by his perceptions of the needs of a reasonable person who will rely on the financial statements.

(f) The Auditor's Responsibility for the Internal Control Structure. In addition to gaining an understanding of the entity's business the auditor has a related responsibility to obtain an understanding of an entity's internal control structure and assess control risk in an audit of the entity's financial statements, which is discussed in SAS No. 55, "Consideration of the Internal Control Structure in a Financial Statement Audit" (AU 319). SAS No. 55 defines the internal control structure as the policies and procedures established to provide reasonable assurance that specific entity objectives will be achieved. These policies and procedures are means of controlling the entity's activities to ensure that it accomplishes the desired objectives. Generally the policies and procedures that are relevant to an audit pertain to the entity's ability to record, process, summarize, and report financial data in the form of financial statements.

(i) Elements of Internal Control Structure. For purposes of an audit, an entity's internal control structure consists of the control environment, the accounting system, and control procedures. The control environment is the collective effect of various factors on establishing, enhancing, or weakening the effectiveness of the entity's accounting system or control procedures and the entity's ability to achieve specific objectives. The accounting system consists of the methods and records established to identify, assemble, classify, record, and report an entity's transactions, and to maintain accountability for the related assets and liabilities. Control procedures are those policies and procedures that management has established, in addition to the control environment and the accounting system, to provide reasonable assurance that specific entity objectives will be achieved. Exhibit 35.2 contains the complete definitions.

The three components of the internal control structure are an important source of information about the types and risks of potential misstatements—including management misrepresentations—that could occur in the financial statements. Additionally, these policies and procedures are a primary source of information about the specific processes, methods, records, and reports used in preparing the entity's financial statements.

For a financial statement audit, an entity's internal control structure comprises the following:

Control Environment

The collective effect of various factors on establishing, enhancing, or mitigating the effectiveness of specific policies or procedures. The control environment includes such factors as:

- Management's philosophy and operating style.
- The entity's organizational structure.
- The functioning of the board of directors and its committees, particularly the audit committee.
- Methods of assigning authority and responsibility.
- Management's control methods for monitoring and following up on performance, including internal auditing.
- Personnel policies and practices.
- Various external influences that affect an entity's operations and practices, such as examinations by bank regulatory agencies.

Accounting System

The methods and records established to identify, assemble, analyze, classify, record, and report an entity's transactions and to maintain accountability for the related assets and liabilities. An effective accounting system gives appropriate consideration to establishing methods and records that will:

- Identify and record all valid transactions.
- Describe on a timely basis the transactions in sufficient detail to permit proper classification of transactions for financial reporting.
- Measure the value of transactions in a manner that permits recording their proper monetary value in the financial statements.
- Determine the time period in which transactions occurred to permit recording of transactions in the proper accounting period.
- Present properly the transactions and related disclosures in the financial statements.

Control Procedures

Those policies and procedures, in addition to the control environment and the accounting system, that management has established to provide reasonable assurance that specific entity objectives will be achieved. Control procedures pertain to:

- Proper authorization of transactions and activities.
- Segregation of duties to reduce the opportunities to allow any person to be in a position to both perpetrate and conceal errors or irregularities in the normal course of his duties—assigning different people the responsibilities of authorizing transactions, recording transactions, and maintaining custody of assets.
- Design and use of adequate documents and records to help ensure proper recording of transactions and events, such as monitoring the use of prenumbered shipping documents.
- Adequate safeguards over access to and use of assets and records, such as secured facilities and authorization for access to computer programs and data files.
- Independent checks on performance and proper valuation of recorded amounts, such as clerical checks, reconciliations, comparisons of assets with recorded accountability, computer-programmed controls, management review of reports that summarize the detail of account balances (for example, an aged trial balance of accounts receivable), and user review of computer-generated reports.

Exhibit 35.2.   Elements of the internal control structure.

(ii) Understanding of Internal Control Structure.   Because this knowledge is so critical to the audit process, SAS No. 55 requires the auditor to obtain an understanding of each element of the internal control structure sufficient to plan the audit. The statement provides specific guidance on the type of information the auditor has to acquire for each element of the control structure. The auditor's understanding of the control environment, for example, should be sufficient to understand the attitude, awareness, and actions of management and the board of

directors concerning the seven control environment factors included in Exhibit 35.2. The auditor should understand the following matters about the accounting system: the classes of transactions that are significant to the entity's financial statements; how an entity's transactions are initiated; the accounting records, supporting documents, computer databases and files, and specific accounts in the financial statements that are involved in processing and reporting transactions; how transactions are accounted for, from initiation to inclusion in the financial statements; and the financial reporting process used to prepare the entity's financial statements.

Auditors generally need to obtain knowledge about the same control environment factors and accounting system components for all audit clients. The control procedures an auditor must understand, however, generally vary from client to client. SAS No. 55 recognizes that, as the auditor obtains an understanding of the control environment and accounting system, he will most likely gain knowledge about some control procedures as well. In some audits, this knowledge is sufficient to plan the audit. In others, the auditor may have to devote additional effort to understanding control procedures.

The auditor obtains the required knowledge of the internal control structure by performing procedures that will provide evidence about the design of the internal control structure policies and procedures and whether they have been placed in operation (that is, the policies and procedures are actually being used). Such procedures include asking questions of management, supervisory and staff personnel, inspecting documents and records, and observing the company's activities and operations. The nature and extent of the auditor's procedures vary depending on the specific internal control structure policy or procedures involved, his assessments of inherent risk, judgments about materiality, and the complexity and sophistication of the entity's systems.

(iii) Assessing Control Risk. After obtaining the necessary understanding, the auditor assesses control risk. Control risk is the risk that a material misstatement that could occur in a financial statement assertion will not be prevented or detected on a timely basis by the entity's internal control structure policies or procedures. More simply stated, control risk is the likelihood that a material misstatement will get through the internal control structure to the financial statements. The auditor assesses this risk by performing tests of controls that provide evidence about the design and operating effectiveness of those policies and procedures in preventing or detecting misstatements. Tests of controls include inquiries of appropriate management, supervisory and other personnel, inspection of documents, observation of the entity's operations, and reperformance.

The assessed level of control risk relates directly to the substantive tests the auditor performs. The more effective the entity's internal control structure, the lower the risk of misstatement in the financial statements. The lower the risk of misstatement, the less evidence the auditor needs from substantive audit procedures to form an opinion on the financial statements.

35.7 OTHER CONDITIONS THAT AFFECT AUDIT PLANNING. When planning the audit, the independent auditor considers other conditions that may require the extension or modification of audit tests, such as the possibility of material errors or irregularities or the existence of related party transactions. The auditor also has responsibility for certain illegal acts that may have occurred and for assessing the entity's ability to continue as a going concern. These areas of special risk are considered in planning the audit and as other audit evidence is accumulated throughout the audit.

(a) Errors and Irregularities. Both errors and irregularities may lead to the material misstatement of financial statements. Errors involve mistakes in judgments, clerical inaccuracies, failure to correctly interpret facts, and misapplication of accounting principles. Errors are unintentional. Irregularities, on the other hand, are caused by acts designed to misstate the financial statements. Irregularities may involve management misrepresentation, the intentional omission or alteration of facts, intentional misapplication of accounting principles, or the misappropriation of assets. SAS No. 53, "The Auditor's Responsibility to Detect and Report Errors and Irregularities" (AU 316) states that:

> The auditor should assess the risk that errors and irregularities may cause the financial statements to contain a material misstatement. Based on that assessment, the auditor should design the audit to provide reasonable assurance of detecting errors and irregularities that are material to the financial statements.

The auditor makes an assessment of risk during planning. The auditor's understanding of the internal control structure either heightens or mitigates his concerns about the risk of material misstatements in the financial statements. The auditor also considers the effect of certain client characteristics, or red flags, on the risk of material misstatements. Examples of some red-flag client characteristics are:

- The client's operating and financing decisions are dominated by a single individual.
- The client's organizational structure is decentralized and monitored inadequately.
- There are many contentious or difficult accounting issues.

The auditor also assesses the risk of management misrepresentation by considering certain factors. For example, evasive responses to audit inquiries may lead the auditor to believe that management may be predisposed to distort the financial statements. In this case, the auditor might alter the overall audit strategy by assigning more experienced staff, expanding the extent of procedures to be performed, or obtaining more persuasive audit evidence. Higher risk also causes the auditor to exercise a higher degree of professional skepticism in conducting the audit.

SAS No. 53 also requires the auditor to make sure that the audit committee or its equivalent is informed about irregularities discovered during the audit unless they are clearly inconsequential. Further, in certain circumstances (for example, in response to a subpoena or in response to inquiries of a successor auditor), the auditor might have to notify persons outside the client about irregularities.

(b) Related Party Transactions.   SAS No. 45, "Related Parties" (AU 334), provides the independent auditor with guidance on procedures to be considered to identify related parties and transactions with such parties. The statement also illustrates procedures for examining identified related party transactions and provides guidance for adequate disclosure. Parties are related when one party has the ability to influence the other(s) to the extent that the other party(s) does not fully pursue its (their) own separate interest (e.g., a parent company and its subsidiary; an entity and its principal shareholders).

Many of the procedures specified in SAS No. 45 are carried out in the ordinary course of an audit. Such procedures may indicate the possible existence of related party transactions, in which case, additional procedures would be required. Other procedures are directed specifically to related party transactions.

(c) Illegal Acts.   The auditor's responsibility for illegal acts is discussed in SAS No. 54, "Illegal Acts by Clients" (AU 317). Although an auditor is not expected to possess the legal background necessary to recognize all possible violations of laws or regulations, he should be familiar with those laws or regulations that directly affect the financial statements. For example, if a client violates the IRC, the income tax provision in its financial statements might be inadequate, which could cause the financial statements to be materially misstated. Therefore, the auditor's responsibility to detect illegal acts that have a direct and material effect on the financial statements is the same as the auditor's responsibility for errors and irregularities in SAS No. 53—to design the audit to provide reasonable assurance that the financial statements are free of material misstatement.

Many other laws and regulations (for example, regulations of the Environmental Protection Agency and the Federal Trade Commission), are highly specialized and complex. The auditor does not ordinarily have a sufficient legal knowledge to always recognize violations of these laws or regulations. Therefore, according to SAS No. 54, the auditor is responsible for these "indirect effect" illegal acts only when information comes to the auditor's attention that suggests an illegal act might have taken place. If information about an illegal act that could have a material effect on the financial statements through a contingent liability comes to the auditor's attention, the auditor must perform procedures to ascertain whether the illegal act has occurred.

SAS No. 54 also requires the auditor to make sure that the audit committee or its equivalent is informed about illegal acts unless they are clearly inconsequential. Further, in certain circumstances (for example, in response to a subpoena or in response to inquiries of a successor auditor), the auditor might have to notify persons not associated with the client about illegal acts.

(d) Going Concern.   Financial statements are ordinarily prepared on the assumption that the entity will continue in business; an auditor does not search for evidence to support this assumption. However, SAS No. 59, "The Auditor's Consideration of an Entity's Ability to Continue as a Going Concern" (AU 341), requires the auditor to consider whether the aggregate results of all audit procedures performed indicate that there could be substantial doubt about the entity's ability to continue as a going concern for a reasonable period of time (not to exceed one year from the date of the audited financial statements). Conditions and events such as recurring operating losses, working capital deficiencies, defaults on loans, or the loss of a principal customer or supplier, might indicate that there is a going concern problem.

If substantial doubt exists, SAS No. 59 directs the auditor to consider management's plans for dealing with the adverse condition. In considering management's plans, the auditor should obtain evidence about whether the adverse condition or event will be mitigated within a reasonable period of time. If, after considering management's plans, the auditor still concludes that there is substantial doubt, he should include an explanatory paragraph in the audit report that describes that doubt (see section 35.14(c)(iv)).

SAS No. 59 recognizes that the auditor is not responsible for predicting the future, and the absence of a reference to substantial doubt in an auditor's report should not be construed as providing assurances about the entity's continued existence.

35.8 EXECUTION OF THE AUDIT PLAN.   After the auditor has obtained the understanding of the entity's internal control structure and assessed control risk, he performs substantive tests to detect any material errors or irregularities that might have occurred and remained undetected in the financial statements. SAS No. 55 defines substantive tests as follows:

> Tests of details and analytical procedures performed to detect material misstatements in the account balance, transaction class, and disclosure components of financial statements.

Substantive tests may be accomplished through inspection, observation, inquiry, confirmation, and computation. The selection of evidence to be obtained and evaluated— hence the audit procedures to be applied—depends on a variety of factors including the reliability, sufficiency, and availability of evidence. Reliability of evidence varies. Evidence obtained from independent sources outside the organization generally is reliable. The degree of reliability of evidence obtained from within the organization generally depends on the system developed by management to produce information. Furthermore, SAS No. 31, "Evidential Matter," indicates that evidence obtained by the auditor through physical examination observation, computation, and inspection is more persuasive than information obtained indirectly (e.g., from the internal control structure). Evidence also must be sufficient to form a reasonable basis for the auditor's opinion.

The auditor selects the most readily available audit evidence, provided it is reliable and sufficient for audit purposes. In some circumstances, reliable and sufficient evidence may be difficult to obtain. Nevertheless, the independent auditor cannot substitute unreliable evidence merely because such evidence happens to be readily available.

Judgment is necessary in choosing the evidence to obtain and evaluate. However, judgment cannot be applied without a thorough knowledge of the entity being audited and the relative importance (materiality) of the specific assertions under study.

(a) Analytical Procedures. SAS No. 56, "Analytical Procedures" (AU 329), defines analytical procedures as comparisons of recorded amounts, or ratios developed from recorded amounts, to expectations developed by the auditor. It requires the auditor to use analytical procedures in the planning and overall review stages of all audits. The nature and extent of procedures performed, however, are up to the auditor.

In the planning stage, an auditor uses analytical procedures to gain an understanding of the client's business and the events and transactions that have occurred since the prior audit. They also help him identify areas in which the risk of material misstatement is high. In the overall review stage, auditors use analytical procedures to ensure that they have obtained explanations for all significant fluctuations in financial statement amounts, that all amounts make sense based on the audit results, and that they are satisfied with the sufficiency of the audit procedures performed.

SAS No. 56 also encourages, but does not require, auditors to use analytical procedures as substantive tests. For some accounts, analytical procedures can be more effective than tests of details in detecting material misstatements in the financial statements. For example, an analytical procedure comparing salaries paid to the total number of employees in a division might indicate unauthorized payments; a test of details might not have uncovered this. In deciding whether to perform analytical procedures or tests of details, the auditor considers factors such as the nature of the assertion and the reliability of and availability of information used to develop the expectation.

(b) Accounting Estimates. Although many users typically see accounting as exact and precise, the truth is accounting estimates are pervasive in a set of financial statements. Because of the fundamental importance of these estimates and the risks associated with their preparation and evaluation, SAS No. 57, "Auditing Accounting Estimates" (AU 342), requires the auditor to obtain sufficient evidence to provide reasonable assurance that all accounting estimates that could be material to the financial statements have been developed, that those estimates are reasonable, and that the estimates conform to GAAP.

(c) Other Required Auditing Procedures. Although the nature, timing, and extent of **auditing** procedures are matters of judgment, certain procedures are required to be applied on all audit engagements. They include **communication with predecessor auditors, confirmation of receivables, observation of inventories, client representations,** and **inquiry of a client's lawyer concerning litigation claims and assessments.** Independent auditors that do not employ these procedures have the burden of justifying the opinion expressed.

(d) Communication with Predecessor Auditors. SAS No. 7, "Communications between Predecessor and Successor Auditors" (AU 315), explains, "[I]nquiry of the predecessor auditor is a necessary procedure because the predecessor may be able to provide the successor with information that will assist him in determining whether to accept the engagement." Those inquiries, which should be made with the prospective client's authorization, should address matters that may bear on the integrity of management, disagreements with management about accounting, auditing, or other significant matters, and on the predecessor auditor's understanding of why a change of auditors is being made. If a prospective client refuses to permit such communication, the reasons should be determined and consideration should be given to whether acceptance of the engagement is appropriate. Other communications, although not required, may be made to facilitate the current audit.

(e) Confirmation of Receivables. *AICPA Professional Standards* (AU 331), states:

> Confirmation of receivables requires direct communication with debtors either during or after the period under audit; the confirmation date, the method of requesting confirmations, and the number to be requested are determined by the independent auditor. Such matters as the effectiveness of internal control structure policies and procedures, the apparent possibility of disputes, inaccuracies or irregularities in the accounts, the probability that requests will receive consideration or that the debtor will be able to confirm the information requested, and the materiality of the amounts involved are factors to be considered by the auditor in selecting the information to be requested and the form of confirmation, as well as the extent and timing of his confirmation procedures.

Two forms of confirmations are used in practice: positive (i.e., the debtor is asked to respond in all cases) and negative (i.e., a response is requested only if there is disagreement). If no response is received to a positive request, the auditor applies alternative procedures such as examination of evidence of subsequent cash receipts, cash remittance advices, and sales and shipping records.

(f) Observation of Inventories. *AICPA Professional Standards,* (AU 331) states:

> When inventory quantities are determined solely by means of a physical count, and all counts are made as of the balance-sheet date or as of a single date within a reasonable time before or after the balance-sheet date, it is ordinarily necessary for the independent auditor to be present at the time of count and, by suitable observation, tests, and inquiries, satisfy himself respecting the effectiveness of the methods of inventory-taking and the measure of reliance which may be placed upon the client's representations about the quantities and physical condition of the inventories.

> When the well-kept perpetual inventory records are checked by the client periodically by comparisons with physical counts, the auditor's observation procedures usually can be performed either during or after the end of the period under audit.

Auditors may become satisfied as to inventory quantities when statistical sampling methods are used to determine those quantities. Except when inventories are held in public warehouses or by other outside custodians (in which case direct confirmation in writing may be acceptable), it will always be necessary for the auditor to make or observe some physical inventory counts.

(g) Client Representations. SAS No. 19, ''Client Representations'' (AU 333), requires that the auditor obtain written representations from management. Management's refusal to furnish a written representation constitutes a limitation on the scope of his audit.

(h) Inquiry of a Client's Lawyer. With respect to litigation, claims, and assessments, auditors obtain evidential matter relevant to the existence of uncertainties that may result in a loss, the period involved, the degree of probability of unfavorable outcome, and the amount or range of potential loss. Gain contingencies also are addressed. Such information is obtained from management and corroborated through a written response by the client's lawyer to the auditor's letter of audit inquiry. SAS No. 12, ''Inquiry of a Client's Lawyer Concerning Litigation, Claims, and Assessments'' (AU 337), provides auditors with detailed guidance related to these matters.

35.9 REVIEW OF AUDIT WORK.   SAS No. 22 requires the review of work performed by assistants. This review is a critical evaluation of the work carried out on the engagement. In general it should include a review of work papers to see that they clearly indicate work performed and that they support conclusions to be expressed in the auditor's report.

35.10 REQUIRED AUDITOR COMMUNICATIONS.   As a by-product of an audit, the auditor is required to communicate certain matters to an audit committee or others with equivalent authority. SAS No. 60, "Communication of Internal Control Structure Related Matters Noted in an Audit" (AU 325), requires the auditor to communicate reportable conditions. Reportable conditions are matters coming to the auditor's attention that, in his judgment, should be communicated (to the audit committee or others, including the board of directors, owners in owner-managed entities, etc.) because they could adversely affect the entity's ability to prepare financial statements. Such deficiencies can occur in any of the three elements of the internal control structure: the control environment, the accounting system, or control procedures.

Under SAS No. 60, the auditor can communicate reportable conditions either orally or in writing, although a written communication is preferable. If the auditor communicates in a written report, that report should:

- State that the purpose of the audit is to report on the financial statements and not to provide assurance on the internal control structure.
- Include the definition of a reportable condition.
- Include a statement that restricts the distribution of the report to the audit committee, board of directors, or owner-manager.

SAS No. 60 does not require the auditor to search for reportable conditions; rather, the auditor is obligated to report those that come to his attention during the audit.

SAS No. 61, "Communications with Audit Committees" (AU 380), requires an auditor to ensure that management is informed about the following matters:

- The scope of the audit and the level of assurance (reasonable, not absolute) that the auditor provides in an audit of financial statements.
- The auditor's responsibility for internal control structure matters.
- Management's initial selection of accounting policies and changes in significant accounting policies or their application.
- The process management uses to formulate sensitive accounting estimates and the basis for the auditor's conclusions about the reasonableness of those estimates.
- Any audit adjustments that could have a significant effect on the entity's financial reporting process.
- The auditor's responsibility for other information in documents containing audited financial statements.
- Disagreements with management about matters that could be significant to the entity's financial statements.
- The auditor's views on significant matters about which management consulted with other accountants.
- Major issues discussed by the auditor with management in connection with his retention.
- Serious difficulties encountered with management in performing the audit (for example, management setting unreasonable timetables or not providing information required by the auditor).

Unlike SAS No. 60, however, the auditor is only required to make these communications to a public company (as defined in the statement) or to entities that either have an audit committee or have formally designated oversight of the financial reporting process to a group equivalent to an audit committee. This means that, in audits of most smaller companies that only have a board of directors, the auditor may, but is not required to, make these communications.

THE INDEPENDENT AUDITOR'S REPORT

35.11 FORMAT OF REPORT DOCUMENT.   The ordinary report document consists of the **basic financial statements** and the **independent auditor's report.** Also, it may include additional information and the independent auditor's report on that supplementary information.

Basic financial statements include the balance sheet, statement of income, statement of retained earnings, statement of cash flows, and related notes. Disclosure of changes in other categories of stockholders' equity presented in financial statement format also are considered basic financial statements.

Although independent auditors may assist in the preparation of the basic financial statements or draft them based on management's accounts and records, the auditor's responsibility is limited to an opinion on the basic financial statements. Management is responsible for the fair presentation of financial position, results of operations, and cash flows in conformity with GAAP.

Notes to financial statements are used to present information considered necessary for informative disclosure concerning the financial statements that generally is not shown on the face of the statements. A **notation** may be included on the basic financial statements to draw the reader's attention to the notes (e.g., "The accompanying notes are an integral part of these financial statements"). Notes to the financial statements are often captioned with a short, but descriptive title of the matter discussed. Often the caption is the same as a balance sheet or income statement caption (e.g., "investments," "property, plant and equipment"). Notes may be numbered or lettered. When both audited and unaudited information is presented, the note information relating to unaudited information is appropriately identified.

Supplementary information, like the basic financial statements, is the responsibility of management. Supplemental information consists of data presented beyond those necessary for presentation of the basic financial statements. Supplemental information may include statistical data, explanatory comments, and other information, some of which may be of a nonaccounting nature. For example, it may include schedules of selling, general, and administrative expenses; statistical data relating to results of operations such as key ratios; analyses of property accounts; or consolidating schedules representing the financial statements of components of the consolidated group. Some supplementary information is required by pronouncements of the FASB and GASB. (The auditor's responsibility for reporting on supplemental information is discussed in a separate section, "Other Reports.")

35.12 THE AUDITOR'S STANDARD REPORT.   The auditor's usual objective in an audit of an entity's financial statements is to express an unqualified or "clean" opinion on those statements. An unqualified opinion states that the financial statements present fairly, in all material respects, the entity's financial position, results of operation, and cash flows in conformity with GAAP. An auditor may give an unqualified opinion only when both of the following conditions are met:

- The audit has been conducted in accordance with GAAS.
- The financial statements are in conformity with GAAP.

An unqualified opinion is most frequently expressed by issuing a **standard report.** The term **standard report** is used because it consists of three paragraphs containing standardized words and phrases having a specific meaning. The use of standardized wording serves two purposes:

INDEPENDENT AUDITOR'S REPORT
Stockholders and Board of Directors
AUD Company

We have audited the accompanying balance sheet of AUD Company as of December 31, 19X1, and the related statements of income, retained earnings, and cash flows for the year then ended. These financial statements are the responsibility of the Company's management. Our responsibility is to express an opinion on these financial statements based on our audit.

We conducted our audit in accordance with generally accepted auditing standards. Those standards require that we plan and perform the audit to obtain reasonable assurance about whether the financial statements are free of material misstatement. An audit includes examining, on a test basis, evidence supporting the amounts and disclosures in the financial statements. An audit also includes assessing the accounting principles used and significant estimates made by management, as well as evaluating the overall financial statement presentation. We believe that our audit provides a reasonable basis for our opinion.

In our opinion, the financial statements referred to above present fairly, in all material respects, the financial position of AUD Company as of December 31, 19X1, and the results of its operations and its cash flows for the year then ended in conformity with generally accepted accounting principles.

Good, Better, & Best CPAs
February 15, 19X2

Exhibit 35.3.   Auditor's standard report.

It helps avoid confusion among report readers, and it helps identify situations in which the auditor has modified the standard report to bring specific circumstances to the reader's attention.

35.13 CONTENT OF THE AUDITOR'S STANDARD REPORT.   SAS No. 58, "Reports on Audited Financial Statements" (AU 508), prescribes the form of the auditor's standard report on the basic financial statements, which includes the following:

1. Title.
2. Addressee.
3. Introductory paragraph.
4. Scope paragraph.
5. Opinion paragraph.
6. Signature.
7. Date.

A typical example of the auditor's standard report is shown in Exhibit 35.3.

(a) Title.   According to SAS No. 58, the title of an auditor's report must include the word **independent.** This informs financial statement users that the report is from an unbiased CPA. It also distinguishes the report from those of others, such as management or internal auditors.

(b) Addressee.   The auditor's report may be addressed to the entity whose financial statements were audited or to its board of directors or stockholders. A report on the financial statements of an unincorporated entity will be addressed as circumstances dictate. For example, such a report might be addressed to the partners, the general partner, or the proprietor. Occasionally, an auditor is retained to audit the financial statements of an entity that is not his client. In such circumstances, the report is customarily addressed to the client and not to the directors or stockholders of the entity whose financial statements are being audited.

(c) Introductory Paragraph.   The introductory paragraph identifies the financial statements that were audited and contrasts management's responsibility for the financial statements with the auditor's responsibility to express an opinion on those statements.

(d) Scope Paragraph.   The scope paragraph makes several important points. First, it states that the auditor performed the audit in accordance with GAAS. Second, it describes the objective of an audit—to obtain reasonable, but not absolute, assurance that the financial statements are free of material errors, irregularities, or fraud and that those statements are in conformity with GAAP. Third, the scope paragraph provides a brief description of what an audit includes by detailing several factors inherent in the audit process that affect the assurance the auditor provides on the financial statements. Last, it clarifies that the procedures performed by the auditor are, in his opinion, sufficient to enable expression of an opinion on the financial statements.

(e) Opinion Paragraph.   In the opinion paragraph, the auditor communicates the results of the audit. This paragraph expresses an informed, expert opinion on the financial statements. It is not an absolute statement because the auditor cannot guarantee that the financial statements are totally accurate.

If an opinion cannot be expressed or if the independent auditor has reservations concerning the expression of an overall opinion, the reasons must be set forth in a separate paragraph and the opinion appropriately modified or disclaimed.

(f) Signature.   The independent auditor generally signs the firm's name on the report manually. In published annual reports, the accountant's name may be printed or the signature reproduced. In filings with the SEC a manual signature may be required.

(g) Date.   The date of the independent auditor's report ordinarily represents the date of completion of all substantive auditing procedures performed at the client's business locations. Usually that date also is the date of the client's written representation as well as the date as of which letters from attorney are requested.

Occasionally, an event requiring disclosure occurs after the report date (i.e., after completion of field work, but before issuance of the report). In such circumstances, SAS No. 1, (AU 530) provides two methods for dating the audit report. The auditor: ". . . may use 'dual dating,' for example, 'February 16, 19X1, except for Note X as to which the date is March 1, 19X1,' or he may date the report as of the later date."

If the later date is used, the auditor's responsibility for the review of events subsequent to the date of the financial statements extends to that later date. If the report is dual dated, the auditor's responsibility for events subsequent to the date of the audit report is limited to specific data disclosed as of the later date.

When an independent auditor's report is reissued (e.g., in a report to a regulatory agency, or to satisfy a request for additional copies), use of the original report date generally is appropriate. However, if an event occurring subsequent to the original report date requiring disclosure in or adjustment of the financial statements comes to the auditor's attention, other dating may be required. Depending on the circumstances, the auditor's report may be:

1. Dual dated.
2. Dated as of the date of a subsequent event disclosed in the notes, in which case the auditor's responsibility for the review of subsequent events is extended to that later date.

3. Dated as of the date of the original report. When this alternative is appropriate, SAS No. 1 (AU 530) provides: "[T]he event may be disclosed in a separate note to the financial statements captioned somewhat as follows: 'Event (Unaudited) Subsequent to the Date of the Report of Independent Auditor.'"

35.14 DEPARTURES FROM THE AUDITOR'S STANDARD REPORT.   Although the auditor's standard report is synonymous with an unqualified opinion, an important distinction exists between an audit report and an audit opinion. An **audit report** represents the entire communication from the auditor about what he did and what he concluded. The audit opinion is only one part of the report—the conclusions reached. In certain circumstances, the auditor can modify the wording of the standard report but still express an unqualified opinion. Under other circumstances, the auditor will not be able to express an unqualified opinion; therefore, he will have to modify the wording of the standard report, **including the opinion.**

(a) Types of Audit Opinions.   As mentioned earlier, two conditions must be met before an auditor can issue an unqualified opinion. If one of these conditions is not met, the auditor will have to issue one of the following opinions.

- *Qualified Opinion*. This type of opinion excludes a specific item from the auditor's opinion. Thus, the auditor expresses an opinion that the financial statements as a whole present fairly in conformity with GAAP, excluding the item or items specified in the report.
- *Adverse Opinion*. This type of opinion states that the financial statements as a whole do *not* present fairly in conformity with GAAP. The auditor expresses this opinion when he believes that the financial statements taken as a whole are misleading.
- *Disclaimer of Opinion*. This is not an opinion but rather a statement by the auditor that an opinion cannot be expressed. That is, the auditor has no opinion on the financial statements taken as a whole.

The specific circumstances encountered in the audit and its materiality generally determine the type of opinion necessary. To avoid obscuring the basic message, the audit report should give a brief explanation of the circumstance in a separate paragraph (preceding the opinion paragraph).

(b) Modification of Both Wording and Opinion.   Three circumstances prevent the auditor from expressing an unqualified opinion:

- *Scope Limitation*. Circumstances may arise in the audit that prevent application of one or more audit procedures the auditor considers necessary.
- *GAAP Departure*. A departure from GAAP, including adequate disclosures, may have a material effect on the financial statements.
- *Lack of Independence*. If the auditor is not independent, he must disclaim an opinion on the financial statements. (If the entity is a nonpublic entity, a compilation report is required.)

Each of these circumstances, when material, precludes the auditor from issuing an unqualified opinion and requires the auditor to modify the report wording not only to express a different type of opinion but also to describe the circumstance causing the change in opinion. These circumstances are discussed below, along with their effect on the type of opinion to be expressed and the modification of report wording.

(i) Scope Limitation.   Circumstances sometimes arise that make it impossible or impracticable to apply certain audit procedures the auditor believes necessary. Such restrictions on the scope of the audit may be imposed by the client, such as refusal to permit confirmation of accounts receivable or refusal to permit inquiry of outside legal counsel. **Scope limitations** may also arise because the client's records are not adequate to permit an audit of the financial statements or because of the timing of the auditor's work, such as when the auditor is appointed too late to observe physical inventory.

Because auditors cannot express an unqualified opinion unless they have been able to apply all of the audit procedures considered necessary, scope limitations require auditors either to express a qualified opinion or to disclaim an opinion. An adverse opinion is inappropriate for scope limitations because such an opinion relates to a deficiency in the financial statements rather than to a deficiency in the scope of the audit.

Opening Paragraph

We have audited the accompanying balance sheet of AUD Company as of December 31, 19X1, and the related statements of income, retained earnings, and cash flows for the year then ended. The financial statements are the responsibility of the Company's management. Our responsibility is to express an opinion on these financial statements based on our audit.

Opening paragraph is the same as in the standard report.

Scope Paragraph

Except as discussed in the following paragraph, we conducted our audit in accordance with generally accepted auditing standards. Those standards require that we plan and perform the audit to obtain reasonable assurance about whether the financial statements are free of material misstatement. An audit includes examining, on a test basis, evidence supporting the amounts and disclosures in the financial statements. An audit also includes assessing the accounting principles used and significant estimates made by management, as well as evaluating the overall financial statement presentation. We believe that our audit provides a reasonable basis for our opinion.

Wording of the scope paragraph is modified to include a restriction affecting the scope of the audit.

Explanatory Paragraph

We were unable to obtain audited financial statements supporting the Company's investment in a foreign affiliate stated at $2,500,000 at December 31, 19X1, or its equity in earnings of that affiliate of $300,000, which is included in net income for the year then ended as described in Note X to the financial statements; nor were we able to satisfy ourselves as to the carrying value of the investment in the foreign affiliate or the equity in its earnings by other auditing procedures.

Separate paragraph is added to explain the nature of the scope limitation.

Opinion Paragraph

In our opinion, *except for the effects of such adjustments, if any, as might have been determined to be necessary had we been able to examine evidence regarding the foreign affiliate investment and earnings,* the financial statements referred to above present fairly, in all material respects, the financial position of AUD Company as of December 31, 19X1, and the results of its operations and its cash flows for the year then ended in conformity with generally accepted accounting principles.

Opinion is qualified "except for" any adjustments the auditor might have found necessary had he been able to examine the records supporting AUD Company's investment in the foreign affiliate.

Exhibit 35.4.   Report with a qualified "except for" opinion due to a limitation on the scope of the engagement. Annotations appear to the right.

Once the auditor has decided that an unqualified opinion is not appropriate, a choice must be made between a qualified opinion and a disclaimer of opinion. This choice is based on the importance of the omitted procedures to the auditor's ability to form an opinion on the financial statements taken as a whole. If the potential effects of the scope limitation are not so material as to preclude the auditor from forming an opinion on the financial statements taken as a whole, the auditor should issue a qualified opinion. Exhibit 35.4 illustrates a qualified opinion for a scope limitation.

If the potential effects of the scope limitation relate to many financial statement items, they may be so material as to preclude the auditor from forming an opinion on the financial statements taken as a whole. Also, if the client imposes the scope limitation, the auditor usually does not express an opinion. Under theses circumstances, a disclaimer of opinion is appropriate.

Opening Paragraph

We have audited the accompanying balance sheet of AUD Company as of December 31, 19X1, and the related statements of income, retained earnings, and cash flows for the year then ended. These financial statements are the responsibility of the Company's management. Our responsibility is to express an opinion on these financial statements based on our audit.

> Opening paragraph is the same as in the standard report.

Scope Paragraph

We conducted our audit in accordance with generally accepted auditing standards. Those standards require that we plan and perform the audit to obtain reasonable assurance about whether the financial statements are free of material misstatement. An audit includes examining, on a test basis, evidence supporting the amounts and disclosures in the financial statements. An audit also includes assessing the accounting priniciples used and significant estimates made by management, as well as evaluating the overall financial statement presentation. We believe that our audit provides a reasonable basis for our opinion.

> Scope paragraph is the same as in the standard report because no limitations have been placed on the scope of the audit.

Explanatory Paragraph

The Company has excluded, from property and debt in the accompanying balance sheets, certain lease obligations which in our opinion, should be capitalized in order to conform with generally accepted accounting principles. If these lease obligations were capitalized, property would be increased by $5,500,000, long-term debt by $7,200,000, and retained earnings would be decreased by $1,700,000 as of December 31, 19X1. Additionally, net income would be decreased by $500,000 and earnings per share would be decreased by $.50 for the year then ended.

> Separate paragraph has been added to explain the departure from GAAP and its effect on the financial statements.

Opinion Paragraph

In our opinion, *except for the effects of not capitalizing certain lease obligations, as discussed in the preceding paragraph,* the financial statements referred to above present fairly, in all material respects, the financial position of AUD Company as of December 31, 19X1, and the results of its operations and its cash flows for the year then ended, in conformity with generally accepted accounting principles.

> Opinion paragraph is qualified "except for" due to the departure from GAAP regarding lease capitalization.

Exhibit 35.5.   Report with a qualified "except for" opinion due to a departure from GAAP. Annotations appear to the right.

(ii) Departure from GAAP.   When a departure from GAAP has a material effect on the financial statements, the auditor cannot express an unqualified opinion. Departures from GAAP include using inappropriate accounting principles, such as valuing property, plant, and equipment in a manufacturing company at current value rather than historical cost; improperly applying accounting methods, such as incorrect application of the LIFO costing method to inventory; and inadequate disclosure, such as failing to disclose the pledging of material amounts of inventory as collateral for a loan.

When the financial statements contain a material departure from GAAP, the auditor should express either a qualified or an adverse opinion. A disclaimer of opinion is inappropriate because the auditor is in a position to express an opinion and cannot avoid disclosing a known departure from GAAP by denying an opinion on the financial statements.

The auditor's choice between a qualified or adverse opinion is based on the materiality of the departure from GAAP. Materiality is evaluated by considering (1) the dollar magnitude of the effects, (2) the significance of the item to the client, (3) the number of financial statement items affected, and (4) the effect of the departure on the financial statements taken as a whole.

If the departure from GAAP is not so material as to cause the financial statement taken as a whole to be misleading, the auditor will express a qualified opinion, as illustrated in Exhibit 35.5.

If the effects of the departure from GAAP are so material that they cause the financial statements as a whole to be misleading, the auditor will express an adverse opinion, as illustrated in Exhibit 35.6.

Consideration of Exhibits 35.5 and 35.6 helps clarify the effect of materiality on the auditor's decision to issue a qualified or adverse opinion. The qualified opinion in Exhibit 35.5 was issued because the client failed to capitalize leased assets that met the requirements for capitalization under GAAP. The effects of this departure caused both the property and the long-term debt accounts to be materially misstated. The misstatements in these accounts, however, when considered in relation to the financial statements as a whole, were not considered to be material enough to cause the statements taken as a whole to be misleading. Therefore, the auditor did not consider an adverse opinion appropriate.

The adverse opinion in Exhibit 35.6 was issued because property, plant, and equipment was stated at appraisal value rather than historical cost and because the client did not provide for deferred income taxes. These departures affected numerous accounts and, in the auditor's judgment, caused the financial statements taken as a whole to be misleading. Thus, the auditor considered an adverse opinion necessary.

(iii) Lack of Independence.   When an accountant is not independent, any procedure performed would not be in accordance with GAAS. Thus, SAS No. 26 (AU 504) requires the accountant who is not independent to issue a special disclaimer of opinion. Exhibit 35.7 illustrates the nonindependent disclaimer for financial statements of a public entity.

(c) Modification of Wording Only.   Circumstances may require modification of the wording of the standard report but not modification of the auditor's opinion on the financial statements. There are six such situations:

- Part of the audit was performed by another independent auditor.
- A departure from a promulgated accounting principle is necessary to keep the financial statements from being misleading.
- A material uncertainty affects the financial statements.
- The auditor has substantial doubt about the entity's ability to continue as a going concern.

Opening Paragraph

We have audited the accompanying balance sheet of AUD Company as of December 31, 19X1, and the related statements of income, retained earnings, and cash flows for the year then ended. These financial statements are the responsibility of the Company's management. Our responsibility is to express an opinion on these financial statements based on our audit.

Opening paragraph is the same as in the standard report.

Scope Paragraph

We conducted our audit in accordance with generally accepted auditing standards. Those standards require that we plan and perform the audit to obtain reasonable assurance about whether the financial statements are free of material misstatement. An audit includes examining, on a test basis, evidence supporting the amounts and disclosures in the financial statements. An audit also includes assessing the accounting principles used and significant estimates made by management, as well as evaluating the overall financial statement presentation. We believe that our audit provides a reasonable basis for our opinion.

Scope paragraph is the same as in the standard report because no limitations have been placed on the scope of the audit.

Explanatory Paragraph 1

As discussed in Note X to the financial statements, the Company carries its property, plant, and equipment accounts at appraisal values, and provides depreciation on the basis of such values. Further, the Company does not provide for income taxes with respect to differences between financial income and taxable income arising because of the use, for income tax purposes, of the installment method of reporting gross profit from certain types of sales. Generally accepted accounting principles require that property, plant, and equipment be stated at an amount not in excess of cost, reduced by depreciation based on such amount, and that deferred income taxes be provided.

Separate paragraphs have been added to explain the departures from GAAP and their effects on the financial statements.

Explanatory Paragraph 2

Because of the departures from generally accepted accounting principles identified above, as of December 31, 19X1, inventories have been increased $450,000 by inclusion in manufacturing overhead of depreciation in excess of that based on cost; property, plant, and equipment, less accumulated depreciation, is carried at $12,500,000 in excess of an amount based on the cost to the Company; and deferred income taxes of $2,500,000 have not been recorded; resulting in an increase of $2,950,000 in retained earnings and in appraisal surplus of $12,500,000. For the year ended December 31, 19X1, cost of goods sold has been increased $350,000 because of the effects of the depreciation accounting referred to above, and deferred income taxes of $1,000,000 have not been provided, resulting in an increase in net income of $650,000.

Opinion Paragraph

In our opinion, *because of the effects of the matters discussed in the preceding paragraphs, the financial statements referred to above do not present fairly,* in conformity with generally accepted accounting principles, the financial position of AUD Company as of December 31, 19X1, or the results of its operations or its cash flows for the year then ended.

Opinion expressed is adverse— the departures from GAAP are so material that the financial statements as a whole are misleading.

Exhibit 35.6. Report with an adverse opinion due to departures from GAAP. Annotations appear to the right.

We are not independent with respect to AUD Company, and the accompanying balance sheet as of December 31, 19X1, and the related statements of income, retained earnings, and cash flows for the year then ended were not audited by us and accordingly, we do not express an opinion on them.	Reason for the lack of independence and any procedures performed should not be described.

Exhibit 35.7. Disclaimer of opinion when not independent (public entity). Annotations appear to the right.

- A material change in accounting principles causes the financial statements to be inconsistent with those of the prior period.
- The auditor wishes to emphasize a matter regarding the financial statements but still express an unqualified opinion.

(i) Part of Audit Performed by Another Independent Auditor. More than one audit firm may participate in an audit, particularly when the entity being audited is widespread geographically. For example, an entity may have its major operations in the Southeast audited by a local CPA firm while having its western subsidiary audited by a different auditor on the West Coast.

When involved in an audit in which part of the audit has been performed by other auditors, the auditor must first decide whether he can serve as **principal auditor** and report on the financial statements even though he has not audited all of the subsidiaries, divisions, branches, or components that will be included in the financial statements. According to *AICPA Professional Standards* (AU 543), ''Part of Audit Performed by Other Independent Auditors,'' in making this decision the auditor should consider

- the materiality of the portion of the financial statements audited in comparison with the portion audited by other auditors.
- knowledge of the overall financial statements.
- the importance of the components audited in relation to the entity as a whole.

The auditor must decide first if it is appropriate to serve as the principal auditor and then, if so, whether to assume responsibility for the work of the other auditor. The principal auditor is never required to assume responsibility for the other auditor's work. However, if the principal auditor does assume responsibility, he must be satisfied as to (1) the independence of the other auditor, (2) the professional reputation of the other auditor, and (3) the other auditor's work.

If a principal auditor decides to accept responsibility for the other auditor's work, the standard report is issued without modification. In such a case, the report expresses an opinion on the financial statements as if the principal auditor had conducted the entire audit; no reference is made to the other auditors or their work in the audit report.

If the principal auditor decides not to assume responsibility for the other auditor's work, the responsibility is shared. Sharing responsibility in no way raises questions about the quality of the other auditor's work, nor does it imply less assurance about the reliability of the financial statements. It means simply that the principal auditor is not in a position to assume responsibility for the other auditor's work as if the principal auditor had done the work.

The indication of shared responsibility is communicated to audit report readers by a modification of the wording of the standard report. The opinion on the financial statements is not affected by the participation of more than one audit firm in the audit. Thus only the report wording—not the opinion—is modified as follows:

- *Opening Paragraph.* The subsidiaries that the principal auditor has not audited are identified, preferably by name, and the magnitude of the portion of the financial statements audited by the other auditor is disclosed by indicating dollar amounts or percentages of appropriate criteria, such as assets or revenues. In addition, the principal auditor specifies that part of the audit was made by other auditors. (The other auditor need not be, and usually is not, identified. The other auditor's permission must be obtained, and his report also must be presented, if he is identified in the principal auditor's report.)

- *Scope Paragraph.* The principal auditor indicates that he believes that his audit **and the report of the other auditors** provide a reasonable basis for the opinion on the consolidated financial statements.

- *Opinion Paragraph.* The prinicipal auditor indicates that the opinion is based in part on the other auditor's audit. The opinion itself is not modified simply because of shared responsibility.

(ii) Departure from a Promulgated Principle.   Rule 203 of the AICPA Code of Professional Conduct precludes the auditor from expressing an unqualified opinion on financial statements that contain a material departure from a promulgated accounting principle. A promulgated accounting principle is one issued by the bodies designated by the AICPA to establish accounting principles. When such a departure exists, the auditor should modify the opinion just as for a departure from any other GAAP.

There is, however, an exception in Rule 203 that permits the auditor to issue an unqualified opinion, despite a departure from a promulgated accounting principle, when the auditor believes that, due to unusual circumstances, the departure is necessary to keep the financial statements from being misleading. When this rare situation exists, the auditor modifies the wording of the report by adding a separate explanatory paragraph, usually between the scope and opinion paragraphs. This paragraph describes the departure, the approximate effects, if practicable, and the reasons compliance with the principle would result in misleading financial statements. The opening, scope, and opinion paragraphs, however, are identical to those in the standard report. The opinion on the financial statements is unqualified.

(iii) Uncertainties.   Sometimes matters exist that affect the financial statements or required disclosures but that have outcomes that cannot be reasonably estimated at the date of the auditor's report. These matters are termed **uncertainties** because it is not possible to determine whether the financial statements should be adjusted or in what amount.

According to SAS No. 58 a matter involving an uncertainty is one that is expected to be resolved at a future date, at which time sufficient evidence concerning its outcome would be expected to become available. Common examples of uncertainties include lawsuits against the client in which legal counsel is unable to form an opinion as to the outcome of the case, such as when the client is sued for patent infringement, and tax claims by tax authorities when precedents are not clear and potential liability cannot be determined, such as when the IRS claims the client owes additional taxes because a particular tax deduction is questionable.

Generally, matters whose outcomes depend on the client's actions and that relate to typical business operations are susceptible to reasonable estimation and, therefore, are estimates inherent in the accounting process, not uncertainties. For example, provisions for losses on uncollectible trade receivables and obsolete inventories, estimates of the useful lives of depreciable assets, and estimates of accruals for income taxes and product warranty obligations are not uncertainties because they normally can be estimated with reasonable accuracy.

When a material uncertainty exists, the auditor must decide whether he has gathered sufficient evidence to support management's assertions about the uncertainty and its presentation or disclosure in the financial statements. If the auditor has not obtained sufficient evidence, he should express a qualified opinion or should issue a disclaimer of opinion on the financial statements.

Similarly, if management has not properly disclosed the uncertainty, has used an inappropriate accounting principle, or has made an unreasonable estimate of a material uncertainty, the auditor should qualify the opinion or express an adverse opinion on the financial statements.

If the auditor has obtained sufficient evidence about the uncertainty and management has accounted for and disclosed the uncertainty in accordance with GAAP, the auditor has to then consider whether to add an explanatory paragraph to the audit report because of the uncertainty. To make that determination, the auditor must consider the likelihood of a material loss resulting from the resolution of the uncertainty. Exhibit 35.8 illustrates the possible outcomes of the auditor's assessment of the uncertainty.

When the auditor decides to add an explanatory paragraph to the report, SAS No. 58 specifies that the explanatory paragraph must follow the opinion paragraph. Note, however, that no reference to the uncertainty is made in the introductory, scope, or opinion paragraphs of the report. An example of an explanatory paragraph that an auditor might add to the report because of an uncertainty follows:

> As discussed in Note X to the financial statements, the Company is a defendant in a lawsuit alleging infringement of certain patent rights and claiming royalties and punitive damages. The Company has filed a counteraction, and preliminary hearings and discovery proceedings on both actions are in progress. The ultimate outcome of the litigation cannot presently be determined. Accordingly, no provision for any liability that may result upon adjudication has been made in the accompanying financial statements.

(iv) Going Concern Matters.   As discussed earlier, SAS No. 59, "The Auditor's Consideration of an Entity's Ability to Continue as a Going Concern" (AU 341), states that the auditor has a responsibility to evaluate whether there is substantial doubt about the entity's ability to continue as a **going concern** for a reasonable period of time.

An auditor might add an explanatory paragraph such as the one below to the report after the opinion paragraph because of an uncertainty about a going concern. The three paragraphs in the auditor's standard report are unchanged.

	Probability of Material Loss		
	Remote	**Reasonably Possible**	**Probable**
Effect of Uncertainty on the Auditor's Report	The auditor will issue a standard unqualified opinion.	The auditor's decision to add an explanatory paragraph depends on the following: 1. The magnitude of the loss relative to materiality. 2. Whether the probability of unfavorable outcome is closer to remote or to probable.	The auditor will add an explanatory paragraph to the report when the amount of the loss cannot be reasonably estimated.

Exhibit 35.8.   Reporting on uncertainties.

The accompanying financial statements have been prepared assuming that the Company will continue as a going concern. As discussed in Note X to the financial statements, the Company has suffered recurring losses from operations and has a net capital deficiency that raise substantial doubt about its ability to continue as a going concern. Management's plans in regard to these matters are also described in Note X. The financial statements do not include any adjustments that might result from the outcome of this uncertainty.

(v) Lack of Consistency. The second standard of reporting (the consistency standard) is concerned with financial statement comparability. This standard requires the auditor to identify changes in accounting principles that have a material effect on the comparability of the financial statements.

Although a change in accounting principle is not the only accounting change that can affect financial statement comparability, it is the only accounting change that requires a report wording modification under the consistency standard. Thus, the factor that determines whether the auditor's report must be modified because of a lack of consistency is whether the accounting change involves a change in accounting principle (including a change in the method of applying a principle). Changes in accounting principle may take the following forms:

- Change from one GAAP to another GAAP, such as changing from the straight-line method to the declining balance method for plant assets.
- Change in the reporting entity covered by the financial statements, such as when consolidated financial statements are presented in place of the statements of individual entities.
- Correction of an error in an accounting principle by changing from a principle that is not generally accepted to one that is, such as changing from an appraisal value basis for property, plant, and equipment to a historical cost basis.

When there is a change in an accounting principle that has a material effect on the financial statements, the auditor should not modify the unqualified opinion on the financial statements. That is, the change in accounting principle, if properly accounted for and disclosed in the financial statement, requires modification of the auditor's standard report, but not qualification or modification of the opinion paragraph.

When a lack of consistency exists, report wording generally is modified by adding an explanatory paragraph to the audit report following the opinion paragraph, identifying the nature of the change and referring the reader to the note in the financial statement that discusses the change in detail. The opening, scope, and opinion paragraphs are not changed. An example of an explanatory paragraph an auditor might add to the report because of a change in accounting follows:

As discussed in Note X to financial statements, the company changed its method of computing depreciation in 19X1.

Two other sets of circumstances relating to the consistency standard occur frequently enough in audit engagements to warrant brief discussion.

1. *First Audit of a Client.* When an auditor has not audited the financial statements of a client for the preceding year, scope limitations may prevent the auditor from forming an opinion on the consistency of the current year with the prior year. The auditor's report should be modified for a scope limitation and the explanatory separate paragraph, which should precede the opinion paragraph, should indicate that an opinion on consistency could not be formed. The opinion is qualified "except for" or disclaimed.

2. *Change in Accounting Principle not in Conformity with GAAP.* A change in accounting principle must meet the three conditions specified in APB Opinion No. 20, "Accounting Changes," to be in conformity with GAAP: (1) the new principle must be a GAAP, (2) the method of accounting for the change must conform with GAAP, and (3) the change must be justified. If one or more of these conditions are not met, the auditor's report on the year of change should be modified because of a departure from GAAP. In this situation, the paragraph explaining the GAAP departure should precede the opinion paragraph, and the opinion is qualified "except for" or is adverse.

(vi) Emphasis of a Matter. Under certain circumstances the auditor may wish to emphasize a specific matter regarding the financial statements even though an unqualified opinion has been expressed. Examples of such matters include important events occurring after the balance sheet date or identification of the entity as a subsidiary of a larger enterprise.

These matters are not deficiencies in the financial statements. They represent matters, properly treated in the financial statements, that are, in the auditor's judgment, sufficiently important to be accentuated in the report. To emphasize matters in the report, the auditor includes a separate explanatory paragraph, usually between the scope and opinion paragraphs of the standard report.

35.15 COMPARATIVE FINANCIAL STATEMENTS. When financial statements of one or more prior periods are presented on a comparative basis with those of the current period, the fourth reporting standard requires a report on those comparative statements. The type of report, its content, and who issues it depend on whether the current auditor is a continuing auditor or is following a predecessor auditor. In addition, the report is affected by (1) whether the opinion(s) on the prior-period statement(s) is the same as or different from the opinion on the current-period statements, (2) whether the opinion on the prior-period statements should be revised in light of new circumstances, and (3) whether the comparative statements are audited or unaudited. SAS No. 58 provides guidance to the auditor on comparative financial statements.

(a) Continuing Auditor. A **continuing auditor** is one who has audited the financial statements of the current period and of one or more consecutive periods immediately preceding the current period. Basically, this means that the auditor must have audited the current period and at least the immediately preceding period to be a continuing auditor.

The reporting responsibilities for a continuing auditor differ from those for one who is not. A continuing auditor has the responsibility to update the report on prior-period financial statements that have been audited and that are presented for comparative purposes. *Updating* requires the auditor to consider whether, based on information obtained in the audit of the current-period statements, the auditor should reexpress the same opinion on prior statements shown on the comparative statements or express a revised opinion on them.

After considering the information obtained during the current audit, an auditor may conclude that the opinion originally expressed on the comparative statements is still appropriate. Exhibit 35.9 illustrates an updated auditor's report when the opinion expressed in the previous period is reexpressed in the updated report. This report is essentially the standard report for a single period expressed in plural form because it both expresses an opinion on the current-period statements and repeats the opinion originally expressed on the prior-period statements. Because the report is updated, the report date for the comparative statements is, in effect, changed to the report date for the current-period statements—the date of the completion of the audit of the most recent financial statements.

In Exhibit 35.9 the opinion expressed on the prior-period statements (19X1) was the same type of opinion expressed on the current-period statements: Both were unqualified opinions. In some audit engagements, the opinion expressed on the prior-period statements might not be the same type of opinion as that expressed on the current-period statements.

Opening Paragraph

We have audited the accompanying *balance sheets* of AUD Company as of December 31, 19X2 and 19X1 and the related statements of income, retained earnings, and cash flows for the *years* then ended. These financial statements are the responsibility of the Company's management. Our responsibility is to express an opinion on these financial statements based on our *audits*.

Opening paragraph is modified to refer to "balance sheets," to cover two (or more) years presented, and to refer to "audits" as plural.

Scope Paragraph

We conducted our *audits* in accordance with generally accepted auditing standards. Those standards require that we plan and perform the audit to obtain reasonable assurance about whether the financial statements are free of material misstatement. An audit includes examining, on a test basis, evidence supporting the amounts and disclosures in the financial statements. An audit also includes assessing the accounting principles used and significant estimates made by management, as well as evaluating the overall financial statement presentation. We believe that our *audits* provide a reasonable basis for our opinion.

Except for the reference to "audits," the scope paragraph is the same as in the standard report.

Opinion Paragraph

In our opinion, the financial statements referred to above present fairly, in all material respects, the financial position of AUD Company as of December 31, 19X2 and 19X1, and the results of its operations and its cash flows *for the years* then ended in conformity with generally accepted accounting principles.

Opinion paragraph is modified to cover two (or more) years.

Exhibit 35.9.   Report on comparative financial statements: Previous opinion reexpressed. Annotations appear to the right.

During the current engagement, the auditor might become aware of circumstances that would cause a change in the type of opinion previously expressed on the prior-period statements. For example, when departures from GAAP in prior-period statements are corrected in the current year by restating those statements, a qualified or adverse opinion on the prior-period statements is no longer appropriate.

The wording of an updated report that expresses a revised opinion on prior-period statements is modified by adding a separate explanatory paragraph, preceding the opinion paragraph, that discloses the following information:

- Date of the auditor's previous report.
- Type of opinion previously expressed.
- Circumstances that caused the revised opinion.
- Statement that the updated opinion differs from the prior opinion.

An example of this explanatory paragraph follows:

In our report dated March 1, 19X2, we expressed an opinion that the 19X1 financial statements did not fairly present financial position, results of operations, and cash flows in conformity with generally accepted accounting principles because of two departures from such principles: (1) the Company carried its property, plant, and equipment at appraisal values, and provided for depreciation on the basis of such values, and (2) the Company did not provide for deferred income taxes with respect to differences between income for financial reporting purposes and taxable income. As described in Note X, the Company has changed its method of accounting for these items and restated its 19X1 financial statements to conform with generally accepted accounting principles. Accordingly, our present opinion on the 19X1 financial statements, as presented herein, is different from that expressed in our previous report.

(b) Predecessor Auditor.   When the current auditor is not a continuing auditor and the client presents comparative statements, two situations can exist: (1) the prior-period statements were reported on by a **predecessor auditor** or (2) the prior-period statements have not been reported on by any auditor.

If one or more prior periods included in the comparative statements have been audited by a predecessor auditor, either of the following reporting approaches may be taken:

- The current (successor) auditor may refer to the predecessor auditor's report in the report on the current-period financial statements.
- The predecessor auditor may reissue his report on the prior-period statements.

Most frequently, the **successor auditor** refers to the predecessor auditor's report. In that circumstance, the successor auditor adds a sentence such as the following to the opening paragraph of the current-period report: "The financial statements of AUD Company as of December 31, 19X1, were audited by other auditors whose report dated March 1, 19X2, expressed an unqualified opinion on those statements."

If a predecessor auditor is asked to reissue the report and agrees to accept that request, the predecessor auditor must perform procedures to determine if the original report is still appropriate: If the predecessor auditor decides that the opinion on the prior-period statements is still appropriate, the previous report should be reissued. The date of the reissued report should be the same as the date of the original report to avoid any implication that any records, transactions, or events after that date have been examined.

If the predecessor auditor believes transactions or events have occurred that may affect the previous opinion on the financial statements, he should perform whatever procedures are believed necessary to determine whether the opinion needs to be revised. If the predecessor auditor concludes that a revised report should be issued, the same reporting guidelines that apply to a continuing auditor's updated report also apply to the predecessor. However, the predecessor's updated report is normally dual dated rather than redated to the report date on the current financial statements.

(c) Prior Period Unaudited.   When the financial statements of the prior period have not been audited, the report on the current period should contain a separate paragraph that includes:

- A statement of the service performed in the prior period.
- The date of the report on that service.
- A description of any material modifications noted in that report.
- A statement that the service was less in scope than an audit and does not provide a reasonable basis for the expression of an opinion on the financial statements taken as a whole.

When the financial statements are those of a public entity, the separate paragraph should include a disclaimer of opinion as discussed in SAS No. 26, "Association with Financial Statements" or a description of a review of the financial statements under SAS No. 36, "Review of Interim Financial Statements" (discussed in section 35.19).

When the financial statements are those of a nonpublic entity and the financial statements were compiled or reviewed, the separate paragraph should contain a description of the compilation or review. These engagements are discussed later in this chapter.

OTHER REPORTS

Sections 35.12 to 35.15 are concerned with audit reports issued by the auditor after an audit of financial statements prepared in accordance with GAAP. However, auditing standards also cover other situations, in which the auditor issues other kinds of reports. These other types of reports include:

- Special reports.
- Reports on internal control structure.
- Involvement with other information.
- Review of interim financial information.
- Reports on financial forecasts and projections.
- Reports on financial statements prepared for use in other countries.
- Reports on the application of accounting principles.

35.16 SPECIAL REPORTS.   SAS No. 62, "Special Reports" (AU 623), identifies the following five types of **special reports:**

1. Reports on financial statements prepared on comprehensive bases of accounting other than GAAP.
2. Reports on specified elements, accounts, or items of a financial statement.
3. Reports on compliance with aspects of contractual agreements or regulatory requirements related to audited financial statements.
4. Reports on financial presentations to comply with contractual agreements or regulatory provisions.
5. Reports on financial information presented in prescribed forms or schedules that require a prescribed form of auditor's report.

In addition, SAS No. 35, "Special Reports: Applying Agreed-Upon Procedures to Specified Elements, Accounts, or Items of a Financial Statement" (AU 622), applies to an engagement in which the scope is limited to applying **agreed-upon procedures** to one or more specified elements, accounts, or items of a financial statement.

(a) Other Comprehensive Bases of Accounting.   Auditors frequently examine financial statements that are prepared on a basis of accounting that differs from GAAP. SAS No. 62 recognizes this and provides reporting guidance to the auditor when financial statements are prepared on **"other comprehensive bases of accounting"** (OCBOA). The auditor's report should provide reasonable assurance that the financial statements conform with OCBOA.

According to SAS No. 62, a measurement basis must meet one of four criteria to be classified as an OCBOA. The measurement must be:

- A basis of accounting that the reporting entity uses to comply with the reporting provisions of a government regulatory agency to whose jurisdiction the entity is subject. For example, insurance companies use bases of accounting pursuant to the rules of state insurance commissions.
- A basis of accounting that the reporting entity uses or expects to use to file its federal income tax return for the period covered by the financial statements.
- The cash receipts and disbursements basis of accounting, and modifications of the cash basis having substantial support, such as recording depreciation on fixed assets or accruing income taxes.

- A definite set of criteria having substantial support that is applied to all material items appearing in the financial statements, such as the price level basis of accounting.

Exhibit 35.10 indicates a sample auditor's report on financial statements prepared on the entity's income tax basis.

(b) Opinions on Specified Elements, Accounts, or Items of a Financial Statement. Sometimes auditors are requested to issue a report on certain aspects of the financial statements. For example, a shopping mall may charge rent to its tenants based on a percentage of the tenants' sales. In this situation, the mall may require a report by the auditor that the sales reported by the tenants are fairly presented in conformity with GAAP. Other examples include reports on royalties and profit participations.

The audit of specified elements, accounts, or items may be undertaken as a separate engagement or in conjunction with an audit of financial statements. In such an engagement, the auditor expresses an opinion on each of the specified elements, accounts, or items encompassed by the report; therefore, the measurement of materiality must be related to each

---

Board of Directors
Diamond Partnership

We have audited the accompanying statements of assets, liabilities, and capital—income tax basis of Diamond Partnership as of December 31, 19X2 and 19X1, and the related statements of revenue and expenses—income tax basis and of changes in partners' capital accounts—income tax basis for the years then ended. These financial statements are the responsibility of the Partnership's management. Our responsibility is to express an opinion on these financial statements based on our audits.	The first paragraph identifies the financial statements audited. The auditor also emphasizes that the financial statements are management's responsibility.
We conducted our audits in accordance with generally accepted auditing standards. Those standards require that we plan and perform the audit to obtain reasonable assurance about whether the financial statements are free of material misstatement. An audit includes examining, on a test basis, evidence supporting the amounts and disclosures in the financial statements. An audit also includes assessing the accounting principles used and significant estimates made by management, as well as evaluating the overall financial statement presentation. We believe that our audits provide a reasonable basis for our opinion.	The scope paragraph states that the audit was conducted in accordance with GAAS.
As described in Note X, these financial statements were prepared on the accounting basis used for income tax purposes, which is a comprehensive basis of accounting other than generally accepted accounting principles.	The third paragraph refers to the note in the financial statements that states the basis of presentation upon which the statements were prepared.
In our opinion, the financial statements referred to above present fairly, in all material respects, the assets, liabilities, and capital of Diamond Partnership as of December 31, 19X2 and 19X1, and its revenue and expenses and changes in partners' capital accounts for the years then ended, on the basis of accounting described in Note X.	The opinion paragraph expresses the auditor's opinion on whether the financial statements are presented fairly, in all material respects, in conformity with the basis described.

Exhibit 35.10.   Financial statements prepared on the entity's income tax basis. Annotations appear to the right.

individual element, account, or item audited rather than to the aggregate thereof or to the financial statements taken as a whole. Consequently, the audit is usually more extensive than if the same information were being considered in conjunction with an audit of the financial statements taken as a whole.

An example of a report related to the amount of sales for the purpose of computing rental charges is shown in Exhibit 35.11.

(c) Applying Agreed-Upon Procedures.   An accountant may undertake an engagement to apply agreed-upon procedures to specified elements, accounts, or items of a financial statement. For example, an individual who is considering purchasing a business may request that the accountant reconcile the bank balances and confirm the accounts receivable of the business. Acceptance of this type of engagement is only permissible if the parties involved have a clear understanding of the procedures to be performed and if distribution of the report is limited to named parties involved.

An engagement to apply agreed-upon procedures does not constitute an audit conducted in accordance with GAAS. Only the three general standards and the first standard of fieldwork apply. When applying agreed-upon procedures, the accountant's report should:

- Indicate the specified elements, accounts, or items to which the agreed-upon procedures were applied.
- Indicate the intended distribution of the report.

We have audited the accompanying schedule of gross sales (as defined in the lease agreement dated March 4, 19X0, between XYZ Company, as lessor, and Stony Stores Corporation, as lessee) of Stony Stores Corporation at its East Street store, Brewster, New York, for the year ended December 31, 19X2. This schedule is the responsibility of the Stony Stores Corp. management. Our responsibility is to express an opinion on this schedule based on our audit.	The first paragraph identifies the sales schedule, the lease agreement, and the parties to the agreement. The auditor also indicates that the schedule is management's responsibility.
We conducted our audit in accordance with generally accepted auditing standards. Those standards require that we plan and perform the audit to obtain reasonable assurance about whether the schedule of gross sales is free of material misstatement. An audit includes examining, on a test basis, evidence supporting the amounts and disclosures in the schedule of gross sales. An audit also includes assessing the accounting principles used and significant estimates made by management, as well as evaluating the overall schedule presentation. We believe that our audit provides a reasonable basis for our opinion.	The scope paragraph states that the audit was conducted in accordance with GAAS.
In our opinion, the schedule of gross sales referred to above presents fairly, in all material respects, the gross sales of Stony Stores Corporation at its East Street store, Brewster, New York, for the year ended December 31, 19X2, as defined in the lease agreement referred to in the first paragraph.	The opinion paragraph expresses the auditor's opinion on whether the schedule presents fairly, in all material respects, the gross sales as defined in the lease agreement.
This report is intended solely for the information and use of the board of directors and management of Stony Stores Corp. and XYZ Company and should not be used for any other purpose.	The final paragraph indicates that distribution of the report is limited to the parties identified.

Exhibit 35.11.   Report relating to amount of sales for the purpose of computing rental. Annotations appear to the right.

- Enumerate the procedures performed.
- State the accountant's findings.
- Disclaim an opinion with respect to the specified elements, accounts, or items.
- State that the report should not be associated with the financial statements of the entity.

(d) Compliance Reports Related to Audited Financial Statements.   Companies may be required by contractual agreements or by regulatory agencies to furnish **compliance reports** by independent auditors. For example, loan agreements usually impose on borrowers a variety of covenants involving matters such as payments into sinking funds, payments of interest, maintenance of current ratio, restriction of dividends payments, and use of the proceeds of sales of property.

Under SAS No. 62, the auditor is allowed to give a negative assurance report on compliance with contractual agreements provided that:

- He has audited the financial statements to which the contractual agreement or regulatory provision relates.
- He has not issued an adverse opinion or disclaimer of opinion on such financial statements.
- He only reports on matters that audit procedures were applied to during the audit of the financial statements.

A report on compliance with contractual provisions is shown in Exhibit 35.12.

(e) Financial Presentations to Comply with Contractual Agreements or Regulatory Provisions. Auditors are sometimes requested to report on special-purpose financial statements prepared to comply with a contractual agreement or regulatory provisions. Generally, these types of reports are intended solely for the use of the parties to the agreement, regulatory bodies, or other specified parties. According to SAS No. 62, ''Special Reports'' (AU623) these types of presentations fall into two categories:

1. Those that do not constitute complete presentation of the entity's assets, liabilities, revenues, and expenses (an incomplete presentation) but are otherwise prepared in conformity with GAAP or an OCBOA.

We have audited, in accordance with generally accepted auditing standards, the balance sheets of Lex Company as of December 31, 19X2 and 19X1, and the related statements of income, retained earnings, and cash flows for the years then ended, and have issued our report thereon dated February 16, 19X3.	The first paragraph identifies the financial statements audited and states that they were audited in accordance with GAAS.
In connection with our audits, nothing came to our attention that caused us to believe that the Company failed to comply with the terms, covenants, provisions, or conditions of sections 10 to 15, inclusive, of the Indenture dated July 21, 19X0, with XYZ Bank insofar as they relate to accounting matters. It should be noted, however, that our audits were not directed primarily toward obtaining knowledge of such noncompliance.	The middle paragraph provides negative assurance about contract violations. The auditor notes that the audit was not directed toward obtaining such knowledge.
This report is intended solely for the information and use of the board of directors and management of Lex Company and XYZ Bank and should not be used for any other purpose.	The last paragraph indicates that distribution of the report is limited to the parties to the contract.

Exhibit 35.12.   Report on compliance with contractual provisions. Annotations appear to the right.

2. Those prepared on a basis of accounting prescribed in an agreement that result in presentations not in conformity with GAAP or an OCBOA.

An auditor may be requested to report on a financial presentation to meet the special purposes of regulatory agencies or parties to an agreement. For example, the SEC may require a schedule of gross income and certain expenses of an entity's real estate operation in which income and expenses are measured in conformity with GAAP, but expenses are defined to exclude certain items such as interest, depreciation, and income taxes. Also, a buy–sell agreement may specify a schedule of gross assets and liabilities of the entity measured in conformity with GAAP but limited to the assets to be sold and liabilities to be transferred pursuant to the agreement. Such financial presentations are regarded as financial statements even though certain items may be excluded. The presentations differ from complete financial statements only to the extent necessary to meet the special purposes for which they are prepared. An example of a special report on such financial presentations is shown in Exhibit 35.13.

An auditor also might be asked to report on a financial presentation prepared to comply with the provisions of a contract or regulatory agreement that results in a presentation not in conformity with GAAP or OCBOA. For example, a loan agreement might call for financial statements prepared in conformity with GAAP except for certain assets, such as inventories and property, plant, and equipment, for which the valuation basis is specified in the

---

We have audited the accompanying statement of net assets sold of Bender Company as of June 8, 19X1. This statement of net assets sold is the responsibility of Bender Company's management. Our responsibility is to express an opinion on the statement of net assets sold based on our audit.

We conducted our audit in accordance with generally accepted auditing standards. Those standards require that we plan and perform the audit to obtain reasonable assurance about whether the statement of net assets sold is free of material misstatement. An audit includes examining, on a test basis, evidence supporting the amounts and disclosures in the statements. An audit also includes assessing the accounting principles used and significant estimates made by management, as well as evaluating the overall presentation of the statement of net assets sold. We believe that our audit provides a reasonable basis for our opinion.

The accompanying statement was prepared to present the net assets of Bender Company sold to XYZ Corporation pursuant to the purchase agreement described in Note X, and is not intended to be a complete presentation of Bender Company's assets and liabilities.

In our opinion, the accompanying statement of net assets sold presents fairly, in all material respects, the net assets sold of Bender Company as of June 8, 19X1, pursuant to the purchase agreement referred to in Note X, in conformity with generally accepted accounting principles.

This report is intended solely for the information and use of the board of directors and management of Bender Company and XYZ Corporation and should not be used for any other purpose.

Annotations (right column):

The first paragraph identifies the audited statement of net assets sold. The auditor emphasizes that the statement is management's responsibility.

The second paragraph states that the audit was conducted in accordance with GAAS.

The third paragraph identifies the note in the statement that describes the basis of presentation as defined in the purchase agreement.

The opinion paragraph states whether the statement is fairly presented in all material respects, pursuant to the agreement in conformity with GAAP.

This paragraph indicates that distribution of the report is limited to the parties to the contract.

Exhibit 35.13.   Report on a statement of assets sold and liabilities transferred to comply with a contractual agreement. Annotations appear to the right.

agreement. These financial statements are not prepared in conformity with GAAP or OCBOA since they do not meet the requirements of being a measurement basis "having substantial support." When reporting on a non-GAAP, non-OCBOA presentation, the auditor would modify the end of the third paragraph in Exhibit 35.13 to read ". . . and are not intended to be a presentation in conformity with generally accepted accounting principles."

(f) Prescribed Forms. Auditors are sometimes requested to complete **prescribed forms** or schedules designed by bodies with which they are to be filed. These forms sometimes also prescribe the wording of the auditor's report. For example, state licensing boards for construction contractors often require the auditor both to complete a prescribed form that presents financial information and to sign a prescribed auditor's report.

Sometimes, these prescribed report forms cannot be signed by the auditor because the report does not conform to the standards of reporting. For example, a report may include a statement that is not consistent with the auditor's responsibility. Sometimes the report can be made acceptable by inserting appropriate additional wording. In other situations, however, the auditor may have to completely reword the form or attach a separate report. In no circumstances should the auditor sign a report that violates professional reporting standards.

35.17 REPORTS ON INTERNAL ACCOUNTING CONTROL.   SAS No. 30, "Reporting on Internal Accounting Control" (AU 642), allows the auditor to perform three different types of engagements on internal accounting control.

- Express an opinion on the entity's system of IAC in effect as of a specified date or a specified period of time.
- Issue a restricted report on all or part of an entity's system based on preestablished criteria of regulatory agencies.
- Issue other restricted-use, special-purpose reports on all or part of an entity's system. (These reports must be restricted to management, another CPA, or other specified third parties. They may be based on a study of system design without tests of compliance or agreed-upon procedures.)

The first two engagements are discussed briefly below.

The study and evaluation of internal accounting control for the purpose of expressing an opinion may be made separately from or in conjunction with an audit of the entity's financial statements. This type of report can be dated differently from the audit report date and can be from a CPA who is not the auditor of the financial statements. In addition, this is the only type of internal accounting control report in which no restrictions are placed on the distribution of the report.

In making a study of internal accounting control for the purpose of expressing an opinion, the auditor should (1) plan the scope of engagement, (2) review the design of the system, (3) test compliance with prescribed procedures, and (4) evaluate the results of the review and tests.

The auditor must obtain a written representation from management that acknowledges management's responsibility for establishing and maintaining the system of internal accounting control and states that management has disclosed to the CPA all material weaknesses in the system of which it is aware. When the study is made as part of a financial statement audit, the auditor is not required to duplicate any procedures that may be performed in the audit.

The accountant's report in this type of engagement should include:

- A description of the scope of the engagement.
- The date to which the opinion relates.

- A statement that the establishment and maintenance of the system is the responsibility of management.
- A brief explanation of the broad objectives and inherent limitations of internal accounting control.
- The accountant's opinion on whether the system as a whole was sufficient to meet the broad objective of internal accounting control, which is the prevention or detection of errors or irregularities material to the financial statements. The opinion may be qualified or disclaimed.

Some government and regulatory agencies require reports on internal accounting control from entities under their jurisdiction. In such cases, specific criteria may be provided for evaluating controls. However, the accountant cannot issue a report unless the criteria are set forth in reasonable detail and in terms susceptible to objective application.

The accountant's report should (1) clearly identify the matters covered by the study, (2) indicate whether the study included tests of compliance with the procedures covered by the study, (3) describe the objectives and limitations of internal accounting control and the accountant's evaluations of it, (4) state the accountant's conclusion, based on the agency's criteria, concerning the adequacy of the procedures studied, with an exception as to any material weaknesses, and (5) state that it is intended for use in connection with the grant or other purpose to which the report refers and that it should not be used for any other purpose.

35.18 INVOLVEMENT WITH OTHER INFORMATION.   Various Statements on Auditing Standards address information that is presented in addition to the basic financial statements. These include SAS No. 8, "Other Information in Documents Containing Audited Financial Statements" (AU 550); SAS No. 52, "Omnibus SAS-1987 (Required Supplementary Information)" (AU 558); and SAS No. 29, "Reporting on Information Accompanying the Basic Financial Statements in Auditor-Submitted Documents."

The auditor has different reporting responsibilities for information appearing in an auditor-submitted document than for information appearing in a client-prepared document.

(a) Client-Prepared Documents.   Client-prepared documents are the responsibility of the client. For example, the annual report to shareholders is usually clearly discernible as the work of the client rather than the auditor. In such documents, the reader would generally expect the auditor's report to cover only the information identified in the report. Other information in the document usually can be clearly identified as furnished by management. For this reason, SAS No. 8 provides that the auditor's responsibility for other information in a client-prepared document containing audited financial statements does not extend beyond the financial information identified in the audit report.

An auditor is not required to perform any audit procedures to substantiate the other information in a client-prepared document. However, SAS No. 8 does require the auditor to read the other information and consider the manner in which it is presented to assess whether it is materially inconsistent with the financial statements. For example, in reading a president's letter in the annual report, the auditor should assess whether the president's comments about operating income are consistent with the income statement. If the auditor does not identify any material inconsistencies, no comment whatsoever is made about the other information. However, if the other information is not consistent with the financial statements, and the financial statements are correct, the auditor would consider taking one of the following steps:

- Requesting the client to revise the information to eliminate the inconsistency.
- Revising the audit report to include an explanatory paragraph describing the inconsistency.

• Withholding the audit report in the document.
• Withdrawing from the engagement.

While reading the other information to determine whether there is a material inconsistency, the auditor may become aware of information that he believes is a material misstatement of fact even though it is not inconsistent with the financial statements. For example, the auditor may note that the president incorrectly states in the annual report that the client is the largest company in its industry. Even though this statement does not contradict the financial statements, the auditor may be aware that the statement is incorrect. SAS No. 8 notes that the auditor may not have the expertise to evaluate the statement, that standards may not exist to assess the statement, and that valid differences of judgment or opinion may exist. However, if the auditor has a valid basis of concern, he should discuss the matter with the client, consider notifying the client in writing, and consider consulting legal counsel.

(b) Auditor-Submitted Documents.   Auditor-submitted documents are bound in the CPA firm's report cover and are sometimes printed on paper bearing the auditor's logo or watermark. The appearance of these documents often leads readers to assume that the auditor is taking some degree of responsibility for all the information in the document. As a result, SAS No. 29 (AU 551) requires the auditor to report on all the information in an auditor-submitted document.

The auditor's report on additional information may be presented separately in the document or may be included as a separate paragraph of the auditor's report on the financial statements. Regardless of the method selected, the report must state that the audit was made for the purpose of forming an opinion on the financial statements taken as a whole, identify the additional information, and indicate that it is presented for purposes of additional analysis and is not a required part of the basic financial statements.

The auditor must either express an opinion on whether the additional information is fairly stated in all material respects to the financial statements as a whole or disclaim an opinion. Expression of an opinion is appropriate only when the information has been subjected to the auditing procedures applied to the financial statements. An auditor has no obligation to apply any auditing procedures to the additional information, and if the additional information in an auditor-submitted document has not been subjected to the auditing procedures applied to the basic financial statements, the auditor should disclaim an opinion on that information.

(c) Supplementary Information Required by the FASB or GASB.   The FASB and the GASB require certain entities to present information supplementary to the financial statements. Currently, these requirements include FASB standards regarding information about oil and gas reserves and a GASB standard on pension disclosures. Required supplementary information is not necessary for the fair presentation of financial statements in conformity with GAAP. However, the information is an essential part of the broader concept of financial reporting in general. For this reason, SAS No. 52 requires an auditor to apply certain limited procedures to this information. These procedures are principally inquiries of management regarding methods of measuring and presenting the supplementary information.

The auditor's reporting responsibility on required supplementary information again depends on whether the information is contained in an auditor-submitted or a client-prepared document. When an auditor-submitted document contains required supplementary information, the auditor should disclaim an opinion on that information unless the auditor has been specifically engaged to audit and express an opinion on the information. The disclaimer is required even though limited procedures must be applied to the information. The following is an illustration of a disclaimer:

> The supplementary oil and gas reserve information is not a required part of the basic financial statements of Horn Company for 19X1, but is supplementary information required by the Financial Accounting Standards Board. We have applied certain limited procedures that consisted principally of inquiries of management regarding the methods of measurement and presentation (or disclosure) of the supplementary information. However, we did not audit the information and we express no opinion on it.

In a client-prepared document, the exception reporting principle applies. SAS No. 52 requires the auditor to report on the required supplementary information only if:

- The required supplementary information is not presented.
- The auditor concludes that the data are not prepared or presented in accordance with FASB or GASB requirements.
- The auditor is unable to perform the limited procedures.
- The auditor has unresolved doubts about the required supplementary information.

When one of the above circumstances causes the auditor to report on the supplementary information in a client-prepared document, the auditor's opinion on the financial statements would not be affected. This is because the required supplementary information is not considered by the FASB or GASB to be part of GAAP and, therefore, does not affect the financial statements.

35.19 REVIEW OF INTERIM FINANCIAL INFORMATION. Interim financial information includes current data during a fiscal year on financial position, results of operations, and cash

---

We have made a review [describe the information or statements reviewed] of Nest Company and consolidated subsidiaries as of September 30, 19X1, and for the three-month and nine-month periods then ended, in accordance with standards established by the American Institute of Certified Public Accountants.	The first paragraph identifies the information or financial statements reviewed and states that the review was made in accordance with standards for such reviews.
A review of interim financial information consists principally of obtaining an understanding of the system for the preparation of interim financial information, applying analytical procedures to financial data, and making inquiries of persons responsible for financial and accounting matters. It is substantially less in scope than an audit performed in accordance with generally accepted auditing standards, the objective of which is the expression of an opinion regarding the financial statements taken as a whole. Accordingly, we do not express such an opinion.	The second paragraph explains that a review consists primarily of analytical procedures and inquiries and is substantially less in scope than an audit made in accordance with GAAS. Therefore, no opinion is given.
Based on our review, we are not aware of any material modification that should be made to the accompanying financial [information or statements] for them to be in conformity with generally accepted auditing standards.	Nothing was found that needs modification for the financial information or statements to be in accordance with GAAP (negative assurance).

Exhibit 35.14. Accountant's report on review of interim financial information for a public entity. Annotations appear to the right.

flows. This information may be issued on a monthly or quarterly basis or at other intervals and can take the form of either complete financial statements, summarized financial statements, or summarized financial data, and may be presented alone or in a note to audited financial statements.

SAS No. 36, "Review of Interim Financial Information," provides guidance to the independent accountant involved with interim financial information. According to SAS No. 36, the objective of a review of interim financial information is to provide the accountant with a basis for reporting whether material modifications should be made for the interim financial information to conform with GAAP. The accountant reaches this conclusion based on the performance of inquiry and analytical procedures.

Exhibit 35.14 is an example of a report on interim financial information.

35.20 PROSPECTIVE FINANCIAL STATEMENTS.   CPAs are increasingly involved with financial information that is future oriented. For example, a client may want a forecast of its earnings for the next year. Or a client may be considering whether to make an investment and therefore may want a projection of future cash flows. Such information that is future oriented is termed *prospective financial information*.

In 1985 the Auditing Standards Board issued a Statement on Standards for Accountants' Services on Prospective Financial Information, "Financial Forecasts and Projections" (AT 100). The statement establishes standards for accountants providing different levels of service on prospective financial statements. Accountants are required under Rule 202 of the Code of Professional Conduct to comply with the new statement when they are performing an engagement involving prospective financial information.

The statement establishes standards for the three types of services that can be provided on prospective financial statements expected to be used by third parties: compilation, application of agreed-upon procedures, and examination. The statement also prohibits the accountant from providing services on prospective financial statements for third-party use if the statements do not disclose the underlying assumptions or if projections (as defined below) appropriate only for limited use are to be distributed to **passive users**—that is, persons who are not negotiating directly with the user.

In addition, in 1986 the Auditing Standards Divisions issued a companion pronouncement, *Guide for Prospective Financial Statements*. This guide establishes preparation and presentation guidelines (analogous to GAAP) for prospective financial statements.

(a) Financial Forecasts and Financial Projections.   The statement (AT 100) defines **financial forecasts** as "prospective financial statements that present, to the best of the responsible party's knowledge and belief, an entity's expected financial position, results of operations, and changes in financial position." Financial forecasts are based on the responsible party's assumptions, reflecting conditions it expects to exist and the course of action it expects to take.

Alternatively, the statement defines **financial projections** as "prospective financial statements that present, to the best of the responsible party's knowledge and belief, given one or more hypothetical assumptions, an entity's expected financial position, results of operations, and changes in financial position." A financial projection is sometimes prepared to present one or more hypothetical courses of action for evaluation, as in response to a question such as, "What would happen if . . .?" A financial projection is based on the responsible party's assumptions reflecting conditions it expects would exist and the course of action it expects would be taken, given one or more hypothetical assumptions.

In a **forecast,** all assumptions are expected to occur. In a **projection,** one or more (hypothetical) assumptions are not necessarily expected to occur (although they may if management chooses a certain course of action). For example, a company may project the construction of a new building without having made the decision to construct the building. All the other assumptions would be expected to occur if the hypothetical assumption occurs.

Prospective financial statements (forecasts or projections) may be presented as complete statements of financial position, results of operations, and cash flows, or may be presented in a summarized or condensed form. Certain items are required for a presentation to qualify as a prospective financial statement, including revenues, gross profit or cost of sales, unusual or infrequent items, income taxes, discontinued operations or extraordinary items, income from continuing operations, net income, earnings per share, and significant changes in financial position. Presentations that omit one or more of these minimum items are called **partial presentations.**

(b) Levels of Service. As noted previously, the statement provides three levels of service on prospective financial statements expected to be used by third parties:

- *Compilation Engagement.* A compilation engagement involves assembling prospective financial statements based on the responsible party's assumptions and considering whether the presentation appears to be presented in conformity with AICPA presentation guidelines and whether it is or is not obviously inappropriate.
- *Agreed-Upon Procedures Engagement.* An agreed-upon procedures engagement is generally an engagement that involves (1) applying to prospective financial statements procedures that have been agreed to or established by specified users of the data (for example, a specific bank) and (2) issuing a report that enumerates the procedures performed, states the accountant's findings, and restricts report distribution to specified parties.
- *Examination.* Examination is generally an audit that involves (1) evaluating the preparation, the support underlying the assumptions, and the presentation of the prospective financial statements for conformity with AICPA presentation guidelines, and (2) issuing an examination report. The examination report expresses a positive opinion on whether the assumptions provide a reasonable basis for the prospective financial statements. An example of a standard report on forecasted financial statements is shown in Exhibit 35.15.

We have examined the accompanying forecasted balance sheet, statements of income, retained earnings, and cash flows of ABC Company as of December 31, 19X1, and for the year then ending. Our examination was made in accordance with standards for an examination of a forecast established by the American Institute of Certified Public Accountants and accordingly, included such procedures as we considered necessary to evaluate both the assumptions used by management and the preparation and presentation of the forecast.	The first paragraph identifies the forecasted statements examined and explains that they were examined in accordance with guidelines established by the AICPA.
In our opinion, the accompanying forecast is presented in conformity with guidelines for presentation of a forecast established by the American Institute of Certified Public Accountants, and the underlying assumptions provide a reasonable basis for management's forecast. However, there will usually be differences between the forecasted and actual results, because events and circumstances frequently do not occur as expected, and those differences may be material. We have no responsibility to update this report for events and circumstances occurring after the date of this report.	The second paragraph expresses an opinion as to whether the forecast is presented in conformity with guidelines set up by the AICPA. It also notes that there are usually differences between actual and forecasted results, and that there is no responsibility to update the report.

Exhibit 35.15.   Accountant's standard report on an examination of a forecast. Annotations appear to the right.

The logic underlying the examination procedures for prospective financial statements is basically the same as that underlying the audit of historical financial statements. However, the literature does contain some distinctive reporting requirements for examinations. If a prospective presentation fails to disclose one or more significant assumptions or if one or more significant assumptions do not have a reasonable basis, an adverse opinion is required. Similarly, if a scope limitation exists—that is, the inability to apply a necessary procedure because of circumstances or client restrictions—a disclaimer is required.

35.21 REPORTING ON FINANCIAL STATEMENTS PREPARED FOR USE IN OTHER COUNTRIES. Most U.S. companies prepare financial statements for use in the United States in conformity with GAAP accepted in the United States. However, some U.S. companies have valid reasons for presenting their financial statements in conformity with accounting principles generally accepted in another country (non-U.S. GAAP). For example, a U.S. company may be a subsidiary of a foreign company or may wish to raise capital abroad.

SAS No. 51, "Reporting on Financial Statements Prepared for Use in Other Countries" (AU 534), provides guidance to a U.S. auditor who expresses an opinion on a U.S. entity's financial statements prepared in conformity with non-U.S. GAAP. The auditor should be familiar with the non-U.S. GAAP used in order to report on the financial statements and should consider consulting with accountants having expertise in such principles. The auditor should also understand and obtain management's written representations about the purpose and use of non-U.S. GAAP financial statements. The auditor should comply with U.S. GAAS but might need to modify certain procedures for assertions embodied in the non-U.S. GAAP financial statements that differ from those in U.S. GAAP financial statements. (For example, some countries require inflation adjustments in financial statements, in which case the U.S. auditor would need to perform procedures to test the inflation restatement.)

According to SAS No. 51 if the non-U.S. GAAP financial statements are prepared for use only outside the United States, the auditor may report using either (1) a U.S.-style report modified to report on the accounting principles of another country or, if appropriate, (2) the report form of another country. When the U.S. auditor uses the report form of another country, he should determine that the report would be used by non-U.S. auditors in similar circumstances and that the attestations contained in the report are appropriate. Non-U.S. GAAP financial statements are ordinarily not useful to U.S. users. Accordingly, if a company's financial statements are needed for use in both another country and the United States, the auditor may report on two sets of financial statements, one prepared using non-U.S. GAAP and the other prepared using U.S. GAAP.

35.22 REPORTS ON THE APPLICATION OF ACCOUNTING PRINCIPLES. Accountants are sometimes engaged by entities, for whom they are not the continuing auditor (that is, the entity is audited by another CPA), to provide consultations regarding a proposed or completed transaction. This type of consultation is often referred to as "opinion shopping" because some infer that the entity will shop around until it finds an accountant who will agree with its position and then hire that accountant as the auditor. There are public perceptions that opinion shopping is not in the public interest because it may compromise the account-ant's objectivity.

As a result of these concerns, the Auditing Standards Board issued SAS No. 50, "Reports on the Application of Accounting Principles" (AU 625). SAS No. 50 applies to accountants who provide reports, written or oral, on the accounting treatments of proposed or completed specific transactions to persons or entities other than continuing clients.

Before providing advice, the accountant should consider the identity of the requestor, the circumstances and purpose of the request, and the use of the resulting report. SAS No. 50 also requires the reporting accountant to exercise due professional care, have adequate technical training and proficiency, properly plan and supervise the engagement, and accumulate sufficient information to provide a reasonable basis for the professional judgment described in the report.

In forming a judgment the accountant should:

- Understand the form and substance of the transaction.
- Review applicable accounting principles.
- Consult with other professionals or experts, as appropriate.
- Perform research and consider precedents and analogies, as appropriate.

Finally, and most important, the reporting accountant is required to consult with the entity's continuing auditor to ascertain all the relevant facts. The continuing auditor can often provide information not otherwise available to the reporting accountant, such as the form and substance of the transaction, how management has applied accounting principles to similar transactions, and whether the method of accounting recommended by the continuing auditor is disputed by management.

COMPILATION AND REVIEW SERVICES

An independent accountant originally engaged to perform an audit of the financial statements of a **nonpublic** entity may be requested to change the engagement to a review or compilation of the financial statements. Before agreeing to change the engagement, consideration should be given to the surrounding circumstances, including:

1. The reason given by the client for changing the engagement, particularly the implications of a restriction on the scope of the audit.
2. The additional audit effort required to complete the audit.
3. The estimated cost to complete the audit. (If auditing procedures are substantially complete or the cost to complete them is relatively insignificant, a change may not be appropriate.)

The reason for the change may result from a change in circumstances (e.g., a decision by the company's banker to accept a review report rather than an audit report). When such situations are present, the request for a change in engagement ordinarily would be considered reasonable.

Whenever financial statements are compiled or reviewed, SSARS No. 1 states that the independent accountant's report should indicate clearly the degree of responsibility taken with respect to those financial statements. These standards apply to financial statements prepared in conformity with GAAP or a comprehensive basis of accounting other than GAAP. The report issued should be appropriate for the highest level of service performed. If statements are processed on a computer controlled by the independent accountant, that accountant should comply with the requirements of SSARS No. 1. However a reporting requirement does not arise merely as a result of consulting with a client on accounting or data-processing matters prior to client submission of data for processing at an outside service center.

35.23 STANDARD COMPILATION REPORT. Compiled financial statements are accompanied by a report that indicates that a compilation has been performed and that such a service is limited to presenting, in financial statement format, information that is the representation of management or owners. The report also states that the financial statements have not been audited or reviewed, thus no opinion or any other form of assurance is expressed on them. No reference is made to any other procedures performed before or during the compilation engagement. The following form of report is appropriate when reporting on a compilation.

> We have compiled the accompanying balance sheets of ABC Co. as of December 31, 19x2 and 19x1 and the related statements of income, retained earnings, and cash flows in accordance with standards established by the American Institute of Certified Public Accountants.
>
> A compilation is limited to presenting in the form of financial statements information that is the representation of management (owners). We have not audited or reviewed the accompanying financial statements and, accordingly, do not express an opinion or any other form of assurance on them.

The report should be dated as of the date the compilation service is completed. Each page of the compiled financial statements should include a reference such as "See accountant's compilation report." On the basic financial statements that notation may be stated somewhat as follows: "See accompanaying notes to the unaudited financial statements and accountant's compilation report."

35.24 STANDARD REVIEW REPORT.   Reviewed financial statements are accompanied by a report that indicates that a review was performed in accordance with AICPA standards. The report describes a review engagement, states that the information in the financial statements is the representation of management (or owners), and disclaims an opinion on the financial statements taken as a whole. Nevertheless, SSARS No. 1 (AR 100) provides the report also should state that: "The accountant is not aware of any material modifications that should be made to the financial statements in order for them to be in conformity with generally accepted accounting principles, other than those modifications, if any, indicated in his report." No reference is made to any other procedures performed before or during the review engagement.

The following form of report is appropriate when reporting on reviewed financial statements. Such a report cannot be issued when the independent accountant is unable to complete inquiry and analytical procedures considered necessary to express the limited assurances described above.

> We have reviewed the accompanying balance sheets of ABC Co. as of December 31, 19X2 and 19X1, and the related statements of income, retained earnings, and cash flows for the years then ended, in accordance with standards established by the American Institute of Certified Public Accountants. All information included in these financial statements is the representation of the management (owners) of ABC Co.
>
> A review consists principally of inquiries of company personnel and analytical procedures applied to financial data. It is substantially less in scope than an audit in accordance with generally accepted auditing standards, the objective of which is the expression of an opinion regarding the financial statements taken as a whole. Accordingly, we do not express such an opinion.
>
> Based on our reviews, we are not aware of any material modifications that should be made to the accompanying financial statements in order for them to be in conformity with generally accepted accounting principles.

The report is dated as of the date inquiry and analytical procedures are completed. Each page of the reviewed financial statements should include a reference such as "See accountant's review report." On the basic financial statements that notation may be stated somewhat as follows: "See accompanying notes to the unaudited financial statements and accountant's review report."

35.25 GAAP DEPARTURES.   If the independent accountant becomes aware of a departure from GAAP (or, if applicable, a comprehensive basis of accounting other than GAAP that appears to be material to the financial statements being compiled or reviewed, and the financial statements are not revised, the standard compilation or review report should be modified by including a separate paragraph that discloses the following:

1. The nature of the departure.
2. The effects of the departure on the financial statements if they have been determined by management or are known as a result of the accountant's procedures; or the fact that the effects of the departure have not been determined by management. The accountant is not required to determine the effects of a departure.

An example of a review report modified to disclose a departure from GAAP follows:

REVIEW REPORT

Standard first paragraph.
Standard second paragraph.

MODIFIED THIRD PARAGRAPH

Based on our review(s), with the exception of the matter(s) described in the following paragraph(s), we are not aware of any material modifications that should be made to the accompanying financial statements in order for them to be in conformity with generally accepted accounting principles.

DESCRIPTION OF DEPARTURE

As disclosed in Note X to the financial statements, generally accepted accounting principles require that inventory cost consist of material, labor, and overhead. Management has informed us that the inventory of finished goods and work in process is stated in the accompanying financial statements as material and labor cost only, and that the effects of this departure from generally accepted accounting principles on the financial position, results of operations, and cash flows have not been determined.

The independent accountant should consider whether modification of the standard review or compilation report is adequate to disclose departures from GAAP. If modification of the standard report does not appear adequate to indicate the deficiencies in the financial statements taken as a whole (e.g., numerous exceptions, or an exception of the type that would lead to an adverse opinion in an audit), the accountant should consider whether to withdraw from the engagement and provide no further services on the financial statements.

(a) Omission of a Statement of Cash Flows. Presentation of a statement of cash flows is required when both a balance sheet and a statement of income and retained earnings are presented. If the statement of cash flows has been omitted, reference to the statement of cash flows should be eliminated from the first paragraph of the accountant's report and a reservation as to presentation should be set forth in a separate paragraph. The reporting for the omission of a statement of cash flows is different if substantially all disclosures are omitted from compiled financial statements. An example of such reporting is provided below.

(b) Omission of Disclosure. The independent accountant may be requested to compile financial statements that **omit substantially all disclosures** required by GAAP (e.g., notes and the disclosures appearing in the body of the financial statements). Independent accountants may compile and report on such financial statements if the omission of substantially all disclosures is not, to their knowledge, undertaken with the intention of misleading users of the compiled statements. For example, it may be misleading for a company to present financial statements without disclosure in the face of a major new uncertainty that has not previously been disclosed in the company's financial statements. The special reporting requirements permitted by SSARS No. 1 apply to the omission of substantially all disclosures. They do not apply to the omission of selected disclosures, in which case a departure from GAAP exists. Further, they do not apply to review engagements. Omission of a required disclosure from reviewed financial statements would result in a GAAP departure.

When compiled financial statements omit substantially all disclosures, the standard report should be modified to indicate that omission. For example, the following paragraph may be added to the standard compilation report when substantially all disclosures have been omitted and the client also omits a statement of changes in financial position:

> Management has elected to omit substantially all the disclosures and the statement of cash flows required by generally accepted accounting principles. If the omitted disclosures and the statement of cash flows were included in the financial statements, they might influence the user's conclusions about the company's financial position, results of operations, and cash flows. Accordingly, these financial statements are not designed for those who are not informed about such matters.

If financial statements compiled in conformity with a comprehensive basis of accounting other than GAAP fail to disclose the basis of accounting used, the basis should be disclosed in the independent accountant's report. If a company wishes to include disclosures concerning only a few matters in the form of notes to the financial statements, such disclosures should be appropriately labeled. For example: "Selected information—Substantially all disclosures required by generally accepted accounting principles are not included."

(c) Uncertainties and Inconsistent Application of GAAP. SSARS No. 1 (AR 100) states:

> Normally, neither an uncertainty nor an inconsistency in the application of accounting principles would cause the accountant to modify the report provided the financial statements appropriately disclose such matters. Nothing in this statement, however, is intended to preclude an accountant from emphasizing in a separate paragraph of his report a matter regarding the financial statements.

(d) Lack of Independence. The lack of independence does not preclude an accountant from issuing a compilation report. In such circumstances, the following should be included as the last paragraph of the report: "We are not independent with respect to ABC Co." The reasons for lack of independence should not be given. On the other hand, the accountant cannot issue a review report if independence is lacking.

SOURCES AND SUGGESTED REFERENCES

AICPA, *AICPA Professional Standards: Vol. 1, U.S. Auditing Standards; and Vol. 2. Accounting and Review Services, Code of Professional Conduct, Bylaws, International Accounting and Auditing, Management Advisory Services, Quality Control, Quality Review, and Tax Practice,* Commerce Clearing House, Chicago, 1990, paperbound annual update. A loose-leaf service that includes the currently effective pronouncements on professional standards issued by the American Institute of Certified Public Accountants as well as the International Accounting Standards of the International Accounting Standards Committee and the International Auditing Guidelines of the International Auditing Practices Committee.

———, *AICPA Audit and Accounting Manual,* Commerce Clearing House, Chicago, 1990, paperbound annual update. A loose-leaf service of nonauthoritative audit tools and illustrations prepared by the AICPA's Technical Information Division, geared primarily to the needs of local practitioners.

———, *AICPA Technical Practice Aids,* Commerce Clearing House, Chicago, 1990, paperbound annual update. A loose-leaf service that includes selected Technical Information Service Inquiries and Replies, Statements of Position of the Auditing and Accounting Standards Divisions of the AICPA, Practice Bulletins by the AcSEC, and a list of issues papers of the Accounting Standards Division of the AICPA.

———, *Public Accountants,* How to Choose and Use a CPA, New York. Booklet answering such questions as: Who needs a CPA? How do you find a CPA? What qualifications should you look for? What do CPAs charge? How can you get the most value from a CPA's services?

————, *The New Auditor's Report—What It Means to You,* New York. Eight-panel brochure explaining the revised auditor's report.

————, *Understanding Audits and the Auditor's Report: A Guide for Financial Statement Users,* New York. Forty-page booklet containing a description of the nature of an audit, illustrative examples of the auditor's standard report, and discussion of the responsibilities of management, the auditor, and users.

————, *What Does a CPA Do? A Guide to CPA Services.* New York. Fifteen-page booklet explaining the various roles of the CPA—as auditor; as small business, management, and tax advisor; and as personal financial planner. The CPA's role in business and industry, education, government, and nonprofit organizations is also explained.

Carmichael, D. R., and Benis, Martin, *Auditing Standards and Procedures Manual,* 1990, Wiley, New York, 1989. A paperbound edition that makes the official language of the SASs easy to read and understandable while separating the minimum requirements of the SASs from advice, observations, and other subordinate information.

Carmichael, D. R., and Willingham, J. J., *Auditing Concepts and Methods,* McGraw-Hill, New York 1989.

Guy, Dan M., Alderman, C. Wayne, and Winters, Alan J., *Auditing,* Harcourt Brace Jovanovich, New York, 1990.

CHAPTER 36

DATA PROCESSING AND MANAGEMENT INFORMATION SYSTEMS

Dennis F. Galletta, PhD, CPA

Joseph M. Katz Graduate School of Business
University of Pittsburgh

CONTENTS

OVERVIEW

Few topics have blossomed like information technology over the past two decades. Virtually every worker has some knowledge of the widespread use of computers in organizations. The proliferation of this technology has led to many changes in how organizations process transactions, handle information inquiries, support decision making, and compete in their markets. This chapter covers data processing and management information systems from an accountant's standpoint.

36.1 DEFINITIONS.   A **management information system** is an "integrated, user-machine system for providing information to support the operations, management, and decision-making functions in an organization. The system utilizes computer hardware and software; manual procedures; models for analysis, planning, control and decision making; and a database" (Davis and Olson, 1985).

A **system** is a set of interacting units organized to support a common goal. Many phenomena can be viewed from a **systems perspective,** where a decision maker attempts to break a complex problem down into those components. Just as physicians cannot properly diagnose a bone marrow problem without considering the respiratory, circulatory, and skeletal subsystems, managers cannot properly diagnose a profitability problem without considering the marketing, production, and logistics subsystems of their firm. For example, any pricing decision must taken into account what the market will bear, costs of production, and availability of distribution channels.

The system exists in an **environment,** and there are many interactions between the system and the environment. These interactions cross the **boundary** of the system and provide linkages to other systems. **Inputs** are used or consumed by the system through some **process,** and **outputs** are produced or discarded by the system. This input-process-output view can be useful for understanding any system, and it is very commonly used when studying information systems in particular. When information systems are developed, for example, many development methodologies concentrate on identifying desired outputs, then determining the inputs that are necessary to produce those outputs, and finally building the processes that will convert those inputs into those outputs. Exhibit 36.1 illustrates the systems view.

The accounting function itself can be considered as an important part of an organization's information system.

The American Accounting Association (1966, p. 64) defines accounting as follows: "Essentially, accounting is an information system. More precisely, it is an application of a general theory of information to the problem of efficient economic operation. It also makes up a large part of the general information systems which provide decision-making information expressed in quantitative terms."

It is difficult to imagine accounting not being an integral part of the formal information systems in any organization. The importance of the role played by accounting systems ultimately depends on the knowledge and flexibility of the accounting profession. Accounting systems must be analyzed in terms of information systems and information theory when decisions are made to change their structure, measurement methods, or underlying concepts.

Information systems are positioned at a curious station: They function in a **probabilistic**

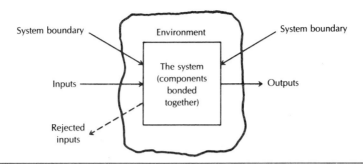

Exhibit 36.1.   System relationships.

environment while they are composed of a set of **deterministic** computer programs. That is, the outcomes and functions desired are uncertain, based on probabilities and intuition. The systems themselves must be written in a computer language, which is based on strict, formal mathematics and logic. As a result, it can be difficult for managers and system developers to communicate, and for business problems to be tackled by a system.

36.2 TECHNOLOGICAL ROOTS.   The first devices that alleviated the limitations of using fingers for arithmetic appeared long ago. The abacus was used for thousands of years until devices of greater power finally appeared in the ninth century A.D. (Deweney, 1988). This early departure from the abacus probably involved a system of elephant-drawn ropes and pulleys and offered significant computational capabilities. During the Renaissance, several calculating devices were proposed and built making use of gears whose teeth represented decimal digits. Eventually, it was discovered that relays and switches could store and manipulate digits. This innovation enabled a shift away from mechanical calculators to electronic devices.

In the 1940s, vacuum tubes replaced switches and relays in the earliest electronic computers. These tubes contain circuits with the ability to process "on" or "off" input impulses and to transmit the results down a wire to other circuits. Several other types of circuits might process these impulses. For example, an "AND" circuit transmits current (i.e., "on") when both of two input wires are "on." An "OR" circuit only needs one of its inputs to be "on" to transmit an "on." A "NOT" circuit takes an input and transmits its opposite (i.e., transmits an "on" when the input is "off"). Although it is not obvious without sketching circuit diagrams, these three circuits can be combined in a fashion that enables addition of binary (base two) numbers. Binary numbers can be electronically converted into decimal numbers. Addition is the basis for all other mathematical operations, since subtraction is addition of negative numbers, multiplication is repeated addition, division is repeated subtraction, and so forth.

Because hundreds of vacuum tubes are necessary to perform simple arithmetic, prospects were grim for more advanced applications of the computer. Further, these tubes burned out at a rapid rate, and it was difficult to locate and replace a burned-out tube. Accordingly, tube-based computers of the 1940s and 1950s were inoperable more than 50% of the time. Finally, the heat, size, and power consumption of tube-based computers made them infeasible for most organizations. Early general-purpose computers included the ENIAC and the UNIVAC I. The latter was used by the Census Bureau to process census results in 1950.

In the late 1950s, transistors replaced vacuum tubes, representing a significant revolution in hardware. Transistors were much smaller, cooler, and more dependable than tubes. In the 1970s, the first microprocessor was produced by photographing a large circuit diagram and reducing the image onto a tiny silicon wafer. The areas exposed to light and dark contain different levels of conductivity and enable performance of transistor functions. The 4004 chip (the first microprocessor) contains the equivalent of 2,300 transistors, the commonly used 80386 chip contains 275,000 transistors (Methvin, 1989), and the 80486 contains 1.2 million transistors (Neff, 1989).

36.3 CURRENT CAPABILITIES.   The high speeds of today's processors enable systems to be constructed to perform a wide variety of functions. Graphics-oriented software requires such speeds, because this software manipulates many more pieces of data per character displayed. As more functions are built into today's systems, users are further removed from the physical characteristics of the devices they use. For example, they no longer have to write programs that estimate the rotation speed of the disk devices so that each piece of data will be written on the disk at just the right spot for quickest retrieval. In today's systems, users are given the necessary building blocks to assure efficient operations of the hardware components.

As speeds of computers increase, demands on them follow suit. Users in the early 1950s were happy simply tabulating counts, but after every hardware improvement, users have always added new function requirements. Today's systems are still playing "catch-up" with user demands. Although applications perform quite satisfactorily, difficulties remain in communicating data between users and between applications. For example, a manager might be interested in analyzing trends in accounting data but may not have any software that allows the mainframe-based accounting data to be transmitted to a microcomputer. As a result, some users spend time retyping data from reports into spreadsheets. Today's challenge for software developers is to provide better integration while maintaining adequate controls.

One method of providing integration is through organization of data formats across equipment and users. A **database management system** serves as a tool to define, store, retrieve, and erase data, controlling access to the data. Today, a growing number of automated accounting systems use database management systems, thus easing integration and control. Many such systems employ easy-to-use **fourth-generation languages,** which allow users to type English-like inquiry commands, and programmers to construct tailored reports more quickly than when using standard programming languages. Such systems also provide facilities for password protection, transaction logging, and backup, necessary ingredients for **control** of systems.

36.4 PROSPECTS FOR THE FUTURE.   Future systems are likely to employ heavy use of graphics, consistency in the ways programs are used, consistency in file formats, screens that display an exact image of what will be printed, and a wide variety of fonts (print styles). Expert systems applications will become more common; experts in many fields will codify their knowledge into computer-readable form to provide assistance to others. Networks will transmit data more reliably and flexibly. All of this will require even faster processors and larger data storage devices than ever before. It will also require intensive efforts in standards development and programming.

One can easily lose sight of the human element in system design by concentrating solely on technical specifications and capabilities. Market shifts toward easier-to-use hardware and software have accelerated each year. The abacus might have been suitable for thousands of years, but today's users are much less patient with their systems. Many users demand significant software upgrades once every year or two. Anxious for more capabilities, many user groups form for the purpose of sharing shortcuts, tips, and enhancement programs. Users seem to have an insatiable appetite for greater functionality.

Future accounting systems should provide greater flexibility on both the input and output side. More systems will allow transactions to be entered using alternatives to the keyboard, for example, bar-code readers, voice inputs, and laser scanners. Because of the importance of maintaining controls, such developments should proceed with caution. It will be a significant challenge to create accounting systems that are easy to use while providing an effective internal control structure.

ORGANIZATIONAL INFORMATION NEEDS

36.5 INTRODUCTION.   Organizations are systems. They consist of a number of separate but interacting parts that work together to achieve a set of goals. The parts may be individuals or groups, and the goals may be specific tasks or more general objectives. Information flows in organizations make harmony between the parts possible. A manager's success depends, to a large degree, on the quality, the amount, and the rate at which relevant information is communicated. Therefore, information flows in organizations are the essence of organizational activity and the bond that holds the organization together.

36.6 ORGANIZATIONAL FUNCTIONS.   There are a number of theories of how organizations should be structured. The classic organizational structure of **functional line and staff** is the military model that places emphasis on the function to be performed. In business this would include elements such as marketing and production. This model also distinguishes between line managers (action takers or decision makers) and staff managers (advisors and information suppliers). The fundamental managerial activities suggested for this structure are **planning, organizing, directing, controlling,** and **staffing.** For more details on this approach see Koontz and O'Donnell (1975).

The disadvantage of a departmentalized functional organization is that it creates barriers between various elements in the organization. Unless heavy emphasis is placed on coordinating functions, it is entirely possible for functions to work at cross-purposes and disrupt the harmony in the organization. Another shortcoming of this approach is its inability to handle effectively long-term, complex projects.

To assist in providing information links between departments, an organization's database and database management system can provide a centralized repository of organizational data. The organization's functions can then share information; any data updated by one function is available to the others. Exhibit 36.2 illustrates a functional view of an organization (Davis and Olson, 1985).

36.7 HIERARCHY OF DECISION MAKING.   Decision making is the rational process of using information in organizations. The type of information required by a decision maker or manager depends not only on the functional area (i.e., marketing, production, etc.) but also on the **kind of decisions** and the **level of decisions.**

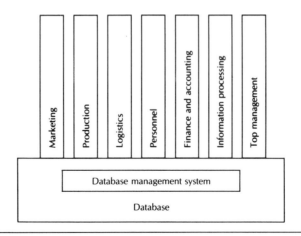

Exhibit 36.2.   Functional view of an organization.

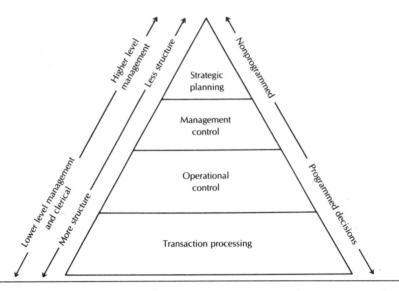

Exhibit 36.3.   Hierarchy of management decisions. *Source:* From G. Davis, *Management Information Systems: Conceptual Foundations, Structure, and Development,* McGraw-Hill, 1974, p. 222. Reproduced by permission.

(a) Kinds of Decisions.   Herbert A. Simon (1960) identified two kinds of decision in organizations—programmed and nonprogrammed.

> **Programmed Decisions.** Simon classified routine, perfunctory decsions made at all levels of management as programmed decisions. These decisions may involve either planning or control actions but more generally control. The programmed decision is known in advance, hence it is easily modeled using operation research techniques. For example, many of the mathematical models in inventory and cash management, as well as production scheduling, represent programmed decisions.
>
> **Nonprogrammed Decisions.** One-time, ill-structured decisions are nonprogrammed. These decisions often involve policy questions and cannot be anticipated, hence they are rarely modeled. Heuristic problem-solving techniques, which involve training decision makers in decision analysis skills, are used to handle these decisions.

(b) Levels of Decisions.   All organizations have a decision hierarchy that identifies the **level of decisions.** The top level in this hierarchy is the **strategic decision,** the middle level is the **tactical decision,** and the lowest level is the **operational decision.** Each level of decision making has different information requirements. Exhibit 36.3 illustrates the interrelationship between programmed decisions and the decision hierarchy.

> **Strategic Decisions.** Decisions at the top level of an organization are concerned with long-range planning, establishing goals, and setting the strategy for the organization. In business this involves major capital expenditures, market share, new product lines, acquisitions and mergers, and product line diversification. The information required for this kind of decision making, according to Burch and Grudnitski (1989) has the following characteristics: (1) Much of it is external information about things like competitive conditions, demographic and economic changes, customer preferences, governmental action, and social changes; (2) it is predictive, with special emphasis on long-term trends in

the areas listed in item 1; and (3) in sophisticated organizations it may be simulated to allow "what if" questions to be asked about changes in variables or assumptions.

Tactical Decisions. Middle managers make tactical decisions that involve the use of resources, the implementation of strategies, and the achievement of goals. In contrast to strategic decisions, which primarily involve planning, tactical decisions have an approximately equal balance of planning and control aspects. Tactical decision makers know the goals set down by the strategic planning activity but still need to set up short-run plans, monitor activities, and take corrective action.

In business, tactical decision makers are division and product line managers who decide such matters as product improvement, manufacturing methods, promotional companies, plant location, personnel acquisition and training, and research and development.

The nature of the decisions made at this level, as in the case of strategic decisions, dictates the information that is necessary. The time horizon of the middle manager is shorter than that of the top manager. The emphasis is on goal achievement. Thus tactical decision makers need **feedback** information on how well plans are going, and on what conditions or assumptions made during the planning have changed (e.g., labor supply, raw material supply, customer interest, product development schedule).

Operating Decisions. These decisions are made by a wide band of lower management, ranging from plant managers to department managers. The operating decision is usually a control decision. Emphasis is on specific and relatively short-run objectives such as meeting production schedules, quality requirements, inventory levels, or sales quotas. The operating decision maker functions on a short time horizon with limited tolerance for delay between action and reaction.

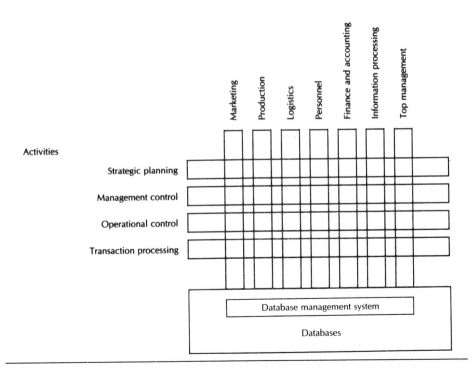

Exhibit 36.4.   Horizontal and vertical differentiation of an information system. *Source:* From G. B. Davis and M. H. Olson, *Management Information Systems: Conceptual Foundations, Structure, and Development,* McGraw-Hill, 1985. Reproduced by permission.

36.8 DIFFERENTIATION OF INFORMATION SYSTEMS.   An information system must support levels of an organization as well as functions. Just as each function suggests the need for different types of information, so does each level. For example, an operational level production information system would differ dramatically from a strategic level marketing system. The former involves many structured, programmed decisions based on internal information; such a system might be devoted to scheduling production for the upcoming weeks. The latter involves unstructured, nonprogrammed decisions based on a variety of information; such a system might be designed to track advertisement patterns of competitors. Exhibit 36.4 combines the concepts of Exhibits 36.2 and 36.3, illustrating the horizontal and vertical differentiation of information systems.

The information systems function should support all levels and functions of an organization. However, bias in supporting certain levels and functions is common. This bias could result from the positioning of the information systems function (many information systems directors report to the controller in manufacturing concerns), from the experience of the developers (many developers are most comfortable developing highly structured systems), or from the users themselves (many users have difficulty expressing their needs in unstructured applications).

THE INFORMATION SYSTEMS FUNCTION

36.9 STRUCTURE AND PLACEMENT

(a) Structure of the Traditional Data Processing Department.   The principal elements or tasks of the data processing department are **systems analysis and design, programming,** and **operations.** The structures vary from classical, formal and functional, to project-directed matrices. Some companies require that analysts be programmers, others separate the two functions. Generally the user deals with the analyst, the analyst with the programmer, and the programmer with the computer. The operations function usually is responsible for input processing, computer operations, output generating and distribution, and maintaining the availability of any online system. Other responsibilities generally include maintenance, library functions, and records retention. The selection of skilled individuals in any of these areas is extremely important. This is especially true for the smaller company, where demonstrated experience is essential. Constant training, evaluation, and attention are essential to maintain effectiveness. As with other organizational groupings, the data processing function should be structured to best meet the needs of the company. No single form is best. The most effective form seems to be one that covers all the required tasks, yet presents data in a form that permits measurement and evaluation.

(b) Reporting Relationship.   The task of performing the computations required by modern business enterprises is considerable. The best organizational location of the computer and the related staff has not been clearly established. Some companies have found the controller's department a satisfactory location; others have established separate information departments reporting to the CEO or to a vice-president for administration. Still other companies have found that independent service bureaus offer the most efficient means of obtaining computer facilities or services.

(c) Controller's Role.   Historically, the controller has been the chief information officer in the business enterprise. Anderson, Schmidt, and McCosh (1973) state that the controller is responsible for three main tasks. These are the preparation of legally required financial reports, the development and implementation of a system of control over the assets of the business, and the preparation of reports for the information of management. More computer applications in business have been attempted in these three areas than in any other field. At the same time, although the principal functions of the controller seem to coincide with the jobs for which the computer has been used, the organizational location of the computer often is not the controller's department.

The controller knows a great deal about the business operation and should put that knowledge to use in the context of the computer age. To do this requires reasonable familiarity with EDP principles and with the most readily available and economical uses of a computer. The computer is increasingly a major factor in the improvement of management information in many companies.

It would be unfortunate if the controller's knowledge were wasted by not employing it in developing the best possible system for the control of information. Diebold (1964) identifies personnel as a major factor causing failures in computer systems. He suggests that the use of technical specialists who fail to acknowledge or even appreciate their own limited understanding of business is a major cause of installation failure.

(d) Chief Information Officer (CIO).   Many firms have named the head of the information systems department the CIO, whereas others use the term *VP of MIS, Director of MIS*, or *Director of Data Processing* (approximately in descending order of executive rank), The CIO position is a strategic one; it exists to assure that corporate strategy and information systems strategy are consistent and advantageous (see Benjamin, Dickinson, and Rockart, 1985). Such a role can help in discovering strategic uses of information systems. However, there is some skepticism about widespread acceptance of this role because of uncertain job expectations, resistance by CEOs and COOs, and a lack of centralized MIS management (see Carlyle, 1988).

(e) Centralization versus Decentralization.   The centralization versus decentralization controversy has brewed for decades. In the early years of information technology, functional professionals (usually physicists or engineers) acquired, programmed, and operated the equipment themselves. The 1960s saw large, centralized data processing departments providing these functions. The end-user computing phenomenon of the 1980s appears in general to be weakening the centralized data processing departments (see Dearden, 1987). However, some organizations appear to be recentralizing, pulling the pendulum back once again (see Carlyle, 1987).

Who should control various information systems functions, including personnel, data, equipment, system development, policies, planning, or operations? All functions need not be centralized or decentralized, and a single function need not be completely centralized or completely decentralized. For example, an organization might have a centralized collection of data that information systems personnel in various organizational locations can access. This data could be stored on a centralized computer but accessed and processed by powerful microcomputer workstations in various sites.

Because of these complications, it is becoming difficult to discuss centralization versus decentralization in a single argument. Centralizing personnel makes it possible to hire specialized staff members and to provide a wider variety of career paths for them, but their functional business expertise may suffer. Centralizing data promotes control and sharability but makes access more difficult for users in various locations. Centralizing equipment allows spreading costs of large computers over more users, but many applications have migrated to smaller computers since the early 1980s. New languages that ease access to data have made it possible for users to develop their own systems, but there are significant difficulties for controlling such applications.

Thus, the question for today and for the future will not be "Should information systems be centralized or decentralized?" but rather "How can our information systems functions be structured and placed to best support the organization's needs?" This is a much more difficult question to address and requires careful study. Selective centralization and decentralization will be the norm, but unfortunately there are few universal principles because much of the answer depends on contextual issues.

36.10 INFORMATION SYSTEMS PLANNING.   Some organizations have discovered difficulties from failing to **plan** for information systems. Overall information systems planning takes place in three stages (Bowman, Davis, and Wetherbe, 1983): (1) Strategy, (2) Organizational Information Requirements, and (3) Resource Allocation.

Strategy for MIS planning involves developing a strategic plan for the MIS department. W. R. King (1978) recommends that this plan be developed in close alliance with the organization's strategic plan. It is important to decide how "strategic" a firm's information technology applications should be (Cash, McFarlan, and McKenney, 1988), using the **strategic grid** shown in Exhibit 36.5.

The strategic grid outlines four general approaches to information systems planning depending on a firm's strategic impact of (1) existing applications and (2) planned applications. If both are nonstrategic, the firm is in a traditional data processing "support" mode, where information systems are not considered vital to a firm's viability. In contrast, if both are strategic, the firm is in a "strategic" mode, where information systems are and have been considered critical to the firm. The other two cells signify changes in strategicity, the "turnaround" cell implying a sudden interest in strategic activity and the "factory" cell describing a firm that has completed strategic activity in the information systems department.

Organizational Information Requirements Planning is the next level of information systems planning. This stage is a more general version of the approach used for each application system and involves identifying key managers' information needs. One technique is the Critical Success Factors method (Rockart, 1979), which asks managers to describe the factors that are critical for success in their positions. Another technique is Business Systems Planning (BSP) (IBM, 1981), which is widely used and is well established. BSP involves performing a top-down analysis of the firm's information requirements by defining business objectives and the processes that contribute to those objectives. The processes are examined in detail, and executives are interviewed to outline key success factors, decisions, and problems. Information is identified that would assist them in these areas. Design clearly follows a top-down orientation, whereas construction follows a bottom-up strategy; individual applications defined by this analysis are developed and combined with other systems, resulting in a system that meets the business objectives that drove the design process.

The **Resource Allocation** stage in systems planning determines which of the individual applications under consideration should be developed and allows scheduling of application development. For this stage, conventional resource allocation tools are used, such as computations of return on investment, payback, and net present value. In addition, rankings by a **steering committee** (an executive-level group that determines which systems should be

	Low	High
High	Factory	Strategic
Low	Support	Turnaround

Strategic impact of existing systems

Strategic impact of applications development portfolio

Exhibit 36.5.   Strategic grid. *Source:* From J. I. Cash, Jr., F. W. McFarlan, and J. L. McKenney, *Corporate Systems Management: The Issues Facing Senior Executives,* Irwin, 1988. Reproduced by permission.

included in the firm's "portfolio" of systems) can be used (see Nolan, 1982). McFarlan (1981) suggests that a firm should maintain a balance between support and strategic applications, between centralized and end-user systems, between high and low risk/payoff, and between systems for highly experienced and novice users.

36.11 INFORMATION SYSTEMS AS COMPETITIVE WEAPONS.   Top executives have found that information systems can be used as weapons against the competition. One of the best-known systems of this type is American Hospital Supply Corporation's ASAP system. The ASAP system was an innovator because it allowed hospitals to order supplies through terminals in their offices. Orders were placed with little effort and were received and processed by American Hospital Supply without delay. After the system was installed in 1978, American Hospital Supply grew at a 17% compound annual rate and enjoyed a profit margin that was four times the industry average. Soon American Hospital Supply dominated the industry, and many analysts credit the system for its swift success (see Canning, 1984).

Many vivid examples illustrate dramatic increases in market share and decreases in the potency of competitors. Wiseman (1988) describes over a hundred published cases of such systems, further emphasizing the importance of investigating potential uses of information technology as competitive weapons; it appears that such an approach is increasingly becoming a tactic for survival.

A framework for identifying areas where a firm can achieve competitive advantage comes from Porter (1980). Porter's framework was applied to information systems by Cash, McFarlan, and McKenney (1988), who developed questions aimed at discovering competitive applications in each of five areas. Potential adopters should ask themselves if they can build barriers to entry, increase customer switching costs, build power in relationships with suppliers, achieve dramatic cost reductions, or generate new products or services.

INFORMATION STORAGE AND RETRIEVAL

36.12 DATA AND INFORMATION.   **Data** may be defined as the raw material from which **information** is derived. The main difference between data and information is that the latter is presented in such a way that it is useful. Processing necessary to achieve a useful presentation of information can include tasks such as summarizing, filtering, and arranging the data.

Files contain important pieces of data. For example, a **customer** file contains **records** with pertinent information about each customer. Each record contains a customer's name, address, phone number, and other important items, called **fields.** Each field contains letters of the alphabet, numbers, or special symbols, called **characters.** When a programmer designs and writes a program that accesses one of these files, he or she must know what the file is called, where it is stored, and how it is structured. The customer file might be called CUSTOMER, be located on a magnetic tape, and contain an 8-character customer ID, a 30-character customer name, a 30-character address, a 15-character city name, a 2-character state name, and a 12-digit current balance field. Thus, the file would contain records with 97 characters, only understandable when using the definitions of the fields shown above.

36.13 DATABASE MANAGEMENT SYSTEMS

(a) Objectives.   A **database** is an organized, centralized collection of data. A **database management system** (DBMS) is a massive computer program that assists in establishing, revising, sharing, and retrieving the data. Such systems are often priced in the hundreds of thousands of dollars, and run on a limited number of computers. Many microcomputer packages are dubbed DBMS, but they are most often used as stand-alone file processors. In most cases, a mainframe or minicomputer is used so that all of the organization's data can be organized to avoid difficulties of **integration, redundancy,** and **flexibility** inherent in processing separate files.

As an illustration, a bank might develop a customer deposit accounting system and an installment loan accounting system. Checking and savings customers, tracked in the former, would function in complete isolation from those in the latter. The fact that many customers have both checking accounts and installment loans would be missing from the bank's information system. If one of these customers changes their address, the bank must remember to update the address in **both** the deposit accounting system and the installment loan system. Only by **defining** explicitly the connections between related data items can a programmer design programs that **process** these connections. Further, if the bank manager decides that a new report would be helpful that listed installment loan customers without checking accounts, a programmer would have to spend a great deal of time discovering the structure of the separate files so that a new program could be built to search through both of them to build the report.

A DBMS allows information about such connections to be defined more easily and flexibly. This promotes integration between separate functions in the customer system. It limits redundancy, because the customer address is only stored and updated **once.** Finally, it provides greater flexibility because tools are provided to automate report generation, and the programmer concentrates more on data by name and meaning rather than on physical location and physical structure.

Everest (1985) provides the following objectives to be achieved in database management.

Shareability is the ability to share data stored in the database. It involves centralization, integration, and coordination of data gathering and storing activity. To reduce redundancy within the database, conflicts between users must be resolved.

Availability is the ability for all users, ranging from managers to technically trained programmers, to access the database either using on-line or batch processing. It also means the ability to define as well as create or modify all parts of the database by all users.

Evolvability is the ability of the database to change over time as the result of the new data items or new demands by the user. This means that the database must be flexible enough to expand to accommodate data not specified as part of it when the base was being created. In addition, it means that as the user needs change, so does the database. For example, a manager may know an item of data exists in the database, such as items sold to a customer, but that this information is identified by product code and not invoice number. Since the record key is the product code, the database appears to be unable to retrieve the present sales to the customer by invoice number or date.

Integrity involves the protection of the database to guarantee data quality, security, backup protection, input control, and loss of data. As the database is updated, it is essential that the data items conform to the strict rules of quality and coding. Therefore, sales by product item should be coded with exact product codes (no blanks, hyphens unless specified), and this code and quantity should be verified.

Data independence is the decoupling of data from processes acting on that data. This enables programs to be changed without affecting the data structure, and data structure to be changed without affecting the programs.

(b) Functions. The general function of a DBMS is to be the custodian of the data. This means that all data storage or retrieval is done through this program. More specifically, the DBMS allows: (1) creating, (2) updating, (3) maintaining, (4) accessing, and (5) controlling the integrity and security of the data. This section describes each of these DBMS functions in more detail.

A DBMS must allow the user to define the structure for a new set of data. This includes not only setting up and naming fields, but also establishing relationships among items throughout the database. To set up fields, a variety of information must be given to certain systems. Many systems require users to define the "width" (number of characters required) and the "type" (numeric, alphanumeric, date, etc.) of each field. Some systems allow the user to define a limited set of values that should fit in a field. For example, the system can be told to accept only "M" or "F" in a gender field; if a user types an "A" by mistake, the system can prompt for a legal value. Finally, some systems allow users to make certain fields mandatory. For example, it wouldn't make sense to permit a blank customer name or ID number when making a credit sale.

Another important DBMS function involves updating data. Updating includes adding new records, inserting new data in the records, or routinely changing or removing information. For example, each sales transaction might be recorded as a new record in the database. New data might be inserted in existing records when scores for makeup tests are entered in student grade records. Routine changes include changing customer addresses. Finally, routine deletions include removing obsolete inventory items.

Maintenance of data in a database involves correction of errors. Errors can be related to **structure** or **content.** Structural errors involve changing the definition of the database, whereas content errors involve changing data values themselves. An example of a structural error is the discovery that there is no field in the customer database to record a credit limit. In that case, a new field would be required to make room for this information. Adding a field could be a formidable task since data for the new field must be entered for each record in the database; if there are 10,000 customers, this modification could create a hefty requirement for data entry.

An important function of DBMS software is that of allowing greater accessibility to data. Most DBMS packages are supplied with **fourth generation languages** (4GLs) that allow users to create reports by entering English-like commands or making simple menu choices. A 4GL is distinguished from lower-level programming languages in that it is nonprocedural in nature, and an entire file can be processed with one command. As such, one does not have to specify **how** something is to be done, just **that** it is to be done. For example, using a 4GL you only need type the word LIST to obtain a full report of the contents of a database file. In a third generation language, it might take a dozen or so commands to create the same report, with the user specifying column headings and spacing, and then specifying how to cycle through each record and how to terminate the "loop." Even more primitive are languages in the first and second generations, which require programmers to process information one character at a time.

The most difficult function of a DBMS is to control the integrity and security of the data contained in the database. The major categories of controls include (1) maintaining conformity to the database definition, (2) controlling simultaneous updates, (3) assuring existence, and (4) controlling accessibility of the data. Conformity is easily enforced by DBMSs that do not permit users to enter data unless it meets the criteria set up by the definition (eg., numeric only, "M" or "F" only, etc.).

Simultaneous updates can be a serious problem when more than one user accesses the same data. For example, if the beginning balance in an inventory account is 180 units, and a sales and purchases program are both running at the same time, a serious error could result. If both programs begin by reading the balance, each marks the balance as 180. If the sales program subtracts 50 units from its 180, the new balance is written as 130. The purchases program then adds 100 units to the 180 it previously read and writes the new balance as 280. The new balance, which should be 230, is written as 280. Control of simultaneous updates is provided by **locking** the files when they are in use. In this case, the purchases program is prevented from reading the previous balance until the sales program is finished with it.

Existence is assured by making backups of the database and recorded transactions. Complete database backups are often called "dumps," and records of transactions are made by "logging" them. If the current database is damaged or destroyed, it can be restored by reading the most recent dump and reprocessing the logged transactions that have occurred since that dump.

Finally, access is controlled by preventing people from entering a facility or from using a

Record #	ID	Name	Phone	etc	ID index	Name index
1	721	Harrison	555-1234	xxxx	4	2
2	514	Anderson	555-4321	xxxx	5	4
3	622	Waters	555-5193	xxxx	2	5
4	101	Barber	555-4444	xxxx	3	1
5	105	Crawford	555-9683	xxxx	1	3

Exhibit 36.6. List structure and two indexes.

remote terminal to examine data. The former might be achieved by locks or guards, where physical access could be gained by using keys, combinations, badges, or fingerprints. The latter might be achieved by using passwords or otherwise limiting users' views of data. For example, if a data-entry clerk were allowed to enter personnel data, salary information could be hidden from view. A manager with a different password could later gain access to the personnel database to enter that sensitive data.

(c) Organization and Access.   A database may be viewed both **physically** and **logically**. Although a database management system insulates a user from the physical organization of data, it is useful to have basic awareness of options for physical organization.

(i) Physical Data Organization.   Data are physically maintained on **computer storage media** such as magnetic disks, drums, or reels, and on sequential media such as magnetic tape. Files are physically organized on the media following patterns such as **sequential, random, indexed sequential,** and **indexed random.** File organization is influenced by the properties of the physical storage medium employed. For example, magnetic tape presents a **sequential or serial order** to the data. To access the data on this kind of file, it is necessary to read the entire file starting with the first record. No specific address is available. Disk storage devices allow **direct access** to a stored record by address and do not require that the entire file be read to locate one address. Data may be sequentially ordered on a disk much like a tape, and direct access is then possible using a binary search procedure. With **random files,** each storage location has an address and can be located by the computer. This means that it is not necessary to sort input data in any sequential order before processing.

(ii) Logical Data Organization.   There are several different approaches to looking at the logical structure of data. Besides viewing data in simple **lists,** other views (**hierarchial, network,** and **relational** models) allow users to model more complex relationships between records and fields.

A **list** structure is a sequential arrangement of data records in a file; the relationships among records are determined purely by their sequential position or by **pointers** that can lead the system from one record to the next. For example, a person manipulating a customer file can create one index for the customer ID field and another index for the customer name field. Using the first index would enable the system to provide a list of customers in ID order and the second would enable the system to print a similar list in alphabetical order. The physical arrangement could be chronological, whereas the indexes provide either logical access. The index simply includes a list of record numbers in the desired order. While printing the records in ID order, for example, the system would consult the index to guide it through the data. Exhibit 36.6 illustrates a small customer data file with corresponding ID and name indexes. Notice that the ID index can guide access by telling the system to pick out record number 4

Exhibit 36.7a.   Hierarchy with each product linked to its parts.

first, then move on to record 5, 2, 3, and then 1. Thus, logical access to the records would be different than the physical ordering of the records.

(d) Types of Database Management Systems

(i) Hierarchical and Network Systems.   Hierarchical and network models allow relationships between data elements to be defined explicitly. Such relationships allow the system to move from one record to another very quickly. For example, an inventory system could keep track of which parts are used in which products that are produced by a firm.

A **hierarchical** view permits a user either to define the parts used by a product or to define the products a part might be used in. These two hierarchical views are shown in Exhibits 36.7a and 36.7b. There are multiple occurrences of the item to which the arrowhead points.

Operationally, records in the single inventory file suggested by Exhibit 36.7a might be defined as follows:

Product number.
Product name.

Exhibit 36.7b.   Hierarchy with each part linked to products.

Product description.

Finished products in stock.

    Part number.

    Part name.

    Part description.

    Quantity in stock.

    Cost.

As users enter information for each product, they enter one product number, name, product description, and number representing quantity in stock. Then for each part used by the product, they enter a part number, name, description, quantity in stock, and cost. After repeating this for each part, they then signify they are finished entering the parts used by that product and move on to the next product. Only then would that single product record be complete. The system would furnish all record numbers, since the user has no knowledge of or interest in them.

If the approach taken instead reflected the structure in Exhibit 36.7b, then information about each product using that part would be entered repeatedly until exhausting the list of products using that part. Choosing an approach (36.7a or 36.7b) would depend on requirements of the user. If the most important report lists parts under products, then the hierarchy in 36.7a is appropriate. If the most important report needed lists parts and the products using those parts, then 36.7b is more appropriate. Unfortunately, only by creating both structures (36.7a and 36.7b) can both reports be generated using the hierarchical model.

One possible physical representation of Exhibit 36.7a that would be stored by the system appears in Exhibit 36.8. Notice that there are in a sense two files. The first includes the products and the second includes the parts. There are pointers from the first to the second.

PRODUCTS

Record #	Prod #	Name etc	Part pointer
1	73	Cabinet . . .	3
2	92	Table . . .	2

PARTS

Record #	Part #	Name etc	Next part
1	114	Sides . . .	7
2	521	Tabletop . . .	6
3	463	Shelf . . .	1
4	781	Legs . . .	0
5	022	Back . . .	0
6	001	Emblem . . .	4
7	001	Emblem . . .	5

Exhibit 36.8. Physical representation—hierarchy of parts under products.

Exhibit 36.9.   Network of products and associated parts.

The system could easily print a report of products and the parts they contain. It would read the information for the first product, the cabinet and would then proceed to parts record 3 to find the first part, the shelf. The "Next part" (1) serves as the "Part pointer" to the next part, the sides. This points to record 7, the emblem, which in turn points to record 5, the back. Finally, record 5 points to 0, or nothing else. The table, product record 2, points to parts record 2, the tabletop. The tabletop would point to record 6, the emblem, which in turn points to record 4, the legs.

A **network** system would support the full complexity of the inventory system; parts can be linked to products and products can be linked to parts. Exhibit 36.9 illustrates the typical graphical representation of a network.

There are multiple occurrences of the data elements at the ends with the arrowheads. In a more complete example, there would be many more boxes on the diagram (such as customers, warehouse locations, sales orders, sales transactions, factories, etc.). Using a network approach, users can thus have both hierarchies described above modeled by the system. Such an approach in the inventory example allows the user to obtain a report of parts used by each product as well as a report of which products use each part. Many network systems simply store pointers for two different hierarchies. A severe disadvantage of the network model, however, is the complexity of using such a system. DBMSs built on the network model have never been advertised as user-oriented and are indeed very confusing for intermittent users.

(ii) Relational Systems.   A **relational** DBMS (RDBMS) is an alternative to hierarchies and networks. This approach is unusual in that it supports both hierarchies and networks. As such, it is not a point on any continuum linking hierarchies to networks; it is a completely different concept. An RDBMS does **not** place actual, physical relationship pointers or links into data files as shown in Exhibit 36.8 for the hierarchical model illustrated. Instead, an RDBMS uses actual **values** to do the "pointing."

An RDBMS caters well to users by arranging data in familiar, uncomplicated tables called **relations.** Relations are very much like simple files. These tables allow the users to take information from one file and pull related information from another file based on their **content** rather than by defining the relationships through pointers. A unique identifier called a **key** is required to unambiguously identify each record in a relation. What is also required is a key that will allow the system to cross-reference to the other relation. This can be accomplished by creating a new relation that simply cross-references the PRODUCTS and PARTS relations, as shown in Exhibit 36.10 (the PRODUCTS-PARTS relation).

PRODUCTS	
Prod #	Name etc
73	Cabinet . . .
92	Table . . .

PARTS	
Part #	Name etc
114	Sides . . .
521	Tabletop . . .
463	Shelf . . .
781	Legs . . .
022	Back . . .
001	Emblem . . .

PRODUCTS–PARTS	
Prod #	Part #
73	463
73	001
73	114
73	022
92	521
92	001
92	781

Exhibit 36.10. Products/parts relations.

By setting up the three relations shown in Exhibit 36.10, the system can make a list of all parts making up each product, or a list of all products using each part. Indeed, this is a network implemented on a relational system. RDBMSs are used because of the straightforward nature of defining and retrieving data. Two generally accepted difficulties with relational systems are efficiency and potential for bad designs. There is widespread (although not universal) perception that relational systems are less efficient than network systems, because of the need to examine the **content** of the data to make necessary connections. The bad design potential is a much more serious point.

It is easy to design relations poorly. Consider a case where a firm wishes to use an RDBMS to record sales transactions. A novice might design one relation that contains all of the pertinent information about each sale, as shown in Exhibit 36.11.

This relation might appear on the surface to make perfect sense. Each sales record would contain the sales date, customer number, customer name, customer address (including fields for city, state, and zip code), quantity purchased, item number purchased, item description, item price, and total (price × quantity).

The difficulties are more apparent when you see some sample data for this relation, shown in Exhibit 36.12.

The biggest problem with this relation is the redundancy within the database. Notice that each time a customer makes a purchase, the user records their complete name and address, as well as the complete item name, description, and price. In the small sample shown, customer 4421 appears several times, and the same customer name and address information appears in the relation. Likewise, nails are sold two times and the same description and price are filled in.

Assuming that each of the 10 fields shown takes up 15 characters, each record in the relation will take up 150 characters of storage space. If there are 10,000 sales per month, a typical sales file for the month will take up 1,500K (1.5 megabytes) of disk storage.

The relation could be improved considerably by removing the two types of redundancy: (1) across records (duplicates of the detailed customer information are unnecessary), and (2)

Date	Cust #	Name	Addr	City etc	Quant	Item #	Descrip	Price	Total

Exhibit 36.11. Massive relation design for all sales information.

Date	Cust #	Name	Addr	City etc	Quant	Item #	Descrip	Price	Total
7/2	4421	Smith, J	1 W.	Omaha, N	1,000	215	nails	.01	$10
7/3	8340	Washin	RD #4	Ames, Iowa	600	215	nails	.01	$6
7/3	4421	Smith, J	1 W.	Omaha, N	10	400	hammers	6.00	$60
7/3	4421	Smith, J	1 W.	Omaha, N	800	314	screws	.04	$32
etc.									

Exhibit 36.12.   Partial contents of the massive sales relation.

within a record (price and quantity give enough information to determine the total—storing a field called "total" is not necessary). Removing the within-record redundancy is simple—the user just drops that field from the relation. However, it is more difficult to remove the between-record redundancy.

Normalizing the relation achieves this. Normalization is actually a simplification tool that involves breaking up a complex relation into several simpler ones. Exhibit 36.13 illustrates a normalized version of the design.

It might appear that the user has made the space problem worse by exploding the file into three. However, assuming that there are still 10 characters per field, the CUSTOMERS relation takes up 40, the ITEMS relation takes up 30, and the SALES record takes up 40 characters per record. Assuming 1,000 customers, 1,000 items, and the same 10,000 sales per month, the three files would take up 40K, 30K, and 400K, respectively. The sum of the three, 470K is less than one-third the size of the unnormalized relation designed in Exhibit 36.11.

Space-saving is important, but it is also important that the files are much more understandable after normalization. It is difficult to give a name to the unnormalized relation because it served three purposes: to record customer information, to record item information, and to

CUSTOMERS

Cust #	Cust name	Cust address	City etc

ITEMS

Item #	Description	Price

SALES

Date	Cust #	Item #	Quantity

Exhibit 36.13.   Normalized version of the massive sales relation.

record sales. Once it is split into the three relations that define the system's purpose, it is much easier to explain what is in each relation.

(e) Administration of Database Management.   Many organizations have discovered the value of data management and DBMS and have placed officials in charge of data for the entire organization, creating a position called **database administrator** (DBA). The DBA is responsible for coordinating the two main DBMS activities performed by users: data definition and data manipulation. **Data definition** involves setting up files, data items, and relationships. This is important work because the DBA's high-level view can prevent users from creating data files that overlap those already established elsewhere in the organization. **Data manipulation** involves retrieving or changing data, usually through a menu system or command language. The DBAs can offer assistance and training to users. There are also technical duties covered by the DBA's office. Updates to the software must be installed and tested. Performance problems must be investigated. New products are evaluated.

The CIO position discussed in an earlier section differs from the DBA position in that the CIO tends to be concerned with positioning information systems in the organization to support business strategy; the DBA takes a more "micro" view and concentrates on data architecture. The CIO would take the place of the information systems director; the DBA complements the information systems director.

SYSTEM DEVELOPMENT

36.14   THE SYSTEMS DEVELOPMENT LIFE CYCLE.   From the moment resources are allocated to solving a business problem through development of a business computer system, careful project planning is needed. This planning takes the form of a series of stages that make up the **systems development life cycle.**

The stages move from definition, to development, then to implementation of the particular system. Within each stage are more specific phases as shown in Exhibit 36.14 (Davis and Olson, 1985).

Before the final stage of implementation, the emphasis shifts from **what** should be done to **how** it should be done. This section discusses each stage in more detail.

36.15   DEFINITION.   The definition stage attempts to discover the nature of the system to be developed. Information systems are complex in nature, and a surprising amount of time is needed to assemble a proposal, assess the project's feasibility, define the users' information requirements, and create a conceptual design (see Exhibit 36.14).

In **proposal definition,** a user has determined that there is an important need, and makes a formal request for consideration. Some firms use request forms that require very rough estimates of benefits and costs associated with the proposed system. This constitutes an initial screening process, forcing the user to think carefully about the potential commitment.

If the proposal receives tentative approval, the **feasibility assessment** phase begins. The goal of this phase is to more carefully estimate and evaluate costs and benefits of the proposed system; it is a major hurdle. There are several kinds of feasibility: **Economic** feasibility considers whether the project is financially worthwhile, **technical** feasibility considers whether the project is technologically possible, **operational** feasibility considers whether the completed system can actually work in the intended environment, **political** feasibility considers whether the project would be supported by upper management, and **schedule** feasibility considers whether the project can be completed in time.

Economic feasibility might appear to be the easiest to determine, but it is in fact very difficult to determine financial costs and benefits of a system. Both benefits and costs could be either tangible or intangible in nature. Intangible benefits and costs do not affect profitability directly, but nevertheless have great potential for indirect effects. For example, improved

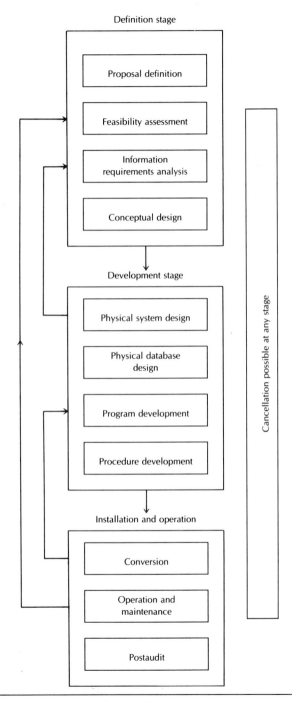

Exhibit 36.14. The application system development life cycle. *Source*: From G. B. Davis and M. H. Olson, *Management Information Systems: Conceptual Foundations, Structure, and Development,* 1985, McGraw-Hill, p. 571. Reproduced by permission.

customer service is an intangible benefit but could result in higher sales. The possibility of clerical bewilderment for a period of time is an intangible cost but could result in high training costs or turnover. The difficulty is that a large proportion of the benefits of a new system are intangible and probabilistic whereas many of the costs are tangible, requiring predetermined expenditures. Many projects are initiated on the faith that the indirect benefits will exceed the direct costs. If the perceived benefits do not exceed the perceived costs, the project ceases at this phase.

Information requirements analysis attempts to pinpoint the precise information that the system needs to provide to the user or users. The goal includes standard and ad hoc reports, but these reporting needs will affect data to be stored and programs to be written. This is a very difficult phase, because often users do not know exactly what information they require to make decisions. The reasons for this problem include human frailties, the complexities of the information requirements, the complexities involved in communicating these require-ments, and unwillingness of some users to provide the requirements (Davis, 1982). To discover the functions that need to be performed and the reports that need to be generated by the proposed system, an analyst must use many tools, such as interviews with potential users, examination of the user's original request, observation of actual work duties, questionnaires and other correspondence with users, and examination of documents used in and generated by the current system (Burch and Grudnitski, 1989).

The **conceptual design** establishes inputs and outputs, general functions to be performed by the new system, and system controls. Much of the work done in the information requirements phase is organized and structured into descriptions of reports needed, inputs needed, general functions to be performed by the system, general flow of processing and operation of the system, outlines of documentation and training materials needed, and control requirements (Davis and Olson, 1985).

The conceptual design sometimes goes through many iterations before it is considered complete. Advocates of structured analysis (Menamin and Palmer, 1984) recommend the use of **data flow diagrams** (DFDs) at this stage to communicate with users. DFDs use four basic labeled symbols to describe system elements. Processes are circles or "bubbles," data flows are arrows, entities are rectangles, and files are parallel lines. For example, Exhibit 36.15 illustrates a DFD for a water billing system (Powers, Adams, and Mills, 1984). This DFD could be used to communicate with users because there are no technical symbols or definitions of exactly how the processes must be performed. It describes the existing billing system; later diagrams (not illustrated) describe the new billing system.

36.16 DEVELOPMENT.   Once the conceptual design is approved by the user, the project can be launched into the **development** stage. In this stage, the user requirements are translated into programming specifications by going through physical system design, physical database design, program development, and procedure development phases.

The **physical system design** phase expands all DFDs to their greatest amount of detail possible. This expansion is performed most meticulously on the DFDs of the **new system,** rather than on the existing system. Each bubble of Exhibit 36.15 can be expanded to describe its internal makeup more clearly. Only then can programming specifications be drafted. One possible expansion of the "apply payment" bubble referred to in Exhibit 36.15 is shown in Exhibit 36.16 (Powers, Adams, and Mills, 1984). Any or all of these bubbles can be further expanded into more and more detailed diagrams until all bubbles appear to have a singular, cohesive purpose for processing requirements to be explicable for development of computer programs. See DeMarco (1978) and Menamin and Palmer (1984) for a discussion of the expansion process.

Some analysts use flowcharting in place of DFDs because a greater variety of symbols can be used. Exhibit 36.17 (Powers, Adams, and Mills, 1984) illustrates a systems flowchart version of the DFD in Exhibit 36.16. The symbols used are described as follows: "transaction batches" illustrates a punched card, "customer-master" depicts a disk file, "edit" is a

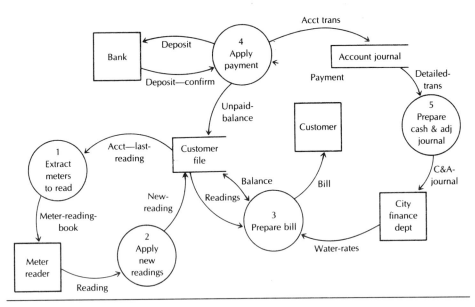

Exhibit 36.15.   Simplified data flow diagram of a water billing system. *Source*: From M. J. Powers, D. R. Adams, and H. Mills, *Computer Information Systems Development: Analysis and Design,* South-Western Publishing, 1984, p. 69. Reproduced by permission.

process, "update log" symbolizes a magnetic tape, and "update summary" represents a printed report. There are several other symbols; a more complete set with usage guidelines can be found in Lucas (1985).

The **physical database design** phase is not independent of the previous phase, but concentrates on the data rather than on processes. Using techniques and approaches described in the "Information Storage and Retrieval" portion of this chapter, files are normalized to the extent feasible. Both processes and data are designed so that the completed system will be understandable to users, and as simple as possible to program. One useful tool that assists in database design was developed by Peter P. Chen (1980). Rishe (1988) offers a useful guide to the design of databases along with processes that operate on the data.

Program development is a major step in system development. Much of this phase is dependent on specific programming languages, but a universal concern is to structure the system so that the resultant program is understandable, flexible, and error-free. Yourdon and Constantine (1978) suggest that the DFDs should be transformed into a **structure chart** that defines program pieces that are (1) cohesive and (2) loosely coupled with other parts of the program. Program pieces that are cohesive contain singular, understandable functions, and when these parts are loosely coupled, changes in one will not affect others. Exhibit 36.18 illustrates a structure chart for a payroll program (from Galletta, 1985).

Highly detailed descriptions of each box in the structure chart are then translated into program code. Many languages are available for this translation, but the most widespread language is **COBOL** (**CO**mmon **B**usiness **O**riented **L**anguage). Some of the thousands of other languages include **ADA, BASIC, C, dBASE,** and **FORTRAN.** There is no doubt a language for every letter of the alphabet.

Other program development approaches include those of Jackson (1983), Warnier (1981), and Orr (1981).

The next phase is **procedure development,** where user documentation is completed. Some advocate that procedure manuals should be developed before programs, so that users can criticize the system's design in time to make important changes. However, this step is usually pushed off to the end and is sometimes severely short-changed. Documentation should be

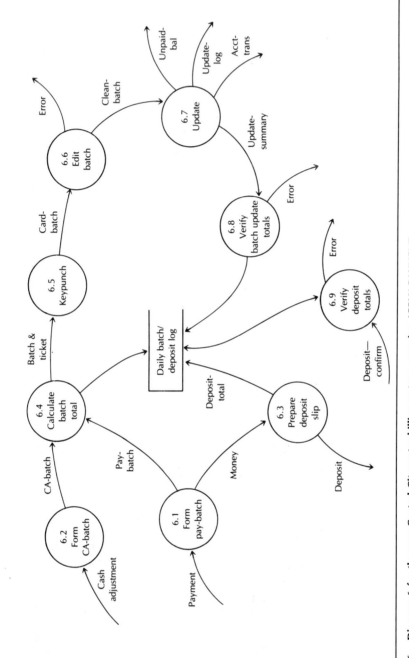

Exhibit 36.16. Diagram 6 for the new Central City water billing system, covering APPLY PAYMENT processing. *Source:* From M. J. Powers, D. R. Adams, and H. Mills, *Computer Information Systems Development: Analysis and Design,* South-Western Publishing, 1984, p. 542. Reproduced by permission.

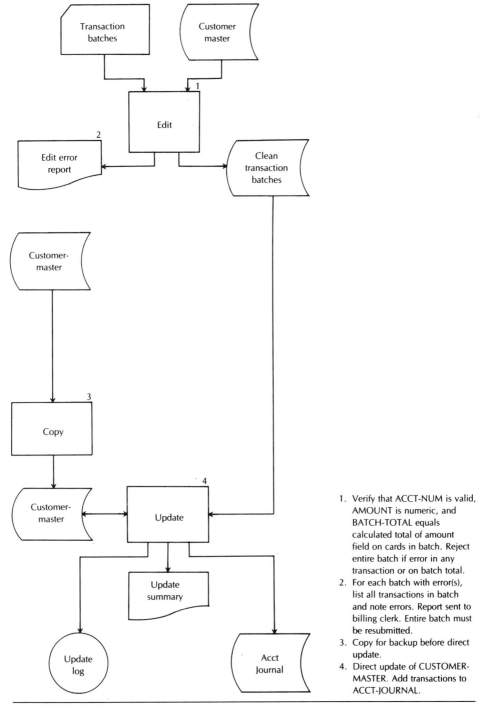

1. Verify that ACCT-NUM is valid, AMOUNT is numeric, and BATCH-TOTAL equals calculated total of amount field on cards in batch. Reject entire batch if error in any transaction or on batch total.
2. For each batch with error(s), list all transactions in batch and note errors. Report sent to billing clerk. Entire batch must be resubmitted.
3. Copy for backup before direct update.
4. Direct update of CUSTOMER-MASTER. Add transactions to ACCT-JOURNAL.

Exhibit 36.17. System flowchart for APPLY PAYMENT processing under the new Central City water billing system. *Source:* From M. J. Powers, D. R. Adams, and H. Mills, *Computer Information Systems Development: Analysis and Design,* South-Western Publishing, 1984, pp. 546-547. Reproduced by permission.

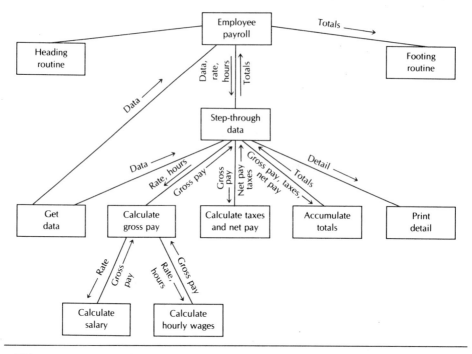

Exhibit 36.18.   Structure Chart. *Source: From D. Galletta, COBOL with an Emphasis on Structured Program Design,* **Prentice-Hall, 1985, p. 129.**

developed for managerial users, clerical personnel, computer operators, and programmers (who might make modifications to the system in the future).

36.17 IMPLEMENTATION.   The final stage in system development is the **implementation** stage. Three phases in this stage are conversion, operation and maintenance, and postauditing.

Conversion involves asking users to accept the system, building files, and training users. This is a critical stage, and users can opt to send the developers "back to the drawing board" if the system is not satisfactory. Most errors made in interpreting user requirements will be discovered during this phase.

An article by Zahniser (1981) describes how the user's problem must be translated into user requirements. These requirements must be used to design the overall system. The system's design determines the design of its individual programs. Finally, the design of each program determines the modules (program pieces) that will be designed. Errors in designing the modules are found when testing the module. Errors in designing the programs will not be found until all modules are designed and tested. Likewise, errors in designing the system will not show up until all programs are assembled. Finally, errors in determining the requirements will not be discovered until the user is asked to accept the system. The point is that the most expensive error is made earliest in the system development process. Exhibit 36.19 illustrates this difficult problem.

File building can be an arduous process. It is most helpful if the old system offers utilities that can store data in such a way that the new system can read it. However, not all data can be found in the old system, and extensive data entry is often needed when building files.

Once the new system is operational, **parallel** operation of the old and new systems is often performed. In parallel operation, both systems are run together, and the outcomes are

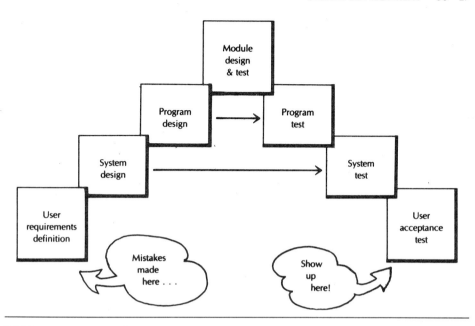

Exhibit 36.19.   Impacts of errors.

compared to build trust in the new system. If this is not possible, a path of **complete cutover** is taken; the old system is disconnected and the new one is launched.

In the **operation and maintenance** phase the system converts the inputs into outputs as designed. During this phase, users may discover that some functions do not operate as smoothly as they originally hoped, or that needed information was overlooked during the initial design. At that stage, a user can place a request for **maintenance** or modification of the system. If the deficiencies are serious enough, the user may request a new system and an entire, new development life cycle can be initiated.

Postaudits are often neglected, but can be a valuable phase in the life cycle. In this phase, a team of users and developers review the application, making recommendations for enhancement, discontinuance, training, or changes in the development process itself. Criteria include timeliness, understandability, accuracy, completeness, and relevance of documentation and reports, as well as ease of use and adequacy of controls. Internal auditors are often instrumental in leading the postaudit.

36.18 ALTERNATIVES TO THE LIFE CYCLE

(a) Alternatives.   Several alternatives to the system development life cycle are available, including the use of service bureaus, consultants, prototyping, and user-developed applications.

(b) Service Bureaus.   The data processing facilities of a service bureau normally include at least one computer. The bureau may also be equipped with a number of standard programs, which are at the disposal of clients, for performing routine accounting work such as payroll and billings. The bureau undertakes to carry out the processing within a certain prescribed time and to return the resulting output to the client. Bureaus have been established by the major computer manufacturers, by many large banks, and by some public accounting firms. Other bureaus are separate operations. Time-shared service bureaus enable the client to store programs in files in the computer permanently, and to run them directly from the client's own offices through the medium of a terminal.

The principal advantage of the service bureau, when compared to ownership of a computer facility, is **cost savings.** The cost of obtaining computer serivce is a variable element, depending on the number of cards read and punched, the number of lines printed, and the number of minutes of computer time used. The standby costs of maintaining the computer are borne by the service bureau operator, who expects, of course, to recoup this outlay through the scale of charges. The cost saving can be substantial if the client has only a few jobs to run on the computer. If the client can use the computer fully, however, a rented or purchased machine normally is cheaper.

The **staff** of the service bureau may be able to provide data processing skills not otherwise available to the user. A small business may not be able to afford the services of a high grade analyst on a full-time basis. The bureau may be able to provide such a person, who will help solve some of the systems problems.

(c) Consulting Firms. The outside organization that provides high quality consulting services can be a valuable contributor to the overall success of a data processing organization. The consulting firms can act as a third-party critical evaluator, or provide a specific task that ordinarily could not be accomplished within the internal structure and time constraints. Problem identification, requirements planning, design specifications, vendor selection, project management, and contingency planning are discrete tasks that can be measured in terms of effort and results. If specialized skills are required and time is a constraint, the consulting organization may provide the solution. Very often the outside consultant can serve as critical evaluator of the *what if* question. That is, in many cases, the consultant will be asked to evaluate the impact of a course of action. This might take the form of a question like "How would you evaluate the impact of relocating our computer center?" Since the third party is perhaps more objective, and has no vested interest, the conclusions can help managers reach critical decisions more objectively.

(d) Prototyping. User requirements might be uncertain when dealing with large systems, complex applications, untrained users, and inexperienced analysts (Davis, 1982). It is then difficult to expect clarity in user requirements, and an experimental strategy called **prototyping** can be used.

Prototyping is described by Naumann and Jenkins (1982), and by Berrisford and Wetherbe (1979). Prototyping involves using report generators and database management systems to develop a system in hours or days that performs the basic tasks the users have described. The users then examine the reports and critique them. Often, problems surface when using the prototype, and revisions can be made quickly. It is possible to use the prototype as the finished system, but Berrisford and Wetherbe warn that controls might be inadequate, and that the prototype should serve only as a simulation tool.

(e) User-Developed Systems. **User-developed** systems have emerged as the newest alternative to the development life cycle. Users have become impatient with development backlogs that can extend to two or more years, and many have acquired training in using a DBMS on the mainframe computer, or have acquired personal computers.

End-user development is "the direct assumption of system development and data processing tasks by the user for his own direct benefit" (Head, 1985). Such activity has advanced rapidly in recent years, and users are short-cutting the development life cycle in record numbers.

However, there are dangers in such development. Davis and Olson (1985) warn that there are many risks involved in such cases. Outside reviews may be nonexistent. Users may have difficulties identifying their requirements. Users' systems may be unstable, error-prone, and undocumented. Information stored by users may not be shared with others who need it. The remedy is to provide sufficient control mechanisms for such systems.

However, there are so many of these systems that it might be difficult to provide external reviews for more than just a few. Serious errors in many of these systems exacerbate the situation. For example, in one experiment 44% of the spreadsheets developed by users were found to contain errors (Brown and Gould, 1987). This number is consistent with much of the literature that warns how common it is to find significant errors in spreadsheets. Control mechanisms of some kind are certainly in order.

SYSTEM CONTROLS

36.19 OVERVIEW

(a) Need for Control.   When accounting systems are automated, several necessary changes in the organization and in the nature of data take place. In the precomputer organization, there is generally an accounting department segmented into various sections: billing and receivables, accounts payable, cost accounting, payroll, and so forth. Each section supervisor is in charge in an area and sees transactions of a certain type entering it, sees changes to (processing of) the transactions, and sees the resulting reports and documents that flow elsewhere. In this organizational environment, segregation of incompatible duties among individuals is possible, and section supervisors have a good view of the entire transaction cycle. These aspects provide control.

When EDP is implemented, the accounting process is organized along functional lines. All types of transactions enter a data control and conversion process, become part of stored data, and are processed by the computer operations function; the results of processing are distributed as appropriate. The parties involved in this organization are the manager of data processing, the systems development function, the computer operations function, the control function, and the users (parties furnishing input data and using output documents and reports).

The effects of these organizational changes are both positive and negative. On the positive side, centralization through EDP often takes the record-keeping function out of the hands of persons having custody of assets (an incompatible function) and places it in EDP. On the negative side, such centralization may eliminate existing segregation of duties and does remove the transaction cycle from the direct review of an immediate supervisor.

A further control problem occurs because EDP is used to prepare simultaneously records that previously served as internal checks. For example, the accounts receivable subsidiary ledger and the general ledger accounts receivable control account may have been arrived at independently under a manual system, but they are prepared from the same data by EDP. Of course, if the **data** are properly controlled and the **processing** of the data is properly controlled, all output records should be reliable.

Thus the emphasis in EDP systems is usually placed on controlling the integrity of the data entering the system and processing such data in a uniform manner. Given the need to contain costs, efficiency is always a paramount concern. As a result, and because EDP systems are generally used for large volumes of data, manually created and handled pieces of information are held to a minimum. As much information as possible is kept in machine-readable form.

From a control standpoint, the absence of visually observable data may cause a reduction in control, because persons who might recognize obvious errors do not have the opportunity to view the material containing them. If centralization is carried so far that key elements of information are very difficult to access, or perhaps even totally removed and missing, certain control activities such as follow-up on customer inquiries or internal audit procedures may be difficult or impossible to perform.

Finally, the information itself is an asset and must be protected and controlled. Should a company have its accounts receivable files destroyed, it could lose a great amount of money because of inability to collect or, at least, because of the cost of reconstruction. Should data such as customer-lead files or trade secrets be stolen, competitive advantage could be lost. These aspects of data that have been highly centralized merit special considerations about control.

(b) Control Objectives.   The general objectives of all internal control structures apply, of course, to automated systems. However, in analyzing whether these are being met, it is helpful to be more specific in their definition. The following six specific EDP control objectives related to processing transactions have been identified (Touche Ross & Co., 1979):

1. Assure that all transactions are **authorized.**
2. Assure that all transactions are **recorded,** and that none are lost or duplicated.
3. Assure that all transactions are properly **valued** and **classified.**
4. Assure that **correct files** are used in processing and that none are lost or destroyed.
5. Assure that **processing** is **accurate and complete.**
6. Assure that **output** is **accurate and complete.**

All EDP and related systems can be analyzed and evaluated in terms of how well they achieve these control objectives. If these are adequately achieved, the broader objectives of internal control will be met as well, at least within the EDP system.

36.20 TYPES OF CONTROLS

(a) Introduction.   There are many good sources of information about EDP internal controls. One well understood source is the AICPA publication "1977 Auditor's Study and Evaluation of Internal Control in EDP Systems." Two other good sources are *Controlling Assets and Transactions* (Touche Ross & Co., 1979) and *Computer Control & Audit* (Mair, Wood, and Davis, 1978).

In the AICPA study, EDP controls are segregated into general controls and application controls. General controls are those that affect all parts of the EDP system. Application controls are those that affect only specific uses of the system, such as payroll or order entry. Within these categories, there are further defined categories of specific control techniques. These are shown in Exhibit 36.20 in matrix format as they affect the objectives above. As the matrix demonstrates, almost all types of control are available to contribute to all control objectives.

(b) General Controls

(i) Organization and Operation Controls.   The key organization controls include authorization policies, segregation of duties, and clear description of responsibilities and job tasks. Authorization policies should be communicated to all affected parties and monitored for compliance. These authorizations would relate to introduction of input into data processing, use of the computer for various purposes, development of and changes to computer programs, acquisition of new EDP equipment, access to data and files, and distribution of the results of processing.

The various duties within the EDP function should be segregated so that no person can manipulate transactions, data and output in an unauthorized manner. The degree and method of segregation will vary with the size of the installation. However, one would expect to see separations of the following EDP functions in most medium-sized or larger installations: systems analysis, programming, computer operation, library, and data control.

Types of Controls	Transactions Are Authorized	Transactions Are Recorded and None Are Lost or Duplicated	Transactions Are Properly Valued and Classified	Correct Files Are Used and None Are Lost or Destroyed	Processing Is Accurate and Complete	Output Is Accurate and Complete
General controls						
Plan of organization and operation of EDP	●			●		
Procedures for systems development and documentation		●	●	●	●	●
Hardware and systems software controls		●	●	●	●	●
Access to equipment and data files controls	●			●		
Application controls						
Input controls	●	●	●	●	●	●
Processing controls	●	●	●	●	●	●
Output controls	●	●	●	●	●	●

Exhibit 36.20. Matrix of control types and objectives.

Descriptions of responsibilities will generally be found in procedural manuals, and instructions for specific operations usually take the form of job run books. In addition to these items, an installation will have in its reference library documentation from vendors relating to the computer and acquired software.

(ii) Procedures for Systems Development and Documentation. Since EDP programs operate with extreme reliability and uniformity, and since many are technically quite complex, it is appropriate to invest significant effort in their development, to assure they are correct. To provide evidence of correct development and to provide a basis for correcting problems and making changes, documentation of the programs must be complete and understandable.

Well-run installations follow standard procedures in developing all systems and programs. These require planning steps, approvals, programming methods, and comprehensive testing. Documentation must be prepared each step of the way, in accordance with specific standards of documentation.

At least two parties outside the EDP function are involved in developing new systems. First to be involved is the function or functions using the results of processing. They are the "customers" of the application and must be satisfied the system will do the job. They should also be responsible for the control requirements of the system.

The second party involved should be the internal auditor. Internal audit often includes persons who are expert in control theory as well as EDP. They provide an objective review and serve as an important developmental control.

(iii) Hardware and Systems Software Controls. Over the years manufacturers have developed extremely reliable hardware and operating systems software. Specific controls are built into the hardware and software so that when something fails, operations are stopped, data are

protected, and the operator is notified. Serious problems from hardware and operating systems failures are very rare. The exception occurs if changes are made to standard operating systems hardware by the installation's systems programmer. Such changes must be carefully controlled.

(iv) Access to Equipment and Data Files Controls.   Since information is valuable and often confidential, it must be physically safeguarded against unauthorized access and intentional or unintentional damage. Thus access devices are designed so that only certain persons can operate them, passwords are used, data are encrypted, computer rooms are locked and protected against fire and heat, files are carefully handled and controlled, data are copied and stored in separate locations, and similar precautions are observed.

(c) Application Controls

(i) Input Controls.   Input controls are essential to assure that only authorized data are introduced into the computer and that such data are correct. Most accountants are familiar with the expression "garbage in, garbage out." Keeping the data "clean" is the function of input controls. The following are three of the more important input controls.

- *Key Verifying.* Most terminals and key-entry devices allow the typist to rekey the data to check for correctness. If a match does not occur, the operator is notified and correction is made. An important control relating to this input step is good forms design, which will motivate accurate key entry.
- *Check Digit.* A check digit is a numeral added to any important number being entered into the computer. Its value is determined by a formula relating it to the contents of the input number in a special way. The computer is programmed to check this relationship when it reads the number and the check digit. If the check digit is absent or is given incorrectly, the inputted transaction is rejected.
- *Control Totals.* Control totals are used to determine whether all the data put into the system were processed. Control totals can be developed and compared at various points of processing manually or automatically. Often the user department performs this function, or it may be performed by the control group in data processing. Control totals may be on any data, meaningful or for control only. For example, a control total of invoice numbers is an unmeaningful total—a so-called hash total.

(ii) Processing Controls.   Processing controls assure reliability throughout a particular EDP application, including the improper addition or deletion of data records. These controls are generally programmed into the system as part of a particular application. Four important processing controls are discussed.

- *Validity Checks.* These routines inspect the contents of individual data fields for the presence of improper items. For example, some fields should always have data present; a blank field would indicate an error condition. Similarly, a field of numeric data could be inspected for the presence of alphabetic characters.
- *Computational Tests.* In many applications, certain data fields should have a fixed computational relationship, and this can be tested. For example, in "accounts receivable," aging categories should sum to the total amount due. These values can be internally cross-added and compared, and exceptions can be identified in processing.
- *Reasonableness Tests.* Although the specific values of many fields of data cannot be precisely determined, as in computational tests, they can be inspected using broader parameters as a test of reasonableness. For example, it may be known that no product shipment should exceed 100 cases, or no employee should work more than 70 hours in a

single week. Such parameters are entered into application programs and compared to data field values during processing. They serve as excellent controls over large errors of many kinds.

- *File Label Controls.* These controls assure that proper files are used in processing, and also serve as a physical control over file accountability. There are two types of file label. **Internal file labels** contain relevant identification data used directly by computer programs. **External file labels** are affixed to the tape or disk itself to identify the file to the computer operator and librarian. There are excellent file management software programs available to provide inventory control over files and their labeling.

(iii) Output Controls.   Although one might surmise that if adequate input and processing controls exist, output will always be reliable, this is not necessarily true. It is always desirable to review the results of processing to determine that it is complete and contains no obvious errors. This may be done by the control group within EDP, by user departments, or by both. Reasonableness parameters may be used for this purpose, and the steps followed may include tying into control totals as discussed earlier.

A special aspect of output controls relates to **error listings.** These are items that were identified as erroneous or questionable by input and processing controls. In some cases, transactions identified on error listings are not included in output, having been completely removed from the data, or stored in a suspense file. In other cases, they are in the output and may be wrong.

It is essential that procedures be established to reprocess all error listing items promptly and accurately. Specific controls must be established to assure this, since the incidence of errors in reprocessing is often far greater than in normal processing. Also, users and management should be aware of the volume and nature of errors as a means of monitoring performance and making improvements in systems.

Finally, **physical controls** should exist to assure the protection and confidentiality of all outputs. For example, checks should be in someone's care at all times, and reports should be distributed promptly, and only to authorized recipients.

EDP AUDITING

36.21 AUDITING COMPUTER SYSTEMS.   It is important to understand that the term ''computer auditing'' and its relatives are umbrella terms covering different types of auditors with different audit objectives. Most larger organizations, for example, are audited by an **independent external auditor,** whose objective is to opine on whether the enterprise's annual financial statements fairly present financial position and results of operations in conformity with GAAP. In doing this, the independent auditor gains an understanding of the client's internal control structure. If the system is automated, some of these controls will be among the types discussed earlier. Similarly, the independent auditor accesses data in performing substantive procedures. If the data are in machine-readable form, the auditor will rely on use of the computer to inspect it and to obtain outputs of it in a form that best meets audit objectives.

It is also common for larger organizations to have **internal auditors.** These persons function as an internal control and as internal project specialists. In their control function, internal auditors review systems in the development phase and they test ongoing systems to determine that control procedures are being followed. As project specialists, they review various operations for efficiency and effectiveness. Since internal audit is a full-time responsibility, they generally probe the areas they touch far more extensively than do the independent auditors (who are concerned only with **material** errors). In automated systems, internal auditors must have significant expertise in EDP to perform their function.

A third group of ''computer auditors'' consists of **computer consultants,** either internal or external, who are brought in to investigate specific, often highly technical areas. Their purpose is always specific, whereas the independent auditor's purpose is almost always general and the internal auditor's falls in both camps.

36.22 COMPUTER-ASSISTED AUDIT TECHNIQUES

(a) Around the Computer.   The auditor has the option to audit "around" the computer, where only the source documents and printed reports are examined as if there were no computer. This assumes that audit trails are visible and intact, and that the system is simple and static (Weber, 1988). If systems are complex or unstable, then the auditor must audit "with" or "through" the computer. (Wilkinson, 1986; Moscove and Simkin, 1984).

(b) With the Computer.   In auditing **with** the computer, the computer is used to assist in certain functions that are otherwise performed manually. For example, the computer can assist in choosing a random sample of transactions to examine, checking files for consistency, printing reports of the contents of various files, and printing confirmations.

(c) Through the Computer.   When auditing **through** the computer, the auditor tests not only the inputs and outputs of the computer, but takes a close look at processing accuracy and procedures. There are many approaches for auditing through the computer. Major methods of auditing through the computer include the (1) test data approach, (2) integrated test facility, (3) program examination, and (4) program substitution.

The **test data approach** allows the auditor to process test transactions, for which the desired result is known. This test data contains errors as well as proper data. The test data is processed using the organization's normal accounting system. After processing, the results are examined and compared with the auditor's expectations. One special advantage is that specially designed test data will be processed by the actual programs used by the client. A disadvantage is that there may be no proof that the programs used for the special processing are the same or behave the same way as when running normal transactions.

The **integrated test facility** allows the auditor to process test transactions along with normal transactions during a regular processing run. Actual results are compared with expected results. Special advantages include the fact that separate test processing is not required and that a full spectrum of the accounting system can be examined (to the point of actually shipping goods). Serious disadvantages are that the auditor is introducing artificial transactions into the system that must be reversed, and that a programmer might discover the special coding scheme used for the test transactions and build statements into the program that detect the false transactions and then behave correctly.

Program examination involves inspecting the computer programs used in the system. Such inspection can be assisted by special commands that allow the auditor to discover what sections of the program are operating at any time, or what sections of the program are not operating at all. If certain parts of the program operate in an inexplicable pattern, there may be a serious error in the program. If certain parts of the program do not ever appear to run, this could be evidence of an error or deliberate scheme; certain functions could be dormant and "awaken" on certain occasions to produce fraudulent transactions. Special advantages are that the auditor gains much deeper understanding of the program, and it is much easier to discover dormant code. Disadvantages are that it is very difficult to read computer programs written by others and that the code that is readable by humans ("source code") might not be the same program as the code that is readable only by the machine ("object code").

In **program substitution** the auditor writes and substitutes his own program for the client's. Actual data records are processed by the substitute program, and the results are compared with the results of the client's actual program. Major advantages of this approach are that any unusual behaviors of the client's program are avoided, and that developing substitute programs is facilitated by modern report generators. This is only possible because substitute programs can use simple designs and do not need much dialogue control or careful user interaction. Simple raw inputs are accepted, and basic outputs are produced. Disadvantages are that even simple programs can take much time to develop.

SOURCES AND SUGGESTED REFERENCES

American Accounting Association, *A Statement of Basic Accounting Theory*, AAA, Sarasota, FL, 1966.

American Institute of Certified Public Accountants, "1977 Auditor's Study and Evaluation of Internal Control in EDP Systems," AICPA, New York, 1977.

Anderson, David R., Schmidt, Leo A., and McCosh, Andrew M., *Practical Controllership*, 3rd ed., Irwin, Homewood, IL, 1973.

Benjamin, R. I., Dickinson, C. Jr., and Rockart, J. F., "Changing Role of the Corporate Information Systems Officer," *Management Information Systems Quarterly*, Vol. 9, No. 3, September 1985, pp. 177–188.

Berrisford, T. R., and Wetherbe, J. C., "Heuristic Development: A Redesign of Systems Design," *Management Information Systems Quarterly*, Vol. 3, No. 1, March 1979, pp. 11–19.

Bowman, B., Davis, G. B., and Wetherbe, J. C., "Three Stage Model of MIS Planning," *Information and Management*, Vol. 6, No. 1, February 1983, pp. 11–25.

Brown, P. S., and Gould, J. D., "An Experimental Study of People Creating Spreadsheets," *ACM Transactions on Office Information Systems*, Vol. 5, No. 3, July 1987, pp. 258–272.

Burch, J. G., and Grudnitski, G., *Information Systems: Theory and Practice*, 5th ed., Wiley, New York, 1989.

Canning, R. G., "Information Systems: New Strategic Role," *EDP Analyzer*, January 1984.

Carlyle, R. E., "CIO: Misfit or Misnomer," *Datamation*, Vol. 34, No. 15, August 1988, pp. 50–53, 56.

———, "Leading IS Shops Shifting to a Centralized Structure," *Datamation*, November 15, 1987, pp. 17–19.

Cash, J. I. Jr., McFarlan, F. W., and McKenney, J. L., *Corporate Information Systems Management: The Issues Facing Senior Executives*, 2nd ed., Irwin, Homewood, IL, 1988.

Chen, Peter P. *Entity-Relationship Approach to System Analysis and Design*, North-Holland, New York, 1980.

Davis, G. B., "Strategies for Information Requirements Determination," *IBM Systems Journal*, Vol. 21, No. 1, 1982, pp. 4–30.

———, *Management Information Systems: Conceptual Foundations, Structure, and Development*, McGraw-Hill, New York, 1974.

———, and Olson, M. H., *Management Information Systems: Conceptual Foundations, Structure, and Development*, McGraw-Hill, New York, 1985.

Dearden, J., "The Withering Away of the IS Organization," *Sloan Management Review*, Summer 1987, pp. 87–91.

DeMarco, T., *Structured Analysis and System Specification*, Prentice-Hall, Englewood Cliffs, NJ, 1978.

Deweney, A. K., "An Ancient Rope-and-Pulley Computer Is Unearthed in the Jungles of Apraphul." *Scientific American*, April 1988, pp. 118–121.

Diebold, J., "ADP—The Still-Sleeping Giant," *Harvard Business Review*, Vol. 42, September–October 1964, pp. 60–65.

Everest, Gordon, *Database Management: Objectives, System Functions, and Administration*, McGraw-Hill, New York, 1985.

Galletta, D., *COBOL with an Emphasis on Structured Program Design*, Prentice-Hall, Englewood Cliffs, NJ, 1985.

Head, R. V., "Information Resource Center: A New Force in End-User Computing," *Journal of Systems Management*, February 1985, p. 24.

IBM, "Business Systems Planning—Information Systems Planning Guide," Application Manual GE20-0527-3, 3rd ed., IBM Corporation, July 1981.

Jackson, M., *System Development*, Prentice-Hall, Englewood Cliffs, NJ, 1983.

King, William R., "Strategic Planning for Management Information Systems," *MIS Quarterly*, Vol. 2, No. 1, March 1978, pp. 27–37.

Koontz, H., & O'Donnell, C., *Principles of Management*, McGraw-Hill, New York, 1975.

Lucas, H. Jr., *The Analysis, Design, and Implementation of Information Systems*, McGraw-Hill, New York, 1985.

Mair, William C., Wood, Donald R., and Davis, Keagle W., *Computer Control & Audit*, Institute of Internal Auditors, Altamonte Springs, FL, 1978.

McFarlan, F. W., "Portfolio Approach to Information Systems," *Harvard Business Review*, September–October 1981, pp. 142–150.

Menamin, S. M. and Palmer, J. F., *Essential Systems Analysis*, Yourdon Press, New York, 1984.

Methvin, D., "The '386 Really Does Have an Edge on the '286," *PC Week Special Report*, April 3, 1989, p. S/3.

Moscove, S. A., and Simkin, M. G., *Accounting Information Systems: Concepts and Practice for Effective Decision Making*, 2nd ed., Wiley, New York, 1984.

Naumann, J. D., and Jenkins, A. M., "Prototyping: the New Paradigm for Systems Development," *Management Information Systems Quarterly*, Vol. 6, No. 3, September 1982, pp. 29–44.

Neff, A., "In the Future, We'll Be Computing on 1 Million Transistors a Day," *PC Week*, July 31, 1989, p. 105.

Nolan R., "Managing Information Systems by Committee," *Harvard Business Review*, July–August 1982, Vol. 60, No. 4, pp. 72–79.

Orr, K., *Structure Requirements Definition*, Ken Orr and Associates, Topeka, KS, 1981.

Porter, Michael E., *Competitive Strategy: Techniques for Analyzing Industries and Competitors*, The Free Press, New York, 1980.

Powers, M. J., Adams, D. R., and Mills, H., *Computer Information Systems Development: Analysis and Design*, South-Western Publishing, Cincinnati, 1984, p. 69.

Rishe, N., *Database Design Fundamentals*, Prentice-Hall, Englewood Cliffs, NJ, 1988.

Rockart, J. F., "Critical Success Factors," *Harvard Business Review*, March–April 1979, pp. 81–91.

Simon, H. A., *Administrative Behavior*, New York: Free Press, 1957.

——, *The New Science of Management Decision*, Harper & Row, New York, 1960.

Touche Ross & Co., *Controlling Assets and Transactions*, Touche Ross, New York, 1979.

Warnier, J., *Logical Construction of Systems*, Van Nostrand Reinhold, New York, 1981.

Weber, R., *EDP Auditing: Conceptual Foundations and Practice*, 2nd ed., McGraw-Hill, New York, 1988.

Wilkinson, J. W., *Accounting and Information Systems*, 2nd ed., Wiley, New York, 1986.

Wiseman, Charles, *Strategic Information Systems*, Irwin, Homewood, IL, 1988.

Yourdon, E., and Constantine L. L., *Structured Design: Fundamentals of a Discipline of Computer Program and Systems Design*, 2nd ed., Yourdon Press, New York, 1978.

Zahniser, R. A., "How to Navigate the User Fog," *Computerworld/InDepth*, March 16, 1981, p. 25.

INDEX